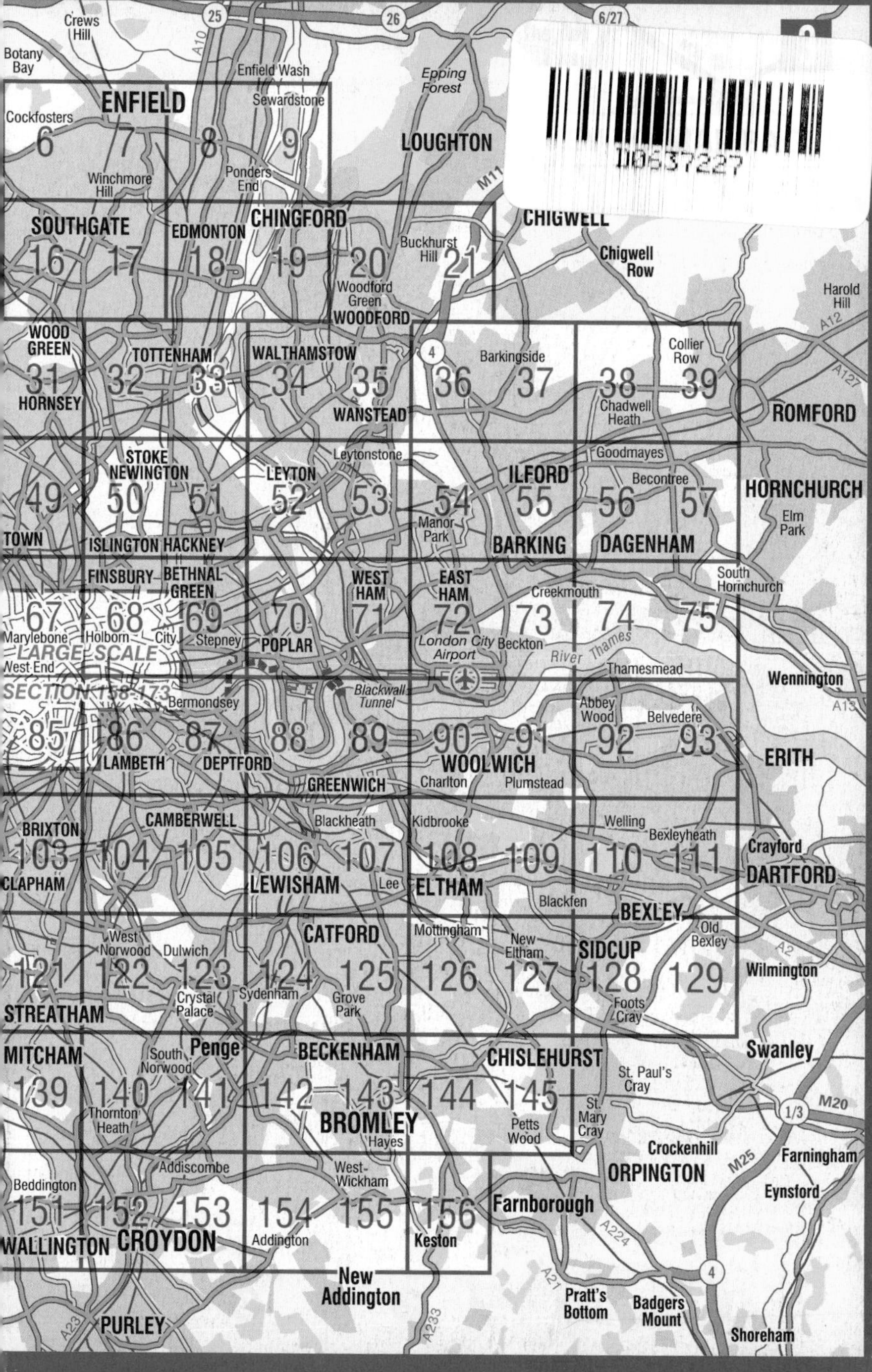

ENFIELD
Cockfosters
Winchmore Hill
Enfield Wash
Sewardstone
Ponders End
Crews Hill
Botany Bay
Epping Forest
LOUGHTON
CHIGWELL
SOUTHGATE
EDMONTON
CHINGFORD
Buckhurst Hill
Woodford Green
WOODFORD
Chigwell Row
Harold Hill
WOOD GREEN
HORNSEY
TOTTENHAM
WALTHAMSTOW
WANSTEAD
Barkingside
Collier Row
Chadwell Heath
ROMFORD
STOKE NEWINGTON
LEYTON
Leytonstone
ILFORD
Goodmayes
Becontree
HORNCHURCH
Elm Park
TOWN
ISLINGTON
HACKNEY
Manor Park
BARKING
DAGENHAM
FINSBURY
BETHNAL GREEN
WEST HAM
EAST HAM
Creekmouth
South Hornchurch
Marylebone
Holborn
City
Stepney
POPLAR
London City Airport
Beckton
River Thames
LARGE SCALE
West End
SECTION 158-173
Bermondsey
Blackwall Tunnel
Thamesmead
Wennington
Abbey Wood
Belvedere
LAMBETH
DEPTFORD
WOOLWICH
GREENWICH
Charlton
Plumstead
ERITH
BRIXTON
CAMBERWELL
Blackheath
Kidbrooke
Welling
Bexleyheath
Crayford
CLAPHAM
LEWISHAM
Lee
ELTHAM
Blackfen
BEXLEY
DARTFORD
West Norwood
Dulwich
CATFORD
Mottingham
New Eltham
SIDCUP
Old Bexley
Wilmington
STREATHAM
Crystal Palace
Sydenham
Grove Park
Foots Cray
MITCHAM
South Norwood
Penge
BECKENHAM
CHISLEHURST
St. Paul's Cray
Swanley
Thornton Heath
BROMLEY
Hayes
Petts Wood
St. Mary Cray
Crockenhill
ORPINGTON
Farningham
Eynsford
Beddington
Addiscombe
West Wickham
Farnborough
WALLINGTON
CROYDON
Addington
Keston
New Addington
Pratt's Bottom
Badgers Mount
PURLEY
Shoreham

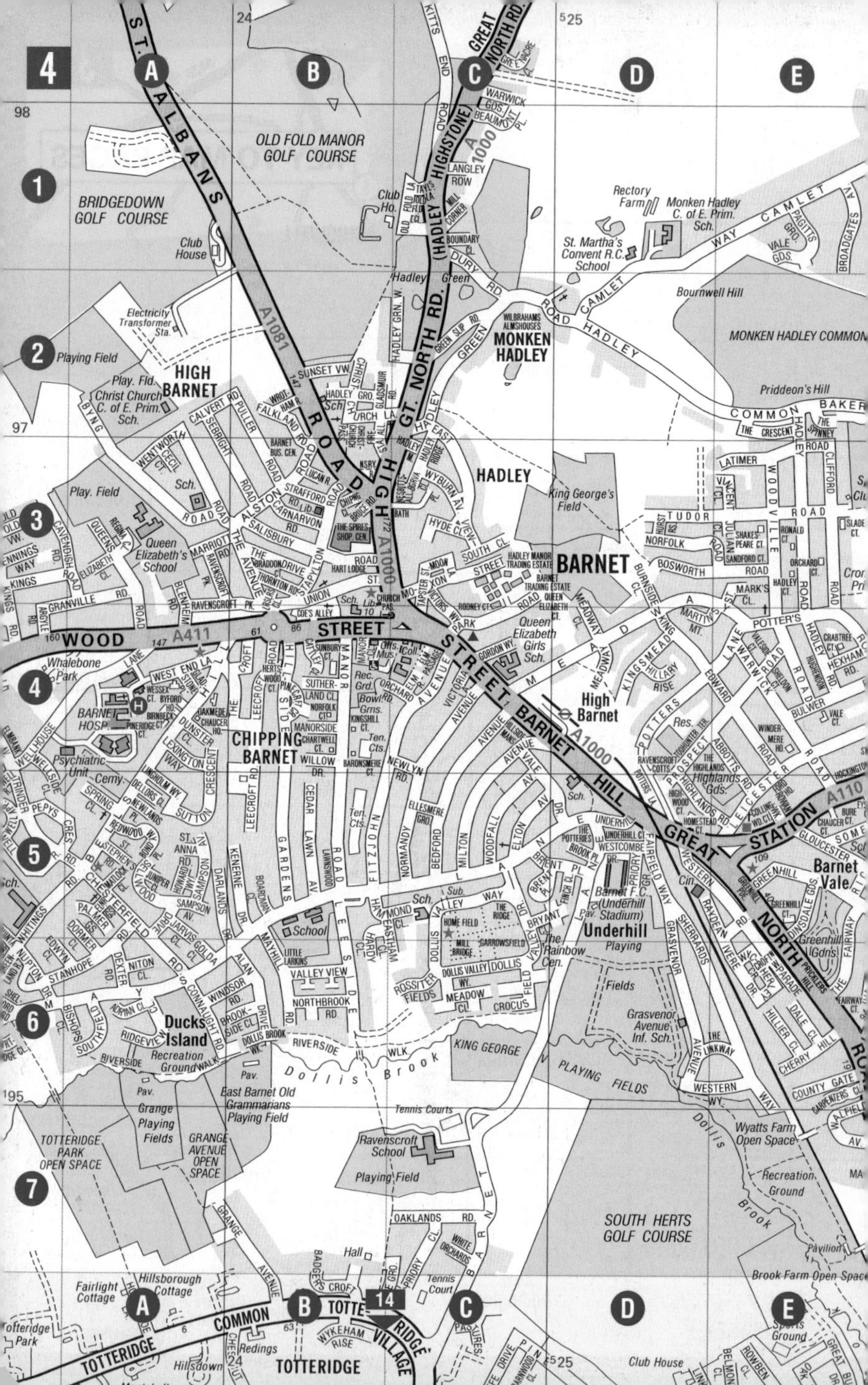
4
A
B
C
D
E
24
525
98
97
195
1
2
3
4
5
6
7
ST. ALBANS ROAD
A1081
GREAT NORTH RD.
HIGHSTONE
(HADLEY HIGHSTONE)
GT. NORTH RD.
A1000
KITTS END ROAD
OLD FOLD MANOR GOLF COURSE
BRIDGEDOWN GOLF COURSE
Club House
Club Ho.
WARWICK GDS.
BEAUMONT PL.
LANGLEY ROW
MILL CORNER
BOUNDARY CL.
DURY RD.
Hadley Green
Rectory Farm
Monken Hadley C. of E. Prim. Sch.
St. Martha's Convent R.C. School
CAMLET WAY
PAGITTS GRO.
VALE GDS.
BROADGATES AV.
Bournwell Hill
MONKEN HADLEY COMMON
HADLEY ROAD
WILBRAHAMS ALMSHOUSES
MONKEN HADLEY
GREEN SLIP RD.
HADLEY GRN. W.
Electricity Transformer Sta.
Playing Field
Play. Fld.
Christ Church C. of E. Prim. Sch.
HIGH BARNET
SUNSET VW.
Prideeon's Hill
COMMON
BAKER
THE CRESCENT
THE SPINNEY
HADLEY ROAD
CLIFFORD
LATIMER
WOODVILLE
VINCENT CL.
HADLEY
HADLEY RIDGE
WYBURN AV.
HYDE CL.
SOUTH CL.
King George's Field
TUDOR
ROAD
HURST
NORFOLK
JULIAN
SHAKESPEARE CT.
SANDFORD CT.
BOSWORTH
RONALD CT.
ORCHARD CT.
HADLEY CT.
SLADE CT.
BYNG
CALVERT RD.
SEBRIGHT
PULLER RD.
WENTWORTH
CECIL CT.
Sch.
FALKLAND RD.
BARNET BUS. CEN.
LUCAN R.
STRAFFORD RD.
CARNARVON RD.
CHIPPING CL.
BRUCE RD.
Lib.
THE SPIRES SHOP. CEN.
BATH
Play. Field
REGINA CT.
QUEENS
CAVENDISH
ELIZABETH CL.
Queen Elizabeth's School
ALSTON ROAD
SALISBURY
MARRIOTT RD.
RAVENSCROFT PK.
THE AVENUE
BRADDON
DRIVE
THORNTON RD.
STAPYLTON
HART LODGE
ROAD
UNION ST.
MOON LA.
TAPSTER ST.
HADLEY MANOR TRADING ESTATE
BARNET TRADING ESTATE
BARNET
BURNSIDE CL.
MEADWAY
QUEEN ELIZABETH CT.
RODNEY CT.
ROAD
PARK
MARK'S CL.
POTTER'S
KINGS
GRANVILLE RD.
ARGYLE
BLENHEIM
RAVENSCROFT PK.
COE'S ALLEY
CHURCH PAS.
Lib.
Sch.
WOOD
A411
STREET
Offs.
Mus.
Coll.
Whalebone Park
WEST END LA.
WESSEX CT.
BYFORD
BIRNBECK CT.
PINERIDGE CT.
BARNET HOSP.
DUNSTER
OAKMEDE
CHAUCER HO.
LEXINGTON WAY
CROFT
LEECROFT
HERTS WOOD CT.
HILLSIDE GR.
PINECROFT CR.
SUNBURY CT.
MANOR
Rec. Grd.
Bowl. Grns.
ORCHARD
SUTHERLAND CL.
NORFOLK CT.
KINGSHILL CT.
MANORSIDE
CHARTWELL CT.
WILLOW DR.
BARONSMERE CT.
Ten. Cts.
NEWLYN RD.
VICTORIA
AVENUE
GORDON WY.
Queen Elizabeth Girls Sch.
STREET
BARNET HILL
A1000
High Barnet
KINGSMEAD
HILLARY RISE
POTTERS
EDWARD
LANE
WARWICK
ROAD
SHELDON
BULWER
VALE CT.
CRABTREE CT.
HEXHAM RD.
WINDERMERE HO.
Res.
RAVENSCROFT COTTS
PROSPECT
THE HIGHLANDS
Highlands Gds.
HIGHWOOD CT.
HOMESTEAD CT.
ABBOTTS RD.
LEICESTER
STATION
A110
COLLINGWOOD CT.
GREAT
NORTH
CHAUCER CT.
GLOUCESTER
Barnet Vale
GREENHILL
DINSDALE GDS.
Greenhill Gdns.
FAIRWAY
CHIPPING BARNET
Psychiatric Unit
Cemy.
WELLHOUSE
WELLSIDE CL.
TRINDER
PEPYS CRES.
SPRING CL.
LINGHOLME WY.
NEWLANDS
ST. STEPHEN'S
REDWOOD WY.
BOND ST.
MATLOCK
ST. ANNA RD.
HOWARD WY.
SAMPSON AV.
JUNIPER CL.
JARVIS CL.
GOLDA CL.
SUTTON
CRESCENT
LEECROFT RD.
KENERNE DR.
DARLANDS DR.
BOARDMAN CL.
GARDENS
CEDAR LAWN AV.
LAWNSWOOD
ROAD
FITZJOHN
NORMANDY AV.
ELLESMERE GRO.
BEDFORD
MILTON
WOODFALL AV.
ELTON AV.
UNDERHILL
THE POTTERIES
BROOK PL.
BRENT PL.
FINCH CL.
WESTCOMBE DR.
PRIORY GR.
FAIRFIELD WAY
Barnet F.C. (Underhill Stadium)
WESTERN
Cin.
RAYDEAN
IVERE DR.
CROFT
PARADE
PRICKLERS HILL
Sch.
CHESTERFIELD RD.
WHITINGS
PALMER GS.
DORMER CL.
EDWYN CL.
STANHOPE RD.
DEXTER RD.
NITON CL.
CONNAUGHT RD.
ALAN DR.
MAYHILL RD.
School
LITTLE LARKINS
VALLEY VIEW
NORTHBROOK RD.
HAMMOND CL.
EASTHAM CL.
HARDY CL.
Sch.
DOLLIS VALLEY WAY
HOME FIELD
THE RIDGE
MILL BRIDGE
GARROWSFIELD
BRYANT CL.
VALLEY DR.
The Rainbow Cen.
Underhill Playing Fields
ROSSITER FIELDS
DOLLIS VALLEY DOLLIS
MEADOW CL.
CROCUS
FIELD
GRASVENOR AVENUE
SHERRARDS
Grasvenor Avenue Inf. Sch.
THE LINKWAY
DALE CL.
HILLIER CL.
CHERRY HILL
WESTERN WY.
COUNTY GATE
CARPENTERS CL.
WALFIELD AV.
Ducks Island Recreation Ground
BISHOPS
SOUTHFIELD
ADRIAN CL.
RIDGEVIEW
RIVERSIDE
WINDSOR RD.
BROOKSIDE CL.
DOLLIS BROOK WK.
RIVERSIDE WLK.
Dollis Brook
KING GEORGE PLAYING FIELDS
Pav.
Grange Playing Fields
East Barnet Old Grammarians Playing Field
TOTTERIDGE PARK OPEN SPACE
GRANGE AVENUE OPEN SPACE
Tennis Courts
Ravenscroft School
Playing Field
BARNET LA.
Wyatts Farm Open Space
Recreation Ground
SOUTH HERTS GOLF COURSE
OAKLANDS RD.
WHITE ORCHARDS
PRIORY CL.
Hall
BADGERS CROFT
Tennis Court
Pavilion
Brook Farm Open Space
Fairlight Cottage
Hillsborough Cottage
GRANGE AVENUE
14
TOTTERIDGE VILLAGE
COMMON
TOTTERIDGE
Totteridge Park
Redings
WYKEHAM RISE
Hillsdown
Sports Ground
Club House
PINE
BELMONT CL.
ROWBEN CL.
GREAT

A-Z LONDON

CONTENTS

Key to Map Pages	2-3	Index to Streets, Areas & selected Places of Interest	178-360
Map Pages @ approx. 3" to 1 mile	4-156	Index to Hospitals & Hospices	361-365
Large Scale Map Pages @ 5¾" to 1 mile	157-173	Index to Stations	366-368
Railway Connections Map	174-175	Underground Railway Map	Back Cover
West End Cinemas & Theatres Maps	176-177		

REFERENCE

- Motorway — M1
- A Road — A2
  - Under Construction
  - Proposed
- B Road — B408
- Dual Carriageway
- One-Way Street
  Traffic flow on A Roads is indicated by a heavy line on the drivers' left.
- Junction Name — MARBLE ARCH
- Restricted Access
- Pedestrianized Road
- Track & Footpath
- Residential Walkway
- Railway — Tunnel; Level Crossing
- Stations:
  - National Rail Network
  - Docklands Light Railway — DLR
  - Underground Station — ⊖ is the registered trade mark of Transport for London
- Croydon Tramlink — Tunnel; Stop
  The boarding of Tramlink trams at stops may be limited to a single direction,indicated by the arrow.
- Map Continuation — 62; Large Scale Map Pages — 160
- Built-Up Area — BANK STREET
- House Numbers A & B Roads only — 51 22 19 48
- Church or Chapel — †
- Fire Station
- Hospital — H
- Information Centre
- National Grid Reference — 530
- Police Station — ▲
- Post Office — ★
- Toilet with facilities for the Disabled
- Educational Establishment
- Hospital or Hospice
- Industrial Building
- Leisure or Recreational Facility
- Place of Interest
- Public Building
- Shopping Centre or Market
- Other Selected Buildings

SCALE
Pages 4-156
2.88 inches to 1 Mile

0 — ¼ — ½ — ¾ Mile
0 — 250 — 500 — 750 Metres — 1 Kilometre

1:22,000
7.31cm to 1 mile
4.55cm to 1 km

Geographers' A-Z Map Company Limited

Head Office : Fairfield Road, Borough Green, Sevenoaks, Kent TN15 8PP Tel: 01732 781000 (General Enquires & Trade Sales)
Showrooms : 44 Gray's Inn Road, London WC1X 8HX Tel: 020 7440 9500 (Retail Sales) www.a-zmaps.co.uk

Ordnance Survey® This product includes mapping data licensed from Ordnance Survey with the permission of the Controller of Her Majesty's Stationery Office.

Edition 5 2001 Edition 5A 2002(Part Revision)

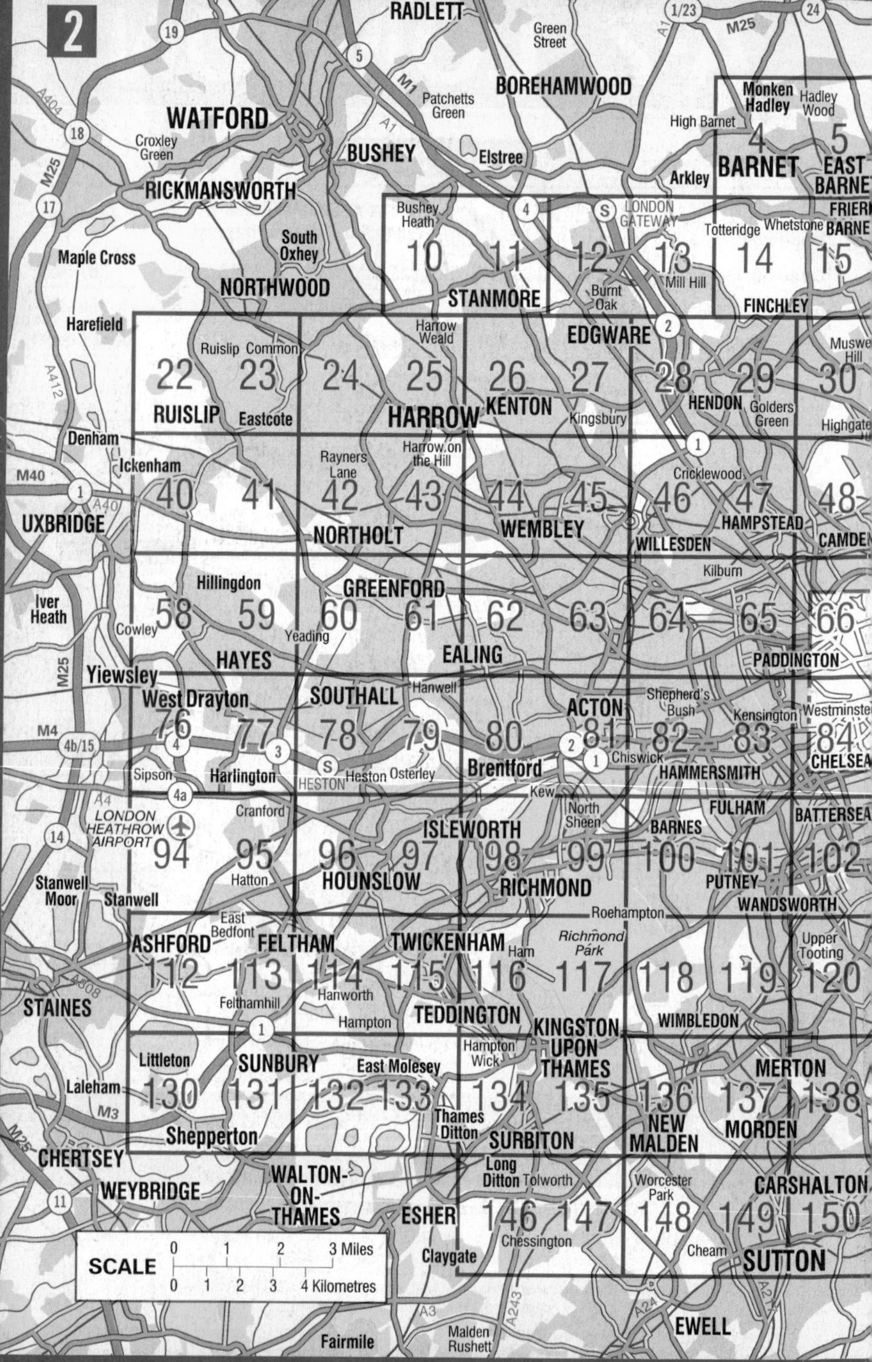
2
RADLETT
Green Street
BOREHAMWOOD
WATFORD
Croxley Green
BUSHEY
Patchetts Green
Elstree
RICKMANSWORTH
Monken Hadley
Hadley Wood
High Barnet
4
BARNET
5
EAST BARNET
Arkley
Bushey Heath
LONDON GATEWAY
Totteridge
Whetstone
FRIERN BARNET
South Oxhey
Maple Cross
10
11
12
13
14
15
Mill Hill
NORTHWOOD
STANMORE
Burnt Oak
FINCHLEY
Harefield
Harrow Weald
EDGWARE
Ruislip Common
Muswell Hill
22
23
24
25
26
27
28
29
30
RUISLIP
Eastcote
HARROW
KENTON
Kingsbury
HENDON
Golders Green
Highgate
Denham
Rayners Lane
Harrow on the Hill
Ickenham
Cricklewood
40
41
42
43
44
45
46
47
48
UXBRIDGE
NORTHOLT
WEMBLEY
WILLESDEN
HAMPSTEAD
CAMDEN
Kilburn
Hillingdon
GREENFORD
Iver Heath
58
59
60
61
62
63
64
65
66
Cowley
Yeading
HAYES
EALING
PADDINGTON
Yiewsley
West Drayton
SOUTHALL
Hanwell
ACTON
Shepherd's Bush
Kensington
Westminster
76
77
78
79
80
81
82
83
84
Sipson
Harlington
HESTON
Heston
Osterley
Brentford
Chiswick
HAMMERSMITH
CHELSEA
Kew
LONDON HEATHROW AIRPORT
Cranford
North Sheen
FULHAM
BATTERSEA
ISLEWORTH
BARNES
94
95
96
97
98
99
100
101
102
Hatton
HOUNSLOW
RICHMOND
PUTNEY
Stanwell Moor
Stanwell
Roehampton
WANDSWORTH
East Bedfont
ASHFORD
FELTHAM
TWICKENHAM
Ham
Richmond Park
Upper Tooting
112
113
114
115
116
117
118
119
120
Hanworth
STAINES
Felthamhill
Hampton
TEDDINGTON
KINGSTON UPON THAMES
WIMBLEDON
Littleton
SUNBURY
East Molesey
Hampton Wick
MERTON
Laleham
130
131
132
133
134
135
136
137
138
Thames Ditton
NEW MALDEN
MORDEN
Shepperton
SURBITON
CHERTSEY
Long Ditton
Tolworth
WALTON-ON-THAMES
WEYBRIDGE
Worcester Park
CARSHALTON
ESHER
146
147
148
149
150
Chessington
Cheam
SUTTON
SCALE
0 1 2 3 Miles
0 1 2 3 4 Kilometres
Claygate
EWELL
Fairmile
Malden Rushett
M25
M1
M40
M4
M3
A1
A40
A4
A404
A412
A308
A3
A243
A24
A217
1/23
24
19
18
17
14
11
4b/15
4a

5
27
28
F
G
H
J
K
1
2
3
4
5
6
7
9
15
Hadley Wood
HADLEY WOOD
Tennis Club
LANCASTER AVENUE
WEST CRESCENT
EAST BEECH HILL
Great Broadgates Hill
WALMAR CL.
Club House
CORBAR CL.
COCKFOSTERS RD.
FERNY HILL
HADLEY RD.
Ash Wood
Ferny Hill Cottage
Ferny Hill Farm
Fernyhill Wood
Rough Lot
TRENT PARK (Country Park)
Seedfield Spinney
Oak Wood
Fish Pond
Lodge
Church Wood
Cemetery
BEECH HILL PARK
HADLEY WOOD GOLF COURSE
Monken Mead Brook
Green Brook
Fish Pond
Sewits Hill
Beech Hill Lake
Newmans Hill
HADLEY WOOD RD.
HILL
TUDOR PARK GOLF COURSE
PARKGATE AVENUE
MUSGRAVE CL.
BEECH HILL WAY
GREENBROOK AV.
NEWMAN'S WAY
COVERT WAY
HILL WOOD AVENUE
GREENOAK PL.
COOMBEHURST CL.
FAIRGREEN
FAIRGREEN EAST
BOURNWELL CL.
A111
Playing Field
East Barnet Sch. 5th. & 6th. Form Centre
Livingstone Prim. Sch.
Play. Fld.
GAMES RD.
NORTHFIELD RD.
ARUNDEL RD.
LINTHORPE ROAD
GROVE ROAD
SOMERCOATES CL.
Playing Fields
Pav.
War Meml.
Cockfosters
COCKFOSTERS
Sch.
BELMONT CL.
CHALK LA.
Spts. Grd.
LANGFORD RD.
MOUNT PLEASANT
HAMILTON CL.
BEVAN RD.
HERTFORD RD.
WESTBROOK CRESCENT
LAWTON RD.
ARMSTRONG CL.
NEW BARNET
Recreation Ground
Ten. Cts.
FORDHAM RD.
BARING RD.
PARK RD.
Pymmes Brook
PYMMES BROOK DR.
CRESCENT ROAD
EDGEWORTH RD.
GLYN AV.
VICTORIA RD.
MARGARET RD.
EAST BARNET RD.
STATION ROAD
ROAD
Mus.
HERONS RI.
ROLFE CL.
SILVERCLIFFE
MOUNT RD.
Brook
HIGH TREES
PILGRIMS RISE
KEELY CL.
Pleasure Ground
EVELYN RD.
NORRY'S RD.
CARSON ROAD
ECCLESTON CL.
HEDDON RD.
HEDDON COURT AVENUE
ASHURST
BELMONT AVENUE
LEYS GDNS.
WESTPOLE AV.
GLOUCESTER
Playing Field
Southgate School
SUSSEX WAY
BRAMLEY RD.
Chicken Shed Theatre
De Bohun Prim. Sch.
Saracens Rugby Football Club
CHASE SIDE
Middlesex University
Oaktree Sch.
Pond
Oakhill College
CANON MOHAN CL.
EAST BARNET
Lib.
CAT HILL
A110
BROOKHILL R.
CHESTNUT GR.
East Barnet Sch.
Play. Fld.
Sch.
LAKESIDE CR.
MANSFIELD
VERNON
DESMOND HO.
BOHUN GRO.
WINDSOR
RIDGEWAY
New Barnet
Lyonsdown
LYONSDOWN RD.
GLOUCESTER RD.
EVERSLEIGH RD.
LONGMORE AV.
B193
CALTON RD.
DALMENY RD.
HOLYROOD RD.
MONKS AV.
NORTHUMBERLAND RD.
WILLENHALL AV.
HIGH ROAD
A1000
NETHERLANDS RD.
THE HOOK
HOLLAND CL.
CHURCH HILL RD.
LITTLEGROVE
BROOKSIDE
CHURCHMEAD CL.
CAPEL RD.
ROSSLYN AV.
OAKHURST AV.
Oakleigh Park
ALVERSTONE AV.
OAKLEIGH PARK
OAKLEIGH RD. NORTH
CEDAR AV.
LOVELACE
ALBEMARLE RD.
RUSHDENE
GALLANTS FARM RD.
BURLINGTON RI.
Sch.
Play. Fld.
HILL
Bandstand
Playground
OAK HILL PARK
Pavilion
Bowling Green
Miniature Golf Course
Monkfrith Prim. Sch.
Tennis Courts
Pav.
PARKSIDE
WOODFIELD AV.
South Barnet
MONKFRITH
FRIARS WAY
MOUNT DRIVE
TEMPLE AVENUE
Playing Field
Tens. Cts.
WHETSTONE
CHANDOS AV.
Queen's Centre Playing Field
DOWNLAND CL.
Warehouse
Works
THE GRANGE
DERWENT
CONNAUGHT AV.
26
Coll.

7
ENFIELD
ENFIELD TOWN
Enfield Town
Chase Side
Gordon Hill
Enfield Chase
Grange Park
GRANGE PARK
Winchmore Hill
WINCHMORE HILL
BUSH HILL PARK
Bush Hill Park
World's End
ENFIELD GOLF COURSE
BUSH HILL PARK GOLF COURSE
Town Park
SLADES HILL
WINDMILL HILL
CHURCH ST.
SOUTHBURY ROAD
RIDGEWAY
LONDON ROAD
RIDGE AV.
A1005
A110
A105
B154
8
17
F
G
H
J
K
1
2
3
4
5
6
7

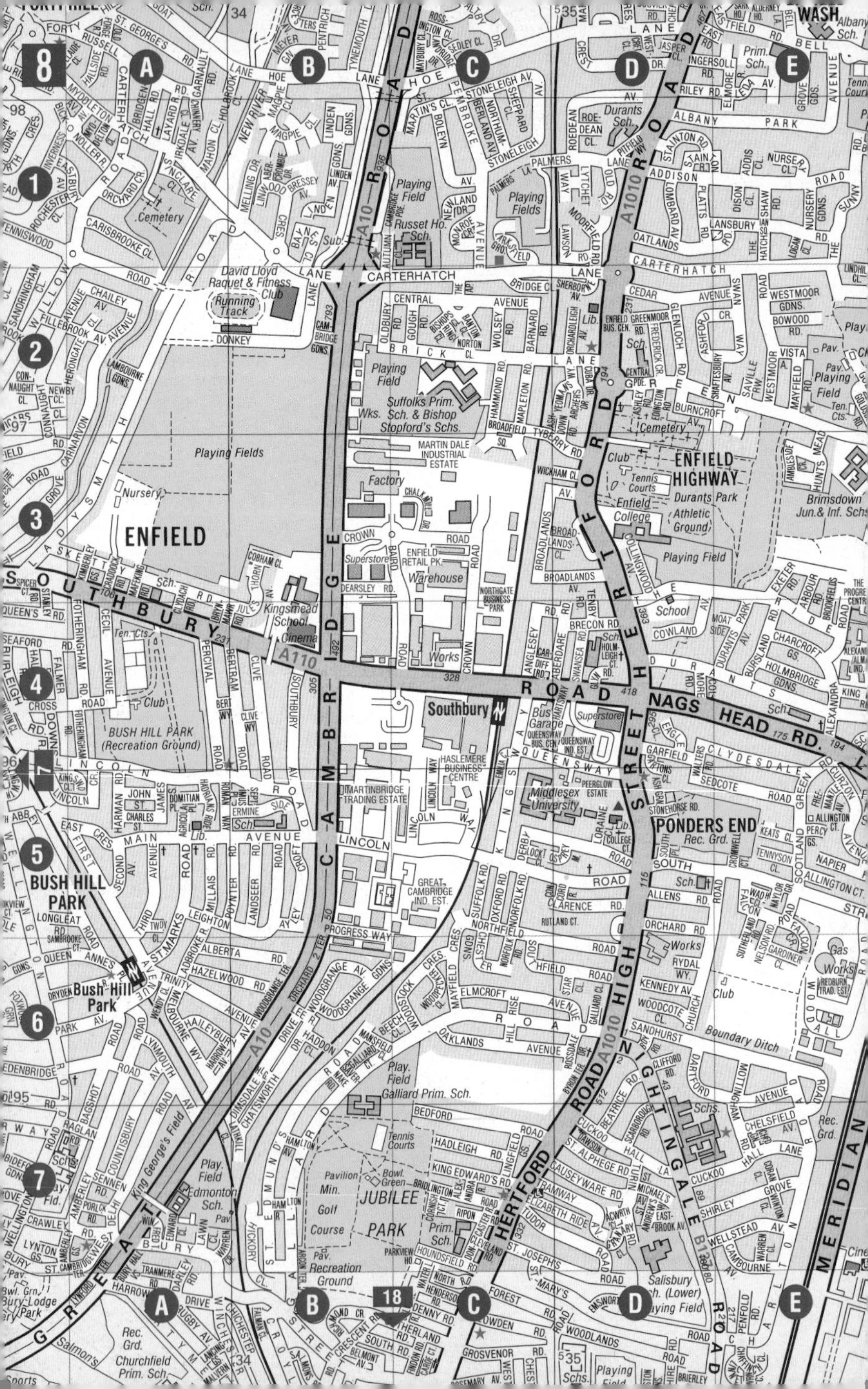

8
A
B
C
D
E
1
2
3
4
5
6
7
98
97
96
95
34
35
18
ENFIELD
ENFIELD HIGHWAY
PONDERS END
BUSH HILL PARK
Bush Hill Park
Southbury
A10
A110
A1010
B112
GREAT CAMBRIDGE ROAD
HERTFORD ROAD
HIGH STREET
SOUTHBURY ROAD
NAGS HEAD RD.
CARTERHATCH LANE
LADYSMITH ROAD
LINCOLN ROAD
MERIDIAN
Cemetery
David Lloyd Raquet & Fitness Club
Running Track
Playing Fields
Playing Field
Russet Ho. Sch.
Durants Sch.
Suffolks Prim. Sch. & Bishop Stopford's Schs.
MARTIN DALE INDUSTRIAL ESTATE
Factory
Superstore
ENFIELD RETAIL PK.
Warehouse
NORTHGATE BUSINESS PARK
Kingsmead School
Cinema
Works
BUSH HILL PARK (Recreation Ground)
HASLEMERE BUSINESS CENTRE
MARTINBRIDGE TRADING ESTATE
GREAT CAMBRIDGE IND. EST.
Middlesex University
PEERGLOW ESTATE
Bus Garage
QUEENSWAY BUS. CEN.
QUEENSWAY IND. EST.
Enfield College
Tennis Courts
Durants Park Athletic Ground
Brimsdown Jun.& Inf. Schs
Ponders End Rec. Grd.
Gas Works
REDBURN TRAD. EST.
Boundary Ditch
Galliard Prim. Sch.
Play. Field
Tennis Courts
Bowl. Green
Pavilion
Min. Golf Course
JUBILEE PARK
Recreation Ground
Prim. Sch.
Edmonton Sch.
King George's Field
Play. Fld.
Rec. Grd.
Churchfield Prim. Sch.
Salmon's
Salisbury Sch. (Lower) Playing Field
Rec. Grd.
Nursery
ENFIELD BUS. CEN.

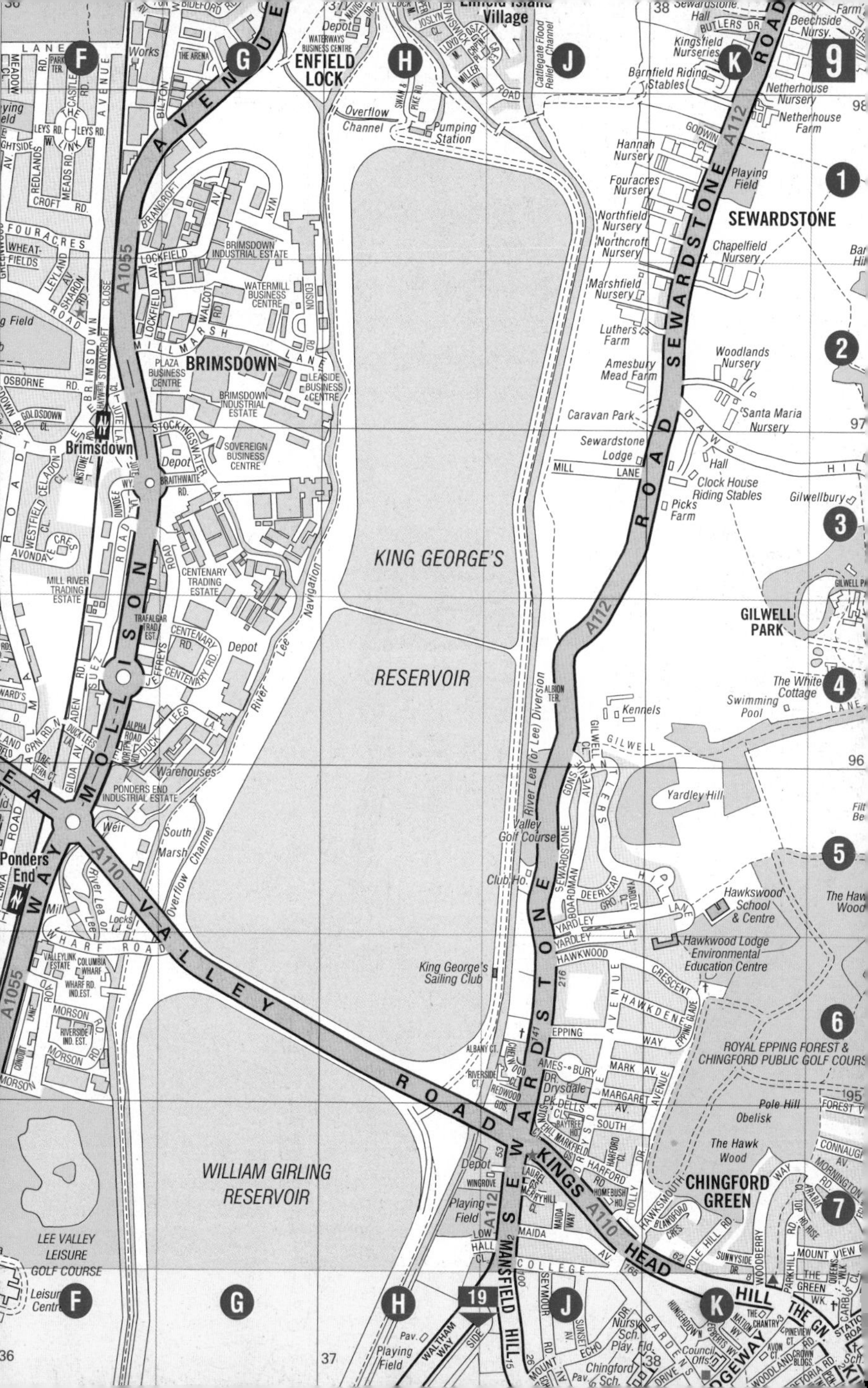
9
ENFIELD LOCK
Enfield Island Village
Waterways Business Centre
Overflow Channel
Pumping Station
Cattlegate Flood Relief Channel
Sewardstone Hall
Kingsfield Nurseries
Barnfield Riding Stables
Beechside Nursy.
Netherhouse Nursery
Netherhouse Farm
Hannah Nursery
Fouracres Nursery
Northfield Nursery
Northcroft Nursery
Marshfield Nursery
Luthers Farm
Amesbury Mead Farm
Playing Field
SEWARDSTONE
Chapelfield Nursery
Woodlands Nursery
Santa Maria Nursery
Caravan Park
Sewardstone Lodge
Clock House Riding Stables
Picks Farm
Gilwellbury
GILWELL PARK
The White Cottage
Swimming Pool
Kennels
Yardley Hill
SEWARDSTONE ROAD
A112
BRIMSDOWN
BRIMSDOWN INDUSTRIAL ESTATE
WATERMILL BUSINESS CENTRE
PLAZA BUSINESS CENTRE
LEASIDE BUSINESS CENTRE
SOVEREIGN BUSINESS CENTRE
Brimsdown
Depot
MILL RIVER TRADING ESTATE
CENTENARY TRADING ESTATE
TRAFALGAR TRAD. EST.
Warehouses
PONDERS END INDUSTRIAL ESTATE
Ponders End
Weir
South Marsh
Locks
River Lee Navigation
KING GEORGE'S RESERVOIR
River Lea (or Lee) Diversion
Valley Golf Course
Club Ho.
King George's Sailing Club
MOLLISON AVENUE
A1055
LEA VALLEY ROAD
A110
WHARF ROAD
VALLEYLINK ESTATE
COLUMBIA WHARF
WHARF RD. IND. EST.
RIVERSIDE IND. EST.
WILLIAM GIRLING RESERVOIR
LEE VALLEY LEISURE GOLF COURSE
Hawkswood School & Centre
Hawkwood Lodge Environmental Education Centre
ROYAL EPPING FOREST & CHINGFORD PUBLIC GOLF COURSE
Pole Hill Obelisk
The Hawk Wood
CHINGFORD GREEN
KINGS HEAD HILL
MANSFIELD HILL
Playing Field
Depot
Pav.
Council Offs.
Chingford Sch.
Nursy. Sch. Play. Fld.
19
F
G
H
J
K
1
2
3
4
5
6
7
36
37
38
95
96
97
98

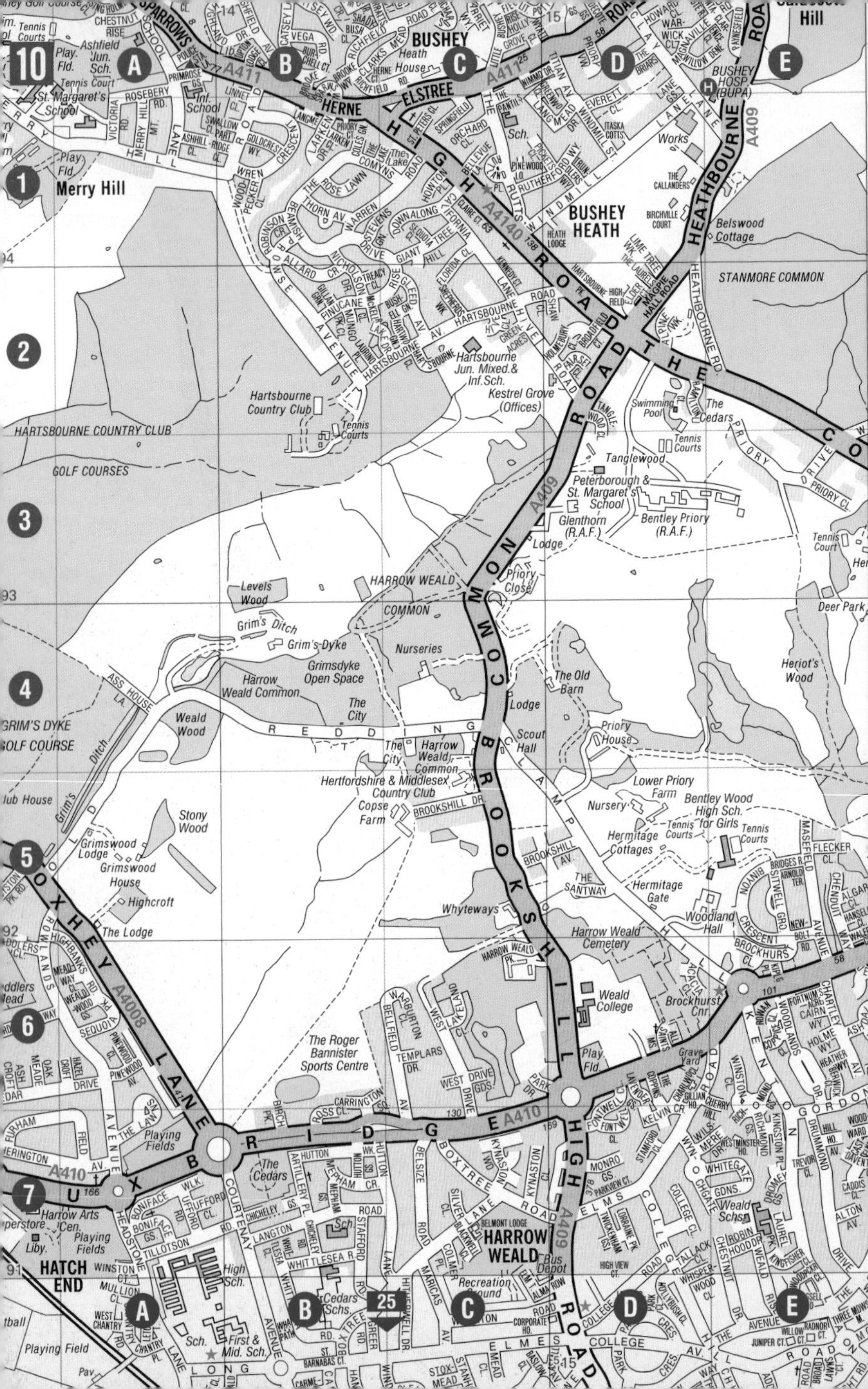
BUSHEY
Bushey Heath
Merry Hill
BUSHEY HEATH
STANMORE COMMON
HARTSBOURNE COUNTRY CLUB
GOLF COURSES
Hartsbourne Country Club
HARROW WEALD
COMMON
Grimsdyke Open Space
Harrow Weald Common
GRIM'S DYKE
GOLF COURSE
Stony Wood
Weald Wood
Levels Wood
Heriot's Wood
Deer Park
Bentley Priory (R.A.F.)
Peterborough & St. Margaret's School
Hertfordshire & Middlesex Country Club
Bentley Wood High Sch. for Girls
Harrow Weald Cemetery
Weald College
The Roger Bannister Sports Centre
HARROW WEALD
HATCH END
Brockhurst Cnr.
A411
A4140
A409
A4008
A410
A = B = C = D = E
25

WATFORD BY-PASS
M1-MOTORWAY
Junction 4
EDGWARE
BROCKLEY
HILL
Elstree Open Space
Norwegian Barn
Brockleyhill Farm
Sports Ground
Brockley Grange
Brockleyhill House
ROYAL NATIONAL ORTHOPAEDIC HOSPITAL
Pear Wood Cottages
Limes House
Wood Farm
Pear Wood
Fish Pond
Newlands
A41 (WATFORD BY-PASS)
(WATLING STREET)
ROMAN ROAD
Cricket Ground
Grove Field
Pavilion
Husaini Shia Islamic Centre
Little Common
Cloisters Wood
Stanmore Hall
Edgwarebury Golf Course
Playing Field
SPUR RD.
Offices
STONEGROVE
LONDON ROAD
Stanmore
St. John's First & Mid. Schs.
Boot Pond
CHURCH RD.
Aylward First & Mid. Sch.
Lake Grove Rec. Grd.
The Lake
North London Collegiate School
STANMORE
Stanmore College
Temple Pond
King George V Memorial Gdns.
CANONS PARK
Club House
Gas Works
Stanmore Marsh
Sports Ground
Whitchurch First & Mid Schs.
STANMORE GOLF COURSE
Stanburn Schs
Canons Park
WHITCHURCH LANE
HONEYPOT LANE
Little Stanmore First & Mid. School
Sports Ground
Prince Edward

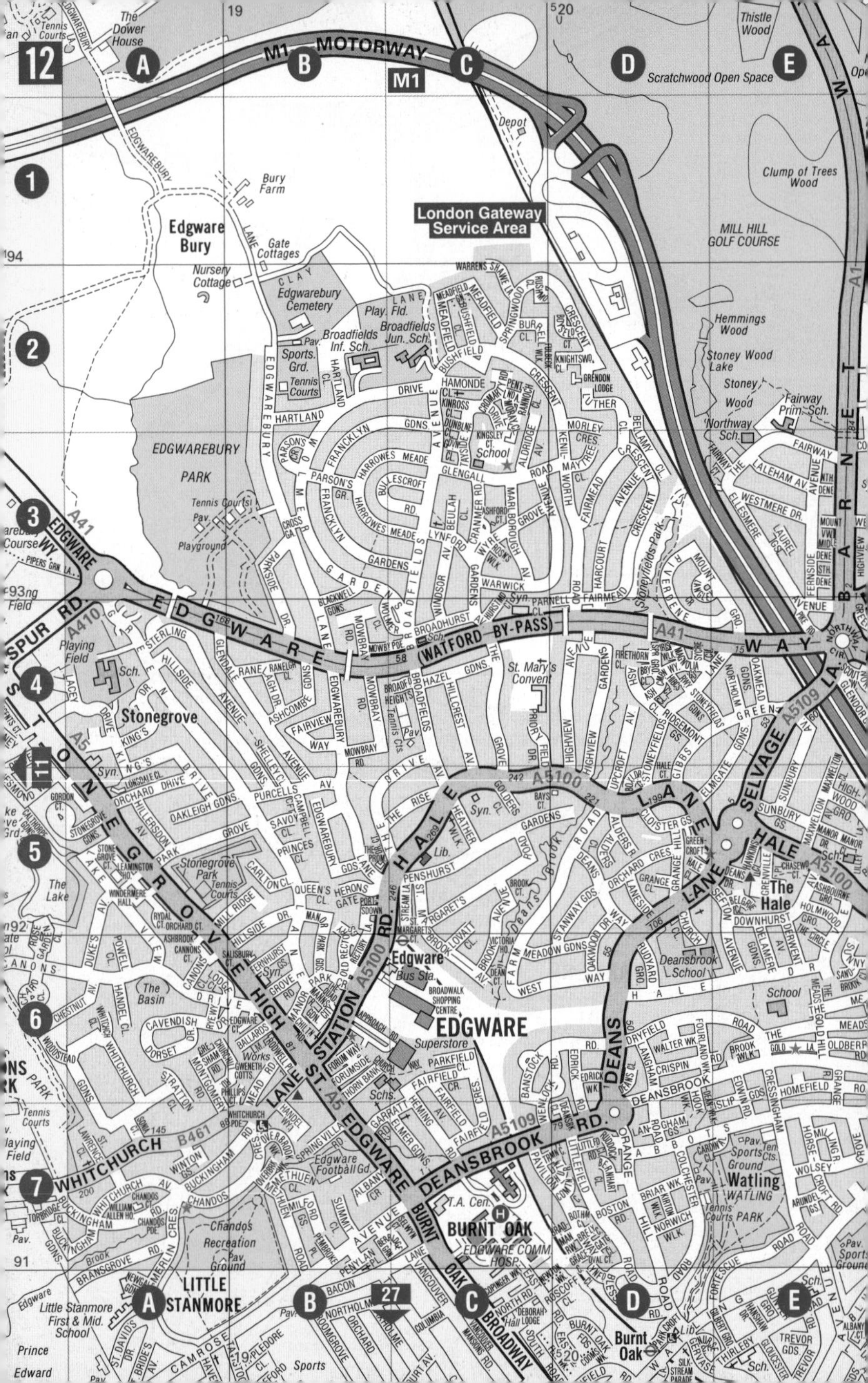

12
M1 MOTORWAY
Scratchwood Open Space
Thistle Wood
Clump of Trees Wood
MILL HILL GOLF COURSE
London Gateway Service Area
Edgware Bury
Bury Farm
Gate Cottages
Nursery Cottage
The Dower House
Edgwarebury Cemetery
Broadfields Inf. Sch.
Broadfields Jun. Sch.
EDGWAREBURY PARK
Hemmings Wood
Stoney Wood Lake
Stoney Wood
Fairway Prim. Sch.
Northway Sch.
EDGWARE WAY (WATFORD BY-PASS)
SPUR RD.
STONEGROVE
Stonegrove
Stonegrove Park
The Lake
The Basin
HALE LANE
SELVAGE LA.
St. Mary's Convent
Edgware
Bus Sta.
BROADWALK SHOPPING CENTRE
EDGWARE
Superstore
The Hale
Deansbrook School
DEANSBROOK RD.
DEANS LANE
HIGH ST.
STATION RD.
WHITCHURCH LANE
Edgware Football Gd.
Chandos Recreation Ground
BURNT OAK
EDGWARE COMM. HOSP.
BURNT OAK BROADWAY
Watling
WATLING PARK
LITTLE STANMORE
Little Stanmore First & Mid. School
Burnt Oak
27
11

13
Hyver Manor
Barnet Gate Wood
Gravel Pit Wood
Tanglewood
HENDON WOOD LANE
BARNET GATE LANE
Allendale
Brent Lodge Farm
Dollis Brook
F
G
H
J
K
HENDON WOOD LANE OPEN SPACE
Sports Ground
Pav.
MOAT MOUNT OPEN SPACE
The Shrubbery
Leg of Mutton Pond
Mote End Farm
Mote Mount
Nut Wood
White Lodge
Tennis Courts
Mill Hill High Sch.
Playing Field
Beech Wood
Highwood Park
The Barn
Highwood Ho.
Hendon Park
CLARK'S LANE
CROWN CL.
Boundary House
Farmleigh
Oak Lodge
Fairlight Cottage
Totteridge Park
Abattoir
St. Edward's College
TOTTERIDGE COMMON
A5109
Ellern Mede Nursing Home
Ellern Mede Farm
Totteridge Common
The Lynch House
Fairlawn
HIGHWOOD HILL
Highwood
Highwood Hill
Highwood Hill Cottage
Holcombe Dale
Holcombe Hill
Folly Brook
Folly Farm
MARSH LANE
RAMILLIES
WORCESTER
NORBURY GRO.
GLENWOOD RD.
LINCOLNS
LAWRENCE GDS.
ABBEY VIEW
HORNBEAM CL.
BRABOURNE HGTS.
AUSTELL GDS.
THE REDDINGS
REDDINGS CL.
SUNNYFIELD
UPHILL RD.
TRETAWN PK.
TRETAWN GARDENS
LAWRENCE AV.
LAWRENCE GROVE
APEX CORNER
WATFORD WAY
A1
Pool
Playing Field
Riding School
Belmont Sch.
Belmont Farm
St. Mary's Abbey & Sch.
The Mill Field
Tennis Courts
DRAPERS' COTTAGE HOMES
CHALET ESTATE
St. Joseph's R.C. College
THE RIDGEWAY
B552
B1461
St. Paul's C. of E. Prim. Sch.
Sports Ground
Cricket Club
Pav.
Nursery
Cemetery
Medical Research Laboratory
Works
St. Vincent's Convent
St. Vincent's School
St. Vincent's R.C. Prim. Sch.
Wentworth Hall
Oakfields
14
SHAKESPEARE RD.
MILTON RD.
TENNYSON RD.
MARSHALE ESTATE
Mill Hill School
HIGH ST.
MILL HILL CIRCUS
VICTORIA RD.
BIRKBECK
BYRON RD.
MARION RD.
HAMMERS LANE
MILL HILL
Playing Field
Ten. Cts.
DAWS LANE
WILLS GROVE
Tennis Court
Ridgeway Ho.
Pavilion
HOLLIES END
VINERIES BANK
MILESPIT HILL
Play. Fld.
The Mount Sch.
Drivers Hill
Watch Tower House
BITTACY PK.
M1 MOTORWAY
THE BROADWAY
Hall
MONTEREY PL. SHOPPING CEN.
Lib.
HARTLEY AV.
FLOWER LANE
Sub.
Garden Centre
Burton Bank
School Park
Featherstone Hill
ARRANDENE OPEN SPACE
Playground
WISE LANE
MILL HILL CEMETERY
RUSHDEN GDS.
WOODCOTE AV.
AVENUE
BITTACY RISE
Ten. Cts.
STANHOPE GDNS.
SYLVAN AV.
OAKLODGE WAY
WISTERIA CL.
Univ.
BARNET BY-PASS
WOODLAND WAY
Tennis Cts.
PARKMEAD GDS.
Cricket Ground
Tennis Courts
MILL HILL PARK
Mill Hill Broadway
GRANARD BUS. CEN.
Lyndhurst Park
LYNDHURST AV.
WOODCROFT AV.
Woodcroft Park
Sports Ground
Pavilion
GRAHAME PARK
BUNNS LANE
M1
RUDDY WAY
MILL HILL IND. EST.
PENTAVIA RETAIL PK.
THE RISE
PARKSIDE
HOLMDENE AV.
GLENMERE AV.
HILLSIDE GRO.
COPTHALL GDNS.
GRENFELL CT.
FEATHERSTONE RD.
MOORLANDS AV.
BROOKFIELD CRES.
BROOKFIELD AV.
Playing Field
Copthall School
TUDOR
HOLLAND CT.
PAGE MDW.
PURSLEY RD.
SALCOMBE
SANDERS LA.
BITTACY RD.
ENGEL PK.
Dollis Jun. & Inf. Schs.
GRANTS CL.
TAVISTOCK AV.
Chase Lodge
Playing Field
Pav.
Powerleague Soccer Centre
Tennis Courts
ROWLANDS
COLENSO
LONGFIELD AVENUE
Club House
Stadium
ASHLEY LANE
ABERDARE
Rugby Club
Copthall Swimming Pool
COPTHALL SPORTS CEN.
HENDON GOLF COURSE
28
Junc. 2
FIVEWAYS CORNER
Pavilion
WATFORD WAY
PAGE ST.
THE WLK.
CLAYTON FIELD
VANGUARD
SATCHELL MEAD
Play. Fld.
Tennis Courts
Hendon Sub. Coll.
MEAD WAY
SOUTH MEAD
LONG MEAD
Grahame Park
MOSTYN GROVE
STORKSMEAD RD.
MAPLE GDNS.
22
23
21

TOTTERIDGE COMMON
A5109
TOTTERIDGE
TOTTERIDGE VILLAGE
SOUTH HERTS GOLF COURSE
Club House
Brook Farm Open Space
Sports Ground
Pavilion
Fairlight Cottage
Hillsborough Cottage
Redings
Hillsdown
Montebello
Burnhams
Chestnut Cottages
The Warren
Copped Hall
Tennis Court
Hall
Waverley
Windyridge
Lyenells
The Croft
Prim. Sch.
Cricket Ground
Darland Lake Nature Reserve
Consolata Missionary College
Laurel Farm
Woodridge Prim. Sch.
Folly Farm
Burtonhole Lane Farm Estate
Nursery
Burtonhole Farm
Works
Oakfields
Partingdale Manor
Mill Hill Sub. Sta.
Riding School
Frith Manor Ho.
Frith Manor Prim. Sch.
FINCHLEY GOLF COURSE
Woodside Park Club
Tennis Courts
Club Ho.
Woodside Park
Sports Ground
Watch Tower House
Inglis Barracks
Depot
Bittacy Hill Park
Playgrd.
BITTACY BUSINESS CENTRE
Mill Hill East
Nether Court (Club House)
Dollis Brook
Folly Brook
West Finchley
Jun. & Inf. Schs.
Victoria Rec. Grd.
Bowling Green
Tennis Courts
Putting Green
Hendon Crematorium
HENDON CEMETERY
HENDON GOLF COURSE
Playing Fields
CHURCH END
FINCHLEY
B552
B1462
A598
RIDGEWAY
BITTACY HILL
DOLLIS ROAD
NETHER ST.
BALLARDS LANE
4
13
29
A B C D E
1 2 3 4 5 6 7
24
25
94
93
92
91

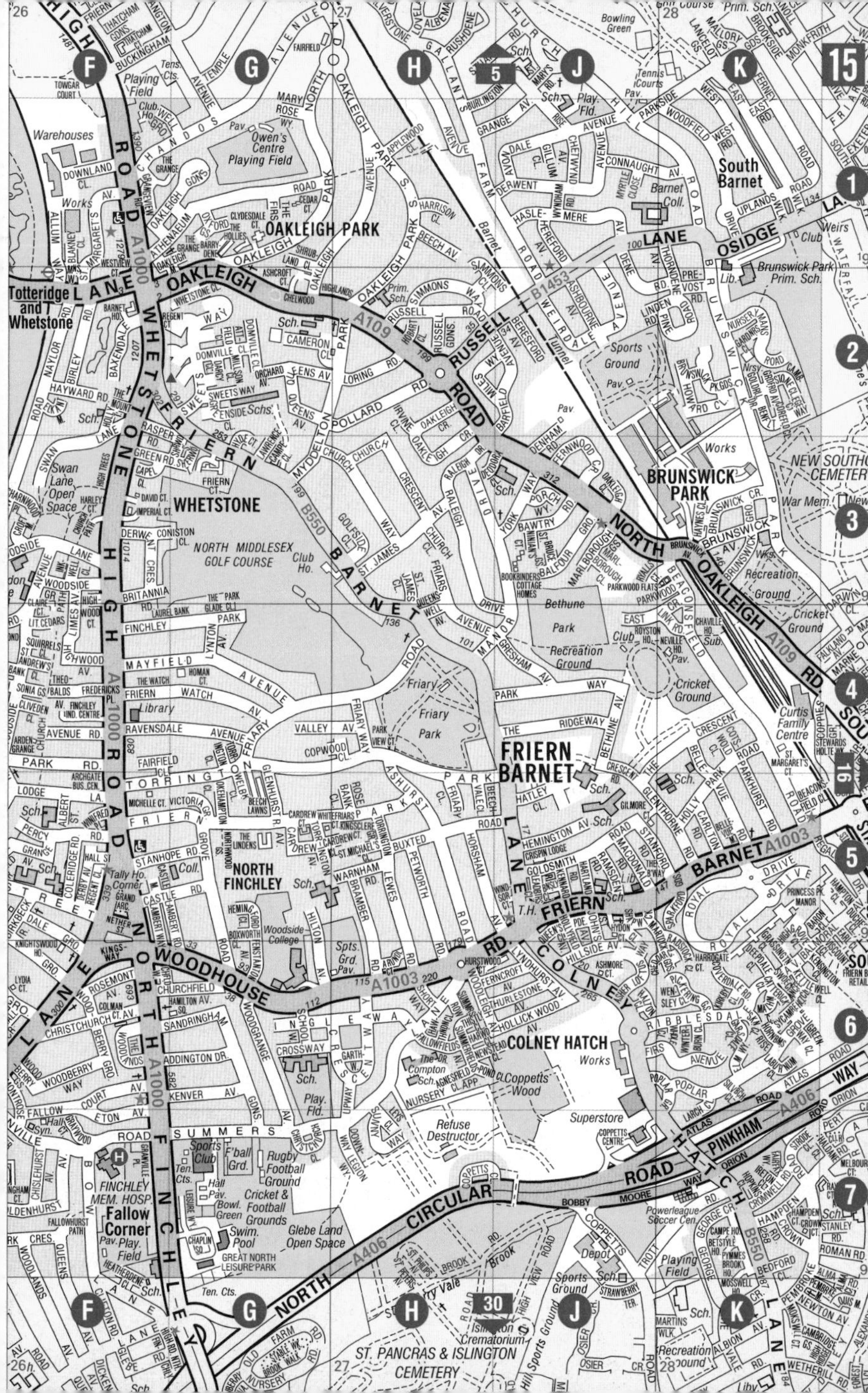

15
OAKLEIGH PARK
Totteridge and Whetstone
WHETSTONE
NORTH MIDDLESEX GOLF COURSE
South Barnet
BRUNSWICK PARK
NEW SOUTHGATE CEMETERY
FRIERN BARNET
NORTH FINCHLEY
COLNEY HATCH
Fallow Corner
FINCHLEY MEM. HOSP.
Friary Park
Bethune Park
Recreation Ground
Owen's Centre Playing Field
Glebe Land Open Space
ST. PANCRAS & ISLINGTON CEMETERY
Islington Crematorium
NORTH CIRCULAR
A406
A1000
A109
A1003
B550
B1453
16
30
5

A
B
C
D
E
1
2
3
4
5
6
7
29
530
6
31
15
SOUTHGATE
OSIDGE
NEW SOUTHGATE
Southgate
GROVELANDS PARK
Bourneside Sports Centre
GROVELANDS PRIORY HOSPITAL
Boating Lake
Pitch & Putt Course
Sports Grd.
Club Ho.
Southgate College
Ashmole Sch.
Osidge Prim. Sch.
Playing Fields
Tennis Courts
Morton Lodge
Southgate Cricket Club Ground
Cemetery
NEW SOUTHGATE CEMETERY
New Southgate Crematorium
Pymme's Brook
Cricket Ground
Factory
Curtis Family Centre
ARNOS PARK
Arnos Grove
Putting Green
Bowl. Green
Tennis Court
Broomfield Park
The Avenue
Bowling Greens
Sports Ground
Broomfield Sch.
Palmers Green
New Southgate
Superstore
Depot
Middlesex Univ.
Bounds Green
Scout Park
Bowes Park
Bowls & Tennis Club
MUSWELL HILL
GOLF
COURSE
Hollickwood Park
Recreation Ground
Club House
CLOCKHOUSE JUNCTION
A111
A1004
A1003
A1110
A109
A406
A105
B1453
B1452
B106
CHASE SIDE
THE BOURNE
BOURNE
WINCHMORE HILL ROAD
HIGH STREET
CANNON HILL
ALDERMANS HILL
WATERFALL ROAD
BOWES ROAD
TELFORD RD.
BOUNDS GREEN ROAD
NORTH CIRCULAR ROAD
WILMER WY.
POWYS LA.
BROWNLOW RD.
GREEN LANES
HIGH RD.
DURNSFORD ROAD
STATION RD.
ROAD

17
WINCHMORE HILL
Winchmore Hill
Prim. Sch.
PALMERS GREEN
TOTTENHAM
White Hart Lane
F
G
H
J
K
1
2
3
4
5
6
7
7
18
32
The Paulin Ground
Highfield Schs.
Winchmore Sch.
City Amenity Site
Clowes Sports Grd.
EDMONTON CEMETERY
Playing Fields
Firs Farm Prim. Sch.
Recreation Playground
Playing Field Latymer School
West Lea Sch.
Haselbury Jun. & Inf. Schs.
Tatem Rec. Grd.
Hollywood Gardens
Aylward School
GREAT CAMBRIDGE JUNCTION
Lib. Arts Cen. & Thtre
THE NORTH MIDDLESEX HOSP.
Wilbury Prim. Sch.
Pymme's Brook
New River
King's Arms Bri.
Sports Ground
Playing Fields
Selby Sports Cen.
Middlesex University
New River Sports and Recreation Centre
Football Ground
White Hart Lane Sch.
TOTTENHAM CEMETERY
BRUCE CASTLE PARK
Bruce Castle & Haringey Mus.
Bury Lodge Park
Nursery
A10
A105
A111
A406
A1080
B154
NORTH CIRCULAR ROAD
GREAT CAMBRIDGE ROAD
GREEN LANES
HEDGE LANE
STERLING WAY
CAMBRIDGE ROAD
THE ROUNDWAY
WHITE HART LANE
CHURCH STREET
BURY STREET
SILVER STREET
FIRS LANE

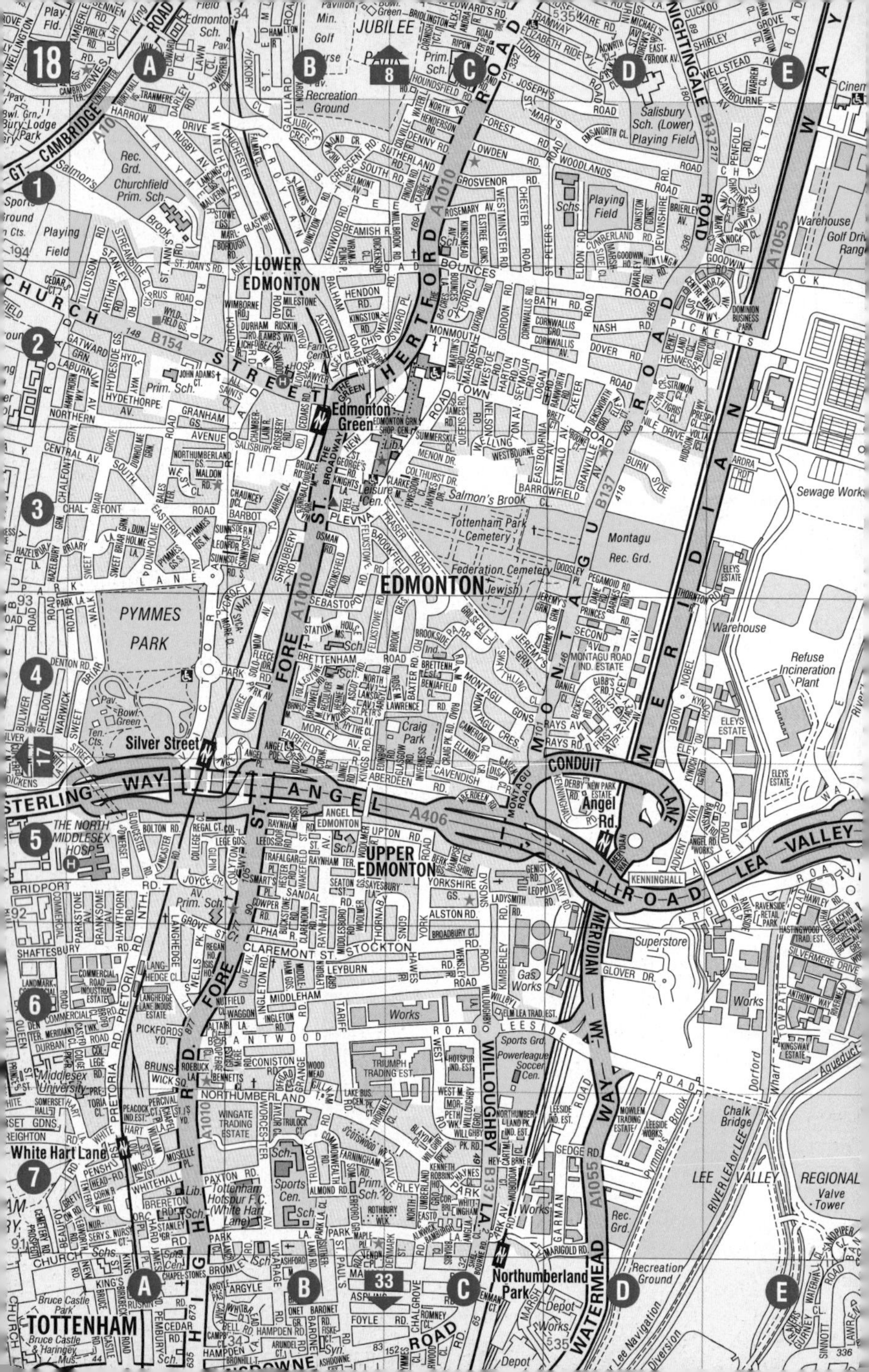

18
A
B
C
D
E
1
2
3
4
5
6
7
8
17
33
JUBILEE
Recreation Ground
Rec. Grd.
Churchfield Prim. Sch.
Playing Field
Salmon's Brook
LOWER EDMONTON
CHURCH STREET
B154
HERTFORD ROAD
A1010
Edmonton Green
Salisbury Sch. (Lower) Playing Field
Playing Field
NIGHTINGALE ROAD
B137
A1055
MERIDIAN WAY
Warehouse
Golf Drive Range
DOMINION BUSINESS PARK
PICKETTS LOCK
Sewage Works
Tottenham Park Cemetery
Montagu Rec. Grd.
Federation Cemetery (Jewish)
EDMONTON
MONTAGU ROAD
PYMMES PARK
FORE ST.
Silver Street
STERLING WAY
ANGEL ROAD
A406
CONDUIT LANE
Angel Rd.
LEA VALLEY ROAD
KENNINGHALL
Refuse Incineration Plant
ELEYS ESTATE
THE NORTH MIDDLESEX HOSP.
UPPER EDMONTON
Superstore
Gas Works
Works
Sports Grd.
Powerleague Soccer Cen.
TRIUMPH TRADING EST.
WINGATE TRADING ESTATE
WILLOUGHBY LA.
WATERMEAD WAY
Chalk Bridge
LEE VALLEY REGIONAL
RIVER LEA or LEE
Valve Tower
Lee Navigation Diversion
Pymme's Brook
Recreation Ground
Northumberland Park
Depot
White Hart Lane
Middlesex University
Tottenham Hotspur F.C. (White Hart Lane)
Sports Cen.
TOTTENHAM
Bruce Castle Park
Bruce Castle & Haringey Mus.
HIGH ROAD

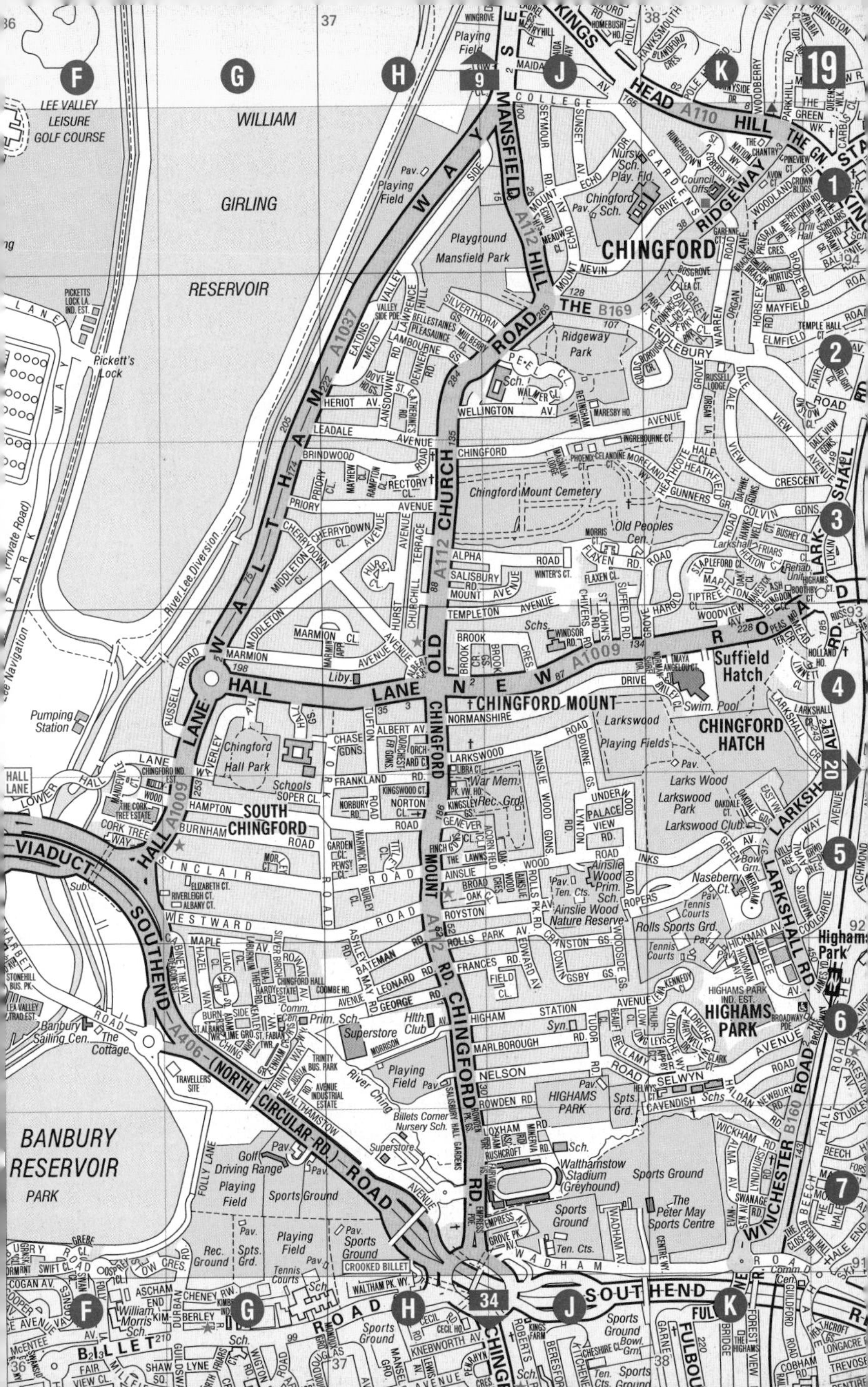

LEE VALLEY LEISURE GOLF COURSE
WILLIAM GIRLING RESERVOIR
Pickett's Lock
PICKETTS LOCK LA. IND. EST.
River Lee Diversion
Pumping Station
CHINGFORD
SOUTH CHINGFORD
CHINGFORD HATCH
CHINGFORD MOUNT
HIGHAMS PARK
BANBURY RESERVOIR
PARK
Playing Field
Playground
Mansfield Park
Ridgeway Park
Chingford Mount Cemetery
Old Peoples Cen.
Suffield Hatch
Swim. Pool
Larkswood Playing Fields
Larks Wood
Larkswood Park
Larkswood Club
Chingford Hall Park
Schools
War Mem. Rec. Grd.
Ainslie Wood Prim. Sch.
Ainslie Wood Nature Reserve
Rolls Sports Grd.
Tennis Courts
Naseberry Ct.
Superstore
Hlth. Club
Prim. Sch.
Comm. Cen.
River Ching
Billets Corner Nursery Sch.
Golf Driving Range
Sports Ground
Rec. Ground
Spts. Grd.
Walthamstow Stadium (Greyhound)
The Peter May Sports Centre
Banbury Sailing Cen.
The Cottage
TRAVELLERS SITE
CROOKED BILLET
WALTHAM WAY
MANSFIELD HILL
OLD CHURCH ROAD
NEW ROAD
HALL LANE
CHINGFORD MOUNT RD.
CHINGFORD RD.
LARKSHALL RD.
WINCHESTER ROAD
KINGS HEAD HILL
THE RIDGEWAY
THE ENDLEBURY
NORTH CIRCULAR RD.
SOUTHEND ROAD
VIADUCT
A1037
A112
A1009
A110
B169
A406
B160
9
20
34
F G H J K
1 2 3 4 5 6 7
36 37 38
Higham Park

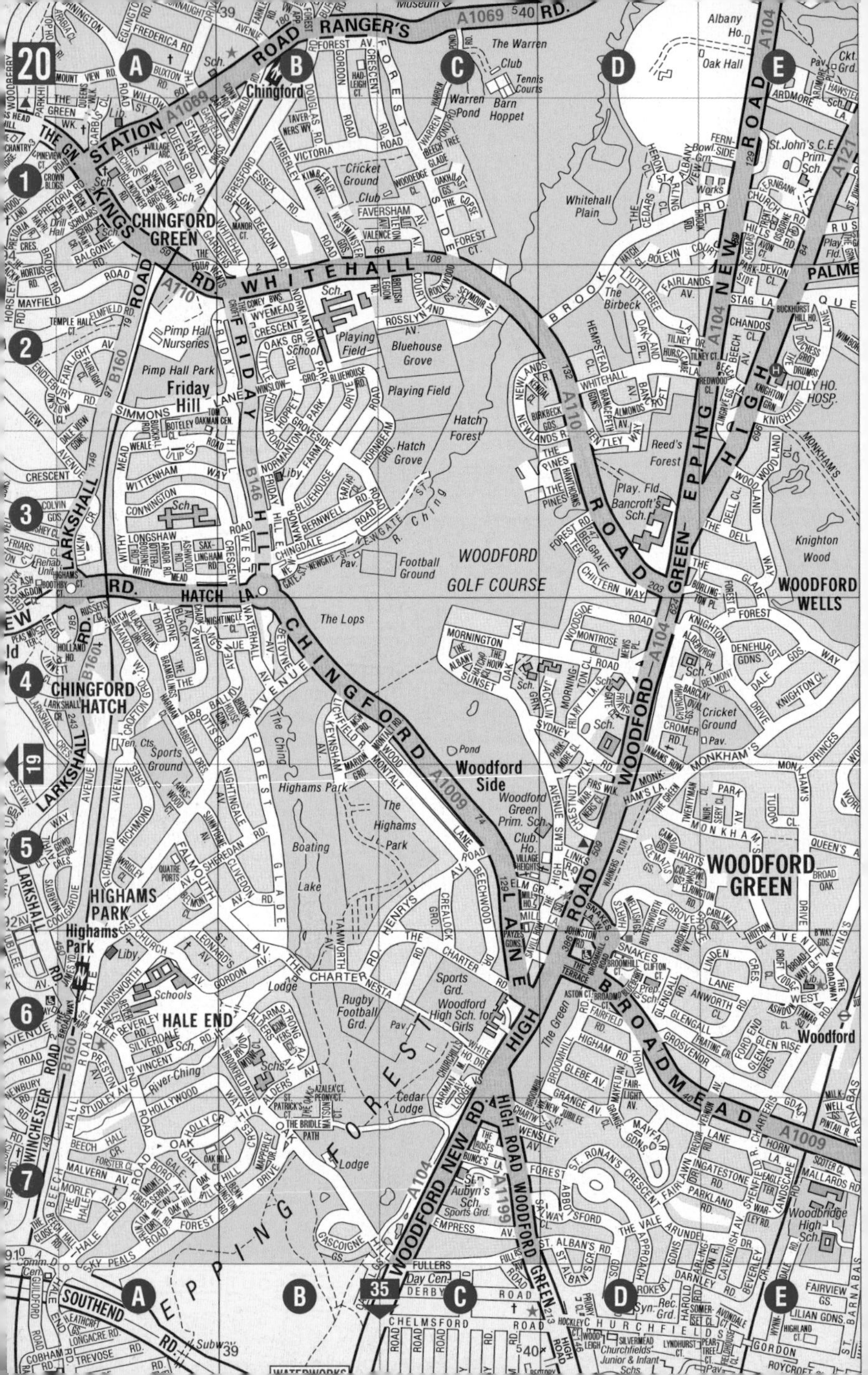

CHINGFORD GREEN
Chingford
RANGER'S RD.
STATION ROAD
KINGS RD.
WHITEHALL RD.
FRIDAY HILL
Friday Hill
Pimp Hall Park
Pimp Hall Nurseries
The Warren
Warren Pond
Barn Hoppet
Cricket Ground
Whitehall Plain
Bluehouse Grove
Playing Field
Hatch Forest
Hatch Grove
The Birbeck
Reed's Forest
Bancroft's Sch.
WOODFORD GOLF COURSE
The Lops
HATCH LA.
CHINGFORD LANE
Football Ground
CHINGFORD HATCH
LARKSHALL RD.
Sports Ground
The Ching
Highams Park
The Highams Park
Boating Lake
Woodford Side
Woodford Green Prim. Sch.
WOODFORD WELLS
Knighton Wood
WOODFORD GREEN
HIGHAMS PARK
HALE END
Rugby Football Grd.
Woodford High Sch. for Girls
Cedar Lodge
EPPING FOREST
WOODFORD NEW RD.
HIGH ROAD WOODFORD GREEN
BROADMEAD RD.
St. Aubyn's Sch.
Woodbridge High Sch.
Woodford
SOUTHEND RD.
CHELMSFORD ROAD
Churchfields Junior & Infant Sch.
HOLLY HO. HOSP.
A
B
C
D
E
1
2
3
4
5
6
7
19
35

F
G
H
J
K
1
2
3
4
5
6
7
43
42
94
93
92
91
Recreation Ground
RODING VALLEY MEADOWS NATURE RESERVE
RODING VALLEY NATURE RESERVE
Lake
David Lloyd Leisure
Ten Cts.
Playing Field
Pav.
College
M11
M11 MOTORWAY
Wakes Hall
RODING LANE
Rodings
CHIGWELL
B170
LEE GROVE
RISE
CHESTER
BROOK RISE
GREAT OWL RD.
BARNABY
DICKENS
Chigwell
COOLGARDIE AV.
CHIGWELL PARK DR.
LYNDHURST RISE
TUDOR CL.
ROAD
A113
CHIGWELL GOLF COURSE
Club House
HATCH SIDE
FOREST LANE
ST. JOHN'S R.C Sch.
ELY PLACE
Convent
Lodge
HIGH ROAD
FOREST TER.
ST. MARY'S WY.
EMMAUS WAY
TURPIN'S LA.
West Hatch High School
Hill House
Playing Fields
LANE
LUXBOROUGH
New Barns Farm
Old Loughtonians Hockey Club
Works
Luxborough
Chigwell Sewage Works
Lake
River Roding
Buckhurst Hill Prim. Sch.
Playing Field
Sports Grd.
Rec. Grd.
RODING RD.
BUCKHURST HILL
Buckhurst Hill
LORD'S BUSHES
Playground
Roding Valley
STATION WAY
FARM WAY
FOREST
AVENUE
WALNUT WAY
CHESTNUT
HORNBEAM
SQUIRRELS LA.
BUCKHURST WAY
CHERRY TREE RISE
Play. Fld.
Bowling Green
Sports Grd.
Tennis Courts
Ray Ho.
Ray Park
Sports Ground
Ray Lodge Prim. Sch.
Gas Works
Football Grd.
WOODFORD
SNAKES LANE
THE RODINGS
DANBURY WAY
RAYLEIGH
ST. ANTHONY'S
SPRING GS.
ROAD
CHIGWELL
Playing Field
NAVESTOCK
WANSFORD ROAD
Winn Bridge
BROADMEAD
River Roding
Dartnalls Playing Field
EAST
A113
CHALFORD WK.
Sewage Works
Cemetery
Sports Ground
Sports
RODING LANE
Playing
WOODFORD BRIDGE
Roding Prim. Sch.
MANOR ROAD
B173
CHIGWELL ROAD
Orchard House
Claybury Hall
Egg Clump
Cocked Hat Plantation
Ash Plantation
Claybury Hospital Woods Nature Reserve
Forest House
Hospital Hill Wood
Hospital Hill
Eden Health Club
ROSEBURY SQUARE
BRANDESBURY SQUARE
TOMSWOOD ROAD
STRADBROKE DR.
CLARENCE
GATE
ROAD
36
Tennis Courts
Playing Fields
WALTHAM
UPLANDS
CANFIELD
HIGHFIELD
VICARAGE
NORTH
GAYNES HILL RD.
Hill Fm.
Swim. Pool
GUYS RETREAT
THE DRIVE
ROEBUCK LANE
LUCTONS AV.
AMBERLEY RD.
THE MEADWAY
SCOTLAND RD.
PALACE GDS.
STRADBROKE
LITTLE PLUCKETT'S WAY
WESTBURY
Liby.
PRINCES
QUEEN'S RD.
THAXTED
BLACKMORE RD.
GREENSTED RD.
ROYDON CL.
RIVER RD.
DENE RD.
HURST RD.

06
07
08
A
B
C
D
E
1
2
3
4
5
6
7
91
90
89
88
Battlers Wells Wood
Shepherds Hill Farm
Shepherds Hill House
John Penrose School
NORTHWOOD ROAD
GROVE
HAREFIELD
Furzefield
Deadman's Grove
Ashain Spring
Scarlet Spring
Raveners Spring
Badminton Shooting Ground
Knightscote Farm & Agricultural Museum
Kiln Pond
Claypits
Dell
Duck's Hill Farm
Ducks Hill Grange
Duck's Hill
Ashby Cottages
Ashby Farm
DUCK'S HILL ROAD
A4180
JACKETS LANE
HURST PL.
MANOR HOUSE DR.
NEAL DR.
VEAGH CL.
DRAKES DR.
FARM END
KINGFISHER CL.
RINGEWOOD CL.
NORTHGATE
SEVENOAKS CT.
BUTTSMEAD
THE COVERT
WOOD WAY
SILVER WOOD CL.
LINKS WAY
COPSE WOOD WAY
OAK GLADE
NICHOLAS WAY
ROGERS RUFF
LOWSWOOD CL.
COPSE CL.
THE BROADWAY
COPSE WOOD
BREAKSPEAR ROAD
Bourne Farm
Breakspear House
Middle Lodge
Nature Reserve
Warren Farm
NORTH RIDING WOOD
YOUNG WOOD
MAD BESS WOOD
Mad Bess Wood Cottage
Youngwood Farm
RUISLIP COMMON
Breakspear Crematorium (Ruislip)
The Lodge
Football Ground
WITHY LA.
BURY
CHELMSINE CT.
BAYHURST WOOD COUNTRY PARK
Willow Tree Farm
Lower Lodge
The Bungalow
The Bungalow
HARVIL ROAD
NEWYEARS GREEN LANE
FINE BUSH LA.
Oak Cottage
St. Leonard's Farm
Pylon Farm
Elm Tree Farm
High View Farm
Highway Farm
Newyears Green
Braemar Farm
Dewes Farm Cotts.
Crows Nest Farm
Old Clack Farm
Newyears Green Covert
BREAKSPEAR ROAD NORTH
BREAKSPEAR ROAD SOUTH
TILE KILN LANE
The Corner
Tile Kiln
Grays Cottages
Dunster Cottage
HOWLETTS LA.
BRICKETT CL.
STOWE CR.
WYTELEAF CL.
ALLINGTON CT.
ST. CATHERINE'S FARM CT.
LEAHOLME WY.
CHERWELL CT.
FLEET CL.
MAYFLOWER DR.
WAYBORNE GRO.
THAMES CL.
WYE CL.
ISIS CL.
STANFORD CL.
LADYGATE LA.
WESTWOOD CL.
WEST WOOD CL.
Whiteheath Jun. & Inf. Schs.
ALLONBY DR.
EAMONT CL.
GREYSTOKE DR.
GLOVERS GROVE
SANDALWOOD DRIVE
LARKSPUR CL.
WHITEHEATH AV.
RAVENS CT. CL.
ARDLEY CL.
GRASMERE AV.
FAIRFIELD CL.
ELLESMERE CL.
WESTCOTE RISE
WOODVILLE GS.
HEATHFIELD RI.
ORCHARD CL.
HILL FARM COTTS.
FIELD WY.
FIELD END
Playground
CLACK LANE
HILL LANE
BOSTON GR.
STANDALE GROVE
BURY AV.
MARLBOROUGH AV.
SKIP LANE
Works
Depot
Birch Farm
40
Gatemead Farm
Brackenbury Barn

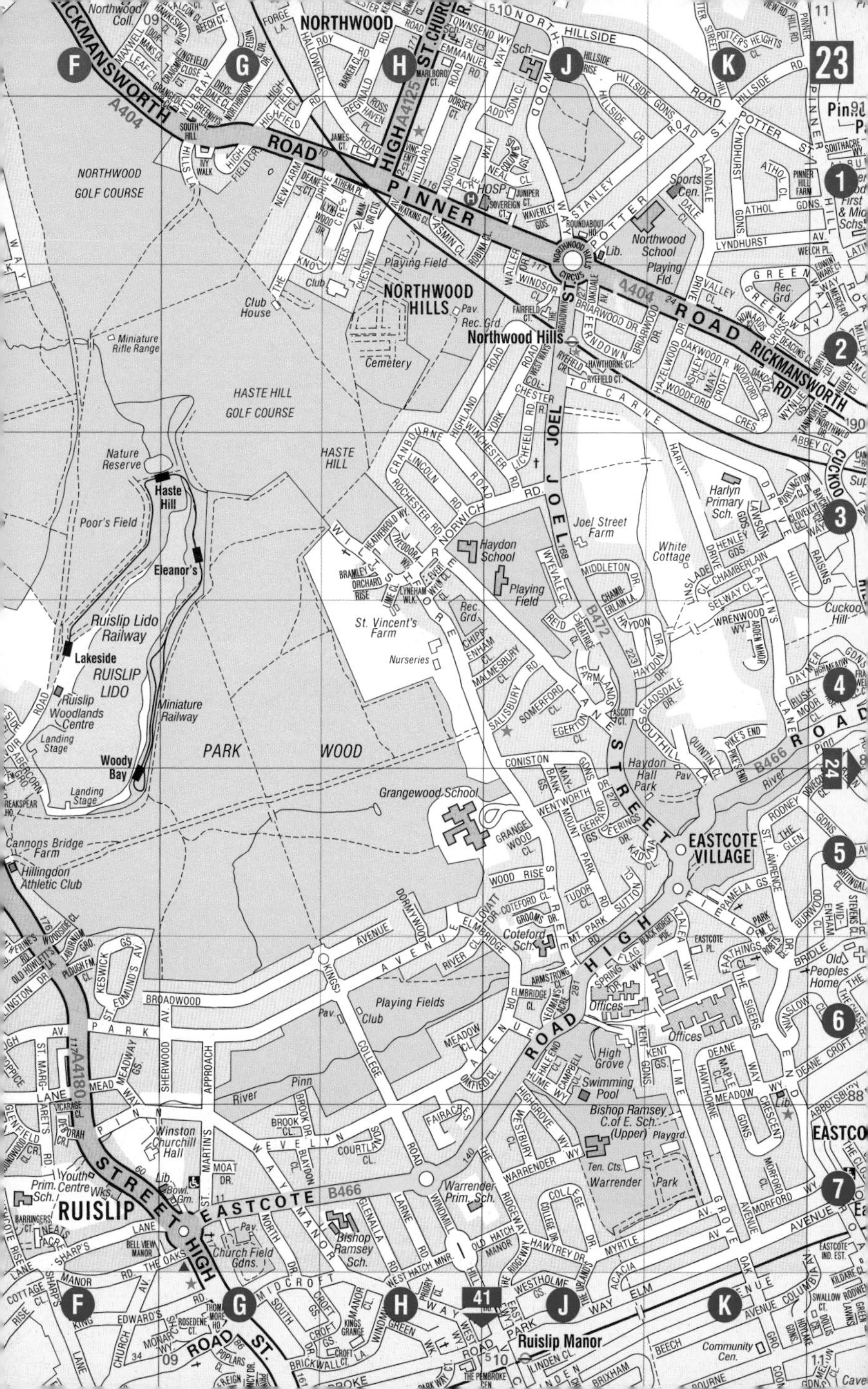

23
NORTHWOOD
Northwood Coll.
RICKMANSWORTH
A404
ROAD
PINNER
HIGH
A4125
ST. CHURCH
NORTHWOOD GOLF COURSE
NORTHWOOD HILLS
Northwood Hills
Playing Field
Club House
Miniature Rifle Range
Cemetery
HASTE HILL GOLF COURSE
HASTE HILL
Nature Reserve
Haste Hill
Poor's Field
Eleanor's
Ruislip Lido Railway
Lakeside
RUISLIP LIDO
Ruislip Woodlands Centre
Landing Stage
Miniature Railway
Woody Bay
PARK
WOOD
Cannons Bridge Farm
Hillingdon Athletic Club
Grangewood School
HOSP.
Lib.
Northwood School
Playing Fld.
Sports Cen.
A4404
ROAD
RICKMANSWORTH RD.
JOEL ST.
JOEL
B472
Haydon School
Playing Field
Rec. Grd.
St. Vincent's Farm
Nurseries
Joel Street Farm
White Cottage
Harlyn Primary Sch.
Cuckoo Hill
Haydon Hall Park
EASTCOTE VILLAGE
STREET
B466
ROAD
River Pinn
Coteford Sch.
Playing Fields
Club
Pav.
Offices
High Grove
Swimming Pool
Bishop Ramsey C.of E. Sch. (Upper)
Warrender Park
Ten. Cts.
Warrender Prim. Sch.
Bishop Ramsey Sch.
Winston Churchill Hall
Youth Centre
Prim. Sch.
RUISLIP
EASTCOTE
STREET
HIGH
A4180
Church Field Gdns.
Old Peoples Home
Lib.
EASTCOTE IND. EST.
Ruislip Manor
Community Cen.
41
24
F
G
H
J
K
1
2
3
4
5
6
7
09
10
11

PINNER HILL GOLF COURSE
A
B
C
D
E
1
2
3
4
5
6
7
Pinnerwood Park
Pinner Wood First & Mid. Schs.
PINNER GREEN
Playing Field
UXBRIDGE ROAD
A404
HATCH END
Superstore
Liby.
Rugby Football Ground
PINNER PARK
Pinner Park Farm
ST. THOMAS' DR.
GEORGE V
AVENUE
River Pinn
Tennis Courts
Little Common
Cemetery
CUCKOO HILL
B466
HIGH RD.
Cuckoo Hill
West Lodge Schs.
Pinner Village Hall
Pinner Memorial Park
Innellan Ho. Sch.
Pinner
PINNER
Reddiford Sch.
Nower Hill
Pinner New Cemetery
Nower Hill High Sch.
Woodlands Open Space
Pinner Village Gardens (Rec. Grd.)
North Harrow
Yeading Brook Open Space
Old Peoples Home
The Croft
Play. Fld.
Cannon Lane First & Mid. Schs.
Heathfield Sch.
Streamside Rec. Grd.
Longfield Schs.
EASTCOTE
Eastcote
Roxborough Rough
Playground
Roxbourne
Rayners Lane
RAYNERS LANE
ALEXANDRA AV.
IMPERIAL
A4090
Sports Ground
Cavendish Recreation
23
42

25
10
26
43
14
15
16
F
G
H
J
K
1
2
3
4
5
6
7
HARROW WEALD
Headstone Lane
Headstone Manor
Harrow Museum & Heritage Cen.
Headstone Manor Recreation Ground
Sports Ground
Model Railway
Tennis Courts
Pinner Park Schs.
Cedars Schs.
High Sch.
First & Mid. Sch.
Salvatorian Coll.
Harrow Crown Court
The Cliveden Cen.
Harrow & Wealdstone
WEALDSTONE
Belmont First & Mid. Schs.
Recreation Ground
Swimming Pool
Leisure Cen.
Harrow Cycling and Safety C
Library
Civic Centre
HEADSTONE
Sports Grd.
GREENHILL
Superstore
Harrow Recreation Ground
Harrow Cemetery
NORTH HARROW
Vaughan Schs.
West Harrow
WEST HARROW
Rec. Grd.
Whitmore High Sch.
Cricket Ground
Harrow-on-the-Hill
Bus Sta.
St. George's Shop. & Leis. Cen.
St. Ann's Shopping Cen.
The Grove Open Space
HARROW
Harrow Hill Golf Course
Miniature Rifle Range
Playing Fields
Music Sch.
Parade Ground
Harrow School Playing Fields
Harrow Sch.
Mus.
Liby.
Yeading Brook
Weald Schs.
Rec. Ground
Bus Depot
Works
A409
A404
A312
B457
HIGH ROAD
ELMES
COLLEGE AV.
MOUNTSIDE
LONG ELMES
HEADSTONE LANE
PINNER PARK
HARROW VIEW
WEALD
HEADSTONE GS.
HEADSTONE DR.
PINNER VIEW
PARKSIDE WAY
KINGSFIELD AV.
CANTERBURY RD.
STATION ROAD
ST. GEORGE GANGE WAY
HIGH MEAD
SHEEPCOTE RD.
ROXBOROUGH PK.
LOWLANDS RD.
KENTON RD.
GROVE HILL
PETERBOROUGH RD.
BESSBOROUGH RD.
PINNER ROAD
VAUGHAN ROAD
WHITMORE ROAD
SHAFTESBURY AV.
RIDGEWAY
DRIVE
WELLDON CRES.
GAYTON ROAD
MARLBOROUGH HILL
HINDES RD.
SUSSEX ROAD
COLLEGE ROAD
WHITEFRIARS AV.
BYRON ROAD
STUART ROAD
CHRISTCHURCH AVENUE
FORWARD DR.
MASONS AV.
HERGA RD.
ROSSLYN CR.
BUTLER AV.
CHURCH HILL
FOOTBALL LA.

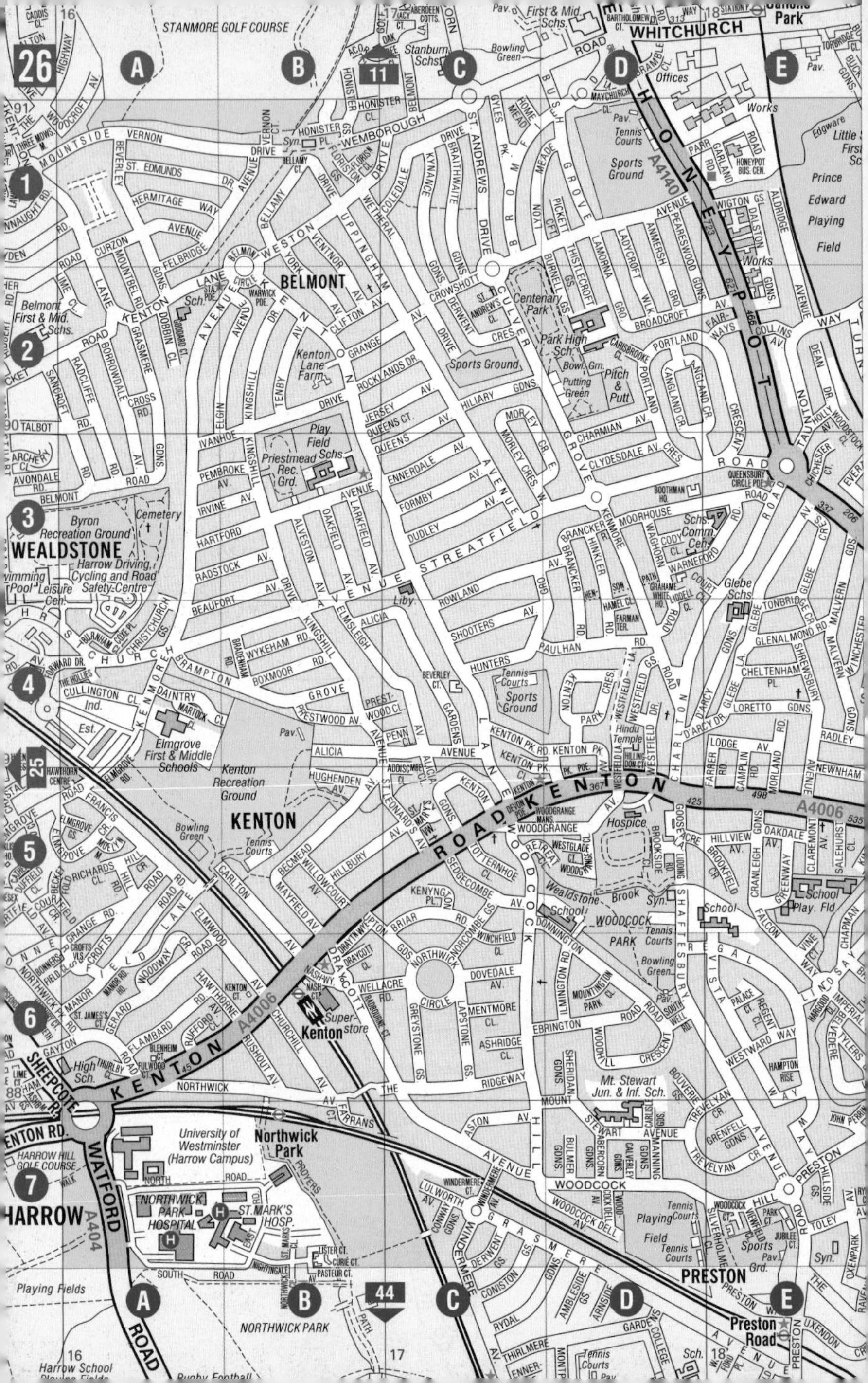

26
A
B
C
D
E
11
44
25
1
2
3
4
5
6
7
STANMORE GOLF COURSE
WHITCHURCH
Canons Park
Stanburn Schs.
First & Mid. Schs.
Offices
Works
Prince Edward Playing Field
Sports Ground
HONEYPOT
A4140
BELMONT
Belmont First & Mid. Schs.
Centenary Park
Park High Sch.
Pitch & Putt
Putting Green
Kenton Lane Farm
Sports Ground
Priestmead Rec. Grd.
Play. Field Schs.
WEALDSTONE
Byron Recreation Ground
Cemetery
Harrow Driving, Cycling and Road Safety Centre
Leisure Cen.
Liby.
Schs. Comm. Cen.
Glebe Schs.
Elmgrove First & Middle Schools
Kenton Recreation Ground
KENTON
Bowling Green
Tennis Courts
Hindu Temple
Hospice
Wealdstone Brook
WOODCOCK PARK
School
School Play. Fld
KENTON ROAD
A4006
Superstore
Kenton
High Sch.
Mt. Stewart Jun. & Inf. Sch.
University of Westminster (Harrow Campus)
Northwick Park
NORTHWICK PARK HOSPITAL
ST. MARK'S HOSP.
HARROW HILL GOLF COURSE
HARROW
WATFORD ROAD
A404
Playing Fields
NORTHWICK PARK
Playing Field
PRESTON
Preston Road
16
17
18
Harrow School Playing Fields

LITTLE STANMORE
Chandos Recreation Ground
BURNT OAK
Burnt Oak
Watling
WATLING PARK
12
Sports Ground
Canons High Sch.
QUEENSBURY
Queensbury
Superstore
BOWMAN TRADING ESTATE
EDGWARE
BROADWAY
Montrose Recreation Ground
COLINDALE HOSPITAL
COLINDALE
COLINDEEP LA.
EUROPEAN BUSINESS CENTRE
COLINDALE BUSINESS PARK
CAPITOL INDUSTRIAL PARK
YAOHAN PLAZA
Roe Green
Recreation Ground
Kingsbury High Sch. Play. Fld.
Roe Grn. Jun. & Inf. Sch.
Kingsbury Manor
Roe Green Park
Kingsbury Manor Studio
KINGSBURY
ROAD
Kingsbury
Police Cadet Training Centre
Sports Ground
Kingsbury Grn. Prim. Sch.
St. Robert Sothwell Sch.
KINGSBURY TRADING ESTATE
Kingsbury Green
Rec. Grd.
Silver Jubilee Park
FRYENT COUNTRY PARK
A4140
A4006
A5
B454
Barn Hill Open Space
Pond
Barn Hill
Field Study Centre
Woodfield Sch.
45
28
F G H J K
1 2 3 4 5 6 7
19 20 21 88 89

Grahame Park
COLINDALE
Colindale
COLINDALE HOSPITAL
Colindale Park
Library
Peel Centre (Metropolitan Police Training Establishment)
Sports Ground
R.A.F. Museum Hendon
Battle of Britain Hall
High Sch.
Hendon Sub. Coll.
Play Field
Tennis Courts
COPTHALL SPORTS CENTRE
Copthall Swimming Pool
Rugby Club
Stadium
Club House
Hasmonean High Sch.
Junction 2
FIVEWAYS CORNER
13
GREAT (BARNET-BY-PASS)
A1
HENDON GOLF COURSE
SUNNY HILL PARK
Playing Fields
Rugby Club
SUNNY GARDENS PDE.
WATFORD WAY
A41
M1 MOTORWAY
COLINDEEP LANE
A5150
M1
EDGWARE ROAD
THE HYDE
A5
Rushgrove Park
Silk Stream
THE HYDE IND. EST.
Superstore
GARRICK INDUSTRIAL ESTATE
KINGSBURY RD.
A4006
HENDON
Middlesex University
St. Mary's C. of E. High Sch.
Museum
Comm. Cen.
THE GARDEN HOSP
BURROUGHS
CHURCH RD.
BRENT ST.
A502
PARSON ST.
B552
QUEENS RD.
B551
Hendon Central
HENDON PARK
Malcolm Park
Hendon
STATION ROAD
A504
WEST HENDON PLAYING FIELDS
Silver Jubilee Park
Brent Reservoir
York Park
Youth Sailing Base
Cool Oak Bridge
COOL OAK LANE
BROADWAY
MOTORWAY
Junc. 1
BRENT CROSS INTERCHANGE
BRENT CROSS SHOPPING CENTRE
Brent Cross
A406 NORTH CIRCULAR ROAD
PRINCE CHARLES DRIVE
WEST HENDON
46
27
WOODFIELD PARK
Rifle Range
BRENT RESERVOIR
STAPLES CORNER
CLAREMONT WAY INDUSTRIAL ESTATE
Depot

29
14
30
47
FINCHLEY
Victoria Rec. Grd.
Bowling Green
Tennis Courts
Putting Green
CHURCH END
Finchley Central
School
Liby.
Pentland Centre
Avenue House Grounds
Sports Ground
Tennis Courts
Play. Fld. Club Ho.
Mus.
St. Marylebone Crematorium
ST. MARYLEBONE CEMETERY
Christ's College
Playing Field
Schs.
Hendon Crematorium
HENDON CEMETERY
HENDON GOLF COURSE
Holders Hill
Windsor Open Space
College
Playing Fields
College Farm
Prim. Sch.
HENLYS CORNER
Mutton Brook
Bowl Grn.
Little Wood
Club
Big Wood
Willifred Green
The Decoy
Monastery
Brent Park Syn.
Temple Fortune
Princes Park
Jewish Cemetery
Kisharon Sch.
GOLDERS GREEN
Golders Green Crematorium
HAMPSTEAD
HEATH
Works
Bus Term.
Golders Green
Brent Cross
Superstores
Sprts. Cen.
Hendon Sch.
Play. Fld.
Tennis Courts
DOLLIS ROAD
NETHER ST.
BALLARDS LANE
REGENTS PARK ROAD
EAST END ROAD
HENDON LANE
HENDON WAY
NORTH CIRCULAR ROAD
FALLODEN WAY
FINCHLEY ROAD
GOLDERS GREEN ROAD
HENDON WAY
NORTH END RD.
HOLDERS HILL ROAD
A1
A406
A504
A598
A502
B552
B1462
F
G
H
J
K
1
2
3
4
5
6
7
24
25
26
88
89
90
91

30
A
B
C
D
E
1
2
3
4
5
6
7
26
27
28
91
90
89
88
15
29
48
FINCHLEY MEM. HOSP.
Fallow Corner
Play. Field
Cricket & Football Grounds
Glebe Open Space
GREEN NORTH LEISURE PARK
Ten. Cts.
NORTH CIRCULAR ROAD
BOBBY MOORE WAY
COLNEY HATCH
Powerleague Soccer Cen.
Depot
Playing Field
Sports Ground
Strawberry Vale
Brook
Islington Crematorium
Muswell Hill Sports Ground
Recreation Ground
HIGH RD. NTH. FINCHLEY
A1000
A406
HIGH ROAD
ST. PANCRAS & ISLINGTON CEMETERY
COLDFALL WOOD
Coldfall Prim. Sch.
Martin Jun. & Inf. School
Fortismere Sch.
EAST FINCHLEY
EAST END ROAD
A504
FORTIS GREEN
FORTIS GREEN
MARYLEBONE CEMETERY
Oak Lodge Sch.
East Finchley
NATIONAL HOSP. FOR NEUROLOGY
Cherry Tree Wood
Rec. Grd.
ST. LUKE'S WOODSIDE HOSP.
St. James C.E. Prim. Sch.
LYTTELTON ROAD
AYLMER ROAD
A1
GREAT NORTH RD.
HAMPSTEAD GARDEN SUBURB
Playing Fields
Stormont Lawn Tennis & Squash Club
HIGHGATE WOOD
HIGHGATE GOLF COURSE
Club House
HIGHGATE PRIVATE HOSP.
NORTH HILL
ARCHWAY RD.
B519
B550
HAMPSTEAD GOLF COURSE
Bunkers Hill
HAMPSTEAD HEATH
Turners Wood
HAMPSTEAD LANE
North Wood
Kenwood House
ATHLONE HOUSE
HIGHGATE
Highgate Jun. Sch.
Playing Field
Sports Ground
Prim. Sch.
The Spaniards
SOUTHWOOD LANE
NORTH RD.

29
31
16
32
49
30
F
G
H
J
K
1
2
3
4
5
6
7
MUSWELL HILL GOLF COURSE
Club House
Recreation Ground
Tennis Courts
Pool
ALBERT RD.
DURNSFORD RD.
BOUNDS GREEN RD.
A109
A105
HIGH ROAD
WOOD GREEN
Wood Green
Shopping City
Alexandra Palace
Blandford Hall
Football Ground
The Lake
Alexandra Pavilion
ALEXANDRA PARK
ALEXANDRA PALACE
Cricket Ground
Reservoir
Filter Beds
Playing Field
Gas Works
Middlesex Univ. (Quicksilver Pl. Campus)
Wood Gn. Common Hall
Depot
STATION RD.
MAYES RD.
PARK RD.
HORNSEY PARK RD.
B138
B151
TURNPIKE LA.
Hornsey
HORNSEY
HORNSEY HIGH ST.
A504
PRIORY RD.
PRIORY PARK
MUSWELL HILL
MUSWELL HILL
ALEXANDRA PARK RD.
B106
B550
DUKE'S AV.
The Grove
Muswell Hill Jun. & Inf. Schs.
Cranley Gardens
QUEEN'S WOOD
HORNSEY CENTRAL HOSPITAL
Swim. Pool
Cricket Ground
Playing Fields
Tennis Courts
Sports Gd.
PARK RD.
A1201
TOTTENHAM LA.
A103
CHURCH LA.
HORNSEY VALE
Stationers Park
Town Hall
The Broadway
CROUCH END
Sports Field
CROUCH END HILL
CROUCH HILL
Crouch Hill
Rec. Cen.
Covered Reservoir
STROUD GREEN
STROUD GRN. RD.
Parkland Walk
Highgate
SHEPHERD'S HILL
A1
HORNSEY LANE
ARCHWAY RD.
B540
HORNSEY RISE
HIGHGATE HILL
HIGH ST.

32
A
B
C
D
E
1
2
3
4
5
6
7
17
31
50
33
TOTTENHAM
TOTTENHAM CEMETERY
WOOD GREEN
Wood Green
NOEL PARK
LORDSHIP RECREATION GROUND
Open Air Theatre
The Moselle
BROADWATER FARM ESTATE
DOWNHILLS PARK
WEST GREEN
HORNSEY
Hornsey
HARRINGAY
Harringay
Harringay Green Lanes
ST. ANN'S HOSPITAL
Chestnuts Rec. Ground
SOUTH TOTTENHAM
Stamford Hill
STROUD GREEN
FINSBURY PARK
Sports Arena
MANOR HOUSE
Manor House
EAST RESERVOIR
WEST RESERVOIR
Sir Thomas Abney Prim. Sch.
LORDSHIP LANE
A109
THE ROUNDWAY
A1080
WESTBURY AVENUE
DOWNHILLS WAY
B155
WEST GREEN ROAD
A504
PHILIP LANE
GREEN LANES
A105
GRAND PARADE
ST. ANN'S ROAD
B152
SEVEN SISTERS ROAD
A503
AMHURST
A107
WIGHTMAN ROAD
B138
TURNPIKE LA.
ENDYMION ROAD
B150
HERMITAGE ROAD

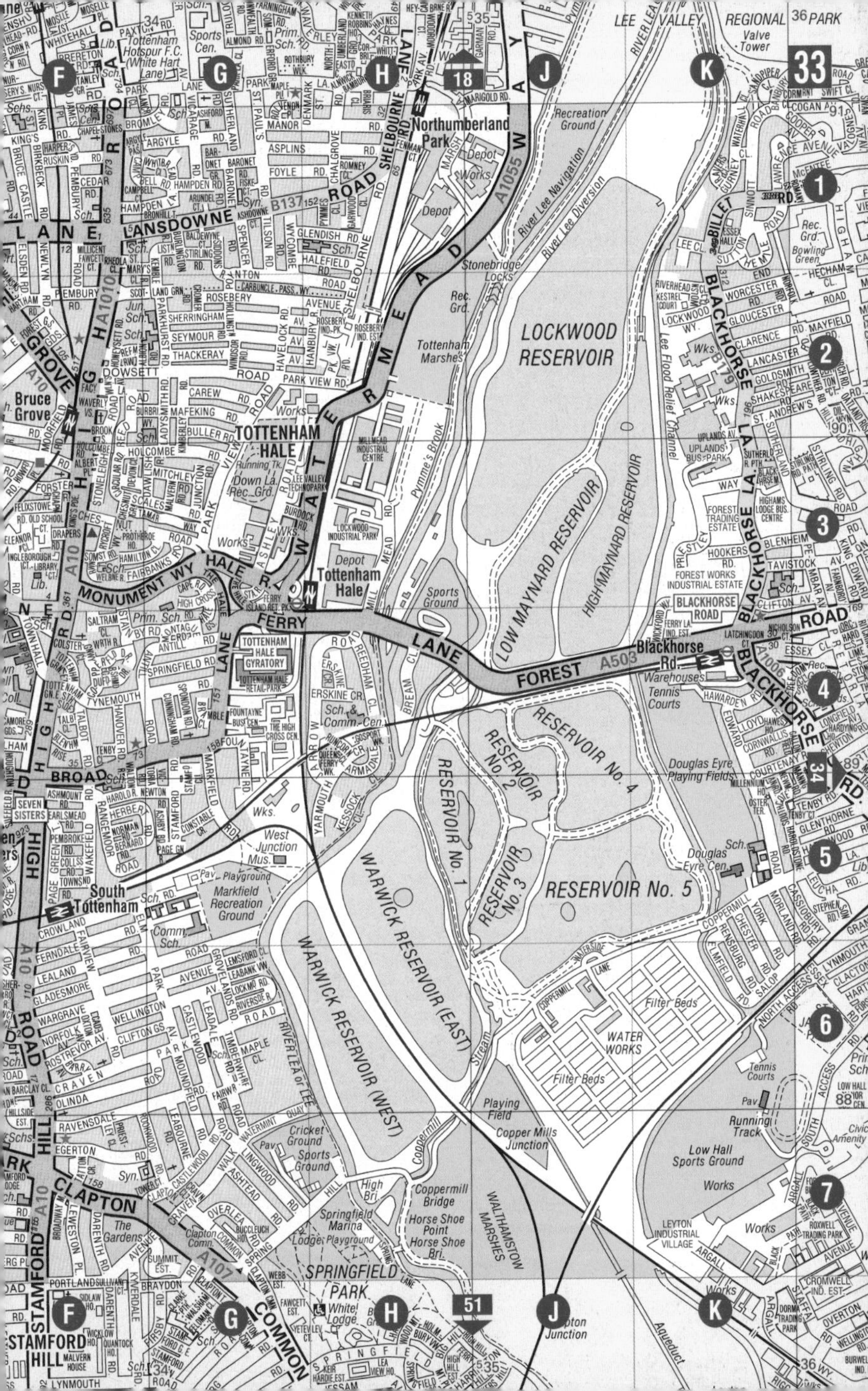
LEE VALLEY REGIONAL PARK
Valve Tower
Tottenham Hotspur F.C. (White Hart Lane)
Northumberland Park
Recreation Ground
River Lee Navigation
River Lee Diversion
Stonebridge Locks
LOCKWOOD RESERVOIR
Lee Flood Relief Channel
Tottenham Marshes
TOTTENHAM HALE
Tottenham Hale
Bruce Grove
LOW MAYNARD RESERVOIR
HIGH MAYNARD RESERVOIR
Blackhorse Rd.
TOTTENHAM HALE GYRATORY
RESERVOIR No. 4
RESERVOIR No. 2
RESERVOIR No. 1
RESERVOIR No. 3
RESERVOIR No. 5
Douglas Eyre Playing Fields
WARWICK RESERVOIR (WEST)
WARWICK RESERVOIR (EAST)
West Junction
South Tottenham
Markfield Recreation Ground
SEVEN SISTERS
Filter Beds
WATER WORKS
Low Hall Sports Ground
Copper Mills Junction
Playing Field
Coppermill Bridge
Horse Shoe Point
Horse Shoe Bri.
WALTHAMSTOW MARSHES
SPRINGFIELD PARK
Springfield Marina
White Lodge
LEYTON INDUSTRIAL VILLAGE
STAMFORD HILL
CLAPTON COMMON
Aqueduct
A10
A1010
A1055
A503
B137
B179
A107
FERRY LANE
FOREST ROAD
BLACKHORSE LANE
BLACKHORSE ROAD
WATERMEAD WAY
MONUMENT WY
BROAD LANE
HIGH ROAD
LANSDOWNE ROAD
LEE VALLEY TECHNOPARK
MILLMEAD INDUSTRIAL CENTRE
LOCKWOOD INDUSTRIAL PARK
FOREST WORKS INDUSTRIAL ESTATE
FOREST TRADING ESTATE
18
34
51
F G H J K
1 2 3 4 5 6 7

34
REGIONAL PARK
BANBURY RESERVOIR
Valve Tower
Playing Field
Sports Ground
Stadium (Greyhound)
Sports Ground
The Peter May Sports Centre
A
B
C
D
E
19
Rec. Ground
Pav. Sports Ground
Tennis Courts
CROOKED BILLET
SOUTHEND RD
WINCHESTER
BANBURY ROAD
SWIFT CL.
COGAN AV.
WADHAM AV.
EMPRESS AV.
GROVE PK. AV.
WALTHAM PK. WY.
SOUTHEND
A406
FULBOURNE RD.
1
BILLET ROAD
B179
William Morris Sch.
Whittingham Prim. Sch.
Rec. Grd.
Bowling Green
HIGHAM HILL
CHINGFORD ROAD
Chapel End
Sports Ground
Sports Grd.
Bowl. Grn.
Ten. Cts.
Sports Ground
Pav.
Bowling Green
BROOKSCROFT RD.
CAZENOVE RD.
A112
LLOYD PARK
Coll.
Playing Field
Athletics Track
Swim. Pool
WALTHAMSTOW
Town Hall
Civic Cen.
College
Gallery
Tennis Cts.
Pav.
Nursery
2
BLACKHORSE
Wks
Works
3
FOREST ROAD
A503
THE BELL
Y.M.C.A.
THORPE COOMBE HOSP.
WOOD ST.
FOREST
Adult Educ. Cen.
4
Disability Cen.
Rec. Grd.
Comm. Cen.
HOE ST.
THE ARCADE
Lib.
Offs.
Walthamstow Central
Bus Sta.
Walthamstow Queens Rd.
ST. MARY
Mus.
33
Prim. Sch.
5
St. James St. Walthamstow
BLACKHORSE RD.
ST. JAMES'S ST.
Liby.
Cemetery
Sch.
SELBORNE
HIGH STREET
A112
MARKHOUSE
6
ST. JAMES'S PARK
Tennis Courts
Kelmscott Leisure Cen.
Prim. Sch.
THE FERGUSON CEN.
LOW HALL MANOR BUS. CEN.
Civic Amenity Site
88
Running Track
A1006
BOUNDARY ROAD
A104
LEA BRIDGE ROAD
BRIDGE
HIGH ST.
Leisure Pool
Bus Sta.
B159
A104
A112
LEYTON
7
FOREST BUS. PK.
ROXWELL TRADING PARK
Playground
Works
Play. Fld.
CROMWELL IND. EST.
DORMA TRADING PARK
BURWELL ROAD IND. EST.
Football Ground
52
Lib.
Leyton Midland Rd.
Tennis Courts
Bowls
Spts. Grd.
Tennis Courts
Rec. Grd.
36
37
38

35
20
36
53
F
G
H
J
K
1
2
3
4
5
6
7
EPPING FOREST
A406
NEW ROAD
WOODFORD NEW ROAD
A104
WATERWORKS CORNER
Subway
Walthamstow Forest
Reservoir (Covered)
NTH. CIRCULAR RD.
SOUTHEND RD.
HIGH ROAD WOODFORD GREEN
A1199
ROAD
A503
Gillbert's Slade
Boating Pond
Community Hall
Horse Ride
Sports Ground
SOUTH WOODFORD
South Woodford
GEORGE LA.
B168
THE VIADUCT
CHIGWELL
A113
HERMON HILL
Snaresbrook Crown Court
SNARESBROOK ROAD
Eagle Pond
SNARESBROOK
Snaresbrook
Hollow Pond (Boating Lake)
Round Pond
WHIPPS CROSS ROAD
A114
WHIPPS CROSS HOSPITAL
Playing Field
Wood St. Walthamstow
UPPER WALTHAMSTOW
B160
LEA BRI. RD.
HOLLYBUSH HILL
NEW WANSTEAD
GREEN MAN ROUNDABOUT
LEYTONSTONE
BUSH ROAD
A12
A106
CAMBRIDGE PARK
EASTERN AV.
Wanstead
George Green
WANSTEAD
BLAKE HALL ROAD
A1008
Recreation Grd.
The Basin (Fish Pond)
Sports Ground
WANSTEAD GOLF COURSE
Reservoir Wood
Shoulder of Mutton Pond
Leytonstone
GAINSBOROUGH RD.
GROVE GRN. RD.
HIGH ROAD
Woodbridge High Sch.
Churchfields Junior & Infant Schs.
Halls of Residence
Superstore
Oakdale Inf. Sch.
Oakdale Jun. Sch.
Nighting Prim. S
Snaresbrk. House
Sports Ground Forest Schs.
St. Aubyn's Sch.
Fullers Day Cen.

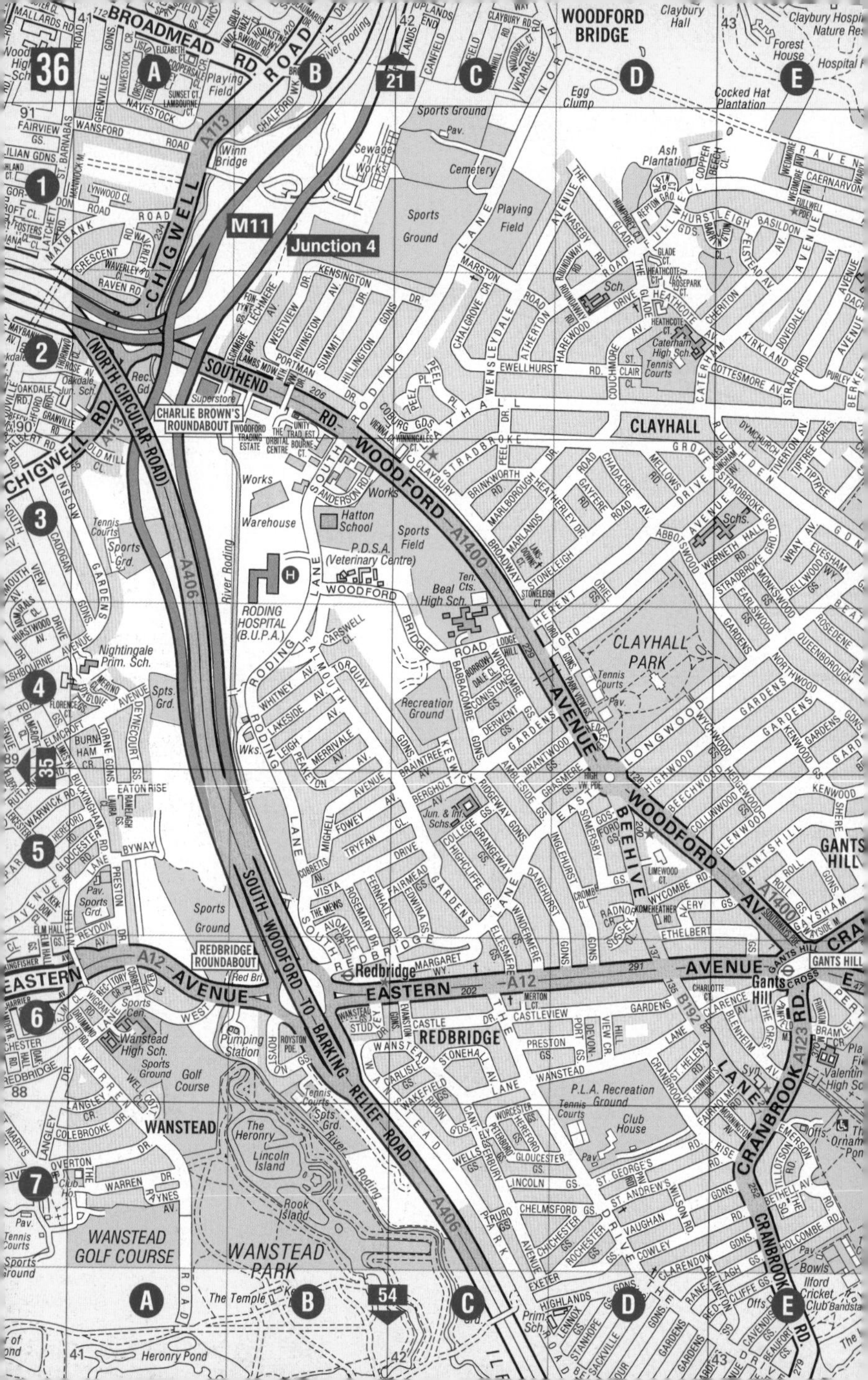

BROADMEAD RD.
WOODFORD BRIDGE
Claybury Hall
Claybury Hospital Nature Reserve
Forest House
Hospital
Egg Clump
Cocked Hat Plantation
Ash Plantation
Playing Field
Sports Ground
Sewage Works
Cemetery
Winn Bridge
M11
Junction 4
CHIGWELL ROAD
A113
21
SOUTHEND RD.
WOODFORD AVENUE
A1400
CHARLIE BROWN'S ROUNDABOUT
Superstore
WOODFORD TRADING ESTATE
THE ORBITAL CENTRE
UNITY TRAD. EST.
NORTH CIRCULAR ROAD
A406
River Roding
Works
Warehouse
Hatton School
P.D.S.A. (Veterinary Centre)
RODING HOSPITAL (B.U.P.A.)
Beal High Sch.
Recreation Ground
Sports Field
CLAYHALL
CLAYHALL PARK
Caterham High Sch.
Tennis Courts
Nightingale Prim. Sch.
Oakdale Jun. Sch.
35
EASTERN AVENUE
A12
REDBRIDGE ROUNDABOUT
Redbridge
REDBRIDGE
SOUTH WOODFORD TO BARKING RELIEF ROAD
Pumping Station
Wanstead High Sch.
Sports Cen.
Golf Course
WANSTEAD
The Heronry
Lincoln Island
Rook Island
WANSTEAD PARK
WANSTEAD GOLF COURSE
The Temple
Heronry Pond
54
P.L.A. Recreation Ground
Club House
BEEHIVE LANE
B192
GANTS HILL
Gants Hill
CRANBROOK RD.
A123
Ilford Cricket Club
Valentines High Sch.

37
Hainault Recreation Grd.
Fairlop Oak Recreation Ground
Powerleague Soccer Cen.
Club Ho.
Club Pavs.
FENCEPIECE RD.
A123
Playing Field
Tennis Courts
Oakfield Sch. Sports Centre
Redbridge Sports Centre
Fairlop
FAIRLOP
Forest Farm Cottages
Forest Farm
FOREST INDUSTRIAL PARK
BRACKEN IND. EST.
School Cen.
Fairlop Lake
Slipways
FAIRLOP WATERS
Country Park
Fairlop Lodge
Activity Centre
King Solomon High Sch.
FOREST ROAD
FAIRLOP WATERS GOLF COURSE
Nature Reserve
Lagoon
Aldborough Hall (School of Riding)
PAINTERS ROAD
NORTH ROAD
Aldborough Hall Farm
ALDBOROUGH HATCH
Aldborough Ho. Farm
Aldborough House
APPLEGARTH DR.
BAWDSEY AV.
RAMSGILL APP.
BURYSIDE CL.
ST. PETER'S CL.
OAKS LANE
38
FULLWELL CROSS
FULLWELL AVENUE
Hospital Hill
Fairlop Prim. Sch.
Playing Field
Ilford High Sch.
Prim. Sch.
Swim Pool
Lib.
Playing Field
Ilford Jewish Prim.Sch.
Barkingside
Football Ground
Cran Brook
BARKINGSIDE
Garden of Rest
Cemetery
Green Elms
Barkingside Rec. Grd.
Court
Pav.
Sports Ground
Barnardos
BARNARDOS VILLAGE
Fullwood Prim. Sch.
HIGH ROAD
MOSSFORD GARDENS
FREMANTLE RD.
TANNERS LA.
CARLTON DR.
STATION RD.
HORNS ROAD
KING GEORGE AV.
Depot
Oaks Park High Sch.
NEWBURY PARK
Newbury Park
Playing Field
Sch.
EASTERN AVENUE
A12
Bowling Green
Sports Ground
Club House
Tennis Courts
Playing Field
SEVEN KINGS PARK
Bandstand
Tennis Courts
Farnham Green Prim.
Newbury Park Prim. Sch.
Timber Mill
Super-store
CENTRAL PARADE
Sports Ground
High Sch.
Playing Field
Tennis Courts
Swim Pool
VALENTINES PARK
Bowling Green
Rec. Grd.
Tennis Courts
SEVEN KINGS
55
Prim. Sch.
R.C. Sch.
HIGH ROAD
Superstore
F
G
H
J
K
1
2
3
4
5
6
7
44
45
46
91
190
88

38
A
B
C
D
E
1
2
3
4
5
6
7
46
47
48
91
90
88
Hainault Rec. Grd.
FOREST
HAINAULT ROAD
Works
Farm Cottages
Hainault Farm
FAIRLOP WATERS
Country Park
Seven Kings Water
Kings Water
PAINTERS ROAD
Aldborough Hall Farm
ALDBOROUGH HATCH
Marks Gate
WHALEBONE LANE
A1112
Furze Cottage
Furze House Farm
ROAD
KINGSTON HILL AV.
Red House Farm
Hainault House
BILLET ROAD
Willow Farm
Playing Field
Little Heath Sch.
Sports Ground
ROSEHATCH AV.
Rec. Grd.
ARNEWAYS AV.
Jun. Sch.
Lib.
Infant Sch.
Chadwell Heath Cemetery
THATCHES
LAWN FARM GRO.
SHEEPCOTES LANE
NORTH
EASTERN AVENUE
A12
AVENUE EAST
EASTERN AV. W.
37
KING GEORGE HOSPITAL
LITTLE HEATH
Nursery
CHADWELL HEATH LANE
Redbridge College
Ethel Davis Sch.
Grove Prim. Sch.
GOODMAYES HOSPITAL
Sports Ground
Club House
CHADWELL HEATH HOSPITAL
The Chadwell Centre
Sports Ground
Tennis Courts
Playing Field
Bowls
Pav.
Playing Field
Brookside
Farnham Green Prim. Sch.
B177
BARLEY LANE
HAVERING GDNS.
TOLWORTH GDNS.
ST. CHAD'S PARK
Playgrd.
Playground
CHADWELL HEATH
MILL LA.
WHALEBONE LA. NORTH
HIGH ROAD
A118
Mayes Brook
Prim. Sch.
Play. Fld.
THACKERAY
Rec. Grd.
Superstores
Superstore
Goodmayes
Chadwell Heath
Works
Warehouse
MIRRAVALE TRADING EST.
SELINAS
FRESHWATER ROAD
CHADWELL HEATH INDUSTRIAL PARK
56
Mayfield Sch. & Coll.
Play. Field
GOODMAYES AV.
KINFAUNS ROAD
KEMP ROAD
Playing

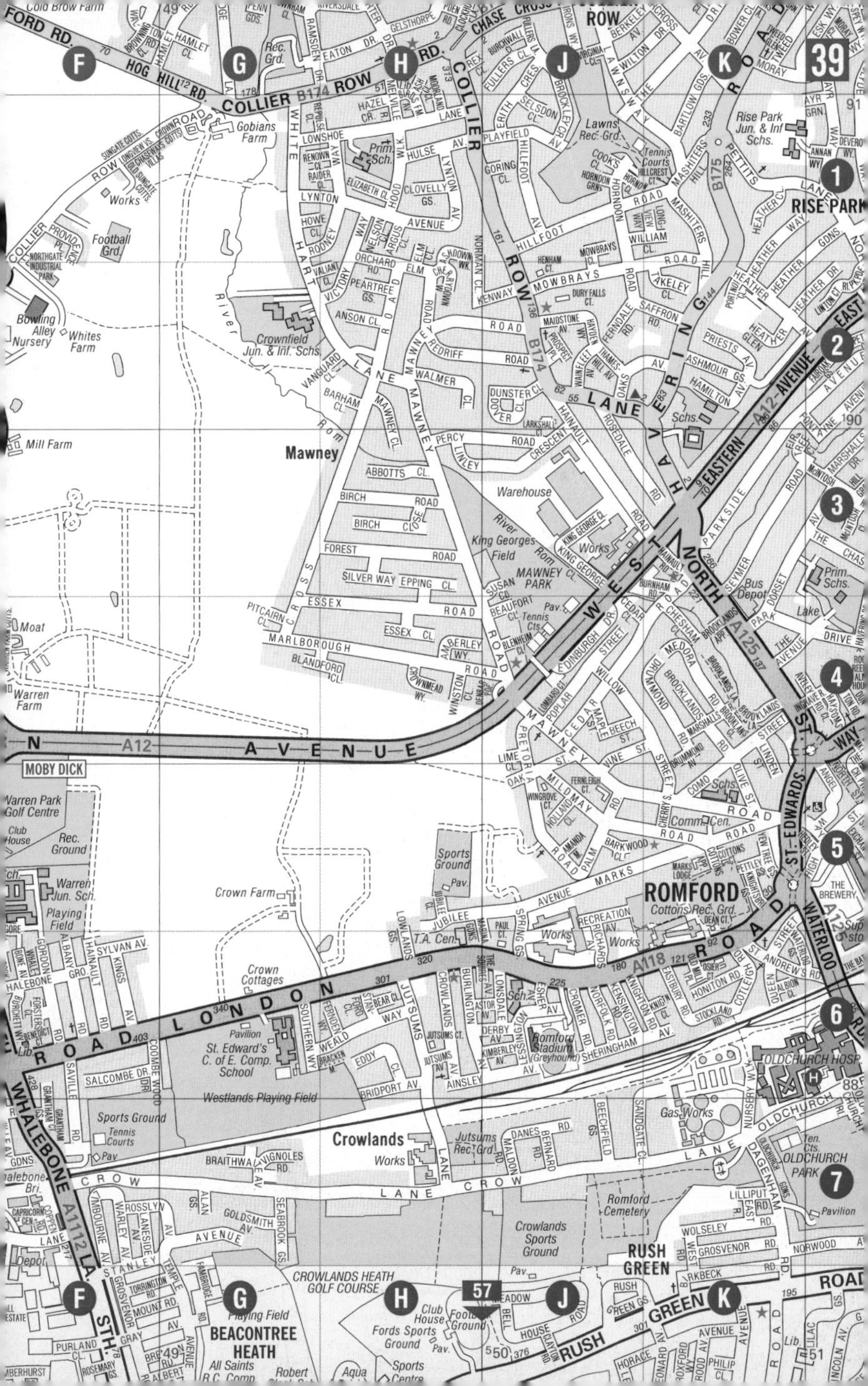

39
F
G
H
J
K
1
2
3
4
5
6
7
COLLIER ROW
CHASE CROSS RD.
HOG HILL RD.
FORD RD.
Gobians Farm
Rec. Grd.
Prim. Sch.
Lawns Rec. Grd.
Tennis Courts
RISE PARK
Rise Park Jun. & Inf Schs.
PETTITS LANE
MASHITERS HILL
B175
B174
HAVERING ROAD
Works
Football Grd.
NORTHGATE INDUSTRIAL PARK
Bowling Alley
Nursery
Whites Farm
Crownfield Jun. & Inf. Schs.
River Rom
Mill Farm
Mawney
MAWNEY ROAD
HAINAULT ROAD
EASTERN AVENUE
A12
Warehouse
King Georges Field
MAWNEY PARK
Works
Schs.
Bus Depot
Prim. Schs.
Lake
NORTH STREET
A125
Moat
Warren Farm
A12
AVENUE
MOBY DICK
Warren Park Golf Centre
Club House
Rec. Ground
Warren Jun. Sch.
Playing Field
Sports Ground
Pav.
Crown Farm
Crown Cottages
LONDON ROAD
A118
ROMFORD
Cottons Rec. Grd.
Comm. Cen.
T.A. Cen.
Works
Romford Stadium (Greyhound)
ST. EDWARDS WAY
WATERLOO RD.
THE BREWERY
OLDCHURCH HOSP.
H
Pavilion
St. Edward's C. of E. Comp. School
Westlands Playing Field
Sports Ground
Tennis Courts
Pav
Crowlands
Works
Jutsums Rec. Grd.
Gas Works
OLDCHURCH PARK
Ten. Cts.
CROW LANE
Romford Cemetery
Crowlands Sports Ground
RUSH GREEN
WHALEBONE LA.
A1112
Depot
BEACONTREE HEATH
Playing Field
CROWLANDS HEATH GOLF COURSE
57
Club House
Football Ground
Fords Sports Ground
Pav.
Sports Centre
RUSH GREEN ROAD
Lib.
All Saints R.C. Comp.

Newyears Green Covert
Old Clack Farm
Works
Depot
Copthall Covert
Research Farm
Grays Cottages
The Corner
Tile Kiln
Dunster Cottage
Gatemead Farm
Brackenbury Barn
Moat
Playground
RUISLIP LANE COURSE
WEST RUISLIP
Golf Driving Range
Club Ho.
Playing Field
Cricket Ground
Club House
Harvil Farm
Copthall Farm
UXBRIDGE GOLF COURSE
HARVIL ROAD
BREAKSPEAR ROAD
SWAKELEYS ROAD
B467
ICKENHAM
HIGH ROAD
Sch.
Play. Fld.
Community Cl.
Lib.
Ickenham
Comm. Cen.
River Pinn
Tennis Courts
Bowling Green
Harrington House
Swakeleys
Sports Ground
Weatherlys Covert
A40
SWAKELEYS ROUNDABOUT
WESTERN AVENUE
Vyners School
Tennis Cts.
The Clump
Park Wood
The Doway Martyrs Sch.
B466
Moat
Ickenham Manor
Play. Flds.
Long Lane Farm
HAREFIELD RD.
Sports Ground
Clare House
Hillingdon Ski Centre
Ski Slope
Uxbridge Common
Cricket Ground
Hillingdon
Sub.
Motel
MASTER BREWER
HILLINGDON CIRCUS
Freezeland Covert
Canal
Playing Field
Hillingdon House Farm Showground
Swimming Pool
Uxbridge College
UXBRIDGE
Prim. Sch.
Superstore
B483
T.A. Centre
Spts. Grd.
LONG LANE
A437
Rec. Grd.
HILLINGDON COURT PARK
Recreation Ground
Bowling Green
Tennis Courts
Playground
American Community School
Convent
R.A.F. STATION
Sports Ground
Tennis Courts
Schs.
Play. Fld.
Playgnd.
Hall

22

58

RUISLIP
EASTCOTE
HIGH ST.
Bishop Ramsey Sch.
23
Ruislip Manor
B466
KINGSEND
Ruislip
Supermarket
Sports Ground
Community Cen.
Ruislip Rugby Club
Sacred Heart R.C. Primary School
RUISLIP MANOR
WEST END
A4180
Bessingby Playing Fields
Works
Playing Field
Recreation Ground
RUISLIP GARDENS
Ruislip Gardens Primary School
Ruislip Gardens
Depot
South Ruislip
42
ODYSSEY BUSINESS PARK
Glebe Primary School
Ickenham Marsh
Yeading Brook
R.A.F. NORTHOLT AERODROME
A V E N U E
A40
POLISH WAR MEMORIAL
C & L Golf & Country Club
Tennis Courts
Cutthroat Wood
Gutteridge Wood
NORTH HILLINGDON
F
G
H
J
K
59
Ten Acres
Cycle Track
SHARVEL LANE
Club House
Moat
The Gorse
Playing Field
1
2
3
4
5
6
7

42
A
B
C
D
E
1
2
3
4
5
6
7
24
41
60
Eastcote
Roxborough Rough
Rayners Lane
RAYNERS LANE
Roxbourne Park
Cavendish Recreation Ground
Pine Gdns.
Bowling Green
Bessingby Playing Fields
Miniature Railway
Roxbourne First & Mid. Schs.
Recreation Ground
Newton Farm First & Mid. Sch.
Newton Park West
Newton Ecology Park
Tennis Courts
Alexandra Sch.
Field End Jun. & Inf. Schs.
Playground
High Sch.
SOUTH RUISLIP
Rec. Grd.
Deane Park
Deanesfield Prim. Sch.
Queensmead Sch.
Playing Fields
Queensmead Sports Cen.
South Ruislip
Earlsmead Sch.
Harrow Borough F.C.
Depot
Warehouses
Victoria Retail Park
Waste Transfer Station
NORTHOLT PARK
Play Centre
Play. Fld.
Northolt High Sch.
Lord Halsbury Memorial Playing Flds.
Willow Tree Prim. Sch.
Com. Cen.
Islips Manor Park
Bourne Primary School
Sports Ground
POLISH WAR MEMORIAL
Priors Fm.
Glebe Farm
War Mem.
WESTERN
A40
A4180
A4090
A312
NORTHOLT
LONDON GOLF COURSE
Bowling Grn.
Walford First & Middle Sch.
Northolt Prim. Sch.
John Chilton Sch.
Walford High Sch.
TARGET ROUNDABOUT
Youth Cen.
Northolt
Swim. Baths
Belvue Park
Golf Club
Golf Range
Club House
Towne Barns Fm.
Moat
ALEXANDRA
AVENUE
MANDEVILLE ROAD
CHURCH
WEST END RD.
IMPERIAL
EASTCOTE
LONG DR.
VICTORIA RD.
FIELD END RD.
85
86
87
185
84
12
13

WEST HARROW
HARROW
HARROW ON THE HILL
ROXETH
SOUTH HARROW
South Harrow
Northolt Pk.
Wood End
Sudbury Hill Harrow
Sudbury Hill
Greenford Green
Greenford
Harrow School
Cricket Ground
Orley Farm Sch.
Harrow Ckt. Club
David Lloyd Raquet & Fitness Club
THE CLEMENTINE CHURCHILL HOSPITAL
Horsenden Hill Rec. Grd.
BERKELEY FIELDS
Nature Reserve
GRAND UNION CANAL
GREENFORD INDUSTRIAL ESTATE
WHITTON AV.
A4090
A4127
A312
A4005
B457
25
44
61

HARROW
44
26
43
62
A
B
C
D
E
1
2
3
4
5
6
7
16
17
18
87
86
85
84
NORTHWICK PARK HOSP.
ST. MARK'S HOSP.
Playing Fields
NORTHWICK PARK
Harrow School Playing Fields
Rugby Football Grounds
Harrow School Farm
WATFORD ROAD
A404
A4127
SUDBURY COURT DRIVE
NORTH WEMBLEY
South Kenton
North Wembley
Preston Road
Preston Park
Byron Ct. Prim. Sch.
Play. Fld.
Wembley High Sch.
EAST LANE
A4088
East Lane Pavilion
Sports Ground
Vale Farm Sports Centre
Wembley Football Club
East Lane Theatre Club
WEMBLEY COMMERCIAL CENTRE
EAST LANE BUSINESS PARK
Playing Fields
KING EDWARD VII PARK
Tennis Courts
HARROW ROAD
A4005
SUDBURY
Maybank Open Space
Sudbury & Harrow Rd.
BARHAM PARK
Library
Sudbury Town
WHITTON AVENUE EAST
A4090
BRIDGEWATER ROAD
HIGH ROAD
EALING ROAD
A4089
Wembley Central
Horsenden Wood
HORSENDEN HILL GOLF COURSE
Horsenden Hill
SUDBURY GOLF COURSE
Club House
Cemetery
Horsenden Farm
GRAND UNION CANAL (PADDINGTON BRANCH)
One Tree Hill Rec. Grd.
Alperton Community Sch.
Alperton
PERIVALE
Perivale Wood Local Nature Reserve
Warehouse
Bus Garage

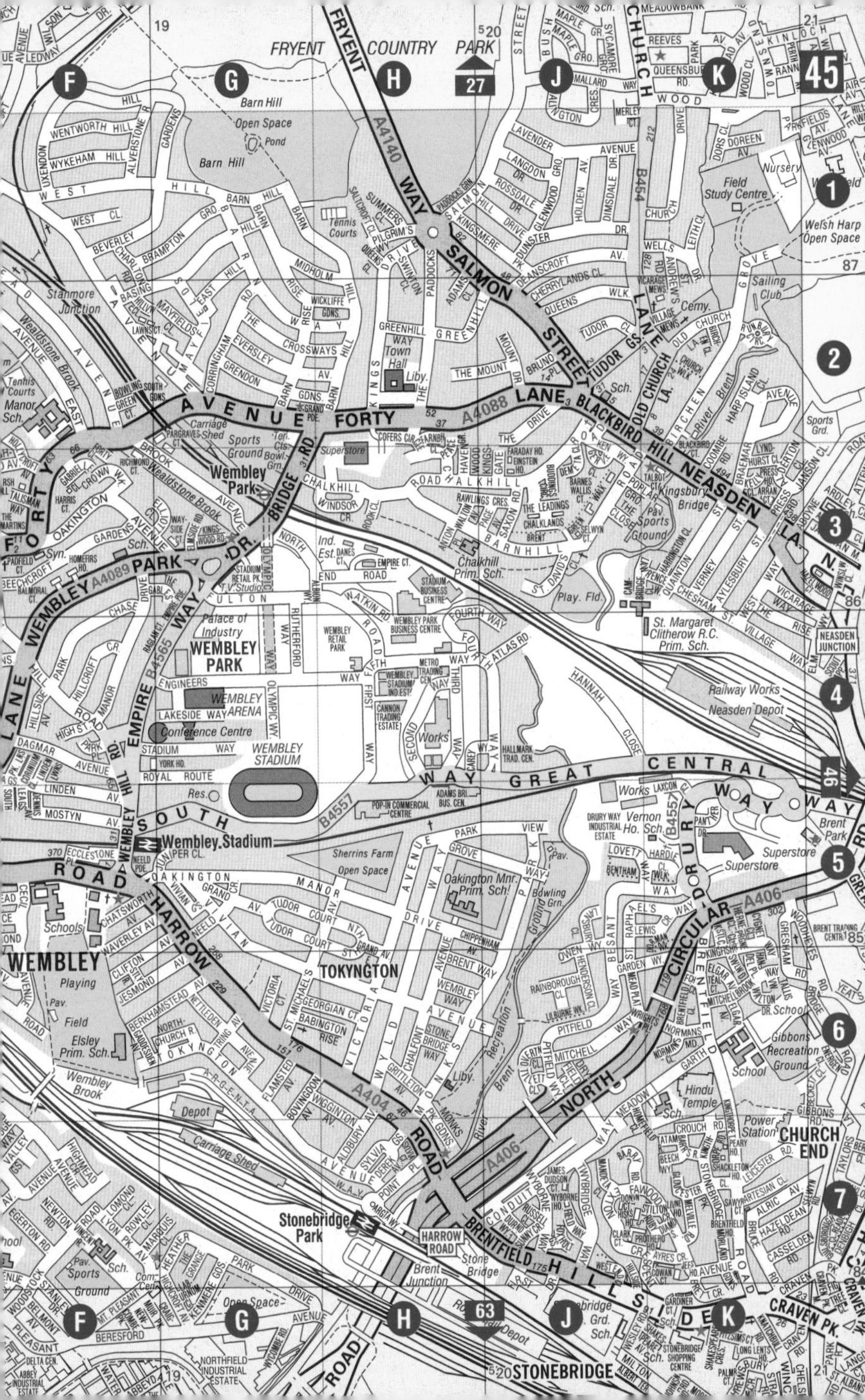
FRYENT COUNTRY PARK
27
Barn Hill
Open Space
Pond
Barn Hill
Field Study Centre
Nursery
Welsh Harp
Open Space
Sailing Club
Sports Grd.
Town Hall
Liby.
Tennis Courts
Stanmore Junction
Wealdstone Brook
Tennis Courts
Manor Sch.
Carriage Shed
Sports Ground
Superstore
Wembley Park
Chalkhill Prim. Sch.
Play. Fld.
Pav. Sports Ground
Kingsbury Bridge
St. Margaret Clitherow R.C. Prim. Sch.
NEASDEN JUNCTION
Railway Works
Neasden Depot
Palace of Industry
WEMBLEY PARK
WEMBLEY ARENA
Conference Centre
WEMBLEY STADIUM
Works
46
Res.
Wembley Stadium
Sherrins Farm Open Space
Oakington Mnr. Prim. Sch.
Vernon Ho. Sch.
Superstore
Brent Park
Bowling Grn.
Schools
WEMBLEY
Playing Field
Pav.
Elsley Prim. Sch.
Wembley Brook
TOKYNGTON
Liby.
River Brent
Recreation Ground
Hindu Temple
Gibbons Recreation Ground
School
Power Station
CHURCH END
Depot
Carriage Shed
Stonebridge Park
HARROW ROAD
Brent Junction
Stone Bridge
63
Depot
Stonebridge Grd. Sch.
STONEBRIDGE
Pav. Sports Ground
Open Space
NORTHFIELD INDUSTRIAL ESTATE
AVENUE FORTY
A4088
FORTY LANE
BLACKBIRD HILL
NEASDEN LANE
SALMON STREET
FRYENT WAY
A4140
CHURCH LANE
B454
WEMBLEY PARK DRIVE
A4089
BRIDGE RD
EMPIRE WAY
B4565
GREAT CENTRAL WAY
SOUTH WAY
B4557
HARROW ROAD
A404
NORTH CIRCULAR ROAD
A406
DRURY WAY
B4557
BRENTFIELD
HILLSIDE
CRAVEN PK.
F
G
H
J
K
1
2
3
4
5
6
7
19
20
21
85
86
87
84

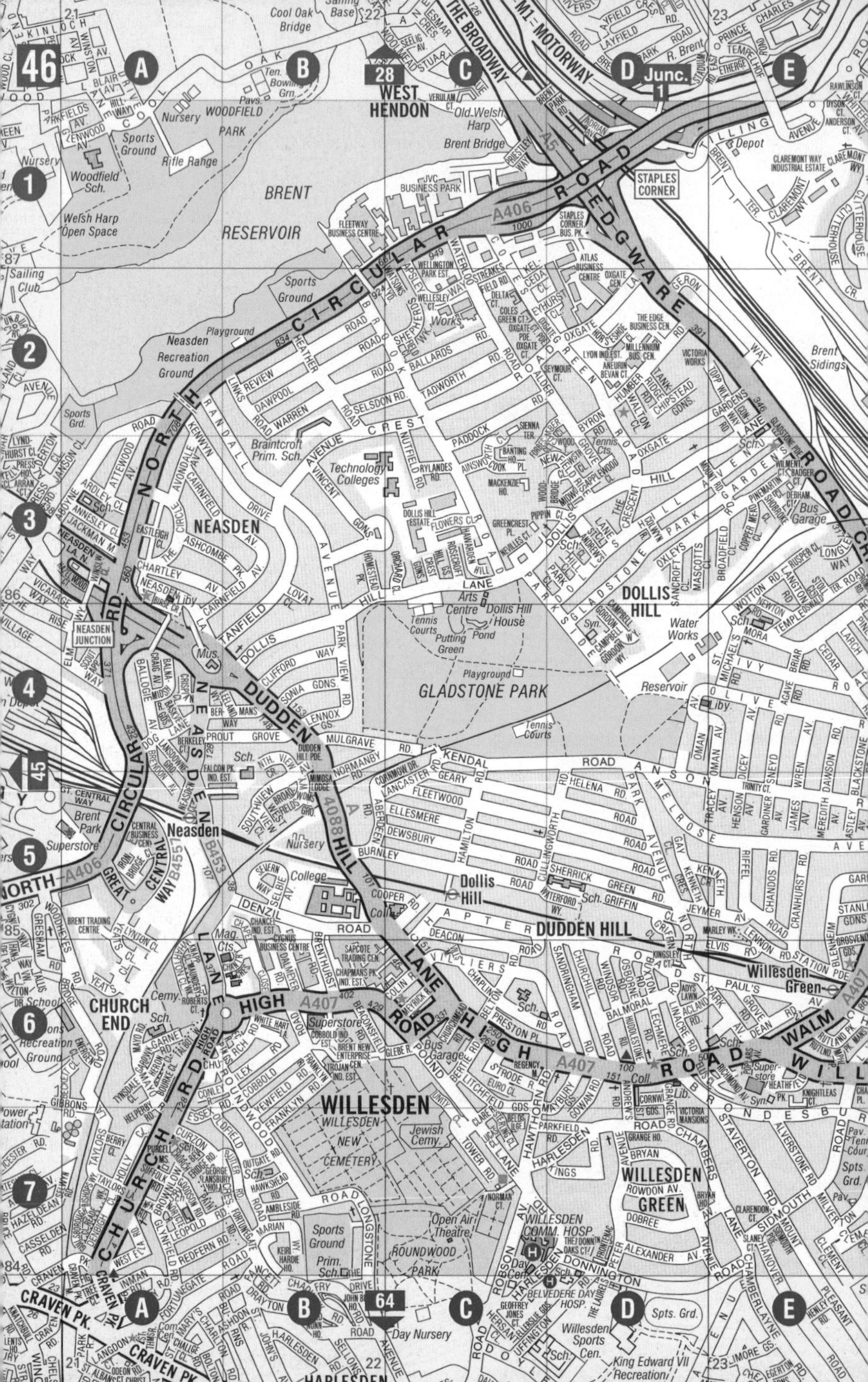

46
A
B
C
D
E
1
2
3
4
5
6
7
28
WEST HENDON
64
45
Junc. 1
M1 MOTORWAY
THE BROADWAY
Cool Oak Bridge
Woodfield Sch.
Sports Ground
WOODFIELD PARK
Nursery
Rifle Range
Welsh Harp Open Space
BRENT
RESERVOIR
Sailing Club
Old Welsh Harp
Brent Bridge
JVC BUSINESS PARK
FLEETWAY BUSINESS CENTRE
STAPLES CORNER
STAPLES CORNER BUS. PK.
ATLAS BUSINESS CENTRE
THE EDGE BUSINESS CEN.
MILLENNIUM BUS. CEN.
VICTORIA WORKS
CLAREMONT WAY INDUSTRIAL ESTATE
Depot
Brent Sidings
NORTH CIRCULAR ROAD
A406
EDGWARE ROAD
A5
Neasden Recreation Ground
Playground
Sports Grd.
NEASDEN
NEASDEN JUNCTION
Braintcroft Prim. Sch.
Technology Colleges
DOLLIS HILL ESTATE
DOLLIS HILL
Arts Centre
Dollis Hill House
Tennis Courts
Putting Green
Pond
Playground
GLADSTONE PARK
Reservoir
Water Works
Bus Garage
DUDDEN HILL LANE
A4088
Brent Park
Superstore
Neasden
CENTRAL BUSINESS CEN.
FALCON PK. IND. EST.
Nursery
College
Dollis Hill
DUDDEN HILL
BRENT TRADING CENTRE
CYGNUS BUSINESS CENTRE
SAPCOTE TRADING CEN.
CHAPMANS PK. IND. EST.
CHURCH END
Mag. Cts.
HIGH ROAD
A407
Superstore
BRENT NEW ENTERPRISE CEN.
Bus Garage
WILLESDEN
WILLESDEN NEW CEMETERY
Jewish Cemy.
Willesden Green
WILLESDEN GREEN
Recreation Ground
Sports Ground
Open Air Theatre
ROUNDWOOD PARK
WILLESDEN COMM. HOSP.
BELVEDERE DAY HOSP.
Willesden Sports Cen.
King Edward VII Recreation
Spts. Grd.
Day Nursery
CRAVEN PK.
HARLESDEN
21
22
23
84
85
86
87

47
HAMPSTEAD
HEATH
Golders Green
GOLDERS GREEN ROAD
NORTH END ROAD
A502
Middlesex University
GOLDERS HILL PARK
Leg of Mutton Pond
West Heath
Jack Straws Castle
CHILD'S HILL
FINCHLEY ROAD
A598
HENDON WAY
A41
Clitterhouse Recreation Ground
Hendon Football Club
Tennis Courts
Basing Hill Park
Childs Hill Park
CRICKLEWOOD
Cricklewood
CRICKLEWOOD BROADWAY
A407
CRICKLEWOOD LANE
WEST HEATH ROAD
PLATT'S LANE
Sports Ground
Hampstead School
Hampstead Cemetery
Fortune Green
FORTUNE GREEN RD.
A41 ARKWRIGHT ROAD
REDINGTON ROAD
WEST HAMPSTEAD
West Hampstead Thameslink
West Hampstead
WEST END LANE
B510
B520
CHICHELE RD.
A5
SHOOT UP HILL
KILBURN HIGH RD.
Kilburn
Brondesbury
BRONDESBURY
Kilburn Grange Park
WILLESDEN LANE
A4003
BRONDESBURY PARK
Brondesbury Park
Willesden Lane Cemetery
SOUTH HAMPSTEAD
BELSIZE ROAD
ABBEY RD.
QUEX RD.
MILL LANE
IVERSON RD.
COMPAYNE GDNS.
Finchley Rd & Frognal
29
48
65
F
G
H
J
K
1
2
3
4
5
6
7
24
25
26

HIGHGATE
HAMPSTEAD HEATH
HAMPSTEAD
PARLIAMENT HILL
VALE OF HEALTH
North End
Kenwood House
KEN WOOD
Open Air Stage
Ladies' Bathing Pond
Highgate Ponds
Hampstead Ponds
East Heath
Sports Ground
Caen Wood Towers Farm
ATHLONE HOUSE
HIGHGATE CEMETERY
William Ellis School
Parliament Hill School
GOSPEL OAK
Gospel Oak
Hampstead Heath
Hampstead
THE ROYAL FREE HOSPITAL
Belsize Pk.
Finchley Rd. & Frognal
Finchley Rd.
SOUTH HAMPSTEAD
Swiss Cottage
South Hampstead
Chalk Farm
PRIMROSE HILL
Reservoir (Covered)
Sigmund Freud Statue
Jack Straws Castle
Whitestone Pond
Camden Arts Centre
HAMPSTEAD HIGH ST.
FITZJOHN'S AVENUE
HAVERSTOCK HILL
ROSSLYN HILL
SPANIARDS ROAD
NORTH END
HEATH ST.
FINCHLEY ROAD
ADELAIDE ROAD
ETON AVENUE
MANSFIELD ROAD
FLEET ROAD
POND ST.
AGINCOURT RD.
MALDEN ROAD
CHALK FARM ROAD
GORDON HOUSE ROAD
HAMPSTEAD LANE
MILLFIELD LA.
HIGHGATE WEST HILL
A502
A41
B519
B518
B511
B509
B517
30
47
66

49
F
G
H
J
K
1
2
3
4
5
6
7
31
50
67
ARCHWAY
HORNSEY
HIGHGATE
CROUCH HILL
Crouch Hill
STROUD GREEN
A1201
WATERLOW PARK
Highgate Wing
HIGHGATE CEMETERY
Middlesex Uni.
WHITTINGTON N.H.S. TRUST
Archway
HOLLOWAY
ST. JOHN'S GR.
Upper Holloway
UPPER HOLLOWAY
Whittington Park
DARTMOUTH PARK
A400
JUNCTION
Tufnell Park
TUFNELL PARK
Halls of Residence
Sports Grd.
MERCERS ROAD
HOLLOWAY
NAG'S HEAD
NAGS HEAD SHOPPING CENTRE
SEVEN SISTERS
A503
A103
TOLLINGTON
HORNSEY RISE
Elthorne Local Park
BRECKNOCK
A5200
CAMDEN
PARKHURST
HILLMARTON
CALEDONIAN
A5203
H.M.P. HOLLOWAY
HILLDROP ESTATE
Holloway Rd.
LOWER HOLLOWAY
KENTISH TOWN
Kentish Town
A400
FORTESS ROAD
YORK WAY
CAMDEN PARK RD.
Caledonian Rd.
Caledonian Park
H.M.P. Pentonville
Paradise Park
BARNSBURY
Caledonian Rd and Barnsbury
CAMDEN TOWN
Camden Rd.
Camden Town
AGAR GROVE
ST. PANCRAS WAY
ROYAL COLLEGE
Channel Tunnel Rail Link (Under Construction)
Driving Range
Warehouse
Oblique Bridge
BRITANNIA JUNC.
PARKWAY
CITIZEN
LIVERPOOL
Depot

A
B
C
D
E
1
2
3
4
5
6
7
FINSBURY PARK
Manor House
MANOR HOUSE
32
49
68
Green Lanes Bridge
WEST RESERVOIR
EAST RESERVOIR
The Castle
Sir Thomas Abney Prim. Sch.
SEVEN SISTERS ROAD
STROUD GREEN ROAD
WOODSTOCK RD.
Finsbury Park
BROWNSWOOD PARK
BLACKSTOCK RD.
BROWNSWOOD RD.
GREEN LANES
LORDSHIP PARK
LORDSHIP RD.
MANOR RD.
CLISSOLD PARK
Council Offices
Clissold Ho.
Paddling Pool
Lake
Tennis Courts
Bowl. Grn.
ABNEY PARK CEMETERY
STOKE NEWINGTON
STOKE NEWINGTON CHURCH ST.
Old Peoples Home
BIRCHMORE HALL
HIGHBURY QUADRANT
Isledon Village
Gillespie Local Park
Arsenal
Arsenal F.C. (Highbury)
ISLEDON RD.
HORNSEY RD.
TOLLINGTON RD.
Drayton Park
HIGHBURY
HIGHBURY PARK
HIGHBURY GROVE
HIGHBURY FIELDS
Highbury Pool
Highbury & Islington
HIGHBURY CNR.
HOLLOWAY RD.
LIVERPOOL RD.
University
Paradise Park
Rec. Grd.
Arts Cen.
Univ.
ST. PAUL'S RD.
BALLS POND RD.
Canonbury
CANONBURY
CANONBURY RD.
UPPER ST.
Essex Rd.
ESSEX RD.
NEW NORTH RD.
NEWINGTON GRN.
NEWINGTON GRN. RD.
ALBION RD.
MILDMAY GROVE NORTH
MILDMAY GROVE SOUTH
Dalston Kingsland
KINGSLAND
DE BEAUVOIR TOWN
BEAUVOIR SQ.
BARNSBURY
ISLINGTON
P.O. Depot
A1
A1199
A1201
A104
A105
A503
A103
B104
B105
B515

51
33
52
69
F
G
H
J
K
1
2
3
4
5
6
7
CLAPTON
STAMFORD HILL
Stoke Newington
SPRINGFIELD PARK
White Lodge
Springfield Marina
Coppermill Bridge
Horse Shoe Point
Horse Shoe Bri.
WALTHAMSTOW
LEYTON INDUSTRIAL VILLAGE
Works
Clapton Junction
MARSHES
Aqueduct
Leyton Marshes
Lea Bridge Riding Sch.
Playing Field
Saw Mill Works
Leeside Wharf
Lee Valley Ice Centre
Filter Beds
Lea Bri.
Middlesex Filter Beds Nature Reserve
LEA BRIDGE
SOUTH MILL FIELDS
South Millfields Rec. Grd.
Power Sta. (Dis.)
NORTH MILLFIELDS Recreation Ground
UPPER CLAPTON
UPPER CLAPTON RD.
COMMON
Clapton
NORTHWOLD
RECTORY ROAD
Rectory Road
STAMFORD HILL
STOKE NEWINGTON HIGH ST.
STOKE NEWINGTON RD.
KINGSLAND HIGH S.
SHACKLEWELL
Kingsland School
LOWER CLAPTON
HACKNEY DOWNS
Stormont House Sch.
Hackney Downs
Hackney Cen.
HOMERTON HOSPITAL
HOMERTON HIGH ST.
Homerton
LEA BRIDGE ROAD
LOWER CLAPTON ROAD
PEMBURY R.
CRICKETFIELD R.
AMHURST
DALSTON LA.
GRAHAM ROAD
MORNING LANE
WICK ROAD
HACKNEY
London Fields
LONDON FIELDS
DALSTON
QUEENSBRIDGE RD.
MARE STREET
WELL ST.
CASSLAND
SOUTH HACKNEY
WELL STREET COMMON
VICTORIA
Victoria Fountain
Royal Gate East
A107
A104
A10
A1207
A102
A106
B111
B113
B108

A
B
C
D
E
34
LEYTON
HACKNEY MARSH
RECREATION GROUND
CLAPTON PARK
HOMERTON
HACKNEY WICK
VICTORIA PARK
SOUTH HACKNEY
OLD FORD
STRATFORD
Stratford Marsh
Temple Mills
LEA INTERCHANGE
ORIENT WAY
RUCKHOLT ROAD
EASTWAY
EAST CROSS ROUTE
HOMERTON HIGH ST.
CARPENTER'S RD.
HIGH ROAD LEYTON
LEA BRIDGE ROAD
Leyton Midland Rd.
Hackney Wick
Homerton
Middlesex Filter Beds Nature Reserve
Cow Bridge
Changing Rooms
River Lea or Lee
River Lee Navigation
Recreation Ground
Football Ground
Running Track
Market Pavilion
New Spitalfields Market
Superstore
Eastway Cycle Circuit
Container Terminal
Cold Stores
Freight Terminal
Warehouses
ROUTE OF CHANNEL TUNNEL RAIL LINK (UNDER CONS
Channelsea River
Waterworks River
City Mill River
Kingsway International Christian Centre
Arena Field Rec. Grd.
Wick Field Recreation Ground
Mabley Green
Leyton Orient F.C. (Brisbane Rd.)
Civic Amenity Tip
Bowling Green
Sports Ground
Victoria Fountain
Royal Gate East
Three Colt Bridge
51
70
A104
A1006
A106
A12
A102
A112
A115
B112
B113
B161
36
37
38

F
G
H
J
K
1
2
3
4
5
6
7
35
54
71
Leytonstone
LEYTONSTONE
Leytonstone High Rd.
GAINSBOROUGH RD.
BUSH RD.
ROUNDABOUT
HALL ROAD
A114
WANSTEAD GOLF COURSE
The Basin (Fish Pond)
Tennis Courts
Sports Ground
Bush Wood
Reservoir Wood
Shoulder of Mutton Pond
WOODLANDS AVENUE
ALDERSBROOK RD.
A116
Horse Ride
Playing Field
WANSTEAD FLATS
CENTRE ROAD
WOODFORD RD.
WOODGRANGE RD.
HIGH ROAD LEYTONSTONE
HIGH RD. LEYTONSTONE
LEYTONSTONE RD.
HARROW ROAD
DAMES ROAD
B161
A12
A106
A11
A112
A118
B164
B165
CATHALL ROAD
GROVE GREEN RD.
St. Patrick's R.C. Cemetery
Depot
Cann Hall
Cemetery
West Ham Cemetery
CANN HALL RD.
Wanstead Park
Forest Gate
FOREST GATE
FOREST LANE
CHOBHAM RD.
LEYTON RD.
ANGEL LANE
Maryland
Stratford
THE GROVE
WATER LANE
ROMFORD RD.
BROADWAY
GREAT EASTERN RD.
HIGH ST.
WEST HAM LA.
VICARAGE LA.
PORTWAY
WEST HAM PARK
Football Ground
Playground
Netball Court
Football Pitch
Tennis Courts
UPTON LANE
UPTON
PLASHET ROAD
WEST HAM
NEW PLAISTOW RD.
GREEN ST.
Upton

WANSTEAD PARK
WANSTEAD GOLF COURSE
Heronry Pond
Perch Pond
ALDERSBROOK
WANSTEAD FLATS
CITY OF LONDON CEMETERY
City of London Crematorium
ILFORD GOLF COURSE
River Roding
CRANBROOK
MANOR PARK
Manor Park Cemetery
Manor Park
Woodgrange Park
LITTLE ILFORD
Little Ilford Park
PLASHET Jewish Cemetery
PLASHET PARK
East Ham
WALLEND
UPTON PARK
Upton Park
SOUTH WOODFORD TO BARKING RELIEF ROAD
NORTH CIRCULAR ROAD
ROMFORD ROAD
HIGH STREET NORTH
ALDERSBROOK
FOREST DRIVE
ILFORD

36
53
72

55
F
G
H
J
K
37
56
73
1
2
3
4
5
6
7
SEVEN KINGS
Seven Kings
ILFORD
LOXFORD
FAIR CROSS
BARKING
Barking
BARKING PARK
SOUTH PARK
The Lake
Loxford Park
Sports Ground
Playing Field
Railway Workshop
Depot
Redbridge Enterprise Cen.
Cemetery
Cricklefield Rec. Grd.
Running Track
Baths Youth Cen.
County
Town Hall
The Exchange
Gordon Fields Prim. Sch.
T.A. Centre
Inf. Sch.
Woodlands Jun. & Inf. Schs.
Loxford Sch. of Science & Technology
Hyleford (Home for the Elderly)
Loxford Water
Playing Water
Swimming Pool
Tennis Courts
Putting Green
Bowling Greens
Miniature Railway
Bus Depot
Barking Hosp.
Upney
Upney Sidings
Barking Abbey Comp. Sch.
Manor Jun. & Inf. Schs.
Vicarage Field Shopping Cen.
Roding Trading Estate
Abbey Retail Park
Superstore
Courts
Barking Abbey (Rem. of)
Prim. Sch.
T.H.
Lib.
Mus.
Valentines Park
Bowling Green
Seabrooke Manor
A118
A108
A1083
A123
A124
HIGH ROAD
HIGH RD.
GREEN LANE
WINSTON WY.
GRIGGS APP.
ILFORD LANE
LONGBRIDGE ROAD
FANSHAWE AV.
BARKING NORTHERN RELIEF RD.
BARKING RELIEF RD.
LONDON RD.
ABBEY RD.
RIPPLE RD.
VICARAGE LANE
CAMERON RD.
BENTON RD.
KINGS GS.
SOUTH PARK DRIVE
SOUTH PARK CRES.
SOUTH PARK TER.
PARKWAY
MEADWAY
LEVETT RD.
DAWLISH DR.
ASHBURTON AV.
UPNEY LANE
ST. PAUL'S RD.
ALDBOROUGH RD.
AUCKLAND RD.
MELBOURNE RD.
BRISBANE RD.
TORONTO RD.
DUNEDIN RD.
COLOMBO RD.
WINCHESTER RD.
GORDON RD.
LITTLEMOOR RD.
CAVENHAM GS.
KINGSTON RD.
HAMPTON RD.
WINDSOR RD.
HENLEY RD.
GRANGE RD.
DUDLEY RD.
RUTLAND RD.
BEDFORD RD.
CLEVELAND RD.
ALBERT RD.
VICTORIA RD.
FAIRFIELD RD.
ROMAN RD.
SAXON RD.
NORMAN RD.
HARVEY RD.
HUNTER RD.
KHARTOUM RD.
WINGATE RD.
ST. LUKE'S AV.
HICKLING RD.
JERSEY RD.
MADRAS RD.
HOWARD RD.
HAMILTON RD.
CECIL RD.
NATAL RD.
PRETORIA RD.
MAYVILLE RD.
TUDOR RD.
VENTNOR GS.
SHIRLEY GDNS.
HURSTBOURNE GDNS.
LYNDHURST GDNS.
STRATHFIELD GDNS.
ALDERSEY GDNS.
WILMINGTON GDNS.
NETHERFIELD GDNS.
SHERWOOD GDNS.
CRANLEIGH GS.
ROSSLYN RD.
SALISBURY AV.
GREENSLADE RD.
ESSEX RD.
SUFFOLK RD.
NORFOLK RD.
SURREY RD.
LAMBOURNE RD.
DAWSON AV.
STUART RD.
DEVON RD.
SISLEY RD.
EASTBURY AV.
WESTROW DR.
OULTON CRES.
DEREHAM RD.
SANDRINGHAM RD.
SHERINGHAM AV.
WOODBRIDGE RD.
MALVERN DR.
THURLESTONE AV.
BROADHURST GDNS.
TAVISTOCK GDNS.
BRIXHAM GDNS.
SEATON AV.
CHESTER RD.
PEMBROKE RD.
ST. ALBANS RD.
LANSDOWNE RD.
CAMBRIDGE RD.
ELGIN RD.
NORFOLK RD.
ASHGROVE RD.
VERNON RD.
FELBRIGGE RD.
AUDLEY GDNS.
OAKWOOD GDNS.
LEAMINGTON RD.
CHARLBURY GDNS.
LYNFORD GDNS.
MORRAB GDNS.
TRENANCE GDNS.
EGERTON GDNS.
BREAMORE RD.
WESTROW GDNS.
TRESCO GDNS.

56
A
B
C
D
E
1
2
3
4
5
6
7
38
55
74
Chadwell Heath
Goodmayes
GOODMAYES
HIGH ROAD
A118
GREEN LANE
A1083
GOODMAYES LANE
GOODMAYES RD.
BARLEY LANE
BENNETTS CASTLE LANE
B191
B177
VALENCE AVENUE
BECONTREE AVENUE
LONGBRIDGE ROAD
A124
WOOD LANE
PORTERS AVENUE
A1153
LODGE AVENUE
RIPPLE ROAD
GALE STREET
HEDGEMANS ROAD
AMESBURY ROAD
WOODWARD ROAD
HEATHWAY
Superstore
Superstores
Works
Warehouse
CHADWELL HEATH INDUSTRIAL PARK
MIRRAVALE TRADING EST.
Play. Field
Playing Field
Mayfield Sch. & Coll.
GOODMAYES PARK
Tennis Courts
Paddling Pool
Playground
Bandstand
Mayespark Prim. Sch.
OAKLEA LODGE
BECONTREE DAY HOSP.
Valence Ho. Mus.
VALENCE PARK
BECONTREE
Youth Cen.
University of East London
Play. Fld.
Football Ground
Running Track
Sports Ground
Barking Abbey Comp. Sch.
Sydney Russell Comp. Sch.
MAYESBROOK PARK
Mayes Brook
Boating Lake
Boat Ho.
PARSLOES PARK
Pavilion
Paddling Pool
Becontree
Goresbrook Park
Goresbrook Leisure Centre
Cemetery
RIPPLE ROAD JUNCTION
47 CASTLE GREEN
Subway
Depot
Train. Cen.
DAGENHAM LEISURE PK
Bingo Hall
Cin.
Prim. Sch.
Schs.
Lib.
Syn.
Pav.
Sch.

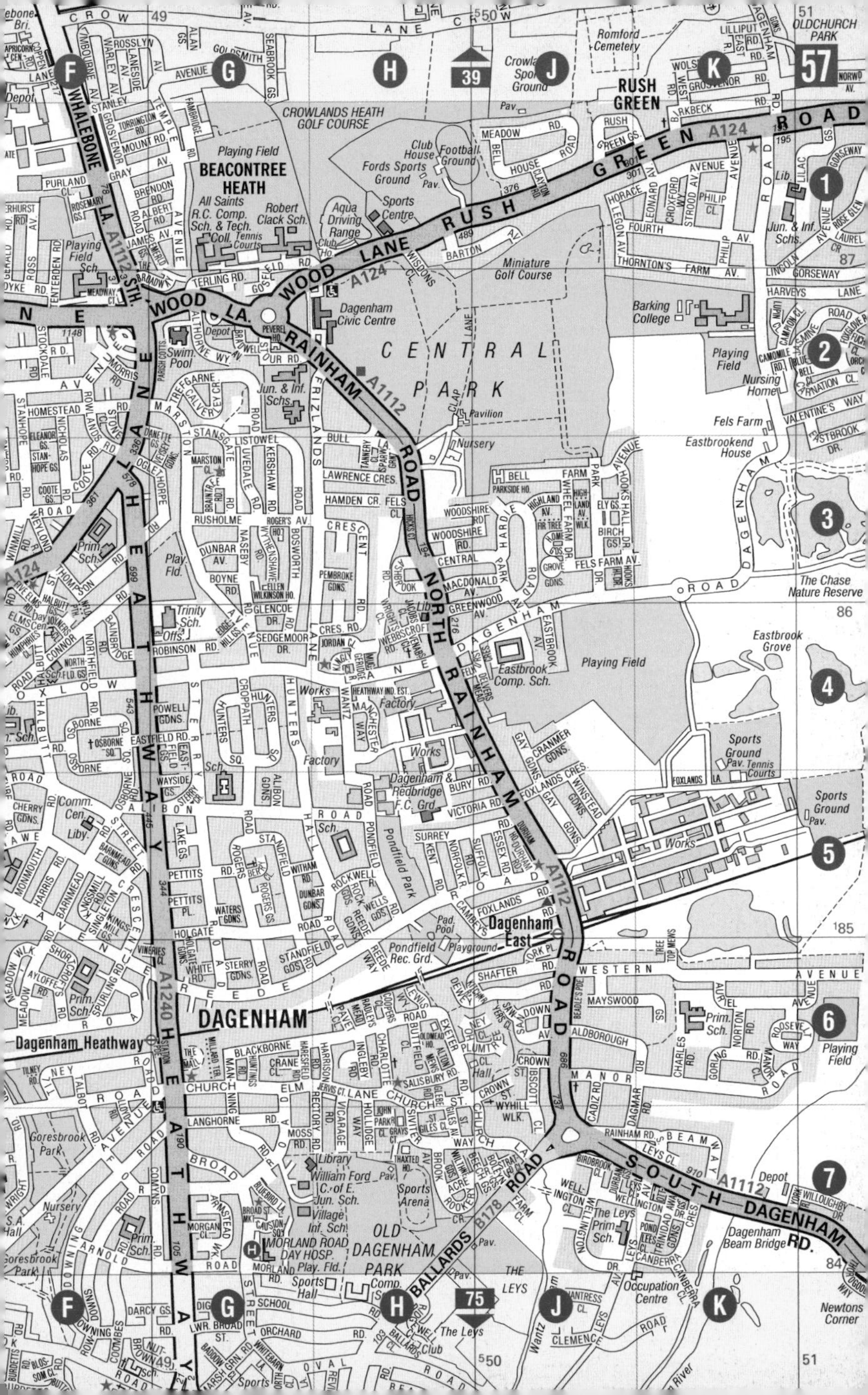

57
39
75
49
50
51
F
G
H
J
K
1
2
3
4
5
6
7
87
86
85
84
OLDCHURCH PARK
Romford Cemetery
Crowlands Sports Ground
RUSH GREEN
CROWLANDS HEATH GOLF COURSE
Playing Field
BEACONTREE HEATH
All Saints R.C. Comp. Sch. & Tech. Coll.
Robert Clack Sch.
Tennis Courts
Club House
Football Ground
Fords Sports Ground
Aqua Driving Range
Sports Centre
RUSH GREEN ROAD
A124
WOOD LANE
Miniature Golf Course
Dagenham Civic Centre
CENTRAL PARK
Pavilion
Nursery
RAINHAM ROAD
A1112
Barking College
Nursing Home
Fels Farm
Eastbrookend House
The Chase Nature Reserve
Eastbrook Grove
Sports Ground
Tennis Courts
Eastbrook Comp. Sch.
Playing Field
NORTH RAINHAM ROAD
DAGENHAM ROAD
Swim. Pool
Jun. & Inf. Schs.
Trinity Sch.
Prim. Sch.
Play. Fld.
HEATHWAY
A1240
Dagenham & Redbridge F.C. Grd.
Pondfield Park
Pondfield Rec. Grd.
Dagenham East
DAGENHAM
Dagenham Heathway
Goresbrook Park
Library
William Ford C. of E. Jun. Sch.
Village Inf. Sch.
MORLAND ROAD DAY HOSP.
Sports Arena
OLD DAGENHAM PARK
Sports Hall
Comp. Sch.
BALLARDS ROAD
B178
THE LEYS
The Leys
The Leys Prim. Sch.
Occupation Centre
Dagenham Beam Bridge
SOUTH DAGENHAM RD.
A1112
Newtons Corner
Depot
WESTERN AVENUE
Playing Field
River

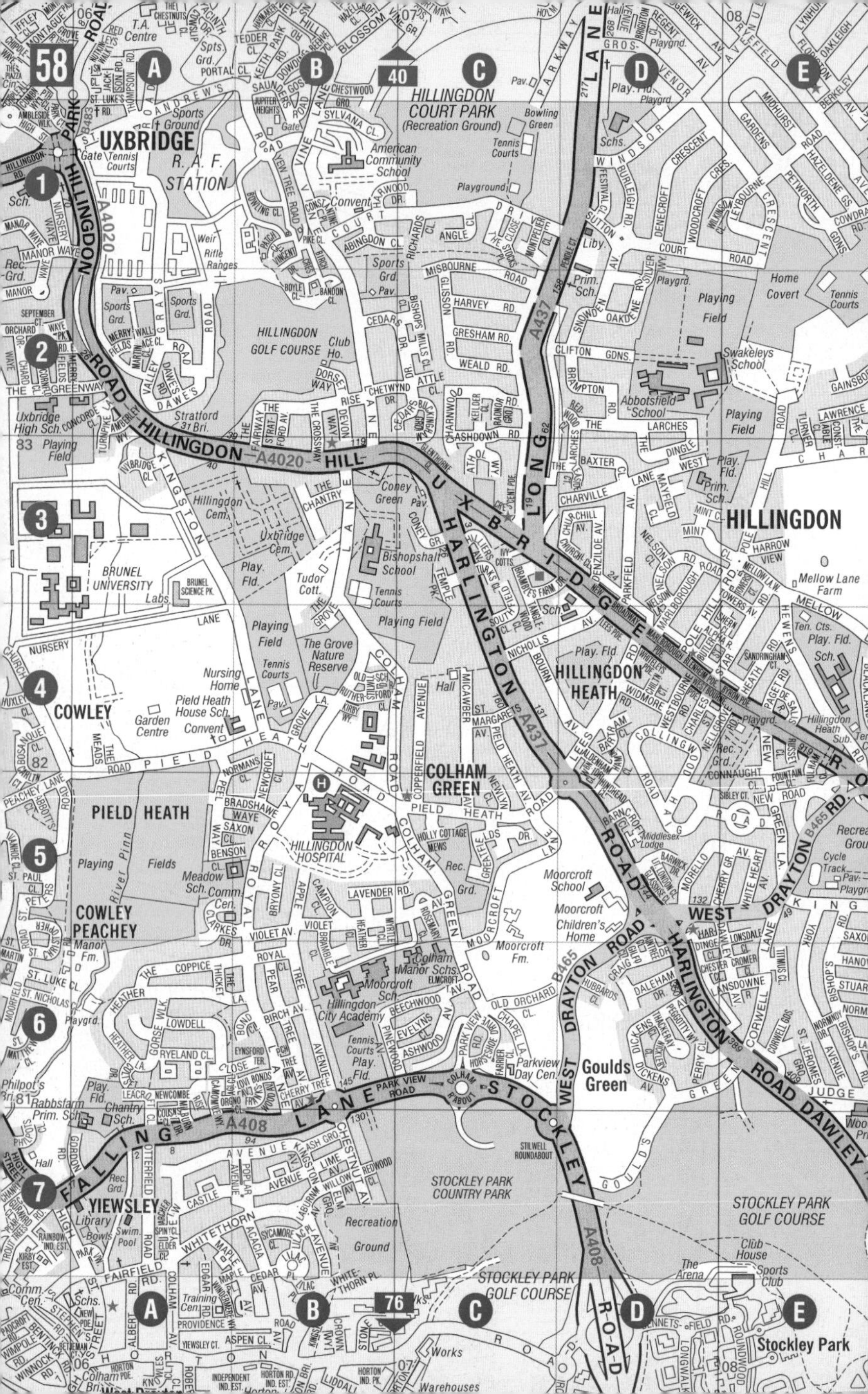

58
A
B
C
D
E
1
2
3
4
5
6
7
40
76
UXBRIDGE
R. A. F. STATION
HILLINGDON COURT PARK (Recreation Ground)
American Community School
HILLINGDON GOLF COURSE
Club Ho.
Uxbridge High Sch.
Playing Field
HILLINGDON ROAD
HILLINGDON HILL
A4020
A437
LONG LANE
UXBRIDGE ROAD
HARLINGTON ROAD
Swakeleys School
Abbotsfield School
HILLINGDON
Mellow Lane Farm
BRUNEL UNIVERSITY
Labs.
BRUNEL SCIENCE PK.
Hillingdon Cem.
Uxbridge Cem.
Bishopshalt School
Playing Field
The Grove Nature Reserve
Tudor Cott.
Coney Green
COWLEY
Garden Centre
Nursing Home
Pield Heath House Sch.
Convent
HILLINGDON HEATH
COLHAM GREEN
PIELD HEATH
Playing Fields
River Pinn
COWLEY PEACHEY
HILLINGDON HOSPITAL
Meadow Sch.
Moorcroft School
Moorcroft Children's Home
Moorcroft Fm.
WEST DRAYTON ROAD
B465
Colham Manor Schs.
Moorcroft Sch.
Hillingdon City Academy
Parkview Day Cen.
Goulds Green
COLHAM R'ABOUT
STOCKLEY
FALLING LANE
A408
STILWELL ROUNDABOUT
STOCKLEY PARK COUNTRY PARK
STOCKLEY PARK GOLF COURSE
Club House
The Arena
Sports Club
Stockley Park
Recreation Ground
YIEWSLEY
Library
Swim. Pool
Rabbsfarm Prim. Sch.
Chantry Sch.
Works
Warehouses
HORTON IND. PK.
INDEPENDENT IND. EST.
HORTON RD IND. EST.
DAWLEY ROAD
Middlesex Lodge
Cycle Track

59
41
60
77
HAYES END
WOOD END GREEN
WOOD END
HAYES
YEADING
NORTH HILLINGDON
UXBRIDGE ROAD
A4020
A437
A312
THE PARKWAY
Ten Acres
The Gorse
Recreation Ground
Cycle Track
Westways Fm.
Lane Covert
West London Shooting Grounds
Grosvenor Playing Field
Corporation Yard
Hedgewood School
Charville Prim. Sch.
Hayes Shrub
Hayes Park
Field House
Home Farm
The Paddocks Fm.
Belmore Primary School
Belmore Playing Fields
Grange Park Jun. & Inf. Schs.
The Hayes Manor Sch.
Hayes Manor Sports Cen.
Hayes Stadium
Sports Centre
Barra Hall
Open-Air Theatre
Town Hall Park
Hayes F.C.
Uxbridge Coll. (Hayes Campus)
Lombardy Retail Park
Essoldo Theatre
Yeading Schs.
Cricket Ground
The Beck Theatre
Norman Leddy Mem. Gdns.
Rosedale Park
Cutthroat Wood
Gutteridge Wood
Hare Plantation
C & L Golf & Country Club
Club House
Moat
Yeading Brook
Canal Feeder

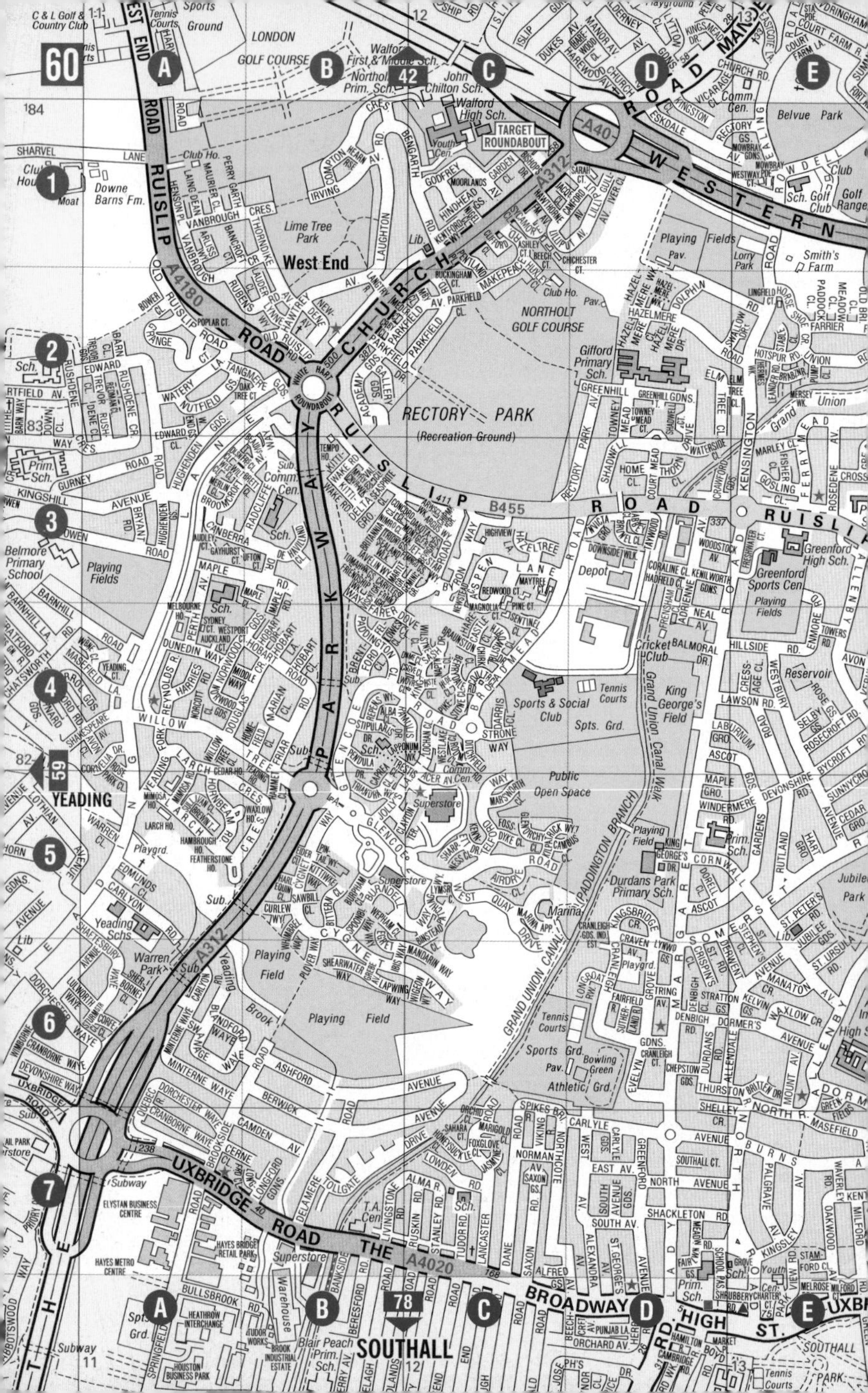
60
C & L Golf & Country Club
Tennis Courts
Sports Ground
LONDON GOLF COURSE
Walford First & Middle Sch.
42
Northolt Prim. Sch.
John Chilton Sch.
Walford High Sch.
TARGET ROUNDABOUT
A40
WESTERN
Belvue Park
Golf Range
Club House
Downe Barns Fm.
Moat
SHARVEL LANE
RUISLIP ROAD
A4180
Lime Tree Park
West End
CHURCH ROAD
A312
WHITE HART ROUNDABOUT
Playing Fields
Smith's Farm
NORTHOLT GOLF COURSE
Gifford Primary Sch.
RECTORY PARK
(Recreation Ground)
PARKWAY
RUISLIP ROAD
B455
Greenford High Sch.
Greenford Sports Cen.
Belmore Primary School
KINGSHILL AVENUE
Depot
Cricket Club
King George's Field
Grand Union Canal Walk
Sports & Social Club
Tennis Courts
Spts. Grd.
Reservoir
Public Open Space
Superstore
YEADING
59
Marina
Durdans Park Primary Sch.
Jubilee Park
Yeading Schs.
Warren Park
Yeading Brook
Playing Field
GRAND UNION CANAL (PADDINGTON BRANCH)
Sports Grd.
Bowling Green
Athletic Grd.
UXBRIDGE ROAD
THE BROADWAY
A4020
ELYSTAN BUSINESS CENTRE
HAYES BRIDGE RETAIL PARK
HAYES METRO CENTRE
HEATHROW INTERCHANGE
Warehouse
78
Blair Peach Prim. Sch.
SOUTHALL
HIGH ST.
SOUTHALL PARK
HOUSTON BUSINESS PARK
BROOK INDUSTRIAL ESTATE
A
B
C
D
E
1
2
3
4
5
6
7
184
83
82
11
12
13

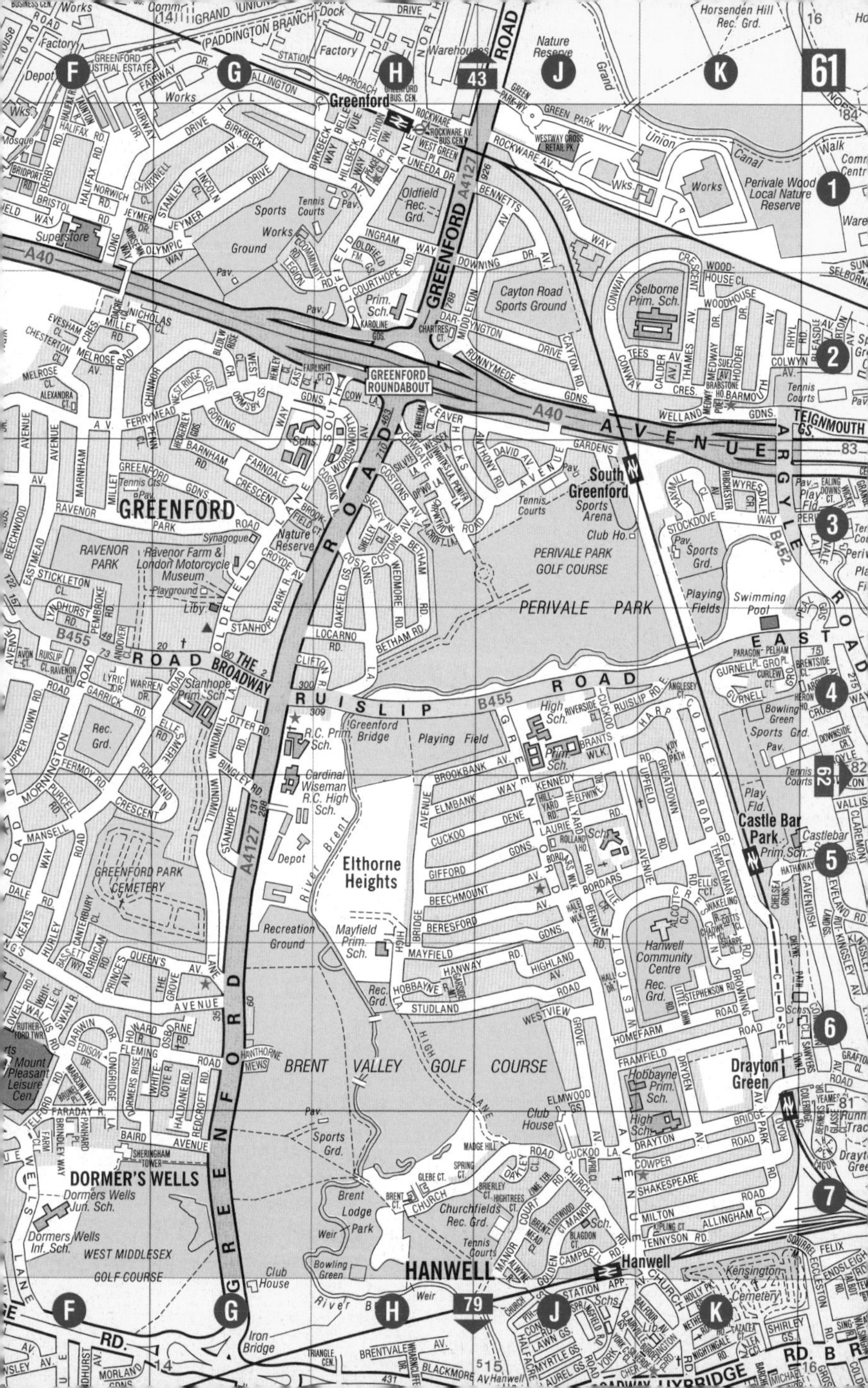

61
F
G
H
J
K
1
2
3
4
5
6
7
43
62
79
GREENFORD
Greenford
GREENFORD ROUNDABOUT
South Greenford
Castle Bar Park
Drayton Green
Hanwell
HANWELL
DORMER'S WELLS
Elthorne Heights
PERIVALE PARK
PERIVALE PARK GOLF COURSE
BRENT VALLEY GOLF COURSE
WEST MIDDLESEX GOLF COURSE
GREENFORD PARK CEMETERY
RAVENOR PARK
Ravenor Farm & London Motorcycle Museum
Perivale Wood Local Nature Reserve
Cayton Road Sports Ground
Oldfield Rec. Grd.
Selborne Prim. Sch.
Hanwell Community Centre
Churchfields Rec. Grd.
Brent Lodge Park
Kensington Cemetery
Cardinal Wiseman R.C. High Sch.
Mayfield Prim. Sch.
Hobbayne Prim. Sch.
Dormers Wells Jun. Sch.
Dormers Wells Inf. Sch.
Stanhope Prim. Sch.
Castlebar Prim. Sch.
Westway Cross Retail Pk.
Grand Union Canal
GREENFORD ROAD
RUISLIP ROAD
RUISLIP ROAD EAST
ARGYLE ROAD
A40
A4127
B455
B452

62
A
B
C
D
E
1
2
3
4
5
6
7
Horsenden Hill
Horsenden Farm
GRAND UNION CANAL
Perivale Wood Local Nature Reserve
PERIVALE
Perivale
Library
Warehouse
Comm. Centre
Sports Ground Comm. Cen.
PERIVALE INDUSTRIAL PARK
Schools
Cemetery
Alperton
Alperton Community Sch.
Teaching Cen.
ALPERTON
Metropolitan Police Traffic Unit
Alperton Sports Ground
Running Track
Superstore
Factory
Subway
HANGER LANE
WESTERN
A40
B452
B455
B456
A4005
A4020
ALPERTON LANE
AVENUE
TEIGNMOUTH GDNS.
EALING GOLF COURSE
Club House
Perivale Bri. Playing Fields
Swimming Pool
RUISLIP RD. E.
Pitshanger Park
Brentham Sports Club
River Brent
GOLF COURSE
Hanger Hill Park
SCOTCH COMMON
Cleveland Park
Castle Bar Park
Drayton Green
CASTLEBAR HILL
High Sch.
Ealing Abbey
R.C. Prim. Sch.
Cricket Ground
Aston Ho. Sch.
HAVEN GRN.
EALING
Town Hall
Ealing Broadway
THE MALL
THE BROADWAY
WEST EALING
West Ealing
UXBRIDGE ROAD
BROADWAY
Kensington Cemetery
Pitshanger Manor Mus.
Ealing Tertiary Coll.
Ealing Studios
WALPOLE PARK
44
61
80

63
45
64
81
F
G
H
J
K
1
2
3
4
5
6
7
19
20
21
Stonebridge Park
HARROW ROAD
Brent Junction
Royal Mail Depot
Stonebridge Rec. Grd.
STONEBRIDGE
HILLSIDE
CRAVEN PK.
STONEBRIDGE SHOPPING CENTRE
Open Space
Sports Ground
NORTHFIELD INDUSTRIAL ESTATE
PARK ROYAL JUNCTION
PREMIER PARK
NORTH CIRCULAR ROAD
A406
A404
Works
Townsend Industrial Estate
Harlesden
Lower Place
GRAND UNION CANAL (Paddington Branch)
Twyford Abbey
Prim. Sch.
Club House
PARK ROYAL
CENTRAL MIDDLESEX HOSPITAL
Power Station
ROYAL LONDON INDUSTRIAL ESTATE
Playing Field
FROGMORE INDUSTRIAL ESTATE
CUMBERLAND BUSINESS PARK
AMC BUSINESS CENTRE
Tennis Courts
Sports Ground
PETER JAMES ENTERPRISE CEN.
Hypermkt.
PARK ROYAL METRO CENTRE
SOVEREIGN PARK TRADING ESTATE
BUSH INDUSTRIAL ESTATE
OAKWOOD BUSINESS PARK
WESTERN AVENUE
A40
NORTH ACTON
Cemetery
North Acton
PILOT INDUSTRIAL CENTRE
Park Royal
Hanger Hill
PARK ROYAL SOUTH LEISURE COMPLEX
CONCORD BUSINESS CENTRE
WESTPOINT TRADING ESTATE
WESTWOOD PARK TRAD. EST.
HERON TRAD. EST.
B4492
A4000
GYPSY CORNER
VICTORIA ROAD
WALES FARM RD.
NORTH ACTON PLAYING FIELDS
West Acton
Sports Grd.
Sports Ground
Nth. Ealing
Acton Main Line
Play. Fld.
School
Japanese Sch. London
HORN LANE
Sports Ground
Prim. Sch.
EALING COMN.
Ealing Common
GUNNERSBURY AV.
ACTON
Sports Cen.
Acton Central
ACTON PARK
Maples Sch.
Cricket Ground
HANGER LANE

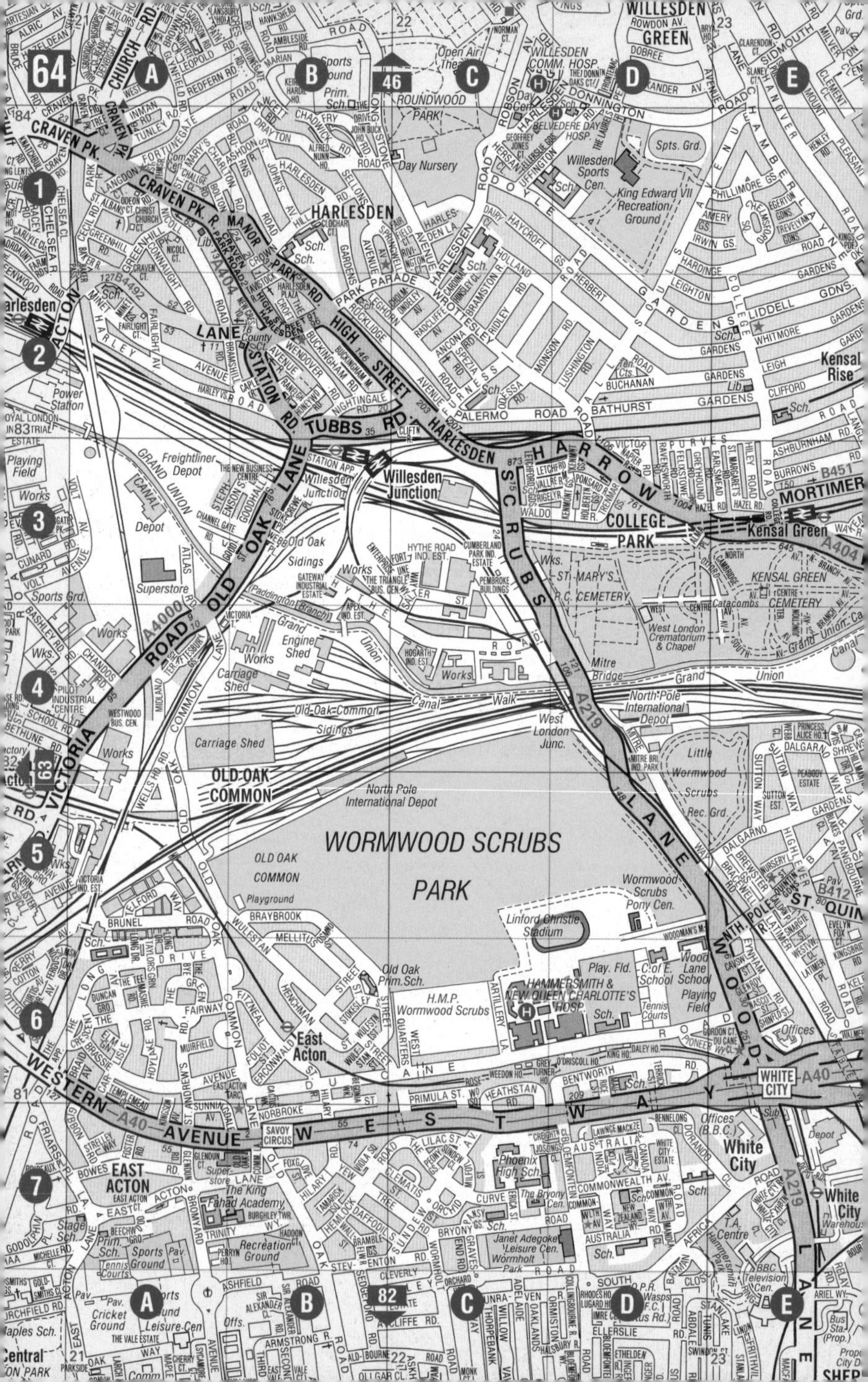
WILLESDEN GREEN
HARLESDEN
Harlesden
Willesden Junction
COLLEGE PARK
Kensal Green
Kensal Rise
KENSAL GREEN CEMETERY
ST. MARY'S R.C. CEMETERY
WORMWOOD SCRUBS PARK
OLD OAK COMMON
Little Wormwood Scrubs Rec. Grd.
Linford Christie Stadium
HAMMERSMITH & NEW QUEEN CHARLOTTE'S HOSP.
H.M.P. Wormwood Scrubs
Old Oak Prim. Sch.
East Acton
EAST ACTON
White City
WHITE CITY
SAVOY CIRCUS
WESTERN AVENUE
WEST WAY
A40
A404
A4000
A219
B451
B412
B4492
CRAVEN PK. RD.
HIGH STREET HARLESDEN
HARROW ROAD
SCRUBS LANE
OLD OAK LANE
VICTORIA ROAD
WOOD LANE
DU CANE ROAD
TUBBS RD.
STATION RD.
ACTON LANE
MANOR PARK RD.
Roundwood Park
Willesden Sports Cen.
King Edward VII Recreation Ground
Willesden Comm. Hosp.
Grand Union Canal
Freightliner Depot
Old Oak Sidings
Old Oak Common Sidings
North Pole International Depot
West London Crematorium & Chapel
Power Station
Carriage Shed
Superstore
Canal Depot
Phoenix High Sch.
The King Fahad Academy
Janet Adegoke Leisure Cen.
Wormholt Park
Offices (B.B.C.)
BBC Television Cen.
Q.P.R. Wasps F.C. (Loftus Rd.)
Hammersmith Park
Wormwood Scrubs Pony Cen.
Recreation Ground
Sports Ground
Cricket Ground
46
63
82
A B C D E
1 2 3 4 5 6 7

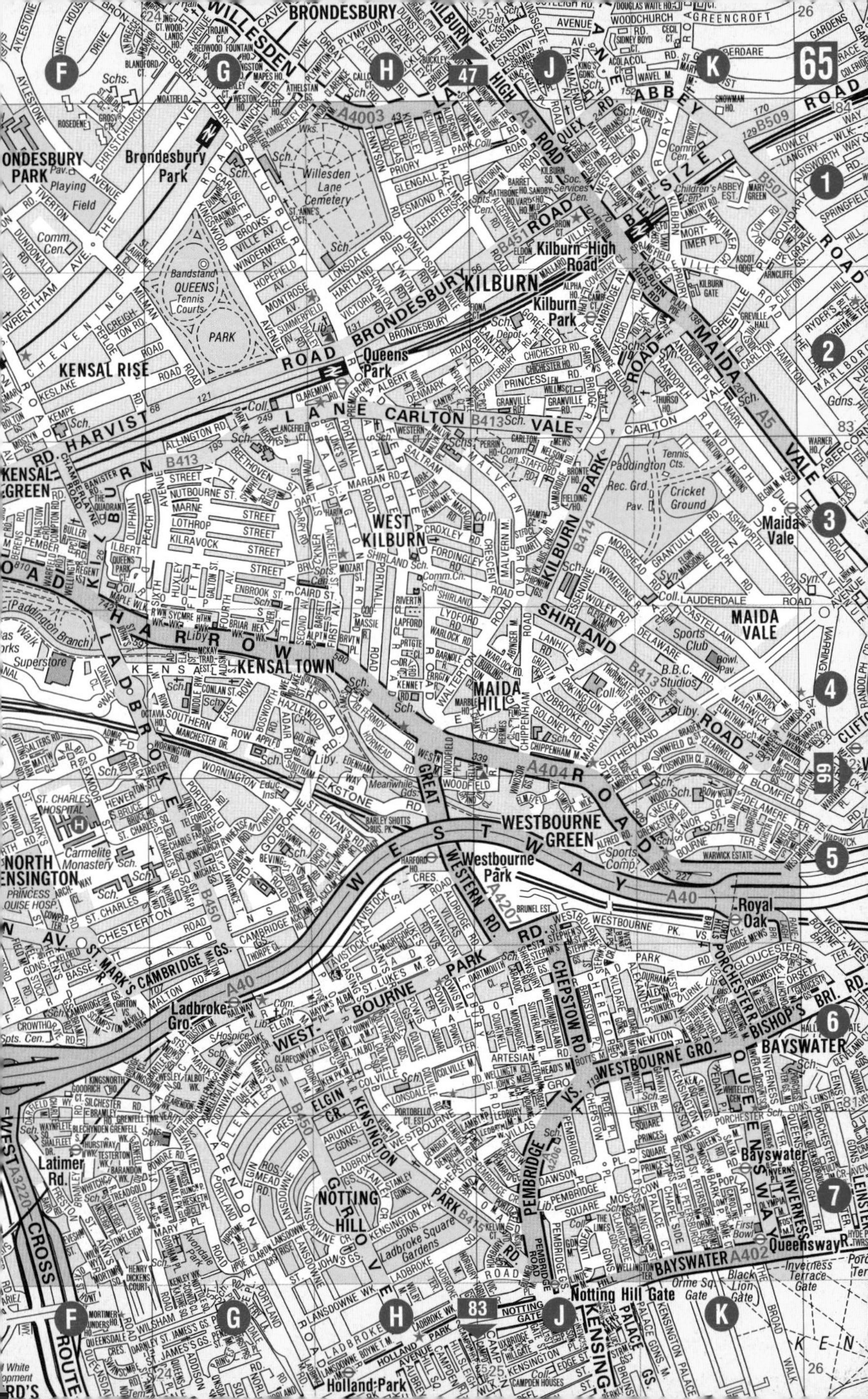

BRONDESBURY
WILLESDEN
KILBURN
47
ABBEY ROAD
BELSIZE
Brondesbury Park
BRONDESBURY PARK
Willesden Lane Cemetery
Kilburn High Road
BRONDESBURY ROAD
Kilburn Park
QUEENS PARK
Queens Park
KENSAL RISE
HARVIST ROAD
CHEVENING ROAD
CARLTON VALE
MAIDA VALE
Maida Vale
WEST KILBURN
KENSAL GREEN
Paddington Rec. Grd.
Cricket Ground
SHIRLAND ROAD
ELGIN AVENUE
HARROW ROAD
KENSAL TOWN
MAIDA HILL
B.B.C. Studios
Sports Club
(Paddington Branch)
Superstore
LADBROKE GROVE
GREAT WESTERN RD.
WESTWAY
WESTBOURNE GREEN
Westbourne Park
Royal Oak
ST. CHARLES HOSPITAL
Carmelite Monastery
NORTH KENSINGTON
PRINCESS LOUISE HOSP.
ST. MARK'S RD.
CAMBRIDGE GS.
Ladbroke Gro.
WESTBOURNE PARK ROAD
CHEPSTOW RD
WESTBOURNE GRO.
BAYSWATER
BISHOP'S BRI. RD.
PORCHESTER RD.
QUEENSWAY
Bayswater
Queensway
Latimer Rd.
WEST CROSS ROUTE
A3220
NOTTING HILL
Ladbroke Square Gardens
KENSINGTON PARK ROAD
PEMBRIDGE VILLAS
BAYSWATER ROAD
Notting Hill Gate
NOTTING HILL GATE
KENSINGTON PALACE
Holland Park
HOLLAND PARK AVENUE
Black Lion Gate
Orme Sq. Gate
Inverness Terrace Gate
83
66
A5
A40
A404
A4207
A402
A4003
B413
B414
B450
B451
B507
B509
F G H J K
1 2 3 4 5 6 7

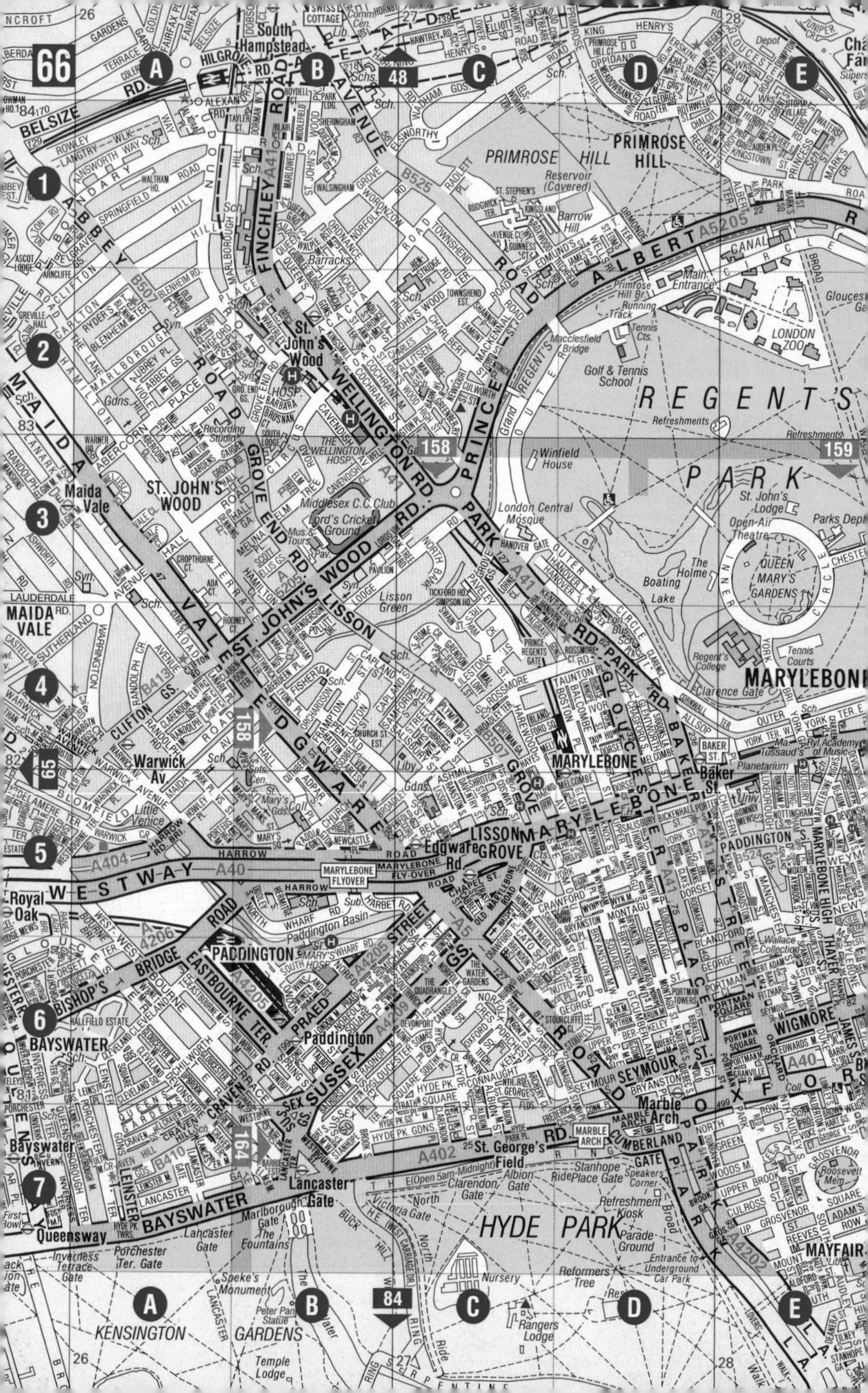

66
South Hampstead
PRIMROSE HILL
PRIMROSE HILL
Reservoir (Covered)
Barrow Hill
ALBERT RD.
LONDON ZOO
Golf & Tennis School
REGENT'S PARK
Winfield House
St. John's Lodge
Open-Air Theatre
QUEEN MARY'S GARDENS
London Central Mosque
Boating Lake
The Holme
Regent's College
Clarence Gate
Hanover Gate
MARYLEBONE
Baker St.
Madame Tussaud's
Planetarium
Ryl. Academy of Music
ST. JOHN'S WOOD
St. John's Wood
Maida Vale
MAIDA VALE
Lord's Cricket Ground
Middlesex C.C. Club
THE WELLINGTON HOSP.
Lisson Green
Warwick Av.
Little Venice
WESTWAY
MARYLEBONE FLYOVER
Edgware Rd.
LISSON GROVE
Royal Oak
Paddington Basin
PADDINGTON
Paddington
BAYSWATER
Bayswater
Queensway
Lancaster Gate
Marble Arch
Wallace Collection
MAYFAIR
HYDE PARK
Speakers Corner
Reformers Tree
Rangers Lodge
KENSINGTON GARDENS
Peter Pan Statue
Speke's Monument
Temple Lodge
The Fountains
St. George's Field

67
CAMDEN TOWN
Camden Town
KENTISH TOWN RD.
CAMDEN RD.
Channel Tunnel Rail Link (Under Construction)
49
F
G
H
J
K
1
2
3
4
5
6
7
BRITANNIA JUNC.
PARKWAY
DELANCEY ST.
ALBANY
Jewish Mus.
PANCRAS WAY
Driving Range
Depot
COPENHAGEN ST.
CALEDONIAN RD.
YORK WAY
CROWNDALE RD.
Mornington Cres.
Barracks
REGENT'S PARK
PANCRAS RD.
Gasholders
Nature Park
London Wildlife Trust
PENTONVILLE
PENTONVILLE RD.
KING'S CROSS
King's Cross Thameslink
SOMERS TOWN
ST. PANCRAS
British Library
EUSTON
EVERSHOLT ST.
HAMPSTEAD RD.
EUSTON RD.
160
161
SWINTON ST.
ACTON ST.
KING'S CROSS RD.
GRAY'S INN RD.
FARRINGDON RD.
CLERKENWELL
Mount Pleasant
ST. PANCRAS
Coram's Fields
Euston Sq.
GOWER ST.
University College
EUSTON UNDERPASS
Regent's Park
Gt. Portland St.
Warren St.
TOTTENHAM COURT RD.
WOBURN PL.
Russell Sq.
BLOOMSBURY
GUILFORD ST.
BERNARD ST.
SOUTHAMPTON ROW
THEOBALDS RD.
British Museum
BEDFORD SQ.
Goodge St.
PORTLAND PL.
GT. PORTLAND ST.
Telecom Twr.
CAVENDISH SQ.
MORTIMER ST.
Oxford Circus
OXFORD ST.
Tottenham Court R.
NEW OXFORD ST.
HIGH HOLBORN
Holborn
HOLBORN
KINGSWAY
CHANCERY LA.
Lincoln's Inn
Law Courts
SOHO
CHARING CROSS RD.
SHAFTESBURY AV.
Covent Gdn.
Leicester Sq.
ALDWYCH
STRAND
Somerset Ho.
Temple
EMBANKMENT
THAMES
RIVER
REGENT ST.
NEW BOND ST.
CONDUIT ST.
Piccadilly Circus
PICCADILLY
HAYMARKET
National Gallery
85
Charing Cross
CHARING CROSS
Embankment
Cleopatra's Needle
VICTORIA EMBANKMENT
WATERLOO BRI.
Royal Festival Hall
Hungerford Bri.
Admiralty Arch
MALL
ST. JAMES'S
Green

68
A
B
C
D
E
1
2
3
4
5
6
7
50
161
162
163
67
86
ISLINGTON
DE BEAUVOIR TOWN
HOXTON
SHOREDITCH
FINSBURY
CLERKENWELL
Angel
Essex Rd.
Old Street
Farringdon
Barbican
Moorgate
LIVERPOOL ST.
CITY
St. Paul's
City Thameslink
Bank
Mansion Ho.
Monument
CANNON STREET
BLACKFRIARS
SOUTHWARK
Temple
ST. LUKE'S
BARBICAN
RIVER THAMES
PENTONVILLE RD.
CITY RD.
NEW NORTH RD.
GOSWELL RD.
UPPER STREET
LIVERPOOL RD.
HOLBORN
FLEET ST.
STRAND
VICTORIA EMBMT.
LONDON WALL
CHEAPSIDE
CORNHILL
BISHOPSGATE
GRACECHURCH ST.
FENCHURCH ST.
LOWER THAMES ST.
UPR. THAMES ST.
QUEEN VICTORIA ST.
FARRINGDON RD.
CLERKENWELL RD.
OLD ST.
SHOREDITCH HIGH ST.
EASTERN ST.
CITY RD.
BEECH ST.
CHISWELL ST.
ALDERSGATE ST.
BLACKFRIARS RD.
SOUTHWARK BRI.
LONDON BR.
Regent's Canal
City Road Basin
Wenlock Basin
Millennium Bridge
Bankside Jetty
Tate Modern
Bunhill Fields Burial Grd.
Charterhouse
Arts Centre
Museum of London
Law Courts
The Temple
H.Q.S. Wellington
H.M.S. President
The London Television Centre
Ryl. National Theatre
London Bri. City Pier
Custom Ho.
Golden Hind
Vinopolis

69
DALSTON
SOUTH HACKNEY
LONDON FIELDS
HAGGERSTON
VICTORIA PARK
Royal Gate East
Victoria Fountain
Cambridge Heath
BETHNAL GREEN
Bethnal Green
GLOBE TOWN
MILE END
Shoreditch
SPITALFIELDS
Old Spitalfields Mkt.
Whitechapel
ROYAL LONDON HOSP.
Stepney Green
STEPNEY
WHITECHAPEL
Aldgate East
Aldgate
Tower Gateway
Tower Hill
THE TOWER
Shadwell
SHADWELL
St. Katharine Docks
Shadwell Basin
King Edward Mem. Park
RIVER THAMES
ROTHERHITHE TUNNEL
Wapping
Queen Mary & Westfields College
F
G
H
J
K
1
2
3
4
5
6
7
51
87
163
169
70

SOUTH HACKNEY
Stratford Marsh
A
B
C
D
E
52
VICTORIA PARK
Victoria Fountain
Bandstand Pav.
Sports Ground
Tennis Courts
Playground
Bowling Green
Three Colt Bridge
Skew Bridge
Crown Gate East
OLD FORD
OLD FORD ROAD
PARNELL RD.
CROSS ROUTE
EAST CROSS ROUTE
A12
BLACKWALL TUNNEL APPROACH
FAIRFIELD RD.
Four Seasons Grn.
Pudding Mill Lane
DLR
BOW INTERCHANGE
Works
Depot
Sun Wharf
City Mill River
MARSHGATE TRADING EST.
VANGUARD TRADING EST.
MARSH GATE BUS. CEN.
HIGH ST.
A118
Three Mills Green
Three-Mills-Wall-River
Bow Creek
T.V. & Film Studio
Superstore
CLOCK HOUSE
1
2
3
4
5
6
7
ROMAN RD.
B135
B118
B142
A1205
MILE END RD.
BOW
BOW ROAD
Bow Rd.
Bow Church
BOW BRIDGE EST.
BROMLEY HIGH ST.
Grove Hall Park
REGENT SQ.
TUNNEL
NORTHERN APPROACH
Bromley-by-Bow
ST. ANDREW'S HOSP.
DEVAS
DEVONS ROAD
Devons Rd.
B140
TWELVE TREES CRESCENT
COVENTRY CROSS
BARRATT IND. PK.
Liby.
MILE END
ROYAL LONDON HOSP. MILE END
Queen Mary & Westfields College
Commercial Wharf
The Green Bri.
Globe Bri.
Mile End
Mile End Park
A11
MILE END
BURDETT RD.
ROYAL LONDON HOSP. ST. CLEMENT'S
TOWER HAMLETS CEMETERY
BOW TRIANGLE BUS. CEN.
BROMLEY
BOW COMMON
BOW COMMON LA.
DEVONS WAY
69
Shandy Park
Gas Works
Ragged Sch. Mus.
MILE END PARK
Stadium
BEN JONSON RD.
ST. PAULS WAY
Furze Grn.
Langdon Park
ZETLAND
LIMEHOUSE FIELDS EST.
RATCLIFF
Bartlett Park
LANSBURY EST.
LIMEHOUSE
Limehouse
COMMERCIAL RD.
A13
Town Hall
EAST INDIA DOCK RD.
All Saints
COTTON ST.
A1203
LIMEHOUSE LINK
Limehouse Basin
NARROW ST.
Westferry
WESTFERRY RD.
POPLAR
POPLAR HIGH ST.
Poplar
ASPEN WAY
A1261
POPLAR BUSINESS PARK
Ratcliff Cross Stairs
VICTORIA WHARF
BLYTH'S WHARF
RIVER THAMES
LIMEHOUSE REACH
Pageant Stairs
Limehouse Hole Stairs
Mus. in Dockland
West India Quay
Billingsgate Fish Market
WEST INDIA DOCKS
Canary Wharf
Canary Wharf Pier
88
WESTFERRY CIRCUS
Ordnance Wharf
Columbia Wharf
Rotherhithe Pier
Sports Grd.
Fisher A.F.C.
CHURCHILL PL.
BLACKWALL BASIN
PRESTON'S RD.
36
37
38

71
53
72
89
F
G
H
J
K
1
2
3
4
5
6
7
WEST HAM
UPTON
WEST HAM PARK
PORTWAY
PLASHET
NEW PLAISTOW RD.
PLAISTOW RD.
HIGH ST.
MANOR RD.
STEPHENSON ST.
BARKING RD.
NEWHAM WAY
PRINCE REGENT LANE
BALAAM ST.
GREENGATE ST.
PLAISTOW
CANNING TOWN
Canning Town
Plaistow
West Ham
East London Crematorium
EAST LONDON CEMETERY
Memorial Recreation Ground
Grange Recreation Ground
Star Park
Recreation Ground
Playing Field
Jubilee Line Depot
Bridge Rd. Depot
Gas Depot
Pumping Station
Mill Meads
Prescott Channel
Channelsea
The London Gas Museum
Gas Works
ABBEY LANE COMMERCIAL ESTATE
PROJECT PARK
CRESCENT COURT BUS. CEN.
THE FORWARD BUS. CEN.
ASHMEAD BUS. CEN.
Superstores
BOW CREEK
BLACKWALL TRAD. EST.
Wharves
LOWER LEA CROSSING
SILVERTOWN WAY
SILVERTOWN VIADUCT
A13
A1011
A112
A114
A124
A1020
B165
B164
B166
B125
LEAMOUTH
East India
Blackwall
BROMLEY
Virginia Quay
Blackwall Pier
Blackwall Point
BLACKWALL TUNNEL
RIVER THAMES
Royal Victoria
Custom House for ExCeL
Prince Regent
ExCeL
ROYAL VICTORIA DOCK
Tidal Basin Watersports Centre
WESTERN BEACH APARTMENTS
VICTORIA DOCK ROAD
London City Airport Pier
Thames Wharf
Brewery
Millennium Mill
Pontoon Dock
NORTH WOOLWICH RD.
Works
Warehouse
Hallsville Prim. Sch.
College
Leisure Cen.
Library
Schools

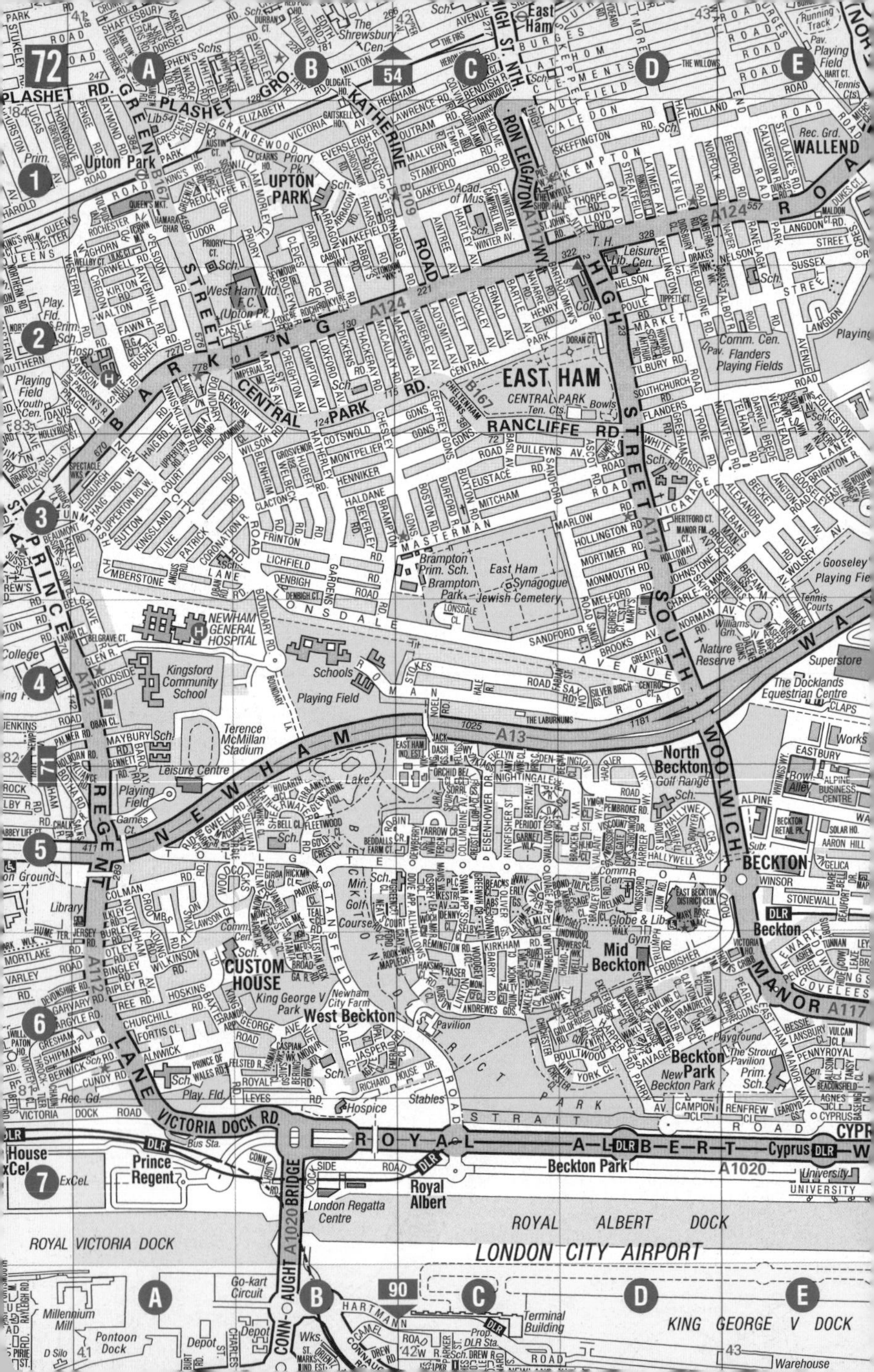

BARKING
Upney
CREEKMOUTH
THAMESMEAD CENTRAL
Gallions Reach
Winsor Park
RIPPLE RD.
ALFRED'S WAY
(EAST HAM AND BARKING BY-PASS)
A13
A123
A406
A1020
A117
CIRCULAR ROAD
ABBEY RD.
DOCKS ROAD
ROYAL DOCKS ROAD
WOOLWICH MANOR WAY
RIVER ROAD
THAMES ROAD
THAMES
RIVER
Beckton Sewage Treatment Works
Sewage Treatment Works
Gas Works
Tanks
Docklands Light Railway Depot
Engine Shed
Barking Creek
Barking Creek Flood Barrier
River Roding
Long Reach
Warpools Reach
Gallions Reach
Margaret or Tripcock Ness
Twin Tumps
Cinema
Bowling Alley
Lagoon
Powerleague Soccer Cen.
Refuse Transfer Station
Hand Trough Creek
Cuckold's Haven
Refuse & Sewage Works
Greatfields Park
Playground
MOVERS LANE
Langdon School
ALBERT BASIN
Gallions Point Marina
Thames House
Newham Coll. of Further Education (Royal Docks Campus)
Custom House
Drawbridge
55
74
91
44
545
46
F
G
H
J
K
1
2
3
4
5
6
7

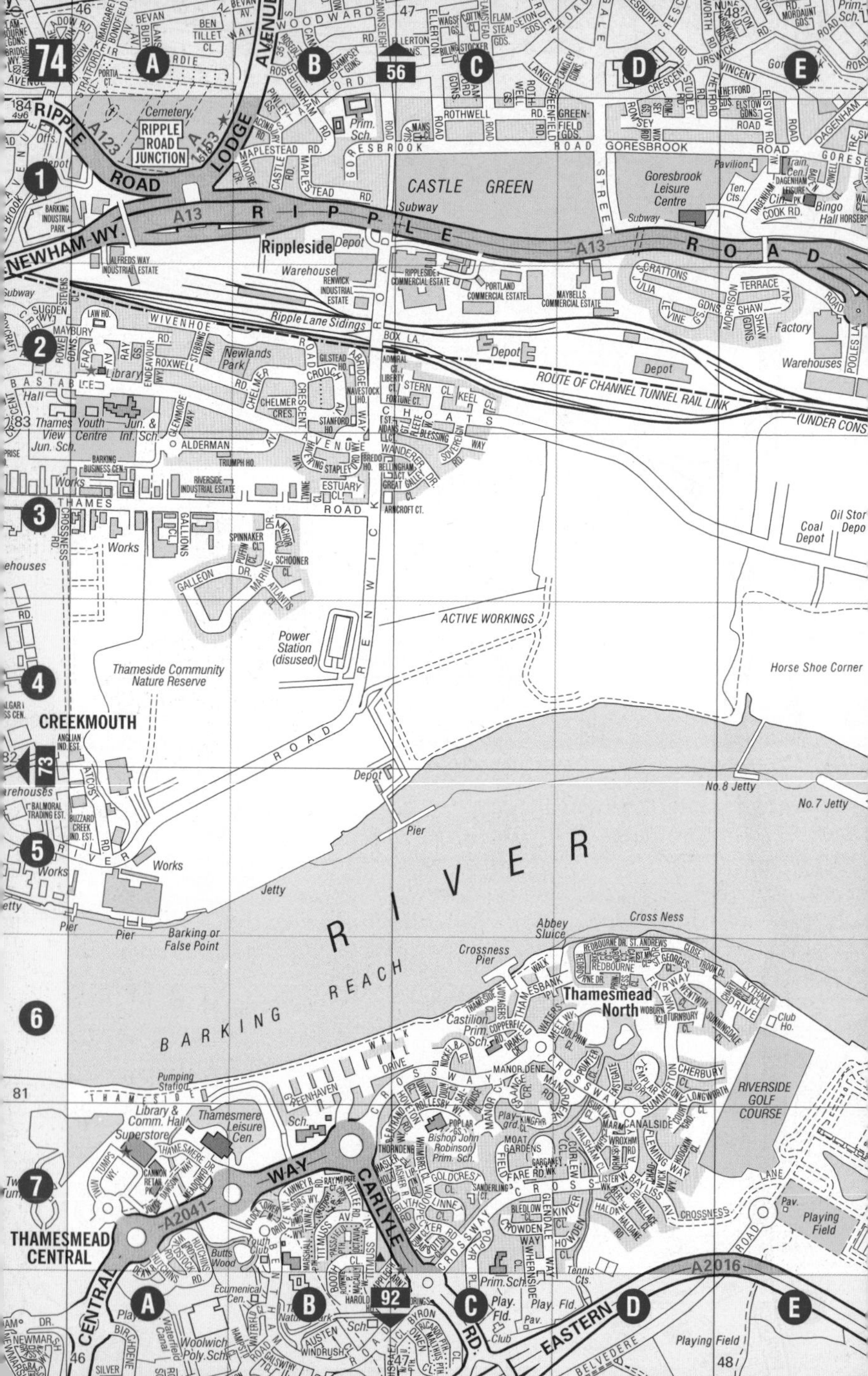
74
56
73
92
A
B
C
D
E
1
2
3
4
5
6
7
RIPPLE ROAD JUNCTION
Cemetery
RIPPLE ROAD
LODGE AVENUE
NEWHAM WY.
A13
RIPPLE ROAD
CASTLE GREEN
Goresbrook Leisure Centre
GORESBROOK ROAD
Rippleside
Warehouse
RENWICK INDUSTRIAL ESTATE
RIPPLESIDE COMMERCIAL ESTATE
PORTLAND COMMERCIAL ESTATE
MAYBELLS COMMERCIAL ESTATE
ALFREDS WAY INDUSTRIAL ESTATE
BARKING INDUSTRIAL PARK
Ripple Lane Sidings
ROUTE OF CHANNEL TUNNEL RAIL LINK
Newlands Park
Library
Thames View Jun. Sch.
Youth Centre
Jun. & Inf. Sch.
BARKING BUSINESS CEN.
RIVERSIDE INDUSTRIAL ESTATE
THAMES ROAD
RENWICK ROAD
Works
Power Station (disused)
ACTIVE WORKINGS
Thameside Community Nature Reserve
CREEKMOUTH
Coal Depot
Oil Stor Depo
Horse Shoe Corner
No.8 Jetty
No.7 Jetty
RIVER ROAD
Depot
Pier
Jetty
Barking or False Point
BARKING REACH
RIVER
Cross Ness
Abbey Sluice
Crossness Pier
Thamesmead North
Castilion Prim. Sch.
Bishop John Robinson Prim. Sch.
Pumping Station
Thamesmere Leisure Cen.
Library & Comm. Hall
Superstore
THAMESMEAD CENTRAL
A2041
CARLYLE WAY
RIVERSIDE GOLF COURSE
Playing Field
A2016
EASTERN WAY
Woolwich Poly. Sch.
Ecumenical Cen.
Butts Wood
Youth Club
Prim. Sch.
Tennis Cts.
Play. Fld.
46
47
48
81
82
83
184
496

SOUTH HORNCHURCH
HORNCHURCH MARSHES
THAMES
Dagenham Dock
GORESBROOK INTERCHANGE
HEATHWAY
RIPPLE ROAD
A1306
A13
NEW ROAD
BALLARDS ROAD
SOUTH DAGENHAM
MOTOR WORKS
Power Station
Dagenham Breach
FORD INDUSTRIAL PARK
Car Compound
Oil Storage Depot
Thunderer Jetty
Landing Stage
Pontoon
Hornchurch Shoot
Old Man's Head
Frog Island
Rainham Steel Mills
Rainham Creek
Timber Yard
Newtons Corner
Mardyke Farm
Beam River
Wantz Stream
THE LEYS
The Leys
Old Dagenham Park
Sports Arena
Dagenham Beam Bridge
Occupation Centre
Goresbrook Park
SEWAGE WORKS
Belvedere Power Sta.
Jenningtree Point
Lighthouse
Wharf
Mill
Pier
Tanks
57
93

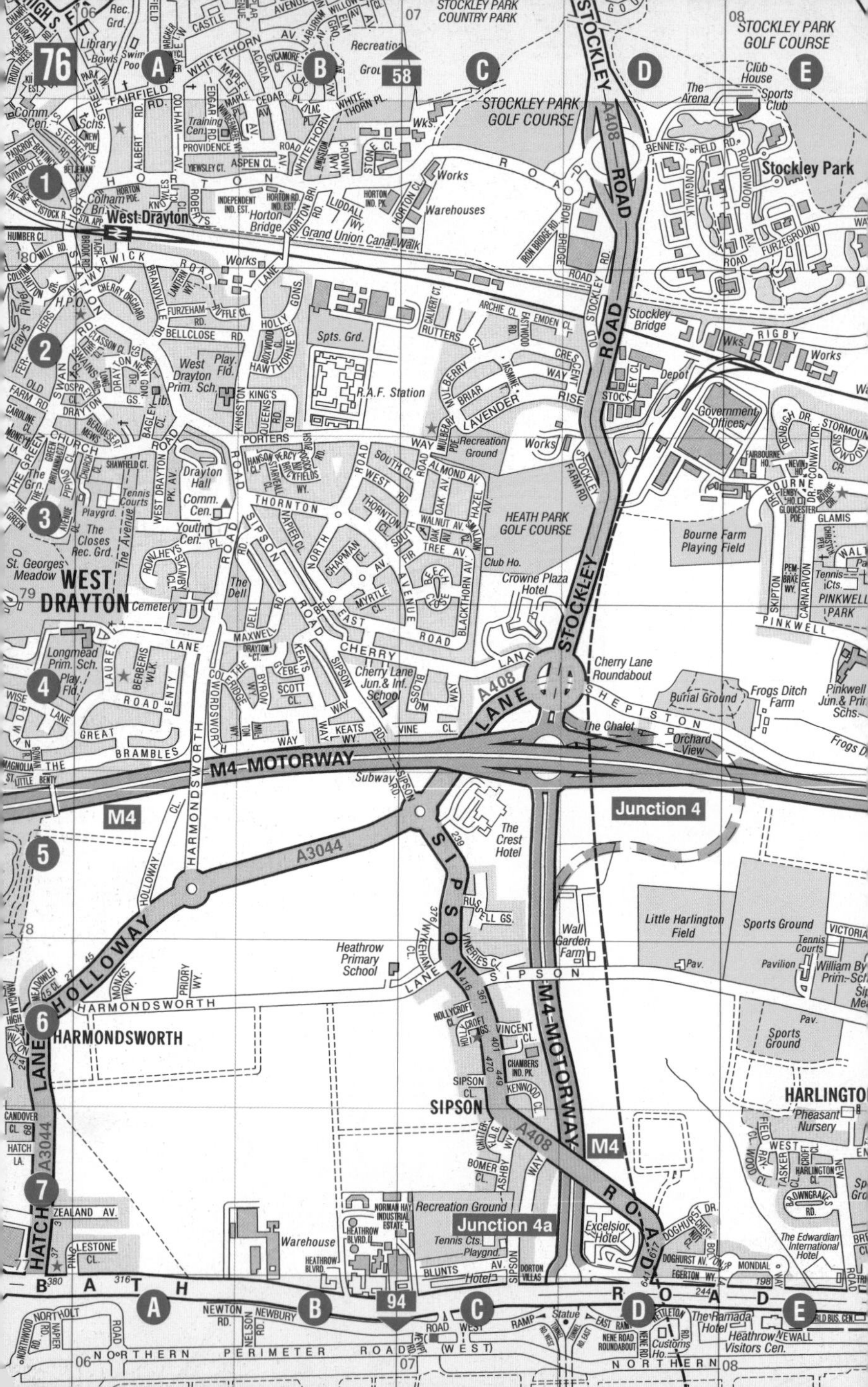
58
94
STOCKLEY PARK COUNTRY PARK
STOCKLEY PARK GOLF COURSE
Stockley Park
West Drayton
WEST DRAYTON
Grand Union Canal Walk
R.A.F. Station
Heath Park Golf Course
Crowne Plaza Hotel
Cherry Lane Roundabout
M4 MOTORWAY
Junction 4
Junction 4a
The Crest Hotel
Heathrow Primary School
Little Harlington Field
Sports Ground
HARMONDSWORTH
SIPSON
HARLINGTON
Excelsior Hotel
The Ramada Hotel
Heathrow Visitors Cen.
The Edwardian International Hotel
BATH ROAD
NORTHERN PERIMETER ROAD (WEST)
Bourne Farm Playing Field
Government Offices
Burial Ground
Frogs Ditch Farm
Longmead Prim. Sch.
Cherry Lane Jun.& Inf. School
Drayton Hall
West Drayton Prim. Sch.
The Closes Rec. Grd.
St. Georges Meadow
Cemetery
A408
A3044
HOLLOWAY
STOCKLEY ROAD
SIPSON ROAD
HATCH LANE

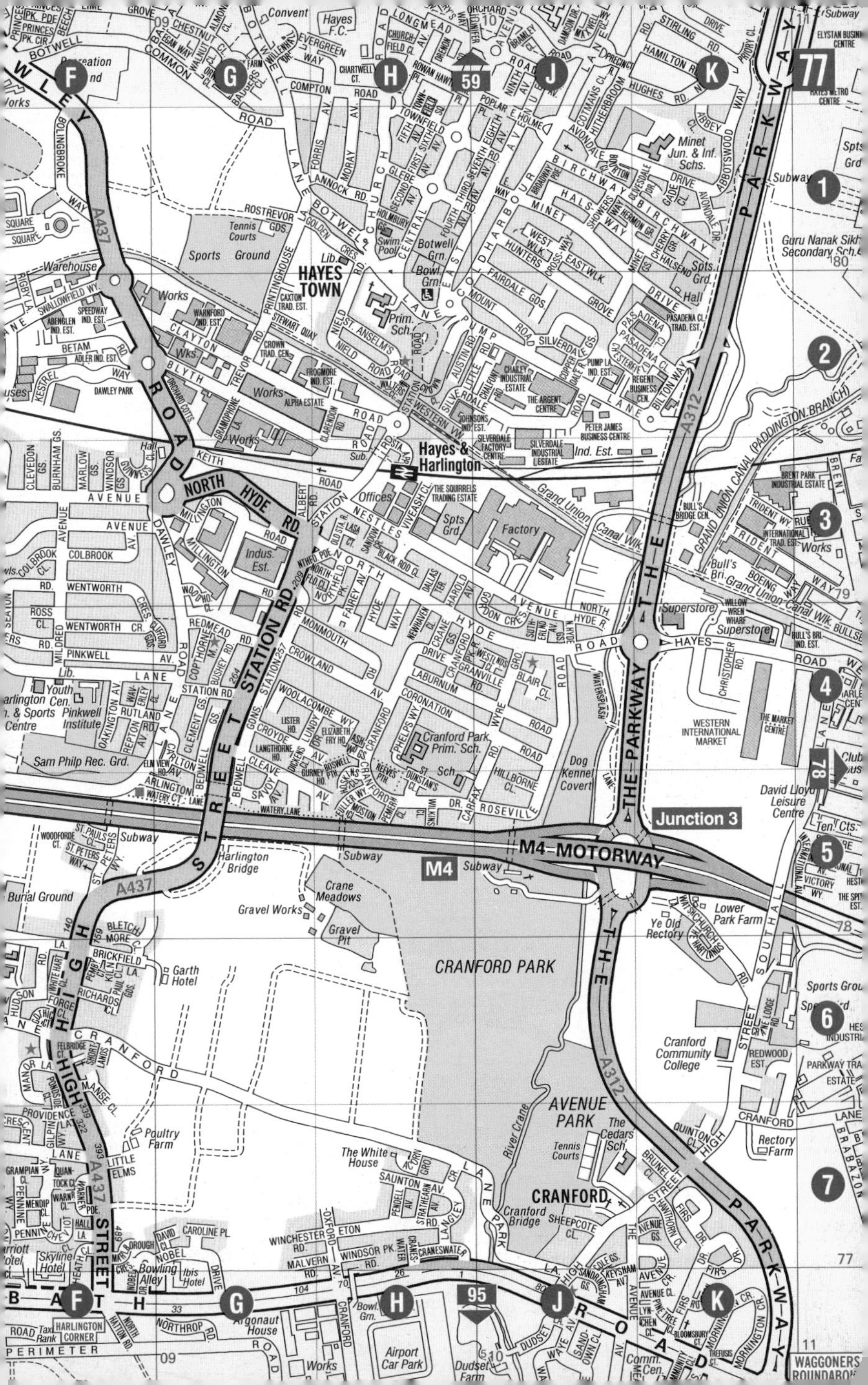

77
HAYES TOWN
Hayes & Harlington
CRANFORD PARK
AVENUE PARK
CRANFORD
M4 MOTORWAY
Junction 3
THE PARKWAY
NORTH HYDE RD.
STATION RD.
HIGH STREET
BATH ROAD
Grand Union Canal
Western International Market
Cranford Community College
Cranford Park Prim. Sch.
Sam Philp Rec. Grd.
Harlington Bridge
Crane Meadows
Gravel Works
Burial Ground
Garth Hotel
Poultry Farm
The White House
Skyline Hotel
Ibis Hotel
Bowling Alley
Argonaut House
Harlington Corner
Airport Car Park
Dudset Farm
Lower Park Farm
Ye Old Rectory
Rectory Farm
David Lloyd Leisure Centre
Dog Kennel Covert
Waggoners Roundabout
59
78
95

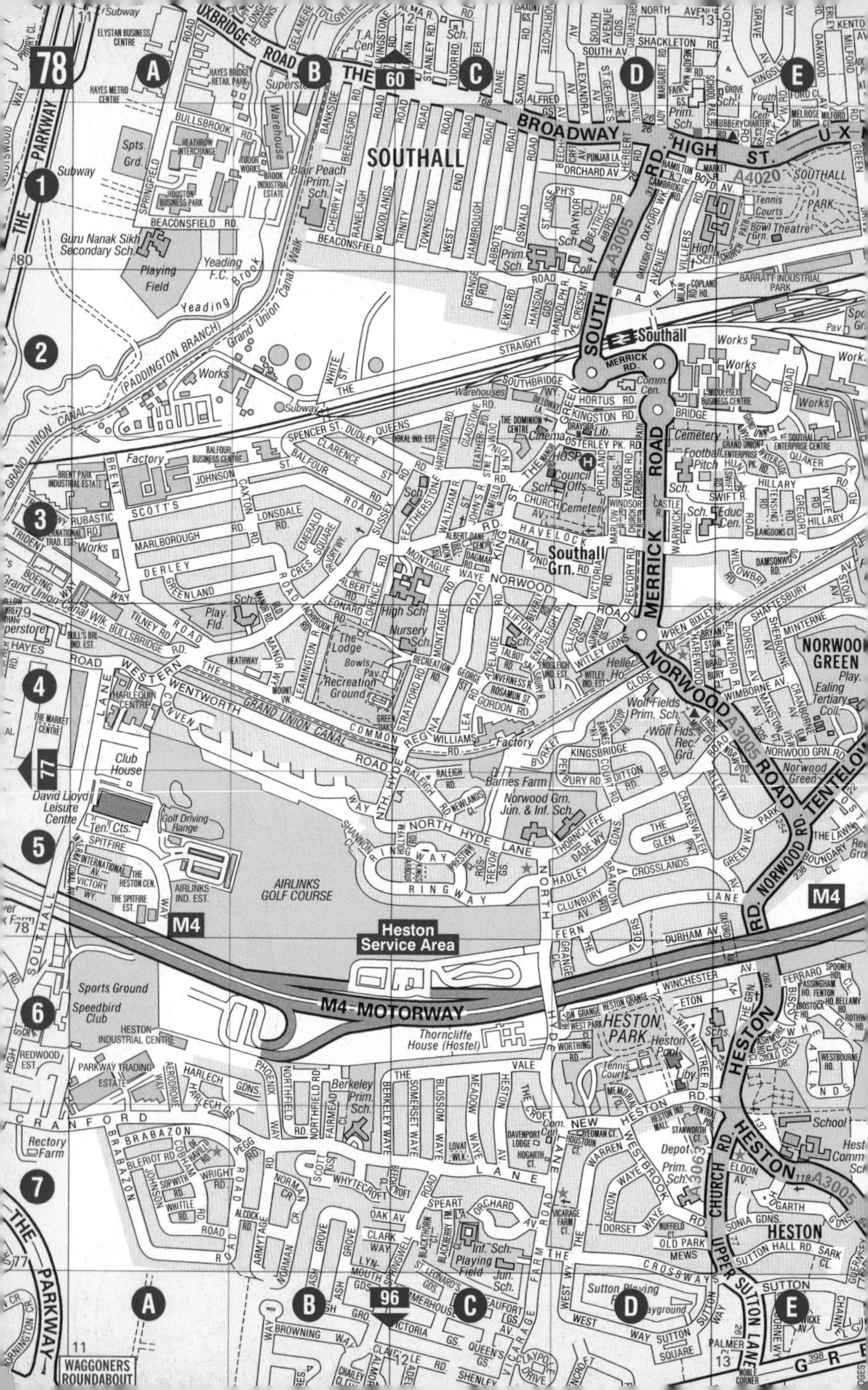

78
77
60
96
A
B
C
D
E
1
2
3
4
5
6
7
11
12
13
UXBRIDGE ROAD
THE BROADWAY
HIGH ST.
A4020
SOUTHALL
SOUTHALL PARK
THE PARKWAY
GRAND UNION CANAL
(PADDINGTON BRANCH)
Grand Union Canal Walk
Yeading Brook
Yeading F.C.
Playing Field
Guru Nanak Sikh Secondary Sch.
Spts. Grd.
HEATHROW INTERCHANGE
HOUSTON BUSINESS PARK
BROOK INDUSTRIAL ESTATE
ELYSTAN BUSINESS CENTRE
HAYES BRIDGE RETAIL PARK
HAYES METRO CENTRE
BEACONSFIELD RD.
Blair Peach Prim. Sch.
Warehouse
Superstore
Subway
SOUTH RD.
A3005
Southall
MERRICK RD.
MERRICK ROAD
NORWOOD ROAD
NORWOOD GREEN
Norwood Green
Ealing Tertiary Coll.
BARRATT INDUSTRIAL PARK
Tennis Courts
Bowl Theatre
Works
MIDDLESEX BUSINESS CENTRE
SOUTHALL ENTERPRISE CENTRE
Cemetery
Football Pitch
Comm. Cen.
THE DOMINION CENTRE
Cinema
Lib.
Hosp.
Council Offs.
THE GREEN
Southall Grn.
KING ST.
HAVELOCK RD.
High Sch.
Nursery Sch.
The Lodge
Bowls Pav.
Recreation Ground
Heller Ho.
Wolf Fields Prim. Sch.
Wolf Fields Rec. Grd.
Factory
Barnes Farm
Norwood Grn. Jun. & Inf. Sch.
NORTH HYDE LANE
NORTH HYDE RD.
BRENT PARK INDUSTRIAL ESTATE
BALFOUR BUSINESS CENTRE
INTERNATIONAL TRAD. EST.
BULL'S BRI. IND. EST.
THE MARKET CENTRE
HARLEQUIN CENTRE
HAYES ROAD
THE WESTERN ROAD
Play. Fld.
Club House
David Lloyd Leisure Centre
Ten. Cts.
Golf Driving Range
AIRLINKS GOLF COURSE
AIRLINKS IND. EST.
THE HESTON CEN.
THE SPITFIRE EST.
M4
Heston Service Area
M4 MOTORWAY
Thorncliffe House (Hostel)
Sports Ground
Speedbird Club
HESTON INDUSTRIAL CENTRE
PARKWAY TRADING ESTATE
CRANFORD LANE
Rectory Farm
Berkeley Prim. Sch.
HESTON PARK
Heston Pool
Tennis Courts
Lby.
Depot
Prim. Sch.
Inf. Sch.
Playing Field
Jun. Sch.
Sutton Playing Field
Playground
HESTON
A3063
HESTON RD.
School
UPPER SUTTON LANE
SUTTON
WAGGONERS ROUNDABOUT

79
DORMER'S WELLS
Dormers Wells Jun. Sch.
WEST MIDDLESEX GOLF COURSE
GREENFORD RD.
A4127
Brent Lodge Park
Churchfields Rec. Grd.
61
Hanwell
Kensington Cemetery
River Brent
Iron Bridge
UXBRIDGE RD.
BROADWAY
A4020
HANWELL
City of Westminster Cemetery
Oaklands Primary Sch.
BOSTON RD.
A3002
ST. BERNARD'S HOSPITAL
EALING HOSP.
Meadow Ho. Hospice
Hanwell Locks
Windmill Bridge
GREAT WESTERN INDUSTRIAL PARK
Grand Union Canal Walk
GRAND UNION CANAL
WINDMILL LANE
B454
Games Courts
Warren Farm School Sports Centre
Sports Ground
WATERSIDE TRADING CENTRE
BOSTON BUSINESS PARK
RIVER BRENT BUSINESS PARK
TRUMPERS WAY
Elthorne Park
Elthorne Park High Sch.
Playing Field
The Aviary Farm
The Aviary
Wincott Farm
Osterley Lock
O S T E R L E Y
M4 MOTORWAY
M4
Trumpers Wood
OSTERLEY LANE
Avenue Lodge
Osterley Park Farm
80
WYKE GREEN GOLF COURSE
Lodges
Wyke Green
Osterley Park House (N.T.)
P A R K
SYON LANE
Club House
Centaurs Rugby Club
West Cross Cen.
OSTERLEY
JERSEY ROAD
Playing Field
Pavilion
GREAT WEST ROAD
A4
Osterley
Running Track
Brunel University
Indian Gymkhana
Sports Ground
Crown Court
97
SPRING GROVE
F
G
H
J
K
1
2
3
4
5
6
7
14
15
16
76
77
78
79
80

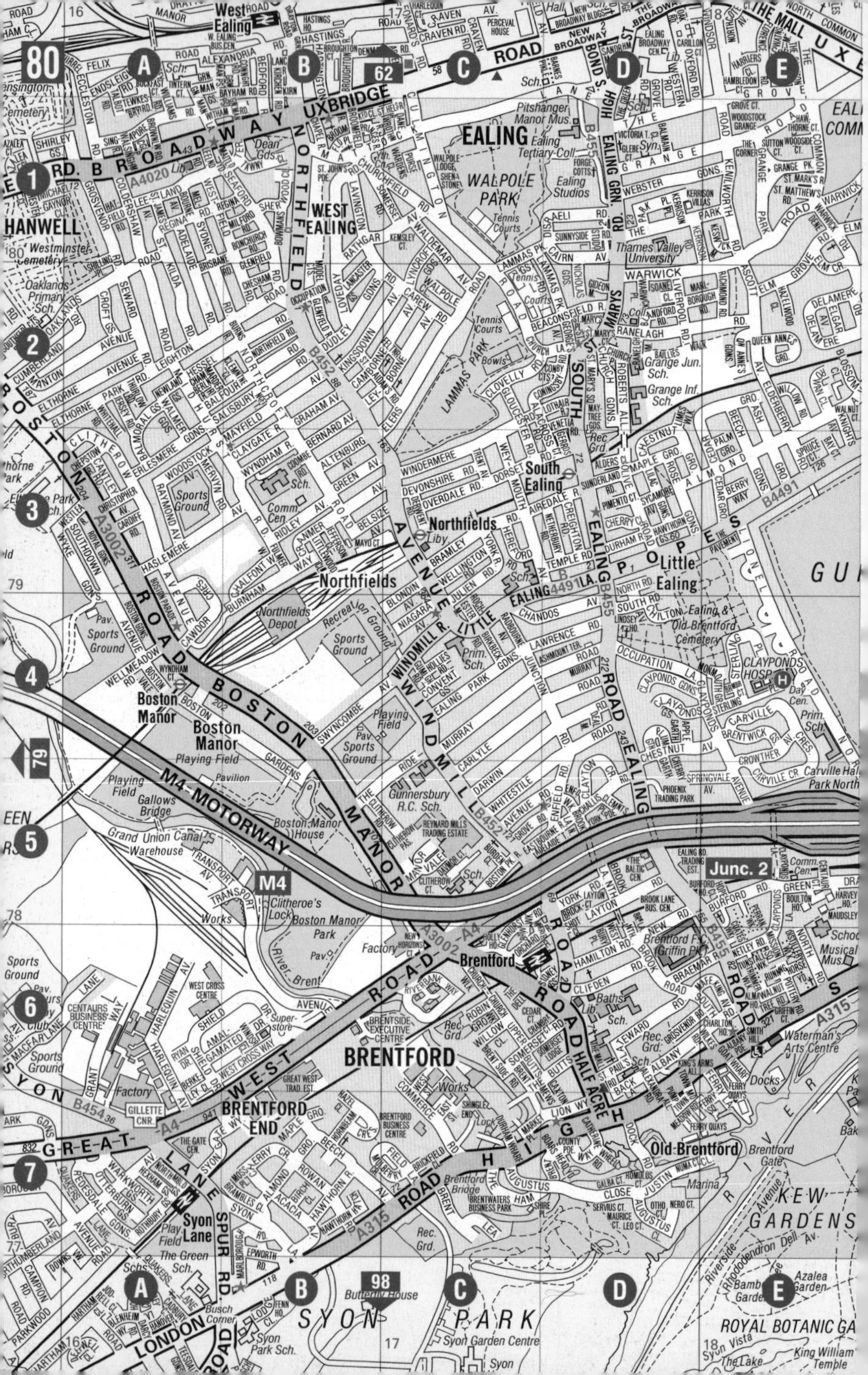
A
B
C
D
E
1
2
3
4
5
6
7
16
17
18
80
79
78
77
62
79
98
West Ealing
EALING
WEST EALING
HANWELL
South Ealing
Little Ealing
Northfields
Boston Manor
BRENTFORD
BRENTFORD END
Old Brentford
Brentford
Syon Lane
SYON PARK
KEW GARDENS
ROYAL BOTANIC GA
UXBRIDGE ROAD
BROADWAY
NEW BROADWAY
NORTHFIELD AVENUE
WINDMILL ROAD
BOSTON MANOR ROAD
BOSTON ROAD
SOUTH EALING ROAD
POPES LANE
M4 MOTORWAY
Junc. 2
M4
GREAT WEST ROAD
HIGH ROAD
HALF ACRE
LONDON ROAD
SPUR RD.
A4020
A3002
B452
B455
B4491
B454
A4
A315
WALPOLE PARK
LAMMAS PARK
Pitshanger Manor Mus.
Ealing Tertiary Coll.
Ealing Studios
Thames Valley University
Westminster Cemetery
Ealing & Old Brentford Cemetery
Northfields Depot
Recreation Ground
Gunnersbury R.C. Sch.
Boston Manor House
Boston Manor Park
Grand Union Canal Warehouse
Clitheroe's Lock
Gallows Bridge
River Brent
Brentford F.C. (Griffin Pk)
Waterman's Arts Centre
CLAYPONDS HOSPITAL
Brentford Gate
Butterfly House
Syon Garden Centre
Syon Park Sch.
Busch Corner
Rhododendron Dell
Azalea Garden
Syon Vista
The Lake
King William Temple
Carville Hall Park North
PHOENIX TRADING PARK
GILLETTE CNR.
CENTAURS BUSINESS CENTRE
WEST CROSS CENTRE
BRENTSIDE EXECUTIVE CENTRE
GREAT WEST TRAD. EST.
BRENTFORD BUSINESS CENTRE
BRENTWATERS BUSINESS PARK
REYNARD MILLS TRADING ESTATE
Marina
Docks

81
EAST ACTON
ACTON
Acton Central
ACTON PARK
SOUTH ACTON
South Acton
Acton Town
ACTON GREEN
BEDFORD PARK
SOUTHFIELD
Southfields Rec. Grd.
Ealing Common
EALING COMN.
GUNNERSBURY
Gunnersbury
CHISWICK PARK
Chiswick Pk.
GUNNERSBURY PARK
NERSBURY
PARK
Museum
Boating Lake
Miniature Golf Course
Kensington Cemetery
Potomac Fish Pond
Refreshment Pavilion
WELLESLEY
Kew Bridge
Steam Mus.
KEW GREEN
KEW
Kew Gardens Gallery
Princess of Wales Conservatory
Plants & People Exhibition
Palm House
Rose Garden
Temple of Bellona
Kew Gds.
Strand on the Green
Oliver's Island
Public Record Office
THAMES
TURNHAM GREEN
CHISWICK
Chiswick House
Chiswick Cemetery
Chiswick Common
Chiswick
GROVE PARK
Sports Ground
M4 MOTORWAY
M4
A4
Junc.1
GT. WEST RD.
CEDARS RD.
ELLESMERE RD.
CHISWICK HIGH RD.
HEATHFIELD TER.
SOUTH PARADE
THE VALE
HIGH ST.
A4020
A4000
A406
A315
A3000
A205
A307
A316
B409
B490
B491
GUNNERSBURY AVENUE
GUNNERSBURY LANE
ACTON LANE
BURLINGTON LANE
GT. CHERTSEY RD.
ALEXANDRA AV.
KEW BRI. RD.
KEW RD.
MORTLAKE RD.
SUTTON COURT RD.
STAVELEY RD.
STEYNE RD.
HORN LANE
63
82
99
F
G
H
J
K
1
2
3
4
5
6
7

A
B
C
D
E
1
2
3
4
5
6
7
64
100
81
ACTON
The King Fahad Academy
Recreation Ground
Sports Ground
Cricket Ground
Leisure Cen.
THE VALE ESTATE
Janet Adegoke Leisure Cen.
Wormholt Park
The Bryony Cen.
Q.P.R. F.C. & Wasps R.U.F.C. (Loftus Rd.)
BBC Television Centre
A219
WOOD LANE
Shepherd's Bush
SHEPHERD'S BUSH GREEN
A4020
THE VALE
UXBRIDGE ROAD
ACTON PARK ESTATE
SOUTHFIELD RD.
THE AVENUE
B491
BEDFORD PARK
Maples Sch.
ASKEW RD.
B408
Wendell Park
Cathnor Park
A402
GOLDHAWK ROAD
Goldhawk Rd.
PADDENSWICK RD.
Adventure Playground
Ravenscourt Park
B409
BATH RD.
STAMFORD BROOK RD.
STH. PDE.
Turnham Green
Stamford Brook
Ravenscourt Park
GLENTHORNE ROAD
Hammersmith
Lyric Theatre
A315
CHISWICK HIGH RD.
KING ST.
A316
CHISWICK LA.
Chiswick Common
Club
Homefield Recreation Ground
A4
GREAT WEST ROAD
HAMMERSMITH
TURNHAM GREEN
HOGARTH LA.
HOGARTH RBT.
Brewery
Chiswick Lodge
Chiswick Eyot
RIVER
Hammersmith Pier
Furnival Gdns.
St. Pauls School
Tennis Courts
Play. Flds.
Playing Field
LILLIAN RD.
GLENTHAM
Riverside Studios
HAMMERSMITH BRI.
CHISWICK
Chiswick House
Temple
Cemy.
Church Wharf
Causeway
Corney Reach
Swedish Sch.
B350
LONSDALE RD.
Nature Reserve
The Harrodian Sch.
Prim. Sch.
Rec. Grd.
Lib.
A306
CASTELNAU
Castelnau
THE WETLANDS CENTRE
THAMES
ALEXANDRA AV.
BURLINGTON LA.
Riverside Recreation Ground
Bowling Green
Sports Ground
Pavilion
Bandstand
Small Profits
Spts. Grd.
Peter Scott Visitor Centre
Barn Elms
Blakes Wharves
Day Cen.
Chiswick Pier

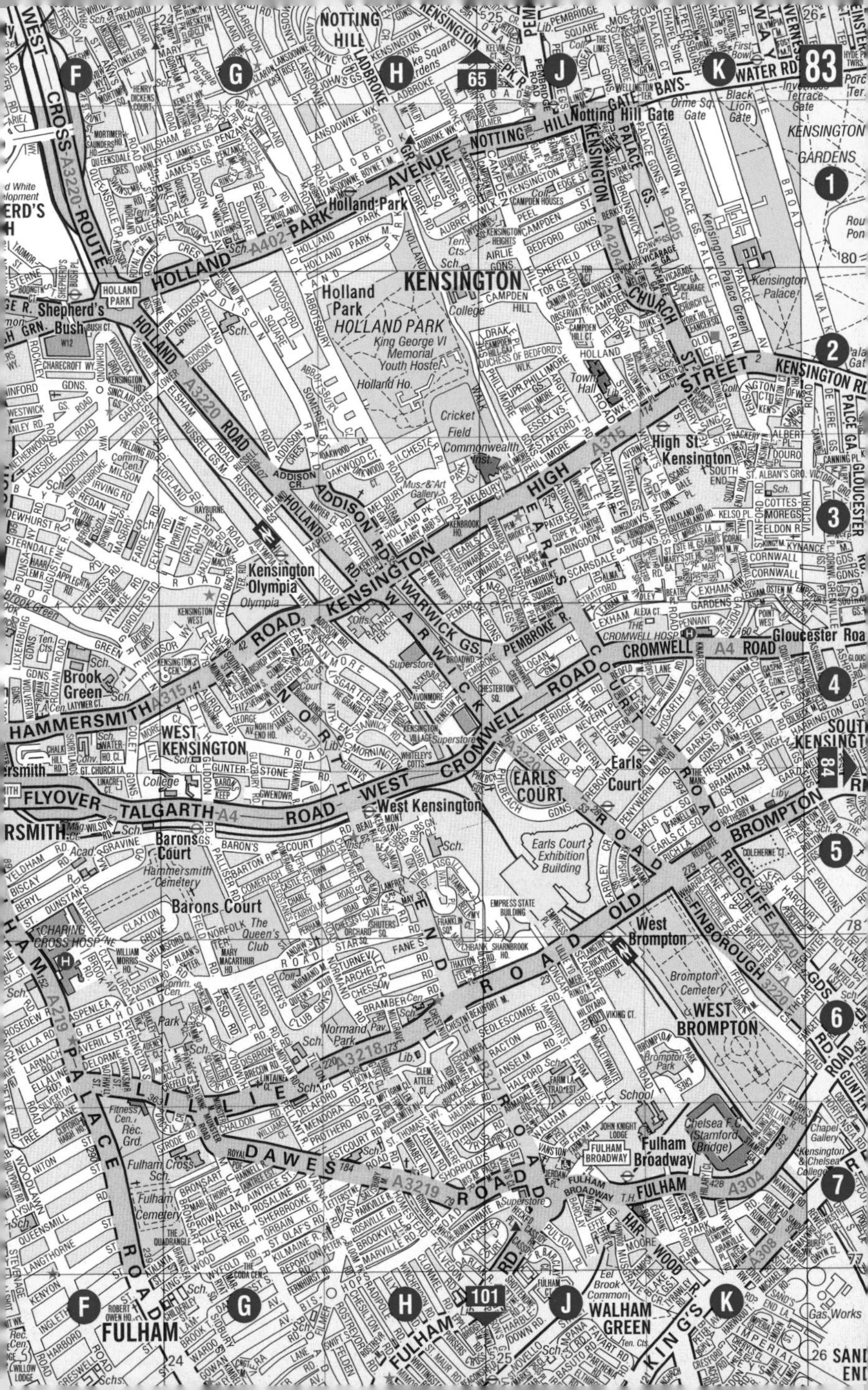

83
F
G
H
J
K
65
NOTTING HILL
Notting Hill Gate
BAYSWATER RD
KENSINGTON GARDENS
Black Lion Gate
Orme Sq. Gate
Kensington Palace
Kensington Palace Green
1
2
3
4
5
6
7
HOLLAND PARK AVENUE
Holland Park
A402
HOLLAND PARK
Holland Park
King George VI Memorial Youth Hostel
Holland Ho.
Cricket Field
Commonwealth Inst.
KENSINGTON
Town Hall
KENSINGTON CHURCH ST.
KENSINGTON HIGH STREET
A315
High St. Kensington
Shepherd's Bush
HOLLAND ROAD
A3220
ADDISON RD.
KENSINGTON ROAD
Kensington Olympia
Olympia
WARWICK RD.
NORTH END RD.
HAMMERSMITH ROAD
Brook Green
WEST KENSINGTON
West Kensington
TALGARTH ROAD
A4
FLYOVER
CROMWELL ROAD
Gloucester Road
THE CROMWELL HOSP.
EARLS COURT
Earls Court
EARLS COURT ROAD
Earls Court Exhibition Building
EMPRESS STATE BUILDING
SOUTH KENSINGTON
84
BROMPTON
REDCLIFFE GDNS.
OLD BROMPTON ROAD
West Brompton
WEST BROMPTON
Brompton Cemetery
FINBOROUGH RD.
Barons Court
Hammersmith Cemetery
The Queen's Club
CHARING CROSS HOSP.
A219
FULHAM PALACE ROAD
LILLIE ROAD
A3218
Normand Park
DAWES ROAD
A3219
Fulham Cross
Fulham Cemetery
FULHAM
FULHAM BROADWAY
Fulham Broadway
FULHAM RD.
A304
Chelsea F.C. (Stamford Bridge)
HARWOOD RD.
A308
Eel Brook Common
WALHAM GREEN
KING'S RD.
101
FULHAM RD.
Gas Works
Chapel Gallery
Kensington & Chelsea College
24
25
26

BAYSWATER RD
Lancaster Gate
Marlborough Gate
The Fountains
Victoria Gate
66
Clarendon Gate
Albion Gate
Place Gate
Refreshment Kiosk
Entrance to Underground Car Park
MAYFAIR
Speke's Monument
The Long Water
Peter Pan Statue
Nursery
Reformers Tree
HYDE PARK
Rangers Lodge
KENSINGTON GARDENS
Round Pond
Temple Lodge
(Open 5am - Midnight)
THE SERPENTINE
Fishermans Keep
Nannies Lawn
Queen Elizabeth Gate
Holocaust Mem. Gdn.
Rose Garden
Kensington Palace
Bandstand
164
Serpentine Gallery
Cafeteria
Rotten Row
Albert Memorial
(Open 5am - Midnight) New Ride
SCOTCH HOUSE
Hyde Park Corner
Palace Gate
Queen's Gate
Alexandra Gate
SOUTH CARRIAGE DRIVE
Prince of Wales Gate
KENSINGTON ROAD
KENSINGTON GORE
A315
KNIGHTSBRIDGE
Knightsbridge
Royal Albert Hall
Imperial College Spts. Cen.
Ryl. Coll. of Music
KNIGHTSBRIDGE
Imperial Coll.
Science Museum
Natural History Mus.
Victoria & Albert Museum
Brompton Oratory
Harrods
BELGRAVE SQ.
GLOUCESTER RD.
CROMWELL RD.
A4
Gloucester Road
THURLOE PL.
BROMPTON
BROMPTON ROAD
SLOANE ST.
PONT ST.
B319
A3216
Sth. Kensington
SOUTH KENSINGTON
170
83
BROMPTON RD.
A3218
SYDNEY ST.
THE ROYAL MARSDEN HOSP.
ROYAL BROMPTON HOSP.
Sloane Square
KING'S ROAD
Duke of York's T.A. H.Q.
Burton's Court
PIMLICO RD.
CHELSEA BRIDGE RD.
Chelsea Barracks
A3308
CHELSEA
THE BOLTONS
REDCLIFFE
ROYAL HOSPITAL RD.
Royal Hospital Chelsea
Ranelagh Gardens
A3216
FULHAM RD.
CHELSEA & WESTMINSTER HOSP.
OAKLEY ST.
B304
A3217
170
EMBANKMENT
171
WEST BROMPTON
CHELSEA EMBANKMENT
CHEYNE WALK
THAMES
RIVER
Cadogan Pier
CHELSEA REACH
Pier
Peace Pagoda
A3031
ALBERT BRIDGE
Childrens Zoo
British Genius Site
Tennis Courts
BATTERSEA PARK
A3220
Chapel Gallery
Kensington & Chelsea College
A308
A3212
WORLDS END EST.
Cremorne Gardens
Chelsea Wharf
Cremorne Wharf
Chelsea Creek
BATTERSEA BRI.
BATTERSEA BRI. RD.
ALBERT BRIDGE ROAD
CENTRAL AVENUE
Boating Lake
Gas Works
SANDS END
102
BATTERSEA
WESTBRIDGE
Wharves
Sun Gate
CARRIAGE DRIVE

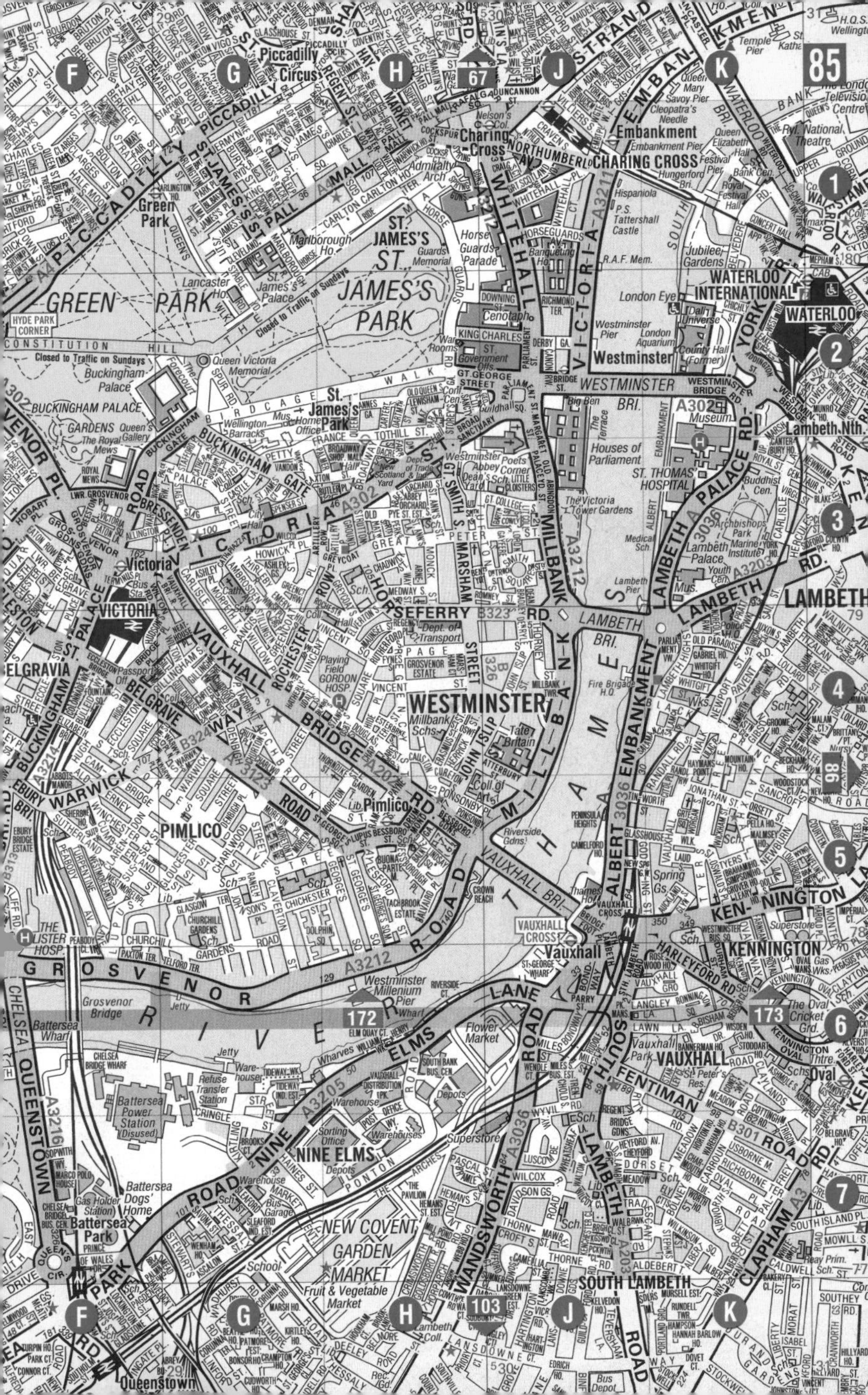
Piccadilly Circus
PICCADILLY
Green Park
GREEN PARK
HYDE PARK CORNER
CONSTITUTION HILL
Closed to Traffic on Sundays
Buckingham Palace
BUCKINGHAM PALACE GARDENS
Queen's Gallery
The Royal Mews
Queen Victoria Memorial
ST. JAMES'S PARK
St. James's Palace
Lancaster Ho.
Marlborough Ho.
Horse Guards Parade
Guards Memorial
Admiralty Arch
Charing Cross
CHARING CROSS
Nelson's Col.
TRAFALGAR SQ.
STRAND
Embankment
Embankment Pier
Cleopatra's Needle
Queen Mary
Savoy Pier
Temple Pier
Queen Elizabeth Hall
Festival Pier
Royal Festival Hall
Hungerford Bri.
Rvl. National Theatre
The London Television Centre
Hispaniola
P.S. Tattershall Castle
R.A.F. Mem.
Jubilee Gardens
London Eye
Dali Universe
Westminster Pier
London Aquarium
County Hall (Former)
WATERLOO INTERNATIONAL
WATERLOO
WHITEHALL
VICTORIA EMBANKMENT
Banqueting Ho.
Cenotaph
Downing St.
War Rooms
Government Offs.
Westminster
WESTMINSTER BRIDGE
Big Ben
Houses of Parliament
The Victoria Tower Gardens
Westminster Abbey
Poets Corner
New Scotland Yard
St. James's Park
Wellington Barracks
Home Office
Victoria
VICTORIA
VICTORIA STREET
BUCKINGHAM GATE
BUCKINGHAM PALACE ROAD
BELGRAVIA
Westminster Cath.
Coach Sta.
ST. THOMAS' HOSPITAL
Museum
Lambeth Nth.
Buddhist Cen.
Archbishops Park
Lambeth Palace
Marine Institute
Youth Cen.
LAMBETH PALACE RD.
LAMBETH RD.
LAMBETH
LAMBETH BRI.
Lambeth Pier
Medical Sch.
Fire Brigade H.Q.
SEFERRY RD.
Dept. of Transport
WESTMINSTER
Millbank Schs.
Tate Britain
Coll. of Art
MILLBANK
ALBERT EMBANKMENT
VAUXHALL BRIDGE RD.
Riverside Gdns.
Playing Field
GORDON HOSP.
GROSVENOR ESTATE
PIMLICO
Pimlico
WARWICK WAY
BELGRAVE RD.
Churchill Gardens
Dolphin Sq.
VAUXHALL BRI.
Crown Reach
VAUXHALL CROSS
Vauxhall
Spring Gs.
KENNINGTON LA.
KENNINGTON
The Oval Cricket Grd.
Oval
VAUXHALL
Vauxhall Park
FENTIMAN RD.
SOUTH LAMBETH ROAD
SOUTH LAMBETH
CLAPHAM RD.
GROSVENOR ROAD
RIVER THAMES
Grosvenor Bridge
Battersea Wharf
Westminster Millenium Pier
NINE ELMS LANE
NINE ELMS
Flower Market
Battersea Power Station (Disused)
Refuse Transfer Station
Sorting Office
Battersea Dogs' Home
Battersea Park
NEW COVENT GARDEN MARKET
Fruit & Vegetable Market
WANDSWORTH ROAD
QUEENSTOWN RD.
Queenstown
CHELSEA BRIDGE
QUEEN'S CIR.
Bus Depot
THE LISTER HOSP.
67
172
173
86
103
F
G
H
J
K
1
2
3
4
5
6
7

RIVER THAMES
BLACKFRIARS
Millennium Bridge
H.Q.S. Wellington
H.M.S. President
68
A
B
C
D
E
CANNON STREET
LOWER THAMES ST.
BYWARD ST.
The London Television Centre
Ryl. National Theatre
Tate Modern
BANKSIDE
SOUTHWARK
SOUTHWARK BRI.
LONDON BRI.
LONDON BRIDGE HOSP.
London Bri. City Pier
H.M.S. Belfast
Tower Millennium Pier
HAY'S GALLERIA
City Hall
STAMFORD ST.
WATERLOO
UPPER GROUND
SOUTHWARK ST.
UNION ST.
THE BOROUGH
GUY'S HOSP.
TOOLEY ST.
LONDON BRI.
ST. THOMAS ST.
Southwark
Waterloo East
THE CUT
WATERLOO
Lambeth Nth.
WESTMINSTER BRI. RD.
BLACKFRIARS RD.
SOUTHWARK BRIDGE RD.
BOROUGH HIGH ST.
Borough
LONG LANE
BERMONDSEY ST.
SNOWSFIELDS
168
169
BOROUGH RD.
LONDON RD.
ST. GEORGE'S RD.
Imperial War Mus.
Geraldine Mary Harmsworth Park
LAMBETH
NEWINGTON
NEWINGTON CAUSEWAY
HARPER RD.
GREAT DOVER ST.
TOWER BRIDGE RD.
GRANGE RD.
Elephant & Castle
NEW KENT RD.
BRICKLAYER'S ARMS
KENNINGTON RD.
KENNINGTON LANE
173
85
WALWORTH RD.
WALWORTH
EAST ST.
OLD KENT RD.
Kennington
KENNINGTON PARK RD.
KENNINGTON
Surrey C.C.G.
The Oval Cricket Grd.
KENNINGTON OVAL
Oval
Kennington Park
CAMBERWELL NEW RD.
CAMBERWELL RD.
ALBANY RD.
Burgess Park
BURGESS PARK
Chumleigh Gdns.
NEATE ST.
SOUTHAMPTON WAY
PECKHAM
CLAPHAM RD.
BRIXTON RD.
104
MEDLAR ST.
CAMBERWELL GREEN
CAMBERWELL
Brunswick Park
St. Gabriel's Manor

87
SHADWELL
TOWER HILL
EAST SMITHFIELD
THE TOWER
St. Katharine Docks
Tower Hotel
Shadwell Basin
King Edward Mem. Park
Shadwell Dock Stairs
RIVER THAMES
Wapping
WAPPING
UPPER POOL
LOWER POOL
BERMONDSEY
Cherry Garden Pier
Rotherhithe
ROTHERHITHE
Canada Water
Surrey Quays
SURREY QUAYS SHOPPING CENTRE
Greenland Dock
Ecological Park
Bellamy's Wharf
Cumberland Wharf
Pelican Stairs
New Crane Stairs
Wapping Old Stairs
Wapping New Stairs
King Henrys Stairs
ROTHERHITHE TUNNEL
A101
JAMAICA ROAD
TOWER BRIDGE ROAD
A100
A200
A2202
A2206
A2208
B205
LOWER ROAD
SALTER RD.
REDRIFF RD.
BRUNEL RD.
SOUTHWARK PARK
SOUTHWARK PARK RD.
RAYMOUTH RD.
ROTHERHITHE NEW RD.
PLOUGH WY.
TRUNDLEYS ROAD
South Bermondsey
MILLWALL F.C. (The Den)
Waste Transfer Station
South Eastern Gas Works
OLD KENT ROAD
A2
TRAFALGAR AV.
ROLLS RD.
DUNTON RD.
CATLIN ST.
PECKHAM PARK RD.
PECKHAM HILL ST.
PECKHAM HIGH ST.
QUEEN'S ROAD
NEW CROSS RD.
NEW CROSS GATE
New Cross Gate
ASYLUM ROAD
POMEROY ST.
KENDER ST.
Brimmington Pk.
Superstore
Bermondsey Spa
Leisure Cen.
Sports Complex
169
69
88
105
F
G
H
J
K
1
2
3
4
5
6
7
34
35
36

70
87
106
LIMEHOUSE REACH
RIVER THAMES
GREENWICH REACH
West India Quay
Canary Wharf
Heron Quays
South Quay
WEST INDIA DOCKS
ISLE OF DOGS
MILLWALL
CUBITT TOWN
Mudchute
MUDCHUTE PARK
MILLWALL PARK
Island Gds.
Crossharbour & London Arena
Poplar
Billingsgate Fish Market
Westferry Circus
WESTFERRY ROAD
MANCHESTER ROAD
PRESTONS ROAD
SALTER ROAD
REDRIFF ROAD
PLOUGH WAY
EVELYN ST.
DEPTFORD
DEPTFORD PARK
CONVOY'S WHARF
Pepys Park
Deptford
New Cross
New Cross Gate
Greenwich
Cutty Sark for Maritime Greenwich
Deptford Bri.
CREEK ROAD
DEPTFORD CHURCH ST.
GREENWICH HIGH RD.
NEW CROSS RD.
BLACKHEATH RD.
Goldsmiths College
Surrey Docks Farm
Greenland Dock
SOUTH DOCK
MILLWALL OUTER DOCK
Printing Works
Ecological Park
Stave Hill
Greenwich Foot Tunnel

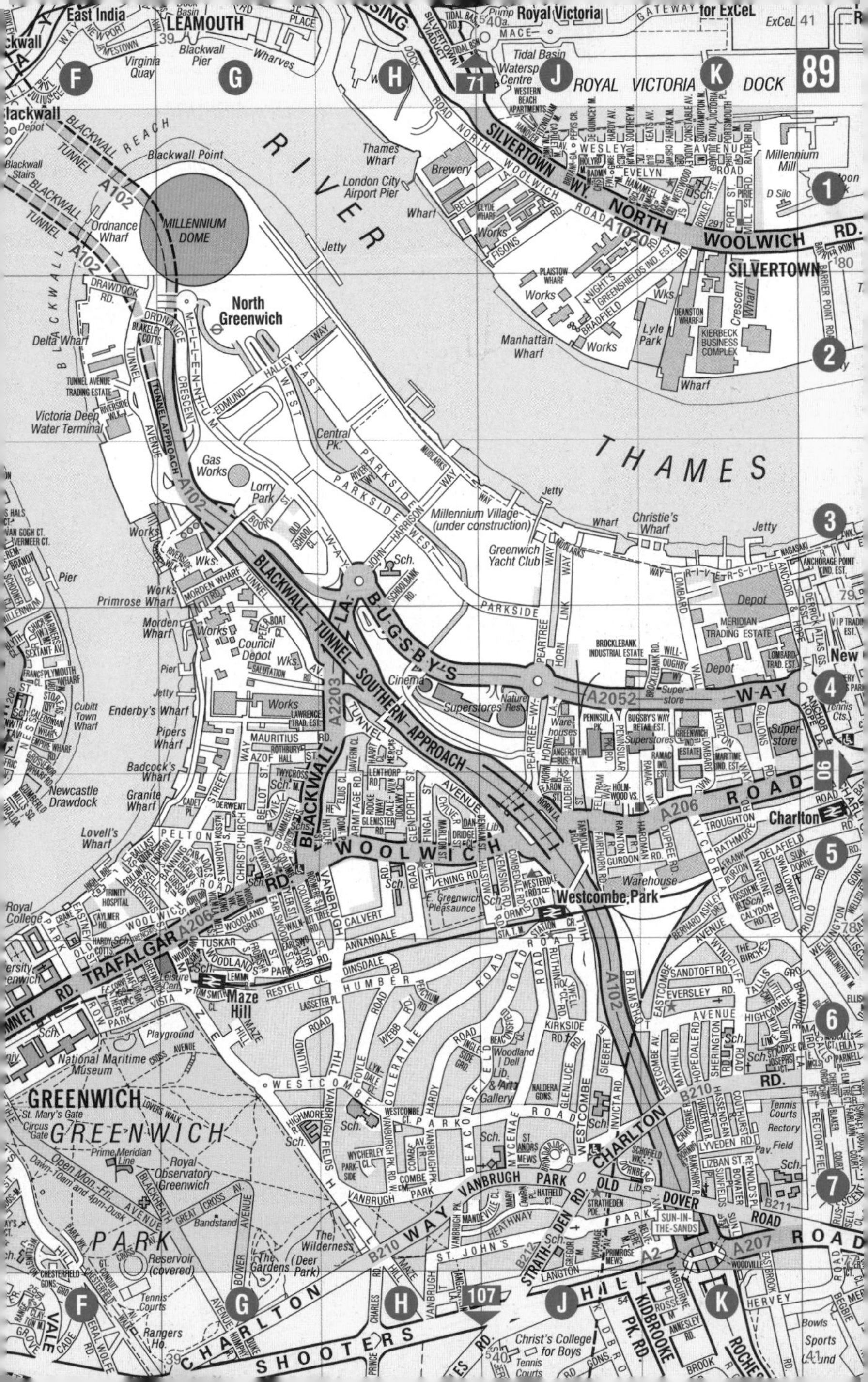
89
ROYAL VICTORIA DOCK
RIVER
THAMES
MILLENNIUM DOME
North Greenwich
GREENWICH
GREENWICH PARK
Royal Observatory Greenwich
National Maritime Museum
Maze Hill
Westcombe Park
Charlton
SILVERTOWN
Millennium Village (under construction)
Greenwich Yacht Club
BLACKWALL TUNNEL SOUTHERN APPROACH
WOOLWICH RD.
TRAFALGAR RD.
BUGSBY'S WAY
NORTH WOOLWICH RD.
SHOOTERS HILL
CHARLTON WAY
OLD DOVER ROAD
Thames Wharf
London City Airport Pier
Lyle Park
Manhattan Wharf
Christie's Wharf
Tidal Basin
71
90
107

ExCeL
Prince Regent
Royal Albert
Beckton Park
ROYAL VICTORIA DOCK
72
ROYAL ALBERT DOCK
LONDON CITY AIRPORT
London Regatta Centre
Go-kart Circuit
Millennium Mill
Pontoon Dock
Terminal Building
KING GEORGE V DOCK
Warehouse
NORTH WOOLWICH RD.
A1020
SILVERTOWN
Thames Barrier Park
Silvertown
THAMES ROAD INDUSTRIAL ESTATE
THAMESIDE INDUSTRIAL ESTATE
Sugar Refinery
FACTORY ROAD
ALBERT RD.
A112
STANDARD INDUSTRIAL ESTATE
North Woolwich
NORTH WOOLWICH
PIER RD.
A117
North Woolwich Pier
WOOLWICH REACH
THAMES FLOOD BARRIER
RIVER
Woolwich Free Ferry
Waterfront Leisure Centre
WOOLWICH HIGH ST.
WOOLWICH CHURCH ST.
Woolwich Dockyard
WOOLWICH ROAD
A206
New Charlton
Charlton
Charlton Athletic F.C. (The Valley)
Maryon Park
MARYON WILSON PARK
WOOLWICH
JOHN WILSON ST.
ARTILLERY PL.
WELLINGTON ST.
LITTLE HEATH
HILL REACH
B210
Museum of Artillery in the Rotunda
Repository Woods
Royal Artillery Barracks
GRAND DEPOT RD.
A205
CHARLTON PARK RD.
CHARLTON
Charlton Ho.
Library
CHARLTON PARK
Cricket Ground
CHARLTON CEMETERY
QUEEN ELIZABETH HOSPITAL
Sports Ground
WOOLWICH COMMON
Old Royal Military Academy
Eaglesfield School
Hornfair Park
SHOOTERS HILL ROAD
A207
108
Recreation Ground
Reservoir (covered)
41
42
43
A
B
C
D
E
1
2
3
4
5
6
7
89

91
73
109
92
F
G
H
J
K
1
2
3
4
5
6
7
THAMESMEAD CENTRAL
THAMESMEAD
Thamesmead South West
THAMESMEAD WEST
PLUMSTEAD MARSHES
THAMES
GALLIONS REACH
WOOLWICH REACH
ALBERT BASIN
Gallions Point Marina
Thames House
Newham Coll. of Further Education (Royal Docks Campus)
Custom House
Drawbridge
Gallions Point
Hoba Wharf
Twin Tumps
Gallions Park
Gallions Lake
Broadwater
Broadwater Green
Crown Ct.
Magistrates Ct.
H. M. P. BELMARSH
WOOLWICH INDUSTRIAL ESTATE
Works
Firepower (Royal Artillery Museum)
Southern Outfall Sewers
Recreation Ground
Bowling Green
Tennis Courts
Plumstead
Woolwich Arsenal
PLUMSTEAD
PLUMSTEAD RD.
PLUMSTEAD HIGH STREET
A206
A2016
A117
WOOLWICH MANOR WAY
WESTERN WAY
PETTMAN CRES.
HARROW MANOR WAY
WICKHAM LA.
Winn's Common
WINNS COMMON
PLUMSTEAD COMMON
Plumstead Common
Bleak Hill
BLEAK HILL LANE
Woolwich Cemetery
Rockliffe Gdns.
Playing Field
Play. Field
SHREWSBURY PARK
SHOOTERS HILL GOLF COURSE
Clothworkers Wood
Greenwood School
Griffin Manor School
Woodlands Abattoir
Lowood Club Ho
East Wickham Open Space
Leisure Cen.
Plumstead Gdns.
Tennis Courts
Bowl Grn.
Sch.
Prim. Sch.
Lib.
Coll.
44
545
46
77
78
79

THAMESMEAD CENTRAL
Twin Tumps
46
47
48
A
B
C
D
E
1
2
3
4
5
6
7
180
79
78
77
74
91
110
THAMESMEAD
Birchmere
Birchmere Park
THAMESMEAD SOUTH
Lakeside Centre
Southmere Lake
Playing Field
Play. Fld.
Woolwich Poly. Sch.
Waterfield Canal
Butts Wood
Youth Club
Ecumenical Cen.
Tump 53 Natural Park
St. Margaret Clitherow R.C. Prim. Sch.
EASTERN WAY
A2016
A2041
CENTRAL WAY
HARROW MANOR WAY
CARLYLE
CROSSWAY
CROSSNESS
HAROLD WILSON HO.
MOORINGS
BELVEDERE
HARTSLOCK DR.
PORTMEADOW WLK.
SEACOURT RD.
Prim. Sch.
TILEHURST POINT
BLEWBURY HO.
TAVY BRIDGE
YARNTON WAY
WOLVERCOTE RD.
HINKSEY PATH
LAKESIDE WAY
LENSBURY
OVERTON ROAD
SEDGEMERE RD.
SYDNEY RD.
RUSHDENE
ALSIKE
Thamesmead Community College
KALE WAY
Birchmere Business Site
HARNESS RD.
NATHAN WAY
PURLAND ROAD
Works
SEWELL ROAD
Abbey Wood Park
Library
Sports Ground
Abbey Wood Sch.
FINCHALE RD.
MOTTISFONT ROAD
FELIXSTOWE ROAD
Abbey Wood
ABBEY WOOD
School
Wks.
THROWLEY CL.
EDINGTON RD.
LUFFIELD RD.
CHALCOMBE RD.
BRACONDALE RD.
BIRKDALE RD.
BLITHDALE RD.
McLEOD RD.
B213
ABBEY WOOD RD.
ABBEY GRO.
KNEE HILL
A2041
Lesnes Abbey Pk.
Remains of Lesnes Abbey
LESNES ABBEY
WOODLAND WAY
FENDYKE
ABBEY RD.
ELSTREE
Rec. Grd.
LEATHER
Tennis Courts
Recreation Ground
MANORWAY
CHURCH
PLUMSTEAD
PLUMSTEAD HIGH ST.
BOSTALL HILL
BOSTALL HEATH
BOSTALL LANE
BASILDON R.
Bostall Gds.
FEDERATION RD.
COMMONWEALTH
Cooperative Woods
ABBEY WOOD CAMPING & CARAVAN SITE
BELVEDERE PRIVATE CLINIC
Hospice
Bostall Ho.
A206
WOOLWICH ROAD
HURST LA.
HARVEL CRES.
FRIARS WLK.
PRIORY DR.
WICKHAM LANE
A209
BOSTALL WOODS
Bowling Green
Heathview Day Centre
Clam Field Recreation Ground
Playing Field
Turpins Cave
LONGLEIGH LA.
BRAMPTON RD.
WEST HEATH
WEST HEATH RD.
GLENVIEW
Bedonwell Prim. & Inf. Schs.
BEDONWELL RD.
Coll.
Bowl. Grn.
Ten. Cts.
Rec. Grd.
AMBERLEY
Bleak Hill
KING'S HIGHWAY
Rockliffe Gds.
SOUTHLAND
Woolwich Cemetery
Play. Field
Hill Grove
PLUMSTEAD CEMETERY
UPPER WICKHAM LANE
EAST WICKHAM
East Wickham Open Space
CHALK STREET
Prim. Sch.
PLYMSTOCK RD.
OKEHAMPTON CRES.
LANSDOWNE LANE
FIRST AVENUE
MADISON CRES.
LESSNESS AV.
KING HAROLDS WAY
Lib.
BOSTALL PARK AV.
LONG LANE
GIPSY ROAD
AXMINSTER CRES.
Stevens Park
CHARMOUTH RD.
SHAKESPEARE RD.
KINGSGATE CL.
GRANITE ST.
GLENDOWN RD.
BASTION RD.
GROSMONT RD.

SEWAGE WORKS
Tanks
RIVER
Wharf
Belvedere Power Sta.
Mill
Jenningtree Point
Lighthouse
ERITH REACH
THAMES
A2016
THAMESMEAD EAST
MARSHES
CROSSNESS
FOOTPATH
EASTERN INDUSTRIAL ESTATE
HAILEY RD.
Depot
WAY
BRONZE
MANORWAY
NORMAN ROAD
Works
Tennis Courts
RIVER WHARF BUSINESS PARK
MULBERRY
ANDERSON WY.
ST. THOMAS RD.
CRABTREE
JENNINGTREE WAY
FISHERS WAY
CALLENDERS COTTS.
Sports Grd.
Pav.
Pier
WORKS
CAPITAL INDUSTRIAL ESTATE
ELBOURNE TRADING ESTATE
KEATS RD.
CABLES CL.
VIKING WAY
HARRON
CENTURION WY.
LEATHERBOTTLE GRN.
ASPEN GRN.
Prim. Sch.
WATERFIELD CL.
SUTHERLAND RD.
MAIDA RD.
CALDY RD.
STATION RD. N.
DOWLING HO.
DYLAN RD.
Belvedere
Superstore
Belvedere Youth Cen.
Belvedere Jun. & Inf. Sch.
New Bri.
GILBERT RD.
PICARDY ST.
LOWER ROAD
B213
B253
PICARDY ROAD
B250
MONARCH RD.
ROAD
WEST STREET
CHURCH MANORWAY
CORINTHIAN MANORWAY
GALLEON CL.
BELVEDERE
HILLSIDE
FRANK'S PARK
Bexley College
VALLEY AVENUE
Trinity Sch. Belvedere
HALT ROBIN RD.
UPPER ABBEY RD.
BOTTLE LANE
GARDENS
KINGSWOOD AV.
WOODS
NELSON RD.
LESSNESS PK.
ERITH ROAD
A206
Liby.
CAMDEN CT.
Play. Fld.
Hall
Coll. Annexe
HOLLY HILL RD.
RIVERDALE RD.
PARKSIDE LODGE
PEMBROKE RD.
ALFORD RD.
ATHOL RD.
FRASER ROAD
Open Space
LESSNESS HEATH
Prim. Sch.
Adult Ed. Cen.
ERITH
Erith
Works
EUROPA TRADING ESTATE
Sub.
Sand and Gravel Pit
ERITH CEMETERY
Lime Wood
A220
CRESCENT ROAD
CHRISTCHURCH AV.
ARRAN CL.
Pav. Sch.
Spts. Grd.
ERITH & DIST. HOSP.
PARK CRES.
LESNEY PARK RD.
MORTIMER RD.
Monastery Prim. Sch.
Cemy.
Hall
BEXLEY ROAD
AVENUE RD.
CARLTON RD.
MANORWAY
Playing Field
Pav.
Club Ho.
Ten. Cts.
Bowl. Grn.
Rec. Grd.
Play-grd.
LOCHMERE CL.
Lib.
LIMEWOOD
Erith Sch.
NORTHUMBERLAND HEATH
Pav. Playing Field
School
NORTHUMBERLAND PK.
BEXLEY ROAD
PARSONAGE MANORWAY
BEDONWELL ROAD
STREAM WAY
NUXLEY ROAD
Belmont Prim. Sch.
BELMONT RD.
IGHTHAM RD.
NURSTEAD RD.
HURLINGHAM RD.
HEATH RD.
ROMNEY GDNS.
CRANBROOK RD.
CHELSEA AV.
DUNWICH
CARTMEL
CRES.
COLYERS LANE
LESNEY FARM ESTATE
Colyers Prim. Sch.
Play. Fld.
Res. (covered)
BIRCHINGTON CL.
ERITH RD.
BARNEHURST
NORTHUMBERLAND
SILECROFT
F
G
H
J
K
1
2
3
4
5
6
7
49
550
51
180
79
78

75
111

LONDON-HEATHROW AIRPORT
Junction 4a
TERMINAL 1
TERMINAL 2
TERMINAL 3
TERMINAL 4
Heathrow Terminals 1,2&3
Heathrow Terminal 4
Heathrow Cen.
Queen's Building
Control Tower
D'Albiac House
Cargo Terminal
Heathrow Express Rail Link
Cargo Tunnel
Vehicle Tunnel
London Heathrow Hilton Hotel
H.M. Customs & Excise
Heathrow Corporate Cen.
Warehouses
WEST BEDFONT
STANWELL
Recreation Ground
Ashford Football Ground
Mentone Farm
Westview Cotts.
Sports Ground
CLOCKHOUSE ROUNDABOUT
Excelsior Hotel
The Ramada Hotel
The Edwardian International Hotel
Heathrow Visitors Cen.
NORTHERN PERIMETER ROAD (WEST)
SOUTHERN PERIMETER ROAD
BATH ROAD
STANWELL ROAD
LONGFORD ROAD
STAINES ROAD
GREAT SOUTH WEST ROAD
A4
A30
M4
76
112

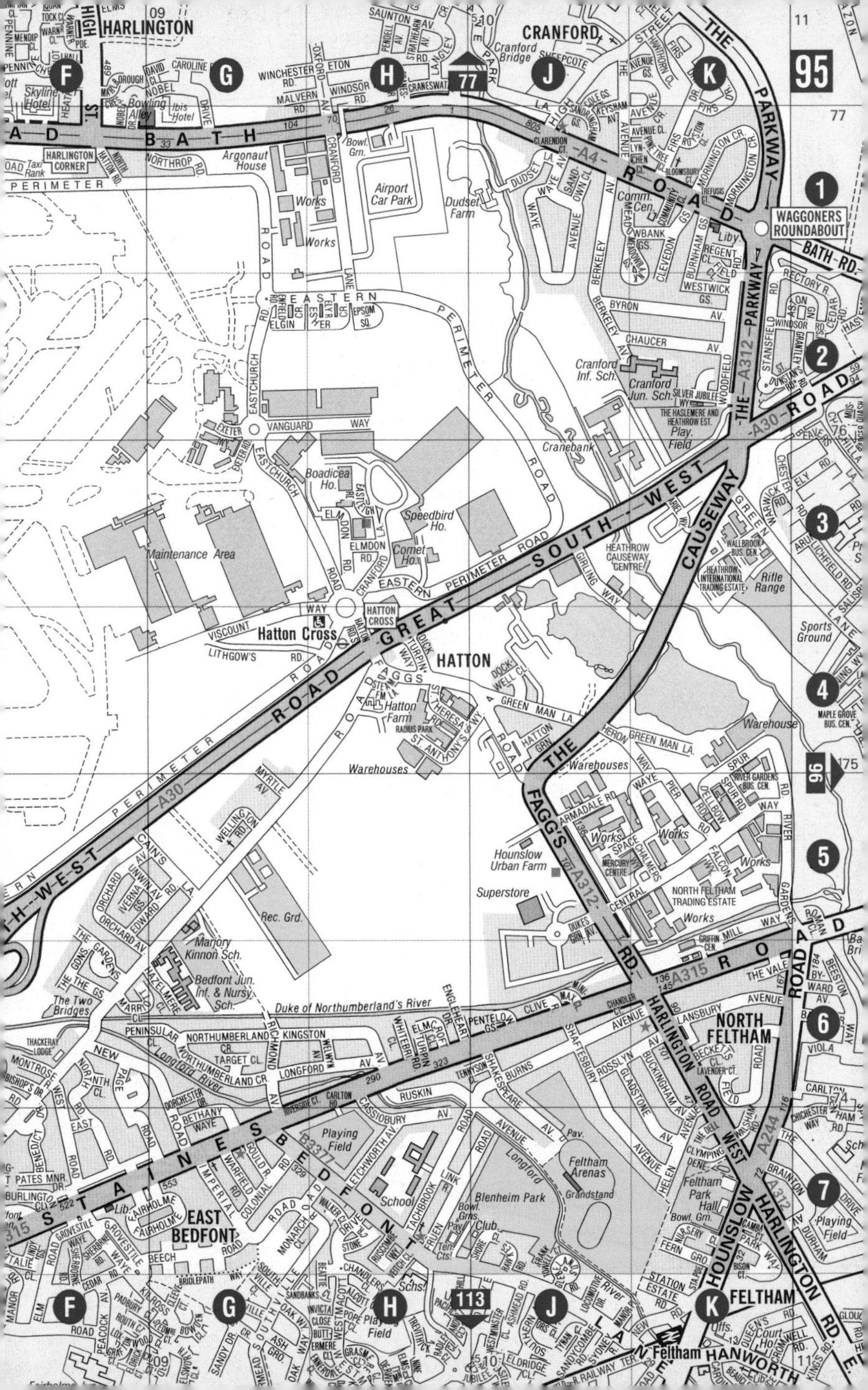
HARLINGTON
CRANFORD
Cranford Bridge
Skyline Hotel
Bowling Alley
Ibis Hotel
BATH ROAD
A4
HARLINGTON CORNER
Taxi Rank
PERIMETER
Argonaut House
Works
Airport Car Park
Dudset Farm
Comm. Cen.
Liby.
WAGGONERS ROUNDABOUT
THE PARKWAY
A312
EASTERN PERIMETER ROAD
Cranford Inf. Sch.
Cranford Jun. Sch.
THE HASLEMERE AND HEATHROW EST.
Play. Field
Cranebank
VANGUARD WAY
Boadicea Ho.
Speedbird Ho.
Comet Ho.
Maintenance Area
EASTCHURCH ROAD
Hatton Cross
HATTON CROSS
VISCOUNT WAY
LITHGOW'S RD.
GREAT SOUTH-WEST ROAD
A30
HEATHROW CAUSEWAY CENTRE
THE CAUSEWAY
WALLBROOK BUS. CEN.
HEATHROW INTERNATIONAL TRADING ESTATE
Rifle Range
Sports Ground
HATTON
Hatton Farm
Warehouses
GREEN MAN LA.
MAPLE GROVE BUS. CEN.
Warehouse
FAGG'S RD.
RIVER GARDENS BUS. CEN.
Works
Hounslow Urban Farm
Superstore
NORTH FELTHAM TRADING ESTATE
Rec. Grd.
Marjory Kinnon Sch.
Bedfont Jun. Inf. & Nursy Sch.
The Two Bridges
Duke of Northumberland's River
Longford River
NORTH FELTHAM
HARLINGTON ROAD WEST
A315
STAINES ROAD
BEDFONT ROAD
B3377
Playing Field
School
EAST BEDFONT
Lib.
Feltham Arenas
Grandstand
Blenheim Park
Feltham Park Hall
Bowl. Grn.
Playing Field
HOUNSLOW ROAD
HARLINGTON RD. E.
A244
STATION ESTATE RD.
FELTHAM
Feltham
HANWORTH
Court Ho.
F
G
H
J
K
1
2
3
4
5
6
7
77
96
113
09
10
11

WAGGONERS ROUNDABOUT
HENLYS ROUNDABOUT
THE PARKWAY
BATH RD.
A4
GREAT SOUTH-WEST ROAD
A30
GREAT WEST ROAD
A3006
A3063
SUTTON LANE
UPPER SUTTON LANE
HESTON
Sutton Playing Field
Playground
CROSSWAYS
SUTTON SQUARE
NOBLE CORNER
Lampton School
Playing Field
Civic Centre
Cemetery
LAMPTON PARK
Bowling Green
BULSTRODE AV.
DENE AV.
Hounslow West
Sports Ground
Club
Pav.
Beaversfield Park
HOUNSLOW WEST
Playing Field
Cavalry Barracks
Schs.
Jun. Sch.
Prim. Sch.
St. Mark's R.C. Sch.
Works
WELLINGTON RD. NTH.
WELLINGTON ROAD SOUTH
A315
STAINES RD.
HEATHROW CORPORATE PARK
Sports Ground
Rifle Range
Warehouse
Lib.
LAWRENCE ESTATE
MAPLE GROVE BUS. CEN.
FREEHOLD INDUSTRIAL ESTATE
CENTRAL PARK ESTATE
Heath Nurseries
Club Ho.
BABER BRI. CARAVAN SITE
Baber Bridge
Weir
HOUNSLOW HEATH GOLF COURSE
HOUNSLOW HEATH
NORTH FELTHAM
Training Centre
Mosque
The Heathland School
Rec. Grd.
A314
NELSON ROAD
Comm. Centre
Hounslow Cemy.
HOWDEN HOUSE
River Crane
Play. Field
Jun. Sch.
Sch.
Playing Field
HANWORTH ROAD
HARLINGTON ROAD EAST
HOUNSLOW ROAD
MILL FARM BUSINESS PARK
South West Middlesex Crematorium
Bridge Farm Nursery
Cemetery
Recre. Grd.
Heathfield Jun. & Inf. Schs.
WYNDHAM CR.
BEAVERS LANE
BARRACK RD.
MARTINDALE RD.
CAMBRIDGE RD.
CROMWELL RD.
ROSEVILLE AV.
VICTORIA AV.
WELLINGTON AV.
78
95
114
A B C D E
1 2 3 4 5 6 7
11 12 13

97
79
98
115
F
G
H
J
K
1
2
3
4
5
6
7
14
15
16
GREAT WEST ROAD
Osterley
Running Track
Play. Fld.
Brunel University
Indian Gymkhana Club Sports Ground
Campion Ho.
Bowl. Gm.
Tennis Cts.
Spts. Grd.
Pavilion
A4
LAMPTON
SPRING GROVE
SPRING GROVE
GROVE RD.
B363
Crown Court
West Thames College
Play Fld.
School
Sports Grd.
Isleworth
LONDON ROAD
A315
Hounslow East
Alexandra School
Hounslow Central
Sports Hall
Bus Depot
Derwent Lodge
Playing Field
WOODLANDS
HIGH STREET
Prim. Sch.
INWOOD PARK
Tennis Courts
HOUNSLOW
Treaty Centre
Lib.
Comm. Cen.
ISLEWORTH
Clock Tower Ind. Est.
Liby. & Isleworth Rec. Cen.
REDLEES PARK
Worton Hall Industrial Estate
Works
Victory Business Centre
West Middlesex Drainage Works
Hounslow
Maswell Park
Heath Bus. Cen.
Queen's Bri.
Superstore
Mogden
Ryde Bridge Retail Park
TWICKENHAM RD.
A310
A3005
A314
B361
Murray Park
Royal Military Sch. of Music (Kneller Hall)
Sports Ground
Playing Field
Duke of Northumberland's River
The Museum of Rugby
Twickenham Trading Estate
Twickenham Rugby Union Football Grd.
Prim. Sch.
London Rd. Roundabout
Chase Bridge
Whitton Rd. R'bout
CHERTSEY ROAD
A316
KNELLER ROAD
WHITTON ROAD
WHITTON
Whitton
Sports Ground
Hall
Richmond upon Thames College
Play. Fld.
Harlequins R.U.F.C. (Stoop Meml. Grd.)
Playing Field
TWICKENHAM
Depot
Kneller Gdns.
Twickenham
Coll.
HOSPITAL BRIDGE RD.
B358

Syon Lane
80
SYON PARK
Butterfly House
Syon Garden Centre
Syon House
DUKE OF NORTHUMBERLAND ESTATE
RIVER THAMES
Syon Reach
ROYAL BOTANIC G
GARDE
Bamboo Garden
Azalea Garden
Syon Vista
The Lake
Arboretum
King William Temple
Isleworth Ferry Gate (Closed)
Water Lily Pond
Evolution House
Temperate House
Conservation Area
Queen Charlotte's Cottage
Cedar Vista
Japanese Gateway & Landscape
King's Steps Gate
OLD DEER PARK
ROYAL MID-SURREY GOLF COURSE
King's Observatory
Royal Mid-Surrey Golf Club
Richmond Athletic Ground
Rugby Grd.
Grand Stand
Tennis Courts
Swimming Baths
Obelisk
Old Deer Park Recreation Ground
Richmond Lock
Old Isleworth
Isleworth Ait
Nazareth Ho.
Brunel Univ.
WEST MIDDLESEX UNIVERSITY HOSP
Cemetery
Busch Corner
Syon Park Sch.
ISLEWORTH
REDLEES PARK
TWICKENHAM ROAD
LONDON ROAD
SPUR RD.
ST. JOHN'S RD.
SOUTH ST.
RICHMOND ROAD
ST. MARGARETS ROAD
THE AVENUE
ST. MARGARETS
St. Margarets
ST. MARGARETS R'BOUT
LONDON RD. ROUNDABOUT
CHERTSEY
Cole Park
Moor Mead Gd.
Twickenham
TWICKENHAM
RICHMOND
Richmond
Richmond Green
RICHMOND CIRCUS
PARADISE RD.
SHEEN
PETERSHAM ROAD
Corporation Island
Asgill Ho.
MARBLE HILL PARK
Marble Hill House
Buccleugh Gdns.
Glover's Island
Petersham Meadows
Petersham Farm
Terrace Gardens
Terrace Fld.
Royal Star & Garter Home
Petersham Common
Orleans Ho. Gallery
York Ho.
Orleans Gdns.
Foot Ferry
116
97
A315
A310
A3004
A316
A305
A307
B321
B363
B454
1
2
3
4
5
6
7
A
B
C
D
E

99
Princess of Wales Conservatory
Public Record Office
Warehouse
81
Chiswick
BURLINGTON
Palm House
The Pond
Rose Garden
Visitor Centre
Victoria Ga.
Temple of Bellona
Berberis Dell
Marianne North Gallery
Cumberland Ga.
KEW GARDENS RD.
Kew Gds.
MORTLAKE ROAD
SANDYCOMBE ROAD
KEW RETAIL PARK
GROVE PARK
University of Westminster Sports Ground
Yacht Basin
Stadium
Sports Ground
Westminster Boathouse
Riverside Lands
Playing Fields
DUKE'S MEADOWS
Sports Ground
Tennis Courts
Driving Range
Tennis Cts.
Pavilion
GREAT CHERTSEY ROAD
A316
RIVER THAMES
Refuse Depot
Mortlake Crematorium
Hammersmith Cemetery
CLIFFORD AV.
CHISWICK BRI.
Playing Field
Recreation Ground
NORTH SHEEN
FULHAM (NORTH SHEEN) CEMETERY
CHALKER'S CORNER
Brewery
Pav. Sports Ground
MORTLAKE
A3003
MORTLAKE HIGH ST
The Green
Mortlake
LOWER RICHMOND ROAD
A205
MORTLAKE RD.
A307
B353
Manor Circus Depot
North Sheen
Holy Trinity C.E.Prim. Sch.
UPPER RICHMOND ROAD
WEST
A305
SHEEN LANE
B351
EAST SHEEN
Day Cen. & Lib.
Sheen Sch. & Sports Centre
100
Pale Well
Pitch and Putt Course
Palewell Common
Palewell Fields
Playing Fields
Sheen Mt. Prim. Sch.
Pesthouse Common
Play. Fld.
Christ's Sch.
East Sheen Cemetery
SHEEN COMMON
Football Ground
Bowling Green
Tennis Courts
Ranger's Gdn.
Richmond Cemetery
King's House Sch.
Bog Gate
Teck Plantation
Sheen Wood
East Sheen Gate
Adam's Pond
Horse Ride
Playing Field
Playing Field
Roehampton Gate
The Bog
Riding Ring
RICHMOND PARK
(Open during daylight hours only)
Sheen Cross Wood
Polo Field
Playing Field
Cambrian Gate
Holly Lodge
Bishop's Pond
Conduit Wood
Barn Wood Pond
Richmond Gate
SAWYER'S HILL
(Open during daylight hours only)
Saw Pit Plantation
Deer Pen
Kidney Wood
Queen's Ride
117
Jubilee Plantation
Duchess' Wood
White Lodge Plantation
SIDMOUTH WOOD
White Lodge
F
G
H
J
K
1
2
3
4
5
6
7
19
20
21
74
75
76
77

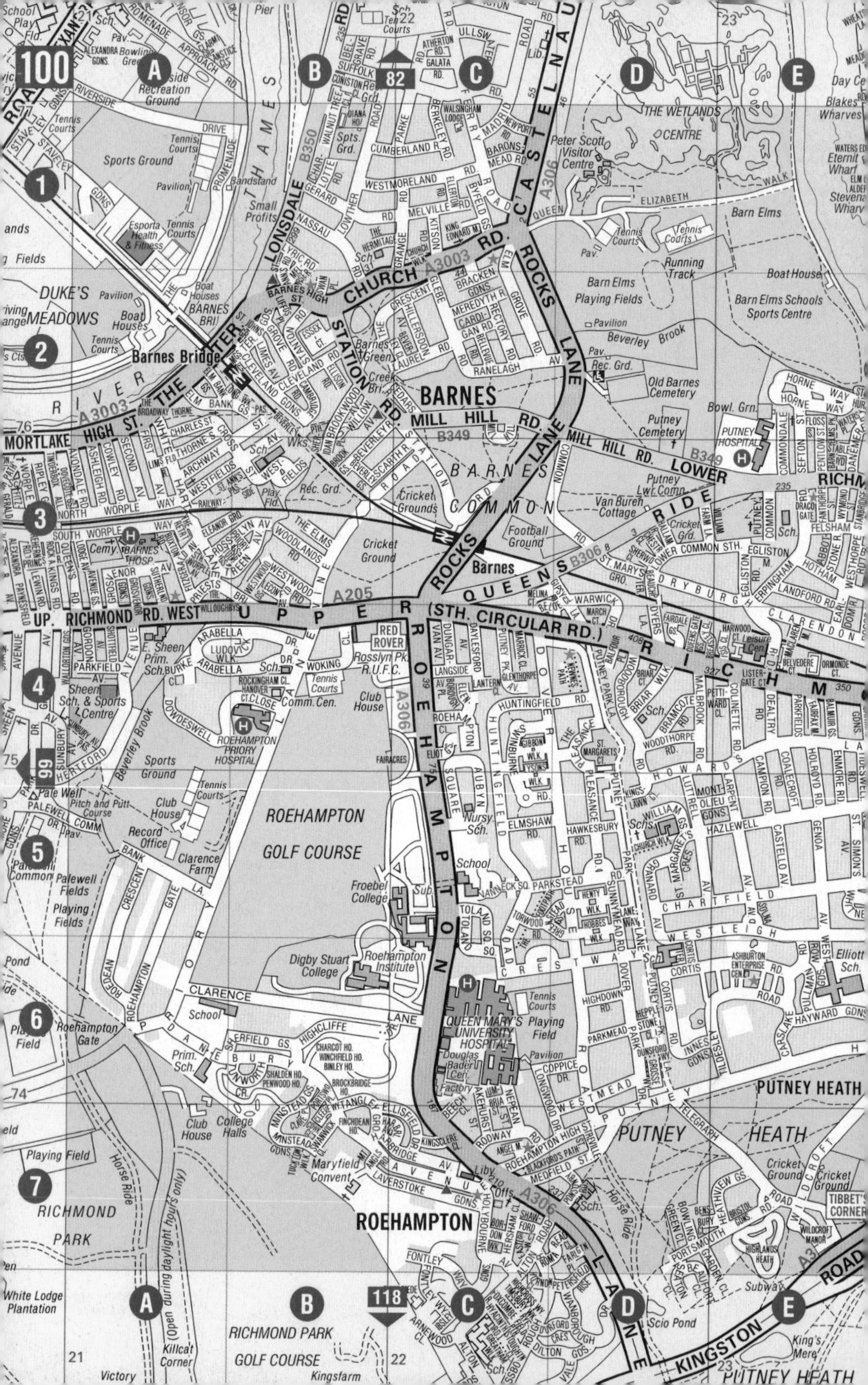
A
B
C
D
E
1
2
3
4
5
6
7
82
118
99
21
22
23
Riverside Recreation Ground
Sports Ground
Esporta Health & Fitness
DUKE'S MEADOWS
Barnes Bridge
RIVER THAMES
MORTLAKE HIGH ST.
A3003
LONSDALE RD.
CHURCH RD.
CASTELNAU
A306
THE WETLANDS CENTRE
Peter Scott Visitor Centre
Barn Elms
Barn Elms Playing Fields
Barn Elms Schools Sports Centre
Boat House
Running Track
Beverley Brook
BARNES
MILL HILL RD.
B349
ROCKS LANE
BARNES COMMON
Old Barnes Cemetery
Putney Cemetery
PUTNEY HOSPITAL
LOWER RICHMOND RD.
Putney Lwr. Comn.
Van Buren Cottage
QUEENS RIDE
B306
Barnes
Football Ground
Cricket Ground
UP. RICHMOND RD. WEST
UPPER (STH. CIRCULAR RD.) RICHMOND RD.
A205
RED ROVER
Rosslyn Pk. R.U.F.C.
ROEHAMPTON LANE
ROEHAMPTON PRIORY HOSPITAL
Sheen Sch. & Sports Centre
Sports Ground
Pitch and Putt Course
ROEHAMPTON GOLF COURSE
Froebel College
Digby Stuart College
Roehampton Institute
Palewell Common
Palewell Fields Playing Fields
Clarence Farm
Record Office
CLARENCE LANE
Roehampton Gate
RICHMOND PARK
QUEEN MARY'S UNIVERSITY HOSPITAL
Douglas Bader Cen.
ROEHAMPTON
ROEHAMPTON HIGH ST.
Maryfield Convent
College Halls
PUTNEY HEATH
Putney Heath
TIBBET'S CORNER
KINGSTON ROAD
Scio Pond
King's Mere
RICHMOND PARK GOLF COURSE
White Lodge Plantation
Killcat Corner
Horse Ride
(Open during daylight hours only)
Kingsfarm
Victory

F
G
H
J
K
1
2
3
4
5
6
7
83
102
119
FULHAM
FULHAM PALACE RD.
Fulham Cemetery
Fulham Palace
Moat Garden
The Warren
Playground
Theatre
BISHOP'S PARK
RIVER
THAMES
Putney Pier
Putney Bri.
PUTNEY BRI.
PUTNEY HIGH ST.
PUTNEY
Putney
Putney Exchange Shop. Cen.
Putney High Sch.
East Putney
PUTNEY HILL
TIBBET'S RIDE
WEST HILL
Royal Hosp. for Neuro-Disability
Roehampton Institute
Playing Fld.
Mosque
Southfields
SOUTHFIELDS
Southfields Comm. Coll.
WANDSWORTH
WANDSWORTH BRIDGE RD.
WANDSWORTH BRI.
Wandsworth Town
WANDSWORTH GYRATORY
WANDSWORTH HIGH ST.
EAST HL.
Wandsworth Shop. Cen.
Wandsworth Park
Leisure Cen.
Solid Waste Transfer Station
Bell Lane Creek
River Wandle
Jetties
Jetty
Hurlingham Wharf
Trinidad Wharf
Dock
HURLINGHAM PARK
Hurlingham
The Hurlingham Club
Running Track
Tennis Courts
Swim. Pool
Ckt. Grd.
SOUTH PARK
PARSONS GRN.
Parsons Grn.
WALHAM GREEN
Eel Brook Common
SANDS END
Gas Works
Townmead Bus. Cen.
Superstore
Fulham Wharf
KING'S RD.
NEW KINGS RD.
FULHAM RD.
MERTON ROAD
BUCKHOLD RD.
GARRATT LANE
King George's Park
Water Scene
Works
Depot
A219
A304
A308
A217
A3209
A205
A3
A218
B306

102
A
B
C
D
E
1
2
3
4
5
6
7
84
101
120
BATTERSEA PARK
SANDS END
Gas Works
Chelsea Creek
Cremorne Gardens
Cremorne Wharf
Chelsea Harbour
Chelsea Harbour Pier
Marina
Bascule Bri.
RIVER THAMES
CHELSEA REACH
Nacovia Wharf
Regent Wharf
Lensbury Wharf
Shell Wharf
London Westland Heliport
Plantation Wharf
Fulham Wharf
Warehouse
Superstore
College
Sports Cen.
General Games Ground
Boating Lake
Sun Gate
BATTERSEA
CLAPHAM JUNCTION
Falcon Park
Open Space
York Gdns.
Wandsworth Town
WANDSWORTH BRI.
Spencer Park
Emanuel School
BOLINGBROKE HOSPITAL
H.M.P. Wandsworth
Cricket Ground
Tennis Courts
Bowling Green
Royal Victoria Patriotic Building
WANDSWORTH COMMON
Wandsworth Common
St. Mary's Cemy.
WANDSWORTH CEMETERY
EARLSFIELD
BALHAM
Rec. Grd.
Playground
CLAPHAM COMMON NORTH SIDE
CLAPHAM COMN. W. SIDE
ALBERT BRIDGE RD.
BATTERSEA BRIDGE RD.
BATTERSEA PARK RD.
LATCHMERE RD.
LAVENDER HILL
ST. JOHN'S HILL
EAST HILL
YORK ROAD
WANDSWORTH ROAD
TRINITY RD.
WINDMILL RD.
SPENCER PARK
NORTHCOTE ROAD
BATTERSEA RISE
BOLINGBROKE GRO.
NIGHTINGALE
WESTBRIDGE
VICARAGE CR.
LOMBARD R.
FALCON RD.
PLOUGH RD.
ELSPETH R.
IMPERIAL ROAD
WANDSWORTH COMMON W. SIDE
NORTH SIDE WANDSWORTH
HUGUENOT PL.
EARLSFIELD RD.
GARRATT LANE
A3
A3031
A3220
A3205
A3036
A3207
A205
A214
A217
B305
B234
B229
B237

NEW COVENT GARDEN MARKET
Fruit & Vegetable Market
Battersea Dogs' Home
Battersea Park
Queenstown Road (Battersea)
Railway Works
Heathbrook Park
SOUTH LAMBETH
Lambeth Coll.
Larkhall Park
Stockwell
Stockwell Park Sch.
Angell Town
STOCKWELL
Wandsworth Rd.
Clapham High St.
Clapham North
LAMBETH HOSPITAL
CLAPHAM
Hospice
Clapham Comn.
CLAPHAM COMMON
BRIXTON
Superstore
CLAPHAM PARK
Windmill Gdns.
Sports Ground
H.M.P. Brixton
Bandstand
Mount Pond
Eagle Pond
Clapham Sth.
Tennis Courts
WANDSWORTH ROAD
CLAPHAM ROAD
STOCKWELL ROAD
CLAPHAM HIGH ST.
COMMON NORTH SIDE
LONG RD.
SOUTH SIDE
CLAPHAM COMMON SOUTH SIDE
CLAPHAM PARK RD.
ACRE LANE
BEDFORD RD.
KING'S AVENUE
BRIXTON HILL
CAVENDISH RD.
POYNDERS RD.
ATKINS RD.
STREATHAM PL.
CHRISTCHURCH RD.
BALHAM HIGH ROAD
CLAPHAM COMMON WEST SIDE
WINDMILL DRIVE
NIGHTINGALE LANE
85
121
104
F G H J K
1 2 3 4 5 6 7

104
A
B
C
D
E
86
1
2
3
4
5
6
7
103
122
SOUTHAMPTON
CAMBERWELL
NEW
MEDLAR ST.
CAMBERWELL GREEN
CAMBERWELL RD.
CAMBERWELL CHURCH STREET
PECKHAM
Angell Town
STOCKWELL
CAMBERWELL
St. Gabriel's Manor
MYATTS FIELDS
Mostyn Gardens
Loughborough Junc.
COLDHARBOUR
COLDHARBOUR
LANE
A2217
Brixton
BRIXTON
DENMARK HILL
Denmark Hill
THE MAUDSLEY HOSP.
KINGS COLLEGE HOSPITAL
CHAMPION PK.
A2216
GROVE LA.
DOG KENNEL HILL
RUSKIN PARK
Superstore
East Dulwich
Dulwich Hamlet F.C.
Sports Ground
Playing Fields
The Charter Sch.
James Allen's Girls Sch.
North Dulwich
EAST DULWICH
HERNE HILL
Herne Hill
HALF MOON LA.
VILLAGE WAY
A2214
DULWICH ROAD
MILKWOOD ROAD
RAILTON ROAD
EFFRA RD.
TULSE HILL
A204
BROCKWELL PARK
Swimming Pool
Bowling Green
Tennis Courts
Open Air Theatre
The Mansion
New Lodge
NORWOOD ROAD
A215
CROXTED ROAD
A2199
Herne Hill Stadium
TURNEY ROAD
Sports Ground
Dulwich Old College
Dulwich Picture Gallery
DULWICH VILLAGE
Old College Gate
Bell House
Boating Lake
Belair
Knight's Hill
Sunray Gdns.
Lettsom Gds.
Lucas Gds.
Brunswick Park

105
F
G
H
J
K
1
2
3
4
5
6
7
87
106
123
PECKHAM
PECKHAM HIGH ST.
QUEEN'S ROAD
A202
Queens Rd. (Peckham)
NEW CROSS GATE
NEW CROSS
NEW CROSS RD.
Bus Garage
HANOVER PK.
RYE LANE
A2215
Peckham Rye
Warwick Gardens
PRINT VILLAGE
CHADWICK
CHOUMERT
Leisure Cen.
Cossall Pk.
Tuke Sch.
Telegraph Hill Park
Telegraph Hill Park
College
Nunhead
EVELINA ROAD
A2214
NUNHEAD LA.
NUNHEAD
NUNHEAD CEMETERY
BROCKLEY
Playing Field
Tennis Courts
Reservoirs (covered)
EAST DULWICH ROAD
EAST DULWICH
Goose Grn.
GROVE VALE
LORDSHIP LANE
A2216
PECKHAM RYE COMMON
PECKHAM RYE PARK
STRAKERS
Piermont Green
School
Pumping Station
AQUARIUS GOLF COURSE
Water Works
Reservoir (covered)
Club House
Playing Field
FOREST HILL
B238
Newlands
Honor Oak Crematorium
New Cemetery
Camberwell
Recreation
Pav. Ground
ONE TREE HILL
HONOR OAK
HONOR OAK ROAD
Honor Oak Park
Brenchley Gardens
Camberwell Old Cemetery
Nature Reserve
Res. (covered)
FOREST HILL
DULWICH PARK
Horse Ride
Court La. Gate
Tennis Cts.
Bowling Grn.
Aviary
Rosebery Lodge Ga.
Queen Mary's Gate
COMMON
DULWICH
THE GROVE
Sports Ground
Horniman Gardens
STANSTEAD
BROCKLEY RISE
B219
B2142
B2227
B218
A2216

New Cross Gate
New Cross
NEW CROSS
NEW CROSS GATE
NEW CROSS ROAD
Goldsmiths College
Laban Cen.
Deptford Bri.
DEPTFORD BROADWAY
GREENWICH HIGH RD.
BLACKHEATH RD.
BLACKHEATH HILL
LEWISHAM WAY
LEWISHAM RD.
BROOKMILL ROAD
ST. JOHNS
St. Johns
Elverson Road
LOAMPIT HILL
LOAMPIT VALE
THURSTON RD.
Lewisham
LEWISHAM
Lewisham College
Telegraph Hill
DRAKEFELL RD.
Brockley
BROCKLEY
BROCKLEY ROAD
HILLY FIELDS PARK
Cricket Ground
Prendergast School
ADELAIDE AV.
LADYWELL RD.
Ladywell
LADYWELL
LEWISHAM UNIVERSITY HOSPITAL
Brockley Cemetery
Ladywell Cemetery
Crofton Park
Crofton Pk.
Honor Oak Crematorium
Honor Oak Pk.
HONOR OAK PARK
HONOR OAK PK.
STONDON PARK
Guy's Hosp. Athletic Grd.
Blythe Hill Fields
Blythe Hill
Lewisham Park
Ladywell Fields
Ladywell Centre
Running Track
Crofton Leisure & Youth Centre
Crofton School
Catford Stadium (Greyhound)
Catford Bridge
Catford
CATFORD GYRATORY
CATFORD
CATFORD RD.
BROWNHILL RD.
RUSHEY GREEN
LEWISHAM HIGH STREET
STANSTEAD ROAD
Playing Fields
88
105
124
A
B
C
D
E
1
2
3
4
5
6
7
36
37
38

107
F
G
H
J
K
GREENWICH PARK
89
108
125
OLD DOVER ROAD
SUN-IN-THE-SANDS
CHARLTON HILL
SHOOTERS HILL ROAD
BLACK HEATH
Blackheath Vale
BLACKHEATH
Blackheath
PRINCE OF WALES RD.
PRINCE CHARLES ROAD
Christ's College for Boys
Morden College
KIDBROOKE PARK RD.
ROCHESTER WAY RELIEF ROAD
Kidbrooke
Thomas Tallis Sch.
BLACKHEATH PARK
LEE HIGH ROAD
LEE TERRACE
ELTHAM ROAD
BURNT ASH RD.
BURNT ASH HILL
LEE
Lee
Manor Park
Manor House Gdns.
Hither Green
HITHER GREEN
SIDCUP ROAD
Horn Park
WESTHORNE AVENUE
ST. MILDREDS ROAD
BARING ROAD
SUTCLIFFE PARK
Sports Grounds
Playing Field
1
2
3
4
5
6
7

SHOOTERS HILL ROAD
A207
90
WOOLWICH COMMON
ACADEMY ROAD
A205
Old Royal Military Academy
Eaglesfield School
Reservoir
Reservoir (covered)
Hornfair Park
Recreation Ground
Bowls
Sports Ground
WRICKLEMARSH ROAD
ROCHESTER WAY RELIEF ROAD
Kidbrooke School
Playing Fields
KIDBROOKE
KIDBROOKE PARK ROAD
Sports Ground
Sam Montague Boys Club
Tennis Courts
CEMETERY
Rec. Grd.
ELTHAM COMMON
MEMORIAL HOSPITAL
CASTLE WOOD
Severndroog Castle
Rose Cottage
JACK WOOD
Thomas Tallis Sch.
Superstore
Kidbrooke
Nature Res.
Spts. Gd.
KIDBROOKE ESTATE
ROCHESTER WAY
A2
WELL HALL ROAD
WELL HALL ROUNDABOUT
ELTHAM PARK
WESTMOUNT ROAD
CROOKSTON
DAIRSIE
ELIBANK ROAD
EARLSHALL
GREENVALE
DUNVEGAN ROAD
ELTHAM PARK
Sports Ground
Bowling Green
Tudor Barn Theatre
KIDBROOKE LA.
AVENUE
Eltham
Meadowside Leisure Cen.
TUDWAY RD.
107
SUTCLIFFE PARK
Harrow Meadow
Running Track
Greenwich Borough F.C.
WESTHORNE AVENUE
ELTHAM ROAD
A210
ELTHAM HILL
YORKSHIRE GREY
Eltham Green Sch.
Playing Field
Moatbridge Sch.
ELTHAM
Eltham Hill Sch.
Swim. Pool
Rec. Grd.
ELTHAM HIGH STREET
A208
COURT ROAD
Supermarket
FOOTSCRAY
Comp. Sch.
SIDCUP ROAD
A20
ELTHAM PALACE RD.
Sports Ground
Spts. Grd.
Quaggy River
Eltham Palace
KING JOHN'S WALK
Institute of Army Education
Club House
ROYAL BLACKHEATH GOLF COURSE
Sports Grd.
Tennis Cts.
Community Centre
126
MOTTINGHAM ROAD
MOTTINGHAM LA.
Carter's Hill
Mottingham Farm
Mottingham
Bird Sanctuary
The Tarn
Horn Park Prim. Sch.
Playing Field
A
B
C
D
E
1
2
3
4
5
6
7
41
42
43
74
75
76
77

109
91
110
127
F
G
H
J
K
1
2
3
4
5
6
7
SHREWSBURY PARK
SHOOTERS HILL
Eaglesfield Rec. Grnd.
Lowood Club Ho
SHOOTERS HILL GOLF COURSE
Clothworkers Wood
Woodlands Abattoir
Woodlands Farm
Garden Centre
Griffin Manor School
Greenwood School
East Wickham Open Space
Council Offices
Jackwood Ho.
Oxleas Meadows
OXLEAS WOOD
Eastcote Prim. Sch.
Falconwood Field
Falconwood
SHEPHERDLEAS WOOD
Playing Field
ELTHAM PARK NORTH
ELTHAM PARK SOUTH
FALCONWOOD
Coll.
Inf. Sch.
Jun. Sch.
Playing Field
Eltham Cemetery
Eltham Crematorium
ELTHAM WARREN GOLF COURSE
Club House
Nature Study Centre
Crown Woods School
University of Greenwich (Avery Hill Campus)
AVERY HILL
AVERY HILL PARK
Sports Ground
(Halls of Residence)
Alderwood Prim. Sch.
Parish Wood
Prim. Sch.
BLACKFEN
Hollyoak Wood Park
Days Lane Prim. Sch.
Willersley Park
Marlborough Sch.
Sparrow's Farm Leisure Cen.
River Sports Ground
Playing Fields
Works
Lamorbey
BELLEGROVE
HILL
A207
A2
A210
A211
B2214
ROCHESTER WAY
EAST ROCHESTER WAY
WELLING WAY
BEXLEY ROAD
BLACKFEN ROAD
AVERY HILL RD.
HALFWAY STREET
ROAD
44
45
46
74
76
77
175

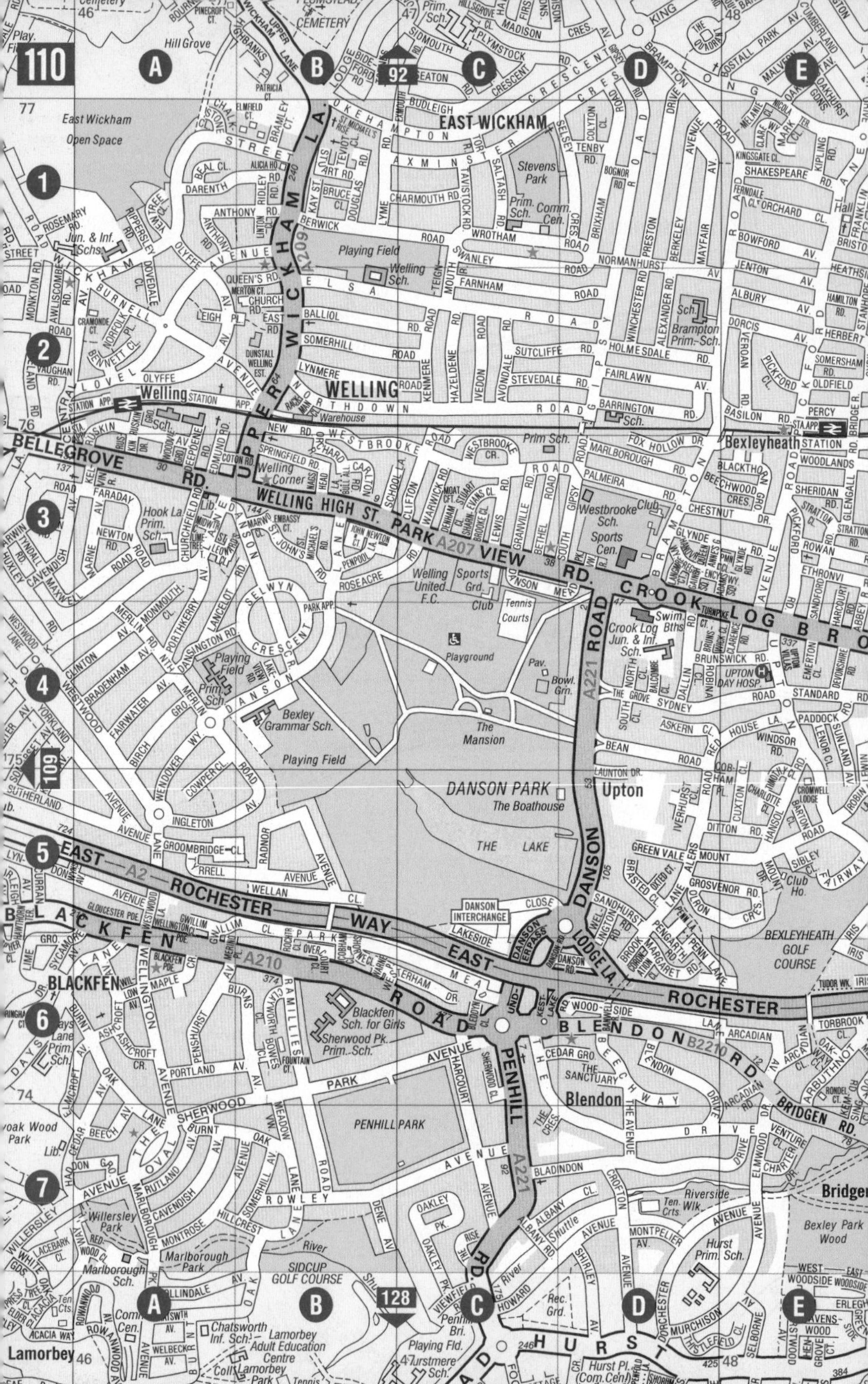
A
B
C
D
E
1
2
3
4
5
6
7
46
47
48
77
76
75
74
92
109
128
Hill Grove
East Wickham
Open Space
EAST WICKHAM
Stevens Park
Prim. Sch.
Comm. Cen.
Playing Field
Welling Sch.
WELLING
Welling STATION
Warehouse
Sch.
Prim Sch.
Brampton Prim. Sch.
Bexleyheath STATION
Welling Corner
Hook La Prim. Sch.
Lib.
Welling United F.C.
Sports Grd.
Club
Tennis Courts
Playground
Pav.
Bowl. Grn.
Westbrooke Sch.
Sports Cen.
Swim. Bths
Crook Log Jun. & Inf. Sch.
UPTON DAY HOSP.
Playing Field
Prim. Sch.
Bexley Grammar Sch.
The Mansion
DANSON PARK
The Boathouse
THE LAKE
Upton
DANSON INTERCHANGE
BEXLEYHEATH GOLF COURSE
Club Ho.
BLACKFEN
Days Lane Prim. Sch.
Blackfen Sch. for Girls
Sherwood Pk. Prim. Sch.
PENHILL PARK
Blendon
Bridgen
Bexley Park Wood
Riverside Wlk.
Ten. Crts.
Hurst Prim. Sch.
Willersley Park
Marlborough Park
Marlborough Sch.
SIDCUP GOLF COURSE
Rec. Grd.
Penhill Bri.
Playing Fld.
Hurstmere Sch.
Chatsworth Inf. Sch.
Lamorbey Adult Education Centre
Lamorbey Park
Lamorbey
Hurst Pl. (Com. Cen.)
Jun. & Inf. Schs.
UPPER WICKHAM LA.
A209
BELLEGROVE RD.
WELLING HIGH ST.
PARK VIEW RD.
A207
CROOK LOG
DANSON ROAD
A221
EAST ROCHESTER WAY
A2
BLACKFEN ROAD
A210
PENHILL
ROCHESTER
BLENDON RD
B2210
BRIDGEN RD.
HURST ROAD
WICKHAM STREET
BRAMPTON ROAD
LONG LANE
EAST WICKHAM CRESCENT
AXMINSTER
NORTHDOWN ROAD
WESTBROOKE ROAD
ELSA ROAD
SELWYN CRESCENT
DANSON LA.
WESTWOOD LANE
WELLINGTON AVENUE
PARK AVENUE
SHERWOOD PARK AVENUE
DANSON MEAD
MOUNT RD.
BLENDON DRIVE
PARKHURST ROAD
LOVEL AVENUE
OLYFFE AVENUE

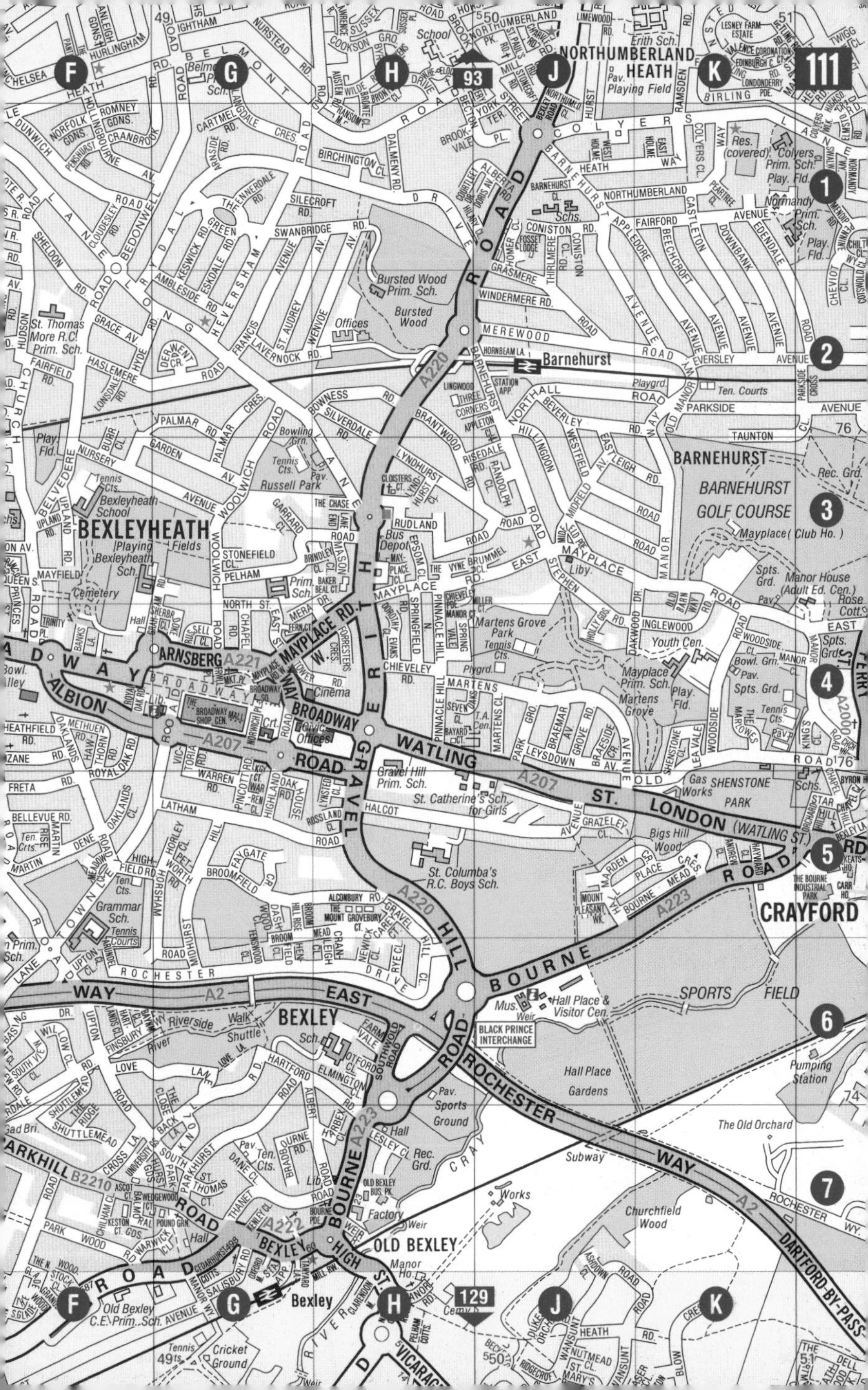

F
G
H
J
K
93
NORTHUMBERLAND HEATH
Erith Sch.
Pav. Playing Field
LESNEY FARM ESTATE
BIRLING PDE.
COLYERS LANE
Colyers Prim. Sch.
Play. Fld.
Res. (covered)
Normandy Prim. Sch.
Play. Fld.
NORTHUMBERLAND AVENUE
BARNEHURST ROAD
Schs.
Bursted Wood Prim. Sch.
Bursted Wood
Offices
Barnehurst
MEREWOOD ROAD
EVERSLEY AVENUE
PARKSIDE AVENUE
TAUNTON
Ten. Courts
BARNEHURST
BARNEHURST GOLF COURSE
Mayplace (Club Ho.)
Manor House (Adult Ed. Cen.)
Rose Cott.
Spts. Grd.
Youth Cen.
Mayplace Prim. Sch.
Play. Fld.
Martens Grove
Martens Grove Park
Liby.
MAYPLACE ROAD EAST
BEXLEYHEATH
Bexleyheath School
Playing Fields
Bexleyheath Sch.
Cemetery
Russell Park
Bowling Grn.
St. Thomas More R.C. Prim. Sch.
Play. Fld.
BROADWAY
ARNSBERG WAY
ALBION ROAD
BROADWAY SHOP. CEN.
Cinema
Civic Offices
Bus Depot
A220
A221
A207
A223
A222
A2
A2000
B2210
WATLING ST.
LONDON ROAD (WATLING ST.)
GRAVEL HILL
Gravel Hill Prim. Sch.
St. Catherine's Sch. for Girls
St. Columba's R.C. Boys Sch.
Gas Works
SHENSTONE PARK
Bigs Hill Wood
BOURNE ROAD
CRAYFORD
THE BOURNE INDUSTRIAL PARK
Grammar Sch.
Tennis Courts
ROCHESTER WAY
EAST ROCHESTER WAY
BEXLEY
Riverside Walk
Shuttle River
Sch.
Mus.
Hall Place & Visitor Cen.
BLACK PRINCE INTERCHANGE
SPORTS FIELD
Hall Place Gardens
Pumping Station
The Old Orchard
Subway
Pav. Sports Ground
Rec. Grd.
CRAY
Works
Churchfield Wood
Factory
OLD BEXLEY BUS. PK.
Weir
OLD BEXLEY
Lib.
Hall
BEXLEY ROAD
PARKHILL ROAD
Old Bexley C.E. Prim. Sch.
Bexley
Manor Ho.
Cricket Ground
Tennis
129
DARTFORD-BY-PASS
1
2
3
4
5
6
7
49
50
51
74
76

112
STANWELL
Recreation Ground
Ashford Football Ground
94
Sports Ground
CLOCKHOUSE ROUNDABOUT
GT. SOUTH-WEST RD.
A315
A30
Old People's Home
HATCHETT RD.
Nursery
Homers Farm
Playing Field
Nurseries
The Holloway Unit
Superstore
ASHFORD HOSP.
Ashford Cemetery
STAINES ROAD
LONDON ROAD
STAINES RESERVOIRS
AVIA PARK
Warehouses
NEW SQUARE
Bedfont Cemetery
BEDFONT LAKE COUNTRY PARK
Visitor Cen.
Bridge Farm
B3003
BEDFONT LAKES COUNTRY PARK
BEDFONT INDUSTRIAL PARK
The Ashford High Sch.
St. David's School
ASHFORD
Ashford
Clarendon Prim. Sch.
CHURCH ROAD
STANWELL ROAD
CLOCKHOUSE LANE
Piggeries
ASHFORD BUSINESS COMPLEX
Recreation Ground
CHATTERN HILL
Playing Field
Spelthorne College
Lib.
B378
FELTHAM ROAD
B377
TOWN TREE RD.
CONVENT RD.
Echelford Prim. Sch.
Salvn. Army Bldng.
Manor House (Club House)
ASHFORD MANOR GOLF COURSE
Manor Cottage
STAINES-BY-PASS
FORDBRIDGE ROUNDABOUT
Fordbridge Park
Ford Bridge
KINGSTON ROAD
A308
STAINES ROAD
Staines Reservoirs Aqueduct
SCHOOL ROAD JUNCTION
Littleton Common
Works
QUEEN MARY RESERVOIR
Gravel Pits
130
SCHOOL ROAD

EAST BEDFONT
Fairholme Jun. Inf. & Nursy. Schs.
Playing Field
Edward Pauling Prim. Sch.
Works
Vineyard Nurseries
H.M. Young Offenders Institution Feltham
Grosvenor Park
FELTHAM
Feltham
Ordnance Depot
Pav. Sports Ground
LEISURE WEST Cinema
FELTHAM BUSINESS COMPLEX
Feltham Hill Inf. Sch.
Feltham Hill Jun. Sch.
LOWER FELTHAM
Cemetery
Croft Farm
Garden Centre
Rugby Football Ground
Club Ho.
Sports Ground
FELTHAMHILL
Kenyngton Manor Prim. Sch.
Laboratories
Spelthorne Jun. & Inf. Schs.
ASHFORD COMMON
SUNBURY COMMON
Warehouse
Junc.1
M3 MOTORWAY
SUNBURY CROSS
Sunbury
KEMPTON PARK RACECOURSE
Grandstand
Pumping Station
Filter Beds
Superstore
Sunbury Manor
Playing Field
HIGH STREET
ASHFORD ROAD
CHERTSEY ROAD
STAINES ROAD WEST
HANWORTH RD.
COUNTRY WAY
HOUNSLOW ROAD
BEDFONT LANE
FELTHAM HILL ROAD
SUNBURY ROAD
VICARAGE ROAD
GROVELY ROAD
STAINES ROAD EAST
95
114
131

96
113
132
A
B
C
D
E
1
2
3
4
5
6
7
12
13
70
71
72
73
FELTHAM
HARLINGTON ROAD EAST
A312
UXBRIDGE ROAD
HANWORTH ROAD
HOUNSLOW ROAD
A314
HAMPTON RD. WEST
GREAT CHERTSEY ROAD
TWICKENHAM RD.
A305
HAMPTON RD. EAST
COUNTRY WAY
A316
South West Middlesex Crematorium
Playing Field
Feltham Community College
Warehouse
Works
Hanworth Park House
HANWORTH PARK
Feltham Airparcs Leisure Centre
Tennis Courts
Mount Corner
Hounslow College
HANWORTH
Rectory Meadow
Castle (Rems.)
Moat
Dairy
Filter Beds
Staines Reservoirs Aqueduct
Reservoir
Half Moon Covert
KEMPTON PARK
RACECOURSE
Grandstand
Kempton Park
Football Ground
Hatherop Park
Oldfield Works
Portlane Bridge
Hydes Field
KINGSWAY BUSINESS PARK
Hampton Community College
Hampton School
TWICKENHAM GOLF COURSE
APEX CORNER
APEX RETAIL PARK
HANWORTH TRAD. EST.
HAMPTON FARM IND. ESTATE
Nature Reserve
Recreation Grd.
Heathfield Jun. & Inf. Schs.
Cemetery
Superstore
Longford River
The Lindon Bennett Sch.
Sports Hall
Comm. Cen.
Bowl. Alley
LEISURE WEST
Cinema
FELTHAM BUSINESS COMPLEX
Sports Ground
MILL FARM BUSINESS PARK
HOWDEN HOUSE
Hounslow Cemy.
STAINES RD. EAST

WHITTON
Whitton
97
Harlequins R.U.F.C. (Stoop Meml. Grd.)
TWICKENHAM
Twickenham Cemetery
Kneller Gdns. Pav.
HOSPITAL BRIDGE ROUNDABOUT
Hospital Bridge
Pav. Sports Ground
River Crane
Twickenham Green
Strawberry Hill
Radnor Gardens
Swan Island
Playing Field Waldegrave Sch. for Girls
St. James' R.C. Prim. Sch.
STRAWBERRY HILL GOLF COURSE
St. Mary's Strawberry Hill
STRAWBERRY HILL
Stanley Jun.& Inf. Schs.
Fulwell Park
FULWELL GOLF COURSE
Fulwell
Club House
Cemetery
Newland Ho.Sch.
116
TEDDINGTON
HAMPTON HILL
Playing Field Lady Eleanor Holles Sch.
Clarendon Sch.
Cricket Grd.
ST. CLARE BUSINESS PARK
Canal Plantation
Works
Pantile Bridge
National Physical Laboratory
Bartons Cottage
Cricket Ground
Bushy House
Teddington
Teddington Lodge
Sports Ground
Bowling Green
Tennis Courts
Carlisle Park
Longford River
Round Plantation
BUSHY PARK
HAMPTON
Hampton & Richmond Borough F.C.
Willow Plantation
133
Broom Clumps
River Lodge
HEATH ROAD
THE GREEN
HAMPTON ROAD
CHERTSEY ROAD
STAINES ROAD
SIXTH CROSS ROAD
WELLINGTON RD.
FULWELL RD.
STANLEY RD.
SHACKLEGATE LANE
CHURCH RD.
WALDEGRAVE ROAD
HIGH STREET
BROAD ST.
PARK ROAD
HAMPTON ROAD
HIGH STREET
CROSS DEEP
A305
A316
A311
A309
A313
A312
B358
B360
F
G
H
J
K
1
2
3
4
5
6
7
14
15
16
170

Twickenham
A
B
C
D
E
98
MARBLE HILL PARK
Marble Hill House
Glover's Island
Petersham Meadows
Star & Garter Home
Petersham Common
Petersham Farm
Orleans Ho. Gallery
Riverside Ho.
York Ho.
Orleans Gdns.
Foot Ferry
RIVER THAMES
WARREN FOOTPATH
RICHMOND RD.
YORK ST.
KING ST.
LONDON RD.
HEATH RD.
CROSS DEEP
STRAWBERRY VALE
TWICKENHAM RD.
Eel Pie Island
TWICKENHAM
Thames Eyot
Radnor Gardens
Swan Island
Cross Deep
Ham Riverside Lands
Nature Reserve
Wood
Ham Fields
Thames Young Mariners Base
Playing Field
Tennis Cts.
Club
Miniature Rifle Range
Ham House
Polo Ground
The German Sch., London
The Russell Prim. Sch.
Strathmore Sch.
The Copse
PETERSHAM
PETERSHAM PARK
SUDBROOK PARK
Sudbrook Park (Club Ho.)
The Wilderness
RICHMOND GOLF COURSE
PETERSHAM RD.
SANDY LANE
HAM STREET
Grey Court School
Ham Green
Convent
HAM
Meadlands Prim. Sch.
C.E. Prim. Sch.
HAM COMMON
HAM GATE
B352
A307
A310
A313
B353
B358
UPPER HAM RD.
RICHMOND RD.
THE CASSEL HOSP.
Dysart Sch.
DUKES AVENUE
DYSART AVENUE
ST. GEORGE'S INDUSTRIAL ESTATE
The Tiffin Girls' Sch.
Fernhill Prim. Sch.
STRAWBERRY HILL
St. Mary's Strawberry Hill
TEDDINGTON
115
Teddington Locks
Teddington Studios
Teddington Weir
Rec. Gd.
Ham Riverside Lands
Sports Ground
Lensbury Club
Trowlock Island
HIGH STREET
KINGSTON ROAD
Athletic Ground
Collis Prim. Sch.
Teddington
Teddington Sch. & Sports Cen.
Recreation Ground
Conifers
The Avenue Centre (Coll.)
Steven's Eyot
Canbury Gardens
LOWER HAM ROAD
KINGSTON UPON THAMES
HAMPTON WICK
Hampton Wick
PARK RD.
SANDY LANE
Teddington Lodge
BUSHY PARK
Warren Plantation
Hawthorn Lodge
Half Moon Plantation
Deer Pen
Leg-of-Mutton Pond
Thatched Cottage
134
UP. TEDDINGTON RD.
Superstore
Mosque
Open 7:30am - 7:00pm
1
2
3
4
5
6
7
16
17
18
70
71
72
73

RICHMOND PARK
SIDMOUTH WOOD
Kidney Wood
Saw Pit Plantation
Jubilee Plantation
Queen's Ride
Duchess' Wood
Deer Pen
White Lodge Plantation
White Lodge (The Royal Ballet School)
Victory Plantation
King Henry VIII Mound
Pen Ponds
Leg of Mutton Pond
Queen Elizabeth's Plantation
Lawn Plantation
Treebox Wood
SPANKERS HILL WOOD
Oak Lodge
DEER PARK
King George V Jubilee Plantation
Playing Fields
Pond Plantation
Whiteash Lodge
Tercentenary Plantation
Horse Ride
Pond Slade
Prince Charles's Spinney
Ham Cross Plantation
Gibbet Wood
Ham Bottom
Peg's Pond
Thomson's Pond
Broomfield Hill
Broomfield Hill Wood
Ham Cross
ISABELLA PLANTATION
Ham Gate
High Wood
Still Pond
Deer Fold
Robin Hood Prim. Sch.
KINGSTON UNIVERSITY
Coronation Plantation
The Flat
Dann's Pond
Ladderstile Gate
Gallows Pond
King's Clump
Warren House
COOMBE HILL GOLF COURSE
COOMBE WOOD GOLF COURSE
COOMBE
Club House
Holy Cross Preparatory R.C. Sch.
Marymount International School
Kingston Gate
KINGSTON HILL A308
QUEENS RD. B351
COOMBE LANE WEST A238
KINGSTON HOSPITAL
Coombe Hill Jun. & Inf. Schools
Sports Ground
R.C. Prim. Sch.
Park Hill Sch.
(Open during daylight hours only)
99
118
135

118
ROEHAMPTON
100
117
136
RICHMOND PARK
GOLF COURSE
Kingsfarm Plantation
Victory Plantation
Killcat Corner
White Lodge Plantation
Treebox Wood
HILL
Playing Fields
Beverley Brook
Horse Ride
(Open during daylight hours only)
Robin Hood Gate
Beverley Bridge
ROEHAMPTON VALE
KINGSTON VALE
STAG LANE
Silver Hill
Chohole Gate
Hyde Park Nursery
PUTNEY HEATH
King's Mere
Scio Pond
Subway
ROEHAMPTON LANE
Jerry's Hill
Stag Ride
Inner Park Ride
Ladies Mile
Putney Vale Crematorium
PUTNEY VALE CEMETERY
Superstore
Newlands Hall
PUTNEY VALE
Kingston University (Roehampton Vale Centre)
Hall School Wimbledon
Memorial Gardens
War Memorial
Playing Fields
ROBIN HOOD
Silent Pools
Stag Bog
Queen's Mere
Wimbledon Postmill & Museum
Club House
Manor Cottage
CLOCKHOUSE CL.
Clock House
WINDMILL RD.
WIMBLEDON
COMMON
Gravelly Ride
Horse Exercise Ring
Gravelly Hill
Horse Exercise Area
Pavilion
WIMBLEDON COMMON & LONDON SCOTTISH GOLF COURSE
White Cottage
Thatched Cottage
ROBIN HOOD ROAD
Farm Bog
Farm Ravine
Horse Ride
Warren Farm
Caesar's Camp
CAMP RD.
Club House
KINGSTON UNIVERSITY
A3 (KINGSTON BY-PASS)
ROBIN HOOD WAY
Tennis Courts
Subway
Fishpond Wood
Mill Corner
ROYAL WIMBLEDON GOLF COURSE
Shadwell Wood
The Warren
Cannizaro House
Cannizaro Park
Lady Jane's Wood
WEST SIDE COMN.
WOODHAYES RD.
COOMBE HILL GOLF COURSE
Club House
Playing Field
Tennis Courts
Rowans Sch.
The Wolfson Rehabilitation Cen.
ATKINSON MORLEY'S HOSP.
COPSE HILL
Sports Grd.
COTTENHAM PARK ROAD
DURHAM
Holland Gdns.
COOMBE LANE WEST
A238
COOMBE LANE
NEW VICTORIA HOSPITAL
TRAPS LA.
Cottenham Park
St. Matthew's C. of E. First Sch.

101
SOUTHFIELDS
King George's Park
Southfields
Library
School
WIMBLEDON PARK
Athletics Ground
Bowling Greens
Putting Green
Tennis Courts
Cricket Ground
Club House
Wimbledon Park
WIMBLEDON PARK GOLF COURSE
Sports Ground
Aorangi Park
WIMBLEDON
All England
Lawn Tennis &
Croquet Club
Earlsfield
River Wandle
Recreation Ground
Depot
Carriage Cleaning Shed
Works
SUMMERSTOWN
Wimbledon Stadium
(Greyhound)
Wimbledon Cemetery
Football Grd.
120
Haydons Road
Bishop Gilpin C.of E. First Sch.
The Priory C. of E. Sch.
South Park Gardens
SOUTH WIMBLEDON
Baths
THE BROADWAY
Wimbledon
WIMBLEDON
Wimbledon High Sch.
Wimbledon Coll.
Ursuline Convent Prep. Sch.
Dundonald Rd.
Dundonald First Sch.
Recreation Ground
137
Merton Park
South Wimbledon
MERTON
MERTON HIGH ST.
NELSON INDUSTRIAL ESTATE
MERANTUN
HIGH ST.
WIMBLEDON HILL RD.
DURNSFORD RD.
HAYDONS ROAD
PLOUGH LANE
GARRATT LANE
ALEXANDRA RD.
HARTFIELD ROAD
KINGSTON ROAD
WORPLE RD.
PARKSIDE
MERTON ROAD
GAP ROAD
A218
A219
A217
A238
B235
B285
F
G
H
J
K
1
2
3
4
5
6
7

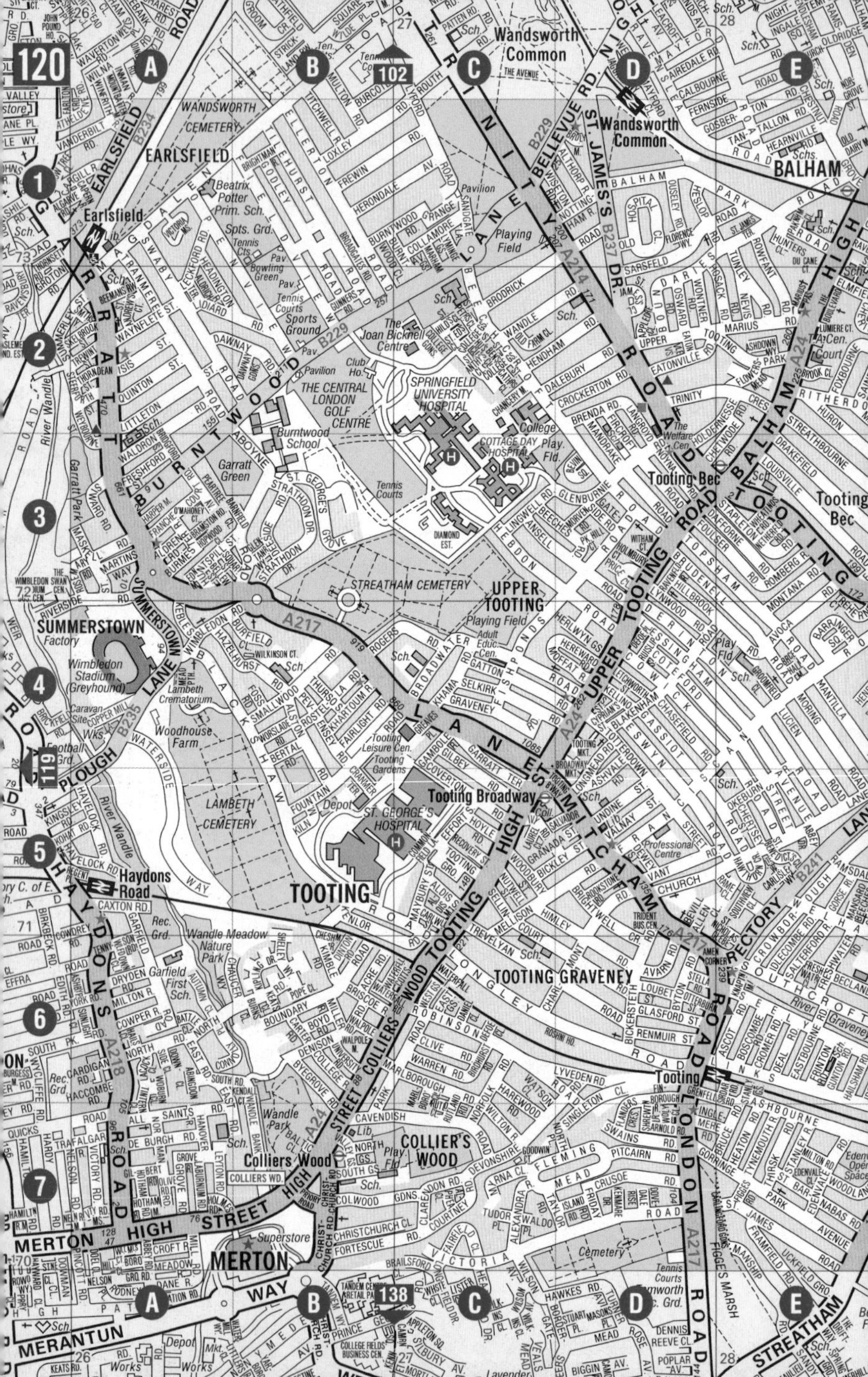

Wandsworth Common
WANDSWORTH CEMETERY
EARLSFIELD
Earlsfield
Beatrix Potter Prim. Sch.
BALHAM
Playing Field
Sports Ground
The Joan Bicknell Centre
THE CENTRAL LONDON GOLF CENTRE
SPRINGFIELD UNIVERSITY HOSPITAL
COTTAGE DAY HOSPITAL
Burntwood School
Garratt Green
Tooting Bec
STREATHAM CEMETERY
UPPER TOOTING
SUMMERSTOWN
Wimbledon Stadium (Greyhound)
Lambeth Crematorium
Woodhouse Farm
LAMBETH CEMETERY
Tooting Leisure Cen.
Tooting Gardens
Tooting Broadway
ST. GEORGE'S HOSPITAL
Professional Centre
Haydons Road
TOOTING
Wandle Meadow Nature Park
Garfield First Sch.
TOOTING GRAVENEY
Tooting
Wandle Park
COLLIER'S WOOD
Colliers Wood
MERTON
Superstore
Cemetery
FIGGE'S MARSH
MERTON HIGH STREET
COLLIERS WOOD HIGH STREET
TOOTING HIGH ST.
UPPER TOOTING ROAD
TRINITY ROAD
BALHAM HIGH ROAD
BURNTWOOD LANE
GARRATT LANE
SUMMERSTOWN
MITCHAM RD.
LONDON ROAD
STREATHAM
A24
A217
A214
A218
A24
B229
B235
B237
B241
102
119
138

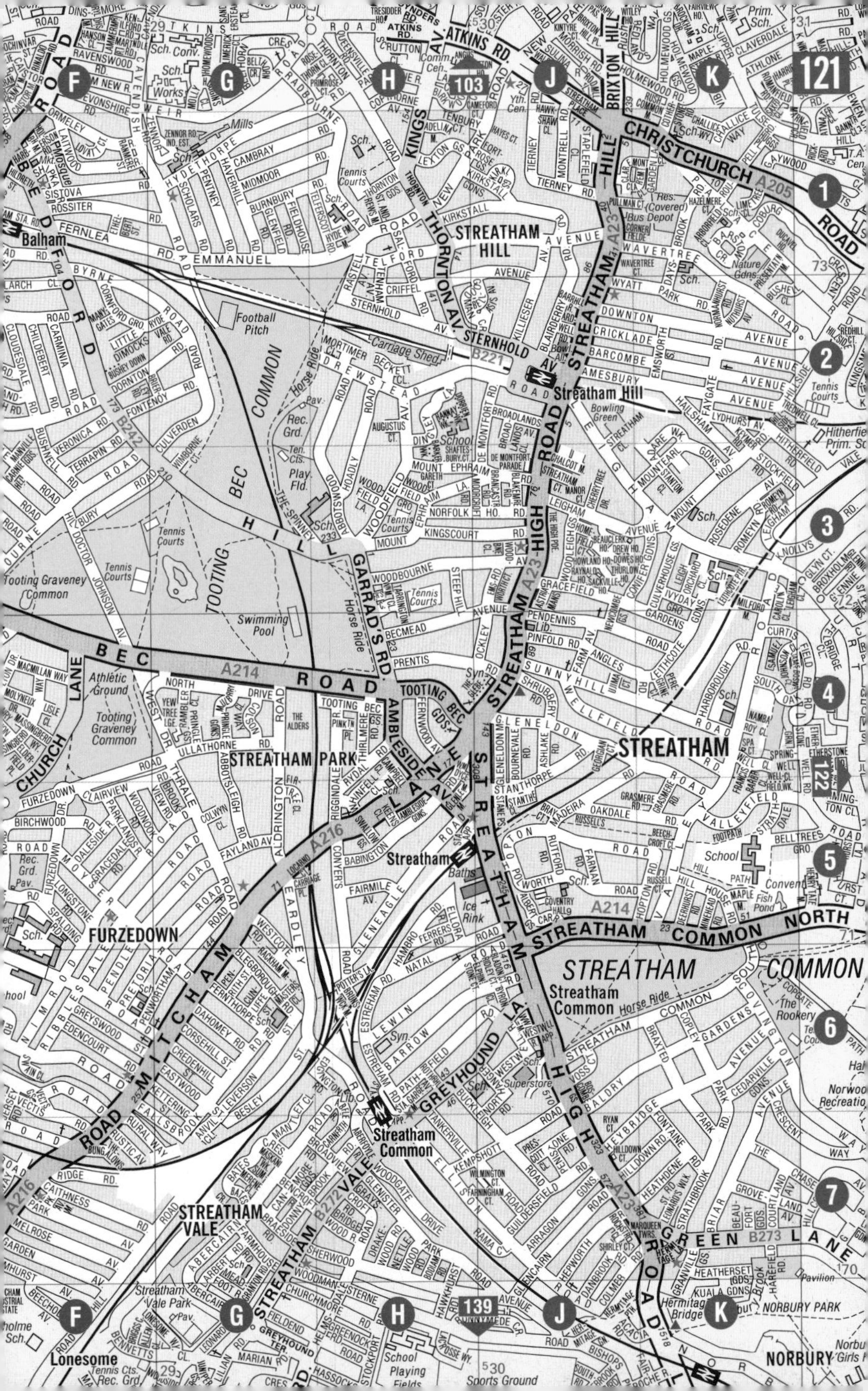

F
G
H
J
K
103
1
2
3
4
5
6
7
122
139
29
530
31
STREATHAM HILL
Streatham Hill
STREATHAM
STREATHAM PARK
FURZEDOWN
STREATHAM VALE
Streatham
Streatham Common
STREATHAM COMMON
Streatham Common
TOOTING BEC COMMON
Tooting Graveney Common
Balham
Lonesome
NORBURY
NORBURY PARK
Streatham Vale Park
Football Pitch
Swimming Pool
Athletic Ground
Ice Rink
Baths
Bus Depot
Bowling Green
Carriage Shed
Horse Ride
The Rookery
Norwood Recreation
Hermitage Bridge
School Playing Fields
Sports Ground
CHRISTCHURCH ROAD
BRIXTON HILL
STREATHAM HILL
STREATHAM HIGH ROAD
A23
A205
A214
A216
B221
B242
B272
B273
BEC ROAD
TOOTING BEC ROAD
BEDFORD HILL
CHURCH LANE
GARRAD'S RD.
AMBLESIDE AV.
MITCHAM LANE
MITCHAM ROAD
STREATHAM COMMON NORTH
STREATHAM COMMON SOUTH
GREYHOUND LA.
GREEN LANE
LONDON ROAD
KINGS AV.
THORNTON AV.
STERNHOLD AV.
ATKINS RD.
EMMANUEL RD.
LEIGHAM AVENUE
LEIGHAM COURT RD.
VALLEY RD.
WAVERTREE RD.
DOWNTON AVENUE
CRICKLADE AVENUE
BARCOMBE AVENUE
AMESBURY AVENUE
SUNNYHILL RD.
WELLFIELD RD.
GLENELDON RD.
ESTREATHAM RD.
EARDLEY RD.
SHERWOOD AV.

122
A
B
C
D
E
1
2
3
4
5
6
7
104
121
140
31
32
33
BROCKWELL PARK
New Lodge
PEABODY ESTATE
CROXTED
TURNEY
Sports Ground
Dulwich Old College
Dulwich Picture Gallery
Tennis Courts
Bell House
Boating Lake
TULSE HILL
NORWOOD ROAD
Knight's Hill
Tulse Hill
CHRISTCHURCH RD.
THURLOW PARK ROAD
DULWICH
West Dulwich
DULWICH COLLEGE
Playing Fields
Belair
Mill Pond
Hitherfield Prim. Sch.
LEIGHAM
KNOLLYS ROAD
ROYAL CIRCUS
Tonge Ho.
ROBSON
CHESTNUT ROAD
Library
West Norwood Cemetery and Crematorium
Catacombs
WEST DULWICH
West Norwood
WEST NORWOOD
AUCKLAND
NORWOOD HIGH ST.
KNIGHTS HILL
ELDER
GIPSY
Kingswood Prim. Sch.
KINGSWOOD ESTATE
NORWOOD PARK
Gipsy Hill
Playing Field
Playground
STREATHAM COMM. NTH.
CROWN LA.
CROWN DALE
CENTRAL HILL
STREATHAM COMMON
The Rookery
St. Joseph's College
St. Joseph's R.C. Jun. & Inf. Schs.
Virgo Fidelis Convent Sch.
Convent Wood
NORWOOD NEW TOWN
Rockmount Prim. Sch.
BEULAH HILL
Norwood Grove Recreation Ground
Bowling Green
Recreation Ground
NORWOOD
Westow Park
Biggin Wood
Downsview Prim. Sch.
Westwood High Sch.
UPPER NORWOOD
NORBURY PARK
NORBURY
Norbury Manor Girls High Sch.
NORBURY WAY
VIRGINIA
FLORIDA
GREEN
B273
A205
A215
A214
A2199
CHURCH

DULWICH & SYDENHAM HILL
GOLF COURSE
DULWICH
Dulwich Wood
Sydenham Hill
UPPER SYDENHAM
Sydenham Wells Park
FOREST HILL
Forest Hill
Horniman Gardens
Horniman Museum
Mayow Park
LOWER SYDENHAM
SYDENHAM
Sydenham
CRYSTAL PALACE PARK
Crystal Palace Museum
Crystal Palace
NATIONAL SPORTS CENTRE
Sports Arena
Sports Hall
Intermediate Lake
Lower Lake
Rockhills Entrance Camping Site
T.V. Transmitter
Site of Crystal Palace
Sydenham Entrance
Penge Entrance
Anerley Entrance
Penge East
Penge West
PENGE
Anerley
Alexandra Rec. Grd.
Alexandra Jun. Sch.
Playing Field
St. Christopher's Hospice
Kent House
City Technology Coll.
Superstore
The Kentwood Cen.
Blenheim Shop. Cen.
THE GROVE
COMMON
LORDSHIP LANE
LONDON ROAD
DARTMOUTH RD.
KIRKDALE
SYDENHAM HILL
WESTWOOD HILL
CRYSTAL PALACE PARK RD.
SYDENHAM ROAD
NEWLANDS PARK
PARISH LANE
HIGH ST.
ANERLEY HILL
ANERLEY ROAD
WALDRAM PK. RD.
PERRY VALE
STANSTEAD RD.
A205
A212
A234
A213
A2216
A2199
B227
105
124
141
F
G
H
J
K
1
2
3
4
5
6
7
34
35
36

124
Blythe Hill
Catford Bridge
Catford
106
STANSTEAD ROAD
A205
CATFORD HILL
CATFORD
BROWNHILL
BROMLEY
A21
RUSHEY GRN.
CATFORD GYRATORY
Council Offs.
Lib.
Powerleague Soccer Cen.
Private Banks Sports Ground
THE PRIORY APARTMENTS
CATFORD TRADING ESTATE
Ravensbourne
River
Pool
Depot
Wks.
Bellingham
BELLINGHAM
Playing Field
BROADMEAD
BELL GREEN
Superstore
Gasholder Station
A212
PERRY HILL
PERRY RISE
B227
PERRY VALE
BELL GRN.
SOUTHEND LA.
STANTON WAY
SOUTHEND LANE
A2218
LWR. SYDENHAM
SYDENHAM RD.
123
Home Park
Britannic Ho. Club
Sports Ground
Lower Sydenham
Southend Park
Secondary School
Beckenham Hill
BECKENHAM HILL ROAD
A2015
Recreation
Ash Plantation
Stumpshill Wood
Beckenham Place Club House
BECKENHAM PLACE PARK
GOLF COURSE
The Cottage
Summerhouse Wood
Club
KANGLEY BUS. CEN.
ORCHARD BUS. CEN.
LWR. SYDENHAM IND. EST.
GARDNER IND. EST.
BECKENHAM BUSINESS CENTRE
THE METRO BUS. CEN.
Alexandra Jun. Sch.
Playing Field
Cricket Grd.
Athletic Grd.
NEW BECKENHAM
New Beckenham
Athletic Ground
Bowling Grn. Sports Ground
CATOR PARK
The Sports Grd.
Kent House
Beckenham Road
142
Beckenham Junc.
SOUTHEND ROAD
BECKENHAM
St. Mary's R.C. Prim. Sch.
Westgate Lodge
A B C D E
1 2 3 4 5 6 7
36 37 38

125
107
126
143
F
G
H
J
K
1
2
3
4
5
6
7
ST. MILDREDS
ROAD
Hither Green Sidings
Northbrook Park
HITHER GREEN CEMETERY
Lewisham Crematorium
Downham Enterprise Centre
Horn Park Prim. Sch.
Playing Field
Carter's Hill
Sports Ground
A2212
GROVE PARK
Grove Park
CHINBROOK RD.
Chinbrook Meadows
Depot
FORSTER MEMORIAL PARK
Playground
Playing Fields
SOUTHEND
Churchdown Christian Centre
Prim. Sch. Downham Fields
Baths
Liby.
DOWNHAM
Shaftesbury Park
Sports Grd.
Bromley Hill Cemy.
A21
BROMLEY ROAD
LONDON ROAD
BURNT ASH LANE
BURNT ASH HILL
PLAISTOW
Parish CE Prim. Sch.
Play. Fld.
King's Meadow Playing Grd.
Hall's Farm
SUNDRIDGE
Golf Club
Cemetery
Sundridge Park
Sports Ground
Playing Field
Golf Course
Ravensbourne
Ravensbourne River
SHORTLANDS GOLF COURSE
BROMLEY PARK
COLLEGE RD.
Bromley Nth.
FARNABY AV.
Quaggy River
Netball Courts

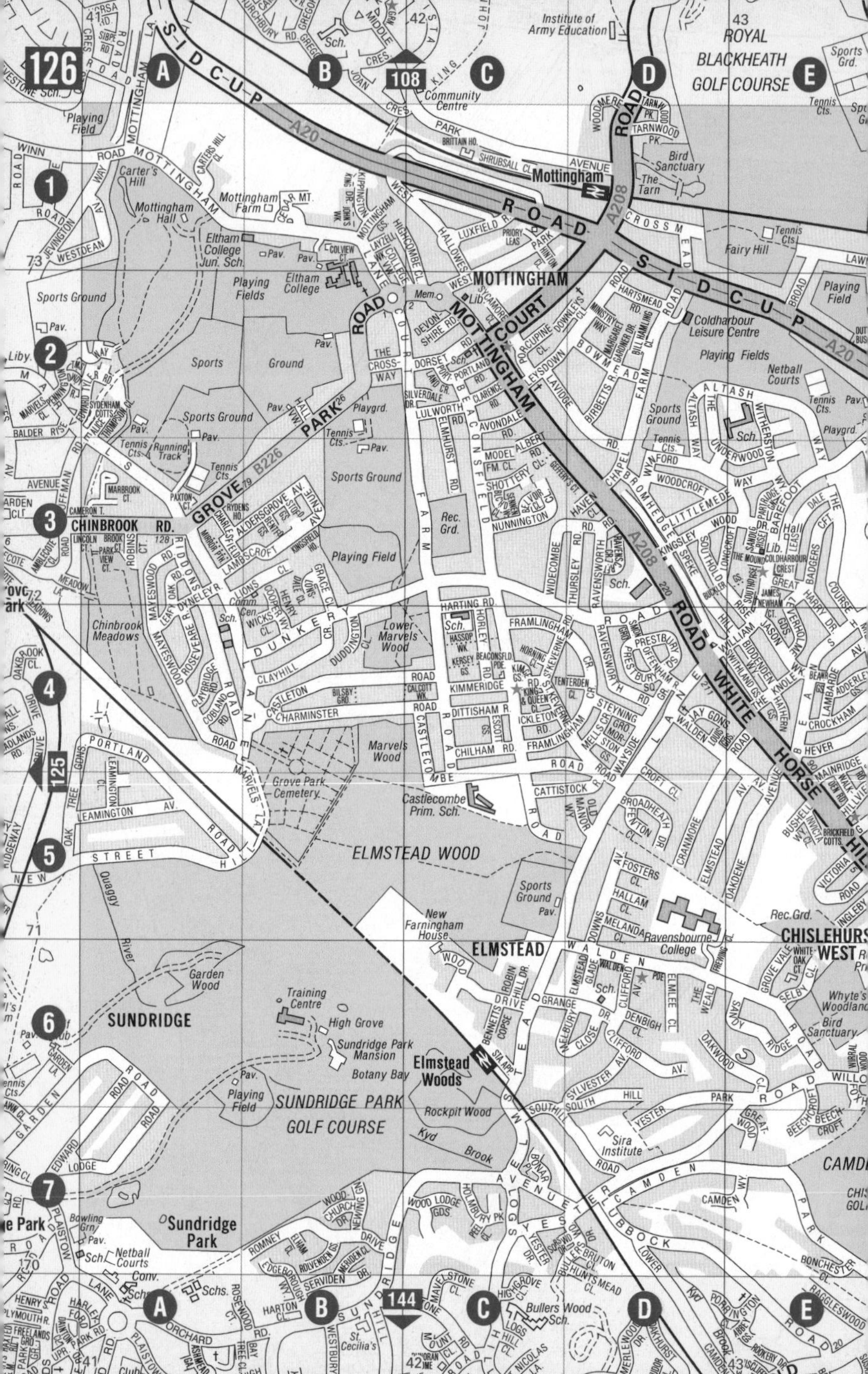

126
A
B
C
D
E
1
2
3
4
5
6
7
108
144
125
SIDCUP ROAD
A20
A208
B226
ROYAL BLACKHEATH GOLF COURSE
Institute of Army Education
Community Centre
Mottingham
Bird Sanctuary
The Tarn
Fairy Hill
Playing Field
Carter's Hill
Mottingham Hall
Mottingham Farm
Eltham College Jun. Sch.
Eltham College
Playing Fields
Sports Ground
MOTTINGHAM
MOTTINGHAM ROAD
COURT ROAD
Coldharbour Leisure Centre
Playing Fields
Netball Courts
GROVE PARK ROAD
CHINBROOK RD.
Chinbrook Meadows
Running Track
Sports Ground
Playing Field
Rec. Grd.
DUNKERY RD.
Lower Marvels Wood
Marvels Wood
Grove Park Cemetery
Castlecombe Prim. Sch.
ELMSTEAD WOOD
WHITE HORSE ROAD
New Farningham House
ELMSTEAD
Ravensbourne College
CHISLEHURST WEST
Whyte's Woodland
Bird Sanctuary
SUNDRIDGE
Garden Wood
Training Centre
High Grove
Sundridge Park Mansion
Botany Bay
Elmstead Woods
SUNDRIDGE PARK GOLF COURSE
Rockpit Wood
Kyd Brook
Sira Institute
Sundridge Park
Bullers Wood Sch.
Quaggy River
NEW STREET HILL
St. Cecilia's

F
G
H
J
K
109
1
2
3
4
5
6
7
128
145
44
45
46
Bowling Grn.
Sports Ground
Playing Fields
Sports Ground
Sparrow's Farm Leisure Cen.
River Sports Ground
Sports Ground
Lamorbey
Marlborough Sch.
Comm. Cen.
Play. Fld.
Baths
Old Farm Park
King George's Rec. Grd.
Marlowe Ho. Offs.
New Eltham
Sports Ground
St. Olave's Prep. School
FIVEWAYS
NEW ELTHAM
Dulverton Prim. Sch.
Wyncham Stream
Works
Wks.
Spts. Grd.
Liby.
Rec. Grd.
Sch.
LONGLANDS
World Of Golf At Sidcup
Flamingo Park Sports Grd.
Pitch & Putt Course
Montbelle Prim. Sch.
Edgebury Prim. Sch.
Kemnal Manor
Ashen Grove
Partridge Shaw
Esporta Health Club
Beaver's Wood
Chislehurst Cemetery
Hoblands Wood
Garden Centre
SIDCUP
Sports Ground
Club
St. Mary & St. Joseph's Catholic Sch.
Playing Field
Foxbury
Lodge
Hall
Mead Rd. Inf. Sch.
Selwood
Westerland
Darul Uloom London Islamic Sch.
Old Elthamians Sports Club
Beaverwood Sch. for Girls
Athletic Ground
Play. Fld.
Sports Ground
Playing Field
FROGNAL CORNER
Spring Shaw
The Lodge
Bank's Shaw
Square Clump
Bushy Clump
SCADBURY PARK WOOD NATURE RESERVE
Farringtons & Stratford House
Tennis Courts
Icehouse Wood
Moat
Archway
Midfield Jun. Sch.
PARK WOOD
Nature Reserve
Hadresham
The Fantails
Holbrook Wood
Lodge
CHISLEHURST
CHISLEHURST COMMON
Camden Place (Golf Club)
Prim. Sch.
Cricket Grd.
Wks.
SIDCUP ROAD
MAIN ROAD
SIDCUP BY-PASS
CRAY ROAD
HALFWAY STREET
STATION RD.
PERRY STREET
BROMLEY RD.
ROYAL PDE.
WATTS LA.
MANOR PARK RD.
HIGH ST.
CENTRE COMN. RD.
A211
A20
A222
A208
B263
B2214

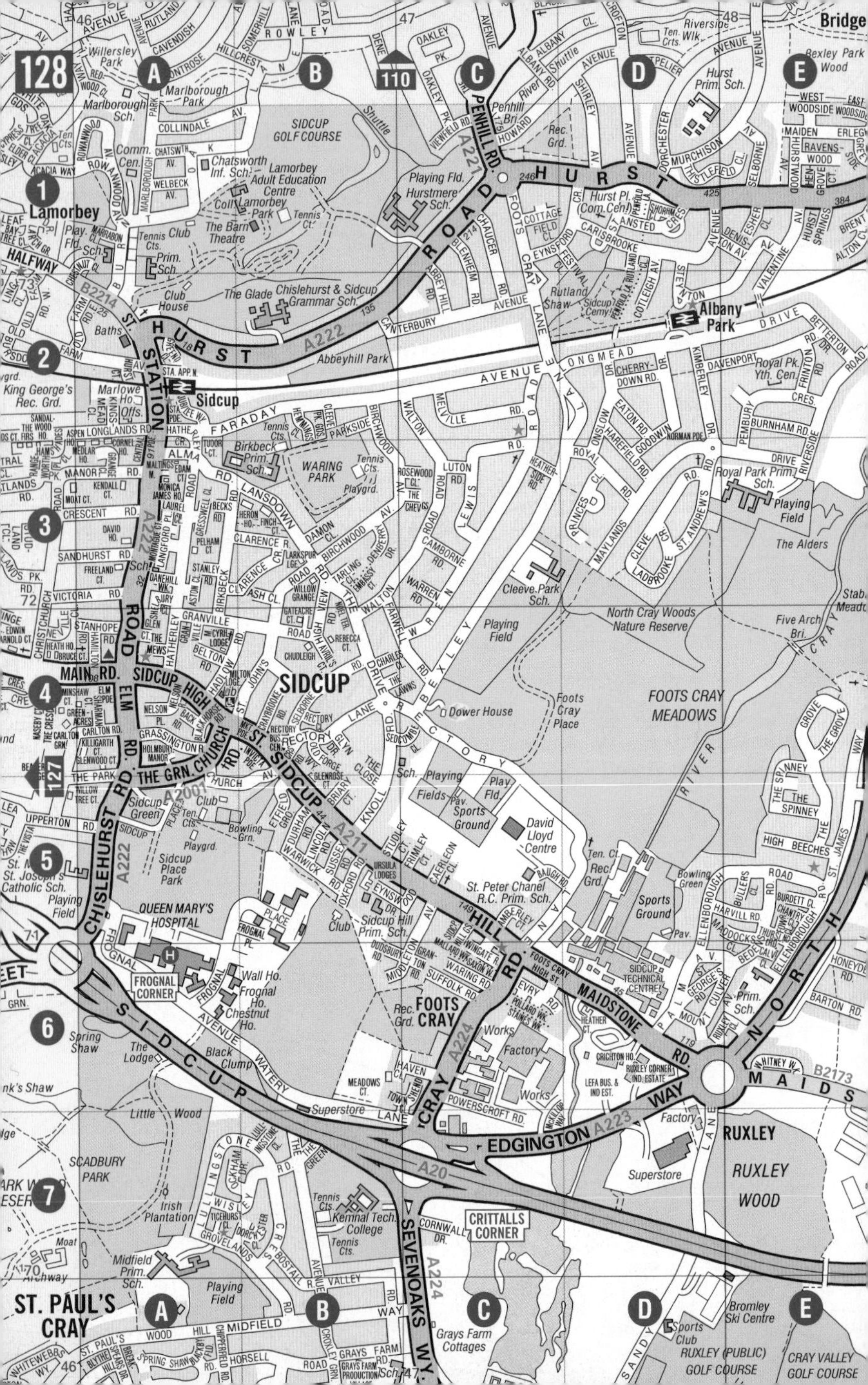
Lamorbey
SIDCUP GOLF COURSE
Lamorbey Adult Education Centre
Chislehurst & Sidcup Grammar Sch.
Abbeyhill Park
Sidcup
King George's Rec. Grd.
WARING PARK
Cleeve Park Sch.
North Cray Woods Nature Reserve
SIDCUP
FOOTS CRAY MEADOWS
Foots Cray Place
Dower House
David Lloyd Centre
QUEEN MARY'S HOSPITAL
FROGNAL CORNER
Sidcup Place Park
FOOTS CRAY
RUXLEY
RUXLEY WOOD
SCADBURY PARK
Kemnal Tech. College
CRITTALLS CORNER
ST. PAUL'S CRAY
Bromley Ski Centre
RUXLEY (PUBLIC) GOLF COURSE
CRAY VALLEY GOLF COURSE
Albany Park
Royal Park Prim. Sch.
Bexley Park Wood
110
127

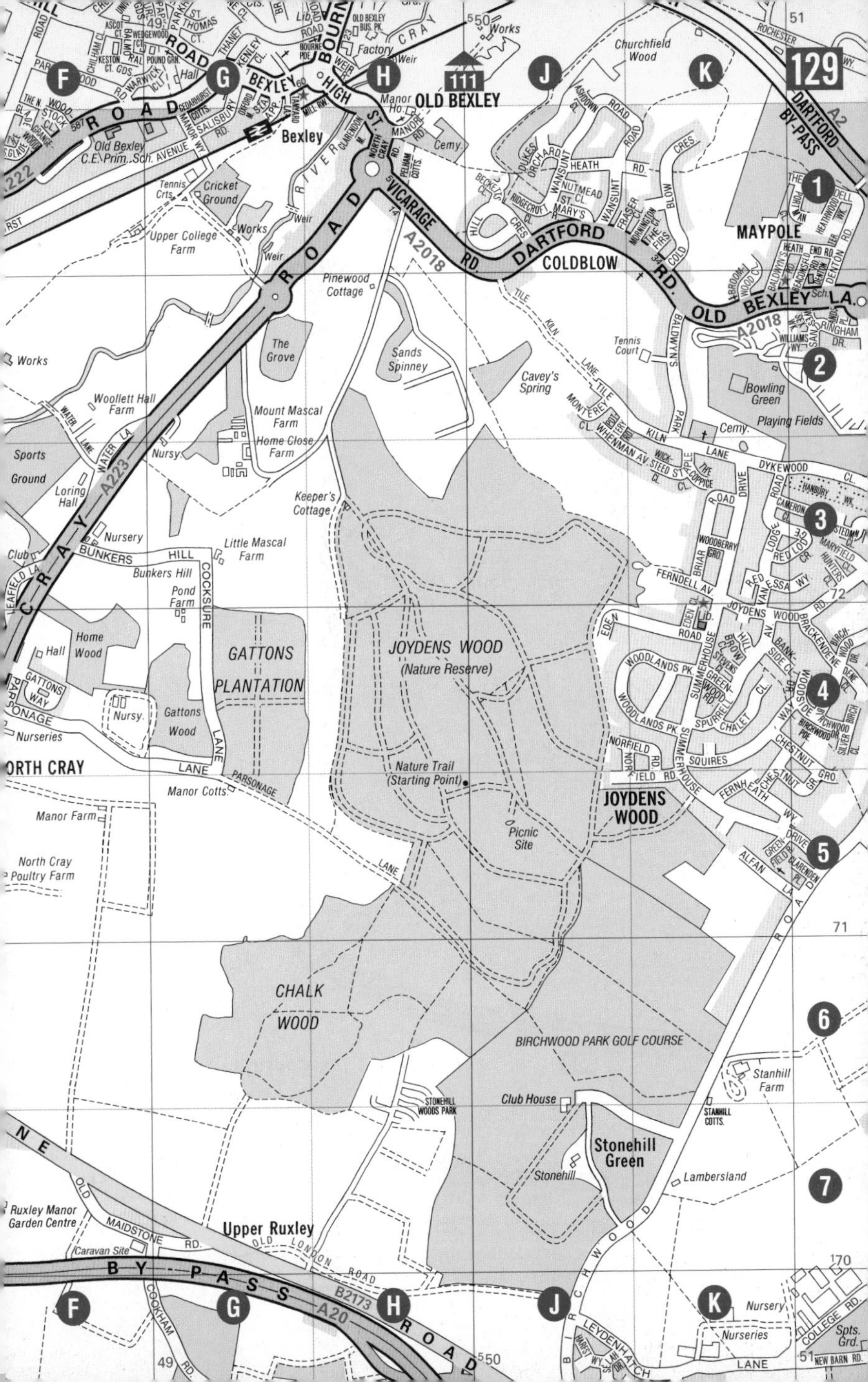
OLD BEXLEY
Bexley
MAYPOLE
COLDBLOW
JOYDENS WOOD
JOYDENS WOOD
(Nature Reserve)
GATTONS PLANTATION
CHALK WOOD
BIRCHWOOD PARK GOLF COURSE
Stonehill Green
Upper Ruxley
NORTH CRAY
Churchfield Wood
Cricket Ground
Upper College Farm
Pinewood Cottage
The Grove
Sands Spinney
Cavey's Spring
Mount Mascal Farm
Home Close Farm
Woollett Hall Farm
Sports Ground
Loring Hall
Keeper's Cottage
Little Mascal Farm
Bunkers Hill
Pond Farm
Home Wood
Gattons Wood
Nature Trail
(Starting Point)
Picnic Site
Manor Cotts.
Manor Farm
North Cray Poultry Farm
Club House
Stonehill
Lambersland
Stanhill Farm
STANHILL COTTS.
STONEHILL WOODS PARK
Ruxley Manor Garden Centre
Caravan Site
Nursery
Nurseries
Bowling Green
Playing Fields
Tennis Court
Old Bexley C.E. Prim. Sch.
DARTFORD BY-PASS
A2
A2018
A223
A222
A20
B2173
VICARAGE RD.
DARTFORD RD.
OLD BEXLEY LA.
CRAY ROAD
BUNKERS HILL
COCKSURE LANE
PARSONAGE LANE
BIRCHWOOD ROAD
MAIDSTONE RD.
OLD LONDON ROAD
BY-PASS ROAD
LEYDENHATCH LANE
TILE KILN LANE
SUMMERHOUSE DRIVE
WOODLANDS PK.
DYKEWOOD CL.
FERNDELL AV.
EDEN ROAD
111
550
51
49
72
71
170
F
G
H
J
K
1
2
3
4
5
6
7

130
112
A
B
C
D
E
1
2
3
4
5
6
7
06
07
08
70
69
68
67
QUEEN MARY
RESERVOIR
Gravel Pits
Intake Channel
Pumping Station
Round Copse
Works
ASHFORD RD.
CAMBRIDGE RD.
ASHDENE CL.
LITTLETON LANE
SPELTHORNE ROAD
QUEEN MARY RD.
HARROW WY.
TREE LODGE WY.
ALMOND CL.
WALNUT TREE CL.
CROSSWELL CL.
CHARLT
Manor Farm
CHARLTON ROAD
NEW ROAD
The Green
LITTLETON
Play. Fld.
OLD MANOR HO. MEWS
Littleton Fm.
RECTORY CL.
Sch.
GODDARD CL.
BRIDGE ROAD
MAGDALENE RD.
SHEPPERTON FILM STUDIOS
STUDIOS ROAD
OBERON WY.
KORDA CL.
LEHAM RD.
STUDIOS RD.
HITCHCOCK CL.
River Ash
NUTTY LANE
Driving Range
Club
SHEPPERTON B376 RD.
Nurseries
Squire's Bridge
Rec. Grd.
CRANWELL GRO.
ASH ROAD
STEWART
HERMITAGE CL.
GLEN AV.
ELLIOTT GS.
FRANCIS CL.
GRANGE CT.
HORNE RD.
PETTS LA.
SHEPPERTON GREEN
WINCHSTONE CL.
SQUIRE'S RD.
BURBIDGE RD.
LEYMOW WY.
HARVEST CT.
WATERSPLASH
WOOD ROAD
FORD CL.
LALEHAM ROAD
387
345
262
150
LANE
MILTON DR.
ASHURST DRIVE
YEW TREES
Gravel Pit
Staines Road Farm
SUNBURY
BRAVINGTON CL.
FAIRVIEW DR.
DRIVE
BRIAR BUSH
ROSEACRE CL.
WRIGHT GS.
ROSEWOOD
BRIAR ROAD
ROAD
MANDEVILLE RD.
WALK
AV.
TANGLYN AV.
Nurseries
B376
ACACIA AV.
PRESTON RD.
PENTLAND AV.
HARRISH CT.
GREENO CR.
JESSIMAN TER.
POOL END CL.
SHEEP WK.
Saxon Prim. Sch.
LOIS DRIVE
BARBARA CL.
CRESCENT RD.
LINDEN WY.
CHARLTON
Shepperton
MARION AV.
SHEPPERTON BUSINESS PK.
GOVETT
STATION RD.
STATION APP.
OLD
PEARMAIN
Sch.
CAREMONT
SHEPHERDS CL.
MANOR FARM AV.
BARTON CL.
GREEN
ST.
THURLESTINE CL.
50
Pool End
Works
MANOR FARM AV.
GRANT CL.
Prim. Sch.
Lib.
KILMISTON AV.
BRUCE
GROVE RD.
BROADLANDS
Playing Field
M3 MOTORWAY
M3
LITTLETON
SHEPPERTON
SCHOOL LA.
HIGH B376
GLEBELAND
96
WAY
RENFREE
CHERTSEY ROAD
B375
ROAD
14
CHERTSEY BRI. RD.
DUMSEY EYOT
Riversleigh Farm
Boat House
Shepperton Range
RIVER THAMES
DOCKETT EDDY LANE
TOWPATH
Mead Farm
FARM CL.
RANGE WAY
ST NICHOLAS DRIVE
Cemetery
CHURCH ROAD
MANOR HO. CT.
CHURCH SQ.
FERRY SQ.
War Close
Pav.
Cricket Ground
Las Palmas Estate
RUSSELL
Lords Bri.
DUNBOE PL.
WADHAM
THAMESFIELD MEWS
CLOSE
Play. Fld.
Halliford Sch.
SANDHILLS MDW.
Sailing Club
FERRY LANE
DESBOROUGH CL.
DESBOROUGH ISLAND
RIVER THAMES
DOCKETT EDDY
Chertsey Meads

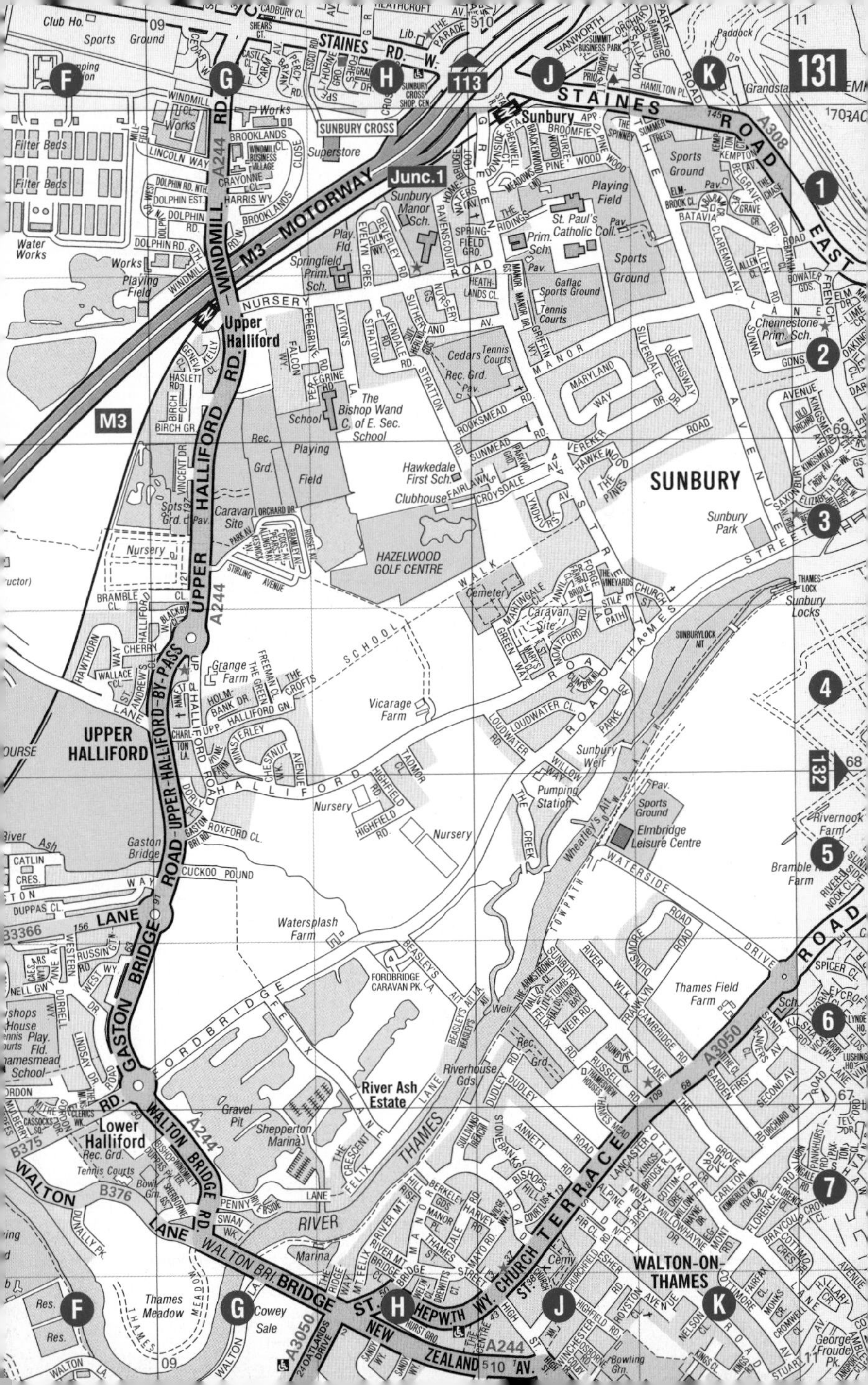
SUNBURY
UPPER HALLIFORD
Upper Halliford
Lower Halliford
WALTON-ON-THAMES
Sunbury Cross
SUNBURY CROSS
M3 MOTORWAY
Junc.1
M3
STAINES RD. W.
STAINES ROAD
A308
A244
A3050
B375
B376
B3366
WINDMILL RD.
UPPER HALLIFORD RD.
UPPER HALLIFORD BY-PASS
GASTON BRIDGE ROAD
WALTON BRIDGE RD.
WALTON LANE
HALLIFORD ROAD
NURSERY ROAD
MANOR LANE
GREEN STREET
THAMES STREET
FORDBRIDGE ROAD
FELIX LANE
CHURCH ST.
NEW ZEALAND AV.
TERRACE ROAD
ROAD
Filter Beds
Water Works
Playing Field
Sunbury Manor Sch.
Springfield Prim. Sch.
St. Paul's Catholic Coll.
Gaflac Sports Ground
Cedars Rec. Grd.
The Bishop Wand C. of E. Sec. School
Hawkedale First Sch.
HAZELWOOD GOLF CENTRE
Cemetery
Caravan Site
Vicarage Farm
Sunbury Park
Sunbury Locks
Sunbury Weir
Pumping Station
Elmbridge Leisure Centre
Thames Field Farm
Watersplash Farm
FORDBRIDGE CARAVAN PK.
River Ash Estate
Gravel Pit
Shepperton Marina
Riverhouse Gds
Thames Meadow
Cowey Sale
Chennestone Prim. Sch.
Rivernook Farm
Bramble Farm
Superstore
Grandstand
Paddock
Res.
RIVER THAMES
113
132
F
G
H
J
K
1
2
3
4
5
6
7
09
10
11
67
68
69
70

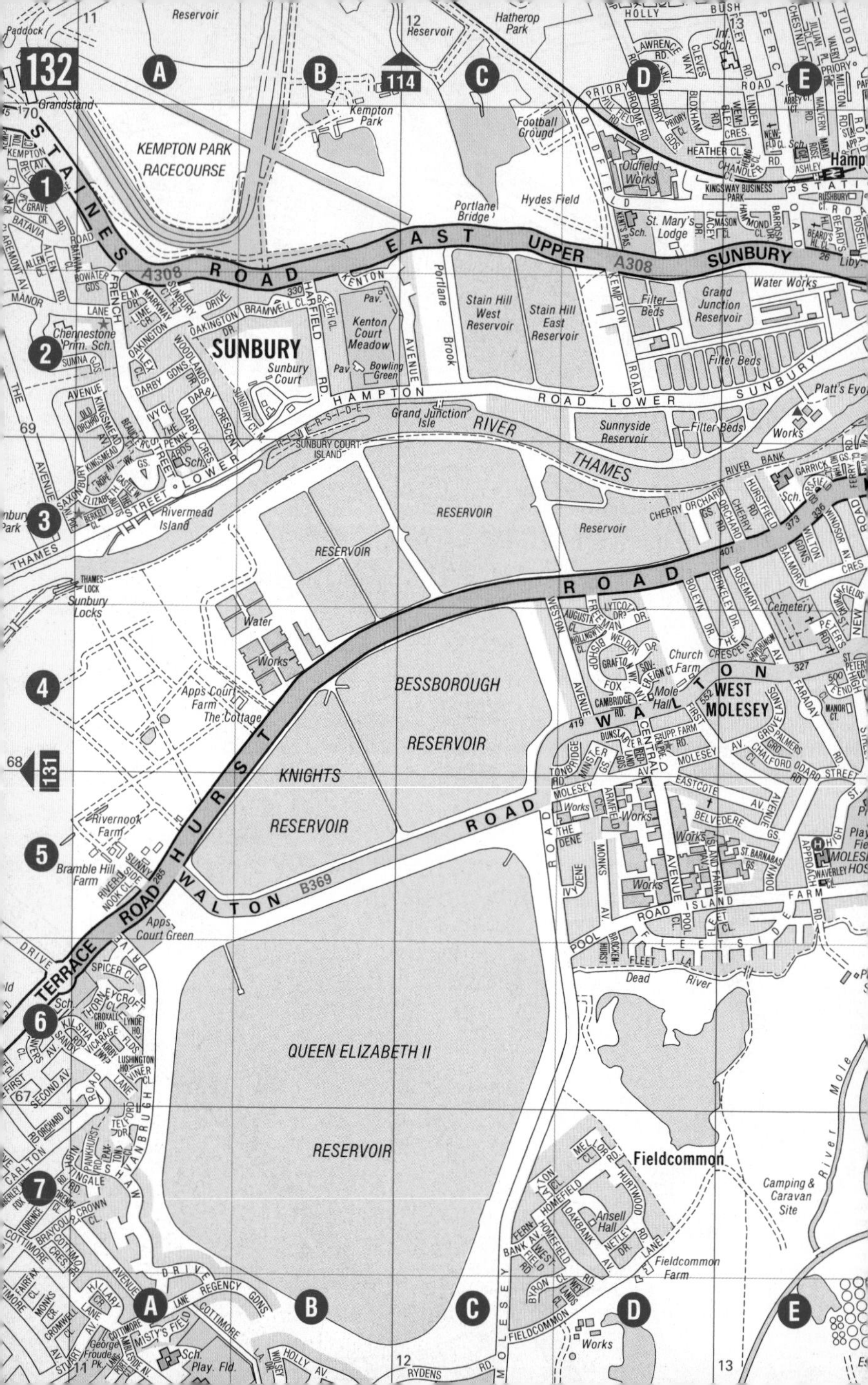

KEMPTON PARK RACECOURSE
Kempton Park
Hatherop Park
Football Ground
Hydes Field
Portlane Bridge
UPPER SUNBURY ROAD EAST
A308
STAINES ROAD
SUNBURY
Sunbury Court
Kenton Court Meadow
Stain Hill West Reservoir
Stain Hill East Reservoir
Grand Junction Reservoir
Water Works
Filter Beds
HAMPTON ROAD LOWER SUNBURY
Grand Junction Isle
RIVER THAMES
Sunnyside Reservoir
Platt's Eyot
Sunbury Court Island
Rivermead Island
LOWER STREET
THAMES STREET
RESERVOIR
Reservoir
Chennestone Prim. Sch.
Sunbury Locks
Thames Lock
Water Works
Apps Court Farm
The Cottage
BESSBOROUGH RESERVOIR
KNIGHTS RESERVOIR
HURST ROAD
WALTON ROAD
B369
Riverrnook Farm
Bramble Hill Farm
Apps Court Green
TERRACE ROAD
WEST MOLESEY
Church Farm
Mole Hall
Cemetery
Works
Dead River
QUEEN ELIZABETH II RESERVOIR
Fieldcommon
Ansell Hall
Fieldcommon Farm
Camping & Caravan Site
River Mole
MOLESEY ROAD
FIELDCOMMON LANE
RYDENS RD.
Misty's Field
George Froude Pk.
Sch.
Play. Fld.

114
131

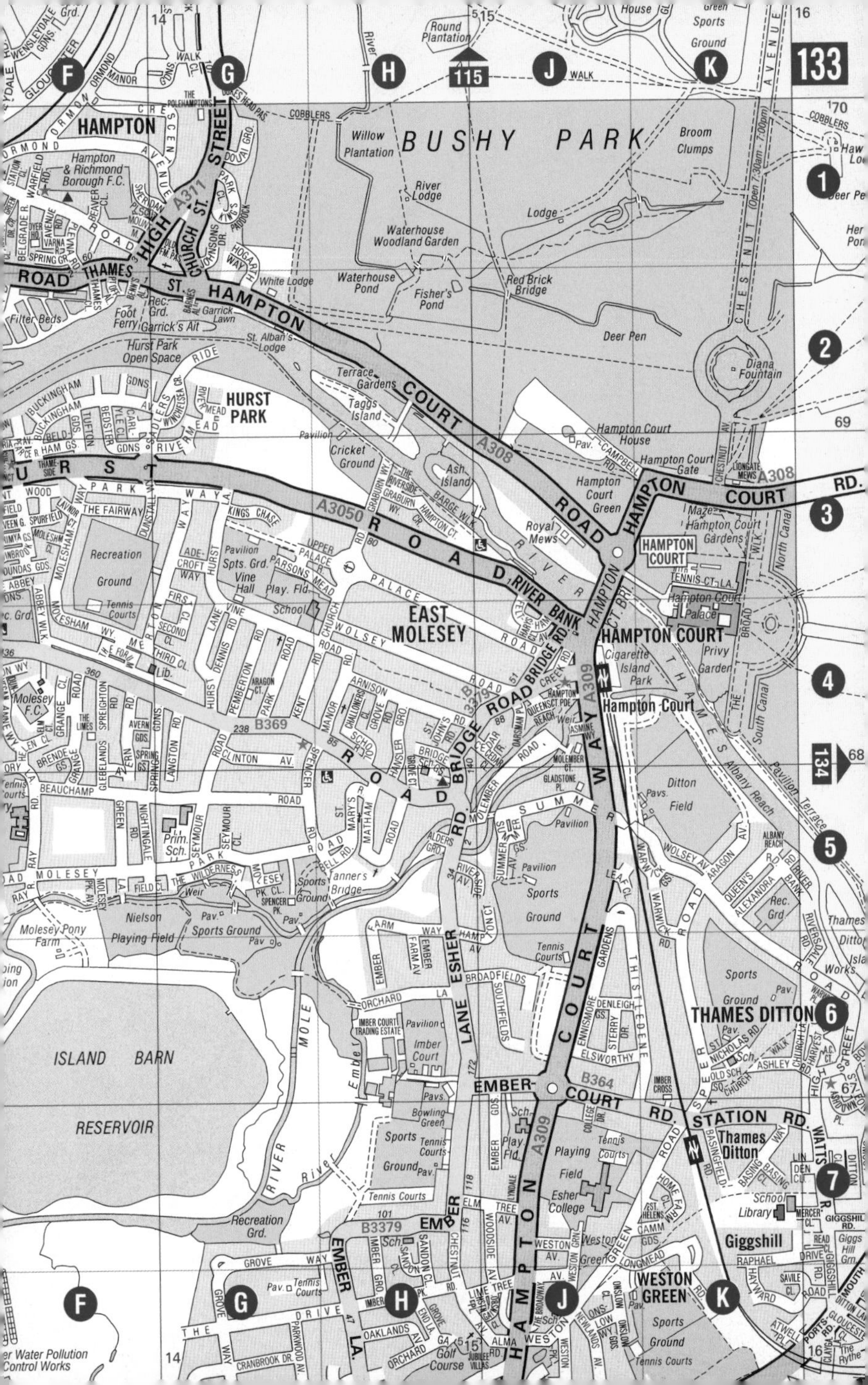
BUSHY PARK
HAMPTON
HURST PARK
EAST MOLESEY
HAMPTON COURT
THAMES DITTON
WESTON GREEN
Giggshill
ISLAND BARN
RESERVOIR
Willow Plantation
Round Plantation
Broom Clumps
River Lodge
Waterhouse Woodland Garden
Waterhouse Pond
Fisher's Pond
Red Brick Bridge
Deer Pen
Diana Fountain
Lodge
White Lodge
Hampton & Richmond Borough F.C.
Filter Beds
Foot Ferry
Garrick's Ait
Garrick Lawn
St. Alban's Lodge
Hurst Park Open Space
Terrace Gardens
Taggs Island
Ash Island
Cricket Ground
Hampton Court House
Hampton Court Gate
Hampton Court Green
Royal Mews
Maze
Hampton Court Gardens
Hampton Court Palace
Privy Garden
Cigarette Island Park
South Canal
North Canal
Ditton Field
Albany Reach
Pavilion Terrace
Recreation Ground
Tennis Courts
Molesey F.C.
Vine Hall
Spts. Grd.
Play. Fld.
Nielson Playing Field
Sports Ground
Molesey Pony Farm
Tanners Bridge
Imber Court Trading Estate
Imber Court
Bowling Green
Recreation Grd.
Esher College
Playing Field
Thames Ditton Island Works
Golf Course
Water Pollution Control Works
HAMPTON COURT ROAD
HAMPTON COURT WAY
HAMPTON COURT RD.
HURST ROAD
THAMES ROAD
WALTON ROAD
BRIDGE ROAD
PALACE ROAD
WOLSEY ROAD
ESHER LANE
EMBER COURT RD.
STATION RD.
HIGH STREET
CHURCH ST.
CHESTNUT AVENUE
RIVER MOLE
River Ember
RIVER THAMES
A308
A3050
A309
A311
B369
B3379
B364
115
134
F
G
H
J
K
1
2
3
4
5
6
7
14
15
16
67
68
69
170

116
133
146
A
B
C
D
E
1
2
3
4
5
6
7
16
17
18
67
68
69
70
BUSHY PARK
Warren Plantation
Hawthorn Lodge
Half Moon Plantation
Deer Pen
Heron Pond
Leg-of-Mutton Pond
Oval Plantation
Thatched Cottage
COBBLERS WALK
CHESTNUT AV.
(Open 7:30am - 7:00pm)
Diana Fountain
The Royal Paddocks
Bushy Lodge
HAMPTON COURT ROAD
A308
HAMPTON WICK
Hampton Wick Royal Cricket Ground
Hampton Wick Pav.
Tennis Courts
The King's Field
Hampton Wick Pond
Hampton Wick
KINGSTON UPON THAMES
KINGSTON BRI.
War Mem.
Boat Yd.
Stud House
HAMPTON COURT PARK
The Long Water
Farm Cottages
The Rick Pond
HOME PARK
GOLF COURSE
Club House
The Wilderness
Parkfield
Raven's Ait
Towing Path
Filter Beds
BARGE WALK
RIVER THAMES
Thames Ditton Island
THE ISLAND
Boyle Farm Island
THAMES DITTON
Seething Wells
Halls of Residence
PORTSMOUTH ROAD
A307
KINGSTON HOUSE ESTATE
Long Ditton Recreation Ground
Rec. Grd.
Play Fld.
LONG DITTON
Giggshill
Giggs Hill Green
GIGGSHILL RD.
B364
Library
Miniature Railway
The Rythe
School
Cockcrow Hill
SOUTHBOROUGH
SURBITON
Surbiton
SURBITON HOSP.
Hillcroft Coll.
The Wood
BRIGHTON ROAD
UPPER BRIGHTON ROAD
A243
VICTORIA RD.
CLAREMONT RD.
B3363
B3370
ST. MARK'S HILL
SURBITON HILL ROAD
SURBITON RD.
PENRHYN RD.
A240
County Hall
Kingston Univ.
HIGH ST.
KINGSTON HALL RD.
WHEATFIELD WAY
Kingston
THE BENTALLS CENTRE
Superstore
KINGSGATE RD.
RICHMOND RD.
CANBURY PASS
Canbury Gardens
Tennis Cts.
TEDDINGTON RD.
HIGH ST.
UP. TEDDINGTON RD.
B358
B359
SANDY LANE
PARK RD.
CHURCH GRO.
Avenue Centre (Coll.)
Synagogue
Crescent Schs.
Miniature Railway
Rec. Grd.
Tennis Courts
Pav.

135
117
136
147
F
G
H
J
K
1
2
3
4
5
6
7
KINGSTON HILL
QUEENS RD.
COOMBE WOOD GOLF COURSE
Holy Cross Preparatory R.C. Sch.
Marymount International School
Rockeby Sch.
WEST LANE
TRAPS LANE
COOMBE LANE
A238
COOMBE ROAD
Coombe Hill Jun. & Inf. Schools
Coombe Girls' Sch.
KINGSTON HOSPITAL
A308
Park Hill Sch.
Norbiton
NORBITON
LONDON ROAD
CAMBRIDGE ROAD
A2043
KINGSTON ROAD
Tiffin Sch.
CLARENCE AVENUE
LANGLEY AVENUE
Corpus Christi R.C. Prim. Sch.
Retail Park
Rec. Grd.
Kingston Cemetery
Kingston upon Thames Crematorium
Running Track
Kingstonian Football Club (Kingsmeadow)
Indoor Bowls Club
Recreation Ground
Sludge Beds
Hogsmill River
Waste Disposal Centre
Sewage Works
Surbiton Cemetery
Berrylands
BERRYLANDS
PARK AVENUE
SURBITON HILL
Recreation Ground
Pavilion
Tennis Courts
Sports Ground
Club House
Bowling Green
Grand Avenue Prim. Sch.
ELMBRIDGE AVENUE
MALDEN WAY
NORTH SOUTH (KINGSTON BY-PASS)
A3
Malden Manor Prim. Sch.
Sports Field
Richard Challoner School
SHEEPHOUSE WAY
A240
EWELL ROAD
ALEXANDRA DRIVE
HOLLYFIELD RD.
ELGAR AVENUE
WARREN DRIVE NORTH
TOLWORTH

COOMBE LA. WEST
COPSE HILL
NEW VICTORIA HOSPITAL
MALDEN GOLF COURSE
COTTENHAM PARK
COOMBE A238
BEVERLEY A3 (KINGSTON BY-PASS)
Raynes Park
A298
New Malden
NEW MALDEN
BURLINGTON
BEVERLEY PARK
RAYNES PARK
SHANNON CORNER
WEST BARNES
Motspur Park
MOTSPUR PARK
MALDEN (KINGSTON BY-PASS)
MALDEN JUNC.
NORTH EAST SURREY CREMATORIUM AND MORDEN CEMETERY
The Sir Joseph Hood Memorial Playing Fields
University of London Athletic Ground
MANOR PARK
Malden Manor
OLD MALDEN
Malden Green
Worcester Park
Merton & Sutton Joint Cemetery
Sewage Works
118
135
148

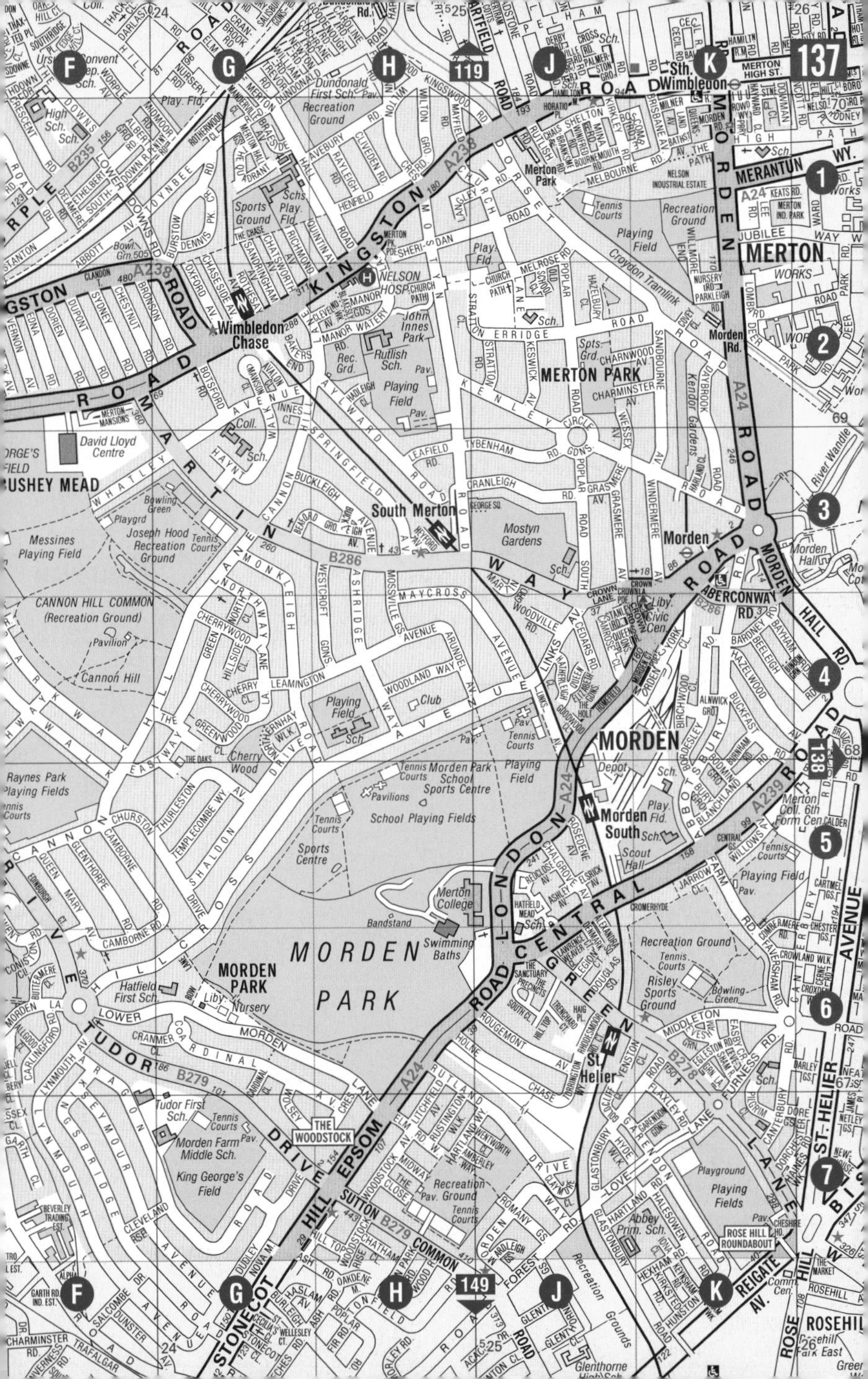
F
G
H
J
K
119
MERTON HIGH ST.
Sth. Wimbledon
MERANTUN WY.
MERTON
Merton Park
NELSON INDUSTRIAL ESTATE
KINGSTON ROAD
A238
NELSON HOSP.
Wimbledon Chase
John Innes Park
Rutlish Sch.
MERTON PARK
Croydon Tramlink
Morden Rd.
MORDEN ROAD
A24
David Lloyd Centre
BUSHEY MEAD
MARTIN WAY
South Merton
Mostyn Gardens
Morden
Morden Hall
River Wandle
Messines Playing Field
Joseph Hood Recreation Ground
CANNON HILL COMMON (Recreation Ground)
Cannon Hill
B286
Civic Cen.
ABERCONWAY RD.
MORDEN HALL RD.
MORDEN
Raynes Park Playing Fields
Cherry Wood
Morden Park School Sports Centre
School Playing Fields
Sports Centre
Merton College
Swimming Baths
Bandstand
MORDEN PARK
LONDON ROAD
Morden South
Scout Hall
CENTRAL ROAD
Recreation Ground
Risley Sports Ground
Hatfield First Sch.
LOWER MORDEN LA.
TUDOR DRIVE
B279
Tudor First Sch.
Morden Farm Middle Sch.
King George's Field
THE WOODSTOCK
EPSOM ROAD
St. Helier
B278
Recreation Pav. Ground
Playing Fields
Abbey Prim. Sch.
ROSE HILL ROUNDABOUT
REIGATE AV.
149
138
A239
ST. HELIER AVENUE
ROSEHILL
Rosehill Park East
STONECOT HILL
SUTTON COMMON ROAD
Recreation Grounds
1
2
3
4
5
6
7
24
25
26
69
67
68

120
137
150
MERTON
MERANTUN WAY
A24
Superstore
Cemetery
Tennis Courts
Tamworth Rec. Grd.
STREATHAM ROAD
A216
A217
WESTERN ROAD
A236
Lavender Pk.
TANDEM CENTRE RETAIL PARK
COLLEGE FIELDS BUSINESS CEN.
MERTON IND. PARK
SAXON BUSINESS CENTRE
Harland First Sch.
Croydon Tramlink
River Wandle
MORDEN HALL PARK
Morden Hall
Morden Cottage
Morden Lodge
Phipps Bridge
MORDEN HALL RD.
A297
MORDEN ROAD
A239
Belgrave Wlk.
Gas Works
Cemy.
Melrose Sch.
Vestry Hall
Cricket Green
CRICKET GRN.
MITCHAM
COMMONSIDE
Beehive Bridge
Running Track
Sports Ground
The Canons Leisure Cen. & Lib.
MADEIRA RD.
Blue Houses Bridge
Cranmer Bri.
CRANMER RD.
R.C.Prim. Sch.
Mitcham
TRAMWAY PATH
Ravensbury Park
LONDON ROAD
CARSHALTON ROAD
A237
Willow Lane Bri.
Mitcham Junction
GOLF
Club House
Watermeads
Sports Ground
Tennis Courts
Poulter Park
Bennett's Hole
Bishopsford House
THE WILLOW BUSINESS CENTRE
WORKS
Depot
Moreton Grn. First Sch.
Bishopsford Comm. Sch.
Moreton Green
ST. HELIER AVENUE
BISHOPSFORD ROAD
Merton Coll. 6th Form Cen.
Playing Field
Open Space
Open Space
ST. HELIER
Hill Ho. Comm. Cen.
Carshalton Sports Arena
Running Track
Pavilion
Playing Fields
Community Hall
Nature Reserves
Mill Green
BEDDINGTON CORNER
ROSE HILL ROUNDABOUT
REIGATE AV.
ROSEHILL
Rosehill Park East
St. Helier Open Space
ST. HELIER HOSPITAL
Greenshaw Wood

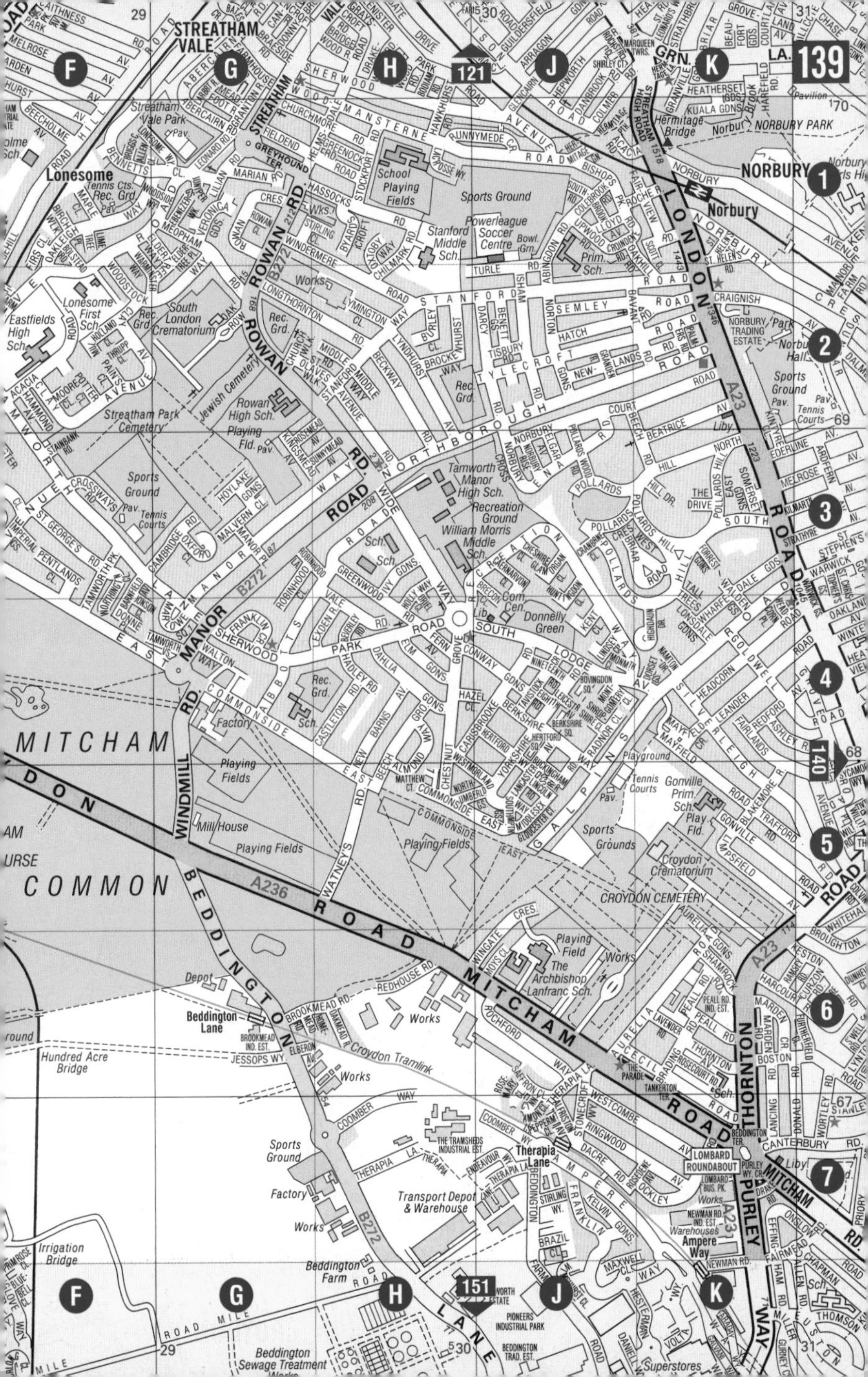
139
STREATHAM VALE
Streatham Vale Park
Lonesome
Lonesome First Sch.
Eastfields High Sch.
South London Crematorium
Jewish Cemetery
Streatham Park Cemetery
Rowan High Sch.
School Playing Fields
Sports Ground
Powerleague Soccer Centre
Stanford Middle Sch.
Tamworth Manor High Sch.
Recreation Ground
William Morris Middle Sch.
Donnelly Green
NORBURY
Norbury
NORBURY PARK
Hermitage Bridge
NORBURY TRADING ESTATE
Norbury Hall
LONDON ROAD
A23
ROWAN ROAD
MANOR ROAD
B272
MITCHAM
COMMON
A236
MITCHAM ROAD
BEDDINGTON LANE
WINDMILL RD.
Mill House
Playing Fields
Gonville Prim. Sch.
Croydon Crematorium
CROYDON CEMETERY
The Archbishop Lanfranc Sch.
Beddington Lane
Hundred Acre Bridge
Croydon Tramlink
Therapia Lane
THE TRAMSHEDS INDUSTRIAL EST.
Transport Depot & Warehouse
LOMBARD ROUNDABOUT
THORNTON ROAD
PURLEY WAY
Ampere Way
Irrigation Bridge
Beddington Farm
Beddington Sewage Treatment Works
PIONEERS INDUSTRIAL PARK
BEDDINGTON TRAD. EST.
Superstores
121
140
151

A
B
C
D
E
1
2
3
4
5
6
7
31
32
33
67
68
69
70
122
139
152
NORBURY
Norbury
NORBURY PARK
Norbury Manor Girls High Sch.
Kensington Avenue Jun. & Inf. Schs.
Sports Ground
Tennis Courts
Norbury Hall
NORBURY TRADING EST.
Biggin Wood
Downsview Prim. Sch.
Westwood High Sch.
Playing Field
UPPER NORWOOD
Playground
David Livingstone Prim. Sch.
R.C. Prim. Sch.
Recreation Ground
Thornton Heath
THORNTON HEATH
THORNTON HEATH POND
Grangewood Recreation Ground
Spurgeon's College
Crystal Palace F.C. & Wimbledon F.C. (Selhurst Park)
T.V. Station
Beaulieu Heights
Cypress Inf. Sch.
St. Chad's R.C. Prim. Sch.
Adult Training Centre
Depot
Selhurst
SELHURST
Playing Field
Ecclesbourne Jun. & Inf. Schs.
Queen's Road Cemetery
Bensham Manor Sch.
MAYDAY UNIVERSITY HOSP.
Works
BROAD GREEN
CROYDON
West Croydon
T.A. Centre
High Sch.
Council Offices
Super.
GREEN LANE
PARCHMORE ROAD
MELFORT AVENUE
CRESCENT
LONDON ROAD
BRIGSTOCK ROAD
HIGH STREET
WHITEHORSE ROAD
ST. JAMES'S ROAD
WINDMILL RD.
NORTHCOTE RD.
SELHURST ROAD
SOUTH NORWOOD HILL
CHURCH ROAD
BEULAH HILL
MITCHAM ROAD
PURLEY WAY
THORNTON ROAD
SUMNER ROAD
LWR. ADDISCOMBE RD.
WELLESLEY RD.
SYDENHAM ROAD
QUEENS ROAD
MAYDAY ROAD
COLLIERS WATER LA.
MANOR ROAD
A23
A235
A236
A212
A213
A215
A222
B266
B273

ANERLEY
PENGE
SOUTH NORWOOD
WOODSIDE
ELMERS END
SOUTH NORWOOD COUNTRY PARK
Birkbeck
Norwood Junc.
Anerley
Beckenham Crematorium
Harris City Technology Coll.
Orchard School Sports Centre
South Norwood Lake
Croydon Sports Arena
Ashburton Playing Fields
SHIRLEY OAKS HOSPITAL
Shirley Oaks
Addiscombe
Blackhorse La.
Woodside
Kent House
Avenue Road
Harrington Rd.
Elmers End
Arena
Croydon Golf Driving Range
Ashburton Park
Ashburton High Sch.
Monks Orchard Prim. Sch.
Davidson Jun. & Inf. Schs.
Heavers Farm Prim. Sch.
Recreation Ground
Pitch & Putt Course
Croydon Tramlink
A214
A213
A215
A222
A234
B243
123
142
153
F
G
H
J
K
1
2
3
4
5
6
7
34
35
36
67
68
69
70

CATOR PARK
Sports Grd.
Kent House
Beckenham Road
Leisure Cen.
Clock House
Beckenham Junc.
BECKENHAM ROAD
A234
A2015
RECTORY ROAD
SOUTHEND ROAD
HIGH STREET
A222
MANOR RD.
BROMLEY RD.
BROMLEY ROAD
WICKHAM ROAD
B230
BECKENHAM HOSPITAL
Recreation Ground
BECKENHAM
Kelsey Park
Elgood Playing Field
Kelsey Park Sch.
Putting Green
HAYES
CROYDON ROAD
UPPER ELMERS END ROAD
ELMERS END
Crease Park
EDEN PARK
PARK LANGLEY
Langley Court (Research Labs)
Langley Park Schools
ELMERS END ROAD
A214
Eden Park
UPPER ELMERS END
Crouch Oak Wood
LINKS WAY
SOUTH EDEN PARK RD.
MONKS ORCHARD
Edenham High Sch.
High Broom Wood
THE BETHLEM ROYAL HOSPITAL
LANGLEY PARK GOLF COURSE
LANGLEY
The Rookery
West Wickham
West Wickham Pools
Blake Recreation Ground
Oak Lodge Prim. Sch.
Nurses' Home
Caravan Park
Parkfields Recreation Ground
124
141
154
A B C D E
1 2 3 4 5 6 7
36 37 38
67 68 69 170

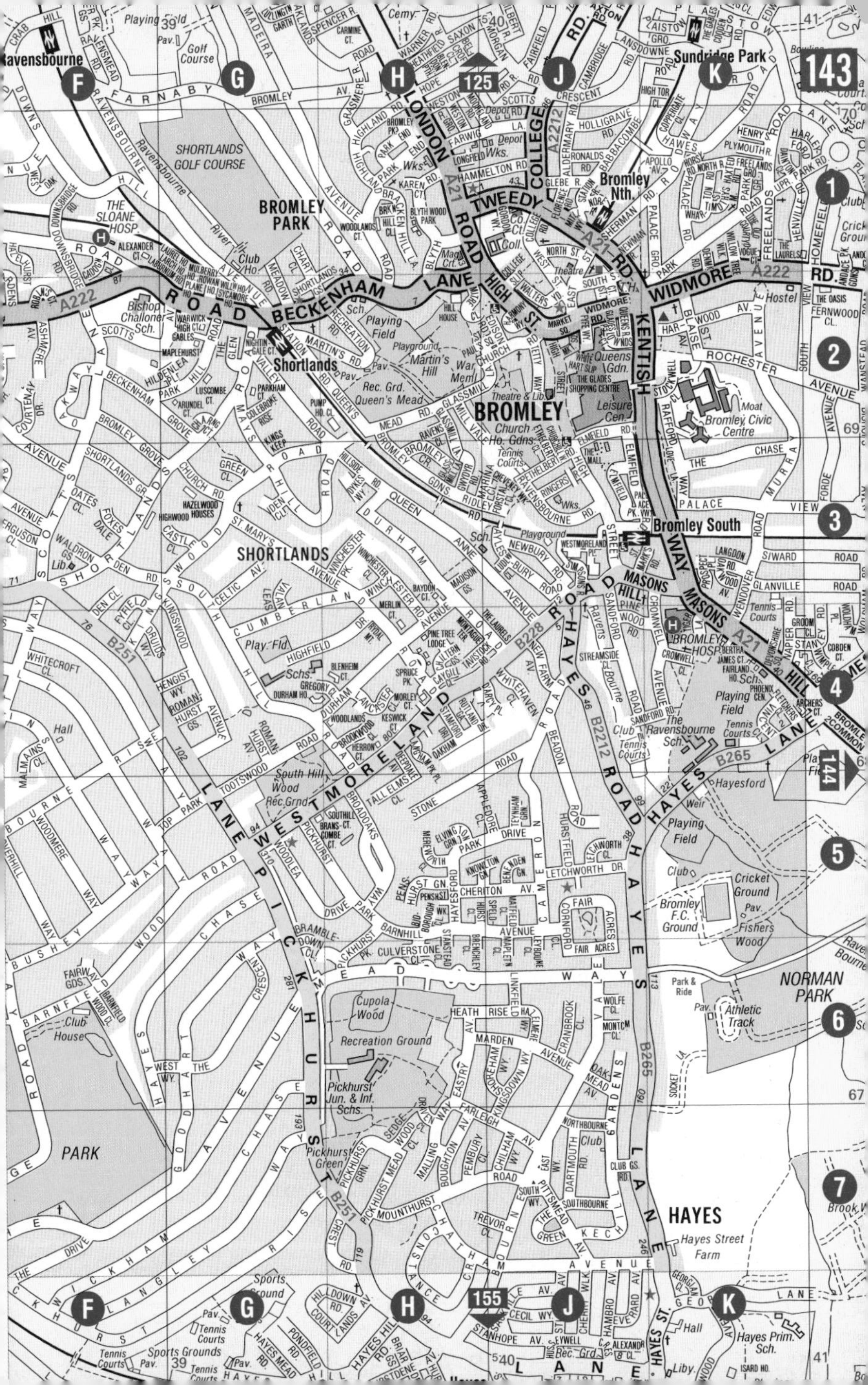

143
125
144
155
F
G
H
J
K
1
2
3
4
5
6
7
39
40
41
Ravensbourne
Sundridge Park
Bromley Nth.
Bromley South
Shortlands
SHORTLANDS GOLF COURSE
Golf Course
Playing Field
BROMLEY PARK
THE SLOANE HOSP.
Bishop Challoner Sch.
BROMLEY
SHORTLANDS
Queens Gdn.
THE GLADES SHOPPING CENTRE
Leisure Cen.
Bromley Civic Centre
Moat
Martin's Hill
War Meml.
Rec. Grd. Queen's Mead
Church Ho. Gdns.
Theatre & Lib.
BROMLEY HOSP.
The Ravensbourne Sch.
Hayesford
South Hill Wood Rec. Grnd
Cupola Wood
Recreation Ground
Pickhurst Jun. & Inf. Schs.
Pickhurst Green
Bromley F.C. Ground
Cricket Ground
Fishers Wood
NORMAN PARK
Athletic Track
Park & Ride
PARK
Club House
Sports Ground
Sports Grounds
Tennis Courts
HAYES
Hayes Street Farm
Hayes Prim. Sch.
Hall
Liby.
Rec. Grd.
A21
A222
A2212
B228
B251
B2212
B265
BECKENHAM LANE
ROAD
LONDON ROAD
HIGH ST.
TWEEDY
COLLEGE
KENTISH WAY
WIDMORE RD.
MASONS HILL
HAYES ROAD
HAYES LANE
WESTMORELAND ROAD
PICKHURST LANE
FARNABY
RAVENSBOURNE
BROMLEY AV.
SHORTLANDS GR.
QUEEN ANNE AVENUE
HIGHFIELD DR.
CUMBERLAND
MEAD WAY
WICKHAM
LANGLEY
CHASE
BUSHEY WAY
HAYES CHASE
WEST WICKHAM
CAMERON
MARDEN AVENUE
BARNHILL AVENUE
CHATHAM AVENUE
KECHILL GARDENS
SOUTHBOURNE
MOUNTHURST
STANHOPE AV.
CECIL WY.

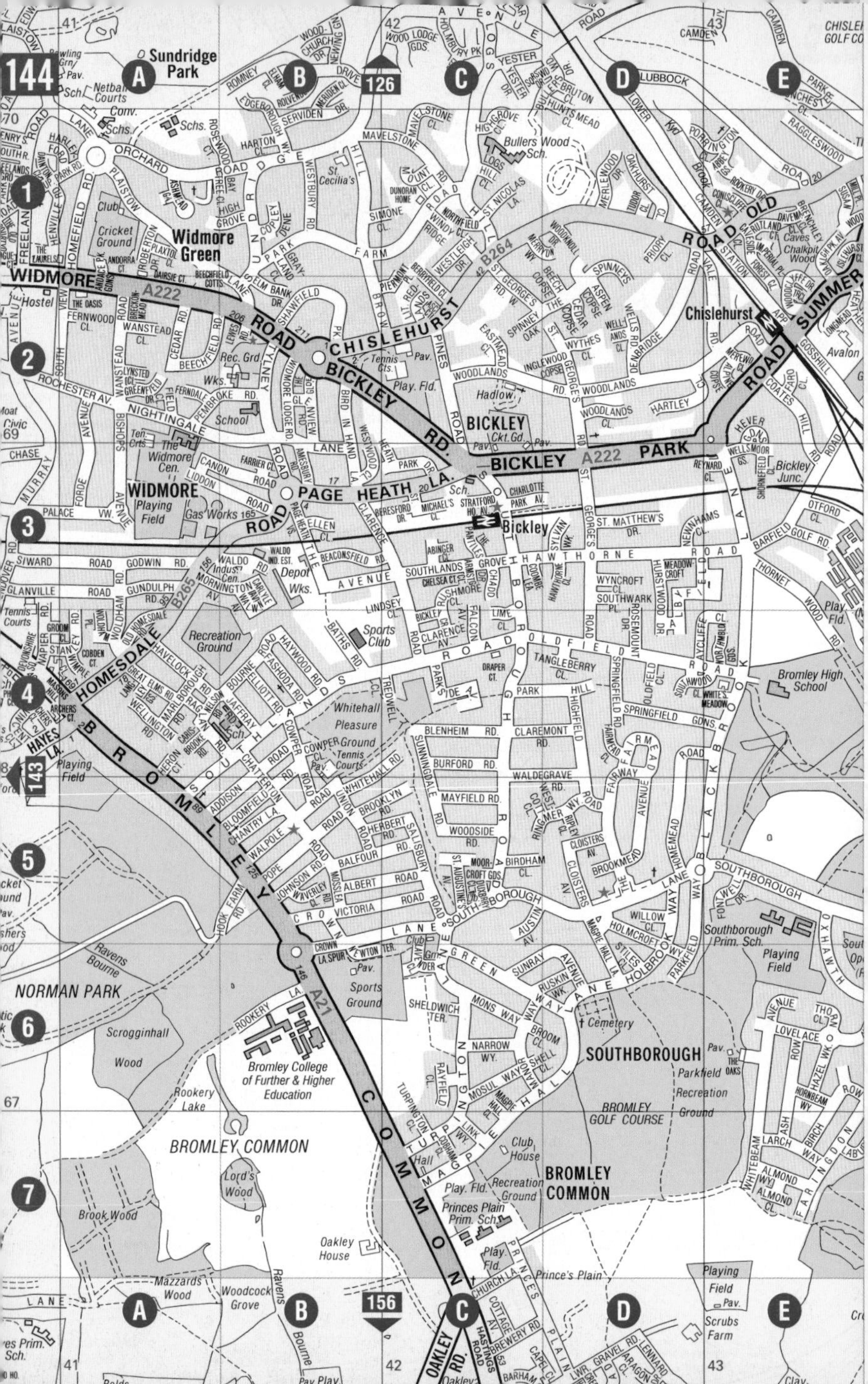
Sundridge Park
Widmore Green
WIDMORE
BICKLEY
Chislehurst
Bickley
Recreation Ground
Sports Club
Whitehall Pleasure Ground
NORMAN PARK
Scrogginhall Wood
Bromley College of Further & Higher Education
SOUTHBOROUGH
BROMLEY GOLF COURSE
BROMLEY COMMON
Rookery Lake
Lord's Wood
Brook Wood
Oakley House
Princes Plain Prim. Sch.
Prince's Plain
Mazzards Wood
Woodcock Grove
Bromley High School
Southborough Prim. Sch.
Parkfield Recreation Ground
Bullers Wood Sch.
WIDMORE ROAD
CHISLEHURST ROAD
BICKLEY PARK ROAD
BICKLEY RD.
PAGE HEATH LA.
HOMESDALE ROAD
BROMLEY COMMON
SOUTHBOROUGH LANE
OLDFIELD ROAD
HAWTHORNE ROAD
MAGPIE HALL LANE
A222
A21
B264
B265
126
143
156

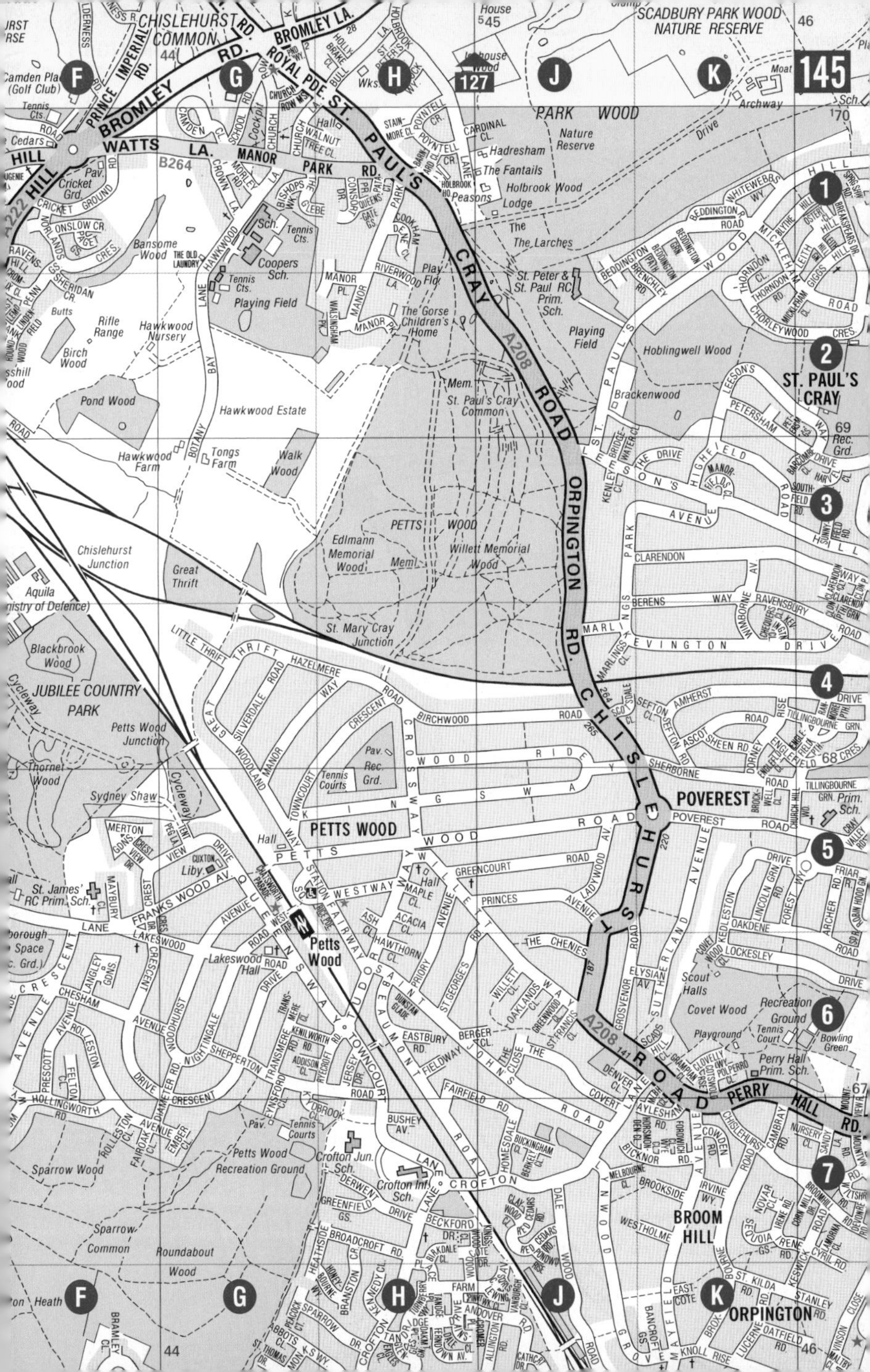
CHISLEHURST COMMON
CHISLEHURST RD.
BROMLEY LA.
SCADBURY PARK WOOD NATURE RESERVE
127
Camden Place (Golf Club)
PRINCE IMPERIAL RD.
BROMLEY RD.
ROYAL PDE.
HOLBROOK LA.
Ice House Wood
Moat
Archway
PARK WOOD
Nature Reserve
Drive
HILL
WATTS LA.
MANOR PARK RD.
B264
A222
Cricket Grd.
Pav.
CRICKET GROUND RD.
ONSLOW CR.
NORLANDS CRES.
CAMDEN CL.
SCHOOL RD.
Cockpit
CHURCH ROW
STAINMORE CL.
POYNTELL CR.
WALNUT TREE CL.
CARDINAL CL.
Hadresham
The Fantails
Holbrook Wood Lodge
Peasons
The Larches
ST. PAUL'S CRAY
A208 ROAD
BISHOPS WK.
THE GLEBE
CONSORT DR.
QUEEN'S MEAD
COOKHAM DENE CL.
Sch.
Tennis Cts.
Coopers Sch.
THE OLD LAUNDRY
HAWKWOOD LANE
Bansome Wood
SHERIDAN CR.
Butts
Rifle Range
Hawkwood Nursery
Birch Wood
Playing Field
MANOR PL.
RIVERWOOD LA.
MANOR PK.
WALSINGHAM PK.
Play Fld.
The Gorse Children's Home
St. Peter & St. Paul RC Prim. Sch.
Playing Field
WHITEWEBBS WY.
BEDDINGTON RD.
BEDDINGTON GRN.
BRENCHLEY RD.
WOOD RD.
MICKLEHAM RD.
THORNDON CL.
THORNDON RD.
GIGGS HILL
LEITH HILL
BREAKSPEARS DR.
CHORLEYWOOD CRES.
Hoblingwell Wood
ST. PAUL'S CRAY
Brackenwood
LEESON'S HILL
PETERSHAM DR.
Rec. Grd.
Pond Wood
Hawkwood Estate
BOTANY BAY LANE
Mem.
St. Paul's Cray Common
Hawkwood Farm
Tongs Farm
Walk Wood
THE DRIVE
KENLEY CL.
HIGHFIELD DR.
MANOR FIELDS CL.
SOUTHFIELD RD.
SUNNYFIELD RD.
PARK AVENUE
ORPINGTON RD.
PETTS WOOD
Edlmann Memorial Wood
Meml.
Willett Memorial Wood
Chislehurst Junction
Great Thrift
Aquila
Ministry of Defence
CLARENDON WAY
BERENS WAY
WIMBORNE AV.
RAVENSBURY RD.
MARLINGS CL.
KEVINGTON DRIVE
St. Mary Cray Junction
Blackbrook Wood
LITTLE THRIFT
HAZELMERE WAY
SILVERDALE ROAD
CRESCENT ROAD
JUBILEE COUNTRY PARK
Cycleway
GREAT WOODLAND
BIRCHWOOD ROAD
CROSSWAY
CHISLEHURST
SEFTON RD.
AMHERST DRIVE
ASCOT RD.
SHEEN RD.
RISE
TILLINGBOURNE GRN.
Petts Wood Junction
Thornet Wood
Pav.
Rec. Grd.
Tennis Courts
TOWNCOURT
WOOD RIDE
SHERBORNE RD.
TILLINGBOURNE GRN. Prim. Sch.
Sydney Shaw
KINGSWAY
POVEREST
POVEREST ROAD
CRAY VALLEY RD.
MERTON GDNS.
CREST VIEW DR.
Hall
PETTS WOOD
WOOD ROAD
LADYWOOD AV.
CUXTON
Liby.
ST. JAMES' RC Prim. Sch.
MAYBURY CL.
FRANKS WOOD AV.
GREENCOURT ROAD
WESTWAY
MAPLE CL.
PRINCES AVENUE
SUTHERLAND AVENUE
DRIVE
LINCOLN GRN.
FOREST WY.
FRIAR RD.
ARCHER RD.
OAKDENE
LANE
LAKESWOOD RD.
Petts Wood
ASH CL.
ACACIA CL.
HAWTHORN CL.
THE CHENIES
COVET WOOD CL.
LOCKESLEY DRIVE
Open Space (Rec. Grd.)
Lakeswood Hall
CRESCENT
CHESHAM AVENUE
LANGLEY GDNS.
WOODHURST AVENUE
NIGHTINGALE
QUEENSWAY
ST. GEORGE'S RD.
WILLETT CL.
OAKLANDS CL.
ELYSIAN AV.
Scout Halls
Covet Wood
Recreation Ground
Playground
Tennis Court
Bowling Green
PRESCOTT AVENUE
ROLLESTON AVENUE
FELTON
SHEPPERTON RD.
TRANSMERE RD.
KENILWORTH RD.
ADDISON CL.
TUDOR WAY
EASTBURY RD.
BERGER CL.
A208 ROAD
ST. FRANCIS CL.
GROSVENOR RD.
Perry Hall Prim. Sch.
PERRY HALL RD.
HOLLINGWORTH RD.
DRIVE CRESCENT
ROLLESTON AVENUE
EMBER CL.
FAIROAK CL.
EYNSFORD CL.
KYDBROOK CL.
JERSEY DR.
BUSHEY AV.
FIELDWAY
JOHNS
FAIRFIELD RD.
COVERT ROAD
DENVER CL.
AYLESHAM RD.
CHISLEHURST ROAD
CAMBRAY RD.
NURSERY CL.
SANDY LA.
Pav.
Tennis Courts
Petts Wood Recreation Ground
Crofton Jun. Sch.
Crofton Inf. Sch.
CROFTON LANE
HOMESDALE RD.
BUCKINGHAM CL.
BERKELEY CL.
BICKNOR RD.
COWDEN RD.
Sparrow Wood
DERWENT DRIVE
GREENFIELD GS.
BECKFORD DR.
CLAYWOOD CL.
RED CEDARS RD.
MELBOURNE CL.
BROOKSIDE
IRVINE WY.
BROOM HILL
NOVAR CL.
SEQUOIA GS.
IRENE RD.
Sparrow Common
Roundabout Wood
HEATHSIDE
BROADCROFT RD.
WESTHOLME
BROOMHILL RD.
KESWICK RD.
CYRIL RD.
Heath
BRANSTON CR.
KENNEDY CL.
FARM
ANDOVER RD.
EAST COTE
ST. KILDA RD.
STANLEY RD.
ORPINGTON
SPARROW DR.
BANCROFT GS.
MAYFIELD
KNOLL RISE
LUCERNE RD.
OATFIELD RD.
BRAMLEY CL.
GROVE
44
45
46
67
68
69
70
1
2
3
4
5
6
7
F
G
H
J
K

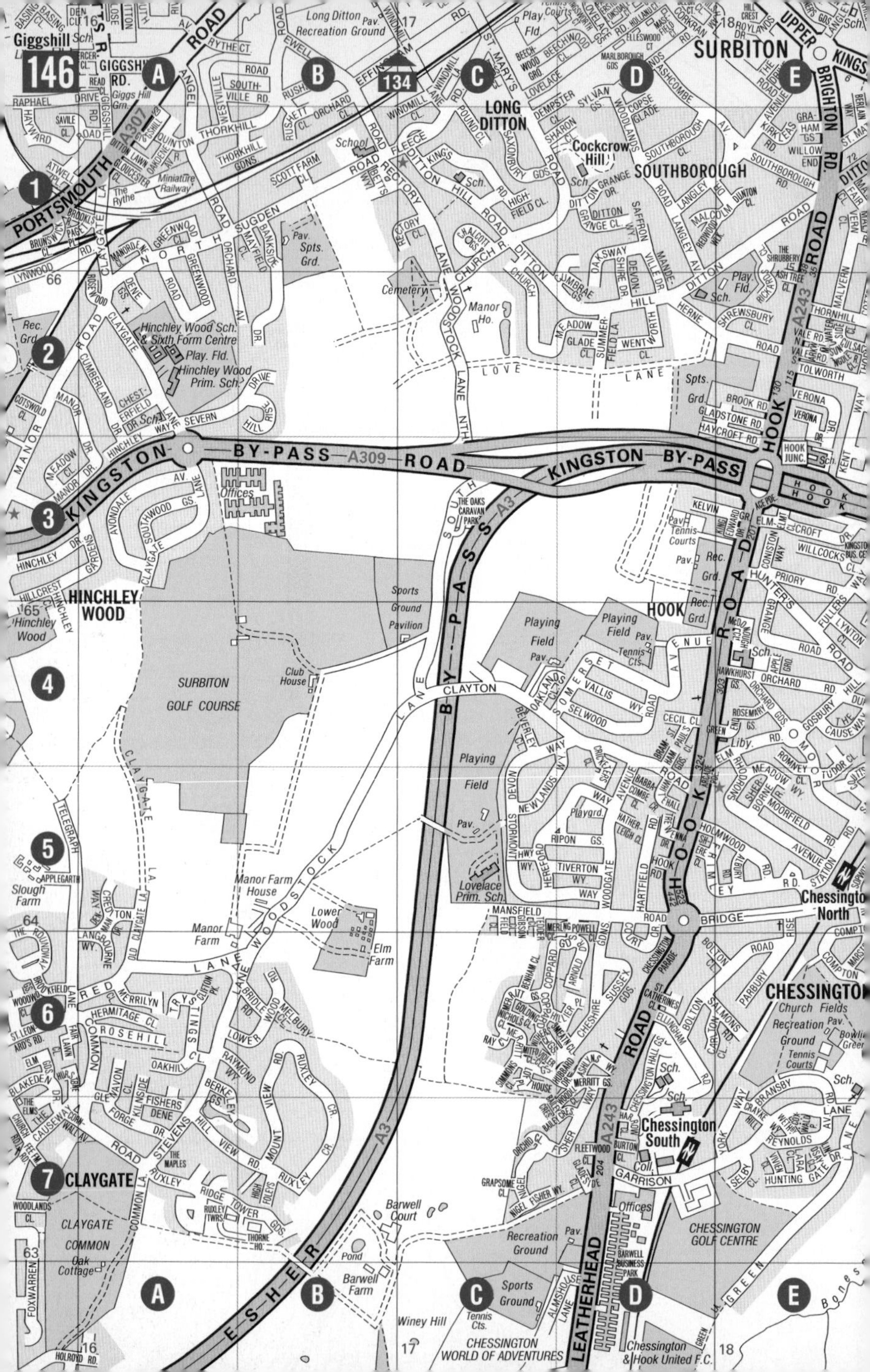
146
Giggshill
GIGGSHILL RD.
SURBITON
LONG DITTON
Cockcrow Hill
SOUTHBOROUGH
HINCHLEY WOOD
HOOK
CHESSINGTON
CLAYGATE
Chessington North
Chessington South
134
A B C D E
1 2 3 4 5 6 7
16 17 18
66 65 64 63
PORTSMOUTH ROAD
A307
KINGSTON BY-PASS
A309
ROAD
A3
ESHER BY-PASS
A243
HOOK ROAD
LEATHERHEAD ROAD
BRIGHTON RD.
UPPER BRIGHTON RD.
DITTON ROAD
DITTON HILL ROAD
Long Ditton Recreation Ground
Pav.
Giggs Hill Grn.
Miniature Railway
The Rythe
Rec. Grd.
Hinchley Wood Sch. & Sixth Form Centre
Play. Fld.
Hinchley Wood Prim. Sch.
Offices
SURBITON GOLF COURSE
Club House
Sports Ground Pavilion
Playing Field
Manor Farm House
Manor Farm
Lower Wood
Elm Farm
Cemetery
Manor Ho.
LOVE LANE
CLAYTON
WOODSTOCK LANE
TELEGRAPH
Slough Farm
APPLEGARTH
Lovelace Prim. Sch.
CLAYGATE COMMON
Oak Cottage
Barwell Court
Barwell Farm
Pond
Winey Hill
Recreation Ground
Sports Ground
Tennis Cts.
CHESSINGTON WORLD OF ADVENTURES
Chessington & Hook United F.C.
CHESSINGTON GOLF CENTRE
Church Fields Recreation Ground
Tennis Courts
Offices
BARWELL BUSINESS PARK
THE OAKS CARAVAN PARK
Spts. Grd.
Liby.
Sch.
Coll.
GARRISON
BRIDGE
RUXLEY
RED LANE
ROSEHILL
FOXWARREN
HOLROYD RD.
Bones

147
135
148
F
G
H
J
K
1
2
3
4
5
6
7
19
20
21
66
65
64
63
TOLWORTH
Tolworth Hosp.
Tolworth
TOLWORTH JUNCTION
KINGSTON BY-PASS
A3
A240
ROAD
KINGSTON RD.
WORCESTER PARK RD.
B284
B2200
ALEXANDRA
Tennis Courts
Recreation Ground
Prim. Sch.
WARREN DRIVE NORTH
WARREN DRIVE SOUTH
KNOLLMEAD
Richard Challoner School
Playing Field
Tennis Courts
Maori Sports Ground
Nursery
MALDEN LANE
CHURCH RD.
Knollmead Prim. Sch.
Sports Ground
Riverhill
Cricket Ground
Linden Bridge Sch. & Spring Cen.
Government Offices
King George's Field Playing Field
Football Pitch
Tolworth Court Farm
Tolworth Court Bridge
Hogsmill River
Riverview C.of E. Prim. Sch.
Play. Fld.
Comm. Cen.
Four Oaks Centre
Buckland Inf. Sch.
Moor Lane Jun. Sch.
Playing Field
Tolworth Rec. Cen.
Epsom & Ewell High Sch.
West Ewell Inf. Sch.
Pack Horse Bri.
King George's Field
Running Track
WEST EWELL
Butcher's Grove
Castle Hill
HORTON COUNTRY PARK
HORTON PARK GOLF & COUNTRY CLUB
Club Ho.
Hook Arena
HOOK RD.
CHESSINGTON RD.
RUXLEY LANE
St. Ebba's Farm Cottage
North Farm Cottage
Gt. Wood
Sports Grd.
Cemetery
Playing Field
ST. EBBA'S

Malden Manor
OLD MALDEN
Malden Green
Worcester Park
WORCESTER PARK
STONELEIGH
Stoneleigh
NONSUCH PARK
WEST EWELL
Ewell West
EWELL
BEGGAR'S HILL
ORGAN CROSSROADS
136
147
MALDEN ROAD
CENTRAL ROAD
CHEAM COMMON ROAD
OLD MALDEN LANE
KINGSTON ROAD
EWELL BY-PASS
LONDON ROAD
Cuddington Recreation Ground
King George's Field
Auriol Park
Oak Plantation
Cherry Orchard Farm
Hogsmill River
Chamber Mead
Playing Fields
Sewage Works

149
137
150
F
G
H
J
K
1
2
3
4
5
6
7
24
25
26
King George's Field
Recreation Ground
Playing Grd.
ROSE HILL ROUNDABOUT
Abbey Prim. Sch.
ROSEHILL
BENHILTON
NORTH CHEAM
CHEAM
SUTTON
BELMONT
CHEAM PARK
STONECOT HILL
LONDON ROAD
MALDEN ROAD
A24
A217
A2043
A232
B279
B2230
B283
SUTTON COMMON ROAD
REIGATE AVENUE
ROSE HILL
ANGEL HILL
ST. DUNSTAN'S HILL
OLDFIELDS ROAD
CHEAM ROAD
EWELL RD.
HIGH ST.
BELMONT RISE
BRIGHTON ROAD
BURDON LANE
MULGRAVE ROAD
CHEAM COMMON ROAD
GANDER GREEN LANE
COLLINGWOOD ROAD
THROWLEY WAY
ST. NICHOLAS WAY
Hospice
ST. ANTHONY'S HOSP.
Sutton Cemetery
Glenthorne High Sch.
Rosehill Recreation Ground
Junior Tennis Centre
Playing Field
Bowling Green
Sutton Common
Superstore
Rec. Grd.
KIMPTON IND. EST.
OLDFIELDS TRAD. EST.
Day Cen.
Westbourne Prim. Sch.
All Weather Pitch
Comm. Hall
QUEEN VICTORIA
Spts. Cen.
Collingwood Road Recreation Ground
Tennis Courts
Sutton United F.C.
West Sutton
Cheam Park Farm Jun. Sch.
Cheam High Sch. Play. Fld.
Water Works
Sutton West Cen.
ST. NICHOLAS CEN.
Civic Cen.
Cen. Lib.
Coll.
Secombe Theatre
Sutton Cricket Ground
Seears Park
Cheam Recreation Ground
Nursery
Cheam
CHEAM VILLAGE
ST. DUNSTAN'S
Nonsuch High Sch. for Girls
Harefield Bri.
Playing Field
Sports Grd.
Glaisdale Sch.
Overton Grange High Sch.
Sports Ground
Stanley Park
Prim. Sch.
School

150
138
149
A
B
C
D
E
1
2
3
4
5
6
7
26
27
28
ROSEHILL
Rosehill Park East
Greenshaw Wood
St. Helier Open Space
Carshalton Sports Arena
Running Track
Pavilion
ST. HELIER HOSPITAL
QUEEN MARY'S HOSPITAL FOR CHILDREN
BENHILTON
Royston Park
THE WRYTHE
Muschamp Prim. Sch.
Playing Field
Limes Grn.
Rushy Meadow Prim. Sch.
Wrythe Rec. Grd.
Carshalton Athletic F.C.
Benhill Rec. Grd.
Carshalton
CARSHALTON
St. Philomenas Convent
Heritage Cen.
Westcroft Leisure Cen.
The Grove
Council Offices
Studio Thea.
Carshalton Coll.
HACKBRIDGE
Hackbridge
Nature Reserve
Wandle Bri.
Nature Reserves
BEDDINGTON CORNER
SUTTON
Sutton
Manor Park
Super-store
Rec. Grd.
The Frying Pan
Hogpit Pond
CARSHALTON PARK
CARSHALTON WAR MEMORIAL HOSP.
Carshalton Beeches
Stanley Pk. Rec. Grd.
Little Holland Ho.
Resrs (covered)
Stowford College
CARSHALTON ON THE HILL
CARSHALTON BEECHES
ROSE HILL
AVENUE
WRYTHE
B278
B277
B271
B2230
A232
CARSHALTON ROAD
NORTH ST.
WEST ST.
HIGH ST.
ACRE LA.
POUND ST.
BEECHES AV.
PARK HILL
RUSKIN ROAD
NIGHTINGALE RD.
HACKBRIDGE RD.
LONDON RD.
BRIGHTON ROAD
BANSTEAD ROAD
WRYTHE LANE
ERSKINE ROAD
BENHILL AV.
WESTMEAD RD.
STANLEY PARK ROAD
GROSVENOR AVENUE
ASHCOMBE AVENUE
THE CROSSWAYS
DOWNSWAY
EAST DRIVE
STANLEY ROAD
SHIRLEY AVENUE
PAGET AVENUE
GASSIOT WAY
MUSCHAMP RD.
BUCKHURST AV.
WINCHCOMBE RD.
THORNTON RD.
WESTMINSTER RD.
CONNAUGHT RD.
PRINCE OF WALES RD.
SAINTS ROAD
GREENHILL WAY
WEST GS.
LOWER RD.
GREYHOUND RD.
THROWLEY WY.
CUMNOR RD.
HILLCROOME RD.
DOWNSIDE RD.
WAVERLEY WY.
GORDON RD.
HARROW RD.
CARSHALTON PK. RD.
BEYNON RD.
WALES AV.
TALBOT RD.
CULVERS AV.
CULVERS WAY
AULTONE WAY
STRAWBERRY LA.
BUTTER HILL
DEVONSHIRE RD.
EGMONT RD.
CHALGROVE RD.
UPLAND RD.
RIDGWAY RD.
MAYFIELD RD.
HIGHWAY
GALLOP
HEATH DR.
THE CAUSEWAY
WOODSTOCK
PARK LA.
BEDDINGTON GDNS.

29
30
31
F
G
H
J
K
139
Irrigation Bridge
Factory
Transport Depot & Warehouse
Works
Beddington Farm
BEDDINGTON
MILE ROAD
Beddington Sewage Treatment Works
ASHWORTH ESTATE
PIONEERS INDUSTRIAL PARK
BEDDINGTON TRAD. EST.
Mile Road Bridge
Hackbridge
A237
LONDON RD.
Tennis Courts
Pavilion
Sports Ground
BEDDINGTON PARK
River Wandle
The Grange
Boating Lake
Carew Manor & Dovecot
Carew Manor Sch.
Church Paddock
Manor Garden
Playing Field
Ampere Way
Superstores
Cinema
Bingo Hall
Superstore
Warehouse
Works
PETERWOOD PARK
THE PROGRESS BUSINESS PARK
THE ORION CENTRE
ANCHOR BUS. CEN.
Electricity Switching Station
BEDDINGTON
WADDON
Waddon Marsh
Waddon Ponds
A23
PURLEY WAY
1
2
3
4
5
6
7
66
165
64
63
A232
CROYDON ROAD
HILLIERS LA.
B272
PLOUGH LANE
Liby.
Retail Park
FIVEWAYS CORNER
152
Sports Ground
Bandon Hill Cemetery
Bandonhill
WALLINGTON
Wallington
Mellows Park
Tennis Courts
Bowling Green
B271
STAFFORD ROAD
Playing Field
Powerleague Soccer Cen.
Wilson's Sch.
Depot
Works
SOUTH BEDDINGTON
Sports Grd.
Foresters Prim. Sch.
Esporta Health & Raquets Club
Roundshaw
Roundshaw Park (Playing Fields)
Amy Johnson Prim. Sch.
WOODCOTE ROAD
MANOR ROAD
FORESTERS DRIVE
SANDY LA.
STANLEY PK. RD.
Court
Superstore
Hostel
Nature Reserve
Sports Ground

152
140
151
A
B
C
D
E
1
2
3
4
5
6
7
CROYDON
West Croydon
East Croydon
South Croydon
Sanderstead
Waddon
WADDON
Waddon Marsh
Wandle Park
WANDLE PARK
SOUTH CROYDON
Reeves Cnr.
Church St.
George St.
Wellesley Rd.
Lebanon Rd.
Croydon Tramlink
Warehouses
Superstore
Council Offices
Depot
Duppas Hill
Sports Ground
Recreation Ground
FIVEWAYS CORNER
Retail Park
Playing Fields
Whitgift Sch.
HALING PARK Play. Flds.
Haling Cott.
War Mem.
PURLEY WAY PLAYING FIELDS
Regina Coeli R.C. Prim. Sch.
Haling Manor High Sch.
St. Giles Sch.
HALING GROVE
Playing Field
Russell Hill Resr. (covered)
Croydon Rec. Grd.
TWIN BRIDGES BUSINESS PARK
Coombe Cliff (Educ. Cen)
Cambridge Tutors Coll.
Park Hill
Fairfield Halls
Law Courts
Croydon Coll.
Lunar Ho.
Theatre
FLYOVER
THE COLONNADES
Bowl Alley
Comm. Cen.
Playground
Factory
Works
Waddon Ponds
THE PURLEY WAY CENTRE
THE PROGRESS BUSINESS PARK
THE WANDLE PARK TRADING ESTATE
A23
A232
A236
A212
A213
A222
A235
B243
B269
B274
B275
PURLEY WAY
DUPPAS HILL RD.
ROMAN WAY
OLD TOWN
WELLESLEY ROAD
PARK LANE
COOMBE ROAD
BRIGHTON ROAD
SOUTH END
SELSDON RD.
CROHAM RD.
WARHAM AV.
DENNING AV.
STAFFORD RD.
EPSOM RD.
SUMNER RD.
ST. JAMES'S RD.
LOWER ADDISCOMBE ROAD
BARCLAY R.
FAIRFIELD RD.
CHEPSTOW ROAD
PARK HILL
CHERRY ORCHARD ROAD
WADDON WAY
HALING PARK ROAD
SANDERSTEAD ROAD
CROYDON R.
MITCHAM ROAD

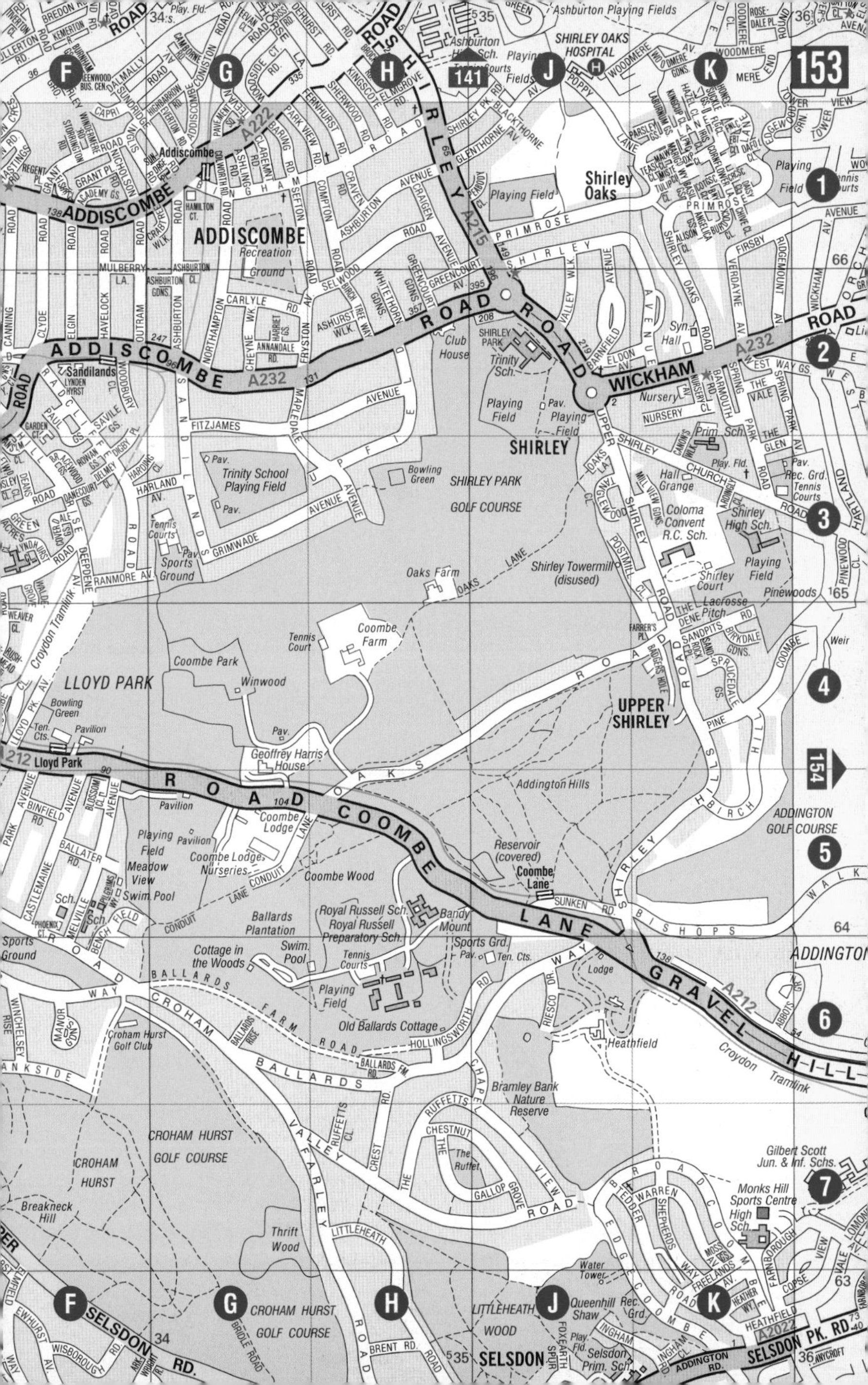

ADDISCOMBE
Addiscombe
Recreation Ground
SHIRLEY
Shirley Oaks
SHIRLEY OAKS HOSPITAL
Ashburton Playing Fields
SHIRLEY PARK GOLF COURSE
Trinity School Playing Field
LLOYD PARK
Coombe Farm
Oaks Farm
Shirley Towermill (disused)
UPPER SHIRLEY
Addington Hills
Reservoir (covered)
Coombe Wood
Ballards Plantation
Royal Russell Sch.
Royal Russell Preparatory Sch.
Bramley Nature Reserve
CROHAM HURST GOLF COURSE
CROHAM HURST
Breakneck Hill
Thrift Wood
LITTLEHEATH WOOD
SELSDON
ADDINGTON GOLF COURSE
ADDINGTON
Gilbert Scott Jun. & Inf. Schs.
Monks Hill Sports Centre
Croydon Tramlink
ADDISCOMBE ROAD
SHIRLEY ROAD
WICKHAM ROAD
COOMBE ROAD
COOMBE LANE
GRAVEL HILL
SELSDON RD.
SELSDON PK. RD.
A222
A232
A215
A212
A2022
141
154

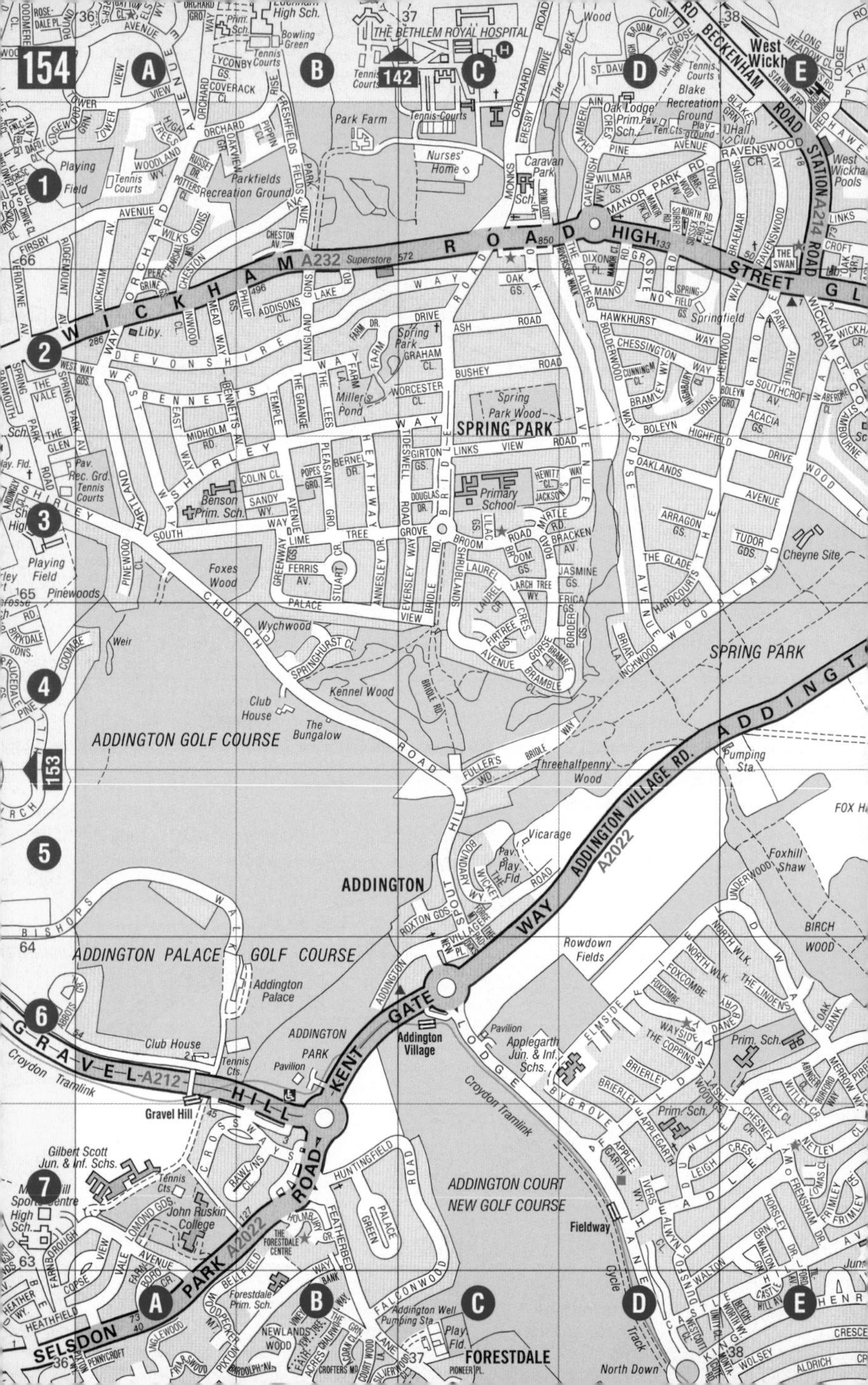
THE BETHLEM ROYAL HOSPITAL
Park Farm
Parkfields Recreation Ground
Playing Field
WICKHAM ROAD A232
HIGH STREET
West Wickham
Blake Recreation Ground
Oak Lodge Prim. Sch.
West Wickham Pools
Springfield
SPRING PARK
Spring Park Wood
Primary School
Benson Prim. Sch.
Foxes Wood
Wychwood
Kennel Wood
Club House
The Bungalow
ADDINGTON GOLF COURSE
Threehalfpenny Wood
Pumping Sta.
Foxhill Shaw
BIRCH WOOD
Cheyne Site
ADDINGTON
ADDINGTON VILLAGE RD. A2022
Vicarage
Rowdown Fields
ADDINGTON PALACE GOLF COURSE
Addington Palace
Club House
GRAVEL HILL A212
Croydon Tramlink
Gravel Hill
ADDINGTON PARK
KENT GATE WAY
Addington Village
Applegarth Jun. & Inf. Schs.
Prim. Sch.
Gilbert Scott Jun. & Inf. Schs.
John Ruskin College
ADDINGTON COURT NEW GOLF COURSE
Fieldway
THE FORESTDALE CENTRE
Forestdale Prim. Sch.
Addington Well Pumping Sta.
FORESTDALE
North Down
SELSDON PARK ROAD A2022
153
142

155
143
156
HAYES
Hayes Farm
HAYES LA.
WEST WICKHAM
CONEY HALL
HAYES COMMON
NASH
NEW ADDINGTON
Hayes
Hayes Prim. Sch.
Playing Field
Baston Pre-Jun. School
Hayes Sch.
HAYES GROVE PRIORY HOSP.
Hayes Court
Hawes Down Jun.& Inf. Schs.
Glebe Sch.
Sports Ground
Sports Grounds
Tennis Courts
Nash Ho.
The Warren
West Wickham Common
Sparrow's Den Playing Fields
Recreation Ground
Lodge
Coney Hall Rec. Grd.
Wickham Court
Emmaus Conference Centre
St. John Rigby R.C. College
Wickham Court Farm
The Cottages
The Bungalows
Hast Hill
Baston Manor
Keston Court Riding School
Rouse Farm
Arlington Orchard
Well Wood
Elm Farm
Fox Hill Nursery
Jackass Shaw
Cooper's Wood
Long Shaw
North Pole Farm
Waytes
Nash Farm
Fuller's Wood
James's Wood
Baldwin Shaw
Bradmanshill Wood
Castlehill Ruffs
Electricity Sub Station
Rushfield Shaw
Broomfieldbank Shaw
Rowdown Wood
Milchden
Five Elms
Gorsewood
CROYDON ROAD
A232
A2022
B251
B265
HAYES LANE
BASTON ROAD
HAYES COMMON
BASTON MANOR RD.
FIVE ELMS ROAD
KESTON ROAD
FOX LANE
JACKASS LANE
NASH LANE
NORTH POLE LANE
NASH ROAD
LAYHAMS ROAD
KINGSWAY
WEST WICKHAM
GATES GREEN ROAD
SYLVAN WAY
CHESTNUT AVENUE
BIRCH TREE AVENUE
CORKSCREW HILL
ADDINGTON RD.
CONEY HILL RD.
PRESTONS ROAD
RIDGEWAY
BOURNE WAY
HAYES HILL
WICKHAM WAY
PICKHURST LANE
GEORGE LANE
HARVEST BANK ROAD
F G H J K
1 2 3 4 5 6 7
39 40 41
63 64 65 66

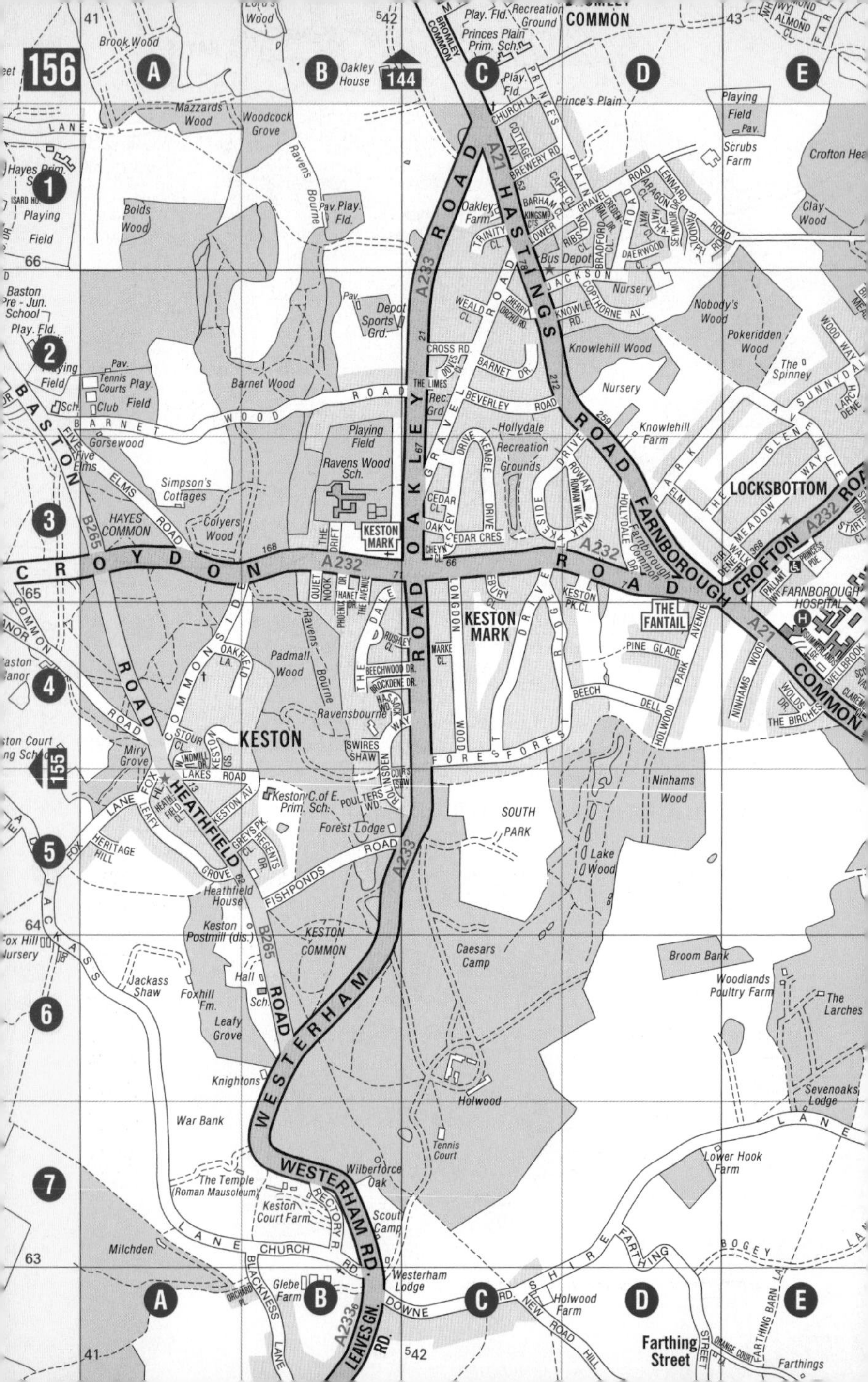
KESTON
KESTON MARK
LOCKSBOTTOM
HAYES COMMON
BROMLEY COMMON
CROYDON ROAD
OAKLEY ROAD
HASTINGS ROAD
FARNBOROUGH
CROFTON ROAD
WESTERHAM ROAD
WESTERHAM RD.
HEATHFIELD
Keston Common
Caesars Camp
Holwood
Farthing Street
Farnborough Hospital
Ravens Wood Sch.
Barnet Wood
Padmall Wood
Ninhams Wood
South Park
Lake Wood
Broom Bank
Woodlands Poultry Farm
Lower Hook Farm
Holwood Farm
Glebe Farm
Keston Court Farm
The Temple (Roman Mausoleum)
Keston Postmill (dis.)
Heathfield House
War Bank
Milchden
Knightons
Jackass Shaw
Foxhill Fm.
Leafy Grove
Miry Grove
Nobody's Wood
Pokeridden Wood
Knowlehill Wood
Scrubs Farm
Clay Wood
Sevenoaks Lodge
The Larches
Wilberforce Oak
Westerham Lodge
Scout Camp
Forest Lodge
Keston C.of E. Prim. Sch.
Hollydale Recreation Grounds
Oakley Farm
Bus Depot
Depot Sports Grd.
Mazzards Wood
Woodcock Grove
Bolds Wood
Brook Wood
Oakley House
Prince's Plain
Princes Plain Prim. Sch.
The Fantail
Farthings

LARGE SCALE SECTION

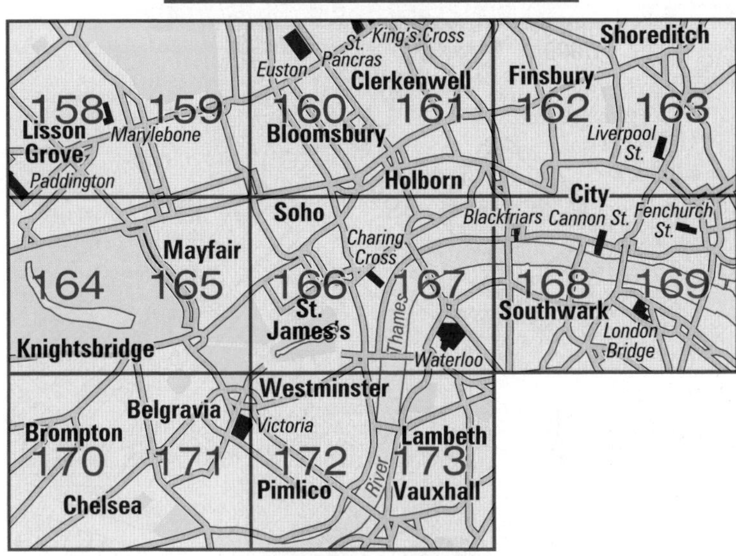

REFERENCE

- **A Road** — A41
- **B Road** — B524
- **Dual Carriageway**
- **One Way Street**
  Traffic flow on A Roads is indicated by a heavy line on the drivers' left.
- **B' road / Minor road**
- **House Numbers** — 37 20 3 14
  A & B Roads only
- **Restricted Access**
- **Pedestrianized Road**
- **Footpath**
- **Residential Walkway**
- **Page Continuation** — Large Scale Map Pages 166 — 66

- **Church or Chapel** — †
- **Fire Station**
- **Information Centre**
- **National Grid Reference** — 527
- **Police Station** — ▲
- **Post Office** — ★
- **National Rail Network**
- **Docklands Light Railway** — DLR
- **Underground Station** — is the registered trade mark of Transport for London
- **Educational Establishment**
- **Hospital or Hospice**
- **Industrial Building**
- **Leisure or Recreational Facility**
- **Place of Interest**
  Open to the Public
- **Public Building**
- **Shopping Centre or Market**
- **Other Selected Building**

SCALE

5¾ inches to 1 mile | **1:11000** | **9.1cm to 1km**

0 50 100 200 300 Yards ¼ ½ Mile

0 50 100 200 300 400 500 750 Metres 1 Kilometre

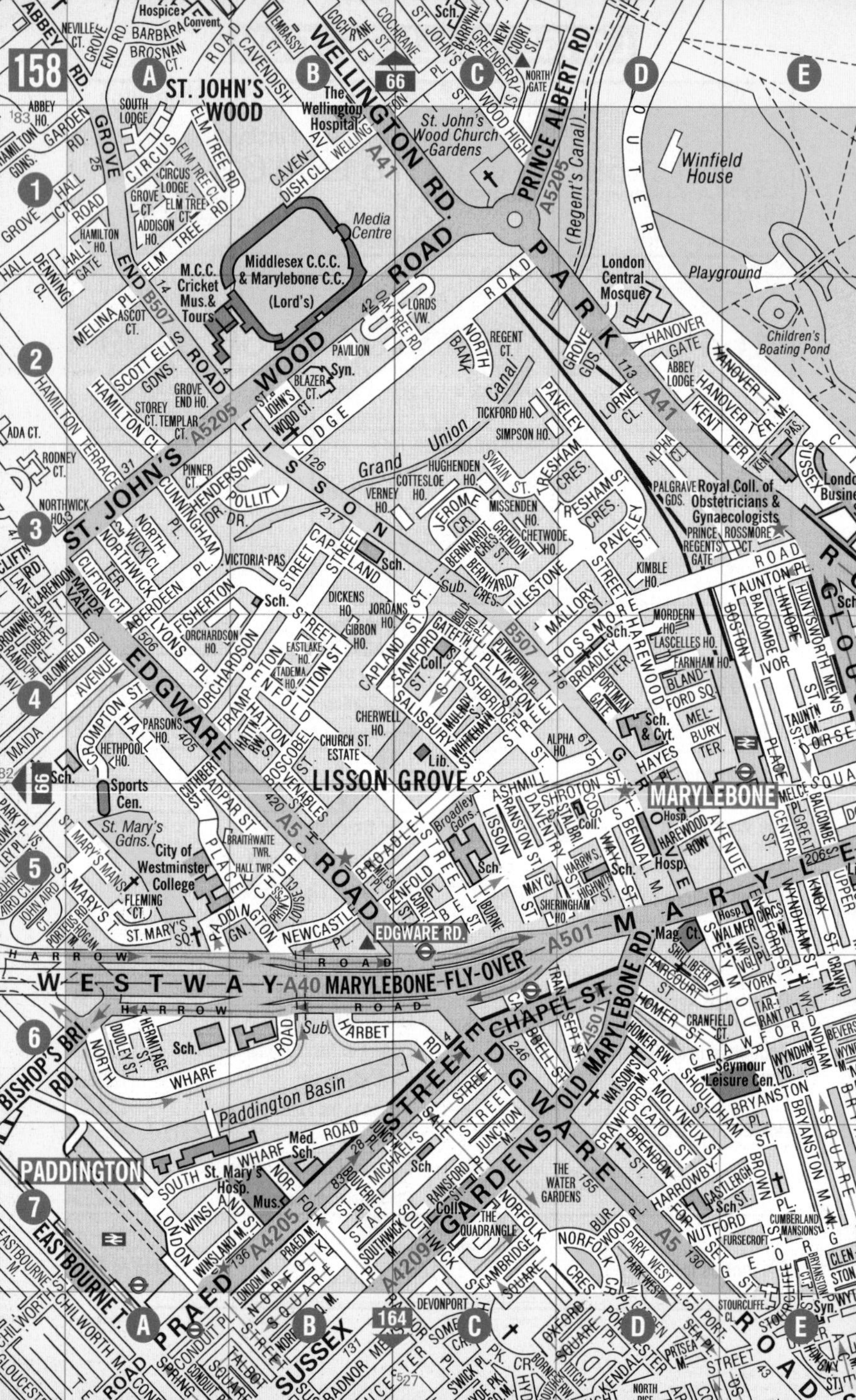

A
B
C
D
E
1
2
3
4
5
6
7
66
164
ST. JOHN'S WOOD
WELLINGTON RD.
A41
PRINCE ALBERT RD.
A5205
(Regent's Canal)
OUTER CIRCLE
Winfield House
Playground
Children's Boating Pond
London Central Mosque
HANOVER GATE
The Wellington Hospital
St. John's Wood Church Gardens
Media Centre
Middlesex C.C.C. & Marylebone C.C. (Lord's)
M.C.C. Cricket Mus.& Tours
ST. JOHN'S WOOD ROAD
GROVE END ROAD
B507
PARK ROAD
LODGE ROAD
Grand Union Canal
LISSON GROVE
Royal Coll. of Obstetricians & Gynaecologists
London Business Sch.
ROSSMORE ROAD
GLOUCESTER PLACE
MARYLEBONE
DORSET SQUARE
MARYLEBONE RD.
A501
EDGWARE ROAD
A5
MAIDA AVENUE
MAIDA VALE
City of Westminster College
Sports Cen.
St. Mary's Gdns.
Broadley Gdns.
EDGWARE RD.
HARROW ROAD
WESTWAY
A40
MARYLEBONE FLY-OVER
CHAPEL ST.
OLD MARYLEBONE RD.
Paddington Basin
NORTH WHARF ROAD
SOUTH WHARF ROAD
BISHOP'S BRI. RD.
PADDINGTON
St. Mary's Hosp.
PRAED ST.
A4205
SUSSEX GARDENS
A4209
THE WATER GARDENS
THE QUADRANGLE
Seymour Leisure Cen.
BRYANSTON SQUARE
GEORGE STREET
NUTFORD PL.
EASTBOURNE T.
CHILWORTH ST.

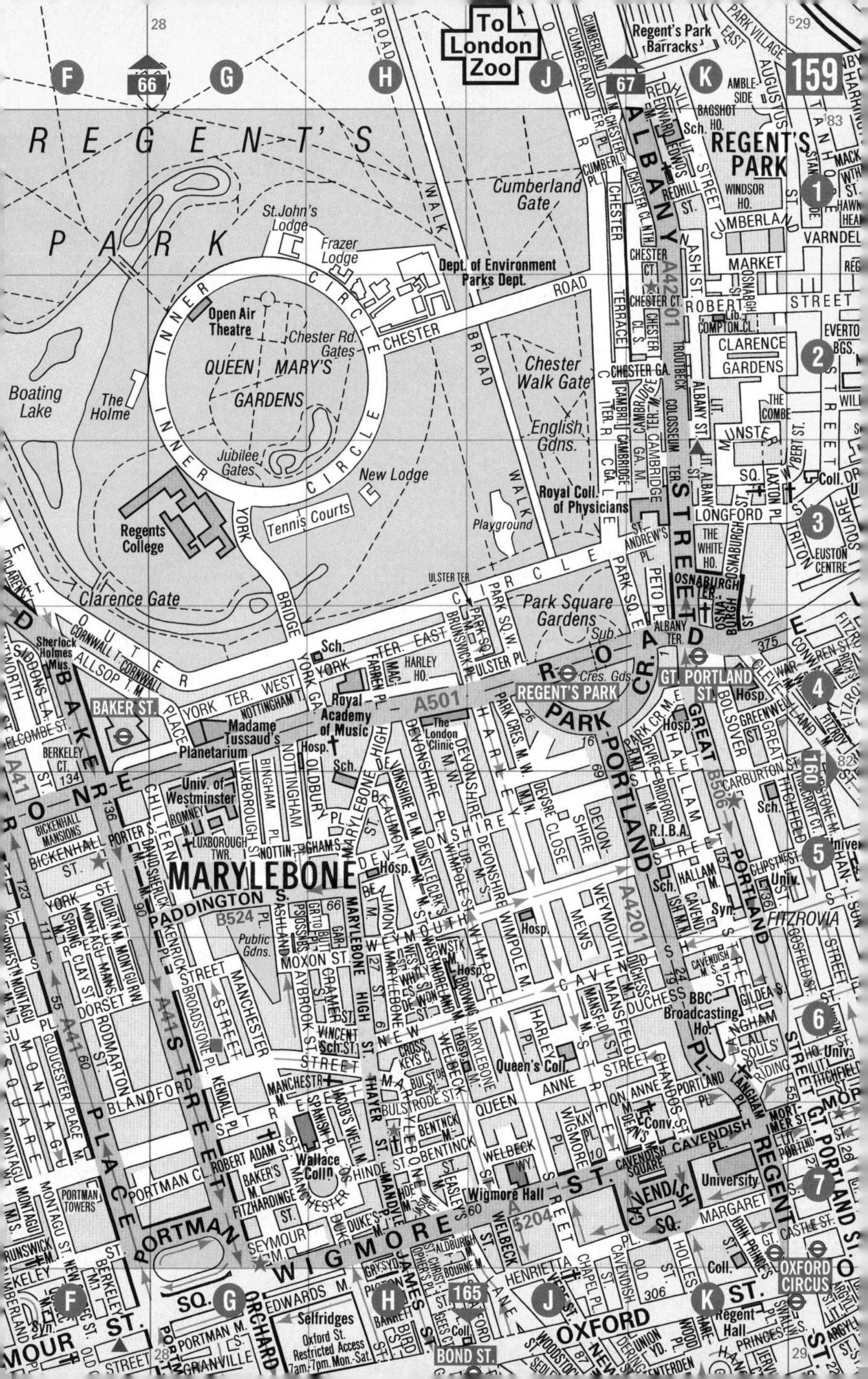
To London Zoo
REGENT'S PARK
Regent's Park Barracks
QUEEN MARY'S GARDENS
Open Air Theatre
Boating Lake
The Holme
Regents College
Cumberland Gate
Chester Walk Gate
English Gdns.
Dept. of Environment Parks Dept.
Royal Coll. of Physicians
Park Square Gardens
Clarence Gate
Sherlock Holmes Mus.
BAKER ST.
Madame Tussaud's
Planetarium
Royal Academy of Music
The London Clinic
REGENT'S PARK
GT. PORTLAND ST.
MARYLEBONE
Univ. of Westminster
Public Gdns.
Wallace Colln
Wigmore Hall
Queen's Coll.
BBC Broadcasting Ho.
FITZROVIA
EUSTON CENTRE
University
OXFORD CIRCUS
Regent Hall
Selfridges
Oxford St. Restricted Access 7am.-7pm. Mon.-Sat.
BOND ST.
MARYLEBONE ROAD
OXFORD ST.
WIGMORE ST.
PORTLAND PLACE
ALBANY STREET
BAKER ST.
GLOUCESTER PLACE
CAVENDISH SQ.
PORTMAN SQ.

REGENT'S PARK
HAMPSTEAD ROAD
A400
EVERSHOLT STREET
A4200
67
SOMERS TOWN
British Library
ST. PANCRAS
KING'S CROSS ST. PANCRAS
EUSTON
St. James's Gardens
EUSTON SQ.
EUSTON ROAD
A501
WARREN STREET
Euston Tower
EUSTON CENTRE
University College
University Coll. Hosp.
Strang Print Room
Percival David Foundation of Chinese Art
TOTTENHAM COURT ROAD
GOWER STREET
TAVISTOCK SQ.
WOBURN PL.
RUSSELL SQUARE
Russell Sq. Gdns.
BLOOMSBURY
Univ. of London Union
Sch. of Oriental & African Studies
Birkbeck Coll.
Sch. of Hygiene & Tropical Med.
Senate House University of London
R.A.D.A.
British Museum
BEDFORD SQUARE
B506
GOODGE STREET
Telecom Tower
FITZROY SQ.
The Middlesex Hospital
FITZROVIA
MORTIMER
OXFORD STREET
A40
OXFORD CIRCUS
REGENT STREET
GT. PORTLAND ST.
The Plaza
NEW OXFORD ST.
TOTTENHAM COURT ROAD
CHARING CROSS RD.
SOHO SQUARE
SHAFTESBURY AV.
HIGH HOLBORN
Sports Cen.
Coll. of Music
Police Ct.
Regent Hall
166
159
A B C D E
1 2 3 4 5 6 7

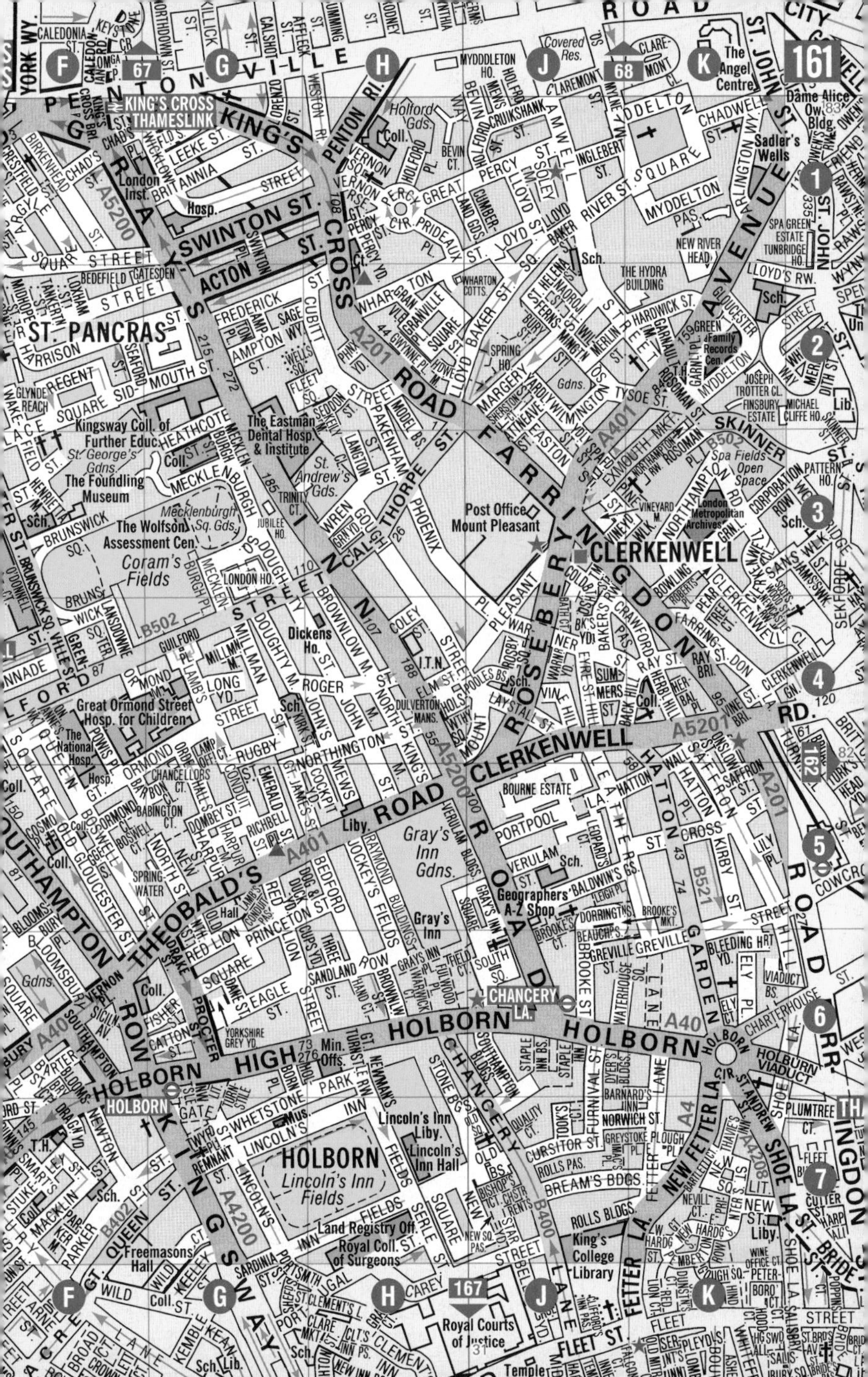

161
F
G
H
J
K
67
68
167
162
1
2
3
4
5
6
7
PENTONVILLE ROAD
KING'S CROSS THAMESLINK
KING'S CROSS ROAD
GRAY'S INN ROAD
A5200
A201
A401
A5201
A40
A4200
A4208
B502
B521
B400
B402
ST. PANCRAS
CLERKENWELL
HOLBORN
Lincoln's Inn Fields
Coram's Fields
Mecklenburgh Sq. Gds.
St. George's Gdns.
St. Andrew's Gdns.
Gray's Inn Gdns.
Gray's Inn
Spa Fields Open Space
Covered Res.
The Angel Centre
Dame Alice Owen's Bldg.
Sadler's Wells
London Inst.
Hosp.
Kingsway Coll. of Further Educ.
The Foundling Museum
The Wolfson Assessment Cen.
The Eastman Dental Hosp. & Institute
Post Office Mount Pleasant
Dickens Ho.
I.T.N.
Great Ormond Street Hosp. for Children
The National Hosp.
London Metropolitan Archives
Family Records Cen.
THE HYDRA BUILDING
NEW RIVER HEAD
Geographers' A-Z Shop
Land Registry Off.
Royal Coll. of Surgeons
Lincoln's Inn Liby.
Lincoln's Inn Hall
Freemasons Hall
King's College Library
Royal Courts of Justice
Temple
CHANCERY LA.
HOLBORN
BOURNE ESTATE
FINSBURY ESTATE
SPA GREEN ESTATE
SWINTON ST.
ACTON ST.
THEOBALD'S ROAD
CLERKENWELL ROAD
FARRINGDON ROAD
ROSEBERY AVENUE
ST. JOHN ST.
HOLBORN VIADUCT
HIGH HOLBORN
KINGSWAY
SOUTHAMPTON ROW
NEW FETTER LA.
FETTER LA.
SHOE LA.
CHANCERY LANE
FLEET ST.
HATTON GARDEN
MYDDELTON SQUARE
BRUNSWICK SQ.

CITY ROAD
GOSWELL ROAD
City Road Basin
WHARF
Wenlock Basin
The Angel Centre
Dame Alice Owen Bldg.
Sadler's Wells
ST. JOHN STREET
WAKLEY ST.
PEREGRINE HO.
MURRAY
Crusoe Ho. Sch.
A501
NILE
SHEPHERDESS WALK
MICAWBER ST.
WELLESLEY TER.
B144
RAWSTORNE
SPA GREEN ESTATE
TUNBRIDGE HO.
LLOYD'S RW.
Moreland Prim. Sch.
PRESIDENT HO.
TURNPIKE HO.
KING SQ.
CENTRAL STREET
DINGLEY RD.
IRONMONGER ROW
Moorfields Eye Hosp.
BATH STREET
GALWAY ST.
PEERLESS
(King's Annexe)
The City University
NORTHAMPTON SQ.
SEBASTIAN ST.
LEVER STREET
B502
Family Records Cen.
Baths
Lib.
Kings Bldg.
BRUNSWICK CLOSE EST.
SKINNER
Spa Fields Open Space
PERCIVAL
FINSBURY
Leisure Cen.
ST. LUKE'S ESTATE
OLD ST
SEWARD
MITCHELL
OLD STREET
A5201
ST. LUKE'S
BUNHILL ROW
FEATHERSTONE
Sch.
COMPTON
Schs.
Spts. Cen.
Halls
DALLINGTON ST.
GOLDEN LANE
WHITECROSS ST.
Bunhill Fields Burial Ground
H.A.C. Ground
CLERKENWELL ROAD
GREAT SUTTON ST.
ALDERSGATE
A1
Coll.
ROSCOE
DUFFERIN
FORTUNE ST.
GOLDEN LANE ESTATE
The Medical Coll. of St. Bartholomew's Hospital
Charterhouse
St. John's Ga.
Northampton Hall City University (Halls of Residence)
CHISWELL STREET
B100
St. John's Gardens
FARRINGDON
BARBICAN
BEECH STREET
CROMWELL TWR.
Lib.
Arts Cen.
ROPEMAKER
COWCROSS
FARRINGDON ROAD
A201
CHARTERHOUSE STREET
Central Markets
LONG LANE
BARBICAN
Sch.
MOORGATE
Ironmongers Hall
Museum
LONDON WALL
A1211
HOLBORN
HOLBORN CIR.
Mus.
St. Bartholomew's Hospital
A40
CITY THAMESLINK
HOLBORN VIADUCT
NEWGATE ST.
KING EDWARD ST.
British Telecom Cen.
Old Bailey
FLEET BUILDING
SHOE LA.
ST. BRIDE ST.
Liby.
Offs.
Clock Mus.
Guildhall
GRESHAM
ST. MARTIN'S LE GRAND
ST. PAUL'S
LUDGATE HILL
St. Paul's Cathedral
CHEAPSIDE
POULTRY
LOTHBURY
Bank of England Offs.
NEW BRIDGE ST.
168
68
161

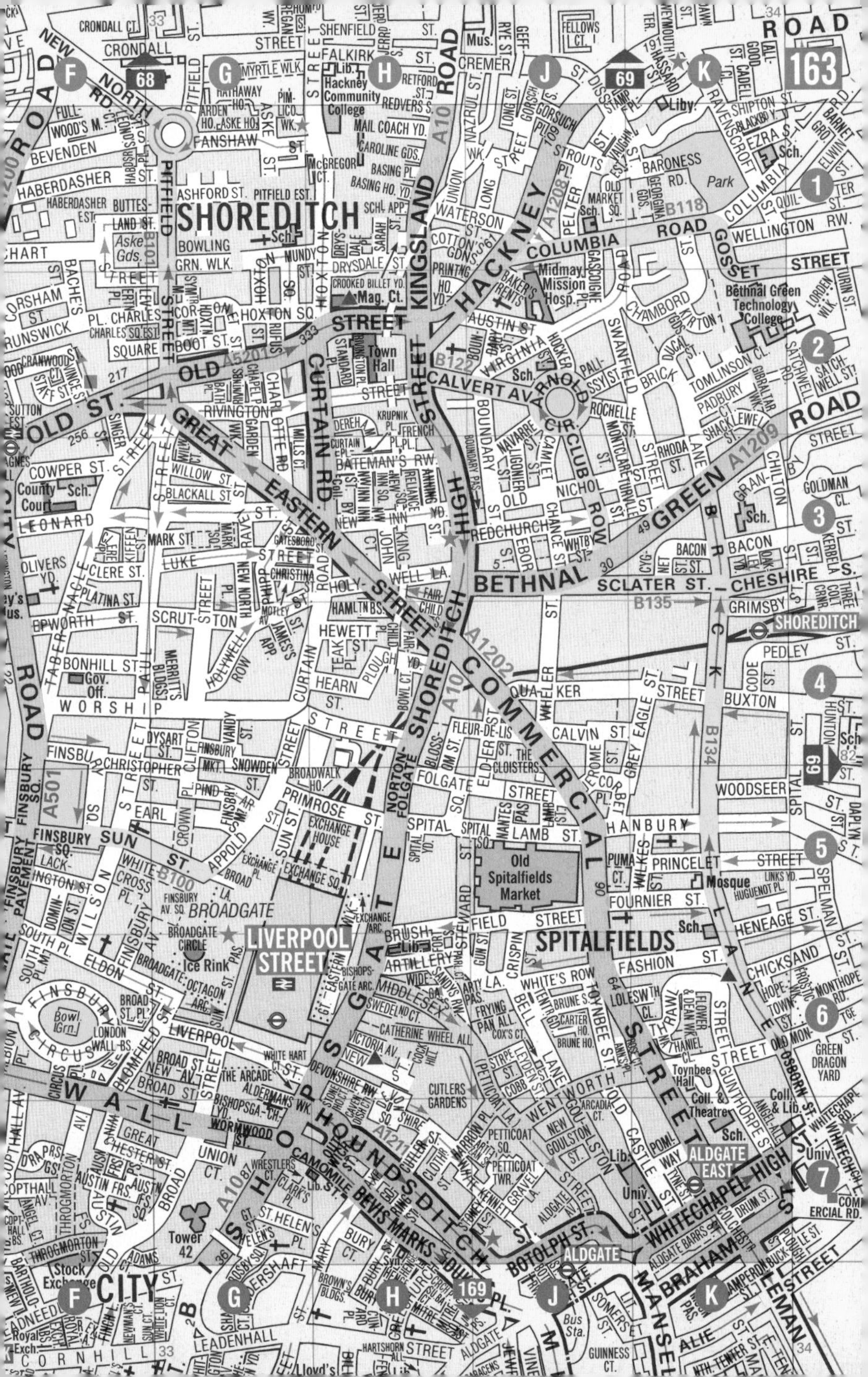
163
68
69
169
SHOREDITCH
SPITALFIELDS
BROADGATE
CITY
LIVERPOOL STREET
ALDGATE
ALDGATE EAST
SHOREDITCH
Hackney Community College
Town Hall
Mag. Ct.
Midmay Mission Hosp.
Bethnal Green Technology College
Old Spitalfields Market
Ice Rink
Broadgate Circle
Tower 42
Stock Exchange
Toynbee Hall
Coll. & Theatre
Mosque
County Court
Gov. Off.
Cutlers Gardens
Bus Sta.
Baroness Park
HACKNEY ROAD
KINGSLAND ROAD
OLD STREET
GREAT EASTERN STREET
CURTAIN RD.
SHOREDITCH HIGH STREET
COMMERCIAL STREET
BETHNAL GREEN ROAD
COLUMBIA ROAD
BISHOPSGATE
HOUNDSDITCH
LONDON WALL
CITY ROAD
WHITECHAPEL HIGH ST.
BRICK LANE
FINSBURY CIRCUS
FINSBURY SQ.
FINSBURY PAVEMENT
SUN ST.
WORSHIP ST.
HOXTON SQ.
CHARLES SQUARE
PITFIELD STREET
SCLATER ST.
CHESHIRE ST.
FASHION ST.
FOURNIER ST.
HANBURY ST.
WENTWORTH ST.
BEVIS MARKS
CAMOMILE ST.
LEADENHALL
CORNHILL
ARNOLD CIR.
BOUNDARY ST.
REDCHURCH ST.
CALVERT AV.
A10
A1202
A1208
A1209
A5201
A501
B100
B101
B118
B122
B134
B135
F
G
H
J
K
1
2
3
4
5
6
7
33
34

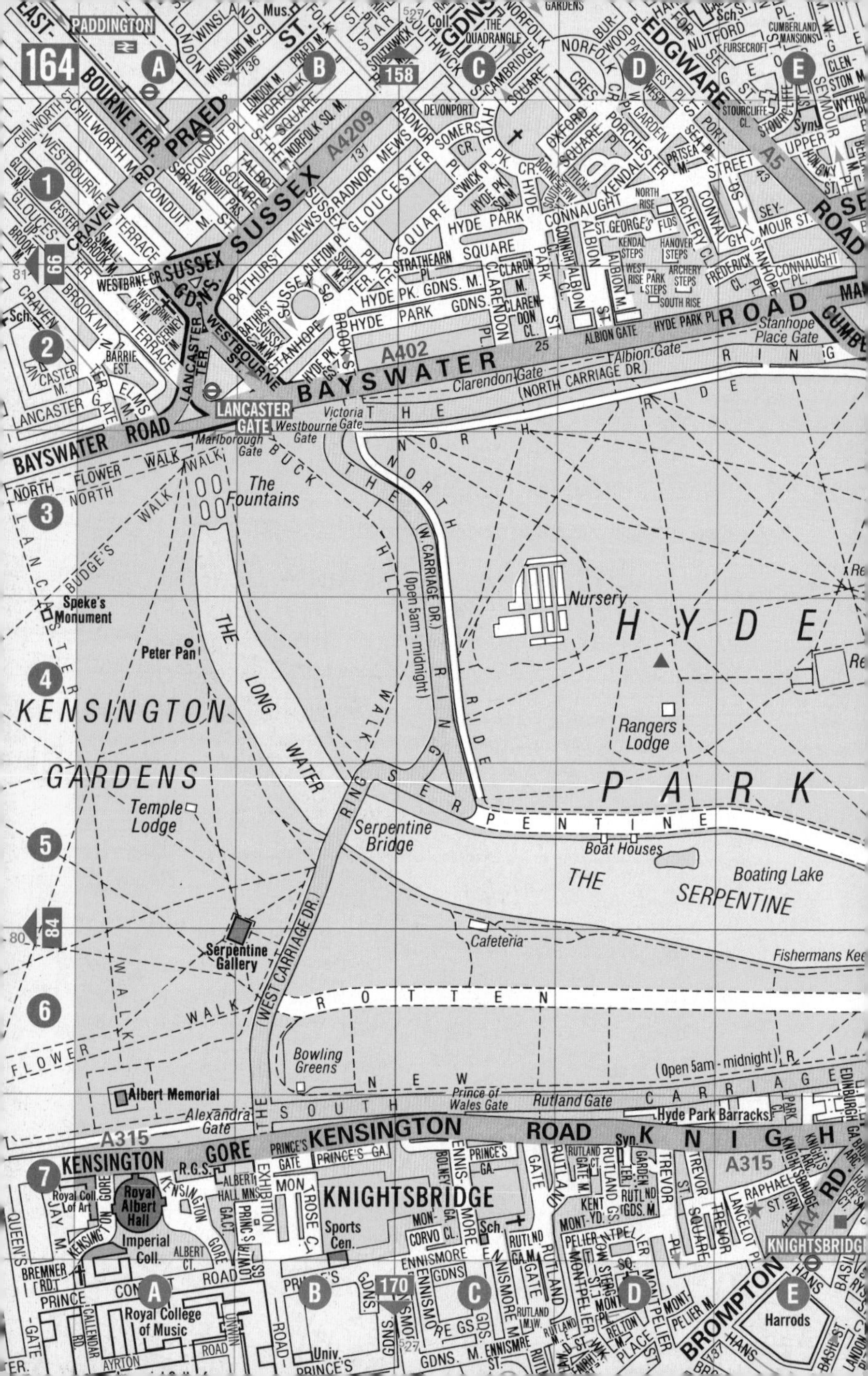

164
PADDINGTON
A
B
C
D
E
158
1
2
3
4
5
6
7
66
84
170
PRAED ST.
SUSSEX GDNS.
SUSSEX SQUARE
BOURNE TER.
CRAVEN RD.
WESTBOURNE TERRACE
GLOUCESTER SQUARE
HYDE PARK SQUARE
CONNAUGHT SQUARE
EDGWARE ROAD
A4209
A5
A402
BAYSWATER ROAD
LANCASTER GATE
Victoria Gate
Westbourne Gate
Marlborough Gate
Clarendon Gate
Albion Gate
Stanhope Place Gate
THE RING
NORTH CARRIAGE DR.
THE NORTH RIDE
BUCK HILL WALK
The Fountains
NORTH FLOWER WALK
LANCASTER WALK
BUDGE'S WALK
Speke's Monument
Peter Pan
THE LONG WATER
KENSINGTON GARDENS
Temple Lodge
Serpentine Bridge
Serpentine Gallery
(W. CARRIAGE DR.)
(Open 5am - midnight)
Nursery
HYDE PARK
Rangers Lodge
SERPENTINE RD
Boat Houses
THE SERPENTINE
Boating Lake
Cafeteria
Fishermans Kee
ROTTEN ROW
Bowling Greens
(WEST CARRIAGE DR.)
FLOWER WALK
SOUTH CARRIAGE DR.
Albert Memorial
Alexandra Gate
Prince of Wales Gate
Rutland Gate
Hyde Park Barracks
A315
KENSINGTON GORE
KENSINGTON ROAD
KNIGHTSBRIDGE
Royal Albert Hall
Royal Coll. of Art
Imperial Coll.
Royal College of Music
Sports Cen.
EXHIBITION RD.
PRINCE'S GATE
ENNISMORE GARDENS
RUTLAND GATE
MONTPELIER SQ.
TREVOR SQUARE
BROMPTON RD.
Harrods

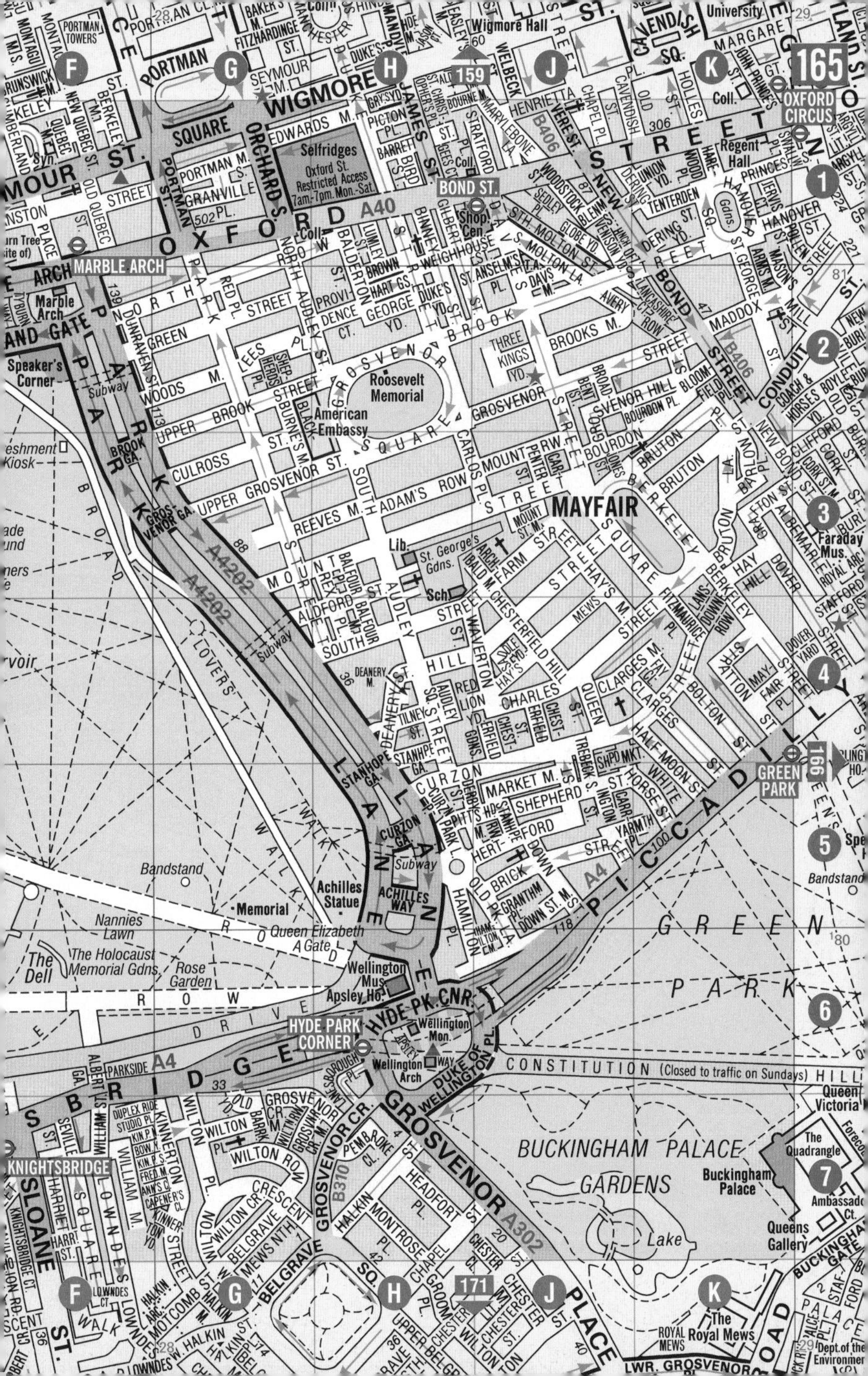
F
G
H
J
K
159
171
166
1
2
3
4
5
6
7
Wigmore Hall
University
Portman Towers
PORTMAN
SQUARE
WIGMORE
ORCHARD ST.
Selfridges
Oxford St. Restricted Access 7am.-7pm. Mon.-Sat.
OXFORD
A40
MARBLE ARCH
Marble Arch
Tyburn Tree (site of)
OXFORD CIRCUS
Regent Hall
BOND ST.
Shop. Cen.
NEW BOND STREET
B406
HENRIETTA
CAVENDISH SQ.
HOLLES
HANOVER SQ.
PRINCES ST.
TENTERDEN
DERING ST.
ST. GEORGE
MADDOX ST.
CONDUIT ST.
BROOK ST.
GROSVENOR SQUARE
Roosevelt Memorial
American Embassy
UPPER BROOK ST.
UPPER GROSVENOR ST.
NORTH AUDLEY ST.
SOUTH AUDLEY ST.
DUKE ST.
DAVIES ST.
GEORGE YD.
THREE KINGS YD.
BROOKS M.
BROOK'S M.
BRUTON ST.
BRUTON PL.
BERKELEY SQUARE
MAYFAIR
MOUNT ST.
ADAM'S ROW
CARLOS PL.
REEVES M.
Lib.
St. George's Gdns.
Sch.
FARM ST.
HAY'S M.
CHESTERFIELD HILL
CHARLES ST.
HILL ST.
WAVERTON ST.
CLARGES ST.
CLARGES M.
BOLTON ST.
HALF MOON ST.
WHITE HORSE ST.
CURZON ST.
SHEPHERD MKT.
SHEPHERD ST.
HERTFORD ST.
BRICK ST.
DOWN ST.
STRATTON ST.
MAY FAIR PL.
DOVER ST.
DOVER YARD
ALBEMARLE ST.
HAY HILL
STAFFORD ST.
Faraday Mus.
GREEN PARK
PICCADILLY
A4
PARK LANE
A4202
Subway
Speaker's Corner
Refreshment Kiosk
Bandstand
Memorial
Nannies Lawn
The Dell
The Holocaust Memorial Gdns.
Rose Garden
Achilles Statue
ACHILLES WAY
CURZON GA.
STANHOPE GA.
GROSVENOR GA.
BROOK GA.
Queen Elizabeth Gate
Wellington Mus.
Apsley Ho.
HYDE PK. CNR.
HYDE PARK CORNER
Wellington Mon.
Wellington Arch
DUKE OF WELLINGTON PL.
CONSTITUTION (Closed to traffic on Sundays) HILL
ROW
DRIVE
KNIGHTSBRIDGE
KNIGHTSBRIDGE
SLOANE ST.
LOWNDES SQUARE
WILTON CRESCENT
WILTON PL.
WILTON ROW
BELGRAVE SQ.
GROSVENOR CR.
GROSVENOR PLACE
A302
B310
HALKIN ST.
MONTROSE PL.
HEADFORT PL.
CHAPEL ST.
CHESTER ST.
BUCKINGHAM PALACE GARDENS
Lake
Buckingham Palace
The Quadrangle
Queen Victoria
Ambassadors Ct.
Queens Gallery
BUCKINGHAM GATE
The Royal Mews
ROYAL MEWS
LWR. GROSVENOR
Dept. of the Environment

OXFORD CIRCUS
OXFORD STREET
160
SOHO SQUARE
CHARING CROSS ROAD
HIGH ST.
ST. GILES
SHAFTESBURY AVENUE
REGENT STREET
Regent Hall
HANOVER SQ.
GREAT MARLBOROUGH ST.
Police Ct.
Coll. of Music
SOHO
BROADWICK ST.
WARDOUR ST.
CAMBRIDGE CIRCUS
SEVEN DIALS
Thomas Neal's
COVENT GARDEN
LONG ACRE
MADDOX ST.
CONDUIT ST.
NEW BURLINGTON ST.
SAVILE ROW
GERRARD ST.
LEICESTER SQ.
Leicester Fields
Trocadero Cen.
PICCADILLY CIRCUS
Eros
GLASSHOUSE ST.
VIGO ST.
Royal Academy Schs.
Royal Academy of Arts
Faraday Mus.
ALBEMARLE ST.
DOVER ST.
OLD BOND ST.
PICCADILLY
JERMYN ST.
HAYMARKET
COVENTRY ST.
National Portrait Gallery
National Gallery
Cent. Lending Lib.
WILLIAM IV ST.
TRAFALGAR SQUARE
Nelson's Column
Canada Ho.
PALL MALL EAST
COCKSPUR ST.
CHARING CROSS
NORTHUMBERLAND AVE.
ST. JAMES'S SQUARE
London Lib.
ST. JAMES'S ST.
GREEN PARK
165
PALL MALL
R.A.C.
CARLTON HOUSE TER.
Mall Galls.
Inst. of Contemp. Arts
Duke of York Mem.
Admiralty Arch.
Old Admiralty Offices
Old War Office
Spencer Ho.
Marlborough Ho.
King George VII Memorial
(Commonwealth Conference Centre)
St. James's Palace
Clarence Ho.
Lancaster Ho.
Stable Yard Gate
THE MALL
(Closed to traffic on Sundays)
HORSE GUARDS RD.
Horse Guards
Horse Guards Parade
Banqueting Ho.
Guards Memorial
WHITEHALL
DOWNING ST.
Foreign Office
Government Offices
Cenotaph
KING CHARLES ST.
Cabinet War Rooms
PARLIAMENT ST.
GREEN PARK
Bandstand
ST. JAMES'S PARK
Duck Island
Lake
Clive Steps
CONSTITUTION HILL
Queen Victoria Mem.
Buckingham Palace
The Quadrangle
The Forecourt
Ambassadors' Ct.
Queens Gallery
SPUR RD.
BIRDCAGE WALK
Queen Anne's Gate
Guards' Mus.
Home Office
Wellington Barracks
BUCKINGHAM GATE
B323
OLD QUEEN ST.
GREAT GEORGE ST.
Q.E.II Conf. Cen.
PARLIAMENT SQ.
Guildhall
BROAD SANCTUARY
Westminster Abbey
Cen. Hall
Caxton Ho.
TOTHILL ST.
ST. JAMES'S PARK
172
Caxton Hall
New Scotland Yard
VICTORIA ST.
Dept. of Trade & Industry
Dept. of the Environment
The Cloisters
The Close
Abbey Garden
New Palace Yard
Westminster Hall

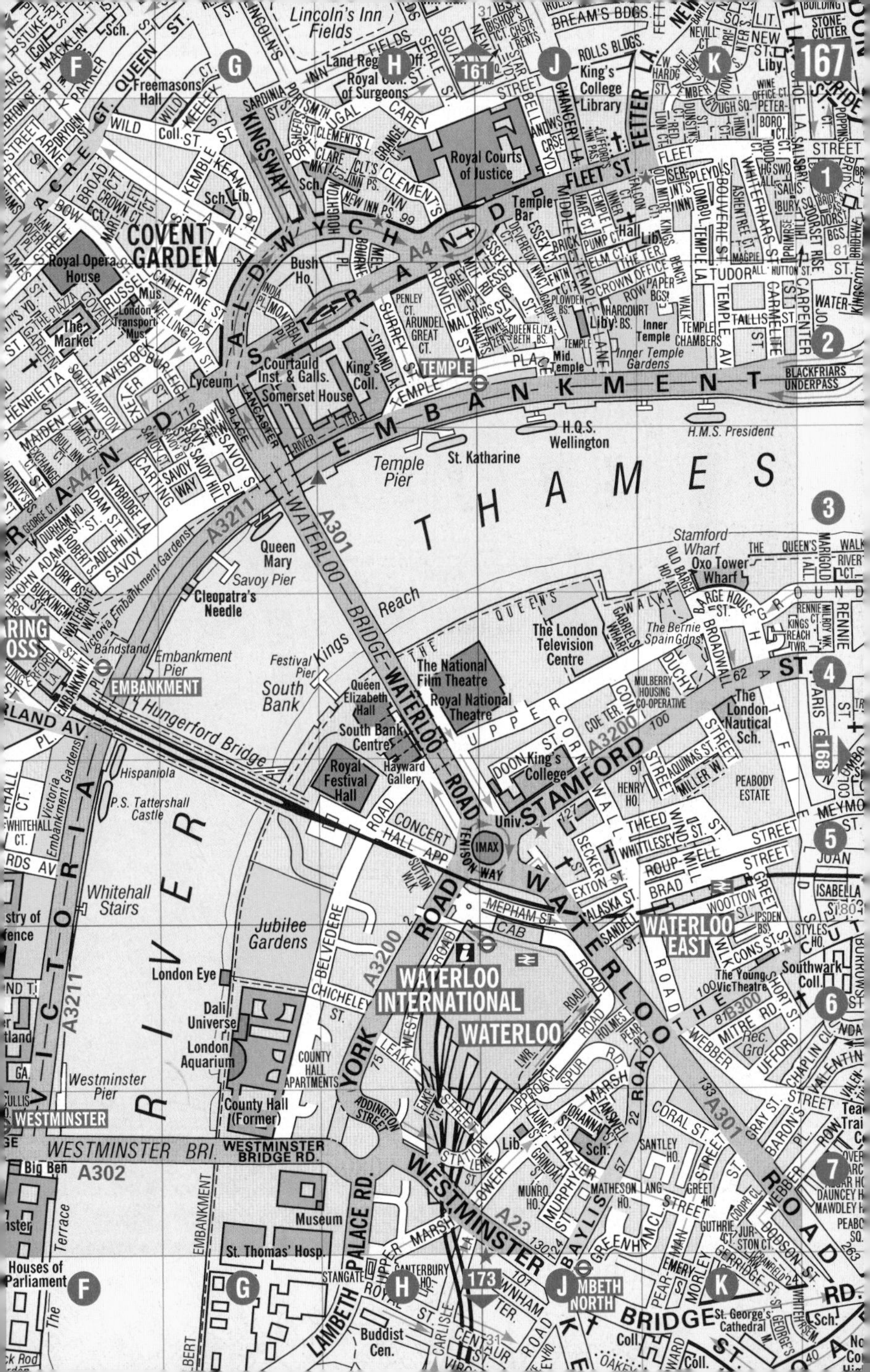

167
Lincoln's Inn Fields
Land Regy. Off.
Royal Coll. of Surgeons
161
Rolls Bldgs.
King's College Library
Freemasons' Hall
Kingsway
Royal Courts of Justice
Fleet St.
Chancery La.
Fetter La.
Temple Bar
COVENT GARDEN
Royal Opera House
The Piazza
The Market
London Transport Mus.
Aldwych
Strand
A4
Bush Ho.
Courtauld Inst. & Galls.
Somerset House
King's Coll.
Lyceum
Savoy
Inner Temple
Mid. Temple
Temple Chambers
Inner Temple Gardens
TEMPLE
Embankment
Blackfriars Underpass
H.Q.S. Wellington
H.M.S. President
St. Katharine
Temple Pier
THAMES
Stamford Wharf
Oxo Tower Wharf
Queen Mary
Savoy Pier
Cleopatra's Needle
Victoria Embankment Gardens
Bandstand
Embankment Pier
EMBANKMENT
Hungerford Bridge
Waterloo Bridge
A301
A3211
Reach
Kings
Festival Pier
South Bank
The London Television Centre
The Bernie Spain Gdns.
Mulberry Housing Co-operative
The National Film Theatre
Royal National Theatre
Queen Elizabeth Hall
South Bank Centre
Hayward Gallery
Royal Festival Hall
King's College
Stamford St.
A3200
The London Nautical Sch.
Peabody Estate
Hispaniola
P.S. Tattershall Castle
IMAX
Tenison Way
Upper Ground
Concert Hall App.
Whitehall Stairs
Jubilee Gardens
London Eye
Dali Universe
London Aquarium
County Hall (Former)
County Hall Apartments
WATERLOO INTERNATIONAL
WATERLOO
WATERLOO EAST
Waterloo Road
York Road
The Young Vic Theatre
Southwark Coll.
B300
The Cut
Westminster Pier
WESTMINSTER
Westminster Bri.
Westminster Bridge Rd.
A302
Big Ben
Houses of Parliament
Museum
St. Thomas' Hosp.
Lambeth Palace Rd.
A23
173
LAMBETH NORTH
St. George's Cathedral
Buddist Cen.
River
Victoria
Thames
1
2
3
4
5
6
7
F
G
H
J
K

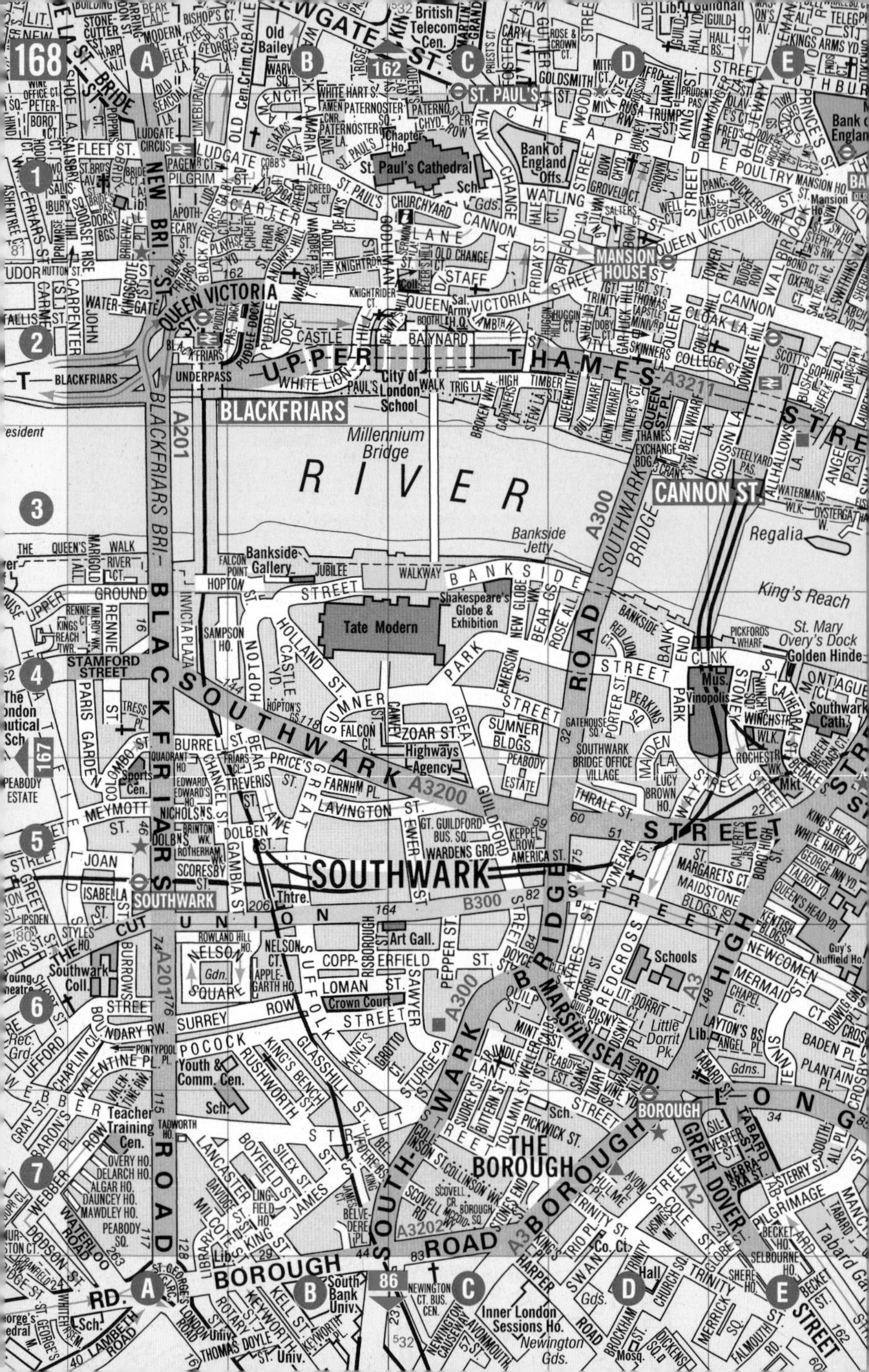
A
B
C
D
E
1
2
3
4
5
6
7
162
167
86
NEWGATE ST.
Old Bailey
British Telecom Cen.
ST. PAUL'S
St. Paul's Cathedral
Chapter Ho.
Bank of England Offs.
Bank of England
CHEAPSIDE
POULTRY
MANSION HOUSE
QUEEN VICTORIA ST.
CANNON ST.
FLEET ST.
LUDGATE CIRCUS
LUDGATE HILL
NEW BRI. ST.
BLACKFRIARS
UPPER THAMES ST.
City of London School
Millennium Bridge
RIVER
Bankside Jetty
Bankside Gallery
Tate Modern
Shakespeare's Globe & Exhibition
King's Reach
St. Mary Overy's Dock
Golden Hinde
Regalia
CANNON ST.
SOUTHWARK BRIDGE
SOUTHWARK BRIDGE ROAD
A300
A201
A3200
A3211
A3202
A3
A2
B300
BLACKFRIARS BRI.
BLACKFRIARS ROAD
SOUTHWARK ST.
STAMFORD STREET
Highways Agency
SOUTHWARK
UNION ST.
Art Gall.
Crown Court
Schools
Little Dorrit Pk.
MARSHALSEA RD.
BOROUGH HIGH ST.
LONG LA.
BOROUGH
THE BOROUGH
BOROUGH ROAD
GREAT DOVER ST.
Southwark Cath.
Mus. Vinopolis
Youth & Comm. Cen.
Teacher Training Cen.
South Bank Univ.
Inner London Sessions Ho.
Newington Gds.
Southwark Coll.
Sports Cen.
NELSON SQUARE
THE CUT
WATERLOO ROAD
LAMBETH ROAD
ST. GEORGE'S CIRCUS

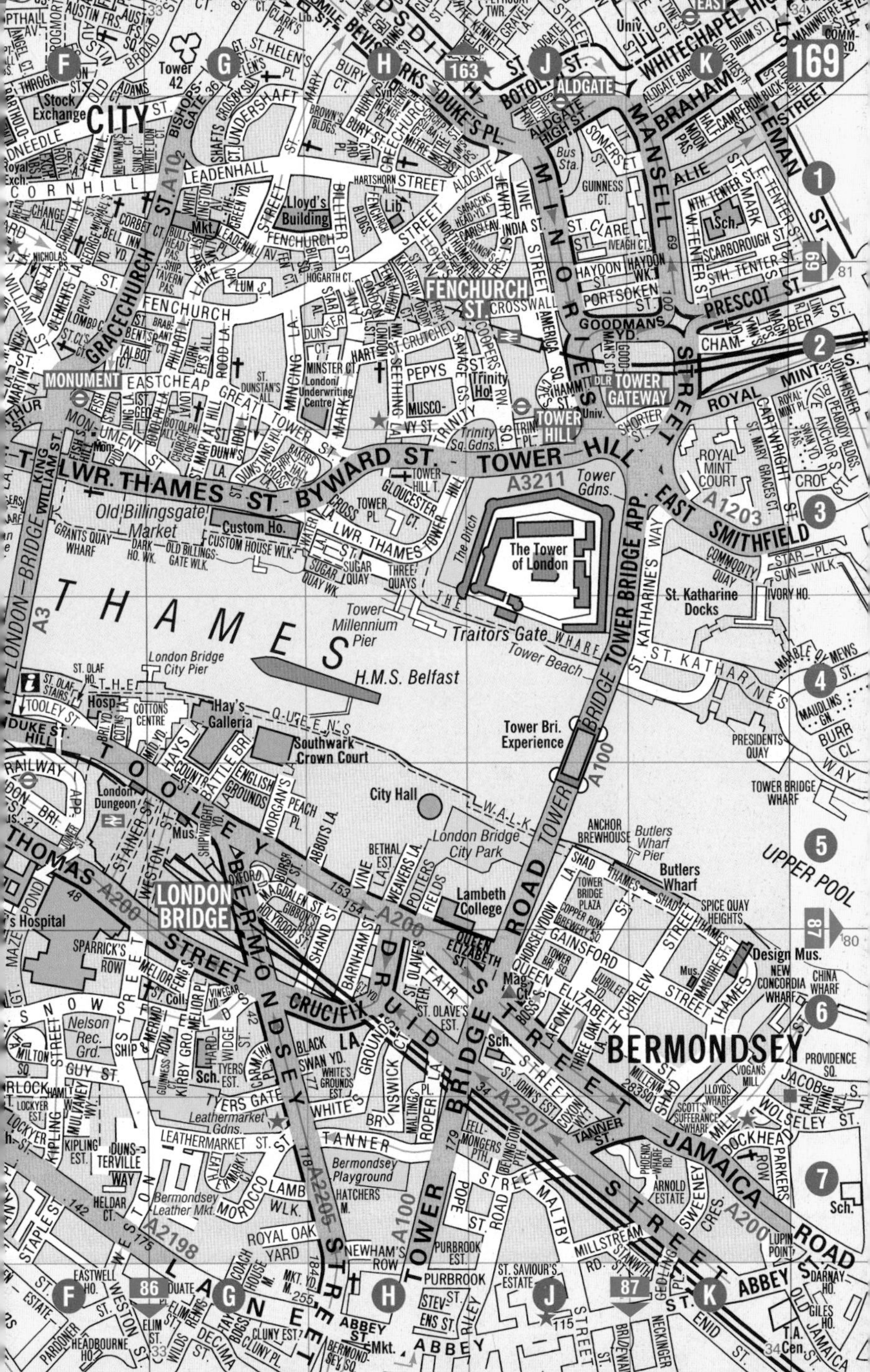
F
G
H
J
K
1
2
3
4
5
6
7
163
69
81
87
80
86
87
CITY
Stock Exchange
Tower 42
Royal Exch.
CORNHILL
LEADENHALL
Lloyd's Building
Mkt.
FENCHURCH
GRACECHURCH
BISHOPSGATE
A10
MONUMENT
EASTCHEAP
GREAT TOWER ST.
LWR. THAMES ST.
BYWARD ST.
TOWER HILL
A3211
FENCHURCH ST.
ALDGATE
WHITECHAPEL HIGH ST.
MINORIES
MANSELL
BRAHAM
LEMAN STREET
ALIE
PRESCOT ST.
ROYAL MINT
TOWER GATEWAY
TOWER HILL
GOODMANS YD.
PEPYS
Trinity Ho.
Trinity Sq. Gdns.
London Underwriting Centre
Custom Ho.
Old Billingsgate Market
Tower Gdns.
The Ditch
The Tower of London
Traitors Gate
WHARF
Tower Beach
Tower Millennium Pier
H.M.S. Belfast
THAMES
London Bridge City Pier
EAST SMITHFIELD
A1203
ROYAL MINT COURT
St. Katharine Docks
ST. KATHARINE'S WAY
TOWER BRIDGE APP.
TOWER BRIDGE ROAD
A100
Tower Bri. Experience
UPPER POOL
Hay's Galleria
Southwark Crown Court
City Hall
QUEENS WALK
London Bridge City Park
TOOLEY ST.
London Dungeon
LONDON BRIDGE
A3
LONDON BRIDGE
KING WILLIAM ST.
THOMAS ST.
A200
ST. THOMAS STREET
BERMONDSEY ST.
A2205
CRUCIFIX LA.
DRUID ST.
Lambeth College
Butlers Wharf
ANCHOR BREWHOUSE
Design Mus.
SHAD THAMES
BERMONDSEY
JAMAICA ROAD
A2207
TANNER ST.
ABBEY ST.
MALTBY ST.
Nelson Rec. Grd.
GUY ST.
SNOWSFIELDS
WESTON ST.
Leathermarket Gdns.
LEATHERMARKET ST.
Bermondsey Playground
Bermondsey Leather Mkt.
A2198
LONG LANE
TOWER BRIDGE ROAD
ST. SAVIOUR'S ESTATE
NECKINGER
ABBEY ST.

170
KENSINGTON
KNIGHTSBRIDGE
164
A
B
C
D
E
1
2
3
4
5
6
7
84
Royal Albert Hall
Imperial Coll.
Royal College of Music
Imperial Coll. of Science, Technology & Medicine
Science Mus.
Natural History Museum
Victoria & Albert Museum
The Oratory
Harrods
Univ.
Sports Cen.
PRINCE CONSORT ROAD
PRINCE'S GDNS.
ENNISMORE GDNS.
RUTLAND GATE
MONTPELIER SQ.
MONTPELIER PL.
BROMPTON ROAD
BROMPTON SQUARE
BROMPTON PL.
BEAUFORT GDNS.
BEAUCHAMP PL.
HANS ROAD
BASIL ST.
WALTON ST.
PONT ST.
OVINGTON SQUARE
OVINGTON GDNS.
YEOMAN'S ROW
EGERTON GDNS.
EGERTON CRESCENT
EGERTON TER.
LENNOX GDNS.
CLABON M.
Juvenile Ct.
QUEEN'S GATE
ELVASTON PL.
IMPERIAL COLLEGE RD.
EXHIBITION RD.
CROMWELL RD.
CROMWELL PLACE
CROMWELL GDNS.
Ismaili Cen.
THURLOE PLACE
THURLOE SQUARE
THURLOE ST.
ALEXANDER SQ.
SOUTH TER.
SOUTH KENSINGTON
BROMPTON
PELHAM STREET
PELHAM CRES.
HARRINGTON RD.
QUEENSBERRY PL.
STANHOPE GDNS.
OLD BROMPTON RD.
ONSLOW SQUARE
ONSLOW GARDENS
SUMNER PL.
SYDNEY ST.
SYDNEY MEWS
DRAYCOTT PL.
DRAYCOTT AVENUE
SLOANE AVENUE
WALTON ST.
MILNER ST.
CADOGAN ST.
ELYSTAN ST.
ELYSTAN PL.
CHELSEA CLOISTERS
SAMUEL LEWIS TRUST DWELLINGS
THE SUTTON ESTATE
IXWORTH PL.
MARLBOROUGH ST.
WHITEHEAD'S GRO.
PETYWARD
JUBILEE PL.
MARKHAM SQUARE
MARKHAM ST.
KINGS WALK SHOP. CEN.
ROSE SQUARE
The Royal Marsden Hosp. (Fulham)
Ryl. Brompton Hosp. Annexe
FULHAM ROAD
CHELSEA
Royal Brompton Hospital
Thamesbrook
Kings College London
Coll. of Art & Design
Dovehouse Grn.
Old Town Hall
Sports Cen.
Reg. Off.
Lib.
KING'S ROAD
DOVEHOUSE ST.
CHELSEA SQUARE
MANRESA RD.
CARLYLE SQUARE
OLD CHURCH ST.
MULBERRY WK.
MALLORD ST.
ELM PARK GDNS.
ELM PARK ROAD
EVELYN GARDENS
SELWOOD PL.
BEAUFORT ST.
CHELSEA PARK GDNS.
PAULTONS SQUARE
GLEBE PL.
OAKLEY STREET
FLOOD ST.
SHAWFIELD ST.
SMITH ST.
ST. LEONARD'S TER.
CHRISTCHURCH ST.
PEABODY EST.
ST. LOO AV.
CHEYNE WALK
CHEYNE ROW
Carlyle's House
ROYAL HOSPITAL RD.
Chelsea Physic Garden
CHELSEA EMBANKMENT
Cadogan Pier
THE PORTICOS
Burial Grnd.
School
A4
A308
A3217
B304
B319

KNIGHTSBRIDGE
GARDENS
Buckingham Palace
Lake
Queen's Gallery
The Royal Mews
ROYAL MEWS
GROSVENOR PLACE
A302
BELGRAVE SQUARE
B310
LWR. GROSVENOR PL.
BRESSENDEN PL.
VICTORIA
VICTORIA
Victoria Place Shopping Cen.
Victoria Coach Station
BELGRAVIA
EATON SQUARE
A3217
ECCLESTON ST.
A3213
BUCKINGHAM PALACE ROAD
A3214
ECCLESTON BRI.
A202
BELGRAVE RD.
SLOANE STREET
A3216
B319
CHESHAM PL.
SLOANE SQ.
SLOANE SQ.
LOWER SLOANE ST.
PIMLICO ROAD
EBURY BRIDGE ROAD
B313
WARWICK WAY
B324
Duke of York's Territorial Army H. Q.
Burton's Court
Chelsea Barracks
CHELSEA BRIDGE ROAD
Royal Hospital Chelsea Mus.
Royal Hospital Chelsea
RANELAGH GARDENS
Monument
Great Hall
National Army Museum
ROYAL HOSPITAL RD.
B302
The Lister Hospital
Grosvenor Canal
Inner Basin
Carriage Shed
GROSVENOR RD.
EMBANKMENT
A3212
CHELSEA BRIDGE
RIVER THAMES
Grosvenor Bri.
Battersea Wharf
CHELSEA BRIDGE WHARF
CARRIAGE DR. NTH.
Pier
165
172
84
85
F G H J K
1 2 3 4 5 6 7
28
29

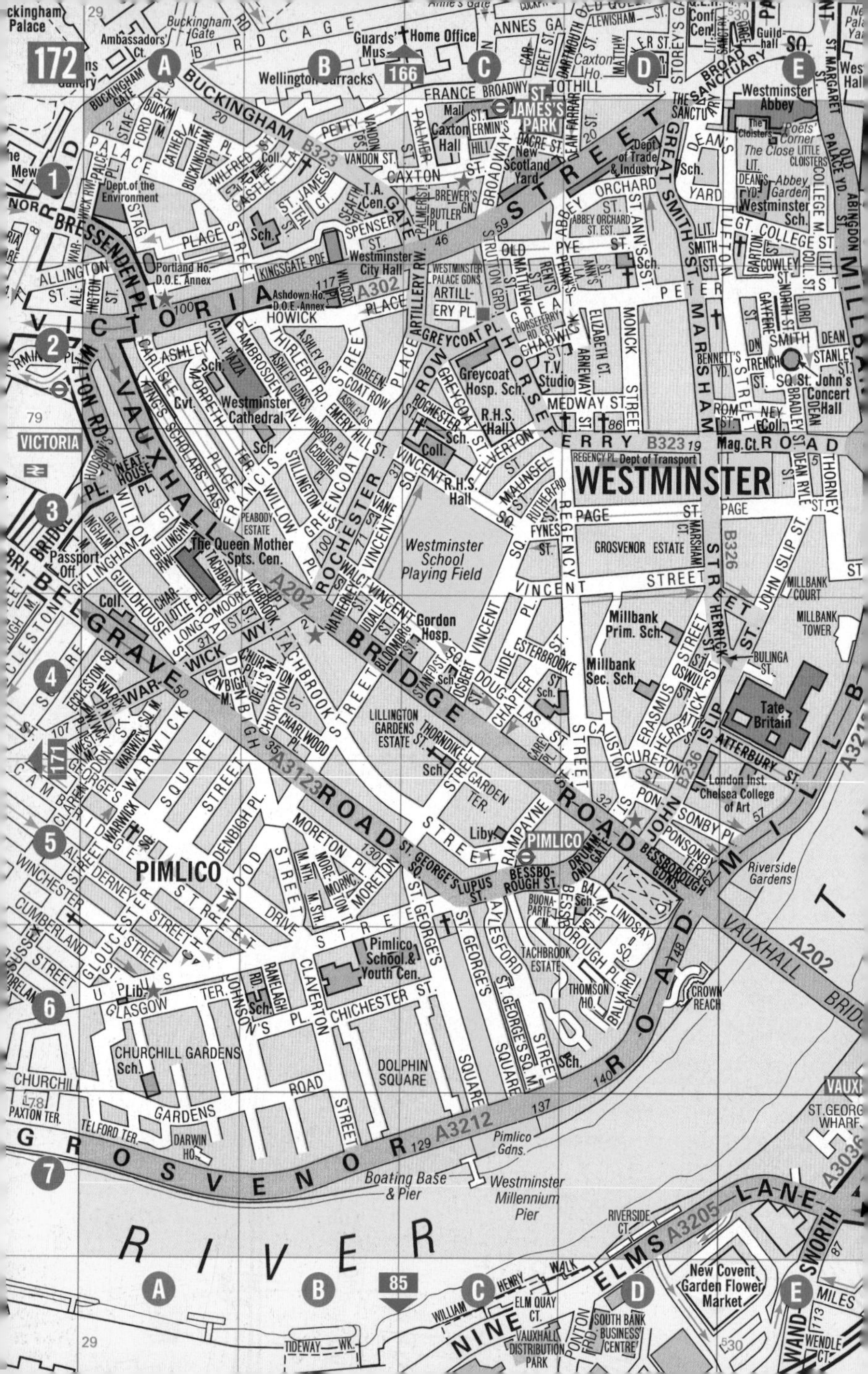

172
Buckingham Palace
Ambassadors' Ct.
Buckingham Gate
BIRDCAGE
Guards' Mus.
Home Office
166
ANNES GA.
LEWISHAM ST.
DARTMOUTH ST.
CARTERET ST.
Caxton Ho.
Guild-hall
BROAD SANCTUARY
SQ.
ST. MARGARET ST.
Wellington Barracks
BUCKINGHAM GATE
BUCKINGHAM
FRANCE BROADWY
TOTHILL
ST. JAMES'S PARK
Mall
Caxton Hall
ST. ERMIN'S HILL
PETTY FRANCE
VANDON ST.
PALMER ST.
DACRE ST.
New Scotland Yard
DEAN FARRAR ST.
THE SANCTUARY
Westminster Abbey
The Cloisters
Poets' Corner
The Close
LITTLE CLOISTERS
Dept. of Trade & Industry
GREAT SMITH ST.
DEAN'S YARD
Sch.
PALACE PL.
STAFFORD PL.
BUCKINGHAM M.
CATHERINE PL.
BUCKINGHAM PL.
WILFRED ST.
CASTLE LA.
Coll.
B323
CAXTON ST.
BREWER'S GN.
BROADWAY
STREET
ABBEY ORCHARD ST.
ABBEY ORCHARD ST. EST.
ST. ANN'S ST.
Abbey Garden
Westminster Sch.
OLD PALACE YD.
ABINGDON ST.
Dept. of the Environment
STAG PLACE
ST. JAMES'S CT.
T.A. Cen.
SEAFORTH PL.
SPENSER ST.
BUTLER PL.
PALMER ST.
CAXTON GATE
46
59
OLD PYE ST.
PERKIN'S RENTS
ST. ANN'S LA.
GT. COLLEGE ST.
COWLEY ST.
BARTON ST.
COLLEGE M.
NORTH ST.
LORD NORTH ST.
MILLBANK
BRESSENDEN PL.
ALLINGTON ST.
Portland Ho. D.O.E. Annex
KINGSGATE PDE.
Westminster City Hall
117
WILCOX PL.
A302
WESTMINSTER PALACE GDNS.
ARTILLERY PL.
ARTILLERY RW.
STRUTTON GRD.
PETER ST.
SMITH SQ.
GAYFERE ST.
DEAN TRENCH ST.
St. John's Concert Hall
VICTORIA
100
Ashdown Ho. D.O.E. Annex
HOWICK PLACE
GREYCOAT PL.
HORSEFERRY RD. EST.
CHADWICK ST.
ELIZABETH CT.
MONCK ST.
MARSHAM ST.
BENNETT'S YD.
STANLEY ST.
WILTON RD.
ASHLEY PL.
CARLISLE PL.
CATH. PIAZZA
AMBROSDEN AV.
THIRLEBY RD.
ASHLEY GDNS.
STREET
GREENCOAT ROW
EMERY HILL ST.
ROCHESTER ROW
Greycoat Hosp. Sch.
T.V. Studio
ARNEWAY
MEDWAY ST.
86
ROMNEY ST.
Coll.
BRADLEY ST.
Mag.Ct.
79
VAUXHALL
KING'S SCHOLARS PAS.
Cvt.
MORPETH TER.
Westminster Cathedral
Sch.
WINDSOR PL.
COBURG CL.
STILLINGTON ST.
ROCHESTER ST.
R.H.S. Hall
ELVERTON ST.
HORSEFERRY ROAD
B323
19
REGENCY PL.
Dept of Transport
WESTMINSTER
DEAN RYLE ST.
THORNEY ST.
HUDSON'S PL.
NEATHOUSE PL.
FRANCIS ST.
WILLOW PL.
GREENCOAT PL.
VANE ST.
VINCENT SQ.
MAUNSEL ST.
RUTHERFORD ST.
PAGE ST.
WILTON RD.
GILLINGHAM ST.
PEABODY ESTATE
The Queen Mother Spts. Cen.
TACHBROOK ST.
VINCENT ST.
Westminster School Playing Field
FYNES ST.
REGENCY ST.
GROSVENOR ESTATE
MARSHAM CT.
B326
JOHN ISLIP ST.
MILLBANK COURT
Passport Off.
BRIDGE PL.
GILLINGHAM ST.
GUILDHOUSE ST.
CHARLOTTE PL.
LONG MOORE ST.
Coll.
A202
WALCOTT ST.
HATHERLEY ST.
UDALL ST.
VINCENT ST.
Gordon Hosp.
VINCENT ST.
HIDE PL.
ESTERBROOKE ST.
Millbank Prim. Sch.
Millbank Sec. Sch.
HERRICK ST.
BULINGA ST.
MILLBANK TOWER
ECCLESTON SQ.
WARWICK WAY
BELGRAVE ROAD
WICK
TACHBROOK ST.
BRIDGE
BLOOMBURG ST.
STANFORD ST.
OSBERT ST.
DOUGLAS ST.
CHAPTER ST.
Sch.
ERASMUS ST.
OSWULF ST.
Tate Britain
50
37
DENBIGH ST.
CHURTON PL.
CHARLWOOD PL.
LILLINGTON GARDENS ESTATE
THORNDIKE ST.
Sch.
CAREY PL.
CAUSTON ST.
CURETON ST.
ATTERBURY ST.
ISLIP ST.
B236
London Inst. Chelsea College of Art
107
WARWICK SQ.
WARWICK SQUARE
ST. GEORGE'S DRIVE
171
CAMBRIDGE ST.
35
A3123
ROAD
GARDEN TER.
RAMPAYNE ST.
Liby.
PIMLICO
JOHN ISLIP ST.
PONSONBY PL.
PONSONBY TER.
57
Riverside Gardens
A3212
CLAREVILLE ST.
WARWICK SQ.
DENBIGH PL.
STREET
MORETON PL.
130
MORETON ST.
ST. GEORGE'S SQ.
LUPUS ST.
BESSBOROUGH ST.
DRUMMOND GATE
BESSBOROUGH GDNS.
VAUXHALL BRIDGE ROAD
VAUXHALL BRIDGE
A202
ALDERNEY ST.
WINCHESTER ST.
CUMBERLAND ST.
SUSSEX ST.
PIMLICO
CHARLWOOD ST.
GLOUCESTER ST.
CHARLWOOD
DRIVE
BUONAPARTE M.
BESSBOROUGH PL.
LINDSAY SQ.
TACHBROOK ESTATE
148
Pimlico School & Youth Cen.
CLAVERTON ST.
ST. GEORGE'S SQUARE
AYLESFORD ST.
ST. GEORGE'S SQ. M.
CROWN REACH
LUPUS ST.
Lib.
GLASGOW TER.
JOHNSON'S PL.
RANELAGH RD.
Sch.
CHICHESTER ST.
THOMSON HO.
BALVAIRD PL.
6
CHURCHILL GARDENS
Sch.
DOLPHIN SQUARE
ROAD
Sch.
140
CHURCHILL GARDENS
PAXTON TER.
TELFORD TER.
DARWIN HO.
137
129
A3212
GROSVENOR ROAD
Pimlico Gdns.
VAUXHALL
ST. GEORGE WHARF
Boating Base & Pier
Westminster Millennium Pier
RIVERSIDE CT.
LANE
A3205
A3036
RIVER
85
HENRY WALK
NINE ELMS
WILLIAM
ELM QUAY CT.
PONTON RD.
SOUTH BANK BUSINESS CENTRE
VAUXHALL DISTRIBUTION PARK
New Covent Garden Flower Market
WANDSWORTH
87
MILES
WENDLE CT.
TIDEWAY WK.
29
530
A B C D E
1 2 3 4 5 6 7

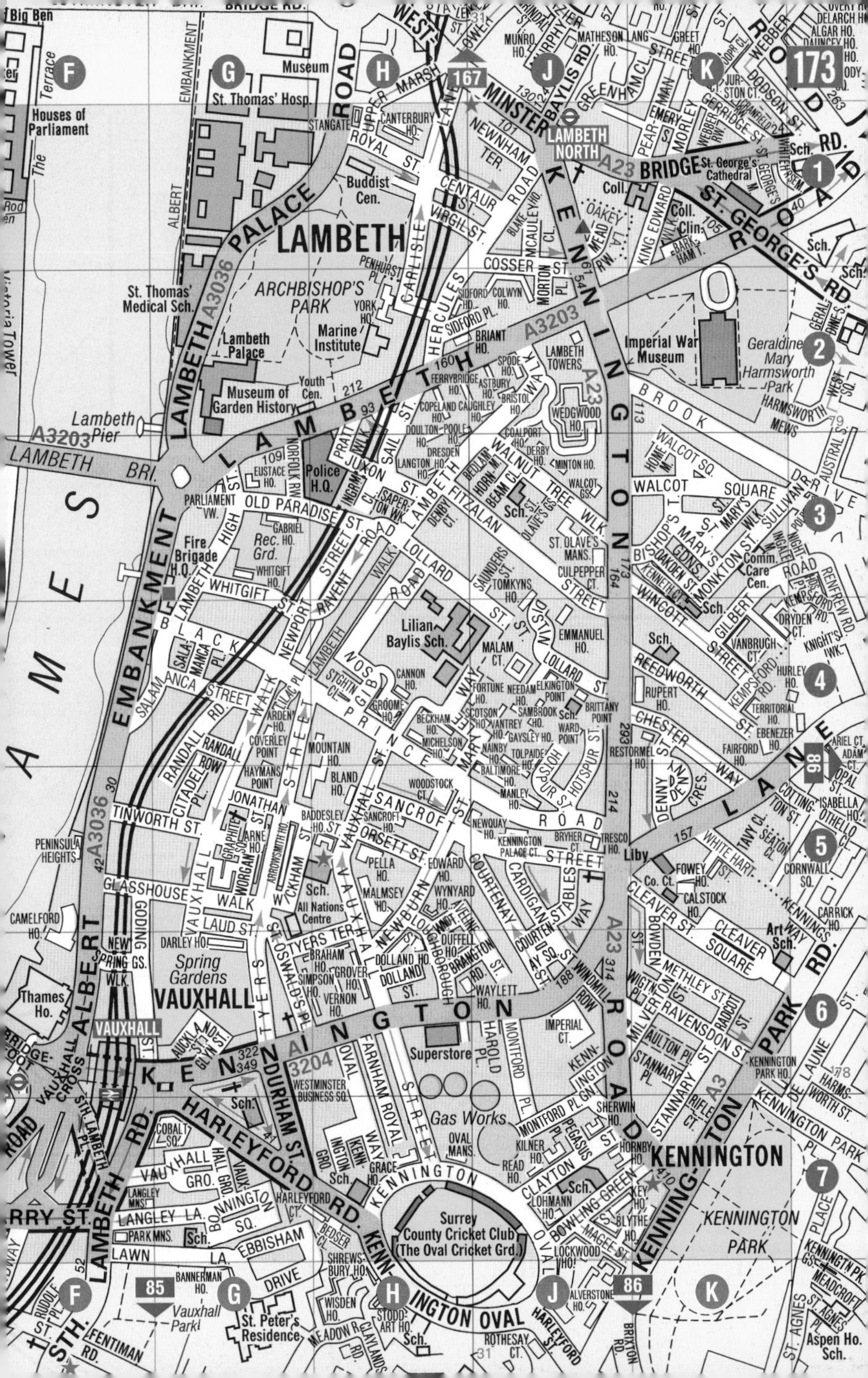
Big Ben
Houses of Parliament
St. Thomas' Hosp.
Museum
LAMBETH
ARCHBISHOP'S PARK
St. Thomas' Medical Sch.
Lambeth Palace
Museum of Garden History
Lambeth Pier
Marine Institute
Buddist Cen.
Youth Cen.
LAMBETH NORTH
St. George's Cathedral
Imperial War Museum
Geraldine Mary Harmsworth Park
LAMBETH TOWERS
WEDGWOOD HO.
Police H.Q.
Fire Brigade H.Q.
Rec. Grd.
Lilian Baylis Sch.
Comm. Care Cen.
Spring Gardens
VAUXHALL
Thames Ho.
PENINSULA HEIGHTS
All Nations Centre
Superstore
Gas Works
WESTMINSTER BUSINESS SQ.
Surrey County Cricket Club (The Oval Cricket Grd.)
KENNINGTON
KENNINGTON PARK
Vauxhall Park
St. Peter's Residence
Art Sch.
Liby.
THAMES
LAMBETH BRIDGE
ALBERT EMBANKMENT
LAMBETH PALACE ROAD
LAMBETH ROAD
KENNINGTON ROAD
KENNINGTON LANE
KENNINGTON OVAL
KENNINGTON PARK ROAD
HARLEYFORD RD.
DURHAM ST.
VAUXHALL WALK
BLACK PRINCE ROAD
WESTMINSTER BRIDGE ROAD
ST. GEORGE'S RD.
BROOK DRIVE
WALCOT SQUARE
CLEAVER SQUARE
A3203
A3036
A23
A3204
A3
85
86
167
F
G
H
J
K
1
2
3
4
5
6
7

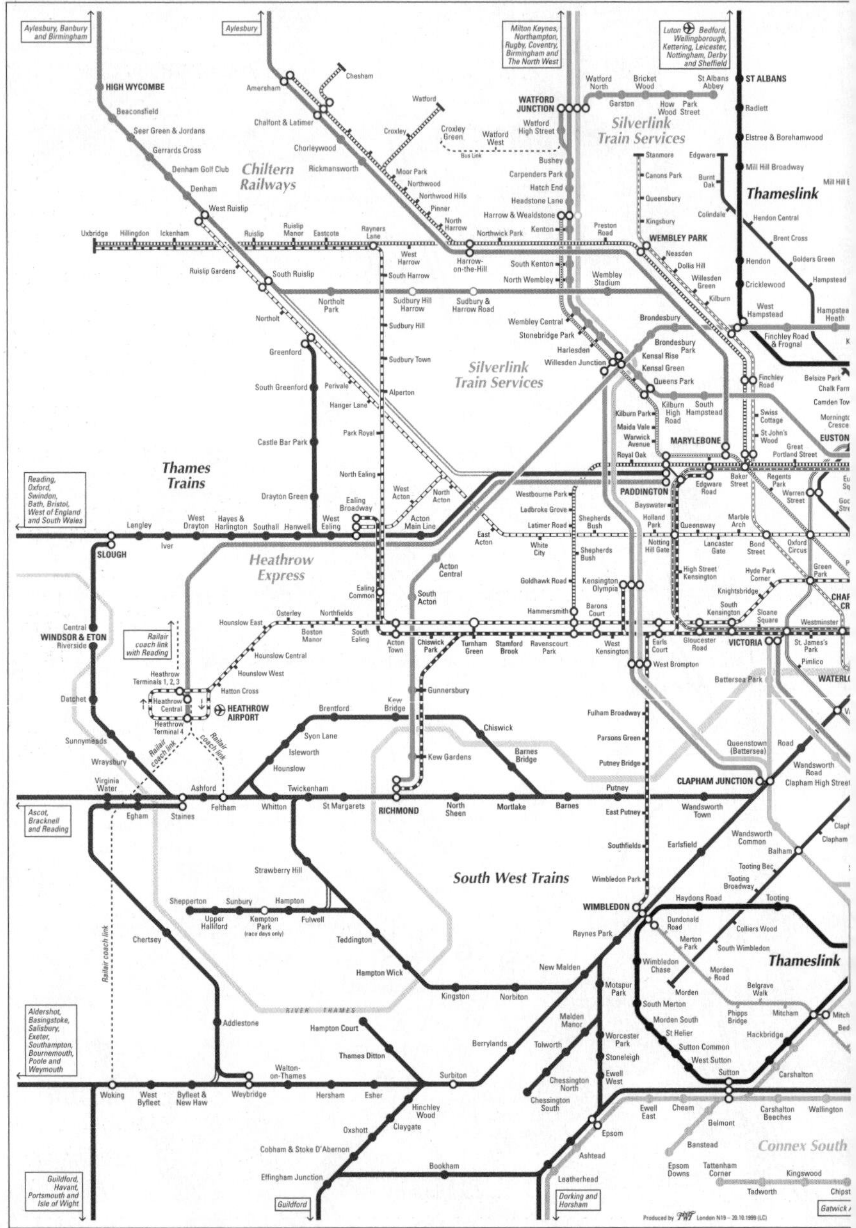

Aylesbury, Banbury and Birmingham
Aylesbury
Milton Keynes, Northampton, Rugby, Coventry, Birmingham and The North West
Luton Bedford, Wellingborough, Kettering, Leicester, Nottingham, Derby and Sheffield
HIGH WYCOMBE
Beaconsfield
Seer Green & Jordans
Gerrards Cross
Denham Golf Club
Denham
West Ruislip
Chiltern Railways
Amersham
Chesham
Chalfont & Latimer
Chorleywood
Rickmansworth
Watford
Croxley
Croxley Green
Watford West
Bus Link
Moor Park
Northwood
Northwood Hills
Pinner
North Harrow
WATFORD JUNCTION
Watford High Street
Watford North
Garston
Bricket Wood
How Wood
Park Street
St Albans Abbey
Silverlink Train Services
ST ALBANS
Radlett
Elstree & Borehamwood
Mill Hill Broadway
Thameslink
Bushey
Carpenders Park
Hatch End
Headstone Lane
Harrow & Wealdstone
Kenton
Stanmore
Canons Park
Queensbury
Kingsbury
Edgware
Burnt Oak
Colindale
Hendon Central
Brent Cross
Golders Green
Hendon
Cricklewood
Hampstead
Uxbridge
Hillingdon
Ickenham
Ruislip
Ruislip Manor
Eastcote
Rayners Lane
West Harrow
Harrow-on-the-Hill
Northwick Park
Preston Road
WEMBLEY PARK
Neasden
Dollis Hill
Willesden Green
Kilburn
Ruislip Gardens
South Ruislip
South Harrow
South Kenton
North Wembley
Wembley Stadium
Northolt Park
Sudbury Hill Harrow
Sudbury & Harrow Road
Northolt
Sudbury Hill
Wembley Central
Stonebridge Park
Harlesden
Willesden Junction
Brondesbury
Brondesbury Park
Kensal Rise
Kensal Green
Queens Park
West Hampstead
Finchley Road & Frognal
Hampstead Heath
Greenford
Sudbury Town
South Greenford
Perivale
Hanger Lane
Alperton
Silverlink Train Services
Finchley Road
Belsize Park
Chalk Farm
Camden Town
Mornington Crescent
Kilburn Park
Kilburn High Road
South Hampstead
Swiss Cottage
St John's Wood
Maida Vale
Warwick Avenue
MARYLEBONE
EUSTON
Great Portland Street
Park Royal
Castle Bar Park
Royal Oak
Thames Trains
North Ealing
Baker Street
Regents Park
Reading, Oxford, Swindon, Bath, Bristol, West of England and South Wales
Drayton Green
West Acton
North Acton
Westbourne Park
PADDINGTON
Edgware Road
Warren Street
Ealing Broadway
Ladbroke Grove
Bayswater
Latimer Road
Shepherds Bush
Holland Park
Queensway
Marble Arch
Langley
West Drayton
Hayes & Harlington
Southall
Hanwell
West Ealing
Acton Main Line
East Acton
White City
Notting Hill Gate
Lancaster Gate
Bond Street
Oxford Circus
SLOUGH
Iver
Heathrow Express
Acton Central
Shepherds Bush
Goldhawk Road
Kensington Olympia
High Street Kensington
Hyde Park Corner
Green Park
Knightsbridge
Ealing Common
South Acton
Hammersmith
Barons Court
South Kensington
Sloane Square
Westminster
Central
WINDSOR & ETON
Riverside
Hounslow East
Osterley
Northfields
Boston Manor
South Ealing
Acton Town
Chiswick Park
Turnham Green
Stamford Brook
Ravenscourt Park
West Kensington
Earls Court
Gloucester Road
VICTORIA
St James's Park
Pimlico
Railair coach link with Reading
Hounslow Central
Hounslow West
Heathrow Terminals 1, 2, 3
Hatton Cross
West Brompton
Battersea Park
Datchet
Heathrow Central
Heathrow Terminal 4
HEATHROW AIRPORT
Brentford
Kew Bridge
Gunnersbury
Fulham Broadway
Sunnymeads
Syon Lane
Isleworth
Hounslow
Chiswick
Barnes Bridge
Kew Gardens
Parsons Green
Putney Bridge
Queenstown Road (Battersea)
Wandsworth Road
Wraysbury
Railair coach link
Railair coach link
Virginia Water
Ashford
Twickenham
Putney
CLAPHAM JUNCTION
Clapham High Street
Egham
Staines
Feltham
Whitton
St Margarets
RICHMOND
North Sheen
Mortlake
Barnes
East Putney
Wandsworth Town
Ascot, Bracknell and Reading
Wandsworth Common
Southfields
Earlsfield
Balham
Strawberry Hill
Tooting Bec
South West Trains
Wimbledon Park
Tooting Broadway
Shepperton
Sunbury
Hampton
Haydons Road
Tooting
Upper Halliford
Kempton Park (race days only)
Fulwell
WIMBLEDON
Dundonald Road
Colliers Wood
Railair coach link
Chertsey
Teddington
Raynes Park
Merton Park
South Wimbledon
Thameslink
Hampton Wick
New Malden
Wimbledon Chase
Morden Road
Morden
Kingston
Norbiton
Motspur Park
South Merton
Belgrave Walk
RIVER THAMES
Aldershot, Basingstoke, Salisbury, Exeter, Southampton, Bournemouth, Poole and Weymouth
Addlestone
Hampton Court
Malden Manor
Morden South
Phipps Bridge
Mitcham
Thames Ditton
Berrylands
Tolworth
Worcester Park
St Helier
Hackbridge
Stoneleigh
Sutton Common
Walton-on-Thames
West Sutton
Sutton
Carshalton
Woking
West Byfleet
Byfleet & New Haw
Weybridge
Hersham
Esher
Surbiton
Chessington North
Ewell West
Hinchley Wood
Chessington South
Ewell East
Cheam
Carshalton Beeches
Wallington
Claygate
Belmont
Oxshott
Epsom
Cobham & Stoke D'Abernon
Banstead
Connex South
Ashtead
Bookham
Epsom Downs
Tattenham Corner
Kingswood
Effingham Junction
Leatherhead
Tadworth
Guildford, Havant, Portsmouth and Isle of Wight
Guildford
Dorking and Horsham
Produced by PWT London N19 – 20.10.1999 (LC)

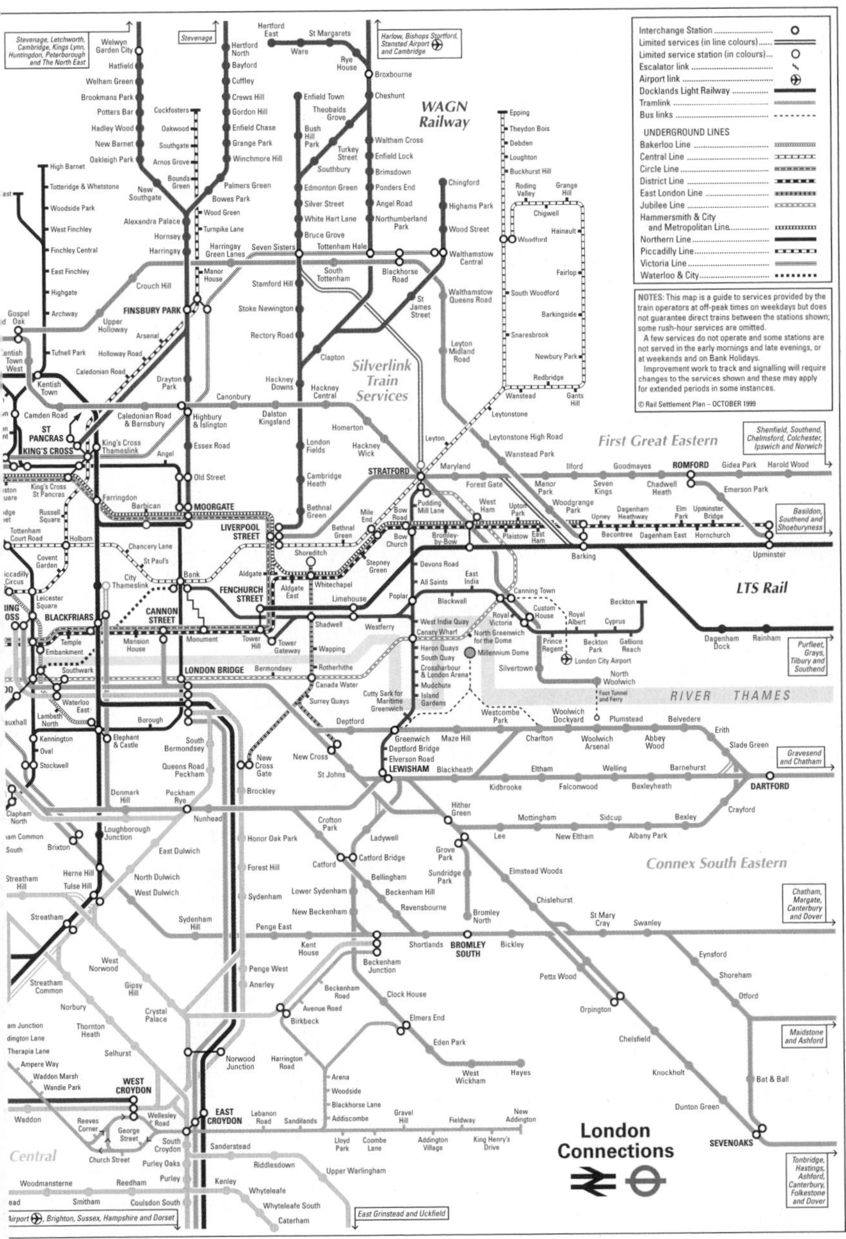

Interchange Station
Limited services (in line colours)
Limited service station (in colours)
Escalator link
Airport link
Docklands Light Railway
Tramlink
Bus links
UNDERGROUND LINES
Bakerloo Line
Central Line
Circle Line
District Line
East London Line
Jubilee Line
Hammersmith & City and Metropolitan Line
Northern Line
Piccadilly Line
Victoria Line
Waterloo & City
NOTES: This map is a guide to services provided by the train operators at off-peak times on weekdays but does not guarantee direct trains between the stations shown; some rush-hour services are omitted.
A few services do not operate and some stations are not served in the early mornings and late evenings, or at weekends and on Bank Holidays.
Improvement work to track and signalling will require changes to the services shown and these may apply for extended periods in some instances.
© Rail Settlement Plan – OCTOBER 1999
Stevenage, Letchworth, Cambridge, Kings Lynn, Huntingdon, Peterborough and The North East
Stevenage
Harlow, Bishops Stortford, Stansted Airport and Cambridge
WAGN Railway
Silverlink Train Services
First Great Eastern
LTS Rail
Connex South Eastern
Central
RIVER THAMES
Shenfield, Southend, Chelmsford, Colchester, Ipswich and Norwich
Basildon, Southend and Shoeburyness
Purfleet, Grays, Tilbury and Southend
Gravesend and Chatham
Chatham, Margate, Canterbury and Dover
Maidstone and Ashford
Tonbridge, Hastings, Ashford, Canterbury, Folkestone and Dover
East Grinstead and Uckfield
Airport, Brighton, Sussex, Hampshire and Dorset
Welwyn Garden City
Hatfield
Welham Green
Brookmans Park
Potters Bar
Hadley Wood
New Barnet
Oakleigh Park
High Barnet
Totteridge & Whetstone
Woodside Park
West Finchley
Finchley Central
East Finchley
Highgate
Archway
Tufnell Park
Kentish Town
Kentish Town West
Gospel Oak
Camden Road
Cockfosters
Oakwood
Southgate
Arnos Grove
Bounds Green
New Southgate
Alexandra Palace
Hornsey
Harringay
Wood Green
Turnpike Lane
Manor House
Harringay Green Lanes
Crouch Hill
Upper Holloway
FINSBURY PARK
Arsenal
Holloway Road
Caledonian Road
Drayton Park
Hertford North
Bayford
Cuffley
Crews Hill
Gordon Hill
Enfield Chase
Grange Park
Winchmore Hill
Palmers Green
Bowes Park
Hertford East
St Margarets
Ware
Rye House
Broxbourne
Cheshunt
Waltham Cross
Enfield Lock
Brimsdown
Ponders End
Angel Road
Northumberland Park
Tottenham Hale
Enfield Town
Theobalds Grove
Bush Hill Park
Turkey Street
Southbury
Edmonton Green
Silver Street
White Hart Lane
Bruce Grove
Seven Sisters
South Tottenham
Stamford Hill
Stoke Newington
Rectory Road
Hackney Downs
Clapton
Blackhorse Road
St James Street
Chingford
Highams Park
Wood Street
Walthamstow Central
Walthamstow Queens Road
Leyton Midland Road
Epping
Theydon Bois
Debden
Loughton
Buckhurst Hill
Roding Valley
Grange Hill
Chigwell
Hainault
Woodford
Fairlop
South Woodford
Barkingside
Snaresbrook
Newbury Park
Redbridge
Wanstead
Gants Hill
Leytonstone
Leytonstone High Road
Wanstead Park
Leyton
Canonbury
Highbury & Islington
Dalston Kingsland
Hackney Central
Homerton
Hackney Wick
London Fields
Cambridge Heath
Bethnal Green
Caledonian Road & Barnsbury
ST PANCRAS
KING'S CROSS
King's Cross Thameslink
Angel
Essex Road
Old Street
MOORGATE
Barbican
Farringdon
King's Cross St Pancras
Russell Square
Tottenham Court Road
Holborn
Chancery Lane
St Paul's
Covent Garden
Leicester Square
City Thameslink
Bank
LIVERPOOL STREET
Aldgate
Aldgate East
FENCHURCH STREET
Shoreditch
Whitechapel
Bethnal Green
Mile End
Stepney Green
Bow Road
Bow Church
Pudding Mill Lane
Bromley-by-Bow
STRATFORD
Maryland
Forest Gate
West Ham
Upton Park
Plaistow
East Ham
Manor Park
Ilford
Seven Kings
Goodmayes
Chadwell Heath
ROMFORD
Gidea Park
Harold Wood
Emerson Park
Woodgrange Park
Upney
Dagenham Heathway
Elm Park
Upminster Bridge
Becontree
Dagenham East
Hornchurch
Barking
Upminster
Devons Road
All Saints
East India
Canning Town
Custom House
Royal Victoria
Royal Albert
Beckton
Cyprus
Gallions Reach
Beckton Park
Prince Regent
London City Airport
Blackwall
Poplar
Limehouse
Westferry
West India Quay
Canary Wharf
Heron Quays
South Quay
Crossharbour & London Arena
Mudchute
Island Gardens
North Greenwich for the Dome
Millennium Dome
Silvertown
North Woolwich
Foot Tunnel and Ferry
Woolwich Dockyard
Westcombe Park
Plumstead
Belvedere
Erith
Slade Green
Dagenham Dock
Rainham
Shadwell
Wapping
Rotherhithe
Canada Water
Surrey Quays
Tower Hill
Tower Gateway
Monument
CANNON STREET
Mansion House
BLACKFRIARS
Temple
Embankment
Southwark
Waterloo East
Lambeth North
Kennington
Oval
Stockwell
Elephant & Castle
Borough
LONDON BRIDGE
Bermondsey
South Bermondsey
Queens Road Peckham
New Cross Gate
New Cross
St Johns
Deptford
Cutty Sark for Maritime Greenwich
Greenwich
Deptford Bridge
Elverson Road
LEWISHAM
Maze Hill
Blackheath
Charlton
Woolwich Arsenal
Abbey Wood
Eltham
Welling
Barnehurst
Kidbrooke
Falconwood
Bexleyheath
DARTFORD
Crayford
Hither Green
Mottingham
Sidcup
Bexley
Lee
New Eltham
Albany Park
Brockley
Crofton Park
Ladywell
Catford
Catford Bridge
Grove Park
Sundridge Park
Bromley North
Elmstead Woods
Chislehurst
St Mary Cray
Swanley
Eynsford
Shoreham
Otford
Bellingham
Beckenham Hill
Ravensbourne
Lower Sydenham
New Beckenham
Honor Oak Park
Forest Hill
Sydenham
Penge East
Kent House
Shortlands
BROMLEY SOUTH
Bickley
Beckenham Junction
Petts Wood
Orpington
Chelsfield
Knockholt
Dunton Green
SEVENOAKS
Bat & Ball
Denmark Hill
Peckham Rye
Nunhead
Loughborough Junction
Brixton
East Dulwich
North Dulwich
West Dulwich
Herne Hill
Tulse Hill
Sydenham Hill
Streatham
West Norwood
Gipsy Hill
Crystal Palace
Penge West
Anerley
Beckenham Road
Avenue Road
Birkbeck
Clock House
Elmers End
Eden Park
West Wickham
Hayes
Norwood Junction
Harrington Road
Arena
Woodside
Blackhorse Lane
Addiscombe
Streatham Common
Norbury
Thornton Heath
Selhurst
WEST CROYDON
EAST CROYDON
Wellesley Road
George Street
Reeves Corner
Church Street
Waddon
Lebanon Road
Sandilands
Lloyd Park
Coombe Lane
Gravel Hill
Addington Village
Fieldway
King Henry's Drive
New Addington
South Croydon
Sanderstead
Purley Oaks
Purley
Riddlesdown
Upper Warlingham
Kenley
Whyteleafe
Whyteleafe South
Caterham
Reedham
Coulsdon South
Smitham
Woodmansterne
Streatham Hill
Clapham North
Vauxhall
Ampere Way
Therapia Lane
Waddon Marsh
Wandle Park
London Connections

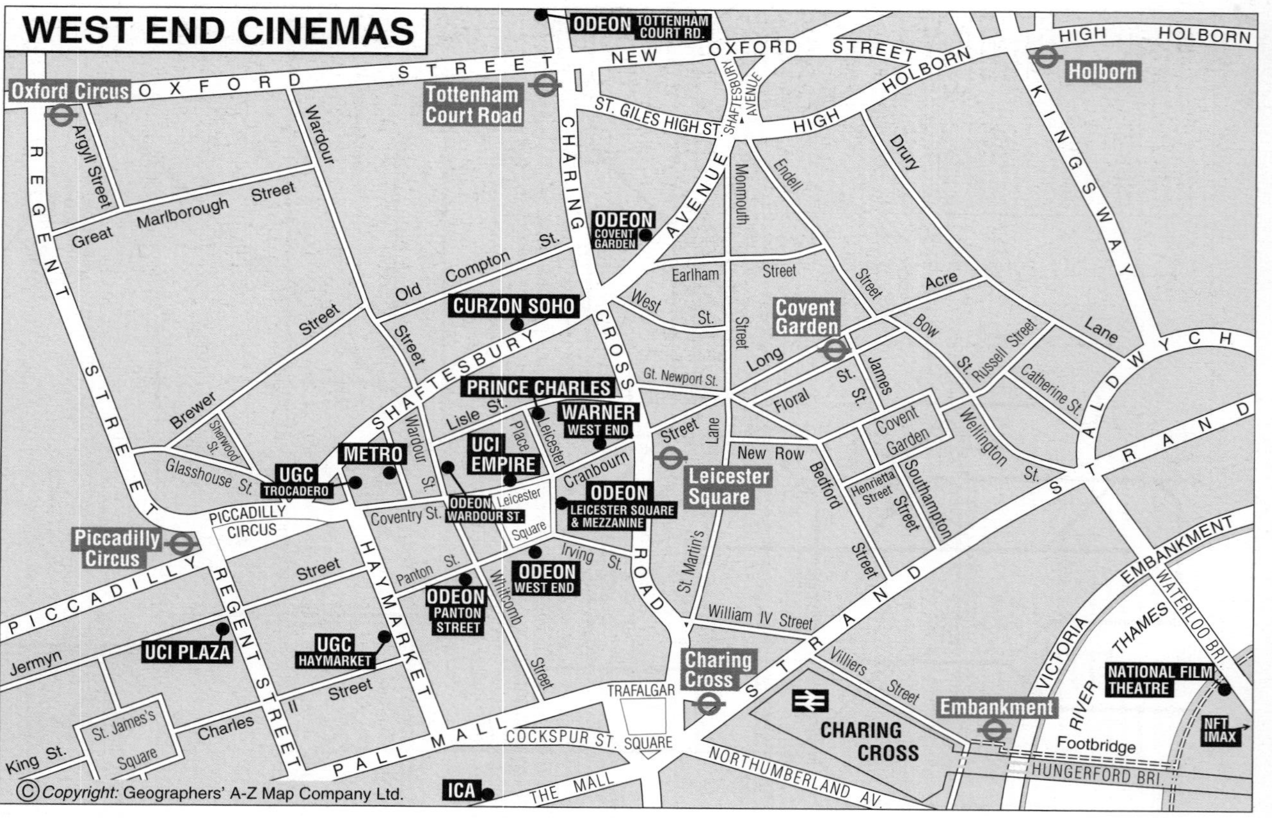
WEST END CINEMAS
ODEON TOTTENHAM COURT RD.
ODEON COVENT GARDEN
CURZON SOHO
PRINCE CHARLES
WARNER WEST END
UCI EMPIRE
METRO
UGC TROCADERO
ODEON WARDOUR ST.
ODEON LEICESTER SQUARE & MEZZANINE
ODEON WEST END
ODEON PANTON STREET
UGC HAYMARKET
UCI PLAZA
ICA
NATIONAL FILM THEATRE
NFT IMAX
Oxford Circus
Tottenham Court Road
Holborn
Covent Garden
Leicester Square
Piccadilly Circus
Charing Cross
Embankment
CHARING CROSS
OXFORD STREET
NEW OXFORD STREET
HIGH HOLBORN
KINGSWAY
ALDWYCH
STRAND
CHARING CROSS ROAD
SHAFTESBURY AVENUE
ST. GILES HIGH ST.
REGENT STREET
PICCADILLY
PICCADILLY CIRCUS
HAYMARKET
PALL MALL
COCKSPUR ST.
TRAFALGAR SQUARE
NORTHUMBERLAND AV.
THE MALL
VICTORIA EMBANKMENT
RIVER THAMES
WATERLOO BRI.
HUNGERFORD BRI.
Footbridge
Argyll Street
Great Marlborough Street
Wardour Street
Old Compton St.
Brewer Street
Sherwood St.
Glasshouse St.
Lisle St.
Wardour St.
Leicester Place
Cranbourn
Leicester Square
Coventry St.
Panton St.
Irving St.
Whitcomb Street
Jermyn Street
Charles II Street
St. James's Square
King St.
Earlham Street
West St.
Gt. Newport St.
Monmouth Street
Endell Street
Drury Lane
Long Acre
Bow St.
Russell Street
Catherine St.
Floral St.
James St.
Covent Garden
Wellington St.
Henrietta Street
Southampton Street
Bedford Street
New Row
St. Martin's Lane
William IV Street
Villiers Street
© Copyright: Geographers' A-Z Map Company Ltd.

WEST END THEATRES

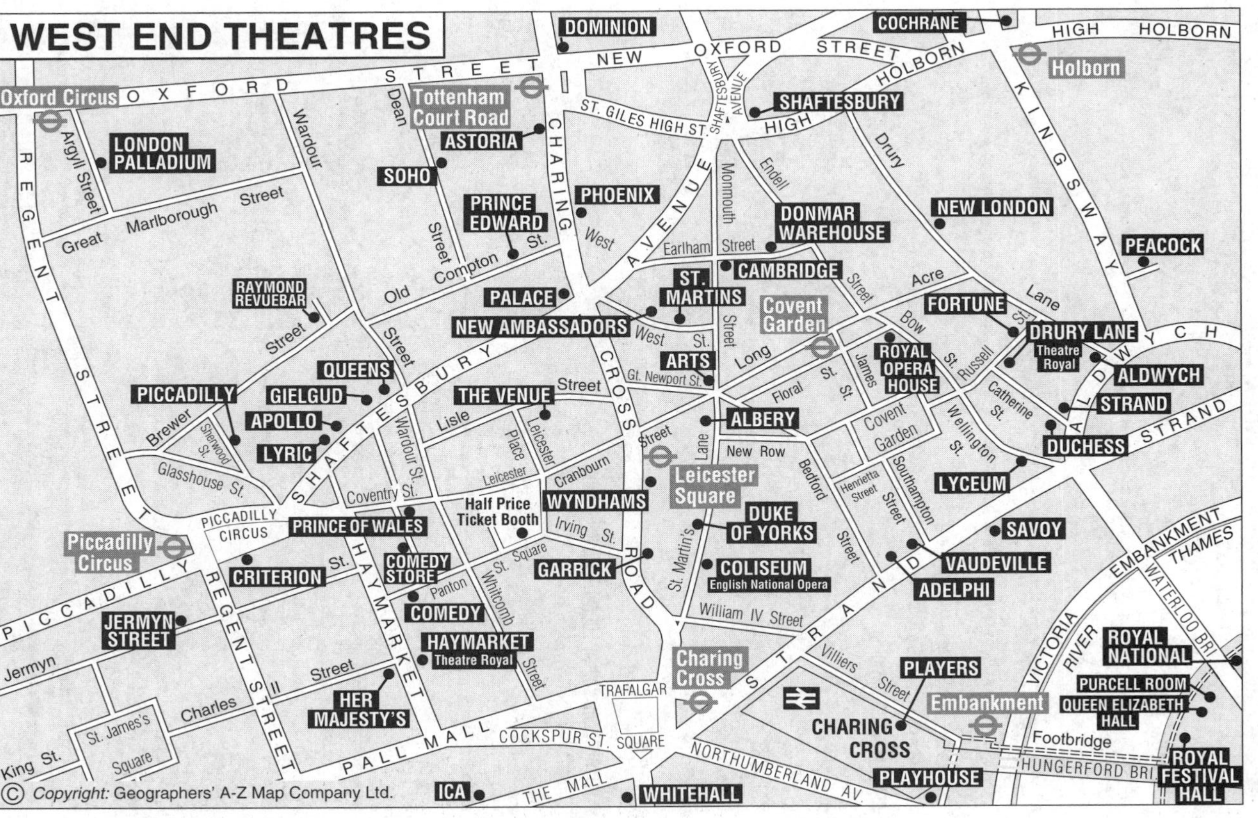

INDEX

Including Streets, Places & Areas, Industrial Estates, Selected Flats & Walkways,
Junction Names and Selected Places of Interest.

HOW TO USE THIS INDEX

1. Each street name is followed by its Postal District (or, if outside the London Postal Districts, by its Posttown or Postal Locality), and then by its map reference; e.g. Abbeville Rd. *SW4* ....6G **103** is in the South West 4 Postal District and is found in square 6G on page **103**. The page number being shown in bold type.

2. A strict alphabetical order is followed in which Av., Rd., St. etc. (though abbreviated) are read in full and as part of the street name; e.g. Abbotsmede Clo. appears after Abbots Mead but before Abbots Pk.

3. Streets and a selection of Subsidiary names not shown on the Maps, appear in this index in *Italics* with the thoroughfare to which it is connected shown in brackets; e.g. *Abbey Ct. NW8 ....2A **66** (off Abbey Rd.)*

4. Places and areas are shown in the index in **bold type** the map reference referring to the actual map square in which the town or area is located and not to the place name; e.g. **Abbey Wood....4C 92**

5. An example of a selected place of interest is ***Admiralty Arch....1H 85 (4D 166)***

6. Map references shown in brackets; e.g. Abbey Orchard St. *SW1* ....3H **85** (1C **172**) refer to entries that also appear on the large scale pages **158-173**.

GENERAL ABBREVIATIONS

All : Alley
App : Approach
Arc : Arcade
Av : Avenue
Bk : Back
Boulevd : Boulevard
Bri : Bridge
B'way : Broadway
Bldgs : Buildings
Bus : Business
Cvn : Caravan
Cen : Centre
Chu : Church
Chyd : Churchyard
Circ : Circle
Cir : Circus
Clo : Close
Comn : Common
Cotts : Cottages
Ct : Court
Cres : Crescent
Cft : Croft
Dri : Drive
E : East
Embkmt : Embankment
Est : Estate
Fld : Field
Gdns : Gardens
Gth : Garth
Ga : Gate
Gt : Great
Grn : Green
Gro : Grove
Ho : House
Ind : Industrial
Info : Information
Junct : Junction
La : Lane
Lit : Little
Lwr : Lower
Mc : Mac
Mnr : Manor
Mans : Mansions
Mkt : Market
Mdw : Meadow
M : Mews
Mt : Mount
Mus : Museum
N : North
Pal : Palace
Pde : Parade
Pk : Park
Pas : Passage
Pl : Place
Quad : Quadrant
Res : Residential
Ri : Rise
Rd : Road
Shop : Shopping
S : South
Sq : Square
Sta : Station
St : Street
Ter : Terrace
Trad : Trading
Up : Upper
Va : Vale
Vw : View
Vs : Villas
Vis : Visitors
Wlk : Walk
W : West
Yd : Yard

POSTTOWN AND POSTAL LOCALITY ABBREVIATIONS

Ashf : Ashford
Bark : Barking
B'side : Barkingside
B'hurst : Barnehurst
Barn : Barnet
Beck : Beckenham
Bedd : Beddington
Bedf : Bedfont
Belv : Belvedere
Bex : Bexley
Bexh : Bexleyheath
Borwd : Borehamwood
Bren : Brentford
Brim : Brimsdown
Brom : Bromley
Buck H : Buckhurst Hill
Bush : Bushey
Bus H : Bushey Heath
Cars : Carshalton
Chad H : Chadwell Heath
Cheam : Cheam
Cher : Chertsey
Chess : Chessington
Chig : Chigwell
Chst : Chislehurst
Clay : Claygate
Cockf : Cockfosters
Col R : Collier Row
Cran : Cranford
Cray : Crayford
Croy : Croydon
Dag : Dagenham
Dart : Dartford
Dit H : Ditton Hill
E Barn : East Barnet
Eastc : Eastcote
E Mol : East Molesey
Edgw : Edgware
Els : Elstree
Enf : Enfield
Eps : Epsom
Eri : Erith
Esh : Esher
Ewe : Ewell
Farnb : Farnborough
Felt : Feltham
Frog : Frogmore
Gnfd : Greenford
Hack : Hackbridge
Ham : Ham
Hamp : Hampton
Hamp H : Hampton Hill
Hamp W : Hampton Wick
Hanw : Hanworth
Hare : Harefield
Harm : Harmondsworth
Harr : Harrow
Har W : Harrow Weald
H End : Hatch End
Hayes : Hayes (Kent)
Hay : Hayes (Middlesex)
H'row : Heathrow
H'row A : London Heathrow Airport
High Bar : High Barnet
Hil : Hillingdon
Hin W : Hinchley Wood
Houn : Hounslow
Ick : Ickenham
Ilf : Ilford
Iswth : Isleworth
Kent : Kenton
Kes : Keston
Kew : Kew
King T : Kingston Upon Thames
L Hth : Little Heath
Lou : Loughton
Mitc : Mitcham
Mit J : Mitcham Junction
Mord : Morden
New Ad : New Addington
New Bar : New Barnet
N Mald : New Malden
N Har : North Harrow
N'holt : Northolt
N Hth : Northumberland Heath
N'wd : Northwood
Orp : Orpington
Pet W : Petts Wood
Pinn : Pinner
Pot B : Potters Bar
Purl : Purley
Rain : Rainham
Rich : Richmond
Ridg : Ridgeway, The
Romf : Romford
Ruis : Ruislip
Rush G : Rush Green
St P : St Pauls Cray
Shep : Shepperton
Short : Shortlands
S'hall : Southall
S Croy : South Croydon
S Harr : South Harrow
S Ruis : South Ruislip
Sidc : Sidcup
Stai : Staines
Stan : Stanmore
Stanw : Stanwell
S'leigh : Stoneleigh
Sun : Sunbury-On-Thames
Surb : Surbiton
Sutt : Sutton
Swan : Swanley
Tedd : Teddington
Th Dit : Thames Ditton
T Hth : Thornton Heath
Twic : Twickenham
Uxb : Uxbridge
Wall : Wallington
Wal A : Waltham Abbey
W on T : Walton-on-Thames
Warl : Warlingham
W'stone : Wealdstone
Well : Welling
Wemb : Wembley
W Dray : West Drayton
W Ewe : West Ewell
W Mol : West Molesey
W W'ck : West Wickham
Wey : Weybridge
Whit : Whitton
Wfd G : Woodford Green
Wor Pk : Worcester Park

INDEX

O2 Centre. *NW3*. 6A **48**
101 Bus. Units. *SW11*. 3D **102**
198 Gallery. ***6B 104***
(off Railton Rd.)

Aaron Hill Rd. *E6*. 5E **72**
*Abady Ho. SW1 . . . 4H **85** (3D **172**)*
(off Page St.)
Abberley M. *SW4*. 3F **103**
Abbess Clo. *E6* 5C **72**
Abbess Clo. *SW2*. 1B **122**
Abbeville M. *SW4* 4H **103**
Abbeville Rd. *N8* 4H **31**
Abbeville Rd. *SW4*. 6G **103**
Abbey Av. *Wemb* 2E **62**
Abbey Bus. Cen.
SW8 . . . . 1G **103**
Abbey Clo. *Hay* 1K **77**
Abbey Clo. *N'holt* 3D **60**
Abbey Clo. *Pinn*. 3K **23**
*Abbey Ct. NW8 . . . . 2A **66***
(off Abbey Rd.)
*Abbey Ct. SE17 . . . . 5C **86***
(off Macleod St.)
Abbey Ct. *Hamp*. 7E **114**
Abbey Cres. *Belv*. 4G **93**
Abbeydale Ct. *E17* 3F **35**
*Abbeydale Ct. S'hall 6F **61***
(off Dormers Ri.)
Abbeydale Rd. *Wemb*. 1F **63**
Abbey Dri. *SW17*. 5E **120**
Abbey Est. *NW8* 1K **65**
Abbeyfield Clo. *Mitc*. 2C **138**
Abbeyfield Est. *SE16* 4J **87**

Abbeyfield Rd. *SE16* 4J 87 (in two parts)
Abbeyfields Clo. *NW10* 2G 63
Abbey Gdns. *NW8* 2A 66
Abbey Gdns. *SE16* 4G 87
Abbey Gdns. *W6* 6G 83
Abbey Gdns. *Chst* 1E 144
Abbey Gro. *SE2* 4B 92
Abbey Hill Rd. *Sidc* 2C 128
Abbey Ho. E15 2G 71 (off Baker's Row)
Abbey Ho. *NW8* 1A 158
Abbey Ind. Est. *Mitc* 5D 138
Abbey Ind. Est. *Wemb* 1F 63
Abbey La. *E15* 2E 70
Abbey La. *Beck* 7C 124
Abbey La. Commercial Est. *E15* 2G 71
Abbey Life Ct. *E16* 5K 71
Abbey Lodge. *NW8* 2D 158
Abbey M. *E17* 5C 34
Abbey Mt. *Belv* 5F 93
Abbey Orchard St. *SW1* 3H 85 (1C 172)
Abbey Orchard St. Est. *SW1* 3H 85 (1D 172) (in two parts)
Abbey Pde. SW19 7A 120 (off Merton High St.)
Abbey Pde. *W5* 3F 63
Abbey Pk. *Beck* 7C 124
Abbey Retail Pk. *Bark* 7F 55
Abbey Rd. *E15* 2F 71
Abbey Rd. *NW6 & NW8* 7K 47 (1A 158)
Abbey Rd. *NW10* 1H 63
Abbey Rd. *SW19* 7A 120
Abbey Rd. *Bark* 7F 55
Abbey Rd. *Belv* 4D 92
Abbey Rd. *Bexh* 4E 110
Abbey Rd. *Croy* 3B 152
Abbey Rd. *Enf* 5K 7
Abbey Rd. *Ilf* 5H 37
Abbey St. *E13* 4J 71
Abbey St. *SE1* 3E 86 (7H 169)
Abbey Ter. *SE2* 4C 92
Abbey Trad. Est. *SE26* 5B 124
Abbey Vw. *NW7* 3G 13
Abbey Wlk. *W Mol* 3F 133
Abbey Wharf Ind. Est. *Bark* 3H 73
Abbey Wood 4C 92
Abbey Wood Camping & Cvn. Site. *SE2* 4C 92
Abbey Wood Rd. *SE2* 4B 92
Abbot Ct. SW8 7J 85 (off Hartington Rd.)
Abbot Ho. E14 7D 70 (off Smythe St.)
Abbotsbury Clo. *E15* 2E 70
Abbotsbury Clo. *W14* 2G 83
Abbotsbury Gdns. *Pinn* 7A 24
Abbotsbury M. *SE15* 3J 105
Abbotsbury Rd. *W14* 2G 83
Abbotsbury Rd. *Brom* 2H 155
Abbotsbury Rd. *Mord* 5K 137
Abbots Clo. *Orp* 7G 145
Abbots Clo. *Ruis* 3B 42
Abbots Dri. *Harr* 2E 42
Abbotsford Av. *N15* 4C 32
Abbotsford Gdns. *Wfd G* 7D 20
Abbotsford Rd. *Ilf* 2A 56
Abbots Gdns. *N2* 4B 30
Abbots Grn. *Croy* 6K 153
Abbotshade Rd. *SE16* 1K 87
Abbotshall Av. *N14* 3B 16
Abbotshall Rd. *SE6* 1F 125
Abbot's Ho. W14 3H 83 (off St Mary Abbots Ter.)
Abbots La. *SE1* 1E 86 (5H 169)
Abbotsleigh Clo. *Sutt* 7K 149
Abbotsleigh Rd. *SW16* 4G 121
Abbots Mnr. *SW1* 4F 85 (5J 171)
Abbots Mead. *Rich* 4D 116
Abbotsmede Clo. *Twic* 2K 115
Abbots Pk. *SW2* 1A 122
Abbot's Pl. *NW6* 1K 65
Abbot's Rd. *E6* 1B 72
Abbots Rd. *Edgw* 7D 12
Abbots Ter. *N8* 6J 31
Abbotstone Rd. *SW15* 3E 100
Abbot St. *E8* 6F 51
Abbots Wlk. *W8* 3K 83
Abbotswell Rd. *SE4* 5B 106
Abbotswood Clo. *Belv* 3E 92
Abbotswood Gdns. *Ilf* 3D 36
Abbotswood Rd. *SE22* 4E 104
Abbotswood Rd. *SW16* 3H 121
Abbotswood Way. *Hay* 1K 77
Abbott Av. *SW20* 1F 137
Abbott Clo. *Hamp* 6C 114
Abbott Clo. *N'holt* 6D 42
Abbott Rd. *E14* 5E 70 (in two parts)
Abbotts Clo. *N1* 6C 50
Abbotts Clo. *SE28* 7C 74
Abbotts Clo. *Romf* 3H 39
Abbott's Clo. *Uxb* 5A 58
Abbotts Cres. *E4* 4A 20
Abbotts Cres. *Enf* 2G 7
Abbotts Dri. *Wemb* 2B 44
Abbotts Ho. SW1 5H 85 (6C 172) (off Aylesford St.)
Abbotts Pk. Rd. *E10* 7E 34
Abbotts Rd. *Mitc* 4G 139 (in two parts)
Abbotts Rd. *New Bar* 4E 4
Abbotts Rd. *S'hall* 1C 78
Abbotts Rd. *Sutt* 4G 149
Abbott's Wlk. *Bexh* 7D 92
Abbotts Wharf. E14 6C 70 (off Stainsby Pl.)
Abby Pk. Ind. Est. *Bark* 2G 73
Abchurch La. *EC4* 7D 68 (2F 169) (in two parts)
Abchurch Yd. *EC4* 7D 68 (2E 168)
Abdale Rd. *W12* 1D 82
Abel Ho. SE11 6A 86 (7K 173) (off Kennington Rd.)
Abenglen Ind. Est. *Hay* 2F 77
Aberavon Rd. *E3* 3A 70
Abercairn Rd. *SW16* 7G 121
Aberconway Rd. *Mord* 4K 137
Abercorn Clo. *NW7* 7B 14
Abercorn Clo. *NW8* 3A 66
Abercorn Commercial Cen. *Wemb* 1D 62
Abercorn Cres. *Harr* 1F 43
Abercorn Gdns. *Harr* 7D 26
Abercorn Gdns. *Romf* 6B 38
Abercorn Gro. *Ruis* 4F 23
Abercorn Ho. SE10 7D 88 (off Tarves Way)
Abercorn Mans. NW8 2A 66 (off Abercorn Pl.)
Abercorn M. *Rich* 4F 99
Abercorn Pl. *NW8* 3A 66
Abercorn Rd. *NW7* 7B 14
Abercorn Rd. *Stan* 7H 11
Abercorn Way. *SE1* 5G 87
Abercrombie Dri. *Enf* 1B 8
Abercrombie St. *SW11* 2C 102
Aberdale Ct. SE16 2K 87 (off Garter Way)
Aberdare Clo. *W Wick* 2E 154
Aberdare Gdns. *NW6* 7K 47
Aberdare Gdns. *NW7* 7A 14
Aberdare Rd. *Enf* 4D 8
Aberdeen Cotts. *Stan* 7H 11
Aberdeen Ct. W9 4A 66 (4A 158) (off Lanark Pl.)
Aberdeen La. *N5* 5C 50
Aberdeen Mans. WC1 4J 67 (3E 160) (off Kenton St.)
Aberdeen Pde. N18 5C 18 (off Aberdeen Rd.)
Aberdeen Pk. *N5* 5C 50
Aberdeen Pl. *NW8* 4B 66 (4A 158)
Aberdeen Rd. *N5* 4C 50
Aberdeen Rd. *N18* 5B 18 (in two parts)
Aberdeen Rd. *NW10* 5B 46
Aberdeen Rd. *Croy* 4C 152
Aberdeen Rd. *Harr* 2K 25
Aberdeen Sq. *E14* 1B 88
Aberdeen Ter. *SE3* 2F 107
Aberdeen Wharf. E1 1H 87 (off Wapping High St.)
Aberdour Rd. *Ilf* 3B 56
Aberdour St. *SE1* 4E 86
Aberfeldy Ho. *SE5* 7B 86 (in two parts)
Aberfeldy St. *E14* 5E 70 (in two parts)
Aberford Gdns. *SE18* 1C 108
Aberfoyle Rd. *SW16* 6H 121 (in two parts)
Abergeldie Rd. *SE12* 6K 107
Abernethy Rd. *SE13* 4G 107
Abersham Rd. *E8* 5F 51
Abery St. *SE18* 4J 91
Abingdon. W14 4H 83 (off Kensington Village)
Abingdon Clo. *NW1* 6H 49
Abingdon Clo. SE1 4F 87 (off Bushwood Dri.)
Abingdon Clo. *SW19* 6A 120
Abingdon Clo. *Uxb* 1B 58
Abingdon Ct. W8 3J 83 (off Abingdon Vs.)
Abingdon Gdns. *W8* 3J 83
Abingdon Ho. E2 4F 69 (3J 163) (off Boundary St.)
Abingdon Lodge. *W8* 3J 83
Abingdon Lodge. Brom 1H 143 (off Beckenham La.)
Abingdon Rd. *N3* 2A 30
Abingdon Rd. *SW16* 2J 139
Abingdon Rd. *W8* 3J 83
Abingdon St. *SW1* 3J 85 (1E 172)
Abingdon Vs. *W8* 3J 83
Abinger Clo. *Bark* 4A 56
Abinger Clo. *Brom* 3C 144
Abinger Clo. *New Ad* 6E 154
Abinger Clo. *Wall* 5J 151
Abinger Ct. *W5* 7C 62
Abinger Ct. *Wall* 5J 151
Abinger Gdns. *Iswth* 3J 97
Abinger Gro. *SE8* 6B 88
Abinger Ho. SE1 2D 86 (7E 168) (off Gt. Dover St.)
Abinger M. *W9* 4J 65
Abinger Rd. *W4* 3A 82
Ablett St. *SE16* 5J 87
Abney Gdns. *N16* 2F 51
Aboyne Dri. *SW20* 2C 136
Aboyne Rd. *NW10* 3A 46
Aboyne Rd. *SW17* 3B 120
Abridge Way. *Bark* 2B 74
Abyssinia Clo. *SW11* 4C 102
Abyssinia Ct. *N8* 5K 31
Abyssinia Rd. *SW11* 4C 102
Acacia Av. *N17* 7J 17
Acacia Av. *Bren* 7B 80
Acacia Av. *Hay* 6H 59
Acacia Av. *Ruis* 1J 41
Acacia Av. *Shep* 5C 130
Acacia Av. *Wemb* 5E 44
Acacia Av. *W Dray* 7B 58
Acacia Bus. Cen. *E11* 3G 53
Acacia Clo. *SE8* 4A 88
Acacia Clo. *SE20* 2G 141
Acacia Clo. *Orp* 5H 145
Acacia Clo. *Stan* 6D 10
Acacia Ct. *Harr* 5F 25
Acacia Dri. *Sutt* 1J 149
Acacia Gdns. *NW8* 2B 66
Acacia Gdns. *W Wick* 2E 154
Acacia Gro. *SE21* 2D 122
Acacia Gro. *N Mald* 3K 135
Acacia Ho. N22 1A 32 (off Douglas Rd.)
Acacia M. *W Dray* 6A 76
Acacia Pl. *NW8* 2B 66
Acacia Rd. *E11* 2G 53
Acacia Rd. *E17* 6A 34
Acacia Rd. *N22* 1A 32
Acacia Rd. *NW8* 2B 66
Acacia Rd. *SW16* 1J 139
Acacia Rd. *W3* 7J 63
Acacia Rd. *Beck* 3B 142
Acacia Rd. *Enf* 1J 7
Acacia Rd. *Hamp* 6E 114
Acacia Rd. *Mitc* 2E 138
Acacias, The. *Barn* 5G 5
Acacia Way. *Sidc* 1K 127
Academy Bldgs. *N1* 1G 163
Academy Ct. E2 3J 69 (off Kirkwall Pl.)
Academy Gdns. *Croy* 1F 153
Academy Gdns. *N'holt* 2B 60
Academy Ho. E3 5D 70 (off Violet Rd.)
Academy Pl. *SE18* 1D 108
Academy Rd. *SE18* 1D 108
Acanthus Dri. *SE1* 5G 87
Acanthus Rd. *SW11* 3E 102
Accommodation Rd. *NW11* 1H 47
Accommodation Rd. *Eps* 5C 148
A.C. Court. *Th Dit* 6A 134
Ace Pde. *Chess* 3E 146
Acer Av. *Hay* 5C 60
Acfold Rd. *SW6* 1K 101
Achilles Clo. *SE1* 5G 87
Achilles Ho. E2 2H 69 (off Old Bethnal Grn. Rd.)
Achilles Rd. *NW6* 5J 47
Achilles St. *SE14* 7A 88
Achilles Way. *W1* 1E 84 (5H 165)
Acklam Rd. *W10* 5G 65 (in two parts)
Acklington Dri. *NW9* 1A 28
Ackmar Rd. *SW6* 1J 101
Ackroyd Dri. *E3* 5B 70
Ackroyd Rd. *SE23* 7K 105
Acland Clo. *SE18* 7H 91
Acland Cres. *SE5* 3D 104
Acland Ho. *SW9* 1K 103
Acland Rd. *NW2* 6D 46
Acle Clo. *Ilf* 1F 37
Acme Ho. *E14* 5E 70
Acock Gro. *N'holt* 4F 43
Acol Ct. *NW6* 7J 47
Acol Cres. *Ruis* 5K 41
Acol Rd. *NW6* 7J 47
Aconbury Rd. *Dag* 1B 74
Acorn Clo. *E4* 5J 19
Acorn Clo. *Chst* 5G 127
Acorn Clo. *Enf* 1G 7
Acorn Clo. *Hamp* 6F 115
Acorn Clo. *Stan* 7G 11
Acorn Ct. *E6* 7C 54
Acorn Ct. *Ilf* 6J 37
Acorn Gdns. *SE19* 1F 141
Acorn Gdns. *W3* 5K 63
Acorn Gro. *Hay* 7H 77
Acorn Gro. *Ruis* 4H 41
Acorn Pde. *SE15* 7H 87
Acorn Production Cen. *N7* 7J 49
Acorn Wlk. *SE16* 1A 88
Acorn Way. *SE23* 3K 123
Acorn Way. *Beck* 5E 142
Acre Dri. *SE22* 4G 105
Acrefield Ho. NW4 4F 29 (off Belle Vue Est.)
Acre La. *SW2* 4J 103
Acre La. *Cars & Wall* 4E 150
Acre Path. N'holt 6C 42 (off Arnold Rd.)
Acre Rd. *SW19* 6B 120
Acre Rd. *Dag* 7H 57
Acre Rd. *King T* 1E 134
Acre Way. *N'wd* 1H 23
Acris St. *SW18* 5A 102
Acropolis Ho. King T 3F 135 (off Winery La.)
Acton 1J 81
Acton Central Ind. Est. *W3* 1H 81
Acton Clo. *N9* 2B 18
Acton Green 3J 81
Acton Hill M. *W3* 1H 81
Acton Ho. E8 1F 69 (off Lee St.)
Acton La. *NW10* 3J 63
Acton La. *W3 & W4* 2J 81 (in three parts)
Acton M. *E8* 1F 69
Acton Pk. Est. *W3* 2K 81
Acton St. *WC1* 3K 67 (2G 161)
Acton Va. Ind. Pk. *W3* 1B 82
Acuba Rd. *SW18* 2K 119
Acworth Clo. *N9* 7D 8
Acworth Ho. SE18 6F 91 (off Barnfield Rd.)
Ada Ct. N1 1C 68 (off Packington St.)
Ada Ct. *W9* 3A 66 (2A 158)
Ada Gdns. *E14* 6F 71
Ada Gdns. *E15* 1H 71
Ada Ho. E2 1G 69 (off Ada Pl.)
Adair Clo. *SE25* 3H 141
Adair Rd. *W10* 4G 65
Adair Tower. W10 4G 65 (off Appleford Rd.)
Ada Kennedy Ct. SE10 7E 88 (off Greenwich S. St.)
Adam & Eve Ct. *W1* 7B 160
Adam & Eve M. *W8* 3J 83
Adam Clo. *SE6* 4B 124
Adam Ct. *SE11* 4K 173
Adam Ct. SW7 4A 84 (off Gloucester Rd.)
Adam Rd. *E4* 6G 19
Adams Bri. Bus. Cen. *Wemb* 5H 45
Adams Clo. *N3* 7D 14
Adams Clo. *NW9* 2H 45
Adams Clo. *Surb* 6F 135
Adams Ct. *E17* 6A 34
Adams Ct. *EC2* 6E 68 (7F 163)
Adams Gdns. Est. *SE16* 2J 87
Adams Ho. E14 6F 71 (off Aberfeldy St.)
Adams M. *N22* 7E 16
Adamson Ct. *N2* 3C 30
Adamson Rd. *E16* 6J 71
Adamson Rd. *NW3* 7B 48
Adams Pl. E14 1D 88 (off N. Colonnade, The)
Adams Pl. *N7* 5K 49
Adamsrill Clo. *Enf* 6J 7
Adamsrill Rd. *SE26* 4K 123
Adams Rd. *N17* 2D 32
Adams Rd. *Beck* 5A 142
Adam's Row. *W1* 7E 66 (3H 165)
Adams Sq. *Bexh* 3E 110
Adam St. *WC2* 7J 67 (3F 167)
Adams Wlk. *King T* 2E 134
Adams Way. *Croy* 6F 141
Adam Wlk. *SW6* 7E 82
Ada Pl. *E2* 1G 69
Adare Wlk. *SW16* 3K 121
Ada Rd. *SE5* 7E 86
Ada Rd. *Wemb* 3D 44
Adastral Ho. WC1 5K 67 (5G 161) (off New North St.)
Ada St. *E8* 1H 69
Ada Workshops. *E8* 1H 69
Adderley Gdns. *SE9* 4E 126

Adderley Gro. SW11 5E 102
Adderley Rd. Harr 1K 25
Adderley St. E14 6E 70
Addey Ho. SE8 7B 88
Addington. 5C 154
Addington Ct. SW14 3K 99
Addington Dri. N12 6G 15
Addington Gro. SE26 4A 124
Addington Ho. SW9 2K 103 *(off Stockwell Rd.)*
Addington Rd. E3 3C 70
Addington Rd. E16 4G 71
Addington Rd. N4 6A 32
Addington Rd. Croy 1A 152
Addington Rd. S Croy 7K 153
Addington Rd. W Wick 4E 154
Addington Sq. SE5 6D 86 (in two parts)
Addington St. SE1 2K 85 (7H 167)
Addington Village Rd. Croy 6B 154 (in two parts)
Addis Clo. Enf 1E 8
Addiscombe. 1G 153
Addiscombe Av. Croy 1G 153
Addiscombe Clo. Harr 5C 26
Addiscombe Ct. Rd. Croy 1E 152
Addiscombe Gro. Croy 2E 152
Addiscombe Rd. Croy 2E 152
Addis Ho. E1 5J 69 *(off Lindley St.)*
Addisland Ct. W14 2G 83 *(off Holland Vs. Rd.)*
Addison Av. N14 6A 6
Addison Av. W11 1G 83
Addison Av. Houn 1G 97
Addison Bri. Pl. W14 4H 83
Addison Clo. N'wd 1J 23
Addison Clo. Orp 6G 145
Addison Cres. W14 3G 83
Addison Dri. SE12 5K 107
Addison Gdns. W14 3F 83
Addison Gdns. Surb 4F 135
Addison Gro. W4 3A 82
Addison Ho. NW8 1A 158
Addison Pk. Mans. W14 3F 83 *(off Richmond Way)*
Addison Pl. SE25 4G 141
Addison Pl. W11 1G 83
Addison Pl. S'hall 7E 60
Addison Rd. E11 6J 35
Addison Rd. E17 5D 34
Addison Rd. SE25 4G 141
Addison Rd. W14 2G 83
Addison Rd. Brom 5A 144
Addison Rd. Enf 1D 8
Addison Rd. Ilf 1G 37
Addison Rd. Tedd 6B 116
Addisons Clo. Croy 2B 154
Addison Ter. W4 4J 81 *(off Chiswick Rd.)*
Addison Way. NW11 4H 29
Addison Way. Hay 6J 59
Addison Way. N'wd 1H 23
Addle Hill. EC4 6B 68 (1B 168)
Addlestone Ho. W10 5E 64 *(off Sutton Way)*
Addle St. EC2 6C 68 (7D 162)
Addy Ho. SE16 4J 87
Adecroft Way. W Mol 3G 133
Adela Av. N Mald 5D 136
Adela Ho. W6 5E 82 *(off Queen Caroline St.)*
Adelaide Av. SE4 4B 106
Adelaide Clo. Enf 1K 7
Adelaide Clo. Stan 4F 11
Adelaide Ct. NW8 2A 66 *(off Abercorn Pl.)*
Adelaide Ct. W7 2K 79
Adelaide Ct. Beck 7B 124
Adelaide Gdns. Romf 5E 38
Adelaide Gro. W12 1C 82
Adelaide Ho. E15 2H 71
Adelaide Ho. E17 2B 34
Adelaide Ho. SE5 2E 104
Adelaide Ho. W11 6H 65 *(off Portobello Rd.)*
Adelaide Rd. E10 3D 52
Adelaide Rd. NW3 7B 48
Adelaide Rd. SW18 5J 101
Adelaide Rd. W13 1A 80
Adelaide Rd. Ashf 5A 112
Adelaide Rd. Chst 5F 127
Adelaide Rd. Houn 1C 96
Adelaide Rd. Ilf 2F 55
Adelaide Rd. Rich 4F 99
Adelaide Rd. S'hall 4C 78
Adelaide Rd. Surb 5E 134
Adelaide Rd. Tedd 6K 115
Adelaide St. WC2 7J 67 (3E 166)
Adelaide Ter. Bren 5D 80
Adelaide Wlk. SW9 4A 104
Adela St. W10 4G 65
Adelina Gro. E1 5J 69
Adelina M. SW12 1H 121
Adeline Pl. WC1 5H 67 (6D 160)
Adeliza Clo. Bark 7G 55
Adelphi Ct. E8 7F 51 *(off Celandine Dri.)*
Adelphi Ct. SE16 2K 87 *(off Garter Way)*
Adelphi Ct. W4 6K 81
Adelphi Cres. Hay 3G 59
Adelphi Ter. WC2 7J 67 (3F 167)
Adelphi Theatre. 7J 67 (3F 167) ***(off Strand)***
Adelphi Way. Hay 3H 59
Adeney Clo. W6 6F 83
Aden Gro. N16 4D 50
Aden Ho. E1 5K 69 *(off Duckett St.)*
Adenmore Rd. SE6 7C 106
Aden Rd. Enf 4F 9
Aden Rd. Ilf 7G 37
Aden Ter. N16 4D 50
Adeyfield Ho. EC1 3D 68 (2F 163) *(off Cranwood St.)*
Adie Rd. W6 3E 82
Adine Rd. E13 4K 71
Adler Ind. Est. Hay 2F 77
Adler St. E1 6G 69
Adley St. E5 5A 52
Adlington Clo. N18 5K 17
Admaston Rd. SE18 7G 91
Admiral Ct. SW10 1A 102 *(off Admiral Sq.)*
Admiral Ct. W1 5E 66 (6G 159) *(off Blandford St.)*
Admiral Ct. Bark 2B 74
Admiral Ct. Cars 1C 150
Admiral Ho. SW1 4G 85 (3B 172) *(off Willow Pl.)*
Admiral Ho. Tedd 4A 116
Admiral Hyson Ind. Est. SE16 5H 87
Admiral M. W10 4F 65
Admiral Pl. SE16 1A 88
Admirals Clo. E18 4K 35
Admirals Ct. E6 6F 73 *(off Trader Rd.)*
Admirals Ct. SE1 1F 87 (5J 169) *(off Horselydown La.)*
Admiral Seymour Rd. SE9 4D 108
Admiral's Ga. SE10 1D 106
Admiral Sq. SW10 1A 102
Admiral St. SE8 2C 106
Admirals Wlk. NW3 3A 48
Admirals Way. E14 2C 88
Admiralty Arch 1H 85 (4D 166)
Admiralty Clo. SE8 7C 88
Admiralty Rd. Tedd 6K 115
Admiralty Way. Tedd 6K 115
Admiral Wlk. W9 5J 65
Adolf St. SE6 4D 124
Adolphus Rd. N4 2B 50
Adolphus St. SE8 7B 88
Adomar Rd. Dag 3D 56
Adpar St. W2 5B 66 (5A 158)
Adrian Av. NW2 1D 46
Adrian Boult Ho. E2 3H 69 *(off Mansford St.)*
Adrian Clo. Barn 6A 4
Adrian Ho. N1 1K 67 *(off Barnsbury Est.)*
Adrian Ho. SW8 7J 85 *(off Wyvil Rd.)*
Adrian M. SW10 6K 83
Adriatic Building. E14 7A 70 *(off Horseferry Rd.)*
Adriatic Ho. E1 4K 69 *(off Ernest St.)*
Adrienne Av. S'hall 4D 60
Adron Ho. SE16 4J 87 *(off Millender Wlk.)*
Adstock Ho. N1 7B 50 *(off Sutton Est., The)*
Advance Rd. SE27 4C 122
Adventurers Ct. E14 7F 71 *(off Newport Av.)*
Advent Way. N18 5D 18
Adys Lawn. NW2 6D 46
Ady's Rd. SE15 3F 105
Aegon Ho. E14 3D 88 *(off Lanark Sq.)*
Aerodrome Rd. NW9 & NW4 3B 28
Aerodrome Way. Houn 6A 78
Aeroville. NW9 2A 28
Affleck St. N1 2K 67 (1G 161)
Afghan Rd. SW11 2C 102
Afsil Ho. EC1 5A 68 (6K 161) *(off Viaduct Bldgs.)*
Agamemnon Rd. NW6 4H 47
Agar Clo. Surb 2F 147
Agar Gro. NW1 7G 49
Agar Gro. Est. NW1 7H 49
Agar Ho. King T 3E 134 *(off Denmark Rd.)*
Agar Pl. NW1 7G 49
Agar St. WC2 7J 67 (3E 166)
Agate Clo. E16 6B 72
Agate Rd. W6 3E 82
Agatha Clo. E1 1H 87
Agaton Rd. SE9 2G 127
Agave Rd. NW2 4E 46
Agdon St. EC1 4B 68 (3A 162)
Agincourt Rd. NW3 4D 48
Agnes Av. Ilf 4E 54
Agnes Clo. E6 7E 72
Agnesfield Clo. N12 6H 15
Agnes Gdns. Dag 4D 56
Agnes Ho. W11 7F 65 *(off St Ann's Rd.)*
Agnes Rd. W3 1B 82
Agnes St. E14 6B 70
Agnew Rd. SE23 7K 105
Agricola Pl. Enf 5A 8
Aidan Clo. Dag 3E 56
Aigburth Mans. SW9 7A 86 *(off Mowll St.)*
Aileen Wlk. E15 7H 53
Ailsa Av. Twic 5A 98
Ailsa Ho. E16 7E 72 *(off University Way)*
Ailsa Rd. Twic 5B 98
Ailsa St. E14 5E 70
Ainger M. NW3 7D 48 *(off Ainger Rd., in two parts)*
Ainger Rd. NW3 7D 48
Ainsdale. NW1 2G 67 (1A 160) *(off Harrington St.)*
Ainsdale Clo. Orp 7H 145
Ainsdale Cres. Pinn 3E 24
Ainsdale Dri. SE1 5G 87
Ainsdale Rd. W5 4D 62
Ainsley Av. Romf 6H 39
Ainsley Clo. N9 1K 17
Ainsley St. E2 3H 69
Ainslie Ct. Wemb 2E 62
Ainslie Wlk. SW12 7F 103
Ainslie Wood Cres. E4 5J 19
Ainslie Wood Gdns. E4 4J 19
Ainslie Wood Rd. E4 5H 19
Ainsty Est. SE16 2K 87
Ainsty St. SE16 2J 87
Ainsworth Clo. NW2 3C 46
Ainsworth Clo. SE15 2E 104
Ainsworth Ho. NW8 1K 65 *(off Ainsworth Way)*
Ainsworth Rd. E9 7J 51
Ainsworth Rd. Croy 1B 152
Ainsworth Way. NW8 1A 66
Aintree Av. E6 1C 72
Aintree Clo. Uxb 6D 58
Aintree Cres. Ilf 2G 37
Aintree Est. SW6 7G 83 *(off Aintree St.)*
Aintree Rd. Gnfd 2B 62
Aintree St. SW6 7G 83
Airbourne Ho. Wall 4G 151 *(off Maldon Rd.)*
Air Call Bus. Cen. NW9 3K 27
Aird Ho. SE1 3C 86 *(off Rockingham St.)*
Airdrie Clo. N1 7K 49
Airdrie Clo. Hay 5C 60
Airedale Av. W4 4B 82
Airedale Av. S. W4 5B 82
Airedale Rd. SW12 7D 102
Airedale Rd. W5 3C 80
Airlie Gdns. W8 1J 83
Airlie Gdns. Ilf 1F 55
Airlinks Ind. Est. Houn 5A 78
Air Pk. Way. Felt 2K 113
Air St. W1 7G 67 (3B 166)
Airthrie Rd. Ilf 2B 56
Aisgill Av. W14 5H 83 (in two parts)
Aisher Rd. SE28 7C 74
Aislibie Rd. SE12 4G 107
Aiten Pl. W6 4C 82
Aithan Ho. E14 6B 70 *(off Copenhagen Pl.)*
Aitken Clo. E8 1G 69
Aitken Clo. Mitc 7D 138
Aitken Rd. SE6 2D 124
Ajax Av. NW9 3A 28
Ajax Ho. E2 2H 69 *(off Old Bethnal Grn. Rd.)*
Ajax Rd. NW6 4H 47
Akabusi Clo. Croy 6G 141
Akbar Ho. E14 4D 88 *(off Cahir St.)*
Akehurst St. SW15 6C 100
Akenside Rd. NW3 5B 48
Akerman Rd. SW9 2B 104
Akerman Rd. Surb 6C 134
Akintaro Ho. SE8 6B 88 *(off Alverton St.)*
Alabama St. SE18 7H 91
Alacross Rd. W5 2C 80
Alandale Dri. Pinn 1K 23
Aland Ct. SE16 3A 88
Alander M. E17 4E 34
Alan Dri. Barn 6B 4
Alan Gdns. Romf 7G 39
Alan Hocken Way. E15 2G 71
Alan Preece Ct. NW6 7F 47
Alan Rd. SW19 5G 119
Alanthus Clo. SE12 6J 107
Alaska Bldgs. SE1 3E 86
Alaska St. SE1 1A 86 (5J 167)
Alastor Ho. E14 3E 88 *(off Strattondale Ho.)*
Alba Clo. Hay 4B 60
Albacore Cres. SE13 6D 106
Alba Gdns. NW11 6G 29
Albain Cres. Ashf 2A 112
Alban Highwalk. EC2 7D 162 (in two parts)
Albany. N12 6E 14
Albany. W1 7G 67 (3A 166)
Albany Clo. N15 4B 32
Albany Clo. SW14 4H 99
Albany Clo. Bex 7C 110
Albany Clo. Uxb 5C 40
Albany Ct. E4 5G 19
Albany Ct. E10 7C 34
Albany Ct. EN3 6H 9
Albany Ct. NW8 2B 66 (1A 158) *(off Abbey Rd.)*
Albany Ct. NW10 3D 64 *(off Trenmar Gdns.)*
Albany Ct. Edgw 1K 27
Albany Courtyard. W1 7G 67 (3B 166)
Albany Cres. Edgw 7B 12
Albany Mans. SW11 7C 84
Albany M. N1 7A 50
Albany M. SE5 6C 86
Albany M. Brom 6J 125
Albany M. King T 6D 116
Albany M. Sutt 5K 149
Albany Pde. Bren 6E 80
Albany Pk. 1F 9
Albany Pk. Av. Enf 1D 8
Albany Pk. Rd. King T 6D 116
Albany Pas. Rich 5E 98
Albany Pl. N7 4A 50
Albany Reach. Th Dit 5K 133
Albany Rd. E10 7C 34
Albany Rd. E12 4B 54
Albany Rd. E17 6A 34
Albany Rd. N4 6A 32
Albany Rd. N18 5D 18
Albany Rd. SE5 6D 86
Albany Rd. SW19 5K 119
Albany Rd. W13 7B 62
Albany Rd. Belv 6F 93
Albany Rd. Bex 7C 110
Albany Rd. Bren 6D 80
Albany Rd. Chst 5F 127
Albany Rd. N Mald 4K 135
Albany Rd. Rich 5F 99
Albany Rd. Romf 6F 39
Albany St. NW1 2F 67 (1K 159)
Albany Ter. NW1 4K 159
Albany Ter. Rich 5F 99 *(off Albany Pas.)*
Albany, The. Wfd G 4C 20
Albany Vw. Buck H 1D 20
Alba Pl. W11 6H 65
Albatross. NW9 2B 28
Albatross St. SE18 7J 91
Albatross Way. SE16 2K 87
Albemarle. SW19 2F 119
Albemarle App. Ilf 6F 37
Albemarle Av. Twic 1D 114
Albemarle Gdns. Ilf 6F 37
Albemarle Gdns. N Mald 4K 135
Albemarle Ho. SE8 4B 88 *(off Foreshore)*
Albemarle Ho. SW9 3A 104
Albemarle Pk. Beck 1D 142
Albemarle Pk. Stan 5H 11
Albemarle Rd. Beck 1D 142
Albemarle Rd. E Barn 7H 5
Albemarle St. W1 7F 67 (3K 165)
Albemarle Way. EC1 4B 68 (4A 162)
Alberon Gdns. NW11 4H 29
Alberta Av. Sutt 4G 149
Alberta Est. SE17 5B 86 *(off Alberta St.)*
Alberta Ho. E14 1E 88 *(off Gaselee St.)*
Alberta Rd. Enf 6A 8
Alberta Rd. Eri 1J 111
Alberta St. SE17 5B 86
Albert Av. E4 4H 19
Albert Av. SW8 7K 85
Albert Barnes Ho. SE1 3C 86 *(off New Kent Rd.)*
Albert Bigg Point. E15 2E 70 *(off Godfrey St.)*
Albert Bri. SW3 & SW11 6C 84
Albert Bri. Rd. SW11 7C 84

Albert Carr Gdns. SW16 5J 121
Albert Clo. E9 1H 69
Albert Clo. N22 1H 31
Albert Cotts. E1 5G 69 (off Deal St.)
Albert Ct. E7 4J 53
Albert Ct. SW7 3B 84 (7A 164)
Albert Ct. Ga. SW1 2D 84 (7E 164) (off Knightsbridge)
Albert Cres. E4 4H 19
Albert Dane Cen. S'hall 3C 78
Albert Dri. SW19 2G 119
Albert Embkmt. SE1 3K 85 (6F 173) (Lambeth Pal. Rd.)
Albert Embkmt. SE1 5J 85 (6F 173) (Vauxhall Cross)
Albert Gdns. E1 6K 69
Albert Ga. SW1 2D 84 (6F 165)
Albert Gray Ho. SW10 7B 84 (off Worlds End Est.)
Albert Gro. SW20 1F 137
Albert Hall Mans. SW7 2B 84 (7A 164) (in two parts)
Albert Ho. E18 3K 35 (off Albert Rd.)
Albert Ho. SE28 2G 91 (off Erebus Dri.)
Albert Mans. Croy 1D 152 (off Lansdowne Rd.)
Albert Memorial 2B 84 (7A 164)
Albert M. E14 7A 70 (off Northey St.)
Albert M. N4 1K 49
Albert M. SE4 4A 106
Albert M. W8 3A 84
Albert Pal. Mans. SW11 1F 103 (off Lurline Gdns.)
Albert Pl. N3 1J 29
Albert Pl. N17 3F 33
Albert Pl. W8 3K 83
Albert Rd. E10 2E 52
Albert Rd. E16 1C 90
Albert Rd. E17 5C 34
Albert Rd. E18 3K 35
Albert Rd. N4 1K 49
Albert Rd. N15 6E 32
Albert Rd. N22 1G 31
Albert Rd. NW4 4F 29
Albert Rd. NW6 2H 65
Albert Rd. NW7 5G 13
Albert Rd. SE9 3C 126
Albert Rd. SE20 6K 123
Albert Rd. SE25 4G 141
Albert Rd. W5 4B 62
Albert Rd. Ashf 5B 112
Albert Rd. Barn 4F 5
Albert Rd. Belv 5F 93
Albert Rd. Bex 6G 111
Albert Rd. Brom 5B 144
Albert Rd. Buck H 2G 21
Albert Rd. Dag 1G 57
Albert Rd. Hamp H 5G 115
Albert Rd. Harr 3G 25
Albert Rd. Hay 3G 77
Albert Rd. Houn 4E 96
Albert Rd. Ilf 3F 55
Albert Rd. King T 2F 135
Albert Rd. Mitc 3D 138
Albert Rd. N Mald 4B 136
Albert Rd. Rich 5E 98
Albert Rd. S'hall 3B 78
Albert Rd. Sutt 5B 150
Albert Rd. Tedd 6K 115
Albert Rd. Twic 1K 115
Albert Rd. W Dray 1A 76
Albert Rd. Est. Belv 5F 93
Albert Sq. E15 5G 53
Albert Sq. SW8 7K 85
Albert Starr Ho. SE8 4K 87 (off Bush Rd.)
Albert St. N12 5F 15
Albert St. NW1 1F 67
Albert Studios. SW11 1D 102
Albert Ter. NW1 1E 66
Albert Ter. NW10 1J 63
Albert Ter. W5 4B 62
Albert Ter. Buck H 2H 21
Albert Ter. M. NW1 1E 66
Albert Victoria Ho. N22 1A 32 (off Pellatt Gro.)
Albert Wlk. E16 2E 90
Albert Way. SE15 7H 87
Albert Westcott Ho. SE17 5B 86
Albert Whicher Ho. E17 4E 34
Albert Yd. SE19 6E 122
Albery Ct. E8 7F 51 (off Middleton Rd.)
Albery Theatre. 7J 67 (2E 166) (off St Martin's La.)
Albion Av. N10 1E 30
Albion Av. SW8 2H 103
Albion Clo. W2 7C 66 (2D 164)
Albion Clo. Romf 6K 39
Albion Ct. W6 4D 82 (off Albion Pl.)
Albion Dri. E8 7F 51 (in two parts)
Albion Est. SE16 2K 87
Albion Gdns. W6 4D 82
Albion Ga. W2 2D 164 (in two parts)
Albion Gro. N16 4E 50
Albion Ho. E16 1F 91 (off Church St.)
Albion Ho. SE8 7C 88 (off Watsons St.)
Albion M. N1 1A 68
Albion M. W2 7C 66 (2D 164)
Albion M. W6 4D 82
Albion Pl. EC1 5B 68 (5A 162)
Albion Pl. EC2 5D 68 (6F 163)
Albion Pl. SE25 3G 141
Albion Pl. W6 4D 82
Albion Rd. E17 3E 34
Albion Rd. N16 4D 50
Albion Rd. N17 2G 33
Albion Rd. Bexh 4F 111
Albion Rd. Hay 6G 59
Albion Rd. Houn 4E 96
Albion Rd. King T 1J 135
Albion Rd. Sutt 6B 150
Albion Rd. Twic 1J 115
Albion Sq. E8 7F 51
Albion St. SE16 2J 87
Albion St. W2 6C 66 (1D 164)
Albion St. Croy 1B 152
Albion Ter. E4 4J 9
Albion Ter. E8 7F 51
Albion Vs. Rd. SE26 3J 123
Albion Way. EC1 5C 68 (6C 162)
Albion Way. SE13 4E 106
Albion Way. Wemb 3G 45
Albion Wharf. SW11 7C 84
Albion Yd. N1 2J 67
Albrighton Rd. SE22 3E 104
Albuhera Clo. Enf 1F 7
Albury Av. Bexh 2E 110
Albury Av. Iswth 7K 79
Albury Clo. Hamp 6F 115
Albury Ct. Mitc 2B 138
Albury Ct. N'holt 3A 60 (off Canberra Dri.)
Albury Ct. S Croy 4C 152 (off Tanfield Rd.)
Albury Ct. Sutt 4A 150
Albury Dri. Pinn 1A 24
Albury Ho. SE1 2B 86 (7B 168) (off Boyfield St.)
Albury M. E12 2A 54
Albury Rd. Chess 5E 146
Albury St. SE8 6C 88
Albyfield. Brom 4D 144
Albyn Rd. SE8 1C 106
Alcester Cres. E5 2H 51
Alcester Rd. Wall 4F 151
Alcock Clo. Wall 7H 151
Alcock Rd. Houn 7B 78
Alconbury. Bexh 5H 111
Alconbury Rd. E5 2G 51
Alcorn Clo. Sutt 2J 149
Alcott Clo. W7 5K 61
Alcott Clo. Felt 1H 113
Alcuin Ct. Stan 7H 11
Aldam Pl. N16 2F 51
Aldborough Ct. Ilf 5K 37 (off Aldborough Rd. N.)
Aldborough Hatch 4K 37
Aldborough Rd. Dag 6J 57
Aldborough Rd. N. Ilf 5K 37
Aldborough Rd. S. Ilf 1J 55 (in two parts)
Aldbourne Rd. W3 1B 82 (in two parts)
Aldbridge St. SE17 5E 86
Aldburgh M. W1 6E 66 (7H 159) (in two parts)
Aldbury Av. Wemb 7H 45
Aldbury Ho. SW3 4C 84 (5C 170) (off Ixworth Pl.)
Aldbury M. N9 7J 7
Aldebert Ter. SW8 7J 85
Aldeburgh Clo. E5 2H 51
Aldeburgh Pl. Wfd G 4D 20
Aldeburgh St. SE10 5J 89
Alden Av. E15 3H 71
Alden Ct. Croy 3E 152
Aldenham Dri. Uxb 4D 58
Aldenham Ho. NW1 2G 67 (1B 160) (off Aldenham St.)
Aldenham St. NW1 2G 67 (1C 160)
Alden Ho. E8 1H 69 (off Duncan Rd.)
Aldensley Rd. W6 3D 82
Alderbrook Rd. SW12 6F 103
Alderbury Rd. SW13 6C 82
Alder Clo. SE15 6F 87
Alder Gro. NW2 2C 46
Aldergrove Gdns. Houn 2C 96
Alderholt Way. SE15 7E 86
Alder Ho. NW3 6D 48
Alder Ho. SE4 3C 106
Alder Ho. SE15 6F 87 (off Alder Clo.)
Alder Lodge. SW6 1E 100
Alderman Av. Bark 3A 74
Aldermanbury. EC2 6C 68 (7D 162)
Aldermanbury Sq. EC2 5C 68 (6D 162)
Alderman Judge Mall. King T 2E 134
Aldermans Hill. N13 4D 16
Aldermans Wlk. EC2 5E 68 (6G 163)
Aldermary Rd. Brom 1J 143
Alder M. N19 2G 49
Aldermoor Rd. SE6 3B 124
Alderney Av. Houn 7F 79
Alderney Gdns. N'holt 7D 42
Alderney Ho. N1 6C 50 (off Arran Wlk.)
Alderney Ho. Enf 1E 8
Alderney Rd. E1 4K 69
Alderney St. SW1 4F 85 (4K 171)
Alder Rd. SW14 3K 99
Alder Rd. Sidc 3K 127
Alders Av. Wfd G 6B 20
Aldersbrook 2K 53
Aldersbrook Av. Enf 2K 7
Aldersbrook Dri. King T 6F 117
Aldersbrook La. E12 3D 54
Aldersbrook Rd. E11 & E12 2K 53
Alders Clo. E11 2K 53
Alders Clo. W5 3D 80
Alders Clo. Edgw 5D 12
Aldersey Gdns. Bark 6H 55
Aldersford Clo. SE4 5K 105
Aldersgate St. EC1 5C 68 (5C 162)
Alders Gro. E Mol 5H 133
Aldersgrove Av. SE9 3B 126
Aldershot Rd. NW6 1H 65
Aldershot Ter. SE18 7E 90
Aldersmead Av. Croy 6K 141
Aldersmead Rd. Beck 7A 124
Alderson Pl. S'hall 1G 79
Alderson St. W10 4G 65
Alders Rd. Edgw 5D 12
Alders, The. N21 6F 7
Alders, The. SW16 4G 121
Alders, The. Felt 4C 114
Alders, The. Houn 6D 78
Alders, The. W Wick 1D 154
Alderton Clo. NW10 3K 45
Alderton Cres. NW4 5D 28
Alderton Rd. SE24 3C 104
Alderton Rd. Croy 7F 141
Alderton Way. NW4 5D 28
Alderville Rd. SW6 2H 101
Alder Wlk. Ilf 5G 55
Alderwick Ct. N7 6K 49 (off Cornelia St.)
Alderwick Dri. Houn 3H 97
Alderwood M. Barn 1F 5
Alderwood Rd. SE9 6H 109
Aldford Ho. W1 1E 84 (4G 165) (off Park St.)
Aldford St. W1 1E 84 (4H 165)
Aldgate. (Junct.) 6F 69 (1J 169)
Aldgate. E1 6F 69 (off Whitechapel High St.)
Aldgate. EC3 6E 68 (1H 169)
Aldgate Av. E1 6F 69 (7J 163)
Aldgate Barrs. E1 6F 69 (7K 163) (off Whitechapel High St.)
Aldgate High St. EC3 6F 69 (1J 169)
Aldgate Triangle. E1 6G 69 (off Coke St.)
Aldham Ho. SE4 2B 106 (off Malpas Rd.)
Aldine Ct. W12 2E 82 (off Aldine St.)
Aldine Pl. W12 2E 82
Aldine St. W12 2E 82
Aldington Clo. Dag 1C 56
Aldington Ct. E8 7G 51 (off London Fld. W. Side)
Aldington Rd. SE18 3B 90
Aldis M. SW17 5C 120
Aldis St. SW17 5C 120
Aldred Rd. NW6 5J 47
Aldren Rd. SW17 3A 120
Aldrich Cres. New Ad 7E 154
Aldriche Way. E4 6K 19
Aldrich Gdns. Sutt 3H 149
Aldrich Ter. SW18 2A 120
Aldrick Ho. N1 1K 67 (off Barnsbury Est.)
Aldridge Av. Edgw 3C 12
Aldridge Av. Ruis 2A 42
Aldridge Av. Stan 1E 26
Aldridge Ri. N Mald 7A 136
Aldridge Rd. Vs. W11 5H 65
Aldridge Wlk. N14 7D 6
Aldrington Rd. SW16 5G 121
Aldsworth Clo. W9 4K 65
Aldwick Clo. SE9 3H 127
Aldwick Rd. Croy 3K 151
Aldworth Gro. SE13 6E 106
Aldworth Rd. E15 7G 53
Aldwych. WC2 6K 67 (2G 167)
Aldwych Av. Ilf 4G 37
Aldwych Ct. E8 7F 51 (off Middleton Rd.)
Aldwych Theatre. 6K 67 (1G 167) (off Aldwych)
Aldwyn Ho. SW8 7J 85 (off Davidson Gdns.)
Alers Rd. Bexh 5D 110
Alesia Clo. N22 7D 16
Alestan Beck Rd. E16 6B 72
Alexa Ct. W8 4J 83
Alexa Ct. Sutt 6J 149
Alexander Av. NW10 7D 46
Alexander Clo. Barn 4G 5
Alexander Clo. Brom 1J 155
Alexander Clo. Sidc 6J 109
Alexander Clo. S'hall 1G 79
Alexander Clo. Twic 2J 115
Alexander Ct. Beck 1F 143
Alexander Ct. Stan 3F 27
Alexander Evans M. SE23 2K 123
Alexander Fleming Mus. 7B 158
Alexander Ho. E14 3C 88 (off Tiller Rd.)
Alexander M. W2 6K 65
Alexander Pl. SW7 4C 84 (3C 170)
Alexander Rd. N19 3J 49
Alexander Rd. Bexh 2D 110
Alexander Rd. Chst 6F 127
Alexander Sq. SW3 4C 84 (3C 170)
Alexander St. W2 6J 65
Alexander Studios. SW11 4B 102 (off Haydon Way)
Alexandra Av. N22 1H 31
Alexandra Av. SW11 1E 102
Alexandra Av. W4 7K 81
Alexandra Av. Harr 1D 42
Alexandra Av. S'hall 7D 60
Alexandra Av. Sutt 3J 149
Alexandra Clo. SE8 6B 88
Alexandra Clo. Ashf 7F 113
Alexandra Clo. Harr 3E 42
Alexandra Cotts. SE14 1B 106
Alexandra Ct. N14 5B 6
Alexandra Ct. SW7 1A 170
Alexandra Ct. W2 7K 65 (off Moscow Rd.)
Alexandra Ct. W9 4A 66 (off Maida Va.)
Alexandra Ct. Ashf 6F 113
Alexandra Ct. Gnfd 2F 61
Alexandra Ct. Houn 2F 97
Alexandra Cres. Brom 6H 125
Alexandra Dri. SE19 5E 122
Alexandra Dri. Surb 7G 135
Alexandra Gdns. N10 4F 31
Alexandra Gdns. W4 7A 82
Alexandra Gdns. Cars 7E 150
Alexandra Gdns. Houn 2F 97
Alexandra Gro. N4 1B 50
Alexandra Gro. N12 5E 14
Alexandra Ho. E16 1K 89 (off Wesley Av.)
Alexandra Ho. W6 5E 82 (off Queen Caroline St.)
Alexandra Mans. SW3 6B 84 (7A 170) (off Moravian Clo.)
Alexandra M. N2 3D 30
Alexandra M. SW19 6H 119
Alexandra Palace 3H 31
Alexandra Pal. Way. N22 4G 31
Alexandra Pde. Harr 4F 43
Alexandra Pk. Rd. N10 2F 31
Alexandra Pk. Rd. N22 1G 31
Alexandra Pl. NW8 1A 66
Alexandra Pl. SE25 5D 140
Alexandra Pl. Croy 1E 152
Alexandra Rd. E6 3E 72
Alexandra Rd. E10 3E 52
Alexandra Rd. E17 6B 34
Alexandra Rd. E18 3K 35
Alexandra Rd. N8 3A 32
Alexandra Rd. N9 7C 8

Alexandra Rd. N10 1F 31
Alexandra Rd. N15 5D 32
Alexandra Rd. NW4 4F 29
Alexandra Rd. NW8 1A 66
Alexandra Rd. SE26 6K 123
Alexandra Rd. SW14 3K 99
Alexandra Rd. SW19 6H 119
Alexandra Rd. W4 2K 81
Alexandra Rd. Ashf 7F 113
Alexandra Rd. Bren 6D 80
Alexandra Rd. Chad H 6E 38
Alexandra Rd. Croy 1E 152
Alexandra Rd. Enf 4E 8
Alexandra Rd. Houn 2F 97
Alexandra Rd. King T 7G 117
Alexandra Rd. Mitc 7C 120
Alexandra Rd. Rich 2F 99
Alexandra Rd. Th Dit 5K 133
Alexandra Rd. Twic 6C 98
Alexandra Rd. Ind. Est. Enf 4E 8
Alexandra Sq. Mord 5J 137
Alexandra St. E16 5J 71
Alexandra St. SE14 7A 88
Alexandra Ter. E14 5D 88 (off Westferry Rd.)
Alexandra Wlk. SE19 5E 122
Alexandra Yd. E9 1K 69
Alexandria Rd. W13 7A 62
Alexis St. SE16 4G 87
Alfan La. Dart 5K 129
Alfearn Rd. E5 4J 51
Alford Ct. N1 2C 68 (1D 162) (off Shepherdess Wlk.)
Alford Grn. New Ad 6F 155
Alford Ho. N6 6G 31
Alford Pl. N1 2C 68 (1D 162) (in two parts)
Alford Rd. Eri 5J 93
Alfoxton Av. N8 4B 32
Alfreda St. SW11 1F 103
Alfred Clo. W4 4K 81
Alfred Finlay Ho. N22 2B 32
Alfred Gdns. S'hall 7C 60
Alfred Ho. E9 5A 52 (off Homerton Rd.)
Alfred Ho. E12 7C 54 (off Tennyson Av.)
Alfred M. W1 5H 67 (5C 160)
Alfred Nunn Ho. NW10 1B 64
Alfred Pl. WC1 5H 67 (5C 160)
Alfred Prior Ho. E12 4E 54
Alfred Rd. E15 5H 53
Alfred Rd. SE25 5G 141
Alfred Rd. W2 5J 65
Alfred Rd. W3 1J 81
Alfred Rd. Belv 5F 93
Alfred Rd. Buck H 2G 21
Alfred Rd. Felt 2A 114
Alfred Rd. King T 3E 134
Alfred Rd. Sutt 5A 150
Alfred's Gdns. Bark 2J 73
Alfred St. E3 3B 70
Alfreds Way. Bark 3F 73
Alfreds Way Ind. Est. Bark 1A 74
Alfreton Clo. SW19 3F 119
Alfriston. Surb 6F 135
Alfriston Av. Croy 7J 139
Alfriston Av. Harr 6E 24
Alfriston Clo. Surb 5F 135
Alfriston Rd. SW11 5D 102
Algar Clo. Iswth 3A 98
Algar Clo. Stan 5E 10
Algar Ho. SE1 7A 168
Algar Rd. Iswth 3A 98
Algarve Rd. SW18 1K 119
Algernon Rd. NW4 6C 28
Algernon Rd. NW6 1J 65
Algernon Rd. SE13 4D 106
Algiers Rd. SE13 4C 106
Alibon Gdns. Dag 5G 57
Alibon Rd. Dag 5F 57
Alice Clo. Barn 4F 5 (off Station App.)
Alice Gilliatt Ct. W14 6H 83 (off Star Rd.)
Alice La. E3 1B 70
Alice M. Tedd 5K 115
Alice Owen Technology Cen. EC1 3B 68 (1A 162) (off Goswell Rd.)
Alice Shepherd Ho. E14 2E 88 (off Manchester Rd.)
Alice St. SE1 3E 86 (in two parts)
Alice Thompson Clo. SE12 2A 126
Alice Walker Clo. SE24 4B 104
Alice Way. Houn 4F 97
Alicia Av. Harr 4B 26
Alicia Clo. Harr 5C 26
Alicia Gdns. Harr 4B 26
Alicia Ho. Well 1B 110
Alie St. E1 6F 69 (1K 169)
Alington Cres. NW9 7J 27
Alington Gro. Wall 7G 151
Alison Clo. E6 6E 72
Alison Clo. Croy 1K 153
Alison Ct. SE1 5G 87
Aliwal Rd. SW11 4C 102
Alkerden Rd. W4 5A 82
Alkham Rd. N16 2F 51
Allan Barclay Clo. N15 6F 33
Allan Clo. N Mald 5K 135
Allandale Av. N3 3G 29
Allanson Ct. E10 2C 52 (off Leyton Grange Est.)
Allan Way. W3 5J 63
Allard Cres. Bus H 1B 10
Allard Gdns. SW4 5H 103
Allardyce St. SW4 4K 103
Allbrook Clo. Tedd 5J 115
Allcott Ho. W12 6D 64 (off Du Cane Rd.)
Allcroft Rd. NW5 5E 48
Allder Way. S Croy 7B 152
Allenby Clo. Gnfd 3E 60
Allenby Rd. SE23 3A 124
Allenby Rd. S'hall 3E 60
Allen Clo. Mitc 1F 139
Allen Clo. Sun 1K 131
Allen Ct. E17 6C 34 (off Yunus Khan Clo.)
Allen Ct. Gnfd 5K 43
Allendale Av. S'hall 6E 60
Allendale Clo. SE5 2D 104
Allendale Clo. SE26 5K 123
Allendale Rd. Gnfd 6B 44
Allen Edwards Dri. SW8 1J 103
Allenford Ho. SW15 6B 100 (off Tunworth Cres.)
Allen Rd. E3 2B 70
Allen Rd. N16 4E 50
Allen Rd. Beck 2K 141
Allen Rd. Croy 1A 152
Allen Rd. Sun 1K 131
Allensbury Pl. NW1 7H 49
Allens Rd. Enf 5D 8
Allen St. W8 3J 83
Allenswood Rd. SE9 3C 108
Allerford Ct. Harr 5G 25
Allerford Rd. SE6 3D 124
Allerton Ho. N1 3D 68 (1E 162) (off Provost Est.)
Allerton Rd. N16 2C 50
Allerton St. N1 3D 68 (1E 162)
Allerton Wlk. N7 2K 49
Allestree Rd. SW6 7G 83
Alleyn Cres. SE21 2D 122
Alleyndale Rd. Dag 2C 56
Alleyn Ho. SE1 3D 86 (off Burbage Clo.)
Alleyn Pk. SE21 2D 122
Alleyn Pk. S'hall 5D 78
Alleyn Rd. SE21 3D 122
Allfarthing La. SW18 6K 101
Allgood Clo. Mord 6F 137
Allgood St. E2 2F 69 (1K 163)
Allhallows La. EC4 7D 68 (3E 168)
Allhallows Rd. E6 5C 72
All Hallows Rd. N17 1E 32
Alliance Clo. Wemb 4D 44
Alliance Ct. W3 5H 63
Alliance Rd. E13 5A 72
Alliance Rd. SE18 6A 92
Alliance Rd. W3 4H 63
Allied Ind. Est. W3 2A 82
Allied Way. W3 2A 82
Allingham Clo. W7 7K 61
Allingham St. N1 2C 68
Allington Av. N17 6K 17
Allington Av. Shep 3G 131
Allington Clo. SW19 5F 119
Allington Clo. Gnfd 7G 43
Allington Ct. SW1 3F 85 (2K 171) (off Allington St.)
Allington Ct. SW8 2G 103
Allington Ct. Enf 5E 8 (in two parts)
Allington Rd. NW4 5D 28
Allington Rd. W10 3G 65
Allington Rd. Harr 5G 25
Allington Rd. Orp 7J 145
Allington St. SW1 3F 85 (2K 171)
Allison Clo. SE10 1E 106
Allison Gro. SE21 1E 122
Allison Rd. N8 5A 32
Allison Rd. W3 6J 63
Alliston Ho. E2 3F 69 (2K 163) (off Gibraltar Wlk.)
Allitsen Rd. NW8 2C 66 (in two parts)
Allnutt Way. SW4 5H 103
Alloa Rd. SE8 5K 87
Alloa Rd. Ilf 2A 56
Allom Ho. W11 7G 65 (off Clarendon Rd.)
Allonby Dri. Ruis 7D 22
Allonby Gdns. Wemb 1C 44
Allonby Ho. E14 5A 70 (off Aston St.)
Allotment Way. NW2 3F 47
Alloway Rd. E3 3A 70
Allport Ho. SE5 3D 104 (off Denmark Hill)
All Saints Clo. N9 2B 18
All Saints Ct. E1 7J 69 (off Johnson St.)
All Saints Ct. SW11 7F 85 (off Prince of Wales Dri.)
All Saints Ct. Houn 1B 96 (off Springwell Rd.)
All Saints Dri. SE3 2G 107 (in two parts)
All Saints Ho. W11 5H 65 (off All Saints Rd.)
All Saints M. Harr 6D 10
All Saints Pas. SW18 5J 101
All Saints Rd. SW19 7A 120 (in two parts)
All Saints Rd. W3 3J 81
All Saints Rd. W11 5H 65
All Saints Rd. Sutt 3K 149
All Saints St. N1 2K 67
All Saints Tower. E10 7D 34
Allsop Pl. NW1 4D 66 (4F 159)
All Souls Av. NW10 2D 64
All Souls' Pl. W1 5F 67 (6K 159)
Allum Way. N20 1F 15
Allwood Clo. SE26 4K 123
Alma Av. E4 7K 19
Alma Birk Ho. NW6 7G 47
Almack Rd. E5 4J 51
Alma Clo. N10 1F 31
Alma Ct. Harr 2H 43
Alma Cres. Sutt 5G 149
Alma Gro. SE1 4F 87
Alma Ho. Bren 6E 80
Alma Pl. NW10 3D 64
Alma Pl. SE19 7F 123
Alma Pl. T Hth 5A 140
Alma Rd. N10 7A 16
Alma Rd. SW18 4A 102
Alma Rd. Cars 5C 150
Alma Rd. Enf 5F 9
Alma Rd. Esh 7J 133
Alma Rd. Sidc 3A 128
Alma Rd. S'hall 7C 60
Alma Rd. Ind. Est. Enf 4E 8
Alma Row. Harr 1H 25
Alma Sq. NW8 2A 66
Alma St. E15 6F 53
Alma St. NW5 6F 49
Alma Ter. SW18 7B 102
Alma Ter. W8 3J 83
Almeida St. N1 1B 68
Almeida Theatre. 1B 68 (off Almeida St.)
Almeric Rd. SW11 4D 102
Almer Rd. SW20 7C 118
Almington St. N4 1K 49
Almond Av. W5 3D 80
Almond Av. Cars 2D 150
Almond Av. Uxb 3D 40
Almond Av. W Dray 3C 76
Almond Clo. SE15 2G 105
Almond Clo. Brom 7E 144
Almond Clo. Felt 1J 113
Almond Clo. Hay 7G 59
Almond Clo. Ruis 3H 41
Almond Clo. Shep 2E 130
Almond Gro. Bren 7B 80
Almond Rd. N17 7B 18
Almond Rd. SE16 4H 87
Almonds Av. Buck H 2D 20
Almond Way. Brom 7E 144
Almond Way. Harr 2F 25
Almond Way. Mitc 5H 139
Almorah Rd. N1 7D 50
Almorah Rd. Houn 1B 96
Almshouse La. Chess 7C 146
Alnmouth Ct. S'hall 6G 61 (off Fleming Rd.)
Alnwick. N17 7C 18
Alnwick Gro. Mord 4K 137
Alnwick Rd. E16 6A 72
Alnwick Rd. SE12 6K 107
Alperton. 2E 62
Alperton La. Gnfd & Wemb 3C 62
Alperton St. W10 4H 65
Alphabet Gdns. Cars 6B 138
Alphabet Sq. E3 5C 70
Alpha Bus. Cen. E17 5B 34
Alpha Clo. NW1 4C 66 (3D 158)
Alpha Est. Hay 2G 77
Alpha Gro. E14 2C 88
Alpha Ho. NW6 2J 65
Alpha Ho. NW8 4C 158
Alpha Ho. SW9 4K 103
Alpha Pl. NW6 2J 65
Alpha Pl. SW3 6C 84 (7D 170)
Alpha Pl. Mord 1F 149
Alpha Rd. E4 3H 19
Alpha Rd. N18 6B 18
Alpha Rd. SE14 1B 106
Alpha Rd. Croy 1E 152
Alpha Rd. Enf 4F 9
Alpha Rd. Surb 6F 135
Alpha Rd. Tedd 5H 115
Alpha Rd. Uxb 4D 58
Alpha St. SE15 2G 105
Alphea Clo. SW19 7C 120
Alpine Av. Surb 2J 147
Alpine Bus. Cen. E6 5E 72
Alpine Clo. Croy 3E 152
Alpine Copse. Brom 2E 144
Alpine Gro. E9 7J 51
Alpine Rd. E10 2D 52
Alpine Rd. SE16 4J 87 (in two parts)
Alpine Rd. W on T 7J 131
Alpine Vw. Cars 5C 150
Alpine Wlk. Stan 2D 10
Alpine Way. E6 5E 72
Alric Av. NW10 7K 45
Alric Av. N Mald 3A 136
Alroy Rd. N4 7A 32
Alsace Rd. SE17 5E 86
Alscot Rd. SE1 4F 87 (in two parts)
Alscot Rd. Ind. Est. SE1 3F 87
Alscot Way. SE1 4F 87
Alsike Rd. SE2 & Eri 3D 92
Alsom Av. Wor Pk 4C 148
Alston Clo. Surb 7B 134
Alston Rd. N18 5C 18
Alston Rd. SW17 4B 120
Alston Rd. Barn 3B 4
Altair Clo. N17 6A 18
Altash Way. SE9 2D 126
Altenburg Av. W13 3B 80
Altenburg Gdns. SW11 4D 102
Alt Gro. SW19 7H 119
Altham Ct. Harr 1F 25
Altham Rd. Pinn 1C 24
Althea St. SW6 2K 101
Althorne Gdns. E18 4H 35
Althorne Way. Dag 2G 57
Althorp Clo. Barn 1H 13
Althorpe M. SW11 1B 102
Althorpe Rd. Harr 5G 25
Althorp Rd. SW17 1D 120
Altior Ct. N6 6G 31
Altmore Av. E6 7D 54
Alton Av. Stan 7E 10
Alton Clo. Bex 1E 128
Alton Clo. Iswth 2K 97
Alton Gdns. Beck 7C 124
Alton Gdns. Twic 7H 97
Alton Rd. N17 3D 32
Alton Rd. SW15 1C 118
Alton Rd. Croy 3A 152
Alton Rd. Rich 4E 98
Alton St. E14 5D 70
Altyre Clo. Beck 5B 142
Altyre Rd. Croy 2D 152
Altyre Way. Beck 5B 142
Aluna Ct. SE15 3J 105
Alvanley Gdns. NW6 5K 47
Alverstone Av. SW19 2J 119
Alverstone Av. Barn 7H 5
Alverstone Gdns. SE9 1G 127
Alverstone Ho. SE11 6A 86 (7J 173)
Alverstone Rd. E12 4E 54
Alverstone Rd. NW2 7E 46
Alverstone Rd. N Mald 4B 136
Alverstone Rd. Wemb 1F 45
Alverston Gdns. SE25 5E 140
Alverton St. SE8 5B 88 (in two parts)
Alveston Av. Harr 3B 26
Alvey St. SE17 5E 86
Alvia Gdns. Sutt 4A 150
Alvington Cres. E8 5F 51
Alway Av. Eps 5K 147
Alwold Cres. SE12 6K 107
Alwyn Av. W4 5K 81
Alwyn Clo. New Ad 7D 154
Alwyne Ho. N1 7B 50 (off Alwyne La.)
Alwyne La. N1 7B 50
Alwyne Pl. N1 6C 50
Alwyne Rd. N1 7C 50
Alwyne Rd. SW19 6H 119
Alwyne Rd. W7 7J 61
Alwyne Sq. N1 6C 50
Alwyne Vs. N1 7B 50
Alwyn Gdns. NW4 4C 28
Alwyn Gdns. W3 6H 63
Alyth Gdns. NW11 6J 29
Alzette Ho. E2 2K 69 (off Mace St.)
Amadeus Ho. Brom 3K 143 (off Elmfield Rd.)
Amalgamated Dri. Bren 6A 80

Amanda M. Romf. 5J 39
Amar Ct. SE18 4K 91
Amar Deep Ct. SE18 5K 91
Amazon St. E1 6G 69
Ambassador Clo. Houn 2C 96
Ambassador Gdns. E6 5D 72
Ambassadors Ct. E8 7F 51 (off Holly St.)
Ambassador's Ct. SW1 5B 166
Ambassador Sq. E14 4D 88
Ambassadors Theatre. 7H 67 (1D 166) (off West St.)
Amber Av. E17 1A 34
Amberden Av. N3 3J 29
Ambergate St. SE17 5B 86
Amber Gro. NW2 1F 47
Amberley Clo. Pinn 3D 24
Amberley Ct. Beck 7B 124
Amberley Ct. Sidc 5C 128
Amberley Gdns. Enf 7K 7
Amberley Gdns. Eps 4B 148
Amberley Gro. SE26 5H 123
Amberley Gro. Croy 7F 141
Amberley Rd. E10 7C 34
Amberley Rd. N13 2E 16
Amberley Rd. SE2 6D 92
Amberley Rd. W9 5J 65
Amberley Rd. Buck H 1F 21
Amberley Rd. Enf 7A 8
Amberley Way. Houn 5A 96
Amberley Way. Mord 7H 137
Amberley Way. Romf 4H 39
Amberley Way. Uxb 2A 58
Amberside Clo. Iswth 6H 97
Amberwood Clo. Wall 5J 151
Amberwood Ri. N Mald 6A 136
Amblecote Clo. SE12 3K 125
Amblecote Meadows. SE12 3K 125
Amblecote Rd. SE12 3K 125
Ambler Rd. N4 3B 50
Ambleside. NW1 1K 159
Ambleside. Brom 6F 125
Ambleside Av. SW16 4H 121
Ambleside Av. Beck 5A 142
Ambleside Av. W on T 7A 132
Ambleside Clo. E9 5J 51
Ambleside Clo. E10 7D 34
Ambleside Cres. Enf 3E 8
Ambleside Dri. Felt 1H 113
Ambleside Gdns. SW16 5H 121
Ambleside Gdns. Ilf 4C 36
Ambleside Gdns. Sutt 6A 150
Ambleside Gdns. Wemb 1D 44
Ambleside Point. SE15 7J 87 (off Tustin Est.)
Ambleside Rd. NW10 7B 46
Ambleside Rd. Bexh 2G 111
Ambleside Wlk. Uxb 1A 58 (off Cumbrian Way)
Ambrooke Rd. Belv 3G 93
Ambrosden Av. SW1 3G 85 (2B 172)
Ambrose Av. NW11 7G 29
Ambrose Clo. E6 5D 72
Ambrose Ho. E14 5C 70 (off Selsey St.)
Ambrose M. SW11 2D 102
Ambrose St. SE16 4H 87
Ambrose Wlk. E3 2C 70
AMC Bus. Cen. NW10 3H 63
Amelia Clo. W3 1H 81
Amelia Ho. W6 5E 82 (off Queen Caroline St.)
Amelia St. SE17 5C 86
Amen Corner. EC4 6B 68 (1B 168)
Amen Corner. SW17 6D 120
Amen Ct. EC4 6B 68 (1B 168)
Amenity Way. Mord 7E 136
American International University of London, The. 7E 98 (in Richmond University)
America Sq. EC3 7F 69 (2J 169)
America St. SE1 1C 86 (5C 168)
Amerland Rd. SW18 5H 101
Amersham Av. N18 6J 17
Amersham Gro. SE14 7B 88
Amersham Rd. SE14 1B 106
Amersham Rd. Croy 6C 140
Amersham Va. SE14 7B 88
Amery Gdns. NW10 1E 64
Amery Ho. SE17 5E 86 (off Kinglake St.)
Amery Rd. Harr 2A 44
Amesbury Av. SW2 2J 121
Amesbury Clo. Wor Pk 1E 148
Amesbury Ct. Enf 2F 7
Amesbury Dri. E4 6J 9
Amesbury Rd. Brom 3B 144
Amesbury Rd. Dag 7D 56
Amesbury Rd. Felt 2B 114
Amesbury Tower. SW8 2G 103
Ames Cotts. E14 5A 70 (off Maroon St.)
Ames Ho. E2 2K 69 (off Mace St.)
Amethyst Clo. N11 7C 16
Amethyst Rd. E15 4F 53
Amherst Av. W13 6C 62
Amherst Dri. Orp 4K 145
Amherst Gdns. W13 6C 62 (off Amherst Rd.)
Amherst Ho. SE16 2K 87 (off Wolfe Cres.)
Amherst Rd. W13 6C 62
Amhurst Gdns. Iswth 2A 98
Amhurst Pk. N16 7D 32
Amhurst Pas. E8 5G 51
Amhurst Rd. N16 & E8 4F 51
Amhurst Ter. E8 4G 51
Amhurst Wlk. SE28 1A 92
Amias Ho. EC1 4C 68 (3C 162) (off Central St.)
Amidas Gdns. Dag 4B 56
Amiel St. E1 4J 69
Amies St. SW11 3D 102
Amigo Ho. SE1 3A 86 (1K 173) (off Morley St.)
Amina Way. SE16 3G 87
Amis Av. Eps 6H 147
Amity Gro. SW20 1D 136
Amity Rd. E15 7H 53
Ammanford Grn. NW9 6A 28
Amner Rd. SW11 6E 102
Amor Rd. W6 3E 82
Amory Ho. N1 1K 67 (off Barnsbury Est.)
Amott Rd. SE15 3G 105
Amoy Pl. E14 6B 70 (in two parts)
Ampere Way. Croy 7J 139 (in two parts)
Ampleforth Rd. SE2 2B 92
Ampthill Est. NW1 2G 67 (1B 160)
Ampton Pl. WC1 3K 67 (2G 161)
Ampton St. WC1 3K 67 (2G 161)
Amroth Clo. SE23 1H 123
Amroth Grn. NW9 6A 28
Amstel Ct. SE15 7F 87 (off Garnies Clo.)
Amsterdam Rd. E14 3E 88
Amundsen Ct. E14 5C 88 (off Napier Av.)
Amundsen Ho. NW10 7K 45 (off Stonebridge Pk.)
Amwell Clo. Enf 5J 7
Amwell Ct. Est. N16 2C 50
Amwell St. EC1 3A 68 (1J 161)
Amyand Cotts. Twic 6B 98
Amyand La. Twic 7B 98
Amyand Pk. Gdns. Twic 7B 98
Amyand Pk. Rd. Twic 7A 98
Amy Clo. Wall 7J 151
Amy Johnson Ct. Edgw 2H 27
Amyruth Rd. SE4 5C 106
Amy's Clo. E16 1K 89 (off Pankhurst Av.)
Amy Warne Clo. E6 4C 72
Anatola Rd. N19 2F 49
Ancaster Cres. N Mald 6C 136
Ancaster M. Beck 3K 141
Ancaster Rd. Beck 3K 141
Ancaster St. SE18 7J 91
Anchor. SW18 4K 101
Anchorage Clo. SW19 5J 119
Anchorage Ho. E14 7F 71 (off Clove Cres.)
Anchorage Point. E14 2B 88 (off Cuba St.)
Anchorage Point Ind. Est. SE7 3A 90
Anchor & Hope La. SE7 3K 89
Anchor Brewhouse. SE1 1F 87 (5J 169)
Anchor Bus. Cen. Croy 3J 151
Anchor Clo. Bark 3B 74
Anchor Ct. SW1 4H 85 (4C 172) (off Vauxhall Bri. Rd.)
Anchor Ct. Enf 5K 7
Anchor Ho. E16 5H 71 (off Barking Rd.)
Anchor Ho. E16 6A 72 (off Prince Regent La.)
Anchor Ho. EC1 4C 68 (3C 162) (off Old St.)
Anchor M. SW12 6F 103
Anchor St. SE16 4H 87
Anchor Ter. E1 4J 69 (off Cephas Av.)
Anchor Wharf. E3 5D 70 (off Yeo St.)
Anchor Yd. EC1 4C 68 (3D 162)
Ancill Clo. W6 6G 83
Ancona Rd. NW10 2C 64
Ancona Rd. SE18 5H 91
Andace Pk. Gdns. Brom 2A 144
Andalus Rd. SW9 3J 103
Andaman Ho. E1 5A 70 (off Duckett St.)
Ander Clo. Wemb 4D 44
Anderson Clo. N21 5E 6
Anderson Clo. W3 6K 63
Anderson Clo. Sutt 1J 149
Anderson Ct. NW2 1E 46
Anderson Dri. Ashf 4E 112
Anderson Ho. E14 7E 70 (off Woolmore St.)
Anderson Ho. W12 6D 64 (off Du Cane Rd.)
Anderson Ho. Bark 1H 73
Anderson Pl. Houn 4F 97
Anderson Rd. E9 6K 51
Anderson Rd. Wfd G 3B 36
Anderson Sq. N1 1B 68 (off Gaskin St.)
Anderson St. SW3 5D 84 (5E 170)
Anderson Way. Belv 2J 93
Anderton Clo. SE5 3D 104
Anderton Ct. N22 2H 31
Andorra Ct. Brom 1A 144
Andover Av. E16 6B 72
Andover Clo. Felt 1H 113
Andover Clo. Gnfd 4F 61
Andover Pl. NW6 2K 65
Andover Rd. N7 2K 49
Andover Rd. Orp 7H 145
Andover Rd. Twic 1H 115
Andoversford Ct. SE15 6E 86 (off Bibury Clo.)
Andreck Ct. Beck 2D 142
Andre St. E8 5G 51
Andrew Borde St. WC2 6H 67 (7D 160)
Andrew Clo. Dart 5K 111
Andrew Ct. SE23 2K 123
Andrewes Gdns. E6 6C 72
Andrewes Highwalk. EC2 6D 162
Andrewes Ho. EC2 6D 162
Andrewes Ho. Sutt 4J 149
Andrew Pl. SW8 7H 85
Andrews Clo. Buck H 2F 21
Andrews Clo. Harr 7H 25
Andrews Clo. Wor Pk 2F 149
Andrews Crosse. WC2 1J 167
Andrews Ho. NW3 7D 48 (off Fellows Rd.)
Andrew's Ho. S Croy 6C 152
Andrews Pl. SE9 6F 109
Andrews Pl. Bex 2K 129
Andrew's Rd. E8 1H 69
Andrew St. E14 6E 70
Andrews Wlk. SE17 6B 86
Andringham Lodge. Brom 1K 143 (off Palace Gro.)
Andwell Clo. SE2 2B 92
Anerley. 2H 141
Anerley Gro. SE19 7F 123
Anerley Hill. SE19 6F 123
Anerley Pk. SE20 7G 123
Anerley Pk. Rd. SE20 7H 123
Anerley Rd. SE19 & SE20 7G 123
Anerley Sta. Rd. SE20 1H 141
Anerley Va. SE19 7F 123
Aneurin Bevan Ct. NW2 2D 46
Aneurin Bevan Ho. N11 7C 16
Anfield Clo. SW12 7G 103
Angel. (Junct.) 2B 68
Angela Davies Ind. Est. SE24 4B 104
Angel All. E1 7K 163
Angel Cen., The. N1 2A 68 (off St John St.)
Angel Clo. N18 5A 18
Angel Corner Pde. N18 4B 18
Angel Ct. EC2 6D 68 (7F 163)
Angel Ct. SW1 1G 85 (5B 166)
Angel Edmonton. (Junct.) 4B 18
Angelfield. Houn 4F 97
Angel Ga. EC1 3B 68 (1B 162) (in three parts)
Angel Hill. Sutt 3K 149 (in two parts)
Angel Hill Dri. Sutt 3K 149
Angelica Clo. W Dray 6A 58
Angelica Dri. E6 5E 72
Angelica Gdns. Croy 1K 153
Angelina Ho. SE15 1G 105 (off Goldsmith Rd.)
Angel La. E15 6F 53
Angel La. Hay 5F 59
Angell Pk. Gdns. SW9 3A 104
Angell Rd. SW9 3A 104
Angell Town. 1A 104
Angell Town Est. SW9 2A 104
Angel M. E1 7H 69
Angel M. N1 2A 68
Angel M. SW15 7C 100
Angel Pas. EC4 7D 68 (3E 168)
Angel Pl. N18 4B 18
Angel Pl. SE1 2D 86 (6E 168)
Angel Rd. N18 5B 18
Angel Rd. Harr 6J 25
Angel Rd. Th Dit 7A 134
Angel Rd. Works. N18 5D 18
Angel Sq. EC1 2A 68
Angel St. EC1 6C 68 (7C 162)
Angel Wlk. W6 4E 82
Angel Way. Romf 5K 39
Angel Yd. N6 1E 48
Angerstein Bus. Pk. SE10 4J 89
Angerstein La. SE3 1H 107
Anglebury. W2 6J 65 (off Talbot Rd.)
Angle Clo. Uxb 1C 58
Angle Grn. Dag 1C 56
Anglers Clo. Rich 4C 116
Angler's La. NW5 6F 49
Anglers Reach. Surb 5D 134
Anglers, The. King T 3D 134 (off High St.)
Anglesea Av. SE18 4F 91
Anglesea Ho. King T 4D 134 (off Anglesea Rd.)
Anglesea Rd. SE18 4F 91
Anglesea Rd. King T 4D 134
Anglesey Clo. Ashf 3C 112
Anglesey Ct. W7 4K 61
Anglesey Ct. Rd. Cars 6E 150
Anglesey Gdns. Cars 6E 150
Anglesey Ho. E14 6C 70 (off Lindfield St.)
Anglesey Rd. Enf 4C 8
Anglesmede Cres. Pinn 3E 24
Anglesmede Way. Pinn 3E 24
Angles Rd. SW16 4J 121
Anglia Clo. N17 7C 18
Anglia Ct. Dag 1D 56 (off Spring Clo.)
Anglia Ho. E14 6A 70 (off Salmon La.)
Anglian Ind. Est. Bark 4K 73
Anglian Rd. E11 3F 53
Anglia Wlk. E6 1E 72 (off Napier Rd.)
Anglo Rd. E3 2B 70
Angrave Ct. E8 1F 69 (off Scriven St.)
Angrave Pas. E8 1F 69
Angus Clo. Chess 5G 147
Angus Dri. Ruis 4A 42
Angus Gdns. NW9 1K 27
Angus Ho. SW2 7H 103
Angus Rd. E13 3A 72
Angus St. SE14 7A 88
Anhalt Rd. SW11 7C 84
Ankerdine Cres. SE18 7F 91
Anlaby Rd. Tedd 5J 115
Anley Rd. W14 2F 83
Anmersh Gro. Stan 1D 26
Annabel Clo. E14 6D 70
Anna Clo. E8 1F 69
Annandale Gro. Uxb 3E 40
Annandale Rd. SE10 6H 89
Annandale Rd. W4 5A 82
Annandale Rd. Croy 2G 153
Annandale Rd. Sidc 7J 109
Anna Neagle Clo. E7 4J 53
Annan Way. Romf 1K 39
Anne Boleyn Ct. SE9 6G 109
Anne Boleyn's Wlk. King T 5E 116
Anne Boleyn's Wlk. Sutt 7F 149
Anne Case M. N Mald 3K 135
Anne Compton M. SE12 7H 107
Anne Goodman Ho. E1 6J 69 (off Jubilee St.)
Anne of Cleeves Ct. SE9 6H 109
Annesley Av. NW9 3K 27
Annesley Clo. NW10 3A 46
Annesley Dri. Croy 3B 154
Annesley Ho. SW9 1A 104
Annesley Rd. SE3 1K 107
Annesley Wlk. N19 2G 49
Anne St. E13 4J 71
Anne Sutherland Ho. Beck 7A 124
Annett Clo. Shep 4G 131
Annette Clo. Harr 2J 25
Annette Rd. N7 3K 49 (in two parts)
Annett Rd. W on T 7J 131
Annetts Cres. N1 7C 50
Anne Way. W Mol 4F 133
Annie Besant Clo. E3 1B 70
Annie Taylor Ho. E12 4E 54 (off Walton Rd.)
Anning St. EC2 4E 68 (3H 163)
Annington Rd. N2 3D 30
Annis Rd. E9 6A 52
Ann La. SW10 6B 84
Ann Moss Way. SE16 3J 87
Ann's Clo. SW1 7F 165
Ann's Pl. E1 6J 163

Ann St. SE18 5G 91 (in two parts)
Annsworthy Av. T Hth 3D 140
Annsworthy Cres. SE25 2D 140
Ansar Gdns. E17 5B 34
Ansdell Rd. SE15 2J 105
Ansdell St. W8 3K 83
Ansdell Ter. W8 3K 83
Ansell Gro. Cars 1E 150
Ansell Ho. E1 5J 69 (off Mile End Rd.)
Ansell Rd. SW17 3C 120
Anselm Clo. Croy 3F 153
Anselm Rd. SW6 6J 83
Anselm Rd. Pinn 1D 24
Ansford Rd. Brom 5E 124
Ansleigh Pl. W11 7F 65
Anson Clo. Romf 2H 39
Anson Ho. E1 4A 70 (off Shandy St.)
Anson Ho. SW1 6G 85 (7A 172) (off Churchill Gdns.)
Anson Pl. SE28 2H 91
Anson Rd. N7 4G 49
Anson Rd. NW2 4D 46
Anson Ter. N'holt 6F 43
Anstey Ct. W3 2H 81
Anstey Ho. E9 1J 69 (off Templecombe Rd.)
Anstey Rd. SE15 3G 105
Anstey Wlk. N15 4B 32
Anstice Clo. W4 7A 82
Anstridge Path. SE9 6H 109
Anstridge Rd. SE9 6H 109
Antelope Rd. SE18 3D 90
Antenor Ho. E2 2H 69 (off Old Bethnal Grn. Rd.)
Anthony Clo. NW7 4F 13
Anthony Cope Ct. N1 3D 68 (1F 163) (off Chart St.)
Anthony Ho. NW8 4C 66 (4C 158) (off Ashbridge St.)
Anthony Rd. SE25 6G 141
Anthony Rd. Gnfd 3J 61
Anthony Rd. Well 1A 110
Anthony St. E1 6H 69
Anthony Way. N18 6E 18
Antigua Wlk. SE19 5D 122
Antilles Bay. E14 2E 88
Antill Rd. E3 3A 70
Antill Rd. N15 4G 33
Antill Ter. E1 6K 69
Antlers Hill. E4 5J 9
Anton Cres. Sutt 3J 149
Antoneys Clo. Pinn 2B 24
Anton Pl. Wemb 3H 45
Anton St. E8 5G 51
Antony Ho. SE14 7K 87 (off Barlborough St.)
Antony Ho. SE16 4J 87 (off Raymouth Rd.)
Antrim Gro. NW3 6D 48
Antrim Rd. NW3 6D 48
Antrobus Clo. Sutt 5H 149
Antrobus Rd. W4 4J 81
Anvil Clo. SW16 7G 121
Anvil Rd. Sun 3J 131
Anworth Clo. Wfd G 6E 20
Apeldoorn Dri. Wall 7J 151
Apex Clo. Beck 1D 142
Apex Corner. (Junct.) 3D 114 (Hanworth)
Apex Corner. (Junct.) 4F 13 (Mill Hill)
Apex Ct. W13 7A 62
Apex Ind. Est. NW10 4B 64
Apex Pde. NW7 4E 12 (off Selvage La.)
Apex Retail Pk. Felt 3D 114
Aphrodite Ct. E14 4C 88 (off Homer Dri.)
Aplin Way. Iswth 1J 97
Apollo Av. Brom 1K 143
Apollo Bus. Cen. SE8 5K 87
Apollo Ct. E1 7G 69 (off Thomas More St.)
Apollo Ct. SW9 1A 104 (off Southey Rd.)
Apollo Ho. E2 2H 69 (off St Jude's Rd.)
Apollo Ho. N6 7D 30
Apollo Ho. SW10 7B 84 (off Riley St.)
Apollo Pl. E11 3G 53
Apollo Pl. SW10 7B 84
Apollo Theatre. 7H 67 (2C 166) (off Shaftesbury Av.)
Apollo Victoria Theatre. 3G 85 (2A 172) (off Wilton Rd.)
Apollo Way. SE28 3H 91
Apostle Way. T Hth 2B 140
Apothecary St. EC4 6B 68 (1A 168)
Appach Rd. SW2 5A 104
Apple Blossom Ct. SW8 7H 85 (off Pascal St.)
Appleby Clo. E4 6K 19
Appleby Clo. N15 5D 32
Appleby Clo. Twic 2H 115
Appleby Gdns. Felt 1H 113
Appleby Rd. E8 7G 51
Appleby Rd. E16 6H 71
Appleby St. E2 2F 69
Appledore Av. Bexh 1J 111
Appledore Av. Ruis 3K 41
Appledore Clo. SW17 2D 120
Appledore Clo. Brom 5H 143
Appledore Clo. Edgw 1G 27
Appledore Cres. Sidc 3J 127
Appleford Ho. W10 4G 65 (off Bosworth Rd.)
Appleford Rd. W10 4G 65
Apple Gth. Bren 4D 80
Applegarth. Clay 5A 146
Applegarth. New Ad 7D 154 (in two parts)
Applegarth Dri. Ilf 4K 37
Applegarth Ho. SE1 6B 168
Applegarth Ho. SE15 7G 87 (off Bird in Bush Rd.)
Applegarth Rd. SE28 1B 92
Applegarth Rd. W14 3F 83
Apple Gro. Chess 4E 146
Apple Gro. Enf 3K 7
Apple Mkt. King T 2D 134
Apple Rd. E11 3G 53
Appleshaw Ho. SE5 3E 104
Appleton Clo. Bexh 2J 111
Appleton Gdns. N Mald 6C 136
Appleton Rd. SE9 3C 108
Appleton Sq. Mitc 1C 138
Apple Tree Av. Uxb & W Dray 5B 58
Appletree Clo. SE20 1H 141
Appletree Gdns. Barn 4H 5
Apple Tree Yd. SW1 1G 85 (4B 166)
Applewood Clo. N20 1H 15 (in two parts)
Applewood Clo. NW2 3D 46
Applewood Clo. Ick 4A 40
Applewood Dri. E13 4K 71
Appold St. EC2 5E 68 (5G 163)
Apprentice Way. E5 4H 51
Approach Clo. N16 4E 50
Approach Rd. E2 2J 69
Approach Rd. SW20 2E 136
Approach Rd. Ashf 6E 112
Approach Rd. Barn 4G 5
Approach Rd. Edgw 6B 12
Approach Rd. W Mol 5E 132
Approach, The. NW4 5F 29
Approach, The. W3 6K 63
Approach, The. Enf 2C 8
Aprey Gdns. NW4 4E 28
April Clo. W7 7J 61
April Clo. Felt 3J 113
April Ct. E2 2G 69 (off Teale St.)
April Glen. SE23 3K 123
April St. E8 4F 51
Apsley Clo. Harr 5G 25
Apsley Ho. E1 5J 69 (off Stepney Way)
Apsley Ho. NW8 2B 66 (off Finchley Rd.)
Apsley Ho. Houn 4D 96
Apsley Rd. SE25 4H 141
Apsley Rd. N Mald 3J 135
Apsley Way. NW2 2C 46
Apsley Way. W1 2E 84 (6H 165) (in two parts)
Aquarius. Twic 1B 116
Aquarius Bus. Pk. NW2 1C 46 (off Priestley Way)
Aquila St. NW8 2B 66
Aquinas St. SE1 1A 86 (5K 167)
Arabella Dri. SW15 4A 100
Arabia Clo. E4 7K 9
Arabian Ho. E1 4A 70 (off Ernest St.)
Arabin Rd. SE4 4A 106
Aragon Av. Th Dit 5K 133
Aragon Clo. Brom 1D 156
Aragon Clo. Enf 1E 6
Aragon Clo. Sun 6H 113
Aragon Ct. E Mol 4G 133
Aragon Dri. Ruis 1B 42
Aragon Ho. E16 1J 89 (off Capulet M.)
Aragon Rd. King T 5E 116
Aragon Rd. Mord 6F 137
Aragon Tower. SE8 4B 88
Aral Ho. E1 4K 69 (off Ernest St.)
Arandora Cres. Romf 7B 38
Aran Dri. Stan 4H 11
Arapiles Ho. E14 6F 71 (off Blair St.)
Arbery Rd. E3 3A 70
Arbon Ct. N1 1C 68 (off Linton St.)
Arbor Clo. Beck 2D 142
Arbor Ct. N16 2D 50
Arboretum Ct. N1 6D 50 (off Dove Rd.)
Arborfield Clo. SW2 1K 121
Arborfield Ho. E14 7C 70 (off E. India Dock Rd.)
Arbor Rd. E4 3A 20
Arbour Ho. E1 6K 69 (off Arbour Sq.)
Arbour Rd. Enf 3E 8
Arbour Sq. E1 6K 69
Arbroath Rd. SE9 3C 108
Arbury Ct. SE20 1H 141
Arbury Ter. SE26 3G 123
Arbuthnot La. Bex 6E 110
Arbuthnot Rd. SE14 2K 105
Arbutus St. E8 1F 69
Arcade. Croy 2C 152
Arcade Pde. Chess 5D 146
Arcade, The. E14 6D 70
Arcade, The. E17 4C 34
Arcade, The. EC2 6G 163
Arcade, The. Bark 7G 55
Arcade, The. Croy 3C 152 (off High St.)
Arcadia Av. N3 2J 29
Arcadia Cen., The. W5 7D 62
Arcadia Clo. Cars 4E 150
Arcadia Ct. E1 7J 163
Arcadian Av. Bex 6E 110
Arcadian Clo. Bex 6E 110
Arcadian Gdns. N22 7E 16
Arcadian Rd. Bex 6E 110
Arcadia St. E14 6C 70
Archangel St. SE16 2K 87
Archbishop's Pl. SW2 7K 103
Archdale Bus. Cen. Harr 2G 43
Archdale Ct. W12 1D 82
Archdale Ho. SE1 3E 86 (7G 169) (off Long La.)
Archdale Pl. King T 3H 135
Archdale Rd. SE22 5F 105
Archel Rd. W14 6H 83
Archer Clo. King T 7E 116
Archer Ho. SE14 1A 106
Archer Ho. SW11 1B 102
Archer Ho. W11 7H 65 (off Westbourne Gro.)
Archer Ho. W13 1B 80 (off Sherwood Clo.)
Archer M. Hamp H 6G 115
Archer Rd. SE25 4H 141
Archer Rd. Orp 5K 145
Archers Ct. Brom 4K 143
Archers Ct. S Croy 5C 152 (off Nottingham Rd.)
Archers Dri. Enf 2D 8
Archers Lodge. SE16 5G 87 (off Culloden Clo.)
Archer Sq. SE14 6A 88
Archer St. W1 7H 67 (2C 166)
Archer Ter. W Dray 7A 58
Archery Clo. W2 6C 66 (1D 164)
Archery Clo. Harr 3K 25
Archery Rd. SE9 5D 108
Archery Steps. W2 2D 164
Arches Bus. Cen., The. S'hall 2D 78 (off Merrick Rd.)
Arches, The. NW1 7F 49
Arches, The. SW8 7H 85
Arches, The. WC2 1J 85 (4F 167) (off Villiers St.)
Arches, The. Harr 2F 43
Archgate Bus. Cen. N12 5F 15
Archibald M. W1 7E 66 (3J 165)
Archibald Rd. N7 4H 49
Archibald St. E3 3C 70
Archie Clo. W Dray 2C 76
Arch St. SE1 3C 86
Archway. (Junct.) 2G 49
Archway Bus. Cen. N19 3H 49
Archway Clo. N19 2G 49
Archway Clo. SW19 3K 119
Archway Clo. W10 5F 65
Archway Clo. Wall 3H 151
Archway Mall. N19 2G 49
Archway M. SW15 4G 101 (off Putney Bri. Rd.)
Archway Rd. N6 & N19 6E 30
Archway St. SW13 3A 100
Arcola St. E8 5F 51
Arcon Ter. N9 7B 8
Arctic St. NW5 5F 49
Arcus Rd. Brom 6G 125
Ardbeg Rd. SE24 5D 104
Arden Clo. SE28 6D 74
Arden Clo. Harr 3H 43
Arden Ct. Gdns. N2 6B 30
Arden Cres. E14 4C 88
Arden Cres. Dag 7C 56
Arden Est. N1 2E 68
Arden Grange. N12 4F 15
Arden Ho. N1 1G 163
Arden Ho. SE11 4G 173
Arden Ho. SW9 2J 103 (off Grantham Rd.)
Arden M. E17 5D 34
Arden Mhor. Pinn 4K 23
Arden Rd. N3 3H 29
Arden Rd. W13 7C 62
Ardent Clo. SE25 3E 140
Ardent Ho. E3 2A 70 (off Roman Rd.)
Ardfern Av. SW16 3A 140
Ardfillan Rd. SE6 1F 125
Ardgowan Rd. SE6 7G 107 (in two parts)
Ardilaun Rd. N5 4C 50
Ardingly Clo. Croy 3K 153
Ardleigh Gdns. Sutt 7J 137
Ardleigh Ho. Bark 1G 73
Ardleigh M. Ilf 3F 55
Ardleigh Rd. E17 1B 34
Ardleigh Rd. N1 6E 50
Ardleigh Ter. E17 1B 34
Ardley Clo. NW10 3A 46
Ardley Clo. SE6 3A 124
Ardley Clo. Ruis 7E 22
Ardlui Rd. SE27 2C 122
Ardmay Gdns. Surb 5E 134
Ardmere Rd. SE13 6F 107
Ardmore La. Buck H 1E 20
Ardmore Pl. Buck H 1E 20
Ardoch Rd. SE6 2F 125
Ardra Rd. N9 3E 18
Ardrossan Gdns. Wor Pk 3C 148
Ardshiel Clo. SW15 3F 101
Ardwell Av. Ilf 5G 37
Ardwell Rd. SW2 2J 121
Ardwick Rd. NW2 4J 47
Arena Bus. Cen. N4 6C 32
Arena Est. N4 6B 32
Arena, The. Enf 1G 9
Ares Ct. E14 4C 88 (off Homer Dri.)
Arethusa Ho. E14 4C 88 (off Cahir St.)
Argali Ho. Eri 3E 92 (off Kale Rd.)
Argall Av. E10 7K 33
Argall Way. E10 1K 51
Argenta Way. Wemb & NW10 6G 45
Argent Cen., The. Hay 2J 77
Argent Ct. Chess 3G 147
Argon M. SW6 7J 83
Argon Rd. N18 5E 18
Argos Ct. SW9 1A 104 (off Caldwell St.)
Argos Ho. E2 2H 69 (off Old Bethnal Grn. Rd.)
Argosy Ho. SE8 4A 88
Argosy La. Stanw 7A 94
Argus Clo. Romf 1H 39
Argus Way. N'holt 3C 60
Argyle Av. Houn 6E 96 (in two parts)
Argyle Clo. W13 4A 62
Argyle Ho. E14 3E 88
Argyle Pas. N17 1F 33
Argyle Pl. W6 4D 82
Argyle Rd. E1 4K 69
Argyle Rd. E15 4G 53
Argyle Rd. E16 6K 71
Argyle Rd. N12 5E 14
Argyle Rd. N17 1G 33
Argyle Rd. N18 4B 18
Argyle Rd. Barn 4A 4
Argyle Rd. Gnfd & W13 3K 61
Argyle Rd. Harr 6F 25
Argyle Rd. Houn 5F 97
Argyle Rd. Ilf 2E 54
Argyle Sq. WC1 3J 67 (1F 161)
Argyle St. WC1 3J 67 (1E 160)
Argyle Wlk. WC1 3J 67 (2F 161)
Argyle Way. SE16 5G 87
Argyll Av. S'hall 1F 79
Argyll Clo. SW9 3K 103
Argyll Gdns. Edgw 2H 27
Argyll Mans. SW3 6B 84 (7B 170)
Argyll Mans. W14 4G 83 (off Hammersmith Rd.)
Argyll Rd. W8 2J 83
Argyll St. W1 6G 67 (1A 166)
Arica Ho. SE16 3H 87 (off Slippers Pl.)
Arica Rd. SE4 4A 106
Ariel Ct. SE11 4B 86 (4K 173)
Ariel Rd. NW6 6J 47
Ariel Way. W12 1E 82

Ariel Way. *Houn.* 3K **95**
Aristotle Rd. *SW4* 3H **103**
Arkell Gro. *SE19* 7B **122**
Arkindale Rd. *SE6* 3E **124**
Arkley Cres. *E17* 5B **34**
Arkley Rd. *E17* 5B **34**
Arklow Ho. SE17 6D **86**
(off Albany Rd.)
Arklow M. *Surb* 2E **146**
Arklow Rd. *SE14* 6B **88**
Arklow Rd. Trad. Est.
SE14 6A **88**
Ark, The. W6 5F **83**
(off Talgarth Rd.)
Arkwright Ho. SW2 7J **103**
(off Streatham Pl.)
Arkwright Rd. *NW3* 5A **48**
Arkwright Rd. *S Croy* 7F **153**
Arlesey Clo. *SW15* 5G **101**
Arlesford Rd. *SW9* 3J **103**
Arlingford Rd. *SW2* 5A **104**
Arlington. *N12* 3D **14**
Arlington Av. *N1* 1C **68**
(in two parts)
Arlington Clo. *SE13* 5F **107**
Arlington Clo. *Sidc* 7J **109**
Arlington Clo. *Sutt* 2J **149**
Arlington Clo. *Twic* 6C **98**
Arlington Ct. W3 2H **81**
(off Mill Hill Rd.)
Arlington Ct. *Hay* 5G **77**
Arlington Dri. *Cars* 2D **150**
Arlington Dri. *Ruis* 6F **23**
Arlington Gdns. *W4* 5J **81**
Arlington Gdns. *Ilf* 1E **54**
Arlington Ho.
EC1 3A **68** (1K **161**)
(off Arlington Way)
Arlington Ho. SE8 6B **88**
(off Evelyn St.)
Arlington Ho.
SW1 1G **85** (4A **166**)
Arlington Ho. W12 1D **82**
(off Tunis Rd.)
Arlington Lodge. *SW2* 4K **103**
Arlington M. *Twic* 6B **98**
Arlington Pk. Mans. W4 5J **81**
(off Sutton La. N.)
Arlington Pas. *Tedd* 4K **115**
Arlington Pl. *SE10* 7E **88**
Arlington Rd. *N14* 2A **16**
Arlington Rd. *NW1* 1F **67**
Arlington Rd. *W13* 6B **62**
Arlington Rd. *Ashf* 5B **112**
Arlington Rd. *Rich* 2D **116**
Arlington Rd. *Surb* 6D **134**
Arlington Rd. *Tedd* 4K **115**
Arlington Rd. *Twic* 6C **98**
Arlington Rd. *Wfd G* 1J **35**
Arlington Sq. *N1* 1C **68**
Arlington St.
SW1 1G **85** (4A **166**)
Arlington Way.
EC1 3A **68** (1K **161**)
Arliss Ho. *Harr* 5K **25**
Arliss Way. *N'holt* 1A **60**
Arlow Rd. *N21* 1F **17**
Armada Ct. *SE8* 6C **88**
Armadale Clo. *N17* 4H **33**
Armadale Rd. *SW6* 7J **83**
Armadale Rd. *Felt* 5J **95**
Armada St. SE8 6C **88**
(off McMillan St.)
Armada Way. *E6* 7F **73**
Armagh Rd. *E3* 1B **70**
Armfield Clo. *W Mol* 5D **132**
Armfield Cres. *Mitc* 2D **138**
Armfield Rd. *Enf* 1J **7**
Arminger Rd. *W12* 1D **82**
Armistice Gdns. *SE25* 3G **141**
Armitage Rd. *NW11* 1G **47**
Armitage Rd. *SE10* 5H **89**
Armour Clo. *N7* 6K **49**
Armoury Rd. *SE8* 2D **106**
Armoury Way. *SW18* 5J **101**
Armsby Ho. E1 5J **69**
(off Stepney Way)
Armstead Wlk. *Dag* 7G **57**
Armstrong Av. *Wfd G* 6B **20**
Armstrong Clo. *E6* 6D **72**
Armstrong Clo. *Brom* 3C **144**
Armstrong Clo. *Dag* 7D **38**
Armstrong Clo. *Pinn* 6J **23**
Armstrong Clo. *W on T* 6J **131**
Armstrong Cres. *Cockf* 3G **5**
Armstrong Rd.
SW7 3B **84** (2A **170**)
Armstrong Rd. *W3* 1B **82**
Armstrong Rd. *Felt* 5C **114**
Armstrong Way. *S'hall* 2F **79**
Armytage Rd. *Houn* 7B **78**
Arnal Cres. *SW18* 7G **101**
Arncliffe. *NW6* 2K **65**
Arncliffe Clo. *N11* 6K **15**
Arncroft Ct. *Bark* 3B **74**
Arndale Wlk. *SW18* 5K **101**
Arne Ho. *SE11* 5G **173**
Arne St. *WC2* 6J **67** (1F **167**)
Arnett Sq. *E4* 6G **19**
Arne Wlk. *SE3* 4H **107**
Arneways Av. *Romf* 3D **38**
Arneway St.
SW1 3H **85** (2D **172**)
Arnewood Clo. *SW15* 1C **118**
Arneys La. *Mitc* 6E **138**
Arngask Rd. *SE6* 7F **107**
Arnhem Pl. *E14* 3C **88**
Arnhem Way. *SE22* 5E **104**
Arnhem Wharf. *E14* 3B **88**
Arnison Rd. *E Mol* 4H **133**
Arnold Cir. *E2* 3F **69** (2J **163**)
Arnold Clo. *Harr* 7F **27**
Arnold Ct. *N22* 7D **16**
Arnold Cres. *Isw* 5H **97**
Arnold Dri. *Chess* 6D **146**
Arnold Est. *SE1* 2F **87** (7K **169**)
(in two parts)
Arnold Gdns. *N13* 5G **17**
Arnold Ho. SE3 7A **90**
(off Shooters Hill Rd.)
Arnold Ho. SE17 5B **86**
(off Doddington Gro.)
Arnold Mans. W14 6H **83**
(off Queen's Club Gdns.)
Arnold Rd. *E3* 3C **70**
Arnold Rd. *N15* 3F **33**
Arnold Rd. *SW17* 7D **120**
Arnold Rd. *Dag* 7F **57**
Arnold Rd. *N'holt* 6C **42**
Arnold Ter. *Stan* 5E **10**
Arnos Gro. *N14* 4C **16**
Arnos Gro. Ct. N11 5B **16**
(off Palmer's Rd.)
Arnos Rd. *N11* 4B **16**
Arnot Ho. SE5 7C **86**
(off Comber Gro.)
Arnott Clo. *SE28* 1C **92**
Arnott Clo. *W4* 4K **81**
Arnould Av. *SE5* 4D **104**
Arnsberg Way. *Bexh* 4G **111**
Arnside Gdns. *Wemb* 1D **44**
Arnside Rd. *Bexh* 1G **111**
Arnside St. *SE17* 6D **86**
Arnulf St. *SE6* 4D **124**
Arnulls Rd. *SW16* 6B **122**
Arodene Rd. *SW2* 6K **103**
Arosa Rd. *Twic* 6D **98**
(in two parts)
Arpley Sq. SE20 7J **123**
(off High St.)
Arragon Gdns. *SW16* 7J **121**
Arragon Gdns. *W Wick* 3D **154**
Arragon Rd. *E6* 1B **72**
Arragon Rd. *SW18* 1J **119**
Arragon Rd. *Twic* 7A **98**
Arran Clo. *Eri* 6K **93**
Arran Clo. *Wall* 4F **151**
Arran Ct. *NW9* 2B **28**
Arran Ct. *NW10* 3K **45**
Arrandene Open Space. **6H 13**
Arran Dri. *E12* 1B **54**
Arran Ho. E14 1E **88**
(off Raleana Rd.)
Arran M. *W5* 1F **81**
Arran Rd. *SE6* 2D **124**
Arran Wlk. *N1* 7C **50**
Arras Av. *Mord* 5A **138**
Arrol Ho. *SE1* 3C **86**
Arrol Rd. *Beck* 3J **141**
Arrow Ct. SW5 4J **83**
(off W. Cromwell Rd.)
Arrowhead Ct. *E11* 6F **35**
Arrow Rd. *E3* 3D **70**
Arrowscout Wlk. *N'holt* 3C **60**
Arrowsmith Ho. *SE11* 5G **173**
Arsenal F.C. (Highbury). **3B 50**
Arsenal Rd. *SE9* 2D **108**
Artemis Ct. E14 4C **88**
(off Homer Dri.)
Arterberry Rd. *SW20* 7E **118**
Artesian Clo. *NW10* 7K **45**
Artesian Gro. *Barn* 4F **5**
Artesian Rd. *W2* 6J **65**
Artesian Wlk. *E11* 3G **53**
Arthingworth St. *E15* 1G **71**
Arthur Ct. *SW11* 1E **102**
Arthur Ct. W2 6K **65**
(off Queensway)
Arthur Ct. W10 6F **65**
(off Silchester Rd.)
Arthur Ct. Croy 3E **152**
(off Fairfield Path)
Arthur Deakin Ho. E1
5G **69** (5K **163**)
(off Hunton St.)
Arthurdon Rd. *SE4* 5C **106**
Arthur Gro. *SE18* 4G **91**
Arthur Henderson Ho.
SW6 2H **101**
(off Fulham Rd.)
Arthur Horsley Wlk. E7 5H **53**
(off Tower Hamlets Rd.)
Arthur Rd. *E6* 2D **72**
Arthur Rd. *N7* 4K **49**
Arthur Rd. *N9* 2A **18**
Arthur Rd. *SW19* 5H **119**
Arthur Rd. *King T* 7G **117**
Arthur Rd. *N Mald* 5D **136**
Arthur Rd. *Romf* 6C **38**
Arthur St. *EC4* 7D **68** (2F **169**)
Artichoke Hill. *E1* 7H **69**
Artichoke M. SE5 1D **104**
(off Artichoke Pl.)
Artichoke Pl. *SE5* 1D **104**
Artillery Clo. *Ilf* 6G **37**
Artillery Ho. *E15* 6G **53**
Artillery Ho. SE18 5E **90**
(off Connaught M.)
Artillery La. *E1* 5E **68** (6H **163**)
Artillery La. *W12* 6C **64**
Artillery Pas. *E1* 6J **163**
Artillery Pl. *SE18* 5D **90**
Artillery Pl. *SW1* 3H **85** (2C **172**)
Artillery Pl. *Harr* 7B **10**
Artillery Row.
SW1 3G **85** (2C **172**)
Artisan Clo. *E6* 6F **73**
Artizan St. *E1* 7J **163**
Arts Theatre. **7J 67 (2E 166)**
(off Up. St Martin's La.)
Arun Ct. *SE25* 5G **141**
Arundale. King T 4D **134**
(off Anglesea Rd.)
Arundel Av. *Mord* 4H **137**
Arundel Bldgs. SE1 3E **86**
(off Swan Mead)
Arundel Clo. *E15* 4G **53**
Arundel Clo. *SW11* 5C **102**
Arundel Clo. *Bex* 6F **111**
Arundel Clo. *Croy* 3B **152**
Arundel Clo. *Hamp H* 5F **115**
Arundel Ct. *N12* 6H **15**
Arundel Ct. *N17* 1G **33**
Arundel Ct. SE16 5H **87**
(off Varcoe Rd.)
Arundel Ct. SW3 5C **84** (5D **170**)
(off Jubilee Pl.)
Arundel Ct. SW13 6D **82**
(off Arundel Ter.)
Arundel Ct. *Brom* 2G **143**
Arundel Ct. *S Harr* 4E **42**
Arundel Dri. *Harr* 4D **42**
Arundel Dri. *Wfd G* 7D **20**
Arundel Gdns. *N21* 1F **17**
Arundel Gdns. *W11* 7H **65**
Arundel Gdns. *Edgw* 7E **12**
Arundel Gdns. *Ilf* 2A **56**
Arundel Gt. Ct.
WC2 7K **67** (2H **167**)
Arundel Gro. *N16* 5E **50**
Arundel Ho. W3 2H **81**
(off Park Rd. N.)
Arundel Ho. Croy 5D **152**
(off Heathfield Rd.)
Arundel Mans. SW6 1H **101**
(off Kelvedon Rd.)
Arundel Pl. *N1* 6A **50**
Arundel Rd. *Cockf* 3H **5**
Arundel Rd. *Croy* 6D **140**
Arundel Rd. *Houn* 3A **96**
Arundel Rd. *King T* 2H **135**
Arundel Rd. *Sutt* 7H **149**
Arundel Sq. *N7* 6A **50**
Arundel St. *WC2* 7K **67** (2H **167**)
Arundel Ter. *SW13* 6D **82**
Arun Ho. *King T* 1D **134**
Arvon Rd. *N5* 5A **50**
(in two parts)
Asa Ct. *Hay* 3H **77**
Asbridge Ct. W6 3D **82**
(off Dalling Rd.)
Ascalon Ho. SW8 7G **85**
(off Thessaly Rd.)
Ascalon St. *SW8* 7G **85**
Ascham Dri. *E4* 7J **19**
Ascham End. *E17* 1A **34**
Ascham St. *NW5* 5G **49**
Aschurch Rd. *Croy* 7F **141**
Ascot Clo. *N'holt* 5E **42**
Ascot Ct. *NW8* 2A **158**
Ascot Ct. *Bex* 7F **111**
Ascot Ct. *Brom* 2C **144**
Ascot Gdns. *S'hall* 4D **60**
Ascot Ho. NW1 3F **67** (1K **159**)
(off Redhill St.)
Ascot Ho. W9 4J **65**
(off Harrow Rd.)
Ascot Lodge. *NW6* 1K **65**
Ascot Pl. *Stan* 5H **11**
Ascot Rd. *E6* 3D **72**
Ascot Rd. *N15* 5D **32**
Ascot Rd. *N18* 4B **18**
Ascot Rd. *SW17* 6E **120**
Ascot Rd. *Felt* 1C **112**
Ascot Rd. *Orp* 4K **145**
Ascott Av. *W5* 2E **80**
Ascott Clo. *Pinn* 4J **23**
Ashbee Ho. E2 3J **69**
(off Portman Pl.)
Ashbourne Av. *E18* 4K **35**
Ashbourne Av. *N20* 2J **15**
Ashbourne Av. *NW11* 5H **29**
Ashbourne Av. *Bexh* 7E **92**
Ashbourne Av. *Harr* 2H **43**
Ashbourne Clo. *N12* 4E **14**
Ashbourne Clo. *W5* 5G **63**
Ashbourne Ct. *E5* 4A **52**
Ashbourne Ct. N12 4E **14**
(off Ashbourne Clo.)
Ashbourne Gro. *NW7* 5E **12**
Ashbourne Gro. *SE22* 4F **105**
Ashbourne Gro. *W4* 5A **82**
Ashbourne Pde. *NW11* 4H **29**
Ashbourne Pde. *W5* 4F **63**
Ashbourne Rd. *W5* 4F **63**
Ashbourne Rd. *Mitc* 7E **120**
Ashbourne Ter. *SW19* 7H **119**
Ashbourne Way. *NW11* 4H **29**
Ashbridge Rd. *E11* 7G **35**
Ashbridge St.
NW8 4C **66** (4C **158**)
Ashbrook. *Edgw* 6A **12**
Ashbrook Rd. *N19* 1H **49**
Ashbrook Rd. *Dag* 3H **57**
Ashburn Gdns. *SW7* 4A **84**
Ashburnham Av. *Harr* 6K **25**
Ashburnham Clo. *N2* 3B **30**
Ashburnham Ct. *Beck* 2E **142**
Ashburnham Ct. *Pinn* 3B **24**
Ashburnham Gdns. *Harr* 6K **25**
Ashburnham Gro. *SE10* 7D **88**
Ashburnham Mans. SW10 7A **84**
(off Ashburnham Rd.)
Ashburnham Pl. *SE10* 7D **88**
Ashburnham Retreat.
SE10 7D **88**
Ashburnham Rd. *NW10* 3E **64**
Ashburnham Rd. *SW10* 7A **84**
Ashburnham Rd. *Belv* 4J **93**
Ashburnham Rd. *Rich* 3B **116**
Ashburnham Tower. SW10 7B **84**
(off Worlds End Est.)
Ashburn Pl. *SW7* 4A **84**
Ashburton Av. *Croy* 1H **153**
Ashburton Av. *Ilf* 5J **55**
Ashburton Clo. *Croy* 1G **153**
Ashburton Enterprise Cen.
SW15 6E **100**
Ashburton Gdns. *Croy* 2G **153**
Ashburton Gro. *N7* 4A **50**
Ashburton Ho. W9 4H **65**
(off Fernhead Rd.)
Ashburton Memorial Homes.
Croy 7H **141**
Ashburton Rd. *E16* 6J **71**
Ashburton Rd. *Croy* 2G **153**
Ashburton Rd. *Ruis* 2J **41**
Ashburton Ter. *E13* 2J **71**
Ashbury Dri. *Uxb* 3D **40**
Ashbury Gdns. *Romf* 5D **38**
Ashbury Pl. *SW19* 6A **120**
Ashbury Rd. *SW11* 3D **102**
Ashby Av. *Chess* 6G **147**
Ashby Ct. NW8 4B **66** (3B **158**)
(off Pollitt Dri.)
Ashby Gro. *N1* 7C **50**
Ashby Ho. N1 7C **50**
(off Essex Rd.)
Ashby Ho. *SW9* 2B **104**
Ashby M. *SE4* 2B **106**
Ashby M. SW2 5J **103**
(off Prague Pl.)
Ashby Rd. *N15* 5G **33**
Ashby Rd. *SE4* 2B **106**
Ashby St. *EC1* 3B **68** (2B **162**)
Ashby Wlk. *Croy* 6C **140**
Ashby Way. *W Dray* 7C **76**
Ashchurch Gro. *W12* 3C **82**
Ashchurch Pk. Vs. *W12* 3C **82**
Ashchurch Ter. *W12* 3C **82**
Ash Clo. *SE20* 2J **141**
Ash Clo. *Cars* 2D **150**
Ash Clo. *Edgw* 4D **12**
Ash Clo. *Hare* 1A **22**
Ash Clo. *N Mald* 2K **135**
Ash Clo. *Orp* 5H **145**
Ash Clo. *Romf* 1H **39**
Ash Clo. *Sidc* 3B **128**
Ash Clo. *Stan* 6F **11**
Ashcombe Av. *Surb* 7D **134**
Ashcombe Gdns. *Edgw* 4B **12**
Ashcombe Pk. *NW2* 3A **46**
Ashcombe Rd. *SW19* 5J **119**
Ashcombe Rd. *Cars* 6E **150**
Ashcombe Sq. *N Mald* 3J **135**
Ashcombe St. *SW6* 2K **101**
Ash Ct. *NW5* 5G **49**
Ash Ct. *SW19* 7G **119**
Ash Ct. *Eps* 4J **147**
Ashcroft. *N14* 2C **16**

Ash Cft. Pinn ... 6A 10
Ashcroft Av. Sidc ... 6A 110
Ashcroft Ct. N20 ... 2G 15
Ashcroft Cres. Sidc ... 6A 110
Ashcroft Ho. SW8 ... 1G 103 (off Wadhurst Rd.)
Ashcroft Rd. E3 ... 3A 70
Ashcroft Rd. Chess ... 3F 147
Ashcroft Sq. W6 ... 4E 82
Ashcroft Theatre. ... 3D 152
Ashdale Clo. Stai ... 2A 112
Ashdale Clo. Twic ... 7G 97
Ashdale Gro. Stan ... 6E 10
Ashdale Ho. N4 ... 7D 32
Ashdale Rd. SE12 ... 1K 125
Ashdale Way. Twic ... 7F 97
Ashdene. SE15 ... 7H 87
Ashdene. Pinn ... 3A 24
Ashdene Clo. Ashf ... 7E 112
Ashdon Clo. Wfd G ... 6E 20
Ashdon Rd. NW10 ... 1B 64
Ashdown. W13 ... 5B 62 (off Clivedon Ct.)
Ashdown Clo. Beck ... 2D 142
Ashdown Clo. Bex ... 7J 111
Ashdown Ct. Sutt ... 6A 150
Ashdown Cres. NW5 ... 5E 48
Ashdowne Ct. N17 ... 1G 33
Ashdown Est. E11 ... 4F 53
Ashdown Ho. SW1 ... 3G 85 (2B 172) (off Victoria St.)
Ashdown Pl. Th Dit ... 7A 134
Ashdown Rd. Enf ... 2D 8
Ashdown Rd. King T ... 2E 134
Ashdown Rd. Uxb ... 2C 58
Ashdown Wlk. E14 ... 4C 88 (off Copeland Dri.)
Ashdown Wlk. Romf ... 1H 39
Ashdown Way. SW17 ... 2E 120
Ashe Ho. Twic ... 6D 98
Ashen. E6 ... 6E 72
Ashenden. SE17 ... 4C 86 (off Deacon Way)
Ashenden Rd. E5 ... 5A 52
Ashen Gro. SW19 ... 3J 119
Ashentree Ct. EC4 ... 1K 167
Asher Loftus Way. N11 ... 6J 15
Asher Way. E1 ... 7G 69
Ashfield Av. Felt ... 1K 113
Ashfield Clo. Beck ... 7C 124
Ashfield Clo. Rich ... 1E 116
Ashfield Ho. W14 ... 5H 83 (off W. Cromwell Rd.)
Ashfield La. Chst ... 6F 127 (in two parts)
Ashfield Pde. N14 ... 1C 16
Ashfield Rd. N4 ... 6C 32
Ashfield Rd. N14 ... 3B 16
Ashfield Rd. W3 ... 1B 82
Ashfield St. E1 ... 5H 69
Ashfield Yd. E1 ... 5J 69
Ashford. ... 4B 112
Ashford Av. N8 ... 4J 31
Ashford Av. Ashf ... 6D 112
Ashford Av. Hay ... 6B 60
Ashford Bus. Complex. Ashf ... 5E 112 (Sandell's Av.)
Ashford Bus. Complex. Ashf ... 4E 112 (Shield Rd.)
Ashford Clo. E17 ... 6B 34
Ashford Clo. Ashf ... 4A 112
Ashford Common. ... 7F 113
Ashford Ct. Edgw ... 3C 12
Ashford Cres. Ashf ... 3A 112
Ashford Cres. Enf ... 2D 8
Ashford Ho. SE8 ... 6B 88
Ashford Ho. SW9 ... 4B 104
Ashford M. N17 ... 1G 33
Ashford Park. ... 4A 112
Ashford Pas. NW2 ... 4F 47
Ashford Rd. E6 ... 7E 54
Ashford Rd. E18 ... 2K 35
Ashford Rd. NW2 ... 4F 47
Ashford Rd. Ashf ... 7E 112
Ashford Rd. Felt ... 4F 113
Ashford Rd. Stai ... 7A 112
Ashford St. N1 ... 3E 68 (1G 163)
Ash Gro. E8 ... 1H 69 (in two parts)
Ash Gro. N13 ... 3H 17
Ash Gro. NW2 ... 4F 47
Ash Gro. SE12 ... 1J 125
Ash Gro. SE20 ... 2J 141
Ash Gro. W5 ... 2E 80
Ash Gro. Enf ... 7K 7
Ash Gro. Felt ... 1G 113
Ash Gro. Hare ... 1A 22
Ash Gro. Hay ... 7F 59
Ash Gro. Houn ... 1B 96
Ash Gro. S'hall ... 5E 60
Ash Gro. Wemb ... 4A 44
Ash Gro. W Dray ... 7B 58
Ash Gro. W Wick ... 2E 154
Ashgrove Ct. W9 ... 5J 65 (off Elmfield Way)
Ashgrove Ho. SW1 ... 5H 85 (5D 172) (off Lindsay Sq.)
Ashgrove Rd. Ashf ... 5E 112
Ashgrove Rd. Brom ... 6F 125
Ashgrove Rd. Ilf ... 1K 55
Ash Hill Clo. Bush ... 1A 10
Ash Hill Dri. Pinn ... 3A 24
Ash Ho. E14 ... 2E 88 (off E. Ferry Rd.)
Ash Ho. SE1 ... 4F 87 (off Longfield Est.)
Ash Ho. W10 ... 4G 65 (off Heather Wlk.)
Ashingdon Clo. E4 ... 3K 19
Ashington Ho. E1 ... 4H 69 (off Barnsley St.)
Ashington Rd. SW6 ... 2H 101
Ashlake Rd. SW16 ... 4J 121
Ashland Pl. W1 ... 5E 66 (5G 159)
Ashlar Pl. SE18 ... 4F 91
Ashleigh Commercial Est. SE7 ... 3A 90
Ashleigh Ct. N14 ... 7B 6
Ashleigh Ct. W5 ... 4D 80 (off Murray Rd.)
Ashleigh Gdns. Sutt ... 2K 149
Ashleigh Point. SE23 ... 3K 123
Ashleigh Rd. SE20 ... 3H 141
Ashleigh Rd. SW14 ... 3A 100
Ashley Av. Ilf ... 2F 37
Ashley Av. Mord ... 5J 137
Ashley Clo. NW4 ... 2E 28
Ashley Clo. Pinn ... 2K 23
Ashley Ct. NW4 ... 2E 28
Ashley Ct. NW9 ... 2B 28 (off Guilfoyle)
Ashley Ct. SW1 ... 3G 85 (2A 172) (off Morpeth Ter.)
Ashley Ct. Barn ... 5F 5
Ashley Ct. N'holt ... 1C 60
Ashley Cres. N22 ... 2A 32
Ashley Cres. SW11 ... 3E 102
Ashley Dri. Iswth ... 6J 79
Ashley Dri. Twic ... 7F 97
Ashley Gdns. N13 ... 4H 17
Ashley Gdns. SW1 ... 3G 85 (2B 172) (in three parts)
Ashley Gdns. Rich ... 2D 116
Ashley Gdns. Wemb ... 2E 44
Ashley La. NW4 ... 7K 13 (in three parts)
Ashley La. Croy ... 4B 152
Ashley Pl. SW1 ... 3G 85 (2A 172) (in two parts)
Ashley Rd. E4 ... 6H 19
Ashley Rd. E7 ... 7A 54
Ashley Rd. N17 ... 3G 33
Ashley Rd. N19 ... 1J 49
Ashley Rd. SW19 ... 6K 119
Ashley Rd. Enf ... 2D 8
Ashley Rd. Hamp ... 1E 132
Ashley Rd. Rich ... 3E 98
Ashley Rd. Th Dit ... 6K 133
Ashley Rd. T Hth ... 4K 139
Ashley Wlk. NW7 ... 7A 14
Ashling Rd. Croy ... 1G 153
Ashlin Rd. E15 ... 4F 53
Ashlone Rd. SW15 ... 3E 100
Ashlyns Way. Chess ... 6D 146
Ashmead. N14 ... 5B 6
Ashmead Bus. Cen. E3 ... 4F 71
Ashmead Ga. Brom ... 1A 144
Ashmead Ho. E9 ... 5A 52 (off Homerton Rd.)
Ashmead M. SE8 ... 2C 106
Ashmead Rd. SE8 ... 2C 106
Ashmead Rd. Felt ... 1J 113
Ashmere Av. Beck ... 2F 143
Ashmere Clo. Sutt ... 5F 149
Ashmere Gro. SW2 ... 4J 103
Ashmill St. NW1 ... 5C 66 (5C 158)
Ashmole Pl. SW8 ... 6K 85 (in two parts)
Ashmole St. SW8 ... 6K 85 (7H 173)
Ashmore. NW1 ... 7H 49 (off Agar Gro.)
Ashmore Clo. SE15 ... 7F 87
Ashmore Ct. N11 ... 6J 15
Ashmore Ct. Houn ... 6E 78
Ashmore Gro. Well ... 3H 109
Ashmore Ho. W14 ... 3G 83 (off Russell Rd.)
Ashmore Rd. W9 ... 2H 65
Ashmount Est. N19 ... 7H 31
Ashmount Rd. N15 ... 5F 33
Ashmount Rd. N19 ... 7G 31
Ashmount Ter. W5 ... 4D 80
Ashmour Gdns. Romf ... 2K 39
Ashneal Gdns. Harr ... 3H 43
Ashness Gdns. Gnfd ... 6B 44
Ashness Rd. SW11 ... 5D 102
Ashpark Ho. E14 ... 6B 70 (off Norbiton Rd.)
Ashridge Clo. Harr ... 6C 26
Ashridge Ct. N14 ... 5B 6
Ashridge Ct. S'hall ... 6G 61 (off Redcroft Rd.)
Ashridge Cres. SE18 ... 7G 91
Ashridge Gdns. N13 ... 5C 16
Ashridge Gdns. Pinn ... 4C 24
Ashridge Way. Mord ... 3H 137
Ashridge Way. Sun ... 6J 113
Ash Rd. E15 ... 5G 53
Ash Rd. Croy ... 2C 154
Ash Rd. Shep ... 4C 130
Ash Rd. Sutt ... 7G 137
Ash Row. Brom ... 7E 144
Ashtead Rd. E5 ... 7G 33
Ashton Clo. Sutt ... 4J 149
Ashton Ct. Harr ... 3K 43
Ashton Gdns. Houn ... 4D 96
Ashton Gdns. Romf ... 6E 38
Ashton Heights. SE23 ... 1J 123
Ashton Ho. SW9 ... 7A 86
Ashton Rd. E15 ... 5F 53
Ashton St. E14 ... 7E 70
Ashtree Av. Mitc ... 2B 138
Ash Tree Clo. Croy ... 6A 142
Ash Tree Clo. Surb ... 2E 146
Ashtree Dell. NW9 ... 5K 27
Ash Tree Way. Croy ... 5K 141
Ashurst Clo. SE20 ... 1H 141
Ashurst Dri. Ilf ... 6F 37
Ashurst Dri. Shep ... 5A 130
Ashurst Gdns. SW2 ... 1A 122
Ashurst Rd. N12 ... 5H 15
Ashurst Rd. Barn ... 5J 5
Ashurst Wlk. Croy ... 2H 153
Ashvale Rd. SW17 ... 5D 120
Ash Vw. Clo. Ashf ... 6A 112
Ash Vw. Gdns. Ashf ... 5A 112
Ashville Rd. E11 ... 2F 53
Ash Wlk. Wemb ... 3C 44
Ashwater Rd. SE12 ... 1J 125
Ashway Cen., The. King T ... 1E 134
Ashwell Clo. E6 ... 6C 72
Ashwin St. E8 ... 6F 51
Ashwood Av. Uxb ... 6C 58
Ashwood Gdns. Hay ... 4H 77
Ashwood Gdns. New Ad ... 6D 154
Ashwood Rd. E4 ... 3A 20
Ashworth Clo. SE5 ... 2D 104
Ashworth Est. Croy ... 1J 151
Ashworth Mans. W9 ... 3K 65 (off Elgin Av.)
Ashworth Rd. W9 ... 3K 65
Aske Ho. N1 ... 1G 163 (in two parts)
Asker Ho. N7 ... 4J 49
Askern Clo. Bexh ... 4D 110
Aske St. N1 ... 3E 68 (1G 163)
Askew Cres. W12 ... 2B 82
Askew Est. W12 ... 1B 82 (off Uxbridge Rd.)
Askew Rd. W12 ... 2B 82
Askham Ct. W12 ... 1C 82
Askham Rd. W12 ... 1C 82
Askill Dri. SW15 ... 5G 101
Askwith Rd. Rain ... 3K 75
Asland Rd. E15 ... 1G 71
Aslett St. SW18 ... 7K 101
Asmara Rd. NW2 ... 5G 47
Asmuns Hill. NW11 ... 5J 29
Asmuns Pl. NW11 ... 5H 29
Asolando Dri. SE17 ... 4C 86
Aspen Clo. N19 ... 2G 49
Aspen Clo. W5 ... 2F 81
Aspen Clo. W Dray ... 1B 76
Aspen Copse. Brom ... 2D 144
Aspen Dri. Wemb ... 3A 44
Aspen Gdns. W6 ... 5D 82
Aspen Gdns. Ashf ... 5E 112
Aspen Gdns. Mitc ... 5E 138
Aspen Grn. Eri ... 3F 93
Aspen Ho. SE15 ... 6J 87 (off Sharratt St.)
Aspen Ho. Sidc ... 3A 128
Aspen La. N'holt ... 3C 60
Aspenlea Rd. W6 ... 6F 83
Aspen Lodge. W8 ... 3K 83 (off Abbots Wlk.)
Aspen Way. E14 ... 7D 70
Aspen Way. Felt ... 3K 113
Aspern Gro. NW3 ... 5C 48
Aspinall Rd. SE4 ... 3K 105 (in two parts)
Aspinden Rd. SE16 ... 4H 87
Aspley Rd. SW18 ... 5K 101
Asplins Rd. N17 ... 1G 33
Asquith Clo. Dag ... 1C 56
Assam St. E1 ... 6G 69
Assata M. N1 ... 6B 50
Assembly Pas. E1 ... 5J 69
Assembly Wlk. Cars ... 7C 138
Ass Ho. La. Harr ... 4A 10
Association Gallery, The. ... 4E 68 (3G 163) (off Leonard St.)
Astall Clo. Harr ... 1J 25
Astbury Bus. Pk. SE15 ... 1J 105
Astbury Ho. SE11 ... 2J 173
Astbury Rd. SE15 ... 1J 105
Astell St. SW3 ... 5C 84 (5D 170)
Aste St. E14 ... 2E 88
Astey's Row. N1 ... 7C 50
Asthall Gdns. Ilf ... 4G 37
Astins Ho. E17 ... 4D 34
Astleham Rd. Shep ... 3A 130
Astle St. SW11 ... 2E 102
Astley Av. NW2 ... 5E 46
Astley Ho. SE1 ... 5F 87 (off Rowcross St.)
Astley Ho. SW13 ... 6D 82 (off Wyatt Dri.)
Aston Av. Harr ... 7C 26
Aston Clo. Sidc ... 3A 128
Aston Ct. Wfd G ... 6D 20
Aston Grn. Houn ... 2A 96
Aston Ho. SW8 ... 1H 103
Aston Ho. W11 ... 7H 65 (off Westbourne Gro.)
Aston M. Romf ... 7C 38
Aston Pl. SW16 ... 6B 122
Aston Rd. SW20 ... 2E 136
Aston Rd. W5 ... 6D 62
Aston St. E14 ... 5A 70
Aston Ter. SW12 ... 6F 103
Astonville St. SW18 ... 1J 119
Astor Av. Romf ... 6J 39
Astor Clo. King T ... 6H 117
Astor Ct. E16 ... 6A 72 (off Ripley Rd.)
Astor Ct. SW6 ... 7A 84 (off Maynard Clo.)
Astoria Mans. SW16 ... 3J 121
Astoria Wlk. SW9 ... 3A 104
Astra Ho. SE14 ... 6B 88 (off Arklow Rd.)
Astrid Ho. Felt ... 2A 114
Astrop M. W6 ... 3E 82
Astrop Ter. W6 ... 2E 82
Astwood M. SW7 ... 4A 84
Asylum Rd. SE15 ... 7H 87
Atalanta St. SW6 ... 7F 83
Atbara Rd. Tedd ... 6B 116
Atcham Rd. Houn ... 4G 97
Atcost Rd. Bark ... 5A 74
Atcraft Cen. Wemb ... 1E 62
Atheldene Rd. SW18 ... 1K 119
Athelney St. SE6 ... 3C 124
Athelstane Gro. E3 ... 2B 70
Athelstane M. N4 ... 1A 50
Athelstan Gdns. NW6 ... 7G 47
Athelstan Ho. King T ... 4F 135 (off Athelstan Rd.)
Athelstan Rd. King T ... 4F 135
Athelstan Way. Orp ... 1K 145
Athelstone Rd. Harr ... 2H 25
Athena Clo. Harr ... 2H 43
Athena Clo. King T ... 3F 135
Athenaeum Ct. N5 ... 4C 50
Athenaeum Pl. N10 ... 3F 31
Athenaeum Rd. N20 ... 1F 15
Athena Pl. N'wd ... 1H 23
Athenia Ho. E14 ... 6F 71 (off Blair St.)
Athenlay Rd. SE15 ... 5K 105
Athens Gdns. W9 ... 4J 65 (off Harrow Rd.)
Atherden Rd. E5 ... 4J 51
Atherfold Rd. SW9 ... 3J 103
Atherley Way. Houn ... 7D 96
Atherstone Ct. W2 ... 5K 65 (off Delamere Ter.)
Atherstone M. SW7 ... 4A 84
Atherton Dri. SW19 ... 4F 119
Atherton Heights. Wemb ... 6C 44
Atherton M. E7 ... 6H 53
Atherton Pl. Harr ... 3H 25
Atherton Pl. S'hall ... 7E 60
Atherton Rd. E7 ... 6H 53
Atherton Rd. SW13 ... 7C 82
Atherton Rd. Ilf ... 2C 36
Atherton St. SW11 ... 2C 102
Athlone Clo. E5 ... 5H 51
Athlone Ct. E17 ... 3F 35
Athlone Ho. E1 ... 6J 69 (off Sidney St.)
Athlone Rd. SW2 ... 7K 103
Athlone St. NW5 ... 6E 48
Athlon Ind. Est. Wemb ... 1D 62
Athlon Rd. Wemb ... 2D 62
Athol Clo. Pinn ... 1K 23
Athole Gdns. Enf ... 5K 7
Athol Gdns. Pinn ... 1K 23
Atholl Ho. W9 ... 3A 66 (off Maida Va.)
Atholl Rd. Ilf ... 7A 38

Athol Rd. Eri 5J 93
Athol Sq. E14 6E 70
Athol Way. Uxb 3C 58
Atkin Building. WC1 5K 67 (5H 161) (off Raymond Bldgs.)
Atkins Dri. W Wick 2F 155
Atkinson Ct. E10 7D 34 (off Kings Clo.)
Atkinson Ho. E2 2G 69 (off Pritchards Rd.)
Atkinson Ho. E13 4H 71 (off Sutton Rd.)
Atkinson Ho. SE17 4D 86 (off Catesby St.)
Atkinson Rd. E16 5A 72
Atkins Rd. E10 6D 34
Atkins Rd. SW12 7G 103
Atlanta Ho. SE16 3A 88 (off Brunswick Quay)
Atlantic Ct. E14 7F 71 (off Jamestown Way)
Atlantic Ho. E1 5A 70 (off Harford St.)
Atlantic Rd. SW9 4A 104
Atlantic Wharf. E1 7K 69 (off Jardine Rd.)
Atlantis Clo. Bark 3B 74
Atlas Bus. Cen. NW2 1D 46
Atlas Gdns. SE7 4A 90
Atlas M. E8 6F 51
Atlas M. N7 6K 49
Atlas Rd. E13 2J 71
Atlas Rd. N11 7K 15
Atlas Rd. NW10 3A 64
Atlas Rd. Wemb 4J 45
Atlas Wharf. E9 6C 52
Atley Rd. E3 1C 70
Atlip Rd. Wemb 1E 62
Atney Rd. SW15 4G 101
Atterbury Rd. N4 6A 32
Atterbury St. SW1 4J 85 (4D 172)
Attewood Av. NW10 3A 46
Attewood Rd. N'holt 6C 42
Attfield Clo. N20 2G 15
Attfield Ct. King T 2F 135 (off Albert Rd.)
Attilburgh Ho. SE1 3F 87 (7J 169) (off Abbey St.)
Attleborough Ct. SE26 2G 123
Attle Clo. Uxb 2C 58
Attlee Clo. Hay 3K 59
Attlee Clo. T Hth 5C 140
Attlee Rd. SE28 7B 74
Attlee Rd. Hay 3J 59
Attlee Ter. E17 4D 34
Attneave St. WC1 3A 68
Atwater Clo. SW2 1A 122
Atwell Clo. E10 6D 34
Atwell Pl. Th Dit 7K 133 & 1A 146
Atwell Rd. SE15 2G 105
Atwood Av. Rich 2G 99
Atwood Ho. W14 4H 83 (off Beckford Clo.)
Atwood Rd. W6 4D 82
Atwoods All. Rich 1G 99
Aubert Ct. N5 4B 50
Aubert Pk. N5 4B 50
Aubert Rd. N5 4B 50
Aubrey Beardsley Ho. SW1 4G 85 (4B 172) (off Vauxhall Bri. Rd.)
Aubrey Mans. NW1 5C 66 (5C 158) (off Lisson St.)
Aubrey Moore Point. E15 2E 70 (off Abbey La.)
Aubrey Pl. NW8 2A 66
Aubrey Rd. E17 3C 34
Aubrey Rd. N8 5J 31
Aubrey Rd. W8 1H 83
Aubrey Wlk. W8 1H 83
Auburn Clo. SE14 7A 88
Aubyn Hill. SE27 4C 122
Aubyn Sq. SW15 5C 100
Auckland Clo. SE19 1F 141
Auckland Ct. Hay 4A 60
Auckland Gdns. SE19 1E 140
Auckland Hill. SE27 4C 122
Auckland Ho. W12 7D 64 (off White City Est.)
Auckland Ri. SE19 1E 140
Auckland Rd. E10 3D 52
Auckland Rd. SE19 1F 141
Auckland Rd. SW11 4C 102
Auckland Rd. Ilf 1F 55
Auckland Rd. King T 4F 135
Auckland St. SE11 5K 85 (6G 173)
Audax. NW9 2B 28
Auden Pl. NW1 1E 66 (in two parts)
Auden Pl. Cheam 4E 148
Audleigh Pl. Chig 6K 21
Audley Clo. N10 7A 16
Audley Clo. SW11 3E 102
Audley Ct. E18 4H 35
Audley Ct. N'holt 3A 60
Audley Ct. Pinn 2A 24
Audley Ct. Twic 3H 115
Audley Dri. E16 1K 89
Audley Gdns. Ilf 2K 55
Audley Pl. Sutt 7K 149
Audley Rd. NW4 5C 28
Audley Rd. W5 5F 63
Audley Rd. Enf 2G 7
Audley Rd. Rich 5F 99
Audley Sq. W1 1E 84 (4H 165)
Audrey Clo. Beck 6D 142
Audrey Gdns. Wemb 2B 44
Audrey Rd. Ilf 3F 55
Audrey St. E2 2G 69
Audric Clo. King T 1G 135
Augurs La. E13 3K 71
Augusta Clo. W Mol 4D 132
Augusta Rd. Twic 2G 115
Augusta St. E14 6D 70
Augustine Rd. W14 3F 83
Augustine Rd. Harr 1F 25
Augustus Clo. W12 2D 82
Augustus Clo. Bren 7C 80
Augustus Ct. SW16 2H 121
Augustus Ct. Felt 4D 114
Augustus Ho. NW1 2F 67 (1A 160) (off Augustus St.)
Augustus Rd. SW19 1F 119
Augustus St. NW1 2F 67 (1K 159)
Aultone Way. Cars 3D 150
Aultone Way. Sutt 2K 149
Aulton Pl. SE11 5A 86 (6K 173)
Aurelia Gdns. Croy 5K 139
Aurelia Rd. Croy 6J 139
Auriel Av. Dag 6K 57
Auriga M. N1 5D 50
Auriol Clo. Wor Pk 3A 148
Auriol Dri. Gnfd 7H 43
Auriol Dri. Uxb 6C 40
Auriol Ho. W12 1D 82 (off Ellerslie Rd.)
Auriol Pk. Rd. Wor Pk 3A 148
Auriol Rd. W14 4G 83
Aurora Ho. E14 6D 70 (off Kerbey St.)
Austell Gdns. NW7 3F 13
Austell Heights. NW7 3F 13 (off Austell Gdns.)
Austen Clo. SE28 1B 92
Austen Ho. NW6 3J 65 (off Cambridge Rd.)
Austen Rd. Eri 7H 93
Austen Rd. Harr 2F 43
Austin Av. Brom 5C 144
Austin Clo. SE23 7A 106
Austin Clo. Twic 5C 98
Austin Ct. E6 1A 72
Austin Ct. SE15 3G 105 (off Philip Wlk.)
Austin Ct. Enf 5K 7
Austin Friars. EC2 6D 68 (7F 163) (in two parts)
Austin Friars Pas. EC2 7F 163
Austin Friars Sq. EC2 7F 163
Austin Ho. SE14 7B 88 (off Achilles St.)
Austin Rd. SW11 1E 102
Austin Rd. Hay 2H 77
Austin's La. Uxb 3E 40 (in two parts)
Austin St. E2 3F 69 (2J 163)
Austin Ter. SE1 3A 86 (1K 173) (off Morley St.)
Austral Clo. Sidc 3K 127
Australia Rd. W12 7D 64
Austral St. SE11 4B 86 (3K 173)
Austyn Gdns. Surb 1H 147
Autumn Clo. SW19 6A 120
Autumn Clo. Enf 1B 8
Autumn Lodge. S Croy 4E 152 (off S. Park Hill Rd.)
Autumn St. E3 1C 70
Avalon Clo. SW20 2G 137
Avalon Clo. W13 5A 62
Avalon Clo. Enf 2F 7
Avalon Rd. SW6 1K 101
Avalon Rd. W13 4A 62
Avarn Rd. SW17 6D 120
Avebury Ct. N1 1D 68 (off Imber St.)
Avebury Pk. Surb 7D 134
Avebury Rd. E11 1F 53
Avebury Rd. SW19 1H 137
Avebury St. N1 1D 68
Aveley Mans. Bark 7F 55 (off Whiting Av.)
Aveley Rd. Romf 4K 39
Aveline St. SE11 5A 86 (5H 173)
Aveling Pk. Rd. E17 2C 34
Ave Maria La. EC4 6B 68 (1B 168)
Avenell Rd. N5 3B 50
Avenfield Ho. W1 7D 66 (2F 165) (off Park La.)
Avening Rd. SW18 7J 101
Avening Ter. SW18 7J 101
Avenons Rd. E13 4J 71
Avenue Clo. N14 6B 6
Avenue Clo. NW8 1C 66
Avenue Clo. Houn 1K 95
Avenue Clo. W Dray 3A 76
Avenue Ct. N14 6B 6
Avenue Ct. NW2 3H 47
Avenue Ct. SW3 4D 84 (4E 170) (off Draycott Av.)
Avenue Cres. W3 2H 81
Avenue Cres. Houn 1K 95
Avenue Elmers. Surb 5E 134
Avenue Gdns. SE25 2G 141
Avenue Gdns. SW14 3A 100
Avenue Gdns. W3 2H 81
Avenue Gdns. Houn 7K 77
Avenue Gdns. Tedd 7K 115
Avenue Ho. NW8 2C 66 (off Allitsen Rd.)
Avenue Ho. NW10 2D 64 (off All Souls Av.)
Avenue Ind. Est. E4 6G 19
Avenue Lodge. NW8 7B 48 (off Avenue Rd.)
Avenue Mans. NW3 5K 47 (off Finchley Rd.)
Avenue M. N10 3F 31
Avenue Pde. N21 7J 7
Avenue Pde. Sun 3K 131
Avenue Pk. Rd. SE27 2B 122
Avenue Rd. E7 4K 53
Avenue Rd. N6 7G 31
Avenue Rd. N12 4F 15
Avenue Rd. N14 7B 6
Avenue Rd. N15 5D 32
Avenue Rd. NW3 & NW8 7B 48
Avenue Rd. NW10 2B 64
Avenue Rd. SE20 & Beck 1J 141
Avenue Rd. SE25 2F 141
Avenue Rd. SW16 2H 139
Avenue Rd. SW20 2D 136
Avenue Rd. W3 2H 81
Avenue Rd. Belv 4J 93
Avenue Rd. Bexh 3E 110
Avenue Rd. Bren 5C 80
Avenue Rd. Chad H 1C 56
Avenue Rd. Eri 7J 93
Avenue Rd. Felt 3H 113
Avenue Rd. Hamp 1F 133
Avenue Rd. Iswth 1K 97
Avenue Rd. King T 3E 134
Avenue Rd. N Mald 4A 136
Avenue Rd. Pinn 3C 24
Avenue Rd. S'hall 1D 78
Avenue Rd. Tedd 7A 116
Avenue Rd. Wall 7G 151
Avenue Rd. Wfd G 6F 21
Avenue S. Surb 7G 135
Avenue Ter. N Mald 3J 135
Avenue, The. E4 6A 20
Avenue, The. E11 6K 35
Avenue, The. N3 2J 29
Avenue, The. N8 3A 32
Avenue, The. N10 2G 31
Avenue, The. N11 5A 16
Avenue, The. N17 3D 32
Avenue, The. NW6 1F 65
Avenue, The. SE9 5D 108
Avenue, The. SE10 7F 89
Avenue, The. SW4 5E 102
Avenue, The. SW18 7C 102
Avenue, The. W4 3A 82
Avenue, The. W13 6B 62
Avenue, The. Barn 3B 4
Avenue, The. Beck 1D 142 (in two parts)
Avenue, The. Bex 7D 110
Avenue, The. Brom 3B 144
Avenue, The. Buck H 2F 21
Avenue, The. Cars 7E 150
Avenue, The. Cran 1J 95
Avenue, The. Croy 3E 152
Avenue, The. Eps & Sutt 7D 148
Avenue, The. Hamp 6D 114
Avenue, The. Harr 1K 25
Avenue, The. Houn 5F 97
Avenue, The. Ick 4C 40
Avenue, The. Kes 4B 156
Avenue, The. Pinn 7D 24
Avenue, The. Rich 2F 99
Avenue, The. Romf 4K 39
Avenue, The. St P 7B 128
Avenue, The. Sun 1K 131
Avenue, The. Surb 6F 135
Avenue, The. Sutt 7G 149
Avenue, The. Twic 5B 98
Avenue, The. Wemb 1E 44
Avenue, The. W Wick 7G 143
Avenue, The. Wor Pk 2B 148
Averil Gro. SW16 6B 122
Averill St. W6 6F 83
Avern Gdns. W Mol 4F 133
Avern Rd. W Mol 4F 133
Avery Farm Row. SW1 4E 84 (4J 171)
Avery Gdns. Ilf 5D 36
Avery Hill. 6H 109
Avery Hill Rd. SE9 6H 109
Avery Row. W1 7F 67 (2J 165)
Avia Pk. Felt 1D 112
Aviary Clo. E16 5H 71
Aviemore Clo. Beck 5B 142
Aviemore Way. Beck 5A 142
Avignon Rd. SE4 3K 105
Avington Ct. SE1 4E 86 (off Old Kent Rd.)
Avington Gro. SE20 7J 123
Avington Way. SE15 7F 87
Avion Cres. NW9 1C 28
Avis Sq. E1 6K 69
Avoca Rd. SW17 4E 120
Avocet Clo. SE1 5G 87
Avocet M. SE28 3H 91
Avon Clo. Hay 4A 60
Avon Clo. Sutt 4A 150
Avon Clo. Wor Pk 2C 148
Avon Ct. E4 1K 19
Avon Ct. N12 5E 14
Avon Ct. W9 5J 65 (off Elmfield Way)
Avon Ct. Buck H 1E 20
Avon Ct. Gnfd 4F 61
Avondale Av. N12 5E 14
Avondale Av. NW2 3A 46
Avondale Av. Barn 1J 15
Avondale Av. Esh 3A 146
Avondale Av. Wor Pk 1B 148
Avondale Ct. E11 1G 53
Avondale Ct. E16 5G 71
Avondale Ct. E18 1K 35
Avondale Cres. Enf 3F 9
Avondale Cres. Ilf 5B 36
Avondale Dri. Hay 1J 77
Avondale Gdns. Houn 5D 96
Avondale Ho. SE1 5G 87 (off Avondale Sq.)
Avondale Pk. Gdns. W11 7G 65
Avondale Pk. Rd. W11 7G 65
Avondale Ri. SE15 3F 105
Avondale Rd. E16 5G 71
Avondale Rd. E17 7C 34
Avondale Rd. N3 1A 30
Avondale Rd. N13 2F 17
Avondale Rd. N15 5B 32
Avondale Rd. SE9 2C 126
Avondale Rd. SW14 3A 100
Avondale Rd. SW19 5K 119
Avondale Rd. Ashf 3A 112
Avondale Rd. Brom 6G 125
Avondale Rd. Harr 3K 25
Avondale Rd. S Croy 6C 152
Avondale Rd. Well 2C 110
Avondale Sq. SE1 5G 87
Avonfield Ct. E17 3F 35
Avon Ho. W8 3J 83 (off Allen St.)
Avon Ho. W14 4H 83 (off Kensington Village)
Avon Ho. King T 1D 134
Avonhurst Ho. NW2 7G 47
Avonley Rd. SE14 7J 87
Avon M. Pinn 1D 24
Avonmore Gdns. W14 4H 83
Avonmore Pl. W14 4G 83
Avonmore Rd. W14 4G 83
Avonmouth St. SE1 3C 86 (7C 168)
Avon Path. S Croy 6C 152
Avon Pl. SE1 2C 86 (7D 168)
Avon Rd. E17 3F 35
Avon Rd. SE4 3C 106
Avon Rd. Gnfd 4E 60
Avon Rd. Sun 7H 113
Avon Way. E18 3J 35
Avonwick Rd. Houn 2F 97
Avril Way. E4 5K 19
Avro Ho. SW8 7F 85 (off Havelock Ter.)
Avro Way. Wall 7J 151
Awlfield Av. N17 1D 32
Awliscombe Rd. Well 2K 109
Axe St. Bark 1G 73 (in two parts)
Axholme Av. Edgw 1G 27
Axminster Cres. Well 1C 110
Axminster Rd. N7 3J 49
Aybrook St. W1 5E 66 (6G 159)
Aycliffe Clo. Brom 4D 144
Aycliffe Rd. W12 1C 82
Ayerst Ct. E10 7E 34

Aylands Clo. Wemb....2E 44
Aylesbury Clo. E7....6H 53
Aylesbury Ct. Sutt....3A 150
Aylesbury Ho. SE15....6G 87 (off Friary Est.)
Aylesbury Rd. SE17....5D 86
Aylesbury Rd. Brom....3J 143
Aylesbury St. EC1....4B 68 (4A 162)
Aylesbury St. NW10....3K 45
Aylesford Av. Beck....5A 142
Aylesford Ho. SE1....2D 86 (7F 169) (off Long La.)
Aylesford St. SW1....5H 85 (5C 172)
Aylesham Cen., The. SE15....1G 105
Aylesham Clo. NW7....7H 13
Aylesham Rd. Orp....7K 145
Ayles Rd. Hay & N'holt....3K 59
Aylestone Av. NW6....7F 47
Aylett Rd. SE25....4H 141
Aylett Rd. Iswth....2J 97
Ayley Cft. Enf....5B 8
Ayliffe Clo. King T....2G 135
Aylmer Clo. Stan....4F 11
Aylmer Ct. N2....5D 30
Aylmer Dri. Stan....4F 11
Aylmer Ho. SE10....5F 89
Aylmer Pde. N2....5D 30
Aylmer Rd. E11....1H 53
Aylmer Rd. N2....5C 30
Aylmer Rd. W12....2B 82
Aylmer Rd. Dag....3E 56
Ayloffe Rd. Dag....6F 57
Aylsham Dri. Uxb....2E 40
Aylton Est. SE16....2J 87
Aylward Rd. SE23....2K 123
Aylward Rd. SW20....2H 137
Aylwards Ri. Stan....4F 11
Aylward St. E1....6J 69 (Jamaica St.)
Aylward St. E1....6J 69 (Jubilee St.)
Aylwin Est. SE1....3E 86
Aynhoe Mans. W14....4F 83 (off Aynhoe Rd.)
Aynhoe Rd. W14....4F 83
Aynscombe Path. SW14....2J 99
Ayr Ct. W3....6G 63
Ayres Clo. E13....3J 71
Ayres Cres. NW10....7K 45
Ayres St. SE1....2C 86 (6D 168)
Ayr Grn. Romf....1K 39
Ayrsome Rd. N16....3E 50
Ayrton Gould Ho. E2....3K 69 (off Roman Rd.)
Ayrton Rd. SW7....3B 84 (1A 170)
Ayr Way. Romf....1K 39
Aysgarth Ct. Sutt....3K 149
Aysgarth Rd. SE21....7E 104
Ayshford Ho. E2....3H 69 (off Viaduct St.)
Ayston Ho. SE16....4K 87 (off Plough Way)
Ayton Ho. SE5....7D 86 (off Edmund St.)
Aytoun Pl. SW9....2K 103
Aytoun Rd. SW9....2K 103
Azalea Clo. W7....1K 79
Azalea Clo. Ilf....5F 55
Azalea Ct. W7....1K 79
Azalea Ct. Wfd G....6B 20
Azalea Ho. SE14....7B 88 (off Achilles St.)
Azalea Wlk. Pinn....5K 23
Azania M. NW5....6F 49
Azenby Rd. SE15....2F 105
Azof St. SE10....4G 89
Azov Ho. E1....4A 70 (off Commodore St.)
Aztec Ho. Ilf....1G 37

Baalbec Rd. N5....5B 50
Babbacombe Clo. Chess....5D 146
Babbacombe Gdns. Ilf....4C 36
Babbacombe Rd. Brom....1J 143
Baber Bri. Cvn. Site. Felt....5A 96
Baber Dri. Felt....6A 96
Babington Ct. WC1....5G 161
Babington Ho. SE1....2C 86 (6D 168) (off Disney St.)
Babington Ri. Wemb....6G 45
Babington Rd. NW4....4D 28
Babington Rd. SW16....5H 121
Babington Rd. Dag....5C 56
Babmaes St. SW1....7H 67 (3C 166)
Bacchus Wlk. N1....2E 68 (off Regan Way)
Bache's St. N1....3D 68 (1F 163)
Back All. EC3....1H 169
Bk. Church La. E1....6G 69
Back Hill. EC1....4A 68 (4K 161)
Backhouse Pl. SE17....4E 86
Back La. N8....5J 31
Back La. NW3....4A 48
Back La. Bark....1G 73
Back La. Bex....7G 111
Back La. Bren....6D 80
Back La. Edgw....1J 27
Back La. Romf....7D 38
Backley Gdns. SE25....6G 141
Back Rd. Sidc....4A 128
Back Rd. Tedd....7J 115
Bacon Gro. SE1....3F 87
Bacon La. NW9....4H 27 (in two parts)
Bacon La. Edgw....1G 27
Bacons La. N6....1E 48
Bacon St. E1 & E2....4F 69 (3K 163)
Bacon Ter. Dag....5B 56
Bacton St. E2....3J 69
Baddesley Ho. SE11....5H 173
Baddow Clo. Dag....1G 75
Baddow Clo. Wfd G....6F 21
Baddow Wlk. N1....1C 68 (off New N. Rd.)
Baden Pl. SE1....2D 86 (6E 168)
Baden Powell Clo. Dag....1E 74
Baden Powell Clo. Surb....2F 147
Baden Powell Ho. SW7....2A 170
Baden Powell Ho. Belv....3G 93 (off Ambrooke Rd.)
Baden Rd. N8....4H 31
Baden Rd. Ilf....5F 55
Badger Clo. Felt....3K 113
Badger Clo. Houn....3A 96
Badger Clo. Ilf....6G 37
Badger Ct. NW2....3E 46
Badgers Clo. Ashf....5B 112
Badgers Clo. Enf....3G 7
Badgers Clo. Harr....6H 25
Badgers Clo. Hay....7G 59
Badgers Copse. Wor Pk....2B 148
Badgers Cft. N20....7B 4
Badgers Cft. SE9....3E 126
Badgers Hole. Croy....4K 153
Badgers Wlk. N Mald....2A 136
Badlis Rd. E17....3C 34
Badminton Clo. Harr....4J 25
Badminton Clo. N'holt....6E 42
Badminton M. E16....1J 89
Badminton Rd. SW12....6E 102
Badsworth Rd. SE5....1C 104
Baffin Way. E14....1E 88
Bagley Clo. W Dray....2A 76
Bagley's La. SW6....1K 101
Bagleys Spring. Romf....4E 38
Bagnigge Ho. WC1....3A 68 (2J 161) (off Margery St.)
Bagshot Ct. SE18....1E 108
Bagshot Ho. NW1....1K 159
Bagshot Rd. Enf....7A 8
Bagshot St. SE17....5E 86
Baildon. E2....2J 69 (off Cyprus St.)
Baildon St. SE8....7B 88
Bailey Clo. E4....4K 19
Bailey Clo. N11....7C 16
Bailey Cres. Chess....7C 146
Bailey M. W4....6H 81 (off Hervert Gdns.)
Bailey Pl. SE26....6K 123
Baillies Wlk. W5....2D 80
Bainbridge Clo. Ham....5E 116
Bainbridge Rd. Dag....4F 57
Bainbridge St. WC1....6H 67 (7D 160)
Baines Clo. S Croy....5D 152
Baird Av. S'hall....7F 61
Baird Clo. E10....1C 52
Baird Clo. NW9....6J 27
Baird Gdns. SE19....4E 122
Baird Ho. W12....7D 64 (off White City Est.)
Baird Memorial Cotts. N14....2C 16 (off Balaams La.)
Baird Rd. Enf....3C 8
Baird St. EC1....4C 68 (3D 162)
Baizdon Rd. SE3....2G 107
Baker Beal Ct. Bexh....3H 111
Baker Ho. W7....1K 79
Baker Ho. WC1....4J 67 (4F 161) (off Colonnade)
Baker La. Mitc....2E 138
Baker Pas. NW10....1A 64
Baker Rd. NW10....1A 64
Baker Rd. SE18....7C 90
Bakers Av. E17....6D 34
Bakers Ct. SE25....3E 140
Bakers End. SW20....2G 137
Baker's Fld. N7....4J 49
Bakers Gdns. Cars....2C 150
Bakers Hall Ct. EC3....3G 169
Bakers Hill. E5....1J 51
Bakers Hill. New Bar....2E 4
Bakers Ho. W5....1D 80 (off Grove, The)
Bakers La. N6....6D 30
Baker's M. W1....6E 66 (7G 159)
Bakers Pas. NW3....4A 48 (off Heath St.)
Baker's Rents. E2....3F 69 (2J 163)
Baker's Row. E15....2G 71
Baker's Row. EC1....4A 68 (4J 161)
Baker Street. (Junct.)....4D 66
Baker St. NW1 & W1....4D 66 (4F 159)
Baker St. Enf....3J 7
Baker's Yd. EC1....4J 161
Bakery Clo. SW9....7K 85
Bakery M. Surb....1G 147
Bakery Path. Edgw....6C 12 (off St Margaret's Rd.)
Bakery Pl. SW11....4D 102
Bakewell Way. N Mald....2A 136
Balaam Ho. Sutt....4J 149
Balaams La. N14....2C 16
Balaam St. E13....4J 71
Balaclava Rd. SE1....4F 87
Balaclava Rd. Surb....7C 134
Bala Grn. NW9....6A 28 (off Ruthin Clo.)
Balcaskie Rd. SE9....5D 108
Balchen Rd. SE3....2B 108
Balchier Rd. SE22....6H 105
Balcombe Clo. Bexh....4D 110
Balcombe Ho. NW1....4C 66 (3E 158) (off Taunton Pl.)
Balcombe St. NW1....4D 66 (3E 158)
Balcon Ct. W5....6F 63
Balcorne St. E9....7J 51
Balder Ri. SE12....2K 125
Balderton Flats. W1....6E 66 (1H 165) (off Balderton St.)
Balderton St. W1....6E 66 (1H 165)
Baldewyne Ct. N17....1G 33
Baldock St. E3....2D 70
Baldrey Ho. SE10....5H 89 (off Blackwall La.)
Baldry Gdns. SW16....6J 121
Baldwin Cres. SE5....1C 104
Baldwin Gdns. Houn....1G 97
Baldwin Ho. SW2....1A 122
Baldwins Gdns. EC1....5A 68 (5J 161)
Baldwin St. EC1....3D 68 (2E 162)
Baldwin Ter. N1....2C 68
Baldwyn Gdns. W3....7K 63
Baldwyn's Pk. Bex....2K 129
Baldwyn's Rd. Bex....2K 129
Bale Rd. E1....5A 70
Bales Ter. N9....3A 18
Balfern Gro. W4....5A 82
Balfern St. SW11....2C 102
Balfe St. N1....2J 67
Balfour Av. W7....1K 79
Balfour Bus. Cen. S'hall....3A 78
Balfour Gro. N20....3J 15
Balfour Ho. W10....5F 65 (off St Charles Sq.)
Balfour M. N9....3B 18
Balfour M. W1....1E 84 (4H 165)
Balfour Pl. SW15....4D 100
Balfour Pl. W1....7E 66 (3H 165)
Balfour Rd. N5....4C 50
Balfour Rd. SE25....5G 141
Balfour Rd. SW19....7K 119
Balfour Rd. W3....5J 63
Balfour Rd. W13....2A 80
Balfour Rd. Brom....5B 144
Balfour Rd. Cars....7D 150
Balfour Rd. Harr....5H 25
Balfour Rd. Houn....3F 97
Balfour Rd. Ilf....2F 55
Balfour Rd. S'hall....3B 78
Balfour St. SE17....4D 86
Balfour Ter. N3....2K 29
Balfron Tower. E14....6E 70
Balgonie Rd. E4....1A 20
Balgowan Clo. N Mald....5A 136
Balgowan Rd. Beck....3A 142
Balgowan St. SE18....4K 91
Balham....1F 121
Balham Continental Mkt. SW12....1F 121 (off Shipka Rd.)
Balham Gro. SW12....7E 102
Balham High Rd. SW17 & SW12....3E 120
Balham Hill. SW12....7F 103
Balham New Rd. SW12....7F 103
Balham Pk. Rd. SW12....1D 120
Balham Rd. N9....2B 18
Balham Sta. Rd. SW12....1F 121
Balin Ho. SE1....2D 86 (6E 168) (off Long La.)
Balkan Wlk. E1....7H 69
Balladier Wlk. E14....5D 70
Ballamore Rd. Brom....3J 125
Ballance Rd. E9....6K 51
Ballantine St. SW18....4A 102
Ballantrae Ho. NW2....4H 47
Ballard Clo. King T....7K 117
Ballard Ho. SE10....6D 88 (off Thames St.)
Ballards Clo. Dag....1H 75
Ballards Farm Rd. S Croy & Croy....6G 153 (in two parts)
Ballards La. N3 & N12....1J 29
Ballards M. Edgw....6B 12
Ballards Ri. S Croy....6G 153
Ballards Rd. NW2....2C 46
Ballards Rd. Dag....2H 75
Ballards Way. S Croy & Croy....6G 153
Ballast Quay. SE10....5F 89
Ballater Rd. SW2....4J 103
Ballater Rd. S Croy....5F 153
Ball Ct. EC3....6D 68 (1F 169) (off Cornhill)
Ballina St. SE23....7K 105
Ballin Ct. E14....2E 88 (off Stewart St.)
Ballingdon Rd. SW11....6E 102
Balliol Av. E4....4B 20
Balliol Rd. N17....1E 32
Balliol Rd. W10....6E 64
Balliol Rd. Well....2B 110
Balloch Rd. SE6....1F 125
Ballogie Av. NW10....4A 46
Ballow Clo. SE5....7E 86
Ball's Pond Pl. N1....6D 50
Balls Pond Rd. N1....6D 50
Balmain Clo. W5....1D 80
Balmain Ct. Houn....1F 97
Balmain Lodge. Surb....4E 134 (off Cranes Pk. Av.)
Balman Ho. SE16....4K 87 (off Rotherhithe New Rd.)
Balmer Rd. E3....2B 70
Balmes Rd. N1....1D 68
Balmoral Av. N11....6K 15
Balmoral Av. Beck....4A 142
Balmoral Clo. SW15....6F 101
Balmoral Ct. SE12....4K 125
Balmoral Ct. SE16....1K 87 (off King & Queen Wharf)
Balmoral Ct. SE27....4C 122
Balmoral Ct. Beck....1E 142 (off Avenue, The)
Balmoral Ct. Sutt....7J 149
Balmoral Ct. Wemb....3F 45
Balmoral Ct. Wor Pk....2D 148
Balmoral Cres. W Mol....3E 132
Balmoral Dri. Hay....4G 59
Balmoral Dri. S'hall....4D 60
Balmoral Gdns. W13....3A 80
Balmoral Gdns. Bex....7F 111
Balmoral Gdns. Ilf....1K 55
Balmoral Gro. N7....6K 49
Balmoral Ho. E14....3D 88 (off Lanark Sq.)
Balmoral Ho. E16....1K 89 (off Keats Av.)
Balmoral Ho. W14....4G 83 (off Windsor Way)
Balmoral M. W12....3B 82
Balmoral Rd. E7....4A 54
Balmoral Rd. E10....2D 52
Balmoral Rd. NW2....6D 46
Balmoral Rd. Harr....4E 42
Balmoral Rd. King T....4F 135
Balmoral Rd. Wor Pk....3D 148
Balmoral Trad. Est. Bark....5K 73
Balmore Cres. Barn....5K 5
Balmore St. N19....2F 49
Balmuir Gdns. SW15....4E 100
Balnacraig Av. NW10....4A 46
Balniel Ga. SW1....5H 85 (5D 172)
Balsam Ho. E14....7D 70 (off E. India Dock Rd.)
Baltic Cen., The. Bren....5D 80
Baltic Clo. SW19....7B 120
Baltic Ct. SE16....2K 87
Baltic Ho. SE5....2C 104
Baltic Pl. N1....1E 68
Baltic St. E. EC1....4C 68 (4C 162)
Baltic St. W. EC1....4C 68 (4C 162)
Baltimore Ho. SE11....5J 173
Baltimore Pl. Well....2K 109
Balvaird Pl. SW1....5H 85 (6D 172)
Balvernie Gro. SW18....7H 101
Balvernie M. SW18....7J 101

Bamber Ho. *Bark* . . . 1H **73**
Bamborough Gdns. *W12* . . . 2E **82**
Bamburgh. *N17* . . . 7C **18**
Bamford Av. *Wemb* . . . 1F **63**
Bamford Ct. *E15* . . . 5D **52**
Bamford Rd. *Bark* . . . 6G **55**
Bamford Rd. *Brom* . . . 5E **124**
Bampfylde Clo. *Wall* . . . 3G **151**
Bampton Ct. *W5* . . . 6D **62**
Bampton Dri. *NW7* . . . 7H **13**
Bampton Rd. *SE23* . . . 3K **123**
Banavie Gdns. *Beck* . . . 1E **142**
Banbury Clo. *Enf* . . . 1G **7**
Banbury Ct. *WC2* . . . 2E **166**
Banbury Ct. *Sutt* . . . 7J **149**
Banbury Ho. *E9* . . . 7K **51**
Banbury Rd. *E9* . . . 7K **51**
Banbury Rd. *E17* . . . 7E **18**
Banbury St. *SW11* . . . 2C **102**
Banbury Wlk. N'holt . . . *2E* **60**
(off Brabazon Rd.)
Banchory Rd. *SE3* . . . 7K **89**
Bancroft Av. *N2* . . . 5C **30**
Bancroft Av. *Buck H* . . . 2D **20**
Bancroft Clo. *Ashf* . . . 5C **112**
Bancroft Ct. SW8 . . . *7J* **85**
(off Allen Edwards Dri.)
Bancroft Ct. *N'holt* . . . 1A **60**
Bancroft Gdns. *Harr* . . . 1G **25**
Bancroft Gdns. *Orp* . . . 7K **145**
Bancroft Ho. E1 . . . *4J* **69**
(off Cephas St.)
Bancroft Rd. *E1* . . . 3J **69**
Bancroft Rd. *Harr* . . . 2G **25**
Bandon Clo. *Uxb* . . . 2B **58**
Bandonhill. . . . 5H 151
Bandon Ri. *Wall* . . . 5H **151**
Banfield Rd. *SE15* . . . 3H **105**
Bangalore St. *SW15* . . . 3E **100**
Bangor Clo. *N'holt* . . . 5F **43**
Banim St. *W6* . . . 4D **82**
Banister Ho. *E9* . . . 5K **51**
Banister Ho. SW8 . . . *1G* **103**
(off Wadhurst Rd.)
Banister Ho. W10 . . . *3G* **65**
(off Bruckner St.)
Banister Rd. *W10* . . . 3F **65**
Bank Av. *Mitc* . . . 2B **138**
Bank Bldgs. E4 . . . *6A* **20**
(off Avenue, The)
Bank End. *SE1* . . . 1C **86** (4D **168**)
Bankfoot Rd. *Brom* . . . 4G **125**
Bankhurst Rd. *SE6* . . . 7B **106**
Bank La. *SW15* . . . 5A **100**
Bank La. *King T* . . . 7E **116**
Bank M. *Sutt* . . . 6A **150**
Bank of England. . . 6D 68 (1E 168)
Bank of England Mus. . . . 1F 169
Bank of England Offices.
EC4 . . . *6C* **68** *(1C* **168***)*
(off New Change)
Banks Ho. SE1 . . . *3C* **86**
(off Rockingham St.)
Banksian Wlk. *Iswth* . . . 1J **97**
Banksia Rd. *N18* . . . 5E **18**
Bankside. *SE1* . . . 7C **68** (3C **168**)
(in two parts)
Bankside. *Enf* . . . 1G **7**
Bankside. *S'hall* . . . 1B **78**
Bankside. *S Croy* . . . 6F **153**
Bankside Art Gallery
. . . 7B 68 (3B 168)
Bankside Av. *N'holt* . . . 2J **59**
Bankside Clo. *Bex* . . . 4K **129**
Bankside Clo. *Cars* . . . 6C **150**
Bankside Clo. *Iswth* . . . 4K **97**
Bankside Dri. *Th Dit* . . . 1B **146**
Bankside Rd. *Ilf* . . . 5G **55**
Bankside Way. *SE19* . . . 6E **122**
Banks La. *Bexh* . . . 4F **111**
Banks Way. *E12* . . . 3E **54**
Bank, The. *N6* . . . 1F **49**
Bankton Rd. *SW2* . . . 4A **104**
Bankwell Rd. *SE13* . . . 4G **107**
Bannerman Ho.
SW8 . . . 6K **85** (7G **173**)
Banner St. *EC1* . . . 4C **68** (4D **162**)
Banning St. *SE10* . . . 5G **89**
Bannister Clo. *SW2* . . . 1A **122**
Bannister Clo. *Gnfd* . . . 5H **43**
Bannister Ho. SE14 . . . *6K* **87**
(off John Williams Clo.)
Bannockburn Rd. *SE18* . . . 4J **91**
Banqueting House.
. . . 1J 85 (5E 166)
Banstead Gdns. *N9* . . . 3K **17**
Banstead Rd. *Cars* . . . 7B **150**
Banstead Rd. S. *Sutt* . . . 7B **150**
Banstead St. *SE15* . . . 3J **105**
Banstead Way. *Wall* . . . 5J **151**
Banstock Rd. *Edgw* . . . 6C **12**
Banting Dri. *N21* . . . 5E **6**
Banting Ho. *NW2* . . . 3C **46**
Bantock Ho. W10 . . . *3G* **65**
(off Third Av.)
Banton Clo. *Enf* . . . 2C **8**
Bantry Ho. E1 . . . *4K* **69**
(off Ernest St.)
Bantry St. *SE5* . . . 7D **86**
Banwell Rd. *Bex* . . . 6D **110**
Banyard Rd. *SE16* . . . 3H **87**
Baptist Gdns. *NW5* . . . 6E **48**
Barandon Rd. *W11* . . . 7F **65**
Barandon Wlk. *W11* . . . 7F **65**
Barbanel Ho. E1 . . . *4J* **69**
(off Cephas St.)
Barbara Brosnan Ct.
NW8 . . . 2B **66** (1A **158**)
Barbara Clo. *Shep* . . . 5D **130**
Barbara Hucklesby Clo.
N22 . . . 2B **32**
Barbauld Rd. *N16* . . . 3E **50**
Barber Beaumont Ho. E1 . . . *3K* **69**
(off Bancroft Rd.)
Barber Clo. *N21* . . . 7F **7**
Barbers All. *E13* . . . 3K **71**
Barbers Rd. *E15* . . . 2D **70**
Barbican Art Gallery.
. . . 5C 68 (5D 162)
(off Barbican)
Barbican Arts Cen.
. . . 5C 68 (5D 162)
Barbican Rd. *Gnfd* . . . 6F **61**
Barbican Theatre.
. . . 5C 68 (5D 162)
(off Silk St.)
Barb M. *W6* . . . 3E **82**
Barbon Clo. *WC1*
. . . 5K **67** (5F **161**)
Barbot Clo. *N9* . . . 3B **18**
Barchard St. *SW18* . . . 5K **101**
Barchester Clo. *W7* . . . 1K **79**
Barchester Rd. *Harr* . . . 2H **25**
Barchester St. *E14* . . . 5D **70**
Barclay Clo. *SW6* . . . 7J **83**
Barclay Ho. E9 . . . *7J* **51**
(off Well St.)
Barclay Oval. *Wfd G* . . . 4D **20**
Barclay Path. *E17* . . . 5E **34**
Barclay Rd. *E11* . . . 1H **53**
(in two parts)
Barclay Rd. *E13* . . . 4A **72**
Barclay Rd. *E17* . . . 5E **34**
Barclay Rd. *N18* . . . 6J **17**
Barclay Rd. *SW6* . . . 7J **83**
Barclay Rd. *Croy* . . . 3D **152**
Barcombe Av. *SW2* . . . 2J **121**
Barcombe Clo. *Orp* . . . 3K **145**
Bardell Ho. SE1 . . . *2G* **87** *(7K* **169***)*
(off Dickens Est.)
Barden St. *SE18* . . . 7J **91**
Bardfield Av. *Romf* . . . 3D **38**
Bardney Rd. *Mord* . . . 4K **137**
Bardolph Av. *Croy* . . . 7A **154**
Bardolph Rd. *N7* . . . 4J **49**
Bardolph Rd. *Rich* . . . 3F **99**
Bard Rd. *W10* . . . 7F **65**
Bardsey Pl. E1 . . . *4J* **69**
(off Mile End Rd.)
Bardsey Wlk. N1 . . . *6C* **50**
(off Douglas Rd. N.)
Bardsley Clo. *Croy* . . . 3F **153**
Bardsley Ho. SE10 . . . *6E* **88**
(off Bardsley La.)
Bardsley La. *SE10* . . . 6E **88**
Barents Ho. E1 . . . *4K* **69**
(off White Horse La.)
Barfett St. *W10* . . . 4H **65**
Barfield Av. *N20* . . . 2J **15**
Barfield Rd. *E11* . . . 1H **53**
Barfield Rd. *Brom* . . . 3E **144**
Barfleur Ho. *SE8* . . . 5B **88**
Barford Clo. *NW4* . . . 2C **28**
Barford St. *N1* . . . 1A **68**
Barforth Rd. *SE15* . . . 3H **105**
Barfreston Way. *SE20* . . . 1H **141**
Bargate Clo. *SE18* . . . 5K **91**
Bargate Clo. *N Mald* . . . 7C **136**
Barge Ho. Rd. *E16* . . . 2F **91**
Barge Ho. St.
SE1 . . . 1A **86** (4K **167**)
Bargery Rd. *SE6* . . . 1D **124**
Barge Wlk. *E Mol* . . . 3H **133**
Barge Wlk. *Hamp W* . . . 1D **134**
Barge Wlk. *King T* . . . 3D **134**
Bargrove Clo. *SE20* . . . 7G **123**
Bargrove Cres. *SE6* . . . 2B **124**
Barham Clo. *Brom* . . . 1C **156**
Barham Clo. *Chst* . . . 5F **127**
Barham Clo. *Romf* . . . 2H **39**
Barham Clo. *Wemb* . . . 6B **44**
Barham Ct. S Croy . . . *4C* **152**
(off Barham Rd.)
Barham Ho. SE17 . . . *5E* **86**
(off Kinglake St.)
Barham Rd. *SW20* . . . 7C **118**
Barham Rd. *Chst* . . . 5F **127**
Barham Rd. *S Croy* . . . 4C **152**
Baring Clo. *SE12* . . . 2J **125**
Baring Ho. E14 . . . *6C* **70**
(off Canton St.)
Baring Rd. *SE12* . . . 7J **107**
Baring Rd. *Cockf* . . . 4G **5**
Baring Rd. *Croy* . . . 1G **153**
Baring St. *N1* . . . 1D **68**
Barker Clo. *N Mald* . . . 4H **135**
Barker Clo. *N'wd* . . . 1H **23**
Barker Dri. *NW1* . . . 7G **49**
Barker M. *SW4* . . . 4F **103**
Barkers Arc. *W8* . . . 2K **83**
Barker St. *SW10* . . . 6A **84**
Barker Wlk. *SW16* . . . 3H **121**
Barkham Rd. *N17* . . . 7J **17**
Barkham Ter. *SE1* . . . 1K **173**
Barking. . . . 7G 55
Barking Bus. Cen. *Bark* . . . 3A **74**
Barking Ind. Pk. *Bark* . . . 1K **73**
Barking Northern Relief Rd.
Bark . . . 7F **55**
Barking Railway
(Miniature Railway)
. . . 6G 55
Barking Rd. *E13 & E6* . . . 2A **72**
Barking Rd. *E16 & E13* . . . 5H **71**
Barkingside. . . . 3G 37
Bark Pl. *W2* . . . 7K **65**
Barkston Gdns. *SW5* . . . 4K **83**
Barkway Ct. *N4* . . . 2C **50**
Barkwith Ho. SE14 . . . *6K* **87**
(off Cold Blow La.)
Barkwood Clo. *Romf* . . . 5J **39**
Barkworth Rd. *SE16* . . . 5H **87**
Barlborough St. *SE14* . . . 7K **87**
Barlby Gdns. *W10* . . . 4F **65**
Barlby Rd. *W10* . . . 5E **64**
Barleycorn Way. *E14* . . . 7B **70**
Barleyfields Clo. *Romf* . . . 6B **38**
Barley La. *Ilf & Romf* . . . 7A **38**
Barley Mow Pas. *EC1* . . . 5B **162**
Barley Mow Pas. *W4* . . . 5K **81**
Barleymow Way. *Shep* . . . 4C **130**
Barley Shotts Bus. Pk.
W10 . . . 5H **65**
Barling. NW1 . . . *6F* **49**
(off Castlehaven Rd.)
Barlings Ho. SE4 . . . *4K* **105**
(off Frendsbury Rd.)
Barlow Clo. *Wall* . . . 6J **151**
Barlow Dri. *SE18* . . . 1C **108**
Barlow Ho. N1 . . . *3D* **68** *(1E* **162***)*
(off Provost Est.)
Barlow Ho. SE16 . . . *4H* **87**
(off Rennie Est.)
Barlow Ho. W11 . . . *7G* **65**
(off Walmer Rd.)
Barlow Pl. *W1* . . . 7F **67** (3K **165**)
Barlow Rd. *NW6* . . . 6H **47**
Barlow Rd. *W3* . . . 1H **81**
Barlow Rd. *Hamp* . . . 7E **114**
Barlow St. *SE17* . . . 4D **86**
Barlow Way. *Rain* . . . 5K **75**
Barmeston Rd. *SE6* . . . 2D **124**
Barmor Clo. *Harr* . . . 2F **25**
Barmouth Av. *Gnfd* . . . 2K **61**
Barmouth Rd. *SW18* . . . 6A **102**
Barmouth Rd. *Croy* . . . 2K **153**
Barnabas Ct. *N21* . . . 4F **7**
Barnabas Rd. *E9* . . . 5K **51**
Barnaby Clo. *Harr* . . . 2G **43**
Barnaby Ct. *NW9* . . . 3A **28**
Barnaby Ct. SE16 . . . *2G* **87**
(off Scott Lidgett Cres.)
Barnaby Pl. *SW7* . . . 4A **170**
Barnaby Way. *Chig* . . . 3K **21**
Barnard Clo. *SE18* . . . 4E **90**
Barnard Clo. *Chst* . . . 1H **145**
Barnard Clo. *Sun* . . . 7K **113**
Barnard Clo. *Wall* . . . 7H **151**
Barnard Gdns. *Hay* . . . 4K **59**
Barnard Gdns. *N Mald* . . . 4C **136**
Barnard Gro. *E15* . . . 7H **53**
Barnard Hill. *N10* . . . 1F **31**
Barnard Ho. E2 . . . *3H* **69**
(off Ellsworth St.)
Barnard Lodge. W9 . . . *5J* **65**
(off Admiral Wlk.)
Barnard Lodge. *New Bar* . . . 4F **5**
Barnard M. *SW11* . . . 4C **102**
Barnardo Dri. *Ilf* . . . 4G **37**
Barnardo Gdns. *E1* . . . 7K **69**
Barnardo St. *E1* . . . 6K **69**
Barnardos Village. *B'side* . . . 3G **37**
Barnard Rd. *SW11* . . . 4C **102**
Barnard Rd. *Enf* . . . 2C **8**
Barnard Rd. *Mitc* . . . 3E **138**
Barnards Ho. SE16 . . . *2B* **88**
(off Wyatt Clo.)
Barnard's Inn. *EC1* . . . 6K **161**
(in two parts)
Barnbrough. NW1 . . . *1G* **67**
(off Camden St.)
Barnby Sq. *E15* . . . 1G **71**
Barnby St. *E15* . . . 1G **71**
Barnby St. *NW1* . . . 2G **67** (1B **160**)
Barn Clo. NW5 . . . *5H* **49**
(off Torriano Av.)
Barn Clo. *Ashf* . . . 5D **112**
Barn Clo. *N'holt* . . . 2A **60**
Barn Cres. *Stan* . . . 6H **11**
Barncroft Clo. *Uxb* . . . 5D **58**
Barneby Clo. *Twic* . . . 1J **115**
Barnehurst. . . . 3J 111
Barnehurst Av.
Eri & Bexh . . . 1J **111**
Barnehurst Clo. *Eri* . . . 1J **111**
Barnehurst Rd. *Bexh* . . . 2J **111**
Barn Elms Pk. *SW15* . . . 3E **100**
Barnes. . . . 2B 100
Barnes All. *Hamp* . . . 2G **133**
Barnes Av. *SW13* . . . 7C **82**
Barnes Av. *S'hall* . . . 4D **78**
Barnes Clo. *E12* . . . 4B **54**
Barnes Ct. *E16* . . . 5A **72**
Barnes Ct. *N1* . . . 7A **50**
Barnes Ct. *Wfd G* . . . 5G **21**
Barnes End. *N Mald* . . . 5C **136**
Barnes High St. *SW13* . . . 2B **100**
Barnes Ho. SE14 . . . *6K* **87**
(off John Williams Clo.)
Barnes Ho. *Bark* . . . 1H **73**
Barnes Pikle. *W5* . . . 7D **62**
Barnes Rd. *N18* . . . 4D **18**
Barnes St. *E14* . . . 6A **70**
Barnes Ter. *SE8* . . . 5B **88**
Barnes Wallis Ct. *Wemb* . . . 3J **45**
Barnet. . . . 3B 4
Barnet Bus. Cen. *Barn* . . . 3B **4**
Barnet By-Pass. *NW7* . . . 6G **13**
Barnet Dri. *Brom* . . . 2C **156**
Barnet F.C. (Underhill Stadium).
. . . 5D 4
Barnet Ga. La. *Barn* . . . 1H **13**
Barnet Gro. *E2* . . . 3G **69** (1K **163**)
Barnet Hill. *Barn* . . . 4C **4**
Barnet Ho. *N20* . . . 2F **15**
Barnet La. *N20 & Barn* . . . 1C **14**
Barnet Trad. Est. *High Bar* . . . 3C **4**
Barnetts Ct. *Harr* . . . 3F **43**
Barnett St. *E1* . . . 6H **69**
Barnet Vale. . . . 5E 4
Barnet Way.
NW7 & Borwd . . . 3E **12**
Barnet Wood Rd. *Brom* . . . 2A **156**
Barney Clo. *SE7* . . . 5A **90**
Barn Fld. *NW3* . . . 5D **48**
Barnfield. *N Mald* . . . 6A **136**
Barnfield Av. *Croy* . . . 2J **153**
Barnfield Av. *King T* . . . 4D **116**
Barnfield Av. *Mitc* . . . 4F **139**
Barnfield Clo. *N4* . . . 7J **31**
Barnfield Clo. *SW17* . . . 3B **120**
Barnfield Gdns. *SE18* . . . 6F **91**
Barnfield Gdns. *King T* . . . 4E **116**
Barnfield Pl. *E14* . . . 4C **88**
Barnfield Rd. *SE18* . . . 6F **91**
(in two parts)
Barnfield Rd. *W5* . . . 4C **62**
Barnfield Rd. *Belv* . . . 6F **93**
Barnfield Rd. *Edgw* . . . 1J **27**
Barnfield Rd. *S Croy* . . . 7E **152**
Barnfield Wood Clo. *Beck* . . . 6F **143**
Barnfield Wood Rd. *Beck* . . . 6F **143**
Barnham Dri. *SE28* . . . 1K **91**
Barnham Rd. *Gnfd* . . . 3G **61**
Barnham St. *SE1* . . . 2E **86** (6H **169**)
Barnhill. *Pinn* . . . 5A **24**
Barn Hill. *Wemb* . . . 1G **45**
Barnhill Av. *Brom* . . . 5H **143**
Barnhill La. *Hay* . . . 3K **59**
Barnhill Rd. *Hay* . . . 3K **59**
Barnhill Rd. *Wemb* . . . 3J **45**
Barningham Way. *NW9* . . . 6K **27**
Barnlea Clo. *Felt* . . . 2C **114**
Barnmead Gdns. *Dag* . . . 5F **57**
Barnmead Rd. *Beck* . . . 1K **141**
Barnmead Rd. *Dag* . . . 5F **57**
Barn M. *S Harr* . . . 3E **42**
Barn Ri. *Wemb* . . . 1G **45**
Barnsbury. . . . 7K 49
Barnsbury Clo. *N Mald* . . . 4J **135**
Barnsbury Cres. *Surb* . . . 1J **147**
Barnsbury Est. *N1* . . . 1K **67**
(in two parts)
Barnsbury Gro. *N7* . . . 7K **49**
Barnsbury Ho. *SW4* . . . 6H **103**
Barnsbury La. *Surb* . . . 2H **147**
Barnsbury Pk. *N1* . . . 7A **50**
Barnsbury Rd. *N1* . . . 2A **68**
Barnsbury Sq. *N1* . . . 7A **50**
Barnsbury St. *N1* . . . 7A **50**
Barnsbury Ter. *N1* . . . 7K **49**
Barnscroft. *SW20* . . . 3D **136**
Barnsdale Av. *E14* . . . 4D **88**
Barnsdale Rd. *W9* . . . 4H **65**
Barnsley St. *E1* . . . 4H **69**
Barnstable La. *SE13* . . . 4E **106**
Barnstaple Ho. SE10 . . . *7D* **88**
(off Devonshire Dri.)

Barnstaple Ho. SE12 . . . . . . 5H 107 (off Taunton Rd.)
Barnstaple Rd. Ruis. 3A 42
Barnston Wlk. N1 . . . . 1C 68 (off Popham St.)
Barn St. N16 . . . . 2E 50
Barn Way. Wemb. 1G 45
Barnwell Ho. SE5. . . . . 1E 104 (off St Giles Rd.)
Barnwell Rd. SW2 . . . . 5A 104
Barnwood Clo. N20 . . . . 1C 14
Barnwood Clo. W9 . . . . 4K 65
Barnwood Clo. Ruis 2F 41
Baron Clo. N11 . . . . 5K 15
Baroness Rd. E2 . . . 3F 69 (1K 163)
Baronet Gro. N17 . . . . 1G 33
Baronet Rd. N17 . . . . 1G 33
Baron Gdns. Ilf 3G 37
Baron Gro. Mitc. 4C 138
Baron Rd. Dag 1D 56
Baronsclere Ct. N6 . . . . 7G 31
Barons Court. 5G 83
Barons Ct. Ilf. 2H 55
Barons Ct. Wall 3H 151
Baron's Ct. Rd. W14 . . . . 5G 83
Barons Court Theatre. . . . . . 5G 83 (off Comeragh Rd.)
Baronsfield Rd. Twic 6B 98
Barons Ga. W4 . . . . 3J 81
Barons Ga. Barn 6H 5
Barons Keep. W14 . . . . 5G 83
Barons Mead. Harr. 4J 25
Baronsmead Rd. SW13 . . . . 1C 100
Baronsmede. W5 . . . . 2F 81
Baronsmere Ct. Barn 4B 4
Baronsmere Rd. N2. . . . . 4C 30
Baron's Pl. SE1 . . . . 2A 86 (7K 167)
Barons, The. Twic 6B 98
Baron St. N1 . . . . 2A 68
Baron's Wlk. Croy 6A 142
Baron Wlk. E16. . . . . 5H 71
Baron Wlk. Mitc. 4C 138
Barque M. SE8 . . . . 6C 88
Barrack Rd. Houn 4B 96
Barra Hall Cir. Hay. 7G 59
Barra Hall Rd. Hay. 7G 59
Barratt Av. N22 . . . . 2K 31
Barratt Ho. N1 . . . . 7B 50 (off Sable St.)
Barratt Ind. Pk. E3. . . . . 4E 70
Barratt Ind. Pk. S'hall. 2E 78
Barratt Way. Harr 2H 25
Barrenger Rd. N10 . . . . 1D 30
Barret Ho. NW6. . . . . 1J 65
Barret Ho. SW9. . . . . 3K 103 (off Benedict Rd.)
Barrett Ho. SE17 . . . . 5C 86 (off Browning St.)
Barrett Rd. E17 . . . . 4E 34
Barrett's Grn. Rd. NW10. . . . . 3J 63
Barrett's Gro. N16 . . . . 5E 50
Barrett St. W1 . . . . . 6E 66 (1H 165)
Barrhill Rd. SW2 . . . . 2J 121
Barrie Ct. New Bar . . . . 5F 5 (off Lyonsdown Rd.)
Barriedale. SE14 . . . . 2A 106
Barrie Est. W2. . . . . 7B 66 (2A 164)
Barrie Ho. W2 . . . . 7A 66 (off Lancaster Ga.)
Barrier App. SE7 . . . . 3B 90
Barrier Point Rd. E16. . . . . . . 1A 90
Barringers Ct. Ruis. 7F 23
Barringer Sq. SW17. . . . . 4E 120
Barrington Clo. NW5 . . . . 5E 48
Barrington Clo. Ilf 1D 36
Barrington Ct. NW5 . . . . 5E 48
Barrington Ct. SW4 . . . . 2J 103
Barrington Ct. W3 . . . . 2H 81 (off Cheltenham Pl.)
Barrington Rd. E12 . . . . 6E 54
Barrington Rd. N8. . . . . 5H 31
Barrington Rd. SW9 . . . . . . 3B 104
Barrington Rd. Bexh 2D 110
Barrington Rd. Sutt 2J 149
Barrington Vs. SE18 . . . . 1E 108
Barrington Wlk. SE19. . . . . . . 6E 122
Barrosa Dri. Hamp. 1E 132
Barrow Av. Cars 7D 150
Barrow Clo. N21 . . . . 3G 17
Barrow Ct. SE6 . . . . 1H 125 (off Cumberland Pl.)
Barrowdene Clo. Pinn 2C 24
Barrowell Grn. N21 . . . . 2G 17
Barrowfield Clo. N9 . . . . 3C 18
Barrowgate Rd. W4 . . . . 5J 81
Barrow Hedges Clo. Cars . . . 7C 150
Barrow Hedges Way. Cars. 7C 150
Barrowhill. Wor Pk 2A 148
Barrowhill Clo. Wor Pk. 2A 148
Barrow Hill Est. NW8. . . . . . . 2C 66 (off Barrow Hill Rd.)
Barrow Hill Rd. NW8 . . . . . . 2C 66 (1C 158)
Barrow Point Av. Pinn 2C 24
Barrow Point La. Pinn 2C 24
Barrow Rd. SW16 . . . . 6H 121
Barrow Rd. Croy 5A 152
Barrow Wlk. Bren 6C 80
Barrs Rd. NW10 . . . . 7K 45
Barry Av. N15 . . . . 6F 33
Barry Av. Bexh. 7E 92
Barrydene. N20. . . . . 1G 15
Barry Ho. SE16. . . . . 4H 87 (off Rennie Est.)
Barry Rd. E6. . . . . 6C 72
Barry Rd. NW10 . . . . 7J 45
Barry Rd. SE22. . . . . 6G 105
Barset Rd. SE15. . . . . 3J 105 (in three parts)
Barson Clo. SE20. . . . . 7J 123
Barston Rd. SE27 . . . . 3C 122
Barstow Cres. SW2 . . . . 1K 121
Barter St. WC1. . . . . 5J 67 (6F 161)
Barters Wlk. Pinn 3C 24
Bartholomew Clo. EC1 . . . . 5C 68 (6B 162) (in two parts)
Bartholomew Clo. SW18 . . . . 4A 102
Bartholomew Ct. E14. . . . . 7F 71 (off Newport Av.)
Bartholomew Ct. EC1 . . . . . . 4C 68 (3D 162) (off Old St.)
Bartholomew Ct. Edgw. 7J 11
Bartholomew La. EC2 . . . . 6D 68 (1F 169)
Bartholomew Pl. EC1. . . . . . . 6C 162
Bartholomew Rd. NW5 . . . . . . 6G 49
Bartholomew Sq. E1 . . . . 4H 69
Bartholomew Sq. EC1 . . . . 4C 68 (3D 162)
Bartholomew St. SE1 . . . . 3D 86
Bartholomew Vs. NW5 . . . . . . 6G 49
Barth Rd. SE18 . . . . 4J 91
Bartle Av. E6 . . . . 2C 72
Bartle Rd. W11 . . . . 6G 65
Bartlett Clo. E14 . . . . 6C 70
Bartlett Ct. EC4 . . . . 6A 68 (7K 161)
Bartlett Houses. Dag . . . . 7H 57 (off Vicarage Rd.)
Bartletts Pas. EC4 . . . . . . 6A 68 (7K 161) (off Fetter La.)
Bartlett St. S Croy 5D 152
Bartlow Gdns. Romf 1K 39
Barton Av. Romf 1H 57
Barton Clo. E6. . . . . 6D 72
Barton Clo. E9 . . . . 5J 51
Barton Clo. NW4 . . . . 5C 28
Barton Clo. SE15. . . . . 3H 105
Barton Clo. Bexh 5E 110
Barton Clo. Shep 6D 130
Barton Ct. W14. . . . . 5G 83 (off Baron's Ct. Rd.)
Barton Grn. N Mald 2K 135
Barton Ho. N1. . . . . 7B 50 (off Sable St.)
Barton Ho. SW6 . . . . 3K 101 (off Wandsworth Bri. Rd.)
Barton Meadows. Ilf. 4F 37
Barton Rd. W14 . . . . 5G 83
Barton Rd. Sidc 6E 128
Barton St. SW1 . . . . 3J 85 (1E 172)
Bartonway. NW8 . . . . 1B 66 (off Queen's Ter.)
Bartram Clo. Uxb. 4D 58
Bartram Rd. SE4 . . . . 5A 106
Bartrams La. Barn 1F 5
Bartrip St. E9. . . . . 6B 52
Barts Clo. Beck 5C 142
Barville Clo. SE4 . . . . 4A 106
Barwell Bus Pk. Chess. 7D 146
Barwell Ho. E2 . . . . 4G 69 (off Menotti St.)
Barwick Dri. Uxb 5D 58
Barwick Ho. W3. . . . . 2J 81 (off Strafford Rd.)
Barwick Rd. E7 . . . . 4K 53
Barwood Av. W Wick 1D 154
Basden Gro. Felt 2E 114
Basden Ho. Felt 2E 114
Basedale Rd. Dag 7B 56
Baseing Clo. E6. . . . . 7E 72
Basevi Way. SE8 . . . . 6C 88
Bashley Rd. NW10 . . . . 4K 63
Basil Av. E6. . . . . 3C 72
Basildene Rd. Houn. 3B 96
Basildon Av. Ilf 1E 36
Basildon Clo. Sutt 7K 149
Basildon Ct. W1 . . . 5E 66 (5H 159) (off Devonshire Rd.)
Basildon Rd. SE2. . . . . 5A 92
Basil Gdns. SE27. . . . . 5C 122
Basil Gdns. Croy 1K 153
Basil Ho. SW8 . . . . 7J 85 (off Wyvil Rd.)
Basilon Rd. Bexh 2E 110
Basil Spence Ho. N22 . . . . . . 1K 31
Basil St. SW3 . . . . . 3D 84 (1E 170)
Basin App. E14 . . . . 6A 70
Basing Clo. Th Dit 7K 133
Basing Ct. SE15. . . . . 1F 105
Basingdon Way. SE5 . . . . . . 4D 104
Basing Dri. Bex 6F 111
Basingfield Rd. Th Dit 7K 133
Basinghall Av. EC2 . . . . . . 6D 68 (7E 162)
Basinghall Gdns. Sutt 7K 149
Basinghall St. EC2. . . . . . . 6D 68 (7E 162)
Basing Hill. NW11. . . . . 1H 47
Basing Hill. Wemb 2F 45
Basing Ho. Bark . . . . 1H 73 (off St Margarets)
Basing Ho. Yd. E2. . . . . 3E 68 (1H 163)
Basing Pl. E2 . . . . . 3E 68 (1H 163)
Basing St. W11. . . . . 6H 65
Basing Way. N3. . . . . 3J 29
Basing Way. Th Dit 7K 133
Basire St. N1. . . . . 1C 68
Baskerville Gdns. NW10 . . . . 4A 46
Baskerville Rd. SW18 . . . . . 7C 102
Basket Gdns. SE9 . . . . 5C 108
Baslow Clo. Harr 1H 25
Baslow Wlk. E5. . . . . 4K 51
Basnett Rd. SW11 . . . . 3E 102
Basque Ct. SE16 . . . . 2K 87 (off Garter Way)
Bassano St. SE22 . . . . 5F 105
Bassant Rd. SE18 . . . . 6K 91
Bassein Pk. Rd. W12. . . . . . . 2B 82
Bassett Gdns. Iswth 7G 79
Bassett Rd. E7. . . . . 4B 54
Bassett Rd. W10 . . . . 6F 65
Bassett St. NW5 . . . . 6E 48
Bassett's Way. Orp. 4E 156
Bassett Way. Gnfd 6F 61
Bassingbourn Ho. N1 . . . . . . 7A 50 (off Sutton Est., The)
Bassingham Rd. SW18 . . . . 7A 102
Bassingham Rd. Wemb. 6D 44
Bassishaw Highwalk. EC2 . . . . 6D 162
Basswood Clo. SE15. . . . . . . 3H 105
Bastable Av. Bark. 2J 73
Basterfield Ho. EC1 . . . . . . 4C 68 (4C 162) (off Golden La. Est.)
Bastion Highwalk. EC2. . . . . 6C 162
Bastion Ho. EC2 . . . . 5C 68 (6D 162) (off London Wall)
Bastion Rd. SE2 . . . . 5A 92
Baston Mnr. Rd. Brom. 3K 155
Baston Rd. Brom. 1K 155
Bastwick St. EC1 . . 4C 68 (3C 162)
Basuto Rd. SW6 . . . . 1J 101
Batavia Clo. Sun 1K 131
Batavia Ho. SE14. . . . . 7A 88 (off Batavia Rd.)
Batavia M. SE14 . . . . 7A 88
Batavia Rd. SE14. . . . . 7A 88
Batavia Rd. Sun. 1K 131
Batchelor St. N1 . . . . 1A 68
Bateman Clo. Bark. 6G 55
Bateman Ho. SE17 . . . . 6B 86 (off Otto St.)
Bateman Rd. E4 . . . . 6H 19
Bateman's Bldgs. W1. . . . . . 1C 166
Bateman's Row. EC2 . . . . 4E 68 (3H 163)
Bateman St. W1 . . . 6H 67 (1C 166)
Bates Cres. SW16 . . . . 7G 121
Bates Cres. Croy 5A 152
Bateson St. SE18. . . . . 4J 91
Bates Point. E13 . . . . 1J 71 (off Pelly Rd.)
Bate St. E14 . . . . 7B 70
Bath Clo. SE15 . . . . 7H 87
Bath Ct. EC1 . . . . 4J 161
Bath Ct. SE26 . . . . 3G 123 (off Droitwich Clo.)
Bathgate Rd. SW19 . . . . 3F 119
Bath Gro. E2 . . . . . . 2G 69 (1K 163) (off Horatio St.)
Bath Ho. E2. . . . . 4G 69 (off Ramsey St.)
Bath Ho. SE1. . . . . 3C 86 (off Bath Ter.)
Bath Ho. Rd. Croy 1J 151
Bath Pas. King T 2D 134
Bath Pl. EC2 . . . . . . 3E 68 (2G 163)
Bath Pl. W6. . . . . 5E 82 (off Fulham Pal. Rd.)
Bath Pl. Barn. 3C 4
Bath Rd. E7. . . . . 6B 54
Bath Rd. N9 . . . . 2C 18
Bath Rd. W4. . . . . 4A 82
Bath Rd. Hay & H'row A 1G 95
Bath Rd. Houn. 1A 96
Bath Rd. Romf. 6E 38
Bath Rd. W Dray & H'row A . . . 1A 94
Baths App. SW6 . . . . 7H 83
Baths Rd. Brom. 4B 144
Bath St. EC1 . . . . . . 3C 68 (2D 162)
Bath Ter. SE1. . . . . 3C 86
Bathurst Av. SW19 . . . . 1K 137
Bathurst Gdns. NW10 . . . . . . 2D 64
Bathurst Ho. W12 . . . . 7D 64 (off White City Est.)
Bathurst M. W2. . . . 6B 66 (2B 164)
Bathurst Rd. Ilf 1F 55
Bathurst St. W2 . . . 7B 66 (2B 164)
Bathway. SE18. . . . . 4E 90
Batley Clo. Mitc. 7D 138
Batley Pl. N16 . . . . 3F 51
Batley Rd. N16. . . . . 3F 51
Batley Rd. Enf. 1H 7
Batman Clo. W12 . . . . 1D 82
Batoum Gdns. W6. . . . . 3E 82
Batson Ho. E1 . . . . 6G 69 (off Fairclough St.)
Batson St. W12. . . . . 2C 82
Batsworth Rd. Mitc 3B 138
Battenberg Wlk. SE19 . . . . . 6E 122
Batten Clo. E6. . . . . 6D 72
Batten Ho. SW4. . . . . 5G 103
Batten Ho. W10. . . . . 3G 65 (off Third Av.)
Batten St. SW11 . . . . 3C 102
Battersby Rd. SE6 . . . . 2F 125
Battersea. 1E 102
Battersea Bri. SW3 & SW11. . . . . . . 7B 84
Battersea Bri. Rd. SW11 . . . . 7C 84
Battersea Bus. Cen. SW11. . . . . 3E 102
Battersea Chu. Rd. SW11. . . 1B 102
Battersea Dogs' Home. 7F 85
Battersea High St. SW11 . . . 1B 102 (in two parts)
Battersea Pk. 7E 84
Battersea Pk. Children's Zoo. 7E 84
Battersea Pk. Rd. SW11 & SW8. . . . . . 2C 102
Battersea Ri. SW11 . . . . 5C 102
Battersea Sq. SW11. . . . . . . 1B 102
Battery Rd. SE28 . . . . 2J 91
Battishill St. N1 . . . . 7B 50
Battis, The. Romf. 6K 39
Battlebridge Ct. N1. . . . . 2J 67 (off Wharfdale Rd.)
Battle Bri. La. SE1 . . . . 1E 86 (5G 169)
Battle Bri. Rd. NW1 . . . . 2J 67
Battle Clo. SW19 . . . . 6A 120
Battledean Rd. N5 . . . . 5B 50
Battle Ho. SE15. . . . . 6G 87 (off Haymerle Rd.)
Battle of Britain Hall. 2B 28
Battle Rd. Belv & Eri 4J 93
Batty St. E1. . . . . 6G 69
Baudene M. NW4 . . . . 4D 28 (off Burroughs, The)
Baudwin Rd. SE6 . . . . 2G 125
Baugh Rd. Sidc 5C 128
Baulk, The. SW18 . . . . 7J 101
Bavant Rd. SW16. . . . . 2J 139
Bavaria Rd. N19. . . . . 2J 49 (in two parts)
Bavent Rd. SE5 . . . . 2C 104
Bawdale Rd. SE22 . . . . 5F 105
Bawdsey Av. Ilf 4K 37
Bawtree Rd. SE14 . . . . 7A 88
Bawtry Rd. N20. . . . . 3J 15
Baxendale. N20 . . . . 2F 15
Baxendale St. E2. . . . . 3G 69
Baxter Clo. S'hall. 3F 79
Baxter Clo. Uxb. 3D 58
Baxter Rd. E16 . . . . 6A 72
Baxter Rd. N1 . . . . 6D 50
Baxter Rd. N18 . . . . 4C 18
Baxter Rd. Ilf 5F 55
Bayard Ct. Bexh. . . . . 4H 111 (off Watling St.)
Bay Ct. E1. . . . . 4K 69 (off Frimley Way)
Bay Ct. W5 . . . . 3E 80
Baycroft Clo. Pinn 3A 24
Baydon Ct. Brom. 3H 143
Bayer Ho. EC1. . . . . 4C 68 (4C 162) (off Golden La. Est.)
Bayes Ct. NW3 . . . . 7D 48 (off Primrose Hill Rd.)
Bayfield Ho. SE4 . . . . 4K 105 (off Coston Wlk.)
Bayfield Rd. SE9 . . . . 4B 108
Bayford M. E8. . . . . 7H 51 (off Bayford St.)
Bayford Rd. NW10. . . . . 3F 65
Bayford St. E8. . . . . 7H 51
Bayford St. Bus. Cen. E8 . . . . 7H 51 (off Sidworth St.)
Baygrove M. Hamp W 1C 134
Bayham Pl. NW1. . . . . 1G 67
Bayham Rd. W4 . . . . 3K 81
Bayham Rd. W13 . . . . 7B 62

Bayham Rd. Mord 4K 137
Bayham St. NW1 . . . . 1G 67
Bayhurst Wood Country Pk. 5B 22
Bayleaf Clo. Hamp H 5H 115
Bayley St. W1 . . . . 5H 67 (6C 160)
Bayley Wlk. SE2 . . . . 5E 92
Baylis Rd. SE1 . . . . 2A 86 (7J 167)
Bayliss Av. SE28 . . . . 7D 74
Bayliss Clo. N21 . . . . 5D 6
Bayliss M. Twic 7A 98
Bayne Clo. E6 . . . . 6D 72
Baynes Clo. Enf 1B 8
Baynes M. NW3 . . . . 6B 48
Baynes St. NW1 . . . . 7G 49
Baynham Clo. Bex 6F 111
Bayonne Rd. W6 . . . . 6G 83
Bays Clo. SE26 . . . . 5J 123
Bays Ct. Edgw 5C 12
Bayshill Ri. N'holt 6F 43
Bayston Rd. N16 . . . . 3F 51
Bayswater. 7A 66
Bayswater Rd. W2 . . . . . . 7K 65 (3A 164)
Baythorne St. E3 . . . . 5B 70
Bayton Ct. E8 . . . . 7G 51 (off Lansdowne Dri.)
Bay Tree Clo. Brom 1B 144
Baytree Clo. Sidc 1K 127
Baytree Ct. SW2 . . . . 4K 103
Baytree Ho. E4 . . . . 7J 9
Baytree Rd. SW2 . . . . 4K 103
Bazalgette Clo. N Mald 5K 135
Bazalgette Gdns. N Mald . . . 5K 135
Bazalgette Ho. NW8 . . . . . . 4B 66 (3B 158) (off Orchardson St.)
Bazeley Ho. SE1 . . . 2B 86 (7A 168) (off Library St.)
Bazely St. E14 . . . . 7E 70
Bazile Rd. N21 . . . . 6F 7
BBC Broadcasting House. 5F 67 (6K 159)
Beacham Clo. SE7 . . . . 5B 90
Beachborough Rd. Brom . . . 4E 124
Beachcroft Rd. E11 . . . . 3G 53
Beachcroft Way. N19 . . . . 1H 49
Beach Gro. Felt 2E 114
Beach Ho. SW5 . . . . 5J 83 (off Philbeach Gdns.)
Beach Ho. Felt 2E 114
Beachy Rd. E3 . . . . 7C 52
Beacon Clo. Uxb 5A 40
Beacon Ga. SE14 . . . . 3K 105
Beacon Gro. Cars 4E 150
Beacon Hill. N7 . . . . 5J 49
Beacon Ho. E14 . . . . 5D 88 (off Burrells Wharf Sq.)
Beacon Ho. SE5 . . . . 7E 86 (off Southampton Way)
Beacon Pl. Croy 3J 151
Beacon Rd. SE13 . . . . 6F 107
Beacon Rd. H'row A 6C 94
Beacons Clo. E6 . . . . 5C 72
Beaconsfield Clo. N11 . . . . . . 5K 15
Beaconsfield Clo. SE3 . . . . . . 6J 89
Beaconsfield Clo. W4 . . . . 5J 81
Beaconsfield Pde. SE9 . . . . . 4C 126
Beaconsfield Rd. E10 . . . . 2E 52
Beaconsfield Rd. E16 . . . . . . 4H 71
Beaconsfield Rd. E17 . . . . 6B 34
Beaconsfield Rd. N9 . . . . 3B 18
Beaconsfield Rd. N11 . . . . . . 3K 15
Beaconsfield Rd. N15 . . . . 4E 32
Beaconsfield Rd. NW10 . . . . . 6B 46
Beaconsfield Rd. SE3 . . . . 7H 89
Beaconsfield Rd. SE9 . . . . . . 2C 126
Beaconsfield Rd. SE17 . . . . . . 5D 86
Beaconsfield Rd. W4 . . . . 3K 81
Beaconsfield Rd. W5 . . . . 2C 80
Beaconsfield Rd. Bex 2K 129
Beaconsfield Rd. Brom 3B 144
Beaconsfield Rd. Croy 6D 140
Beaconsfield Rd. Hay 1A 78
Beaconsfield Rd. N Mald . . . 2K 135
Beaconsfield Rd. S'hall 1B 78
Beaconsfield Rd. Surb 7F 135
Beaconsfield Rd. Twic 6B 98
Beaconsfield Ter. Romf 6D 38
Beaconsfield Ter. Rd. W14 . . . 3G 83
Beaconsfield Wlk. E6 . . . . 6E 72
Beaconsfield Wlk. SW6 . . . . 1H 101
Beacontree Av. E17 . . . . 1F 35
Beacontree Heath. 2G 57
Beacontree Rd. E11 . . . . 1H 53
Beadle's Pde. Dag 6J 57
Beadlow Clo. Cars 6B 138
Beadman St. SE27 . . . . 4B 122
Beadnell Rd. SE23 . . . . 1K 123
Beadon Rd. W6 . . . . 4E 82
Beadon Rd. Brom 4J 143
Beaford Gro. SW20 . . . . 3G 137
Beagle Clo. Felt 4K 113
Beak St. W1 . . . . . . 7G 67 (2B 166)
Beal Clo. Well 1A 110
Beale Clo. N13 . . . . 5G 17
Beale Pl. E3 . . . . 2B 70
Beale Rd. E3 . . . . 1B 70
Beal Rd. Ilf 2E 54
Beam Av. Dag 1H 75
Beaminster Gdns. Ilf 2F 37
Beaminster Ho. SW8 . . . . 7K 85 (off Dorset Rd.)
Beamish Dri. Bus H 1B 10
Beamish Ho. SE16 . . . . 4H 87 (off Rennie Est.)
Beamish Rd. N9 . . . . 1B 18
Beam Vs. Dag 2J 75
Beamway. Dag 7K 57
Beanacre Clo. E9 . . . . 6B 52
Bean Rd. Bexh 4D 110
Beanshaw. SE9 . . . . 4E 126
Beansland Gro. Romf 2E 38
Bear All. EC4 . . . . . . 6B 68 (7A 162)
Bear Clo. Romf 6H 39
Beardell St. SE19 . . . . 6F 123
Beardow Gro. N14 . . . . 6B 6
Beard Rd. King T 5F 117
Beardsfield. E13 . . . . 2J 71
Beard's Hill. Hamp 1E 132
Beard's Hill Clo. Hamp 1E 132
Beardsley Ter. Dag . . . . 5B 56 (off Fitzstephen Rd.)
Beardsley Way. W3 . . . . 2K 81
Beard's Rd. Ashf 6G 113
Bearfield Rd. King T 7E 116
Bear Gdns. SE1 . . . . 1C 86 (4C 168)
Bear La. SE1 . . . . . . 1B 86 (4B 168)
Bear Rd. Felt 4B 114
Bearsted Ri. SE4 . . . . 5B 106
Bearsted Ter. Beck 1C 142
Bear St. WC2 . . . . . 7H 67 (2D 166)
Beasley's Ait. Sun 6H 131
Beasley's Ait La. Sun 6H 131
Beaton Clo. SE15 . . . . 1F 105
Beatrice Av. SW16 . . . . 3K 139
Beatrice Av. Wemb 5E 44
Beatrice Clo. E13 . . . . 4J 71
Beatrice Clo. Pinn 4J 23
Beatrice Ct. Buck H 2G 21
Beatrice Ho. W6 . . . . 5E 82 (off Queen Caroline St.)
Beatrice Pl. W8 . . . . 3K 83
Beatrice Rd. E17 . . . . 5C 34
Beatrice Rd. N4 . . . . 7A 32
Beatrice Rd. N9 . . . . 7D 8
Beatrice Rd. SE1 . . . . 4G 87
Beatrice Rd. Rich 5F 99
Beatrice Rd. S'hall 1D 78
Beatrix Ho. SW5 . . . . 5K 83 (off Old Brompton Rd.)
Beatson Wlk. SE16 . . . . 1A 88 (in two parts)
Beattie Clo. Felt 7H 95
Beattie Ho. SW8 . . . . 1G 103
Beattock Ri. N10 . . . . 4F 31
Beatty Ho. E14 . . . . 2C 88 (off Admirals Way)
Beatty Ho. NW1 . . . 4G 67 (3A 160)
Beatty Ho. SW1 . . . 5G 85 (6B 172) (off Dolphin Sq.)
Beatty Rd. N16 . . . . 4E 50
Beatty Rd. Stan 6H 11
Beatty St. NW1 . . . . 2G 67
Beattyville Gdns. Ilf 4E 36
Beauchamp Clo. W4 . . . . 3J 81
Beauchamp Ct. Stan 5H 11
Beauchamp Pl. SW3 . . . . . . 3C 84 (1D 170)
Beauchamp Rd. E7 . . . . 7K 53
Beauchamp Rd. SE19 . . . . . 1D 140
Beauchamp Rd. SW11 . . . . . 4C 102
Beauchamp Rd. Sutt 4J 149
Beauchamp Rd. Twic 7A 98
Beauchamp Rd. W Mol & E Mol 5F 133
Beauchamp St. EC1 . . . . 5A 68 (6J 161)
Beauchamp Ter. SW15 . . . . . 3D 100
Beauclerc Ct. Sun 2A 132
Beauclerc Rd. W6 . . . . 3D 82
Beauclerk Clo. Felt 1K 113
Beauclerk Ho. SW16 . . . . . . 3J 121
Beaudesert M. W Dray 2A 76
Beaufort Av. Harr 4A 26
Beaufort Clo. E4 . . . . 6J 19
Beaufort Clo. SW15 . . . . 7D 100
Beaufort Clo. W5 . . . . 5F 63
Beaufort Clo. Romf 4J 39
Beaufort Ct. E14 . . . . 2C 88 (off Admirals Way)
Beaufort Ct. N11 . . . . 5A 16 (off Limes Av., The)
Beaufort Ct. New Bar 5F 5
Beaufort Ct. Rich 4C 116
Beaufort Dri. E6 . . . . 5E 72
Beaufort Dri. NW11 . . . . 4J 29
Beaufort Gdns. NW4 . . . . 6E 28
Beaufort Gdns. SW3 . . . . . . 3C 84 (1D 170)
Beaufort Gdns. SW16 . . . . . 7K 121
Beaufort Gdns. Houn 1C 96
Beaufort Gdns. Ilf 1E 54
Beaufort Ho. E16 . . . . 1K 89 (off Fairfax M.)
Beaufort Ho. SW1 . . . . . . 5H 85 (6C 172) (off Aylesford St.)
Beaufort M. SW6 . . . . 6H 83
Beaufort Pk. NW11 . . . . 4J 29
Beaufort Rd. W5 . . . . 5F 63
Beaufort Rd. King T 4E 134
Beaufort Rd. Rich 4C 116
Beaufort Rd. Ruis 2F 41
Beaufort Rd. Twic 7C 98
Beaufort St. SW3 . . . . . . 6B 84 (7A 170)
Beaufort Ter. E14 . . . . 5E 88 (off Ferry St.)
Beaufort Way. Eps 7C 148
Beaufoy Ho. SE27 . . . . 3B 122
Beaufoy Ho. SW8 . . . . 7K 85 (off Rita Rd.)
Beaufoy Rd. N17 . . . . 7K 17
Beaufoy Wlk. SE11 . . . . . . 4K 85 (4H 173)
Beaulieu Av. E16 . . . . 1K 89
Beaulieu Av. SE26 . . . . 4H 123
Beaulieu Clo. NW9 . . . . 4A 28
Beaulieu Clo. SE5 . . . . 3D 104
Beaulieu Clo. Houn 5D 96
Beaulieu Clo. Mitc 1E 138
Beaulieu Clo. Twic 6D 98
Beaulieu Ct. W5 . . . . 5E 62
Beaulieu Dri. Pinn 6B 24
Beaulieu Gdns. N21 . . . . 7H 7
Beaulieu Lodge. E14 . . . . 3F 89 (off Schooner Clo.)
Beaulieu Pl. W4 . . . . 3J 81
Beaumanor Gdns. SE9 . . . . . 4E 126
Beaumaris Dri. Wfd G 7G 21
Beaumaris Grn. NW9 . . . . 6A 28
Beaumaris Tower. W3 . . . . . . 2H 81 (off Park Rd. N.)
Beaumont. W14 . . . . 4H 83 (off Kensington Village)
Beaumont Av. W14 . . . . 5H 83
Beaumont Av. Harr 6F 25
Beaumont Av. Rich 3F 99
Beaumont Av. Wemb 5C 44
Beaumont Bldgs. WC2 . . . . . . 6J 67 (1F 167) (off Martlett Ct.)
Beaumont Clo. King T 7G 117
Beaumont Ct. E5 . . . . 3H 51
Beaumont Ct. NW9 . . . . 2B 28 (off Cherry Clo.)
Beaumont Ct. W1 . . . . 5E 66 (5H 159) (off Beaumont St.)
Beaumont Ct. W4 . . . . 5J 81
Beaumont Ct. Wemb 5C 44
Beaumont Cres. W14 . . . . 5H 83
Beaumont Dri. Ashf 5F 113
Beaumont Gdns. NW3 . . . . 3J 47
Beaumont Gro. E1 . . . . 4K 69
Beaumont Ho. E10 . . . . 7D 34
Beaumont Ho. E15 . . . . 1H 71 (off John St.)
Beaumont Lodge. E8 . . . . 6G 51 (off Greenwood Rd.)
Beaumont M. W1 . . . . 5E 66 (5H 159)
Beaumont M. Pinn 3C 24
Beaumont Pl. W1 . . . . 4G 67 (3B 160)
Beaumont Pl. Barn 1C 4
Beaumont Pl. Iswth 5K 97
Beaumont Ri. N19 . . . . 1H 49
Beaumont Rd. E10 . . . . 7D 34 (in three parts)
Beaumont Rd. E13 . . . . 3K 71
Beaumont Rd. SE19 . . . . 6C 122
Beaumont Rd. SW19 . . . . . . 7G 101
Beaumont Rd. W4 . . . . 3J 81
Beaumont Rd. Orp 6H 145
Beaumont Sq. E1 . . . . 5K 69
Beaumont St. W1 . . . . 5E 66 (5H 159)
Beaumont Ter. SE13 . . . . 7G 107 (off Wellmeadow Rd.)
Beaumont Wlk. NW3 . . . . 7D 48
Beauvais Ter. N'holt 3B 60
Beauvale. NW1 . . . . 7E 48 (off Ferdinand St.)
Beauval Rd. SE22 . . . . 6F 105
Beaux Arts Building. N7 . . . . . 3J 49
Beaverbank Rd. SE9 . . . . . . 1H 127
Beaver Clo. SE20 . . . . 7G 123
Beaver Clo. Hamp 1F 133
Beaver Ct. Beck 7D 124
Beaver Gro. N'holt 3C 60
Beavers Cres. Houn 4A 96
Beavers La. Houn 2A 96
Beavers Lodge. Sidc 4K 127
Beaverwood Rd. Chst 5J 127
Beavor Gro. W6 . . . . 5C 82 (off Beavor La.)
Beavor La. W6 . . . . 5C 82
Bebbington Rd. SE18 . . . . 4J 91
Beccles Dri. Bark 6J 55
Beccles St. E14 . . . . 6B 70
Bec Clo. Ruis 3B 42
Bechervaise Ct. E10 . . . . 1D 52 (off Leyton Grange Est.)
Bechtel Ho. W6 . . . . 4F 83 (off Hammersmith Rd.)
Beck Clo. SE13 . . . . 1D 106
Beck Ct. Beck 3K 141
Beckenham. 1C 142
Beckenham Bus. Cen. Beck 6A 124
Beckenham Crematorium. Beck 3J 141
Beckenham Gdns. N9 . . . . 3K 17
Beckenham Gro. Brom 2F 143
Beckenham Hill Est. Beck 5D 124
Beckenham Hill Rd. Beck & SE6 . . . . 6D 124
Beckenham La. Brom 2G 143
Beckenham Pl. Pk. Beck . . . 7D 124
Beckenham Rd. Beck 1K 141
Beckenham Rd. W Wick . . . 7D 142
Beckers, The. N16 . . . . 4G 51
Becket Av. E6 . . . . 3E 72
Becket Clo. SE25 . . . . 6G 141
Becket Clo. SW19 . . . . 7K 119 (off High Path)
Becket Fold. Harr 5K 25
Becket Ho. E16 . . . . 1K 89 (off Constable Av.)
Becket Ho. SE1 . . . . 7E 168
Becket Rd. N18 . . . . 4D 18
Becket St. SE1 . . . . 3D 86 (7E 168)
Beckett Clo. NW10 . . . . 6A 46
Beckett Clo. SW16 . . . . 2H 121
Beckett Clo. Belv 3F 93
Beckett Ho. E1 . . . . 5J 69 (off Jubilee St.)
Beckett Ho. SW9 . . . . 2J 103
Becketts Clo. Bex 1J 129
Becketts Clo. Felt 6K 95
Becketts Ho. Ilf 3E 54
Becketts Pl. Hamp W 1D 134
Beckett Wlk. Beck 6A 124
Beckfoot. NW1 . . . . 2G 67 (1B 160) (off Ampthill Est.)
Beckford Clo. W14 . . . . 4H 83
Beckford Dri. Orp 7H 145
Beckford Ho. N16 . . . . 5E 50
Beckford Pl. SE17 . . . . 5C 86
Beckford Rd. Croy 6F 141
Beckham Ho. SE11 . . . . . . 4K 85 (4H 173)
Beck La. Beck 3K 141
Becklow Gdns. W12 . . . . 2C 82 (off Becklow Rd.)
Becklow M. W12 . . . . 2C 82 (off Becklow Rd.)
Becklow Rd. W12 . . . . 2B 82 (in two parts)
Beck River Pk. Beck 1C 142
Beck Rd. E8 . . . . 1H 69
Becks Rd. Sidc 3A 128
Beck Theatre, The. 6H 59
Beckton. 6D 72
Beckton Park. 6D 72
Beckton Retail Pk. E6 . . . . . . 5E 72
Beckton Rd. E16 . . . . 5H 71
Beckton Triangle Retail Pk. E6 . . . . 4F 73
Beck Way. Beck 3B 142
Beckway Rd. SW16 . . . . 2H 139
Beckway St. SE17 . . . . 4E 86 (in two parts)
Beckwith Rd. SE24 . . . . 5D 104
Beclands Rd. SW17 . . . . 6E 120
Becmead Av. SW16 . . . . 4H 121
Becmead Av. Harr 5B 26
Becondale Rd. SE19 . . . . 5E 122
Becontree. 2E 56
Becontree Av. Dag 4B 56
Bective Pl. SW15 . . . . 4H 101
Bective Rd. E7 . . . . 4J 53
Bective Rd. SW15 . . . . 4H 101
Becton Pl. Eri 7H 93
Bedale Rd. Enf 1H 7
Bedale St. SE1 . . . . 1D 86 (5E 168)
Beddalls Farm Ct. E6 . . . . 5B 72
Beddington. 3J 151
Beddington Corner. 7E 138
Beddington Farm Rd. Croy 7J 139
Beddington Gdns. Cars & Wall . . . . 6E 150 (in two parts)
Beddington Grn. Orp 1K 145
Beddington Gro. Wall 5H 151
Beddington La. Croy 5G 139

Beddington Pk. Cotts. Wall 3H 151
Beddington Path. Orp 1K 145
Beddington Rd. Ilf 7K 37
Beddington Rd. Orp 1J 145
Beddington Ter. Croy 7K 139
Beddington Trad. Est. Croy 1J 151
Bede Clo. Pinn 1B 24
Bedefield. WC1 3J 67 (2F 161)
Bede Ho. SE4 1B 106 (off Clare Rd.)
Bedens Rd. Sidc 6E 128
Bede Rd. Romf 6C 38
Bedfont Clo. Felt 6E 94
Bedfont Clo. Mitc 2E 138
Bedfont Grn. Clo. Felt 1E 112
Bedfont Ind. Pk. Ashf 3E 112
Bedfont Lakes Country Pk. 2E 112
Bedfont La. Felt 7H 95
Bedfont Pk. Ind. Est. Ashf 3E 112
Bedfont Rd. Felt 1E 112
Bedfont Rd. Stanw 6A 94
Bedford Av. WC1 5H 67 (6D 160)
Bedford Av. Barn 5C 4
Bedford Av. Hay 6K 59
Bedfordbury. WC2 7J 67 (2E 166)
Bedford Clo. N10 7K 15
Bedford Clo. W4 6A 82
Bedford Corner. W4 4A 82 (off South Pde.)
Bedford Ct. WC2 7J 67 (3E 166) (in two parts)
Bedford Ct. Croy 1C 152 (off Tavistock Rd.)
Bedford Ct. Mans. WC1 6D 160
Bedford Gdns. W8 1J 83
Bedford Hill. SW12 & SW16 1F 121
Bedford Ho. SW4 4J 103 (off Solon New Rd. Est.)
Bedford M. N2 3C 30
Bedford Park 3K 81
Bedford Pk. Croy 1C 152
Bedford Pk. Corner. W4 4A 82
Bedford Pk. Mans. W4 4K 81
Bedford Pas. SW6 7G 83 (off Dawes Rd.)
Bedford Pas. W1 5G 67 (5B 160)
Bedford Pl. WC1 5J 67 (5E 160)
Bedford Pl. Croy 1D 152
Bedford Rd. E6 1E 72
Bedford Rd. E17 2C 34
Bedford Rd. E18 2J 35
Bedford Rd. N2 3C 30
Bedford Rd. N8 6H 31
Bedford Rd. N9 7C 8
Bedford Rd. N15 4E 32
Bedford Rd. N22 1J 31
Bedford Rd. NW7 2F 13
Bedford Rd. SW4 4J 103
Bedford Rd. W4 3K 81
Bedford Rd. W13 7B 62
Bedford Rd. Harr 6G 25
Bedford Rd. Ilf 3F 55
Bedford Rd. Ruis 4H 41
Bedford Rd. Sidc 3J 127
Bedford Rd. Twic 3H 115
Bedford Rd. Wor Pk 2E 148
Bedford Row. WC1 5K 67 (5H 161)
Bedford Sq. WC1 5H 67 (6D 160)
Bedford St. WC2 7J 67 (2E 166)
Bedford Ter. SW4 5J 103
Bedford Way. WC1 4H 67 (4D 160)
Bedgebury Gdns. SW19 2G 119
Bedgebury Rd. SE9 4B 108
Bedivere Rd. Brom 3J 125
Bedlam M. SE11 4A 86 (3J 173) (off Walnut Tree Wlk.)
Bedlow Way. Croy 4K 151
Bedmond Ho. SW3 5C 84 (5C 170) (off Ixworth Pl.)
Bedonwell Rd. SE2 & Belv 6E 92
Bedonwell Rd. Belv 6E 92
Bedonwell Rd. Bexh 1F 111
Bedser Clo. SE11 6K 85 (7H 173)
Bedser Clo. T Hth 3C 140
Bedser Dri. Gnfd 5H 43
Bedster Gdns. W Mol 2F 133
Bedwardine Rd. SE19 7E 122
Bedwell Ct. Romf 7D 38 (off Broomfield Rd.)
Bedwell Gdns. Hay 5G 77 (in two parts)
Bedwell Ho. SW9 2A 104
Bedwell Rd. N17 1E 32
Bedwell Rd. Belv 5G 93
Beeby Rd. E16 5K 71
Beech Av. N20 1H 15
Beech Av. W3 1A 82
Beech Av. Bren 7B 80
Beech Av. Buck H 2E 20
Beech Av. Ruis 1K 41
Beech Av. Sidc 7A 110
Beech Clo. N9 6B 8
Beech Clo. SE8 6C 88
Beech Clo. SW15 7C 100
Beech Clo. SW19 6E 118
Beech Clo. Ashf 5F 113
Beech Clo. Cars 2D 150
Beech Clo. Sun 2B 132
Beech Clo. W Dray 3C 76
Beech Copse. Brom 1D 144
Beech Copse. S Croy 5E 152
Beech Ct. W9 5J 65 (off Elmfield Way)
Beech Ct. Beck 7B 124
Beech Ct. Brom 1H 143 (off Blyth Rd.)
Beech Ct. N'holt 1C 60
Beech Ct. N'wd 1G 23
Beech Ct. Surb 7D 134
Beech Cres. Ct. N5 4B 50
Beechcroft. Chst 7E 126
Beechcroft Av. NW11 7H 29
Beechcroft Av. Bexh 1K 111
Beechcroft Av. Harr 7E 24
Beechcroft Av. N Mald 1J 135
Beechcroft Av. S'hall 1D 78
Beechcroft Clo. SW16 5K 121
Beechcroft Clo. Houn 7C 78
Beechcroft Ct. NW11 7H 29 (off Beechcroft Av.)
Beechcroft Ct. Sutt 7A 150
Beechcroft Gdns. Wemb 3F 45
Beechcroft Ho. W5 5E 62
Beechcroft Rd. E18 2K 35
Beechcroft Rd. SW14 3J 99
Beechcroft Rd. SW17 2C 120
Beechcroft Rd. Chess 3F 147
Beechdale. N21 2E 16
Beechdale Rd. SW2 6K 103
Beech Dell. Kes 4D 156
Beechdene. SE15 1H 105 (off Carlton Gro.)
Beech Dri. N2 2D 30
Beechen Cliff Way. Iswth 2K 97
Beechen Gro. Pinn 3D 24
Beechen Pl. SE23 2K 123
Beeches Av. Cars 7C 150
Beeches Clo. SE20 1J 141
Beeches Rd. SW17 3C 120
Beeches Rd. Sutt 1G 149
Beeches, The. E12 7C 54
Beeches, The. Houn 1F 97
Beeches, The. S Croy 5D 152 (off Blunt Rd.)
Beeches Wlk. Cars 7B 150
Beechey Ho. E1 1H 87 (off Watts St.)
Beechfield Cotts. Brom 1A 144
Beechfield Ct. S Croy 4C 152 (off Bramley Hill)
Beechfield Gdns. Romf 7J 39
Beechfield Rd. N4 6C 32
Beechfield Rd. SE6 1B 124
Beechfield Rd. Brom 2A 144
Beechfield Rd. Eri 7K 93
Beech Gdns. EC2 5C 68 (5C 162) (off Beech St.)
Beech Gdns. W5 2E 80
Beech Gdns. Dag 7J 57
Beech Gro. Mitc 5H 139 (in two parts)
Beech Gro. N Mald 3K 135
Beech Hall Cres. E4 7A 20
Beech Hall Rd. E4 7K 19
Beech Haven Ct. Dart 5K 111 (off London Rd.)
Beech Hill. Barn 1G 5
Beech Hill Av. Barn 1F 5
Beech Hill Pk. 1G 5
Beech Ho. E17 3F 35
Beech Ho. SE16 2J 87 (off Ainsty Est.)
Beech Ho. Rd. Croy 3D 152
Beechhill Rd. SE9 5E 108
Beech La. Buck H 2E 20
Beech Lawns. N12 5G 15
Beechmont Clo. Brom 5G 125
Beechmore Gdns. Sutt 2F 149
Beechmore Rd. SW11 1D 102
Beechmount Av. W7 5H 61
Beecholme. N12 5E 14
Beecholme Av. Mitc 1F 139
Beecholme Est. E5 3H 51
Beech Rd. N11 6D 16
Beech Rd. SW16 2J 139
Beech Rd. Felt 7G 95
Beechrow. Ham 4E 116
Beech St. EC2 5C 68 (5C 162)
Beech St. Romf 4J 39
Beech Tree Clo. N1 7A 50
Beech Tree Clo. Stan 5H 11
Beech Tree Glade. E4 1C 20
Beech Tree Pl. Sutt 5K 149
Beechvale Clo. N12 5H 15
Beech Wlk. NW7 6F 13
Beech Way. NW10 7K 45
Beechway. Bex 6D 110
Beech Way. Twic 3E 114
Beechwood Av. N3 3H 29
Beechwood Av. Gnfd 3F 61
Beechwood Av. Harr 3F 43
Beechwood Av. Hay 7F 59
Beechwood Av. Rich 1G 99
Beechwood Av. Ruis 2H 41
Beechwood Av. Sun 6J 113
Beechwood Av. T Hth 4B 140
Beechwood Av. Uxb 6C 58
Beechwood Circ. Harr 3F 43
Beechwood Clo. N2 4D 30 (off Western Rd.)
Beechwood Clo. NW7 5F 13
Beechwood Clo. Surb 7C 134
Beechwood Ct. W4 6K 81
Beechwood Ct. Cars 4D 150
Beechwood Ct. Sun 6J 113
Beechwood Cres. Bexh 3D 110
Beechwood Dri. Kes 4B 156
Beechwood Dri. Wfd G 5C 20
Beechwood Gdns. NW10 3F 63
Beechwood Gdns. Harr 3F 43
Beechwood Gdns. Ilf 5D 36
Beechwood Gro. W3 7A 64
Beechwood Gro. Surb 7C 134
Beechwood Hall. N3 3H 29
Beechwood Ho. E2 2G 69 (off Teale St.)
Beechwood M. N9 2B 18
Beechwood Pk. E18 3J 35
Beechwood Ri. Chst 4F 127
Beechwood Rd. E8 6F 51
Beechwood Rd. N8 4H 31
Beechwood Rd. S Croy 7E 152
Beechwoods Ct. SE19 5F 123
Beechworth. NW6 7G 47
Beechworth Clo. NW3 2J 47
Beecroft La. SE4 5A 106
Beecroft M. SE4 5A 106
Beecroft Rd. SE4 5A 106
Beehive Clo. E8 7F 51
Beehive Clo. Uxb 7B 40
Beehive La. Ilf 5D 36
Beehive Pl. SW9 3A 104
Beeleigh Rd. Mord 4K 137
Beemans Row. SW18 2A 120
Bee Pas. EC3 6E 68 (1G 169) (off Lime St.)
Beeston Clo. E8 5G 51
Beeston Ho. SE1 3D 86 (off Burbage Clo.)
Beeston Pl. SW1 3F 85 (1K 171)
Beeston Rd. Barn 6G 5
Beeston Way. Felt 6A 96
Beethoven St. W10 3G 65
Beeton Clo. Pinn 1E 24
Begbie Rd. SE3 1A 108
Beggar's Hill. (Junct.) 6B 148
Beggar's Hill. Eps 7B 148
Beggars Roost La. Sutt 6J 149
Begonia Clo. E6 5D 72
Begonia Pl. Hamp 6E 114
Begonia Wlk. W12 6B 64
Beira St. SW12 7F 103
Bekesbourne St. E14 6A 70
Belcroft Clo. Brom 7H 125
Beldanes Lodge. NW10 7C 46
Beldham Gdns. W Mol 2F 133
Belfairs Dri. Romf 7C 38
Belfast Rd. N16 2F 51
Belfast Rd. SE25 4H 141
Belfield Rd. Eps 7K 147
Belfont Wlk. N7 4J 49 (in two parts)
Belford Gro. SE18 4E 90
Belford Ho. E8 1F 69
Belfort Rd. SE15 2J 105
Belfry Clo. SE16 5H 87
Belgrade Rd. N16 4E 50
Belgrade Rd. Hamp 1F 133
Belgrave Clo. N14 5B 6
Belgrave Clo. NW7 5E 12
Belgrave Clo. W3 2H 81
Belgrave Ct. E13 4A 72
Belgrave Ct. E14 7B 70 (off Westferry Cir.)
Belgrave Ct. SW8 7G 85 (off Ascalon St.)
Belgrave Ct. W4 5J 81
Belgrave Cres. Sun 1K 131
Belgrave Gdns. N14 4C 6
Belgrave Gdns. NW8 1K 65
Belgrave Gdns. Stan 5H 11
Belgrave Heights. E11 1J 53
Belgrave Ho. SW9 7A 86
Belgrave M. N. SW1 2E 84 (7G 165)
Belgrave M. S. SW1 3E 84 (1H 171)
Belgrave M. W. SW1 3E 84 (1G 171)
Belgrave Pl. SW1 3E 84 (1H 171)
Belgrave Rd. E10 1E 52
Belgrave Rd. E11 2J 53
Belgrave Rd. E13 4A 72
Belgrave Rd. E17 5C 34
Belgrave Rd. SE25 4F 141
Belgrave Rd. SW1 4F 85 (4K 171)
Belgrave Rd. SW13 7B 82
Belgrave Rd. Houn 3D 96
Belgrave Rd. Ilf 1D 54
Belgrave Rd. Mitc 3B 138
Belgrave Rd. Sun 1K 131
Belgrave Sq. SW1 3E 84 (1G 171)
Belgrave St. E1 5K 69
Belgrave Ter. Wfd G 3D 20
Belgrave Wlk. Mitc 3B 138
Belgrave Yd. SW1 2J 171
Belgravia 3E 84 (2H 171)
Belgravia Clo. Barn 3C 4
Belgravia Ct. SW1 2J 171
Belgravia Gdns. Brom 6G 125
Belgravia Ho. SW1 3E 84 (1G 171) (off Halkin Pl.)
Belgravia Ho. SW4 6H 103
Belgravia M. King T 4D 134
Belgravia Workshops. N19 2J 49 (off Marlborough Rd.)
Belgrove St. WC1 3J 67 (1F 161)
Belham Wlk. SE5 1D 104
Belinda Rd. SW9 3B 104
Belitha Vs. N1 7K 49
Bellamine Clo. SE28 1K 91
Bellamy Clo. E14 2C 88
Bellamy Clo. W14 5H 83
Bellamy Clo. Edgw 2D 12
Bellamy Clo. Uxb 3C 40
Bellamy Ct. Stan 1B 26
Bellamy Dri. Stan 1B 26
Bellamy Ho. Houn 6E 78
Bellamy Rd. E4 6J 19
Bellamy Rd. Enf 2J 7
Bellamy's Ct. SE16 1K 87 (off Abbotshade Rd.)
Bellamy St. SW12 7F 103
Bellasis Av. SW2 2J 121
Bell Av. W Dray 4B 76
Bell Clo. Pinn 2A 24
Bell Clo. Ruis 3H 41
Bellclose Rd. W Dray 2A 76
Bell Ct. NW4 4E 28
Bell Dri. SW18 7G 101
Bellefields Rd. SW9 3K 103
Bellegrove Clo. Well 2K 109
Bellegrove Pde. Well 3K 109
Bellegrove Rd. Well 2H 109
Bellenden Rd. SE15 1F 105
Bellestaines Pleasaunce. E4 2H 19
Belleville Rd. SW11 5C 102
Belle Vue. Gnfd 1H 61
Belle Vue Est. NW4 4F 29
Bellevue La. Bus H 1C 10
Bellevue M. N11 5K 15
Bellevue Pk. T Hth 3C 140
Bellevue Pl. E1 4J 69
Belle Vue Rd. E17 2F 35
Bellevue Rd. N11 4K 15
Belle Vue Rd. NW4 4F 29
Bellevue Rd. SW13 2C 100
Bellevue Rd. SW17 1C 120
Bellevue Rd. W13 4B 62
Bellevue Rd. Bexh 5F 111
Bellevue Rd. King T 3E 134 (in two parts)
Bellew St. SW17 3A 120
Bell Farm Av. Dag 3J 57
Bellfield. Croy 7A 154
Bellfield Av. Harr 6C 10
Bellflower Clo. E6 5C 72
Bell Gdns. E10 1C 52 (off Church Rd.)
Bellgate M. NW5 4F 49
Bell Green 4A 124
Bell Grn. SE26 4B 124
Bell Grn. La. SE26 5B 124
Bell Hill. Croy 2C 152
Bell Ho. SE10 6E 88 (off Haddo St.)
Bellhouse Cotts. Hay 7G 59
Bell Ho. Rd. Romf 1J 57
Bellina M. NW5 4F 49
Bell Ind. Est. W4 4J 81
Bellingham 3D 124

Bellingham. N17 . . . 7C 18 (off Park La.)
Bellingham Ct. Bark . . . 3B 74
Bellingham Grn. SE6 . . . 3C 124
Bellingham Rd. SE6 . . . 3D 124
Bellingham Trad. Est. SE6 . . . 3D 124
Bell Inn Yd. EC3 . . . 6D 68 (1F 169)
Bell Junct. Houn . . . 3F 97
Bell La. E1 . . . 5F 69 (6J 163)
Bell La. E16 . . . 1H 89
Bell La. NW4 & NW11 . . . 4F 29
Bell La. Enf . . . 1E 8
Bell La. Twic . . . 1A 116
Bell La. Wemb . . . 3D 44
Bellmaker Ct. E3 . . . 5C 70
Bell Mdw. SE19 . . . 5E 122
Bell Moor. NW3 . . . 3A 48 (off E. Heath Rd.)
Bello Clo. SE24 . . . 7B 104
Bellot Gdns. SE10 . . . 5G 89 (off Bellot St.)
Bellot St. SE10 . . . 5G 89
Bellring Clo. Belv . . . 6G 93
Bell Rd. E Mol . . . 5H 133
Bell Rd. Enf . . . 1J 7
Bell Rd. Houn . . . 3F 97
Bells All. SW6 . . . 2J 101
Bells Hill. Barn . . . 5A 4
Bell St. NW1 . . . 5C 66 (5C 158)
Bell St. SE18 . . . 1C 108
Bell, The. (Junct.) . . . 3C 34
Belltrees Gro. SW16 . . . 5K 121
Bell Vw. Mnr. Ruis . . . 7F 23
Bell Water Ga. SE18 . . . 3E 90
Bell Wharf La. EC4 . . . 7C 68 (3D 168)
Bellwood Rd. SE15 . . . 4K 105
Bell Yd. WC2 . . . 6A 68 (1J 167)
Belmarsh Rd. SE28 . . . 2J 91
Belmont. . . . 2B 26
Belmont Av. N9 . . . 1B 18
Belmont Av. N13 . . . 5E 16
Belmont Av. N17 . . . 3C 32
Belmont Av. Barn . . . 5J 5
Belmont Av. N Mald . . . 4C 136
Belmont Av. S'hall . . . 3C 78
Belmont Av. Well . . . 2J 109
Belmont Av. Wemb . . . 1F 63
Belmont Circ. Harr . . . 1B 26
Belmont Clo. E4 . . . 5A 20
Belmont Clo. N20 . . . 1E 14
Belmont Clo. SW4 . . . 3G 103
Belmont Clo. Cockf . . . 4J 5
Belmont Clo. Uxb . . . 6A 40
Belmont Clo. Wfd G . . . 4E 20
Belmont Ct. N5 . . . 4C 50
Belmont Ct. NW11 . . . 5H 29
Belmont Gro. SE13 . . . 3F 107
Belmont Gro. W4 . . . 4K 81
Belmont Hall Ct. SE13 . . . 3F 107
Belmont Hill. SE13 . . . 3E 106
Belmont La. Chst . . . 5F 127 (in two parts)
Belmont La. Stan . . . 1C 26
Belmont Lodge. Har W . . . 7C 10
Belmont M. SW19 . . . 2F 119
Belmont Pde. NW11 . . . 5H 29
Belmont Pde. Chst . . . 5G 127
Belmont Pk. SE13 . . . 4F 107
Belmont Pk. Clo. SE13 . . . 4G 107
Belmont Pk. Rd. E10 . . . 6D 34
Belmont Ri. Sutt . . . 6H 149
Belmont Rd. N15 & N17 . . . 4C 32
Belmont Rd. SE25 . . . 5H 141
Belmont Rd. SW4 . . . 3G 103
Belmont Rd. W4 . . . 4K 81
Belmont Rd. Beck . . . 2A 142
Belmont Rd. Chst . . . 5F 127
Belmont Rd. Eri . . . 7G 93
Belmont Rd. Harr . . . 3K 25
Belmont Rd. Ilf . . . 3G 55
Belmont Rd. Twic . . . 2H 115
Belmont Rd. Uxb . . . 7A 40
Belmont Rd. Wall . . . 5F 151
Belmont St. NW1 . . . 7E 48
Belmont Ter. W4 . . . 4K 81
Belmore Av. Hay . . . 6J 59
Belmore La. N7 . . . 5H 49
Belmore St. SW8 . . . 1H 103
Beloe Clo. SW15 . . . 4C 100
Belsham St. E9 . . . 6J 51
Belsize Av. N13 . . . 6E 16
Belsize Av. NW3 . . . 6B 48
Belsize Av. W13 . . . 3B 80
Belsize Ct. NW3 . . . 5B 48
Belsize Ct. Garages. NW3 . . . 5B 48 (off Belsize La.)
Belsize Cres. NW3 . . . 5B 48
Belsize Gdns. Sutt . . . 4K 149
Belsize Gro. NW3 . . . 6C 48
Belsize La. NW3 . . . 6B 48
Belsize M. NW3 . . . 6B 48
Belsize Pk. NW3 . . . 6B 48
Belsize Pk. Gdns. NW3 . . . 6B 48
Belsize Pk. M. NW3 . . . 6B 48
Belsize Pl. NW3 . . . 5B 48
Belsize Rd. NW6 . . . 1K 65
Belsize Rd. Harr . . . 7C 10
Belsize Sq. NW3 . . . 6B 48
Belsize Ter. NW3 . . . 6B 48
Belson Rd. SE18 . . . 4D 90
Beltane Dri. SW19 . . . 3F 119
Belthorn Cres. SW12 . . . 7G 103
Belton Rd. E7 . . . 7K 53
Belton Rd. E11 . . . 4G 53
Belton Rd. N17 . . . 3E 32
Belton Rd. NW2 . . . 6C 46
Belton Rd. Sidc . . . 4A 128
Belton Way. E3 . . . 5C 70
Beltran Rd. SW6 . . . 2K 101
Beltwood Rd. Belv . . . 4J 93
Belvedere. . . . 3H 93
Belvedere Av. SW19 . . . 5G 119
Belvedere Av. Ilf . . . 2F 37
Belvedere Bldgs. SE1 . . . 2B 86 (7B 168)
Belvedere Clo. Tedd . . . 5J 115
Belvedere Ct. NW2 . . . 6F 47 (off Willesden La.)
Belvedere Ct. SW15 . . . 4E 100
Belvedere Ct. Belv . . . 3F 93
Belvedere Dri. SW19 . . . 5G 119
Belvedere Gdns. W Mol . . . 5D 132
Belvedere Gro. SW19 . . . 5G 119
Belvedere M. SE3 . . . 7K 89
Belvedere M. SE15 . . . 3J 105
Belvedere Pl. SE1 . . . 2B 86 (7B 168)
Belvedere Pl. SW2 . . . 4K 103
Belvedere Rd. E10 . . . 1A 52
Belvedere Rd. SE1 . . . 1K 85 (6H 167)
Belvedere Rd. SE2 . . . 1C 92
Belvedere Rd. SE19 . . . 7F 123
Belvedere Rd. W7 . . . 3K 79
Belvedere Rd. Bexh . . . 3F 111
Belvedere Sq. SW19 . . . 5G 119
Belvedere Strand. NW9 . . . 2B 28
Belvedere, The. SW10 . . . 1A 102 (off Chelsea Harbour)
Belvedere Way. Harr . . . 6E 26
Belvoir Clo. SE9 . . . 3C 126
Belvoir Rd. SE22 . . . 7G 105
Belvue Bus. Cen. N'holt . . . 7F 43
Belvue Clo. N'holt . . . 7E 42
Belvue Rd. N'holt . . . 7E 42
Bembridge Clo. NW6 . . . 7G 47
Bembridge Gdns. Ruis . . . 2F 41
Bembridge Ho. SE8 . . . 4B 88 (off Longshore)
Bemersyde Point. E13 . . . 3K 71 (off Dongola Rd. W.)
Bemerton Est. N1 . . . 7J 49
Bemerton St. N1 . . . 1K 67
Bemish Rd. SW15 . . . 3F 101
Bempton Dri. Ruis . . . 2K 41
Bemsted Rd. E17 . . . 3B 34
Benares Rd. SE18 . . . 4K 91
Benbow Ct. W6 . . . 3E 82 (off Benbow Rd.)
Benbow Ho. SE8 . . . 6C 88 (off Benbow St.)
Benbow Rd. W6 . . . 3D 82
Benbow St. SE8 . . . 6C 88
Benbury Clo. Brom . . . 5E 124
Bence Ho. SE8 . . . 5A 88
Bench Fld. S Croy . . . 6F 153
Bench, The. Rich . . . 3C 116
Bencroft Rd. SW16 . . . 7G 121
Bencurtis Pk. W Wick . . . 3F 155
Bendall M. NW1 . . . 5D 158
Bendemeer Rd. SW15 . . . 3F 101
Benden Ho. SE13 . . . 5E 106 (off Monument Gdns.)
Bendish Point. SE28 . . . 2G 91 (off Erebus Dri.)
Bendish Rd. E6 . . . 7C 54
Bendmore Av. SE2 . . . 5A 92
Bendon Valley. SW18 . . . 7K 101
Benedict Clo. Belv . . . 3E 92
Benedict Ct. Romf . . . 6F 39
Benedict Dri. Felt . . . 7F 95
Benedict Rd. SW9 . . . 3K 103
Benedict Rd. Mitc . . . 3B 138
Benedict Way. N2 . . . 3A 30
Benedict Wharf. Mitc . . . 3B 138
Benenden Grn. Brom . . . 5J 143
Benett Gdns. SW16 . . . 2J 139
Ben Ezra Ct. SE17 . . . 4C 86 (off Asolando Dri.)
Benfleet Clo. Sutt . . . 3A 150
Benfleet Ct. E8 . . . 1F 69
Benfleet Way. N11 . . . 2K 15
Bengal Ct. EC3 . . . 6D 68 (1F 169) (off Birchin La.)
Bengal Ho. E1 . . . 5K 69 (off Duckett St.)
Bengal Rd. Ilf . . . 4F 55
Bengarth Dri. Harr . . . 2H 25
Bengarth Rd. N'holt . . . 1C 60
Bengeworth Rd. SE5 . . . 3C 104
Bengeworth Rd. Harr . . . 2A 44
Ben Hale Clo. Stan . . . 5G 11
Benham Clo. SW11 . . . 3B 102
Benham Clo. Chess . . . 6C 146
Benham Gdns. Houn . . . 5D 96
Benham Rd. W7 . . . 5J 61
Benham's Pl. NW3 . . . 4A 48
Benhill Av. Sutt . . . 4K 149
Benhill Rd. SE5 . . . 7D 86
Benhill Rd. Sutt . . . 3A 150
Benhill Wood Rd. Sutt . . . 3A 150
Benhilton. . . . 3A 150
Benhilton Gdns. Sutt . . . 3K 149
Benhurst Ct. SW16 . . . 5A 122
Benhurst La. SW16 . . . 5A 122
Benin St. SE13 . . . 7F 107
Benjafield Clo. N18 . . . 4C 18
Benjamin Clo. E8 . . . 1G 69
Benjamin Ct. Belv . . . 6F 93
Benjamin Franklin House. . . . 1J 85 (4E 166) (off Craven St.)
Benjamin St. EC1 . . . 5B 68 (5A 162)
Ben Jonson Ct. N1 . . . 2E 68
Ben Jonson Ho. EC2 . . . 5D 162
Ben Jonson Pl. EC2 . . . 5D 162
Ben Jonson Rd. E1 . . . 5K 69
Benledi St. E14 . . . 6F 71
Bennelong Clo. W12 . . . 7D 64
Bennerley Rd. SW11 . . . 5C 102
Bennets Fld. Rd. Uxb . . . 1D 76
Bennet's Hill. EC4 . . . 7C 68 (2B 168)
Bennet St. SW1 . . . 1G 85 (4A 166)
Bennett Clo. Hamp W . . . 1C 134
Bennett Clo. N'wd . . . 1H 23
Bennett Clo. Well . . . 2A 110
Bennett Ct. N7 . . . 3K 49
Bennett Gro. SE13 . . . 1D 106
Bennett Ho. SW1 . . . 4H 85 (3D 172) (off Page St.)
Bennett Pk. SE3 . . . 3H 107
Bennett Rd. E13 . . . 4A 72
Bennett Rd. N16 . . . 4E 50
Bennett Rd. Romf . . . 6E 38
Bennetts Av. Croy . . . 2A 154
Bennetts Av. Gnfd . . . 1J 61
Bennett's Castle La. Dag . . . 2C 56
Bennetts Clo. N17 . . . 6A 18
Bennetts Clo. Mitc . . . 1F 139
Bennetts Copse. Chst . . . 6C 126
Bennett St. W4 . . . 6A 82
Bennetts Way. Croy . . . 2A 154
Bennett's Yd. SW1 . . . 3H 85 (2D 172)
Benningholme Rd. Edgw . . . 6F 13
Bennington Rd. N17 . . . 1E 32
Bennington Rd. Wfd G . . . 7B 20
Benn's All. Hamp . . . 2F 133
Benn St. E9 . . . 6A 52
Benns Wlk. Rich . . . 4E 98 (off Michelsdale Dri.)
Benrek Clo. Ilf . . . 1G 37
Bensbury Clo. SW15 . . . 7D 100
Bensham Clo. T Hth . . . 4C 140
Bensham Gro. T Hth . . . 2C 140
Bensham La. T Hth & Croy . . . 5B 140
Bensham Mnr. Rd. T Hth . . . 4C 140
Bensley Clo. N11 . . . 5J 15
Ben Smith Way. SE16 . . . 3G 87
Benson Av. E6 . . . 2A 72
Benson Clo. Houn . . . 4E 96
Benson Clo. Uxb . . . 5A 58
Benson Ho. E2 . . . 4F 69 (3J 163) (off Ligonier St.)
Benson Ho. SE1 . . . 1B 86 (5K 167) (off Hatfields)
Benson Quay. E1 . . . 7J 69
Benson Rd. SE23 . . . 1J 123
Benson Rd. Croy . . . 3A 152
Bentalls Cen., The. King T . . . 2D 134
Bentfield Gdns. SE9 . . . 3B 126
Benthal Rd. N16 . . . 3G 51
Bentham Ct. N1 . . . 7C 50 (off Ecclesbourne Rd.)
Bentham Ct. SE1 . . . 3D 86 (off Falmouth Rd.)
Bentham Rd. E9 . . . 6K 51
Bentham Rd. SE28 . . . 7B 74
Bentham Wlk. NW10 . . . 5J 45
Ben Tillet Clo. E16 . . . 1D 90
Ben Tillet Clo. Bark . . . 7A 56
Ben Tillet Ho. N15 . . . 3B 32
Bentinck Clo. NW8 . . . 2C 66
Bentinck Ho. W12 . . . 7D 64 (off White City Est.)
Bentinck M. W1 . . . 6E 66 (7H 159)
Bentinck Rd. W Dray . . . 1A 76
Bentinck St. W1 . . . 6E 66 (7H 159)
Bentley Dri. NW2 . . . 3H 47
Bentley Dri. Ilf . . . 6G 37
Bentley Ho. SE5 . . . 1E 104 (off Peckham Rd.)
Bentley Rd. N1 . . . 6E 50
Bentley Way. Stan . . . 5F 11
Bentley Way. Wfd G . . . 3D 20
Benton Rd. Ilf . . . 1H 55
Bentons La. SE27 . . . 4C 122
Benton's Ri. SE27 . . . 5D 122
Bentry Clo. Dag . . . 2E 56
Bentry Rd. Dag . . . 2E 56
Bentworth Clo. W12 . . . 6D 64 (off Bentworth Rd.)
Bentworth Ct. E2 . . . 4G 69 (3K 163) (off Granby St.)
Bentworth Rd. W12 . . . 6D 64
Benville Ho. SW8 . . . 7K 85 (off Oval Pl.)
Benwell Ct. Sun . . . 1J 131
Benwell Rd. N7 . . . 4A 50
Benwick Clo. SE16 . . . 4H 87
Benwood Ct. Sutt . . . 3A 150
Benworth St. E3 . . . 3B 70
Benyon Ct. N1 . . . 1E 68 (off De Beauvoir Est.)
Benyon Ho. EC1 . . . 3A 68 (1K 161) (off Myddelton Pas.)
Benyon Rd. N1 . . . 1D 68
Berberis Ct. Ilf . . . 6F 55
Berberis Ho. E3 . . . 5C 70 (off Gale St.)
Berberis Wlk. W Dray . . . 4A 76
Berber Pl. E14 . . . 7C 70
Berber Rd. SW11 . . . 5D 102
Berberry Clo. Edgw . . . 4D 12
Bercta Rd. SE9 . . . 2G 127
Berenger Tower. SW10 . . . 7B 84 (off Worlds End Est.)
Berenger Wlk. SW10 . . . 7B 84 (off Worlds End Est.)
Berens Ct. Sidc . . . 4K 127
Berens Rd. NW10 . . . 3F 65
Berens Way. Chst . . . 3K 145
Beresford Av. N20 . . . 2J 15
Beresford Av. W7 . . . 5H 61
Beresford Av. Surb . . . 1H 147
Beresford Av. Twic . . . 6C 98
Beresford Av. Wemb . . . 1F 63
Beresford Dri. Brom . . . 3C 144
Beresford Dri. Wfd G . . . 4F 21
Beresford Gdns. Enf . . . 4K 7
Beresford Gdns. Houn . . . 5D 96
Beresford Gdns. Romf . . . 5E 38
Beresford Rd. E4 . . . 1B 20
Beresford Rd. E17 . . . 1D 34
Beresford Rd. N2 . . . 3C 30
Beresford Rd. N5 . . . 5D 50
Beresford Rd. N8 . . . 5A 32
Beresford Rd. Harr . . . 5H 25
Beresford Rd. King T . . . 1F 135
Beresford Rd. N Mald . . . 4J 135
Beresford Rd. S'hall . . . 1B 78
Beresford Rd. Sutt . . . 7H 149
Beresford Sq. SE18 . . . 4F 91
Beresford St. SE18 . . . 3F 91
Beresford Ter. N5 . . . 5C 50
Berestede Rd. W4 . . . 5B 82
Bere St. E1 . . . 7K 69
Bergen Ho. SE5 . . . 2C 104 (off Carew St.)
Bergen Sq. SE16 . . . 3A 88
Berger Clo. Orp . . . 6H 145
Berger Rd. E9 . . . 6K 51
Berghem M. W14 . . . 3F 83
Bergholt Av. Ilf . . . 5C 36
Bergholt Cres. N16 . . . 7E 32
Bergholt M. NW1 . . . 7G 49
Berglen Ct. E14 . . . 6A 70
Bering Sq. E14 . . . 5C 88
Bering Wlk. E16 . . . 6B 72
Berisford M. SW18 . . . 6A 102
Berkeley Av. Bexh . . . 1D 110
Berkeley Av. Gnfd . . . 6J 43
Berkeley Av. Houn . . . 1J 95
Berkeley Av. Ilf . . . 2E 36
Berkeley Av. Romf . . . 1J 39
Berkeley Clo. Bren . . . 6A 80
Berkeley Clo. King T . . . 7E 116
Berkeley Clo. Orp . . . 7J 145
Berkeley Clo. Ruis . . . 3J 41
Berkeley Clo. Twic . . . 3J 115 (off Wellesley Rd.)
Berkeley Ct. N3 . . . 1K 29
Berkeley Ct. N14 . . . 6B 6
Berkeley Ct. NW1 . . . 4F 159
Berkeley Ct. NW10 . . . 4A 46
Berkeley Ct. NW11 . . . 7H 29 (off Ravenscroft Av.)
Berkeley Ct. W5 . . . 7C 62 (off Gordon Rd.)
Berkeley Ct. Croy . . . 4D 152 (off Coombe Rd.)
Berkeley Ct. Surb . . . 7D 134

Berkeley Ct. Wall 3G 151
Berkeley Cres. Barn 5G 5
Berkeley Dri. W Mol 3D 132
Berkeley Gdns. N21 7J 7
Berkeley Gdns. W8 1J 83
Berkeley Gdns. Clay 6A 146
Berkeley Gdns. W on T 7H 131
Berkeley Ho. SE8 5B 88 (off Grove St.)
Berkeley Ho. Bren 6D 80 (off Albany Rd.)
Berkeley M. W1 6D 66 (1F 165)
Berkeley Pl. SW19 6F 119
Berkeley Rd. E12 5C 54
Berkeley Rd. N8 5H 31
Berkeley Rd. N15 6D 32
Berkeley Rd. NW9 4G 27
Berkeley Rd. SW13 1C 100
Berkeley Rd. Uxb 7E 40
Berkeley Sq. W1 7F 67 (3K 165)
Berkeley St. W1 7F 67 (3K 165)
Berkeley Tower. E14 1B 88 (off Westferry Cir.)
Berkeley Wlk. N7 2K 49 (off Durham Rd.)
Berkeley Waye. Houn 6B 78
Berkely Clo. Sun 3A 132
Berkhampstead Rd. Belv 5G 93
Berkhamsted Av. Wemb 6F 45
Berkley Gro. NW1 7E 48
Berkley Rd. NW1 7D 48
Berkshire Ct. W7 4K 61 (off Copley Clo.)
Berkshire Gdns. N13 6F 17
Berkshire Gdns. N18 5C 18
Berkshire Ho. SE6 4C 124
Berkshire Rd. E9 6B 52
Berkshire Sq. Mitc 4J 139
Berkshire Way. Mitc 4J 139
Bermans Way. NW10 4A 46
Bermondsey. 2G 87 (7K 169)
Bermondsey Sq. SE1 3E 86 (7H 169)
Bermondsey St. SE1 1E 86 (5G 169)
Bermondsey Trad. Est. SE16 5J 87
Bermondsey Wall E. SE16 2G 87
Bermondsey Wall W. SE16 2G 87 (6K 169)
Bernal Clo. SE28 7D 74
Bernard Angell Ho. SE10 6F 89 (off Trafalgar Rd.)
Bernard Ashley Dri. SE7 5K 89
Bernard Av. W13 3B 80
Bernard Cassidy St. E16 5H 71
Bernard Gdns. SW19 5H 119
Bernard Mans. WC1 4J 67 (4E 160) (off Bernard St.)
Bernard Rd. N15 5F 33
Bernard Rd. Romf 7J 39
Bernard Rd. Wall 4F 151
Bernard Shaw Ct. NW1 7G 49 (off St Pancras Way)
Bernard St. WC1 4J 67 (4E 160)
Bernard Sunley Ho. SW9 7A 86 (off S. Island Pl.)
Bernays Clo. Stan 6H 11
Bernays Gro. SW9 4K 103
Bernel Dri. Croy 3B 154
Berne Rd. T Hth 5C 140
Berners Dri. W13 7A 62
Berners Ho. N1 2A 68 (off Barnsbury Est.)
Berners M. W1 5G 67 (6B 160)
Berners Pl. W1 6G 67 (7B 160)
Berners Rd. N1 1B 68
Berners Rd. N22 1A 32
Berners St. W1 5G 67 (6B 160)
Berner Ter. E1 6G 69 (off Fairclough St.)
Berney Ho. Beck 5A 142
Berney Rd. Croy 7D 140
Bernhardt Cres. NW8 4C 66 (3C 158)
Bernhart Clo. Edgw 7D 12
Bernville Way. Harr 5F 27
Bernwell Rd. E4 3B 20
Berridge Grn. Edgw 7B 12
Berridge M. NW6 5J 47
Berridge Rd. SE19 5D 122
Berriman Rd. N7 3K 49
Berriton Rd. Harr 1D 42
Berrybank Clo. E4 2K 19
Berry Clo. N21 1G 17
Berry Clo. NW10 7A 46
Berry Clo. Dag 5G 57
Berry Ct. Houn 5D 96
Berrydale Rd. Hay 4C 60
Berryfield Clo. E17 4D 34
Berryfield Clo. Brom 1C 144
Berryfield Rd. SE17 5B 86
Berryhill. SE9 4F 109
Berry Hill. Stan 4J 11
Berryhill Gdns. SE9 4F 109
Berry Ho. E1 4H 69 (off Headlam St.)
Berrylands. 6G 135
Berrylands. SW20 3E 136
Berrylands. Surb 6F 135
Berrylands Rd. Surb 6F 135
Berry La. SE21 4D 122
Berryman Clo. Dag 3C 56
Berryman's La. SE26 4K 123
Berrymead Gdns. W3 1J 81
Berrymede Rd. W4 3K 81
Berry Pl. EC1 3B 68 (2B 162)
Berry St. EC1 4B 68 (3B 162)
Berry Way. W5 3E 80
Bertal Rd. SW17 4B 120
Bertha Hollamby Ct. Sidc 5C 128 (off Sidcup Hill)
Bertha James Ct. Brom 4K 143
Berthons Gdns. E17 5F 35 (off Wood St.)
Berthon St. SE8 7C 88
Bertie Rd. NW10 6C 46
Bertie Rd. SE26 6K 123
Bertram Cotts. SW19 7J 119
Bertram Rd. NW4 6C 28
Bertram Rd. Enf 4B 8
Bertram Rd. King T 7G 117
Bertram St. N19 2F 49
Bertrand Ho. SW16 3J 121 (off Leigham Av.)
Bertrand St. SE13 3D 106
Bertrand Way. SE28 7B 74
Bert Rd. T Hth 5C 140
Bert Way. Enf 4A 8
Berwick Av. Hay 6B 60
Berwick Clo. Stan 6E 10
Berwick Cres. Sidc 7J 109
Berwick Ho. N2 2B 30
Berwick Rd. E16 6K 71
Berwick Rd. N22 1B 32
Berwick Rd. Well 1B 110
Berwick St. W1 6G 67 (7B 160)
Berwyn Av. Houn 1F 97
Berwyn Rd. SE24 1B 122
Berwyn Rd. Rich 4H 99
Beryl Av. E6 5C 72
Beryl Rd. W6 5F 83
Berystede. King T 7H 117
Besant Clo. NW2 3G 47
Besant Ct. N1 5D 50
Besant Ho. NW8 1A 66 (off Boundary Rd.)
Besant Rd. NW2 4G 47
Besant Wlk. N7 2K 49
Besant Way. NW10 5J 45
Besford Ho. E2 2G 69 (off Pritchard's Rd.)
Besley St. SW16 6G 121
Bessant Dri. Rich 1G 99
Bessborough Gdns. SW1 5H 85 (5D 172)
Bessborough Pl. SW1 5H 85 (5D 172)
Bessborough Rd. SW15 1C 118
Bessborough Rd. Harr 1H 43
Bessborough St. SW1 5H 85 (5C 172)
Bessemer Ct. NW1 7G 49 (off Rochester Sq.)
Bessemer Rd. SE5 2C 104
Bessie Lansbury Clo. E6 6E 72
Bessingby Rd. Ruis 2K 41
Bessingham Wlk. SE4 4K 105 (off Aldersford Clo.)
Besson St. SE14 1J 105
Bessy St. E2 3J 69
Bestwood St. SE8 4K 87
Beswick M. NW6 6K 47
Betam Rd. Hay 2F 77
Beta Pl. SW9 4K 103
Betchworth Clo. Sutt 5B 150
Betchworth Rd. Ilf 2J 55
Betchworth Way. New Ad 7E 154
Bethal Est. SE1 5H 169
Betham Rd. Gnfd 3H 61
Bethany Waye. Felt 7G 95
Bethecar Rd. Harr 5J 25
Bethell Av. E16 4H 71
Bethell Av. Ilf 7E 36
Bethel Rd. Well 3C 110
Bethersden Clo. Beck 7B 124
Bethersden Ho. SE17 5E 86 (off Kinglake St.)
Bethlehem Ho. E14 7B 70 (off Limehouse Causeway)
Bethnal Green. 3H 69
Bethnal Green Mus. of Childhood. 3J 69
Bethnal Grn. Rd. E1 & E2 4F 69 (3J 163)
Bethune Av. N11 4J 15
Bethune Clo. N16 1E 50
Bethune Rd. N16 7D 32
Bethune Rd. NW10 4K 63
Bethwin Rd. SE5 7B 86
Betjeman Clo. Pinn 4E 24
Betjeman Ct. W Dray 1A 76
Betony Clo. Croy 1K 153
Betoyne Av. E4 4B 20
Betsham Ho. SE1 2D 86 (6E 168) (off Newcomen St.)
Betstyle Cir. N11 4A 16
Betstyle Ho. N10 7K 15
Betstyle Rd. N11 4A 16
Betterton Dri. Sidc 2E 128
Betterton Ho. WC2 6J 67 (1F 167) (off Betterton St.)
Betterton Rd. Rain 3K 75
Betterton St. WC2 6J 67 (1E 166)
Bettons Pk. E15 1G 71
Bettridge Rd. SW6 2H 101
Betts Clo. Beck 2A 142
Betts Ho. E1 7H 69 (off Betts St.)
Betts M. E17 6B 34
Betts Rd. E16 7K 71
Betts St. E1 7H 69
Betts Way. SE20 1H 141
Betts Way. Surb 1B 146
Betty Brooks Ho. E11 3F 53
Betty May Gray Ho. E14 4E 88 (off Pier St.)
Beulah Av. T Hth 2C 140
Beulah Clo. Edgw 3C 12
Beulah Cres. T Hth 2C 140
Beulah Gro. Croy 6C 140
Beulah Hill. SE19 6B 122
Beulah Path. E17 5E 34
Beulah Rd. E17 5D 34
Beulah Rd. SW19 7H 119
Beulah Rd. Sutt 4J 149
Beulah Rd. T Hth 3C 140
Bevan Av. Bark 7A 56
Bevan Ct. Croy 5A 152
Bevan Ho. WC1 5J 67 (5F 161) (off Boswell St.)
Bevan Ho. Twic 6D 98
Bevan Rd. SE2 5B 92
Bevan Rd. Barn 4J 5
Bevan St. N1 1C 68
Bev Callender Clo. SW8 3F 103
Bevenden St. N1 3D 68 (1F 163)
Bevercote Wlk. Belv 6F 93
Beveridge Rd. NW10 7A 46
Beverley Av. SW20 1B 136
Beverley Av. Houn 4D 96
Beverley Av. Sidc 7K 109
Beverley Clo. N21 1H 17
Beverley Clo. SW11 4B 102
Beverley Clo. SW13 2C 100
Beverley Clo. Chess 4C 146
Beverley Clo. Enf 4K 7
Beverley Cotts. SW15 3A 118
Beverley Ct. N2 4D 30 (off Western Rd.)
Beverley Ct. N14 7B 6
Beverley Ct. SE4 3B 106 (in two parts)
Beverley Ct. W4 5J 81
Beverley Ct. Harr 3H 25
Beverley Ct. Houn 4D 96
Beverley Ct. Kent 4C 26
Beverley Cres. Wfd G 1K 35
Beverley Dri. Edgw 3G 27
Beverley Gdns. NW11 7G 29
Beverley Gdns. SW13 3B 100
Beverley Gdns. Stan 1A 26
Beverley Gdns. Wemb 1F 45
Beverley Gdns. Wor Pk 1C 148
Beverley Ho. Brom 5F 125 (off Brangbourne Rd.)
Beverley La. SW15 3B 118
Beverley La. King T 7A 118
Beverley M. E4 6A 20
Beverley Path. SW13 2B 100
Beverley Rd. E4 6A 20
Beverley Rd. E6 3B 72
Beverley Rd. SE20 2H 141
Beverley Rd. SW13 3B 100
Beverley Rd. W4 5B 82
Beverley Rd. Bexh 2J 111
Beverley Rd. Brom 2C 156
Beverley Rd. Dag 4E 56
Beverley Rd. King T 1C 134
Beverley Rd. Mitc 4H 139
Beverley Rd. N Mald 4C 136
Beverley Rd. Ruis 2J 41
Beverley Rd. S'hall 4C 78
Beverley Rd. Sun 1H 131
Beverley Rd. Wor Pk 2E 148
Beverley Trad. Est. Mord 7F 137
Beverley Way. SW20 & N Mald 1B 136
Beversbrook Rd. N19 3H 49
Beverstone Rd. SW2 5K 103
Beverstone Rd. T Hth 4A 140
Beverston M. W1 6E 158
Bevill Allen Clo. SW17 5D 120
Bevill Clo. SE25 3G 141
Bevin Clo. SE16 1A 88
Bevin Ct. WC1 3K 67 (1H 161)
Bevington Path. SE1 2F 87 (7J 169) (off Tanner St.)
Bevington Rd. W10 5G 65
Bevington Rd. Beck 2D 142
Bevington St. SE16 2G 87
Bevin Ho. E2 3J 69 (off Butler St.)
Bevin Rd. Hay 3J 59
Bevin Sq. SW17 3D 120
Bevin Way. WC1 2A 68 (1J 161)
Bevis Marks. EC3 6E 68 (7H 163)
Bewcastle Gdns. Enf 4D 6
Bew Ct. SE22 7G 105
Bewdley St. N1 7A 50
Bewick M. SE15 7H 87
Bewick St. SW8 2F 103
Bewley Ho. E1 7H 69 (off Bewley St.)
Bewley St. E1 7J 69
Bewlys Rd. SE27 5B 122
Bexhill Clo. Felt 2C 114
Bexhill Rd. N11 5C 16
Bexhill Rd. SE4 6B 106
Bexhill Rd. SW14 3J 99
Bexhill Wlk. E15 1G 71
Bexley. 7G 111
Bexley Gdns. N9 3J 17
Bexley Gdns. Chad H 5B 38
Bexley Hall Place Vis. Cen. (Hall Place). 6J 111
Bexleyheath. 4G 111
Bexley High St. Bex 7G 111
Bexley Ho. SE4 4A 106
Bexley La. Dart 5K 111
Bexley La. Sidc 4C 128
Bexley Local Studies & Archive Cen. 6J 111 (Hall Place)
Bexley Rd. SE9 5F 109
Bexley Rd. Eri 1J 111 (in two parts)
Beynon Rd. Cars 5D 150
Bianca Rd. SE15 6G 87
Bibsworth Rd. N3 2H 29
Bibury Clo. SE15 6E 86 (in two parts)
Bicester Rd. Rich 3G 99
Bickenhall Mans. W1 5F 159 (in two parts)
Bickenhall St. W1 5D 66 (5F 159)
Bickersteth Rd. SW17 6D 120
Bickerton Rd. N19 2G 49
Bickley. 3C 144
Bickley Cres. Brom 4C 144
Bickley Pk. Rd. Brom 3C 144
Bickley Rd. E10 7D 34
Bickley Rd. Brom 2B 144
Bickley St. SW17 5C 120
Bicknell Ho. E1 6G 69 (off Ellen St.)
Bicknell Rd. SE5 3C 104
Bicknoller Rd. Enf 1K 7
Bicknor Rd. Orp 7J 145
Bidborough Clo. Brom 5H 143
Bidborough St. WC1 3J 67 (2E 160)
Biddenden Way. SE9 4E 126
Biddenham Ho. SE16 4K 87 (off Plough Way)
Bidder St. E16 5G 71 (in two parts)
Biddesden Ho. SW3 4D 84 (4E 170) (off Cadogan St.)
Biddestone Rd. N7 4K 49
Biddulph Ho. SE18 4D 90
Biddulph Mans. W9 3K 65 (off Elgin Av.)
Biddulph Rd. W9 3K 65
Bideford Av. Gnfd 2B 62
Bideford Clo. Edgw 1G 27
Bideford Clo. Felt 3D 114
Bideford Gdns. Enf 7K 7
Bideford Rd. Brom 3H 125
Bideford Rd. Enf 1G 9
Bideford Rd. Ruis 3K 41
Bideford Rd. Well 7B 92
Bidwell Gdns. N11 7B 16
Bidwell St. SE15 1H 105
Big Ben. 2J 85 (7F 167)
Bigbury Clo. N17 7J 17
Biggerstaff Rd. E15 1E 70

Biggerstaff St. N4 . . . 2A 50
Biggin Av. Mitc . . . 1D 138
Biggin Hill. SE19 . . . 1B 140
Biggin Hill Clo. King T . . . 5C 116
Biggin Way. SE19 . . . 7B 122
Bigginwood Rd. SW16 . . . 7B 122
Biggs Row. SW15 . . . 3F 101
Big Hill. E5 . . . 1H 51
Bigland St. E1 . . . 6H 69
Bignell Rd. SE18 . . . 5F 91
Bignold Rd. E7 . . . 4J 53
Bigwood Ct. NW11 . . . 5K 29
Bigwood Rd. NW11 . . . 5K 29
Bilberry Ho. E3 . . . 5C 70 (off Watts Gro.)
Billet Clo. Romf . . . 3D 38
Billet Rd. E17 . . . 1K 33
Billet Rd. Romf . . . 3B 38
Billets Hart Clo. W7 . . . 2J 79
Bill Hamling Clo. SE9 . . . 2D 126
Billing Clo. Dag . . . 7C 56
Billingford Clo. SE4 . . . 4K 105
Billing Ho. E1 . . . 6K 69 (off Bower St.)
Billingley. NW1 . . . 1G 67 (off Pratt St.)
Billing Pl. SW10 . . . 7K 83
Billing Rd. SW10 . . . 7K 83
Billingsgate Fish Market. . . . 1D 88
Billing St. SW6 . . . 7K 83
Billington Rd. SE14 . . . 7K 87
Billinton Hill. Croy . . . 2D 152
Billiter Sq. EC3 . . . 1H 169
Billiter St. EC3 . . . 6E 68 (1H 169)
Bill Nicholson Way. N17 . . . 7A 18 (off High Rd.)
Billockby Clo. Chess . . . 6F 147
Billson St. E14 . . . 4E 88
Bilsby Gro. SE9 . . . 4B 126
Bilsby Lodge. Wemb . . . 3J 45 (off Chalklands)
Bilton Cen., The. Gnfd . . . 1B 62
Bilton Rd. Gnfd . . . 1A 62
Bilton Towers. W1 . . . 6D 66 (1F 165) (off Gt. Cumberland Pl.)
Bilton Way. Enf . . . 1F 9
Bilton Way. Hay . . . 2K 77
Bina Gdns. SW5 . . . 4A 84
Binbrook Ho. W10 . . . 5E 64 (off Sutton Way)
Bincote Rd. Enf . . . 3E 6
Binden Rd. W12 . . . 3B 82
Bindon Grn. Mord . . . 4K 137
Binfield Rd. SW8 . . . 1J 103
Binfield Rd. S Croy . . . 5F 153
Bingfield St. N1 . . . 1J 67 (in two parts)
Bingham Ct. N1 . . . 7B 50 (off Halton Rd.)
Bingham Pl. W1 . . . 5E 66 (5G 159)
Bingham Rd. Croy . . . 1G 153
Bingham St. N1 . . . 6D 50
Bingley Rd. E16 . . . 6A 72
Bingley Rd. Gnfd . . . 4G 61
Bingley Rd. Sun . . . 7J 113
Binley Ho. SW15 . . . 6B 100
Binney St. W1 . . . 6E 66 (1H 165)
Binnie Ct. SE10 . . . 7D 88 (off Greenwich High Rd.)
Binnie Ho. SE1 . . . 3C 86 (off Bath Ter.)
Binns Rd. W4 . . . 5A 82
Binns Ter. W4 . . . 5A 82
Binsey Wlk. SE2 . . . 2C 92
Binstead Clo. Hay . . . 5C 60
Binyon Cres. Stan . . . 5E 10
Birbetts Rd. SE9 . . . 2D 126
Bircham Path. SE4 . . . 4K 105 (off Aldersford Clo.)
Birchanger Rd. SE25 . . . 5G 141
Birch Av. N13 . . . 3H 17
Birch Av. W Dray . . . 6B 58
Birch Clo. E16 . . . 5G 71
Birch Clo. N19 . . . 2G 49
Birch Clo. SE15 . . . 2G 105 (off Bournemouth Clo.)
Birch Clo. Bren . . . 7B 80
Birch Clo. Buck H . . . 3G 21
Birch Clo. Houn . . . 2H 97
Birch Clo. Romf . . . 3H 39
Birch Clo. Shep . . . 2G 131
Birch Clo. Tedd . . . 5A 116
Birch Ct. Wall . . . 4F 151
Birch Cres. Uxb . . . 1B 58
Birchdale Gdns. Romf . . . 7D 38
Birchdale Rd. E7 . . . 5A 54
Birchdene Dri. SE28 . . . 1A 92
Birchen Clo. NW9 . . . 2K 45
Birchend Clo. S Croy . . . 6D 152
Birchen Gro. NW9 . . . 2K 45
Birches Clo. Mitc . . . 3D 138
Birches Clo. Pinn . . . 5C 24
Birches, The. E12 . . . 4C 54
Birches, The. N21 . . . 6E 6
Birches, The. SE7 . . . 6K 89
Birches, The. Brom . . . 4H 143 (off Durham Av.)
Birches, The. Houn . . . 7D 96
Birches, The. Orp . . . 4E 156
Birchfield Ho. E14 . . . 7C 70 (off Birchfield St.)
Birchfield St. E14 . . . 7C 70
Birch Gdns. Dag . . . 3J 57
Birch Grn. NW9 . . . 7F 13
Birch Gro. E11 . . . 4G 53
Birch Gro. SE12 . . . 7H 107
Birch Gro. W3 . . . 1G 81
Birch Gro. Shep . . . 2G 131
Birch Gro. Well . . . 4A 110
Birch Hill. Croy . . . 5K 153
Birch Ho. N22 . . . 1A 32 (off Acacia Rd.)
Birch Ho. SE14 . . . 1B 106
Birch Ho. SW2 . . . 6A 104 (off Tulse Hill)
Birch Ho. W10 . . . 4G 65 (off Droop St.)
Birchington Clo. Bexh . . . 1H 111
Birchington Ct. NW6 . . . 1K 65 (off W. End La.)
Birchington Ho. E5 . . . 5H 51
Birchington Rd. N8 . . . 6H 31
Birchington Rd. NW6 . . . 1J 65
Birchington Rd. Surb . . . 7F 135
Birchin La. EC3 . . . 6D 68 (1F 169)
Birchlands Av. SW12 . . . 7D 102
Birchmead. Orp . . . 2E 156
Birchmead Av. Pinn . . . 4A 24
Birchmere Bus. Site. SE28 . . . 2A 92
Birchmere Lodge. SE16 . . . 5H 87 (off Sherwood Gdns.)
Birchmere Row. SE3 . . . 2H 107
Birchmore Hall. N5 . . . 3C 50
Birchmore Wlk. N5 . . . 3C 50
Birch Pk. Harr . . . 7B 10
Birch Rd. Felt . . . 5B 114
Birch Rd. Romf . . . 3H 39
Birch Row. Brom . . . 7E 144
Birch Tree Av. W Wick . . . 5H 155
Birch Tree Way. Croy . . . 2H 153
Birch Va. Ct. NW8 . . . 4B 66 (3B 158) (off Pollitt Dri.)
Birchville Ct. Bus H . . . 1D 10
Birch Wlk. Eri . . . 6J 93
Birch Wlk. Mitc . . . 1F 139
Birchway. Hay . . . 1J 77
Birchwood Av. N10 . . . 3E 30
Birchwood Av. Beck . . . 4B 142
Birchwood Av. Sidc . . . 2B 128
Birchwood Av. Wall . . . 3E 150
Birchwood Clo. Mord . . . 4K 137
Birchwood Ct. N13 . . . 5G 17
Birchwood Ct. Edgw . . . 2J 27
Birchwood Dri. NW3 . . . 3K 47
Birchwood Dri. Dart . . . 4K 129
Birchwood Gro. Hamp . . . 6E 114
Birchwood Pde. Dart . . . 4K 129
Birchwood Rd. SW17 . . . 5F 121
Birchwood Rd. Orp . . . 4H 145
Birchwood Rd. Swan & Dart . . . 7J 129
Birdbrook Clo. Dag . . . 7J 57
Birdbrook Ho. N1 . . . 7C 50 (off Popham Rd.)
Birdbrook Rd. SE3 . . . 4A 108
Birdcage Wlk. SW1 . . . 2G 85 (7A 166)
Birdham Clo. Brom . . . 5C 144
Birdhurst Av. S Croy . . . 4D 152
Birdhurst Gdns. S Croy . . . 4D 152
Birdhurst Ri. S Croy . . . 5E 152
Birdhurst Rd. SW18 . . . 5A 102
Birdhurst Rd. SW19 . . . 6C 120
Birdhurst Rd. S Croy . . . 5E 152
Bird in Bush Rd. SE15 . . . 7G 87
Bird in Hand La. Brom . . . 2B 144
Bird-in-Hand Pas. SE23 . . . 2J 123
Bird in Hand Yd. NW3 . . . 4A 48
Birdlip Clo. SE15 . . . 6E 86
Birdsall Ho. SE5 . . . 3E 104
Birds Farm Av. Romf . . . 1H 39
Birdsfield La. E3 . . . 1B 70
Bird St. W1 . . . 6E 66 (1H 165)
Bird Wlk. Twic . . . 1D 114
Birdwood Clo. Tedd . . . 4J 115
Birkbeck Av. W3 . . . 7J 63
Birkbeck Av. Gnfd . . . 1G 61
Birkbeck College. . . . 5H 67 (5D 160)
Birkbeck Ct. W3 . . . 1K 81
Birkbeck Gdns. Wfd G . . . 2D 20
Birkbeck Gro. W3 . . . 2K 81
Birkbeck Hill. SE21 . . . 1B 122
Birkbeck M. E8 . . . 5F 51
Birkbeck M. W3 . . . 1K 81
Birkbeck Pl. SE21 . . . 2C 122
Birkbeck Rd. E8 . . . 5F 51
Birkbeck Rd. N8 . . . 4J 31
Birkbeck Rd. N12 . . . 5F 15
Birkbeck Rd. N17 . . . 1F 33
Birkbeck Rd. NW7 . . . 5G 13
Birkbeck Rd. SW19 . . . 5K 119
Birkbeck Rd. W3 . . . 1K 81
Birkbeck Rd. W5 . . . 4C 80
Birkbeck Rd. Beck . . . 2J 141
Birkbeck Rd. Enf . . . 1J 7
Birkbeck Rd. Ilf . . . 5H 37
Birkbeck Rd. Romf . . . 1K 57
Birkbeck Rd. Sidc . . . 3A 128
Birkbeck St. E2 . . . 3H 69
Birkbeck Way. Gnfd . . . 1H 61
Birkdale Av. Pinn . . . 3E 24
Birkdale Clo. SE16 . . . 5H 87
Birkdale Clo. SE28 . . . 6D 74
Birkdale Clo. Orp . . . 7H 145
Birkdale Ct. S'hall . . . 6G 61 (off Redcroft Rd.)
Birkdale Gdns. Croy . . . 4K 153
Birkdale Rd. SE2 . . . 4A 92
Birkdale Rd. W5 . . . 4E 62
Birkenhead Av. King T . . . 2F 135
Birkenhead St. WC1 . . . 3J 67 (1F 161)
Birkhall Rd. SE6 . . . 1F 125
Birkwood Clo. SW12 . . . 7H 103
Birley Lodge. NW8 . . . 2B 66 (off Acacia Rd.)
Birley Rd. N20 . . . 2F 15
Birley St. SW11 . . . 2E 102
Birling Rd. Eri . . . 7K 93
Birnam Rd. N4 . . . 2K 49
Birnbeck Ct. NW11 . . . 5H 29
Birnbeck Ct. Barn . . . 4A 4
Birrell Ho. SW9 . . . 2K 103 (off Stockwell Rd.)
Birse Cres. NW10 . . . 3A 46
Birstall Rd. N15 . . . 5E 32
Biscay Ho. E1 . . . 4K 69 (off Mile End Rd.)
Biscay Rd. W6 . . . 5F 83
Biscoe Clo. Houn . . . 6E 78
Biscoe Way. SE13 . . . 3F 107
Biscott Ho. E3 . . . 4D 70
Bisenden Rd. Croy . . . 2E 152
Bisham Clo. Cars . . . 1D 150
Bisham Gdns. N6 . . . 1E 48
Bishop Ct. N12 . . . 4E 14
Bishop Ct. Rich . . . 3E 98
Bishop Duppas Pk. Shep . . . 7G 131
Bishop Fox Way. W Mol . . . 4D 132
Bishop Ken Rd. Harr . . . 2K 25
Bishop King's Rd. W14 . . . 4G 83
Bishop Rd. N14 . . . 7A 6
Bishop's Av. E13 . . . 1K 71
Bishop's Av. SW6 . . . 2F 101
Bishops Av. Brom . . . 2A 144
Bishops Av. Romf . . . 6C 38
Bishops Av., The. N2 . . . 6B 30
Bishop's Bri. Rd. W2 . . . 6K 65 (6A 158)
Bishops Clo. E17 . . . 4D 34
Bishop's Clo. N19 . . . 3G 49
Bishop's Clo. SE9 . . . 2G 127
Bishops Clo. W4 . . . 5J 81
Bishops Clo. Barn . . . 6A 4
Bishops Clo. Enf . . . 2C 8
Bishops Clo. Rich . . . 3D 116
Bishop's Clo. Sutt . . . 3J 149
Bishops Clo. Uxb . . . 2C 58
Bishop's Ct. EC4 . . . 7A 162
Bishops Ct. W2 . . . 6K 65 (off Bishop's Bri. Rd.)
Bishop's Ct. WC2 . . . 7J 161
Bishops Ct. Wemb . . . 4B 44
Bishopsdale Ho. NW6 . . . 1J 65 (off Kilburn Va.)
Bishop's Dri. Felt . . . 6F 95
Bishops Dri. N'holt . . . 1C 60
Bishopsford Rd. Mord . . . 7A 138
Bishopsgate. EC2 . . . 6E 68 (1G 169)
Bishopsgate Arc. EC2 . . . 6H 163
Bishopsgate Chyd. EC2 . . . 5E 68 (7G 163)
Bishopsgate Institute & Libraries. . . . 6H 163
Bishops Grn. Brom . . . 1K 143 (off Up. Park Rd.)
Bishops Gro. N2 . . . 6C 30
Bishop's Gro. Hamp . . . 4D 114
Bishops Gro. Cvn. Site. Hamp . . . 4E 114
Bishop's Hall. King T . . . 2D 134
Bishops Hill. W on T . . . 7J 131
Bishops Ho. SW8 . . . 7J 85 (off S. Lambeth Rd.)
Bishop's Mans. SW6 . . . 2F 101 (in two parts)
Bishops Mead. SE5 . . . 7C 86 (off Camberwell Rd.)
Bishop's Pk. Rd. SW6 . . . 2F 101
Bishops Pk. Rd. SW16 . . . 1J 139
Bishops Rd. N6 . . . 6E 30
Bishops Rd. SW6 . . . 1G 101
Bishop's Rd. SW11 . . . 7C 84
Bishops Rd. W7 . . . 2J 79
Bishop's Rd. Croy . . . 7B 140
Bishop's Rd. Hay . . . 6E 58
Bishop's Ter. SE11 . . . 4A 86 (3K 173)
Bishopsthorpe Rd. SE26 . . . 4K 123
Bishop St. N1 . . . 1C 68
Bishops Vw. Ct. N10 . . . 4F 31
Bishops Wlk. Chst . . . 1G 145
Bishops Wlk. Croy . . . 5K 153
Bishops Wlk. Pinn . . . 3C 24
Bishop's Way. E2 . . . 2H 69
Bishopswood Rd. N6 . . . 7D 30
Bishop Way. NW10 . . . 7A 46
Bishop Wilfred Wood Clo. SE15 . . . 2G 105
Bishop Wilfred Wood Ct. E13 . . . 2A 72 (off Pragel St.)
Bisley Clo. Wor Pk . . . 1E 148
Bison Ct. Felt . . . 7K 95
Bispham Rd. NW10 . . . 3F 63
Bissextile Ho. SE8 . . . 2D 106
Bisson Rd. E15 . . . 2E 70
Bisterne Av. E17 . . . 3F 35
Bittacy Bus. Cen. NW7 . . . 6B 14
Bittacy Clo. NW7 . . . 6A 14
Bittacy Ct. NW7 . . . 7B 14
Bittacy Hill. NW7 . . . 6A 14
Bittacy Pk. Av. NW7 . . . 5A 14
Bittacy Ri. NW7 . . . 6K 13
Bittacy Rd. NW7 . . . 6A 14
Bittern Clo. Hay . . . 5B 60
Bittern Ct. NW9 . . . 2A 28
Bittern Ct. SE8 . . . 6C 88
Bittern Ho. SE1 . . . 2C 86 (7C 168) (off Gt. Suffolk St.)
Bittern Pl. N22 . . . 2K 31
Bittern St. SE1 . . . 2C 86 (7C 168)
Bittoms Ct. King T . . . 3D 134
Bittoms, The. King T . . . 3D 134 (in two parts)
Bixley Clo. S'hall . . . 4D 78
Blackall St. EC2 . . . 4E 68 (3G 163)
Blackberry Clo. Shep . . . 4G 131
Blackberry Farm Clo. Houn . . . 7C 78
Blackbird Ct. NW9 . . . 3K 45
Blackbird Hill. NW9 . . . 2J 45
Blackbird Yd. E2 . . . 3F 69 (1K 163)
Blackborne Rd. Dag . . . 6G 57
Black Boy La. N15 . . . 5C 32
Blackbrook La. Brom . . . 5D 144
Blackburn. NW9 . . . 2B 28
Blackburne's M. W1 . . . 7E 66 (2G 165)
Blackburn Rd. NW6 . . . 6K 47
Blackbush Av. Romf . . . 5D 38
Blackbush Clo. Sutt . . . 7K 149
Blackdown Clo. N2 . . . 2A 30
Blackett St. SW15 . . . 3F 101
Black Fan Clo. Enf . . . 1H 7
Blackfen. . . . 6A 110
Blackfen Pde. Sidc . . . 6A 110
Blackfen Rd. Sidc . . . 6J 109
Blackford Clo. S Croy . . . 7B 152
Blackford's Path. SW15 . . . 7C 100
Blackfriars Bri. EC4 . . . 7B 68 (2A 168)
Blackfriars Bri. SE1 & EC4 . . . 7B 68
Blackfriars Ct. EC4 . . . 2A 168
Black Friars La. EC4 . . . 6B 68 (2A 168) (in two parts)
Blackfriars Pas. EC4 . . . 7B 68 (2A 168)
Blackfriars Rd. SE1 . . . 2B 86 (4A 168)
Blackfriars Underpass. EC4 . . . 7A 68 (2A 168)
Black Gates. Pinn . . . 3D 24
Blackheath. . . . 2H 107
Blackheath Av. SE10 . . . 7F 89
Blackheath Bus. Est. SE10 . . . 1E 106 (off Blackheath Hill)
Blackheath Gro. SE3 . . . 2H 107
Blackheath Hill. SE10 . . . 1E 106
Blackheath Park. . . . 4J 107
Blackheath Pk. SE3 . . . 3H 107
Blackheath Ri. SE13 . . . 2E 106
Blackheath Rd. SE10 . . . 1D 106
Blackheath Vale. . . . 2H 107
Blackheath Va. SE3 . . . 2G 107
Blackheath Village. SE3 . . . 2H 107
Black Horse Ct. SE1 . . . 3D 86 (off Gt. Dover St.)

Blackhorse Lane. (Junct.) 4K 33
Blackhorse La. E17 2K 33
Black Horse La. Croy 7G 141
Blackhorse M. E17 3K 33
Black Horse Pde. Eastc 5K 23
Blackhorse Rd. E17 4K 33
Blackhorse Rd. SE8 6A 88
Blackhorse Rd. Sidc 4A 128
Blacklands Dri. Hay 4E 58
Blacklands Rd. SE6 4E 124
Blacklands Ter. SW3 4D 84 (4E 170)
Black Lion La. W6 4C 82
Black Lion M. W6 4C 82
Blackmans Yd. E2 4G 69 (3K 163) (off Grimsby St.)
Blackmore Av. S'hall 1H 79
Blackmore Ho. N1 1K 67 (off Barnsbury Est.)
Blackmore Rd. Buck H 1H 21
Blackmore's Gro. Tedd 6A 116
Blackmore Tower. W3 3J 81 (off Stanley Rd.)
Blackness La. Kes 7B 156
Black Path. E10 7A 34
Blackpool Gdns. Hay 4G 59
Blackpool Rd. SE15 2H 105
Black Prince Interchange. (Junct.) 6H 111
Black Prince Rd. SE1 & SE11 4K 85 (4G 173)
Black Rod Clo. Hay 3H 77
Blackshaw Rd. SW17 4A 120
Blacksmiths Clo. Romf 6C 38
Blacksmiths Ho. E17 4C 34 (off Gillards M.)
Blacks Rd. W6 5E 82
Blackstock M. N4 2B 50
Blackstock Rd. N4 & N5 2B 50
Blackstone Est. E8 7G 51
Blackstone Ho. SW1 5G 85 (6A 172) (off Churchill Gdns.)
Blackstone Rd. NW2 5E 46
Black Swan Yd. SE1 2E 86 (6H 169)
Blackthorn Av. W Dray 4C 76
Blackthorn Ct. Houn 7C 78
Blackthorne Av. Croy 1J 153
Blackthorne Ct. SE15 7F 87 (off Cator St.)
Blackthorne Ct. S'hall 1F 79 (off Dormer's Wells La.)
Blackthorne Dri. E4 4A 20
Blackthorn Gro. Bexh 3E 110
Blackthorn St. E3 4C 70
Blacktree M. SW9 3A 104
Blackwall. 7E 70
Blackwall La. SE10 5G 89 (in two parts)
Blackwall Trad. Est. E14 5F 71
Blackwall Tunnel. E14 & SE10 1F 89 (in two parts)
Blackwall Tunnel App. E14 6E 70
Blackwall Tunnel Northern App. E3 & E14 2C 70
Blackwall Tunnel Southern App. SE10 3G 89
Blackwall Way. E14 1E 88
Blackwater Clo. E7 4H 53
Blackwater Clo. Rain 5K 75
Blackwater Ho. NW8 5B 66 (5B 158) (off Church St.)
Blackwater St. SE22 5F 105
Blackwell Clo. E5 4K 51
Blackwell Clo. Harr 7C 10
Blackwell Gdns. Edgw 4B 12
Blackwell Ho. SW4 6H 103
Blackwood Av. N18 5E 18
Blackwood Ho. E1 4H 69 (off Collingwood St.)
Blackwood St. SE17 5D 86
Blade M. SW15 4H 101
Bladen Ho. E1 6K 69 (off Dunelm St.)
Blades Ct. SW15 4H 101
Blades Ct. W6 5D 82 (off Lower Mall)
Blades Ho. SE11 6A 86 (7J 173) (off Kennington Oval)
Bladindon Dri. Bex 7C 110
Bladon Ct. SW16 6J 121
Bladon Gdns. Harr 6F 25
Blagdens Clo. N14 2C 16
Blagdens La. N14 2C 16
Blagdon Ct. W7 7J 61
Blagdon Rd. SE13 6D 106
Blagdon Rd. N Mald 4B 136 (in two parts)
Blagdon Wlk. Tedd 6C 116
Blagrove Rd. W10 5G 65
Blair Av. NW9 7A 28
Blair Clo. N1 6C 50
Blair Clo. Hay 4J 77
Blair Clo. Sidc 5J 109
Blair Ct. NW8 1B 66
Blair Ct. SE6 1H 125
Blair Ct. Beck 1D 142
Blairderry Rd. SW2 2J 121
Blair Ho. SW9 2K 103
Blair St. E14 6E 70
Blake Av. Bark 1J 73
Blake Clo. Cars 1C 150
Blake Clo. Well 1J 109
Blake Ct. NW6 3J 65 (off Stafford Clo.)
Blake Ct. SE16 5H 87 (off Stubbs Dri.)
Blakeden Dri. Clay 6A 146
Blake Gdns. SW6 1K 101
Blake Hall Cres. E11 1J 53
Blake Hall Rd. E11 7J 35
Blakehall Rd. Cars 6D 150
Blake Ho. E14 2C 88 (off Admirals Way)
Blake Ho. SE1 3A 86 (1J 173)
Blake Ho. SE8 6C 88 (off New King St.)
Blakeley Cotts. SE10 2F 89
Blakemore Rd. SW16 3J 121
Blakemore Rd. T Hth 5K 139
Blakemore Way. Belv 3E 92
Blakeney Av. Beck 1B 142
Blakeney Clo. E8 5G 51
Blakeney Clo. N20 1F 15
Blakeney Clo. NW1 7H 49
Blakeney Rd. Beck 7B 124
Blakenham Rd. SW17 4D 120
Blaker Ct. SE7 7A 90 (in two parts)
Blake Rd. E16 4H 71
Blake Rd. N11 7B 16
Blake Rd. Croy 2E 152
Blake Rd. Mitc 3C 138
Blaker Rd. E15 1E 70
Blakes Av. N Mald 5B 136
Blakes Clo. W10 5E 64
Blake's Grn. W Wick 1E 154
Blakes La. N Mald 5B 136
Blakesley Av. W5 6C 62
Blakesley Wlk. SW20 2H 137
Blake's Rd. SE15 7E 86
Blakes Ter. N Mald 5C 136
Blakesware Gdns. N9 7J 7
Blakewood Clo. Felt 4A 114
Blanchard Clo. SE9 3C 126
Blanchard Ho. Twic 6D 98 (off Clevedon Rd.)
Blanchard Way. E8 6G 51
Blanch Clo. SE15 7J 87
Blanchedowne. SE5 4D 104
Blanche St. E16 4H 71
Blanchland Rd. Mord 5K 137
Blandfield Rd. SW12 7E 102
Blandford Av. Beck 2A 142
Blandford Av. Twic 1F 115
Blandford Clo. N2 4A 30
Blandford Clo. Croy 3J 151
Blandford Clo. Romf 4G 39
Blandford Ct. E8 7E 50 (off St Peter's Way)
Blandford Ct. NW6 7F 47
Blandford Cres. E4 7K 9
Blandford Ho. SW8 7K 85 (off Richborne Ter.)
Blandford Rd. W4 3A 82
Blandford Rd. W5 2D 80
Blandford Rd. Beck 3J 141
Blandford Rd. S'hall 4E 78
Blandford Rd. Tedd 5H 115
Blandford Sq. NW1 4C 66 (4D 158)
Blandford St. W1 6D 66 (7F 159)
Blandford Waye. Hay 6A 60
Bland Ho. SE11 5H 173
Bland St. SE9 4B 108
Blaney Cres. E6 3F 73
Blanmerle Rd. SE9 1F 127
Blann Clo. SE9 6B 108
Blantyre St. SW10 7B 84
Blantyre Tower. SW10 7B 84 (off Blantyre St.)
Blantyre Wlk. SW10 7B 84 (off Worlds End Est.)
Blashford. NW3 7D 48 (off Adelaide Rd.)
Blashford St. SE13 7F 107
Blasker Wlk. E14 5D 88
Blawith Rd. Harr 4J 25
Blaxland Ho. W12 7D 64 (off White City Est.)
Blaydon Clo. N17 7C 18
Blaydon Clo. Ruis 7G 23
Blaydon Ct. N'holt 6E 42
Blazer Ct. NW8 2B 158
Bleak Hill La. SE18 6K 91
Blean Gro. SE20 7J 123
Bleasdale Av. Gnfd 2A 62
Blechynden Ho. W10 6F 65 (off Kingsdown Clo.)
Blechynden St. W10 7F 65
Bleddyn Clo. Sidc 6C 110
Bledlow Clo. SE28 7C 74
Bledlow Ho. NW8 4B 66 (4B 158) (off Capland St.)
Bledlow Ri. Gnfd 2G 61
Bleeding Heart Yd. EC1 6K 161
Blegborough Rd. SW16 6G 121
Blemundsbury. WC1 5K 67 (5G 161) (off Dombey St.)
Blendon. 6D 110
Blendon Dri. Bex 6D 110
Blendon Path. Brom 7H 125
Blendon Rd. Bex 6D 110
Blendon Row. SE17 4D 86 (off Townley St.)
Blendon Ter. SE18 5G 91
Blendworth Way. SE15 7E 86 (off Clanfield Way)
Blenheim Av. Ilf 6E 36
Blenheim Clo. N21 1H 17
Blenheim Clo. SW20 3E 136
Blenheim Clo. Gnfd 2H 61
Blenheim Clo. Romf 4J 39
Blenheim Clo. Wall 7G 151
Blenheim Ct. N19 2J 49
Blenheim Ct. SE16 1K 87 (off King & Queen Wharf)
Blenheim Ct. Brom 4H 143
Blenheim Ct. Kent 6A 26
Blenheim Ct. Sidc 3H 127
Blenheim Ct. Sutt 6A 150
Blenheim Cres. W11 7G 65
Blenheim Cres. Ruis 2F 41
Blenheim Cres. S Croy 7C 152
Blenheim Dri. Well 1K 109
Blenheim Gdns. NW2 6E 46
Blenheim Gdns. SW2 6K 103
Blenheim Gdns. King T 7H 117
Blenheim Gdns. Wall 6G 151
Blenheim Gdns. Wemb 3E 44
Blenheim Gro. SE15 2G 105
Blenheim Ho. E16 1K 89 (off Constable Av.)
Blenheim Ho. Houn 3E 96
Blenheim Pde. Uxb 4D 58
Blenheim Pk. Rd. S Croy 7C 152
Blenheim Pas. NW8 2A 66 (in two parts)
Blenheim Ri. N15 4F 33
Blenheim Rd. E6 3B 72
Blenheim Rd. E15 4G 53
Blenheim Rd. E17 3K 33
Blenheim Rd. NW8 2A 66
Blenheim Rd. SE20 7J 123
Blenheim Rd. SW20 3E 136
Blenheim Rd. W4 3A 82
Blenheim Rd. Barn 3A 4
Blenheim Rd. Brom 4C 144
Blenheim Rd. Harr 6F 25
Blenheim Rd. N'holt 6F 43
Blenheim Rd. Sidc 1C 128
Blenheim Rd. Sutt 3J 149
Blenheim Shop. Cen. SE20 7J 123
Blenheim St. W1 6F 67 (1J 165)
Blenheim Ter. NW8 2A 66
Blenheim Way. Iswth 1A 98
Blenkarne Rd. SW11 6D 102
Bleriot. NW9 2B 28 (off Belvedere Strand)
Bleriot Rd. Houn 7A 78
Blessbury Rd. Edgw 1J 27
Blessington Clo. SE13 3F 107
Blessington Rd. SE13 3F 107
Blessing Way. Bark 3C 74
Bletchingley Clo. T Hth 4B 140
Bletchley Ct. N1 1E 162 (in two parts)
Bletchley St. N1 2D 68 (1D 162)
Bletchmore Clo. Hay 5F 77
Bletsoe Wlk. N1 2C 68
Blewbury Ho. SE2 2D 92
Blick Ho. SE16 3J 87 (off Neptune St.)
Blincoe Clo. SW19 2F 119
Bliss Cres. SE13 2D 106
Blissett St. SE10 1E 106
Bliss M. W10 3G 65
Blisworth Clo. Hay 4C 60
Blisworth Ho. E2 1G 69 (off Whiston Rd.)
Blithbury Rd. Dag 6B 56
Blithdale Rd. SE2 4A 92
Blithfield St. W8 3K 83
Blockley Rd. Wemb 2B 44
Bloemfontein Av. W12 1D 82
Bloemfontein Rd. W12 7D 64
Bloemfontein Way. W12 1D 82
Blomfield Ct. W9 4A 66 (3A 158) (off Maida Va.)
Blomfield Mans. W12 1E 82 (off Stanlake Rd.)
Blomfield Rd. W9 5K 65 (4A 158)
Blomfield St. EC2 5D 68 (6F 163)
Blomfield Vs. W2 5K 65
Blomville Rd. Dag 3E 56
Blondel St. SW11 2E 102
Blondin Av. W5 4C 80
Blondin St. E3 2C 70
Bloomburg St. SW1 4H 85 (4B 172)
Bloomfield Ct. N6 6E 30
Bloomfield Cres. Ilf 6F 37
Bloomfield Ho. E1 5G 69 (off Old Montague St.)
Bloomfield Pl. W1 2K 165
Bloomfield Rd. N6 6E 30
Bloomfield Rd. SE18 6F 91
Bloomfield Rd. Brom 5B 144
Bloomfield Rd. King T 4E 134
Bloomfields, The. Bark 6G 55
Bloomfield Ter. SW1 5E 84 (5H 171)
Bloom Gro. SE27 3B 122
Bloomhall Rd. SE19 5D 122
Bloom Pk. Rd. SW6 7H 83
Bloomsbury. 5J 67 (5E 160)
Bloomsbury Clo. NW7 7H 13
Bloomsbury Clo. W5 7F 63
Bloomsbury Ct. WC1 6F 161
Bloomsbury Ct. Houn 1K 95
Bloomsbury Ct. Pinn 3D 24
Bloomsbury Ho. SW4 6H 103
Bloomsbury Pl. SW18 5A 102
Bloomsbury Pl. WC1 5J 67 (5F 161)
Bloomsbury Sq. WC1 5J 67 (6F 161)
Bloomsbury St. WC1 5H 67 (6D 160)
Bloomsbury Theatre. 3C 160
Bloomsbury Way. WC1 5J 67 (6E 160)
Blore Clo. SW8 1H 103
Blore Ct. W1 1C 166
Blossom Clo. W5 2E 80
Blossom Clo. Dag 1F 75
Blossom Clo. S Croy 5F 153
Blossom La. Enf 1H 7
Blossom St. E1 4E 68 (4H 163)
Blossom Way. Uxb 7B 40
Blossom Way. W Dray 4C 76
Blossom Waye. Houn 6C 78
Blount Ho. E14 5A 70 (off Maroon St.)
Blount St. E14 6A 70
Bloxam Gdns. SE9 5C 108
Bloxhall Rd. E10 1B 52
Bloxham Cres. Hamp 7D 114
Bloxworth Clo. Wall 3G 151
Blucher Rd. SE5 7C 86
Blue Anchor All. Rich 4E 98
Blue Anchor La. SE16 4G 87
Blue Anchor Yd. E1 7G 69 (3K 169)
Blue Ball Yd. SW1 1G 85 (5A 166)
Bluebell Av. E12 5B 54
Bluebell Clo. E9 1J 69
Bluebell Clo. SE26 4F 123
Bluebell Clo. Rush G 2K 57
Bluebell Clo. Wall 1F 151
Bluebell Way. Ilf 6F 55
Blueberry Clo. Wfd G 6D 20
Bluebird La. Dag 7G 57
Bluebird Way. SE28 2H 91
Bluefield Clo. Hamp 5E 114
Bluegate M. E1 7H 69
Bluegates. Ewe 7C 148
Bluehouse Rd. E4 2B 20
Blue Riband Ind. Est. Croy 2B 152
Blue Water. SW18 4K 101
Blundell Rd. Edgw 1K 27
Blundell St. N7 7J 49
Blunden Clo. Dag 1C 56
Blunt Rd. S Croy 5D 152
Blunts Av. W Dray 7C 76
Blunts Rd. SE9 5E 108
Blurton Rd. E5 4J 51
Blydon Ct. N21 5E 6 (off Chaseville Pk. Rd.)
Blyth Clo. E14 4F 89
Blyth Clo. Twic 6K 97
Blyth Ct. Brom 1H 143 (off Blyth Rd.)
Blythe Clo. SE6 7B 106

Blythe Hill. 7B 106
Blythe Hill. SE6 7B 106
Blythe Hill. Orp 1K 145 & 7A 128
Blythe Hill La. SE6 7B 106
Blythe Ho. SE11 6A 86 (7J 173)
Blythe M. W14 3F 83
Blythendale Ho. E2 2G 69 (off Mansford St.)
Blythe Rd. W14 3F 83 (in two parts)
Blythe St. E2 3H 69
Blythe Va. SE6 1B 124
Blyth Hill Pl. SE23 7A 106 (off Brockley Pk.)
Blyth Rd. E17 7B 34
Blyth Rd. SE28 7C 74
Blyth Rd. Brom 1H 143
Blyth Rd. Hay 2G 77
Blyth's Wharf. E14 7A 70 (off Narrow St.)
Blythswood Rd. Ilf 1A 56
Blyth Wood Pk. Brom 1H 143
Blythwood Rd. N4 7J 31
Blythwood Rd. Pinn 1B 24
Boades M. NW3 4B 48
Boadicea St. N1 1K 67
Boakes Clo. NW9 4J 27
Boardman Av. E4 5J 9
Boardman Clo. Barn 5B 4
Boardwalk Pl. E14 1E 88
Boarhound. NW9 2B 28 (off Further Acre)
Boarley Ho. SE17 4E 86 (off Massinger St.)
Boars Head Yd. Bren 7D 80
Boathouse Cen., The. W10 4F 65 (off Canal Clo.)
Boathouse Wlk. SE15 7F 87 (in two parts)
Boat Lifter Way. SE16 4A 88
Bob Anker Clo. E13 3J 71
Bobbin Clo. SW4 3G 103
Bobby Moore Way. N12 7J 15
Bob Marley Way. SE24 4A 104
Bockhampton Rd. King T 7F 117
Bocking St. E8 1H 69
Boddicott Clo. SW19 2G 119
Boddington Ho. SE14 1J 105 (off Pomeroy St.)
Boddington Ho. SW13 6D 82 (off Wyatt Dri.)
Bodeney Ho. SE5 1E 104 (off Peckham Rd.)
Boden Ho. E1 5G 69 (5K 163) (off Woodseer St.)
Bodiam Clo. Enf 2K 7
Bodiam Rd. SW16 7H 121
Bodicea M. Houn 6D 96
Bodington Ct. W12 2F 83
Bodley Clo. N Mald 5A 136
Bodley Mnr. Way. SW2 7A 104
Bodley Rd. N Mald 6K 135
Bodmin. NW9 2B 28 (off Further Acre)
Bodmin Clo. Harr 3D 42
Bodmin Gro. Mord 5K 137
Bodmin Pl. SE27 4B 122
Bodmin St. SW18 1J 119
Bodnant Gdns. SW20 3C 136
Bodney Rd. E8 5H 51
Boeing Way. S'hall 3K 77
Boevey Path. Belv 5F 93
Bogart Ct. E14 7C 70 (off Premiere Pl.)
Bogey La. Orp 7E 156
Bognor Rd. Well 1D 110
Bohemia Pl. E8 6J 51
Bohn Rd. E1 5A 70
Bohun Gro. Barn 6H 5
Boileau Pde. W5 6F 63 (off Boileau Rd.)
Boileau Rd. SW13 7C 82
Boileau Rd. W5 6F 63
Boisseau Ho. E1 5J 69 (off Stepney Way)
Bolden St. SE8 2D 106
Boldero Pl. NW8 4C 158
Bolderwood Way. W Wick 2D 154
Boldmere Rd. Pinn 7A 24
Boleyn Av. Enf 1C 8
Boleyn Clo. E17 4C 34
Boleyn Ct. Buck H 1D 20
Boleyn Dri. Ruis 2B 42
Boleyn Dri. W Mol 3D 132
Boleyn Gdns. Dag 7J 57
Boleyn Gdns. W Wick 2D 154
Boleyn Gro. W Wick 2E 154
Boleyn Ho. E16 1J 89 (off Southey M.)
Boleyn Rd. E6 2B 72
Boleyn Rd. E7 7J 53
Boleyn Rd. N16 5E 50
Boleyn Way. Barn 3F 5
Bolina Rd. SE16 5J 87
Bolingbroke Gro. SW11 4C 102
Bolingbroke Rd. W14 3F 83
Bolingbroke Wlk. SW11 1B 102
Bolingbroke Way. Hay 1F 77
Bolliger Ct. NW10 4J 63
Bollo Bri. Rd. W3 3H 81
Bollo Ct. W3 3J 81 (off Bollo Bri. Rd.)
Bollo La. W3 & W4 2H 81
Bolney Ga. SW7 2C 84 (7C 164)
Bolney St. SW8 7K 85
Bolney Way. Felt 3C 114
Bolsover St. W1 4F 67 (4K 159)
Bolstead Rd. Mitc 1F 139
Bolster Gro. N22 7C 16
Bolt Ct. EC4 6A 68 (1K 167)
Boltmore Clo. NW4 3F 29
Bolton Clo. SE20 2G 141
Bolton Clo. Chess 6D 146
Bolton Cres. SE5 7B 86
Bolton Gdns. NW10 2F 65
Bolton Gdns. SW5 5K 83
Bolton Gdns. Brom 6H 125
Bolton Gdns. Tedd 6A 116
Bolton Gdns. M. SW10 5A 84
Bolton Ho. SE10 5G 89 (off Trafalgar Rd.)
Bolton Pl. NW8 1K 65 (off Bolton Rd.)
Bolton Rd. E15 6H 53
Bolton Rd. N18 5A 18
Bolton Rd. NW8 1K 65
Bolton Rd. NW10 1A 64
Bolton Rd. W4 7J 81
Bolton Rd. Chess 6D 146
Bolton Rd. Harr 4G 25
Boltons Ct. SW5 5K 83 (off Old Brompton Rd.)
Bolton's La. Hay 7D 76
Boltons Pl. SW5 5A 84
Boltons, The. SW10 5A 84
Boltons, The. Wemb 4K 43
Bolton St. W1 1F 85 (4K 165)
Bolton Studios. SW10 5A 84
Bolton Wlk. N7 2K 49 (off Durham Rd.)
Bombay St. SE16 4H 87
Bomer Clo. W Dray 7C 76
Bomore Rd. W11 7G 65
Bonar Pl. Chst 7C 126
Bonar Rd. SE15 7G 87
Bonchester Clo. Chst 7E 126
Bonchurch Clo. Sutt 7K 149
Bonchurch Rd. W10 5G 65
Bonchurch Rd. W13 1B 80
Bond Clo. W Dray 6B 58
Bond Ct. EC4 7D 68 (2E 168)
Bondfield Av. Hay 3J 59
Bondfield Rd. E6 5D 72
Bond Gdns. Wall 4G 151
Bond Ho. NW6 2H 65 (off Rupert Rd.)
Bond Ho. SE14 7A 88 (off Goodwood Rd.)
Bonding Yd. Wlk. SE16 3A 88
Bond Rd. Mitc 2C 138
Bond Rd. Surb 2F 147
Bond St. E15 5G 53
Bond St. W4 4K 81
Bond St. W5 7D 62
Bondway. SW8 6J 85 (7F 173)
Boneta Rd. SE18 3D 90
Bonfield Rd. SE13 4E 106
Bonham Gdns. Dag 2D 56
Bonham Rd. SW2 5K 103
Bonham Rd. Dag 2D 56
Bonheur Rd. W4 2K 81
Bonhill St. EC2 4D 68 (4F 163)
Boniface Gdns. Harr 7A 10
Boniface Rd. Uxb 3D 40
Boniface Wlk. Harr 7A 10
Bonita M. SE4 3K 105
Bon Marche Ter. M. SE27 4E 122
Bonner Hill Rd. King T 2F 135 (in two parts)
Bonner Rd. E2 2J 69
Bonnersfield Clo. Harr 6K 25
Bonnersfield La. Harr 6K 25
Bonner St. E2 2J 69
Bonneville Gdns. SW4 6G 103
Bonnington Ct. N'holt 2B 60 (off Gallery Gdns.)
Bonnington Ho. N1 2K 67
Bonnington Sq. SW8 6K 85 (7G 173)
Bonny St. NW1 7G 49
Bonser Rd. Twic 2K 115
Bonsor Ho. SW8 1G 103
Bonsor St. SE5 7E 86
Bonville Gdns. NW4 4D 28
Bonville Rd. Brom 5H 125
Bookbinders Cottage Homes. N20 3J 15
Booker Clo. E14 5B 70
Booker Rd. N18 5B 18
Bookham Ct. SW19 3B 138
Boone Ct. N9 3D 18
Boones Rd. SE13 4G 107
Boone St. SE13 4G 107
Boord St. SE10 3G 89
Boothby Ct. E4 3K 19
Boothby Rd. N19 2H 49
Booth Clo. E9 1H 69
Booth Clo. SE28 1B 92
Booth Dri. Stai 6A 112
Booth La. EC4 2C 168
Boothman Ho. Kent 3D 26
Booth Rd. NW9 2K 27
Booth Rd. Croy 2B 152
Booth's Pl. W1 5G 67 (6B 160)
Boot Pde. Edgw 6B 12 (off High St.)
Boot St. N1 3E 68 (2G 163)
Bordars Rd. W7 5J 61
Bordars Wlk. W7 5J 61
Borden Av. Enf 6J 7
Border Cres. SE26 5H 123
Border Gdns. Croy 4D 154
Bordergate. Mitc 1C 138
Border Rd. SE26 5H 123
Bordesley Rd. Mord 5K 137
Bordeston Ct. Bren 7C 80 (off Augustus Clo.)
Bordon Wlk. SW15 7C 100
Boreas Wlk. N1 1B 162
Boreham Av. E16 6J 71
Boreham Clo. E11 1E 52
Boreham Rd. N22 2C 32
Boreman Ho. SE10 6E 88 (off Thames St.)
Borgard Rd. SE18 4D 90
Borland Rd. SE15 4J 105
Borland Rd. Tedd 7B 116
Borneo St. SW15 3E 100
Borough High St. SE1 2C 86 (7D 168)
Borough Hill. Croy 3B 152
Borough Rd. SE1 3B 86 (7B 168)
Borough Rd. Iswth 1J 97
Borough Rd. King T 1G 135
Borough Rd. Mitc 2C 138
Borough Sq. SE1 7C 168
Borough, The. 2D 86 (6E 168)
Borrett Clo. SE17 5C 86
Borrodaile Rd. SW18 6K 101
Borrowdale. NW1 3G 67 (2A 160) (off Robert St.)
Borrowdale Av. Harr 2A 26
Borrowdale Clo. Ilf 4C 36
Borrowdale Ct. Enf 1H 7
Borthwick M. E15 4G 53
Borthwick Rd. E15 4G 53
Borthwick Rd. NW9 6B 28
Borthwick St. SE8 5C 88
Borwick Av. E17 3B 34
Bosanquet Clo. Uxb 4A 58
Bosbury Rd. SE6 3E 124
Boscastle Rd. NW5 3F 49
Boscobel Ho. E8 6H 51
Boscobel Pl. SW1 4E 84 (3H 171)
Boscobel St. NW8 4B 66 (4B 158)
Boscombe Av. E10 7F 35
Boscombe Clo. E5 5A 52
Boscombe Gdns. SW16 6J 121
Boscombe Ho. Croy 1D 152 (off Sydenham Rd.)
Boscombe Rd. SW17 6E 120
Boscombe Rd. SW19 1K 137
Boscombe Rd. W12 1C 82
Boscombe Rd. Wor Pk 1E 148
Bose Clo. N3 1G 29
Bosgrove. E4 2K 19
Boss Ho. SE1 2F 87 (6J 169) (off Boss St.)
Boss St. SE1 2F 87 (6J 169)
Bostall Hill. SE2 5A 92
Bostall La. SE2 4B 92
Bostall Mnr. Way. SE2 4B 92
Bostall Pk. Av. Bexh 7E 92
Bostall Rd. Orp 7B 128
Bostock Ho. Houn 6E 78
Boston Bus. Pk. W7 3J 79
Boston Gdns. W4 6A 82
Boston Gdns. W7 4A 80
Boston Gdns. Bren 4A 80
Boston Gro. Ruis 6E 22
Boston Manor. 4A 80
Boston Manor House. 5B 80
Boston Mnr. Rd. Bren 4B 80
Boston Pde. W7 3A 80
Boston Pk. Rd. Bren 5C 80
Boston Pl. NW1 4D 66 (4E 158)
Boston Rd. E6 3C 72
Boston Rd. E17 6C 34
Boston Rd. W7 1J 79
Boston Rd. Croy 6K 139
Boston Rd. Edgw 7D 12
Bostonthorpe Rd. W7 2J 79
Boston Va. W7 4A 80
Bosun Clo. E14 2C 88
Boswell Ct. W14 3F 83 (off Blythe Rd.)
Boswell Ct. WC1 5J 67 (5F 161)
Boswell Ct. King T 1F 135 (off Clifton Rd.)
Boswell Ho. WC1 5J 67 (5F 161) (off Boswell St.)
Boswell Path. Hay 4H 77
Boswell Rd. T Hth 4C 140
Boswell St. WC1 5J 67 (5F 161)
Bosworth Clo. E17 1B 34
Bosworth Ho. W10 4G 65 (off Bosworth Rd.)
Bosworth Rd. N11 6C 16
Bosworth Rd. W10 4G 65
Bosworth Rd. Barn 3D 4
Bosworth Rd. Dag 3G 57
Botany Bay La. Chst 3G 145
Botany Clo. Barn 4H 5
Boteley Clo. E4 2A 20
Botham Clo. Edgw 7D 12
Botha Rd. E13 5K 71
Bothwell Clo. E16 5H 71
Bothwell St. W6 6F 83
Botolph All. EC3 2G 169
Botolph La. EC3 7E 68 (3G 169)
Botsford Rd. SW20 2G 137
Botts M. W2 6J 65
Botwell Comn. Rd. Hay 7F 59
Botwell Cres. Hay 6G 59
Botwell La. Hay 7G 59
Boucher Clo. Tedd 5K 115
Bouchier Ho. N2 2B 30
Boughton Av. Brom 7H 143
Boughton Ho. SE1 2D 86 (6E 168) (off Tennis St.)
Boughton Rd. SE28 3J 91
Boulcott St. E1 6K 69
Boulevard, The. SW17 2E 120
Boulevard, The. SW18 4K 101
Boulevard, The. Pinn 4E 24 (in two parts)
Boulevard, The. Wfd G 6K 21
Boulogne Ho. SE1 3F 87 (7J 169) (off Abbey St.)
Boulogne Rd. Croy 6C 140
Boulter Ho. SE14 1J 105 (off Kender St.)
Boulton Ho. Bren 5E 80
Boulton Rd. Dag 2E 56
Boultwood Rd. E6 6D 72
Bounces La. N9 2C 18
Bounces Rd. N9 2C 18
Boundaries Rd. SW12 2D 120
Boundaries Rd. Felt 1A 114
Boundary Av. E17 7B 34
Boundary Bus. Ct. Mitc 3B 138
Boundary Clo. SE25 2G 141
Boundary Clo. Barn 1C 4
Boundary Clo. Ilf 4J 55
Boundary Clo. King T 3H 135
Boundary Clo. S'hall 5E 78
Boundary Ct. N18 6A 18 (off Snells Pk.)
Boundary Ho. SE5 7C 86
Boundary La. E13 3B 72 (in two parts)
Boundary La. SE17 6C 86
Boundary M. NW8 1A 66 (off Boundary Rd.)
Boundary Pas. E1 4F 69 (3J 163)
Boundary Rd. E13 2A 72
Boundary Rd. E17 7B 34
Boundary Rd. N2 1B 30
Boundary Rd. N9 6D 8
Boundary Rd. N22 3B 32
Boundary Rd. NW8 1K 65
Boundary Rd. SW19 6B 120
Boundary Rd. Bark 2G 73 (in two parts)
Boundary Rd. Cars & Wall 6F 151
Boundary Rd. Pinn 7B 24
Boundary Rd. Sidc 5J 109
Boundary Rd. Wemb 3E 44
Boundary Row. SE1 2B 86 (6A 168)
Boundary St. E2 3F 69 (2J 163) (in two parts)
Boundary Way. Croy 5C 154
Boundfield Rd. SE6 3G 125
Bounds Green. 6C 16

Bounds Grn. Ct. N11 6C 16 (off Bounds Grn. Rd.)
Bounds Grn. Ind. Est. N11 6B 16
Bounds Grn. Rd. N11 & N22 6B 16
Bourbon Ho. SE6 5E 124
Bourchier St. W1 7H 67 (2C 166) (in two parts)
Bourdon Pl. W1 2K 165
Bourdon Rd. SE20 2J 141
Bourdon St. W1 7F 67 (3J 165)
Bourke Clo. NW10 6A 46
Bourke Clo. SW4 6J 103
Bourlet Clo. W1 5G 67 (6A 160)
Bourn Av. N15 4D 32
Bourn Av. Uxb 4C 58
Bournbrook Rd. SE3 3B 108
Bourne Av. N14 2D 16
Bourne Av. Barn 5G 5
Bourne Av. Hay 3E 76
Bourne Av. Ruis 5A 42
Bourne Cir. Hay 3E 76
Bourne Ct. W4 6J 81
Bourne Ct. S Ruis 5K 41
Bourne Ct. Wfd G 3B 36
Bourne Dri. Mitc 2B 138
Bourne Est. EC1 5A 68 (5J 161)
Bourne Gdns. E4 4J 19
Bourne Hall Mus. 7B 148
Bourne Hill. N14 1D 16
Bourne Hill Clo. N13 2E 16
Bourne Ind. Pk., The. Dart 5K 111
Bourne Mead. Bex 5J 111
Bournemead Av. N'holt 2J 59
Bournemead Clo. N'holt 3J 59
Bournemead Way. N'holt 2K 59
Bourne M. W1 6E 66 (1H 165)
Bournemouth Clo. SE15 2G 105
Bournemouth Rd. SE15 2G 105
Bournemouth Rd. SW19 1J 137
Bourne Pde. Bex 7H 111
Bourne Pl. W4 5K 81
Bourne Rd. E7 3H 53
Bourne Rd. N8 6J 31
Bourne Rd. Bex & Dart 7H 111
Bourne Rd. Brom 4B 144
Bournes Ho. N15 6E 32 (off Chisley Rd.)
Bourneside Cres. N14 1C 16
Bourneside Gdns. SE6 5E 124
Bourne St. SW1 4E 84 (4G 171)
Bourne St. Croy 2B 152
Bourne Ter. W2 5K 65
Bourne, The. N14 1C 16
Bourne Va. Brom 1H 155
Bournevale Rd. SW16 4J 121
Bourne Vw. Gnfd 6K 43
Bourne Way. Brom 2H 155
Bourne Way. Eps 4J 147
Bourne Way. Sutt 5H 149
Bournewood Rd. SE18 7A 92
Bournville Rd. SE6 7C 106
Bournwell Clo. Barn 3J 5
Bourton Clo. Hay 1J 77
Bousfield Rd. SE14 2K 105
Boutflower Rd. SW11 4C 102
Boutique Hall. SE13 4E 106
Bouverie Gdns. Harr 6D 26
Bouverie M. N16 2E 50
Bouverie Pl. W2 6B 66 (7B 158)
Bouverie Rd. N16 2E 50
Bouverie Rd. Harr 6G 25
Bouverie St. EC4 6A 68 (1K 167)
Bouvier Rd. Enf 1D 8
Boveney Rd. SE23 7K 105
Bovill Rd. SE23 7K 105
Bovingdon Av. Wemb 6G 45
Bovingdon Clo. N19 2G 49
Bovingdon La. NW9 1A 28
Bovingdon Rd. SW6 1K 101
Bovingdon Sq. Mitc 4J 139
Bow. 3C 70
Bowater Clo. NW9 5K 27
Bowater Clo. SW2 6J 103
Bowater Gdns. Sun 2A 132
Bowater Ho. EC1 4C 68 (4C 162) (off Golden La. Est.)
Bowater Pl. SE3 7K 89
Bowater Rd. SE18 3B 90
Bow Bri. Est. E3 3D 70
Bow Brook, The. E2 2K 69 (off Mace St.)
Bow Chyd. EC4 1D 168
Bow Common. 5C 70
Bow Comn. La. E3 4B 70
Bowden Clo. Felt 1G 113
Bowden St. SE11 5A 86 (6K 173)
Bowditch. SE8 4B 88 (in two parts)
Bowdon Rd. E17 7C 34
Bowen Dri. SE21 3E 122
Bowen Rd. Harr 7G 25
Bowen St. E14 6D 70
Bower Av. SE10 1G 107
Bower Clo. N'holt 2A 60
Bower Clo. Romf 1K 39
Bower Ct. E4 1K 19 (off Ridgeway, The)
Bowerdean St. SW6 1K 101
Bower Ho. SE14 1K 105 (off Besson St.)
Bowerman Av. SE14 6A 88
Bowerman Ct. N19 2H 49 (off St John's Way)
Bower St. E1 6K 69
Bowers Wlk. E6 6D 72
Bowes Clo. Sidc 6B 110
Bowe's Ho. Bark 7F 55
Bowes-Lyon Hall. E16 1J 89 (off Wesley Av., in two parts)
Bowes Park. 7D 16
Bowes Rd. N11 & N13 5B 16
Bowes Rd. W3 7A 64
Bowes Rd. Dag 4C 56
Bowfell Rd. W6 6E 82
Bowford Av. Bexh 1E 110
Bowhill Clo. SW9 7A 86
Bowie Clo. SW4 7H 103
Bow Ind. Pk. E15 7C 52
Bow Interchange. (Junct.) 3E 70
Bowland Rd. SW4 4H 103
Bowland Rd. Wfd G 5F 21
Bowland Yd. SW1 7F 165
Bow La. EC4 6C 68 (1D 168)
Bow La. N12 7F 15
Bow La. Mord 6G 137
Bowl Ct. EC2 4E 68 (4H 163)
Bowles Rd. SE1 6G 87
Bowley Clo. SE19 6F 123
Bowley Ho. SE16 3G 87
Bowley La. SE19 5F 123
Bowling Clo. Uxb 1B 58
Bowling Grn. Clo. SW15 7D 100
Bowling Grn. Ct. Wemb 2F 45
Bowling Grn. La. EC1 4A 68 (3K 161)
Bowling Grn. Pl. SE1 2D 86 (6E 168)
Bowling Grn. Row. SE18 3D 90
Bowling Grn. St. SE11 6A 86 (7J 173)
Bowling Grn. Wlk. N1 3E 68 (1G 163)
Bowls Clo. Stan 5G 11
Bowman Av. E16 7H 71
Bowman M. SW18 1H 119
Bowman's Bldgs. NW1 5C 66 (5C 158) (off Penfold Pl.)
Bowmans Clo. W13 1B 80
Bowmans Lea. SE23 7J 105
Bowmans Mdw. Wall 3F 151
Bowman's M. E1 7G 69
Bowman's M. N7 3J 49
Bowman's Pl. N7 3J 49
Bowman Trad. Est. NW9 4G 27
Bowmead. SE9 2D 126
Bowmore Wlk. NW1 7H 49
Bowness Clo. E8 6F 51 (off Beechwood Rd.)
Bowness Cres. SW15 5A 118
Bowness Dri. Houn 4C 96
Bowness Ho. SE15 7J 87 (off Hillbeck Clo.)
Bowness Rd. SE6 7D 106
Bowness Rd. Bexh 2H 111
Bowood Rd. SW11 5E 102
Bowood Rd. Enf 2E 8
Bow Rd. E3 3B 70
Bowrons Av. Wemb 7D 44
Bowry Ho. E14 5B 70 (off Wallwood St.)
Bowsley Ct. Felt 2J 113
Bowsprit Point. E14 3C 88 (off Westferry Rd.)
Bow St. E15 5G 53
Bow St. WC2 6J 67 (1F 167)
Bow Triangle Bus. Cen. E3 4C 70
Bowyer Clo. E6 5D 72
Bowyer Ho. N1 1E 68 (off Whitmore Est.)
Bowyer Pl. SE5 7C 86
Bowyer St. SE5 7C 86
Boxall Rd. SE21 6E 104
Boxelder Clo. Edgw 5D 12
Boxgrove Rd. SE2 2B 92
Box La. Bark 2B 74
Boxley Rd. Mord 4A 138
Boxley St. E16 1K 89
Boxmoor Ho. W11 1F 83 (off Queensdale Cres.)
Boxmoor Rd. Harr 4B 26
Boxoll Rd. Dag 4F 57
Boxted Clo. Buck H 1H 21
Box Tree Ho. SE8 6A 88
Boxtree La. Harr 1G 25
Boxtree Rd. Harr 7C 10
Boxwood Clo. W Dray 2B 76
Boxworth Clo. N12 5G 15
Boxworth Gro. N1 1K 67
Boyard Rd. SE18 5F 91
Boyce Ho. W10 3H 65 (off Bruckner St.)
Boyce Way. E13 4J 71
Boycroft Av. NW9 6J 27
Boyd Av. S'hall 1D 78
Boyd Clo. King T 7G 117
Boydell Ct. NW8 7B 48 (in two parts)
Boyden Ho. E17 3E 34
Boyd Rd. SW19 6B 120
Boyd St. E1 6G 69
Boyfield St. SE1 2B 86 (7B 168)
Boyland Rd. Brom 5H 125
Boyle Av. Stan 6F 11
Boyle Clo. Uxb 2B 58
Boyle Farm Rd. Th Dit 6A 134
Boyle St. W1 7G 67 (2A 166)
Boyne Av. NW4 4F 29
Boyne Rd. SE13 3E 106
Boyne Rd. Dag 3G 57
Boyne Ter. M. W11 1H 83
Boyseland Ct. Edgw 2D 12
Boyson Rd. SE17 6C 86 (in two parts)
Boyson Wlk. SE17 6D 86
Boyton Clo. E1 4J 69
Boyton Clo. N8 3J 31
Boyton Ho. NW8 2B 66 (off Wellington Rd.)
Boyton Rd. N8 3J 31
Brabant Ct. EC3 2G 169
Brabant Rd. N22 2K 31
Brabazon Av. Wall 7J 151
Brabazon Rd. Houn 7A 78
Brabazon Rd. N'holt 2E 60
Brabazon St. E14 6D 70
Brabner Ho. E2 3G 69 (1K 163) (off Wellington Row)
Brabourne Clo. SE19 5E 122
Brabourne Cres. Bexh 6F 93
Brabourne Heights. NW7 3F 13
Brabourne Ri. Beck 5E 142
Brabourn Gro. SE15 2J 105
Brabrook Ct. Wall 4F 151
Brabstone Ho. Gnfd 2K 61
Bracer Ho. N1 2E 68 (off Whitmore Est.)
Bracewell Av. Gnfd 5K 43
Bracewell Rd. W10 5E 64
Bracewood Gdns. Croy 3F 153
Bracey M. N4 2J 49
Bracey St. N4 2J 49
Bracken Av. SW12 6E 102
Bracken Av. Croy 3C 154
Brackenbridge Dri. Ruis 3B 42
Brackenbury. N4 1A 50 (off Osborne Rd.)
Brackenbury Gdns. W6 3D 82
Brackenbury Rd. N2 3A 30
Brackenbury Rd. W6 3D 82
Bracken Clo. E6 5D 72
Bracken Clo. Sun 6H 113
Bracken Clo. Twic 7E 96
Brackendale. N21 2E 16
Brackendale Clo. Houn 1F 97
Brackendene. Dart 4K 129
Bracken End. Iswth 5H 97
Brackenfield Clo. E5 3H 51
Bracken Gdns. SW13 2C 100
Brackenhill. Ruis 4C 42
Bracken Hill Clo. Brom 1H 143
Bracken Hill La. Brom 1H 143
Bracken Ho. E3 5C 70 (off Devons Rd.)
Bracken Ind. Est. Ilf 1J 37
Bracken M. E4 1K 19
Bracken M. Romf 6H 39
Brackens. Beck 7C 124
Brackens, The. Enf 7K 7
Bracken, The. E4 2K 19
Brackenwood. Sun 1J 131
Brackenwood Lodge. Barn 4D 4 (off Prospect Rd.)
Brackley Clo. Wall 7J 151
Brackley Ct. NW8 4B 66 (3B 158) (off Henderson Dri.)
Brackley Rd. W4 5A 82
Brackley Rd. Beck 7B 124
Brackley Sq. Wfd G 7G 21
Brackley St. EC1 4C 68 (5D 162)
Brackley Ter. W4 5A 82
Bracklyn Ct. N1 2D 68
Bracklyn St. N1 2D 68
Bracknell Clo. N22 1A 32
Bracknell Gdns. NW3 4K 47
Bracknell Ga. NW3 5K 47
Bracknell Way. NW3 4K 47
Bracondale Rd. SE2 4A 92
Bradbeer Ho. E2 3J 69 (off Cornwall Av.)
Bradbourne Rd. Bex 7G 111
Bradbourne St. SW6 2J 101
Bradbury Clo. S'hall 4D 78
Bradbury M. N16 5E 50 (off Bradbury St.)
Bradbury St. N16 5E 50
Braddock Clo. Iswth 2K 97
Braddon Ct. Barn 3B 4
Braddon Rd. Rich 3F 99
Braddyll St. SE10 5G 89
Bradenham. SE17 6D 86 (off Bradenham Clo.)
Bradenham Av. Well 4A 110
Bradenham Clo. SE17 6D 86
Bradenham Rd. Harr 4B 26
Bradenham Rd. Hay 3G 59
Braden St. W9 4K 65
Bradfield Ct. NW1 7F 49 (off Hawley Rd.)
Bradfield Dri. Bark 5A 56
Bradfield Rd. E16 2J 89
Bradfield Rd. Ruis 5C 42
Bradford Clo. N17 6A 18
Bradford Clo. SE26 4H 123
Bradford Clo. Brom 1D 156
Bradford Dri. Eps 6B 148
Bradford Ho. W14 3F 83 (off Spring Va. Ter.)
Bradford Rd. W3 2A 82
Bradford Rd. Ilf 1H 55
Bradgate Rd. SE6 6D 106
Brading Cres. E11 2K 53
Brading Rd. SW2 7K 103
Brading Rd. Croy 6K 139
Brading Ter. W12 3C 82
Bradiston Rd. W9 3H 65
Bradley Clo. N7 6J 49
Bradley Gdns. W13 6B 62
Bradley Ho. E2 2G 69 (off Claredale St.)
Bradley Ho. SE16 4J 87 (off Raymouth Rd.)
Bradley M. SW17 1D 120
Bradley Rd. N22 2K 31
Bradley Rd. SE19 6C 122
Bradley's Clo. N1 2A 68
Bradley Stone Rd. E6 5D 72
Bradman Row. Edgw 7D 12
Bradmead. SW8 7F 85
Bradmore Pk. Rd. W6 4D 82
Bradshaw Clo. SW19 6J 119
Bradshawe Waye. Uxb 5B 58
Bradshaws Clo. SE25 3G 141
Bradstock Ho. E9 7K 51
Bradstock Rd. E9 6K 51
Bradstock Rd. Eps 5C 148
Brad St. SE1 1A 86 (5K 167)
Bradwell Av. Dag 2G 57
Bradwell Clo. E18 4H 35
Bradwell Ho. NW6 1K 65 (off Mortimer Cres.)
Bradwell M. N18 4B 18
Bradwell Rd. Buck H 1H 21
Brady Ct. Dag 1D 56
Brady Ho. SW8 1G 103 (off Corunna Rd.)
Bradymead. E6 6E 72
Brady St. E1 4H 69
Braeburn Ct. Barn 4G 5
Braemar Av. N22 1J 31
Braemar Av. NW10 3K 45
Braemar Av. SW19 2J 119
Braemar Av. Bexh 4J 111
Braemar Av. S Croy 7C 152
Braemar Av. T Hth 3A 140
Braemar Av. Wemb 7D 44
Braemar Clo. SE16 5H 87 (off Masters Dri.)
Braemar Ct. SE6 1H 125
Braemar Gdns. NW9 1K 27
Braemar Gdns. Sidc 3H 127
Braemar Gdns. W Wick 1E 154
Braemar Ho. W9 3A 66 (off Maida Va.)
Braemar Rd. E13 4H 71
Braemar Rd. N15 5E 32
Braemar Rd. Bren 6D 80
Braemar Rd. Wor Pk 3D 148
Braeside. Beck 5C 124
Braeside Av. SW19 1G 137
Braeside Cres. Bexh 4J 111
Braeside Rd. SW16 7G 121
Braes St. N1 7B 50
Braesyde Clo. Belv 4F 93
Brafferton Rd. Croy 4C 152
Braganza St. SE17 5B 86
Bragg Clo. Dag 6B 56
Bragg Rd. Tedd 6J 115

Braham Ho. SE11 ... 5K 85 (6H 173)
Braham St. E1 ... 6F 69 (1K 169)
Braid Av. W3 ... 6A 64
Braid Clo. Felt ... 2D 114
Braid Ho. SE10 ... 1E 106 (off Blackheath Hill)
Braidwood Pas. EC1 ... 5C 68 (5C 162) (off Aldersgate St.)
Braidwood Rd. SE6 ... 1F 125
Brailsford Clo. SW19 ... 7C 120
Brailsford Rd. SW2 ... 5A 104
Brainton Av. Felt ... 7K 95
Braintree Av. Ilf ... 4C 36
Braintree Ho. E1 ... 4J 69 (off Malcolm Rd.)
Braintree Rd. Dag ... 3G 57
Braintree Rd. Ruis ... 4K 41
Braintree St. E2 ... 3J 69
Braithwaite Av. Romf ... 7G 39
Braithwaite Gdns. Stan ... 1C 26
Braithwaite Ho. E14 ... 6F 71
Braithwaite Ho. EC1 ... 4D 68 (3E 162) (off Bunhill Row)
Braithwaite Rd. Enf ... 3G 9
Braithwaite Tower. W2 ... 5B 158
Bramah Grn. SW9 ... 1A 104
Bramah Tea & Coffee Mus. ... 6K 169
Bramalea Clo. N6 ... 6E 30
Bramall Clo. E15 ... 5H 53
Bramall Ct. N7 ... 5K 49 (off George's Rd.)
Bramber. WC1 ... 2E 160
Bramber Ct. W5 ... 4E 80
Bramber Rd. N12 ... 5H 15
Bramber Rd. W14 ... 6H 83
Brambleacres Clo. Sutt ... 7J 149
Bramblebury Rd. SE18 ... 5G 91
Bramble Clo. N15 ... 4G 33
Bramble Clo. Beck ... 5E 142
Bramble Clo. Croy ... 4C 154
Bramble Clo. Shep ... 3F 131
Bramble Clo. Stan ... 7J 11
Bramble Clo. Uxb ... 6B 58
Bramble Cft. Eri ... 4J 93
Brambledown Clo. W Wick ... 5G 143
Brambledown Rd. Cars & Wall ... 7E 150
Brambledown Rd. S Croy ... 7E 152
Bramble Gdns. W12 ... 7B 64
Bramble Ho. E3 ... 5C 70 (off Devons Rd.)
Bramble La. Hamp ... 6D 114
Brambles Clo. Iswth ... 7B 80
Brambles Farm Dri. Uxb ... 3C 58
Brambles, The. SW19 ... 5H 119 (off Woodside)
Brambles, The. W Dray ... 4A 76
Bramblewood Clo. Cars ... 1C 150
Brambling Ct. SE8 ... 6B 88 (off Abinger Gro.)
Bramblings, The. E4 ... 4A 20
Bramcote Av. Mitc ... 4D 138
Bramcote Gro. SE16 ... 5J 87
Bramcote Rd. SW15 ... 4D 100
Bramdean Cres. SE12 ... 1J 125
Bramdean Gdns. SE12 ... 1J 125
Bramerton. NW6 ... 7F 47 (off Willesden La.)
Bramerton Rd. Beck ... 3B 142
Bramerton St. SW3 ... 6C 84 (7C 170)
Bramfield Ct. N4 ... 3C 50 (off Queens Dri.)
Bramfield Rd. SW11 ... 6C 102
Bramford Ct. N14 ... 2C 16
Bramford Rd. SW18 ... 4A 102
Bramham Gdns. SW5 ... 5K 83
Bramham Gdns. Chess ... 4D 146
Bramham Ho. SE15 ... 3F 105
Bramhope La. SE7 ... 6K 89
Bramlands Clo. SW11 ... 3C 102
Bramley Av. Shep ... 3G 131
Bramley Clo. E17 ... 2A 34
Bramley Clo. N14 ... 5A 6
Bramley Clo. Eastc ... 3H 23
Bramley Clo. Hay ... 7J 59
Bramley Clo. Orp ... 7F 145
Bramley Clo. S Croy ... 5C 152
Bramley Clo. Twic ... 6G 97
Bramley Clo. Wfd G ... 7F 21
Bramley Ct. E4 ... 1K 19 (off Ridgeway, The)
Bramley Ct. Barn ... 4H 5
Bramley Ct. Mitc ... 2B 138
Bramley Ct. S'hall ... 7G 61 (off Baird Av.)
Bramley Ct. Well ... 1B 110
Bramley Cres. SW8 ... 7H 85
Bramley Cres. Ilf ... 6E 36
Bramley Hill. S Croy ... 5B 152
Bramley Ho. SW15 ... 6B 100 (off Tunworth Cres.)
Bramley Ho. W10 ... 6F 65
Bramley Ho. Houn ... 4D 96
Bramleyhyrst. S Croy ... 4C 152 (off Bramley Hill)
Bramley Pde. N14 ... 4B 6
Bramley Rd. N14 ... 5A 6
Bramley Rd. W5 ... 3C 80
Bramley Rd. W10 ... 6F 65 (in two parts)
Bramley Rd. Cheam ... 7F 149
Bramley Rd. Sutt ... 5B 150
Bramley Way. Houn ... 5D 96
Bramley Way. W Wick ... 2D 154
Brampton. WC1 ... 5K 67 (6G 161) (off Red Lion Sq.)
Brampton Clo. E5 ... 2H 51
Brampton Ct. NW4 ... 4D 28
Brampton Gdns. N15 ... 5C 32
Brampton Gro. NW4 ... 4D 28
Brampton Gro. Harr ... 4A 26
Brampton Gro. Wemb ... 1G 45
Brampton La. NW4 ... 4E 28
Brampton Pk. Rd. N8 ... 3A 32
Brampton Rd. E6 ... 3B 72
Brampton Rd. N15 ... 5C 32
Brampton Rd. NW9 ... 4G 27
Brampton Rd. SE2 & Bexh ... 6C 92
Brampton Rd. Croy ... 7F 141
Brampton Rd. Uxb ... 2D 58
Bramshaw Ri. N Mald ... 6A 136
Bramshaw Rd. E9 ... 6K 51
Bramshill Gdns. NW5 ... 3F 49
Bramshill Rd. NW10 ... 2B 64
Bramshot Av. SE7 ... 6J 89
Bramshurst. NW8 ... 1K 65 (off Abbey Rd.)
Bramston Rd. NW10 ... 2C 64
Bramston Rd. SW17 ... 3A 120
Bramwell Clo. Sun ... 2B 132
Bramwell Ho. SE1 ... 3C 86
Bramwell Ho. SW1 ... 5G 85 (6A 172) (off Churchill Gdns.)
Bramwell M. N1 ... 1K 67
Brancaster Dri. NW7 ... 7H 13
Brancaster Ho. E1 ... 3K 69 (off Moody St.)
Brancaster Rd. E12 ... 4D 54
Brancaster Rd. SW16 ... 3J 121
Brancaster Rd. Ilf ... 6J 37
Brancepeth Gdns. Buck H ... 2D 20
Branch Hill. NW3 ... 3A 48
Branch Hill Ho. NW3 ... 3K 47
Branch Pl. N1 ... 1D 68
Branch Rd. E14 ... 7A 70
Branch St. SE15 ... 7E 86
Brancker Clo. Wall ... 7J 151
Brancker Rd. Harr ... 3D 26
Brancroft Way. Enf ... 1F 9
Brand Clo. N4 ... 1B 50
Brandesbury Sq. Wfd G ... 7K 21
Brandlehow Rd. SW15 ... 4H 101
Brandon. NW9 ... 2B 28 (off Further Acre)
Brandon Est. SE17 ... 6B 86
Brandon Ho. Beck ... 5D 124 (off Beckenham Hill Rd.)
Brandon Mans. W14 ... 6G 83 (off Queen's Club Gdns.)
Brandon M. EC2 ... 6E 162
Brandon Rd. E17 ... 4E 34
Brandon Rd. N7 ... 7J 49
Brandon Rd. S'hall ... 5D 78
Brandon Rd. Sutt ... 4K 149
Brandon St. SE17 ... 4C 86 (in three parts)
Brandram M. SE13 ... 4G 107 (off Brandram Rd.)
Brandram Rd. SE13 ... 3G 107
Brandreth Ct. Harr ... 6K 25
Brandreth Rd. E6 ... 6D 72
Brandreth Rd. SW17 ... 2F 121
Brandries, The. Wall ... 3H 151
Brand St. SE10 ... 7E 88
Brandville Gdns. Ilf ... 4F 37
Brandville Rd. W Dray ... 2A 76
Brandy Way. Sutt ... 7J 149
Brangbourne Rd. Brom ... 5E 124
Brangton Rd. SE11 ... 5K 85 (6H 173)
Brangwyn Ct. W14 ... 3G 83 (off Blythe Rd.)
Brangwyn Cres. SW19 ... 1A 138
Branham Ho. SE18 ... 5F 91
Branksea St. SW6 ... 7G 83
Branksome Av. N18 ... 6A 18
Branksome Clo. Tedd ... 4H 115
Branksome Ho. SW8 ... 7K 85 (off Meadow Rd.)
Branksome Rd. SW2 ... 5J 103
Branksome Rd. SW19 ... 1J 137
Branksome Way. Harr ... 6F 27
Branksome Way. N Mald ... 1J 135
Branksone Ct. N2 ... 3A 30
Bransby Rd. Chess ... 6E 146
Branscombe. NW1 ... 1G 67 (off Plender St.)
Branscombe Ct. Brom ... 5H 143
Branscombe Gdns. N21 ... 7F 7
Branscombe St. SE13 ... 3D 106
Bransdale Clo. NW6 ... 1J 65
Bransgrove Rd. Edgw ... 1F 27
Branston Cres. Orp ... 7H 145
Branstone Rd. Rich ... 1F 99
Brants Wlk. W7 ... 4J 61
Brantwood Av. Eri ... 7J 93
Brantwood Av. Iswth ... 4A 98
Brantwood Clo. E17 ... 3D 34
Brantwood Gdns. Enf ... 4D 6
Brantwood Gdns. Ilf ... 4C 36
Brantwood Ho. SE5 ... 7C 86 (off Wyndam Est.)
Brantwood Rd. N17 ... 6B 18
Brantwood Rd. SE24 ... 5C 104
Brantwood Rd. Bexh ... 2H 111
Brantwood Rd. S Croy ... 7C 152
Branxholme Ct. Brom ... 1H 143 (off Highland Rd.)
Brasenose Dri. SW13 ... 6E 82
Brasher Clo. Gnfd ... 5H 43
Brassett Point. E15 ... 1G 71 (off Abbey Rd.)
Brassey Clo. Felt ... 1J 113
Brassey Ho. E14 ... 4D 88 (off Cahir St.)
Brassey Rd. NW6 ... 6H 47
Brassey Sq. SW11 ... 3E 102
Brassie Av. W3 ... 6A 64
Brass Talley All. SE16 ... 2K 87
Brasted Clo. SE26 ... 4J 123
Brasted Clo. Bexh ... 5D 110
Brasted Lodge. Beck ... 7C 124
Brathay. NW1 ... 2G 67 (1B 160) (off Ampthill Est.)
Brathway Rd. SW18 ... 7J 101
Bratley St. E1 ... 4G 69
Bratten Ct. Croy ... 6D 140
Braund Av. Gnfd ... 4F 61
Braundton Av. Sidc ... 1K 127
Braunston Dri. Hay ... 4C 60
Bravington Clo. Shep ... 5B 130
Bravington Pl. W9 ... 4H 65
Bravington Rd. W9 ... 2H 65
Brawne Ho. SE17 ... 6B 86 (off Brandon Est.)
Braxfield Rd. SE4 ... 4A 106
Braxted Pk. SW16 ... 6K 121
Bray. NW3 ... 7C 48
Brayards Rd. SE15 ... 2H 105
Brayards Rd. Est. SE15 ... 2J 105 (off Brayards Rd.)
Braybourne Dri. Iswth ... 7K 79
Braybrooke Gdns. SE19 ... 7E 122
Braybrook St. W12 ... 5B 64
Brayburne Av. SW4 ... 2G 103
Bray Ct. SW16 ... 5J 121
Braycourt Av. W on T ... 7K 131
Bray Cres. SE16 ... 2K 87
Braydon Rd. N16 ... 1G 51
Bray Dri. E16 ... 7H 71
Brayfield Ter. N1 ... 7A 50
Brayford Sq. E1 ... 6J 69
Bray Pas. E16 ... 7J 71
Bray Pl. SW3 ... 4D 84 (4E 170)
Bray Rd. NW7 ... 6A 14
Brayton Gdns. Enf ... 4C 6
Braywood Rd. SE9 ... 4H 109
Brazil Clo. Bedd ... 7J 139
Breach La. Dag ... 3G 75
Bread St. EC4 ... 6C 68 (1D 168) (in two parts)
Breakspear Crematorium. Ruis ... 5E 22
Breakspear Ho. Ruis ... 5F 23
Breakspear M. Hare ... 3A 22
Breakspear Rd. Ruis ... 7D 22
Breakspear Rd. N. Hare ... 3A 22
Breakspear Rd. S. Uxb & Hare ... 3B 40
Breakspears Dri. Orp ... 7A 128 & 1K 145
Breakspears M. SE4 ... 2B 106
Breakspears Rd. SE4 ... 4B 106
Bream Clo. N17 ... 4H 33
Bream Gdns. E6 ... 3E 72
Breamore Clo. SW15 ... 1C 118
Breamore Ho. SE15 ... 7G 87 (off Friary Est.)
Breamore Rd. Ilf ... 2K 55
Bream's Bldgs. EC4 ... 6A 68 (7J 161)
Bream St. E3 ... 7C 52
Breamwater Gdns. Rich ... 3B 116
Brearley Clo. Edgw ... 7D 12
Brearley Clo. Uxb ... 6A 40
Breasley Clo. SW15 ... 4D 100
Breasy Pl. NW4 ... 4D 28 (off Burroughs Gdns.)
Brechin Pl. SW7 ... 4A 84
Brecknock Rd. N19 & N7 ... 4G 49
Brecknock Rd. Est. N19 ... 4G 49
Breckonmead. Brom ... 2A 144
Brecon Clo. Mitc ... 3J 139
Brecon Clo. Wor Pk ... 2E 148
Brecon Grn. NW9 ... 6A 28
Brecon Ho. W2 ... 6A 66 (off Hallfield Est.)
Brecon M. NW5 ... 5H 49
Brecon Rd. W6 ... 6G 83
Brecon Rd. Enf ... 4D 8
Brede Clo. E6 ... 3E 72
Bredel Ho. E14 ... 5C 70 (off St Paul's Way)
Bredgar Rd. N19 ... 2G 49
Bredhurst Clo. SE20 ... 6J 123
Bredo Ho. Bark ... 3B 74
Bredon Rd. Croy ... 7F 141
Breer St. SW6 ... 3K 101
Breezers Ct. E1 ... 7G 69 (off Highway, The)
Breezer's Hill. E1 ... 7G 69
Brember Rd. Harr ... 2G 43
Bremer M. E17 ... 4D 34
Bremner Rd. SW7 ... 3A 84 (1A 170)
Brenchley Clo. Brom ... 6H 143
Brenchley Clo. Chst ... 1E 144
Brenchley Gdns. SE23 ... 6J 105
Brenchley Rd. Orp ... 2K 145
Brenda Rd. SW17 ... 2D 120
Brende Gdns. W Mol ... 4F 133
Brendon Av. NW10 ... 4A 46
Brendon Clo. Hay ... 7E 76
Brendon Ct. S'hall ... 4F 79
Brendon Gdns. Harr ... 4F 43
Brendon Gdns. Ilf ... 5J 37
Brendon Gro. N2 ... 2A 30
Brendon Rd. SE9 ... 2H 127
Brendon Rd. Dag ... 1F 57
Brendon St. W1 ... 6C 66 (7D 158)
Brendon Vs. N21 ... 1H 17
Brendon Way. Enf ... 7K 7
Brenley Clo. Mitc ... 3E 138
Brenley Gdns. SE9 ... 4B 108
Brenley Ho. SE1 ... 2D 86 (6E 168) (off Tennis St.)
Brennand Ct. N19 ... 3G 49
Brent Clo. Bex ... 1E 128
Brentcot Clo. W13 ... 4B 62
Brent Ct. NW11 ... 7F 29
Brent Ct. W7 ... 7H 61
Brent Cres. NW10 ... 2F 63
Brent Cross. ... 7E 28
Brent Cross Fly-Over. NW4 ... 7F 29
Brent Cross Gdns. NW4 ... 6F 29
Brent Cross Interchange. (Junct.) ... 6E 28
Brent Cross Shop. Cen. NW4 ... 7E 28
Brentfield. NW10 ... 7H 45
Brentfield Clo. NW10 ... 6K 45
Brentfield Gdns. NW2 ... 7F 29
Brentfield Ho. NW10 ... 7K 45
Brentfield Rd. NW10 ... 6K 45
Brentford. ... 6D 80
Brentford Bus. Cen. Bren ... 7C 80
Brentford Clo. Hay ... 4B 60
Brentford End. ... 7B 80
Brentford F.C. (Griffin Pk.) ... 6D 80
Brentford Ho. Twic ... 7B 98
Brentford Musical Mus. ... 6E 80
Brent Grn. NW4 ... 5E 28
Brent Grn. Wlk. Wemb ... 3J 45
Brentham Way. W5 ... 4D 62
Brent Ho. E9 ... 6J 51 (off Frampton Pk. Rd.)
Brenthouse Rd. E9 ... 7J 51
Brenthurst Rd. NW10 ... 6B 46
Brent Lea. Bren ... 7C 80
Brentmead Clo. W7 ... 7J 61
Brentmead Gdns. NW10 ... 2F 63
Brentmead Pl. NW11 ... 6F 29
Brent New Enterprise Cen. NW10 ... 6B 46
Brenton St. E14 ... 6A 70
Brent Pk. Ind. Est. S'hall ... 3K 77
Brent Pk. Rd. NW4 ... 7D 28 (in two parts)
Brent Pl. Barn ... 5C 4
Brent Rd. E16 ... 6J 71
Brent Rd. SE18 ... 7F 91
Brent Rd. Bren ... 6C 80
Brent Rd. S'hall ... 3A 78
Brent Rd. S Croy ... 7H 153
Brent Side. Bren ... 6C 80
Brentside Clo. W13 ... 4A 62
Brentside Executive Cen. Bren ... 6B 80

Brent St. NW4 4E 28
Brent Ter. NW2 1E 46 (in two parts)
Brent Trad. Cen. NW10 5A 46
Brentvale Av. S'hall 1H 79
Brentvale Av. Wemb 1F 63
Brent Vw. Rd. NW9 6C 28
Brentwaters Bus. Pk. Bren 7C 80
Brent Way. N3 6D 14
Brent Way. Bren 7D 80
Brent Way. Wemb 6H 45
Brentwick Gdns. Bren 4E 80
Brentwood Clo. SE9 1G 127
Brentwood Ho. SE18 7B 90 (off Portway Gdns.)
Brentwood Lodge. NW4 5F 29 (off Holmdale Gdns.)
Brereton Rd. N17 7A 18
Bressenden Pl. SW1 3F 85 (1K 171)
Bressey Av. Enf 1B 8
Bressey Gro. E18 2H 35
Breton Highwalk. EC1 5C 68 (5D 162) (off Golden La.)
Breton Ho. EC1 4D 162
Breton Ho. SE1 3F 87 (7J 169) (off Abbey St.)
Brett Clo. N16 2E 50
Brett Clo. N'holt 3B 60
Brett Ct. N9 2D 18
Brett Cres. NW10 1K 63
Brettell St. SE17 5D 86
Brettenham Av. E17 1C 34
Brettenham Rd. E17 2C 34
Brettenham Rd. N18 4B 18
Brett Gdns. Dag 7E 56
Brett Ho. Clo. SW15 7F 101
Brettinghurst. SE1 5G 87 (off Avondale Sq.)
Brett Pas. E8 5H 51
Brett Rd. E8 5H 51
Brewer's Grn. SW1 1C 172
Brewer's Hall Garden. EC2 5C 68 (6D 162) (off London Wall)
Brewers La. Rich 5D 98
Brewer St. W1 7G 67 (2B 166)
Brewery Clo. Wemb 5A 44
Brewery Ind. Est., The. N1 2C 68 (1D 162) (off Wenlock Rd.)
Brewery La. Twic 7K 97
Brewery M. Cen. Iswth 3A 98
Brewery Rd. N7 7J 49
Brewery Rd. SE18 5H 91
Brewery Rd. Brom 1C 156
Brewery Sq. SE1 5J 169
Brewery, The. Romf 5K 39
Brewhouse La. E1 1H 87
Brewhouse Rd. SE18 4D 90
Brewhouse St. SW15 3G 101
Brewhouse Wlk. SE16 1A 88
Brewhouse Yd. EC1 4B 68 (3A 162)
Brewin Ter. Hay 5A 60
Brewood Rd. Dag 6B 56
Brewster Gdns. W10 5E 64
Brewster Ho. E14 7B 70 (off Three Colt St.)
Brewster Ho. SE1 4F 87 (off Dunton Rd.)
Brewster Rd. E10 1D 52
Brian Rd. Romf 5C 38
Briant Ho. SE1 2J 173
Briants Clo. Pinn 2D 24
Briant St. SE14 1K 105
Briar Av. SW16 7K 121
Briarbank Rd. W13 6A 62
Briar Clo. N2 3K 29
Briar Clo. N13 3H 17
Briar Clo. Buck H 2G 21
Briar Clo. Hamp 5D 114
Briar Clo. Iswth 5K 97
Briar Ct. SW15 4D 100
Briar Ct. Sutt 4E 148
Briar Cres. N'holt 6F 43
Briardale Gdns. NW3 3J 47
Briarfield Av. N2 3K 29
Briarfield Av. N3 2K 29
Briar Gdns. Brom 1H 155
Briaris Clo. N17 7C 18
Briar La. Croy 4D 154
Briar Rd. NW2 4E 46
Briar Rd. SW16 3J 139
Briar Rd. Bex 3K 129
Briar Rd. Harr 5C 26
Briar Rd. Shep 5B 130
Briar Rd. Twic 1J 115
Briars, The. Bush 1D 10
Briar Wlk. SW15 4D 100
Briar Wlk. W10 4G 65
Briar Wlk. Edgw 7D 12
Briar Way. W Dray 2C 76
Briarwood Clo. NW9 6J 27
Briarwood Clo. Felt 4G 113
Briarwood Ct. Wor Pk 1C 148 (off Avenue, The)
Briarwood Dri. N'wd 2J 23
Briarwood Rd. SW4 5H 103
Briarwood Rd. Eps 6C 148
Briary Clo. NW3 7C 48
Briary Ct. Sidc 5B 128
Briary Gdns. Brom 5K 125
Briary Gro. Edgw 2H 27
Briary La. N9 3A 18
Briary Lodge. Beck 1E 142
Brickbarn Clo. SW10 7A 84 (off King's Barn)
Brick Ct. EC4 6A 68 (1J 167)
Brickett Clo. Ruis 5E 22
Brick Farm Clo. Rich 1H 99
Brickfield Clo. Bren 7C 80
Brickfield Cotts. SE18 7K 91
Brickfield Cotts. Chst 5E 126
Brickfield La. Hay 6F 77
Brickfield Rd. SW19 4K 119
Brickfield Rd. T Hth 1B 140
Brickfields. Harr 2H 43 (in two parts)
Brickfields Way. W Dray 3B 76
Brick La. E2 & E1 3F 69 (2K 163)
Brick La. Enf 2C 8
Brick La. Stan 7J 11
Brick Lane Music Hall. 3E 68 (2H 163) (off Curtain Rd.)
Bricklayer's Arms. (Junct.) 4D 86
Bricklayers Arms Bus. Cen. SE1 4E 86
Brick St. W1 1F 85 (5J 165)
Brickwall La. Ruis 1G 41
Brickwood Clo. SE26 3H 123
Brickwood Rd. Croy 2E 152
Brideale Clo. SE15 6F 87
Bride Ct. EC4 1A 168
Bride La. EC4 6B 68 (1A 168)
Bridel M. N1 1B 68 (off Colebrook Row)
Bride St. N7 6K 49
Bridewain St. SE1 3F 87 (7J 169) (in two parts)
Bridewell Pl. E1 1H 87
Bridewell Pl. EC4 6B 68 (1A 168)
Bridewell, The. (Theatre) 6B 68 (1A 168) (off Bridewell Pl.)
Bridford M. W1 5F 67 (5K 159)
Bridge App. NW1 7E 48
Bridge Av. W6 4E 82
Bridge Av. W7 5H 61
Bridge Av. Mans. W6 5E 82 (off Bridge Av.)
Bridge Clo. W10 6F 65
Bridge Clo. Enf 2C 8
Bridge Clo. Tedd 4K 115
Bridge Clo. W on T 7H 131
Bridge Ct. E10 1B 52
Bridgedown Golf Course. 1A 4
Bridge Dri. N13 4E 16
Bridge End. E17 1E 34
Bridgefield Rd. Sutt 6J 149
Bridgefoot. SE1 5J 85 (6F 173)
Bridgefoot. Sun 1H 131
Bridge Gdns. Ashf 7E 112
Bridge Gdns. E Mol 4H 133
Bridge Ga. N21 7H 7
Bridge Ho. E9 6K 51 (off Shepherds La.)
Bridge Ho. NW3 7E 48 (off Adelaide Rd.)
Bridge Ho. NW10 2F 65 (off Chamberlayne Rd.)
Bridge Ho. SE4 4B 106
Bridge Ho. SW1 5F 85 (5J 171) (off Ebury Bri.)
Bridge Ho. Sutt 6K 149 (off Bridge Rd.)
Bridgehouse Ct. SE1 2B 86 (7A 168) (off Blackfriars Rd.)
Bridge Ho. Quay. E14 1E 88
Bridgeland Rd. E16 7J 71
Bridge La. NW11 4G 29
Bridge La. SW11 1C 102
Bridgeman Ho. E9 7J 51 (off Frampton Pk. Rd.)
Bridgeman Rd. N1 7K 49
Bridgeman Rd. Tedd 6A 116
Bridgeman St. NW8 2C 66
Bridge Meadows. SE14 6K 87
Bridgen. 7E 110
Bridgend Rd. SW18 4A 102
Bridgenhall Rd. Enf 1A 8
Bridgen Ho. E1 6H 69 (off Nelson St.)
Bridgen Rd. Bex 7E 110
Bridge Pde. N21 7H 7 (off Ridge Av.)
Bridgepark. SW18 5J 101
Bridge Pl. SW1 4F 85 (3K 171)
Bridge Pl. Croy 1D 152
Bridgeport Pl. E1 1G 87
Bridge Rd. E6 7D 54
Bridge Rd. E15 7F 53
Bridge Rd. E17 7B 34
Bridge Rd. N9 3B 18
Bridge Rd. N22 1J 31
Bridge Rd. NW10 6A 46
Bridge Rd. Beck 7B 124
Bridge Rd. Bexh 2E 110
Bridge Rd. Chess 5E 146
Bridge Rd. E Mol 4H 133
Bridge Rd. Houn & Iswth 3H 97
Bridge Rd. S'hall 2D 78
Bridge Rd. Sutt 6K 149
Bridge Rd. Twic 6B 98
Bridge Rd. Wall 5F 151
Bridge Rd. Wemb 3G 45
Bridge Row. Croy 1D 152
Bridges Ct. SW11 3B 102 (in two parts)
Bridges Ho. SE5 7D 86 (off Elmington Est.)
Bridgeside Ho. N1 2C 68 (off Wharf Rd.)
Bridges La. Croy 4J 151
Bridges Pl. SW6 1H 101
Bridges Rd. SW19 6K 119
Bridges Rd. Stan 5E 10
Bridges Rd. M. SW19 6K 119
Bridge St. SW1 2J 85 (7E 166)
Bridge St. W4 4K 81
Bridge St. Pinn 3C 24
Bridge St. Rich 5D 98
Bridge St. W on T 7G 131
Bridge Ter. E15 7F 53 (in two parts)
Bridge, The. Harr 4K 25
Bridgetown Clo. SE19 5E 122
Bridge Vw. W6 5E 82
Bridgewalk Heights. SE1 2D 86 (6F 169) (off Weston St.)
Bridgewater Clo. Chst 3J 145
Bridgewater Gdns. Edgw 2F 27
Bridgewater Highwalk. EC2 5C 162
Bridgewater Rd. E15 1E 70
Bridgewater Rd. Ruis 4J 41
Bridgewater Rd. Wemb 6C 44
Bridgewater Sq. EC2 5C 68 (5C 162)
Bridgewater St. EC2 5C 68 (5C 162)
Bridge Way. N11 3B 16
Bridge Way. NW11 5H 29
Bridgeway. Bark 7K 55
Bridge Way. Twic 7G 97
Bridge Way. Uxb 5D 40
Bridge Way. Wemb 7E 44
Bridgeway St. NW1 2G 67
Bridge Wharf. E2 2K 69
Bridge Wharf Rd. Iswth 3B 98
Bridgewood Clo. SE20 7H 123
Bridgewood Rd. SW16 7H 121
Bridgewood Rd. Wor Pk 4C 148
Bridge Yd. SE1 1D 86 (4F 169)
Bridgford St. SW18 3A 120
Bridgman Rd. W4 3J 81
Bridgnorth Ho. SE15 6G 87 (off Friary Est.)
Bridgwater Ho. W2 6A 66 (off Hallfield Est.)
Bridle Clo. Eps 5K 147
Bridle Clo. King T 4D 134
Bridle Clo. Sun 3J 131
Bridle La. W1 7G 67 (2B 166)
Bridle La. Twic 6B 98
Bridle Path. Croy 3J 151 (in two parts)
Bridle Path, The. Wfd G 7B 20
Bridlepath Way. Felt 1G 113
Bridle Rd. Clay 6B 146
Bridle Rd. Croy 3C 154 (in two parts)
Bridle Rd. Pinn 6K 23
Bridle Rd. S Croy 7G 153
Bridle Way. Croy 4C 154
Bridleway, The. Wall 5G 151
Bridlington Rd. N9 7C 8
Bridport. SE17 5D 86 (off Date St.)
Bridport Av. Romf 6H 39
Bridport Ho. N1 1D 68 (off Bridport Pl.)
Bridport Pl. N1 1D 68 (in two parts)
Bridport Rd. N18 5K 17
Bridport Rd. Gnfd 1F 61
Bridport Rd. T Hth 3A 140
Bridstow Pl. W2 6J 65
Brief St. SE5 1B 104
Brierfield. NW1 1G 67 (off Arlington Rd.)
Brierley. New Ad 6D 154 (in two parts)
Brierley Av. N9 1D 18
Brierley Clo. SE25 4G 141
Brierley Ct. W7 7J 61
Brierley Rd. E11 4F 53
Brierley Rd. SW12 2G 121
Brierly Gdns. E2 2J 69
Brigade Clo. Harr 2H 43
Brigade St. SE3 2H 107 (off Tranquil Va.)
Brigadier Av. Enf 1H 7
Brigadier Hill. Enf 1H 7
Briggeford Clo. E5 2G 51
Briggs Clo. Mitc 1F 139
Briggs Ho. E2 3F 69 (1K 163) (off Chambord St.)
Bright Clo. Belv 4D 92
Brightfield Rd. SE12 5G 107
Brightling Rd. SE4 6B 106
Brightlingsea Pl. E14 7B 70
Brightman Rd. SW18 1B 120
Brighton Av. E17 5B 34
Brighton Bldgs. SE1 3E 86 (off Tower Bri. Rd.)
Brighton Clo. Uxb 7D 40
Brighton Dri. N'holt 6E 42
Brighton Gro. SE14 1A 106
Brighton Rd. E6 3E 72 (in two parts)
Brighton Rd. N2 2A 30
Brighton Rd. N16 4E 50
Brighton Rd. S Croy 5C 152
Brighton Rd. Surb 6C 134
Brighton Rd. Sutt 7K 149
Brighton Ter. SW9 4K 103
Brightside Rd. SE13 6F 107
Brightside, The. Enf 1E 8
Bright St. E14 6D 70
Brightwell Clo. Croy 1A 152
Brightwell Cres. SW17 5D 120
Brig M. SE8 6C 88
Brigstock Ho. SE5 2C 104
Brigstock Rd. Belv 4H 93
Brigstock Rd. T Hth 5A 140
Brill Pl. NW1 2H 67 (1D 160)
Brim Hill. N2 4A 30
Brimpsfield Clo. SE2 3B 92 (in two parts)
Brimsdown. 2F 9
Brimsdown Av. Enf 2F 9
Brimsdown Ho. E3 4D 70
Brimsdown Ind. Est. Enf 1G 9 (in two parts)
Brimstone Ho. E15 7G 53 (off Victoria St.)
Brindle Ga. Sidc 1J 127
Brindley Clo. Bexh 3G 111
Brindley Clo. Gnfd 1D 62
Brindley St. SE14 1B 106
Brindley Way. Brom 5J 125
Brindley Way. S'hall 7F 61
Brindwood Rd. E4 3G 19
Brinkburn Clo. SE2 4A 92
Brinkburn Clo. Edgw 3H 27
Brinkburn Gdns. Edgw 3G 27
Brinkley Rd. Wor Pk 2D 148
Brinklow Cres. SE18 7F 91
Brinklow Ho. W2 5K 65 (off Torquay St.)
Brinkworth Rd. Ilf 3C 36
Brinkworth Way. E9 6B 52
Brinsdale Rd. NW4 3F 29
Brinsley Ho. E1 6J 69 (off Tarling St.)
Brinsley Rd. Harr 2H 25
Brinsley St. E1 6H 69
Brinsworth Clo. Twic 1H 115
Brinsworth Ho. Twic 2H 115
Brinton Wlk. SE1 5A 168
Brion Pl. E14 5E 70
Brisbane Av. SW19 1K 137
Brisbane Ho. W12 7D 64 (off White City Est.)
Brisbane Rd. E10 2D 52
Brisbane Rd. W13 2A 80
Brisbane Rd. Ilf 7F 37
Brisbane St. SE5 7D 86
Briscoe Clo. E11 2H 53
Briscoe Rd. SW19 6B 120
Briset Rd. SE9 3B 108
Briset St. EC1 5B 68 (5A 162)
Briset Way. N7 2K 49
Bristol Clo. Stanw 6A 94
Bristol Clo. Wall 7J 151
Bristol Ct. Stanw 6A 94
Bristol Gdns. SW15 7E 100
Bristol Gdns. W9 4K 65
Bristol Ho. SE11 2J 173
Bristol Ho. Bark 7A 56 (off Margaret Bondfield Av.)

Bristol M. W9 . . . 4K 65
Bristol Pk. Rd. E17 . . . 4A 34
Bristol Rd. E7 . . . 6A 54
Bristol Rd. Gnfd . . . 1F 61
Bristol Rd. Mord . . . 5A 138
Briston Gro. N8 . . . 6J 31
Briston M. NW7 . . . 7H 13
Bristowe Clo. SW2 . . . 6A 104
Bristow Rd. SE19 . . . 5E 122
Bristow Rd. Bexh . . . 1E 110
Bristow Rd. Croy . . . 4J 151
Bristow Rd. Houn . . . 3G 97
***Britain Vis. Cen.* . . . 1H 85 (4C 166) (off Regent St.)**
Britannia Bus. Cen. NW2 . . . 4F 47
Britannia Clo. SW4 . . . 4H 103
Britannia Clo. N'holt . . . 3B 60
Britannia Ct. W Dray . . . 3A 76
Britannia Ga. E16 . . . 1J 89
Britannia Junction. (Junct.) . . . 7F 49
Britannia La. Twic . . . 7G 97
Britannia Rd. E14 . . . 4C 88
Britannia Rd. N12 . . . 3F 15
Britannia Rd. SW6 . . . 7K 83 (in two parts)
Britannia Rd. Ilf . . . 3F 55
Britannia Rd. Surb . . . 7F 135
Britannia Row. N1 . . . 1B 68
Britannia St. WC1 . . . 3K 67 (1G 161)
Britannia Wlk. N1 . . . 2D 68 (1E 162) (in two parts)
Britannia Way. NW10 . . . 4H 63
Britannia Way. SW6 . . . 7K 83 (off Britannia Rd.)
Britannia Way. Stanw . . . 7A 94
Britannic Highwalk. EC2 . . . 5D 68 (6E 162) (off Moor La.)
Britannic Tower. EC2 . . . 5E 162
British Gro. W4 . . . 5B 82
British Gro. Pas. W4 . . . 5B 82
British Gro. S. W4 . . . 5B 82
British Legion Rd. E4 . . . 2C 20
***British Library.* . . . 3H 67 (1D 160)**
***British Mus.* . . . 5J 67 (6E 160)**
British St. E3 . . . 3B 70
British Telecom Cen. EC1 . . . 6C 68 (7C 162) (off Newgate St.)
British Wharf Ind. Est. SE14 . . . 5K 87
Britley Ho. E14 . . . 6B 70 (off Copenhagen Pl.)
Brittain Ho. SE9 . . . 1C 126
Brittain Rd. Dag . . . 3E 56
Brittany Point. SE11 . . . 4A 86 (4J 173)
Britten Clo. NW11 . . . 1K 47
Britten Ct. E15 . . . 2F 71
Britten Dri. S'hall . . . 6E 60
Britten St. SW3 . . . 5C 84 (6C 170)
Britton Clo. SE6 . . . 7F 107
Britton St. EC1 . . . 4B 68 (4A 162)
Brixham Cres. Ruis . . . 1J 41
Brixham Gdns. Ilf . . . 5J 55
Brixham Rd. Well . . . 1D 110
Brixham St. E16 . . . 1E 90
Brixton. . . . 4K 103
Brixton Hill. SW2 . . . 7J 103
Brixton Hill Ct. SW2 . . . 5K 103
Brixton Hill Pl. SW2 . . . 7J 103
Brixton Oval. SW9 . . . 4A 104
Brixton Rd. SW9 & SE11 . . . 4A 104 (7J 173)
Brixton Sta. Rd. SW9 . . . 3A 104
Brixton Water La. SW2 . . . 5K 103
Broadacre Clo. Uxb . . . 3D 40
Broadbent Clo. N6 . . . 1F 49
Broadbent St. W1 . . . 7F 67 (2J 165)
Broadbridge Clo. SE3 . . . 7J 89
Broadbury Ct. N18 . . . 6C 18
Broad Comn. Est. N16 . . . 1G 51 (off Osbaldeston Rd.)
Broadcoombe. S Croy . . . 7K 153
Broad Ct. WC2 . . . 6J 67 (1F 167)
Broadcroft Av. Stan . . . 2D 26
Broadcroft Rd. Orp . . . 7H 145
Broadeaves Clo. S Croy . . . 5E 152
Broadfield. NW6 . . . 6K 47
Broadfield Clo. NW2 . . . 3E 46
Broadfield Clo. Croy . . . 2K 151
Broadfield Ct. Bus H . . . 2D 10
Broadfield Ct. N Har . . . 1F 25 (off Broadfields)
Broadfield Heights. Edgw . . . 4C 12
Broadfield La. NW1 . . . 7J 49
Broadfield Pde. Edgw . . . 3C 12 (off Glengall Rd.)
Broadfield Rd. SE6 . . . 7G 107
Broadfields. E Mol . . . 6J 133
Broadfields. Harr . . . 2F 25
Broadfields Av. N21 . . . 6F 7
Broadfields Av. Edgw . . . 4C 12
Broadfield Sq. Enf . . . 2C 8
Broadfields Way. NW10 . . . 5B 46
Broadfield Way. Buck H . . . 3F 21
Broadford Ho. E1 . . . 4A 70 (off Commodore St.)
Broadgate. EC2 . . . 5E 68 (6G 163) (off Broadgate Cir.)
Broadgate Circ. EC2 . . . 5E 68 (6G 163)
Broadgate Rd. E16 . . . 6B 72
Broadgates Av. Barn . . . 1E 4
Broadgates Ct. SE11 . . . 5A 86 (6K 173) (off Cleaver St.)
Broadgates Rd. SW18 . . . 1B 120
Broad Green. . . . 7B 140
Broad Grn. Av. Croy . . . 7B 140
Broadhead Strand. NW9 . . . 2B 28
Broadheath Dri. Chst . . . 5D 126
Broadhinton Rd. SW4 . . . 3F 103
Broadhurst Av. Edgw . . . 4C 12
Broadhurst Av. Ilf . . . 4K 55
Broadhurst Clo. NW6 . . . 6A 48
Broadhurst Clo. Rich . . . 5F 99
Broadhurst Gdns. NW6 . . . 6K 47
Broadhurst Gdns. Ruis . . . 2A 42
Broadlands. E17 . . . 3A 34
Broadlands. Hanw . . . 3E 114
Broadlands Av. SW16 . . . 2J 121
Broadlands Av. Enf . . . 3C 8
Broadlands Av. Shep . . . 6E 130
Broadlands Clo. N6 . . . 7E 30
Broadlands Clo. SW16 . . . 2J 121
Broadlands Clo. Enf . . . 3D 8
Broadlands Ct. Rich . . . 7G 81 (off Kew Gdns. Rd.)
Broadlands Lodge. N6 . . . 7D 30
Broadlands Rd. N6 . . . 7D 30
Broadlands Rd. Brom . . . 4K 125
Broadlands Way. N Mald . . . 6B 136
Broad La. EC2 . . . 5E 68 (5G 163) (in two parts)
Broad La. N8 . . . 5K 31
Broad La. N15 . . . 4F 33
Broad La. Hamp . . . 7D 114
Broad Lawn. SE9 . . . 2E 126
Broadlawns Ct. Harr . . . 1K 25
Broadley St. NW8 . . . 5B 66 (5B 158)
Broadley Ter. NW1 . . . 4C 66 (4D 158)
Broadmayne. SE17 . . . 5D 86 (off Portland St.)
Broadmead. SE6 . . . 3C 124
Broadmead. W14 . . . 4G 83
Broadmead Av. Wor Pk . . . 7C 136
Broadmead Clo. Hamp . . . 6E 114
Broadmead Clo. Pinn . . . 1C 24
Broadmead Ct. Wfd G . . . 6D 20
Broadmead Rd. Hay & N'holt . . . 4C 60
Broadmead Rd. Wfd G . . . 6D 20
Broadoak. Sun . . . 6H 113
Broad Oak. Wfd G . . . 5E 20
Broad Oak Clo. E4 . . . 5H 19
Broadoak Ct. SW9 . . . 3A 104
Broadoak Ho. NW6 . . . 1K 65 (off Mortimer Cres.)
Broadoak Rd. Eri . . . 7K 93
Broadoaks. Surb . . . 2H 147
Broadoaks Way. Brom . . . 5H 143
Broad Sanctuary. SW1 . . . 2H 85 (7D 166)
Broadstone Ho. SW8 . . . 7K 85 (off Dorset Rd.)
Broadstone Pl. W1 . . . 5E 66 (6G 159)
Broad St. Dag . . . 7G 57
Broad St. Tedd . . . 6K 115
Broad St. Av. EC2 . . . 5E 68 (6G 163)
Broad St. Mkt. Dag . . . 7G 57
Broad St. Pl. EC2 . . . 6F 163
Broad Vw. NW9 . . . 6G 27
Broadview Rd. SW16 . . . 7H 121
Broadwalk. E18 . . . 3H 35
Broad Wlk. N21 . . . 2E 16
Broad Wlk. NW1 . . . 1E 66 (1H 159)
Broad Wlk. SE3 . . . 2A 108
Broad Wlk. W1 . . . 7D 66 (3F 165)
Broadwalk. Harr . . . 5E 24
Broad Wlk. Houn . . . 1B 96
Broad Wlk. Rich . . . 7F 81
Broadwalk Clo. E14 . . . 1E 88 (off Broadwalk Pl.)
Broadwalk Ct. W8 . . . 1J 83 (off Palace Gdns. Ter.)
Broadwalk Ho. EC2 . . . 4E 68 (5G 163)
Broadwalk Ho. SW7 . . . 2A 84 (off Hyde Pk. Ga.)
Broad Wlk. La. NW11 . . . 7H 29
Broadwalk Shop. Cen. Edgw . . . 6C 12
Broad Wlk., The. W8 . . . 1K 83
Broad Wlk., The. E Mol . . . 4K 133
Broadwalk, The. N'wd . . . 2E 22
Broadwall. SE1 . . . 1A 86 (4K 167)
Broadwater Farm Est. N17 . . . 2D 32
Broadwater Rd. N17 . . . 1E 32
Broadwater Rd. SE28 . . . 3H 91
Broadwater Rd. SW17 . . . 4C 120
Broadway. E13 . . . 2K 71
Broadway. E15 . . . 7F 53 (in two parts)
Broadway. SW1 . . . 3H 85 (7C 166)
Broadway. W7 . . . 1J 79
Broadway. W13 . . . 1A 80
Broadway. Bark . . . 1G 73
Broadway. Bexh . . . 4E 110 (in three parts)
Broadway Arc. W6 . . . 4E 82 (off Hammersmith B'way.)
Broadway Av. Croy . . . 5D 140
Broadway Av. Twic . . . 6B 98
Broadway Cen., The. W6 . . . 4E 82
Broadway Chambers. W6 . . . 4E 82 (off Hammersmith B'way.)
Broadway Clo. Wfd G . . . 6E 20
Broadway Ct. SW19 . . . 6J 119
Broadway Ct. Beck . . . 3E 142
Broadway Gdns. Mitc . . . 4C 138
Broadway Gdns. Wfd G . . . 6E 20
Broadway Ho. E8 . . . 1H 69
Broadway Ho. Brom . . . 5F 125 (off Bromley Rd.)
Broadway Mkt. E8 . . . 1H 69
Broadway Mkt. SW17 . . . 4D 120
Broadway Mkt. Ilf . . . 2H 37 (in two parts)
Broadway Mkt. M. E8 . . . 1G 69
Broadway M. N13 . . . 5E 16
Broadway M. N16 . . . 7F 33 (in two parts)
Broadway M. N21 . . . 1G 17
Broadway Pde. E4 . . . 6K 19
Broadway Pde. N8 . . . 6J 31
Broadway Pde. Harr . . . 5F 25
Broadway Pde. Hay . . . 1J 77
Broadway Pl. SW19 . . . 6H 119
Broadway Shop. Cen. Bexh . . . 4G 111
Broadway Shop. Mall. SW1 . . . 3H 85 (1C 172)
Broadway Sq. Bexh . . . 4G 111
Broadway, The. E4 . . . 6A 20
Broadway, The. N8 . . . 6J 31
Broadway, The. N9 . . . 3B 18
Broadway, The. N11 . . . 5K 15 (off Stanford Rd.)
Broadway, The. N14 . . . 1C 16 (off Southgate Cir.)
Broadway, The. N22 . . . 2A 32
Broadway, The. NW7 . . . 7H 13 (off Colenso Dri.)
Broadway, The. NW7 . . . 5F 13 (Watford Way)
Broadway, The. NW9 . . . 6B 28
Broadway, The. SW14 . . . 2A 100
Broadway, The. SW19 . . . 6H 119
Broadway, The. W3 . . . 2G 81
Broadway, The. W5 . . . 7D 62
Broadway, The. Cheam . . . 6G 149
Broadway, The. Croy . . . 4J 151
Broadway, The. Dag . . . 2F 57
Broadway, The. Gnfd . . . 4G 61
Broadway, The. N'wd . . . 2J 23
Broadway, The. S'hall . . . 7B 60
Broadway, The. Stan . . . 5H 11
Broadway, The. Sutt . . . 5A 150
Broadway, The. Th Dit . . . 7J 133
Broadway, The. W'stone . . . 2J 25
Broadway, The. Wemb . . . 3E 44
Broadway, The. Wfd G . . . 6E 20
Broadway Theatre, The. . . . 7D 106 (off Catford Broadway)
Broadwell Ct. Houn . . . 1B 96 (off Springwell Rd.)
Broadwick St. W1 . . . 7G 67 (2B 166)
Broadwood Av. Ruis . . . 6G 23
Broadwood Ter. W14 . . . 4H 83 (off Warwick Rd.)
Broad Yd. EC1 . . . 4B 68 (4A 162)
Brocas Clo. NW3 . . . 7C 48
Brockbridge Ho. SW15 . . . 6B 100
Brockdene Dri. Kes . . . 4B 156
Brockdish Av. Bark . . . 5K 55
Brockenhurst. W Mol . . . 5D 132
Brockenhurst Av. Wor Pk . . . 1A 148
Brockenhurst Gdns. NW7 . . . 5F 13
Brockenhurst Gdns. Ilf . . . 5G 55
Brockenhurst M. N18 . . . 4B 18
Brockenhurst Rd. Croy . . . 7H 141
Brockenhurst Way. SW16 . . . 2H 139
Brocket Ho. SW8 . . . 2H 103
Brockham Clo. SW19 . . . 5H 119
Brockham Cres. New Ad . . . 7F 155
Brockham Dri. SW2 . . . 7K 103
Brockham Dri. Ilf . . . 6F 37
Brockham Ho. NW1 . . . 1G 67 (off Bayham Pl.)
Brockham Ho. SW2 . . . 7K 103 (off Brockham Dri.)
Brockham St. SE1 . . . 3C 86 (7D 168)
Brockhurst Clo. Stan . . . 6E 10
Brockill Cres. SE4 . . . 4A 106
Brocklebank Ho. E16 . . . 1E 90 (off Glenister St.)
Brocklebank Ind. Est. SE7 . . . 4J 89
Brocklebank Rd. SE7 . . . 4K 89
Brocklebank Rd. SW18 . . . 7A 102
Brocklehurst St. SE14 . . . 7K 87
Brocklesby Rd. SE25 . . . 4H 141
Brockley. . . . 4B 106
Brockley Av. Stan . . . 3K 11
Brockley Clo. Stan . . . 4K 11
Brockley Cres. Romf . . . 1J 39
Brockley Cross. SE4 . . . 3A 106
Brockley Cross Bus. Cen. SE4 . . . 3A 106
Brockley Footpath. SE4 . . . 5A 106 (in two parts)
Brockley Footpath. SE15 . . . 4J 105
Brockley Gdns. SE4 . . . 2B 106
Brockley Gro. SE4 . . . 5B 106
Brockley Hall Rd. SE4 . . . 5A 106
Brockley Hill. Stan . . . 1H 11
Brockley M. SE4 . . . 5A 106
Brockley Pk. SE23 . . . 7A 106
Brockley Ri. SE23 . . . 1A 124
Brockley Rd. SE4 . . . 3B 106
Brockley Side. Stan . . . 4K 11
Brockley Vw. SE23 . . . 7A 106
Brockley Way. SE4 . . . 5K 105
Brockman Ri. Brom . . . 4F 125
Brockmer Ho. E1 . . . 7H 69 (off Crowder St.)
Brock Pl. E3 . . . 4D 70
Brock Rd. E13 . . . 5K 71
Brocks Dri. Sutt . . . 3G 149
Brockshot Clo. Bren . . . 5D 80
Brock St. SE15 . . . 3J 105
Brockway Clo. E11 . . . 2G 53
Brockweir. E2 . . . 2J 69 (off Cyprus St.)
Brockwell Clo. Orp . . . 5K 145
Brockwell Ct. SW2 . . . 5A 104
Brockwell Ho. SE11 . . . 6K 85 (7H 173) (off Vauxhall St.)
Brockwell Pk. Gdns. SE24 . . . 7A 104
Brockwell Pk. Row. SW2 . . . 7A 104
Brodia Rd. N16 . . . 3E 50
Brodie Ho. SE1 . . . 5F 87 (off Cooper's Rd.)
Brodie Rd. E4 . . . 1K 19
Brodie Rd. Enf . . . 1H 7
Brodie St. SE1 . . . 5F 87
Brodlove La. E1 . . . 7K 69
Brodrick Gro. SE2 . . . 4B 92
Brodrick Rd. SW17 . . . 2C 120
Brograve Gdns. Beck . . . 2D 142
Broken Wharf. EC4 . . . 7C 68 (2C 168)
Brokesley St. E3 . . . 3B 70
Broke Wlk. E8 . . . 1F 69
Bromar Rd. SE5 . . . 3E 104
Bromefield. Stan . . . 1C 26
Bromell's Rd. SW4 . . . 4G 103
Brome Rd. SE9 . . . 3D 108
Bromfelde Rd. SW4 . . . 3H 103
Bromfelde Wlk. SW4 . . . 2H 103
Bromfield St. N1 . . . 1A 68
Bromhall Rd. Dag . . . 6B 56
Bromhead Rd. E1 . . . 6J 69 (off Jubilee St.)
Bromhead St. E1 . . . 6J 69
Bromhedge. SE9 . . . 3D 126
Bromholm Rd. SE2 . . . 3B 92
Bromleigh Ct. SE23 . . . 2G 123
Bromleigh Ho. SE1 . . . 3F 87 (7J 169) (off Abbey St.)
Bromley. . . . 3D 70 (Bow)
Bromley. . . . 2J 143 (Chislehurst)
Bromley Av. Brom . . . 7G 125
Bromley Common. . . . 1C 156
Bromley Comn. Brom . . . 4A 144
Bromley Cres. Brom . . . 3H 143
Bromley Cres. Ruis . . . 4H 41
Bromley F.C. . . . 5K 143
Bromley Gdns. Brom . . . 3H 143
Bromley Gro. Brom . . . 2F 143

Bromley Hall Rd. E14 5E 70
Bromley High St. E3 3D 70
Bromley Hill. Brom 6G 125
Bromley Ind. Cen. Brom 3B 144 (off Waldo Rd.)
Bromley La. Chst 7G 127
Bromley Park. 1G 143
Bromley Pk. Brom 1H 143
Bromley Pl. W1 5G 67 (5A 160)
Bromley Rd. E10 6D 34
Bromley Rd. E17 3C 34
Bromley Rd. N17 1F 33
Bromley Rd. N18 3J 17
Bromley Rd. SE6 & Brom 1D 124
Bromley Rd. Beck & Short 1D 142
Bromley Rd. Chst 1F 145
Bromley St. E1 5K 69
Brompton. 3C 84 (2D 170)
Brompton Arc. SW3 7E 164
Brompton Clo. SE20 2G 141
Brompton Clo. Houn 5D 96
Brompton Gro. N2 4C 30
Brompton Pk. Cres. SW6 6K 83
Brompton Pl. SW3 3C 84 (1D 170)
Brompton Rd. SW3 & SW1 4C 84 (3C 170)
Brompton Sq. SW3 3C 84 (1C 170)
Brompton Ter. SE18 1D 108
Bromwich Av. N6 2E 48
Bromyard Av. W3 7A 64
Bromyard Ho. SE15 7H 87 (off Commercial Way)
Bron Ct. NW6 1J 65
Brondesbury. 7H 47
Brondesbury Ct. NW2 6F 47
Brondesbury M. NW6 7J 47
Brondesbury Park. 1G 65
Brondesbury Pk. NW2 & NW6 6D 46
Brondesbury Rd. NW6 2H 65
Brondesbury Vs. NW6 2H 65
Bronhill Ter. N17 1G 33
Bronsart Rd. SW6 7G 83
Bronson Rd. SW20 2F 137
Bronte Clo. E7 4J 53
Bronte Clo. Eri 7H 93
Bronte Clo. Ilf 4E 36
Bronte Ct. W14 3F 83 (off Girdler's Rd.)
Bronte Ho. N16 5E 50
Bronte Ho. NW6 3J 65
Bronte Ho. SW4 7G 103
Bronti Clo. SE17 5C 86
Bronwen Ct. NW8 3B 66 (2A 158) (off Grove End Rd.)
Bronze Age Way. Belv & Eri 2H 93
Bronze St. SE8 7C 88
Brook Av. Dag 7H 57
Brook Av. Edgw 6C 12
Brook Av. Wemb 3G 45
Brookbank Av. W7 5H 61
Brookbank Rd. SE13 3C 106
Brook Clo. NW7 7B 14
Brook Clo. SW17 2E 120
Brook Clo. SW20 3D 136
Brook Clo. W5 1G 81
Brook Clo. Ruis 7G 23
Brook Clo. Stanw 7B 94
Brook Ct. E11 3G 53
Brook Ct. E15 5D 52 (off Clays La.)
Brook Ct. E17 3A 34
Brook Ct. SE12 3A 126
Brook Ct. Beck 1B 142
Brook Ct. Edgw 5C 12
Brook Cres. E4 4H 19
Brook Cres. N18 4C 18
Brookdale. N11 4B 16
Brookdale Rd. E17 3C 34
Brookdale Rd. SE6 7D 106 (in two parts)
Brookdale Rd. Bex 6E 110
Brookdales. NW4 4G 29
Brookdene Rd. SE18 4J 91
Brook Dri. SE11 3A 86 (2K 173)
Brook Dri. Harr 4G 25
Brook Dri. Ruis 7G 23
Brooke Av. Harr 3G 43
Brooke Clo. Bush 1B 10
Brooke Ho. SE14 1A 106
Brookehowse Rd. SE6 2C 124
Brookend Rd. Sidc 1J 127
Brooke Rd. E5 3G 51
Brooke Rd. E17 4E 34
Brooke Rd. N16 3F 51
Brooke's Ct. EC1 5A 68
Brooke's Mkt. EC1 5K 161
Brooke St. EC1 5A 68 (6J 161)
Brooke Way. Bush 1B 10
Brookfield. N6 3E 48
Brookfield Av. E17 4E 34
Brookfield Av. NW7 6J 13
Brookfield Av. W5 4D 62
Brookfield Av. Sutt 4C 150
Brookfield Clo. NW7 6J 13
Brookfield Ct. Gnfd 3G 61
Brookfield Cres. NW7 6J 13
Brookfield Cres. Harr 5E 26
Brookfield Gdns. Clay 6A 146
Brookfield Pk. NW5 3F 49
Brookfield Path. Wfd G 6B 20
Brookfield Rd. E9 6A 52
Brookfield Rd. N9 3B 18
Brookfield Rd. W4 2K 81
Brookfields. Enf 4E 8
Brookfields Av. Mitc 5C 138
Brook Gdns. E4 4J 19
Brook Gdns. SW13 3B 100
Brook Gdns. King T 1J 135
Brook Ga. W1 7D 66 (3F 165)
Brook Green. 4F 83
Brook Grn. W6 3F 83
Brook Grn. Flats. W14 3F 83 (off Dunsany Rd.)
Brookhill Clo. SE18 5F 91
Brookhill Clo. E Barn 5H 5
Brookhill Rd. SE18 6F 91
Brookhill Rd. Barn 5H 5
Brook Ho. W6 4E 82 (off Shepherd's Bush Rd.)
Brookhouse Gdns. E4 4B 20
Brook Houses. NW1 2G 67 (off Cranleigh St.)
Brook Ind. Est. Hay 1B 78
Brooking Rd. E7 5J 53
Brookland Clo. NW11 4J 29
Brookland Gth. NW11 4J 29
Brookland Hill. NW11 4K 29
Brookland Ri. NW11 4J 29
Brooklands App. Romf 4K 39
Brooklands Av. SW19 2K 119
Brooklands Av. Sidc 2H 127
Brooklands Clo. Romf 4K 39
Brooklands Clo. Sun 1G 131
Brooklands Ct. N21 5J 7
Brooklands Ct. NW6 7H 47
Brooklands Ct. King T 4D 134 (off Surbiton Rd.)
Brooklands Ct. Mitc 2B 138
Brooklands Dri. Gnfd 1C 62
Brooklands La. Romf 4K 39 (in two parts)
Brooklands Pk. SE3 3J 107
Brooklands Pas. SW8 1H 103
Brooklands Rd. Romf 4K 39
Brooklands Rd. Th Dit 1A 146
Brooklands, The. Iswth 1H 97
Brook La. SE3 2K 107
Brook La. Bex 6D 110
Brook La. Brom 6J 125
Brook La. Bus. Cen. Bren 5D 80
Brook La. N. Bren 5D 80 (in three parts)
Brooklea Clo. NW9 1A 28
Brook Lodge. Romf 4K 39 (off Medora Rd.)
Brooklyn Av. SE25 4H 141
Brooklyn Clo. Cars 2C 150
Brooklyn Gro. SE25 4H 141
Brooklyn Rd. SE25 4H 141
Brooklyn Rd. Brom 5B 144
Brookmarsh Ind. Est. SE8 7D 88
Brook Mead. Eps 6A 148
Brookmead Av. Brom 5D 144
Brookmead Ind. Est. Croy 6G 139
Brook Mdw. N12 3E 14
Brook Mdw. Clo. Wfd G 6B 20
Brookmead Rd. Croy 6G 139
Brook M. WC2 6H 67 (1D 166)
Brook M. N. W2 7A 66 (2A 164)
Brookmill Rd. SE8 1C 106
Brook Pde. Chig 3K 21
Brook Pk. Clo. N21 5G 7
Brook Pl. Barn 5D 4
Brook Ri. Chig 3K 21
Brook Rd. N2 7H 15
Brook Rd. N8 4J 31
Brook Rd. N22 3K 31
Brook Rd. NW2 2B 46
Brook Rd. Buck H 2D 20
Brook Rd. Ilf 6J 37
Brook Rd. Surb 2E 146
Brook Rd. T Hth 4C 140
Brook Rd. Twic 6A 98
Brook Rd. S. Bren 6D 80
Brooks Av. E6 4D 72
Brooksbank St. E9 6J 51
Brooksby M. N1 7A 50
Brooksby St. N1 7A 50
Brooksby's Wlk. E9 5K 51
Brooks Clo. SE9 2E 126
Brooks Ct. SW8 7G 85
Brookscroft. E17 3D 34 (off Forest Rd.)
Brookscroft Rd. E17 1D 34 (in two parts)
Brookshill. Harr 5C 10
Brookshill Av. Harr 5C 10
Brookshill Dri. Harr 5C 10
Brookside. N21 6E 6
Brookside. Cars 5E 150
Brookside. E Barn 6H 5
Brookside. Orp 7K 145
Brookside. Uxb 7B 40
Brookside Clo. Barn 6B 4
Brookside Clo. Felt 3J 113
Brookside Clo. Kent 5D 26
Brookside Clo. S Harr 4C 42
Brookside Cres. Wor Pk 1C 148
Brookside Rd. N9 4C 18 (in two parts)
Brookside Rd. N19 2G 49
Brookside Rd. NW11 6G 29
Brookside Rd. Hay 7A 60
Brookside S. E Barn 7K 5
Brookside Wlk. N12 6D 14
Brookside Wlk. NW11 4G 29
Brookside Way. Croy 6K 141
Brooks La. W4 6G 81
Brooks Lodge. N1 2E 68 (off Hoxton St.)
Brooks M. W1 7F 67 (2J 165)
Brooks Rd. E13 1J 71
Brooks Rd. W4 5G 81
Brook St. N17 2F 33
Brook St. W1 7F 67 (2J 165)
Brook St. W2 7B 66 (2B 164)
Brook St. Belv & Eri 5H 93
Brook St. King T 2E 134
Brooksville Av. NW6 1G 65
Brooks Wlk. N3 3G 29
Brook Va. Eri 1H 111
Brookview Ct. Enf 5K 7
Brookview Rd. SW16 5G 121
Brookville Rd. SW6 7H 83
Brook Wlk. N2 1B 30
Brook Wlk. Edgw 6E 12
Brookway. SE3 3J 107
Brook Way. Chig 3K 21
Brookwood Av. SW13 2B 100
Brookwood Clo. Brom 4H 143
Brookwood Ho. SE1 2B 86 (7B 168) (off Webber St.)
Brookwood Rd. SW18 1H 119
Brookwood Rd. Houn 2F 97
Broom Clo. Brom 6C 144
Broom Clo. Tedd 7D 116
Broomcroft Av. N'holt 3A 60
Broome Rd. Hamp 7D 114
Broome Way. SE5 7D 86
Broomfield. E17 7B 34
Broomfield. NW1 7E 48 (off Ferdinand St.)
Broomfield. Sun 1J 131
Broomfield Av. N13 5E 16
Broomfield Ct. SE16 3G 87 (off Ben Smith Way)
Broomfield Ho. SE17 4E 86 (off Massinger St.)
Broomfield Ho. Stan 3F 11 (off Stanmore Hill)
Broomfield La. N13 4D 16
Broomfield Pl. W13 1B 80
Broomfield Rd. N13 5D 16
Broomfield Rd. W13 1B 80
Broomfield Rd. Beck 3A 142
Broomfield Rd. Bexh 5G 111
Broomfield Rd. Rich 1F 99
Broomfield Rd. Romf 7D 38
Broomfield Rd. Surb 1F 147
Broomfield Rd. Tedd 6C 116
Broomfield St. E14 5C 70
Broom Gdns. Croy 3C 154
Broomgrove Gdns. Edgw 1G 27
Broomgrove Rd. SW9 2K 103
Broomhall Rd. S Croy 7D 152
Broom Hill. 7K 145
Broomhill Ct. Wfd G 6D 20
Broom Hill Ri. Bexh 5G 111
Broomhill Rd. SW18 5J 101
Broomhill Rd. Ilf 2A 56
Broomhill Rd. Orp 7K 145
Broomhill Rd. Wfd G 6D 20 (in two parts)
Broomhill Wlk. Wfd G 6C 20
Broomhouse La. SW6 2J 101
Broomhouse Rd. SW6 2J 101
Broomleigh. Brom 1J 143 (off Tweedy Rd.)
Broomloan La. Sutt 2J 149
Broom Lock. Tedd 6C 116
Broom Mead. Bexh 6G 111
Broom Pk. Tedd 7D 116
Broom Rd. Croy 3C 154
Broom Rd. Tedd 5B 116
Broomsleigh Bus. Pk. SE26 5B 124
Broomsleigh St. NW6 5H 47
Broom Water. Tedd 6C 116
Broom Water W. Tedd 5C 116
Broomwood Clo. Bex 2K 129
Broomwood Clo. Croy 5K 141
Broomwood Rd. SW11 6D 102
Broseley Gro. SE26 5A 124
Broster Gdns. SE25 3F 141
Brougham Rd. E8 1G 69
Brougham Rd. W3 6J 63
Brougham St. SW11 2D 102
Brough Clo. SW8 7J 85
Brough Clo. King T 5D 116
Broughton Av. N3 3G 29
Broughton Av. Rich 3B 116
Broughton Ct. W13 7B 62
Broughton Dri. SW9 4A 104
Broughton Gdns. N6 6G 31
Broughton Rd. SW6 2K 101
Broughton Rd. W13 7B 62
Broughton Rd. T Hth 6A 140
Broughton St. SW8 2E 102
Broughton St. Ind. Est. SW11 2E 102
Brouncker Rd. W3 2J 81
Browells La. Felt 2K 113 (in two parts)
Brown Bear Ct. Felt 4B 114
Brown Clo. Wall 7J 151
Browne Ho. SE8 7C 88 (off Deptford Chu. St.)
Brownfield Area. E14 6D 70
Brownfield St. E14 6D 70
Browngraves Rd. Hay 7E 76
Brown Hart Gdns. W1 7E 66 (2H 165)
Brownhill Rd. SE6 7D 106
Browning Av. W7 6K 61
Browning Av. Sutt 4C 150
Browning Av. Wor Pk 1D 148
Browning Clo. E17 4E 34
Browning Clo. W9 4A 66 (4A 158)
Browning Clo. Col R 1F 39
Browning Clo. Hamp 4D 114
Browning Clo. Well 1J 109
Browning Ho. SE14 1A 106 (off Loring Rd.)
Browning Ho. W12 6E 64 (off Wood La.)
Browning M. W1 5F 67 (6H 159)
Browning Rd. E11 7H 35
Browning Rd. E12 5D 54
Browning Rd. Enf 1J 7
Browning St. SE17 5C 86
Browning Way. Houn 1B 96
Brownlea Gdns. Ilf 2A 56
Brownlow Ct. N2 5A 30
Brownlow Ct. N11 6D 16 (off Brownlow Rd.)
Brownlow Ho. SE16 2G 87 (off George Row)
Brownlow M. WC1 4K 67 (4H 161)
Brownlow Rd. E7 4J 53
Brownlow Rd. E8 1F 69
Brownlow Rd. N3 7E 14
Brownlow Rd. N11 6D 16
Brownlow Rd. NW10 7A 46
Brownlow Rd. W13 1A 80
Brownlow Rd. Croy 4E 152
Brownlow St. WC1 5K 67 (6H 161)
Brownrigg Rd. Ashf 4C 112
Browns Arc. W1 7G 67 (3B 166) (off Regent St.)
Brown's Bldgs. EC3 6E 68 (1H 169)
Browns La. NW5 5F 49
Brownspring Dri. SE9 4F 127
Browns Rd. E17 3C 34
Brown's Rd. Surb 7F 135
Brown St. W1 6D 66 (7E 158)
Brownswell Rd. N2 2B 30
Brownswood Park. 2B 50
Brownswood Rd. N4 3B 50
Broxash Rd. SW11 6E 102
Broxbourne Av. E18 4K 35
Broxbourne Rd. E7 3J 53
Broxbourne Rd. Orp 7K 145
Broxholme Ho. SW6 1K 101 (off Harwood Rd.)
Broxholm Rd. SE27 3A 122
Broxted Rd. SE23 2B 124
Broxwood Way. NW8 1C 66
Bruce Av. Shep 6E 130
Bruce Castle Ct. N17 1F 33 (off Lordship La.)
Bruce Castle Mus. 1E 32
Bruce Castle Rd. N17 1F 33
Bruce Clo. W10 5F 65
Bruce Clo. Well 1B 110
Bruce Ct. Sidc 4K 127

Bruce Gdns. N20 . . . . 3J 15
Bruce Gro. N17 . . . . 1E 32
Bruce Hall M. SW17 . . . . 4E 120
Bruce Ho. W10 . . . . 5F 65
Bruce Rd. E3 . . . . 3D 70
Bruce Rd. NW10 . . . . 7K 45
Bruce Rd. SE25 . . . . 4D 140
Bruce Rd. Barn 3B 4
Bruce Rd. Harr 2J 25
Bruce Rd. Mitc 7E 120
Bruckner St. W10 . . . . 3G 65
Brudenell Rd. SW17 . . . . 3D 120
Bruffs Mdw. N'holt 6C 42
Bruges Pl. NW1 . . . . 7G 49 (off Randolph St.)
Brumfield Rd. Eps 5J 147
Brummel Clo. Bexh 3J 111
Brune Ho. E1 . . . . 6J 163
Brunei Gallery. . . . 5H 67 (5D 160)
Brunel Clo. SE19 . . . . 6F 123
Brunel Clo. Houn 7K 77
Brunel Clo. N'holt 3D 60
Brunel Est. W2 . . . . 5J 65
Brunel Ho. E14 . . . . 5D 88 (off Ship Yd.)
Brunel Pl. S'hall 6F 61
Brunel Rd. E17 . . . . 6A 34
Brunel Rd. SE16 . . . . 2J 87
Brunel Rd. W3 . . . . 5A 64
Brunel Rd. Wfd G 5J 21
Brunel Science Pk. Uxb 3A 58
Brunel St. E16 . . . . 6H 71
Brunel University. (Borough Rd., Isleworth) 7J 79
Brunel University. (St Margaret's Rd.) 4B 98
Brunel University. (Uxbridge) 3A 58
Brunel Wlk. N15 . . . . 4E 32
Brunel Wlk. Twic 7E 96
Brune St. E1 . . . . 5F 69 (6J 163)
Brunlees Ho. SE1 . . . . 3C 86 (off Bath Ter.)
Brunner Clo. NW11 . . . . 5K 29
Brunner Ho. SE6 . . . . 4E 124
Brunner Rd. E17 . . . . 5A 34
Brunner Rd. W5 . . . . 4D 62
Bruno Pl. NW9 . . . . 2J 45
Brunswick Av. N11 . . . . 3K 15 (in two parts)
Brunswick Cen. WC1 . . . . 4J 67 (3E 160)
Brunswick Clo. Bexh 4D 110
Brunswick Clo. Pinn 6C 24
Brunswick Clo. Th Dit 1A 146
Brunswick Clo. Twic 3H 115
Brunswick Clo. Est. EC1 . . . . 3B 68 (2A 162)
Brunswick Ct. EC1 . . . . 3B 68 (2A 162) (off Tompion St.)
Brunswick Ct. SE1 . . . . 2E 86 (7H 169)
Brunswick Ct. SW1 . . . . 4H 85 (4D 172) (off Regency St.)
Brunswick Ct. Barn 5G 5
Brunswick Ct. Sutt 4K 149
Brunswick Cres. N11 . . . . 3K 15
Brunswick Gdns. W5 . . . . 4E 62
Brunswick Gdns. W8 . . . . 1J 83
Brunswick Gdns. Ilf 1G 37
Brunswick Gro. N11 . . . . 3K 15
Brunswick Ho. E2 . . . . 2F 69 (off Thurtle Rd.)
Brunswick Ho. N3 . . . . 1H 29
Brunswick Ho. SE16 . . . . 3A 88 (off Brunswick Quay)
Brunswick Ind. Pk. N11 . . . . 4A 16
Brunswick Mans. WC1 . . . . 4J 67 (3F 161) (off Handel St.)

Brunswick M. SW16 . . . . 6H 121
Brunswick M. W1 . . . . 6D 66 (7F 159)
Brunswick Park. 3K 15
Brunswick Pk. SE5 . . . . 1E 104
Brunswick Pk. Gdns. N11 . . . . 2K 15
Brunswick Pk. Rd. N11 . . . . 2K 15
Brunswick Pl. N1 . . . . 3D 68 (2F 163)
Brunswick Pl. NW1 . . . . 4E 66 (4H 159) (in two parts)
Brunswick Pl. SE19 . . . . 7G 123
Brunswick Quay. SE16 . . . . 3K 87
Brunswick Rd. E10 . . . . 1E 52
Brunswick Rd. E14 . . . . 6E 70
Brunswick Rd. N15 . . . . 4E 32 (in two parts)
Brunswick Rd. W5 . . . . 4D 62
Brunswick Rd. Bexh 4D 110
Brunswick Rd. Enf 1H 9
Brunswick Rd. King T 1G 135
Brunswick Rd. Sutt 4K 149
Brunswick Sq. N17 . . . . 6A 18
Brunswick Sq. WC1 . . . . 4J 67 (3F 161)
Brunswick St. E17 . . . . 5E 34
Brunswick Vs. SE5 . . . . 1E 104
Brunswick Way. N11 . . . . 4A 16
Brunton Pl. E14 . . . . 6A 70
Brushfield St. E1 . . . . 5E 68 (5H 163) (in two parts)
Brussels Rd. SW11 . . . . 4B 102
Bruton Clo. Chst 7D 126
Bruton La. W1 . . . . 7F 67 (3K 165)
Bruton Pl. W1 . . . . 7F 67 (3K 165)
Bruton Rd. Mord 4A 138
Bruton St. W1 . . . . 7F 67 (3K 165)
Bruton Way. W13 . . . . 5A 62
Brutus Ct. SE11 . . . . 4B 86 (off Kennington La.)
Bryan Av. NW10 . . . . 7D 46
Bryan Clo. Sun 7J 113
Bryan Ho. NW10 . . . . 7D 46
Bryan Ho. SE16 . . . . 2B 88
Bryan Rd. SE16 . . . . 2B 88
Bryan's All. SW6 . . . . 2K 101
Bryanston Av. Twic 1F 115
Bryanston Clo. S'hall 4D 78
Bryanston Ct. W1 . . . . 7E 158 (in two parts)
Bryanstone Ct. Sutt 3A 150
Bryanstone Rd. N8 . . . . 6H 31
Bryanston Mans. W1 . . . . 5D 66 (5E 158) (off York St.)
Bryanston M. E. W1 . . . . 5D 66 (6E 158)
Bryanston M. W. W1 . . . . 5D 66 (6E 158)
Bryanston Pl. W1 . . . . 5D 66 (6E 158)
Bryanston Sq. W1 . . . . 6D 66 (6E 158)
Bryanston St. W1 . . . . 6D 66 (1E 164)
Bryant Clo. Barn 5C 4
Bryant Ct. E2 . . . . 2F 69 (off Whiston Rd., in two parts)
Bryant Ct. W3 . . . . 1K 81
Bryant Rd. N'holt 3A 60
Bryant St. E15 . . . . 7F 53
Bryantwood Rd. N7 . . . . 5A 50
Brycedale Cres. N14 . . . . 4B 16
Bryce Ho. SE14 . . . . 6K 87 (off John Williams Clo.)
Bryce Rd. Dag 4C 56
Brydale Ho. SE16 . . . . 4K 87 (off Rotherhithe New Rd.)
Bryden Clo. SE26 . . . . 5A 124
Brydges Pl. WC2 . . . . 7J 67 (3E 166)
Brydges Rd. E15 . . . . 5F 53
Brydon Wlk. N1 . . . . 1J 67
Bryer Ct. EC2 . . . . 5C 162

Bryet Rd. N7 . . . . 3J 49
Bryher Ct. SE11 . . . . 5J 173
Brymay Clo. E3 . . . . 2C 70
Brynmaer Rd. SW11 . . . . 1D 102
Brynmawr Rd. Enf 4A 8
Bryony Clo. Uxb 5B 58
Bryony Rd. W12 . . . . 7C 64
Bryony Way. Sun 6J 113
Buccleugh Ho. E5 . . . . 7G 33
Buchanan Clo. N21 . . . . 5E 6
Buchanan Ct. SE16 . . . . 4K 87 (off Worgan St.)
Buchanan Gdns. NW10 . . . . 2D 64
Buchan Rd. SE15 . . . . 3J 105
Bucharest Rd. SW18 . . . . 7A 102
Buckden Clo. N2 . . . . 4D 30
Buckden Clo. SE12 . . . . 6J 107
Buckfast Ct. W13 . . . . 7A 62
Buckfast Rd. Mord 4K 137
Buckfast St. E2 . . . . 3G 69
Buck Hill Wlk. W2 . . . . 7B 66 (3B 164)
Buckhold Rd. SW18 . . . . 6J 101
Buckhurst Av. Cars 1C 150
Buckhurst Ct. Buck H . . . . 2G 21 (off Albert Rd.)
Buckhurst Hill. 2G 21
Buckhurst Hill Ho. Buck H 2E 20
Buckhurst Ho. N7 . . . . 5H 49
Buckhurst St. E1 . . . . 4H 69
Buckhurst Ter. Buck H 1G 21
Buckhurst Way. Buck H 4G 21
Buckingham Arc. WC2 . . . . 3E 166
Buckingham Av. N20 . . . . 7F 5
Buckingham Av. Felt 6K 95
Buckingham Av. Gnfd 1A 62
Buckingham Av. T Hth 1A 140
Buckingham Av. Well 4J 109
Buckingham Av. W Mol 2F 133
Buckingham Chambers. SW1 . . . . 4G 85 (3B 172) (off Greencoat Pl.)
Buckingham Clo. W5 . . . . 5C 62
Buckingham Clo. Enf 2K 7
Buckingham Clo. Hamp 5D 114
Buckingham Clo. Orp 7J 145
Buckingham Ct. NW4 . . . . 3C 28
Buckingham Ct. W7 . . . . 4K 61 (off Copley Clo.)
Buckingham Ct. N'holt 2C 60
Buckingham Dri. Chst 4G 127
Buckingham Gdns. Edgw 7K 11
Buckingham Gdns. T Hth 2A 140
Buckingham Gdns. W Mol 2F 133
Buckingham Ga. SW1 . . . . 3G 85 (1A 172)
Buckingham Gro. Uxb 2C 58
Buckingham La. SE23 . . . . 7A 106
Buckingham Mans. NW6 . . . . 5K 47 (off W. End La.)
Buckingham M. N1 . . . . 6E 50
Buckingham M. NW10 . . . . 2B 64
Buckingham M. SW1 . . . . 1A 172
Buckingham Palace. 2F 85 (7K 165)
Buckingham Pal. Rd. SW1 . . . . 4F 85 (4J 171)
Buckingham Pde. Stan 5H 11
Buckingham Pl. SW1 . . . . 3G 85 (1A 172)
Buckingham Rd. E10 . . . . 3D 52
Buckingham Rd. E11 . . . . 5A 36
Buckingham Rd. E15 . . . . 5H 53
Buckingham Rd. E18 . . . . 1H 35
Buckingham Rd. N1 . . . . 6E 50
Buckingham Rd. N22 . . . . 1J 31
Buckingham Rd. NW10 . . . . 2B 64
Buckingham Rd. Edgw 7A 12
Buckingham Rd. Hamp 4D 114
Buckingham Rd. Harr 5H 25
Buckingham Rd. Ilf 2H 55
Buckingham Rd. King T 4F 135

Buckingham Rd. Mitc 4J 139
Buckingham Rd. Rich 2D 116
Buckingham St. WC2 . . . . 7J 67 (4F 167)
Buckingham Way. Wall 7G 151
Buckland Ct. N1 . . . . 2E 68 (off St Johns Est.)
Buckland Ct. Ick 2E 40
Buckland Cres. NW3 . . . . 7B 48
Buckland Ri. Pinn 1A 24
Buckland Rd. E10 . . . . 2E 52
Buckland Rd. Chess 5F 147
Bucklands Rd. Tedd 6C 116
Buckland St. N1 . . . . 2D 68
Buckland's Wharf. King T 2D 134
Buckland Wlk. W3 . . . . 2J 81
Buckland Wlk. Mord 4A 138
Buckland Way. Wor Pk 1E 148
Buck La. NW9 . . . . 5K 27
Bucklebury. NW1 . . . . 4G 67 (3A 160) (off Stanhope St.)
Buckleigh Av. SW20 . . . . 3G 137
Buckleigh Rd. SW16 . . . . 6H 121
Buckleigh Way. SE19 . . . . 7F 123
Buckler Gdns. SE9 . . . . 3D 126
Bucklers All. SW6 . . . . 6H 83 (in two parts)
Bucklersbury. EC4 . . . . 1E 168
Bucklersbury Pas. EC2 & EC4 . . . . 6D 68
Buckler's Way. Cars 3D 150
Buckles Ct. Belv 4D 92
Buckle St. E1 . . . . 6F 69 (7K 163)
Buckley Clo. SE23 . . . . 7H 105
Buckley Ct. NW6 . . . . 7H 47
Buckley Rd. NW6 . . . . 7H 47
Buckmaster Clo. SW9 . . . . 3A 104 (off Stockwell Pk. Rd.)
Buckmaster Ho. N7 . . . . 4K 49
Buckmaster Rd. SW11 . . . . 4C 102
Bucknall St. WC2 . . . . 6J 67 (7D 160)
Bucknall Way. Beck 4D 142
Bucknell Clo. SW9 . . . . 4K 103
Buckner Rd. SW2 . . . . 4K 103
Bucknill Ho. SW1 . . . . 5F 85 (5J 171) (off Ebury Bri. Rd.)
Buckrell Rd. E4 . . . . 2A 20
Buckridge Ho. EC1 . . . . 5A 68 (5J 161) (off Portpool La.)
Buckstone Clo. SE23 . . . . 6J 105
Buckstone Rd. N18 . . . . 5B 18
Buck St. NW1 . . . . 7F 49
Buckters Rents. SE16 . . . . 1A 88
Buckthorne Rd. SE4 . . . . 5A 106
Buckthorn Ho. Sidc . . . . 3K 127 (off Longlands Rd.)
Buck Wlk. E17 . . . . 4F 35
Buckwheat Ct. Eri 3D 92
Budd Clo. N12 . . . . 4E 14
Buddings Circ. Wemb 3J 45
Budd's All. Twic 5C 98
Bude Clo. E17 . . . . 5B 34
Budge La. Mitc 7D 138
Budge Row. EC4 . . . . 7D 68 (1E 168)
Budge's Wlk. W2 . . . . 3A 164
Budleigh Cres. Well 1C 110
Budleigh Ho. SE15 . . . . 7G 87 (off Bird in Bush Rd.)
Budoch Ct. Ilf 2A 56
Budoch Dri. Ilf 2A 56
Buer Rd. SW6 . . . . 2G 101
Bugsby's Way. SE10 & SE7 . . . . 4H 89
Bugsby's Way Retail Est. SE7 . . . . 4J 89 (off Bugsby's Way)
Bulbarrow. NW8 . . . . 1K 65 (off Abbey Rd.)

Bulganak Rd. T Hth 4C 140
Bulinga St. SW1 . . . . 4E 172
Bullace Row. SE5 . . . . 1D 104
Bull All. Well 3B 110
Bullard Rd. Tedd 6J 115
Bullard's Pl. E2 . . . . 3K 69
Bullbanks Rd. Belv 4J 93
Bulleid Way. SW1 . . . . 4F 85 (4K 171)
Bullen Ho. E1 . . . . 4H 69 (off Collingwood St.)
Bullen St. SW11 . . . . 2C 102
Buller Clo. SE15 . . . . 7G 87
Buller Rd. N17 . . . . 2G 33
Buller Rd. N22 . . . . 2A 32
Buller Rd. NW10 . . . . 3F 65
Buller Rd. Bark 7J 55
Buller Rd. T Hth 2D 140
Bullers Clo. Sidc 5E 128
Bullers Wood Dri. Chst 7D 126
Bullescroft Rd. Edgw 3B 12
Bullingham Mans. W8 . . . . 2J 83 (off Pitt St. La.)
Bull Inn Ct. WC2 . . . . 3F 167
Bullivant St. E14 . . . . 7E 70
Bull La. N18 . . . . 5K 17
Bull La. Chst 7H 127
Bull La. Dag 3H 57
Bull Rd. E15 . . . . 2H 71
Bullrush Clo. Cars 2C 150
Bullrush Clo. Croy 6E 140
Bull's All. SW14 . . . . 2K 99
Bull's Bri. Cen. Hay 3K 77
Bull's Bri. Ind. Est. S'hall 4A 78
Bullsbridge Rd. S'hall 4A 78
Bullsbrook Rd. Hay 1A 78
Bulls Gdns. SW3 . . . . 4C 84 (3D 170) (in two parts)
Bulls Head Pas. EC3 . . . . 1G 169
Bull Wharf La. EC4 . . . . 7C 68 (3D 168)
Bull Yd. SE15 . . . . 1G 105
Bulmer Gdns. Harr 7D 26
Bulmer M. W11 . . . . 7J 65
Bulmer Pl. W11 . . . . 1J 83
Bulow Est. SW6 . . . . 1K 101 (off Pearscroft Rd.)
Bulstrode Av. Houn 2D 96
Bulstrode Gdns. Houn 3E 96
Bulstrode Pl. W1 . . . . 5E 66 (6H 159)
Bulstrode Rd. Houn 3E 96
Bulstrode St. W1 . . . . 6E 66 (7H 159)
Bulwer Ct. E11 . . . . 1F 53
Bulwer Ct. Rd. E11 . . . . 1F 53
Bulwer Gdns. Barn 4F 5
Bulwer Rd. E11 . . . . 7F 35
Bulwer Rd. N18 . . . . 4K 17
Bulwer Rd. Barn 4E 4
Bulwer St. W12 . . . . 1E 82
Bunbury Ho. SE15 . . . . 7G 87 (off Fenham Rd.)
Bunce's La. Wfd G 7C 20
Bungalow Rd. SE25 . . . . 4E 140
Bungalows, The. E10 . . . . 6E 34
Bungalows, The. SW16 . . . . 7F 121
Bungalows, The. Ilf 1J 37
Bungalows, The. Wall 5F 151
Bunhill Row. EC1 . . . . 4D 68 (3E 162)
Bunhouse Pl. SW1 . . . . 5E 84 (5H 171)
Bunkers Hill. NW11 . . . . 7A 30
Bunkers Hill. Belv 4G 93
Bunkers Hill. Sidc 3F 129
Bunning Way. N7 . . . . 7J 49
Bunns La. NW7 . . . . 6F 13 (in two parts)
Bunsen Ho. E3 . . . . 2A 70 (off Grove Rd.)
Bunsen St. E3 . . . . 2A 70
Buntingbridge Rd. Ilf 5H 37

Bunting Clo. N9 1E 18
Bunting Clo. Mitc 5D 138
Bunting Ct. NW9 2A 28
Bunton St. SE18 3E 90
Bunyan Ct. EC2 5C 162
Bunyan Rd. E17 3A 34
Buonaparte M. SW1 5H 85 (5C 172)
Burbage Clo. SE1 3D 86
Burbage Clo. Hay 6F 59
Burbage Ho. N1 1D 68 (off Poole St.)
Burbage Ho. SE14 6K 87 (off Samuel Clo.)
Burbage Rd. SE24 & SE21 6C 104
Burberry Clo. N Mald 2A 136
Burbidge Rd. Shep 4C 130
Burbridge Way. N17 2G 33
Burcham St. E14 6D 70
Burcharbro Rd. SE2 6D 92
Burchell Ct. Bush 1B 10
Burchell Ho. SE11 5K 85 (5H 173) (off Jonathan St.)
Burchell Rd. E10 1D 52
Burchell Rd. SE15 1H 105
Burchetts Way. Shep 6D 130
Burchett Way. Romf 6F 39
Burchwall Clo. Romf 1J 39
Burcote Rd. SW18 7B 102
Burden Clo. Bren 5C 80
Burden Ho. SW8 7J 85 (off Thorncroft St.)
Burdenshott Av. Rich 4H 99
Burden Way. E11 2K 53
Burder Clo. N1 6E 50
Burder Rd. N1 6E 50
Burdett Av. SW20 1C 136
Burdett Clo. W7 1K 79
Burdett Clo. Sidc 5E 128
Burdett M. NW3 6B 48
Burdett M. W2 6K 65
Burdett Rd. E3 & E14 4A 70
Burdett Rd. Croy 6D 140
Burdett Rd. Rich 2F 99
Burdetts Rd. Dag 1F 75
Burdock Clo. Croy 1K 153
Burdock Rd. N17 3G 33
Burdon La. Sutt 7G 149
Burdon Pk. Sutt 7H 149
Bure Ct. New Bar 5E 4
Burfield Clo. SW17 4B 120
Burford Clo. Dag 3C 56
Burford Clo. Ilf 4G 37
Burford Clo. Uxb 4A 40
Burford Gdns. N13 3E 16
Burford Ho. Bren 5D 80
Burford Rd. E6 3C 72
Burford Rd. E15 1F 71
Burford Rd. SE6 2B 124
Burford Rd. Bren 5E 80
Burford Rd. Brom 4C 144
Burford Rd. Sutt 2J 149
Burford Rd. Wor Pk 7B 136
Burford Wlk. SW6 7A 84
Burford Way. New Ad 6E 154
Burge Rd. E7 4B 54
Burges Gro. SW13 7D 82
Burges Rd. E6 7C 54
Burgess Av. NW9 6K 27
Burgess Clo. Felt 4C 114
Burgess Ct. E6 7E 54
Burgess Ct. S'hall 6F 61 (off Fleming Rd.)
Burgess Hill. NW2 4J 47
Burgess Ind. Pk. SE5 7D 86
Burgess M. SW19 6K 119
Burgess Pk. 6E 86
Burgess Rd. E6 7E 54
Burgess Rd. E15 4G 53
Burgess Rd. Sutt 4K 149
Burgess St. E14 5C 70
Burge St. SE1 3D 86
Burghill Rd. SE26 4A 124
Burghley Av. N Mald 1K 135
Burghley Hall Clo. SW19 1G 119
Burghley Pl. Mitc 5D 138
Burghley Rd. E11 1G 53
Burghley Rd. N8 3A 32
Burghley Rd. NW5 4F 49
Burghley Rd. SW19 4F 119
Burghley Tower. W3 7B 64
Burgh St. N1 2B 68
Burgon St. EC4 6B 68 (1B 168)
Burgos Clo. Croy 6A 152
Burgos Gro. SE10 1D 106
Burgoyne Rd. N4 6B 32
Burgoyne Rd. SE25 4F 141
Burgoyne Rd. SW9 3K 103
Burgoyne Rd. Sun 6H 113
Burham Clo. SE20 7J 123
Burhill Gro. Pinn 2C 24
Burke Clo. SW15 4A 100
Burke Lodge. E13 3K 71
Burke St. E16 5H 71 (in two parts)
Burket Clo. S'hall 4C 78
Burland Rd. SW11 5D 102
Burleigh Av. Sidc 5K 109
Burleigh Av. Wall 3E 150
Burleigh Gdns. N14 1B 16
Burleigh Gdns. Ashf 5E 112
Burleigh Ho. SW3 7B 170
Burleigh Ho. W10 5G 65 (off St Charles Sq.)
Burleigh Pde. N14 1C 16
Burleigh Pl. SW15 5F 101
Burleigh Rd. Enf 4K 7
Burleigh Rd. Sutt 1G 149
Burleigh Rd. Uxb 1D 58
Burleigh St. WC2 7K 67 (2G 167)
Burleigh Wlk. SE6 1E 124
Burleigh Way. Enf 3J 7
Burley Clo. E4 5H 19
Burley Clo. SW16 2H 139
Burley Ho. E1 6K 69 (off Chudleigh St.)
Burley Rd. E16 6A 72
Burlington Arc. W1 7G 67 (3A 166)
Burlington Av. Rich 1G 99
Burlington Av. Romf 6H 39
Burlington Clo. E6 6C 72
Burlington Clo. W9 4J 65
Burlington Clo. Felt 7F 95
Burlington Clo. Pinn 3K 23
Burlington Gdns. SW6 2G 101
Burlington Gdns. W1 7G 67 (3A 166)
Burlington Gdns. W3 1J 81
Burlington Gdns. W4 5J 81
Burlington Gdns. Romf 7E 38
Burlington La. W4 7J 81
Burlington M. SW15 5H 101
Burlington M. W3 1J 81
Burlington Pl. SW6 2G 101
Burlington Pl. Wfd G 3E 20
Burlington Ri. E Barn 1H 15
Burlington Rd. N10 3E 30
Burlington Rd. N17 1G 33
Burlington Rd. SW6 2G 101
Burlington Rd. W4 5J 81
Burlington Rd. Enf 1J 7
Burlington Rd. Iswth 1H 97
Burlington Rd. N Mald 4B 136
Burlington Rd. T Hth 2C 140
Burma M. N16 4D 50
Burma Rd. N16 4D 50
Burmarsh Ct. SE20 1J 141
Burma Ter. SE19 5E 122
Burmester Rd. SW17 3A 120
Burnaby Cres. W4 6J 81
Burnaby Gdns. W4 6H 81
Burnaby St. SW10 7A 84
Burnand Ho. W14 3F 83 (off Redan St.)
Burnard Pl. N7 5K 49
Burnaston Ho. E5 3G 51
Burnbrae Clo. N12 6E 14
Burnbury Rd. SW12 1G 121
Burncroft Av. Enf 2D 8
Burndell Way. Hay 5B 60
Burne Jones Ho. W14 4G 83
Burnell Av. Rich 5C 116
Burnell Av. Well 2A 110
Burnell Gdns. Stan 2D 26
Burnell Rd. Sutt 4K 149
Burnell Wlk. SE1 5F 87 (off Abingdon Clo.)
Burnels Av. E6 3E 72
Burness Clo. N7 6K 49
Burne St. NW1 5C 66 (5C 158)
Burnett Clo. E9 5J 51
Burnett Ho. SE13 2E 106 (off Lewisham Hill)
Burney Av. Surb 5F 135
Burney St. SE10 7E 88
Burnfoot Av. SW6 1G 101
Burnham. NW3 7C 48
Burnham Av. Uxb 4E 40
Burnham Clo. NW7 7H 13
Burnham Clo. SE1 4F 87
Burnham Clo. Enf 1K 7
Burnham Clo. W'stone 4A 26
Burnham Ct. W2 7K 65 (off Moscow Rd.)
Burnham Cres. E11 4A 36
Burnham Dri. Wor Pk 2F 149
Burnham Est. E2 3J 69 (off Burnham St.)
Burnham Gdns. Croy 7F 141
Burnham Gdns. Hay 3F 77
Burnham Gdns. Houn 1K 95
Burnham Rd. E4 5G 19
Burnham Rd. Dag 7B 56
Burnham Rd. Mord 4K 137
Burnham Rd. Romf 3K 39
Burnham Rd. Sidc 2E 128
Burnham St. E2 3J 69
Burnham St. King T 1G 135
Burnham Way. SE26 5B 124
Burnham Way. W13 4B 80
Burnhill Rd. Beck 2C 142
Burnley Rd. NW10 5B 46
Burnley Rd. SW9 2K 103
Burnsall St. SW3 5C 84 (6D 170)
Burns Av. Chad H 7C 38
Burns Av. Felt 6J 95
Burns Av. Sidc 6B 110
Burns Av. S'hall 7E 60
Burns Clo. E17 4E 34
Burns Clo. SW19 6B 120
Burns Clo. Hay 5H 59
Burns Clo. Well 1K 109
Burns Ho. E2 3J 69 (off Cornwall Av.)
Burns Ho. SE17 5B 86 (off Doddington Gro.)
Burn Side. N9 3D 18
Burnside Av. E4 6G 19
Burnside Clo. SE16 1K 87
Burnside Clo. Barn 3D 4
Burnside Clo. Twic 6A 98
Burnside Cres. Wemb 1D 62
Burnside Rd. Dag 2C 56
Burns Rd. NW10 1B 64
Burns Rd. SW11 2D 102
Burns Rd. W13 2B 80
Burns Rd. Wemb 2E 62
Burns Way. Houn 2B 96
Burnt Ash Hill. SE12 6H 107 (in two parts)
Burnt Ash La. Brom 7J 125
Burnt Ash Rd. SE12 5H 107
Burnthwaite Rd. SW6 7H 83
Burnt Oak. 2J 27
Burnt Oak B'way. Edgw 7C 12
Burnt Oak Fields. Edgw 1J 27
Burnt Oak La. Sidc 6A 110
Burntwood Clo. SW18 1C 120
Burntwood Grange Rd. SW18 1B 120
Burntwood La. SW17 3A 120
Burntwood Vw. SE19 5F 123
Buross St. E1 6H 69
Burpham Clo. Hay 5B 60
Burrage Ct. SE16 4K 87 (off Worgan St.)
Burrage Gro. SE18 4G 91
Burrage Pl. SE18 5F 91
Burrage Rd. SE18 6G 91
Burrard Rd. E16 6K 71
Burrard Rd. NW6 5J 47
Burr Clo. E1 1G 87 (4K 169)
Burr Clo. Bexh 3F 111
Burrell Clo. Croy 6A 142
Burrell Clo. Edgw 2C 12
Burrell Row. Beck 2C 142
Burrell St. SE1 1B 86 (4A 168)
Burrells Wharf Sq. E14 5C 88
Burrell Towers. E10 7C 34
Burrhill Ct. SE16 3K 87 (off Worgan St.)
Burritt Rd. King T 2G 135
Burroughs Cotts. E14 5A 70 (off Halley St.)
Burroughs Gdns. NW4 4D 28
Burroughs Pde. NW4 4D 28
Burroughs, The. NW4 4D 28
Burrow Ho. SW9 2A 104 (off Stockwell Pk. Rd.)
Burrow Rd. SE22 4E 104
Burrows M. SE1 2B 86 (6A 168)
Burrows Rd. NW10 3E 64
Burrow Wlk. SE21 7C 104
Burr Rd. SW18 1J 119
Bursar St. SE1 1E 86 (5G 169)
Bursdon Clo. Sidc 2K 127
Bursland Rd. Enf 4E 8
Burslem St. E1 6G 69
Burstock Rd. SW15 4G 101
Burston Rd. SW15 5F 101
Burstow Rd. SW20 1G 137
Burtenshaw Rd. Th Dit 7A 134
Burtley Clo. N4 1C 50
Burton Bank. N1 7D 50 (off Yeate St.)
Burton Clo. Chess 7D 146
Burton Clo. T Hth 3D 140
Burton Ct. SE20 2J 141
Burton Ct. SW3 5D 84 (5F 171) (off Turks Row, in two parts)
Burton Gdns. Houn 1D 96
Burton Gro. SE17 5D 86
Burtonhole Clo. NW7 4A 14
Burtonhole La. NW7 5K 13 (in two parts)
Burton Ho. SE16 2H 87 (off Cherry Garden St.)
Burton La. SW9 2A 104 (in two parts)
Burton M. SW1 4E 84 (4H 171)
Burton Pl. WC1 4H 67 (2D 160)
Burton Rd. E18 3K 35
Burton Rd. NW6 7H 47
Burton Rd. SW9 2B 104 (Akerman Rd.)
Burton Rd. SW9 2A 104 (Brixton Rd.)
Burton Rd. King T 7E 116
Burton's Rd. Hamp H 4F 115
Burton St. WC1 3H 67 (2D 160)
Burtonwood Ho. N4 7D 32
Burt Rd. E16 1A 90
Burtt Ho. N1 3E 68 (1G 163) (off Aske St.)
Burtwell La. SE27 4D 122
Burwash Ho. SE1 2D 86 (7F 169) (off Kipling Est.)
Burwash Rd. SE18 5H 91
Burwell. King T 2G 135 (off Excelsior Rd.)
Burwell Av. Gnfd 6J 43
Burwell Clo. E1 6H 69
Burwell Rd. E10 1A 52
Burwell Rd. Ind. Est. E10 1A 52
Burwell Wlk. E3 4C 70
Burwood Av. Brom 2K 155
Burwood Av. Pinn 5K 23
Burwood Clo. Surb 1G 147
Burwood Ho. SW9 4B 104
Burwood Pl. W2 6C 66 (7D 158)
Burwood Pl. Barn 1F 5
Bury Av. Hay 2G 59
Bury Av. Ruis 6E 22
Bury Clo. SE16 1K 87
Bury Ct. EC3 6E 68 (7H 163)
Bury Gro. Mord 5K 137
Bury Hall Vs. N9 7A 8
Bury Pl. WC1 5J 67 (6E 160)
Bury Rd. E4 1B 20
Bury Rd. N22 2A 32
Bury Rd. Dag 5H 57
Buryside Clo. Ilf 4K 37
Bury St. EC3 6E 68 (1H 169)
Bury St. N9 7A 8
Bury St. SW1 1G 85 (4B 166)
Bury St. Ruis 5E 22
Bury St. W. N9 7J 7
Bury Wlk. SW3 4C 84 (4C 170)
Busbridge Ho. E14 5C 70 (off Brabazon St.)
Busby M. NW5 6H 49
Busby Pl. NW5 6H 49
Busch Clo. Iswth 1B 98
Bushbaby Clo. SE1 3E 86
Bushberry Rd. E9 6A 52
Bush Clo. Ilf 5H 37
Bush Cotts. SW18 5J 101
Bush Ct. N14 1C 16
Bush Ct. W12 2F 83
Bushell Clo. SW2 2K 121
Bushell Grn. Bus H 2C 10
Bushell St. E1 1G 87
Bushell Way. Chst 5E 126
Bushey Av. E18 3H 35
Bushey Av. Orp 7H 145
Bushey Clo. E4 3K 19
Bushey Clo. Uxb 2C 40
Bushey Ct. SW20 3D 136
Bushey Down. SW12 2F 121
Bushey Heath. 1C 10
Bushey Hill Rd. SE5 1E 104
Bushey La. Sutt 4J 149
Bushey Mead. 2F 137
Bushey Rd. E13 2A 72
Bushey Rd. N15 6E 32
Bushey Rd. SW20 3D 136
Bushey Rd. Croy 2C 154
Bushey Rd. Hay 4G 77
Bushey Rd. Sutt 4J 149
Bushey Rd. Uxb 2C 40
Bushey Way. Beck 6F 143
Bush Fair Ct. N14 6A 6
Bushfield Clo. Edgw 2C 12
Bushfield Cres. Edgw 2C 12
Bush Gro. NW9 7J 27
Bush Gro. Stan 1D 26
Bushgrove Rd. Dag 4D 56
Bush Hill. N21 7H 7
Bush Hill Pde. N9 7J 7
Bush Hill Park. 6A 8
Bush Hill Pk. 4A 8
Bush Hill Pk. Golf Course. 5H 7
Bush Hill Rd. N21 6J 7
Bush Hill Rd. Harr 6F 27
Bush Ind. Est. N19 3G 49
Bush Ind. Est. NW10 4K 63
Bush La. EC4 7D 68 (2E 168)
Bushmead Clo. N15 4F 33
Bushmoor Cres. SE18 7F 91
Bushnell Rd. SW17 2F 121
Bush Rd. E8 1H 69
Bush Rd. E11 7H 35
Bush Rd. SE8 4K 87

Bush Rd. Buck H 4G 21
Bush Rd. Rich 6F 81
Bush Rd. Shep 5B 130
Bushway. Dag 4D 56
Bushwood. E11 1H 53
Bushwood Dri. SE1 4F 87
Bushwood Rd. Rich 6G 81
Bushy Ct. King T 1C 134
(off Up. Teddington Rd.)
Bushy Lees. Sidc 6K 109
Bushy Pk. Gdns. Tedd 5H 115
Bushy Pk. Rd. Tedd 7B 116
(in two parts)
Bushy Rd. Tedd 6K 115
Butcher Row. E14 & E1 7K 69
Butchers Rd. E16 6J 71
Bute Av. Rich 2E 116
Bute Ct. Wall 5G 151
Bute Gdns. W6 4F 83
Bute Gdns. Rich 1E 116
Bute Gdns. Wall 5G 151
Bute Gdns. W. Wall 5G 151
Bute M. NW11 5A 30
Bute Rd. Croy 1A 152
Bute Rd. Ilf 5F 37
Bute Rd. Wall 4G 151
Bute St. SW7 4B 84 (3A 170)
Bute Wlk. N1 6D 50
Butfield Ho. E9 6J 51
(off Stevens Av.)
Butler Av. Harr 7H 25
Butler Ct. Wemb 4A 44
Butler Ho. E2 3J 69
(off Bacton St.)
Butler Ho. E14 6B 70
(off Burdett St.)
Butler Ho. SW9 1B 104
(off Lothian Rd.)
Butler Pl. SW1 1C 172
Butler Rd. NW10 7B 46
Butler Rd. Dag 4B 56
Butler Rd. Harr 7G 25
Butlers & Colonial Wharf. SE1 2F 87 (6K 169)
(off Shad Thames)
Butlers Dri. E4 1K 9
Butler St. E2 3J 69
Butler St. Uxb 4D 58
Butlers Wharf. SE1 6K 169
Butley Ct. E3 2A 70
(off Ford St.)
Butterfield Clo. N17 6H 17
Butterfield Clo. SE16 2H 87
Butterfield Clo. Twic 6K 97
Butterfields. E17 5E 34
Butterfield Sq. E6 6D 72
Butterfly La. SE9 6F 109
Butterfly Wlk. SE5 2D 104
(off Denmark Hill)
Butter Hill. Cars 3E 150
Butteridges Clo. Dag 1F 75
Buttermere. NW1 3F 67 (1K 159)
(off Augustus St.)
Buttermere Clo. E15 4F 53
Buttermere Clo. SE1 4F 87
Buttermere Clo. Felt 1H 113
Buttermere Clo. Mord 6F 137
Buttermere Ct. NW8 1B 66
(off Boundary Rd.)
Buttermere Dri. SW15 5G 101
Buttermere Wlk. E8 6F 51
Butterwick. W6 4F 83
Butterworth Gdns. Wfd G 6D 20
Buttesland St. N1 3D 68 (1F 163)
Buttfield Clo. Dag 6H 57
Buttmarsh Clo. SE18 5F 91
Buttsbury Rd. Ilf 5G 55
(in two parts)
Butts Cotts. Felt 3C 114
Butts Cres. Hanw 3E 114
Buttsmead. N'wd 1E 22
Butts Piece. N'holt 2K 59
Butts Rd. Brom 5G 125
Butts, The. Bren 6C 80
Butts, The. Sun 3A 132
Buxhall Cres. E9 6B 52
Buxted Rd. E8 7F 51
Buxted Rd. N12 5H 15
Buxted Rd. SE22 4E 104
Buxton Clo. N9 2D 18
Buxton Clo. Wfd G 6G 21
Buxton Ct. N1 1D 162
(in two parts)
Buxton Cres. Sutt 4G 149
Buxton Dri. E11 4G 35
Buxton Dri. N Mald 2K 135
Buxton Gdns. W3 7H 63
Buxton Ho. E11 4G 35
Buxton Rd. E4 1A 20
Buxton Rd. E6 3C 72
Buxton Rd. E15 5G 53
Buxton Rd. E17 4A 34
Buxton Rd. N19 1H 49
Buxton Rd. NW2 6D 46
Buxton Rd. SW14 3A 100
Buxton Rd. Ashf 5A 112
Buxton Rd. Eri 7K 93
Buxton Rd. Ilf 6J 37
Buxton Rd. T Hth 5B 140
Buxton St. E1 4F 69 (4K 163)
Buzzard Creek Ind. Est. Bark 5A 74
Byam St. SW6 2A 102
Byards Ct. SE16 4K 87
(off Worgan St.)
Byards Cft. SW16 1H 139
Byatt Wlk. Hamp 6C 114
Bychurch End. Tedd 5K 115
Bycroft Rd. S'hall 4E 60
Bycroft St. SE20 7K 123
Bycullah Av. Enf 3G 7
Bycullah Rd. Enf 2G 7
Byegrove Rd. SW19 6B 120
Byelands Clo. SE16 1K 87
Bye, The. W3 6A 64
Byeways. Twic 3F 115
Byeways, The. Surb 5G 135
Byeway, The. SW14 3J 99
Bye Way, The. Harr 1J 25
Byfeld Gdns. SW13 1C 100
Byfield Clo. SE16 2B 88
Byfield Pas. Iswth 3A 98
Byfield Rd. Iswth 3A 98
Byford Clo. E15 7G 53
Byford Ho. Barn 4A 4
Bygrove. New Ad 6D 154
Bygrove St. E14 6D 70
(in two parts)
Byland Clo. N21 7E 6
Bylands Clo. SE2 3B 92
Byne Rd. SE26 6J 123
Byne Rd. Cars 2C 150
Bynes Rd. S Croy 7D 152
Byng Pl. WC1 4H 67 (4D 160)
Byng Rd. Barn 2A 4
Byng St. E14 2C 88
Bynon Av. Bexh 3F 111
Byre Rd. N14 6A 6
Byrne Rd. SW12 1F 121
Byron Av. E12 6C 54
Byron Av. E18 3H 35
Byron Av. NW9 4H 27
Byron Av. Houn 2J 95
Byron Av. N Mald 5C 136
Byron Av. Sutt 4B 150
Byron Av. E. Sutt 4B 150
Byron Clo. E8 1G 69
Byron Clo. SE20 3H 141
Byron Clo. SE26 4A 124
Byron Clo. SE28 1C 92
Byron Clo. SW16 6J 121
Byron Clo. Hamp 4D 114
Byron Clo. W on T 7C 132
Byron Ct. E11 4K 35
(off Makepeace Rd.)
Byron Ct. NW6 7A 48
(off Fairfax Rd.)
Byron Ct. SE22 1G 123
Byron Ct. W7 4A 80
(off Boston Rd.)
Byron Ct. W9 4J 65
(off Lanhill Rd.)
Byron Ct. WC1 4K 67 (3G 161)
(off Mecklenburgh Sq.)
Byron Ct. Enf 2G 7
Byron Ct. Harr 6J 25
Byron Dri. N2 6B 30
Byron Dri. Eri 7H 93
Byron Gdns. Sutt 4B 150
Byron Hill Rd. Harr 1H 43
Byron Ho. Dart 5K 111
Byron M. NW3 5D 48
Byron M. W9 4J 65
Byron Pde. Uxb 4E 58
Byron Rd. E10 1D 52
Byron Rd. E17 3C 34
Byron Rd. NW2 2D 46
Byron Rd. NW7 5H 13
Byron Rd. W5 1F 81
Byron Rd. Harr 6J 25
Byron Rd. W'stone 2K 25
Byron Rd. Wemb 2C 44
Byron St. E14 6E 70
Byron Ter. N9 6D 8
Byron Way. Hay 4H 59
Byron Way. N'holt 3C 60
Byron Way. W Dray 4B 76
Bysouth Clo. N15 4D 32
Bysouth Clo. Ilf 1F 37
Bythorn St. SW9 3K 103
Byton Rd. SW17 6D 120
Byward Av. Felt 6A 96
Byward St. EC3 7E 68 (3H 169)
Bywater Ho. SE18 3C 90
Bywater Pl. SE16 1A 88
Bywater St. SW3 5D 84 (5E 170)
Byway. E11 5A 36
Byway, The. Eps 4B 148
Byway, The. Sutt 7B 150
Bywell Pl. W1 6A 160
Bywood Av. Croy 6J 141
Byworth Wlk. N19 1J 49

Cabbell St. NW1 5C 66 (6C 158)
Cabinet War Rooms. 2H 85 (6D 166)
Cabinet Way. E4 6G 19
Cable Ho. WC1 3A 68 (1J 161)
(off Gt. Percy St.)
Cable Pl. SE10 1E 106
Cables Clo. Belv 3J 93
Cable St. E1 7G 69
Cable Trade Pk. SE7 4A 90
Cabot Ct. SE16 4K 87
(off Worgan St.)
Cabot Sq. E14 1C 88
Cabot Way. E6 1B 72
Cab Rd. SE1 6J 167
Cabul Rd. SW11 2C 102
Caci Ho. W14 4H 83
(off Avonmore Rd.)
Cactus Clo. SE15 2E 104
Cactus Wlk. W12 6B 64
Cadbury Clo. Iswth 1A 98
Cadbury Clo. Sun 7G 113
Cadbury Rd. Sun 7G 113
Cadbury Way. SE16 3F 87
(in two parts)
Caddington Clo. Barn 5H 5
Caddington Rd. NW2 3G 47
Caddis Clo. Stan 7E 10
Cadell Clo. E2 2F 69 (1K 163)
Cade Rd. SE10 1F 107
Cader Rd. SW18 6A 102
Cadet Dri. SE1 4F 87
Cadet Pl. SE10 5G 89
Cadiz Ct. Dag 7K 57
(off Rainham Rd. S.)
Cadiz Rd. Dag 7J 57
Cadiz St. SE17 5C 86
Cadley Ter. SE23 2J 123
Cadman Clo. SW9 7B 86
Cadman Ct. W4 5H 81
(off Chaseley Dri.)
Cadmer Clo. N Mald 4A 136
Cadmore Ho. N1 7B 50
(off Sutton Est., The)
Cadmus Clo. SW4 3H 103
Cadmus Ct. SW9 1A 104
(off Southey Rd.)
Cadnam Lodge. E14 3E 88
(off Schooner Clo.)
Cadogan Clo. E9 7B 52
Cadogan Clo. Beck 1F 143
Cadogan Clo. Harr 4F 43
Cadogan Clo. Tedd 5J 115
Cadogan Ct. SW3 4D 84 (4E 170)
(off Draycott Av.)
Cadogan Ct. Sutt 6K 149
Cadogan Gdns. E18 3K 35
Cadogan Gdns. N3 1K 29
Cadogan Gdns. N21 5F 7
Cadogan Gdns. SW3 4D 84 (3F 171)
Cadogan Ga. SW1 4D 84 (3F 171)
Cadogan Ho. SW3 7B 170
Cadogan La. SW1 3E 84 (2G 171)
Cadogan Mans. SW3 4D 84 (4F 171)
(off Cadogan Gdns.)
Cadogan Pl. SW1 3D 84 (1F 171)
Cadogan Rd. Surb 5D 134
Cadogan Sq. SW1 3D 84 (2E 170)
Cadogan St. SW3 4D 84 (4E 170)
Cadogan Ter. E9 6B 52
Cadoxton Av. N15 6F 33
Cadwallon Rd. SE9 2F 127
Caedmon Rd. N7 4K 49
Caerleon Clo. Sidc 5C 128
Caerleon Ter. SE2 4B 92
Caernafon Ho. Stan 5F 11
Caernarvon Clo. Mitc 3J 139
Caernarvon Dri. Ilf 1E 36
Caernarvon Ho. E16 1K 89
(off Audley Dri.)
Caernarvon Ho. W2 6A 66
(off Hallfield Est.)
Caesars Wlk. Mitc 5D 138
Caesars Way. Shep 6F 131
Café Gallery. 3J 87
Cahill St. EC1 4C 68 (4D 162)
Cahir St. E14 4D 88
Cain Ct. W5 5C 62
(off Castlebar M.)
Caine Ho. W3 2H 81
(off Hanbury Rd.)
Cain's La. Felt 5G 95
Caird St. W10 3G 65
Cairn Av. W5 1D 80
Cairncross M. N8 6J 31
(off Felix Av.)
Cairndale Clo. Brom 7H 125
Cairnfield Av. NW2 3A 46
Cairngorm Clo. Tedd 5A 116
Cairns Av. Wfd G 6H 21
Cairns Rd. SW11 5C 102
Cairn Way. Stan 6E 10
Cairo New Rd. Croy 2B 152
Cairo Rd. E17 4C 34
Caister Ho. N7 6K 49
Caistor Ho. E15 1H 71
(off Caistor Pk. Rd.)
Caistor M. SW12 7F 103
Caistor Pk. Rd. E15 1H 71
Caistor Rd. SW12 7F 103
Caithness Gdns. Sidc 6K 109
Caithness Ho. N1 1K 67
(off Twyford St.)
Caithness Rd. W14 3F 83
Caithness Rd. Mitc 7F 121
Calabria Rd. N5 6B 50
Calais Ga. SE5 1B 104
Calais St. SE5 1B 104
Calbourne Rd. SW12 7D 102
Calcott Ct. W14 3G 83
(off Blythe Rd.)
Calcott Wlk. SE9 4C 126
Calcraft Ho. E2 2J 69
(off Bonner Rd.)
Caldbeck Av. Wor Pk 2C 148
Caldecote. King T 2G 135
(off Excelsior Clo.)
Caldecote Gdns. Bush 1D 10
Caldecot Rd. SE5 2C 104
Caldecott Way. E5 3K 51
Calder Av. Gnfd 2K 61
Calder Clo. Enf 3K 7
Calder Ct. SE16 1B 88
Calder Gdns. Edgw 3G 27
Calderon Ho. NW8 2C 66
(off Townshend Est.)
Calderon Pl. W10 5E 64
Calderon Rd. E11 4E 52
Calder Rd. Mord 5A 138
Caldervale Rd. SW4 5H 103
Calderwood St. SE18 4E 90
Caldew Ct. NW7 7H 13
Caldew St. SE5 7D 86
Caldicot Grn. NW9 6A 28
Caldwell Ho. SW13 7E 82
(off Trinity Chu. Rd.)
Caldwell St. SW9 7K 85
Caldy Rd. Belv 3H 93
Caldy Wlk. N1 7C 50
Caleb St. SE1 2C 86 (6C 168)
Caledonia Ct. Bark 2C 74
(off Keel Clo.)
Caledonia Ho. E14 6A 70
(off Salmon La.)
Caledonian Clo. Ilf 1B 56
Caledonian Rd. N7 & N1 4K 49
Caledonian Wharf. E14 4F 89
Caledonia Rd. Stai 1A 112
Caledonia St. N1 2J 67 (1F 161)
Caledon Rd. E6 1D 72
Caledon Rd. Wall 4E 150
Cale St. SW3 5C 84 (5C 170)
Caletock Way. SE10 5H 89
Calgarth. NW1 2G 67 (1B 160)
(off Ampthill Est.)
Calgary Ct. SE16 2J 87
(off Canada Est.)
Caliban Tower. N1 2E 68
(off Arden Est.)
Calico Ho. EC4 6C 68 (1D 168)
(off Well Ct.)
Calico Row. SW11 3A 102
Calidore Clo. SW2 6K 103
California La. Bus H 1C 10
California Pl. Bush 1C 10
(off High Rd.)
California Rd. N Mald 4H 135
Callaby Ter. N1 6D 50
Callaghan Clo. SE13 4G 107
Callahan Cotts. E1 5J 69
(off Lindley St.)
Callander Rd. SE6 2D 124
Callanders, The. Bush 1D 10
Callard Av. N13 4G 17
Callcott Ct. NW6 7H 47
Callcott Rd. NW6 7H 47
Callcott St. W8 1J 83
Callendar Rd. SW7 3B 84 (1A 170)
Callenders Cotts. Belv 2K 93
Callingham Clo. E14 5B 70
Callis Farm Clo. Stanw 6A 94
Callis Rd. E17 6B 34

Callonfield. E17 4K 33
Callow St. SW3 6B 84 (7A 170)
Calmington Rd. SE5 6E 86
Calmont Rd. Brom 6F 125
Calne Av. Ilf 1F 37
Calonne Rd. SW19 4F 119
Calshot Ho. N1 2K 67 (off Calshot St.)
Calshot Rd. H'row A 2C 94 (in two parts)
Calshot St. N1 2K 67 (1G 161)
Calshot Way. Enf 3G 7
Calshot Way. H'row A 2C 94 (in two parts)
Calstock. NW1 1G 67 (off Royal College St.)
Calstock Ho. SE11 5K 173
Calthorpe Gdns. Edgw 5K 11
Calthorpe Gdns. Sutt 3A 150
Calthorpe St. WC1 4K 67 (3H 161)
Calton Av. SE21 6E 104
Calton Rd. New Bar 6F 5
Calverley Clo. Beck 6D 124
Calverley Cres. Dag 2G 57
Calverley Gdns. Harr 7D 26
Calverley Gro. N19 1H 49
Calverley Rd. Eps 6C 148
Calvert Av. E1 & E2 3E 68 (2H 163)
Calvert Clo. Belv 4G 93
Calvert Clo. Sidc 6E 128
Calvert Ho. W12 7D 64 (off White City Est.)
Calverton. SE5 6E 86 (off Albany Rd.)
Calverton Rd. E6 1E 72
Calvert Rd. SE10 5H 89
Calvert Rd. Barn 2A 4
Calvert's Bldgs. SE1 1D 86 (5E 168)
Calvert St. NW1 1E 66
Calvin St. E1 4F 69 (4J 163)
Calydon Rd. SE7 5K 89
Calypso Way. SE16 3B 88
Camac Rd. Twic 1H 115
Cambalt Rd. SW15 5F 101
Cambay Ho. E1 4A 70 (off Harford St.)
Camber Ho. SE15 6J 87
Camberley Av. SW20 2D 136
Camberley Av. Enf 4K 7
Camberley Clo. Sutt 3F 149
Camberley Ho. NW1 2F 67 (off Redhill St.)
Camberley Rd. H'row A 3C 94
Cambert Way. SE3 4K 107
Camberwell. 1D 104
Camberwell Chu. St. SE5 1D 104
Camberwell Glebe. SE5 1E 104
Camberwell Green. (Junct.) 1D 104
Camberwell Grn. SE5 1D 104
Camberwell Gro. SE5 1D 104
Camberwell New Rd. SE5 6A 86
Camberwell Pl. SE5 1C 104
Camberwell Rd. SE5 & SE17 6C 86
Camberwell Sta. Rd. SE5 1C 104
Camberwell Trad. Est. SE5 1B 104
Cambeys Rd. Dag 5H 57
Camborne Av. W13 2B 80
Camborne Clo. H'row A 3C 94
Camborne Rd. SW18 7J 101
Camborne Rd. Croy 7G 141
Camborne Rd. Mord 5F 137
Camborne Rd. Sidc 3C 128
Camborne Rd. Sutt 7J 149
Camborne Rd. Well 2J 109
Camborne Way. Houn 1E 96
Cambourne Av. N9 7E 8
Cambourne M. W11 6G 65 (off St Mark's Rd.)
Cambourne Rd. H'row A 3C 94
Cambourne Wlk. Rich 6D 98
Cambrai Ct. N13 3D 16
Cambray Rd. SW12 1G 121
Cambray Rd. Orp 7K 145
Cambria Clo. Houn 4E 96
Cambria Clo. Sidc 1H 127
Cambria Ct. Felt 7K 95
Cambria Gdns. Stai 7A 94 (in two parts)
Cambria Ho. E14 6A 70 (off Salmon La.)
Cambria Ho. SE26 4G 123 (off High Level Dri.)
Cambrian Av. Ilf 5J 37
Cambrian Clo. SE27 3B 122
Cambrian Grn. NW9 5A 28 (off Snowden Dri.)
Cambrian Rd. E10 7C 34
Cambrian Rd. Rich 6F 99
Cambria Rd. SE5 3C 104
Cambria St. SW6 7K 83
Cambridge Arc. E9 7J 51 (off Elsdale St.)
Cambridge Av. NW6 2J 65
Cambridge Av. NW10 3E 64
Cambridge Av. Gnfd 5K 43
Cambridge Av. N Mald 3A 136 (in two parts)
Cambridge Av. Well 4K 109
Cambridge Barracks Rd. SE18 4D 90
Cambridge Cir. WC2 6H 67 (1D 166)
Cambridge Clo. E17 6B 34
Cambridge Clo. N22 1A 32
Cambridge Clo. NW10 3J 45
Cambridge Clo. SW20 1D 136
Cambridge Clo. Houn 4C 96
Cambridge Cotts. Rich 6G 81
Cambridge Ct. E2 2H 69 (off Cambridge Heath Rd.)
Cambridge Ct. N15 7E 32 (off Amhurst Pk.)
Cambridge Ct. NW6 2J 65 (off Cambridge Av., in three parts)
Cambridge Ct. W2 5C 66 (6C 158) (off Edgware Rd.)
Cambridge Ct. W6 4E 82 (off Shepherd's Bush Rd.)
Cambridge Cres. E2 2H 69
Cambridge Cres. Tedd 5A 116
Cambridge Dri. SE12 5J 107
Cambridge Dri. Ruis 2A 42
Cambridge Gdns. N10 1E 30
Cambridge Gdns. N17 7J 17
Cambridge Gdns. N21 7J 7
Cambridge Gdns. NW6 2J 65
Cambridge Gdns. W10 6F 65
Cambridge Gdns. Enf 2B 8
Cambridge Gdns. King T 2G 135
Cambridge Ga. NW1 4F 67 (3J 159)
Cambridge Ga. M. NW1 4F 67 (3K 159)
Cambridge Grn. SE9 1F 127
Cambridge Gro. SE20 1H 141
Cambridge Gro. W6 4D 82
Cambridge Gro. Rd. King T 3G 135 (in two parts)
Cambridge Heath Rd. E1 & E2 5H 69
Cambridge Ho. W6 4D 82 (off Cambridge Gro.)
Cambridge Ho. W13 6A 62
Cambridge Lodge Vs. E8 1H 69
Cambridge Pde. Enf 1B 8
Cambridge Pk. E11 7J 35
Cambridge Pk. Twic 6C 98
Cambridge Pk. Ct. Twic 7D 98
Cambridge Pl. W8 2K 83
Cambridge Rd. E4 1A 20
Cambridge Rd. E11 6H 35
Cambridge Rd. NW6 2J 65 (in two parts)
Cambridge Rd. SE20 3H 141
Cambridge Rd. SW11 1D 102
Cambridge Rd. SW13 2B 100
Cambridge Rd. SW20 1C 136
Cambridge Rd. W7 2K 79
Cambridge Rd. Ashf 7E 112
Cambridge Rd. Bark 7G 55
Cambridge Rd. Brom 7J 125
Cambridge Rd. Cars 6C 150
Cambridge Rd. Hamp 7D 114
Cambridge Rd. Harr 5E 24
Cambridge Rd. Houn 4C 96
Cambridge Rd. Ilf 1J 55
Cambridge Rd. King T 2F 135
Cambridge Rd. Mitc 3G 139
Cambridge Rd. N Mald 4K 135
Cambridge Rd. Rich 7G 81
Cambridge Rd. Sidc 4J 127
Cambridge Rd. S'hall 1D 78
Cambridge Rd. Tedd 4K 115
Cambridge Rd. Twic 6D 98
Cambridge Rd. W on T 6K 131
Cambridge Rd. W Mol 4D 132
Cambridge Rd. N. W4 5H 81
Cambridge Rd. S. W4 5H 81
Cambridge Row. SE18 5F 91
Cambridge Sq. W2 6C 66 (7C 158)
Cambridge St. SW1 4F 85 (4K 171)
Cambridge Ter. N9 7K 7
Cambridge Ter. NW1 3F 67 (2J 159)
Cambridge Ter. M. NW1 3F 67 (2K 159)
Cambridge Theatre. 6J 67 (1E 166) (off Earlham St.)
Cambridge Yd. W7 2K 79
Cambstone Clo. N11 2K 15
Cambus Clo. Hay 5C 60
Cambus Rd. E16 5J 71
Cam Ct. SE15 6F 87
Camdale Rd. SE18 7K 91
Camden Arts Cen. 5K 47
Camden Av. Felt 1A 114
Camden Av. Hay 7B 60
Camden Clo. Chst 1G 145
Camden Ct. NW1 7G 49 (off Rousden St.)
Camden Ct. Belv 5G 93
Camden Gdns. NW1 7F 49
Camden Gdns. Sutt 5K 149
Camden Gdns. T Hth 3B 140
Camden Gro. Chst 6F 127
Camden High St. NW1 7F 49
Camden Hill Rd. SE19 6E 122
Camden Ho. SE8 5B 88
Camdenhurst St. E14 6A 70
Camden La. N7 5H 49
Camden Lock Market. 7F 49
Camden Lock Pl. NW1 7F 49
Camden M. NW1 7G 49
Camden Pk. Rd. NW1 6H 49
Camden Pk. Rd. Chst 7D 126
Camden Passage. 1B 68
Camden Pas. N1 1B 68 (in two parts)
Camden Peoples Theatre. 4G 67 (3A 160) (off Hampstead Rd.)
Camden Rd. E11 6K 35
Camden Rd. E17 6B 34
Camden Rd. NW1 & N7 7G 49
Camden Rd. Bex 1F 129
Camden Rd. Cars 4D 150
Camden Rd. Sutt 5K 149
Camden Row. SE3 2G 107
Camden Row. Pinn 3A 24
Camden Sq. NW1 7H 49 (in two parts)
Camden St. NW1 7G 49
Camden Studios. NW1 1G 67 (off Camden St.)
Camden Ter. NW1 6H 49
Camden Town. 1F 67
Camden Wlk. N1 1B 68 (in two parts)
Camden Way. Chst 7D 126
Camden Way. T Hth 3B 140
Cameford Ct. SW12 7J 103
Camelford. NW1 1G 67 (off Royal College St.)
Camelford Ct. W11 6G 65
Camelford Ho. SE1 5J 85 (5F 173)
Camelford Wlk. W11 6G 65
Camel Gro. King T 5D 116
Camellia Ho. SE8 7B 88 (off Idonia St.)
Camellia Pl. Twic 7F 97
Camellia St. SW8 7J 85
Camelot Clo. SE28 2H 91
Camelot Clo. SW19 4H 119
Camelot Ho. NW1 6H 49
Camel Rd. E16 1B 90
Camera Pl. SW10 6B 84 (7A 170)
Cameret Ct. W14 2F 83 (off Holland Rd.)
Cameron Clo. N18 4C 18
Cameron Clo. N20 2G 15
Cameron Clo. Bex 3K 129
Cameron Ho. NW8 2C 66 (off St John's Wood Ter.)
Cameron Ho. SE5 7C 86
Cameron Pl. E1 6H 69
Cameron Rd. SE6 2B 124
Cameron Rd. Brom 5J 143
Cameron Rd. Croy 6B 140
Cameron Rd. Ilf 1J 55
Cameron Sq. Mitc 1C 138
Cameron Ter. SE12 3K 125
Camerton Clo. E8 6F 51
Camilla Clo. Sun 6H 113
Camilla Rd. SE16 4H 87
Camille Clo. SE25 3G 141
Camlan Rd. Brom 4H 125
Camlet St. E2 4F 69 (3J 163)
Camlet Way. Barn 2D 4
Camley St. NW1 7H 49
Camm Gdns. King T 2F 135
Camm Gdns. Th Dit 7K 133
Camomile Av. Mitc 1D 138
Camomile Rd. Rush G 2K 57
Camomile St. EC3 6E 68 (7H 163)
Camomile Way. W Dray 6A 58
Campana Rd. SW6 1J 101
Campania Building. E1 7K 69 (off Jardine Rd.)
Campbell Av. Ilf 4F 37
Campbell Clo. SE18 1E 108 (in two parts)
Campbell Clo. SW16 4H 121
Campbell Clo. Ruis 6J 23
Campbell Clo. Twic 1H 115
Campbell Ct. N17 1F 33
Campbell Ct. SE21 1G 123
Campbell Ct. SW7 3A 84 (off Gloucester Rd.)
Campbell Cft. Edgw 5B 12
Campbell Gordon Way. NW2 4D 46
Campbell Ho. SW1 5G 85 (6A 172) (off Churchill Gdns.)
Campbell Ho. W12 7D 64 (off White City Est.)
Campbell Rd. E3 3C 70
Campbell Rd. E6 1C 72
Campbell Rd. E15 4H 53
Campbell Rd. E17 4B 34
Campbell Rd. N17 1F 33
Campbell Rd. W7 7J 61
Campbell Rd. Croy 7B 140
Campbell Rd. E Mol 3J 133
Campbell Rd. Twic 2H 115
Campbell Wlk. N1 1J 67 (off Outram Pl.)
Campdale Rd. N7 3H 49
Campden Cres. Dag 4B 56
Campden Cres. Wemb 3B 44
Campden Gro. W8 2J 83
Campden Hill. W8 2J 83
Campden Hill Ct. W8 2J 83
Campden Hill Gdns. W8 1J 83
Campden Hill Ga. W8 2J 83
Campden Hill Mans. W8 1J 83 (off Edge St.)
Campden Hill Pl. W11 1H 83
Campden Hill Rd. W8 1J 83
Campden Hill Sq. W8 1H 83
Campden Ho. NW6 7B 48 (off Harben Rd.)
Campden Ho. W8 1J 83 (off Sheffield Ter.)
Campden Ho. Clo. W8 2J 83
Campden Houses. W8 1J 83
Campden Rd. S Croy 5E 152
Campden Rd. Uxb 3B 40
Campden St. W8 1J 83
Campe Ho. N10 7K 15
Campen Clo. SW19 2G 119
Camperdown Ho. Wall 6F 151 (off Stanley Pk. Rd.)
Camperdown St. E1 6F 69 (1K 169)
Campfield Rd. SE9 7B 108
Campion Clo. E6 7D 72
Campion Clo. Harr 6F 27
Campion Clo. Rush G 2K 57
Campion Clo. S Croy 4E 152
Campion Clo. Uxb 5B 58
Campion Ct. Wemb 2E 62
Campion Gdns. Wfd G 5D 20
Campion Pl. SE28 1A 92
Campion Rd. SW15 4E 100
Campion Rd. Iswth 1K 97
Campion Ter. NW2 3F 47
Campion Way. Edgw 4D 12
Camplin Rd. Harr 5E 26
Camplin St. SE14 7K 87
Camp Rd. SW19 5D 118 (in two parts)
Campsbourne Rd. N8 3J 31 (in two parts)
Campsbourne, The. N8 4J 31
Campsey Gdns. Dag 7B 56
Campsey Rd. Dag 7B 56
Campsfield Rd. N8 3J 31
Campshill Pl. SE13 5E 106
Campshill Rd. SE13 5E 106
Campus Rd. E17 6B 34
Campus Way. NW4 3D 28
Camp Vw. SW19 5D 118
Cam Rd. E15 1F 71
Camrose Av. Edgw 2F 27
Camrose Av. Eri 6H 93
Camrose Av. Felt 4A 114
Camrose Clo. Croy 7A 142
Camrose Clo. Mord 4J 137
Camrose St. SE2 5A 92
Canada Av. N18 6H 17
Canada Cres. W3 5J 63
Canada Est. SE16 3J 87
Canada Gdns. SE13 5E 106
Canada Ho. SE16 3A 88 (off Brunswick Quay)
Canada Rd. W3 5J 63
Canada Sq. E14 1D 88
Canada St. SE16 2K 87
Canada Way. W12 7D 64
Canada Wharf. SE16 1B 88
Canadian Av. SE6 1D 124
Canal App. SE8 5A 88
Canal Bridge. (Junct.) 6G 87

Canal Building. N1 . . . . 2C 68
(off Shepherdess Wlk.)
Canal Clo. E1 . . . . 4A 70
Canal Clo. W10 . . . . 4F 65
Canal Gro. SE15 . . . . 6H 87
Canal Path. E2 . . . . 1F 69
Canalside. SE28 . . . . 7D 74
Canal St. SE5 . . . . 6D 86
Canal Wlk. N1 . . . . 1D 68
Canal Wlk. NW10 . . . . 7J 45
(off Westend Clo.)
Canal Wlk. SE25 . . . . 6E 140
Canal Wlk. SE26 . . . . 5J 123
Canal Way. W10 . . . . 4F 65
Canary Wharf. 1D 88
Canary Wharf Pier. E14 . . . . . 1B 88
(off Westferry Cir.)
Canberra Clo. NW4 . . . . 3C 28
Canberra Clo. Dag 7K 57
Canberra Cres. Dag 7K 57
Canberra Dri. N'holt 3A 60
Canberra Rd. E6 . . . . 1D 72
Canberra Rd. SE7 . . . . 6A 90
Canberra Rd. Bexh 6D 92
Canberra Rd. H'row A 3C 94
Canbury Av. King T 1F 135
Canbury Bus. Cen. King T
. . . . 1E 134
Canbury Bus. Pk. King T . . . 1E 134
(off Canbury Pk. Rd.)
Canbury M. SE26 . . . . 3G 123
Canbury Pk. Rd. King T 1E 134
Canbury Pas. King T 1D 134
Cancell Rd. SW9 . . . . 1A 104
Candahar Rd. SW11 . . . . . . 2C 102
Candida Ct. NW1 . . . . 7F 49
Candid Ho. NW10 . . . . 3D 64
(off Trenmar Gdns.)
Candler M. Twic 7A 98
Candler St. N15 . . . . 6D 32
Candover Clo. W Dray 7A 76
Candover St. W1
. . . . 5G 67 (6A 160)
Candy St. E3 . . . . 1B 70
Caney M. NW2 . . . . 2F 47
Canfield Dri. Ruis 5K 41
Canfield Gdns. NW6 . . . . 7K 47
Canfield Ho. N15 . . . . 6E 32
(off Albert Rd.)
Canfield Pl. NW6 . . . . 6A 48
Canfield Rd. Wfd G 7H 21
Canford Av. N'holt 1D 60
Canford Clo. Enf 2F 7
Canford Gdns. N Mald 6A 136
Canford Pl. Tedd 6C 116
Canford Rd. SW11 . . . . 5E 102
Canham Rd. SE25 . . . . 3E 140
Canham Rd. W3 . . . . 2A 82
Canmore Gdns. SW16 . . . . . 7G 121
Cann Hall. 4G 53
Cann Hall Rd. E11 . . . . 4G 53
Cann Ho. W14 . . . . 3G 83
(off Russell Rd.)
Canning Cres. N22 . . . . 1K 31
Canning Cross. SE5 . . . . . . 2E 104
Canning Ho. W12 . . . . 7D 64
(off Australia Rd.)
Canning Pas. W8 . . . . 3A 84
(in two parts)
Canning Pl. W8 . . . . 3A 84
Canning Pl. M. W8 . . . . 3A 84
(off Canning Pl.)
Canning Rd. E15 . . . . 2G 71
Canning Rd. E17 . . . . 4A 34
Canning Rd. N5 . . . . 3B 50
Canning Rd. Croy 2F 153
Canning Rd. Harr 3J 25
Cannington Rd. Dag 6C 56
Canning Town. 6H 71
Canning Town. (Junct.) 6F 71
Cannizaro Rd. SW19 . . . . . . 6E 118
Cannock Ho. N4 . . . . 7C 32
Cannonbury Av. Pinn 6B 24
Cannon Clo. SW20 . . . . 3E 136
Cannon Clo. Hamp 6F 115
Cannon Dri. E14 . . . . 7C 70
Cannon Hill. N14 . . . . 3D 16
Cannon Hill. NW6 . . . . 5J 47
Cannon Hill La. SW20 . . . . . 5F 137
Cannon Hill M. N14 . . . . 3D 16
Cannon Ho. SE11 . . . . 4H 173
Cannon La. NW3 . . . . 3B 48
Cannon La. Pinn 5C 24
Cannon Pl. NW3 . . . . 3B 48
Cannon Pl. SE7 . . . . 5C 90
Cannon Retail Pk. SE28 . . . . 7A 74
Cannon Rd. N14 . . . . 3D 16
Cannon Rd. Bexh 1E 110
Cannon St. EC4 . . . . 6C 68 (1C 168)
Cannon St. Rd. E1 . . . . 6H 69
Cannon Trad. Est. Wemb . . . 4H 45
Cannon Way. W Mol 4E 132
Cannon Wharf Bus. Cen. SE8
. . . . 4A 88
Cannon Workshops. E14 . . . . 7C 70
(off Cannon Dri.)
Canon All. EC4 . . . . 6C 68 (1C 168)
(off Queen's Head Pas.)
Canon Av. Romf 5C 38
Canon Beck Rd. SE16 . . . . . . 2J 87
Canonbie Rd. SE23 . . . . 7J 105
Canonbury. 6C 50
Canonbury Bus. Cen. N1 . . . . 1C 68
Canonbury Ct. N1 . . . . 7B 50
(off Hawes St.)
Canonbury Cres. N1 . . . . 7C 50
Canonbury Gro. N1 . . . . 7C 50
Canonbury Heights. N1 . . . . . 6D 50
(off Dove Rd.)
Canonbury La. N1 . . . . 7B 50
Canonbury Pk. N. N1 . . . . . . 6C 50
Canonbury Pk. S. N1 . . . . . . 6C 50
Canonbury Pl. N1 . . . . 6B 50
(in two parts)
Canonbury Rd. N1 . . . . 6B 50
Canonbury Rd. Enf 1K 7
Canonbury Sq. N1 . . . . 7B 50
Canonbury St. N1 . . . . 7C 50
Canonbury Vs. N1 . . . . 7B 50
Canon Mohan Clo. N14 . . . . . . 6K 5
Canon Rd. Brom 3A 144
Canon Row. SW1
. . . . 2J 85 (7E 166)
(in two parts)
Canon's Clo. N2 . . . . 7B 30
Canons Clo. Edgw 6A 12
Canons Corner. Edgw 4K 11
Canons Ct. Edgw 6A 12
Canons Dri. Edgw 6K 11
Canonsleigh Rd. Dag 7B 56
Canons Park. 7J 11
Canons Pk. 6K 11
Canons Pk. Stan 6J 11
Canons Pk. Clo. Edgw 7K 11
Canon St. N1 . . . . 1C 68
Canon's Wlk. Croy 3K 153
Canopus Way. Stai 7A 94
Canrobert St. E2 . . . . 2H 69
Cantelowes Rd. NW1 . . . . . . 6H 49
(in two parts)
Canterbury Av. Ilf 7C 36
Canterbury Av. Sidc 2B 128
Canterbury Clo. E6 . . . . 6D 72
Canterbury Clo. SE5 . . . . . . 2C 104
(off Lilford Rd.)
Canterbury Clo. Beck 1D 142
Canterbury Clo. Gnfd 5F 61
Canterbury Ct. NW6 . . . . 2J 65
(off Canterbury Rd.)
Canterbury Ct. NW9 . . . . 2A 28
Canterbury Ct. SE12 . . . . . . 3K 125
Canterbury Cres. SW9 . . . . 3A 104
Canterbury Gro. SE27 . . . . . 4A 122
Canterbury Ho. SE1
. . . . 3K 85 (1H 173)
Canterbury Ho. SW9 . . . . 7A 86
Canterbury Ho. Bark 7A 56
(off Margaret Bondfield Av.)
Canterbury Ho. Croy 1D 152
(off Sydenham Rd.)
Canterbury Ind. Pk. SE15 . . . 6J 87
Canterbury Pl. SE17 . . . . 5B 86
Canterbury Rd. E10 . . . . 7E 34
Canterbury Rd. NW6 . . . . 2H 65
(in two parts)
Canterbury Rd. Croy 7K 139
Canterbury Rd. Felt 2C 114
Canterbury Rd. Harr 5F 25
Canterbury Rd. Mord 7K 137
Canterbury Ter. NW6 . . . . 2J 65
Cantium Retail Pk. SE1 . . . . . 6G 87
Cantley Gdns. SE19 . . . . . . 1F 141
Cantley Gdns. Ilf 6G 37
Cantley Rd. W7 . . . . 3A 80
Canton St. E14 . . . . 6C 70
Cantrell Rd. E3 . . . . 4B 70
Cantwell Rd. SE18 . . . . 7F 91
Canute Gdns. SE16 . . . . 4K 87
Canvey St. SE1 . . . . 1C 86 (4C 168)
Cape Clo. Bark 7F 55
Cape Henry Ct. E14 . . . . 7F 71
(off Jamestown Way)
Cape Ho. E8 . . . . 6F 51
(off Dalston La.)
Capel Av. Wall 5K 151
Capel Clo. N20 . . . . 3F 15
Capel Clo. Brom 1C 156
Capel Ct. EC2 . . . . . 6D 68 (1F 169)
(off Bartholomew La.)
Capel Ct. SE20 . . . . 1J 141
Capel Gdns. Ilf 4K 55
Capel Gdns. Pinn 4D 24
Capel Ho. E9 . . . . 7J 51
(off Loddiges Rd.)
Capel Rd. E7 & E12 . . . . 4K 53
Capel Rd. Barn 6H 5
Capener's Clo. SW1 . . . . 7F 165
Capern Rd. SW18 . . . . 1A 120
Cape Rd. N17 . . . . 3G 33
Cape Yd. E1 . . . . 7G 69
Capital Bus. Cen. Wemb 2D 62
Capital Ind. Est. Belv 3H 93
Capital Ind. Est. Mitc 5D 138
Capital Interchange Way. Bren
. . . . 5G 81
Capital Pl. Croy 5K 151
Capital Wharf. E1 . . . . 1G 87
Capitol Ind. Pk. NW9 . . . . 3J 27
Capitol Way. NW9 . . . . 3J 27
Capland Ho. NW8
. . . . 4B 66 (3B 158)
(off Capland St.)
Capland St. NW8
. . . . 4B 66 (3B 158)
Caple Ho. SW10 . . . . 7A 84
(off King's Rd.)
Caple Rd. NW10 . . . . 2B 64
Capper St. W1 . . . . 4G 67 (4B 160)
Caprea Clo. Hay 5B 60
Capricorn Cen. Dag 7F 39
Capri Ho. E17 . . . . 2B 34
Capri Rd. Croy 1F 153
Capstan Clo. Romf 6B 38
Capstan Ct. E1 . . . . 7J 69
(off Wapping Wall)
Capstan Ho. E14 . . . . 4E 88
(off Stebondale St.)
Capstan Ho. E14 . . . . 7F 71
(off Clove Cres.)
Capstan Ride. Enf 2F 7
Capstan Rd. SE8 . . . . 4B 88
Capstan Sq. E14 . . . . 2E 88
Capstan Way. SE16 . . . . 1A 88
Capstone Rd. Brom 4H 125
Capthorne Av. Harr 1C 42
Capuchin Clo. Stan 6G 11
Capulet M. E16 . . . . 1J 89
Capworth St. E10 . . . . 1C 52
Caradoc Clo. W2 . . . . 6J 65
Caradoc Evans Clo. N11 . . . . 5A 16
(off Springfield Rd.)
Caradoc St. SE10 . . . . 5G 89
Caradon Clo. E11 . . . . 1G 53
Caradon Way. N15 . . . . 4D 32
Caranday Villas. W11 . . . . . . 1F 83
(off Norland Rd.)
Caravel Clo. E14 . . . . 3C 88
Caravelle Gdns. N'holt 3B 60
Caravel M. SE8 . . . . 6C 88
Caraway Clo. E13 . . . . 5K 71
Caraway Heights. E14 . . . . . . 7E 70
(off Poplar High St.)
Caraway Pl. Wall 3F 151
Carberry Rd. SE19 . . . . 6E 122
Carbery Av. W3 . . . . 2F 81
Carbis Clo. E4 . . . . 1A 20
Carbis Rd. E14 . . . . 6B 70
Carbrooke Ho. E9 . . . . 1J 69
(off Templecombe Rd.)
Carbuncle Pas. Way. N17 . . . 2G 33
Carburton St. W1
. . . . 5F 67 (5K 159)
Cardale St. E14 . . . . 2E 88
Carden Rd. SE15 . . . . 3H 105
Cardiff Ho. SE15 . . . . 6G 87
(off Friary Est.)
Cardiff Rd. W7 . . . . 3A 80
Cardiff Rd. Enf 4C 8
Cardiff St. SE18 . . . . 7J 91
Cardigan Ct. W7 . . . . 4K 61
(off Copley Clo.)
Cardigan Gdns. Ilf 2A 56
Cardigan Pl. SE3 . . . . 2F 107
Cardigan Rd. E3 . . . . 2B 70
Cardigan Rd. SW13 . . . . . . 2C 100
Cardigan Rd. SW19 . . . . . . 6A 120
Cardigan Rd. Rich 6E 98
Cardigan St. SE11
. . . . 5A 86 (5J 173)
Cardigan Wlk. N1 . . . . 7C 50
(off Ashby Gro.)
Cardinal Av. King T 5E 116
Cardinal Av. Mord 6G 137
Cardinal Bourne St. SE1 . . . . 3D 86
Cardinal Cap All. SE1
. . . . 1C 86 (3C 168)
Cardinal Clo. Chst 1H 145
Cardinal Clo. Edgw 7E 12
Cardinal Clo. Mord 6G 137
Cardinal Clo. Wor Pk 4C 148
Cardinal Ct. E1 . . . . 7G 69
(off Thomas More St.)
Cardinal Cres. N Mald 2J 135
Cardinal Hinsley Clo. NW10
. . . . 2C 64
Cardinal Pl. SW15 . . . . 4F 101
Cardinal Rd. Felt 1K 113
Cardinal Rd. Ruis 1B 42
Cardinals Wlk. Hamp 7G 115
Cardinals Wlk. Sun 6G 113
Cardinals Way. N19 . . . . 1H 49
Cardinal Way. Harr 3J 25
Cardine M. SE15 . . . . 7H 87
Cardington Rd. H'row A 3D 94
Cardington Sq. Houn 4B 96
Cardington St. NW1
. . . . 3G 67 (1B 160)
Cardozo Rd. N7 . . . . 5J 49
Cardrew Av. N12 . . . . 5G 15
Cardrew Clo. N12 . . . . 5H 15
Cardrew Ct. N12 . . . . 5G 15
Cardross Ho. W6 . . . . 3D 82
(off Cardross St.)
Cardross St. W6 . . . . 3D 82
Cardwell Rd. N7 . . . . 4J 49
Career Ct. SE16 . . . . 2K 87
(off Christopher Clo.)
Carew Clo. N7 . . . . 2K 49
Carew Ct. SE14 . . . . 6K 87
(off Samuel Clo.)
Carew Ct. Sutt 7K 149
Carew Manor & Dovecote.
. . . . 3G 151
Carew Mnr. Cotts. Wall 3H 151
Carew Rd. N17 . . . . 2G 33
Carew Rd. W13 . . . . 2C 80
Carew Rd. Ashf 6E 112
Carew Rd. Mitc 2E 138
Carew Rd. T Hth 4B 140
Carew Rd. Wall 6G 151
Carew St. SE5 . . . . 2C 104
Carey Ct. SE5 . . . . 7C 86
Carey Ct. Bexh 5H 111
Carey Gdns. SW8 . . . . 1G 103
Carey La. EC2 . . . . . . 6C 68 (7C 162)
Carey Mans. SW1
. . . . 4H 85 (3C 172)
(off Rutherford St.)
Carey Pl. SW1 . . . . 4H 85 (4C 172)
Carey Rd. Dag 4E 56
Carey St. WC2 . . . . 6K 67 (1H 167)
Carey Way. Wemb 4H 45
Carfax Pl. SW4 . . . . 4H 103
Carfax Rd. Hay 5H 77
Carfree Clo. N1 . . . . 7A 50
Cargill Rd. SW18 . . . . 1K 119
Cargreen Pl. SE25 . . . . 4F 141
Cargreen Rd. SE25 . . . . 4F 141
Cargrey Ho. Stan 5H 11
Carholme Rd. SE23 . . . . 1B 124
Carillon Ct. W5 . . . . 7D 62
Carina M. SE27 . . . . 4C 122
Carinthia Ct. SE16 . . . . 4A 88
(off Plough Way)
Carisbrooke Av. Bex 1D 128
Carisbrooke Clo. Enf 1A 8
Carisbrooke Clo. Stan 2D 26
Carisbrooke Ct. W3 . . . . 2J 81
(off Brouncker Rd.)
Carisbrooke Ct. Cheam 7H 149
Carisbrooke Ct. N'holt 1D 60
(off Eskdale Av.)
Carisbrooke Gdns. SE15 . . . . 7F 87
Carisbrooke Rd. E17 . . . . 4A 34
Carisbrooke Rd. Brom 4A 144
Carisbrooke Rd. Mitc 4H 139
Carker's La. NW5 . . . . 5F 49
Carleton Av. Wall 7H 151
Carleton Clo. Esh 7H 133
Carleton Gdns. N19 . . . . 5G 49
Carleton Rd. N7 . . . . 5H 49
Carleton Vs. NW5 . . . . 5G 49
Carlile Clo. E3 . . . . 2B 70
Carlina Gdns. Wfd G 5E 20
Carlingford Gdns. Mitc 7D 120
Carlingford Rd. N8 . . . . 3B 32
Carlingford Rd. NW3 . . . . 4B 48
Carlingford Rd. Mord 6F 137
Carlisle Av. EC3 . . . . 6F 69 (1J 169)
Carlisle Av. W3 . . . . 6A 64
Carlisle Clo. King T 1G 135
Carlisle Clo. Pinn 1C 42
Carlisle Gdns. Harr 7D 26
Carlisle Gdns. Ilf 6C 36
Carlisle La. SE1 . . . 3K 85 (2H 173)
Carlisle Mans. SW1
. . . . 4G 85 (3A 172)
(off Carlisle Pl.)
Carlisle M. King T 1G 135
Carlisle Pl. N11 . . . . 4A 16
Carlisle Pl. SW1 . . . 3G 85 (2A 172)
Carlisle Rd. E10 . . . . 1C 52
Carlisle Rd. N4 . . . . 7A 32
Carlisle Rd. NW6 . . . . 1G 65
Carlisle Rd. NW9 . . . . 3J 27
Carlisle Rd. Hamp 7F 115
Carlisle Rd. Sutt 6H 149
Carlisle St. W1 . . . . 6H 67 (1C 166)
Carlisle Wlk. E8 . . . . 6F 51
Carlisle Way. SW17 . . . . 5E 120
Carlos Pl. W1 . . . . . 7E 66 (3H 165)
Carlow St. NW1 . . . . 2G 67
Carlson Ct. SW15 . . . . 4H 101
Carlton Av. N14 . . . . 5C 6
Carlton Av. Felt 6A 96
Carlton Av. Harr 5B 26
Carlton Av. Hay 4G 77
Carlton Av. S Croy 7E 152
Carlton Av. E. Wemb 2D 44
Carlton Av. W. Wemb 2B 44

Carlton Clo. NW3 2J 47
Carlton Clo. Chess 6D 146
Carlton Clo. Edgw 5B 12
Carlton Clo. N'holt 5G 43
Carlton Ct. SE20 1H 141
Carlton Ct. SW9 1B 104
Carlton Ct. W9 2K 65 (off Maida Va.)
Carlton Ct. Ilf 3H 37
Carlton Ct. Uxb 5A 58
Carlton Cres. Sutt 4G 149
Carlton Dri. SW15 5F 101
Carlton Dri. Ilf 3H 37
Carlton Gdns. SW1 1H 85 (5C 166)
Carlton Gdns. W5 6C 62
Carlton Grn. Sidc 4K 127
Carlton Gro. SE15 1H 105
Carlton Hill. NW8 2K 65
Carlton Ho. NW6 2J 65 (off Canterbury Ter., in five parts)
Carlton Ho. SE16 2K 87 (off Wolfe Cres.)
Carlton Ho. Felt 6H 95
Carlton Ho. Houn 6E 96
Carlton Ho. Ter. SW1 1H 85 (5C 166)
Carlton Lodge. N4 7A 32 (off Carlton Rd.)
Carlton Mans. NW6 7J 47 (off W. End La.)
Carlton Mans. W9 3K 65
Carlton M. NW6 3J 65
Carlton Pde. Wemb 2E 44
Carlton Pk. Av. SW20 2F 137
Carlton Rd. E11 1H 53
Carlton Rd. E12 4B 54
Carlton Rd. E17 1A 34
Carlton Rd. N4 7A 32
Carlton Rd. N11 5K 15
Carlton Rd. SW14 3J 99
Carlton Rd. W4 2K 81
Carlton Rd. W5 7C 62
Carlton Rd. Eri 6H 93
Carlton Rd. N Mald 2A 136
Carlton Rd. Sidc 5K 127
Carlton Rd. S Croy 6D 152
Carlton Rd. Sun 7H 113
Carlton Rd. W on T 7K 131
Carlton Rd. Well 3B 110
Carlton Sq. E1 4K 69 (in two parts)
Carlton St. SW1 7H 67 (3C 166)
Carlton Ter. E7 7A 54
Carlton Ter. E11 5K 35
Carlton Ter. N18 3J 17
Carlton Ter. SE26 3J 123
Carlton Tower Pl. SW1 3D 84 (1F 171)
Carlton Va. NW6 2H 65
Carlwell St. SW17 5C 120
Carlyle Av. Brom 3B 144
Carlyle Av. S'hall 7D 60
Carlyle Clo. N2 6A 30
Carlyle Clo. NW10 1K 63
Carlyle Clo. W Mol 2F 133
Carlyle Ct. SW6 1K 101 (off Imperial Rd.)
Carlyle Ct. SW10 1A 102 (off Chelsea Harbour)
Carlyle Gdns. S'hall 7D 60
Carlyle M. E1 4K 69
Carlyle Pl. SW15 4F 101
Carlyle Rd. E12 4C 54
Carlyle Rd. SE28 7B 74
Carlyle Rd. W5 5C 80
Carlyle Rd. Croy 2G 153
Carlyle's House. 6C 84 (7C 170) (off Cheyne Row)
Carlyle Sq. SW3 5B 84 (6B 170)
Carlyon Av. Harr 4D 42
Carlyon Clo. Wemb 1E 62
Carlyon Rd. Hay 5A 60 (in two parts)
Carlyon Rd. Wemb 2E 62
Carlys Clo. Beck 2K 141
Carmalt Gdns. SW15 4E 100
Carmarthen Ct. W7 4K 61 (off Copley Clo.)
Carmarthen Grn. NW9 5A 28
Carmarthen Pl. SE1 2E 86 (6G 169)
Carmel Ct. W8 2K 83 (off Holland St.)
Carmelite Clo. Harr 1G 25
Carmelite Rd. Harr 1G 25
Carmelite St. EC4 7A 68 (2K 167)
Carmelite Wlk. Harr 1G 25
Carmelite Way. Harr 2G 25
Carmen St. E14 6D 70
Carmichael Clo. SW11 3B 102
Carmichael Ct. SW13 2B 100 (off Grove Rd.)
Carmichael Ho. E14 7E 70 (off Poplar High St.)
Carmichael M. SW18 7B 102
Carmichael Rd. SE25 5F 141
Carmine Ct. Brom 7H 125
Carminia Rd. SW17 2F 121
Carnaby St. W1 6G 67 (1A 166)
Carnac St. SE27 4D 122
Carnanton Rd. E17 1F 35
Carnarvon Av. Enf 3A 8
Carnarvon Dri. Hay 3E 76
Carnarvon Rd. E10 5E 34
Carnarvon Rd. E15 6H 53
Carnarvon Rd. E18 1H 35
Carnarvon Rd. Barn 3B 4
Carnation Clo. Rush G 2K 57
Carnation St. SE2 5B 92
Carnbrook Rd. SE3 3B 108
Carnecke Gdns. SE9 5C 108
Carnegie Clo. Surb 2F 147
Carnegie Pl. SW19 3F 119
Carnegie Rd. Harr 7K 25
Carnegie St. N1 1K 67
Carnforth Clo. Eps 6H 147
Carnforth Rd. SW16 7H 121
Carnie Hall. SW17 3F 121
Carnival Ho. SE1 2F 87 (6K 169) (off Gainsford St.)
Carnoustie Clo. SE28 6D 74
Carnoustie Dri. N1 7K 49 (in two parts)
Carnwath Rd. SW6 3J 101
Caroe Ct. N9 1C 18
Carol Clo. NW4 4F 29
Carolina Clo. E15 5G 53
Carolina Rd. T Hth 2B 140
Caroline Clo. N10 2F 31
Caroline Clo. SW16 3K 121
Caroline Clo. W2 7K 65 (off Bayswater Rd.)
Caroline Clo. Croy 4E 152
Caroline Clo. Iswth 7H 79
Caroline Clo. W Dray 2A 76
Caroline Ct. SE6 4F 125
Caroline Ct. Ashf 6D 112
Caroline Ct. Stan 6F 11
Caroline Gdns. E2 3E 68 (1H 163)
Caroline Gdns. SE15 7H 87
Caroline Ho. W6 5E 82 (off Queen Caroline St.)
Caroline Pl. SW11 2E 102
Caroline Pl. W2 7K 65
Caroline Pl. Hay 7G 77
Caroline Pl. M. W2 7K 65
Caroline Rd. SW19 7H 119
Caroline St. E1 6K 69
Caroline Ter. SW1 4E 84 (4G 171)
Caroline Wlk. W6 6G 83 (off Lillie Rd.)
Carol St. NW1 1G 67
Caronia Ct. SE16 4A 88 (off Plough Way)
Carpenter Gdns. N21 2G 17
Carpenter Ho. E14 5C 70 (off Burgess St.)
Carpenter Ho. NW11 6A 30
Carpenters Clo. Barn 6E 4
Carpenters Ct. NW1 1G 67 (off Pratt St.)
Carpenters Ct. Twic 2J 115
Carpenters M. N7 5J 49
Carpenters Pl. SW4 4H 103
Carpenter's Rd. E15 6C 52
Carpenter St. W1 7F 67 (3J 165)
Carradale Ho. E14 6E 70 (off St Leonard's Rd.)
Carrara M. E8 6G 51
Carrara Wlk. SE24 4A 104
Carrara Wharf. SW6 3G 101
Carr Gro. SE18 4C 90
Carr Ho. Dart 5K 111
Carriage Dri. E. SW11 7E 84
Carriage Dri. N. SW11 7D 84 (7H 171) (in two parts)
Carriage Dri. S. SW11 1D 102
Carriage Dri. W. SW11 7D 84
Carriage M. Ilf 2G 55
Carriage Pl. N16 3D 50
Carriage Pl. SW16 5G 121
Carrick Clo. Iswth 3A 98
Carrick Dri. Ilf 1G 37
Carrick Gdns. N17 7K 17
Carrick Ho. N7 6K 49 (off Caledonian Rd.)
Carrick Ho. SE11 5A 86 (5K 173)
Carrick M. SE8 6C 88
Carrill Way. Belv 4D 92
Carrington Av. Houn 5F 97
Carrington Clo. Croy 7A 142
Carrington Clo. King T 5J 117
Carrington Ct. SW11 4C 102 (off Barnard Rd.)
Carrington Gdns. E7 4J 53
Carrington Ho. W1 1F 85 (5J 165) (off Carrington St.)
Carrington Rd. Rich 4G 99
Carrington Sq. Harr 6B 10
Carrington St. W1 1F 85 (5J 165)
Carrol Clo. NW5 4F 49
Carroll Clo. E15 5H 53
Carroll Ct. W3 3H 81 (off Osborne Rd.)
Carroll Ho. W2 7B 66 (2A 164) (off Craven Ter.)
Carronade Pl. SE28 3G 91
Carron Clo. E14 6D 70
Carroun Rd. SW8 7K 85
Carroway La. Gnfd 3H 61
Carrow Rd. Dag 7B 56
Carr Rd. E17 2B 34
Carr Rd. N'holt 6E 42
Carrs La. N21 5H 7
Carr St. E14 5A 70 (in two parts)
Carshalton. 4E 150
Carshalton Athletic F.C. 3C 150
Carshalton Beeches. 7C 150
Carshalton Gro. Sutt 4B 150
Carshalton on the Hill. 7E 150
Carshalton Pk. Rd. Cars 5D 150
Carshalton Pl. Cars 5E 150
Carshalton Rd. Mitc 4E 138
Carshalton Rd. Sutt & Cars 5A 150
Carslake Rd. SW15 6E 100
Carson Rd. E16 4J 71
Carson Rd. SE21 2D 122
Carson Rd. Cockf 4J 5
Carstairs Rd. SE6 3E 124
Carston Clo. SE12 5H 107
Carswell Clo. Ilf 4B 36
Carswell Rd. SE6 7E 106
Carter Clo. Wall 7H 151
Carter Ct. EC4 1A 168
Carter Dri. Romf 1H 39
Carteret Ho. W12 7D 64 (off White City Est.)
Carteret St. SW1 2H 85 (7C 166)
Carteret Way. SE8 4A 88
Carterhatch La. Enf 1A 8
Carterhatch Rd. Enf 1D 8
Carter Ho. E1 6J 163
Carter La. EC4 6B 68 (1B 168)
Carter Pl. SE17 5C 86
Carter Rd. E13 1K 71
Carter Rd. SW19 6B 120
Carters Clo. NW5 5H 49 (off Torriano Av.)
Carters Clo. Wor Pk 2F 149
Carters Hill Clo. SE9 1A 126
Carters La. SE23 2A 124
Carter St. SE17 6C 86
Carter's Yd. SW18 5J 101
Carthew Rd. W6 3D 82
Carthew Vs. W6 3D 82
Carthusian St. EC1 5B 68 (5C 162)
Cartier Circ. E14 1D 88
Carting La. WC2 7J 67 (3F 167)
Cart La. E4 1B 20
Cartmel. NW1 3G 67 (1A 160) (off Hampstead Rd.)
Cartmel Clo. N17 7C 18
Cartmel Ct. N'holt 6C 42
Cartmel Gdns. Mord 5A 138
Cartmel Rd. Bexh 1G 111
Carton Ho. SE16 7K 169
Carton Ho. W11 1F 83 (off St Ann's Rd.)
Cartwright Gdns. WC1 3J 67 (2E 160)
Cartwright Ho. SE1 3C 86 (off County St.)
Cartwright Rd. Dag 7F 57
Cartwright St. E1 7F 69 (2K 169)
Cartwright Way. SW13 7D 82
Carvel Ho. E14 5E 88 (off Manchester Rd.)
Carver Clo. W4 3J 81
Carver Rd. SE24 6C 104
Carville Cres. Bren 4E 80
Cary Rd. E11 4G 53
Carysfort Rd. N8 5H 31
Carysfort Rd. N16 3D 50
Casby Ho. SE16 3G 87 (off Marine St.)
Cascade Av. N10 4G 31
Cascade Clo. Buck H 2G 21
Cascade Rd. Buck H 2G 21
Cascades Tower. E14 1B 88
Casella Rd. SE14 7K 87
Casewick Rd. SE27 5A 122
Casimir Rd. E5 2J 51
Casino Av. SE24 5C 104
Caspian Ho. E1 5K 69 (off Shandy St.)
Caspian St. SE5 7D 86
Caspian Wlk. E16 6B 72
Cassandra Clo. N'holt 4H 43
Casselden Rd. NW10 7K 45
Cassell Ho. SW9 2J 103 (off Stockwell Gdns. Est.)
Cassidy Rd. SW6 7J 83 (in two parts)
Cassilda Rd. SE2 4A 92
Cassilis Rd. Twic 5B 98
Cassiobury Av. Felt 7H 95
Cassiobury Rd. E17 5A 34
Cassland Rd. E9 7K 51
Cassland Rd. T Hth 4D 140
Casslee Rd. SE6 7B 106
Cassocks Sq. Shep 7F 131
Casson Ho. E1 5G 69 (5K 163) (off Spelman St.)
Casson St. E1 5G 69
Castalia Sq. E14 2E 88
Castellain Mans. W9 4K 65 (off Castellain Rd., in two parts)
Castellain Rd. W9 4K 65
Castellane Clo. Stan 7E 10
Castell Ho. SE8 7C 88
Castello Av. SW15 5E 100
Castelnau. 6D 82
Castelnau. SW13 1C 100
Castelnau Gdns. SW13 6D 82
Castelnau Mans. SW13 6D 82 (off Castelnau, in two parts)
Castelnau Row. SW13 6D 82
Casterbridge. NW6 1K 65 (off Abbey Rd.)
Casterbridge. W11 6H 65 (off Dartmouth Clo.)
Casterbridge Rd. SE3 3J 107
Casterton St. E8 6H 51
Castile Rd. SE18 4E 90
Castillon Rd. SE6 2G 125
Castlands Rd. SE6 2B 124
Castleacre. W2 6C 66 (1C 164) (off Hyde Pk. Cres.)
Castle Av. E4 5A 20
Castle Av. Eps 7C 148
Castle Av. W Dray 7A 58
Castlebar Ct. W5 5C 62
Castlebar Hill. W5 5C 62
Castlebar M. W5 5C 62
Castlebar Pk. W5 5B 62
Castlebar Rd. W5 5C 62
Castle Baynard St. EC4 7B 68 (2B 168)
Castlebrook Ct. SE11 4B 86
Castle Clo. E9 5A 52
Castle Clo. SW19 3F 119
Castle Clo. W3 2H 81
Castle Clo. Brom 3G 143
Castle Clo. Sun 7G 113
Castlecombe Dri. SW19 7F 101
Castlecombe Rd. SE9 4C 126
Castle Ct. EC3 6D 68 (1F 169) (off Birchin La.)
Castle Ct. SE26 4A 124
Castledine Rd. SE20 7H 123
Castle Dri. Ilf 6C 36
Castleford Av. SE9 1F 127
Castleford Clo. N17 6A 18
Castleford Ct. NW8 4B 66 (3B 158) (off Henderson Dri.)
Castlegate. Rich 3F 99
Castlehaven Rd. NW1 7F 49
Castle Hill Av. New Ad 7D 154
Castle Hill Pde. W13 7B 62 (off Avenue, The)
Castle Ho. SE1 4C 86 (off Walworth Rd.)
Castle Ho. SW8 7J 85 (off S. Lambeth Rd.)
Castle Ind. Est. SE17 4C 86
Castle La. SW1 3G 85 (1B 172)
Castleleigh Ct. Enf 5J 7
Castlemaine. SW11 2D 102
Castlemaine Av. Eps 7D 148
Castlemaine Av. S Croy 5F 153
Castle Mead. SE5 7C 86
Castle M. N12 5F 15
Castle M. NW1 6F 49
Castle Pde. Eps 7C 148
Castle Pl. NW1 6F 49
Castle Pl. W4 4A 82
Castle Point. E13 2A 72 (off Boundary Rd.)
Castlereagh St. W1 6D 66 (7E 158)
Castle Rd. N12 5F 15
Castle Rd. NW1 6F 49
Castle Rd. Dag 1B 74
Castle Rd. Enf 1F 9

Castle Rd. Iswth 2K 97
Castle Rd. N'holt 6F 43
Castle Rd. S'hall 3D 78
Castle Row. W4 5K 81
Castle St. E6 2A 72
Castle St. King T 2E 134
Castleton Av. Bexh 1K 111
Castleton Av. Wemb 4E 44
Castleton Clo. Croy 6A 142
Castleton Gdns. Wemb 3E 44
Castleton Ho. E14 4E 88 (off Pier St.)
Castleton Rd. E17 2F 35
Castleton Rd. SE9 4B 126
Castleton Rd. Ilf 1A 56
Castleton Rd. Mitc 4H 139 (in two parts)
Castleton Rd. Ruis 1B 42
Castletown Rd. W14 5G 83
Castleview Clo. N4 2C 50
Castleview Gdns. Ilf 6C 36
Castle Wlk. Sun 3A 132
Castle Way. SW19 3F 119
Castle Way. Felt 4A 114
Castle Wharf. E14 7G 71 (off Orchard Pl.)
Castlewood Dri. SE9 2D 108
Castlewood Rd. N15 & N16 6G 33
Castlewood Rd. Cockf 3G 5
Castle Yd. N6 7E 30
Castle Yd. SE1 1B 86 (4B 168)
Castle Yd. Rich 5D 98
Castor La. E14 7D 70
Catalina Rd. H'row A 2D 94
Caterham Av. Ilf 2D 36
Caterham Rd. SE13 3F 107
Catesby Ho. E9 7J 51 (off Frampton Pk. Rd.)
Catesby St. SE17 4D 86
Catford. 7D 106
Catford B'way. SE6 7D 106
Catford Greyhound Stadium. 6C 106
Catford Gyratory. (Junct.) 1D 124
Catford Hill. SE6 1B 124
Catford Island. SE6 7D 106
Catford M. SE6 7D 106
Catford Rd. SE6 7C 106
Catford Trad. Est. SE6 2D 124
Cathall Rd. E11 2F 53
Cathay Ho. SE16 2H 87
Cathay St. SE16 2H 87
Cathay Wlk. N'holt 2E 60 (off Brabazon Rd.)
Cathcart Dri. Orp 7J 145
Cathcart Hill. N19 3G 49
Cathcart Rd. SW10 6K 83
Cathcart St. NW5 6F 49
Cathedral Lodge. EC1 5C 68 (5C 162) (off Aldersgate St.)
Cathedral Mans. SW1 4G 85 (3A 172) (off Vauxhall Bri. Rd.)
Cathedral Piazza. SW1 3G 85 (2A 172)
Cathedral St. SE1 1D 86 (4E 168)
Catherall Rd. N5 3C 50
Catherine Ct. N14 5B 6
Catherine Ct. SW19 5H 119
Catherine Ct. Ilf 6G 37
Catherine Dri. Rich 4E 98
Catherine Dri. Sun 6H 113
Catherine Gdns. Houn 4H 97
Catherine Griffiths Ct. EC1 4A 68 (3K 161) (off Pine St.)
Catherine Gro. SE10 1D 106
Catherine Ho. N1 1E 68 (off Whitmore Est.)
Catherine Howard Ct. SE9 6H 109
Catherine of Aragon Ct. SE9 6G 109
Catherine Parr Ct. SE9 6H 109
Catherine Pl. SW1 3G 85 (1A 172)
Catherine Pl. Harr 5K 25
Catherine Rd. Surb 5D 134
Catherine St. WC2 7K 67 (2G 167)
Catherine Wheel All. E1 5E 68 (6H 163) (in two parts)
Catherine Wheel Rd. Bren 7D 80
Catherine Wheel Yd. SW1 5A 166
Catherwood Ct. N1 1E 162 (in two parts)
Cat Hill. Barn 6H 5
Cathles Rd. SW12 6F 103
Cathnor Rd. W12 2D 82
Catlin Cres. Shep 5F 131
Catling Clo. SE23 3J 123
Catlin's La. Pinn 3K 23
Catlin St. SE16 5G 87
Cator La. Beck 1B 142
Cato Rd. SW4 3H 103
Cator Rd. SE26 6K 123
Cator Rd. Cars 5D 150
Cator St. SE15 7F 87 (Commercial Way)
Cator St. SE15 6F 87 (St George's Way)
Cato St. W1 5C 66 (6D 158)
Catsey La. Bush 1B 10
Catsey Wood. Bush 1B 10
Catterick Clo. N11 6K 15
Cattistock Rd. SE9 5C 126
Cattley Clo. Barn 4B 4
Catton St. WC1 5K 67 (6G 161)
Caudwell Ter. SW18 6B 102
Caughley Ho. SE11 2J 173
Caulfield Rd. E6 1C 72
Caulfield Rd. SE15 2H 105
Causeway, The. N2 4C 30
Causeway, The. SW18 5K 101 (in two parts)
Causeway, The. SW19 5E 118
Causeway, The. Cars 3E 150
Causeway, The. Chess 4E 146
Causeway, The. Clay 7A 146
Causeway, The. Felt & Houn 4J 95
Causeway, The. Sutt 7A 150
Causeway, The. Tedd 6K 115
Causeyware Rd. N9 7D 8
Causton Cotts. E14 6A 70
Causton Ho. SE5 6C 86
Causton Rd. N6 7F 31
Causton Sq. Dag 7G 57
Causton St. SW1 4H 85 (4D 172)
Cautley Av. SW4 5G 103
Cavalier Clo. Romf 4D 38
Cavalier Ct. Surb 6F 135
Cavalier Gdns. Hay 6F 59
Cavalry Cres. Houn 4B 96
Cavalry Gdns. SW15 5H 101
Cavan Pl. Pinn 1D 24
Cavaye Pl. SW10 5A 84 (6A 170)
Cavell Dri. Enf 2F 7
Cavell Ho. N1 1E 68 (off Colville Est.)
Cavell Rd. N17 7J 17
Cavell St. E1 5H 69
Cavendish Av. N3 2J 29
Cavendish Av. NW8 2B 66 (1B 158)
Cavendish Av. W13 5A 62
Cavendish Av. Eri 6J 93
Cavendish Av. Harr 4H 43
Cavendish Av. N Mald 5C 136
Cavendish Av. Ruis 5K 41
Cavendish Av. Sidc 7A 110
Cavendish Av. Well 3K 109
Cavendish Av. Wfd G 1K 35
Cavendish Clo. N18 5C 18
Cavendish Clo. NW6 6H 47
Cavendish Clo. NW8 3B 66 (1B 158)
Cavendish Clo. Hay 5G 59
Cavendish Clo. Sun 6H 113
Cavendish Ct. EC3 7H 163
Cavendish Ct. Sun 6H 113
Cavendish Dri. E11 1F 53
Cavendish Dri. Edgw 6A 12
Cavendish Gdns. SW4 6G 103
Cavendish Gdns. Bark 5J 55
Cavendish Gdns. Ilf 1E 54
Cavendish Gdns. Romf 5E 38
Cavendish Ho. NW8 2B 66 (1B 158) (off Wellington Rd.)
Cavendish Mans. EC1 4A 68 (4J 161) (off Rosebery Av.)
Cavendish Mans. NW6 5J 47
Cavendish M. N. W1 5F 67 (5K 159)
Cavendish M. S. W1 5F 67 (6K 159)
Cavendish Pde. SW12 6F 103 (off Clapham Comn. S. Side)
Cavendish Pde. Houn 2C 96
Cavendish Pl. SW4 5H 103
Cavendish Pl. W1 6F 67 (7K 159)
Cavendish Rd. E4 6K 19
Cavendish Rd. N4 6B 32
Cavendish Rd. N18 5C 18
Cavendish Rd. NW6 7G 47
Cavendish Rd. SW12 6F 103
Cavendish Rd. SW19 7B 120
Cavendish Rd. W4 1J 99
Cavendish Rd. Barn 3A 4
Cavendish Rd. Croy 1B 152
Cavendish Rd. N Mald 4B 136
Cavendish Rd. Sun 6H 113
Cavendish Rd. Sutt 7A 150
Cavendish Sq. W1 6F 67 (7K 159)
Cavendish St. N1 2D 68
Cavendish Ter. Felt 2J 113
Cavendish Way. W Wick 1D 154
Cavenham Gdns. Ilf 3H 55
Caverleigh Way. Wor Pk 1C 148
Cave Rd. E13 3K 71
Cave Rd. Rich 4C 116
Caversham Av. N13 3F 17
Caversham Av. Sutt 2G 149
Caversham Ct. N11 2K 15
Caversham Ho. N15 4C 32 (off Caversham Rd.)
Caversham Ho. SE15 6G 87 (off Haymerle Rd.)
Caversham Ho. King T 2E 134 (off Lady Booth Rd.)
Caversham Rd. N15 4C 32
Caversham Rd. NW5 6G 49
Caversham Rd. King T 2F 135
Caversham St. SW3 6D 84 (7E 170)
Caverswall St. W12 6E 64
Caveside Clo. Chst 1E 144
Cavour Ho. SE17 5B 86 (off Alberta Est.)
Cawdor Cres. W7 4A 80
Cawnpore St. SE19 5E 122
Caxton Ct. SW11 2C 102
Caxton Gro. E3 3C 70
Caxton M. Bren 6D 80
Caxton Pl. Ilf 3E 54
Caxton Rd. N22 2K 31
Caxton Rd. SW19 5A 120
Caxton Rd. W12 2F 83
Caxton Rd. S'hall 3B 78
Caxton St. SW1 3G 85 (1C 172)
Caxton St. N. E16 6H 71
Caxton Trad. Est. Hay 2G 77
Caxton Wlk. WC2 6H 67 (1D 166)
Caygill Clo. Brom 4H 143
Cayley Clo. Wall 7J 151
Cayley Rd. S'hall 3F 79
Cayton Pl. EC1 2E 162
Cayton Rd. Gnfd 2J 61
Cayton St. EC1 3D 68 (2E 162)
Cazenove Rd. E17 1C 34
Cazenove Rd. N16 2F 51
Cearns Ho. E6 1B 72
Cecil Av. Bark 7H 55
Cecil Av. Enf 4A 8
Cecil Av. Wemb 5F 45
Cecil Clo. W5 5D 62
Cecil Clo. Ashf 7E 112
Cecil Clo. Chess 4D 146
Cecil Ct. NW6 7K 47
Cecil Ct. SW10 6A 84 (off Fawcett St.)
Cecil Ct. WC2 7J 67 (3E 166)
Cecil Ct. Barn 3A 4
Cecil Ct. Enf 4J 7
Cecile Pk. N8 6J 31
Cecil Ho. E17 1C 34
Cecilia Clo. N2 3A 30
Cecilia Rd. E8 5F 51
Cecil Pk. Pinn 4C 24
Cecil Pl. Mitc 5D 138
Cecil Rhodes Ho. NW1 2H 67 (off Goldington St.)
Cecil Rd. E11 3H 53
Cecil Rd. E13 1J 71
Cecil Rd. E17 1C 34
Cecil Rd. N10 2F 31
Cecil Rd. N14 1B 16
Cecil Rd. NW9 3A 28
Cecil Rd. NW10 1A 64
Cecil Rd. SW19 7K 119
Cecil Rd. W3 5J 63
Cecil Rd. Ashf 7E 112
Cecil Rd. Croy 6J 139
Cecil Rd. Enf 3H 7
Cecil Rd. Harr 3J 25
Cecil Rd. Houn 2G 97
Cecil Rd. Ilf 4F 55
Cecil Rd. Romf 7D 38
Cecil Rd. Sutt 6H 149
Cecil Rosen Ct. Wemb 3B 44
Cecil Way. Brom 1J 155
Cedar Av. Barn 7H 5
Cedar Av. Enf 2D 8
Cedar Av. Hay 6J 59
Cedar Av. Romf 5E 38
Cedar Av. Ruis 5A 42
Cedar Av. Sidc 7A 110
Cedar Av. Twic 6F 97
Cedar Av. W Dray 7B 58
Cedar Clo. SE21 1C 122
Cedar Clo. SW15 4K 117
Cedar Clo. Brom 3C 156
Cedar Clo. Buck H 2G 21
Cedar Clo. Cars 6D 150
Cedar Clo. E Mol 4J 133
Cedar Clo. Romf 4J 39
Cedar Copse. Brom 2D 144
Cedar Ct. E18 1J 35
Cedar Ct. N1 7C 50
Cedar Ct. N10 2E 30
Cedar Ct. N11 5B 16
Cedar Ct. N20 1G 15
Cedar Ct. SE7 6A 90
Cedar Ct. SW19 3F 119
Cedar Ct. Bren 6C 80
Cedar Ct. Sutt 6A 150
Cedar Cres. Brom 3C 156
Cedarcroft Rd. Chess 4F 147
Cedar Dri. N2 4C 30
Cedar Gdns. Sutt 6A 150
Cedar Grange. Enf 5K 7
Cedar Gro. W5 3E 80
Cedar Gro. Bex 6D 110
Cedar Gro. S'hall 5E 60
Cedar Heights. NW2 6H 47
Cedar Heights. Rich 1E 116
Cedar Ho. E14 2E 88 (off Manchester Rd.)
Cedar Ho. N22 1A 32 (off Acacia Rd.)
Cedar Ho. SE14 1K 105
Cedar Ho. SE16 2K 87 (off Woodland Cres.)
Cedar Ho. W8 3K 83 (off Marloes Rd.)
Cedar Ho. Hay 4A 60
Cedarhurst. Brom 7G 125
Cedarhurst Cotts. Bex 7G 111
Cedarhurst Dri. SE9 5A 108
Cedarland Ter. SW20 7D 118
Cedar Lawn Av. Barn 5B 4
Cedar Mt. SE9 1B 126
Cedarne Rd. SW6 7K 83
Cedar Pk. Gdns. Romf 7D 38
Cedar Pk. Rd. Enf 1H 7
Cedar Pl. SE7 5A 90
Cedar Ri. N14 7K 5
Cedar Rd. N17 1F 33
Cedar Rd. NW2 4E 46
Cedar Rd. Brom 2A 144
Cedar Rd. Croy 2D 152
Cedar Rd. E Mol 4J 133
Cedar Rd. Enf 1G 7
Cedar Rd. Felt 1F 113
Cedar Rd. Houn 2A 96
Cedar Rd. Romf 4J 39
Cedar Rd. Sutt 6A 150
Cedar Rd. Tedd 5A 116
Cedars Av. E17 5C 34
Cedars Av. Mitc 4E 138
Cedars Clo. NW4 3F 29
Cedars Clo. SE13 3F 107
Cedars Ct. N9 2K 17
Cedars Dri. Uxb 2B 58
Cedars Ho. E17 3D 34
Cedars M. SW4 4F 103 (in two parts)
Cedars Rd. E15 6G 53
Cedars Rd. N9 2B 18
Cedars Rd. N21 2G 17
Cedars Rd. SW4 3F 103
Cedars Rd. SW13 2C 100
Cedars Rd. W4 6J 81
Cedars Rd. Beck 2A 142
Cedars Rd. Croy 3J 151
Cedars Rd. Hamp W 1C 134
Cedars Rd. Mord 4J 137
Cedars, The. E15 7H 53
Cedars, The. W13 6C 62
Cedars, The. Buck H 1D 20
Cedars, The. Tedd 6K 115
Cedars, The. Wall 4G 151
Cedar Ter. Rich 4E 98
Cedar Tree Gro. SE27 5B 122
Cedar Vw. King T 3D 134 (off Milner Rd.)
Cedarville Gdns. SW16 6K 121
Cedar Way. NW1 7H 49
Cedar Way. Sun 7G 113
Cedar Way Ind. Est. NW1 7H 49
Cedra Ct. N16 1G 51
Cedric Rd. SE9 3G 127
Celadon Clo. Enf 3F 9
Celandine Clo. E3 5C 70
Celandine Ct. E4 3J 19
Celandine Dri. E8 7F 51
Celandine Dri. SE28 1B 92
Celandine Way. E15 3G 71
Celbridge M. W2 5K 65
Celestial Gdns. SE13 4F 107
Celia Cres. Ashf 6A 112
Celia Ho. N1 2E 68 (off Arden Est.)
Celia Rd. N19 4G 49
Celtic Av. Brom 3G 143
Celtic St. E14 5D 70

Cemetery La. SE7 6C 90
Cemetery Rd. E7 5H 53
Cemetery Rd. N17 7K 17
Cemetery Rd. SE2 7B 92
Cenacle Clo. NW3 3J 47
Cenotaph. 2J 85 (6E 166)
Centaur Ct. Bren 5E 80
Centaurs Bus. Cen. Iswth 6A 80
Centaur St. SE1 3K 85 (1H 173)
Centenary Rd. Enf 4G 9
Centenary Trad. Est. Enf 3G 9
Centennial Av. Els 1H 11
Central Av. E11 2F 53
Central Av. N2 2B 30 (East Finchley)
Central Av. N2 4K 29 (St Marylebone Cemetery)
Central Av. N9 3K 17
Central Av. SW11 7D 84
Central Av. Enf 2C 8
Central Av. Hay 1H 77
Central Av. Houn 4G 97
Central Av. Pinn 6D 24
Central Av. Wall 5J 151
Central Av. Well 2K 109
Central Av. W Mol 4D 132
Central Bus. Cen. NW10 5A 46
Central Cir. NW4 5D 28
Central Criminal Court. (Old Bailey) 6B 68 (7B 162)
Central Gdns. Mord 5K 137
Central Hill. SE19 5C 122
Central Ho. E15 2E 70
Central Mans. NW4 5D 28 (off Watford Way)
Central Markets. (Smithfield) 5B 68 (6A 162) (off Charterhouse St.)
Central Pde. E17 4C 34
Central Pde. SE20 7K 123 (off High St.)
Central Pde. W3 2H 81
Central Pde. Enf 2D 8
Central Pde. Felt 7A 96
Central Pde. Gnfd 3A 62
Central Pde. Harr 5K 25
Central Pde. Houn 7D 78
Central Pde. Ilf 6H 37
Central Pde. Sidc 3A 128
Central Pde. Surb 6E 134
Central Pde. W Mol 4D 132
Central Pk. Av. Dag 3H 57
Central Pk. Est. Houn 5B 96
Central Pk. Rd. E6 2B 72
Central Pl. SE25 5G 141
Central Rd. Mord 6J 137
Central Rd. Wemb 5B 44
Central Rd. Wor Pk 1C 148
Central School Path. SW14 3J 99
Central Sq. NW11 6K 29
Central Sq. Wemb 5E 44
Central St. EC1 3C 68 (1C 162)
Central Ter. Beck 3K 141
Central Way. NW10 3J 63
Central Way. SE28 1A 92
Central Way. Cars 7C 150
Central Way. Felt 5J 95
Centre Av. N2 2C 30
Centre Av. NW10 3E 64
Centre Av. W3 1K 81
Centre Comn. Rd. Chst 6G 127
Centre Ct. Shop. Cen. SW19 6H 119
Centre Dri. E7 4A 54
Cen. for the Magic Arts. 4G 67 (3B 160) (off Stephenson Way)
Centre Heights. NW3 7B 48 (off Finchley Rd.)
Centre Point. SE1 5G 87
Centrepoint. WC2 6H 67 (off St Giles High St.)
Centre Point Ho. WC2 6H 67 (7D 160) (off St Giles High St.)
Centre Rd. E11 & E7 2J 53
Centre Rd. Dag 2H 75
Centre St. E2 2H 69
Centre, The. Felt 2J 113
Centre, The. Houn 3F 97
Centre, The. W on T 7H 131
Centre Way. E17 7K 19
Centre Way. N9 2D 18
Centre Way. Ilf 2G 55
Centric Clo. NW1 1E 66
Centro Ct. E6 4D 72
Centurion Clo. N7 7K 49
Centurion Ct. Hack 2F 151
Centurion La. E3 1B 70
Centurion Way. Eri 3F 93
Century Clo. NW4 5F 29
Century Ho. SW15 4F 101
Century M. E5 4J 51
Century Rd. E17 3A 34
Century Yd. SE23 2J 123
Cephas Av. E1 4J 69
Cephas Ho. E1 4J 69 (off Doveton St.)
Cephas St. E1 4J 69
Ceres Rd. SE18 4K 91
Cerise Rd. SE15 1G 105
Cerne Clo. Hay 7A 60
Cerne Rd. Mord 6A 138
Cerney M. W2 7B 66 (2A 164)
Cervantes Ct. W2 6K 65
Cester St. E2 1G 69
Ceylon Rd. W14 3F 83
Chadacre Av. Ilf 3D 36
Chadacre Ct. E15 1J 71 (off Vicars Clo.)
Chadacre Ho. SW9 4B 104 (off Loughborough Pk.)
Chadacre Rd. Eps 6D 148
Chadbourn St. E14 5D 70
Chadbury Ct. NW7 7H 13
Chadd Dri. Brom 3C 144
Chadd Grn. E13 1J 71 (in two parts)
Chadston Ho. N1 7B 50 (off Halton Rd.)
Chadswell. WC1 3J 67 (2F 161) (off Cromer St.)
Chadview Ct. Romf 7D 38
Chadville Gdns. Romf 5D 38
Chadway. Dag 1C 56
Chadwell Av. Romf 7B 38
Chadwell Heath. 7D 38
Chadwell Heath Ind. Pk. Dag 1E 56
Chadwell Heath La. Chad H & Romf 4B 38
Chadwell St. EC1 3A 68 (1K 161)
Chadwick Av. E4 4A 20
Chadwick Av. N21 5E 6
Chadwick Av. SW19 6J 119
Chadwick Clo. SW15 7B 100
Chadwick Clo. W7 5K 61
Chadwick Clo. Tedd 6A 116
Chadwick Pl. Surb 7C 134
Chadwick Rd. E11 6G 35
Chadwick Rd. NW10 1B 64
Chadwick Rd. SE15 2F 105
Chadwick Rd. Ilf 3F 55
Chadwick St. SW1 3H 85 (2C 172)
Chadwick Way. SE28 7D 74
Chadwin Rd. E13 5K 71
Chadworth Ho. EC1 3C 68 (2C 162) (off Lever St.)
Chadworth Ho. N4 1C 50
Chaffinch Av. Croy 6K 141
Chaffinch Bus. Pk. Beck 4K 141
Chaffinch Clo. N9 1E 18
Chaffinch Clo. Croy 5K 141
Chaffinch Clo. Surb 3G 147
Chaffinch Rd. Beck 1A 142
Chafford Way. Romf 4C 38
Chagford St. NW1 4D 66 (4E 158)
Chailey Av. Enf 2A 8
Chailey Clo. Houn 1B 96
Chailey Ind. Est. Hay 2J 77
Chailey St. E5 3J 51
Chalbury Wlk. N1 2K 67
Chalcombe Rd. SE2 3B 92
Chalcot Clo. Sutt 7J 149
Chalcot Cres. NW1 1D 66
Chalcot Gdns. NW3 6D 48
Chalcot M. SW16 3J 121
Chalcot Rd. NW1 7E 48
Chalcot Sq. NW1 7E 48 (in two parts)
Chalcott Gdns. Surb 1C 146
Chalcroft Rd. SE13 5G 107
Chaldon Ct. SE19 1D 140
Chaldon Rd. SW6 7G 83
Chale Rd. SW2 6J 103
Chalet Clo. Bex 4K 129
Chalet Est. NW7 4H 13
Chalfont Av. Wemb 6H 45
Chalfont Ct. NW1 4D 66 (4F 159) (off Baker St.)
Chalfont Ct. NW9 3B 28
Chalfont Ct. Harr 6K 25 (off Northwick Pk. Rd.)
Chalfont Grn. N9 3K 17
Chalfont Ho. SE16 3H 87 (off Keetons Rd.)
Chalfont Rd. N9 3K 17
Chalfont Rd. SE25 3F 141
Chalfont Rd. Hay 2J 77
Chalfont Wlk. Pinn 2A 24
Chalfont Way. W13 3B 80
Chalford. NW3 6A 48 (off Finchley Rd.)
Chalford Clo. W Mol 4E 132
Chalford Rd. SE21 4D 122
Chalford Wlk. Wfd G 1B 36
Chalgrove Av. Mord 5J 137
Chalgrove Cres. Ilf 2C 36
Chalgrove Gdns. N3 3G 29
Chalgrove Rd. N17 1H 33
Chalgrove Rd. Sutt 7B 150
Chalice Clo. Wall 6H 151
Chalice Ct. N2 4C 30
Chalkenden Clo. SE20 7H 123
Chalker's Corner. (Junct.) 3H 99
Chalk Farm. 7E 48
Chalk Farm Rd. NW1 7E 48
Chalk Hill Rd. W6 4F 83
Chalkhill Rd. Wemb 3G 45 (in two parts)
Chalklands. Wemb 3J 45
Chalk La. Barn 3J 5
Chalkley Clo. Mitc 2D 138
Chalkmill Dri. Enf 3C 8
Chalk Pit Way. Sutt 6A 150
Chalk Rd. E13 5K 71
Chalkstone Clo. Well 1A 110
Chalkwell Ho. E1 6K 69 (off Pitsea St.)
Chalkwell Pk. Av. Enf 4K 7
Challenge Clo. NW10 1A 64
Challenger Ho. E14 7A 70 (off Victory Pl.)
Challenge Rd. Ashf 3F 113
Challice Way. SW2 1K 121
Challin St. SE20 1J 141
Challis Rd. Bren 5D 80
Challoner Clo. N2 2B 30
Challoner Cres. W14 5H 83
Challoners Clo. E Mol 4H 133
Challoner St. W14 5H 83
Chalmers Ho. E17 5D 34
Chalmers Rd. Ashf 5D 112
Chalmers Rd. E. Ashf 4D 112
Chalmers Wlk. SE17 6B 86 (off Hillingdon St.)
Chalmers Way. Felt 5K 95
Chalsey Rd. SE4 4B 106
Chalton Dri. N2 6B 30
Chalton Ho. NW1 3H 67 (1C 160) (off Chalton St.)
Chalton St. NW1 2G 67 (1C 160) (in three parts)
Chamberlain Clo. SE28 3H 91
Chamberlain Cotts. SE5 1D 104
Chamberlain Cres. W Wick 1D 154
Chamberlain Gdns. Houn 1G 97
Chamberlain Ho. E1 7J 69 (off Cable St.)
Chamberlain Ho. NW1 1D 160
Chamberlain Ho. SE1 2A 86 (7J 167) (off Westminster Bri. Rd.)
Chamberlain La. Pinn 4J 23
Chamberlain Pl. E17 3A 34
Chamberlain Rd. N2 2A 30
Chamberlain Rd. N9 3B 18
Chamberlain Rd. W13 2A 80
Chamberlain St. NW1 7D 48
Chamberlain Wlk. Felt 4C 114 (off Swift Rd.)
Chamberlain Way. Pinn 3K 23
Chamberlain Way. Surb 7E 134
Chamberlayne Av. Wemb 3E 44
Chamberlayne Mans. NW10 3F 65 (off Chamberlayne Rd.)
Chamberlayne Rd. NW10 1E 64
Chambers Gdns. N2 1B 30
Chambers Ind. Pk. W Dray 6C 76
Chambers La. NW10 7D 46
Chambers Pl. S Croy 7D 152
Chambers Rd. N7 4J 49
Chambers St. SE16 2G 87
Chambers, The. SW10 1A 102 (off Chelsea Harbour)
Chamber St. E1 7F 69 (2K 169)
Chambers Wlk. Stan 5G 11
Chambers Wharf. SE16 2G 87
Chambon Pl. W6 4C 82
Chambord St. E2 3F 69 (1K 163)
Chamomile Ct. E17 6C 34 (off Yunus Khan Clo.)
Champion Cres. SE26 4A 124
Champion Gro. SE5 3D 104
Champion Hill. SE5 3D 104
Champion Hill Est. SE5 3E 104
Champion Pk. SE5 2D 104
Champion Rd. SE26 4A 124
Champlain Ho. W12 7D 64 (off White City Est.)
Champness Clo. SE27 4D 122
Champneys Clo. Sutt 7H 149
Chancel Ind. Est. NW10 5B 46
Chancellor Gdns. S Croy 7B 152
Chancellor Gro. SE21 2C 122
Chancellor Ho. E1 1H 87 (off Green Bank)
Chancellor Pas. E14 1C 88
Chancellor Pl. NW9 2B 28
Chancellors Ct. WC1 5G 161
Chancellor's Rd. W6 5E 82
Chancellor's St. W6 5E 82
Chancellors Wharf. W6 5E 82
Chancelot Rd. SE2 4B 92
Chancel St. SE1 1B 86 (5A 168)
Chancery Bldgs. E1 7H 69 (off Lowood St.)
Chancery La. WC2 6A 68 (6H 161)
Chancery La. Beck 2D 142
Chancery M. SW17 2C 120
Chance St. E2 & E1 4F 69 (3J 163)
Chanctonbury Clo. SE9 3F 127
Chanctonbury Gdns. Sutt 7K 149
Chanctonbury Way. N12 4C 14
Chandler Av. E16 5J 71
Chandler Clo. Hamp 1E 132
Chandler Ct. Felt 6J 95
Chandler Ho. NW6 1H 65 (off Willesden La.)
Chandler Ho. WC1 4J 67 (4F 161) (off Colonnade)
Chandlers Clo. Felt 7H 95
Chandlers Ct. SE12 1K 125
Chandlers Dri. Eri 4K 93
Chandlers M. E14 2C 88
Chandler St. E1 1H 87
Chandlers Way. SW2 7A 104
Chandler Way. SE15 7F 87 (Diamond St.)
Chandler Way. SE15 6E 86 (St George's Way)
Chandlery Ho. E1 6G 69 (off Bk. Church La.)
Chandlery, The. SE1 3A 86 (1K 173) (off Gerridge St.)
Chandon Lodge. Sutt 7A 150
Chandos Av. E17 2C 34
Chandos Av. N14 3B 16
Chandos Av. N20 1F 15
Chandos Av. W5 4C 80
Chandos Clo. Buck H 2E 20
Chandos Ct. N14 2C 16
Chandos Ct. Edgw 7A 12
Chandos Cres. Edgw 7A 12
Chandos Pde. Edgw 7A 12
Chandos Pl. WC2 7J 67 (3E 166)
Chandos Rd. E15 5F 53
Chandos Rd. N2 2B 30
Chandos Rd. N17 2E 32
Chandos Rd. NW2 5E 46
Chandos Rd. NW10 4A 64
Chandos Rd. Harr 5G 25
Chandos Rd. Pinn 7B 24
Chandos St. W1 5F 67 (6K 159)
Chandos Way. NW11 1K 47
Change All. EC3 6D 68 (1F 169)
Channel Clo. Houn 1E 96
Channel Ga. Rd. NW10 3A 64
Channel Ho. E14 5A 70 (off Aston St.)
Channel Islands Est. N1 6C 50 (off Guernsey Rd.)
Channelsea Path. E15 1F 71
Channelsea Rd. E15 1F 71
Channon Ct. Surb 5E 134 (off Maple Rd)
Chantress Clo. Dag 1J 75
Chantrey Rd. SW9 3K 103
Chantry Clo. W9 4J 65
Chantry Clo. Enf 1H 7
Chantry Clo. Harr 5F 27
Chantry Clo. Sidc 5E 128
Chantry Clo. W Dray 7A 58
Chantry Ct. Cars 3C 150
Chantry La. Brom 5B 144
Chantry Pl. Harr 1F 25
Chantry Rd. Chess 5F 147
Chantry Rd. Harr 1F 25
Chantry Sq. W8 3K 83
Chantry St. N1 1B 68
Chantry, The. E4 1K 19
Chantry, The. Uxb 3B 58
Chantry Way. Mitc 3B 138
Chantry Way. Rain 2K 75
Chant Sq. E15 7F 53
Chant St. E15 7F 53
Chapel Clo. NW10 5B 46
Chapel Clo. Dart 5K 111
Chapel Ct. N2 3C 30

Chapel Ct. SE1 . . . 2D 86 (6E 168)
Chapel Ct. Hay . . . 7H 59
Chapel End. . . . **1C 34**
Chapel Farm Rd. SE9 . . . 3D 126
Chapel Hill. N2 . . . 2C 30
Chapel Hill. Dart . . . 5K 111
Chapel Ho. St. E14 . . . 5D 88
Chapel La. Pinn . . . 3B 24
Chapel La. Romf . . . 7D 38
Chapel La. Uxb . . . 6C 58
Chapel Mkt. N1 . . . 2A 68
Chapel M. Wfd G . . . 6K 21
Chapel of St John the Evangelist. . . . ***3J 169*** ***(in Tower of London, The, White Tower, The)***
Chapel Path. E11 . . . *6K 35* *(off Woodbine Pl.)*
Chapel Pl. EC2 . . . 3E 68 (2G 163)
Chapel Pl. N1 . . . 2A 68
Chapel Pl. N17 . . . 7A 18
Chapel Pl. W1 . . . 6F 67 (1J 165)
Chapel Rd. SE27 . . . 4B 122
Chapel Rd. W13 . . . 1B 80
Chapel Rd. Bexh . . . 4G 111
Chapel Rd. Houn . . . 3F 97
Chapel Rd. Ilf . . . 3E 54
Chapel Rd. Twic . . . 7B 98
Chapel Side. W2 . . . 7K 65
Chapel Stones. N17 . . . 1F 33
Chapel St. NW1 . . . 5C 66 (6C 158)
Chapel St. SW1 . . . 3E 84 (1H 171)
Chapel St. Enf . . . 3H 7
Chapel Vw. S Croy . . . 6J 153
Chapel Wlk. NW4 . . . 4D 28 (in two parts)
Chapel Wlk. Croy . . . 2C 152
Chapel Way. N7 . . . 3K 49
Chapel Yd. SW18 . . . *5J 101* *(off Wandsworth High St.)*
Chaplemount Rd. Wfd G . . . 6J 21
Chaplin Clo. SE1 . . . 2A 86 (6K 167)
Chaplin Clo. Wemb . . . 6D 44
Chaplin Cres. Sun . . . 6G 113
Chaplin Rd. E15 . . . 2H 71
Chaplin Rd. N17 . . . 3F 33
Chaplin Rd. NW2 . . . 6C 46
Chaplin Rd. Dag . . . 7E 56
Chaplin Rd. Wemb . . . 6C 44
Chaplin Sq. N12 . . . 7G 15
Chapman Clo. W Dray . . . 3B 76
Chapman Cres. Harr . . . 6E 26
Chapman Ho. E1 . . . *6H 69* *(off Bigland St.)*
Chapman Rd. E9 . . . 6B 52
Chapman Rd. Belv . . . 5H 93
Chapman Rd. Croy . . . 1A 152
Chapmans Grn. N22 . . . 1A 32
Chapman's La. SE2 & Belv . . . 4C 92
Chapmans Pk. Ind. Est. NW10 . . . 6B 46
Chapman Sq. SW19 . . . 2F 119
Chapman St. E1 . . . 7H 69
Chapman Ter. N22 . . . *1B 32* *(off Perth Rd.)*
Chapone Pl. W1 . . . 6H 67 (1C 166)
Chapter Chambers. SW1 . . . *4H 85 (4C 172)* *(off Chapter St.)*
Chapter Clo. W4 . . . 3J 81
Chapter Clo. Uxb . . . 7B 40
Chapter Rd. NW2 . . . 5C 46
Chapter Rd. SE17 . . . 5B 86
Chapter St. SW1 . . . 4H 85 (4C 172)
Chapter Way. Hamp . . . 4E 114
Chara Pl. W4 . . . 6K 81
Charcot Ho. SW15 . . . 6B 100
Charcroft Ct. W14 . . . *2F 83* *(off Minford Gdns.)*
Charcroft Gdns. Enf . . . 4E 8
Chardin Ho. SW9 . . . *1A 104* *(off Gosling Way)*
Chardin Rd. W4 . . . 4A 82
Chardmore Rd. N16 . . . 1G 51
Chard Rd. H'row A . . . 2D 94
Chardwell Clo. E6 . . . 6D 72
Charecroft Way. W12 & W14 . . . 2F 83
Charfield Ct. W9 . . . *4K 65* *(off Shirland Rd.)*
Charford Rd. E16 . . . 5J 71
Chargeable La. E13 . . . 4H 71
Chargeable St. E16 . . . 4H 71
Chargrove Clo. SE16 . . . 2K 87
Charing Ct. Brom . . . 2G 143
Charing Cross. SW1 . . . 4E 166
Charing Cross Rd. WC2 . . . 6H 67 (7D 160)
Charing Ho. SE1 . . . *2A 86 (6K 167)* *(off Windmill Wlk.)*
Charlbert Ct. NW8 . . . *2C 66* *(off Charlbert St.)*
Charlbert St. NW8 . . . 2C 66
Charlbury Av. Stan . . . 5J 11
Charlbury Gdns. Ilf . . . 2K 55
Charlbury Gro. W5 . . . 6C 62
Charlbury Rd. Uxb . . . 3B 40
Charldane Rd. SE9 . . . 3F 127
Charlecote Gro. SE26 . . . 3H 123
Charlecote Rd. Dag . . . 3E 56
Charlemont Rd. E6 . . . 4D 72
Charles Auffray Ho. E1 . . . *5J 69* *(off Smithy St.)*
Charles Barry Clo. SW4 . . . 3G 103
Charles Bradlaugh Ho. N17 . . . *7C 18* *(off Haynes Clo.)*
Charles Clo. Sidc . . . 4B 128
Charles Cobb Gdns. Croy . . . 5A 152
Charles Coveney Rd. SE5 . . . 1F 105
Charles Cres. Harr . . . 7H 25 (in two parts)
Charles Curran Ho. Uxb . . . 3D 40
Charles Darwin Ho. E2 . . . *3H 69* *(off Canrobert St.)*
Charles Dickens Ho. E2 . . . *3G 69* *(off Mansford St.)*
Charle Sevright Dri. NW7 . . . 5A 14
Charlesfield. SE9 . . . 3A 126
Charles Flemwell M. E16 . . . 1J 89
Charles Gardner Ct. N1 . . . *3D 68 (1F 163)* *(off Haberdasher Est.)*
Charles Grinling Wlk. SE18 . . . 4E 90
Charles Haller St. SW2 . . . 7A 104
Charles Harrod Ct. SW13 . . . *6E 82* *(off Somerville Av.)*
Charles Hocking Ho. W3 . . . *2J 81* *(off Bollo Bri. Rd.)*
Charles Ho. N17 . . . *7A 18* *(off Love La.)*
Charles La. NW8 . . . 2C 66
Charles MacKenzie Ho. SE16 . . . *4G 87* *(off Linsey St.)*
Charles Pl. NW1 . . . 3G 67 (2B 160)
Charles Rd. E7 . . . 7A 54
Charles Rd. SW19 . . . 1J 137
Charles Rd. W13 . . . 6A 62
Charles Rd. Dag . . . 6K 57
Charles Rd. Romf . . . 6D 38
Charles Rd. Stai . . . 6A 112
Charles Rowan Ho. WC1 . . . *3A 68 (2J 161)* *(off Margery St.)*
Charles II Pl. SW3 . . . 5D 84 (6E 170)
Charles II St. SW1 . . . 1H 85 (4C 166)
Charles Simmons Ho. WC1 . . . *3K 67 (2J 161)* *(off Margery St.)*
Charles Sq. N1 . . . 3D 68 (2F 163)
Charles Sq. Est. N1 . . . 2F 163
Charles St. E16 . . . 1A 90
Charles St. SW13 . . . 2A 100
Charles St. W1 . . . 1F 85 (4J 165)
Charles St. Croy . . . 3C 152
Charles St. Enf . . . 5A 8
Charles St. Houn . . . 2D 96
Charles St. Uxb . . . 4D 58
Charleston Clo. Felt . . . 3J 113
Charleston St. SE17 . . . 4C 86
Charles Townsend Ho. EC1 . . . *3B 68 (2A 162)* *(off Finsbury Est.)*
Charles Uton Ct. E8 . . . 4G 51
Charles Whinchup Rd. E16 . . . 1K 89
Charlesworth Ho. E14 . . . *6C 70* *(off Dod St.)*
Charleville Cir. SE26 . . . 5G 123
Charleville Mans. W14 . . . *5G 83* *(off Charleville Rd.)*
Charleville Rd. W14 . . . 5G 83
Charlie Brown's Roundabout. (Junct.) . . . 1A 36
Charlie Chaplin Wlk. SE1 . . . 1K 85 (5H 167)
Charlieville Rd. Eri . . . 7J 93
Charlmont Rd. SW17 . . . 6C 120
Charlotte Clo. Bexh . . . 5E 110
Charlotte Clo. Ilf . . . 1G 37
Charlotte Ct. N8 . . . 6H 31
Charlotte Ct. SE1 . . . *4E 86* *(off Old Kent Rd.)*
Charlotte Ct. Ilf . . . 6D 36
Charlotte Despard Av. SW11 . . . 1E 102
Charlotte Ho. E16 . . . *1K 89* *(off Fairfax M.)*
Charlotte Ho. W6 . . . *5E 82* *(off Queen Caroline St.)*
Charlotte M. W1 . . . 5G 67 (5B 160)
Charlotte M. W10 . . . 6F 65
Charlotte M. W14 . . . 4G 83
Charlotte Pk. Av. Brom . . . 3C 144
Charlotte Pl. NW9 . . . 5J 27
Charlotte Pl. SW1 . . . 4G 85 (4A 172)
Charlotte Pl. W1 . . . 5G 67 (6B 160)
Charlotte Rd. EC2 . . . 3E 68 (2G 163)
Charlotte Rd. SW13 . . . 1B 100
Charlotte Rd. Dag . . . 6H 57
Charlotte Rd. Wall . . . 6G 151
Charlotte Row. SW4 . . . 3G 103
Charlotte Sq. Rich . . . 6F 99
Charlotte St. W1 . . . 5G 67 (5B 160)
Charlotte Ter. N1 . . . 1K 67
Charlow Clo. SW6 . . . 2A 102
Charlton. . . . **3E 130** **(Shepperton)**
Charlton. . . . **6B 90** **(Woolwich)**
Charlton Athletic F.C. ***(Valley, The)*** . . . ***5A 90***
Charlton Chu. La. SE7 . . . 5A 90
Charlton Clo. Uxb . . . 2D 40
Charlton Ct. E2 . . . 1F 69
Charlton Cres. Bark . . . 2K 73
Charlton Dene. SE7 . . . 7A 90
Charlton Ho. Bren . . . 6E 80
Charlton King's Rd. NW5 . . . 5H 49
Charlton La. SE7 . . . 4B 90 (in two parts)
Charlton La. Shep . . . 3E 130 (in two parts)
Charlton Pk. La. SE7 . . . 7B 90
Charlton Pk. Rd. SE7 . . . 6B 90
Charlton Pl. N1 . . . 2B 68
Charlton Rd. N9 . . . 1E 18
Charlton Rd. NW10 . . . 1A 64
Charlton Rd. SE3 & SE7 . . . 7J 89
Charlton Rd. Harr . . . 4D 26
Charlton Rd. Shep . . . 3E 130
Charlton Rd. Wemb . . . 1F 45
Charlton Way. SE3 . . . 1G 107
Charlwood. Croy . . . 7B 154
Charlwood Clo. Harr . . . 6D 10
Charlwood Ho. SW1 . . . *4H 85 (4C 172)* *(off Vauxhall Bri. Rd.)*
Charlwood Houses. WC1 . . . *3J 67 (2F 161)* *(off Midhope St.)*
Charlwood Pl. SW1 . . . 4G 85 (4B 172)
Charlwood Rd. SW15 . . . 4F 101
Charlwood Sq. Mitc . . . 3B 138
Charlwood St. SW1 . . . 5G 85 (6A 172) (in two parts)
Charlwood Ter. SW15 . . . 4F 101
Charmans Ho. SW8 . . . *7J 85* *(off Wandsworth Rd.)*
Charmian Av. Stan . . . 3D 26
Charminster Av. SW19 . . . 2J 137
Charminster Ct. Surb . . . 7D 134
Charminster Rd. SE9 . . . 4B 126
Charminster Rd. Wor Pk . . . 1F 149
Charmouth Ct. Rich . . . 5F 99
Charmouth Ho. SW8 . . . 7K 85
Charmouth Rd. Well . . . 1C 110
Charnock Ho. W12 . . . *7D 64* *(off White City Est.)*
Charnock Rd. E5 . . . 3H 51
Charnwood Av. SW19 . . . 2J 137
Charnwood Clo. N Mald . . . 4A 136
Charnwood Dri. E18 . . . 3K 35
Charnwood Gdns. E14 . . . 4C 88
Charnwood Pl. N20 . . . 3F 15
Charnwood Rd. SE25 . . . 5D 140
Charnwood Rd. Uxb . . . 2C 58
Charnwood St. E5 . . . 2H 51
Charrington Rd. Croy . . . 2C 152
Charrington St. NW1 . . . 2H 67
Charsley Rd. SE6 . . . 2D 124
Chart Clo. Brom . . . 1G 143
Chart Clo. Croy . . . 6J 141
Chart Clo. Mitc . . . 4D 138
Charter Av. Ilf . . . 1H 55
Charter Ct. N4 . . . 1A 50
Charter Ct. N22 . . . 1H 31
Charter Ct. N Mald . . . 3A 136
Charter Ct. S'hall . . . 1E 78
Charter Cres. Houn . . . 4C 96
Charter Dri. Bex . . . 7E 110
Charter Ho. WC2 . . . *6J 67 (1F 167)* *(off Crown Ct.)*
Charter Ho. Sutt . . . *6K 149* *(off Mulgrave Rd.)*
Charterhouse Av. Wemb . . . 4C 44
Charterhouse Bldgs. EC1 . . . 4C 68 (4B 162)
Charterhouse M. EC1 . . . 5B 68 (5B 162)
Charterhouse Rd. E8 . . . 5G 51
Charterhouse Sq. EC1 . . . 5B 68 (5B 162)
Charterhouse St. EC1 . . . 5A 68 (6K 161)
Charteris Rd. N4 . . . 1A 50
Charteris Rd. NW6 . . . 1H 65
Charteris Rd. Wfd G . . . 7E 20
Charter Quay. King T . . . *2D 134* *(off Wadbrook St.)*
Charter Rd. King T . . . 3H 135
Charter Rd., The. Wfd G . . . 6B 20
Charters Clo. SE19 . . . 5E 122
Charter Sq. King T . . . 2H 135
Charter Way. N3 . . . 4H 29
Charter Way. N14 . . . 6B 6
Chartes Ho. SE1 . . . *3E 86 (7H 169)* *(off Stevens St.)*
Chartfield Av. SW15 . . . 5D 100
Chartfield Sq. SW15 . . . 5F 101
Chartham Ct. SW9 . . . *3A 104* *(off Canterbury Cres.)*
Chartham Gro. SE27 . . . 3B 122
Chartham Ho. SE1 . . . *3D 86 (7F 169)* *(off Weston St.)*
Chartham Rd. SE25 . . . 3H 141
Chart Hills Clo. SE28 . . . 6E 74
Chart Ho. E14 . . . *5D 88* *(off Burrells Wharf Sq.)*
Chartley Av. NW2 . . . 3A 46
Chartley Av. Stan . . . 6E 10
Charton Clo. Belv . . . 6F 93
Chartres Ct. Gnfd . . . 2H 61
Chartridge. SE17 . . . *6D 86* *(off Westmoreland Rd.)*
Chart St. N1 . . . 3D 68 (1F 163)
Chartwell Clo. SE9 . . . 2H 127
Chartwell Clo. Croy . . . 1D 152
Chartwell Clo. Gnfd . . . 1F 61
Chartwell Ct. Barn . . . 4B 4
Chartwell Ct. Hay . . . 7H 59
Chartwell Ct. Wfd G . . . 7C 20
Chartwell Gdns. Sutt . . . 3G 149
Chartwell Lodge. Beck . . . 7C 124
Chartwell Pl. Harr . . . 2H 43
Chartwell Pl. Sutt . . . 3H 149
Chartwell Way. SE20 . . . 1H 141
Charville Ct. Harr . . . 6K 25
Charville La. Hay . . . 3E 58
Charville La. W. Uxb . . . 3D 58
Char Wood. SW16 . . . 4A 122
Chase Bank Ct. N14 . . . *6B 6* *(off Avenue Rd.)*
Chase Cen., The. NW10 . . . 3K 63
Chase Ct. Iswth . . . 2A 98
Chase Ct. Gdns. Enf . . . 3H 7
Chase Cross Rd. Romf . . . 1J 39
Chasefield Rd. SW17 . . . 4D 120
Chase Gdns. E4 . . . 4H 19
Chase Gdns. Twic . . . 7H 97
Chase Grn. Enf . . . 3H 7
Chase Grn. Av. Enf . . . 2G 7
Chase Hill. Enf . . . 3H 7
Chase La. Ilf . . . 5H 37 (in two parts)
Chaseley Dri. W4 . . . 5H 81
Chaseley St. E14 . . . 6A 70
Chasemore Clo. Mitc . . . 7D 138
Chasemore Gdns. Croy . . . 5A 152
Chasemore Ho. SW6 . . . *7G 83* *(off Williams Clo.)*
Chase Ridings. Enf . . . 2F 7
Chase Rd. N14 . . . 5B 6
Chase Rd. NW10 . . . 4K 63
Chase Rd. Trad. Est. NW10 . . . 4K 63
Chase Side. . . . **2H 7**
Chase Side. N14 . . . 6K 5
Chase Side. Enf . . . 3H 7
Chaseside Av. SW20 . . . 1G 137
Chase Side Av. Enf . . . 2H 7
Chase Side Cres. Enf . . . 1H 7
Chase Side Ind. Est. N14 . . . 7C 6
Chase Side Pl. Enf . . . 2H 7
Chase, The. E12 . . . 4B 54
Chase, The. SW4 . . . 3F 103
Chase, The. SW16 . . . 7K 121
Chase, The. SW20 . . . 1G 137
Chase, The. Bexh . . . 3H 111
Chase, The. Brom . . . 3K 143
Chase, The. Chad H . . . 6E 38
Chase, The. Eastc . . . 6A 24
Chase, The. Edgw . . . 1H 27
Chase, The. Pinn . . . 4D 24
Chase, The. Romf . . . 3K 39
Chase, The. Stan . . . 6F 11
Chase, The. Sun . . . 1K 131
Chase, The. Uxb . . . 5C 40
Chase, The. Wall . . . 5J 151
Chaseville Pde. N21 . . . 5E 6
Chaseville Pk. Rd. N21 . . . 5D 6
Chase Way. N14 . . . 2A 16
Chaseways Vs. Romf . . . 1F 39
Chasewood Av. Enf . . . 2G 7
Chasewood Ct. NW7 . . . 5E 12
Chasewood Pk. Harr . . . 3K 43

Chaston St. NW5 5E 48 (off Grafton Ter.)
Chater Ho. E2 3K 69 (off Roman Rd.)
Chatfield Rd. SW11 3A 102
Chatfield Rd. Croy 1B 152
Chatham Av. Brom 7H 143
Chatham Clo. NW11 5J 29
Chatham Clo. Sutt 7H 137
Chatham Pl. E9 6J 51
Chatham Rd. E17 3A 34
Chatham Rd. E18 2H 35
Chatham Rd. SW11 6D 102
Chatham Rd. King T 2G 135
Chatham St. SE17 4D 86
Chatsfield Pl. W5 6E 62
Chatsworth Av. NW4 2E 28
Chatsworth Av. SW20 1G 137
Chatsworth Av. Brom 4K 125
Chatsworth Av. Sidc 1A 128
Chatsworth Av. Wemb 5F 45
Chatsworth Clo. NW4 2E 28
Chatsworth Clo. W4 6J 81
Chatsworth Clo. W Wick 2H 155
Chatsworth Ct. W8 4J 83 (off Pembroke Rd.)
Chatsworth Ct. Stan 5H 11
Chatsworth Cres. Houn 4H 97
Chatsworth Dri. Enf 7B 8
Chatsworth Est. E5 4K 51
Chatsworth Gdns. W3 1H 81
Chatsworth Gdns. Harr 1F 43
Chatsworth Gdns. N Mald 5B 136
Chatsworth Ho. E16 1K 89 (off Wesley Av.)
Chatsworth Ho. Brom 4J 143 (off Westmoreland Rd.)
Chatsworth Lodge. W4 5K 81 (off Bourne Pl.)
Chatsworth Pde. Orp 5G 145
Chatsworth Pl. NW2 6E 46
Chatsworth Pl. Mitc 3D 138
Chatsworth Pl. Tedd 4A 116
Chatsworth Ri. W5 4F 63
Chatsworth Rd. E5 3J 51
Chatsworth Rd. E15 5H 53
Chatsworth Rd. NW2 6E 46 (in two parts)
Chatsworth Rd. W4 6J 81
Chatsworth Rd. W5 4F 63
Chatsworth Rd. Croy 4D 152
Chatsworth Rd. Hay 4K 59
Chatsworth Rd. Sutt 5F 149
Chatsworth Way. SE27 3B 122
Chattern Hill. 4D 112
Chattern Hill. Ashf 4D 112
Chattern Rd. Ashf 4E 112
Chatterton Ct. Rich 2F 99
Chatterton M. N4 3B 50 (off Chatterton Rd.)
Chatterton Rd. N4 3B 50
Chatterton Rd. Brom 4B 144
Chatto Rd. SW11 5D 102
Chaucer Av. Hay 5J 59
Chaucer Av. Houn 2K 95
Chaucer Av. Rich 3G 99
Chaucer Clo. N11 5B 16
Chaucer Ct. New Bar 5E 4
Chaucer Dri. SE1 4F 87
Chaucer Gdns. Sutt 3J 149 (in two parts)
Chaucer Grn. Croy 7H 141
Chaucer Ho. SW1 5G 85 (6A 172) (off Churchill Gdns.)
Chaucer Ho. Barn 4A 4
Chaucer Ho. Sutt 3J 149 (off Chaucer Gdns.)
Chaucer Mans. W14 6G 83 (off Queen's Club Gdns.)
Chaucer Rd. E7 6J 53
Chaucer Rd. E11 6J 35
Chaucer Rd. E17 2E 34
Chaucer Rd. SE24 5A 104
Chaucer Rd. W3 1J 81
Chaucer Rd. Ashf 4A 112
Chaucer Rd. Sidc 1C 128
Chaucer Rd. Sutt 4J 149
Chaucer Rd. Well 1J 109
Chaucer Theatre. 6F 69 (7K 163) (off Braham St.)
Chaucer Way. SW19 6A 120
Chaulden Ho. EC1 3D 68 (2F 163) (off Cranwood St.)
Chauncey Clo. N9 3B 18
Chaundrye Clo. SE9 6D 108
Chauntler Clo. E16 6K 71
Chaville Ho. N11 4K 15
Cheadle Ct. NW8 4B 66 (3B 158) (off Henderson Dri.)
Cheadle Ho. E14 6B 70 (off Copenhagen Pl.)
Cheam. 6G 149
Cheam Comn. Rd. Wor Pk 2D 148
Cheam Mans. Sutt 7G 149
Cheam Pk. Way. Sutt 6G 149
Cheam Rd. Eps & Ewe 7F 149
Cheam Rd. Sutt 6H 149
Cheam St. SE15 3J 105
Cheam Village. (Junct.) 6G 149
Cheapside. EC2 6C 68 (1D 168)
Cheapside. N13 4J 17
Cheapside. N22 3A 32
Chearsley. SE17 4C 86 (off Deacon Way)
Cheddar Clo. N11 6J 15
Cheddar Waye. Hay 6K 59
Cheddington Ho. E2 1G 69 (off Whiston Rd.)
Cheddington Rd. N18 3K 17
Chedworth Clo. E16 6H 71
Cheeseman Clo. Hamp 6C 114
Cheesemans Ter. W14 5H 83 (in two parts)
Chelford Rd. Brom 5F 125
Chelmer Cres. Bark 2B 74
Chelmer Rd. E9 5K 51
Chelmsford Clo. E6 6D 72
Chelmsford Clo. W6 6F 83
Chelmsford Ct. N14 7C 6 (off Chelmsford Rd.)
Chelmsford Gdns. Ilf 7C 36
Chelmsford Ho. N7 4K 49 (off Holloway Rd.)
Chelmsford Rd. E11 1F 53
Chelmsford Rd. E17 6C 34
Chelmsford Rd. E18 1H 35
Chelmsford Rd. N14 7B 6
Chelmsford Sq. NW10 1E 64
Chelmsine Ct. Ruis 5E 22
Chelsea. 5C 84 (6C 170)
Chelsea Bri. SW1 & SW8 6F 85 (7J 171)
Chelsea Bri. Bus. Cen. SW8 7F 85
Chelsea Bri. Rd. SW1 5E 84 (5G 171)
Chelsea Bri. Wharf. SW8 6F 85 (7K 171)
Chelsea Cinema. 5C 84 (6D 170)
Chelsea Cloisters. SW3 4C 84 (4D 170)
Chelsea Clo. NW10 1K 63
Chelsea Clo. Edgw 2G 27
Chelsea Clo. Hamp H 5G 115
Chelsea Clo. Wor Pk 7C 136
Chelsea College of Art & Design. 5C 84 (6C 170)
Chelsea Ct. Brom 3C 144
Chelsea Cres. NW2 6H 47
Chelsea Cres. SW10 1A 102
Chelsea Embkmt. SW3 6C 84 (7D 170)
Chelsea Farm Ho. Studios. SW10 6B 84 (off Milman's St.)
Chelsea F.C. (Stamford Bridge) 7K 83
Chelsea Gdns. SW1 5E 84 (6H 171)
Chelsea Gdns. W13 5K 61
Chelsea Gdns. Sutt 4G 149
Chelsea Ga. SW1 6H 171
Chelsea Harbour Design Cen. SW10 1A 102 (off Chelsea Harbour)
Chelsea Harbour Dri. SW10 1A 102
Chelsea Lodge. SW3 6D 84 (7F 171) (off Tite St.)
Chelsea Mnr. Ct. SW3 6C 84 (7D 170)
Chelsea Mnr. Gdns. SW3 5C 84 (6D 170)
Chelsea Mnr. St. SW3 5C 84 (6D 170)
Chelsea Pk. Gdns. SW3 6B 84 (7A 170)
Chelsea Physic Garden. 6D 84 (7E 170)
Chelsea Reach Tower. SW10 7B 84 (off Worlds End Est.)
Chelsea Sq. SW3 5B 84 (5B 170)
Chelsea Studios. SW6 7K 83 (off Fulham Rd.)
Chelsea Towers. SW3 7D 170
Chelsea Village. SW6 7K 83 (off Fulham Rd.)
Chelsea Wharf. SW10 7B 84 (off Lots Rd.)
Chelsfield Av. N9 7E 8
Chelsfield Gdns. SE26 3J 123
Chelsfield Grn. N9 7E 8
Chelsfield Ho. SE17 4E 86 (off Massinger St.)
Chelsham Rd. SW4 3H 103
Chelsham Rd. S Croy 7D 152
Chelsiter Ct. Sidc 4K 127
Chelston App. Ruis 2J 41
Chelston Rd. Ruis 1J 41
Chelsworth Dri. SE18 6H 91
Cheltenham Av. Twic 7A 98
Cheltenham Clo. N Mald 3J 135
Cheltenham Clo. N'holt 6F 43
Cheltenham Ct. Stan 5H 11 (off Marsh La.)
Cheltenham Gdns. E6 2C 72
Cheltenham Pl. W3 1H 81
Cheltenham Pl. Harr 4E 26
Cheltenham Rd. E10 6E 34
Cheltenham Rd. SE15 4J 105
Cheltenham Ter. SW3 5D 84 (5F 171)
Chelverton Rd. SW15 4F 101
Chelwood. N20 2G 15
Chelwood Clo. E4 6J 9
Chelwood Gdns. Rich 2G 99
Chelwood Gdns. Pas. Rich 2G 99
Chelwood Ho. W2 6B 66 (1B 164) (off Gloucester Sq.)
Chelwood Wlk. SE4 4A 106
Chenappa Clo. E13 3J 71
Chenduit Way. Stan 5E 10
Cheney Ct. SE23 1K 123
Cheney Rd. NW1 2J 67 (1E 160)
Cheney Row. E17 1B 34
Cheneys Rd. E11 3G 53
Cheney St. Pinn 4A 24
Chenies Ho. W4 7B 82 (off Corney Reach Way)
Chenies M. WC1 4H 67 (4C 160)
Chenies Pl. NW1 2H 67
Chenies St. WC1 5H 67 (5C 160)
Chenies, The. NW1 2H 67 (off Pancras Rd.)
Chenies, The. Orp 6J 145
Cheniston Gdns. W8 3K 83
Chepstow Clo. SW15 6G 101
Chepstow Corner. W2 6J 65 (off Chepstow Pl.)
Chepstow Ct. W11 7J 65 (off Chepstow Vs.)
Chepstow Cres. W11 7J 65
Chepstow Cres. Ilf 6J 37
Chepstow Gdns. S'hall 6D 60
Chepstow Pl. W2 6J 65
Chepstow Ri. Croy 3E 152
Chepstow Rd. W2 6J 65
Chepstow Rd. W7 3A 80
Chepstow Rd. Croy 3E 152
Chepstow Vs. W11 7H 65
Chequers. Buck H 1E 20
Chequers Clo. NW9 3A 28
Chequers Clo. Orp 4K 145
Chequers Ct. EC1 4D 68 (3E 162) (off Chequer St.)
Chequers Ho. NW8 4C 66 (3C 158) (off Jerome Cres.)
Chequers La. Dag 5F 75
Chequers Pde. N13 5H 17
Chequers Pde. SE9 6D 108 (off Eltham High St.)
Chequers Pde. Dag 1F 75
Chequers, The. Pinn 3B 24
Chequer St. EC1 4C 68 (4D 162) (in two parts)
Chequers Way. N13 5G 17
Cherbury Clo. SE28 6D 74
Cherbury Ct. N1 2D 68 (off St John's Est.)
Cherbury St. N1 2D 68
Cherchefelle M. Stan 5G 11
Cherimoya Gdns. W Mol 3F 133
Cherington Rd. W7 1J 79
Cheriton Av. Brom 5H 143
Cheriton Av. Ilf 2D 36
Cheriton Clo. W5 5C 62
Cheriton Clo. Barn 3J 5
Cheriton Ct. SE12 7J 107
Cheriton Dri. SE18 7H 91
Cheriton Sq. SW17 2E 120
Cherry Av. S'hall 1B 78
Cherry Blossom Clo. N13 5G 17
Cherry Clo. E17 5D 34
Cherry Clo. NW9 2A 28
Cherry Clo. SW2 7A 104
Cherry Clo. W5 3D 80
Cherry Clo. Cars 2D 150
Cherry Clo. Mord 4G 137
Cherry Clo. Ruis 3H 41
Cherry Ct. W3 1A 82
Cherry Ct. Pinn 2B 24
Cherry Cres. Bren 7B 80
Cherrydown Av. E4 3G 19
Cherrydown Clo. E4 3H 19
Cherrydown Rd. Sidc 2D 128
Cherrydown Wlk. Romf 2H 39
Cherry Garden Ho. SE16 2H 87 (off Cherry Garden St.)
Cherry Gdns. Dag 5F 57
Cherry Gdns. N'holt 7F 43
Cherry Garden St. SE16 2H 87
Cherry Gth. Bren 5D 80
Cherry Gro. Hay 1K 77
Cherry Gro. Uxb 5D 58
Cherry Hill. Harr 6E 10
Cherry Hill. New Bar 6E 4
Cherry Hill Gdns. Croy 4K 151
Cherrylands Clo. NW9 2J 45
Cherry La. W Dray 4B 76
Cherry Laurel Wlk. SW2 6K 103
Cherry Orchard. SE7 6A 90
Cherry Orchard. W Dray 2A 76
Cherry Orchard Gdns. Croy 1D 152
Cherry Orchard Gdns. W Mol 3D 132
Cherry Orchard Rd. Brom 2C 156
Cherry Orchard Rd. Croy 2D 152
Cherry Orchard Rd. W Mol 3E 132
Cherry Rd. Enf 1D 8
Cherry St. Romf 5K 39
Cherry Tree Av. W Dray 6B 58
Cherry Tree Clo. E9 1J 69
Cherry Tree Clo. Wemb 4A 44
Cherry Tree Ct. NW1 7G 49 (off Camden Rd.)
Cherry Tree Ct. NW9 4J 27
Cherry Tree Ct. SE7 6A 90
Cherrytree Dri. SW16 3J 121
Cherry Tree Hill. N2 5C 30
Cherry Tree Ho. N22 7D 16
Cherry Tree Ri. Buck H 4F 21
Cherry Tree Rd. E15 5G 53
Cherry Tree Rd. N2 4D 30
Cherry Tree Wlk. EC1 4C 68 (4D 162)
Cherry Tree Wlk. Beck 4B 142
Cherry Tree Wlk. W Wick 4H 155
Cherrytree Way. Stan 6G 11
Cherry Wlk. Brom 1J 155
Cherry Way. Eps 6K 147
Cherry Way. Shep 4F 131
Cherrywood Clo. E3 3A 70
Cherry Wood Clo. King T 7G 117
Cherrywood Ct. Tedd 5A 116
Cherrywood Dri. SW15 5F 101
Cherrywood La. Mord 4G 137
Cherry Wood Way. W5 5G 63
Chertsey Bri. Rd. Cher 7A 130
Chertsey Ct. SW14 3H 99
Chertsey Dri. Sutt 2G 149
Chertsey Rd. E11 2F 53
Chertsey Rd. Ashf 7F 113
Chertsey Rd. Felt 5G 113
Chertsey Rd. Ilf 4H 55
Chertsey Rd. Shep 7A 130
Chertsey Rd. Twic 2F 115
Chertsey St. SW17 5E 120
Chervil Clo. Felt 3J 113
Chervil M. SE28 1B 92
Cherwell Ct. Eps 4J 147
Cherwell Ho. NW8 4B 158
Cherwell Way. Ruis 6E 22
Cheryls Clo. SW6 1K 101
Cheseman St. SE26 3H 123
Chesfield Rd. King T 7E 116
Chesham Av. Orp 6F 145
Chesham Clo. SW1 2G 171
Chesham Clo. Romf 4K 39
Chesham Cres. SE20 1J 141
Chesham Flats. W1 7E 66 (2H 165) (off Brown Hart Gdns.)
Chesham M. SW1 1G 171
Chesham Pl. SW1 3E 84 (2G 171) (in two parts)
Chesham Rd. SE20 2J 141
Chesham Rd. SW19 5B 120
Chesham Rd. King T 2G 135
Chesham St. NW10 3K 45
Chesham St. SW1 3E 84 (2G 171)
Chesham Ter. W13 2B 80
Cheshire Clo. E17 1D 34
Cheshire Clo. SE4 2B 106

Cheshire Clo. Mitc 3J 139
Cheshire Ct. EC4 . . . 6A 68 (1K 167) (off Fleet St.)
Cheshire Gdns. Chess 6D 146
Cheshire Ho. Mord 7K 137
Cheshire Rd. N22 . . . . 7E 16
Cheshire St. E2 . . . . 4F 69 (3K 163)
Cheshir Ho. NW4 . . . . 4E 28
Chesholm Rd. N16 . . . . 3E 50
Cheshunt Ho. NW6 . . . . 1K 65 (off Mortimer Cres.)
Cheshunt Rd. E7 . . . . 6K 53
Cheshunt Rd. Belv 5G 93
Chesil Ct. E2 . . . . 2J 69 (off Bishop's Way)
Chesil Ct. SW3 . . . . 7D 170
Chesilton Rd. SW6 . . . . 1H 101
Chesil Way. Hay 3H 59
Chesley Gdns. E6 . . . . 2B 72
Chesney Ct. W9 . . . . 4J 65 (off Shirland Rd.)
Chesney Cres. New Ad 7E 154
Chesney Ho. SE13 . . . . 4F 107 (off Mercator Rd.)
Chesney St. SW11 . . . . 1E 102
Chesnut Gro. N17 . . . . 3F 33
Chesnut Rd. N17 . . . . 3F 33
Chesnut Row. N3 . . . . 7D 14
Chessell Clo. T Hth 4B 140
Chessholme Rd. Ashf 6E 112
Chessing Ct. N2 . . . . 3D 30 (off Fortis Grn.)
Chessington. 5F 147
Chessington Av. N3 . . . . 3G 29
Chessington Av. Bexh 7E 92
Chessington Clo. Eps 6J 147
Chessington Ct. N3 . . . . 3H 29 (off Charter Way)
Chessington Ct. Pinn 4D 24
Chessington Hall Gdns. Chess 7D 146
Chessington Hill Pk. Chess 5G 147
Chessington Ho. SW8 . . . . . 2H 103
Chessington Lodge. N3 . . . . 3H 29
Chessington Mans. E10 . . . . 7C 34
Chessington Mans. E11 . . . . 7G 35
Chessington Pde. Chess 6D 146
Chessington Rd. Eps & Ewe 6G 147
Chessington Way. W Wick 2D 154
Chessington World of Adventures. 7C 146
Chesson Rd. W14 . . . . 6H 83
Chesswood Way. Pinn 2B 24
Chestbrook Ct. Enf . . . . 5K 7 (off Forsyth Pl.)
Chester Av. Rich 6F 99
Chester Av. Twic 1D 114
Chester Clo. SW1 . . . . 2F 85 (7J 165)
Chester Clo. SW13 . . . . 3D 100
Chester Clo. Ashf 5F 113
Chester Clo. Rich 6F 99
Chester Clo. Sutt 2J 149
Chester Clo. Uxb 6D 58
Chester Clo. N. NW1 . . . . 3F 67 (1K 159)
Chester Clo. S. NW1 . . . . 3F 67 (2K 159)
Chester Cotts. SW1 . . . . . . 4G 171
Chester Ct. NW1 . . . 3F 67 (1K 159)
Chester Ct. SE5 . . . . 7D 86 (off Lomond Gro.)
Chester Ct. SE8 . . . . 5K 87
Chester Ct. Brom . . . . 4J 143 (off Durham Rd.)
Chester Cres. E8 . . . . 5F 51
Chester Dri. Harr 6D 24
Chesterfield Clo. SE13 . . . . . 2F 107
Chesterfield Ct. Surb . . . . . . 5E 134 (off Cranes Pk.)
Chesterfield Dri. Esh 2A 146
Chesterfield Flats. Barn . . . . . . 5A 4 (off Bells Hill)
Chesterfield Gdns. N4 . . . . . . 5B 32
Chesterfield Gdns. SE10 . . . 1F 107
Chesterfield Gdns. W1 . . . . 1F 85 (4J 165)
Chesterfield Gro. SE22 . . . . 5F 105
Chesterfield Hill. W1 . . . . 1F 85 (4J 165)
Chesterfield Ho. W1 . . . . 1E 84 (4H 165) (off Chesterfield Gdns.)
Chesterfield Lodge. N21 . . . . . 7E 6 (off Church Hill)
Chesterfield M. Ashf 4A 112
Chesterfield Rd. E10 . . . . 6E 34
Chesterfield Rd. N3 . . . . 6D 14
Chesterfield Rd. W4 . . . . 6J 81
Chesterfield Rd. Ashf 4A 112
Chesterfield Rd. Barn 5A 4
Chesterfield Rd. Eps 7K 147
Chesterfield St. W1 . . . . 1F 85 (4J 165)
Chesterfield Wlk. SE10 . . . . 1F 107
Chesterfield Way. SE15 . . . . . 7J 87
Chesterfield Way. Hay 2J 77
Chesterford Gdns. NW3 . . . . 4K 47
Chesterford Ho. SE18 . . . . . . 1B 108 (off Tellson Av.)
Chesterford Rd. E12 . . . . 5D 54
Chester Gdns. W13 . . . . 6B 62
Chester Gdns. Enf 6C 8
Chester Gdns. Mord 6A 138
Chester Ga. NW1 . . . 3F 67 (2J 159)
Chester Ho. SE8 . . . . 6B 88
Chester Ho. SW1 . . . . 4F 85 (3J 171) (off Eccleston Pl.)
Chester Ho. SW9 . . . . 7A 86 (off Brixton Rd.)
Chesterman Ct. W4 . . . . 7A 82 (off Corney Reach Way)
Chester M. E17 . . . . 2C 34
Chester M. SW1 . . . 3F 85 (1J 171)
Chester Pl. NW1 . . . 3F 67 (1J 159)
Chester Rd. E7 . . . . 7B 54
Chester Rd. E11 . . . . 6K 35
Chester Rd. E16 . . . . 4G 71
Chester Rd. E17 . . . . 5K 33
Chester Rd. N9 . . . . 1C 18
Chester Rd. N17 . . . . 3D 32
Chester Rd. N19 . . . . 2F 49
Chester Rd. NW1 . . . . 3E 66 (2H 159)
Chester Rd. SW19 . . . . 6E 118
Chester Rd. Chig 3K 21
Chester Rd. Houn 3K 95
Chester Rd. Ilf 1K 55
Chester Rd. H'row A 3C 94
Chester Rd. N'wd 1H 23
Chester Rd. Sidc . . . . 5J 109 (in two parts)
Chester Row. SW1 . . . . 4E 84 (4G 171)
Chester Sq. SW1 . . . . 4E 84 (3H 171)
Chester Sq. M. SW1 . . . . . . 2J 171
Chesters, The. N Mald 1A 136
Chester St. E2 . . . . 4G 69
Chester St. SW1 . . . 3E 84 (1H 171)
Chester Ter. NW1 . . . . 3F 67 (1J 159) (in three parts)
Chester Ter. Bark 6H 55
Chesterton Clo. SW18 . . . . . . 5J 101
Chesterton Clo. Gnfd 2F 61
Chesterton Ct. W3 . . . . 3H 81 (off Bollo Bri. Rd.)
Chesterton Ct. W5 . . . . 5D 62
Chesterton Dri. Stai 1B 112
Chesterton Ho. Croy . . . . . . 4D 152 (off Heathfield Rd.)
Chesterton Rd. E13 . . . . 3J 71
Chesterton Rd. W10 . . . . 5F 65
Chesterton Sq. W8 . . . . 4J 83
Chesterton Ter. E13 . . . . 3J 71
Chesterton Ter. King T 2G 135
Chester Way. SE11 . . . . 4A 86 (4K 173)
Chesthunte Rd. N17 . . . . 1C 32
Chestnut All. SW6 . . . . 6H 83
Chestnut Av. E7 . . . . 4K 53
Chestnut Av. N8 . . . . 5J 31
Chestnut Av. SW14 . . . . 3K 99
Chestnut Av. Bren 4D 80
Chestnut Av. Buck H 3G 21
Chestnut Av. E Mol & Tedd 3K 133
Chestnut Av. Edgw 6K 11
Chestnut Av. Eps 4A 148
Chestnut Av. Esh 7H 133
Chestnut Av. Hamp 7E 114
Chestnut Av. N'wd 2H 23
Chestnut Av. Wemb 5B 44
Chestnut Av. W Dray 7B 58
Chestnut Av. W Wick 5G 155
Chestnut Av. N. E17 . . . . 4F 35
Chestnut Av. S. E17 . . . . 5E 34
Chestnut Clo. N14 . . . . 5B 6
Chestnut Clo. N16 . . . . 2D 50
Chestnut Clo. SE6 . . . . 5E 124
Chestnut Clo. SE14 . . . . 1B 106
Chestnut Clo. SW16 . . . . . . 4A 122
Chestnut Clo. Ashf 4D 112
Chestnut Clo. Buck H 2G 21
Chestnut Clo. Cars 1D 150
Chestnut Clo. Hay 7G 59
Chestnut Clo. Sidc 1A 128
Chestnut Clo. Sun 6H 113
Chestnut Clo. W Dray 7D 76
Chestnut Ct. N8 . . . . 5J 31
Chestnut Ct. SW6 . . . . 6H 83
Chestnut Ct. W8 . . . . 3K 83 (off Abbots Wlk.)
Chestnut Ct. Felt 5B 114
Chestnut Ct. S Croy . . . . . . 4C 152 (off Bramley Hill)
Chestnut Dri. E11 . . . . 6J 35
Chestnut Dri. Bexh 3D 110
Chestnut Dri. Harr 7E 10
Chestnut Dri. Pinn 6B 24
Chestnut Gro. SE20 . . . . . . 7H 123
Chestnut Gro. SW12 . . . . . . 7E 102
Chestnut Gro. W5 . . . . 3D 80
Chestnut Gro. Barn 5J 5
Chestnut Gro. Dart 4K 129
Chestnut Gro. Iswth 4A 98
Chestnut Gro. Mitc 5H 139
Chestnut Gro. N Mald 3K 135
Chestnut Gro. S Croy 7H 153
Chestnut Gro. Wemb 5B 44
Chestnut Ho. W4 . . . . 4A 82 (off Orchard, The)
Chestnut La. N20 . . . . 1B 14
Chestnut Ri. SE18 . . . . 6H 91
Chestnut Ri. Bush 1A 10
Chestnut Rd. SE27 . . . . 3B 122
Chestnut Rd. SW20 . . . . 2F 137
Chestnut Rd. Ashf 4D 112
Chestnut Rd. King T 7E 116
Chestnut Rd. Twic 2J 115
Chestnuts, The. N5 . . . . 4C 50 (off Highbury Grange)
Chestnuts, The. Pinn 1D 24
Chestnuts, The. Uxb 7A 40
Chestnut Ter. Sutt 4K 149
Chestnut Wlk. Shep 4G 131
Chestnut Wlk. Wfd G 5D 20
Chestnut Way. Felt 3K 113
Cheston Av. Croy 2A 154
Chestwood Gro. Uxb 7B 40
Chettle Clo. SE1 . . . . 3D 86 (off Spurgeon St.)
Chettle Ct. N8 . . . . 6A 32
Chetwode Ho. NW8 . . . . 3C 158
Chetwode Rd. SW17 . . . . . . 3D 120
Chetwood Wlk. E6 . . . . 5C 72 (off Greenwich Cres.)
Chetwynd Av. E Barn 1J 15
Chetwynd Dri. Uxb 2B 58
Chetwynd Rd. NW5 . . . . 4F 49
Chevalier Clo. Stan 4K 11
Cheval Pl. SW7 . . . 3C 84 (1D 170)
Cheval St. E14 . . . . 3C 88
Cheveney Wlk. Brom 3J 143
Chevening Rd. NW6 . . . . 2F 65
Chevening Rd. SE10 . . . . 5H 89
Chevening Rd. SE19 . . . . . . 6D 122
Chevenings, The. Sidc 3C 128
Cheverell Ho. E2 . . . . 2G 69 (off Pritchard's Rd.)
Cheverton Rd. N19 . . . . 1H 49
Chevet St. E9 . . . . 5A 52
Chevington. NW2 . . . . 6H 47
Cheviot. N17 . . . . 7C 18 (off Northumberland Gro.)
Cheviot Clo. Bexh 2K 111
Cheviot Clo. Enf 2J 7
Cheviot Clo. Hay 7F 77
Cheviot Ct. SE14 . . . . 6J 87 (off Avonley Rd.)
Cheviot Ct. S'hall 4F 79
Cheviot Gdns. NW2 . . . . 2F 47
Cheviot Gdns. SE27 . . . . . . 4B 122
Cheviot Ga. NW2 . . . . 2G 47
Cheviot Ho. E1 . . . . 6H 69 (off Commercial Rd.)
Cheviot Rd. SE27 . . . . 5A 122
Cheviot Way. Ilf 4J 37
Chevron Clo. E16 . . . . 6J 71
Chevy Rd. S'hall 2G 79
Chewton Rd. E17 . . . . 4A 34
Cheylesmore Ho. SW1 . . . . 5F 85 (6J 171) (off Ebury Bri. Rd.)
Cheyne Av. E18 . . . . 3H 35
Cheyne Av. Twic 1D 114
Cheyne Clo. NW4 . . . . 5E 28
Cheyne Clo. Brom 3C 156
Cheyne Ct. SW3 . . . 6D 84 (7E 170)
Cheyne Gdns. SW3 . . . . 6C 84 (7D 170)
Cheyne Hill. Surb 4F 135
Cheyne M. SW3 . . . 6C 84 (7D 170)
Cheyne Path. W7 . . . . 5K 61
Cheyne Pl. SW3 . . . 6D 84 (7E 170)
Cheyne Rd. Ashf 7F 113
Cheyne Row. SW3 . . . . 6C 84 (7C 170)
Cheyne Wlk. N21 . . . . 5G 7
Cheyne Wlk. NW4 . . . . 6E 28
Cheyne Wlk. SW10 & SW3 . . . . 7B 84 (7C 170) (in three parts)
Cheyne Wlk. Croy 2G 153
Cheyneys Av. Edgw 6J 11
Chichele Gdns. Croy 4E 152
Chichele Rd. NW2 . . . . 5F 47
Chicheley Gdns. Harr . . . . . . 7B 10 (in two parts)
Chicheley Rd. Harr 7B 10
Chicheley St. SE1 . . . . 2K 85 (6H 167)
Chichester Av. Ruis 2F 41
Chichester Clo. E6 . . . . 6C 72
Chichester Clo. SE3 . . . . 7A 90
Chichester Clo. Hamp 6D 114
Chichester Ct. Edgw . . . . 6B 12 (off Whitchurch La.)
Chichester Ct. Eps 7B 148
Chichester Ct. N'holt 1C 60
Chichester Ct. Stan 3E 26
Chichester Gdns. Ilf 7C 36
Chichester Ho. NW6 . . . . 2J 65
Chichester Ho. SW9 . . . . 7A 86 (off Brixton Rd.)
Chichester M. SE27 . . . . . . 4A 122
Chichester Rents. WC2 . . . . . 7J 161
Chichester Rd. E11 . . . . 3G 53
Chichester Rd. N9 . . . . 1B 18
Chichester Rd. NW6 . . . . 2J 65
Chichester Rd. W2 . . . . 5K 65
Chichester Rd. Croy 3E 152
Chichester St. SW1 . . . . 5G 85 (6B 172)
Chichester Way. E14 . . . . 4F 89
Chichester Way. Felt 7A 96
Chicken Shed Theatre. 5K 5
Chicksand Ho. E1 . . . . 5G 69 (5K 163) (off Chicksand St.)
Chicksand St. E1 . . . . 5F 69 (6K 163) (in two parts)
Chiddingfold. N12 . . . . 3D 14
Chiddingstone. SE13 . . . . . . 5E 106
Chiddingstone Av. Bexh 7F 93
Chiddingstone St. SW6 . . . . . 2J 101
Chieveley Pde. Bexh . . . . . . 4H 111 (off Chieveley Rd.)
Chieveley Pde. Bexh . . . . . . 3H 111 (Mayplace Rd. E.)
Chieveley Rd. Bexh 4H 111
Chignell Pl. W13 . . . . 1A 80
Chigwell. 3K 21
Chigwell Hill. E1 . . . . 7H 69
Chigwell Hurst Ct. Pinn 3B 24
Chigwell Pk. Chig 4K 21
Chigwell Pk. Dri. Chig 4K 21
Chigwell Ri. Chig 2K 21
Chigwell Rd. E18 & Wfd G 3K 35
Chilcot Clo. E14 . . . . 6D 70
Chilcott Clo. Wemb 4C 44
Childebert Rd. SW17 . . . . . . 2F 121
Childeric Rd. SE14 . . . . 7A 88
Childerley St. SW6 . . . . 1G 101
Childers St. SE8 . . . . 6A 88
Childers, The. Wfd G 5J 21
Childs Ct. Hay 7J 59
Child's Hill. 3J 47
Childs Hill Wlk. NW2 . . . . 3H 47 (off Cricklewood La.)
Child's La. SE19 . . . . 6E 122
Child's Pl. SW5 . . . . 4J 83
Child's St. SW5 . . . . 4J 83
Child's Wlk. SW5 . . . . 4J 83 (off Child's St.)
Childs Way. NW11 . . . . 5H 29
Chilham Clo. Bex 7F 111
Chilham Clo. Gnfd 2A 62
Chilham Ho. SE1 . . . . 3D 86
Chilham Ho. SE15 . . . . 6J 87
Chilham Rd. SE9 . . . . 4C 126
Chilham Way. Brom 7J 143
Chilianwalla Memorial . . . 7G 171 (in Royal Hospital Chelsea)
Chillerton Rd. SW17 . . . . . . 5E 120
Chillingworth Gdns. Twic 3K 115
Chillingworth Rd. N7 . . . . 5A 50
Chilmark Gdns. N Mald 6C 136
Chilmark Rd. SW16 . . . . 2H 139
Chiltern Av. Twic 1E 114
Chiltern Clo. Bexh 1K 111
Chiltern Clo. Croy 3E 152
Chiltern Clo. Uxb 2C 40
Chiltern Clo. Wor Pk 1E 148
Chiltern Ct. N10 . . . . 2E 30
Chiltern Ct. NW1 . . . . 4D 66 (4F 159) (off Baker St.)
Chiltern Ct. SE14 . . . . 7J 87 (off Avonley Rd.)
Chiltern Ct. Harr 5H 25
Chiltern Ct. New Bar 5F 5
Chiltern Ct. Uxb 4D 58
Chiltern Dene. Enf 4E 6
Chiltern Dri. Surb 6G 135
Chiltern Gdns. NW2 . . . . 3F 47
Chiltern Gdns. Brom 4H 143
Chiltern Ho. SE17 . . . . 6D 86 (off Portland St.)
Chiltern Ho. W5 . . . . 5E 62

Chiltern Rd. E3 4C 70
Chiltern Rd. Ilf 5J 37
Chiltern Rd. Pinn 5A 24
Chilterns, The. Brom 2K 143 (off Murray Av.)
Chiltern St. W1 5E 66 (5G 159)
Chiltern Way. Wfd G 3D 20
Chilthorne Clo. SE6 7B 106
Chilton Av. W5 4D 80
Chilton Ct. N22 7D 16 (off Truro Rd.)
Chilton Gro. SE8 4K 87
Chiltonian Ind. Est. SE12 6H 107
Chilton Rd. Edgw 6B 12
Chilton Rd. Rich 3G 99
Chiltons, The. E18 2J 35
Chilton St. E2 4F 69 (3K 163)
Chilvers Clo. Twic 2J 115
Chilver St. SE10 5H 89
Chilworth Ct. SW19 1F 119
Chilworth Gdns. Sutt 3A 150
Chilworth M. W2 6B 66 (1A 164)
Chilworth St. W2 6A 66 (1A 164)
Chimes Av. N13 5F 17
Chimney Ct. E1 1H 87 (off Brewhouse La.)
China Ct. E1 1H 87 (off Asher Way)
China M. SW2 7K 103
China Wharf. SE1 2G 87 (6K 169)
Chinbrook Cres. SE12 3K 125
Chinbrook Rd. SE12 3K 125
Chinchilla Dri. Houn 2A 96
Chine, The. N10 4G 31
Chine, The. N21 6G 7
Chine, The. Wemb 5B 44
Ching Ct. WC2 6J 67 (1E 166) (off Monmouth St.)
Chingdale Rd. E4 3B 20
Chingford. 1B 20
Chingford Av. E4 3H 19
Chingford Green. 1A 20
Chingford Hall Est. E4 6G 19
Chingford Hatch. 4A 20
Chingford Ind. Est. E4 4F 19
Chingford La. Wfd G 4B 20
Chingford Mount. 4H 19
Chingford Mt. Rd. E4 4H 19
Chingford Rd. E4 6H 19
Chingford Rd. E17 1D 34
Chingley Clo. Brom 6G 125
Ching Way. E4 6G 19 (in two parts)
Chinnery Clo. Enf 1A 8
Chinnock's Wharf. E14 7A 70 (off Narrow St.)
Chinnor Cres. Gnfd 2F 61
Chipka St. E14 2E 88 (in two parts)
Chipley St. SE14 6A 88
Chipmunk Gro. N'holt 3C 60
Chippendale All. Uxb 7A 40
Chippendale Ho. SW1 5F 85 (6K 171) (off Churchill Gdns.)
Chippendale St. E5 3K 51
Chippendale Waye. Uxb 7A 40
Chippenham. King T 2F 135 (off Excelsior Clo.)
Chippenham Av. Wemb 5H 45
Chippenham Clo. Pinn 4H 23
Chippenham Gdns. NW6 3J 65
Chippenham M. W9 4J 65
Chippenham Rd. W9 4J 65
Chipperfield Ho. SW3 5C 84 (5C 170) (off Ixworth Pl.)
Chipping Barnet. 4B 4
Chipping Clo. Barn 3B 4
Chipstead Av. T Hth 4B 140
Chipstead Clo. SE19 7F 123
Chipstead Clo. Sutt 7K 149
Chipstead Gdns. NW2 2D 46
Chipstead Rd. H'row A 3C 94
Chipstead St. SW6 1J 101
Chip St. SW4 3H 103
Chirk Clo. Hay 4C 60
Chisenhale Rd. E3 2A 70
Chisholm Ct. W6 5C 82
Chisholm Rd. Croy 2E 152
Chisholm Rd. Rich 6F 99
Chisledon Wlk. E9 6B 52 (off Osborne Rd.)
Chislehurst. 6F 127
Chislehurst Av. N12 7F 15
Chislehurst Caves. 1E 144
Chislehurst Rd. Brom & Chst 2B 144
Chislehurst Rd. Orp 4J 145
Chislehurst Rd. Rich 5E 98
Chislehurst Rd. Sidc 5A 128
Chislehurst West. 5E 126
Chislet Clo. Beck 7C 124
Chisley Rd. N15 6E 32
Chiswell Sq. SE3 2K 107
Chiswell St. EC1 5C 68 (5E 162)
Chiswick. 5K 81
Chiswick Bri. SW14 & W4 2J 99
Chiswick Clo. Croy 3K 151
Chiswick Comn. Rd. W4 4K 81
Chiswick Ct. W4 4H 81
Chiswick Ct. Pinn 3D 24
Chiswick High Rd. Bren & W4 5G 81 (in two parts)
Chiswick House. 6A 82
Chiswick La. W4 5A 82
Chiswick La. S. W4 6B 82
Chiswick Mall. W4 & W6 6B 82
Chiswick Pk. W4 4H 81
Chiswick Plaza. W4 6J 81
Chiswick Quay. W4 1J 99
Chiswick Rd. N9 2B 18
Chiswick Rd. W4 4J 81
Chiswick Roundabout. (Junct.) 5G 81
Chiswick Sq. W4 6A 82
Chiswick Staithe. W4 1J 99
Chiswick Ter. W4 4J 81 (off Chiswick Rd.)
Chiswick Village. W4 6G 81
Chiswick Wharf. W4 6B 82
Chitterfield Ga. W Dray 7C 76
Chitty's La. Dag 2D 56
Chitty St. W1 5G 67 (5B 160)
Chivalry Rd. SW11 5C 102
Chive Clo. Croy 1K 153
Chivenor Gro. King T 5D 116
Chivers Rd. E4 3J 19
Choats Rd. Bark & Dag 2C 74
Chobham Gdns. SW19 2F 119
Chobham Rd. E15 5F 53
Cholmeley Cres. N6 7F 31
Cholmeley Lodge. N6 1F 49
Cholmeley Pk. N6 1F 49
Cholmley Gdns. NW6 5J 47
Cholmley Rd. Th Dit 6B 134
Cholmondeley Av. NW10 2C 64
Cholmondeley Wlk. Rich 5C 98 (in two parts)
Choppin's Ct. E1 1H 87
Chopwell Clo. E15 7F 53
Chorleywood Cres. Orp 2K 145
Choumert Gro. SE15 2G 105
Choumert Rd. SE15 3F 105
Choumert Sq. SE15 2G 105
Chow Sq. E8 5F 51
Chrisp Ho. SE10 6G 89 (off Maze Hill)
Chrisp St. E14 5D 70 (in two parts)
Christabel Clo. Isw th 3J 97
Christchurch Av. N12 6F 15
Christchurch Av. NW6 1F 65
Christchurch Av. Eri 6K 93
Christchurch Av. Harr 4K 25
Christchurch Av. Tedd 5A 116
Christchurch Av. Wemb 6E 44
Christchurch Clo. N12 7G 15
Christchurch Clo. SW19 7B 120
Christchurch Clo. Enf 2H 7
Christchurch Ct. EC4 6B 68 (7B 162) (off Warwick La.)
Christ Church Ct. NW10 1A 64
Christchurch Ct. Hay 4A 60 (off Dunedin Way)
Christchurch Flats. Rich 3E 98
Christchurch Gdns. Harr 4A 26
Christchurch Grn. Wemb 6E 44
Christchurch Hill. NW3 3B 48
Christchurch Ho. SW2 1K 121 (off Christchurch Rd.)
Christchurch La. Barn 2B 4
Christchurch Lodge. Barn 4J 5
Christchurch Pk. Sutt 7A 150
Christchurch Pas. NW3 3A 48
Christchurch Pas. High Bar 2B 4
Christchurch Path. Hay 3E 76
Christchurch Pl. SW8 2H 103
Christchurch Rd. N8 6J 31
Christchurch Rd. SW2 1K 121
Christ Chu. Rd. SW14 5H 99
Christchurch Rd. SW19 7B 120
Christ Chu. Rd. Beck 2C 142
Christchurch Rd. Ilf 1F 55
Christchurch Rd. H'row A 3C 94
Christchurch Rd. Sidc 4K 127
Christchurch Rd. Surb 6F 135
Christchurch Sq. E9 1J 69
Christchurch St. SW3 6D 84 (7E 170)
Christchurch Ter. SW3 7E 170
Christchurch Way. SE10 5G 89
Christian Ct. SE16 1B 88
Christian Fields. SW16 7A 122
Christian Pl. E1 6G 69 (off Burslem St.)
Christian St. E1 6G 69
Christie Ct. N19 2J 49
Christie Dri. Croy 5G 141
Christie Gdns. Romf 6B 38
Christie Ho. SE10 5H 89 (off Blackwall La.)
Christie Rd. E9 6A 52
Christina Sq. N4 1B 50
Christina St. EC2 4E 68 (3G 163)
Christine Worsley Clo. N21 1G 17
Christopher Av. W7 3A 80
Christopher Clo. SE16 2K 87
Christopher Clo. Sidc 5K 109
Christopher Gdns. Dag 5D 56
Christopher Ho. Sidc 2A 128 (off Station Rd.)
Christopher Pl. NW1 3H 67 (1D 160)
Christopher Rd. S'hall 4K 77
Christophers M. W11 1G 83
Christopher St. EC2 4D 68 (4F 163)
Chryssell Rd. SW9 7A 86
Chubworthy St. SE14 6A 88
Chudleigh. Sidc 4B 128
Chudleigh Cres. Ilf 4J 55
Chudleigh Gdns. Sutt 3A 150
Chudleigh Rd. NW6 7F 47
Chudleigh Rd. SE4 5B 106
Chudleigh Rd. Twic 6J 97 (in two parts)
Chudleigh St. E1 6K 69
Chudleigh Way. Ruis 1J 41
Chulsa Rd. SE26 5H 123
Chumleigh St. SE5 6E 86
Chumleigh Wlk. Surb 4F 135
Church All. Croy 1A 152
Church App. SE21 3D 122
Church Av. E4 6A 20
Church Av. N2 2B 30
Church Av. NW1 6F 49
Church Av. SW14 3K 99
Church Av. Beck 1C 142
Church Av. N'holt 7D 42
Church Av. Pinn 6C 24
Church Av. Ruis 1F 41
Church Av. Sidc 5A 128
Church Av. S'hall 3C 78
Churchbank. E17 4C 34 (off Teresa M.)
Churchbury Clo. Enf 2K 7
Churchbury La. Enf 3J 7
Churchbury Rd. SE9 7B 108
Churchbury Rd. Enf 2K 7
Church Cloisters. EC3 3G 169
Church Clo. N20 3H 15
Church Clo. W8 2K 83
Church Clo. Edgw 5D 12
Church Clo. Hay 5F 59
Church Clo. Houn 2C 96
Church Clo. N'wd 1H 23
Church Clo. W Dray 3A 76
Church Ct. SE16 2B 88 (off Rotherhithe St.)
Church Ct. Rich 5D 98
Church Ct. Wfd G 6F 21
Church Cres. E9 7K 51
Church Cres. N3 1H 29
Church Cres. N10 4F 31
Church Cres. N20 3H 15
Churchcroft Clo. SW12 7E 102
Churchdown. Brom 4G 125
Church Dri. NW9 1K 45
Church Dri. Harr 6E 24
Church Dri. W Wick 3G 155
Church Elm La. Dag 6G 57
Church End. 1H 29 **(Finchley)**
Church End. 6A 46 **(Willesden)**
Church End. E17 4D 34
Church End. NW4 3D 28
Church Entry. EC4 1B 168
Church Est. Almshouses. Rich 4F 99 (off Sheen Rd.)
Church Farm House Mus. 3D 28
Church Farm La. Sutt 6G 149
Churchfield Av. N12 6G 15
Churchfield Clo. Harr 4G 25
Churchfield Clo. Hay 7H 59
Churchfield Mans. SW6 2H 101 (off New Kings Rd.)
Churchfield Rd. W3 1J 81
Churchfield Rd. W7 2J 79
Churchfield Rd. W13 1B 80
Churchfield Rd. W on T 7J 131
Churchfield Rd. Well 3A 110
Churchfields. E18 1J 35
Churchfields. SE10 6E 88
Churchfields. W Mol 3E 132
Churchfields Av. Felt 3D 114
Churchfields Rd. Beck 2K 141
Churchfield Way. N12 6F 15
Church Gdns. W5 2D 80
Church Gdns. Wemb 4A 44
Church Gth. N19 2H 49 (off St John's Gro.)
Church Ga. SW6 3G 101
Church Grn. SW9 1A 104
Church Grn. Hay 6H 59
Church Gro. SE13 5D 106
Church Gro. King T 1C 134
Church Hill. E17 4C 34
Church Hill. N21 7E 6
Church Hill. SE18 3D 90
Church Hill. SW19 5H 119
Church Hill. Cars 5D 150
Church Hill. Cray 4K 111
Church Hill. Harr 1J 43
Church Hill Rd. E17 4D 34
Church Hill Rd. Barn & E Barn 6H 5
Church Hill Rd. Surb 5E 134
Church Hill Rd. Sutt 3F 149
Church Hill Wood. Orp 5K 145
Church Ho. SW1 3H 85 (1D 172) (off Gt. Smith St.)
Church Hyde. SE18 6J 91
Churchill Av. Harr 6B 26
Churchill Av. Uxb 3D 58
Churchill Clo. Felt 1H 113
Churchill Clo. Uxb 3D 58
Churchill Ct. N4 7A 32
Churchill Ct. W5 4F 63
Churchill Ct. N'holt 5E 42
Churchill Ct. Pinn 1C 24
Churchill Ct. S Harr 5F 25
Churchill Gdns. SW1 6A 172 (in three parts)
Churchill Gdns. W3 6G 63
Churchill Gdns. Rd. SW1 5F 85 (6K 171)
Churchill Pl. E14 1D 88
Churchill Pl. Harr 4J 25
Churchill Rd. E16 6A 72
Churchill Rd. NW2 6D 46
Churchill Rd. NW5 4F 49
Churchill Rd. Edgw 6A 12
Churchill Rd. S Croy 7C 152
Churchill Ter. E4 4H 19
Churchill Theatre. 2J 143
Churchill Wlk. E9 5J 51
Churchill Way. Brom 2J 143
Churchill Way. Sun 5J 113
Church La. E11 1G 53
Church La. E17 4D 34
Church La. N2 3B 30
Church La. N8 4K 31
Church La. N9 2B 18
Church La. N17 1E 32
Church La. NW9 6J 27
Church La. SW17 5D 120
Church La. SW19 1H 137
Church La. W5 2C 80
Church La. Brom 1C 156
Church La. Chess 6F 147
Church La. Chst 1G 145
Church La. Dag 7J 57
Church La. Enf 3J 7
Church La. Harr 1K 25
Church La. Pinn 3C 24
Church La. Rich 1E 116
Church La. Tedd 5K 115
Church La. Th Dit 6K 133
Church La. Twic 1A 116
Church La. Wall 3H 151
Churchley Rd. SE26 4H 123
Church Manorway. SE2 5A 92
Church Manorway. Eri 3K 93
Church Mead. SE5 7C 86 (off Camberwell Rd.)
Churchmead Clo. E Barn 6H 5
Church Mdw. Surb 2C 146
Churchmead Rd. NW10 6C 46
Churchmore Rd. SW16 1G 139
Church Mt. N2 5B 30
Chu. Paddock Ct. Wall 3H 151
Church Pde. Ashf 4B 112
Church Pas. EC2 6C 68 (7D 162) (off Guildhall Yd.)
Church Pas. Barn 3B 4
Church Pas. Surb 5E 134
Church Pas. Twic 1B 116
Church Path. E11 5J 35
Church Path. E17 4D 34
Church Path. N5 5B 50
Church Path. N12 4F 15
Church Path. N17 1E 32
Church Path. NW10 7A 46
Church Path. SW14 3K 99 (in two parts)

Church Path. SW19 2H 137 (in two parts)
Church Path. W3 & W4 2J 81 (in two parts)
Church Path. W7 1J 79
Church Path. Bark 1G 73
Church Path. Barn 4B 4
Church Path. Croy 2C 152 (in two parts)
Church Path. Mitc 3C 138 (in two parts)
Church Path. Romf 5K 39
Church Path. S'hall (UB1) 1E 78
Church Path. S'hall (UB2) 3D 78 (in two parts)
Church Pl. SW1 7G 67 (3B 166)
Church Pl. W5 2D 80
Church Pl. Ick 3E 40
Church Pl. Mitc 3C 138
Church Ri. SE23 2K 123
Church Ri. Chess 6F 147
Church Rd. E10 1C 52
Church Rd. E12 5C 54
Church Rd. E17 2A 34
Church Rd. N1 6C 50 (off Marquess Rd. S.)
Church Rd. N6 6E 30
Church Rd. N17 1E 32 (in two parts)
Church Rd. NW4 4D 28
Church Rd. NW10 7A 46
Church Rd. SE19 1E 140
Church Rd. SW13 2B 100
Church Rd. SW19 & Mitc 1B 138 (Christchurch Rd.)
Church Rd. SW19 5G 119 (High St.)
Church Rd. W3 1J 81
Church Rd. W7 7H 61
Church Rd. Ashf 3B 112
Church Rd. Bark 6G 55
Church Rd. Bexh 2F 111
Church Rd. Brom 2J 143
Church Rd. Buck H 1E 20
Church Rd. Clay 7A 146
Church Rd. Croy 3C 152 (in two parts)
Church Rd. E Mol 4H 133
Church Rd. Enf 6D 8
Church Rd. Eri 5K 93
Church Rd. Felt 5B 114
Church Rd. Ham & Rich 4D 116
Church Rd. Hay 1H 77
Church Rd. Houn 5K 77 (High St.)
Church Rd. Houn 7E 78 (Up. Sutton La.)
Church Rd. Ilf 6J 37
Church Rd. Iswth 1H 97
Church Rd. Kes 7B 156
Church Rd. King T 2F 135
Church Rd. N'holt 2B 60
Church Rd. N'wd 1H 23
Church Rd. Rich 4E 98
Church Rd. Shep 7D 130
Church Rd. Short 3G 143
Church Rd. Sidc 4A 128
Church Rd. S'hall 3D 78
Church Rd. Stan 5G 11
Church Rd. Surb 1C 146
Church Rd. Sutt 6G 149
Church Rd. Tedd 4J 115
Church Rd. Uxb 4A 58
Church Rd. Wall 3H 151
Church Rd. Well 2B 110
Church Rd. W Dray 3A 76
Church Rd. W Ewe 7K 147
Church Rd. Wor Pk 1A 148
Church Rd. Almshouses. E10 2D 52 (off Church Rd.)
Church Rd. Ind. Est. E10 1C 52
Church Rd. N. N2 2B 30
Church Rd. S. N2 2B 30
Church Row. NW3 4A 48
Church Row. Chst 1G 145
Church Row M. Chst 7G 127
Church Sq. Shep 7D 130
Church St. E15 1G 71
Church St. E16 1F 91
Church St. N9 7J 7
Church St. W2 & NW8 5B 66 (5B 158)
Church St. W4 6B 82
Church St. Croy 3B 152
Church St. Dag 6H 57
Church St. Enf 3H 7
Church St. Eps 7C 148
Church St. Hamp 1G 133
Church St. Iswth 3B 98
Church St. King T 2D 134
Church St. Sun 3K 131
Church St. Sutt 5K 149
Church St. Twic 1A 116
Church St. W on T 7J 131
Church St. Est. NW8 4B 66 (4B 158) (in two parts)
Church St. N. E15 1G 71
Church St. Pas. E15 1G 71
Church Stretton Rd. Houn 5G 97
Church Ter. NW4 3D 28
Church Ter. SE13 3G 107
Church Ter. Rich 5D 98
Church Va. N2 3D 30
Church Va. SE23 2K 123
Church Vw. Rich 5E 98
Churchview Rd. Twic 1H 115
Church Wlk. N6 3E 48
Church Wlk. N16 3D 50 (in three parts)
Church Wlk. NW2 3H 47
Church Wlk. NW4 3E 28
Church Wlk. NW9 2K 45
Church Wlk. SW13 1C 100
Church Wlk. SW15 5D 100
Church Wlk. SW16 2G 139
Church Wlk. SW20 3E 136
Church Wlk. Bren 6C 80 (in two parts)
Church Wlk. Enf 3J 7
Church Wlk. Hay 6G 59 (in three parts)
Church Wlk. Rich 5D 98
Church Wlk. Th Dit 6K 133
Church Wlk. W on T 7J 131
Churchward Ho. W14 5H 83 (off Ivatt Pl.)
Church Way. N20 3H 15
Churchway. NW1 3H 67 (1D 160) (in two parts)
Church Way. Barn 4J 5
Church Way. Edgw 6B 12
Churchwell Path. E9 5J 51
Churchwood Gdns. Wfd G 4D 20
Churchyard Pas. SE5 2D 104
Churchyard Row. SE11 4B 86
Churnfield. N4 2A 50
Churston Av. E13 1K 71
Churston Clo. SW2 1A 122
Churston Dri. Mord 5F 137
Churston Gdns. N11 6B 16
Churton Pl. SW1 4G 85 (4B 172)
Churton St. SW1 4G 85 (4B 172)
Chusan Pl. E14 6B 70
Chute Ho. SW9 2A 104 (off Stockwell Pk. Rd.)
Chyngton Clo. Sidc 3K 127
Cibber Rd. SE23 2K 123
Cicada Rd. SW18 6A 102
Cicely Ho. NW8 2B 66 (off Cochrane St.)
Cicely Rd. SE15 1G 105
Cinderella Path. NW11 1K 47
Cinderford Way. Brom 4G 125
Cinnabar Wharf Central. E1 1G 87 (off Wapping High St.)
Cinnabar Wharf E. E1 1G 87 (off Wapping High St.)
Cinnabar Wharf W. E1 1G 87 (off Wapping High St.)
Cinnamon Clo. Croy 7J 139
Cinnamon Row. SW11 3A 102
Cinnamon St. E1 1H 87
Cinnamon Wharf. SE1 6K 169
Cintra Pk. SE19 7F 123
Circle Gdns. SW19 2J 137
Circle, The. NW2 3A 46
Circle, The. NW7 6E 12
Circle, The. SE1 2F 87 (6J 169) (off Queen Elizabeth St.)
Circuits, The. Pinn 4A 24
Circular Rd. N2 2B 30
Circular Rd. N17 3F 33
Circular Way. SE18 6D 90
Circus Lodge. NW8 1A 158
Circus M. W1 5E 158
Circus Pl. EC2 5D 68 (6F 163)
Circus Rd. NW8 3B 66 (1A 158)
Circus St. SE10 7E 88
Cirencester St. W2 5K 65
Cirrus Clo. Wall 7J 151
Cissbury Ho. SE26 3G 123
Cissbury Ring N. N12 5C 14
Cissbury Ring S. N12 5C 14
Cissbury Rd. N15 5D 32
Citadel Pl. SE11 5K 85 (5G 173)
Citizen Rd. N7 4A 50
Citrus Ho. SE8 5B 88 (off Alverton St.)
City Airport. 1C 90
City Bus. Cen. SE16 3J 87
City Central Est. EC1 3C 68 (2C 162) (off Seward St.)
City Garden Row. N1 2B 68 (1B 162)
City Harbour. E14 3D 88 (off Selsdon Way)
City Heights. SE1 1E 86 (5H 169) (off Weavers La.)
City Ho. Wall 1E 150 (off Corbet Clo.)
City of London. 6D 68 (7E 162)
City of London Almshouses. SW9 4K 103
City of London Crematorium. E12 3C 54
City Pavilion. EC1 5B 68 (5A 162) (off Britton St.)
City Rd. EC1 2B 68 (1A 162)
City Tower. EC2 5D 68 (6E 162) (off Basinghall St.)
City University. 3B 68 (2A 162)
City Vw. Ct. SE22 7G 105
Civic Way. Ilf 4G 37
Civic Way. Ruis 5B 42
Clabon M. SW1 3D 84 (2E 170)
Clack La. Ruis 1E 40
Clack St. SE16 2J 87
Clacton Rd. E13 3B 72
Clacton Rd. E17 6A 34
Clacton Rd. N17 2F 33
Claigmar Gdns. N3 1K 29
Claire Ct. N12 4F 15
Claire Ct. NW2 6G 47
Claire Ct. Bush 1C 10
Claire Gdns. Stan 5H 11
Claire Ho. Edgw 2J 27 (off Burnt Oak B'way.)
Claire Pl. E14 3C 88
Clairvale Rd. Houn 1B 96
Clairview Rd. SW16 5F 121
Clairville Gdns. W7 1J 79
Clairville Point. SE23 3K 123 (off Dacres Rd.)
Clamp Hill. Stan 4C 10
Clancarty Rd. SW6 2J 101
Clandeboye Ho. E15 1H 71 (off John St.)
Clandon Clo. W3 2H 81
Clandon Clo. Eps 6B 148
Clandon Gdns. N3 3J 29
Clandon Ho. SE1 2B 86 (7B 168) (off Webber St.)
Clandon Rd. Ilf 2J 55
Clandon St. SE8 2C 106
Clandon Ter. SW20 2F 137
Clanfield Way. SE15 7E 86
Clanricarde Gdns. W2 7J 65
Clapham. 4G 103
Clapham Common. (Junct.) 4H 103
Clapham Comn. N. Side. SW4 4D 102
Clapham Comn. S. Side. SW4 6F 103
Clapham Comn. W. Side. SW4 4D 102 (in five parts)
Clapham Cres. SW4 4H 103
Clapham High St. SW4 4H 103
Clapham Junction. 3C 102
Clapham Junct. App. SW11 3C 102
Clapham Mnr. Ct. SW4 3G 103
Clapham Mnr. St. SW4 3G 103
Clapham Park. 6H 103
Clapham Pk. Est. SW4 6H 103
Clapham Pk. Rd. SW4 4G 103
Clapham Pk. Ter. SW4 5J 103 (off Kings Av.)
Clapham Rd. SW4 & SW9 3J 103
Clapham Rd. Est. SW4 3J 103
Clap La. Dag 2H 57
Claps Ga. La. E6 4E 72
Clapton Comn. E5 7F 33 (in four parts)
Clapton Park. 4K 51
Clapton Pk. Est. E5 4K 51
Clapton Pas. E5 5J 51
Clapton Sq. E5 5J 51
Clapton Ter. N16 1G 51
Clapton Way. E5 4G 51
Clara Grant Ho. E14 3C 88 (off Mellish St.)
Clara Nehab Ho. NW11 5H 29 (off Leeside Cres.)
Clara Pl. SE18 4E 90
Clare Clo. N2 3A 30
Clare Corner. SE9 7F 109
Clare Ct. WC1 3J 67 (2F 161) (off Judd St.)
Claredale Ho. E2 2H 69 (off Claredale St.)
Claredale St. E2 2G 69
Clare Gdns. E7 4J 53
Clare Gdns. W11 6G 65
Clare Gdns. Bark 6K 55
Clare Ho. E16 7E 72 (off University Way)
Clare La. N1 7C 50
Clare Lawn Av. SW14 5J 99
Clare Mkt. WC2 6K 67 (1H 167)
Clare M. SW6 7K 83
Claremont. Shep 6D 130
Claremont Av. Harr 5E 26
Claremont Av. N Mald 5C 136
Claremont Av. Sun 1K 131
Claremont Clo. E16 1E 90
Claremont Clo. N1 2A 68 (1K 161)
Claremont Clo. SW2 1J 121
Claremont Clo. Orp 4E 156
Claremont Gdns. Ilf 2J 55
Claremont Gdns. Surb 5E 134
Claremont Gro. W4 7A 82
Claremont Gro. Wfd G 6F 21
Claremont Pk. N3 1G 29
Claremont Rd. E7 5K 53
Claremont Rd. E11 3F 53
Claremont Rd. E17 2A 34
Claremont Rd. N6 7G 31
Claremont Rd. NW2 7F 29
Claremont Rd. W9 2G 65
Claremont Rd. W13 5A 62
Claremont Rd. Brom 4C 144
Claremont Rd. Croy 1G 153
Claremont Rd. Harr 2J 25
Claremont Rd. Surb 5E 134
Claremont Rd. Tedd 5K 115
Claremont Rd. Twic 7B 98
Claremont Sq. N1 2A 68 (1J 161)
Claremont St. E16 2E 90
Claremont St. N18 6B 18
Claremont St. SE10 6D 88
Claremont Ter. Th Dit 7B 134
Claremont Way. NW2 1E 46 (in two parts)
Claremont Way Ind. Est. NW2 1E 46
Clarence Av. SW4 7H 103
Clarence Av. Brom 4C 144
Clarence Av. Ilf 6E 36
Clarence Av. N Mald 2J 135
Clarence Clo. Barn 5G 5
Clarence Clo. Bus H 1E 10
Clarence Ct. NW7 5F 13
Clarence Ct. W6 4D 82 (off Cambridge Gro.)
Clarence Cres. SW4 6H 103
Clarence Cres. Sidc 3B 128
Clarence Gdns. NW1 3F 67 (2K 159)
Clarence Ga. Wfd G 6J 21 (in four parts)
Clarence Ga. Gdns. NW1 4D 66 (4F 159) (off Glentworth St.)
Clarence House. 6B 166
Clarence La. SW15 6A 100
Clarence M. E5 5H 51
Clarence M. SE16 1K 87
Clarence M. SW12 7F 103
Clarence Pas. NW1 2J 67
Clarence Pl. E5 5H 51
Clarence Rd. E5 4H 51
Clarence Rd. E12 4B 54
Clarence Rd. E16 4G 71
Clarence Rd. E17 2K 33
Clarence Rd. N15 5C 32
Clarence Rd. N22 7D 16
Clarence Rd. NW6 7H 47
Clarence Rd. SE8 6D 88
Clarence Rd. SE9 2C 126
Clarence Rd. SW19 6K 119
Clarence Rd. W4 5G 81
Clarence Rd. Bexh 4E 110
Clarence Rd. Brom 3B 144
Clarence Rd. Croy 7D 140
Clarence Rd. Enf 5D 8
Clarence Rd. Rich 1F 99
Clarence Rd. Sidc 3B 128
Clarence Rd. Sutt 5K 149
Clarence Rd. Tedd 6K 115
Clarence Rd. Wall 5F 151
Clarence St. King T 2D 134 (in three parts)
Clarence St. Rich 4E 98
Clarence St. S'hall 3B 78
Clarence Ter. NW1 4D 66 (3F 159)
Clarence Ter. Houn 4F 97
Clarence Wlk. SW4 2J 103
Clarence Way. NW1 7F 49
Clarenden Pl. Dart 5K 129

Clarendon Clo. E9 7J 51
Clarendon Clo. W2 7C 66 (2C 164)
Clarendon Clo. Orp 3K 145
Clarendon Ct. NW2 7E 46
Clarendon Ct. NW11 4H 29
Clarendon Ct. Beck 1D 142 (off Albemarle Rd.)
Clarendon Ct. Houn 1J 95
Clarendon Ct. Rich 1F 99
Clarendon Cres. Twic 3H 115
Clarendon Cross. W11 7G 65
Clarendon Dri. SW15 4E 100
Clarendon Flats. W1 6E 66 (1H 165) (off Balderton St.)
Clarendon Gdns. NW4 3C 28
Clarendon Gdns. W9 4A 66
Clarendon Gdns. Ilf 7D 36
Clarendon Gdns. Wemb 3D 44
Clarendon Grn. Orp 4K 145
Clarendon Gro. NW1 3H 67 (1C 160)
Clarendon Gro. Mitc 3D 138
Clarendon Ho. NW1 2G 67 (off Werrington St.)
Clarendon M. W2 7C 66 (2C 164)
Clarendon M. Bex 1H 129
Clarendon Path. Orp 4K 145 (in two parts)
Clarendon Pl. W2 7C 66 (2C 164)
Clarendon Ri. SE13 4E 106
Clarendon Rd. E11 1F 53
Clarendon Rd. E17 6D 34
Clarendon Rd. E18 3J 35
Clarendon Rd. N8 3K 31
Clarendon Rd. N15 4C 32
Clarendon Rd. N18 6B 18
Clarendon Rd. N22 2K 31
Clarendon Rd. SW19 7C 120
Clarendon Rd. W5 3E 62
Clarendon Rd. W11 7G 65
Clarendon Rd. Ashf 4B 112
Clarendon Rd. Croy 2B 152
Clarendon Rd. Harr 6J 25
Clarendon Rd. Hay 2H 77
Clarendon Rd. Wall 6G 151
Clarendon St. SW1 5F 85 (5K 171)
Clarendon Ter. W9 4A 66 (3A 158)
Clarendon Wlk. W11 6G 65
Clarendon Way. N21 6H 7
Clarendon Way. Chst & Orp 3K 145
Clarens St. SE6 2B 124
Clare Pl. SW15 7B 100
Clare Rd. E11 6F 35
Clare Rd. NW10 7C 46
Clare Rd. SE14 1B 106
Clare Rd. Gnfd 6H 43
Clare Rd. Houn 3D 96
Clare Rd. Stanw 1A 112
Clare St. E2 2H 69
Claret Gdns. SE25 3E 140
Clareville Gro. SW7 4A 84 (4A 170)
Clareville Gro. M. SW7 4A 170
Clareville St. SW7 4A 84 (4A 170)
Clare Way. Bexh 1E 110
Clarewood Ct. W1 5D 66 (6E 158) (off Seymour Pl.)
Clarewood Wlk. SW9 4A 104
Clarges M. W1 1F 85 (4J 165)
Clarges St. W1 1F 85 (4K 165)
Claribel Rd. SW9 2B 104
Clarice Way. Wall 7J 151
Claridge Ct. SW6 2H 101
Claridge Rd. Dag 1D 56
Clarion Ho. E3 2A 70 (off Roman Rd.)
Clarion Ho. SW1 5G 85 (5B 172) (off Moreton Pl.)
Clarion Ho. W1 6H 67 (1C 166) (off St Anne's Ct.)
Clarissa Ho. E14 6D 70 (off Cordela St.)
Clarissa Rd. Romf 7D 38
Clarissa St. E8 1F 69
Clark Ct. NW10 7J 45
Clarke Mans. Bark 7K 55 (off Upney La.)
Clarke M. N9 3C 18
Clarke Path. N16 1G 51
Clarkes Av. Wor Pk 1F 149
Clarkes Dri. Uxb 5A 58
Clarke's M. W1 5E 66 (5H 159)
Clarks Mead. Bush 1B 10
Clarkson Rd. E16 6H 71
Clarkson Row. NW1 2G 67 (off Mornington Ter.)
Clarksons, The. Bark 2G 73
Clarkson St. E2 3H 69
Clark's Pl. EC2 6E 68 (7G 163)
Clarks Rd. Ilf 2H 55
Clark St. E1 5H 69
Clark Way. Houn 7B 78
Classic Mans. E9 7H 51 (off Wells St.)
Classon Clo. W Dray 2A 76
Claude Rd. E10 2E 52
Claude Rd. E13 1K 71
Claude Rd. SE15 2H 105
Claude St. E14 4C 88
Claudia Jones Ho. N17 1C 32
Claudia Jones Way. SW2 6J 103
Claudia Pl. SW19 1G 119
Claughton Rd. E13 2A 72
Clauson Av. N'holt 5F 43
Clavell St. SE10 6E 88
Claverdale Rd. SW2 7K 103
Clavering Av. SW13 6D 82
Clavering Clo. Twic 4A 116
Clavering Ho. SE13 4F 107 (off Blessington Rd.)
Clavering Ind. Est. N9 2D 18 (off Montagu Rd.)
Clavering Rd. E12 1B 54
Claverley Gro. N3 1K 29
Claverley Vs. N3 7E 14
Claverton St. SW1 5G 85 (6B 172)
Clave St. E1 1J 87
Claxton Gro. W6 5F 83
Claxton Path. SE4 4K 105 (off Coston Wlk.)
Clay Av. Mitc 2F 139
Claybank Gro. SE13 3D 106
Claybourne M. SE19 7E 122
Claybridge Rd. SE12 4A 126
Claybrook Clo. N2 3B 30
Claybrook Rd. W6 6F 83
Claybury. Bush 1A 10
Claybury B'way. Ilf 3C 36
Claybury Rd. Wfd G 7H 21
Clay Ct. E17 3F 35
Claydon. SE17 4C 86 (off Deacon Way)
Claydon Dri. Croy 4J 151
Claydon Ho. NW4 2F 29 (off Holders Hill Rd.)
Claydown M. SE18 5E 90
Clay Farm Rd. SE9 2G 127
Claygate Cres. New Ad 6E 154
Claygate La. Esh 2A 146 (in two parts)
Claygate La. Th Dit 1A 146
Claygate Rd. W13 3B 80
Clayhall. 2D 36
Clayhall Av. Ilf 3C 36
Clayhill. Surb 5G 135
Clayhill Cres. SE9 4B 126
Claylands Pl. SW8 7A 86
Claylands Rd. SW8 6K 85 (7H 173)
Clay La. Bus H 1D 10
Clay La. Edgw 2B 12
Clay La. Stanw 7B 94
Claymore Clo. Mord 7J 137
Claypole Ct. E17 5C 34 (off Yunus Khan Clo.)
Claypole Dri. Houn 1C 96
Claypole Rd. E15 2E 70
Clayponds Av. W5 & Bren 4D 80
Clayponds Gdns. W5 4D 80 (in two parts)
Clayponds La. Bren 5E 80 (in two parts)
Clays La. E15 5D 52
Clays La. Clo. E15 5D 52
Clay St. W1 5D 66 (6F 159)
Clayton Av. Wemb 7E 44
Clayton Clo. E6 6D 72
Clayton Ct. E17 2A 34
Clayton Cres. Bren 5D 80
Clayton Fld. NW9 7F 13
Clayton Ho. E9 7J 51 (off Frampton Pk. Rd.)
Clayton Ho. SW13 7E 82 (off Trinity Chu. Rd.)
Clayton M. SE10 1F 107
Clayton Rd. SE15 1G 105
Clayton Rd. Chess 4C 146
Clayton Rd. Hay 2G 77
Clayton Rd. Iswth 3J 97
Clayton Rd. Romf 1J 57
Clayton St. SE11 6A 86 (7J 173)
Clayton Ter. Hay 5C 60
Claywood Clo. Orp 7J 145
Clayworth Clo. Sidc 6B 110
Cleanthus Clo. SE18 1F 109
Cleanthus Rd. SE18 2F 109
Clearbrook Way. E1 6J 69
Clearwater Pl. Surb 6C 134
Clearwater Ter. W11 2G 83 (off Lorne Gdns.)
Clearwell Dri. W9 4K 65
Cleave Av. Hay 4G 77
Cleaveland Rd. Surb 5D 134
Cleaverholme Clo. SE25 6H 141
Cleaver Ho. NW3 7D 48 (off Adelaide Rd.)
Cleaver Sq. SE11 5A 86 (6K 173)
Cleaver St. SE11 5A 86 (5K 173)
Cleaves Almshouses. King T 2E 134 (off London Rd.)
Cleeve Ct. Felt 1G 113
Cleeve Hill. SE23 1H 123
Cleeve Pk. Gdns. Sidc 2B 128
Cleeve Way. SW15 7B 100
Cleeve Workshops. E2 3E 68 (2H 163) (off Boundary Rd.)
Clegg Ho. SE3 4K 107
Clegg Ho. SE16 3J 87 (off Moodkee St.)
Clegg St. E1 1H 87
Clegg St. E13 2J 71
Cleland Ho. E2 2J 69 (off Sewardstone Rd.)
Clematis Gdns. Wfd G 5D 20
Clematis St. W12 7C 64
Clem Attlee Ct. SW6 6H 83
Clem Attlee Pde. SW6 6H 83 (off N. End Rd.)
Clemence Rd. Dag 1J 75
Clemence St. E14 5B 70
Clement Av. SW4 4H 103
Clement Clo. NW6 7E 46
Clement Clo. W4 4K 81
Clement Gdns. Hay 4G 77
Clementhorpe Rd. Dag 6C 56
Clement Ho. SE8 4A 88
Clement Ho. W10 5E 64 (off Dalgarno Gdns.)
Clementina Rd. E10 1B 52
Clementine Clo. W13 2B 80
Clement Rd. SW19 5G 119
Clement Rd. Beck 2K 141
Clement's Av. E16 7J 71
Clements Ct. Houn 4B 96
Clements Ct. Ilf 3F 55
Clement's Inn. WC2 6K 67 (1H 167)
Clement's Inn Pas. WC2 1H 167
Clements La. EC4 7D 68 (2F 169)
Clements La. Ilf 3F 55
Clements Pl. Bren 5D 80
Clements Rd. E6 7C 54
Clement's Rd. SE16 3G 87
Clements Rd. Ilf 3F 55
Clemson Ho. E8 1F 69
Clendon Way. SE18 4H 91
Clennam St. SE1 2C 86 (6D 168)
Clensham Ct. Sutt 2J 149
Clensham La. Sutt 2J 149
Clenston M. W1 6D 66 (7E 158)
Cleopatra's Needle. 7K 67 (3G 167)
Clephane Rd. N1 6C 50 (in two parts)
Clephane Rd. N. N1 6C 50
Clere Pl. EC2 4D 68 (3F 163)
Clere St. EC2 4D 68 (3F 163)
Clerics Wlk. Shep 7F 131
Clerkenwell. 4A 68 (4A 162)
Clerkenwell Clo. EC1 4A 68 (3K 161) (in two parts)
Clerkenwell Grn. EC1 4A 68 (4K 161)
Clerkenwell Rd. EC1 4A 68 (4J 161)
Clermont Rd. E9 1J 69
Cleveden Ct. S Croy 5E 152
Clevedon Clo. N16 3F 51
Clevedon Gdns. Hay 3F 77
Clevedon Gdns. Houn 1K 95
Clevedon Mans. NW5 4E 48
Clevedon Pas. N16 2F 51
Clevedon Rd. SE20 1K 141
Clevedon Rd. King T 2G 135
Clevedon Rd. Twic 6D 98 (in two parts)
Cleve Ho. NW6 7K 47
Cleveland Av. SW20 2H 137
Cleveland Av. W4 4B 82
Cleveland Av. Hamp 7D 114
Cleveland Ct. W13 5B 62
Cleveland Gdns. N4 5C 32
Cleveland Gdns. NW2 2F 47
Cleveland Gdns. SW13 2B 100
Cleveland Gdns. W2 6A 66
Cleveland Gdns. Wor Pk 2A 148
Cleveland Gro. E1 4J 69
Cleveland Ho. N2 2B 30 (off Grange, The)
Cleveland La. N9 7C 8
Cleveland Mans. SW9 7A 86 (off Mowll St.)
Cleveland Mans. W9 4J 65
Cleveland M. W1 5G 67 (5A 160)
Cleveland Pk. Stai 6A 94
Cleveland Pk. Av. E17 4C 34
Cleveland Pk. Cres. E17 4C 34
Cleveland Pl. SW1 1G 85 (4B 166)
Cleveland Ri. Mord 7F 137
Cleveland Rd. E18 3J 35
Cleveland Rd. N1 7D 50
Cleveland Rd. SW13 2B 100
Cleveland Rd. W4 3J 81
Cleveland Rd. W13 5A 62
Cleveland Rd. Ilf 3F 55
Cleveland Rd. Iswth 4A 98
Cleveland Rd. N Mald 4A 136
Cleveland Rd. Well 2K 109
Cleveland Rd. Wor Pk 2A 148
Cleveland Row. SW1 1G 85 (5A 166)
Cleveland Sq. W2 6A 66
Clevelands, The. Bark 6G 55
Cleveland St. W1 4F 67 (4K 159)
Cleveland Ter. W2 6A 66
Cleveland Way. E1 4J 69
Cleveley Clo. SE7 4B 90
Cleveley Cres. W5 2E 62
Cleveleys Rd. E5 3H 51
Cleverly Est. W12 1C 82
Cleve Rd. NW6 7K 47
Cleve Rd. Sidc 3D 128
Cleves Av. Eps 7D 148
Cleves Ho. E16 1K 89 (off Southey M.)
Cleves Rd. E6 1B 72
Cleves Rd. Rich 3C 116
Cleves Wlk. Ilf 1G 37
Cleves Way. Hamp 7D 114
Cleves Way. Ruis 1B 42
Cleves Way. Sun 6H 113
Clewer Ct. E10 1C 52 (off Leyton Grange Est.)
Clewer Cres. Harr 1H 25
Clewer Ho. SE2 2D 92 (off Wolvercote Rd.)
Cley Ho. SE4 4K 105
Clichy Est. E1 5J 69
Clichy Ho. E1 5J 69 (off Stepney Way)
Clifden Rd. E5 5J 51
Clifden Rd. Bren 6D 80
Clifden Rd. Twic 1K 115
Cliffe Ho. SE10 5H 89 (off Blackwall La.)
Cliffe Rd. S Croy 5D 152
Cliffe Wlk. Sutt 5A 150 (off Greyhound Rd.)
Clifford Av. SW14 3H 99 (in two parts)
Clifford Av. Chst 6D 126
Clifford Av. Ilf 1F 37
Clifford Av. Wall 4G 151
Clifford Clo. N'holt 1C 60
Clifford Ct. W2 5K 65 (off Westbourne Pk. Vs.)
Clifford Dri. SW9 4B 104
Clifford Gdns. NW10 2E 64
Clifford Gdns. Hay 4G 77
Clifford Gro. Ashf 4C 112
Clifford Haigh Ho. SW6 7F 83
Clifford Ho. W14 4H 83 (off Edith Vs.)
Clifford Rd. E16 4H 71
Clifford Rd. E17 2E 34
Clifford Rd. N1 1E 68
Clifford Rd. N9 6D 8
Clifford Rd. SE25 4G 141
Clifford Rd. Barn 3E 4
Clifford Rd. Houn 3B 96
Clifford Rd. Rich 2D 116
Clifford Rd. Wemb 7D 44
Clifford's Inn Pas. EC4 6A 68 (1J 167)
Clifford St. W1 7G 67 (3A 166)
Clifford Way. NW10 4B 46
Cliff Rd. NW1 6H 49
Cliffsend Ho. SW9 1A 104 (off Cowley Rd.)
Cliff Ter. SE8 2C 106
Cliffview Rd. SE13 3C 106
Cliff Vs. NW1 6H 49
Cliff Wlk. E16 5H 71 (in two parts)
Clifton Av. E17 3K 33
Clifton Av. N3 1H 29
Clifton Av. W12 1B 82

Clifton Av. Felt 3A 114
Clifton Av. Stan 2B 26
Clifton Av. Wemb 6F 45
Clifton Ct. N4 . . . . 2A 50
Clifton Ct. NW8 . . . . 3A 158
Clifton Ct. SE15 . . . . 7H 87
Clifton Ct. Beck 1D 142
Clifton Ct. Stanw 6A 94
Clifton Ct. Wfd G 6D 20
Clifton Cres. SE15 . . . . 7H 87
Clifton Est. SE15 . . . . 1H 105
Clifton Gdns. N15 . . . . 6F 33
Clifton Gdns. NW11 . . . . . . 6H 29
Clifton Gdns. W4 . . . . 4K 81 (in two parts)
Clifton Gdns. W9 . . . . 4A 66
Clifton Gdns. Enf 4D 6
Clifton Gdns. Uxb 2D 58
Clifton Gro. E8 . . . . 6G 51
Clifton Hill. NW6 . . . . 2K 65
Clifton Ho. E2 . . . . . 4F 69 (3J 163) (off Club Row)
Clifton Ho. E11 . . . . 2G 53
Clifton Pde. Felt 4A 114
Clifton Pk. Av. SW20 . . . . . 2E 136
Clifton Pl. SE16 . . . . 2J 87
Clifton Pl. W2 . . . . . 6B 66 (1B 164)
Clifton Ri. SE14 . . . . 7A 88 (in two parts)
Clifton Rd. E7 . . . . 6B 54
Clifton Rd. E16 . . . . 5G 71
Clifton Rd. N3 . . . . 1A 30
Clifton Rd. N8 . . . . 6H 31
Clifton Rd. N22 . . . . 1G 31
Clifton Rd. NW10 . . . . 2C 64
Clifton Rd. SE25 . . . . 4E 140
Clifton Rd. SW19 . . . . 6F 119
Clifton Rd. W9 . . . . 4A 66 (3A 158)
Clifton Rd. Gnfd 4G 61
Clifton Rd. Harr 4F 27
Clifton Rd. Ilf 6H 37
Clifton Rd. Iswth 2J 97
Clifton Rd. King T 7F 117
Clifton Rd. Sidc 4J 127
Clifton Rd. S'hall 4C 78
Clifton Rd. Tedd 4J 115
Clifton Rd. Wall 5F 151
Clifton Rd. Well 3C 110
Clifton St. EC2 . . . . 4E 68 (5G 163) (in two parts)
Clifton Ter. N4 . . . . 2A 50
Clifton Vs. W9 . . . . 5A 66
Cliftonville Ct. SE12 . . . . . . 1J 125
Clifton Wlk. W6 . . . . 4D 82 (off King St.)
Clifton Way. SE15 . . . . 7H 87
Clifton Way. H'row A 3D 94
Clifton Way. Wemb 1E 62
Climsland Ho. SE1 . . . . 1A 86 (4K 167)
Clinch Ct. E16 . . . . 5J 71 (off Plymouth Rd., in two parts)
Cline Rd. N11 . . . . 6B 16
Clinger Ct. N1 . . . . 1E 68 (off Hobbs Pl. Est.)
Clink Exhibition, The. . . . . 1D 86 (4E 168) (off Clink St.)
Clink St. SE1 . . . . . 1D 86 (4E 168)
Clink Wharf. SE1 . . . . 1D 86 (4E 168) (off Clink St.)
Clinton Av. E Mol 4G 133
Clinton Av. Well 4A 110
Clinton Rd. E3 . . . . 3A 70
Clinton Rd. E7 . . . . 4J 53
Clinton Rd. N15 . . . . 4D 32
Clipper Clo. SE16 . . . . 2K 87
Clipper Ho. E14 . . . . 5E 88 (off Manchester Rd.)
Clipper Way. SE13 . . . . 4E 106
Clippesby Clo. Chess 6F 147
Clipstone M. W1 . . . . 5G 67 (5A 160)
Clipstone Rd. Houn 3E 96
Clipstone St. W1 . . . 5F 67 (5K 159)
Clissold Clo. N2 . . . . 3D 30
Clissold Ct. N4 . . . . 2C 50
Clissold Cres. N16 . . . . 3D 50
Clissold Rd. N16 . . . . 3D 50
Clitheroe Av. Harr 1E 42
Clitheroe Rd. SW9 . . . . 2J 103
Clitherow Av. W7 . . . . 3A 80
Clitherow Ct. Bren 5C 80
Clitherow Pas. Bren 5C 80
Clitherow Rd. Bren 5B 80
Clitterhouse Cres. NW2 . . . . . 1E 46
Clitterhouse Rd. NW2 . . . . . . 1E 46
Clive Av. N18 . . . . 6B 18
Clive Ct. W9 . . . . 4A 66 (off Maida Va.)
Cliveden Clo. N12 . . . . 4F 15
Cliveden Ho. E16 . . . . 1J 89 (off Fitzwilliam M.)
Cliveden Pl. SW1 . . . . 4E 84 (3G 171)
Cliveden Pl. Shep 6E 130
Cliveden Rd. SW19 . . . . 1H 137
Clivedon Ct. W13 . . . . 5B 62
Clivedon Rd. E4 . . . . 5B 20
Clive Ho. SE10 . . . . 6E 88 (off Haddo St.)
Clive Lloyd Ho. N15 . . . . 5C 32 (off Woodlands Pk. Rd.)
Clive Lodge. NW4 . . . . 6F 29
Clive Pas. SE21 . . . . 3D 122
Clive Rd. SE21 . . . . 3D 122
Clive Rd. SW19 . . . . 6C 120
Clive Rd. Belv 4G 93
Clive Rd. Enf 4B 8
Clive Rd. Felt 6J 95
Clive Rd. Twic 4K 115
Clivesdale Dri. Hay 1K 77
Clive Way. Enf 4B 8
Cloak La. EC4 . . . . 7C 68 (2D 168)
Clochar Ct. NW10 . . . . 1B 64
Clock Ho. E3 . . . . 3E 70
Clock Ho. E17 . . . . 4F 35 (off Wood St.)
Clockhouse Av. Bark 1G 73
Clockhouse Clo. SW19 . . . . 2E 118
Clockhouse Ct. Beck 2A 142
Clockhouse Junction. (Junct.) 5E 16
Clockhouse La. Ashf & Felt 4C 112
Clockhouse La. Romf 1H 39
Clock Ho. Pde. E11 . . . . 5K 35
Clockhouse Pde. N13 . . . . . . 5F 17
Clockhouse Pl. SW15 . . . . . 6G 101
Clock Ho. Rd. Beck 3A 142
Clockhouse Roundabout. (Junct.) 1E 112
Clock Mus., The. 7D 162
Clock Pde. Enf 5J 7
Clock Pl. SE11 . . . . 4B 86 (off Newington Butts)
Clock Tower Ind. Est. Iswth 3K 97
Clock Tower M. N1 . . . . 1C 68
Clock Tower M. SE28 . . . . . . 7B 74
Clock Tower Pl. N7 . . . . 6J 49
Clock Tower Rd. Iswth 3K 97
Cloister Clo. Tedd 5B 116
Cloister Gdns. SE25 . . . . . . 6H 141
Cloister Gdns. Edgw 5D 12
Cloister Rd. NW2 . . . . 3H 47
Cloister Rd. W3 . . . . 5J 63
Cloisters Av. Brom 5D 144
Cloisters Bus. Cen. SW8 . . . . 7F 85 (off Battersea Pk. Rd.)
Cloisters Ct. Bexh 3H 111
Cloisters Mall. King T 2E 134
Cloisters, The. . . . . 1E 172 (in Westminster Abbey)
Cloisters, The. E1 . . . . 4J 163
Cloisters, The. SW9 . . . . . . 1A 104
Clonbrock Rd. N16 . . . . 4E 50
Cloncurry St. SW6 . . . . 2F 101
Clonmel Clo. Harr 2H 43
Clonmell Rd. N17 . . . . 3D 32
Clonmel Rd. SW6 . . . . 7H 83
Clonmel Rd. Tedd 4H 115
Clonmore St. SW18 . . . . . . 1H 119
Clorane Gdns. NW3 . . . . 3J 47
Close, The. E4 . . . . 7K 19
Close, The. N10 . . . . 2F 31
Close, The. N14 . . . . 2C 16
Close, The. N20 . . . . 2C 14
Close, The. SE3 . . . . 2F 107
Close, The. SE25 . . . . 6G 141
Close, The. Beck 4A 142
Close, The. Bex 6G 111
Close, The. Cars 7C 150
Close, The. E Barn 6J 5
Close, The. Eastc 7A 24
Close, The. Harr 2G 25
Close, The. Ilf 6J 37
Close, The. Iswth 2H 97
Close, The. Mitc 4D 138
Close, The. N Mald 2J 135
Close, The. Orp 6J 145
Close, The. Pinn 7D 24
Close, The. Rich 3H 99
Close, The. Romf 6E 38
Close, The. Sidc 4B 128
Close, The. Surb 6E 134
Close, The. Sutt 7H 137
Close, The. Uxb 1C 58
Close, The. Wemb (HA0) 6E 44
Close, The. Wemb (HA9) 3J 45
Cloth Ct. EC1 . . . . 6B 162
Cloth Fair. EC1 . . . . 5B 68 (6B 162)
Clothier St. E1 . . . . 6E 68 (7H 163)
Cloth St. EC1 . . . . . 5C 68 (5C 162)
Clothworkers Rd. SE18 . . . . . 7H 91
Cloudesdale Rd. SW17 . . . . 2F 121
Cloudesley Pl. N1 . . . . 1A 68
Cloudesley Rd. N1 . . . . 1A 68 (in two parts)
Cloudesley Rd. Bexh 1F 111
Cloudesley Sq. N1 . . . . 1A 68
Cloudesley St. N1 . . . . 1A 68
Clouston Clo. Wall 5J 151
Clova Rd. E7 . . . . 6H 53
Clove Cres. E14 . . . . 7E 70
Clove Hitch Quay. SW11 . . . 3A 102
Clovelly Av. NW9 . . . . 4B 28
Clovelly Av. Uxb 4E 40
Clovelly Clo. Pinn 3K 23
Clovelly Clo. Uxb 4E 40
Clovelly Gdns. SE19 . . . . . . 1F 141
Clovelly Gdns. Enf 7K 7
Clovelly Gdns. Romf 1H 39
Clovelly Ho. W2 . . . . 6A 66 (off Hallfield Est.)
Clovelly Rd. N8 . . . . 4H 31
Clovelly Rd. W4 . . . . 2K 81
Clovelly Rd. W5 . . . . 2C 80
Clovelly Rd. Bexh 6E 92
Clovelly Rd. Houn 2E 96
Clovelly Way. E1 . . . . 6J 69
Clovelly Way. Orp 6K 145
Clovelly Way. S Harr 2D 42
Clover Clo. E11 . . . . 2F 53
Cloverdale Gdns. Sidc 6K 109
Clover M. SW3 . . . . 6D 84 (7F 171)
Clover Way. Wall 1E 150
Clove St. E13 . . . . 4J 71
Clowders Rd. SE6 . . . . 3B 124
Clowser Clo. Sutt 5A 150
Cloysters Grn. E1 . . . . 1G 87
Cloyster Wood. Edgw 7J 11
Club Gdns. Rd. Brom 7J 143
Club Row. E2 & E1 . . . . 4F 69 (3J 163)
Clumps, The. Ashf 4F 113
Clunbury Av. S'hall 5D 78
Clunbury St. N1 . . . . 2D 68
Cluny Est. SE1 . . . 3E 86 (7G 169)
Cluny M. SW5 . . . . 4J 83
Cluny Pl. SE1 . . . . 3E 86 (7G 169)
Cluse Ct. N1 . . . . 2C 68 (off St Peters St., in two parts)
Clutton St. E14 . . . . 5D 70
Clydach Rd. Enf 4A 8
Clyde Cir. N15 . . . . 4E 32
Clyde Ct. NW1 . . . . 2H 67 (off Hampden Clo.)
Clyde Flats. SW6 . . . . 7H 83 (off Rhylston Rd.)
Clyde Ho. King T 1D 134
Clyde Pl. E10 . . . . 7D 34
Clyde Rd. N15 . . . . 4E 32
Clyde Rd. N22 . . . . 1H 31
Clyde Rd. Croy 2F 153
Clyde Rd. Stai 1A 112
Clyde Rd. Sutt 5J 149
Clyde Rd. Wall 6G 151
Clydesdale. Enf 4E 8
Clydesdale Av. Stan 3D 26
Clydesdale Clo. Iswth 3K 97
Clydesdale Ct. N20 . . . . 1G 15
Clydesdale Gdns. Rich 4H 99
Clydesdale Ho. W11 . . . . 6H 65 (off Clydesdale Rd.)
Clydesdale Ho. Eri . . . . 2E 92 (off Kale Rd.)
Clydesdale Rd. W11 . . . . 6H 65
Clyde St. SE8 . . . . 6B 88
Clyde Ter. SE23 . . . . 2J 123
Clyde Va. SE23 . . . . 2J 123
Clyde Way. Romf 1K 39
Clyde Wharf. E16 . . . . 1J 89
Clydon Clo. Eri 6K 93
Clyfford Rd. Ruis 4H 41
Clymping Dene. Felt 7K 95
Clynes Ho. E2 . . . . 3K 69 (off Knottisford St.)
Clynes Ho. Dag . . . . 3G 57 (off Uvedale Rd.)
Clyston St. SW8 . . . . 2G 103
Coach & Horses Yd. W1 . . . . 7G 67 (2K 165)
Coach Ho. La. N5 . . . . 4B 50
Coach Ho. La. SW19 . . . . . . 4F 119
Coach Ho. M. SE1 . . . . 2E 86 (7G 169)
Coach Ho. M. SE20 . . . . 7H 123
Coach Ho. M. SE23 . . . . 6K 105
Coach Ho. Yd. NW3 . . . . 4A 48 (off Hampstead High St.)
Coach Ho. Yd. SW18 . . . . . 4K 101
Coachmaker M. SW4 . . . . . . 3J 103 (off Fenwick Pl.)
Coach Yd. M. N19 . . . . 1J 49
Coaldale Wlk. SE21 . . . . 7C 104
Coalecroft Rd. SW15 . . . . . 4E 100
Coalport Ho. SE11 . . . . 2J 173
Coates Av. SW18 . . . . 6C 102
Coates Hill Rd. Brom 2E 144
Coate St. E2 . . . . 2G 69
Coates Wlk. Bren 6E 80
Cobalt Sq. SW8 . . . . 7G 173
Cobbett Rd. SE9 . . . . 3C 108
Cobbett Rd. Twic 1E 114
Cobbetts Av. Ilf 5B 36
Cobbett St. SW8 . . . . 7K 85
Cobble La. N1 . . . . 7B 50
Cobble M. N4 . . . . 3C 50
Cobblers Wlk. Hamp & Tedd . . . . 1G 133 (in two parts)
Cobblestone Pl. Croy 1C 152
Cobbold Ct. SW1 . . . . 4H 85 (3C 172) (off Elverton St.)
Cobbold Ind. Est. NW10 . . . . 6B 46
Cobbold M. W12 . . . . 2B 82
Cobbold Rd. E11 . . . . 3H 53
Cobbold Rd. NW10 . . . . 6B 46
Cobbold Rd. W12 . . . . 2A 82
Cobb's Ct. EC4 . . . . 1B 168
Cobb's Hall. SW6 . . . . 6F 83 (off Fulham Pal. Rd.)
Cobb's Rd. Houn 4D 96
Cobbsthorpe Vs. SE26 . . . . 4K 123
Cobb St. E1 . . . . . . 5F 69 (6J 163)
Cobden Ct. Brom 4A 144
Cobden Ho. E2 . . . . 3G 69 (off Nelson Gdns.)
Cobden Ho. NW1 . . . . 2G 67 (off Arlington Rd.)
Cobden M. SE26 . . . . 5H 123
Cobden Rd. E11 . . . . 3G 53
Cobden Rd. SE25 . . . . 5G 141
Cobham Av. N Mald 5C 136
Cobham Clo. SW11 . . . . 6C 102
Cobham Clo. Brom 7C 144
Cobham Clo. Edgw 2H 27
Cobham Clo. Enf 3B 8
Cobham Clo. Sidc 6B 110
Cobham Clo. Wall 6J 151
Cobham Ct. Mitc 2B 138
Cobham Ho. Bark . . . . 1G 73 (in two parts)
Cobham M. NW1 . . . . 7H 49
Cobham Pl. Bexh 5D 110
Cobham Rd. E17 . . . . 1E 34
Cobham Rd. N22 . . . . 3B 32
Cobham Rd. Houn 7A 78
Cobham Rd. Ilf 2J 55
Cobham Rd. King T 2G 135
Cobland Rd. SE12 . . . . 4A 126
Coborn Rd. E3 . . . . 2B 70
Coborn St. E3 . . . . 3B 70
Cobourg Rd. SE5 . . . . 6F 87
Cobourg St. NW1 . . . . 3G 67 (2B 160)
Coburg Clo. SW1 . . . . 3B 172
Coburg Cres. SW2 . . . . 1K 121
Coburg Dwellings. E1 . . . . . . 6J 69 (off Hardinge St.)
Coburg Gdns. Ilf 2B 36
Coburg Rd. N22 . . . . 3K 31
Cochrane Clo. NW8 . . . . . . 1B 158
Cochrane Ct. E10 . . . . 1C 52 (off Leyton Grange Est.)
Cochrane Ho. E14 . . . . 2C 88 (off Admirals Way)
Cochrane M. NW8 . . . . 2B 66
Cochrane Rd. SW19 . . . . . . 7G 119
Cochrane St. NW8 . . . . 2B 66 (1B 158)
Cochrane Theatre, The. . . . . 5J 67 (6F 161) (off Theobald's Rd.)
Cockburn Ho. SW1 . . . . 5H 85 (6D 172) (off Aylesford St.)
Cockcrow Hill. 1D 146
Cockerell Rd. E17 . . . . 7A 34
Cockfosters. 4K 5
Cockfosters Pde. Barn 4K 5
Cockfosters Rd. Pot B & Barn 1H 5
Cock Hill. E1 . . . . . 5E 68 (6H 163)
Cock La. EC1 . . . . . 5B 68 (6A 162)
Cockpit Steps. SW1 . . . . 7C 166
Cockpit Theatre. . . . . 4C 66 (4C 158) (off Gateforth St.)
Cockpit Yd. WC1 . . . 5K 67 (5H 161)
Cocks Cres. N Mald 4B 136
Cockspur Ct. SW1 . . . . 1H 85 (4D 166)
Cockspur St. SW1 . . . . 1H 85 (4D 166)
Cocksure La. Sidc 3G 129
Coda Cen., The. SW6 . . . . . . 7G 83
Code St. E1 . . . . . . 4F 69 (4K 163)
Codicote Ho. SE8 . . . . 4K 87 (off Chilton Gro.)
Codicote Ter. N4 . . . . 2C 50
Codling Clo. E1 . . . . 1G 87
Codling Way. Wemb 4D 44
Codrington Ct. E1 . . . . 4H 69
Codrington Ct. SE16 . . . . 7A 70
Codrington Hill. SE23 . . . . . 7A 106
Codrington M. W11 . . . . 6G 65

Cody Clo. Harr 3D 26
Cody Clo. Wall 7H 151
Cody Rd. E16 4F 71
Coe Av. SE25 6G 141
Coe's All. Barn 4B 4
Cofers Circ. Wemb 2H 45
Coffey St. SE8 7C 88
Cogan Av. E17 1A 34
Coin St. SE1 1A 86 (4J 167)
(in two parts)
Coity Rd. NW5 6E 48
Cokers La. SE21 1D 122
Coke St. E1 6G 69
Colas M. NW6 1J 65
Colbeck M. SW7 4K 83
Colbeck Rd. Harr 7G 25
Colberg Pl. N16 7F 33
Colborne Ho. E14 7C 70
(off E. India Dock Rd.)
Colborne Way. Wor Pk 3E 148
Colbrook Av. Hay 3F 77
Colbrook Clo. Hay 3F 77
Colburn Way. Sutt 3B 150
Colby M. SE19 5E 122
Colby Rd. SE19 5E 122
Colby Rd. W on T 7J 131
Colchester Av. E12 4D 54
Colchester Dri. Pinn 5B 24
Colchester Rd. E10 7E 34
Colchester Rd. E17 6C 34
Colchester Rd. Edgw 7D 12
Colchester Rd. N'wd 2J 23
Colchester St. E1
6F 69 (7K 163)
Coldbath Sq. EC1
4A 68 (3J 161)
Coldbath St. SE13 1D 106
(in two parts)
Coldblow. 1J 129
Cold Blow Cres. Bex 1K 129
Cold Blow La. SE14 7K 87
(in two parts)
Cold Blows. Mitc 3D 138
Coldershaw Rd. W13 1A 80
Coldfall Av. N10 2E 30
Coldham Ct. N22 1B 32
Coldharbour. E14 2E 88
Coldharbour Crest. SE9 3E 126
Coldharbour La. SW9 & SE5
4A 104
Coldharbour La. Hay 1J 77
Coldharbour Pl. SE5 2C 104
Coldharbour Rd. Croy 5A 152
Coldharbour Way. Croy 5A 152
Coldstream Gdns. SW18 6H 101
Colebeck M. N1 6B 50
Colebert Av. E1 4J 69
Colebert Ho. E1 4J 69
(off Colebert Av.)
Colebrook Clo. SW15 7F 101
Colebrook Ct. SW3
4C 84 (4D 170)
(off Makins St.)
Colebrooke Av. W13 6B 62
Colebrooke Ct. Sidc 4B 128
(off Granville Rd.)
Colebrooke Dri. E11 7A 36
Colebrooke Pl. N1 1B 68
Colebrooke Ri. Brom 2G 143
Colebrooke Row. N1
2B 68 (1A 162)
Colebrook Ho. E14 6D 70
(off Ellesmere St.)
Colebrook Rd. SW16 1J 139
Colebrook Way. N11 5A 16
Coleby Path. SE5 7D 86
Colechurch Ho. SE1 5G 87
(off Avondale Sq.)
Cole Clo. SE28 1B 92
Cole Ct. Twic 7A 98
Coledale Dri. Stan 1C 26
Coleford Rd. SW18 5A 102
Cole Gdns. Houn 7J 77
Colegrave Rd. E15 5F 53
Colegrove Rd. SE15 6F 87
Coleherne Ct. SW5 5K 83
Coleherne Mans. SW5 5K 83
(off Old Brompton Rd.)
Coleherne M. SW10 5K 83
Coleherne Rd. SW10 5K 83
Colehill Gdns. SW6 2G 101
Colehill La. SW6 1G 101
Cole Ho. SE1 2A 86 (7J 167)
(off Baylis Rd.)
Coleman Clo. SE25 2G 141
Coleman Fields. N1 1C 68
Coleman Mans. N8 7J 31
Coleman Rd. SE5 7E 86
Coleman Rd. Belv 4G 93
Coleman Rd. Dag 6E 56
Colemans Heath. SE9 3E 126
Coleman St. EC2
6D 68 (7E 162)
Coleman St. Bldgs. EC2 7E 162
Colenso Dri. NW7 7H 13
Colenso Rd. E5 4J 51
Colenso Rd. Ilf 1J 55
Cole Park. 6A 98
Cole Pk. Gdns. Twic 5A 98
Cole Pk. Rd. Twic 5A 98
Cole Pk. Vw. Twic 6A 98
Colepits Wood Rd. SE9 5G 109
Coleraine Rd. N8 3A 32
Coleraine Rd. SE3 6H 89
Coleridge Av. E12 6C 54
Coleridge Av. Sutt 4C 150
Coleridge Clo. SW8 2F 103
Coleridge Ct. W14 3F 83
(off Blythe Rd.)
Coleridge Ct. New Bar 5E 4
(off Station Rd.)
Coleridge Gdns. NW6 7A 48
Coleridge Ho. SE17 5C 86
(off Browning St.)
Coleridge Ho. SW1
5G 85 (6B 172)
(off Churchill Gdns.)
Coleridge La. N8 6J 31
Coleridge Rd. E17 4B 34
Coleridge Rd. N4 2A 50
Coleridge Rd. N8 6H 31
Coleridge Rd. N12 5F 15
Coleridge Rd. Ashf 4A 112
Coleridge Rd. Croy 7J 141
Coleridge Sq. W13 6A 62
Coleridge Wlk. NW11 4J 29
Coleridge Way. Hay 6J 59
Coleridge Way. W Dray 4A 76
Cole Rd. Twic 6A 98
Colesburg Rd. Beck 3B 142
Coles Cres. Harr 2F 43
Coles Grn. Bus H 1B 10
Coles Grn. Ct. NW2 2C 46
Coles Grn. Rd. NW2 1C 46
Coleshill Flats. SW1 4H 171
Coleshill Rd. Tedd 6J 115
Colestown St. SW11 2C 102
Cole St. SE1 2C 86 (7D 168)
Colesworth Ho. Edgw 2J 27
(off Burnt Oak B'way.)
Colet Clo. N13 6G 17
Colet Ct. W6 4F 83
(off Hammersmith Rd.)
Colet Gdns. W14 4F 83
Colet Ho. SE17 5B 86
(off Doddington Gro.)
Colette Ct. SE16 2K 87
(off Eleanor Clo.)
Coley St. WC1 4K 67 (4H 161)
Colfe & Hatcliffe Glebe. SE13
5D 106
(off Lewisham High St.)
Colfe Rd. SE23 1A 124
Colham Av. W Dray 1A 76
Colham Green. 5C 58
Colham Grn. Rd. Uxb 5C 58
Colham Mill Rd. W Dray 2A 76
Colham Rd. Uxb 4B 58
Colham Roundabout. Uxb 6C 58
Colina M. N15 4B 32
Colina Rd. N8 5B 32
Colin Clo. NW9 4A 28
Colin Clo. Croy 3B 154
Colin Clo. W Wick 3H 155
Colin Cres. NW9 4B 28
Colindale. 3K 27
Colindale Av. NW9 3K 27
Colindale Bus. Pk. NW9 3J 27
Colindeep Gdns. NW4 4C 28
Colindeep La. NW9 & NW4
3A 28
Colin Dri. NW9 5B 28
Colinette Rd. SW15 4E 100
Colin Gdns. NW9 4B 28
Colin Pde. NW9 4A 28
Colin Pk. Rd. NW9 4A 28
Colin Rd. NW10 6C 46
Colinton Rd. Ilf 2B 56
Colin Winter Ho. E1 4J 69
(off Nicholas Rd.)
Coliston Pas. SW18 7J 101
Coliston Rd. SW18 7J 101
Collamore Av. SW18 1C 120
Collapit Clo. Harr 6F 25
Collard Pl. NW1 7F 49
Collards Almshouses.
E17 5E 34
(off Maynard Rd.)
College App. SE10 6E 88
College Arts Collection, The.
4H 67 (3C 160)
(off Gower St.,
Strang Print Room)
College Av. Harr 1J 25
College Clo. E5 5J 51
College Clo. N18 5A 18
College Clo. Harr 7D 10
College Clo. Twic 1H 115
College Ct. NW3 6B 48
(off College Cres.)
College Ct. SW3 6F 171
College Ct. W5 7E 62
College Ct. W6 5E 82
(off Queen Caroline St.)
College Ct. Enf 5D 8
College Cres. NW3 6A 48
College Cross. N1 7A 50
College Dri. Ruis 7J 23
College Dri. Th Dit 7J 133
College E. E1 5F 69 (6K 163)
College Fields Bus. Cen.
SW19 1B 138
College Gdns. E4 7J 9
College Gdns. N18 5A 18
College Gdns. SE21 1E 122
College Gdns. SW17 2C 120
(in three parts)
College Gdns. Enf 1J 7
College Gdns. Ilf 5C 36
College Gdns. N Mald 5B 136
College Grn. SE19 7E 122
College Gro. NW1 1G 67
College Hill. EC4
7C 68 (2D 168)
College Hill Rd. Harr 7D 10
College La. NW5 4F 49
College Mans. NW6 1G 65
(off Winchester Av.)
College M. N1 7A 50
(off College Cross)
College M. SW1 1E 172
College M. SW18 5K 101
College of Arms. 2C 168
College Pde. NW6 1G 65
College Park. 3D 64
College Pk. Clo. SE13 4F 107
College Pk. Rd. N17 6A 18
College Pl. E17 4G 35
College Pl. NW1 1G 67
College Pl. SW10 7A 84
(off Hortensia Rd.)
College Point. E15 6H 53
College Rd. E17 5E 34
College Rd. N17 6A 18
College Rd. N21 2F 17
College Rd. NW10 2E 64
College Rd. SE21 & SE19
7E 104
College Rd. SW19 6B 120
College Rd. W13 6B 62
College Rd. Brom 1J 143
College Rd. Croy 2D 152
College Rd. Enf 2J 7
College Rd. Harr 6J 25
College Rd. Har W 1J 25
College Rd. Iswth 1K 97
College Rd. Swan 7K 129
College Rd. Wemb 1D 44
College Roundabout. King T
3E 134
College Row. E9 5K 51
College Slip. Brom 1J 143
(in two parts)
College St. EC4 7C 68 (2D 168)
College Ter. E3 3B 70
College Ter. N3 2H 29
College Vw. SE9 1B 126
College Wlk. King T 3E 134
College Way. Ashf 4B 112
College Way. Hay 7J 59
College Yd. NW5 4F 49
Collent St. E9 6J 51
Collerston Ho. SE10 5H 89
(off Armitage Rd.)
Colless Rd. N15 5F 33
Collett Rd. SE16 3G 87
Collett Way. S'hall 2F 79
Collier Clo. E6 7F 73
Collier Clo. Eps 6G 147
Collier Dri. Edgw 2G 27
Collier Row. 1H 39
Collier Row La. Romf 1H 39
Collier Row Rd. Romf 1F 39
Colliers Ct. Croy 4D 152
Colliers Shaw. Kes 5B 156
Collier St. N1 2K 67
Colliers Water La. T Hth 5A 140
Collier's Wood. 7B 120
Colliers Wood. (Junct.) 7B 120
Collindale Av. Eri 7H 93
Collindale Av. Sidc 1A 128
Collingbourne Rd. W12 1D 82
Collingham Gdns. SW5 4K 83
Collingham Pl. SW5 4K 83
Collingham Rd. SW5 4K 83
Collings Clo. N22 6E 16
Collington St. SE10 5F 89
Collingtree Rd. SE26 4J 123
Collingwood Av. N10 3E 30
Collingwood Av. Surb 1J 147
Collingwood Clo. SE20 1H 141
Collingwood Clo. Twic 7E 96
Collingwood Ct. W5 5F 63
Collingwood Ct. New Bar 5E 4
Collingwood Ho. E1 4H 69
(off Darling Row)
Collingwood Ho. SE16 2H 87
(off Cherry Garden St.)
Collingwood Ho. SW1
5H 85 (6C 172)
(off Dolphin Sq.)
Collingwood Ho. W1
5G 67 (5A 160)
(off Clipstone St.)
Collingwood Rd. E17 6C 34
Collingwood Rd. N15 4E 32
Collingwood Rd. Mitc
3C 138
Collingwood Rd. Sutt 3J 149
Collingwood Rd. Uxb 4D 58
Collingwood St. E1 4H 69
Collins Av. Stan 2E 26
Collins Ct. E8 6G 51
Collins Dri. Ruis 2A 42
Collins Ho. E14 7E 70
(off Newby Pl.)
Collins Ho. E15 1H 71
(off John St.)
Collins Ho. SE10 5H 89
(off Armitage Rd.)
Collinson Ct. SE1
2C 86 (7C 168)
(off Gt. Suffolk St.)
Collinson Ho. SE15 7G 87
(off Peckham Pk. Rd.)
Collinson St. SE1
2C 86 (7C 168)
Collinson Wlk. SE1
2C 86 (7C 168)
Collins Path. Hamp 6D 114
Collins Rd. N5 4C 50
Collins Sq. SE3 2H 107
Collins St. SE3 2G 107
(in two parts)
Collin's Yd. N1 1B 68
Collinwood Av. Enf 3D 8
Collinwood Gdns. Ilf 5D 36
Collis All. Twic 1J 115
Coll's Rd. SE15 1J 105
Collyer Av. Croy 4J 151
Collyer Pl. SE15 1G 105
Collyer Rd. Croy 4J 151
Colman Ct. N12 6F 15
Colman Ct. Stan 6G 11
Colman Pde. Enf 3K 7
Colman Rd. E16 5A 72
Colmans Wharf. E14 5D 70
(off Morris Rd.)
Colmar Clo. E1 4K 69
Colmer Pl. Harr 7C 10
Colmer Rd. SW16 1J 139
Colmore M. SE15 1H 105
Colmore Rd. Enf 4D 8
Colnbrook St. SE1 3B 86
Colne Ct. W7 6H 61
(off High La.)
Colne Ct. Eps 4J 147
Colnedale Rd. Uxb 5A 40
Colne Ho. Bark 7F 55
Colne Rd. E5 4A 52
Colne Rd. N21 7J 7
Colne Rd. Twic 1J 115
Colne St. E13 3J 71
Colney Hatch. 6J 15
Colney Hatch La. N11 & N10
6J 15
Cologne Rd. SW11 4B 102
Colombo Rd. Ilf 1G 55
Colombo St. SE1
1B 86 (5A 168)
Colomb St. SE10 5G 89
Colonel's Wlk. Enf 3G 7
Colonial Av. Twic 6G 97
Colonial Dri. W4 4J 81
Colonial Rd. Felt 7G 95
Colonnade. WC1
4J 67 (4F 161)
Colonnades, The. W2 6K 65
Colonnades, The. Croy 6A 152
Colonnade, The. SE8 4B 88
Colonnade Wlk. SW1
4F 85 (4J 171)
Colosseum Ter. NW1 2K 159
Colour Ct. SW1 5B 166
Colroy Ct. NW11 5G 29
Colson Rd. Croy 2E 152
Colson Way. SW16 4G 121
Colstead Ho. E1 6H 69
(off Watney Mkt.)
Colsterworth Rd. N15 4F 33
(in two parts)
Colston Av. Cars 4C 150
Colston Ct. Cars 4D 150
(off West St.)
Colston Rd. E7 6B 54
Colston Rd. SW14 4J 99
Colthurst Cres. N4 2B 50
Colthurst Dri. N9 3C 18
Coltman Ho. E14 6A 70
(off Maroon St.)

Coltman Ho. SE10 6E 88 (off Welland St.)
Coltness Cres. SE2 5B 92
Colton Gdns. N17 3C 32
Colton Rd. Harr 5J 25
Coltsfoot Dri. W Dray 6A 58
Columbas Dri. NW3 1B 48
Columbia Av. Edgw 1H 27
Columbia Av. Ruis 1K 41
Columbia Av. Wor Pk 7B 136
Columbia Point. SE16 3J 87 (off Surrey Quays Rd.)
Columbia Rd. E2 3F 69 (1J 163)
Columbia Rd. E13 4H 71
Columbia Rd. Market. 3F 69 (1K 163) (off Columbia Rd.)
Columbia Sq. SW14 4J 99
Columbia Wharf. Enf 6F 9
Columbine Av. E6 5C 72
Columbine Av. S Croy 7B 152
Columbine Way. SE13 2E 106
Columbus Ct. SE16 1J 87 (off Rotherhithe St.)
Columbus Ct. Yd. E14 1C 88
Columbus Gdns. N'wd 1J 23
Colva Wlk. N19 2F 49
Colverson Ho. E1 5J 69 (off Lindley St.)
Colvestone Cres. E8 5F 51
Colview Ct. SE9 1B 126
Colville Est. N1 1E 68
Colville Est. W. E2 3F 69 (2K 163) (off Turin St.)
Colville Gdns. W11 6H 65 (in two parts)
Colville Houses. W11 6H 65
Colville M. W11 6H 65
Colville Pl. W1 5G 67 (6B 160)
Colville Rd. E11 3E 52
Colville Rd. E17 2A 34
Colville Rd. N9 1C 18
Colville Rd. W3 3H 81
Colville Rd. W11 6H 65
Colville Sq. W11 6H 65
Colville Ter. W11 6H 65
Colvin Clo. SE26 5J 123
Colvin Gdns. E4 3K 19
Colvin Gdns. E18 4K 35
Colvin Gdns. Ilf 1G 37
Colvin Rd. E6 7C 54
Colvin Rd. T Hth 5A 140
Colwall Gdns. Wfd G 5D 20
Colwell Rd. SE22 5F 105
Colwick Clo. N6 7H 31
Colwith Rd. W6 6E 82
Colwood Gdns. SW19 7B 120
Colworth Gro. SE17 4C 86
Colworth Rd. E11 6G 35
Colworth Rd. Croy 1G 153
Colwyn Av. Gnfd 2K 61
Colwyn Clo. SW16 5G 121
Colwyn Cres. Houn 1G 97
Colwyn Grn. NW9 6A 28 (off Snowdon Dri.)
Colwyn Ho. SE1 3A 86 (2J 173)
Colwyn Rd. NW2 3D 46
Colyer Clo. N1 2K 67
Colyer Clo. SE9 2F 127
Colyers Clo. Eri 1K 111
Colyers La. Eri 1J 111
Colyers Wlk. Eri 1K 111
Colyton Clo. Well 1D 110
Colyton Clo. Wemb 6C 44
Colyton Rd. SE22 5H 105
Colyton Way. N18 5B 18
Combe Av. SE3 7H 89
Combedale Rd. SE10 5J 89
Combe Dene. Brom 4H 143 (off Cumberland Rd.)
Combemartin Rd. SW18 7G 101
Combe M. SE3 7H 89
Comber Clo. NW2 2D 46
Comber Gro. SE5 7C 86
Comber Ho. SE5 7C 86
Combermere Rd. SW9 3K 103
Combermere Rd. Mord 6K 137
Comberton. King T 2G 135 (off Eureka Rd.)
Comberton Rd. E5 2H 51
Combeside. SE18 7K 91
Combe, The. NW1 3F 67 (2K 159) (in two parts)
Combwell Cres. SE2 3A 92
Comedy Store. 7H 67 (3C 166) (off Oxendon St.)
Comedy Theatre. 7H 67 (3C 166) (off Panton St.)
Comely Bank Rd. E17 5E 34
Comeragh M. W14 5G 83
Comeragh Rd. W14 5G 83
Comer Cres. S'hall 2G 79 (off Windmill Av.)
Comerell Pl. SE10 5H 89
Comerford Rd. SE4 4A 106
Comet Clo. E12 4B 54
Comet Pl. SE8 7C 88 (in two parts)
Comet Rd. Stanw 7A 94
Comet St. SE8 7C 88
Commerce Rd. N22 1K 31
Commerce Rd. Bren 6C 80
Commerce Way. Croy 2K 151
Commercial Dock Path. SE16 3B 88 (off Gulliver St.)
Commercial Rd. E1 6G 69 (7K 163)
Commercial Rd. N18 5K 17
Commercial Rd. Ind. Est. N18 6A 18
Commercial St. E1 4F 69 (4J 163)
Commercial Way. NW10 2H 63
Commercial Way. SE15 7F 87
Commerell St. SE10 5G 89
Commodity Quay. E1 7F 69 (3K 169)
Commodore Ct. SE8 1C 106 (off Albyn Rd.)
Commodore Ho. E14 7E 70 (off Poplar High St.)
Commodore Sq. SW10 1A 102
Commodore St. E1 4A 70
Commondale. SW15 3E 100
Commonfield La. SW17 5C 120
Common La. Clay 7A 146
Common Rd. SW13 3D 100
Common Rd. Clay 6A 146
Common Rd. Stan 4C 10
Commonside. Kes 4A 156
Commonside E. Mitc 3E 138 (in two parts)
Commonside W. Mitc 3D 138
Common, The. E15 6G 53 (in two parts)
Common, The. W5 7E 62 (in two parts)
Common, The. S'hall 4A 78
Common, The. Stan 2D 10
Commonwealth Av. W12 7D 64 (in three parts)
Commonwealth Av. Hay 6F 59
Commonwealth Institute. 3H 83
Commonwealth Rd. N17 7B 18
Commonwealth Way. SE2 5B 92
Community Clo. Houn 1K 95
Community Clo. Uxb 3D 40
Community La. N7 5H 49
Community Rd. E15 5F 53
Community Rd. Gnfd 1G 61
Como Rd. SE23 2A 124
Como St. Romf 5K 39
Compass Ct. SE1 1F 87 (5J 169) (off Shad Thames)
Compass Hill. Rich 6D 98
Compass Ho. SW18 4K 101
Compass Point. E14 7B 70 (off Grenade St.)
Compayne Gdns. NW6 7K 47
Compton Av. E6 2B 72
Compton Av. N1 6B 50
Compton Av. N6 7C 30
Compton Av. Wemb 4C 44
Compton Clo. E3 5C 70
Compton Clo. NW1 2K 159
Compton Clo. NW11 3F 47
Compton Clo. SE15 7G 87
Compton Clo. W13 6A 62
Compton Clo. Edgw 7D 12
Compton Ct. SE19 6E 122
Compton Ct. Sutt 4A 150
Compton Cres. N17 7H 17
Compton Cres. W4 6J 81
Compton Cres. Chess 5E 146
Compton Cres. N'holt 1B 60
Compton Pas. EC1 4B 68 (3B 162)
Compton Pl. WC1 4J 67 (3E 160)
Compton Ri. Pinn 5C 24
Compton Rd. N1 6B 50
Compton Rd. N21 1F 17
Compton Rd. NW10 3F 65
Compton Rd. SW19 6H 119
Compton Rd. Croy 1H 153
Compton Rd. Hay 7G 59
Compton St. EC1 4B 68 (3A 162)
Compton Ter. N1 6B 50
Compton Ter. N21 1F 17
Comreddy Clo. Enf 1G 7
Comus Ho. SE17 4E 86 (off Comus Pl.)
Comus Pl. SE17 4E 86
Comyn Rd. SW11 4C 102
Comyns Clo. E16 5H 71
Comyns Rd. Dag 7G 57
Comyns, The. Bush 1B 10
Conant Ho. SE11 6B 86 (7K 173) (off St Agnes Pl.)
Conant M. E1 7G 69
Concanon Rd. SW2 4K 103
Concert Hall App. SE1 1K 85 (5H 167)
Concord Bus. Cen. W3 4H 63
Concord Clo. N'holt 3B 62
Concord Ct. King T 3F 135 (off Winery La.)
Concorde Clo. Houn 2F 97
Concorde Clo. Uxb 2A 58
Concorde Dri. E6 5D 72
Concord Ho. N17 7A 18 (off Park La.)
Concordia Wharf. E14 1E 88 (off Coldharbour)
Concord Rd. W3 4H 63
Concord Rd. Enf 5D 8
Concourse, The. N9 2C 18 (off Plevna Rd.)
Concourse, The. NW9 1A 28
Condell Rd. SW8 1G 103
Conder St. E14 6A 70
Condor Path. N'holt 2E 60 (off Union Rd.)
Condover Cres. SE18 7F 91
Condray Pl. SW11 7C 84
Conduit Av. SE10 1F 107
Conduit Ct. WC2 2E 166
Conduit La. N18 5D 18
Conduit La. Enf 6F 9
Conduit La. S Croy 5G 153 (in two parts)
Conduit M. W2 6B 66 (1A 164)
Conduit Pas. W2 1A 164
Conduit Pl. W2 6B 66 (1A 164)
Conduit Rd. SE18 5F 91
Conduit St. W1 7F 67 (2K 165)
Conduit Way. NW10 7J 45
Conewood St. N5 3B 50
Coney Acre. SE21 1C 122
Coney Burrows. E4 2B 20
Coney Gro. Uxb 3C 58
Coneygrove Path. N'holt 6C 42 (off Arnold Rd.)
Coney Hall. 4G 155
Coney Hall Pde. W Wick 3G 155
Coney Hill Rd. W Wick 2G 155
Coney Way. SW8 6K 85
Conference Clo. E4 2K 19
Conference Rd. SE2 4C 92
Congers Ho. SE8 7C 88
Congleton Gro. SE18 5G 91
Congo Rd. SE18 5H 91
Congress Rd. SE2 4C 92
Congreve Ho. N16 5E 50
Congreve Rd. SE9 3D 108
Congreve St. SE17 4E 86
Congreve Wlk. E16 5B 72 (off Fulmer Rd.)
Conical Corner. Enf 2H 7
Conifer Gdns. SW16 3J 121
Conifer Gdns. Enf 6K 7
Conifer Gdns. Sutt 2K 149
Conifer Ho. SE4 4B 106 (off Brockley Rd.)
Conifers Clo. Tedd 7B 116
Conifer Way. Hay 7J 59
Conifer Way. Wemb 3C 44
Coniffe Ct. SE9 5F 109
Coniger Rd. SW6 2J 101
Coningham Ct. SW10 7A 84 (off King's Rd.)
Coningham M. W12 1C 82
Coningham Rd. W12 1D 82
Coningsby Cotts. W5 2D 80
Coningsby Gdns. E4 6J 19
Coningsby Rd. N4 7B 32
Coningsby Rd. W5 2D 80
Coningsby Rd. S Croy 7C 152
Conington Rd. SE13 2D 106
Conisbee Ct. N14 5B 6
Conisborough Cres. SE6 3E 124
Conisbrough. NW1 1G 67 (off Bayham St.)
Coniscliffe Clo. Chst 1E 144
Coniscliffe Rd. N13 3H 17
Coniston. NW1 3G 67 (1A 160) (off Harrington St.)
Coniston Av. Bark 7J 55
Coniston Av. Gnfd 3B 62
Coniston Av. Well 3J 109
Coniston Clo. N20 3F 15
Coniston Clo. SW13 7B 82
Coniston Clo. SW20 6F 137
Coniston Clo. W4 7J 81
Coniston Clo. Bark 7J 55
Coniston Clo. Bexh 1J 111
Coniston Clo. Eri 7K 93
Coniston Ct. SE16 2K 87 (off Eleanor Clo.)
Coniston Ct. W2 6C 66 (1D 164) (off Kendal St.)
Conistone Way. N7 7J 49
Coniston Gdns. N9 1D 18
Coniston Gdns. NW9 5K 27
Coniston Gdns. Ilf 4C 36
Coniston Gdns. Pinn 4J 23
Coniston Gdns. Sutt 6B 150
Coniston Gdns. Wemb 1C 44
Coniston Ho. E3 4B 70 (off Southern Gro.)
Coniston Ho. SE5 7C 86 (off Wyndham Rd.)
Coniston Rd. N10 2F 31
Coniston Rd. N17 6B 18
Coniston Rd. Bexh 1J 111
Coniston Rd. Brom 6G 125
Coniston Rd. Croy 7G 141
Coniston Rd. Twic 6F 97
Coniston Wlk. E9 5J 51
Coniston Way. Chess 3E 146
Conlan St. W10 4G 65
Conley Rd. NW10 6A 46
Conley St. SE10 5G 89
Connaught Av. E4 7K 9 & 1A 20
Connaught Av. SW14 3J 99
Connaught Av. Ashf 4A 112
Connaught Av. E Barn 1J 15
Connaught Av. Enf 2K 7
Connaught Av. Houn 4C 96
Connaught Bri. E16 1B 90
Connaught Bus. Cen. NW9 5B 28
Connaught Bus. Cen. Mitc 5D 138
Connaught Clo. E10 2K 51
Connaught Clo. W2 1D 164
Connaught Clo. Enf 2K 7
Connaught Clo. Sutt 2B 150
Connaught Clo. Uxb 4E 58
Connaught Ct. E17 4D 34 (off Orford Rd.)
Connaught Dri. NW11 4J 29
Connaught Gdns. N10 5F 31
Connaught Gdns. N13 4G 17
Connaught Gdns. Mord 4A 138
Connaught Ho. NW10 3D 64 (off Trenmar Gdns.)
Connaught Ho. W1 7F 67 (3J 165) (off Davies St.)
Connaught La. Ilf 2G 55
Connaught Lodge. N4 7A 32 (off Connaught Rd.)
Connaught M. NW3 4C 48
Connaught M. SE11 4A 86 (3K 173) (off Walcot Sq.)
Connaught M. SE18 5E 90
Connaught M. SW6 1G 101
Connaught Pl. W2 7D 66 (2E 164)
Connaught Rd. E4 1B 20
Connaught Rd. E11 1F 53
Connaught Rd. E16 1B 90 (Albert Rd.)
Connaught Rd. E16 7B 72 (Connaught Bri.)
Connaught Rd. E17 5C 34
Connaught Rd. N4 7A 32
Connaught Rd. NW10 1A 64
Connaught Rd. SE18 5E 90
Connaught Rd. W13 7B 62
Connaught Rd. Barn 6A 4
Connaught Rd. Harr 1K 25
Connaught Rd. Ilf 2H 55
Connaught Rd. N Mald 4A 136
Connaught Rd. Rich 5F 99
Connaught Rd. Sutt 2B 150
Connaught Rd. Tedd 5H 115
Connaught Roundabout. (Junct.) 7B 72
Connaught Sq. W2 6D 66 (1D 164)
Connaught St. W2 6C 66 (1D 164)
Connaught Way. N13 4G 17
Connell Ct. SE14 6K 87 (off Myers La.)
Connell Cres. W5 4F 63
Connett Ho. E2 2G 69 (off Mansford St.)
Connington Cres. E4 3A 20
Connolly Pl. SW19 6A 120
Connor Clo. E11 7G 35
Connor Clo. Ilf 1G 37
Connor Ct. SW11 1F 103
Connor Rd. Dag 4F 57
Connor St. E9 1K 69
Conolly Rd. W7 1J 79
Conrad Dri. Wor Pk 1E 148

Conrad Ho. E14 7A 70 (off Victory Pl.)
Conrad Ho. E16 1K 89 (off Wesley Av.)
Conrad Ho. N16 5E 50 (off Matthias Rd.)
Conrad Ho. SW8 7J 85 (off Wyvil Rd.)
Conrad Tower. W3 3H 81 (off Bollo La.)
Consec Farriers M. SE15 3J 105
Consfield Av. N Mald 4C 136
Consort Ho. E14 5D 88 (off St Davids Sq.)
Consort Ho. W2 7K 65 (off Queensway)
Consort Lodge. NW8 1D 66 (off Prince Albert Rd.)
Consort M. Iswth 5H 97
Consort Rd. SE15 1H 105
Cons St. SE1 2A 86 (6K 167)
Constable Av. E16 1K 89
Constable Clo. NW11 6K 29
Constable Clo. Hay 2E 58
Constable Ct. SE16 5H 87 (off Stubbs Dri.)
Constable Ct. W4 5H 81 (off Chaseley Dri.)
Constable Cres. N15 5G 33
Constable Gdns. Edgw 1G 27
Constable Gdns. Iswth 5H 97
Constable Ho. NW3 7D 48
Constable Ho. N'holt 2B 60 (off Gallery Gdns.)
Constable M. Dag 4B 56
Constable Wlk. SE21 3E 122
Constance Allen Ho. W10 6F 65 (off Bridge Clo.)
Constance Cres. Brom 7H 143
Constance Rd. Croy 7B 140
Constance Rd. Enf 6K 7
Constance Rd. Sutt 4A 150
Constance Rd. Twic 7F 97
Constance St. E16 1C 90
Constant Ho. E14 7D 70 (off Harrow La.)
Constantine Pl. Hil 1B 58
Constantine Rd. NW3 4C 48
Constitution Hill. SW1 2F 85 (6J 165)
Constitution Ri. SE18 1E 108
Content St. SE17 4D 86
Control Tower Rd. H'row A 3C 94
Convair Wlk. N'holt 3B 60
Convent Clo. Beck 7E 124
Convent Gdns. W5 4C 80
Convent Gdns. W11 6G 65
Convent Hill. SE19 6C 122
Convent Lodge. Ashf 5D 112
Convent Rd. Ashf 5C 112
Convent Way. S'hall 4A 78
Conway Clo. Stan 6F 11
Conway Cres. Gnfd 2J 61
Conway Cres. Romf 6C 38
Conway Dri. Ashf 6E 112
Conway Dri. Hay 3E 76
Conway Dri. Sutt 6K 149
Conway Gdns. Enf 1K 7
Conway Gdns. Mitc 4J 139
Conway Gdns. Wemb 7C 26
Conway Gro. W3 5K 63
Conway Ho. E14 4C 88 (off Cahir St.)
Conway Ho. E17 5A 34 (off Mission Gro.)
Conway M. W1 4A 160
Conway Rd. N14 3D 16
Conway Rd. N15 5B 32
Conway Rd. NW2 2E 46
Conway Rd. SE18 4H 91
Conway Rd. SW20 1E 136
Conway Rd. Felt 5B 114
Conway Rd. Houn 7D 96
Conway Rd. H'row A 3D 94
Conway St. W1 4G 67 (4A 160) (in two parts)
Conway Wlk. Hamp 6D 114
Conybeare. NW3 7C 48
Conyers Clo. Wfd G 6B 20
Conyer's Rd. SW16 5H 121
Conyer St. E3 2A 70
Cooden Clo. Brom 7K 125
Cook Ct. SE16 1J 87 (off Rotherhithe St.)
Cookes Clo. E11 2H 53
Cookes La. Sutt 6G 149
Cookham Clo. S'hall 3F 79
Cookham Cres. SE16 2K 87
Cookham Dene Clo. Chst 1H 145
Cookham Ho. E2 4F 69 (3J 163) (off Montclare St.)
Cookham Rd. Swan 7G 129
Cookhill Rd. SE2 2B 92
Cook Rd. Dag 1E 74
Cook's Clo. Romf 1J 39
Cooks Hole Rd. Enf 1H 7
Cookson Gro. Eri 7H 93
Cook's Rd. E15 2D 70
Cook's Rd. SE17 6B 86
Coolfin Rd. E16 6J 71
Coolgardie Av. E4 5A 20
Coolgardie Av. Chig 3K 21
Coolgardie Rd. Ashf 5E 112
Coolhurst Rd. N8 6H 31
Cool Oak La. NW9 1A 46
Coomassie Rd. W9 4H 65
Coombe. 7K 117
Coombe Av. Croy 4E 152
Coombe Bank. King T 1A 136
Coombe Clo. Edgw 2F 27
Coombe Clo. Houn 4E 96
Coombe Corner. N21 1G 17
Coombe Ct. Croy 4D 152 (off St Peter's Rd.)
Coombe Cres. Hamp 7D 114
Coombe Dri. Ruis 1K 41
Coombe End. King T 7K 117
Coombefield Clo. N Mald 5A 136
Coombe Gdns. SW20 2C 136
Coombe Gdns. N Mald 4B 136
Coombe Hill Glade. King T 7A 118
Coombe Hill Rd. King T 7A 118
Coombe Ho. E4 6G 19
Coombe Ho. N7 5H 49
Coombe Ho. Chase. N Mald 1K 135
Coombehurst Clo. Barn 2J 5
Coombe Lane. (Junct.) 7B 118
Coombe La. SW20 1B 136
Coombe La. Croy 5H 153
Coombe La. Flyover. SW20 1B 136
Coombe La. W. King T 1H 135
Coombe Lea. Brom 3C 144
Coombe Lodge. SE7 6A 90
Coombe Neville. King T 7K 117
Coombe Pk. King T 5J 117
Coomber Ho. SW6 3K 101 (off Wandsworth Bri. Rd.)
Coombe Ridings. King T 5J 117
Coombe Ri. King T 1J 135
Coombe Rd. N22 2A 32
Coombe Rd. NW10 3K 45
Coombe Rd. SE26 4H 123
Coombe Rd. W4 5A 82
Coombe Rd. W13 3B 80
Coombe Rd. Croy 4D 152
Coombe Rd. Hamp 6D 114
Coombe Rd. King T 1G 135
Coombe Rd. N Mald 2A 136
Coomber Way. Croy 7H 139 (in two parts)
Coombes Rd. Dag 1F 75
Coombe Wlk. Sutt 3K 149
Coombe Wood Dri. Romf 6F 39
Coombewood Rd. King T 5J 117
Coombs St. N1 2B 68 (1B 162)
Coomer M. SW6 6H 83
Coomer Pl. SW6 6H 83
Coomer Rd. SW6 6H 83
Cooms Wlk. Edgw 1J 27
Cooperage Clo. N17 6A 18
Cooper Av. E17 1A 34
Cooper Clo. SE1 2A 86 (7K 167)
Cooper Ct. E15 5D 52
Cooper Ct. SE18 6F 91
Cooper Cres. Cars 3D 150
Cooper Ho. NW8 4B 66 (4A 158) (off Lyons Pl.)
Cooper Ho. Houn 3D 96
Cooper Rd. NW4 6F 29
Cooper Rd. NW10 5B 46
Cooper Rd. Croy 4B 152
Coopersale Clo. Wfd G 7F 21
Coopersale Rd. E9 5K 51
Coopers Clo. E1 4J 69
Coopers Clo. Dag 6H 57
Coopers Ct. W3 1J 81 (off Church Rd.)
Coopers Ct. Iswth 2K 97 (off Woodlands Rd.)
Coopers La. E10 1D 52
Coopers La. NW1 2H 67
Cooper's La. SE12 2K 125
Coopers Lodge. SE1 2F 87 (6J 169) (off Tooley St.)
Cooper's Rd. SE1 5F 87
Coopers Row. EC3 7F 69 (2J 169)
Cooper St. E16 5H 71
Coopers Wlk. E15 5G 53
Cooper's Yd. SE19 6E 122
Coote Gdns. Dag 3F 57
Coote Rd. Bexh 1F 111
Coote Rd. Dag 3F 57
Cope Ho. EC1 2D 162
Copeland Dri. E14 4C 88
Copeland Ho. SE11 2H 173
Copeland Rd. E17 6D 34
Copeland Rd. SE15 2G 105
Copeman Clo. SE26 5J 123
Copenhagen Gdns. W4 2K 81
Copenhagen Ho. N1 1K 67 (off Barnsbury Est.)
Copenhagen Pl. E14 6B 70 (in two parts)
Copenhagen St. N1 1J 67
Cope Pl. W8 3J 83
Copers Cope Rd. Beck 7B 124
Cope St. SE16 4K 87
Copford Clo. Wfd G 6H 21
Copford Wlk. N1 1C 68 (off Popham St.)
Copgate Path. SW16 6K 121
Copinger Wlk. Edgw 1H 27
Copland Av. Wemb 5D 44
Copland Clo. Wemb 5C 44
Copland Ho. S'hall 2D 78
Copland M. Wemb 6E 44
Copland Rd. Wemb 6E 44
Copleston M. SE15 2F 105
Copleston Pas. SE5 2F 105
Copleston Rd. SE15 3F 105
Copley Clo. SE17 6C 86
Copley Clo. W7 4K 61
Copley Dene. Brom 1B 144
Copley Pk. SW16 6K 121
Copley Rd. Stan 5H 11
Copley St. E1 5K 69
Copnor Way. SE15 7E 86
Coppard Gdns. Chess 6C 146
Coppelia Rd. SE3 4H 107
Coppen Rd. Dag 7F 39
Copperas St. SE8 6D 88
Copperbeech Clo. NW3 5B 48
Copper Beech Clo. Ilf 1D 36
Copper Beeches Ct. Iswth 1H 97
Copper Clo. SE19 7F 123
Copperdale Rd. Hay 2J 77
Copperfield Av. Uxb 5C 58
Copperfield Dri. N15 4F 33
Copperfield Ho. SE1 2G 87 (7K 169) (off Wolseley St.)
Copperfield Ho. W1 5E 66 (5H 159) (off Marylebone High St.)
Copperfield Ho. W11 1F 83 (off St Ann's Rd.)
Copperfield M. N18 4K 17
Copperfield Rd. E3 4A 70
Copperfield Rd. SE28 6C 74
Copperfields. Beck 1E 142
Copperfields. Harr 7J 25
Copperfields Ct. W3 2G 81
Copperfield St. SE1 2B 86 (6B 168)
Copperfield Way. Chst 6G 127
Copperfield Way. Pinn 4D 24
Coppergate Clo. Brom 1K 143
Copper Mead Clo. NW2 3E 46
Copper Mill Dri. Iswth 2K 97
Coppermill La. E17 6J 33
Copper Mill La. SW17 4A 120
Copper Row. SE1 5J 169
Coppetts Cen. N11 7J 15
Coppetts Clo. N12 7H 15
Coppetts Rd. N10 7J 15
Coppice Clo. SW20 3E 136
Coppice Clo. Beck 4D 142
Coppice Clo. Ruis 6F 23
Coppice Clo. Stan 6E 10
Coppice Dri. SW15 6D 100
Coppice, The. Ashf 6D 112
Coppice, The. Bex 3K 129
Coppice, The. Enf 4G 7
Coppice, The. New Bar 6E 4 (off Gt. North Rd.)
Coppice, The. W Dray 6A 58
Coppice Wlk. N20 3D 14
Coppice Way. E18 4H 35
Coppies Gro. N11 4A 16
Copping Clo. Croy 4E 152
Coppins, The. Harr 6D 10
Coppins, The. New Ad 6D 154
Coppock Clo. SW11 2C 102
Coppsfield. W Mol 3E 132
Copse Av. W Wick 3D 154
Copse Clo. SE7 6K 89
Copse Clo. N'wd 2E 22
Copse Glade. Surb 7D 134
Copse Hill. 7D 118
Copse Hill. SW20 1C 136
Copse Hill. Sutt 7K 149
Copse, The. E4 1C 20
Copse, The. N2 3D 30
Copse Vw. S Croy 7K 153
Copsewood Clo. Sidc 6J 109
Copse Wood Way. N'wd 1D 22
Coptefield Dri. Belv 3D 92
Copthall Av. EC2 6D 68 (7F 163) (in three parts)
Copthall Bldgs. EC2 7F 163
Copthall Clo. EC2 6D 68 (7E 162)
Copthall Dri. NW7 7H 13
Copthall Gdns. NW7 7H 13
Copthall Gdns. Twic 1K 115
Copthall Rd. E. Uxb 2C 40
Copthall Rd. W. Uxb 2C 40
Copthall Sports Cen. 1D 28
Copthorne Av. SW12 7H 103
Copthorne Av. Brom 2D 156
Copthorne Chase. Ashf 4B 112
Copthorne Clo. Shep 6E 130
Copthorne M. Hay 4G 77
Coptic St. WC1 5J 67 (6E 160)
Copwood Clo. N12 4G 15
Coral Clo. Romf 4C 38
Coral Ho. E1 4A 70 (off Harford St.)
Coraline Clo. S'hall 3D 60
Coralline Wlk. SE2 2C 92
Coral Row. SW11 3A 102
Coral St. SE1 2A 86 (7K 167)
Coram Ho. W4 5A 82 (off Wood St.)
Coram Ho. WC1 3E 160
Coram St. WC1 4J 67 (4E 160)
Coran Clo. N9 7E 8
Corban Rd. Houn 3E 96
Corbar Clo. Barn 1G 5
Corbden Clo. SE15 1F 105
Corbet Clo. Wall 1E 150
Corbet Ct. EC3 6D 68 (1F 169)
Corbet Ho. N1 2A 68 (off Barnsbury Est.)
Corbet Pl. E1 5F 69 (5J 163)
Corbett Ct. SE26 4B 124
Corbett Gro. N22 7D 16
Corbett Ho. SW10 6A 84 (off Cathcart Rd.)
Corbett Rd. E11 6A 36
Corbett Rd. E17 3E 34
Corbetts La. SE16 4J 87 (in two parts)
Corbetts Pas. SE16 4J 87 (off Corbetts La.)
Corbetts Wharf. SE16 2H 87 (off Bermondsey Wall E.)
Corbicum. E11 7G 35
Corbidge Ct. SE8 6D 88 (off Glaisher St.)
Corbiere Ct. SW19 6F 119
Corbiere Ho. N1 1E 68 (off De Beauvoir Est.)
Corbins La. Harr 3F 43
Corbridge. N17 7C 18
Corbridge Cres. E2 2H 69
Corby Cres. Enf 4D 6
Corbylands Rd. Sidc 7J 109
Corbyn St. N4 1J 49
Corby Rd. NW10 2K 63
Corby Way. E3 4C 70
Cordelia Clo. SE24 4B 104
Cordelia Gdns. Stai 7A 94
Cordelia Ho. N1 2E 68 (off Arden Est.)
Cordelia Rd. Stai 7A 94
Cordelia St. E14 6D 70
Cordell Ho. N15 5G 33 (off Newton Rd.)
Cordingley Rd. Ruis 2F 41
Cording St. E14 5D 70
Cordwainers Ct. E9 7H 51 (off St Thomas's Sq.)
Cordwainers Wlk. E13 2J 71
Cord Way. E14 3C 88
Cordwell Rd. SE13 5G 107
Corefield Clo. N11 2K 15
Corelli Ct. SW5 4J 83 (off W. Cromwell Rd.)
Corelli Rd. SE3 2C 108
Corfe Av. Harr 4E 42
Corfe Clo. Hay 6A 60
Corfe Ho. SW8 7K 85 (off Dorset Rd.)
Corfe Tower. W3 2H 81
Corfield Rd. N21 5E 6
Corfield St. E2 3H 69
Corfton Lodge. W5 5E 62
Corfton Rd. W5 6E 62
Coriander Av. E14 6F 71
Cories Clo. Dag 2D 56
Corinium Clo. Wemb 4F 45
Corinne Rd. N19 4G 49
Corinthian Manorway. Eri 4K 93
Corinthian Rd. Eri 4K 93
Corinthian Way. Stanw 7A 94
Corkers Path. Ilf 2G 55
Corker Wlk. N7 2K 49
Corkran Rd. Surb 7D 134
Corkscrew Hill. W Wick 2E 154

Cork Sq. E1 . . . 1H 87
Cork St. W1 . . . 7G 67 (3A 166)
Cork St. M. W1 . . . 3A 166
Cork Tree Est., The. E4 . . . 5F 19
Cork Tree Ho. SE27 . . . 5B 122
(off Lakeview Rd.)
Cork Tree Way. E4 . . . 5F 19
Corlett St. NW1 . . . 5C 66 (5C 158)
Cormont Rd. SE5 . . . 1B 104
Cormorant Clo. E17 . . . 7F 19
Cormorant Ct. SE8 . . . 6B 88
(off Pilot Clo.)
Cormorant Pl. Sutt . . . 5H 149
Cormorant Rd. E7 . . . 5H 53
Cornbury Ho. SE8 . . . 6B 88
(off Evelyn St.)
Cornbury Rd. Edgw . . . 7J 11
Cornel Ho. Sidc . . . 3A 128
Cornelia Dri. Hay . . . 4A 60
Cornelia Ho. Twic . . . 6D 98
(off Denton Rd.)
Cornelia St. N7 . . . 6K 49
Cornell Building. E1 . . . 6G 69
(off Coke St.)
Cornell Clo. Sidc . . . 6E 128
Cornell Ho. S Harr . . . 3D 42
Cornercroft. Sutt . . . 5F 149
(off Wickham Av.)
Corner Fielde. SW2 . . . 1K 121
Corner Grn. SE3 . . . 2J 107
Corner Ho. St. WC2 . . . 4E 166
Corner Mead. NW9 . . . 7G 13
Cornerside. Ashf . . . 7E 112
Cornerstone Ho. Croy . . . 7C 140
Corner, The. W5 . . . 1E 80
Corney Reach Way. W4 . . . 7A 82
Corney Rd. W4 . . . 6A 82
Cornfield Clo. Uxb . . . 2A 58
Cornflower La. Croy . . . 1K 153
Cornflower Ter. SE22 . . . 6H 105
Cornford Clo. Brom . . . 5J 143
Cornford Gro. SW12 . . . 2F 121
Cornhill. EC3 . . . 6D 68 (1F 169)
Cornick Ho. SE16 . . . 3H 87
(off Slippers Pl.)
Cornish Ct. N9 . . . 7C 8
Cornish Gro. SE20 . . . 1H 141
Cornish Ho. SE17 . . . 6B 86
(off Brandon Est.)
Cornish Ho. Bren . . . 5F 81
Corn Mill Dri. Orp . . . 7K 145
Cornmill La. SE13 . . . 3E 106
Cornmow Dri. NW10 . . . 5B 46
Cornshaw Rd. Dag . . . 1D 56
Cornthwaite Rd. E5 . . . 3J 51
Cornwall Av. E2 . . . 3J 69
Cornwall Av. N3 . . . 7D 14
Cornwall Av. N22 . . . 1J 31
Cornwall Av. Clay . . . 7A 146
Cornwall Av. S'hall . . . 5D 60
Cornwall Av. Well . . . 3J 109
Cornwall Clo. Bark . . . 6K 55
Cornwall Ct. W7 . . . 4K 61
(off Copley Clo.)
Cornwall Ct. Pinn . . . 1D 24
Cornwall Cres. W11 . . . 6G 65
Cornwall Dri. Orp . . . 7C 128
Cornwall Gdns. NW10 . . . 6D 46
Cornwall Gdns. SE25 . . . 4F 141
Cornwall Gdns. SW7 . . . 3K 83
Cornwall Gdns. Wlk. SW7 . . . 3K 83
Cornwall Gro. W4 . . . 5A 82
Cornwallis Av. N9 . . . 2C 18
Cornwallis Av. SE9 . . . 2H 127
Cornwallis Ct. SW8 . . . 1J 103
(off Lansdowne Grn.)
Cornwallis Gro. N9 . . . 2C 18
Cornwallis Ho. SE16 . . . 2H 87
(off Cherry Garden St.)
Cornwallis Ho. W12 . . . 7D 64
(off India Way)
Cornwallis Rd. E17 . . . 4K 33
Cornwallis Rd. N9 . . . 2C 18
Cornwallis Rd. N19 . . . 2J 49
Cornwallis Rd. Dag . . . 4D 56
Cornwallis Sq. N19 . . . 2J 49
Cornwallis Wlk. SE9 . . . 3D 108
Cornwall Mans. SW10 . . . 7A 84
(off Cremorne Rd.)
Cornwall Mans. W14 . . . 3F 83
(off Blythe Rd.)
Cornwall M. S. SW7 . . . 3A 84
Cornwall M. W. SW7 . . . 3K 83
Cornwall Rd. N4 . . . 7A 32
Cornwall Rd. N15 . . . 5D 32
Cornwall Rd. N18 . . . 5B 18
Cornwall Rd. SE1
. . . 1A 86 (4J 167)
Cornwall Rd. Croy . . . 2B 152
Cornwall Rd. Harr . . . 6G 25
Cornwall Rd. Pinn . . . 1D 24
Cornwall Rd. Ruis . . . 3H 41
Cornwall Rd. Sutt . . . 7H 149
Cornwall Rd. Twic . . . 7A 98
Cornwall Rd. Uxb . . . 6A 40
Cornwall Sq. SE11 . . . 5K 173
Cornwall St. E1 . . . 7H 69
Cornwall Ter. NW1
. . . 4D 66 (4F 159)
Cornwall Ter. M. NW1 . . . 4F 159
Corn Way. E11 . . . 3F 53
Cornwell Cres. E7 . . . 4A 54
Cornwood Clo. N2 . . . 5B 30
Cornwood Dri. E1 . . . 6J 69
Cornworthy Rd. Dag . . . 5C 56
Corona Rd. SE12 . . . 7J 107
Coronation Av. N16 . . . 4F 51
Coronation Clo. Bex . . . 6D 110
Coronation Clo. Ilf . . . 4G 37
Coronation Ct. E15 . . . 6H 53
Coronation Ct. W10 . . . 5E 64
(off Brewster Gdns.)
Coronation Ct. Eri . . . 7K 93
Coronation Rd. E13 . . . 3A 72
Coronation Rd. NW10 . . . 3F 63
Coronation Rd. Hay . . . 4H 77
Coronation Vs. NW10 . . . 4H 63
Coronation Wlk. Twic . . . 1E 114
Coronet Pde. Wemb . . . 6E 44
Coronet St. N1 . . . 3E 68 (2G 163)
Corporate Dri. Felt . . . 3K 113
Corporate Ho. Har W . . . 1H 25
Corporation Av. Houn . . . 4C 96
Corporation Row. EC1
. . . 4A 68 (3K 161)
Corporation St. E15 . . . 2G 71
Corporation St. N7 . . . 5J 49
Corrance Rd. SW2 . . . 4J 103
Corri Av. N14 . . . 4C 16
Corrib Ct. N13 . . . 3E 16
Corrib Dri. Sutt . . . 5C 150
Corrigan Clo. NW4 . . . 3E 28
Corringham Ct. NW11 . . . 7J 29
Corringham Ho. E1 . . . 6K 69
(off Pitsea St.)
Corringham Rd. NW11 . . . 7J 29
Corringham Rd. Wemb . . . 2G 45
Corringway. NW11 . . . 7K 29
Corringway. W5 . . . 4G 63
Corris Grn. NW9 . . . 5A 28
Corry Ho. E14 . . . 7D 70
(off Wade's Pl.)
Corsair Clo. Stai . . . 7A 94
Corsair Rd. Stai . . . 7A 94
Corscombe Clo. King T . . . 5J 117
Corsehill St. SW16 . . . 6G 121
Corsham St. N1 . . . 3D 68 (2F 163)
Corsica St. N5 . . . 6B 50
Corsley Way. E9 . . . 6B 52
(off Osborne Rd.)
Cortayne Ct. Twic . . . 2J 115
Cortayne Rd. SW6 . . . 2H 101
Cortis Rd. SW15 . . . 6D 100
Cortis Ter. SW15 . . . 6D 100
Corunna Rd. SW8 . . . 1G 103
Corunna Ter. SW8 . . . 1G 103
Corvette Sq. SE10 . . . 6F 89
Corwell Gdns. Uxb . . . 6E 58
Corwell La. Uxb . . . 6E 58
(in two parts)
Coryton Path. W9 . . . 4H 65
(off Ashmore Rd.)
Cosbycote Av. SE24 . . . 5C 104
Cosdach Av. Wall . . . 7H 151
Cosedge Cres. Croy . . . 5A 152
Cosgrove Clo. N21 . . . 2H 17
Cosgrove Clo. Hay . . . 4C 60
Cosgrove Ho. E2 . . . 1G 69
(off Whiston Rd.)
Cosmo Pl. WC1 . . . 5J 67 (5F 161)
Cosmur Clo. W12 . . . 3B 82
Cossall Wlk. SE15 . . . 2H 105
Cossar M. SW2 . . . 5A 104
Cosser St. SE1 . . . 3A 86 (1J 173)
Costa St. SE15 . . . 2G 105
Costons Av. Gnfd . . . 3H 61
Costons La. Gnfd . . . 3H 61
Coston Wlk. SE4 . . . 4K 105
Cosway Mans. NW1
. . . 5C 66 (5D 158)
(off Shroton St.)
Cosway St. NW1
. . . 5C 66 (5D 158)
Cotall St. E14 . . . 5C 70
Coteford Clo. Pinn . . . 5J 23
Coteford St. SW17 . . . 4D 120
Cotelands. Croy . . . 3E 152
Cotesbach Rd. E5 . . . 3J 51
Cotes Ho. NW8 . . . 4C 66 (4C 158)
(off Broadley St.)
Cotesmore Gdns. Dag . . . 4C 56
Cotford Rd. T Hth . . . 4C 140
Cotham St. SE17 . . . 4C 86
Cotherstone Rd. SW2 . . . 1K 121
Cotleigh Av. Bex . . . 2D 128
Cotleigh Rd. NW6 . . . 7J 47
Cotleigh Rd. Romf . . . 6K 39
Cotman Clo. NW11 . . . 6A 30
Cotman Clo. SW15 . . . 6F 101
Cotman Gdns. Edgw . . . 2G 27
Cotman Ho. NW8 . . . 2C 66
(off Townshend Est.)
Cotman Ho. N'holt . . . 2B 60
(off Academy Gdns.)
Cotman M. Dag . . . 5C 56
(off Highgrove Rd.)
Cotmans Clo. Hay . . . 1J 77
Coton Rd. Well . . . 3A 110
Cotsford Av. N Mald . . . 5J 135
Cotswold Clo. N11 . . . 4K 15
Cotswold Clo. Bexh . . . 2K 111
Cotswold Clo. Hin W . . . 2A 146
Cotswold Clo. King T . . . 6J 117
Cotswold Ct. EC1 . . . 3C 162
Cotswold Ct. Gnfd . . . 2K 61
(off Hodder Dri.)
Cotswold Gdns. E6 . . . 3B 72
Cotswold Gdns. NW2 . . . 2F 47
Cotswold Gdns. Ilf . . . 7H 37
Cotswold Ga. NW2 . . . 1G 47
Cotswold Grn. Enf . . . 4E 6
Cotswold M. SW11 . . . 1B 102
Cotswold Ri. Orp . . . 6K 145
Cotswold Rd. Hamp . . . 5E 114
Cotswold St. SE27 . . . 4B 122
Cotswold Way. Enf . . . 3E 6
Cotswold Way. Wor Pk . . . 2E 148
Cottage Av. Brom . . . 1C 156
Cottage Clo. E1 . . . 4J 69
(off Hayfield Pas.)
Cottage Clo. Ruis . . . 1F 41
Cottage Fld. Clo. Sidc . . . 1C 128
Cottage Grn. SE5 . . . 7D 86
Cottage Gro. SW9 . . . 3J 103
Cottage Gro. Surb . . . 6D 134
Cottage Pl. SW3 . . . 3C 84 (1C 170)
Cottage Rd. Eps . . . 7K 147
Cottage St. E14 . . . 7D 70
Cottage Wlk. N16 . . . 3F 51
Cottenham Dri. SW20 . . . 7D 118
Cottenham Pde. SW20 . . . 2D 136
Cottenham Park. . . . 1D 136
Cottenham Pk. Rd. SW20
. . . 1C 136
(in two parts)
Cottenham Pl. SW20 . . . 7D 118
Cottenham Rd. E17 . . . 4B 34
Cotterill Rd. Surb . . . 2E 146
Cottesbrook St. SE14 . . . 7A 88
Cottesloe Ho. NW8 . . . 3C 158
Cottesloe M. SE1
. . . 3A 86 (1K 173)
(off Emery St.)
Cottesloe Theatre. . . . 4J 167
(in Royal National Theatre)
Cottesmore Av. Ilf . . . 2E 36
Cottesmore Ct. W8 . . . 3K 83
(off Stanford Rd.)
Cottesmore Gdns. W8 . . . 3K 83
Cottimore Av. W on T . . . 7K 131
Cottimore Cres. W on T . . . 7K 131
Cottimore La. W on T . . . 7K 131
(in two parts)
Cottimore Ter. W on T . . . 7K 131
Cottingham Chase. Ruis . . . 3J 41
Cottingham Rd. SE20 . . . 7K 123
Cottingham Rd. SW8 . . . 7K 85
Cottington Rd. Felt . . . 4B 114
Cottington St. SE11
. . . 5A 86 (5K 173)
Cottle Way. SE16 . . . 2H 87
(off Paradise St.)
Cotton Av. W3 . . . 6K 63
Cotton Clo. Dag . . . 7C 56
Cottongrass Clo. Croy . . . 1K 153
Cotton Hill. Brom . . . 4E 124
Cotton Ho. SW2 . . . 7J 103
Cotton Row. SW11 . . . 3A 102
Cottons App. Romf . . . 5K 39
Cottons Cen. SE1
. . . 1E 86 (4G 169)
Cottons Ct. Romf . . . 5K 39
Cotton's Gdns. E2
. . . 3E 68 (1H 163)
Cottons La. SE1 . . . 1D 86 (4F 169)
Cotton St. E14 . . . 7E 70
Cotts Clo. W7 . . . 5K 61
Couchmore Av. Ilf . . . 2D 36
Coulgate St. SE4 . . . 3A 106
Coulson Clo. Dag . . . 1C 56
Coulson St. SW3
. . . 5D 84 (5E 170)
Coulter Clo. Hay . . . 4C 60
Coulter Rd. W6 . . . 3D 82
Coulthurst Ct. SW16 . . . 7J 121
(off Heybridge Av.)
Councillor St. SE5 . . . 7C 86
Counter Ct. SE1 . . . 1D 86 (5E 168)
(off Borough High St.)
Counter St. SE1 . . . 1E 86 (5G 169)
Countess Rd. NW5 . . . 5G 49
Countisbury Av. Enf . . . 7A 8
Country Way. Hanw . . . 6K 113
County Gdns. Bark . . . 2J 73
County Ga. SE9 . . . 3G 127
County Ga. New Bar . . . 6E 4
County Gro. SE5 . . . 1C 104
County Hall Apartments. SE1
. . . 6G 167
County Pde. Bren . . . 7D 80
County Rd. E6 . . . 5F 73
County Rd. T Hth . . . 2B 140
County St. SE1 . . . 3C 86
Coupland Pl. SE18 . . . 5G 91
Courcy Rd. N8 . . . 3A 32
Courland Gro. SW8 . . . 1H 103
Courland St. SW8 . . . 1H 103
(in two parts)
Course, The. SE9 . . . 3E 126
Courtauld Clo. SE28 . . . 1A 92
Courtauld Ho. E2 . . . 1G 69
(off Goldsmiths Row)
Courtauld Institute Galleries.
. . . 2G 167
Courtauld Rd. N19 . . . 1J 49
Court Av. Belv . . . 5F 93
Court Clo. Harr . . . 3E 26
Court Clo. Twic . . . 3F 115
Court Clo. Wall . . . 7H 151
Court Clo. Av. Twic . . . 3F 115
Court Cres. Chess . . . 5D 146
Court Downs Rd. Beck . . . 2D 142
Court Dri. Croy . . . 4K 151
Court Dri. Stan . . . 4K 11
Court Dri. Sutt . . . 4C 150
Court Dri. Uxb . . . 1B 58
Courtenay Av. N6 . . . 7C 30
Courtenay Av. Harr . . . 7B 10
Courtenay Av. Sutt . . . 7J 149
Courtenay Dri. Beck . . . 2F 143
Courtenay Gdns. Harr . . . 2G 25
Courtenay M. E17 . . . 5A 34
Courtenay Pl. E17 . . . 5A 34
Courtenay Rd. E11 . . . 3H 53
Courtenay Rd. E17 . . . 4K 33
Courtenay Rd. SE20 . . . 6K 123
Courtenay Rd. Wemb . . . 3D 44
Courtenay Rd. Wor Pk . . . 3E 148
Courtenay Sq. SE11
. . . 5A 86 (6J 173)
Courtenay St. SE11
. . . 5A 86 (5J 173)
Courtens M. Stan . . . 7H 11
Court Farm Av. Eps . . . 5K 147
Court Farm La. N'holt . . . 7E 42
Court Farm Rd. SE9 . . . 2B 126
Court Farm Rd. N'holt . . . 7E 42
Courtfield. W5 . . . 5C 62
Courtfield Av. Harr . . . 5K 25
Courtfield Cres. Harr . . . 5K 25
Courtfield Gdns. SW5 . . . 4K 83
Courtfield Gdns. W13 . . . 6A 62
Courtfield Gdns. Ruis . . . 2H 41
Courtfield Ho. EC1 . . . 5A 68
(off Baldwins Gdns.)
Courtfield M. SW5 . . . 4A 84
Courtfield Ri. W Wick . . . 3F 155
Courtfield Rd. SW7 . . . 4A 84
Courtfield Rd. Ashf . . . 6D 112
Court Gdns. N7 . . . 6A 50
(in two parts)
Courthill Rd. SE13 . . . 4E 106
Courthope Ho. SE16 . . . 3J 87
(off Lower Rd.)
Courthope Ho. SW8 . . . 7J 85
(off Hartington Rd.)
Courthope Rd. NW3 . . . 4D 48
Courthope Rd. SW19 . . . 5G 119
Courthope Rd. Gnfd . . . 2H 61
Courthope Vs. SW19 . . . 7G 119
Court Ho. Gdns. N3 . . . 6D 14
Courthouse Rd. N12 . . . 6E 14
Courtland Av. E4 . . . 2C 20
Courtland Av. NW7 . . . 3E 12
Courtland Av. SW16 . . . 7K 121
Courtland Av. Ilf . . . 2D 54
Courtland Gro. SE28 . . . 7D 74
Courtland Rd. E6 . . . 1C 72
Courtlands. Rich . . . 5G 99
Courtlands. W on T . . . 7J 131
Courtlands Av. SE12 . . . 5K 107
Courtlands Av. Brom . . . 1G 155
Courtlands Av. Hamp . . . 6D 114
Courtlands Av. Rich . . . 2H 99
Courtlands Clo. Ruis . . . 7H 23
Courtlands Dri. Eps . . . 6A 148
Courtlands Rd. Surb . . . 7G 135
Court La. SE21 . . . 6E 104
Court La. Gdns. SE21 . . . 7E 104
Courtleet Dri. Eri . . . 1H 111
Courtleigh. NW11 . . . 5H 29
Courtleigh Gdns. NW11 . . . 4G 29
Court Lodge. Belv . . . 5G 93
Courtman Rd. N17 . . . 7H 17
Court Mead. N'holt . . . 3D 60
Courtmead Clo. SE24 . . . 6C 104
Courtnell St. W2 . . . 6J 65
Courtney Clo. SE19 . . . 6E 122
Courtney Ct. N7 . . . 5A 50
Courtney Cres. Cars . . . 7D 150

Courtney Ho. NW4 3E 28 (off Mulberry Clo.)
Courtney Ho. W14 3G 83 (off Russell Rd.)
Courtney Pl. Croy 3A 152
Courtney Rd. N7 5A 50
Courtney Rd. SW19 7C 120
Courtney Rd. Croy 3A 152
Courtney Rd. H'row A 3C 94
Court Pde. Wemb 3B 44 (in two parts)
Courtrai Rd. SE23 6A 106
Court Rd. SE9 6D 108
Court Rd. SE25 2F 141
Court Rd. S'hall 4D 78
Court Rd. Uxb 5D 40
Courtside. N8 6H 31
Courtside. SE26 3H 123
Court St. E1 5H 69
Court St. Brom 2J 143
Court, The. Ruis 4C 42
Courtville Ho. W10 3G 65 (off Third Av.)
Court Way. NW9 4A 28
Court Way. W3 5J 63
Court Way. Ilf 3G 37
Court Way. Twic 7K 97
Court Way. Wfd G 5F 21
Court Wood La. Croy 7B 154
Court Yd. SE9 6C 108
Courtyard, The. N1 7K 49
Courtyard, The. NW1 7E 48
Courtyard Theatre. 2J 67 (1F 161) (off York Way)
Cousin La. EC4 7D 68 (3E 168)
Cousins Clo. W Dray 7A 58
Couthurst Rd. SE3 6K 89
Coutts Av. Chess 5E 146
Coutt's Cres. NW5 3E 48
Couzens Ho. E3 5B 70 (off Weatherley Clo.)
Coval Gdns. SW14 4H 99
Coval La. SW14 4H 99
Coval Pas. SW14 4J 99
Coval Rd. SW14 4H 99
Covelees Wall. E6 6E 72
Covell Ct. SE8 7C 88
Covell Ct. Enf 1E 6 (off Ridgeway, The)
Covent Garden. 7J 67 (2F 167)
Covent Garden. WC2 7J 67 (2F 167)
Coventry Clo. E6 6D 72
Coventry Clo. NW6 2J 65
Coventry Cross. E3 4E 70
Coventry Hall. SW16 5J 121
Coventry Rd. E1 & E2 4H 69
Coventry Rd. SE25 4G 141
Coventry Rd. Ilf 2F 55
Coventry St. W1 7H 67 (3C 166)
Coverack Clo. N14 6B 6
Coverack Clo. Croy 7A 142
Coverdale Clo. Stan 5G 11
Coverdale Gdns. Croy 3F 153
Coverdale Rd. N11 6K 15
Coverdale Rd. NW2 7F 47
Coverdale Rd. W12 2D 82
Coverdales, The. Bark 2H 73
Coverley Clo. E1 5G 69
Coverley Point. SE11 4K 85 (4G 173) (off Tyers St.)
Coverton Rd. SW17 5C 120
Covert, The. SE19 7F 123 (off Fox Hill)
Covert, The. N'wd 1E 22
Covert, The. Orp 6J 145
Covert Way. Barn 2F 5
Covet Wood Clo. Orp 6K 145
Covey Clo. SW19 2K 137
Covington Gdns. SW16 7B 122
Covington Way. SW16 6K 121 (in two parts)
Cowan Clo. E6 5C 72
Cowan Ct. NW10 7K 45
Cowbridge La. Bark 7F 55
Cowbridge Rd. Harr 4F 27
Cowcross St. EC1 5B 68 (5A 162)
Cowdenbeath Path. N1 1K 67
Cowden Rd. Orp 7K 145
Cowden St. SE6 4C 124
Cowdray Rd. Uxb 1E 58
Cowdrey Clo. Enf 2K 7
Cowdrey Rd. SW19 5K 119
Cowen Av. Harr 2H 43
Cowgate Rd. Gnfd 3H 61
Cowick Rd. SW17 4D 120
Cowings Mead. N'holt 6C 42
Cowland Av. Enf 4D 8
Cow La. Gnfd 2H 61
Cow Leaze. E6 6E 72
Cowleaze Rd. King T 1E 134
Cowley La. E11 3G 53
Cowley Peachey. 6A 58
Cowley Pl. NW4 5E 28
Cowley Rd. E11 5K 35
Cowley Rd. SW9 1A 104
Cowley Rd. SW14 3A 100
Cowley Rd. W3 1B 82
Cowley Rd. Ilf 7D 36
Cowley St. SW1 3J 85 (1E 172)
Cowling Clo. W11 1G 83
Cowper Av. E6 7C 54
Cowper Av. Sutt 4B 150
Cowper Clo. Brom 4B 144
Cowper Clo. Well 5A 110
Cowper Gdns. N14 6A 6
Cowper Gdns. Wall 6G 151
Cowper Ho. SE17 5C 86 (off Browning St.)
Cowper Ho. SW1 5H 85 (6C 172) (off Aylesford St.)
Cowper Rd. N14 1A 16
Cowper Rd. N16 5E 50
Cowper Rd. N18 5B 18
Cowper Rd. SW19 6A 120
Cowper Rd. W3 1K 81
Cowper Rd. W7 7K 61
Cowper Rd. Belv 4F 93
Cowper Rd. Brom 4B 144
Cowper Rd. King T 5F 117
Cowper's Ct. EC3 1F 169
Cowper St. EC2 4D 68 (3F 163)
Cowper Ter. W10 5F 65
Cowslip Clo. Uxb 7A 40
Cowslip Rd. E18 2K 35
Cowthorpe Rd. SW8 1H 103
Cox Ct. Barn 4H 5
Coxe Pl. W'stone 4A 26
Cox Ho. W6 6G 83 (off Field Rd.)
Cox La. Chess 4F 147
Cox La. Eps 5H 147
Coxmount Rd. SE7 5B 90
Coxs Av. Shep 3G 131
Cox's Ct. E1 6J 163
Coxson Way. SE1 2F 87 (7J 169)
Cox's Wlk. SE21 & SE26 1G 123
Coxwell Rd. SE18 5H 91
Coxwell Rd. SE19 7E 122
Coxwold Path. Chess 7E 146
Crab Hill. Beck 7F 125
Crabtree Av. Romf 4D 38
Crabtree Av. Wemb 2E 62
Crabtree Clo. E2 2F 69
Crabtree Ct. E15 5D 52
Crabtree Ct. New Bar 4E 4
Crabtree La. SW6 7E 82 (in two parts)
Crabtree Manorway N. Belv 2J 93
Crabtree Manorway S. Belv 3J 93
Crabtree Wlk. SE15 1F 105 (off Peckham Rd.)
Crabtree Wlk. Croy 1G 153
Crace St. NW1 3H 67 (1C 160)
Craddock Rd. Enf 3A 8
Craddock St. NW5 6E 48
Cradley Rd. SE9 1H 127
Crafts Council & Gallery. 2A 68
Cragie Ho. SE1 4F 87 (off Balaclava Rd.)
Craig Dri. Uxb 6D 58
Craigen Av. Croy 1H 153
Craigerne Rd. SE3 7K 89
Craig Gdns. E18 2H 35
Craigholm. SE18 2E 108
Craigmore Ct. N'wd 1G 23
Craigmuir Pk. Wemb 1F 63
Craignair Rd. SW2 7A 104
Craignish Av. SW16 2K 139
Craig Pk. Rd. N18 4C 18
Craig Rd. Rich 4C 116
Craig's Ct. SW1 1J 85 (4E 166)
Craigton Rd. SE9 4D 108
Craigweil Clo. Stan 5J 11
Craigweil Dri. Stan 5J 11
Craigwell Av. Felt 3J 113
Craik Ct. NW6 2H 65 (off Carlton Va.)
Crail Row. SE17 4D 86
Crales Ho. SE18 3C 90
Cramer St. W1 5E 66 (6H 159)
Crammond Clo. W6 6G 83
Cramond Ct. Felt 1G 113
Cramonde Ct. Well 2A 110
Crampton Ho. SW8 1G 103
Crampton Rd. SE20 6J 123
Crampton St. SE17 4C 86
Cranberry Clo. N'holt 2B 60
Cranberry La. E16 4G 71
Cranborne Av. S'hall 4E 78
Cranborne Av. Surb 3G 147
Cranborne Rd. Bark 1H 73
Cranborne Waye. Hay 6K 59 (in two parts)
Cranbourn All. WC2 7H 67 (2D 166) (off Cranbourn St.)
Cranbourne Av. E11 4K 35
Cranbourne Clo. SW16 3J 139
Cranbourne Dri. Pinn 5B 24
Cranbourne Gdns. NW11 5G 29
Cranbourne Gdns. Ilf 3G 37
Cranbourne Pas. SE16 2H 87
Cranbourne Rd. E12 5C 54
Cranbourne Rd. E15 4E 52
Cranbourne Rd. N10 2F 31
Cranbourne Rd. N'wd 3H 23
Cranbourn Ho. SE16 2H 87 (off Marigold St.)
Cranbourn St. WC2 7H 67 (2D 166)
Cranbrook. 1D 54
Cranbrook. NW1 1G 67 (off Camden St.)
Cranbrook Clo. Brom 6J 143
Cranbrook Ct. Bren 6C 80
Cranbrook Dri. Esh 7G 133
Cranbrook Dri. Twic 1F 115
Cranbrook Est. E2 2K 69
Cranbrook La. N11 4A 16
Cranbrook M. E17 5B 34
Cranbrook Pk. N22 1A 32
Cranbrook Ri. Ilf 6D 36
Cranbrook Rd. SE8 1C 106
Cranbrook Rd. SW19 7G 119
Cranbrook Rd. W4 5A 82
Cranbrook Rd. Barn 6G 5
Cranbrook Rd. Bexh 1F 111
Cranbrook Rd. Houn 4D 96
Cranbrook Rd. Ilf 7E 36
Cranbrook Rd. T Hth 2C 140
Cranbrook St. E2 2K 69
Cranbury Rd. SW6 2K 101
Crandley Ct. SE8 4A 88
Crane Av. W3 7J 63
Crane Av. Iswth 5A 98
Cranebank M. Twic 4A 98
Cranebrook. Twic 2G 115
Crane Clo. Dag 6G 57
Crane Clo. Harr 3G 43
Crane Ct. EC4 6A 68 (1K 167)
Crane Ct. Eps 4J 147
Craneford Clo. Twic 7K 97
Craneford Way. Twic 7J 97
Crane Gdns. Hay 4H 77
Crane Gro. N7 6A 50
Crane Ho. E3 2A 70 (off Roman Rd.)
Crane Ho. SE15 1F 105
Crane Ho. Felt 3E 114
Crane Lodge Rd. Houn 6K 77
Crane Mead. SE16 4K 87
Crane Mead Ct. Twic 7K 97
Crane Pk. Rd. Twic 2F 115
Crane Rd. Twic 1J 115
Cranesbill Clo. NW9 3K 27
Cranes Dri. Surb 4E 134
Cranes Pk. Surb 4E 134
Cranes Pk. Av. Surb 4E 134
Cranes Pk. Cres. Surb 4F 135
Crane St. SE10 5F 89
Crane St. SE15 1F 105
Craneswater. Hay 7H 77
Craneswater Pk. S'hall 5D 78
Crane Way. Twic 7G 97
Cranfield Clo. SE27 3C 122
Cranfield Ct. W1 6D 158
Cranfield Dri. NW9 7F 13
Cranfield Ho. WC1 5E 160
Cranfield Rd. SE4 3B 106
Cranfield Rd. E. Cars 7E 150
Cranfield Rd. W. Cars 7D 150
Cranfield Row. SE1 1K 173
Cranford. 1J 95
Cranford Av. N13 5D 16
Cranford Av. Stai 7A 94
Cranford Clo. SW20 7D 118
Cranford Clo. Stai 7A 94
Cranford Cotts. E1 7K 69 (off Cranford St.)
Cranford Dri. Hay 4H 77
Cranford La. Hay 6F 77
Cranford La. H'row 1H 95 (in two parts)
Cranford La. Houn 7K 77
Cranford La. H'row A 3H 95
Cranford Pk. Rd. Hay 4H 77
Cranford St. E1 7K 69
Cranford Way. N8 4K 31
Cranhurst Rd. NW2 5E 46
Cranleigh Clo. SE20 2H 141
Cranleigh Clo. Bex 6H 111
Cranleigh Ct. Mitc 3B 138
Cranleigh Ct. Rich 3G 99
Cranleigh Ct. S'hall 6D 60
Cranleigh Gdns. N21 5F 7
Cranleigh Gdns. SE25 3E 140
Cranleigh Gdns. Bark 7H 55
Cranleigh Gdns. Harr 5E 26
Cranleigh Gdns. King T 6F 117
Cranleigh Gdns. S'hall 6D 60
Cranleigh Gdns. Sutt 2K 149
Cranleigh Gdns. Ind. Est. S'hall 5D 60
Cranleigh Houses. NW1 2G 67 (off Cranleigh St.)
Cranleigh M. SW11 2C 102
Cranleigh Rd. N15 5C 32
Cranleigh Rd. SW19 3J 137
Cranleigh Rd. Felt 4H 113
Cranleigh St. NW1 2G 67
Cranley Dene Ct. N10 4F 31
Cranley Dri. Ilf 7G 37
Cranley Dri. Ruis 2H 41
Cranley Gardens. 4F 31
Cranley Gdns. N10 4F 31
Cranley Gdns. N13 3E 16
Cranley Gdns. SW7 5A 84 (5A 170)
Cranley Gdns. Wall 7G 151
Cranley M. SW7 5A 84 (5A 170)
Cranley Pde. SE9 4C 126 (off Beaconsfield Rd.)
Cranley Pl. SW7 4B 84 (4A 170)
Cranley Rd. E13 5K 71
Cranley Rd. Ilf 6G 37
Cranmer Av. W13 3B 80
Cranmer Clo. Mord 6F 137
Cranmer Clo. Ruis 1B 42
Cranmer Clo. Stan 7H 11
Cranmer Ct. N3 2G 29
Cranmer Ct. SW3 4C 84 (4D 170)
Cranmer Ct. SW4 3H 103
Cranmere Ct. SE5 1C 104
Cranmere Ct. Enf 2F 7
Cranmer Farm Clo. Mitc 4D 138
Cranmer Gdns. Dag 4J 57
Cranmer Ho. SW9 7A 86 (off Brixton Rd.)
Cranmer Rd. E7 4K 53
Cranmer Rd. SW9 7A 86
Cranmer Rd. Croy 3B 152
Cranmer Rd. Edgw 3C 12
Cranmer Rd. Hamp H 5F 115
Cranmer Rd. Hay 6F 59
Cranmer Rd. King T 5E 116
Cranmer Rd. Mitc 4D 138
Cranmer Ter. SW17 5B 120
Cranmore Av. Iswth 7G 79
Cranmore Rd. Brom 3H 125
Cranmore Rd. Chst 5D 126
Cranmore Way. N10 4G 31
Cranston Clo. Houn 2C 96
Cranston Clo. Uxb 2F 41
Cranston Est. N1 2D 68
Cranston Gdns. E4 6J 19
Cranston Rd. SE23 1A 124
Cranswick Rd. SE16 5H 87
Crantock Rd. SE6 2D 124
Cranwell Clo. E3 4D 70
Cranwell Gro. Shep 4B 130
Cranwell Rd. H'row A 2D 94
Cranwich Av. N21 7J 7
Cranwich Rd. N16 7D 32
Cranwood Ct. EC1 2F 163
Cranwood St. EC1 3D 68 (2F 163)
Cranworth Cres. E4 1A 20
Cranworth Gdns. SW9 1A 104
Craster Rd. SW2 7K 103
Crathie Rd. SE12 6K 107
Cravan Av. Felt 2J 113
Craven Av. W5 7C 62
Craven Av. S'hall 5D 60
Craven Clo. N16 7G 33
Craven Clo. Hay 6J 59
Craven Ct. NW10 1A 64
Craven Ct. Romf 6E 38
Craven Gdns. SW19 5J 119
Craven Gdns. Bark 2J 73
Craven Gdns. Ilf 2H 37
Craven Hill. W2 7A 66
Craven Hill Gdns. W2 7A 66 (in two parts)
Craven Hill M. W2 7A 66
Craven Ho. N2 2B 30 (off Central Av.)
Craven Lodge. W2 7A 66 (off Craven Hill)
Craven M. SW11 3E 102
Craven Pk. NW10 1K 63
Craven Pk. M. NW10 7A 46
Craven Pk. Rd. N15 6F 33
Craven Pk. Rd. NW10 1A 64
Craven Pas. WC2 1J 85 (4E 166) (off Craven St.)
Craven Rd. NW10 1K 63
Craven Rd. W2 7A 66 (2A 164)
Craven Rd. W5 7C 62

Craven Rd. *Croy* 1H 153
Craven Rd. *King T* 1F 135
Craven St. *WC2* . . . 1J 85 (4E 166)
Craven Ter. *W2* 7A 66 (2A 164)
Craven Wlk. *N16* 7G 33
Crawford Av. *Wemb* 5D 44
Crawford Bldgs. W1
. . . . *5C 66 (6D 158)*
(off Homer St.)
Crawford Clo. *Iswth* 2J 97
Crawford Est. *SE5* 2C 104
Crawford Gdns. *N13* 3G 17
Crawford Gdns. *N'holt* 3D 60
Crawford Mans. W1
. . . . *5C 66 (6D 158)*
(off Crawford St.)
Crawford M. *W1* . . . 5D 66 (6E 158)
Crawford Pas. *EC1*
. . . . 4A 68 (4K 161)
Crawford Pl. *W1*
. . . . 6C 66 (7D 158)
Crawford Point. E16 . . . . *6H 71*
(off Wouldham Rd.)
Crawford Rd. *SE5* 1C 104
Crawford St. *W1* . . . 5C 66 (6E 158)
Crawley Rd. *E10* 1D 52
Crawley Rd. *N22* 2C 32
Crawley Rd. *Enf* 7K 7
Crawshay Ct. *SW9* 1A 104
Crawthew Gro. *SE22* 4F 105
Craybrooke Rd. *Sidc* 4B 128
Craybury End. *SE9* 2G 127
Crayford Clo. *E6* 6C 72
Crayford Ho. SE1
. . . . *2D 86 (7F 169)*
(off Long La.)
Crayford Rd. *N7* 4H 49
Crayke Hill. *Chess* 7E 146
Crayle Ho. EC1 . . . . *4B 68 (3B 162)*
(off Malta St.)
Crayonne Clo. *Sun* 1G 131
Cray Rd. *Belv* 6G 93
Cray Rd. *Sidc* 6C 128
Cray Valley Rd. *Orp* 5K 145
Crealock Gro. *Wfd G* 5C 20
Crealock St. *SW18* 6K 101
Creasy Est. *SE1* 3E 86
Crebor St. *SE22* 6G 105
Credenhall Dri. *Brom* 1D 156
Credenhill Ho. *SE15* 7H 87
Credenhill St. *SW16* 6G 121
Crediton Hill. *NW6* 5K 47
Crediton Rd. *E16* 6J 71
Crediton Rd. *NW10* 1F 65
Crediton Way. *Clay* 5A 146
Credon Rd. *E13* 2A 72
Credon Rd. *SE16* 5H 87
Creechurch La. *EC3*
. . . . 6E 68 (1H 169)
(in two parts)
Creechurch Pl. *EC3* 1H 169
Creed Ct. *EC4* 1B 168
Creed La. *EC4* 6B 68 (1B 168)
Creek Ho. W14 . . . . *3G 83*
(off Russell Rd.)
Creekmouth. **4K 73**
Creek Rd. *SE8 & SE10* 6C 88
Creek Rd. *Bark* 3K 73
Creek Rd. *E Mol* 4J 133
Creekside. *SE8* 7D 88
Creek, The. *Sun* 5J 131
Creek Way. *Rain* 5K 75
Creeland Gro. *SE6* 1B 124
Crefeld Clo. *W6* 6G 83
Creffield Rd. *W5 & W3* 7F 63
Creighton Av. *E6* 2B 72
Creighton Av. *N2 & N10* 3C 30
Creighton Clo. *W12* 7C 64
Creighton Rd. *N17* 7K 17
Creighton Rd. *NW6* 2F 65
Creighton Rd. *W5* 3D 80
Cremer Bus. Cen. E2
. . . . *2F 69 (1J 163)*
(off Cremer St.)
Cremer Ho. SE8 . . . . *7C 88*
(off Deptford Chu. St.)
Cremer St. *E2* 2F 69 (1J 163)
Cremorne Est. *SW10* 6B 84
Cremorne Rd. *SW10* 7A 84
Creon Ct. SW9 . . . . *7A 86*
(off Caldwell St.)
Crescent. *EC3* 7F 69 (2J 169)
Crescent Ct. *Surb* 5D 134
Crescent Ct. Bus. Cen. *E16*
. . . . 4F 71
Crescent Dri. *Orp* 5F 145
Crescent E. *Barn* 1F 5
Crescent Gdns. *SW19* 3J 119
Crescent Gdns. *Ruis* 7K 23
Crescent Gro. *SW4* 4G 103
Crescent Gro. *Mitc* 4C 138
Crescent Ho. EC1
. . . . *4C 68 (4C 162)*
(off Golden La. Est.)
Crescent Ho. *SE8* 2D 106
Crescent La. *SW4* 4G 103
Crescent M. *N22* 1J 31
Crescent Pde. *Uxb* 3C 58
Crescent Pl. *SW3*
. . . . 4C 84 (3D 170)
Crescent Ri. *N3* 1H 29
Crescent Ri. *N22* 1H 31
Crescent Ri. *Barn* 5H 5
Crescent Rd. *E4* 1B 20
Crescent Rd. *E6* 1A 72
Crescent Rd. *E10* 2D 52
Crescent Rd. *E13* 1J 71
Crescent Rd. *E18* 1A 36
Crescent Rd. *N3* 1H 29
Crescent Rd. *N8* 6H 31
Crescent Rd. *N9* 1B 18
Crescent Rd. *N11* 4J 15
Crescent Rd. *N15* 3B 32
Crescent Rd. *N22* 1H 31
Crescent Rd. *SE18* 5F 91
Crescent Rd. *SW20* 1F 137
Crescent Rd. *Barn* 4G 5
Crescent Rd. *Beck* 2D 142
Crescent Rd. *Brom* 7J 125
Crescent Rd. *Dag* 3H 57
Crescent Rd. *Enf* 4G 7
Crescent Rd. *King T* 7G 117
Crescent Rd. *Shep* 5E 130
Crescent Rd. *Sidc* 3K 127
Crescent Row. *EC1*
. . . . 4C 68 (4C 162)
Crescent Stables. *SW15* . . . 5G 101
Crescent St. *N1* 7K 49
Crescent, The. *E17* 6A 34
Crescent, The. *N9* 2C 18
Crescent, The. *N11* 4J 15
Crescent, The. *NW2* 3D 46
Crescent, The. *SW13* 2B 100
Crescent, The. *SW19* 3J 119
Crescent, The. *W3* 6A 64
Crescent, The. *Ashf* 5B 112
Crescent, The. *Barn* 2E 4
Crescent, The. *Beck* 1C 142
Crescent, The. *Bex* 7C 110
Crescent, The. *Croy* 6D 140
Crescent, The. *Harr* 1G 43
Crescent, The. *Hay* 7F 77
Crescent, The. *Ilf* 6E 36
Crescent, The. *N Mald* 3J 135
Crescent, The. *Shep* 7H 131
Crescent, The. *Sidc* 4K 127
Crescent, The. *S'hall* 2D 78
Crescent, The. *Surb* 5E 134
Crescent, The. *Sutt* 5B 150
Crescent, The. *Wemb* 2B 44
Crescent, The. *W Mol* 4E 132
Crescent, The. *W Wick* 6G 143
Crescent Way. *N12* 6H 15
Crescent Way. *SE4* 3C 106
Crescent Way. *SW16* 6K 121
Crescent W. *Barn* 1F 5
Crescent Wharf. E16 . . . . *1K 89*
(off N. Woolwich Rd., in two parts)
Crescent Wood Rd. *SE26*
. . . . 3G 123
Cresford Rd. *SW6* 1K 101
Crespigny Rd. *NW4* 6D 28
Cressage Clo. *S'hall* 4E 60
Cressage Ho. Bren *6E 80*
(off Ealing Rd.)
Cressal Ho. E14 . . . . *3C 88*
(off Tiller Rd.)
Cresset Rd. *E9* 6J 51
Cresset St. *SW4* 3H 103
Cressfield Clo. *NW5* 5E 48
Cressida Rd. *N19* 1G 49
Cressingham Gdns. Est. *SW2*
. . . . 7A 104
Cressingham Gro. *Sutt* 4A 150
Cressingham Rd. *SE13* 3E 106
Cressingham Rd. *Edgw* 6E 12
Cressington Clo. *N16* 5E 50
Cress M. *Brom* 5F 125
Cresswell. *NW9* 2B 28
Cresswell Gdns. *SW5* 5A 84
Cresswell Pk. *SE3* 3H 107
Cresswell Pl. *SW10* 5A 84
Cresswell Rd. *SE25* 4G 141
Cresswell Rd. *Felt* 3C 114
Cresswell Rd. *Twic* 6D 98
Cresswell Way. *N21* 7F 7
Cressy Ct. *E1* 5J 69
Cressy Ct. *W6* 3D 82
Cressy Houses. E1 . . . . *5J 69*
(off Hannibal Rd.)
Cressy Pl. *E1* 5J 69
Cressy Rd. *NW3* 5D 48
Cresta Ct. *W5* 4F 63
Cresta Ho. NW3 . . . . *7B 48*
(off Finchley Rd.)
Crestbrook Av. *N13* 3G 17
Crestbrook Pl. N13 . . . . *3G 17*
(off Green Lanes)
Crest Ct. *NW4* 5E 28
Crest Dri. *Enf* 1D 8
Crestfield St. *WC1*
. . . . 3J 67 (1F 161)
Crest Gdns. *Ruis* 3A 42
Creston Way. *Wor Pk*
. . . . 1F 149
Crest Rd. *NW2* 2C 46
Crest Rd. *Brom* 7H 143
Crest Rd. *S Croy* 7H 153
Crest, The. *N13* 4F 17
Crest, The. *NW4* 5E 28
Crest, The. *Surb* 5G 135
Crest Vw. *Pinn* 4B 24
Crest Vw. Dri. *Orp* 5F 145
Crestway. *SW15* 6C 100
Crestwood Way. *Houn* 5C 96
Creswick Ct. *W3* 7H 63
Creswick Rd. *W3* 7H 63
Creswick Wlk. *E3* 3C 70
Creswick Wlk. *NW11* 4H 29
Creton St. *SE18* 3E 90
Crewdson Rd. *SW9* 7A 86
Crewe Pl. *NW10* 3B 64
Crewkerne Ct. SW11 . . . . *1B 102*
(off Bolingbroke Wlk.)
Crews St. *E14* 4C 88
Crewys Rd. *NW2* 2H 47
Crewys Rd. *SE15* 2H 105
Crichton Av. *Wall* 5H 151
Crichton Ho. *Sidc* 6D 128
Crichton Rd. *Cars* 6D 150
Crichton St. *SW8* 2G 103
Cricketers Arms Rd. *Enf* 2H 7
Cricketers Clo. *N14* 7B 6
Cricketers Clo. *Chess* 4D 146
Cricketers Clo. *Eri* 5K 93
Cricketers Ct. SE11 . . . . *4B 86*
(off Kennington La.)
Cricketers M. *SW18* 5K 101
Cricketers Ter. *Cars* 3C 150
Cricketers Wlk. *SE26* 5J 123
Cricketfield Rd. *E5* 4H 51
Cricket Grn. *Mitc* 3D 138
Cricket Ground Rd. *Chst* . . . 1F 145
(in two parts)
Cricket La. *Beck* 6A 124
Cricklade Av. *SW2* 2J 121
Cricklewood. **3G 47**
Cricklewood B'way. *NW2* 3E 46
Cricklewood La. *NW2* 4F 47
Cridland St. *E15* 1H 71
Crieff Ct. *Tedd* 7C 116
Crieff Rd. *SW18* 6A 102
Criffel Av. *SW2* 2H 121
Crimscott St. *SE1* 3E 86
Crimsworth Rd. *SW8* 1H 103
Crinan St. *N1* 2J 67
Cringle St. *SW8* 7G 85
Cripplegate St. *EC2*
. . . . 5C 68 (5D 162)
Cripps Grn. *Hay* 4K 59
Crispe Ho. N1 . . . . *1K 67*
(off Barnsbury Est.)
Crispe Ho. *Bark* 2H 73
Crispen Rd. *Felt* 4C 114
Crispian Clo. *NW10* 4A 46
Crispin Clo. *Croy* 2J 151
Crispin Cres. *Croy* 3H 151
Crispin Lodge. *N11* 5J 15
Crispin Rd. *Edgw* 6D 12
Crispin St. *E1* 5F 69 (6J 163)
Crispin Ter. *Wfd G* 6G 21
Crisp Rd. *W6* 5E 82
Cristowe Rd. *SW6* 2H 101
Criterion Ct. E8 . . . . *7F 51*
(off Middleton Rd.)
Criterion M. *N19* 2H 49
Criterion Theatre.
. . . . ***7G 67 (3C 166)***
(off Piccadilly)
Crittall's Corner. (Junct.)
. . . . 7B 128
Crockerton Rd. *SW17* 2D 120
Crockham Way. *SE9* 4E 126
Crocus Clo. *Croy* 1K 153
Crocus Fld. *Barn* 6C 4
Croft Av. *W Wick* 1E 154
Croft Clo. *NW7* 3F 13
Croft Clo. *Belv* 5F 93
Croft Clo. *Chst* 5D 126
Croft Clo. *Hay* 7E 76
Croft Clo. *Uxb* 7C 40
Croft Ct. *SE13* 6E 106
Croft Ct. *Ruis* 1H 41
Croftdown Rd. *NW5* 3E 48
Croft End Clo. Chess *3F 147*
(off Ashcroft Rd.)
Crofters Clo. *Iswth* 5H 97
Crofters Ct. SE8 . . . . *4A 88*
(off Croft St.)
Crofters Mead. *Croy* 7B 154
Crofters Way. *NW1* 1H 67
Croft Gdns. *W7* 2A 80
Croft Gdns. *Ruis* 1G 41
Croft Ho. *E17* 4D 34
Croft Ho. W10 . . . . *3G 65*
(off Third Av.)
Croft Lodge Clo. *Wfd G* 6E 20
Croft M. *N12* 3F 15
Crofton Av. *W4* 7K 81
Crofton Av. *Bex* 7D 110
Croftongate Way. *SE4* 5A 106
Crofton Gro. *E4* 4A 20
Crofton La. *Orp* 7H 145
Crofton Park. **5B 106**
Crofton Pk. Rd. *SE4* 6B 106
Crofton Rd. *E13* 4K 71
Crofton Rd. *SE5* 1E 104
Crofton Rd. *Orp* 3E 156
Crofton Ter. *E5* 5A 52
Crofton Ter. *Rich* 4F 99
Crofton Way. *Barn* 6E 4
Crofton Way. *Enf* 2F 7
Croft Rd. *SW16* 1A 140
Croft Rd. *SW19* 7A 120
Croft Rd. *Brom* 6J 125
Croft Rd. *Enf* 1F 9
Croft Rd. *Sutt* 5C 150
Crofts Ho. E2 . . . . *2G 69*
(off Teale St.)
Croftside, The. *SE25* 3G 141
Crofts La. *N22* 7F 17
Crofts Rd. *Harr* 6A 26
Crofts St. *E1* 7G 69 (2K 169)
Crofts, The. *Shep* 4G 131
Croft St. *SE8* 4A 88
Crofts Vs. *Harr* 6A 26
Croft, The. *E4* 2B 20
Croft, The. *NW10* 2B 64
Croft, The. *W5* 5E 62
Croft, The. *Barn* 4B 4
Croft, The. *Houn* 6C 78
Croft, The. *Pinn* 7D 24
Croft, The. *Ruis* 4A 42
Croft, The. *Wemb* 5C 44
Croftway. *NW3* 4J 47
Croftway. *Rich* 3B 116
Croft Way. *Sidc* 3J 127
Crogsland Rd. *NW1* 7E 48
Croham Clo. *S Croy* 7E 152
Croham Mnr. Rd. *S Croy* . . . 7E 152
Croham Mt. *S Croy* 7E 152
Croham Pk. Av. *S Croy* 5E 152
Croham Rd. *S Croy* 5D 152
Croham Valley Rd. *S Croy*
. . . . 6G 153
Croindene Rd. *SW16* 1J 139
Crokesley Ho. Edgw *2J 27*
(off Burnt Oak B'way.)
Cromartie Rd. *N19* 7H 31
Cromarty Ct. *SW2* 5K 103
Cromarty Ho. E1 . . . . *5A 70*
(off Ben Jonson Rd.)
Cromarty Rd. *Edgw* 2C 12
Cromberdale Ct. N17 . . . . *1G 33*
(off Spencer Rd.)
Crombie Clo. *Ilf* 5D 36
Crombie M. *SW11* 2C 102
Crombie Rd. *Sidc* 1H 127
Crome Ho. N'holt *2C 60*
(off Parkfield Dri.)
Cromer Clo. *Uxb* 6E 58
Cromerhyde. *Mord* 5K 137
Cromer Pl. *Orp* 7J 145
Cromer Rd. *E10* 7F 35
Cromer Rd. *N17* 2G 33
Cromer Rd. *SE25* 3H 141
Cromer Rd. *SW17* 6E 120
Cromer Rd. *Chad H* 6E 38
Cromer Rd. *H'row A* 2C 94
Cromer Rd. *New Bar* 4F 5
Cromer Rd. *Romf* 6J 39
Cromer Rd. *Wfd G* 4D 20
Cromer Rd. W. *H'row A* 3C 94
Cromer St. *WC1* . . . 3J 67 (2E 160)
Cromer Ter. *E8* 5G 51
Cromer Vs. Rd. *SW18* 6H 101
Cromford Path. *E5* 4K 51
Cromford Rd. *SW18* 5J 101
Cromford Way. *N Mald* 1K 135
Cromlix Clo. *Chst* 2F 145
Crompton Ho. SE1 . . . . *3C 86*
(off County St.)
Crompton Ho. W2
. . . . *4B 66 (4A 158)*
(off Hall Pl.)
Crompton Pl. *Enf* 1H 9
Crompton St. *W2*
. . . . 4B 66 (4A 158)
Cromwell Av. *N6* 1F 49
Cromwell Av. *W6* 5D 82
Cromwell Av. *Brom* 4K 143
Cromwell Av. *N Mald* 5B 136
Cromwell Cen. *NW10* 3K 63
Cromwell Cen., The. Dag *7F 39*
(off Selinas La.)
Cromwell Clo. *E1* 1G 87
Cromwell Clo. *N2* 4B 30
Cromwell Clo. *W3* 1J 81
(in two parts)
Cromwell Clo. *Brom* 4K 143

Cromwell Clo. W on T 7K 131
Cromwell Ct. Enf 5E 8
Cromwell Cres. SW5 4J 83
Cromwell Gdns. SW7 3B 84 (2B 170)
Cromwell Gro. W6 3E 82
Cromwell Highwalk. EC2 5D 162
Cromwell Ho. Croy 3B 152
Cromwell Ind. Est. E10 1A 52
Cromwell Lodge. E1 4J 69 (off Cleveland Gro.)
Cromwell Lodge. Bexh 5E 110
Cromwell M. SW7 4B 84 (3B 170)
Cromwell Pl. EC2 5C 68 (5D 162) (off Beech St.)
Cromwell Pl. N6 1F 49
Cromwell Pl. SW7 4B 84 (3B 170)
Cromwell Pl. SW14 3J 99
Cromwell Rd. E7 7A 54
Cromwell Rd. E17 5E 34
Cromwell Rd. N3 1A 30
Cromwell Rd. N10 7K 15 (in two parts)
Cromwell Rd. SW5 & SW7 4J 83 (3A 170)
Cromwell Rd. SW9 1B 104
Cromwell Rd. SW19 5J 119
Cromwell Rd. Beck 2A 142
Cromwell Rd. Croy 7D 140
Cromwell Rd. Felt 1K 113
Cromwell Rd. Hay 6F 59
Cromwell Rd. Houn 4E 96
Cromwell Rd. King T 1E 134
Cromwell Rd. Tedd 6A 116
Cromwell Rd. Wemb 2E 62
Cromwell Rd. Wor Pk 3K 147
Cromwell St. Houn 4E 96
Cromwell Tower. EC2 5D 162
Crondace Rd. SW6 1J 101
Crondall Ct. N1 1F 163
Crondall St. N1 2D 68 (1F 163)
Crone Ct. NW6 2H 65 (off Denmark Rd.)
Cronin St. SE15 7F 87
Crooked Billet. (Junct.) 1C 34
Crooked Billet. SW19 6E 118
Crooked Billet Yd. E2 3E 68 (2H 163)
Crooked Usage. N3 3G 29
Crooke Rd. SE8 5A 88
Crookham Rd. SW6 1H 101
Crook Log. Bexh 3D 110
Crookston Rd. SE9 3E 108
Croombs Rd. E16 5A 72
Croom's Hill. SE10 7E 88
Croom's Hill Gro. SE10 7E 88
Cropley Ct. N1 2D 68 (off Cropley St., in two parts)
Cropley St. N1 2D 68 (1E 162)
Croppath Rd. Dag 4G 57
Cropthorne Ct. W9 3A 66
Crosbie. NW9 2B 28
Crosbie Ho. E17 3E 34 (off Prospect Hill)
Crosby Clo. Felt 3C 114
Crosby Ct. SE1 6E 168
Crosby Ho. E7 6J 53
Crosby Ho. E14 3E 88 (off Manchester Rd.)
Crosby Rd. E7 6J 53
Crosby Rd. Dag 2H 75
Crosby Row. SE1 2D 86 (7E 168)
Crosby Sq. EC3 6E 68 (1G 169)
Crosby Wlk. E8 6F 51
Crosby Wlk. SW2 7A 104
Crosby Way. SW2 7A 104
Crosier Clo. SE3 1C 108
Crosier Rd. Ick 4E 40
Crosier Way. Ruis 3G 41
Crosland Pl. SW11 3E 102
Cross Av. SE10 6F 89
Crossbow Ho. W13 1B 80 (off Sherwood Clo.)
Crossbrook Rd. SE3 2C 108
Cross Clo. SE15 2H 105
Cross Deep. Twic 2K 115
Cross Deep Gdns. Twic 2K 115
Crossfield Ho. W11 7G 65 (off Mary Pl.)
Crossfield Rd. N17 3C 32
Crossfield Rd. NW3 6B 48
Crossfield St. SE8 7C 88 (in two parts)
Crossford St. SW9 2K 103
Cross Ga. Edgw 3B 12
Crossgate. Gnfd 6B 44
Cross Keys Clo. N9 2B 18 (off Lacey Clo.)
Cross Keys Clo. W1 5E 66 (6H 159)
Cross Keys Sq. EC1 5C 68 (6C 162) (off Little Britain)
Cross Lances Rd. Houn 4F 97
Crossland Rd. T Hth 6B 140
Crosslands Av. W5 1F 81
Crosslands Av. S'hall 5D 78
Crosslands Rd. Eps 6K 147
Cross La. EC3 7E 68 (3G 169)
Cross La. N8 3K 31 (in two parts)
Cross La. Bex 7F 111
Crossleigh Ct. SE14 7B 88 (off New Cross Rd.)
Crosslet St. SE17 4D 86
Crosslet Va. SE10 1D 106
Crossley St. N7 6A 50
Crossmead. SE9 1D 126
Crossmead Av. Gnfd 3E 60
Crossmount Ho. SE5 7C 86 (off Bowyer St.)
Crossness Footpath. Eri 1F 93
Crossness La. SE28 7D 74
Crossness Rd. Bark 3K 73
Cross Rd. E4 1A 20
Cross Rd. N11 5A 16
Cross Rd. N22 7F 17
Cross Rd. SE5 2E 104
Cross Rd. SW19 7J 119
Cross Rd. Brom 2C 156
Cross Rd. Chad H 7C 38
Cross Rd. Croy 1D 152
Cross Rd. Enf 4K 7
Cross Rd. Felt 4C 114
Cross Rd. Harr 4H 25
Cross Rd. King T 7F 117
Cross Rd. Romf 4G 39
Cross Rd. Sidc 4B 128
Cross Rd. S Harr 3F 43
Cross Rd. Sutt 5B 150
Cross Rd. W'stone 2A 26
Cross Rd. Wfd G 6J 21
Cross St. N1 1B 68
Cross St. N18 5B 18
Cross St. SE5 3D 104
Cross St. SW13 2A 100
Cross St. Hamp H 5G 115
Crossthwaite Av. SE5 4D 104
Crosswall. EC3 7F 69 (2J 169)
Crossway. N12 6G 15
Crossway. N16 5E 50
Crossway. NW9 4B 28
Crossway. SE28 6B 74
Crossway. SW20 4E 136
Crossway. W13 4A 62
Crossway. Dag 3C 56
Crossway. Enf 7K 7
Crossway. Hay 1J 77
Crossway. Orp 4H 145
Cross Way. Pinn 2K 23
Crossway. Ruis 4A 42
Cross Way. Wfd G 4F 21
Crossway Ct. SE4 2A 106
Crossways. N21 6H 7
Crossways. S Croy 7A 154
Crossways. Sun 7H 113
Crossways. Sutt 7B 150
Crossways Rd. Beck 4C 142
Crossways Rd. Mitc 3F 139
Crossways Ter. E5 4J 51
Crossways, The. Houn 7D 78
Crossways, The. Surb 1H 147
Crossways, The. Wemb 2G 45
Crossway, The. N22 7G 17
Crossway, The. SE9 2B 126
Cross Way, The. Harr 2J 25
Crossway, The. Uxb 2B 58
Crosswell Clo. Shep 2E 130
Croston St. E8 1G 69
Crothall Clo. N13 3E 16
Crouch Av. Bark 2B 74
Crouch Clo. Beck 6C 124
Crouch Cft. SE9 3E 126
Crouch End. 7H 31
Crouch End Hill. N8 7H 31
Crouch Hall Ct. N19 1J 49
Crouch Hall Rd. N8 6H 31
Crouch Hill. N8 & N4 6J 31
Crouchman's Clo. SE26 3F 123
Crouch Rd. NW10 7K 45
Crowborough Rd. SW17 6E 120
Crowden Way. SE28 7C 74
Crowder St. E1 7H 69
Crowfield Ho. N5 4C 50
Crowfoot Clo. E9 5B 52
Crowhurst Clo. SW9 2A 104
Crowhurst Ho. SW9 2K 103 (off Aytoun Rd.)
Crowland Av. Hay 4G 77
Crowland Gdns. N14 7D 6
Crowland Ho. NW8 1A 66 (off Springfield Rd.)
Crowland Rd. N15 5F 33
Crowland Rd. T Hth 4D 140
Crowlands Av. Romf 6H 39
Crowland Ter. N1 7D 50
Crowland Wlk. Mord 6K 137
Crow La. Romf 7F 39
Crowley Cres. Croy 5A 152
Crowline Wlk. N1 6C 50
Crowmarsh Gdns. SE23 7J 105
Crown Arc. King T 2D 134
Crownbourne Ct. Sutt 4K 149 (off St Nicholas Way)
Crown Bldgs. E4 1K 19
Crown Clo. E3 1C 70
Crown Clo. NW6 6K 47
Crown Clo. NW7 2G 13
Crown Clo. Hay 2H 77
Crown Clo. W on T 7A 132
Crown Clo. Bus. Cen. E3 1C 70 (off Crown Clo.)
Crown Cotts. Romf 1G 39
Crown Ct. EC4 1D 168
Crown Ct. N10 7K 15
Crown Ct. SE12 6K 107
Crown Ct. WC2 6J 67 (1F 167)
Crown Dale. SE19 6B 122
Crowndale Ct. NW1 2H 67 (off Crowndale Rd.)
Crowndale Rd. NW1 2G 67
Crownfield Av. Ilf 6J 37
Crownfield Rd. E15 4F 53
Crown Hill. Croy 2C 152
Crown Hill Rd. NW10 1B 64
Crownhill Rd. Wfd G 7H 21
Crown Ho. Ruis 1J 41
Crown La. N14 1B 16
Crown La. SW16 5A 122
Crown La. Brom 5B 144
Crown La. Chst 1G 145
Crown La. Mord 4J 137
Crown La. Gdns. SW16 5A 122
Crown La. Spur. Brom 6B 144
Crown Lodge. SW3 4C 84 (4D 170)
Crownmead Way. Romf 4H 39
Crown M. E13 1A 72
Crown M. W6 4C 82
Crown Office Row. EC4 7A 68 (2J 167)
Crown Pde. N14 1B 16
Crown Pde. SE19 6B 122
Crown Pde. Mord 3J 137
Crown Pas. SW1 1G 85 (5B 166)
Crown Pas. King T 2D 134
Crown Pl. EC2 5E 68 (5G 163) (in two parts)
Crown Pl. NW5 6F 49
Crown Reach. SW1 5H 85 (6D 172)
Crown Rd. N10 7K 15
Crown Rd. Enf 4C 8
Crown Rd. Ilf 4H 37
Crown Rd. Mord 4K 137
Crown Rd. N Mald 1J 135
Crown Rd. Ruis 5B 42
Crown Rd. Sutt 4K 149
Crown Rd. Twic 6B 98
Crownstone Ct. SW2 5A 104
Crownstone Rd. SW2 5A 104
Crown St. SE5 7C 86
Crown St. W3 1H 81
Crown St. Dag 6J 57 (in two parts)
Crown St. Harr 1H 43
Crown Ter. N14 1C 16 (off Crown La.)
Crown Ter. Rich 4F 99
Crown Trad. Cen. Hay 2G 77
Crowntree Clo. Iswth 6K 79
Crown Wlk. Wemb 3F 45
Crown Way. W Dray 1B 76
Crown Wharf. E14 1E 88 (off Coldharbour)
Crown Wharf. SE8 5B 88 (off Grove St.)
Crown Woods. SE18 2F 109
Crown Woods Way. SE9 5H 109
Crown Yd. Houn 3G 97
Crowshott Av. Stan 2C 26
Crows Rd. E15 3F 71
Crows Rd. Bark 6F 55
Crowther Av. Bren 4E 80
Crowther Clo. SW6 6H 83 (off Buckers All.)
Crowther Rd. SE25 5G 141
Crowthorne Clo. SW18 7H 101
Crowthorne Rd. W10 6F 65
Croxall Ho. W on T 6A 132
Croxden Clo. Edgw 3G 27
Croxden Wlk. Mord 6A 138
Croxford Gdns. N22 7G 17
Croxford Way. Romf 1K 57
Croxley Rd. W9 3H 65
Croxted Clo. SE21 7C 104
Croxted M. SE24 6C 104
Croxted Rd. SE24 & SE21 6C 104
Croxteth Ho. SW8 2H 103
Croyde Av. Gnfd 3G 61
Croyde Av. Hay 4G 77
Croyde Clo. Sidc 7H 109
Croydon. 2C 152
Croydon. N17 2D 32 (off Gloucester Rd.)
Croydon Clock Tower. 3C 152 (off Katherine St.)
Croydon Crematorium. Croy 5K 139
Croydon Flyover, The. Croy 3C 152
Croydon Gro. Croy 1B 152
Croydon Ho. SE1 1A 86 (6K 167) (off Wootton St.)
Croydon Rd. E13 4H 71
Croydon Rd. SE20 2H 141
Croydon Rd. Beck 4K 141
Croydon Rd. Brom & Kes 3A 156
Croydon Rd. H'row A 2D 94
Croydon Rd. Mitc & Croy 4E 138
Croydon Rd. Wall & Croy 4F 151
Croydon Rd. W Wick & Brom 3G 155
Croydon Rd. Ind. Est. Beck 4K 141
Croyland Rd. N9 1B 18
Croylands Dri. Surb 7E 134
Croysdale Av. Sun 3J 131
Crozier Ho. SE3 3K 107
Crozier Ho. SW8 7K 85 (off Wilkinson St.)
Crozier Ter. E9 5K 51
Crucible Clo. Romf 6B 38
Crucifix La. SE1 2E 86 (6H 169)
Cruden Ho. SE17 6B 86 (off Brandon Est.)
Cruden St. N1 1B 68
Cruikshank Ho. NW8 2C 66 (off Townshend Rd.)
Cruikshank Rd. E15 4G 53
Cruikshank St. WC1 3A 68 (1J 161)
Crummock Gdns. NW9 5A 28
Crumpsall St. SE2 4C 92
Crundale Av. NW9 5G 27
Crunden Rd. S Croy 7D 152
Crusader Gdns. Croy 3E 152
Crusoe M. N16 2D 50
Crusoe Rd. Eri 5K 93
Crusoe Rd. Mitc 7D 120
Crutched Friars. EC3 7E 68 (2H 169)
Crutchley Rd. SE6 2G 125
Crystal Palace. 6F 123
Crystal Palace F.C. (Selhurst Pk.). 4E 140
Crystal Palace Mus. 6F 123
Crystal Palace National Sports Cen. 6G 123
Crystal Pal. Pde. SE19 6F 123
Crystal Pal. Pk. Rd. SE26 5G 123
Crystal Pal. Rd. SE22 6F 105
Crystal Pal. Sta. Rd. SE19 6G 123
Crystal Ter. SE19 6D 122
Crystal Vw. Ct. Brom 4F 125
Crystal Way. Dag 1C 56
Crystal Way. Harr 5K 25
Cuba Dri. Enf 2D 8
Cuba St. E14 2C 88
Cubitt Ho. SW4 6G 103
Cubitt Sq. S'hall 1G 79
Cubitt Steps. E14 1C 88
Cubitt St. WC1 3K 67 (2H 161)
Cubitt St. Croy 5K 151
Cubitt's Yd. WC2 2F 167
Cubitt Ter. SW4 3G 103
Cubitt Town. 4E 88
Cuckoo Av. W7 4J 61
Cuckoo Dene. W7 5H 61
Cuckoo Hall La. N9 7D 8
Cuckoo Hall Rd. N9 7D 8
Cuckoo Hill. Pinn 3A 24
Cuckoo Hill Dri. Pinn 3A 24
Cuckoo Hill Rd. Pinn 4A 24
Cuckoo La. W7 7J 61
Cuckoo Pound. Shep 5G 131
Cudas Clo. Eps 4B 148
Cuddington. SE17 4C 86 (off Deacon Way)
Cuddington Av. Wor Pk 3B 148
Cudham St. SE6 7E 106
Cudworth Ho. SW8 1G 103
Cudworth St. E1 4H 69
Cuff Cres. SE9 6B 108
Cuffley Ho. W10 5E 64 (off Sutton Way)
Cuff Point. E2 3F 69 (1J 163) (off Columbia Rd.)

Culford Gdns. SW3 4D 84 (4F 171)
Culford Gro. N1 6E 50
Culford Mans. SW3 4D 84 (4F 171)
Culford M. N1 6E 50
Culford Rd. N1 7E 50 (in two parts)
Culgaith Gdns. Enf 4D 6
Culham Ho. E2 3F 69 (2J 163) (off Palissy St.)
Cullen Way. NW10 4J 63
Culling Rd. SE16 3J 87
Cullington Clo. Harr 4A 26
Cullingworth Rd. NW10 5C 46
Culloden Clo. SE16 5G 87
Culloden Rd. Enf 2G 7
Cullum St. EC3 7E 68 (2G 169)
Cullum Welch Ct. N1 3D 68 (1F 163) (off Haberdasher St.)
Cullum Welch Ho. EC1 4C 68 (4C 162) (off Goswell Rd.)
Culmington Pde. W13 1C 80 (off Uxbridge Rd.)
Culmington Rd. W13 1C 80
Culmington Rd. S Croy 7C 152
Culmore Rd. SE15 7H 87
Culmstock Rd. SW11 5E 102
Culpeper Ho. E14 6A 70
Culpepper Ct. SE11 3J 173
Culross Bldgs. NW1 2J 67 (off Battle Bri. Rd.)
Culross Clo. N15 4C 32
Culross Ho. W10 6F 65 (off Bridge Clo.)
Culross St. W1 7E 66 (3G 165)
Culsac Rd. Surb 2E 146
Culverden Rd. SW12 2G 121
Culver Gro. Stan 2C 26
Culverhouse. WC1 5K 67 (6G 161) (off Red Lion Sq.)
Culverhouse Gdns. SW16 3K 121
Culverlands Clo. Stan 4G 11
Culverley Rd. SE6 1D 124
Culvers Av. Cars 2D 150
Culvers Retreat. Cars 1D 150
Culverstone Clo. Brom 6H 143
Culvers Way. Cars 2D 150
Culvert Pl. SW11 2E 102
Culvert Rd. N15 5E 32
Culvert Rd. SW11 2D 102
Culworth Ho. NW8 2C 66 (off Allitsen Rd.)
Culworth St. NW8 2C 66
Culzean Clo. SE27 3B 122
Cumberland Av. NW10 3H 63
Cumberland Av. Well 3J 109
Cumberland Bus. Pk. NW10 3H 63
Cumberland Clo. E8 6F 51
Cumberland Clo. SW20 7F 119
Cumberland Clo. Ilf 1G 37
Cumberland Clo. Twic 6B 98
Cumberland Ct. SW1 5F 85 (5K 171) (off Cumberland St.)
Cumberland Ct. Croy 1D 152
Cumberland Ct. Harr 3J 25 (off Princes Dri.)
Cumberland Ct. Well 2J 109
Cumberland Cres. W14 4G 83 (in two parts)
Cumberland Dri. Bexh 7E 92
Cumberland Dri. Chess 3F 147
Cumberland Dri. Esh 2A 146
Cumberland Gdns. NW4 2G 29
Cumberland Gdns. WC1 3A 68 (1J 161)
Cumberland Ga. W1 7D 66 (2E 164)
Cumberland Ho. E16 1J 89 (off Wesley Av.)
Cumberland Ho. N9 1D 18 (off Cumberland Rd.)
Cumberland Ho. SE28 2G 91 (off Erebus Dri.)
Cumberland Ho. King T 7H 117
Cumberland Mans. W1 7E 158
Cumberland Mkt. NW1 3F 67 (1K 159)
Cumberland Mills Sq. E14 5F 89
Cumberland Pk. W3 7J 63
Cumberland Pk. Ind. Est. NW10 3C 64
Cumberland Pl. NW1 3F 67 (1J 159)
Cumberland Pl. SE6 1H 125
Cumberland Pl. Sun 4J 131
Cumberland Rd. E12 4B 54
Cumberland Rd. E13 5K 71
Cumberland Rd. E17 2A 34
Cumberland Rd. N9 1D 18
Cumberland Rd. N22 2K 31
Cumberland Rd. SE25 6H 141
Cumberland Rd. SW13 1B 100
Cumberland Rd. W3 7J 63
Cumberland Rd. W7 2K 79
Cumberland Rd. Ashf 3A 112
Cumberland Rd. Brom 4G 143
Cumberland Rd. Harr 5F 25
Cumberland Rd. Rich 7G 81
Cumberland Rd. Stan 3F 27
Cumberland St. SW1 5F 85 (5K 171)
Cumberland Ter. NW1 2F 67 (1J 159)
Cumberland Ter. M. NW1 1J 159
Cumberland Vs. W3 7J 63 (off Cumberland Rd.)
Cumberlow Av. SE25 3F 141
Cumbernauld Gdns. Sun 5H 113
Cumberton Rd. N17 1D 32
Cumbrae Gdns. Surb 2D 146
Cumbrian Gdns. NW2 2F 47
Cumbrian Way. Uxb 7A 40
Cuming Mus. 4C 86 (off Walworth Rd.)
Cumming St. N1 2K 67 (1H 161)
Cumnor Clo. SW9 2K 103 (off Robsart St.)
Cumnor Gdns. Eps 6C 148
Cumnor Rd. Sutt 6A 150
Cunard Cres. N21 6J 7
Cunard Pl. EC3 6E 68 (1H 169)
Cunard Rd. NW10 3K 63
Cunard Wlk. SE16 4K 87
Cundy Rd. E16 6A 72
Cundy St. SW1 4E 84 (4H 171)
Cunliffe Pde. Eps 4B 148
Cunliffe Rd. Eps 4B 148
Cunliffe St. SW16 6G 121
Cunningham Clo. Romf 5C 38
Cunningham Clo. W Wick 2D 154
Cunningham Ho. SE5 7D 86 (off Elmington Est.)
Cunningham Pk. Harr 5G 25
Cunningham Pl. NW8 4B 66 (3A 158)
Cunningham Rd. N15 4G 33
Cunnington St. W4 3J 81
Cupar Rd. SW11 1E 102
Cupola Clo. Brom 5K 125
Cureton St. SW1 4H 85 (4D 172)
Curfew Ho. Bark 1G 73
Curie Ct. Harr 7B 26
Curie Gdns. NW9 2A 28
Curlew Clo. SE28 7D 74
Curlew Clo. Ilf 3E 36
Curlew Ct. W13 4K 61
Curlew Ct. Surb 3G 147
Curlew Ho. SE4 4A 106 (off St Norbert Rd.)
Curlew Ho. SE15 1F 105
Curlew St. SE1 2F 87 (6K 169)
Curlew Way. Hay 5B 60
Curnick's La. SE27 4C 122
Curran Av. Sidc 5K 109
Curran Av. Wall 3E 150
Curran Ho. SW3 4C 84 (4C 170) (off Lucan Pl.)
Currey Rd. Gnfd 6H 43
Curricle St. W3 1A 82
Currie Hill Clo. SW19 4H 119
Currie Ho. E14 6F 71 (off Abbott Rd.)
Curry Ri. NW7 6A 14
Cursitor St. EC4 6A 68 (7J 161)
Curtain Pl. EC2 3H 163
Curtain Rd. EC2 4E 68 (2H 163) (in two parts)
Curthwaite Gdns. Enf 4C 6
Curtis Dri. W3 6K 63
Curtis Fld. Rd. SW16 4K 121
Curtis Ho. SE17 5D 86 (off Morecambe St.)
Curtis La. Wemb 5E 44
Curtis Rd. Eps 4J 147
Curtis Rd. Houn 7D 96
Curtis St. SE1 4F 87
Curtis Way. SE1 4F 87
Curtis Way. SE28 7B 74
Curtlington Ho. Edgw 2J 27 (off Burnt Oak B'way.)
Curve, The. W12 7C 64
Curwen Av. E7 4K 53
Curwen Rd. W12 2C 82
Curzon Av. Enf 5E 8
Curzon Av. Stan 1A 26
Curzon Ct. SW6 1K 101 (off Maltings Pl.)
Curzon Cres. NW10 7A 46
Curzon Cres. Bark 3K 73
Curzon Ga. W1 1E 84 (5H 165)
Curzon Pl. W1 1E 84 (5H 165)
Curzon Pl. Pinn 5A 24
Curzon Rd. N10 2F 31
Curzon Rd. W5 4B 62
Curzon Rd. T Hth 6A 140
Curzon St. W1 1E 84 (5H 165)
Cusack Clo. Twic 4K 115
Custance Ho. N1 2D 68 (1E 162) (off Provost Est.)
Custance St. N1 3D 68 (1E 162)
Custom House. 6A 72
Custom House. 7E 68 (3G 169)
Custom Ho. Reach. SE16 2B 88
Custom Ho. Wlk. EC3 7E 68 (3G 169)
Cutbush Ho. N7 5H 49
Cutcombe Rd. SE5 2C 104
Cuthberga Clo. Bark 7G 55
Cuthbert Gdns. SE25 3E 140
Cuthbert Harrowing Ho. EC1 4C 68 (4C 162) (off Golden La. Est.)
Cuthbert Ho. W2 5B 66 (5A 158) (off Hall Pl.)
Cuthbert Rd. E17 3E 34
Cuthbert Rd. N18 5B 18
Cuthbert Rd. Croy 2B 152
Cuthbert St. W2 5B 66 (5A 158)
Cuthill Wlk. SE5 1D 104
Cutlers Gdns. E1 6H 163
Cutlers Sq. E14 4C 88
Cutler St. E1 6E 68 (7H 163)
Cut, The. SE1 2A 86 (6K 167)
Cutthroat All. Rich 2C 116
Cutty Sark Clipper Ship. 6E 88
Cutty Sark Gdns. SE10 6E 88 (off King William Wlk.)
Cuxton. Orp 5G 145
Cuxton Clo. Bexh 5E 110
Cyclamen Clo. Hamp 6E 114
Cyclamen Way. Eps 5J 147
Cyclops M. E14 4C 88
Cygnet Av. Felt 7A 96
Cygnet Clo. NW10 5K 45
Cygnets, The. Felt 4C 114
Cygnet St. E1 4F 69 (3K 163)
Cygnet Way. Hay 5B 60
Cygnus Bus. Cen. NW10 5B 46
Cymbeline Ct. Harr 6K 25 (off Gayton Rd.)
Cynthia St. N1 2K 67 (1H 161)
Cyntra Pl. E8 7H 51
Cypress Av. Twic 7G 97
Cypress Gdns. SE4 5A 106
Cypress Ho. SE14 1K 105
Cypress Ho. SE16 2K 87 (off Woodland Cres.)
Cypress Pl. W1 4G 67 (4B 160)
Cypress Rd. SE25 2E 140
Cypress Rd. Harr 2H 25
Cypress Tree Clo. Sidc 1K 127
Cyprus. 7E 72
Cyprus Av. N3 2G 29
Cyprus Clo. N4 6B 32
Cyprus Gdns. N3 2G 29
Cyprus Pl. E2 2J 69
Cyprus Pl. E6 7E 72
Cyprus Rd. N3 2H 29
Cyprus Rd. N9 2A 18
Cyprus St. E2 2J 69 (in two parts)
Cyrena Rd. SE22 6F 105
Cyril Lodge. Sidc 4A 128
Cyril Mans. SW11 1D 102
Cyril Rd. Bexh 2E 110
Cyril Rd. Orp 7K 145
Cyrus Ho. EC1 4B 68 (3B 162) (off Cyrus St.)
Cyrus St. EC1 3B 162
Czar St. SE8 6C 88

Dabbs Hill La. N'holt 6D 42 (in two parts)
Dabbs La. EC1 4A 68 (4K 161) (off Farringdon Rd.)
Dabin Cres. SE10 1E 106
Dacca St. SE8 6B 88
Dace Rd. E3 1C 70
Dacre Av. Ilf 2E 36
Dacre Clo. Gnfd 2F 61
Dacre Gdns. SE13 4G 107
Dacre Ho. SW3 7B 170
Dacre Pk. SE13 3G 107
Dacre Pl. SE13 3G 107
Dacre Rd. E11 1H 53
Dacre Rd. E13 1K 71
Dacre Rd. Croy 7J 139
Dacres Ho. SW4 3F 103
Dacres Rd. SE23 2K 123
Dacre St. SW1 3H 85 (1C 172)
Dade Way. S'hall 5D 78
Daerwood Clo. Brom 1D 156
Daffodil Clo. Croy 1K 153
Daffodil Gdns. Ilf 5F 55
Daffodil Pl. Hamp 6E 114
Daffodil St. W12 7B 64
Dafforne Rd. SW17 3E 120
Da Gama Pl. E14 5C 88
Dagenham. 6G 57
Dagenham & Redbridge F.C. 5H 57
Dagenham Av. Dag 1E 74 (in two parts)
Dagenham Leisure Pk. Dag 1E 74
Dagenham Rd. E10 1B 52
Dagenham Rd. Dag 4J 57
Dagenham Rd. Rain 7K 57
Dagenham Rd. Romf 7K 39
Dagmar Av. Wemb 4F 45
Dagmar Ct. E14 3E 88
Dagmar Gdns. NW10 2F 65
Dagmar M. S'hall 3C 78 (off Dagmar Rd.)
Dagmar Pas. N1 1B 68 (off Cross St.)
Dagmar Rd. N4 7A 32
Dagmar Rd. N15 4D 32
Dagmar Rd. N22 1H 31
Dagmar Rd. SE5 1E 104
Dagmar Rd. SE25 5E 140
Dagmar Rd. Dag 7J 57
Dagmar Rd. King T 1F 135
Dagmar Rd. S'hall 3C 78
Dagmar Ter. N1 1B 68
Dagnall Pk. SE25 6E 140
Dagnall Rd. SE25 5E 140
Dagnall St. SW11 2D 102
Dagnan Rd. SW12 7F 103
Dagobert Ho. E1 5J 69 (off Smithy St.)
Dagonet Gdns. Brom 3J 125
Dagonet Rd. Brom 3J 125
Dahlia Gdns. Ilf 6F 55
Dahlia Gdns. Mitc 4H 139
Dahlia Rd. SE2 4B 92
Dahomey Rd. SW16 6G 121
Daimler Way. Wall 7J 151
Dain Ct. W8 4J 83 (off Lexham Gdns.)
Daines Clo. E12 3D 54
Dainford Clo. Brom 5F 125
Dainton Clo. Brom 1K 143
Daintry Clo. Harr 4A 26
Daintry Way. E9 6B 52
Dairsie Ct. Brom 1A 144
Dairsie Rd. SE9 3E 108
Dairy Clo. NW10 1C 64
Dairy Clo. Brom 7K 125
Dairy Clo. T Hth 2C 140
Dairy La. SE18 4D 90
Dairyman Clo. NW2 3F 47
Dairy M. SW9 3J 103
Dairy Wlk. SW19 4G 119
Daisy Clo. Croy 1K 153
Daisy Dobbings Wlk. N19 7J 31 (off Jessie Blythe La.)
Daisy La. SW6 3J 101
Daisy Rd. E16 4G 71
Daisy Rd. E18 2K 35
Dakota Clo. Wall 7K 151
Dakota Gdns. E6 4C 72
Dakota Gdns. N'holt 3C 60
Dalberg Rd. SW2 4A 104 (in two parts)
Dalberg Way. SE2 3D 92
Dalby Rd. SW18 4A 102
Dalbys Cres. N17 6K 17
Dalby St. NW5 6F 49
Dalcross Rd. Houn 2C 96
Dale Av. Edgw 1F 27
Dale Av. Houn 3C 96
Dalebury Rd. SW17 2D 120
Dale Clo. SE3 3J 107
Dale Clo. New Bar 6E 4
Dale Clo. Pinn 1K 23
Dale Ct. King T 7F 117 (off York Rd.)
Dale Dri. Hay 4H 59
Dale Gdns. Wfd G 4E 20
Dale Grn. Rd. N11 3A 16
Dale Gro. N12 5F 15
Daleham Dri. Uxb 6D 58
Daleham Gdns. NW3 5B 48
Daleham M. NW3 6B 48
Dalehead. NW1 2G 67 (1A 160) (off Harrington Sq.)
Dale Ho. NW8 1A 66 (off Boundary Rd.)
Dale Ho. SE4 4A 106
Dale Lodge. N6 6G 31
Dalemain M. E16 1J 89
Dale Pk. Av. Cars 2D 150
Dale Pk. Rd. SE19 1C 140
Dale Rd. NW5 5E 48
Dale Rd. SE17 6B 86

Dale Rd. Gnfd 5F 61
Dale Rd. Sun 7H 113
Dale Rd. Sutt 4H 149
Dale Rd. W on T 7H 131
Dale Row. W11 6G 65
Daleside Rd. SW16 5F 121
Daleside Rd. Eps 6K 147
Dale St. W4 5A 82
Dale, The. Kes 4B 156
Dale Vw. Av. E4 2K 19
Dale Vw. Cres. E4 2K 19
Dale Vw. Gdns. E4 3A 20
Daleview Rd. N15 6E 32
Dalewood Gdns. Wor Pk 2D 148
Dale Wood Rd. Orp 7J 145
Daley Ho. W12 6D 64
Daley St. E9 6K 51
Daley Thompson Way. SW8 2F 103
Dalgarno Gdns. W10 5E 64
Dalgarno Way. W10 4E 64
Dalgleish St. E14 6A 70
Daling Way. E3 1A 70
Dali Universe. 2K 85 (6G 167)
Dalkeith Ct. SW1 4H 85 (3D 172) (off Vincent St.)
Dalkeith Gro. Stan 5J 11
Dalkeith Ho. SW9 1B 104 (off Lothian Rd.)
Dalkeith Rd. SE21 1C 122
Dalkeith Rd. Ilf 3G 55
Dallas Rd. NW4 7C 28
Dallas Rd. SE26 3H 123
Dallas Rd. W5 5F 63
Dallas Rd. Sutt 6G 149
Dallas Ter. Hay 3H 77
Dallega Clo. Hay 7F 59
Dallinger Rd. SE12 6H 107
Dalling Rd. W6 4D 82
Dallington St. EC1 4B 68 (3B 162)
Dallin Rd. SE18 7F 91
Dallin Rd. Bexh 4D 110
Dalmain Rd. SE23 1K 123
Dalmally Rd. Croy 7F 141
Dalmeny Av. N7 4H 49
Dalmeny Av. SW16 2A 140
Dalmeny Clo. Wemb 6C 44
Dalmeny Cres. Houn 4H 97
Dalmeny Rd. N7 3H 49 (in three parts)
Dalmeny Rd. Cars 7E 150
Dalmeny Rd. Eri 1H 111
Dalmeny Rd. New Bar 6F 5
Dalmeny Rd. Wor Pk 3D 148
Dalmeyer Rd. NW10 6B 46
Dalmore Rd. SE21 2C 122
Dalo Lodge. E3 5C 70 (off Gale St.)
Dalrymple Clo. N14 7C 6
Dalrymple Rd. SE4 4A 106
Dalston. 6F 51
Dalston Gdns. Stan 1E 26
Dalston La. E8 6F 51
Dalton Av. Mitc 2C 138
Dalton Clo. Hay 4F 59
Dalton Ho. SE14 6K 87 (off John Williams Clo.)
Dalton Ho. SW1 5F 85 (5J 171) (off Ebury Bri. Rd.)
Dalton Ho. Stan 5F 11
Dalton Rd. W'stone 2H 25
Dalton St. SE27 2B 122
Dalwood St. SE5 1E 104
Daly Ct. E15 5D 52
Dalyell Rd. SW9 3K 103
Damascene Wlk. SE21 1C 122
Damask Cres. E16 4G 71
Damer Ter. SW10 7A 84
Dames Rd. E7 3J 53
Dame St. N1 2C 68
Damien Ct. E1 6H 69 (off Damien St.)
Damien St. E1 6H 69
Damon Clo. Sidc 3B 128
Damory Ho. SE16 4H 87 (off Abbeyfield Est.)
Damson Dri. Hay 7J 59
Damsonwood Rd. S'hall 3E 78
Danbrook Rd. SW16 1J 139
Danbury Clo. Romf 3D 38
Danbury Mans. Bark 7F 55 (off Whiting Av.)
Danbury M. Wall 4F 151
Danbury St. N1 2B 68
Danbury Way. Wfd G 6F 21
Danby Ct. Enf 3H 7 (off Horseshoe La.)
Danby Ho. E9 7J 51 (off Frampton Pk. Rd.)
Danby St. SE15 3F 105
Dancer Rd. SW6 1H 101
Dancer Rd. Rich 3G 99
Dando Cres. SE3 3K 107
Dandridge Clo. SE10 5H 89
Dandridge Ho. E1 5F 69 (5J 163) (off Lamb St.)
Danebury. New Ad 6E 154
Danebury Av. SW15 6A 100 (in two parts)
Daneby Rd. SE6 3D 124
Dane Clo. Bex 7G 111
Danecourt Gdns. Croy 3F 153
Danecroft Rd. SE24 5C 104
Danehill Wlk. Sidc 3A 128
Danehurst Gdns. Ilf 5C 36
Danehurst St. SW6 1G 101
Daneland. Barn 6J 5
Danemead Gro. N'holt 5F 43
Danemere St. SW15 3E 100
Dane Pl. E3 2A 70
Dane Rd. N18 3D 18
Dane Rd. SW19 1A 138
Dane Rd. W13 1C 80
Dane Rd. Ashf 6E 112
Dane Rd. Ilf 5G 55
Dane Rd. S'hall 7C 60
Danesbury Rd. Felt 1K 113
Danescombe. SE12 1J 125
Danes Ct. NW8 1D 66 (off St Edmund's Ter.)
Danes Ct. Wemb 3H 45
Danescourt Cres. Sutt 2A 150
Danescroft. NW4 5F 29
Danescroft Av. NW4 5F 29
Danescroft Gdns. NW4 5F 29
Danesdale Rd. E9 6A 52
Danesfield. SE5 6E 86 (off Albany Rd.)
Danes Ga. Harr 3J 25
Danes Ho. W10 5E 64 (off Sutton Way)
Danes Rd. Romf 7J 39
Dane St. WC1 5K 67 (6G 161)
Daneswood Av. SE6 3E 124
Danethorpe Rd. Wemb 6D 44
Danetree Clo. Eps 7J 147
Danetree Rd. Eps 7J 147
Danette Gdns. Dag 2G 57
Daneville Rd. SE5 1D 104
Dangan Rd. E11 6J 35
Daniel Bolt Clo. E14 5D 70
Daniel Clo. N18 4D 18
Daniel Clo. SW17 6C 120
Daniel Clo. Houn 7D 96
Daniel Ct. NW9 1A 28
Daniel Gdns. SE15 7F 87
Daniel Ho. N1 2D 68 (off Cranston Est.)
Daniell Way. Croy 1J 151
Daniel Pl. NW4 7D 28
Daniel Rd. W5 7F 63
Daniels Rd. SE15 3J 105
Danleigh Ct. N14 7C 6
Dan Leno Wlk. SW6 7K 83
Dansey Pl. W1 2C 166
Dansington Rd. Well 4A 110
Danson Cres. Well 3A 110
Danson Interchange. (Junct.) 5C 110
Danson La. Well 4B 110
Danson Mead. Well 3C 110
Danson Rd. SE17 5B 86
Danson Rd. Bex & Bexh 6C 110 (in two parts)
Danson Underpass. Sidc 6C 110 (in two parts)
Dante Pl. SE11 4B 86 (off Dante Rd.)
Dante Rd. SE11 4B 86
Danube Ct. SE15 7F 87 (off Daniel Gdns.)
Danube St. SW3 5C 84 (5D 170)
Danvers Ho. E1 6G 69 (off Christian St.)
Danvers Rd. N8 4H 31
Danvers St. SW3 6B 84 (7B 170)
Da Palma Ct. SW6 6J 83 (off Anselm Rd.)
Daphne Ct. Wor Pk 2A 148
Daphne Gdns. E4 3K 19
Daphne Ho. N22 1A 32 (off Acacia Rd.)
Daphne St. SW18 6A 102
Daplyn St. E1 5G 69 (5K 163)
D'Arblay St. W1 6G 67 (1B 166)
Darby Cres. Sun 2A 132
Darby Gdns. Sun 2A 132
Darcy Av. Wall 4G 151
Darcy Clo. N20 2G 15
D'Arcy Dri. Harr 4D 26
Darcy Gdns. Dag 1F 75
D'Arcy Gdns. Harr 4E 26
Darcy Ho. E8 1H 69 (off London Fields E. Side)
D'Arcy Pl. Brom 4J 143
Darcy Rd. SW16 2J 139
Darcy Rd. Iswth 1A 98
D'Arcy Rd. Sutt 4F 149
Dare Ct. E10 7E 34
Dare Gdns. Dag 3E 56
Darell Rd. Rich 3G 99
Darent Ho. NW8 5B 66 (5B 158) (off Church St. Est.)
Darent Ho. Brom 5F 125
Darenth Rd. N16 7F 33
Darenth Rd. Well 1A 110
Darfield. NW1 1G 67 (off Bayham St.)
Darfield Rd. SE4 5B 106
Darfield Way. W10 6F 65
Darfur St. SW15 3F 101
Dargate Clo. SE19 7F 123
Darien Ho. E1 5K 69 (off Shandy St.)
Darien Rd. SW11 3B 102
Daring Ho. E3 2A 70 (off Roman Rd.)
Dark Ho. Wlk. EC3 7D 68 (3G 169)
Darland Lake Nature Reserve. 3B 14
Darlands Dri. Barn 5A 4
Darlan Rd. SW6 7H 83
Darlaston Rd. SW19 7F 119
Darley Clo. Croy 6A 142
Darley Dri. N Mald 2K 135
Darley Gdns. Mord 6A 138
Darley Ho. SE11 6G 173
Darley Rd. N9 1A 18
Darley Rd. SW11 6D 102
Darling Ho. Twic 6D 98
Darling Rd. SE4 3C 106
Darling Row. E1 4H 69
Darlington Ct. SE12 1H 125
Darlington Ho. SW8 7H 85 (off Hemans St.)
Darlington Rd. SE27 5B 122
Darmaine Clo. S Croy 7C 152
Darnall Ho. SE10 1E 106 (off Royal Hill)
Darnay Ho. SE16 3G 87 (7K 169)
Darndale Clo. E17 2B 34
Darnley Ho. E14 6A 70 (off Camdenhurst St.)
Darnley Rd. E9 6J 51
Darnley Rd. Wfd G 1J 35
Darnley Ter. W11 1F 83
Darrell Charles Ct. Uxb 7A 40
Darrell Rd. SE22 5G 105
Darren Clo. N4 7K 31
Darris Clo. Hay 4C 60
Darsley Dri. SW8 1H 103
Dartford Av. N9 6D 8
Dartford By-Pass. Bex & Dart 7K 111
Dartford Gdns. Chad H 5B 38
Dartford Heath. (Junct.) 1K 129
Dartford Ho. SE1 4F 87 (off Longfield Est.)
Dartford Rd. Bex 1J 129
Dartford St. SE17 6C 86
Dartington. NW1 1G 67 (off Plender St.)
Dartington Ho. SW8 2H 103 (off Union Gro.)
Dartington Ho. W2 5K 65 (off Senior St.)
Dartle Ct. SE16 2G 87 (off Scott Lidgett Cres.)
Dartmoor Wlk. E14 4C 88 (off Charnwood Gdns.)
Dartmouth Clo. W11 6H 65
Dartmouth Ct. SE10 1E 106
Dartmouth Gro. SE10 1E 106
Dartmouth Hill. SE10 1E 106
Dartmouth Park. 3F 49
Dartmouth Pk. Av. NW5 3F 49
Dartmouth Pk. Hill. N19 & NW5 1F 49
Dartmouth Pk. Rd. NW5 4F 49
Dartmouth Pl. SE23 2J 123
Dartmouth Pl. W4 6A 82
Dartmouth Rd. NW2 6F 47
Dartmouth Rd. NW4 6C 28
Dartmouth Rd. SE26 & SE23 3H 123
Dartmouth Rd. Brom 7J 143
Dartmouth Rd. Ruis 3J 41
Dartmouth Row. SE10 2E 106
Dartmouth St. SW1 2H 85 (7D 166)
Dartmouth Ter. SE10 1F 107
Dartnell Rd. Croy 7F 141
Darton Ct. W3 1J 81
Dartrey Tower. SW10 7A 84 (off Worlds End Est.)
Dartrey Wlk. SW10 7A 84
Dart St. W10 3G 65
Darville Rd. N16 3F 51
Darwell Clo. E6 2E 72
Darwin Clo. N11 3A 16
Darwin Ct. NW1 1E 66 (in three parts)
Darwin Dri. S'hall 6F 61
Darwin Ho. SW1 7A 172
Darwin Rd. N22 1B 32
Darwin Rd. W5 5C 80
Darwin Rd. Well 3K 109
Darwin St. SE17 4D 86 (in two parts)
Daryngton Dri. Gnfd 2H 61
Daryngton Ho. SW8 7J 85 (off Hartington Rd.)
Dashwood Clo. Bexh 5G 111
Dashwood Rd. N8 6K 31
Dassett Rd. SE27 5B 122
Data Point Bus. Cen. E16 4F 71
Datchelor Pl. SE5 1D 104
Datchet Ho. NW1 3F 67 (1K 159) (off Augustus St.)
Datchet Rd. SE6 2B 124
Datchworth Ct. Enf 5K 7
Datchworth Ho. N1 7B 50 (off Sutton Est., The)
Date St. SE17 5D 86
Daubeney Gdns. N17 7H 17
Daubeney Rd. E5 4A 52
Daubeney Rd. N17 7H 17
Daubeney Tower. SE8 5B 88 (off Bowditch)
Dault Rd. SW18 6A 102
Dauncey Ho. SE1 7A 168
Davema Clo. Chst 1E 144
Davenant Rd. N19 2H 49
Davenant Rd. Croy 4B 152
Davenant St. E1 5G 69
Davenport Clo. Tedd 6A 116
Davenport Ho. SE11 4A 86 (3J 173) (off Walnut Tree Wlk.)
Davenport Lodge. Houn 7C 78
Davenport Rd. SE6 6D 106
Davenport Rd. Sidc 2E 128
Daventer Dri. Stan 7E 10
Daventry Av. E17 6C 34
Daventry St. NW1 5C 66 (5C 158)
Daver Ct. SW3 5C 84 (5D 170)
Daver Ct. W5 4D 62
Davern Clo. SE10 4H 89
Davey Clo. N7 6K 49
Davey Clo. N13 5E 16
Davey Rd. E9 7C 52
Davey's Ct. WC2 2E 166
Davey St. SE15 6F 87
David Av. Gnfd 3J 61
David Clo. Hay 7G 77
David Coffer Ct. Belv 4H 93
David Ct. N20 3F 15
Davidge Ho. SE1 2A 86 (7K 167) (off Coral St.)
Davidge St. SE1 2B 86 (7A 168)
David Ho. E14 5D 70 (off Uamvar St.)
David Ho. SW8 7J 85 (off Wyvil Rd.)
David Ho. Sidc 3A 128
David Lee Point. E15 1G 71 (off Leather Gdns.)
David Lloyd Leisure. 2B 8
David M. W1 5D 66 (5F 159)
David Rd. Dag 2E 56
David's Ct. S'hall 6G 61 (off Whitecote Rd.)
Davidson Gdns. SW8 7J 85
Davidson La. Harr 7K 25
Davidson Rd. Croy 1E 152
Davidson Terraces. E7 5K 53 (off Claremont Rd., in two parts)
Davidson Tower. Brom 5K 125
David's Rd. SE23 1J 123
David St. E15 6F 53
David Twigg Clo. King T 1E 134
Davies Clo. Croy 6F 141
Davies La. E11 2G 53
Davies M. W1 7F 67 (2J 165)
Davies St. W1 6F 67 (1J 165)
Davies Wlk. Iswth 1H 97
Da Vinci Ct. SE16 5H 87 (off Rossetti Rd.)
Davington Gdns. Dag 5B 56
Davington Rd. Dag 6B 56
Davinia Clo. Wfd G 6J 21
Davis Ho. W12 7D 64 (off White City Est.)
Davis Rd. W3 1B 82
Davis Rd. Chess 4G 147
Davis St. E13 2K 71
Davisville Rd. W12 2C 82
Davmor Ct. Bren 5C 80

Dawes Av. Iswth 5A 98
Dawes Ho. SE17 4D 86 (off Orb St.)
Dawes Rd. SW6 7G 83
Dawe's Rd. Uxb 2A 58
Dawes St. SE17 5D 86
Dawley Av. Uxb 5E 58
Dawley Pde. Hay 7E 58
Dawley Pk. Hay 2F 77
Dawley Rd. Hay 7E 58
Dawlish Av. N13 4D 16
Dawlish Av. SW18 2K 119
Dawlish Av. Gnfd 2A 62
Dawlish Dri. Ilf 4J 55
Dawlish Dri. Pinn 5C 24
Dawlish Dri. Ruis 2J 41
Dawlish Rd. E10 1E 52
Dawlish Rd. N17 3G 33
Dawlish Rd. NW2 6F 47
Dawnay Gdns. SW18 2B 120
Dawnay Rd. SW18 2A 120
Dawn Clo. Houn 3C 96
Dawn Cres. E15 1F 71
Dawpool Rd. NW2 2B 46
Daws Hill. E4 3K 9
Daws La. NW7 5G 13
Dawson Av. Bark 7J 55
Dawson Clo. SE18 4G 91
Dawson Clo. Hay 5F 59
Dawson Gdns. Bark 7K 55
Dawson Ho. E2 3J 69 (off Sceptre Rd.)
Dawson Pl. W2 7J 65
Dawson Rd. NW2 5E 46
Dawson Rd. King T 3F 135
Dawson St. E2 2F 69 (1K 163)
Dawson Ter. N9 7D 8
Daybrook Rd. SW19 2K 137
Day Ho. SE5 7C 86 (off Bethwin Rd.)
Daylesford Av. SW15 4C 100
Daymer Gdns. Pinn 4K 23
Daysbrook Rd. SW2 1K 121
Days La. Sidc 7J 109
Dayton Gro. SE15 1J 105
Deaconess Ct. N15 4F 33 (off Tottenham Grn. E.)
Deacon Est., The. E4 6G 19
Deacon Ho. SE11 4K 85 (4H 173) (off Black Prince Rd.)
Deacon M. N1 7D 50
Deacon Rd. NW2 5C 46
Deacon Rd. King T 1F 135
Deacons Clo. Pinn 2K 23
Deacons Ct. Twic 2K 115
Deacon's Ri. N2 5B 30
Deacons Wlk. Hamp 4E 114
Deacon Way. SE17 4C 86
Deacon Way. Wfd G 7J 21
Deal Ct. NW9 2B 28 (off Hazel Clo.)
Deal Ct. S'hall 6G 61 (off Haldane Rd.)
Deal Ho. SE15 6K 87 (off Lovelinch La.)
Deal M. W5 4D 80
Deal Porters Wlk. SE16 2K 87
Deal Porters Way. SE16 3J 87
Deal Rd. SW17 6E 120
Deal's Gateway. SE10 1C 106
Deal St. E1 5G 69
Dealtry Rd. SW15 4E 100
Deal Wlk. SW9 7A 86
Dean Abbott Ho. SW1 4H 85 (3C 172) (off Vincent St.)
Dean Bradley St. SW1 3J 85 (2E 172)
Dean Clo. E9 5J 51
Dean Clo. SE16 1K 87
Dean Clo. Uxb 7B 40
Dean Ct. SW8 7J 85 (off Thorncroft St.)
Dean Ct. W3 6K 63
Dean Ct. Edgw 6C 12
Dean Ct. Romf 5K 39
Dean Ct. Wemb 3B 44
Deancross St. E1 6J 69
Dean Dri. Stan 2E 26
Deane Av. Ruis 5A 42
Deane Ct. N'wd 1G 23
Deane Cft. Rd. Pinn 6A 24
Deanery Clo. N2 4C 30
Deanery M. W1 4H 165
Deanery Rd. E15 6G 53
Deanery St. W1 1E 84 (4H 165)
Deane Way. Ruis 6K 23
Dean Farrar St. SW1 3H 85 (1D 172)
Deanfield Gdns. Croy 4D 152
Dean Gdns. E17 4F 35
Deanhill Ct. SW14 4H 99
Deanhill Rd. SW14 4H 99
Dean Ho. E1 6J 69 (off Tarling St.)
Dean Ho. SE14 7A 88 (off New Cross Rd.)
Dean Rd. NW2 6E 46
Dean Rd. SE28 1A 92
Dean Rd. Croy 4D 152
Dean Rd. Hamp 5E 114
Dean Rd. Houn 5F 97
Dean Ryle St. SW1 4J 85 (3E 172)
Deansbrook Clo. Edgw 7D 12
Deansbrook Rd. Edgw 7C 12
Dean's Bldgs. SE17 4D 86
Deans Clo. W4 6H 81
Deans Clo. Croy 3F 153
Deans Clo. Edgw 6D 12
Dean's Ct. EC4 6B 68 (1B 168)
Deanscroft Av. NW9 1J 45
Deans Dri. N13 6G 17
Deans Dri. Edgw 5E 12
Deans Ga. Clo. SE23 3K 123
Deanshanger Ho. SE8 4K 87 (off Chilton Gro.)
Deans La. W4 6H 81 (off Deans Clo.)
Deans La. Edgw 6D 12
Dean's M. W1 6F 67 (7K 159)
Deans Rd. W7 1K 79
Deans Rd. Sutt 3K 149
Dean Stanley St. SW1 3J 85 (2E 172)
Deanston Wharf. E16 2K 89 (in two parts)
Dean St. E7 5J 53
Dean St. W1 6H 67 (7C 160)
Deansway. N2 4B 30
Deansway. N9 3K 17
Deans Way. Edgw 5D 12
Deanswood. N11 6C 16
Dean's Yd. SW1 1D 172
Dean Trench St. SW1 3J 85 (2E 172)
Dean Wlk. Edgw 6D 12
Dean Way. S'hall 2F 79
Dearne Clo. Stan 5F 11
Dearn Gdns. Mitc 3C 138
Dearsley Rd. Enf 3B 8
Deason St. E15 1E 70
Deauville Ct. SE16 2K 87 (off Eleanor Clo.)
Deauville Ct. SW4 6G 103
De Barowe M. N5 4B 50
Debdale Ho. E2 1G 69 (off Whiston Rd.)
Debden. N17 2D 32 (off Gloucester Rd.)
Debden Clo. King T 5D 116
Debden Clo. Wfd G 7G 21
De Beauvoir Ct. N1 7D 50 (off Northchurch Rd.)
De Beauvoir Cres. N1 1E 68
De Beauvoir Est. N1 1E 68
De Beauvoir Pl. N1 6E 50
De Beauvoir Rd. N1 1E 68
De Beauvoir Sq. N1 7E 50
De Beauvoir Town. 1E 68
Debenham Ct. E8 1G 69 (off Pownall Rd.)
Debham Ct. NW2 3E 46
Debnams Rd. SE16 4J 87
De Bohun Av. N14 6A 6
Deborah Clo. Iswth 1J 97
Deborah Ct. E18 3K 35 (off Victoria Rd.)
Deborah Cres. Ruis 7F 23
Deborah Lodge. Edgw 1H 27
Debrabant Clo. Eri 6K 93
De Brome Rd. Felt 1A 114
De Bruin Ct. E14 5E 88 (off Ferry St.)
De Burgh Rd. SW19 7A 120
Debussy. NW9 2B 28
Decima St. SE1 3E 86 (7G 169)
Decimus Clo. T Hth 4D 140
Deck Clo. SE16 1K 87
Decoy Av. NW11 5G 29
De Crespigny Pk. SE5 2D 104
Dee Ct. W7 6H 61 (off Hobbayne Rd.)
Deeley Rd. SW8 1H 103
Deena Clo. W3 6F 63
Deepdale. SW19 4F 119
Deepdale Av. Brom 4H 143
Deepdale Clo. N11 6K 15
Deepdale Ct. S Croy 4D 152 (off Birdhurst Av.)
Deep Dene. W5 4F 63
Deepdene Av. Croy 3F 153
Deepdene Clo. E11 4J 35
Deepdene Ct. N21 6G 7
Deepdene Gdns. SW2 7K 103
Deepdene Point. SE23 3K 123
Deepdene Rd. SE5 4D 104
Deepdene Rd. Well 3A 110
Deepway. SE8 5A 88 (off Evelyn St.)
Deepwell Clo. Iswth 1A 98
Deepwood La. Gnfd 3H 61
Deerbrook Rd. SE24 1B 122
Deerdale Rd. SE24 4C 104
Deerfield Cotts. NW9 5B 28
Deerhurst Clo. Felt 4K 113
Deerhurst Cres. Hamp H 5G 115
Deerhurst Ho. SE15 6G 87 (off Haymerle Rd.)
Deerhurst Rd. NW2 6F 47
Deerhurst Rd. SW16 5K 121
Deerings Dri. Pinn 5J 23
Deerleap Gro. E4 5J 9
Dee Rd. Rich 4F 99
Deer Pk. Clo. King T 7H 117
Deer Pk. Gdns. Mitc 4B 138
Deer Pk. Rd. SW19 2K 137
Deer Pk. Way. W Wick 2H 155
Deeside Rd. SW17 3B 120
Dee St. E14 6E 70
Defiance Wlk. SE18 3D 90
Defiant. NW9 2B 28 (off Further Acre)
Defiant Way. Wall 7J 151
Defoe Av. Rich 7G 81
Defoe Clo. SE16 2B 88
Defoe Clo. SW17 6C 120
Defoe Ho. EC2 5D 162
Defoe Pl. EC2 5C 68 (5C 162) (off Beech St.)
Defoe Pl. SW17 4D 120
Defoe Rd. N16 3E 50
De Frene Rd. SE26 4K 123
Degema Rd. Chst 5F 127
Dehar Cres. NW9 7B 28
De Havilland Clo. N'holt 3B 60
De Havilland Rd. Edgw 2H 27
De Havilland Rd. Houn 7A 78
De Havilland Way. Stanw 6A 94
Dekker Ho. SE5 7D 86 (off Elmington Est.)
Dekker Rd. SE21 6E 104
Delacourt Rd. SE3 7K 89
Delafield Ho. E1 6G 69 (off Christian St.)
Delafield Rd. SE7 5K 89
Delaford Rd. SE16 5H 87
Delaford St. SW6 7G 83
Delamare Cres. Croy 6J 141
Delamere Gdns. NW7 6E 12
Delamere Rd. SW20 1F 137
Delamere Rd. W5 2E 80
Delamere Rd. Hay 7B 60
Delamere St. W2 5K 65
Delamere Ter. W2 5K 65
Delancey Pas. NW1 1F 67 (off Delancey St.)
Delancey St. NW1 1F 67
Delancey Studios. NW1 1F 67
Delany Ho. SE10 6E 88 (off Thames St.)
Delarch Ho. SE1 7A 168
De Laune St. SE17 5B 86 (6K 173)
Delaware Mans. W9 4K 65 (off Delaware Rd.)
Delaware Rd. W9 4K 65
Delawyk Cres. SE24 6C 104
Delcombe Av. Wor Pk 1E 148
Delderfield Ho. Romf 2K 39 (off Portnoi Clo.)
Delft Ho. King T 7F 117 (off Acre Rd.)
Delft Way. SE22 5E 104
Delhi Rd. Enf 7A 8
Delhi St. N1 1J 67 (in two parts)
Delia St. SW18 7K 101
Delisle Rd. SE28 2J 91 (in two parts)
Delius Gro. E15 2F 71
Della Path. E5 3G 51
Dellbow Rd. Felt 5K 95
Dell Clo. E15 1F 71
Dell Clo. Wall 4G 151
Dell Clo. Wfd G 3E 20
Dell Farm Rd. Ruis 5F 23
Dellfield Clo. Beck 1E 142
Dell La. Eps 5C 148
Dellors Clo. Barn 5A 4
Dellow Clo. Ilf 7H 37
Dellow Ho. E1 7H 69 (off Dellow St.)
Dellow St. E1 7H 69
Dell Rd. Eps 6C 148
Dell Rd. W Dray 4B 76
Dells Clo. E4 7J 9
Dells Clo. Tedd 6K 115
Dell's M. SW1 4B 172
Dell, The. SE2 5A 92
Dell, The. SE19 1F 141
Dell, The. Bex 1K 129
Dell, The. Bren 6C 80
Dell, The. Felt 7K 95
Dell, The. Pinn 2B 24
Dell, The. Wemb 5B 44
Dell, The. Wfd G 3E 20
Dell Wlk. N Mald 2A 136
Dell Way. W13 6C 62
Dellwood Gdns. Ilf 3E 36
Delmaine Ho. E14 6A 70 (off Maroon St.)
Delmare Clo. SW9 4K 103
Delme Cres. SE3 2K 107
Delmerend Ho. SW3 5C 84 (5C 170) (off Ixworth Pl.)
Delmey Clo. Croy 3F 153
Deloraine Ho. SE8 1C 106
Delorme St. W6 6F 83
Delroy Ct. N20 7F 5
Delta Building. E14 6E 70 (off Ashton St.)
Delta Cen. Wemb 1F 63
Delta Clo. Wor Pk 3B 148
Delta Ct. NW2 2C 46
Delta Est. E2 3G 69
Delta Gro. N'holt 3B 60
Delta Pk. SW18 4K 101
Delta Point. Croy 1C 152 (off Wellesley Rd.)
Delta Rd. Wor Pk 3A 148
Delta St. E2 3G 69 (1K 163)
De Luci Rd. Eri 5J 93
De Lucy St. SE2 4B 92
Delvan Clo. SE18 7E 90
Delvers Mead. Dag 4J 57
Delverton Ho. SE17 5B 86 (off Delverton Rd.)
Delverton Rd. SE17 5B 86
Delvino Rd. SW6 1J 101
Demesne Rd. Wall 4H 151
Demeta Clo. Wemb 3J 45
De Montfort Pde. SW16 3J 121
De Montfort Rd. SW16 3J 121
De Morgan Rd. SW6 3K 101
Dempster Clo. Surb 1C 146
Dempster Rd. SW18 5A 102
Denbar Pde. Romf 4H 39
Denberry Dri. Sidc 3B 128
Denbigh Clo. NW10 7A 46
Denbigh Clo. W11 7H 65
Denbigh Clo. Chst 6D 126
Denbigh Clo. Ruis 2H 41
Denbigh Clo. S'hall 6D 60
Denbigh Clo. Sutt 5H 149
Denbigh Ct. E6 3B 72
Denbigh Ct. W7 5K 61 (off Copley Clo.)
Denbigh Dri. Hay 2E 76
Denbigh Gdns. Rich 5F 99
Denbigh Ho. SW1 3D 84 (1F 171) (off Hans Pl.)
Denbigh Ho. W11 7H 65 (off Westbourne Gro.)
Denbigh M. SW1 4A 172
Denbigh Pl. SW1 5G 85 (5A 172)
Denbigh Rd. E6 3B 72
Denbigh Rd. W11 7H 65
Denbigh Rd. W13 7B 62
Denbigh Rd. Houn 2F 97
Denbigh Rd. S'hall 6D 60
Denbigh St. SW1 4G 85 (4A 172) (in two parts)
Denbigh Ter. W11 7H 65
Denbridge Rd. Brom 2D 144
Denby Ct. SE11 3H 173
Dence Ho. E2 3G 69 (2K 163) (off Turin St.)
Denchworth Ho. SW9 2A 104
Dencliffe. Ashf 5C 112
Den Clo. Beck 3F 143
Dene Av. Houn 3D 96
Dene Av. Sidc 7B 110
Dene Clo. SE4 3A 106
Dene Clo. Brom 1H 155
Dene Clo. Dart 4K 129
Dene Clo. Wor Pk 2B 148
Dene Ct. W5 5C 62
Dene Ct. S Croy 5C 152 (off Warham Rd.)
Denecroft Cres. Uxb 1D 58
Dene Gdns. Stan 5H 11
Dene Gdns. Th Dit 2A 146
Dene Ho. N14 7C 6
Denehurst Gdns. NW4 6E 28
Denehurst Gdns. W3 1H 81
Denehurst Gdns. Rich 4G 99
Denehurst Gdns. Twic 7H 97
Denehurst Gdns. Wfd G 4E 20
Dene Rd. N11 1J 15
Dene Rd. Buck H 1G 21
Denesmead. SE24 5C 104
Dene, The. W13 5B 62
Dene, The. Croy 4K 153
Dene, The. Wemb 4E 44

Dene, The. W Mol 5D 132
Denewood. New Bar 5F 5
Denewood Rd. N6 6D 30
Denford St. SE10 5H 89 (off Glenforth St.)
Dengie Wlk. N1 1C 68 (off Basire St.)
Denham Clo. Well 3C 110
Denham Ct. SE26 3H 123 (off Kirkdale)
Denham Ct. S'hall 7G 61 (off Baird Av.)
Denham Cres. Mitc 4D 138
Denham Dri. Ilf 6G 37
Denham Ho. W12 7D 64 (off White City Est.)
Denham Rd. N20 3J 15
Denham Rd. Felt 7A 96
Denham St. SE10 5J 89
Denham Way. Bark 1K 73
Denholme Rd. W9 3H 65
Denison Clo. N2 3A 30
Denison Ho. E14 6C 70 (off Farrance St.)
Denison Rd. SW19 6B 120
Denison Rd. W5 4C 62
Denison Rd. Felt 4H 113
Deniston Av. Bex 1E 128
Denis Way. SW4 3H 103
Denland Ho. SW8 7K 85 (off Dorset Rd.)
Denleigh Gdns. N21 7F 7
Denleigh Gdns. Th Dit 6J 133
Denman Dri. NW11 5J 29
Denman Dri. Ashf 6D 112
Denman Dri. Clay 5A 146
Denman Dri. N. NW11 5J 29
Denman Dri. S. NW11 5J 29
Denman Pl. W1 2C 166
Denman Rd. SE15 1F 105
Denman St. W1 7H 67 (3C 166)
Denmark Av. SW19 7G 119
Denmark Ct. Mord 6J 137
Denmark Gdns. Cars 3D 150
Denmark Gro. N1 2A 68
Denmark Hill. SE5 1D 104
Denmark Hill Dri. NW9 3C 28
Denmark Hill Est. SE5 4D 104
Denmark Mans. SE5 2C 104 (off Coldharbour La.)
Denmark Path. SE25 5H 141
Denmark Pl. WC2 6H 67 (7D 160)
Denmark Rd. N8 4A 32
Denmark Rd. NW6 2H 65 (in two parts)
Denmark Rd. SE5 1C 104
Denmark Rd. SE25 5G 141
Denmark Rd. SW19 6F 119
Denmark Rd. W13 7B 62
Denmark Rd. Brom 1K 143
Denmark Rd. Cars 3D 150
Denmark Rd. King T 3E 134
Denmark Rd. Twic 3H 115
Denmark St. E11 3G 53
Denmark St. E13 5K 71
Denmark St. N17 1H 33
Denmark St. WC2 6H 67 (7D 160)
Denmark Ter. N2 3D 30
Denmark Wlk. SE27 4C 122
Denmead Ho. SW15 6B 100 (off Highcliffe Dri.)
Denmead Rd. Croy 1B 152
Denmead Way. SE15 7F 87 (off Pentridge St.)
Denmore Ct. Wall 5F 151
Dennan Rd. Surb 1F 147
Dennard Way. F'boro 4E 156
Denner Rd. E4 2H 19
Denne Ter. E8 1F 69
Dennett Rd. Croy 1A 152
Dennett's Gro. SE14 1J 105
Denning Av. Croy 4A 152
Denning Clo. NW8 3A 66 (1A 158)
Denning Clo. Hamp 5D 114
Denning Point. E1 6F 69 (7K 163) (off Commercial St.)
Denning Rd. NW3 4B 48
Dennington Clo. E5 2J 51
Dennington Pk. Rd. NW6 6J 47
Denningtons, The. Wor Pk 2A 148
Dennis Av. Wemb 5F 45
Dennis Clo. Ashf 7F 113
Dennis Gdns. Stan 5H 11
Dennis Ho. Sutt 4J 149
Dennis La. Stan 3G 11
Dennison Point. E15 7E 52
Dennis Pde. N14 1C 16
Dennis Pk. Cres. SW20 1G 137
Dennis Reeve Clo. Mitc 1D 138
Dennis Rd. E Mol 4G 133
Denny Clo. E6 5C 72
Denny Cres. SE11 5A 86 (5K 173)
Denny Gdns. Dag 7B 56
Denny Rd. N9 1C 18
Denny St. SE11 5A 86 (5K 173)
Den Rd. Brom 3F 143
Densham Ho. NW8 2B 66 (1B 158) (off Cochrane St.)
Densham Rd. E15 1G 71
Densole Clo. Beck 1A 142
Denstone Ho. SE15 6G 87 (off Haymerle Rd.)
Densworth Gro. N9 2D 18
Dent Ho. SE17 4E 86 (off Tatum St.)
Denton. NW1 6E 48
Denton Ho. N1 7B 50 (off Halton Rd.)
Denton Rd. N8 5K 31
Denton Rd. N18 4K 17
Denton Rd. Bex 2K 129
Denton Rd. Twic 6D 98
Denton Rd. Well 7C 92
Denton St. SW18 6K 101
Denton Ter. Bex 2K 129
Denton Way. E5 3K 51
Dents Rd. SW11 6D 102
Denver Clo. Orp 6J 145
Denver Rd. N16 7E 32
Denwood. SE23 3K 123
Denyer St. SW3 4C 84 (4D 170)
Denys Ho. EC1 5A 68 (5J 161) (off Bourne Est.)
Denziloe Av. Uxb 3D 58
Denzil Rd. NW10 5B 46
Deodar Rd. SW15 4G 101
Deodora Clo. N20 3H 15
Depot App. NW2 4F 47
Depot Rd. W12 7E 64
Depot Rd. Houn 3H 97
Depot St. SE5 6D 86
Deptford. 7C 88
Deptford B'way. SE8 1C 106
Deptford Bus. Pk. SE15 6J 87
Deptford Chu. St. SE8 6C 88 (in two parts)
Deptford Creek Bri. SE8 6D 88 (off Creek Rd.)
Deptford Ferry Rd. E14 4C 88
Deptford Grn. SE8 6C 88
Deptford High St. SE8 6C 88
Deptford Pk. Bus. Cen. SE8 5A 88
Deptford Strand. SE8 4B 88
Deptford Trad. Est. SE8 5A 88
Deptford Wharf. SE8 4B 88 (in two parts)
De Quincey Ho. SW1 5G 85 (6A 172) (off Lupus St.)
De Quincey M. E16 1J 89
De Quincey Rd. N17 1D 32
Derby Av. N12 5F 15
Derby Av. Harr 1H 25
Derby Av. Romf 6J 39
Derby Ga. SW1 2J 85 (6E 166) (in two parts)
Derby Hill. SE23 2J 123
Derby Hill Cres. SE23 2J 123
Derby Ho. SE11 3J 173
Derby Ho. Pinn 2B 24
Derby Lodge. N3 2H 29
Derby Lodge. WC1 3K 67 (1G 161) (off Britannia St.)
Derby Rd. E7 7B 54
Derby Rd. E9 1K 69
Derby Rd. E18 1H 35
Derby Rd. N18 5D 18
Derby Rd. SW14 4H 99
Derby Rd. SW19 7J 119
Derby Rd. Croy 1B 152
Derby Rd. Enf 5C 8
Derby Rd. Gnfd 1F 61
Derby Rd. Houn 4F 97
Derby Rd. Surb 1G 147
Derby Rd. Sutt 6H 149
Derbyshire St. E2 3G 69 (in two parts)
Derby St. W1 1E 84 (5H 165)
Dereham Ho. SE4 4K 105 (off Frendsbury Rd.)
Dereham Pl. EC2 3E 68 (2H 163)
Dereham Rd. Bark 5K 55
Derek Av. Eps 6G 147
Derek Av. Wall 4F 151
Derek Av. Wemb 7H 45
Derek Clo. Ewe 5H 147
Derek Walcott Clo. SE24 5B 104
Dericote St. E8 1H 69
Deridene Clo. Stanw 6A 94
Derifall Clo. E6 5D 72
Dering Pl. S Croy 4C 152
Dering Rd. Croy 4C 152
Dering St. W1 6F 67 (1J 165)
Dering Yd. W1 6F 67 (1K 165)
Derinton Rd. SW17 4D 120
Derley Rd. S'hall 3A 78
Dermody Gdns. SE13 5F 107
Dermody Rd. SE13 5F 107
Deronda Est. SW2 1B 122
Deronda Rd. SE24 1B 122
Deroy Clo. Cars 6D 150
Derrick Gdns. SE7 3A 90
Derrick Rd. Beck 3B 142
Derry Rd. Croy 3J 151
Derry St. W8 2K 83
Dersingham Av. E12 4D 54
Dersingham Rd. NW2 3G 47
Derwent. NW1 3G 67 (2A 160) (off Robert St.)
Derwent Av. N18 5J 17
Derwent Av. NW7 6E 12
Derwent Av. NW9 5A 28
Derwent Av. SW15 4A 118
Derwent Av. Barn 1J 15
Derwent Av. Uxb 2C 40
Derwent Clo. Felt 1H 113
Derwent Ct. SE16 2K 87 (off Eleanor Clo.)
Derwent Cres. N12 3F 15
Derwent Cres. Bexh 2G 111
Derwent Cres. Stan 2C 26
Derwent Dri. Hay 5G 59
Derwent Dri. Orp 7H 145
Derwent Gdns. Ilf 4C 36
Derwent Gdns. Wemb 7C 26
Derwent Gro. SE22 4F 105
Derwent Ho. E3 4B 70 (off Southern Gro.)
Derwent Ho. SE20 2H 141 (off Derwent Rd.)
Derwent Ho. SW7 4A 84 (3A 170) (off Cromwell Rd.)
Derwent Lodge. Iswth 2H 97
Derwent Lodge. Wor Pk 2D 148
Derwent Ri. NW9 6A 28
Derwent Rd. N13 4E 16
Derwent Rd. SE20 2G 141
Derwent Rd. SW20 5F 137
Derwent Rd. W5 3C 80
Derwent Rd. S'hall 6D 60
Derwent Rd. Twic 6F 97
Derwent St. SE10 5G 89
Derwent Wlk. Wall 7F 151
Derwentwater Rd. W3 1J 81
Derwent Yd. W13 3C 80 (off Derwent Rd.)
De Salis Rd. Uxb 4E 58
Desborough Clo. W2 5K 65
Desborough Clo. Shep 7C 130
Desborough Ho. W14 6H 83 (off N. End Rd.)
Desenfans Rd. SE21 6E 104
Desford Ct. Ashf 2C 112
Desford Rd. E16 4G 71
Desford Way. Ashf 2B 112
Design Mus. 2F 87 (6K 169)
Desmond Ho. Barn 6H 5
Desmond St. SE14 6A 88
Despard Rd. N19 1G 49
Dethick Ct. E3 1A 70
Detling Ho. SE17 4E 86 (off Congreve St.)
Detling Rd. Brom 5J 125
Detling Rd. Eri 7K 93
Detmold Rd. E5 2J 51
Devalls Clo. E6 7F 73
Devana End. Cars 3D 150
Devas Rd. SW20 1E 136
Devas St. E3 4D 70
Devenay Rd. E15 7H 53
Devenish Rd. SE2 2A 92
Deventer Cres. SE22 5E 104
De Vere Gdns. W8 2A 84
De Vere Gdns. Ilf 2D 54
Deverell St. SE1 3D 86
De Vere M. W8 3A 84 (off De Vere Gdns.)
Devereux Ct. WC2 1J 167
Devereux La. SW13 7D 82
Devereux Rd. SW11 6D 102
Deveron Way. Romf 1K 39
Devey Clo. King T 7B 118
Devitt Ho. E14 7D 70 (off Wade's Pl.)
Devizes St. N1 1D 68
Devon Av. Twic 1G 115
Devon Clo. N17 3F 33
Devon Clo. Buck H 2E 20
Devon Clo. Gnfd 1C 62
Devon Ct. W7 5K 61 (off Copley Clo.)
Devon Ct. Hamp 7E 114
Devoncroft Gdns. Twic 7A 98
Devon Gdns. N4 6B 32
Devon Ho. E17 2B 34
Devonhurst Pl. W4 5K 81
Devonia Gdns. N18 6H 17
Devonia Rd. N1 2B 68
Devon Mans. SE1 2F 87 (6J 169) (off Tooley St.)
Devon Mans. Harr 5C 26 (off Woodcock Hill)
Devon Pde. Harr 5C 26
Devonport. W2 6C 66 (1C 164)
Devonport Gdns. Ilf 6D 36
Devonport M. W12 2D 82
Devonport Rd. W12 1D 82 (in two parts)
Devonport St. E1 6K 69
Devon Ri. N2 4B 30
Devon Rd. Bark 1J 73
Devon Rd. Sutt 7G 149
Devons Est. E3 3D 70
Devonshire Av. Sutt 7A 150
Devonshire Clo. E15 4G 53
Devonshire Clo. N13 3F 17
Devonshire Clo. W1 5F 67 (5J 159)
Devonshire Ct. E1 3J 69 (off Bancroft Rd.)
Devonshire Ct. WC1 5J 67 (5F 161) (off Boswell St.)
Devonshire Ct. Pinn 1D 24 (off Devonshire Rd.)
Devonshire Cres. NW7 7A 14
Devonshire Dri. SE10 7D 88
Devonshire Dri. Surb 1D 146
Devonshire Gdns. N17 6H 17
Devonshire Gdns. N21 7H 7
Devonshire Gdns. W4 7J 81
Devonshire Gro. SE15 6H 87
Devonshire Hall. E9 6J 51 (off Frampton Pk. Rd.)
Devonshire Hill La. N17 6G 17 (in two parts)
Devonshire Ho. NW6 6H 47 (off Kilburn High Rd.)
Devonshire Ho. SE1 3C 86 (off Bath Ter.)
Devonshire Ho. SW1 5H 85 (5D 172) (off Lindsay Sq.)
Devonshire Ho. Sutt 7A 150
Devonshire Ho. Bus. Cen. Brom 4K 143 (off Devonshire Sq.)
Devonshire M. N13 4F 17
Devonshire M. SW10 6B 84 (7A 170) (off Camera Pl.)
Devonshire M. W4 5A 82
Devonshire M. N. W1 5F 67 (5J 159)
Devonshire M. S. W1 5F 67 (5J 159)
Devonshire M. W. W1 4E 66 (4H 159)
Devonshire Pas. W4 5A 82
Devonshire Pl. NW2 3J 47
Devonshire Pl. W1 4E 66 (4H 159)
Devonshire Pl. W8 3K 83
Devonshire Pl. M. W1 5E 66 (4H 159)
Devonshire Rd. E16 6K 71
Devonshire Rd. E17 6C 34
Devonshire Rd. N9 1D 18
Devonshire Rd. N13 4E 16
Devonshire Rd. N17 6H 17
Devonshire Rd. NW7 7A 14
Devonshire Rd. SE9 2C 126
Devonshire Rd. SE23 1J 123
Devonshire Rd. SW19 7C 120
Devonshire Rd. W4 5A 82
Devonshire Rd. W5 3C 80
Devonshire Rd. Bexh 4E 110
Devonshire Rd. Cars 4E 150
Devonshire Rd. Croy 7D 140
Devonshire Rd. Eastc 6A 24
Devonshire Rd. Felt 3C 114
Devonshire Rd. Harr 6H 25
Devonshire Rd. Ilf 7J 37
Devonshire Rd. Orp 7K 145
Devonshire Rd. Pinn 1D 24
Devonshire Rd. S'hall 5E 60
Devonshire Rd. Sutt 7A 150
Devonshire Row. EC2 5E 68 (6H 163)
Devonshire Row M. W1 4K 159
Devonshire Sq. EC2 & EC1 6E 68 (6H 163)
Devonshire Sq. Brom 4K 143
Devonshire St. W1 5E 66 (5H 159)
Devonshire St. W4 5A 82

Devonshire Ter. W2 6A 66
Devonshire Way. Croy 2A 154
Devonshire Way. Hay 6K 59
Devons Rd. E3 3D 70
Devon St. SE15 6H 87
Devon Way. Chess 5C 146
Devon Way. Eps 5H 147
Devon Way. Uxb 2B 58
Devon Waye. Houn 7D 78
Devon Wharf. E14 5E 70
(off Leven Rd.)
De Walden Ho. NW8 2C 66
(off Allitsen Rd.)
De Walden St. W1 5E 66 (6H 159)
Dewar St. SE15 3G 105
Dewberry Gdns. E6 5C 72
Dewberry St. E14 5E 70
Dewey Rd. N1 2A 68
Dewey Rd. Dag 6H 57
Dewey St. SW17 5D 120
Dewhurst Rd. W14 3F 83
Dewsbury Clo. Pinn 6C 24
Dewsbury Ct. W4 4J 81
Dewsbury Gdns. Wor Pk 3C 148
Dewsbury Rd. NW10 5C 46
Dewsbury Ter. NW1 1F 67
Dexter Ho. Eri 3E 92
(off Kale Rd.)
Dexter Rd. Barn 6A 4
Deyncourt Rd. N17 1C 32
Deynecourt Gdns. E11 4A 36
D'Eynsford Rd. SE5 1D 104
Dhonau Ho. SE1 4F 87
(off Longfield Est.)
Diadem Ct. W1 7C 160
Dial Wlk., The. W8 2K 83
(off Broad Wlk., The)
Diameter Rd. Orp 7F 145
Diamond Clo. Dag 1C 56
Diamond Est. SW17 3C 120
Diamond Ho. E3 2A 70
(off Roman Rd.)
Diamond Rd. Ruis 4B 42
Diamond St. NW10 7K 45
Diamond St. SE15 7E 86
Diamond Ter. SE10 1E 106
Diamond Way. SE8 6C 88
Diana Clo. E18 1K 35
Diana Clo. SE8 6B 88
Diana Gdns. Surb 2F 147
Diana Ho. SW13 1B 100
Diana Rd. E17 3B 34
Dianne Way. Barn 4H 5
Dianthus Clo. SE2 5B 92
Dibden Ho. SE5 7E 86
Dibden St. N1 1C 68
Dibdin Clo. Sutt 3J 149
Dibdin Ho. NW6 2K 65
Dibdin Rd. Sutt 3J 149
Dicey Av. NW2 4E 46
Dickens Av. N3 1A 30
Dickens Av. Uxb 6D 58
Dickens Clo. Eri 7H 93
Dickens Clo. Hay 4G 77
Dickens Clo. Rich 2E 116
Dickens Ct. E11 4J 35
(off Makepeace Rd.)
Dickens Dri. Chst 6G 127
Dickens Est. SE1 & SE16 2G 87 (7K 169)
Dickens Est. SE16 3G 87
Dickens House. 4K 67 (4H 161)
Dickens Ho. NW6 3J 65
(off Malvern Rd.)
Dickens Ho. NW8 3B 158
Dickens Ho. SE17 5B 86
(off Doddington Gro.)
Dickens Ho. WC1 3E 160
Dickens La. N18 5K 17
Dickens M. EC1 5B 68 (5A 162)
(off Turnmill St.)
Dickenson Clo. N9 1B 18
Dickenson Ho. N8 6K 31
Dickenson Rd. N8 7J 31
Dickenson Rd. Felt 5A 114
Dickensons La. SE25 5G 141
(in two parts)
Dickensons Pl. SE25 6G 141
Dickens Ri. Chig 3K 21
Dickens Rd. E6 2B 72
Dickens Sq. SE1 3C 86 (7D 168)
Dickens St. SW8 2F 103
Dickenswood Clo. SE19 7B 122
Dickerage La. N Mald 3J 135
Dickerage Rd. King T 1J 135
Dicksee Ho. NW8 4B 66 (4A 158)
(off Lyons Pl.)
Dickson Fold. Pinn 4B 24
Dickson Ho. E1 6H 69
(off Philpot St.)
Dickson Rd. SE9 3C 108
Dick Turpin Way. Felt 4H 95
Didsbury Clo. E6 1D 72
Digby Bus. Cen. E9 6K 51
(off Digby Rd.)
Digby Cres. N4 2C 50
Digby Gdns. Dag 1G 75
Digby Mans. W6 5D 82
(off Hammersmith Bri. Rd.)
Digby Pl. Croy 3F 153
Digby Rd. E9 6K 51
Digby Rd. Bark 7K 55
Digby St. E2 3J 69
Diggon St. E1 5K 69
Dighton Ct. SE5 6C 86
Dighton Rd. SW18 5A 102
Dignum St. N1 2A 68
Digswell St. N7 6A 50
Dilhorne Clo. SE12 3K 125
Dilke St. SW3 6D 84 (7F 171)
Dilloway La. S'hall 2C 78
Dillwyn Clo. SE26 4A 124
Dilston Clo. N'holt 3A 60
Dilston Gro. SE16 4J 87
Dilton Gdns. SW15 1C 118
Dilwyn Ct. E17 2A 34
Dimes Pl. W6 4D 82
Dimmock Dri. Gnfd 5H 43
Dimond Clo. E7 4J 53
Dimsdale Dri. NW9 1J 45
Dimsdale Dri. Enf 7B 8
Dimsdale Wlk. E13 2J 71
Dimson Cres. E3 3C 70
Dingle Gdns. E14 7C 70
Dingle Rd. Ashf 5D 112
Dingles Ct. Pinn 1B 24
Dingle, The. Uxb 3D 58
Dingley La. SW16 2H 121
Dingley Pl. EC1 3C 68 (2D 162)
Dingley Rd. EC1 3C 68 (2C 162)
Dingwall Av. Croy & New Ad 2C 152
Dingwall Gdns. NW11 6J 29
Dingwall Rd. SW18 7A 102
Dingwall Rd. Cars 7D 150
Dingwall Rd. Croy 1D 152
Dinmont Est. E2 2G 69
Dinmont Ho. E2 2G 69
(off Pritchard's Rd.)
Dinmont St. E2 2H 69
Dinmore Ho. E9 1J 69
(off Templecombe Rd.)
Dinnington Ho. E1 4H 69
(off Coventry Rd.)
Dinsdale Gdns. SE25 5E 140
Dinsdale Gdns. New Bar 5E 4
Dinsdale Rd. SE3 6H 89
Dinsmore Rd. SW12 7F 103
Dinton Ho. NW8 4C 66 (3C 158)
(off Lilestone St.)
Dinton Rd. SW19 6B 120
Dinton Rd. King T 7F 117
Diploma Av. N2 4C 30
Diploma Ct. N2 4C 30
Dirleton Rd. E15 1H 71
Disbrowe Rd. W6 6G 83
Discovery Bus. Pk. SE16 3G 87
(off St James's Rd.)
Discovery Ho. E14 7E 70
(off Newby Pl.)
Discovery Wlk. E1 1H 87
Dishforth La. NW9 7F 13
Disley Ct. S'hall 6F 61
(off Howard Rd.)
Disney Pl. SE1 2C 86 (6D 168)
Disney St. SE1 2C 86 (6D 168)
Dison Clo. Enf 1E 8
Disraeli Clo. SE28 1C 92
Disraeli Clo. W4 3K 81
Disraeli Gdns. SW15 4H 101
Disraeli Rd. E7 6J 53
Disraeli Rd. NW10 2K 63
Disraeli Rd. SW15 4G 101
Disraeli Rd. W5 1D 80
Diss St. E2 3F 69 (1J 163)
Distaff La. EC4 7C 68 (2C 168)
Distillery La. W6 5E 82
Distillery Rd. W6 5E 82
Distillery Wlk. Bren 6E 80
Distin St. SE11 4A 86 (4J 173)
District Rd. Wemb 5B 44
Ditch All. SE10 1D 106
Ditchburn St. E14 7E 70
Ditchfield Rd. Hay 4C 60
Ditchley Ct. W7 5K 61
(off Templeman Rd.)
Dittisham Rd. SE9 4C 126
Ditton Clo. Th Dit 7A 134
Dittoncroft Clo. Croy 4E 152
Ditton Grange Clo. Surb 1D 146
Ditton Grange Dri. Surb 1D 146
Ditton Hill. Surb 1C 146
Ditton Hill Rd. Surb 1C 146
Ditton Lawn. Th Dit 1A 146
Ditton Pl. SE20 1H 141
Ditton Reach. Th Dit 6B 134
Ditton Rd. Bexh 5D 110
Ditton Rd. S'hall 5D 78
Ditton Rd. Surb 2D 146
Divis Way. SW15 6D 100
(off Dover Pk. Dri.)
Dixon Clark Ct. N1 6B 50
Dixon Clo. E6 6D 72
Dixon Ho. W10 6F 65
(off Darfield Way)
Dixon Pl. W Wick 1D 154
Dixon Rd. SE14 1A 106
Dixon Rd. SE25 3E 140
Dixon's All. SE16 2H 87
Dobbin Clo. Harr 2A 26
Dobell Rd. SE9 5D 108
Dobree Av. NW10 7D 46
Dobson Clo. NW6 7B 48
Dobson Ho. SE5 7D 86
(off Edmund St.)
Dobson Ho. SE14 6K 87
(off John Williams Clo.)
Doby Ct. EC4 2D 168
Dock Cotts. E1 7J 69
(off Highway, The)
Dockers Tanner Rd. E14 3C 88
Dockett Eddy. Cher 7A 130
Dockett Eddy La. Shep 7B 130
Dockhead. SE1 2F 87 (7K 169)
Dockhead Wharf. SE1 2F 87 (7K 169)
(off Shad Thames)
Dock Hill Av. SE16 1K 87
Dockland St. E16 1E 90
(in two parts)
Dockley Rd. SE16 3G 87
Dockley Rd. Ind. Est. SE16 3G 87
(off Dockley Rd.)
Dock Offices. SE16 3J 87
(off Surrey Quays Rd.)
Dock Rd. E16 7H 71
Dock Rd. Bren 7D 80
Dockside Rd. E16 7B 72
Dock St. E1 7G 69
Dockwell Clo. Felt 4J 95
Doctor Johnson Av. SW17 3F 121
Doctors Clo. SE26 5J 123
Docwra's Bldgs. N1 6E 50
Dodbrooke Rd. SE27 3A 122
Dodd Ho. SE16 4H 87
(off Rennie Est.)
Doddington Gro. SE17 6B 86
Doddington Pl. SE17 6B 86
Dodsley Pl. N9 3D 18
Dodson St. SE1 2A 86 (7K 167)
Dod St. E14 6B 70
Doebury Wlk. SE18 6A 92
(off Prestwood Clo.)
Doel Clo. SW19 7A 120
Dog & Duck Yd. WC1 5G 161
Doggett Rd. SE6 7C 106
Doggetts Courts. Barn 5H 5
Doghurst Av. Hay 7D 76
Doghurst Dri. W Dray 7D 76
Dog Kennel Hill. SE22 3E 104
Dog Kennel Hill Est. SE22 3E 104
(off Albrighton Rd.)
Dog La. NW10 4A 46
Doherty Rd. E13 4J 71
Dokal Ind. Est. S'hall 3C 78
Dolben Ct. SE8 4B 88
Dolben St. SE1 1B 86 (5A 168)
(in two parts)
Dolby Rd. SW6 2H 101
Dolland Ho. SE11 6H 173
Dolland St. SE11 5K 85 (6H 173)
Dollar Bay Ct. E14 2E 88
(off Lawn Ho. Clo.)
Dollary Pde. King T 3H 135
(off Kingston Rd.)
Dollis Av. N3 1H 29
Dollis Brook Wlk. Barn 6B 4
Dollis Cres. Ruis 1A 42
Dolliscroft. NW7 7B 14
Dollis Hill. 2D 46
Dollis Hill Av. NW2 3D 46
Dollis Hill Est. NW2 3C 46
Dollis Hill La. NW2 4B 46
Dollis M. N3 1J 29
Dollis Pk. N3 1H 29
Dollis Rd. NW7 & N3 7B 14
Dollis Valley Dri. Barn 6C 4
Dollis Valley Way. Barn 6C 4
Dolman Clo. N3 1A 30
Dolman Rd. W4 4K 81
Dolman St. SW4 4K 103
Dolphin Clo. SE16 2K 87
Dolphin Clo. SE28 6D 74
Dolphin Clo. Surb 5D 134
Dolphin Ct. NW11 6G 29
Dolphin Ct. SE8 6B 88
(off Wotton Rd.)
Dolphin Est. Sun 1G 131
Dolphin Ho. SW18 4K 101
Dolphin La. E14 7D 70
Dolphin Rd. N'holt 2D 60
Dolphin Rd. Sun 1G 131
Dolphin Rd. N. Sun 1G 131
Dolphin Rd. S. Sun 1G 131
Dolphin Rd. W. Sun 1G 131
Dolphin Sq. SW1 5G 85 (6B 172)
Dolphin Sq. W4 7A 82
Dolphin St. King T 2E 134
Dolphin Tower. SE8 6B 88
(off Abinger Gro.)
Dombey Ho. SE1 2G 87 (7K 169)
(off Wolseley St.)
Dombey Ho. W11 1F 83
(off St Ann's Rd.)
Dombey St. WC1 5K 67 (5G 161)
(in two parts)
Dome Hill Pk. SE26 4F 123
Domett Clo. SE5 4D 104
Domfe Pl. E5 4J 51
Domingo St. EC1 4C 68 (3C 162)
Dominica Clo. E13 3A 72
Dominion Bus. Pk. N9 2E 18
Dominion Cen., The. S'hall 2C 78
Dominion Ct. E8 7F 51
(off Middleton Rd.)
Dominion Ho. E14 5D 88
(off St Davids Sq.)
Dominion Pde. Harr 5K 25
Dominion Rd. Croy 7F 141
Dominion Rd. S'hall 2C 78
Dominion St. EC2 5D 68 (5F 163)
Dominion Theatre. 6H 67 (7D 160)
(off Tottenham Ct. Rd.)
Domitian Pl. Enf 5A 8
Domonic Dri. SE9 4F 127
Domville Clo. N20 2G 15
Donald Dri. Romf 5C 38
Donald Hunter Ho. E7 5K 53
(off Post Office App., in two parts)
Donald Rd. E13 1K 71
Donald Rd. Croy 7K 139
Donaldson Rd. NW6 1H 65
Donaldson Rd. SE18 1E 108
Donald Woods Gdns. Surb 2H 147
Doncaster Dri. N'holt 5D 42
Doncaster Gdns. N4 6C 32
Doncaster Gdns. N'holt 5D 42
Doncaster Rd. N9 7C 8
Donegal Ho. E1 4H 69
(off Cambridge Heath Rd.)
Donegal St. N1 2K 67
Doneraile Ho. SW1 5F 85 (6J 171)
(off Ebury Bri. Rd.)
Doneraile St. SW6 2F 101
Dongola Rd. E1 5A 70
Dongola Rd. E13 3K 71
Dongola Rd. N17 3E 32
Dongola Rd. W. E13 3K 71
Donington Av. Ilf 5G 37
Donkey All. SE22 7G 105
Donkey La. Enf 2B 8
Donkin Ho. SE16 4H 87
(off Rennie Est.)
Donmar Warehouse Theatre. 6J 67 (1E 166)
(off Earlham St.)
Donnatt's Rd. SE14 1B 106
Donne Ct. SE24 6C 104
Donnefield Av. Edgw 7K 11
Donne Ho. E14 6C 70
(off Dod St.)
Donne Ho. SE14 6K 87
(off Samuel Clo.)
Donnelly Ct. SW6 7G 83
(off Dawes Rd.)
Donne Pl. SW3 4C 84 (3D 170)
Donne Pl. Mitc 4F 139
Donne Rd. Dag 2C 56
Donnington Ct. NW1 7F 49
(off Castlehaven Rd.)
Donnington Ct. NW10 7D 46
Donnington Mans. NW10 1E 64
(off Donnington Rd.)
Donnington Rd. NW10 7D 46
Donnington Rd. Harr 5D 26
Donnington Rd. Wor Pk 2C 148
Donnybrook Rd. SW16 7G 121
Donoghue Cotts. E14 5A 70
(off Galsworthy Av.)
Donovan Av. N10 2F 31
Donovan Ct. NW10 7J 45

Donovan Ct. SW10 5B 84 (6A 170) (off Drayton Gdns.)
Donovan Ho. E1 7J 69 (off Cable St.)
Donovan Pl. N21 5E 6
Don Phelan Clo. SE5 1D 104
Doone Clo. Tedd 6A 116
Doon St. SE1 1A 86 (5J 167)
Dora Ho. E14 6B 70 (off Rhodeswell Rd.)
Dora Ho. W11 7F 65 (off St Ann's Rd.)
Doral Way. Cars 5D 150
Doran Ct. E6 2D 72
Dorando Clo. W12 7D 64
Doran Gro. SE18 7J 91
Doran Mnr. N2 5D 30 (off Gt. North Rd.)
Doran Wlk. E15 7E 52
Dora Rd. SW19 5J 119
Dora St. E14 6B 70
Dorchester Av. N13 4H 17
Dorchester Av. Bex 1D 128
Dorchester Av. Harr 6G 25
Dorchester Clo. N'holt 5F 43
Dorchester Clo. Orp 7B 128
Dorchester Ct. E18 1H 35 (off Buckingham Rd.)
Dorchester Ct. N1 7E 50 (off Englefield Rd.)
Dorchester Ct. N10 3F 31
Dorchester Ct. N14 7A 6
Dorchester Ct. NW2 3F 47
Dorchester Ct. SE24 5C 104
Dorchester Dri. SE24 5C 104
Dorchester Dri. Felt 6G 95
Dorchester Gdns. E4 4H 19
Dorchester Gdns. NW11 4J 29
Dorchester Gro. W4 5A 82
Dorchester M. N Mald 4K 135
Dorchester M. Twic 6C 98
Dorchester Rd. Mord 7K 137
Dorchester Rd. N'holt 5F 43
Dorchester Rd. Wor Pk 1E 148
Dorchester Ter. NW2 3F 47 (off Gratton Ter.)
Dorchester Way. Harr 6F 27
Dorchester Waye. Hay 6K 59 (in two parts)
Dorcis Av. Bexh 2E 110
Dordrecht Rd. W3 1A 82
Dore Av. E12 5E 54
Doreen Av. NW9 1K 45
Doreen Capstan Ho. E11 3G 53 (off Apollo Pl.)
Dore Gdns. Mord 7K 137
Dorell Clo. S'hall 5D 60
Doria Rd. SW6 2H 101
Doric Ho. E2 2K 69 (off Mace St.)
Doric Way. NW1 3H 67 (1C 160)
Dorien Rd. SW20 2F 137
Doris Av. Eri 1J 111
Doris Emmerton Ct. SW11 4A 102
Doris Rd. E7 7J 53
Doris Rd. Ashf 6F 113
Doritt M. N18 5K 17
Dorking Clo. SE8 6B 88
Dorking Clo. Wor Pk 2F 149
Dorking Ct. N17 1G 33 (off Hampden La.)
Dorking Ho. SE1 3D 86
Dorlcote Rd. SW18 7C 102
Dorly Clo. Shep 5G 131
Dorman Pl. N9 2B 18
Dormans Clo. N'wd 1F 23
Dorman Wlk. NW10 5K 45
Dorman Way. NW8 1B 66
Dorma Trad. Pk. E10 1K 51
Dormay St. SW18 5K 101
Dormer Clo. E15 6H 53
Dormer Clo. Barn 5A 4
Dormer's Av. S'hall 6E 60
Dormers Ct. E14 6C 70
Dormers Ri. S'hall 6F 61
Dormer's Wells. 7F 61
Dormer's Wells La. S'hall 6E 60
Dormstone Ho. SE17 4E 86 (off Beckway St.)
Dormywood. Ruis 5H 23
Dornberg Clo. SE3 7J 89
Dornberg Rd. SE3 7K 89
Dorncliffe Rd. SW6 2G 101
Dorney. NW3 7C 48
Dorney Ri. Orp 4K 145
Dorney Way. Houn 5C 96
Dornfell St. NW6 5H 47
Dornton Rd. SW12 2F 121
Dornton Rd. S Croy 6D 152
Dorothy Av. Wemb 7E 44
Dorothy Evans Clo. Bexh 4H 111
Dorothy Gdns. Dag 4B 56
Dorothy Pettingell Ho. Sutt 3K 149 (off Angel Hill)
Dorothy Rd. SW11 3D 102
Dorrell Pl. SW9 3A 104
Dorrien Wlk. SW16 2H 121
Dorrington Ct. SE25 1E 140
Dorrington St. EC1 5A 68 (5J 161)
Dorrit Ho. W11 1F 83 (off St Ann's Rd.)
Dorrit St. SE1 2C 86 (6D 168)
Dorrit Way. Chst 6G 127
Dorryn Ct. SE26 5K 123
Dors Clo. NW9 1K 45
Dorset Av. Hay 3G 59
Dorset Av. Romf 4K 39
Dorset Av. S'hall 4E 78
Dorset Av. Well 4K 109
Dorset Bldgs. EC4 6B 68 (1A 168)
Dorset Clo. NW1 5D 66 (5E 158)
Dorset Clo. Hay 3G 59
Dorset Ct. N1 7E 50 (off Hertford Rd.)
Dorset Ct. W7 5K 61 (off Copley Clo.)
Dorset Ct. N'wd 1H 23
Dorset Dri. Edgw 6A 12
Dorset Gdns. Mitc 4K 139
Dorset Ho. NW1 4D 66 (5F 159) (off Gloucester Pl.)
Dorset M. N3 1J 29
Dorset Pl. E15 6F 53
Dorset Ri. EC4 6B 68 (1A 168)
Dorset Rd. E7 7A 54
Dorset Rd. N15 4D 32
Dorset Rd. N22 1J 31
Dorset Rd. SE9 2C 126
Dorset Rd. SW8 7J 85
Dorset Rd. SW19 1J 137
Dorset Rd. W5 3C 80
Dorset Rd. Ashf 3A 112
Dorset Rd. Beck 3K 141
Dorset Rd. Harr 6G 25
Dorset Rd. Mitc 2C 138
Dorset Sq. NW1 4D 66 (4E 158)
Dorset St. W1 5D 66 (6F 159)
Dorset Way. Twic 1H 115
Dorset Way. Uxb 2B 58
Dorset Waye. Houn 7D 78
Dorton Clo. SE15 7E 86
Dorton Vs. W Dray 7C 76
Dorville Cres. W6 3D 82
Dorville Rd. SE12 5H 107
Dothill Rd. SE18 7G 91
Douai Gro. Hamp 1G 133
Doughty Ct. E1 1H 87 (off Prusom St.)
Doughty Ho. SW10 6A 84 (off Netherton Gro.)
Doughty M. WC1 4K 67 (4G 161)
Doughty St. WC1 4K 67 (3G 161)
Douglas Av. E17 1B 34
Douglas Av. N Mald 4D 136
Douglas Av. Wemb 7E 44
Douglas Clo. Stan 5F 11
Douglas Clo. Wall 6J 151
Douglas Ct. NW6 7J 47 (off Quex Rd.)
Douglas Ct. King T 4E 134 (off Geneva Rd.)
Douglas Cres. Hay 4A 60
Douglas Dri. Croy 3C 154
Douglas Est. N1 6C 50 (off Marquess Rd.)
Douglas Ho. Surb 1F 147
Douglas Johnstone Ho. SW6 6H 83 (off Clem Attlee Ct.)
Douglas Mans. Houn 3F 97
Douglas M. NW2 3G 47
Douglas Pl. SW1 4H 85 (4C 172) (off Douglas St.)
Douglas Rd. E4 1B 20
Douglas Rd. E16 5J 71
Douglas Rd. N1 7C 50
Douglas Rd. N22 1A 32
Douglas Rd. NW6 1H 65
Douglas Rd. Houn 3F 97
Douglas Rd. Ilf 7A 38
Douglas Rd. King T 2H 135
Douglas Rd. Stanw 6A 94
Douglas Rd. Surb 2F 147
Douglas Rd. Well 1B 110
Douglas Rd. N. N1 6C 50
Douglas Rd. S. N1 6C 50
Douglas Robinson Ct. SW16 7J 121 (off Streatham High Rd.)
Douglas Sq. Mord 6J 137
Douglas St. SW1 4H 85 (4C 172)
Douglas Ter. E17 1B 34
Douglas Waite Ho. NW6 7J 47
Douglas Way. SE8 7B 88 (Amersham Va., in two parts)
Douglas Way. SE8 7C 88 (Idonia St.)
Doulton Ho. SE11 2H 173
Doulton M. NW6 6K 47
Dounesforth Gdns. SW18 1K 119
Douro Pl. W8 3K 83
Douro St. E3 2C 70
Douthwaite Sq. E1 1G 87
Dove App. E6 5C 72
Dove Clo. NW7 7G 13
Dove Clo. N'holt 4B 60
Dove Clo. Wall 7K 151
Dove Commercial Cen. NW5 5G 49
Dovecot Clo. Pinn 5A 24
Dovecote Av. N22 3A 32
Dovecote Gdns. SW14 3K 99
Dove Ct. EC2 1E 168
Dovedale Av. Harr 6C 26
Dovedale Av. Ilf 2E 36
Dovedale Clo. Well 2A 110
Dovedale Ri. Mitc 7D 120
Dovedale Rd. SE22 5H 105
Dovedon Clo. N14 2D 16
Dovehouse Ct. N'holt 3B 60 (off Delta Gro.)
Dove Ho. Gdns. E4 2H 19
Dovehouse Mead. Bark 2H 73
Dovehouse St. SW3 5B 84 (5B 170)
Dove M. SW5 4A 84
Dove Pk. Pinn 1E 24
Dover Clo. NW2 2F 47
Dover Clo. Romf 2J 39
Dovercourt Av. T Hth 5A 140
Dovercourt Est. N1 6D 50
Dovercourt Gdns. Stan 5K 11
Dovercourt La. Sutt 3A 150
Dovercourt Rd. SE22 6E 104
Doverfield Rd. SW2 7J 103
Dover Flats. SE1 4E 86
Dover Gdns. Cars 3D 150
Dover Ho. SE15 6J 87
Dover Ho. Rd. SW15 4C 100
Doveridge Gdns. N13 4G 17
Dove Rd. N1 6D 50
Dove Row. E2 1G 69
Dover Pk. Dri. SW15 6D 100
Dover Patrol. SE3 2K 107
Dover Rd. E12 2A 54
Dover Rd. N9 2D 18
Dover Rd. SE19 6D 122
Dover Rd. Romf 6E 38
Dover St. W1 7F 67 (3K 165)
Dover Ter. Rich 2F 99 (off Sandycombe Rd.)
Dover Yd. W1 4A 166
Doves Clo. Brom 2C 156
Doves Yd. N1 1A 68
Doveton Ho. E1 4J 69 (off Doveton St.)
Doveton Rd. S Croy 5D 152
Doveton St. E1 4J 69
Dove Wlk. SW1 5E 84 (5G 171)
Dovey Lodge. N1 7A 50 (off Bewdley St.)
Dowanhill Rd. SE6 1F 125
Dowdeswell Clo. SW15 4A 100
Dowding Ho. N6 7E 30 (off Hillcrest)
Dowding Pl. Stan 6F 11
Dowding Rd. Uxb 7B 40
Dowdney Clo. NW5 5G 49
Dowe Ho. SE3 3G 107
Dower Av. Wall 7F 151
Dowes Ho. SW16 3J 121
Dowgate Hill. EC4 7D 68 (2E 168)
Dowland St. W10 3G 65
Dowlas St. SE5 7E 86
Dowler Ct. King T 1E 134 (off Burton Rd.)
Dowler Ho. E1 6G 69 (off Burslem St.)
Dowling Ho. Belv 3F 93
Dowman Clo. SW19 1K 137
Downage. NW4 3E 28
Downalong. Bus H 1C 10
Downbank Av. Bexh 1K 111
Down Barns Rd. Ruis 3B 42
Downbury M. SW18 5J 101
Down Clo. N'holt 2K 59
Downderry Rd. Brom 3F 125
Downe Clo. Well 7C 92
Down End. SE18 7F 91
Downend Ct. SE15 6E 86 (off Longhope Clo.)
Downe Rd. Kes 7C 156
Downe Rd. Mitc 2D 138
Downer's Cottage. SW4 4G 103
Downes Clo. Twic 6B 98
Downes Ct. N21 1F 17
Downes Ho. Croy 4B 152 (off Violet La.)
Downe Ter. Rich 6E 98
Downey Ho. E1 4K 69 (off Globe Rd.)
Downfield. Wor Pk 1B 148
Downfield Clo. W9 4K 65
Down Hall Rd. King T 1D 134
Downham. 5F 125
Downham Clo. Romf 1G 39
Downham Enterprise Cen. SE6 2H 125
Downham La. Brom 5F 125
Downham Rd. N1 7D 50
Downham Way. Brom 5F 125
Downhills Av. N17 3D 32
Downhills Pk. Rd. N17 3C 32
Downhills Way. N17 3C 32
Downhurst Av. NW7 5E 12
Downhurst Ct. NW4 3E 28
Downing Clo. Harr 3G 25
Downing Dri. Gnfd 1H 61
Downing Rd. Dag 1F 75
Downings. E6 6E 72
Downing St. SW1 2J 85 (6E 166)
Downland Clo. N20 1F 15
Downleys Clo. SE9 2C 126
Downman Rd. SE9 3C 108
Down Pl. W6 4D 82
Down Rd. Tedd 6B 116
Downs Av. Chst 5D 126
Downs Av. Pinn 6C 24
Downsbridge Rd. Beck 1F 143
Downsell Rd. E15 4E 52
Downsfield Rd. E17 6A 34
Downshall Av. Ilf 6J 37
Downs Hill. Beck 7F 125
Downshire Hill. NW3 4B 48
Downside. Sun 1J 131
Downside. Twic 3K 115
Downside Clo. SW19 6A 120
Downside Cres. NW3 5C 48
Downside Cres. W13 4A 62
Downside Rd. Sutt 6B 150
Downside Wlk. Bren 6D 80 (off Windmill Rd.)
Downside Wlk. N'holt 3D 60
Downs La. E5 4H 51
Downs Pk. Rd. E8 & E5 5F 51
Downs Rd. E5 4G 51
Downs Rd. Beck 2D 142 (in two parts)
Downs Rd. Enf 4K 7
Downs Rd. T Hth 1C 140
Downs, The. SW20 7F 119
Down St. W1 1F 85 (5J 165)
Down St. W Mol 5E 132
Down St. M. W1 1F 85 (5J 165)
Downs Vw. Iswth 1K 97
Downsview Gdns. SE19 7B 122
Downsview Rd. SE19 7C 122
Downsway, The. Sutt 7A 150
Downton Av. SW2 2J 121
Downtown Rd. SE16 2A 88
Downway. N12 7H 15
Down Way. N'holt 2K 59
Dowrey St. N1 1A 68
Dowsett Rd. N17 2F 33
Dowson Clo. SE5 4D 104
Dowson Ho. E1 6K 69 (off Bower St.)
Doyce St. SE1 2C 86 (6C 168)
Doyle Gdns. NW10 1C 64
Doyle Ho. SW13 7E 82 (off Trinity Chu. Rd.)
Doyle Rd. SE25 4G 141
D'Oyley St. SW1 4E 84 (3G 171)
Doynton St. N19 2F 49
Draco Ga. SW15 3E 100
Draco St. SE17 6C 86
Dragonfly Clo. E13 3K 71
Dragon Rd. SE15 6E 86
Dragon Yd. WC1 7F 161
Dragoon Rd. SE8 5B 88
Dragor Rd. NW10 4J 63
Drake Clo. SE16 2K 87
Drake Ct. W12 2E 82 (off Scott's Rd.)
Drake Ct. Surb 4E 134 (off Cranes Pk. Av.)
Drake Cres. SE28 6C 74
Drakefell Rd. SE14 & SE4 2K 105
Drakefield Rd. SW17 3E 120
Drake Hall. E16 1K 89 (off Wesley Av., in two parts)
Drake Ho. E1 5J 69 (off Stepney Way)

Drake Ho. E14 7A 70 (off Victory Pl.)
Drake Ho. SW1 6H 85 (7C 172) (off Dolphin Sq.)
Drakeland Ho. W9 4H 65 (off Fernhead Rd.)
Drakeley Ct. N5 4B 50
Drake Rd. SE4 3C 106
Drake Rd. Chess 5G 147
Drake Rd. Croy 7K 139
Drake Rd. Harr 2D 42
Drake Rd. Mitc 6E 138
Drakes Ct. SE23 1J 123
Drakes Courtyard. NW6 7H 47
Drakes Dri. N'wd 1D 22
Drake St. WC1 5K 67 (6G 161)
Drake St. Enf 1J 7
Drakes Wlk. E6 1D 72 (in two parts)
Drakewood Rd. SW16 7H 121
Draper Clo. Belv 4F 93
Draper Clo. Iswth 2H 97
Draper Ct. Brom 4C 144
Draper Ho. SE1 4B 86 (off Elephant & Castle)
Draper Pl. N1 1B 68 (off Dagmar Ter.)
Drapers' Cottage Homes. NW7 4H 13 (in two parts)
Drapers Gdns. EC2 6D 68 (7F 163)
Drapers Rd. E15 4F 53
Drapers Rd. N17 3F 33
Drapers Rd. Enf 2G 7
Drappers Way. SE16 4G 87
Draven Clo. Brom 7H 143
Drawdock Rd. SE10 2F 89
Drawell Clo. SE18 5J 91
Drax Av. SW20 7C 118
Draycot Rd. E11 6K 35
Draycot Rd. Surb 1G 147
Draycott Av. SW3 4C 84 (3D 170)
Draycott Av. Harr 6B 26
Draycott Clo. NW2 3F 47
Draycott Clo. Harr 6B 26
Draycott Pl. SW3 4D 84 (4E 170)
Draycott Ter. SW3 4D 84 (4F 171)
Dray Ct. Wor Pk 1B 148
Drayford Clo. W9 4H 65
Dray Gdns. SW2 5K 103
Draymans Way. Iswth 3K 97
Drayside M. S'hall 2D 78
Drayson M. W8 2J 83
Drayton Av. W13 7A 62
Drayton Bri. Rd. W7 & W13 7K 61
Drayton Clo. Houn 5D 96
Drayton Clo. Ilf 1H 55
Drayton Ct. W Dray 4B 76
Drayton Gdns. N21 7G 7
Drayton Gdns. SW10 5A 84 (6A 170)
Drayton Gdns. W13 7A 62
Drayton Gdns. W Dray 2A 76
Drayton Grn. W13 7A 62
Drayton Grn. Rd. W13 7B 62
Drayton Gro. W13 7A 62
Drayton Ho. E11 1F 53
Drayton Ho. SE5 7D 86 (off Elmington Rd.)
Drayton Pk. N5 4A 50
Drayton Pk. M. N5 5A 50
Drayton Rd. E11 1F 53
Drayton Rd. N17 2E 32
Drayton Rd. NW10 1B 64
Drayton Rd. W13 7A 62
Drayton Rd. Croy 2B 152
Drayton Waye. Harr 6B 26
Dreadnought Wharf. SE10 6D 88 (off Thames St.)
Drenon Sq. Hay 7H 59
Dresden Clo. NW6 6K 47
Dresden Ho. SE11 3H 173
Dresden Rd. N19 1G 49
Dressington Av. SE4 6C 106
Drew Av. NW7 6B 14
Drewery Ct. SE3 3G 107
Drewett Ho. E1 6G 69 (off Christian St.)
Drew Gdns. Gnfd 6K 43
Drew Ho. SW16 3J 121
Drewitts Ct. W on T 7H 131
Drew Rd. E16 1B 90 (in three parts)
Drewstead Rd. SW16 2H 121
Driffield Ct. NW9 1A 28 (off Pageant Av.)
Driffield Rd. E3 2A 70
Drift, The. Brom 3B 156
Driftway, The. Mitc 1E 138
Drill Hall Arts Cen. 5H 67 (5C 160) (off Chenies St.)
Drinkwater Ho. SE5 7D 86 (off Picton St.)
Drinkwater Rd. Harr 2F 43
Drive Ct. Edgw 5B 12
Drive Mans. SW6 2G 101 (off Fulham Rd.)
Drive, The. E4 1A 20
Drive, The. E17 3D 34
Drive, The. E18 4J 35
Drive, The. N2 5D 30
Drive, The. N3 7D 14
Drive, The. N7 6K 49 (in two parts)
Drive, The. N11 6C 16
Drive, The. NW10 1B 64
Drive, The. NW11 7G 29
Drive, The. SW6 2G 101
Drive, The. SW16 3K 139
Drive, The. SW20 7E 118
Drive, The. W3 6J 63
Drive, The. Ashf 7F 113
Drive, The. Bark 7K 55
Drive, The. Beck 2C 142
Drive, The. Bex 6C 110
Drive, The. Buck H 1F 21
Drive, The. Chst 3K 145
Drive, The. Col R 1K 39
Drive, The. Edgw 5B 12
Drive, The. Enf 1J 7
Drive, The. Eps 6B 148
Drive, The. Eri 7H 93
Drive, The. Esh 7G 133
Drive, The. Felt 7A 96
Drive, The. Harr 7E 24
Drive, The. High Bar 3B 4
Drive, The. Houn & Iswth 2H 97
Drive, The. Ilf 6C 36
Drive, The. King T 7J 117
Drive, The. Mord 5A 138
Drive, The. New Bar 6F 5
Drive, The. N'wd 2G 23
Drive, The. Sidc 3B 128
Drive, The. Surb 7E 134
Drive, The. T Hth 4D 140
Drive, The. Uxb 3A 40
Drive, The. Wemb 2J 45
Drive, The. W Wick 7F 143
Driveway, The. E17 6D 34 (off Hoe St.)
Dr Johnson's House. 6A 68 (7K 161) (off Pemberton Row)
Droitwich Clo. SE26 3G 123
Dromey Gdns. Harr 7E 10
Dromore Rd. SW15 6G 101
Dronfield Gdns. Dag 5C 56
Dron Ho. E1 5J 69 (off Adelina Gro.)
Droop St. W10 3F 65
Drovers Ct. King T 2E 134 (off Fairfield E.)
Drovers Pl. SE15 7J 87
Drovers Rd. S Croy 5D 152
Druce Rd. SE21 6E 104
Druid St. SE1 2E 86 (6H 169)
Druids Way. Brom 4F 143
Drumaline Ridge. Wor Pk 2A 148
Drummond Av. Romf 4K 39
Drummond Cen., The. Croy 2C 152
Drummond Cres. NW1 3H 67 (1C 160)
Drummond Dri. Stan 7E 10
Drummond Ga. SW1 5H 85 (5D 172)
Drummond Ho. E2 2G 69 (off Goldsmiths Row)
Drummond Pl. Twic 7B 98
Drummond Rd. E11 6A 36
Drummond Rd. SE16 3H 87
Drummond Rd. Croy 2C 152 (in two parts)
Drummond Rd. Romf 4K 39
Drummonds, The. Buck H 2E 20
Drummond St. NW1 4G 67 (3A 160)
Drum St. E1 6F 69 (7K 163)
Drury Cres. Croy 2A 152
Drury Ho. SW8 1G 103
Drury La. WC2 6J 67 (7F 161)
Drury Lane Theatre. 7K 67 (1G 167) (off Catherine St.)
Drury Rd. Harr 7G 25
Drury Way. NW10 5K 45
Drury Way Ind. Est. NW10 5J 45
Dryad St. SW15 3F 101
Dryburgh Gdns. NW9 3G 27
Dryburgh Ho. SW1 5F 85 (5K 171) (off Abbots Mnr.)
Dryburgh Rd. SW15 3D 100
Dryden Av. W7 6K 61
Dryden Ct. SE11 4B 86 (4K 173)
Dryden Mans. W14 6G 83 (off Queen's Club Gdns.)
Dryden Rd. SW19 6A 120
Dryden Rd. Enf 6K 7
Dryden Rd. Harr 1K 25
Dryden Rd. Well 1K 109
Dryden St. WC2 6J 67 (1F 167)
Dryfield Clo. NW10 6J 45
Dryfield Rd. Edgw 6D 12
Dryfield Wlk. SE8 6C 88
Dryhill Rd. Belv 6F 93
Drylands Rd. N8 6J 31
Drysdale Av. E4 7J 9
Drysdale Clo. N'wd 1G 23
Drysdale Ho. N1 3E 68 (1H 163) (off Drysdale St.)
Drysdale Pl. N1 3E 68 (1H 163)
Drysdale St. N1 3E 68 (1H 163)
Dublin Av. E8 1G 69
Dublin Ct. S Harr 2H 43 (off Northolt Rd.)
Du Burstow Ter. W7 2J 79
Ducal St. E2 3F 69 (2K 163)
Du Cane Clo. W12 6E 64
Du Cane Ct. SW17 1E 120
Du Cane Rd. W12 6B 64
Ducavel Ho. SW2 1K 121
Duchess Clo. N11 5A 16
Duchess Clo. Sutt 4A 150
Duchess Gro. Buck H 2E 20
Duchess M. W1 5F 67 (6K 159)
Duchess of Bedford Ho. W8 2J 83 (off Duchess of Bedford's Wlk.)
Duchess of Bedford's Wlk. W8 2J 83
Duchess St. W1 5F 67 (6K 159)
Duchess Theatre. 7K 67 (2G 167) (off Catherine St.)
Duchy Rd. Barn 1G 5
Duchy St. SE1 1A 86 (4K 167) (in two parts)
Ducie St. SW4 4K 103
Duckett M. N4 6B 32
Duckett Rd. N4 6A 32
Duckett St. E1 4K 69
Ducking Stool Ct. Romf 4K 39
Duck La. W1 1C 166
Duck Lees La. Enf 4F 9
Duck's Hill Rd. N'wd & Ruis 1D 22
Ducks Island. 6A 4
Ducks Wlk. Twic 5C 98
Du Cros Dri. Stan 6J 11
Du Cros Rd. W3 1A 82
Dudden Hill. 5D 46
Dudden Hill La. NW10 4B 46
Dudden Hill Pde. NW10 4B 46
Duddington Clo. SE9 4B 126
Dudley Av. Harr 3C 26
Dudley Ct. NW11 4H 29
Dudley Ct. W1 6D 66 (1E 164) (off Up. Berkeley St.)
Dudley Ct. WC2 6J 67 (7E 160)
Dudley Dri. Mord 1G 149
Dudley Dri. Ruis 5K 41
Dudley Gdns. W13 2B 80
Dudley Gdns. Harr 1H 43
Dudley Ho. W2 5B 66 (6A 158) (off N. Wharf Rd.)
Dudley Rd. E17 2C 34
Dudley Rd. N3 2K 29
Dudley Rd. NW6 2G 65
Dudley Rd. SW19 6J 119
Dudley Rd. Ashf 5B 112
Dudley Rd. Felt 1E 112
Dudley Rd. Harr 2G 43
Dudley Rd. Ilf 4F 55
Dudley Rd. King T 3F 135
Dudley Rd. Rich 2F 99
Dudley Rd. S'hall 2B 78
Dudley Rd. W on T 6J 131
Dudley St. W2 5B 66 (6A 158)
Dudlington Rd. E5 2J 51
Dudmaston M. SW3 5B 170
Dudrich M. SE5 7C 86 (off Pitman St.)
Dudrich M. Enf 1G 7
Dudsbury Rd. Sidc 6B 128
Dudset La. Houn 1J 95
Duffell Ho. SE11 6H 173
Dufferin Av. EC1 4E 162
Dufferin Ct. EC1 4D 68 (4E 162) (off Dufferin St.)
Dufferin St. EC1 4C 68 (4D 162)
Duffield Clo. Harr 5K 25
Duffield Dri. N15 4F 33
Duff St. E14 6D 70
Dufour's Pl. W1 6G 67 (1B 166)
Dugard Way. SE11 4B 86 (3K 173)
Duke Gdns. Ilf 4H 37
Duke Humphrey Rd. SE3 1G 107 (in two parts)
Duke of Cambridge Clo. Twic 6H 97
Duke of Edinburgh Rd. Sutt 2B 150
Duke of Wellington Pl. SW1 2E 84 (6H 165)
Duke of York Memorial. 5D 166
Duke of York's Theatre. 7J 67 (3E 166) (off St Martin's La.)
Duke of York St. SW1 1G 85 (4B 166)
Duke Rd. W4 5K 81
Duke Rd. Ilf 4H 37
Dukes Av. N3 1K 29
Duke's Av. N10 3F 31
Duke's Av. W4 5K 81
Duke's Av. Edgw 6A 12
Dukes Av. Harr 4J 25
Dukes Av. Houn 4C 96
Dukes Av. N Mald 3A 136
Dukes Av. N Har 6D 24
Dukes Av. N'holt 7C 42
Dukes Av. Rich 4C 116
Dukes Clo. Ashf 4E 112
Dukes Clo. Hamp 5D 114
Dukes Ct. E6 1E 72
Dukes Ct. SE13 2E 106
Dukes Ga. W4 4J 81
Dukes Grn. Av. Felt 5J 95
Dukes Head Pas. Hamp 7G 115
Duke's Head Yd. N6 1F 49
Duke Shore Wharf. E14 7B 70
Duke's Ho. SW1 4H 85 (3D 172) (off Vincent St.)
Dukes La. W8 2K 83
Dukes M. N10 3F 31
Duke's M. W1 7H 159
Dukes Orchard. Bex 1J 129
Duke's Pas. E17 4E 34
Duke's Pl. EC3 6E 68 (1H 169)
Dukes Ride. Uxb 4A 40
Dukes Rd. E6 1E 72
Dukes Rd. W3 4G 63
Duke's Rd. WC1 3H 67 (2D 160)
Dukesthorpe Rd. SE26 4K 123
Duke St. SW1 1G 85 (4B 166)
Duke St. W1 6E 66 (7H 159)
Duke St. Rich 4D 98
Duke St. Sutt 4B 150
Duke St. Hill. SE1 1D 86 (4F 169)
Duke St. Mans. W1 6E 66 (1H 165) (off Duke St.)
Dukes Way. W Wick 3G 155
Duke's Yd. W1 7E 66 (2H 165)
Dulas St. N4 1K 49
Dulford St. W11 7G 65
Dulka Rd. SW11 5D 102
Dulverton. NW1 1G 67 (off Royal College St.)
Dulverton Mans. WC1 4H 161
Dulverton Rd. SE9 2G 127
Dulverton Rd. Ruis 1J 41
Dulwich. 2E 122
Dulwich Comn. SE21 1E 122
Dulwich Hamlet F.C. 4E 104
Dulwich Lawn Clo. SE22 5F 105
Dulwich Oaks Pl. SE21 3E 122
Dulwich Picture Gallery. 7D 104
Dulwich Ri. Gdns. SE22 5F 105
Dulwich Rd. SE24 5A 104
Dulwich Village. 7E 104
Dulwich Village. SE21 6D 104
Dulwich Wood Av. SE19 4E 122
Dulwich Wood Pk. SE19 4E 122
Dumain Ct. SE11 4B 86 (off Opal St.)
Dumbarton Ct. SW2 6J 103
Dumbarton Rd. SW2 6J 103
Dumbleton Clo. King T 1H 135
Dumbreck Rd. SE9 4D 108
Dumont Rd. N16 3E 50
Dumpton Pl. NW1 7E 48
Dumsey Eyot. Cher 7A 130
Dunally Pk. Shep 7F 131
Dunbar Av. SW16 2A 140
Dunbar Av. Beck 4A 142
Dunbar Av. Dag 3G 57
Dunbar Clo. Hay 6K 59
Dunbar Ct. Brom 4J 143 (off Durham Rd.)
Dunbar Ct. Sutt 5B 150
Dunbar Gdns. Dag 5G 57
Dunbar Rd. E7 6J 53

Dunbar Rd. N22 1A 32
Dunbar Rd. N Mald 4J 135
Dunbar St. SE27 3C 122
Dunbar Wharf. E14 7B 70
(off Narrow St.)
Dunblane Clo. Edgw 2C 12
Dunblane Rd. SE9 3C 108
Dunboe Pl. Shep 7E 130
Dunboyne Rd. NW3 5D 48
Dunbridge Ho. SW15 6B 100
(off Highcliffe Dri.)
Dunbridge St. E2 4G 69
Duncan Clo. Barn 4F 5
Duncan Ct. N21 1G 17
Duncan Gro. W3 6A 64
Duncan Ho. NW3 7D 48
(off Fellows Rd.)
Duncan Ho. SW1
5G 85 (6B 172)
(off Dolphin Sq.)
Duncannon Ho. SW1
5H 85 (6D 172)
(off Lindsay Sq.)
Duncannon St. WC2
7J 67 (3E 166)
Duncan Rd. E8 1H 69
Duncan Rd. Rich 4E 98
Duncan St. N1 2B 68
Duncan Ter. N1 2B 68
(in two parts)
Dunch St. E1 6H 69
Duncombe Hill. SE23 7A 106
Duncombe Rd. N19 1H 49
Duncrievie Rd. SE13 6F 107
Duncroft. SE18 7J 91
Dundalk Ho. E1 6J 69
(off Clark St.)
Dundalk Rd. SE4 3A 106
Dundas Gdns. W Mol 3F 133
Dundas Rd. SE15 2J 105
Dundee Ct. E1 1H 87
(off Wapping High St.)
Dundee Ho. W9 3A 66
(off Maida Va.)
Dundee Rd. E13 2K 71
Dundee Rd. SE25 5H 141
Dundee St. E1 1H 87
Dundee Way. Enf 3F 9
Dundee Wharf. E14 7B 70
Dundela Gdns. Wor Pk 4D 148
Dundonald Clo. E6 6C 72
Dundonald Ho. E14 2D 88
(off Admirals Way)
Dundonald Rd. NW10 1F 65
Dundonald Rd. SW19 7G 119
Dundry Ho. SE26 3G 123
Dunedin Ho. E16 1D 90
(off Manwood St.)
Dunedin Rd. E10 3D 52
Dunedin Rd. Ilf 1G 55
Dunedin Way. Hay 4A 60
Dunelm Gro. SE27 3C 122
Dunelm St. E1 6K 69
Dunfield Gdns. SE6 5D 124
Dunfield Rd. SE6 5D 124
(in two parts)
Dunford Ct. Pinn 1D 24
Dunford Rd. N7 4K 49
Dungarvan Av. SW15 4C 100
Dunheved Clo. T Hth 6A 140
Dunheved Rd. N. T Hth 6A 140
Dunheved Rd. S. T Hth 6A 140
Dunheved Rd. W. T Hth 6A 140
Dunholme Grn. N9 3A 18
Dunholme La. N9 3A 18
Dunholme Rd. N9 3A 18
Dunkeld Ho. E14 6F 71
(off Abbott Rd.)
Dunkeld Rd. SE25 4D 140
Dunkeld Rd. Dag 2B 56
Dunkery Rd. SE9 4B 126
Dunkirk St. SE27 4C 122
Dunlace Rd. E5 4J 51
Dunleary Clo. Houn 7D 96
Dunley Dri. New Ad 7D 154
Dunlin Ho. SE16 4K 87
(off Tawny Way)
Dunloe Av. N17 3D 32
Dunloe Ct. E2 2F 69
Dunloe St. E2 2F 69
Dunlop Pl. SE16 3F 87
Dunmore Point. E2
3F 69 (2J 163)
(off Gascoigne Pl.)
Dunmore Rd. NW6 1G 65
Dunmore Rd. SW20 1E 136
Dunmow Clo. Felt 3C 114
Dunmow Clo. Romf 5C 38
Dunmow Ho. SE11
5K 85 (5H 173)
(off Newburn St.)
Dunmow Rd. E15 4F 53
Dunmow Wlk. N1 1C 68
(off Popham St.)
Dunnage Cres. SE16 4A 88
(in two parts)
Dunnico Ho. SE17 5E 86
(off East St.)
Dunn Mead. NW9 7G 13
Dunnock Clo. E6 6C 72
Dunnock Clo. N9 1E 18
Dunn's Pas. WC1 7F 161
Dunn St. E8 5F 51
Dunollie Pl. NW5 5G 49
Dunollie Rd. NW5 5G 49
Dunoon Gdns. SE23 7K 105
Dunoon Ho. N1 1K 67
(off Bemerton Est.)
Dunoon Rd. SE23 7J 105
Dunoran Home. Brom 1C 144
Dunraven Dri. Enf 2F 7
Dunraven Rd. W12 1C 82
Dunraven St. W1
7D 66 (2F 165)
Dunsany Rd. W14 3F 83
Dunsfold Way. New Ad 7D 154
Dunsford Way. SW15 6D 100
Dunsmore Clo. Hay 4C 60
Dunsmore Rd. W on T 6K 131
Dunsmure Rd. N16 1E 50
Dunspring La. Ilf 2F 37
Dunstable M. W1
5E 66 (5H 159)
Dunstable Rd. Rich 4E 98
Dunstable Rd. W Mol 4D 132
Dunstall Rd. SW20 6D 118
Dunstall Way. W Mol 3F 133
Dunstall Welling Est. Well
2B 110
Dunstan Clo. N2 3A 30
Dunstan Glade. Orp 6H 145
Dunstan Houses. E1 5J 69
(off Stepney Grn.)
Dunstan Rd. NW11 1H 47
Dunstan's Gro. SE22 6H 105
Dunstan's Rd. SE22 7G 105
Dunster Av. Mord 1F 149
Dunster Clo. Barn 4A 4
Dunster Clo. Romf 2J 39
Dunster Ct. EC3 7E 68 (2H 169)
Dunster Dri. NW9 1J 45
Dunster Gdns. NW6 7H 47
Dunster Ho. SE6 3E 124
Dunsterville Way. SE1
2D 86 (7F 169)
Dunster Way. Harr 3C 42
Dunston Rd. E8 1F 69
Dunston Rd. SW11 2E 102
Dunston St. E8 1E 68
Dunton Clo. Surb 1E 146
Dunton Ct. SE23 2H 123
Dunton Rd. E10 7D 34
Dunton Rd. SE1 5F 87
Dunton Rd. Romf 4K 39
Duntshill Rd. SW18 1K 119
Dunvegan Clo. W Mol 4F 133
Dunvegan Rd. SE9 4D 108
Dunwich Rd. Bexh 1F 111
Dunworth M. W11 6H 65
Duplex Ride. SW1
2D 84 (7F 165)
Dupont Rd. SW20 2F 137
Duppas Av. Croy 4B 152
Duppas Clo. Shep 5F 131
Duppas Ct. Croy 3B 152
(off Duppas Hill Ter.)
Duppas Hill La. Croy 4B 152
Duppas Hill Rd. Croy 4A 152
Duppas Hill Ter. Croy 3B 152
Duppas Rd. Croy 3A 152
Dupree Rd. SE7 5K 89
Duraden Clo. Beck 7D 124
Durand Clo. Cars 1D 150
Durand Gdns. SW9 1K 103
Durands Wlk. SE16 2B 88
Durand Way. NW10 7J 45
Durants Pk. Av. Enf 4E 8
Durants Rd. Enf 4D 8
Durant St. E2 2G 69
Durban Ct. E7 7B 54
Durban Gdns. Dag 7J 57
Durban Ho. W12 7D 64
(off White City Est.)
Durban Rd. E15 3G 71
Durban Rd. E17 1B 34
Durban Rd. N17 6K 17
Durban Rd. SE27 4C 122
Durban Rd. Beck 2B 142
Durban Rd. Ilf 1J 55
Durbin Rd. Chess 4E 146
Durdan Cotts. S'hall 6D 60
(off Denbigh Rd.)
Durdans Ho. NW1 7F 49
(off Farrier St.)
Durdans Rd. S'hall 6D 60
Durell Gdns. Dag 5D 56
Durell Ho. SE16 2K 87
(off Wolfe Cres.)
Durell Rd. Dag 5D 56
Durfey Ho. SE5 7D 86
(off Edmund St.)
Durford Cres. SW15 1D 118
Durham Av. Brom 4H 143
Durham Av. Houn 5D 78
Durham Av. Wfd G 5G 21
Durham Clo. SW20 2D 136
Durham Ct. NW6 2J 65
(off Kilburn Pk. Rd., in five parts)
Durham Ct. Tedd 4J 115
Durham Hill. Brom 4H 125
Durham Ho. Bark 7A 56
(off Margaret Bondfield Av.)
Durham Ho. Brom 4G 143
Durham Ho. Dag 5J 57
Durham Ho. St. WC2 3F 167
Durham Pl. SW3
5D 84 (6E 170)
Durham Pl. Ilf 4G 55
Durham Ri. SE18 5G 91
Durham Rd. E12 4B 54
Durham Rd. E16 4G 71
Durham Rd. N2 3C 30
Durham Rd. N7 2K 49
Durham Rd. N9 2B 18
Durham Rd. SW20 1D 136
Durham Rd. W5 3D 80
Durham Rd. Brom 3H 143
Durham Rd. Dag 5J 57
Durham Rd. Felt 7A 96
Durham Rd. Harr 5F 25
Durham Rd. Sidc 5B 128
Durham Row. E1 5K 69
Durham St. SE11
6K 85 (6G 173)
Durham Ter. W2 6K 65
Durham Wharf. Bren 7C 80
Durham Yd. E2 3H 69
Durley Av. Pinn 7C 24
Durley Rd. N16 7E 32
Durliston Rd. E5 2G 51
Durlston Rd. King T 6E 116
Durnford Ho. SE6 3E 124
Durnford St. N15 5E 32
Durnford St. SE10 6E 88
Durning Rd. SE19 5D 122
Durnsford Av. SW19 2J 119
Durnsford Rd. N11 1H 31
Durnsford Rd. SW19 2J 119
Durrant Ct. Har W 2J 25
Durrell Rd. SW6 1H 101
Durrell Way. Shep 6F 131
Durrels Ho. W14 4H 83
(off Warwick Gdns.)
Durrington Av. SW20 7E 118
Durrington Pk. Rd. SW20
1E 136
Durrington Rd. E5 4A 52
Durrington Tower. SW8 2G 103
Durrisdeer Ho. NW2 4H 47
(off Lyndale)
Dursley Clo. SE3 2A 108
Dursley Ct. SE15 7E 86
(off Lydney Clo.)
Dursley Gdns. SE3 1B 108
Dursley Rd. SE3 2A 108
Durward St. E1 5H 69
Durweston M. W1 5F 159
Durweston St. W1
5D 66 (6F 159)
Dury Falls Ct. Romf 2J 39
Dury Rd. Barn 1C 4
Dutch Barn Clo. Stanw 6A 94
Dutch Gdns. King T 6H 117
Dutch Yd. SW18 5J 101
Dutton Bus. Pk. SE9 2E 126
Dutton St. SE10 1E 106
Duxberry Av. Felt 3A 114
Duxberry Clo. Brom 5C 144
Duxford Ho. SE2 2D 92
(off Wolvercote Rd.)
Dye Ho. La. E3 1C 70
Dyer Ho. Hamp 1F 133
Dyer's Bldgs. EC1
5A 68 (6J 161)
Dyers Hall Rd. E11 1G 53
Dyers Hill Rd. E11 2F 53
Dyers La. SW15 4D 100
Dykes Way. Brom 3H 143
Dykewood Clo. Bex 3K 129
Dylan Rd. SE24 4B 104
Dylan Rd. Belv 3G 93
Dylan Thomas Ho. N8 4K 31
Dylways. SE5 4D 104
Dymchurch Clo. Ilf 2E 36
Dymes Path. SW19 2F 119
Dymock Ct. SE15 7E 86
(off Lydney Clo.)
Dymock St. SW6 3K 101
Dyneley Rd. SE12 3A 126
Dyne Rd. NW6 7G 47
Dynevor Rd. N16 3E 50
Dynevor Rd. Rich 5E 98
Dynham Rd. NW6 7J 47
Dyott St. WC1 6H 67 (7D 160)
Dysart Av. King T 5C 116
Dysart St. EC2 4D 68 (4G 163)
Dyson Ct. NW2 1E 46
Dyson Ct. Wemb 4A 44
Dyson Ho. SE10 5H 89
(off Blackwall La.)
Dyson Rd. E11 6G 35
Dyson Rd. E15 6H 53
Dysons Rd. N18 5C 18

Eade Rd. N4 7C 32
Eagans Clo. N2 3B 30
Eagle Av. Romf 6E 38
Eagle Clo. SE16 5J 87
Eagle Clo. Enf 4D 8
Eagle Clo. Wall 6J 151
Eagle Ct. E11 4J 35
Eagle Ct. EC1
5B 68 (5A 162)
Eagle Dri. NW9 2A 28
Eagle Hill. SE19 6D 122
Eagle Ho. E1 4H 69
(off Headlam St.)
Eagle Ho. N1 2D 68
(off Eagle Wharf Rd.)
Eagle La. E11 4J 35
Eagle Lodge. NW11 7H 29
Eagle M. N1 6E 50
Eagle Pl. SW1 3B 166
Eagle Pl. SW7 5A 84
(off Rolandway)
Eagle Rd. Wemb 7D 44
Eaglesfield Rd. SE18 1F 109
Eagle St. WC1 5K 67 (6G 161)
Eagle Ter. Wfd G 7E 20
Eagle Trad. Est. Mitc 6D 138
Eagle Wharf Ct. SE1
1F 87 (5J 169)
(off Lafone St.)
Eagle Wharf E. E14 7A 70
(off Narrow St.)
Eagle Wharf Rd. N1 2C 68
Eagle Wharf W. E14 7A 70
(off Narrow St.)
Ealdham Sq. SE9 4A 108
Ealing. 7D 62
Ealing B'way. Cen. W5 7D 62
Ealing Common. (Junct.) 1F 81
Ealing Downs Ct. Gnfd 3A 62
Ealing Grn. W5 1D 80
Ealing Pk. Gdns. W5 4C 80
Ealing Rd. Bren 4D 80
Ealing Rd. N'holt 1E 60
Ealing Rd. Wemb 6E 44
Ealing Rd. Trad. Est. Bren 5D 80
Ealing Village. W5 6E 62
Eamont Clo. Ruis 7D 22
Eamont Ct. NW8 2C 66
(off Eamont St.)
Eamont St. NW8 2C 66
Eardley Cres. SW5 5J 83
Eardley Rd. SW16 5G 121
Eardley Rd. Belv 5G 93
Earl Clo. N11 5A 16
Earldom Rd. SW15 4E 100
Earle Gdns. King T 7E 116
Earlham Gro. E7 5H 53
Earlham Gro. N22 7E 16
Earlham St. WC2
6J 67 (1D 166)
Earl Ho. NW1 4C 66 (4D 158)
(off Lisson Gro.)
Earlom Ho. WC1 3A 68 (2J 161)
(off Margery St.)
Earl Ri. SE18 5H 91
Earl Rd. SW14 4J 99
Earl's Court. 5J 83
Earl's Court Exhibition Building.
5J 83
Earls Ct. Gdns. SW5 4K 83
Earls Ct. Rd. W8 & SW5 3J 83
Earl's Ct. Sq. SW5 5K 83
Earls Cres. Harr 4J 25
Earlsdown Ho. Bark 2H 73
Earlsferry Way. N1 7J 49
(in two parts)
Earlsfield. 1A 120
Earlsfield Rd. SW18 1A 120
Earlshall Rd. SE9 4D 108
Earlsmead. Harr 4D 42
Earlsmead Rd. N15 5F 33
Earlsmead Rd. NW10 3E 64
Earls Ter. W8 3H 83
Earlsthorpe M. SW12 6E 102
Earlsthorpe Rd. SE26 4K 123
Earlstoke St. EC1
3B 68 (1A 162)
Earlston Gro. E9 1H 69
Earl St. EC2 5D 68 (5G 163)
Earls Wlk. W8 3J 83
Earl's Wlk. Dag 4B 56
Earlswood Av. T Hth 5A 140
Earlswood Clo. SE10 6G 89
Earlswood Gdns. Ilf 3E 36
Earlswood St. SE10 5G 89

Early M. *NW1* 1F **67**
Earnshaw St. *WC2* 6H **67** (7D **160**)
Earsby St. *W14* 4G **83** (in three parts)
Easby Cres. *Mord* 6K **137**
Easebourne Rd. *Dag* 5C **56**
Easleys M. *W1* 6E **66** (7H **159**)
East Acton. 7A 64
E. Acton Arc. *W3* 6A **64**
E. Acton Ct. *W3* 7A **64**
E. Acton La. *W3* 1A **82**
E. Arbour St. *E1* 6K **69**
East Av. *E12* 7C **54**
East Av. *E17* 4D **34**
East Av. *N2* 4K **29**
East Av. *Hay* 1H **77**
East Av. *S'hall* 7D **60**
East Av. *Wall* 5K **151**
East Bank. *N16* 7E **32**
Eastbank Rd. *Hamp H* 5G **115**
East Barnet. 6H 5
E. Barnet Rd. *Barn* 4G **5**
E. Beckton District Cen. *E6* 5D **72**
East Bedfont. 7G 95
East Block. SE1 2K 85 (6H 167) (off York Rd.)
E. Boundary Rd. *E12* 3D **54**
Eastbourne Av. *W3* 6K **63**
Eastbourne Gdns. *SW14* 3J **99**
Eastbourne M. *W2* 6A **66** (7A **158**)
Eastbourne Rd. *E6* 3E **72** (in two parts)
Eastbourne Rd. *E15* 1G **71**
Eastbourne Rd. *N15* 6E **32**
Eastbourne Rd. *SW17* 6E **120**
Eastbourne Rd. *W4* 6J **81**
Eastbourne Rd. *Bren* 5C **80**
Eastbourne Rd. *Felt* 2B **114**
Eastbourne Ter. *W2* 6A **66** (7A **158**)
Eastbournia Av. *N9* 3C **18**
Eastbrook Av. *N9* 7D **8**
Eastbrook Av. *Dag* 4J **57**
Eastbrook Dri. *Romf* 3K **57**
Eastbrook Rd. *SE3* 1K **107**
Eastbury Av. *Bark* 1J **73**
Eastbury Av. *Enf* 1A **8**
Eastbury Ct. *Bark* 1J **73**
Eastbury Ct. New Bar 5F 5 (off Lyonsdown Rd.)
Eastbury Gro. *W4* 5A **82**
Eastbury Rd. *E6* 4E **72**
Eastbury Rd. *King T* 7E **116**
Eastbury Rd. *Orp* 6H **145**
Eastbury Rd. *Romf* 6K **39**
Eastbury Sq. *Bark* 1K **73**
Eastbury Ter. *E1* 4K **69**
Eastcastle St. *W1* 6G **67** (7A **160**)
Eastcheap. *EC3* 7E **68** (2G **169**)
E. Churchfield Rd. *W3* 1K **81**
Eastchurch Rd. *H'row A* 2G **95**
East Clo. *W5* 4G **63**
East Clo. *Barn* 4K **5**
East Clo. *Gnfd* 2G **61**
Eastcombe Av. *SE7* 6K **89**
Eastcote. 7K 23
Eastcote. *Orp* 7K **145**
Eastcote Av. *Gnfd* 5A **44**
Eastcote Av. *Harr* 2F **43**
Eastcote Av. *W Mol* 5D **132**
Eastcote Ind. Est. *Ruis* 7A **24**
Eastcote La. *Harr* 4C **42**
Eastcote La. *N'holt* 5D **42** (in three parts)
Eastcote La. N. *N'holt* 6D **42**
Eastcote Pl. *Pinn* 6K **23**
Eastcote Rd. *Harr* 3G **43**
Eastcote Rd. *Pinn* 5B **24**
Eastcote Rd. *Ruis* 7G **23**
Eastcote Rd. *Well* 2H **109**
Eastcote St. *SW9* 2K **103**
Eastcote Vw. *Pinn* 4A **24**
Eastcote Village. 5K 23
East Ct. *Wemb* 2C **44**
East Cres. *N11* 4J **15**
East Cres. *Enf* 5A **8**
Eastcroft Rd. *Eps* 7A **148**
E. Cross Cen. *E15* 6C **52**
E. Cross Route. *E9 & E3* 7B **52**
Eastdown Ct. *SE13* 4F **107**
Eastdown Ho. *E8* 4G **51**
Eastdown Pk. *SE13* 4F **107**
East Dri. *Cars* 7C **150**
E. Duck Lees La. *Enf* 4F **9**
East Dulwich. 4F 105
E. Dulwich Gro. *SE22* 5E **104**
E. Dulwich Rd. *SE22 & SE15* 4F **105**
E. End Farm. *Pinn* 3D **24**
E. End Rd. *N3 & N2* 2J **29**
E. End Way. *Pinn* 3C **24**
East Entrance. *Dag* 2H **75**
Eastern Av. *E11 & Ilf* 6K **35**
Eastern Av. *Pinn* 7B **24**
Eastern Av. E. *Romf* 3K **39**
Eastern Av. W. *Romf* 4E **38** (in two parts)
Eastern Ind. Est. *Eri* 2G **93**
Eastern Perimeter Rd. *H'row A* 2H **95**
Eastern Rd. *E13* 2K **71**
Eastern Rd. *E17* 5E **34**
Eastern Rd. *N2* 3D **30**
Eastern Rd. *N22* 1J **31**
Eastern Rd. *SE4* 4C **106**
Easternville Gdns. *Ilf* 6G **37**
Eastern Way. *SE28* 2A **92**
E. Ferry Rd. *E14* 4D **88**
Eastfield Gdns. *Dag* 4G **57**
Eastfield Rd. *E17* 4C **34**
Eastfield Rd. *N8* 3J **31**
Eastfield Rd. *Dag* 4F **57**
Eastfield Rd. *Enf* 1E **8**
Eastfields. *Pinn* 5A **24**
Eastfields Rd. *W3* 5J **63**
Eastfields Rd. *Mitc* 2E **138**
Eastfield St. *E14* 5A **70**
East Finchley. 4C 30
East Gdns. *SW17* 6C **120**
Eastgate Clo. *SE28* 6D **74**
Eastglade. *Pinn* 3D **24**
East Ham. 1D 72
E. Ham and Barking By-Pass. *Bark* 2J **73**
Eastham Clo. *Barn* 5C **4**
E. Ham Ind. Est. *E6* 4C **72**
E. Ham Mnr. Way. *E6* 6E **72**
E. Harding St. *EC4* 6A **68** (7K **161**)
E. Heath Rd. *NW3* 3A **48**
East Hill. *SW18* 5K **101**
East Hill. *Wemb* 2G **45**
Eastholm. *NW11* 4K **29**
East Holme. *Eri* 1K **111**
East Holme. *Hay* 1J **77**
E. India Bldgs. E14 7C 70 (off Saltwell St.)
E. India Dock Ho. *E14* 6E **70**
E. India Dock Rd. *E14* 6C **70**
Eastlake Ho. *NW8* 4B **158**
Eastlake Rd. *SE5* 2C **104**
Eastlands Cres. *SE21* 6F **105**
East La. *SE16* 2G **87** (Chambers St.)
East La. *SE16* 2G **87** (Scott Lidgett Cres.)
East La. *King T* 3D **134**
East La. *Wemb* 3B **44**
East La. Bus. Pk. *Wemb* 2D **44**
Eastlea M. *E16* 4G **71**
Eastleigh Av. *Harr* 2F **43**
Eastleigh Clo. *NW2* 3A **46**
Eastleigh Clo. *Sutt* 7K **149**
Eastleigh Rd. *E17* 2B **34**
Eastleigh Rd. *Bexh* 3J **111**
Eastleigh Rd. *H'row A* 3H **95**
Eastleigh Wlk. *SW15* 7C **100**
Eastleigh Way. *Felt* 1J **113**
East Lodge. E16 1J 89 (off Wesley Av.)
East London Crematorium. *E13* 3H **71**
Eastman Ho. *SW4* 6G **103**
Eastman Rd. *W3* 2K **81**
East Mascalls. *SE7* 6A **90**
East Mead. *Ruis* 3B **42**
Eastmead Av. *Gnfd* 3F **61**
Eastmead Clo. *Brom* 2C **144**
Eastmearn Rd. *SE27* 2C **122**
East Molesey. 4H 133
Eastmoor Pl. *SE7* 3B **90**
Eastmoor St. *SE7* 3B **90**
E. Mount St. *E1* 5H **69** (in two parts)
Eastney Rd. *Croy* 1B **152**
Eastney St. *SE10* 5F **89**
Eastnor Rd. *SE9* 1G **127**
Easton St. *WC1* 4A **68** (3J **161**)
East Pk. Clo. *Romf* 5D **38**
East Parkside. *SE10* 2G **89**
East Pas. *EC1* 5C **162**
East Pl. *SE27* 4C **122**
East Point. *SE1* 5G **87**
E. Pole Cotts. *Barn* 4C **6**
E. Poultry Av. *EC1* 5B **68** (6A **162**)
East Ramp. *H'row A* 1D **94**
East Rd. *E15* 1J **71**
East Rd. *N1* 3D **68** (2E **162**)
East Rd. *N2* 1C **30**
East Rd. *SW19* 6A **120**
East Rd. *Barn* 1K **15**
East Rd. *Chad H* 5E **38**
East Rd. *Edgw* 1H **27**
East Rd. *Enf* 1D **8**
East Rd. *Felt* 7F **95**
East Rd. *Harr* 7B **26**
East Rd. *King T* 1E **134**
East Rd. *Rush G* 7K **39**
East Rd. *Well* 2B **110**
East Rd. *W Dray* 4B **76**
E. Rochester Way. *Sidc & Bex* 4J **109**
East Row. *E11* 6J **35**
East Row. *W10* 4G **65**
Eastry Av. *Brom* 6H **143**
Eastry Ho. SW8 7J 85 (off Hartington Rd.)
Eastry Rd. *Eri* 7G **93**
East Sheen. 4J 99
E. Sheen Av. *SW14* 5K **99**
Eastside Rd. *NW11* 4H **29**
East Smithfield. *E1* 7F **69** (3K **169**)
East St. *SE17* 5C **86**
East St. *Bark* 1G **73**
East St. *Bexh* 4G **111**
East St. *Bren* 7C **80**
East St. *Brom* 2J **143**
E. Surrey Gro. *SE15* 7F **87**
E. Tenter St. *E1* 6F **69** (1K **169**)
East Ter. *Sidc* 1J **127**
East Towers. *Pinn* 5B **24**
East Va. *W3* 1B **82**
East Vw. *E4* 5K **19**
East Vw. *Barn* 2C **4**
Eastview Av. *SE18* 7J **91**
Eastville Av. *NW11* 6H **29**
East Wlk. *E Barn* 7K **5**
East Wlk. *Hay* 1J **77**
Eastway. *E9* 6B **52** (in two parts)
East Way. *E11* 5K **35**
East Way. *Brom* 7J **143**
East Way. *Croy* 2A **154**
East Way. *Hay* 1J **77**
Eastway. *Mord* 5F **137**
East Way. *Ruis* 1J **41**
Eastway. *Wall* 4G **151**
Eastwell Clo. *Beck* 7A **124**
Eastwell Ho. *SE1* 7F **169**
E. W. Link Rd. *King T* 1D **134**
East Wickham. 1C 110
Eastwood Clo. *E18* 2J **35**
Eastwood Clo. *N17* 7C **18**
Eastwood Rd. *E18* 2J **35**
Eastwood Rd. *N10* 2E **30**
Eastwood Rd. *Ilf* 7A **38**
Eastwood Rd. *W Dray* 2C **76**
East Woodside. *Bex* 1E **128**
Eastwood St. *SW16* 6G **121**
Eatington Rd. *E10* 5F **35**
Eaton Clo. *SW1* 4E **84** (4G **171**)
Eaton Clo. *Stan* 4G **11**
Eaton Dri. *SW9* 4B **104**
Eaton Dri. *King T* 7G **117**
Eaton Dri. *Romf* 1H **39**
Eaton Gdns. *Dag* 7E **56**
Eaton Ga. *SW1* 4E **84** (3G **171**)
Eaton Gro. *N19* 3H **49**
Eaton Ho. E14 7B 70 (off Westferry Cir.)
Eaton Ho. *SW11* 1B **102**
Eaton La. *SW1* 3F **85** (2K **171**)
Eaton Mans. SW1 4E 84 (4G 171) (off Bourne St.)
Eaton M. N. *SW1* 4E **84** (3G **171**)
Eaton M. S. *SW1* 4E **84** (3H **171**)
Eaton M. W. *SW1* 4E **84** (3H **171**)
Eaton Pk. Rd. *N13* 2F **17**
Eaton Pl. *SW1* 4E **84** (2G **171**)
Eaton Ri. *E11* 5A **36**
Eaton Ri. *W5* 5D **62**
Eaton Rd. *NW4* 5E **28**
Eaton Rd. *Enf* 3K **7**
Eaton Rd. *Houn* 4H **97**
Eaton Rd. *Sidc* 2D **128**
Eaton Rd. *Sutt* 6A **150**
Eaton Row. *SW1* 3F **85** (2J **171**)
Eatons Mead. *E4* 2H **19**
Eaton Sq. *SW1* 4E **84** (3G **171**)
Eaton Ter. *E3* 3A **70**
Eaton Ter. *SW1* 4E **84** (3G **171**)
Eaton Ter. M. *SW1* 3G **171**
Eatonville Rd. *SW17* 2D **120**
Eatonville Vs. *SW17* 2D **120**
Ebbisham Dri. *SW8* 6K **85** (7G **173**)
Ebbisham Rd. *Wor Pk* 2E **148**
Ebbsfleet Rd. *NW2* 5G **47**
Ebdon Way. *SE3* 3K **107**
Ebenezer Ho. *SE11* 4B **86** (4K **173**)
Ebenezer Mussel Ho. E2 2J 69 (off Patriot Sq.)
Ebenezer St. *N1* 3D **68** (1E **162**)
Ebenezer Wlk. *SW16* 1G **139**
Ebley Clo. *SE15* 6F **87**
Ebner St. *SW18* 5K **101**
Ebor Cotts. *SW15* 3A **118**
Ebor St. *E1* 4F **69** (3J **163**)
Ebrington Rd. *Harr* 6D **26**
Ebsworth St. *SE23* 7K **105**
Eburne Rd. *N7* 3J **49**
Ebury Bri. *SW1* 5F **85** (5J **171**)
Ebury Bri. Est. *SW1* 5F **85** (5J **171**)
Ebury Bri. Rd. *SW1* 5E **84** (6H **171**)
Ebury Clo. *Kes* 3C **156**
Ebury M. *SE27* 3B **122**
Ebury M. *SW1* 4F **85** (3J **171**)
Ebury M. E. *SW1* 3F **85** (2J **171**)
Ebury Sq. *SW1* 4E **84** (4H **171**)
Ebury St. *SW1* 4E **84** (4H **171**)
Ecclesbourne Clo. *N13* 5F **17**
Ecclesbourne Gdns. *N13* 5F **17**
Ecclesbourne Rd. *N1* 7C **50**
Ecclesbourne Rd. *T Hth* 5C **140**
Eccleshill. Brom 4H 143 (off Durham Rd.)
Eccles Rd. *SW11* 4D **102**
Eccleston Bri. *SW1* 4F **85** (3K **171**)
Eccleston Clo. *Cockf* 4J **5**
Eccleston Cres. *Romf* 7B **38**
Ecclestone Ct. *Wemb* 5E **44**
Ecclestone M. *Wemb* 5E **44**
Ecclestone Pl. *Wemb* 5F **45**
Eccleston Ho. *SW2* 6A **104**
Eccleston M. *SW1* 3E **84** (2H **171**)
Eccleston Pl. *SW1* 4F **85** (3J **171**)
Eccleston Rd. *W13* 7A **62**
Eccleston Sq. *SW1* 4F **85** (4K **171**)
Eccleston Sq. M. *SW1* 4F **85** (4K **171**)
Eccleston St. *SW1* 3F **85** (2J **171**)
Echelforde Dri. *Ashf* 4C **112**
Echo Heights. *E4* 1J **19**
Eckford St. *N1* 2A **68**
Eckington Ho. N15 6D 32 (off Fladbury Rd.)
Eckstein Rd. *SW11* 4C **102**
Eclipse Rd. *E13* 5K **71**
Ector Rd. *SE6* 2G **125**
Edam Ct. *Sidc* 3A **128**
Edans Ct. *W12* 2B **82**
Edbrooke Rd. *W9* 4J **65**
Eddington St. *N4* 1A **50**
Eddisbury Ho. *SE26* 3G **123**
Eddiscombe Rd. *SW6* 2H **101**
Eddy Clo. *Romf* 6H **39**
Eddystone Rd. *SE4* 5A **106**
Eddystone Tower. *SE8* 5A **88**
Eddystone Wlk. *Stai* 7A **94**
Ede Clo. *Houn* 3D **96**
Edenbridge Clo. SE16 5H 87 (off Masters Dri.)
Edenbridge Rd. *E9* 7K **51**
Edenbridge Rd. *Enf* 6K **7**
Eden Clo. *NW3* 2J **47**
Eden Clo. *W8* 3J **83**
Eden Clo. *Bex* 4K **129**
Eden Clo. *Wemb* 1D **62**
Edencourt Rd. *SW16* 6F **121**
Edendale. *W3* 7H **63**
Edendale Rd. *Bexh* 1K **111**
Edenfield Gdns. *Wor Pk* 3B **148**
Eden Gro. *E17* 5D **34**
Eden Gro. *N7* 5K **49**
Edenham Way. *W10* 4H **65**
Eden Ho. NW8 4C 66 (4C 158) (off Church St.)
Edenhurst Av. *SW6* 3H **101**
Eden Lodge. *NW6* 7F **47**
Eden M. *SW17* 3A **120**
Eden Park. 5C 142
Eden Pk. Av. *Beck* 4A **142** (in two parts)
Eden Rd. *E17* 5D **34**
Eden Rd. *SE27* 4B **122**
Eden Rd. *Beck* 4A **142**
Eden Rd. *Bex* 4J **129**
Eden Rd. *Croy* 4D **152**
Edensor Gdns. *W4* 7A **82**
Edensor Rd. *W4* 7A **82**
Eden St. *King T* 2D **134**
Edenvale Clo. *Mitc* 7E **120**
Edenvale Rd. *Mitc* 7E **120**
Edenvale St. *SW6* 2K **101**
Eden Wlk. *King T* 2E **134**
Eden Way. *Beck* 5B **142**
Ederline Av. *SW16* 3K **139**
Edgar Ct. *N Mald* 2A **136**
Edgar Ho. E9 5A 52 (off Homerton Rd.)

Edgar Ho. E11 . . . 7J 35
Edgar Ho. SW8 . . . 7J 85
(off Wyvil Rd.)
Edgar Kail Way. SE22 . . . 4E 104
Edgarley Ter. SW6 . . . 1G 101
Edgar Rd. E3 . . . 3D 70
Edgar Rd. Houn . . . 7D 96
Edgar Rd. Romf . . . 7D 38
Edgar Rd. W Dray . . . 7A 58
Edgcott Ho. W10 . . . 5E 64
(off Sutton Way)
Edgeborough Way. Brom . . . 7B 126
Edgebury. Chst . . . 4F 127
Edgebury Wlk. Chst . . . 4G 127
Edge Bus. Cen., The. NW2 . . . 2D 46
Edgecombe Ho. SE5 . . . 2E 104
Edgecoombe. S Croy . . . 7J 153
Edgecoombe Clo. King T . . . 7K 117
Edgecote Clo. W3 . . . 1J 81
Edgecot Gro. N15 . . . 5E 32
Edgefield Av. Bark . . . 7K 55
Edgefield Ct. Bark . . . 7K 55
(off Edgefield Av.)
Edge Hill. SE18 . . . 6F 91
Edge Hill. SW19 . . . 7F 119
Edge Hill Av. N3 . . . 4J 29
Edge Hill Ct. SW19 . . . 7F 119
Edge Hill Ct. Sidc . . . 4K 127
Edgehill Gdns. Dag . . . 4G 57
Edgehill Ho. SW9 . . . 2B 104
Edgehill Rd. W13 . . . 5C 62
Edgehill Rd. Chst . . . 3G 127
Edgehill Rd. Mitc . . . 1F 139
Edgeley La. SW4 . . . 3H 103
Edgeley Rd. SW4 . . . 3H 103
Edgel St. SW18 . . . 4K 101
Edgepoint Clo. SE27 . . . 5B 122
Edge St. W8 . . . 1J 83
Edgewood Grn. Croy . . . 1K 153
Edgeworth Av. NW4 . . . 5C 28
Edgeworth Clo. NW4 . . . 5C 28
Edgeworth Ct. Barn . . . 4H 5
(off Fordham Rd.)
Edgeworth Cres. NW4 . . . 5C 28
Edgeworth Ho. NW8 . . . 1A 66
(off Boundary Rd.)
Edgeworth Rd. SE9 . . . 4A 108
Edgeworth Rd. Cockf . . . 4H 5
Edgington Rd. SW16 . . . 6H 121
Edgington Way. Sidc . . . 7C 128
Edgson Ho. SW1 . . . 5F 85 (5J 171)
(off Ebury Bri. Rd.)
Edgware. . . . 6B 12
Edgware Bury. . . . 3C 12
Edgwarebury Gdns. Edgw . . . 5B 12
Edgwarebury Golf Course. . . . 3K 11
Edgwarebury La. Edgw . . . 1A 12
(in two parts)
Edgwarebury Pk. . . . 3A 12
Edgware Ct. Edgw . . . 6B 12
Edgware Rd. NW2 . . . 1D 46
Edgware Rd. NW9 . . . 2J 27
Edgware Rd. W2 . . . 4B 66 (4A 158)
Edgware Way. Edgw & NW7 . . . 4A 12
Edgware Way. Els . . . 1J 11
Edinburgh Clo. E2 . . . 2J 69
Edinburgh Clo. Pinn . . . 7B 24
Edinburgh Clo. Uxb . . . 4D 40
Edinburgh Ct. SE16 . . . 1K 87
(off Rotherhithe St.)
Edinburgh Ct. SW20 . . . 5F 137
Edinburgh Ct. Eri . . . 7K 93
Edinburgh Ct. King T . . . 3E 134
(off Watersplash Clo.)
Edinburgh Dri. Romf . . . 4J 39
Edinburgh Dri. Uxb . . . 4D 40
Edinburgh Ga. SW1 . . . 2D 84 (6E 164)
Edinburgh Ho. NW4 . . . 3E 28
Edinburgh Ho. W9 . . . 3K 65
(off Maida Va.)
Edinburgh Rd. E13 . . . 2K 71
Edinburgh Rd. E17 . . . 5C 34
Edinburgh Rd. N18 . . . 5B 18
Edinburgh Rd. W7 . . . 2K 79
Edinburgh Rd. Sutt . . . 2A 150
Edington. NW5 . . . 6E 48
Edington Rd. SE2 . . . 3B 92
Edington Rd. Enf . . . 2D 8
Edison Building. E14 . . . 2C 88
Edison Clo. E17 . . . 5C 34
Edison Dri. S'hall . . . 6F 61
Edison Dri. Wemb . . . 3E 44
Edison Gro. SE18 . . . 7K 91
Edison Ho. Wemb . . . 3J 45
(off Barnhill Rd.)
Edison Rd. N8 . . . 6H 31
Edison Rd. Brom . . . 2J 143
Edison Rd. Enf . . . 2G 9
Edison Rd. Well . . . 1K 109
Edis St. NW1 . . . 1E 66
Edith Brinson Ho. E14 . . . 6F 71
(off Oban St.)
Edith Cavell Clo. N19 . . . 7J 31
Edith Gdns. Surb . . . 7H 135
Edith Gro. SW10 . . . 6A 84
Edith Ho. W6 . . . 5E 82
(off Queen Caroline St.)
Edithna St. SW9 . . . 3J 103
Edith Neville Cotts. NW1 . . . 3H 67 (1C 160)
(off Crace St.)
Edith Ramsay Ho. E1 . . . 5A 70
(off Duckett St.)
Edith Rd. E6 . . . 7B 54
Edith Rd. E15 . . . 5F 53
Edith Rd. N11 . . . 7C 16
Edith Rd. SE25 . . . 5D 140
Edith Rd. SW19 . . . 6K 119
Edith Rd. W14 . . . 4G 83
Edith Rd. Romf . . . 7D 38
Edith Row. SW6 . . . 1K 101
Edith St. E2 . . . 2G 69
Edith Summerskill Ho. SW6 . . . 7H 83
(off Clem Attlee Est.)
Edith Ter. SW10 . . . 7A 84
Edith Vs. W14 . . . 4H 83
Edith Yd. SW10 . . . 7A 84
Edmansons Clo. N17 . . . 1F 33
Edmeston Clo. E9 . . . 6A 52
Edmond Ct. SE14 . . . 1J 105
Edmonscote. W13 . . . 5A 62
Edmonton. . . . 4B 18
Edmonton Ct. SE16 . . . 3J 87
(off Canada Est.)
Edmonton Grn. Shop. Cen. N9 . . . 2B 18
Edmund Halley Way. SE10 . . . 2G 89
Edmund Ho. SE17 . . . 6B 86
Edmund Hurst Dri. E6 . . . 5F 73
Edmund Rd. Mitc . . . 3C 138
Edmund Rd. Well . . . 3A 110
Edmundsbury Ct. Est. SW9 . . . 4K 103
Edmunds Clo. Hay . . . 5A 60
Edmund St. SE5 . . . 7D 86
Edmunds Wlk. N2 . . . 4C 30
Ednam Ho. SE15 . . . 6G 87
(off Haymerle Rd.)
Edna Rd. SW20 . . . 2F 137
Edna St. SW11 . . . 1C 102
Edred Ho. E9 . . . 4A 52
(off Lindisfarne Way)
Edrich Ho. SW4 . . . 1J 103
Edric Ho. SW1 . . . 4H 85 (3D 172)
(off Page St.)
Edrick Rd. Edgw . . . 6D 12
Edrick Wlk. Edgw . . . 6D 12
Edric Rd. SE14 . . . 7K 87
Edridge Rd. Croy . . . 3C 152
Edward Av. E4 . . . 6J 19
Edward Av. Mord . . . 5B 138
Edward Bond Ho. WC1 . . . 3J 67 (2F 161)
(off Cromer St.)
Edward Clo. N9 . . . 7A 8
Edward Clo. NW2 . . . 4F 47
Edward Clo. Hamp H . . . 5G 115
Edward Clo. N'holt . . . 2A 60
Edward Ct. E16 . . . 5J 71
Edward Dodd Ct. N1 . . . 3D 68 (1F 163)
(off Haberdasher St.)
Edward Edward's Ho. SE1 . . . 5A 168
Edwardes Pl. W8 . . . 3H 83
Edwardes Sq. W8 . . . 3H 83
Edward Gro. Barn . . . 5G 5
Edward Ho. SE11 . . . 5H 173
Edward Mann Clo. E1 . . . 6K 69
(off Caroline St.)
Edward Mans. Bark . . . 7K 55
(off Upney La.)
Edward M. NW1 . . . 3F 67 (1K 159)
Edward Pl. SE8 . . . 6B 88
Edward Rd. E17 . . . 4K 33
Edward Rd. SE20 . . . 7K 123
Edward Rd. Barn . . . 5G 5
Edward Rd. Brom . . . 7K 125
Edward Rd. Chst . . . 5F 127
Edward Rd. Croy . . . 7E 140
Edward Rd. Felt . . . 5F 95
Edward Rd. Hamp H . . . 5G 115
Edward Rd. Harr . . . 3G 25
Edward Rd. N'holt . . . 2A 60
Edward Rd. Romf . . . 6E 38
Edward Robinson Ho. SE14 . . . 7K 87
(off Reaston St.)
Edward's Av. Ruis . . . 6K 41
Edwards Clo. Wor Pk . . . 2F 149
Edward's Cotts. N1 . . . 6B 50
Edwards Ct. S Croy . . . 4D 152
(off S. Park Hill Rd.)
Edwards Dri. N11 . . . 7C 16
Edward VII Mans. NW10 . . . 3F 65
(off Chamberlayne Rd.)
Edward's La. N16 . . . 2D 50
Edwards M. N1 . . . 7A 50
Edwards M. W1 . . . 6E 66 (1G 165)
Edward Sq. N1 . . . 1K 67
Edward Sq. SE16 . . . 1A 88
Edwards Rd. Belv . . . 4G 93
Edward St. E16 . . . 4J 71
Edward St. SE14 & SE8 . . . 7A 88
Edwards Yd. Wemb . . . 1E 62
Edward Temme Av. E15 . . . 7H 53
Edward Tyler Rd. SE12 . . . 2A 126
Edward Way. Ashf . . . 2B 112
Edwina Gdns. Ilf . . . 5C 36
Edwin Arnold Ct. Sidc . . . 4K 127
Edwin Av. E6 . . . 2E 72
(in two parts)
Edwin Clo. Bexh . . . 6F 93
Edwin Ho. SE15 . . . 7G 87
Edwin Pl. Croy . . . 1E 152
(off Leslie Gro.)
Edwin Rd. Edgw . . . 6E 12
Edwin Rd. Twic . . . 1J 115
(in two parts)
Edwin's Mead. E9 . . . 4A 52
Edwinstray Ho. Felt . . . 2E 114
Edwin St. E1 . . . 4J 69
Edwin St. E16 . . . 5J 71
Edwin Ware Ct. Pinn . . . 2A 24
Edwyn Clo. Barn . . . 6A 4
Effie Pl. SW6 . . . 7J 83
Effie Rd. SW6 . . . 7J 83
Effingham Clo. Sutt . . . 7K 149
Effingham Lodge. King T . . . 4D 134
Effingham Rd. N8 . . . 5A 32
Effingham Rd. SE12 . . . 5G 107
Effingham Rd. Croy . . . 7K 139
Effingham Rd. Surb . . . 7B 134
Effort St. SW17 . . . 5C 120
Effra Clo. SW19 . . . 6K 119
Effra Ct. SW2 . . . 5K 103
(off Brixton Hill)
Effra Pde. SW2 . . . 5A 104
Effra Rd. SW2 . . . 4A 104
Effra Rd. SW19 . . . 6K 119
Effra Rd. Retail Pk. SW2 . . . 5A 104
Egan Way. Hay . . . 7G 59
Egbert St. NW1 . . . 1E 66
Egbury Ho. SW15 . . . 6B 100
(off Tangley Gro.)
Egerton Clo. Pinn . . . 4J 23
Egerton Ct. E11 . . . 7F 35
Egerton Cres. SW3 . . . 4C 84 (3D 170)
Egerton Dri. SE10 . . . 1D 106
Egerton Gdns. NW4 . . . 4D 28
Egerton Gdns. NW10 . . . 1E 64
Egerton Gdns. SW3 . . . 4C 84 (2C 170)
Egerton Gdns. W13 . . . 6B 62
Egerton Gdns. Ilf . . . 3K 55
Egerton Gdns. M. SW3 . . . 3C 84 (2D 170)
Egerton Pl. SW3 . . . 3C 84 (2D 170)
Egerton Rd. N16 . . . 7F 33
Egerton Rd. SE25 . . . 3E 140
Egerton Rd. N Mald . . . 4B 136
Egerton Rd. Twic . . . 7J 97
Egerton Rd. Wemb . . . 7F 45
Egerton Ter. SW3 . . . 3C 84 (2D 170)
Egerton Way. Hay . . . 7D 76
Eggardon Ct. N'holt . . . 6F 43
Egham Clo. SW19 . . . 2G 119
Egham Clo. Sutt . . . 2G 149
Egham Cres. Sutt . . . 3G 149
Egham Rd. E13 . . . 5K 71
Eglantine Rd. SW18 . . . 5A 102
Egleston Rd. Mord . . . 6K 137
Eglington Ct. SE17 . . . 6C 86
Eglington Rd. E4 . . . 7K 9 & 1A 20
Eglinton Hill. SE18 . . . 6F 91
Eglinton Rd. SE18 . . . 6E 90
Egliston M. SW15 . . . 3E 100
Egliston Rd. SW15 . . . 3E 100
Eglon M. NW1 . . . 7D 48
Egmont Av. Surb . . . 1F 147
Egmont Rd. N Mald . . . 4B 136
Egmont Rd. Surb . . . 1F 147
Egmont Rd. Sutt . . . 7A 150
Egmont Rd. W on T . . . 7K 131
Egmont St. SE14 . . . 7K 87
Egremont Ho. SE13 . . . 2D 106
(off Russett Way)
Egremont Rd. SE27 . . . 3A 122
Egret Ho. SE16 . . . 4K 87
(off Tawny Way)
Egret Way. Hay . . . 5B 60
Eider Clo. E7 . . . 5H 53
Eider Clo. Hay . . . 5B 60
Eider Ct. SE8 . . . 6B 88
(off Pilot Clo.)
Eighteenth Rd. Mitc . . . 4J 139
Eighth Av. E12 . . . 4D 54
Eighth Av. Hay . . . 1J 77
Eileen Rd. SE25 . . . 5D 140
Eindhoven Clo. Cars . . . 1E 150
Einstein Ho. Wemb . . . 3J 45
Eisenhower Dri. E6 . . . 5C 72
Elaine Gro. NW5 . . . 5E 48
Elam Clo. SE5 . . . 2B 104
Elam St. SE5 . . . 2B 104
Elan Ct. E1 . . . 5H 69
Eland Pl. Croy . . . 3B 152
Eland Rd. SW11 . . . 3D 102
Eland Rd. Croy . . . 3B 152
Elba Pl. SE17 . . . 4C 86
Elberon Av. Croy . . . 6G 139
Elbe St. SW6 . . . 2A 102
Elborough Rd. SE25 . . . 5G 141
Elborough St. SW18 . . . 1J 119
Elbourne Ct. SE16 . . . 3K 87
(off Worgan St.)
Elbourne Trad. Est. Belv . . . 3H 93
Elbourn Ho. SW3 . . . 5C 84 (5C 170)
(off Cale St.)
Elbury Dri. E16 . . . 6J 71
Elcho St. SW11 . . . 7C 84
Elcot Av. SE15 . . . 7H 87
Eldenwall Ind. Est. Dag . . . 1E 56
Elder Av. N8 . . . 5J 31
Elderberry Gro. SE27 . . . 4C 122
Elderberry Rd. W5 . . . 2E 80
Elder Clo. N20 . . . 2E 14
Elder Clo. Sidc . . . 1K 127
Elder Clo. W Dray . . . 7A 58
Elder Ct. Bush . . . 2D 10
Elderfield Ho. E14 . . . 7C 70
Elderfield Pl. SW17 . . . 4F 121
Elderfield Rd. E5 . . . 4K 51
Elderfield Wlk. E11 . . . 5K 35
Elderflower Way. E15 . . . 7G 53
Elder Gdns. SE27 . . . 5C 122
Elder Oak Clo. SE20 . . . 1H 141
Elder Oak Ct. SE20 . . . 1H 141
(off Anerley Ct.)
Elder Rd. SE27 . . . 4C 122
Elderslie Clo. Beck . . . 5C 142
Elderslie Rd. SE9 . . . 5E 108
Elder St. E1 . . . 4F 69 (5J 163)
(in two parts)
Elderton Rd. SE26 . . . 4A 124
Eldertree Pl. Mitc . . . 1G 139
Eldertree Way. Mitc . . . 1G 139
Elder Wlk. N1 . . . 1B 68
(off Popham St.)
Elderwood Pl. SE27 . . . 5C 122
Eldon Av. Croy . . . 2J 153
Eldon Av. Houn . . . 7E 78
Eldon Ct. NW6 . . . 1J 65
Eldon Gro. NW3 . . . 5B 48
Eldon Pk. SE25 . . . 4H 141
Eldon Rd. E17 . . . 4B 34
Eldon Rd. N9 . . . 1D 18
Eldon Rd. N22 . . . 1B 32
Eldon Rd. W8 . . . 3K 83
Eldon St. EC2 . . . 5D 68 (6F 163)
Eldon Way. NW10 . . . 3H 63
Eldred Rd. Bark . . . 1J 73
Eldrick Ct. Felt . . . 1F 113
Eldridge Clo. Felt . . . 1J 113
Eldridge Ct. SE16 . . . 3G 87
Eleanora Ter. Sutt . . . 5A 150
(off Lind Rd.)
Eleanor Clo. N15 . . . 3F 33
Eleanor Clo. SE16 . . . 2K 87
Eleanor Cres. NW7 . . . 5A 14
Eleanor Gdns. Barn . . . 5A 4
Eleanor Gdns. Dag . . . 2F 57
Eleanor Gro. SW13 . . . 3A 100
Eleanor Gro. Ick . . . 3D 40
Eleanor Ho. W6 . . . 5E 82
(off Queen Caroline St.)
Eleanor Rd. E8 . . . 6H 51
Eleanor Rd. E15 . . . 6H 53
Eleanor Rd. N11 . . . 6D 16
Eleanor St. E3 . . . 3C 70
Eleanor Wlk. SE18 . . . 4C 90
Electric Av. SW9 . . . 4A 104
Electric La. SW9 & SW2 . . . 4A 104
(in two parts)
Electric Pde. E18 . . . 2J 35
(off George La.)
Electric Pde. Ilf . . . 2J 55
Electric Pde. Surb . . . 6D 134
Elephant & Castle. (Junct.) . . . 3B 86
Elephant & Castle. SE1 . . . 4B 86
Elephant La. SE16 . . . 2J 87
Elephant Rd. SE17 . . . 4C 86
Elers Rd. W13 . . . 2C 80
Elers Rd. Hay . . . 4F 77
Eley Rd. N18 . . . 4D 18
Eleys Est. N9 . . . 3E 18

Eleys Est. N18 4E 18
(in two parts)
Elfindale Rd. SE24 5C 104
Elfin Gro. Tedd 5K 115
Elford Clo. SE3 4K 107
Elford M. SW4 5G 103
Elfort Rd. N5 4A 50
Elfrida Cres. SE6 4C 124
Elf Row. E1 7J 69
Elfwine Rd. W7 5J 61
Elgar. N8 3J 31
(off Boyton Clo.)
Elgar Av. NW10 6K 45
(in two parts)
Elgar Av. SW16 3J 139
Elgar Av. W5 2E 80
Elgar Av. Surb 1G 147
Elgar Clo. E13 2A 72
Elgar Clo. SE8 7C 88
Elgar Clo. Buck H 2G 21
Elgar Clo. Uxb 2C 40
Elgar Ct. W14 3G 83
(off Blythe Rd.)
Elgar Ho. NW6 7A 48
(off Fairfax Rd.)
Elgar Ho. SW1 5F 85 (6K 171)
(off Churchill Gdns.)
Elgar St. SE16 3A 88
Elgin Av. W9 4H 65
Elgin Av. W12 2D 82
Elgin Av. Ashf 6E 112
Elgin Av. Harr 2B 26
Elgin Ct. W9 4K 65
Elgin Ct. S Croy 4C 152
(off Bramley Hill)
Elgin Cres. W11 7G 65
Elgin Cres. H'row A 2G 95
Elgin Dri. N'wd 1G 23
Elgin Est. W9 4J 65
(off Elgin Av.)
Elgin Ho. E14 6D 70
(off Ricardo St.)
Elgin Mans. W9 3K 65
Elgin M. W11 6G 65
Elgin M. N. W9 3K 65
Elgin M. S. W9 3K 65
Elgin Rd. N22 2G 31
Elgin Rd. Croy 2F 153
Elgin Rd. Ilf 1J 55
Elgin Rd. Sutt 3A 150
Elgin Rd. Wall 6G 151
Elgood Clo. W11 7G 65
Elgood Ho. NW8 2B 66
(off Wellington Rd.)
Elham Clo. Brom 7B 126
Elham Ho. E5 5H 51
Elia M. N1 2B 68 (1A 162)
Elias Pl. SW8 6A 86
Elia St. N1 2B 68 (1B 162)
Elibank Rd. SE9 4D 108
Elim Est. SE1 3E 86 (7G 169)
Elim St. SE1 7F 169
(in two parts)
Elim Way. E13 3H 71
Eliot Bank. SE23 2H 123
Eliot Cotts. SE3 2G 107
Eliot Dri. Harr 2F 43
Eliot Gdns. SW15 4C 100
Eliot Hill. SE13 2E 106
Eliot M. NW8 2A 66
Eliot Pk. SE13 2E 106
Eliot Pl. SE3 2G 107
Eliot Rd. Dag 4D 56
Eliot Va. SE3 2F 107
Elis David Almshouses. Croy 3B 152
Elizabethan Clo. Stanw 7A 94
Elizabethan Way. Stanw 7A 94
Elizabeth Av. N1 1C 68
Elizabeth Av. Enf 3G 7
Elizabeth Av. Ilf 2H 55
Elizabeth Av. Stai 7A 112
Elizabeth Barnes Ct. SW6 2K 101
(off Marinefield Rd.)
Elizabeth Blackwell Ho. N22 1A 32
(off Progress Way)
Elizabeth Bri. SW1 4F 85 (4J 171)
Elizabeth Clo. E14 6D 70
Elizabeth Clo. W9 4A 66
Elizabeth Clo. Barn 3A 4
Elizabeth Clo. Romf 1H 39
Elizabeth Clo. Sutt 4H 149
Elizabeth Clyde Clo. N15 4E 32
Elizabeth Cotts. Kew 1F 99
Elizabeth Ct. E4 5G 19
Elizabeth Ct. SW1 2D 172
Elizabeth Ct. SW10 6B 84
(off Milman's St.)
Elizabeth Ct. Brom 1H 143
(off Highland Rd.)
Elizabeth Ct. Tedd 5J 115
Elizabeth Ct. Wfd G 7F 21
Elizabeth Fry Ho. Hay 4H 77
Elizabeth Fry M. E8 7H 51
Elizabeth Fry Pl. SE18 1C 108
Elizabeth Gdns. W3 1B 82
Elizabeth Gdns. Stan 6H 11
Elizabeth Gdns. Sun 3A 132
Elizabeth Garrett Anderson Ho. Belv 3G 93
(off Ambrook Rd.)
Elizabeth Ho. SE11 4A 86 (4K 173)
(off Reedworth St.)
Elizabeth Ho. W6 5E 82
(off Queen Caroline St.)
Elizabeth Ind. Est. SE14 6K 87
Elizabeth M. NW3 6C 48
Elizabeth M. Harr 6J 25
Elizabeth Newcomen Ho. SE1 2D 86 (6E 168)
(off Newcomen St.)
Elizabeth Pl. N15 4D 32
Elizabeth Ride. N9 7C 8
Elizabeth Rd. E6 1B 72
Elizabeth Rd. N15 5E 32
Elizabeth Sq. SE16 7A 70
(off Sovereign Cres.)
Elizabeth St. SW1 4E 84 (3H 171)
Elizabeth Ter. SE9 6D 108
Elizabeth Way. SE19 7D 122
Elizabeth Way. Felt 4A 114
Elkanet M. N20 2F 15
Elkington Point. SE11 4J 173
Elkington Rd. E13 4K 71
Elkstone Ct. SE15 6E 86
(off Birdlip Clo.)
Elkstone Rd. W10 5H 65
Ellaline Rd. W6 6F 83
Ella M. NW3 4D 48
Ellanby Cres. N18 4C 18
Elland Ho. E14 6B 70
(off Copenhagen Pl.)
Elland Rd. SE15 4J 105
Ella Rd. N8 7J 31
Ellement Clo. Pinn 5B 24
Ellena Ct. N14 3D 16
(off Conway Rd.)
Ellenborough Ho. W12 7D 64
(off White City Est.)
Ellenborough Pl. SW15 4C 100
Ellenborough Rd. N22 1C 32
Ellenborough Rd. Sidc 5D 128
Ellenbridge Way. S Croy 7E 152
Ellen Clo. Brom 3B 144
Ellen Ct. E4 1K 19
(off Ridgeway, The)
Ellen Ct. N9 2D 18
Ellen St. E1 6G 69
Ellen Webb Dri. W'stone 3J 25
Ellen Wilkinson Ho. E2 3K 69
(off Usk St.)
Ellen Wilkinson Ho. SW6 6H 83
(off Clem Attlee Ct.)
Ellen Wilkinson Ho. Dag 3G 57
Elleray Rd. Tedd 6K 115
Ellerby St. SW6 1F 101
Ellerdale Clo. NW3 4A 48
Ellerdale Rd. NW3 5A 48
Ellerdale St. SE13 4D 106
Ellerdine Rd. Houn 4G 97
Ellerker Gdns. Rich 6E 98
Ellerman Av. Twic 1D 114
Ellerslie Gdns. NW10 1C 64
Ellerslie Rd. W12 1D 82
Ellerslie Sq. Ind. Est. SW2 5J 103
Ellerton Gdns. Dag 7C 56
Ellerton Lodge. N3 2J 29
Ellerton Rd. SW13 1C 100
Ellerton Rd. SW18 1B 120
Ellerton Rd. SW20 7C 118
Ellerton Rd. Dag 7C 56
Ellerton Rd. Surb 2F 147
Ellery Ho. SE17 4D 86
Ellery Rd. SE19 7D 122
Ellery St. SE15 2H 105
Ellesmere Av. NW7 3E 12
Ellesmere Av. Beck 2D 142
Ellesmere Clo. E11 5H 35
Ellesmere Clo. Ruis 7E 22
Ellesmere Ct. W4 5K 81
Ellesmere Gdns. Ilf 5C 36
Ellesmere Gro. Barn 5C 4
Ellesmere Rd. E3 2A 70
Ellesmere Rd. NW10 5C 46
Ellesmere Rd. W4 6J 81
Ellesmere Rd. Gnfd 4G 61
Ellesmere Rd. Twic 6C 98
Ellesmere St. E14 6D 70
Elleswood Ct. Surb 7D 134
Ellie M. Ashf 2A 112
Ellingfort Rd. E8 7H 51
Ellingham Rd. E15 4F 53
Ellingham Rd. W12 2C 82
Ellingham Rd. Chess 6D 146
Ellington Ct. N14 2C 16
Ellington Ho. SE1 3C 86
Ellington Rd. N10 4F 31
Ellington Rd. Felt 4H 113
Ellington Rd. Houn 2F 97
Ellington St. N7 6A 50
Elliot Clo. E15 7G 53
Elliot Ho. W1 5C 66 (6D 158)
(off Cato St.)
Elliot Rd. NW4 6D 28
Elliott Av. Ruis 2K 41
Elliott Clo. Wemb 3G 45
Elliott Clo. Wfd G 6G 21
Elliott Gdns. Shep 4C 130
Elliott Rd. SW9 1B 104
Elliott Rd. W4 4A 82
Elliott Rd. Brom 4B 144
Elliott Rd. Stan 6F 11
Elliott Rd. T Hth 4B 140
Elliott's Pl. N1 1B 68
Elliott Sq. NW3 7C 48
Elliotts Row. SE11 4B 86
Ellis Clo. NW10 6D 46
Ellis Clo. SE9 2G 127
Ellis Clo. Edgw 6F 13
Elliscombe Mt. SE7 6A 90
Elliscombe Rd. SE7 5A 90
Ellis Ct. W7 5K 61
Ellisfield Dri. SW15 7C 100
Ellis Franklin Ct. NW8 2A 66
(off Abbey Rd.)
Ellis Ho. SE17 5D 86
(off Brandon St.)
Ellison Gdns. S'hall 4D 78
Ellison Ho. SE13 2D 106
(off Lewisham Rd.)
Ellison Rd. SW13 2B 100
Ellison Rd. SW16 7H 121
Ellison Rd. Sidc 1H 127
Ellis Rd. Mitc 6D 138
Ellis Rd. S'hall 1G 79
Ellis St. SW1 4E 84 (3F 171)
Ellora Rd. SW16 5H 121
Ellsworth St. E2 3H 69
Ellwood Ct. W9 4K 65
(off Clearwell Dri.)
Elmar Rd. N15 4D 32
Elm Av. W5 1E 80
Elm Av. Ashf 2A 112
Elm Av. Ruis 1J 41
Elm Bank. N14 7D 6
Elmbank Av. Barn 4A 4
Elm Bank Dri. Brom 2B 144
Elm Bank Gdns. SW13 2A 100
Elmbank Way. W7 5H 61
Elmbourne Dri. Belv 4H 93
Elmbourne Rd. SW17 3E 120
Elmbridge Av. Surb 5H 135
Elmbridge Clo. Ruis 6J 23
Elmbridge Dri. Ruis 5H 23
Elmbridge Wlk. E8 7G 51
Elmbrook Clo. Sun 1K 131
Elmbrook Gdns. SE9 4C 108
Elmbrook Rd. Sutt 4H 149
Elm Clo. E11 6K 35
Elm Clo. N19 2G 49
Elm Clo. NW4 5F 29
Elm Clo. SW20 4E 136
Elm Clo. Buck H 2G 21
Elm Clo. Cars 1D 150
Elm Clo. Harr 6F 25
Elm Clo. Hay 6J 59
Elm Clo. Romf 1H 39
Elm Clo. S Croy 6E 152
Elm Clo. Surb 7J 135
Elm Clo. Twic 2F 115
Elmcote. Pinn 2B 24
Elm Cotts. Mitc 2D 138
Elm Ct. EC4 1J 167
Elm Ct. SE13 3F 107
Elm Ct. W9 5J 65
(off Admiral Wlk.)
Elm Ct. W Mol 4F 133
Elmcourt Rd. SE27 2B 122
Elm Cres. W5 1E 80
Elm Cres. King T 1E 134
Elmcroft. N6 7G 31
Elmcroft Av. E11 5K 35
Elmcroft Av. N9 6C 8
Elmcroft Av. NW11 7H 29
Elmcroft Av. Sidc 7K 109
Elmcroft Clo. E11 4K 35
Elmcroft Clo. N8 5K 31
Elmcroft Clo. W5 6D 62
Elmcroft Clo. Chess 3E 146
Elmcroft Clo. Felt 6H 95
Elmcroft Cres. NW11 7G 29
Elmcroft Cres. Harr 3E 24
Elmcroft Dri. Ashf 5C 112
Elmcroft Dri. Chess 3E 146
Elmcroft Gdns. NW9 4G 27
Elmcroft St. E5 4J 51
Elmcroft Ter. Uxb 6C 58
Elmdale Rd. N13 5E 16
Elmdene. Surb 1J 147
Elmdene Clo. Beck 6B 142
Elmdene Rd. SE18 5F 91
Elmdon Rd. Houn 2B 96
Elmdon Rd. H'row A 3H 95
Elm Dri. Harr 6F 25
Elm Dri. Sun 2A 132
Elmer Clo. Enf 3E 6
Elmer Gdns. Edgw 7C 12
Elmer Gdns. Iswth 3H 97
Elmer Ho. NW8 5C 66 (5C 158)
(off Broadley St.)
Elmer Rd. SE6 7E 106
Elmers Dri. Tedd 6B 116
Elmers End. 4A 142
Elmers End Rd. SE20 & Beck 2J 141
Elmerside Rd. Beck 4A 142
Elmers Rd. SE25 7G 141
Elmfield Av. N8 5J 31
Elmfield Av. Mitc 1E 138
Elmfield Av. Tedd 5K 115
Elmfield Clo. Harr 2J 43
Elmfield Ct. Well 1B 110
Elmfield Ho. N2 2B 30
(off Grange, The)
Elmfield Pk. Brom 3J 143
Elmfield Rd. E4 2K 19
Elmfield Rd. E17 6K 33
Elmfield Rd. N2 3B 30
Elmfield Rd. SW17 2E 120
Elmfield Rd. Brom 2J 143
Elmfield Rd. S'hall 3C 78
Elmfield Way. W9 5J 65
Elmfield Way. S Croy 7F 153
Elm Friars Wlk. NW1 7H 49
Elm Gdns. N2 3A 30
Elm Gdns. Clay 6A 146
Elm Gdns. Mitc 4H 139
Elmgate Av. Felt 3K 113
Elmgate Gdns. Edgw 5D 12
Elm Grn. W3 6A 64
Elm Gro. N8 6J 31
Elm Gro. NW2 4F 47
Elm Gro. SE15 2F 105
Elm Gro. SW19 7G 119
Elm Gro. Eri 7K 93
Elm Gro. Harr 7E 24
Elm Gro. King T 1E 134
Elm Gro. Sutt 4K 149
Elm Gro. W Dray 7B 58
Elm Gro. Wfd G 5C 20
Elmgrove Cres. Harr 5K 25
Elmgrove Gdns. Harr 5A 26
Elm Gro. Pde. Wall 3E 150
Elm Gro. Rd. SW13 1C 100
Elm Gro. Rd. W5 2E 80
Elmgrove Rd. Croy 7H 141
Elmgrove Rd. Harr 5K 25
Elmgrove Rd. Kent 5A 26
Elm Hall Gdns. E11 5K 35
(in two parts)
Elm Ho. E14 2E 88
(off E. Ferry Rd.)
Elm Ho. W10 4G 65
(off Briar Wlk.)
Elm Ho. King T 7F 117
(off Elm Rd.)
Elmhurst. Belv 6E 92
Elmhurst Av. N2 3B 30
Elmhurst Av. Mitc 7F 121
Elmhurst Ct. Croy 4D 152
Elmhurst Dri. E18 2J 35
Elmhurst Lodge. Sutt 7A 150
Elmhurst Mans. SW4 3H 103
Elmhurst Rd. E7 7K 53
Elmhurst Rd. N17 2F 33
Elmhurst Rd. SE9 2C 126
Elmhurst St. SW4 3H 103
Elmington Clo. Bex 6H 111
Elmington Est. SE5 7D 86
Elmington Rd. SE5 7D 86
Elmira St. SE13 3D 106
Elm La. SE6 2B 124
Elm Lawn Clo. Uxb 7A 40
Elmlea Dri. Hay 5G 59
Elm Lea Trad. Est. N17 6C 18
Elmlee Clo. Chst 6D 126
Elmley Clo. E6 5C 72
Elmley St. SE18 5H 91
(in two parts)
Elm Lodge. SW6 1E 100
Elmore Clo. Wemb 2E 62
Elmore Ho. SW9 2B 104
Elmore Rd. E11 3E 52
Elmore Rd. Enf 1E 8
Elmore St. N1 7C 50
Elm Pde. Sidc 4A 128
Elm Pk. SW2 6K 103
Elm Pk. Stan 5G 11
Elm Pk. Av. N15 5F 33
Elm Pk. Chambers. SW10 5B 84 (6A 170)
(off Elm Pk. Gdns.)

Elm Pk. Ct. Pinn 3A 24
Elm Pk. Gdns. NW4 . . . . . 5F 29
Elm Pk. Gdns. SW10 . . . . . 5B 84 (6A 170)
Elm Pk. Ho. SW10 . . . . . 5B 84 (6A 170)
Elm Pk. La. SW3 . . . . . 5B 84 (6A 170)
Elm Pk. Mans. SW10 . . . . . 7A 170
Elm Pk. Rd. E10 . . . . . 1A 52
Elm Pk. Rd. N3 . . . . . 7C 14
Elm Pk. Rd. N21 . . . . . 7H 7
Elm Pk. Rd. SE25 . . . . . 3F 141
Elm Pk. Rd. SW3 . . . . . 6B 84 (7A 170)
Elm Pk. Rd. Pinn 2A 24
Elm Pas. Barn 4C 4
Elm Pl. SW7 . . . . . 5B 84 (5A 170)
Elm Quay Ct. SW8 . . . . . 6H 85 (7C 172)
Elm Rd. E7 . . . . . 6H 53
Elm Rd. E11 . . . . . 2F 53
Elm Rd. E17 . . . . . 5E 34
Elm Rd. N22 . . . . . 1B 32
Elm Rd. SW14 . . . . . 3J 99
Elm Rd. Barn 4C 4
Elm Rd. Beck 2B 142
Elm Rd. Chess 4E 146
Elm Rd. Eps 6B 148
Elm Rd. Felt 1F 113
Elm Rd. King T 1F 135
Elm Rd. N Mald 2K 135
Elm Rd. Romf 2H 39
Elm Rd. Sidc 4A 128
Elm Rd. T Hth 4D 140
Elm Rd. Wall 1E 150
Elm Rd. Wemb 5E 44
Elm Rd. W. Sutt 7H 137
Elm Row. NW3 . . . . . 3A 48
Elms Av. N10 . . . . . 3F 31
Elms Av. NW4 . . . . . 5F 29
Elmscott Gdns. N21 . . . . . 6H 7
Elmscott Rd. Brom 5G 125
Elms Ct. Wemb 4A 44
Elms Cres. SW4 . . . . . 6G 103
Elmsdale Rd. E17 . . . . . 4B 34
Elms Gdns. Dag 4F 57
Elms Gdns. Wemb 4A 44
Elmshaw Rd. SW15 . . . . . 5C 100
Elmshurst Cres. N2 . . . . . 4B 30
Elmside. New Ad 6D 154
Elmside Rd. Wemb 3G 45
Elms La. Wemb 3A 44
Elmsleigh Av. Harr 4B 26
Elmsleigh Ct. Sutt 3K 149
Elmsleigh Ho. Twic 2H 115
(off Staines Rd.)
Elmsleigh Rd. Twic 2H 115
Elmslie Clo. Wfd G 6J 21
Elmslie Point. E3 . . . . . 5B 70
(off Leopold St.)
Elms M. W2 . . . . . 7B 66 (2A 164)
Elms Pk. Av. Wemb 4A 44
Elms Rd. SW4 . . . . . 5G 103
Elms Rd. Harr 7D 10
Elmstead. 6D 126
Elmstead Av. Chst 5D 126
Elmstead Av. Wemb 1E 44
Elmstead Clo. N20 . . . . . 2D 14
Elmstead Clo. Eps 5A 148
Elmstead Gdns. Wor Pk . . . 3C 148
Elmstead Glade. Chst 6D 126
Elmstead La. Chst 7C 126
Elmstead Rd. Eri 1K 111
Elmstead Rd. Ilf 2J 55
Elmsted Cres. Well 6C 92
Elms, The. E12 . . . . . 6B 54
Elms, The. SW13 . . . . . 3B 100
Elms, The. Clay 7A 146
Elms, The. Croy 1C 152
(off Tavistock Rd.)
Elmstone Rd. SW6 . . . . . 1J 101
Elm St. WC1 . . . . . 4K 67 (4H 161)
Elmsway. Ashf 5C 112
Elmsworth Av. Houn 2F 97
Elm Ter. NW2 . . . . . 3J 47
Elm Ter. NW3 . . . . . 4C 48
Elm Ter. SE9 . . . . . 6E 108
Elm Ter. Harr 1H 25
Elm Ter. Stan 5H 11
Elmton Ct. NW8 . . . 4B 66 (3A 158)
(off Cunningham Pl.)
Elmton Way. E5 . . . . . 3G 51
Elm Tree Av. Esh 7H 133
Elm Tree Clo. NW8 . . . . . 3B 66 (1A 158)
Elm Tree Clo. Ashf 5D 112
Elm Tree Clo. N'holt 2D 60
Elm Tree Ct. NW8 . . . . . 1A 158
Elm Tree Ct. SE7 . . . . . 6A 90
Elm Tree Rd. NW8 . . . . . 3B 66 (1A 158)
Elmtree Rd. Tedd 4J 115
Elm Vw. Ct. S'hall 4E 78
Elm Vw. Ho. Hay 4F 77
Elm Wlk. NW3 . . . . . 2J 47
Elm Wlk. SW20 . . . . . 4E 136
Elm Wlk. Orp 3D 156
Elm Way. N11 . . . . . 6K 15
Elm Way. NW10 . . . . . 4A 46
Elm Way. Eps 5K 147
Elm Way. Wor Pk 3E 148
Elmwood Av. N13 . . . . . 5D 16
Elmwood Av. Felt 2J 113
Elmwood Av. Harr 5A 26
Elmwood Clo. Eps 7C 148
Elmwood Clo. Wall 2F 151
Elmwood Ct. E10 . . . . . 1C 52
(off Goldsmith Rd.)
Elmwood Ct. SW11 . . . . . 1F 103
Elmwood Ct. Wemb 3A 44
Elmwood Cres. NW9 . . . . . 4J 27
Elmwood Dri. Bex 7E 110
Elmwood Dri. Eps 6C 148
Elmwood Gdns. W7 . . . . . 6J 61
Elmwood Ho. NW10 . . . . . 2D 64
(off All Souls Av.)
Elmwood Rd. SE24 . . . . . 5D 104
Elmwood Rd. W4 . . . . . 6J 81
Elmwood Rd. Croy 7B 140
Elmwood Rd. Mitc 3D 138
Elmworth Gro. SE21 . . . . . 2D 122
Elnathan M. W9 . . . . . 4K 65
Elphinstone Ct. SW16 . . . . . 6J 121
Elphinstone Rd. E17 . . . . . 2B 34
Elphinstone St. N5 . . . . . 4B 50
Elrington Rd. E8 . . . . . 6G 51
Elrington Rd. Wfd G 5D 20
Elsa Cotts. E14 . . . . . 5A 70
(off Halley St.)
Elsa Ct. Beck 1B 142
Elsa Rd. Well 2B 110
Elsa St. E1 . . . . . 5A 70
Elsdale St. E9 . . . . . 6J 51
Elsden M. E2 . . . . . 2J 69
Elsden Rd. N17 . . . . . 1F 33
Elsenham Rd. E12 . . . . . 5E 54
Elsenham St. SW18 . . . . . 1H 119
Elsham Rd. E11 . . . . . 3G 53
Elsham Rd. W14 . . . . . 2G 83
Elsham Ter. W14 . . . . . 3G 83
(off Elsham Rd.)
Elsiedene Rd. N21 . . . . . 7H 7
Elsie La. Ct. W2 . . . . . 5J 65
(off Westbourne Pk. Vs.)
Elsiemaud Rd. SE4 . . . . . 5B 106
Elsie Rd. SE22 . . . . . 4F 105
Elsinore Av. Stai 7A 94
Elsinore Gdns. NW2 . . . . . 3G 47
Elsinore Ho. N1 . . . . . 1A 68
(off Denmark Gro.)
Elsinore Ho. SE5 . . . . . 2C 104
(off Denmark Rd.)
Elsinore Ho. W6 . . . . . 5E 82
(off Fulham Pal. Rd.)
Elsinore Rd. SE23 . . . . . 1A 124
Elsinore Way. Rich 3H 99
Elsley Rd. SW11 . . . . . 3D 102
Elspeth Rd. SW11 . . . . . 4D 102
Elspeth Rd. Wemb 5E 44
Elsrick Av. Mord 5J 137
Elstan Way. Croy 7A 142
Elstead Ct. Sutt 1G 149
Elstead Ho. SW2 . . . . . 7K 103
(off Redlands Way)
Elsted St. SE17 . . . . . 4D 86
Elstow Clo. SE9 . . . . . 5D 108
(in two parts)
Elstow Clo. Ruis 7B 24
Elstow Gdns. Dag 1E 74
Elstow Grange. NW6 . . . . . 7F 47
Elstow Rd. Dag 7E 56
Elstree Gdns. N9 . . . . . 1C 18
Elstree Gdns. Belv 4E 92
Elstree Gdns. Ilf 5G 55
Elstree Hill. Brom 7G 125
Elstree Hill S. Els 1J 11
Elstree Rd. Bus H & Els . . . 1C 10
Elswick Rd. SE13 . . . . . 2D 106
Elswick St. SW6 . . . . . 2A 102
Elsworth Clo. Felt 1G 113
Elsworthy. Th Dit 6J 133
Elsworthy Ri. NW3 . . . . . 7C 48
Elsworthy Rd. NW3 . . . . . 1C 66
Elsworthy Ter. NW3 . . . . . 7C 48
Elsynge Rd. SW18 . . . . . 5B 102
Eltham. 6D 108
Eltham Crematorium. SE9 . . . . . 4H 109
Eltham Grn. SE9 . . . . . 5B 108
Eltham Grn. Rd. SE9 . . . . . 4A 108
Eltham High St. SE9 . . . . . 6D 108
Eltham Hill. SE9 . . . . . 5B 108
Eltham Palace. 7C 108
Eltham Pal. Rd. SE9 . . . . . 6A 108
Eltham Park. 4E 108
Eltham Pk. Gdns. SE9 . . . . . 4E 108
Eltham Rd. SE12 & SE9 . . . 5H 107
Elthiron Rd. SW6 . . . . . 1J 101
Elthorne Av. W7 . . . . . 2K 79
Elthorne Ct. Felt 1A 114
Elthorne Heights. 5H 61
Elthorne Pk. Rd. W7 . . . . . 2K 79
Elthorne Rd. N19 . . . . . 2H 49
Elthorne Rd. NW9 . . . . . 7K 27
Elthorne Way. NW9 . . . . . 6K 27
Elthruda Rd. SE13 . . . . . 6F 107
Eltisley Rd. Ilf 4F 55
Elton Av. Barn 5C 4
Elton Av. Gnfd 6J 43
Elton Av. Wemb 5B 44
Elton Clo. King T 7C 116
Elton Ho. E3 . . . . . 1B 70
(off Candy St.)
Elton Pl. N16 . . . . . 5E 50
Elton Rd. King T 1F 135
Eltringham St. SW18 . . . . . 4A 102
Elvaston M. SW7 . . . . . 3A 84 (2A 170)
Elvaston Pl. SW7 . . . . . 3A 84 (1A 170)
Elveden Ho. SE24 . . . . . 5B 104
Elveden Pl. NW10 . . . . . 2G 63
Elveden Rd. NW10 . . . . . 2G 63
Elvendon Rd. N13 . . . . . 6D 16
Elver Gdns. E2 . . . . . 3G 69
Elverson Rd. SE8 . . . . . 2D 106
Elverton St. SW1 . . . . . 4H 85 (3C 172)
Elvington Grn. Brom 5H 143
Elvington La. NW9 . . . . . 1A 28
Elvino Rd. SE26 . . . . . 5A 124
Elvis Rd. NW2 . . . . . 6E 46
Elwill Way. Beck 4E 142
Elwin St. E2 . . . . . 3G 69 (1K 163)
Elwood St. N5 . . . . . 3B 50
Elworth Ho. SW8 . . . . . 7K 85
(off Oval Pl.)
Elwyn Gdns. SE12 . . . . . 7J 107
Ely Clo. N Mald 2B 136
Ely Cotts. SW8 . . . . . 7K 85
Ely Ct. EC1 . . . . . 6K 161
Ely Ct. NW6 . . . . . 2J 65
(off Chichester Rd.)
Ely Gdns. Dag 3J 57
Ely Gdns. Ilf 7C 36
Ely Ho. SE15 . . . . . 7G 87
(off Friary Est.)
Elyne Rd. N4 . . . . . 6A 32
Ely Pl. EC1 . . . . . 5A 68 (6K 161)
Ely Pl. Wfd G 6K 21
Ely Rd. E10 . . . . . 6E 34
Ely Rd. Croy 5D 140
Ely Rd. Houn 3A 96
Ely Rd. H'row A 2H 95
Elysian Av. Orp 6K 145
Elysium Pl. SW6 . . . . . 2H 101
(off Elysium St.)
Elysium St. SW6 . . . . . 2H 101
Elystan Bus. Cen. Hay 7A 60
Elystan Clo. Wall 7G 151
Elystan Pl. SW3 . . . 5C 84 (5D 170)
Elystan St. SW3 . . . 4C 84 (4C 170)
Elystan Wlk. N1 . . . . . 1A 68
Emanuel Av. W3 . . . . . 6J 63
Emanuel Dri. Hamp 5D 114
Embankment. SW15 . . . . . 2F 101
(in three parts)
Embankment Gdns. SW3 . . . . . 6D 84 (7F 171)
Embankment Pl. WC2 . . . . . 1J 85 (4F 167)
Embankment, The. Twic . . . 1A 116
Embassy Ct. N11 . . . . . 6C 16
(off Bounds Grn. Rd.)
Embassy Ct. NW8 . . . . . 1B 158
Embassy Ct. W5 . . . . . 7F 63
Embassy Ct. Sidc 3B 128
Embassy Ct. Wall 6F 151
Embassy Ct. Well 3B 110
Embassy Gdns. Beck 1B 142
Embassy Ho. NW6 . . . . . 7K 47
Emba St. SE16 . . . . . 2G 87
Ember Clo. Orp 7G 145
Ember Ct. NW9 . . . . . 2A 28
Embercourt Rd. Th Dit 6J 133
Ember Farm Av. E Mol 6H 133
Ember Farm Way. E Mol . . . 6H 133
Ember Gdns. Th Dit 7J 133
Ember La. Esh & E Mol 7H 133
Emberton. SE5 . . . . . 6E 86
(off Albany Rd.)
Emberton Ct. EC1 . . . . . 3B 68 (2A 162)
(off Tompion St.)
Embleton Rd. SE13 . . . . . 4D 106
Embleton Wlk. Hamp 5D 114
Embley Point. E5 . . . . . 4H 51
(off Tiger Way)
Embroidery Bus. Cen. Wfd G 2B 36
(off Southend Rd.)
Embry Clo. Stan 4F 11
Embry Dri. Stan 6F 11
Embry Way. Stan 5F 11
Emden Clo. W Dray 2C 76
Emden St. SW6 . . . . . 1K 101
Emerald Clo. E16 . . . . . 6B 72
Emerald Gdns. Dag 1G 57
Emerald Sq. S'hall 3B 78
Emerald St. WC1 . . . . . 5K 67 (5G 161)
Emerson Gdns. Harr 6F 27
Emerson Rd. Ilf 7E 36
Emerson St. SE1 . . . . . 1C 86 (4C 168)
Emerson Ter. Wfd G 6G 21
Emerton Clo. Bexh 4E 110
Emery Hill St. SW1 . . . . . 3G 85 (2B 172)
Emery St. SE1 . . . 3A 86 (1K 173)
Emes Rd. Eri 7J 93
Emilia Clo. Enf 5C 8
Emily Pl. N7 . . . . . 4A 50
Emily St. E16 . . . . . 6H 71
(off Jude St.)
Emlyn Gdns. W12 . . . . . 2A 82
Emlyn Rd. W12 . . . . . 2A 82
Emmanuel Ct. E10 . . . . . 7D 34
Emmanuel Ho. SE11 . . . . . 4A 86 (4J 173)
Emmanuel Rd. SW12 . . . . . 1G 121
Emmanuel Rd. N'wd 1H 23
Emma Rd. E13 . . . . . 2H 71
Emma St. E2 . . . . . 2H 69
Emmaus Way. Chig 5K 21
Emminster. NW6 . . . . . 1K 65
(off Abbey Rd.)
Emmott Av. Ilf 5G 37
Emmott Clo. E1 . . . . . 4A 70
Emmott Clo. NW11 . . . . . 6A 30
Emms Pas. King T 2D 134
Emperor's Ga. SW7 . . . . . 3A 84
Empingham Ho. SE8 . . . . . 4K 87
(off Chilton Ho.)
Empire Av. N18 . . . . . 5H 17
Empire Ct. Wemb 3H 45
Empire Pde. N18 . . . . . 6J 17
Empire Pde. Wemb 3G 45
Empire Rd. Gnfd 1B 62
Empire Sq. N7 . . . . . 3J 49
Empire Sq. SE20 . . . . . 7K 123
(off High St.)
Empire Way. Wemb 4F 45
Empire Wharf. E3 . . . . . 1A 70
(off Old Ford Rd.)
Empire Wharf Rd. E14 . . . . . 4F 89
Empress Av. E4 . . . . . 7J 19
Empress Av. E12 . . . . . 2A 54
Empress Av. Ilf 2D 54
Empress Av. Wfd G 7C 20
Empress Dri. Chst 6F 127
Empress M. SE5 . . . . . 2C 104
Empress Pde. E4 . . . . . 7H 19
Empress Pl. SW6 . . . . . 5J 83
Empress State Building. W14 . . . . . 5J 83
Empress St. SE17 . . . . . 6C 86
Empson St. E3 . . . . . 4D 70
Emsworth Clo. N9 . . . . . 1D 18
Emsworth Ct. SW16 . . . . . 3J 121
Emsworth Rd. Ilf 2F 37
Emsworth St. SW2 . . . . . 2K 121
Emu Rd. SW8 . . . . . 2F 103
Ena Rd. SW16 . . . . . 3J 139
Enbrook St. W10 . . . . . 3G 65
Endale Clo. Cars 2D 150
Endeavour Way. SW19 . . . . . 4K 119
Endeavour Way. Bark 2A 74
Endeavour Way. Croy 7J 139
Endell St. WC2 . . . . 6J 67 (7E 160)
Enderby St. SE10 . . . . . 5F 89
Enderley Clo. Harr 2J 25
Enderley Rd. Harr 1J 25
Endersleigh Gdns. NW4 . . . . 4C 28
Endlebury Rd. E4 . . . . . 2K 19
Endlesham Rd. SW12 . . . . . 7E 102
Endsleigh Gdns. WC1 . . . . . 4H 67 (3C 160)
Endsleigh Gdns. Ilf 2D 54
Endsleigh Gdns. Surb 6C 134
Endsleigh Ind. Est. S'hall . . . 4C 78
Endsleigh Pl. WC1 . . . . . 4H 67 (3D 160)
Endsleigh Rd. W13 . . . . . 7A 62
Endsleigh Rd. S'hall 4C 78
Endsleigh St. WC1 . . . . . 4H 67 (3D 160)
End Way. Surb 7G 135
Endwell Rd. SE4 . . . . . 2A 106
Endymion Rd. N4 . . . . . 7A 32
Endymion Rd. SW2 . . . . . 6K 103
Energen Clo. NW10 . . . . . 6A 46
Enfield. 3J 7
Enfield Bus. Cen. Enf 2D 8
Enfield Cloisters. N1 . . . . . 3E 68 (1G 163)
(off Fanshaw St.)
Enfield Golf Course. 4F 7
Enfield Highway. 2E 8

Enfield Ho. SW9 2J 103 (off Stockwell Rd.)
Enfield Retail Pk. Enf 3C 8
Enfield Rd. N1 7E 50
Enfield Rd. W3 2H 81
Enfield Rd. Bren 5D 80
Enfield Rd. Enf 4C 6
Enfield Rd. H'row A 2G 95
Enfield Town. 3J 7
Enfield Wlk. Bren 5D 80
Enford St. W1 5D 66 (5E 158)
Engadine Clo. Croy 3F 153
Engadine St. SW18 1H 119
Engate St. SE13 4E 106
Engel Pk. NW7 6K 13
Engine Ct. SW1 1G 85 (5B 166) (off Ambassadors' Ct.)
Engineer Clo. SE18 6E 90
Engineers Way. Wemb 4G 45
England's La. NW3 6D 48
England Way. N Mald 4H 135
Englefield. NW1 3G 67 (2A 160) (off Clarence Gdns.)
Englefield Clo. Croy 6C 140
Englefield Clo. Enf 2F 7
Englefield Clo. Orp 5K 145
Englefield Cres. Orp 4K 145
Englefield Path. Orp 4K 145
Englefield Rd. N1 7D 50
Engleheart Dri. Felt 6H 95
Engleheart Rd. SE6 7D 106
Englewood Rd. SW12 6F 103
English Grounds. SE1 1E 86 (5G 169)
English St. E3 4B 70
Enid St. SE16 3F 87 (7K 169)
Enmore Av. SE25 5G 141
Enmore Gdns. SW14 5K 99
Enmore Rd. SE25 5G 141
Enmore Rd. SW15 4E 100
Enmore Rd. S'hall 4E 60
Ennerdale. NW1 3G 67 (1A 160) (off Varndell St.)
Ennerdale Av. Stan 3C 26
Ennerdale Clo. Felt 1H 113
Ennerdale Clo. Sutt 4H 149
Ennerdale Dri. NW9 5A 28
Ennerdale Gdns. Wemb 1C 44
Ennerdale Ho. E3 4B 70
Ennerdale Rd. Bexh 1G 111
Ennerdale Rd. Rich 2F 99
Ennersdale Rd. SE13 5F 107
Ennis Ho. E14 6D 70 (off Vesey Path)
Ennismore Av. W4 4B 82
Ennismore Av. Gnfd 6J 43
Ennismore Gdns. SW7 2C 84 (7C 164)
Ennismore Gdns. Th Dit 6J 133
Ennismore Gdns. M. SW7 3C 84 (1C 170)
Ennismore M. SW7 3C 84 (7C 164)
Ennismore St. SW7 3C 84 (1C 170)
Ennis Rd. N4 1A 50
Ennis Rd. SE18 6G 91
Ennor Ct. Sutt 4E 148
Ensbury Ho. SW8 7K 85 (off Carroun Rd.)
Ensign Clo. Stanw 1A 112
Ensign Dri. N13 3H 17
Ensign Ho. E14 2C 88 (off Admirals Way)
Ensign Ind. Cen. E1 7G 69 (off Ensign St.)
Ensign St. E1 7G 69
Ensign Way. Stanw 1A 112
Ensign Way. Wall 7J 151
Enslin Rd. SE9 7E 108
Ensor M. SW7 5B 84 (5A 170)
Enstone Rd. Enf 3F 9
Enstone Rd. Uxb 3B 40
Enterprise Bus. Pk. E14 2D 88
Enterprise Cen., The. Beck 5A 124 (off Cricket La.)
Enterprise Clo. Croy 1A 152
Enterprise Ho. E9 7J 51 (off Tudor Gro.)
Enterprise Ho. E14 5D 88 (off St Davids Sq.)
Enterprise Ho. Bark 3K 73
Enterprise Ind. Est. SE16 5J 87
Enterprise Way. NW10 3B 64
Enterprise Way. SW18 4J 101
Enterprise Way. Tedd 6K 115
Enterprize Way. SE8 4B 88
Epcot M. NW10 3F 65
Epirus M. SW6 7J 83
Epirus Rd. SW6 7H 83
Epping Clo. E14 4C 88
Epping Clo. Romf 3H 39
Epping Glade. E4 6K 9
Epping New Rd. Buck H & Lou 2E 20
Epping Pl. N1 6A 50
Epping Way. E4 6J 9
Epple Rd. SW6 1H 101
Epsom Clo. Bexh 3H 111
Epsom Clo. N'holt 5D 42
Epsom Rd. E10 6E 34
Epsom Rd. Croy 4A 152
Epsom Rd. Ilf 6K 37
Epsom Rd. Sutt 7H 137
Epsom Sq. H'row A 2H 95
Epstein Rd. SE28 1A 92
Epworth Rd. Iswth 7B 80
Epworth St. EC2 4D 68 (4F 163)
Equity Sq. E2 3F 69 (2K 163) (off Shacklewell St.)
Erasmus St. SW1 4H 85 (4D 172)
Erconwald St. W12 6B 64
Erebus Dri. SE28 2G 91
Eresby Dri. Beck 1C 154
Eresby Ho. SW7 2C 84 (7D 164) (off Rutland Ga.)
Eresby Pl. NW6 7J 47
Erica Gdns. Croy 3D 154
Erica Ho. N22 1A 32 (off Acacia Rd.)
Erica Ho. SE4 3B 106
Erica St. W12 7C 64
Eric Clarke La. Bark 4F 73
Eric Clo. E7 4J 53
Ericcson Clo. SW18 5J 101
Eric Fletcher Ct. N1 7C 50 (off Essex Rd.)
Eric Rd. E7 4J 53
Eric Rd. NW10 6B 46
Eric Rd. Romf 7D 38
Ericson Ho. SE13 4F 107 (off Blessington Rd.)
Eric St. E3 4B 70 (in two parts)
Eric Wilkins Ho. SE1 5G 87 (off Old Kent Rd.)
Eridge Rd. W4 3K 81
Erin Clo. Brom 7G 125
Erin Clo. Ilf 6A 38
Erindale. SE18 6H 91
Erindale Ter. SE18 6H 91
Erith Cres. Romf 1J 39
Erith Rd. Belv & Eri 5G 93
Erith Rd. Bexh & N Hth 4H 111
Erlanger Rd. SE14 1K 105
Erlesmere Gdns. W7 3A 80
Erlich Cotts. E1 5J 69 (off Sidney St.)
Ermine Clo. Houn 2A 96
Ermine Rd. N15 6F 33
Ermine Rd. SE13 4D 106
Ermine Side. Enf 5B 8
Ermington Rd. SE9 2G 127
Ernald Av. E6 2C 72
Erncroft Way. Twic 6K 97
Ernest Av. SE27 4B 122
Ernest Clo. Beck 5C 142
Ernest Cotts. Eps 7B 148
Ernest Gdns. W4 6H 81
Ernest Gro. Beck 5B 142
Ernest Harriss Ho. W9 4J 65 (off Elgin Av.)
Ernest Rd. King T 2H 135
Ernest Sq. King T 2H 135
Ernest St. E1 4K 69
Ernle Rd. SW20 7D 118
Ernshaw Pl. SW15 5G 101
Eros. 7H 67 (3C 166)
Eros Ho. Shops. SE6 7D 106 (off Brownhill Rd.)
Erpingham Rd. SW15 3E 100
Erridge Rd. SW19 2J 137
Errington Rd. W9 4H 65
Errol Gdns. Hay 4K 59
Errol Gdns. N Mald 4C 136
Errol St. EC1 4C 68 (4D 162)
Erskine Clo. Sutt 3C 150
Erskine Cres. N17 4H 33
Erskine Hill. NW11 4J 29
Erskine Ho. SW1 5G 85 (6A 172) (off Churchill Gdns.)
Erskine M. NW3 7D 48 (off Erskine Rd.)
Erskine Rd. E17 4B 34
Erskine Rd. NW3 7D 48
Erskine Rd. Sutt 4B 150
Erwood Rd. SE7 5C 90
Esam Way. SW16 5A 122
Escot Rd. Sun 7H 113
Escott Gdns. SE9 4C 126
Escreet Gro. SE18 4E 90
Esher Av. Romf 6J 39
Esher Av. Sutt 3F 149
Esher Av. W on T 7J 131
Esher By-Pass. Clay & Chess 7B 146
Esher Clo. Bex 1E 128
Esher Cres. H'row A 2H 95
Esher Gdns. SW19 2F 119
Esher M. Mitc 3E 138
Esher Rd. E Mol 6H 133
Esher Rd. Ilf 3J 55
Eskdale. NW1 2G 67 (1A 160) (off Stanhope St.)
Eskdale Av. N'holt 1D 60
Eskdale Clo. Wemb 2D 44
Eskdale Rd. Bexh 2G 111
Eskmont Ridge. SE19 7D 122
Esk Rd. E13 4J 71
Esk Way. Romf 1K 39
Esmar Cres. NW9 7C 28
Esmeralda Rd. SE1 4G 87
Esmond Ct. W8 3K 83 (off Thackeray St.)
Esmond Gdns. W4 4K 81
Esmond Rd. NW6 1H 65
Esmond Rd. W4 4K 81
Esmond St. SW15 4G 101
Esparto St. SW18 7K 101
Essan Ho. W5 5B 62
Essenden Rd. Belv 5G 93
Essenden Rd. S Croy 7E 152
Essendine Rd. W9 3J 65
Essex Av. Iswth 3J 97
Essex Clo. E17 4A 34
Essex Clo. Mord 7F 137
Essex Clo. Romf 4H 39
Essex Clo. Ruis 1B 42
Essex Ct. SW13 2B 100
Essex Ct. WC2 6A 68 (off Brick Ct.)
Essex Gdns. N4 6B 32
Essex Gro. SE19 6D 122
Essex Hall. E17 1K 33
Essex Ho. E14 6D 70 (off Giraud St.)
Essex Mans. E11 7F 35
Essex Pk. N3 6E 14
Essex Pk. M. W3 1A 82
Essex Pl. W4 4J 81 (in two parts)
Essex Pl. Sq. W4 4K 81
Essex Rd. E4 1B 20
Essex Rd. E10 6E 34
Essex Rd. E12 5C 54
Essex Rd. E17 6A 34
Essex Rd. E18 2K 35
Essex Rd. N1 1B 68
Essex Rd. NW10 7A 46
Essex Rd. W3 7J 63
Essex Rd. W4 4K 81 (in two parts)
Essex Rd. Bark 7H 55
Essex Rd. Chad H 7C 38
Essex Rd. Dag 5J 57
Essex Rd. Enf 4J 7
Essex Rd. Romf 4H 39
Essex Rd. S. E11 7F 35
Essex St. E7 5J 53
Essex St. SE18 3G 91
Essex St. WC2 6A 68 (1J 167)
Essex Vs. W8 2J 83
Essex Wharf. E5 2K 51
Essian St. E1 5A 70
Essoldo Way. Edgw 3F 27
Estate Way. E10 1B 52
Estcourt Rd. SE25 6H 141
Estcourt Rd. SW6 7H 83
Estella Av. N Mald 4D 136
Estella Ho. W11 7F 65 (off St Ann's Rd.)
Estelle Rd. NW3 4D 48
Esterbrooke St. SW1 4H 85 (4C 172)
Este Rd. SW11 3C 102
Esther Clo. N21 7F 7
Esther Rd. E11 7G 35
Estoria Clo. SW2 7A 104
Estorick Collection of Modern Italian Art. 6B 50
Estreham Rd. SW16 6H 121
Estridge Clo. Houn 4E 96
Estuary Clo. Bark 3B 74
Eswyn Rd. SW17 4D 120
Etal Ho. N1 7B 50 (off Sutton Est., The)
Etchingham Ct. N3 7E 14
Etchingham Pk. Rd. N3 7E 14
Etchingham Rd. E15 4E 52
Eternit Wlk. SW6 1E 100
Etfield Gro. Sidc 5B 128
Ethelbert Clo. Brom 2J 143
Ethelbert Ct. Brom 3J 143 (off Ethelbert Rd.)
Ethelbert Gdns. Ilf 5D 36
Ethelbert Rd. SW20 1F 137
Ethelbert Rd. Brom 3J 143
Ethelbert Rd. Eri 7J 93
Ethelbert St. SW12 1F 121
Ethel Brooks Ho. SE18 6F 91
Ethelburga St. SW11 1C 102
Ethelburga Tower. SW11 1C 102 (off Maskelyne Clo.)
Etheldene Av. N10 4G 31
Ethelden Rd. W12 1D 82
Ethel Rd. E16 6K 71
Ethel Rd. Ashf 5A 112
Ethel St. SE17 4C 86
Etheridge Rd. NW4 7E 28 (in two parts)
Etherley Rd. N15 5C 32
Etherow St. SE22 7G 105
Etherstone Grn. SW16 4A 122
Etherstone Rd. SW16 4A 122
Ethnard Rd. SE15 6H 87
Ethronvi Rd. Bexh 3E 110
Etloe Rd. E10 2C 52
Eton Av. N12 7F 15
Eton Av. NW3 7B 48
Eton Av. Barn 6H 5
Eton Av. Houn 6D 78
Eton Av. N Mald 5K 135
Eton Av. Wemb 4B 44
Eton Clo. SW18 7K 101
Eton College Rd. NW3 6D 48
Eton Ct. NW3 7B 48 (off Eton Av.)
Eton Ct. Wemb 4C 44
Eton Garages. NW3 6C 48
Eton Gro. NW9 3G 27
Eton Gro. SE13 3G 107
Eton Hall. NW3 6D 48
Eton Ho. N5 4B 50 (off Leigh Rd.)
Eton Mnr. Ct. E10 2C 52 (off Leyton Grange Est.)
Eton Pl. NW3 7E 48
Eton Ri. NW3 6D 48
Eton Rd. NW3 7D 48
Eton Rd. Hay 7H 77
Eton Rd. Ilf 4G 55
Eton St. Rich 5E 98
Eton Vs. NW3 6D 48
Etta St. SE8 6A 88
Ettrick St. E14 6E 70 (in two parts)
Etwell Pl. Surb 6F 135
Eugene Cotter Ho. SE17 4D 86 (off Tatum St.)
Eugenia Rd. SE16 4J 87
Eugenie M. Chst 1F 145
Eureka Rd. King T 2G 135
Euro Clo. NW10 6C 46
Eurolink Bus. Cen. SW2 5A 104
Europa Pl. EC1 3C 68 (2C 162)
Europa Trad. Est. Eri 5K 93
European Bus. Cen. NW9 3J 27 (Carlisle Rd.)
European Bus. Cen. NW9 3K 27 (Edgware Rd.)
Europe Rd. SE18 3D 90
Eustace Ho. SE11 3G 173
Eustace Pl. SE18 4D 90
Eustace Rd. E6 3C 72
Eustace Rd. SW6 7J 83
Eustace Rd. Romf 7D 38
Euston Cen. NW1 4G 67 (3A 160) (in two parts)
Euston Gro. NW1 2C 160
Euston Rd. NW1 & N1 4F 67 (3A 160)
Euston Rd. Croy 1A 152
Euston Sq. NW1 3H 67 (2C 160) (in two parts)
Euston Sta. Colonnade. NW1 3H 67 (2C 160)
Euston St. NW1 3G 67 (2B 160)
Euston Tower. NW1 4G 67 (3A 160)
Euston Underpass. (Junct.) 3F 67 (3A 160)
Evandale Rd. SW9 2A 104
Evangelist Ho. EC4 6B 68 (1A 168) (off Black Friars La.)
Evangelist Rd. NW5 4F 49
Evans Clo. E8 6F 51
Evans Gro. Felt 2E 114
Evans Ho. SW8 7H 85 (off Wandsworth Rd.)
Evans Ho. W12 7D 64 (off White City Est.)
Evans Ho. Felt 2E 114
Evans Rd. SE6 2G 125
Evanston Av. E4 7K 19
Evanston Gdns. Ilf 6C 36
Eva Rd. Romf 7C 38
Evelina Mans. SE5 7D 86
Evelina Rd. SE15 3J 105
Evelina Rd. SE20 7J 123
Eveline Rd. Mitc 1D 138
Evelyn Av. NW9 4K 27
Evelyn Av. Ruis 7G 23
Evelyn Clo. Twic 7F 97
Evelyn Ct. E8 4G 51

Evelyn Ct. N1 2D 68 (1E 162) (off Evelyn Wlk., in two parts)
Evelyn Cres. Sun 1H 131
Evelyn Denington Ct. N1 7B 50 (off Sutton Est., The)
Evelyn Denington Rd. E6 4C 72
Evelyn Dri. Pinn 1B 24
Evelyn Fox Ct. W10 5E 64
Evelyn Gdns. SW7 5A 84 (6A 170)
Evelyn Gdns. Rich 4E 98
Evelyn Gro. W5 1F 81
Evelyn Gro. S'hall 6D 60
Evelyn Ho. SE14 1A 106 (off Loring Rd.)
Evelyn Ho. W12 2B 82 (off Cobbold Rd.)
Evelyn Lowe Est. SE16 3G 87
Evelyn Mans. SW1 3G 85 (2A 172) (off Carlisle Pl.)
Evelyn Mans. W14 6G 83 (off Queen's Club Gdns.)
Evelyn Rd. E16 1J 89
Evelyn Rd. E17 4E 34
Evelyn Rd. SW19 5K 119
Evelyn Rd. W4 3K 81
Evelyn Rd. Cockf 4J 5
Evelyn Rd. Ham 3C 116
Evelyn Rd. Rich 3E 98
Evelyns Clo. Uxb 6C 58
Evelyn St. SE8 4A 88
Evelyn Ter. Rich 3E 98
Evelyn Wlk. N1 2D 68 (1E 162)
Evelyn Way. Sun 1H 131
Evelyn Way. Wall 4H 151
Evelyn Yd. W1 6H 67 (7C 160)
Evening Hill. Beck 7E 124
Evenlode Ho. SE2 2C 92 (off Coralline Wlk.)
Evenwood Clo. SW15 5G 101
Everard Av. Brom 1J 155
Everard Ct. N13 3E 16
Everard Ho. E1 6G 69 (off Boyd St.)
Everard Way. Wemb 3E 44
Everatt Clo. SW18 6H 101
Everdon Rd. SW13 6C 82
Everest Pl. E14 5E 70
Everest Rd. SE9 5D 108
Everest Rd. Stanw 7A 94
Everett Clo. Bus H 1D 10
Everett Clo. Pinn 3H 23
Everett Ho. SE17 5D 86 (off East St.)
Everett Wlk. Belv 5F 93
Everglade Ho. E17 2B 34
Everglade Strand. NW9 1B 28
Evergreen Clo. SE20 7J 123
Evergreen Way. Hay 7G 59
Everilda St. N1 1K 67
Evering Rd. N16 & E5 3F 51
Everington Rd. N10 2D 30
Everington St. W6 6F 83 (in two parts)
Everitt Rd. NW10 3K 63
Everleigh St. N4 1K 49
Eve Rd. E11 4G 53
Eve Rd. E15 2G 71
Eve Rd. N17 3E 32
Eve Rd. Iswth 4A 98
Eversfield Gdns. NW7 6F 13
Eversfield Rd. Rich 2F 99
Evershed Wlk. W4 3J 81
Eversholt St. NW1 2G 67 (1B 160)
Evershot Rd. N4 1K 49
Eversleigh Rd. E6 1B 72
Eversleigh Rd. N3 7C 14
Eversleigh Rd. SW11 3D 102
Eversleigh Rd. New Bar 5F 5
Eversley Av. Bexh 2K 111
Eversley Av. Wemb 2G 45
Eversley Clo. N21 6E 6
Eversley Cres. N21 6E 6
Eversley Cres. Iswth 1H 97
Eversley Cres. Ruis 2G 41
Eversley Ho. E2 3G 69 (2K 163) (off Gossett St.)
Eversley Mt. N21 6E 6
Eversley Pk. SW19 6D 118
Eversley Pk. Rd. N21 6E 6
Eversley Rd. SE7 6K 89
Eversley Rd. SE19 7D 122
Eversley Rd. Surb 4F 135
Eversley Way. Croy 4C 154
Everthorpe Rd. SE15 3F 105
Everton Bldgs. NW1 3G 67 (2A 160)
Everton Dri. Stan 3E 26
Everton Rd. Croy 1G 153
Evesham Av. E17 2C 34
Evesham Clo. Gnfd 2F 61
Evesham Clo. Sutt 7J 149
Evesham Ct. W13 1A 80 (off Tewkesbury Rd.)
Evesham Ct. Rich 6F 99
Evesham Grn. Mord 6K 137
Evesham Ho. E2 2J 69 (off Old Ford Rd.)
Evesham Ho. NW8 1A 66 (off Abbey Rd.)
Evesham Rd. E15 7H 53
Evesham Rd. N11 5B 16
Evesham Rd. Mord 6K 137
Evesham St. W11 7F 65
Evesham Ter. Surb 6D 134
Evesham Wlk. SE5 2D 104
Evesham Wlk. SW9 2A 104
Evesham Way. SW11 3E 102
Evesham Way. Ilf 3E 36
Evry Rd. Sidc 6C 128
Ewald Rd. SW6 2H 101
Ewanrigg Ter. Wfd G 5F 21
Ewart Gro. N22 1A 32
Ewart Pl. E3 2B 70
Ewart Rd. SE23 7K 105
Ewe Clo. N7 6J 49
Ewell. 7B 148
Ewell By-Pass. Eps 7C 148
Ewell Ct. Av. Eps & Ewe 5A 148
Ewellhurst Rd. Ilf 2C 36
Ewell Pk. Gdns. Eps 7C 148
Ewell Pk. Way. Ewe 6C 148
Ewell Rd. Surb 7B 134 (Effingham Rd.)
Ewell Rd. Surb 6E 134 (Surbiton Hill Rd.)
Ewell Rd. Sutt 7F 149
Ewelme Rd. SE23 1J 123
Ewen Cres. SW2 7A 104
Ewen Ho. N1 1K 67 (off Barnsbury Est.)
Ewer St. SE1 1C 86 (5C 168)
Ewesdon Clo. N9 3C 18
Ewhurst Av. S Croy 7F 153
Ewhurst Clo. E1 5J 69
Ewhurst Ct. Mitc 3B 138
Ewhurst Rd. SE4 6B 106
Exbury Ho. E9 7J 51
Exbury Ho. SW1 5H 85 (5C 172) (off Rampayne St.)
Exbury Rd. SE6 2C 124
ExCeL. 7K 71
Excel Ct. WC2 3D 166
Excelsior Clo. King T 2G 135
Excelsior Gdns. SE13 2E 106
Excelsior Ind. Est. SE15 6J 87
Exchange Arc. EC2 5E 68 (5H 163)
Exchange Building. E1 4F 69 (4J 163) (off Commercial St.)
Exchange Clo. N11 2K 15
Exchange Ct. WC2 7J 67 (3F 167)
Exchange Ho. EC2 5H 163
Exchange Mans. NW11 7H 29
Exchange Pl. EC2 5E 68 (5G 163)
Exchange Sq. EC2 5E 68 (5G 163)
Exchange St. EC1 3C 68 (2C 162)
Exchange St. Romf 5K 39
Exchange, The. Ilf 2F 55
Exeforde Av. Ashf 4C 112
Exeter Clo. E6 6D 72
Exeter Ct. NW6 2J 65 (off Cambridge Rd., in four parts)
Exeter Ct. Surb 5E 134 (off Maple Rd.)
Exeter Gdns. Ilf 1C 54
Exeter Ho. SE15 6G 87 (off Friary Est.)
Exeter Ho. W2 6A 66 (off Hallfield Est.)
Exeter Ho. Bark 7A 56 (off Margaret Bondfield Av.)
Exeter Ho. Felt 2D 114 (off Watermill Way)
Exeter Mans. NW2 6G 47
Exeter M. NW6 6K 47
Exeter M. SW6 7J 83
Exeter Rd. E16 5J 71
Exeter Rd. E17 5C 34
Exeter Rd. N9 2D 18
Exeter Rd. N14 1A 16
Exeter Rd. NW2 5G 47
Exeter Rd. Croy 7E 140
Exeter Rd. Dag 6H 57
Exeter Rd. Enf 3E 8
Exeter Rd. Felt 3D 114
Exeter Rd. Harr 2C 42
Exeter Rd. H'row A 3G 95
Exeter Rd. Well 2J 109
Exeter St. WC2 7J 67 (2F 167)
Exeter Way. SE14 7B 88
Exeter Way. H'row A 2G 95
Exford Gdns. SE12 1K 125
Exford Rd. SE12 2K 125
Exhibition Clo. W12 7E 64
Exhibition Rd. SW7 2B 84 (7B 164)
Exmoor Clo. Ilf 1F 37
Exmoor Ho. E3 2A 70 (off Gernon Rd.)
Exmoor St. W10 4F 65
Exmouth Ho. E14 4D 88 (off Cahir St.)
Exmouth Ho. EC1 4A 68 (3J 161) (off Pine St.)
Exmouth Mkt. EC1 4A 68 (3J 161)
Exmouth M. NW1 3G 67 (2B 160)
Exmouth Pl. E8 7H 51
Exmouth Rd. E17 5B 34
Exmouth Rd. Hay 3G 59
Exmouth Rd. Ruis 3A 42
Exmouth Rd. Well 1C 110
Exmouth St. E1 6J 69
Exning Rd. E16 4H 71
Exonbury. NW8 1K 65 (off Abbey Rd.)
Exon St. SE17 5E 86
Explorer Av. Stai 1A 112
Express Dri. Ilf 1B 56
Express Newspapers. SE1 1B 86 (4A 168) (off Blackfriars Rd.)
Express Wharf. E14 2C 88
Exton Cres. NW10 7J 45
Exton Gdns. Dag 5C 56
Exton St. SE1 1A 86 (5J 167)
Eyebright Clo. Croy 1K 153
Eyhurst Clo. NW2 2C 46
Eylewood Rd. SE27 5C 122
Eynella Rd. SE22 7F 105
Eynham Rd. W12 6E 64
Eynsford Clo. Orp 7G 145
Eynsford Cres. Bex 1C 128
Eynsford Ho. SE1 2D 86 (7E 168) (off Crosby Row)
Eynsford Ho. SE15 6J 87
Eynsford Ho. SE17 4E 86 (off Beckway St.)
Eynsford Rd. Ilf 2J 55
Eynsford Ter. W Dray 6B 58
Eynsham Dri. SE2 4A 92
Eynswood Dri. Sidc 5B 128
Eyot Gdns. W6 5B 82
Eyot Grn. W4 5B 82
Eyre Ct. NW8 2B 66
Eyre St. Hill. EC1 4A 68 (4J 161)
Eysham Ct. New Bar 5E 4
Eythorne Rd. SW9 1A 104
Ezra St. E2 3F 69 (1K 163)

Faber Gdns. NW4 5C 28
Fabian Rd. SW6 7H 83
Fabian St. E6 4D 72
Facade, The. SE23 2J 123
Factory La. N17 2F 33
Factory La. Croy 1A 152
Factory Rd. E16 1B 90
Factory Sq. SW16 6J 121 (off Streatham High Rd.)
Factory Yd. W7 1J 79
Fagg's Rd. Felt 4H 95
Fairacre. N Mald 3A 136
Fairacre Ct. N'wd 1G 23
Fairacres. SW15 4B 100
Fair Acres. Brom 5J 143
Fair Acres. Croy 7B 154
Fairacres. Ruis 7H 23
Fairbairn Grn. SW9 1B 104
Fairbank Av. Orp 2E 156
Fairbank Est. N1 2D 68 (1E 162)
Fairbanks Rd. N17 3F 33
Fairbourne Ho. Hay 3E 76
Fairbourne Rd. N17 3E 32
Fairbridge Rd. N19 2H 49
Fairbrook Clo. N13 5F 17
Fairbrook Rd. N13 6F 17
Fairburn Ct. SW15 5G 101
Fairburn Ho. W14 5H 83 (off Ivatt Pl.)
Fairby Ho. SE1 4F 87 (off Longfield Est.)
Fairby Rd. SE12 5K 107
Faircharm Trad. Est. SE8 7D 88
Fairchild Clo. SW11 2B 102
Fairchild Ho. E9 7J 51 (off Frampton Pk. Rd.)
Fairchild Ho. N1 3E 68 (1G 163) (off Fanshaw St.)
Fairchild Ho. N3 1J 29
Fairchild Pl. EC2 4H 163
Fairchild St. EC2 & E1 4E 68 (3H 163)
Fair Clo. Bush 1A 10
Fairclough St. E1 6G 69
Faircroft Ct. Tedd 6A 116
Fair Cross. 5J 55
Faircross Av. Bark 6G 55
Faircross Av. Romf 1K 39
Faircross Pde. Bark 5J 55
Fairdale Gdns. SW15 4D 100
Fairdale Gdns. Hay 2J 77
Fairey Av. Hay 4H 77
Fairfax Av. Eps & Ewe 7D 148
Fairfax Clo. W on T 7K 131
Fairfax Gdns. SE3 1A 108
Fairfax Ho. King T 3F 135 (off Livesey Clo.)
Fairfax Mans. NW3 6A 48 (off Finchley Rd.)
Fairfax M. E16 1K 89
Fairfax M. SW15 4E 100
Fairfax Pl. NW6 7A 48
Fairfax Rd. N8 4A 32
Fairfax Rd. NW6 7A 48
Fairfax Rd. W4 3A 82
Fairfax Rd. Tedd 6A 116
Fairfax Way. N10 7K 15
Fairfield. E1 5J 69 (off Redman's Rd.)
Fairfield. N20 7G 5
Fairfield. NW1 1G 67 (off Arlington Rd.)
Fairfield Av. NW4 6D 28
Fairfield Av. Edgw 6C 12
Fairfield Av. Ruis 7E 22
Fairfield Av. Twic 1F 115
Fairfield Clo. N12 4F 15
Fairfield Clo. Enf 4E 8
Fairfield Clo. Ewe 5A 148
Fairfield Clo. Mitc 7C 120
Fairfield Clo. Sidc 6K 109
Fairfield Ct. NW10 1C 64
Fairfield Ct. N'wd 2J 23
Fairfield Ct. Ruis 1F 41
Fairfield Cres. Edgw 6C 12
Fairfield Dri. SW18 5K 101
Fairfield Dri. Gnfd 1C 62
Fairfield Dri. Harr 3G 25
Fairfield E. King T 2E 134
Fairfield Gdns. N8 5J 31
Fairfield Gro. SE7 6B 90
Fairfield Halls. 3D 152
Fairfield Ind. Est. King T 3F 135
Fairfield N. King T 2E 134
Fairfield Path. Croy 3D 152
Fairfield Pl. King T 3E 134
Fairfield Rd. E3 2C 70
Fairfield Rd. E17 2A 34
Fairfield Rd. N8 5J 31
Fairfield Rd. N18 4B 18
Fairfield Rd. Beck 2C 142
Fairfield Rd. Bexh 2F 111
Fairfield Rd. Brom 7J 125
Fairfield Rd. Croy 3D 152
Fairfield Rd. Ilf 6F 55
Fairfield Rd. King T 2E 134
Fairfield Rd. Orp 6H 145
Fairfield Rd. S'hall 6D 60
Fairfield Rd. Uxb 6A 40
Fairfield Rd. W Dray 7A 58
Fairfield Rd. Wfd G 6D 20
Fairfields Clo. NW9 5J 27
Fairfields Cres. NW9 4J 27
Fairfields S. King T 2E 134
Fairfields Rd. Houn 3G 97
Fairfield St. SW18 5K 101
Fairfield Way. Barn 5D 4
Fairfield Way. Eps 5A 148
Fairfield W. King T 2E 134
Fairfoot Rd. E3 4C 70
Fairford. SE6 1C 124
Fairford Av. Bexh 1K 111
Fairford Av. Croy 5K 141
Fairford Clo. Croy 5A 142
Fairford Ct. Sutt 7K 149
Fairford Gdns. Wor Pk 2B 148
Fairford Ho. SE11 4A 86 (4K 173)
Fairgreen. Barn 3J 5
Fairgreen Ct. Barn 3J 5
Fairgreen E. Barn 3J 5
Fairgreen Rd. T Hth 5B 140
Fairhaven Av. Croy 6K 141
Fairhaven Ct. S Croy 5C 152 (off Warham Rd.)
Fairhazel Gdns. NW6 6K 47
Fairhazel Mans. NW6 7A 48 (off Fairhazel Gdns.)
Fairholme. Felt 7F 95
Fairholme Clo. N3 4G 29
Fairholme Cres. Hay 4H 59
Fairholme Gdns. N3 3G 29
Fairholme Rd. W14 5G 83
Fairholme Rd. Ashf 5A 112
Fairholme Rd. Croy 7A 140
Fairholme Rd. Harr 5K 25

Fairholme Rd. *Ilf* 7D **36**
Fairholme Rd. *Sutt* 6H **149**
Fairholt Clo. *N16* 1E **50**
Fairholt Rd. *N16* 1D **50**
Fairholt St. *SW7* 3C **84** (1D **170**)
Fairland Ho. *Brom* 4K **143**
Fairland Rd. *E15* 6H **53**
Fairlands Av. *Buck H* 2D **20**
Fairlands Av. *Sutt* 2J **149**
Fairlands Av. *T Hth* 4K **139**
Fairlands Ct. *SE9* 6E **108**
Fairlawn. *SE7* 7A **90**
Fairlawn Av. *N2* 4C **30**
Fairlawn Av. *W4* 4J **81**
Fairlawn Av. *Bexh* 2D **110**
Fairlawn Clo. *N14* 6B **6**
Fair Lawn Clo. *Clay* 6A **146**
Fairlawn Clo. *Felt* 4D **114**
Fairlawn Clo. *King T* 6J **117**
Fairlawn Ct. *SE7* 7A **90**
(in two parts)
Fairlawn Ct. *W4* 4J **81**
Fairlawn Dri. *Wfd G* 7D **20**
Fairlawn Gdns. *S'hall* 7D **60**
Fairlawn Gro. *W4* 4J **81**
Fairlawn Mans. *SE14* 1K **105**
Fairlawn Pk. *SE26* 5A **124**
Fairlawn Rd. *SW19* 7H **119**
Fairlawns. *Pinn* 2B **24**
Fairlawns. *Sun* 3H **131**
Fairlawns. *Twic* 6C **98**
Fairlawns. *Wall* 5F **151**
Fairlea Pl. *W5* 4C **62**
Fairlie Gdns. *SE23* 7J **105**
Fairlight Av. *E4* 2A **20**
Fairlight Av. *NW10* 2A **64**
(in two parts)
Fairlight Av. *Wfd G* 6D **20**
Fairlight Clo. *E4* 2A **20**
Fairlight Clo. *Wor Pk* 4E **148**
Fairlight Ct. *NW10* 2A **64**
Fairlight Ct. *Gnfd* 2G **61**
Fairlight Rd. *SW17* 4B **120**
Fairline Ct. *Beck* 2E **142**
Fairlop. **1J 37**
Fairlop Ct. *E11* 1F **53**
Fairlop Gdns. *Ilf* 1G **37**
Fairlop Rd. *E11* 7F **35**
Fairlop Rd. *Ilf* 2G **37**
Fairman Ter. *Kent* 4D **26**
Fairmark Dri. *Uxb* 6C **40**
Fairmead. *Brom* 4D **144**
Fairmead. *Surb* 1H **147**
Fairmead Clo. *Brom* 4D **144**
Fairmead Clo. *Houn* 7B **78**
Fairmead Clo. *N Mald* 3K **135**
Fairmead Ct. *Rich* 2H **99**
Fairmead Cres. *Edgw* 3D **12**
Fairmead Gdns. *Ilf* 5C **36**
Fairmead Ho. *E9* 4A **52**
Fairmead Rd. *N19* 3H **49**
Fairmead Rd. *Croy* 7K **139**
Fairmile Av. *SW16* 5H **121**
Fairmile Ho. *Tedd* 4A **116**
Fairmont Clo. *Belv* 5F **93**
Fairmount Rd. *SW2* 6K **103**
Fairoak Clo. *Orp* 7F **145**
Fairoak Dri. *SE9* 5H **109**
Fairoak Gdns. *Romf* 2K **39**
Fair Oak Pl. *Ilf* 2G **37**
Fairseat Clo. *Bus H* 2D **10**
Fairstead Wlk. N1 *1C* ***68***
(off Popham St.)
Fair St. *SE1* 2E **86** (6H **169**)
Fair St. *Houn* 3G **97**
Fairthorn Rd. *SE7* 5J **89**
Fairview. *Ruis* 4A **42**
Fairview Av. *Wemb* 6D **44**
Fairview Clo. *E17* 1A **34**
Fairview Clo. *SE26* 5A **124**
Fairview Ct. *NW4* 2F **29**
Fairview Ct. *Ashf* 5C **112**
Fairview Cres. *Harr* 1E **42**
Fairview Dri. *Shep* 5B **130**
Fairview Gdns. *Wfd G* 1K **35**
Fairview Ho. *SW2* 7K **103**
Fairview Ind. Pk. *Rain* 5K **75**
Fairview Pl. *SW2* 7K **103**
Fairview Rd. *N15* 5F **33**
Fairview Rd. *SW16* 1K **139**
Fairview Rd. *Enf* 1F **7**
Fairview Rd. *Sutt* 5B **150**
Fairview Vs. *E4* 7J **19**
Fairview Way. *Edgw* 4B **12**
Fairwall Ho. *SE5* 1E **104**
Fairwater Av. *Well* 4A **110**
Fairwater Ho. *Tedd* 4A **116**
Fairway. *SW20* 3E **136**
Fairway. *Bexh* 5E **110**
Fairway. *Orp* 5H **145**
Fair Way. *Wfd G* 5F **21**
Fairway Av. *NW9* 3H **27**
Fairway Clo. *NW11* 7A **30**
Fairway Clo. *Croy* 5A **142**
Fairway Clo. *Eps* 4J **147**
Fairway Clo. *Houn* 5A **96**
Fairway Ct. *NW7* 3E **12**
Fairway Ct. SE16 *2K* ***87***
(off Christopher Clo.)
Fairway Ct. *New Bar* 6E **4**
Fairway Dri. *SE28* 6D **74**
Fairway Dri. *Gnfd* 7F **43**
Fairway Gdns. *Beck* 6F **143**
Fairway Gdns. *Ilf* 5G **55**
Fairways. *E17* 4E **34**
Fairways. *Ashf* 6D **112**
Fairways. *Isw th* 1H **97**
Fairways. *Stan* 2E **26**
Fairways. *Tedd* 7D **116**
Fairways Bus. Pk. *E10* 2A **52**
Fairway, The. *N13* 3H **17**
Fairway, The. *N14* 6A **6**
Fairway, The. *NW7* 3E **12**
Fairway, The. *W3* 6A **64**
Fairway, The. *Brom* 5D **144**
Fairway, The. *New Bar* 6E **4**
Fairway, The. *N Mald* 1K **135**
Fairway, The. *N'holt* 6G **43**
Fairway, The. *Ruis* 4A **42**
Fairway, The. *Uxb* 2B **58**
Fairway, The. *Wemb* 3B **44**
Fairway, The. *W Mol* 3F **133**
Fairweather Clo. *N15* 4E **32**
Fairweather Ct. *N13* 4E **16**
Fairweather Rd. *N16* 6G **33**
Fairwyn Rd. *SE26* 4A **124**
Fakenham Clo. *NW7* 7H **13**
Fakenham Clo. *N'holt* 6D **42**
Fakruddin St. *E1* 4G **69**
Falcon. WC1 *5J* ***67*** *(5F* ***161****)*
(off Old Gloucester St.)
Falcon Av. *Brom* 4C **144**
Falconberg Ct. *W1*
6H **67** (7D **160**)
Falconberg M. *W1*
6H **67** (7D **160**)
Falcon Clo. *SE1* 1B **86** (4B **168**)
Falcon Clo. *W4* 6J **81**
Falcon Clo. *N'wd* 1G **23**
Falcon Ct. E18 *3K* ***35***
(off Albert Rd.)
Falcon Ct. *EC4* 6A **68** (1K **167**)
Falcon Ct. N1 *2B* ***68***
(off City Garden Row)
Falcon Ct. *New Bar* 4F **5**
Falcon Ct. *Ruis* 2G **41**
Falcon Cres. *Enf* 5E **8**
Falcon Dri. *Stanw* 6A **94**
Falconer Ct. *N17* 7H **17**
Falconer Wlk. *N7* 2K **49**
Falconet Ct. E1 *1H* ***87***
(off Wapping High St.)
Falcon Gro. *SW11* 3C **102**
Falcon Ho. E14 *5D* ***88***
(off St Davids Sq.)
Falcon La. *SW11* 3C **102**
Falcon Lodge. W9 *5J* ***65***
(off Admiral Wlk.)
Falcon Pk. Ind. Est. *NW10*
4A **46**
Falcon Point. *SE1*
7B **68** (3B **168**)
Falcon Rd. *SW11* 2C **102**
Falcon Rd. *Enf* 5E **8**
Falcon Rd. *Hamp* 7D **114**
Falconry Ct. King T *3E* ***134***
(off Fairfield S.)
Falcon St. *E13* 4H **71**
Falcon Ter. *SW11* 3C **102**
Falcon Way. *E11* 4J **35**
Falcon Way. *E14* 4D **88**
Falcon Way. *NW9* 2A **28**
Falcon Way. *Felt* 5K **95**
Falcon Way. *Harr* 5E **26**
Falcon Way. *Sun* 2G **131**
Falconwood. **4K 109**
Falconwood. (Junct.) 4G **109**
Falconwood Av. *Well* 2H **109**
Falconwood Ct. SE3 *2H* ***107***
(off Montpelier Row)
Falconwood Pde. *Well* 4J **109**
Falconwood Rd. *Croy* 7B **154**
Falcourt Clo. *Sutt* 5K **149**
Falkirk Ct. SE16 *1K* ***87***
(off Rotherhithe St.)
Falkirk Ho. W9 *2K* ***65***
(off Maida Va.)
Falkirk St. *N1* 2E **68** (1H **163**)
Falkland Av. *N3* 7D **14**
Falkland Av. *N11* 4A **16**
Falkland Ho. *SE6* 4E **124**
Falkland Ho. *W8* 3K **83**
Falkland Ho. W14 *5H* ***83***
(off Edith Vs.)
Falkland Pk. Av. *SE25* 3E **140**
Falkland Pl. *NW5* 5G **49**
Falkland Rd. *N8* 4A **32**
Falkland Rd. *NW5* 5G **49**
Falkland Rd. *Barn* 2B **4**
Fallaize Av. *Ilf* 4F **55**
Falling La. *W Dray* 7A **58**
Falloden Way. *NW11* 4J **29**
Fallodon Ho. W11 *5H* ***65***
(off Tavistock Cres.)
Fallow Corner. **7F 15**
Fallow Ct. SE16 *5G* ***87***
(off Argyle Way)
Fallow Ct. Av. *N12* 7F **15**
Fallowfield. *Stan* 4F **11**
Fallowfield Ct. *Stan* 3F **11**
Fallowfields Dri. *N12* 6H **15**
Fallowhurst Path. *N12* 7F **15**
Fallows Clo. *N2* 2B **30**
Fallsbrook Rd. *SW16* 6F **121**
Falman Clo. *N9* 1B **18**
Falmer Rd. *E17* 3D **34**
Falmer Rd. *N15* 5C **32**
Falmer Rd. *Enf* 4K **7**
Falmouth Av. *E4* 5A **20**
Falmouth Clo. *N22* 7E **16**
Falmouth Clo. *SE12* 5H **107**
Falmouth Gdns. *Ilf* 4B **36**
Falmouth Ho. SE11
5A ***86*** *(5K* ***173****)*
(off Seaton Clo.)
Falmouth Ho. W2
7C ***66*** *(2C* ***164****)*
(off Clarendon Pl.)
Falmouth Ho. *Pinn* 1D **24**
Falmouth Rd. *SE1*
3C **86** (7E **168**)
Falmouth St. *E15* 5F **53**
Falstaff Ct. SE11 *4B* ***86***
(off Opal St.)
Falstaff Ho. N1 *2E* ***68*** *(1G* ***163****)*
(off Arden Est.)
Falstaff M. Hamp H *5H* ***115***
(off Parkside)
Fambridge Clo. *SE26* 4B **124**
Fambridge Ct. Romf *5K* ***39***
(off Marks Rd.)
Fambridge Rd. *Dag* 1G **57**
Fane Ho. *E2* 1J **69**
Fane St. *W14* 6H **83**
Fan Mus. ***7E 88***
Fann St. *EC2 & EC1* 4C **68**
(in two parts)
Fanshawe Av. *Bark* 6G **55**
Fanshawe Cres. *Dag* 5E **56**
Fanshawe Rd. *Rich* 4C **116**
Fanshaw St. *N1* 3E **68** (1G **163**)
Fantail, The. (Junct.) 4D **156**
Fanthorpe St. *SW15* 3E **100**
Faraday Av. *Sidc* 2A **128**
Faraday Clo. *N7* 6K **49**
Faraday Ho. E14 *7B* ***70***
(off Brightlingsea Pl.)
Faraday Ho. *Wemb* 3J **45**
Faraday Mans. W14 *6G* ***83***
(off Queen's Club Gdns.)
Faraday Mus. ***7G 67 (3A 166)***
Faraday Rd. *E15* 6H **53**
Faraday Rd. *SW19* 6J **119**
Faraday Rd. *W3* 7J **63**
Faraday Rd. *W10* 5G **65**
Faraday Rd. *S'hall* 7F **61**
Faraday Rd. *Well* 3A **110**
Faraday Rd. *W Mol* 4E **132**
Faraday Way. *SE18* 3B **90**
Faraday Way. *Croy* 1K **151**
Fareham Rd. *Felt* 7A **96**
Fareham St. *W1* 6H **67** (7C **160**)
Farewell Pl. *Mitc* 1C **138**
Faringdon Av. *Brom* 7E **144**
Faringford Rd. *E15* 7G **53**
Farjeon Ho. NW3 *7B* ***48***
(off Hilgrove Rd.)
Farjeon Rd. *SE3* 1B **108**
Farleigh Av. *Brom* 7H **143**
Farleigh Ct. *S Croy* 5C **152**
Farleigh Pl. *N16* 4F **51**
Farleigh Rd. *N16* 4F **51**
Farley Ct. NW1 *4D* ***66*** *(4G* ***159****)*
(off Allsop Pl.)
Farley Dri. *Ilf* 1J **55**
Farley Ho. *SE26* 3H **123**
Farley Pl. *SE25* 4G **141**
Farley Rd. *SE6* 7D **106**
Farley Rd. *S Croy* 7H **153**
Farlington Pl. *SW15* 7D **100**
Farlow Rd. *SW15* 3F **101**
Farlton Rd. *SW18* 1K **119**
Farman Gro. *N'holt* 3B **60**
Farm Av. *NW2* 3G **47**
Farm Av. *SW16* 4J **121**
Farm Av. *Harr* 7D **24**
Farm Av. *Wemb* 6C **44**
Farmborough Clo. *Harr* 7H **25**
Farm Clo. *N14* 6A **6**
Farm Clo. *SW6* 7J **83**
Farm Clo. *Buck H* 3F **21**
Farm Clo. *Dag* 7J **57**
Farm Clo. *Shep* 7C **130**
Farm Clo. *S'hall* 7F **61**
Farm Clo. *Sutt* 7B **150**
Farm Clo. *Uxb* 2D **40**
Farm Clo. *W Wick* 3H **155**
Farmcote Rd. *SE12* 1J **125**
Farm Ct. *NW4* 3C **28**
Farmdale Rd. *SE10* 5J **89**
Farmdale Rd. *Cars* 7C **150**
Farm Dri. *Croy* 2B **154**
Farm End. *N'wd* 1D **22**
Farmer Rd. *E10* 1D **52**
Farmer's Rd. *SE5* 7B **86**
Farmer St. *W11 & W8* 1J **83**
Farmfield Rd. *Brom* 5G **125**
Farm Ho. Ct. *NW7* 7H **13**
Farmhouse Rd. *SW16* 7G **121**
Farmilo Rd. *E17* 7B **34**
Farmington Av. *Sutt* 3B **150**
Farmlands. *Enf* 1F **7**
Farmlands. *Pinn* 4J **23**
Farmlands, The. *N'holt* 6D **42**
Farmland Wlk. *Chst* 5F **127**
Farm La. *SW6* 6J **83**
Farm La. *Croy* 2B **154**
Farm La. Trad. Est. *SW6* 6J **83**
Farmleigh. *N14* 7B **6**
Farmleigh Ho. *SW9* 5B **104**
Farm M. *Mitc* 2F **139**
Farm Pl. *W8* 1J **83**
Farm Rd. *N21* 1H **17**
Farm Rd. *NW10* 1K **63**
Farm Rd. *Edgw* 6C **12**
Farm Rd. *Houn* 1C **114**
Farm Rd. *Mord* 5K **137**
Farm Rd. *Sutt* 7B **150**
Farmstead Rd. *SE6* 4D **124**
Farmstead Rd. *Harr* 1H **25**
Farm St. *W1* 7F **67** (3J **165**)
Farm Va. *Bex* 6H **111**
Farm Wlk. *NW11* 5H **29**
Farm Way. *Buck H* 4F **21**
Farmway. *Dag* 3C **56**
Farm Way. *Wor Pk* 3E **148**
Farnaby Ho. W10 *3H* ***65***
(off Bruckner St.)
Farnaby Rd. *SE9* 4A **108**
Farnaby Rd. *Brom* 7F **125**
Farnan Av. *E17* 2C **34**
Farnan Rd. *SW16* 5J **121**
Farnborough Av. *E17* 3A **34**
Farnborough Av. *S Croy* 7K **153**
Farnborough Clo. *Wemb* 2H **45**
Farnborough Comn. *Orp* 3D **156**
Farnborough Cres. *Brom*
1H **155**
Farnborough Cres. *S Croy*
7A **154**
Farnborough Way. *SE15* 7E **86**
Farncombe St. *SE16* 2G **87**
Farndale Av. *N13* 3G **17**
Farndale Cres. *Gnfd* 3G **61**
Farndale Ho. NW6 *1K* ***65***
(off Kilburn Va.)
Farnell M. *SW5* 5K **83**
Farnell Rd. *Isw th* 3H **97**
Farnham Clo. *N20* 7F **5**
Farnham Ct. S'hall *7G* ***61***
(off Redcroft Rd.)
Farnham Ct. *Sutt* 6G **149**
Farnham Gdns. *SW20* 2D **136**
Farnham Ho. *NW1* 4D **158**
Farnham Pl. *SE1*
1B **86** (5B **168**)
Farnham Rd. *Ilf* 7K **37**
Farnham Rd. *Well* 2C **110**
Farnham Royal. *SE11*
5K **85** (6H **173**)
Farningham Ct. *SW16* 7H **121**
Farningham Ho. *N4* 7D **32**
Farningham Rd. *N17* 7B **18**
Farnley Ho. *SW8* 2H **103**
Farnley Rd. *E4* 1B **20**
Farnley Rd. *SE25* 4D **140**
Farnworth Ho. E14 *4F* ***89***
(off Manchester Rd.)
Faro Clo. *Brom* 2E **144**
Faroe Rd. *W14* 3F **83**
Farorna Wlk. *Enf* 1F **7**
Farquhar Rd. *SE19* 5F **123**
Farquhar Rd. *SW19* 3J **119**
Farquharson Rd. *Croy* 1C **152**
Farrance Rd. *Romf* 6E **38**
Farrance St. *E14* 6C **70**
Farrans Ct. *Harr* 7B **26**
Farrant Av. *N22* 2A **32**
Farr Av. *Bark* 2A **74**
Farrell Ho. E1 *6J* ***69***
(off Ronald St.)
Farren Rd. *SE23* 2A **124**
Farrer Ct. *Twic* 7D **98**
Farrer Ho. *SE8* 7C **88**
Farrer M. *N8* 4G **31**
Farrer Rd. *N8* 4G **31**
Farrer Rd. *Harr* 5E **26**
Farrer's Pl. *Croy* 4K **153**
Farrier Clo. *Brom* 3B **144**
Farrier Clo. *Sun* 3J **131**

Farrier Clo. Uxb 6C 58
Farrier Rd. N'holt 2E 60
Farriers Ho. EC1 4C 68 (4D 162) (off Errol St.)
Farrier St. NW1 7F 49
Farrier Wlk. SW10 6A 84
Farringdon La. EC1 4A 68 (4K 161)
Farringdon Rd. EC1 4A 68 (3J 161)
Farringdon St. EC4 5B 68 (6A 162)
Farrington Pl. Chst 7H 127
Farrins Rents. SE16 1A 88
Farrow La. SE14 7J 87
Farrow Pl. SE16 3A 88
Farr Rd. Enf 1J 7
Farthingale Wlk. E15 7F 53
Farthing All. SE1 2G 87 (7K 169)
Farthing Barn La. Orp 7E 156
Farthing Fields. E1 1H 87
Farthings Clo. E4 3B 20
Farthings Clo. Pinn 6K 23
Farthings, The. King T 1G 135
Farthing Street. 7D 156
Farthing St. Orp 7D 156
Farwell Rd. Sidc 4B 128
Farwig La. Brom 1H 143
Fashion St. E1 5F 69 (6K 163)
Fashoda Rd. Brom 4B 144
Fassett Rd. E8 6G 51
Fassett Rd. King T 4E 134
Fassett Sq. E8 6G 51
Fauconberg Ct. W4 6J 81 (off Fauconberg Rd.)
Fauconberg Rd. W4 6J 81
Faulkner Clo. Dag 7D 38
Faulkners All. EC1 5B 68 (5A 162)
Faulkner St. SE14 1J 105
Fauna Clo. Romf 6C 38
Faunce Ho. SE17 6B 86 (off Doddington Gro.)
Faunce St. SE17 5B 86
Favart Rd. SW6 1J 101
Faversham Av. E4 1B 20
Faversham Av. Enf 6J 7
Faversham Ho. NW1 1G 67 (off Bayham Pl.)
Faversham Ho. SE17 5E 86 (off Kinglake St.)
Faversham Rd. SE6 7B 106
Faversham Rd. Beck 2B 142
Faversham Rd. Mord 6K 137
Fawcett Clo. SW11 2B 102
Fawcett Clo. SW16 5A 122
Fawcett Est. E5 1G 51
Fawcett Rd. NW10 7B 46
Fawcett Rd. Croy 3C 152
Fawcett St. SW10 6A 84
Fawe Pk. M. SW15 4H 101
Fawe Pk. Rd. SW15 4H 101
Fawe St. E14 5D 70
Fawkham Ho. SE1 4F 87 (off Longfield Est.)
Fawley Lodge. E14 4F 89 (off Millennium Dri.)
Fawley Rd. NW6 5K 47
Fawnbrake Av. SE24 5B 104
Fawn Rd. E13 2A 72
Fawns Mnr. Clo. Felt 1E 112
Fawns Mnr. Rd. Felt 1F 113
Fawood Av. NW10 7J 45
Faygate Cres. Bexh 5G 111
Faygate Rd. SW2 2K 121
Fayland Av. SW16 5G 121
Fazeley Ct. W9 5J 65 (off Elmfield Way)
Fearnley Cres. Hamp 5C 114
Fearnley Ho. SE5 2E 104
Fearon St. SE10 5J 89
Featherbed La. Croy & Warl 7B 154
Feathers Pl. SE10 6F 89
Featherstone Av. SE23 2H 123
Featherstone Ho. Hay 5A 60
Featherstone Ind. Est. S'hall 2C 78 (off Straight, The)
Featherstone Rd. NW7 6J 13
Featherstone Rd. S'hall 3C 78
Featherstone St. EC1 4D 68 (3E 162)
Featherstone Ter. S'hall 3C 78
Featley Rd. SW9 3B 104
Federal Rd. Gnfd 1C 62
Federation Rd. SE2 4B 92
Fee Farm Rd. Clay 7A 146
Felbridge Av. Stan 1A 26
Felbridge Clo. SW16 4A 122
Felbridge Clo. Sutt 7K 149
Felbridge Ct. Felt 1K 113 (off High St.)
Felbridge Ct. Hay 6F 77
Felbridge Ho. SE22 3E 104
Felbrigge Rd. Ilf 2K 55
Felday Rd. SE13 6D 106
Felden Clo. Pinn 1C 24
Felden St. SW6 1H 101
Feldman Clo. N16 1G 51
Felgate M. W6 4D 82
Felhampton Rd. SE9 2F 127
Felhurst Cres. Dag 4H 57
Feline Ct. Barn 6H 5
Felix Av. N8 6J 31
Felix Ct. E17 5D 34
Felix Ho. E16 7E 72 (off University Way)
Felix La. Shep 6G 131
Felix Mnr. Chst 6J 127
Felix Rd. W13 7A 62
Felix Rd. W on T 6J 131
Felixstowe Ct. E16 1F 91
Felixstowe Rd. N9 3B 18
Felixstowe Rd. N17 3F 33
Felixstowe Rd. NW10 3D 64
Felixstowe Rd. SE2 3B 92
Felix St. E2 2H 69
Fellbrigg Rd. SE22 5F 105
Fellbrigg St. E1 4H 69
Fellbrook. Rich 3B 116
Fellmongers Path. SE1 7J 169
Fellmongers Yd. Croy 3C 152 (off Surrey St.)
Fellowes Clo. Hay 4B 60
Fellowes Rd. Cars 3C 150
Fellows Ct. E2 2F 69 (1J 163) (in two parts)
Fellows Rd. NW3 7B 48
Fell Rd. Croy 3C 152 (in two parts)
Felltram Way. SE7 5J 89
Fell Wlk. Edgw 1J 27
Felmersham Clo. SW4 4J 103
Felmingham Rd. SE20 2J 141
Felnex Trad. Est. NW10 2K 63
Felsberg Rd. SW2 6J 103
Fels Clo. Dag 3H 57
Fels Farm Av. Dag 3J 57
Felsham M. SW15 3F 101 (off Felsham Rd.)
Felsham Rd. SW15 3E 100
Felspar Clo. SE18 5K 91
Felstead Av. Ilf 1E 36
Felstead Gdns. E14 5E 88
Felstead Rd. E9 6B 52
Felstead Rd. E11 7J 35
Felstead St. E9 6B 52
Felstead Wharf. E14 5E 88
Felsted Rd. E16 6B 72
Feltham. 2J 113
Feltham Av. E Mol 4J 133
Felthambrook Ind. Est. Felt 3K 113
Felthambrook Way. Felt 3K 113
Feltham Bus. Complex. Felt 2K 113
Felthamhill. 5H 113
Feltham Hill Rd. Ashf 5C 112
Felthamhill Rd. Felt 4J 113
Feltham Rd. Ashf 4C 112
Feltham Rd. Mitc 2D 138
Felton Clo. Orp 6F 145
Felton Gdns. Bark 1J 73
Felton Ho. N1 1D 68 (off Colville Est.)
Felton Ho. SE3 4K 107
Felton Lea. Sidc 5K 127
Felton Rd. W13 2C 80
Felton Rd. Bark 2J 73
Felton St. N1 1D 68
Fencepiece Rd. Chig & Ilf 1G 37
Fenchurch Av. EC3 6E 68 (1G 169)
Fenchurch Bldgs. EC3 6E 68 (1H 169)
Fenchurch Pl. EC3 6E 68 (2H 169)
Fenchurch St. EC3 7E 68 (2G 169)
Fen Ct. EC3 6E 68 (2G 169)
Fendall Rd. Eps 5J 147
Fendall St. SE1 3E 86 (in two parts)
Fendt Clo. E16 6H 71
Fendyke Rd. Belv 4D 92
Fenelon Pl. W14 4H 83
Fen Gro. Sidc 5K 109
Fenham Rd. SE15 7G 87
Fenman Ct. N17 1H 33
Fenman Gdns. Ilf 1B 56
Fenn Clo. Brom 6J 125
Fennel Clo. E16 4G 71
Fennel Clo. Croy 1K 153
Fennells Mead. Eps 7B 148
Fennell St. SE18 6E 90
Fenner Clo. SE16 4H 87
Fenner Ho. E1 1H 87 (off Watts St.)
Fenner Sq. SW11 3B 102
Fenn Ho. Iswth 1B 98
Fenning St. SE1 2E 86 (6G 169)
Fenn St. E9 5J 51
Fenstanton. N4 1K 49 (off Marquis Rd.)
Fenstanton Av. N12 6G 15
Fen St. E16 7H 71
Fenswood Clo. Bex 6G 111
Fentiman Rd. SW8 6J 85 (7F 173)
Fenton Clo. E8 6F 51
Fenton Clo. SW9 2K 103
Fenton Clo. Chst 5D 126
Fenton House. 3A 48 (off Windmill Hill)
Fenton Ho. SE14 7A 88
Fenton Ho. Houn 6E 78
Fenton Rd. N17 7H 17
Fentons Av. E13 3K 71
Fenton St. E1 6H 69
Fenwick Clo. SE18 6E 90
Fenwick Gro. SE15 3G 105
Fenwick Pl. SW9 3J 103
Fenwick Pl. S Croy 7B 152
Fenwick Rd. SE15 3G 105
Ferby Ct. SE9 3H 127 (off Main Rd.)
Ferdinand Ho. NW1 7E 48 (off Ferdinand Pl.)
Ferdinand Pl. NW1 7E 48
Ferdinand St. NW1 7E 48
Ferguson Av. Surb 5F 135
Ferguson Cen., The. E17 6A 34
Ferguson Clo. E14 4C 88
Ferguson Clo. Brom 3F 143
Ferguson Dri. W3 6K 63
Ferguson Ho. SE10 1E 106
Fergus Rd. N5 5B 50
Fermain Ct. E. N1 1E 68 (off De Beauvoir Est.)
Fermain Ct. N. N1 1E 68 (off De Beauvoir Est.)
Fermain Ct. W. N1 1E 68 (off De Beauvoir Est.)
Ferme Pk. Rd. N8 & N4 5J 31
Fermor Rd. SE23 1A 124
Fermoy Rd. W9 4H 65
Fermoy Rd. Gnfd 4F 61
Fern Av. Mitc 4H 139
Fernbank. Buck H 1E 20
Fernbank Av. W on T 7C 132
Fernbank Av. Wemb 4K 43
Fernbank M. SW12 6F 103
Fernbrook Av. Sidc 5J 109
Fernbrook Cres. SE13 6G 107 (off Leahurst Rd.)
Fernbrook Dri. Harr 7F 25
Fernbrook Rd. SE13 5G 107
Ferncliff Rd. E8 5G 51
Fern Clo. N1 2E 68
Fern Ct. SE14 2K 105
Fern Ct. Bexh 4G 111
Ferncroft Av. N12 6J 15
Ferncroft Av. NW3 3J 47
Ferncroft Av. Ruis 2A 42
Ferndale. Brom 2A 144
Ferndale Av. E17 5F 35
Ferndale Av. Houn 3C 96
Ferndale Clo. Bexh 1E 110
Ferndale Rd. E7 7K 53
Ferndale Rd. E11 2G 53
Ferndale Rd. N15 6F 33
Ferndale Rd. SE25 5H 141
Ferndale Rd. SW4 & SW9 4J 103
Ferndale Rd. Ashf 5A 112
Ferndale Rd. Romf 2J 39
Ferndale St. E6 7F 73
Ferndale Ter. Harr 4K 25
Ferndell Av. Bex 3K 129
Fern Dene. W13 5B 62
Ferndene Rd. SE24 4C 104
Fernden Way. Romf 6H 39
Ferndown. N'wd 2J 23
Ferndown Av. Orp 7H 145
Ferndown Clo. Pinn 1C 24
Ferndown Clo. Sutt 6B 150
Ferndown Ct. S'hall 6G 61 (off Haldane Rd.)
Ferndown Lodge. E14 3E 88 (off Manchester Rd.)
Ferndown Rd. SE9 7B 108
Ferney Meade Way. Iswth 2A 98
Ferney Rd. E Barn 7K 5
Fern Gro. Felt 7K 95
Fernhall Dri. Ilf 5B 36
Fernham Rd. T Hth 3C 140
Fernhead Rd. W9 2H 65
Fernheath Way. Dart 5K 129
Fernhill Ct. E17 2F 35
Fernhill Gdns. King T 5D 116
Fernhill St. E16 1D 90
Fernholme Rd. SE15 5K 105
Fernhurst Gdns. Edgw 6B 12
Fernhurst Rd. SW6 1G 101
Fernhurst Rd. Ashf 4E 112
Fernhurst Rd. Croy 7H 141
Fern La. Houn 5D 78
Fernlea Rd. SW12 1F 121
Fernlea Rd. Mitc 2E 138
Fernleigh Clo. Croy 4A 152
Fernleigh Ct. Harr 2F 25
Fernleigh Ct. Romf 5J 39
Fernleigh Ct. Wemb 2E 44
Fernleigh Rd. N21 2F 17
Fernsbury St. WC1 3A 68 (2J 161)
Fernshaw Clo. SW10 6A 84
Fernshaw Rd. SW10 6A 84
Fernside. NW11 2J 47
Fernside. Buck H 1E 20
Fernside Av. NW7 3E 12
Fernside Av. Felt 4K 113
Fernside Ct. NW4 2F 29 (off Holders Hill Rd.)
Fernside Rd. SW12 1D 120
Ferns Rd. E15 6H 53
Fern St. E3 4C 70
Fernthorpe Rd. SW16 6G 121
Ferntower Rd. N5 5D 50
Fern Wlk. SE16 5G 87
Fern Wlk. Ashf 5A 112
Fernways. Ilf 4F 55
Fernwood. Croy 7A 154
Fernwood Av. SW16 4H 121
Fernwood Av. Wemb 6C 44
Fernwood Clo. Brom 2A 144
Fernwood Cres. N20 3J 15
Ferny Hill. Barn 1J 5
Ferranti Clo. SE18 3B 90
Ferraro Clo. Houn 6E 78
Ferrers Av. Wall 4H 151
Ferrers Av. W Dray 2A 76
Ferrers Rd. SW16 5H 121
Ferrestone Rd. N8 4K 31
Ferrey M. SW9 2A 104
Ferriby Clo. N1 7A 50
Ferrier Ind. Est. SW18 4K 101 (off Ferrier St.)
Ferrier Point. E16 5J 71 (off Forty Acre La.)
Ferrier St. SW18 4K 101
Ferring Clo. Harr 1G 43
Ferrings. SE21 3E 122
Ferris Av. Croy 3B 154
Ferris Rd. SE22 4G 105
Ferron Rd. E5 3H 51
Ferry App. SE18 3E 90
Ferrybridge Ho. SE11 2H 173
Ferrydale Lodge. NW4 4E 28 (off Church Rd.)
Ferry Ho. E5 1H 51 (off High Hill Ferry)
Ferry Island Retail Pk. N17 3G 33
Ferry La. N17 4G 33
Ferry La. SW13 6B 82
Ferry La. Bren 6E 80
Ferry La. Rich 6F 81
Ferry La. Shep 7C 130
Ferry La. Ind. Est. E17 4K 33
Ferrymead Av. Gnfd 3E 60
Ferrymead Dri. Gnfd 2E 60
Ferrymead Gdns. Gnfd 2F 61
Ferrymoor. Rich 3B 116
Ferry Pl. SE18 3E 90
Ferry Quays. Bren 7D 80 (in two parts)
Ferry Rd. SW13 7C 82
Ferry Rd. Tedd 5B 116
Ferry Rd. Th Dit 6B 134
Ferry Rd. Twic 1B 116
Ferry Rd. W Mol 3E 132
Ferry Sq. Bren 7E 80
Ferry Sq. Shep 7D 130
Ferry St. E14 5E 88
Festing Rd. SW15 3F 101
Festival Clo. Bex 1D 128
Festival Clo. Uxb 1D 58
Festival Ct. E8 7F 51 (off Holly St.)
Festival Wlk. Cars 5D 150
Fetter La. EC4 6A 68 (1K 167) (in two parts)
Fettes Ho. NW8 2B 66 (off Wellington Rd.)
Ffinch St. SE8 7C 88
Field Clo. E4 6J 19
Field Clo. Brom 2A 144
Field Clo. Buck H 3F 21
Field Clo. Chess 5C 146
Field Clo. Hay 7E 76
Field Clo. Houn 1K 95
Field Clo. Ruis 1E 40
Field Clo. Uxb 2D 40
Field Clo. W Mol 5F 133
Fieldcommon. 7D 132

Fieldcommon La. W on T 7C 132
Field Ct. SW19 3J 119
Field Ct. WC1 5K 67 (6H 161)
Field End. N'holt 6C 42
Field End. Ruis 6A 42
Field End. Twic 4K 115
Fieldend Rd. SW16 1G 139
Field End Rd. Pinn & Ruis 5K 23
Fielders Clo. Enf 4K 7
Fielders Clo. Harr 1G 43
Fieldfare Rd. SE28 7C 74
Fieldgate La. Mitc 2C 138
Fieldgate Mans. E1 5G 69 (off Fieldgate St., in two parts)
Fieldgate St. E1 5G 69
Field Ho. NW6 3F 65 (off Harvist Rd.)
Fieldhouse Clo. E18 1K 35
Fieldhouse Rd. SW12 1G 121
Fielding Av. Twic 3G 115
Fielding Ho. NW6 3J 65
Fielding Ho. W4 6A 82 (off Devonshire Rd.)
Fielding M. SW13 6D 82 (off Jenner Pl.)
Fielding Rd. W4 3K 81
Fielding Rd. W14 3F 83
Fieldings, The. SE23 1J 123
Fielding St. SE17 6C 86
Fielding Ter. W5 7F 63
Field La. Bren 7C 80
Field La. Tedd 5A 116
Field Mead. NW7 7F 13
Field Pl. N Mald 6B 136
Field Point. E7 4J 53
Field Rd. E7 4H 53
Field Rd. N17 3D 32
Field Rd. W6 5G 83
Field Rd. Felt 6K 95
Fieldsend Rd. Sutt 5G 149
Fields Est. E8 7G 51
Fieldside Rd. Brom 5F 125
Fields Pk. Cres. Romf 5D 38
Field St. WC1 3K 67 (1G 161)
Fieldsway Ho. N5 5A 50
Fieldview. SW18 1B 120
Field Vw. Felt 4F 113
Fieldview Cotts. N14 2C 16 (off Balaams La.)
Field Way. NW10 7J 45
Fieldway. Dag 3C 56
Field Way. Gnfd 1F 61
Fieldway. New Ad 7D 154
Fieldway. Orp 6H 145
Field Way. Ruis 1E 40
Fieldway Cres. N5 5A 50
Fiennes Clo. Dag 1C 56
Fifehead Clo. Ashf 6A 112
Fife Rd. E16 5J 71
Fife Rd. N22 7G 17
Fife Rd. SW14 5J 99
Fife Rd. King T 2E 134 (in two parts)
Fife Ter. N1 2K 67
Fifield Path. SE23 3K 123
Fifth Av. E12 4D 54
Fifth Av. W10 3G 65
Fifth Av. Hay 1H 77
Fifth Cross Rd. Twic 2H 115
Fifth Way. Wemb 4H 45
Figges Rd. Mitc 7E 120
Fig Tree Clo. NW10 1A 64
Figure Ct. SW3 6F 171
Filanco Ct. W7 1K 79 (off Uxbridge Rd.)
Filby Rd. Chess 6F 147
Filey Av. N16 1G 51
Filey Clo. Sutt 7A 150
Filey Waye. Ruis 2J 41
Filigree Ct. SE16 1B 88
Fillebrook Av. Enf 2K 7
Fillebrook Rd. E11 1F 53
Filmer Rd. SW6 1G 101
Filston Rd. Eri 5J 93
Filton Ct. SE14 7J 87 (off Farrow La.)
Finborough Ho. SW10 6A 84 (off Finborough Rd.)
Finborough Rd. SW10 5K 83
Finborough Rd. SW17 6D 120
Finborough Theatre, The. 6K 83 (off Finborough Rd.)
Finchale Rd. SE2 3A 92
Fincham Clo. Uxb 3E 40
Finch Av. SE27 4D 122
Finch Clo. NW10 6K 45
Finch Clo. Barn 5D 4
Finch Ct. Sidc 3B 128
Finchdean Ho. SW15 7B 100
Finch Dri. Felt 7B 96
Finch Gdns. E4 5H 19
Finch Ho. SE8 7D 88 (off Bronze St.)
Finchingfield Av. Wfd G 7F 21
Finch La. EC3 6D 68 (1F 169)
Finchley. 1J 29
Finchley Ct. N3 6E 14
Finchley Golf Course. 5C 14
Finchley Ind. Est. N12 4F 15
Finchley La. NW4 4E 28
Finchley Pk. N12 4F 15
Finchley Pl. NW8 2B 66
Finchley Rd. NW3 4J 47
Finchley Rd. NW8 & NW3 1B 66
Finchley Rd. NW11 & NW2 4H 29
Finchley Way. N3 7D 14
Finch Lodge. W9 5J 65 (off Admiral Wlk.)
Finch M. SE15 1F 105
Finch's Ct. E14 7D 70
Finden Rd. E7 5A 54
Findhorn Av. Hay 5K 59
Findhorn St. E14 6E 70
Findon Clo. SW18 6J 101
Findon Clo. Harr 3F 43
Findon Rd. N9 1C 18
Findon Rd. W12 2C 82
Fine Bush La. Hare 6D 22
Fingal St. SE10 5H 89
Fingest Ho. NW8 4C 66 (3C 158) (off Lilestone St.)
Finians Clo. Uxb 7B 40
Finland Rd. SE4 3A 106
Finland St. SE16 3A 88
Finlays Clo. Chess 5G 147
Finlay St. SW6 1F 101
Finmere Ho. N4 7C 32
Finnemore Ho. N1 1C 68 (off Britannia Row)
Finney La. Iswth 1A 98
Finn Ho. N1 3D 68 (1F 163) (off Bevenden St.)
Finnis St. E2 3H 69
Finnymore Rd. Dag 7E 56
Finsbury. 3A 68 (2K 161)
Finsbury Av. EC2 5D 68 (6F 163) (in two parts)
Finsbury Av. Sq. EC2 5G 163
Finsbury Cir. EC2 5D 68 (6F 163)
Finsbury Cotts. N22 7D 16
Finsbury Est. EC1 3A 68 (2K 161)
Finsbury Ho. N22 1J 31
Finsbury Mkt. EC2 4E 68 (4G 163) (in two parts)
Finsbury Park. 1A 50
Finsbury Pk. Av. N4 6C 32
Finsbury Pk. Rd. N4 2B 50
Finsbury Pavement. EC2 5D 68 (5F 163)
Finsbury Rd. N22 7E 16
Finsbury Sq. EC2 4D 68 (4F 163)
Finsbury St. EC2 & EC1 5D 68 (5E 162)
Finsbury Way. Bex 6F 111
Finsen Rd. SE5 4C 104
Finstock Rd. W10 6F 65
Finucane Ri. Bus H 2B 10
Finwhale Ho. E14 3D 88 (off Glengall Gro.)
Fiona Ct. NW6 2J 65
Fiona Ct. Enf 3G 7
Firbank Clo. E16 5B 72
Firbank Clo. Enf 4H 7
Firbank Rd. SE15 2H 105
Fir Clo. W on T 7J 131
Fircroft Gdns. Harr 3J 43
Fircroft Rd. SW17 2D 120
Fircroft Rd. Chess 4F 147
Fir Dene. Orp 3D 156
Firdene. Surb 1J 147
Fire Bell La. Surb 6E 134
Firecrest Dri. NW3 3K 47
Firefly Clo. Wall 7J 151
Firefly Gdns. E6 4C 72
Firemans Flats. N22 7D 16
Fire Sta. All. High Bar 3B 4
Fire Sta. M. Beck 1C 142
Firethorn Clo. Edgw 4D 12
Fir Gro. N Mald 6B 136
Firhill Rd. SE6 4C 124
Fir Ho. W10 4G 65 (off Droop St.)
Firle Ho. W10 5E 64 (off Sutton Way)
Fir Rd. Felt 5B 114
Fir Rd. Sutt 1H 149
Firs Av. N10 3E 30
Firs Av. N11 6J 15
Firs Av. SW14 4J 99
Firsby Av. Croy 1K 153
Firsby Rd. N16 1G 51
Firs Clo. N10 4E 30
Firs Clo. SE23 7A 106
Firs Clo. Mitc 1F 139
Firscroft. N13 3H 17
Firs Dri. Houn 7K 77
Firs Ho. N22 1A 32 (off Acacia Rd.)
Firside Gro. Sidc 1K 127
Firs La. N13 & N21 3H 17
Firs La. N21 7H 7
Firs Pk. Av. N21 1H 17
Firs Pk. Gdns. N21 1H 17
First Av. E12 4C 54
First Av. E13 3J 71
First Av. E17 5C 34
First Av. N18 4D 18
First Av. NW4 4E 28
First Av. SW14 3A 100
First Av. W3 1B 82
First Av. W10 4H 65
First Av. Bexh 7C 92
First Av. Dag 2H 75
First Av. Enf 5A 8
First Av. Eps 7A 148
First Av. Hay 1H 77
First Av. Romf 5C 38
First Av. W on T 6K 131
First Av. Wemb 2D 44
First Av. W Mol 4D 132
First Bowl. 7K 65
First Clo. W Mol 3G 133
First Cross Rd. Twic 2J 115
First Dri. NW10 7J 45
Firs, The. E6 7C 54
Firs, The. N20 1G 15
Firs, The. SE26 5J 123 (Homecroft Rd.)
Firs, The. SE26 5H 123 (Lawrie Pk. Gdns.)
Firs, The. W5 5D 62
Firs, The. Bex 1K 129
Firs, The. Sidc 3K 127
First St. SW3 4C 84 (3D 170)
Firstway. SW20 2E 136
First Way. Wemb 4H 45
Firs Wlk. Wfd G 5D 20
Firswood Av. Eps 5A 148
Firth Gdns. SW6 1G 101
Firth Ho. E2 3G 69 (off Barnet Gro.)
Firtree Av. Mitc 2E 138
Fir Tree Av. W Dray 3C 76
Firtree Clo. SW16 5G 121
Fir Tree Clo. W5 6E 62
Firtree Clo. Ewe 4B 148
Fir Tree Clo. Romf 3K 39
Firtree Gdns. Croy 4C 154
Fir Tree Gro. Cars 7D 150
Fir Tree Ho. SE14 7J 87 (off Avonley Rd.)
Fir Tree Pl. Ashf 5C 112
Fir Tree Rd. Houn 4C 96
Fir Trees Clo. SE16 1A 88
Fir Tree Wlk. Dag 3J 57
Fir Tree Wlk. Enf 3J 7
Fir Wlk. Sutt 6F 149
Fisher Athletic F.C. 1K 87
Fisher Clo. Croy 1F 153
Fisher Clo. Gnfd 3E 60
Fisher Ho. E1 7J 69 (off Cable St.)
Fisher Ho. N1 1A 68 (off Barnsbury Est.)
Fisherman Clo. Rich 4B 116
Fishermans Dri. SE16 2K 87
Fisherman's Pl. W4 6B 82
Fisherman's Wlk. E14 1C 88
Fishermans Wlk. SE28 2J 91
Fisher Rd. Harr 2K 25
Fisher's Clo. SW16 3H 121
Fishers Ct. SE14 1K 105
Fishers Dene. Clay 7A 146
Fisher's La. W4 4K 81
Fisher St. E16 5J 71
Fisher St. WC1 5K 67 (6G 161)
Fishers Way. Belv 1J 93
Fisherton St. NW8 4B 66 (4A 158)
Fishguard Way. E16 1F 91 (in two parts)
Fishmongers Hall Wharf. EC4 3E 168
Fishponds Rd. SW17 4C 120
Fishponds Rd. Kes 5B 156
Fish St. Hill. EC3 7D 68 (3F 169)
Fish Wharf. EC3 7D 68 (3F 169) (off Lwr. Thames St.)
Fiske Ct. N17 1G 33
Fiske Ct. Bark 2H 73
Fisons Rd. E16 1J 89
Fitzalan Rd. N3 3G 29
Fitzalan St. SE11 4A 86 (3H 173)
Fitzgeorge Av. W14 4G 83
Fitzgeorge Av. N Mald 1K 135
Fitzgerald Av. SW14 3A 100
Fitzgerald Ct. E10 1D 52 (off Leyton Grange Est.)
Fitzgerald Ho. E14 6D 70 (off E. India Dock Rd.)
Fitzgerald Ho. SW9 2A 104
Fitzgerald Rd. E11 5J 35
Fitzgerald Rd. SW14 3K 99
Fitzgerald Rd. Th Dit 6A 134
Fitzhardinge Ho. W1 6E 66 (7G 159) (off Portman Sq.)
Fitzhardinge St. W1 6E 66 (7G 159)
Fitzhugh Gro. SW18 6B 102
Fitzjames Av. W14 4G 83
Fitzjames Av. Croy 2G 153
Fitzjohn Av. Barn 5B 4
Fitzjohn's Av. NW3 4A 48
Fitzmaurice Ho. SE16 4H 87 (off Rennie Est.)
Fitzmaurice Pl. W1 1F 85 (4K 165)
Fitzneal St. W3 6B 64
Fitzrovia. 5F 67 (5K 159)
Fitzroy Clo. N6 1D 48
Fitzroy Ct. N6 6G 31
Fitzroy Ct. W1 4B 160
Fitzroy Ct. Croy 7D 140
Fitzroy Cres. W4 7K 81
Fitzroy Gdns. SE19 7E 122
Fitzroy Ho. E14 5B 70 (off Wallwood St.)
Fitzroy Ho. SE1 5F 87 (off Coopers La.)
Fitzroy M. W1 4A 160
Fitzroy Pk. N6 1D 48
Fitzroy Rd. NW1 1E 66
Fitzroy Sq. W1 4G 67 (4A 160)
Fitzroy St. W1 4G 67 (4A 160) (in two parts)
Fitzroy Yd. NW1 1E 66
Fitzsimmons Ct. NW10 1K 63
Fitzstephen Rd. Dag 5B 56
Fitzwarren Gdns. N19 1G 49
Fitzwilliam Av. Rich 2F 99
Fitzwilliam Heights. SE23 2J 123
Fitzwilliam Ho. Rich 4D 98
Fitzwilliam M. E16 1J 89
Fitzwilliam Rd. SW4 3G 103
Fitzwygram Clo. Hamp H 5G 115
Five Acre. NW9 2B 28
Fiveacre Clo. T Hth 6A 140
Five Bell All. E14 6B 70 (off Three Colt St.)
Five Elms Rd. Brom 2K 155
Five Elms Rd. Dag 3F 57
Fives Ct. SE11 3B 86
Fiveways. (Junct.) 2F 127
Fiveways. SE9 2F 127
Five Ways Bus. Cen. Felt 3K 113
Fiveways Corner. (Junct.) 4K 151 (Croydon)
Fiveways Corner. (Junct.) 1D 28 (Hendon)
Fiveways Rd. SW9 2A 104
Flack Ct. E10 7D 34
Fladbury Rd. N15 6D 32
Fladgate Rd. E11 6G 35
Flag Clo. Croy 1K 153
Flag Wlk. Pinn 6J 23
Flambard Rd. Harr 6A 26
Flamborough Ho. SE15 1G 105 (off Clayton Rd.)
Flamborough Rd. Ruis 3J 41
Flamborough St. E14 6A 70
Flamborough Wlk. E14 6A 70 (off Flamborough St.)
Flamingo Ct. SE8 7C 88 (off Hamilton St.)
Flamingo Gdns. N'holt 3C 60
Flamstead Gdns. Dag 7C 56
Flamstead Ho. SW3 5C 84 (5C 170) (off Cale St.)
Flamstead Rd. Dag 7C 56
Flamsted Av. Wemb 6G 45
Flamsteed Rd. SE7 5C 90
Flanchford Rd. W12 3B 82
Flanders Ct. E17 7A 34
Flanders Cres. SW17 7D 120
Flanders Mans. W4 4B 82
Flanders Rd. E6 2D 72
Flanders Rd. W4 4A 82
Flanders Way. E9 6K 51
Flank St. E1 7G 69
Flansham Ho. E14 6B 70 (off Clemence St.)
Flask Wlk. NW3 4A 48
Flatford Ho. SE6 4E 124
Flatiron Yd. SE1 1C 86 (5D 168) (off Union St.)
Flavell M. SE10 5G 89

Flaxen Clo. E4 3J 19
Flaxen Rd. E4 3J 19
Flaxley Rd. Mord 7K 137
Flaxman Ct. W1 1C 166
Flaxman Ct. WC1 3H 67 (2D 160) (off Flaxman Ter.)
Flaxman Ct. Belv 5G 93 (off Hoddesdon Rd.)
Flaxman Ho. W4 5A 82 (off Devonshire St.)
Flaxman Rd. SE5 3B 104
Flaxman Ter. WC1 3H 67 (2D 160)
Flaxton Rd. SE18 1H 109
Flecker Clo. Stan 5E 10
Flecker Ho. SE5 7D 86 (off Lomond Gro.)
Fleece Dri. N9 4B 18
Fleece Rd. Surb 1C 146
Fleece Wlk. N7 6J 49
Fleeming Clo. E17 2B 34
Fleeming Rd. E17 2B 34
Fleetbank Ho. EC4 6A 68 (1K 167) (off Salisbury Sq.)
Fleet Building. EC4 7A 162
Fleet Clo. Ruis 6E 22
Fleet Clo. W Mol 5D 132
Fleetfield. WC1 3J 67 (1F 161) (off Birkenhead St.)
Fleet Ho. E14 7A 70 (off Victory Pl.)
Fleet La. W Mol 6D 132
Fleet Pl. EC4 7A 162 (in two parts)
Fleet Rd. NW3 5C 48
Fleetside. W Mol 5D 132
Fleet Sq. WC1 3K 67 (2H 161)
Fleet St. EC4 6A 68 (1J 167)
Fleet St. Hill. E1 4G 69
Fleetway. WC1 3J 67 (1F 161) (off Birkenhead St.)
Fleetway Bus. Cen. NW2 1B 46
Fleetway W. Bus. Pk. Gnfd 2B 62
Fleetwood Clo. E16 5B 72
Fleetwood Clo. Chess 7D 146
Fleetwood Clo. Croy 3F 153
Fleetwood Ct. E6 5D 72 (off Evelyn Dennington Rd., in three parts)
Fleetwood Ct. Stanw 6A 94
Fleetwood Rd. NW10 5C 46
Fleetwood Rd. King T 3H 135
Fleetwood Sq. King T 3H 135
Fleetwood St. N16 2E 50
Fleming. N8 3J 31 (off Boyton Clo.)
Fleming Clo. W9 4J 65
Fleming Ct. W2 5A 158
Fleming Ct. Croy 5A 152
Fleming Dri. N21 5E 6
Fleming Ho. N4 1C 50
Fleming Ho. SE16 2G 87 (off George Row)
Fleming Ho. Wemb 3J 45 (off Barnhill Rd.)
Fleming Lodge. W9 5J 65 (off Admiral Wlk.)
Fleming Mead. Mitc 7C 120
Fleming Rd. SE17 6B 86
Fleming Rd. S'hall 6F 61
Fleming Wlk. NW9 3A 28
Fleming Way. SE28 7D 74
Fleming Way. Iswth 4K 97
Flemming Av. Ruis 1K 41
Flempton Rd. E10 1A 52
Fletcher Bldgs. WC2 6J 67 (1F 167) (off Martlett Ct.)
Fletcher Clo. E6 6F 73
Fletcher La. E10 7E 34
Fletcher Path. SE8 7C 88
Fletcher Rd. W4 3J 81
Fletchers Clo. Brom 4K 143
Fletcher St. E1 7G 69
Fletching Rd. E5 3J 51
Fletching Rd. SE7 6A 90
Fletton Rd. N11 7D 16
Fleur-de-Lis St. E1 4F 69 (4H 163)
Fleur Gates. SW19 7F 101
Flexmere Gdns. N17 1D 32
Flexmere Rd. N17 1D 32
Flight App. NW9 2B 28
Flimwell Clo. Brom 5G 125
Flinders Ho. E1 1H 87 (off Green Bank)
Flintmill Cres. SE3 2C 108 (in three parts)
Flinton St. SE17 5E 86
Flint St. SE17 4D 86
Flitcroft St. WC2 6H 67 (1D 166)
Flitton Ho. N1 7B 50 (off Sutton Est., The)
Flock Mill Pl. SW18 1K 119
Flockton St. SE16 2G 87
Flodden Rd. SE5 1C 104
Flood La. Twic 1A 116
Flood Pas. SE18 3C 90
Flood St. SW3 5C 84 (6D 170)
Flood Wlk. SW3 6C 84 (7D 170)
Flora Clo. E14 6D 70
Flora Gdns. W6 4D 82 (off Albion Gdns.)
Flora Gdns. Romf 6C 38
Floral Pl. N1 5D 50
Floral St. WC2 7J 67 (2E 166)
Flora St. Belv 5F 93
Florence Av. Enf 3H 7
Florence Av. Mord 5A 138
Florence Clo. W on T 7K 131
Florence Ct. E5 3G 51
Florence Ct. E11 4K 35
Florence Ct. N1 7B 50 (off Florence St.)
Florence Ct. SW19 6G 119
Florence Ct. W9 3A 66 (off Maida Va.)
Florence Dri. Enf 3H 7
Florence Elson Clo. E12 3E 54 (off Grantham Rd.)
Florence Gdns. W4 6J 81
Florence Ho. SE16 5H 87 (off Rotherhithe New Rd.)
Florence Ho. W11 7F 65 (off St Ann's Rd.)
Florence Ho. King T 7F 117 (off Florence Rd)
Florence Mans. NW4 5D 28 (off Vivian Av.)
Florence Nightingale Mus. 2K 85 (7G 167)
Florence Rd. E6 1A 72
Florence Rd. E13 2H 71
Florence Rd. N4 7K 31 (in two parts)
Florence Rd. SE2 4C 92
Florence Rd. SE14 1B 106
Florence Rd. SW19 6K 119
Florence Rd. W4 3K 81
Florence Rd. W5 7E 62
Florence Rd. Beck 2A 142
Florence Rd. Brom 1J 143
Florence Rd. Felt 1K 113
Florence Rd. King T 7F 117
Florence Rd. S'hall 4B 78
Florence Rd. S Croy 7D 152
Florence Rd. W on T 7K 131
Florence St. E16 4H 71
Florence St. N1 7B 50
Florence St. NW4 4E 28
Florence Ter. SE14 1B 106
Florence Ter. SW15 3A 118
Florence Way. SW12 1D 120
Flores Ho. E1 5K 69 (off Shandy St.)
Florey Lodge. W9 5J 65 (off Admiral Wlk.)
Florfield Pas. E8 6H 51 (off Florfield Rd.)
Florfield Rd. E8 6H 51
Florian. SE5 1E 104
Florian Av. Sutt 4B 150
Florian Rd. SW15 4G 101
Florida Clo. Bus H 2C 10
Florida Ct. Brom 4H 143 (off Westmoreland Rd.)
Florida Rd. T Hth 1B 140
Florida St. E2 3G 69
Florin Ct. N18 4K 17
Florin Ct. SE1 2F 87 (7J 169) (off Tanner St.)
Floris Pl. SW4 3G 103
Floriston Av. Uxb 7E 40
Floriston Clo. Stan 1B 26
Floriston Ct. N'holt 5F 43
Floriston Gdns. Stan 1B 26
Floss St. SW15 2E 100
Flower & Dean Wlk. E1 5F 69 (6K 163)
Flower La. NW7 5G 13
Flowerpot Clo. N15 6F 33
Flowers Clo. NW2 3C 46
Flowersmead. SW17 2E 120
Flowers M. N19 2G 49
Flower Wlk., The. SW7 2A 84 (6A 164)
Floyd Rd. SE7 5A 90
Fludyer St. SE13 4G 107
Flynn Ct. E14 7C 70 (off Garford St.)
Foley Ho. E1 6J 69 (off Tarling St.)
Foley St. W1 5G 67 (6A 160)
Folgate St. E1 5E 68 (5H 163) (in two parts)
Foliot Ho. N1 2K 67 (off Priory Grn. Est.)
Foliot St. W3 6B 64
Folkestone Ct. N'holt 5F 43 (off Newmarket Av.)
Folkestone Rd. E6 2E 72
Folkestone Rd. E17 4D 34
Folkestone Rd. N18 4B 18
Folkingham La. NW9 1K 27
Folkington Corner. N12 5C 14
Folland. NW9 2B 28 (off Hundred Acre)
Follett Ho. SW10 7B 84 (off Worlds End Est.)
Follett St. E14 6E 70
Follingham Ct. N1 3E 68 (1H 163) (off Drysdale Pl.)
Folly La. E17 1A 34 (in two parts)
Folly M. W11 6H 65
Folly Wall. E14 2E 88
Fonda Ct. E14 7C 70 (off Premiere Pl.)
Fontaine Rd. SW16 7K 121
Fontarabia Rd. SW11 4E 102
Fontayne Av. Romf 2K 39
Fontenelle Gdns. SE5 1E 104
Fontenoy Ho. SE11 4B 86 (off Kennington La.)
Fontenoy Rd. SW12 2F 121
Fonteyne Gdns. Wfd G 2B 36
Fonthill Clo. SE20 2G 141
Fonthill M. N4 2K 49
Fonthill Rd. N4 1K 49
Font Hills. N2 2A 30
Fontley Way. SW15 7C 100
Fontmell Clo. Ashf 5C 112
Fontmell Pk. Ashf 5B 112
Fontwell Clo. Harr 7D 10
Fontwell Clo. N'holt 6E 42
Fontwell Dri. Brom 5E 144
Football La. Harr 1K 43
Footpath, The. SW15 6C 100
Foots Cray. 6C 128
Foots Cray High St. Sidc 6C 128
Foots Cray La. Sidc 1C 128
Footscray Rd. SE9 6E 108
Forber Ho. E2 3J 69 (off Cornwall Av.)
Forbes Clo. NW2 3C 46
Forbes St. E1 6G 69
Forbes Way. Ruis 2K 41
Forburg Rd. N16 1G 51
Fordbridge Cvn. Pk. Sun 6H 131
Fordbridge Ct. Ashf 6A 112
Fordbridge Rd. Ashf 6A 112
Fordbridge Rd. Sun 6G 131
Fordbridge Roundabout. (Junct.) 6A 112
Ford Clo. E3 2A 70
Ford Clo. Ashf 6A 112
Ford Clo. Harr 7H 25
Ford Clo. Shep 4C 130
Ford Clo. T Hth 5B 140
Forde Av. Brom 3A 144
Fordel Rd. SE6 1E 124
Ford End. Wfd G 6E 20
Fordham. King T 2G 135 (off Excelsior Clo.)
Fordham Clo. Barn 3H 5
Fordham Rd. Barn 3G 5
Fordham St. E1 6G 69
Fordhook Av. W5 1F 81
Ford Ho. Barn 5E 4
Ford Ind. Pk. Dag 4H 75
Fordingley Rd. W9 3H 65
Fordington Ho. SE26 3G 123
Fordington Rd. N6 5D 30
Fordmill Rd. SE6 2C 124
Ford Rd. E3 2B 70
Ford Rd. Ashf 4B 112
Ford Rd. Dag 7F 57
Fords Gro. N21 1H 17
Fords Pk. Rd. E16 5J 71
Ford Sq. E1 5H 69
Ford St. E3 1A 70
Ford St. E16 6H 71
Fordwich Clo. Orp 7K 145
Fordwych Rd. NW2 4G 47
Fordyce Rd. SE13 6E 106
Fordyke Rd. Dag 2F 57
Foreign St. SE5 2B 104
Foreland Ct. NW4 1F 29
Foreland Ho. W11 7G 65 (off Walmer Rd.)
Foreland St. SE18 4H 91
Foreman Ct. Twic 1K 115
Foreshore. SE8 4B 88
Forest App. E4 1B 20
Forest App. Wfd G 7D 20
Forest Av. E4 1B 20
Forest Av. Chig 5K 21
Forest Bus. Pk. E10 7A 34
Forest Clo. E11 5J 35
Forest Clo. N10 1F 31
Forest Clo. Chst 1E 144
Forest Clo. Wfd G 3E 20
Forest Ct. E4 1C 20
Forest Ct. E11 4G 35
Forest Ct. N12 5E 14
Forest Cft. SE23 2H 123
Forestdale. 7B 154
Forestdale. N14 4C 16
Forestdale Cen., The. Croy 7B 154
Forest Dene Ct. Sutt 6A 150
Forest Dri. E12 3B 54
Forest Dri. Kes 4C 156
Forest Dri. Sun 7H 113
Forest Dri. Wfd G 7A 20
Forest Dri. E. E11 7F 35
Forest Dri. W. E11 7E 34
Forest Edge. Buck H 4F 21
Forester Rd. SE15 3H 105
Foresters Clo. Wall 7H 151
Foresters Dri. E17 4F 35
Foresters Dri. Wall 7H 151
Forest Gdns. N17 2F 33
Forest Gate. 5K 53
Forest Ga. NW9 4A 28
Forest Glade. E4 4B 20
Forest Glade. E11 6G 35
Forest Gro. E8 6F 51
Forest Hill. 2J 123
Forest Hill Bus. Cen. SE23 2J 123 (off Clyde Va.)
Forest Hill Ind. Est. SE23 2J 123
Forest Hill Rd. SE22 & SE23 5H 105
Forestholme Clo. SE23 2J 123
Forest Ind. Pk. Ilf 1J 37
Forest La. E15 & E7 5G 53
Forest La. Chig 5K 21
Forest Lodge. SE26 3J 123 (off Dartmouth Rd.)
Forest Mt. Rd. Wfd G 7A 20
Forest Point. E7 5K 53 (off Windsor Rd.)
Fore St. EC2 5C 68 (6D 162)
Fore St. N18 & N9 6A 18
Fore St. Pinn 3H 23
Fore St. Av. EC2 5D 68 (6E 162)
Forest Ridge. Beck 3C 142
Forest Ridge. Kes 4C 156
Forest Ri. E17 3F 35 (in three parts)
Forest Rd. E7 4J 53
Forest Rd. E8 6F 51
Forest Rd. E11 7F 35
Forest Rd. N9 1C 18
Forest Rd. N17 & E17 4J 33
Forest Rd. Felt 2A 114
Forest Rd. Ilf 2H 37
Forest Rd. Rich 7G 81
Forest Rd. Romf 3H 39
Forest Rd. Sutt 1J 149
Forest Rd. Wfd G 3D 20
Forest Side. E4 1C 20
Forest Side. E7 4K 53
Forest Side. Buck H 1F 21
Forest Side. Wor Pk 1B 148
Forest St. E7 5J 53
Forest Ter. Chig 5K 21
Forest, The. E11 4G 35
Forest Trad. Est. E17 3K 33
Forest Vw. E4 7K 9 & 1B 20
Forest Vw. E11 7H 35
Forest Vw. Av. E10 5F 35
Forest Vw. Rd. E12 4C 54
Forest Vw. Rd. E17 1E 34
Forest Way. N19 2G 49
Forest Way. Orp 5K 145
Forest Way. Sidc 7H 109
Forest Way. Wfd G 4E 20
Forest Works Ind. Est. E17 3K 33
Forfar Rd. N22 1B 32
Forfar Rd. SW11 1E 102
Forge Clo. Brom 1J 155
Forge Clo. Hay 6F 77
Forge Cotts. W5 1D 80
Forge Dri. Clay 7A 146
Forge La. Felt 5C 114
Forge La. N'wd 1G 23
Forge La. Sun 3J 131
Forge La. Sutt 7G 149
Forge M. Croy 5C 154
Forge Pl. NW1 6E 48
Forman Pl. N16 4F 51
Formation, The. E16 2F 91 (off Woolwich Mnr. Way)
Formby Av. Stan 3C 26
Formby Ct. N7 5A 50 (off Morgan Rd.)
Former County Hall. 2K 85 (6G 167)
Formosa Ho. E1 4A 70 (off Ernest St.)

Formosa St. W9 4K 65
Formunt Clo. E16 5H 71
Forres Gdns. NW11 6J 29
Forrester Path. SE26 4J 123
Forresters Cres. Bexh 4H 111
Forrest Gdns. SW16 3K 139
Forris Av. Hay 1H 77
Forset Ct. W2 6C 66 (7D 158) (off Harrowby St.)
Forset St. W1 6C 66 (7D 158)
Forstal Clo. Brom 3J 143
Forster Clo. E4 7A 20
Forster Ho. Brom 4F 125
Forster Rd. E17 6A 34
Forster Rd. N17 3F 33
Forster Rd. SW12 7J 103
Forster Rd. Beck 3A 142
Forsters Clo. Romf 6F 39
Forsters Way. Hay 6K 59
Forston St. N1 2C 68
Forsyte Cres. SE19 1E 140
Forsythe Shades Ct. Beck 1E 142
Forsyth Gdns. SE17 6B 86
Forsyth Ho. E9 7J 51 (off Frampton Pk. Rd.)
Forsyth Ho. SW1 5G 85 (5B 172) (off Tachbrook St.)
Forsythia Clo. Ilf 5F 55
Forsyth Pl. Enf 5K 7
Forterie Gdns. Ilf 3A 56
Fortescue Av. E8 7H 51
Fortescue Av. Twic 3G 115
Fortescue Rd. SW19 7B 120
Fortescue Rd. Edgw 1K 27
Fortess Gro. NW5 5G 49
Fortess Rd. NW5 5F 49
Fortess Wlk. NW5 5F 49
Fortess Yd. NW5 4F 49
Forthbridge Rd. SW11 4E 102
Fortis Clo. E16 6A 72
Fortis Ct. N10 3E 30
Fortis Green. 4D 30
Fortis Grn. N2 & N10 4C 30
Fortis Grn. Av. N2 3D 30
Fortis Grn. Rd. N10 3E 30
Fortismere Av. N10 3E 30
Fortnam Rd. N19 2H 49
Fortnum's Acre. Stan 6E 10
Fort Rd. SE1 4F 87
Fort Rd. N'holt 7E 42
Fortrose Gdns. SW2 1J 121
Fort St. E1 5E 68 (6H 163)
Fort St. E16 1K 89
Fortuna Clo. N7 6K 49
Fortune Ct. Bark 2C 74
Fortunegate Rd. NW10 1A 64
Fortune Green. 4J 47
Fortune Grn. Rd. NW6 4J 47
Fortune Ho. EC1 4C 68 (4D 162) (off Fortune St.)
Fortune Ho. SE11 4J 173
Fortunes Mead. N'holt 6C 42
Fortune St. EC1 4C 68 (4D 162)
Fortune Theatre. 6J 67 (1F 167) (off Russell St.)
Fortune Wlk. SE28 3H 91 (off Broadwater Rd.)
Fortune Way. NW10 3C 64
Forty Acre La. E16 5J 71
Forty Av. Wemb 3F 45
Forty Clo. Wemb 3F 45
Forty Footpath. SW14 3J 99
Forty Foot Way. SE9 7G 109
Forty Hill. 1K 7
Forty Hill. Enf 1K 7
Forty La. Wemb 2H 45
Forum Magnum Sq. SE1 2K 85 (6H 167) (off York Rd.)
Forumside. Edgw 6B 12
Forum, The. W Mol 4F 133
Forum Way. Edgw 6B 12
Forval Clo. Mitc 5D 138
Forward Bus. Cen. E16 4F 71
Forward Dri. Harr 4K 25
Fosbrooke Ho. SW8 7J 85 (off Davidson Gdns.)
Fosbury M. W2 7K 65
Foscote M. W9 4J 65
Foscote Rd. NW4 6D 28
Foskett Ho. N2 2B 30
Foskett Rd. SW6 2H 101
Foss Av. Croy 5A 152
Fossdene Rd. SE7 5K 89
Fossdyke Clo. Hay 5C 60
Fosset Lodge. Bexh 1J 111
Fosse Way. W13 5A 62
Fossil Rd. SE13 3C 106
Fossington Rd. Belv 4D 92
Foss Rd. SW17 4B 120
Fossway. Dag 2C 56
Foster Ct. E16 7H 71 (off Tarling Rd.)
Foster Ct. NW1 7G 49 (off Royal College St.)
Foster Ct. NW4 4E 28
Foster Ho. SE14 1B 106
Foster La. EC2 6C 68 (7C 162)
Foster Rd. E13 4J 71
Foster Rd. W3 7A 64
Foster Rd. W4 5K 81
Fosters Clo. E18 1K 35
Fosters Clo. Chst 5D 126
Foster St. NW4 4E 28
Foster's Way. SW18 1K 119
Foster Wlk. NW4 4E 28
Fothergill Clo. E13 2J 71
Fothergill Dri. N21 5D 6
Fotheringham Rd. Enf 4A 8
Foubert's Pl. W1 6G 67 (1A 166)
Foulden Rd. N16 4F 51
Foulden Ter. N16 4F 51
Foulis Ter. SW7 5B 84 (5B 170)
Foulser Rd. SW17 3D 120
Foulsham Rd. T Hth 3C 140
Founder Clo. E6 6F 73
Founders Ct. EC2 7E 162
Founders Gdns. SE19 7C 122
Founders Ho. SW1 5H 85 (6C 172) (off Aylesford St.)
Foundling Ct. WC1 4J 67 (3E 160) (off Brunswick Cen.)
Foundry Clo. SE16 1A 88
Foundry Ho. E14 5D 70 (off Morris Rd.)
Foundry M. NW1 3B 160
Foundry Pl. SW18 7K 101
Fountain Clo. Uxb 5E 58
Fountain Ct. EC4 7A 68 (2J 167)
Fountain Ct. SE23 2K 123
Fountain Ct. SW1 4F 85 (4J 171) (off Buckingham Pal. Rd.)
Fountain Ct. Sidc 6B 110
Fountain Dri. SE19 4F 123
Fountain Dri. Cars 7D 150
Fountain Grn. Sq. SE16 2G 87
Fountain Ho. NW6 7G 47
Fountain Ho. W1 1E 84 (4G 165) (off Park St.)
Fountain M. N5 4C 50 (off Highbury Grange)
Fountain M. NW3 6D 48
Fountain Pl. SW9 1A 104
Fountain Rd. SW17 5B 120
Fountain Rd. T Hth 3C 140
Fountain Roundabout. N Mald 4A 136
Fountains Av. Felt 3D 114
Fountains Clo. Felt 2D 114 (in two parts)
Fountains Cres. N14 7D 6
Fountain Sq. SW1 4F 85 (3K 171)
Fountains, The. N3 7E 14 (off Ballards La.)
Fountayne Bus. Cen. N15 4G 33
Fountayne Rd. N15 4G 33
Fountayne Rd. N16 2G 51
Fount St. SW8 7H 85
Fouracres. NW1 3G 67 (2A 160) (off Stanhope St.)
Fouracres. Enf 1F 9
Fourland Wlk. Edgw 6D 12
Fournier St. E1 5F 69 (5J 163)
Four Seasons Clo. E3 2C 70
Four Seasons Cres. Sutt 2H 149
Four Sq. Ct. Houn 6E 96
Fourth Av. E12 4D 54
Fourth Av. W10 4G 65
Fourth Av. Hay 1H 77
Fourth Av. Romf 1K 57
Fourth Cross Rd. Twic 2H 115
Fourth Way. Wemb 4H 45
Four Wents, The. E4 2A 20
Fovant Ct. SW8 2G 103
Fowey Av. Ilf 5B 36
Fowey Clo. E1 1H 87
Fowey Ho. SE11 5K 173
Fowler Clo. SW11 3B 102
Fowler Ho. N15 5D 32 (off South Gro.)
Fowler Rd. E7 4J 53
Fowler Rd. N1 1B 68
Fowler Rd. Mitc 2E 138
Fowlers Clo. Sidc 5E 128
Fowler's Wlk. W5 4D 62
Fownes St. SW11 3C 102
Fox & Knot St. EC1 5B 162
Foxberry Rd. SE4 3A 106
Foxborough Gdns. SE4 5C 106
Foxbourne Rd. SW17 2E 120
Foxbury Av. Chst 6H 127
Foxbury Clo. Brom 6K 125
Foxbury Rd. Brom 6J 125
Fox Clo. E1 4J 69
Fox Clo. E16 5J 71
Foxcombe. New Ad 6D 154 (in two parts)
Foxcombe Clo. E6 2B 72
Foxcombe Rd. SW15 1C 118
Foxcote. SE5 5E 86
Foxcroft. WC1 2K 67 (1H 161) (off Penton Ri.)
Foxcroft Rd. SE18 1F 109
Foxearth Spur. S Croy 7J 153
Foxes Dale. SE3 3J 107
Foxes Dale. Brom 3F 143
Foxfield. NW1 1F 67 (off Arlington Rd.)
Foxglove Clo. S'hall 7C 60
Foxglove Ct. Wemb 2E 62
Foxglove Gdns. E11 4A 36
Foxglove La. Chess 4G 147
Foxglove Rd. Rush G 2K 57
Foxglove St. W12 7B 64
Foxglove Way. Wall 1F 151
Foxgrove. N14 3D 16
Fox Gro. W on T 7K 131
Foxgrove Av. Beck 7D 124
Foxgrove Rd. Beck 7D 124
Foxham Rd. N19 3H 49
Fox Hill. SE19 7F 123
Fox Hill. Kes 5A 156
Fox Hill Gdns. SE19 7F 123
Foxhole Rd. SE9 5C 108
Fox Hollow Clo. SE18 5J 91
Fox Hollow Dri. Bexh 3D 110
Foxholt Gdns. NW10 7J 45
Foxhome Clo. Chst 6E 126
Fox Ho. Rd. Belv 5H 93 (in two parts)
Foxlands Cres. Dag 5J 57
Foxlands La. Dag 5K 57
Foxlands Rd. Dag 5J 57
Fox La. N13 2E 16
Fox La. W5 4E 62 (in two parts)
Fox La. Kes 5K 155
Foxleas Ct. Brom 7G 125
Foxlees. Wemb 4A 44
Foxley Clo. E8 5G 51
Foxley Ct. Sutt 7A 150
Foxley Rd. SW9 7A 86
Foxley Rd. T Hth 4B 140
Foxley Sq. SW9 1B 104
Foxmead Clo. Enf 3E 6
Foxmore St. SW11 1D 102
Fox Rd. E16 5H 71
Fox's Path. Mitc 2C 138
Foxton Gro. Mitc 2B 138
Foxton Ho. E16 2E 90 (off Albert Rd.)
Foxwarren. Clay 7A 146
Foxwell M. SE4 3A 106
Foxwell St. SE4 3A 106
Foxwood Clo. NW7 4F 13
Foxwood Clo. Felt 3K 113
Foxwood Grn. Clo. Enf 6K 7
Foxwood Rd. SE3 4H 107
Foyle Rd. N17 1G 33
Foyle Rd. SE3 6H 89
Framfield Clo. N12 3D 14
Framfield Ct. Enf 6K 7 (off Queen Annes Gdns.)
Framfield Rd. N5 5B 50
Framfield Rd. W7 6J 61
Framfield Rd. Mitc 7E 120
Framlingham Clo. E5 2J 51
Framlingham Cres. SE9 4C 126
Frampton. NW1 7H 49 (off Wrotham Rd.)
Frampton Clo. Sutt 7J 149
Frampton Ct. W3 2J 81 (off Avenue Rd.)
Frampton Ho. NW8 4B 66 (4B 158) (off Frampton St.)
Frampton Pk. Est. E9 7J 51
Frampton Pk. Rd. E9 6J 51
Frampton Rd. Houn 5C 96
Frampton St. NW8 4B 66 (4B 158)
Francemary Rd. SE4 5C 106
Frances Ct. E17 6C 34
Frances Rd. E4 6H 19
Frances St. SE18 3D 90
Franche Ct. Rd. SW17 3A 120
Francis Av. Bexh 2G 111
Francis Av. Felt 3J 113
Francis Av. Ilf 2H 55
Francis Barber Clo. SW16 5K 121
Franciscan Rd. SW17 5D 120
Francis Chichester Way. SW11 1E 102
Francis Clo. E14 4F 89
Francis Clo. Eps 4K 147
Francis Clo. Shep 4C 130
Francis Ct. EC1 5A 162
Francis Ct. NW7 5G 13 (off Watford Way)
Francis Ct. SE14 6K 87 (off Myers La.)
Francis Ct. Surb 4E 134 (off Cranes Pk. Av.)
Francis Gro. SW19 6H 119 (in two parts)
Francis Ho. E17 6B 34
Francis Ho. N1 1E 68 (off Colville Est.)
Francis M. SE12 7J 107
Francis Rd. E10 1E 52
Francis Rd. N2 4D 30
Francis Rd. Croy 7B 140
Francis Rd. Gnfd 2B 62
Francis Rd. Harr 5A 26
Francis Rd. Houn 2B 96
Francis Rd. Ilf 2H 55
Francis Rd. Pinn 5A 24
Francis Rd. Wall 6G 151
Francis St. E15 5G 53
Francis St. SW1 4G 85 (3A 172)
Francis St. Ilf 2H 55
Francis Ter. N19 3G 49
Francis Wlk. N1 1K 67
Francklyn Gdns. Edgw 3B 12
Franconia Rd. SW4 5H 103
Frank Bailey Wlk. E12 5E 54
Frank Beswick Ho. SW6 6H 83 (off Clem Attlee Ct.)
Frank Burton Clo. SE7 5K 89
Frank Dixon Clo. SE21 7E 104
Frank Dixon Way. SE21 1E 122
Frankfurt Rd. SE24 5C 104
Frankham Ho. SE8 7C 88 (off Frankham St.)
Frankham St. SE8 7C 88
Frank Ho. SW8 7J 85 (off Wyvil Rd.)
Frankland Clo. SE16 3H 87
Frankland Clo. Wfd G 5F 21
Frankland Rd. E4 5H 19
Frankland Rd. SW7 3B 84 (2A 170)
Franklin Building. E14 2C 88
Franklin Clo. N20 7F 5
Franklin Clo. SE13 1D 106
Franklin Clo. SE27 3B 122
Franklin Clo. King T 3G 135
Franklin Cotts. Stan 4G 11
Franklin Cres. Mitc 4G 139
Franklin Ho. E1 1H 87 (off Watts St.)
Franklin Pas. SE9 3C 108
Franklin Rd. SE20 7J 123
Franklin Rd. Bexh 1E 110
Franklins M. Harr 2G 43
Franklin Sq. W14 5H 83
Franklin's Row. SW3 5D 84 (5F 171)
Franklin St. E3 3D 70
Franklin St. N15 6E 32
Franklin Way. Croy 7J 139
Franklyn Rd. NW10 6B 46
Franklyn Rd. W on T 6J 131
Franks Av. N Mald 4J 135
Frank Soskice Ho. SW6 6H 83 (off Clem Attlee Ct.)
Frank St. E13 4J 71
Franks Wood Av. Orp 5F 145
Frankswood Av. W Dray 6B 58
Frank Towell Ct. Felt 7J 95
Frank Welsh Ct. Pinn 4A 24
Frank Whymark Ho. SE16 2J 87 (off Rupack St.)
Franlaw Cres. N13 4H 17
Fransfield Gro. SE26 3H 123
Frans Hals Ct. E14 3F 89
Frant Clo. SE20 7J 123
Franthorne Way. SE6 2D 124
Frant Rd. T Hth 5B 140
Fraser Clo. E6 6C 72
Fraser Clo. Bex 1J 129
Fraser Ct. E14 5E 88 (off Ferry St.)
Fraser Ho. Bren 5F 81
Fraser Rd. E17 5D 34
Fraser Rd. N9 3C 18
Fraser Rd. Eri 5J 93
Fraser Rd. Gnfd 1B 62
Fraser St. W4 5A 82
Frating Cres. Wfd G 6E 20
Frazer Av. Ruis 5A 42
Frazier St. SE1 2A 86 (7J 167)
Frean St. SE16 3G 87
Frearson Ho. WC1 3K 67 (1H 161) (off Penton Ri.)
Freda Corbett Clo. SE15 7G 87
Frederica Rd. E4 1A 20
Frederica St. N7 7K 49

Frederick Charrington Ho. E1 4J 69 (off Wickford St.)
Frederick Clo. W2 7D 66 (2D 164)
Frederick Clo. Sutt 4H 149
Frederick Cres. SW9 7B 86
Frederick Cres. Enf 2D 8
Frederick Gdns. Croy 6B 140
Frederick Gdns. Sutt 4H 149
Frederick Pl. SE18 5F 91
Frederick Rd. SE17 6B 86
Frederick Rd. Rain 2K 75
Frederick Rd. Sutt 5H 149
Frederick's Pl. EC2 6D 68 (1E 168)
Fredericks Pl. N12 4F 15
Frederick Sq. SE16 7A 70 (off Sovereign Cres.)
Frederick's Row. EC1 3B 68 (1A 162)
Frederick St. WC1 3K 67 (2G 161)
Frederick Ter. E8 7F 51
Frederic M. SW1 7F 165
Frederic St. E17 5A 34
Fredora Av. Hay 4H 59
Fred Styles Ho. SE7 6A 90
Fred White Wlk. N7 6J 49
Freedom Clo. E17 4K 33
Freedom Rd. N17 2D 32
Freedom St. SW11 2D 102
Freegrove Rd. N7 5J 49 (in two parts)
Freehold Ind. Est. Houn 5A 96
Freeland Ct. Sidc 3A 128
Freeland Pk. NW4 2G 29
Freeland Rd. W5 7F 63
Freelands Av. S Croy 7K 153
Freelands Gro. Brom 1K 143
Freelands Rd. Brom 1K 143
Freeling Ho. NW8 1B 66 (off Dorman Way)
Freeling St. N1 7K 49 (Carnoustie Dri.)
Freeling St. N1 7J 49 (Pembroke St.)
Freeman Clo. N'holt 7C 42
Freeman Clo. Shep 4G 131
Freeman Dri. W Mol 4D 132
Freeman Rd. Mord 5B 138
Freemans La. Hay 7G 59
Freemantle Av. Enf 5E 8
Freemantle St. SE17 5E 86
Freemasons Rd. E16 5K 71
Freemasons Rd. Croy 1E 152
Freethorpe Clo. SE19 7D 122
Free Trade Wharf. E1 7K 69
Freezeland Way. Hil 6D 40
Freke Rd. SW11 3E 102
Fremantle Ho. E1 4H 69 (off Somerford St.)
Fremantle Rd. Belv 4G 93
Fremantle Rd. Ilf 2F 37
Fremont St. E9 1H 69 (in two parts)
French Ordinary Ct. EC3 2H 169
French Pl. E1 3E 68 (2H 163)
French St. Sun 2A 132
Frendsbury Rd. SE4 4A 106
Frensham Clo. S'hall 4D 60
Frensham Dri. SW15 3B 118 (in two parts)
Frensham Dri. New Ad 7E 154
Frensham Rd. SE9 2H 127
Frensham St. SE15 6G 87
Frere St. SW11 2C 102
Fresham Ho. Brom 3H 143 (off Durham Rd.)
Freshfield Av. E8 7F 51
Freshfield Clo. SE13 4F 107
Freshfield Dri. N14 7A 6
Freshfields. Croy 1B 154
Freshford St. SW17 3A 120
Freshwater Clo. SW17 6E 120
Freshwater Ct. W1 5C 66 (6D 158) (off Crawford St.)
Freshwater Ct. S'hall 3E 60
Freshwater Rd. SW17 6E 120
Freshwater Rd. Dag 1D 56
Freshwell Av. Romf 4C 38
Fresh Wharf Rd. Bark 1F 73
Freshwood Clo. Beck 1D 142
Freshwood Way. Wall 7F 151
Freston Gdns. Barn 5K 5
Freston Pk. N3 2H 29
Freston Rd. W10 & W11 7F 65
Freswick Ho. SE8 4K 87 (off Chilton Gro.)
Freta Rd. Bexh 5F 111
Freud Mus., The. 6A 48
Frewell Ho. EC1 5A 68 (5J 161) (off Bourne Est.)
Frewing Clo. Chst 6D 126
Frewin Rd. SW18 1B 120
Friar M. SE27 3B 122
Friar Rd. Hay 4B 60
Friar Rd. Orp 5K 145
Friars Av. N20 3H 15
Friars Av. SW15 3B 118
Friars Clo. E4 3K 19
Friars Clo. SE1 5B 168
Friars Clo. Ilf 1H 55
Friars Clo. N'holt 3B 60
Friars Ct. E17 1B 34
Friars Gdns. W3 6K 63
Friars Ga. Clo. Wfd G 4D 20
Friars La. Rich 5D 98
Friars Mead. E14 3E 88
Friars M. SE9 5E 108
Friars Pl. La. W3 7K 63
Friars Rd. E6 1B 72
Friars Stile Pl. Rich 6E 98
Friars Stile Rd. Rich 6E 98
Friar St. EC4 6B 68 (1B 168)
Friars Wlk. N14 7A 6
Friars Wlk. SE2 5D 92
Friars Way. W3 6K 63
Friarswood. Croy 7A 154
Friary Clo. N12 5H 15
Friary Ct. SW1 5B 166
Friary Est. SE15 6G 87 (in two parts)
Friary La. Wfd G 4D 20
Friary Pk. Ct. W3 6J 63
Friary Rd. N12 4G 15
Friary Rd. SE15 7G 87
Friary Rd. W3 6J 63
Friary Way. N12 4H 15
Friday Hill. 2B 20
Friday Hill. E4 2B 20
Friday Hill E. E4 3B 20
Friday Hill W. E4 2B 20
Friday Rd. Eri 5K 93
Friday Rd. Mitc 7D 120
Friday St. EC4 7C 68 (2C 168)
Frideswide Pl. NW5 5G 49
Friendly Pl. SE13 1D 106
Friendly St. SE8 2C 106
Friendly St. M. SE8 2C 106
Friendship Wlk. N'holt 3B 60
Friends Rd. Croy 3D 152
Friend St. EC1 3B 68 (1A 162)
Friern Barnet. 5J 15
Friern Barnet La. N20 & N11 2G 15
Friern Barnet Rd. N11 5J 15
Friern Bri. Retail Pk. N11 6A 16
Friern Ct. N20 3G 15
Friern Mt. Dri. N20 7F 5
Friern Pk. N12 5F 15
Friern Rd. SE22 7G 105
Friern Watch Av. N12 4F 15
Frigate Ho. E14 4E 88 (off Stebondale St.)
Frigate M. SE8 6C 88
Frimley Av. Wall 5J 151
Frimley Clo. SW19 2G 119
Frimley Clo. New Ad 7E 154
Frimley Ct. Sidc 5C 128
Frimley Cres. New Ad 7E 154
Frimley Gdns. Mitc 3C 138
Frimley Rd. Chess 5D 146
Frimley Rd. Ilf 3J 55
Frimley St. E1 4K 69 (off Frimley Way)
Frimley Way. E1 4K 69
Fringewood Clo. N'wd 1D 22
Frinstead Ho. W10 7F 65 (off Freston Rd.)
Frinsted Rd. Eri 7K 93
Frinton Ct. W13 5B 62 (off Hardwick Grn.)
Frinton Dri. Wfd G 7A 20
Frinton M. Ilf 6E 36
Frinton Rd. E6 3B 72
Frinton Rd. N15 6E 32
Frinton Rd. SW17 6E 120
Frinton Rd. Sidc 2E 128
Friston St. SW6 2K 101
Friswell Pl. Bexh 4G 111
Fritham Clo. N Mald 6A 136
Frith Ct. NW7 7B 14
Frith Ho. NW8 4B 66 (4B 158) (off Frampton St.)
Frith La. NW7 7B 14
Frith Rd. E11 4E 52
Frith Rd. Croy 2C 152
Frith St. W1 6H 67 (1C 166)
Frithville Ct. W12 1E 82 (off Frithville Gdns.)
Frithville Gdns. W12 1E 82
Frizlands La. Dag 2H 57
Frobisher Clo. Pinn 7B 24
Frobisher Ct. NW9 2A 28
Frobisher Ct. SE10 6F 89 (off Old Woolwich Rd.)
Frobisher Ct. SE23 2H 123
Frobisher Ct. W12 2E 82 (off Lime Gro.)
Frobisher Ct. Sutt 7G 149
Frobisher Cres. EC2 5C 68 (5D 162) (off Beech St.)
Frobisher Cres. Stai 7A 94
Frobisher Gdns. E10 7D 34
Frobisher Gdns. Stai 7A 94
Frobisher Ho. E1 1H 87 (off Watts St.)
Frobisher Ho. SW1 6H 85 (7C 172) (off Dolphin Sq.)
Frobisher M. Enf 4J 7
Frobisher Pas. E14 1C 88
Frobisher Rd. E6 6D 72
Frobisher Rd. N8 4A 32
Frobisher St. SE10 6G 89
Frog La. Frog 5K 75
Frogley Rd. SE22 4F 105
Frogmore. SW18 5J 101
Frogmore Av. Hay 4G 59
Frogmore Clo. Sutt 3F 149
Frogmore Ct. S'hall 4D 78
Frogmore Gdns. Hay 4G 59
Frogmore Gdns. Sutt 4G 149
Frogmore Ind. Est. N5 5C 50
Frogmore Ind. Est. NW10 3J 63
Frogmore Ind. Est. Hay 2G 77
Frognal. NW3 4A 48
Frognal Av. Harr 4K 25
Frognal Av. Sidc 6A 128
Frognal Clo. NW3 5A 48
Frognal Corner. (Junct.) 6K 127
Frognal Ct. NW3 6A 48
Frognal Gdns. NW3 4A 48
Frognal La. NW3 5K 47
Frognal Pde. NW3 6A 48
Frognal Pl. Sidc 6A 128
Frognal Ri. NW3 3A 48
Frognal Way. NW3 4A 48
Froissart Rd. SE9 5B 108
Frome Ho. SE15 4H 105
Frome Rd. N15 3B 32
Frome St. N1 2C 68
Fromondes Rd. Sutt 5G 149
Frontenac. NW10 7D 46
Frostic Wlk. E1 5G 69 (6K 163)
Froude St. SW8 2F 103
Fruen Rd. Felt 7H 95
Fruiterers Pas. EC4 3D 168
Fryatt Rd. N17 7J 17 (in two parts)
Fryent Clo. NW9 6G 27
Fryent Country Pk. 7G 27
Fryent Cres. NW9 6A 28
Fryent Fields. NW9 6A 28
Fryent Gro. NW9 6A 28
Fryent Way. NW9 5G 27
Fry Ho. E7 7A 54
Frying Pan All. E1 6J 163
Fry Rd. E6 7B 54
Fry Rd. NW10 1B 64
Fry Rd. Ashf 4A 112
Fryston Av. Croy 2G 153
Fuchsia Clo. Rush G 2K 57
Fuchsia St. SE2 5B 92
Fulbeck Dri. NW9 1A 28
Fulbeck Ho. N7 6K 49 (off Sutterton St.)
Fulbeck Rd. N19 4G 49
Fulbeck Wlk. Edgw 2C 12
Fulbeck Way. Harr 2G 25
Fulbourn. King T 2G 135 (off Eureka Rd.)
Fulbourne Rd. E17 1E 34
Fulbourne St. E1 5H 69
Fulbrook M. N19 4G 49
Fulcher Ho. N1 1E 68 (off Colville Ho.)
Fulcher Ho. SE8 5B 88
Fulford Ho. Eps 7K 147
Fulford Rd. Eps 7K 147
Fulford St. SE16 2H 87
Fulham. 2G 101
Fulham Broadway. (Junct.) 7J 83
Fulham B'way. SW6 7J 83
Fulham Clo. Uxb 4E 58
Fulham Ct. SW6 1J 101
Fulham F.C. (Craven Cottage) 1F 101
Fulham High St. SW6 2G 101
Fulham Pal. Rd. W6 & SW6 5E 82
Fulham Pk. Gdns. SW6 2H 101
Fulham Pk. Rd. SW6 2H 101
Fulham Rd. SW6 & SW10,SW3 2G 101 (in two parts)
Fullbrooks Av. Wor Pk 1B 148
Fuller Clo. E2 4G 69 (off Cheshire St.)
Fuller Rd. Dag 3B 56
Fullers Av. E18 7C 20
Fullers Av. Surb 2F 147
Fullers Clo. Romf 1J 39
Fuller's Griffin Brewery & Vis. Cen. 6B 82
Fullers La. Romf 1J 39
Fullers Rd. E18 7C 20
Fuller St. NW4 4E 28
Fullers Way N. Surb 3F 147
Fullers Way S. Chess 4E 146
Fuller's Wood. Croy 5C 154
Fullerton Ct. Tedd 6A 116
Fullerton Rd. SW18 5K 101
Fullerton Rd. Cars 7C 150
Fullerton Rd. Croy 7F 141
Fuller Way. Hay 5H 77
Fullwell Av. Ilf 1D 36
Fullwell Cross. Ilf 2H 37
Fullwell Pde. Ilf 1E 36
Fullwood's M. N1 3D 68 (1F 163)
Fulmar Ct. Surb 6F 135
Fulmar Ho. SE16 4K 87 (off Tawny Way)
Fulmead St. SW6 1K 101
Fulmer Clo. Hamp 5C 114
Fulmer Ho. NW8 4C 66 (4C 158) (off Rossmore Rd.)
Fulmer Rd. E16 5B 72
Fulmer Way. W13 3B 80
Fulneck. E1 5J 69 (off Mile End Rd.)
Fulready Rd. E10 5F 35
Fulstone Clo. Houn 4D 96
Fulthorp Rd. SE3 2H 107
Fulton M. W2 7A 66 (off Porchester Ter.)
Fulton Rd. Wemb 3G 45
Fulwell. 4H 115
Fulwell Ct. S'hall 7G 61 (off Baird Av.)
Fulwell Cross. 2G 37
Fulwell Pk. Av. Twic 2F 115
Fulwell Rd. Tedd 4H 115
Fulwood Av. Wemb 2F 63
Fulwood Clo. Hay 6H 59
Fulwood Ct. Kent 6A 26
Fulwood Gdns. Twic 6K 97
Fulwood Pl. WC1 5K 67 (6H 161)
Fulwood Wlk. SW19 1G 119
Furber St. W6 3D 82
Furham Fld. Pinn 7A 10
Furley Ho. SE15 7G 87 (off Peckham Pk. Rd.)
Furley Rd. SE15 7G 87
Furlong Clo. Wall 1F 151
Furlong Path. N'holt 6C 42 (off Cowings Mead)
Furlong Rd. N7 6A 50
Furmage St. SW18 7K 101
Furneaux Av. SE27 5B 122
Furness Ho. SW1 5F 85 (5J 171) (off Abbots Mnr.)
Furness Rd. NW10 2C 64
Furness Rd. SW6 2K 101
Furness Rd. Harr 7F 25
Furness Rd. Mord 6K 137
Furnival Mans. W1 5G 67 (6A 160) (off Wells St.)
Furnival St. EC4 6A 68 (7J 161)
Furrow La. E9 5J 51
Fursby Av. N3 6D 14
Fursecroft. W1 7E 158
Further Acre. NW9 2B 28
Furtherfield Clo. Croy 6A 140
Further Grn. Rd. SE6 7G 107
Furzedown. 5F 121
Furzedown Dri. SW17 5F 121
Furzedown Rd. SW17 5F 121
Furze Farm Clo. Romf 2E 38
Furzefield Clo. Chst 6F 127
Furzefield Rd. SE3 6K 89
Furzeground Way. Uxb 1E 76
Furzeham Rd. W Dray 2A 76
Furze Rd. T Hth 3C 140
Furze St. E3 5C 70
Furzewood. Sun 1J 131
Fye Foot La. EC4 7C 68 (2C 168) (off Queen Victoria St., in two parts)
Fyfe Way. Brom 2J 143
Fyfield. N4 2A 50 (off Six Acres Est.)
Fyfield Clo. Brom 4F 143
Fyfield Ct. E7 6J 53
Fyfield Ho. E6 1C 72 (off Ron Leighton Way)
Fyfield Rd. E17 3F 35
Fyfield Rd. SW9 3A 104
Fyfield Rd. Enf 3K 7

Fyfield Rd. Wfd G . . . 7F 21
Fynes St. SW1 . . . 4H 85 (3C 172)

Gable Clo. Pinn . . . 1E 24
Gable Ct. SE26 . . . 4H 123
Gables Av. Ashf . . . 5B 112
Gables Clo. SE5 . . . 1E 104
Gables Clo. SE12 . . . 1J 125
Gables Lodge. Barn . . . 1F 5
Gables, The. N10 . . . 3E 30 (off Fortis Grn.)
Gables, The. Bark . . . 6G 55
Gables, The. Brom . . . 7K 125
Gables, The. Wemb . . . 3G 45
Gabriel Clo. Felt . . . 4C 114
Gabriel Ho. SE11 . . . 4K 85 (3G 173)
Gabrielle Clo. Wemb . . . 3F 45
Gabrielle Ct. NW3 . . . 6B 48
Gabriel St. SE23 . . . 7K 105
Gabriels Wharf. SE1 . . . 1A 86 (4J 167)
Gad Clo. E13 . . . 3K 71
Gaddesden Av. Wemb . . . 6F 45
Gaddesden Ho. EC1 . . . 3D 68 (2F 163) (off Cranwood St.)
Gadebridge Ho. SW3 . . . 5C 84 (5C 170) (off Cale St.)
Gade Clo. Hay . . . 1K 77
Gadesden Rd. Eps . . . 6J 147 (in two parts)
Gadsbury Clo. NW9 . . . 6B 28
Gadsden Ho. W10 . . . 4G 65 (off Hazlewood Cres.)
Gadwall Clo. E16 . . . 6K 71
Gadwall Way. SE28 . . . 2H 91
Gage Brown Ho. W10 . . . 6F 65 (off Bridge Clo.)
Gage Rd. E16 . . . 5G 71
Gage St. WC1 . . . 5J 67 (5F 161)
Gainford Ho. E2 . . . 3H 69 (off Ellsworth St.)
Gainford St. N1 . . . 1A 68
Gainsboro Gdns. Gnfd . . . 5J 43
Gainsborough Av. E12 . . . 5E 54
Gainsborough Clo. Beck . . . 7C 124
Gainsborough Clo. Esh . . . 7J 133
Gainsborough Ct. N12 . . . 5E 14
Gainsborough Ct. SE16 . . . 5H 87 (off Stubbs Dri.)
Gainsborough Ct. SE21 . . . 2E 122
Gainsborough Ct. W4 . . . 5H 81 (off Chaseley Dri.)
Gainsborough Ct. W12 . . . 2E 82
Gainsborough Gdns. NW3 . . . 3B 48
Gainsborough Gdns. NW11 . . . 7H 29
Gainsborough Gdns. Edgw . . . 2F 27
Gainsborough Gdns. Iswth . . . 5H 97
Gainsborough Ho. E14 . . . 7A 70 (off Victory Pl.)
Gainsborough Ho. SW1 . . . 4H 85 (4D 172) (off Erasmus St.)
Gainsborough Ho. Dag . . . 4B 56 (off Gainsborough Rd.)
Gainsborough Lodge. Harr . . . 5K 25 (off Hindes Rd.)
Gainsborough Mans. W14 . . . 6G 83 (off Queen's Club Gdns.)
Gainsborough M. SE26 . . . 3H 123
Gainsborough Rd. E11 . . . 7G 35
Gainsborough Rd. E15 . . . 3G 71
Gainsborough Rd. N12 . . . 5E 14
Gainsborough Rd. W4 . . . 4B 82
Gainsborough Rd. Dag . . . 4B 56
Gainsborough Rd. Hay . . . 2E 58
Gainsborough Rd. N Mald . . . 6K 135
Gainsborough Rd. Rich . . . 2F 99
Gainsborough Rd. Wfd G . . . 6H 21
Gainsborough Sq. Bexh . . . 3D 110
Gainsborough Ter. Sutt . . . 7H 149 (off Belmont Ri.)
Gainsborough Tower. N'holt . . . 2B 60 (off Academy Gdns.)
Gainsfield Ct. E11 . . . 3G 53
Gainsford Rd. E17 . . . 4B 34
Gainsford St. SE1 . . . 2F 87 (6J 169)
Gairloch Ho. NW1 . . . 7H 49 (off Stratford Vs.)
Gairloch Rd. SE5 . . . 2E 104
Gaisford St. NW5 . . . 6G 49
Gaitskell Ct. SW11 . . . 2C 102
Gaitskell Ho. E6 . . . 1B 72
Gaitskell Ho. E17 . . . 3D 34
Gaitskell Ho. SE17 . . . 6E 86 (off Villa St.)
Gaitskell Rd. SE9 . . . 1G 127
Galahad Rd. Brom . . . 4J 125
Galata Rd. SW13 . . . 7C 82
Galatea Sq. SE15 . . . 3H 105
Galba Ct. Bren . . . 7D 80
Galbraith St. E14 . . . 3E 88
Galdana Av. Barn . . . 3F 5
Galeborough Av. Wfd G . . . 7A 20
Gale Clo. Hamp . . . 6C 114
Gale Clo. Mitc . . . 3B 138
Galena Ho. W6 . . . 4D 82 (off Galena Rd.)
Galena Rd. W6 . . . 4D 82
Galen Pl. WC1 . . . 5J 67 (6F 161)
Galesbury Rd. SW18 . . . 6A 102
Gales Gdns. E2 . . . 3H 69
Gale St. E3 . . . 5C 70
Gale St. Dag . . . 5C 56
Gales Way. Wfd G . . . 7H 21
Galgate Clo. SW19 . . . 1F 119
Gallants Farm Rd. E Barn . . . 7H 5
Galleon Clo. SE16 . . . 2K 87
Galleon Clo. Eri . . . 4K 93
Galleon Dri. Bark . . . 3A 74
Galleon Ho. E14 . . . 4E 88 (off Glengarnock Av.)
Gallery Ct. SE1 . . . 2D 86 (7E 168) (off Pilgrimage St.)
Gallery Ct. SW10 . . . 6A 84 (off Gunter Gro.)
Gallery Gdns. N'holt . . . 2B 60
Gallery Rd. SE21 . . . 1D 122
Galleywall Rd. SE16 . . . 4H 87
Galleywall Rd. Trad. Est. SE16 . . . 4H 87 (off Galleywall Rd.)
Galleywood Ho. W10 . . . 5E 64 (off Sutton Way)
Galliard Clo. N9 . . . 6D 8
Galliard Ct. N9 . . . 6B 8
Galliard Rd. N9 . . . 7B 8
Gallia Rd. N5 . . . 5B 50
Gallions Clo. Bark . . . 3A 74
Gallions Entrance. E16 . . . 1G 91
Gallions Rd. SE7 . . . 4K 89 (in two parts)
Gallions Vw. Rd. SE28 . . . 2J 91
Galliver Pl. E5 . . . 4H 51
Gallon Clo. SE7 . . . 4A 90
Gallop, The. S Croy . . . 7H 153
Gallop, The. Sutt . . . 7B 150
Gallosson Rd. SE18 . . . 4J 91
Galloway Path. Croy . . . 4D 152
Galloway Rd. W12 . . . 1C 82
Gallus Clo. N21 . . . 6E 6
Gallus Sq. SE3 . . . 3K 107
Galpin's Rd. T Hth . . . 5J 139
Galsworthy Av. E14 . . . 5A 70
Galsworthy Av. Romf . . . 7B 38
Galsworthy Clo. NW2 . . . 4G 47
Galsworthy Clo. SE28 . . . 1B 92
Galsworthy Ct. W3 . . . 3H 81 (off Bollo Bri. Rd.)
Galsworthy Cres. SE3 . . . 1A 108
Galsworthy Ho. W11 . . . 6G 65 (off Elgin Cres.)
Galsworthy Rd. NW2 . . . 4G 47
Galsworthy Rd. King T . . . 7H 117
Galsworthy Ter. N16 . . . 3E 50
Galton St. W10 . . . 3G 65
Galva Clo. Barn . . . 4K 5
Galvani Way. Croy . . . 1K 151
Galveston Ho. E1 . . . 4A 70 (off Harford St.)
Galveston Rd. SW15 . . . 5H 101
Galway Clo. SE16 . . . 5H 87 (off Masters Dri.)
Galway Ho. E1 . . . 5K 69 (off White Horse La.)
Galway Ho. EC1 . . . 2D 162
Galway St. EC1 . . . 3C 68 (2D 162)
Galy. NW9 . . . 2B 28
Gambetta St. SW8 . . . 2F 103
Gambia St. SE1 . . . 1B 86 (5B 168)
Gambier Ho. EC1 . . . 3C 68 (2D 162) (off Mora St.)
Gambole Rd. SW17 . . . 4C 120
Games Rd. Barn . . . 3J 5
Gamlen Rd. SW15 . . . 4F 101
Gamuel Clo. E17 . . . 6C 34
Gander Grn. Cres. Hamp . . . 1E 132
Gander Grn. La. Sutt . . . 2G 149
Gandhi Clo. E17 . . . 6C 34
Gandolfi St. SE15 . . . 6E 86
Ganton St. W1 . . . 7G 67 (2A 166)
Gants Hill. . . . 6E 36
Gants Hill. (Junct.) . . . 5E 36
Gantshill Cres. Ilf . . . 5E 36
Gants Hill Cross. Ilf . . . 6E 36
Gap Rd. SW19 . . . 5J 119
Garage Rd. W3 . . . 6G 63
Garbett Ho. SE17 . . . 6B 86 (off Doddington Gro.)
Garbutt Pl. W1 . . . 5E 66 (5H 159)
Garden Av. Bexh . . . 3G 111
Garden Av. Mitc . . . 7F 121
Garden City. Edgw . . . 6B 12
Garden Clo. E4 . . . 5H 19
Garden Clo. SE12 . . . 3K 125
Garden Clo. SW15 . . . 7E 100
Garden Clo. Ashf . . . 6E 112
Garden Clo. Hamp . . . 5D 114
Garden Clo. N'holt . . . 1C 60
Garden Clo. Ruis . . . 2G 41
Garden Clo. Wall . . . 5J 151
Garden Ct. EC4 . . . 2J 167
Garden Ct. W4 . . . 3J 81
Garden Ct. Croy . . . 2F 153
Garden Ct. Hamp . . . 5D 114
Garden Ct. Rich . . . 1F 99
Garden Ct. Stan . . . 5H 11
Gardener Gro. Felt . . . 2D 114
Gardeners Clo. N11 . . . 2K 15
Gardeners Rd. Croy . . . 1B 152
Garden Ho. N2 . . . 2B 30 (off Grange, The)
Gardenia Rd. Enf . . . 6K 7
Gardenia Way. Wfd G . . . 6D 20
Garden La. SW2 . . . 1K 121
Garden La. Brom . . . 6K 125
Garden M. W2 . . . 7J 65
Garden Pl. E8 . . . 1F 69
Garden Rd. NW8 . . . 3A 66 (1A 158)
Garden Rd. SE20 . . . 1J 141
Garden Rd. Brom . . . 7K 125
Garden Rd. Rich . . . 3G 99
Garden Rd. W on T . . . 6K 131
Garden Row. SE1 . . . 3B 86
Gardens, The. N8 . . . 4J 31 (in two parts)
Gardens, The. SE22 . . . 4G 105
Gardens, The. Beck . . . 1E 142
Gardens, The. Felt . . . 5F 95
Gardens, The. Harr . . . 6G 25
Gardens, The. Pinn . . . 6D 24
Gardens, The. Uxb . . . 2A 40
Garden St. E1 . . . 5K 69
Garden Ter. SW1 . . . 5H 85 (5C 172)
Garden Ter. SW7 . . . 7D 164
Garden Vw. E7 . . . 4A 54
Garden Wlk. EC2 . . . 3E 68 (2G 163)
Garden Wlk. Beck . . . 1B 142
Garden Way. NW10 . . . 6J 45
Gardiner Av. NW2 . . . 5E 46
Gardiner Clo. Enf . . . 6E 8
Gardiner Ct. NW10 . . . 1K 63
Gardiner Ct. S Croy . . . 6C 152
Gardiners Clo. Dag . . . 4D 56
Gardner Clo. E11 . . . 6K 35
Gardner Ho. Felt . . . 2D 114
Gardner Ho. S'hall . . . 7B 60 (off Broadway, The)
Gardner Ind. Est. SE26 . . . 5B 124
Gardner Rd. E13 . . . 4K 71
Gardners La. EC4 . . . 7C 68 (2C 168)
Gardnor Rd. NW3 . . . 4B 48
Gard St. EC1 . . . 3B 68 (1B 162)
Garendon Gdns. Mord . . . 7K 137
Garendon Rd. Mord . . . 7K 137
Garenne Ct. E4 . . . 1K 19
Gareth Clo. Wor Pk . . . 2F 149
Gareth Ct. SW16 . . . 3H 121
Gareth Gro. Brom . . . 4J 125
Garfield. Enf . . . 5J 7 (off Private Rd.)
Garfield Ct. NW6 . . . 7F 47 (off Willesden La.)
Garfield M. SW11 . . . 3E 102
Garfield Rd. E4 . . . 1A 20
Garfield Rd. E13 . . . 4H 71
Garfield Rd. SW11 . . . 3E 102
Garfield Rd. SW19 . . . 5A 120
Garfield Rd. Enf . . . 4D 8
Garfield Rd. Twic . . . 1A 116
Garford St. E14 . . . 7C 70
Garganey Ct. NW10 . . . 6K 45 (off Elgar Av.)
Garganey Wlk. SE28 . . . 7C 74
Garibaldi St. SE18 . . . 4J 91
Garland Ct. E14 . . . 7C 70 (off Premiere Pl.)
Garland Rd. SE18 . . . 7H 91
Garland Rd. Stan . . . 1E 26
Garlands Ct. Croy . . . 4D 152 (off Chatsworth Rd.)
Garlick Hill. EC4 . . . 7C 68 (2D 168)
Garlies Rd. SE23 . . . 3A 124
Garlinge Rd. NW2 . . . 6H 47
Garman Clo. N18 . . . 5J 17
Garman Rd. N17 . . . 7D 18
Garnault M. EC1 . . . 2K 161
Garnault Pl. EC1 . . . 3A 68 (2K 161)
Garnault Rd. Enf . . . 1A 8
Garner Clo. Dag . . . 1D 56
Garner Rd. E17 . . . 1E 34
Garner St. E2 . . . 2G 69
Garnet Ho. E1 . . . 1J 87 (off Garnet St.)
Garnet Rd. NW10 . . . 6A 46
Garnet Rd. T Hth . . . 4C 140
Garnet St. E1 . . . 7J 69
Garnett Clo. SE9 . . . 3D 108
Garnett Rd. NW3 . . . 5D 48
Garnett Way. E17 . . . 1A 34 (off Swansland Gdns.)
Garnet Wlk. E6 . . . 5C 72
Garnham Clo. N16 . . . 2F 51
Garnham St. N16 . . . 2F 51
Garnies Clo. SE15 . . . 7F 87
Garrad's Rd. SW16 . . . 3H 121
Garrard Clo. Bexh . . . 3G 111
Garrard Clo. Chst . . . 5F 127
Garrard Wlk. NW10 . . . 6A 46
Garratt Clo. Croy . . . 4J 151
Garratt Ct. SW18 . . . 7K 101
Garratt La. SW18 & SW17 . . . 6K 101
Garratt Rd. Edgw . . . 7B 12
Garratts Rd. Bush . . . 1B 10
Garratt Ter. SW17 . . . 4C 120
Garraway Ct. SW13 . . . 7E 82 (off Wyatt Dri.)
Garrett Clo. W3 . . . 5K 63
Garrett Ho. W12 . . . 6D 64 (off Du Cane Rd.)
Garrett St. EC1 . . . 4C 68 (3D 162)
Garrick Av. NW11 . . . 6G 29
Garrick Clo. SW18 . . . 4A 102
Garrick Clo. W5 . . . 4E 62
Garrick Clo. Rich . . . 5D 98
Garrick Cres. Croy . . . 2E 152
Garrick Dri. NW4 . . . 2E 28
Garrick Dri. SE28 . . . 3H 91
Garrick Gdns. W Mol . . . 3E 132
Garrick Ho. W1 . . . 1F 85 (5J 165)
Garrick Ho. W4 . . . 6A 82
Garrick Ho. King T . . . 4E 134 (off Surbiton Rd.)
Garrick Ind. Est. NW9 . . . 5B 28
Garrick Pk. NW4 . . . 2F 29
Garrick Rd. NW9 . . . 6B 28
Garrick Rd. Gnfd . . . 4F 61
Garrick Rd. Rich . . . 2G 99
Garricks Ho. King T . . . 2D 134 (off Wadbrook St.)
Garrick St. WC2 . . . 7J 67 (2E 166)
Garrick Theatre. . . . 7H 67 (3E 166) (off Charing Cross Rd.)
Garrick Way. NW4 . . . 4F 29
Garrick Yd. WC2 . . . 2E 166
Garrison Clo. SE18 . . . 7E 90
Garrison Clo. Houn . . . 5D 96
Garrison La. Chess . . . 7D 146
Garrowsfield. Barn . . . 6C 4
Garry Way. Romf . . . 1K 39
Garsdale Clo. N11 . . . 6K 15
Garsdale Ter. W14 . . . 5H 83 (off Aisgill Av.)
Garside Clo. SE28 . . . 3H 91
Garside Clo. Hamp . . . 6F 115
Garsington M. SE4 . . . 3B 106
Garson Ho. W2 . . . 7B 66 (2A 164) (off Gloucester Ter.)
Garston Ho. N1 . . . 7B 50 (off Sutton Est., The)
Garter Way. SE16 . . . 2K 87
Garth Clo. W4 . . . 5K 81
Garth Clo. King T . . . 5F 117
Garth Clo. Mord . . . 7F 137
Garth Clo. Ruis . . . 1B 42
Garth Ct. W4 . . . 5K 81
Garth Ct. Harr . . . 6K 25 (off Northwick Pk. Rd.)
Garth M. W5 . . . 4E 62
Garthorne Rd. SE23 . . . 7K 105
Garth Rd. NW2 . . . 2H 47
Garth Rd. W4 . . . 5K 81
Garth Rd. King T . . . 5F 117
Garth Rd. Mord . . . 6E 136
Garth Rd. Ind. Est. Mord . . . 1F 149
Garthside. Ham . . . 5E 116
Garth, The. Hamp . . . 6F 115
Garth, The. Harr . . . 6F 27
Garthway. N12 . . . 6H 15
Gartmoor Gdns. SW19 . . . 1H 119
Gartmore Rd. Ilf . . . 2K 55
Garton Pl. SW18 . . . 6A 102
Gartons Clo. Enf . . . 4D 8
Gartons Way. SW11 . . . 3A 102
Garvary Rd. E16 . . . 6K 71
Garway Rd. W2 . . . 6K 65
Garwood Clo. N17 . . . 1H 33
Gascoigne Gdns. Wfd G . . . 7B 20
Gascoigne Pl. E2 . . . 3F 69 (1J 163) (in two parts)
Gascoigne Rd. Bark . . . 1G 73
Gascoigne Rd. New Ad . . . 7F 155

Gascony Av. NW6 7J 47
Gascoyne Ho. E9 7A 52
Gascoyne Rd. E9 7K 51
Gaselee St. E14 1E 88 (off Baffin Way)
Gaskarth Rd. SW12 6F 103
Gaskarth Rd. Edgw 1J 27
Gaskell Rd. N6 6D 30
Gaskell St. SW4 2J 103
Gaskin St. N1 1B 68
Gaspar Clo. SW5 4K 83 (off Courtfield Gdns.)
Gaspar M. SW5 4K 83
Gassiot Rd. SW17 4D 120
Gassiot Way. Sutt 3B 150
Gasson Ho. SE14 6K 87 (off John Williams Clo.)
Gastein Rd. W6 6F 83
Gastigny Ho. EC1 2D 162
Gaston Bell Clo. Rich 3F 99
Gaston Bri. Rd. Shep 6F 131
Gaston Rd. Mitc 3E 138
Gaston Way. Shep 5F 131
Gataker Ho. SE16 3H 87 (off Slippers Pl.)
Gataker St. SE16 3H 87
Gatcombe Ct. Beck 7C 124
Gatcombe Ho. SE22 3E 104
Gatcombe M. W5 7F 63
Gatcombe Rd. E16 1J 89
Gatcombe Rd. N19 3H 49
Gatcombe Way. Barn 3J 5
Gateacre Ct. Sidc 4B 128
Gate Cen., The. Bren 7A 80
Gateforth St. NW8 4C 66 (4C 158)
Gate Hill Ct. W11 1H 83 (off Ladbroke Ter.)
Gatehouse Clo. King T 7J 117
Gatehouse Sq. SE1 4D 168
Gateley Ho. SE4 4K 105 (off Coston Wlk.)
Gateley Rd. SW9 3K 103
Gate Lodge. W9 5J 65 (off Admiral Wlk.)
Gate M. SW7 7D 164
Gater Dri. Enf 1J 7
Gates. NW9 2B 28
Gatesborough St. EC2 4E 68 (3G 163)
Gates Ct. SE17 5C 86
Gatesden. WC1 3J 67 (2G 161)
Gates Grn. Rd. W Wick & Kes 3H 155
Gateside Rd. SW17 3D 120
Gatestone Rd. SE19 6E 122
Gate St. WC2 6K 67 (7G 161)
Gate Theatre, The. 1J 83 (off Pembridge Rd.)
Gateway. SE17 6C 86
Gateway Arc. N1 2B 68 (off Upper St.)
Gateway Ho. Bark 1G 73
Gateway Ind. Est. NW10 3B 64
Gateway M. E8 5F 51
Gateway Retail Pk. E6 4F 73
Gateway Rd. E10 3D 52
Gateways. Surb 5E 134 (off Surbiton Hill Rd.)
Gateways Ct. Wall 5F 151
Gateways, The. SW3 4D 170
Gateways, The. Rich 4D 98 (off Park La.)
Gatfield Gro. Felt 2E 114
Gatfield Ho. Felt 2D 114
Gathorne Rd. N22 2A 32
Gathorne St. E2 2K 69
Gatley Av. Eps 5H 147
Gatliff Clo. SW1 6J 171
Gatliff Rd. SW1 5F 85 (6J 171) (in two parts)
Gatling Rd. SE2 5A 92
Gatonby St. SE15 1F 105
Gatting Clo. Edgw 7D 12
Gatting Way. Uxb 6A 40
Gattis Wharf. N1 2J 67 (off New Wharf Rd.)
Gatton Rd. SW17 4C 120
Gattons Way. Sidc 4F 129
Gatward Clo. N21 6G 7
Gatward Grn. N9 2A 18
Gatwick Ho. E14 6B 70 (off Clemence St.)
Gatwick Rd. SW18 7H 101
Gauden Clo. SW4 3H 103
Gauden Rd. SW4 2H 103
Gaugin Ct. SE16 5H 87 (off Stubbs Dri.)
Gaumont Ter. W12 2E 82 (off Lime Gro.)
Gauntlet. NW9 2B 28 (off Five Acre)
Gauntlet Clo. N'holt 7C 42
Gauntlett Ct. Wemb 5B 44
Gauntlett Rd. Sutt 5B 150
Gaunt St. SE1 3C 86
Gautrey Rd. SE15 2J 105
Gautrey Sq. E6 6D 72
Gavel St. SE17 4D 86
Gavestone Cres. SE12 7K 107
Gavestone Rd. SE12 7K 107
Gaviller Pl. E5 4H 51
Gavina Clo. Mord 5C 138
Gawber St. E2 3J 69
Gawsworth Clo. E15 5H 53
Gawthorne Av. NW7 5B 14
Gay Clo. NW2 5D 46
Gaydon Ho. W2 5K 65 (off Bourne Ter.)
Gaydon La. NW9 1A 28
Gayfere Rd. Eps 5C 148
Gayfere Rd. Ilf 3D 36
Gayfere St. SW1 3J 85 (2E 172)
Gayford Rd. W12 2B 82
Gay Gdns. Dag 4J 57
Gay Ho. N16 5E 50
Gayhurst. SE17 6D 86 (off Hopwood Rd.)
Gayhurst Ct. N'holt 3A 60
Gayhurst Ho. NW8 4C 66 (3C 158) (off Mallory St.)
Gayhurst Rd. E8 7G 51
Gaylor Rd. N'holt 5D 42
Gaymead. NW8 1K 65 (off Abbey Rd.)
Gaynesford Rd. SE23 2K 123
Gaynesford Rd. Cars 7D 150
Gaynes Hill Rd. Wfd G 6H 21
Gay Rd. E15 2F 71
Gaysham Av. Ilf 5E 36
Gaysham Hall. Ilf 3F 37
Gaysley Ho. SE11 4J 173
Gay St. SW15 3F 101
Gayton Ct. Harr 6K 25
Gayton Cres. NW3 4B 48
Gayton Rd. NW3 4B 48
Gayton Rd. SE2 3C 92
Gayton Rd. Harr 6K 25
Gayville Rd. SW11 6D 102
Gaywood Clo. SW2 1K 121
Gaywood Rd. E17 3C 34
Gaywood St. SE1 3B 86
Gaza St. SE17 5B 86
Gaze Ho. E14 6F 71 (off Blair St.)
Geariesville Gdns. Ilf 4F 37
Geary Rd. NW10 5C 46
Geary St. N7 5K 49
Geddes Pl. Bexh 4G 111 (off Arnsberga Way)
Gedeney Rd. N17 1C 32
Gedling Pl. SE1 3F 87 (7K 169)
Geere Rd. E15 1H 71
Gees Ct. W1 6E 66 (1H 165)
Gee St. EC1 4C 68 (3C 162)
Geffery's Ct. SE9 3C 126
Geffrye Ct. N1 2E 68
Geffrye Est. N1 2E 68
Geffrye Mus. 2F 69
Geffrye St. E2 2F 69 (1J 163)
Geldart Rd. SE15 7H 87
Geldeston Rd. E5 2G 51
Gellatly Rd. SE14 2J 105
Gell Clo. Uxb 3B 40
Gelsthorpe Rd. Romf 1H 39
Gemini Bus. Cen. E16 4F 71
Gemini Bus. Est. SE14 5K 87
Gemini Ct. E1 7G 69 (off Vaughan Way)
Gemini Gro. N'holt 3C 60
General Gordon Pl. SE18 4F 91
General Wolfe Rd. SE10 1F 107
Genesis Clo. Stanw 1B 112
Genesta Rd. SE18 6F 91
Geneva Clo. Shep 2G 131
Geneva Ct. NW9 5B 28
Geneva Dri. SW9 4A 104
Geneva Gdns. Romf 5E 38
Geneva Rd. King T 4E 134
Geneva Rd. T Hth 5C 140
Genever Clo. E4 5H 19
Genista Rd. N18 5C 18
Genoa Av. SW15 5E 100
Genoa Ho. E1 4K 69 (off Ernest St.)
Genoa Rd. SE20 1J 141
Genotin Rd. Enf 3J 7
Genotin Ter. Enf 4J 7
Gentlemans Row. Enf 3H 7
Gentry Gdns. E13 4J 71
Geoffrey Clo. SE5 2C 104
Geoffrey Ct. SE4 2B 106
Geoffrey Gdns. E6 2C 72
Geoffrey Ho. SE1 3D 86 (7F 169) (off Pardoner St.)
Geoffrey Jones Ct. NW10 1C 64
Geoffrey Rd. SE4 3B 106
Geographers' A-Z Shop. 5A 68 (5J 161)
George Beard Rd. SE8 4B 88
George Belt Ho. E2 3K 69 (off Smart St.)
George Comberton Wlk. E12 5E 54
George Ct. WC2 3F 167
George Cres. N10 7K 15
George Downing Est. N16 2F 51
George Eliot Ho. SW1 4G 85 (4B 172) (off Vauxhall Bri. Rd.)
George Elliston Ho. SE1 5G 87 (off Old Kent Rd.)
George Eyre Ho. NW8 2B 66 (off Cochrane St.)
George V Av. Pinn 2D 24
George V Clo. Pinn 3E 24
George V Way. Gnfd 1B 62
George Gange Way. Harr 3J 25
George Gillett Ct. EC1 3D 162
George Gro. Rd. SE20 1G 141
George Inn Yd. SE1 1D 86 (5E 168)
George La. E18 2J 35 (in two parts)
George La. SE13 6D 106
George La. Brom 1K 155
George Lansbury Ho. N22 1A 32 (off Progress Way)
George Lansbury Ho. NW10 7A 46
George Lindgren Ho. SW6 7H 83 (off Clem Attlee Ct.)
George Loveless Ho. E2 3F 69 (1K 163) (off Diss St.)
George Lowe Ct. W2 5K 65 (off Bourne Ter.)
George Mathers Rd. SE11 4B 86
George M. NW1 2B 160
George M. Enf 3J 7 (off Town, The)
George Peabody Ct. NW1 5C 66 (5C 158) (off Bell St.)
George Pl. N17 3E 32
George Potter Ho. SW11 2B 102 (off George Potter Way)
George Potter Way. SW11 2B 102
George Rd. E4 6H 19
George Rd. King T 7H 117 (in two parts)
George Rd. N Mald 4B 136
George Row. SE16 2G 87
George Sq. SW19 3J 137
George's Rd. N7 5K 49
George's Sq. SW6 6H 83 (off N. End Rd.)
George St. E16 6H 71
George St. W1 6D 66 (7E 158)
George St. W7 1J 79
George St. Bark 7G 55
George St. Croy 2C 152
George St. Houn 2D 96
George St. Rich 5D 98
George St. S'hall 4C 78
George Tingle Ho. SE1 3F 87 (off Grange Wlk.)
Georgetown Clo. SE19 5E 122
Georgette Pl. SE10 7E 88
Georgeville Gdns. Ilf 4F 37
George Walter Ct. SE16 4J 87 (off Millender Wlk.)
George Wyver Clo. SW19 7G 101
George Yd. EC3 6D 68 (1F 169)
George Yd. W1 7E 66 (2H 165)
Georgiana St. NW1 1G 67
Georgian Clo. Brom 1K 155
Georgian Clo. Stan 7F 11
Georgian Clo. Uxb 4A 40
Georgian Ct. E9 1J 69
Georgian Ct. N3 1H 29
Georgian Ct. NW4 5D 28
Georgian Ct. SW16 4J 121
Georgian Ct. Croy 1D 152 (off Cross Rd.)
Georgian Ct. New Bar 4F 5
Georgian Ct. Wemb 6G 45
Georgian Ho. E16 1J 89 (off Capulet M.)
Georgian Way. Harr 2H 43
Georgia Rd. N Mald 4J 135
Georgia Rd. T Hth 1B 140
Georgina Gdns. E2 3F 69 (1K 163)
Geraint Rd. Brom 4J 125
Geraldine Rd. SW18 5A 102
Geraldine Rd. W4 6G 81
Geraldine St. SE11 3B 86 (2K 173)
Gerald M. SW1 3H 171
Gerald Rd. E16 4H 71
Gerald Rd. SW1 4E 84 (3H 171)
Gerald Rd. Dag 2F 57
Gerard Av. Houn 7E 96
Gerard Gdns. Rain 2K 75
Gerard Rd. SW13 1B 100
Gerard Rd. Harr 6A 26
Gerards Clo. SE16 5J 87
Gerda Rd. SE9 2G 127
Germander Way. E15 3G 71
Gernon Rd. E3 2A 70
Geron Way. NW2 2D 46
Gerrard Gdns. Pinn 5J 23
Gerrard Ho. SE14 7J 87 (off Briant St.)
Gerrard Pl. W1 7H 67 (2D 166)
Gerrard Rd. N1 2B 68
Gerrards Clo. N14 5B 6
Gerrards Ct. W5 3D 80
Gerrard St. W1 7H 67 (2D 166)
Gerridge Ct. SE1 3A 86 (1K 173) (off Gerridge St.)
Gerridge St. SE1 3A 86 (1K 173)
Gerry Raffles Sq. E15 7F 53
Gertrude Rd. Belv 4G 93
Gertrude St. SW10 6A 84 (7A 170)
Gervase Clo. Wemb 3J 45
Gervase Rd. Edgw 1J 27
Gervase St. SE15 7H 87
Gervis Ct. Houn 7G 79
Ghent St. SE6 2C 124
Ghent Way. E8 6F 51
Giant Arches Rd. SE24 7C 104
Giant Tree Hill. Bus H 1C 10
Gibbfield Clo. Romf 3E 38
Gibbings Ho. SE1 2B 86 (7B 168) (off King James St.)
Gibbins Rd. E15 7E 52 (in three parts)
Gibbon Ho. NW8 4B 66 (4B 158) (off Fisherton St.)
Gibbon Rd. SE15 2J 105
Gibbon Rd. W3 7A 64
Gibbon Rd. King T 1E 134
Gibbon's Rents. SE1 5G 169
Gibbons Rd. NW10 6A 46
Gibbon Wlk. SW15 4C 100
Gibbs Av. SE19 5D 122
Gibbs Clo. SE19 6D 122
Gibbs Grn. W14 5H 83 (in two parts)
Gibbs Grn. Edgw 4D 12
Gibbs Grn. Clo. W14 5H 83
Gibbs Ho. Brom 1H 143 (off Longfield)
Gibb's Rd. N18 4D 18
Gibbs Sq. SE19 5D 122
Gibney Ter. Brom 4H 125
Gibraltar Wlk. E2 2K 163
Gibson Clo. E1 4J 69
Gibson Clo. N21 6F 7
Gibson Clo. Chess 5C 146
Gibson Clo. Iswth 3J 97
Gibson Gdns. N16 2F 51
Gibson Ho. Sutt 4J 149
Gibson M. Twic 6C 98
Gibson Rd. SE11 4K 85 (4H 173)
Gibson Rd. Dag 1C 56
Gibson Rd. Sutt 5K 149
Gibson Rd. Uxb 4B 40
Gibsons Hill. SW16 7A 122
Gibson Sq. N1 1A 68
Gibson St. SE10 5G 89
Gideon Clo. Belv 4H 93
Gideon M. W5 2D 80
Gideon Rd. SW11 3E 102
Gielgud Theatre. 7H 67 (2C 166) (off Shaftesbury Av.)
Giesbach Rd. N19 2H 49
Giffard Rd. N18 6K 17
Giffen Sq. Mkt. SE8 7C 88 (off Giffen St.)
Giffin St. SE8 7C 88
Gifford Gdns. W7 5H 61
Gifford Ho. SE10 5F 89 (off Eastney St.)
Gifford Ho. SW1 5G 85 (6A 172) (off Churchill Gdns.)
Gifford St. N1 7J 49
Gift La. E15 1H 71
Giggshill. 7A 134
Giggs Hill. Orp 2K 145
Giggshill Gdns. Th Dit 1A 146
Giggshill Rd. Th Dit 7A 134
Gilbert Bri. EC2 5C 68 (5D 162) (off Gilbert Ho.)
Gilbert Clo. SE18 1D 108

Gilbert Clo. SW19 . . . 7K 119
(off High Path)
Gilbert Collection. . . . 7K 67 (2G 167)
(off Lancaster Pl.)
Gilbert Ct. W5 . . . 6F 63
(off Green Va.)
Gilbert Gro. Edgw . . . 1K 27
Gilbert Ho. E2 . . . 3K 69
(off Usk St.)
Gilbert Ho. E17 . . . 3D 34
Gilbert Ho. EC2 . . . 5D 162
Gilbert Ho. SE8 . . . 6C 88
Gilbert Ho. SW1 . . . 5F 85 (6K 171)
(off Churchill Gdns.)
Gilbert Ho. SW8 . . . 7J 85
(off Wyvil Rd.)
Gilbert Ho. SW13 . . . 7D 82
(off Trinity Chu. Rd.)
Gilbert Pl. WC1 . . . 5J 67 (6E 160)
Gilbert Rd. SE11 . . . 4A 86 (4K 173)
Gilbert Rd. SW19 . . . 7A 120
Gilbert Rd. Belv . . . 3G 93
Gilbert Rd. Brom . . . 7J 125
Gilbert Rd. Hare . . . 2A 22
Gilbert Rd. Pinn . . . 4B 24
Gilbert Sheldon Ho. W2 . . . 5B 66 (5B 158)
(off Edgware Rd.)
Gilbertson Ho. E14 . . . 3C 88
(off Mellish St.)
Gilbert St. E15 . . . 4G 53
Gilbert St. W1 . . . 6E 66 (1H 165)
Gilbert St. Houn . . . 3G 97
Gilbert Way. Croy . . . 2K 151
Gilbey Clo. Uxb . . . 4D 40
Gilbey Rd. SW17 . . . 4C 120
Gilbeys Yd. NW1 . . . 7E 48
Gilbourne Rd. SE18 . . . 6K 91
Gilda Av. Enf . . . 5F 9
Gilda Ct. NW7 . . . 1C 28
Gilda Cres. N16 . . . 1G 51
Gildea Clo. Pinn . . . 1E 24
Gildea St. W1 . . . 5F 67 (6K 159)
Gilden Cres. NW5 . . . 5E 48
Gildersome St. SE18 . . . 6E 90
Gilders Rd. Chess . . . 7F 147
Giles Coppice. SE19 . . . 4F 123
Giles Ho. SE16 . . . 7K 169
Gilesmead. SE5 . . . 1D 104
Gilfrid Clo. Uxb . . . 6D 58
Gilkes Cres. SE21 . . . 6E 104
Gilkes Pl. SE21 . . . 6E 104
Gillam Ho. SE16 . . . 4J 87
(off Silwood St.)
Gillan Ct. SE12 . . . 3K 125
Gillan Grn. Bus H . . . 2B 10
Gillards M. E17 . . . 4C 34
Gillards Way. E17 . . . 4C 34
Gill Av. E16 . . . 6J 71
Gillender St. E3 & E14 . . . 4E 70
Gillespie Rd. N5 . . . 3A 50
Gillett Av. E6 . . . 2C 72
Gillette Corner. (Junct.) . . . 7A 80
Gillett Ho. N8 . . . 3J 31
(off Campsfield Rd.)
Gillett Pl. N16 . . . 5E 50
Gillett Rd. T Hth . . . 4D 140
Gillett St. N16 . . . 5E 50
Gillfoot. NW1 . . . 2G 67 (1A 160)
(off Hampstead Rd.)
Gillham Ter. N17 . . . 6B 18
Gillian Ho. Har W . . . 6D 10
Gillian Pk. Rd. Sutt . . . 1H 149
Gillian St. SE13 . . . 5D 106
Gillies St. NW5 . . . 5E 48
Gilling Ct. NW3 . . . 6C 48
Gillingham M. SW1 . . . 4G 85 (3A 172)
Gillingham Rd. NW2 . . . 3G 47
Gillingham Row. SW1 . . . 4G 85 (3A 172)
Gillingham St. SW1 . . . 4G 85 (3A 172)
Gillings Ct. Barn . . . 4B 4
(off Wood St.)
Gillison Wlk. SE16 . . . 3H 87
Gillman Dri. E15 . . . 1H 71
Gillman Ho. E2 . . . 2G 69
(off Pritchard's Rd.)
Gill St. E14 . . . 6B 70
Gillum Clo. E Barn . . . 1J 15
Gilmore Clo. Uxb . . . 3C 40
Gilmore Ct. N11 . . . 5J 15
Gilmore Cres. Ashf . . . 5C 112
Gilmore Rd. SE13 . . . 4F 107
Gilpin Av. SW14 . . . 4K 99
Gilpin Clo. Mitc . . . 2C 138
Gilpin Cres. N18 . . . 5A 18
Gilpin Cres. Twic . . . 7F 97
Gilpin Rd. E5 . . . 4A 52
Gilpin Way. Hay . . . 7F 77
Gilray Ho. W2 . . . 7B 66 (2A 164)
(off Gloucester Ter.)
Gilsland Rd. T Hth . . . 4D 140
Gilstead Ho. Bark . . . 2B 74
Gilstead Rd. SW6 . . . 2K 101
Gilston Rd. SW10 . . . 5A 84 (7A 170)
Gilton Rd. SE6 . . . 3G 125
Giltspur St. EC1 . . . 6B 68 (7B 162)
Gilwell Clo. E4 . . . 4J 9
Gilwell La. E4 . . . 4J 9
(in two parts)
Gilwell Park. . . . 4K 9
Gilwell Pk. E4 . . . 3K 9
Ginsburg Yd. NW3 . . . 4A 48
Gippeswyck Clo. Pinn . . . 1B 24
Gipsy Hill. SE19 . . . 4E 122
Gipsy La. SW15 . . . 3D 100
Gipsy Rd. SE27 . . . 4C 122
Gipsy Rd. Well . . . 7D 92
Gipsy Rd. Gdns. SE27 . . . 4C 122
Giralda Clo. E16 . . . 5B 72
Giraud St. E14 . . . 6D 70
Girdler's Rd. W14 . . . 4F 83
Girdlestone Wlk. N19 . . . 2G 49
Girdwood Rd. SW18 . . . 7G 101
Girling Ho. N1 . . . 1E 68
(off Colville Est.)
Girling Way. Felt . . . 3J 95
Gironde Rd. SW6 . . . 7H 83
Girtin Ho. N'holt . . . 2B 60
(off Academy Gdns.)
Girton Av. NW9 . . . 3G 27
Girton Clo. N'holt . . . 6G 43
Girton Gdns. Croy . . . 3C 154
Girton Rd. SE26 . . . 5K 123
Girton Rd. N'holt . . . 6G 43
Girton Vs. W10 . . . 6F 65
Gisbourne Clo. Wall . . . 3H 151
Gisburn Ho. SE15 . . . 6G 87
(off Friary Est.)
Gisburn Rd. N8 . . . 4K 31
Gissing Wlk. N1 . . . 7A 50
Gittens Clo. Brom . . . 4H 125
Given Wilson Wlk. E13 . . . 2H 71
Glacier Way. Wemb . . . 2D 62
Gladbeck Way. Enf . . . 4G 7
Gladding Rd. E12 . . . 4B 54
Glade Clo. Surb . . . 2D 146
Glade Ct. Ilf . . . 1D 36
Glade Gdns. Croy . . . 7A 142
Glade La. S'hall . . . 2F 79
Glade Rd. E12 . . . 3D 54
Gladeside. N21 . . . 6E 6
Gladeside. Croy . . . 6K 141
Gladeside Clo. Chess . . . 7D 146
Gladesmore Rd. N15 . . . 6F 33
Glades Pl. Brom . . . 2J 143
Glades Shop. Cen., The. Brom . . . 2J 143
Gladeswood Rd. Belv . . . 4H 93
Glade, The. N20 . . . 3G 15
Glade, The. N21 . . . 6E 6
Glade, The. SE7 . . . 7A 90
Glade, The. Brom . . . 2B 144
Glade, The. Croy . . . 6A 142
Glade, The. Enf . . . 3F 7
Glade, The. Eps . . . 6C 148
Glade, The. Ilf . . . 1D 36
Glade, The. Sutt . . . 7G 149
Glade, The. W Wick . . . 3D 154
Glade, The. Wfd G . . . 3E 20
Gladiator St. SE23 . . . 7A 106
Glading Ter. N16 . . . 3F 51
Gladioli Clo. Hamp . . . 6E 114
Gladsdale Dri. Pinn . . . 4J 23
Gladsmuir Rd. N19 . . . 1G 49
Gladsmuir Rd. Barn . . . 2B 4
Gladstone Av. E12 . . . 7C 54
Gladstone Av. N22 . . . 2A 32
Gladstone Av. Felt . . . 6J 95
Gladstone Av. Twic . . . 1H 115
Gladstone Ct. SW1 . . . 4H 85 (4D 172)
(off Regency St.)
Gladstone Ct. Bus. Cen. SW8 . . . 1F 103
(off Pagden St.)
Gladstone Gdns. Houn . . . 1G 97
Gladstone Ho. E14 . . . 6C 70
(off E. India Dock Rd.)
Gladstone M. N22 . . . 2A 32
Gladstone M. NW6 . . . 7H 47
(off Cavendish Rd.)
Gladstone M. SE20 . . . 7J 123
Gladstone Pde. NW2 . . . 2E 46
Gladstone Pk. Gdns. NW2 . . . 3D 46
Gladstone Pl. E3 . . . 2B 70
Gladstone Pl. Barn . . . 4A 4
Gladstone Pl. E Mol . . . 5J 133
Gladstone Rd. SW19 . . . 7J 119
Gladstone Rd. W4 . . . 3K 81
Gladstone Rd. Buck H . . . 1F 21
Gladstone Rd. Croy . . . 7D 140
Gladstone Rd. King T . . . 3G 135
Gladstone Rd. S'hall . . . 2C 78
Gladstone Rd. Surb . . . 2D 146
Gladstone St. SE1 . . . 3B 86 (1K 173)
Gladstone Ter. SE27 . . . 5C 122
(off Bentons La.)
Gladstone Ter. SW8 . . . 1F 103
Gladstone Way. Harr . . . 3J 25
Gladwell Rd. N8 . . . 6K 31
Gladwell Rd. Brom . . . 6J 125
Gladwin Ho. NW1 . . . 2G 67 (1B 160)
(off Cranleigh St.)
Gladwyn Rd. SW15 . . . 3F 101
Gladys Dimson Ho. E7 . . . 5H 53
Gladys Rd. NW6 . . . 7J 47
Glaisher St. SE8 . . . 6C 88
Glamis Ct. W3 . . . 2H 81
Glamis Cres. Hay . . . 3E 76
Glamis Pl. E1 . . . 7J 69
Glamis Rd. E1 . . . 7J 69
Glamis Way. N'holt . . . 6G 43
Glamorgan Clo. Mitc . . . 3J 139
Glamorgan Ct. W7 . . . 5K 61
(off Copley Clo.)
Glamorgan Rd. King T . . . 7C 116
Glanfield Rd. Beck . . . 4B 142
Glanleam Rd. Stan . . . 4J 11
Glanville Rd. SW2 . . . 5J 103
Glanville Rd. Brom . . . 3K 143
Glasbrook Av. Twic . . . 1D 114
Glasbrook Rd. SE9 . . . 7B 108
Glaserton Rd. N16 . . . 7E 32
Glasford St. SW17 . . . 6D 120
Glasfryn Ct. Harr . . . 2H 43
(off Roxeth Hill)
Glasfryn Ho. Harr . . . 2H 43
(off Roxeth Hill)
Glasgow Ho. W9 . . . 2K 65
(off Maida Va.)
Glasgow Rd. E13 . . . 2K 71
Glasgow Rd. N18 . . . 5C 18
Glasgow Ter. SW1 . . . 5G 85 (6A 172)
Glasier Ct. E15 . . . 7G 53
Glasse Clo. W13 . . . 7A 62
Glasshill St. SE1 . . . 2B 86 (6B 168)
Glasshouse Clo. Uxb . . . 5D 58
Glasshouse Fields. E1 . . . 7K 69
Glasshouse St. W1 . . . 7G 67 (3B 166)
Glasshouse Wlk. SE11 . . . 5J 85 (5F 173)
Glasshouse Yd. EC1 . . . 4C 68 (4C 162)
Glasslyn Rd. N8 . . . 5H 31
Glassmill La. Brom . . . 2H 143
(in two parts)
Glass St. E2 . . . 4H 69
Glass Yd. SE18 . . . 3E 90
Glastonbury Av. Wfd G . . . 7G 21
Glastonbury Ct. SE14 . . . 7J 87
(off Farrow La.)
Glastonbury Ct. W13 . . . 1A 80
(off Talbot Rd.)
Glastonbury Ho. SE12 . . . 5H 107
(off Wantage Rd.)
Glastonbury Ho. SW1 . . . 5F 85 (5J 171)
(off Abbots Mnr.)
Glastonbury Pl. E1 . . . 6J 69
Glastonbury Rd. N9 . . . 1B 18
Glastonbury Rd. Mord . . . 7J 137
Glastonbury St. NW6 . . . 5H 47
Glaston Ct. W5 . . . 1D 80
(off Grange Rd.)
Glaucus St. E3 . . . 5D 70
Glazbury Rd. W14 . . . 4G 83
Glazebrook Clo. SE21 . . . 2D 122
Glazebrook Rd. Tedd . . . 7K 115
Glebe Av. Enf . . . 3G 7
Glebe Av. Harr . . . 4E 26
Glebe Av. Mitc . . . 2C 138
Glebe Av. Ruis . . . 6K 41
Glebe Av. Uxb . . . 3E 40
Glebe Av. Wfd G . . . 6D 20
Glebe Clo. W4 . . . 5A 82
Glebe Clo. Uxb . . . 4E 40
Glebe Cotts. Felt . . . 3E 114
Glebe Ct. N13 . . . 3F 17
Glebe Ct. SE3 . . . 3G 107
(off Glebe, The)
Glebe Ct. W5 . . . 1D 80
Glebe Ct. W7 . . . 7H 61
Glebe Ct. Mitc . . . 3D 138
Glebe Ct. Stan . . . 5H 11
Glebe Cres. NW4 . . . 4E 28
Glebe Cres. Harr . . . 3E 26
Glebe Gdns. N Mald . . . 7A 136
Glebe Ho. SE16 . . . 3H 87
(off Slippers Pl.)
Glebe Ho. Dri. Brom . . . 1K 155
Glebe Hyrst. SE19 . . . 4E 122
Glebeland Gdns. Shep . . . 6E 130
Glebelands. E10 . . . 2D 52
Glebelands. W Mol . . . 5F 133
Glebelands Av. E18 . . . 2J 35
Glebelands Av. Ilf . . . 7H 37
Glebelands Clo. SE5 . . . 3E 104
Glebelands Rd. Felt . . . 1J 113
Glebe La. Harr . . . 4E 26
Glebe Path. Mitc . . . 3D 138
Glebe Pl. SW3 . . . 6C 84 (7C 170)
Glebe Rd. E8 . . . 7F 51
Glebe Rd. N3 . . . 1A 30
Glebe Rd. N8 . . . 4K 31
Glebe Rd. NW10 . . . 6C 46
Glebe Rd. SW13 . . . 2C 100
Glebe Rd. Brom . . . 1J 143
Glebe Rd. Cars . . . 6D 150
Glebe Rd. Dag . . . 6H 57
Glebe Rd. Hay . . . 1H 77
Glebe Rd. Stan . . . 5H 11
Glebe Rd. Sutt . . . 7G 149
Glebe Side. Twic . . . 6K 97
Glebe Sq. Mitc . . . 3D 138
Glebe St. W4 . . . 5A 82
Glebe Ter. E3 . . . 3D 70
Glebe Ter. W4 . . . 5A 82
Glebe, The. SE3 . . . 3G 107
Glebe, The. SW16 . . . 4H 121
Glebe, The. Chst . . . 1G 145
Glebe, The. W Dray . . . 4B 76
Glebe, The. Wor Pk . . . 1B 148
Glebe Way. Hanw . . . 3E 114
Glebe Way. W Wick . . . 2E 154
Glebe Way. Wfd G . . . 5F 21
Gledhow Gdns. SW5 . . . 4A 84
Gledstanes Rd. W14 . . . 5G 83
Gledwood Av. Hay . . . 5H 59
Gledwood Cres. Hay . . . 5H 59
Gledwood Dri. Hay . . . 5H 59
Gledwood Gdns. Hay . . . 5H 59
Gleed Av. Bus H . . . 2C 10
Glegg Pl. SW15 . . . 4F 101
Glenaffric Av. E14 . . . 4E 88
Glen Albyn Rd. SW19 . . . 2F 119
Glenallan Ho. W14 . . . 4H 83
(off N. End Cres.)
Glenalla Rd. Ruis . . . 7H 23
Glenalmond Rd. Harr . . . 4E 26
Glenalvon Way. SE18 . . . 4C 90
Glena Mt. Sutt . . . 4A 150
Glenarm Rd. E5 . . . 4J 51
Glen Av. Ashf . . . 4C 112
Glenavon Clo. Clay . . . 6A 146
Glenavon Ct. Wor Pk . . . 2D 148
Glenavon Lodge. Beck . . . 7C 124
Glenavon Rd. E15 . . . 7G 53
Glenbarr Clo. SE9 . . . 3F 109
Glenbow Rd. Brom . . . 6G 125
Glenbrook N. Enf . . . 4E 6
Glenbrook Rd. NW6 . . . 5J 47
Glenbrook S. Enf . . . 4E 6
Glenbuck Rd. Surb . . . 6D 134
Glenburnie Rd. SW17 . . . 3D 120
Glencairn Dri. W5 . . . 4C 62
Glencairne Clo. E16 . . . 5B 72
Glencairn Rd. SW16 . . . 1J 139
Glen Clo. Shep . . . 4C 130
Glencoe Av. Ilf . . . 7H 37
Glencoe Dri. Dag . . . 4G 57
Glencoe Mans. SW9 . . . 7A 86
(off Mowll St.)
Glencoe Rd. Hay . . . 5B 60
Glen Ct. Sidc . . . 4A 128
Glen Cres. Wfd G . . . 6E 20
Glendale Av. N22 . . . 7F 17
Glendale Av. Edgw . . . 4A 12
Glendale Av. Romf . . . 7C 38
Glendale Clo. SE9 . . . 3E 108
Glendale Dri. SW19 . . . 5H 119
Glendale Gdns. Wemb . . . 1D 44
Glendale M. Beck . . . 1D 142
Glendale Rd. Eri . . . 4J 93
Glendale Way. SE28 . . . 7C 74
Glendall St. SW9 . . . 4K 103
Glendarvon St. SW15 . . . 3F 101
Glendevon Clo. Edgw . . . 3C 12
Glendish Rd. N17 . . . 1H 33
Glendor Gdns. NW7 . . . 4E 12
Glendower Gdns. SW14 . . . 3K 99
Glendower Pl. SW7 . . . 4B 84 (3A 170)
Glendower Rd. E4 . . . 1A 20
Glendower Rd. SW14 . . . 3K 99
Glendown Ho. E8 . . . 5G 51
Glendown Rd. SE2 . . . 5A 92
Glendun Ct. W3 . . . 7A 64
Glendun Rd. W3 . . . 7A 64
Gleneagle M. SW16 . . . 5H 121
Gleneagle Rd. SW16 . . . 5H 121
Gleneagles. W13 . . . 5B 62
(off Malvern Way)
Gleneagles. Stan . . . 7G 11
Gleneagles Clo. SE16 . . . 5H 87
Gleneagles Clo. Orp . . . 7H 145
Gleneagles Grn. Orp . . . 7H 145
Gleneagles Tower. S'hall . . . 6G 61
(off Fleming Rd.)

Gleneldon M. SW16 4J 121
Gleneldon Rd. SW16 4J 121
Glenelg Rd. SW2 5J 103
Glenesk Rd. SE9 3E 108
Glenfarg Rd. SE6 1E 124
Glenfield Cres. Ruis 7F 23
Glenfield Rd. SW12 1G 121
Glenfield Rd. W13 2B 80
Glenfield Rd. Ashf 6D 112
Glenfield Ter. W13 2B 80
Glenfinlas Way. SE5 7B 86
Glenforth St. SE10 5H 89
Glengall Causeway. E14 3C 88
Glengall Gro. E14 3D 88
Glengall Pas. NW6 1J 65 (off Priory Pk. Rd., in two parts)
Glengall Rd. NW6 1H 65
Glengall Rd. SE15 5F 87
Glengall Rd. Bexh 3E 110
Glengall Rd. Edgw 3C 12
Glengall Rd. Wfd G 6D 20
Glengall Ter. SE15 6F 87
Glen Gdns. Croy 3A 152
Glengarnock Av. E14 4E 88
Glengarry Rd. SE22 5E 104
Glenham Dri. Ilf 5F 37
Glenhead Clo. SE9 3F 109
Glenhill Clo. N3 2J 29
Glen Ho. E16 1E 90 (off Storey St.)
Glenhouse Rd. SE9 5E 108
Glenhurst. Beck 1E 142
Glenhurst Av. NW5 4E 48
Glenhurst Av. Bex 1F 129
Glenhurst Av. Ruis 7E 22
Glenhurst Ri. SE19 7C 122
Glenhurst Rd. N12 5G 15
Glenhurst Rd. Bren 6C 80
Glenilla Rd. NW3 6C 48
Glenister Pk. Rd. SW16 7H 121
Glenister Rd. SE10 5H 89
Glenister St. E16 1E 90
Glenkerry Ho. E14 6E 70 (off Burcham St.)
Glenlea Rd. SE9 5D 108
Glenloch Rd. NW3 6C 48
Glenloch Rd. Enf 2D 8
Glenluce Rd. SE3 6J 89
Glenlyon Rd. SE9 5E 108
Glenmead. Buck H 1F 21
Glenmere Av. NW7 7H 13
Glenmill. Hamp 5D 114
Glenmore Lawns. W13 6A 62
Glenmore Lodge. Beck 1D 142
Glenmore Pde. Wemb 1E 62
Glenmore Rd. NW3 6C 48
Glenmore Rd. Well 7K 91
Glenmore Way. Bark 2A 74
Glenmount Path. SE18 5G 91
Glennie Ct. SE22 1G 123
Glennie Ho. SE10 1E 106 (off Blackheath Hill)
Glennie Rd. SE27 3A 122
Glenny Rd. Bark 6G 55
Glenorchy Clo. Hay 5C 60
Glenparke Rd. E7 6K 53
Glenridding. NW1 2G 67 (1B 160) (off Ampthill Est.)
Glen Ri. Wfd G 6E 20
Glen Rd. E13 4A 72
Glen Rd. E17 5B 34
Glen Rd. Chess 4F 147
Glen Rd. End. Wall 7F 151
Glenrosa St. SW6 2A 102
Glenrose Ct. Sidc 5B 128
Glenroy St. W12 6E 64
Glensdale Rd. SE4 3B 106
Glenshaw Mans. SW9 7A 86 (off Brixton Rd.)
Glenshiel Rd. SE9 5E 108
Glentanner Way. SW17 3B 120
Glen Ter. E14 2E 88 (off Manchester Rd.)
Glentham Gdns. SW13 6D 82
Glentham Rd. SW13 6C 82
Glen, The. Brom 2G 143
Glen, The. Croy 3K 153
Glen, The. Eastc 5K 23
Glen, The. Enf 4G 7
Glen, The. Orp 3D 156
Glen, The. Pinn 7C 24
Glen, The. S'hall 5D 78
Glen, The. Wemb 4E 44
Glenthorne Av. Croy 1H 153
Glenthorne Clo. Sutt 1J 149
Glenthorne Clo. Uxb 3C 58
Glenthorne Gdns. Ilf 3E 36
Glenthorne Gdns. Sutt 1J 149
Glenthorne M. W6 4D 82
Glenthorne Rd. E17 5A 34
Glenthorne Rd. N11 5J 15
Glenthorne Rd. W6 4D 82
Glenthorne Rd. King T 4F 135
Glenthorpe Av. SW15 4C 100
Glenthorpe Rd. Mord 5F 137
Glenton Rd. SE13 4G 107
Glentworth St. NW1 4D 66 (4F 159)
Glenure Rd. SE9 5E 108
Glenview. SE2 6D 92
Glenview Rd. Brom 2B 144
Glenville Av. Enf 1H 7
Glenville Gro. SE8 7B 88
Glenville M. SW18 7K 101
Glenville Rd. King T 1G 135
Glen Wlk. Iswth 5H 97
Glenwood Av. NW9 1A 46
Glenwood Clo. Harr 5K 25
Glenwood Ct. E18 3J 35
Glenwood Ct. Sidc 4A 128
Glenwood Gdns. Ilf 5E 36
Glenwood Gro. NW9 1J 45
Glenwood Rd. N15 5B 32
Glenwood Rd. NW7 3F 13
Glenwood Rd. SE6 1B 124
Glenwood Rd. Eps 6C 148
Glenwood Rd. Houn 3H 97
Glenwood Way. Croy 6K 141
Glenworth Av. E14 4F 89
Gliddon Rd. W14 4G 83
Glimpsing Grn. Eri 3E 92
Glisson Rd. Uxb 2C 58
Global App. E3 2D 70
Globe Pond Rd. SE16 1A 88
Globe Rd. E2 & E1 3J 69 (in two parts)
Globe Rd. E15 5H 53
Globe Rd. Wfd G 6F 21
Globe Rope Wlk. E14 4D 88 (off E. Ferry Rd.)
Globe St. SE1 3D 86 (7E 168)
Globe Ter. E2 3J 69
Globe Town. 3K 69
Globe Town Mkt. E2 3K 69
Globe Wharf. SE16 7K 69
Globe Yd. W1 1J 165
Glossop Rd. S Croy 7D 152
Gloster Rd. N Mald 4A 136
Gloucester Arc. SW7 4A 84
Gloucester Av. NW1 7E 48
Gloucester Av. Sidc 2J 127
Gloucester Av. Well 4K 109
Gloucester Cir. SE10 7E 88
Gloucester Clo. NW10 7K 45
Gloucester Clo. Th Dit 1A 146
Gloucester Ct. EC3 7E 68 (3H 169)
Gloucester Ct. NW11 7H 29 (off Golders Grn. Rd.)
Gloucester Ct. W7 5K 61 (off Copley Clo.)
Gloucester Ct. Harr 3J 25
Gloucester Ct. Mitc 5J 139
Gloucester Ct. Rich 7G 81
Gloucester Cres. NW1 1F 67
Gloucester Cres. Stai 6A 112
Gloucester Dri. N4 2B 50
Gloucester Dri. NW11 4J 29
Gloucester Gdns. NW11 7H 29
Gloucester Gdns. W2 6A 66
Gloucester Gdns. Cockf 4K 5
Gloucester Gdns. Ilf 7C 36
Gloucester Gdns. Sutt 2K 149
Gloucester Ga. NW1 2F 67 (in two parts)
Gloucester Ga. M. NW1 2F 67
Gloucester Gro. Edgw 1K 27
Gloucester Ho. E16 1J 89 (off Gatcombe Rd.)
Gloucester Ho. NW6 2J 65 (off Cambridge Rd.)
Gloucester Ho. SE5 7A 86
Gloucester Ho. Rich 5G 99
Gloucester M. E10 7C 34
Gloucester M. W2 6A 66 (1A 164)
Gloucester M. W. W2 6A 66
Gloucester Pde. Hay 3E 76
Gloucester Pde. Sidc 5A 110
Gloucester Pl. NW1 & W1 4D 66 (4E 158)
Gloucester Pl. M. W1 5D 66 (6F 159)
Gloucester Rd. E10 7C 34
Gloucester Rd. E11 5K 35
Gloucester Rd. E12 3D 54
Gloucester Rd. E17 2K 33
Gloucester Rd. N17 2D 32
Gloucester Rd. N18 5A 18
Gloucester Rd. SW7 3A 84 (4A 170)
Gloucester Rd. W3 2J 81
Gloucester Rd. W5 2C 80
Gloucester Rd. Barn 5E 4
Gloucester Rd. Belv 5F 93
Gloucester Rd. Croy 1D 152
Gloucester Rd. Enf 1H 7
Gloucester Rd. Felt 1A 114
Gloucester Rd. Hamp 7F 115
Gloucester Rd. Harr 5F 25
Gloucester Rd. Houn 4C 96
Gloucester Rd. King T 2G 135
Gloucester Rd. Rich 7G 81
Gloucester Rd. Tedd 5J 115
Gloucester Rd. Twic 1G 115
Gloucester Sq. E2 1G 69
Gloucester Sq. W2 6B 66 (1B 164)
Gloucester St. SW1 5G 85 (6A 172)
Gloucester Ter. N14 1C 16 (off Crown La.)
Gloucester Ter. W2 6K 65
Gloucester Wlk. W8 2J 83
Gloucester Way. EC1 3A 68 (2K 161)
Glover Clo. SE2 4C 92
Glover Dri. N18 6D 18
Glover Ho. NW6 7A 48 (off Harben Rd.)
Glover Ho. SE15 4H 105
Glover Rd. Pinn 6B 24
Glovers Gro. Ruis 7D 22
Gloxinia Wlk. Hamp 6E 114
Glycena Rd. SW11 3D 102
Glyn Av. Barn 4G 5
Glyn Clo. SE25 2E 140
Glyn Ct. SW16 3A 122
Glyndale Grange. Sutt 6K 149
Glyndebourne Ct. N'holt 3A 60 (off Canberra Dri.)
Glynde M. SW3 2D 170
Glynde Reach. WC1 2F 161
Glynde Rd. Bexh 3D 110
Glynde St. SE4 6B 106
Glyndon Rd. SE18 4G 91 (in two parts)
Glyn Dri. Sidc 4B 128
Glynfield Rd. NW10 7A 46
Glynne Rd. N22 2A 32
Glyn Rd. E5 3K 51
Glyn Rd. Enf 4D 8
Glyn Rd. Wor Pk 2F 149
Glyn St. SE11 5K 85 (6G 173)
Glynwood Ct. SE23 2J 123
Goater's All. SW6 7H 83 (off Dawes Rd.)
Goat Ho. Bri. SE25 3G 141
Goat La. Enf 1A 8
Goat Rd. Mitc 7E 138
Goat Wharf. Bren 6E 80
Gobions Av. Romf 1K 39
Godalming Av. Wall 5J 151
Godalming Rd. E14 5D 70
Godbold Rd. E15 4G 71
Goddard Clo. Shep 3B 130
Goddard Ct. W'stone 2A 26
Goddard Pl. N19 3G 49
Goddard Rd. Beck 4K 141
Goddards Way. Ilf 1H 55
Goddarts Ho. E17 3C 34
Godfrey Av. N'holt 1C 60
Godfrey Av. Twic 7H 97
Godfrey Hill. SE18 4C 90
Godfrey Ho. EC1 2E 162
Godfrey Rd. SE18 4D 90
Godfrey St. E15 2E 70
Godfrey St. SW3 5C 84 (5D 170)
Godfrey Way. Houn 7C 96
Goding St. SE11 5J 85 (5F 173)
Godley Rd. SW18 1B 120
Godliman St. EC4 6B 68 (1B 168)
Godman Rd. SE15 2H 105
Godolphin Clo. N13 6G 17
Godolphin Ho. NW3 7C 48 (off Fellows Rd.)
Godolphin Pl. W3 7K 63
Godolphin Rd. W12 1D 82 (in two parts)
Godric Cres. New Ad 7F 155
Godson Rd. Croy 3A 152
Godstone Ho. SE1 3D 86 (7F 169) (off Pardoner St.)
Godstone Rd. Sutt 4A 150
Godstone Rd. Twic 6B 98
Godstow Rd. SE2 2B 92
Godwin Clo. E4 1K 9
Godwin Clo. N1 2C 68
Godwin Clo. Eps 6J 147
Godwin Ct. NW1 2G 67 (off Chalton St.)
Godwin Ho. NW6 2K 65 (off Tollgate Gdns., in three parts)
Godwin Rd. E7 4K 53
Godwin Rd. Brom 3A 144
Goffers Rd. SE3 1G 107
Goffs Rd. Ashf 6F 113
Goidel Clo. Wall 4H 151
Golborne Gdns. W10 4G 65
Golborne Ho. W10 4G 65 (off Adair Rd.)
Golborne M. W10 5G 65
Golborne Rd. W10 5G 65
Golda Clo. Barn 6A 4
Golda Ct. N3 2H 29
Goldbeaters Gro. Edgw 6F 13
Goldcliff Clo. Mord 7J 137
Goldcrest Clo. E16 5B 72
Goldcrest Clo. SE28 7C 74
Goldcrest M. W5 5D 62
Goldcrest Way. Bush 1B 10
Goldcrest Way. New Ad 7F 155
Golden Ct. Barn 4H 5
Golden Ct. Rich 5D 98
Golden Cres. Hay 1H 77
Golden Cross M. W11 6H 65 (off Portobello Rd.)
Golden Hinde Educational Mus. 1D 86 (4E 168)
Golden Hind Pl. SE8 4B 88 (off Grove St.)
Golden La. EC1 4C 68 (3C 162)
Golden La. Est. EC1 4C 68 (4C 162)
Golden Mnr. W7 7J 61
Golden M. SE20 1J 141
Golden Pde. E17 3E 34 (off Wood St.)
Golden Plover Clo. E16 6J 71
Golden Sq. W1 7G 67 (2B 166)
Golden Yd. NW3 4A 48 (off Holly Mt.)
Golders Clo. Edgw 5C 12
Golders Ct. NW11 7H 29
Golders Gdns. NW11 7G 29
Golders Green. 6G 29
Golders Green Crematorium. NW11 7J 29
Golders Grn. Cres. NW11 7H 29
Golders Grn. Rd. NW11 6G 29
Golderslea. NW11 1J 47
Golders Mnr. Dri. NW11 6F 29
Golders Pk. Clo. NW11 1J 47
Golders Ri. NW4 5F 29
Golders Way. NW11 7H 29
Golderton. NW4 4D 28 (off Prince of Wales Clo.)
Goldfinch Rd. SE28 3H 91
Goldhawk Ind. Est. W6 3D 82
Goldhawk M. W12 2D 82
Goldhawk Rd. W6 & W12 4B 82
Goldhaze Clo. Wfd G 7G 21
Gold Hill. Edgw 6E 12
Goldhurst Ter. NW6 7K 47
Goldie Ho. N19 7H 31
Golding Clo. Chess 6C 146
Golding Ct. Ilf 3E 54
Golding St. E1 6G 69
Golding Ter. E1 6G 69
Golding Ter. SW11 2E 102
Goldington Ct. NW1 1H 67 (off Royal College St.)
Goldington Cres. NW1 2H 67
Goldington St. NW1 2H 67
Gold La. Edgw 6E 12
Goldman Clo. E2 4G 69 (3K 163)
Goldmark Ho. SE3 3K 107
Goldney Rd. W9 4J 65
Goldrill Dri. N11 2K 15
Goldsboro' Rd. SW8 1H 103
Goldsborough Cres. E4 2J 19
Goldsborough Ho. E14 5D 88 (off St Davids Sq.)
Goldsdown Clo. Enf 2F 9
Goldsdown Rd. Enf 2E 8
Goldsmid St. SE18 5J 91
Goldsmith Av. E12 6C 54
Goldsmith Av. NW9 5A 28
Goldsmith Av. W3 7K 63
Goldsmith Av. Romf 7G 39
Goldsmith Clo. Harr 1F 43
Goldsmith Ct. WC2 6J 67 (7F 161) (off Stukeley St.)
Goldsmith La. NW9 4H 27
Goldsmith Rd. E10 1C 52
Goldsmith Rd. E17 2K 33
Goldsmith Rd. N11 5J 15
Goldsmith Rd. SE15 1G 105
Goldsmith Rd. W3 1K 81
Goldsmith's Bldgs. W3 1K 81
Goldsmiths Clo. W3 1K 81
Goldsmith's Pl. NW6 1K 65 (off Springfield La.)
Goldsmith's Row. E2 2G 69
Goldsmith's Sq. E2 2G 69
Goldsmith St. EC2 6C 68 (7D 162)
Goldsworthy Gdns. SE16 5J 87
Goldthorpe. NW1 1G 67 (off Camden St.)
Goldwell Ho. SE22 3E 104
Goldwell Rd. T Hth 4K 139
Goldwin Clo. SE14 1J 105
Goldwing Clo. E16 6J 71

Golf Clo. Stan 7H 11
Golf Clo. T Hth 1A 140
Golf Club Dri. King T 7K 117
Golfe Rd. Ilf 3H 55
Golf Rd. W5 6F 63
Golf Rd. Brom 3E 144
Golf Side. Twic 3H 115
Golfside Clo. N20 3H 15
Golfside Clo. N Mald 2A 136
Goliath Clo. Wall 7J 151
Gollogly Ter. SE7 5A 90
Gomer Gdns. Tedd 6A 116
Gomer Pl. Tedd 6A 116
Gomm Rd. SE16 3J 87
Gomshall Av. Wall 5J 151
Gondar Gdns. NW6 5H 47
Gonson St. SE8 6D 88
Gonston Clo. SW19 2G 119
Gonville Cres. N'holt 6F 43
Gonville Rd. T Hth 5K 139
Gonville St. SW6 3G 101
Gooch Ho. E5 3H 51
Gooch Ho. EC1 5A 68 (5J 161) (off Portpool La.)
Goodall Ho. SE4 4K 105
Goodall Rd. E11 3E 52
Gooden Ct. Harr 3J 43
Goodenough Rd. SW19 7H 119
Goodey Rd. Bark 7J 55
Goodfaith Ho. E14 7D 70 (off Simpson's Rd.)
Goodge Pl. W1 5G 67 (6B 160)
Goodge St. W1 5G 67 (6B 160)
Goodhall Clo. Stan 6G 11
Goodhall St. NW10 3B 64 (in two parts)
Goodhart Pl. E14 7A 70
Goodhart Way. W Wick 7G 143
Goodhew Rd. Croy 6G 141
Goodhope Ho. E14 7D 70 (off Poplar High St.)
Gooding Clo. N Mald 4J 135
Goodinge Clo. N7 6J 49
Gooding Ho. SE7 5A 90
Goodman Cres. SW2 2J 121
Goodman Rd. E10 7E 34
Goodman's Ct. E1 2J 169
Goodmans Ct. Wemb 4D 44
Goodman's Stile. E1 6G 69 (7K 163)
Goodmans Yd. E1 7F 69 (2J 169)
Goodmayes. 1A 56
Goodmayes Av. Ilf 1A 56
Goodmayes La. Ilf 4A 56
Goodmayes Rd. Ilf 1A 56
Goodrich Ct. W10 6F 65
Goodrich Ho. E2 2J 69 (off Sewardstone Rd.)
Goodrich Rd. SE22 6F 105
Goodson Rd. NW10 7A 46
Goodson St. N1 2A 68
Goodspeed Ho. E14 7D 70 (off Simpson's Rd.)
Goods Way. NW1 2J 67
Goodway Gdns. E14 6F 71
Goodwill Ho. E14 7D 70 (off Simpson's Rd.)
Goodwin Clo. SE16 3F 87
Goodwin Clo. Mitc 3B 138
Goodwin Ct. N8 3J 31 (off Campsbourne Rd.)
Goodwin Ct. SW19 7C 120
Goodwin Ct. Barn 6H 5
Goodwin Dri. Sidc 3D 128
Goodwin Gdns. Croy 6B 152
Goodwin Ho. N9 1D 18
Goodwin Rd. N9 1E 18
Goodwin Rd. W12 2C 82
Goodwin Rd. Croy 5B 152
Goodwins Ct. WC2 7J 67 (2E 166)
Goodwin St. N4 2A 50
Goodwood Clo. Mord 4J 137
Goodwood Clo. Stan 5H 11
Goodwood Ct. W1 5F 67 (5K 159) (off Devonshire St.)
Goodwood Dri. N'holt 6E 42
Goodwood Ho. SE14 1A 106 (off Goodwood St.)
Goodwood Pde. Beck 4A 142
Goodwood Rd. SE14 7A 88
Goodwyn Av. NW7 5F 13
Goodwyns Va. N10 1E 30
Goodyear Ho. N2 2B 30 (off Grange, The)
Goodyear Pl. SE5 6C 86
Goodyer Ho. SW1 5H 85 (5C 172) (off Tachbrook St.)
Goodyers Gdns. NW4 5F 29
Goosander Way. SE28 3H 91
Gooseacre La. Harr 5D 26
Goose Grn. Trad. Est. SE22 4F 105
Gooseley La. E6 3E 72 (in three parts)
Goosens Clo. Sutt 5A 150
Goose Sq. E6 6D 72
Gophir La. EC4 7D 68 (2E 168)
Gopsall St. N1 1D 68
Gordon Av. E4 6B 20
Gordon Av. SW14 4A 100
Gordon Av. Stan 7E 10
Gordon Av. Twic 5A 98
Gordonbrock Rd. SE4 5C 106
Gordon Clo. E17 6C 34
Gordon Clo. N19 1G 49
Gordon Ct. W12 6E 64
Gordon Ct. Edgw 5K 11
Gordon Cres. Croy 1E 152
Gordon Cres. Hay 4J 77
Gordondale Rd. SW19 2J 119
Gordon Dri. Shep 7F 131
Gordon Gdns. Edgw 2H 27
Gordon Gro. SE5 2B 104
Gordon Hill. Enf 1H 7
Gordon Ho. E1 7J 69 (off Glamis Rd.)
Gordon Ho. SE10 7D 88 (off Tarves Way)
Gordon Ho. W5 3E 62
Gordon Ho. Rd. NW5 4E 48
Gordon Mans. W14 3F 83 (off Addison Gdns.)
Gordon Mans. WC1 4H 67 (4C 160) (off Torrington Pl.)
Gordon Pl. W8 2J 83
Gordon Rd. E4 1B 20
Gordon Rd. E11 6J 35
Gordon Rd. E15 4E 52
Gordon Rd. E18 1K 35
Gordon Rd. N3 7C 14
Gordon Rd. N9 2C 18
Gordon Rd. N11 7C 16
Gordon Rd. SE15 2H 105
Gordon Rd. W4 6H 81
Gordon Rd. W13 & W5 7B 62
Gordon Rd. Ashf 3A 112
Gordon Rd. Bark 1J 73
Gordon Rd. Beck 3B 142
Gordon Rd. Belv 4J 93
Gordon Rd. Cars 6D 150
Gordon Rd. Chad H 6F 39
Gordon Rd. Enf 1H 7
Gordon Rd. Harr 3J 25
Gordon Rd. Houn 4G 97
Gordon Rd. Ilf 3H 55
Gordon Rd. King T 1F 135
Gordon Rd. Rich 2F 99
Gordon Rd. Shep 6F 131
Gordon Rd. Sidc 5J 109
Gordon Rd. S'hall 4C 78
Gordon Rd. Surb 7F 135
Gordon Rd. W Dray 7A 58
Gordon Sq. WC1 4H 67 (3C 160)
Gordon St. E13 3J 71
Gordon St. WC1 4H 67 (3C 160)
Gordon Way. Barn 4C 4
Gordon Way. Brom 1J 143
Gore Ct. NW9 5G 27
Gorefield Ho. NW6 2J 65 (off Gorefield Pl., in three parts)
Gorefield Pl. NW6 2J 65
Gore Rd. E9 1J 69
Gore Rd. SW20 2E 136
Goresbrook Rd. Dag 1B 74
Gore St. SW7 3A 84
Gorham Ho. SE16 2K 87 (off Wolfe Cres.)
Gorham Pl. W11 7G 65
Goring Clo. Romf 1J 39
Goring Gdns. Dag 4C 56
Goring Rd. N11 6D 16
Goring Rd. Dag 6K 57
Goring St. EC3 7H 163
Goring Way. Gnfd 2G 61
Gorleston Rd. N15 5D 32
Gorleston St. W14 4G 83 (in two parts)
Gorman Rd. SE18 4D 90
Gorringe Pk. Av. Mitc 7D 120
Gorse Clo. E16 6J 71
Gorsefield Ho. E14 7C 70 (off E. India Dock Rd.)
Gorse Ri. SW17 5E 120
Gorse Rd. Croy 4C 154
Gorse Wlk. W Dray 6A 58
Gorseway. Romf 1K 57
Gorst Rd. NW10 4J 63
Gorst Rd. SW11 6D 102
Gorsuch Pl. E2 3F 69 (1J 163)
Gorsuch St. E2 2F 69 (1J 163)
Gosberton Rd. SW12 1D 120
Gosbury Hill. Chess 4E 146
Gosfield Rd. Dag 2G 57
Gosfield St. W1 5G 67 (6A 160)
Gosford Gdns. Ilf 5D 36
Goshawk Gdns. Hay 3G 59
Goslett Yd. WC2 6H 67 (1D 166)
Gosling Clo. Gnfd 3E 60
Gosling Ho. E1 7J 69 (off Sutton St.)
Gosling Way. SW9 1A 104
Gospatrick Rd. N17 7H 17
Gospel Oak. 4E 48
Gospel Oak Est. NW5 5D 48
Gosport Rd. E17 5B 34
Gosport Wlk. N17 4H 33
Gosport Way. SE15 7F 87
Gossage Rd. SE18 5H 91
Gossage Rd. Uxb 7B 40
Gosset St. E2 3F 69 (1K 163)
Gosshill Rd. Chst 2E 144
Gossington Clo. Chst 4F 127
Gosterwood St. SE8 6A 88
Gostling Rd. Twic 1E 114
Goston Gdns. T Hth 3A 140
Goswell Pl. EC1 2B 162
Goswell Rd. EC1 2B 68 (1A 162)
Gothic Cotts. Enf 2H 7 (off Chase Grn. Av.)
Gothic Ct. SE5 7C 86 (off Wyndham Rd.)
Gothic Ct. Hay 6F 77
Gothic Rd. Twic 2H 115
Gottfried M. NW5 4G 49
Goudhurst Rd. Brom 5G 125
Gough Ho. N1 1B 68 (off Windsor St.)
Gough Ho. King T 2E 134 (off Eden St.)
Gough Rd. E15 4H 53
Gough Rd. Enf 2C 8
Gough Sq. EC4 6A 68 (7K 161)
Gough St. WC1 4K 67 (3H 161)
Gough Wlk. E14 6C 70
Goulden Ho. SW11 2C 102
Goulden Ho. App. SW11 2C 102
Goulding Gdns. T Hth 2C 140
Gouldman Ho. E1 4J 69 (off Wyllen Clo.)
Gould Rd. Felt 7G 95
Gould Rd. Twic 1J 115
Goulds Green. 6D 58
Gould's Grn. Uxb 7D 58
Gould Ter. E8 5H 51
Goulston St. E1 6F 69 (7J 163)
Goulton Rd. E5 4H 51
Gourley Pl. N15 5E 32
Gourley St. N15 5E 32
Gourock Rd. SE9 5E 108
Govan St. E2 1G 69
Gover Ct. SW4 2J 103
Govett Av. Shep 5E 130
Govier Clo. E15 7G 53
Gowan Av. SW6 1G 101
Gowan Ho. E2 3F 69 (2K 163) (off Chambord St.)
Gowan Rd. NW10 6D 46
Gower Clo. SW4 6G 103
Gower Ct. WC1 4H 67 (3C 160)
Gower Ho. E17 3D 34
Gower Ho. SE17 5C 86 (off Morecambe St.)
Gower M. WC1 5H 67 (6D 160)
Gower M. Mans. WC1 5H 67 (5D 160) (off Gower M.)
Gower Pl. WC1 4H 67 (3B 160)
Gower Rd. E7 6J 53
Gower Rd. Iswth 6K 79
Gower St. WC1 4G 67 (3B 160)
Gower's Wlk. E1 6G 69
Gowland Pl. Beck 2B 142
Gowlett Rd. SE15 3G 105
Gowrie Rd. SW11 3E 102
Graburn Way. E Mol 3H 133
Grace Av. Bexh 2F 111
Gracechurch St. EC3 7D 68 (2F 169)
Grace Clo. SE9 3B 126
Grace Clo. Edgw 7D 12
Grace Ct. Croy 3B 152 (off Waddon Rd.)
Gracedale Rd. SW16 5F 121
Gracefield Gdns. SW16 3J 121
Gracehill. E1 5J 69 (off Hannibal Rd.)
Grace Ho. SE11 7H 173
Grace Jones Clo. E8 6G 51
Grace M. SE20 2J 141 (off Marlow Rd.)
Grace Path. SE26 4J 123
Grace Pl. E3 3D 70
Grace Rd. Croy 6C 140
Graces All. E1 7G 69
Graces M. NW8 2A 66
Grace's M. SE5 2D 104
Grace's Rd. SE5 2E 104
Grace St. E3 3D 70
Gradient, The. SE26 4G 123
Graduate Pl. SE1 3E 86 (7G 169) (off Long La.)
Graeme Rd. Enf 2J 7
Graemesdyke Av. SW14 3H 99
Grafely Way. SE15 7F 87
Grafton Clo. W13 6A 62
Grafton Clo. Houn 1C 114
Grafton Clo. Wor Pk 3A 148
Grafton Ct. Felt 1F 113
Grafton Cres. NW1 6F 49
Grafton Gdns. N4 6C 32
Grafton Gdns. Dag 2E 56
Grafton Ho. SE8 5B 88
Grafton M. N1 2C 68 (off Frome St.)
Grafton M. W1 4G 67 (4A 160)
Grafton Pk. Rd. Wor Pk 2A 148
Grafton Pl. NW1 3H 67 (2D 160)
Grafton Rd. NW5 5E 48
Grafton Rd. W3 7J 63
Grafton Rd. Croy 1A 152
Grafton Rd. Dag 1E 56
Grafton Rd. Enf 3E 6
Grafton Rd. Harr 5G 25
Grafton Rd. N Mald 3A 136
Grafton Rd. Wor Pk 3K 147
Grafton Sq. SW4 3G 103
Graftons, The. NW2 3J 47
Grafton St. W1 7F 67 (3K 165)
Grafton Ter. NW5 5D 48
Grafton Way. W1 & WC1 4G 67 (4A 160)
Grafton Way. W Mol 4D 132
Grafton Yd. NW5 6F 49
Graham Av. W13 2B 80
Graham Av. Mitc 1E 138
Graham Clo. Croy 2C 154
Graham Ct. SE14 6K 87 (off Myers La.)
Graham Ct. N'holt 5D 42
Grahame Park. 1B 28
Grahame Pk. Est. NW9 1A 28
Grahame Pk. Way. NW7 & NW9 7G 13
Grahame White Ho. Kent 3D 26
Graham Gdns. Surb 1E 146
Graham Ho. N9 1D 18 (off Cumberland Rd.)
Graham Lodge. NW4 6D 28
Graham Mans. Bark 7A 56 (off Lansbury Av.)
Graham Rd. E8 6G 51
Graham Rd. E13 3J 71
Graham Rd. N15 3B 32
Graham Rd. NW4 6D 28
Graham Rd. SW19 7H 119
Graham Rd. W4 3K 81
Graham Rd. Bexh 4G 111
Graham Rd. Hamp 4E 114
Graham Rd. Harr 3J 25
Graham Rd. Mitc 1E 138
Graham St. N1 2B 68 (1C 162)
Graham Ter. SW1 4E 84 (4G 171)
Graham Ter. Sidc 6B 110 (off Westerham Dri.)
Grainger Clo. N'holt 5F 43
Grainger Ct. SE5 7C 86
Grainger Rd. N22 1C 32
Grainger Rd. Iswth 2K 97
Gramer Clo. E11 2F 53
Gramophone La. Hay 2G 77
Grampian Clo. Hay 7F 77
Grampian Clo. Orp 6K 145
Grampian Gdns. NW2 1G 47
Grampians, The. W6 2F 83 (off Shepherd's Bush Rd.)
Grampion Clo. Sutt 7A 150
Granada St. SW17 5C 120
Granard Av. SW15 5D 100
Granard Bus. Cen. NW7 6F 13
Granard Ho. E9 6K 51
Granard Rd. SW12 7D 102
Granary Clo. N9 7D 8
Granary Mans. SE28 2G 91 (off Erebus Dri.)
Granary Rd. E1 4H 69
Granary Sq. N1 6A 50
Granary St. NW1 1H 67
Granby Pl. SE1 2A 86 (7J 167) (off Station App. Rd.)
Granby Rd. SE9 2D 108
Granby St. E2 4G 69 (3K 163) (in two parts)
Granby Ter. NW1 2G 67 (1A 160)
Grand Arc. N12 5F 15
Grand Av. EC1 5B 68 (5B 162) (in three parts)
Grand Av. N10 4E 30

Grand Av. Surb 5H 135
Grand Av. Wemb 5G 45
Grand Av. E. Wemb 5H 45
Grand Depot Rd. SE18 5E 90
Grand Dri. SW20 2E 136
Grand Dri. S'hall 2G 79
Granden Rd. SW16 2J 139
Grandfield Ct. W4 6K 81
Grandison Rd. SW11 5D 102
Grandison Rd. Wor Pk 2E 148
Grand Junct. Wharf. N1 2C 68
Grand Pde. N4 5B 32
Grand Pde. SW14 4J 99 (off Up. Richmond Rd. W.)
Grand Pde. Surb 1G 147
Grand Pde. Wemb 2G 45
Grand Pde. M. SW15 5G 101
Grand Union Cen. W10 4F 65 (off West Row)
Grand Union Clo. W9 5H 65
Grand Union Cres. E8 1G 69
Grand Union Enterprise Pk. S'hall 3E 78
Grand Union Ind. Est. NW10 2H 63
Grand Union Wlk. NW1 7F 49 (off Kentish Town Rd.)
Grand Union Way. S'hall 2E 78
Grand Vitesse Ind. Cen. SE1 1B 86 (5B 168) (off Dolben St.)
Grand Wlk. E1 4A 70
Granfield St. SW11 1B 102
Grange Av. N12 5F 15
Grange Av. N20 7B 4
Grange Av. SE25 2E 140
Grange Av. E Barn 1H 15
Grange Av. Stan 2B 26
Grange Av. Twic 2J 115
Grange Av. Wfd G 6D 20
Grangecliffe Gdns. SE25 2E 140
Grange Clo. Edgw 5D 12
Grange Clo. Hay 5G 59
Grange Clo. Houn 6D 78
Grange Clo. Sidc 3A 128
Grange Clo. W Mol 4F 133
Grange Clo. Wfd G 7D 20
Grange Ct. NW10 3A 46 (off Neasden La.)
Grange Ct. WC2 6K 67 (1H 167)
Grange Ct. Harr 3K 43
Grange Ct. N'holt 2A 60
Grange Ct. Pinn 3C 24
Grange Ct. Shep 4C 130
Grange Ct. Sutt 7K 149
Grangecourt Rd. N16 1E 50
Grange Cres. SE28 6C 74
Grangedale Clo. N'wd 1G 23
Grange Dri. Chst 6C 126
Grange Farm Clo. Harr 2G 43
Grangefield. NW1 7H 49 (off Marquis Rd.)
Grange Gdns. N14 1C 16
Grange Gdns. NW3 3K 47
Grange Gdns. SE25 2E 140
Grange Gdns. Pinn 3C 24
Grange Gro. N1 6C 50
Grange Hill. SE25 2E 140
Grange Hill. Edgw 5D 12
Grangehill Pl. SE9 3D 108
Grangehill Rd. SE9 4D 108
Grange Ho. NW10 7D 46
Grange Ho. SE1 3F 87
Grange La. SE21 2F 123
Grange Lodge. SW19 6F 119
Grange Mans. Eps 7B 148
Grange M. Felt 4J 113
Grangemill Rd. SE6 3C 124
Grangemill Way. SE6 2C 124
Grange Mus. of Community History. 4A 46
Grange Park. 6G 7
Grange Pk. W5 1E 80
Grange Pk. Av. N21 6H 7
Grange Pk. Pl. SW20 7D 118
Grange Pk. Rd. E10 1D 52
Grange Pk. Rd. T Hth 4D 140
Grange Pl. NW6 7J 47
Grange Rd. E10 1C 52
Grange Rd. E13 3H 71
Grange Rd. E17 5A 34 (in two parts)
Grange Rd. N6 6E 30
Grange Rd. N17 & N18 6B 18
Grange Rd. NW10 6D 46
Grange Rd. SE1 3E 86
Grange Rd. SW13 1C 100
Grange Rd. W4 5H 81
Grange Rd. W5 1D 80
Grange Rd. Chess 4E 146
Grange Rd. Edgw 6E 12
Grange Rd. Harr 5A 26
Grange Rd. Hay 6G 59
Grange Rd. Ilf 4F 55
Grange Rd. King T 3E 134
Grange Rd. S'hall 2C 78
Grange Rd. S Croy 7C 152
Grange Rd. S Harr 2H 43
Grange Rd. Sutt 7J 149
Grange Rd. T Hth & SE25 4D 140
Grange Rd. W Mol 4F 133
Grange St. N1 1D 68
Grange, The. E17 5A 34 (off Grange Rd.)
Grange, The. N2 2B 30
Grange, The. N20 1G 15 (Athenaeum Rd.)
Grange, The. N20 1F 15 (Chandos Av.)
Grange, The. SE1 3F 87
Grange, The. SW19 6F 119
Grange, The. W3 2H 81
Grange, The. W4 5H 81
Grange, The. W13 5C 62
Grange, The. W14 4H 83
Grange, The. Croy 2B 154
Grange, The. N Mald 5B 136
Grange, The. Wemb 7G 45
Grange, The. Wor Pk 3K 147
Grange Va. Sutt 7K 149
Grangeview Rd. N20 1F 15
Grange Wlk. SE1 3E 86
Grange Wlk. M. SE1 3E 86 (off Grange Wlk.)
Grange Way. N12 4E 14
Grange Way. NW6 7J 47
Grange Way. Wfd G 4F 21
Grangeway Gdns. Ilf 5C 36
Grangeway, The. N21 6G 7
Grangewood. Bex 1F 129
Grangewood Clo. Pinn 5J 23
Grangewood Dri. Sun 7H 113
Grangewood La. Beck 6B 124
Grangewood St. E6 1B 72
Grangewood Ter. SE25 2D 140
Grange Yd. SE1 3F 87
Granham Gdns. N9 2A 18
Granite St. SE18 5K 91
Granleigh Rd. E11 2G 53
Gransden Av. E8 7H 51
Gransden Ho. SE8 5B 88
Gransden Rd. W12 2B 82
Grantbridge St. N1 2B 68
Grantchester. King T 2G 135 (off St Peters Rd.)
Grantchester Clo. Harr 3K 43
Grant Clo. N14 7B 6
Grant Clo. Shep 6D 130
Grant Ct. E4 1K 19 (off Ridgeway, The)
Grant Ct. NW9 2B 28 (off Hazel Clo.)
Grantham Clo. Edgw 3K 11
Grantham Ct. SE16 2K 87 (off Eleanor Clo.)
Grantham Ct. King T 5D 116
Grantham Ct. Romf 7F 39
Grantham Gdns. Romf 6F 39
Grantham Ho. SE15 6G 87 (off Friary Est.)
Grantham Pl. W1 1F 85 (5J 165)
Grantham Rd. E12 4E 54
Grantham Rd. SW9 2J 103
Grantham Rd. W4 7A 82
Grantley Ho. SE14 6K 87 (off Myers La.)
Grantley Rd. Houn 2A 96
Grantley St. E1 3K 69
Grantock Rd. E17 1F 35
Granton Rd. SW16 1G 139
Granton Rd. Ilf 1A 56
Granton Rd. Sidc 6C 128
Grant Pl. Croy 1F 153
Grant Rd. SW11 4B 102
Grant Rd. Croy 1F 153
Grant Rd. Harr 3K 25
Grants Clo. NW7 7K 13
Grants Quay Wharf. EC3 7D 68 (3F 169)
Grant St. E13 3J 71
Grant St. N1 2A 68
Grantully Rd. W9 3K 65
Grant Way. Iswth 6A 80
Granville Arc. SW9 4A 104
Granville Av. N9 3D 18
Granville Av. Felt 2J 113
Granville Av. Houn 5E 96
Granville Clo. Croy 2E 152
Granville Ct. N1 1E 68 (off Colville Est.)
Granville Ct. SE14 7A 88 (off Nynehead St.)
Granville Gdns. SW16 1K 139
Granville Gdns. W5 1F 81
Granville Gro. SE13 3E 106
Granville Ho. E14 6C 70 (off E. India Dock Rd.)
Granville Mans. W12 2E 82 (off Shepherd's Bush Grn.)
Granville M. Sidc 4A 128
Granville M. Stan 5F 11
Granville Pk. SE13 3E 106
Granville Pl. N12 7F 15
Granville Pl. SW6 7K 83
Granville Pl. W1 6E 66 (1G 165)
Granville Pl. Pinn 3B 24
Granville Point. NW2 2H 47
Granville Rd. E17 6D 34
Granville Rd. E18 2K 35
Granville Rd. N4 6K 31
Granville Rd. N12 7F 15
Granville Rd. N13 6E 16
Granville Rd. N22 1B 32
Granville Rd. NW2 2H 47
Granville Rd. NW6 2J 65 (in two parts)
Granville Rd. SW18 7H 101
Granville Rd. SW19 7J 119
Granville Rd. Barn 4A 4
Granville Rd. Hay 4H 77
Granville Rd. Ilf 1F 55
Granville Rd. Sidc 4A 128
Granville Rd. Uxb 6D 40
Granville Rd. Well 3C 110
Granville Sq. SE15 7E 86
Granville Sq. WC1 3K 67 (2H 161)
Granville St. WC1 3K 67 (2H 161)
Granwood Ct. Iswth 1J 97
Grape St. WC2 6J 67 (7E 160)
Graphite Sq. SE11 5K 85 (5G 173)
Grapsome Clo. Chess 7C 146
Grasdene Rd. SE18 7A 92
Grasgarth Clo. W3 7J 63
Grasmere. NW1 3F 67 (2K 159) (off Osnaburgh St.)
Grasmere Av. SW15 4K 117
Grasmere Av. SW19 3J 137
Grasmere Av. W3 7K 63
Grasmere Av. Houn 6F 97
Grasmere Av. Orp 3E 156
Grasmere Av. Ruis 7E 22
Grasmere Av. Wemb 7C 26
Grasmere Clo. Felt 1H 113
Grasmere Ct. N22 6E 16
Grasmere Ct. SE26 5G 123
Grasmere Ct. SW13 6C 82 (off Verdun Rd.)
Grasmere Ct. Sutt 6A 150
Grasmere Gdns. Harr 2A 26
Grasmere Gdns. Ilf 5D 36
Grasmere Gdns. Orp 3E 156
Grasmere Point. SE15 7J 87 (off Old Kent Rd.)
Grasmere Rd. E13 2J 71
Grasmere Rd. N10 1F 31
Grasmere Rd. N17 6B 18
Grasmere Rd. SE25 6H 141
Grasmere Rd. SW16 5K 121
Grasmere Rd. Bexh 2J 111
Grasmere Rd. Brom 1H 143
Grasshaven Way. SE28 1K 91 (in two parts)
Grassington Clo. N11 6K 15
Grassington Rd. Sidc 4A 128
Grassmount. SE23 2H 123
Grass Pk. N3 1H 29
Grass Way. Wall 4G 151
Grasvenor Av. Barn 5D 4
Gratton Rd. W14 3G 83
Gratton Ter. NW2 3F 47
Gravel Hill. N3 2H 29
Gravel Hill. Bexh 5H 111
Gravel Hill. Croy 6K 153
Gravel Hill. Uxb 5A 40
Gravel Hill Clo. Bexh 5H 111
Gravel La. E1 6F 69 (7J 163)
Gravel Pit La. SE9 5F 109
Gravel Rd. Brom 3C 156
Gravel Rd. Twic 1J 115
Gravelwood Clo. Chst 3G 127
Gravely Ho. SE8 4A 88 (off Chilton Gro.)
Gravenel Gdns. SW17 5C 120 (off Nutwell St.)
Graveney Gro. SE20 7J 123
Graveney Rd. SW17 4C 120
Gravesend Rd. W12 7C 64
Gray Av. Dag 1F 57
Grayham Cres. N Mald 4K 135
Grayham Rd. N Mald 4K 135
Gray Ho. SE17 5C 86 (off King & Queen St.)
Grayland Clo. Brom 1B 144
Grayling Clo. E16 4G 71
Grayling Ct. W5 1D 80 (off Grange Rd.)
Grayling Rd. N16 2D 50
Grayling Sq. E2 3G 69 (off Nelson Gdns.)
Grays Ct. Dag 7H 57
Grayscroft Rd. SW16 7H 121
Grayshott Rd. SW11 2E 102
Gray's Inn. 5K 67 (5H 161)
Gray's Inn Bldgs. EC1 4A 68 (4J 161) (off Rosebery Av.)
Gray's Inn Pl. WC1 5K 67 (6H 161)
Gray's Inn Rd. WC1 3J 67 (1F 161)
Gray's Inn Sq. WC1 5K 67 (5J 161)
Grays La. Ashf 4D 112
Grayson Ho. EC1 2D 162
Grays Rd. Uxb 2A 58
Gray St. SE1 2A 86 (7K 167)
Grayswood Gdns. SW20 2D 136
Gray's Yd. W1 1H 165
Graywood Ct. N12 7F 15
Grazebrook Rd. N16 2D 50
Grazeley Clo. Bexh 5J 111
Grazeley Ct. SE19 5E 122
Gt. Acre Ct. SW4 4H 103
Gt. Arthur Ho. EC1 4C 68 (4C 162) (off Golden La. Est.)
Gt. Bell All. EC2 6D 68 (7E 162)
Great Benty. W Dray 4A 76
Great Brownings. SE21 4F 123
Gt. Bushey Dri. N20 1E 14
Gt. Cambridge Ind. Est. Enf 5C 8
Great Cambridge Junction. (Junct.) 5H 17
Gt. Cambridge Rd. N18 & N9 4J 17
Gt. Castle St. W1 6F 67 (7K 159)
Gt. Central Av. Ruis 5A 42
Gt. Central St. NW1 5D 66 (5E 158)
Gt. Central Way. Wemb & NW10 4J 45
Gt. Chapel St. W1 6H 67 (7C 160)
Gt. Chertsey Rd. W4 2J 99
Gt. Chertsey Rd. Felt & Twic 3D 114
Gt. Church La. W6 4F 83
Gt. College St. SW1 3J 85 (1E 172)
Great Cft. WC1 3J 67 (2F 161) (off Cromer St.)
Gt. Cross Av. SE10 7F 89 (in three parts)
Gt. Cumberland M. W1 6D 66 (1E 164)
Gt. Cumberland Pl. W1 6D 66 (7E 158)
Gt. Dover St. SE1 2C 86 (7D 168)
Greatdown Rd. W7 4K 61
Gt. Eastern Bldgs. E1 5G 69 (off Fieldgate St.)
Gt. Eastern Enterprise Cen. E14 2D 88
Gt. Eastern Rd. E15 7F 53
Gt. Eastern St. EC2 3E 68 (2G 163)
Gt. Eastern Wlk. EC2 6H 163
Gt. Eastern Wharf. SW11 7C 84
Gt. Elms Rd. Brom 4A 144
Great Fld. NW9 1A 28
Greatfield Av. E6 4D 72
Greatfield Clo. N19 4G 49
Greatfield Clo. SE4 4C 106
Greatfields Dri. Uxb 5C 58
Greatfields Rd. Bark 1H 73
Gt. Fleete Way. Bark 2C 74
Gt. Galley Clo. Bark 3B 74
Gt. Gatton Clo. Croy 7A 142
Gt. George St. SW1 2H 85 (7D 166)
Gt. Guildford Bus. Sq. SE1 5C 168
Gt. Guildford St. SE1 1C 86 (4C 168)
Greatham Wlk. SW15 1C 118
Gt. Harry Dri. SE9 3E 126
Gt. James St. WC1 5K 67 (5G 161)
Gt. Marlborough St. W1 6G 67 (1A 166)
Gt. Maze Pond. SE1 2D 86 (5F 169) (in two parts)
Gt. Newport St. WC2 7J 67 (2E 166)
Gt. New St. EC4 6A 68 (7K 161)
Gt. N. Leisure Pk. N12 7G 15
Gt. North Rd. N2 & N6 5C 30
Gt. North Rd. Barn 2C 4
Gt. North Rd. New Bar 5D 4
Gt. North Way. NW4 2D 28
Greatorex Ho. E1 5G 69 (off Greatorex St.)

Greatorex St. *E1* . . . 5G **69**
Gt. Ormond St. *WC1* . . . 5J **67** (5F **161**)
Gt. Owl Rd. *Chig* . . . 3K **21**
Gt. Percy St. *WC1* . . . 3K **67** (1H **161**)
Gt. Peter St. *SW1* . . . 3H **85** (2C **172**)
Gt. Portland St. *W1* . . . 4F **67** (4K **159**)
Gt. Pulteney St. *W1* . . . 7G **67** (2B **166**)
Gt. Queen St. *WC2* . . . 6J **67** (1F **167**)
Gt. Russell St. *WC1* . . . 6H **67** (7D **160**)
Gt. St Helen's. *EC3* . . . 6E **68** (7G **163**)
Gt. St Thomas Apostle. *EC4* . . . 7C **68** (2D **168**)
Gt. Scotland Yd. *SW1* . . . 1J **85** (5E **166**)
Gt. Smith St. *SW1* . . . 3H **85** (1D **172**)
Gt. South W. Rd. *Bedf & Felt* . . . 7E **94**
Great Spilmans. *SE22* . . . 5E **104**
Great Strand. *NW9* . . . 1B **28**
Gt. Suffolk St. *SE1* . . . 1B **86** (5B **168**)
Gt. Sutton St. *EC1* . . . 4B **68** (4B **162**)
Gt. Swan All. *EC2* . . . 6D **68** (7E **162**) (in two parts)
Great Thrift. *Orp* . . . 4G **145**
Gt. Titchfield St. *W1* . . . 4F **67** (4K **159**)
Gt. Tower St. *EC3* . . . 7E **68** (2G **169**)
Gt. Trinity La. *EC4* . . . 7C **68** (2D **168**)
Great Turnstile. *WC1* . . . 5K **67** (6H **161**)
Gt. Western Ind. Pk. *S'hall* . . . 2F **79**
Gt. Western Rd. *W9 & W11* . . . 5H **65**
Gt. West Rd. *W4 & W6* . . . 5B **82**
Gt. West Rd. *Houn* . . . 2B **96**
Gt. West Rd. *Iswth & Bren* . . . 7J **79**
Gt. West Trad. Est. *Bren* . . . 6B **80**
Gt. Winchester St. *EC2* . . . 6D **68** (7F **163**)
Gt. Windmill St. *W1* . . . 7H **67** (2C **166**)
Greatwood. *Chst* . . . 7E **126**
Great Yd. *SE1* . . . 6H **169**
Greaves Clo. *Bark* . . . 7H **55**
Greaves Cotts. *E14* . . . 5A **70**
Greaves Pl. *SW17* . . . 4C **120**
Greaves Tower. SW10 . . . 7A 84 (off Worlds End Est.)
Grebe Av. *Hay* . . . 6B **60**
Grebe Clo. *E7* . . . 5H **53**
Grebe Clo. *E17* . . . 7F **19**
Grebe Ct. E14 . . . 2E 88 (off River Barge Clo.)
Grebe Ct. SE8 . . . 6B 88 (off Dorking Clo.)
Grebe Ct. *Sutt* . . . 5H **149**
Grebe Ter. *King T* . . . 3E **134**
Grecian Cres. *SE19* . . . 6B **122**
Greek Ct. *W1* . . . 6H **67** (1D **166**)
Greek St. *W1* . . . 6H **67** (1D **166**)
Greenacre Clo. *Barn* . . . 1C **4**
Greenacre Clo. *N'holt* . . . 5D **42**
Greenacre Gdns. *E17* . . . 4E **34**
Greenacre Pl. *Hack* . . . 2F **151**
Greenacres. *N3* . . . 2H **29**
Greenacres. *SE9* . . . 6E **108**
Greenacres. *Bus H* . . . 2C **10**
Green Acres. *Croy* . . . 3F **153**
Greenacres. *Sidc* . . . 4A **128**
Greenacres Av. *Uxb* . . . 3B **40**
Greenacres Dri. *Stan* . . . 6G **11**
Greenacre Sq. *SE16* . . . 2K **87**
Greenacre Wlk. *N14* . . . 3C **16**
Grn. Arbour Ct. *EC4* . . . 7A **162**
Green Av. *NW7* . . . 4E **12**
Green Av. *W13* . . . 3B **80**
Greenaway Av. *N18* . . . 6E **18**
Greenaway Gdns. *NW3* . . . 4K **47**
Greenaway Ho. NW8 . . . 1A 66 (off Boundary Rd.)
Greenaway Ho. WC1 . . . 3A 68 (2J 161) (off Fernsbury St.)
Green Bank. *E1* . . . 1H **87**
Greenbank. *N12* . . . 4E **14**
Greenbank Av. *Wemb* . . . 5A **44**
Grn. Bank Clo. *E4* . . . 2K **19**
Greenbank Cres. *NW4* . . . 4G **29**
Greenbanks. *Harr* . . . 4J **43**
Greenbay Rd. *SE7* . . . 7B **90**
Greenberry St. *NW8* . . . 2C **66** (1C **158**)
Greenbrook Av. *Barn* . . . 1F **5**
Green Clo. *E15* . . . 1G **71**
Green Clo. *NW9* . . . 6J **27**
Green Clo. *NW11* . . . 7A **30**
Green Clo. *Brom* . . . 3G **143**
Green Clo. *Cars* . . . 2D **150**
Green Clo. *Felt* . . . 5C **114**
Greencoat Mans. SW1 . . . 3G 85 (2B 172) (off Greencoat Row)
Greencoat Pl. *SW1* . . . 4G **85** (2B **172**)
Greencoat Row. *SW1* . . . 3G **85** (2B **172**)
Greencourt Av. *Croy* . . . 2H **153**
Greencourt Av. *Edgw* . . . 1H **27**
Greencourt Gdns. *Croy* . . . 1H **153**
Greencourt Ho. E1 . . . 4K 69 (off Mile End Rd.)
Greencourt Rd. *Orp* . . . 5H **145**
Greencrest Pl. *NW2* . . . 3C **46**
Greencroft. *Edgw* . . . 5D **12**
Greencroft Av. *Ruis* . . . 2A **42**
Greencroft Clo. *E6* . . . 5B **72**
Greencroft Gdns. *NW6* . . . 7K **47**
Greencroft Gdns. *Enf* . . . 3K **7**
Greencroft Rd. *Houn* . . . 1D **96**
Greendale. *NW7* . . . 4F **13**
Green Dale. *SE5* . . . 4D **104**
Green Dale. *SE22* . . . 5E **104**
Grn. Dale Clo. *SE22* . . . 5E **104**
Grn. Dragon Ct. *SE1* . . . 4E **168**
Grn. Dragon La. *N21* . . . 6F **7**
Grn. Dragon La. *Bren* . . . 5E **80**
Grn. Dragon Yd. *E1* . . . 5G **69** (6K **163**)
Green Dri. *S'hall* . . . 1E **78**
Greene Ct. SE14 . . . 6K 87 (off Samuel Clo.)
Greene Ho. SE1 . . . 3D 86 (off Burbage Clo.)
Green End. *N21* . . . 2G **17**
Green End. *Chess* . . . 4E **146**
Greenend Rd. *W4* . . . 2A **82**
Greener Ho. *SW4* . . . 3H **103**
Greenfell Mans. *SE8* . . . 6D **88**
Greenfield Av. *Surb* . . . 7H **135**
Greenfield Dri. *N2* . . . 4D **30**
Greenfield Dri. *Brom* . . . 2A **144**
Greenfield Gdns. *NW2* . . . 2G **47**
Greenfield Gdns. *Dag* . . . 1D **74**
Greenfield Gdns. *Orp* . . . 7H **145**
Greenfield Rd. *E1* . . . 5G **69**
Greenfield Rd. *N15* . . . 5E **32**
Greenfield Rd. *Dag* . . . 7C **56**
Greenfield Rd. *Dart* . . . 5K **129**
Greenfields. *S'hall* . . . 6E **60**
Greenfield Way. *Harr* . . . 3F **25**
Greenford. . . . 3G 61
Greenford Av. *W7* . . . 4J **61**
Greenford Av. *S'hall* . . . 7D **60**
Greenford Bus. Cen. *Gnfd* . . . 7H **43**
Greenford Gdns. *Gnfd* . . . 3F **61**
Greenford Green. . . . 6J 43
Greenford Ind. Est. *N'holt* . . . 7F **43**
Greenford Rd. *S'hall* . . . 1G **79**
Greenford Rd. *Sutt* . . . 4K **149** (in two parts)
Greenford Roundabout. (Junct.) . . . 2H **61**
Greengate. *Gnfd* . . . 6B **44**
Greengate Lodge. E13 . . . 2K 71 (off Hollybush St.)
Greengate St. *E13* . . . 2K **71**
Greenhalgh Wlk. *N2* . . . 4A **30**
Greenham Clo. *SE1* . . . 2A **86** (7J **167**)
Greenham Cres. *E4* . . . 6G **19**
Greenham Ho. E9 . . . 1J 69 (off Templecombe Rd.)
Greenham Ho. *Houn* . . . 3H **97**
Greenham Rd. *N10* . . . 2E **30**
Greenhaven Dri. *SE28* . . . 6B **74**
Greenheath Bus. Cen. E2 . . . 4H 69 (off Three Colts La.)
Green Hedge. *Twic* . . . 5C **98**
Greenheys Clo. *N'wd* . . . 1G **23**
Greenheys Dri. *E18* . . . 3H **35**
Greenhill. . . . 5J 25
Greenhill. *NW3* . . . 4B **48**
Green Hill. *SE18* . . . 5D **90**
Greenhill. *Buck H* . . . 1F **21**
Greenhill. *Sutt* . . . 2A **150**
Greenhill. *Wemb* . . . 2H **45**
Greenhill Ct. *SE18* . . . 5D **90**
Greenhill Ct. *New Bar* . . . 5E **4**
Greenhill Gdns. *N'holt* . . . 2D **60**
Greenhill Gro. *E12* . . . 4C **54**
Greenhill Pde. *New Bar* . . . 5E **4**
Greenhill Pk. *NW10* . . . 1A **64**
Greenhill Pk. *New Bar* . . . 5E **4**
Greenhill Rd. *NW10* . . . 1A **64**
Greenhill Rd. *Harr* . . . 6J **25**
Greenhill's Rents. *EC1* . . . 5B **68** (5A **162**)
Greenhills Ter. *N1* . . . 6D **50**
Greenhill Ter. *SE18* . . . 5D **90**
Greenhill Ter. *N'holt* . . . 2D **60**
Greenhill Way. *Harr* . . . 6J **25**
Greenhill Way. *Wemb* . . . 2H **45**
Greenhithe Clo. *Sidc* . . . 7J **109**
Greenholm Rd. *SE9* . . . 5F **109**
Grn. Hundred Rd. *SE15* . . . 6G **87**
Greenhurst Rd. *SE27* . . . 5A **122**
Greening St. *SE2* . . . 4C **92**
Greenland Cres. *S'hall* . . . 3A **78**
Greenland Ho. E1 . . . 4A 70 (off Ernest St.)
Greenland M. *SE8* . . . 5K **87**
Greenland Pl. *NW1* . . . 1F **67**
Greenland Quay. *SE16* . . . 4K **87**
Greenland Rd. *NW1* . . . 1G **67**
Greenland Rd. *Barn* . . . 6A **4**
Greenland St. *NW1* . . . 1F **67**
Green La. *NW4* . . . 4F **29**
Green La. *SE9 & Chst* . . . 1F **127**
Green La. *SE20* . . . 7K **123**
Green La. *SW16 & T Hth* . . . 7K **121**
Green La. *W7* . . . 2J **79**
Green La. *Chess* . . . 7D **146** (in two parts)
Green La. *Edgw* . . . 4A **12**
Green La. *Felt* . . . 5C **114**
Green La. *Harr* . . . 3J **43**
Green La. *Houn* . . . 3K **95**
Green La. *Ilf* . . . 2H **55**
Green La. *Mord* . . . 7E **136** (Battersea Cemetery)
Green La. *Mord* . . . 6J **137** (Morden)
Green La. *N Mald* . . . 5J **135**
Green La. *Shep* . . . 6E **130**
Green La. *Stan* . . . 4G **11**
Green La. *Sun* . . . 7H **113**
Green La. *Uxb* . . . 5E **58**
Green La. *W Mol* . . . 5F **133**
Green La. *Wor Pk* . . . 1C **148**
Green La. Cotts. *Stan* . . . 4G **11**
Green La. Gdns. *T Hth* . . . 2C **140**
Green Lanes. *N8 & N4* . . . 3B **32**
Green Lanes. *N13 & N21* . . . 3F **17**
Green Lanes. *Eps* . . . 7A **148** (in two parts)
Greenlaw Ct. W5 . . . 6D 62 (off Mt. Park Rd.)
Greenlaw Gdns. *N Mald* . . . 7B **136**
Greenlawns. *N12* . . . 6E **14**
Green Lawns. *Ruis* . . . 1A **42**
Greenlaw St. *SE18* . . . 3E **90**
Grn. Leaf Av. *Wall* . . . 4H **151**
Greenleaf Clo. *SW2* . . . 7A **104**
Greenleafe Dri. *Ilf* . . . 3F **37**
Greenleaf Rd. *E6* . . . 1A **72**
Greenleaf Rd. *E17* . . . 3B **34**
Green Leas. King T . . . 3E 134 (off Mill St.)
Green Leas. *Sun* . . . 6H **113**
Grn. Leas Clo. *Sun* . . . 6H **113**
Greenleaves Ct. *Ashf* . . . 6D **112**
Grn. Man Gdns. *W13* . . . 7A **62**
Grn. Man La. *W13* . . . 7A **62**
Grn. Man La. *Felt* . . . 4J **95** (Faggs Rd.)
Grn. Man La. *Felt* . . . 4K **95** (Heron Way)
Grn. Man Pas. *W13* . . . 7B **62** (in two parts)
Green Man Roundabout. (Junct.) . . . 6H **35**
Greenman St. *N1* . . . 7C **50**
Greenmead. *Eri* . . . 3E **92**
Greenmead Clo. *SE25* . . . 5G **141**
Green Moor Link. *N21* . . . 7G **7**
Greenmoor Rd. *Enf* . . . 2D **8**
Greenoak Pl. *Cockf* . . . 2J **5**
Green Oaks. *S'hall* . . . 4B **78**
Greenoak Way. *SW19* . . . 4F **119**
Greenock Rd. *SW16* . . . 1H **139**
Greenock Rd. *W3* . . . 3H **81**
Greeno Cres. *Shep* . . . 5C **130**
Green Pde. *Houn* . . . 5F **97**
Green Pk. . . . 2F 85 (5K 165)
Greenpark Ct. *Wemb* . . . 7C **44**
Grn. Park Way. *Gnfd* . . . 7J **43** (in two parts)
Green Point. *E15* . . . 6G **53**
Grn. Pond Clo. *E17* . . . 3A **34**
Grn. Pond Rd. *E17* . . . 3A **34**
Green Rd. *N14* . . . 6A **6**
Green Rd. *N20* . . . 3F **15**
Green's Ct. *W1* . . . 2C **166**
Green's End. *SE18* . . . 4F **91**
Greenshank Clo. *E17* . . . 7F **19**
Greenshields Ind. Est. *E16* . . . 2J **89**
Greenside. *Bex* . . . 1E **128**
Green Side. *Dag* . . . 1C **56**
Greenside Clo. *N20* . . . 2G **15**
Greenside Clo. *SE6* . . . 2F **125**
Greenside Rd. *W12* . . . 3C **82**
Greenside Rd. *Croy* . . . 7A **140**
Greenslade Rd. *Bark* . . . 7H **55**
Grn. Slip Rd. *Barn* . . . 2C **4**
Greenstead Av. *Wfd G* . . . 7F **21**
Greenstead Clo. *Wfd G* . . . 6F **21**
Greenstead Gdns. *SW15* . . . 5D **100**
Greenstead Gdns. *Wfd G* . . . 6F **21**
Greensted Rd. *Lou* . . . 1H **21**
Greenstone M. *E11* . . . 6J **35**
Green St. *E7 & E13* . . . 6K **53**
Green St. *W1* . . . 7E **66** (2G **165**)
Green St. *Enf* . . . 2D **8**
Green St. *Sun* . . . 1J **131**
Greenstreet Hill. *SE14* . . . 2K **105**
Green Ter. *EC1* . . . 3A **68** (2K **161**)
Green, The. *E4* . . . 1K **19**
Green, The. *E11* . . . 6K **35**
Green, The. *E15* . . . 6G **53**
Green, The. *N9* . . . 2B **18**
Green, The. *N14* . . . 2C **16**
Green, The. *N17* . . . 6H **17**
Green, The. *N21* . . . 7F **7**
Green, The. *SW19* . . . 5F **119**
Green, The. *W3* . . . 6A **64**
Green, The. *W5* . . . 1D **80**
Green, The. *Bexh* . . . 1G **111**
Green, The. *Brom* . . . 3J **125** (in two parts)
Green, The. *Buck H* . . . 1E **20**
Green, The. *Cars* . . . 4E **150**
Green, The. *Croy* . . . 7B **154**
Green, The. *Felt* . . . 2K **113**
Green, The. *Hayes* . . . 7J **143**
Green, The. *Houn* . . . 6E **78**
Green, The. *Ick* . . . 2E **40**
Green, The. *Mord* . . . 4G **137**
Green, The. *N Mald* . . . 3K **135**
Green, The. *Orp* (BR5) . . . 7B **128**
Green, The. *Orp* (BR6) . . . 4E **156**
Green, The. *Rich* . . . 5D **98**
Green, The. *Shep* . . . 4G **131**
Green, The. *Sidc* . . . 4A **128**
Green, The. *S'hall* . . . 3C **78**
Green, The. *Sutt* . . . 3K **149**
Green, The. *Twic* . . . 1J **115**
Green, The. *Well* . . . 4J **109**
Green, The. *Wemb* . . . 2A **44**
Green, The. *W Dray* . . . 3A **76**
Green, The. *Wfd G* . . . 5D **20**
Green Va. *W5* . . . 6F **63**
Green Va. *Bexh* . . . 5D **110**
Greenvale Rd. *SE9* . . . 4D **108**
Green Verges. *Stan* . . . 7J **11**
Green Vw. *Chess* . . . 7F **147**
Greenview Av. *Beck* . . . 6A **142**
Greenview Av. *Croy* . . . 6A **142**
Greenview Clo. *W3* . . . 1A **82**
Greenview Ct. *Ashf* . . . 4B **112**
Green Wlk. *NW4* . . . 5F **29**
Green Wlk. *SE1* . . . 3E **86**
Green Wlk. *Hamp* . . . 6D **114**
Green Wlk. *Lou* . . . 1H **21**
Green Wlk. *Ruis* . . . 1H **41**
Green Wlk. *S'hall* . . . 5E **78**
Green Wlk. *Wfd G* . . . 6H **21**
Green Wlk., The. *E4* . . . 1A **20**
Greenway. *N14* . . . 2D **16**
Greenway. *N20* . . . 2D **14**
Green Way. *SE9* . . . 5B **108**
Greenway. *SW20* . . . 4E **136**
Green Way. *Brom* . . . 6C **144**
Greenway. *Chst* . . . 5E **126**
Greenway. *Dag* . . . 2C **56**
Greenway. *Hay* . . . 3J **59**
Greenway. *Kent* . . . 5E **26**
Greenway. *Pinn* . . . 2K **23**
Green Way. *Sun* . . . 4J **131**
Green Way. *Wall* . . . 4G **151**
Green Way. *Wfd G* . . . 5F **21**
Greenway Av. *E17* . . . 4F **35**
Greenway Clo. *N4* . . . 2C **50**
Greenway Clo. *N11* . . . 6K **15**
Greenway Clo. *N15* . . . 4F **33**
Greenway Clo. *N20* . . . 2D **14**
Greenway Clo. *NW9* . . . 2K **27**
Greenway Gdns. *NW9* . . . 2K **27**
Greenway Gdns. *Croy* . . . 3B **154**
Greenway Gdns. *Gnfd* . . . 3E **60**
Greenway Gdns. *Harr* . . . 2J **25**
Greenways. *Beck* . . . 3C **142**
Greenways, The. *Twic* . . . 6A **98**
Greenway, The. *NW9* . . . 2K **27**
Greenway, The. *Houn* . . . 4D **96**
Greenway, The. *Ick* . . . 2E **40**
Green Way, The. *Pinn* . . . 6D **24**
Greenway, The. *Uxb* . . . 2A **58**
Green Way, The. *W'stone* . . . 1J **25**
Greenwell St. *W1* . . . 4F **67** (4K **159**)
Greenwich. . . . 7E 88
Greenwich Bus. Pk. *SE10* . . . 7D **88**
Greenwich Chu. St. *SE10* . . . 6E **88**

Greenwich Commercial Cen. SE10 7D 88
Greenwich Ct. E1 6H 69 (off Cavell St.)
Greenwich Cres. E6 5C 72
Greenwich Gateway Vis. Cen. 6E 88
Greenwich High Rd. SE10 1D 106
Greenwich Ind. Est. SE7 4K 89
Greenwich Ind. Est. SE10 7D 88
Greenwich Mkt. SE10 6E 88
Greenwich Pk. 7F 89
Greenwich Pk. St. SE10 6F 89
Greenwich Quay. SE8 6D 88
Greenwich S. St. SE10 1D 106
Greenwich University. 3E 90 (Beresford St.)
Greenwich University. 6G 109 (Besley Rd., Avery Hill Campus)
Greenwich University. 4E 90 (Wellington St.)
Greenwich Vw. Pl. E14 3D 88
Greenwood Av. Dag 4H 57
Greenwood Av. Enf 2F 9
Greenwood Bus. Cen. Croy 7F 141
Greenwood Clo. Bus H 1D 10
Greenwood Clo. Mord 4G 137
Greenwood Clo. Orp 6J 145
Greenwood Clo. Sidc 2A 128
Greenwood Clo. Th Dit 1A 146
Greenwood Dri. E4 5A 20
Greenwood Gdns. N13 3G 17
Greenwood Gdns. Ilf 1G 37
Greenwood Ho. N22 1A 32
Greenwood Ho. SE4 4K 105
Greenwood La. Hamp H 5F 115
Greenwood Mans. Bark 7A 56 (off Lansbury Av.)
Greenwood Pk. King T 7A 118
Greenwood Pl. NW5 5F 49
Greenwood Rd. E8 6G 51
Greenwood Rd. E13 2H 71
Greenwood Rd. Bex 4K 129
Greenwood Rd. Croy 7B 140
Greenwood Rd. Iswth 3K 97
Greenwood Rd. Mitc 3H 139
Greenwood Rd. Th Dit 1A 146
Greenwoods, The. S Harr 3G 43
Greenwood Ter. NW10 1K 63
Green Wrythe Cres. Cars 1C 150
Green Wrythe La. Cars 6B 138
Green Yd. WC1 3H 161
Green Yd., The. EC3 1G 169
Greer Rd. Harr 1G 25
Greet Ho. SE1 7K 167
Greet St. SE1 1A 86 (5K 167)
Greg Clo. E10 6E 34
Gregory Clo. Brom 4G 143
Gregory Cres. SE9 7B 108
Gregory Pl. W8 2K 83
Gregory Rd. Romf 4D 38
Gregory Rd. S'hall 3E 78
Greig Clo. N8 5J 31
Greig Ter. SE17 6B 86
Grenaby Av. Croy 7D 140
Grenaby Rd. Croy 7D 140
Grenada Ho. E14 7B 70 (off Limehouse Causeway)
Grenada Rd. SE7 7A 90
Grenade St. E14 7B 70
Grenadier St. E16 1E 90
Grena Gdns. Rich 4F 99
Grenard Clo. SE15 7G 87
Grena Rd. Rich 4F 99
Grendon Gdns. Wemb 2G 45
Grendon Ho. E9 7J 51 (off Shore Pl.)
Grendon Ho. N1 2K 67 (off Calshot St.)
Grendon Lodge. Edgw 2D 12
Grendon St. NW8 4C 66 (3C 158)
Grenfell Ct. NW7 6J 13
Grenfell Gdns. Harr 7E 26
Grenfell Gdns. Ilf 5K 37
Grenfell Ho. SE5 7C 86
Grenfell Rd. SW17 6D 120
Grenfell Rd. W11 7F 65
Grenfell Tower. W11 7F 65
Grenfell Wlk. W11 7F 65
Grenier Apartments. SE15 7H 87
Grennell Clo. Sutt 2B 150
Grennell Rd. Sutt 2A 150
Grenoble Gdns. N13 6F 17
Grenville Clo. N3 1G 29
Grenville Clo. Surb 1J 147
Grenville Ct. W13 5B 62
Grenville Gdns. Wfd G 1A 36
Grenville Ho. E3 2A 70 (off Arbery Rd.)
Grenville Ho. SE8 6C 88 (off New King St.)
Grenville Ho. SW1 6H 85 (7C 172) (off Dolphin Sq.)
Grenville M. SW7 4A 84 (off Harrington Gdns.)
Grenville M. Hamp 5F 115
Grenville Pl. NW7 5E 12
Grenville Pl. SW7 3A 84
Grenville Rd. N19 1J 49
Grenville St. WC1 4J 67 (4F 161)
Gresham Av. N20 4J 15
Gresham Clo. Bex 6E 110
Gresham Clo. Enf 3H 7
Gresham Dri. Romf 5B 38
Gresham Gdns. NW11 1G 47
Gresham Lodge. E17 5D 34
Gresham M. W4 3J 81
Gresham Rd. E6 2D 72
Gresham Rd. E16 6K 71
Gresham Rd. NW10 5K 45
Gresham Rd. SE25 4G 141
Gresham Rd. SW9 3A 104
Gresham Rd. Beck 2A 142
Gresham Rd. Edgw 6A 12
Gresham Rd. Hamp 6E 114
Gresham Rd. Houn 1G 97
Gresham Rd. Uxb 2C 58
Gresham St. EC2 6C 68 (7C 162)
Gresham Way. SW19 3K 119
Gresley Clo. E17 6A 34
Gresley Clo. N15 4D 32
Gresley Rd. N19 1G 49
Gressenhall Rd. SW18 6H 101
Gresse St. W1 6H 67 (6C 160)
Gresswell Clo. Sidc 3A 128
Greswell St. SW6 1F 101
Gretton Ho. E2 3J 69 (off Globe Rd.)
Gretton Rd. N17 7A 18
Greville Clo. Twic 7B 98
Greville Ct. E5 4H 51 (off Napoleon Rd.)
Greville Ct. Harr 4J 43
Greville Hall. NW6 2K 65
Greville Lodge. E13 1K 71
Greville Lodge. N12 5E 14
Greville Lodge. Edgw 4C 12 (off Broadhurst Av.)
Greville M. NW6 1K 65 (off Greville Rd.)
Greville Pl. NW6 2K 65
Greville Rd. E17 4E 34
Greville Rd. NW6 2K 65
Greville Rd. Rich 6F 99
Greville St. EC1 5A 68 (6J 161) (in two parts)
Grey Clo. NW11 6A 30
Greycoat Gdns. SW1 3H 85 (2C 172) (off Greycoat St.)
Greycoat Pl. SW1 3H 85 (2C 172)
Greycoat St. SW1 3H 85 (2C 172)
Greycot Rd. Beck 5C 124
Grey Eagle St. E1 4F 69 (4K 163)
Greyfell Clo. Stan 5H 11
Greyfriars. SE26 3G 123 (off Wells Pk. Rd.)
Greyfriars Pas. EC1 6B 68 (7B 162)
Greyhound Ct. WC2 7K 67 (2H 167)
Greyhound Hill. NW4 3C 28
Greyhound La. SW16 6H 121
Greyhound Mans. W6 6G 83 (off Greyhound Rd.)
Greyhound Rd. N15 3E 32
Greyhound Rd. NW10 3D 64
Greyhound Rd. W6 & W14 6F 83
Greyhound Rd. Sutt 5A 150
Greyhound Ter. SW16 1G 139
Grey Ho. W12 7D 64 (off White City Est.)
Greyladies Gdns. SE10 2E 106
Greys Pk. Clo. Kes 5B 156
Greystead Rd. SE23 7J 105
Greystoke Av. Pinn 3E 24
Greystoke Ct. W5 4E 62
Greystoke Dri. Ruis 7D 22
Greystoke Gdns. W5 4E 62
Greystoke Gdns. Enf 4C 6
Greystoke Ho. SE15 6G 87 (off Peckham Pk. Rd.)
Greystoke Ho. W5 4E 62
Greystoke Lodge. W5 4F 63 (off Hanger La.)
Greystoke Pk. Ter. W5 3D 62
Greystoke Pl. EC4 6A 68 (7J 161)
Greystone Gdns. Harr 6C 26
Greystone Gdns. Ilf 2G 37
Greystone Path. E11 7H 35 (off Mornington Rd.)
Greyswood Av. N18 6E 18
Greyswood St. SW16 6F 121
Grey Turner Ho. W12 6C 64
Grierson Rd. SE23 7K 105
Griffin Cen. Felt 5K 95
Griffin Cen., The. King T 2D 134 (off Market Pl.)
Griffin Clo. NW10 5D 46
Griffin Ct. W4 5B 82
Griffin Ct. Bren 6E 80
Griffin Ho. E14 6D 70 (off Ricardo St.)
Griffin Ho. W6 4F 83 (off Hammersmith Rd.)
Griffin Mnr. Way. SE28 3H 91
Griffin Rd. N17 2E 32
Griffin Rd. SE18 5H 91
Griffins Clo. N21 7J 7
Griffin Way. Sun 2J 131
Griffith Clo. Dag 7C 38
Griffiths Clo. Wor Pk 2D 148
Griffiths Rd. SW19 7J 119
Griggs App. Ilf 2G 55
Grigg's Pl. SE1 3E 86
Griggs Rd. E10 6E 34
Grilse Clo. N9 4C 18
Grimaldi Ho. N1 2K 67 (off Calshot St.)
Grimsby Gro. E16 2F 91
Grimsby St. E2 4F 69 (4K 163)
Grim's Dyke Golf Course. 4A 10
Grimsdyke Rd. Pinn 1D 24
Grimsel Path. SE5 7B 86
Grimshaw Clo. N6 7E 30
Grimston Rd. SW6 2H 101
Grimthorpe Ho. EC1 3A 162
Grimwade Av. Croy 3G 153
Grimwade Clo. SE15 3J 105
Grimwood Rd. Twic 7K 97
Grindall Clo. Croy 4B 152
Grindall Ho. E1 4H 69 (off Darling Row)
Grindal St. SE1 2A 86 (7J 167)
Grindleford Av. N11 2K 15
Grindley Gdns. Croy 6F 141
Grindley Ho. E3 5B 70 (off Leopold St.)
Grinling Pl. SE8 6C 88
Grinstead Rd. SE8 5A 88
Grisedale. NW1 3G 67 (1A 160) (off Cumberland Mkt.)
Grittleton Av. Wemb 6H 45
Grittleton Rd. W9 4J 65
Grizedale Ter. SE23 2H 123
Grocer's Hall Ct. EC2 6D 68 (1E 168)
Grocer's Hall Gdns. EC2 1E 168
Grogan Clo. Hamp 6D 114
Groombridge Clo. Well 5A 110
Groombridge Rd. E9 7K 51
Groom Clo. Brom 4K 143
Groom Cres. SW18 7B 102
Groome Ho. SE11 4K 85 (4H 173)
Groomfield Clo. SW17 4E 120
Groom Pl. SW1 3E 84 (1H 171)
Grooms Dri. Pinn 5J 23
Grosmont Rd. SE18 6K 91
Grosse Way. SW15 6D 100
Grosvenor Av. N5 5C 50
Grosvenor Av. SW14 3A 100
Grosvenor Av. Cars 6D 150
Grosvenor Av. Harr 6F 25
Grosvenor Av. Hay 2H 59
Grosvenor Av. Rich 5E 98
Grosvenor Cotts. SW1 4E 84 (3G 171)
Grosvenor Ct. E10 1D 52
Grosvenor Ct. N14 7B 6
Grosvenor Ct. NW6 1F 65
Grosvenor Ct. NW7 5E 12 (off Hale La.)
Grosvenor Ct. SE5 6C 86
Grosvenor Ct. W3 1G 81
Grosvenor Ct. W5 7E 62 (off Grove, The)
Grosvenor Ct. Mans. W2 6D 66 (1E 164) (off Edgware Rd.)
Grosvenor Cres. NW9 4G 27
Grosvenor Cres. SW1 2E 84 (7H 165)
Grosvenor Cres. Uxb 7D 40
Grosvenor Cres. M. SW1 2E 84 (7G 165)
Grosvenor Est. SW1 4H 85 (3D 172)
Grosvenor Gdns. E6 3B 72
Grosvenor Gdns. N10 3G 31
Grosvenor Gdns. N14 5C 6
Grosvenor Gdns. NW2 5E 46
Grosvenor Gdns. NW11 6H 29
Grosvenor Gdns. SW1 3F 85 (1J 171)
Grosvenor Gdns. SW14 3A 100
Grosvenor Gdns. King T 6D 116
Grosvenor Gdns. Wall 7G 151
Grosvenor Gdns. Wfd G 6D 20
Grosvenor Gdns. M. E. SW1 1K 171
Grosvenor Gdns. M. N. SW1 2J 171
Grosvenor Gdns. M. S. SW1 2K 171
Grosvenor Ga. W1 7E 66 (3G 165)
Grosvenor Hill. SW19 6G 119
Grosvenor Hill. W1 7F 67 (2J 165)
Grosvenor Hill Ct. W1 7F 67 (2J 165) (off Bourdon St.)
Grosvenor Pde. W5 1G 81 (off Uxbridge Rd.)
Grosvenor Pk. SE5 7C 86
Grosvenor Pk. Rd. E17 5C 34
Grosvenor Pl. SW1 2E 84 (7H 165)
Grosvenor Ri. E. E17 5D 34
Grosvenor Rd. E6 1B 72
Grosvenor Rd. E7 6K 53
Grosvenor Rd. E10 1E 52
Grosvenor Rd. E11 5K 35
Grosvenor Rd. N3 7C 14
Grosvenor Rd. N9 1C 18
Grosvenor Rd. N10 1F 31
Grosvenor Rd. SE25 4F 141
Grosvenor Rd. SW1 6F 85 (7J 171)
Grosvenor Rd. W4 5H 81
Grosvenor Rd. W7 1A 80
Grosvenor Rd. Belv 6G 93
Grosvenor Rd. Bexh 5D 110
Grosvenor Rd. Bren 6D 80
Grosvenor Rd. Dag 1F 57
Grosvenor Rd. Houn 3D 96
Grosvenor Rd. Ilf 3G 55
Grosvenor Rd. Orp 6J 145
Grosvenor Rd. Rich 5E 98
Grosvenor Rd. Romf 7K 39
Grosvenor Rd. S'hall 3D 78
Grosvenor Rd. Twic 1A 116
Grosvenor Rd. Wall 6F 151
Grosvenor Rd. W Wick 1D 154
Grosvenor Sq. W1 7E 66 (2H 165)
Grosvenor St. W1 7F 67 (2J 165)
Grosvenor Ter. SE5 7C 86
Grosvenor Va. Ruis 2H 41
Grosvenor Way. E5 2J 51
Grosvenor Wharf Rd. E14 4F 89
Grotes Bldgs. SE3 2G 107
Grote's Pl. SE3 2G 107
Groton Rd. SW18 2K 119
Grotto Ct. SE1 2B 86 (6B 168)
Grotto Pas. W1 5E 66 (5H 159)
Grotto Rd. Twic 2K 115
Grove Av. N3 7D 14
Grove Av. N10 2G 31
Grove Av. W7 6J 61
Grove Av. Pinn 4C 24
Grove Av. Sutt 6J 149
Grove Av. Twic 1K 115
Grovebury Clo. Eri 6K 93
Grovebury Ct. N14 7C 6
Grovebury Ct. Bexh 5H 111
Grovebury Rd. SE2 2B 92
Grove Clo. N14 7B 6
Grove Clo. SE23 1A 124
Grove Clo. Brom 2J 155
Grove Clo. Felt 4C 114
Grove Clo. King T 4F 135
Grove Clo. Uxb 5C 40
Grove Cotts. W4 6A 82
Grove Ct. NW8 1A 158
Grove Ct. SW10 5A 84 (6A 170) (off Drayton Gdns.)
Grove Ct. W5 1E 80
Grove Ct. E Mol 4H 133
Grove Ct. Houn 4E 96
Grove Ct. King T 3E 134 (off Grove Cres.)
Grove Cres. E18 2H 35
Grove Cres. NW9 4J 27
Grove Cres. Felt 4C 114
Grove Cres. King T 3E 134
Grove Cres. W on T 7K 131
Grove Cres. Rd. E15 6F 53
Grovedale Rd. N19 2H 49
Grove Dwellings. E1 5J 69
Grove End. E18 2H 35
Grove End. NW5 4F 49

Grove End Gdns. NW8 2B 66
Grove End Ho. NW8 2A 158
Grove End La. Esh 7H 133
Grove End Rd. NW8 2B 66 (1A 158)
Grovefield. N11 4A 16 (off Coppies Gro.)
Grove Footpath. Surb 4E 134
Grove Gdns. NW4 5C 28
Grove Gdns. NW8 3C 66 (2D 158)
Grove Gdns. Dag 3J 57
Grove Gdns. Enf 1E 8
Grove Gdns. Rich 6F 99
Grove Gdns. Tedd 4A 116
Grove Grn. Rd. E10 3E 52
Grove Hall Ct. NW8 3A 66 (1A 158)
Grove Hill. E18 2H 35
Grove Hill. Harr 7J 25
Grovehill Ct. Brom 6H 125
Grove Hill Rd. SE5 3E 104
Grove Hill Rd. Harr 7K 25
Grove Ho. SW3 6C 84 (7D 170) (off Chelsea Manor St.)
Grove Ho. Rd. N8 4J 31
Groveland Av. SW16 7K 121
Groveland Ct. EC4 1D 168
Groveland Rd. Beck 3B 142
Grovelands. King T 4D 134 (off Palace Rd.)
Grovelands. W Mol 4E 132
Grovelands Clo. SE5 2E 104
Grovelands Clo. Harr 3F 43
Grovelands Ct. N14 7C 6
Grovelands Pk. 1E 16
Grovelands Rd. N13 4E 16
Grovelands Rd. N15 6G 33
Grovelands Rd. Orp 7A 128
Groveland Way. N Mald 5J 135
Grove La. SE5 1D 104
Grove La. King T 4E 134
Grove La. Uxb 4B 58
Grove La. Ter. SE5 2D 104
Groveley Rd. Sun 5H 113
Grove Mans. W6 2E 82 (off Hammersmith Gro.)
Grove Mkt. Pl. SE9 6D 108
Grove M. W6 3E 82
Grove Mill Pl. Cars 3E 150
Grove Nature Reserve, The. 4B 58
Grove Park. 3K 125 (Bromley)
Grove Park. 1J 99 (Chiswick)
Grove Pk. E11 6K 35
Grove Pk. NW9 4J 27
Grove Pk. SE5 2E 104
Gro. Park Av. E4 7J 19
Gro. Park Bri. W4 7J 81
Gro. Park Gdns. W4 7H 81
Gro. Park Ind. Est. NW9 4K 27
Gro. Park M. W4 7J 81
Gro. Park Rd. N15 4E 32
Gro. Park Rd. SE9 3A 126
Gro. Park. Rd. W4 7H 81
Gro. Park Ter. W4 7H 81 (in two parts)
Grove Pas. E2 2H 69
Grove Pl. NW3 3B 48
Grove Pl. SW12 7F 103
Grove Pl. W3 1J 81
Grove Pl. Bark 7G 55
Grover Ct. SE13 2D 106
Grover Ho. SE11 5K 85 (6H 173)
Grove Rd. E3 1K 69
Grove Rd. E4 4K 19
Grove Rd. E11 7H 35
Grove Rd. E17 6D 34
Grove Rd. E18 2H 35
Grove Rd. N11 5A 16
Grove Rd. N12 5G 15
Grove Rd. N15 5E 32
Grove Rd. NW2 6E 46
Grove Rd. SW13 2B 100
Grove Rd. SW19 7A 120
Grove Rd. W3 1J 81
Grove Rd. W5 7D 62
Grove Rd. Belv 6F 93
Grove Rd. Bexh 4J 111
Grove Rd. Bren 5C 80
Grove Rd. Chad H 7B 38
Grove Rd. Cockf 3H 5
Grove Rd. E Mol 4H 133
Grove Rd. Edgw 6B 12
Grove Rd. Houn 4E 96
Grove Rd. Iswth 1J 97
Grove Rd. Mitc 3E 138 (in two parts)
Grove Rd. Pinn 5D 24
Grove Rd. Rich 6F 99
Grove Rd. Shep 6E 130
Grove Rd. Surb 5D 134
Grove Rd. Sutt 6J 149
Grove Rd. T Hth 4A 140
Grove Rd. Twic 3H 115
Grove Rd. Uxb 7A 40
Groveside Clo. W3 5G 63
Groveside Clo. Cars 2C 150
Groveside Rd. E4 2B 20
Grovestile Waye. Felt 7F 95
Grove St. N18 5A 18
Grove St. SE8 4B 88
Grove Ter. NW5 3F 49
Grove Ter. S'hall 7E 60
Grove Ter. Tedd 4A 116
Grove Ter. M. NW5 3F 49
Grove, The. (Junct.) 1G 123
Grove, The. E15 6G 53
Grove, The. N3 1J 29
Grove, The. N4 7K 31
Grove, The. N6 1E 48
Grove, The. N8 5H 31
Grove, The. N13 4F 17 (in two parts)
Grove, The. N14 5B 6
Grove, The. NW9 5K 27
Grove, The. NW11 7G 29
Grove, The. W5 1D 80
Grove, The. Bexh 4D 110
Grove, The. Edgw 4C 12
Grove, The. Enf 2F 7
Grove, The. Gnfd 6G 61
Grove, The. Iswth 1J 97
Grove, The. Sidc 4E 128
Grove, The. Stan 2F 11
Grove, The. Tedd 4A 116
Grove, The. Twic 6B 98
Grove, The. Uxb (UB8) 4B 58
Grove, The. Uxb (UB10) 5C 40
Grove, The. W on T 7K 131
Grove, The. W Wick 3D 154
Grove Va. SE22 4F 105
Grove Va. Chst 6E 126
Grove Vs. E14 7D 70
Groveway. SW9 1K 103
Groveway. Dag 3D 56
Grove Way. Esh 7G 133
Grove Way. Uxb 7A 40
Grove Way. Wemb 5H 45
Grovewood. Rich 1G 99
Grovewood Pl. Wfd G 6J 21
Grummant Rd. SE15 1F 105
Grundy St. E14 6D 70
Gruneisen Rd. N3 7E 14
Guardian Ct. SE12 5G 107
Guards' Mus. 2G 85 (7B 166)
Gubyon Av. SE24 5B 104
Guerin Sq. E3 3B 70
Guernsey Clo. Houn 7E 78
Guernsey Gro. SE24 7C 104
Guernsey Ho. N1 6C 50 (off Douglas Rd. N.)
Guernsey Ho. Enf 1E 8 (off Eastfield Rd.)
Guernsey Rd. E11 1F 53
Guernsey Rd. N1 6C 50
Guibal Rd. SE12 7K 107
Guildersfield Rd. SW16 7J 121
Guildford Av. Felt 2H 113
Guildford Ct. SW8 7J 85 (off Guildford Rd.)
Guildford Gro. SE10 1D 106
Guildford Rd. E6 6D 72
Guildford Rd. E17 1E 34
Guildford Rd. SW8 1J 103
Guildford Rd. Croy 6D 140
Guildford Rd. Ilf 2J 55
Guildford Way. Wall 5J 151
Guildhall. 6C 68 (7D 162)
Guildhall Art Gallery. 6D 68 (7E 162)
Guildhall Bldgs. EC2 7E 162
Guildhall Library. 6C 68 (7D 162)
Guildhall Offices. EC2 6C 68 (7D 162) (off Basinghall St.)
Guildhall School of Music & Drama. 5C 68 (5D 162) (off Silk St.)
Guildhall Yd. EC2 7D 162
Guildhouse St. SW1 4G 85 (3A 172)
Guildown Av. N12 4E 14
Guild Rd. SE7 6B 90
Guildsway. E17 1B 34
Guilford Av. Surb 5F 135
Guilford Pl. WC1 4K 67 (4G 161)
Guilford St. WC1 4J 67 (4E 160)
Guilfoyle. NW9 2B 28
Guillemot Pl. N22 2K 31
Guilsborough Clo. NW10 7A 46
Guinness Clo. E9 7A 52
Guinness Clo. Hay 3F 77
Guinness Ct. E1 1J 169
Guinness Ct. EC1 2D 162
Guinness Ct. NW8 1C 66
Guinness Ct. SE1 6G 169
Guinness Ct. SW3 4D 84 (4E 170)
Guinness Ct. Croy 2F 153
Guinness Sq. SE1 4E 86
Guinness Trust Bldgs. SE11 5B 86
Guinness Trust Bldgs. W6 5F 83 (off Fulham Pal. Rd.)
Guinness Trust Est. E15 1H 71
Guinness Trust Est. N16 1E 50
Guion Rd. SW6 2H 101
Gulland Wlk. N1 7C 50 (off Oronsay Wlk.)
Gull Clo. Wall 7J 151
Gulliver Clo. N'holt 1D 60
Gulliver Rd. Sidc 2H 127
Gulliver's Ho. EC1 4C 162
Gulliver St. SE16 3A 88
Gulston Wlk. SW3 4F 171
Gumleigh Rd. W5 4C 80
Gumley Gdns. Iswth 3A 98
Gundulph Rd. Brom 3A 144
Gun Ho. E1 1H 87 (off Wapping High St.)
Gunmaker's La. E3 1A 70
Gunnell Clo. SE26 4G 123
Gunnell Clo. Croy 6F 141
Gunner La. SE18 5E 90
Gunnersbury. 5H 81
Gunnersbury Av. W5, W3 & W4 1F 81
Gunnersbury Clo. W4 5H 81
Gunnersbury Ct. W3 2H 81
Gunnersbury Cres. W3 2G 81
Gunnersbury Dri. W5 2F 81
Gunnersbury Gdns. W3 2G 81
Gunnersbury La. W3 3G 81
Gunnersbury Mnr. W5 1F 81
Gunnersbury M. W4 5H 81
Gunnersbury Park. (Junct.) 3G 81
Gunnersbury Pk. Mus. 3G 81
Gunners Gro. E4 3K 19
Gunners Rd. SW18 2B 120
Gunning St. SE18 4J 91
Gunpowder Sq. EC4 6A 68 (7K 161) (off Gough Sq., in two parts)
Gunstor Rd. N16 4E 50
Gun St. E1 5F 69 (6J 163)
Gunter Gro. SW10 6A 84
Gunter Gro. Edgw 1K 27
Gunterstone Rd. W14 4G 83
Gunthorpe St. E1 5F 69 (6K 163)
Gunton Rd. E5 3H 51
Gunton Rd. SW17 6E 120
Gunwhale Clo. SE16 1K 87
Gun Wharf. E1 1J 87 (off Wapping High St.)
Gun Wharf Bus. Cen. E3 1A 70 (off Old Ford Rd.)
Gurdon Ho. E14 6C 70 (off Dod St.)
Gurdon Rd. SE7 5J 89
Gurnard Clo. W Dray 7A 58
Gurnell Gro. W13 4K 61
Gurney Clo. E15 5G 53
Gurney Clo. E17 1K 33
Gurney Clo. Bark 6F 55
Gurney Cres. Croy 1K 151
Gurney Dri. N2 4A 30
Gurney Ho. E2 2G 69 (off Goldsmith Row)
Gurney Ho. Hay 5G 77
Gurney Rd. E15 5G 53
Gurney Rd. SW6 3A 102
Gurney Rd. Cars 4E 150
Gurney Rd. N'holt 3K 59
Guthrie Ct. SE1 7K 167
Guthrie St. SW3 5B 84 (5C 170)
Gutter La. EC2 6C 68 (7C 162)
Guyatt Gdns. Mitc 2E 138
Guy Barnett Gro. SE3 3J 107
Guy Rd. Wall 3H 151
Guyscliff Rd. SE13 5E 106
Guys Retreat. Buck H 1F 21
Guy St. SE1 2D 86 (6F 169)
Gwalior Rd. SW15 4F 101
Gwendolen Av. SW15 4F 101
Gwendolen Clo. SW15 5F 101
Gwendoline Av. E13 1K 71
Gwendwr Rd. W14 5G 83
Gweneth Cotts. Edgw 6B 12
Gwent Ct. SE16 1K 87 (off Rotherhithe St.)
Gwillim Clo. Sidc 5A 110
Gwilym Maries Ho. E2 3H 69 (off Blythe St.)
Gwydor Rd. Beck 3K 141
Gwydyr Rd. Brom 3H 143
Gwyn Clo. SW6 7A 84
Gwynne Av. Croy 7K 141
Gwynne Clo. W4 6B 82
Gwynne Ho. E1 5H 69 (off Turner St.)
Gwynne Ho. WC1 3A 68 (2J 161) (off Lloyd Baker St.)
Gwynne Pk. Av. Wfd G 6J 21
Gwynne Pl. WC1 3K 67 (2H 161)
Gwynne Rd. SW11 2B 102
Gylcote Clo. SE5 4D 104
Gyles Pk. Stan 1C 26
Gyllyngdune Gdns. Ilf 2K 55
Gypsy Corner. (Junct.) 5J 63

Haarlem Rd. W14 3F 83
Haberdasher Est. N1 3D 68 (1F 163)
Haberdasher Pl. N1 1F 163
Haberdashers Ct. SE14 3K 105
Haberdasher St. N1 3D 68 (1F 163)
Habington Ho. SE5 7D 86 (off Notley St.)
Haccombe Rd. SW19 6A 120
Hackbridge. 2E 150
Hackbridge Grn. Wall 2E 150
Hackbridge Pk. Gdns. Cars 2D 150
Hackbridge Rd. Wall 2E 150
Hackford Rd. SW9 1K 103
Hackford Wlk. SW9 1K 103
Hackington Cres. Beck 6C 124
Hackney. 6H 51
Hackney Gro. E8 6H 51
Hackney Rd. E2 3E 68 (2J 163)
Hackney Wick. 6C 52
Hackney Wick. (Junct.) 6A 52
Hadar Clo. N20 1D 14
Hadden Rd. SE28 3J 91
Hadden Way. Gnfd 6H 43
Haddington Ct. SE10 7D 88 (off Tarves Way)
Haddington Rd. Brom 3F 125
Haddo Ho. SE10 6D 88 (off Haddo St.)
Haddon Clo. Enf 6B 8
Haddon Clo. N Mald 5B 136
Haddon Ct. NW4 3E 28
Haddon Ct. W3 7B 64
Haddonfield. SE8 4K 87
Haddon Gro. Sidc 7K 109
Haddon Rd. Sutt 4K 149
Haddo St. SE10 6D 88
Haden Ct. N4 2A 50
Haden La. N11 4B 16
Hadfield Clo. S'hall 3D 60
Hadfield Ho. E1 6G 69 (off Ellen St.)
Hadleigh Clo. E1 4J 69
Hadleigh Clo. SW20 2H 137
Hadleigh Ct. E4 1B 20
Hadleigh Ho. E1 4J 69 (off Hadleigh Clo.)
Hadleigh Rd. N9 7C 8
Hadleigh St. E2 3J 69
Hadleigh Wlk. E6 6C 72
Hadley. 3C 4
Hadley Clo. N21 6F 7
Hadley Comn. Barn 2D 4
Hadley Ct. N16 1G 51
Hadley Ct. New Bar 3E 4
Hadley Gdns. W4 5K 81
Hadley Gdns. S'hall 5D 78
Hadley Grn. Rd. Barn 2C 4
Hadley Grn. W. Barn 2C 4
Hadley Gro. Barn 2B 4
Hadley Highstone. Barn 1C 4
Hadley Mnr. Trad. Est. Barn 3C 4
Hadley M. Barn 3C 4
Hadley Pde. Barn 3B 4 (off High St.)
Hadley Ridge. Barn 3C 4
Hadley Rd. Barn & Enf (EN4,EN2) 1K 5
Hadley Rd. Barn (EN5) 2E 4
Hadley Rd. Belv 4F 93
Hadley Rd. Mitc 4H 139
Hadley St. NW1 6F 49 (in two parts)
Hadley Way. N21 6F 7
Hadley Wood. 1F 5
Hadley Wood Golf Course. 1G 5
Hadley Wood Rd. Barn 2F 5
Hadlow Ho. SE17 5E 86 (off Kinglake Est.)
Hadlow Pl. SE19 7G 123
Hadlow Rd. Sidc 4A 128
Hadlow Rd. Well 7C 92
Hadrian Clo. Stai 7A 94
Hadrian Ct. Sutt 7K 149
Hadrian Est. E2 2G 69

Hadrians Ride. Enf 5A 8
Hadrian St. SE10 5G 89
Hadrian Way. Stanw 7A 94 (in two parts)
Hadstock Ho. NW1 3H 67 (1D 160) (off Ossulston St.)
Hadyn Pk. Ct. W12 2C 82 (off Curwen Rd.)
Hadyn Pk. Rd. W12 2C 82
Hafer Rd. SW11 4D 102
Hafton Rd. SE6 1G 125
Haggard Rd. Twic 7B 98
Hagger Ct. E17 3F 35
Haggerston. 2F 69
Haggerston Rd. E8 & E2 7F 51
Hague St. E2 3G 69
Ha Ha Rd. SE18 6D 90
Haig Ho. E2 2G 69 (1K 163) (off Shipton St.)
Haig Pl. Mord 6J 137
Haig Rd. Stan 5H 11
Haig Rd. Uxb 5D 58
Haig Rd. E. E13 3A 72
Haig Rd. W. E13 3A 72
Haigville Gdns. Ilf 4F 37
Hailes Clo. SW19 6A 120
Haileybury Av. Enf 6A 8
Hailey Rd. Eri 2G 93
Hailsham Av. SW2 2K 121
Hailsham Clo. Surb 7D 134
Hailsham Cres. Bark 6K 55
Hailsham Dri. Harr 3H 25
Hailsham Rd. SW17 6E 120
Hailsham Ter. N18 5J 17
Haimo Rd. SE9 5B 108
Hainault Ct. E17 4F 35
Hainault Gore. Romf 5E 38
Hainault Rd. E11 1E 52
Hainault Rd. Chad H 6F 39
Hainault Rd. Col R 2J 39
Hainault Rd. Romf 1B 38
Hainault St. SE9 1F 127
Hainault St. Ilf 2G 55
Haines St. SW8 7G 85
Haines Wlk. Mord 7K 137
Hainford Clo. SE4 4K 105
Haining Clo. W4 5G 81
Hainthorpe Rd. SE27 3B 122
Hainton Clo. E1 6H 69
Halberd M. E5 2H 51
Halbutt Gdns. Dag 3F 57
Halbutt St. Dag 4F 57
Halcomb St. N1 1E 68
Halcot Av. Bexh 5H 111
Halcrow St. E1 5H 69
Halcyon. Enf 5K 7 (off Private Rd.)
Halcyon Wharf. E1 1G 87 (off Hermitage Wall)
Haldane Clo. N10 7A 16
Haldane Pl. SW18 1K 119
Haldane Rd. E6 3B 72
Haldane Rd. SE28 7D 74
Haldane Rd. SW6 7H 83
Haldane Rd. S'hall 7G 61
Haldan Rd. E4 6K 19
Haldon Rd. SW18 6H 101
Hale Clo. E4 3K 19
Hale Clo. Edgw 5D 12
Hale Ct. Edgw 5D 12
Hale Dri. NW7 6D 12
Hale End. 6A 20
Hale End Clo. Ruis 6J 23
Hale End Rd. E4 & Wfd G 6A 20
Halefield Rd. N17 1H 33
Hale Gdns. N17 4G 33
Hale Gdns. W3 1G 81
Hale Gro. Gdns. NW7 5F 13
Hale Ho. SW1 5H 85 (5D 172) (off Lindsay Sq.)
Hale La. NW7 5E 12
Hale La. Edgw 5C 12
Hale Path. SE27 4B 122
Hale Rd. E6 4C 72
Hale Rd. N17 3G 33
Halesowen Rd. Mord 7K 137
Hales Prior. N1 2K 67 (1G 161) (off Calshot St.)
Hales St. SE8 7C 88
Hale St. E14 7D 70
Halesworth Clo. E5 2J 51
Halesworth Rd. SE13 3D 106
Hale, The. 5D 12
Hale, The. E4 7A 20
Hale, The. N17 3G 33
Hale Wlk. W7 5J 61
Haley Rd. NW4 6E 28
Half Acre. Bren 6D 80
Half Acre. Stan 6H 11
Half Acre Rd. W7 1J 79
Half Moon Ct. EC1 6C 162
Half Moon Cres. N1 2K 67 (in two parts)
Half Moon La. SE24 6C 104
Half Moon Pas. E1 6F 69 (1K 169) (in two parts)
Half Moon St. W1 1F 85 (4K 165)
Halford Clo. Edgw 2H 27
Halford Rd. E10 5F 35
Halford Rd. SW6 6J 83
Halford Rd. Rich 5E 98
Halford Rd. Uxb 4C 40
Halfway St. Sidc 7H 109
Haliburton Rd. Twic 5A 98
Haliday Ho. N1 6D 50 (off Mildmay St.)
Haliday Wlk. N1 6D 50
Halidon Clo. E9 5J 51
Halifax. NW9 2B 28
Halifax Clo. Tedd 6J 115
Halifax Rd. Enf 2H 7
Halifax Rd. Gnfd 1F 61
Halifax St. SE26 3H 123
Halifield Dri. Belv 3E 92
Haling Down Pas. Purl 7C 152 (in two parts)
Haling Gro. S Croy 7C 152
Haling Pk. Gdns. Croy 6B 152
Haling Pk. Rd. S Croy 5B 152
Haling Rd. S Croy 6D 152
Haliwell Ho. NW6 1K 65 (off Mortimer Cres.)
Halkin Arc. SW1 3D 84 (1F 171) (in two parts)
Halkin M. SW1 3E 84 (1G 171)
Halkin Pl. SW1 3E 84 (1G 171)
Halkin St. SW1 2E 84 (7H 165)
Hallam Clo. Chst 5D 126
Hallam Ct. W1 5F 67 (5K 159) (off Hallam St.)
Hallam Gdns. Pinn 1C 24
Hallam Ho. SW1 5G 85 (6B 172) (off Churchill Gdns.)
Hallam M. W1 5F 67 (5K 159)
Hallam Rd. N15 4B 32
Hallam Rd. SW13 3D 100
Hallam St. W1 4F 67 (4K 159)
Hallane Ho. SE27 5C 122
Hall Clo. W5 5E 62
Hall Ct. Tedd 5K 115
Hall Dri. SE26 5J 123
Hall Dri. W7 6J 61
Halley Gdns. SE13 4F 107
Halley Ho. E2 2G 69 (off Pritchards Rd.)
Halley Ho. SE10 5H 89 (off Armitage Rd.)
Halley Rd. E7 & E12 6A 54
Halley St. E14 5A 70
Hall Farm Clo. Stan 4G 11
Hall Farm Dri. Twic 7H 97
Hallfield Est. W2 6A 66 (in two parts)
Hall Gdns. E4 4G 19
Hall Ga. NW8 3B 66 (1A 158)
Halliards, The. W on T 6J 131
Halliday Sq. S'hall 1H 79
Halliford Clo. Shep 4F 131
Halliford Rd. Shep & Sun 5G 131
Halliford St. N1 7C 50
Hallingbury Ct. E17 3D 34
Halliwell Ct. SE22 5G 105
Halliwell Rd. SW2 6K 103
Halliwick Ct. Pde. N12 6J 15 (off Woodhouse Rd.)
Halliwick Rd. N10 1E 30
Hall Lane. (Junct.) 4E 18
Hall La. E4 5F 19
Hall La. NW4 1C 28
Hall La. Hay 7F 77
Hallmark Trad. Cen. Wemb 4J 45
Hallmead Rd. Sutt 3K 149
Hall Oak Wlk. NW6 6H 47
Hallowell Av. Croy 4J 151
Hallowell Clo. Mitc 3E 138
Hallowell Rd. N'wd 1G 23
Hallowfield Way. Mitc 3C 138
Hall Place. 6J 111
Hall Pl. W2 4B 66 (4A 158) (in two parts)
Hall Pl. Cres. Bex 5J 111
Hall Place Mus. 6J 111
Hall Rd. E6 1D 72
Hall Rd. E15 4F 53
Hall Rd. NW8 3A 66 (1A 158)
Hall Rd. Chad H 6C 38
Hall Rd. Iswth 5H 97
Hall Rd. Wall 7F 151
Hallside Rd. Enf 1A 8
Hall St. EC1 3B 68 (1B 162)
Hall St. N12 5F 15
Hallsville Rd. E16 6H 71
Hallswelle Pde. NW11 5H 29
Hallswelle Rd. NW11 5H 29
Hall, The. SE3 3J 107
Hall Tower. W2 5B 158
Hall Vw. SE9 2B 126
Hallywell Cres. E6 5D 72
Halons Rd. SE9 7E 108
Halpin Pl. SE17 4D 86
Halsbrook Rd. SE3 3A 108
Halsbury Clo. Stan 4G 11
Halsbury Ct. Stan 5G 11
Halsbury Rd. W12 1D 82
Halsbury Rd. E. N'holt 4G 43
Halsbury Rd. W. N'holt 5F 43
Halsend. Hay 1K 77
Halsey M. SW3 4D 84 (3E 170)
Halsey St. SW3 4D 84 (3E 170)
Halsmere Rd. SE5 1B 104
Halstead Clo. Croy 3C 152
Halstead Ct. E17 7B 34
Halstead Ct. N1 2D 68 (1F 163) (off Fairbank Est.)
Halstead Gdns. N21 1J 17
Halstead Rd. E11 5J 35
Halstead Rd. N21 1J 17
Halstead Rd. Enf 4K 7
Halston Clo. SW11 6D 102
Halstow Rd. NW10 3F 65
Halstow Rd. SE10 5J 89
Halsway. Hay 1J 77
Halton Clo. N11 6J 15
Halton Cross St. N1 1B 68
Halton Mans. N1 7B 50
Halton Pl. N1 1C 68
Halton Rd. N1 7B 50
Halt Robin La. Belv 4H 93
Halt Robin Rd. Belv 4G 93 (in two parts)
Halyard Ho. E14 3E 88
Ham. 3C 116
Hamara Ghar. E13 1A 72
Hambalt Rd. SW4 5G 103
Hamble Clo. Ruis 2G 41
Hambleden Pl. SE21 1E 122
Hambledon. SE17 6D 86 (off Villa St.)
Hambledon Clo. Uxb 4D 58
Hambledon Ct. SE22 4E 104
Hambledon Ct. W5 7E 62
Hambledon Gdns. SE25 3F 141
Hambledon Rd. SW18 7H 101
Hambledown Rd. Sidc 7H 109
Hamblehyrst. Beck 2D 142
Hamble St. SW6 3K 101
Hambleton Clo. Wor Pk 2E 148
Hamble Wlk. N'holt 2E 60 (off Brabazon Rd.)
Hambley Ho. SE16 4H 87 (off Camilla Rd.)
Hamblin Ho. S'hall 7C 60 (off Broadway, The)
Hambridge Way. SW2 7A 104
Hambro Av. Brom 1J 155
Hambrook Rd. SE25 3H 141
Hambro Rd. SW16 6H 121
Hambrough Ho. Hay 5A 60
Hambrough Rd. S'hall 1C 78
Ham Clo. Rich 3C 116 (in two parts)
Ham Comn. Rich 3D 116
Ham Ct. NW9 2A 28
Hamden Cres. Dag 3H 57
Hamel Clo. Harr 4D 26
Hame Way. E6 4E 72
Ham Farm Rd. Rich 4D 116
Hamfrith Rd. E15 6H 53
Ham Ga. Av. Rich 3D 116
Ham House. 1C 116
Hamilton Av. N9 7B 8
Hamilton Av. Ilf 4F 37
Hamilton Av. Romf 2K 39
Hamilton Av. Surb 2G 147
Hamilton Av. Sutt 2G 149
Hamilton Bldgs. EC2 4H 163
Hamilton Clo. N17 3F 33
Hamilton Clo. NW8 3B 66 (2A 158)
Hamilton Clo. SE16 2A 88
Hamilton Clo. Cockf 4H 5
Hamilton Clo. Felt 5H 113
Hamilton Clo. Stan 2D 10
Hamilton Ct. SE6 1H 125
Hamilton Ct. SW15 3G 101
Hamilton Ct. W5 7E 62
Hamilton Ct. W9 3A 66 (off Maida Va.)
Hamilton Ct. Croy 1G 153
Hamilton Cres. N13 4F 17
Hamilton Cres. Harr 3D 42
Hamilton Cres. Houn 5F 97
Hamilton Gdns. NW8 3A 66 (1A 158)
Hamilton Ho. E14 7B 70 (off Victory Pl.)
Hamilton Ho. E14 5D 88 (off St Davids Sq.)
Hamilton Ho. NW8 1A 158
Hamilton Ho. W4 6A 82
Hamilton La. N5 4B 50
Hamilton Lodge. E1 4J 69 (off Cleveland Gro.)
Hamilton M. SW18 1J 119
Hamilton M. SW19 7J 119
Hamilton M. W1 2F 85 (6J 165)
Hamilton Pde. Felt 4H 113
Hamilton Pk. N5 4B 50
Hamilton Pk. W. N5 4B 50
Hamilton Pl. W1 1E 84 (5H 165)
Hamilton Pl. Sun 7K 113
Hamilton Rd. E15 3G 71
Hamilton Rd. E17 2A 34
Hamilton Rd. N2 3A 30
Hamilton Rd. N9 7B 8
Hamilton Rd. NW10 5C 46
Hamilton Rd. NW11 7F 29
Hamilton Rd. SE27 4D 122
Hamilton Rd. SW19 7K 119
Hamilton Rd. W4 2A 82
Hamilton Rd. W5 7E 62
Hamilton Rd. Bexh 2E 110
Hamilton Rd. Bren 6D 80
Hamilton Rd. Cockf 4H 5
Hamilton Rd. Felt 4H 113
Hamilton Rd. Harr 5J 25
Hamilton Rd. Hay 7K 59
Hamilton Rd. Ilf 4F 55
Hamilton Rd. Sidc 4A 128
Hamilton Rd. S'hall 1D 78
Hamilton Rd. T Hth 3D 140
Hamilton Rd. Twic 1J 115
Hamilton Rd. Ind. Est. SE27 4D 122 (off Hamilton Rd.)
Hamilton Rd. M. SW19 7K 119
Hamilton Sq. N12 6G 15
Hamilton Sq. SE1 6F 169
Hamilton St. SE8 6C 88
Hamilton Ter. NW8 2K 65 (2A 158)
Hamilton Way. N3 6D 14
Hamilton Way. N13 4G 17
Hamilton Way. Wall 7H 151
Hamlea Clo. SE12 5J 107
Hamlet Clo. SE13 4G 107
Hamlet Clo. Romf 1G 39
Hamlet Ct. SE11 5B 86 (off Opal St.)
Hamlet Ct. W6 4C 82
Hamlet Ct. Enf 5K 7
Hamlet Gdns. W6 4C 82
Hamlet Ind. Est. E9 7C 52
Hamlet Rd. SE19 7F 123
Hamlet Rd. Romf 1G 39
Hamlet Sq. NW2 3G 47
Hamlets Way. E3 4B 70 (in two parts)
Hamlet, The. SE5 3D 104
Hamlet Way. SE1 2D 86 (6F 169)
Hamlin Cres. Pinn 5A 24
Hamlyn Clo. Edgw 3K 11
Hamlyn Gdns. SE19 7E 122
Hammelton Ct. Brom 1H 143 (off London Rd.)
Hammelton Grn. SW9 1B 104
Hammelton Rd. Brom 1H 143
Hammerfield Ho. SW3 5C 84 (5D 170) (off Marlborough St.)
Hammers La. NW7 5H 13
Hammersley Ho. SE14 7J 87 (off Pomeroy St.)
Hammersmith. 4E 82
Hammersmith Bri. SW13 & W6 6D 82
Hammersmith Bri. Rd. W6 5E 82
Hammersmith Broadway. (Junct.) 3E 82
Hammersmith B'way. W6 4E 82
Hammersmith Flyover. (Junct.) 5E 82
Hammersmith Flyover. W6 5E 82
Hammersmith Gro. W6 2E 82
Hammersmith Ind. Est. W6 6E 82
Hammersmith Rd. W6 & W14 4F 83
Hammersmith Ter. W6 5C 82
Hammet Clo. Hay 5B 60
Hammett St. EC3 7F 69 (2J 169)
Hammond Av. Mitc 2F 139
Hammond Clo. Barn 5B 4
Hammond Clo. Gnfd 5H 43
Hammond Clo. Hamp 1E 132
Hammond Ct. E10 2D 52 (off Crescent Rd.)
Hammond Ct. E17 5A 34 (off Maude Rd.)

Hammond Ho. E14 3C 88
(off Tiller Rd.)
Hammond Ho. SE14 7J 87
(off Lubbock St.)
Hammond Lodge. W9 5J 65
(off Admiral Wlk.)
Hammond Rd. Enf 2C 8
Hammond Rd. S'hall 3C 78
Hammonds Clo. Dag 3C 56
Hammond St. NW5 6G 49
Hammond Way. SE28 7B 74
Hamond Clo. S Croy 7B 152
Hamonde Clo. Edgw 2C 12
Hamond Sq. N1 2E 68
(off Hoxton St.)
Ham Pk. Rd. E15 & E7 7H 53
Hampden Av. Beck 2A 142
Hampden Clo. NW1 2H 67
Hampden Ct. N10 7K 15
Hampden Gurney St. W1 6D 66 (1E 164)
Hampden Ho. SW9 2A 104
Hampden La. N17 1F 33
Hampden Rd. N8 4A 32
Hampden Rd. N10 7K 15
Hampden Rd. N17 1G 33
Hampden Rd. N19 2H 49
Hampden Rd. Beck 2A 142
Hampden Rd. Harr 1G 25
Hampden Rd. King T 3G 135
Hampden Rd. Romf 1H 39
Hampden Sq. N14 1A 16
Hampden Way. N14 1A 16
Hampshire Clo. N18 5C 18
Hampshire Hog La. W6 5D 82
Hampshire Rd. N22 7E 16
Hampshire St. NW5 6H 49
Hampson Way. SW8 1K 103
Hampstead. 4B 48
Hampstead Clo. SE28 1B 92
Hampstead Gdns. NW11 6J 29
Hampstead Gdns. Chad H 5B 38
Hampstead Garden Suburb. 5A 30
Hampstead Grn. NW3 5C 48
Hampstead Gro. NW3 3A 48
Hampstead Heath. 2B 48
Hampstead Heights. N2 3A 30
Hampstead High St. NW3 4B 48
Hampstead Hill Gdns. NW3 4B 48
Hampstead La. NW3 & N6 1B 48
Hampstead Mus. 4B 48
(off New End Sq.)
Hampstead Rd. NW1 2G 67 (1A 160)
Hampstead Sq. NW3 3A 48
Hampstead Theatre Club. 7B 48
(off Avenue Rd.)
Hampstead Wlk. E3 1B 70
Hampstead Way. NW11 5H 29
Hampstead W. NW6 6J 47
Hampton. 1F 133
Hampton & Richmond Borough F.C. 1F 133
Hampton Clo. N11 5A 16
Hampton Clo. NW6 3J 65
Hampton Clo. SW20 7E 118
Hampton Court. 4J 133
Hampton Court. (Junct.) 3J 133
Hampton Ct. N1 6B 50
Hampton Ct. N22 1G 31
Hampton Ct. SE16 7K 69
(off King & Queen Wharf)
Hampton Ct. Av. E Mol 6H 133
Hampton Ct. Bri. E Mol 4J 133
Hampton Ct. Cres. E Mol 3H 133
Hampton Court Palace. 4K 133
Hampton Ct. Pde. E Mol 4J 133
Hampton Ct. Rd. E Mol & King T 3K 133
Hampton Ct. Rd. Hamp & E Mol 2G 133
Hampton Ct. Way. Th Dit & E Mol 7J 133
Hampton Farm Ind. Est. Felt 3C 114
Hampton Hill. 5G 115
Hampton Ho. Bexh 2H 111
(off Erith Rd.)
Hampton La. Felt 4C 114
Hampton M. NW10 3K 63
Hampton Ri. Harr 6E 26
Hampton Rd. E4 5G 19
Hampton Rd. E7 5K 53
Hampton Rd. E11 1F 53
Hampton Rd. Croy 6C 140
Hampton Rd. Ilf 4G 55
Hampton Rd. Tedd 5H 115
Hampton Rd. Twic 3H 115
Hampton Rd. Wor Pk 2C 148
Hampton Rd. E. Felt 4D 114
Hampton Rd. W. Felt 3C 114
Hampton St. SE17 & SE1 4B 86
Hampton Wick. 1C 134
Ham Ridings. Rich 5F 117
Hamshades Clo. Sidc 3K 127
Ham St. Rich 1B 116
Ham, The. Bren 7C 80
Ham Vw. Croy 6A 142
Ham Yd. W1 7H 67 (2C 166)
Hanah Ct. SW19 7F 119
Hanameel St. E16 1J 89
Hanbury Clo. NW4 3E 28
Hanbury Ct. Harr 6K 25
Hanbury Dri. N21 5E 6
Hanbury Ho. E1 5G 69
(off Hanbury St.)
Hanbury Ho. SW8 7J 85
(off Regent's Bri. Gdns.)
Hanbury M. N1 1C 68
Hanbury Rd. N17 2H 33
Hanbury Rd. W3 2H 81
Hanbury St. E1 5F 69 (5J 163)
Hanbury Wlk. Bex 3K 129
Hancock Nunn Ho. NW3 6D 48
(off Fellows Rd.)
Hancock Rd. E3 3E 70
Hancock Rd. SE19 6D 122
Handa Wlk. N1 6D 50
Hand Ct. WC1 5K 67 (6H 161)
Handcroft Rd. Croy 7B 140
Handel Clo. Edgw 6A 12
Handel House Mus. 5F 67 (2J 165)
(off Brook St.)
Handel Mans. SW13 7E 82
Handel Mans. WC1 4J 67 (3F 161)
(off Handel St.)
Handel Pde. Edgw 7B 12
(off Whitchurch La.)
Handel Pl. NW10 6K 45
Handel St. WC1 4J 67 (3E 160)
Handel Way. Edgw 7B 12
Handen Rd. SE12 5G 107
Handforth Rd. SW9 7A 86
Handforth Rd. Ilf 3F 55
Handley Gro. NW2 3F 47
Handley Page Rd. Wall 7K 151
Handley Rd. E9 7J 51
Handowe Clo. NW4 4C 28
Handside Clo. Wor Pk 1F 149
Hands Wlk. E16 6J 71
Handsworth Av. E4 6A 20
Handsworth Rd. N17 3D 32
Handtrough Way. Bark 2F 73
Hanford Clo. SW18 1J 119
Hanford Row. SW19 6E 118
Hanger Ct. W5 4F 63
Hanger Grn. W5 4G 63
Hanger Hill. 4F 63
Hanger Lane. (Junct.) 4F 63
Hanger La. W5 2E 62
Hanger Va. La. W5 6F 63
(in two parts)
Hanger Vw. Way. W3 6G 63
Hanging Sword All. EC4 1K 167
Hankey Pl. SE1 2D 86 (7F 169)
Hankins La. NW7 2F 13
Hanley Gdns. N4 1K 49
Hanley Pl. Beck 7C 124
Hanley Rd. N4 1J 49
Hanmer Wlk. N7 2K 49
Hannah Barlow Ho. SW8 1K 103
Hannah Clo. NW10 4J 45
Hannah Clo. Beck 3E 142
Hannah Mary Way. SE1 4G 87
Hannah M. Wall 7G 151
Hannay La. N8 7H 31
Hannay Wlk. SW16 2H 121
Hannell Rd. SW6 7G 83
Hannen Rd. SE27 3B 122
Hannibal Rd. E1 5J 69
Hannibal Rd. Stanw 7A 94
Hannibal Way. Croy 5K 151
Hannington Point. E9 6B 52
(off Eastway)
Hannington Rd. SW4 3F 103
Hanover Av. E16 1J 89
Hanover Av. Felt 1J 113
Hanover Circ. Hay 6E 58
Hanover Clo. Rich 7G 81
Hanover Clo. Sutt 4G 149
Hanover Ct. NW9 3A 28
Hanover Ct. SW15 4B 100
Hanover Ct. W12 1C 82
(off Uxbridge Rd.)
Hanover Ct. Ruis 3J 41
Hanover Dri. Chst 4G 127
Hanover Flats. W1 7E 66 (2H 165)
(off Binney St., in two parts)
Hanover Gdns. SE11 6A 86
Hanover Gdns. Ilf 1G 37
Hanover Ga. NW8 & NW1 3C 66 (2D 158)
Hanover Ga. Mans. NW1 4C 66 (3D 158)
Hanover Ho. E14 1B 88
(off Westferry Cir.)
Hanover Ho. NW8 1C 158
Hanover Ho. SW9 3A 104
Hanover Mans. SW2 5A 104
Hanover Mead. NW11 5G 29
Hanover Pk. SE15 1G 105
Hanover Pl. E3 3B 70
Hanover Pl. WC2 6J 67 (1F 167)
Hanover Rd. N15 4F 33
Hanover Rd. NW10 7E 46
Hanover Rd. SW19 7A 120
Hanover Sq. W1 6F 67 (1K 165)
Hanover Steps. W2 1D 164
Hanover St. W1 6F 67 (1K 165)
Hanover St. Croy 3B 152
Hanover Ter. NW1 3C 66 (2E 158)
Hanover Ter. Iswth 1A 98
Hanover Ter. M. NW1 3C 66 (2D 158)
Hanover Trad. Est. N7 5J 49
Hanover Way. Bexh 3D 110
Hanover W. Ind. Est. NW10 3K 63
Hanover Yd. N1 2C 68
(off Noel Rd.)
Hansard M. W14 2F 83
(in two parts)
Hansart Way. Enf 1F 7
Hanscomb M. SW4 4G 103
Hans Cres. SW1 3D 84 (1E 170)
Hanselin Clo. Stan 5E 10
Hansen Dri. N21 5E 6
Hanshaw Dri. Edgw 1K 27
Hansler Gro. E Mol 4H 133
Hansler Rd. SE22 5F 105
Hansol Rd. Bexh 5E 110
Hansom Ter. Brom 1K 143
(off Freelands Gro.)
Hanson Clo. SW12 7F 103
Hanson Clo. SW14 3J 99
Hanson Clo. Beck 6D 124
Hanson Clo. W Dray 3B 76
Hanson Ct. E17 6D 34
Hanson Gdns. S'hall 2C 78
Hanson St. W1 5G 67 (5A 160)
Hans Pl. SW1 3D 84 (1F 171)
Hans Rd. SW3 3D 84 (1E 170)
Hans St. SW1 3D 84 (2F 171)
Hanway Pl. W1 6H 67 (7C 160)
Hanway Rd. W7 6H 61
Hanway St. W1 6H 67 (7C 160)
Hanwell. 1K 79
Hanworth. 5C 114
Hanworth Ho. SE5 7B 86
(in two parts)
Hanworth Rd. Felt 1K 113
Hanworth Rd. Hamp 4D 114
Hanworth Rd. Houn 1C 114
Hanworth Rd. Sun 7J 113
(in two parts)
Hanworth Ter. Houn 4F 97
Hanworth Trad. Est. Felt 3C 114
Hapgood Clo. Gnfd 5H 43
Harad's Pl. E1 7G 69
Harben Pde. NW3 7A 48
(off Finchley Rd.)
Harben Rd. NW6 7A 48
Harberson Rd. E15 1H 71
Harberson Rd. SW12 1F 121
Harberton Rd. N19 1G 49
Harbet Rd. N18 & E4 5F 19
Harbet Rd. W2 5B 66 (6B 158)
Harbex Clo. Bex 7H 111
Harbinger Rd. E14 4D 88
Harbledown Ho. SE1 2D 86 (7E 168)
(off Manciple St.)
Harbledown Rd. SW6 1J 101
Harbord Clo. SE5 2D 104
Harbord Ho. SE16 4K 87
(off Cope St.)
Harbord St. SW6 1F 101
Harborough Av. Sidc 7J 109
Harborough Rd. SW16 4K 121
Harbour Av. SW10 1A 102
Harbour Exchange Sq. E14 2D 88
Harbour Quay. E14 1E 88
Harbour Rd. SE5 3C 104
Harbour Yd. SW10 1A 102
Harbridge Av. SW15 7B 100
Harbury Rd. Cars 7C 150
Harbut Rd. SW11 4B 102
(in two parts)
Harcombe Rd. N16 3E 50
Harcourt Av. E12 4D 54
Harcourt Av. Edgw 3D 12
Harcourt Av. Sidc 6C 110
Harcourt Av. Wall 4F 151
Harcourt Bldgs. EC4 2J 167
Harcourt Clo. Iswth 3A 98
Harcourt Fld. Wall 4F 151
Harcourt Lodge. Wall 4F 151
Harcourt Rd. E15 2H 71
Harcourt Rd. N22 1H 31
Harcourt Rd. SE4 3B 106
Harcourt Rd. SW19 7J 119
Harcourt Rd. Bexh 4E 110
Harcourt Rd. T Hth 6K 139
Harcourt Rd. Wall 4F 151
Harcourt St. W1 5C 66 (6D 158)
Harcourt Ter. SW10 5K 83
Hardcastle Clo. Croy 6G 141
Hardcastle Ho. SE14 1A 106
(off Loring Rd.)
Hardcourts Clo. W Wick 3D 154
Hardel Ri. SW2 1B 122
Hardel Wlk. SW2 7A 104
Harden Ct. SE7 4C 90
Harden Ho. SE5 2E 104
Harden's Manorway. SE7 3B 90
(in three parts)
Harders Rd. SE15 2H 105
Hardess St. SE24 3C 104
Hardie Clo. NW10 5K 45
Hardie Rd. Dag 3J 57
Harding Clo. SE17 6C 86
Harding Clo. Croy 3F 153
Hardinge Clo. Uxb 5D 58
Hardinge La. E1 6J 69
(in two parts)
Hardinge Rd. N18 6K 17
Hardinge Rd. NW10 1D 64
Harding Ho. SW13 6D 82
(off Wyatt Dri.)
Harding Ho. Hay 6K 59
Harding Rd. Bexh 2F 111
Harding's Clo. King T 1F 135
Hardings La. SE20 6K 123
Hardington. NW1 7E 48
(off Belmont St.)
Hardman Rd. SE7 5K 89
Hardman Rd. King T 2E 134
Hardwick Clo. Stan 5H 11
Hardwick Ct. Eri 6K 93
Hardwicke Av. Houn 1E 96
Hardwicke M. WC1 3K 67 (2H 161)
(off Lloyd Baker M.)
Hardwicke Rd. N13 6D 16
Hardwicke Rd. W4 4K 81
Hardwicke Rd. Rich 4C 116
Hardwicke St. Bark 1G 73
Hardwick Grn. W13 5B 62
Hardwick Ho. NW8 4C 66 (3D 158)
(off Lilestone St.)
Hardwick St. EC1 3A 68 (2K 161)
Hardwicks Way. SW18 5J 101
Hardwidge St. SE1 2E 86 (6G 169)
Hardy Av. E16 1J 89
Hardy Av. Ruis 5K 41
Hardy Clo. SE16 2K 87
Hardy Clo. Barn 6B 4
Hardy Clo. Pinn 7B 24
Hardy Cotts. SE10 6F 89
Hardy Ho. SW4 7G 103
Hardying Ho. E17 4A 34
Hardy Rd. E4 6G 19
Hardy Rd. SE3 7H 89
Hardy Rd. SW19 7K 119
Hardys Clo. E Mol 4J 133
Hardy Way. Enf 1F 7
Hare & Billet Rd. SE3 1F 107
Harebell Dri. E6 5E 72
Harecastle Clo. Hay 4C 60
Hare Ct. EC4 6A 68 (1J 167)
Harecourt Rd. N1 6C 50
Haredale Rd. SE24 4C 104
Haredon Clo. SE23 7K 105
Harefield Clo. Enf 1F 7
Harefield Grn. NW7 6K 13
Harefield M. SE4 3B 106
Harefield Rd. N8 5H 31
Harefield Rd. SE4 3B 106
Harefield Rd. SW16 7K 121
Harefield Rd. Sidc 3D 128
Harefield Rd. Uxb 5A 40
Hare Marsh. E2 4G 69
Hare Pl. EC4 6A 68 (1K 167)
(off Pleydell St.)
Hare Row. E2 2H 69
Haresfield Rd. Dag 6G 57
Hare St. SE18 3E 90
Hare Wlk. N1 2E 68
(in two parts)
Harewood Av. NW1 4C 66 (4D 158)
Harewood Av. N'holt 7D 42
Harewood Clo. N'holt 7D 42
Harewood Dri. Ilf 2D 36

Harewood Pl. W1 6F 67 (1K 165)
Harewood Rd. SW19 6C 120
Harewood Rd. Iswth 7K 79
Harewood Rd. S Croy 6E 152
Harewood Row. NW1 5C 66 (5D 158)
Harewood Ter. S'hall 4D 78
Harfield Gdns. SE5 3E 104
Harfield Rd. Sun 2B 132
Harfleur Ct. SE11 4B 86 (off Opal St.)
Harford Clo. E4 7J 9
Harford Ho. SE5 6C 86 (off Bethwin Rd.)
Harford Ho. W11 5H 65
Harford M. N19 3H 49
Harford Rd. E4 7J 9
Harford St. E1 4A 70
Harford Wlk. N2 4B 30
Harfst Way. Swan 7J 129
Hargood Clo. Harr 6E 26
Hargood Rd. SE3 1A 108
Hargrave Mans. N19 2H 49
Hargrave Pk. N19 2G 49
Hargrave Pl. NW5 5H 49
Hargrave Rd. N19 2G 49
Hargraves Ho. W12 7D 64 (off White City Est.)
Hargwyne St. SW9 3K 103
Haringey Pk. N8 6J 31
Haringey Pas. N8 4A 32
Haringey Rd. N8 4J 31
Harington Ter. N13 3J 17
Harkett Clo. Harr 2K 25
Harkett Ct. W'stone 2K 25
Harkness Ho. E1 6G 69 (off Christian St.)
Harland Av. Croy 3F 153
Harland Av. Sidc 3H 127
Harland Clo. SW19 3K 137
Harland Rd. SE12 1J 125
Harlech Gdns. Houn 6A 78
Harlech Gdns. Pinn 1B 42
Harlech Rd. N14 3D 16
Harlech Tower. W3 2J 81
Harlequin Av. Bren 6A 80
Harlequin Cen. S'hall 4A 78
Harlequin Clo. Hay 5B 60
Harlequin Clo. Iswth 5J 97
Harlequin Ct. NW10 6K 45 (off Mitchellbrook Way)
Harlequin Ct. W5 7C 62
Harlequin Ho. Eri 3E 92 (off Kale Rd.)
Harlequin Rd. Tedd 7B 116
Harlequins R.U.F.C. (Stoop Memorial Ground). 7J 97
Harlescott Rd. SE15 4K 105
Harlesden. 2B 64
Harlesden Gdns. NW10 1B 64
Harlesden La. NW10 1C 64
Harlesden Plaza. NW10 2B 64
Harlesden Rd. NW10 1C 64
Harleston Clo. E5 2J 51
Harley Clo. Wemb 6D 44
Harley Ct. E11 7J 35
Harley Ct. N20 3F 15
Harley Ct. Harr 4H 25
Harley Cres. Harr 4H 25
Harleyford. Brom 1K 143
Harleyford Ct. SE11 7G 173
Harleyford Mnr. W3 1J 81 (off Edgecote Clo.)
Harleyford Rd. SE11 6K 85 (7G 173)
Harleyford St. SE11 6A 86 (7J 173)
Harley Gdns. SW10 5A 84
Harley Gro. E3 3B 70
Harley Ho. E11 7F 35
Harley Ho. NW1 4H 159
Harley Pl. W1 5F 67 (6J 159)
Harley Rd. NW3 7B 48
Harley Rd. NW10 2A 64
Harley Rd. Harr 4H 25
Harley St. W1 4F 67 (4J 159)
Harley Vs. NW10 2A 64
Harling Ct. SW11 2D 102
Harlinger St. SE18 3C 90
Harlington. 6F 77
Harlington Clo. Hay 7E 76
Harlington Corner. (Junct.) 1F 95
Harlington Rd. Bexh 3E 110
Harlington Rd. Uxb 3C 58
Harlington Rd. E. Felt 7K 95
Harlington Rd. W. Felt 6K 95
Harlowe Clo. E8 1G 69
Harlowe Ho. E8 1F 69 (off Clarissa St.)
Harlow Mans. Bark 7F 55 (off Whiting Av.)
Harlow Rd. N13 3J 17
Harlyn Dri. Pinn 3K 23
Harlynwood. SE5 7C 86 (off Wyndham Rd.)
Harman Av. Wfd G 6C 20
Harman Clo. E4 4A 20
Harman Clo. NW2 3G 47
Harman Clo. SE1 5G 87
Harman Dri. NW2 3G 47
Harman Dri. Sidc 6K 109
Harman Rd. Enf 5A 8
Harmondsworth La. W Dray 6A 76
Harmondsworth Rd. W Dray 5A 76
Harmon Ho. SE8 4B 88
Harmont Ho. W1 5F 67 (6J 159) (off Harley St.)
Harmony Clo. NW11 5G 29
Harmony Clo. Wall 7H 151
Harmony Way. NW4 4E 28
Harmony Way. Brom 2J 143
Harmood Gro. NW1 7F 49
Harmood Ho. NW1 7F 49 (off Harmood St.)
Harmood Pl. NW1 7F 49
Harmood St. NW1 6F 49
Harmsworth M. SE11 3A 86 (2K 173)
Harmsworth St. SE17 5B 86 (6K 173)
Harmsworth Way. N20 1C 14
Harness Rd. SE28 2A 92
Harold Av. Belv 5F 93
Harold Av. Hay 3H 77
Harold Ct. SE16 2K 87 (off Christopher Clo.)
Harold Est. SE1 3E 86
Harold Gibbons Ct. SE7 6A 90
Harold Ho. E2 2K 69 (off Mace St.)
Harold Laski Ho. EC1 3B 68 (2B 162) (off Percival St.)
Harold Maddison Ho. SE17 5B 86 (off Penton Pl.)
Harold Pl. SE11 5A 86 (6J 173)
Harold Rd. E4 4K 19
Harold Rd. E11 1G 53
Harold Rd. E13 1K 71
Harold Rd. N8 5K 31
Harold Rd. N15 5F 33
Harold Rd. NW10 3K 63
Harold Rd. SE19 7D 122
Harold Rd. Sutt 4B 150
Harold Rd. Wfd G 1J 35
Haroldstone Rd. E17 5K 33
Harold Wilson Ho. SE28 1B 92
Harold Wilson Ho. SW6 6H 83 (off Clem Attlee Ct.)
Harp All. EC4 6B 68 (7A 162)
Harp Bus. Cen. NW2 1C 46 (off Apsley Way)
Harpenden Rd. E12 2A 54
Harpenden Rd. SE27 3B 122
Harpenmead Point. NW2 2H 47
Harper Clo. N14 5B 6
Harper Ho. SW9 3B 104
Harper M. SW17 3A 120
Harper Rd. E6 6D 72
Harper Rd. SE1 3C 86 (7C 168)
Harper's Yd. N17 1F 33
Harp Island Clo. NW10 2K 45
Harp La. EC3 7E 68 (3G 169)
Harpley Sq. E1 4J 69
Harpour Rd. Bark 6G 55
Harp Rd. W7 4K 61
Harpsden St. SW11 1E 102
Harpur M. WC1 5K 67 (5G 161)
Harpur St. WC1 5K 67 (5G 161)
Harraden Rd. SE3 1A 108
Harrier Av. E11 6K 35
Harrier Ct. Houn 3C 96
Harrier M. SE28 2H 91
Harrier Rd. NW9 2A 28
Harriers Clo. W5 7E 62
Harrier Way. E6 5D 72
Harries Rd. Hay 4A 60
Harriet Clo. E8 1G 69
Harriet Gdns. Croy 2G 153
Harriet Ho. SW6 7K 83 (off Wandon Rd.)
Harriet St. SW1 2D 84 (7F 165)
Harriet Tubman Clo. SW2 7K 103
Harriet Wlk. SW1 2D 84 (7F 165)
Harriet Way. Bush 1C 10
Harringay. 5B 32
Harringay Gdns. N8 4B 32
Harringay Rd. N15 5B 32 (in two parts)
Harrington Clo. NW10 3K 45
Harrington Clo. Croy 2J 151
Harrington Ct. W10 3H 65
Harrington Ct. Croy 2D 152
Harrington Gdns. SW7 4K 83
Harrington Hill. E5 1H 51
Harrington Ho. NW1 3G 67 (1A 160) (off Harrington St.)
Harrington Ho. Uxb 4D 40
Harrington Rd. E11 1G 53
Harrington Rd. SE25 4G 141
Harrington Rd. SW7 4B 84 (3A 170)
Harrington Sq. NW1 2G 67
Harrington St. NW1 2G 67 (1A 160) (in two parts)
Harrington Way. SE18 3B 90
Harriott Clo. SE10 4H 89
Harriott Ho. E1 5J 69 (off Jamaica St.)
Harris Bldgs. E1 6G 69 (off Burslem St.)
Harris Clo. Enf 1G 7
Harris Clo. Houn 1E 96
Harris Ct. Wemb 3F 45
Harris Ho. SW9 3A 104 (off St James's Cres.)
Harris Lodge. SE6 1E 124
Harrison Clo. N20 1H 15
Harrison Ct. Shep 5D 130
Harrison Ho. SE17 5D 86 (off Brandon St.)
Harrison Rd. Dag 6H 57
Harrisons Ct. SE14 6K 87 (off Myers La.)
Harrison's Ri. Croy 3B 152
Harrison St. WC1 3J 67 (2F 161)
Harris Rd. Bexh 1E 110
Harris Rd. Dag 5F 57
Harris St. E17 7B 34
Harris St. SE5 7D 86
Harris Way. Sun 1G 131
Harrods. 3D 84 (1E 170)
Harrogate Ct. N11 6K 15
Harrogate Ct. SE12 7J 107
Harrogate Ct. SE26 3G 123 (off Droitwich Clo.)
Harrold Ho. NW6 7B 48
Harrold Rd. Dag 5B 56
Harrovian Bus. Village. Harr 7J 25
Harrow. 6J 25
Harrow Av. Enf 6A 8
Harroway Rd. SW11 2B 102
Harrow Borough F.C. 4E 42
Harrowby St. W1 6C 66 (7D 158)
Harrow Clo. Chess 7D 146
Harrowdene Clo. Wemb 4D 44
Harrowdene Gdns. Tedd 6A 116
Harrowdene Rd. Wemb 3D 44
Harrow Dri. N9 1A 18
Harrowes Meade. Edgw 3B 12
Harrow Fields Gdns. Harr 3J 43
Harrowgate Ho. E9 6K 51
Harrowgate Rd. E9 6A 52
Harrow Grn. E11 3G 53
Harrow La. E14 7D 70
Harrow Lodge. NW8 4B 66 (3A 158) (off Northwick Ter.)
Harrow Mnr. Way. SE2 1C 92
Harrow Mus. & Heritage Cen. 3G 25
Harrow on the Hill. 1J 43
Harrow Pk. Harr 2J 43
Harrow Pl. E1 6E 68 (7H 163)
Harrow Road. (Junct.) 6H 45
Harrow Rd. E6 1C 72
Harrow Rd. E11 3G 53
Harrow Rd. NW10 3D 64 (6A 158)
Harrow Rd. W2 & NW1 5A 66 (in two parts)
Harrow Rd. W10 & W9 4G 65
Harrow Rd. Bark 1J 73
Harrow Rd. Cars 6C 150
Harrow Rd. Felt 2C 112
Harrow Rd. Ilf 4G 55
Harrow Rd. Wemb (HA0) 4K 43 (in two parts)
Harrow Rd. Wemb (HA9) 5G 45
Harrow Rd. Bri. W2 5A 66
Harrow School Old Speech Room Gallery. 1J 43 (off High St., in Harrow School)
Harrow St. NW1 5D 158
Harrow Vw. Harr 2G 25
Harrow Vw. Hay 6J 59
Harrow Vw. Uxb 3E 58
Harrow Vw. Rd. W5 4B 62
Harrow Way. Shep 2E 130
Harrow Weald. 1J 25
Harrow Weald Pk. Harr 6C 10
Harry Hinkins Ho. SE17 5C 86 (off Bronti Clo.)
Harry Lambourn Ho. SE15 7H 87 (off Gervase St.)
Hartcliff Ct. W7 2K 79
Hart Ct. E6 7E 54
Harte Rd. Houn 2D 96
Hartfield Av. N'holt 2K 59
Hartfield Cres. SW19 7H 119
Hartfield Cres. W Wick 3J 155
Hartfield Gro. SE20 1J 141
Hartfield Ho. N'holt 2K 59 (off Hartfield Av.)
Hartfield Rd. SW19 7H 119
Hartfield Rd. Chess 5D 146
Hartfield Rd. W Wick 4J 155
Hartfield Ter. E3 2C 70
Hartford Av. Harr 3A 26
Hartford Rd. Bex 6G 111
Hartford Rd. Eps 6H 147
Hart Gro. W5 1G 81
Hart Gro. S'hall 5E 60
Hart Gro. Ct. W5 1G 81
Hartham Clo. N7 5J 49
Hartham Clo. Iswth 1A 98
Hartham Rd. N7 5J 49
Hartham Rd. N17 2F 33
Hartham Rd. Iswth 1K 97
Harting Rd. SE9 3C 126
Hartington Clo. Harr 4J 43
Hartington Ct. SW8 1J 103
Hartington Ct. W4 7H 81
Hartington Ho. SW1 5H 85 (5D 172) (off Drummond Ga.)
Hartington Rd. E16 6K 71
Hartington Rd. E17 6A 34
Hartington Rd. SW8 1J 103
Hartington Rd. W4 7H 81
Hartington Rd. W13 7B 62
Hartington Rd. S'hall 3C 78
Hartington Rd. Twic 7B 98
Hartismere Rd. SW6 7H 83
Hartlake Rd. E9 6K 51
Hartland. NW1 1G 67 (off Royal College St.)
Hartland Clo. N21 6H 7
Hartland Clo. Edgw 2B 12
Hartland Ct. N11 5J 15 (off Hartland Rd.)
Hartland Dri. Edgw 2B 12
Hartland Dri. Ruis 3K 41
Hartland Rd. E15 7H 53
Hartland Rd. N11 5J 15
Hartland Rd. NW1 7F 49
Hartland Rd. NW6 2H 65
Hartland Rd. Hamp H 4F 115
Hartland Rd. Iswth 3A 98
Hartland Rd. Mord 7J 137
Hartlands Clo. Bex 6F 111
Hartlands, The. Houn 6K 77
Hartland Way. Croy 3A 154
Hartland Way. Mord 7H 137
Hartlepool Ct. E16 1F 91
Hartley Av. E6 1C 72
Hartley Av. NW7 5G 13
Hartley Clo. NW7 5G 13
Hartley Clo. Brom 2D 144
Hartley Ho. SE1 4F 87 (off Longfield Est.)
Hartley Rd. E11 1H 53
Hartley Rd. Croy 7C 140
Hartley Rd. Well 7C 92
Hartley St. E2 3J 69 (in two parts)
Hart Lodge. High Bar 3B 4
Hartmann Rd. E16 1B 90
Hartnoll St. N7 5K 49
Harton Clo. Brom 1B 144
Harton Rd. N9 2C 18
Harton St. SE8 1C 106
Hartop Point. SW6 7G 83 (off Pellant Rd.)
Hartsbourne Av. Bus H 2B 10
Hartsbourne Clo. Bus H 2C 10
Hartsbourne Country Club Golf Courses. 2A 10
Hartsbourne Ct. S'hall 6G 61 (off Fleming Rd.)
Hartsbourne Pk. Bush 2D 10
Hartsbourne Rd. Bus H 2C 10
Harts Gro. Wfd G 5D 20
Hartshill Clo. Uxb 7D 40
Hartshorn All. EC3 1H 169
Hartshorn Gdns. E6 4E 72
Hart's La. SE14 1A 106
Harts La. Bark 6F 55
Hartslock Dri. SE2 2D 92
Hartsmead Rd. SE9 2D 126
Hart St. EC3 7E 68 (2H 169)
Hartsway. Enf 4D 8
Hartswood Gdns. W12 3B 82
Hartswood Rd. W12 2B 82
Hartsworth Clo. E13 2H 71
Hartville Rd. SE18 4J 91

Hartwell Dri. E4 .... 6K 19
Hartwell Ho. SE7 .... 5K 89
(off Troughton Rd.)
Hartwell St. E8 .... 6F 51
Hartwood Grn. Bush 2C 10
Harvard Ct. NW6 .... 5K 47
Harvard Hill. W4 .... 6H 81
Harvard Ho. SE17 .... 6B 86
(off Doddington Gro.)
Harvard La. W4 .... 5J 81
Harvard Rd. SE13 .... 5E 106
Harvard Rd. W4 .... 5H 81
Harvard Rd. Iswth 1J 97
Harvel Clo. Orp 3K 145
Harvel Cres. SE2 .... 5D 92
Harvest Bank Rd. W Wick
.... 3H 155
Harvest Ct. Shep 4C 130
Harvesters Clo. Iswth 5H 97
Harvest La. Th Dit 6A 134
Harvest Rd. Felt 4J 113
Harvey Ct. E17 .... 5C 34
Harvey Dri. Hamp 1F 133
Harvey Gdns. E11 .... 1H 53
Harvey Gdns. SE7 .... 5A 90
Harvey Ho. E1 .... 4H 69
(off Brady St.)
Harvey Ho. N1 .... 1D 68
(off Colville Est.)
Harvey Ho. SW1
.... 5H 85 (6D 172)
(off Aylesford St.)
Harvey Ho. Bren 5E 80
Harvey Ho. Romf 4D 38
Harvey Lodge. W9 .... 5J 65
(off Admiral Wlk.)
Harvey Point. E16 .... 5J 71
(off Fife Rd.)
Harvey Rd. E11 .... 1G 53
Harvey Rd. N8 .... 5K 31
Harvey Rd. SE5 .... 1D 104
(in two parts)
Harvey Rd. Houn 7D 96
Harvey Rd. Ilf 5F 55
Harvey Rd. N'holt 7A 42
Harvey Rd. Uxb 2C 58
Harvey Rd. W on T 7H 131
Harvey's Bldgs. WC2
.... 7J 67 (3F 167)
Harveys La. Romf 2K 57
Harvey St. N1 .... 1D 68
Harvill Rd. Sidc 5E 128
Harvil Rd. Hare & Uxb 6A 22
Harvington Wlk. E8 .... 7G 51
Harvist Est. N7 .... 4A 50
Harvist Rd. NW6 .... 2F 65
Harwell Clo. Ruis 1F 41
Harwell Pas. N2 .... 4D 30
Harwood Av. Brom 2K 143
Harwood Av. Mitc 3C 138
Harwood Clo. N12 .... 6H 15
Harwood Clo. Wemb 4D 44
Harwood Ct. N1 .... 1D 68
(off Colville Est.)
Harwood Ct. SW15 .... 4E 100
Harwood Dri. Uxb 1B 58
Harwood M. SW6 .... 7J 83
Harwood Point. SE16 .... 2B 88
Harwood Rd. SW6 .... 7J 83
Harwoods Yd. N21 .... 7F 7
Harwood Ter. SW6 .... 1K 101
Haselbury Rd. N18 & N9 .... 4K 17
Haseley End. SE23 .... 7J 105
Haselrigge Rd. SW4 .... 4H 103
Haseltine Rd. SE26 .... 4B 124
Haselwood Dri. Enf 4G 7
Haskard Rd. Dag 4D 56
Hasker St. SW3
.... 4C 84 (3D 170)
Haslam Av. Sutt 1G 149
Haslam Clo. N1 .... 7A 50
Haslam Clo. Uxb 2E 40
Haslam Ct. N11 .... 4A 16
Haslam St. SE15 .... 7F 87
Haslemere and Heathrow Est., The.
Houn 2K 95
Haslemere Av. NW4 .... 6F 29
Haslemere Av. SW18 .... 2K 119
Haslemere Av. W7 & W13 .... 3A 80
Haslemere Av. Barn 1J 15
Haslemere Av. Houn 2A 96
Haslemere Av. Mitc 2B 138
Haslemere Bus. Cen. Enf 4C 8
Haslemere Clo. Hamp 5D 114
Haslemere Clo. Wall 5J 151
Haslemere Gdns. N3 .... 3H 29
Haslemere Ind. Est. SW18
.... 2K 119
Haslemere Rd. N8 .... 7H 31
Haslemere Rd. N21 .... 2G 17
Haslemere Rd. Bexh 2F 111
Haslemere Rd. Ilf 2K 55
Haslemere Rd. T Hth 5B 140
Hasler Clo. SE28 .... 7B 74
Haslers Wharf. E3 .... 1A 70
(off Old Ford Rd.)
Haslett Rd. Shep 2G 131
Hasluck Gdns. New Bar 6E 4
Hassard St. E2 .... 2F 69 (1K 163)
Hassendean Rd. SE3 .... 6K 89
Hassett Rd. E9 .... 6K 51
Hassocks Clo. SE26 .... 3H 123
Hassocks Rd. SW16 .... 1H 139
Hassock Wood. Kes 4B 156
Hassop Rd. NW2 .... 4F 47
Hassop Wlk. SE9 .... 4C 126
Hasted Rd. SE7 .... 5B 90
Haste Hill Golf Course. 2G 23
Hastings Av. Ilf 4G 37
Hastings Clo. SE15 .... 7G 87
Hastings Clo. Barn 4F 5
Hastings Clo. Wemb 4C 44
Hastings Ct. Tedd 5H 115
Hastings Dri. Surb 6C 134
Hastings Ho. SE18 .... 4D 90
(off Mulgrave Rd.)
Hastings Ho. W12 .... 7D 64
(off White City Est.)
Hastings Ho. W13 .... 7B 62
Hastings Ho. WC1
.... 3J 67 (2E 160)
(off Hastings St.)
Hastings Rd. N11 .... 5B 16
Hastings Rd. N17 .... 3D 32
Hastings Rd. W13 .... 7B 62
Hastings Rd. Brom 1C 156
Hastings Rd. Croy 1F 153
Hastings St. WC1
.... 3J 67 (2E 160)
Hastingwood Ct. E17 .... 5D 34
Hastingwood Trad. Est. N18
.... 5E 18
Hastoe Clo. Hay 4C 60
Hat & Mitre Ct. EC1 .... 4B 162
Hatcham M. Bus. Cen. SE14
.... 1K 105
Hatcham Pk. M. SE14 .... 1K 105
Hatcham Pk. Rd. SE14
.... 1K 105
Hatcham Rd. SE15 .... 6J 87
Hatchard Rd. N19 .... 2H 49
Hatchcroft. NW4 .... 3D 28
Hatch End. 1D 24
Hatchers M. SE1
.... 2E 86 (7H 169)
(off Bermondsey St.)
Hatchett Rd. Felt 1E 112
Hatchfield Ho. N15 .... 6E 32
(off Albert Rd.)
Hatch Gro. Romf 4E 38
Hatch La. E4 .... 4A 20
(in two parts)
Hatch La. W Dray 7A 76
Hatch Pl. King T 5F 117
Hatch Rd. SW16 .... 2J 139
Hatch Side. Chig 5K 21
Hatch, The. Enf 1E 8
Hatchwood Clo. Wfd G 4C 20
Hatcliffe Almshouses. SE10
.... 5G 89
(off Tuskar St.)
Hatcliffe Clo. SE3 .... 3H 107
Hatcliffe St. SE10 .... 5H 89
Hatfield Clo. SE14 .... 7K 87
Hatfield Clo. Ilf 3F 37
Hatfield Clo. Mitc 4B 138
Hatfield Ct. SE3 .... 7J 89
Hatfield Ct. N'holt 3A 60
(off Canberra Dri.)
Hatfield Ho. EC1
.... 4C 68 (4C 162)
(off Golden La. Est.)
Hatfield Mead. Mord 5J 137
Hatfield Rd. E15 .... 5G 53
Hatfield Rd. W4 .... 2K 81
Hatfield Rd. W13 .... 1A 80
Hatfield Rd. Dag 6E 56
Hatfields. SE1 .... 1A 86 (4K 167)
Hathaway Clo. Brom 1D 156
Hathaway Clo. Ruis 4H 41
Hathaway Clo. Stan 5F 11
Hathaway Cres. E12 .... 6D 54
Hathaway Gdns. W13 .... 5A 62
Hathaway Gdns. Romf 5D 38
Hathaway Ho. N1
.... 2E 68 (1G 163)
Hathaway Rd. Croy 7B 140
Hatherleigh Clo. Chess 5D 146
Hatherleigh Clo. Mord 4J 137
Hatherleigh Rd. Ruis 2J 41
Hatherley Ct. W2 .... 6K 65
(off Hatherley Gro.)
Hatherley Cres. Sidc 2A 128
Hatherley Gdns. E6 .... 3B 72
Hatherley Gdns. N8 .... 6J 31
Hatherley Gro. W2 .... 6K 65
Hatherley Ho. E17 .... 4C 34
Hatherley M. E17 .... 4C 34
Hatherley Rd. E17 .... 4B 34
Hatherley Rd. Rich 1F 99
Hatherley Rd. Sidc 4A 128
Hatherley St. SW1
.... 4G 85 (4B 172)
Hathern Gdns. SE9 .... 4E 126
Hatherop Rd. Hamp 7D 114
Hathersage Ct. N1 .... 5D 50
Hathorne Clo. SE15 .... 2H 105
Hathway St. SE15 .... 2K 105
Hathway Ter. SE15 .... 2K 105
(off Hathway St.)
Hatley Av. Ilf 4G 37
Hatley Clo. N11 .... 5J 15
Hatley Rd. N4 .... 2K 49
Hatteraick St. SE16 .... 2J 87
Hattersfield Clo. Belv 4F 93
Hatton. 4H 95
Hatton Clo. SE18 .... 7H 91
Hatton Cross. (Junct.) 3H 95
Hatton Garden. EC1
.... 5A 68 (5K 161)
Hatton Gdns. Mitc 5D 138
Hatton Grn. Felt 4J 95
Hatton Gro. W Dray 2A 76
Hatton Ho. King T 2F 135
(off Victoria Rd.)
Hatton Pl. EC1 .... 5A 68 (5K 161)
Hatton Rd. Croy 1A 152
Hatton Rd. Felt 7E 94
Hatton Rd. S. Felt 4H 95
Hatton Row. NW8 .... 4B 158
Hatton St. NW8 .... 4B 66 (4B 158)
Hatton Wall. EC1
.... 5A 68 (5K 161)
Haughmond. N12 .... 4E 14
Haunch of Venison Yd. W1
.... 6F 67 (1J 165)
Hauteville Ct. Gdns. W6 .... 3B 82
(off South Side)
Havana Rd. SW19 .... 2J 119
Havannah St. E14 .... 2C 88
Havant Rd. E17 .... 3E 34
Havelock Clo. W12 .... 7D 64
Havelock Ct. S'hall 3D 78
(off Havelock Rd.)
Havelock Ho. SE23 .... 1J 123
Havelock Pl. Harr 6J 25
Havelock Rd. N17 .... 2G 33
Havelock Rd. SW19 .... 5A 120
Havelock Rd. Belv 4F 93
Havelock Rd. Brom 4A 144
Havelock Rd. Croy 2F 153
Havelock Rd. Harr 3J 25
Havelock Rd. S'hall 3C 78
Havelock St. N1 .... 1J 67
Havelock St. Ilf 2F 55
Havelock Ter. SW8 .... 1F 103
Havelock Wlk. SE23 .... 1J 123
Haven Clo. SE9 .... 3D 126
Haven Clo. SW19 .... 3F 119
Haven Clo. Hay 4G 59
Haven Clo. Sidc 6C 128
Haven Ct. Beck 2E 142
Haven Ct. Surb 6F 135
Haven Grn. W5 .... 6D 62
Haven Grn. Ct. W5 .... 6D 62
Havenhurst Ri. Enf 2F 7
Haven La. W5 .... 6E 62
Haven Lodge. Enf 6K 7
(off Village Rd.)
Haven M. E3 .... 5B 70
Haven Pl. W5 .... 7D 62
Havenpool. NW8 .... 1K 65
(off Abbey Rd.)
Haven Rd. Ashf 3D 112
Haven St. NW1 .... 7F 49
Haven, The. N14 .... 6A 6
Haven, The. Rich 3G 99
Haven, The. Sun 7J 113
Haven Wood. Wemb 3H 45
Haverfield Gdns. Rich 7G 81
Haverfield Rd. E3 .... 3A 70
Haverford Way. Edgw 1F 27
Haverhill Rd. E4 .... 1K 19
Haverhill Rd. SW12 .... 1G 121
Havering. NW1 .... 7F 49
(off Castlehaven Rd.)
Havering Dri. Romf 4K 39
Havering Gdns. Romf 5C 38
Havering Rd. Romf 3K 39
Havering St. E1 .... 6K 69
Havering Way. Bark 3B 74
Haversham Clo. Twic 6D 98
Haversham Ct. Gnfd 6K 43
Haversham Pl. N6 .... 2D 48
Haverstock Hill. NW3 .... 5C 48
Haverstock Pl. N1
.... 3B 68 (1B 162)
(off Haverstock St.)
Haverstock Rd. NW5 .... 5E 48
Haverstock St. N1
.... 2B 68 (1B 162)
Havil St. SE5 .... 7E 86
Havisham Ho. SE16 .... 2G 87
Havisham Pl. SE19 .... 7B 122
Hawarden Gro. SE24 .... 7C 104
Hawarden Hill. NW2 .... 3C 46
Hawarden Rd. E17 .... 4K 33
Hawbridge Rd. E11 .... 1F 53
Hawes Ho. E17 .... 4K 33
Hawes La. W Wick 1E 154
Hawes Rd. N18 .... 6C 18
Hawes Rd. Brom 1K 143
(in two parts)
Hawes St. N1 .... 7B 50
Hawgood St. E3 .... 5C 70
Hawkdene. E4 .... 6J 9
Hawke Ct. Hay 4A 60
(off Perth Av.)
Hawke Ho. E1 .... 4K 69
(off Ernest St.)
Hawke Pk. Rd. N22 .... 3B 32
Hawke Pl. SE16 .... 2K 87
Hawker Ct. King T 2F 135
(off Church Rd.)
Hawke Rd. SE19 .... 6D 122
Hawkesbury Rd. SW15 .... 5D 100
Hawkesfield Rd. SE23 .... 2A 124
Hawkesley Clo. Twic 4A 116
Hawkes Rd. Felt 7J 95
Hawkes Rd. Mitc 1D 138
Hawkesworth Clo. N'wd 1G 23
Hawke Tower. SE14 .... 6A 88
Hawkewood Rd. Sun 3J 131
Hawkfield Ct. Iswth 2J 97
Hawkhurst Gdns. Chess 4E 146
Hawkhurst Rd. SW16 .... 1H 139
Hawkhurst Way. N Mald 5K 135
Hawkhurst Way. W Wick 2D 154
Hawkinge. N17 .... 2D 32
(off Gloucester Rd.)
Hawkins Clo. NW7 .... 5E 12
Hawkins Clo. Harr 7H 25
Hawkins Ct. SE18 .... 4C 90
Hawkins Ho. SE8 .... 6C 88
(off New King St.)
Hawkins Ho. SW1
.... 6G 85 (7B 172)
(off Dolphin Sq.)
Hawkins Rd. Tedd 6B 116
Hawkins Way. SE6 .... 5C 124
Hawkley Gdns. SE27 .... 2B 122
Hawkridge Clo. Romf 6C 38
Hawksbrook La. Beck 6D 142
(in two parts)
Hawkshaw Clo. SW2 .... 7J 103
Hawkshead. NW1 .... 1A 160
Hawkshead Clo. Brom
.... 7G 125
Hawkshead Rd. NW10 .... 7B 46
Hawkshead Rd. W4 .... 2A 82
Hawkslade Rd. SE15 .... 5K 105
Hawksley Rd. N16 .... 3E 50
Hawks M. SE10 .... 7E 88
Hawksmoor Clo. E6 .... 6C 72
Hawksmoor Clo. SE18 .... 5J 91
Hawksmoor Ho. E14 .... 5A 70
(off Aston St.)
Hawksmoor M. E1 .... 7H 69
Hawksmoor Pl. E2
.... 4G 69 (3K 163)
(off Cheshire St.)
Hawksmoor St. W6 .... 6F 83
Hawksmouth. E4 .... 7K 9
Hawks Pas. King T 2F 135
(off Minerva Rd.)
Hawks Rd. King T 2F 135
Hawkstone Rd. SE16 .... 4J 87
Hawkwell Ct. E4 .... 3K 19
Hawkwell Wlk. N1 .... 1C 68
(off Maldon Rd.)
Hawkwood Cres. E4 .... 6J 9
Hawkwood La. Chst 1G 145
Hawkwood Mt. E5 .... 1H 51
Hawlands Dri. Pinn 7C 24
Hawley Clo. Hamp 6D 114
Hawley Cres. NW1 .... 7F 49
Hawley M. NW1 .... 7F 49
Hawley Rd. N18 .... 5E 18
Hawley Rd. NW1 .... 7F 49
(in two parts)
Hawley St. NW1 .... 7F 49
Hawley Way. Ashf 5C 112
Hawstead Rd. SE6 .... 6D 106
Hawsted. Buck H 1E 20
Hawter. NW9 .... 1B 28
Hawthorn Av. E3 .... 1B 70
Hawthorn Av. N13 .... 5D 16
Hawthorn Cen. Harr 5K 25
Hawthorn Clo. Hamp 5E 114
Hawthorn Clo. Houn 7K 77
Hawthorn Clo. Orp 6H 145
Hawthorn Cotts. Well 3A 110
(off Hook La.)
Hawthorn Ct. Pinn 2A 24
(off Rickmansworth Rd.)
Hawthorn Ct. Rich 1H 99
Hawthorn Cres. SW17 .... 5E 120
Hawthornden Clo. N12 .... 6H 15
Hawthorndene Clo. Brom
.... 2H 155

Hawthorndene Rd. *Brom* 2H **155**
Hawthorn Dri. *Harr* 6E **24**
Hawthorn Dri. *W Wick* 4G **155**
Hawthorne Av. *Cars* 7E **150**
Hawthorne Av. *Harr* 6A **26**
Hawthorne Av. *Mitc* 2B **138**
Hawthorne Av. *Ruis* 6K **23**
Hawthorne Av. *T Hth* 1B **140**
Hawthorne Clo. *N1* 6E **50**
Hawthorne Clo. *Brom* 3D **144**
Hawthorne Clo. *Sutt* 2A **150**
Hawthorne Ct. *W5* 1E **80**
Hawthorne Ct. *N'wd* 2J **23**
Hawthorne Cres. *W Dray* 2B **76**
Hawthorne Farm Av. *N'holt* 1C **60**
Hawthorne Gro. *NW9* 7J **27**
*Hawthorne Ho. SW1 5G **85** (6B 172)*
(off Churchill Gdns.)
Hawthorne M. *Gnfd* 6G **61**
Hawthorne Pl. *Hay* 7H **59**
Hawthorne Rd. *E17* 3C **34**
Hawthorne Rd. *Brom* 3C **144**
Hawthorn Gdns. *W5* 3D **80**
Hawthorn Gro. *SE20* 7H **123**
Hawthorn Gro. *Enf* 1J **7**
Hawthorn Hatch. *Bren* 7B **80**
Hawthorn M. *NW7* 1G **29**
Hawthorn Pl. *Eri* 5J **93**
Hawthorn Rd. *N8* 3H **31**
Hawthorn Rd. *N18* 6A **18**
Hawthorn Rd. *NW10* 7C **46**
Hawthorn Rd. *Bexh* 4F **111**
Hawthorn Rd. *Bren* 7B **80**
Hawthorn Rd. *Buck H* 4G **21**
Hawthorn Rd. *Sutt* 6C **150**
Hawthorn Rd. *Wall* 7F **151**
*Hawthorns. S Croy 4B **152***
(off Bramley Hill)
Hawthorns. *Wfd G* 3D **20**
Hawthorns, The. *Eps* 7B **148**
Hawthorn Ter. *Sidc* 5K **109**
Hawthorn Wlk. *W10* 4G **65**
Hawthorn Way. *N9* 2K **17**
Hawthorn Way. *Shep* 4F **131**
Hawtrey Av. *N'holt* 2B **60**
Hawtrey Dri. *Ruis* 7J **23**
Hawtrey Rd. *NW3* 7C **48**
Haxted Rd. *Brom* 1K **143**
Hay Clo. *E15* 7G **53**
Haycroft Gdns. *NW10* 1C **64**
Haycroft Rd. *SW2* 5J **103**
Haycroft Rd. *Surb* 2D **146**
Hay Currie St. *E14* 6D **70**
Hayday Rd. *E16* 5J **71**
Haydens M. *W3* 6J **63**
Hayden's Pl. *W11* 6H **65**
Hayden Way. *Romf* 2J **39**
Haydock Av. *N'holt* 6E **42**
Haydock Grn. *N'holt* 6E **42**
*Haydock Grn. Flats. N'holt 6E **42***
(off Haydock Grn.)
Haydon Clo. *NW9* 4J **27**
Haydon Clo. *Enf* 6K **7**
Haydon Dri. *Pinn* 4J **23**
Haydon Pk. Rd. *SW19* 5J **119**
Haydon Rd. *Dag* 2C **56**
Haydons Rd. *SW19* 5K **119**
Haydon St. *EC3* 7F **69** (2J **169**)
Haydon Wlk. *E1* 6F **69** (1K **169**)
Haydon Way. *SW11* 4B **102**
Hayes. 1J 155
(Bromley)
Hayes. 6G 59
(Hillingdon)
Hayes Bri. Retail Pk. *Hay* 7A **60**
Hayes Chase. *W Wick* 6F **143**
Hayes Clo. *Brom* 2J **155**
*Hayes Ct. SE5 7C **86***
(off Camberwell New Rd.)
Hayes Ct. *SW2* 1J **121**
Hayes Cres. *NW11* 5H **29**
Hayes Cres. *Sutt* 4F **149**
Hayes End. 5F 59
Hayes End Clo. *Hay* 5F **59**
Hayes End Dri. *Hay* 4F **59**
Hayes End Rd. *Hay* 4F **59**
Hayes F.C. 7H 59
Hayesford Pk. Dri. *Brom* 5H **143**
Hayes Garden. *Brom* 2J **155**
Hayes Hill. *Brom* 1G **155**
Hayes Hill Rd. *Brom* 1H **155**
Hayes La. *Beck* 3E **142**
Hayes La. *Brom* 5J **143**
Hayes Mead Rd. *Brom* 1G **155**
Hayes Metro Cen. *Hay* 7A **60**
Hayes Pl. *NW1* 4C **66** (4D **158**)
Hayes Rd. *Brom* 4J **143**
Hayes Rd. *S'hall* 4K **77**
Hayes St. *Brom* 1K **155**
Hayes Town. 2H 77
Hayes Way. *Beck* 4E **142**
Hayes Wood Av. *Brom* 1K **155**
Hayfield Pas. *E1* 4J **69**
Hayfield Yd. *E1* 4J **69**
Haygarth Pl. *SW19* 5F **119**
Haygreen Clo. *King T* 6H **117**
Hay Hill. *W1* 7F **67** (3K **165**)
Hayland Clo. *NW9* 4K **27**
Hay La. *NW9* 4J **27**
*Hayles Bldgs. SE11 4B **86***
(off Elliotts Row)
Hayles St. *SE11* 4B **86**
Haylett Gdns. *King T* 4D **134**
Hayling Av. *Felt* 3J **113**
Hayling Clo. *N16* 5E **50**
Hayling Ct. *Sutt* 4E **148**
Haymaker Clo. *Uxb* 7B **40**
Hayman Cres. *Hay* 2F **59**
Haymans Point. *SE11* 4K **85** (4G **173**)
Hayman St. *N1* 7B **50**
Haymarket. *SW1* 7H **67** (3C **166**)
Haymarket Arc. *SW1* 3C **166**
Haymarket Theatre Royal. 7H 67 (4D 166)
(off Haymarket)
Haymer Gdns. *Wor Pk* 3C **148**
*Haymerle Ho. SE15 6G **87***
(off Haymerle Rd.)
Haymerle Rd. *SE15* 6G **87**
Haymill Clo. *Gnfd* 3K **61**
*Hayne Ho. W11 1G **83***
(off Penzance Pl.)
Hayne Rd. *Beck* 2B **142**
Haynes Clo. *N11* 3K **15**
Haynes Clo. *N17* 7C **18**
Haynes Clo. *SE3* 3G **107**
Haynes Dri. *N9* 3C **18**
Haynes La. *SE19* 6E **122**
Haynes Rd. *Wemb* 7E **44**
Hayne St. *EC1* 5B **68** (5B **162**)
Haynt Wlk. *SW20* 3G **137**
Hay's Galleria. *SE1* 1E **86** (4G **169**)
Hays La. *SE1* 1E **86** (4G **169**)
Haysleigh Gdns. *SE20* 2G **141**
Hay's M. *W1* 1F **85** (4J **165**)
Haysoms Clo. *Romf* 4K **39**
Haystall Clo. *Hay* 2G **59**
Hay St. *E2* 1G **69**
Hayter Ct. *E11* 2K **53**
Hayter Rd. *SW2* 5J **103**
Hayton Clo. *E8* 6F **51**
Hayward Clo. *SW19* 7K **119**
Hayward Clo. *Dart* 5K **111**
*Hayward Ct. SW9 2J **103***
(off Clapham Rd.)
Hayward Gallery. 5H 167
Hayward Gdns. *SW15* 6E **100**
Hayward Rd. *N20* 2F **15**
Hayward Rd. *Th Dit* 7K **133** & 1A **146**
Haywards Clo. *Chad H* 5B **38**
Hayward's Pl. *EC1* 4B **68** (3A **162**)
*Haywards Yd. SE4 5B **106***
(off Lindal Rd.)
Haywood Clo. *Pinn* 2B **24**
*Haywood Lodge. N11 6D **16***
(off Oak La.)
Haywood Rd. *Brom* 4B **144**
Hayworth Clo. *Enf* 2F **9**
Hazel Av. *W Dray* 3C **76**
Hazel Bank. *SE25* 2E **140**
Hazel Bank. *Surb* 1J **147**
Hazelbank Rd. *SE6* 2F **125**
Hazelbourne Rd. *SW12* 6F **103**
Hazelbury Clo. *SW19* 2J **137**
Hazelbury Grn. *N9* 3K **17**
Hazelbury La. *N9* 3K **17**
Hazel Clo. *N13* 3J **17**
Hazel Clo. *N19* 2G **49**
Hazel Clo. *NW9* 2A **28**
Hazel Clo. *SE15* 2G **105**
Hazel Clo. *Bren* 7B **80**
Hazel Clo. *Croy* 7K **141**
Hazel Clo. *Mitc* 4H **139**
Hazel Clo. *Twic* 7G **97**
Hazel Ct. *W5* 7E **62**
Hazel Cres. *Romf* 1H **39**
Hazel Cft. *Pinn* 6A **10**
Hazelcroft Clo. *Uxb* 7B **40**
Hazeldean Rd. *NW10* 7K **45**
Hazeldene Dri. *Pinn* 3A **24**
Hazeldene Gdns. *Uxb* 1E **58**
Hazeldene Rd. *Ilf* 2B **56**
Hazeldene Rd. *Well* 2C **110**
Hazeldon Rd. *SE4* 5A **106**
Hazeleigh Gdns. *Wfd G* 5H **21**
Hazel Gdns. *Edgw* 4C **12**
Hazelgreen Clo. *N21* 1G **17**
Hazel Gro. *SE26* 4K **123**
Hazel Gro. *Felt* 1J **113**
Hazel Gro. *Orp* 2E **156**
Hazel Gro. *Romf* 3E **38**
Hazel Gro. *Wemb* 1E **62**
Hazelhurst. *Beck* 1F **143**
*Hazelhurst Ct. SE6 5E **124***
(off Beckenham Hill Rd.)
Hazelhurst Rd. *SW17* 4A **120**
Hazel La. *Rich* 2E **116**
Hazellville Rd. *N19* 7H **31**
Hazelmere Clo. *Felt* 6G **95**
Hazelmere Clo. *N'holt* 2D **60**
Hazelmere Ct. *SW2* 1K **121**
Hazelmere Dri. *N'holt* 2D **60**
Hazelmere Rd. *NW6* 1H **65**
Hazelmere Rd. *N'holt* 2D **60**
Hazelmere Rd. *Orp* 4G **145**
Hazelmere Wlk. *N'holt* 2D **60**
(in two parts)
Hazelmere Way. *Brom* 6J **143**
Hazel Rd. *E15* 5G **53**
Hazel Rd. *NW10* 3D **64**
(in two parts)
Hazeltree La. *N'holt* 3C **60**
Hazel Wlk. *Brom* 6E **144**
Hazel Way. *E4* 6G **19**
Hazel Way. *SE1* 4F **87**
Hazelwood Av. *Mord* 4K **137**
Hazelwood Clo. *W5* 2E **80**
Hazelwood Clo. *Harr* 4F **25**
*Hazelwood Ct. N13 4F **17***
(off Hazelwood La.)
Hazelwood Ct. *NW10* 3A **46**
Hazelwood Ct. *Surb* 6E **134**
Hazelwood Cres. *N13* 4F **17**
Hazelwood Dri. *Pinn* 2K **23**
Hazelwood Ho. *SE8* 4A **88**
Hazelwood Houses. *Short* 3G **143**
Hazelwood La. *N13* 4F **17**
Hazelwood Rd. *E17* 5A **34**
Hazelwood Rd. *Enf* 6A **8**
Hazlebury Rd. *SW6* 2K **101**
Hazledean Rd. *Croy* 2D **152**
Hazledene Rd. *W4* 6J **81**
Hazlemere Gdns. *Wor Pk* 1C **148**
Hazlewell Rd. *SW15* 5E **100**
Hazlewood Clo. *E5* 3A **52**
Hazlewood Cres. *W10* 4G **65**
*Hazlewood Tower. W10 4G **65***
(off Golborne Gdns.)
Hazlitt Clo. *Felt* 4C **114**
Hazlitt M. *W14* 3G **83**
Hazlitt Rd. *W14* 3G **83**
Heacham Av. *Uxb* 3E **40**
Headbourne Ho. *SE1* 3D **86** (7F **169**)
Headcorn Pl. *T Hth* 4K **139**
Headcorn Rd. *N17* 7A **18**
Headcorn Rd. *Brom* 5H **125**
Headcorn Rd. *T Hth* 4K **139**
Headfort Pl. *SW1* 2E **84** (7H **165**)
*Headington Ct. Croy 4C **152***
(off Tanfield Rd.)
Headington Rd. *SW18* 2A **120**
Headlam Rd. *SW4* 6H **103**
(in two parts)
Headlam St. *E1* 4H **69**
Headley App. *Ilf* 5F **37**
Headley Av. *Wall* 5K **151**
Headley Clo. *Eps* 6G **147**
Headley Ct. *SE26* 5J **123**
Headley Dri. *Ilf* 6F **37**
Headley Dri. *New Ad* 7D **154**
Head's M. *W11* 6J **65**
Headstone. 4G 25
Headstone Dri. *Harr* 3H **25**
Headstone Gdns. *Harr* 4G **25**
Headstone La. *Harr* 7A **10**
Headstone Pde. *Harr* 4H **25**
Headstone Rd. *Harr* 5J **25**
Head St. *E1* 6K **69**
(in two parts)
Headway Clo. *Rich* 4C **116**
Heald St. *SE14* 1C **106**
Healey Ho. *SW9* 7A **86**
Healey St. *NW1* 6F **49**
Hearne Rd. *W4* 6G **81**
Hearn Ri. *N'holt* 1B **60**
Hearn's Bldgs. *SE17* 4D **86**
*Hearnshaw Ho. E14 5A **70***
(off Halley St.)
Hearn St. *EC2* 4E **68** (4H **163**)
Hearnville Rd. *SW12* 1E **120**
Heatham Pk. *Twic* 7K **97**
Heath Av. *Bexh* 6D **92**
Heathbourne Rd. *Bus H* 1D **10**
Heath Brow. *NW3* 3A **48**
Heath Bus. Cen. *Houn* 4G **97**
Heath Clo. *NW11* 7K **29**
Heath Clo. *W5* 4F **63**
Heath Clo. *Hay* 7F **77**
*Heathcock Ct. WC2 7J **67** (3F 167)*
(off Exchange Ct.)
Heathcote Av. *Ilf* 2D **36**
Heathcote Ct. *Ilf* 1D **36**
(in two parts)
Heathcote Gro. *E4* 3K **19**
Heathcote Rd. *Twic* 6B **98**
Heathcote St. *WC1* 4K **67** (3G **161**)
*Heath Ct. Croy 4D **152***
(off Heathfield Rd.)
Heath Ct. *Houn* 4D **96**
Heath Ct. *Uxb* 7A **40**
Heathcroft. *NW11* 1K **47**
Heathcroft. *W5* 4F **63**
Heathcroft Av. *Sun* 7H **113**
Heathcroft Gdns. *E17* 1F **35**
Heathdale Av. *Houn* 3C **96**
Heathdene Dri. *Belv* 4H **93**
Heathdene Rd. *SW16* 7K **121**
Heathdene Rd. *Wall* 7F **151**
Heath Dri. *NW3* 4K **47**
Heath Dri. *SW20* 4E **136**
Heath Dri. *Sutt* 7A **150**
Heathedge. *SE26* 2H **123**
Heath End Rd. *Bex* 1K **129**
Heather Av. *Romf* 2K **39**
Heatherbank. *SE9* 2D **108**
Heatherbank. *Chst* 2E **144**
Heather Clo. *E6* 6E **72**
Heather Clo. *N7* 3K **49**
Heather Clo. *SE13* 7F **107**
Heather Clo. *SW8* 3F **103**
Heather Clo. *Hamp* 1D **132**
Heather Clo. *Iswth* 5H **97**
Heather Clo. *Romf* 1K **39**
Heather Clo. *Uxb* 5B **58**
Heather Ct. *Sidc* 6D **128**
Heatherdale Clo. *King T* 6G **117**
Heatherdene Clo. *N12* 7F **15**
Heatherdene Clo. *Mitc* 4B **138**
Heather Dri. *Enf* 2G **7**
Heather Dri. *Romf* 2K **39**
Heatherfold Way. *Pinn* 3H **23**
Heather Gdns. *NW11* 6G **29**
Heather Gdns. *Romf* 2K **39**
Heather Gdns. *Sutt* 6J **149**
Heather Glen. *Romf* 2K **39**
*Heather Ho. E14 6E **70***
(off Dee St.)
Heatherlands. *Sun* 6J **113**
Heather La. *W Dray* 6A **58**
Heatherley Ct. *E5* 3G **51**
Heatherley Dri. *Ilf* 3C **36**
Heather Pk. Dri. *Wemb* 7G **45**
*Heather Pk. Pde. Wemb 7F **45***
(off Heather Pk. Dri.)
Heather Rd. *E4* 6G **19**
Heather Rd. *NW2* 2B **46**
Heather Rd. *SE12* 2J **125**
Heatherset Gdns. *SW16* 7K **121**
Heatherside Rd. *Eps* 7K **147**
Heatherside Rd. *Sidc* 3C **128**
Heathers, The. *Stai* 7B **94**
Heatherton Ter. *N3* 2K **29**
Heather Wlk. *W10* 4G **65**
Heather Wlk. *Edgw* 5C **12**
*Heather Wlk. Twic 7E **96***
(off Stephenson Rd.)
Heather Way. *Romf* 2K **39**
Heather Way. *S Croy* 7K **153**
Heather Way. *Stan* 6E **10**
Heatherwood Clo. *E12* 2A **54**
Heatherwood Dri. *Hay* 2F **59**
Heathfield. *E4* 3K **19**
Heathfield. *Chst* 6G **127**
Heathfield. *Harr* 7K **25**
Heathfield Av. *SW18* 7B **102**
Heathfield Clo. *E16* 5B **72**
Heathfield Clo. *Kes* 5A **156**
Heathfield Ct. *SE20* 7J **123**
Heathfield Ct. *W4* 5K **81**
Heathfield Dri. *Mitc* 1C **138**
Heathfield Gdns. *NW11* 6F **29**
*Heathfield Gdns. SE3 2G **107***
(off Baizdon Rd.)
Heathfield Gdns. *SW18* 6B **102**
Heathfield Gdns. *W4* 5J **81**
Heathfield Gdns. *Croy* 4D **152**
Heathfield Ho. *SE3* 2G **107**
Heathfield La. *Chst* 6F **127**
Heathfield N. *Twic* 7J **97**
Heathfield Pk. *NW2* 6E **46**
Heathfield Pk. Dri. *Romf* 5B **38**
Heathfield Ri. *Ruis* 7E **22**
Heathfield Rd. *SW18* 6A **102**
Heathfield Rd. *W3* 2H **81**
Heathfield Rd. *Bexh* 4F **111**
Heathfield Rd. *Brom* 7H **125**
Heathfield Rd. *Croy* 4D **152**
Heathfield Rd. *Kes* 5A **156**
Heathfields Ct. *Houn* 5C **96**
Heathfield S. *Twic* 7K **97**
Heathfield Sq. *SW18* 7B **102**
*Heathfield St. W11 7G **65***
(off Portland Rd.)
Heathfield Ter. *SE18* 6J **91**
Heathfield Ter. *W4* 5J **81**

Heathfield Va. S Croy 7K 153
Heath Gdns. Twic 1K 115
Heathgate. NW11 6K 29
Heathgate Pl. NW3 5D 48
Heath Gro. SE20 7J 123
Heath Gro. Sun 7H 113
Heath Ho. Sidc 4K 127
Heath Hurst Rd. NW3 4C 48
Heathhurst Rd. S Croy 7E 152
Heathland Rd. N16 1E 50
Heathlands Clo. Sun 2J 131
Heathlands Clo. Twic 2K 115
Heathlands Way. Houn 5C 96
Heath La. SE3 2F 107 (in two parts)
Heathlee Rd. SE3 4H 107
Heathley End. Chst 6G 127
Heath Lodge. Bush 1D 10
Heathmans Rd. SW6 1H 101
Heath Mead. SW19 3F 119
Heath Pk. Dri. Brom 3C 144
Heath Pas. NW3 2K 47
Heathpool Ct. E1 4H 69
Heath Ri. SW15 6F 101
Heath Ri. Brom 6H 143
Heath Rd. SW8 2F 103
Heath Rd. Bex 1J 129
Heath Rd. Harr 7G 25
Heath Rd. Houn 4F 97
Heath Rd. Romf 7D 38
Heath Rd. T Hth 3C 140
Heath Rd. Twic 1K 115
Heath Rd. Uxb 4E 58
Heathrow Airport. 3D 94
Heathrow Boulevd. W Dray 7B 76 (in two parts)
Heathrow Causeway Cen. Houn 3J 95
Heathrow Corporate Pk. Houn 3A 96
Heathrow Interchange. Hay 1A 78
Heathrow International Trad. Est. Houn 3K 95
Heaths Clo. Enf 2K 7
Heath Side. NW3 4B 48
Heathside. NW11 1J 47
Heathside. SE13 2E 106
Heathside. Houn 7D 96
Heathside. Orp 7G 145
Heathside Av. Bexh 1E 110
Heathstan Rd. W12 6C 64
Heath St. NW3 3A 48
Heath, The. W7 1J 79
Heath Vw. N2 4A 30
Heathview. NW5 4E 48
Heath Vw. Clo. N2 4A 30
Heathview Dri. SE2 6D 92
Heathview Gdns. SW15 7E 100
Heathview Rd. T Hth 4A 140
Heath Vs. NW3 3B 48
Heath Vs. SE18 5K 91
Heathville Rd. N19 7J 31
Heathwall St. SW11 3D 102
Heathway. (Junct.) 2G 75
Heathway. SE3 7J 89
Heathway. Croy 3B 154
Heathway. Dag 3F 57
Heath Way. Eri 1J 111
Heathway. S'hall 4B 78
Heath Way. Wfd G 5F 21
Heathway Ct. NW11 2J 47
Heathway Ind. Est. Dag 4H 57
Heathwood Gdns. SE7 4C 90
Heathwood Point. SE23 3K 123
Heathwood Wlk. Bex 1K 129
Heaton Clo. E4 3K 19
Heaton Rd. SE15 2H 105
Heaton Rd. Mitc 7E 120
Heaven Tree Clo. N1 6C 50
Heaver Rd. SW11 3B 102
Heavitree Clo. SE18 5H 91
Heavitree Rd. SE18 5H 91 (in two parts)
Hebden Ct. E2 1F 69
Hebden Ter. N17 6K 17
Hebdon Rd. SW17 3C 120
Heber Mans. W14 6G 83 (off Queen's Club Gdns.)
Heber Rd. NW2 5F 47
Heber Rd. SE22 6F 105
Hebron Rd. W6 3E 82
Hecham Clo. E17 2A 34
Heckfield Pl. SW6 7J 83
Heckford Ho. E14 6D 70 (off Grundy St.)
Heckford St. E1 7K 69
Hector. NW9 1B 28 (off Five Acre)
Hector Ct. SW9 7A 86 (off Caldwell St.)
Hector Ho. E2 2H 69 (off Old Bethnal Grn. Rd.)
Hector St. SE18 4J 91
Heddington Gro. N7 5K 49
Heddon Clo. Iswth 4A 98
Heddon Ct. Av. Barn 5J 5
Heddon Ct. Pde. Barn 5K 5
Heddon Rd. Cockf 5J 5
Heddon St. W1 7G 67 (2A 166) (in two parts)
Hedgegate Ct. W11 6H 65
Hedge Hill. Enf 1G 7
Hedge La. N13 3G 17
Hedgemans Rd. Dag 7D 56
Hedgemans Way. Dag 6E 56
Hedgerley Gdns. Gnfd 2G 61
Hedgers Gro. E9 6A 52
Hedger St. SE11 4B 86
Hedge Wlk. SE6 5D 124
Hedgewood Gdns. Ilf 5E 36
Hedgley. Ilf 4D 36
Hedgley M. SE12 5H 107
Hedgley St. SE12 5H 107
Hedingham Clo. N1 7C 50
Hedingham Rd. Dag 5B 56
Hedley Ho. E14 3E 88 (off Stewart St.)
Hedley Rd. Twic 7E 96
Hedley Row. N5 5D 50
Hedley St. Romf 5K 39
Hedsor Ho. E2 4F 69 (3J 163) (off Ligonier St.)
Heenan Clo. Bark 6G 55
Heene Rd. Enf 1J 7
Hega Ho. E14 5E 70 (off Ullin St.)
Heidegger Cres. SW13 7D 82
Heigham Rd. E6 1B 72
Heighton Gdns. Croy 5B 152
Heights Clo. SW20 7D 118
Heights, The. SE7 5A 90
Heights, The. Beck 7E 124 (in two parts)
Heights, The. N'holt 5D 42
Heiron St. SE17 6B 86
Helby Rd. SW4 6H 103
Heldar Ct. SE1 2D 86 (7F 169)
Helder Gro. SE12 7H 107
Helder St. S Croy 6D 152
Heldmann Clo. Houn 4H 97
Helena Ct. W5 5D 62
Helena Pl. E9 1H 69
Helena Rd. E13 2H 71
Helena Rd. E17 5C 34
Helena Rd. NW10 5D 46
Helena Rd. W5 5D 62
Helena Sq. SE16 7A 70 (off Sovereign Cres.)
Helen Av. Felt 7K 95
Helen Clo. N2 3A 30
Helen Clo. W Mol 4F 133
Helen Gladstone Ho. SE1 2B 86 (6A 168) (off Surrey Row)
Helen Ho. E2 2H 69 (off Old Bethnal Grn. Rd.)
Helen Mackay Ho. E14 6F 71 (off Blair St.)
Helen Peele Cotts. SE16 3J 87 (off Lower Rd.)
Helenslea Av. NW11 1J 47
Helen's Pl. E2 3J 69
Helen St. SE18 4F 91
Helen Taylor Ho. SE16 3G 87 (off Evelyn Lowe Est.)
Helford Clo. Ruis 2G 41
Helgiford Gdns. Sun 7G 113
Heliport Ind. Est. SW11 2B 102
Helix Gdns. SW2 6K 103
Helix Rd. SW2 6K 103
Hellings St. E1 1G 87
Helme Clo. SW19 5H 119
Helmet Row. EC1 4C 68 (3D 162) (in two parts)
Helmore Rd. Bark 7K 55
Helmsdale Clo. Hay 4C 60
Helmsdale Ho. NW6 2K 65 (off Carlton Va.)
Helmsdale Rd. SW16 1H 139
Helmsley Pl. E8 7H 51
Helmsley St. E8 7H 51
Helperby Rd. NW10 7A 46
Helsby Ct. NW8 4B 66 (3A 158) (off Pollitt Dri.)
Helsinki Sq. SE16 3A 88
Helston. NW1 1G 67 (off Camden St.)
Helston Clo. Pinn 1D 24
Helston Ct. N15 5E 32 (off Culvert Rd.)
Helston Ho. SE11 5A 86 (5K 173) (off Kennings Way)
Helvetia St. SE6 2B 124
Helwys Ct. E4 6J 19
Hemans St. SW8 7H 85
Hemans St. Est. SW8 7H 85
Hemberton Rd. SW9 3J 103
Hemery Rd. Gnfd 5H 43
Hemingford Clo. N12 5G 15
Hemingford Rd. N1 1K 67
Hemingford Rd. Sutt 4E 148
Heming Rd. Edgw 7C 12
Hemington Av. N11 5J 15
Hemingway Clo. NW5 4E 48
Hemlington Ho. E14 5A 70 (off Aston St.)
Hemlock Rd. W12 7B 64 (in two parts)
Hemmen La. Hay 6H 59
Hemming Clo. Hamp 1E 132
Hemmings Clo. Sidc 2B 128
Hemming St. E1 4G 69
Hempstead Clo. Buck H 2D 20
Hempstead Rd. E17 3F 35
Hemp Wlk. SE17 4D 86
Hemsby Rd. Chess 6F 147
Hemstal Rd. NW6 7J 47
Hemsted Rd. Eri 7K 93
Hemswell Dri. NW9 1A 28
Hemsworth Ct. N1 2E 68
Hemsworth St. N1 2E 68
Hemus Pl. SW3 5C 84 (6D 170)
Hen & Chicken Ct. EC4 6A 68 (1J 167) (off Fleet St.)
Henchman St. W12 6B 64
Hendale Av. NW4 3D 28
Henderson Clo. NW10 6J 45
Henderson Ct. SE14 6K 87 (off Myers La.)
Henderson Dri. NW8 4B 66 (3A 158)
Henderson Ho. Dag 3G 57 (off Kershaw Rd.)
Henderson Rd. E7 6A 54
Henderson Rd. N9 1C 18
Henderson Rd. SW18 7C 102
Henderson Rd. Croy 6D 140
Henderson Rd. Hay 3J 59
Hendham Rd. SW17 2C 120
Hendon. 5D 28
Hendon Av. N3 1G 29
Hendon Crematorium. NW4 1F 29
Hendon F.C. 1F 47
Hendon Golf Course. 1E 28
Hendon Hall Ct. NW4 3F 29
Hendon Ho. NW4 5F 29
Hendon La. N3 3G 29
Hendon Lodge. NW4 3D 28
Hendon Pk. Mans. NW4 5E 28
Hendon Pk. Row. NW11 6H 29
Hendon Rd. N9 2B 18
Hendon Way. NW4 & NW2 6D 28
Hendon Wood La. NW7 1G 13
Hendren Clo. Gnfd 5H 43
Hendre Rd. SE1 4E 86
Hendrick Av. SW12 7D 102
Heneage La. EC3 6E 68 (1H 169)
Heneage Pl. EC3 6E 68 (1H 169)
Heneage St. E1 5F 69 (5K 163)
Henfield Clo. N19 1G 49
Henfield Clo. Bex 6G 111
Henfield Rd. SW19 1H 137
Hengelo Gdns. Mitc 4B 138
Hengist Rd. SE12 7K 107
Hengist Rd. Eri 7H 93
Hengist Way. Brom 4G 143
Hengrave Rd. SE23 6J 105
Hengrove Ct. Bex 1E 128
Hengrove Cres. Ashf 3A 112
Henham Ct. Romf 1J 39
Henley Av. Sutt 3G 149
Henley Clo. SE16 2J 87 (off St Marychurch St.)
Henley Clo. Gnfd 2G 61
Henley Clo. Iswth 1K 97
Henley Ct. N14 7B 6
Henley Ct. NW2 6F 47
Henley Dri. SE1 4F 87
Henley Dri. King T 7B 118
Henley Gdns. Pinn 3K 23
Henley Gdns. Romf 5E 38
Henley Ho. E2 4F 69 (3K 163) (off Swanfield St.)
Henley Prior. N1 2K 67 (1G 161) (off Collier St.)
Henley Rd. E16 2D 90
Henley Rd. N18 4K 17
Henley Rd. NW10 1E 64
Henley Rd. Ilf 4G 55
Henley St. SW11 2E 102
Henley Way. Felt 5B 114
Henlow Pl. Rich 2D 116
Henlys Corner. (Junct.) 4H 29
Henlys Roundabout. (Junct.) 2A 96
Hennel Clo. SE23 3J 123
Hennessey Rd. N9 2D 18
Henniker Gdns. E6 3B 72
Henniker M. SW3 6B 84 (7A 170)
Henniker Point. E15 5G 53 (off Leytonstone Rd.)
Henniker Rd. E15 5F 53
Henningham Rd. N17 1D 32
Henning St. SW11 1C 102
Henrietta Clo. SE8 6C 88
Henrietta Ct. Twic 7C 98 (off Richmond Rd.)
Henrietta Ho. N15 6E 32 (off St Ann's Rd.)
Henrietta Ho. W6 5E 82 (off Queen Caroline St.)
Henrietta M. WC1 4J 67 (3F 161)
Henrietta Pl. W1 6F 67 (1J 165)
Henrietta St. E15 5E 52
Henrietta St. WC2 7J 67 (2F 167)
Henriques St. E1 6G 69
Henry Addlington Clo. E6 5F 73
Henry Clo. Enf 1K 7
Henry Cooper Way. SE9 3B 126
Henry Darlot Dri. NW7 5A 14
Henry Dickens Ct. W11 7F 65
Henry Doulton Dri. SW17 4E 120
Henry Hatch Wlk. Sutt 7A 150
Henry Ho. SE1 1A 86 (5J 167)
Henry Ho. SW8 7J 85 (off Wyvil Rd.)
Henry Jackson Rd. SW15 3F 101
Henry Macaulay Av. King T 1D 134
Henry Peters Dri. Tedd 5J 115 (off Somerset Gdns.)
Henry Purcell Ho. E16 1K 89 (off Evelyn Rd.)
Henry Rd. E6 2C 72
Henry Rd. N4 1C 50
Henry Rd. Barn 5G 5
Henrys Av. Wfd G 5C 20
Henryson Rd. SE4 5C 106
Henry St. Brom 1K 143
Henry's Wlk. Ilf 1H 37
Henry Tate M. SW16 5A 122
Henry Wise Ho. SW1 4G 85 (4B 172) (off Vauxhall Bri. Rd.)
Hensford Gdns. SE26 4H 123
Henshall St. N1 6D 50
Henshawe Rd. Dag 3D 56
Henshaw St. SE17 4D 86
Henslowe Rd. SE22 5G 105
Henslow Ho. SE15 7G 87 (off Peckham Pk. Rd.)
Henson Av. NW2 5E 46
Henson Path. Harr 3D 26
Henson Pl. N'holt 1A 60
Henstridge Pl. NW8 1C 66
Henty Clo. SW11 7C 84
Henty Wlk. SW15 5D 100
Henville Rd. Brom 1K 143
Henwick Rd. SE9 3B 108
Henwood Side. Wfd G 6J 21
Hepburn Gdns. Brom 1G 155
Hepburn M. SW11 5D 102
Hepple Clo. Iswth 2B 98
Hepplestone Clo. SW15 6D 100
Hepscott Rd. E9 6C 52
Hepworth Ct. N1 1B 68 (off Gaskin St.)
Hepworth Ct. NW3 5C 48
Hepworth Ct. Sutt 1J 149
Hepworth Gdns. Bark 5A 56
Hepworth Rd. SW16 7J 121
Hepworth Way. W on T 7H 131
Heracles. NW9 1B 28 (off Five Acre)
Heracles Clo. Wall 7J 151
Hera Ct. E14 4C 88 (off Homer Dri.)
Herald Gdns. Wall 2F 151
Herald's Pl. SE11 4B 86 (3K 173)
Herald St. E2 4H 69
Herbal Hill. EC1 4A 68 (4K 161)
Herbal Hill Gdns. EC1 4A 68 (4K 161)
Herbal Pl. EC1 4A 68 (4K 161) (off Herbal Hill)
Herbert Cres. SW1 3D 84 (1F 171)
Herbert Gdns. NW10 2D 64
Herbert Gdns. W4 6H 81
Herbert Gdns. Romf 7D 38
Herbert Ho. E1 6F 69 (7J 163) (off Old Castle St.)

Herbert Morrison Ho. SW6 6H 83 (off Clem Attlee Ct.)
Herbert Pl. SE18 6F 91
Herbert Rd. E12 4C 54
Herbert Rd. E17 7B 34
Herbert Rd. N11 7D 16
Herbert Rd. N15 5F 33
Herbert Rd. NW9 6C 28
Herbert Rd. SE18 7E 90 (in two parts)
Herbert Rd. SW19 7H 119 (in two parts)
Herbert Rd. Bexh 2E 110
Herbert Rd. Brom 5B 144
Herbert Rd. Ilf 2J 55
Herbert Rd. King T 3F 135
Herbert Rd. S'hall 1D 78
Herbert St. E13 2J 71
Herbert St. NW5 6E 48
Herbrand Est. WC1 4J 67 (3E 160)
Herbrand St. WC1 4J 67 (3E 160)
Hercies Rd. Uxb 7B 40
Hercules Pl. N7 3J 49 (in two parts)
Hercules Rd. SE1 3K 85 (2H 173)
Hercules St. N7 3J 49
Hercules Tower. SE14 6A 88
Hercules Wharf. E14 7G 71 (off Orchard Pl.)
Hercules Yd. N7 3J 49
Hereford Av. Barn 1J 15
Hereford Bldgs. SW3 6B 84 (7B 170) (off Old Church St.)
Hereford Ct. W7 5K 61 (off Copley Clo.)
Hereford Ct. Harr 4J 25
Hereford Ct. Sutt 7J 149
Hereford Gdns. SE13 5G 107
Hereford Gdns. Ilf 7C 36
Hereford Gdns. Pinn 5C 24
Hereford Gdns. Twic 1G 115
Hereford Ho. NW6 2J 65 (off Carlton Va.)
Hereford Ho. SW3 3C 84 (1D 170) (off Old Brompton Rd.)
Hereford Ho. SW10 7K 83 (off Fulham Rd.)
Hereford M. W2 6J 65
Hereford Pl. SE14 7B 88
Hereford Retreat. SE15 7G 87
Hereford Rd. E11 5K 35
Hereford Rd. W2 6J 65
Hereford Rd. W3 7H 63
Hereford Rd. W5 3C 80
Hereford Rd. Felt 1A 114
Hereford Sq. SW7 4A 84
Hereford St. E2 4G 69
Hereford Way. Chess 5C 146
Herent Dri. Ilf 4C 36
Hereward Gdns. N13 5F 17
Hereward Rd. SW17 4D 120
Herga Ct. Harr 3J 43
Herga Rd. Harr 4K 25
Heriot Av. E4 2H 19
Heriot Rd. NW4 5E 28
Heriots Clo. Stan 4F 11
Heritage Clo. SW9 3B 104
Heritage Ct. SE8 5K 87 (off Trundley's Rd.)
Heritage Hill. Kes 5A 156
Heritage Vw. Harr 3K 43
Herlwyn Av. Ruis 2G 41
Herlwyn Gdns. SW17 4D 120
Her Majesty's Theatre. 1H 85 (4C 166) (off Haymarket)
Herm Clo. Iswth 7G 79
Hermes Clo. W9 4J 65
Hermes Ct. SW9 1A 104 (off Southey Rd.)
Hermes St. N1 2A 68 (1J 161)
Hermes Wlk. N'holt 2E 60
Hermes Way. Wall 7H 151
Herm Ho. N1 6C 50
Herm Ho. Enf 1E 8
Hermiston Av. N8 5J 31
Hermitage Clo. E18 4H 35
Hermitage Clo. Clay 6A 146
Hermitage Clo. Enf 2G 7
Hermitage Clo. Shep 4C 130
Hermitage Ct. E1 1G 87 (off Knighten St.)
Hermitage Ct. E18 4J 35
Hermitage Ct. NW2 3J 47
Hermitage Gdns. NW2 3J 47
Hermitage Gdns. SE19 7C 122
Hermitage Grn. SW16 1J 139
Hermitage La. N18 5J 17
Hermitage La. NW2 3J 47
Hermitage La. SE25 6G 141 (in two parts)
Hermitage La. SW16 7K 121
Hermitage Path. SW16 1J 139
Hermitage Rd. N4 & N15 7B 32
Hermitage Rd. SE19 7C 122
Hermitage Rooms. 7K 67 (2H 167) (off Embankment)
Hermitage Row. E8 5G 51
Hermitage St. W2 5B 66 (6A 158)
Hermitage, The. SE13 2E 106
Hermitage, The. SE23 1J 123
Hermitage, The. SW13 1B 100
Hermitage, The. Felt 3H 113
Hermitage, The. King T 4D 134
Hermitage, The. Rich 5E 98
Hermitage, The. Uxb 6A 40
Hermitage Wlk. E18 4H 35
Hermitage Wall. E1 1G 87
Hermitage Waterside. E1 1G 87 (off Thomas More St.)
Hermitage Way. Stan 1A 26
Hermit Pl. NW6 1K 65
Hermit Rd. E16 5H 71
Hermit St. EC1 3B 68 (1A 162)
Hermon Gro. Hay 1J 77
Hermon Hill. E11 & E18 5J 35
Herndon Rd. SW18 5A 102
Herne Clo. NW10 5K 45
Herne Ct. Bush 1B 10
Herne Hill. 5C 104
Herne Hill. SE24 6C 104
Herne Hill Ho. SE24 6B 104 (off Railton Rd.)
Herne Hill Rd. SE24 3C 104
Herne Hill Stadium. 4D 104
Herne M. N18 4B 18
Herne Pl. SE24 5B 104
Herne Rd. Surb 2D 146
Heron Clo. E17 2B 34
Heron Clo. NW10 6A 46
Heron Clo. Buck H 1D 20
Heron Clo. Sutt 5H 149
Heron Ct. E14 3E 88 (off New Union Clo.)
Heron Ct. Brom 4A 144
Heron Ct. Ilf 2F 55
Heron Ct. King T 3E 134
Heron Ct. Ruis 2F 41
Heron Cres. Sidc 3J 127
Herondale Av. SW18 1B 120
Heron Dri. N4 2C 50
Herongate Clo. Enf 2A 8
Herongate Rd. E12 2A 54
Heron Hill. Belv 5F 93
Heron Ho. E6 7C 54
Heron Ho. NW8 2C 66 (1C 158) (off Barrow Hill Est.)
Heron Ho. SW11 7C 84 (off Searles Clo.)
Heron Ho. W13 4A 62
Heron Ho. Sidc 3B 128
Heron Ind. Est. E15 2D 70
Heron Mead. Enf 1H 9
Heron M. Ilf 2F 55
Heron Pl. SE16 1A 88
Heron Pl. W1 6E 66 (7H 159) (off Thayer St.)
Heron Quay. E14 1C 88
Heron Rd. SE24 4C 104
Heron Rd. Croy 2E 152
Heron Rd. Twic 4A 98
Heronsforde. W13 6C 62
Herons Ga. Edgw 5B 12
Heron's Lea. N6 6D 30
Heronslea Dri. Stan 5K 11
Heron's Pl. Iswth 3B 98
Heron Sq. Rich 5D 98
Herons Ri. New Bar 4H 5
Herons, The. E11 6H 35
Heron Trad. Est. W3 5H 63
Heron Way. Felt 4J 95
Heron Way. Wfd G 4F 21
Herrick Ho. SE5 7D 86 (off Elmington Est.)
Herrick Rd. N5 3C 50
Herrick St. SW1 4H 85 (4D 172)
Herries St. W10 2G 65
Herringham Rd. SE7 3A 90
Herron Ct. Brom 4H 143
Hersant Clo. NW10 1C 64
Herschell M. SE5 3C 104
Herschell Rd. SE23 7A 106
Hersham Clo. SW15 7C 100
Hershell Ct. SW14 4H 99
Hertford Av. SW14 5K 99
Hertford Clo. Barn 3G 5
Hertford Ct. E6 3D 72 (off Vicarage La.)
Hertford Ct. N13 3F 17
Hertford Pl. W1 4G 67 (4B 160)
Hertford Rd. N1 1E 68 (in two parts)
Hertford Rd. N2 3C 30
Hertford Rd. N9 2C 18
Hertford Rd. Bark 7E 54
Hertford Rd. Barn 3F 5
Hertford Rd. Ilf 6J 37
Hertfordshire & Middlesex Country Club. 5B 10
Hertford Sq. Mitc 4J 139
Hertford St. W1 1F 85 (5J 165)
Hertford Wlk. Belv 5G 93
Hertford Way. Mitc 4J 139
Hertslet Rd. N7 3K 49
Hertsmere Ho. E14 7C 70 (off Hertsmere Rd.)
Hertsmere Rd. E14 1C 88
Hertswood Ct. Barn 4B 4
Hervey Clo. N3 1J 29
Hervey Pk. Rd. E17 4A 34
Hervey Rd. SE3 1K 107
Hervey Way. N3 1J 29
Hesa Rd. Hay 6J 59
Hesewall Clo. SW4 2G 103
Hesketh Pl. W11 7G 65
Hesketh Rd. E7 3J 53
Heslop Rd. SW12 1D 120
Hesper M. SW5 4K 83
Hesperus Clo. E14 4D 88
Hesperus Cres. E14 4D 88
Hessel Rd. W13 2A 80
Hessel St. E1 6H 69
Hestercombe Av. SW6 2G 101
Hesterman Way. Croy 1K 151
Hester Rd. N18 5B 18
Hester Rd. SW11 7C 84
Hester Ter. Rich 3G 99
Heston. 7E 78
Heston Av. Houn 6C 78
Heston Cen., The. Houn 5A 78
Heston Grange. Houn 6D 78
Heston Grange La. Houn 6D 78
Heston Ho. SE8 1C 106
Heston Ind. Cen. Houn 6A 78
Heston Ind. Mall. Houn 7D 78
Heston Rd. Houn 7E 78
Heston St. SE14 1C 106
Hetherington Rd. SW4 4J 103
Hetherington Rd. Shep 2E 130
Hetherington Way. Uxb 4A 40
Hethpool Ho. W2 4A 158
Hetley Gdns. SE19 7F 123
Hetley Rd. W12 1D 82
Heton Gdns. NW4 4D 28
Hevelius Clo. SE10 5H 89
Hever Cft. SE9 4E 126
Hever Gdns. Brom 2E 144
Heverham Rd. SE18 4J 91
Hever Ho. SE15 6K 87 (off Lovelinch Clo.)
Heversham Ho. SE15 6J 87
Heversham Rd. Bexh 2G 111
Hewens Rd. Uxb 4E 58
Hewer St. W10 5F 65
Hewett Clo. Stan 4G 11
Hewett Rd. Dag 5D 56
Hewett St. EC2 4E 68 (4H 163)
Hewish Rd. N18 4K 17
Hewison St. E3 2B 70
Hewitt Av. N22 2B 32
Hewitt Clo. Croy 3C 154
Hewitt Rd. N8 5A 32
Hewlett Ho. SW8 7F 85 (off Havelock Ter.)
Hewlett Rd. E3 2A 70
Hexagon, The. N6 1D 48
Hexal Rd. SE6 3G 125
Hexham Gdns. Iswth 7A 80
Hexham Rd. SE27 2C 122
Hexham Rd. Barn 4E 4
Hexham Rd. Mord 1K 149
Heybourne Rd. N17 7C 18
Heybridge. NW1 6F 49 (off Lewis St.)
Heybridge Av. SW16 7J 121
Heybridge Dri. Ilf 2H 37
Heybridge Way. E10 7A 34
Heydon Ho. SE14 1J 105 (off Kender St.)
Heyford Av. SW8 7J 85
Heyford Av. SW20 3H 137
Heyford Rd. Mitc 2C 138
Heyford Ter. SW8 7J 85
Heygate St. SE17 4C 86
Heylyn Sq. E3 3B 70
Heynes Rd. Dag 4C 56
Heysham La. NW3 3K 47
Heysham Rd. N15 6D 32
Heythorp St. SW18 1H 119
Heythrop College. 3K 83 (off Kensington Sq., University of London)
Heythrop Dri. Ick 4B 40
Heywood Av. NW9 1A 28
Heywood Ct. Stan 5H 11
Heywood Ho. SE14 6K 87 (off Myers La.)
Heyworth Rd. E5 4H 51
Heyworth Rd. E15 5H 53
Hibbert Ho. E14 3C 88 (off Tiller Rd.)
Hibbert Rd. E17 7B 34
Hibbert Rd. Harr 2K 25
Hibbert St. SW11 3B 102
Hibernia Gdns. Houn 4E 96
Hibernia Point. SE2 2D 92 (off Wolvercote Rd.)
Hibernia Rd. Houn 4E 96
Hibiscus Clo. Edgw 4D 12
Hichisson Rd. SE15 5J 105
Hickes Ho. NW6 7B 48
Hickey's Almshouses. Rich 4F 99
Hickin Clo. SE7 4B 90
Hickin St. E14 3E 88
Hickleton. NW1 1G 67 (off Camden St.)
Hickling Ho. SE16 3H 87 (off Slippers Pl.)
Hickling Rd. Ilf 5F 55
Hickman Av. E4 6K 19
Hickman Clo. E16 5B 72
Hickman Rd. Romf 7C 38
Hickmore Wlk. SW4 3H 103
Hickory Clo. N9 7B 8
Hicks Av. Gnfd 3H 61
Hicks Clo. SW11 3C 102
Hicks Ct. Dag 3H 57
Hicks St. SE8 5A 88
Hidcote Gdns. SW20 3D 136
Hide. E6 6E 72
Hide Pl. SW1 4H 85 (4C 172)
Hider Ct. SE3 7A 90
Hide Rd. Harr 4G 25
Hides St. N7 6K 49
Hide Tower. SW1 4H 85 (4C 172) (off Regency St.)
Higgins Ho. N1 1E 68 (off Colville Est.)
Higginson Ho. NW3 7D 48 (off Fellows Rd.)
Higgins Wlk. Hamp 6C 114 (off Abbott Clo.)
Higgs Ind. Est. SE24 3B 104
High Acres. Enf 3G 7
Higham Hill. 2A 34
Higham Hill Rd. E17 1A 34
Higham Path. E17 3A 34
Higham Pl. E17 3A 34
Higham Rd. N17 3D 32
Higham Rd. Wfd G 6D 20
Highams Ct. E4 3A 20
Highams Lodge Bus. Cen. E17 3K 33
Highams Park. 6A 20
Highams Pk. Ind. Est. E4 6K 19
Highams Sta. Av. E4 6H 19
Highams, The. E17 1E 34
Higham St. E17 3A 34
Highbanks Clo. Well 7B 92
Highbanks Rd. Pinn 6A 10
Highbank Way. N8 6A 32
High Barnet. 2A 4
Highbarrow Rd. Croy 1G 153
High Beech. N21 6E 6
High Beech. S Croy 7E 152
High Beeches. Sidc 5E 128
High Birch Ct. New Bar 4H 5 (off Park Rd.)
High Bri. SE10 5F 89
Highbridge Ct. SE14 7J 87 (off Farrow La.)
Highbridge Rd. Bark 1F 73
High Bri. Wharf. SE10 5F 89 (off High Bri.)
Highbrook Rd. SE3 3B 108
High Broom Cres. W Wick 7D 142
Highbury. 4B 50
Highbury Av. T Hth 2A 140
Highbury Barn. N5 4C 50
Highbury Clo. N Mald 4J 135
Highbury Clo. W Wick 2D 154
Highbury Corner. (Junct.) 6A 50
Highbury Cres. N5 5B 50
Highbury Est. N5 5C 50
Highbury Gdns. Ilf 2J 55
Highbury Grange. N5 4C 50
Highbury Gro. N5 5B 50
Highbury Gro. Ct. N5 6C 50
Highbury Hill. N5 3A 50
Highbury New Pk. N5 5C 50
Highbury Pk. N5 3B 50
Highbury Pk. M. N5 4C 50
Highbury Pl. N5 6B 50
Highbury Quad. N5 3C 50
Highbury Rd. SW19 5G 119
Highbury Sta. Rd. N1 6A 50
Highbury Ter. N5 5B 50

Highbury Ter. M. *N5* ... 5B **50**
High Cedar Dri. *SW20* ... 7E **118**
Highclere Rd. *N Mald* ... 3K **135**
Highclere St. *SE26* ... 4A **124**
Highcliffe. W13 ... 5B 62
(off Clivedon Ct.)
Highcliffe Dri. *SW15* ... 6B **100**
(in two parts)
Highcliffe Gdns. *Ilf* ... 5C **36**
Highcombe. *SE7* ... 6K **89**
Highcombe Clo. *SE9* ... 1B **126**
High Coombe Pl. *King T* ... 6K **117**
Highcroft. *NW9* ... 5A **28**
Highcroft Av. *Wemb* ... 7G **45**
Highcroft Est. *N19* ... 7J **31**
Highcroft Gdns. *NW11* ... 6H **29**
Highcroft Rd. *N19* ... 7J **31**
High Cross Cen., The. *N15* ... 4G **33**
High Cross Rd. *N17* ... 3G **33**
Highcross Way. *SW15* ... 1C **118**
Highdaun Dri. *SW16* ... 4K **139**
Highdown. *Wor Pk* ... 2A **148**
Highdown Rd. *SW15* ... 6D **100**
High Dri. *N Mald* ... 1J **135**
High Elms. *Wfd G* ... 5D **20**
Highfield. *Bus H* ... 2D **10**
Highfield Av. *NW9* ... 5J **27**
Highfield Av. *NW11* ... 7F **29**
Highfield Av. *Eri* ... 6H **93**
Highfield Av. *Gnfd* ... 5J **43**
Highfield Av. *Pinn* ... 5D **24**
Highfield Av. *Wemb* ... 3F **45**
Highfield Clo. *N22* ... 1A **32**
Highfield Clo. *NW9* ... 5J **27**
Highfield Clo. *SE13* ... 6F **107**
Highfield Clo. *N'wd* ... 1G **23**
Highfield Clo. *Surb* ... 1C **146**
Highfield Ct. *N14* ... 6B **6**
Highfield Ct. *NW11* ... 6G **29**
Highfield Cres. *N'wd* ... 1G **23**
Highfield Dri. *Brom* ... 4G **143**
Highfield Dri. *Eps* ... 6B **148**
Highfield Dri. *Uxb* ... 4A **40**
Highfield Dri. *W Wick* ... 2D **154**
Highfield Gdns. *NW11* ... 6G **29**
Highfield Hill. *SE19* ... 7D **122**
Highfield Rd. *N21* ... 2G **17**
Highfield Rd. *NW11* ... 6G **29**
Highfield Rd. *W3* ... 5H **63**
Highfield Rd. *Bexh* ... 5F **111**
Highfield Rd. *Brom* ... 4D **144**
Highfield Rd. *Chst* ... 3K **145**
Highfield Rd. *Felt* ... 2J **113**
(in two parts)
Highfield Rd. *Iswth* ... 1K **97**
Highfield Rd. *N'wd* ... 1G **23**
Highfield Rd. *Sun* ... 5H **131**
Highfield Rd. *Surb* ... 7J **135**
Highfield Rd. *Sutt* ... 5C **150**
Highfield Rd. *W on T* ... 7J **131**
Highfield Rd. *Wfd G* ... 7H **21**
Highfields. *Sutt* ... 2J **149**
Highfields Gro. *N6* ... 1D **48**
High Foleys. *Clay* ... 7B **146**
High Gables. *Brom* ... 2G **143**
Highgate. ... 1F 49
Highgate Av. *N6* ... 7F **31**
Highgate Cemetery. ... 2F 49
Highgate Clo. *N6* ... 7E **30**
Highgate Edge. *N2* ... 5C **30**
Highgate Heights. *N6* ... 6G **31**
Highgate High St. *N6* ... 1E **48**
Highgate Hill. *N6 & N19* ... 1F **49**
Highgate Ho. *SE26* ... 3G **123**
Highgate Rd. *NW5* ... 3E **48**
Highgate Spinney. *N8* ... 6H **31**
Highgate Wlk. *SE23* ... 2J **123**
Highgate W. Hill. *N6* ... 2E **48**
High Gro. *SE18* ... 7H **91**
High Gro. *Brom* ... 1B **144**
Highgrove Clo. *N11* ... 5K **15**
Highgrove Clo. *Chst* ... 1C **144**
Highgrove Ct. *Beck* ... 7C **124**
Highgrove Ct. *Sutt* ... 6J **149**
Highgrove M. *Cars* ... 3D **150**
Highgrove Rd. *Dag* ... 5C **56**
Highgrove Way. *Ruis* ... 6J **23**
High Hill Est. *E5* ... 1H **51**
High Hill Ferry. *E5* ... 1H **51**
High Holborn. *WC1* ... 6J **67** (7E **160**)
Highland Av. *W7* ... 6J **61**
Highland Av. *Dag* ... 3J **57**
Highland Cotts. *Wall* ... 4G **151**
Highland Ct. *E18* ... 1K **35**
Highland Cft. *Beck* ... 5D **124**
Highland Dri. *Bush* ... 1A **10**
Highland Pk. *Felt* ... 4H **113**
Highland Rd. *SE19* ... 6E **122**
Highland Rd. *Bexh* ... 5G **111**
Highland Rd. *Brom* ... 1H **143**
Highland Rd. *N'wd* ... 2H **23**
Highlands. *N20* ... 2G **15**
Highlands Av. *N21* ... 5E **6**
Highlands Av. *W3* ... 7J **63**
Highlands Clo. *N4* ... 7J **31**
Highlands Clo. *Houn* ... 1F **97**
Highlands Ct. *SE19* ... 6E **122**
Highlands Gdns. *Ilf* ... 1D **54**
Highlands Heath. *SW15* ... 7E **100**
Highlands Rd. *Barn* ... 5D **4**
Highlands, The. *Barn* ... 4D **4**
Highlands, The. *Edgw* ... 2H **27**
Highlands Village. ... 5E 6
Highland Ter. SE13 ... 3D 106
(off Algernon Rd.)
High La. *W7* ... 5H **61**
(in two parts)
Highlawn Hall. *Harr* ... 3J **43**
Highlea Clo. *NW9* ... 7F **13**
High Level Dri. *SE26* ... 4G **123**
Highlever Rd. *W10* ... 5E **64**
Highmead. N18 ... 5B 18
(off Alpha Rd.)
Highmead. *SE18* ... 7K **91**
High Mead. *Harr* ... 5J **25**
High Mead. *W Wick* ... 2F **155**
Highmead Cres. *Wemb* ... 7F **45**
High Mdw. Clo. *Pinn* ... 4A **24**
High Mdw. Cres. *NW9* ... 5K **27**
High Meads Rd. *E16* ... 6B **72**
Highmore Rd. *SE3* ... 7G **89**
High Mt. *NW4* ... 6C **28**
High Oaks. *Enf* ... 1E **6**
High Pde., The. *SW16* ... 3J **121**
High Pk. Av. *Rich* ... 1G **99**
High Pk. Rd. *Rich* ... 1G **99**
High Path. *SW19* ... 1K **137**
Highpoint. *N6* ... 7E **30**
High Point. *SE9* ... 3F **127**
High Ridge. *N10* ... 1F **31**
High Ridge Pl. Enf ... 1E 6
(off Oak Av.)
High Rd. *E18* ... 1J **35**
High Rd. *N11* ... 5A **16**
High Rd. *N15 & N17* ... 5F **33**
High Rd. *N22* ... 1K **31**
High Rd. *NW10* ... 6A **46**
High Rd. *Buck H* ... 2E **20**
High Rd. *Bus H* ... 1C **10**
High Rd. *Chig* ... 5K **21**
High Rd. *Eastc* ... 6J **23**
High Rd. *Harr* ... 7D **10**
High Rd. *Hay* ... 5G **59**
High Rd. *Ick* ... 3E **40**
High Rd. *Ilf & Romf* ... 3F **55**
(in five parts)
High Rd. *Romf* ... 7D **38**
High Rd. *Wemb* ... 5D **44**
High Rd. E. Finchley. *N2* ... 1B **30**
High Rd. Leyton. *E10 & E15* ... 6D **34**
High Rd. Leytonstone. *E11 & E15* ... 4G **53**
High Rd. N. Finchley. *N12* ... 3F **15**
High Rd. Whetstone. *N20* ... 7F **5**
High Rd. Woodford Grn. *Wfd G* ... 6C **20**
High Sheldon. *N6* ... 6D **30**
Highshore Rd. *SE15* ... 2F **105**
(in two parts)
Highstead Cres. *Eri* ... 1K **111**
Highstone Av. *E11* ... 6J **35**
Highstone Ct. E11 ... 6H 35
(off New Wanstead)
Highstone Mans. NW1 ... 7G 49
(off Camden Rd.)
High St. *E11* ... 5J **35**
High St. *E13* ... 2J **71**
High St. *E15* ... 2E **70**
High St. *E17* ... 5A **34**
High St. *N8* ... 4J **31**
High St. *N14* ... 1C **16**
High St. *NW7* ... 5J **13**
High St. *SE20* ... 6J **123**
High St. *SE25* ... 4F **141**
High St. *SW19* ... 5F **119**
High St. *W3* ... 1H **81**
High St. *W5* ... 1D **80**
High St. *B'side* ... 3G **37**
High St. *Barn* ... 3B **4**
High St. *Beck* ... 2C **142**
High St. *Bren* ... 7C **80**
High St. *Brom* ... 2J **143**
(in two parts)
High St. *Cars* ... 5E **150**
High St. *Cheam* ... 6G **149**
High St. *Chst* ... 6F **127**
High St. *Cran* ... 1J **95**
High St. *Croy* ... 2C **152**
(in two parts)
High St. *Edgw* ... 6B **12**
High St. *Enf* ... 6D **8**
High St. *Ewe* ... 7B **148**
High St. *Felt* ... 3H **113**
High St. *Hamp* ... 1G **133**
High St. *Hamp H* ... 6G **115**
High St. *Hamp W* ... 1C **134**
High St. *Harm* ... 6A **76**
High St. *Harr* (HA1) ... 1J **43**
High St. *Harr* (HA3) ... 2J **25**
High St. *Hay* ... 6F **77**
High St. *Houn* ... 3F **97**
(in three parts)
High St. *King T* ... 3D **134**
High St. *N Mald* ... 4A **136**
High St. *N'wd* ... 1H **23**
High St. *Pinn* ... 3C **24**
High St. *Romf* ... 5K **39**
High St. *Ruis* ... 7G **23**
High St. *Shep* ... 6D **130**
High St. *S'hall* ... 1D **78**
High St. *Stanw* ... 6A **94**
High St. *Sutt* ... 4K **149**
High St. *Tedd* ... 5K **115**
High St. *Th Dit* ... 6A **134**
High St. *T Hth* ... 4C **140**
High St. *Uxb* ... 1A **58**
(in two parts)
High St. *W on T* ... 7J **131**
High St. *Wemb* ... 4F **45**
High St. *W Dray* ... 7A **58**
High St. *W Mol* ... 4E **132**
High St. *W Wick* ... 1D **154**
High St. *Whit* ... 7G **97**
High St. Colliers Wood. *SW19* ... 7B **120**
High St. Harlesden. *NW10* ... 2B **64**
High St. M. *SW19* ... 5G **119**
High St. N. *E12 & E6* ... 5C **54**
High St. S. *E6* ... 2D **72**
High Timber St. *EC4* ... 7C **68** (2C **168**)
High Tor Clo. *Brom* ... 7K **125**
High Trees. *N20* ... 3F **15**
High Trees. *SW2* ... 1A **122**
High Trees. *Barn* ... 5H **5**
High Trees. *Croy* ... 1A **154**
Hightrees Ct. *W7* ... 7J **61**
Highview. *N6* ... 6G **31**
Highview. *NW7* ... 3E **12**
Highview. *N'holt* ... 3C **60**
High Vw. *Pinn* ... 4A **24**
Highview Av. *Edgw* ... 4D **12**
Highview Av. *Wall* ... 5K **151**
High Vw. Clo. *SE19* ... 2F **141**
High Vw. Ct. *Har W* ... 7D **10**
Highview Gdns. *N3* ... 3G **29**
Highview Gdns. *N11* ... 5B **16**
Highview Gdns. *Edgw* ... 4D **12**
Highview Ho. *Romf* ... 4E **38**
Highview Lodge. Enf ... 3G 7
(off Ridgeway, The)
High Vw. Pde. *Ilf* ... 5D **36**
High Vw. Rd. *E18* ... 2H **35**
High Vw. Rd. *N2* ... 1D **30**
Highview Rd. *SE19* ... 6D **122**
Highview Rd. *W13* ... 5A **62**
High Vw. Rd. *Sidc* ... 4B **128**
Highway Bus. Pk., The. E1 ... 7K 69
(off Heckford St.)
Highway, The. *E1 & E14* ... 7G **69**
Highway, The. *Stan* ... 1K **25**
Highway, The. *Sutt* ... 7A **150**
Highway Trad. Cen., The. E1 ... 7K 69
(off Heckford St.)
Highwood. *Brom* ... 3G **143**
Highwood Av. *N12* ... 4F **15**
Highwood Ct. *N12* ... 3F **15**
Highwood Ct. *Barn* ... 5D **4**
Highwood Gdns. *Ilf* ... 5D **36**
Highwood Gro. *NW7* ... 5E **12**
Highwood Hill. ... 3G 13
Highwood Hill. *NW7* ... 2G **13**
Highwood Rd. *N19* ... 3J **49**
High Worple. *Harr* ... 7D **24**
Highworth Rd. *N11* ... 6C **16**
Highworth St. *NW1* ... 5D **158**
Hi-Gloss Cen. *SE8* ... 5A **88**
Hilary Av. *Mitc* ... 3E **138**
Hilary Clo. *E11* ... 5J **35**
Hilary Clo. *SW6* ... 7K **83**
Hilary Clo. *Eri* ... 1H **111**
Hilary Dennis Ct. *E11* ... 4J **35**
Hilary Rd. *W12* ... 6B **64**
(in two parts)
Hilbert Rd. *Sutt* ... 3F **149**
Hilborough Ct. *E8* ... 7F **51**
Hilda Ct. *Surb* ... 7D **134**
Hilda Rd. *E6* ... 7B **54**
Hilda Rd. *E16* ... 4G **71**
Hilda Ter. *SW9* ... 2A **104**
Hilda Va. Clo. *Orp* ... 4E **156**
Hilda Va. Rd. *Orp* ... 4E **156**
Hildenborough Gdns. *Brom* ... 6G **125**
Hildenborough Ho. Beck ... 7B 124
(off Bethersden Clo.)
Hildenlea Pl. *Brom* ... 2F **143**
Hilderley Ho. King T ... 3F 135
(off Winery La.)
Hildreth St. *SW12* ... 1F **121**
Hildyard Rd. *SW6* ... 6J **83**
Hiley Rd. *NW10* ... 3E **64**
Hilgrove Rd. *NW6* ... 7A **48**
Hiliary Gdns. *Stan* ... 2C **26**
Hillary. N8 ... 3J 31
(off Boyton Clo.)
Hillary Ct. W12 ... 2E 82
(off Titmuss St.)
Hillary Cres. *W on T* ... 7A **132**
Hillary Dri. *Iswth* ... 5K **97**
Hillary Ri. *Barn* ... 4D **4**
Hillary Rd. *S'hall* ... 3E **78**
Hillbeck Clo. *SE15* ... 7J **87**
Hillbeck Ho. SE15 ... 6J 87
(off Hillbeck Clo.)
Hillbeck Way. *Gnfd* ... 1H **61**
Hillborne Clo. *Hay* ... 5J **77**
Hillboro Ct. *E11* ... 7F **35**
Hillborough Clo. *SW19* ... 7A **120**
Hillbrook Rd. *SW17* ... 3D **120**
Hill Brow. *Brom* ... 1B **144**
Hillbrow. *N Mald* ... 3B **136**
Hill Brow Clo. *Bex* ... 4K **129**
Hillbrow Rd. *Brom* ... 7G **125**
Hillbury Av. *Harr* ... 5B **26**
Hillbury Rd. *SW17* ... 3F **121**
Hill Clo. *NW2* ... 3D **46**
Hill Clo. *NW11* ... 6J **29**
Hill Clo. *Chst* ... 5F **127**
Hill Clo. *Harr* ... 3J **43**
Hill Clo. *Stan* ... 4G **11**
Hillcote Av. *SW16* ... 7A **122**
Hill Ct. *W5* ... 4F **63**
Hill Ct. *Barn* ... 4H **5**
Hill Ct. *N'holt* ... 5E **42**
Hillcourt Av. *N12* ... 6E **14**
Hillcourt Est. *N16* ... 1D **50**
Hillcourt Rd. *SE22* ... 6H **105**
Hill Cres. *N20* ... 2E **14**
Hill Cres. *Bex* ... 1J **129**
Hill Cres. *Harr* ... 5A **26**
Hill Cres. *Surb* ... 5F **135**
Hill Cres. *Wor Pk* ... 2E **148**
Hillcrest. *N6* ... 7E **30**
Hillcrest. *N21* ... 7F **7**
Hillcrest. *SE5* ... 4D **104**
Hillcrest. *Sidc* ... 7A **110**
Hill Crest. *Surb* ... 7E **134**
Hillcrest Av. *NW11* ... 5H **29**
Hillcrest Av. *Edgw* ... 4C **12**
Hillcrest Av. *Pinn* ... 4B **24**
Hillcrest Clo. *SE26* ... 4G **123**
Hillcrest Clo. *Beck* ... 6B **142**
Hillcrest Ct. *Romf* ... 1K **39**
Hillcrest Ct. *Sutt* ... 6B **150**
Hillcrest Gdns. *N3* ... 4G **29**
Hill Crest Gdns. *NW2* ... 3C **46**
Hillcrest Gdns. *Esh* ... 3A **146**
Hillcrest Rd. *E17* ... 2F **35**
Hillcrest Rd. *E18* ... 2J **35**
Hillcrest Rd. *W3* ... 1H **81**
Hillcrest Rd. *W5* ... 5E **62**
Hillcrest Rd. *Brom* ... 5J **125**
Hillcrest Vw. *Beck* ... 6B **142**
Hillcroft Av. *Pinn* ... 6D **24**
Hillcroft Cres. *W5* ... 6E **62**
Hillcroft Cres. *Ruis* ... 3B **42**
Hillcroft Cres. *Wemb* ... 4F **45**
Hillcroft Rd. *E6* ... 5F **73**
Hillcroome Rd. *Sutt* ... 6B **150**
Hillcross Av. *Mord* ... 6F **137**
Hilldale Rd. *Sutt* ... 4H **149**
Hilldown Ct. *SW16* ... 7J **121**
Hilldown Rd. *SW16* ... 7J **121**
Hilldown Rd. *Brom* ... 1G **155**
Hill Dri. *NW9* ... 1J **45**
Hill Dri. *SW16* ... 3K **139**
Hilldrop Cres. *N7* ... 5H **49**
Hilldrop Est. *N7* ... 4H **49**
Hilldrop La. *N7* ... 5H **49**
Hilldrop Rd. *N7* ... 5H **49**
Hilldrop Rd. *Brom* ... 6K **125**
Hillend. *SE18* ... 1E **108**
Hiller Ho. NW1 ... 7H 49
(off Camden Sq.)
Hillersden Ho. SW1 ... 5F 85 (5J 171)
(off Ebury Bri. Rd.)
Hillersdon Av. *SW13* ... 2C **100**
Hillersdon Av. *Edgw* ... 5A **12**
Hillery Clo. *SE17* ... 4D **86**
Hill Farm Cotts. *Ruis* ... 7E **22**
Hill Farm Rd. *W10* ... 5E **64**
Hill Farm Rd. *Uxb* ... 4F **41**
Hillfield Av. *N8* ... 5J **31**
Hillfield Av. *NW9* ... 5A **28**
Hillfield Av. *Mord* ... 6C **138**
Hillfield Av. *Wemb* ... 7E **44**
Hillfield Clo. *Harr* ... 4G **25**
Hillfield Ct. *NW3* ... 5C **48**
Hillfield Ho. *N5* ... 5C **50**
Hillfield Pk. *N10* ... 4F **31**
Hillfield Pk. *N21* ... 2F **17**

Hillfield Pk. M. *N10* 4F **31**
Hillfield Rd. *NW6* 5H **47**
Hill Fld. Rd. *Hamp* 7D **114**
Hillfoot Av. *Romf* 1J **39**
Hillfoot Rd. *Romf* 1J **39**
Hillgate Pl. *SW12* 7F **103**
Hillgate Pl. *W8* 1J **83**
Hillgate St. *W8* 1J **83**
Hill Gro. *Felt* 2D **114**
Hill Gro. *Romf* 3K **39**
Hill Ho. E5 1H **51** *(off Harrington Hill)*
Hill Ho. *Brom* 2H **143**
Hillhouse Av. *Stan* 7E **10**
Hill Ho. Clo. *N21* 7F **7**
Hill Ho. Dri. *Hamp* 1E **132**
Hill Ho. Rd. *SW16* 5K **121**
Hilliard Ho. E1 1H **87** *(off Prusom St.)*
Hilliard Rd. *N'wd* 1H **23**
Hilliards Ct. *E1* 1J **87**
Hillier Clo. *New Bar* 6E **4**
Hillier Gdns. *Croy* 5A **152**
Hillier Lodge. *Tedd* 5H **115**
Hillier Pl. *Chess* 6D **146**
Hillier Rd. *SW11* 6D **102**
Hilliers Av. *Uxb* 3C **58**
Hilliers La. *Croy* 3J **151**
Hillingdon. 3C **58**
Hillingdon Av. *Stai* 1A **112**
Hillingdon Cir. *Hil* 6D **40**
Hillingdon Ct. *Harr* 4D **26**
Hillingdon Heath. 4D **58**
Hillingdon Hill. *Uxb* 2A **58**
Hillingdon Rd. *Bexh* 2J **111**
Hillingdon Rd. *Uxb* 1A **58**
Hillingdon St. *SE5 & SE17* 6B **86** (in two parts)
Hillington Gdns. *Wfd G* 2B **36**
Hill La. *Ruis* 1E **40**
Hillman Clo. *Uxb* 5A **40**
Hillman Dri. *W10* 4E **64**
Hillman St. *E8* 6H **51**
Hillmarton Rd. *N7* 5J **49**
Hillmead Dri. *SW9* 4B **104**
Hillmore Ct. SE13 3F **107** *(off Belmont Hill)*
Hillmore Gro. *SE26* 5A **124**
Hill Path. *SW16* 5K **121**
Hillreach. *SE18* 5D **90**
Hill Ri. *N9* 6C **8**
Hill Ri. *NW11* 4K **29**
Hill Ri. *SE23* 1H **123**
Hill Ri. *Esh* 2B **146**
Hill Ri. *Gnfd* 7G **43**
Hill Ri. *Rich* 5D **98**
Hill Ri. *Ruis* 1E **40**
Hill Ri. *W on T* 7H **131**
Hillrise Mans. N19 7J **31** *(off Warltersville Rd.)*
Hillrise Rd. *N19* 7J **31**
Hill Rd. *N10* 1D **30**
Hill Rd. *NW8* 3A **66**
Hill Rd. *Cars* 6C **150**
Hill Rd. *Harr* 5A **26**
Hill Rd. *Mitc* 1F **139**
Hill Rd. *Pinn* 5C **24**
Hill Rd. *Sutt* 5K **149**
Hill Rd. *Wemb* 3B **44**
Hillsboro' Rd. *SE22* 5E **104**
Hillsborough Ct. NW6 1K **65** *(off Mortimer Cres.)*
Hillsgrove Clo. *Well* 7C **92**
Hillside. 4J **93**
Hillside. *N8* 6H **31**
Hillside. *NW5* 3E **48**
Hillside. *NW9* 4K **27**
Hillside. *NW10* 7J **45**
Hillside. SE10 7F **89** *(off Crooms Hill)*
Hillside. *SW19* 6F **119**
Hillside. *Eri* 4J **93**
Hillside. *New Bar* 5F **5**
Hillside Av. *N11* 6J **15**
Hillside Av. *Wemb* 4F **45**
Hillside Av. *Wfd G* 6F **21**
Hillside Clo. *NW8* 2K **65**
Hillside Clo. *Mord* 4G **137**
Hillside Clo. *Wfd G* 5F **21**
Hillside Cres. *Harr* 1G **43**
Hillside Cres. *N'wd* 1J **23**
Hillside Dri. *Edgw* 6B **12**
Hillside Est. *N15* 6F **33**
Hillside Gdns. *E17* 3F **35**
Hillside Gdns. *N6* 6F **31**
Hillside Gdns. *N11* 6B **16**
Hillside Gdns. *SW2* 2A **122**
Hillside Gdns. *Barn* 4B **4**
Hillside Gdns. *Edgw* 4A **12**
Hillside Gdns. *Harr* 7E **26**
Hillside Gdns. *N'wd* 1J **23**
Hillside Gdns. *Wall* 7G **151**
Hillside Gro. *N14* 7C **6**
Hillside Gro. *NW7* 7H **13**
Hillside Ho. Croy 4B **152** *(off Violet La.)*
Hillside La. *Brom* 2H **155** (in two parts)
Hillside Mans. *Barn* 4C **4**
Hillside Pas. *SW16* 2K **121**
Hillside Ri. *N'wd* 1J **23**
Hillside Rd. *N16* 7E **32**
Hillside Rd. *SW2* 2K **121**
Hillside Rd. *W5* 5E **62**
Hillside Rd. *Brom* 3H **143**
Hillside Rd. *Croy* 5B **152**
Hillside Rd. *N'wd* 1J **23**
Hillside Rd. *Pinn* 1K **23**
Hillside Rd. *S'hall* 4E **60**
Hillside Rd. *Surb* 4F **135**
Hillside Rd. *Sutt* 7H **149**
Hills La. *N'wd* 1G **23**
Hillsleigh Rd. *W8* 1H **83**
Hills M. *W5* 7E **62**
Hills Pl. *W1* 6G **67** (1A **166**)
Hills Rd. *Buck H* 1E **20**
Hillstowe St. *E5* 3J **51**
Hill St. *W1* 1E **84** (4H **165**)
Hill St. *Rich* 5D **98**
Hilltop. *E17* 3D **34**
Hilltop. *NW11* 4K **29**
Hill Top. *Mord* 6J **137**
Hill Top. *Sutt* 7H **137**
Hilltop Ct. NW8 7A **48** *(off Alexandra Rd.)*
Hill Top Ct. *Wfd G* 6J **21**
Hilltop Gdns. *NW4* 2D **28**
Hilltop Rd. *NW6* 7J **47**
Hill Top Vw. *Wfd G* 6J **21**
Hilltop Way. *Stan* 3F **11**
Hillview. *SW20* 7D **118**
Hillview Av. *Harr* 5E **26**
Hillview Clo. *Wemb* 2F **45**
Hill Vw. Cres. *Ilf* 6D **36**
Hill Vw. Dri. *SE28* 1J **91**
Hill Vw. Dri. *Well* 2J **109**
Hillview Gdns. *NW4* 4F **29**
Hill Vw. Gdns. *NW9* 5K **27**
Hillview Gdns. *Harr* 3E **24**
Hillview Rd. *NW7* 4A **14**
Hillview Rd. *Chst* 5E **126**
Hill Vw. Rd. *Clay* 7A **146**
Hillview Rd. *Pinn* 1D **24**
Hillview Rd. *Sutt* 3A **150**
Hill Vw. Rd. *Twic* 6A **98**
Hillway. *N6* 2E **48**
Hillway. *NW9* 1A **46**
Hillwood Ho. NW1 2G **67** (1B **160**) *(off Polygon Rd.)*
Hillworth. *Beck* 2D **142**
Hillworth Rd. *SW2* 7A **104**
Hillyard Ho. *SW9* 1A **104**
Hillyard Rd. *W7* 5J **61**
Hillyard St. *SW9* 1A **104**
Hillyfield. *E17* 2A **34**
Hilly Fields Cres. *SE4* 3C **106**
Hilsea St. *E5* 4J **51**
Hilton Av. *N12* 5G **15**
Hilton Ho. *SE4* 4K **105**
Hilton Wharf. SE10 6D **88** *(off Norman Rd.)*
Hilversum Cres. *SE22* 5E **104**
Himley Rd. *SW17* 5C **120**
Hinchinbrook Ho. NW6 1K **65** *(off Mortimer Cres.)*
Hinchley Clo. *Esh* 4A **146**
Hinchley Dri. *Esh* 3A **146**
Hinchley Way. *Esh* 3A **146**
Hinckley Rd. *SE15* 4G **105**
Hind Ct. *EC4* 6A **68** (1K **167**)
Hind Cres. *Eri* 6K **93**
Hinde Ho. W1 6E **66** (7H **159**) *(off Hinde St.)*
Hinde M. *W1* 7H **159**
Hindes Rd. *Harr* 5H **25**
Hinde St. *W1* 6E **66** (7H **159**)
Hind Gro. *E14* 6C **70**
Hindhead Clo. *N16* 1E **50**
Hindhead Clo. *Uxb* 5D **58**
Hindhead Gdns. *N'holt* 1C **60**
Hindhead Way. *Wall* 5J **151**
Hind Ho. SE14 6K **87** *(off Myers La.)*
Hindlip Ho. *SW8* 1H **103**
Hindmans Rd. *SE22* 5G **105**
Hindmans Way. *Dag* 4F **75**
Hindmarsh Clo. *E1* 7G **69**
Hindrey Rd. *E5* 5H **51**
Hindsley's Pl. *SE23* 2J **123**
Hinkler Rd. *Harr* 3D **26**
Hinksey Path. *SE2* 2D **92**
Hinstock. NW6 1K **65** *(off Belsize Rd.)*
Hinstock Rd. *SE18* 6G **91**
Hinton Av. *Houn* 4B **96**
Hinton Clo. *SE9* 1C **126**
Hinton Ct. E10 2D **52** *(off Leyton Grange Est.)*
Hinton Ho. *W5* 6C **62**
Hinton Rd. *N18* 4K **17**
Hinton Rd. *SW9* 3B **104**
Hinton Rd. *Wall* 6G **151**
Hippodrome M. *W11* 7G **65**
Hippodrome Pl. *W11* 7G **65**
Hiroshima Promenade. *SE7* 3A **90**
Hissocks Ho. NW10 7J **45** *(off Stilton Cres.)*
Hitcham Rd. *E17* 7B **34**
Hitchcock Clo. *Shep* 3B **130**
Hitchin Sq. *E3* 2A **70**
Hitherbroom Rd. *Hay* 1J **77**
Hither Farm Rd. *SE3* 3A **108**
Hitherfield Rd. *SW16* 2K **121**
Hitherfield Rd. *Dag* 2E **56**
Hither Green. 6G **107**
Hither Grn. La. *SE13* 5E **106**
Hitherwell Dri. *Harr* 1H **25**
Hitherwood Dri. *SE19* 4F **123**
Hive Clo. *Bus H* 2C **10**
Hive Rd. *Bus H* 2C **10** (in two parts)
HMS Belfast. ***1E 86 (4H 169)***
Hoadly Rd. *SW16* 3H **121**
Hobart Clo. *N20* 2H **15**
Hobart Clo. *Hay* 4B **60**
Hobart Ct. S Croy 5D **152** *(off S. Park Hill Rd.)*
Hobart Dri. *Hay* 4B **60**
Hobart Gdns. *T Hth* 3D **140**
Hobart La. *Hay* 4B **60**
Hobart Pl. *SW1* 3F **85** (1J **171**)
Hobart Pl. *Rich* 7F **99**
Hobart Rd. *Dag* 4D **56**
Hobart Rd. *Hay* 4B **60**
Hobart Rd. *Ilf* 2G **37**
Hobart Rd. *Wor Pk* 3D **148**
Hobbayne Rd. *W7* 6H **61**
Hobbes Wlk. *SW15* 5D **100**
Hobbs Ct. SE1 2F **87** (6K **169**) *(off Mill St.)*
Hobbs Grn. *N2* 3A **30**
Hobbs M. *Ilf* 2K **55**
Hobbs Pl. *N1* 1E **68**
Hobbs Pl. Est. N1 1E **68** *(off Hobbs Pl.)*
Hobbs Rd. *SE27* 4C **122**
Hobday St. *E14* 6D **70**
Hobill Wlk. *Surb* 6F **135**
Hoblands End. *Chst* 6J **127**
Hobson's Pl. *E1* 5G **69**
Hobury St. *SW10* 6A **84** (7A **170**)
Hocker St. *E2* 3F **69** (2J **163**)
Hockett Clo. *SE8* 4A **88**
Hockington Ct. *New Bar* 4E **4**
Hockley Av. *E6* 2C **72**
Hockley Ct. *E18* 1J **35**
Hockley M. *Bark* 3J **73**
Hockliffe Ho. W10 5E **64** *(off Sutton Way)*
Hockney Ct. SE16 5H **87** *(off Rossetti Rd.)*
Hocroft Av. *NW2* 3H **47**
Hocroft Ct. *NW2* 3H **47**
Hocroft Rd. *NW2* 3H **47**
Hocroft Wlk. *NW2* 3H **47**
Hodder Dri. *Gnfd* 2K **61**
Hoddesdon Rd. *Belv* 5G **93**
Hodes Row. *NW3* 4E **48**
Hodford Rd. *NW11* 1H **47**
Hodgkin Clo. *SE28* 7D **74**
Hodister Clo. *SE5* 7C **86**
Hodnet Gro. *SE16* 4K **87**
Hodson Clo. *Harr* 3D **42**
Hoecroft Ct. Enf 1D **8** *(off Hoe La.)*
Hoe La. *Enf* 1B **8**
Hoe St. *E17* 4C **34**
Hoever Ho. *SE6* 4E **124**
Hofland Rd. *W14* 3G **83**
Hogan M. *W2* 5A **66** (5A **158**)
Hogan Way. *E5* 2G **51**
Hogarth Av. *Ashf* 6E **112**
Hogarth Bus. Cen. *W4* 6A **82**
Hogarth Clo. *E16* 5B **72**
Hogarth Clo. *W5* 5E **62**
Hogarth Ct. E1 6G **69** *(off Batty St.)*
Hogarth Ct. *EC3* 6E **68** (2H **169**)
Hogarth Ct. NW1 7G **49** *(off St Pancras Way)*
Hogarth Ct. *SE19* 4F **123**
Hogarth Ct. *Houn* 7C **78**
Hogarth Cres. *SW19* 1B **138**
Hogarth Cres. *Croy* 7C **140**
Hogarth Gdns. *Houn* 7E **78**
Hogarth Hill. *NW11* 4H **29**
Hogarth Ho. SW1 ***4H 85 (4D 172)*** ***(off Erasmus St.)***
Hogarth Ho. N'holt 2B **60** *(off Gallery Gdns.)*
Hogarth Ind. Est. *NW10* 4C **64**
Hogarth La. *W4* 6A **82**
Hogarth Pl. SW5 4K **83** *(off Hogarth Rd.)*
Hogarth Rd. *SW5* 4K **83**
Hogarth Rd. *Dag* 5B **56**
Hogarth Rd. *Edgw* 2G **27**
Hogarth Roundabout. (Junct.) 6B **82**
Hogarth's House. 6A **82** *(off Hogarth La.)*
Hogarth Ter. *W4* 6A **82**
Hogarth Way. *Hamp* 1G **133**
Hog Hill Rd. *Romf* 1F **39**
Hogshead Pas. E1 7H **69** *(off Reunion Row)*
Hogsmill Ho. King T 3F **135** *(off Vineyard Clo.)*
Hogsmill Wlk. King T 3E **134** *(off Penrhyn Rd.)*
Hogsmill Way. *Eps* 5J **147**
Holbeach Gdns. *Sidc* 6J **109**
Holbeach M. *SW12* 1F **121**
Holbeach Rd. *SE6* 7C **106**
Holbeck Row. *SE15* 7G **87**
Holbein Ho. SW1 5E **84** (5G **171**) *(off Holbein M.)*
Holbein M. *SW1* 5E **84** (5G **171**)
Holbein Pl. *SW1* 4E **84** (4G **171**)
Holbein Ter. Dag 4C **56** *(off Marlborough Rd.)*
Holberton Gdns. *NW10* 3D **64**
Holborn. **5A 68 (6J 161)**
Holborn. *EC1* 5A **68** (6J **161**)
Holborn Cir. *EC1* 5A **68** (6K **161**)
Holborn Pl. *WC2* 6G **161**
Holborn Rd. *E13* 5K **71**
Holborn Viaduct. *EC4 & EC1* 5A **68**
Holborn Way. *Mitc* 2D **138**
Holbrook Clo. *N19* 1F **49**
Holbrook Clo. *Enf* 1A **8**
Holbrooke Ct. *N7* 3J **49**
Holbrooke Pl. *Rich* 5D **98**
Holbrook Ho. *Chst* 1H **145**
Holbrook La. *Chst* 7H **127**
Holbrook Rd. *E15* 2H **71**
Holbrook Way. *Brom* 6D **144**
Holburne Clo. *SE3* 1A **108**
Holburne Gdns. *SE3* 1B **108**
Holburne Rd. *SE3* 1A **108**
Holcombe Hill. *NW7* 3H **13**
Holcombe Ho. SW9 3J **103** *(off Landor Rd.)*
Holcombe Pl. SE4 3A **106** *(off St Asaph Rd.)*
Holcombe Rd. *N17* 3F **33** (in two parts)
Holcombe Rd. *Ilf* 7E **36**
Holcombe St. *W6* 4D **82**
Holcote Clo. *Belv* 3E **92**
Holcroft Ct. *W1* 5A **160**
Holcroft Ho. *SW11* 3B **102**
Holcroft Rd. *E9* 7J **51**
Holden Av. *N12* 5E **14**
Holden Av. *NW9* 1J **45**
Holdenby Rd. *SE4* 5A **106**
Holden Clo. *Dag* 3B **56**
Holden Ho. N1 1C **66** *(off Prebend St.)*
Holden Ho. *SE8* 7C **88**
Holdenhurst Av. *N12* 7F **15**
Holden Rd. *N12* 5E **14**
Holden St. *SW11* 2E **102**
Holder Clo. *N3* 7E **14**
Holdernesse Clo. *Iswth* 1A **98**
Holdernesse Rd. *SW17* 3D **120**
Holderness Ho. *SE5* 3E **104**
Holderness Way. *SE27* 5B **122**
Holders Hill. 2F **29**
Holder's Hill Av. *NW4* 2F **29**
Holders Hill Cir. *NW7* 7B **14**
Holders Hill Cres. *NW4* 2F **29**
Holders Hill Dri. *NW4* 3F **29**
Holder's Hill Gdns. *NW4* 2G **29**
Holders Hill Pde. *NW4* 1G **29**
Holders Hill Rd. *NW4 & NW7* 2F **29**
Holford Ho. SE16 4H **87** *(off Camilla Rd.)*
Holford M. *WC1* 1J **161**
Holford Pl. *WC1* 3K **67** (1H **161**)
Holford Rd. *NW3* 3A **48**
Holford St. *WC1* 3K **67** (1J **161**)
Holford Yd. WC1 2A **68** (1J **161**) *(off Cruikshank St.)*
Holgate Av. *SW11* 3B **102**
Holgate Gdns. *Dag* 6G **57**
Holgate Rd. *Dag* 5G **57**
Holgate St. *SE7* 3B **90**
Hollam Ho. *N8* 4K **31**

Holland Av. SW20 1B 136
Holland Av. Sutt 7J 149
Holland Clo. Brom 2H 155
Holland Clo. New Bar 7G 5
Holland Clo. Romf 5J 39
Holland Clo. Stan 5G 11
Holland Ct. E17 4E 34
(off Evelyn Rd.)
Holland Ct. NW7 6H 13
Holland Ct. Surb 7D 134
Holland Dri. SE23 3A 124
Holland Gdns. W14 3G 83
Holland Gro. SW9 7A 86
Holland Ho. E4 4A 20
Holland Ho. NW10 2D 64
(off Holland Rd.)
Holland Park. 1H 83
Holland Pk. 2H 83
Holland Pk. W11 1G 83
Holland Pk. Av. W11 2G 83
Holland Pk. Av. Ilf 6J 37
Holland Pk. Gdns. W14 2G 83
Holland Pk. M. W11 1G 83
Holland Pk. Rd. W14 3H 83
Holland Park Roundabout. (Junct.) 2G 83
Holland Pk. Theatre. 2H 83
(off Holland Pk., Open Air)
Holland Pas. N1 1C 68
(off Basire St.)
Holland Pl. W8 2K 83
(off Kensington Chu. St.)
Holland Pl. Chambers. W8 2K 83
(off Holland Pl.)
Holland Ri. Ho. SW9 7K 85
(off Clapham Rd.)
Holland Rd. E6 1D 72
Holland Rd. E15 3G 71
Holland Rd. NW10 1C 64
Holland Rd. SE25 5G 141
Holland Rd. W14 2F 83
Holland Rd. Wemb 6D 44
Hollands, The. Felt 4B 114
Hollands, The. Wor Pk 1B 148
Holland St. SE1 1B 86 (4B 168)
Holland St. W8 2J 83
Holland Vs. Rd. W14 2G 83
Holland Wlk. N19 1H 49
Holland Wlk. W8 1H 83
(off Holland Pk. Av.)
Holland Wlk. Stan 5F 11
Holland Way. Brom 2H 155
Hollar Rd. N16 3F 51
Hollen St. W1 6H 67 (7C 160)
Holles Clo. Hamp 6E 114
Holles Ho. SW9 2A 104
Holles St. W1 6F 67 (7K 159)
Holley Rd. W3 2A 82
Hollick Wood Av. N12 6J 15
Holliday Sq. SW11 3B 102
(off Fowler Clo.)
Hollidge Way. Dag 7H 57
Hollies Av. Sidc 2K 127
Hollies Clo. SW16 6A 122
Hollies Clo. Twic 2K 115
Hollies End. NW7 5J 13
Hollies Rd. W5 4C 80
Hollies, The. E11 5J 35
(off New Wanstead)
Hollies, The. N20 1G 15
Hollies, The. Harr 4A 26
Hollies Way. SW12 7E 102
Holligrave Rd. Brom 1J 143
Hollingbourne Av. Bexh 1F 111
Hollingbourne Gdns. W13 5B 62
Hollingbourne Rd. SE24 5C 104
Hollingsworth Ct. Surb 7D 134
Hollingsworth Rd. Croy 6H 153
Hollington Ct. Chst 6F 127
Hollington Cres. N Mald 6B 136
Hollington Rd. E6 3D 72
Hollington Rd. N17 2G 33
Hollingworth Clo. W Mol 4D 132
Hollingworth Rd. Orp 6F 145
Hollins Ho. N7 4J 49
Hollisfield. WC1 3J 67 (2F 161)
(off Cromer St.)
Hollman Gdns. SW16 6B 122
Holloway. 3J 49
Holloway Clo. W Dray 5A 76
Holloway Ho. NW2 3E 46
(off Stoll Clo.)
Holloway La. W Dray 6A 76
Holloway Rd. E6 3D 72
Holloway Rd. E11 3F 53
Holloway Rd. N19 & N7 2H 49
Holloway St. Houn 3F 97
Hollowfield Wlk. N'holt 7C 42
Hollows, The. Bren 6F 81
Hollow, The. Wfd G 4C 20
Holly Av. Stan 2E 26
Holly Av. W on T 7B 132
Hollybank Clo. Hamp 5E 114
Hollyberry La. NW3 4A 48
Hollybrake Clo. Chst 7H 127
Hollybush Clo. E11 5J 35
Hollybush Clo. Harr 1J 25
Hollybush Gdns. E2 3H 69
Hollybush Hill. E11 6H 35
Hollybush Hill. NW3 4A 48
Hollybush Ho. E2 3H 69
Holly Bush La. Hamp 7D 114
Hollybush Pl. E2 3H 69
Hollybush Rd. King T 5E 116
Hollybush Steps. NW3 4A 48
(off Holly Mt.)
Hollybush St. E13 3K 71
Holly Bush Va. NW3 4A 48
Hollybush Wlk. SW9 4B 104
Holly Clo. NW10 7A 46
Holly Clo. Beck 4E 142
Holly Clo. Buck H 3G 21
Holly Clo. Felt 5C 114
Holly Clo. Wall 7F 151
Holly Cottage M. Uxb 5C 58
Holly Ct. N15 4E 32
Holly Ct. Sidc 4B 128
(off Sidcup Hill)
Holly Ct. Sutt 7J 149
Holly Cres. Beck 5B 142
Holly Cres. Wfd G 7A 20
Hollycroft Av. NW3 3J 47
Hollycroft Av. Wemb 2F 45
Hollycroft Clo. S Croy 5E 152
Hollycroft Clo. W Dray 6C 76
Hollycroft Gdns. W Dray 6C 76
Hollydale Clo. N'holt 4F 43
Hollydale Dri. Brom 3D 156
Hollydale Rd. SE15 1J 105
Holly Dene. SE15 1H 105
Hollydene. Brom 1H 143
(off Beckenham Rd.)
Hollydown Way. E11 3F 53
Holly Dri. E4 7J 9
Holly Farm Rd. S'hall 5C 78
Hollyfield Av. N11 5J 15
Hollyfield Rd. Surb 7F 135
Holly Gdns. Bexh 4J 111
Holly Gdns. W Dray 2B 76
Holly Gro. NW9 7J 27
Holly Gro. SE15 2F 105
Hollygrove. Bush 1C 10
Holly Gro. Pinn 1C 24
Hollygrove Clo. Houn 4D 96
Holly Hedge Ter. SE13 5F 107
Holly Hill. N21 6E 6
Holly Hill. NW3 4A 48
Holly Hill Rd. Belv 5H 93
Holly Ho. W10 4G 65
(off Hawthorn Wlk.)
Holly Ho. Iswth 6C 80
Holly Lodge. Harr 5H 25
Holly Lodge Gdns. N6 2E 48
Holly Lodge Mans. N6 2E 48
Hollymead. Cars 3D 150
Holly M. SW10 6A 170
Holly Mt. NW3 4A 48
Hollymount Clo. SE10 1E 106
Holly Pk. N3 3H 29
Holly Pk. N4 7J 31
(in two parts)
Holly Pk. Est. N4 7K 31
Holly Pk. Gdns. N3 3J 29
Holly Pk. Rd. N11 5K 15
Holly Pk. Rd. W7 1K 79
Holly Pl. NW3 4A 48
(off Holly Berry La.)
Holly Rd. E11 7H 35
Holly Rd. W4 4K 81
Holly Rd. Hamp 6G 115
Holly Rd. Houn 4F 97
Holly Rd. Twic 1K 115
Holly St. E8 7F 51
Holly Ter. N6 1E 48
Holly Ter. N20 2F 15
Holly Tree Clo. SW19 1F 119
Holly Tree Ho. SE4 3B 106
(off Brockley Rd.)
Hollytree Pde. Sidc 6C 128
(off Sidcup Hill)
Holly Vw. Clo. NW4 6C 28
Holly Village. N6 2F 49
Holly Wlk. NW3 4A 48
Holly Wlk. Enf 3H 7
Holly Way. Mitc 4H 139
Hollywood Ct. W5 7F 63
Hollywood Gdns. Hay 6K 59
Hollywood M. SW10 6A 84
Hollywood Rd. E4 5F 19
Hollywood Rd. SW10 6A 84
Hollywood Way. Wfd G 7A 20
Holman Ct. Eps 7C 148
Holman Ho. E2 3K 69
(off Roman Rd.)
Holman Hunt Ho. W6 5G 83
(off Field Rd.)
Holman Rd. SW11 2B 102
Holman Rd. Eps 5J 147
Holmbank Dri. Shep 4G 131
Holmbridge Gdns. Enf 4E 8
Holmbrook. NW1 2G 67
(off Eversholt St.)
Holmbrook Dri. NW4 5F 29
Holmbury Ct. SW17 3D 120
Holmbury Ct. S Croy 5E 152
Holmbury Gdns. Hay 1H 77
Holmbury Gro. Croy 7B 154
Holmbury Ho. SE24 5B 104
Holmbury Mnr. Sidc 4A 128
Holmbury Pk. Brom 7C 126
Holmbury Vw. E5 1H 51
Holmbush Rd. SW15 6G 101
Holmcote Gdns. N5 5C 50
Holm Ct. SE12 3K 125
Holmcroft Ho. E17 4D 34
Holmcroft Way. Brom 5D 144
Holmdale Gdns. NW4 5F 29
Holmdale Rd. NW6 5J 47
Holmdale Rd. Chst 5G 127
Holmdale Ter. N15 7E 32
Holmdene. N12 5E 14
Holmdene Av. NW7 6H 13
Holmdene Av. SE24 5C 104
Holmdene Av. Harr 3F 25
Holmdene Clo. Beck 2E 142
Holmead Rd. SW6 7K 83
Holmebury Clo. Bush 2D 10
Holme Lacey Rd. SE12 6H 107
Holme Rd. E6 1C 72
Holmes Av. E17 3B 34
Holmes Av. NW7 5B 14
Holmesdale Av. SW14 3H 99
Holmesdale Clo. SE25 3F 141
Holmesdale Ho. NW6 1J 65
(off Kilburn Va.)
Holmesdale Rd. N6 7F 31
Holmesdale Rd. Bexh 2D 110
Holmesdale Rd. Croy & SE25 5D 140
Holmesdale Rd. Rich 1F 99
Holmesdale Rd. Tedd 7C 116
Holmesley Rd. SE23 6A 106
Holmes Pl. SW10 6A 84
Holmes Rd. NW5 5F 49
Holmes Rd. SW19 7A 120
Holmes Rd. Twic 2K 115
Holmes Ter. SE1 6J 167
Holmeswood Ct. N22 2A 32
Holme Way. Stan 6E 10
Holmewood Gdns. SW2 7K 103
Holmewood Rd. SE25 3E 140
Holmewood Rd. SW2 7J 103
Holmfield Av. NW4 5F 29
Holmfield Ct. NW3 5C 48
Holm Gro. Uxb 7C 40
Holmhurst Rd. Belv 5H 93
Holmlea Ct. Croy 4D 152
(off Chatsworth Rd.)
Holmleigh Ct. Enf 4D 8
Holmleigh Rd. N16 1E 50
Holmleigh Rd. Est. N16 1E 50
Holmoak Clo. SW15 6H 101
Holm Oak M. SW4 5J 103
Holmoaks Ho. Beck 2E 142
Holmsdale Ho. E14 7D 70
(off Poplar High St.)
Holmsdale Ho. N11 4A 16
(off Coppies Gro.)
Holmshaw Clo. SE26 4A 124
Holmside Rd. SW12 6E 102
Holmsley Clo. N Mald 6B 136
Holmsley Ho. SW15 7B 100
(off Tangley Gro.)
Holmstall Av. Edgw 3J 27
Holmstall Pde. Edgw 2J 27
Holm Wlk. SE3 2J 107
Holmwood Clo. Harr 3G 25
Holmwood Clo. N'holt 6F 43
Holmwood Clo. Sutt 7F 149
Holmwood Gdns. N3 2J 29
Holmwood Gdns. Wall 6F 151
Holmwood Gro. NW7 5E 12
Holmwood Rd. Chess 5D 146
Holmwood Rd. Ilf 2J 55
Holmwood Rd. Sutt 7E 148
Holmwood Vs. SE7 5J 89
Holne Chase. N2 6A 30
Holne Chase. Mord 6H 137
Holness Rd. E15 6H 53
Holroyd Rd. SW15 4E 100
Holst Ct. SE1 3A 86 (1J 173)
(off Westminster Bri. Rd.)
Holstein Way. Eri 3D 92
Holst Mans. SW13 6E 82
Holstock Rd. Ilf 2G 55
Holsworth Clo. Harr 5G 25
Holsworthy Sq. WC1 4H 161
Holsworthy Way. Chess 5C 146
Holt Clo. N10 4E 30
Holt Clo. SE28 7B 74
Holt Ct. E15 5E 52
Holt Ho. SW2 6A 104
Holton St. E1 4K 69
Holt Rd. E16 1C 90
Holt Rd. Wemb 3B 44
Holt, The. Mord 4J 137
Holt, The. Wall 4G 151
Holtwhites Av. Enf 2H 7
Holtwhite's Hill. Enf 1G 7
Holwell Pl. Pinn 4C 24
Holwood Pk. Av. Orp 4D 156
Holwood Pl. SW4 4H 103
Holybourne Av. SW15 7C 100
Holyhead Clo. E3 3C 70
Holyhead Clo. E6 5D 72
Holyhead Ct. King T 4D 134
(off Anglesea Rd.)
Holyoake Ct. SE16 2B 88
Holyoake Ho. W5 4C 62
Holyoake Wlk. N2 3A 30
Holyoake Wlk. W5 4C 62
Holyoak Rd. SE11 4B 86
Holyport Rd. SW6 7F 83
Holyrood Av. Harr 4C 42
Holyrood Gdns. Edgw 3H 27
Holyrood M. E16 1J 89
(off Badminton M.)
Holyrood Rd. New Bar 6F 5
Holyrood St. SE1 1E 86 (5G 169)
Holywell Clo. SE3 6J 89
Holywell Clo. SE16 5H 87
Holywell Clo. Stai 1A 112
Holywell La. EC2 4E 68 (3H 163)
Holywell Row. EC2 4E 68 (4G 163)
Holywell Way. Stai 1A 112
Homan Ct. N12 4G 15
Homebush Ho. E4 7J 9
Home Clo. Cars 2D 150
Home Clo. N'holt 3D 60
Home Ct. Surb 5D 134
Homecroft Rd. N22 1C 32
Homecroft Rd. SE26 5J 123
Home Farm Clo. Shep 4G 131
Home Farm Clo. Th Dit 7K 133
Homefarm Rd. W7 6J 61
Home Fld. Barn 5C 4
Homefield. Mord 4J 137
Homefield Av. Ilf 5J 37
Homefield Clo. NW10 6J 45
Homefield Clo. Hay 4B 60
Homefield Ct. SW16 3J 121
Homefield Gdns. N2 3B 30
Homefield Gdns. Mitc 2A 138
Homefield Ho. SE23 3K 123
Homefield M. Beck 1C 142
Homefield Pk. Sutt 6K 149
Homefield Rd. SW19 6F 119
Homefield Rd. W4 4B 82
Homefield Rd. Brom 1A 144
Homefield Rd. Edgw 6E 12
Homefield Rd. W on T 7C 132
Homefield Rd. Wemb 4B 44
Homefield St. N1 2E 68 (1G 163)
Homefirs Ho. Wemb 3F 45
Home Gdns. Dag 3J 57
Homeland Dri. Sutt 7K 149
Homelands Dri. SE19 7E 122
Homeleigh Rd. SE15 5K 105
Home Mead. Stan 1C 26
Homemead Rd. Brom 5D 144
Homemead Rd. Croy 6G 139
Home Pk. Ct. King T 4D 134
(off Palace Rd.)
Home Pk. Pde. King T 2D 134
(off High St.)
Home Pk. Rd. SW19 4H 119
Home Pk. Ter. King T 2D 134
(off Hampton Ct. Rd.)
Home Pk. Wlk. King T 4D 134
Homer Clo. Bexh 1J 111
Homer Dri. E14 4C 88
Home Rd. SW11 2C 102
Homer Rd. E9 6A 52
Homer Rd. Croy 6K 141
Homer Row. W1 5C 66 (6D 158)
Homersham Rd. King T 2G 135
Homer St. W1 5C 66 (6D 158)
Homerton. 5K 51
Homerton Gro. E9 5K 51
Homerton High St. E9 5K 51
Homerton Rd. E9 5A 52
Homerton Row. E9 5J 51
Homerton Ter. E9 6J 51
(in two parts)
Homesdale Clo. E11 5J 35
Homesdale Rd. Brom 4A 144
Homesdale Rd. Orp 7J 145
Homesfield. NW11 5J 29
Homestall Rd. SE22 5J 105
Homestead Ct. Barn 5D 4
Homestead Paddock. N14 5A 6
Homestead Pk. NW2 3B 46
Homestead Rd. SW6 7H 83
Homestead Rd. Dag 2F 57

Homesteads, The. N11 . . . 4A 16
Homewaters Av. Sun . . . 1H 131
Homewillow Clo. N21 . . . 6G 7
Homewood Clo. Hamp . . . 6D 114
Homewood Cres. Chst . . . 6J 127
Homewoods. SW12 . . . 7G 103
Homildon Ho. SE26 . . . 3G 123
Honduras St. EC1 . . . 4C 68 (3C 162)
Honeybourne Rd. NW6 . . . 5K 47
Honeybourne Way. Orp . . . 7H 145
Honeybrook Rd. SW12 . . . 7G 103
Honey Clo. Dag . . . 6H 57
Honeycroft Hill. Uxb . . . 7A 40
Honeyden Rd. Sidc . . . 6E 128
Honey Hill. Uxb . . . 7B 40
Honey La. EC2 . . . 1D 168
Honeyman Clo. NW6 . . . 7F 47 (in two parts)
Honeymead. N8 . . . 3J 31 (off Campsfield Rd.)
Honeypot Bus. Cen. Stan . . . 1E 26
Honeypot Clo. NW9 . . . 4F 27
Honeypot La. Stan & NW9 . . . 7J 11
Honeysett Rd. N17 . . . 2F 33
Honeysuckle Clo. S'hall . . . 7C 60
Honeysuckle Ct. E12 . . . 6F 55
Honeysuckle Gdns. Croy . . . 7K 141
Honeysuckle La. N22 . . . 2C 32
Honeywell Rd. SW11 . . . 6D 102
Honeywood Heritage Cen. . . . 4D 150
Honeywood Rd. NW10 . . . 2B 64
Honeywood Rd. Iswth . . . 4A 98
Honeywood Wlk. Cars . . . 4D 150
Honister Clo. Stan . . . 1B 26
Honister Gdns. Stan . . . 7G 11
Honister Pl. Stan . . . 1B 26
Honiton Gdns. SE15 . . . 2J 105 (off Gibbon Rd.)
Honiton Rd. NW6 . . . 2H 65
Honiton Rd. Romf . . . 6K 39
Honiton Rd. Well . . . 2K 109
Honley Rd. SE6 . . . 7D 106
Honnor Gdns. Iswth . . . 2H 97
Honor Oak. . . . 6J 105
Honor Oak Crematorium. SE23 . . . 5A 106
Honor Oak Park. . . . 7A 106
Honor Oak Pk. SE23 . . . 6J 105
Honor Oak Ri. SE23 . . . 6J 105
Honor Oak Rd. SE23 . . . 1J 123
Hood Av. N14 . . . 6A 6
Hood Av. SW14 . . . 5J 99
Hood Clo. Croy . . . 1B 152
Hoodcote Gdns. N21 . . . 7G 7
Hood Ct. EC4 . . . 1K 167
Hood Ho. SE5 . . . 7D 86 (off Elmington Est.)
Hood Ho. SW1 . . . 5H 85 (6C 172) (off Dolphin Sq.)
Hood Rd. SW20 . . . 7B 118
Hood Wlk. Romf . . . 1H 39
Hook. . . . 5D 146
Hooke Ho. E3 . . . 2A 70 (off Gernon Rd.)
Hookers Rd. E17 . . . 3K 33
Hook Farm Rd. Brom . . . 5B 144
Hookham Ct. SW8 . . . 1H 103
Hooking Grn. Harr . . . 5F 25
Hook Junction. (Junct.) . . . 3D 146
Hook La. Well . . . 5K 109
Hook Ri. Bus. Cen. Chess . . . 3G 147
Hook Ri. N. Surb . . . 3E 146
Hook Ri. S. Surb . . . 3E 146
Hook Ri. S. Ind. Pk. Chess . . . 3F 147
Hook Rd. Chess & Surb . . . 5D 146
Hook Rd. Eps . . . 7J 147
Hooks Clo. SE15 . . . 1H 105
Hookshall Dri. Dag . . . 3J 57
Hookstone Way. Wfd G . . . 7G 21
Hook, The. New Bar . . . 6G 5
Hook Wlk. Edgw . . . 6D 12
Hooper Rd. E16 . . . 6J 71
Hooper's Ct. SW3 . . . 2D 84 (7E 164)
Hooper's M. W3 . . . 1J 81
Hooper Sq. E1 . . . 6G 69 (off Hooper St.)
Hooper St. E1 . . . 6G 69
Hoop La. NW11 . . . 7H 29 (in two parts)
Hope Clo. N1 . . . 6C 50
Hope Clo. SE12 . . . 3K 125
Hope Clo. Bren . . . 5E 80
Hope Clo. Chad H . . . 4D 38
Hope Clo. Sutt . . . 5A 150
Hope Clo. Wfd G . . . 6F 21
Hope Ct. NW10 . . . 3F 65 (off Chamberlayne Rd.)
Hopedale Rd. SE7 . . . 6K 89
Hopefield Av. NW6 . . . 2G 65
Hope Ho. Croy . . . 4E 152 (off Steep Hill)
Hope Pk. Brom . . . 7H 125
Hopes Clo. Houn . . . 6E 78
Hope St. SW11 . . . 3B 102
Hopetown St. E1 . . . 5F 69 (6K 163)
Hopewell St. SE5 . . . 7D 86
Hopewell Yd. SE5 . . . 7D 86 (off Hopewell St.)
Hope Wharf. SE16 . . . 2J 87
Hop Gdns. WC2 . . . 7J 67 (3E 166)
Hopgood St. W12 . . . 1E 82
Hopkins Clo. N10 . . . 7K 15
Hopkins Ho. E14 . . . 6C 70 (off Canton St.)
Hopkins M. E15 . . . 1H 71
Hopkinsons Pl. NW1 . . . 1E 66
Hopkins St. W1 . . . 6G 67 (1B 166)
Hoppers Rd. N21 . . . 2F 17
Hoppett Rd. E4 . . . 2B 20
Hopping La. N1 . . . 6B 50
Hoppingwood Av. N Mald . . . 3A 136
Hoppner Rd. Hay . . . 2F 59
Hopton Ct. Brom . . . 1K 155
Hopton Gdns. N Mald . . . 6C 136
Hopton Rd. SW16 . . . 5J 121
Hopton's Gdns. SE1 . . . 4B 168
Hopton St. SE1 . . . 1B 86 (4B 168)
Hoptree Clo. N12 . . . 5E 14
Hopwood Clo. SW17 . . . 3A 120
Hopwood Rd. SE17 . . . 6D 86
Hopwood Wlk. E8 . . . 7G 51
Horace Av. Romf . . . 1J 57
Horace Rd. E7 . . . 4K 53
Horace Rd. Ilf . . . 3G 37
Horace Rd. King T . . . 3F 135
Horatio Ct. SE16 . . . 1J 87 (off Rotherhithe St.)
Horatio Ho. E2 . . . 2F 69 (1K 163) (off Horatio St.)
Horatio Ho. W6 . . . 5F 83 (off Fulham Pal. Rd.)
Horatio Pl. E14 . . . 1E 88 (off Preston's Rd.)
Horatio Pl. SW19 . . . 1J 137
Horatio St. E2 . . . 2F 69 (in two parts)
Horatius Way. Croy . . . 5K 151
Horbury Cres. W11 . . . 7J 65
Horbury M. W11 . . . 7H 65
Horder Rd. SW6 . . . 1G 101
Hordle Promenade E. SE15 . . . 7F 87
Hordle Promenade N. SE15 . . . 7F 87
Hordle Promenade S. SE15 . . . 7F 87 (off Quarley Way)
Hordle Promenade W. SE15 . . . 7E 86 (off Clanfield Way)
Horizon Building. E14 . . . 7C 70 (off Hertsmere Rd.)
Horizon Way. SE7 . . . 4K 89
Horle Wlk. SW9 . . . 2B 104
Horley Clo. Bexh . . . 5G 111
Horley Rd. SE9 . . . 4C 126
Hormead Rd. W9 . . . 4H 65
Hornbeam Clo. NW7 . . . 3G 13
Hornbeam Clo. SE11 . . . 4A 86 (3J 173)
Hornbeam Clo. Buck H . . . 3G 21
Hornbeam Clo. Ilf . . . 5H 55
Hornbeam Clo. N'holt . . . 5D 42
Hornbeam Cres. Bren . . . 7B 80
Hornbeam Gro. E4 . . . 3B 20
Hornbeam Ho. Buck H . . . 3G 21
Hornbeam La. Bexh . . . 2J 111
Hornbeam Rd. Buck H . . . 3G 21
Hornbeam Rd. Hay . . . 5A 60
Hornbeams Ri. N11 . . . 6K 15
Hornbeam Ter. Cars . . . 1C 150
Hornbeam Wlk. Rich . . . 2F 117
Hornbeam Way. Brom . . . 6E 144
Hornblower Clo. SE16 . . . 3A 88
Hornbuckle Clo. Harr . . . 2H 43
Hornby Clo. NW3 . . . 7B 48
Hornby Ho. SE11 . . . 7J 173
Horncastle Clo. SE12 . . . 7J 107
Horncastle Rd. SE12 . . . 7J 107
Hornchurch. N17 . . . 2D 32 (off Gloucester Rd.)
Hornchurch Clo. King T . . . 4D 116
Horndean Clo. SW15 . . . 1C 118
Horndon Clo. Romf . . . 1J 39
Horndon Grn. Romf . . . 1J 39
Horndon Rd. Romf . . . 1J 39
Horner Ho. N1 . . . 1E 68 (off Whitmore Est.)
Horner La. Mitc . . . 2B 138
Horne Rd. Shep . . . 4C 130
Horne Way. SW15 . . . 2E 100
Hornfair Rd. SE7 . . . 6A 90
Horniman Dri. SE23 . . . 1H 123
Horniman Mus. . . . 1H 123
Horning Clo. SE9 . . . 4C 126
Horn La. SE10 . . . 5J 89 (in two parts)
Horn La. W3 . . . 7J 63 (in two parts)
Horn La. Wfd G . . . 6D 20
Horn Link Way. SE10 . . . 4J 89
Horn Park. . . . 5K 107
Horn Pk. Clo. SE12 . . . 5K 107
Hornpark La. SE12 . . . 5K 107
Horns End Pl. Pinn . . . 4A 24
Hornsey. . . . 4J 31
Hornsey La. N6 . . . 1F 49
Hornsey La. Est. N19 . . . 7H 31
Hornsey La. Gdns. N6 . . . 7G 31
Hornsey Pk. Rd. N8 . . . 3K 31
Hornsey Ri. N19 . . . 7H 31
Hornsey Ri. Gdns. N19 . . . 7H 31
Hornsey Rd. N19 & N7 . . . 1J 49
Hornsey St. N7 . . . 5K 49
Hornsey Vale. . . . 5K 31
Hornshay St. SE15 . . . 6J 87
Horns Rd. Ilf . . . 4H 37
Hornton Ct. W8 . . . 2J 83 (off Kensington High St.)
Hornton Pl. W8 . . . 2K 83
Hornton St. W8 . . . 2J 83
Horsa Rd. SE12 . . . 7A 108
Horsa Rd. Eri . . . 7H 93
Horse & Dolphin Yd. W1 . . . 2D 166
Horsebridge Clo. Dag . . . 1E 74
Horsecroft Rd. Edgw . . . 7E 12
Horse Fair. King T . . . 2D 134
Horseferry Pl. SE10 . . . 6E 88
Horseferry Rd. E14 . . . 7A 70
Horseferry Rd. SW1 . . . 3H 85 (2C 172)
Horseferry Rd. Est. SW1 . . . 2C 172
Horseguards Av. SW1 . . . 1J 85 (5E 166)
Horse Guards Rd. SW1 . . . 1H 85 (5D 166)
Horse Leaze. E6 . . . 6E 72
Horsell Rd. N5 . . . 5A 50 (in two parts)
Horselydown La. SE1 . . . 2F 87 (6J 169)
Horselydown Mans. SE1 . . . 2F 87 (6J 169) (off Lafone St.)
Horsemongers M. SE1 . . . 7D 168
Horsenden Av. Gnfd . . . 5K 43
Horsenden Cres. Gnfd . . . 5K 43
Horsenden La. N. Gnfd . . . 6J 43
Horsenden La. S. Gnfd . . . 1A 62
Horse Ride. SW1 . . . 1G 85 (5C 166)
Horseshoe Clo. E14 . . . 5E 88
Horseshoe Clo. NW2 . . . 2D 46
Horse Shoe Cres. N'holt . . . 2E 60
Horseshoe Dri. Uxb . . . 6C 58
Horse Shoe Grn. Sutt . . . 2K 149
Horseshoe La. N20 . . . 1A 14
Horseshoe La. Enf . . . 3H 7
Horseshoe Wharf. SE1 . . . 1D 86 (4E 168) (off Clink St.)
Horse Yd. N1 . . . 1B 68 (off Essex Rd.)
Horsfeld Gdns. SE9 . . . 5C 108
Horsfeld Rd. SE9 . . . 5B 108
Horsfield Ho. N1 . . . 7C 50 (off Northampton St.)
Horsford Rd. SW2 . . . 5K 103
Horsham Av. N12 . . . 5H 15
Horsham Ct. N17 . . . 1G 33 (off Lansdowne Rd.)
Horsham Rd. Bexh . . . 5G 111
Horsham Rd. Felt . . . 6E 94
Horsley Dri. King T . . . 5D 116
Horsley Dri. New Ad . . . 7E 154
Horsley Rd. E4 . . . 2K 19
Horsley Rd. Brom . . . 1K 143
Horsley St. SE17 . . . 6D 86
Horsman Ho. SE5 . . . 6C 86 (off Bethwin Rd.)
Horsman St. SE5 . . . 6C 86
Horsmonden Clo. Orp . . . 7K 145
Horsmonden Rd. SE4 . . . 5B 106
Hortensia Ho. SW10 . . . 7A 84 (off Hortensia Rd.)
Hortensia Rd. SW10 . . . 7A 84
Horticultural Pl. W4 . . . 5K 81
Horton Av. NW2 . . . 4G 47
Horton Bri. Rd. W Dray . . . 1B 76
Horton Clo. W Dray . . . 1C 76
Horton Country Pk. . . . 7G 147
Horton Ho. SE15 . . . 6J 87
Horton Ho. SW8 . . . 7K 85
Horton Ho. W6 . . . 5G 83 (off Field Rd.)
Horton Ind. Pk. W Dray . . . 1B 76
Horton La. Eps . . . 7H 147
Horton Pde. W Dray . . . 1A 76
Horton Rd. E8 . . . 6H 51
Horton Rd. W Dray . . . 1A 76
Horton Rd. Ind. Est. W Dray . . . 1B 76
Horton St. SE13 . . . 3D 106
Horton Way. Croy . . . 5K 141
Hortus Rd. E4 . . . 2K 19
Hortus Rd. S'hall . . . 2D 78
Horwood Ho. E2 . . . 3H 69 (off Pott St.)
Horwood Ho. NW8 . . . 4C 66 (3D 158) (off Paveley St.)
Hosack Rd. SW17 . . . 2E 120
Hoser Av. SE12 . . . 2J 125
Hosier La. EC1 . . . 5B 68 (6A 162)
Hoskins Clo. E16 . . . 6A 72
Hoskins Clo. Hay . . . 5H 77
Hoskins St. SE10 . . . 5F 89
Hospital Bri. Rd. Twic . . . 7F 97
Hospital Bridge Roundabout. (Junct.) . . . 2F 115
Hospital Rd. E9 . . . 5K 51
Hospital Rd. Houn . . . 3E 96
Hospital Way. SE13 . . . 6F 107
Hotham Clo. W Mol . . . 3E 132
Hotham Rd. SW15 . . . 3E 100
Hotham Rd. SW19 . . . 7A 120
Hotham Rd. M. SW19 . . . 7A 120
Hotham St. E15 . . . 1G 71
Hothfield Pl. SE16 . . . 3J 87
Hotspur Ind. Est. N17 . . . 6C 18
Hotspur Rd. N'holt . . . 2E 60
Hotspur St. SE11 . . . 4A 86 (5J 173)
Houblon Rd. Rich . . . 5E 98
Houghton Clo. E8 . . . 6F 51
Houghton Clo. Hamp . . . 6C 114
Houghton Rd. N15 . . . 4F 33
Houghton St. WC2 . . . 6K 67 (1H 167) (in two parts)
Houlder Cres. Croy . . . 6B 152
Houndsden Rd. N21 . . . 6E 6
Houndsditch. EC3 . . . 6E 68 (7H 163)
Houndsfield Rd. N9 . . . 7C 8
Hounslow. . . . 3F 97
Hounslow Av. Houn . . . 5F 97
Hounslow Bus. Pk. Houn . . . 4E 96
Hounslow Cen. Houn . . . 3F 97
Hounslow Gdns. Houn . . . 5F 97
Hounslow Rd. Felt . . . 1K 113
Hounslow Rd. Hanw . . . 4B 114
Hounslow Rd. Twic . . . 6F 97
Hounslow Urban Farm. . . . 5J 95
Hounslow West. . . . 2C 96
Houseman Way. SE5 . . . 7D 86
Houses of Parliament. . . . 3J 85 (1F 173)
Houston Bus. Pk. Hay . . . 1A 78
Houston Pl. Esh . . . 7H 133
Houston Rd. SE23 . . . 2A 124
Houston Rd. Surb . . . 6B 134
Houstoun Ct. Houn . . . 7D 78
Hove Av. E17 . . . 5B 34
Hoveden Rd. NW2 . . . 5G 47
Hove Gdns. Sutt . . . 1K 149
Hove St. SE15 . . . 7J 87 (off Culmore Rd.)
Hoveton Rd. SE28 . . . 6C 74
Hoveton Way. Ilf . . . 1F 37
Howard Av. Bex . . . 1C 128
Howard Clo. N11 . . . 2K 15
Howard Clo. NW2 . . . 4G 47
Howard Clo. W3 . . . 6H 63
Howard Clo. Bus H . . . 1D 10
Howard Clo. Hamp . . . 7G 115
Howard Clo. Sun . . . 6H 113
Howard Ct. Bark . . . 1H 73
Howard Ho. E16 . . . 1K 89 (off Wesley Av.)
Howard Ho. SE8 . . . 6B 88 (off Evelyn St.)
Howard Ho. SW1 . . . 5G 85 (6B 172) (off Dolphin Sq.)
Howard Ho. SW9 . . . 3B 104 (off Barrington Rd.)
Howard Ho. W1 . . . 4F 67 (4K 159) (off Cleveland St.)
Howard M. N5 . . . 4B 50
Howard Rd. E6 . . . 2D 72
Howard Rd. E11 . . . 3G 53
Howard Rd. E17 . . . 3C 34
Howard Rd. N15 . . . 6E 32
Howard Rd. N16 . . . 4D 50
Howard Rd. NW2 . . . 4F 47
Howard Rd. SE20 . . . 1J 141
Howard Rd. SE25 . . . 5G 141
Howard Rd. Ashf . . . 4A 112
Howard Rd. Bark . . . 1H 73

Howard Rd. Brom 7J 125
Howard Rd. Ilf 4F 55
Howard Rd. Iswth 3K 97
Howard Rd. N Mald 3A 136
Howard Rd. S'hall 6F 61
Howard Rd. Surb 6F 135
Howards Clo. Pinn 2K 23
Howards Crest Clo. Beck 2E 142
Howard's La. SW15 4D 100
Howards Rd. E13 3J 71
Howard St. Th Dit 7B 134
Howard Wlk. N2 4A 30
Howard Way. Barn 5A 4
Howarth Ct. E15 5D 52
Howarth Rd. SE2 5A 92
Howberry Clo. Edgw 6J 11
Howberry Rd. Stan & Edgw 6J 11
Howberry Rd. T Hth 1D 140
Howbury Rd. SE15 3J 105
Howcroft Cres. N3 7D 14
Howcroft La. Gnfd 3H 61
Howden Clo. SE28 7D 74
Howden Ho. Houn 7C 96
Howden Rd. SE25 2F 141
Howden St. SE15 3G 105
Howe Clo. Romf 1G 39
Howell Clo. Romf 5D 38
Howell Ct. E10 7D 34
Howell Wlk. SE1 4B 86
Howerd Way. SE18 1C 108 (in two parts)
Howes Clo. N3 3J 29
Howeth Ct. N11 6J 15 (off Ribblesdale Av.)
Howfield Pl. N17 3F 33
Howgate Rd. SW14 3K 99
Howick Pl. SW1 3G 85 (2B 172)
Howie St. SW11 7C 84
Howitt Clo. N16 4E 50
Howitt Clo. NW3 6C 48
Howitt Rd. NW3 6C 48
Howland Est. SE16 3J 87
Howland Ho. SW16 3J 121
Howland M. E. W1 5G 67 (5B 160)
Howland St. W1 5G 67 (5A 160)
Howland Way. SE16 2A 88
Howletts La. Ruis 5E 22
Howlett's Rd. SE24 6C 104
Howley Pl. W2 5A 66 (5A 158)
Howley Rd. Croy 3B 152
Howsman Rd. SW13 6C 82
Howson Rd. SE4 4A 106
Howson Ter. Rich 6E 98
How's St. E2 2F 69
Howton Pl. Bus H 1C 10
Hoxton. 2E 68
***Hoxton Hall Theatre.* 2E 68 (off Hoxton Rd.)**
Hoxton Mkt. N1 2G 163
Hoxton Sq. N1 3E 68 (2G 163)
Hoxton St. N1 1E 68 (2H 163)
Hoylake Cres. Uxb 2C 40
Hoylake Gdns. Mitc 3G 139
Hoylake Gdns. Ruis 1K 41
Hoylake Rd. W3 6A 64
Hoyland Clo. SE15 7H 87
Hoyle Rd. SW17 5C 120
Hoy St. E16 6H 71
Hubbard Dri. Chess 6D 146
Hubbard Rd. SE27 4C 122
Hubbards Clo. Uxb 6D 58
Hubbard St. E15 1G 71
Huberd Ho. SE1 3D 86 (7F 169) (off Manciple St.)
Hubert Clo. SW19 1A 138 (off Nelson Gro. Rd.)
Hubert Gro. SW9 3J 103
Hubert Ho. NW8 4C 66 (4C 158) (off Ashbridge St.)
Hubert Rd. E6 3B 72
Hucknall Ct. NW8 4B 66 (3A 158) (off Cunningham Pl.)
Huddart St. E3 5B 70 (in two parts)
Huddleston Clo. E2 2J 69
Huddlestone Rd. E7 4H 53
Huddlestone Rd. NW2 6D 46
Huddleston Rd. N7 3G 49
Hudson. NW9 1B 28 (off Near Acre)
Hudson Clo. W12 7D 64
Hudson Ct. E14 5C 88 (off Maritime Quay)
Hudson Pl. SE18 5G 91
Hudson Rd. Bexh 2F 111
Hudson Rd. Hay 6F 77
Hudson's Pl. SW1 3A 172
Hudson Way. N9 3D 18
Huggin Ct. EC4 2C 168
Huggin Hill. EC4 7C 68 (2D 168)
Huggins Pl. SW2 1K 121
Hughan Rd. E15 5F 53
Hugh Astor Ct. SE1 3B 86 (7B 168) (off Keyworth St.)
Hugh Clark Ho. W13 1A 80 (off Singapore Rd.)
Hugh Dalton Av. SW6 6H 83
Hughenden Av. Harr 5B 26
Hughenden Gdns. N'holt 3A 60 (in two parts)
Hughenden Ho. NW8 3C 158
Hughenden Rd. Wor Pk 7C 136
Hughendon. New Bar 4E 4
Hughendon Ter. E15 4E 52
Hughes Ct. N7 5H 49
Hughes Ho. E2 3J 69 (off Sceptre Ho.)
Hughes Ho. SE8 6C 88 (off Benbow St.)
Hughes Ho. SE17 4B 86 (off Peacock St.)
Hughes Mans. E1 4G 69
Hughes M. SW11 5D 102
Hughes Rd. Ashf 6E 112
Hughes Rd. Hay 7K 59
Hughes Ter. E16 5H 71 (off Clarkson Rd.)
Hughes Wlk. Croy 7C 140
Hugh Gaitskell Clo. SW6 6H 83
Hugh Gaitskell Ho. N16 2F 51
Hugh Herland Ho. King T 3E 134
Hugh M. SW1 4F 85 (4K 171)
Hugh Platt Ho. E2 2H 69 (off Patriot Sq.)
Hugh St. SW1 4F 85 (4K 171)
Hugon Rd. SW6 3K 101
Hugo Rd. N19 4G 49
Huguenot Pl. E1 5F 69 (5K 163)
Huguenot Pl. SW18 5A 102
Huguenot Sq. SE15 3H 105
Hullbridge M. N1 1D 68
Hull Clo. SE16 2K 87
Hull Pl. E16 1G 91
Hull St. EC1 3C 68 (2C 162)
Hulme Pl. SE1 2C 86 (7D 168)
Hulse Av. Bark 6H 55
Hulse Av. Romf 1H 39
Hulverston Clo. Sutt 7K 149
Humber Clo. W Dray 1A 76
Humber Ct. W7 6H 61 (off Hobbayne Rd.)
Humber Dri. W10 4F 65
Humber Rd. NW2 2D 46
Humber Rd. SE3 6H 89
Humberstone Rd. E13 3A 72
Humberton Clo. E9 5A 52
Humbolt Rd. W6 6G 83
Hume Ct. N1 7B 50 (off Hawes St.)
Hume Ho. W11 1F 83 (off Queensdale Cres.)
Humes Av. W7 3J 79
Hume Ter. E16 5K 71
Hume Way. Ruis 6J 23
Humphrey Clo. Ilf 1D 36
Humphrey St. SE1 5F 87
Humphries Clo. Dag 4F 57
Hundred Acre. NW9 2B 28
Hungerdown. E4 1K 19
Hungerford Ho. SW1 6G 85 (7B 172) (off Churchill Gdns.)
Hungerford La. WC2 4F 167 (in two parts)
Hungerford Rd. N7 6H 49
Hungerford St. E1 6H 69
Hunsdon Clo. Dag 6E 56
Hunsdon Rd. SE14 7K 87
Hunslett St. E2 3J 69
Hunstanton Ho. NW1 5C 66 (5D 158) (off Cosway St.)
Hunston Rd. Mord 1K 149
Hunt Ct. N14 7A 6
Hunt Ct. N'holt 2B 60 (off Gallery Gdns.)
Hunter Clo. SE1 3D 86
Hunter Clo. Wall 7J 151
Hunter Ho. SE1 2B 86 (7B 168) (off Lancaster St.)
Hunter Ho. SW5 5J 83 (off Old Brompton Rd.)
Hunter Ho. SW8 7H 85 (off Fount St.)
Hunter Ho. WC1 4J 67 (3F 161) (off Hunter St.)
***Hunterian Mus., The.* 6K 67 (1H 167) (off Portugal St.)**
Hunter Lodge. W9 5J 65 (off Admiral Wlk.)
Hunter Rd. SW20 1E 136
Hunter Rd. Ilf 5F 55
Hunter Rd. T Hth 3D 140
Hunters Clo. SW12 1E 120
Hunters Clo. Bex 3K 129
Hunters Ct. Rich 5D 98
Hunters Gro. Harr 4C 26
Hunters Gro. Hay 1J 77
Hunters Hall Rd. Dag 4G 57
Hunters Hill. Ruis 3A 42
Hunters Mdw. SE19 4E 122
Hunter's Rd. Chess 3E 146
Hunters Sq. Dag 4G 57
Hunter St. WC1 4J 67 (3F 161)
Hunter's Way. Croy 4E 152
Hunters Way. Enf 1F 7
Hunter Wlk. E13 2J 71
Huntingdon Clo. Mitc 3J 139
Huntingdon Gdns. W4 7J 81
Huntingdon Gdns. Wor Pk 3E 148
Huntingdon Rd. N2 3C 30
Huntingdon Rd. N9 1D 18
Huntingdon St. E16 6H 71
Huntingdon St. N1 7K 49
Huntingfield. Croy 7B 154
Huntingfield Rd. SW15 4C 100
Hunting Ga. Clo. Enf 3F 7
Hunting Ga. Dri. Chess 7E 146
Hunting Ga. M. Sutt 3K 149
Hunting Ga. M. Twic 1J 115
Huntings Farm. Ilf 2J 55
Huntings Rd. Dag 6G 57
Huntley Dri. N3 6D 14
Huntley St. WC1 4G 67 (4B 160)
Huntley Way. SW20 2C 136
Huntly Rd. SE25 4E 140
Hunton St. E1 5G 69 (4K 163)
Hunt Rd. S'hall 3E 78
Hunt's Clo. SE3 2J 107
Hunt's Ct. WC2 7H 67 (3D 166)
Hunts La. E15 2E 70
Huntsmans Clo. Felt 4K 113
Huntsman St. SE17 4E 86
Hunts Mead. Enf 3E 8
Huntsmead Clo. Chst 7D 126
Huntsmoor Rd. Eps 5K 147
Huntspill St. SW17 3A 120
Hunts Slip Rd. SE21 3E 122
Hunt St. W11 1F 83
Huntsworth M. NW1 4D 66 (3E 158)
Hurdwick Pl. NW1 2G 67 (off Hampstead Rd.)
Hurleston Ho. SE8 5B 88
Hurley Ct. W5 6C 62
Hurley Cres. SE16 2K 87
Hurley Ho. SE11 4B 86 (4K 173)
Hurley Rd. Gnfd 6F 61
Hurlingham. 3K 101
Hurlingham Bus. Pk. SW6 3J 101
Hurlingham Ct. SW6 3H 101
Hurlingham Gdns. SW6 3H 101
Hurlingham Retail Pk. SW6 3K 101
Hurlingham Rd. SW6 2H 101
Hurlingham Rd. Bexh 7F 93
Hurlingham Sq. SW6 3J 101
Hurlock St. N5 3B 50
Hurlstone Rd. SE25 5E 140
Hurn Ct. Houn 2B 96
Hurn Ct. Rd. Houn 2B 96
Huron Rd. SW17 2E 120
Hurren Clo. SE3 3G 107
Hurricane Rd. Wall 7J 151
Hurry Clo. E15 7G 53
Hurst Av. E4 4H 19
Hurst Av. N6 6G 31
Hurstbourne. Clay 6A 146
Hurstbourne Gdns. Bark 6J 55
Hurstbourne Ho. SW15 6B 100 (off Tangley Gro.)
Hurstbourne Rd. SE23 1A 124
Hurst Clo. E4 3H 19
Hurst Clo. NW11 6K 29
Hurst Clo. Brom 1H 155
Hurst Clo. Chess 5G 147
Hurst Clo. N'holt 6D 42
Hurstcombe. Buck H 2D 20
Hurst Ct. E6 5B 72 (off Tollgate Rd.)
Hurst Ct. Sidc 2A 128
Hurstcourt Rd. Sutt 2K 149
Hurstdene Av. Brom 1H 155
Hurstdene Gdns. N15 7E 32
Hurstfield. Brom 5J 143
Hurstfield Cres. Hay 4G 59
Hurstfield Rd. W Mol 3E 132
Hurst Gro. W on T 7H 131
Hurst Ho. WC1 2K 67 (1H 161) (off Penton Ri.)
Hurst La. SE2 5D 92
Hurst La. E Mol 4G 133
Hurst La. Est. SE2 5D 92
Hurstleigh Gdns. Ilf 1D 36
Hurstmead Ct. Edgw 4C 12
Hurst Park. 2G 133
Hurst Pl. N'wd 1D 22
Hurst Ri. Barn 3D 4
Hurst Rd. E17 3D 34
Hurst Rd. N21 1F 17
Hurst Rd. Buck H 1G 21
Hurst Rd. Croy 5D 152
Hurst Rd. Eri 1J 111
Hurst Rd. Sidc & Bex 2A 128
Hurst Rd. W on T & W Mol 5A 132
Hurst Springs. Bex 1E 128
Hurst St. SE24 6B 104
Hurstview Grange. S Croy 7B 152
Hurst Vw. Rd. S Croy 7E 152
Hurst Way. S Croy 6E 152
Hurstway Rd. W10 7F 65
Hurstway Wlk. W11 7F 65
Hurstwood Av. E18 4K 35
Hurstwood Av. Bex 1E 128
Hurstwood Ct. N12 6H 15
Hurstwood Ct. NW11 4H 29 (off Finchley Rd.)
Hurstwood Dri. Brom 3D 144
Hurstwood Rd. NW11 4G 29
Hurtwood Rd. W on T 7D 132
Husborne Ho. SE8 4A 88 (off Chilton Gro.)
Huson Clo. NW3 7C 48
Hussain Clo. Harr 4K 43
Hussars Clo. Houn 3C 96
Husseywell Cres. Brom 1J 155
Hutchings St. E14 2C 88
Hutchings Wlk. NW11 4K 29
Hutchings Wharf. E14 2C 88 (off Hutchings St.)
Hutchins Clo. E15 7E 52
Hutchinson Ct. Romf 4D 38
Hutchinson Ho. NW3 7D 48
Hutchinson Ho. SE14 7J 87
Hutchinson Ter. Wemb 3D 44
Hutchins Rd. SE28 7A 74
Hutton Clo. Gnfd 5H 43
Hutton Clo. Wfd G 6E 20
Hutton Ct. N4 1K 49 (off Victoria Rd.)
Hutton Ct. N9 7D 8 (off Tramway Av.)
Hutton Ct. W5 5B 62
Hutton Gdns. Harr 7B 10
Hutton Gro. N12 5E 14
Hutton La. Harr 7B 10
Hutton Row. Edgw 7D 12
Hutton St. EC4 6B 68 (2K 167)
Hutton Wlk. Harr 7B 10
Huxbear St. SE4 5B 106
Huxley Clo. N'holt 2C 60
Huxley Clo. Uxb 4A 58
Huxley Dri. Romf 7B 38
Huxley Gdns. NW10 3F 63
Huxley Ho. NW8 4B 66 (4B 158) (off Fisherton St.)
Huxley Pde. N18 5J 17
Huxley Pl. N13 3G 17
Huxley Rd. E10 2E 52
Huxley Rd. N18 4J 17
Huxley Rd. Well 3K 109
Huxley Sayze. N18 5J 17
Huxley S. N18 5J 17
Huxley St. W10 3G 65
Hyacinth Clo. Hamp 6E 114
Hyacinth Clo. Ilf 6F 55
Hyacinth Dri. Uxb 7A 40
Hyacinth Rd. SW15 1C 118
Hyde Clo. E13 2J 71
Hyde Clo. Ashf 6G 113
Hyde Clo. Barn 3C 4
Hyde Ct. N20 3G 15
Hyde Cres. NW9 5A 28
Hyde Est. Rd. NW9 5B 28
Hyde Farm M. SW12 1H 121
Hydefield Clo. N21 1J 17
Hydefield Ct. N9 2K 17
Hyde Ind. Est., The. NW9 5B 28
Hyde La. SW11 1C 102
***Hyde Pk.* 1C 84 (3D 164)**
Hyde Pk. Av. N21 2H 17
Hyde Park Corner. (Junct.) 2F 85 (6H 165)
Hyde Pk. Corner. W1 2E 84 (6H 165)
Hyde Pk. Cres. W2 6C 66 (1C 164)
Hyde Pk. Gdns. N21 1H 17
Hyde Pk. Gdns. W2 7B 66 (2B 164)
Hyde Pk. Gdns. M. W2 7B 66 (2B 164) (in two parts)
Hyde Pk. Ga. SW7 2A 84 (in two parts)
Hyde Pk. Ga. M. SW7 2A 84

Hyde Pk. Mans. NW1 5C 66 (6C 158) (off Cabbell St., in two parts)
Hyde Pk. Pl. W2 7C 66 (2D 164)
Hyde Pk. Sq. W2 6C 66 (1C 164)
Hyde Pk. Sq. M. W2 1C 164
Hyde Pk. St. W2 6C 66 (1C 164)
Hyde Pk. Towers. W2 7A 66
Hyderbad Way. E15 7G 53
Hyde Rd. N1 1E 68
Hyde Rd. Bexh 2F 111
Hyde Rd. Rich 5F 99
Hydeside Gdns. N9 2A 18
Hyde's Pl. N1 7B 50
Hyde St. SE8 6C 88
Hyde Ter. Ashf 6G 113
Hyde, The. 5B 28
Hyde, The. NW9 5A 28
Hydethorpe Av. N9 2A 18
Hydethorpe Rd. SW12 1G 121
Hyde Va. SE10 7E 88
Hyde Wlk. Mord 7J 137
Hyde Way. N9 2A 18
Hyde Way. Hay 4H 77
Hydon Ct. N11 5J 15
Hydra Building, The. EC1 2K 161
Hylands Rd. E17 2F 35
Hylton St. SE18 4K 91
Hyndewood. SE23 3K 123
Hyndman Ho. Dag 3G 57 (off Kershaw Rd.)
Hyndman St. SE15 6H 87
Hynton Rd. Dag 2C 56
Hyperion Ho. E3 2A 70 (off Arbery Rd.)
Hyperion Ho. SW2 6K 103
Hyrstdene. S Croy 4B 152
Hyson Rd. SE16 5H 87
Hythe Av. Bexh 7E 92
Hythe Clo. N18 4B 18
Hythe Ho. SE16 2J 87 (off Swan Rd.)
Hythe Ho. W6 4E 82 (off Shepherd's Bush Rd.)
Hythe Rd. NW10 3B 64
Hythe Rd. T Hth 2D 140
Hythe Rd. Ind. Est. NW10 3C 64

Ian Bowater Ct. N1 3D 68 (1F 163) (off East Rd.)
Ian Ct. SE23 2J 123
Ian Sq. Enf 1E 8
Ibberton Ho. SW8 7K 85 (off Meadow Rd.)
Ibberton Ho. W14 3G 83 (off Russell Rd.)
Ibbotson Av. E16 6H 71
Ibbott St. E1 4J 69
Iberia Ho. N19 7H 31
Iberian Av. Wall 4H 151
Ibis Ct. SE8 6B 88 (off Edward Pl.)
Ibis La. W4 1J 99
Ibis Way. Hay 6B 60
Ibrox Ct. Buck H 2F 21
Ibscott Clo. Dag 6J 57
Ibsley Gdns. SW15 1C 118
Ibsley Way. Cockf 5H 5
Iceland Rd. E3 1C 70
Ice Wharf Marina. N1 2J 67 (off New Wharf Rd.)
Ickburgh Est. E5 2H 51
Ickburgh Rd. E5 3H 51
Ickenham. 3D 40
Ickenham Clo. Ruis 2F 41
Ickenham Grn. Uxb 1D 40
Ickenham Rd. Ruis 2E 40
Ickleton Rd. SE9 4C 126
Icknield Dri. Ilf 5F 37
Icknield Ho. SW3 5C 84 (5D 170) (off Marlborough St.)
Ickworth Pk. Rd. E17 4A 34
Ida Rd. N15 4D 32
Ida St. E14 6E 70 (in three parts)
Iden Clo. Brom 3G 143
Idlecombe Rd. SW17 6E 120
Idmiston Rd. E15 4H 53
Idmiston Rd. SE27 3C 122
Idmiston Rd. Wor Pk 7B 136
Idmiston Sq. Wor Pk 7B 136
Idol La. EC3 7E 68 (3G 169)
Idonia St. SE8 7C 88
Iffley Clo. Uxb 7A 40
Iffley Rd. W6 3D 82
Ifield Rd. SW10 6K 83
Ifor Evans Pl. E1 4K 69
Ightham Ho. SE17 4E 86 (off Comus Pl.)
Ightham Ho. Beck 7B 124 (off Bethersden Clo.)
Ightham Rd. Eri 7G 93
Ilbert St. W10 3F 65
Ilchester Gdns. W2 7K 65
Ilchester Pl. W14 3H 83
Ilchester Rd. Dag 5B 56
Ildersly Gro. SE21 2D 122
Ilderton Rd. SE16 & SE15 5J 87
Ilderton Wharf. SE15 6J 87 (off Rollins St.)
Ilex Clo. Sun 2A 132
Ilex Rd. NW10 6B 46
Ilex Way. SW16 5A 122
Ilford. 3F 55
Ilford Hill. Ilf 3E 54
Ilford Ho. N1 6D 50 (off Dove Rd.)
Ilford La. Ilf 3F 55
Ilfracombe Flats. SE1 2C 86 (6D 168) (off Marshalsea Rd.)
Ilfracombe Gdns. Romf 7B 38
Ilfracombe Rd. Brom 3H 125
Iliffe St. SE17 5B 86
Iliffe Yd. SE17 5B 86 (off Crampton St.)
Ilkeston Ct. E5 4K 51 (off Clapton Pk. Est.)
Ilkley Clo. SE19 6D 122
Ilkley Rd. E16 5A 72
Illingworth Clo. Mitc 3B 138
Illingworth Way. Enf 5K 7
Ilmington Rd. Harr 6D 26
Ilminster Gdns. SW11 4C 102
Imani Mans. SW11 2B 102
IMAX Cinema. 1A 86 (5J 167)
Imber Clo. N14 7B 6
Imber Ct. Trad. Est. E Mol 6H 133
Imber Cross. Th Dit 6K 133
Imber Gro. Esh 7H 133
Imber Pk. Rd. Esh 7H 133
Imber St. N1 1D 68
Impact Bus. Pk. Gnfd 2B 62
Impact Ct. SE20 2H 141
Imperial Av. N16 4E 50
Imperial Clo. Harr 6E 24
Imperial College. 3B 84 (1A 170)
Imperial College Rd. SW7 3B 84 (2A 170)
Imperial Ct. N6 6G 31
Imperial Ct. N20 3F 15
Imperial Ct. NW8 2C 66 (off Prince Albert Rd.)
Imperial Ct. SE11 5A 86 (6J 173)
Imperial Ct. S Harr 7E 24
Imperial Dri. Harr 7E 24
Imperial Gdns. Mitc 3F 139
Imperial Ho. E3 3A 70 (off Grove Rd.)
Imperial Ho. E14 7B 70 (off Victory Pl.)
Imperial M. E6 2B 72
Imperial Pde. EC4 6B 68 (1A 168) (off New Bri. St.)
Imperial Pl. Chst 1E 144
Imperial Rd. N22 7D 16 (in two parts)
Imperial Rd. SW6 1K 101
Imperial Rd. Felt 7G 95
Imperial Sq. SW6 1K 101
Imperial St. E3 3E 70
Imperial War Mus. 3A 86 (2K 173)
Imperial Way. Chst 3G 127
Imperial Way. Croy 6K 151
Imperial Way. Harr 6E 26
Imre Clo. W12 1D 82
Inca Dri. SE9 7F 109
Inchmery Rd. SE6 2D 124
Inchwood. Croy 4D 154
Independent Ind. Est. W Dray 1A 76
Independent Pl. E8 5F 51
Independents Rd. SE3 3H 107
Inderwick Rd. N8 5K 31
Indescon Ct. E14 2C 88
India Pl. WC2 2G 167
India St. EC3 6F 69 (1J 169)
India Way. W12 7D 64
Indigo M. E14 7E 70
Indigo M. N16 3D 50
Indus Rd. SE7 7A 90
Infirmary Ct. SW3 7F 171
Ingal Rd. E13 4J 71
Ingate Pl. SW8 1F 103
Ingatestone Rd. E12 1A 54
Ingatestone Rd. SE25 4H 141
Ingatestone Rd. Wfd G 7E 20
Ingelow Ho. W8 2K 83 (off Holland St.)
Ingelow Rd. SW8 2F 103
Ingersoll Rd. W12 1D 82
Ingersoll Rd. Enf 1D 8
Ingestre Pl. W1 6G 67 (1B 166)
Ingestre Rd. E7 4J 53
Ingestre Rd. NW5 4F 49
Ingham Clo. S Croy 7K 153
Ingham Rd. NW6 4J 47
Ingham Rd. S Croy 7J 153
Inglebert St. EC1 3A 68 (1J 161)
Ingleborough Ct. N17 3F 33
Ingleborough St. SW9 2A 104
Ingleby Dri. Harr 3H 43
Ingleby Rd. N7 3J 49
Ingleby Rd. Dag 6H 57
Ingleby Rd. Ilf 1F 55
Ingleby Way. Chst 5E 126
Ingleby Way. Wall 7H 151
Ingle Clo. Pinn 3C 24
Ingledew Rd. SE18 5H 91
Inglefield Sq. E1 1H 87 (off Prusom St.)
Inglehurst Gdns. Ilf 5D 36
Inglemere Rd. SE23 3K 123
Inglemere Rd. Mitc 7D 120
Inglesham Wlk. E9 6B 52
Ingleside Clo. Beck 7C 124
Ingleside Gro. SE3 6H 89
Inglethorpe St. SW6 1F 101
Ingleton Av. Well 5A 110
Ingleton Rd. N18 6B 18
Ingleton Rd. Cars 7C 150
Ingleton St. SW9 2A 104
Ingleway. N12 6G 15
Inglewood. Croy 7A 154
Inglewood Clo. E14 4C 88
Inglewood Copse. Brom 2C 144
Inglewood Rd. NW6 5J 47
Inglewood Rd. Bexh 4K 111
Inglis Rd. W5 7F 63
Inglis Rd. Croy 1F 153
Inglis St. SE5 1B 104
Ingoldisthorpe Gro. SE15 6F 87
Ingram Av. NW11 7A 30
Ingram Clo. SE11 4K 85 (3H 173)
Ingram Clo. Stan 5H 11
Ingram Ho. E3 1A 70
Ingram Rd. N2 4C 30
Ingram Rd. T Hth 1C 140
Ingram Way. Gnfd 1H 61
Ingrave Rd. Romf 4K 39
Ingrave St. SW11 3B 102
Ingrebourne Ct. E4 3J 19
Ingrebourne Ho. NW8 5B 66 (5B 158) (off Broadley St.)
Ingrebourne Ho. Brom 5F 125 (off Brangbourne Rd.)
Ingress St. W4 5A 82
Inigo Jones Rd. SE7 7C 90
Inigo Pl. WC2 2E 166
Inkerman Rd. NW5 6F 49
Inkerman Ter. W8 3J 83 (off Allen St.)
Inks Grn. E4 5K 19
Inkwell Clo. N12 3F 15
Inman Rd. NW10 1A 64
Inman Rd. SW18 7A 102
Inmans Row. Wfd G 4D 20
Inner Circ. NW1 3E 66 (2G 159)
Inner Pk. Rd. SW19 1F 119
Inner Ring E. H'row A 3D 94
Inner Ring W. H'row A 3C 94
Inner Temple Hall. 6A 68 (2K 167) (off Middle Temple La.)
Inner Temple La. EC4 6A 68 (1J 167)
Innes Clo. SW20 2G 137
Innes Gdns. SW15 6D 100
Innes Yd. Croy 3C 152
Innis Ho. SE17 5E 86 (off East St.)
Inniskilling Rd. E13 2A 72
Innovation Cen., The. E14 2E 88 (off Marsh Wall)
Innovation Clo. Wemb 1E 62
Inskip Clo. E10 2D 52
Inskip Rd. Dag 1D 56
Institute for English Studies. 5D 160 (in University of London, Senate House)
Institute of Advanced Legal Studies. 4J 67 (4E 160) (off Russell Sq.)
Institute of Classical Studies. 5D 160 (in University of London, Senate House)
Institute of Commonwealth Studies. 5J 67 (5E 160) (off Russell Sq.)
Institute of Contemporary Arts. 5D 166
Institute of Education. 4H 67 (4D 160) (off Bedford Way)
Institute of Germanic Studies. 5J 67 (5E 160) (off Russell Sq.)
Institute of Historical Research. 5D 160 (in University of London, Senate House)
Institute of Latin American Studies. 4H 67 (3D 160)
Institute of Romance Studies. 5D 160 (in University of London, Senate House)
Institute of United States Studies. 5D 160 (in University of London, Senate House)
Institute Pl. E8 5H 51
Integer Gdns. E11 7F 35
Interface Ho. Houn 3E 96 (off Staines Rd.)
International Av. Houn 5A 78
International Ho. E1 7F 69 (3K 169) (off St Katharine's Way)
International Trad. Est. S'hall 3K 77
Inverary Pl. SE18 6H 91
Inver Clo. E5 2J 51
Inverclyde Gdns. Romf 4C 38 (in two parts)
Inver Ct. W2 6K 65
Inveresk Gdns. Wor Pk 3C 148
Inverforth Clo. NW3 2A 48
Inverforth Rd. N11 5A 16
Invergarry Ho. NW6 2K 65 (off Carlton Va.)
Inverine Rd. SE7 5K 89
Invermore Pl. SE18 4G 91
Inverness Av. Enf 1K 7
Inverness Ct. SE6 1H 125
Inverness Gdns. W8 1K 83
Inverness M. E16 1G 91
Inverness M. W2 7K 65
Inverness Pl. W2 7K 65
Inverness Rd. N18 5C 18
Inverness Rd. Houn 4D 96
Inverness Rd. S'hall 4C 78
Inverness Rd. Wor Pk 1F 149
Inverness St. NW1 1F 67
Inverness Ter. W2 6K 65
Inverton Rd. SE15 4K 105
Invicta Clo. Chst 5E 126
Invicta Clo. Felt 1H 113
Invicta Gro. N'holt 3D 60
Invicta Pde. Sidc 4B 128
Invicta Plaza. SE1 1B 86 (4A 168)
Invicta Rd. SE3 7J 89
Inville Rd. SE17 5D 86
Inville Wlk. SE17 5D 86
Inwen Ct. SE8 5A 88 (in three parts)
Inwood Av. Houn 3G 97
Inwood Clo. Croy 2A 154
Inwood Ct. NW1 7G 49 (off Rochester Sq.)
Inwood Rd. Houn 4F 97
Inworth St. SW11 2C 102
Inworth Wlk. N1 1C 68 (off Popham St.)
Iona Clo. SE6 7C 106
Iona Clo. Mord 7K 137
Ion Ct. E2 2G 69
Ionian Building. E14 7A 70
Ionian Ho. E1 4K 69 (off Duckett St.)
Ion Sq. E2 2G 69
Ipsden Bldgs. SE1 5K 167
Ipswich Ho. SE4 5K 105
Ipswich Rd. SW17 6E 120
Ireland Clo. E6 5D 72
Ireland Pl. N22 7D 16
Ireland Yd. EC4 6B 68 (1B 168)
Irene M. W7 1K 79 (off Uxbridge Rd.)
Irene Rd. SW6 1J 101
Irene Rd. Orp 7K 145
Ireton Clo. N10 7K 15
Ireton St. E3 3C 70
Iris Av. Bex 6E 110
Iris Clo. E6 5C 72
Iris Clo. Croy 1K 153
Iris Clo. Surb 7F 135
Iris Ct. SE14 1J 105 (off Briant St.)
Iris Cres. Bexh 6F 93

Iris Rd. W Ewe . . . 5H 147
Iris Wlk. Edgw . . . 4D 12
Iris Way. E4 . . . 6G 19
Irkdale Av. Enf . . . 1A 8
Iron Bri. Clo. NW10 . . . 5A 46
Ironbridge Clo. S'hall . . . 1G 79
Iron Bri. Ho. NW1 . . . 7D 48
Iron Bri. Rd. W Dray . . . 1C 76
Iron Mill Pl. SW18 . . . 6K 101
Iron Mill Rd. SW18 . . . 6K 101
Ironmonger La. EC2 . . . 6C 68 (1D 168)
Ironmonger Pas. EC1 . . . 3C 68 (2D 162) (off Ironmonger Row)
Ironmonger Row. EC1 . . . 3C 68 (2D 162)
Ironmongers Pl. E14 . . . 4C 88
Ironside Clo. SE16 . . . 2K 87
Ironside Ho. E9 . . . 4A 52
Irons Way. Romf . . . 1J 39
Irvine Av. Harr . . . 3A 26
Irvine Clo. N20 . . . 2H 15
Irvine Ho. E14 . . . 5D 70 (off Uamvar St.)
Irvine Ho. N7 . . . 6K 49 (off Caledonian Rd.)
Irvine Way. Orp . . . 7K 145
Irving Av. N'holt . . . 1B 60
Irving Gro. SW9 . . . 2K 103
Irving Ho. SE17 . . . 5B 86 (off Doddington Gro.)
Irving Mans. W14 . . . 6G 83 (off Queen's Club Gdns.)
Irving M. N1 . . . 6C 50
Irving Rd. W14 . . . 3F 83
Irving St. WC2 . . . 7H 67 (3D 166)
Irving Way. NW9 . . . 5C 28
Irwell Ct. W7 . . . 6H 61 (off Hobbayne Rd.)
Irwell Est. SE16 . . . 3J 87
Irwin Av. SE18 . . . 7J 91
Irwin Clo. Uxb . . . 3C 40
Irwin Gdns. NW10 . . . 1D 64
Isabel Hill Clo. Hamp . . . 2F 133
Isabella Clo. N14 . . . 7B 6
Isabella Ct. Rich . . . 6F 99 (off Kings Mead)
Isabella Ho. SE11 . . . 5K 173
Isabella Ho. W6 . . . 5E 82 (off Queen Caroline St.)
Isabella Plantation. . . . 4H 117
Isabella Rd. E9 . . . 5J 51
Isabella St. SE1 . . . 1B 86 (5A 168)
Isabel St. SW9 . . . 1K 103
Isambard M. E14 . . . 3E 88
Isambard Pl. SE16 . . . 1J 87
Isard Ho. Brom . . . 1K 155
Isel Way. SE22 . . . 5E 104
Isham Rd. SW16 . . . 2J 139
Isis Clo. SW15 . . . 4E 100
Isis Clo. Ruis . . . 6E 22
Isis Ct. W4 . . . 7H 81
Isis Ho. N18 . . . 6A 18
Isis Ho. NW8 . . . 4B 66 (4B 158) (off Church St. Est.)
Isis St. SW18 . . . 2A 120
Island Farm Av. W Mol . . . 5D 132
Island Farm Rd. W Mol . . . 5D 132
Island Rd. Mitc . . . 7D 120
Island Row. E14 . . . 6B 70
Island, The. Th Dit . . . 6A 134
Isla Rd. SE18 . . . 6G 91
Islay Gdns. Houn . . . 5B 96
Isleden Ho. N1 . . . 1C 68 (off Prebend St.)
Isledon Rd. N7 . . . 3A 50
Isledon Village. . . . 3A 50
Islehurst Clo. Chst . . . 1E 144
Isleworth. . . . 3A 98
Isleworth Bus. Complex. Iswth . . . 2K 97
Isleworth Promenade. Twic . . . 4B 98
Isley Ct. SW8 . . . 2G 103
Islington. . . . 7B 50
Islington Crematorium. N2 . . . 1D 30
Islington Grn. N1 . . . 1B 68
Islington High St. N1 . . . 2A 68 (in two parts)
Islington Pk. M. N1 . . . 7B 50
Islington Pk. St. N1 . . . 7A 50
Islip Gdns. Edgw . . . 7E 12
Islip Gdns. N'holt . . . 7C 42
Islip Mnr. Rd. N'holt . . . 7C 42
Islip St. NW5 . . . 5G 49
Ismailia Rd. E7 . . . 7K 53
Isobel Ho. Harr . . . 5K 25
Isom Clo. E13 . . . 3K 71
Itaska Cotts. Bush . . . 1D 10
Ivanhoe Clo. Uxb . . . 5A 58
Ivanhoe Dri. Harr . . . 3A 26
Ivanhoe Ho. E3 . . . 2A 70 (off Grove Rd.)
Ivanhoe Rd. SE5 . . . 3F 105
Ivanhoe Rd. Houn . . . 3B 96
Ivatt Pl. W14 . . . 5H 83
Ivatt Way. N17 . . . 3B 32
Iveagh Av. NW10 . . . 2G 63
Iveagh Clo. E9 . . . 1K 69
Iveagh Clo. NW10 . . . 2G 63
Iveagh Clo. N'wd . . . 1D 22
Iveagh Ct. E1 . . . 1J 169
Iveagh Ct. Beck . . . 3E 142
Iveagh Ho. SW9 . . . 2B 104
Iveagh Ho. SW10 . . . 7A 84 (off King's Rd.)
Iveagh Ter. NW10 . . . 2G 63 (off Iveagh Av.)
Ivedon Rd. Well . . . 2C 110
Ive Farm Clo. E10 . . . 2C 52
Ive Farm La. E10 . . . 2C 52
Iveley Rd. SW4 . . . 2G 103
Ivere Dri. New Bar . . . 6E 4
Iverhurst Clo. Bexh . . . 5D 110
Iverna Ct. W8 . . . 3J 83
Iverna Gdns. W8 . . . 3J 83
Iverna Gdns. Felt . . . 5F 95
Iverson Rd. NW6 . . . 6H 47
Ivers Way. New Ad . . . 7D 154
Ives Rd. E16 . . . 5G 71
Ives St. SW3 . . . 4C 84 (3D 170)
Ivestor Ter. SE23 . . . 7J 105
Ivimey St. E2 . . . 3G 69
Ivinghoe Clo. Enf . . . 1K 7
Ivinghoe Ho. N7 . . . 5H 49
Ivinghoe Rd. Dag . . . 5B 56
Ivor Ct. N8 . . . 6J 31
Ivor Ct. NW1 . . . 4D 66 (3E 158) (off Gloucester Pl.)
Ivor Gro. SE9 . . . 1F 127
Ivories, The. N1 . . . 7C 50 (off Northampton St.)
Ivor Pl. NW1 . . . 4D 66 (4E 158)
Ivor St. NW1 . . . 7G 49
Ivory Ct. Felt . . . 2J 113
Ivorydown. Brom . . . 4J 125
Ivory Ho. E1 . . . 1F 87 (3K 169)
Ivory Sq. SW11 . . . 3A 102
Ivybridge Clo. Twic . . . 7A 98
Ivybridge Clo. Uxb . . . 3A 58
Ivybridge Ct. NW1 . . . 7F 49 (off Lewis St.)
Ivybridge Ct. Chst . . . 1E 144 (off Sutton Way)
Ivybridge Ho. SE22 . . . 6G 105 (off Old Hill)
Ivybridge La. WC2 . . . 7J 67 (3F 167)
Ivy Bri. Retail Pk. Iswth . . . 5K 97
Ivychurch Clo. SE20 . . . 7J 123
Ivychurch La. SE17 . . . 5F 87
Ivy Clo. Harr . . . 4D 42
Ivy Clo. Pinn . . . 7A 24
Ivy Clo. Sun . . . 2A 132
Ivy Cotts. E14 . . . 7E 70
Ivy Cotts. Uxb . . . 3C 58
Ivy Ct. SE16 . . . 5G 87 (off Argyle Way)
Ivy Cres. W4 . . . 4J 81
Ivydale Rd. SE15 . . . 3K 105
Ivydale Rd. Cars . . . 2D 150
Ivyday Gro. SW16 . . . 3K 121
Ivydene. W Mol . . . 5D 132
Ivydene Clo. Sutt . . . 4A 150
Ivy Gdns. N8 . . . 6J 31
Ivy Gdns. Mitc . . . 3H 139
Ivyhouse Rd. Dag . . . 6D 56
Ivyhouse Rd. Uxb . . . 3D 40
Ivy La. Houn . . . 4D 96
Ivymount Rd. SE27 . . . 3A 122
Ivy Rd. E16 . . . 6J 71
Ivy Rd. E17 . . . 6C 34
Ivy Rd. N14 . . . 7B 6
Ivy Rd. NW2 . . . 4E 46
Ivy Rd. SE4 . . . 4B 106
Ivy Rd. SW17 . . . 5C 120
Ivy Rd. Houn . . . 4F 97
Ivy Rd. Surb . . . 1G 147
Ivy St. N1 . . . 2E 68
Ivy Wlk. Dag . . . 6E 56
Ivy Wlk. N'wd . . . 1G 23
Ixworth Pl. SW3 . . . 5C 84 (5C 170)
Izane Rd. Bexh . . . 4F 111
Jacaranda Clo. N Mald . . . 3A 136
Jacaranda Gro. E8 . . . 7F 51
Jackass La. Kes . . . 5K 155
Jack Barnett Way. N22 . . . 2K 31
Jack Clow Rd. E15 . . . 2G 71
Jack Cook Ho. Bark . . . 7F 55
Jack Cornwell St. E12 . . . 4E 54
Jack Dash Ho. E14 . . . 2E 88 (off Lawn Ho. Clo.)
Jack Dash Way. E6 . . . 4C 72
Jackets La. Hare & N'wd . . . 1D 22 (in two parts)
Jack Goodchild Way. King T . . . 3H 135
Jacklin Grn. Wfd G . . . 4D 20
Jackman Ho. E1 . . . 1H 87 (off Watts St.)
Jackman M. NW10 . . . 3A 46
Jackman St. E8 . . . 1H 69
Jackson Clo. E9 . . . 7J 51
Jackson Clo. Uxb . . . 7A 40
Jackson Ct. E7 . . . 6K 53
Jackson Rd. N7 . . . 4K 49
Jackson Rd. Bark . . . 1H 73
Jackson Rd. Barn . . . 6H 5
Jackson Rd. Brom . . . 2D 156
Jackson Rd. Uxb . . . 7A 40
Jacksons La. N6 . . . 7E 30
Jacksons Pl. Croy . . . 1D 152
Jackson St. SE18 . . . 6E 90
Jackson's Way. Croy . . . 3C 154
Jackson Way. S'hall . . . 2F 79
Jack Walker Ct. N5 . . . 4B 50
Jacob Ho. Eri . . . 2D 92
Jacobin Lodge. N7 . . . 5J 49
Jacobs Clo. Dag . . . 4H 57
Jacobs Ho. E13 . . . 3A 72 (off New City Rd.)
Jacob St. SE1 . . . 2G 87 (6K 169)
Jacob's Well M. W1 . . . 5E 66 (6H 159)
Jacotts Ho. W10 . . . 4E 64 (off Sutton Way)
Jacqueline Clo. N'holt . . . 1C 60
Jacqueline Creft Ter. N6 . . . 6E 30 (off Grange Rd.)
Jacqueline Vs. E17 . . . 5E 34 (off Shernhall St.)
Jade Clo. E16 . . . 6B 72
Jade Clo. NW2 . . . 7F 29
Jade Clo. Dag . . . 1C 56
Jade Ter. NW6 . . . 7A 48
Jaffe Rd. Ilf . . . 1H 55
Jaffray Pl. SE27 . . . 4B 122
Jaffray Rd. Brom . . . 4B 144
Jaggard Way. SW12 . . . 7D 102
Jagger Ho. SW11 . . . 1D 102 (off Rosenau Rd.)
Jago Clo. SE18 . . . 6G 91
Jago Wlk. SE5 . . . 7D 86
Jamaica Rd. SE1 & SE16 . . . 2F 87 (7K 169)
Jamaica Rd. T Hth . . . 6B 140
Jamaica St. E1 . . . 6J 69
James Anderson Ct. N1 . . . 2E 68 (off Kingsland Rd.)
James Av. NW2 . . . 5E 46
James Av. Dag . . . 1F 57
James Bedford Clo. Pinn . . . 2A 24
James Boswell Clo. SW16 . . . 4K 121
James Brine Ho. E2 . . . 3F 69 (1K 163) (off Ravenscroft St.)
James Campbell Ho. E2 . . . 2J 69 (off Old Ford Rd.)
James Clo. E13 . . . 2J 71
James Clo. NW11 . . . 6G 29
James Collins Clo. W9 . . . 4H 65
James Ct. N1 . . . 1C 68 (off Raynor Pl.)
James Ct. NW9 . . . 2A 28
James Ct. N'holt . . . 2C 60 (off Church Rd.)
James Ct. N'wd . . . 1H 23
James Docherty Ho. E2 . . . 2H 69 (off Patriot Sq.)
James Dudson Ct. NW10 . . . 7J 45
James Est. Mitc . . . 2D 138
James Gdns. N22 . . . 7G 17
James Hammett Ho. E2 . . . 3F 69 (1K 163) (off Ravenscroft St.)
James Ho. E1 . . . 4A 70 (off Solebay St.)
James Ho. SE16 . . . 2K 87 (off Wolfe Cres.)
James Joyce Wlk. SE24 . . . 4B 104
James La. E10 & E11 . . . 7E 34
James Lind Ho. SE8 . . . 4B 88 (off Grove St.)
James Middleton Ho. E2 . . . 3H 69 (off Middleton St.)
James Newham Ct. SE9 . . . 3E 126
Jameson Clo. W3 . . . 2J 81
Jameson Ct. E2 . . . 2J 69 (off Russia La.)
Jameson Ho. SE11 . . . 5K 85 (5G 173) (off Glasshouse Wlk.)
Jameson Lodge. N6 . . . 6G 31
Jameson St. W8 . . . 1J 83
James Pl. N17 . . . 1F 33
James's Cotts. Rich . . . 7G 81
James Stewart Ho. NW6 . . . 7H 47
James St. W1 . . . 6E 66 (1H 165)
James St. WC2 . . . 7J 67 (1F 167)
James St. Bark . . . 7G 55
James St. Enf . . . 5A 8
James St. Houn . . . 3H 97
James Stroud Ho. SE17 . . . 5C 86 (off Bronti Clo.)
James Ter. SW14 . . . 3K 99 (off Church Path)
James Terry Ct. S Croy . . . 5C 152 (off Warham Rd.)
Jamestown Rd. NW1 . . . 1F 67
Jamestown Way. E14 . . . 7F 71
James Yd. E4 . . . 6A 20
Jamieson Ho. Houn . . . 6D 96
Jamilah Ho. E16 . . . 7F 73 (off University Way)
Jamuna Clo. E14 . . . 5A 70
Jane Austen Hall. E16 . . . 1K 89 (off Wesley Av., in two parts)
Jane Austen Ho. SW1 . . . 5G 85 (6A 172) (off Churchill Gdns.)
Jane Seymour Ct. SE9 . . . 7G 109
Jane St. E1 . . . 6H 69
Janet St. E14 . . . 3C 88
Janeway Pl. SE16 . . . 2H 87
Janeway St. SE16 . . . 2G 87
Janice M. Ilf . . . 2F 55
Jansen Wlk. SW11 . . . 3B 102
Janson Clo. E15 . . . 5G 53
Janson Clo. NW10 . . . 3A 46
Janson Rd. E15 . . . 5G 53
Jansons Rd. N15 . . . 3E 32
Japan Cres. N4 . . . 1K 49
Japan Rd. Chad H . . . 6D 38
Jardine Rd. E1 . . . 7K 69
Jarman Ho. E1 . . . 5J 69 (off Jubilee St.)
Jarman Ho. SE16 . . . 4K 87 (off Hawkstone Rd.)
Jarrett Clo. SW2 . . . 1B 122
Jarrow Clo. Mord . . . 5K 137
Jarrow Rd. N17 . . . 4H 33
Jarrow Rd. SE16 . . . 4J 87
Jarrow Rd. Romf . . . 6C 38
Jarrow Way. E9 . . . 4B 52
Jarvis Clo. Bark . . . 1H 73
Jarvis Clo. Barn . . . 5A 4
Jarvis Rd. SE22 . . . 4E 104
Jarvis Rd. S Croy . . . 6D 152
Jashoda Ho. SE18 . . . 5E 90 (off Connaught M.)
Jasmin Clo. N'wd . . . 1H 23
Jasmin Ct. SE12 . . . 6H 107
Jasmine Clo. Ilf . . . 5F 55
Jasmine Clo. Orp . . . 2E 156
Jasmine Clo. S'hall . . . 7C 60
Jasmine Ct. SW19 . . . 5J 119
Jasmine Gdns. Croy . . . 3D 154
Jasmine Gdns. Harr . . . 2E 42
Jasmine Gro. SE20 . . . 1H 141
Jasmine Rd. Rush G . . . 2K 57
Jasmine Ter. W Dray . . . 2C 76
Jasmine Way. E Mol . . . 4J 133
Jasmin Lodge. SE16 . . . 5H 87 (off Sherwood Gdns.)
Jasmin Rd. Eps . . . 5H 147
Jason Ct. SW9 . . . 1A 104 (off Southey Rd.)
Jason Ct. W1 . . . 7H 159
Jason Wlk. SE9 . . . 4E 126
Jasper Clo. Enf . . . 1D 8
Jasper Pas. SE19 . . . 6F 123
Jasper Rd. E16 . . . 6B 72
Jasper Rd. SE19 . . . 5F 123
Jasper Wlk. N1 . . . 3D 68 (1E 162)
Java Wharf. SE1 . . . 6K 169
Javelin Way. N'holt . . . 3B 60
Jaycroft. Enf . . . 1F 7
Jay Gdns. Chst . . . 4D 126
Jay M. SW7 . . . 2A 84 (7A 164)
Jazzfern Ter. Wemb . . . 5A 44
Jean Batten Clo. Wall . . . 7K 151
Jean Darling Ho. SW10 . . . 6B 84 (off Milman's St.)
Jean Pardies Ho. E1 . . . 5J 69 (off Jubilee St.)
Jebb Av. SW2 . . . 6J 103 (in two parts)
Jebb St. E3 . . . 2C 70
Jedburgh Rd. E13 . . . 3A 72
Jedburgh St. SW11 . . . 4E 102
Jeddo M. W3 . . . 2B 82
Jeddo Rd. W12 . . . 2B 82
Jefferson Building. E14 . . . 2C 88
Jefferson Clo. W13 . . . 3B 80
Jefferson Clo. Ilf . . . 5F 37
Jefferson Wlk. SE18 . . . 6E 90
Jeffrey Row. SE12 . . . 5K 107
Jeffrey's Pl. NW1 . . . 7G 49
Jeffreys Rd. SW4 . . . 2J 103
Jeffreys Rd. Enf . . . 4F 9
Jeffrey's St. NW1 . . . 7G 49
Jeffries Ho. NW10 . . . 7K 45
Jeffs Clo. Hamp . . . 6F 115
Jeffs Rd. Sutt . . . 4H 149
Jeger Av. E2 . . . 1F 69
Jeken Rd. SE9 . . . 4A 108

Jelf Rd. SW2 5A 104
Jellicoe Gdns. Stan 6E 10
Jellicoe Ho. E2 2G 69 (1K 163) (off Ropley St.)
Jellicoe Ho. NW1 4F 67 (4K 159)
Jellicoe Rd. E13 4J 71
Jellicoe Rd. N17 7J 17
Jemmett Clo. King T 1H 135
Jemotts Ct. SE14 6K 87 (off Myers La.)
Jem Paterson Ct. Harr 4J 43
Jengar Clo. Sutt 4K 149
Jenkins La. Bark 2G 73
Jenkinson Ho. E2 3K 69 (off Usk St.)
Jenkins Rd. E13 4K 71
Jenner Av. W3 5K 63
Jenner Ho. SE3 6G 89 (off Restell Clo.)
Jenner Ho. WC1 4J 67 (3F 161) (off Hunter St.)
Jenner Pl. SW13 6D 82
Jenner Rd. N16 3F 51
Jennett Rd. Croy 3A 152
Jennifer Ho. SE11 4A 86 (4K 173) (off Reedworth St.)
Jennifer Rd. Brom 3H 125
Jenningsbury Ho. SW3 5C 84 (5D 170) (off Marlborough St.)
Jennings Clo. Surb 7C 134
Jennings Ho. SE10 5F 89 (off Old Woolwich Rd.)
Jennings Rd. SE22 6F 105
Jennings Way. Barn 3A 4
Jenningtree Way. Belv 2J 93
Jenny Hammond Clo. E11 3H 53
Jenson Way. SE19 7F 123
Jenton Av. Bexh 1E 110
Jephson Ct. SW4 2J 103
Jephson Ho. SE17 6B 86 (off Doddington Gro.)
Jephson Rd. E7 7A 54
Jephson St. SE5 1D 104
Jephtha Rd. SW18 6J 101
Jeppos La. Mitc 4D 138
Jepson Ho. SW6 1K 101 (off Pearscroft Rd.)
Jerdan Pl. SW6 7J 83
Jeremiah St. E14 6D 70
Jeremy Bentham Ho. E2 3G 69 (off Mansford St.)
Jeremy's Grn. N18 4C 18
Jermyn St. SW1 1G 85 (4A 166)
Jermyn Street Theatre. 7H 67 (3B 166) (off Jermyn St.)
Jerningham Av. Ilf 2F 37
Jerningham Ct. SE14 1A 106
Jerningham Rd. SE14 2A 106
Jerome Cres. NW8 4C 66 (3C 158)
Jerome Ho. NW1 5C 66 (5D 158) (off Lisson Gro.)
Jerome Ho. SW7 4B 84 (3A 170) (off Glendower Pl.)
Jerome Ho. Hamp W 2D 134 (off Old Bri. St.)
Jerome St. E1 4F 69 (5J 163)
Jerome Tower. W3 2H 81
Jerrard St. SE13 3D 106
Jerrold St. N1 2E 68 (1H 163)
Jersey Av. Stan 2B 26
Jersey Dri. Orp 6H 145
Jersey Ho. N1 6C 50
Jersey Ho. Enf 1E 8 (off Eastfield Rd.)
Jersey Rd. E11 1F 53
Jersey Rd. E16 6A 72
Jersey Rd. N1 6C 50
Jersey Rd. SW17 6F 121
Jersey Rd. W7 2A 80
Jersey Rd. Houn & Iswth 1F 97
Jersey Rd. Ilf 4F 55
Jersey St. E2 3H 69
Jerusalem Pas. EC1 4B 68 (4A 162)
Jervis Bay Ho. E14 6F 71 (off Blair St.)
Jervis Ct. SE10 1E 106 (off Blissett St.)
Jervis Ct. W1 1K 165
Jervis Ct. Dag 6H 57
Jerviston Gdns. SW16 6A 122
Jerwood Space Art Gallery. 6C 168
Jesmond Av. Wemb 6F 45
Jesmond Clo. Mitc 3F 139
Jesmond Rd. Croy 7F 141
Jesmond Way. Stan 5K 11
Jessam Av. E5 1H 51
Jessamine Rd. W7 1K 79
Jessel Ho. SW1 4H 85 (3D 172) (off Page St.)
Jessel Ho. WC1 3J 67 (2E 160) (off Judd St.)
Jessel Mans. W14 6G 83 (off Queen's Club Gdns.)
Jesse Rd. E10 1E 52
Jessett Clo. Eri 4K 93
Jessica Rd. SW18 6A 102
Jessie Blythe La. N19 7J 31
Jessie Wood Ct. SW9 7A 86 (off Caldwell St.)
Jessiman Ter. Shep 5C 130
Jesson Ho. SE17 4D 86 (off Orb St.)
Jessop Av. S'hall 4D 78
Jessop Ct. N1 2B 68
Jessop Rd. SE24 4B 104
Jessop Sq. E14 1C 88 (off Heron Quay)
Jessops Way. Croy 6G 139
Jessup Clo. SE18 4G 91
Jetstar Way. N'holt 3C 60
Jevington Way. SE12 1K 125
Jewel House. 3J 169 (in Tower of London, The)
Jewel Rd. E17 3C 34
Jewel Tower. 3J 85 (1E 172) (off College M.)
Jewish Mus. 1F 67 (Camden Town)
Jewish Mus., The. 2K 29 (off E. End Rd., Finchley)
Jewry St. EC3 6F 69 (1J 169)
Jew's Row. SW18 4K 101
Jews' Wlk. SE26 4H 123
Jeymer Av. NW2 5D 46
Jeymer Dri. Gnfd 1F 61 (in two parts)
Jeypore Pas. SW18 6A 102
Jeypore Rd. SW18 7A 102
Jillian Clo. Hamp 7E 114
Jim Bradley Clo. SE18 4E 90
Jim Griffiths Ho. SW6 6H 83 (off Clem Attlee Ct.)
Joan Cres. SE9 7B 108
Joan Gdns. Dag 2E 56
Joanna Ho. W6 5E 82 (off Queen Caroline St.)
Joan Rd. Dag 2E 56
Joan St. SE1 1B 86 (5A 168)
Jocelin Ho. N1 1K 67 (off Barnsbury Est.)
Jocelyn Rd. Rich 3E 98
Jocelyn St. SE15 1G 105
Jockey's Fields. WC1 5K 67 (5H 161)
Jodane St. SE8 4B 88
Jodrell Clo. Iswth 1A 98
Jodrell Rd. E3 1B 70
Joe Hunte Ct. SE27 5B 122
Joel St. N'wd & Pinn 2J 23
Johanna St. SE1 2A 86 (7J 167)
John Adams Ct. N9 2A 18
John Adam St. WC2 7J 67 (3F 167)
John Aird Ct. W2 5A 158 (in two parts)
John Archer Way. SW18 6B 102
John Ashby Clo. SW2 6J 103
John Austin Clo. King T 1F 135
John Baird Ct. SE26 4J 123
John Barker Ct. NW6 7G 47 (off Brondesbury Pk.)
John Barnes Wlk. E15 6H 53
John Betts' Ho. W12 3B 82
John Bradshaw Rd. N14 1C 16
John Brent Ho. SE8 4K 87 (off Bush Rd.)
John Buck Ho. NW10 1B 64
John Burns Dri. Bark 7J 55
John Campbell Rd. N16 5E 50
John Carpenter St. EC4 7B 68 (2A 168)
John Cartwright Ho. E2 3H 69 (off Old Bethnal Grn. Rd.)
John Drinkwater Clo. E11 7H 35
John Felton Rd. SE16 2G 87
John Fielden Ho. E2 3H 69 (off Canrobert St.)
John Fisher St. E1 7G 69 (2K 169)
John Goddard Way. Felt 2K 113
John Gooch Dri. Enf 1G 7
John Harrison Way. SE10 3H 89
John Islip St. SW1 4H 85 (5D 172)
John Kennedy Ct. N1 6D 50 (off Newington Grn. Rd.)
John Kennedy Ho. SE16 4K 87 (off Rotherhithe Old Rd.)
John Kirk Ho. E6 6E 72 (off Pearl Clo.)
John Knight Lodge. SW6 7J 83
John Lamb Ct. Harr 1J 25
John Masefield Ho. N15 6D 32 (off Fladbury Rd.)
John Maurice Clo. SE17 4D 86
John McDonald Ho. E14 3E 88 (off Glengall Gro.)
John McKenna Wlk. SE16 3G 87
John Newton Ct. Well 3B 110
John Parker Clo. Dag 7H 57
John Parker Sq. SW11 3B 102
John Parry Ct. N1 2E 68 (off Hare Wlk.)
John Penn Ho. SE14 7B 88 (off Amersham Va.)
John Penn St. SE13 1D 106
John Perrin Pl. Harr 7E 26
John Pound Ho. SW18 7K 101
John Prince's St. W1 6F 67 (7K 159)
John Pritchard Ho. E1 4G 69 (off Buxton St.)
John Ratcliffe Ho. NW6 3J 65 (off Chippenham Gdns.)
John Rennie Wlk. E1 7H 69
John Roll Way. SE16 3G 87
John Ruskin St. SE5 7B 86
John's Av. NW4 4E 28
John's Clo. Ashf 4E 112
John's Ct. Sutt 6K 149
John Scurr Ho. E14 6A 70 (off Ratcliffe La.)
John Silkin La. SE8 5K 87
John's La. Mord 5A 138
John's M. WC1 4K 67 (4H 161)
John Smith Av. SW6 7H 83
Johnson Clo. E8 1G 69
Johnson Ho. E2 3G 69 (off Roberta St.)
Johnson Ho. NW1 2G 67 (off Cranleigh St.)
Johnson Ho. NW3 7D 48 (off Adelaide Rd.)
Johnson Ho. SW1 4E 84 (4H 171) (off Cundy St.)
Johnson Ho. SW8 7H 85 (off Wandsworth Rd.)
Johnson Lodge. W9 5J 65 (off Admiral Wlk.)
Johnson Mans. W14 6G 83 (off Queen's Club Gdns.)
Johnson Rd. NW10 1K 63
Johnson Rd. Brom 5B 144
Johnson Rd. Croy 7D 140
Johnson Rd. Houn 7A 78
Johnsons Clo. Cars 2D 150
Johnson's Ct. EC4 6A 68 (1K 167)
Johnsons Dri. Hamp 1G 133
Johnsons Ind. Est. Hay 2H 77
Johnson's Pl. SW1 5G 85 (6A 172)
Johnson St. E1 7J 69
Johnson St. S'hall 3A 78
Johnsons Way. NW10 4H 63
John Spencer Sq. N1 6B 50
John's Pl. E1 6H 69
John's Ter. Croy 1E 152
Johnston Clo. SW9 1K 103
Johnstone Ho. SE13 3F 107 (off Belmont Hill)
Johnstone Rd. E6 3D 72
Johnston Rd. Wfd G 6D 20
Johnston Ter. NW2 3F 47
John Strachey Ho. SW6 6H 83 (off Clem Attlee Ct.)
John St. E15 1H 71
John St. SE25 4G 141
John St. WC1 4K 67 (4H 161)
John St. Enf 5A 8
John St. Houn 2C 96
John Strype Ct. E10 1D 52
John Trundle Ct. EC2 5C 162
John Trundle Highwalk. EC2 5C 68 (5C 162) (off Beech St.)
John Tucker Ho. E14 3C 88 (off Mellish St.)
John Watkin Clo. Eps 7H 147
John Wesley Ct. Twic 1A 116
John Wesley Highwalk. EC1 5C 68 (6C 162) (off Barbican)
John Wheatley Ho. SW6 6H 83 (off Clem Attlee Ct.)
John Williams Clo. SE14 6K 87
John Williams Clo. King T 1D 134
John Wilson St. SE18 3E 90
John Woolley Clo. SE13 4G 107
Joiners Arms Yd. SE5 1D 104
Joiners Pl. N5 4D 50
Joiner St. SE1 1D 86 (5F 169)
Joint Rd. N2 1C 30
Jollys La. Harr 1H 43
Jollys La. Hay 5B 60
Jonathan St. SE11 5K 85 (5G 173)
Jones Ho. E14 6F 71 (off Blair St.)
Jones M. SW15 4G 101
Jones Rd. E13 5K 71
Jones St. W1 7F 67 (3J 165)
Jones Wlk. Rich 6F 99
Jonquil Gdns. Hamp 6E 114
Jonson Clo. Hay 5J 59
Jonson Clo. Mitc 4F 139
Jonson Ho. SE1 3D 86 (off Burbage Clo.)
Jordan Clo. Dag 4H 57
Jordan Clo. Harr 3D 42
Jordan Ho. N1 1D 68 (off Colville Est.)
Jordan Ho. SE4 4K 105 (off St Norbert Rd.)
Jordan Rd. Gnfd 1B 62
Jordans Clo. Iswth 1J 97
Jordans Ho. NW8 3B 158
Jordans M. Twic 2J 115
Joscoyne Ho. E1 6H 69 (off Philpot St.)
Joseph Av. W3 6K 63
Joseph Conrad Ho. SW1 4G 85 (4B 172) (off Tachbrook St.)
Joseph Ct. N15 6E 32 (off Amhurst Pk.)
Joseph Gdns. SE18 3C 90
Joseph Hardcastle Clo. SE14 7K 87
Josephine Av. SW2 5K 103
Joseph Irwin Ho. E14 7B 70 (off Gill St.)
Joseph Lister Ct. E7 7J 53
Joseph Powell Clo. SW12 6F 103
Joseph Priestley Ho. E2 3H 69 (off Canrobert St.)
Joseph Ray Rd. E11 2G 53
Joseph St. E3 4B 70
Joseph Trotter Clo. EC1 2K 161
Joshua Clo. S Croy 7B 152
Joshua St. E14 6E 70
Joslings Clo. W12 7C 64
Joslyn Clo. Enf 1H 9
Josseline Ct. E3 2A 70 (off Ford St.)
Joubert St. SW11 2D 102
Jowett St. SE15 7F 87
Jowitt Ho. E2 3K 69 (off Morpeth St.)
Joyce Av. N18 5A 18
Joyce Butler Ho. N22 1K 31
Joyce Dawson Way. SE28 7A 74
Joyce Page Clo. SE7 6B 90
Joyce Wlk. SW2 6A 104
Joydens Wood. 4K 129
Joydens Wood Rd. Bex 4K 129
Joydon Dri. Romf 6B 38
Joyners Clo. Dag 4F 57
Joystone Ct. New Bar 4H 5 (off Park Rd.)
Jubb Powell Ho. N15 6E 32
Jubilee Av. E4 6K 19
Jubilee Av. Romf 5H 39
Jubilee Av. Twic 1G 115
Jubilee Bldgs. NW8 1B 66
Jubilee Clo. NW9 6K 27
Jubilee Clo. King T 1C 134
Jubilee Clo. Pinn 2A 24
Jubilee Clo. Romf 5H 39
Jubilee Ct. N10 3E 30
Jubilee Ct. Harr 7E 26
Jubilee Ct. Houn 3G 97 (off Bristow Rd.)
Jubilee Cres. E14 3E 88
Jubilee Cres. N9 1B 18
Jubilee Dri. Ruis 4B 42
Jubilee Gdns. S'hall 5E 60
Jubilee Ho. SE11 4A 86 (4K 173) (off Reedworth St.)
Jubilee Ho. WC1 3G 161
Jubilee Ho. Stan 5J 11
Jubilee Mans. E1 6J 69 (off Jubilee St.)
Jubilee Mkt. Wfd G 6F 21
Jubilee Pde. Wfd G 6F 21
Jubilee Pl. SW3 5C 84 (5D 170)
Jubilee Rd. Gnfd 1B 62
Jubilee Rd. Sutt 7F 149
Jubilee St. E1 6J 69
Jubilee, The. SE10 7D 88
Jubilee Vs. Esh 7H 133
Jubilee Walkway. SE1 7B 68 (3B 168)
Jubilee Way. SW19 1K 137

Jubilee Way. Chess 4G 147
Jubilee Way. Felt 1J 113
Jubilee Way. Sidc 2A 128
Jubilee Yd. SE1 6J 169
Judd St. WC1 3J 67 (2E 160)
Jude St. E16 6H 71
Judge Heath La. Hay 6E 58
Judges Wlk. NW3 3A 48
Juer Ho. SW11 7C 84 (off Juer St.)
Juer St. SW11 7C 84
Jules Thorn Av. Enf 4B 8
Julia Ct. E17 5D 34
Julia Gdns. Bark 2D 74
Julia Garfield M. E16 1K 89
Juliana Clo. N2 2A 30
Julian Av. W3 7H 63
Julian Clo. New Bar 3E 4
Julian Hill. Harr 2J 43
Julian Pl. E14 5D 88
Julian Taylor Path. SE23 2H 123
Julia St. NW5 4E 48
Julien Rd. W5 3C 80
Juliet Ho. N1 2E 68 (off Arden Est.)
Juliette Rd. E13 2J 71
Julius Nyerere Clo. N1 1K 67 (off Copenhagen St.)
Junction App. SE13 3E 106
Junction App. SW11 3C 102
Junction Av. NW10 4E 64
Junction M. W2 6C 66 (7C 158)
Junction Pl. W2 7B 158
Junction Rd. E13 2K 71
Junction Rd. N9 1B 18
Junction Rd. N17 3G 33
Junction Rd. N19 4G 49
Junction Rd. W5 4C 80
Junction Rd. Ashf 5E 112
Junction Rd. Harr 6J 25
Junction Rd. S Croy 5D 152
Junction Rd. E. Romf 7E 38
Junction Rd. W. Romf 7E 38
Juniper Clo. Barn 5A 4
Juniper Clo. Chess 5F 147
Juniper Clo. Wemb 5G 45
Juniper Ct. W8 3K 83 (off St Mary's Pl.)
Juniper Ct. Harr 1K 25
Juniper Ct. Houn 4F 97 (off Grove Rd.)
Juniper Ct. N'wd 1J 23
Juniper Ct. Romf 6B 38
Juniper Cres. NW1 7E 48
Juniper Gdns. SW16 1G 139
Juniper Gdns. Sun 6H 113
Juniper Ho. SE15 7J 87
Juniper Ho. W10 4G 65 (off Fourth Av.)
Juniper La. E6 5C 72
Juniper Rd. Ilf 3E 54
Juniper St. E1 7J 69
Juniper Way. Hay 7F 59
Juno Ct. SW9 7A 86 (off Caldwell St.)
Juno Way. SE14 6K 87
Juno Way Ind. Est. SE14 6K 87
Jupiter Ct. SW9 7A 86 (off Caldwell St.)
Jupiter Ct. N'holt 3B 60 (off Seasprite Clo.)
Jupiter Heights. Uxb 1B 58
Jupiter Ho. E14 5D 88 (off St Davids Sq.)
Jupiter Way. N7 6K 49
Jupp Rd. E15 7F 53
Jupp Rd. W. E15 1F 71
Jura Ho. SE16 4K 87 (off Plough Way)
Jurston Ct. SE1 7K 167
Justice Wlk. SW3 7C 170
Justin Clo. Bren 7D 80
Justin Rd. E4 6G 19
Jute La. Brim 2F 9 (in two parts)
Jutland Clo. N19 1J 49
Jutland Ho. SE5 2C 104
Jutland Rd. E13 4J 71
Jutland Rd. SE6 7E 106
Jutsums Av. Romf 6H 39
Jutsums Ct. Romf 6H 39
Jutsums La. Romf 6H 39
Juxon Clo. Harr 1F 25
Juxon St. SE11 4K 85 (3H 173)
JVC Bus. Pk. NW2 1C 46

Kaduna Clo. Pinn 5J 23
Kale Rd. Eri 2E 92
Kambala Rd. SW11 3B 102
Kangley Bri. Rd. SE26 6B 124
Kangley Bus. Cen. SE26 5B 124
Kaplan Dri. N21 5E 6
Kara Way. NW2 4F 47
Karen Ct. Brom 1H 143
Karen Ter. E11 2H 53
Karoline Gdns. Gnfd 2H 61
Kashgar Rd. SE18 4K 91
Kashmir Rd. SE7 7B 90
Kassala Rd. SW11 1D 102
Katharine Ho. Croy 3C 152 (off Katharine St.)
Katharine St. Croy 3C 152
Katherine Clo. SE16 1K 87
Katherine Ct. SE23 1H 123
Katherine Gdns. SE9 4B 108
Katherine Rd. E7 & E6 5A 54
Katherine Rd. Twic 1A 116
Katherine Sq. W11 1G 83
Kathleen Av. W3 5J 63
Kathleen Av. Wemb 7E 44
Kathleen Godfree Ct. SW19 6J 119
Kathleen Rd. SW11 3D 102
Kayemoor Rd. Sutt 6B 150
Kay Rd. SW9 2J 103
Kay St. E2 2G 69
Kay St. E15 7F 53
Kay St. Well 1B 110
Kay Ter. E18 1H 35
Kay Way. SE10 7E 88 (off Greenwich High Rd.)
Kean Ho. SE17 6B 86
Kean Ho. Twic 6D 98 (off Arosa Rd.)
Kean St. WC2 6K 67 (1G 167)
Keatley Grn. E4 6G 19
Keats Av. E16 1K 89
Keats Clo. E11 5K 35
Keat's Clo. NW3 4C 48
Keats Clo. SE1 4F 87
Keats Clo. SW19 6B 120
Keats Clo. Enf 5E 8
Keats Clo. Hay 5J 59
Keat's Gro. NW3 4C 48
Keats House. 4C 48
Keats Ho. E2 3J 69 (off Roman Rd.)
Keats Ho. SE5 7C 86 (off Elmington Est.)
Keats Ho. SW1 6G 85 (7B 172) (off Churchill Gdns.)
Keats Ho. Cray 5K 111
Keats Pde. N9 2B 18 (off Church St.)
Keats Pl. EC2 5D 68 (6E 162) (off Moorfields)
Keats Rd. Belv 3J 93
Keats Rd. Well 1J 109
Keats Way. Croy 6J 141
Keats Way. Gnfd 5F 61
Keats Way. W Dray 4B 76
Kebbell Ter. E7 5K 53 (off Claremont Rd.)
Keble Clo. N'holt 5G 43
Keble Clo. Wor Pk 1B 148
Keble Pl. SW13 6D 82
Keble St. SW17 4A 120
Kechill Gdns. Brom 7J 143
Kedeston Ct. Sutt 1K 149
Kedge Ho. E14 3C 88 (off Tiller Rd.)
Kedleston Dri. Orp 6K 145
Kedleston Wlk. E2 3H 69
Kedyngton Ho. Edgw 2J 27 (off Burnt Oak B'way.)
Keeble Clo. SE18 6F 91
Keedonwood Rd. Brom 5G 125
Keel Clo. SE16 1K 87
Keel Clo. Bark 2C 74
Keeley Rd. Croy 2C 152
Keeley St. WC2 6K 67 (1G 167)
Keeling Ho. E2 2H 69 (off Claredale St.)
Keeling Rd. SE9 5B 108
Keely Clo. Barn 5H 5
Keemor Clo. SE18 7E 90
Keens Clo. SW16 5H 121
Keens Rd. Croy 4C 152
Keen's Yd. N1 6B 50
Keepers Ct. S Croy 5C 152 (off Warham Rd.)
Keepers M. Tedd 6C 116
Keepier Wharf. E14 7K 69 (off Narrow St.)
Keep, The. SE3 2J 107
Keep, The. King T 6F 117
Keeton's Rd. SE16 3H 87 (in two parts)
Keevil Dri. SW19 7F 101
Keighley Clo. N7 5J 49
Keightley Dri. SE9 1G 127
Keilder Clo. Uxb 2C 58
Keildon Rd. SW11 4D 102
Keir Hardie Ct. NW10 7B 46
Keir Hardie Est. E5 1H 51
Keir Hardie Ho. N19 7H 31
Keir Hardie Ho. W6 6F 83 (off Fulham Pal. Rd.)
Keir Hardie Way. Bark 7A 56
Keir Hardie Way. Hay 3J 59
Keir, The. SW19 5E 118
Keith Connor Clo. SW8 3F 103
Keith Gro. W12 2C 82
Keith Ho. NW6 3K 65 (off Carlton Va.)
Keith Pk. Rd. Uxb 7B 40
Keith Rd. E17 1B 34
Keith Rd. Bark 2H 73
Keith Rd. Hay 3G 77
Kelbrook Rd. SE3 2C 108
Kelby Ho. N7 6K 49 (off Sutterton St.)
Kelby Path. SE9 3F 127
Kelceda Clo. NW2 2C 46
Kelf Gro. Hay 6H 59
Kelfield Ct. W10 6F 65
Kelfield Gdns. W10 6E 64
Kelfield M. W10 6F 65
Kelland Clo. N8 5H 31
Kelland Rd. E13 4J 71
Kellaway Rd. SE3 2B 108
Keller Cres. E12 4B 54
Kellerton Rd. SE13 5G 107
Kellet Houses. WC1 3J 67 (2F 161) (off Tankerton St.)
Kellett Ho. N1 1E 68 (off Colville Est.)
Kellett Rd. SW2 4A 104
Kelling Gdns. Croy 7B 140
Kellino St. SW17 4D 120
Kellner Rd. SE28 3K 91
Kellogg Tower. Gnfd 5J 43
Kellow Ho. SE1 2D 86 (6E 168) (off Tennis St.)
Kell St. SE1 3B 86 (7B 168)
Kelly Av. SE15 7F 87
Kelly Clo. NW10 3K 45
Kelly Clo. Shep 2G 131
Kelly Ct. E14 7C 70 (off Garford St.)
Kelly M. W9 4H 65
Kelly Rd. NW7 6B 14
Kelly St. NW1 6F 49
Kelly Way. Romf 5E 38
Kelman Clo. SW4 2H 103
Kelmore Gro. SE22 4G 105
Kelmscott Clo. E17 1B 34
Kelmscott Gdns. W12 3C 82
Kelmscott Rd. SW11 5C 102
Kelross Pas. N5 4C 50
Kelross Rd. N5 4C 50
Kelsall Clo. SE3 2K 107
Kelsey Ga. Beck 2D 142
Kelsey La. Beck 2C 142 (in two parts)
Kelsey Pk. Av. Beck 2D 142
Kelsey Pk. Rd. Beck 2C 142
Kelsey Sq. Beck 2C 142
Kelsey St. E2 4G 69
Kelsey Way. Beck 3C 142
Kelson Ho. E14 3E 88
Kelso Pl. W8 3K 83
Kelso Rd. Cars 7A 138
Kelston Rd. Ilf 2F 37
Kelvedon Clo. King T 6G 117
Kelvedon Ho. SW8 1J 103
Kelvedon Rd. SW6 7H 83
Kelvedon Way. Wfd G 6J 21
Kelvin Av. N13 6E 16
Kelvin Av. Tedd 6J 115
Kelvinbrook. W Mol 3F 133
Kelvin Clo. Eps 6G 147
Kelvin Ct. SE20 1H 141
Kelvin Ct. W11 7J 65
Kelvin Ct. Iswth 2J 97
Kelvin Cres. Harr 7D 10
Kelvin Dri. Twic 6B 98
Kelvin Gdns. Croy 7J 139
Kelvin Gdns. S'hall 6E 60
Kelvin Gro. SE26 3H 123
Kelvin Gro. Chess 3D 146
Kelvington Clo. Croy 7A 142
Kelvington Rd. SE15 5K 105
Kelvin Rd. N5 4C 50
Kelvin Rd. Well 3A 110
Kember St. N1 7K 49
Kemble Ct. SE15 7E 86 (off Lydney Clo.)
Kemble Dri. Brom 3C 156
Kemble Ho. SW9 3B 104 (off Barrington Rd.)
Kemble Rd. N17 1G 33
Kemble Rd. SE23 1K 123
Kemble Rd. Croy 3B 152
Kemble St. WC2 6K 67 (1G 167)
Kemerton Rd. SE5 3C 104
Kemerton Rd. Beck 2D 142
Kemerton Rd. Croy 7F 141
Kemeys St. E9 5A 52
Kemnal Rd. Chst 4H 127 (in two parts)
Kemp. NW9 1B 28 (off Concourse, The)
Kemp Ct. SW8 7J 85 (off Hartington Rd.)
Kempe Ho. SE1 3D 86 (off Burge St.)
Kempe Rd. NW6 2F 65
Kemp Gdns. Croy 6C 140
Kemp Ho. E2 2K 69 (off Sewardstone Rd.)
Kemp Ho. E6 6E 54
Kemp Ho. W1 7H 67 (2C 166) (off Berwick St.)
Kempis Way. SE22 5E 104
Kemplay Rd. NW3 4B 48
Kemp Rd. Dag 1D 56
Kemps Ct. W1 6H 67 (1C 166) (off Hopkins St.)
Kemps Dri. E14 7C 70
Kemps Dri. N'wd 1H 23
Kempsford Gdns. SW5 5J 83
Kempsford Rd. SE11 4A 86 (4K 173) (Reedworth St.)
Kempsford Rd. SE11 4B 86 (4K 173) (Renfrew Rd.)
Kemps Gdns. SE13 5E 106
Kempshott Rd. SW16 7H 121
Kempson Rd. SW6 1J 101
Kempthorne Rd. SE8 4B 88
Kempton Av. N'holt 6E 42
Kempton Av. Sun 1K 131
Kempton Clo. Eri 6J 93
Kempton Clo. Uxb 4E 40
Kempton Ct. E1 5H 69
Kempton Ct. Sun 1K 131
Kempton Pk. Racecourse. 7A 114
Kempton Rd. E6 1D 72
Kempton Rd. Hamp 2D 132 (in three parts)
Kempton Wlk. Croy 6A 142
Kempt St. SE18 6E 90
Kemsing Clo. Bex 7E 110
Kemsing Clo. Brom 2H 155
Kemsing Clo. T Hth 4C 140
Kemsing Ho. SE1 2D 86 (7F 169) (off Long La.)
Kemsing Rd. SE10 5J 89
Kemsley Ct. W13 1C 80
Kenbrook Ho. W14 3H 83
Kenbury Clo. Uxb 3C 40
Kenbury Gdns. SE5 2C 104
Kenbury Mans. SE5 2C 104 (off Kenbury St.)
Kenbury St. SE5 2C 104
Kenchester Clo. SW8 7J 85
Kencot Way. Eri 2F 93
Kendal. NW1 3F 67 (1K 159) (off Augustus St.)
Kendal Av. N18 4J 17
Kendal Av. W3 4G 63 (in two parts)
Kendal Av. Bark 1J 73
Kendal Clo. SW9 7B 86
Kendal Clo. Felt 1H 113
Kendal Clo. Hay 2G 59
Kendal Clo. Wfd G 2C 20
Kendal Ct. W3 5G 63
Kendale Rd. Brom 5G 125
Kendal Gdns. N18 4J 17
Kendal Gdns. Sutt 2A 150
Kendal Ho. E9 1J 69
Kendal Ho. N1 2K 67 (off Priory Grn. Est.)
Kendal Ho. SE20 2G 141 (off Derwent Rd.)
Kendall Av. Beck 2A 142
Kendall Ct. SW19 6B 120
Kendall Ct. Sidc 3A 128
Kendall Lodge. Brom 1K 143 (off Willow Tree Wlk.)
Kendall Pl. W1 5E 66 (6G 159)
Kendall Rd. SE18 1C 108
Kendall Rd. Beck 2A 142
Kendall Rd. Iswth 2A 98
Kendalmere Clo. N10 1F 31
Kendal Pde. N18 4J 17
Kendal Pl. SW9 7B 86 (off Kendal Clo.)
Kendal Pl. SW15 5H 101
Kendal Rd. NW10 4C 46
Kendal Steps. W2 1D 164
Kendal St. W2 6C 66 (1D 164)
Kender St. SE14 7J 87
Kendoa Rd. SW4 4H 103
Kendon Clo. E11 5K 35
Kendra Hall Rd. S Croy 7B 152
Kendrey Gdns. Twic 7J 97
Kendrick Ct. SE15 1H 105 (off Woods Rd.)
Kendrick M. SW7 4B 84 (3A 170)

Kendrick Pl. SW7 4B 84 (4A 170)
Kenelm Clo. Harr 3A 44
Kenerne Dri. Barn 5B 4
Kenilford Rd. SW12 7F 103
Kenilworth Av. E17 2C 34
Kenilworth Av. SW19 5J 119
Kenilworth Av. Harr 4D 42
Kenilworth Cres. Enf 1K 7
Kenilworth Gdns. SE18 2F 109
Kenilworth Gdns. Hay 5H 59
Kenilworth Gdns. Ilf 2K 55
Kenilworth Gdns. S'hall 3D 60
Kenilworth Rd. E3 2A 70
Kenilworth Rd. NW6 1H 65
Kenilworth Rd. SE20 1K 141
Kenilworth Rd. W5 1E 80
Kenilworth Rd. Ashf 3A 112
Kenilworth Rd. Edgw 3D 12
Kenilworth Rd. Eps 5C 148
Kenilworth Rd. Orp 6G 145
Kenley Av. NW9 1A 28
Kenley Clo. Barn 4H 5
Kenley Clo. Bex 7G 111
Kenley Clo. Chst 3J 145
Kenley Gdns. T Hth 4B 140
Kenley Rd. SW19 2J 137
Kenley Rd. King T 2H 135
Kenley Rd. Twic 6B 98
Kenley Wlk. W11 7G 65
Kenley Wlk. Sutt 4F 149
Kenlor Rd. SW17 5B 120
Kenmare Dri. Mitc 7D 120
Kenmare Gdns. N13 4H 17
Kenmare Rd. T Hth 6A 140
Kenmere Gdns. Wemb 1G 63
Kenmere Rd. Well 2C 110
Kenmont Gdns. NW10 3D 64
Kenmore Av. Harr 4A 26
Kenmore Clo. Rich 7G 81
Kenmore Cres. Hay 3H 59
Kenmore Gdns. Edgw 2H 27
Kenmore Rd. Harr 3D 26
Kenmure Rd. E8 5H 51
Kenmure Yd. E8 5H 51
Kennacraig Clo. E16 1J 89
Kennard Ho. SW11 2E 102
Kennard Rd. E15 7F 53
Kennard Rd. N11 5J 15
Kennard St. E16 1D 90
Kennard St. SW11 1E 102
Kennedy Av. Enf 6D 8
Kennedy Clo. E13 2J 71
Kennedy Clo. Mitc 1E 138
Kennedy Clo. Orp 7H 145
Kennedy Ct. Beck 6B 142
Kennedy Ct. Bush 2C 10
Kennedy Cox Ho. E16 5H 71 (off Burke St.)
Kennedy Ho. SE11 5K 85 (5G 173) (off Vauxhall Wlk.)
Kennedy Path. W7 4K 61
Kennedy Rd. W7 5J 61
Kennedy Rd. Bark 1J 73
Kennedy Wlk. SE17 4D 86 (off Elsted St.)
Kennet Clo. SW11 4B 102
Kennet Ct. W9 5J 65 (off Elmfield Way)
Kenneth Av. Ilf 4F 55
Kenneth Campbell Ho. NW8 4B 66 (3B 158) (off Orchardson St.)
Kenneth Ct. SE11 4A 86 (3K 173)
Kenneth Cres. NW2 5D 46
Kenneth Gdns. Stan 6F 11
Kenneth More Rd. Ilf 3F 55
Kenneth More Theatre. 3F 55
Kennet Ho. NW8 4B 66 (4B 158) (off Church St. Est.)
Kenneth Rd. Romf 7D 38
Kenneth Robbins Ho. N17 7C 18
Kenneth Younger Ho. SW6 6H 83 (off Clem Attlee Ct.)
Kennet Rd. W9 4H 65
Kennet Rd. Iswth 3K 97
Kennet Sq. SW19 1B 138
Kennet St. E1 1G 87
Kennett Ct. W4 7H 81
Kennett Dri. Hay 5C 60
Kennett Wharf La. EC4 7C 68 (3D 168)
Kenninghall. (Junct.) 5D 18
Kenninghall Rd. E5 3G 51
Kenninghall Rd. N18 5D 18
Kenning Ho. N1 1E 68 (off Colville Est.)
Kenning St. SE16 2J 87
Kennings Way. SE11 5A 86 (5K 173)
Kennington. 6A 86 (7K 173)
Kennington Grn. SE11 5A 86 (6J 173)
Kennington Gro. SE11 6K 85 (7H 173)
Kennington La. SE11 5K 85 (6G 173)
Kennington Oval. (Junct.) 6A 86
Kennington Oval. SE11 6K 85 (7H 173)
Kennington Pal. Ct. SE11 5J 173
Kennington Pk. Gdns. SE11 6B 86 (7K 173)
Kennington Pk. Ho. SE11 6K 173
Kennington Pk. Pl. SE11 6A 86 (7K 173)
Kennington Pk. Rd. SE11 6A 86 (7K 173)
Kennington Rd. SE1 & SE11 3A 86 (1J 173)
Kennistoun Ho. NW5 5G 49
Kenny Dri. Cars 7E 150
Kennyland Ct. NW4 6D 28 (off Hendon Way)
Kenny Rd. NW7 6B 14
Kenrick Pl. W1 5E 66 (6G 159)
Kensal Green. 3E 64
Kensal Ho. W10 4F 65 (off Ladbroke Gro.)
Kensal Rise. 2F 65
Kensal Rd. W10 4G 65
Kensal Town. 4G 65
Kensington. 2K 83
Kensington Arc. W8 2K 83 (off Kensington High St.)
Kensington Av. E12 6C 54
Kensington Av. T Hth 1A 140
Kensington Cen. W14 4G 83 (in two parts)
Kensington Chu. Ct. W8 2K 83
Kensington Chu. St. W8 1J 83
Kensington Chu. Wlk. W8 2K 83 (in two parts)
Kensington Clo. N11 6K 15
Kensington Ct. SE16 1K 87 (off King & Queen Wharf)
Kensington Ct. W8 2K 83
Kensington Ct. Gdns. W8 3K 83 (off Kensington Ct. Pl.)
Kensington Ct. M. W8 3K 83 (off Kensington Ct. Pl.)
Kensington Ct. Pl. W8 3K 83
Kensington Dri. Wfd G 2B 36
Kensington Gardens. 1A 84
Kensington Gdns. Ilf 1D 54
Kensington Gdns. King T 3D 134 (in two parts)
Kensington Gdns. Sq. W2 6K 65 (in two parts)
Kensington Ga. W8 3A 84
Kensington Gore. SW7 2A 84 (7A 164)
Kensington Hall Gdns. W14 5H 83
Kensington Heights. W8 1J 83
Kensington Heights. Harr 6K 25 (off Sheepcote Rd.)
Kensington High St. W14 & W8 3H 83
Kensington Ho. W14 2F 83
Kensington Mall. W8 1J 83
Kensington Mans. SW5 5J 83 (off Trebovir Rd., in two parts)
Kensington Palace. 2K 83
Kensington Pal. Gdns. W8 1K 83
Kensington Pk. Gdns. W11 7H 65
Kensington Pk. M. W11 6H 65
Kensington Pk. Rd. W11 6H 65
Kensington Pl. W8 1J 83
Kensington Rd. W8 & SW7 2A 84
Kensington Rd. N'holt 3E 60
Kensington Rd. Romf 6J 39
Kensington Sq. W8 3K 83
Kensington Ter. S Croy 7D 152
Kensington Village. W14 4H 83
Kensington W. W14 4G 83
Kenswick Ct. SE13 5D 106
Kensworth Ho. EC1 3D 68 (2F 163) (off Cranwood St.)
Kent Av. W13 5B 62
Kent Av. Dag 4G 75
Kent Av. Well 5K 109
Kent Clo. Mitc 4J 139
Kent Ct. E2 2F 69
Kent Ct. NW9 2A 28
Kent Dri. Cockf 4K 5
Kent Dri. Tedd 5J 115
Kentford Way. N'holt 1C 60
Kent Gdns. W13 5B 62
Kent Gdns. Ruis 6J 23
Kent Ga. Way. Croy 6B 154
Kent Ho. SE1 5F 87
Kent Ho. SW1 5H 85 (5C 172) (off Aylesford St.)
Kent Ho. W4 5A 82 (off Devonshire St.)
Kent Ho. La. Beck 6A 124
Kent Ho. Rd. SE26 & Beck 5A 124
Kentish Bldgs. SE1 2D 86 (5E 168)
Kentish Rd. Belv 4G 93
Kentish Town. 5F 49
Kentish Town Ind. Est. NW5 5F 49
Kentish Town Rd. NW1 & NW5 7F 49
Kentish Way. Brom 2J 143
Kentlea Rd. SE28 2J 91
Kentmere Ho. SE15 6J 87
Kentmere Mans. W5 4B 62
Kentmere Rd. SE18 4J 91
Kenton. 5C 26
Kenton Av. Harr 7K 25
Kenton Av. S'hall 7E 60
Kenton Av. Sun 2B 132
Kenton Ct. SE26 4A 124 (off Adamsrill Rd.)
Kenton Ct. W14 3H 83
Kenton Ct. Kent 6B 26
Kenton Ct. Twic 6D 98
Kentone Ct. SE25 4H 141
Kenton Gdns. Harr 5C 26
Kenton Ho. E1 4J 69 (off Mantus Clo.)
Kenton La. Harr 6E 10
Kenton Pk. Av. Harr 4D 26
Kenton Pk. Clo. Harr 4C 26
Kenton Pk. Cres. Harr 4D 26
Kenton Pk. Mans. Kent 5C 26 (off Kenton Rd.)
Kenton Pk. Pde. Harr 5C 26
Kenton Pk. Rd. Harr 4C 26
Kenton Rd. E9 6K 51
Kenton Rd. Harr 7K 25
Kenton St. WC1 4J 67 (3E 160)
Kenton Way. Hay 3G 59
Kent Pk. Ind. Est. SE15 6H 87
Kent Pas. NW1 4D 66 (3E 158)
Kent Rd. N21 1J 17
Kent Rd. W4 3J 81
Kent Rd. Dag 5H 57
Kent Rd. E Mol 4G 133
Kent Rd. King T 3D 134
Kent Rd. Rich 7G 81
Kent Rd. W Wick 1D 154
Kent's Pas. Hamp 1D 132
Kent St. E2 2F 69
Kent St. E13 3K 71
Kent Ter. NW1 3C 66 (2D 158)
Kent Vw. Gdns. Ilf 2J 55
Kent Wlk. SW9 4B 104
Kent Way. Surb 3E 146
Kentwell Clo. SE4 4A 106
Kent Wharf. SE8 7D 88 (off Creekside)
Kentwode Grn. SW13 7C 82
Kent Yd. SW7 2C 84 (7D 164)
Kenver Av. N12 6G 15
Kenward Rd. SE9 5A 108
Kenway. Romf 2J 39
Ken Way. Wemb 3J 45
Kenway Rd. SW5 4K 83
Ken Wilson Ho. E2 2G 69 (off Pritchards Rd.)
Kenwood Av. N14 5C 6
Kenwood Clo. NW3 1B 48
Kenwood Clo. W Dray 6C 76
Kenwood Dri. Beck 3E 142
Kenwood Gdns. E18 3K 35
Kenwood Gdns. Ilf 4E 36
Kenwood House. 1C 48
Kenwood Ho. SW9 4B 104
Kenwood Rd. N6 6D 30
Kenwood Rd. N9 1B 18
Kenworthy Rd. E9 5A 52
Kenwrick Ho. N1 1K 67 (off Barnsbury Est.)
Kenwyn Dri. NW2 2A 46
Kenwyn Lodge. N2 4D 30
Kenwyn Rd. SW4 4H 103
Kenwyn Rd. SW20 1E 136
Kenya Rd. SE7 7B 90
Kenyngton Ct. Sun 5J 113
Kenyngton Dri. Sun 5J 113
Kenyngton Pl. Harr 5C 26
Kenyon Mans. W14 6G 83 (off Queen's Club Gdns.)
Kenyon St. SW6 1F 101
Keogh Rd. E15 6G 53
Kepler Ho. SE10 5H 89 (off Armitage Rd.)
Kepler Rd. SW4 4J 103
Keppel Ho. SE8 5B 88
Keppel Rd. E6 7D 54
Keppel Rd. Dag 4E 56
Keppel Row. SE1 1C 86 (5C 168)
Keppel St. WC1 5H 67 (5D 160)
Kerbela St. E2 4G 69 (3K 163)
Kerbey St. E14 6D 70
Kerfield Cres. SE5 1D 104
Kerfield Pl. SE5 1D 104
Kerridge Ct. N1 6E 50 (off Balls Pond Rd.)
Kerrington Ct. W12 2E 82 (off Uxbridge Rd.)
Kerrison Pl. W5 1D 80
Kerrison Rd. E15 1F 71
Kerrison Rd. SW11 3C 102
Kerrison Rd. W5 1D 80
Kerrison Vs. W5 1D 80
Kerry. N7 6J 49
Kerry Av. Stan 4H 11
Kerry Clo. E16 6K 71
Kerry Clo. N13 2E 16
Kerry Ct. Stan 4J 11
Kerry Ho. E1 6J 69 (off Sidney St.)
Kerry Path. SE14 6B 88
Kerry Rd. SE14 6B 88
Kersey Gdns. SE9 4C 126
Kersfield Rd. SW15 6F 101
Kershaw Clo. SW18 6B 102
Kershaw Rd. Dag 3G 57
Kersley M. SW11 1D 102
Kersley Rd. N16 2E 50
Kersley St. SW11 2D 102
Kerstin Clo. Hay 7H 59
Kerswell Clo. N15 5E 32
Kerwick Clo. N7 7J 49
Keslake Mans. NW10 2F 65 (off Station Ter.)
Keslake Rd. NW6 2F 65
Kessock Clo. N17 5H 33
Kestlake Rd. Bex 6C 110
Keston. 5A 156
Keston Av. Kes 5A 156
Keston Clo. N18 3J 17
Keston Clo. Well 7C 92
Keston Ct. Bex 7F 111
Keston Ct. Surb 5F 135 (off Cranes Pk.)
Keston Gdns. Kes 4A 156
Keston Ho. SE17 5E 86 (off Kinglake St.)
Keston Mark. 4C 156
Keston Mark. (Junct.) 4B 156
Keston Pk. Clo. Kes 3D 156
Keston Rd. N17 3D 32
Keston Rd. SE15 3G 105
Keston Rd. T Hth 6A 140
Kestrel Av. E6 5C 72
Kestrel Av. SE24 5B 104
Kestrel Clo. NW9 2A 28
Kestrel Clo. NW10 5K 45
Kestrel Clo. King T 4D 116
Kestrel Ct. E17 2K 33
Kestrel Ct. Ruis 2F 41
Kestrel Ct. S Croy 6C 152
Kestrel Ho. EC1 3C 68 (1C 162) (off Pickard St.)
Kestrel Pl. SE14 6A 88
Kestrel Way. Hay 2F 77
Kestrel Way. New Ad 7F 155
Keswick Av. SW15 5A 118
Keswick Av. SW19 2J 137
Keswick Av. Shep 3G 131
Keswick Clo. Sutt 4A 150
Keswick Ct. SE6 1H 125
Keswick Ct. Brom 4H 143
Keswick Gdns. Ilf 4C 36
Keswick Gdns. Ruis 6F 23
Keswick Gdns. Wemb 4E 44
Keswick Ho. SE5 2C 104
Keswick M. W5 1E 80
Keswick Rd. SW15 5G 101
Keswick Rd. Bexh 1G 111
Keswick Rd. Orp 7K 145
Keswick Rd. Twic 6G 97
Keswick Rd. W Wick 2G 155
Kettering St. SW16 6G 121
Kett Gdns. SW2 5K 103
Kettlebaston Rd. E10 1B 52
Kettleby Ho. SW9 3B 104 (off Barrington Rd.)
Kettlewell Clo. N11 6K 15
Ketton Ho. W10 4E 64 (off Sutton Way)
Kevan Ct. E17 4C 34
Kevan Ho. SE5 7C 86
Kevelioc Rd. N17 1C 32
Kevin Clo. Houn 2B 96
Kevington Clo. Orp 4K 145
Kevington Dri. Chst & Orp 4J 145
Kew. 7G 81

Kew Bridge. (Junct.) 6G 81
Kew Bri. Bren 6F 81
Kew Bri. Arches. Rich 6G 81
Kew Bri. Ct. W4 5G 81
Kew Bri. Distribution Cen. Bren 5F 81
Kew Bri. Rd. Bren 6F 81
Kew Bridge Steam Mus. 5F 81
Kew Cres. Sutt 3G 149
Kew Foot Rd. Rich 4E 98
Kew Gardens Plants & People Exhibition. 7F 81
Kew Gdns. Rd. Rich 7F 81
Kew Green. (Junct.) 7F 81
Kew Grn. Rich 6F 81
Kew Mdw. Path. Rich 2J 99 (Thames Bank)
Kew Mdw. Path. Rich 1H 99 (W. Park Av.)
Kew Palace. 7E 80
Kew Retail Pk. Rich 1H 99
Kew Rd. Rich 6G 81
Keybridge Ho. SW8 6J 85 (7F 173) (off Miles St.)
Key Clo. E1 4J 69
Keyes Ho. SW1 5H 85 (6C 172) (off Dolphin Sq.)
Keyes Rd. NW2 5F 47
Key Ho. SE11 6A 86 (7K 173)
Keymer Rd. SW2 2K 121
Keynes Clo. N2 4D 30
Keynsham Av. Wfd G 4B 20
Keynsham Gdns. SE9 5C 108
Keynsham Rd. SE9 5B 108
Keynsham Rd. Mord 1K 149
Keynsham Wlk. Mord 1K 149
Keys Ct. Croy 3D 152 (off Beech Ho. Rd.)
Keyse Rd. SE1 3F 87
Keysham Av. Houn 1J 95
Keystone Cres. N1 2J 67 (1F 161)
Keywood Dri. Sun 6J 113
Keyworth Clo. E5 4A 52
Keyworth Pl. SE1 7B 168
Keyworth St. SE1 3B 86 (7B 168)
Kezia St. SE8 5A 88
Khama Rd. SW17 4C 120
Khartoum Rd. E13 3K 71
Khartoum Rd. SW17 4B 120
Khartoum Rd. Ilf 5F 55
Khyber Rd. SW11 2C 102
Kibworth St. SW8 7K 85
Kidbrooke. 2K 107
Kidbrooke Est. SE3 3A 108
Kidbrooke Gdns. SE3 2J 107
Kidbrooke Gro. SE3 1J 107
Kidbrooke La. SE9 4C 108
Kidbrooke Pk. Clo. SE3 1K 107
Kidbrooke Pk. Rd. SE3 1K 107
Kidbrooke Way. SE3 2K 107
Kidderminster Pl. Croy 1B 152
Kidderminster Rd. Croy 1B 152
Kidderpore Av. NW3 4J 47
Kidderpore Gdns. NW3 4J 47
Kidd Pl. SE7 5C 90
Kidlington Way. NW9 2K 27
Kierbeck Bus. Complex. E16 2K 89
Kiffen St. EC2 4D 68 (3F 163)
Kilberry Clo. Iswth 1H 97
Kilbrennan Ho. E14 6E 70 (off Findhorn St.)
Kilburn. 1J 65
Kilburn Bri. NW6 1J 65
Kilburn Ga. NW6 2K 65
Kilburn High Rd. NW6 7H 47
Kilburn Ho. NW6 2H 65 (off Malvern Pl.)
Kilburn La. W10 & W9 3F 65
Kilburn Pk. Rd. NW6 3J 65
Kilburn Pl. NW6 1J 65
Kilburn Priory. NW6 1K 65
Kilburns Mill Clo. Wall 2F 151
Kilburn Sq. NW6 1J 65
Kilburn Va. NW6 1K 65
Kilburn Va. Est. NW6 1K 65 (off Kilburn Va.)
Kildare Clo. Ruis 1A 42
Kildare Gdns. W2 6J 65
Kildare Rd. E16 5J 71
Kildare Ter. W2 6J 65
Kildare Wlk. E14 6C 70
Kildoran Rd. SW2 5J 103
Kildowan Rd. Ilf 1A 56
Kilgour Rd. SE23 6A 106
Kilkie St. SW6 2A 102
Killarney Rd. SW18 6A 102
Killearn Rd. SE6 1F 125
Killester Gdns. Wor Pk 4D 148
Killick Ho. Sutt 4K 149
Killick St. N1 2K 67 (1G 161)
Killieser Av. SW2 2J 121
Killigarth Ct. Sidc 4A 128
Killip Clo. E16 6H 71
Killoran Ho. E14 3E 88 (off Galbraith St.)
Killowen Av. N'holt 5G 43
Killowen Rd. E9 6K 51
Killyon Rd. SW8 2G 103
Killyon Ter. SW8 2G 103
Kilmaine Rd. SW6 7G 83
Kilmarnock Gdns. Dag 3C 56
Kilmarsh Rd. W6 4E 82
Kilmartin Av. SW16 3A 140
Kilmartin Rd. Ilf 2A 56
Kilmington Rd. SW13 6C 82
Kilmiston Av. Shep 6E 130
Kilmore Ho. E14 6D 70 (off Vesey Path)
Kilmorey Gdns. Twic 5B 98
Kilmorey Rd. Twic 4B 98
Kilmorie Rd. SE23 1A 124
Kilmuir Ho. SW1 4E 84 (4H 171) (off Bury St.)
Kiln Clo. Hay 6F 77
Kiln Ct. E14 7B 70 (off Newell St.)
Kilner Ho. E16 5K 71 (off Freemasons Rd.)
Kilner Ho. SE11 7J 173
Kilner St. E14 5C 70
Kiln M. SW17 5B 120
Kiln Pl. NW5 5E 48
Kilnside. Clay 7A 146
Kilpatrick Way. Hay 5C 60
Kilravock St. W10 3G 65
Kilronan. W3 6K 63
Kilross Rd. Felt 1F 113
Kilsby Wlk. Dag 6B 56
Kilsha Rd. W on T 6A 132
Kimbell Gdns. SW6 1G 101
Kimbell Pl. SE3 4A 108
Kimberley Av. E6 2C 72
Kimberley Av. SE15 2H 105
Kimberley Av. Ilf 7H 37
Kimberley Av. Romf 6J 39
Kimberley Dri. Sidc 2D 128
Kimberley Gdns. N4 5B 32
Kimberley Gdns. Enf 3A 8
Kimberley Ga. Brom 7G 125
Kimberley Ho. E14 3E 88 (off Galbraith St.)
Kimberley Ind. Est. E17 1B 34
Kimberley Rd. E4 1B 20
Kimberley Rd. E11 2F 53
Kimberley Rd. E16 4H 71
Kimberley Rd. E17 1A 34
Kimberley Rd. N17 2G 33
Kimberley Rd. N18 6C 18
Kimberley Rd. NW6 1G 65
Kimberley Rd. SW9 2J 103
Kimberley Rd. Beck 2K 141
Kimberley Rd. Croy 6B 140
Kimberley Wlk. W on T 7K 131
Kimberley Way. E4 1B 20
Kimber Rd. SW18 7J 101
Kimble Cres. Bush 1B 10
Kimble Ho. NW8 3D 158
Kimble Rd. SW19 6B 120
Kimbolton Clo. SE12 6H 107
Kimbolton Ct. SW3 4C 84 (4C 170) (off Fulham Rd.)
Kimbolton Row. SW3 4C 84 (4C 170) (off Fulham Rd.)
Kimmeridge Gdns. SE9 4C 126
Kimmeridge Rd. SE9 4C 126
Kimpton Ind. Est. Sutt 2H 149
Kimpton Rd. SE5 1D 104
Kimpton Rd. Sutt 2H 149
Kinburn St. SE16 2K 87
Kincaid Rd. SE15 7H 87
Kincardine Gdns. W9 4J 65 (off Harrow Rd.)
Kincha Lodge. King T 1F 135 (off Elm Rd.)
Kinch Gro. Wemb 7F 27
Kinder Clo. SE28 7D 74
Kinder Ho. N1 2D 68 (off Cranston Est.)
Kindersley Ho. E1 6G 69 (off Pinchin St.)
Kinder St. E1 6H 69
Kinefold Ho. N7 6J 49
Kinfauns Rd. SW2 2A 122
Kinfauns Rd. Ilf 1A 56
King Alfred Av. SE6 4C 124 (in two parts)
King & Queen Clo. SE9 4C 126
King & Queen St. SE17 5C 86
King & Queen Wharf. SE16 7K 69
King Arthur Clo. SE15 7J 87
King Charles Ct. SE17 6B 86 (off Royal Rd.)
King Charles Cres. Surb 7F 135
King Charles Ho. SW6 7K 83 (off Wandon Rd.)
King Charles Rd. Surb 5F 135
King Charles's Ct. SE10 6E 88 (off Park Row)
King Charles St. SW1 2H 85 (6D 166)
King Charles Ter. E1 7H 69 (off Sovereign Clo.)
King Charles Wlk. SW19 1G 119
King Ct. E10 7D 34
Kingcup Clo. Croy 7K 141
King David La. E1 7J 69
Kingdon Ho. E14 3E 88 (off Galbraith St.)
Kingdon Rd. NW6 6J 47
King Edward Building. EC1 6B 68 (7C 162)
King Edward Dri. Chess 3E 146
King Edward Mans. E8 1H 69 (off Mare St.)
King Edward M. SW13 1C 100
King Edward Rd. E10 1E 52
King Edward Rd. E17 3A 34
King Edward Rd. Barn 4D 4
King Edward's Gdns. W3 1G 81
King Edwards Gro. Tedd 6B 116
King Edwards Mans. SW6 7J 83 (off Fulham Rd.)
King Edward's Pl. W3 1G 81
King Edward's Rd. E8 & E9 1H 69
King Edward's Rd. N9 7C 8
King Edwards Rd. Bark 1H 73
King Edward's Rd. Enf 4E 8
King Edward's Rd. Ruis 1F 41
King Edward St. EC1 6C 68 (7C 162)
King Edward III M. SE16 2H 87
King Edward Wlk. SE1 3A 86 (1K 173)
Kingfield Rd. W5 4D 62
Kingfield St. E14 4E 88
Kingfisher Av. E11 6K 35
Kingfisher Clo. SE28 7C 74
Kingfisher Clo. Har W 7E 10
Kingfisher Clo. N'wd 1D 22
Kingfisher Ct. E14 2E 88 (off River Barge Clo.)
Kingfisher Ct. SW19 2F 119
Kingfisher Ct. Enf 1E 6
Kingfisher Ct. Houn 5F 97
Kingfisher Dri. Rich 4B 116
Kingfisher M. SE13 4C 106
Kingfisher Pl. N22 2K 31
Kingfisher Sq. SE8 6B 88 (off Clyde St.)
Kingfisher St. E6 5C 72
Kingfisher Wlk. NW9 2A 28
Kingfisher Way. NW10 6K 45
Kingfisher Way. Beck 5K 141
King Frederick IX Tower. SE16 3B 88
King Gdns. Croy 5B 152
King George Av. E16 6A 72
King George Av. Ilf 5H 37
King George Clo. Romf 3J 39
King George Clo. Sun 5G 113
King George's Dri. S'hall 5D 60
King George VI Av. Mitc 4D 138
King George Sq. Rich 6F 99
King George's Trad. Est. Chess 4G 147
King George St. SE10 7E 88
Kingham Clo. SW18 7A 102
Kingham Clo. W11 2G 83 (off Holland Pk. Av.)
King Harolds Way. Bexh & Belv 7D 92
King Henry's Dri. New Ad 7D 154
King Henry's Reach. W6 6E 82
King Henry's Rd. NW3 7C 48
King Henry's Rd. King T 3H 135
King Henry St. N16 5E 50
King Henry's Wlk. N1 6E 50
King Henry Ter. E1 7H 69 (off Sovereign Clo.)
Kinghorn St. EC1 5C 68 (6C 162)
King Ho. W12 6D 64
King James Ct. SE1 7B 168
King James St. SE1 2B 86 (7B 168)
King John Ct. EC2 4E 68 (3H 163)
King John St. E1 5K 69
King John's Wlk. SE9 7C 108 (Middle Pk. Av., in two parts)
King John's Wlk. SE9 1B 126 (Mottingham La.)
Kinglake Est. SE17 5E 86
Kinglake St. SE17 5E 86 (in two parts)
Kingly Ct. W1 2B 166
Kingly St. W1 6G 67 (1A 166)
Kingsand Rd. SE12 2J 125
Kings Arbour. S'hall 5C 78
King's Arms All. Bren 6D 80
Kings Arms Ct. E1 5G 69 (6K 163)
Kings Arms Yd. EC2 6D 68 (7E 162)
Kingsash Dri. Hay 4C 60
King's Av. N10 3E 30
Kings Av. N21 1G 17
Kings Av. SW12 & SW4 1H 121
Kings Av. W5 6D 62
Kings Av. Brom 6H 125
King's Av. Buck H 2G 21
King's Av. Cars 7C 150
King's Av. Gnfd 5F 61
Kings Av. Houn 1F 97
Kings Av. N Mald 4A 136
Kings Av. Romf 6F 39
King's Av. Sun 5H 113
King's Av. Wfd G 6E 20
King's Bench St. SE1 2B 86 (6B 168)
King's Bench Wlk. EC4 6A 68 (1K 167)
Kingsbridge Av. W5 2F 81
Kingsbridge Ct. E14 3C 88 (off Dockers Tanner Rd.)
Kingsbridge Ct. NW1 7F 49 (off Castlehaven Rd.)
Kingsbridge Cres. S'hall 5D 60
Kingsbridge Rd. W10 6E 64
Kingsbridge Rd. Bark 2H 73
Kingsbridge Rd. Mord 6F 137
Kingsbridge Rd. S'hall 4D 78
Kingsbridge Rd. W on T 7K 131
Kingsbridge Way. Hay 3G 59
Kingsbury. 7K 27
Kingsbury Circ. NW9 5G 27
Kingsbury Green. 5J 27
Kingsbury Rd. N1 6E 50
Kingsbury Rd. NW9 5G 27
Kingsbury Ter. N1 6E 50
Kingsbury Trad. Est. NW9 6K 27
Kings Chase. E Mol 3G 133
Kings Chase Vw. Ridg 2F 7
Kingsclere Clo. SW15 7C 100
Kingsclere Ct. N12 5H 15
Kingsclere Pl. Enf 2H 7
Kingscliffe Gdns. SW19 1H 119
Kings Clo. E10 7D 34
King's Clo. NW4 4F 29
King's Clo. Dart 4K 111
Kings Clo. Stai 7A 112
Kings Clo. Th Dit 6A 134
Kings Clo. W on T 7K 131
Kings College Ct. NW3 7C 48
King's College London. 5B 84 (6B 170) (Chelsea Campus)
King's College London. 7K 67 (2H 167) (Strand Campus)
King's College London. 1A 86 (5J 167) (Waterloo Campus)
King's College London Dental Institute. 2D 104
King's College Rd. NW3 7C 48
Kings College Rd. Ruis 6H 23
King's College School of Medicine & Dentistry. 2C 104
Kingscote Rd. W4 3K 81
Kingscote Rd. Croy 7H 141
Kingscote Rd. N Mald 3K 135
Kingscote St. EC4 7B 68 (2A 168)
King's Ct. E13 1K 71
Kings Ct. N7 7K 49 (off Caledonian Rd.)
Kings Ct. NW8 1D 66 (off Prince Albert Rd.)
King's Ct. SE1 2B 86 (6B 168)
Kings Ct. W6 4C 82
Kings Ct. Buck H 2G 21
Kings Ct. N. SW3 5C 84 (6C 170)
Kingscourt Rd. SW16 3H 121
Kings Ct. S. SW3 6C 170
King's Cres. N4 3C 50
Kings Cres. Est. N4 2C 50
Kingscroft. SW4 6J 103
Kingscroft Rd. NW2 6H 47
King's Cross. 2J 67
King's Cross. (Junct.) 2J 67 (1E 160)
King's Cross Bri. N1 1F 161
King's Cross Rd. WC1 3K 67 (1G 161)
Kingsdale Gdns. W11 1F 83
Kingsdale Rd. SE18 7K 91
Kingsdale Rd. SE20 7K 123
Kingsdown Av. W3 7A 64

Kingsdown Av. W13 2B 80
Kingsdown Av. S Croy 7C 152
Kingsdown Clo. SE16 5H 87 (off Masters Dri.)
Kingsdown Clo. W10 6F 65
Kingsdowne Rd. Surb 7E 134
Kingsdown Ho. E8 5G 51
Kingsdown Rd. E11 3G 53
Kingsdown Rd. N19 2J 49
Kingsdown Rd. Sutt 5G 149
Kingsdown Way. Brom 7J 143
King's Dri. Edgw 4A 12
Kings Dri. Surb 7G 135
Kings Dri. Tedd 5H 115
Kings Dri. Th Dit 7B 134
Kings Dri. Wemb 2H 45
Kingsend. Ruis 1F 41
Kingsend Ct. Ruis 1G 41
Kings Farm. E17 1D 34
Kings Farm Av. Rich 4G 99
Kingsfield Av. Harr 4F 25
Kingsfield Ho. SE9 3B 126
Kingsfield Rd. Harr 7H 25
Kingsfield Ter. Harr 1H 43
Kingsford St. NW5 5D 48
Kingsford Way. E6 5D 72
King's Gdns. NW6 7J 47
Kings Gdns. Ilf 1H 55
Kings Gth. M. SE23 2J 123
Kingsgate. Wemb 3J 45
Kingsgate Av. N3 3J 29
Kingsgate Bus. Cen. King T 1E 134 (off Kingsgate Rd.)
Kingsgate Clo. Bexh 1E 110
Kingsgate Est. N1 6E 50
Kingsgate Ho. SW9 1A 104
Kingsgate Mans. WC1 5K 67 (6G 161) (off Red Lion Sq.)
Kingsgate Pde. SW1 2B 172
Kingsgate Pl. NW6 7J 47
Kingsgate Rd. NW6 7J 47
Kingsgate Rd. King T 1E 134
Kings Grange. Ruis 1H 41
Kingsground. SE9 7B 108
King's Gro. SE15 7H 87 (in two parts)
Kingshall M. SE13 3E 106
Kings Hall Rd. Beck 7A 124
Kings Head Hill. E4 7J 9
Kings Head Pas. SW4 4H 103 (off Clapham Pk. Rd.)
Kings Head Theatre. 1B 68 (off Upper St.)
King's Head Yd. SE1 1D 86 (5E 168)
King's Highway. SE18 6J 91
Kingshill. SE17 4C 86
Kingshill Av. Harr 4B 26
Kingshill Av. Hay & N'holt 3G 59
Kingshill Av. Wor Pk 7C 136
Kingshill Ct. Barn 4B 4
Kingshill Dri. Harr 2B 26
Kingshold Rd. E9 7J 51
Kingsholm Gdns. SE9 4B 108
Kings Ho. SW8 7J 85 (off S. Lambeth Rd.)
Kingshurst Rd. SE12 7J 107
Kings Keep. SW15 5F 101
Kings Keep. Brom 3G 143
Kings Keep. King T 4E 134
Kingsland. 6E 50
Kingsland. NW8 1C 66
Kingsland Grn. E8 6E 50
Kingsland High St. E8 6F 51
Kingsland Pas. E8 6E 50
Kingsland Rd. E2 & E8 3E 68 (2H 163)
Kingsland Rd. E13 3A 72
Kingsland Shop. Cen. E8 6F 51
Kings La. Sutt 6B 150
Kingslawn Clo. SW15 5D 100
Kingsleigh Pl. Mitc 3D 138
Kingsleigh Wlk. Brom 4H 143 (off Stamford Dri.)
Kingsley Av. W13 5A 62
Kingsley Av. Houn 2G 97
Kingsley Av. S'hall 7E 60
Kingsley Av. Sutt 4B 150
Kingsley Clo. N2 5A 30
Kingsley Clo. Dag 4H 57
Kingsley Ct. NW2 6D 46
Kingsley Ct. Bexh 5G 111
Kingsley Ct. Edgw 3C 12
Kingsley Ct. Sutt 7K 149
Kingsley Ct. Wor Pk 2B 148 (off Avenue, The)
Kingsley Dri. Wor Pk 2B 148
Kingsley Flats. SE1 4E 86 (off Old Kent Rd.)
Kingsley Gdns. E4 5H 19
Kingsley Ho. SW3 6B 84 (off Beaufort St.)
Kingsley Mans. W14 6G 83 (off Greyhound Rd.)
Kingsley M. E1 7H 69
Kingsley M. W8 3K 83
Kingsley M. Chst 6F 127
Kingsley Pl. N6 7E 30
Kingsley Rd. E7 7J 53
Kingsley Rd. E17 2E 34
Kingsley Rd. N13 4F 17
Kingsley Rd. NW6 1H 65
Kingsley Rd. SW19 5K 119
Kingsley Rd. Croy 1A 152
Kingsley Rd. Harr 4G 43
Kingsley Rd. Houn 1F 97
Kingsley Rd. Ilf 1G 37
Kingsley Rd. Pinn 4D 24
Kingsley St. SW11 3D 102
Kingsley Way. N2 6A 30
Kingsley Wood Dri. SE9 3D 126
Kingslyn Cres. SE19 1E 140
Kings Mall. W6 4E 82
Kingsman Pde. SE18 3D 90
Kingsman St. SE18 3D 90
Kingsmead. Barn 4D 4
Kings Mead. Rich 6F 99
Kingsmead Av. N9 1C 18
Kingsmead Av. NW9 7K 27
Kingsmead Av. Mitc 3G 139
Kingsmead Av. Sun 2A 132
Kingsmead Av. Surb 2G 147
Kingsmead Av. Wor Pk 2D 148
Kingsmead Clo. Eps 7K 147
Kingsmead Clo. Sidc 2A 128
Kingsmead Clo. Tedd 6B 116
Kingsmead Cotts. Brom 1C 156
Kingsmead Ct. N6 7H 31
Kingsmead Dri. N'holt 7D 42
Kingsmead Ho. E9 4A 52
Kingsmead Rd. SW2 2A 122
King's Mead Way. E9 4A 52
Kingsmere Clo. SW15 3F 101
Kingsmere Pk. NW9 1H 45
Kingsmere Pl. N16 1D 50
Kingsmere Rd. SW19 2F 119
King's M. SW4 5J 103
King's M. WC1 4K 67 (4H 161)
Kingsmill. NW8 2B 66 (off Kingsmill Ter.)
Kingsmill Bus. Pk. King T 3F 135
Kingsmill Gdns. Dag 5F 57
Kingsmill Ho. SW3 5C 84 (5D 170) (off Marlborough St.)
Kingsmill Rd. Dag 5F 57
Kingsmill Ter. NW8 2B 66
Kingsnorth Ho. W10 6F 65
Kingsnympton Pk. King T 7H 117
King's Orchard. SE9 6C 108
King's Paddock. Hamp 1G 133
Kings Pde. N17 3F 33
Kings Pde. NW10 1E 64
Kings Pde. W12 3C 82
King's Pde. Cars 3D 150 (off Wrythe La.)
King's Pde. Edgw 5B 12 (off Edgwarebury La.)
Kingspark Ct. E18 3J 35
Kings Pas. E11 7G 35
Kings Pas. King T (KT1) 2D 134
King's Pas. King T (KT2) 1D 134
King's Pl. SE1 2C 86 (7C 168)
King's Pl. W4 5J 81
Kings Pl. Buck H 2F 21
King Sq. EC1 3C 68 (2C 162)
King's Quay. SW10 1A 102 (off Chelsea Harbour)
Kings Reach Tower. SE1 4K 167
Kings Ride Ga. Rich 4G 99
Kingsridge. SW19 2G 119
Kings Rd. E4 1A 20
King's Rd. E6 1A 72
Kings Rd. E11 7G 35
King's Rd. N17 1F 33
Kings Rd. N18 5B 18
Kings Rd. N22 1K 31
Kings Rd. NW10 7D 46
Kings Rd. SE25 3G 141
King's Rd. SW6 & SW10,SW3 7K 83 (7A 170)
Kings Rd. SW14 3K 99
Kings Rd. SW19 6J 119
Kings Rd. W5 5D 62
Kings Rd. Bark 7G 55
Kings Rd. Barn 3A 4
Kings Rd. Felt 1A 114
Kings Rd. Harr 2D 42
King's Rd. King T 1E 134
Kings Rd. Mitc 3E 138
Kings Rd. Rich 6F 99
King's Rd. Surb 1C 146
King's Rd. Tedd 5H 115
Kings Rd. Twic 6B 98
Kings Rd. W on T 7K 131
King's Rd. W Dray 2B 76
Kings Rd. Bungalows. S Harr 4D 42
King's Scholars' Pas. SW1 2A 172
King Stairs Clo. SE16 2H 87
King's Ter. NW1 1G 67
King's Ter. Iswth 4A 98
Kingsthorpe Rd. SE26 4K 123
Kingston Av. Felt 6G 95
Kingston Av. Sutt 3G 149
Kingston Av. W Dray 7B 58 (in three parts)
Kingston Bri. King T 2D 134
Kingston Bus. Cen. Chess 3E 146
Kingston By-Pass. SW15 & SW20 4A 118
Kingston By-Pass. N Mald 5A 136
Kingston By-Pass. Surb 3D 146
Kingston By-Pass Rd. Esh & Surb 3A 146
Kingston Clo. N'holt 1D 60
Kingston Clo. Romf 3E 38 (in two parts)
Kingston Clo. Tedd 6B 116
Kingston Cres. Beck 1B 142
Kingston Gdns. Croy 3J 151
Kingston Hall Rd. King T 3D 134
Kingston Hill. King T 1G 135
Kingston Hill Av. Romf 3E 38
Kingston Hill Pl. King T 4J 117
Kingston Ho. NW6 7G 47
Kingston Ho. King T 4D 134 (off Surbiton Rd.)
Kingston Ho. E. SW7 2C 84 (7C 164) (off Prince's Ga.)
Kingston Ho. Est. Surb 6B 134
Kingston Ho. N. SW7 2C 84 (7C 164) (off Prince's Ga.)
Kingston Ho. S. SW7 2C 84 (7C 164) (off Ennismore Gdns.)
Kingstonian F.C. 3G 135
Kingston La. Tedd 5A 116
Kingston La. Uxb 3A 58
Kingston La. W Dray 2B 76
Kingston Mus. 2E 134
Kingston Mus. & Art Gallery. 2E 134
Kingston Pl. Harr 7E 10
Kingston Rd. N9 2B 18
Kingston Rd. SW15 & SW19 2C 118
Kingston Rd. SW20 & SW19 2F 137
Kingston Rd. Barn 5G 5
Kingston Rd. Eps 7B 148
Kingston Rd. Ilf 4F 55
Kingston Rd. King T & N Mald 3H 135
Kingston Rd. S'hall 2D 78
Kingston Rd. Stai & Ashf 6A 112 (in two parts)
Kingston Rd. Surb & Eps 2H 147
Kingston Rd. Tedd 5B 116
Kingston Sq. SE19 5D 122
Kingston University. 3E 134 (Grange Rd.)
Kingston University. 5K 117 (Kingston Hill)
Kingston University. 4E 134 (Penrhyn Rd.)
Kingston Upon Thames. 2D 134
Kingston upon Thames Crematorium. King T 3G 135
Kingston upon Thames Library, Art Gallery and Mus. 2E 134
Kingston Vale. 4A 118
Kingston Va. SW15 4K 117
Kingstown St. NW1 1E 66 (in two parts)
King St. E13 4J 71
King St. EC2 6C 68 (1D 168)
King St. N2 3B 30
King St. N17 1F 33
King St. SW1 1G 85 (5B 166)
King St. W3 1J 81
King St. W6 4C 82
King St. WC2 7J 67 (2E 166)
King St. Rich 5D 98
King St. S'hall 3C 78
King St. Twic 1A 116
King St. Cloisters. W6 4D 82 (off King St.)
King St. Pde. Twic 1A 116 (off King St.)
Kings Wlk. Shop. Cen. SW3 5D 84 (5E 170)
Kingswater Pl. SW11 7C 84
Kingsway. N12 6F 15
Kingsway. SW14 3H 99
Kingsway. WC2 6K 67 (7G 161)
King's Way. Croy 5K 151
Kingsway. Enf 5C 8
Kings Way. Harr 4J 25
Kingsway. Hay 5E 58
Kingsway. N Mald 4E 136
Kingsway. Orp 5H 145
Kingsway. Stai 1A 112
Kingsway. Wemb 4E 44
Kingsway. W Wick 3G 155
Kings Way. Wfd G 5F 21
Kingsway Bus. Pk. Hamp 1D 132
Kingsway Cres. Harr 4G 25
Kingsway Est. N18 6E 18
Kingsway Mans. WC1 5K 67 (6G 161) (off Red Lion Sq.)
Kingsway Pl. EC1 4A 68 (3K 161) (off Corporation Row)
Kingsway Rd. Sutt 7G 149
Kingswear Rd. NW5 3F 49
Kingswear Rd. Ruis 2J 41
Kingswood. E2 2J 69 (off Cyprus St.)
Kingswood Av. NW6 1G 65
Kingswood Av. Belv 4F 93
Kingswood Av. Brom 3G 143
Kingswood Av. Hamp 6F 115
Kingswood Av. Houn 1D 96
Kingswood Av. T Hth 5A 140
Kingswood Clo. N20 7F 5
Kingswood Clo. SW8 7J 85
Kingswood Clo. Enf 5K 7
Kingswood Clo. N Mald 6B 136
Kingswood Clo. Orp 7J 145
Kingswood Clo. Surb 7E 134
Kingswood Ct. E4 5H 19
Kingswood Ct. NW6 7J 47 (off W. End La.)
Kingswood Dri. SE19 4E 122
Kingswood Dri. Cars 1D 150
Kingswood Dri. Sutt 7K 149
Kingswood Est. SE21 4E 122
Kingswood Pk. N3 1H 29
Kingswood Pl. SE13 4G 107
Kingswood Rd. E11 7G 35
Kingswood Rd. SE20 6J 123
Kingswood Rd. SW2 6J 103
Kingswood Rd. SW19 7H 119
Kingswood Rd. W4 3J 81
Kingswood Rd. Brom 4F 143
Kingswood Rd. Ilf 1A 56
Kingswood Rd. Wemb 3G 45
Kingswood Ter. W4 3J 81
Kingswood Way. Wall 5J 151
Kingsworth Clo. Beck 5A 142
Kingsworthy Clo. King T 3F 135
Kings Yd. E9 6C 52
Kings Yd. SW15 3E 100 (off Lwr. Richmond Rd.)
Kingthorpe Rd. NW10 7K 45
Kingthorpe Ter. NW10 6K 45
Kington Ho. NW6 1K 65 (off Mortimer Cres.)
Kingward Ho. E1 5G 69 (off Hanbury St.)
Kingweston Clo. NW2 3G 47
King William IV Gdns. SE20 6J 123
King William La. SE10 5G 89
King William's Ct. SE10 6F 89 (off Park Row)
King William St. EC4 6D 68 (1E 168)
King William Wlk. SE10 6E 88 (in two parts)
Kingwood Rd. SW6 1G 101
Kinlet Rd. SE18 1G 109
Kinloch Dri. NW9 7K 27
Kinloch St. N7 3K 49
Kinloss Ct. N3 4H 29
Kinloss Gdns. N3 3H 29
Kinloss Rd. Cars 7A 138
Kinnaird Av. W4 7J 81
Kinnaird Av. Brom 6H 125
Kinnaird Clo. Brom 6H 125
Kinnaird Way. Wfd G 6J 21
Kinnear Rd. W12 2B 82
Kinnerton Pl. N. SW1 7F 165
Kinnerton Pl. S. SW1 7F 165
Kinnerton St. SW1 2E 84 (7G 165)
Kinnerton Yd. SW1 7G 165
Kinnoul Rd. W6 6G 83
Kinross Av. Wor Pk 2C 148
Kinross Clo. Edgw 2C 12
Kinross Clo. Harr 5F 27
Kinross Clo. Sun 5H 113
Kinross Ct. SE6 1H 125

Kinross Ct. Brom 1H 143
(off Highland Rd.)
Kinross Dri. Sun 5H 113
Kinross Ter. E17 2B 34
Kinsale Rd. SE15 3G 105
Kinsella Gdns. SW19 5D 118
Kinsham Ho. E2 4G 69
(off Ramsey St.)
Kintore Way. SE1 4F 87
Kintyre Clo. SW16 2K 139
Kintyre Ct. SW2 7J 103
Kintyre Ho. E14 1E 88
(off Coldharbour)
Kinveachy Gdns. SE7 5C 90
Kinver Rd. SE26 4J 123
Kipling Ct. W7 7K 61
Kipling Dri. SW19 6B 120
Kipling Est. SE1 2D 86 (7F 169)
Kipling Ho. E16 1K 89
(off Southampton M.)
Kipling Ho. SE5 7D 86
(off Elmington Est.)
Kipling Pl. Stan 6E 10
Kipling Rd. Bexh 1E 110
Kipling St. SE1 2D 86 (7F 169)
Kipling Ter. N13 3J 17
Kipling Tower. W3 3J 81
(off Palmerston Rd.)
Kippington Dri. SE9 1B 126
Kirby Clo. Eps 5B 148
Kirby Est. SE16 3H 87
Kirby Est. W Dray 7A 58
Kirby Gro. SE1 2E 86 (6G 169)
Kirby St. EC1 5A 68 (5K 161)
Kirby Way. Uxb 4B 58
Kirby Way. W on T 6A 132
Kirchen Rd. W13 7B 62
Kirkby Clo. N11 6K 15
Kirkdale. SE26 2H 123
Kirkdale Corner. SE26 4J 123
Kirkdale Rd. E11 1G 53
Kirkeby Ho. EC1 5A 68 (5J 161)
(off Leather La.)
Kirkfield Clo. W13 1B 80
Kirkham Rd. E6 6C 72
Kirkham St. SE18 6J 91
Kirkland Av. Ilf 2E 36
Kirkland Clo. Sidc 6J 109
Kirkland Dri. Enf 1H 7
Kirkland Ho. E14 5D 88
(off Westferry Rd.)
Kirkland Ho. E14 5D 88
(off St Davids Sq.)
Kirkland Wlk. E8 6F 51
Kirk La. SE18 6G 91
Kirkleas Rd. Surb 1E 146
Kirklees Rd. Dag 5C 56
Kirklees Rd. T Hth 5A 140
Kirkley Rd. SW19 1J 137
Kirkman Pl. W1 6C 160
Kirkmichael Rd. E14 6E 70
Kirk Ri. Sutt 3K 149
Kirk Rd. E17 6B 34
Kirkside Rd. SE3 6J 89
Kirkstall Av. N17 4D 32
Kirkstall Gdns. SW2 1J 121
Kirkstall Rd. SW2 1H 121
Kirksted Rd. Mord 1K 149
Kirkstone. NW1 3G 67 (1A 160)
(off Harrington St.)
Kirkstone Way. Brom 7G 125
Kirk St. WC1 4G 161
Kirkton Rd. N15 4E 32
Kirkwall Pl. E2 3J 69
Kirkwood Pl. NW1 7E 48
Kirkwood Rd. SE15 2H 105
Kirn Rd. W13 7B 62
Kirrane Clo. N Mald 5B 136
Kirtley Ho. SW8 1G 103
Kirtley Rd. SE26 4A 124
Kirtling St. SW8 7G 85
Kirton Clo. W4 4K 81
Kirton Gdns. E2 3F 69 (2K 163)
(in two parts)
Kirton Lodge. SW18 6K 101
Kirton Rd. E13 2A 72
Kirton Wlk. Edgw 7D 12
Kirwyn Way. SE5 7B 86
Kitcat Ter. E3 3C 70
Kitchener Rd. E7 6K 53
Kitchener Rd. E17 1D 34
Kitchener Rd. N2 3C 30
Kitchener Rd. N17 3E 32
Kitchener Rd. Dag 6H 57
Kitchener Rd. T Hth 3D 140
Kite Pl. E2 3G 69
(off Lampern Sq.)
Kite Yd. SW11 1D 102
(off Cambridge Rd.)
Kitley Gdns. SE19 1F 141
Kitson Rd. SE5 7D 86
Kitson Rd. SW13 1C 100
Kittiwake Ct. SE8 6B 88
(off Abinger Gro.)
Kittiwake Pl. Sutt 5H 149
Kittiwake Rd. N'holt 3B 60
Kittiwake Way. Hay 5B 60
Kitto Rd. SE14 2K 105
Kitts End Rd. Barn 1C 4
Kiver Rd. N19 2H 49
Klea Av. SW4 6G 103
Klein's Wharf. E14 3C 88
(off Westferry Rd.)
Knapdale Clo. SE23 2H 123
Knapmill Rd. SE6 2C 124
Knapmill Way. SE6 2D 124
Knapp Clo. NW10 6A 46
Knapp Rd. E3 4C 70
Knapp Rd. Ashf 4B 112
Knapton M. SW17 6E 120
Knaresborough Dri. SW18 1K 119
Knaresborough Pl. SW5 4K 83
Knatchbull Rd. NW10 1K 63
Knatchbull Rd. SE5 2B 104
Knebworth Av. E17 1C 34
Knebworth Ho. SW8 2H 103
Knebworth Rd. N16 4E 50
Knee Hill. SE2 4C 92
Kneehill Cres. SE2 4C 92
Kneller Gdns. Iswth 6H 97
Kneller Ho. N'holt 2B 60
(off Academy Gdns.)
Kneller Rd. SE4 4A 106
Kneller Rd. N Mald 7A 136
Kneller Rd. Twic 6G 97
Knight Clo. Dag 2C 56
Knight Ct. E4 1K 19
(off Ridgeway, The)
Knight Ct. N15 5E 32
Knighten St. E1 1H 87
Knighthead Point. E14 2C 88
Knight Ho. SE17 4E 86
(off Tatum St.)
Knightland Rd. E5 2H 51
Knightleas Ct. NW2 6E 46
Knighton Clo. Romf 6K 39
Knighton Clo. S Croy 7B 152
Knighton Clo. Wfd G 4E 20
Knighton Dri. Wfd G 4E 20
Knighton Grn. Buck H 2E 20
Knighton La. Buck H 2E 20
Knighton Pk. Rd. SE26 5K 123
Knighton Rd. E7 3J 53
Knighton Rd. Romf 6J 39
Knightrider Ct. EC4 2B 168
Knightrider St. EC4 6B 68 (2B 168)
Knights Arc. SW1 7E 164
Knights Av. W5 2E 80
Knightsbridge. 2C 84 (7E 164)
Knightsbridge. SW7 & SW1 2D 84 (7D 164)
Knightsbridge Ct. SW1 7F 165
Knightsbridge Gdns. Romf 5K 39
Knightsbridge Grn. SW1 2D 84 (7E 164)
(in two parts)
Knights Clo. E9 5J 51
Knightscote Farm & Agricultural Mus. 2A 22
Knights Ct. Brom 3H 125
Knights Ct. King T 3E 134
Knights Hill. SE27 5B 122
Knight's Hill Sq. SE27 4B 122
Knights Ho. SW8 7J 85
(off S. Lambeth Rd.)
Knights La. N9 3B 18
Knight's Pk. King T 3E 134
Knight's Pl. Twic 1J 115
Knight's Rd. E16 2J 89
Knights Rd. Stan 4H 11
Knight's Wlk. SE11 4B 86 (4K 173)
(in two parts)
Knightswood Clo. Edgw 2D 12
Knightswood Ct. N6 7H 31
Knightswood Ho. N12 6F 15
Knightwood Cres. N Mald 6A 136
Knivet Rd. SW6 6J 83
Knobs Hill Rd. E15 1D 70
Knockholt Rd. SE9 5B 108
Knole Clo. Croy 6J 141
Knole Ct. N'holt 3A 60
(off Broomcroft Av.)
Knole Ga. Sidc 3J 127
Knole, The. SE9 4E 126
Knoll Cres. N'wd 1G 23
(in two parts)
Knoll Dri. N14 7K 5
Knoll Ho. NW8 2A 66
(off Carlton Hill)
Knollmead. Surb 1J 147
Knoll Ri. Orp 7K 145
Knoll Rd. SW18 5A 102
Knoll Rd. Bex 7G 111
Knoll Rd. Sidc 5B 128
Knolls Clo. Wor Pk 3D 148
Knoll, The. W13 5C 62
Knoll, The. Beck 1D 142
Knoll, The. Brom 2J 155
Knollys Clo. SW16 3A 122
Knolly's Ho. WC1 4J 67 (3E 160)
(off Tavistock Pl.)
Knollys Rd. SW16 3K 121
Knottisford St. E2 3J 69
Knotts Grn. M. E10 6D 34
Knotts Grn. Rd. E10 6D 34
Knowlden Ho. E1 7J 69
(off Cable St.)
Knowle Av. Bexh 7E 92
Knowle Clo. SW9 3A 104
Knowle Rd. Brom 2D 156
Knowle Rd. Twic 1J 115
Knowles Clo. W Dray 1A 76
Knowles Ct. Harr 6K 25
(off Gayton Rd.)
Knowles Hill Cres. SE13 5F 107
Knowles Wlk. SW4 3G 103
Knowlton Grn. Brom 5H 143
Knowlton Ho. SW9 1A 104
(off Cowley Rd.)
Knowsley Av. S'hall 1F 79
Knowsley Rd. SW11 2D 102
Knox Ct. SW4 2J 103
Knox Rd. E7 6H 53
Knox St. NW1 5D 66 (5E 158)
Knoyle St. SE14 6A 88
Koblenz Ho. N8 3J 31
(off Newland Rd.)
Kohat Rd. SW19 5K 119
Komeheather Ho. Ilf 5D 36
Korda Clo. Shep 3B 130
Kossuth St. SE10 5G 89
Kotree Way. SE1 4G 87
Kramer M. SW5 5J 83
Kreedman Wlk. E8 5G 51
Kreisel Wlk. Rich 6F 81
Kristina Ct. Sutt 6J 149
(off Overton Rd.)
Krupnik Pl. EC2 2H 163
Kuala Gdns. SW16 1K 139
Kubrick Bus. Est. E7 4K 53
(off Station App.)
Kuhn Way. E7 5J 53
Kwame Ho. E16 7F 73
(off University Way)
Kydbrook Clo. Orp 7G 145
Kylemore Clo. E6 2B 72
Kylemore Rd. NW6 7J 47
Kylestrome Ho. SW1 4E 84 (4H 171)
(off Cundy St.)
Kymberley Rd. Harr 6J 25
Kymes Ct. S Harr 2H 43
Kynance Gdns. Stan 1C 26
Kynance M. SW7 3K 83
Kynance Pl. SW7 3A 84
Kynaston Av. N16 3F 51
Kynaston Av. T Hth 5C 140
Kynaston Clo. Harr 7C 10
Kynaston Cres. T Hth 5C 140
Kynaston Rd. N16 3E 50
Kynaston Rd. Brom 5J 125
Kynaston Rd. Enf 1J 7
Kynaston Rd. T Hth 5C 140
Kynaston Wood. Harr 7C 10
Kynnersley Clo. Cars 3D 150
Kynoch Rd. N18 4D 18
Kyrle Rd. SW11 6E 102
Kyverdale Rd. N16 1F 51

Laburnum Av. N9 2A 18
Laburnum Av. N17 7J 17
Laburnum Av. Sutt 3C 150
Laburnum Av. W Dray 7B 58
Laburnum Clo. E4 6G 19
Laburnum Clo. N11 6K 15
Laburnum Clo. SE15 7J 87
Laburnum Clo. Wemb 1G 63
Laburnum Ct. E2 1F 69
Laburnum Ct. SE16 2J 87
(off Albion St.)
Laburnum Ct. SE19 1F 141
Laburnum Ct. Harr 6F 25
Laburnum Ct. Stan 4H 11
Laburnum Cres. Sun 1K 131
Laburnum Gdns. N21 2H 17
Laburnum Gdns. Croy 7K 141
Laburnum Gro. N21 2H 17
Laburnum Gro. NW9 7J 27
Laburnum Gro. Houn 4D 96
Laburnum Gro. N Mald 2K 135
Laburnum Gro. Ruis 6F 23
Laburnum Gro. S'hall 4D 60
Laburnum Ho. Short 1F 143
Laburnum Lodge. N3 2H 29
Laburnum Pl. SE9 5E 108
Laburnum Rd. SW19 7A 120
Laburnum Rd. Hay 4H 77
Laburnum Rd. Mitc 2E 138
Laburnums, The. E6 4C 72
Laburnum St. E2 1F 69
Laburnum Way. Brom 7E 144
Laburnum Way. Stai 1B 112
La Caye Apartments. E14 4F 89
(off Glenaffric Av.)
Lacebark Clo. Sidc 7K 109
Lacey Clo. N9 2B 18
Lacey Dri. Edgw 4A 12
Lacey Dri. Hamp 1D 132
Lacey Wlk. E3 2C 70
Lacine Ct. SE16 2K 87
(off Christopher Clo.)
Lackington St. EC2 5D 68 (5F 163)
Lackland Ho. SE1 5F 87
(off Rowcross St.)
Lacland Ho. SW10 7B 84
(off Worlds End Est.)
Lacock Clo. SW19 6A 120
Lacock Ct. W13 1A 80
(off Tewkesbury Rd.)
Lacon Ho. WC1 5K 67 (5G 161)
(off Theobalds Rd.)
Lacon Rd. SE22 4G 105
Lacrosse Way. SW16 1H 139
Lacy Dri. Dag 3C 56
Lacy Rd. SW15 4F 101
(in two parts)
Ladas Rd. SE27 4C 122
Ladbroke Cres. W11 6G 65
Ladbroke Gdns. W11 7H 65
Ladbroke Gro. W10 & W11 4F 65
Ladbroke Gro. Ho. W11 7H 65
(off Ladbroke Gro.)
Ladbroke M. W11 1G 83
Ladbroke Rd. W11 1H 83
Ladbroke Rd. Enf 6A 8
Ladbroke Sq. W11 7H 65
Ladbroke Ter. W11 7H 65
Ladbroke Wlk. W11 1H 83
Ladbrook Clo. Pinn 5D 24
Ladbrooke Cres. Sidc 3D 128
Ladbrook Rd. SE25 4D 140
Ladderstile Ride. King T 5H 117
Ladderswood Way. N11 5B 16
Ladlands. SE22 7G 105
Lady Aylesford Av. Stan 5F 11
Lady Booth Rd. King T 2E 134
Ladycroft Rd. SE13 3D 106
Ladycroft Wlk. Stan 1D 26
Lady Dock Wlk. SE16 2A 88
Lady Elizabeth Ho. SW14 3J 99
Lady Forsdyke Way. Eps 7G 147
Ladygate La. Ruis 6D 22
Lady Harewood Way. Eps 7G 147
Lady Hay. Wor Pk 2B 148
Lady Margaret Rd. NW5 & N19 5G 49
Lady Margaret Rd. S'hall 7D 60
Lady Micos Almshouses. E1 6J 69
(off Aylward St.)
Lady Sarah Ho. N11 6J 15
(off Asher Loftus Way)
Lady Shaw Ct. N13 2E 16
Ladyship Ter. SE22 7G 105
Ladysmith Av. E6 2C 72
Ladysmith Av. Ilf 7J 37
Ladysmith Clo. NW7 7H 13
Ladysmith Rd. E16 3H 71
Ladysmith Rd. N17 2G 33
Ladysmith Rd. N18 5C 18
Ladysmith Rd. SE9 6E 108
Ladysmith Rd. Enf 3K 7
(in two parts)
Ladysmith Rd. Harr 2J 25
Lady Somerset Rd. NW5 4F 49
Ladywell. 5D 106
Ladywell Clo. SE4 5C 106
Ladywell Heights. SE4 6B 106
Ladywell Rd. SE13 5C 106
Ladywell St. E15 1H 71
Ladywood Av. Orp 5J 145
Ladywood Rd. Surb 2G 147
Lafone Av. Felt 2A 114
Lafone St. SE1 2F 87 (6J 169)
Lagado M. SE16 1K 87
Laidlaw Dri. N21 5E 6
Laing Dean. N'holt 1A 60
Laing Ho. SE5 7C 86
Laings Av. Mitc 2D 138
Lainlock Pl. Houn 1F 97
Lainson St. SW18 7J 101
Lairdale Clo. SE21 1C 122
Laird Ho. SE5 7C 86
(off Redcar St.)
Lairs Clo. N7 5J 49
Laitwood Rd. SW12 1F 121
Lakanal. SE5 1E 104
(off Dalwood St.)

Lake Av. *Brom* . . . 6J **125**
Lake Bus. Cen. *N17* . . . 7B **18**
Lake Clo. *SW19* . . . 5H **119**
Lakedale Rd. *SE18* . . . 6J **91**
Lake Dri. *Bush* . . . 2C **10**
Lakefield Clo. *SE20* . . . 7H **123**
Lakefield Rd. *N22* . . . 2B **32**
Lake Footpath. *SE2* . . . 2D **92**
Lake Gdns. *Dag* . . . 5G **57**
Lake Gdns. *Rich* . . . 2B **116**
Lake Gdns. *Wall* . . . 3F **151**
Lakehall Gdns. *T Hth* . . . 5B **140**
Lakehall Rd. *T Hth* . . . 5B **140**
Lake Ho. SE1 . . . 2C 86 (7C 168)
(off Southwark Bri. Rd.)
Lake Ho. Rd. *E11* . . . 3J **53**
Lakehurst Rd. *Eps* . . . 5A **148**
Lakeland Clo. *Harr* . . . 6C **10**
Lakenheath. *N14* . . . 5C **6**
Laker Ct. *SW4* . . . 1J **103**
Laker Ind. Est. SE26 . . . 5A 124
(off Kent Ho. La.)
Lake Rd. *SW19* . . . 5H **119**
Lake Rd. *Croy* . . . 2B **154**
Lake Rd. *Romf* . . . 4D **38**
Laker Pl. *SW15* . . . 6G **101**
Lakeside. *N3* . . . 2K **29**
Lakeside. *W13* . . . 6C **62**
Lakeside. *Beck* . . . 3D **142**
Lakeside. *Enf* . . . 4C **6**
Lakeside. *Eps* . . . 6A **148**
Lakeside. *Wall* . . . 4F **151**
Lakeside Av. *SE28* . . . 2A **92**
Lakeside Av. *Ilf* . . . 4B **36**
Lakeside Clo. *SE25* . . . 2G **141**
Lakeside Clo. *Ruis* . . . 4E **22**
Lakeside Clo. *Sidc* . . . 5C **110**
Lakeside Ct. *N4* . . . 2C **50**
Lakeside Cres. *Barn* . . . 5J **5**
Lakeside Dri. *Brom* . . . 3C **156**
Lakeside Rd. *N13* . . . 4E **16**
Lakeside Rd. *W14* . . . 3F **83**
Lakeside Ter. *EC2* . . . 5D **162**
Lakeside Way. *SE2* . . . 3D **92**
Lakeside Way. *Wemb* . . . 4G **45**
Lakes Rd. *Kes* . . . 5A **156**
Lakeswood Rd. *Orp* . . . 6F **145**
Lake, The. *Bush* . . . 1C **10**
Lake Vw. *Edgw* . . . 5A **12**
Lake Vw. Ct. SW1 . . . 3F 85 (1K 171)
(off Bressenden Pl.)
Lake Vw. Est. *E3* . . . 2A **70**
Lakeview Rd. *SE27* . . . 5A **122**
Lakeview Rd. *Well* . . . 4B **110**
Lake Vw. Ter. N18 . . . 4A 18
(off Sweet Briar Wlk.)
Lakis Clo. *NW3* . . . 4A **48**
Laleham Av. *NW7* . . . 3E **12**
Laleham Ho. E2 . . . 4F 69 (3J 163)
(off Camlet St.)
Laleham Rd. *SE6* . . . 7E **106**
Laleham Rd. *Shep* . . . 4B **130**
Lalor St. *SW6* . . . 2G **101**
Lambarde Av. *SE9* . . . 4E **126**
Lambard Ho. SE10 . . . 7E 88
(off Langdale Rd.)
Lamb Ct. E14 . . . 7A 70
(off Narrow St.)
Lamberhurst Ho. *SE15* . . . 6J **87**
Lamberhurst Rd. *SE27* . . . 4A **122**
Lamberhurst Rd. *Dag* . . . 1F **57**
Lambert Av. *Rich* . . . 3G **99**
Lambert Ct. Eri . . . 6J 93
(off Park Cres.)
Lambert Jones M. *EC2* . . . 5C **162**
Lambert Lodge. Bren . . . 5D 80
(off Layton Rd.)
Lambert Rd. *E16* . . . 6K **71**
Lambert Rd. *N12* . . . 5G **15**
Lambert Rd. *SW2* . . . 5J **103**
Lambert's Pl. *Croy* . . . 1D **152**
Lamberts Rd. *Surb* . . . 5E **134**
Lambert St. *N1* . . . 7A **50**
Lambert Wlk. *Wemb* . . . 3D **44**
Lambert Way. *N12* . . . 5F **15**
Lambeth. . . . 3K 85 (2G 173)
Lambeth Bri. *SW1 & SE1* . . . 4J **85** (3F **173**)
Lambeth Crematorium. *SW17* . . . 4A **120**
Lambeth High St. *SE1* . . . 4K **85** (4G **173**)
Lambeth Hill. *EC4* . . . 7C **68** (2C **168**)
Lambeth Pal. Rd. *SE1* . . . 3K **85** (2G **173**)
Lambeth Rd. *SE1 & SE11* . . . 4K **85** (3G **173**)
Lambeth Rd. *Croy* . . . 7A **140**
Lambeth Towers. *SE11* . . . 2J **173**
Lambeth Wlk. *SE1 & SE11* . . . 4K **85**
(in two parts)
Lambfold Ho. *N7* . . . 6J **49**
Lamb Ho. SE5 . . . 7C 86
(off Elmington Est.)
Lamb Ho. SE10 . . . 6E 88
(off Haddo St.)
Lamb La. *E8* . . . 7H **51**
Lamble St. *NW5* . . . 5E **48**
Lambley Rd. *Dag* . . . 6B **56**
Lambolle Pl. *NW3* . . . 6C **48**
Lambolle Rd. *NW3* . . . 6C **48**
Lambourn Clo. *NW5* . . . 4G **49**
Lambourn Clo. *W7* . . . 2K **79**
Lambourn Clo. *S Croy* . . . 7B **152**
Lambourne Av. *SW19* . . . 4H **119**
Lambourne Ct. *Wfd G* . . . 7F **21**
Lambourne Gdns. *E4* . . . 2H **19**
Lambourne Gdns. *Bark* . . . 7K **55**
Lambourne Gdns. *Enf* . . . 2A **8**
Lambourne Ho. NW8 . . . 5B 66 (5B 158)
(off Broadley St.)
Lambourne Ho. *SE16* . . . 4K **87**
Lambourne Pl. *SE3* . . . 1K **107**
Lambourne Rd. *E11* . . . 7E **34**
Lambourne Rd. *Bark* . . . 7J **55**
Lambourne Rd. *Ilf* . . . 2J **55**
Lambourn Gro. *King T* . . . 2H **135**
Lambourn Rd. *SW4* . . . 3F **103**
Lambrook Ho. *SE15* . . . 1G **105**
Lambrook Ter. *SW6* . . . 1G **101**
Lamb's Bldgs. *EC1* . . . 4D **68** (4E **162**)
Lamb's Clo. *N9* . . . 2B **18**
Lamb's Conduit Pas. *WC1* . . . 5K **67** (5G **161**)
Lamb's Conduit St. *WC1* . . . 4K **67** (4G **161**)
(in three parts)
Lambscroft Av. *SE9* . . . 3A **126**
Lambs Mdw. *Wfd G* . . . 2B **36**
Lamb's M. *N1* . . . 1B **68**
Lamb's Pas. *EC1* . . . 4D **68** (5E **162**)
Lambs Ter. *N9* . . . 2J **17**
Lamb St. *E1* . . . 5E **68** (5J **163**)
Lamb's Wlk. *Enf* . . . 2H **7**
Lambton Pl. *W11* . . . 7H **65**
Lambton Rd. *N19* . . . 1J **49**
Lambton Rd. *SW20* . . . 1E **136**
Lamb Wlk. *SE1* . . . 2E **86** (7G **169**)
LAMDA Theatre. . . . 4J 83
(off Logan Pl.)
Lamerock Rd. *Brom* . . . 4H **125**
Lamerton Rd. *Ilf* . . . 2F **37**
Lamerton St. *SE8* . . . 6C **88**
Lamford Clo. *N17* . . . 7J **17**
Lamington St. *W6* . . . 4D **82**
Lamlash St. *SE11* . . . 4B **86**
Lamley Ho. SE10 . . . 7D 88
(off Ashburnham Pl.)
Lammas Av. *Mitc* . . . 2E **138**
Lammas Grn. *SE26* . . . 3H **123**
Lammas Pk. Gdns. *W5* . . . 1C **80**
Lammas Pk. Rd. *W5* . . . 2D **80**
Lammas Rd. *E9* . . . 7K **51**
Lammas Rd. *E10* . . . 2A **52**
Lammas Rd. *Rich* . . . 4C **116**
Lammermoor Rd. *SW12* . . . 7F **103**
Lamont Rd. *SW10* . . . 6B **84** (7A **170**)
Lamont Rd. Pas. *SW10* . . . 7A **170**
Lamorbey. . . . 1K 127
Lamorbey Clo. *Sidc* . . . 1K **127**
Lamorna Clo. *E17* . . . 2E **34**
Lamorna Clo. *Orp* . . . 7K **145**
Lamorna Gro. *Stan* . . . 1D **26**
Lampard Gro. *N16* . . . 1F **51**
Lampern Sq. *E2* . . . 3G **69**
Lampeter Clo. *NW9* . . . 6A **28**
Lampeter Sq. *W6* . . . 6G **83**
Lamplighter Clo. *E1* . . . 4J **69**
Lampmead Rd. *SE12* . . . 5H **107**
Lamp Office Ct. *WC1* . . . 4G **161**
Lamport Clo. *SE18* . . . 4D **90**
Lamps Ct. *SE5* . . . 7C **86**
Lampton. . . . 1F 97
Lampton Av. *Houn* . . . 1F **97**
Lampton Ct. *Houn* . . . 1F **97**
Lampton Ho. Clo. *SW19* . . . 4F **119**
Lampton Pk. Rd. *Houn* . . . 2F **97**
Lampton Rd. *Houn* . . . 2F **97**
Lanacre Av. *HA8* . . . 1K **27**
Lanain Ct. *SE12* . . . 7H **107**
Lanark Clo. *W5* . . . 5C **62**
Lanark Ct. N'holt . . . 5E 42
(off Newmarket Av.)
Lanark Ho. SE1 . . . 5G 87
(off Old Kent Rd.)
Lanark Mans. W9 . . . 4A 66
(off Lanark Rd.)
Lanark Mans. W12 . . . 2E 82
(off Pennard Rd.)
Lanark M. *W9* . . . 3A **66**
Lanark Pl. *W9* . . . 4A **66** (3A **158**)
Lanark Rd. *W9* . . . 2K **65**
Lanark Sq. *E14* . . . 3D **88**
Lanata Wlk. Hay . . . 4B 60
(off Alba Clo.)
Lanbury Rd. *SE15* . . . 4K **105**
Lancashire Ct. *W1* . . . 2K **165**
Lancaster Av. *E18* . . . 4K **35**
Lancaster Av. *SE27* . . . 2B **122**
Lancaster Av. *SW19* . . . 5F **119**
Lancaster Av. *Bark* . . . 7J **55**
Lancaster Av. *Barn* . . . 1G **5**
Lancaster Av. *Mitc* . . . 5J **139**
Lancaster Clo. *N1* . . . 7E **50**
Lancaster Clo. *N17* . . . 7B **18**
Lancaster Clo. *NW9* . . . 7G **13**
Lancaster Clo. *SE27* . . . 2B **122**
Lancaster Clo. W2 . . . 7K 65
(off St Petersburgh Pl.)
Lancaster Clo. *Ashf* . . . 4A **112**
Lancaster Clo. *Brom* . . . 4H **143**
Lancaster Clo. *King T* . . . 5D **116**
Lancaster Clo. *Stanw* . . . 6A **94**
Lancaster Cotts. *Rich* . . . 6E **98**
Lancaster Ct. *SE27* . . . 2B **122**
Lancaster Ct. *SW6* . . . 7H **83**
Lancaster Ct. W2 . . . 7A 66 (2A 164)
(off Lancaster Ga.)
Lancaster Ct. Sutt . . . 7J 149
(off Mulgrave Rd.)
Lancaster Ct. *W on T* . . . 7J **131**
Lancaster Dri. *E14* . . . 1E **88**
Lancaster Dri. *NW3* . . . 6C **48**
Lancaster Gdns. *SW19* . . . 5G **119**
Lancaster Gdns. *W13* . . . 2B **80**
Lancaster Gdns. *King T* . . . 5D **116**
Lancaster Ga. *W2* . . . 7A **66** (2A **164**)
Lancaster Gro. *NW3* . . . 6B **48**
Lancaster Hall. E16 . . . 1J 89
(off Wesley Av., in two parts)
Lancaster Ho. *Enf* . . . 1J **7**
Lancaster Lodge. W11 . . . 6G 65
(off Lancaster Rd.)
Lancaster M. *SW18* . . . 5K **101**
Lancaster M. *W2* . . . 7A **66** (2A **164**)
Lancaster M. *Rich* . . . 6E **98**
Lancaster Pk. *Rich* . . . 5E **98**
Lancaster Pl. *SW19* . . . 5F **119**
Lancaster Pl. *WC2* . . . 7K **67** (2G **167**)
Lancaster Pl. *Houn* . . . 2A **96**
Lancaster Pl. *Ilf* . . . 5G **55**
Lancaster Pl. *Twic* . . . 6A **98**
Lancaster Rd. *E7* . . . 7J **53**
Lancaster Rd. *E11* . . . 2G **53**
Lancaster Rd. *E17* . . . 2K **33**
Lancaster Rd. *N4* . . . 7K **31**
Lancaster Rd. *N11* . . . 6C **16**
Lancaster Rd. *N18* . . . 5A **18**
Lancaster Rd. *NW10* . . . 5C **46**
Lancaster Rd. *SE25* . . . 2F **141**
Lancaster Rd. *SW19* . . . 5F **119**
Lancaster Rd. *W11* . . . 6G **65**
Lancaster Rd. *Barn* . . . 4G **5**
(in two parts)
Lancaster Rd. *Enf* . . . 1J **7**
Lancaster Rd. *Harr* . . . 5E **24**
Lancaster Rd. *N'holt* . . . 6G **43**
Lancaster Rd. *S'hall* . . . 7C **60**
Lancaster Stables. *NW3* . . . 6C **48**
Lancaster St. *SE1* . . . 2B **86** (7A **168**)
Lancaster Ter. *W2* . . . 7B **66** (2A **164**)
Lancaster Wlk. *W2* . . . 1A **84** (3A **164**)
Lancaster Wlk. *Hay* . . . 6E **58**
Lancastrian Rd. *Wall* . . . 7J **151**
Lancefield Ct. *W10* . . . 2G **65**
Lancefield Ho. *SE15* . . . 4H **105**
Lancefield St. *W10* . . . 3H **65**
Lancell St. *N16* . . . 2E **50**
Lancelot Av. *Wemb* . . . 4D **44**
Lancelot Cres. *Wemb* . . . 4D **44**
Lancelot Gdns. *E Barn* . . . 7K **5**
Lancelot Pl. *SW7* . . . 2D **84** (7E **164**)
Lancelot Rd. *Well* . . . 4A **110**
Lancelot Rd. *Wemb* . . . 4D **44**
Lance Rd. *Harr* . . . 7G **25**
Lancer Sq. *W8* . . . 2K **83**
Lancey Clo. *SE7* . . . 4C **90**
Lanchester Ct. W2 . . . 6D 66 (1E 164)
(off Seymour St.)
Lanchester Rd. *N6* . . . 5D **30**
Lancing Gdns. *N9* . . . 1A **18**
Lancing Ho. Croy . . . 4D 152
(off Coombe Rd.)
Lancing Rd. *W13* . . . 7B **62**
Lancing Rd. *Croy* . . . 7K **139**
Lancing Rd. *Felt* . . . 2H **113**
Lancing Rd. *Ilf* . . . 6H **37**
Lancing St. *NW1* . . . 3H **67** (2C **160**)
Lancresse Ct. N1 . . . 1E 68
(off De Beauvoir Est.)
Landale Ho. SE16 . . . 3J 87
(off Lower Rd.)
Landau Ct. S Croy . . . 5C 152
(off Warham Rd.)
Landcroft Rd. *SE22* . . . 5F **105**
Landells Rd. *SE22* . . . 6F **105**
Landford Rd. *SW15* . . . 3E **100**
Landgrove Rd. *SW19* . . . 5J **119**
Landin Ho. E14 . . . 6C 70
(off Thomas Rd.)
Landleys Fld. NW5 . . . 5H 49
(off Long Mdw.)
Landmann Ho. SE16 . . . 4H 87
(off Rennie Est.)
Landmann Way. *SE14* . . . 5K **87**
Landmark Commercial Cen. *N18* . . . 6K **17**
Landmark Ho. W6 . . . 5E 82
(off Hammersmith Bri. Rd.)
Landon Pl. *SW1* . . . 3D **84** (1E **170**)
Landon's Clo. *E14* . . . 1E **88**
Landon Wlk. *E14* . . . 7D **70**
Landon Way. *Ashf* . . . 6D **112**
Landor Ho. SE5 . . . 7D 86
(off Elmington Est.)
Landor Rd. *SW4* . . . 3J **103**
Landor Wlk. *W12* . . . 2C **82**
Landra Gdns. *N21* . . . 6G **7**
Landrake. NW1 . . . 1G 67
(off Plender St.)
Landridge Dri. *Enf* . . . 1C **8**
Landridge Rd. *SW6* . . . 2H **101**
Landrock Rd. *N8* . . . 6J **31**
Landscape Rd. *Wfd G* . . . 7E **20**
Landseer Av. *E12* . . . 5E **54**
Landseer Clo. *SW19* . . . 1A **138**
Landseer Clo. *Edgw* . . . 2G **27**
Landseer Ct. *Hay* . . . 2F **59**
Landseer Ho. NW8 . . . 4B 66 (3B 158)
(off Frampton St.)
Landseer Ho. SW1 . . . 4H 85 (4D 172)
(off Herrick St.)
Landseer Ho. *SW11* . . . 1E **102**
Landseer Ho. N'holt . . . 2B 60
(off Parkfield Dri.)
Landseer Rd. *N19* . . . 3J **49**
(in two parts)
Landseer Rd. *Enf* . . . 5B **8**
Landseer Rd. *N Mald* . . . 7K **135**
Landseer Rd. *Sutt* . . . 6J **149**
Landstead Rd. *SE18* . . . 7H **91**
Landulph Ho. SE11 . . . 5A 86 (5K 173)
(off Kennings Way)
Landward Ct. W1 . . . 6C 66 (7D 158)
(off Harrowby St.)
Lane App. *NW7* . . . 5B **14**
Lane Clo. *NW2* . . . 3D **46**
Lane End. *SW15* . . . 6F **101**
Lane End. *Bexh* . . . 3H **111**
Lane Gdns. *Bus H* . . . 1D **10**
La. Jane Ct. King T . . . 2F 135
(off London Rd.)
Lane M. *E12* . . . 3D **54**
Lanercost Clo. *SW2* . . . 2A **122**
Lanercost Gdns. *N14* . . . 7D **6**
Lanercost Rd. *SW2* . . . 2A **122**
Lanesborough Pl. *SW1* . . . 6H **165**
Laneside. *Chst* . . . 5F **127**
Laneside. *Edgw* . . . 5D **12**
Laneside Av. *Dag* . . . 7F **39**
Lane, The. *NW8* . . . 2A **66**
Lane, The. *SE3* . . . 3J **107**
Laneway. *SW15* . . . 5D **100**
Laney Ho. EC1 . . . 5A 68 (5J 161)
(off Leather La.)
Lanfranc Ct. *Harr* . . . 3K **43**
Lanfranc Rd. *E3* . . . 2A **70**
Lanfrey Pl. *W14* . . . 5H **83**
Langbourne Av. *N6* . . . 2E **48**
Langbourne Ct. *E17* . . . 6A **34**
Langbourne Mans. *N6* . . . 2E **48**
Langbourne Pl. *E14* . . . 5D **88**
Langbourne Way. *Clay* . . . 6A **146**
Langbrook Rd. *SE3* . . . 3B **108**
Langcroft Clo. *Cars* . . . 3D **150**
Langdale. NW1 . . . 3G 67 (1A 160)
(off Stanhope St.)
Langdale Av. *Mitc* . . . 3D **138**
Langdale Clo. *SE17* . . . 6C **86**
Langdale Clo. *SW14* . . . 4H **99**
Langdale Clo. *Dag* . . . 1C **56**
Langdale Clo. *Orp* . . . 3E **156**
Langdale Cres. *Bexh* . . . 7G **93**
Langdale Dri. *Hay* . . . 2G **59**
Langdale Gdns. *Gnfd* . . . 3B **62**
Langdale Ho. SW1 . . . 5G 85 (6A 172)
(off Churchill Gdns.)
Langdale Pde. *Mitc* . . . 3D **138**

Langdale Rd. SE10 7E 88
Langdale Rd. T Hth 4A 140
Langdale St. E1 6H 69
Langdon Ct. EC1 2B 68 (1B 162) (off City Rd.)
Langdon Ct. NW10 1A 64
Langdon Cres. E6 2E 72
Langdon Dri. NW9 1J 45
Langdon Ho. E14 6E 70
Langdon Pk. Rd. N6 7G 31
Langdon Pl. SW14 3J 99
Langdon Rd. E6 1E 72
Langdon Rd. Brom 3K 143
Langdon Rd. Mord 5A 138
Langdons Ct. S'hall 3E 78
Langdon Shaw. Sidc 5K 127
Langdon Wlk. Mord 5A 138
Langdon Way. SE1 4G 87
Langford Clo. E8 5G 51
Langford Clo. NW8 2A 66
Langford Clo. W3 2H 81
Langford Ct. NW8 2A 66 (off Abbey Rd.)
Langford Cres. Cockf 4J 5
Langford Grn. SE5 3E 104
Langford Ho. SE8 6C 88
Langford Pl. NW8 2A 66
Langford Pl. Sidc 3A 128
Langford Rd. SW6 2K 101
Langford Rd. Cockf 4J 5
Langford Rd. Wfd G 6F 21
Langfords. Buck H 2G 21
Langham Clo. N15 3B 32 (off Langham Rd.)
Langham Ct. NW4 5F 29
Langham Ct. Ruis 5K 41
Langham Dri. Romf 6B 38
Langham Gdns. N21 5F 7
Langham Gdns. W13 7B 62
Langham Gdns. Edgw 7D 12
Langham Gdns. Rich 4C 116
Langham Gdns. Wemb 2C 44
Langham Ho. Clo. Rich 4D 116
Langham Mans. SW5 5K 83 (off Earl's Ct. Sq.)
Langham Pl. N15 3B 32
Langham Pl. W1 5F 67 (6K 159)
Langham Pl. W4 6A 82
Langham Rd. N15 3B 32
Langham Rd. SW20 1E 136
Langham Rd. Edgw 6D 12
Langham Rd. Tedd 5B 116
Langham St. W1 5F 67 (6K 159)
Langhedge Clo. N18 6A 18
Langhedge La. N18 6A 18
Langhedge La. Ind. Est. N18 6A 18
Langholm Clo. SW12 7H 103
Langholme. Bush 1B 10
Langhorn Dri. Twic 7J 97
Langhorne Ct. NW8 7B 48 (off Dorman Way)
Langhorne Rd. Dag 7G 57
Lang Ho. SW8 7J 85 (off Hartington Rd.)
Langland Cres. Stan 2D 26
Langland Dri. Pinn 1C 24
Langland Gdns. NW3 5K 47
Langland Gdns. Croy 2B 154
Langland Ho. SE5 7D 86 (off Edmund St.)
Langler Rd. NW10 2E 64
Langley Av. Ruis 2K 41
Langley Av. Surb 1D 146
Langley Av. Wor Pk 1F 149
Langley Ct. WC2 7J 67 (2E 166)
Langley Cres. E11 7A 36
Langley Cres. Dag 7C 56
Langley Cres. Edgw 3D 12
Langley Cres. Hay 7H 77
Langley Dri. E11 7K 35
Langley Dri. W3 2H 81
Langley Gdns. Brom 4A 144
Langley Gdns. Dag 7D 56
Langley Gdns. Orp 6F 145
Langley Gro. N Mald 2A 136
Langley La. SW8 6J 85 (7F 173)
Langley Mans. SW8 7F 173
Langley Pk. NW7 6F 13
Langley Pk. Rd. Sutt 5A 150
Langley Rd. SW19 1H 137
Langley Rd. Beck 4A 142
Langley Rd. Iswth 2K 97
Langley Rd. Surb 7E 134
Langley Rd. Well 6C 92
Langley Row. Barn 1C 4
Langley St. WC2 6J 67 (1E 166)
Langley Way. W Wick 1F 155
Langmead Dri. Bus H 1D 10
Langmead St. SE27 4B 122
Langmore Ct. Bexh 3D 110
Langmore Ho. E1 6G 69 (off Stutfield St.)
Langport Ct. W on T 7A 132
Langport Ho. SW9 2B 104
Langridge M. Hamp 6D 114
Langroyd Rd. SW17 2D 120
Langside Av. SW15 4C 100
Langside Cres. N14 3C 16
Langston Hughes Clo. SE24 4B 104
Lang St. E1 4J 69
Langthorn Ct. EC2 6D 68 (7E 162)
Langthorne Ct. SE6 4E 124
Langthorne Ho. Hay 4G 77
Langthorne Rd. E11 3E 52
Langthorne St. SW6 7F 83
Langton Av. E6 3E 72
Langton Av. N20 7F 5
Langton Clo. WC1 4K 67 (3H 161)
Langton Ho. SE11 3H 173
Langton Pl. SW18 1J 119
Langton Ri. SE23 7H 105
Langton Rd. NW2 3E 46
Langton Rd. SW9 7B 86
Langton Rd. Harr 7B 10
Langton Rd. W Mol 4G 133
Langton St. SW10 6A 84
Langton Way. SE3 1H 107
Langton Way. Croy 3E 152
Langtry Pl. SW6 6J 83
Langtry Rd. NW8 1K 65
Langtry Rd. N'holt 2B 60
Langtry Wlk. NW8 1K 65
Langwood Chase. Tedd 6C 116
Langworth Dri. Hay 6J 59
Lanhill Rd. W9 4J 65
Lanier Rd. SE13 6F 107
Lanigan Dri. Houn 5F 97
Lankaster Gdns. N2 1B 30
Lankers Dri. Harr 6D 24
Lankton Clo. Beck 1E 142
Lannock Rd. Hay 1H 77
Lannoy Point. SW6 7G 83 (off Pellant Rd.)
Lannoy Rd. SE9 1G 127
Lanrick Ho. E14 6F 71 (off Lanrick Rd.)
Lanrick Rd. E14 6F 71
Lanridge Rd. SE2 3D 92
Lansbury Av. N18 5J 17
Lansbury Av. Bark 7A 56
Lansbury Av. Felt 6K 95
Lansbury Av. Romf 5E 38
Lansbury Clo. NW10 5J 45
Lansbury Dri. Hay 2G 59
Lansbury Est. E14 6D 70
Lansbury Gdns. E14 6F 71
Lansbury Rd. Enf 1E 8
Lansbury Way. N18 5K 17
Lanscombe Wlk. SW8 1J 103
Lansdell Ho. SW2 6A 104 (off Tulse Hill)
Lansdell Rd. Mitc 2E 138
Lansdowne Av. Bexh 7D 92
Lansdowne Av. Orp 7F 145
Lansdowne Clo. SW20 7F 119
Lansdowne Clo. Surb 2H 147
Lansdowne Clo. Twic 1K 115
Lansdowne Ct. W11 7G 65 (off Lansdowne Ri.)
Lansdowne Ct. Ilf 3C 36
Lansdowne Ct. Wor Pk 2C 148
Lansdowne Cres. W11 7G 65
Lansdowne Dri. E8 6G 51
Lansdowne Gdns. SW8 1J 103
Lansdowne Grn. Est. SW8 1J 103
Lansdowne Gro. NW10 4A 46
Lansdowne Hill. SE27 3B 122
Lansdowne La. SE7 6B 90
Lansdowne M. SE7 5B 90
Lansdowne M. W11 1H 83
Lansdowne Pl. SE1 3D 86
Lansdowne Pl. SE19 7F 123
Lansdowne Ri. W11 7G 65
Lansdowne Rd. E4 2H 19
Lansdowne Rd. E11 2H 53
Lansdowne Rd. E17 6C 34
Lansdowne Rd. E18 3J 35
Lansdowne Rd. N3 7D 14
Lansdowne Rd. N10 2G 31
Lansdowne Rd. N17 1F 33
Lansdowne Rd. SW20 7E 118
Lansdowne Rd. W11 7G 65
Lansdowne Rd. Brom 7J 125
Lansdowne Rd. Croy 2D 152
Lansdowne Rd. Eps 7J 147
Lansdowne Rd. Harr 7J 25
Lansdowne Rd. Houn 3F 97
Lansdowne Rd. Ilf 1K 55
Lansdowne Rd. Stan 6H 11
Lansdowne Rd. Uxb 6E 58
Lansdowne Row. W1 1F 85 (4K 165)
Lansdowne Ter. WC1 4J 67 (4F 161)
Lansdowne Wlk. W11 1H 83
Lansdowne Way. SW8 1H 103
Lansdowne Wood Clo. SE27 3B 122
Lansdowne Workshops. SE7 5A 90
Lansdown Rd. E7 7A 54
Lansdown Rd. Sidc 3B 128
Lansfield Av. N18 4B 18
Lantern Clo. SW15 4C 100
Lantern Clo. Wemb 5D 44
Lanterns Ct. E14 3C 88
Lantern Way. W Dray 2A 76
Lant Ho. SE1 2C 86 (7C 168) (off Toulmin St.)
Lantry Ct. W3 1H 81
Lant St. SE1 2C 86 (6C 168)
Lanvanor Rd. SE15 2J 105
Lanyard Ho. SE8 4B 88
Lapford Clo. W9 4H 65
Lapponum Wlk. Hay 4B 60
Lapse Wood Wlk. SE23 1H 123
Lapstone Gdns. Harr 6C 26
Lapwing Ct. Surb 3G 147
Lapwing Tower. SE8 6B 88 (off Taylor Clo.)
Lapwing Way. Hay 6B 60
Lapworth. N11 4A 16 (off Coppies Gro.)
Lapworth Ct. W2 5K 65 (off Chichester Rd.)
Lara Clo. SE13 6E 106
Lara Clo. Chess 7E 146
Larbert Rd. SW16 7G 121
Larch Av. W3 1A 82
Larch Clo. E13 4K 71
Larch Clo. N11 7K 15
Larch Clo. N19 2G 49
Larch Clo. SE8 6B 88
Larch Clo. SW12 2F 121
Larch Ct. W9 5J 65 (off Admiral Wlk.)
Larch Cres. Eps 6H 147
Larch Cres. Hay 5A 60
Larch Dene. Orp 2E 156
Larch Dri. W4 5G 81
Larches Av. SW14 4K 99
Larches, The. N13 3H 17
Larches, The. Uxb 3D 58
Larch Grn. NW9 1A 28
Larch Gro. Sidc 1K 127
Larch Ho. SE16 2J 87 (off Ainsty Est.)
Larch Ho. W10 4G 65 (off Rowan Wlk.)
Larch Ho. Hay 5A 60
Larch Ho. Short 1G 143
Larch Rd. E10 2C 52
Larch Rd. NW2 4E 46
Larch Tree Way. Croy 3C 154
Larchvale Ct. Sutt 7K 149
Larch Way. Brom 7E 144
Larchwood Rd. SE9 2F 127
Larcombe Clo. Croy 4F 153
Larcombe Ct. Sutt 7K 149 (off Worcester Rd.)
Larcom St. SE17 4C 86
Larden Rd. W3 1A 82
Largewood Av. Surb 2G 147
Larissa St. SE17 5D 86
Larkbere Rd. SE26 4A 124
Larken Clo. Bush 1B 10
Larken Dri. Bush 1B 10
Larkfield Av. Harr 3B 26
Larkfield Clo. Brom 2H 155
Larkfield Rd. Rich 4E 98
Larkfield Rd. Sidc 3K 127
Larkhall La. SW4 2H 103
Larkhall Ri. SW4 3G 103
Larkham Clo. Felt 3G 113
Lark Row. E2 1J 69
Larksfield Gro. Enf 1C 8
Larks Gro. Bark 7J 55
Larkshall Ct. Romf 2J 39
Larkshall Cres. E4 4K 19
Larkshall Rd. E4 5K 19
Larkspur Clo. E6 5C 72
Larkspur Clo. N17 7J 17
Larkspur Clo. NW9 5H 27
Larkspur Clo. Ruis 7E 22
Larkspur Gro. Edgw 4D 12
Larkspur Lodge. Sidc 3B 128
Larkspur Way. Eps 5J 147
Larkswood Ct. E4 5A 20
Larkswood Ri. Pinn 4A 24
Larkswood Rd. E4 4H 19
Lark Way. Cars 7C 138
Larkway Clo. NW9 4K 27
Larnach Rd. W6 6F 83
Larne Rd. Ruis 7H 23
Larpent Av. SW15 5E 100
Larwood Clo. Gnfd 5H 43
Lascelles Av. Harr 7H 25
Lascelles Clo. E11 2F 53
Lascelles Ho. NW1 4D 158
Lascotts Rd. N22 6E 16
Laseron Ho. N15 4F 33 (off Tottenham Grn. E.)
Lassa Rd. SE9 5C 108
Lassell St. SE10 5F 89
Lasseter Pl. SE3 6G 89
Latchett Rd. E18 1K 35
Latchingdon Ct. E17 4K 33
Latchingdon Gdns. Wfd G 6H 21
Latchmere Clo. Rich 5E 116
Latchmere La. King T 6F 117
Latchmere Pas. SW11 2C 102
Latchmere Rd. SW11 2D 102
Latchmere Rd. King T 7E 116
Latchmere St. SW11 2D 102
Lateward Rd. Bren 6D 80
Latham Clo. E6 5C 72
Latham Clo. Twic 7A 98
Latham Ct. SW5 4J 83 (off W. Cromwell Rd.)
Latham Ct. N'holt 3B 60 (off Seasprite Clo.)
Latham Ho. E1 6K 69 (off Chudleigh St.)
Latham Rd. Bexh 5G 111
Latham Rd. Twic 7K 97
Latham's Way. Croy 1K 151
Lathkill Clo. Enf 7B 8
Lathkill Ct. Beck 1B 142
Lathom Rd. E6 7C 54
Latimer Av. E6 1D 72
Latimer Clo. Pinn 1A 24
Latimer Clo. Wor Pk 4D 148
Latimer Ct. Brom 4H 143 (off Durham Rd.)
Latimer Gdns. Pinn 1A 24
Latimer Ho. E9 6K 51
Latimer Ho. W11 7H 65 (off Kensington Pk. Rd.)
Latimer Pl. W10 6E 64
Latimer Rd. E7 4K 53
Latimer Rd. N15 6E 32
Latimer Rd. SW19 6K 119
Latimer Rd. W10 5E 64 (in two parts)
Latimer Rd. Barn 3E 4
Latimer Rd. Croy 3B 152
Latimer Rd. Tedd 5K 115
Latona Ct. SW9 7A 86 (off Caldwell St.)
Latona Rd. SE15 6G 87
Lattimer Pl. W4 7A 82
Latton Clo. W on T 7C 132
Latymer Ct. W6 4F 83
Latymer Gdns. N3 2G 29
Latymer Rd. N9 1A 18
Latymer Way. N9 2K 17
Lauder Clo. N'holt 2B 60
Lauder Ct. N14 7D 6
Lauderdale Dri. Rich 3D 116
Lauderdale Ho. SW9 1A 104 (off Gosling Way)
Lauderdale Mans. W9 3K 65 (off Lauderdale Rd., in two parts)
Lauderdale Pl. EC2 5C 68 (5C 162) (off Beech St.)
Lauderdale Rd. W9 3K 65
Lauderdale Tower. EC2 5C 162
Laud St. SE11 5K 85 (5G 173)
Laud St. Croy 3C 152
Laughton Rd. N'holt 1B 60
Launcelot Rd. Brom 4J 125
Launcelot St. SE1 2A 86 (7J 167)
Launceston Gdns. Gnfd 1C 62
Launceston Pl. W8 3A 84
Launceston Rd. Gnfd 1C 62
Launch St. E14 3E 88
Laundress La. N16 3G 51
Laundry La. N1 1C 68
Laundry M. SE23 7A 106
Laundry Rd. W6 6G 83
Launton Dri. Bexh 5D 110
Laura Clo. E11 5A 36
Laura Clo. Enf 5K 7
Lauradale Rd. N2 4D 30
Laura Pl. E5 4J 51
Laurel Av. Twic 1K 115
Laurel Bank. N12 4F 15
Laurel Bank Gdns. SW6 2H 101
Laurel Bank Rd. Enf 1H 7
Laurel Bank Vs. W7 2J 79 (off Lwr. Boston Rd.)
Laurelbrook. SE6 3G 125
Laurel Clo. N19 2G 49
Laurel Clo. SW17 5C 120
Laurel Clo. Sidc 3A 128
Laurel Ct. S Croy 4E 152 (off S. Park Hill Rd.)
Laurel Ct. Wemb 2E 62
Laurel Cres. Croy 3C 154
Laurel Cres. Romf 1K 57
Laurel Dri. N21 7F 7

Laurel Gdns. E4 7J 9
Laurel Gdns. NW7 3E 12
Laurel Gdns. W7 1J 79
Laurel Gdns. Houn 4C 96
Laurel Gro. SE20 7H 123
Laurel Gro. SE26 4K 123
Laurel Ho. SE8 6B 88
Laurel Ho. Short 1G 143
Laurel La. W Dray 4A 76
Laurel Mnr. Sutt 7A 150
Laurel Pk. Harr 7E 10
Laurel Rd. SW13 2C 100
Laurel Rd. SW20 1D 136
Laurel Rd. Hamp H 5H 115
Laurels, The. NW10 1D 64
Laurels, The. Brom (BR1) 1K 143
Laurels, The. Brom (BR2) 4J 143
Laurels, The. Buck H 1F 21
Laurels, The. Bush 2D 10
Laurel St. E8 6F 51
Laurel Vw. N12 3E 14
Laurel Way. E18 4H 35
Laurel Way. N20 3D 14
Laurence Ct. E10 7D 34
Laurence M. W12 2C 82
Laurence Pountney Hill. EC4 7D 68 (2E 168)
Laurence Pountney La. EC4 7D 68 (2E 168)
Laurie Gro. SE14 1A 106
Laurie Ho. SE1 3B 86 (off St George's Rd.)
Laurie Rd. W7 5J 61
Laurier Rd. NW5 3F 49
Laurier Rd. Croy 7F 141
Laurimel Clo. Stan 6G 11
Laurino Pl. Bush 2B 10
Lauriston Ho. E9 7J 51 (off Lauriston Rd.)
Lauriston Rd. E9 7J 51
Lauriston Rd. SW19 6F 119
Lausanne Rd. N8 4A 32
Lausanne Rd. SE15 1J 105
Lavell St. N16 4D 50
Lavender Av. NW9 1J 45
Lavender Av. Mitc 1C 138
Lavender Av. Wor Pk 3E 148
Lavender Clo. SW3 6B 84 (7B 170)
Lavender Clo. Brom 6C 144
Lavender Clo. Cars 4F 151
Lavender Ct. Felt 6K 95
Lavender Ct. W Mol 3F 133
Lavender Gdns. SW11 4D 102
Lavender Gdns. Enf 1G 7
Lavender Gdns. Har W 6D 10
Lavender Gro. E8 7G 51
Lavender Gro. Mitc 1C 138
Lavender Hill. SW11 4C 102
Lavender Hill. Enf 1F 7
Lavender Ho. SE16 1K 87 (off Rotherhithe St.)
Lavender Pl. Ilf 5F 55
Lavender Ri. W Dray 2C 76
Lavender Rd. SE16 1A 88
Lavender Rd. SW11 3B 102
Lavender Rd. Cars 4E 150
Lavender Rd. Croy 6K 139
Lavender Rd. Enf 1J 7
Lavender Rd. Eps 5H 147
Lavender Rd. Sutt 4B 150
Lavender Rd. Uxb 5B 58
Lavender Sq. E11 3F 53
Lavender St. E15 6G 53
Lavender Sweep. SW11 4D 102
Lavender Ter. SW11 3C 102
Lavender Va. Wall 6H 151
Lavender Wlk. SW11 4D 102
Lavender Wlk. Mitc 3E 138
Lavender Way. Croy 6K 141
Lavendon Ho. NW8 4C 66 (3D 158) (off Paveley St.)
Lavengro Rd. SE27 2C 122
Lavenham Rd. SW18 2H 119
Lavernock Rd. Bexh 2G 111
Lavers Rd. N16 3E 50
Laverstoke Gdns. SW15 7B 100
Laverton M. SW5 4K 83
Laverton Pl. SW5 4K 83
Lavidge Rd. SE9 2C 126
Lavina Gro. N1 2K 67
Lavington Clo. E9 6B 52
Lavington Rd. W13 1B 80
Lavington Rd. Croy 3K 151
Lavington St. SE1 1B 86 (5B 168)
Lavisham Ho. Brom 5J 125
Lawdons Gdns. Croy 4B 152
Lawford Clo. Wall 7J 151
Lawford Rd. N1 7E 50
Lawford Rd. NW5 6G 49
Lawford Rd. W4 7J 81
Law Ho. Bark 2A 74
Lawless Ho. E14 7E 70 (off Bazely St.)
Lawless St. E14 7D 70
Lawley Ho. Twic 6D 98
Lawley Rd. N14 7A 6
Lawley St. E5 4J 51
Lawn Clo. N9 7A 8
Lawn Clo. Brom 7K 125
Lawn Clo. N Mald 2A 136
Lawn Clo. Ruis 3H 41
Lawn Cres. Rich 2G 99
Lawn Dri. E7 4B 54
Lawn Farm Gro. Romf 4E 38
Lawn Gdns. W7 1J 79
Lawn Ho. Clo. E14 2E 88
Lawn La. SW8 6J 85 (7F 173)
Lawn Rd. NW3 5D 48
Lawn Rd. Beck 7B 124
Lawns Ct. Wemb 2F 45
Lawnside. SE3 4H 107
Lawns, The. E4 5H 19
Lawns, The. SE3 3H 107
Lawns, The. SE19 1D 140
Lawns, The. SW19 5H 119
Lawns, The. Pinn 7A 10
Lawns, The. Sidc 4B 128
Lawns, The. Sutt 7G 149
Lawnsway. Romf 1J 39
Lawnswood. Barn 5B 4
Lawn Ter. SE3 3G 107
Lawn, The. S'hall 5E 78
Lawn Va. Pinn 2C 24
Lawrence Av. E12 4E 54
Lawrence Av. E17 1K 33
Lawrence Av. N13 4G 17
Lawrence Av. NW7 4F 13
Lawrence Av. N Mald 6K 135
Lawrence Bldgs. N16 3F 51
Lawrence Campe Clo. N20 3G 15
Lawrence Clo. E3 3C 70
Lawrence Clo. N15 4E 32
Lawrence Clo. W12 7D 64
Lawrence Ct. NW7 5F 13
Lawrence Ct. W3 3J 81 (off Stanley Rd.)
Lawrence Cres. Dag 3H 57
Lawrence Cres. Edgw 2G 27
Lawrence Dri. Uxb 4E 40
Lawrence Est. Houn 4A 96
Lawrence Gdns. NW7 3G 13
Lawrence Hill. E4 2H 19
Lawrence Ho. SW1 4H 85 (4D 172) (off Cureton St.)
Lawrence La. EC2 6C 68 (7D 162)
Lawrence Pde. Iswth 3B 98 (off Lower Sq.)
Lawrence Pl. N1 1J 67 (off Brydon Wlk.)
Lawrence Rd. E6 1C 72
Lawrence Rd. E13 1K 71
Lawrence Rd. N15 4E 32
Lawrence Rd. N18 4C 18 (in two parts)
Lawrence Rd. SE25 4F 141
Lawrence Rd. W5 4C 80
Lawrence Rd. Eri 7H 93
Lawrence Rd. Hamp 7D 114
Lawrence Rd. Hay 2E 58
Lawrence Rd. Houn 4A 96
Lawrence Rd. Pinn 6B 24
Lawrence Rd. Rich 4C 116
Lawrence Rd. W Wick 4J 155
Lawrence St. E16 5H 71
Lawrence St. NW7 4G 13
Lawrence St. SW3 6C 84 (7C 170)
Lawrence Trad. Est. SE10 4G 89
Lawrence Way. NW10 3K 45
Lawrence Weaver Clo. Mord 6J 137
Lawrence Yd. N15 4E 32
Lawrie Pk. Av. SE26 5H 123
Lawrie Pk. Cres. SE26 5H 123
Lawrie Pk. Gdns. SE26 4H 123
Lawrie Pk. Rd. SE26 6H 123
Lawson Clo. E16 5A 72
Lawson Clo. SW19 3F 119
Lawson Ct. N4 1K 49 (off Lorne Rd.)
Lawson Ct. Surb 7D 134
Lawson Gdns. Pinn 3K 23
Lawson Ho. SE18 6E 90 (off Nightingale Pl.)
Lawson Ho. W12 7D 64 (off White City Est.)
Lawson Rd. Enf 1D 8
Lawson Rd. S'hall 4E 60
Law St. SE1 3D 86
Lawton Rd. E3 3A 70
Lawton Rd. E10 1E 52
Lawton Rd. Cockf 3G 5
Laxcon Clo. NW10 5K 45
Laxfield Ct. E8 1G 69 (off Pownall Rd.)
Laxford Ho. SW1 4E 84 (4H 171) (off Cundy St.)
Laxley Clo. SE5 7B 86
Laxton Pl. NW1 4F 67 (3K 159)
Layard Rd. SE16 4H 87
Layard Rd. Enf 1A 8
Layard Rd. T Hth 2D 140
Layard Sq. SE16 4H 87
Laybourne Ho. E14 2C 88 (off Admirals Way)
Laybrook Lodge. E18 4H 35
Laycock St. N1 6A 50
Layer Gdns. W3 7G 63
Layfield Clo. NW4 7D 28
Layfield Cres. NW4 7D 28
Layfield Ho. SE10 5J 89 (off Kemsing Rd.)
Layfield Rd. NW4 7D 28
Layhams Rd. W Wick & Kes 3F 155
Laymarsh Clo. Belv 3F 93
Laymead Clo. N'holt 6C 42
Laystall Ct. WC1 4A 68 (4J 161) (off Mount Pleasant)
Laystall St. EC1 4A 68 (4J 161)
Layton Ct. Bren 5D 80
Layton Cres. Croy 5A 152
Layton Pl. Kew 1G 99
Layton Rd. Bren 5D 80
Layton Rd. Houn 4F 97
Layton's Bldgs. SE1 2D 86 (6E 168)
Layton's La. Sun 2H 131
Layzell Wlk. SE9 1B 126
Lazar Wlk. N7 2K 49
Lazenby Ct. WC2 2E 166
Leabank Clo. Harr 3J 43
Leabank Sq. E9 6C 52
Leabank Vw. N15 6G 33
Lea Bon Ct. E15 1H 71 (off Plaistow Gro.)
Leabourne Rd. N16 7G 33
Lea Bridge. 3K 51
Lea Bri. Ind. Cen. E10 1A 52
Lea Bri. Rd. E5 & E10 3J 51
Lea Clo. Twic 7D 96
Lea Ct. E4 2K 19
Lea Ct. E13 3J 71
Lea Cres. Ruis 4H 41
Leacroft Av. SW12 7D 102
Leacroft Clo. W Dray 6A 58
Leadale Av. E4 2H 19
Leadale Rd. N15 & N16 6G 33
Leadbeaters Clo. N11 5J 15
Leadbetter Ct. NW10 7K 45 (off Melville Rd.)
Leadenhall Market. 6E 68 (1G 169)
Leadenhall Pl. EC3 6E 68 (1G 169)
Leadenhall St. EC3 6E 68 (1G 169)
Leadenham Ct. E3 4C 70
Leader Av. E12 5E 54
Leadings, The. Wemb 3J 45
Leaf Clo. N'wd 1F 23
Leaf Clo. Th Dit 5J 133
Leaf Gro. SE27 5A 122
Leafield Clo. SW16 6B 122
Leafield La. Sidc 3F 129
Leafield Rd. SW20 3H 137
Leafield Rd. Sutt 2J 149
Leafy Gro. Kes 5A 156
Leafy Oak Rd. SE12 4A 126
Leafy Way. Croy 2F 153
Lea Gdns. Wemb 4F 45
Leagrave St. E5 3J 51
Lea Hall Gdns. E10 1C 52
Lea Hall Rd. E10 1C 52
Leaholme Way. Ruis 6E 22
Lea Ho. NW8 4C 66 (4C 158) (off Salisbury St.)
Leahurst Rd. SE13 5F 107
Lea Interchange. (Junct.) 5C 52
Leake Ct. SE1 2K 85 (7H 167)
Leake St. SE1 2K 85 (6H 167) (in two parts)
Lealand Rd. N15 6F 33
Leamington Av. E17 5C 34
Leamington Av. Brom 5A 126
Leamington Av. Mord 4G 137
Leamington Clo. E12 5C 54
Leamington Clo. Brom 4A 126
Leamington Clo. Houn 5G 97
Leamington Cres. Harr 3C 42
Leamington Gdns. Ilf 2K 55
Leamington Ho. Edgw 5A 12
Leamington Pk. W3 5K 63
Leamington Pl. Hay 4H 59
Leamington Rd. S'hall 4B 78
Leamington Rd. Vs. W11 5H 65
Leamore St. W6 4E 82
Leamouth. 7G 71
Leamouth Rd. E6 5C 72
Leamouth Rd. E14 6F 71
Leander Ct. NW9 1A 28
Leander Ct. SE8 1C 106
Leander Ct. Surb 7D 134
Leander Rd. SW2 6K 103
Leander Rd. N'holt 2E 60
Leander Rd. T Hth 4K 139
Lea Pk. Trad. Est. E10 1B 52 (off Warley Clo.)
Leapold M. E9 1J 69
Learner Dri. Harr 2E 42
Lea Rd. Beck 2C 142
Lea Rd. Enf 1J 7
Lea Rd. S'hall 4C 78
Learoyd Gdns. E6 7E 72
Leary Ho. SE11 5K 85 (6H 173)
Leas Clo. Chess 7F 147
Leas Dale. SE9 3E 126
Leas Grn. Chst 6K 127
Leaside Av. N10 3E 30
Leaside Bus. Cen. Enf 2G 9
Leaside Ct. Uxb 3D 58
Leaside Mans. N10 3E 30 (off Fortis Grn.)
Leaside Rd. E5 1J 51
Leasowes Rd. E10 1C 52
Leatherbottle Grn. Eri 3F 93
Leather Bottle La. Belv 4E 92
Leather Clo. Mitc 2E 138
Leatherdale St. E1 4J 69 (in two parts)
Leather Gdns. E15 1G 71
Leatherhead Clo. N16 1F 51
Leatherhead Rd. Chess 7D 146
Leather La. EC1 5A 68 (5J 161) (in two parts)
Leathermarket Ct. SE1 2E 86 (7G 169)
Leathermarket St. SE1 2E 86 (7G 169)
Leathersellers Clo. Barn 3B 4
Leathsail Rd. Harr 3F 43
Leathwaite Rd. SW11 4D 102
Leathwell Rd. SE8 2D 106
Lea Va. Dart 4K 111
Lea Valley Rd. Enf & E4 5F 9
Lea Valley Trad. Est. N18 6E 18
Lea Valley Viaduct. N18 & E4 5E 18
Leaveland Clo. Beck 4C 142
Leaver Gdns. Gnfd 2H 61
Leavesden Rd. Stan 6F 11
Leaves Grn. Rd. Kes 7B 156
Lea Vw. Ho. E5 1H 51
Leaway. E10 1K 51
Lebanon Av. Felt 5B 114
Lebanon Gdns. SW18 6J 101
Lebanon Pk. Twic 7B 98
Lebanon Rd. SW18 5J 101
Lebanon Rd. Croy 1E 152
Lebrun Sq. SE3 4K 107
Lebus Ho. NW8 2C 66 (1C 158) (off Cochrane St.)
Le Chateau. Croy 3D 152 (off Chatsworth Rd.)
Lechmere App. Wfd G 2A 36
Lechmere Av. Wfd G 2B 36
Lechmere Rd. NW2 6D 46
Leckford Rd. SW18 2A 120
Leckhampton Pl. SW2 7A 104
Leckwith Av. Bexh 6E 92
Lecky St. SW7 5B 84 (5A 170)
Leclair Ho. SE3 3K 107
Leconfield Av. SW13 3B 100
Leconfield Ho. SE5 4E 104
Leconfield Rd. N5 4D 50
Leda Av. Enf 1E 8
Leda Ct. SW9 7A 86 (off Caldwell St.)
Ledam Ho. EC1 5A 68 (5J 161) (off Bourne Est.)
Leda Rd. SE18 3D 90
Ledbury Ho. SE22 3E 104
Ledbury Ho. W11 6H 65 (off Colville Rd.)
Ledbury M. N. W11 7J 65
Ledbury M. W. W11 7J 65
Ledbury Pl. Croy 4C 152
Ledbury Rd. W11 6H 65
Ledbury Rd. Croy 4D 152
Ledbury St. SE15 7G 87
Ledrington Rd. SE19 6G 123
Ledway Dri. Wemb 7F 27
Lee. 5H 107
Lee Av. Romf 6E 38
Lee Bri. SE13 3E 106
Leechcroft Av. Sidc 5K 109
Leechcroft Rd. Wall 3E 150
Lee Chu. St. SE13 4G 107
Lee Clo. E17 1K 33
Lee Clo. Barn 4F 5
Lee Conservancy Rd. E9 5B 52

Lee Ct. SE13 4F 107
(off Lee High Rd.)
Leecroft Rd. Barn 5B 4
Leeds Pl. N4 1K 49
Leeds Rd. Ilf 1H 55
Leeds St. N18 5B 18
Leefern Rd. W12 2C 82
Leegate. SE12 5H 107
Lee Green. (Junct.) 5H 107
Lee Gro. Chig 2K 21
Lee High Rd. SE13 & SE12 3E 106
Lee Ho. EC2 5C 68 (6D 162)
(off Monkwell Sq.)
Leeke St. WC1 3K 67 (1G 161)
Leeland Rd. W13 1A 80
Leeland Ter. W13 1A 80
Leeland Way. NW10 4B 46
Leemount Clo. NW4 4F 29
Leemount Ho. NW4 4F 29
Lee Pk. SE3 4H 107
Lee Pk. Way. N18 & N9 4E 18
Leerdam Dri. E14 3E 88
Lee Rd. NW7 7A 14
Lee Rd. SE3 3H 107
Lee Rd. SW19 1K 137
Lee Rd. Enf 6B 8
Lee Rd. Gnfd 1C 62
Lees Av. N'wd 1H 23
Lees Ct. W1 7E 66 (2G 165)
(off Lees Pl.)
Leeside. Barn 5B 4
Leeside Ct. SE16 1K 87
(off Rotherhithe St.)
Leeside Cres. NW11 6G 29
Leeside Ind. Est. N17 7D 18
Leeside Rd. N17 6C 18
Leeside Works. N17 7D 18
Leeson Ho. Twic 7B 98
Leeson Rd. SE24 4A 104
Leesons Hill. Chst & Orp 3J 145
Leeson's Way. Orp 2K 145
Lees Pde. Uxb 4D 58
Lees Pl. W1 7E 66 (2G 165)
Lees Rd. Uxb 4D 58
Lees, The. Croy 2B 154
Lee St. E8 1F 69
Lee Ter. SE3 3G 107
Lee Valley Ice Cen. 2K 51
Lee Valley Leisure Golf Course. 7F 9
Lee Valley Technopark. N17 3G 33
Lee Vw. Enf 1G 7
Leeward Ct. E1 7G 69
Leeward Gdns. SW19 5G 119
Leeway. SE8 5B 88
Leeway Clo. H End 1D 24
Leeways, The. Sutt 6G 149
Leewood Clo. SE12 6H 107
Lefa Bus. & Ind. Est. Sidc 6D 128
Lefevre Wlk. E3 1B 70
Leff Ho. NW6 1G 65
Lefroy Ho. SE1 2C 86 (7C 168)
(off Southwark Bri. Rd.)
Lefroy Rd. W12 2B 82
Legard Rd. N5 3B 50
Legatt Rd. SE9 5B 108
Leggatt Rd. E15 2E 70
Legge St. SE13 5E 106
Leghorn Rd. NW10 2B 64
Leghorn Rd. SE18 5H 91
Legion Clo. N1 7A 50
Legion Ct. Mord 6J 137
Legion Rd. Gnfd 1G 61
Legion Ter. E3 1B 70
Legion Way. N12 7H 15
Legon Av. Romf 1J 57
Legrace Av. Houn 2B 96
Leicester Av. Mitc 4J 139
Leicester Clo. Wor Pk 4E 148
Leicester Ct. W9 5J 65
(off Elmfield Way)
Leicester Ct. WC2 2D 166
Leicester Ct. Twic 6D 98
(off Clevedon Rd.)
Leicester Fields. WC2 7H 67 (3D 166)
(off Leicester Sq.)
Leicester Gdns. Ilf 7J 37
Leicester Ho. SW9 3B 104
(off Loughborough Rd.)
Leicester M. N2 3C 30
Leicester Pl. WC2 7H 67 (2D 166)
Leicester Rd. E11 5K 35
Leicester Rd. N2 3C 30
Leicester Rd. NW10 7K 45
Leicester Rd. Barn 5E 4
Leicester Rd. Croy 7E 140
Leicester Sq. WC2 7H 67 (3D 166)
Leicester St. WC2 7H 67 (2D 166)
Leigham Av. SW16 3J 121
Leigham Clo. SW16 3K 121
Leigham Ct. Rd. SW16 2J 121
Leigham Dri. Iswth 7J 79
Leigham Hall Pde. SW16 3J 121
(off Streatham High Rd.)
Leigham Va. SW16 & SW2 3K 121
Leigh Av. Ilf 4B 36
Leigh Clo. N Mald 4J 135
Leigh Clo. Ind. Est. N Mald 4K 135
Leigh Ct. Harr 1J 43
Leigh Cres. New Ad 7D 154
Leigh Gdns. NW10 2E 64
Leigh Hunt Dri. N14 1C 16
Leigh Orchard Clo. SW16 3K 121
Leigh Pl. EC1 5A 68 (5J 161)
Leigh Pl. Well 2A 110
Leigh Rd. E6 6E 54
Leigh Rd. E10 7E 34
Leigh Rd. N5 4B 50
Leigh Rd. Houn 4H 97
Leigh St. WC1 3J 67 (2E 160)
Leighton Av. E12 5E 54
Leighton Av. Pinn 3C 24
Leighton Clo. Edgw 2G 27
Leighton Cres. NW5 5G 49
Leighton Gdns. NW10 2D 64
Leighton Gdns. Croy 1B 152
Leighton Gro. NW5 5G 49
Leighton Ho. SW1 4H 85 (4D 172)
(off Herrick St.)
Leighton House Mus. & Art Galley. 3H 83
Leighton Mans. W14 6G 83
(off Greyhound Rd.)
Leighton Pl. NW5 5G 49
Leighton Rd. NW5 5G 49
Leighton Rd. W13 2A 80
Leighton Rd. Enf 5A 8
Leighton Rd. Har W 2H 25
Leighton St. Croy 1B 152
Leila Parnell Pl. SE7 6A 90
Leinster Av. SW14 3J 99
Leinster Gdns. W2 6A 66
Leinster M. W2 7A 66
Leinster Pl. W2 6A 66
Leinster Rd. N10 4F 31
Leinster Sq. W2 6J 65
(in two parts)
Leinster Ter. W2 7A 66
Leisure Way. N12 7G 15
Leisure West. Felt 2K 113
Leith Clo. NW9 1K 45
Leithcote Gdns. SW16 4K 121
Leithcote Path. SW16 3K 121
Leith Hill. Orp 1K 145
Leith Hill Grn. Orp 1K 145
Leith Mans. W9 3K 65
(off Grantully Rd.)
Leith Rd. N22 1B 32
Leith Towers. Sutt 7K 149
Lela Av. Houn 2A 96
Lelita Clo. E8 1G 69
Lely Ho. N'holt 2B 60
(off Academy Gdns.)
Leman Pas. E1 6G 69
(off Leman St.)
Leman St. E1 6F 69 (1K 169)
Lemark Clo. Stan 6H 11
Le May Av. SE12 3K 125
Lemmon Rd. SE10 6G 89
Lemna Rd. E11 7H 35
Le Moal Ho. E1 5J 69
(off Stepney Way)
Lemon Gro. Felt 1J 113
Lemonwell Dri. SE9 6G 109
Lemsford Clo. N15 6G 33
Lemsford Ct. N4 2C 50
Lemuel St. SW18 6A 102
Lena Cres. N9 2D 18
Lena Gdns. W6 3E 82
Lena Kennedy Clo. E4 6K 19
Lenanton Steps. E14 2C 88
(off Manilla St.)
Len Clifton Ho. SE18 4D 90
(off Cambridge Barracks Rd.)
Lendal Ter. SW4 3H 103
Lenelby Rd. Surb 1G 147
Len Freeman Pl. SW6 6H 83
Lenham Ho. SE1 3D 86 (7F 169)
(off Long La.)
Lenham Rd. SE12 4H 107
Lenham Rd. Bexh 6F 93
Lenham Rd. Sutt 4K 149
Lenham Rd. T Hth 2D 140
Lennard Av. W Wick 2G 155
Lennard Clo. W Wick 2G 155
Lennard Rd. SE20 & Beck 6K 123
Lennard Rd. Brom 1D 156
Lennard Rd. Croy 1C 152
Lennon Rd. NW2 5E 46
Lennox Gdns. NW10 4B 46
Lennox Gdns. SW1 3D 84 (2E 170)
Lennox Gdns. Croy 4B 152
Lennox Gdns. Ilf 1D 54
Lennox Gdns. M. SW1 3D 84 (2E 170)
Lennox Ho. Belv 3G 93
(off Picardy St.)
Lennox Ho. Twic 6D 98
(off Clevedon Rd.)
Lennox Lewis Cen. E5 2J 51
Lennox Rd. E17 6B 34
Lennox Rd. N4 2K 49
Lenor Clo. Bexh 4E 110
Lensbury Way. SE2 3C 92
Lens Rd. E7 7A 54
Lenthall Ho. SW1 5G 85 (6B 172)
(off Churchill Gdns.)
Lenthall Rd. E8 7G 51
Lenthorp Rd. SE10 4H 89
Lentmead Rd. Brom 3H 125
Lenton Path. SE18 6H 91
Lenton Ri. Rich 3E 98
Lenton Rd. SE18 4H 91
Len Williams Ct. NW6 2J 65
Leo Ct. Bren 7D 80
Leof Cres. SE6 5D 124
Leominster Rd. Mord 6A 138
Leominster Wlk. Mord 6A 138
Leonard Av. Mord 5A 138
Leonard Av. Romf 1K 57
Leonard Ct. WC1 4H 67 (3D 160)
Leonard Ct. Har W 1J 25
Leonard Rd. E4 6H 19
Leonard Rd. E7 4J 53
Leonard Rd. N9 3A 18
Leonard Rd. SW16 1G 139
Leonard Rd. S'hall 3B 78
Leonard Robbins Path. SE28 7B 74
(off Tawney Rd.)
Leonard St. E16 1C 90
Leonard St. EC2 4D 68 (3F 163)
Leonora Ho. W9 4A 66
(off Lanark Rd.)
Leontine Clo. SE15 7G 87
Leopards Ct. EC1 5J 161
Leopold Av. SW19 5H 119
Leopold Bldgs. E2 3F 69 (1J 163)
(off Columbia Rd.)
Leopold Rd. E17 5C 34
Leopold Rd. N2 3B 30
Leopold Rd. N18 5C 18
Leopold Rd. NW10 7A 46
Leopold Rd. SW19 4H 119
Leopold Rd. W5 1F 81
Leopold St. E3 5B 70
Leopold Ter. SW19 5H 119
Leo St. SE15 7H 87
Leo Yd. EC1 4B 162
Leppoc Rd. SW4 5H 103
Leroy St. SE1 4E 86
Lerry Clo. W14 6H 83
Lerwick Ct. Enf 5K 7
Lescombe Clo. SE23 3A 124
Lescombe Rd. SE23 3A 124
Lesley Clo. Bex 7H 111
Leslie Gdns. Sutt 6J 149
Leslie Gro. Croy 1E 152
Leslie Gro. Pl. Croy 1E 152
Leslie Pk. Rd. Croy 1E 152
Leslie Prince Ct. SE5 7D 86
Leslie Rd. E11 4E 52
Leslie Rd. E16 6K 71
Leslie Rd. N2 3B 30
Leslie Smith Sq. SE18 6E 90
Lesnes Abbey (Remains of). 4D 92
Lesney Farm Est. Eri 7K 93
Lesney Pk. Eri 6K 93
Lesney Pk. Rd. Eri 6K 93
Lessar Av. SW4 6G 103
Lessingham Av. SW17 4D 120
Lessingham Av. Ilf 3E 36
Lessing St. SE23 7A 106
Lessington Av. Romf 6J 39
Lessness Av. Bexh 7D 92
Lessness Heath. 5G 93
Lessness Pk. Belv 5F 93
Lessness Rd. Belv 6G 93
Lessness Rd. Mord 6A 138
Lester Av. E15 4G 71
Leswin Pl. N16 3F 51
Leswin Rd. N16 3F 51
Letchford Gdns. NW10 3C 64
Letchford M. NW10 3C 64
Letchford Ter. Harr 1F 25
Letchmore Ho. W10 4E 64
(off Sutton Way)
Letchworth Av. Felt 7H 95
Letchworth Clo. Brom 5J 143
Letchworth Dri. Brom 5J 143
Letchworth St. SW17 4D 120
Lethbridge Clo. SE13 1E 106
Letterstone Rd. SW6 7H 83
Lettice St. SW6 1H 101
Lett Rd. E15 7F 53
Lettsom St. SE5 2E 104
Lettsom Wlk. E13 2J 71
Leucha Rd. E17 5A 34
Levana Clo. SW19 1G 119
Levant Ho. E1 4K 69
(off Ernest St.)
Levehurst Ho. SE27 5C 122
Levendale Rd. SE23 2A 124
Levenhurst Way. SW4 2J 103
Leven Rd. E14 5E 70
Leven Way. Hay 6G 59
Leverett St. SW3 4C 84 (3D 170)
Leverholme Gdns. SE9 3E 126
Leverington Pl. N1 2F 163
Leverson St. SW16 6G 121
Leverstock Ho. SW3 5C 84 (5D 170)
(off Cale St.)
Lever St. EC1 3B 68 (2B 162)
Leverton Pl. NW5 5G 49
Leverton St. NW5 5G 49
Levett Gdns. Ilf 4K 55
Levett Rd. Bark 6J 55
Levine Gdns. Bark 2D 74
Levison Way. N19 1H 49
Levita Ho. NW1 1D 160
(in two parts)
Lewes Clo. N'holt 6E 42
Lewesdon Clo. SW19 1F 119
Lewes Ho. SE1 2E 86 (6H 169)
(off Druid St.)
Lewes Ho. SE15 6G 87
(off Friary Est.)
Lewes Rd. N12 5H 15
Lewes Rd. Brom 2B 144
Leweston Pl. N16 7F 33
Lewey Ho. E3 4B 70
(off Joseph St.)
Lewgars Av. NW9 6J 27
Lewing Clo. Orp 7J 145
Lewin Rd. SW14 3K 99
Lewin Rd. SW16 6H 121
Lewin Rd. Bexh 5E 110
Lewis Av. E17 1C 34
Lewis Clo. N14 7B 6
Lewis Ct. SE16 5H 87
(off Stubbs Dri.)
Lewis Cres. NW10 5K 45
Lewis Gdns. N2 2B 30
Lewis Gro. SE13 4E 106
Lewisham. 3E 106
Lewisham Bus. Cen. SE14 6K 87
Lewisham Cen. SE13 4E 106
Lewisham Crematorium. SE6 2H 125
Lewisham Heights. SE23 1J 123
Lewisham High St. SE13 3E 106
(Lewisham Rd.)
Lewisham High St. SE13 6D 106
(Rushey Grn.)
Lewisham Hill. SE13 2E 106
Lewisham Model Mkt. SE13 4E 106
(off Lewisham High St.)
Lewisham Pk. SE13 5E 106
Lewisham Rd. SE13 1D 106
Lewisham St. SW1 2H 85 (7D 166)
(in two parts)
Lewisham Way. SE14 & SE4 1B 106
Lewis Ho. E14 1E 88
(off Coldharbour)
Lewis Pl. E8 5G 51
Lewis Rd. Mitc 2B 138
(in two parts)
Lewis Rd. Rich 5D 98
Lewis Rd. Sidc 3C 128
Lewis Rd. S'hall 2C 78
Lewis Rd. Sutt 4K 149
Lewis Rd. Well 3C 110
Lewis Silkin Ho. SE15 6J 87
(off Lovelinch Clo.)
Lewis St. NW1 6F 49
(in two parts)
Lewis Way. Dag 6H 57
Lexden Dri. Romf 6B 38
Lexden Rd. W3 7H 63
Lexden Rd. Mitc 4H 139
Lexham Gdns. W8 4J 83
Lexham Gdns. M. W8 3K 83
Lexham Ho. Bark 1H 73
(off St Margarets)
Lexham M. W8 4J 83
Lexham Wlk. W8 3K 83
Lexington Apartments. EC1 4D 68 (3F 163)
Lexington St. W1 7G 67 (2B 166)
Lexington Way. Barn 4A 4
Lexton Gdns. SW12 1H 121
Leyborne Av. W13 2B 80
Leyborne Pk. Rich 1G 99
Leybourne Clo. Brom 6J 143

Leybourne Ho. E14 . . . . 6B 70
Leybourne Ho. SE15 . . . . 6J 87
Leybourne Rd. E11 . . . . 1H 53
Leybourne Rd. NW1 . . . . 7F 49
Leybourne Rd. NW9 . . . . 5G 27
Leybourne Rd. Uxb 1E 58
Leybourne St. NW1 . . . . 7F 49
Leybridge Ct. SE12 . . . . 5J 107
Leyburn Clo. E17 . . . . 4D 34
Leyburn Gdns. Croy 2E 152
Leyburn Gro. N18 . . . . 6B 18
Leyburn Rd. N18 . . . . 6B 18
Leydenhatch La. Swan 7J 129
Leyden Mans. N19 . . . . 7J 31
Leyden St. E1 . . . . . 5F 69 (6J 163)
Leydon Clo. SE16 . . . . 1K 87
Leyes Rd. E16 . . . . 7B 72
Leyfield. Wor Pk 1A 148
Leyland Av. Enf 2F 9
Leyland Gdns. Wfd G 5F 21
Leyland Ho. E14 . . . . 7D 70
(off Hale St.)
Leyland Rd. SE12 . . . . 5J 107
Leylang Rd. SE14 . . . . 7K 87
Leys Av. Dag 1J 75
Leys Clo. Dag 7K 57
(in two parts)
Leys Clo. Harr 5H 25
Leys Ct. SW9 . . . . 2A 104
Leysdown Av. Bexh 4J 111
Leysdown Ho. SE17 . . . . 5E 86
(off Madron St.)
Leysdown Rd. SE9 . . . . 2C 126
Leysfield Rd. W12 . . . . 3C 82
Leys Gdns. Barn 5K 5
Leyspring Rd. E11 . . . . 1H 53
Leys Rd. E. Enf 1F 9
Leys Rd. W. Enf 1F 9
Leys Sq. N3 . . . . 1K 29
Leys, The. N2 . . . . 4A 30
Leys, The. Harr 6F 27
Ley St. Ilf 2F 55
Leyswood Dri. Ilf 5J 37
Leythe Rd. W3 . . . . 2J 81
Leyton 3E 52
Leyton Bus. Cen. E10 . . . . . . 2C 52
Leyton Ct. SE23 . . . . 1J 123
Leyton Grange Est. E10 . . . . . 2C 52
Leyton Grn. Rd. E10 . . . . 6E 34
Leyton Ind. Village. E17 . . . . . 7K 33
Leyton Orient F.C. (Brisbane Rd.) 3D 52
Leyton Pk. Rd. E10 . . . . 3E 52
Leyton Rd. E15 . . . . 5E 52
Leyton Rd. SW19 . . . . 7A 120
Leytonstone 1G 53
Leytonstone Rd. E15 . . . . 4G 53
Leyton Way. E11 . . . . 7G 35
Leywick St. E15 . . . . 2G 71
Liardet St. SE14 . . . . 6A 88
Liberia Rd. N5 . . . . 6B 50
Liberty Av. SW19 . . . . 1A 138
Liberty Ct. Bark 2B 74
Liberty M. N22 . . . . 1B 32
Liberty M. SW12 . . . . 6F 103
Liberty St. SW9 . . . . 1K 103
Libra Ct. E4 . . . . 4H 19
Libra Rd. E3 . . . . 2B 70
Libra Rd. E13 . . . . 2J 71
Library Ct. N17 . . . . 3F 33
Library Mans. W12 . . . . 2E 82
(off Pennard Rd.)
Library Pde. NW10 . . . . 1A 64
(off Craven Pk. Rd.)
Library Pl. E1 . . . . 7H 69
Library St. SE1 . . . . 2B 86 (7A 168)
Library Way. Twic 7G 97
Lichfield Clo. Barn 3J 5
Lichfield Ct. Rich 4E 98
Lichfield Ct. Surb 5E 134
(off Claremont Rd.)
Lichfield Gdns. Rich 4E 98
Lichfield Gro. N3 . . . . 1J 29
Lichfield Rd. E3 . . . . 3A 70
Lichfield Rd. E6 . . . . 3B 72
Lichfield Rd. N9 . . . . 2B 18
Lichfield Rd. NW2 . . . . 4G 47
Lichfield Rd. Dag 4B 56
Lichfield Rd. Houn 3A 96
Lichfield Rd. N'wd 3J 23
Lichfield Rd. Rich 1F 99
Lichfield Rd. Wfd G 4B 20
Lichfield Ter. Rich 5E 98
Lickey Ho. W14 . . . . 6H 83
(off N. End Rd.)
Lidbury Rd. NW7 . . . . 6B 14
Lidcote Gdns. SW9 . . . . 2K 103
Liddall Way. W Dray 1B 76
Liddell Clo. Harr 3D 26
Liddell Gdns. NW10 . . . . 2E 64
Liddell Rd. NW6 . . . . 6J 47
Lidding Rd. Harr 5D 26
Liddington Rd. E15 . . . . 1H 71
Liddon Rd. E13 . . . . 3K 71
Liddon Rd. Brom 3A 144
Liden Clo. E17 . . . . 7B 34
Lidfield Rd. N16 . . . . 4D 50
Lidgate Rd. SE15 . . . . 7F 87
Lidiard Rd. SW18 . . . . 2A 120
Lidlington Pl. NW1 . . . . 2G 67
Lido Sq. N17 . . . . 2D 32
Lidyard Rd. N19 . . . . 1G 49
Lifetimes Mus. 3C 152
(off High St.)
Liffler Rd. SE18 . . . . 5J 91
Liffords Pl. SW13 . . . . 2B 100
Lifford St. SW15 . . . . 4F 101
Lightcliffe Rd. N13 . . . . 4F 17
Lighter Clo. SE16 . . . . 4A 88
Lighterman Ho. E14 . . . . 7E 70
Lighterman M. E1 . . . . 6K 69
Lightermans Rd. E14 . . . . 2C 88
Lightermans Wlk. SW18 . . . . 4J 101
Lightfoot Rd. N8 . . . . 5J 31
Light Horse Ct. SW3 . . . . . . 6G 171
Lightley Clo. Wemb 1E 62
Ligonier St. E2 . . . . . 4F 69 (3J 163)
Lilac Clo. E4 . . . . 6G 19
Lilac Ct. E13 . . . . 1A 72
Lilac Ct. Tedd 4K 115
Lilac Gdns. W5 . . . . 3D 80
Lilac Gdns. Croy 3C 154
Lilac Gdns. Hay 6G 59
Lilac Gdns. Romf 1K 57
Lilac Ho. SE4 . . . . 3C 106
Lilac Pl. SE11 . . . . . 4K 85 (4G 173)
Lilac Pl. W Dray 7B 58
Lilac St. W12 . . . . 7C 64
Lilburne Gdns. SE9 . . . . 5C 108
Lilburne Rd. SE9 . . . . 5C 108
Lilburne Wlk. NW10 . . . . 6J 45
Lile Cres. W7 . . . . 5J 61
Lilestone Ho. NW8 . . . . 4B 66 (3B 158)
(off Frampton St.)
Lilestone St. NW8 . . . . 4C 66 (3C 158)
Lilford Ho. SE5 . . . . 2C 104
Lilford Rd. SE5 . . . . 2B 104
Lilian Barker Clo. SE12 . . . . 5J 107
Lilian Board Way. Gnfd 5H 43
Lilian Clo. N16 . . . . 3E 50
Lilian Gdns. Wfd G 1K 35
Lilian Rd. SW16 . . . . 1G 139
Lillechurch Rd. Dag 6B 56
Lilleshall Rd. Mord 6B 138
Lilley Clo. E1 . . . . 1G 87
Lilley La. NW7 . . . . 5E 12
Lillian Av. W3 . . . . 2G 81
Lillian Rd. SW13 . . . . 6C 82
Lillie Mans. SW6 . . . . 6G 83
(off Lillie Rd.)
Lillie Rd. SW6 . . . . 6G 83
Lillieshall Rd. SW4 . . . . 3F 103
Lillie Yd. SW6 . . . . 6J 83
Lillington Gdns. Est. SW1 . . . . 4B 172
Lilliput Av. N'holt 1C 60
Lilliput Ct. SE12 . . . . 5K 107
Lilliput Rd. Romf 7K 39
Lily Clo. W14 . . . . 4F 83
(in two parts)
Lily Gdns. Wemb 2C 62
Lily Nichols Ho. E16 . . . . 1B 90
(off Connaught Rd.)
Lily Pl. EC1 . . . . . . 5A 68 (5K 161)
Lily Rd. E17 . . . . 6C 34
Lilyville Rd. SW6 . . . . 1H 101
Limberg Ho. SE8 . . . . 4B 88
Limborough Ho. E14 . . . . 5C 70
(off Thomas Rd.)
Limbourne Av. Dag 7F 39
Limburg Rd. SW11 . . . . 4C 102
Lime Av. W Dray 7B 58
Limeburner La. EC4 . . . . 6B 68 (1A 168)
Lime Clo. E1 . . . . 1G 87
Lime Clo. Brom 4C 144
Lime Clo. Buck H 2G 21
Lime Clo. Cars 2D 150
Lime Clo. Harr 2A 26
Lime Clo. Pinn 3H 23
Lime Clo. Romf 4J 39
Lime Ct. E11 . . . . 2G 53
(off Trinity Clo.)
Lime Ct. E17 . . . . 5E 34
Lime Ct. SE9 . . . . 2F 127
Lime Ct. Harr 6K 25
Lime Ct. Mitc 2B 138
Lime Cres. Sun 2A 132
Limecroft Clo. Eps 7K 147
Limedene Clo. Pinn 1B 24
Lime Gro. E4 . . . . 6G 19
Lime Gro. N20 . . . . 1C 14
Lime Gro. W12 . . . . 2E 82
Lime Gro. Hay 7F 59
Lime Gro. N Mald 3K 135
Lime Gro. Ruis 6K 23
Lime Gro. Sidc 6K 109
Lime Gro. Twic 6K 97
Limeharbour. E14 . . . . 3D 88
Limehouse 6B 70
Limehouse Causeway. E14 . . . 7B 70
Limehouse Ct. E14 . . . . 6C 70
(off Dod St.)
Limehouse Cut. E14 . . . . 5D 70
(off Morris Rd.)
Limehouse Fields Est. E1 . . . . 5A 70
Limehouse Link. E14 . . . . 6A 70
Lime Kiln Dri. SE7 . . . . 6K 89
Limekiln Pl. SE19 . . . . 7F 123
Limerick Clo. SW12 . . . . 7G 103
Lime Rd. Eri 3F 93
Lime Rd. Rich 4F 99
Lime Row. Eri 3F 93
Limerston St. SW10 . . . . 6A 84 (7A 170)
Limes Av. E11 . . . . 4K 35
Limes Av. E12 . . . . 3C 54
Limes Av. N12 . . . . 4F 15
Limes Av. NW7 . . . . 6F 13
Limes Av. NW11 . . . . 7G 29
Limes Av. SE20 . . . . 7H 123
Limes Av. SW13 . . . . 2B 100
Limes Av. Cars 1D 150
Limes Av. Croy 3A 152
Limes Av., The. N11 . . . . 5A 16
Limes Clo. N11 . . . . 5B 16
Limes Clo. Ashf 5C 112
Limes Ct. NW6 . . . . 7G 47
(off Brondesbury Pk.)
Limesdale Gdns. Edgw 2J 27
Limes Fld. Rd. SW14 . . . . . . 3A 100
Limesford Rd. SE15 . . . . . . 4K 105
Limes Gdns. SW18 . . . . 6J 101
Limes Gro. SE13 . . . . 4E 106
Limes Pl. Croy 7D 140
Limes Rd. Beck 2D 142
Limes Rd. Croy 6D 140
Limes, The. SW18 . . . . 6J 101
Limes, The. W2 . . . . 7J 65
Limes, The. Brom 2C 156
Limes, The. E Mol 4F 133
Limestone Wlk. Eri 2D 92
Lime St. E17 . . . . 4A 34
Lime St. EC3 . . . . . 7E 68 (2G 169)
Lime St. Pas. EC3 . . . . 6E 68 (1G 169)
Limes Wlk. SE15 . . . . 4J 105
Limes Wlk. W5 . . . . 2D 80
Lime Ter. W7 . . . . 7J 61
Lime Tree Av. Esh 7H 133
Limetree Clo. SW2 . . . . 1K 121
Lime Tree Ct. S Croy 6C 152
Lime Tree Gro. Croy 3B 154
Lime Tree Pl. Mitc 1F 139
Lime Tree Rd. Houn 1F 97
Limetree Ter. SE6 . . . . 1B 124
Limetree Ter. Well 3A 110
Limetree Wlk. SW17 . . . . . . 5E 120
Lime Tree Wlk. Bush 1D 10
Lime Tree Wlk. Enf 1H 7
Lime Tree Wlk. W Wick 4H 155
Lime Wlk. E15 . . . . 1G 71
Limewood Clo. E17 . . . . 4B 34
Limewood Clo. W13 . . . . 6B 62
Limewood Clo. Beck 5E 142
Limewood Ct. Ilf 5D 36
Limewood Rd. Eri 7J 93
Limpsfield Av. SW19 . . . . . . 2F 119
Limpsfield Av. T Hth 5K 139
Linacre Clo. SE15 . . . . 3H 105
Linacre Ct. W6 . . . . 5F 83
Linacre Rd. NW2 . . . . 6D 46
Linale Ho. N1 . . . . 1E 162
Linberry Wlk. SE8 . . . . 4B 88
Linchmere Rd. SE12 . . . . . . 7H 107
Lincoln Av. N14 . . . . 3B 16
Lincoln Av. SW19 . . . . 3F 119
Lincoln Av. Romf 2K 57
Lincoln Av. Twic 2G 115
Lincoln Clo. SE25 . . . . 6G 141
Lincoln Clo. Gnfd 1G 61
Lincoln Clo. Harr 5D 24
Lincoln Ct. N16 . . . . 7D 32
Lincoln Ct. SE12 . . . . 3A 126
Lincoln Ct. S Croy 5C 152
(off Warham Rd.)
Lincoln Cres. Enf 5K 7
Lincoln Gdns. Ilf 7C 36
Lincoln Grn. Rd. Orp 5K 145
Lincoln Ho. SW3 . . . 2D 84 (7E 164)
Lincoln Ho. SW9 & SE5 . . . . . 7A 86
Lincoln M. NW6 . . . . 1H 65
Lincoln M. SE21 . . . . 2D 122
Lincoln Pde. N2 . . . . 3C 30
Lincoln Rd. E7 . . . . 6B 54
Lincoln Rd. E13 . . . . 4K 71
Lincoln Rd. E18 . . . . 1H 35
Lincoln Rd. N2 . . . . 3C 30
Lincoln Rd. SE25 . . . . 3H 141
Lincoln Rd. Enf 4K 7
Lincoln Rd. Felt 3D 114
Lincoln Rd. Harr 5D 24
Lincoln Rd. Mitc 5J 139
Lincoln Rd. N Mald 3J 135
Lincoln Rd. N'wd 3H 23
Lincoln Rd. Sidc 5B 128
Lincoln Rd. Wemb 6D 44
Lincoln Rd. Wor Pk 1D 148
Lincolns Inn Fields. WC2 . . . . 6K 67 (7G 161)
Lincoln's Inn Hall. 6K 67 (7H 161)
Lincolns, The. NW7 . . . . 3G 13
Lincoln St. E11 . . . . 2G 53
Lincoln St. SW3 . . . 4D 84 (4E 170)
Lincoln Way. Enf 5C 8
Lincoln Way. Sun 1G 131
Lincombe Rd. Brom 3H 125
Lindal Cres. Enf 4D 6
Lindal Rd. SE4 . . . . 5B 106
Lindbergh Rd. Wall 7J 151
Linden Av. NW10 . . . . 2F 65
Linden Av. Enf 1B 8
Linden Av. Houn 5F 97
Linden Av. Ruis 1J 41
Linden Av. T Hth 4B 140
Linden Av. Wemb 5F 45
Linden Clo. N14 . . . . 6B 6
Linden Clo. Ruis 1J 41
Linden Clo. Stan 5G 11
Linden Clo. Th Dit 7K 133
Linden Ct. W12 . . . . 1E 82
Linden Ct. Sidc 4J 127
Linden Cres. Gnfd 6K 43
Linden Cres. King T 2F 135
Linden Cres. Wfd G 6E 20
Lindenfield. Chst 2F 145
Linden Gdns. W2 . . . . 7J 65
Linden Gdns. W4 . . . . 5A 82
Linden Gdns. Enf 1B 8
Linden Gro. SE15 . . . . 3H 105
Linden Gro. SE26 . . . . 6J 123
Linden Gro. N Mald 3A 136
Linden Gro. Tedd 5K 115
Linden Ho. SE8 . . . . 6B 88
(off Abinger Gro.)
Linden Ho. SE15 . . . . 3H 105
Linden Ho. Hamp 6E 114
Linden Lawns. Wemb 4F 45
Linden Lea. N2 . . . . 5A 30
Linden Leas. W Wick 2F 155
Linden M. N1 . . . . 5D 50
Linden M. W2 . . . . 7J 65
Linden Pl. Mitc 4C 138
Linden Rd. N10 . . . . 4F 31
Linden Rd. N11 . . . . 2J 15
Linden Rd. N15 . . . . 4C 32
Linden Rd. Hamp 7E 114
Lindens, The. E17 . . . . 4D 34
(off Prospect Hill)
Lindens, The. N12 . . . . 5G 15
Lindens, The. W4 . . . . 1J 99
Lindens, The. New Ad 6E 154
Linden St. Romf 4K 39
Linden Wlk. N19 . . . . 2G 49
Linden Way. N14 . . . . 6B 6
Linden Way. Shep 5E 130
Lindeth Clo. Stan 6G 11
Lindfield Gdns. NW3 . . . . 5K 47
Lindfield Rd. W5 . . . . 4C 62
Lindfield Rd. Croy 6F 141
Lindfield St. E14 . . . . 6C 70
Lindhill Clo. Enf 2E 8
Lindholme Ct. NW9 . . . . 1A 28
(off Pageant Av.)
Lindisfarne Rd. SW20 . . . . . 7C 118
Lindisfarne Rd. Dag 3C 56
Lindisfarne Way. E9 . . . . 4A 52
Lindley Ct. King T 1C 134
Lindley Est. SE15 . . . . 7G 87
Lindley Ho. E1 . . . . 5J 69
(off Lindley St.)
Lindley Ho. SE15 . . . . 7G 87
(off Peckham Pk. Rd.)
Lindley Pl. Kew 1G 99
Lindley Rd. E10 . . . . 2E 52
Lindley St. E1 . . . . 5J 69
Lindop Ho. E1 . . . . 4A 70
(off Mile End Rd.)
Lindore Rd. SW11 . . . . 4D 102
Lindores Rd. Cars 7A 138
Lindo St. SE15 . . . . 2J 105
Lind Rd. Sutt 5A 150
Lindrop St. SW6 . . . . 2A 102
Lindsay Clo. Chess 7E 146
Lindsay Clo. Stanw 5A 94
Lindsay Ct. Croy 4D 152
(off Eden Rd.)
Lindsay Dri. Harr 6E 26
Lindsay Dri. Shep 6F 131
Lindsay Rd. Hamp H 4F 115
Lindsay Rd. Wor Pk 2D 148
Lindsay Sq. SW1 . . . . 5H 85 (5D 172)
Lindsell St. SE10 . . . . 1E 106
Lindsey Clo. Brom 3B 144
Lindsey Clo. Mitc 4J 139
Lindsey Ct. N13 . . . . 3F 17
(off Green Lanes)
Lindsey Gdns. Felt 7F 95
Lindsey Ho. W5 . . . . 4D 80
Lindsey M. N1 . . . . 7C 50
Lindsey Rd. Dag 4C 56

Lindsey St. EC1 . . . . 5B 68 (5B 162)
Lind St. SE8 . . . . 2C 106
Lindum Rd. Tedd 7C 116
Lindway. SE27 . . . . 5B 122
Lindwood Clo. E6 . . . . 6D 72
Linfield. WC1 . . . . . 3K 67 (2G 161) (off Sidmouth St.)
Linfield Clo. NW4 . . . . 4E 28
Linford Christie Stadium. 5C 64
Linford Rd. E17 . . . . 3E 34
Linford St. SW8 . . . . 1G 103
Lingard Ho. E14 . . . . 3E 88 (off Marshfield St.)
Lingards Rd. SE13 . . . . 4E 106
Lingey Clo. Sidc 2K 127
Lingfield Av. King T 4E 134
Lingfield Clo. Enf 6K 7
Lingfield Clo. N'wd 1G 23
Lingfield Ct. N'holt 2E 60
Lingfield Cres. SE9 . . . . 4H 109
Lingfield Gdns. N9 . . . . 7C 8
Lingfield Ho. SE1 . . . . 7B 168
Lingfield Rd. SW19 . . . . 5F 119
Lingfield Rd. Wor Pk 3E 148
Lingham St. SW9 . . . . 2J 103
Lingholm Way. Barn 5A 4
Ling Rd. E16 . . . . 5J 71
Ling Rd. Eri 6J 93
Lingrove Gdns. Buck H 2E 20
Lings Coppice. SE21 . . . . . . 2D 122
Lingwell Rd. SW17 . . . . 3C 120
Lingwood. Bexh 2H 111
Lingwood Gdns. Iswth 7J 79
Lingwood Rd. E5 . . . . 7G 33
Linhope St. NW1 . . . 4D 66 (3E 158)
Linkenholt Mans. W6 . . . . 4B 82 (off Stamford Brook Av.)
Linkfield. Brom 6J 143
Linkfield. W Mol 3F 133
Linkfield Rd. Iswth 2K 97
Link Ho. E3 . . . . 2D 70
Link Ho. W10 . . . . 6F 65 (off Kingsdown Clo.)
Link La. Wall 6H 151
Linklea Clo. NW9 . . . . 7F 13
Link Rd. E1 . . . . . . 7G 69 (2K 169)
Link Rd. N8 . . . . 3A 32 (in two parts)
Link Rd. N11 . . . . 4K 15
Link Rd. Dag 2H 75
Link Rd. Felt 7H 95
Link Rd. Wall 1E 150
Links Av. Mord . . . . 4J 137 (in two parts)
Linkscroft Av. Ashf 6D 112
Links Dri. N20 . . . . 1D 14
Links Gdns. SW16 . . . . 7A 122
Linkside. N12 . . . . 6D 14
Linkside. N Mald 2A 136
Linkside Clo. Enf 3E 6
Linkside Gdns. Enf 3E 6
Links Rd. NW2 . . . . 2B 46
Links Rd. SW17 . . . . 6E 120
Links Rd. W3 . . . . 6G 63
Links Rd. Ashf 5A 112
Links Rd. W Wick 1E 154
Links Rd. Wfd G 5D 20
Links Side. Enf 3E 6
Links, The. E17 . . . . 4A 34
Link St. E9 . . . . 6J 51
Linksview. N2 . . . . 5D 30 (off Gt. North Rd.)
Links Vw. N3 . . . . 7C 14
Links Vw. Clo. Stan 7F 11
Links Vw. Ct. Hamp 4H 115
Links Vw. Rd. Croy 3C 154
Links Vw. Rd. Hamp H 5G 115
Linksway. NW4 . . . . 2F 29
Links Way. Beck 6C 142
Links Way. N'wd 1E 22
Links Yd. E1 . . . . 5K 163
Link, The. SE9 . . . . 3E 126 (off William Barefoot Dri.)
Link, The. W3 . . . . 6H 63
Link, The. Enf 1F 9
Link, The. N'holt 5D 42
Link, The. Pinn 7A 24
Link, The. Tedd 6K 115
Link, The. Wemb 1C 44
Linkway. N4 . . . . 7C 32
Linkway. SW20 . . . . 4D 136
Link Way. Brom 7C 144
Linkway. Dag 4C 56
Link Way. Pinn 1B 24
Linkway. Rich 2B 116
Linkway, The. Barn 6E 4
Linkwood Wlk. NW1 . . . . 7H 49
Linley Ct. Sutt 4A 150
Linley Cres. Romf 3H 39
Linley Rd. N17 . . . . 2E 32
Linley Sambourne House. . . . . 3J 83 (off Stafford Ter.)
Linnell Clo. NW11 . . . . 6K 29
Linnell Dri. NW11 . . . . 6K 29
Linnell Ho. E1 . . . . . 5F 69 (5J 163) (off Folgate St.)
Linnell Rd. N18 . . . . 5B 18
Linnell Rd. SE5 . . . . 2E 104
Linnet Clo. N9 . . . . 1E 18
Linnet Clo. SE28 . . . . 7C 74
Linnet Clo. Bush 1B 10
Linnet M. SW12 . . . . 7E 102
Linnett Clo. E4 . . . . 4K 19
Linom Rd. SW4 . . . . 4J 103
Linscott Rd. E5 . . . . 4J 51
Linsdell Rd. Bark 1G 73
Linsey Ct. E10 . . . . 1C 52 (off Grange Rd.)
Linsey St. SE16 . . . . 4G 87 (in two parts)
Linslade Clo. Houn 5C 96
Linslade Clo. Pinn 3K 23
Linslade Ho. E2 . . . . 1G 69
Linslade Ho. NW8 . . . . 4C 66 (3D 158) (off Paveley St.)
Linstead St. NW6 . . . . 7J 47
Linstead Way. SW18 . . . . . . 7G 101
Lintaine Clo. W6 . . . . 6G 83
Linthorpe Av. Wemb 6C 44
Linthorpe Rd. N16 . . . . 7E 32
Linthorpe Rd. Cockf 3H 5
Linton Clo. SE7 . . . . 5A 90
Linton Clo. Mitc 7D 138
Linton Clo. Well 1B 110
Linton Ct. Romf 2K 39
Linton Gdns. E6 . . . . 6C 72
Linton Gro. SE27 . . . . 5B 122
Linton Ho. E3 . . . . 5C 70 (off St Paul's Way)
Linton Rd. Bark 7G 55
Lintons, The. Bark 7G 55
Linton St. N1 . . . . 1C 68 (in two parts)
Lintott Ct. Stanw 6A 94
Linver Rd. SW6 . . . . 2J 101
Linwood Clo. SE5 . . . . 2F 105
Linwood Cres. Enf 1B 8
Linzee Rd. N8 . . . . 4J 31
Lion Av. Twic 1K 115
Lion Clo. SE4 . . . . 6C 106
Lion Clo. Shep 3A 130
Lion Ct. E1 . . . . 7K 69 (off Highway, The)
Lion Ct. N1 . . . . 1K 67 (off Copenhagen St.)
Lion Ct. SE1 . . . . . . 1E 86 (5H 169) (off Magdalen St.)
Lionel Gdns. SE9 . . . . 5B 108
Lionel Mans. W14 . . . . 3F 83 (off Haarlem Rd.)
Lionel M. W10 . . . . 5G 65
Lionel Rd. SE9 . . . . 5B 108
Lionel Rd. N. Bren 3E 80
Lionel Rd. S. Bren 5F 81
Lion Ga. Gdns. Rich 3F 99
Lion Gate M. SW18 . . . . 7J 101
Liongate M. E Mol 3K 133
Lion Mills. E2 . . . . 2G 69
Lion Pk. Av. Chess 4G 147
Lion Rd. E6 . . . . 5D 72
Lion Rd. N9 . . . . 2B 18
Lion Rd. Bexh 4E 110
Lion Rd. Croy 5C 140
Lion Rd. Twic 1K 115
Lions Clo. SE9 . . . . 3B 126
Lion Way. Bren 7D 80
Lion Wharf Rd. Iswth 3B 98
Lion Yd. SW4 . . . . 4H 103
Liphook Cres. SE23 . . . . . . 7J 105
Lipton Clo. SE28 . . . . 7C 74
Lipton Rd. E1 . . . . 6K 69
Lisbon Av. Twic 2G 115
Lisbon Clo. E17 . . . . 2B 34
Lisburne Rd. NW3 . . . . 4D 48
Lisford St. SE15 . . . . 1F 105
Lisgar Ter. W14 . . . . 4H 83
Liskeard Clo. Chst 6G 127
Liskeard Gdns. SE3 . . . . . . 1J 107
Liskeard Ho. SE11 . . . . 5A 86 (5K 173) (off Kennings Way)
Lisle Clo. SW17 . . . . 4F 121
Lisle Ct. NW2 . . . . 3G 47
Lisle St. WC2 . . . . . 7H 67 (2D 166)
Lismore. SW19 . . . . 5H 119 (off Woodside)
Lismore Cir. NW5 . . . . 5E 48
Lismore Clo. Iswth 2A 98
Lismore Ho. SE15 . . . . 3H 105
Lismore Rd. N17 . . . . 3D 32
Lismore Rd. S Croy 6E 152
Lismore Wlk. N1 . . . . 6C 50 (off Clephane Rd.)
Lisselton Ho. NW4 . . . . 4F 29 (off Belle Vue Est.)
Lissenden Gdns. NW5 . . . . . . 4E 48 (in two parts)
Lissenden Mans. NW5 . . . . . . 4E 48
Lisson Grn. Est. NW8 . . . . 4C 66 (3C 158) (off Tresham Cres.)
Lisson Grove. 5C 66 (5D 158)
Lisson Gro. NW8 & NW1 . . . . 4B 66 (3B 158)
Lisson Ho. NW1 . . . 5C 66 (5C 158) (off Lisson St.)
Lisson St. NW1 . . . . 5C 66 (5C 158)
Lister Clo. W3 . . . . 5K 63
Lister Clo. Mitc 1C 138
Lister Ct. Harr 7B 26
Lister Gdns. N18 . . . . 5H 17
Listergate Ct. SW15 . . . . . . 4E 100
Lister Ho. E1 . . . . 5G 69
Lister Ho. SE3 . . . . 6G 89 (off Restell Clo.)
Lister Ho. Hay 4G 77
Lister Ho. Wemb . . . . 3J 45 (off Barnhill Rd.)
Lister Lodge. W2 . . . . 5J 65 (off Admiral Wlk.)
Lister M. N7 . . . . 4K 49
Lister Rd. E11 . . . . 1G 53
Lister Wlk. SE28 . . . . 7D 74
Liston Rd. N17 . . . . 1G 33
Liston Rd. SW4 . . . . 3G 103
Liston Way. Wfd G 7F 21
Listowel Clo. SW9 . . . . 7A 86
Listowel Rd. Dag 3G 57
Listria Pk. N16 . . . . 2E 50
Litcham Ho. E1 . . . . 3K 69 (off Longnor Rd.)
Litchfield Av. E15 . . . . 6G 53
Litchfield Av. Mord 7H 137
Litchfield Ct. E17 . . . . 6C 34
Litchfield Gdns. NW10 . . . . . . 6C 46
Litchfield Rd. Sutt 4A 150
Litchfield St. WC2 . . . . 7H 67 (2D 166)
Litchfield Way. NW11 . . . . . . 5K 29
Lithgow's Rd. H'row A 4G 95
Lithos Rd. NW3 . . . . 6K 47
Little Acre. Beck 3C 142
Lit. Albany St. NW1 . . . . 2K 159 (in two parts)
Little Angel Theatre. . . . . . 1B 68 (off Dagmar Pas.)
Lit. Argyll St. W1 . . . . 6G 67 (1A 166)
Little Benty. W Dray 5A 76
Little Birches. Sidc 2J 127
Lit. Boltons, The. SW5 & SW10 . . . . 5K 83
Little Bornes. SE21 . . . . 4E 122
Littlebourne. SE13 . . . . 7G 107
Little Britain. EC1 . . . 5B 68 (6B 162)
Littlebrook Clo. Croy 6K 141
Little Brownings. SE23 . . . . 2H 123
Littlebury Rd. SW4 . . . . 3H 103
Lit. Bury St. N9 . . . . 1J 17
Lit. Bushey La. Bush 1C 10
Little Cedars. N12 . . . . 4F 15
Lit. Chester St. SW1 . . . . 3F 85 (1J 171)
Little Cloisters. SW1 . . . . 3J 85 (1E 172)
Lit. College La. EC4 . . . . 7D 68 (2E 168) (off College St.)
Lit. College St. SW1 . . . . 3J 85 (1E 172)
Littlecombe. SE7 . . . . 6K 89
Littlecombe Clo. SW15 . . . . . 6F 101
Little Common. Stan 3F 11
Littlecote Clo. SW19 . . . . . . 7G 101
Littlecote Pl. Pinn 1C 24
Little Ct. W Wick 2G 155
Little Cft. SE9 . . . . 3E 108
Littledale. SE2 . . . . 6A 92
Lit. Dean's Yd. SW1 . . . . 1E 172
Little Dimocks. SW12 . . . . . . 2F 121
Lit. Dorrit Ct. SE1 . . . . 2C 86 (6D 168)
Little Ealing. 3D 80
Lit. Ealing La. W5 . . . . 4C 80
Lit. Edward St. NW1 . . . . 3F 67 (1K 159)
Little Elms. Hay 7F 77
Lit. Essex St. WC2 . . . . 2J 167
Lit. Ferry Rd. Twic 1B 116
Littlefield Clo. N19 . . . . 4G 49
Littlefield Clo. King T 2E 134
Littlefield Ho. King T . . . . . . 2E 134 (off Littlefield Clo)
Littlefield Rd. Edgw 7D 12
Lit. Friday Rd. E4 . . . . 2B 20
Little Gearies. Ilf 4F 37
Lit. George St. SW1 . . . . 2J 85 (7E 166)
Little Grange. Gnfd 3A 62
Little Grn. Rich 4D 98
Lit. Green St. NW5 . . . . 4F 49
Littlegrove. E Barn 6H 5
Little Halliards. W on T 6J 131
Little Heath. 4B 38
Little Heath. SE7 . . . . 6C 90
Little Heath. Chad H 4B 38
Lit. Heath Rd. Bexh 1F 111
Littleheath Rd. S Croy 7H 153
Little Holt. E11 . . . . 5J 35
Little Ilford. 4E 54
Lit. Ilford La. E12 . . . . 4D 54
Lit. John Rd. W7 . . . . 6K 61
Little Larkins. Barn 6B 4
Lit. London Clo. Uxb 5D 58
Lit. London Ct. SE1 . . . . 2F 87 (7K 169) (off Wolseley St.)
Lit. Marlborough St. W1 . . . 1A 166
Littlemede. SE9 . . . . 3D 126
Littlemoor Rd. Ilf 3H 55
Littlemore Rd. SE2 . . . . 2A 92
Lit. Moss La. Pinn 2C 24
Lit. Newport St. WC2 . . . . 7H 67 (2D 166)
Lit. New St. EC4 . . . . 6A 68 (7K 161)
Lit. Orchard Clo. Pinn 2C 24
Lit. Park Dri. Felt 2C 114
Lit. Park Gdns. Enf 3H 7
Lit. Pluckett's Way. Buck H 1G 21
Lit. Portland St. W1 . . . . 6G 67 (7K 159)
Little Potters. Bush 1C 10
Lit. Queen's Rd. Tedd 6K 115
Little Redlands. Brom 2C 144
Little Rd. Hay 2H 77
Littlers Clo. SW19 . . . . 1A 138
Lit. Russell St. WC1 . . . . 5J 67 (6E 160)
Lit. St James's St. SW1 . . . . 1G 85 (5A 166)
Lit. St Leonard's. SW14 . . . . . 3J 99
Little Sanctuary. SW1 . . . . 2H 85 (7D 166)
Lit. Smith St. SW1 . . . . 3H 85 (1D 172)
Lit. Somerset St. E1 . . . . 6F 69 (1J 169)
Little Stanmore. 7A 12
Littlestone Clo. Beck 6C 124
Little Strand. NW9 . . . . 2B 28
Little Theatre, The. 1J 143
Little Thrift. Orp 4G 145
Lit. Titchfield St. W1 . . . . 5G 67 (6A 160)
Littleton. 3C 130
Littleton Av. E4 . . . . 1C 20
Littleton Common. 7E 112
Littleton Cres. Harr 2K 43
Littleton Ho. SW1 . . . . 5G 85 (6A 172) (off Lupus St.)
Littleton La. Shep 6A 130
Littleton Rd. Ashf 7E 112
Littleton Rd. Harr 2K 43
Littleton St. SW18 . . . . 2A 120
Lit. Trinity La. EC4 . . . . 7C 68 (2D 168)
Little Turnstile. WC1 . . . . 5K 67 (6G 161)
Lit. Warkworth Ho. Iswth 2B 98
Littlewood. SE13 . . . . 6E 106
Littlewood Clo. W13 . . . . 3B 80
Lit. Wood St. King T 2D 134
Livermere Ct. E8 . . . . 1F 69 (off Queensbridge Rd.)
Livermere Rd. E8 . . . . 1F 69
Liverpool Gro. SE17 . . . . 5C 86
Liverpool Rd. E10 . . . . 6E 34
Liverpool Rd. E16 . . . . 5G 71
Liverpool Rd. N7 & N1 . . . . . 5A 50
Liverpool Rd. W5 . . . . 2D 80
Liverpool Rd. King T 7G 117
Liverpool Rd. T Hth 3C 140
Liverpool St. EC2 . . . . 5E 68 (6G 163)
Livesey Clo. King T 3F 135
Livesey Mus. 6H 87
Livesey Pl. SE15 . . . . 6G 87
Livesley Clo. SE28 . . . . 2G 91
Livingstone College Towers. E10 . . . . 6E 34
Livingstone Ct. E10 . . . . 6E 34
Livingstone Ct. W'stone 3K 25
Livingstone Ho. NW10 . . . . . . 7K 45
Livingstone Ho. SE5 . . . . 7C 86 (off Wyndham Rd.)
Livingstone Lodge. W9 . . . . . . 5J 65 (off Admiral Wlk.)
Livingstone Mans. W14 . . . . . 6G 83 (off Queen's Club Gdns.)
Livingstone Pl. E14 . . . . 5E 88
Livingstone Rd. E15 . . . . 1E 70
Livingstone Rd. E17 . . . . 6D 34
Livingstone Rd. N13 . . . . 6D 16
Livingstone Rd. SW11 . . . . . 3B 102
Livingstone Rd. Houn 4G 97
Livingstone Rd. S'hall 7B 60
Livingstone Rd. T Hth 2C 140
Livonia St. W1 . . . . 6G 67 (1B 166)
Lizard St. EC1 . . . . 3C 68 (2D 162)
Lizban St. SE3 . . . . 7K 89

Llandovery Ho. E14 . . . . 2E 88 (off Chipka St.)
Llanelly Rd. NW2 . . . . 2H 47
Llanover Rd. SE18. . . . . 6E 90
Llanover Rd. Wemb. 3D 44
Llanthony Rd. Mord. 5B 138
Llanvanor Rd. NW2. . . . . 2H 47
Llewellyn Ct. SE20. . . . . 1J 141
Llewellyn St. SE16 . . . . 2G 87
Lloyd Av. SW16. . . . . 1J 139
Lloyd Baker St. WC1 . . . . 3K 67 (2H 161) (in two parts)
Lloyd Ct. Pinn 5B 24
Lloyd M. Enf 1H 9
Lloyd Pk. Av. Croy 4F 153
Lloyd Pk. Ho. E17 . . . . 3C 34
Lloyd Rd. E6. . . . . 1D 72
Lloyd Rd. E17 . . . . 4K 33
Lloyd Rd. Dag 6F 57
Lloyd Rd. Wor Pk 3E 148
Lloyd's Av. EC3. . . . 6E 68 (1H 169)
Lloyds Building. 6E 68 (1G 169)
Lloyd's Pl. SE3 . . . . 2G 107
Lloyd Sq. WC1 . . . . 3A 68 (1J 161)
Lloyd's Row. EC1 . . . . 3A 68 (2K 161)
Lloyd St. WC1. . . . . 3A 68 (1J 161)
Lloyds Way. Beck 5A 142
Lloyds Wharf. SE1. . . . . 7K 169
Lloyd Thomas Ct. N22. . . . . . 7E 16
Lloyd Vs. SE4 . . . . 2C 106 (off Lewisham Way)
Loampit Hill. SE13. . . . . 2C 106
Loampit Vale. (Junct.) 3E 106
Loampit Va. SE13 . . . . 3D 106
Loanda Clo. E8 . . . . 1F 69
Loats Rd. SW2. . . . . 6J 103
Lobelia Clo. E6 . . . . 5C 72
Locarno Ct. SW16. . . . . 5G 121
Locarno Rd. W3. . . . . 1J 81
Locarno Rd. Gnfd 4H 61
Lochaber Rd. SE13 . . . . 4G 107
Lochaline St. W6 . . . . 6E 82
Lochan Clo. Hay 4C 60
Lochinvar St. SW12. . . . . . . 7F 103
Lochleven Ho. N2 . . . . 2B 30 (off Grange, The)
Lochmere Clo. Eri. 6H 93
Lochmore Ho. SW1 . . . . 4E 84 (4H 171) (off Cundy St.)
Lochnagar St. E14. . . . . 5E 70
Lockbridge Ct. W9. . . . . 5J 65 (off Elmfield Way)
Lock Chase. SE3 . . . . 3G 107
Lock Clo. S'hall. 2G 79
Locke Ho. SW8. . . . . 1G 103 (off Wadhurst Rd.)
Lockesley Dri. Orp 6K 145
Lockesley Sq. Surb 6D 134
Locket Rd. Harr. 3J 25
Lockfield Av. Brim 2F 9
Lockgate Clo. E9 . . . . 5B 52
Lockhart Clo. N7 . . . . 6K 49
Lockhart Clo. Enf. 5C 8
Lockhart Ho. SE10 . . . . 7D 88 (off Tarves Way)
Lockhart St. E3. . . . . 4B 70
Lockhurst St. E5 . . . . 4K 51
Lockie Pl. SE25. . . . . 3G 141
Lockier Wlk. Wemb. 3D 44
Lockington Rd. SW8 . . . . . . 1F 103
Lock Keepers Quay. SE16 . . . 3K 87 (off Brunswick Quay)
Lockmead Rd. N15 . . . . 6G 33
Lockmead Rd. SE13 . . . . . . 3E 106
Lock Rd. Rich 4C 116
Locksbottom. 3E 156
Locksfield Pl. E14 . . . . 5D 88
Locksfields. SE17 . . . . 4D 86 (off Catesby St.)
Lockside. E14 . . . . 7A 70 (off Narrow St.)
Locks La. Mitc. 1D 138
Locksley Est. E14 . . . . 6B 70
Locksley St. E14. . . . . 5B 70
Locksmeade Rd. Rich 4C 116
Lockswood Clo. Barn. 4J 5
Lock Vw. Ct. E14. . . . . 7A 70 (off Narrow St.)
Lockwood Clo. SE26 . . . . . . 4K 123
Lockwood Ho. SE11 . . . . 6A 86 (7J 173)
Lockwood Ind. Pk. N17. . . . . 3H 33
Lockwood Sq. SE16 . . . . 3H 87
Lockwood Way. E17 . . . . 2K 33
Lockwood Way. Chess. 5G 147
Lockyer Est. SE1 . . . . 7F 169 (in two parts)
Lockyer Ho. SE10 . . . . 5H 89 (off Armitage Rd.)
Lockyer Ho. SW8 . . . . 7H 85 (off Wandsworth Rd.)
Lockyer Ho. SW15. . . . . 3F 101
Lockyer St. SE1. . . . 2D 86 (7F 169)
Locomotive Dri. Felt. 1J 113
Locton Grn. E3 . . . . 1B 70
Loddiges Ho. E9 . . . . 7J 51
Loddiges Rd. E9 . . . . 7J 51
Loder St. SE15 . . . . 7J 87
Lodge Av. SW14 . . . . 3A 100
Lodge Av. Croy 3A 152
Lodge Av. Dag. 1A 74
Lodge Av. Harr 4E 26
Lodge Clo. N18. . . . . 5H 17
Lodge Clo. Edgw 6A 12
Lodge Clo. Iswth. 1B 98
Lodge Clo. Wall 1E 150
Lodge Ct. Wemb 6E 44
Lodge Dri. N13 . . . . 4F 17
Lodge Gdns. Beck 5B 142
Lodge Hill. Ilf. 4C 36
Lodge Hill. Well. 7B 92
Lodgehill Pk. Clo. Harr. 2F 43
Lodge La. N12. . . . . 5F 15
Lodge La. Bex. 6D 110
Lodge La. New Ad 6C 154
Lodge La. Romf 1G 39
Lodge Pl. Sutt 5K 149
Lodge Rd. NW4. . . . . 4E 28
Lodge Rd. NW8 . . . 3B 66 (2B 158)
Lodge Rd. Brom 7K 125
Lodge Rd. Croy 6B 140
Lodge Rd. Wall 5F 151
Lodge Vs. Wfd G. 6C 20
Lodge Way. Ashf 2A 112
Lodge Way. Shep. 2E 130
Lodore Gdns. NW9. . . . . 5A 28
Lodore Grn. Uxb 3A 40
Lodore St. E14 . . . . 6E 70
Loft Ho. Pl. Chess 6C 146
Loftie St. SE16 . . . . 2G 87
Lofting Rd. N1. . . . . 7K 49
Loftus Rd. W12. . . . . 1D 82
Logan Clo. Enf. 1E 8
Logan Clo. Houn 3D 96
Logan M. W8. . . . . 4J 83
Logan Pl. W8. . . . . 4J 83
Logan Rd. N9 . . . . 2C 18
Logan Rd. Wemb 2D 44
Loggetts. SE21 . . . . 2E 122
Logs Hill. Chst. 7C 126
Logs Hill Clo. Chst. 1C 144
Lohmann Ho. SE11 . . . . 7J 173
Lois Dri. Shep. 5D 130
Lolesworth Clo. E1 . . . . 5F 69 (6J 163)
Lollard St. SE11 . . . 4K 85 (3H 173) (in two parts)
Loman St. SE1 . . . . 2B 86 (6B 168)
Lomas Clo. Croy 7E 154
Lomas St. E1 . . . . 5G 69
Lombard Av. Enf. 1D 8
Lombard Av. Ilf 1J 55
Lombard Bus. Cen., The. SW11 . . . . 2B 102
Lombard Bus. Pk. Croy 7K 139
Lombard Ct. EC3. . . 7D 68 (2F 169)
Lombard Ct. W3 . . . . 1H 81
Lombard Ct. Romf. . . . . 4J 39 (off Poplar St.)
Lombard La. EC4 . . . . 6A 68 (1K 167)
Lombard Rd. N11 . . . . 5A 16
Lombard Rd. SW11. . . . . . . 2B 102
Lombard Rd. SW19. . . . . . . 2K 137
Lombard Roundabout. (Junct.) 7K 139
Lombard St. EC3. . . 6D 68 (1F 169)
Lombard Trad. Est. SE7. . . . . 4K 89
Lombard Wall. SE7 . . . . 3K 89 (in two parts)
Lombardy Pl. W2 . . . . 7K 65
Lombardy Retail Pk. Hay 7K 59
Lomond Clo. N15 . . . . 5E 32
Lomond Clo. Wemb. 7F 45
Lomond Gdns. S Croy 7A 154
Lomond Gro. SE5 . . . . 7D 86
Lomond Ho. SE5. . . . . 7D 86
Loncroft Rd. SE5. . . . . 6E 86
Londesborough Rd. N16 . . . . 4E 50
Londinium Tower. E1 . . . . 7F 69 (2K 169) (off W. Tenter St.)
London Aquarium. 2K 85 (6G 167)
London Arena. 3D 88
London Bri. SE1 & EC4 . . . . 1D 86 (4F 169)
London Bri. St. SE1 . . . . 1D 86 (5F 169)
London Bri. Wlk. SE1 . . . . 1D 86 (4F 169) (off Duke St. Hill)
London Broncos Rugby League Football Club (Brentford F.C.) 6D 80
London Business School. 4D 66 (3E 158)
London Butterfly House. . . . 1B 98
London Canal Mus. 2J 67
London City Airport. 1C 90
London City College. . . . . 1A 86 (5J 167) (in Schiller University)
London Coliseum. . . . . 7J 67 (3E 166) (off St Martin's La.)
Londonderry Pde. Eri. 7K 93
London Dungeon. 5F 169
London Eye. 2K 85 (6G 167)
London Fields E. Side. E8 . . . 7H 51 (in two parts)
London Fields W. Side. E8 . . . 7G 51
London Fruit Exchange. E1 . . . . 5F 69 (6J 163) (off Brushfield St.)
London Guildhall University. . . . . 6G 69 (Commercial Rd.)
London Guildhall University. . . . . 6F 69 (1J 169) (Jewry St.)
London Guildhall University. . . . . 5D 68 (6F 163) (Moorgate)
London Guildhall University. . . . . 6G 69 (Whitechapel High St., Central Ho.)
London Heathrow Airport. 3D 94
London Ho. NW8. . . . . 2C 66 (off Avenue Rd.)
London Ho. WC1 . . . . 4K 67 (3G 161)
London Ind. Pk., The. E6. . . . 5F 73
London Knights Ice Hockey (London Arena) 3D 88
London La. E8. . . . . 7H 51
London La. Brom 7H 125
London Leopards Basketball (London Arena) 3D 88
London Master Bakers Almshouses. E10 . . . 6D 34
London M. W2 . . . . 6B 66 (7B 158)
London Motorcycle Mus. . . . 3G 61
London Palladium. . . . . 6G 67 (1A 166) (off Argyll St.)
London Planetarium. 4E 66 (4G 159)
London Rd. E13. . . . . 2J 71
London Rd. SE1 . . . . 3B 86 (7A 168)
London Rd. SE23 . . . . 1H 123
London Rd. SW16. . . . . 1K 139
London Rd. SW17 & Mitc 7D 120
London Rd. Bark 7F 55
London Rd. Brom 7H 125
London Rd. Cray 5K 111
London Rd. Enf. 3J 7
London Rd. Ewe & Sutt 7B 148
London Rd. Harr 2J 43
London Rd. Houn & Iswth. . . 3G 97
London Rd. Iswth & Twic . . . 5A 98 (Linkfield Rd.)
London Rd. Iswth & Bren . . . 2K 97 (Twickenham Rd.)
London Rd. King T. . . . . . . 2F 135 (in two parts)
London Rd. Mitc & Wall. . . . 7E 138
London Rd. Mord 5J 137
London Rd. Romf 6G 39
London Rd. Stai & Ashf. . . . 2A 112
London Rd. Stan. 5H 11
London Rd. T Hth & Croy 5A 140
London Rd. Wemb. 5E 44
London Road Roundabout. (Junct.) 6A 98
London School of Economics & Politics, The. 6K 67 (1H 167)
London Scottish R.U.F.C. 3D 98
London Stile. W4 . . . . 5G 81
London St. EC3. . . . 7E 68 (2H 169)
London St. W2 . . . . 6B 66 (7A 158)
London Ter. E2 . . . . 2G 69
London Towers Basketball (Crystal Palace National Sports Cen.) 6G 123
London Transport Mus. 7J 67 (2F 167)
London Underwriting Cen. EC3 . . . . 2H 169
London Wall. EC2 . . . . 5C 68 (6D 162)
London Wall Bldgs. EC2. . . . 6F 163
London Westland Heliport. 2B 102
London Wharf. E2. . . . . 1H 69 (off Wharf Pl.)
London Zoo. 2E 66
Lonesome. 1G 139
Lonesome Way. SW16. . . . . 1F 139
Long Acre. WC2 . . . 7J 67 (2E 166)
Longacre Clo. Enf 3H 7
Long Acre Ct. W13 . . . . 5A 62
Longacre Pl. Cars 6E 150
Longacre Rd. E17 . . . . 1F 35
Longbeach Rd. SW11 . . . . . 3D 102
Longberrys. NW2 . . . . 3H 47
Longboat Row. S'hall 6D 60
Longbridge Ho. Dag . . . . 4B 56 (off Gainsborough Rd.)
Longbridge Rd. Bark 6H 55
Longbridge Way. SE13. . . . 5E 106
Longcroft. SE9 . . . . 3D 126
Longcrofte Rd. Edgw 7J 11
Long Deacon Rd. E4 . . . . 1B 20
Long Ditton. 1C 146
Longdon Wood. Kes 3C 156
Longdown Rd. SE6 . . . . 4C 124
Long Dri. W3. . . . . 6A 64
Long Dri. Gnfd. 1F 61
Long Dri. Ruis. 5A 42
Long Dri. W Dray 2A 76
Long Elmes. Harr. 1F 25
Longfellow Rd. E17. . . . . 6B 34
Longfellow Rd. Wor Pk 2C 148
Longfellow Way. SE1 . . . . 4F 87
Long Fld. NW9. . . . . 7F 13
Longfield. Brom 1H 143
Longfield Av. E17 . . . . 4A 34
Longfield Av. NW7. . . . . 7H 13
Longfield Av. W5. . . . . 7C 62
Longfield Av. Wall 1E 150
Longfield Av. Wemb. 1E 44
Longfield Cres. SE26 . . . . . . 3J 123
Longfield Dri. SW14 . . . . 5H 99
Longfield Dri. Mitc. 7C 120
Longfield Est. SE1 . . . . 4F 87
Longfield Rd. W5 . . . . 6C 62
Longfield St. SW18 . . . . 7J 101
Longfield Wlk. W5. . . . . 6C 62
Longford Av. Felt. 6G 95
Longford Av. S'hall. 7F 61
Longford Av. Stai. 1A 112
Longford Clo. Hamp H. 4E 114
Longford Clo. Hanw. 3C 114
Longford Clo. Hay 7B 60
Longford Ct. NW4 . . . . 4F 29
Longford Ct. Eps 4J 147
Longford Ct. S'hall. . . . . 1E 78 (off Uxbridge Rd.)
Longford Gdns. Hay 7B 60
Longford Gdns. Sutt 3A 150
Longford Ho. E1 . . . . 6J 69 (off Jubilee St.)
Longford Ho. Brom . . . . 5F 125 (off Brangbourne Rd.)
Longford Ho. Hamp. 4E 114
Longford Rd. Twic. 1E 114
Longford St. NW1 . . . . . 4F 67 (3K 159)
Longford Wlk. SW2. . . . . . . 7A 104
Longford Way. Stai 1A 112
Longhayes Av. Romf 4D 38
Longhayes Ct. Romf 4D 38
Longheath Gdns. Croy 5J 141
Longhedge Ho. SE26. . . . . . 4G 123 (off High Level Dri.)
Long Hedges. Houn. 2E 96
Longhedge St. SW11. . . . . . 2E 102
Longhill Rd. SE6 . . . . 2F 125
Longhook Gdns. N'holt 2J 59
Longhope Clo. SE15 . . . . 6E 86
Longhurst Rd. SE13. . . . . . . 5F 107
Longhurst Rd. Croy. 6H 141
Longland Ct. SE1 . . . . 5G 87
Longland Dri. N20. . . . . 3E 14
Longlands. 3H 127
Longlands Ct. W11 . . . . 7H 65 (off Westbourne Gro.)
Longlands Ct. Sidc 3K 127
Longlands Pk. Cres. Sidc . . . 3J 127
Longlands Rd. Sidc 3J 127
Long La. EC1 . . . . . 5B 68 (6B 162)
Long La. N3 & N2. . . . . 1K 29 (in two parts)
Long La. SE1 . . . . . 2D 86 (7E 168)
Long La. Bexh. 7D 92
Long La. Croy 6H 141
Long La. Hil 6D 40
Long La. Stai & Stanw. 2B 112
Long La. Uxb. 3C 58
Longleat Ho. SW1 . . . . 5H 85 (5C 172) (off Rampayne St.)
Longleat Rd. Enf 5K 7
Longleat Way. Felt 7F 95
Longleigh Ho. SE5. . . . . 1E 104 (off Peckham Rd.)
Longleigh La. SE2. . . . . 6C 92
Long Lents Ho. NW10. . . . . . 1K 63
Longley Av. Wemb 1F 63
Longley Ct. SW8 . . . . 1J 103
Longley Rd. SW17. . . . . 6C 120
Longley Rd. Croy. 7B 140
Longley Rd. Harr. 5G 25

Long Leys. E4 ... 6J 19
Longley St. SE1 ... 4G 87
Longley Way. NW2 ... 3E 46
Longman Ho. E2 ... 2K 69
(off Mace St.)
Longman Ho. E8 ... 1F 69
(off Haggerston Rd.)
Long Mark Rd. E16 ... 5B 72
Long Mead. NW9 ... 1B 28
Longmead. Chst ... 2E 144
Longmead Dri. Sidc ... 2D 128
Longmead Ho. SE27 ... 5C 122
Long Mdw. NW5 ... 5H 49
Long Mdw. Clo. W Wick ... 7E 142
Longmeadow Rd. Sidc ... 1J 127
Longmead Rd. SW17 ... 5D 120
Longmead Rd. Hay ... 7H 59
Longmead Rd. Th Dit ... 7J 133
Longmoore St. SW1 ... 4G 85 (4A 172)
Longmore Av. Barn & E Barn ... 6F 5
Longnor Est. E1 ... 3K 69
Longnor Rd. E1 ... 3K 69
Long Pond Rd. SE3 ... 1G 107
Longreach Ct. Bark ... 2H 73
Long Reach Rd. Bark ... 4K 73
Longridge Ho. SE1 ... 3C 86
Longridge La. S'hall ... 6F 61
Longridge Rd. SW5 ... 4J 83
Longridge Rd. Bark ... 7G 55
Long Ridges. N10 ... 3E 30
(off Fortis Grn.)
Long Rd. SW4 ... 4F 103
Long's Ct. WC2 ... 3D 166
Longs Ct. Rich ... 4F 99
Longshaw Rd. E4 ... 3A 20
Longshore. SE8 ... 4B 88
Longshott Ct. SW5 ... 4J 83
(off W. Cromwell Rd.)
Longstaff Cres. SW18 ... 6J 101
Longstaff Rd. SW18 ... 6J 101
Longstone Av. NW10 ... 7B 46
Longstone Rd. SW17 ... 5F 121
Long St. E2 ... 3F 69 (1J 163)
Longthornton Rd. SW16 ... 2G 139
Longton Av. SE26 ... 4G 123
Longton Gro. SE26 ... 4H 123
Longview Vs. Romf ... 1F 39
Longview Way. Romf ... 1K 39
Longville Rd. SE11 ... 4B 86
Long Wlk. SE1 ... 3E 86
Long Wlk. SE18 ... 6F 91
Long Wlk. SW13 ... 2A 100
Long Wlk. N Mald ... 3J 135
Longwalk Rd. Uxb ... 1D 76
Long Wall. E15 ... 3F 71
Longwater Ho. King T ... 3D 134
(off Portsmouth Rd.)
Longwood Dri. SW15 ... 6C 100
Longwood Gdns. Ilf ... 4D 36
Longworth Clo. SE28 ... 6D 74
Long Yd. WC1 ... 4K 67 (4G 161)
Loning, The. NW9 ... 4B 28
Lonsdale Av. E6 ... 4B 72
Lonsdale Av. Romf ... 6J 39
Lonsdale Av. Wemb ... 5E 44
Lonsdale Clo. E6 ... 4C 72
Lonsdale Clo. SE9 ... 3B 126
Lonsdale Clo. Edgw ... 5A 12
Lonsdale Clo. Pinn ... 1C 24
Lonsdale Clo. Uxb ... 5E 58
Lonsdale Ct. Surb ... 7D 134
Lonsdale Cres. Ilf ... 6F 37
Lonsdale Dri. Enf ... 4C 6
Lonsdale Gdns. SW16 ... 4K 139
Lonsdale Ho. W11 ... 6H 65
(off Lonsdale Rd.)
Lonsdale M. W11 ... 6H 65
(off Lonsdale Rd.)
Lonsdale M. Rich ... 1G 99
Lonsdale Pl. N1 ... 7A 50
Lonsdale Rd. E11 ... 6H 35
Lonsdale Rd. NW6 ... 1H 65
Lonsdale Rd. SE25 ... 4H 141
Lonsdale Rd. SW13 ... 1B 100
Lonsdale Rd. W4 ... 4B 82
Lonsdale Rd. W11 ... 6H 65
Lonsdale Rd. Bexh ... 2F 111
Lonsdale Rd. S'hall ... 3B 78
Lonsdale Sq. N1 ... 7A 50
Lonsdale Yd. W11 ... 7J 65
Loobert Rd. N15 ... 3E 32
Looe Gdns. Ilf ... 3F 37
Loop Rd. Chst ... 6G 127
Lopen Rd. N18 ... 4K 17
Lopez Ho. SW9 ... 3J 103
Lorac Ct. Sutt ... 7J 149
Loraine Clo. Enf ... 5D 8
Loraine Ct. Chst ... 5F 127
Loraine Ho. Wall ... 4F 151
Loraine Rd. N7 ... 4K 49
Loraine Rd. W4 ... 6H 81
Lord Amory Way. E14 ... 2E 88
Lord Av. Ilf ... 4D 36
Lord Chancellor Wlk. King T ... 1J 135
Lordell Pl. SW19 ... 6E 118
Lorden Wlk. E2 ... 3G 69 (2K 163)
Lord Gdns. Ilf ... 4C 36
Lord Hills Bri. W2 ... 5K 65
Lord Hills Rd. W2 ... 5K 65
Lord Holland La. SW9 ... 2A 104
Lord Knyvetts Ct. Stanw ... 6A 94
Lord Napier Pl. W6 ... 5C 82
Lord N. St. SW1 ... 3J 85 (2E 172)
Lord Roberts M. SW6 ... 7K 83
Lord Robert's Ter. SE18 ... 5E 90
Lords Clo. SE21 ... 2C 122
Lords Clo. Felt ... 2C 114
Lord's Cricket Ground. ... 3B 66 (2B 158)
Lordship Gro. N16 ... 2D 50
Lordship La. N22 & N17 ... 2A 32
Lordship La. SE22 ... 4F 105
Lordship La. Est. SE21 ... 7G 105
Lordship Pk. N16 ... 2C 50
Lordship Pk. M. N16 ... 2C 50
Lordship Pl. SW3 ... 6C 84 (7C 170)
Lordship Rd. N16 ... 1D 50
Lordship Rd. N'holt ... 7C 42
Lordship Ter. N16 ... 2D 50
Lordsmead Rd. N17 ... 1E 32
Lord St. E16 ... 1C 90
Lords Vw. NW8 ... 3B 66 (2C 158)
Lord Warwick St. SE18 ... 3D 90
Loreburn Ho. N7 ... 4K 49
Lorenzo St. WC1 ... 3K 67 (1G 161)
Loretto Gdns. Harr ... 4E 26
Lorian Clo. N12 ... 4E 14
Loring Rd. N20 ... 2H 15
Loring Rd. SE14 ... 1A 106
Loring Rd. Iswth ... 2K 97
Loris Rd. W6 ... 3E 82
Lorn Ct. SW9 ... 2A 104
Lorne Av. Croy ... 7K 141
Lorne Clo. NW8 ... 3C 66 (2D 158)
Lorne Gdns. E11 ... 4A 36
Lorne Gdns. W11 ... 2F 83
Lorne Gdns. Croy ... 7K 141
Lorne Ho. E1 ... 5A 70
(off Ben Jonson Rd.)
Lorne Rd. E7 ... 4K 53
Lorne Rd. E17 ... 5C 34
Lorne Rd. N4 ... 1K 49
Lorne Rd. Harr ... 2K 25
Lorne Rd. Rich ... 5F 99
Lorne Ter. N3 ... 2H 29
Lorn Rd. SW9 ... 2K 103
Lorraine Ct. NW1 ... 7F 49
Lorraine Pk. Harr ... 7D 10
Lorrimore Rd. SE17 ... 6B 86
Lorrimore Sq. SE17 ... 6B 86
Lorton Ho. NW6 ... 1J 65
(off Kilburn Va.)
Lothair Rd. W5 ... 2D 80
Lothair Rd. N. N4 ... 6B 32
Lothair Rd. S. N4 ... 7A 32
Lothbury. EC2 ... 6D 68 (7E 162)
Lothian Av. Hay ... 5K 59
Lothian Clo. Wemb ... 4A 44
Lothian Rd. SW9 ... 1B 104
Lothrop St. W10 ... 3G 65
Lots Rd. SW10 ... 7A 84
Lotus Clo. SE21 ... 3D 122
Loubet St. SW17 ... 6D 120
Loudoun Av. Ilf ... 5F 37
Loudoun Rd. NW8 ... 1A 66
Loudwater Clo. Sun ... 4J 131
Loudwater Rd. Sun ... 4J 131
Loughborough Est. SW9 ... 3B 104
Loughborough Junction. (Junct.) ... 3B 104
Loughborough Pk. SW9 ... 4B 104
Loughborough Rd. SW9 ... 2A 104
Loughborough St. SE11 ... 5K 85 (5H 173)
Lough Rd. N7 ... 5K 49
Loughton Way. Buck H ... 1G 21
Louisa Ct. Twic ... 2J 115
Louisa Gdns. E1 ... 4K 69
Louisa St. E1 ... 4K 69
Louise Bennett Clo. SE24 ... 4B 104
Louise Ct. N22 ... 1A 32
Louise De Marillac Ho. E1 ... 5J 69
(off Smithy St.)
Louise Rd. E15 ... 6G 53
Louise White Ho. N19 ... 1H 49
Louis Gdns. Chst ... 4D 126
Louis M. N10 ... 1F 31
Louisville Rd. SW17 ... 3E 120
Lousada Lodge. N14 ... 6B 6
(off Avenue Rd.)
Louvaine Rd. SW11 ... 4B 102
Lovage App. E6 ... 5C 72
Lovat Clo. NW2 ... 3B 46
Lovat La. EC3 ... 7E 68 (3G 169)
(in two parts)
Lovatt Clo. Edgw ... 6C 12
Lovatt Ct. SW12 ... 1F 121
Lovatt Dri. Ruis ... 5J 23
Lovat Wlk. Houn ... 7C 78
Loveday Rd. W13 ... 2B 80
Lovegrove St. SE1 ... 5G 87
Lovegrove Wlk. E14 ... 1E 88
Lovekyn Clo. King T ... 2E 134
Lovelace Av. Brom ... 6E 144
Lovelace Gdns. Bark ... 4A 56
Lovelace Gdns. Surb ... 7D 134
Lovelace Grn. SE9 ... 3D 108
Lovelace Ho. E8 ... 1F 69
(off Haggerston Rd.)
Lovelace Rd. SE21 ... 2C 122
Lovelace Rd. Barn ... 7H 5
Lovelace Rd. Surb ... 7C 134
Loveland Mans. Bark ... 7K 55
(off Upney La.)
Love La. EC2 ... 6C 68 (7D 162)
Love La. N17 ... 7A 18
Love La. SE18 ... 4E 90
Love La. SE25 ... 3H 141
(in two parts)
Love La. Bex ... 6F 111
(in two parts)
Love La. Brom ... 3K 143
(off Elmfield Rd., in two parts)
Love La. Mitc ... 3C 138
(in two parts)
Love La. Mord ... 7J 137
Love La. Pinn ... 2B 24
Love La. Surb ... 2C 146
Love La. Sutt ... 6G 149
Love La. Wfd G ... 6J 21
Lovel Av. Well ... 2A 110
Lovelinch Clo. SE15 ... 6J 87
Lovell Ho. E8 ... 1G 69
(off Shrubland Rd.)
Lovell Pl. SE16 ... 3A 88
Lovell Rd. Rich ... 3C 116
Lovell Rd. S'hall ... 6F 61
Loveridge M. NW6 ... 6H 47
Loveridge Rd. NW6 ... 6H 47
Lovers Wlk. N3 ... 7D 14
Lovers Wlk. NW7 & N3 ... 6C 14
Lovers Wlk. SE10 ... 6F 89
Lovers' Wlk. W1 ... 1E 84 (4G 165)
Lovett Dri. Cars ... 7A 138
Lovett Way. NW10 ... 5J 45
Love Wlk. SE5 ... 2D 104
Lovibonds Av. W Dray ... 6B 58
Lowbrook Rd. Ilf ... 4F 55
Low Cross Wood La. SE21 ... 3F 123
Lowdell Clo. W Dray ... 6A 58
Lowden Rd. N9 ... 1C 18
Lowden Rd. SE24 ... 4B 104
Lowden Rd. S'hall ... 7C 60
Lowder Ho. E1 ... 1H 87
(off Wapping La.)
Lowe Av. E16 ... 5J 71
Lowell Ho. SE5 ... 7C 86
(off Wyndham Est.)
Lowell St. E14 ... 6A 70
Lowen Rd. Rain ... 2K 75
Lwr. Addiscombe Rd. Croy ... 1E 152
Lwr. Addison Gdns. W14 ... 2G 83
Lwr. Belgrave St. SW1 ... 3F 85 (2J 171)
Lwr. Boston Rd. W7 ... 1J 79
Lwr. Broad St. Dag ... 1G 75
Lower Camden. Chst ... 7D 126
Lwr. Church St. Croy ... 2B 152
Lower Clapton. ... 4H 51
Lwr. Clapton Rd. E5 ... 3H 51
Lwr. Clarendon Wlk. W11 ... 6G 65
(off Clarendon Rd.)
Lwr. Common S. SW15 ... 3D 100
Lwr. Coombe St. Croy ... 4C 152
Lwr. Downs Rd. SW20 ... 1F 137
Lwr. Drayton Pl. Croy ... 2B 152
Lower Edmonton. ... 3B 18
Lower Feltham. ... 3H 113
Lower Fosters. NW4 ... 5E 28
(off New Brent St.)
Lwr. George St. Rich ... 5D 98
Lwr. Gravel Rd. Brom ... 1C 156
Lwr. Green Gdns. Wor Pk ... 1C 148
Lwr. Green W. Mitc ... 3C 138
Lwr. Grosvenor Pl. SW1 ... 3F 85 (1K 171)
Lwr. Grove Rd. Rich ... 6F 99
Lower Halliford. ... 6F 131
Lwr. Hall La. E4 ... 5F 19
(in two parts)
Lwr. Hampton Rd. Sun ... 3A 132
Lwr. Ham Rd. King T ... 5D 116
Lower Holloway. ... 5K 49
Lwr. James St. W1 ... 7G 67 (2B 166)
Lwr. John St. W1 ... 7G 67 (2B 166)
Lwr. Kenwood Av. Enf ... 5D 6
Lwr. Lea Crossing. E14 ... 7G 71
Lwr. Maidstone Rd. N11 ... 6B 16
Lower Mall. W6 ... 5D 82
Lwr. Mardyke Av. Rain ... 2J 75
Lower Marsh. SE1 ... 2A 86 (7J 167)
Lwr. Marsh La. King T ... 4F 135
(in two parts)
Lwr. Merton Ri. NW3 ... 7C 48
Lower Mill. Eps ... 7B 148
Lwr. Morden La. Mord ... 6E 136
Lwr. Mortlake Rd. Rich ... 4E 98
Lwr. Park Rd. N11 ... 5B 16
Lwr. Park Rd. Belv ... 4G 93
Lwr. Park Trad. Est. W3 ... 4J 63
Lower Place. ... 2J 63
Lwr. Place Bus. Cen. NW10 ... 2K 63
(off Steele Rd.)
Lwr. Queen's Rd. Buck H ... 2G 21
Lwr. Richmond Rd. SW15 ... 3D 100
Lwr. Richmond Rd. Rich & SW14 ... 3G 99
Lower Rd. SE1 ... 2A 86 (6J 167)
Lower Rd. SE16 & SE8 ... 2J 87
(in two parts)
Lower Rd. Belv ... 3H 93
Lower Rd. Harr ... 1H 43
Lower Rd. Sutt ... 4A 150
Lwr. Sloane St. SW1 ... 4E 84 (4G 171)
Lower Sq. Iswth ... 3B 98
Lower Sq., The. Sutt ... 5K 149
Lower Strand. NW9 ... 2B 28
Lwr. Sunbury Rd. Hamp ... 2D 132
Lower Sydenham. ... 4K 123
Lwr. Sydenham Ind. Est. SE26 ... 5B 124
Lwr. Teddington Rd. King T ... 1D 134
Lower Ter. NW3 ... 3A 48
Lwr. Thames St. EC3 ... 7D 68 (3F 169)
Lowerwood Ct. W11 ... 6G 65
(off Westbourne Pk. Rd.)
Lwr. Wood Rd. Clay ... 6B 146
Lowestoft Clo. E5 ... 2J 51
(off Mt. Pleasant Hill)
Lowestoft M. E16 ... 2F 91
Loweswater Clo. Wemb ... 2D 44
Loweswater Ho. E3 ... 4B 70
Lowfield Rd. NW6 ... 7J 47
Lowfield Rd. W3 ... 6H 63
Low Hall Clo. E4 ... 7J 9
Low Hall La. E17 ... 6A 34
Low Hall Mnr. Bus. Cen. E17 ... 6A 34
Lowick Rd. Harr ... 4J 25
Lowlands Gdns. Romf ... 5H 39
Lowlands Rd. Harr ... 6J 25
Lowlands Rd. Pinn ... 7A 24
Lowman Rd. N7 ... 4K 49
Lowndes Clo. SW1 ... 3E 84 (2H 171)
Lowndes Ct. SW1 ... 3D 84 (1F 171)
Lowndes Ct. W1 ... 1A 166
Lowndes Pl. SW1 ... 3E 84 (2G 171)
Lowndes Sq. SW1 ... 2D 84 (7F 165)
Lowndes St. SW1 ... 3E 84 (1F 171)
Lownds Ct. Brom ... 2J 143
Lowood Ho. E1 ... 7J 69
(off Bewley St.)
Lowood St. E1 ... 7H 69
Lowry Clo. Eri ... 4K 93
Lowry Ct. SE16 ... 5H 87
(off Stubbs Dri.)
Lowry Cres. Mitc ... 2C 138
Lowry Ho. N17 ... 1F 33
(off Pembury Rd.)
Lowry Rd. Dag ... 5B 56
Lowshoe La. Romf ... 1G 39
Lowswood Clo. N'wd ... 1E 22
Lowther Dri. Enf ... 4D 6
Lowther Gdns. SW7 ... 2B 84 (1B 170)
Lowther Hill. SE23 ... 7A 106
Lowther Ho. E8 ... 1F 69
(off Clarissa St.)
Lowther Ho. SW1 ... 5G 85 (6B 172)
(off Churchill Gdns.)
Lowther Rd. E17 ... 2A 34
Lowther Rd. N7 ... 5A 50
Lowther Rd. SW13 ... 1B 100
Lowther Rd. King T ... 1F 135
Lowther Rd. Stan ... 3F 27
Lowth Rd. SE5 ... 1C 104
Loxford. ... 5G 55
Loxford Av. E6 ... 2B 72
Loxford La. Ilf ... 5G 55
Loxford Rd. Bark ... 6F 55
Loxford Ter. Bark ... 6G 55
Loxham Rd. E4 ... 7J 19
Loxham St. WC1 ... 3J 67 (2F 161)
Loxley Clo. SE26 ... 5K 123

Loxley Rd. SW18 1B 120
Loxley Rd. Hamp 4D 114
Loxton Rd. SE23 1K 123
Loxwood Clo. Felt 1F 113
Loxwood Rd. N17 3E 32
Lubbock Ho. E14 7D 70 (off Poplar High St.)
Lubbock Rd. Chst 7D 126
Lubbock St. SE14 7J 87
Lucan Ho. N1 1D 68 (off Colville Est.)
Lucan Pl. SW3 4C 84 (4C 170)
Lucan Rd. Barn 3B 4
Lucas Av. E13 1K 71
Lucas Av. Harr 2E 42
Lucas Clo. NW10 7C 46
Lucas Ct. SE26 5A 124
Lucas Ct. SW11 1E 102
Lucas Gdns. N2 2A 30
Lucas Rd. SE20 6J 123
Lucas Sq. NW11 6J 29
Lucas St. SE8 1C 106
Lucerne Clo. N13 3D 16
Lucerne Ct. Eri 3E 92
Lucerne Gro. E17 4F 35
Lucerne M. W8 1J 83
Lucerne Rd. N5 4B 50
Lucerne Rd. Orp 7K 145
Lucerne Rd. T Hth 5B 140
Lucey Rd. SE16 3G 87
Lucey Way. SE16 3G 87 (in two parts)
Lucie Av. Ashf 6D 112
Lucien Rd. SW17 4E 120
Lucien Rd. SW19 2K 119
Lucinda Ct. Enf 5K 7
Lucknow St. SE18 7J 91
Lucorn Clo. SE12 6H 107
Luctons Av. Buck H 1F 21
Lucy Brown Ho. SE1 1C 86 (5D 168) (off Park St.)
Lucy Cres. W3 5J 63
Lucy Gdns. Dag 3E 56
Luddesdon Rd. Eri 7G 93
Ludford Clo. NW9 2A 28
Ludford Clo. Croy 3B 152
Ludgate B'way. EC4 6B 68 (1A 168)
Ludgate Cir. EC4 6B 68 (1A 168)
Ludgate Hill. EC4 6B 68 (1A 168)
Ludgate Sq. EC4 6B 68 (1B 168)
Ludham Clo. SE28 6C 74
Ludham Clo. Ilf 1G 37
Ludlow Clo. Brom 3J 143
Ludlow Clo. Harr 4D 42
Ludlow Ct. W3 2J 81
Ludlow Rd. W5 4C 62
Ludlow Rd. Felt 4J 113
Ludlow St. EC1 4C 68 (3C 162)
Ludlow Way. N2 4A 30
Ludovick Wlk. SW15 4A 100
Ludwick M. SE14 7A 88
Luffield Rd. SE2 3B 92
Luffman Rd. SE12 3K 125
Lugard Ho. W12 1D 82
Lugard Rd. SE15 2H 105
Lugg App. E12 3E 54
Luke Ho. E1 6H 69 (off Tillman St.)
Luke St. EC2 4E 68 (3G 163)
Lukin Cres. E4 3A 20
Lukin St. E1 6J 69
Lullingstone Clo. Orp 7B 128
Lullingstone Cres. Orp 7A 128
Lullingstone Ho. SE15 6J 87 (off Lovelinch Clo.)
Lullingstone La. SE13 6F 107
Lullingstone Rd. Belv 6F 93
Lullington Gth. N12 5C 14
Lullington Gth. Brom 7G 125
Lullington Rd. SE20 7G 123
Lullington Rd. Dag 7E 56
Lulot Gdns. N19 2F 49
Lulworth. NW1 7H 49 (off Wrotham Rd.)
Lulworth. SE17 5D 86 (off Portland St.)
Lulworth Av. Houn 1F 97
Lulworth Av. Wemb 7C 26
Lulworth Clo. Harr 3D 42
Lulworth Ct. N1 7E 50 (off St Peter's Way)
Lulworth Cres. Mitc 2C 138
Lulworth Dri. Pinn 6B 24
Lulworth Gdns. Harr 2C 42
Lulworth Ho. SW8 7K 85
Lulworth Rd. SE9 2C 126
Lulworth Rd. SE15 2H 105
Lulworth Rd. Well 2K 109
Lulworth Waye. Hay 6K 59
Lumen Rd. Wemb 2D 44
Lumiere Building, The. E7 5B 54 (off Romford Rd.)
Lumiere Ct. SW17 2E 120
Lumley Clo. Belv 5G 93
Lumley Ct. WC2 7J 67 (3F 167)
Lumley Flats. SW1 5E 84 (5G 171) (off Holbein Pl.)
Lumley Gdns. Sutt 5G 149
Lumley Rd. Sutt 5G 149
Lumley St. W1 6E 66 (1H 165)
Lumsdon. NW8 1K 65 (off Abbey Rd.)
Luna Rd. T Hth 3C 140
Lund Point. E15 1E 70
Lundy Dri. Hay 4G 77
Lundy Wlk. N1 6C 50
Lunham Rd. SE19 6E 122
Luntley Pl. E1 5G 69 (6K 163)
Lupin Clo. SW2 2B 122
Lupin Clo. Croy 1K 153
Lupin Clo. Rush G 2K 57
Lupin Cres. Ilf 6F 55
Lupin Point. SE1 7K 169
Lupton Clo. SE12 3K 125
Lupton St. NW5 4G 49 (in two parts)
Lupus St. SW1 5F 85 (6K 171)
Luralda Gdns. E14 5F 89
Lurgan Av. W6 6F 83
Lurline Gdns. SW11 1E 102
Luscombe Ct. Brom 2G 143
Luscombe Way. SW8 7J 85
Lushington Ho. W on T 6A 132
Lushington Rd. NW10 2D 64
Lushington Rd. SE6 4D 124
Lushington Ter. E8 5G 51 (off Wayland Av.)
Lutea Ho. Sutt 7A 150 (off Walnut M.)
Luther Clo. Edgw 2D 12
Luther King Clo. E17 6B 34
Luther Rd. Tedd 5K 115
Luton Ho. E13 4J 71 (off Luton Rd.)
Luton Pl. SE10 7E 88
Luton Rd. E13 4J 71
Luton Rd. E17 3B 34
Luton Rd. Sidc 3C 128
Luton St. NW8 4B 66 (4B 158)
Lutton Ter. NW3 4A 48 (off Heath St.)
Luttrell Av. SW15 5D 100
Lutwyche Rd. SE6 2B 124
Lutyens Ho. SW1 5G 85 (6K 171) (off Churchill Gdns.)
Luxborough Ho. W1 5E 66 (5G 159) (off Luxborough St.)
Luxborough La. Chig 3H 21
Luxborough St. W1 5E 66 (5G 159)
Luxborough Tower. W1 5G 159
Luxemburg Gdns. W6 4F 83
Luxfield Rd. SE9 1C 126
Luxford St. SE16 4K 87
Luxmore St. SE4 1B 106
Luxor St. SE5 3C 104
Lyall Av. SE21 4E 122
Lyall M. SW1 3E 84 (2G 171)
Lyall M. W. SW1 3E 84 (2G 171)
Lyall St. SW1 3E 84 (2G 171)
Lyal Rd. E3 2A 70
Lycett Pl. W12 2C 82
Lyceum Theatre. 7K 67 (2G 167) (off Strand)
Lychgate Mnr. Harr 7J 25
Lych Ga. Wlk. Hay 7H 59 (in two parts)
Lyconby Gdns. Croy 7A 142
Lydd Clo. Sidc 3J 127
Lydden Gro. SW18 7K 101
Lydden Rd. SW18 7K 101
Lydd Rd. Bexh 7F 93
Lydeard Rd. E6 7D 54
Lydford. NW1 1G 67 (off Royal College St.)
Lydford Clo. N16 5E 50 (off Pellerin Rd.)
Lydford Rd. N15 5D 32
Lydford Rd. NW2 6E 46
Lydford Rd. W9 4H 65
Lydhurst Av. SW2 2K 121
Lydia Ct. N12 6F 15
Lydney Clo. SE15 7E 86
Lydney Clo. SW19 2G 119
Lydon Rd. SW4 3G 103
Lydstep Rd. Chst 4E 126
Lyford Rd. SW18 7B 102
Lyford St. SE7 4C 90
Lygon Ho. E2 3F 69 (1K 163) (off Gosset St.)
Lygon Ho. SW6 1G 101 (off Fulham Pal. Rd.)
Lygon Pl. SW1 3F 85 (2J 171)
Lyham Clo. SW2 6J 103
Lyham Rd. SW2 5J 103
Lyle Clo. Mitc 7E 138
Lyly Ho. SE1 3D 86 (off Burbage Clo.)
Lyme Farm Rd. SE12 4J 107
Lyme Gro. E9 7J 51
Lyme Gro. Ho. E9 7J 51 (off Lyme Gro.)
Lymer Av. SE19 5F 123
Lyme Rd. Well 1B 110
Lymescote Gdns. Sutt 2J 149
Lyme St. NW1 7G 49
Lyme Ter. NW1 7G 49
Lyminge Clo. Sidc 4K 127
Lyminge Gdns. SW18 1C 120
Lymington Av. N22 2A 32
Lymington Clo. E6 5D 72
Lymington Clo. SW16 2H 139
Lymington Ct. Sutt 3K 149
Lymington Dri. Ruis 2F 41
Lymington Gdns. Eps 5B 148
Lymington Lodge. E14 3F 89 (off Schooner Clo.)
Lymington Rd. NW6 6K 47
Lymington Rd. Dag 1D 56
Lyminster Clo. Hay 5C 60
Lympne. N17 2D 32 (off Gloucester Rd.)
Lympstone Gdns. SE15 7G 87
Lynbridge Gdns. N13 4G 17
Lynbrook Clo. Rain 2K 75
Lynch Clo. SE3 2H 107
Lynchen Clo. Houn 1K 95
Lynch Wlk. SE8 6B 88 (off Dacca St.)
Lyncott Cres. SW4 4F 103
Lyncourt. SE3 2F 107
Lyncroft Av. Pinn 5C 24
Lyncroft Gdns. NW6 5J 47
Lyncroft Gdns. W13 2C 80
Lyncroft Gdns. Houn 5G 97
Lyncroft Mans. NW6 5J 47
Lyndale. NW2 4H 47
Lyndale. Th Dit 7J 133
Lyndale Av. NW2 3H 47
Lyndale Clo. SE3 6H 89
Lynde Ho. SW4 3H 103
Lynde Ho. W on T 6A 132
Lynden Hyrst. Croy 2F 153
Lyndhurst Av. N12 6J 15
Lyndhurst Av. NW7 6F 13
Lyndhurst Av. SW16 2H 139
Lyndhurst Av. Pinn 1K 23
Lyndhurst Av. S'hall 1F 79
Lyndhurst Av. Sun 3J 131
Lyndhurst Av. Surb 1H 147
Lyndhurst Av. Twic 1D 114
Lyndhurst Clo. NW10 3K 45
Lyndhurst Clo. Bexh 3H 111
Lyndhurst Clo. Croy 3F 153
Lyndhurst Ct. E18 1J 35
Lyndhurst Ct. NW8 1B 66 (off Finchley Rd.)
Lyndhurst Ct. Sutt 7J 149 (off Grange Rd.)
Lyndhurst Dri. E10 7E 34
Lyndhurst Dri. N Mald 7A 136
Lyndhurst Gdns. N3 1G 29
Lyndhurst Gdns. NW3 5B 48
Lyndhurst Gdns. Bark 6J 55
Lyndhurst Gdns. Enf 4K 7
Lyndhurst Gdns. Ilf 6H 37
Lyndhurst Gdns. Pinn 1K 23
Lyndhurst Gro. SE15 2E 104
Lyndhurst Lodge. E14 4F 89 (off Millennium Dri.)
Lyndhurst Ri. Chig 4K 21
Lyndhurst Rd. E4 7K 19
Lyndhurst Rd. N18 4B 18
Lyndhurst Rd. N22 6F 17
Lyndhurst Rd. NW3 5B 48
Lyndhurst Rd. Bexh 3H 111
Lyndhurst Rd. Gnfd 4F 61
Lyndhurst Rd. T Hth 4A 140
Lyndhurst Sq. SE15 1F 105
Lyndhurst Ter. NW3 5B 48
Lyndhurst Way. SE15 1F 105
Lyndhurst Way. Sutt 7J 149
Lyndon Av. Sidc 5K 109
Lyndon Av. Wall 3E 150
Lyndon Rd. Belv 4G 93
Lyne Cres. E17 1B 34
Lynegrove Av. Ashf 5E 112
Lyneham Wlk. E5 5A 52
Lyneham Wlk. Pinn 3H 23
Lynette Av. SW4 6F 103
Lynford Clo. Edgw 1J 27
Lynford Ct. Croy 4E 152 (off Coombe Rd.)
Lynford Gdns. Edgw 3C 12
Lynford Gdns. Ilf 2K 55
Lynford Ter. N9 1A 18
Lynhurst Cres. Uxb 7E 40
Lynhurst Rd. Uxb 7E 40
Lynmere Rd. Well 2B 110
Lyn M. E3 3B 70
Lyn M. N16 4E 50
Lynmouth Av. Enf 6A 8
Lynmouth Av. Mord 6F 137
Lynmouth Dri. Ruis 2K 41
Lynmouth Gdns. Gnfd 1B 62
Lynmouth Gdns. Houn 7B 78
Lynmouth Rd. E17 6A 34
Lynmouth Rd. N2 3D 30
Lynmouth Rd. N16 1F 51
Lynmouth Rd. Gnfd 1B 62
Lynn Clo. Ashf 5F 113
Lynn Clo. Harr 2H 25
Lynne Clo. SE23 7B 106
Lynne Ct. S Croy 4E 152 (off Birdhurst Rd.)
Lynnett Rd. Dag 2D 56
Lynne Way. N'holt 2B 60
Lynn Ho. SE15 6H 87 (off Friary Est.)
Lynn M. E11 2G 53
Lynn Rd. E11 2G 53
Lynn Rd. SW12 7F 103
Lynn Rd. Ilf 7H 37
Lynn St. Enf 1J 7
Lynscott Way. S Croy 7B 152
Lynstead Ct. Beck 2A 142
Lynsted Clo. Bexh 5H 111
Lynsted Clo. Brom 2A 144
Lynsted Gdns. SE9 3B 108
Lynton Av. N12 4G 15
Lynton Av. NW9 4B 28
Lynton Av. W13 6A 62
Lynton Av. Romf 1G 39
Lynton Clo. NW10 5A 46
Lynton Clo. Chess 4E 146
Lynton Clo. Iswth 4K 97
Lynton Cres. Ilf 6F 37
Lynton Est. SE1 4G 87
Lynton Gdns. N11 6C 16
Lynton Gdns. Enf 7K 7
Lynton Grange. N2 3D 30
Lynton Ho. W2 6A 66 (off Hallfield Est.)
Lynton Ho. Ilf 2G 55
Lynton Mans. SE1 3A 86 (1J 173) (off Kennington Rd.)
Lynton Mead. N20 3D 14
Lynton Rd. E4 5J 19
Lynton Rd. N8 5H 31 (in two parts)
Lynton Rd. NW6 2H 65
Lynton Rd. SE1 4F 87
Lynton Rd. W3 7G 63
Lynton Rd. Croy 6A 140
Lynton Rd. Harr 2C 42
Lynton Rd. N Mald 5K 135
Lynton Ter. W3 6J 63
Lynton Wlk. Hay 3G 59
Lynwood Clo. E18 1A 36
Lynwood Clo. Harr 3C 42
Lynwood Ct. King T 2H 135
Lynwood Dri. N'wd 1H 23
Lynwood Dri. Wor Pk 2C 148
Lynwood Gdns. Croy 4K 151
Lynwood Gdns. S'hall 6D 60
Lynwood Gro. N21 1F 17
Lynwood Gro. Orp 7J 145
Lynwood Rd. SW17 3D 120
Lynwood Rd. W5 3D 62
Lynwood Rd. Th Dit 2A 146
Lyon Bus. Pk. Bark 2J 73
Lyon Ct. Ruis 1H 41
Lyon Ho. NW8 4C 66 (4C 158) (off Broadley St.)
Lyon Ind. Est. NW2 2D 46
Lyon Meade. Stan 1C 26
Lyon Pk. Av. Wemb 6E 44 (in two parts)
Lyon Rd. SW19 1A 138
Lyon Rd. Harr 6K 25
Lyonsdown. 5F 5
Lyonsdown Av. New Bar 6F 5
Lyonsdown Rd. Barn 6F 5
Lyons Pl. NW8 4B 66 (4A 158)
Lyon St. N1 7K 49
Lyons Wlk. W14 4G 83
Lyon Way. Gnfd 1J 61
Lyric Dri. Gnfd 4F 61
Lyric M. SE26 4J 123
Lyric Rd. SW13 1B 100
Lyric Theatre. 4E 82 (Hammersmith)
Lyric Theatre. 7H 67 (2C 166) (off Shaftesbury Av., Westminster)
Lysander. NW9 1B 28
Lysander Gdns. Surb 6F 135
Lysander Gro. N19 1H 49
Lysander Ho. E2 2H 69 (off Temple St.)
Lysander M. N19 1G 49
Lysander Rd. Croy 6K 151
Lysander Rd. Ruis 2F 41
Lysia Ct. SW6 7E 82 (off Lysia St.)
Lysias Rd. SW12 6F 103
Lysia St. SW6 7F 83
Lysons Wlk. SW15 4C 100
Lytchet Rd. Brom 7J 125

Lytchet Way. Enf 1D 8
Lytchgate Clo. S Croy 7E 152
Lytcott Dri. W Mol 3D 132
Lytcott Gro. SE22 5E 104
Lytham Clo. SE28 6E 74
Lytham Ct. S'hall 6F 61
(off Whitecote Rd.)
Lytham Gro. W5 3F 63
Lytham St. SE17 5D 86
Lyttelton Clo. NW3 7C 48
Lyttelton Ct. N2 5A 30
Lyttelton Ho. E9 7J 51
(off Well St.)
Lyttelton Rd. E10 3D 52
Lyttelton Rd. N2 5A 30
Lyttelton Theatre 4J 167
(in Royal National Theatre)
Lyttleton Ct. Hay 4A 60
(off Dunedin Way)
Lyttleton Rd. N8 3A 32
Lytton Av. N13 2F 17
Lytton Av. Enf 1F 9
Lytton Clo. N2 6B 30
Lytton Clo. N'holt 7D 42
Lytton Gdns. Wall 4H 151
Lytton Gro. SW15 5F 101
Lytton Rd. E11 7G 35
Lytton Rd. Barn 4F 5
Lytton Rd. Pinn 1C 24
Lytton Strachey Path. SE28
7B 74
Lyveden Rd. SE3 7K 89
Lyveden Rd. SW17 6D 120

M

Mabbett Ho. SE18 6E 90
(off Nightingale Pl.)
Mabel Evetts Ct. Hay 7K 59
Maberley Cres. SE19 7G 123
Maberley Rd. SE19 1F 141
Maberley Rd. Beck 3K 141
Mabledon Ct. WC1
3H 67 (2D 160)
(off Mabledon Pl.)
Mabledon Pl. WC1
3H 67 (2D 160)
Mablethorpe Rd. SW6 7G 83
Mabley St. E9 5A 52
Mablin Lodge. Buck H 1F 21
McAdam Dri. Enf 2G 7
Macaret Clo. N20 7E 4
Macarthur Clo. E7 6J 53
MacArthur Clo. Eri 5K 93
Macarthur Ter. SE7 6B 90
Macartney Ho. SE10 7F 89
(off Chesterfield Wlk.)
Macartney Ho. SW9 1A 104
(off Gosling Way)
Macaulay Ct. SW4 3F 103
Macaulay Rd. E6 2B 72
Macaulay Rd. SW4 3F 103
Macaulay Sq. SW4 4F 103
Macaulay Way. SE28 1B 92
McAuley Clo. SE1
3A 86 (1J 173)
McAuley Clo. SE9 5F 109
Macauley M. SE13 1E 106
Macbean St. SE18 3F 91
Macbeth Ho. N1 2E 68
Macbeth St. W6 5D 82
McCall Clo. SW4 2J 103
McCall Cres. SE7 5C 90
McCall Ho. N7 4J 49
McCarthy Rd. Felt 5B 114
Macclesfield Ho. EC1
3C 68 (2C 162)
(off Central St.)
Macclesfield Rd. EC1
3C 68 (1C 162)
Macclesfield Rd. SE25 5J 141
Macclesfield St. W1
7H 67 (2D 166)
McCoid Way. SE1
2C 86 (7C 168)
McCrone M. NW3 6B 48
McCullum Rd. E3 1B 70
McDermott Clo. SW11 3C 102
McDermott Rd. SE15 3G 105
Macdonald Av. Dag 3H 57
Macdonald Rd. E7 4J 53
Macdonald Rd. E17 2E 34
Macdonald Rd. N11 5J 15
Macdonald Rd. N19 2G 49
McDonough Clo. Chess 4E 146
McDowall Clo. E16 5H 71
McDowall Rd. SE5 1C 104
Macduff Rd. SW11 1E 102
Mace Clo. E1 1H 87
Mace Gateway. E16 7J 71
McEntee Av. E17 1A 34
Mace St. E2 2K 69
McEwen Way. E15 1F 71
Macey St. SE10 6E 88
(off Thames St.)
Macfarlane La. Isw'th 6K 79
Macfarlane Rd. W12 1E 82
Macfarren Pl. NW1
4E 66 (4H 159)
McGlashon Ho. E1
4G 69 (4K 163)
(off Hunton St.)
McGrath Rd. E15 5H 53
McGregor Ct. N1 1H 163
MacGregor Rd. E16 5A 72
McGregor Rd. W11 6H 65
Machell Rd. SE15 3J 105
McIndoe Ct. N1 1D 68
(off Sherborne St.)
McIntosh Clo. Romf 3K 39
McIntosh Clo. Wall 7J 151
McIntosh Ho. SE16 4J 87
(off Millender Wlk.)
Macintosh Ho. W1
5E 66 (5H 159)
(off Beaumont St.)
McIntosh Rd. Romf 3K 39
McIntyre Ct. SE18 4C 90
(off Prospect Va.)
Mackay Ho. W12 7D 64
(off White City Est.)
Mackay Rd. SW8 3F 103
McKay Rd. SW20 7D 118
McKay Trad. Est. W10 4G 65
McKellar Clo. Bus H 2B 10
Mackennal St. NW8 2C 66
Mackenzie Clo. W12 7D 64
Mackenzie Ho. NW2 3C 46
Mackenzie Rd. N7 6K 49
Mackenzie Rd. Beck 2J 141
Mackenzie Wlk. E14 1C 88
McKerrell Rd. SE15 1G 105
Mackeson Rd. NW3 4D 48
Mackie Rd. SW2 7A 104
McKillop Way. Sidc 7C 128
Mackintosh La. E9 5K 51
Macklin St. WC2 6J 67 (7F 161)
Mackonochie Ho. EC1
5A 68 (5J 161)
(off Baldwins Gdns.)
Mackrow Wlk. E14 7E 70
Mack's Rd. SE16 4G 87
Mackworth Ho. NW1
3G 67 (1A 160)
(off Augustus St.)
Mackworth St. NW1
3G 67 (1A 160)
Maclaren M. SW15 4E 100
Maclean Rd. SE23 6A 106
McLeod Ct. SE22 1G 123
Macleod Rd. N21 5D 6
McLeod Rd. SE2 4B 92
McLeod's M. SW7 4K 83
(in two parts)
Macleod St. SE17 5C 86
Maclise Ho. SW1 4J 85 (4E 172)
(off Marsham St.)
Maclise Rd. W14 3G 83
Macmillan Ct. S Harr 1E 42
McMillan Ho. SE4 3A 106
(off Arica Rd.)
McMillan Ho. SE14 1A 106
McMillan St. SE8 6C 88
Macmillan Way. SW17 4F 121
McNair Rd. S'hall 3F 79
Macnamara Ho. SW10 7B 84
(off Worlds End Est.)
McNeil Rd. SE5 2E 104
McNicol Dri. NW10 2J 63
Macoma Rd. SE18 6H 91
Macoma Ter. SE18 6H 91
Maconochies Rd. E14 5D 88
Macquarie Way. E14 4D 88
McRae La. Mitc 7D 138
Macready Ho. W1
5C 66 (6E 158)
(off Crawford St.)
Macready Pl. N7 4J 49
Macroom Rd. W9 3H 65
Macs Ho. E17 3D 34
Mac's Pl. EC4 7J 161
Madame Tussaud's
4E 66 (4G 159)
Maddams St. E3 4D 70
Maddison Clo. Tedd 6K 115
Maddocks Clo. Sidc 5E 128
Maddocks Ho. E1 7H 69
(off Cornwall St.)
Maddock Way. SE17 6B 86
Maddox St. W1 7F 67 (2K 165)
Madeira Av. Brom 7G 125
Madeira Gro. Wfd G 6F 21
Madeira Rd. E11 1F 53
Madeira Rd. N13 4G 17
Madeira Rd. SW16 5J 121
Madeira Rd. Mitc 4D 138
Madeleine Clo. Romf 6C 38
Madeley Rd. W5 6D 62
Madeline Gro. Ilf 5H 55
Madeline Rd. SE20 7G 123
Madge Gill Way. E6 1C 72
(off High St. N.)
Madge Hill. W7 7H 61
Madinah Rd. E8 6G 51
Madison Cres. Bexh 7C 92
Madison Gdns. Bexh 7C 92
Madison Gdns. Brom 3H 143
Madison Ho. E14 7B 70
(off Victory Pl.)
Madison, The. SE1
2D 86 (6E 168)
(off Long La.)
Madras Pl. N7 6A 50
Madras Rd. Ilf 4F 55
Madrid Rd. SW13 1C 100
Madrigal La. SE5 7B 86
Madron St. SE17 5E 86
Mafeking Av. E6 2C 72
Mafeking Av. Bren 6E 80
Mafeking Av. Ilf 7H 37
Mafeking Rd. E16 4H 71
Mafeking Rd. N17 2G 33
Mafeking Rd. Enf 3A 8
Magdala Av. N19 2G 49
Magdala Rd. Isw'th 3A 98
Magdala Rd. S Croy 7D 152
Magdalene Clo. SE15 2H 105
Magdalene Gdns. E6 4E 72
Magdalene Rd. Shep 4B 130
Magdalen Ho. E16 1K 89
(off Keats Av.)
Magdalen Pas. E1
7F 69 (2K 169)
Magdalen Rd. SW18 1A 120
Magdalen St. SE1
1E 86 (5G 169)
Magee St. SE11 6A 86 (7J 173)
Magellan Ct. NW10 7K 45
(off Stonebridge Pk.)
Magellan Ho. E1 4K 69
(off Ernest St.)
Magellan Pl. E14 4C 88
Magnaville Rd. Bus H 1D 10
Magnet Rd. Wemb 2D 44
Magnin Clo. E8 1G 69
Magnolia Clo. E10 2C 52
Magnolia Clo. King T 6H 117
Magnolia Ct. Felt 1J 113
Magnolia Ct. Harr 7F 27
Magnolia Ct. N'holt 4C 60
Magnolia Ct. Rich 1H 99
Magnolia Ct. Sutt 7J 149
(off Grange Rd.)
Magnolia Ct. Uxb 6D 40
Magnolia Ct. Wall 5F 151
Magnolia Gdns. E10 2C 52
Magnolia Gdns. Edgw 4D 12
Magnolia Ho. SE8 6B 88
(off Evelyn St.)
Magnolia Lodge. E4 3J 19
Magnolia Lodge. W8 3K 83
(off St Mary's Ga.)
Magnolia Pl. SW4 5J 103
Magnolia Pl. W5 5D 62
Magnolia Rd. W4 6H 81
Magnolia St. W Dray 4A 76
Magnolia Way. Eps 5J 147
Magpie All. EC4 6A 68 (1K 167)
Magpie Clo. E7 5H 53
Magpie Clo. NW9 2A 28
Magpie Clo. Enf 1B 8
Magpie Hall Clo. Brom 6C 144
Magpie Hall La. Brom 7C 144
Magpie Hall Rd. Bus H 2D 10
Magpie Pl. SE14 6A 88
Magri Wlk. E1 5J 69
Maguire Dri. Rich 4C 116
Maguire St. SE1 2F 87 (6K 169)
Mahatma Gandhi Ind. Est.
SE24 4B 104
Mahlon Av. Ruis 5K 41
Mahogany Clo. SE16 1A 88
Mahon Clo. Enf 1A 8
Maida Av. E4 7J 9
Maida Av. W2 5A 66 (4A 158)
Maida Hill 4H 65
Maida Rd. Belv 3G 93
Maida Vale 3K 65
Maida Va. W9 2K 65 (3A 158)
Maida Way. E4 7J 9
Maiden Erlegh Av. Bex 1E 128
Maiden La. NW1 7H 49
Maiden La. SE1 1C 86 (5D 168)
Maiden La. WC2 7J 67 (3F 167)
Maiden Pl. NW5 3G 49
Maiden Rd. E15 7G 53
Maidenstone Hill. SE10 1E 106
Maids of Honour Row.
Rich 5D 98
Maidstone Av. Romf 2J 39
Maidstone Bldgs. SE1
1C 86 (5D 168)
Maidstone Ho. E14 6D 70
(off Carmen St.)
Maidstone Rd. N11 6B 16
Maidstone Rd. Sidc 6D 128
Mail Coach Yd. E2
3E 68 (1H 163)
Main Av. Enf 5A 8
Main Dri. Wemb 3D 44
Mainridge Rd. Chst 4E 126
Main Rd. Sidc 3H 127
Main St. Felt 5B 114
Mais Ho. SE26 2H 123
Maismore St. SE15 6G 87
Maisonettes, The. Sutt 5H 149
Maitland Clo. SE10 7D 88
Maitland Clo. Houn 3D 96
Maitland Ct. W2 7B 66 (2A 164)
(off Lancaster Ter.)
Maitland Ho. SW1
6G 85 (7A 172)
(off Churchill Gdns.)
Maitland Pk. Est. NW3 6D 48
Maitland Pk. Rd. NW3 6D 48
Maitland Pk. Vs. NW3 6D 48
Maitland Pl. E5 4H 51
Maitland Rd. E15 6H 53
Maitland Rd. SE26 6K 123
Maitland Yd. W13 1A 80
Maize Row. E14 7B 70
Majendie Rd. SE18 5H 91
Majestic Way. Mitc 2D 138
Major Rd. E15 5F 53
Major Rd. SE16 3G 87
Makepeace Av. N6 2E 48
Makepeace Mans. N6 2E 48
Makepeace Rd. E11 4J 35
Makepeace Rd. N'holt 2C 60
Makinen Ho. Buck H 1F 21
Makins St. SW3 4C 84 (4D 170)
Malabar Ct. W12 7D 64
(off India Way)
Malabar St. E14 2C 88
Malam Ct. SE11 4A 86 (4J 173)
Malam Gdns. E14 7D 70
Malbrook Rd. SW15 4D 100
Malcolm Ct. E7 6H 53
Malcolm Ct. NW4 6C 28
Malcolm Ct. Stan 5H 11
Malcolm Cres. NW4 6C 28
Malcolm Dri. Surb 1D 146
Malcolm Ho. N1 2E 68
(off Arden Est.)
Malcolm Pl. E2 4J 69
Malcolm Rd. E1 4J 69
Malcolm Rd. SE20 7J 123
Malcolm Rd. SE25 6G 141
Malcolm Rd. SW19 6G 119
Malcolm Rd. Uxb 4B 40
Malcolm Sargent Ho. E16 1K 89
(off Evelyn Rd.)
Malcolmson Ho. SW1
5H 85 (6C 172)
(off Aylesford St.)
Malcolm Way. E11 5J 35
Malcombs Way. N14 5B 6
Malden Av. SE25 4H 141
Malden Av. Gnfd 5J 43
Malden Ct. N4 6C 32
Malden Ct. N Mald 3D 136
Malden Cres. NW5 6E 48
Malden Green 1C 148
Malden Grn. Av. Wor Pk 1B 148
Malden Hill. N Mald 3B 136
Malden Hill Gdns. N Mald
3B 136
Malden Junction. (Junct.) 5A 136
Malden Pk. N Mald 6B 136
Malden Pl. NW5 5E 48
Malden Rd. NW5 5D 48
Malden Rd. N Mald 5A 136
Malden Rd. Sutt 4E 148
Malden Way. N Mald 6K 135
Maldon Clo. E15 5G 53
Maldon Clo. N1 1C 68
Maldon Clo. SE5 3E 104
Maldon Ct. E6 1E 72
Maldon Ct. Wall 5G 151
Maldon Rd. N9 3A 18
Maldon Rd. W3 7J 63
Maldon Rd. Romf 7J 39
Maldon Rd. Wall 5F 151
Maldon Wlk. Wfd G 6F 21
Malet Pl. WC1 4H 67 (4C 160)
Malet St. WC1 4H 67 (4C 160)
Maley Av. SE27 2B 122
Malford Ct. E18 2J 35
Malford Gro. E18 4H 35
Malfort Rd. SE5 3E 104
Malham Clo. N11 6K 15
Malham Rd. SE23 1K 123
Malham Ter. N18 6C 18
(off Dysons Rd.)
Malibu Ct. SE26 3H 123
Mallams M. SW9 3B 104
Mallard Clo. E9 6B 52
Mallard Clo. NW6 2J 65
Mallard Clo. W7 2J 79
Mallard Clo. New Bar 6G 5
Mallard Clo. Twic 7E 96
Mallard Ct. E17 3F 35
Mallard Ho. NW8 2C 66
(off Barrow Hill Est.)
Mallard Path. SE28 3H 91
(off Goosander Way)

Mallard Pl. N22 . . . . 2K 31
Mallard Pl. Twic. 3A 116
Mallards. E11. . . . . 7J 35
(off Blake Hall Rd.)
Mallards Rd. Wfd G 7E 20
Mallard Wlk. Beck 5K 141
Mallard Wlk. Sidc 6C 128
Mallard Way. NW9 . . . . 7J 27
Mallard Way. Wall 7G 151
Mall Chambers. W8 . . . . 1J 83
(off Kensington Mall)
Mallet Dri. N'holt 5D 42
Mallet Rd. SE13 . . . . 6F 107
Mall Galleries. 4D 166
Mall Gallery. WC2 . . . 6J 67 (1E 166)
(off Thomas Neals Shop. Mall)
Malling Clo. Croy 6J 141
Malling Gdns. Mord 6A 138
Malling Way. Brom 7H 143
Mallinson Rd. SW11 . . . . 5C 102
Mallinson Rd. Croy 3H 151
Mallon Gdns. E1 . . . . 6F 69 (7K 163)
(off Commercial St.)
Mallord St. SW3 . . . 6B 84 (7B 170)
Mallory Clo. SE4 . . . . 4A 106
Mallory Gdns. E Barn 7K 5
Mallory Ho. E14 . . . . 5D 70
(off Teviot St.)
Mallory St. NW8 . . . 4C 66 (3D 158)
Mallow Clo. Croy 1K 153
Mallow Mead. NW7 . . . . 7B 14
Mallows, The. Uxb 3D 40
Mallow St. EC1 . . . . 4D 68 (3E 162)
Mall Rd. W6 . . . . 5D 82
Mall, The. E15 . . . . 7F 53
Mall, The. N14 . . . . 3D 16
Mall, The. SW1 . . . . 2G 85 (5D 166)
Mall, The. SW14 . . . . 5J 99
Mall, The. W5 . . . . 7E 62
Mall, The. Bexh 4G 111
Mall, The. Bren 6D 80
Mall, The. Brom 3J 143
Mall, The. Croy 2C 152
Mall, The. Dag 6G 57
Mall, The. Harr 6F 27
Mall, The. Surb 5D 134
Malmains Clo. Beck 4F 143
Malmains Way. Beck 4E 142
Malmesbury. E2 . . . . 2J 69
(off Cyprus St.)
Malmesbury Clo. Pinn 4H 23
Malmesbury Rd. E3 . . . . 3B 70
Malmesbury Rd. E16 . . . . 5G 71
Malmesbury Rd. E18 . . . . 1H 35
Malmesbury Rd. Mord 7A 138
Malmesbury Ter. E16 . . . . 5H 71
Malmsey Ho. SE11
. . . . 5K 85 (5H 173)
Malpas Dri. Pinn 5B 24
Malpas Rd. E8 . . . . 5H 51
Malpas Rd. SE4 . . . . 2B 106
Malpas Rd. Dag 6D 56
Malsmead Ho. E9 . . . . 5B 52
(off Homerton Rd.)
Malta Rd. E10 . . . . 1C 52
Malta St. EC1 . . . . . 4B 68 (3A 162)
Maltby Clo. Orp 7K 145
Maltby Dri. Enf 1C 8
Maltby Rd. Chess 6G 147
Maltby St. SE1 . . . . . 2F 87 (7J 169)
Malthouse Dri. W4 . . . . 6B 82
Malthouse Dri. Felt 5B 114
Malthouse Pas. SW13 . . . . . 2B 100
(off Maltings Clo.)
Malthus Path. SE28 . . . . 1C 92
Malting Ho. E14 . . . . 7B 70
(off Oak La.)
Maltings. W4 . . . . 5G 81
Maltings Clo. SW13 . . . . 2B 100
Maltings Lodge. W4 . . . . 6A 82
(off Corney Reach Way)
Maltings M. Sidc 3A 128
Maltings Pl. SE1 . . . . 7H 169
Maltings Pl. SW6 . . . . 1K 101
Malting Way. Iswth 3K 97
Malton M. SE18 . . . . 6J 91
Malton M. W10 . . . . 6G 65
Malton Rd. W10 . . . . 6G 65
Malton St. SE18 . . . . 6J 91
Maltravers St. WC2
. . . . 7K 67 (2H 167)
Malt St. SE1 . . . . 6G 87
Malva Clo. SW18 . . . . 5K 101
Malvern Av. E4 . . . . 7A 20
Malvern Av. Bexh 7E 92
Malvern Av. Harr 3C 42
Malvern Clo. SE20 . . . . 2G 141
Malvern Clo. W10 . . . . 5H 65
Malvern Clo. Mitc 3G 139
Malvern Clo. Surb 1E 146
Malvern Clo. Uxb 2C 40
Malvern Ct. SW7 . . . 4B 84 (3B 170)
(off Onslow Sq.)
Malvern Ct. W12 . . . . 2C 82
(off Hadyn Pk. Rd.)
Malvern Ct. Sutt 7J 149
Malvern Dri. Felt 5B 114
Malvern Dri. Ilf 4K 55
Malvern Dri. Wfd G 5F 21
Malvern Gdns. NW2 . . . . 2G 47
Malvern Gdns. Harr 4E 26
Malvern Ho. N16 . . . . 1F 51
Malvern M. NW6 . . . . 3J 65
Malvern Pl. NW6 . . . . 3H 65
Malvern Rd. E6 . . . . 1C 72
Malvern Rd. E8 . . . . 7G 51
Malvern Rd. E11 . . . . 2G 53
Malvern Rd. N8 . . . . 3A 32
Malvern Rd. N17 . . . . 3G 33
Malvern Rd. NW6 . . . . 3J 65
(in two parts)
Malvern Rd. Hamp 7E 114
Malvern Rd. Hay 7G 77
Malvern Rd. Surb 2E 146
Malvern Rd. T Hth 4A 140
Malvern Ter. N1 . . . . 1A 68
Malvern Ter. N9 . . . . 1A 18
Malvern Way. W13 . . . . 5B 62
Malwood Rd. SW12 . . . . 6F 103
Malyons Rd. SE13 . . . . 6D 106
Malyons Ter. SE13 . . . . 5D 106
Malyons, The. Shep 6F 131
Managers St. E14 . . . . 1E 88
Manatee Pl. Wall 3H 151
Manaton Clo. SE15 . . . . 3H 105
Manaton Cres. S'hall 6E 60
Manbey Gro. E15 . . . . 6G 53
Manbey Pk. Rd. E15 . . . . 6G 53
Manbey Rd. E15 . . . . 6G 53
Manbey St. E15 . . . . 6G 53
Manbre Rd. W6 . . . . 6E 82
Manbrough Av. E6 . . . . 3E 72
Manchester Ct. E16 . . . . 6K 71
(off Garvary Rd.)
Manchester Dri. W10 . . . . 4G 65
Manchester Gro. E14 . . . . 5E 88
Manchester Ho. SE17 . . . . . . 5C 86
Manchester M. W1 . . . . 6G 159
Manchester Rd. E14 . . . . 5E 88
Manchester Rd. N15 . . . . 6D 32
Manchester Rd. T Hth 3C 140
Manchester Sq. W1
. . . . 6E 66 (7G 159)
Manchester St. W1
. . . . 5E 66 (6G 159)
Manchester Way. Dag 4H 57
Manchuria Rd. SW11 . . . . . . 6E 102
Manciple St. SE1 . . . 2D 86 (7E 168)
Mandalay Rd. SW4 . . . . 5G 103
Mandarin Ct. NW10 . . . . 6K 45
(off Mitchellbrook Way)
Mandarin Ct. SE8 . . . . 6B 88
Mandarin St. E14 . . . . 7C 70
Mandarin Way. Hay 6C 60
Mandela Clo. NW10 . . . . 7J 45
Mandela Clo. W12 . . . . 7D 64
Mandela Ho. E2 . . . . 3F 69 (2J 163)
(off Virginia Rd.)
Mandela Ho. SE5 . . . . 2B 104
Mandela Rd. E16 . . . . 6J 71
Mandela St. NW1 . . . . 1G 67
Mandela St. SW9 . . . . 7A 86
(in two parts)
Mandela Way. SE1 . . . . 4E 86
Mandeville Clo. SE3 . . . . 7H 89
Mandeville Clo. SW20 . . . . . 7G 119
Mandeville Ct. E4 . . . . 5F 19
Mandeville Dri. Surb 1D 146
Mandeville Ho. SE1 . . . . 5F 87
(off Rolls Rd.)
Mandeville Ho. SW4 . . . . . . 5G 103
Mandeville M. SW4 . . . . 4H 103
Mandeville Pl.
W1 . . . . 6E 66 (7H 159)
Mandeville Rd. N14 . . . . 2A 16
Mandeville Rd. Iswth 2A 98
Mandeville Rd. N'holt 7E 42
Mandeville Rd. Shep 5C 130
Mandeville St. E5 . . . . 3A 52
Mandrake Rd. SW17 . . . . . . 3D 120
Mandrake Way. E15 . . . . 7G 53
Mandrell Rd. SW2 . . . . 5J 103
Manesty Ct. N14 . . . . 7C 6
(off Ivy Rd.)
Manette St. W1 . . . . 6H 67 (1D 166)
Manfred Rd. SW15 . . . . 5H 101
Manger Rd. N7 . . . . 6J 49
Mangold Way. Eri 3D 92
Manilla St. E14 . . . . 2C 88
Man in the Moon Theatre.
. . . . 6B 84 (7A 170)
Manister Rd. SE2 . . . . 3A 92
Manitoba Ct. SE16 . . . . 2J 87
(off Canada Est.)
Manley Ct. N16 . . . . 3F 51
Manley Ho. SE11 . . . . 4A 86 (5J 173)
Manley St. NW1 . . . . 1E 66
Mann Clo. Croy 3C 152
Manneby Prior. N1
. . . . 2K 67 (1H 161)
(off Cumming St.)
Manningford Clo. EC1
. . . . 3B 68 (1A 162)
Manning Gdns. Harr 7D 26
Manning Pl. Rich 6F 99
Manning Rd. E17 . . . . 5A 34
Manning Rd. Dag 6G 57
Manningtree Clo. SW19 . . . . 1G 119
Manningtree Rd. Ruis 4K 41
Manningtree St. E1 . . . . 6G 69
Mannin Rd. Romf 7B 38
Mannock M. E18 . . . . 1A 36
Mannock Rd. N22 . . . . 3B 32
Mann's Clo. Iswth 5K 97
Manns Rd. Edgw 6B 12
Manny Shinwell Ho. SW6 . . . 6H 83
(off Clem Attlee Ct.)
Manoel Rd. Twic 3G 115
Manor Av. E7 . . . . 4A 54
Manor Av. SE4 . . . . 2B 106
Manor Av. Houn 3B 96
Manor Av. N'holt 7D 42
Manor Brook. SE3 . . . . 4J 107
Manor Circus. (Junct.) 3F 99
Manor Clo. E17 . . . . 1A 34
Manor Clo. NW7 . . . . 5E 12
Manor Clo. NW9 . . . . 5H 27
Manor Clo. SE28 . . . . 7C 74
Manor Clo. Barn 4B 4
Manor Clo. Cray 4K 111
Manor Clo. Dag 6K 57
Manor Clo. Ruis 1H 41
Manor Clo. Wor Pk 1A 148
Manor Cotts. N2 . . . . 2A 30
(off Manor Cotts. App.)
Manor Cotts. N'wd 1H 23
Manor Cotts. App. N2 . . . . . . 2A 30
Manor Ct. E4 . . . . 1B 20
Manor Ct. E10 . . . . 1D 52
Manor Ct. N2 . . . . 5D 30
(off Aylmer Rd.)
Manor Ct. N14 . . . . 2C 16
Manor Ct. N20 . . . . 3J 15
(off York Way)
Manor Ct. SW2 . . . . 5K 103
Manor Ct. SW6 . . . . 1K 101
Manor Ct. SW16 . . . . 3J 121
Manor Ct. W3 . . . . 4G 81
Manor Ct. Bark 7K 55
Manor Ct. Bexh 4H 111
Manor Ct. Harr 6K 25
Manor Ct. King T 1G 135
Manor Ct. Twic 2G 115
Manor Ct. Wemb 5E 44
Manor Ct. W Mol 4E 132
Manor Ct. W Wick 1D 154
Manor Ct. Rd. W7 . . . . 7J 61
Manor Cres. Surb 6G 135
Manor Dene. SE28 . . . . 6C 74
Manordene Clo. Th Dit 1A 146
Manordene Rd. SE28 . . . . 6D 74
Manor Dri. N14 . . . . 1A 16
Manor Dri. N20 . . . . 4J 15
Manor Dri. NW7 . . . . 5E 12
Manor Dri. Eps 6A 148
Manor Dri. Esh 2A 146
Manor Dri. Felt 5B 114
Manor Dri. Sun 2J 131
Manor Dri. Surb 6F 135
Manor Dri. Wemb 4F 45
Manor Dri. N.
N Mald & Wor Pk . . 7K 135
Manor Dri., The. Wor Pk . . . 1A 148
Manor Est. SE16 . . . . 4H 87
Mnr. Farm Av. Shep 6D 130
Mnr. Farm Clo. Wor Pk 1A 148
Mnr. Farm Ct. E6 . . . . 3D 72
(off Holloway Rd.)
Mnr. Farm Dri. E4 . . . . 3B 20
Mnr. Farm Rd. SW16 . . . . . . 2A 140
Mnr. Farm Rd. Wemb 2D 62
Manorfield Clo. N19 . . . . 4G 49
(off Fulbrook M.)
Manor Fields. SW15 . . . . 6F 101
Manorfields Clo. Chst 3K 145
Manor Gdns. N7 . . . . 3J 49
Manor Gdns. SW4 . . . . 2G 103
(off Larkhall Ri.)
Manor Gdns. SW20 . . . . 2H 137
Manor Gdns. W3 . . . . 4G 81
Manor Gdns. W4 . . . . 5A 82
Manor Gdns. Hamp 7F 115
Manor Gdns. Rich 4F 99
Manor Gdns. Ruis 5A 42
Manor Gdns. S Croy 6F 153
Manor Gdns. Sun 1J 131
Manor Ga. N'holt 7C 42
Manorgate Rd. King T 1G 135
Manor Gro. SE15 . . . . 6J 87
Manor Gro. Beck 2D 142
Manor Gro. Rich 4G 99
Mnr. Hall Av. NW4 . . . . 2F 29
Mnr. Hall Dri. NW4 . . . . 2F 29
Manorhall Gdns. E10 . . . . 1C 52
Manor House. (Junct.) 1C 50
Manor Ho. NW1 . . . 5C 66 (5D 158)
(off Marylebone Rd.)
Manor Ho. S'hall 3C 78
Manor Ho. Ct. W9 . . . . 4A 66
(off Warrington Gdns.)
Manor Ho. Ct. Shep 7D 130
Mnr. House Dri. NW6 . . . . 7F 47
Manor Ho. Dri. N'wd 1D 22
Manor Ho. Est. Stan 6G 11
Mnr. Ho. Garden. E11 . . . . . . 6K 35
Manor Ho. Way. Iswth 3B 98
Manor La. SE13 & SE12 . . . 5G 107
Manor La. Felt 2J 113
Manor La. Hay 6F 77
Manor La. Sun 2J 131
Manor La. Sutt 5A 150
Manor La. Ter. SE13 . . . . . . 4G 107
Manor M. NW6 . . . . 2J 65
(off Cambridge Av., in two parts)
Manor M. SE4 . . . . 2B 106
Manor Mt. SE23 . . . . 1J 123
Manor Pde. N16 . . . . 2F 51
Manor Pde. NW10 . . . . 2B 64
(off High St.)
Manor Pde. Harr 6K 25
Manor Park. 4C 54
Manor Pk. SE13 . . . . 4F 107
Manor Pk. Chst 2H 145
Manor Pk. Rich 4F 99
Mnr. Park Clo. W Wick 1D 154
Manor Park Crematorium.
E7 . . . . 4A 54
Mnr. Park Cres. Edgw 6B 12
Mnr. Park Dri. Harr 3F 25
Mnr. Park Gdns. Edgw 5B 12
Mnr. Park Pde. SE13 . . . . . . 4F 107
(off Lee High Rd.)
Mnr. Park Rd. E12 . . . . 4B 54
Mnr. Park Rd. N2 . . . . 3A 30
Mnr. Park Rd. NW10 . . . . 1B 64
Mnr. Park Rd. Chst 1G 145
Mnr. Park Rd. Sutt 5A 150
Mnr. Park Rd. W Wick 1D 154
Manor Pl. SE17 . . . . 5B 86
Manor Pl. Chst 2H 145
Manor Pl. Felt 1J 113
Manor Pl. Mitc 3G 139
Manor Pl. Sutt 4K 149
Manor Pl. W on T 7J 131
(off Thames St., in two parts)
Manor Rd. E10 . . . . 7C 34
Manor Rd. E15 & E16 . . . . . . 2G 71
Manor Rd. E17 . . . . 2A 34
Manor Rd. N16 . . . . 2D 50
Manor Rd. N17 . . . . 1G 33
Manor Rd. N22 . . . . 6D 16
Manor Rd. SE25 . . . . 4G 141
Manor Rd. SW20 . . . . 2H 137
Manor Rd. W13 . . . . 7A 62
Manor Rd. Ashf 5B 112
Manor Rd. Bark 6K 55
Manor Rd. Barn 4B 4
Manor Rd. Beck 2D 142
Manor Rd. Bex 1H 129
Manor Rd. Chad H 6D 38
Manor Rd. Dag 6J 57
Manor Rd. Dart 4K 111
Manor Rd. E Mol 4H 133
Manor Rd. Enf 2H 7
Manor Rd. Harr 6A 26
Manor Rd. Hay 6J 59
Manor Rd. Mitc 4G 139
Manor Rd. Rich 4G 99
Manor Rd. Ruis 1F 41
Manor Rd. Sidc 3K 127
Manor Rd. Sutt 7H 149
Manor Rd. Tedd 5A 116
(in two parts)
Manor Rd. Twic 2G 115
Manor Rd. Wall 4F 151
Manor Rd. W on T 7H 131
Manor Rd. W Wick 2D 154
Manor Rd. Wfd G & Chig 6J 21
Manor Rd. Ho. Harr 6A 26
Manor Rd. N. Esh 3A 146
Manor Rd. N. Wall 4F 151
Manorside. Barn 4B 4
Manorside Clo. SE2 . . . . 4C 92
Manor Sq. Dag 2C 56
Manor Va. Bren 5C 80
Manor Vw. N3 . . . . 2K 29
Manor Way. E4 . . . . 4A 20
Manor Way. NW9 . . . . 4A 28
Manor Way. SE3 . . . . 4H 107
Manor Way. Beck 2C 142
Manor Way. Bex 1G 129
Manor Way. Bexh 3K 111
Manor Way. Brom 6C 144
Manorway. Enf 7K 7
Manor Way. Harr 4F 25
Manor Way. Mitc 3G 139
Manor Way. Orp 4G 145
Manor Way. Rain 4K 75
Manor Way. Ruis 7G 23
Manor Way. S'hall 4B 78
Manor Way. S Croy 6E 152
Manor Way. Wfd G 5F 21
Manor Way. Wor Pk 1A 148
Manor Way Bus. Cen.
Rain 5K 75

Manor Waye. Uxb 1A 58
Manor Way, The. Wall 4F 151
Manpreet Ct. E12 5D 54
Manresa Rd. SW3 5C 84 (6C 170)
Mansard Beeches. SW17 5E 120
Mansard Clo. Pinn 3B 24
Manse Clo. Hay 6F 77
Mansel Gro. E17 1C 34
Mansell Rd. W3 2K 81
Mansell Rd. Gnfd 5F 61
Mansell St. E1 6F 69 (1K 169)
Mansel Rd. SW19 6G 119
Mansergh Clo. SE18 7C 90
Manse Rd. N16 3F 51
Manser Rd. Rain 3K 75
Mansfield Av. N15 4D 32
Mansfield Av. Barn 6J 5
Mansfield Av. Ruis 1K 41
Mansfield Clo. N9 6B 8
Mansfield Ct. E2 1F 69 (off Whiston Rd.)
Mansfield Dri. Hay 4G 59
Mansfield Heights. N2 5C 30
Mansfield Hill. E4 7J 9
Mansfield M. W1 5F 67 (6J 159)
Mansfield Pl. NW3 4A 48
Mansfield Pl. S Croy 6D 152
Mansfield Rd. E11 6K 35
Mansfield Rd. E17 4B 34
Mansfield Rd. NW3 5D 48
Mansfield Rd. W3 4H 63
Mansfield Rd. Chess 5C 146
Mansfield Rd. Ilf 2E 54
Mansfield Rd. S Croy 6D 152
Mansfield St. W1 5F 67 (6J 159)
Mansford St. E2 2G 69
Manship Rd. Mitc 7E 120
Mansion Clo. SW9 1A 104 (in two parts)
Mansion Gdns. NW3 3K 47
Mansion House. 6D 68 (1E 168)
Mansion Ho. Pl. EC4 6D 68 (1E 168)
Mansion Ho. St. EC4 1E 168
Mansions, The. SW5 5K 83
Manson M. SW7 4B 84 (4A 170)
Manson Pl. SW7 4B 84 (4A 170)
Mansted Gdns. Romf 7C 38
Manston. N17 2D 32 (off Adams Rd.)
Manston. NW1 7G 49 (off Agar Gro.)
Manston Av. S'hall 4E 78
Manston Clo. SE20 1J 141
Manstone Rd. NW2 5G 47
Manston Gro. King T 5D 116
Manston Ho. W14 3G 83 (off Russell Rd.)
Manthorp Rd. SE18 5G 91
Mantilla Rd. SW17 4E 120
Mantle Rd. SE4 3A 106
Mantlet Clo. SW16 7G 121
Mantle Way. E15 7G 53
Manton Av. W7 2K 79
Manton Clo. Hay 7G 59
Manton Rd. SE2 4A 92
Mantua St. SW11 3B 102
Mantus Clo. E1 4J 69
Mantus Rd. E1 4J 69
Manus Way. N20 2F 15
Manville Gdns. SW17 3F 121
Manville Rd. SW17 2E 120
Manwood Rd. SE4 5B 106
Manwood St. E16 1D 90
Manygate La. Shep 7E 130
Manygate Mobile Home Est. Shep 6F 131 (off Mitre Clo.)
Manygates. SW12 2F 121
Mapesbury Rd. NW2 7G 47
Mapeshill Pl. NW2 6E 46
Mapes Ho. NW6 7G 47
Mape St. E2 4H 69
Maple Av. E4 5G 19
Maple Av. W3 1A 82
Maple Av. Harr 2F 43
Maple Av. W Dray 7A 58
Maple Clo. N3 6D 14
Maple Clo. N16 6G 33
Maple Clo. SW4 6H 103
Maple Clo. Buck H 3G 21
Maple Clo. Hamp 6C 114
Maple Clo. Hay 3B 60
Maple Clo. Mitc 1F 139
Maple Clo. Orp 5H 145
Maple Clo. Ruis 6K 23
Maple Ct. E6 5E 72
Maple Ct. SE6 1D 124
Maple Ct. Croy 4C 152 (off Lwr. Coombe St.)
Maple Ct. Croy 4C 152 (off Waldrons, The)
Maple Ct. N Mald 3K 135
Maple Cres. Sidc 6A 110
Maplecroft Clo. E6 6B 72
Mapledale Av. Croy 2G 153
Mapledene. Chst 5G 127
Mapledene Est. E8 7G 51
Mapledene Rd. E8 7F 51
Maple Gdns. Edgw 7F 13
Maple Gdns. Stai 2A 112
Maple Gro. NW9 7J 27
Maple Gro. W5 3D 80
Maple Gro. Bren 7B 80
Maple Gro. S'hall 5D 60
Maple Gro. Bus. Cen. Houn 4A 96
Maple Ho. E17 3D 34
Maple Ho. SE8 7B 88 (off Idonia St.)
Maple Ho. King T 5E 134 (off Maple Rd.)
Maplehurst. Brom 2G 143
Maplehurst Clo. King T 4E 134
Maple Ind. Est. Felt 3J 113
Maple Leaf Dri. Sidc 1K 127
Mapleleafe Gdns. Ilf 3F 37
Maple Leaf Sq. SE16 2K 87
Maple Lodge. W8 3K 83 (off Abbots Wlk.)
Maple M. NW6 2K 65
Maple M. SW16 5K 121
Maple Pl. N17 7B 18
Maple Pl. W1 4G 67 (5B 160)
Maple Pl. W Dray 1A 76
Maple Rd. E11 6G 35
Maple Rd. SE20 1H 141
Maple Rd. Hay 3A 60
Maple Rd. Surb 6D 134
Maples Pl. E1 5H 69
Maplestead Rd. SW2 7K 103
Maplestead Rd. Dag 1B 74
Maples, The. Clay 7A 146
Maples, The. King T 7C 116
Maple St. W1 5G 67 (5A 160)
Maple St. Romf 4J 39
Maplethorpe Rd. T Hth 4A 140
Mapleton Clo. Brom 6J 143
Mapleton Cres. SW18 6K 101
Mapleton Cres. Enf 1D 8
Mapleton Rd. E4 3K 19
Mapleton Rd. SW18 6J 101 (in two parts)
Mapleton Rd. Enf 2C 8
Maple Wlk. W10 3F 65
Maple Way. Felt 3J 113
Maplin Clo. N21 6E 6
Maplin Ho. SE2 2D 92 (off Wolvercote Rd.)
Maplin Rd. E16 6J 71
Maplin St. E3 3B 70
Mapperley Clo. E11 6H 35
Mapperley Dri. Wfd G 7B 20
Maran Way. Eri 3D 92
Marathon Ho. NW1 5D 66 (5E 158) (off Marylebone Rd.)
Marathon Way. SE28 2K 91
Marban Rd. W9 3H 65
Marble Arch. (Junct.) 7C 66 (2E 164)
Marble Arch. 2F 165
Marble Arch. W1 7D 66 (2E 164)
Marble Arch Apartments. W1 6D 66 (7E 158) (off Harrowby St.)
Marble Clo. W3 1H 81
Marble Dri. NW2 1F 47
Marble Hill Clo. Twic 7B 98
Marble Hill Gdns. Twic 7B 98
Marble Hill House. 7C 98
Marble Ho. W9 4H 65
Marble Quay. E1 1G 87 (4K 169)
Marbrook Ct. SE12 3A 126
Marcella Rd. SW9 2A 104
March. NW9 1B 28 (off Concourse, The)
Marchant Ct. SE1 5F 87
Marchant Rd. E11 2F 53
Marchant St. SE14 6A 88
Marchbank Rd. W14 6H 83
March Ct. SW15 4D 100
Marchmont Rd. Rich 5F 99
Marchmont Rd. Wall 7G 151
Marchmont St. WC1 4J 67 (3E 160)
March Rd. Twic 7A 98
Marchside Clo. Houn 1B 96
Marchwood Clo. SE5 7E 86
Marchwood Cres. W5 6C 62
Marcia Rd. SE1 4E 86
Marcilly Rd. SW18 5B 102
Marcon Ct. E8 5H 51 (off Amhurst Rd.)
Marconi Pl. N11 4A 16
Marconi Rd. E10 1C 52
Marconi Way. S'hall 6F 61
Marcon Pl. E8 5H 51
Marco Polo Ho. SW8 7F 85
Marco Rd. W6 3E 82
Marcourt Lawns. W5 4E 62
Marcus Ct. E15 1G 71
Marcus Garvey M. SE22 6H 105
Marcus Garvey Way. SE24 4A 104
Marcus St. E15 1G 71
Marcus St. SW18 6K 101
Marcus Ter. SW18 6K 101
Mardale Ct. NW7 7H 13
Mardale Dri. NW9 5K 27
Mardell Rd. Croy 5K 141
Marden Av. Brom 6H 143
Marden Cres. Bex 5J 111
Marden Cres. Croy 6K 139
Marden Ho. E5 5H 51
Marden Rd. N17 2E 32
Marden Rd. Croy 6K 139
Marden Sq. SE16 3H 87
Marder Rd. W13 2A 80
Mardyke Ho. SE17 4D 86 (off Mason St.)
Marechal Niel Av. Sidc 3H 127
Marechal Niel Pde. Sidc 3H 127 (off Main Rd.)
Maresby Ho. E4 2J 19
Mares Fld. Croy 3E 152
Maresfield Gdns. NW3 5A 48
Mare St. E8 & E2 5H 51
Marfleet Clo. Cars 2C 150
Margaret Av. E4 6J 9
Margaret Bondfield Av. Bark 7A 56
Margaret Bldgs. N16 1F 51
Margaret Ct. W1 7A 160
Margaret Ct. Barn 4G 5
Margaret Gardner Dri. SE9 2D 126
Margaret Herbison Ho. SW6 6H 83 (off Clem Attlee Ct.)
Margaret Ho. W6 5E 82 (off Queen Caroline St.)
Margaret Ingram Clo. SW6 6H 83 (off Rylston Rd.)
Margaret Lockwood Clo. King T 4F 135
Margaret Rd. N16 1F 51
Margaret Rd. Barn 4G 5
Margaret Rd. Bex 6D 110
Margaret St. W1 6F 67 (7K 159)
Margaretta Ter. SW3 6C 84 (7C 170)
Margaretting Rd. E12 1A 54
Margaret Way. Ilf 6C 36
Margaret White Ho. NW1 3H 67 (1D 160) (off Chalton St.)
Margate Rd. SW2 5J 103
Margery Fry Ct. N7 3J 49
Margery Pk. Rd. E7 6J 53
Margery Rd. Dag 3D 56
Margery St. WC1 3A 68 (2J 161)
Margin Dri. SW19 5F 119
Margravine Gdns. W6 5F 83
Margravine Rd. W6 5F 83
Marham Gdns. SW18 1C 120
Marham Gdns. Mord 6A 138
Maria Clo. SE1 4H 87
Marian Clo. Hay 4B 60
Marian Ct. E9 5J 51
Marian Ct. Sutt 5K 149
Marian Pl. E2 2H 69
Marian Rd. SW16 1G 139
Marian Sq. E2 2H 69
Marian St. E2 2H 69
Marian Way. NW10 7B 46
Maria Ter. E1 5K 69
Maria Theresa Clo. N Mald 5K 135
Maribor. SE10 7E 88 (off Burney St.)
Maricas Av. Harr 1H 25
Marie Curie. SE5 1E 104
Marie Lloyd Gdns. N19 7J 31
Marie Lloyd Ho. N1 2D 68 (1E 162) (off Murray Gro.)
Marie Lloyd Wlk. E8 6F 51
Mariette Way. Wall 7J 151
Marigold All. SE1 3A 168
Marigold Clo. S'hall 7C 60
Marigold Rd. N17 7D 18
Marigold St. SE16 2H 87
Marigold Way. Croy 1K 153
Marina App. Hay 5C 60
Marina Av. N Mald 5D 136
Marina Clo. Brom 3J 143
Marina Dri. Well 2J 109
Marina Gdns. Romf 5H 39
Marina Way. Tedd 7D 116
Marine Dri. SE18 4D 90
Marine Dri. Bark 3B 74
Marinefield Rd. SW6 2K 101
Marinel Ho. SE5 7C 86
Mariner Gdns. Rich 3C 116
Mariner Rd. E12 4E 54
Mariners M. E14 4F 89
Marine St. SE16 3G 87 (7K 169)
Marine Tower. SE8 6B 88 (off Abinger Gro.)
Marion Av. Shep 5D 130
Marion Gro. Wfd G 5B 20
Marion Rd. NW7 5H 13
Marion Rd. T Hth 5C 140
Marischal Rd. SE13 3F 107
Maritime Ind. Est. SE7 4K 89
Maritime Quay. E14 5C 88
Maritime St. E3 4B 70
Marius Pas. SW17 2E 120
Marius Rd. SW17 2E 120
Marjorie Gro. SW11 4D 102
Marjorie M. E1 6K 69
Mark Av. E4 6J 9
Mark Clo. Bexh 1E 110
Mark Clo. S'hall 7F 61
Marke Clo. Kes 4C 156
Market Cen., The. S'hall 4K 77
Market Chambers. Enf 3J 7 (off Church St.)
Market Ct. W1 7A 160
Market Entrance. SW8 7G 85
Market Est. N7 6J 49
Market Hill. SE18 3E 90
Market La. Edgw 1J 27
Market Link. Romf 4K 39
Market M. W1 1F 85 (5J 165)
Market Pde. E10 6E 34 (off High Rd. Leyton)
Market Pde. E17 3B 34 (off Forest Rd.)
Market Pde. N9 2B 18 (off Winchester Rd.)
Market Pde. Brom 1J 143 (off East St.)
Market Pde. Felt 3C 114
Market Pde. Sidc 4B 128
Market Pavilion. E10 3C 52
Market Pl. N2 3C 30
Market Pl. NW11 4K 29
Market Pl. SE16 4G 87 (in two parts)
Market Pl. W1 6G 67 (7A 160)
Market Pl. W3 1J 81
Market Pl. Bexh 4G 111
Market Pl. Bren 7C 80
Market Pl. Enf 3J 7
Market Pl. King T 2D 134
Market Pl. S'hall 1D 78
Market Rd. N7 6J 49
Market Rd. Rich 3G 99
Market Row. SW9 4A 104
Market Sq. E14 6D 70
Market Sq. Brom 2J 143 (in two parts)
Market Sq., The. N9 2C 18 (off Plevna Rd.)
Market St. E6 2D 72
Market St. SE18 4E 90
Market Ter. Bren 6E 80 (off Albany Rd.)
Market, The. Sutt 1A 150
Market Way. E14 6D 70
Market Way. Wemb 5E 44
Market Yd. M. SE1 2E 86 (7G 169)
Markfield Gdns. E4 7J 9
Markfield Rd. N15 4G 33
Markham Ho. Dag 3G 57 (off Uvedale Rd.)
Markham Pl. SW3 5D 84 (5E 170)
Markham Sq. SW3 5D 84 (5E 170)
Markham St. SW3 5C 84 (5D 170)
Markhole Clo. Hamp 7D 114
Mark Ho. E2 2K 69 (off Sewardstone Rd.)
Markhouse Av. E17 6A 34
Markhouse Pas. E17 6B 34 (off Markhouse Rd.)
Markhouse Rd. E17 6B 34
Markland Ho. W10 7F 65 (off Darfield Way)
Mark La. EC3 7E 68 (2H 169)
Mark Lodge. Cockf 4H 5 (off Edgeworth Rd.)
Markmanor Av. E17 7A 34
Mark Rd. N22 1B 32
Marksbury Av. Rich 3G 99
Marks Gate. 1E 38
Marks Lodge. Romf 5K 39
Mark Sq. EC2 4E 68 (3G 163)
Marks Rd. Romf 5J 39 (in two parts)
Markstone Ho. SE1 2B 86 (7A 168) (off Lancaster St.)
Mark St. E15 7G 53
Mark St. EC2 4E 68 (3G 163)
Markway. Sun 2A 132

Markwell Clo. SE26 . . . 4H 123
Markyate Ho. W10 . . . 4E 64
(off Sutton Way)
Markyate Rd. Dag . . . 5B 56
Marlands Rd. Ilf . . . 3C 36
Marlborough Av. E8 . . . 1G 69
(in three parts)
Marlborough Av. N14 . . . 3B 16
Marlborough Av. Edgw . . . 3C 12
Marlborough Av. Ruis . . . 6E 22
Marlborough Clo. N20 . . . 3J 15
Marlborough Clo. SE17 . . . 4C 86
Marlborough Clo. SW19 . . . 6C 120
Marlborough Clo. Orp . . . 6K 145
Marlborough Ct. W1 . . . 2A 166
Marlborough Ct. W8 . . . 4J 83
(off Pembroke Rd.)
Marlborough Ct. Buck H. . . . 2F 21
Marlborough Ct. Enf . . . 5K 7
Marlborough Ct. Harr . . . 4H 25
Marlborough Ct. N'wd . . . 1H 23
Marlborough Ct. S Croy . . . 4E 152
(off Birdhurst Rd.)
Marlborough Ct. Wall . . . 7G 151
Marlborough Cres. W4 . . . 3K 81
Marlborough Cres. Hay . . . 7F 77
Marlborough Dri. Ilf . . . 3C 36
Marlborough Flats. SW3 . . . 3D 170
Marlborough Gdns. N20 . . . 3J 15
Marlborough Gdns. Surb . . . 7D 134
Marlborough Gro. SE1 . . . 5G 87
Marlborough Hill. NW8 . . . 2A 66
Marlborough Hill. Harr . . . 4H 25
Marlborough House. . . . 1G 85 (5B 166)
Marlborough Ho. E16 . . . 1J 89
(off Hardy Av.)
Marlborough Ho. NW1 . . . 4F 67 (3K 159)
(off Osnaburgh St.)
Marlborough La. SE7 . . . 6A 90
Marlborough Mans. NW6 . . . 5K 47
(off Canon Hill)
Marlborough M. SW2 . . . 4K 103
Marlborough Pde. Edgw . . . 3C 12
(off Marlborough Av.)
Marlborough Pde. Uxb . . . 4D 58
Marlborough Pk. Av. Sidc . . . 7A 110
Marlborough Pl. NW8 . . . 2A 66
Marlborough Rd. E4 . . . 6J 19
Marlborough Rd. E7 . . . 7A 54
Marlborough Rd. E15 . . . 4G 53
Marlborough Rd. E18 . . . 2J 35
(in two parts)
Marlborough Rd. N9 . . . 1A 18
Marlborough Rd. N19 . . . 2H 49
(in two parts)
Marlborough Rd. N22 . . . 7D 16
Marlborough Rd. SW1 . . . 1G 85 (5B 166)
Marlborough Rd. SW19 . . . 6C 120
Marlborough Rd. W4 . . . 5J 81
Marlborough Rd. W5 . . . 2D 80
Marlborough Rd. Ashf . . . 5A 112
Marlborough Rd. Bexh . . . 3D 110
Marlborough Rd. Brom . . . 4A 144
Marlborough Rd. Dag . . . 4B 56
Marlborough Rd. Felt . . . 2B 114
Marlborough Rd. Hamp . . . 6E 114
Marlborough Rd. Iswth . . . 1B 98
Marlborough Rd. Rich . . . 6F 99
Marlborough Rd. Romf . . . 4G 39
Marlborough Rd. S'hall . . . 3A 78
Marlborough Rd. S Croy . . . 7C 152
Marlborough Rd. Sutt . . . 3J 149
Marlborough Rd. Uxb . . . 4D 58
Marlborough St. SW3 . . . 4C 84 (4C 170)
Marlborough Yd. N19 . . . 2H 49
Marlbury. NW8 . . . 1K 65
(off Abbey Rd.)
Marler Rd. SE23 . . . 1A 124
Marley Av. Bexh . . . 6D 92
Marley Clo. N15 . . . 4B 32
Marley Clo. Gnfd . . . 3E 60
Marley Ho. W11 . . . 7F 65
(off St Ann's Rd.)
Marley Wlk. NW2 . . . 5E 46
Marlfield Clo. Wor Pk . . . 1C 148
Marlin Clo. Sun . . . 6G 113
Marlingdene Clo. Hamp . . . 6E 114
Marlings Clo. Chst . . . 4J 145
Marlings Pk. Av. Chst . . . 4J 145
Marlins Clo. Sutt . . . 5A 150
Marloes Clo. Wemb . . . 4D 44
Marloes Rd. W8 . . . 3K 83
Marlow Clo. SE20 . . . 3H 141
Marlow Ct. N14 . . . 7B 6
Marlow Ct. NW6 . . . 7F 47
Marlow Ct. NW9 . . . 3B 28
Marlow Cres. Twic . . . 6K 97
Marlow Dri. Sutt . . . 2F 149
Marlowe Bus. Cen. SE14 . . . 7A 88
(off Batavia Rd.)
Marlowe Clo. Chst . . . 6H 127
Marlowe Clo. Ilf . . . 1G 37
Marlowe Ct. SW3 . . . 4C 84 (4D 170)
(off Petyward)
Marlowe Gdns. SE9 . . . 6E 108
Marlowe Ho. SE8 . . . 5B 88
(off Bowditch)
Marlowe Ho. King T . . . 4D 134
(off Portsmouth Rd.)
Marlowe Rd. E17 . . . 4E 34
Marlowe Sq. Mitc . . . 4G 139
Marlowes, The. NW8 . . . 1B 66
Marlowes, The. Dart . . . 4K 111
Marlowe Way. Croy . . . 2J 151
Marlow Gdns. Hay . . . 3F 77
Marlow Ho. E2 . . . 3F 69 (2J 163)
(off Calvert Av.)
Marlow Ho. SE1 . . . 3F 87 (7J 169)
(off Maltby St.)
Marlow Ho. W2 . . . 6K 65
(off Bishop's Bri. Rd.)
Marlow Ho. Surb . . . 5E 134
(off Cranes Pk.)
Marlow Ho. Tedd . . . 4A 116
Marlow Rd. E6 . . . 3D 72
Marlow Rd. SE20 . . . 3H 141
Marlow Rd. S'hall . . . 3D 78
Marlow Way. SE16 . . . 2K 87
Marl Rd. SW18 . . . 4A 102
Marlton St. SE10 . . . 5H 89
Marlwood Clo. Sidc . . . 2J 127
Marmadon Rd. SE18 . . . 4K 91
Marmion App. E4 . . . 4H 19
Marmion Av. E4 . . . 4G 19
Marmion Clo. E4 . . . 4G 19
Marmion M. SW11 . . . 3E 102
Marmion Rd. SW11 . . . 4E 102
Marmont Rd. SE15 . . . 1G 105
Marmora Ho. E1 . . . 5A 70
(off Ben Jonson Rd.)
Marmora Rd. SE22 . . . 6J 105
Marmot Rd. Houn . . . 3B 96
Marne Av. N11 . . . 4A 16
Marne Av. Well . . . 3A 110
Marnell Way. Houn . . . 3B 96
Marne St. W10 . . . 3G 65
Marney Rd. SW11 . . . 4E 102
Marnfield Cres. SW2 . . . 1A 122
Marnham Av. NW2 . . . 4G 47
Marnham Ct. Wemb . . . 5C 44
Marnham Cres. Gnfd . . . 3F 61
Marnock Ho. SE17 . . . 5D 86
(off Brandon St.)
Marnock Rd. SE4 . . . 5B 106
Maroon Ho. E14 . . . 5A 70
Maroon St. E14 . . . 5A 70
Maroons Way. SE6 . . . 4C 124
Marqueen Towers. SW16 . . . 7K 121
Marquess Rd. N1 . . . 6D 50
Marquess Rd. N. N1 . . . 6D 50
Marquess Rd. S. N1 . . . 6C 50
Marquis Clo. Wemb . . . 7F 45
Marquis Ct. N4 . . . 1K 49
(off Marquis Rd.)
Marquis Ct. Bark . . . 5J 55
Marquis Ct. King T . . . 4D 134
(off Anglesea Rd.)
Marquis Rd. N4 . . . 1K 49
Marquis Rd. N22 . . . 6E 16
Marquis Rd. NW1 . . . 6H 49
Marrabon Clo. Sidc . . . 1A 128
Marrick Clo. SW15 . . . 4C 100
Marrick Ho. NW6 . . . 1K 65
(off Mortimer Cres.)
Marriett Ho. SE6 . . . 4E 124
Marrilyne Av. Enf . . . 1G 9
Marriner Ct. Hay . . . 7G 59
(off Barra Hall Rd.)
Marriott Clo. Felt . . . 6F 95
Marriott Rd. E15 . . . 1G 71
Marriott Rd. N4 . . . 1K 49
Marriott Rd. N10 . . . 1D 30
Marriott Rd. Barn . . . 3A 4
Marriotts Clo. NW9 . . . 6B 28
Marryat Clo. Houn . . . 4D 96
Marryat Ho. SW1 . . . 5G 85 (6A 172)
(off Churchill Gdns.)
Marryat Pl. SW19 . . . 4G 119
Marryat Rd. SW19 . . . 5F 119
Marryat Sq. SW6 . . . 1G 101
Marsala Rd. SE13 . . . 4D 106
Marsden Rd. N9 . . . 2C 18
Marsden Rd. SE15 . . . 3F 105
Marsden St. NW5 . . . 6E 48
(in two parts)
Marshall Clo. SW18 . . . 6A 102
Marshall Clo. Harr . . . 7H 25
Marshall Clo. Houn . . . 5D 96
Marshall Dri. Hay . . . 5H 59
Marshall Est. NW7 . . . 4H 13
Marshall Ho. N1 . . . 2D 68
(off Cranston Est.)
Marshall Ho. NW6 . . . 2H 65
(off Albert Rd.)
Marshall Ho. SE1 . . . 3E 86
(off Page's Wlk.)
Marshall Ho. SE17 . . . 5D 86
(off East St.)
Marshall Path. SE28 . . . 7B 74
Marshall Rd. E10 . . . 3D 52
Marshall Rd. N17 . . . 1D 32
Marshalls Clo. N11 . . . 4A 16
Marshalls Dri. Romf . . . 3K 39
Marshalls Gro. SE18 . . . 4C 90
Marshall's Pl. SE16 . . . 3F 87
Marshalls Rd. Romf . . . 4K 39
Marshall's Rd. Sutt . . . 4K 149
Marshall St. W1 . . . 6G 67 (1B 166)
Marshall Way. E10 . . . 3D 52
Marshalsea Rd. SE1 . . . 2C 86 (6D 168)
Marsham Clo. Chst . . . 5F 127
Marsham Ct. SW1 . . . 4H 85 (3D 172)
Marsham Ho. Eri . . . 2D 92
Marsham St. SW1 . . . 3H 85 (2D 172)
Marsh Av. Mitc . . . 2D 138
Marshbrook Clo. SE3 . . . 3B 108
Marsh Cen., The. E1 . . . 6F 69 (7K 163)
(off Whitechapel High St.)
Marsh Clo. NW7 . . . 3G 13
Marsh Ct. E8 . . . 6G 51
(off St Philip's Rd.)
Marsh Dri. NW9 . . . 6B 28
Marsh Farm Rd. Twic . . . 1K 115
Marshfield St. E14 . . . 3E 88
Marsh Ga. Bus. Cen. E15 . . . 1E 70
Marshgate La. E15 . . . 7D 52
Marshgate Path. SE28 . . . 3G 91
Marshgate Trad. Est. E15 . . . 7D 52
Marsh Grn. Rd. Dag . . . 1G 75
Marsh Hall. Wemb . . . 3F 45
Marsh Hill. E9 . . . 5A 52
Marsh Ho. SW1 . . . 5H 85 (6D 172)
(off Aylesford St.)
Marsh Ho. SW8 . . . 1G 103
Marsh La. E10 . . . 2B 52
Marsh La. N17 . . . 1H 33
Marsh La. NW7 . . . 3F 13
Marsh La. Stan . . . 5H 11
Marsh Rd. Pinn . . . 4C 24
Marsh Rd. Wemb . . . 3D 62
Marshside Clo. N9 . . . 1D 18
Marsh St. E14 . . . 4D 88
Marsh Wall. E14 . . . 1C 88
Marsh Way. Rain . . . 3K 75
(in two parts)
Marshwood Ho. NW6 . . . 1J 65
(off Kilburn Va.)
Marsland Clo. SE17 . . . 5B 86
Marsom Ho. N1 . . . 2D 68 (1E 162)
(off Provost Est.)
Marston Av. Chess . . . 6E 146
Marston Av. Dag . . . 2G 57
Marston Clo. NW6 . . . 7A 48
Marston Clo. Dag . . . 3G 57
Marston Ho. SW9 . . . 2A 104
Marston Rd. Ilf . . . 1C 36
Marston Rd. Tedd . . . 5B 116
Marston Way. SE19 . . . 7B 122
Marsworth Av. Pinn . . . 1B 24
Marsworth Clo. Hay . . . 5C 60
Marsworth Ho. E2 . . . 1G 69
(off Whiston Rd.)
Martaban Rd. N16 . . . 2F 51
Martello St. E8 . . . 7H 51
Martello Ter. E8 . . . 7H 51
Martell Rd. SE21 . . . 3D 122
Martel Pl. E8 . . . 6F 51
Marten Rd. E17 . . . 2C 34
Martens Av. Bexh . . . 4H 111
Martens Clo. Bexh . . . 4J 111
Martha Ct. E2 . . . 2H 69
Martham Clo. SE28 . . . 7D 74
Martham Clo. Ilf . . . 1F 37
Martha Rd. E15 . . . 6G 53
Martha's Bldgs. EC1 . . . 4D 68 (3E 162)
Martha St. E1 . . . 6J 69
Marthorne Cres. Harr . . . 2H 25
Martin Bowes Rd. SE9 . . . 3D 108
Martinbridge Trad. Est. Enf . . . 5B 8
Martin Clo. N9 . . . 1E 18
Martin Clo. Uxb . . . 2A 58
Martin Ct. E14 . . . 2E 88
(off River Barge Clo.)
Martin Ct. S Croy . . . 5D 152
(off Birdhurst Rd.)
Martin Cres. Croy . . . 1A 152
Martindale. SW14 . . . 5J 99
Martindale Av. E16 . . . 7J 71
Martindale Ho. E14 . . . 7D 70
(off Poplar High St.)
Martin Dale Ind. Est. Enf . . . 3C 8
Martindale Rd. SW12 . . . 7F 103
Martindale Rd. Houn . . . 3C 96
Martin Dene. Bexh . . . 5F 111
Martin Dri. N'holt . . . 5D 42
Martineau Est. E1 . . . 7J 69
Martineau Ho. SW1 . . . 5G 85 (6A 172)
(off Churchill Gdns.)
Martineau M. N5 . . . 4B 50
Martineau Rd. N5 . . . 4B 50
Martingale Clo. Sun . . . 4J 131
Martingales Clo. Rich . . . 3D 116
Martin Gdns. Dag . . . 4C 56
Martin Gro. Mord . . . 3J 137
Martin Ho. SE1 . . . 3C 86
Martin Ho. SW8 . . . 7J 85
(off Wyvil Rd.)
Martin La. EC4 . . . 7D 68 (2F 169)
(in two parts)
Martin Pl. SE28 . . . 1J 91
(off Martin St.)
Martin Ri. Bexh . . . 5F 111
Martin Rd. Dag . . . 4C 56
Martins Clo. W Wick . . . 1F 155
Martins Mt. New Bar . . . 4D 4
Martin's Rd. Brom . . . 2G 143
Martins, The. Wemb . . . 3F 45
Martin St. SE28 . . . 1J 91
Martins Wlk. N10 . . . 1E 30
Martin Wlk. SE28 . . . 1J 91
(off Martin St.)
Martin Way. SW20 & Mord . . . 2F 137
Martlesham. N17 . . . 2E 32
(off Adams Rd.)
Martlet Gro. N'holt . . . 3B 60
Martlett Ct. WC2 . . . 6J 67 (1F 167)
Martley Dri. Ilf . . . 5F 37
Martock Clo. Harr . . . 4A 26
Martock Gdns. N11 . . . 5J 15
Marton Clo. SE6 . . . 3C 124
Marton Rd. N16 . . . 2E 50
Martynside. NW9 . . . 1B 28
Martys Yd. NW3 . . . 4B 48
Marvell Av. Hay . . . 5J 59
Marvell Ho. SE5 . . . 7D 86
(off Camberwell Rd.)
Marvels Clo. SE12 . . . 2K 125
Marvels La. SE12 . . . 2K 125
(in two parts)
Marville Rd. SW6 . . . 7H 83
Marvin St. E8 . . . 6H 51
Marwell Clo. W Wick . . . 2H 155
Marwood Clo. Well . . . 3B 110
Mary Adelaide Clo. SW15 . . . 4A 118
Mary Ann Gdns. SE8 . . . 6C 88
Mary Ann Pl. SE8 . . . 6C 88
(off Mary Ann Gdns.)
Maryatt Av. Harr . . . 2F 43
Mary Bank. SE18 . . . 4D 90
Mary Clo. Stan . . . 4F 27
Mary Datchelor Clo. SE5 . . . 1D 104
Maryfield Clo. Bex . . . 3K 129
Mary Flux Ct. SW5 . . . 5K 83
(off Bramham Gdns.)
Mary Grn. NW8 . . . 1K 65
Mary Ho. W6 . . . 5E 82
(off Queen Caroline St.)
Mary Jones Ho. E14 . . . 7C 70
(off Garford St.)
Maryland Ho. E15 . . . 6G 53
(off Manbey Pk. Rd.)
Maryland Ind. Est. E15 . . . 5G 53
(off Maryland Rd.)
Maryland Pk. E15 . . . 5G 53
Maryland Point. E15 . . . 6G 53
(off Grove, The)
Maryland Rd. E15 . . . 5F 53
Maryland Rd. N22 . . . 6E 16
Maryland Rd. T Hth . . . 1B 140
Maryland Sq. E15 . . . 5G 53
Marylands Rd. W9 . . . 4J 65
Maryland St. E15 . . . 5F 53
Maryland Wlk. N1 . . . 1C 68
(off Popham St.)
Maryland Way. Sun . . . 2J 131
Mary Lawrenson Pl. SE3 . . . 7J 89
Marylebone. . . . 5E 66 (5H 159)
Marylebone Cricket Club. . . . 3B 66 (1B 158)
Marylebone Flyover. (Junct.) . . . 5B 66 (6C 158)
Marylebone Fly-Over. W2 . . . 5B 66 (6B 158)
Marylebone High St. W1 . . . 5E 66 (5H 159)
Marylebone La. W1 . . . 5E 66 (6H 159)
Marylebone M. W1 . . . 5F 67 (6J 159)
Marylebone Pas. W1 . . . 6G 67 (7B 160)
Marylebone Rd. NW1 . . . 5C 66 (5D 158)
Marylebone St. W1 . . . 5E 66 (6H 159)
Marylee Way. SE11 . . . 4K 85 (4H 173)
Mary MacArthur Ho. E2 . . . 3K 69
(off Warley St.)
Mary Macarthur Ho. W6 . . . 6G 83

Mary Macarthur Ho. Dag....3G 57
(off Wythenshawe Rd.)
Maryon Gro. SE7.......4C 90
Maryon M. NW3.......4C 48
Maryon Rd. SE7 & SE18....4C 90
Mary Peters Dri. Gnfd.....5H 43
Mary Pl. W11.......7G 65
Mary Rose Clo. Hamp.....1E 132
Mary Rose Mall. E6.......5D 72
Mary Rose Way. N20.......1G 15
Mary Seacole Clo. E8.......1F 69
Mary Smith Ct. SW5.......4J 83
(off Trebovir Rd.)
Marysmith Ho. SW1
.......5H 85 (5D 172)
(off Cureton St.)
Mary's Ter. Twic.......7A 98
(in two parts)
Mary St. E16.......5H 71
Mary St. N1.......1C 68
Mary Ter. NW1.......1F 67
Maryville. Well.......2K 109
Mary Wharrie Ho.
NW3.......7D 48
(off Fellows Rd.)
Marzena Ct. Houn.......6G 97
Masault Ct. Rich.......4E 98
(off Kew Foot Rd.)
Masbro' Rd. W14.......3F 83
Mascalls Ct. SE7.......6A 90
Mascalls Rd. SE7.......6A 90
Mascotte Rd. SW15.......4F 101
Mascotts Clo. NW2.......3D 46
Masefield Av. S'hall.......7E 60
Masefield Av. Stan.......5E 10
Masefield Ct. New Bar.......4F 5
Masefield Ct. Surb.......7D 134
Masefield Cres. N14.......5B 6
Masefield Gdns. E6.......4E 72
Masefield Ho. NW6.......3J 65
(off Stafford Rd.)
Masefield La. Hay.......4K 59
Masefield Rd. Hamp.......4D 114
Masefield Way. Stai.......1B 112
Mashie Rd. W3.......6A 64
Mashiters Hill. Romf.......1K 39
Maskall Clo. SW2.......1A 122
Maskani Wlk. SW16.......7G 121
Maskell Rd. SW17.......3A 120
Maskelyne Clo. SW11.......1C 102
Mason Clo. E16.......7J 71
Mason Clo. SE16.......5G 87
Mason Clo. Bexh.......3H 111
Mason Clo. Hamp.......1D 132
Mason Ho. E9.......7J 51
(off Frampton Pk. Rd.)
Mason Rd. Sutt.......5K 149
Mason Rd. Wfd G.......4B 20
Mason's Arms M. W1
.......6F 67 (1K 165)
Mason's Av. EC2....6D 68 (7E 162)
Mason's Av. Croy.......3C 152
Masons Av. Harr.......4K 25
Mason's Grn. La. W5.......4G 63
(in two parts)
Masons Hill. SE18.......4F 91
Masons Hill. Brom.......3J 143
Mason's Pl. EC1...3C 68 (1C 162)
Masons Pl. Mitc.......1D 138
Mason St. SE17.......4D 86
Mason's Yd. SW1
.......1G 85 (4B 166)
Mason's Yd. SW19.......5F 119
Massey Clo. N11.......5A 16
Massey Ct. E6.......1A 72
(off Florence Rd.)
Massie Rd. E8.......6G 51
Massingberd Way. SW17....4F 121
Massinger St. SE17.......4E 86
Massingham St. E1.......4K 69
Masson Av. Ruis.......6A 42
Mast Ct. SE16.......4A 88
(off Boat Lifter Way)
Master Brewer. (Junct.).....5D 40
Master Gunners Pl. SE18....7C 90
Masterman Ho. SE5.......7D 86
(off Elmington Est.)
Masterman Rd. E6.......3C 72
Masters Clo. SW16.......6G 121
Masters Dri. SE16.......5H 87
Masters Lodge. E1.......6J 69
(off Johnson St.)
Masters St. E1.......5K 69
Mast Ho. Ter. E14.......4C 88
(in two parts)
Mastmaker Ct. E14.......2C 88
Mastmaker Rd. E14.......2C 88
Maswell Park.......5G 97
Maswell Pk. Cres. Houn.....5G 97
Maswell Pk. Rd. Houn.......5F 97
Matcham Ct. Twic.......6D 98
(off Clevedon Rd.)
Matcham Rd. E11.......3G 53
Matchless Dri. SE18.......7E 90
Matfield Clo. Brom.......5J 143
Matfield Rd. Belv.......6G 93
Matham Gro. SE22.......4F 105
Matham Rd. E Mol.......5H 133
Matheson Lang Ho. SE1....7J 167
Matheson Rd. W14.......4H 83
Mathews Av. E6.......2E 72
Mathews Pk. Av. E15.......6H 53
Mathews Yd. WC2
.......6J 67 (1E 166)
Mathieson Ct. SE1
.......2B 86 (7B 168)
(off King James St.)
Matilda Clo. SE19.......7D 122
Matilda Ho. E1.......1G 87
(off St Katherine's Way)
Matilda St. N1.......1K 67
Matlock Clo. SE24.......4C 104
Matlock Clo. Barn.......5A 4
Matlock Ct. SE5.......4D 104
Matlock Cres. Sutt.......4G 149
Matlock Gdns. Sutt.......4G 149
Matlock Pl. Sutt.......4G 149
Matlock Rd. E10.......6E 34
Matlock St. E14.......6A 70
Matlock Way. N Mald.......1K 135
Maton Ho. SW6.......7H 83
(off Estcourt Rd.)
Matrimony Pl. SW8.......2G 103
Matson Ct. Wfd G.......7B 20
Matson Ho. SE16.......3H 87
Matthew Clo. W10.......4F 65
Matthew Ct. E17.......3E 34
Matthew Ct. Mitc.......5H 139
Matthew Parker St. SW1
.......2H 85 (7D 166)
Matthews Ct. E17.......1C 34
(off Chingford Rd.)
Matthews Ho. E14.......5C 70
(off Burgess St.)
Matthews Rd. Gnfd.......5H 43
Matthews St. SW11.......2D 102
Matthias Rd. N16.......5E 50
Mattingley Way. SE15.......7F 87
Mattison Rd. N4.......6A 32
Mattock La. W13 & W5.....1B 80
Maud Cashmore Way.
SE18.......3D 90
Maude Ho. E2.....2G 69 (1K 163)
(off Ropley St.)
Maude Rd. E17.......5A 34
Maude Rd. SE5.......1E 104
Maude Ter. E17.......5A 34
Maud Gdns. E13.......1H 71
Maud Gdns. Bark.......2K 73
Maudlins Grn. E1
.......1G 87 (4K 169)
Maud Rd. E10.......3E 52
Maud Rd. E13.......2H 71
Maudslay Rd. SE9.......3D 108
Maudsley Ho. Bren.......5E 80
Maud St. E16.......5H 71
Maudsville Cotts. W7.......1J 79
Maud Wilkes Clo. NW5.......5G 49
Maugham Ct. W3.......3J 81
(off Palmerston Rd.)
Mauleverer Rd. SW2.......5J 103
Maundeby Wlk. NW10.......6A 46
Maunder Rd. W7.......1K 79
Maunsel St. SW1
.......4H 85 (3C 172)
Maureen Ct. Beck.......2J 141
Mauretania Building. E1.....7K 69
(off Jardine Rd.)
Maurice Av. N22.......2B 32
Maurice Bishop Ter. N6.....6E 30
(off View Rd.)
Maurice Brown Clo. NW7....5A 14
Maurice Ct. Bren.......7D 80
Maurice Drummond Ho.
SE10.......1D 106
(off Catherine Gro.)
Maurice St. W12.......6D 64
Maurice Wlk. NW11.......4A 30
Maurier Clo. N'holt.......1A 60
Mauritius Rd. SE10.......4G 89
Maury Rd. N16.......2G 51
Mauveine Gdns. Houn.......4E 96
Mavelstone Clo. Brom.....1C 144
Mavelstone Rd. Brom.....1B 144
Maverton Rd. E3.......1C 70
Mavis Av. Eps.......5A 148
Mavis Clo. Eps.......5A 148
Mavis Wlk. E6.......5C 72
(off Greenwich Cres.)
Mavor Ho. N1.......1K 67
(off Barnsbury Est.)
Mawbey Ho. SE1.......5F 87
Mawbey Pl. SE1.......5F 87
Mawbey Rd. SE1.......5F 87
Mawbey St. SW8.......7J 85
Mawdley Ho. SE1.......7A 168
Mawney.......4J 39
Mawney Clo. Romf.......2H 39
Mawney Rd. Romf.......2H 39
Mawson Clo. SW20.......2G 137
Mawson Ho. EC1....5A 68 (5J 161)
(off Baldwins Gdns.)
Mawson La. W4.......6B 82
Maxden Ct. SE15.......3F 105
Maxey Gdns. Dag.......4E 56
Maxey Rd. SE18.......4G 91
Maxey Rd. Dag.......5E 56
Maxfield Clo. N20.......7F 5
Maxilla Wlk. W10.......6F 65
(off Westway)
Maximfeldt Rd. Eri.......5K 93
Maxim Rd. N21.......6F 7
Maxim Rd. Eri.......4K 93
Maxted Pk. Harr.......7J 25
Maxted Rd. SE15.......3F 105
Maxwell Clo. Croy.......1J 151
Maxwell Clo. Hay.......7J 59
Maxwell Ct. SE22.......1G 123
Maxwell Ct. SW4.......5H 103
Maxwell Rd. SW6.......7K 83
Maxwell Rd. Ashf.......6E 112
Maxwell Rd. N'wd.......1F 23
Maxwell Rd. Well.......3K 109
Maxwell Rd. W Dray.......4B 76
Maxwelton Av. NW7.......5E 12
Maxwelton Clo. NW7.......5E 12
Maya Angelou Ct. E4.......4K 19
Maya Clo. SE15.......2H 105
Mayall Rd. SE24.......5B 104
Maya Rd. N2.......4A 30
Maybank Av. E18.......2K 35
Maybank Av. Wemb.......5K 43
Maybank Gdns. Pinn.......5J 23
Maybank Rd. E18.......1K 35
May Bate Av. King T.......1D 134
Maybells Commercial Est.
Bark.......2D 74
Mayberry Ct. Beck.......7B 124
(off Copers Cope Rd.)
Mayberry Pl. Surb.......7F 135
Maybourne Clo. SE26.......6H 123
Maybury Clo. Enf.......1C 8
Maybury Clo. Orp.......5F 145
Maybury Ct. W1...5E 66 (6H 159)
(off Marylebone St.)
Maybury Ct. Harr.......6H 25
Maybury Ct. S Croy.......5B 152
(off Haling Pk. Rd.)
Maybury Gdns. NW10.......6D 46
Maybury M. N6.......7G 31
Maybury Rd. E13.......4A 72
Maybury Rd. Bark.......2K 73
Maybury St. SW17.......5C 120
Maychurch Clo. Stan.......7J 11
May Clo. Chess.......6F 147
Maycroft. Pinn.......2K 23
Maycross Av. Mord.......4H 137
Mayday Gdns. SE3.......2C 108
Mayday Rd. T Hth.......6B 140
Maydew Ho. SE16.......4J 87
(off Abbeyfield Est.)
Maydwell Ho. E14.......5C 70
(off Thomas Rd.)
Mayerne Rd. SE9.......5B 108
Mayesbrook Rd. Bark.......1K 73
Mayesbrook Rd. Ilf.......3A 56
Mayesford Rd. Romf.......7C 38
Mayes Rd. N22.......2K 31
Mayeswood Rd. SE12.....4A 126
Mayfair.......7F 67 (3J 165)
Mayfair Av. Bexh.......1D 110
Mayfair Av. Ilf.......2D 54
Mayfair Av. Romf.......6D 38
Mayfair Av. Twic.......7G 97
Mayfair Av. Wor Pk.......1C 148
Mayfair Clo. Beck.......1D 142
Mayfair Clo. Surb.......1E 146
Mayfair Gdns. N17.......6H 17
Mayfair Gdns. Wfd G.......7D 20
Mayfair M. NW1.......7D 48
(off Regents Pk. Rd.)
Mayfair Pl. W1....1F 85 (4K 165)
Mayfair Ter. N14.......7C 6
Mayfield. Bexh.......3F 111
Mayfield Av. N12.......4F 15
Mayfield Av. N14.......2C 16
Mayfield Av. W4.......4A 82
Mayfield Av. W13.......3B 80
Mayfield Av. Harr.......5B 26
Mayfield Av. Orp.......7K 145
Mayfield Av. Wfd G.......6D 20
Mayfield Clo. E8.......6F 51
Mayfield Clo. SE20.......1H 141
Mayfield Clo. SW4.......5H 103
Mayfield Clo. Ashf.......6D 112
Mayfield Clo. Th Dit.......1B 146
Mayfield Clo. Uxb.......3D 58
Mayfield Cres. N9.......6C 8
Mayfield Cres. T Hth.......4K 139
Mayfield Dri. Pinn.......4D 24
Mayfield Gdns. NW4.......6F 29
Mayfield Gdns. W7.......6H 61
Mayfield Ho. E2.......2H 69
(off Cambridge Heath Rd.)
Mayfield Rd. E4.......2K 19
Mayfield Rd. E8.......7F 51
Mayfield Rd. E13.......4H 71
Mayfield Rd. E17.......2A 34
Mayfield Rd. N8.......5K 31
Mayfield Rd. SW19.......1H 137
Mayfield Rd. W3.......7H 63
Mayfield Rd. W12.......2A 82
Mayfield Rd. Belv.......4J 93
Mayfield Rd. Brom.......5C 144
Mayfield Rd. Dag.......1C 56
Mayfield Rd. Enf.......2E 8
Mayfield Rd. S Croy.......7D 152
Mayfield Rd. Sutt.......6B 150
Mayfield Rd. T Hth.......4K 139
Mayfield Rd. Flats. N8.......6K 31
Mayfields. Wemb.......2G 45
Mayfields Clo. Wemb.......2G 45
Mayflower Clo. SE16.......4K 87
Mayflower Clo. Ruis.......6E 22
Mayflower Ho. Bark.......1H 73
(off Westbury Rd.)
Mayflower Rd. SW9.......3J 103
Mayflower St. SE16.......2J 87
Mayfly Clo. Eastc.......7A 24
Mayfly Gdns. N'holt.......3B 60
Mayford. NW1.......2G 67
(in three parts)
Mayford Clo. SW12.......7D 102
Mayford Clo. Beck.......3K 141
Mayford Rd. SW12.......7D 102
May Gdns. Wemb.......3C 62
Maygood St. N1.......2A 68
Maygrove Rd. NW6.......6H 47
Mayhew Clo. E4.......3H 19
Mayhew Ct. SE5.......4D 104
Mayhill Rd. SE7.......6K 89
Mayhill Rd. Barn.......6B 4
Mayland Mans. Bark.......7F 55
(off Whiting Av.)
Maylands Dri. Sidc.......3D 128
Maylands Ho. SW3
.......4C 84 (4D 170)
(off Elystan St.)
Maynard Clo. N15.......5E 32
Maynard Clo. SW6.......7K 83
Maynard Path. E17.......5E 34
Maynard Rd. E17.......5E 34
Maynards Quay. E1.......7J 69
Mayne Ct. SE26.......5H 123
Maynooth Gdns. Cars.......7D 138
Mayo Ct. W13.......3B 80
Mayo Ho. E1.......5J 69
(off Lindley St.)
Mayola Rd. E5.......4J 51
Mayo Rd. NW10.......6A 46
Mayo Rd. Croy.......5D 140
Mayo Rd. W on T.......7J 131
Mayow Rd. SE26 & SE23
.......4K 123
Mayplace Clo. Bexh.......3H 111
Mayplace La. SE18.......6F 91
(in two parts)
Mayplace Rd. E. Bexh.....3H 111
Mayplace Rd. W. Bexh.....4G 111
Maypole.......1K 129
Maypole Ct. S'hall.......2D 78
(off Merrick Rd.)
May Rd. E4.......6H 19
May Rd. E13.......2J 71
May Rd. Twic.......1J 115
Mayroyd Av. Surb.......2G 147
May's Bldgs. M. SE10.....7E 88
May's Ct. SE10.......7F 89
Mays Ct. WC2.....7J 67 (3E 166)
Mays Hill Rd. Brom.......2G 143
Mays La. Barn.....1H 13 & 6A 4
Maysoule Rd. SW11.......4B 102
Mays Rd. Tedd.......5H 115
Mayston M. SE10.......5J 89
(off Ormiston Rd.)
May St. W14.......5H 83
Mayswood Gdns. Dag.......6J 57
Mayton St. N7.......3K 49
Maytree Clo. Edgw.......3D 12
Maytree Ct. N'holt.......3C 60
Maytree Gdns. W5.......2D 80
May Tree Ho. SE4.......3B 106
(off Wickham Rd.)
Maytree La. Stan.......7F 11
Maytree Wlk. SW2.......2A 122
Mayville Est. N16.......5E 50
Mayville Rd. E11.......2G 53
Mayville Rd. Ilf.......5F 55
May Wlk. E13.......2K 71
Mayward Ho. SE5.......1E 104
(off Peckham Rd.)
Maywood Clo. Beck.......7D 124
May Wynne Ho. E16.......7K 71
(off Murray Sq.)
Maze Hill. SE10 & SE3.....6G 89
Maze Hill Lodge. SE10.....6F 89
(off Park Vista)
Mazenod Av. NW6.......7J 47
Maze Rd. Rich.......7G 81
M.C.C. Cricket Mus. & Tours.
.......3B 66 (2A 158)
Mead Clo. NW1.......6E 48
Mead Clo. Harr.......1H 25
Mead Ct. NW9.......5J 27
Mead Cres. E4.......4K 19

Mead Cres. Sutt. . . . 3C 150
Meadcroft Rd. SE11 . . . 6B 86 (7K 173) (in two parts)
Meade Clo. W4 . . . 6G 81
Meader Ct. SE14 . . . 7K 87
Meadfield. Edgw . . . 2C 12 (in two parts)
Mead Fld. Harr . . . 3D 42
Meadfield Grn. Edgw . . . 2C 12
Meadfoot Rd. SW16 . . . 7G 121
Meadgate Av. Wfd G . . . 5H 21
Mead Gro. Romf . . . 3D 38
Mead Ho. W11 . . . 1H 83 (off Ladbroke Rd.)
Mead Ho. La. Hay . . . 4F 59
Meadhurst Pk. Sun . . . 6G 113
Meadlands Dri. Rich . . . 2D 116
Mead Lodge. W4 . . . 2K 81
Meadow Av. Croy . . . 6K 141
Meadow Bank. N21 . . . 6E 6
Meadowbank. NW3 . . . 7D 48
Meadowbank. Surb . . . 6F 135
Meadowbank Clo. SW6 . . . 7E 82
Meadowbank Gdns. Houn . . . 1J 95
Meadowbank Rd. NW9 . . . 7K 27
Meadowbrook Ct. Iswth . . . 3J 97
Meadow Clo. E4 . . . 1J 19
Meadow Clo. E9 . . . 5B 52
Meadow Clo. SE6 . . . 5C 124
Meadow Clo. SW20 . . . 4E 136
Meadow Clo. Barn . . . 6C 4
Meadow Clo. Bexh . . . 5F 111
Meadow Clo. Chst . . . 5F 127
Meadow Clo. Enf . . . 1F 9
Meadow Clo. Esh . . . 3A 146
Meadow Clo. Houn . . . 6E 96
Meadow Clo. N'holt . . . 2E 60
Meadow Clo. Rich . . . 1E 116
Meadow Clo. Ruis . . . 6H 23
Meadow Clo. Sutt . . . 2A 150
Meadow Ct. N1 . . . 2E 68
Meadow Ct. Houn . . . 6F 97
Meadowcourt Rd. SE3 . . . 4H 107
Meadowcroft. W4 . . . 5G 81 (off Brooks Rd.)
Meadowcroft. Brom . . . 3D 144
Meadowcroft Clo. N13 . . . 2F 17
Meadowcroft Rd. N13 . . . 2F 17
Meadow Dri. N10 . . . 3F 31
Meadow Dri. NW4 . . . 2E 28
Meadowford Clo. SE28 . . . 7A 74
Meadow Gdns. Edgw . . . 6C 12
Meadow Gth. NW10 . . . 6J 45 (in two parts)
Meadow Hill. N Mald . . . 6A 136
Meadow La. SE12 . . . 3K 125
Meadowlea Clo. Harm . . . 6A 76
Meadow M. SW8 . . . 6K 85
Meadow Pl. SW8 . . . 7J 85
Meadow Pl. W4 . . . 7A 82
Meadow Rd. SW8 . . . 7K 85 (7H 173)
Meadow Rd. SW19 . . . 7A 120
Meadow Rd. Ashf . . . 5F 113
Meadow Rd. Bark . . . 7K 55
Meadow Rd. Brom . . . 2G 143
Meadow Rd. Dag . . . 6F 57
Meadow Rd. Felt . . . 2C 114
Meadow Rd. Pinn . . . 4B 24
Meadow Rd. Romf . . . 1J 57
Meadow Rd. S'hall . . . 7D 60
Meadow Rd. Sutt . . . 4C 150
Meadow Row. SE1 . . . 3C 86
Meadows Clo. E10 . . . 2C 52
Meadows Ct. Sidc . . . 6B 128
Meadows End. Sun . . . 1J 131
Meadowside. SE9 . . . 4A 108
Meadowside. Twic . . . 7D 98
Meadow Stile. Croy . . . 3C 152
Meadowsweet Clo. E16 . . . 5B 72
Meadowsweet Clo. SW20 . . . 4E 136
Meadow, The. N10 . . . 3E 30
Meadow, The. Chst . . . 6G 127
Meadow Vw. Harr . . . 1J 43
Meadow Vw. Sidc . . . 7B 110
Meadowview Rd. SE6 . . . 5B 124
Meadowview Rd. Bex . . . 6E 110
Meadowview Rd. Eps . . . 7A 148
Meadow Vw. Rd. Hay . . . 4F 59
Meadow Vw. Rd. T Hth . . . 5B 140
Meadow Wlk. E18 . . . 4J 35
Meadow Wlk. Dag . . . 6F 57
Meadow Wlk. Eps . . . 6A 148 (in two parts)
Meadow Wlk. Wall . . . 3F 151
Meadow Way. NW9 . . . 5K 27
Meadow Way. Chess . . . 5E 146
Meadow Way. Orp . . . 3E 156
Meadow Way. Ruis . . . 6K 23
Meadow Way. Wemb . . . 4D 44
Meadow Waye. Houn . . . 6C 78
Meadow Way, The. Harr . . . 1J 25
Mead Path. SW17 . . . 4A 120
Mead Pl. E9 . . . 6J 51
Mead Pl. Croy . . . 1C 152
Mead Plat. NW10 . . . 6J 45
Mead Rd. Chst . . . 6G 127
Mead Rd. Edgw . . . 6B 12
Mead Rd. Rich . . . 3C 116
Mead Row. SE1 . . . 3A 86 (1J 173)
Meads Ct. E15 . . . 6H 53
Meadside Clo. Beck . . . 1A 142
Meads La. Ilf . . . 7J 37
Meads Rd. N22 . . . 2B 32
Meads Rd. Enf . . . 1F 9
Meads, The. Edgw . . . 6E 12
Meads, The. Mord . . . 5C 138
Meads, The. Sutt . . . 3G 149
Meads, The. Uxb . . . 4A 58
Mead Ter. Wemb . . . 4D 44
Mead, The. N2 . . . 2A 30
Mead, The. W13 . . . 5B 62
Mead, The. Beck . . . 1E 142
Mead, The. Uxb . . . 2C 40
Mead, The. Wall . . . 6H 151
Mead, The. W Wick . . . 1F 155
Meadvale Rd. W5 . . . 4B 62
Meadvale Rd. Croy . . . 7F 141
Meadway. N14 . . . 2C 16
Meadway. NW11 . . . 6J 29
Mead Way. SW20 . . . 4E 136
Meadway. Ashf . . . 4C 112
Meadway. Barn . . . 4D 4
Meadway. Beck . . . 1E 142
Mead Way. Brom . . . 6H 143
Mead Way. Croy . . . 2A 154
Meadway. Ilf . . . 4J 55
Mead Way. Ruis . . . 6F 23
Meadway. Surb . . . 1J 147
Meadway. Twic . . . 1H 115
Mead Way. Wfd G . . . 5F 21
Meadway Clo. NW11 . . . 6K 29
Meadway Clo. Barn . . . 4D 4
Meadway Clo. Pinn . . . 6A 10
Meadway Ct. NW11 . . . 6K 29
Meadway Ct. W5 . . . 4F 63
Meadway Ct. Dag . . . 2F 57
Meadway Ct. Tedd . . . 5C 116
Meadway Gdns. Ruis . . . 6F 23
Meadway Ga. NW11 . . . 6J 29
Meadway, The. SE3 . . . 2F 107
Meadway, The. Buck H . . . 1G 21
Meaford Way. SE20 . . . 7H 123
Meakin Est. SE1 . . . 3E 86
Meanley Rd. E12 . . . 4C 54
Meard St. W1 . . . 6H 67 (1C 166) (in two parts)
Meath Rd. E15 . . . 2H 71
Meath Rd. Ilf . . . 3G 55
Meath St. SW11 . . . 1F 103
Mechanic's Path. SE8 . . . 7C 88 (off Deptford High St.)
Mecklenburgh Pl. WC1 . . . 4K 67 (3G 161)
Mecklenburgh Sq. WC1 . . . 4K 67 (3G 161)
Mecklenburgh St. WC1 . . . 4K 67 (3G 161)
Medburn St. NW1 . . . 2H 67
Medcroft Gdns. SW14 . . . 4J 99
Medebourne Clo. SE3 . . . 3J 107
Mede Ho. Brom . . . 5K 125 (off Pike Clo.)
Medesenge Way. N13 . . . 6G 17
Medfield St. SW15 . . . 7C 100
Medhurst Clo. E3 . . . 2A 70
Median Rd. E5 . . . 5J 51
Medina Gro. N7 . . . 3A 50
Medina Rd. N7 . . . 3A 50
Medland Clo. Wall . . . 1E 150
Medland Ho. E14 . . . 7A 70
Medlar Clo. N'holt . . . 2B 60
Medlar Ho. Sidc . . . 3A 128
Medlar St. SE5 . . . 1C 104
Medley Rd. NW6 . . . 6J 47
Medora Rd. SW2 . . . 7K 103
Medora Rd. Romf . . . 4K 39
Medusa Rd. SE6 . . . 6D 106
Medway Bldgs. E3 . . . 2A 70 (off Medway Rd.)
Medway Clo. Croy . . . 6J 141
Medway Clo. Ilf . . . 5G 55
Medway Ct. WC1 . . . 3J 67 (2E 160) (off Judd St.)
Medway Dri. Gnfd . . . 2K 61
Medway Gdns. Wemb . . . 4A 44
Medway Ho. NW8 . . . 4C 66 (4C 158) (off Penfold St.)
Medway Ho. SE1 . . . 2D 86 (7F 169) (off Hankey Pl.)
Medway Ho. King T . . . 1D 134
Medway M. E3 . . . 2A 70
Medway Pde. Gnfd . . . 2K 61
Medway Rd. E3 . . . 2A 70
Medway St. SW1 . . . 3H 85 (2D 172)
Medwin St. SW4 . . . 4K 103
Meerbrook Rd. SE3 . . . 3A 108
Meeson Rd. E15 . . . 7H 53
Meeson St. E5 . . . 4A 52
Meeting Fld. Path. E9 . . . 6J 51
Meeting Ho. All. E1 . . . 1H 87
Meeting Ho. La. SE15 . . . 1H 105
Mehetabel Rd. E9 . . . 5J 51
Meister Clo. Ilf . . . 1H 55
Melancholy Wlk. Rich . . . 2C 116
Melanda Clo. Chst . . . 5D 126
Melanie Clo. Bexh . . . 1E 110
Melba Way. SE13 . . . 1D 106
Melbourne Av. N13 . . . 6E 16
Melbourne Av. W13 . . . 1A 80
Melbourne Av. Pinn . . . 3F 25
Melbourne Clo. SE20 . . . 7G 123
Melbourne Clo. Orp . . . 7J 145
Melbourne Clo. Uxb . . . 4C 40
Melbourne Clo. Wall . . . 5G 151
Melbourne Ct. N10 . . . 7A 16
Melbourne Ct. W9 . . . 4A 66 (off Randolph Av.)
Melbourne Gdns. Romf . . . 5E 38
Melbourne Gro. SE22 . . . 4E 104
Melbourne Ho. W8 . . . 1J 83 (off Kensington Pl.)
Melbourne Ho. Hay . . . 4A 60
Melbourne Mans. W14 . . . 6G 83 (off Musard Rd.)
Melbourne M. SE6 . . . 7E 106
Melbourne M. SW9 . . . 1A 104
Melbourne Pl. WC2 . . . 6K 67 (1H 167)
Melbourne Rd. E6 . . . 2D 72
Melbourne Rd. E10 . . . 7D 34
Melbourne Rd. E17 . . . 4A 34
Melbourne Rd. SW19 . . . 1J 137
Melbourne Rd. Ilf . . . 1F 55
Melbourne Rd. Tedd . . . 6C 116
Melbourne Rd. Wall . . . 5F 151
Melbourne Sq. SW9 . . . 1A 104
Melbourne Ter. SW6 . . . 7K 83 (off Moore Pk. Rd.)
Melbourne Way. Enf . . . 6A 8
Melbray M. SW6 . . . 2H 101
Melbreak Ho. SE22 . . . 3E 104
Melbury Av. S'hall . . . 3F 79
Melbury Clo. Chst . . . 6C 126
Melbury Clo. Clay . . . 6B 146
Melbury Ct. W8 . . . 3H 83
Melbury Dri. SE5 . . . 7E 86
Melbury Gdns. SW20 . . . 1D 136
Melbury Ho. SW8 . . . 7K 85 (off Richborne Ter.)
Melbury Rd. W14 . . . 3H 83
Melbury Rd. Harr . . . 5F 27
Melbury Ter. NW1 . . . 4C 66 (4D 158)
Melchester. W11 . . . 6H 65 (off Ledbury Rd.)
Melchester Ho. N19 . . . 3H 49 (off Wedmore St.)
Melcombe Ct. NW1 . . . 5D 66 (5E 158) (off Melcombe Pl.)
Melcombe Gdns. Harr . . . 6F 27
Melcombe Ho. SW8 . . . 7K 85 (off Dorset Rd.)
Melcombe Pl. NW1 . . . 5D 66 (5E 158)
Melcombe Regis Ct. W1 . . . 5E 66 (6H 159) (off Weymouth St.)
Melcombe St. NW1 . . . 4D 66 (4F 159)
Meldex Clo. NW7 . . . 6K 13 (off Prince of Wales Clo.)
Meldon Clo. SW6 . . . 1K 101
Meldone Clo. Surb . . . 7H 135
Meldrum Rd. Ilf . . . 2A 56
Melfield Gdns. SE6 . . . 4E 124
Melford Av. Bark . . . 6J 55
Melford Clo. Chess . . . 5F 147
Melford Ct. SE1 . . . 3E 86 (off Fendall St.)
Melford Ct. SE22 . . . 1G 123
Melford Pas. SE22 . . . 7G 105
Melford Rd. E6 . . . 4D 72
Melford Rd. E11 . . . 2G 53
Melford Rd. E17 . . . 4A 34
Melford Rd. SE22 . . . 7G 105
Melford Rd. Ilf . . . 2H 55
Melfort Av. T Hth . . . 3B 140
Melfort Rd. T Hth . . . 3B 140
Melgund Rd. N5 . . . 5A 50
Melina Clo. Hay . . . 5F 59
Melina Ct. SW15 . . . 3C 100
Melina Pl. NW8 . . . 3B 66 (2A 158)
Melina Rd. W12 . . . 2D 82
Melior Ct. N6 . . . 6G 31
Melior Pl. SE1 . . . 2E 86 (6G 169)
Melior St. SE1 . . . 2E 86 (6G 169)
Meliot Rd. SE6 . . . 2F 125
Meller Clo. Croy . . . 3J 151
Melling Dri. Enf . . . 1B 8
Melling St. SE18 . . . 6J 91
Mellish Clo. Bark . . . 1K 73
Mellish Flats. E10 . . . 7C 34
Mellish Gdns. Wfd G . . . 5D 20
Mellish Ho. E1 . . . 6H 69 (off Varden St.)
Mellish Ind. Est. SE18 . . . 3B 90
Mellish St. E14 . . . 3C 88
Mellison Rd. SW17 . . . 5C 120
Mellitus St. W12 . . . 5B 64
Mellor Clo. W on T . . . 7D 132
Mellow La. E. Hay . . . 3E 58
Mellow La. W. Uxb . . . 3E 58
Mellows Rd. Ilf . . . 3D 36
Mellows Rd. Wall . . . 5H 151
Mells Cres. SE9 . . . 4D 126
Mell St. SE10 . . . 5G 89
Melody La. N5 . . . 5C 50
Melody Rd. SW18 . . . 5A 102
Melon Pl. W8 . . . 2J 83
Melon Rd. E11 . . . 3G 53
Melon Rd. SE15 . . . 1G 105
Melrose Av. N22 . . . 1B 32
Melrose Av. NW2 . . . 5D 46
Melrose Av. SW16 . . . 3K 139
Melrose Av. SW19 . . . 2H 119
Melrose Av. Gnfd . . . 2F 61
Melrose Av. Mitc . . . 7F 121
Melrose Av. Twic . . . 7F 97
Melrose Clo. SE12 . . . 1J 125
Melrose Clo. Gnfd . . . 2F 61
Melrose Clo. Hay . . . 5J 59
Melrose Dri. S'hall . . . 1E 78
Melrose Gdns. W6 . . . 3E 82
Melrose Gdns. Edgw . . . 3H 27
Melrose Gdns. N Mald . . . 3K 135
Melrose Ho. E14 . . . 3D 88 (off Lanark Sq.)
Melrose Ho. NW6 . . . 3J 65 (off Carlton Va.)
Melrose Rd. SW13 . . . 2B 100
Melrose Rd. SW18 . . . 6H 101
Melrose Rd. SW19 . . . 2J 137
Melrose Rd. W3 . . . 3J 81
Melrose Rd. Pinn . . . 4D 24
Melrose Ter. W6 . . . 3E 82
Melrose Tudor. Wall . . . 5J 151 (off Plough La.)
Melsa Rd. Mord . . . 6A 138
Melthorne Dri. Ruis . . . 3A 42
Melthorpe Gdns. SE3 . . . 1C 108
Melton Clo. Ruis . . . 1A 42
Melton Ct. SW7 . . . 4B 84 (4B 170) (in two parts)
Melton Ct. Sutt . . . 7A 150
Melton St. NW1 . . . 3G 67 (2B 160)
Melville Av. SW20 . . . 7C 118
Melville Av. Gnfd . . . 5K 43
Melville Av. S Croy . . . 5F 153
Melville Clo. Uxb . . . 2F 41
Melville Ct. SE8 . . . 4A 88
Melville Ct. W12 . . . 3D 82 (off Goldhawk Rd.)
Melville Gdns. N13 . . . 5G 17
Melville Ho. SE10 . . . 1E 106
Melville Ho. New Bar . . . 5G 5
Melville Pl. N1 . . . 7C 50
Melville Rd. E17 . . . 3B 34
Melville Rd. NW10 . . . 7K 45
Melville Rd. SW13 . . . 1C 100
Melville Rd. Romf . . . 1H 39
Melville Rd. Sidc . . . 2C 128
Melville Vs. Rd. W3 . . . 1J 81
Melvin Rd. SE20 . . . 1J 141
Melwood Ho. E1 . . . 6H 69 (off Watney Mkt.)
Melyn Clo. N7 . . . 4G 49
Memel Ct. EC1 . . . 4C 162
Memel St. EC1 . . . 4C 68 (4C 162)
Memess Path. SE18 . . . 6E 90
Memorial Av. E15 . . . 3G 71
Memorial Clo. Houn . . . 6D 78
Mendham Ho. SE1 . . . 3E 86 (7G 169) (off Cluny Pl.)
Mendip Clo. SE26 . . . 4J 123
Mendip Clo. SW19 . . . 2G 119
Mendip Clo. Hay . . . 7F 77
Mendip Clo. Wor Pk. . . . 1E 148
Mendip Ct. SE14 . . . 6J 87 (off Avonley Rd.)
Mendip Ct. SW18 . . . 3A 102
Mendip Dri. NW2 . . . 2G 47
Mendip Houses. E2 . . . 3J 69 (off Welwyn St.)
Mendip Rd. SW11 . . . 3A 102
Mendip Rd. Bexh . . . 1K 111
Mendip Rd. Ilf . . . 5J 37
Mendora Rd. SW6 . . . 7G 83
Menelik Rd. NW2 . . . 4G 47
Menlo Gdns. SE19 . . . 7D 122
Menlo Lodge. N13 . . . 3E 16 (off Crothall Clo.)
Menon Dri. N9 . . . 3C 18
Menotti St. E2 . . . 4G 69
Menteath Ho. E14 . . . 6C 70 (off Dod St.)
Mentmore Clo. Harr . . . 6C 26
Mentmore Ter. E8 . . . 7H 51
Meon Ct. Iswth . . . 2J 97
Meon Rd. W3 . . . 2J 81

Meopham Rd. Mitc ... 1G 139
Mepham Cres. Harr ... 7B 10
Mepham Gdns. Harr ... 7B 10
Mepham St. SE1 ... 1A 86 (5J 167)
Mera Dri. Bexh ... 4G 111
Merantun Way. SW19 ... 1K 137
Merbury Clo. SE13 ... 5F 107
Merbury Rd. SE28 ... 2J 91
Mercator Pl. E14 ... 5C 88
Mercator Rd. SE13 ... 4F 107
Mercer Clo. Th Dit ... 7A 134
Mercer Ho. SW1 ... 5F 85 (5J 171)
(off Ebury Bri. Rd.)
Merceron Houses. E2 ... 3J 69
(off Globe Rd.)
Merceron St. E1 ... 4H 69
Mercer Pl. Pinn ... 2A 24
Mercers Clo. SE10 ... 4H 89
Mercer's Cotts. E1 ... 6A 70
(off White Horse Rd.)
Mercers Pl. W6 ... 4F 83
Mercers Rd. N19 ... 3H 49
(in two parts)
Mercer St. WC2 ... 6J 67 (1E 166)
Merchant Ct. E1 ... 1J 87
(off Wapping Wall)
Merchant Ind. Ter. NW10 ... 4J 63
Merchants Lodge. E17 ... 4C 34
(off Westbury Rd.)
Merchant St. E3 ... 3B 70
Merchiston Rd. SE6 ... 2F 125
Merchland Rd. SE9 ... 1G 127
Mercia Gro. SE13 ... 4E 106
Mercia Ho. SE5 ... 2C 104
(off Denmark Rd.)
Mercier Rd. SW15 ... 5G 101
Mercury. NW9 ... 1B 28
(off Concourse, The)
Mercury Cen. Felt ... 5J 95
Mercury Ct. E14 ... 4C 88
(off Homer Dri.)
Mercury Ho. Bren ... 6C 80
(off Glenhurst Rd.)
Mercury Rd. Bren ... 6C 80
Mercury Way. SE14 ... 6K 87
Mercy Ter. SE13 ... 5D 106
Merebank La. Croy ... 5K 151
Mere Clo. SW15 ... 7F 101
Meredith Av. NW2 ... 5E 46
Meredith Clo. Pinn ... 1B 24
Meredith Ho. N16 ... 5E 50
Meredith M. SE4 ... 4B 106
Meredith St. E13 ... 3J 71
Meredith St. EC1 ... 3B 68 (2A 162)
Meredyth Rd. SW13 ... 2C 100
Mere End. Croy ... 7K 141
Mere Rd. Shep ... 6D 130
Meretone Clo. SE4 ... 4A 106
Merevale Cres. Mord ... 6A 138
Mereway Rd. Twic ... 1H 115
Merewood Clo. Brom ... 2E 144
Merewood Rd. Bexh ... 2J 111
Mereworth Clo. Brom ... 5H 143
Mereworth Dri. SE18 ... 7F 91
Mereworth Ho. SE15 ... 6J 87
Merganser Ct. SE8 ... 6B 88
(off Edward St.)
Merganser Gdns. SE28 ... 3H 91
Meriden Clo. Brom ... 7B 126
Meriden Clo. Ilf ... 1G 37
Meriden Ct. SW3 ... 6C 170
Meridian Ga. E14 ... 2E 88
Meridian Ho. SE10 ... 4G 89
(off Azof St.)
Meridian Ho. SE10 ... 7E 88
(off Royal Hill)
Meridian Pl. E14 ... 2D 88
Meridian Rd. SE7 ... 7B 90
Meridian Sq. E15 ... 7F 53
Meridian Trad. Est. SE7 ... 4K 89
Meridian Wlk. N17 ... 6K 17
Meridian Way. N18 & N9 ... 5D 18
Merifield Rd. SE9 ... 4A 108
Merino Clo. E11 ... 4A 36
Merino Pl. Sidc ... 6A 110
Merioneth Ct. W7 ... 5K 61
(off Copley Clo.)
Merivale Rd. SW15 ... 4G 101
Merivale Rd. Harr ... 7G 25
Merlewood Dri. Chst ... 1D 144
Merlewood Pl. SE9 ... 5D 108
Merley Ct. NW9 ... 1J 45
Merlin. NW9 ... 1B 28
(off Concourse, The)
Merlin Clo. Croy ... 4E 152
Merlin Clo. Mitc ... 3C 138
Merlin Clo. N'holt ... 3A 60
Merlin Clo. Wall ... 6K 151
Merlin Ct. Brom ... 3H 143
Merlin Ct. Ruis ... 2F 41
Merlin Cres. Edgw ... 1F 27
Merlin Gdns. Brom ... 3J 125
Merling Clo. Chess ... 5C 146
Merlin Gro. Beck ... 4B 142
Merlin Rd. E12 ... 2B 54
Merlin Rd. Well ... 4A 110
Merlin Rd. N. Well ... 4A 110
Merlins Av. Harr ... 3D 42
Merlins Ct. WC1 ... 3A 68 (2J 161)
(off Margery St.)
Merlin St. WC1 ... 3A 68 (2J 161)
Mermaid Ct. E8 ... 7F 51
(off Celandine Dri.)
Mermaid Ct. SE1 ... 2D 86 (6E 168)
Mermaid Ct. SE16 ... 1B 88
Mermaid Ho. E14 ... 7E 70
(off Bazely St.)
Mermaid Tower. SE8 ... 6B 88
(off Abinger Gro.)
Meroe Ct. N16 ... 2E 50
Merredene St. SW2 ... 6K 103
Merriam Clo. E4 ... 5K 19
Merrick Rd. S'hall ... 2D 78
Merrick Sq. SE1 ... 3D 86 (7E 168)
Merridene. N21 ... 6G 7
Merrielands Cres. Dag ... 2F 75
Merrielands Retail Pk. Dag ... 1F 75
Merrilands Rd. Wor Pk ... 1E 148
Merrilees Rd. Sidc ... 1J 127
Merrilyn Clo. Clay ... 6A 146
Merriman Rd. SE3 ... 1A 108
Merrington Rd. SW6 ... 6J 83
Merrion Av. Stan ... 5J 11
Merritt Gdns. Chess ... 6C 146
Merritt Rd. SE4 ... 5B 106
Merritt's Bldgs. EC2 ... 4G 163
Merrivale. N14 ... 6C 6
Merrivale. NW1 ... 1G 67
(off Camden St.)
Merrivale Av. Ilf ... 4B 36
Merrow Ct. Mitc ... 2B 138
Merrow Rd. Sutt ... 7F 149
Merrow St. SE17 ... 5D 86
Merrow Wlk. SE17 ... 5D 86
Merrow Way. New Ad ... 6E 154
Merrydown Way. Chst ... 1C 144
Merryfield. SE3 ... 2H 107
Merryfield Gdns. Stan ... 5H 11
Merryfield Ho. SE9 ... 3A 126
(off Gro. Park Rd.)
Merryfields. Uxb ... 2A 58
(in two parts)
Merryfields Way. SE6 ... 7D 106
Merry Hill ... 1A 10
Merryhill Clo. E4 ... 7J 9
Merry Hill Mt. Bush ... 1A 10
Merry Hill Rd. Bush ... 1A 10
Merryhills Ct. N14 ... 5B 6
Merryhills Dri. Enf ... 4C 6
Merryweather Ct. N19 ... 3G 49
Merryweather Ct. N Mald ... 5A 136
Mersea Ho. Bark ... 6F 55
Mersey Ct. King T ... 1D 134
Mersey Rd. E17 ... 3B 34
Mersey Wlk. N'holt ... 2E 60
Mersham Dri. NW9 ... 5G 27
Mersham Pl. SE20 ... 1H 141
Mersham Rd. T Hth ... 3D 140
Merten Rd. Romf ... 7E 38
Merthyr Ter. SW13 ... 6D 82
Merton ... 7A 120
Merton Av. W4 ... 4B 82
Merton Av. N'holt ... 5G 43
Merton Av. Uxb ... 7D 40
Merton Ct. Ilf ... 6C 36
Merton Ct. Well ... 2B 110
Merton Gdns. Orp ... 5F 145
Merton Hall Gdns. SW20 ... 1G 137
Merton Hall Rd. SW19 ... 7G 119
Merton High St. SW19 ... 7K 119
Merton Ind. Pk. SW19 ... 1K 137
Merton La. N6 ... 2D 48
Merton Lodge. New Bar ... 5F 5
Merton Mans. SE8 ... 1C 106
(off Brookmill Rd.)
Merton Mans. SW20 ... 2F 137
Merton Park ... 2J 137
Merton Pk. Pde. SW19 ... 1H 137
Merton Pl. SW19 ... 1A 138
(off Nelson Gro. Rd.)
Merton Ri. NW3 ... 7C 48
(in two parts)
Merton Rd. E17 ... 5E 34
Merton Rd. SE25 ... 5G 141
Merton Rd. SW18 ... 6J 101
Merton Rd. SW19 ... 7K 119
Merton Rd. Bark ... 7K 55
Merton Rd. Enf ... 1J 7
Merton Rd. Harr ... 1G 43
Merton Rd. Ilf ... 7K 37
Merton Way. Uxb ... 7D 40
Merton Way. W Mol ... 4F 133
Mertoun Ter. W1 ... 5D 66 (7E 158)
(off Seymour Pl.)
Merttins Rd. SE15 & SE4 ... 5K 105
Meru Clo. NW5 ... 4E 48
Mervan Rd. SW2 ... 4A 104
Mervyn Av. SE9 ... 3G 127
Mervyn Rd. W13 ... 3A 80
Mervyn Rd. Shep ... 7E 130
Messaline Av. W3 ... 6J 63
Messent Rd. SE9 ... 5A 108
Messeter Pl. SE9 ... 6E 108
Messina Av. NW6 ... 7J 47
Messiter Ho. N1 ... 1K 67
(off Barnsbury Est.)
Metcalf Rd. Ashf ... 5D 112
Metcalf Wlk. Felt ... 4C 114
Meteor St. SW11 ... 4E 102
Meteor Way. Wall ... 7J 151
Metheringham Way. NW9 ... 1A 28
Methley St. SE11
... 5A 86 (6K 173)
Methuen Clo. Edgw ... 7B 12
Methuen Pk. N10 ... 3F 31
Methuen Rd. Belv ... 4H 93
Methuen Rd. Bexh ... 4F 111
Methuen Rd. Edgw ... 7B 12
Methwold Rd. W10 ... 5F 65
Metro Bus. Cen., The.
SE26 ... 6B 124
Metro Central Heights. SE1
... 3C 86
(off Newington Causeway)
Metro Cinema ... 7H 67 (2C 166)
(off Rupert St.)
Metro Ind. Cen. Iswth ... 2J 97
Metropolis. SE11 ... 3B 86
(off Oswin St.)
Metropolitan Bus. Cen. N1 ... 7E 50
(off Enfield Rd.)
Metropolitan Clo. E14 ... 5C 70
Metropolitan Wharf. E1 ... 1J 87
Metro Trad. Est. Wemb ... 4H 45
Mews Pl. Wfd G ... 4D 20
Mews St. E1 ... 1G 87 (4K 169)
Mews, The. N1 ... 1C 68
Mews, The. N8 ... 3A 32
Mews, The. Ilf ... 5B 36
Mews, The. Romf ... 4K 39
Mews, The. Sidc ... 4A 128
Mews, The. Twic ... 6B 98
Mexborough. NW1 ... 1G 67
Mexfield Rd. SW15 ... 5H 101
Meyer Grn. Enf ... 1B 8
Meyer Rd. Eri ... 6K 93
Meymott St. SE1 ... 1B 86 (5A 168)
Meynell Cres. E9 ... 7K 51
Meynell Gdns. E9 ... 7K 51
Meynell Rd. E9 ... 7K 51
Meyrick Ho. E14 ... 5C 70
(off Burgess St.)
Meyrick Rd. NW10 ... 6C 46
Meyrick Rd. SW11 ... 3B 102
Miah Ter. E1 ... 1G 87
Miall Wlk. SE26 ... 4A 124
Micawber Av. Uxb ... 4C 58
Micawber Ct. N1 ... 3C 68 (1D 162)
(off Windsor Ter.)
Micawber Ho. SE16 ... 2G 87
(off Llewellyn St.)
Micawber St. N1 ... 3C 68 (1D 162)
Michael Cliffe Ho. EC1 ... 2A 162
Michael Faraday Ho. SE17 ... 5E 86
(off Beaconsfield Rd.)
Michael Gaynor Clo. W7 ... 1K 79
Michael Manley Ind. Est.
SW8 ... 2G 103
(off Clyston St.)
Michaelmas Clo. SW20 ... 3E 136
Michael Rd. E11 ... 1H 53
Michael Rd. SE25 ... 3E 140
Michael Rd. SW6 ... 1K 101
Michaels Clo. SE13 ... 4G 107
Michael Stewart Ho. SW6 ... 6H 83
(off Clem Attlee Ct.)
Michelangelo Ct. SE16 ... 5H 87
(off Stubbs Dri.)
Micheldever Rd. SE12 ... 6G 107
Michelham Gdns. Twic ... 3K 115
Michelle Ct. N12 ... 5F 15
Michelle Ct. W3 ... 7K 63
Michelle Ct. Brom ... 1H 143
(off Blyth Rd.)
Michelsdale Dri. Rich ... 4E 98
Michelson Ho. SE11 ... 4H 173
Michel's Row. Rich ... 4E 98
(off Michelsdale Dri.)
Michigan Av. E12 ... 4D 54
Michigan Ho. E14 ... 4C 88
Michleham Down. N12 ... 4C 14
Mickledore. NW1
... 2G 67 (1B 160)
(off Ampthill Est.)
Mickleham Clo. Orp ... 2K 145
Mickleham Gdns. Sutt ... 6G 149
Mickleham Rd. Orp ... 1K 145
Mickleham Way. New Ad ... 7F 155
Micklethwaite Rd. SW6 ... 6J 83
Midas Metropolitan Ind. Est.
Mord ... 7E 136
Mid Beckton ... 6D 72
Midcroft. Ruis ... 1G 41
Middle Dene. NW7 ... 3E 12
Middlefield. NW8 ... 1B 66
Middlefielde. W13 ... 5B 62
Middlefield Gdns. Ilf ... 6F 37
Middle Grn. Clo. Surb ... 6F 135
Middleham Gdns. N18 ... 6B 18
Middleham Rd. N18 ... 6B 18
Middle La. N8 ... 5J 31
Middle La. Tedd ... 6K 115
Middle La. M. N8 ... 5J 31
Middle Mill Hall. King T ... 3F 135
Middle Pk. Av. SE9 ... 6B 108
Middle Path. Harr ... 1H 43
Middle Rd. E13 ... 2J 71
Middle Rd. SW16 ... 2H 139
Middle Rd. E Barn ... 6H 5
Middle Rd. Harr ... 2H 43
Middle Row. W10 ... 4G 65
Middlesborough Rd. N18 ... 6B 18
Middlesex Bus. Cen. S'hall ... 2D 78
Middlesex County Cricket Club.
... 3B 66 (1B 158)
Middlesex Ct. W4 ... 5B 82
Middlesex Ct. Harr ... 5K 25
Middlesex Pas. EC1 ... 6B 162
Middlesex Pl. E9 ... 6J 51
(off Elsdale St.)
Middlesex Rd. Mitc ... 5J 139
Middlesex St. E1 ... 5E 68 (6H 163)
Middlesex University
(Bounds Grn. Campus)
... 6B 16
Middlesex University
(Enfield Campus) ... 5C 8
Middlesex University
(Hendon Campus) ... 4D 28
Middlesex University
(Tottenham Campus)
... 6K 17
Middlesex Wharf. E5 ... 2J 51
Middle St. EC1 ... 5C 68 (5C 162)
Middle St. Croy ... 2C 152
(in two parts)
Middle Temple Hall.
... 7A 68 (2J 167)
(off Middle Temple La.)
Middle Temple La. EC4
... 6A 68 (1J 167)
Middleton Av. E4 ... 4G 19
Middleton Av. Gnfd ... 2H 61
Middleton Av. Sidc ... 6B 128
Middleton Bldgs. W1 ... 6A 160
Middleton Clo. E4 ... 3G 19
Middleton Dri. SE16 ... 2K 87
Middleton Dri. Pinn ... 3J 23
Middleton Gdns. Ilf ... 6F 37
Middleton Gro. N7 ... 5J 49
Middleton Ho. E8 ... 7F 51
Middleton Ho. SE1 ... 3D 86
(off Burbage Clo.)
Middleton Ho. SW1
... 4H 85 (4D 172)
(off Causton St.)
Middleton M. N7 ... 5J 49
Middleton Rd. E8 ... 7F 51
Middleton Rd. NW11 ... 7J 29
Middleton Rd. Hay ... 5F 59
Middleton Rd. Mord ... 6K 137
Middleton Rd. N Mald ... 3J 135
Middleton St. E2 ... 3H 69
Middleton Way. SE13 ... 4F 107
Middleway. NW11 ... 5K 29
Middle Way. SW16 ... 2H 139
Middle Way. Eri ... 3E 92
Middle Way. Hay ... 4A 60
Middle Way, The. Harr ... 2K 25
Middle Yd. SE1 ... 1E 86 (4G 169)
Midfield Av. Bexh ... 3J 111
Midfield Pde. Bexh ... 3J 111
Midfield Way. Orp ... 7B 128
Midford Ho. NW4 ... 4F 29
(off Belle Vue Est.)
Midford Pl. W1 ... 4G 67 (4B 160)
Midholm. Wemb ... 1G 45
Midholm Clo. NW11 ... 4K 29
Midholm Rd. Croy ... 3A 154
Midhope Ho. WC1
... 3J 67 (2F 161)
(off Midhope St.)
Midhope St. WC1 ... 3J 67 (2F 161)
Midhurst. SE26 ... 6J 123
Midhurst Av. N10 ... 3E 30
Midhurst Av. Croy ... 7A 140
Midhurst Gdns. Uxb ... 1E 58
Midhurst Hill. Bexh ... 6G 111
Midhurst Ho. E14 ... 6B 70
(off Salmon La.)
Midhurst Pde. N10 ... 3E 30
(off Fortis Grn.)
Midhurst Rd. W13 ... 2A 80
Midhurst Way. E5 ... 4G 51
Midland Cres. NW3 ... 6A 48
Midland Pde. NW6 ... 6K 47
Midland Pl. E14 ... 5E 88
Midland Rd. E10 ... 7E 34
Midland Rd. NW1
... 2H 67 (1D 160)
Midland Ter. NW2 ... 3F 47
Midland Ter. NW10 ... 4A 64
(in two parts)
Midmoor Rd. SW12 ... 1G 121
Midmoor Rd. SW19 ... 1F 137

Midship Clo. SE16 1K 87
Midship Point. E14 2C 88 (off Quarterdeck, The)
Midstrath Rd. NW10 4A 46
Midsummer Av. Houn 4D 96
Midway. Sutt 7H 137
Midway Ho. EC1 1A 162
Midwinter Clo. Well 3A 110
Midwood Clo. NW2 3D 46
Miers Clo. E6 1E 72
Mighell Av. Ilf 5B 36
Milan Rd. S'hall 2D 78
Milborne Gro. SW10 5A 84 (6A 170)
Milborne St. E9 6J 51
Milborough Cres. SE12 6G 107
Milburn Dri. W Dray 7A 58
Milcote St. SE1 2B 86 (7A 168)
Mildenhall Rd. E5 4J 51
Mildmay Av. N1 6D 50
Mildmay Gro. N. N1 5D 50
Mildmay Gro. S. N1 5D 50
Mildmay Pk. N1 5D 50
Mildmay Pl. N16 5E 50
Mildmay Rd. N1 5D 50
Mildmay Rd. Ilf 3F 55
Mildmay Rd. Romf 5J 39
Mildmay St. N1 6D 50
Mildred Av. Hay 4F 77
Mildred Av. N'holt 5F 43
Mildred Rd. Eri 5K 93
Mildura Ct. N8 4K 31
Mile End 4B 70
Mile End Pk. 3A 70
Mile End Pl. E1 4K 69
Mile End Rd. E1 & E3 5J 69
Mile End, The. E17 1K 33
Mile Rd. Wall 1F 151
Miles Bldgs. NW1 5C 66 (5C 158) (off Penfold Pl.)
Miles Ct. E1 6H 69 (off Tillman St.)
Miles Ct. Croy 2B 152 (off Cuthbert Rd.)
Miles Dri. SE28 1J 91
Miles Ho. SE10 5G 89 (off Tuskar St.)
Miles Lodge. Harr 5H 25
Milespit Hill. NW7 5J 13
Miles Pl. NW1 5B 158
Miles Pl. Surb 4F 135
Miles Rd. N8 3J 31
Miles Rd. Mitc 3C 138
Miles St. SW8 6J 85 (7E 172) (in two parts)
Miles St. Bus. Est. SW8 6J 85 (7F 173)
Milestone Clo. N9 2B 18
Milestone Clo. Sutt 7B 150
Milestone Green. (Junct.) 4K 99
Milestone Ho. King T 3D 134 (off Surbiton Rd.)
Milestone Rd. SE19 6F 123
Miles Way. N20 2H 15
Milfoil St. W12 7C 64
Milford Clo. SE2 6E 92
Milford Ct. S'hall 1E 78
Milford Gdns. Croy 5J 141
Milford Gdns. Edgw 7B 12
Milford Gdns. Wemb 4D 44
Milford Gro. Sutt 4A 150
Milford La. WC2 7A 68 (2H 167)
Milford M. SW16 3K 121
Milford Rd. W13 1B 80
Milford Rd. S'hall 7E 60
Milford Towers. SE6 7D 106
Milk St. E16 1F 91
Milk St. EC2 6C 68 (1D 168)
Milk St. Brom 6K 125
Milkwell Gdns. Wfd G 7E 20
Milkwell Yd. SE5 1C 104
Milkwood Rd. SE24 5B 104
Milk Yd. E1 7J 69
Millais Av. E12 5E 54
Millais Ct. N'holt 2B 60 (off Academy Gdns.)
Millais Gdns. Edgw 2G 27
Millais Ho. SW1 4J 85 (4E 172) (off Marsham St.)
Millais Rd. E11 4E 52
Millais Rd. Enf 5A 8
Millais Rd. N Mald 7A 136
Millais Way. Eps 4J 147
Millard Clo. N16 5E 50
Millard Ho. SE8 5B 88 (off Leeway)
Millard Ter. Dag 6G 57
Millbank. SW1 3J 85 (2E 172)
Millbank Ct. SW1 3E 172
Millbank Tower. SW1 4J 85 (4E 172)
Millbank Way. SE12 5J 107
Millbourne Rd. Felt 4C 114
Mill Bri. Barn 6C 4
Millbrook Av. Well 4H 109
Millbrook Gdns. Chad H 6F 39
Millbrook Ho. SE15 6G 87 (off Peckham Pk. Rd.)
Millbrook Pas. SW9 3B 104
Millbrook Pl. NW1 2G 67 (off Hampstead Rd.)
Millbrook Rd. N9 1C 18
Millbrook Rd. SW9 3B 104
Mill Clo. Cars 2E 150
Mill Corner. Barn 1C 4
Mill Ct. E10 3E 52
Millcroft Ho. SE6 4E 124 (off Melfield Gdns.)
Millender Wlk. SE16 4J 87
Millennium Bridge. 7B 68 (3B 168)
Millennium Bus. Cen. NW2 2D 46
Millennium Clo. E16 6K 71
Millennium Dri. E14 4F 89
Millennium Ho. E17 5K 33
Millennium Pl. E2 2H 69
Millennium Sq. SE1 2F 87 (6K 169)
Millennium Way. SE10 2G 89
Miller Av. Enf 1H 9
Miller Clo. Mitc 7D 138
Miller Clo. Pinn 2A 24
Miller Ct. Bexh 3J 111
Miller Rd. SW19 6B 120
Miller Rd. Croy 1K 151
Miller's Av. E8 5F 51
Millers Clo. NW7 4H 13
Miller's Ct. W4 5B 82
Millers Ct. Wemb 2E 62 (off Vicars Bri. Clo.)
Millers Grn. Clo. Enf 3G 7
Millers Mdw. Clo. SE3 5H 107
Miller's Ter. E8 5F 51
Miller St. NW1 2G 67 (in two parts)
Millers Way. W6 2E 82
Millers Wharf Ho. E1 1G 87 (off St Katherine's Way)
Miller Wlk. SE1 1A 86 (5K 167)
Millet Rd. Gnfd 2F 61
Mill Farm Av. Sun 7G 113
Mill Farm Bus. Pk. Houn 7C 96
Mill Farm Clo. Pinn 2A 24
Mill Farm Cres. Houn 1C 114
Millfield. N4 2A 50
Millfield. King T 3F 135
Millfield. Sun 1F 131
Millfield Av. E17 1A 34
Millfield La. N6 1C 48 (in two parts)
Millfield Pl. N6 2E 48
Millfield Rd. Edgw 2J 27
Millfield Rd. Houn 1C 114
Millfields Rd. E5 4J 51
Mill Gdns. SE26 3H 123
Mill Grn. Mitc 7E 138
Mill Grn. Bus. Pk. Mitc 7E 138
Mill Grn. Rd. Mitc 7E 138
Millgrove St. SW11 1E 102
Millharbour. E14 2D 88
Millhaven Clo. Romf 6B 38
Mill Hill. 5F 13
Mill Hill. SW13 2C 100
Mill Hill Circus. (Junct.) 5G 13
Mill Hill Golf Course. 1E 12
Mill Hill Gro. W3 1J 81
Mill Hill Ind. Est. NW7 6G 13
Mill Hill Pk. 6G 13
Mill Hill Rd. SW13 2C 100
Mill Hill Rd. W3 2H 81
Mill Hill Ter. W3 1H 81
Mill Hill Yd. W3 2H 81
Mill Ho. Wfd G 5C 20
Millhouse Pl. SE27 4B 122
Millicent Fawcett Ct. N17 1F 33
Millicent Rd. E10 1B 52
Milligan St. E14 7B 70
Milling Rd. Edgw 7E 12
Millington Ho. N16 3D 50
Millington Rd. Hay 3G 77
Mill La. E4 3J 9
Mill La. NW6 5H 47
Mill La. SE18 5E 90
Mill La. Cars 4D 150
Mill La. Croy 3K 151
Mill La. Eps 7B 148
Mill La. Romf 6E 38
Mill La. Wfd G 5C 20
Millman M. WC1 4K 67 (4G 161)
Millman Pl. WC1 4K 67 (4H 161) (off Millman St.)
Millman St. WC1 4K 67 (4G 161)
Millmark Gro. SE14 2A 106
Millmarsh La. Brim 2F 9
Millmead Ind. Cen. N17 2H 33
Mill Mead Rd. N17 3H 33
Mill Meads. 2F 71
Mill Pl. E14 6A 70
Mill Pl. Chst 1F 145
Mill Pl. King T 3F 135
Mill Plat. Iswth 2A 98 (in two parts)
Mill Plat Av. Iswth 2A 98
Mill Pond Clo. SW8 7H 85
Millpond Est. SE16 2H 87
Mill Ridge. Edgw 5A 12
Mill River Trad. Est. Enf 3F 9
Mill Rd. E16 1K 89
Mill Rd. SW19 7A 120
Mill Rd. Eri 7J 93
Mill Rd. Ilf 3E 54
Mill Rd. Twic 2G 115
Mill Row. N1 1E 68
Mill Row. Bex 1H 129
Mills Clo. Uxb 2C 58
Mills Ct. EC2 3G 163
Mills Gro. E14 6E 70
Mills Gro. NW4 3F 29
Millshot Clo. SW6 1E 100
Mills Ho. E17 3F 35
Mills Ho. SW8 1G 103 (off Thessaly Rd.)
Millside. Cars 2D 150
Millside Pl. Iswth 2B 98
Millson Clo. N20 2G 15
Mills Row. W4 4K 81
Millstream Clo. N13 5F 17
Millstream Ho. SE16 2H 87 (off Jamaica Rd.)
Millstream Rd. SE1 2F 87 (7J 169)
Mill St. SE1 2F 87 (7K 169)
Mill St. W1 7F 67 (2A 166)
Mill St. King T 3E 134
Mill Trad. Est., The. NW10 3J 63
Mill Va. Brom 2H 143
Mill Vw. Clo. Ewe 7B 148
Mill Vw. Gdns. Croy 3K 153
Millwall. 4C 88
Millwall Dock Rd. E14 3C 88
Millwall F.C. (New Den, The) 5J 87
Millway. NW7 4F 13
Mill Way. Felt 5K 95
Millway Gdns. N'holt 6D 42
Millwood Rd. Houn 5G 97
Millwood St. W10 5G 65
Mill Yd. E1 7G 69
Milman Clo. Pinn 3B 24
Milman Rd. NW6 2F 65
Milman's St. SW10 6B 84 (7A 170)
Milne Gdns. SE9 5C 108
Milne Ho. SE18 4D 90 (off Ogilby St.)
Milner Dri. Twic 7H 97
Milner Pl. N1 1A 68
Milner Pl. Cars 4E 150
Milner Rd. E15 3G 71
Milner Rd. SW19 1K 137
Milner Rd. Dag 2C 56
Milner Rd. King T 3D 134
Milner Rd. Mord 5B 138
Milner Rd. T Hth 3D 140
Milner Sq. N1 7B 50
Milner St. SW3 4D 84 (3E 170)
Milner Wlk. Sidc 2H 127
Milnthorpe Rd. W4 6K 81
Milo Gdns. SE22 6F 105
Milo Rd. SE22 6F 105
Milrood Ho. E1 5K 69 (off Stepney Grn.)
Milroy Wlk. SE1 1B 86 (4A 168)
Milson Rd. W14 3F 83
Milstead Ho. E5 5H 51
Milton Av. E6 7B 54
Milton Av. N6 7G 31
Milton Av. NW9 3J 27
Milton Av. NW10 1J 63
Milton Av. Barn 5C 4
Milton Av. Croy 7D 140
Milton Av. Sutt 3B 150
Milton Clo. N2 5A 30
Milton Clo. SE1 4F 87
Milton Clo. Hay 6J 59
Milton Clo. Sutt 3B 150
Milton Ct. E17 4C 34
Milton Ct. EC2 5D 68 (5E 162)
Milton Ct. SE14 6B 88
Milton Ct. SW18 5J 101
Milton Ct. Chad H 7C 38
Milton Ct. Twic 3J 115
Milton Ct. Uxb 3D 40
Milton Ct. Rd. SE14 6A 88
Milton Ct. Wlk. EC2 5D 68 (5E 162) (off Silk St.)
Milton Cres. Ilf 7F 37
Milton Dri. Shep 4A 130
Milton Garden Est. N16 4D 50
Milton Gdns. Stai 1B 112
Milton Gro. N11 5B 16
Milton Gro. N16 4D 50
Milton Ho. E2 3J 69 (off Roman Rd.)
Milton Ho. E17 4C 34
Milton Ho. SE5 7D 86 (off Elmington Est.)
Milton Ho. Sutt 3J 149
Milton Lodge. Sidc 4A 128
Milton Lodge. Twic 7K 97
Milton Mans. W14 6G 83 (off Queen's Club Gdns.)
Milton Pk. N6 7G 31
Milton Pl. N7 5A 50
Milton Rd. E17 4C 34
Milton Rd. N6 7G 31
Milton Rd. N15 4B 32
Milton Rd. NW7 5H 13
Milton Rd. NW9 7C 28
Milton Rd. SE24 5B 104
Milton Rd. SW14 3K 99
Milton Rd. SW19 6A 120
Milton Rd. W3 1K 81
Milton Rd. W7 7K 61
Milton Rd. Belv 4G 93
Milton Rd. Croy 1D 152
Milton Rd. Hamp 7E 114
Milton Rd. Harr 4J 25
Milton Rd. Mitc 7E 120
Milton Rd. Sutt 3J 149
Milton Rd. Uxb 4D 40
Milton Rd. Wall 6G 151
Milton Rd. Well 1K 109
Milton St. EC2 5D 68 (5E 162)
Milton Way. W Dray 4B 76
Milverton Dri. Uxb 4E 40
Milverton Gdns. Ilf 2K 55
Milverton Ho. SE23 3A 124
Milverton Rd. NW6 7E 46
Milverton St. SE11 5A 86 (6K 173)
Milverton Way. SE9 4E 126
Milward Wlk. E1 5H 69
Milward Wlk. SE18 6E 90
Mimosa Ho. Hay 5A 60
Mimosa Lodge. NW10 5B 46
Mimosa Rd. Hay 5A 60
Mimosa St. SW6 1H 101
Minard Rd. SE6 7G 107 (in two parts)
Mina Rd. SE17 5E 86
Mina Rd. SW19 1J 137
Minchenden Ct. N14 2C 16
Minchenden Cres. N14 3B 16
Minchin Ho. E14 6C 70 (off Dod St.)
Mincing La. EC3 7E 68 (2G 169)
Minden Rd. SE20 1H 141
Minden Rd. Sutt 2H 149
Minehead Rd. SW16 5K 121
Minehead Rd. Harr 3E 42
Mineral St. SE18 4J 91
Minera M. SW1 4E 84 (3G 171)
Minerva Clo. SW9 7A 86 (in two parts)
Minerva Clo. Sidc 4J 127
Minerva Rd. E4 7J 19
Minerva Rd. NW10 4J 63
Minerva Rd. King T 2F 135
Minerva St. E2 2H 69
Minerva Wlk. EC1 6B 68 (7B 162)
Minet Av. NW10 2A 64
Minet Dri. Hay 1J 77
Minet Gdns. NW10 2A 64
Minet Gdns. Hay 1K 77
Minet Rd. SW9 2B 104
Minford Gdns. W14 2F 83
Minford Ho. W14 2F 83 (off Minford Gdns.)
Mingard Wlk. N7 2K 49
Ming St. E14 7C 70
Minimax Clo. Felt 6J 95
Ministry Way. SE9 2D 126
Miniver Pl. EC4 2D 168
Mink Ct. Houn 2A 96
Minniedale. Surb 5F 135
Minnow St. SE17 4E 86
Minnow Wlk. SE17 4E 86
Minories. EC3 6F 69 (1J 169)
Minshaw Ct. Sidc 4K 127
Minshill St. SW8 1H 103
Minshull Pl. Beck 7C 124
Minson Rd. E9 1K 69
Minstead Gdns. SW15 7B 100
Minstead Way. N Mald 6A 136
Minster Av. Sutt 2J 149
Minster Ct. EC3 2H 169
Minster Ct. W5 4E 62
Minster Dri. Croy 4E 152
Minster Gdns. W Mol 4D 132
Minsterley Av. Shep 4G 131
Minster Pavement. EC3 7E 68 (2H 169) (off Mincing La.)
Minster Rd. NW2 5G 47
Minster Rd. Brom 7K 125
Minster Wlk. N8 4J 31
Minstrel Gdns. Surb 4F 135
Mint Bus. Pk. E16 5K 71
Mint Clo. Hil 3D 58
Mintern Clo. N13 3G 17

Minterne Av. S'hall 4E 78
Minterne Rd. Harr 5F 27
Minterne Waye. Hay 6A 60
Mintern St. N1 2D 68
Minton Ho. SE11 3J 173
Minton M. NW6 6K 47
Mint Rd. Wall 4F 151
Mint St. SE1 2C 86 (6C 168)
Mint Wlk. Croy 3C 152
Mirabel Rd. SW6 7H 83
Miranda Clo. E1 5J 69
Miranda Ct. W3 6F 63
Miranda Rd. N19 1G 49
Mirfield St. SE7 4B 90
Miriam Rd. SE18 5J 91
Mirravale Trad. Est. Dag 7E 38
Mirren Clo. Harr 4D 42
Mirror Path. SE9 3A 126
Misbourne Rd. Uxb 1C 58
Missenden. SE17 5D 86 (off Roland Way)
Missenden Clo. Felt 1H 113
Missenden Gdns. Mord 6A 138
Missenden Ho. NW8 3C 158
Mission Gro. E17 5A 34
Mission Pl. SE15 1G 105
Mission Sq. Bren 6E 80
Mission, The. E14 6B 70 (off Commercial Rd.)
Mistletoe Clo. Croy 1K 153
Mistral. SE5 1E 104
Misty's Fld. W on T 7A 132
Mitali Pas. E1 6G 69 (in two parts)
Mitcham. 3D 138
Mitcham Garden Village. Mitc 5E 138
Mitcham Ho. SE5 1C 104
Mitcham Ind. Est. Mitc 1F 139
Mitcham La. SW16 6G 121
Mitcham Pk. Mitc 4C 138
Mitcham Rd. E6 3C 72
Mitcham Rd. SW17 5D 120
Mitcham Rd. Croy 6J 139
Mitcham Rd. Ilf 7K 37
Mitchell. NW9 1B 28 (off Concourse, The)
Mitchellbrook Way. NW10 6K 45
Mitchell Clo. SE2 4C 92
Mitchell Clo. Belv 3J 93
Mitchell Ho. W12 7D 64 (off White City Est.)
Mitchell Rd. N13 5H 17
Mitchell's Pl. SE21 6E 104 (off Aysgarth Rd.)
Mitchell St. EC1 4C 68 (3C 162) (in two parts)
Mitchell Wlk. E6 5C 72 (off Neats Ct. Rd.)
Mitchell Wlk. E6 5D 72 (Elmley Clo.)
Mitchell Way. NW10 6J 45
Mitchell Way. Brom 1J 143
Mitchison Rd. N1 6D 50
Mitchley Rd. N17 3G 33
Mitford Clo. Chess 6C 146
Mitford Rd. N19 2J 49
Mitre Av. E17 3C 34
Mitre Bri. Ind. Pk. W10 4D 64
Mitre Clo. Brom 2H 143
Mitre Clo. Shep 6F 131
Mitre Clo. Sutt 7A 150
Mitre Ct. EC2 7D 162
Mitre Rd. E15 2G 71
Mitre Rd. SE1 2A 86 (6K 167)
Mitre Sq. EC3 6E 68 (1H 169)
Mitre St. EC3 6E 68 (1H 169)
Mitre, The. E14 7B 70
Mitre Way. NW10 & W10 4D 64
Mitre Yd. SW3 4C 84 (3D 170)
Moat Ct. SE9 6D 108
Moat Ct. Sidc 3K 127
Moat Cres. N3 3K 29
Moat Cft. Well 3C 110
Moat Dri. E13 2A 72
Moat Dri. Harr 4G 25
Moat Dri. Ruis 7G 23
Moat Farm Rd. N'holt 6D 42
Moatfield. NW6 7G 47
Moat Gdns. SE28 7C 74
Moatlands Ho. WC1 3J 67 (2F 161) (off Cromer St.)
***Moat Mount Open Space.** 1F 13*
Moat Pl. SW9 3K 103
Moat Pl. W3 6H 63
Moat Side. Enf 4E 8
Moat Side. Felt 4A 114
Moat, The. N Mald 1A 136
Moberley Rd. SW4 7H 103
Mobil Ct. WC2 6K 67 (1H 167) (off Clement's Inn)
Mobile Way. W3 5K 63
Moby Dick. (Junct.) 4E 38
Mocatta Ho. E1 4H 69 (off Brady St.)
Modbury Gdns. NW5 6E 48
Modder Pl. SW15 4F 101
Model Bldgs. WC1 2H 161
Model Cotts. SW14 4J 99
Model Cotts. W13 2B 80
Model Farm Clo. SE9 3C 126
Modern Ct. EC4 7A 162
Modling Ho. E2 2K 69 (off Mace St.)
Moelwyn. N7 5H 49
Moelyn M. Harr 5A 26
Moffat Ct. SW19 5J 119
Moffat Ho. SE5 7C 86
Moffat Rd. N13 6D 16
Moffat Rd. SW17 4D 120
Moffat Rd. T Hth 2C 140
Mogden La. Iswth 5K 97
Mohammedi Pk. N'holt 1E 60
Mohawk Ho. E3 2A 70 (off Gernon Rd.)
Mohmmad Khan Rd. E11 1H 53
Moineau. NW9 1B 28 (off Concourse, The)
Moira Clo. N17 2E 32
Moira Rd. SE9 4D 108
Mokswell Ct. N10 1E 30
Moland Mead. SE16 5K 87 (in two parts)
Molasses Ho. SW11 3A 102 (off Clove Hitch Quay)
Molasses Row. SW11 3A 102
Mole Abbey Gdns. W Mol 3F 133
Mole Ct. Eps 4J 147
Molember Ct. E Mol 4J 133
Molember Rd. E Mol 5J 133
Molescroft. SE9 3G 127
Molesey Av. W Mol 5D 132
Molesey Dri. Sutt 2G 149
Molesey Pk. Av. W Mol 5F 133
Molesey Pk. Clo. E Mol 5G 133
Molesey Pk. Rd. W Mol 5F 133
Molesey Rd. W on T & W Mol 7C 132
Molesford Rd. SW6 1J 101
Molesham Clo. W Mol 3F 133
Molesham Way. W Mol 3F 133
Molesworth Ho. SE17 6B 86 (off Brandon Est.)
Molesworth St. SE13 4E 106
Moliner Ct. Beck 7C 124
Mollis Ho. E3 5C 70 (off Gale St.)
Mollison Av. Enf 4F 9
Mollison Dri. Wall 7H 151
Mollison Way. Edgw 2F 27
Molly Huggins Clo. SW12 7G 103
Molton Ho. N1 1K 67 (off Barnsbury Est.)
Molyneux Dri. SW17 4F 121
Molyneux St. W1 5C 66 (6D 158)
Monarch Clo. Felt 7G 95
Monarch Clo. W Wick 4H 155
Monarch Ct. N2 5B 30
Monarch Dri. E16 5B 72
Monarch M. E17 6D 34
Monarch M. SW16 5A 122
Monarch Pde. Mitc 2D 138
Monarch Pl. Buck H 2F 21
Monarch Rd. Belv 3G 93
Monarchs Way. Ruis 1F 41
Mona Rd. SE15 2J 105
Monastery Gdns. Enf 2J 7
Mona St. E16 5H 71
Monaveen Gdns. W Mol 3F 133
Moncks Row. SW18 6H 101
Monck St. SW1 3H 85 (2D 172)
Monclar Rd. SE5 4D 104
Moncorvo Clo. SW7 7C 164
Moncrieff Clo. E6 6C 72
Moncrieff Pl. SE15 2G 105
Moncrieff St. SE15 2G 105
Mondial Way. Hay 7E 76
Monega Rd. E7 & E12 6A 54
Monet Ct. SE16 5H 87 (off Stubbs Dri.)
Moneyer Ho. N1 2D 68 (1E 162) (off Provost Est.)
Money La. W Dray 3A 76
Mongers Almshouses. E9 7K 51 (off Church Cres.)
Mongomery Ct. W4 7J 81
Monica Ct. Enf 5K 7
Monica James Ho. Sidc 3A 128
Monica Shaw Ct. NW1 2H 67 (1D 160) (off Purchese St., in two parts)
Monier Rd. E3 7C 52
Monivea Rd. Beck 7B 124
Monk Ct. W12 1C 82
Monk Dri. E16 7J 71
Monken Hadley. 2C 4
***Monken Hadley Common.** 2E 4*
Monkfrith Av. N14 6A 6
Monkfrith Clo. N14 7A 6
Monkfrith Way. N14 7K 5
Monkham's Av. Wfd G 5E 20
Monkham's Dri. Wfd G 5E 20
Monkham's La. Buck H 3E 20
Monkham's La. Wfd G 5D 20 (in two parts)
Monkleigh Rd. Mord 3G 137
Monk Pas. E16 7J 71 (off Monk Dri.)
Monks Av. Barn 6F 5
Monks Av. W Mol 5D 132
Monks Clo. SE2 4D 92
Monks Clo. Enf 2H 7
Monks Clo. Harr 2E 42
Monks Clo. Ruis 4B 42
Monks Cres. W on T 7K 131
Monksdene Gdns. Sutt 3K 149
Monks Dri. W3 5G 63
Monks Orchard. 7A 142
Monks Orchard Rd. Beck 1C 154
Monks Pk. Wemb 6H 45
Monks Pk. Gdns. Wemb 7H 45
Monks Rd. Enf 2G 7
Monk St. SE18 4E 90
Monks Way. NW11 4H 29
Monks Way. Beck 6C 142
Monks Way. Orp 7G 145
Monks Way. W Dray 6A 76
Monkswood Gdns. Ilf 3E 36
Monkton Ho. E5 5H 51
Monkton Ho. SE16 2K 87 (off Wolfe Cres.)
Monkton Rd. Well 2K 109
Monkton St. SE11 4A 86 (3K 173)
Monkville Av. NW11 4H 29
Monkville Pde. NW11 4H 29
Monkwell Sq. EC2 5C 68 (6D 162)
Monmouth Av. E18 3K 35
Monmouth Av. King T 7C 116
Monmouth Clo. W4 3J 81
Monmouth Clo. Mitc 4J 139
Monmouth Clo. Well 4A 110
Monmouth Ct. W7 5K 61 (off Copley Clo.)
Monmouth Gro. W5 4E 80
Monmouth Pl. W2 6K 65 (off Monmouth Rd.)
Monmouth Rd. E6 3D 72
Monmouth Rd. N9 2C 18
Monmouth Rd. W2 6J 65
Monmouth Rd. Dag 5F 57
Monmouth Rd. Hay 4G 77
Monmouth St. WC2 6J 67 (1E 166)
Monnery Rd. N19 3G 49
Monnow Rd. SE1 5G 87
Mono La. Felt 2K 113
Monoux Almshouses. E17 4D 34
Monoux Gro. E17 1C 34
Monroe Cres. Enf 1C 8
Monroe Dri. SW14 5H 99
Monro Gdns. Harr 7D 10
Monsell Ct. N4 3B 50
Monsell Rd. N4 3A 50
Monson Rd. NW10 2C 64
Monson Rd. SE14 7K 87
Mons Way. Brom 6C 144
Montacute Rd. SE6 7B 106
Montacute Rd. Bus H 1E 10
Montacute Rd. Mord 6B 138
Montacute Rd. New Ad 7E 154
Montagu Cres. N18 4C 18
Montague Av. SE4 4B 106
Montague Av. W7 1K 79
Montague Clo. SE1 1D 86 (4E 168)
Montague Clo. W on T 7K 131
Montague Ct. Sidc 3A 128
Montague Gdns. W3 7G 63
Montague Ho. E16 1K 89 (off Wesley Av.)
Montague Pas. Uxb 7A 40
Montague Pl. WC1 5H 67 (5D 160)
Montague Rd. E8 5G 51
Montague Rd. E11 2H 53
Montague Rd. N8 5K 31
Montague Rd. N15 4G 33
Montague Rd. SW19 7K 119
Montague Rd. W7 1K 79
Montague Rd. W13 6B 62
Montague Rd. Croy 1B 152
Montague Rd. Houn 3F 97
Montague Rd. Rich 6E 98
Montague Rd. S'hall 4C 78
Montague Rd. Uxb 7A 40
Montague Sq. SE15 7J 87
Montague St. EC1 5C 68 (6C 162)
Montague St. WC1 5J 67 (5E 160)
Montague Ter. Brom 4H 143
Montague Waye. S'hall 3C 78
Montagu Gdns. N18 4C 18
Montagu Gdns. Wall 4G 151
Montagu Mans. W1 5D 66 (5F 159)
Montagu M. N. W1 5D 66 (6F 159)
Montagu M. S. W1 6D 66 (7F 159)
Montagu M. W. W1 6D 66 (7F 159)
Montagu Pl. W1 5D 66 (6E 158)
Montagu Rd. N18 & N9 5C 18
Montagu Rd. NW4 6C 28
Montagu Rd. Ind. Est. N18 4D 18
Montagu Row. W1 5D 66 (6F 159)
Montagu Sq. W1 5D 66 (6F 159)
Montagu St. W1 6D 66 (7F 159)
Montalt Rd. Wfd G 4C 20
Montana Gdns. SE26 5B 124
Montana Gdns. Sutt 5A 150
Montana Rd. SW17 3E 120
Montana Rd. SW20 1E 136
Montbelle Rd. SE9 3F 127
Montcalm Clo. Brom 6J 143
Montcalm Clo. Hay 3K 59
Montcalm Ho. E14 4B 88
Montcalm Rd. SE7 7B 90
Montclare St. E2 4F 69 (3J 163)
Monteagle Av. Bark 6G 55
Monteagle Ct. N1 2E 68
Monteagle Way. E5 3G 51
Monteagle Way. SE15 3H 105
Montefiore St. SW8 2F 103
Montego Clo. SE24 4A 104
Montem Rd. SE23 7B 106
Montem Rd. N Mald 4A 136
Montem St. N4 1K 49
Montenotte Rd. N8 5G 31
Monterey Clo. Bex 2J 129
Monterey Pl. Shop. Cen. NW7 5F 13
Montesole Ct. Pinn 2A 24
Montesquieu Ter. E16 6H 71 (off Clarkson Rd.)
Montevetro. SW11 1B 102
Montford Pl. SE11 5A 86 (6J 173)
Montford Rd. Sun 4J 131
Montfort Ho. E2 3J 69 (off Victoria Pk. Sq.)
Montfort Ho. E14 3E 88 (off Galbraith St.)
Montfort Pl. SW19 1F 119
Montgolfier Wlk. N'holt 3C 60
Montgomery Clo. Mitc 4J 139
Montgomery Clo. Sidc 6K 109
Montgomery Ct. S Croy 5E 152 (off Birdhurst Rd.)
Montgomery Lodge. E1 4J 69 (off Cleveland Gro.)
Montgomery Rd. W4 4J 81
Montgomery Rd. Edgw 6A 12
Montholme Rd. SW11 6D 102
Monthope Rd. E1 5G 69 (6K 163)
Montolieu Gdns. SW15 5D 100
Montpelier Av. W5 5C 62
Montpelier Av. Bex 7D 110
Montpelier Clo. Uxb 1C 58
Montpelier Ct. W5 5D 62
Montpelier Ct. Brom 4H 143 (off Westmoreland Rd.)
Montpelier Gdns. E6 3B 72
Montpelier Gdns. Romf 7C 38
Montpelier Gro. NW5 5G 49
Montpelier M. SW7 3C 84 (1D 170)
Montpelier Pl. E1 6J 69
Montpelier Pl. SW7 3C 84 (1D 170)
Montpelier Ri. NW11 7G 29
Montpelier Ri. Wemb 1D 44
Montpelier Rd. N3 1A 30
Montpelier Rd. SE15 1H 105
Montpelier Rd. W5 5D 62
Montpelier Rd. Sutt 4A 150
Montpelier Row. SE3 2H 107
Montpelier Row. Twic 7C 98
Montpelier Sq. SW7 2C 84 (7D 164)
Montpelier St. SW7 3C 84 (1D 170)
Montpelier Ter. SW7 2C 84 (7D 164)
Montpelier Va. SE3 2H 107
Montpelier Wlk. SW7 3C 84 (1D 170)
Montpelier Way. NW11 7G 29
Montrave Rd. SE20 6J 123
Montreal Pl. WC2 7K 67 (2G 167)
Montreal Rd. Ilf 7G 37
Montrell Rd. SW2 1J 121
Montrose Av. NW6 2G 65
Montrose Av. Edgw 2J 27

Montrose Av. Sidc. . . . 7A 110
Montrose Av. Twic 7F 97
Montrose Av. Well. . . . 3H 109
Montrose Clo. Ashf 6E 112
Montrose Clo. Well 3K 109
Montrose Clo. Wfd G. . . . 4D 20
Montrose Ct. NW9. . . . 2J 27
Montrose Ct. NW11. . . . 4H 29
Montrose Ct. SE6 . . . . 1H 125
Montrose Ct. SW7 . . . . 2B 84 (7B 164)
Montrose Ct. Harr 5F 25
Montrose Cres. N12. . . . 6F 15
Montrose Cres. Wemb. . . . 6E 44
Montrose Gdns. Mitc. . . . 2D 138
Montrose Gdns. Sutt 2K 149
Montrose Ho. E14. . . . 3C 88
Montrose Pl. SW1 . . . . 2E 84 (7H 165)
Montrose Rd. Felt 6F 95
Montrose Rd. Harr. . . . 2J 25
Montrose Wlk. Stan. . . . 6G 11
Montrose Way. SE23. . . . 1K 123
Montserrat Av. Wfd G 7A 20
Montserrat Clo. SE19 . . . . 5D 122
Montserrat Rd. SW15 . . . . 4G 101
Monument Gdns. SE13 . . . . 5E 106
Monument St. EC3 . . . . 7D 68 (2F 169)
Monument, The. . . . 2F 169
Monument Way. N17. . . . 3F 33
Monza St. E1 . . . . 7J 69
Moodkee St. SE16. . . . 3J 87
Moody Rd. SE15 . . . . 1F 105
Moody St. E1 . . . . 3K 69
Moon Ct. SE12. . . . 4J 107
Moon La. Barn 3C 4
Moon St. N1 . . . . 1B 68
Moorcroft. Edgw 1H 27
Moorcroft Gdns. Brom. . . . 5C 144
Moorcroft La. Uxb 5C 58
Moorcroft Rd. SW16 . . . . 3J 121
Moorcroft Way. Pinn 5C 24
Moordown. SE18. . . . 7F 91
Moore Clo. SW14 . . . . 3J 99
Moore Clo. Mitc 2F 139
Moore Clo. Wall. . . . 7J 151
Moore Ct. N1. . . . 1B 68 (off Gaskin St.)
Moore Cres. Dag 1B 74
Moorehead Way. SE3. . . . 3J 107
Moore Ho. E1 . . . . 7J 69 (off Cable St.)
Moore Ho. E2 . . . . 3J 69 (off Roman Rd.)
Moore Ho. N8 . . . . 4J 31 (off Pembroke Rd.)
Moore Ho. SE10 . . . . 5H 89 (off Armitage Rd.)
Mooreland Rd. Brom. . . . 7H 125
Moore Pk. Ct. SW6 . . . . 7K 83 (off Fulham Rd.)
Moore Pk. Rd. SW6. . . . 7J 83
Moore Rd. SE19 . . . . 6C 122
Moore St. SW3. . . . 4D 84 (3E 170)
Moore Wlk. E7. . . . 4J 53
Moore Way. Sutt 7J 149
Moorey Clo. E15 . . . . 1H 71
Moorfield Av. W5 . . . . 4D 62
Moorfield Rd. N17. . . . 2F 33
Moorfield Rd. Chess 5E 146
Moorfield Rd. Enf 1D 8
Moorfield Rd. Uxb. . . . 6A 58
Moorfields. EC2 . . . . 5D 68 (6E 162)
Moorfields Highwalk. EC2 . . . . 5D 68 (6E 162) (off Moor La., in two parts)
Moorgate. EC2 . . . . 6D 68 (7E 162)
Moorgate Pl. EC2. . . . 7E 162
Moorgreen Ho. EC1. . . . 1A 162
Moorhouse. NW9 . . . . 1B 28
Moorhouse Rd. W2 . . . . 6J 65
Moorhouse Rd. Harr 3D 26
Moorings, The. E16. . . . 5A 72 (off Prince Regent La.)
Moorland Clo. Romf 1H 39
Moorland Clo. Twic 7E 96
Moorland M. N1 . . . . 7A 50
Moorland Rd. SW9 . . . . 4B 104
Moorlands. N'holt 1C 60
Moorlands Av. NW7. . . . 6J 13
Moor La. EC2 . . . . 5D 68 (6E 162) (in two parts)
Moor La. Chess 4E 146
Moormead Dri. Eps 5A 148
Moor Mead Rd. Twic. . . . 6A 98
Moor Pk. Gdns. King T 7A 118
Moor Pl. EC2 . . . . 5D 68 (6E 162)
Moorside Rd. Brom. . . . 3G 125
Moor St. W1. . . . 6H 67 (1D 166)
Moot Ct. NW9. . . . 5G 27
Moran Ho. E1 . . . . 1H 87 (off Wapping La.)
Morant Pl. N22 . . . . 1K 31
Morant St. E14 . . . . 7C 70
Mora Rd. NW2 . . . . 4E 46
Mora St. EC1 . . . . 3C 68 (2D 162)
Morat St. SW9. . . . 1K 103
Moravian Clo. SW10 . . . . 6B 84 (7A 170)
Moravian Pl. SW10. . . . 6B 84
Moravian St. E2. . . . 2J 69
Moray Av. Hay. . . . 1H 77
Moray Clo. Edgw. . . . 2C 12
Moray Clo. Romf. . . . 1K 39
Moray Ct. S Croy. . . . 5C 152 (off Warham Rd.)
Moray Ho. E1 . . . . 4A 70 (off Harford St.)
Moray M. N7. . . . 2K 49
Moray Rd. N4 . . . . 2K 49
Moray Way. Romf 1K 39
Mordaunt Gdns. Dag. . . . 7E 56
Mordaunt Ho. NW10 . . . . 1K 63
Mordaunt Rd. NW10 . . . . 1K 63
Mordaunt St. SW9. . . . 3K 103
Morden. . . . 3K 137
Morden Ct. Mord. . . . 4K 137
Morden Ct. Pde. Mord 4K 137
Morden Gdns. Gnfd. . . . 5K 43
Morden Gdns. Mitc 4B 138
Morden Hall Rd. Mord 3K 137
Morden Hill. SE13 . . . . 2E 106 (in two parts)
Morden La. SE13. . . . 1E 106
Morden Park. . . . 6G 137
Morden Rd. SE3 . . . . 2J 107
Morden Rd. SW19. . . . 1K 137
Morden Rd. Mord & Mitc. . . . 4A 138
Morden Rd. Romf 7E 38
Morden Rd. M. SE3. . . . 2J 107
Morden St. SE13. . . . 1D 106
Morden Way. Sutt 7J 137
Morden Wharf. SE10. . . . 3G 89 (off Morden Wharf Rd.)
Morden Wharf Rd. SE10 . . . . 3G 89
Mordern Ho. NW1. . . . 3D 158
Mordon Rd. Ilf. . . . 7K 37
Mordred Rd. SE6 . . . . 2G 125
Morecambe Clo. E1. . . . 5K 69
Morecambe Gdns. Stan 4J 11
Morecambe St. SE17. . . . 4C 86
Morecambe Ter. N18 . . . . 4J 17 (off Gt. Cambridge Rd.)
More Clo. E16. . . . 6H 71
More Clo. W14 . . . . 4F 83
Morecoombe Clo. King T. . . . 7H 117
Moree Way. N18 . . . . 4B 18
Moreland Ct. NW2 . . . . 3J 47
Moreland St. EC1 . . . . 3B 68 (1B 162)
Moreland Way. E4 . . . . 3J 19
Morella Rd. SW12. . . . 7D 102
Morello Av. Uxb. . . . 5D 58
Moremead Rd. SE6 . . . . 4B 124
Morena St. SE6. . . . 7D 106
Moresby Av. Surb 7H 135
Moresby Rd. E5 . . . . 1H 51
Moresby Wlk. SW8 . . . . 2G 103
More's Garden. SW3 . . . . 6B 84 (off Cheyne Wlk.)
Moreton Av. Iswth 1J 97
Moreton Clo. E5 . . . . 2H 51
Moreton Clo. N15 . . . . 6D 32
Moreton Clo. NW7. . . . 6K 13
Moreton Clo. SW1. . . . 5B 172
Moreton Gdns. Wfd G 5H 21
Moreton Ho. SE16. . . . 3H 87
Moreton Pl. SW1 . . . . 5G 85 (5B 172)
Moreton Rd. N15 . . . . 6D 32
Moreton Rd. S Croy 5D 152
Moreton Rd. Wor Pk 2C 148
Moreton St. SW1 . . . . 5G 85 (5B 172)
Moreton Ter. SW1 . . . . 5G 85 (5B 172)
Moreton Ter. M. N. SW1 . . . . 5G 85 (5B 172)
Moreton Ter. M. S. SW1 . . . . 5G 85 (5B 172)
Moreton Tower. W3. . . . 1H 81
Morford Clo. Ruis 7K 23
Morford Way. Ruis 7K 23
Morgan Av. E17. . . . 4F 35
Morgan Clo. Dag. . . . 7G 57
Morgan Ct. Ashf 5D 112
Morgan Ct. Cars 4D 150
Morgan Ho. SW1 . . . . 4G 85 (4B 172) (off Vauxhall Bri. Rd.)
Morgan Ho. SW8 . . . . 1G 103 (off Wadhurst Rd.)
Morgan Mans. N7. . . . 5A 50 (off Morgan Rd.)
Morgan Rd. N7. . . . 5A 50
Morgan Rd. W10. . . . 5H 65
Morgan Rd. Brom 7J 125
Morgan Rd. Tedd. . . . 6J 115
Morgan's La. SE1 . . . . 1E 86 (5G 169)
Morgan's La. Hay. . . . 5F 59
Morgan St. E3. . . . 3A 70
Morgan St. E16. . . . 5H 71
Morgan Wlk. Beck. . . . 4D 142
Morgan Way. Wfd G 6H 21
Moriatry Clo. N7 . . . . 4J 49
Morie St. SW18. . . . 5K 101
Morieux Rd. E10. . . . 1B 52
Moring Rd. SW17 . . . . 4E 120
Morkyns Wlk. SE21 . . . . 3E 122
Morland Av. Croy. . . . 1E 152
Morland Clo. NW11. . . . 1K 47
Morland Clo. Hamp. . . . 5D 114
Morland Clo. Mitc 3C 138
Morland Ct. W12. . . . 2D 82 (off Coningham Rd.)
Morland Est. E8. . . . 7G 51
Morland Gdns. NW10 . . . . 7K 45
Morland Gdns. S'hall 1F 79
Morland Ho. NW1 . . . . 2G 67 (1B 160) (off Cranleigh St.)
Morland Ho. NW6 . . . . 1J 65
Morland Ho. SW1 . . . . 4J 85 (3E 172) (off Marsham St.)
Morland Ho. W11 . . . . 6G 65 (off Lancaster Rd.)
Morland Rd. E17 . . . . 5K 33
Morland Rd. SE20. . . . 6K 123
Morland Rd. Croy 1E 152
Morland Rd. Dag. . . . 7G 57
Morland Rd. Harr. . . . 5E 26
Morland Rd. Ilf 2F 55
Morland Rd. Sutt. . . . 5A 150
Morley Av. E4 . . . . 7A 20
Morley Av. N18 . . . . 4B 18
Morley Av. N22 . . . . 2A 32
Morley Ct. E4 . . . . 5G 19
Morley Ct. Brom 4H 143
Morley Cres. Edgw 2D 12
Morley Cres. Ruis 2A 42
Morley Cres. E. Stan 2C 26
Morley Cres. W. Stan. . . . 3C 26
Morley Hill. Enf 1J 7
Morley Ho. N16. . . . 2G 51
Morley Rd. E10 . . . . 1E 52
Morley Rd. E15. . . . 2H 71
Morley Rd. SE13 . . . . 4E 106
Morley Rd. Bark 1H 73
Morley Rd. Chst 1G 145
Morley Rd. Romf 5E 38
Morley Rd. Sutt. . . . 1H 149
Morley Rd. Twic 6D 98
Morley St. SE1 . . . . 3A 86 (1K 173)
Morna Rd. SE5 . . . . 2C 104
Morning La. E9 . . . . 6J 51
Morningside Rd. Wor Pk 2D 148
Mornington Av. W14 . . . . 4H 83
Mornington Av. Brom 3A 144
Mornington Av. Ilf 7E 36
Mornington Clo. Wfd G 4D 20
Mornington Ct. NW1 . . . . 2G 67 (off Mornington Cres.)
Mornington Ct. Bex 1K 129
Mornington Cres. NW1 . . . . 2G 67
Mornington Cres. Houn. . . . 1K 95
Mornington Gro. E3. . . . 3C 70
Mornington M. SE5. . . . 1C 104
Mornington Pl. NW1 . . . . 2G 67
Mornington Pl. SE8. . . . 7B 88 (off Mornington Rd.)
Mornington Rd. E4. . . . 7K 9 & 1A 20
Mornington Rd. E11 . . . . 7H 35 (in two parts)
Mornington Rd. SE8 . . . . 7B 88
Mornington Rd. Ashf 5E 112
Mornington Rd. Gnfd 5F 61
Mornington Rd. Wfd G 4C 20
Mornington St. NW1 . . . . 2F 67
Mornington Ter. NW1. . . . 1F 67
Mornington Wlk. Rich 4C 116
Morocco St. SE1. . . . 2E 86 (7G 169)
Morpeth Gro. E9 . . . . 1K 69
Morpeth Mans. SW1 . . . . 4G 85 (3A 172) (off Morpeth Ter.)
Morpeth Rd. E9. . . . 1K 69
Morpeth St. E2 . . . . 3J 69
Morpeth Ter. SW1 . . . . 3G 85 (2A 172)
Morpeth Wlk. N17. . . . 7C 18
Morrab Gdns. Ilf 3K 55
Morrel Ct. E2. . . . 2G 69 (off Goldsmiths Row)
Morrell Clo. New Bar 3F 5
Morris Av. E12 . . . . 5D 54
Morris Blitz Ct. N16. . . . 4F 51
Morris Clo. Croy 5A 142
Morris Ct. E4 . . . . 3J 19
Morris Gdns. SW18 . . . . 7J 101
Morris Ho. E2 . . . . 3J 69 (off Roman Rd.)
Morris Ho. NW8 . . . . 4C 66 (4C 158) (off Salisbury St.)
Morrish Rd. SW2. . . . 7J 103
Morrison Av. E4 . . . . 6H 19
Morrison Av. N17 . . . . 3E 32
Morrison Bldgs. N. E1. . . . 6G 69 (off Commercial Rd.)
Morrison Bldgs. S. E1. . . . 6G 69 (off Commercial Rd.)
Morrison Ct. Barn . . . . 4B 4 (off Manor Way)
Morrison Rd. Bark. . . . 2E 74
Morrison Rd. Hay 3K 59
Morrison St. SW11 . . . . 3E 102
Morris Pl. N4. . . . 2A 50
Morris Rd. E14 . . . . 5D 70
Morris Rd. E15 . . . . 4G 53
Morris Rd. Dag 2F 57
Morris Rd. Iswth 3K 97
Morriss Ho. SE16 . . . . 2H 87 (off Cherry Garden St.)
Morris St. E1. . . . 6H 69
Morritt Ho. Wemb . . . . 5D 44 (off Talbot Rd.)
Morse Clo. E13 . . . . 3J 71
Morshead Mans. W9 . . . . 3J 65 (off Morshead Rd.)
Morshead Rd. W9 . . . . 3J 65
Morson Rd. Enf. . . . 6F 9
Morston Gdns. SE9. . . . 4D 126
Mortain Ho. SE16 . . . . 4H 87 (off Roseberry St.)
Morten Clo. SW4. . . . 6H 103
Morteyne Rd. N17. . . . 1D 32
Mortgramit Sq. SE18 . . . . 3E 90
Mortham St. E15. . . . 1G 71
Mortimer Clo. NW2. . . . 2H 47
Mortimer Clo. SW16 . . . . 2H 121
Mortimer Ct. NW8 . . . . 2A 66 (1A 158) (off Abbey Rd.)
Mortimer Cres. NW6 . . . . 1K 65
Mortimer Cres. Wor Pk 3K 147
Mortimer Dri. Enf. . . . 6J 7
Mortimer Est. NW6 . . . . 1K 65 (off Mortimer Pl.)
Mortimer Ho. W11 . . . . 1F 83
Mortimer Ho. W14 . . . . 4G 83 (off N. End Rd.)
Mortimer Mkt. WC1 . . . . 4G 67 (4B 160)
Mortimer Mkt. Cen. WC1 . . . . 4G 67 (4B 160) (off Mortimer Mkt.)
Mortimer Pl. NW6. . . . 1K 65
Mortimer Rd. E6. . . . 3D 72
Mortimer Rd. N1 . . . . 7E 50 (in two parts)
Mortimer Rd. NW10 . . . . 3E 64
Mortimer Rd. W13 . . . . 6C 62
Mortimer Rd. Eri. . . . 6K 93
Mortimer Rd. Mitc. . . . 1D 138
Mortimer Sq. W11 . . . . 7F 65
Mortimer St. W1. . . . 6G 67 (7K 159)
Mortimer Ter. NW5 . . . . 4F 49
Mortlake. . . . 3K 99
Mortlake Clo. Croy. . . . 3J 151
Mortlake Crematorium. Rich 2J 99
Mortlake Dri. Mitc 1C 138
Mortlake High St. SW14 . . . . 3K 99
Mortlake Rd. E16. . . . 6K 71
Mortlake Rd. Ilf. . . . 4G 55
Mortlake Rd. Rich 7G 81
Mortlake Ter. Rich . . . . 7G 81 (off Mortlake Rd.)
Mortlock Clo. SE15 . . . . 1H 105
Mortlock Ct. E7 . . . . 4B 54
Morton Clo. Wall. . . . 7K 151
Morton Ct. N'holt 5G 43
Morton Cres. N14 . . . . 4C 16
Morton Gdns. Wall 5G 151
Morton M. SW5. . . . 4K 83
Morton Pl. SE1 . . . . 3A 86 (2J 173)
Morton Rd. E15. . . . 7H 53
Morton Rd. N1 . . . . 7C 50
Morton Rd. Mord 5B 138
Morton Way. N14 . . . . 3B 16
Morvale Clo. Belv. . . . 4F 93
Morval Rd. SW2 . . . . 5A 104
Morven Rd. SW17. . . . 3D 120
Morville St. E3. . . . 2C 70
Morwell St. WC1. . . . 5H 67 (6C 160)
Moscow Pl. W2. . . . 7K 65
Moscow Rd. W2 . . . . 7J 65
Mosedale. NW1 . . . . 3G 67 (2K 159) (off Cumberland Mkt.)
Moselle Av. N22 . . . . 2A 32
Moselle Clo. N8. . . . 3K 31
Moselle Ho. N17 . . . . 7A 18 (off William St.)
Moselle Pl. N17. . . . 7A 18
Moselle St. N17. . . . 7A 18
Mossborough Clo. N12 . . . . 6E 14
Mossbury Rd. SW11 . . . . 3C 102
Moss Clo. E1. . . . 5G 69
Moss Clo. Pinn 2D 24
Mossdown Clo. Belv 4G 93
Mossford Ct. Ilf 2F 37
Mossford Grn. Ilf. . . . 3F 37

Mossford La. *Ilf* 2F **37**
Mossford St. *E3* 4B **70**
Moss Gdns. *Felt* 2J **113**
Moss Gdns. *S Croy* 7K **153**
Moss Hall Ct. *N12* 6E **14**
Moss Hall Cres. *N12* 6E **14**
Moss Hall Gro. *N12* 6E **14**
Mossington Gdns. *SE16* 4J **87**
Moss La. *Pinn* 1C **24**
Mosslea Rd. *SE20* . . . . 6J **123** (in two parts)
Mosslea Rd. *Brom* 5B **144**
Mossop St. *SW3* . . . 4C **84** (3D **170**)
Moss Rd. *Dag* 7G **57**
Mossville Gdns. *Mord* 3H **137**
Mosswell Ho. *N10* 1E **30**
Moston Clo. *Hay* 5H **77**
Mostyn Av. *Wemb* 5F **45**
Mostyn Gdns. *NW10* 3F **65**
Mostyn Gro. *E3* 2C **70**
Mostyn Rd. *SW9* 1A **104**
Mostyn Rd. *SW19* 1H **137**
Mostyn Rd. *Edgw* 7F **13**
Mosul Way. *Brom* 6C **144**
Mota M. *N3* 1J **29**
Motcomb St. *SW1* 3E **84** (1G **171**)
Moth Clo. *Wall* 7J **151**
Mothers Sq. *E5* 4H **51**
Motley Av. *EC2* 4G **163**
Motley St. *SW8* 2G **103**
Motspur Park. **6C 136**
Motspur Pk. *N Mald* 6B **136**
Mottingham. **2C 126**
Mottingham Gdns. *SE9* 1B **126**
Mottingham La. *SE9* 1A **126**
Mottingham Rd. *N9* 6E **8**
Mottingham Rd. *SE9* 2C **126**
Mottisfont Rd. *SE2* 3A **92**
Mott St. *E4* 1K **9**
Moules Ct. *SE5* 7C **86**
Moulins Rd. *E9* 7J **51**
Moulsford Ho. *N7* 5H **49**
Moulton Av. *Houn* 2C **96**
Moundfield Rd. *N16* 6G **33**
Mound, The. *SE9* 3E **126**
Mounsey Ho. W10 . . . . *3G* **65** *(off Third Av.)*
Mountacre Clo. *SE26* 4F **123**
Mt. Adon Pk. *SE22* 7G **105**
Mountague Pl. *E14* 7E **70**
Mountain Ho. *SE11* 4K **85** (4H **173**)
Mt. Angelus Rd. *SW15* 7B **100**
Mt. Ararat Rd. *Rich* 5E **98**
Mount Arlington. Brom . . . . *2G* **143** *(off Pk. Hill Rd.)*
Mt. Ash Rd. *SE26* 3H **123**
Mount Av. *E4* 3H **19**
Mount Av. *W5* 5C **62**
Mount Av. *S'hall* 6E **60**
Mountbatten Clo. *SE18* 6J **91**
Mountbatten Clo. *SE19* 5E **122**
Mountbatten Ct. SE16 . . . . . . *1J* **87** *(off Rotherhithe St.)*
Mountbatten Ct. *Buck H* 2G **21**
Mountbatten Gdns. *Beck* . . . 4A **142**
Mountbatten Ho. N6 . . . . *7E* **30** *(off Hillcrest)*
Mountbatten M. *SW18* 7A **102**
Mountbel Rd. *Stan* 1A **26**
Mt. Carmel Chambers. W8 . . . *2J* **83** *(off Dukes La.)*
Mount Clo. *W5* 5C **62**
Mount Clo. *Brom* 1C **144**
Mount Clo. *Cars* 7E **150**
Mount Clo. *Cockf* 4K **5**
Mountcombe Clo. *Surb* 7E **134**
Mount Ct. *SW15* 3G **101**
Mount Ct. *W Wick* 2G **155**
Mt. Culver Av. *Sidc* 6D **128**
Mount Dri. *Bexh* 5E **110**
Mount Dri. *Harr* 5D **24**
Mount Dri. *Wemb* 2J **45**
Mountearl Gdns. *SW16* 3K **121**
Mt. Eaton Ct. W5 . . . . *5C* **62** *(off Mount Av.)*
Mt. Echo Av. *E4* 2J **19**
Mt. Echo Dri. *E4* 1J **19**
Mt. Ephraim La. *SW16* 3H **121**
Mt. Ephraim Rd. *SW16* 3H **121**
Mount Felix. *W on T* 7H **131**
Mountfield Clo. *SE6* 7F **107**
Mountfield Rd. *E6* 2E **72**
Mountfield Rd. *N3* 3H **29**
Mountfield Rd. *W5* 6D **62**
Mountford Rd. *E8* 5G **51**
Mountford St. *E1* 6G **69**
Mountfort Cres. *N1* 7A **50**
Mountfort Ter. *N1* 7A **50**
Mount Gdns. *SE26* 3H **123**
Mount Gro. *Edgw* 3D **12**
Mountgrove Rd. *N5* 3B **50**
Mounthurst Rd. *Brom* 7H **143**
Mountington Pk. Clo. *Harr* . . . 6D **26**
Mountjoy Clo. EC2 . . . . *5C* **68** *(6D* **162***)* *(off Thomas More Highwalk)*
Mountjoy Clo. *SE2* 2B **92**
Mountjoy Ho. *EC2* 6C **162**
Mount Lodge. *N6* 6G **31**
Mount M. *Hamp* 1F **133**
Mount Mills. *EC1* 3B **68** (2B **162**)
Mt. Nod Rd. *SW16* 3K **121**
Mt. Olive Ct. *W7* 2J **79**
Mount Pde. *Barn* 4H **5**
Mount Pk. *Cars* 7E **150**
Mt. Park Av. *Harr* 2H **43**
Mt. Park Av. *S Croy* 7B **152**
Mt. Park Cres. *W5* 6D **62**
Mt. Park Rd. *W5* 5D **62**
Mt. Park Rd. *Harr* 3H **43**
Mt. Park Rd. *Pinn* 5J **23**
Mount Pl. *W3* 1H **81**
Mount Pleasant. N14 . . . . *7C* **6** *(off Wells, The)*
Mount Pleasant. *SE27* 4C **122**
Mount Pleasant. *WC1* 4A **68** (4J **161**)
Mount Pleasant. *Barn* 4H **5**
Mount Pleasant. *Ilf* 5G **55**
Mount Pleasant. *Ruis* 2A **42**
Mount Pleasant. *Wemb* 1E **62**
Mt. Pleasant Cres. *N4* 1K **49**
Mt. Pleasant Hill. *E5* 2H **51**
Mt. Pleasant La. *E5* 1H **51**
Mt. Pleasant Pl. *SE18* 4H **91**
Mt. Pleasant Rd. *E17* 2A **34**
Mt. Pleasant Rd. *N17* 2E **32**
Mt. Pleasant Rd. *NW10* 7E **46**
Mt. Pleasant Rd. *SE13* 6D **106**
Mt. Pleasant Rd. *W5* 4C **62**
Mt. Pleasant Rd. *N Mald* . . . 3J **135**
Mt. Pleasant Vs. *N4* 7K **31**
Mt. Pleasant Wlk. *Bex* 5J **111**
Mount Rd. *NW2* 3D **46**
Mount Rd. *NW4* 6C **28**
Mount Rd. *SW19* 2J **119**
Mount Rd. *Barn* 5H **5**
Mount Rd. *Chess* 5F **147**
Mount Rd. *Dag* 1F **57**
Mount Rd. *Felt* 3C **114**
Mount Rd. *Hay* 2J **77**
Mount Rd. *Mitc* 2B **138**
Mount Rd. *N Mald* 3K **135**
Mount Row. *W1* 7F **67** (3J **165**)
Mountsfield Ct. *SE13* 6F **107**
Mountside. *Stan* 1K **25**
Mounts Pond Rd. *SE3* . . . . . 2F **107** (in two parts)
Mount Sq., The. *NW3* 3A **48**
Mounts Rd. *Bexh* 5D **110**
Mt. Stewart Av. *Harr* 7D **26**
Mount St. *W1* 7E **66** (3G **165**)
Mount St. M. *W1* . . . 7F **67** (3J **165**)
Mount Ter. *E1* 5H **69**
Mount, The. *E5* . . . . 2H **51** (in two parts)
Mount, The. *N20* 2F **15**
Mount, The. *NW3* 3A **48**
Mount, The. *W3* 1J **81**
Mount, The. *Bexh* 5H **111**
Mount, The. *N Mald* 3B **136**
Mount, The. *N'holt* 5F **43**
Mount, The. S Croy . . . . *5C* **152** *(off Warham Rd.)*
Mount, The. *Wemb* 2H **45**
Mount, The. *Wor Pk* 4D **148**
Mount Vernon. *NW3* 4A **48**
Mount Vw. *NW7* 3E **12**
Mount Vw. *W5* 4D **62**
Mount Vw. *Enf* 1E **6**
Mount Vw. *S'hall* 4B **78**
Mountview Clo. *NW11* 1K **47**
Mountview Ct. *N8* 4B **32**
Mount Vw. Rd. *E4* . . . 7K **9** & 1A **20**
Mount Vw. Rd. *N4* 7J **31**
Mount Vw. Rd. *NW9* 5K **27**
Mount Vw. Rd. *Clay* 7B **146**
Mountview Rd. *Orp* . . . . 7K **145** (in two parts)
Mount Vs. *SE27* 3B **122**
Mount Way. *Cars* 7E **150**
Mount Wood. *W Mol* 3F **133**
Movers Lane. (Junct.) 2J **73**
Movers La. *Bark* 1H **73**
Mowat Ct. Wor Pk . . . . *2B* **148** *(off Avenue, The)*
Mowatt Clo. *N19* 2H **49**
Mowbray Ct. *N22* 1A **32**
Mowbray Ct. *SE19* 7F **123**
Mowbray Gdns. *N'holt* 1E **60**
Mowbray Ho. N2 . . . . *2B* **30** *(off Grange, The)*
Mowbray Pde. *Edgw* 4B **12**
Mowbray Pde. *N'holt* 1E **60**
Mowbray Rd. *NW6* 7G **47**
Mowbray Rd. *SE19* 1F **141**
Mowbray Rd. *Edgw* 4B **12**
Mowbray Rd. *New Bar* 5F **5**
Mowbray Rd. *Rich* 3C **116**
Mowbrays Clo. *Romf* 1J **39**
Mowbrays Rd. *Romf* 2J **39**
Mowlem St. *E2* 2H **69**
Mowlem Trad. Est. *N17* 7D **18**
Mowll St. *SW9* 7A **86**
Moxon Clo. *E13* 2H **71**
Moxon St. *W1* 5E **66** (6G **159**)
Moxon St. *Barn* 3C **4**
Moye Clo. *E2* 2G **69**
Moyers Rd. *E10* 7E **34**
Moylan Rd. *W6* 6G **83**
Moyle Ho. SW1 . . . . *5G* **85** *(6B* **172***)* *(off Churchill Gdns.)*
Moyne Ho. *SW9* 5B **104**
Moyne Pl. *NW10* 2G **63**
Moynihan Dri. *N21* 5D **6**
Moys Clo. *Croy* 6J **139**
Moyser Rd. *SW16* 5F **121**
Mozart St. *W10* 3H **65**
Mozart Ter. *SW1* . . . 4E **84** (4H **171**)
Muchelney Rd. *Mord* 6A **138**
Mudlarks Way. *SE10 & SE7* . . . . 3H **89** (in two parts)
Muggeridge Clo. *S Croy* 5D **152**
Muggeridge Rd. *Dag* 4H **57**
Muirdown Av. *SW14* 4K **99**
Muir Dri. *SW18* 6C **102**
Muirfield. *W3* 6A **64**
Muirfield Clo. *SE16* 5H **87**
Muirfield Cres. *E14* 3D **88**
Muirkirk Rd. *SE6* 1E **124**
Muir Rd. *E5* 4G **51**
Muir St. *E16* . . . . 1C **90** (in two parts)
Mulberry Av. *Stai* 1A **112**
Mulberry Bus. Cen. *SE16* 2K **87**
Mulberry Clo. *E4* 2H **19**
Mulberry Clo. *N8* 5J **31**
Mulberry Clo. *NW3* 4B **48**
Mulberry Clo. *NW4* 3E **28**
Mulberry Clo. *SE7* 6B **90**
Mulberry Clo. *SE22* 5G **105**
Mulberry Clo. *SW3* 6B **84** (7B **170**)
Mulberry Clo. *SW16* 4G **121**
Mulberry Clo. *Barn* 4G **5**
Mulberry Clo. *N'holt* 2C **60**
Mulberry Ct. EC1 . . . *3B* **68** *(2B* **162***)* *(off Tompion St.)*
Mulberry Ct. *Bark* 7K **55**
Mulberry Ct. *Surb* 7D **134**
Mulberry Ct. *Twic* 3K **115**
Mulberry Cres. *Bren* 7B **80**
Mulberry Cres. *W Dray* 2C **76**
Mulberry Ho. E2 . . . . *3J* **69** *(off Victoria Pk. Sq.)*
Mulberry Ho. *SE8* 6B **88**
Mulberry Ho. *Short* 1G **143**
Mulberry Housing Co-operative. *SE1* 4K **167**
Mulberry La. *Croy* 1F **153**
Mulberry M. *SE14* 1B **106**
Mulberry M. *Wall* 6G **151**
Mulberry Pde. *W Dray* 3C **76**
Mulberry Pl. E14 . . . . *7E* **70** *(off Clove Cres.)*
Mulberry Pl. *W6* 5C **82**
Mulberry Rd. *E8* 7F **51**
Mulberry St. *E1* 6G **69**
Mulberry Trees. *Shep* 7F **131**
Mulberry Wlk. *SW3* 6B **84** (7B **170**)
Mulberry Way. *E18* 2K **35**
Mulberry Way. *Belv* 2J **93**
Mulberry Way. *Ilf* 4G **37**
Mulgrave Ct. Sutt . . . . *6K* **149** *(off Mulgrave Rd.)*
Mulgrave Rd. *NW10* 4B **46**
Mulgrave Rd. *SE18* 4D **90**
Mulgrave Rd. *SW6* 6H **83**
Mulgrave Rd. *W5* 3D **62**
Mulgrave Rd. *Croy* 3D **152**
Mulgrave Rd. *Harr* 2A **44**
Mulgrave Rd. *Sutt* 7H **149**
Mulholland Clo. *Mitc* 2F **139**
Mulkern Rd. *N19* 1H **49**
Mullards Clo. *Mitc* 1D **150**
Mullen Tower. EC1 . . . . *4A* **68** *(4J* **161***)* *(off Mount Pleasant)*
Muller Ho. *SE18* 5E **90**
Muller Rd. *SW4* 6H **103**
Mullet Gdns. *E2* 3G **69**
Mulletsfield. WC1 . . . *3J* **67** *(2F* **161***)* *(off Cromer St.)*
Mullins Path. *SW14* 3K **99**
Mullion Clo. *Harr* 1F **25**
Mull Wlk. N1 . . . . *6C* **50** *(off Clephane Rd.)*
Mulready Ho. SW1 . . . . *4J* **85** *(4E* **172***)* *(off Marsham St.)*
Mulready St. *NW8* 4C **66** (4C **158**)
Multimedia Ho. *NW10* 4J **63**
Multi Way. *W3* 2A **82**
Multon Ho. *E9* 7J **51**
Multon Rd. *SW18* 7B **102**
Mulvaney Way. *SE1* . . . . 2D **86** (7F **169**) (in two parts)
Mumford Ct. *EC2* 6C **68** (7D **162**)
Mumford Rd. *SE24* 5B **104**
Muncaster Clo. *Ashf* 4C **112**
Muncaster Rd. *SW11* 5D **102**
Muncaster Rd. *Ashf* 5D **112**
Muncies M. *SE6* 2E **124**
Mundania Rd. *SE22* 6H **105**
Munday Ho. SE1 . . . . *3D* **86** *(off Deverell St.)*
Munday Rd. *E16* 7J **71**
Munden St. *W14* 4G **83**
Mundford Rd. *E5* 2J **51**
Mundon Gdns. *Ilf* 1H **55**
Mund St. *W14* 5H **83**
Mundy Ho. *W10* 3G **65**
Mundy St. *N1* 3E **68** (1G **163**)
Mungo Pk. Clo. *Bus H* 2B **10**
Munnings Gdns. *Iswth* 5H **97**
Munnings Ho. E16 . . . . *1K* **89** *(off Portsmouth M.)*
Munro Dri. *N11* 6B **16**
Munro Ho. *SE1* 2A **86** (7J **167**)
Munro M. *W10* . . . . 5G **65** (in two parts)
Munro Ter. *SW10* 7B **84**
Munslow Gdns. *Sutt* 4B **150**
Munster Av. *Houn* 5C **96**
Munster Ct. *SW6* 2H **101**
Munster Ct. *Tedd* 6C **116**
Munster Gdns. *N13* 4G **17**
Munster M. *SW6* 7G **83**
Munster Rd. *SW6* 7G **83**
Munster Rd. *Tedd* 6B **116**
Munster Sq. *NW1* 3F **67** (2K **159**)
Munton Rd. *SE17* 4C **86**
Murchison Av. *Bex* 1D **128**
Murchison Rd. *E10* 2E **52**
Murdoch Ho. SE16 . . . . *3J* **87** *(off Moodkee St.)*
Murdock Clo. *E16* 6H **71**
Murdock St. *SE15* 6H **87**
Murfett Clo. *SW19* 2G **119**
Muriel Ct. *E10* 7D **34**
Muriel St. *N1* . . . . 2K **67** (in two parts)
Murillo Rd. *SE13* 4F **107**
Murphy Ho. SE1 . . . *3B* **86** *(7B* **168***)* *(off Borough Rd.)*
Murphy St. *SE1* 2A **86** (7J **167**)
Murray Av. *Brom* 3K **143**
Murray Av. *Houn* 5F **97**
Murray Ct. *Harr* 6K **25**
Murray Ct. *Twic* 2H **115**
Murray Cres. *Pinn* 1B **24**
Murray Gro. *N1* 2C **68** (1D **162**)
Murray Ho. SE18 . . . . *4D* **90** *(off Rideout St.)*
Murray M. *NW1* 7H **49**
Murray Rd. *SW19* 6F **119**
Murray Rd. *W5* 4C **80**
Murray Rd. *N'wd* 1G **23**
Murray Rd. *Rich* 2B **116**
Murray Sq. *E16* 6J **71**
Murray St. *NW1* 7G **49**
Murray Ter. *NW3* 4A **48**
Murray Ter. *W5* 4D **80**
Mursell Est. *SW8* 1K **103**
Musard Rd. *W6* 6G **83**
Musbury St. *E1* 6J **69**
Muscal. W6 . . . . *6G* **83** *(off Field Rd.)*
Muscatel Pl. *SE5* 1E **104**
Muschamp Rd. *SE15* 3F **105**
Muschamp Rd. *Cars* 2C **150**
Muscovy Ho. Eri . . . . *3E* **92** *(off Kale Rd.)*
Muscovy St. *EC3* . . . 7E **68** (2H **169**)
Museum Chambers. WC1 . . . . *5J* **67** *(6E* **160***)* *(off Bury Pl.)*
Mus. in Docklands. ***7C 70***
Museum La. *SW7* 2B **170**
Mus. of Artillery in the Rotunda. ***5D 90***
Mus. of Classical Art. . . . . ***4H 67 (3C 160)*** ***(off Gower Pl.)***
Mus. of Fulham Palace. ***2G 101***
Mus. of Garden History. . . . . ***3K 85 (2G 173)***
Mus. of London. . . . . ***5C 68 (6C 162)***
Mus. of Methodism. . . . . ***4D 68 (4F 163)***
Mus. of Richmond. . . . . ***5D 98*** ***(off Whittaker Av.)***
Mus. of Rugby, The. ***6J 97***

Mus. of the Order of St John, The. 4B 68 (4A 162)
(off St John's La.)
Museum Pas. E2 3J 69
Museum St. WC1 5J 67 (6E 160)
Musgrave Clo. Barn 1F 5
Musgrave Ct. SW11 1C 102
Musgrave Cres. SW6 7J 83
Musgrave Rd. Iswth 1K 97
Musgrove Rd. SE14 1K 105
Musjid Rd. SW11 2B 102
Musket Clo. E Barn 6G 5
Musquash Way. Houn 2A 96
Muston Rd. E5 2H 51
Mustow Pl. SW6 2H 101
Muswell Av. N10 1F 31
Muswell Hill. 3F 31
Muswell Hill. N10 3F 31
Muswell Hill B'way. N10 3F 31
Muswell Hill Pl. N10 4F 31
Muswell Hill Rd. N6 6E 30
Muswell M. N10 3F 31
Muswell Rd. N10 3F 31
Mutrix Rd. NW6 1J 65
Mutton Pl. NW1 6E 48
Muybridge Rd. N Mald 2J 135
Myatt Rd. SW9 1B 104
Myatts Fields S. SW9 2A 104
(off St Lawrence Way)
Mycenae Rd. SE3 7J 89
Myddelton Av. Enf 1K 7
Myddelton Clo. Enf 1A 8
Myddelton Gdns. N21 7H 7
Myddelton Pk. N20 3G 15
Myddelton Pas. EC1 3A 68 (1K 161)
Myddelton Rd. N8 3J 31
Myddelton Sq. EC1 3A 68 (1K 161)
Myddelton St. EC1 3A 68 (2K 161)
Myddleton Av. N4 2C 50
Myddleton Ho. N1 2A 68 (1J 161)
(off Pentonville Rd.)
Myddleton M. N22 7D 16
Myddleton Rd. N22 7D 16
Myers La. SE14 6K 87
Mylis Clo. SE26 4H 123
Mylius Clo. SE14 7J 87
Mylne Clo. W6 5C 82
Mylne St. EC1 3A 68 (1J 161)
Myra St. SE2 5A 92
Myrdle St. E1 5G 69
Myrna Clo. SW19 7C 120
Myron Pl. SE13 3E 106
Myrtle Av. Felt 5G 95
Myrtle Av. Ruis 7J 23
Myrtleberry Clo. E8 6F 51
(off Beechwood Rd.)
Myrtle Clo. E Barn 1J 15
Myrtle Clo. Uxb 5B 58
Myrtle Clo. W Dray 3B 76
Myrtledene Rd. SE2 5A 92
Myrtle Gdns. W7 1J 79
Myrtle Gro. Enf 1J 7
Myrtle Gro. N Mald 2J 135
Myrtle Rd. E6 1D 72
Myrtle Rd. E17 6A 34
Myrtle Rd. N13 3H 17
Myrtle Rd. W3 1J 81
Myrtle Rd. Croy 3C 154
Myrtle Rd. Hamp H 6G 115
Myrtle Rd. Houn 2G 97
Myrtle Rd. Ilf 2F 55
Myrtle Rd. Sutt 5A 150
Myrtle Wlk. N1 2E 68 (1G 163)
Mysore Rd. SW11 3D 102
Myton Rd. SE21 3D 122
Mytton Ho. SW8 7K 85
(off St Stephens Ter.)

Nadine Ct. Wall 7G 151
Nadine St. SE7 5A 90
Nagasaki Wlk. SE7 3K 89
Nagle Clo. E17 2F 35
Nag's Head. (Junct.) 3J 49
Nags Head Ct. EC1 4D 162
Nags Head La. Well 3B 110
Nags Head Rd. Enf 4D 8
Nags Head Shop. Cen. N7 4K 49
Nailsworth Ct. SE15 6E 86
(off Birdlip Clo.)
Nainby Ho. SE11 4J 173
Nairne Gro. SE24 5D 104
Nairn Rd. Ruis 6A 42
Nairn St. E14 5E 70
Naish Ct. N1 1J 67
(in three parts)
Naldera Gdns. SE3 6J 89
Nallhead Rd. Felt 5A 114
Namba Roy Clo. SW16 4K 121
Namton Dri. T Hth 4K 139
Nan Clark's La. NW7 2F 13
Nankin St. E14 6C 70
Nansen Ho. NW10 7K 45
(off Stonebridge Pk.)
Nansen Rd. SW11 3E 102
Nansen Village. N12 4E 14
Nant Ct. NW2 2H 47
Nantes Clo. SW18 4A 102
Nantes Pas. E1 5F 69 (5J 163)
Nant Rd. NW2 2H 47
Nant St. E2 3H 69
Naoroji St. WC1 3A 68 (2J 161)
Napier. NW9 1B 28
Napier Av. E14 5C 88
Napier Av. SW6 3H 101
Napier Clo. SE8 7B 88
Napier Clo. W14 3G 83
Napier Clo. W Dray 3B 76
Napier Ct. N1 2D 68
(off Cropley St.)
Napier Ct. SW6 3H 101
(off Ranelagh Gdns.)
Napier Ct. Hay 4A 60
(off Dunedin Way)
Napier Gro. N1 2C 68
Napier Pl. W14 3H 83
Napier Rd. E6 1E 72
Napier Rd. E11 4G 53
Napier Rd. E15 2G 71
(in two parts)
Napier Rd. N17 3E 32
Napier Rd. NW10 3D 64
Napier Rd. SE25 4H 141
Napier Rd. W14 3G 83
Napier Rd. Ashf 7F 113
Napier Rd. Belv 4F 93
Napier Rd. Brom 4K 143
Napier Rd. Enf 5E 8
Napier Rd. Iswth 4A 98
Napier Rd. H'row A 1A 94
Napier Rd. S Croy 7D 152
Napier Rd. Wemb 6D 44
Napier St. SE8 7B 88
(off Napier Clo.)
Napier Ter. N1 7B 50
Napier Wlk. Ashf 7F 113
Napoleon Rd. E5 3H 51
Napoleon Rd. Twic 7B 98
Napton Clo. Hay 4C 60
Narbonne Av. SW4 5G 103
Narborough Clo. Uxb 2E 40
Narborough St. SW6 2K 101
Narcissus Rd. NW6 5J 47
Nardini. NW9 1B 28
(off Concourse, The)
Naresby Fold. Stan 6H 11
Narford Rd. E5 3G 51
Narrow Boat Clo. SE28 2H 91
Narrow St. E14 7K 69
(off Highway, The)
Narrow St. W3 1H 81
Narrow Way. Brom 6C 144
Narvic Ho. SE5 2C 104
Nascot St. W12 6E 64
Naseby Clo. NW6 7A 48
Naseby Clo. Iswth 1J 97
Naseby Ct. Sidc 4K 127
Naseby Rd. SE19 6D 122
Naseby Rd. Dag 3G 57
Naseby Rd. Ilf 1D 36
Nash. 6J 155
Nash Clo. Sutt 3B 150
Nash Ct. E14 1D 88
(off Nash Pl.)
Nash Ct. Kent 6B 26
Nashe Ho. SE1 3D 86
(off Burbage Clo.)
Nash Grn. Brom 6J 125
Nash Ho. E17 3D 34
Nash Ho. SW1 5F 85 (6K 171)
(off Lupus St.)
Nash La. Kes 7J 155
Nash Pl. E14 1D 88
Nash Rd. N9 2D 18
Nash Rd. SE4 4A 106
Nash Rd. Chad H 4D 38
Nash St. NW1 3F 67 (1K 159)
Nash Way. Kent 6B 26
Nasmyth St. W6 3D 82
Nassau Path. SE28 1C 92
Nassau Rd. SW13 1B 100
Nassau St. W1 5G 67 (6A 160)
Nassington Rd. NW3 4D 48
Natalie Clo. Felt 7F 95
Natalie M. Twic 3H 115
Natal Rd. N11 6D 16
Natal Rd. SW16 6H 121
Natal Rd. Ilf 4F 55
Natal Rd. T Hth 3D 140
Nathan Ct. N9 7D 8
(off Causeyware Rd.)
Nathan Ho. SE11 4A 86 (4K 173)
(off Reedworth St.)
Nathaniel Clo. E1 5F 69 (6K 163)
Nathaniel Ct. E17 7A 34
Nathans Rd. Wemb 1C 44
Nathan Way. SE28 4H 91
National Army Mus. 6D 84 (7F 171)
National Film Theatre, The. 4H 167
National Gallery. 7H 67 (3D 166)
National Gallery (Sainsbury Wing). 3D 166
National Maritime Mus. 6F 89
National Portrait Gallery. 3E 166
Nation Way. E4 1K 19
Natural History Mus. 3B 84 (2A 170)
Nautilus Building, The. EC1 3A 68 (1K 161)
(off Myddelton Pas.)
Naval Ho. E14 7F 71
(off Quixley St.)
Naval Row. E14 7E 70
Naval Wlk. Brom 2J 143
(off Mitre Clo.)
Navarino Gro. E8 6G 51
Navarino Mans. E8 6G 51
Navarino Rd. E8 6G 51
Navarre Rd. E6 2C 72
Navarre St. E2 4F 69 (3J 163)
Navenby Wlk. E3 4C 70
Navestock Clo. E4 3K 19
Navestock Cres. Wfd G 7F 21
Navestock Ho. Bark 2B 74
Navigation Dri. Enf 1H 9
Navigator Dri. S'hall 2G 79
Navy St. SW4 3H 103
Nayland Ho. SE6 4E 124
Naylor Gro. Enf 5E 8
Naylor Ho. W10 3G 65
Naylor Rd. N20 2F 15
Naylor Rd. SE15 7H 87
Nazareth Gdns. SE15 2H 105
Nazrul St. E2 3F 69 (1J 163)
Neagle Ho. NW2 3E 46
(off Stoll Clo.)
Neal Av. S'hall 4D 60
Neal Clo. N'wd 1J 23
Nealden St. SW9 3K 103
Neale Clo. N2 3A 30
Neal St. WC2 6J 67 (1E 166)
Neal's Yd. WC2 6J 67 (1E 166)
Near Acre. NW9 1B 28
Neasden. 3A 46
Neasden Clo. NW10 5A 46
Neasden Junction. (Junct.) 4K 45
Neasden La. NW10 3A 46
(in two parts)
Neasden La. N. NW10 3K 45
Neasham Rd. Dag 5B 56
Neate St. SE5 6E 86
(in two parts)
Neath Gdns. Mord 6A 138
Neath Ho. SE24 6B 104
(off Dulwich Rd.)
Neathouse Pl. SW1 4G 85 (3A 172)
Neats Acre. Ruis 7F 23
Neatscourt Rd. E6 5B 72
Nebraska St. SE1 2D 86 (7E 168)
Neckinger. SE16 3F 87
Neckinger Est. SE16 3F 87
Neckinger St. SE1 2F 87 (7K 169)
Nectarine Way. SE13 2D 106
Needham Ho. SE11 4J 173
Needham Rd. W11 6J 65
Needham Ter. NW2 3F 47
Needleman St. SE16 2K 87
Needwood Ho. N4 1C 50
Neela Clo. Uxb 4D 40
Neeld Cres. NW4 5D 28
Neeld Cres. Wemb 5G 45
Neeld Pde. Wemb 5F 45
Neil Clo. Ashf 5E 112
Neil Wates Cres. SW2 1A 122
Nelgarde Rd. SE6 7C 106
Nella Rd. W6 6F 83
Nelldale Rd. SE16 4J 87
Nellgrove Rd. Uxb 4D 58
Nell Gwynne Av. Shep 6F 131
Nello James Gdns. SE27 4D 122
Nelson Clo. NW6 3J 65
(off Cambridge Rd.)
Nelson Clo. Croy 1B 152
Nelson Clo. Felt 1H 113
Nelson Clo. Romf 1H 39
Nelson Clo. Uxb 3D 58
Nelson Clo. W on T 7K 131
Nelson Ct. SE1 2B 86 (6B 168)
Nelson Ct. SE16 1J 87
(off Brunel Rd.)
Nelson Gdns. E2 3G 69
Nelson Gdns. Houn 6E 96
Nelson Gro. Rd. SW19 1A 138
Nelson Ho. SW1 6G 85 (7B 172)
(off Dolphin Sq.)
Nelson Ind. Est. SW19 1K 137
Nelson La. Uxb 3D 58
Nelson Mandela Clo. N10 2E 30
Nelson Mandela Rd. SE3 3A 108
Nelson Pas. EC1 3C 68 (1D 162)
Nelson Pl. N1 2B 68 (1B 162)
Nelson Pl. Sidc 4A 128
Nelson Rd. E4 6J 19
Nelson Rd. E11 4J 35
Nelson Rd. N8 5K 31
Nelson Rd. N9 2C 18
Nelson Rd. N15 4E 32
Nelson Rd. SE10 6E 88
Nelson Rd. SW19 7K 119
Nelson Rd. Ashf 5A 112
Nelson Rd. Belv 5F 93
Nelson Rd. Brom 4A 144
Nelson Rd. Enf 6E 8
Nelson Rd. Harr 1H 43
Nelson Rd. Houn & Twic 6E 96
Nelson Rd. H'row A 1B 94
Nelson Rd. N Mald 5K 135
Nelson Rd. Sidc 4A 128
Nelson Rd. Stan 6H 11
Nelson Rd. Uxb 3D 58
Nelson Rd. M. SW19 7K 119
Nelson's Column. 1J 85 (4E 166)
Nelson Sq. SE1 2B 86 (6A 168)
Nelson's Row. SW4 4H 103
Nelson St. E1 6H 69
Nelson St. E6 2D 72
(in two parts)
Nelson St. E16 7H 71
(in two parts)
Nelsons Yd. NW1 2G 67
(off Mornington Cres.)
Nelson Ter. N1 2B 68
Nelson Wlk. SE16 1A 88
Nelson Wlk. Eps 7G 147
Nemoure Rd. W3 7J 63
Nene Gdns. Felt 2D 114
Nene Rd. H'row A 1D 94
Nene Rd. Roundabout. H'row A 1D 94
Nepaul Rd. SW11 2C 102
Nepean St. SW15 6C 100
Neptune Ct. E14 4C 88
(off Homer Dri.)
Neptune Ho. SE16 3J 87
(off Moodkee St.)
Neptune Rd. Harr 6H 25
Neptune Rd. H'row A 1E 94
Neptune St. SE16 3J 87
Neptune Wlk. Eri 4K 93
Nero Ct. Bren 7D 80
Nesbit Rd. SE9 4B 108
Nesbitt Clo. SE3 3G 107
Nesbitts All. Barn 3C 4
Nesbitt Sq. SE19 7E 122
Nesham St. E1 7G 69
Ness St. SE16 3G 87
Nesta Rd. Wfd G 6B 20
Nestles Av. Hay 3H 77
Nestor Av. N21 6G 7
Nestor Ho. E2 2H 69
(off Old Bethnal Grn. Rd.)
Netheravon Rd. W4 4B 82
Netheravon Rd. W7 1K 79
Netheravon Rd. S. W4 5B 82
Netherbury Rd. W5 3D 80
Netherby Gdns. Enf 4D 6
Netherby Rd. SE23 7J 105
Nether Clo. N3 7D 14
Nethercourt Av. N3 6D 14
Netherfield Gdns. Bark 6H 55
Netherfield Rd. N12 5E 14
Netherfield Rd. SW17 3E 120
Netherford Rd. SW4 2G 103
Netherhall Gdns. NW3 6A 48
Netherhall Way. NW3 5A 48
Netherlands Rd. Barn 6G 5
Netherleigh Clo. N6 1F 49
Nether St. N3 & N12 1J 29
Netherton Gro. SW10 6A 84
Netherton Rd. N15 6D 32
Netherton Rd. Twic 5A 98
Netherwood. N2 2B 30
Netherwood Pl. W14 3F 83
(off Netherwood Rd.)
Netherwood Rd. W14 3F 83
Netherwood St. NW6 7H 47
Nethewode Ct. Belv 3H 93
(off Lwr. Park Rd.)
Netley. SE5 1E 104
(off Redbridge Gdns.)
Netley Clo. Cheam 5F 149
Netley Clo. New Ad 7E 154
Netley Dri. W on T 7D 132
Netley Gdns. Mord 7A 138
Netley Rd. E17 5B 34
Netley Rd. Bren 6E 80
Netley Rd. Ilf 5H 37
Netley Rd. Mord 7A 138
Netley St. NW1 3G 67 (2A 160)

Nettlecombe. NW1 7H 49 (off Agar Gro.)
Nettleden Av. Wemb 6G 45
Nettleden Ho. SW3 4C 84 (4D 170) (off Marlborough St.)
Nettlefold Pl. SE27 3B 122
Nettlestead Clo. Beck 7B 124
Nettleton Ct. EC2 5C 68 (6C 162) (off London Wall)
Nettleton Rd. SE14 1K 105
Nettleton Rd. H'row A 1D 94
Nettleton Rd. Uxb 4B 40
Nettlewood Rd. SW16 7H 121
Neuchatel Rd. SE6 2B 124
Nevada Clo. N Mald 4J 135
Nevada St. SE10 6E 88
Nevern Mans. SW5 5J 83 (off Warwick Rd.)
Nevern Pl. SW5 4J 83
Nevern Rd. SW5 4J 83
Nevern Sq. SW5 4J 83
Nevil Ho. SW9 2B 104 (off Loughborough Est.)
Nevill Ct. EC4 6A 68 (7K 161) (off E. Harding St.)
Neville Av. N Mald 1K 135
Neville Clo. E11 3H 53
Neville Clo. NW1 2H 67
Neville Clo. NW6 2H 65
Neville Clo. SE15 1G 105
Neville Clo. W3 2J 81
Neville Clo. Houn 2F 97
Neville Clo. Sidc 4K 127
Neville Ct. NW8 1A 158
Neville Dri. N2 6A 30
Neville Gdns. Dag 3D 56
Neville Gill Clo. SW18 6J 101
Neville Ho. N11 4K 15
Neville Ho. N22 1K 31 (off Neville Pl.)
Neville Ho. Yd. King T 2E 134
Neville Pl. N22 1K 31
Neville Rd. E7 7J 53
Neville Rd. NW6 2H 65
Neville Rd. W5 4D 62
Neville Rd. Croy 7D 140
Neville Rd. Dag 2D 56
Neville Rd. Ilf 1G 37
Neville Rd. King T 2G 135
Neville Rd. Rich 3C 116
Nevilles Ct. NW2 3C 46
Neville St. SW7 5B 84 (5A 170)
Neville Ter. SW7 5B 84 (5A 170)
Neville Wlk. Cars 7C 138
Nevill Rd. N16 4E 50
Nevin Dri. E4 1J 19
Nevin Ho. Hay 3E 76
Nevinson Clo. SW18 6B 102
Nevis Rd. SW17 2E 120
Nevitt Ho. N1 2D 68 (off Cranston Est.)
New Acres Rd. SE28 2J 91 (in three parts)
Newall Ho. SE1 3C 86 (off Bath Ter.)
Newall Rd. H'row A 1E 94
Newark Cres. NW10 3K 63
Newarke Ho. SW9 2B 104
Newark Knok. E6 6E 72
Newark Pde. NW4 3C 28
Newark Rd. S Croy 6D 152
Newark St. E1 5H 69 (in two parts)
Newark Way. NW4 4C 28
New Ash Clo. N2 3B 30
New Atlas Wharf. E14 3C 88 (off Arnhem Pl.)
New Baltic Wharf. SE8 5A 88 (off Evelyn St.)
New Barn Clo. Wall 6K 151
New Barnet 4G 5
New Barn Rd. Swan 7K 129
New Barns Av. Mitc 4H 139 (in two parts)
New Barn St. E13 4J 71
New Barns Way. Chig 3K 21
New Beckenham 6B 124
New Bentham Ct. N1 7C 50 (off Ecclesbourne Rd.)
Newbery Ho. N1 7C 50 (off Northampton St.)
Newbold Cotts. E1 6J 69
Newbolt Av. Sutt 5E 148
Newbolt Ho. SE17 5D 86 (off Brandon St.)
Newbolt Rd. Stan 5E 10
New Bond St. W1 6F 67 (1J 165)
Newborough Grn. N Mald 4K 135
New Brent St. NW4 5E 28
Newbridge Point. SE23 3K 123 (off Windrush La.)
New Bri. St. EC4 6B 68 (1A 168)
New Broad St. EC2 5E 68 (6G 163)
New B'way. W5 7D 62
New B'way. Hamp H 5H 115
New B'way. Uxb 3D 58
Newburgh Rd. W3 1J 81
Newburgh St. W1 6G 67 (1B 166)
New Burlington M. W1 7G 67 (2A 166)
New Burlington Pl. W1 7G 67 (2A 166)
New Burlington St. W1 7G 67 (2A 166)
Newburn Ho. SE11 5K 85 (5H 173) (off Newburn St.)
Newburn St. SE11 5K 85 (5H 173)
Newbury Clo. N'holt 6D 42
Newbury Ct. Sidc 4K 127
Newbury Gdns. Eps 4B 148
Newbury Ho. N22 1J 31
Newbury Ho. SW9 2B 104
Newbury Ho. W2 6K 65 (off Hallfield Est.)
Newbury M. NW5 6E 48
Newbury Park 5G 37
Newbury Rd. E4 6K 19
Newbury Rd. Brom 3J 143
Newbury Rd. Ilf 6J 37
Newbury Rd. H'row A 1B 94
Newbury St. EC1 5C 68 (6C 162)
Newbury Way. N'holt 6C 42
New Bus. Cen., The. NW10 3B 64
New Butt La. SE8 7C 88
New Butt La. N. SE8 7C 88 (off Hales St.)
New B'way Bldgs. W5 7D 62
Newby. NW1 3G 67 (2A 160) (off Robert St.)
Newby Clo. Enf 2K 7
Newby Ho. E14 7E 70 (off Newby Pl.)
Newby Pl. E14 7E 70
Newby St. SW8 3F 103
New Caledonian Wharf. SE16 3B 88
Newcastle Clo. EC4 6B 68 (7A 162)
Newcastle Ct. EC4 7C 68 (2D 168) (off College Hill)
Newcastle Ho. W1 5E 66 (5G 159) (off Luxborough St.)
Newcastle Pl. W2 5B 66 (5B 158)
Newcastle Row. EC1 4A 68 (4K 161)
New Cavendish St. W1 5E 66 (6H 159)
New Change. EC4 6C 68 (1C 168)
New Chapel Sq. Felt 1K 113
New Charles St. EC1 3B 68 (1B 162)
New Charlton 4A 90
New Chu. Rd. SE5 7C 86 (in three parts)
New City Rd. E13 3A 72
New Clo. SW19 3A 138
New Clo. Felt 5C 114
New Colebrooke Ct. Cars 7E 150 (off Stanley Rd.)
New College Ct. NW3 6A 48 (off Finchley Rd.)
New College M. N1 7A 50
New College Pde. NW3 6B 48 (off College Cres.)
Newcombe Gdns. SW16 4J 121
Newcombe Gdns. Houn 4D 96
Newcombe Pk. NW7 5F 13
Newcombe Pk. Wemb 1F 63
Newcombe Ri. W Dray 6A 58
Newcombe St. W8 1J 83
Newcomen Rd. E11 3H 53
Newcomen Rd. SW11 3B 102
Newcomen St. SE1 2D 86 (6E 168)
New Compton St. WC2 6H 67 (1D 166)
New Concordia Wharf. SE1 2G 87 (6K 169)
New Ct. EC4 2J 167
New Ct. N'holt 5F 43
Newcourt Ho. E2 3H 69 (off Pott St.)
Newcourt St. NW8 2C 66 (1C 158)
New Covent Garden Market 7H 85
New Coventry St. W1 7H 67 (3D 166)
New Crane Pl. E1 1J 87
New Crane Wharf. E1 1J 87 (off New Crane Pl.)
New Cres. Yd. NW10 2B 64
Newcroft Clo. Uxb 5B 58
New Cross 7B 88
New Cross. (Junct.) 1A 106
New Cross Gate 1K 105
New Cross Gate. (Junct.) 1K 105
New Cross Rd. SE15 & SE14 7J 87
Newdales Clo. N9 2B 18
Newdene Av. N'holt 2B 60
Newdigate Ho. E14 6B 70 (off Norbiton Rd.)
Newell St. E14 6B 70
New Eltham 2G 127
New End. NW3 4A 48
New End Sq. NW3 4B 48
New England Ind. Est. Bark 2G 73
Newent Clo. SE15 7E 86
New Era Est. N1 1E 68 (off Phillipp St.)
New Farm Av. Brom 4J 143
New Farm La. N'wd 1G 23
New Fetter La. EC4 6A 68 (7K 161)
Newfield Clo. Hamp 1E 132
Newfield Ri. NW2 3D 46
New Forest La. Chig 6K 21
Newgale Gdns. Edgw 1F 27
New Garden Dri. W Dray 2A 76
Newgate. Croy 1C 152
Newgate Clo. Felt 2C 114
Newgate St. E4 3B 20 (in two parts)
Newgate St. EC1 6B 68 (7B 162)
New Globe Wlk. SE1 1C 86 (4C 168)
New Goulston St. E1 6F 69 (7J 163)
New Grn. Pl. SE19 6E 122
Newham Grn. N22 1A 32
Newham's Row. SE1 2E 86 (7H 169)
Newham Way. E16 & E6 5H 71
Newhaven Clo. Hay 4H 77
Newhaven Cres. Ashf 5F 113
Newhaven Gdns. SE9 4B 108
Newhaven La. E16 4H 71
Newhaven Rd. SE25 5D 140
New Heston Rd. Houn 7D 78
New Horizons Ct. Bren 6C 80
Newhouse Av. Romf 3D 38
Newhouse Clo. N Mald 7A 136
Newhouse Wlk. Mord 7A 138
Newick Clo. Bex 6H 111
Newick Rd. E5 4H 51
Newing Grn. Brom 7B 126
Newington 3C 86
Newington Barrow Way. N7 3K 49
Newington Butts. SE11 & SE1 4B 86
Newington Causeway. SE1 3B 86 (7C 168)
Newington Ct. Bus. Cen. SE1 7C 168
Newington Grn. N1 & N16 5D 50
Newington Grn. Mans. N16 5D 50
Newington Grn. Rd. N1 6D 50
Newington Ind. Est. SE17 4C 86 (off Crampton St.)
New Inn B'way. EC2 4E 68 (3H 163)
New Inn Pas. WC2 1H 167
New Inn Sq. EC2 3H 163
New Inn St. EC2 4E 68 (3H 163)
New Inn Yd. EC2 4E 68 (3H 163)
New Jubilee Ct. Wfd G 7D 20
New Jubilee Wharf. E1 1J 87 (off Wapping Wall)
New Kelvin Av. Tedd 6J 115
New Kent Rd. SE1 3C 86
New Kings Rd. SW6 2H 101
New King St. SE8 6C 88
Newland Ct. EC1 2E 162
Newland Dri. Enf 1C 8
Newland Gdns. W13 2A 80
Newland Ho. N8 3J 31 (off Newland Rd.)
Newland Ho. SE14 6K 87 (off John Williams Clo.)
Newland Rd. N8 3J 31
Newlands 5K 105 **(Brockley)**
Newlands 3K 11 **(Edgware)**
Newlands. NW1 3G 67 (1A 160) (off Harrington St.)
Newlands Av. Th Dit 7J 133
Newlands Clo. Edgw 3K 11
Newlands Clo. S'hall 5C 78
Newlands Clo. Wemb 6C 44
Newlands Ct. SE9 6E 108
Newlands Pk. SE26 6J 123
Newlands Pl. Barn 5A 4
Newlands Quay. E1 7J 69
Newlands Rd. SW16 2J 139
Newlands Rd. Wfd G 2C 20
Newlands, The. Wall 7G 151
Newland St. E16 1C 90
Newlands Way. Chess 5C 146
Newlands Wood. Croy 7B 154
Newling Clo. E6 6D 72
New London St. EC3 2H 169
New London Theatre 6J 67 (7F 161) (off Drury La.)
New Lydenburg Commercial Est. SE7 3A 90
New Lydenburg St. SE7 3A 90
Newlyn. NW1 1G 67 (off Plender St.)
Newlyn Clo. Uxb 5C 58
Newlyn Gdns. Harr 7D 24
Newlyn Ho. Pinn 1D 24
Newlyn Rd. N17 1F 33
Newlyn Rd. Barn 4C 4
Newlyn Rd. Well 2K 109
New Malden 4A 136
Newman Pas. W1 5G 67 (6B 160)
Newman Rd. E13 3K 71
Newman Rd. E17 5K 33
Newman Rd. Brom 1J 143
Newman Rd. Croy 1K 151
Newman Rd. Hay 7K 59
Newman Rd. Ind. Est. Croy 7K 139
Newman's Ct. EC3 1F 169
Newmans La. Surb 6D 134
Newman's Row. WC2 5K 67 (6H 161)
Newman St. W1 5G 67 (6B 160)
Newman's Way. Barn 1F 5
Newman Yd. W1 6G 67 (7C 160)
Newmarket Av. N'holt 5E 42
Newmarket Grn. SE9 7B 108
Newmarsh Rd. SE28 1K 91
Newmill Ho. E3 4E 70
Newminster Rd. Mord 6A 138
New Mt. St. E15 7F 53
Newnes Path. SW15 4D 100
Newnet Clo. Cars 1D 150
Newnham Av. Ruis 1A 42
Newnham Clo. N'holt 6G 43
Newnham Clo. T Hth 2C 140
Newnham Gdns. N'holt 6G 43
Newnham Lodge. Belv 5G 93 (off Erith Rd.)
Newnham M. N22 7E 16
Newnham Rd. N22 1K 31
Newnhams Clo. Brom 3D 144
Newnham Ter. SE1 3A 86 (1J 173)
Newnham Way. Harr 5E 26
New N. Pl. EC2 4E 68 (3G 163)
New N. Rd. N1 7C 50 (1F 163)
New N. Rd. Ilf 1G 37
New N. St. WC1 5K 67 (5G 161)
Newnton Clo. N4 7D 32 (in two parts)
New Oak Rd. N2 2A 30
New Orleans Wlk. N19 7H 31
New Oxford St. WC1 6H 67 (7D 160)
New Pde. Ashf 4B 112
New Pde. W Dray 1A 76
New Pk. Av. N13 3H 17
New Pk. Clo. N'holt 6C 42
New Pk. Est. N18 5D 18
New Pk. Ho. N13 4E 16
New Pk. Pde. SW2 7J 103 (off New Pk. Rd.)
New Pk. Rd. SW2 1H 121
New Pk. Rd. Ashf 5E 112
New Pl. Croy 6C 154
New Pl. Sq. SE16 3H 87
New Plaistow Rd. E15 1G 71
New Pond Pde. Ruis 3J 41
Newport Av. E13 4K 71
Newport Av. E14 7F 71
Newport Ct. WC2 7H 67 (2D 166)
Newport Ho. E3 3A 70 (off Strahan Rd.)
Newport Lodge. Enf 5K 7 (off Village Rd.)
Newport Pl. WC2 7H 67 (2D 166)
Newport Rd. E10 2E 52
Newport Rd. E17 4A 34
Newport Rd. SW13 1C 100
Newport Rd. Hay 5F 59
Newport Rd. H'row A 1C 94
Newport St. SE11 4K 85 (4G 173)
New Priory Ct. NW6 7J 47 (off Mazenod Av.)
Newquay Cres. Harr 2C 42

Newquay Ho. SE11 5A 86 (5J 173)
Newquay Rd. SE6 2D 124
New Quebec St. W1 6D 66 (1F 165)
New Ride. SW7 & SW1 2C 84 (6C 164)
New River Ct. N5 4C 50
New River Cres. N13 4G 17
New River Head. EC1 3A 68 (2K 161)
New River Wlk. N1 6C 50
New River Way. N4 7D 32
New Rd. E1 5H 69
New Rd. E4 4J 19
New Rd. N8 5J 31
New Rd. N9 3B 18
New Rd. N17 1F 33
New Rd. N22 1C 32
New Rd. NW7 7B 14
New Rd. SE2 4D 92
New Rd. Bedf 1K 113
New Rd. Bren 6D 80
New Rd. Dag 2G 75
New Rd. Felt 6F 95
New Rd. Hanw 5C 114
New Rd. Harr 4K 43
New Rd. Hay 7E 76
New Rd. Houn 4F 97
New Rd. Ilf 2J 55
New Rd. King T 7G 117
New Rd. Mitc 1D 150
New Rd. Rich 4C 116
New Rd. Shep 3C 130
New Rd. Uxb 4E 58
New Rd. Well 2B 110
New Rd. W Mol 4E 132
New Rd. Hill. Kes & Orp 7C 156
New Rochford St. NW5 5D 48
New Row. WC2 7J 67 (2E 166)
Newry Rd. Twic 5A 98
Newsam Av. N15 5D 32
Newsholme Av. N21 5E 6
New Southgate 5A 16
New Southgate Crematorium. N11 3A 16
New Southgate Ind. Est. N11 5B 16
New Spitalfields Market 3D 52
New Spring Gdns. Wlk. SE1 & SE11 5J 85
New Sq. WC2 6A 68 (7J 161)
New Sq. Felt 1E 112
New Sq. Pas. WC2 7J 161
Newstead Clo. N12 6H 15
Newstead Ct. N'holt 3C 60
Newstead Rd. SE12 7H 107
Newstead Wlk. Cars 7A 138
Newstead Way. SW19 4F 119
New St. EC2 5E 68 (6H 163)
New St. Hill. Brom 5K 125
New St. Sq. EC4 6A 68 (7K 161)
Newton Av. N10 1E 30
Newton Av. W3 2J 81
Newton Clo. E17 6A 34
Newton Clo. Harr 2E 42
Newton Gro. W4 4A 82
Newton Ho. E1 7H 69 (off Cornwall St.)
Newton Ho. E17 3D 34 (off Prospect Hill)
Newton Ho. NW8 1K 65 (off Abbey Rd.)
Newton Ho. SE20 7K 123
Newton Ind. Est. Romf 4D 38
Newton Mans. W14 6G 83 (off Queen's Club Gdns.)
Newton Pl. E14 4C 88
Newton Point. E16 6H 71 (off Clarkson Rd.)
Newton Rd. E15 5F 53
Newton Rd. N15 5G 33
Newton Rd. NW2 4E 46
Newton Rd. SW19 7G 119
Newton Rd. W2 6K 65
Newton Rd. Harr 2J 25
Newton Rd. Isw th 2K 97
Newton Rd. H'row A 1A 94
Newton Rd. Well 3A 110
Newton Rd. Wemb 7F 45
Newton St. WC2 6J 67 (7F 161)
Newton's Yd. SW18 5J 101
Newton Ter. Brom 6B 144
Newton Wlk. Edgw 1H 27
Newton Way. N18 5H 17
New Tower Bldgs. E1 1H 87
Newtown St. SW11 1F 103
New Trinity Rd. N2 3B 30
New Turnstile. WC1 5K 67 (off High Holborn)
New Union Clo. E14 3E 88
New Union St. EC2 5D 68 (6E 162)
New Wanstead. E11 6H 35
New Way Rd. NW9 4A 28
New Wharf Rd. N1 2J 67
Newyears Green 7B 22
Newyears Grn. La. Hare 6A 22
New Zealand Av. W on T 7H 131
New Zealand Way. W12 7D 64
Niagara Av. W5 4C 80
Niagra Clo. N1 2C 68
Niagra Ct. SE16 3J 87 (off Canada Est.)
Nibthwaite Rd. Harr 5J 25
Nicholas Clo. Gnfd 2F 61
Nicholas Ct. W4 6A 82 (off Corney Reach Way)
Nicholas Gdns. W5 2D 80
Nicholas La. EC4 7D 68 (2F 169) (in two parts)
Nicholas M. W4 6A 82
Nicholas Pas. EC4 1F 169
Nicholas Rd. E1 4J 69
Nicholas Rd. Croy 4J 151
Nicholas Rd. Dag 2F 57
Nicholas Stacey Ho. SE7 5K 89 (off Frank Burton Clo.)
Nicholas Way. N'wd 1E 22
Nichola Ter. Bexh 1E 110
Nicholay Rd. N19 1H 49
Nichol Clo. N14 1C 16
Nicholes Rd. Houn 4E 96
Nichol La. Brom 7J 125
Nicholl Ho. N4 1C 50
Nicholls Av. Uxb 4C 58
Nichollsfield Wlk. N7 5K 49
Nicholls Point. E13 1J 71 (off Park Gro.)
Nicholl St. E2 1G 69
Nichols Clo. N4 1A 50 (off Osborne Rd.)
Nichols Clo. Chess 6C 146
Nichols Grn. W5 5E 62
Nicholson Ct. E17 4A 34
Nicholson Dri. Bush 1B 10
Nicholson Ho. SE17 5D 86
Nicholson M. King T 4E 134
Nicholson Rd. Croy 1F 153
Nicholson St. SE1 1B 86 (5A 168)
Nickelby Clo. SE28 6C 74
Nickleby Clo. Uxb 6D 58
Nickleby Ho. SE16 2G 87 (7K 169) (off George Row)
Nicola Clo. Harr 2H 25
Nicola Clo. S Croy 6C 152
Nicol Clo. Twic 6B 98
Nicoll Ct. N10 7A 16
Nicoll Ct. NW10 1A 64
Nicoll Pl. NW4 6D 28
Nicoll Rd. NW10 1A 64
Nicolson. NW9 1A 28
Nicosia Rd. SW18 7C 102
Niederwald Rd. SE26 4A 124
Nield Rd. Hay 2H 77
Nigel Clo. N'holt 1C 60
Nigel Ct. N3 7E 14
Nigel Fisher Way. Chess 7C 146
Nigel Ho. EC1 5A 68 (5J 161) (off Portpool La.)
Nigel M. Ilf 4F 55
Nigel Playfair Av. W6 4D 82
Nigel Rd. E7 5A 54
Nigel Rd. SE15 3G 105
Nigeria Rd. SE7 7A 90
Nighthawk. NW9 1B 28
Nightingale Av. E4 5B 20
Nightingale Av. Harr 1B 44
Nightingale Clo. E4 4A 20
Nightingale Clo. W4 6J 81
Nightingale Clo. Cars 2E 150
Nightingale Clo. Pinn 5A 24
Nightingale Ct. E14 2E 88 (off Ovex Clo.)
Nightingale Ct. N4 2K 49 (off Tollington Pk.)
Nightingale Ct. SW6 1K 101 (off Maltings Pl.)
Nightingale Ct. Short 2G 143
Nightingale Dri. Eps 6H 147
Nightingale Gro. SE13 5F 107
Nightingale Heights. SE18 6F 91
Nightingale Ho. E1 1G 87 (off Thomas More St.)
Nightingale Ho. N1 1E 68 (off Wilmer Gdns.)
Nightingale Ho. SE18 5E 90 (off Connaught M.)
Nightingale Ho. W12 6E 64 (off Du Cane Rd.)
Nightingale La. E11 4K 35
Nightingale La. N8 4J 31
Nightingale La. SW12 & SW4 7D 102
Nightingale La. Brom 2A 144
Nightingale La. Rich 7E 98
Nightingale Lodge. W9 5J 65 (off Admiral Wlk.)
Nightingale M. E3 2K 69
Nightingale M. SE11 4B 86 (3K 173)
Nightingale M. King T 3D 134 (off South La.)
Nightingale Pl. SE18 6E 90
Nightingale Pl. SW10 6A 84 (7A 170)
Nightingale Rd. E5 3H 51
Nightingale Rd. N9 6D 8
Nightingale Rd. N22 7D 16
Nightingale Rd. NW10 2B 64
Nightingale Rd. W7 1K 79
Nightingale Rd. Cars 3D 150
Nightingale Rd. Hamp 5E 114
Nightingale Rd. Orp 6G 145
Nightingale Rd. W on T 7A 132
Nightingale Rd. W Mol 5F 133
Nightingale Sq. SW12 7E 102
Nightingales, The. Stai 7B 94
Nightingale Va. SE18 6E 90
Nightingale Wlk. SW4 6F 103
Nightingale Way. E6 5C 72
Nikols Wlk. SW18 4K 101
Nile Clo. N16 3F 51
Nile Dri. N9 2D 18
Nile Path. SE18 6E 90
Nile Rd. E13 2A 72
Nile St. N1 3C 68 (1D 162)
Nile Ter. SE15 5F 87
Nimegen Way. SE22 5E 104
Nimmo Dri. Bus H 1C 10
Nimrod. NW9 1A 28
Nimrod Clo. N'holt 3B 60
Nimrod Ho. E16 5K 71 (off Vanguard Clo.)
Nimrod Pas. N1 6E 50
Nimrod Rd. SW16 6F 121
Nina Mackay Clo. E15 1G 71
Nine Acres Clo. E12 5C 54
Nine Elms 7G 85
Nine Elms Clo. Felt 1H 113
Nine Elms La. SW8 7G 85 (7C 172)
Nineteenth Rd. Mitc 4J 139
Ninhams Wood. Orp 4E 156
Ninth Av. Hay 7J 59
Nita Ct. SE12 1J 125
Nithdale Rd. SE18 7F 91
Nithsdale Gro. Uxb 3E 40
Niton Clo. Barn 6A 4
Niton Rd. Rich 3G 99
Niton St. SW6 7F 83
Nobel Dri. Hay 1F 95
Nobel Ho. SE5 2C 104
Nobel Rd. N18 4D 18
Noble Corner. Houn 1E 96
Noble Ct. E1 7H 69
Noble Ct. Mitc 2B 138
Noblefield Heights. N2 5C 30
Noble St. EC2 6C 68 (7C 162)
Noel. NW9 1A 28
Noel Ct. Houn 3D 96
Noel Coward Ho. SW1 4G 85 (4B 172) (off Vauxhall Bri. Rd.)
Noel Ho. NW3 7B 48 (off Harben Rd.)
Noel Park 2B 32
Noel Pk. Rd. N22 2A 32
Noel Rd. E6 4C 72
Noel Rd. N1 2B 68
Noel Rd. W3 7G 63
Noel Sq. Dag 4C 56
Noel St. W1 6G 67 (1B 166)
Noel Ter. SE23 2J 123
Noel Ter. Sidc 4B 128
Nolan Way. E5 4G 51
Nolton Pl. Edgw 1F 27
Nonsuch Pl. Sutt 7F 149
Nonsuch Wlk. Sutt 7F 149 (in two parts)
Nora Gdns. NW4 4F 29
Norbiton 2G 135
Norbiton Av. King T 1G 135
Norbiton Comn. Rd. King T 3H 135
Norbiton Hall. King T 2F 135
Norbiton Rd. E14 6B 70
Norbreck Gdns. NW10 3F 63
Norbreck Pde. NW10 3E 62
Norbroke St. W12 7B 64
Norburn St. W10 5G 65
Norbury 2K 139
Norbury Av. SW16 1K 139
Norbury Av. Houn 4H 97
Norbury Clo. SW16 1A 140
Norbury Ct. Rd. SW16 3J 139
Norbury Cres. SW16 1K 139
Norbury Cross. SW16 3J 139
Norbury Gdns. Romf 5D 38
Norbury Gro. NW7 3F 13
Norbury Hill. SW16 7A 122
Norbury Ri. SW16 3J 139
Norbury Rd. E4 5H 19
Norbury Rd. T Hth 2C 140
Norbury Trad. Est. SW16 2K 139
Norcombe Gdns. Harr 6C 26
Norcombe Ho. N19 3H 49 (off Wedmore St.)
Norcott Clo. Hay 4A 60
Norcott Rd. N16 2G 51
Norcroft Gdns. SE22 7G 105
Norcutt Rd. Twic 1J 115
Nordenfeldt Rd. Eri 5K 93
Norden Ho. E2 3H 69 (off Pott St.)
Norfield Rd. Dart 4J 129
Norfolk Av. N13 6G 17
Norfolk Av. N15 6F 33
Norfolk Clo. N2 3C 30
Norfolk Clo. N13 6G 17
Norfolk Clo. Barn 4K 5
Norfolk Clo. Twic 6B 98
Norfolk Ct. Barn 4B 4
Norfolk Cres. W2 6C 66 (7C 158)
Norfolk Cres. Sidc 7J 109
Norfolk Gdns. Bexh 1F 111
Norfolk Gdns. Houn 5D 96
Norfolk Ho. SE3 6G 89 (off Restell Clo.)
Norfolk Ho. SE8 1C 106
Norfolk Ho. SE20 1J 141
Norfolk Ho. SW1 4H 85 (3D 172) (off Page St.)
Norfolk Ho. Rd. SW16 3H 121
Norfolk Mans. SW11 1D 102 (off Prince of Wales Dri.)
Norfolk M. W10 5H 65 (off Blagrove Rd.)
Norfolk Pl. W2 6B 66 (7B 158) (in two parts)
Norfolk Pl. Well 2A 110
Norfolk Rd. E6 1D 72
Norfolk Rd. E17 2K 33
Norfolk Rd. NW8 1B 66
Norfolk Rd. NW10 7A 46
Norfolk Rd. SW19 7C 120
Norfolk Rd. Bark 7J 55
Norfolk Rd. Barn 3D 4
Norfolk Rd. Dag 5H 57
Norfolk Rd. Enf 6C 8
Norfolk Rd. Felt 1A 114
Norfolk Rd. Harr 5F 25
Norfolk Rd. Ilf 1J 55
Norfolk Rd. Romf 6J 39
Norfolk Rd. T Hth 3C 140
Norfolk Rd. Uxb 6A 40
Norfolk Row. SE1 4K 85 (3G 173) (in two parts)
Norfolk Sq. W2 6B 66 (1B 164)
Norfolk Sq. M. W2 1B 164
Norfolk St. E7 5J 53
Norfolk Ter. W6 5G 83
Norgrove St. SW12 7E 102
Norhyrst Av. SE25 3F 141
Norland Ho. W11 1F 83 (off Queensdale Cres.)
Norland Pl. W11 1G 83
Norland Rd. W11 1F 83 (off Queensdale Cres.)
Norlands Cres. Chst 1F 145
Norland Sq. W11 1G 83
Norland Sq. Mans. W11 1G 83 (off Norland Sq.)
Norley Va. SW15 1C 118
Norlington Rd. E10 1E 52
Norman Av. N22 1B 32
Norman Av. Felt 2C 114
Norman Av. S'hall 7C 60
Norman Av. Twic 7C 98
Normanby Clo. SW15 5H 101
Normanby Rd. NW10 4B 46
Norman Clo. N22 1C 32
Norman Clo. Romf 1H 39
Norman Ct. N4 7A 32
Norman Ct. NW10 7C 46
Norman Ct. W13 1B 80 (off Kirkfield Clo.)
Norman Ct. Brom 1J 143 (off Tweedy Rd.)
Norman Ct. Ilf 7H 37
Norman Cres. Houn 7B 78
Norman Cres. Pinn 1A 24
Normand Gdns. W14 6G 83 (off Greyhound Rd.)
Normand M. W14 6G 83
Normand Rd. W14 6H 83
Normandy Av. Barn 5C 4
Normandy Clo. SE26 3A 124
Normandy Dri. Hay 6E 58
Normandy Ho. E14 2E 88 (off Plevna St.)
Normandy Rd. SW9 1A 104
Normandy Ter. E16 6K 71
Normandy Way. Eri 1K 111
Norman Gro. E3 2A 70
Norman Hay Ind. Est. W Dray 7B 76
Norman Ho. SW8 7J 85 (off Wyvil Rd.)

Norman Ho. Felt . . . . . 2D 114 (off Watermill Way)
Normanhurst. Ashf 5C 112
Normanhurst Av. Bexh. 1D 110
Normanhurst Dri. Twic. 5A 98
Normanhurst Rd. SW2 . . . . 2K 121
Norman Pde. Sidc 2D 128
Norman Rd. E6 . . . . . 4D 72
Norman Rd. E11 . . . . . 2F 53
Norman Rd. N15 . . . . . 5F 33
Norman Rd. SE10 . . . . . 7D 88
Norman Rd. SW19 . . . . . 7A 120
Norman Rd. Ashf 6F 113
Norman Rd. Belv . . . . . 3H 93 (in two parts)
Norman Rd. Ilf 5F 55
Norman Rd. Sutt 5J 149
Norman Rd. T Hth 5B 140
Norman's Clo. NW10 . . . . . 6K 45
Normans Clo. Uxb 4B 58
Normansfield Av. Tedd 7C 116
Normanshire Dri. E4 . . . . . 4H 19
Norman's Mead. NW10 . . . . . 6K 45
Norman St. EC1 . . . 3C 68 (2D 162)
Normanton Av. SW19 . . . . . 2J 119
Normanton Pk. E4 . . . . . 2B 20
Normanton Rd. S Croy 5E 152
Normanton St. SE23 . . . . . 2K 123
Norman Way. N14 . . . . . 2D 16
Norman Way. W3 . . . . . 5H 63
Normington Clo. SW16 . . . . 5A 122
Norrice Lea. N2 . . . . . 5B 30
Norris. NW9 . . . . . 1B 28 (off Concourse, The)
Norris Ho. E9 . . . . . 1J 69 (off Handley Rd.)
Norris Ho. N1 . . . . . 1E 68 (off Colville Est.)
Norris Ho. SE8 . . . . . 5B 88 (off Grove St.)
Norris St. SW1 . . . . 7H 67 (3C 166)
Norroy Rd. SW15 . . . . . 4F 101
Norry's Clo. Cockf 4J 5
Norry's Rd. Cockf 4J 5
Norseman Clo. Ilf 1B 56
Norseman Way. Gnfd 1F 61
Norstead Pl. SW15 . . . . . 2C 118
N. Access Rd. E17 . . . . . 6K 33
North Acre. NW9 . . . . . 1A 28
North Acton. 4K 63
N. Acton Rd. NW10 . . . . . 2K 63
Northall Rd. Bexh 2J 111
Northampton Gro. N1 . . . . . 5C 50
Northampton Pk. N1 . . . . . 6C 50
Northampton Rd. EC1 . . . . . 4A 68 (3K 161)
Northampton Rd. Croy 2G 153
Northampton Rd. Enf 4F 9
Northampton Row. EC1 . . . . 3K 161
Northampton Sq. EC1 . . . . . 3B 68 (2A 162)
Northampton St. N1 . . . . . 7C 50
Northanger Rd. SW16 . . . . . 6J 121
N. Audley St. W1 . . . 6E 66 (1G 165)
North Av. N18 . . . . . 4B 18
North Av. NW10 . . . . . 3E 64
North Av. W13 . . . . . 5B 62
North Av. Cars 7E 150
North Av. Harr 6F 25
North Av. Hay 7J 59
North Av. Rich 1G 99
North Av. S'hall 7D 60
North Bank. NW8 . . . . . 3C 66 (2C 158)
Northbank Rd. E17 . . . . . 2E 34
North Beckton. 5C 72
N. Birkbeck Rd. E11 . . . . . 3F 53
North Block. SE1 . . . . . 2K 85 (6H 167) (off York Rd.)
Northborough Rd. SW16 . . . 3H 139
Northbourne. Brom 7J 143
Northbourne Rd. SW4 . . . . . 5H 103
N. Branch Av. NW10 . . . . . 3E 64
Northbrook Dri. N'wd 1G 23
Northbrook Rd. N22 . . . . . 7D 16
Northbrook Rd. SE13 . . . . . 5G 107
Northbrook Rd. Barn 6B 4
Northbrook Rd. Croy 5D 140
Northbrook Rd. Ilf 2E 54
Northburgh St. EC1 . . . . . 4B 68 (4B 162)
N. Carriage Dri. W2 . . . . . 2C 164
North Cheam. 3F 149
Northchurch. SE17 . . . . . 5D 86 (in three parts)
Northchurch Rd. N1 . . . . . 7D 50 (in two parts)
Northchurch Rd. Wemb 6G 45
Northchurch Ter. N1 . . . . . 7E 50 (in two parts)
N. Circular Rd. E4 . . . . . 6G 19
N. Circular Rd. N3 & N12 . . . 3J 29
N. Circular Rd. N13 . . . . . 5F 17
N. Circular Rd. NW2 . . . . . 3A 46
N. Circular Rd. NW4 . . . . . 7E 28
N. Circular Rd. NW10 . . . . . 2F 63
Northcliffe Clo. Wor Pk 3A 148
Northcliffe Dri. N20 . . . . . 1C 14
North Clo. Bexh 4D 110
North Clo. Dag 1G 75
North Clo. Felt 6F 95
North Clo. Mord 4G 137
N. Colonnade, The. E14 . . . . 1C 88
N. Common Rd. W5 . . . . . 7E 62
N. Common Rd. Uxb 5A 40
Northcote. Pinn 2A 24
Northcote Av. W5 . . . . . 7E 62
Northcote Av. Iswth 5A 98
Northcote Av. S'hall 7C 60
Northcote Av. Surb 7H 135
Northcote M. SW11 . . . . . 4C 102
Northcote Rd. E17 . . . . . 4A 34
Northcote Rd. NW10 . . . . . 7A 46
Northcote Rd. SW11 . . . . . 5C 102
Northcote Rd. Croy 6D 140
Northcote Rd. N Mald 3J 135
Northcote Rd. Sidc 4J 127
Northcote Rd. Twic 5A 98
Northcott Av. N22 . . . . . 1J 31
N. Countess Rd. E17 . . . . . 2B 34
North Ct. SE24 . . . . . 3B 104
North Ct. SW1 . . . . 3J 85 (2E 172) (off Gt. Peter St.)
North Ct. W1 . . . . 5G 67 (5B 160)
North Ct. Brom . . . . . 1J 143 (off Palace Gro.)
North Cray. 5E 128
N. Cray Rd. Sidc & Bex 6E 128
North Cres. E16 . . . . . 4F 71
North Cres. N3 . . . . . 2H 29
North Cres. WC1 . . . 5H 67 (5C 160)
Northcroft Ct. W12 . . . . . 2C 82
Northcroft Rd. W13 . . . . . 2B 80
Northcroft Rd. Eps 7A 148
North Crofts. SE23 . . . . . 1H 123
Northcroft Ter. W13 . . . . . 2B 80
N. Cross Rd. SE22 . . . . . 5F 105
N. Cross Rd. Ilf 4G 37
Northdale Ct. SE25 . . . . . 3F 141
North Dene. NW7 . . . . . 3E 12
North Dene. Houn 1F 97
Northdene Gdns. N15 . . . . . 6F 33
Northdown Clo. Ruis 3H 41
Northdown Gdns. Ilf 5J 37
Northdown Rd. Well 2B 110
Northdown St. N1 . . . . . 2J 67 (1G 161)
North Dri. SW16 . . . . . 4G 121
North Dri. Beck 4D 142
North Dri. Houn 2G 97
North Dri. Ruis 7G 23
North East Surrey Crematorium. Mord 6E 136
North End. 2A 48
North End. NW3 . . . . . 2A 48
North End. Buck H 1F 21
North End. Croy 2C 152
N. End Av. NW3 . . . . . 2A 48 (in two parts)
N. End Cres. W14 . . . . . 4H 83
N. End Ho. W14 . . . . . 4G 83
N. End Pde. W14 . . . . . 4G 83 (off N. End Rd.)
N. End Rd. NW11 . . . . . 1J 47
N. End Rd. W14 & SW6 . . . . 4G 83
N. End Rd. Wemb 3G 45
N. End Way. NW3 . . . . . 2A 48
Northern Av. N9 . . . . . 2K 17
Northernhay Wlk. Mord 4G 137
Northern Perimeter Rd. H'row A 1D 94
Northern Perimeter Rd. W. H'row A 1A 94
Northern Rd. E13 . . . . . 2K 71
Northesk Ho. E1 . . . . . 4H 69 (off Tent St.)
N. Eyot Gdns. W6 . . . . . 5B 82
Northey St. E14 . . . . . 7A 70
North Feltham. 6K 95
N. Feltham Trad. Est. Felt 5K 95
Northfield Av. W13 & W5 . . . . 1B 80
Northfield Av. Pinn 4B 24
Northfield Clo. Brom 1C 144
Northfield Clo. Hay 3H 77
Northfield Cres. Sutt 4G 149
Northfield Gdns. Dag 4F 57
Northfield Ho. SE15 . . . . . 6G 87
Northfield Ind. Est. NW10 . . . 3G 63
Northfield Ind. Est. Wemb . . . 1G 63
Northfield Pde. Hay 3G 77
Northfield Pk. Hay 3H 77
Northfield Path. Dag 4F 57
Northfield Rd. E6 . . . . . 7D 54
Northfield Rd. N16 . . . . . 7E 32
Northfield Rd. W13 . . . . . 2B 80
Northfield Rd. Barn 3H 5
Northfield Rd. Dag 4F 57
Northfield Rd. Enf 5C 8
Northfield Rd. Houn 6B 78
Northfields. 3B 80
Northfields. SW18 . . . . . 4J 101
Northfields Prospect Bus. Cen. SW18 . . . . . 4J 101
Northfields Rd. W3 . . . . . 5H 63
North Finchley. 5F 15
Northfleet Ho. SE1 . . . . . 2D 86 (6E 168) (off Tennis St.)
N. Flock St. SE16 . . . . . 2G 87
N. Flower Wlk. W2 . . . . . 3A 164
North Garden. E14 . . . . . 1B 88
North Gdns. SW19 . . . . . 7B 120
North Ga. NW8 . . . . . 1C 158
Northgate. N'wd 1E 22
Northgate Bus. Pk. Enf 3C 8
Northgate Dri. NW9 . . . . . 6A 28
Northgate Ho. E14 . . . . . 7C 70 (off E. India Dock Rd.)
Northgate Ind. Pk. Romf 1F 39
N. Glade, The. Bex 7F 111
N. Gower St. NW1 . . . . . 3G 67 (2B 160)
North Grn. NW9 . . . . . 7F 13
North Gro. N6 . . . . . 1E 30
North Gro. N15 . . . . . 5D 32
North Harrow. 5F 25
N. Hatton Rd. H'row A 1F 95
North Hill. N6 . . . . . 6D 30
N. Hill Av. N6 . . . . . 6E 30
North Hillingdon. 7E 40
North Ho. SE8 . . . . . 5B 88
N. Hyde Gdns. Hay 4J 77
N. Hyde La. S'hall 5B 78
N. Hyde Rd. Hay 3G 77
Northiam. N12 . . . . . 4D 14 (in two parts)
Northiam. WC1 . . . . 3J 67 (2F 161) (off Cromer St.)
Northiam St. E9 . . . . . 1H 69
Northington St. WC1 . . . . . 4K 67 (4H 161)
North Kensington. 5F 65
Northlands St. SE5 . . . . . 2C 104
North La. Tedd 6K 115
Northleach Ct. SE15 . . . . . 6E 86 (off Birdlip Clo.)
North Lodge. E16 . . . . . 1K 89 (off Wesley Av.)
North Lodge. New Bar 5F 5
N. Lodge Clo. SW15 . . . . . 5F 101
North Mall. N9 . . . . . 2C 18 (off Plevna Rd.)
North M. WC1 . . . . 4K 67 (4H 161)
North Mt. N20 . . . . . 2F 15 (off High Rd.)
Northolm. Edgw 4E 12
Northolme Gdns. Edgw 1G 27
Northolme Rd. N5 . . . . . 4C 50
Northolt. 7E 42
Northolt. N17 . . . . . 2E 32 (off Griffin Rd.)
Northolt Av. Ruis 5K 41
Northolt Gdns. Gnfd 5K 43
Northolt Rd. Harr 4F 43
Northolt Rd. H'row A 1A 94
Northover. Brom 3H 125
North Pde. Chess 5F 147
North Pde. Edgw 2G 27
North Pde. S'hall . . . . . 6E 60 (off North Rd.)
North Pk. SE9 . . . . . 6D 108
North Pl. SW18 . . . . . 5J 101
North Pl. Mitc 7D 120
North Pl. Tedd 6K 115
N. Pole La. Kes 6H 155
N. Pole Rd. W10 . . . . . 5E 64
Northport St. N1 . . . . . 1D 68
North Ride. W2 . . . 7C 66 (3C 164)
North Ri. W2 . . . . 6C 66 (1D 164)
North Rd. N2 . . . . . 2C 30
North Rd. N6 . . . . . 7E 30
North Rd. N7 . . . . . 6J 49
North Rd. N9 . . . . . 1C 18
North Rd. SE18 . . . . . 4J 91
North Rd. SW19 . . . . . 6A 120
North Rd. W5 . . . . . 3D 80
North Rd. Belv 3H 93
North Rd. Bren 6E 80
North Rd. Brom 1K 143
North Rd. Chad H 5E 38
North Rd. Edgw 1H 27
North Rd. Felt 6F 95
North Rd. Harr 7A 26
North Rd. Hay 5F 59
North Rd. Ilf 2J 55
North Rd. Rich 3G 99
North Rd. S'hall 6E 60
North Rd. Surb 6D 134
North Rd. W Dray 3B 76
North Rd. W Wick 1D 154
Northrop Rd. H'row A 1G 95
North Row. W1 . . . . 7D 66 (2F 165)
N. Row Bldgs. W1 . . . . . 7E 66 (2G 165) (off North Row)
North Several. SE3 . . . . . 2F 107
North Sheen. 3G 99
Northside Rd. Brom 1J 143
N. Side Wandsworth Comn. SW18 . . . . . 5B 102
Northspur Rd. Sutt 3J 149
North Sq. N9 . . . . . 2C 18 (off Hertford Rd.)
North Sq. NW11 . . . . . 5J 29
Northstead Rd. SW2 . . . . . 2A 122
North St. E13 . . . . . 2K 71
North St. NW4 . . . . . 5E 28
North St. SW4 . . . . . 3G 103
North St. Bark . . . . . 6F 55 (Barking Northern Relief Rd.)
North St. Bark . . . . . 7G 55 (London Rd.)
North St. Bexh 4G 111
North St. Brom 1J 143
North St. Cars 3D 150
North St. Iswth 3A 98
North St. Romf . . . . . 3K 39 (in two parts)
N. Street Pas. E13 . . . . . 2K 71
N. Tenter St. E1 . . . . 6F 69 (1K 169)
North Ter. SW3 . . . . 3C 84 (2C 170)
Northumberland All. EC3 . . . . . 6E 68 (1H 169) (in two parts)
Northumberland Av. E12 . . . . 1A 54
Northumberland Av. WC2 . . . . . 1J 85 (4E 166)
Northumberland Av. Enf 1C 8
Northumberland Av. Iswth . . . 1K 97
Northumberland Av. Well . . . 4H 109
Northumberland Clo. Eri 7J 93
Northumberland Clo. Stanw 6A 94
Northumberland Cres. Felt . . 6G 95
Northumberland Gdns. N9 . . . 3A 18
Northumberland Gdns. Brom 4E 144
Northumberland Gdns. Iswth 7A 80
Northumberland Gdns. Mitc 5H 139
Northumberland Gro. N17 . . . 7C 18
Northumberland Heath. . . . 7J 93
Northumberland Ho. WC2 . . . . . 1J 85 (4E 166) (off Northumberland Av.)
Northumberland Pk. N17 . . . . 7A 18
Northumberland Pk. Eri 7J 93
Northumberland Pk. Ind. Est. N17 . . . . . 7C 18
Northumberland Pl. W2 . . . . 6J 65
Northumberland Pl. Rich 5D 98
Northumberland Rd. E6 . . . . 6C 72
Northumberland Rd. E17 . . . . 7C 34
Northumberland Rd. Harr . . . 5D 24
Northumberland Rd. New Bar 6F 5
Northumberland Row. Twic 1J 115
Northumberland St. WC2 . . . . . 1J 85 (4E 166)
Northumberland Way. Eri . . . 1J 111
Northumbria St. E14 . . . . . 6C 70
N. Verbena Gdns. W6 . . . . . 5C 82
Northview. N7 . . . . . 3J 49
North Vw. SW19 . . . . . 5E 118
North Vw. W5 . . . . . 4C 62
North Vw. Pinn 7A 24
N. View Cres. NW10 . . . . . 4B 46
Northview Dri. Wfd G 2B 36
N. View Rd. N8 . . . . . 4H 31
North Vs. NW1 . . . . . 6H 49
North Wlk. W8 & W2 . . . . . 7K 65 (off Bayswater Rd.)
North Wlk. New Ad . . . . . 6D 154 (in two parts)
North Way. N9 . . . . . 2E 18
North Way. N11 . . . . . 6B 16
North Way. NW9 . . . . . 3H 27
Northway. NW11 . . . . . 5K 29
Northway. Mord 3G 137
North Way. Pinn 4B 24
North Way. Uxb 7A 40
Northway. Wall 4G 151
Northway Cir. NW7 . . . . . 4E 12
Northway Cres. NW7 . . . . . 4E 12
Northway Gdns. NW11 . . . . . 5K 29
Northway Rd. SE5 . . . . . 3C 104
Northway Rd. Croy 6F 141
Northways Pde. NW3 . . . . . 7B 48 (off College Cres., in two parts)
Northweald La. King T 5D 116
North Wembley. 3D 44
N. Western Commercial Cen. NW1 . . . . . 7J 49
Northwest Pl. N1 . . . . . 2A 68
North Wharf. E14 . . . . . 1E 88 (off Coldharbour)
N. Wharf Rd. W2 . . . . . 5B 66 (6A 158)
Northwick Av. Harr 6A 26
Northwick Circ. Harr 6C 26
Northwick Clo. NW8 . . . . . 4B 66 (3A 158)

Northwick Clo. *Harr* 1B **44**
Northwick Ho. *NW8* 3A **158**
Northwick Pk. Rd. *Harr* 6K **25**
Northwick Rd. *Wemb* 1D **62**
Northwick Ter. *NW8* 4B **66** (3A **158**)
Northwick Wlk. *Harr* 7K **25**
Northwold Dri. *Pinn* 2A **24**
Northwold Est. *E5* 2G **51**
Northwold Rd. *N16 & E5* 2F **51**
N. Wood Ct. *SE25* 3G **141**
Northwood Gdns. *N12* 5G **15**
Northwood Gdns. *Gnfd* 5K **43**
Northwood Gdns. *Ilf* 4E **36**
Northwood Golf Course *1F 23*
Northwood Hills 2J 23
Northwood Hills Cir. *N'wd* 1J **23**
Northwood Ho. *SE27* 4D **122**
Northwood Pl. *Eri* 3F **93**
Northwood Rd. *N6* 7F **31**
Northwood Rd. *SE23* 1B **124**
Northwood Rd. *Cars* 6E **150**
Northwood Rd. *Hare* 1A **22**
Northwood Rd. *H'row A* 1A **94**
Northwood Rd. *T Hth* 2B **140**
Northwood Way. *SE19* 6D **122**
Northwood Way. *Hare* 1A **22**
Northwood Way. *N'wd* 1J **23**
North Woolwich 1E 90
North Woolwich Old Station Mus. *2E 90*
N. Woolwich Rd. *E16* 1H **89**
N. Worple Way. *SW14* 3K **99**
Norton Av. *Surb* 7H **135**
Norton Clo. *E4* 5H **19**
Norton Clo. *Enf* 2C **8**
Norton Folgate. *E1* 5E **68** (5H **163**)
Norton Folgate Houses. E1 5F 69 (5J 163)
(off Puma Ct.)
Norton Gdns. *SW16* 2J **139**
Norton Ho. E1 6H 69
(off Bigland St.)
Norton Ho. E2 2K 69
(off Mace St.)
Norton Ho. SW1 3H 85 (2D 172)
(off Arneway St.)
Norton Ho. SW9 2K 103
(off Aytoun Rd.)
Norton Rd. *E10* 1B **52**
Norton Rd. *Dag* 6K **57**
Norton Rd. *Wemb* 6D **44**
Norval Rd. *Wemb* 2B **44**
Norway Ga. *SE16* 3A **88**
Norway Pl. *E14* 6B **70**
Norway St. *SE10* 6D **88**
Norway Wharf. E14 6B 70
(off Norway Pl.)
Norwich Ho. E14 6D 70
(off Cordelia St.)
Norwich M. *Ilf* 1A **56**
Norwich Pl. *Bexh* 4G **111**
Norwich Rd. *E7* 5J **53**
Norwich Rd. *Dag* 2G **75**
Norwich Rd. *Gnfd* 1F **61**
Norwich Rd. *N'wd* 3H **23**
Norwich Rd. *T Hth* 3C **140**
Norwich St. *EC4* 6A **68** (7J **161**)
Norwich Wlk. *Edgw* 7D **12**
Norwood 6E 122
Norwood Av. *Romf* 7K **39**
Norwood Av. *Wemb* 1F **63**
Norwood Clo. *NW2* 3G **47**
Norwood Clo. *S'hall* 4E **78**
Norwood Clo. *Twic* 2H **115**
Norwood Dri. *Harr* 6D **24**
Norwood Gdns. *Hay* 4A **60**
Norwood Gdns. *S'hall* 4D **78**
Norwood Green 4E 78
Norwood Grn. Rd. *S'hall* 4E **78**
Norwood High St. *SE27* 3B **122**
Norwood Ho. E14 7D 70
(off Poplar High St.)
Norwood New Town 6C 122
Norwood Pk. Rd. *SE27* 5C **122**
Norwood Rd. *SE24* 1B **122**
Norwood Rd. *SE27* 2B **122**
Norwood Rd. *S'hall* 3C **78**
Norwood Ter. *S'hall* 4F **79**
Notley St. *SE5* 7D **86**
Notson Rd. *SE25* 4H **141**
Notting Barn Rd. *W10* 4F **65**
Nottingdale Sq. *W11* 1G **83**
Nottingham Av. *E16* 5A **72**
Nottingham Ct. *WC2* 6J **67** (1E **166**)
Nottingham Ho. WC2 6J 67 (1E 166)
(off Shorts Gdns.)
Nottingham Pl. *W1* 5E **66** (4G **159**)
Nottingham Rd. *E10* 6E **34**
Nottingham Rd. *SW17* 1D **120**
Nottingham Rd. *Iswth* 2K **97**
Nottingham Rd. *S Croy* 4C **152**
Nottingham St. *W1* 5E **66** (5G **159**)
Nottingham Ter. *NW1* 4G **159**
Notting Hill 7H 65
Notting Hill Ga. *W11* 1J **83**
Nottingwood Ho. W11 7G 65
(off Clarendon Rd.)
Nova M. *Sutt* 1G **149**
Novar Clo. *Orp* 7K **145**
Nova Rd. *Croy* 1B **152**
Novar Rd. *SE9* 1G **127**
Novello St. *SW6* 1J **101**
Nowell Rd. *SW13* 6C **82**
Nower Ct. *Pinn* 4D **24**
Nower Hill. *Pinn* 4D **24**
Noyna Rd. *SW17* 3D **120**
Nubia Way. *Brom* 3G **125**
Nuding Clo. *SE13* 3C **106**
Nuffield Ct. *Houn* 7D **78**
Nuffield Lodge. *N6* 6G **31**
Nuffield Lodge. W9 5J 65
(off Admiral Wlk.)
Nugent Rd. *N19* 1J **49**
Nugent Rd. *SE25* 3F **141**
Nugents Ct. *Pinn* 1C **24**
Nugent's Pk. *Pinn* 1C **24**
Nugent Ter. *NW8* 2A **66**
Numa Ct. *Bren* 7D **80**
Nun Ct. *EC2* 6E **162**
Nuneaton Rd. *Dag* 7E **56**
Nunhead 3H 105
Nunhead Cres. *SE15* 3H **105**
Nunhead Est. *SE15* 4H **105**
Nunhead Grn. *SE15* 3H **105**
Nunhead Gro. *SE15* 3H **105**
Nunhead La. *SE15* 3H **105**
Nunhead Pas. *SE15* 3G **105**
Nunnington Clo. *SE9* 3C **126**
Nunns Rd. *Enf* 2H **7**
Nupton Dri. *Barn* 6A **4**
Nurse Clo. *Edgw* 1J **27**
Nursery App. *N12* 6H **15**
Nursery Av. *N3* 2A **30**
Nursery Av. *Bexh* 3F **111**
Nursery Av. *Croy* 2K **153**
Nursery Clo. *SE4* 2B **106**
Nursery Clo. *SW15* 4F **101**
Nursery Clo. *Croy* 2K **153**
Nursery Clo. *Enf* 1E **8**
Nursery Clo. *Felt* 7K **95**
(in two parts)
Nursery Clo. *Orp* 7K **145**
Nursery Clo. *Romf* 6D **38**
Nursery Clo. *Wfd G* 5E **20**
Nursery Ct. *N17* 7A **18**
Nursery Ct. *W13* 5A **62**
Nursery Gdns. *Chst* 6F **127**
Nursery Gdns. *Enf* 1E **8**
Nursery Gdns. *Hamp* 4D **114**
Nursery Gdns. *Houn* 5D **96**
Nursery Gdns. *Sun* 2H **131**
Nursery La. *E2* 1F **69**
Nursery La. *E7* 6J **53**
Nursery La. *W10* 5E **64**
Nursery La. *Uxb* 4A **58**
Nurserymans Rd. *N11* 2K **15**
Nursery Rd. *E9* 6J **51**
Nursery Rd. *N2* 1B **30**
Nursery Rd. *N14* 7B **6**
Nursery Rd. *SW9* 4K **103**
Nursery Rd. *SW19* 2K **137**
(Merton)
Nursery Rd. *SW19* 7G **119**
(Wimbledon)
Nursery Rd. *Pinn* 3A **24**
Nursery Rd. *Sun* 2G **131**
Nursery Rd. *Sutt* 4A **150**
Nursery Rd. *T Hth* 4D **140**
Nursery Row. *Barn* 3B **4**
Nursery St. *N17* 7A **18**
Nursery Wlk. *NW4* 3E **28**
Nursery Wlk. *Romf* 7K **39**
Nursery Waye. *Uxb* 1A **58**
Nurstead Rd. *Eri* 7G **93**
Nutbourne St. *W10* 3G **65**
Nutbrook St. *SE15* 3G **105**
Nutbrowne Rd. *Dag* 1F **75**
Nutcroft Rd. *SE15* 7H **87**
Nutfield Clo. *N18* 6A **18**
Nutfield Clo. *Cars* 3C **150**
Nutfield Gdns. *Ilf* 2K **55**
Nutfield Gdns. *N'holt* 2A **60**
Nutfield Rd. *E15* 4E **52**
Nutfield Rd. *NW2* 3C **46**
Nutfield Rd. *SE22* 4F **105**
Nutfield Rd. *T Hth* 4B **140**
Nutford Pl. *W1* 6D **66** (7D **158**)
Nuthatch Clo. *Stai* 1B **112**
Nuthatch Gdns. *SE28* 2H **91**
(in two parts)
Nuthurst Av. *SW2* 2K **121**
Nutkin Wlk. *Uxb* 7A **40**
Nutley Ter. *NW3* 6A **48**
Nutmead Clo. *Bex* 1J **129**
Nutmeg Clo. *E16* 4G **71**
Nutmeg La. *E14* 6F **71**
Nuttall St. *N1* 2E **68**
Nutter La. *E11* 6A **36**
Nutt Gro. *Edgw* 2J **11**
Nutt St. *SE15* 7F **87**
Nutty La. *Shep* 3E **130**
Nutwell St. *SW17* 5C **120**
Nuxley Rd. *Belv* 6F **93**
Nyanza St. *SE18* 6H **91**
Nye Bevan Est. *E5* 3K **51**
Nye Bevan Ho. SW6 7H 83
(off St Thomas's Way)
Nylands Av. *Rich* 1G **99**
Nymans Gdns. *SW20* 3D **136**
Nynehead St. *SE14* 7A **88**
Nyon Gro. *SE6* 2B **124**
Nyssa Clo. *Wfd G* 6J **21**
Nyssa Ct. E15 3G 71
(off Teasel Way)
Nyton Clo. *N19* 1J **49**

Oak Apple Ct. *SE12* 1J **125**
Oak Av. *N8* 4J **31**
Oak Av. *N10* 7A **16**
Oak Av. *N17* 7J **17**
Oak Av. *Croy* 1C **154**
Oak Av. *Enf* 1E **6**
Oak Av. *Hamp* 5C **114**
Oak Av. *Houn* 7B **78**
Oak Av. *Uxb* 2D **40**
Oak Av. *W Dray* 3C **76**
Oak Bank. *New Ad* 6E **154**
Oakbank Av. *W on T* 7D **132**
Oakbank Gro. *SE24* 4C **104**
Oakbrook Clo. *Brom* 4K **125**
Oakbury Rd. *SW6* 2K **101**
Oak Clo. *N14* 7A **6**
Oak Clo. *Sutt* 2A **150**
Oakcombe Clo. *N Mald* 1A **136**
Oak Cottage Clo. *SE6* 1H **125**
Oak Cotts. *W7* 2J **79**
Oak Ct. SE15 7F 87
(off Sumner Rd.)
Oak Cres. *E16* 5G **71**
Oakcroft Bus. Cen. *Chess* 4F **147**
Oakcroft Clo. *Pinn* 2K **23**
Oakcroft Rd. *SE13* 2F **107**
Oakcroft Rd. *Chess* 4F **147**
Oakcroft Vs. *Chess* 4F **147**
Oakdale. *N14* 1A **16**
Oakdale Av. *Harr* 5E **26**
Oakdale Av. *N'wd* 2J **23**
Oakdale Ct. *E4* 5K **19**
Oakdale Gdns. *E4* 5K **19**
Oakdale Rd. *E7* 7K **53**
Oakdale Rd. *E11* 2F **53**
Oakdale Rd. *E18* 2K **35**
Oakdale Rd. *N4* 6C **32**
Oakdale Rd. *SE15 & SE4* 3J **105**
Oakdale Rd. *SW16* 5J **121**
Oakdale Rd. *Eps* 7K **147**
Oakdale Way. *Mitc* 7E **138**
Oakdene. *SE15* 1H **105**
Oakdene. *W13* 5B **62**
Oakdene Av. *Chst* 5E **126**
Oakdene Av. *Eri* 6J **93**
Oakdene Av. *Th Dit* 1A **146**
Oakdene Clo. *Pinn* 1D **24**
Oakdene Dri. *Surb* 7J **135**
Oakdene M. *Sutt* 1H **149**
Oakdene Pk. *N3* 7C **14**
Oakdene Rd. *Orp* 5K **145**
Oakdene Rd. *Uxb* 2D **58**
Oakden St. *SE11* 4A **86** (3K **173**)
Oake Ct. *SW15* 5G **101**
Oakeford Ho. W14 3G 83
(off Russell Rd.)
Oakend Ho. *N4* 7D **32**
Oakenholt Ho. *SE2* 1D **92**
Oakenshaw Clo. *Surb* 7E **134**
Oakes Clo. *E6* 6D **72**
Oakeshott Av. *N6* 2E **48**
Oakey La. *SE1* 3A **86** (1J **173**)
Oakfield. *E4* 5J **19**
Oakfield Av. *Harr* 3B **26**
Oakfield Cen. *SE20* 7H **123**
Oakfield Clo. *N Mald* 5B **136**
Oakfield Clo. *Ruis* 6H **23**
Oakfield Ct. *N8* 7J **31**
Oakfield Ct. *NW11* 7F **29**
Oakfield Gdns. *N18* 4K **17**
Oakfield Gdns. *SE19* 5E **122**
(in two parts)
Oakfield Gdns. *Beck* 5D **142**
Oakfield Gdns. *Cars* 1C **150**
Oakfield Gdns. *Gnfd* 4H **61**
Oakfield Ho. E3 5C 70
(off Gale St.)
Oakfield La. *Kes* 4A **156**
Oakfield Lodge. Ilf 3F 55
(off Albert Rd.)
Oakfield Rd. *E6* 1C **72**
Oakfield Rd. *E17* 2A **34**
Oakfield Rd. *N3* 1K **29**
Oakfield Rd. *N8* 6A **32**
Oakfield Rd. *N14* 2D **16**
Oakfield Rd. *SE20* 7H **123**
Oakfield Rd. *SW19* 3F **119**
Oakfield Rd. *Ashf* 5D **112**
Oakfield Rd. *Croy* 1C **152**
Oakfield Rd. *Ilf* 3F **55**
Oakfield Rd. Ind. Est. *SE20* 7H **123**
Oakfields Rd. *NW11* 6G **29**
Oakfield St. *SW10* 6A **84**
Oakford Rd. *NW5* 4G **49**
Oak Gdns. *Croy* 2C **154**
Oak Gdns. *Edgw* 2H **27**
Oak Glade. *N'wd* 1D **22**
Oak Gro. *NW2* 4G **47**
Oak Gro. *Ruis* 7K **23**
Oak Gro. *Sun* 7K **113**
Oak Gro. *W Wick* 1E **154**
Oak Gro. Rd. *SE20* 1J **141**
Oakhall Ct. *E11* 6K **35**
Oakhall Dri. *Sun* 5H **113**
Oak Hall Rd. *E11* 6K **35**
Oakham Clo. *SE6* 2B **124**
Oakham Clo. *Barn* 3J **5**
Oakham Dri. *Brom* 4H **143**
Oakham Ho. W10 4E 64
(off Sutton Way)
Oakhampton Rd. *NW7* 7A **14**
Oakhill. *Clay* 6A **146**
Oakhill. *Surb* 7E **134**
Oak Hill. *Wfd G* 7A **20**
Oakhill Av. *NW3* 4K **47**
Oakhill Av. *Pinn* 2C **24**
Oak Hill Clo. *Wfd G* 7A **20**
Oakhill Ct. *SE23* 6J **105**
Oakhill Ct. *SW19* 7F **119**
Oak Hill Ct. *Wfd G* 7A **20**
Oakhill Cres. *Surb* 7E **134**
Oak Hill Cres. *Wfd G* 7A **20**
Oakhill Dri. *Surb* 7E **134**
Oak Hill Gdns. *Wfd G* 1G **35**
Oakhill Gro. *Surb* 6E **134**
Oak Hill Pk. *NW3* 4K **47**
Oak Hill Pk. M. *NW3* 4A **48**
Oakhill Path. *Surb* 6E **134**
Oakhill Pl. *SW15* 5J **101**
Oakhill Rd. *SW15* 5H **101**
Oakhill Rd. *SW16* 1J **139**
Oakhill Rd. *Beck* 2E **142**
Oakhill Rd. *Surb* 6E **134**
Oakhill Rd. *Sutt* 3K **149**
Oak Hill Way. *NW3* 4A **48**
Oak Ho. *N2* 2B **30**
Oak Ho. W10 4G 65
(off Sycamore Wlk.)
Oakhouse Rd. *Bexh* 5G **111**
Oakhurst Av. *Barn* 7H **5**
Oakhurst Av. *Bexh* 7E **92**
Oakhurst Clo. *E17* 4G **35**
Oakhurst Clo. *Chst* 1D **144**
Oakhurst Clo. *Ilf* 1F **37**
Oakhurst Clo. *Tedd* 5J **115**
Oakhurst Ct. E17 4G 35
(off Woodford New Rd.)
Oakhurst Gdns. *E4* 1C **20**
Oakhurst Gdns. *E17* 4G **35**
Oakhurst Gdns. *Bexh* 7E **92**
Oakhurst Gro. *SE22* 4G **105**
Oakhurst Rd. *Eps* 6J **147**
Oakington Av. *Harr* 7E **24**
Oakington Av. *Hay* 4F **77**
Oakington Av. *Wemb* 3F **45**
Oakington Ct. Enf 2G 7
(off Ridgeway, The)
Oakington Dri. *Sun* 2A **132**
Oakington Mnr. Dri. *Wemb* 5G **45**
Oakington Rd. *W9* 4J **65**
Oakington Way. *N8* 7J **31**
Oakland Pl. *Buck H* 2D **20**
Oakland Rd. *E15* 4F **53**
Oaklands. *N13* 2E **16**
Oaklands. *W13* 5A **62**
Oaklands. *Beck* 1D **142**
Oaklands Av. *N9* 6C **8**
Oaklands Av. *Esh* 7H **133**
Oaklands Av. *Iswth* 6K **79**
Oaklands Av. *Sidc* 7K **109**
Oaklands Av. *T Hth* 4A **140**
Oaklands Av. *W Wick* 3D **154**
Oaklands Clo. *Bexh* 5F **111**
Oaklands Clo. *Chess* 4C **146**
Oaklands Clo. *Orp* 6J **145**
Oaklands Clo. *Wemb* 5D **44**
Oaklands Ct. NW10 1A 64
(off Nicoll Rd.)
Oaklands Ct. SE20 7J 123
(off Chestnut Gro.)
Oaklands Ct. *Wemb* 5D **44**
Oaklands Dri. *Twic* 7G **97**
Oaklands Est. *SW4* 6G **103**
Oaklands Gro. *W12* 1C **82**
Oaklands M. NW2 4F 47
(off Oaklands Rd.)
Oaklands Pk. Av. *Ilf* 2G **55**
Oaklands Pas. NW2 4F 47
(off Oaklands Rd.)
Oaklands Pl. *SW4* 4G **103**

Oaklands Rd. N20 . . . 7C 4
Oaklands Rd. NW2 . . . 4F 47
Oaklands Rd. SW14 . . . 3K 99
Oaklands Rd. W7 . . . 2K 79 (in two parts)
Oaklands Rd. Bexh . . . 4F 111
Oaklands Rd. Brom . . . 7G 125
Oaklands Way. Wall . . . 7H 151
Oakland Way. Eps . . . 6A 148
Oak La. E14 . . . 7B 70
Oak La. N2 . . . 2B 30
Oak La. N11 . . . 6C 16
Oak La. Iswth . . . 4J 97
Oak La. Twic . . . 7A 98
Oak La. Wfd G . . . 4C 20
Oakleafe Gdns. Ilf . . . 3F 37
Oaklea Lodge. Ilf . . . 3A 56
Oaklea Pas. King T . . . 3D 134
Oakleigh Av. N20 . . . 2G 15
Oakleigh Av. Edgw . . . 2H 27
Oakleigh Av. Surb . . . 1G 147
Oakleigh Clo. N20 . . . 3J 15
Oakleigh Ct. Barn . . . 6H 5
Oakleigh Ct. Edgw . . . 2J 27
Oakleigh Ct. S'hall . . . 1D 78
Oakleigh Cres. N20 . . . 2H 15
Oakleigh Gdns. N20 . . . 1F 15
Oakleigh Gdns. Edgw . . . 5A 12
Oakleigh M. N20 . . . 1F 15
Oakleigh Park. . . . 1G 15
Oakleigh Pk. Av. Chst . . . 1E 144
Oakleigh Pk. N. N20 . . . 1G 15
Oakleigh Pk. S. N20 . . . 7H 5
Oakleigh Rd. Uxb . . . 7E 40
Oakleigh Rd. N. N20 . . . 2G 15
Oakleigh Rd. S. N11 . . . 3K 15
Oakleigh Way. Mitc . . . 1F 139
Oakleigh Way. Surb . . . 1G 147
Oakley Av. W5 . . . 7G 63
Oakley Av. Bark . . . 7K 55
Oakley Av. Croy . . . 4K 151
Oakley Clo. E4 . . . 3K 19
Oakley Clo. E6 . . . 6C 72
Oakley Clo. W7 . . . 7J 61
Oakley Clo. Iswth . . . 1H 97
Oakley Cres. EC1 . . . 2B 68 (1B 162)
Oakley Dri. SE9 . . . 1H 127
Oakley Dri. SE13 . . . 6F 107
Oakley Dri. Brom . . . 3C 156
Oakley Gdns. N8 . . . 5K 31
Oakley Gdns. SW3 . . . 6C 84 (7D 170)
Oakley Grange. Harr . . . 3G 43
Oakley Ho. SW1 . . . 4D 84 (3F 171)
Oakley Ho. W3 . . . 7G 63
Oakley Pk. Bex . . . 7C 110
Oakley Pl. SE1 . . . 5F 87
Oakley Rd. N1 . . . 7D 50
Oakley Rd. SE25 . . . 5H 141
Oakley Rd. Brom . . . 3C 156
Oakley Rd. Harr . . . 6J 25
Oakley Sq. NW1 . . . 2G 67
Oakley St. SW3 . . . 6C 84 (7C 170)
Oakley Wlk. W6 . . . 6F 83
Oakley Yd. E2 . . . 3K 163
Oak Lodge. E11 . . . 6J 35
Oak Lodge. W8 . . . 3K 83 (off Chantry Sq.)
Oak Lodge Clo. Stan . . . 5H 11
Oak Lodge Dri. W Wick . . . 7D 142
Oaklodge Way. NW7 . . . 5G 13
Oakmead Av. Brom . . . 6J 143
Oakmead Ct. Stan . . . 4H 11
Oak Meade. Pinn . . . 6A 10
Oakmead Gdns. Edgw . . . 4E 12
Oakmead Pl. Mitc . . . 1C 138
Oakmead Rd. SW12 . . . 1E 120
Oakmead Rd. Croy . . . 6H 139
Oakmede. Barn . . . 4A 4
Oakmere Rd. SE2 . . . 6A 92
Oakmont Pl. Orp . . . 7H 145
Oak Pk. Gdns. SW19 . . . 1F 119
Oak Pk. M. N16 . . . 3F 51
Oak Pl. SW18 . . . 5K 101
Oakridge Dri. N2 . . . 3B 30
Oakridge La. Brom . . . 5F 125
Oakridge Rd. Brom . . . 4F 125
Oak Ri. Buck H . . . 3G 21
Oak Rd. W5 . . . 7D 62
Oak Rd. Eri . . . 7J 93
Oak Rd. N Mald . . . 2K 135
Oak Row. SW16 . . . 2G 139
Oaks Av. SE19 . . . 5E 122
Oaks Av. Felt . . . 2C 114
Oaks Av. Romf . . . 2J 39
Oaks Av. Wor Pk . . . 3D 148
Oaks Cvn. Pk., The. Chess . . . 3C 146
Oaksford Av. SE26 . . . 3H 123
Oaks Gro. E4 . . . 2B 20
Oakshade Rd. Brom . . . 4F 125
Oakshaw Rd. SW18 . . . 7K 101
Oakshott Ct. NW1 . . . 2H 67 (1C 160) (in two parts)
Oaks La. Croy . . . 3J 153 (in two parts)
Oaks La. Ilf . . . 5J 37
Oaks Rd. Croy . . . 5H 153
Oaks Rd. Stanw . . . 5A 94
Oaks Shop. Cen., The. W3 . . . 1J 81
Oaks, The. N12 . . . 4E 14
Oaks, The. NW6 . . . 7F 47 (off Brondesbury Pk.)
Oaks, The. NW10 . . . 7D 46
Oaks, The. SE18 . . . 5G 91
Oaks, The. Brom . . . 6E 144
Oaks, The. Enf . . . 3G 7 (off Bycullah Rd.)
Oaks, The. Hay . . . 2E 58
Oaks, The. Mord . . . 4G 137
Oaks, The. Ruis . . . 7G 23
Oaks, The. Wfd G . . . 7B 20
Oak St. E14 . . . 2E 88 (off Stewart St.)
Oak St. Romf . . . 5J 39
Oaks Way. Cars . . . 7D 150
Oaksway. Surb . . . 1D 146
Oakthorpe Ct. N13 . . . 5H 17
Oakthorpe Pk. Est. N13 . . . 5H 17
Oakthorpe Rd. N13 . . . 5F 17
Oaktree Av. N13 . . . 3G 17
Oak Tree Clo. W5 . . . 6C 62
Oak Tree Clo. Stan . . . 7H 11
Oak Tree Ct. W3 . . . 7H 63
Oak Tree Ct. N'holt . . . 2A 60
Oak Tree Dell. NW9 . . . 5K 27
Oak Tree Dri. N20 . . . 1E 14
Oak Tree Gdns. Brom . . . 5K 125
Oaktree Gro. Ilf . . . 5H 55
Oak Tree Ho. W9 . . . 4J 65 (off Shirland Rd.)
Oak Tree Rd. NW8 . . . 3C 66 (2B 158)
Oakview Gdns. N2 . . . 4B 30
Oakview Gro. Croy . . . 1A 154
Oakview Lodge. NW11 . . . 7H 29 (off Beechcroft Av.)
Oakview Rd. SE6 . . . 5D 124
Oak Village. NW5 . . . 4E 48
Oak Vs. NW11 . . . 6H 29 (off Hendon Pk. Row)
Oak Way. N14 . . . 7A 6
Oak Way. SW20 . . . 4E 136
Oak Way. W3 . . . 1A 82
Oakway. Brom . . . 2F 143
Oak Way. Croy . . . 6K 141
Oak Way. Felt . . . 1G 113
Oakway Clo. Bex . . . 6E 110
Oakways. SE9 . . . 6F 109
Oakwood. . . . 5B 6
Oakwood. Wall . . . 7F 151
Oakwood Av. N14 . . . 7C 6
Oakwood Av. Beck . . . 2E 142
Oakwood Av. Brom . . . 3K 143
Oakwood Av. Mitc . . . 2B 138
Oakwood Av. S'hall . . . 7E 60
Oakwood Bus. Pk. NW10 . . . 4K 63
Oakwood Clo. N14 . . . 6B 6
Oakwood Clo. Chst . . . 6D 126
Oakwood Clo. Wfd G . . . 6H 21
Oakwood Ct. E6 . . . 7C 54
Oakwood Ct. W14 . . . 3H 83
Oakwood Ct. Harr . . . 6H 25
Oakwood Cres. N21 . . . 6D 6
Oakwood Cres. Gnfd . . . 6A 44
Oakwood Dri. SE19 . . . 6D 122
Oakwood Dri. Bexh . . . 4J 111
Oakwood Dri. Edgw . . . 6D 12
Oakwood Gdns. Ilf . . . 2K 55
Oakwood Gdns. Sutt . . . 2J 149
Oakwood La. W14 . . . 3H 83
Oakwood Lodge. N14 . . . 6B 6 (off Avenue Rd.)
Oakwood Pk. . . . 6D 6
Oakwood Pk. Rd. N14 . . . 7C 6
Oakwood Pl. Croy . . . 6A 140
Oakwood Rd. NW11 . . . 4J 29
Oakwood Rd. SW20 . . . 1C 136
Oakwood Rd. Croy . . . 6A 140
Oakwood Rd. Pinn . . . 2K 23
Oakwood Vw. N14 . . . 6C 6
Oakworth Rd. W10 . . . 5E 64
Oarsman Pl. E Mol . . . 4J 133
Oasis, The. Brom . . . 2A 144
Oast Ct. E14 . . . 7B 70 (off Newell St.)
Oast Lodge. W4 . . . 7A 82 (off Corney Reach Way)
Oates Clo. Brom . . . 3F 143
Oatfield Ho. N15 . . . 6E 32 (off Perry Ct.)
Oatfield Rd. Orp . . . 7K 145
Oatland Ri. E17 . . . 2A 34
Oatlands Dri. Wey . . . 7G 131
Oatlands Rd. Enf . . . 1D 8
Oat La. EC2 . . . 6C 68 (7D 162)
Oatwell Ho. SW3 . . . 5C 84 (4D 170) (off Marlborough St.)
Oban Clo. E13 . . . 4A 72
Oban Ho. E14 . . . 6F 71 (off Oban St.)
Oban Ho. Bark . . . 2H 73
Oban Rd. E13 . . . 3A 72
Oban Rd. SE25 . . . 4D 140
Oban St. E14 . . . 6F 71
Oberon Ho. N1 . . . 2E 68 (off Arden Est.)
Oberon Way. Shep . . . 3A 130
Oberstein Rd. SW11 . . . 4B 102
Oborne Clo. SE24 . . . 5B 104
O'Brien Ho. E2 . . . 3K 69 (off Roman Rd.)
Observatory Gdns. W8 . . . 2J 83
Observatory M. E14 . . . 4F 89
Observatory Rd. SW14 . . . 4J 99
Occupation La. SE18 . . . 1F 109
Occupation La. W5 . . . 4D 80
Occupation Rd. SE17 . . . 5C 86
Occupation Rd. W13 . . . 2B 80
Occupation Rd. Eps . . . 7K 147
Ocean Est. E1 . . . 5A 70 (Ben Jonson Rd.)
Ocean Est. E1 . . . 4K 69 (Ernest St.)
Ocean St. E1 . . . 5K 69
Ocean Wharf. E14 . . . 2B 88
Ockbrook. E1 . . . 5J 69 (off Hannibal Rd.)
Ockenden M. N1 . . . 6D 50
Ockendon Rd. N1 . . . 6D 50
Ockham Dri. Orp . . . 7A 128
Ockley Ct. Sidc . . . 3J 127
Ockley Ct. Sutt . . . 4A 150
Ockley Rd. SW16 . . . 4J 121
Ockley Rd. Croy . . . 7K 139
Octagon Arc. EC2 . . . 5E 68 (6G 163)
Octagon Ct. SE16 . . . 1K 87 (off Rotherhithe St.)
Octavia Clo. Mitc . . . 5C 138
Octavia Ho. SW1 . . . 3H 85 (2C 172) (off Medway St.)
Octavia Ho. W10 . . . 4G 65
Octavia Rd. Iswth . . . 3J 97
Octavia St. SW11 . . . 1C 102
Octavia Way. SE28 . . . 7B 74
Octavius St. SE8 . . . 7C 88
October Pl. NW4 . . . 3F 29
Odard Rd. W Mol . . . 4E 132
Oddmark Rd. Bark . . . 2H 73
Odeon Cinema. . . . 6H 67 (1D 166) (off Shaftesbury Av.)
Odeon Ct. E16 . . . 5J 71
Odeon Ct. NW10 . . . 1A 64
Odeon Leicester Square Cinema. . . . 7H 67 (3D 166) (off Leicester Sq.)
Odeon Pde. Gnfd . . . 6B 44 (off Allendale Rd.)
Odeon Swiss Cen. Cinema. . . . 7H 67 (2D 166) (off Leicester St.)
Odeon West End Cinema. . . . 7H 67 (3D 166) (off Panton St.)
Odessa Rd. E7 . . . 3H 53
Odessa Rd. NW10 . . . 2C 64
Odessa St. SE16 . . . 2B 88
Odette Duval Ho. E1 . . . 5J 69 (off Stepney Way)
Odger St. SW11 . . . 2D 102
Odhams Wlk. WC2 . . . 6J 67 (1F 167)
Odin Ho. SE5 . . . 2C 104
O'Donnell Ct. WC1 . . . 4J 67 (3F 161)
Odontological Mus., The. . . . 6K 67 (7H 161) (off Lincoln's Inn Fields, Royal College of Surgeons)
O'Driscoll Ho. W12 . . . 6D 64
Odyssey Bus. Pk. Ruis . . . 5K 41
Offa's Mead. E9 . . . 4B 52
Offenbach Ho. E2 . . . 2K 69 (off Mace St.)
Offenham Rd. SE9 . . . 4D 126
Offers Ct. King T . . . 3F 135
Offerton Rd. SW4 . . . 3G 103
Offham Ho. SE17 . . . 4E 86 (off Beckway St.)
Offham Slope. N12 . . . 5C 14
Offley Pl. Iswth . . . 2H 97
Offley Rd. SW9 . . . 7A 86
Offord Clo. N17 . . . 6B 18
Offord Rd. N1 . . . 7K 49
Offord St. N1 . . . 7K 49
Ogden Ho. Felt . . . 3C 114
Ogilby St. SE18 . . . 4D 90
Ogilvie Ho. E1 . . . 6K 69 (off Stepney Causeway)
Oglander Rd. SE15 . . . 4F 105
Ogle St. W1 . . . 5G 67 (5A 160)
Oglethorpe Rd. Dag . . . 3F 57
O'Gorman Ho. SW10 . . . 7A 84 (off King's Rd.)
O'Grady Ho. E17 . . . 3D 34
Ohio Cotts. Pinn . . . 2A 24
Ohio Rd. E13 . . . 4H 71
Oil Mill La. W6 . . . 5C 82
Okeburn Rd. SW17 . . . 5E 120
Okehampton Clo. N12 . . . 5G 15
Okehampton Cres. Well . . . 1B 110
Okehampton Rd. NW10 . . . 1E 64
Olaf St. W11 . . . 7F 65
Oldacre M. SW12 . . . 7E 102
Old Bailey. EC4 . . . 6B 68 (1B 168)
Old Barge Ho. All. SE1 . . . 3K 167
Old Barn Clo. Sutt . . . 7G 149
Old Barn Way. Bexh . . . 3K 111
Old Barrack Yd. SW1 . . . 2E 84 (7G 165) (in two parts)
Old Barrowfield. E15 . . . 1G 71
Old Bellgate Wharf. E14 . . . 3B 88
Oldberry Rd. Edgw . . . 6E 12
Old Bethnal Grn. Rd. E2 . . . 3G 69
Old Bexley. . . . 7H 111
Old Bexley Bus. Pk. Bex . . . 7H 111
Old Bexley La. Bex & Dart . . . 2K 129 (in two parts)
Old Billingsgate Mkt. EC3 . . . 7E 68 (3G 169) (off Lwr. Thames St.)
Old Billingsgate Wlk. EC3 . . . 7E 68 (3G 169)
Old Bond St. W1 . . . 7G 67 (3A 166)
Oldborough Rd. Wemb . . . 3C 44
Old Brentford. . . . 7D 80
Old Brewer's Yd. WC2 . . . 6J 67 (1E 166)
Old Brewery M. NW3 . . . 4B 48
Old Bri. Clo. N'holt . . . 2E 60
Old Bri. St. Hamp W . . . 2D 134
Old Broad St. EC2 . . . 6D 68 (7F 163)
Old Bromley Rd. Brom . . . 5F 125
Old Brompton Rd. SW5 & SW7 . . . 5J 83
Old Bldgs. WC2 . . . 7J 161
Old Burlington St. W1 . . . 7G 67 (2A 166)
Oldbury Pl. W1 . . . 5E 66 (5H 159)
Oldbury Rd. Enf . . . 2B 8
Old Canal M. SE15 . . . 5F 87 (off Trafalgar Av.)
Old Castle St. E1 . . . 6F 69 (7J 163)
Old Cavendish St. W1 . . . 6F 67 (7J 159)
Old Change Ct. EC4 . . . 1C 168
Old Chapel Pl. SW9 . . . 2A 104
Old Charlton Rd. Shep . . . 5E 130
Old Chelsea M. SW3 . . . 6C 84 (7C 170)
Old Chiswick Yd. W4 . . . 6A 82 (off Pumping Sta. Rd.)
Old Church Ct. N11 . . . 5A 16
Oldchurch Gdns. Romf . . . 7K 39
Old Church La. NW9 . . . 2K 45
Old Church La. Gnfd . . . 3A 62
Old Church La. Stan . . . 5G 11
Oldchurch Ri. Romf . . . 7K 39
Old Church Rd. E1 . . . 6K 69
Old Church Rd. E4 . . . 4H 19
Oldchurch Rd. Romf . . . 7K 39
Old Church St. SW3 . . . 5B 84 (6B 170)
Old Claygate La. Clay . . . 6A 146
Old Compton St. W1 . . . 7H 67 (2C 166)
Old Cote Dri. Houn . . . 6E 78
Old Ct. Ho. W8 . . . 2K 83 (off Old Ct. Pl.)
Old Ct. Pl. W8 . . . 2K 83
Old Courtyard, The. Brom . . . 1K 143
Old Dairy M. NW5 . . . 6F 49
Old Dairy M. SW12 . . . 1E 120
Old Deer Pk. Gdns. Rich . . . 3E 98
Old Devonshire Rd. SW12 . . . 7F 103
Old Dock Clo. Rich . . . 6G 81
Old Dover Rd. SE3 . . . 7J 89
Oldegate Ho. E6 . . . 7B 54
Old Farm Av. N14 . . . 7B 6
Old Farm Av. Sidc . . . 1H 127
Old Farm Clo. SW17 . . . 2C 120
Old Farm Clo. Houn . . . 4D 96
Old Farm Pas. Hamp . . . 1G 133
Old Farm Rd. N2 . . . 1B 30
Old Farm Rd. Hamp . . . 6D 114 (in two parts)
Old Farm Rd. W Dray . . . 2A 76
Old Farm Rd. E. Sidc . . . 2A 128
Old Farm Rd. W. Sidc . . . 2K 127
Oldfield Clo. Brom . . . 4D 144
Oldfield Clo. Gnfd . . . 5J 43
Oldfield Clo. Stan . . . 5F 11
Oldfield Ct. Surb . . . 4F 135 (off Cranes Pk. Cres.)
Oldfield Farm Gdns. Gnfd . . . 1H 61
Oldfield Gro. SE16 . . . 4K 87
Oldfield Ho. W4 . . . 5A 82 (off Devonshire Rd.)
Oldfield La. N. Gnfd . . . 2H 61
Oldfield La. S. Gnfd . . . 4G 61

Oldfield M. N6 7G 31
Oldfield Rd. N16 3E 50
Oldfield Rd. NW10 7B 46
Oldfield Rd. SW19 6G 119
Oldfield Rd. W3 2B 82
Oldfield Rd. Bexh 2E 110
Oldfield Rd. Brom 4C 144
Oldfield Rd. Hamp 1D 132
Oldfields Cir. N'holt 6G 43
Oldfields Rd. Sutt 3H 149
Oldfields Trad. Est. Sutt 3J 149
Old Fish St. Hill. EC4 7C 68 (2C 168) (off Victoria St.)
Old Fleet La. EC4 6B 68 (7A 162)
Old Fold Clo. Barn 1C 4
Old Fold La. Barn 1C 4
Old Fold Manor Golf Course. 1A 4
Old Fold Vw. Barn 3A 4
Old Ford. 1B 70
Old Ford. (Junct.) 1C 70
Old Ford Rd. E2 & E3 3J 69
Old Forge Clo. Stan 4F 11
Old Forge Cres. Shep 6D 130
Old Forge M. W12 2D 82
Old Forge Rd. Enf 1A 8
Old Forge Way. Sidc 4B 128
Old Gloucester St. WC1 5J 67 (5F 161)
Old Hall Clo. Pinn 1C 24
Old Hall Dri. Pinn 1C 24
Oldham Ter. W3 1J 81 (in two parts)
Old Hatch Mnr. Ruis 7H 23
Old Hill. Chst 1E 144
Oldhill St. N16 1G 51
Old Homesdale Rd. Brom 4A 144
Old Hospital Clo. SW17 1D 120
Old Ho. Clo. SW19 5G 119
Old Ho. Gdns. Twic 6C 98
Old Howlett's La. Ruis 6F 23
Old Isleworth. 3B 98
Old Jamaica Rd. SE16 3G 87 (7K 169)
Old James St. SE15 3H 105
Old Jewry. EC2 6D 68 (1E 168)
Old Kenton La. NW9 5H 27
Old Kent Rd. SE1 & SE15 4E 86
Old Kingston Rd. Wor Pk 2J 147
Old Laundry, The. Chst 1G 145
Old Lodge Pl. Twic 6B 98
Old Lodge Way. Stan 5F 11
Old London Rd. King T 2E 134
Old London Rd. Sidc 7G 129
Old Maidstone Rd. Sidc 7F 129
Old Malden. 1A 148
Old Malden La. Wor Pk 3K 147
Old Mnr. Ct. NW8 2A 66
Old Mnr. Dri. Iswth 6G 97
Old Mnr. Ho. M. Shep 3C 130
Old Mnr. Rd. S'hall 4B 78
Old Mnr. Way. Bexh 2K 111
Old Mnr. Way. Chst 5D 126
Old Mnr. Yd. SW5 4K 83
Old Mkt. Sq. E2 3F 69 (1J 163)
Old Marylebone Rd. NW1 5C 66 (6D 158)
Oldmead Ho. Dag 6H 57
Old M. Harr 5J 25
Old Mill Clo. E18 3A 36
Old Mill Pl. Romf 6K 39
Old Mill Rd. SE18 6H 91
Old Mitre Ct. EC4 6A 68 (1K 167)
Old Montague St. E1 5G 69 (6K 163)
Old Nichol St. E2 4F 69 (3J 163)
Old N. St. WC1 5G 161
Old Nursery Pl. Ashf 5D 112
Old Oak Clo. Chess 4F 147
Old Oak Common. 4A 64
Old Oak Comn. La. W3 & NW10 5A 64
Old Oak La. NW10 3A 64
Old Oak Rd. W3 7B 64
Old Orchard. Sun 2A 132
Old Orchard Clo. Barn 1G 5
Old Orchard Clo. Uxb 6C 58
Old Orchard, The. NW3 4D 48
Old Pal. La. Rich 5C 98
Old Pal. Rd. Croy 3B 152
Old Pal. Ter. Rich 5D 98
Old Pal. Yd. SW1 3J 85 (1E 172)
Old Pal. Yd. Rich 5C 98
Old Paradise St. SE11 4K 85 (3G 173)
Old Pk. Av. SW12 6E 102
Old Pk. Av. Enf 5H 7
Old Pk. Gro. Enf 4H 7
Old Pk. La. W1 1F 85 (5J 165)
Old Pk. M. Houn 7D 78
Old Pk. Ridings. N21 6G 7
Old Pk. Rd. N13 4E 16
Old Pk. Rd. SE2 5A 92
Old Pk. Rd. Enf 3G 7
Old Pk. Rd. S. Enf 4G 7
Old Pk. Vw. Enf 3F 7
Old Perry St. Chst 6J 127
Old Pound Clo. Iswth 2A 98
Old Pye St. SW1 3H 85 (1C 172)
Old Pye St. Est. SW1 3H 85 (1C 172) (off Old Pye St.)
Old Quebec St. W1 6D 66 (1F 165)
Old Queen St. SW1 2H 85 (7D 166)
Old Rectory Gdns. Edgw 6B 12
Old Redding. Harr 5A 10
Old Red Lion Theatre. 2A 68 (1K 161) (off St John St.)
Oldridge Rd. SW12 7E 102
Old River Works. N17 6H 17
Old Rd. SE13 4G 107
Old Rd. Dart 5K 111
Old Rd. Enf 1D 8
Old Royal Free Pl. N1 1A 68
Old Royal Free Sq. N1 1A 68
Old Royal Naval College 5F 89
Old Ruislip Rd. N'holt 2A 60
Old School Clo. SE10 3G 89
Old School Clo. SW19 2J 137
Old School Clo. Beck 2K 141
Old School Ct. N17 3F 33
Old School Cres. E7 6J 53
Old School Rd. Uxb 4B 58
Old Schools La. Eps 7B 148
Old School Sq. E14 6C 70 (off Pelling St.)
Old School Sq. Th Dit 6K 133
Old Seacoal La. EC4 6B 68 (1A 168)
Old S. Clo. H End 1B 24
Old S. Lambeth Rd. SW8 7J 85
Old Spitalfields Market. 5F 69 (5J 163)
Old Sq. WC2 6K 67 (7J 161)
Old Stable M. N5 3C 50
Old Sta. Gdns. Tedd 6A 116 (off Victoria Rd.)
Old Sta. Rd. Hay 3H 77
Oldstead Rd. Brom 4E 124
Old Stockley Rd. W Dray 2D 76
Old Street. (Junct.) 4C 68 (2E 162)
Old St. E13 2K 71
Old St. EC1 4C 68 (3C 162)
Old Sungate Cotts. Romf 1F 39
Old Sun Wharf. E14 7A 70 (off Narrow St.)
Old Swan Wharf. SW11 1B 102
Old Swan Yd. Cars 4D 150
Old Thackeray School. SW8 2F 103
Old Theatre Ct. SE1 1C 86 (4D 168) (off Porter St.)
Old Town. SW4 3G 103
Old Town. Croy 3B 152
Old Tramyard. SE18 4J 91
Old Vic Theatre. 2A 86 (6K 167) (off Cut, The)
Old Woolwich Rd. SE10 6F 89
Old York Rd. SW18 5K 101
O'Leary Sq. E1 5J 69
Olga St. E3 2A 70
Olinda Rd. N16 6F 33
Oliphant St. W10 3F 65
Oliver Av. SE25 3F 141
Oliver Bus. Pk. NW10 2J 63
Oliver Clo. W4 6H 81
Oliver Ct. SE18 4G 91
Oliver Gdns. E6 5C 72
Oliver Goldsmith Est. SE15 1G 105
Oliver Gro. SE25 4F 141
Oliver Ho. SE16 2G 87 (off George Row)
Oliver Ho. SW8 7J 85 (off Wyvil Rd.)
Oliver M. SE15 2G 105
Olive Rd. E13 3A 72
Olive Rd. NW2 4E 46
Olive Rd. SW19 7A 120
Olive Rd. W5 3D 80
Oliver Rd. E10 2D 52
Oliver Rd. E17 5E 34
Oliver Rd. NW10 2J 63
Oliver Rd. N Mald 2J 135
Oliver Rd. Sutt 4B 150
Olivers Wharf. E1 1H 87 (off Wapping High St.)
Olivers Yd. EC1 4D 68 (3F 163)
Olive St. Romf 5K 39
Olive Tree Ho. SE15 6J 87 (off Sharratt St.)
Olivette St. SW15 3F 101
Olive Waite Ho. NW6 7J 47
Olivia Ct. Enf 1H 7 (off Chase Side)
Olivier Theatre. 4J 167 (in Royal National Theatre)
Ollerton Grn. E3 1B 70
Ollerton Rd. N11 5C 16
Olley Clo. Wall 7J 151
Ollgar Clo. W12 1B 82
Olliffe St. E14 3E 88
Olmar St. SE1 6G 87
Olney Ho. NW8 4C 66 (3D 158) (off Tresham Cres.)
Olney Rd. SE17 6B 86 (in two parts)
Olron Cres. Bexh 5D 110
Olven Rd. SE18 6G 91
Olveston Wlk. Cars 6B 138
Olwen M. Pinn 2B 24
Olyffe Av. Well 1A 110
Olympia. 3G 83
Olympia Ind. Est. N22 3K 31
Olympia M. W2 7K 65
Olympian Ct. E14 4C 88 (off Homer Dri.)
Olympia Way. W14 3G 83
Olympic Way. Gnfd 1G 61
Olympic Way. Wemb 3G 45 (in three parts)
Olympus Sq. E5 3G 51
O'Mahoney Ct. SW17 3A 120
Oman Av. NW2 4E 46
O'Meara St. SE1 1C 86 (5D 168)
Omega Clo. E14 3D 88
Omega Pl. N1 1F 161
Omega St. SE14 1C 106
Ommaney Rd. SE14 1K 105
Omnibus Way. E17 2C 34
Ondine Rd. SE15 4F 105
Onega Ga. SE16 3A 88
O'Neill Ho. NW8 2C 66 (1C 158) (off Cochrane St.)
O'Neill Path. SE18 6E 90
One Owen St. EC1 2B 68 (1A 162) (off Goswell St.)
One Tree Clo. SE23 6J 105
Ongar Clo. Romf 5C 38
Ongar Rd. SW6 6J 83
Onra Rd. E17 7C 34
Onslow Av. Rich 5E 98
Onslow Clo. E4 2K 19
Onslow Clo. Th Dit 7J 133
Onslow Cres. Chst 1F 145
Onslow Dri. Sidc 2D 128
Onslow Gdns. E18 3K 35
Onslow Gdns. N10 5F 31
Onslow Gdns. N21 5F 7
Onslow Gdns. SW7 4B 84 (4A 170)
Onslow Gdns. Th Dit 7J 133
Onslow Gdns. Wall 6G 151
Onslow Ho. King T 1F 135 (off Acre Rd.)
Onslow M. E. SW7 4B 84 (4A 170)
Onslow M. W. SW7 4B 84 (4A 170)
Onslow Mills Trad. Est. W Dray 7A 58
Onslow Pde. N14 1A 16
Onslow Rd. Croy 7K 139
Onslow Rd. N Mald 4C 136
Onslow Rd. Rich 5E 98
Onslow Sq. SW7 4B 84 (4B 170)
Onslow St. EC1 4A 68 (4K 161)
Onslow Way. Th Dit 7J 133
Ontario St. SE1 3B 86
Ontario Way. E14 7C 70 (in two parts)
Opal Clo. E16 6B 72
Opal M. NW6 1H 65
Opal M. Ilf 2F 55
Opal St. SE11 5B 86 (5K 173)
Openshaw Rd. SE2 4B 92
Open University, The. (Parsifal College) 4J 47
Openview. SW18 1A 120
Opera Ct. N19 3H 49 (off Wedmore St.)
Operating Theatre Mus. 5F 169
Ophelia Gdns. NW2 3G 47
Ophelia Ho. W6 5F 83 (off Fulham Pal. Rd.)
Ophir Ter. SE15 1G 105
Opie Ho. NW8 2C 66 (off Townshend Est.)
Opossum Way. Houn 3A 96
Oppenheim Rd. SE13 2E 106
Oppidans Rd. NW3 7D 48
Orange Ct. La. Orp 7E 156
Orange Gro. E11 3G 53 (in two parts)
Orange Hill Rd. Edgw 7D 12
Orange Pl. SE16 3J 87
Orangery La. SE9 5D 108
Orangery, The. Rich 2C 116
Orange St. WC2 7H 67 (3D 166)
Orange Tree Ct. SE5 7E 86 (off Havil St.)
Orange Yd. W1 1D 166
Oransay Rd. N1 6C 50
Oratory La. SW3 5B 170
Oratory, The. 3C 84 (2C 170)
Orbain Rd. SW6 7G 83
Orbel St. SW11 1C 102
Orbital Cen., The. Wfd G 2B 36
Orb St. SE17 4D 86
Orchard Av. N3 3J 29
Orchard Av. N14 6B 6
Orchard Av. N20 2G 15
Orchard Av. Ashf 6E 112
Orchard Av. Belv 6E 92
Orchard Av. Croy 2A 154
Orchard Av. Felt 5F 95
Orchard Av. Houn 7C 78
Orchard Av. Mitc 1E 150
Orchard Av. N Mald 2A 136
Orchard Av. S'hall 1D 78
Orchard Av. Th Dit 1A 146
Orchard Bus. Cen. SE26 5B 124
Orchard Clo. E4 4H 19
Orchard Clo. E11 4K 35
Orchard Clo. N1 7C 50
Orchard Clo. NW2 3C 46
Orchard Clo. SE23 6J 105
Orchard Clo. SW20 4E 136
Orchard Clo. W10 5H 65
Orchard Clo. Ashf 6E 112
Orchard Clo. Bexh 1E 110
Orchard Clo. Bus H 1C 10
Orchard Clo. Edgw 6K 11
Orchard Clo. N'holt 6G 43
Orchard Clo. Ruis 7E 22
Orchard Clo. Surb 1B 146
Orchard Clo. W on T 7K 131
Orchard Clo. Wemb 1E 62
Orchard Clo. W Ewe 6H 147
Orchard Cotts. Hay 2G 77
Orchard Cotts. King T 1F 135
Orchard Ct. E10 1D 52
Orchard Ct. N14 6B 6
Orchard Ct. Edgw 5A 12
Orchard Ct. Iswth 7H 79
Orchard Ct. New Bar 3E 4
Orchard Ct. Twic 2H 115
Orchard Ct. Wall 5F 151
Orchard Ct. Wor Pk 1C 148
Orchard Cres. Edgw 5D 12
Orchard Cres. Enf 1A 8
Orchard Dri. SE3 2F 107
Orchard Dri. Edgw 5A 12
Orchard Dri. Shep 3G 131
Orchard Gdns. Chess 4E 146
Orchard Gdns. Sutt 5J 149
Orchard Ga. NW9 4A 28
Orchard Ga. Esh 7H 133
Orchard Ga. Gnfd 6B 44
Orchard Gro. SE20 7G 123
Orchard Gro. Croy 7A 142
Orchard Gro. Edgw 1G 27
Orchard Gro. Harr 5F 27
Orchard Hill. SE13 2D 106
Orchard Hill. Cars 5D 150
Orchard Hill. Dart 5K 111
Orchard Ho. SE5 1C 104 (off County Gro.)
Orchard Ho. SE16 3J 87
Orchard Ho. SW6 7G 83 (off Varna Rd.)
Orchard Ho. W1 6E 66 (7G 159) (off Fitzhardinge St.)
Orchard Ho. W12 1C 82
Orchard La. SW20 1D 136
Orchard La. E Mol 6H 133
Orchard La. Wfd G 4F 21
Orchardleigh Av. Enf 2D 8
Orchard Mead Ho. NW2 2J 47
Orchardmede. N21 6J 7
Orchard M. N1 7D 50
Orchard Pl. E14 7G 71 (in two parts)
Orchard Pl. N17 7A 18
Orchard Pl. Kes 7A 156
Orchard Ri. Croy 1A 154
Orchard Ri. King T 1J 135
Orchard Ri. Pinn 3H 23
Orchard Ri. Rich 4H 99
Orchard Ri. E. Sidc 5J 109
Orchard Ri. W. Sidc 5J 109
Orchard Rd. N6 7F 31
Orchard Rd. SE3 2G 107
Orchard Rd. SE18 4H 91
Orchard Rd. Barn 4C 4
Orchard Rd. Belv 4G 93
Orchard Rd. Bren 6C 80
Orchard Rd. Brom 1A 144
Orchard Rd. Chess 4E 146
Orchard Rd. Dag 1G 75
Orchard Rd. Enf 5D 8
Orchard Rd. Felt 1J 113
Orchard Rd. Hamp 7D 114

Orchard Rd. Hay 7J 59
Orchard Rd. Houn 5D 96
Orchard Rd. King T 2E 134
Orchard Rd. Mitc 1E 150
Orchard Rd. Rich 3G 99
Orchard Rd. Romf 1H 39
Orchard Rd. Sidc 4J 127
Orchard Rd. Sun 7K 113
Orchard Rd. Sutt 5J 149
Orchard Rd. Twic 5A 98
Orchard Rd. Well 3B 110
Orchardson Ho. NW8 4A 158
Orchardson St. NW8 4B 66 (4A 158)
Orchard Sq. W14 5H 83
Orchard St. E17 4A 34
Orchard St. W1 6E 66 (1G 165)
Orchard Studios. W6 4F 83 (off Brook Grn.)
Orchard Ter. Enf 6B 8
Orchard, The. N14 5A 6
Orchard, The. N21 6J 7
Orchard, The. NW11 5J 29
Orchard, The. SE3 2F 107
Orchard, The. W4 4K 81
Orchard, The. W5 5D 62 (off Montpelier Rd.)
Orchard, The. Eps 7B 148
Orchard, The. Houn 2G 97
Orchard Way. Ashf 2B 112
Orchard Way. Croy 1A 154
Orchard Way. Enf 3K 7
Orchard Way. Sutt 4B 150
Orchard Waye. Uxb 2A 58
Orchard Wharf. E14 7G 71 (off Orchard Pl.)
Orchid Clo. E6 5C 72
Orchid Clo. Chess 7C 146
Orchid Clo. S'hall 7C 60
Orchid Ct. Rush G 2K 57
Orchid Ct. Wemb 2E 44
Orchid Grange. N14 7B 6
Orchid Rd. N14 7B 6
Orchid St. W12 7C 64
Orde. NW9 1B 28
Orde Hall St. WC1 4K 67 (4G 161)
Ordell Rd. E3 2B 70
Ordnance Clo. Felt 2J 113
Ordnance Cres. SE10 2F 89
Ordnance Hill. NW8 1B 66
Ordnance M. NW8 2B 66
Ordnance Rd. E16 5H 71
Ordnance Rd. SE18 6E 90
Oregano Clo. W Dray 6A 58
Oregano Dri. E14 6F 71
Oregon Av. E12 4D 54
Oregon Clo. N Mald 4J 135
Orestes M. NW6 5J 47
Orford Ct. SE27 2B 122
Orford Ct. Stan 6H 11
Orford Gdns. Twic 2K 115
Orford Rd. E17 5C 34
Orford Rd. E18 3K 35
Orford Rd. SE6 3D 124
Organ Crossroads. (Junct.) 7C 148
Organ La. E4 2K 19 (in two parts)
Oriana Ho. E14 7B 70 (off Victory Pl.)
Oriel Clo. Mitc 4H 139
Oriel Ct. NW3 4A 48
Oriel Ct. Croy 1D 152
Oriel Dri. SW13 6E 82
Oriel Gdns. Ilf 3D 36
Oriel Pl. NW3 4A 48 (off Heath St.)
Oriel Rd. E9 6K 51
Oriel Way. N'holt 7F 43
Oriental Rd. E16 1B 90
Oriental St. E14 7C 70 (off Pennyfields)
Orient Ind. Pk. E10 2C 52
Orient St. SE11 4B 86 (3K 173)
Orient Way. E5 3K 51
Orient Way. E10 1A 52
Orient Wharf. E1 1H 87 (off Wapping High St.)
Oriole Way. SE28 7B 74
Orion Bus. Cen. SE14 5K 87
Orion Cen., The. Croy 2J 151
Orion Ho. E1 4H 69 (off Coventry Rd.)
Orion Rd. N11 7K 15
Orissa Rd. SE18 5J 91
Orkney Ho. N1 1K 67 (off Bemerton Est.)
Orkney St. SW11 2E 102
Orlando Rd. SW4 3G 103
Orleans Ct. Twic 7B 98
Orleans House Gallery. 1B 116
Orleans Rd. SE19 6D 122
Orleans Rd. Twic 7B 98
Orleston M. N7 6A 50
Orleston Rd. N7 6A 50
Orley Ct. Harr 4K 43
Orley Farm Rd. Harr 3J 43
Orlop St. SE10 5G 89
Ormanton Rd. SE26 4G 123
Orme Ct. W2 7K 65
Orme Ct. M. W2 7K 65 (off Orme La.)
Orme Ho. E8 1F 69
Orme La. W2 7K 65
Ormeley Rd. SW12 1F 121
Orme Rd. King T 2H 135
Ormerod Gdns. Mitc 2E 138
Ormesby Clo. SE28 7D 74
Ormesby Way. Harr 6F 27
Orme Sq. W2 7K 65
Ormiston Gro. W12 1D 82
Ormiston Rd. SE10 5J 89
Ormond Av. Hamp 1F 133
Ormond Av. Rich 5D 98
Ormond Clo. WC1 5J 67 (5F 161)
Ormond Cres. Hamp 1F 133
Ormond Dri. Hamp 7F 115
Ormonde Ct. SW15 4E 100
Ormonde Ga. SW3 5D 84 (6F 171)
Ormonde Pl. SW1 4E 84 (4G 171)
Ormonde Ri. Buck H 1F 21
Ormonde Rd. SW14 3J 99
Ormonde Ter. NW8 1D 66
Ormond M. WC1 4J 67 (4F 161)
Ormond Rd. N19 1J 49
Ormond Rd. Rich 5D 98
Ormond Yd. SW1 1G 85 (4B 166)
Ormsby. Sutt 7K 149
Ormsby Gdns. Gnfd 2G 61
Ormsby Lodge. W4 3A 82
Ormsby Pl. N16 3F 51
Ormsby St. E2 2F 69
Ormside St. SE15 6J 87
Ornan Rd. NW3 5C 48
Orpen Wlk. N16 3E 50
Orpheus St. SE5 1D 104
Orpington. 7K 145
Orpington Gdns. N18 3K 17
Orpington Mans. N21 1G 17
Orpington Rd. N21 1G 17
Orpington Rd. Chst 3J 145
Orpwood Clo. Hamp 6D 114
Orsett M. W2 6K 65 (in two parts)
Orsett St. SE11 5K 85 (5H 173)
Orsett Ter. W2 6K 65
Orsett Ter. Wfd G 7F 21
Orsman Rd. N1 1E 68
Orton St. E1 1G 87
Orville Rd. SW11 2B 102
Orwell Clo. Hay 7G 59
Orwell Clo. Rain 5K 75
Orwell Ct. E8 1G 69 (off Pownall Rd.)
Orwell Ct. N5 4C 50
Orwell Rd. E13 2A 72
Osbaldeston Rd. N16 2G 51
Osberton Rd. SE12 5J 107
Osbert St. SW1 4H 85 (4C 172)
Osborn Clo. E8 1G 69
Osborne Av. Stai 1B 112
Osborne Clo. Barn 3J 5
Osborne Clo. Beck 4A 142
Osborne Clo. Felt 5B 114
Osborne Ct. E10 7D 34
Osborne Ct. W5 5E 62
Osborne Gdns. T Hth 2C 140
Osborne Gro. E17 4B 34
Osborne Gro. N4 1A 50
Osborne Ho. E16 1J 89 (off Wesley Av.)
Osborne M. E17 4B 34
Osborne Pl. Sutt 5B 150
Osborne Rd. E7 5K 53
Osborne Rd. E9 6B 52
Osborne Rd. E10 2D 52
Osborne Rd. N4 1A 50
Osborne Rd. N13 3F 17
Osborne Rd. NW2 6D 46
Osborne Rd. W3 3H 81
Osborne Rd. Belv 5F 93
Osborne Rd. Buck H 1E 20
Osborne Rd. Dag 5F 57
Osborne Rd. Enf 2F 9
Osborne Rd. Houn 3D 96
Osborne Rd. King T 7E 116
Osborne Rd. S'hall 6G 61
Osborne Rd. T Hth 2C 140
Osborne Rd. W on T 7J 131
Osborne Sq. Dag 4F 57
Osborne Ter. SW17 5D 120 (off Church La.)
Osborne Way. Chess 5F 147 (off Bridge Rd.)
Osborn Gdns. NW7 7A 14
Osborn La. SE23 7A 106
Osborn St. E1 5F 69 (6K 163)
Osborn Ter. SE3 4H 107
Osbourne Ct. Harr 4F 25
Osbourne Ho. Twic 2G 115
Oscar Faber Pl. N1 7E 50
Oscar St. SE4 2C 106 (in two parts)
Oseney Cres. NW5 5G 49
O'Shea Gro. E3 1B 70
Osidge. 1A 16
Osidge La. N14 1K 15
Osier Ct. E1 4K 69 (off Osier St.)
Osier Ct. Bren 6E 80 (off Ealing Rd.)
Osier Ct. Romf 6K 39
Osier Cres. N10 1D 30
Osier M. W4 6A 82
Osiers Ct. King T 1D 134 (off Steadfast Rd.)
Osiers Rd. SW18 4J 101
Osier St. E1 4J 69
Osier Way. E10 3D 52
Osier Way. Mitc 5D 138
Oslac Rd. SE6 5D 124
Oslo Ct. NW8 2C 66 (off Prince Albert Rd.)
Oslo Ho. SE5 2C 104 (off Carew St.)
Oslo Sq. SE16 3A 88
Osman Clo. N15 6D 32
Osman Rd. N9 3B 18
Osman Rd. W6 3E 82
Osmington Ho. SW8 7K 85 (off Dorset Rd.)
Osmond Clo. Harr 2G 43
Osmond Gdns. Wall 5G 151
Osmund St. W12 5B 64
Osnaburgh St. NW1 4F 67 (4K 159) (Longford St.)
Osnaburgh Ter. NW1 4F 67 (3K 159)
Osney Ho. SE2 2D 92
Osney Wlk. Cars 6B 138
Osprey. NW9 1B 28
Osprey Clo. E6 5C 72
Osprey Clo. E11 4J 35
Osprey Clo. E17 7F 19
Osprey Clo. Sutt 5H 149
Osprey Clo. W Dray 2A 76
Osprey Ct. Beck 7C 124
Osprey Ho. E14 7A 70 (off Victory Pl.)
Osprey M. Enf 5D 8
Ospringe Clo. SE20 7J 123
Ospringe Ho. SE1 2A 86 (6K 167) (off Wootton St.)
Ospringe Rd. NW5 4G 49
Osram Ct. W6 3E 82
Osram Rd. Wemb 3D 44
Osric Path. N1 2E 68
Ossian M. N4 7K 31
Ossian Rd. N4 7K 31
Ossington Bldgs. W1 5E 66 (5G 159)
Ossington Clo. W2 7J 65
Ossington St. W2 7J 65
Ossory Rd. SE1 6G 87
Ossulston St. NW1 2H 67 (1D 160)
Ossulton Pl. N2 3A 30
Ossulton Way. N2 4A 30
Ostade Rd. SW2 7K 103
Ostell Cres. Enf 1H 9
Ostend Pl. SE1 4C 86
Osten M. SW7 3K 83
Osterley. 7H 79
Osterley Av. Iswth 7H 79
Osterley Clo. Orp 1K 145
Osterley Ct. Iswth 1H 97
Osterley Ct. N'holt 3A 60 (off Canberra Dri.)
Osterley Cres. Iswth 1J 97
Osterley Gdns. S'hall 2G 79
Osterley Gdns. T Hth 2C 140
Osterley Ho. E14 6D 70 (off Girauld St.)
Osterley La. S'hall & Iswth 5E 78 (in two parts)
Osterley Lodge. Iswth 7J 79 (off Church Rd.)
Osterley Pk. House. 6G 79
Osterley Pk. Rd. S'hall 3D 78
Osterley Pk. Vw. Rd. W7 2J 79
Osterley Rd. N16 4E 50
Osterley Rd. Iswth 7J 79
Osterley Views. S'hall 1G 79
Oster Ter. E17 5K 33
Ostliffe Rd. N13 5H 17
Oswald Rd. S'hall 1C 78
Oswald's Mead. E9 4A 52
Oswald St. E5 3K 51
Oswald Ter. NW2 3E 46
Osward Pl. N9 2C 18
Osward Rd. SW17 2D 120
Oswell Ho. E1 1H 87 (off Farthing Fields)
Oswin St. SE11 4B 86
Oswyth Rd. SE5 2E 104
Otford Clo. SE20 1J 141
Otford Clo. Bex 6H 111
Otford Clo. Brom 3E 144
Otford Cres. SE4 6B 106
Otford Ho. SE1 2D 86 (7F 169) (off Staple St.)
Otford Ho. SE15 6J 87 (off Lovelinch Clo.)
Othello Clo. SE11 5B 86 (5K 173)
Otho Ct. Bren 7D 80
Otis St. E3 3E 70
Otley App. Ilf 6F 37
Otley Dri. Ilf 5F 37
Otley Ho. N4 3A 50
Otley Rd. E16 6A 72
Otley Ter. E5 3K 51
Ottawa Gdns. Dag 7K 57
Ottaway Ct. E5 3G 51
Ottaway St. E5 3G 51
Otterbourne Rd. E4 3A 20
Otterbourne Rd. Croy 2C 152
Otterburn Gdns. Iswth 7A 80
Otterburn Ho. SE5 7C 86 (off Sultan St.)
Otterburn St. SW17 6D 120
Otter Clo. E15 1E 70
Otterden St. SE6 4C 124
Otterfield Rd. W Dray 7A 58
Otter Rd. Gnfd 4G 61
Otto Clo. SE26 3H 123
Otto St. SE17 6B 86
Otway Gdns. Bush 1D 10
Oulton Clo. E5 2J 51
Oulton Clo. SE28 6C 74
Oulton Cres. Bark 5K 55
Oulton Rd. N15 5D 32
Ouseley Rd. SW12 1D 120
Outer Circ. NW1 2C 66 (1D 158)
Outgate Rd. NW10 7B 46
Outram Pl. N1 1J 67
Outram Rd. E6 1C 72
Outram Rd. N22 1H 31
Outram Rd. Croy 2F 153
Outwich St. EC3 7H 163
Outwood Ho. SW2 7K 103 (off Deepdene Gdns.)
Oval Ct. Edgw 7D 12
Oval Cricket Ground. (Surrey County Cricket Club) 6K 85 (7H 173)
Oval Ho. Croy 1E 152 (off Oval Rd.)
Oval House Theatre. 6A 86 (7J 173)
Oval Mans. SE11 6K 85 (7H 173)
Oval Pl. SW8 7K 85
Oval Rd. NW1 1F 67
Oval Rd. Croy 2D 152
Oval Rd. N. Dag 1H 75
Oval Rd. S. Dag 2H 75
Oval, The. E2 2H 69
Oval, The. Sidc 7A 110
Oval Way. SE11 5K 85 (6H 173)
Overbrae. Beck 6C 124
Overbrook Wlk. Edgw 7B 12 (in two parts)
Overbury Av. Beck 3D 142
Overbury Rd. N15 6D 32
Overbury St. E5 4K 51
Overcliff Rd. SE13 3C 106
Overcourt Clo. Sidc 6B 110
Overdale Av. N Mald 2J 135
Overdale Rd. W5 3C 80
Overdown Rd. SE6 4C 124
Overhill Rd. SE22 7G 105
Overhill Way. Beck 5F 143
Overlea Rd. E5 7G 33
Overmead. SE9 7H 109
Oversley Ho. W2 5J 65 (off Alfred Rd.)
Overstand Clo. Beck 5C 142
Overstone Gdns. Croy 7B 142
Overstone Ho. E14 6C 70 (off E. India Dock Rd.)
Overstone Rd. W6 3E 82
Overstrand Mans. SW11 1D 102
Overton Clo. NW10 6J 45
Overton Clo. Iswth 1K 97
Overton Ct. E11 7J 35
Overton Ct. Sutt 7J 149
Overton Dri. E11 7J 35
Overton Dri. Romf 7C 38
Overton Ho. SW15 7B 100 (off Tangley Gro.)
Overton Rd. E10 1A 52
Overton Rd. N14 5D 6
Overton Rd. SE2 3C 92
Overton Rd. SW9 2A 104
Overton Rd. Sutt 6J 149
Overton Rd. E. SE2 3D 92
Overton's Yd. Croy 3C 152

Overy Ho. SE1 2B 86 (7A 168)
Ovesdon Av. Harr 1D 42
Ovett Clo. SE19 6E 122
Ovex Clo. E14 2E 88
Ovington Gdns. SW3 3C 84 (2D 170)
Ovington M. SW3 2D 170
Ovington Sq. SW3 3C 84 (2D 170)
Ovington St. SW3 4C 84 (3D 170)
Owen Clo. SE28 1C 92
Owen Clo. Croy 6D 140
Owen Clo. Hay 3K 59
Owen Gdns. Wfd G 6H 21
Owen Ho. Twic 7B 98
Owenite St. SE2 4B 92
Owen Mans. W14 6G 83 (off Queen's Club Gdns.)
Owen Rd. N13 5H 17
Owen Rd. Hay 3K 59
Owen's Ct. EC1 3B 68 (1A 162)
Owen's Row. EC1 3B 68 (1A 162)
Owen St. EC1 2B 68 (1A 162) (in two parts)
Owens Way. SE23 7A 106
Owen Wlk. SE20 1G 141
Owen Way. NW10 6J 45
Owgan Clo. SE5 7D 86
Oxberry Av. SW6 2G 101
Oxendon St. SW1 7H 67 (3C 166)
Oxenford St. SE15 3F 105
Oxenham Ho. SE8 6C 88 (off Benbow St.)
Oxenholme. NW1 2G 67 (1A 160) (off Harrington Sq.)
Oxenpark Av. Wemb 7E 26
Oxestall's Rd. SE8 5A 88
Oxford & Cambridge Mans. NW1 5C 66 (6D 158) (off Old Marylebone Rd.)
Oxford Av. NW10 3D 64
Oxford Av. SW20 2G 137
Oxford Av. Hay 7H 77
Oxford Av. Houn 5E 78
Oxford Cir. W1 6G 67 (1A 166) (off Oxford St.)
Oxford Cir. Av. W1 6G 67 (1A 166)
Oxford Clo. N9 2C 18
Oxford Clo. Ashf 7E 112
Oxford Clo. Mitc 3G 139
Oxford Ct. EC4 2E 168
Oxford Ct. W3 6G 63
Oxford Ct. W4 5H 81
Oxford Ct. W7 5K 61 (off Copley Clo.)
Oxford Ct. W9 5J 65 (off Elmfield Way)
Oxford Ct. Felt 4B 114
Oxford Cres. N Mald 6K 135
Oxford Dri. SE1 1E 86 (5G 169)
Oxford Dri. Ruis 2A 42
Oxford Gdns. N20 1G 15
Oxford Gdns. N21 7H 7
Oxford Gdns. W4 5G 81
Oxford Gdns. W10 6E 64
Oxford Ga. W6 4F 83
Oxford M. Bex 7G 111
Oxford Pl. NW10 3K 45 (off Press Rd.)
Oxford Rd. E15 6F 53 (in two parts)
Oxford Rd. N4 1A 50
Oxford Rd. N9 2C 18
Oxford Rd. NW6 2J 65
Oxford Rd. SE19 6D 122
Oxford Rd. SW15 4G 101
Oxford Rd. W5 7D 62
Oxford Rd. Cars 6C 150
Oxford Rd. Enf 5C 8
Oxford Rd. Harr 6G 25
Oxford Rd. Ilf 5G 55
Oxford Rd. Sidc 5B 128
Oxford Rd. Tedd 5H 115
Oxford Rd. Wall 5G 151
Oxford Rd. W'stone 3K 25
Oxford Rd. Wfd G 5G 21
Oxford Rd. N. W4 5H 81
Oxford Rd. S. W4 5G 81
Oxford Sq. W2 6C 66 (1D 164)
Oxford St. W1 6E 66 (1G 165)
Oxford Wlk. S'hall 1D 78
Oxford Way. Felt 4B 114
Oxgate Cen. NW2 2D 46
Oxgate Ct. NW2 2C 46
Oxgate Gdns. NW2 3D 46
Oxgate La. NW2 2D 46
Oxgate Pde. NW2 2C 46
Oxhawth Cres. Brom 5E 144
Oxleas. E6 6F 73
Oxleas Clo. Well 2H 109
Oxleay Rd. Harr 1E 42
Oxleigh Clo. N Mald 5A 136
Oxley Clo. SE1 5F 87
Oxleys Rd. NW2 3D 46
Oxlip Clo. Croy 1K 153
Oxlow La. Dag 4F 57
Oxonian St. SE22 4F 105
Oxo Tower Wharf. 7A 68 (3K 167)
Oxted Clo. Mitc 3B 138
Oxtoby Way. SW16 1H 139
Oystercatchers Clo. E16 6K 71
Oystergate Wlk. EC4 3E 168
Oyster Row. E1 6J 69
Ozolins Way. E16 6J 71

Pablo Neruda Clo. SE24 4B 104
Pace Pl. E1 6H 69
Pacific Clo. Felt 1H 113
Pacific Ho. E1 4K 69 (off Ernest St.)
Pacific Rd. E16 6J 71
Pacific Wharf. SE16 1K 87
Packenham Ho. E2 3F 69 (1K 163) (off Wellington Row)
Packington Rd. W3 3J 81
Packington Sq. N1 1C 68 (in three parts)
Packington St. N1 1B 68
Packmores Rd. SE9 5H 109
Padbury. SE17 5E 86 (off Bagshot St.)
Padbury Clo. Felt 1F 113
Padbury Ct. E2 3F 69 (2K 163)
Padbury Ho. NW8 4C 66 (3D 158) (off Tresham Cres.)
Padcroft Rd. W Dray 1A 76
Paddenswick Rd. W6 3C 82
Paddington. 6B 66 (1A 164)
Paddington Clo. Hay 4B 60
Paddington Ct. W7 5K 61 (off Copley Clo.)
Paddington Grn. W2 5B 66 (5A 158)
Paddington St. W1 5E 66 (5G 159)
Paddock Clo. SE3 2J 107
Paddock Clo. SE26 4K 123
Paddock Clo. N'holt 2E 60
Paddock Clo. Wor Pk 1A 148
Paddock Gdns. SE19 6E 122
Paddock Lodge. Enf 5K 7 (off Village Rd.)
Paddock Pas. SE19 6E 122 (off Paddock Gdns.)
Paddock Rd. NW2 3C 46
Paddock Rd. Bexh 4E 110
Paddock Rd. Ruis 3B 42
Paddocks Clo. Harr 4F 43
Paddocks Grn. NW9 1H 45
Paddocks, The. W5 3D 80 (off Popes La.)
Paddocks, The. Cockf 3J 5
Paddocks, The. Croy 6C 154
Paddocks, The. Wemb 2H 45
Paddock, The. NW9 5G 27
Paddock, The. Uxb 4D 40
Paddock Way. Chst 7H 127
Padfield Ct. Wemb 3F 45
Padfield Rd. SE5 3C 104
Padley Clo. Chess 5F 147
Padnall Ct. Romf 3D 38
Padnall Rd. Chad H 3D 38
Padstow Ho. E14 7B 70 (off Three Colt St.)
Padstow Rd. Enf 1G 7
Padstow Wlk. Felt 1H 113
Padua Rd. SE20 1J 141
Pagden St. SW8 1F 103
Pageant Av. NW9 1K 27
Pageant Cres. SE16 1A 88
Pageantmaster Ct. EC4 1A 168
Pageant Wlk. Croy 3E 152
Page Av. Wemb 3J 45
Page Clo. Dag 5E 56
Page Clo. Hamp 6C 114
Page Clo. Harr 6F 27
Page Cres. Croy 5B 152
Page Grn. Rd. N15 5G 33
Page Grn. Ter. N15 5F 33
Page Heath La. Brom 3B 144
Page Heath Vs. Brom 3B 144
Page Ho. SE10 6E 88 (off Welland St.)
Pagehurst Rd. Croy 7H 141
Page Mdw. NW7 7J 13
Page Rd. Felt 6F 95
Pages Hill. N10 2E 30
Pages La. N10 2E 30
Page St. NW7 1C 28
Page St. SW1 4H 85 (3D 172)
Page's Wlk. SE1 4E 86
Pages Yd. W4 6B 82
Paget Av. Sutt 3B 150
Paget Clo. Hamp 4H 115
Paget Gdns. Chst 1F 145
Paget La. Iswth 3H 97
Paget Pl. King T 6J 117
Paget Pl. Th Dit 1A 146
Paget Ri. SE18 6E 90
Paget Rd. N16 1D 50
Paget Rd. Ilf 4F 55
Paget Rd. Uxb 4E 58
Paget St. EC1 3B 68 (1A 162)
Paget Ter. SE18 6F 91
Pagham Ho. W10 4E 64 (off Sutton Way)
Pagin Ho. N15 5E 32 (off Braemar Rd.)
Pagitts Gro. Barn 1E 4
Pagnell St. SE14 7B 88
Pagoda Av. Rich 3F 99
Pagoda Gdns. SE3 2F 107
Paignton Rd. N15 6E 32
Paignton Rd. Ruis 3J 41
Paines Clo. Pinn 3C 24
Paines La. Pinn 1C 24
Pain's Clo. Mitc 2F 139
Painsthorpe Rd. N16 3E 50
Painswick Ct. SE15 7F 87 (off Daniel Gdns.)
Painters Rd. Ilf 3K 37
Paisley Rd. N22 1B 32
Paisley Rd. Cars 1B 150
Pakeman Ho. SE1 2B 86 (6B 168) (off Surrey Row)
Pakeman St. N7 3K 49
Pakenham Clo. SW12 1E 120
Pakenham St. WC1 3K 67 (2H 161)
Pakington Ho. SW9 2J 103 (off Stockwell Gdns. Est.)
Palace Av. W8 2K 83
Palace Ct. NW3 5K 47
Palace Ct. W2 7K 65 (off Moscow Rd., in two parts)
Palace Ct. Brom 1K 143 (off Palace Gro.)
Palace Ct. Harr 6E 26
Palace Ct. Gdns. N10 3G 31
Palace Gdns. Buck H 1G 21
Palace Gdns. Enf 4J 7
Palace Gdns. M. W8 1K 83
Palace Gdns. Shop. Cen. Enf 4J 7 (off Palace Gdns.)
Palace Gdns. Ter. W8 1J 83
Palace Ga. W8 2A 84
Palace Gates Rd. N22 1H 31
Palace Grn. W8 1K 83
Palace Grn. Croy 7B 154
Palace Gro. SE19 7F 123
Palace Gro. Brom 1K 143
Palace Mans. W14 4G 83 (off Hammersmith Rd.)
Palace Mans. King T 4D 134 (off Palace Rd.)
Palace M. E17 4B 34
Palace M. SW1 4H 171
Palace M. SW6 7J 83
Palace M. Enf 3J 7
Palace Pde. E17 4B 34
Palace Pl. SW1 3G 85 (1A 172)
Palace Pl. Mans. W8 2K 83 (off Kensington Ct.)
Palace Rd. N8 5H 31 (in two parts)
Palace Rd. N11 7D 16
Palace Rd. SE19 7F 123
Palace Rd. SW2 1K 121
Palace Rd. Brom 1K 143
Palace Rd. E Mol 3H 133
Palace Rd. King T 4D 134
Palace Rd. Ruis 4C 42
Palace Sq. SE19 7F 123
Palace St. SW1 3G 85 (1A 172)
Palace Theatre. 6H 67 (1D 166) (off Shaftesbury Av.)
Palace Vw. SE12 2J 125
Palace Vw. Brom 3K 143 (in two parts)
Palace Vw. Croy 4B 154
Palace Vw. Rd. E4 5J 19
Palace Wharf. W6 7E 82 (off Rainville Rd.)
Palamon Ct. SE1 5F 87 (off Cooper's Rd.)
Palamos Rd. E10 1C 52
Palatine Av. N16 4E 50
Palatine Rd. N16 4E 50
Palermo Rd. NW10 2C 64
Palestine Gro. SW19 1B 138
Palewell Comn. Dri. SW14 5K 99
Palewell Pk. SW14 5K 99
Palfrey Pl. SW8 7K 85
Palgrave Av. S'hall 7E 60
Palgrave Gdns. NW1 4C 66 (3D 158)
Palgrave Ho. SE5 7C 86 (off Wyndham Est.)
Palgrave Ho. Twic 7G 97
Palgrave Rd. W12 3B 82
Palissy St. E2 3F 69 (2J 163) (in two parts)
Pallant Ho. SE1 3D 86 (off Tabard St.)
Pallant Way. Orp 3E 156
Pallett Way. SE18 1C 108
Palliser Ct. W14 5G 83 (off Palliser Rd.)
Palliser Ho. E1 4K 69 (off Ernest St.)
Palliser Ho. SE10 6F 89 (off Trafalgar Rd.)
Palliser Rd. W14 5G 83
Pall Mall. SW1 1G 85 (5B 166)
Pall Mall E. SW1 1H 85 (4D 166)
Pall Mall Pl. SW1 5B 166
Palmar Cres. Bexh 3G 111
Palmar Rd. Bexh 2G 111
Palm Av. Sidc 6D 128
Palm Clo. E10 3D 52
Palm Ct. SE15 7F 87 (off Garnies Clo.)
Palmeira Rd. Bexh 3D 110
Palmer Av. Sutt 4E 148
Palmer Clo. Houn 1E 96
Palmer Clo. W Wick 3F 155
Palmer Ct. NW10 1K 63 (in two parts)
Palmer Cres. King T 3E 134
Palmer Gdns. Barn 5A 4
Palmer Pl. N7 5A 50
Palmer Rd. E13 4K 71
Palmer Rd. Dag 1D 56
Palmer's Ct. N11 5B 16 (off Palmer's Rd.)
Palmers Green. 4F 17
Palmers Gro. W Mol 4E 132
Palmers La. Enf 1C 8 (in two parts)
Palmers Pas. SW14 3J 99 (off Palmers Rd.)
Palmer's Rd. E2 2K 69
Palmer's Rd. N11 5B 16
Palmers Rd. SW14 3J 99
Palmers Rd. SW16 2K 139
Palmerston Cen. W'stone 3K 25
Palmerston Ct. E3 2K 69 (off Old Ford Rd.)
Palmerston Ct. Buck H 1F 21
Palmerston Ct. Surb 7D 134
Palmerston Cres. N13 5E 16
Palmerston Cres. SE18 6G 91
Palmerston Gro. SW19 7J 119
Palmerston Ho. SE1 2A 86 (7J 167) (off Westminster Bri. Rd.)
Palmerston Ho. W8 1J 83 (off Kensington Pl.)
Palmerston Mans. W14 6G 83 (off Queen's Club Gdns.)
Palmerston Rd. E7 6K 53
Palmerston Rd. E17 3B 34
Palmerston Rd. N22 7E 16
Palmerston Rd. NW6 7H 47 (in two parts)
Palmerston Rd. SW14 4J 99
Palmerston Rd. SW19 7J 119
Palmerston Rd. W3 3J 81
Palmerston Rd. Buck H 2E 20
Palmerston Rd. Cars 4D 150
Palmerston Rd. Croy 5D 140
Palmerston Rd. Harr 3J 25
Palmerston Rd. Houn 1G 97
Palmerston Rd. Sutt 5A 150
Palmerston Rd. Twic 6J 97
Palmerston Way. SW8 7F 85
Palmer St. SW1 3H 85 (1C 172) (in two parts)
Palm Gro. W5 3E 80
Palm Rd. Romf 5J 39
Palm Tree Ho. SE14 7K 87 (off Barlborough St.)
Pamela Ct. N3 6E 14
Pamela Gdns. Pinn 5K 23
Pamela Ho. E8 1F 69 (off Haggerston Rd.)
Pampisford Rd. Purl 7B 152
Pams Way. Eps 5K 147
Panama Ho. E1 5K 69 (off Beaumont Sq.)
Pancras La. EC4 6C 68 (1E 168)
Pancras Rd. NW1 2H 67 (1E 160)
Pandora Rd. NW6 6J 47
Panfield M. Ilf 6E 36
Panfield Rd. SE2 3A 92
Pangbourne. NW1 3G 67 (2A 160) (off Stanhope St.)
Pangbourne Av. W10 5E 64
Pangbourne Dri. Stan 5J 11

Panhard Pl. S'hall 7F 61
Pank Av. Barn 5F 5
Pankhurst Av. E16 1K 89
Pankhurst Clo. SE14 7K 87
Pankhurst Clo. Iswth 3K 97
Pankhurst Rd. W on T 7A 132
Panmuir Rd. SW20 1D 136
Panmure Clo. N5 4B 50
Panmure Ct. S'hall 6G 61
(off Osborne Rd.)
Panmure Rd. SE26 3H 123
Panorama Ct. N6 6G 31
Pansy Gdns. W12 7C 64
Panther Dri. NW10 5K 45
Pantiles Clo. N13 5G 17
Pantiles, The. NW11 5H 29
Pantiles, The. Bexh 7F 93
Pantiles, The. Brom 3C 144
Pantiles, The. Bush 1C 10
Panton St. SW1 7H 67 (3C 166)
Paper Bldgs. EC4 2K 167
Papermill Clo. Cars 4E 150
Paper Mill Wharf. E14 7A 70
Papillons Wlk. SE3 2J 107
Papworth Gdns. N7 5K 49
Papworth Way. SW2 7A 104
Parade Mans. NW4 5D 28
Parade M. SE27 2B 122
Parade, The. N4 1A 50
Parade, The. SE4 2B 106
(off Up. Brockley Rd.)
Parade, The. SE26 3H 123
(off Wells Pk. Rd.)
Parade, The. SW11 7D 84
Parade, The. Cars 5D 150
(off Beynon Rd.)
Parade, The. Croy 6J 139
Parade, The. Gnfd 5B 44
Parade, The. Hamp 5H 115
Parade, The. King T 2E 134
(off London Rd.)
Parade, The. Sun 7H 113
Parade, The. Sutt 3H 149
Parade, The. Wor Pk 4B 148
Paradise Pas. N7 5A 50
Paradise Pl. SE18 4C 90
Paradise Rd. SW4 2J 103
Paradise Rd. Rich 5D 98
Paradise Row. E2 3H 69
Paradise St. SE16 2H 87
Paradise Wlk. SW3 6D 84 (7F 171)
Paragon Clo. E16 6J 71
Paragon Gro. Surb 6F 135
Paragon M. SE1 4D 86
Paragon Pl. SE3 2H 107
Paragon Pl. W13 4K 61
Paragon Pl. Surb 6F 135
Paragon Rd. E9 6J 51
Paragon, The. SE3 2H 107
Paramount Building. EC1 4B 68 (3A 162)
(off St John St.)
Paramount Ct. WC1 4B 160
Parbury Ri. Chess 6E 146
Parbury Rd. SE23 6A 106
Parchmore Rd. T Hth 2B 140
Parchmore Way. T Hth 2B 140
Pardoner Ho. SE1 3D 86
(off Pardoner St.)
Pardoner St. SE1 3D 86 (7F 169)
(in two parts)
Pardon St. EC1 4B 68 (3B 162)
Parfett St. E1 5G 69
(in two parts)
Parfitt Clo. NW3 1A 48
Parfrey St. W6 6E 82
Pargreaves Ct. Wemb 2G 45
Parham Dri. Ilf 6F 37
Parham Way. N10 2G 31
Paris Garden. SE1 1B 86 (4A 168)
Parish Cotts. Dag 2G 57
Parish Ct. Surb 5E 134
Parish Ga. Dri. Sidc 6J 109
Parish La. SE20 6K 123
Parish M. SE20 7K 123
Paris Ho. E2 2H 69
(off Old Bethnal Grn. Rd.)
Parish Wharf Pl. SE18 4C 90
Park App. SE16 3H 87
Park App. Well 4B 110
Park Av. E6 1E 72
Park Av. E15 6G 53
Park Av. N3 1K 29
Park Av. N13 3F 17
Park Av. N18 4B 18
Park Av. N22 2J 31
Park Av. NW2 6E 46
Park Av. NW10 2F 63
(in two parts)
Park Av. NW11 1K 47
Park Av. SW14 4K 99
Park Av. Bark 6G 55
Park Av. Brom 6H 125
Park Av. Cars 6E 150
Park Av. Enf 5J 7
Park Av. Houn 6F 97
Park Av. Ilf 1E 54
Park Av. Mitc 7F 121
Park Av. Orp 3D 156
Park Av. Ruis 6F 23
Park Av. Shep 3G 131
Park Av. S'hall 2D 78
Park Av. W Wick 2E 154
Park Av. Wfd G 5E 20
Park Av. E. Eps 6C 148
Park Av. M. Mitc 7F 121
Park Av. N. N8 3H 31
Park Av. N. NW10 5D 46
Park Av. Rd. N17 7C 18
Park Av. S. N8 4H 31
Park Av. W. Eps 6C 148
Park Bus. Cen. NW6 3J 65
Park Chase. Wemb 4F 45
Park Clo. E9 1J 69
Park Clo. N20 3G 15
Park Clo. NW2 3D 46
Park Clo. NW10 3F 63
Park Clo. SW1 2D 84 (7E 164)
Park Clo. W4 6K 81
Park Clo. W14 3H 83
Park Clo. Cars 6D 150
Park Clo. Hamp 1G 133
Park Clo. Harr 1J 25
Park Clo. Houn 5G 97
Park Clo. King T 1G 135
Park Ct. E4 2K 19
Park Ct. E17 5D 34
Park Ct. N11 7C 16
Park Ct. N17 7B 18
Park Ct. SE26 6H 123
Park Ct. SW11 1F 103
Park Ct. Hamp W 1C 134
Park Ct. Harr 7E 26
Park Ct. N Mald 4K 135
Park Ct. S Croy 5C 152
(off Warham Rd.)
Park Ct. Uxb 1A 58
Park Ct. Wemb 5E 44
Park Cres. N3 7F 15
Park Cres. W1 4F 67 (4J 159)
Park Cres. Enf 4J 7
Park Cres. Eri 6J 93
Park Cres. Harr 1J 25
Park Cres. Twic 1H 115
Park Cres. M. E. W1 4F 67 (4K 159)
Park Cres. M. W. W1 4F 67 (4J 159)
Park Cres. Rd. Eri 6K 93
Park Cft. Edgw 1J 27
Parkcroft Rd. SE12 7H 107
Parkdale. N11 6C 16
Parkdale Cres. Wor Pk 3K 147
Parkdale Rd. SE18 5J 91
Park Dri. N21 6H 7
Park Dri. NW11 1K 47
Park Dri. SE7 6C 90
Park Dri. SW14 5K 99
Park Dri. W3 3G 81
Park Dri. Dag 3J 57
Park Dri. Har W 6C 10
Park Dri. N Har 7E 24
Park Dri. Romf 4K 39
Park Dwellings. NW3 5D 48
Park End. NW3 4C 48
Park End. Brom 1H 143
Parker Clo. E16 1C 90
Parker Clo. Cars 6D 150
Parker Ho. E14 2C 88
(off Admirals Way)
Parker M. WC2 6J 67 (7F 161)
Parke Rd. SW13 1C 100
Parke Rd. Sun 4J 131
Parker Rd. Croy 4C 152
Parkers Row. SE1 2G 87 (7K 169)
Parker St. E16 1C 90
Parker St. WC2 6J 67 (7F 161)
Pk. Farm Clo. N2 3A 30
Pk. Farm Clo. Pinn 5K 23
Pk. Farm Ct. Hay 7G 59
Pk. Farm Rd. Brom 1B 144
Pk. Farm Rd. King T 7E 116
Parkfield. Iswth 1J 97
Parkfield Av. SW14 4A 100
Parkfield Av. Felt 3J 113
Parkfield Av. Harr 2G 25
Parkfield Av. Hil 3D 58
Parkfield Av. N'holt 2B 60
Parkfield Clo. Edgw 6C 12
Parkfield Clo. N'holt 2C 60
Parkfield Ct. SE14 1B 106
(off Parkfield Rd.)
Parkfield Cres. Felt 3J 113
Parkfield Cres. Harr 2G 25
Parkfield Cres. Ruis 2C 42
Parkfield Dri. N'holt 2B 60
Parkfield Gdns. Harr 3F 25
Parkfield Ho. N Har 1F 25
Parkfield Ind. Est. SW11 2E 102
Parkfield Pde. Felt 3J 113
Parkfield Rd. NW10 7D 46
Parkfield Rd. SE14 1B 106
Parkfield Rd. Felt 3J 113
Parkfield Rd. Harr 3G 43
Parkfield Rd. N'holt 2C 60
Parkfield Rd. Uxb & Ick 2D 40
Parkfields. SW15 4E 100
Parkfields. Croy 1B 154
Parkfields Av. NW9 1K 45
Parkfields Av. SW20 1D 136
Parkfields Clo. Cars 4E 150
Parkfields Rd. King T 5F 117
Parkfield St. N1 2A 68
Parkfield Way. Brom 6D 144
Park Gdns. E10 1C 52
Park Gdns. NW9 3H 27
Park Gdns. Eri 4K 93
Park Gdns. King T 5F 117
Park Ga. N2 3B 30
Park Ga. N21 7E 6
Park Ga. SE3 3H 107
Park Ga. W5 5D 62
Parkgate Av. Barn 1F 5
Pk. Gate Clo. King T 6H 117
Pk. Gate Ct. Hamp H 6G 115
Parkgate Cres. Barn 1F 5
Parkgate Gdns. SW14 5K 99
Parkgate M. N6 7G 31
Parkgate Rd. SW11 7C 84
Parkgate Rd. Wall 5E 150
Park Gates. Harr 4E 42
Park Gro. E15 1J 71
Park Gro. N11 7C 16
Park Gro. Bexh 4J 111
Park Gro. Brom 1K 143
Park Gro. Edgw 5A 12
Park Gro. Rd. E11 2G 53
Park Hall. SE10 7F 89
(off Crooms Hill)
Parkhall Rd. N2 4C 30
Pk. Hall Rd. SE21 3C 122
Pk. Hall Trad. Est. SE21 3C 122
Parkham Ct. Brom 2G 143
Parkham St. SW11 1C 102
Park Hill. SE23 2H 123
Park Hill. SW4 5H 103
Park Hill. W5 5D 62
Park Hill. Brom 4C 144
Park Hill. Cars 6C 150
Park Hill. Rich 6F 99
Pk. Hill Clo. Cars 5C 150
Pk. Hill Ct. SW17 3D 120
Pk. Hill M. S Croy 5D 152
(off S. Park Hill Rd.)
Pk. Hill Ri. Croy 2E 152
Parkhill Rd. E4 1K 19
Parkhill Rd. NW3 5D 48
Parkhill Rd. Bex 7F 111
Pk. Hill Rd. Brom 2G 143
Pk. Hill Rd. Croy 2E 152
Pk. Hill Rd. Sidc 3H 127
Pk. Hill Rd. Wall 7F 151
Parkhill Wlk. NW3 5D 48
Parkholme Rd. E8 6G 51
Park Ho. E9 7J 51
(off Shore Rd.)
Park Ho. N21 7E 6
Park Ho. Gdns. Twic 5C 98
Park Ho. Pas. N6 7E 30
Parkhouse St. SE5 7D 86
Parkhurst Ct. N7 4J 49
Parkhurst Gdns. Bex 7G 111
Parkhurst Rd. E12 4E 54
Parkhurst Rd. E17 4A 34
Parkhurst Rd. N7 4J 49
Parkhurst Rd. N11 5K 15
Parkhurst Rd. N17 2G 33
Parkhurst Rd. N22 6E 16
Parkhurst Rd. Bex 7G 111
Parkhurst Rd. Sutt 4B 150
Parkinson Ho. E9 7J 51
(off Frampton Pk. Rd.)
Parkinson Ho. SW1 4G 85 (5C 172)
(off Tachbrook St.)
Parkland Ct. E15 5G 53
(off Maryland Pk.)
Parkland Gdns. SW19 1F 119
Parkland Gro. Ashf 4C 112
Parkland Rd. N22 2K 31
Parkland Rd. Ashf 4C 112
Parkland Rd. Wfd G 7E 20
Parklands. N6 1F 49
Parklands. Surb 5F 135
Parklands Clo. SW14 5J 99
Parklands Clo. Barn 1G 5
Parklands Clo. Ilf 7G 37
Parklands Ct. Houn 2B 96
Parklands Dri. N3 3G 29
Parklands Gro. Iswth 1K 97
Parklands Pde. Houn 2B 96
Parklands Rd. SW16 5F 121
Parklands Way. Wor Pk 2A 148
Park La. E15 1F 71
Park La. N9 3K 17
Park La. N17 7A 18
(in two parts)
Park La. W1 7D 66 (2F 165)
Park La. Cars 4E 150
Park La. Chad H 6D 38
Park La. Cran 7J 77
Park La. Croy 3D 152
Park La. Harr 3F 43
Park La. Hay 5G 59
Park La. Rich 4D 98
Park La. Stan 3F 11
Park La. Sutt 6G 149
Park La. Tedd 6K 115
Park La. Wemb 5E 44
Park La. Clo. N17 7B 18
Park La. Mans. Croy 3D 152
(off Edridge Rd.)
Park Langley 4E 142
Park Lawns. Wemb 4F 45
Parklea Clo. NW9 1A 28
Pk. Lee Ct. N16 7E 32
Parkleigh Rd. SW19 2K 137
Parkleys. Rich 4D 116
Parkleys Pde. Rich 4D 116
Park Lodge. NW8 7B 48
Park Lofts. SW2 5J 103
(off Mandrell Rd.)
Park Lorne. NW8 3C 66 (2D 158)
(off Park Rd.)
Park Mnr. Sutt 7A 150
(off Christchurch Pk.)
Park Mans. NW4 5D 28
Park Mans. NW8 2C 66
(off Allitsen Rd.)
Park Mans. SW1 2D 84 (7E 164)
(off Knightsbridge)
Park Mans. SW8 6J 85 (7F 173)
Park Mans. SW11 1D 102
(off Prince of Wales Dri.)
Parkmead. SW15 6D 100
Park Mead. Harr 3F 43
Park Mead. Sidc 5B 110
Parkmead Gdns. NW7 6G 13
Park M. SE24 7C 104
Park M. W10 2G 65
Park M. Chst 6F 127
Park M. Stanw 7B 94
Parkmore Clo. Wfd G 4D 20
Park Pde. NW10 2B 64
Park Pde. W5 3G 81
Park Pde. Hay 6G 59
Park Pl. E14 1C 88
Park Pl. SW1 1G 85 (5A 166)
Park Pl. W3 4G 81
Park Pl. W5 1D 80
Park Pl. Brom 1K 143
(off Park Rd.)
Park Pl. Hamp H 6G 115
Park Pl. Wemb 4F 45
Park Pl. Vs. W2 5A 66 (5A 158)
Park Ridings. N8 3A 32
Park Ri. SE23 1A 124
Park Ri. Harr 1J 25
Park Ri. Rd. SE23 1A 124
Park Rd. E6 1A 72
Park Rd. E10 1C 52
Park Rd. E12 1K 53
Park Rd. E15 1J 71
Park Rd. E17 5B 34
Park Rd. N2 3B 30
Park Rd. N8 4G 31
Park Rd. N11 7C 16
Park Rd. N14 1C 16
Park Rd. N15 4B 32
Park Rd. N18 4B 18
Park Rd. NW4 7C 28
Park Rd. NW8 & NW1 3C 66 (2D 158)
Park Rd. NW9 7K 27
Park Rd. NW10 1A 64
Park Rd. SE25 4E 140
Park Rd. SW19 6B 120
Park Rd. W4 7J 81
Park Rd. W7 7K 61
Park Rd. Ashf 5D 112
Park Rd. Barn 4G 5
Park Rd. Beck 7B 124
Park Rd. Brom 1K 143
Park Rd. Cheam 6G 149
Park Rd. Chst 6F 127
Park Rd. E Mol 4G 133
Park Rd. Felt 4B 114
Park Rd. Hack 2F 151
Park Rd. Hamp H 4F 115
Park Rd. Hamp W 1C 134
Park Rd. Hay 5G 59
Park Rd. High Bar 4C 4
Park Rd. Houn 5F 97
Park Rd. Ilf 3H 55
Park Rd. Iswth 1B 98
Park Rd. King T 5F 117
Park Rd. N Mald 4K 135
Park Rd. Rich 6F 99
Park Rd. Sun 7K 113
Park Rd. Surb 6F 135
Park Rd. Tedd 6K 115

Park Rd. Twic 6C 98
Park Rd. Uxb. 7A 40
Park Rd. Wall. 5F 151
Park Rd. Wemb 6E 44
Park Rd. E. W3 2H 81
Park Rd. E. Uxb. 2A 58
Park Rd. Ho. King T. 7G 117
Park Rd. N. W3 2H 81
Park Rd. N. W4 5K 81
Park Row. SE10 5F 89
Park Royal 3H 63
Park Royal Junction. (Junct.) 1H 63
Pk. Royal Metro Cen. NW10 4H 63
Pk. Royal Rd. NW10 & W3 3J 63
Pk. Royal S. Leisure Complex. W3 4G 63
Parkshot. Rich 4D 98
Parkside. N3 1K 29
Parkside. NW2 3C 46
Parkside. NW7 6H 13
Parkside. SE3 7H 89
Parkside. SW1 6F 165
Parkside. SW19 3F 119
Parkside. W3 1A 82
Parkside. W5 7E 62
Parkside. Buck H 2E 20
Parkside. Hamp H 5H 115
Parkside. Hay 7G 59
Parkside. Sidc 2B 128
Parkside. Sutt 6G 149
Parkside Av. SW19 5F 119
Parkside Av. Bexh 2K 111
Parkside Av. Brom 4C 144
Parkside Av. Romf 3K 39
Parkside Bus. Est. SE8 6A 88 (Blackhorse Rd.)
Parkside Bus. Est. SE8 6A 88 (Rolt St.)
Parkside Clo. SE20 7J 123
Parkside Ct. E11 6J 35 (off Wanstead Pl.)
Parkside Ct. N22 6E 16
Parkside Cres. N7 3A 50
Parkside Cres. Surb 6J 135
Parkside Cross. Bexh 2K 111
Parkside Dri. Edgw 3B 12
Parkside Est. E9 1J 69
Parkside Gdns. SW19 4F 119
Parkside Gdns. E Barn 1J 15
Parkside Ho. Dag 3J 57
Parkside Lodge. Belv 5J 93
Parkside Rd. SW11 1E 102
Parkside Rd. Belv 4H 93
Parkside Rd. Houn 5F 97
Parkside Ter. N18 4J 17
Parkside Way. Harr 4F 25
Park Sq. E. NW1 4F 67 (3J 159)
Park Sq. M. NW1 4J 159
Park Sq. W. NW1 4F 67 (3J 159)
Parkstead Rd. SW15 5C 100
Park Steps. W2 2D 164
Parkstone Av. N18 6A 18
Parkstone Rd. E17 3E 34
Parkstone Rd. SE15 2G 105
Park St. SE1 1C 86 (4C 168)
Park St. W1 7E 66 (2G 165)
Park St. Croy 3C 152
Park St. Tedd 6J 115
Park Ter. Cars 3C 150
Park Ter. Enf 1F 9
Park Ter. Wor Pk 1C 148
Park, The. N6 6E 30
Park, The. NW11 1K 47
Park, The. SE19 7E 122
Park, The. SE23 1J 123
Park, The. W5 1D 80
Park, The. Cars 5D 150
Park, The. Sidc 5A 128
Parkthorne Clo. Harr 6F 25
Parkthorne Dri. Harr 6E 24
Parkthorne Rd. SW12 7H 103
Park Towers. W1 1F 85 (5J 165) (off Brick St.)
Park Vw. N5 4C 50
Park Vw. N21 7E 6
Park Vw. W3 5J 63
Park Vw. Chad H 6D 38
Parkview. Eri 3D 92
Parkview. Gnfd 3A 62 (off Perivale La.)
Park Vw. N Mald 3B 136
Park Vw. Pinn 1D 24
Park Vw. Wemb 5H 45
Park Vw. W Dray 7A 58
Pk. View Ct. N12 4H 15
Pk. View Ct. SE20 1H 141
Parkview Ct. SW6 2G 101
Parkview Ct. SW18 5J 101
Parkview Ct. Har W 7D 10
Pk. View Cres. N11 4A 16
Pk. View Est. E2 2K 69
Pk. View Gdns. N22 1A 32
Pk. View Gdns. NW4 5E 28
Pk. View Gdns. Bark 2J 73
Pk. View Gdns. Ilf 4D 36
Pk. View Ho. E4 5H 19
Parkview Ho. N9 7C 8
Pk. View Ho. SE24 6B 104 (off Hurst St.)
Pk. View Mans. N4 7B 32
Pk. View Rd. N3 1K 29
Pk. View Rd. N17 3G 33
Pk. View Rd. NW10 4B 46
Parkview Rd. SE9 1F 127
Pk. View Rd. W5 5E 62
Pk. View Rd. Croy 1G 153
Pk. View Rd. S'hall 1E 78
Pk. View Rd. Uxb 6B 58
Pk. View Rd. Well 3C 110
Pk. Village E. NW1 2F 67 (1K 159)
Pk. Village W. NW1 2F 67
Park Vs. Romf 6D 38
Parkville Rd. SW6 7H 83
Park Vista. SE10 6F 89
Park Wlk. N6 7E 30
Park Wlk. SE10 7F 89
Park Wlk. SW10 6A 84 (7A 170)
Park Wlk. Barn 3G 5
Parkway. N14 2D 16
Park Way. N20 4J 15
Parkway. NW1 1F 67
Park Way. NW11 5G 29
Parkway. SW20 4F 137
Park Way. Edgw 1H 27
Park Way. Enf 2F 7
Parkway. Eri 3E 92
Park Way. Felt 7K 95
Parkway. Ilf 3K 55
Park Way. Ruis 1J 41
Parkway. Uxb 7C 40
Park Way. W Mol 3F 133
Park Way. Wfd G 5F 21
Pk. Way Ct. Ruis 1H 41
Parkway, The. Hay (UB3) 3K 77
Parkway, The. Hay & N'holt (UB4,UB5) 6A 60
Parkway, The. Houn 6J 77 (Church Rd.)
Parkway, The. Houn & S'hall 5J 77 (Watersplash La.)
Parkway Trad. Est. Houn 6A 78
Park West. W2 7D 158
Park W. Pl. W2 6C 66 (7D 158)
Park Wharf. SE8 5A 88 (off Evelyn St.)
Parkwood. N20 3J 15
Parkwood. NW8 1D 66 (off St Edmund's Ter.)
Parkwood. Beck 7C 124
Parkwood Av. Esh 7G 133
Parkwood Flats. N20 3J 15
Parkwood Gro. Sun 3J 131
Parkwood M. N6 6F 31
Parkwood Rd. SW19 5H 119
Pk. Wood Rd. Bex 7F 111
Parkwood Rd. Iswth 1K 97
Parliament Ct. E1 6H 163
Parliament Hill. 3D 48
Parliament Hill. NW3 4C 48
Parliament Hill Mans. NW5 4E 48
Parliament M. SW14 2J 99
Parliament Sq. SW1 2J 85 (7E 166)
Parliament St. SW1 2J 85 (6E 166)
Parliament Vw. SE1 4K 85 (3G 173)
Parma Cres. SW11 4D 102
Parmiter Ind. Est. E2 2H 69 (off Parmiter St.)
Parmiter St. E2 2H 69
Parmoor Ct. EC1 3C 162
Parndon Ho. Lou 1H 21
Parnell Clo. W12 3D 82
Parnell Clo. Edgw 4C 12
Parnell Ho. WC1 5H 67 (6D 160)
Parnell Rd. E3 1B 70 (in two parts)
Parnham St. E14 6A 70 (in two parts)
Parolles Rd. N19 1G 49
Paroma Rd. Belv 3G 93
Parr Clo. N9 & N18 4C 18
Parr Ct. N1 2D 68 (off New N. Rd.)
Parr Ct. Felt 4A 114
Parr Ho. E16 1K 89 (off Beaulieu Av.)
Parrington Ho. SW4 6H 103
Parr Rd. E6 1B 72
Parr Rd. Stan 1D 26
Parrs Clo. S Croy 7D 152
Parrs Pl. Hamp 7E 114
Parr St. N1 2D 68
Parry Av. E6 6D 72
Parry Clo. Eps 7D 148
Parry Ho. E1 1H 87 (off Green Bank)
Parry Pl. SE18 4F 91
Parry Rd. SE25 3E 140
Parry Rd. W10 3G 65 (in two parts)
Parry St. SW8 6J 85 (7F 173)
Parsifal Rd. NW6 5J 47
Parsley Gdns. Croy 1K 153
Parsloes Av. Dag 4D 56
Parsonage Clo. Hay 6H 59
Parsonage Gdns. Enf 2H 7
Parsonage La. Enf 2H 7
Parsonage La. Sidc 4F 129
Parsonage Manorway. Belv 6G 93
Parsonage St. E14 4E 88
Parson's Cres. Edgw 3B 12
Parsons Green. 1J 101
Parson's Grn. SW6 1J 101
Parson's Grn. La. SW6 1J 101
Parson's Gro. Edgw 3B 12
Parsons Hill. SE18 3E 90 (off Powis St.)
Parsons Ho. W2 4A 158
Parsons Lodge. NW6 7K 47 (off Priory Rd.)
Parson's Mead. Croy 1B 152
Parsons Mead. E Mol 3G 133
Parson's Rd. E13 2A 72
Parson St. NW4 4E 28
Parthenia Rd. SW6 1J 101
Partingdale La. NW7 5A 14
Partington Clo. N19 1H 49
Partridge Clo. E16 5B 72
Partridge Clo. Barn 6A 4
Partridge Clo. Bush 1B 10
Partridge Clo. Stan 4K 11
Partridge Ct. EC1 3A 162
Partridge Grn. SE9 3E 126
Partridge Rd. Hamp 6D 114
Partridge Rd. Sidc 3J 127
Partridge Sq. E6 5C 72
Partridge Way. N22 1J 31
Pasadena Clo. Hay 2J 77
Pasadena Clo. Trad. Est. Hay 2K 77
Pascall Ho. SE17 6C 86 (off Draco St.)
Pascal St. SW8 7H 85
Pascoe Rd. SE13 5F 107
Pasley Clo. SE17 5B 86
Pasquier Rd. E17 3A 34
Passage, The. Rich 5E 98
Passey Pl. SE9 6D 108
Passfield Dri. E14 5D 70
Passfield Path. SE28 7B 74
Passfields. SE6 3D 124
Passfields. W14 5H 83 (off Star St.)
Passing All. EC1 4B 162
Passingham Ho. Houn 6E 78
Passmore Gdns. N11 6C 16
Passmore St. SW1 5E 84 (5G 171)
Pasteur Clo. NW9 2A 28
Pasteur Ct. Harr 1B 44
Pasteur Gdns. N18 5G 17
Paston Clo. E5 3K 51
Paston Clo. Wall 3G 151
Paston Cres. SE12 7K 107
Pastor Ct. N6 6G 31
Pastor St. SE11 4B 86 (in two parts)
Pasture Clo. Wemb 3B 44
Pasture Rd. SE6 1H 125
Pasture Rd. Dag 4F 57
Pasture Rd. Wemb 2B 44
Pastures Mead. Uxb 6C 40
Pastures, The. N20 1C 14
Patcham Ter. SW8 1F 103
Patch Clo. Uxb 1B 58
Patching Way. Hay 5C 60
Patchway Ct. SE15 6E 86 (off Newent Clo.)
Patent Ho. E14 5D 70 (off Morris Rd.)
Paternoster La. EC4 6B 68 (1B 168)
Paternoster Row. EC4 6C 68 (1C 168)
Paternoster Sq. EC4 6B 68 (7B 162)
Paterson Ct. EC1 2E 162
Pater St. W8 3J 83
Pates Mnr. Dri. Felt 7F 95
Pathfield Rd. SW16 6H 121
Path, The. SW19 1K 137
Patience Rd. SW11 2C 102
Patio Clo. SW4 6H 103
Patmore Est. SW8 1G 103
Patmore Ho. N16 5E 50
Patmore Lodge. N6 4D 30
Patmore St. SW8 1G 103
Patmos Lodge. SW9 1B 104 (off Elliott Rd.)
Patmos Rd. SW9 7B 86
Paton Clo. E3 3C 70
Paton Ho. SW9 2K 103 (off Stockwell Rd.)
Paton St. EC1 3C 68 (2C 162)
Patricia Ct. Chst 1H 145
Patricia Ct. Well 7B 92
Patrick Coman Ho. EC1 3B 68 (2A 162) (off Finsbury Est.)
Patrick Connolly Gdns. E3 3D 70
Patrick Pas. SW11 2C 102
Patrick Rd. E13 3A 72
Patriot Sq. E2 2H 69
Patrol Pl. SE6 6D 106
Pat Shaw Ho. E1 4K 69 (off Globe Rd.)
Patshull Pl. NW5 6G 49
Patshull Rd. NW5 6G 49
Patten All. Rich 5D 98
Pattenden Rd. SE6 1B 124
Patten Ho. N16 1C 50
Patten Rd. SW18 7C 102
Patterdale. NW1 3F 67 (2K 159) (off Osnaburgh St.)
Patterdale Clo. Brom 6H 125
Patterdale Rd. SE15 7J 87
Pattern Ho. EC1 4B 68 (3A 162)
Patterson Ct. SE19 7F 123
Patterson Rd. SE19 6F 123
Pattina Wlk. SE16 1A 88 (off Capstan Way)
Pattinson Point. E16 5J 71 (off Fife Rd.)
Pattison Ho. E1 6K 69 (off Wellesley St.)
Pattison Ho. SE1 2C 86 (6D 168) (off Redcross Way)
Pattison Rd. NW2 3J 47
Pattison Wlk. SE18 5G 91
Paul Byrne Ho. N2 3A 30
Paul Clo. E15 7G 53
Paul Ct. N18 4B 18 (off Fairfield Rd.)
Paul Ct. Romf 5J 39
Paulet Rd. SE5 2B 104
Paul Gdns. Croy 2F 153
Paul Gdns. Hay 6F 77
Paulhan Rd. Harr 4D 26
Paulin Dri. N21 7F 7
Pauline Cres. Twic 1G 115
Pauline Ho. E1 5G 69 (off Old Montague St.)
Paul Julius Clo. E14 7F 71
Paul Robeson Clo. E6 3E 72
Pauls Ho. E3 5B 70 (off Timothy Rd.)
Paul St. E15 1G 71
Paul St. EC2 4D 68 (4F 163)
Paul's Wlk. EC4 7C 68 (2B 168)
Paultons Sq. SW3 6B 84 (7B 170)
Paultons St. SW3 6B 84 (7B 170)
Pauntley St. N19 1G 49
Pavan Ct. E2 3J 69 (off Sceptre Rd.)
Paved Ct. Rich 5D 98
Paveley Dri. SW11 7C 84
Paveley Ho. N1 2K 67 (off Priory Grn. Est.)
Paveley St. NW8 3C 66 (2C 158)
Pavement M. Romf 7D 38
Pavement Sq. Croy 1G 153
Pavement, The. E11 1E 52 (off Hainault Rd.)
Pavement, The. SW4 4G 103
Pavement, The. W5 3E 80
Pavement, The. Iswth 3A 98 (off South St.)
Pavet Clo. Dag 6H 57
Pavilion. NW8 3B 66 (2B 158)
Pavilion Ct. NW6 3J 65 (off Stafford Rd.)
Pavilion Lodge. Harr 1H 43
Pavilion M. N3 3J 29
Pavilion Rd. SW1 3D 84 (7F 165)
Pavilion Rd. Ilf 7D 36
Pavilion St. SW1 3D 84 (2F 171)
Pavilion Ter. W12 6E 64 (off Wood La.)
Pavilion Ter. Ilf 5J 37
Pavilion, The. SW8 7H 85
Pavilion Way. Edgw 7C 12
Pavilion Way. Ruis 2A 42
Pawleyne Clo. SE20 7J 123
Pawsey Clo. E13 1K 71
Pawsons Rd. Croy 6C 140
Paxfold. Stan 5J 11
Paxford Rd. Wemb 2B 44
Paxton Clo. Rich 2F 99
Paxton Clo. W on T 7A 132
Paxton Ct. SE12 3A 126
Paxton Ct. SE26 4A 124 (off Adamsrill Rd.)
Paxton Pl. SE27 4E 122
Paxton Rd. N17 7A 18

Paxton Rd. SE23 . . . . 3A 124
Paxton Rd. W4 . . . . 6A 82
Paxton Rd. Brom 7J 125
Paxton Ter. SW1 . . . 6F 85 (7K 171)
Paymal Ho. E1 . . . . 5J 69
(off Stepney Way)
Payne Clo. Bark 7K 55
Payne Ho. N1 . . . . 1K 67
(off Barnsbury Est.)
Paynell Ct. SE3 . . . . 3G 107
Payne Rd. E3 . . . . 2D 70
Paynesfield Av. SW14 . . . . . . 3K 99
Paynesfield Rd. Bus H 1E 10
Payne St. SE8 . . . . 7B 88
Paynes Wlk. W6 . . . . 6G 83
Payzes Gdns. Wfd G 6C 20
Peabody Av. SW1 . . . 5F 85 (5J 171)
Peabody Bldgs. E1 . . . . 2K 169
Peabody Bldgs. EC1
. . . . 4C 68 (4D 162)
(off Roscoe St.)
Peabody Bldgs. SW3 . . . . . . 7C 170
Peabody Clo. SE10 . . . . 1D 106
Peabody Clo. SW1
. . . . 5F 85 (7K 171)
Peabody Clo. Croy 1J 153
Peabody Cotts. N17 . . . . 1E 32
Peabody Ct. EC1 . . . 4C 68 (4D 162)
(off Roscoe St.)
Peabody Ct. SE5 . . . . 1D 104
(off Kimpton Rd.)
Peabody Est. E1 . . . . 7K 69
(off Glasmis Pl.)
Peabody Est. E2 . . . . 2H 69
(off Minerva St.)
Peabody Est. EC1
. . . . 4C 68 (4K 161)
(off Whitecross St., in two parts)
Peabody Est. EC1
. . . . 4A 68 (4K 161)
(off Farringdon La.)
Peabody Est. N1 . . . . 1C 68
Peabody Est. SE1
. . . . 1A 86 (5K 167)
(Hatfield St.)
Peabody Est. SE1 . . . . 5K 167
(Mint St.)
Peabody Est. SE1
. . . . 1C 86 (5K 167)
(Southwark St.)
Peabody Est. SE24 . . . . 7B 104
Peabody Est. SW1 . . . . 3B 172
Peabody Est. SW3
. . . . 6C 84 (7D 170)
Peabody Est. SW6 . . . . 6J 83
(off Lillie Rd.)
Peabody Est. SW11 . . . . 4C 102
Peabody Est. W6 . . . . 5E 82
Peabody Est. W10 . . . . 5E 64
Peabody Hill. SE21 . . . . 1B 122
Peabody Sq. SE1
. . . . 2B 86 (7A 168)
(in two parts)
Peabody Tower. EC1
. . . . 4C 68 (4D 162)
(off Golden La.)
Peabody Trust. SE17 . . . . 4D 86
Peabody Yd. N1 . . . . 1C 68
Peace Clo. N14 . . . . 5A 6
Peace Clo. SE25 . . . . 4E 140
Peace Clo. Gnfd 1H 61
Peace Gro. Wemb 3H 45
Peace St. SE18 . . . . 6E 90
Peaches Clo. Sutt 7G 149
Peachey Edwards Ho. E2 . . . . 3H 69
(off Teesdale St.)
Peachey La. Uxb 5A 58
Peach Rd. W10 . . . . 3F 65
Peach Rd. Felt 1J 113
Peach Tree Av. W Dray 6B 58
Peachum Rd. SE3 . . . . 6H 89
(in two parts)
Peachwalk M. E3 . . . . 2K 69
Peacock Av. Felt 1F 113
Peacock Clo. Dag 1C 56
Peacock Ind. Est. N17 . . . . . . 7A 18
Peacock St. SE17 . . . . 4B 86
Peacock Theatre.
. . . . 6K 67 (1G 167)
(off Portugal St.)
Peacock Wlk. E16 . . . . 6K 71
(off Mortlake Rd.)
Peacock Wlk. N6 . . . . 7F 31
Peacock Yd. SE17 . . . . 5B 86
(off Iliffe St.)
Peaketon Av. Ilf 4B 36
Peak Hill. SE26 . . . . 4J 123
Peak Hill Av. SE26 . . . . 4J 123
Peak Hill Gdns. SE26 . . . . . . 4J 123
Peak Ho. N4 . . . . 1C 50
(off Woodberry Down Est.)
Peak, The. SE26 . . . . 3J 123
Peal Gdns. W13 . . . . 3A 62
Peall Rd. Croy 6K 139
Peall Rd. Ind. Est. Croy 6K 139
Pearce Clo. Mitc 2E 138
Pearcefield Av. SE23 . . . . . . 1J 123
Pearce Rd. W Mol 3F 133
Pear Clo. NW9 . . . . 4K 27
Pear Clo. SE14 . . . . 7A 88
Pear Ct. SE15 . . . . 7F 87
(off Thruxton Way)
Pearcroft Rd. E11 . . . . 2F 53
Peardon St. SW8 . . . . 2F 103
Peareswood Gdns. Stan 1D 26
Pearfield Rd. SE23 . . . . 3A 124
Pearl Clo. E6 . . . . 6E 72
Pearl Clo. NW2 . . . . 7F 29
Pearl Rd. E17 . . . . 3C 34
Pearl St. E1 . . . . 1H 87
Pearmain Clo. Shep 5D 130
Pearman St. SE1 . . . 3A 86 (1K 173)
Pear Pl. SE1 . . . . . . 2A 86 (6J 167)
Pear Rd. E11 . . . . 3F 53
Pears Av. Shep 3G 131
Pearscroft Ct. SW6 . . . . 1K 101
Pearscroft Rd. SW6 . . . . 1K 101
Pearse St. SE15 . . . . 6E 86
Pearson's Av. SE14 . . . . 1C 106
Pearson St. E2 . . . . 2F 69
Pears Rd. Houn 3G 97
Peartree. SE26 . . . . 5A 124
Peartree Av. SW17 . . . . 3A 120
Pear Tree Av. W Dray 6B 58
Pear Tree Clo. E2 . . . . 1F 69
Pear Tree Clo. Chess 5G 147
Peartree Clo. Eri 1K 111
Peartree Clo. Mitc 2C 138
Pear Tree Ct. E18 . . . . 1K 35
Pear Tree Ct. EC1
. . . . 4A 68 (4K 161)
Peartree Gdns. Dag 4B 56
Peartree Gdns. Romf 2H 39
Pear Tree Ho. SE4 . . . . 3B 106
Peartree La. E1 . . . . 7J 69
Pear Tree Rd. Ashf 5E 112
Peartree Rd. Enf 3K 7
Peartrees. W Dray 7A 58
Pear Tree St. EC1
. . . . 4C 68 (3B 162)
Pear Tree Way. SE10 . . . . 4J 89
Peary Ho. NW10 . . . . 7K 45
Peary Pl. E2 . . . . 3J 69
Peas Mead Ter. E4 . . . . 4K 19
Peatfield Clo. Sidc 3J 127
Pebble Way. W3 . . . . 1H 81
(off Steyne Rd.)
Pebworth Rd. Harr 2A 44
Peckarmans Wood. SE26 . . . 3G 123
Peckett Sq. N5 . . . . 4C 50
Peckford Pl. SW9 . . . . 2A 104
Peckham. 1G 105
Peckham Gro. SE15 . . . . 7E 86
Peckham High St. SE15 . . . . 1G 105
Peckham Hill St. SE15 . . . . . . 7G 87
Peckham Pk. Rd. SE15 . . . . . . 7G 87
Peckham Rd. SE5 & SE15
. . . . 1E 104
Peckham Rye.
SE15 & SE22 . . . . . . 3G 105
Peckham Sq. SE15 . . . . 1G 105
Pecks Yd. E1 . . . . . . 5F 69 (5J 163)
(off Hanbury St.)
Peckwater St. NW5 . . . . 5G 49
Pedhoulas. N14 . . . . 3D 16
Pedlar's Wlk. N7 . . . . 5K 49
Pedley Rd. Dag 1C 56
Pedley St. E1 . . . . . 4F 69 (4K 163)
Pedro St. E5 . . . . 3K 51
Pedworth Gdns. SE16 . . . . . . 4J 87
Peebles Ct. S'hall 6G 61
(off Haldane Rd.)
Peek Cres. SW19 . . . . 5F 119
Peel Clo. E4 . . . . 2J 19
Peel Clo. N9 . . . . 3B 18
Peel Dri. Ilf 3C 36
Peel Gro. E2 . . . . 2J 69
(in two parts)
Peel La. NW9 . . . . 3C 28
Peel Pas. W8 . . . . 1J 83
(off Peel St.)
Peel Pl. Ilf 2C 36
Peel Precinct. NW6 . . . . 2J 65
Peel Rd. E18 . . . . 1H 35
Peel Rd. Harr 3K 25
(in two parts)
Peel Rd. Wemb 3D 44
Peel St. W8 . . . . 1J 83
Peel Way. Uxb 5A 58
Peerglow Est. Enf 5D 8
Peerless St. EC1 . . . 3D 68 (2E 162)
Pegamoid Rd. N18 . . . . 3D 18
Pegasus Clo. N5 . . . . 4D 50
Pegasus Ct. NW10 . . . . 3D 64
(off Trenmar Gdns.)
Pegasus Ct. Bren 5F 81
Pegasus Ct. King T 3D 134
Pegasus Ho. E1 . . . . 4K 69
(off Beaumont Sq.)
Pegasus Pl. SE11
. . . . 6A 86 (7J 173)
Pegasus Pl. SW6 . . . . 1J 101
Pegasus Way. N11 . . . . 6A 16
Peggotty Way. Uxb 6D 58
Pegg Rd. Houn 7B 78
Pegley Gdns. SE12 . . . . 2J 125
Pegwell St. SE18 . . . . 7J 91
Pekin Clo. E14 . . . . 6C 70
(off Pekin St.)
Pekin St. E14 . . . . 6C 70
Pelabon Ho. Twic 6D 98
(off Clevedon Rd.)
Peldon Ct. Rich 4F 99
Peldon Pas. Rich 4F 99
Peldon Wlk. N1 . . . . 1B 68
(off Popham St.)
Pelham Av. Bark 1K 73
Pelham Clo. SE5 . . . . 3E 104
Pelham Cotts. Bex 1H 129
Pelham Ct. SW3 . . . 4C 84 (4C 170)
(off Fulham Rd.)
Pelham Ct. Sidc 3A 128
Pelham Cres. SW7
. . . . 4C 84 (4C 170)
Pelham Ho. W14 . . . . 4H 83
(off Mornington Av.)
Pelham Pl. SW7 . . . 4C 84 (3C 170)
Pelham Pl. W13 . . . . 4K 61
Pelham Rd. E18 . . . . 3K 35
Pelham Rd. N15 . . . . 4F 33
Pelham Rd. N22 . . . . 2A 32
Pelham Rd. SW19 . . . . 7J 119
Pelham Rd. Beck 2J 141
Pelham Rd. Bexh 3G 111
Pelham Rd. Ilf 2H 55
Pelham St. SW7 . . . 4B 84 (3B 170)
Pelican Est. SE15 . . . . 1F 105
Pelican Ho. SE8 . . . . 4B 88
Pelican Pas. E1 . . . . 4J 69
Pelican Wlk. SW9 . . . . 4B 104
Pelican Wharf. E1 . . . . 1J 87
(off Wapping Wall)
Pelier St. SE17 . . . . 6C 86
Pelinore Rd. SE6 . . . . 2G 125
Pella Ho. SE11 . . . . 5K 85 (5H 173)
Pellant Rd. SW6 . . . . 7G 83
Pellatt Gro. N22 . . . . 1A 32
Pellatt Rd. SE22 . . . . 5F 105
Pellatt Rd. Wemb 2D 44
(in two parts)
Pellerin Rd. N16 . . . . 5E 50
Pellew Ho. E1 . . . . 4H 69
(off Somerford St.)
Pelling St. E14 . . . . 6C 70
Pellipar Clo. N13 . . . . 3F 17
Pellipar Gdns. SE18 . . . . 5D 90
Pellipar Rd. SE18 . . . . 5D 90
Pelly Rd. E13 . . . . 1J 71
(in two parts)
Pelter St. E2 . . . . . . 3F 69 (1J 163)
(in two parts)
Pelton Rd. SE10 . . . . 5G 89
Pembar Av. E17 . . . . 3A 34
Pemberley Chase.
W Ewe 5H 147
Pemberley Clo. W Ewe 5H 147
Pember Rd. NW10 . . . . 3F 65
Pemberton Ct. E1 . . . . 3K 69
(off Portelet Rd.)
Pemberton Gdns. N19 . . . . . . 3G 49
Pemberton Gdns. Romf 5E 38
Pemberton Ho. SE26 . . . . . . 4G 123
(off High Level Dri.)
Pemberton Pl. E8 . . . . 7H 51
Pemberton Rd. N4 . . . . 5A 32
Pemberton Rd. E Mol 4G 133
Pemberton Row. EC4
. . . . 6A 68 (7K 161)
Pemberton Ter. N19 . . . . 3G 49
Pembridge Av. Twic 1D 114
Pembridge Cres. W11 . . . . . . 7J 65
Pembridge Gdns. W2 . . . . 7J 65
Pembridge M. W11 . . . . 7J 65
Pembridge Pl. SW15 . . . . . . 5J 101
Pembridge Pl. W2 . . . . 7J 65
Pembridge Rd. W11 . . . . 7J 65
Pembridge Sq. W2 . . . . 7J 65
Pembridge Vs. W11 & W2 . . . 7J 65
Pembroke Av. Enf 1C 8
Pembroke Av. Harr 3A 26
Pembroke Av. Pinn 1B 42
Pembroke Av. Surb 5H 135
Pembroke Bldgs. NW10 . . . . . 3C 64
Pembroke Cen., The. Ruis . . . 1H 41
Pembroke Clo. SW1
. . . . 2E 84 (7H 165)
Pembroke Cotts. W8 . . . . 3J 83
(off Pembroke Sq.)
Pembroke Ct. W7 . . . . 6K 61
(off Copley Clo.)
Pembroke Gdns. W8 . . . . 4H 83
Pembroke Gdns. Dag 3H 57
Pembroke Gdns. Clo. W8 . . . . 3J 83
Pembroke Hall. NW4 . . . . 3E 28
(off Mulberry Clo.)
Pembroke Ho. W2 . . . . 6K 65
(off Hallfield Est.)
Pembroke Ho. W3 . . . . 2J 81
(off Park Rd. E.)
Pembroke Lodge. Stan 6H 11
Pembroke M. E3 . . . . 3A 70
Pembroke M. N10 . . . . 1F 31
Pembroke M. W8 . . . . 3J 83
Pembroke Pde. Eri 5J 93
Pembroke Pl. W8 . . . . 3J 83
Pembroke Pl. Edgw 7B 12
Pembroke Pl. Iswth 2J 97
Pembroke Rd. E6 . . . . 5D 72
Pembroke Rd. E17 . . . . 5D 34
Pembroke Rd. N8 . . . . 4J 31
Pembroke Rd. N10 . . . . 1E 30
Pembroke Rd. N13 . . . . 3H 17
Pembroke Rd. N15 . . . . 5F 33
Pembroke Rd. SE25 . . . . 4E 140
Pembroke Rd. W8 . . . . 4H 83
Pembroke Rd. Brom 2A 144
Pembroke Rd. Eri 5J 93
Pembroke Rd. Gnfd 4F 61
Pembroke Rd. Ilf 1K 55
Pembroke Rd. Mitc 2E 138
Pembroke Rd. Ruis 1G 41
Pembroke Rd. Wemb 3D 44
Pembroke Sq. W8 . . . . 3J 83
Pembroke St. N1 . . . . 7J 49
(in two parts)
Pembroke Vs. W8 . . . . 4J 83
Pembroke Vs. Rich 4D 98
Pembroke Wlk. W8 . . . . 4J 83
Pembroke Way. Hay 3E 76
Pembrook M. SW11 . . . . 4B 102
Pembry Clo. SW9 . . . . 1A 104
Pembury Av. Wor Pk 1C 148
Pembury Clo. E5 . . . . 5H 51
Pembury Clo. Brom 7H 143
Pembury Ct. Hay 6F 77
Pembury Cres. Sidc 2E 128
Pembury Pl. E5 . . . . 5H 51
Pembury Rd. E5 . . . . 5H 51
Pembury Rd. N17 . . . . 1F 33
Pembury Rd. SE25 . . . . 4G 141
Pembury Rd. Bexh 7E 92
Pemdevon Rd. Croy 7A 140
Pemell Clo. E1 . . . . 4J 69
Pemell Ho. E1 . . . . 4J 69
(off Pemell Clo.)
Pemerich Clo. Hay 5H 77
Pempath Pl. Wemb 2D 44
Penally Pl. N1 . . . . 1D 68
Penang Ho. E1 . . . . 1H 87
(off Prusom St.)
Penang St. E1 . . . . 1H 87
Penard Rd. S'hall 3F 79
Penarth Cen. SE15 . . . . 6J 87
Penarth St. SE15 . . . . 6J 87
Penberth Rd. SE6 . . . . 2E 124
Penbury Rd. S'hall 4D 78
Pencombe M. W11 . . . . 7H 65
Pencraig Way. SE15 . . . . 6H 87
Pendall Clo. Barn 4H 5
Penda Rd. Eri 7H 93
Pendarves Rd. SW20 . . . . . . 1E 136
Penda's Mead. E9 . . . . 4A 52
Pendell Av. Hay 7H 77
Pendennis Ho. SE8 . . . . 4A 88
Pendennis Rd. N17 . . . . 3D 32
Pendennis Rd. SW16 . . . . . . 4J 121
Penderel Rd. Houn 5E 96
Penderry Ri. SE6 . . . . 2F 125
Penderyn Way. N7 . . . . 4H 49
Pendlebury Ct. Surb 4E 134
(off Cranes Pk.)
Pendle Ct. Uxb 1D 58
Pendle Ho. SE26 . . . . 3G 123
Pendle Rd. SW16 . . . . 6F 121
Pendlestone Rd. E17 . . . . 5D 34
Pendragon Rd. Brom 3H 125
Pendragon Wlk. NW9 . . . . 6A 28
Pendrell Ho. WC2
. . . . 6H 67 (1D 166)
(off New Compton St.)
Pendrell Rd. SE4 . . . . 2A 106
Pendrell St. SE18 . . . . 6H 91
Pendula Dri. Hay 4B 60
Pendulum M. E8 . . . . 5F 51
Penerley Rd. SE6 . . . . 1D 124
Penfield Lodge. W9 . . . . 5J 65
(off Admiral Wlk.)
Penfields Ho. N7 . . . . 6J 49
Penfold Clo. Croy 3A 152
Penfold La. Bex 2D 128
(in two parts)
Penfold Pl. NW1 . . . 5C 66 (5C 158)
Penfold Rd. N9 . . . . 1E 18
Penfold St. NW8 & NW1
. . . . 4B 66 (4B 158)
Penford Gdns. SE9 . . . . 3B 108
Penford St. SE5 . . . . 2B 104
Pengarth Rd. Bex 5D 110
Penge. 7J 123
Penge Ho. SW11 . . . . 3B 102
Penge La. SE20 . . . . 7J 123
Penge Rd. E13 . . . . 1A 72
Penge Rd. SE25 & SE20 . . . 3G 141
Penhall Rd. SE7 . . . . 4B 90
Penhill Rd. Bex 6C 110

Penhurst Pl. SE1 1H 173
Penhurst Rd. Ilf 1F 37
Penifather La. Gnfd 3H 61
Peninsula Ct. E14 3D 88 (off E. Ferry Rd.)
Peninsula Heights. SE1 5J 85 (5F 173)
Peninsula Pk. SE7 4J 89 (off Peninsula Pk. Rd., in two parts)
Peninsula Pk. Rd. SE7 4J 89
Peninsular Clo. Felt 6F 95
Penistone Rd. SW16 7J 121
Penketh Dri. Harr 3H 43
Penley Ct. WC2 7K 67 (2H 167)
Penmayne Ho. SE11 5A 86 (5K 173) (off Kennings Way)
Penmon Rd. SE2 3A 92
Pennack Rd. SE15 6F 87
Penn Almshouses. SE10 1E 106 (off Greenwich S. St.)
Pennant M. W8 4K 83
Pennant Ter. E17 2B 34
Pennard Mans. W12 2E 82 (off Goldhawk Rd.)
Pennard Rd. W12 2E 82
Pennards, The. Sun 3A 132
Penn Clo. Gnfd 2F 61
Penn Clo. Harr 4C 26
Penn Ct. NW9 3K 27
Penner Clo. SW19 2G 119
Penners Gdns. Surb 7E 134
Pennethorne Clo. E9 1J 69
Pennethorne Ho. SW11 3B 102
Pennethorne Rd. SE15 7H 87
Penn Gdns. Chst 2F 145
Penn Gdns. Romf 1G 39
Penn Ho. NW8 4C 66 (4C 158) (off Mallory St.)
Pennine Dri. NW2 2F 47
Pennine La. NW2 2G 47
Pennine Pde. NW2 2G 47
Pennine Way. Bexh 1K 111
Pennine Way. Hay 7F 77
Pennington Clo. SE27 4D 122
Pennington Ct. SE16 1A 88
Pennington Dri. N21 5D 6
Pennington Lodge. Surb 5E 134 (off Cranes Dri.)
Pennington St. E1 7H 69
Pennington Way. SE12 2K 125
Penniston Clo. N17 2C 32
Penn La. Bex 5D 110 (in two parts)
Penn Rd. N7 5J 49
Penn St. N1 1D 68
Pennycroft. Croy 7A 154
Pennyfather La. Enf 3H 7
Pennyfields. E14 7C 70 (in two parts)
Pennyford Ct. NW8 4B 66 (3A 158) (off St John's Wood Rd.)
Penny La. Shep 7G 131
Penny M. SW12 7F 103
Pennymoor Wlk. W9 4H 65 (off Ashmore Rd.)
Penny Rd. NW10 3H 63
Penny Royal. Wall 6H 151
Pennyroyal Av. E6 6E 72
Penpoll Rd. E8 6H 51
Penpool La. Well 3B 110
Penrhyn Av. E17 1B 34
Penrhyn Cres. E17 1C 34
Penrhyn Cres. SW14 4J 99
Penrhyn Gdns. King T 4D 134
Penrhyn Gro. E17 1C 34
Penrhyn Rd. King T 4E 134
Penrith Clo. SW15 5G 101
Penrith Clo. Beck 1D 142
Penrith Clo. Uxb 7A 40
Penrith Pl. SE27 2B 122
Penrith Rd. N15 5D 32
Penrith Rd. N Mald 4K 135
Penrith Rd. T Hth 2C 140
Penrith St. SW16 6G 121
Penrose Gro. SE17 5C 86
Penrose Ho. SE17 5C 86 (in two parts)
Penrose St. SE17 5C 86
Penryn Ho. SE11 5K 173
Penryn St. NW1 2H 67
Penry St. SE1 4E 86
Pensbury Pl. SW8 2G 103
Pensbury St. SW8 2G 103
Pensford Av. Rich 2G 99
Penshurst. NW5 6E 48
Penshurst Av. Sidc 6A 110
Penshurst Gdns. Edgw 5C 12
Penshurst Grn. Brom 5H 143
Penshurst Ho. SE15 6J 87 (off Lovelinch Clo.)
Penshurst Rd. E9 7K 51
Penshurst Rd. N17 7A 18
Penshurst Rd. Bexh 1F 111
Penshurst Rd. T Hth 5B 140
Penshurst Wlk. Brom 5H 143
Penshurst Way. Sutt 7J 149
Pensilver Clo. Barn 4H 5
Penstemon Clo. N3 6D 14
Pentagon, The. W13 7A 62
Pentavia Retail Pk. NW7 7G 13
Pentelow Gdns. Felt 6J 95
Pentire Rd. E17 1F 35
Pentland Av. Edgw 2C 12
Pentland Av. Shep 5C 130
Pentland Clo. N9 2D 18
Pentland Clo. NW11 2G 47
Pentland Gdns. SW18 6A 102
Pentland Pl. N'holt 1C 60
Pentlands Clo. Mitc 3F 139
Pentland St. SW18 6A 102
Pentland Way. Uxb 3E 40
Pentlow St. SW15 3E 100
Pentlow Way. Buck H 1H 21
Pentney Rd. E4 1A 20
Pentney Rd. SW12 1G 121
Pentney Rd. SW19 1G 137
Penton Gro. N1 2A 68
Penton Ho. N1 2A 68 (1J 161) (off Donegal St.)
Penton Ho. SE2 1D 92
Penton Pl. SE17 5B 86
Penton Ri. WC1 3K 67 (1H 161)
Penton St. N1 2A 68
Pentonville. 2K 67
Pentonville Rd. N1 2K 67 (1F 161)
Pentrich Av. Enf 1B 8
Pentridge St. SE15 7F 87
Pentyre Av. N18 5J 17
Penwerris Av. Iswth 7G 79
Penwerris Ct. Houn 7G 79
Penwith Rd. SW18 2J 119
Penwood Ct. Pinn 4D 24
Penwood Ho. SW15 6B 100
Penwortham Ct. N22 2K 31
Penwortham Rd. SW16 6F 121
Penylan Pl. Edgw 7B 12
Penywern Rd. SW5 5J 83
Penzance Ho. SE11 5A 86 (5K 173) (off Seaton Clo.)
Penzance Pl. W11 1G 83
Penzance St. W11 1G 83
Peony Ct. Wfd G 6B 20
Peony Gdns. W12 7C 64
Peperfield. WC1 3K 67 (2G 161) (off Cromer St.)
Pepler Ho. W10 4G 65 (off Wornington Rd.)
Pepler M. SE5 5F 87
Peploe Rd. NW6 2F 65 (in two parts)
Peplow Clo. W Dray 1A 76
Pepper Clo. E6 5D 72
Peppercorn Clo. T Hth 2D 140
Peppermead Sq. SE4 5C 106
Peppermint Clo. Croy 7J 139
Peppermint Pl. E11 3G 53
Pepper St. E14 3D 88
Pepper St. SE1 2C 86 (6C 168)
Peppie Clo. N16 2E 50 (in two parts)
Pepys Clo. Uxb 4D 40
Pepys Cres. E16 1J 89
Pepys Cres. Barn 5A 4
Pepys Ho. E2 3J 69 (off Kirkwall Pl.)
Pepys Rd. SE14 1K 105
Pepys Rd. SW20 1E 136
Pepys St. EC3 7E 68 (2H 169)
Perceval Av. NW3 5C 48
Perceval Ct. N'holt 5E 42
Perceval Ho. W5 7C 62
Percheron Clo. Iswth 3K 97
Perch St. E8 4F 51
Percival Ct. N17 7A 18
Percival David Foundation of Chinese Art. 3D 160
Percival Gdns. Romf 6C 38
Percival Rd. SW14 4J 99
Percival Rd. Enf 4A 8
Percival Rd. Felt 2H 113
Percival St. EC1 4B 68 (3A 162)
Percival Way. Eps 4K 147
Percy Av. Ashf 5C 112
Percy Bryant Rd. Sun 7G 113
Percy Bush Rd. W Dray 3B 76
Percy Cir. WC1 3K 67 (1H 161)
Percy Gdns. Enf 5E 8
Percy Gdns. Hay 3G 59
Percy Gdns. Iswth 3A 98
Percy Gdns. Wor Pk 1A 148
Percy M. W1 6C 160
Percy Pas. W1 6C 160
Percy Rd. E11 7G 35
Percy Rd. E16 5G 71
Percy Rd. N12 5F 15
Percy Rd. N21 7H 7
Percy Rd. SE20 1K 141
Percy Rd. SE25 5G 141
Percy Rd. W12 2C 82
Percy Rd. Bexh 2E 110
Percy Rd. Hamp 7E 114
Percy Rd. Ilf 7A 38
Percy Rd. Iswth 4A 98
Percy Rd. Mitc 7E 138
Percy Rd. Romf 3H 39
Percy Rd. Twic 1F 115
Percy St. W1 5H 67 (6C 160)
Percy Way. Twic 1G 115
Percy Yd. WC1 3K 67 (1H 161)
Peregrine Clo. NW10 5K 45
Peregrine Ct. SE8 6C 88 (off Edward St.)
Peregrine Ct. SW16 4K 121
Peregrine Ct. Well 1K 109
Peregrine Gdns. Croy 2A 154
Peregrine Ho. EC1 1B 162
Peregrine Rd. Sun 2H 131
Peregrine Way. SW19 7E 118
Perham Rd. W14 5G 83
Peridot St. E6 5C 72
Perifield. SE21 1C 122
Perimeade Rd. Gnfd 2C 62
Periton Rd. SE9 4B 108
Perivale. 1C 62
Perivale Gdns. W13 4B 62
Perivale Grange. Gnfd 3A 62
Perivale Ind. Pk. Gnfd 2B 62
Perivale La. Gnfd 3A 62
Perivale Lodge. Gnfd 3A 62 (off Perivale La.)
Perivale New Bus. Cen. Gnfd 2C 62
Perkin Clo. Houn 4E 96
Perkin Clo. Wemb 5B 44
Perkins Ct. Ashf 5B 112
Perkins Ho. E14 5B 70 (off Wallwood St.)
Perkin's Rents. SW1 3H 85 (2C 172)
Perkins Rd. Ilf 5H 37
Perkins Sq. SE1 1C 86 (4D 168)
Perks Clo. SE3 3G 107
Perley Ho. E3 5B 70 (off Weatherley Clo.)
Perpins Rd. SE9 6H 109
Perran Rd. SW2 1B 122
Perran Wlk. Bren 5E 80
Perren St. NW5 6F 49
Perrers Rd. W6 4D 82
Perrin Clo. Ashf 5B 112
Perring Est. E3 5C 70 (off Gale St.)
Perrin Ho. NW6 3J 65
Perrin Rd. Wemb 4B 44
Perrin's Ct. NW3 4A 48
Perrin's La. NW3 4A 48
Perrin's Wlk. NW3 4A 48
Perronet Ho. SE1 3B 86 (off Princess St.)
Perrott St. SE18 4G 91
Perry Av. W3 6K 63
Perry Clo. Rain 2K 75
Perry Clo. Uxb 6D 58
Perry Ct. E14 5C 88 (off Maritime Quay)
Perry Ct. N15 6E 32
Perryfield Way. NW9 6B 28
Perryfield Way. Rich 3B 116
Perry Gdns. N9 3J 17
Perry Gth. N'holt 1A 60
Perry Hall Rd. Orp 6K 145
Perry Hill. SE6 3B 124
Perry How. Wor Pk 1B 148
Perrymans Farm Rd. Ilf 6H 37
Perry Mead. Enf 2G 7
Perrymead St. SW6 1J 101
Perryn Ct. Twic 6A 98
Perryn Ho. W3 7A 64
Perryn Rd. SE16 3H 87
Perryn Rd. W3 1K 81
Perry Ri. SE23 3A 124
Perry Rd. Dag 5F 75
Perry's Pl. W1 6H 67 (7C 160)
Perry St. Chst 6H 127
Perry St. Dart 4K 111
Perry St. Gdns. Chst 6J 127
Perry St. Shaw. Chst 7J 127
Perry Va. SE23 2J 123
Persant Rd. SE6 2G 125
Perseverance Pl. SW9 7A 86
Perseverance Pl. Rich 4E 98
Perseverance Works. E2 3E 68 (1H 163) (off Kingsland Rd.)
Pershore Clo. Ilf 5F 37
Pershore Gro. Cars 6B 138
Pert Clo. N10 7A 16
Perth Av. NW9 7K 27
Perth Av. Hay 4A 60
Perth Clo. SE5 4D 104
Perth Clo. SW20 2B 136
Perth Ho. N1 7K 49 (off Bemerton Est.)
Perth Rd. E10 1A 52
Perth Rd. E13 2K 71
Perth Rd. N4 1A 50
Perth Rd. N22 1B 32
Perth Rd. Bark 2H 73
Perth Rd. Beck 2E 142
Perth Rd. Ilf 6E 36
Perth Ter. Ilf 7G 37
Perwell Av. Harr 1D 42
Perystreete. SE23 2J 123
Petavel Rd. Tedd 6J 115
Peter Av. NW10 7D 46
Peter Best Ho. E1 6H 69 (off Nelson St.)
Peterboat Clo. SE10 4G 89
Peterborough Ct. EC4 6A 68 (1K 167)
Peterborough Gdns. Ilf 7C 36
Peterborough M. SW6 2J 101
Peterborough Rd. E10 5E 34
Peterborough Rd. SW6 2J 101
Peterborough Rd. Cars 6C 138
Peterborough Rd. Harr 1J 43
Peterborough Vs. SW6 1K 101
Peter Butler Ho. SE1 2G 87 (7K 169) (off Wolseley St.)
Peterchurch Ho. SE15 6H 87 (off Commercial Way)
Petergate. SW11 4A 102
Peterhead Ct. S'hall 6G 61 (off Osborne Rd.)
Peter Heathfield Ho. E15 1F 71 (off Wise Rd.)
Peter Ho. SW8 7J 85 (off Luscombe Way)
Peter James Bus. Cen. Hay 2J 77
Peter James Enterprise Cen. NW10 3J 63
Peterley Bus. Cen. E2 2H 69
Peter Pan. 1B 84 (4A 164)
Peters Clo. Dag 1D 56
Peters Clo. Stan 6J 11
Peters Clo. Well 2J 109
Peter Scott Vis. Cen., The. 1D 100
Peters Ct. W2 6K 65 (off Porchester Rd.)
Petersfield Clo. N18 5H 17
Petersfield Ri. SW15 1D 118
Petersfield Rd. W3 2J 81
Petersham. 1E 116
Petersham Clo. Rich 2D 116
Petersham Clo. Sutt 5H 149
Petersham Dri. Orp 2K 145
Petersham Gdns. Orp 2K 145
Petersham Ho. SW7 4B 84 (3A 170) (off Kendrick M.)
Petersham La. SW7 3A 84
Petersham M. SW7 3A 84
Petersham Pl. SW7 3A 84
Petersham Rd. Rich 6D 98
Petersham Ter. Croy 3J 151 (off Richmond Grn.)
Peter's Hill. EC4 7C 68 (2C 168)
Peter Shore Ct. E1 5K 69 (off Beaumont Sq.)
Peter's La. EC1 5B 68 (5B 162)
Peter's Path. SE26 4H 123
Peterstone Rd. SE2 2B 92
Peterstow Clo. SW19 2G 119
Peter St. W1 7H 67 (2C 166)
Peterwood Pk. Croy 2K 151
Peterwood Way. Croy 2K 151
Petherton Ct. NW10 1F 65 (off Tiverton Rd.)
Petherton Ct. Harr 6K 25 (off Gayton Rd.)
Petherton Ho. N4 1C 50 (off Woodberry Down Est.)
Petherton Rd. N5 5C 50
Petiver Clo. E9 7J 51
Petley Rd. W6 6F 83
Peto Pl. NW1 4F 67 (3K 159)
Peto St. N. E16 6H 71
Petrie Clo. NW2 6G 47
Petrie Ho. SE18 6E 90 (off Woolwich Comn.)
Petrie Mus. of Egyptian Archaeology. 4H 67 (4C 160)
Petros Gdns. NW3 6A 48
Petticoat La. E1 5E 68 (6J 163)
Petticoat Lane Market. 6F 69 (6J 163) (in Middlesex St.)
Petticoat Sq. E1 6F 69 (7J 163)
Petticoat Tower. E1 6F 69 (7J 163) (off Petticoat Sq.)
Pettits Clo. Romf 2K 39
Pettits La. N. Romf 1K 39
Pettits Pl. Dag 5G 57
Pettits Rd. Dag 5G 57
Pettiward Clo. SW15 4E 100

Pettley Gdns. Romf 5K 39
Pettman Cres. SE28 3H 91
Pettsgrove Av. Wemb 5C 44
Pett's Hill. N'holt 5F 43
Petts La. Shep 4C 130
Pett St. SE18 4C 90
Petts Wood. 5G 145
Petts Wood Rd. Orp 5G 145
Petty France. SW1 3G 85 (1B 172)
Petworth Clo. N'holt 7D 42
Petworth Gdns. SW20 3D 136
Petworth Gdns. Uxb 1E 58
Petworth Rd. N12 5H 15
Petworth Rd. Bexh 5G 111
Petworth St. SW11 1C 102
Petyt Pl. SW3 6C 84
Petyward. SW3 4C 84 (4D 170)
Pevensey Av. N11 5C 16
Pevensey Av. Enf 2K 7
Pevensey Clo. Iswth 7G 79
Pevensey Ct. W3 2H 81
Pevensey Ho. E1 5K 69 (off Ben Jonson Rd.)
Pevensey Rd. E7 4H 53
Pevensey Rd. SW17 4B 120
Pevensey Rd. Felt 1C 114
Peverel. E6 6E 72
Peverel Ho. Dag 2G 57
Peveret Clo. N11 5A 16
Peveril Dri. Tedd 5H 115
Peveril Ho. SE1 3D 86 (off Rephidim St.)
Pewsey Clo. E4 5H 19
Peyton Pl. SE10 7E 88
Pharamond. NW2 6F 47
Pharaoh Clo. Mitc 7D 138
Pheasant Clo. E16 6K 71
Phelp St. SE17 6D 86
Phelps Way. Hay 4H 77
Phene St. SW3 6C 84 (7D 170)
Philadelphia Ct. SW10 7A 84 (off Uverdale Rd.)
Philbeach Gdns. SW5 5H 83
Phil Brown Pl. SW8 3F 103 (off Wandsworth Rd.)
Philchurch Pl. E1 6G 69
Philimore Clo. SE18 5J 91
Philip Av. Romf 1K 57
Philip Clo. Romf 1K 57
Philip Ct. W2 5B 66 (5A 158) (off Hall Pl.)
Philip Gdns. Croy 2B 154
Philip Ho. NW6 1K 65 (off Mortimer Pl.)
Philip La. N15 4D 32
Philipot Path. SE9 6D 108
Philippa Gdns. SE9 5B 108
Philips Clo. Cars 1E 150
Philip St. E13 4J 71
Philip Wlk. SE15 3G 105 (in two parts)
Phillimore Gdns. NW10 1E 64
Phillimore Gdns. W8 2J 83
Phillimore Gdns. Clo. W8 3J 83
Phillimore Pl. W8 2J 83
Phillimore Ter. W8 3J 83 (off Allen St.)
Phillimore Wlk. W8 3J 83
Phillipp St. N1 1E 68 (in two parts)
Phillips Ct. Edgw 6B 12
Philosophy Programme. 5D 160 (in University of London, Senate House)
Philpot La. EC3 7E 68 (2G 169)
Philpot Path. Ilf 3G 55
Philpots Clo. W Dray 7A 58
Philpot Sq. SW6 3K 101
Philpot St. E1 6H 69
Phineas Pett Rd. SE9 3C 108
Phipps Bri. Rd. SW19 2A 138
Phipps Hatch La. Enf 1H 7
Phipps Ho. SE7 5K 89 (off Woolwich Rd.)
Phipps Ho. W12 7D 64 (off White City Est.)
Phipp St. EC2 4E 68 (3G 163)
Phoebeth Rd. SE13 5C 106
Phoenix Bus. Cen. E3 5C 70
Phoenix Cen. Brom 4K 143
Phoenix Clo. E8 1F 69
Phoenix Clo. W Wick 2F 155
Phoenix Ct. E4 3J 19
Phoenix Ct. E14 4C 88
Phoenix Ct. NW1 2H 67 (off Purchese St.)
Phoenix Ct. SE14 6A 88 (off Chipley St.)
Phoenix Ct. Houn 5B 96
Phoenix Ct. S Croy 5F 153
Phoenix Dri. Kes 4B 156
Phoenix Ho. Sutt 4K 149
Phoenix Ind. Est. Harr 4K 25
Phoenix Lodge Mans. W6 4E 82 (off Brook Grn.)
Phoenix Pl. WC1 4K 67 (3H 161)
Phoenix Rd. NW1 3H 67 (1C 160)
Phoenix Rd. SE20 6J 123
Phoenix St. WC2 6H 67 (1D 166)
Phoenix Theatre. 6H 67 (1D 166) (off Charing Cross Rd.)
Phoenix Trad. Est. Gnfd 1C 62
Phoenix Trad. Pk. Bren 5D 80
Phoenix Way. Houn 6B 78
Phoenix Wharf. E1 1H 87 (off Wapping High St.)
Phoenix Wharf Rd. SE1 7K 169
Phoenix Yd. WC1 2H 161
Photographers' Gallery. 7J 67 (2E 166) (off Gt. Newport St.)
Phyllis Av. N Mald 5D 136
Phyllis Ho. Croy 4B 152 (off Ashley La.)
Physic Pl. SW3 6D 84 (7E 170)
Piazza, The. WC2 2F 167 (in two parts)
Piazza, The. Uxb 7A 40
Picardy Manorway. Belv 3H 93
Picardy Rd. Belv 5G 93
Picardy St. Belv 3G 93
Piccadilly. W1 1F 85 (5K 165)
Piccadilly Arc. SW1 4A 166
Piccadilly Circus. 7H 67 (3C 166)
Piccadilly Cir. W1 7H 67 (3C 166)
Piccadilly Pl. W1 3B 166
Piccadilly Theatre. 7G 67 (2B 166)
Pickard St. EC1 3B 68 (1B 162)
Pickering Av. E6 2E 72
Pickering Clo. E9 7K 51
Pickering Gdns. N11 6K 15
Pickering Gdns. Croy 6F 141
Pickering Ho. W2 6A 66 (off Hallfield Est.)
Pickering Ho. W5 4C 80 (off Windmill Rd.)
Pickering M. W2 6K 65
Pickering Pl. SW1 5B 166
Pickering St. N1 1B 68
Pickets Clo. Bus H 1C 10
Pickets St. SW12 7F 103
Pickett Cft. Stan 1D 26
Picketts Lock La. N9 2D 18
Picketts Lock La. Ind. Est. N9 2F 19
Picketts Ter. SE22 5G 105
Pickford Clo. Bexh 2E 110
Pickford La. Bexh 2E 110
Pickford Rd. Bexh 3E 110
Pickfords Wharf. N1 2C 68
Pickfords Wharf. SE1 1D 86 (4E 168)
Pickfords Yd. N17 6A 18
Pickhurst Grn. Brom 7H 143
Pickhurst La. W Wick & Brom 5G 143
Pickhurst Mead. Brom 7H 143
Pickhurst Pk. Brom 5G 143
Pickhurst Ri. W Wick 7E 142
Pickwick Clo. Houn 5C 96
Pickwick Ho. SE16 2G 87 (off George Row)
Pickwick Ho. W11 1F 83 (off St Ann's Rd.)
Pickwick M. N18 4K 17
Pickwick Pl. Harr 7J 25
Pickwick Rd. SE21 7D 104
Pickwick St. SE1 2C 86 (7C 168)
Pickwick Way. Chst 6G 127
Pickworth Clo. SW8 7J 85
Picton Pl. W1 6E 66 (1H 165)
Picton St. SE5 7D 86
Pied Bull Yd. WC1 6E 160
Piedmont Rd. SE18 5H 91 (in two parts)
Pield Heath. 5A 58
Pield Heath Av. Uxb 4C 58
Pield Heath Rd. Uxb 4A 58
Pier Head. E1 1H 87 (in two parts)
Pierhead Wharf. E1 1H 87 (off Wapping High St.)
Pier Ho. SW3 6C 84 (7D 170)
Piermont Pl. Brom 2C 144
Piermont Rd. SE22 5H 105
Pier Pde. E16 1E 90 (off Pier Rd.)
Pierpoint Building. E14 2B 88
Pierrepoint Rd. W3 7H 63
Pierrepont Arc. N1 2B 68 (off Pierrepont Row)
Pierrepont Row. N1 2B 68 (off Camden Pas.)
Pier Rd. E16 2D 90
Pier Rd. Felt 5K 95
Pier St. E14 4E 88 (in two parts)
Pier Ter. SW18 4K 101
Pier Way. SE28 2G 91
Pigeon La. Hamp 4E 114
Piggott Ho. E2 2K 69 (off Sewardstone Rd.)
Pigott St. E14 6C 70
Pike Clo. Brom 5K 125
Pike Clo. Uxb 1B 58
Pikemans Ct. SW5 4J 83 (off W. Cromwell Rd.)
Pike Rd. NW7 4E 12
Pike's End. Pinn 4K 23
Pikestone Clo. Hay 4C 60
Pikethorne. SE23 2K 123
Pilgrimage St. SE1 2D 86 (7E 168)
Pilgrim Clo. Mord 7K 137
Pilgrim Hill. SE27 4C 122
Pilgrim Ho. SE1 3D 86 (off Lansdowne Pl.)
Pilgrims Cloisters. SE5 7E 86 (off Sedgmoor Pl.)
Pilgrims Clo. N13 4E 16
Pilgrims Clo. N'holt 5G 43
Pilgrim's La. NW3 4B 48
Pilgrims M. E14 7G 71
Pilgrim's Pl. NW3 4B 48
Pilgrims Ri. Barn 5H 5
Pilgrim St. EC4 6B 68 (1A 168)
Pilgrims Way. E6 1C 72
Pilgrims Way. N19 1H 49
Pilgrims Way. S Croy 5F 153
Pilgrim's Way. Wemb 1H 45
Pilkington Rd. SE15 2H 105
Pillions La. Hay 4F 59
Pilot Clo. SE8 6B 88
Pilot Ind. Cen. NW10 4K 63
Pilsden Clo. SW19 1F 119
Pilton Est., The. Croy 2B 152
Pilton Pl. SE17 5C 86 (off Pingle St.)
Pilton Pl. Est. SE17 5C 86
Pimento Ct. W5 3D 80
Pimlico. 5G 85 (6A 172)
Pimlico Ho. SW1 5F 85 (5J 171) (off Ebury Bri. Rd.)
Pimlico Rd. SW1 5E 84 (5G 171)
Pimlico Wlk. N1 1G 163
Pinchin St. E1 7G 69
Pincombe Ho. SE17 5D 86
Pincott Pl. SE4 3K 105
Pincott Rd. SW19 7A 120
Pincott Rd. Bexh 5G 111
Pindar St. EC2 5E 68 (5G 163)
Pindock M. W9 4K 65
Pineapple Ct. SW1 1B 172
Pine Av. E15 5F 53
Pine Av. W Wick 1D 154
Pine Clo. E10 2D 52
Pine Clo. N14 7B 6
Pine Clo. N19 2G 49
Pine Clo. SE20 1J 141
Pine Clo. Stan 4G 11
Pine Coombe. Croy 4K 153
Pine Ct. N21 5E 6
Pine Ct. N'holt 4C 60
Pinecroft Ct. Well 7A 92
Pinecroft Cres. Barn 4B 4
Pinedene. SE15 1H 105
Pinefield Clo. E14 7C 70
Pine Gdns. Ruis 1K 41
Pine Gdns. Surb 6G 135
Pine Glade. Orp 4D 156
Pine Gro. N4 2J 49
Pine Gro. N20 1C 14
Pine Gro. SW19 5H 119
Pine Ho. SE16 2J 87 (off Ainsty Est.)
Pine Ho. W10 4G 65 (off Droop St.)
Pinehurst Ct. W11 6H 65 (off Colville Gdns.)
Pinehurst Wlk. Orp 7H 145
Pinemartin Clo. NW2 3E 46
Pine M. NW10 2F 65
Pine Pl. Hay 4H 59
Pine Ridge. Cars 7E 150
Pineridge Ct. Barn 4A 4
Pine Rd. N11 2K 15
Pine Rd. NW2 4E 46
Pines Rd. Brom 2C 144
Pines, The. N14 5B 6
Pines, The. SE19 7B 122
Pines, The. Sun 3J 131
Pines, The. Wfd G 3D 20
Pine St. EC1 4A 68 (3K 161)
Pine Tree Clo. Houn 1K 95
Pine Tree Ho. SE14 7K 87 (off Reaston St.)
Pine Tree Lodge. Brom 4H 143
Pine Trees Dri. Uxb 4A 40
Pineview Ct. E4 1K 19
Pine Wlk. Surb 6G 135
Pine Wood. Sun 1J 131
Pinewood Av. Pinn 6A 10
Pinewood Av. Sidc 1J 127
Pinewood Av. Uxb 6B 58
Pinewood Clo. Croy 3A 154
Pinewood Clo. Pinn 6A 10
Pinewood Ct. SW4 6H 103
Pinewood Ct. Enf 3G 7
Pinewood Gro. W5 6C 62
Pinewood Lodge. Bush 1C 10
Pinewood Pl. Eps 4K 147
Pinewood Rd. SE2 6D 92
Pinewood Rd. Brom 4J 143
Pinewood Rd. Felt 3K 113
Pinfold Rd. SW16 4J 121
Pinglestone Clo. W Dray 7A 76
Pinkcoat Clo. Felt 3K 113
Pinkerton Pl. SW16 4H 121
Pinkham Mans. W4 5G 81
Pinkham Way. N11 7K 15
Pinkwell Av. Hay 4F 77
Pinkwell La. Hay 4E 76
Pinley Gdns. Dag 1B 74
Pinnace Ho. E14 3E 88 (off Manchester Rd.)
Pinnacle Hill. Bexh 4H 111
Pinnacle Hill N. Bexh 3H 111
Pinnacle Pl. Stan 4G 11
Pinnell Rd. SE9 4B 108
Pinner. 4C 24
Pinner Ct. NW8 3A 158
Pinner Ct. Pinn 4E 24
Pinner Green. 2A 24
Pinner Grn. Pinn 2A 24
Pinner Gro. Pinn 4C 24
Pinner Hill Farm. Pinn 1K 23
Pinner Hill Golf Course. 1A 24
Pinner Hill Rd. Pinn 1K 23
Pinner Pk. 1E 24
Pinner Pk. Pinn 2E 24
Pinner Pk. Av. Harr 3F 25
Pinner Pk. Gdns. Harr 2G 25
Pinner Rd. Harr 4E 24
Pinner Rd. N'wd & Pinn 1H 23
Pinner Rd. Pinn 4D 24
Pinner Vw. Harr 4G 25
Pinnerwood Park. 1A 24
Pinn Way. Ruis 7F 23
Pintail Clo. E6 5C 72
Pintail Ct. SE8 6B 88 (off Pilot Clo.)
Pintail Rd. Wfd G 7E 20
Pintail Way. Hay 5B 60
Pinter Ho. SW9 2J 103 (off Grantham Rd.)
Pinto Way. SE3 4K 107
Pioneer Mkt. Ilf 3F 55 (off Winston Way)
Pioneers Ind. Pk. Croy 1J 151
Pioneer St. SE15 1G 105
Pioneer Way. W12 6D 64
Piper Clo. N7 5K 49
Piper Rd. King T 3G 135
Piper's Gdns. Croy 7A 142
Pipers Grn. NW9 5J 27
Pipers Grn. La. Edgw 3K 11 (in two parts)
Pipewell Rd. Cars 6C 138
Pippin Clo. NW2 3C 46
Pippin Clo. Croy 1B 154
Pippins Clo. W Dray 3A 76
Pippins Ct. Ashf 6D 112
Piquet Rd. SE20 2J 141
Pirbright Cres. New Ad 6E 154
Pirbright Rd. SW18 1H 119
Pirie Clo. SE5 3D 104
Pirie St. E16 1K 89
Pitcairn Clo. Romf 4G 39
Pitcairn Ho. E8 7J 51
Pitcairn Rd. Mitc 7D 120
Pitcairn's Path. Harr 3G 43
Pitchford St. E15 7F 53
Pitfield Cres. SE28 1A 92
Pitfield Est. N1 3E 68 (1G 163)
Pitfield St. N1 3E 68 (1G 163)
Pitfield Way. NW10 6J 45
Pitfield Way. Enf 1D 8
Pitfold Clo. SE12 6J 107
Pitfold Rd. SE12 6J 107
Pitlake. Croy 2B 152
Pitman Ho. SE8 1C 106
Pitman St. SE5 7C 86 (in two parts)
Pitmaston Ho. SE13 2E 106 (off Lewisham Rd.)
Pitsea Pl. E1 6K 69
Pitsea St. E1 6K 69
Pitshanger La. W5 4B 62
Pitshanger Manor. 1D 80
Pitt Cres. SW19 4K 119
Pittman Gdns. Ilf 5G 55
Pitt Rd. T Hth & Croy 5C 140
Pitt's Head M. W1 1E 84 (5H 165)
Pittsmead Av. Brom 7J 143

Pitt St. W8 2J **83**
Pittville Gdns. SE25 3G **141**
Pixfield Ct. Brom 2H ***143*** *(off Beckenham La.)*
Pixley St. E14 6B **70**
Pixton Way. Croy 7A **154**
Place Farm Av. Orp 7H **145**
Place, The. 3H 67 (2D 160) (off Flaxman Ter.)
Plaisterers Highwalk. EC2 5C ***68*** *(6C 162) (off Noble St.)*
Plaistow. 7J 125 (Bromley)
Plaistow. 3K 71 (West Ham)
Plaistow Gro. E15 1H **71**
Plaistow Gro. Brom 7K **125**
Plaistow La. Brom 7J **125** (in two parts)
Plaistow Pk. Rd. E13 2K **71**
Plaistow Rd. E15 & E13 1H **71**
Plaistow Wharf. E16 1J **89**
Plane Ho. Short 2G **143**
Plane St. SE26 3H **123**
Planetree Ct. W6 4F ***83*** *(off Brook Grn.)*
Plane Tree Cres. Felt 3K **113**
Plane Tree Ho. SE8 6A ***88*** *(off Etta St.)*
Plane Tree Wlk. N2 3C **30**
Plane Tree Wlk. SE19 6E **122**
Plantagenet Clo. Wor Pk 4K **147**
Plantagenet Gdns. Romf 7D **38**
Plantagenet Ho. SE18 3D ***90*** *(off Leda Rd.)*
Plantagenet Pl. Romf 7D **38**
Plantagenet Rd. Barn 4F **5**
Plantain Gdns. E11 3F ***53*** *(off Hollydown Way, in two parts)*
Plantain Pl. SE1 2D **86** (6E 168)
Plantation, The. SE3 2J **107**
Plantation Wharf. SW11 3A **102**
Plasel Ct. E13 1K ***71*** *(off Pawsey Clo.)*
Plashet. 6C 54
Plashet Gro. E6 1A **72**
Plashet Rd. E13 1J **71**
Plassy Rd. SE6 7D **106**
Plate Ho. E14 5D ***88*** *(off Burrells Wharf Sq.)*
Platina St. EC2 3F **163**
Plato Rd. SW2 4J **103**
Platt Halls. NW9 2B **28**
Platt's La. NW3 4J **47**
Platts Rd. Enf 1D **8**
Platt St. NW1 2H **67**
Platt, The. SW15 3F **101**
Plawsfield Rd. Beck 1K **141**
Plaxtol Clo. Brom 1A **144**
Plaxtol Rd. Eri 7G **93**
Plaxton Ct. E11 3H **53**
Players Theatre. 1J 85 (4F 167) (off Hungerford La.)
Playfair Ho. E14 6C ***70*** *(off Saracen St.)*
Playfair Mans. W14 6G ***83*** *(off Queen's Club Gdns.)*
Playfair St. W6 5E **82**
Playfield Av. Romf 1J **39**
Playfield Cres. SE22 5F **105**
Playfield Rd. Edgw 2J **27**
Playford Rd. N4 2K **49** (in two parts)
Playgreen Way. SE6 3C **124**
Playground Clo. Beck 2K **141**
Playhouse Theatre. 1J 85 (4F 167) (off Northumberland Av.)
Playhouse Yd. EC4 6B **68** (1A 168)
Plaza Bus. Cen. Enf 2F **9**
Plaza Pde. NW6 2K **65**
Plaza Shop. Cen., The. W1 6G **67** (7B 160)
Pleasance Rd. SW15 5D **100**
Pleasance, The. SW15 4D **100**
Pleasant Gro. Croy 3B **154**
Pleasant Pl. N1 7B **50**
Pleasant Pl. S Harr 1H **43**
Pleasant Row. NW1 1F **67**
Pleasant Way. Wemb 2C **62**
Plender Pl. NW1 1G ***67*** *(off Plender St.)*
Plender St. NW1 1G **67**
Pleshey Rd. N7 4H **49**
Plesman Way. Wall 7J **151**
Plevna Cres. N15 6E **32**
Plevna Rd. N9 3B **18**
Plevna Rd. Hamp 1F **133**
Plevna St. E14 3E **88**
Pleydell Av. SE19 7F **123**
Pleydell Av. W6 4B **82**
Pleydell Ct. EC4 6A ***68*** *(1K 167) (off Lombard La.)*
Pleydell Est. EC1 2D **162**
Pleydell St. EC4 1K **167**
Plimsoll Clo. E14 6D **70**
Plimsoll Rd. N4 3A **50**
Plough Ct. EC3 7D **68** (2F 169)
Plough Farm Clo. Ruis 6F **23**
Plough La. SE22 6F **105**
Plough La. SW19 & SW17 5K **119**
Plough La. Purl 7J **151**
Plough La. Tedd 5A **116**
Plough La. Wall 4J **151**
Plough La. Clo. Wall 5J **151**
Ploughmans Clo. NW1 1H **67**
Ploughmans End. Iswth 5H **97**
Ploughmans Wlk. N2 2A ***30*** *(off Long La.)*
Plough Pl. EC4 6A **68** (7K 161)
Plough Rd. SW11 3B **102**
Plough Rd. Eps 7K **147**
Plough St. E1 6F **69** (7K 163)
Plough Ter. SW11 4B **102**
Plough Way. SE16 4K **87**
Plough Yd. EC2 4E **68** (4H 163)
Plover Ho. SW9 7A ***86*** *(off Brixton Rd.)*
Plover Way. SE16 3A **88**
Plover Way. Hay 6B **60**
Plowden Bldgs. EC4 2J **167**
Plowman Clo. N18 5J **17**
Plowman Way. Dag 1C **56**
Plumber's Row. E1 5G **69**
Plumbridge St. SE10 1D **106**
Plum Clo. Felt 1J **113**
Plume Ho. SE10 6D ***88*** *(off Creek Rd.)*
Plum Gth. Bren 4D **80**
Plum La. SE18 7F **91**
Plummer La. Mitc 2D **138**
Plummer Rd. SW4 7H **103**
Plumpton Clo. N'holt 6E **42**
Plumpton Way. Cars 3C **150**
Plumstead. 4J 91
Plumstead Common. 6H 91
Plumstead Comn. Rd. SE18 6F **91**
Plumstead High St. SE18 4H **91**
Plumstead Rd. SE18 4F **91**
Plumtree Clo. Dag 6H **57**
Plumtree Clo. Wall 7H **151**
Plumtree Ct. EC4 6B **68** (7A 162)
Plymouth Ct. Surb 4E ***134*** *(off Cranes Pk. Av.)*
Plymouth Ho. SE10 7D ***88*** *(off Devonshire Dri.)*
Plymouth Ho. Bark 7A ***56*** *(off Keir Hardie Way)*
Plymouth Rd. E16 5J **71**
Plymouth Rd. Brom 1K **143**
Plymouth Wharf. E14 4F **89**
Plympton Av. NW6 7H **47**
Plympton Clo. Belv 3E **92**
Plympton Pl. NW8 4C **66** (4C 158)
Plympton Rd. NW6 7H **47**
Plympton St. NW8 4C **66** (4C 158)
Plymstock Rd. Well 7C **92**
Pocklington Clo. NW9 2A **28**
Pocklington Clo. W12 3C ***82*** *(off Ashchurch Pk. Vs.)*
Pocklington Lodge. W12 3C **82**
Pocock Av. W Dray 3B **76**
Pocock St. SE1 2B **86** (6A 168)
Podmore Rd. SW18 4A **102**
Poet's Rd. N5 5D **50**
Poets Way. Harr 4J **25**
Pointalls Clo. N3 2A **30**
Point Clo. SE10 1E **106**
Pointer Clo. SE28 6D **74**
Pointers Clo. E14 5D **88**
Pointers Cotts. Rich 2C **116**
Point Hill. SE10 7E **88**
Point Pl. Wemb 7H **45**
Point Pleasant. SW18 4J **101**
Point Ter. E7 5K ***53*** *(off Claremont Rd.)*
Point, The. Ruis 4J **41**
Point West. SW7 4K **83**
Poland St. W1 6G **67** (1B 166)
Polebrook Rd. SE3 3A **108**
Pole Cat All. Brom 2H **155**
Polecroft La. SE6 2B **124**
Polehamptons, The. Hamp 7G **115**
Pole Hill Rd. E4 7K **9**
Pole Hill Rd. Uxb & Hil 4D **58**
Polesden Gdns. SW20 2D **136**
Polesworth Ho. W2 5J ***65*** *(off Alfred Rd.)*
Polesworth Rd. Dag 7D **56**
Police Sta. La. Bush 1A **10**
Polish War Memorial. (Junct.) 6A **42**
Pollard Clo. E16 7J **71**
Pollard Clo. N7 4K **49**
Pollard Ho. N1 2K ***67*** *(1G 161) (off Northdown St.)*
Pollard Rd. N20 2H **15**
Pollard Rd. Mord 5B **138**
Pollard Row. E2 3G **69**
Pollards Cres. SW16 3J **139**
Pollards Hill E. SW16 3K **139**
Pollards Hill N. SW16 3J **139**
Pollards Hill S. SW16 3J **139**
Pollards Hill W. SW16 3K **139**
Pollard St. E2 3G **69**
Pollards Wood Rd. SW16 3J **139**
Pollard Wlk. Sidc 6C **128**
Pollen St. W1 6G **67** (1A 166)
Pollitt Dri. NW8 4B **66** (3B 158)
Pollock Ho. W10 4G ***65*** *(off Kensal Rd.)*
Pollock's Toy Mus. 5G 67 (5B 160)
Polperro Clo. Orp 6K **145**
Polperro M. SE11 4B **86** (3K 173)
Polsted Rd. SE6 7B **106**
Polthorne Gro. SE18 4G **91**
Polworth Rd. SW16 5J **121**
Polygon Rd. NW1 2H **67** (1C 160)
Polygon, The. NW8 1B ***66*** *(off Avenue Rd.)*
Polygon, The. SW4 4G **103**
Polytechnic St. SE18 4E **90**
Pomell Way. E1 6F **69** (7K 163)
Pomeroy Ho. E2 2K ***69*** *(off St James's Av.)*
Pomeroy Ho. W11 6G ***65*** *(off Lancaster Rd.)*
Pomeroy St. SE14 7J **87**
Pomfret Rd. SE5 3B **104**
Pomoja La. N19 2J **49**
Pomona Ho. SE8 4A ***88*** *(off Evelyn St.)*
Pond Clo. N12 6H **15**
Pond Clo. SE3 2J **107**
Pond Cottage La. Beck 1C **154**
Pond Cotts. SE21 1E **122**
Ponders End. 5D 8
Ponders End Ind. Est. Enf 5F **9**
Ponder St. N7 7K **49** (in two parts)
Pond Farm Est. E5 3J **51**
Pondfield Ho. SE27 5C **122**
Pondfield Rd. Brom 1G **155**
Pondfield Rd. Dag 5H **57**
Pond Grn. Ruis 2G **41**
Pond Hill Gdns. Sutt 6G **149**
Pond Ho. SW3 4C **84** (4C 170)
Pond Ho. Stan 6G **11**
Pond Lees Clo. Dag 7K **57**
Pond Mead. SE21 6D **104**
Pond Path. Chst 6F **127**
Pond Pl. SW3 4C **84** (4C 170)
Pond Rd. E15 2G **71**
Pond Rd. SE3 2H **107**
Pondside Clo. Hay 6F **77**
Pond Sq. N6 1E **48**
Pond St. NW3 5C **48**
Pond Way. Tedd 6C **116**
Pondwood Ri. Orp 7J **145**
Ponler St. E1 6H **69**
Ponsard Rd. NW10 3D **64**
Ponsford St. E9 6J **51**
Ponsonby Pl. SW1 5H **85** (5D 172)
Ponsonby Rd. SW15 7D **100**
Ponsonby Ter. SW1 5H **85** (5D 172)
Pontefract Ct. N'holt 5F ***43*** *(off Newmarket Av.)*
Pontefract Rd. Brom 5H **125**
Ponton Rd. SW8 7H **85**
Pont St. SW1 3D **84** (2E 170)
Pont St. M. SW1 3D **84** (2E 170)
Pontypool Pl. SE1 2B **86** (6A 168)
Pool Clo. Beck 5C **124**
Pool Clo. W Mol 5D **132**
Pool Ct. SE6 2C **124**
Poole Clo. Ruis 2G **41**
Poole Ct. N1 7E ***50*** *(off St Peter's Way)*
Poole Ct. Houn 2C **96**
Poole Ct. Rd. Houn 2C **96**
Poole Ho. SE11 3H **173**
Pool End. 5C 130
Pool End Clo. Shep 5C **130**
Poole Rd. E9 6K **51**
Poole Rd. Eps 6K **147**
Pooles Bldgs. WC1 4J **161**
Pooles Cotts. Rich 2D **116**
Pooles La. SW10 7A **84**
Pooles La. Dag 2E **74**
Pooles Pk. N4 2A **50**
Poole St. N1 1D **68**
Poole Way. Hay 3G **59**
Pool Ho. NW8 5B ***66*** *(5C 158) (off Penfold St.)*
Poolmans St. SE16 2K **87**
Pool Rd. Harr 7H **25**
Pool Rd. W Mol 5D **132**
Poolsford Rd. NW9 4A **28**
Poonah St. E1 6J **69**
Pope Clo. SW19 6B **120**
Pope Clo. Felt 1H **113**
Pope Ho. SE5 7D ***86*** *(off Elmington Est.)*
Pope Ho. SE16 4H ***87*** *(off Manor Est.)*
Pope Rd. Brom 5B **144**
Popes Av. Twic 2J **115**
Popes Ct. Twic 2J **115**
Popes Dri. N3 1J **29**
Popes Gro. Croy 3B **154**
Popes Gro. Twic 2J **115**
Pope's Head All. EC3 6D **68** (1F 169)
Popes La. W5 3D **80**
Pope's Rd. SW9 3A **104**
Pope St. SE1 2E **86** (7H 169)
Popham Clo. Hanw 3D **114**
Popham Gdns. Rich 3G **99**
Popham Rd. N1 1C **68**
Popham St. N1 1B **68** (in two parts)
Pop-In Commercial Cen. Wemb 5H **45**
Popinjays Row. Cheam 5F ***149*** *(off Netley Clo.)*
Poplar. 7D 70
Poplar Av. Mitc 1D **138**
Poplar Av. S'hall 3F **79**
Poplar Av. W Dray 7B **58**
Poplar Bath St. E14 6D **70**
Poplar Bus. Pk. E14 7E **70**
Poplar Clo. E9 5B **52**
Poplar Clo. Pinn 1B **24**
Poplar Ct. SW19 5J **119**
Poplar Ct. N'holt 2A **60**
Poplar Ct. Twic 6C **98**
Poplar Cres. Eps 6J **147**
Poplar Farm Clo. Eps 6J **147**
Poplar Gdns. SE28 7C **74**
Poplar Gdns. N Mald 2K **135**
Poplar Gro. N11 6K **15**
Poplar Gro. W6 2E **82**
Poplar Gro. N Mald 2K **135**
Poplar Gro. Wemb 3J **45**
Poplar High St. E14 7D **70**
Poplar Ho. SE4 4B ***106*** *(off Wickham Rd.)*
Poplar Ho. SE16 2K ***87*** *(off Woodland Cres.)*
Poplar M. W12 1E **82**
Poplar Mt. Belv 4H **93**
Poplar Pl. SE28 7C **74**
Poplar Pl. W2 7K **65**
Poplar Pl. Hay 7J **59**
Poplar Rd. SE24 4C **104**
Poplar Rd. SW19 2J **137**
Poplar Rd. Ashf 5E **112**
Poplar Rd. Sutt 1H **149**
Poplar Rd. S. SW19 3J **137**
Poplars Av. NW2 6E **46**
Poplars Clo. Ruis 1G **41**
Poplars Rd. E17 6D **34**
Poplars, The. N14 5A **6**
Poplar St. Romf 4J **39**
Poplar Vw. Wemb 2D **44**
Poplar Wlk. SE24 3C **104** (in two parts)
Poplar Wlk. Croy 2C **152**
Poplar Way. Felt 3J **113**
Poplar Way. Ilf 4G **37**
Poppins Ct. EC4 6B **68** (1A 168)
Poppleton Rd. E11 6G **35**
Poppy Clo. Belv 3H **93**
Poppy Clo. Wall 1E **150**
Poppy La. Croy 7J **141**
Porchester Clo. SE5 4C **104**
Porchester Ct. W2 7K ***65*** *(off Porchester Gdns.)*
Porchester Gdns. W2 7K **65**
Porchester Gdns. M. W2 6K **65**
Porchester Ga. W2 7K ***65*** *(off Bayswater Rd., in two parts)*
Porchester Ho. E1 6H ***69*** *(off Philpot St.)*
Porchester Mead. Beck 6C **124**
Porchester M. W2 6K **65**
Porchester Pl. W2 6C **66** (1D 164)
Porchester Rd. W2 6K **65**
Porchester Rd. King T 2H **135**
Porchester Sq. W2 6K **65**
Porchester Ter. W2 7A **66**
Porchester Ter. N. W2 6K **65**
Porch Way. N20 3J **15**
Porcupine Clo. SE9 2C **126**
Porden Rd. SW2 4K **103**
Porlock Av. Harr 1G **43**
Porlock Ho. SE26 3G **123**
Porlock Rd. W10 4F **65**

Porlock Rd. Enf 7A 8
Porlock St. SE1 2D 86 (6F 169)
Porrington Clo. Chst 1D 144
Porson Ct. SE13 3D 106
Portal Clo. SE27 3A 122
Portal Clo. Ruis 4J 41
(in two parts)
Portal Clo. Uxb 7A 40
(in two parts)
Portbury Clo. SE15 1G 105
Port Cres. E13 4K 71
Portcullis Ho. SW1 7E 166
Portcullis Lodge Rd. Enf 3J 7
Portelet Ct. N1 1E 68
(off De Beauvoir Est.)
Portelet Rd. E1 3K 69
Porten Houses. W14 3G 83
(off Porten Rd.)
Porten Rd. W14 3G 83
Porter Rd. E6 6D 72
Porters & Walters Almshouses. N22 7E 16
(off Nightingale Rd.)
Porters Av. Dag 6B 56
Porter Sq. N19 1J 49
Porter St. SE1 1C 86 (4D 168)
Porter St. W1 5D 66 (5F 159)
Porters Wlk. E1 7H 69
(off Balkan Wlk.)
Porters Way. W Dray 3B 76
Porteus Rd. W2 5A 66 (5A 158)
Portgate Clo. W9 4H 65
Porthcawe Rd. SE26 4A 124
Porthkerry Av. Well 4A 110
Port Ho. E14 5D 88
(off Burrells Wharf Sq.)
Portia Ct. SE11 5B 86
(off Opal St.)
Portia Ct. Bark 7A 56
Portia Way. E3 4B 70
Porticos, The. SW3 7A 170
Portinscale Rd. SW15 5G 101
Portland Av. N16 7F 33
Portland Av. N Mald 7B 136
Portland Av. Sidc 6A 110
Portland Clo. Romf 5E 38
Portland Commercial Est. Bark 2C 74
Portland Ct. N1 7E 50
(off St Peter's Way)
Portland Ct. SE1 3D 86 (7E 168)
(off Gt. Dover St.)
Portland Ct. SE14 6A 88
(off Whitcher Clo.)
Portland Cres. SE9 2C 126
Portland Cres. Felt 4F 113
Portland Cres. Gnfd 4F 61
Portland Cres. Stan 2D 26
Portland Dri. Enf 1K 7
Portland Gdns. N4 6B 32
Portland Gdns. Romf 5D 38
Portland Gro. SW8 1K 103
Portland Ho. SW1 3G 85 (2A 172)
(off Stag Pl.)
Portland M. W1 6G 67 (1B 166)
Portland Pl. SE25 4G 141
(off Portland Rd.)
Portland Pl. W1 4F 67 (4J 159)
Portland Ri. N4 1B 50
Portland Ri. Est. N4 1C 50
Portland Rd. N15 4F 33
Portland Rd. SE9 2C 126
Portland Rd. SE25 4G 141
Portland Rd. W11 7G 65
Portland Rd. Ashf 3A 112
Portland Rd. Brom 4A 126
Portland Rd. Hay 3G 59
Portland Rd. King T 3E 134
Portland Rd. Mitc 2C 138
Portland Rd. S'hall 3D 78
Portland Sq. E1 1H 87
Portland St. SE17 5D 86
Portland Ter. Rich 4D 98
Portland Wlk. SE17 6D 86
Portman Av. SW14 3K 99
Portman Clo. W1 6D 66 (7F 159)
Portman Clo. Bex 1K 129
Portman Clo. Bexh 3E 110
Portman Dri. Wfd G 2B 36
Portman Gdns. NW9 2K 27
Portman Gdns. Uxb 7C 40
Portman Ga. NW1 4D 158
Portman Mans. W1 5D 66 (5F 159)
(off Chiltern St.)
Portman M. S. W1 6E 66 (1G 165)
Portman Pl. E2 3J 69
Portman Rd. King T 2F 135
Portman Sq. W1 6E 66 (7G 159)
Portman St. W1 6E 66 (1G 165)
Portman Towers. W1 6D 66 (7F 159)
Portmeadow Wlk. SE2 2D 92
Port Meers Clo. E17 6B 34
Portnall Rd. W9 2H 65
Portnoi Clo. Romf 2K 39
Portobello Ct. Est. W11 6H 65
Portobello M. W11 7J 65
Portobello Rd. W10 5G 65
Portobello Rd. W11 6H 65
Portobello Road Market 5G 65
Portpool La. EC1 5A 68
Portree Clo. N22 7E 16
Portree St. E14 6F 71
Portrush Ct. S'hall 6G 61
(off Whitecote Rd.)
Portsdown. Edgw 5B 12
Portsdown Av. NW11 6H 29
Portsdown M. NW11 6H 29
Portsea Hall. W2 6D 66 (1D 164)
(off Portsea Pl.)
Portsea M. W2 1D 164
Portsea Pl. W2 6C 66 (1D 164)
Portslade Rd. SW8 2G 103
Portsmouth Av. Th Dit 7A 134
Portsmouth M. E16 1K 89
Portsmouth Rd. SW15 7D 100
Portsmouth Rd. Th Dit, Surb & King T 1A 146
Portsmouth St. WC2 6K 67 (1G 167)
Portsoken St. E1 7F 69 (2J 169)
Portswood Pl. SW15 6B 100
Portugal Gdns. Twic 2G 115
Portugal St. WC2 6K 67 (1G 167)
Portway. E15 1H 71
Portway Gdns. SE18 7B 90
Pory Ho. SE11 4K 85 (4H 173)
Poseidon Ct. E14 4C 88
(off Homer Dri.)
Postern Grn. Enf 2F 7
Postern, The. EC2 6D 162
Post La. Twic 1H 115
Postmill Clo. Croy 3J 153
Post Office All. Hamp 2F 133
Post Office App. E7 5K 53
Post Office Ct. EC4 6D 68 (1F 169)
(off Barbican)
Post Office Way. SW8 7H 85
Post Rd. S'hall 3F 79
Postway M. Ilf 3F 55
(in two parts)
Potier St. SE1 3D 86
Potter Clo. Mitc 2F 139
Potteries, The. Barn 5D 4
Potterne Clo. SW19 7F 101
Potters Clo. Croy 1A 154
Potters Fld. Enf 4K 7
(off Lincoln Rd.)
Potters Fields. SE1 1E 86 (5H 169)
Potters Gro. N Mald 4J 135
Potters Heights Clo. Pinn 1K 23
Potter's La. SW16 6H 121
Potters La. Barn 4D 4
(in two parts)
Potters Lodge. E14 5E 88
(off Manchester Rd.)
Potters Rd. SW6 2A 102
Potter's Rd. Barn 4E 4
Potter St. N'wd 1J 23
Potter St. Pinn 1K 23
Potter St. Hill. Pinn 1K 23
Pottery La. W11 1G 83
Pottery Rd. Bex 2J 129
Pottery Rd. Bren 6E 80
Pottery St. SE16 2H 87
Pott St. E2 3H 69
Poulett Gdns. Twic 1A 116
Poulett Rd. E6 2D 72
Poulters Wood. Kes 5B 156
Poulton Av. Sutt 3B 150
Poulton Clo. E8 6H 51
Poultry. EC2 6D 68 (1E 168)
Pound Clo. Surb 1C 146
Pound Grn. Bex 7G 111
Pound La. NW10 6C 46
Pound Pk. Rd. SE7 4B 90
Pound Pl. SE9 6E 108
Pound St. Cars 5D 150
Pound Way. Chst 7G 127
Pountney Rd. SW11 3E 102
Poverest 5K 145
Poverest Rd. Orp 5K 145
Povey Ho. SE17 4E 86
(off Tatum St.)
Powder Mill La. Twic 7D 96
Powell Clo. Chess 5D 146
Powell Clo. Edgw 6A 12
Powell Clo. Wall 7J 151
Powell Ct. E17 3D 34
Powell Ct. S Croy 4B 152
(off Bramley Hill)
Powell Gdns. Dag 4G 57
Powell Rd. E5 3H 51
Powell Rd. Buck H 1F 21
Powell's Wlk. W4 6A 82
Powergate Bus. Pk. NW10 3K 63
Power Rd. W4 4G 81
Powers Ct. Twic 7D 98
Powerscroft Rd. E5 4J 51
Powerscroft Rd. Sidc 6C 128
Powis Ct. W11 6H 65
(off Powis Gdns.)
Powis Ct. Bus H 1C 10
(off Rutherford Way)
Powis Gdns. NW11 7H 29
Powis Gdns. W11 6H 65
Powis M. W11 6H 65
Powis Pl. WC1 4J 67 (4F 161)
Powis Rd. E3 3D 70
Powis Sq. W11 6H 65
(in two parts)
Powis St. SE18 3E 90
Powis Ter. W11 6H 65
Powlett Ho. NW1 6F 49
(off Powlett Pl.)
Powlett Pl. NW1 7E 48
Pownall Gdns. Houn 4F 97
Pownall Rd. E8 1G 69
Pownall Rd. Houn 4F 97
Pownsett Ter. Ilf 5G 55
Powster Rd. Brom 5J 125
Powys Clo. Bexh 6D 92
Powys Ct. N11 5D 16
Powys La. N14 & N13 4D 16
Poynders Ct. SW4 6G 103
Poynders Gdns. SW4 7G 103
Poynders Rd. SW4 6G 103
Poynings Rd. N19 3G 49
Poynings Way. N12 5D 14
Poyntell Cres. Chst 1H 145
Poynter Ct. N'holt 2B 60
(off Gallery Gdns.)
Poynter Ho. NW8 4B 66 (3A 158)
(off Fisherton St.)
Poynter Ho. W11 1F 83
(off Queensdale Cres.)
Poynter Rd. Enf 5A 8
Poynton Rd. N17 2G 33
Poyntz Rd. SW11 2D 102
Poyser St. E2 2H 69
Praed M. W2 6B 66 (7B 158)
Praed St. W2 6B 66 (1A 164)
Pragel St. E13 2A 72
Pragnell Rd. SE12 2K 125
Prague Pl. SW2 5J 103
Prah Rd. N4 2A 50
Prairie St. SW8 2E 102
Pratt M. NW1 1G 67
Pratts Pas. King T 2E 134
Pratt St. NW1 1G 67
Pratt Wlk. SE11 4K 85 (3H 173)
Prayle Gro. NW2 1F 47
Preachers Ct. EC1 4B 68 (4B 162)
(off Charterhouse Sq.)
Prebend Gdns. W6 & W4 4B 82
(in two parts)
Prebend Mans. W4 4B 82
(off Chiswick High Rd.)
Prebend St. N1 1C 68
Precinct Rd. Hay 7J 59
Precincts, The. Mord 6J 137
Precinct, The. N1 1C 68
(in two parts)
Precinct, The. W Mol 3F 133
Premier Corner. W9 2H 65
Premier Ct. Enf 1D 8
Premiere Pl. E14 7C 70
Premier Ho. N1 7B 50
(off Waterloo Ter.)
Premier Pk. NW10 1H 63
Premier Pk. Rd. NW10 2H 63
Premier Pl. SW15 4G 101
Prendergast Rd. SE3 3G 107
Prentice Ct. SW19 5H 119
Prentis Rd. SW16 4H 121
Prentiss Ct. SE7 4B 90
Presburg Rd. N Mald 5A 136
Presburg St. E5 3K 51
Prescelly Pl. Edgw 1F 27
Prescot St. E1 7F 69 (2K 169)
Prescott Av. Orp 6F 145
Prescott Clo. SW16 7J 121
Prescott Ho. SE17 6B 86
(off Hillingdon St.)
Prescott Pl. SW4 3H 103
Presentation M. SW2 2K 121
Preshaw Cres. Mitc 3C 138
President Dri. E1 1H 87
President Ho. EC1 3B 68 (2B 162)
President Quay. E1 4K 169
President St. EC1 1C 162
Prespa Clo. N9 2D 18
Press Ho. NW10 3K 45
Press Rd. NW10 3K 45
Prestage Way. E14 7E 70
Prestbury Rd. E7 7A 54
Prestbury Sq. SE9 4D 126
Prested Rd. SW11 4C 102
Prestige Way. NW4 5E 28
Preston 1E 44
Preston Av. E4 6A 20
Preston Clo. SE1 4E 86
Preston Clo. Twic 3J 115
Preston Ct. New Bar 4F 5
Preston Ct. Sidc 4K 127
(off Crescent, The)
Preston Dri. E11 5A 36
Preston Dri. Bexh 1D 110
Preston Dri. Eps 6A 148
Preston Gdns. NW10 6B 46
Preston Gdns. Ilf 6C 36
Preston Hill. Harr 7E 26
Preston Ho. SE1 4E 86
(off Preston Clo.)
Preston Ho. SE1 3F 87
(off Stanworth St.)
Preston Ho. Dag 3G 57
(off Uvedale Rd.)
Preston Pl. NW2 6C 46
Preston Pl. Rich 5E 98
Preston Rd. E11 6G 35
Preston Rd. SE19 6B 122
Preston Rd. SW20 7B 118
Preston Rd. Shep 5C 130
Preston Rd. Wemb 1E 44
Preston's Rd. E14 7E 70
Prestons Rd. Brom 3J 155
Preston St. E2 2K 69
Preston Waye. Harr 1E 44
Prestwich Ter. SW4 5G 103
Prestwick Clo. S'hall 5C 78
Prestwick Ct. S'hall 7G 61
(off Baird Av.)
Prestwood Av. Harr 4B 26
Prestwood Clo. SE18 6A 92
Prestwood Clo. Harr 4B 26
Prestwood Gdns. Croy 7C 140
Prestwood Ho. SE16 3H 87
(off Drummond Rd.)
Prestwood St. N1 2C 68 (1D 162)
Pretoria Av. E17 4A 34
Pretoria Clo. N17 7A 18
Pretoria Cres. E4 1K 19
Pretoria Rd. E4 1K 19
Pretoria Rd. E11 1F 53
Pretoria Rd. E16 4H 71
Pretoria Rd. N17 7A 18
Pretoria Rd. SW16 6F 121
Pretoria Rd. Ilf 5F 55
Pretoria Rd. Romf 4J 39
Pretoria Rd. N. N18 6A 18
Prevost Rd. N11 2K 15
Priam Ho. E2 2H 69
(off Old Bethnal Grn. Rd.)
Price Clo. NW7 6B 14
Price Clo. SW17 3D 120
Price' Ct. SW11 3B 102
Price Ho. N1 1C 68
(off Britannia Row)
Price Rd. Croy 5B 152
Price's St. SE1 1B 86 (5B 168)
Price's Yd. N1 1K 67
Price Way. Hamp 6C 114
Prichard Ct. N7 6K 49
Pricklers Hill. Barn 6E 4
Prickley Wood. Brom 1H 155
Priddy's Yd. Croy 2C 152
Prideaux Pl. W3 7K 63
Prideaux Pl. WC1 3K 67 (1H 161)
Prideaux Rd. SW9 3J 103
Pridham Rd. T Hth 4D 140
Priestfield Rd. SE23 3A 124
Priestlands Pk. Rd. Sidc 3K 127
Priestley Clo. N16 7F 33
Priestley Gdns. Romf 6B 38
Priestley Ho. EC1 4C 68 (3D 162)
(off Old St.)
Priestley Ho. Wemb 3J 45
(off Barnhill Rd.)
Priestley Rd. Mitc 2E 138
Priestley Way. E17 3K 33
Priestley Way. NW2 1C 46
Priest Pk. Av. Harr 2E 42
Priests Av. Romf 2K 39
Priest's Bri. SW14 & SW15 3A 100
Priest's Ct. EC2 7C 162
Prima Rd. SW9 7A 86
Prime Meridian Line, The. 7F 89
(Greenwich Royal Observatory)
Primrose Av. Enf 1J 7
Primrose Av. Romf 7B 38
Primrose Clo. N3 2K 29
Primrose Clo. SE6 5E 124
Primrose Clo. Harr 3D 42
Primrose Clo. Wall 7F 139
Primrose Ct. SW12 7H 103
Primrose Gdns. NW3 6C 48
Primrose Gdns. Bush 1A 10
Primrose Gdns. Ruis 5A 42
Primrose Hill 1E 66

Primrose Hill. EC4 6A 68 (1K 167)
Primrose Hill Ct. NW3 7D 48
Primrose Hill Rd. NW3 7D 48
Primrose Hill Studios. NW1 1E 66
Primrose La. Croy 1J 153
Primrose Mans. SW11 1E 102
Primrose M. NW1 7D 48 (off Sharpleshall St.)
Primrose M. SE3 7J 89
Primrose Rd. E10 1D 52
Primrose Rd. E18 2K 35
Primrose Sq. E9 7J 51
Primrose St. EC2 5E 68 (5G 163)
Primrose Wlk. SE14 7A 88
Primrose Wlk. Eps 7B 148
Primrose Way. Wemb 2D 62
Primula St. W12 6C 64
Prince Albert Ct. NW8 1D 66 (off Prince Albert Rd.)
Prince Albert Rd. NW1 & NW8 3C 66 (1C 158)
Prince Arthur M. NW3 4A 48
Prince Arthur Rd. NW3 5A 48
Prince Charles Cinema. 7H 67 (2D 166) (off Leicester Pl.)
Prince Charles Dri. NW4 7E 28
Prince Charles Rd. SE3 2H 107
Prince Charles Way. Wall 3F 151
Prince Consort Dri. Chst 1H 145
Prince Consort Rd. SW7 3A 84 (1A 170)
Princedale Rd. W11 1G 83
Prince Edward Mans. W2 7J 65 (off Hereford Rd.)
Prince Edward Rd. E9 6B 52
Prince Edward Theatre. 6H 67 (1D 166) (off Old Compton St.)
Prince George Av. N14 5B 6
Prince George Rd. N16 4E 50
Prince George's Av. SW20 2E 136
Prince George's Rd. SW19 1B 138
Prince Henry Rd. SE7 7B 90
Prince Imperial Rd. SE18 1D 108
Prince Imperial Rd. Chst 1F 145
Prince John Rd. SE9 5C 108
Princelet St. E1 5F 69 (5K 163)
Prince of Wales Clo. NW4 4D 28
Prince of Wales Dri. SW11 & SW8 1C 102
Prince of Wales Mans. SW11 1E 102
Prince of Wales Pas. NW1 2A 160
Prince of Wales Rd. E16 6A 72
Prince of Wales Rd. NW5 6E 48
Prince of Wales Rd. SE3 2H 107
Prince of Wales Rd. Sutt 2B 150
Prince of Wales Ter. W4 5A 82
Prince of Wales Ter. W8 2K 83
Prince of Wales Theatre. 7H 67 (3C 166) (off Coventry St.)
Prince Regent Ct. NW8 2C 66 (off Avenue Rd.)
Prince Regent Ct. SE16 7A 70 (off Edward Sq.)
Prince Regent La. E13 & E16 3K 71
Prince Regent M. NW1 2A 160
Prince Regent Rd. Houn 3G 97
Prince Regents Ga. NW8 4C 66 (3D 158)
Prince Rd. SE25 5E 140
Prince Rupert Rd. SE9 4D 108
Princes Arc. SW1 4B 166
Princes Av. N3 1J 29
Princes Av. N10 3F 31
Princes Av. N13 5F 17
Princes Av. N22 1H 31
Princes Av. NW9 4G 27
Princes Av. W3 3G 81
Princes Av. Cars 7D 150
Prince's Av. Gnfd 6F 61
Princes Av. Orp 5J 145
Princes Av. Surb 1G 147
Princes Av. Wfd G 4E 20
Princes Cir. WC2 6J 67 (7E 160)
Princes Clo. N4 1B 50
Princes Clo. NW9 4G 27
Princes Clo. SW4 3G 103
Princes Clo. Edgw 5B 12
Princes Clo. Sidc 3D 128
Prince's Clo. Tedd 4H 115
Prince's Ct. SE16 3B 88
Prince's Ct. SW3 3D 84 (1E 170) (off Brompton Rd.)
Princes Ct. Wemb 5E 44
Princes Ct. Bus. Cen. E1 7H 69
Princes Dri. Harr 3J 25
Prince's Gdns. SW7 3B 84 (1B 170)
Princes Gdns. W3 5G 63
Princes Gdns. W5 4C 62
Prince's Ga. SW7 2B 84 (7B 164) (in six parts)
Prince's Ga. Ct. SW7 2B 84 (7A 164)
Prince's Ga. M. SW7 3B 84 (1B 170)
Princes La. N10 3F 31
Prince's M. W2 7K 65
Princes M. W6 5D 82 (off Down Pl.)
Princes M. Houn 4E 96
Princes Pde. NW11 6G 29 (off Golders Grn. Rd.)
Princes Pk. Av. NW11 6G 29
Princes Pk. Av. Hay 7F 59
Princes Pk. Circ. Hay 7F 59
Princes Pk. Clo. Hay 7F 59
Princes Pk. La. Hay 7F 59
Princes Pk. Pde. Hay 7F 59
Princes Pl. SW1 4B 166
Princes Pl. W11 1G 83
Prince's Plain. Brom 7C 144
Prince's Ri. SE13 2E 106
Princes Riverside Rd. SE16 1K 87
Princes Rd. N18 4D 18
Princes Rd. SE20 6K 123
Princes Rd. SW14 3K 99
Prince's Rd. SW19 6J 119
Princes Rd. W13 1B 80
Princes Rd. Ashf 5B 112
Princes Rd. Buck H 2F 21
Princes Rd. Felt 2H 113
Princes Rd. Ilf 4H 37
Princes Rd. Kew 1F 99
Princes Rd. King T 7G 117
Princes Rd. Rich 5F 99
Prince's Rd. Tedd 4H 115
Princessa Ct. Enf 5J 7
Princess Alice Ho. W10 4E 64
Princess Alice Way. SE28 2H 91
Princess Av. Wemb 2E 44
Princess Clo. SE28 6D 74
Princess Ct. N6 7G 31
Princess Ct. W1 5D 66 (6E 158) (off Bryanston Pl.)
Princess Ct. W2 7K 65 (off Queensway)
Princess Ct. King T 3F 135 (off Horace Rd.)
Princess Cres. N4 2B 50
Princess La. Ruis 1G 41
Princess Louise Clo. W2 5B 66 (5B 158)
Princess Mary Ho. SW1 4H 85 (3D 172) (off Vincent St.)
Princess May Rd. N16 4E 50
Princess M. NW3 5B 48
Princess M. King T 3F 135
Princess Pde. Dag 2G 75
Princess Pde. Orp 3E 156
Princess Pk. Mnr. N11 5K 15
Prince's Sq. W2 7K 65 (in two parts)
Princess Rd. NW1 1E 66
Princess Rd. NW6 2J 65
Princess Rd. Croy 6C 140
Princess St. SE1 3B 86
Prince's St. EC2 6D 68 (1E 168)
Princes St. N17 6K 17
Princes St. W1 6F 67 (1K 165)
Princes St. Bexh 3F 111
Princes St. Rich 4E 98
Princes St. Sutt 4B 150
Princes Ter. E13 1K 71
Prince's Tower. SE16 2J 87 (off Elephant La.)
Prince St. SE8 6B 88
Princes Way. SW19 7F 101
Princes Way. Buck H 2F 21
Princes Way. Croy 5K 151
Princes Way. Ruis 4C 42
Princes Way. W Wick 4H 155
Prince's Yd. W11 1G 83 (off Princedale Rd.)
Princethorpe Ho. W2 5K 65 (off Woodchester Sq.)
Princethorpe Rd. SE26 4K 123
Princeton Ct. SW15 3F 101
Princeton M. King T 1G 135
Princeton St. WC1 5K 67 (6G 161)
Principal Sq. E9 5K 51
Pringle Gdns. SW16 4G 121 (in two parts)
Printers Inn Ct. EC4 6A 68 (7J 161)
Printers M. E3 1A 70
Printer St. EC4 6A 68 (7K 161)
Printinghouse La. Hay 2G 77
Printing Ho. Yd. E2 3E 68 (1H 163)
Printon Ho. E14 5B 70 (off Wallwood St.)
Print Village. SE15 2F 105
Printwork Apartments. SE1 3E 86 (7G 169) (off Long La.)
Priolo Rd. SE7 5A 90
Prior Av. Sutt 7C 150
Prior Bolton St. N1 6B 50
Prioress Rd. SE27 3B 122
Prioress St. SE1 3E 86
Prior Rd. Ilf 3E 54
Priors Cft. E17 2A 34
Priors Fld. N'holt 6C 42
Priors Gdns. Ruis 5A 42
Priors Mead. Enf 1K 7
Prior St. SE10 7E 88
Priory Apartments, The. SE6 1D 124
Priory Av. E4 3G 19
Priory Av. E17 5C 34
Priory Av. N8 4H 31
Priory Av. W4 4A 82
Priory Av. Orp 6H 145
Priory Av. Sutt 4F 149
Priory Av. Wemb 4K 43
Priory Clo. E4 3G 19
Priory Clo. E18 1J 35
Priory Clo. N3 1H 29
Priory Clo. N14 5A 6
Priory Clo. N20 7C 4
Priory Clo. SW19 1K 137
Priory Clo. Beck 3A 142
Priory Clo. Chst 1D 144
Priory Clo. Hamp 1D 132
Priory Clo. Hay 7K 59
Priory Clo. Ruis 1H 41
Priory Clo. Stan 3E 10
Priory Clo. Sun 7J 113
Priory Clo. Wemb 4K 43
Priory Ct. E6 1A 72
Priory Ct. E9 5K 51
Priory Ct. E17 2B 34
Priory Ct. EC4 6B 68 (1B 168) (off Pilgrim St.)
Priory Ct. SW8 1H 103
Priory Ct. Bush 1B 10
Priory Ct. Eps 7B 148
Priory Ct. Houn 3F 97
Priory Ct. King T 3E 134 (off Denmark Rd.)
Priory Ct. Sutt 4G 149
Priory Ct. Wemb 2E 62
Priory Ct. Est. E17 2B 34
Priory Cres. SE19 7C 122
Priory Cres. Sutt 4F 149
Priory Cres. Wemb 3A 44
Priory Dri. SE2 5D 92
Priory Dri. Stan 3E 10
Priory Field Dri. Edgw 4C 12
Priory Gdns. N6 6F 31
Priory Gdns. SE25 4F 141
Priory Gdns. SW13 3B 100
Priory Gdns. W4 4A 82
Priory Gdns. W5 3E 62
Priory Gdns. Ashf 5F 113
Priory Gdns. Hamp 7D 114
Priory Gdns. Wemb 4A 44
Priory Grange. N2 3D 30 (off Fortis Grn.)
Priory Grn. Est. N1 2K 67
Priory Gro. SW8 1J 103
Priory Gro. Barn 5D 4
Priory Hill. Wemb 4A 44
Priory Ho. E1 5F 69 (5J 163) (off Folgate St.)
Priory Ho. EC1 4B 68 (3K 161) (off Sans Wlk.)
Priory Ho. SW1 5H 85 (5C 172) (off Rampayne St.)
Priory La. SW15 6A 100
Priory La. Rich 7G 81
Priory La. W Mol 4F 133
Priory Leas. SE9 1C 126
Priory M. SW8 1J 103
Priory Pk. SE3 3H 107
Priory Pk. Rd. NW6 1H 65 (in two parts)
Priory Pk. Rd. Wemb 4A 44
Priory Rd. E6 1B 72
Priory Rd. N8 4G 31
Priory Rd. NW6 1K 65
Priory Rd. SW19 7B 120
Priory Rd. W4 3K 81
Priory Rd. Bark 7H 55
Priory Rd. Chess 3E 146
Priory Rd. Croy 7A 140
Priory Rd. Hamp 7D 114
Priory Rd. Houn 5G 97
Priory Rd. Rich 6G 81
Priory Rd. Sutt 4F 149
Priory St. E3 3D 70
Priory Ter. NW6 1K 65
Priory Ter. Sun 7J 113
Priory, The. SE3 4H 107 (in two parts)
Priory, The. Croy 4A 152
Priory Vw. Bus H 1D 10
Priory Vs. N11 6J 15 (off Colney Hatch La.)
Priory Wlk. SW10 5A 84
Priory Way. Harr 4F 25
Priory Way. S'hall 3B 78
Priory Way. W Dray 6A 76
Pritchard Ho. E2 2H 69 (off Ada Pl.)
Pritchard's Rd. E2 1G 69
Priter Rd. SE16 3G 87
Priter Way. SE16 3G 87
Private Rd. Enf 5J 7
Probert Rd. SW2 5A 104
Probyn Ho. SW1 4H 85 (3D 172) (off Page St.)
Probyn Rd. SW2 2B 122
Procter Ho. SE1 5G 87 (off Avondale Sq.)
Procter Ho. SE5 7D 86 (off Picton St.)
Procter St. WC1 5K 67 (6G 161)
Proctor Clo. Mitc 1E 138
Proctors Clo. Felt 1J 113
Progress Bus. Pk., The. Croy 2K 151
Progress Cen., The. N9 3K 17
Progress Cen., The. Enf 3E 8
Progress Way. N22 1A 32
Progress Way. Croy 2K 151
Progress Way. Enf 5B 8
Project Pk. E3 4F 71
Promenade App. Rd. W4 7A 82
Promenade, The. W4 2A 100
Promenade, The. Edgw 5B 12
Prospect Clo. SE26 4H 123
Prospect Clo. Belv 4G 93
Prospect Clo. Houn 1D 96
Prospect Clo. Ruis 7B 24
Prospect Cotts. SW18 4J 101
Prospect Cres. Twic 6G 97
Prospect Hill. E17 4D 34
Prospect Ho. E17 3E 34 (off Prospect Hill)
Prospect Ho. N1 2A 68 (off Donegal St.)
Prospect Ho. SE1 3B 86 (off Gaywood St.)
Prospect Ho. W10 6F 65 (off Bridge Clo.)
Prospect Pl. E1 1J 87 (in two parts)
Prospect Pl. N2 4B 30
Prospect Pl. N7 4J 49
Prospect Pl. N17 7K 17
Prospect Pl. NW2 3H 47
Prospect Pl. NW3 4A 48
Prospect Pl. SE8 6B 88 (off Evelyn St.)
Prospect Pl. SW20 7D 118
Prospect Pl. W4 5K 81
Prospect Pl. Brom 3K 143
Prospect Pl. Romf 2J 39
Prospect Quay. SW18 4J 101 (off Lightermans Wlk.)
Prospect Ring. N2 3B 30
Prospect Rd. NW2 3H 47
Prospect Rd. Barn 4D 4
Prospect Rd. Surb 6C 134
Prospect Rd. Wfd G 6F 21
Prospect St. SE16 3H 87
Prospect Va. SE18 4C 90
Prospect Wharf. E1 7J 69
Prospero Rd. N19 1H 49
Protea Clo. E16 4H 71
Protheroe Ho. N17 3F 33
Prothero Gdns. NW4 5D 28
Prothero Ho. NW10 7K 45
Prothero Rd. SW6 7G 83
Prout Gro. NW10 4A 46
Prout Rd. E5 3H 51
Provence St. N1 2C 68
Providence Clo. E9 1K 69
Providence Ct. W1 7E 66 (2H 165)
Providence La. Hay 7F 77
Providence Pl. N1 1B 68
Providence Pl. Romf 1F 39
Providence Rd. W Dray 1A 76
Providence Row. N1 1G 161
Providence Row Clo. E2 3H 69
Providence Sq. SE1 2G 87 (6K 169)
Providence Tower. SE16 2G 87 (off Bermondsey Wall W.)
Providence Yd. E2 3G 69 (1K 163) (off Ezra St.)
Provost Ct. NW3 6D 48 (off Eton Rd.)
Provost Est. N1 1E 162
Provost Rd. NW3 7D 48
Provost St. N1 2D 68 (1E 162)
Prowse Av. Bus H 1B 10

Prowse Pl. *NW1* ... 7G **49**
Proyers Path. *Harr.* ... 7B **26**
Pruden Clo. *N14* ... 2B **16**
Prudent Pas. *EC2* ... 7D **162**
*Prusom's Island. E1 ... 1J **87** (off Cinnamon St.)*
Prusom St. *E1* ... 1H **87**
Pryors, The. *NW3* ... 3B **48**
Public Record Office. ... 7H 81
Pudding La. *EC3* ... 7D **68** (3F **169**)
Pudding Mill La. *E15* ... 1D **70**
Puddle Dock. *EC4* ... 7B **68** (2A **168**) (in two parts)
Puffin Clo. *Bark* ... 3B **74**
Puffin Clo. *Beck* ... 5K **141**
*Pugin Ct. N1 ... 7A **50** (off Liverpool Rd.)*
Pulborough Rd. *SW18* ... 7H **101**
Pulborough Way. *Houn* ... 4A **96**
Pulford Rd. *N15* ... 6D **32**
Pulham Av. *N2* ... 4A **30**
*Pulham Ho. SW8 ... 7K **85** (off Dorset Rd.)*
*Pullen's Bldgs. SE17 ... 5B **86** (off Iliffe St.)*
Puller Rd. *Barn* ... 2B **4**
Pulleyns Av. *E6* ... 3C **72**
Pullman Ct. *SW2* ... 1J **121**
Pullman Gdns. *SW15* ... 6E **100**
Pullman M. *SE12* ... 3K **125**
Pullman Pl. *SE9* ... 5C **108**
Pulross Rd. *SW9* ... 3K **103**
Pulteney Clo. *E3* ... 1B **70**
Pulteney Gdns. *E18* ... 3K **35**
Pulteney Rd. *E18* ... 3K **35**
Pulteney Ter. *N1* ... 1K **67** (in two parts)
*Pulton Ho. SE4 ... 4A **106** (off Turnham Rd.)*
Pulton Pl. *SW6* ... 7J **83**
Puma Ct. *E1* ... 5F **69** (5J **163**)
Pump All. *Bren* ... 7D **80**
Pump Clo. *N'holt* ... 2E **60**
Pump Ct. *EC4* ... 6A **68** (1J **167**)
*Pumphandle Path. N2 ... 2B **30** (off Oak La.)*
Pump Ho. Clo. *SE16* ... 2J **87**
Pump Ho. Clo. *Brom* ... 2G **143**
Pumping Sta. Rd. *W4* ... 7A **82**
Pump La. *SE14* ... 7J **87**
Pump La. *Hay* ... 2J **77**
Pump La. Ind. Est. *Hay* ... 2J **77**
Pump Pail N. *Croy* ... 3C **152**
Pump Pail S. *Croy* ... 3C **152**
Punderson's Gdns. *E2* ... 3H **69**
Punjab La. *S'hall* ... 1D **78**
Purbeck Av. *N Mald* ... 6B **136**
Purbeck Dri. *NW2* ... 2F **47**
*Purbeck Ho. SW8 ... 7K **85** (off Bolney St.)*
Purbrook Est. *SE1* ... 2E **86** (7H **169**)
Purbrook St. *SE1* ... 3E **86** (7H **169**)
Purcell Cres. *SW6* ... 7F **83**
*Purcell Ho. SW10 ... 6B **84** (off Milman's St.)*
*Purcell Mans. W14 ... 6G **83** (off Queen's Club Gdns.)*
Purcell M. *NW10* ... 7A **46**
Purcell Rd. *Gnfd* ... 5F **61**
Purcell Room. ... 1K 85 (4H 167) (off Waterloo Rd.)
Purcells Av. *Edgw* ... 5B **12**
Purcell St. *N1* ... 2E **68**
Purchese St. *NW1* ... 2H **67** (1D **160**)
*Purdon Ho. SE15 ... 1G **105** (off Peckham High St.)*
Purdy Ct. *Wor Pk* ... 2C **148**
Purdy St. *E3* ... 4D **70**
*Purelake M. SE13 ... 3F **107** (off Marischal Rd.)*
Purland Clo. *Dag* ... 1F **57**
Purland Rd. *SE28* ... 2K **91**
Purleigh Av. *Wfd G* ... 6H **21**
Purley Av. *NW2* ... 2G **47**
Purley Clo. *Ilf* ... 2E **36**
Purley Pl. *N1* ... 7B **50**
Purley Rd. *N9* ... 3K **17**
Purley Rd. *S Croy* ... 7D **152**
*Purley Vw. Ter. S Croy ... 7D **152** (off Sanderstead Rd.)*
Purley Way. *Croy* ... 7K **139**
Purley Way Cen., The. *Croy* ... 2A **152**
Purley Way Corner. *Croy* ... 7K **139**
Purley Way Cres. *Croy* ... 7K **139**
Purneys Rd. *SE9* ... 4B **108**
Purrett Rd. *SE18* ... 5K **91**
*Purser Ho. SW2 ... 6A **104** (off Tulse Hill)*
Pursers Cross Rd. *SW6* ... 1H **101** (in two parts)
Purse Wardens Clo. *W13* ... 1C **80**
Pursley Rd. *NW7* ... 7J **13**
Purves Rd. *NW10* ... 3D **64**
*Pusey Ho. E14 ... 6C **70** (off Saracen St.)*
*Puteaux Ho. E2 ... 2K **69** (off Mace St.)*
Putney. ... 4G 101
Putney Bri. *SW15 & SW6* ... 3G **101**
Putney Bri. App. *SW6* ... 3G **101**
Putney Bri. Rd. *SW15 & SW18* ... 4G **101**
Putney Comn. *SW15* ... 3E **100**
Putney Exchange Shop. Cen. *SW15* ... 4F **101**
Putney Gdns. *Chad H* ... 5B **38**
Putney Heath. ... 6E 100
Putney Heath. *SW15* ... 7D **100**
Putney Heath La. *SW15* ... 6F **101**
Putney High St. *SW15* ... 4F **101**
Putney Hill. *SW15* ... 7F **101** (in two parts)
Putney Pk. Av. *SW15* ... 4C **100**
Putney Pk. La. *SW15* ... 4D **100**
Putney Vale. ... 3C 118
Putney Vale Crematorium. *SW15* ... 2C **118**
Pycroft Way. *N9* ... 4A **18**
Pyecombe Corner. *N12* ... 4C **14**
Pylbrook Rd. *Sutt* ... 3J **149**
Pylon Trad. Est. *E16* ... 4G **71**
Pylon Way. *Croy* ... 1J **151**
Pym Clo. *E Barn* ... 5G **5**
Pymers Mead. *SE21* ... 1C **122**
Pymmes Brook Ho. *N10* ... 7K **15**
Pymmes Clo. *N13* ... 5E **16**
Pymmes Clo. *N17* ... 1H **33**
Pymmes Gdns. N. *N9* ... 3A **18**
Pymmes Gdns. S. *N9* ... 3A **18**
Pymmes Grn. Rd. *N11* ... 4A **16**
Pymmes Rd. *N13* ... 6D **16**
Pymms Brook Dri. *Barn* ... 4H **5**
Pynchester Clo. *Uxb* ... 2C **40**
Pyne Rd. *Surb* ... 1G **147**
Pynfolds. *SE16* ... 2H **87**
Pynham Clo. *SE2* ... 3B **92**
Pynnacles Clo. *Stan* ... 5G **11**
Pynnersmead. *SE24* ... 5C **104**
Pyramid Ho. *Houn* ... 2C **96**
Pyrford Ho. *SW9* ... 4B **104**
Pyrland Rd. *N5* ... 5D **50**
Pyrland Rd. *Rich* ... 6F **99**
Pyrmont Gro. *SE27* ... 3B **122**
Pyrmont Rd. *W4* ... 6G **81**
Pytchley Cres. *SE19* ... 6C **122**
Pytchley Rd. *SE22* ... 3E **104**

Quadrangle Clo. *SE1* ... 4E **86**
Quadrangle, The. *SE24* ... 5C **104**
Quadrangle, The. *SW6* ... 7G **83**
Quadrangle, The. *SW10* ... 1A **102**
Quadrangle, The. *W2* ... 6C **66** (7C **158**)
*Quadrangle, The. W12 ... 6D **64** (off Du Cane Rd.)*
Quadrangle, The. *Stan* ... 7H **11**
Quadrant Arc. *W1* ... 3B **166**
Quadrant Clo. *NW4* ... 5D **28**
Quadrant Gro. *NW5* ... 5D **48**
Quadrant Ho. *SE1* ... 4A **168**
Quadrant Rd. *Rich* ... 4D **98**
Quadrant Rd. *T Hth* ... 4B **140**
Quadrant, The. *NW4* ... 4E **28**
Quadrant, The. *SW20* ... 1G **137**
Quadrant, The. *W10* ... 3F **65**
Quadrant, The. *Bexh* ... 7D **92**
Quadrant, The. *Edgw* ... 6B **12**
Quadrant, The. *Harr* ... 3H **25**
Quadrant, The. *Rich* ... 4D **98**
Quadrant, The. *Sutt* ... 6A **150**
Quad Rd. *Wemb* ... 3D **44**
Quaggy Wlk. *SE3* ... 4J **107**
*Quain Mans. W14 ... 6G **83** (off Queen's Club Gdns.)*
Quainton St. *NW10* ... 3K **45**
*Quaker Ct. E1 ... 4F **69** (4J **163**) (off Quaker St.)*
Quaker Ct. *EC1* ... 3E **162**
Quaker La. *S'hall* ... 3E **78**
Quakers Course. *NW9* ... 1B **28**
Quakers La. *Iswth* ... 7A **80** (in three parts)
Quakers Pl. *E7* ... 5B **54**
Quaker St. *E1* ... 4F **69** (4J **163**)
Quakers Wlk. *N21* ... 6J **7**
Quality Ct. *WC2* ... 7J **161**
Quantock Clo. *Hay* ... 7F **77**
Quantock Dri. *Wor Pk* ... 2E **148**
Quantock Gdns. *NW2* ... 2F **47**
Quantock Ho. *N16* ... 1F **51**
Quarley Way. *SE15* ... 7F **87**
Quarrendon St. *SW6* ... 2J **101**
Quarr Rd. *Cars* ... 6B **138**
Quarry Pk. Rd. *Sutt* ... 6H **149**
Quarry Ri. *Sutt* ... 6H **149**
Quarry Rd. *SW18* ... 6A **102**
Quarterdeck, The. *E14* ... 2C **88**
Quarter Mile La. *E10* ... 4D **52**
*Quastel Ho. SE1 ... 2D **86** (7E **168**) (off Long La.)*
Quatre Ports. *E4* ... 5A **20**
*Quay Ho. E14 ... 2C **88** (off Admirals Way)*
*Quayside Cotts. E1 ... 1G **87** (off Mew St.)*
*Quayside Ct. SE16 ... 1K **87** (off Abbotshade Rd.)*
Quayside Ho. *E14* ... 1B **88**
*Quay Vw. Apartments. E14 ... 3C **88** (off Arden Cres.)*
Quebec M. *W1* ... 6D **66** (1F **165**)
Quebec Rd. *Hay* ... 6A **60**
Quebec Rd. *Ilf* ... 7F **37**
Quebec Way. *SE16* ... 2K **87**
Quebec Way Ind. Est. *SE16* ... 2A **88**
*Quedgeley Ct. SE15 ... 6F **87** (off Ebley Clo.)*
Queen Adelaide Ct. *SE20* ... 6J **123**
Queen Adelaide Rd. *SE20* ... 6J **123**
*Queen Alexandra Mans. WC1 ... 3J **67** (2E **160**) (off Bidborough St.)*
Queen Alexandra's Ct. *SW19* ... 5H **119**
Queen Anne Av. *Brom* ... 3H **143**
*Queen Anne Ho. E16 ... 1J **89** (off Hardy Av.)*
Queen Anne M. *W1* ... 5F **67** (6K **159**)
Queen Anne Rd. *E9* ... 6K **51**
Queen Anne's Clo. *Twic* ... 3H **115**
*Queen Anne's Ct. SE10 ... 5F **89** (off Park Row)*
Queen Anne's Gdns. *W4* ... 3A **82**
Queen Anne's Gdns. *W5* ... 2E **80**
Queen Anne's Gdns. *Enf* ... 6K **7**
Queen Anne's Gdns. *Mitc* ... 3D **138**
Queen Anne's Ga. *SW1* ... 2H **85** (7C **166**)
Queen Anne's Ga. *Bexh* ... 3D **110**
Queen Anne's Gro. *W4* ... 3A **82**
Queen Anne's Gro. *W5* ... 2E **80**
Queen Anne's Gro. *Enf* ... 7J **7**
Queen Anne's Pl. *Enf* ... 6K **7**
Queen Anne St. *W1* ... 6F **67** (7J **159**)
Queen Anne's Wlk. *WC1* ... 4F **161**
*Queen Anne Ter. E1 ... 7H **69** (off Sovereign Clo.)*
Queenborough Gdns. *Chst* ... 6H **127**
Queenborough Gdns. *Ilf* ... 4E **36**
Queen Caroline St. *W6* ... 5E **82** (in two parts)
*Queen Catherine Ho. SW6 ... 7K **83** (off Wandon Rd.)*
Queen Charlotte's Cottage. ... 2D 98
Queen Elizabeth Bldgs. *EC4* ... 2J **167**
Queen Elizabeth Ct. *High Bar* ... 3C **4**
Queen Elizabeth Gdns. *Mord* ... 4J **137**
Queen Elizabeth Hall. ... 1K 85 (4G 167)
Queen Elizabeth Ho. *SW12* ... 7E **102**
Queen Elizabeth II Conference Cen. ... 2H 85 (7D 166)
Queen Elizabeth Rd. *E17* ... 3A **34**
Queen Elizabeth Rd. *King T* ... 2F **135**
Queen Elizabeth's Clo. *N16* ... 2D **50**
Queen Elizabeth's College. *SE10* ... 7E **88**
Queen Elizabeth's Dri. *N14* ... 1D **16**
Queen Elizabeth's Dri. *New Ad* ... 7F **155**
Queen Elizabeth St. *SE1* ... 2E **86** (6H **169**)
Queen Elizabeth's Wlk. *N16* ... 1D **50**
Queen Elizabeth's Wlk. *Wall* ... 4H **151**
Queen Elizabeth Wlk. *SW13* ... 1C **100** (in two parts)
Queengate Ct. *N12* ... 5E **14**
Queenhithe. *EC4* ... 7C **68** (2D **168**)
*Queen Isabella Way. EC1 ... 6B **68** (7B **162**) (off King Edward St.)*
*Queen Margaret Flats. E2 ... 3H **69** (off St Jude's Rd.)*
Queen Margaret's Gro. *N1* ... 5E **50**
Queen Mary Av. *Mord* ... 5F **137**
Queen Mary Clo. *Surb* ... 3H **147**
*Queen Mary Ho. E16 ... 1K **89** (off Wesley Av.)*
Queen Mary Rd. *SE19* ... 6B **122**
Queen Mary Rd. *Shep* ... 2E **130**
Queen Mary's Av. *Cars* ... 7D **150**
*Queen Marys Bldgs. SW1 ... 4G **85** (3B **172**) (off Stillington St.)*
*Queen Mary's Ct. SE10 ... 6F **89** (off Park Row)*
Queen of Denmark Ct. *SE16* ... 3B **88**
Queens Acre. *Sutt* ... 7F **149**
Queens Av. *N3* ... 7F **15**
Queens Av. *N10* ... 3E **30**
Queens Av. *N20* ... 2G **15**
Queens Av. *N21* ... 1G **17**
Queens Av. *Felt* ... 4A **114**
Queen's Av. *Gnfd* ... 6F **61**
Queens Av. *Stan* ... 3C **26**
Queen's Av. *Wfd G* ... 5E **20**
Queensberry M. W. *SW7* ... 4B **84** (3A **170**)
Queensberry Pl. *E12* ... 5B **54**
Queensberry Pl. *SW7* ... 4B **84** (3A **170**)
Queensberry Way. *SW7* ... 4B **84** (3A **170**)
*Queensborough Ct. NW11 ... 4H **29** (off N. Circular Rd.)*
Queensborough M. *W2* ... 7A **66**
*Queensborough Pas. W2 ... 7A **66** (off Queensborough M.)*
*Queensborough Studios. W2 ... 7A **66** (off Queensborough M.)*
Queensborough Ter. *W2* ... 7K **65**
*Queensbridge Ct. E2 ... 1F **69** (off Queensbridge Rd.)*
Queensbridge Pk. *Iswth* ... 5J **97**
Queensbridge Rd. *E8 & E2* ... 6F **51**
Queensbury. ... 3E 26
Queensbury Circ. Pde. *Harr* ... 3E **26**
Queensbury Ho. *Rich* ... 5C **98**
Queensbury Rd. *NW9* ... 7K **27**
Queensbury Rd. *Wemb* ... 2F **63**
Queensbury Sta. Pde. *Edgw* ... 3F **27**
Queensbury St. *N1* ... 7C **50**
Queen's Cir. *SW8* ... 7F **85**
Queens Clo. *Edgw* ... 5B **12**
Queens Clo. *Wall* ... 5F **151**
Queen's Club Gdns. *W14* ... 6G **83**
Queen's Club (Tennis). ... 5G 83
Queens Ct. *NW6* ... 5K **47**
*Queen's Ct. NW8 ... 2B **66** (off Queen's Ter.)*
Queens Ct. *NW11* ... 5H **29**
Queens Ct. *SE23* ... 2H **123**
*Queens Ct. W2 ... 7K **65** (off Queensway)*
Queens Ct. *Rich* ... 6F **99**
*Queens Ct. S Croy ... 5C **152** (off Warham Rd.)*
Queens Ct. *W'stone* ... 2B **26**
Queenscourt. *Wemb* ... 4E **44**
Queen's Cres. *NW5* ... 6E **48**
Queen's Cres. *Rich* ... 5F **99**
Queenscroft Rd. *SE9* ... 5B **108**
Queensdale Cres. *W11* ... 1F **83**
Queensdale Pl. *W11* ... 1G **83**
Queensdale Rd. *W11* ... 1F **83**
Queensdale Wlk. *W11* ... 1G **83**
Queensdown Rd. *E5* ... 4H **51**
Queens Dri. *E10* ... 7C **34**
Queen's Dri. *N4* ... 2B **50**
Queens Dri. *W5 & W3* ... 6F **63**
Queen's Dri. *Surb* ... 7G **135**
Queen's Dri. *Th Dit* ... 6A **134**
*Queen's Elm Pde. SW3 ... 5B **84** (5B **170**) (off Old Church St.)*
Queen's Elm Sq. *SW3* ... 5B **84** (6A **170**)
Queens Ferry Wlk. *N17* ... 4H **33**
Queensfield Ct. *Sutt* ... 4E **148**
Queens Gallery ... 2F 85 (7K 165)
Queen's Gdns. *NW4* ... 5E **28**
Queen's Gdns. *W2* ... 7A **66**
Queen's Gdns. *W5* ... 4C **62**
Queen's Gdns. *Houn* ... 1C **96**
Queen's Gdns. *Rain* ... 2K **75**
Queen's Ga. *SW7* ... 2A **84** (7A **164**)
Queen's Ga. Gdns. *SW7* ... 3A **84**
Queens Ga. Gdns. *SW15* ... 4D **100**
Queensgate Gdns. *Chst* ... 1H **145**
Queen's Ga. M. *SW7* ... 3A **84**
Queensgate Pl. *NW6* ... 7J **47**
Queen's Ga. Pl. *SW7* ... 3A **84**
Queen's Ga. Pl. M. *SW7* ... 3A **84** (2A **170**)
Queen's Ga. Ter. *SW7* ... 3A **84** (1A **170**)
Queens Ga. Vs. *E9* ... 7A **52**

Queen's Gro. NW8 1B 66
Queens Gro. Rd. E4 1A 20
Queen's Gro. Studios. NW8 1B 66
Queen's Head Pas. EC4 6C 68 (7C 162)
Queen's Head St. N1 1B 68
Queen's Head Yd. SE1 5E 168
Queens Ho. SW8 7J 85 (off S. Lambeth Rd.)
Queens Ho. Tedd 6K 115
Queen's House, The. 6F 89 (off National Maritime Mus.)
Queen's Ice Club 7K 65
Queen's Keep. Twic 6C 98
Queensland Av. N18 6H 17
Queensland Av. SW19 1K 137
Queensland Ho. E16 1E 90 (off Rymill St.)
Queensland Pl. N7 4A 50
Queensland Rd. N7 4A 50
Queens La. N10 3F 31
Queens La. Ashf 4B 112
Queen's Mans. W6 4F 83 (off Brook Grn.)
Queen's Mkt. E13 1A 72
Queensmead. NW8 1B 66
Queen's Mead Rd. Brom 2H 143
Queensmere Clo. SW19 2F 119
Queensmere Ct. SW13 7B 82
Queensmere Rd. SW19 2F 119
Queen's M. W2 7K 65 (in two parts)
Queensmill Rd. SW6 7F 83
Queens Pde. N8 4B 32
Queen's Pde. N11 5J 15 (off Friern Barnet Rd.)
Queen's Pde. NW2 6E 46 (off Walm La.)
Queens Pde. NW4 5E 28 (off Queens Rd.)
Queens Pde. W5 6F 63
Queens Pde. Clo. N11 5J 15
Queens Pk. Ct. W10 3F 65
Queen's Pk. Gdns. Felt 3H 113
Queen's Park Rangers F.C. (Loftus Rd.) 1D 82
Queens Pas. Chst 6F 127
Queens Pl. Mord 4J 137
Queen's Promenade. King T 4D 134
Queen Sq. WC1 4J 67 (4F 161)
Queen Sq. Pl. WC1 4F 161
Queen's Quay. EC4 7C 68 (2C 168) (off Up. Thames St.)
Queens Reach. E Mol 4J 133
Queens Reach. King T 2D 134
Queens Ride. SW13 & SW15 3C 100
Queens Ri. Rich 6F 99
Queens Rd. E11 7F 35
Queens Rd. E13 1K 71
Queen's Rd. E17 6B 34
Queens Rd. N3 1A 30
Queens Rd. N9 3C 18
Queens Rd. N11 7D 16
Queens Rd. NW4 5E 28
Queen's Rd. SE15 & SE14 1H 105
Queen's Rd. SW14 3K 99
Queens Rd. SW19 6H 119
Queen's Rd. W5 6E 62
Queens Rd. Bark 6G 55
Queens Rd. Barn 3A 4
Queens Rd. Beck 2A 142
Queens Rd. Brom 2J 143
Queen's Rd. Buck H 2E 20
Queens Rd. Chst 6F 127
Queens Rd. Croy 6B 140
Queen's Rd. Enf 4K 7
Queen's Rd. Felt 1K 113
Queen's Rd. Hamp H 4F 115
Queens Rd. Hay 6G 59
Queen's Rd. Houn 3F 97
Queens Rd. King T 7G 117
Queens Rd. Mord 4J 137
Queens Rd. N Mald 4B 136
Queen's Rd. Rich 7F 99
Queens Rd. S'hall 2B 78
Queen's Rd. Tedd 6K 115
Queen's Rd. Th Dit 5K 133
Queens Rd. Twic 1A 116
Queens Rd. Wall 5F 151
Queen's Rd. Well 2A 110
Queens Rd. W Dray 2B 76
Queens Rd. W. E13 2J 71
Queen's Row. SE17 6D 86
Queens Ter. E1 4J 69
Queen's Ter. E13 1K 71
Queen's Ter. NW8 1B 66
Queens Ter. Iswth 4A 98
Queen's Ter. Cotts. W7 2J 79
Queen's Theatre. 7H 67 (2C 166) (off Shaftesbury Av.)
Queensthorpe Rd. SE26 4K 123
Queenstown M. SW11 2F 103
Queenstown Rd. SW8 6F 85 (7J 171)
Queen St. EC4 7C 68 (2D 168) (in two parts)
Queen St. N17 6K 17
Queen St. W1 1F 85 (4J 165)
Queen St. Bexh 3F 111
Queen St. Croy 4C 152
Queen St. Romf 6K 39
Queen St. Pl. EC4 7C 68 (2D 168)
Queensville Rd. SW12 7H 103
Queens Wlk. E4 1A 20
Queens Wlk. NW9 2J 45
Queen's Wlk. SW1 1G 85 (5A 166)
Queen's Wlk. W5 4C 62
Queen's Wlk. Ashf 4A 112
Queens Wlk. Harr 4J 25
Queens Wlk. Ruis 2A 42
Queens Wlk. Ter. Ruis 3A 42
Queen's Wlk., The. SE1 7A 68 (4F 169) (Barge Ho. St.)
Queen's Wlk., The. SE1 1E 86 (4F 169) (Morgan's La.)
Queen's Wlk., The. SE1 1K 85 (4F 169) (Waterloo Rd.)
Queen's Way. NW4 5E 28
Queensway. W2 6K 65
Queensway. Croy 6K 151
Queensway. Enf 4C 8
Queens Way. Felt 4A 114
Queensway. Orp 5G 145
Queensway. Sun 2K 131
Queensway. W Wick 3G 155
Queensway Bus. Cen. Enf 4C 8
Queensway Ind. Est. Enf 4D 8
Queenswell Av. N20 3H 15
Queens Wharf. W6 5E 82
Queenswood Av. E17 1E 34
Queenswood Av. Hamp 6F 115
Queenswood Av. Houn 2D 96
Queenswood Av. T Hth 5A 140
Queenswood Av. Wall 4H 151
Queenswood Ct. SE27 4D 122
Queenswood Ct. SW4 5J 103
Queenswood Gdns. E11 1K 53
Queenswood Pk. N3 2G 29
Queens Wood Rd. N10 6F 31
Queenswood Rd. SE23 3K 123
Queenswood Rd. Sidc 5K 109
Queen's Yd. W1 5G 67 (4B 160)
Queen Victoria. (Junct.) 3E 148
Queen Victoria Av. Wemb 7D 44
Queen Victoria Memorial. 2G 85 (7A 166)
Queen Victoria Seaman's Rest. E14 6D 70 (off E. India Dock Rd.)
Queen Victoria St. EC4 7B 68 (2A 168)
Queen Victoria Ter. E1 7H 69 (off Sovereign Clo.)
Quemerford Rd. N7 5K 49
Quendon Ho. W10 4E 64 (off Sutton Way)
Quenington Ct. SE15 6F 87
Quentin Ho. SE1 2A 86 (7K 167) (off Gray St., in two parts)
Quentin Pl. SE13 3G 107
Quentin Rd. SE3 3G 107
Quernmore Clo. Brom 6J 125
Quernmore Rd. N4 6A 32
Quernmore Rd. Brom 6J 125
Querrin St. SW6 2A 102
Quested Ct. E8 5H 51 (off Brett Rd.)
Quex M. NW6 1J 65
Quex Rd. NW6 1J 65
Quick Rd. W4 5A 82
Quicks Rd. SW19 7K 119
Quick St. N1 2B 68
Quick St. M. N1 2B 68
Quickswood. NW3 7C 48
Quiet Nook. Brom 3B 156
Quill La. SW15 4F 101
Quill St. N4 3A 50
Quill St. W5 2E 62
Quilp St. SE1 2C 86 (6C 168) (in two parts)
Quilter Ho. W10 3H 65 (off Dart St.)
Quilter St. E2 3G 69 (1K 163)
Quilter St. SE18 5K 91
Quilting Ct. SE16 2K 87 (off Garter Way)
Quinta Dri. Barn 5A 4
Quintin Av. SW20 1H 137
Quintin Clo. Pinn 4K 23
Quinton Clo. Beck 3E 142
Quinton Clo. Houn 7K 77
Quinton Clo. Wall 4F 151
Quinton Ho. SW8 7J 85 (off Wyvil Rd.)
Quinton Rd. Th Dit 1A 146
Quinton St. SW18 2A 120
Quixley St. E14 7F 71
Quorn Rd. SE22 4E 104

Rabbit Row. W8 1J 83
Rabbits Rd. E12 4C 54
Rabournmead Dri. N'holt 5C 42
Raby Rd. N Mald 4K 135
Raby St. E14 6A 70
Raccoon Way. Houn 2A 96
Rachel Clo. Ilf 3H 37
Rachel Point. E5 4G 51
Racine. SE5 1E 104 (off Peckham Rd.)
Rackham M. SW16 6G 121
Rackman Clo. Well 2B 110
Rackstraw Ho. NW3 7D 48
Racton Rd. SW6 6J 83
Radbourne Av. W5 4C 80
Radbourne Clo. E5 4K 51
Radbourne Ct. Harr 6B 26
Radbourne Cres. E17 2F 35
Radbourne Rd. SW12 7G 103
Radcliffe Av. NW10 2C 64
Radcliffe Av. Enf 1H 7
Radcliffe Gdns. Cars 7C 150
Radcliffe Ho. SE16 4H 87 (off Anchor St.)
Radcliffe M. Hamp H 5G 115
Radcliffe Path. SW8 2F 103
Radcliffe Rd. N21 1G 17
Radcliffe Rd. SE1 3E 86
Radcliffe Rd. Croy 2F 153
Radcliffe Rd. Harr 2A 26
Radcliffe Sq. SW15 6F 101
Radcliffe Way. N'holt 3B 60
Radcot Point. SE23 3K 123
Radcot St. SE11 5A 86 (6K 173)
Raddington Rd. W10 5G 65
Radfield Way. Sidc 7H 109 (in two parts)
Radford Ho. E14 5D 70 (off St Leonard's Rd.)
Radford Ho. N7 5K 49
Radford Rd. SE13 6E 106
Radford Way. Bark 3K 73
Radipole Rd. SW6 1H 101
Radius Pk. Felt 4H 95
Radland Rd. E16 6H 71
Radlet Av. SE26 3H 123
Radlett Clo. E7 6H 53
Radlett Pl. NW8 1C 66
Radley Av. Ilf 4A 56
Radley Clo. Felt 1H 113
Radley Ct. SE16 2K 87
Radley Gdns. Harr 4E 26
Radley Ho. NW1 4D 66 (3E 158) (off Gloucester Pl.)
Radley Ho. SE2 2D 92 (off Wolvercote Rd.)
Radley M. W8 3J 83
Radley Rd. N17 2E 32
Radley's La. E18 2J 35
Radleys Mead. Dag 6H 57
Radley Sq. E5 2J 51
Radley Ter. E16 5H 71 (off Hermit Rd.)
Radlix Rd. E10 1C 52
Radnor Av. Harr 5J 25
Radnor Av. Well 5B 110
Radnor Clo. Chst 6J 127
Radnor Clo. Mitc 4J 139
Radnor Ct. W7 6K 61 (off Copley Clo.)
Radnor Ct. Har W 1K 25
Radnor Cres. SE18 7A 92
Radnor Cres. Ilf 5D 36
Radnor Gdns. Enf 1K 7
Radnor Gdns. Twic 2K 115
Radnor Gro. Uxb 2C 58
Radnor M. W2 6B 66 (1B 164)
Radnor Pl. W2 6C 66 (1C 164)
Radnor Rd. NW6 1G 65
Radnor Rd. SE15 7G 87
Radnor Rd. Harr 5H 25
Radnor Rd. Twic 1K 115
Radnor St. EC1 3C 68 (2D 162)
Radnor Ter. W14 4H 83
Radnor Ter. Sutt 7J 149
Radnor Wlk. E14 4C 88 (off Barnsdale Av.)
Radnor Wlk. SW3 5C 84 (6D 170)
Radnor Wlk. Croy 6A 142
Radnor Way. NW10 4H 63
Radstock Av. Harr 3A 26
Radstock Clo. N11 6K 15
Radstock St. SW11 7C 84 (in two parts)
Raeburn Av. Surb 1H 147
Raeburn Clo. NW11 6A 30
Raeburn Clo. King T 7D 116
Raeburn Ho. N'holt 2B 60 (off Academy Gdns.)
Raeburn Rd. Edgw 1G 27
Raeburn Rd. Hay 2F 59
Raeburn Rd. Sidc 6J 109
Raeburn St. SW2 4J 103
Raffles Ct. NW4 4D 28
Raffles Sq. E15 7F 53
Rafford Way. Brom 2K 143
R.A.F. Mus. Hendon. 2C 28
R.A.F. Northolt. 6H 41
Raggleswood. Chst 1E 144
Raglan Clo. Houn 5D 96
Raglan Ct. SE12 5J 107
Raglan Ct. S Croy 5B 152
Raglan Ct. Wemb 4F 45
Raglan Rd. E17 5E 34
Raglan Rd. SE18 5F 91
Raglan Rd. Belv 4F 93
Raglan Rd. Brom 4A 144
Raglan Rd. Enf 7A 8
Raglan St. NW5 6F 49
Raglan Ter. Harr 4F 43
Raglan Way. N'holt 6G 43
Ragley Clo. W3 2J 81
Raider Clo. Romf 1G 39
Railey M. NW5 5G 49
Railshead Rd. Iswth 4B 98
Railton Rd. SE24 4A 104
Railway App. N4 6A 32
Railway App. SE1 1D 86 (5F 169)
Railway App. Harr 4K 25
Railway App. Twic 7A 98
Railway App. Wall 5F 151
Railway Arches. E7 4J 53 (off Winchelsea Rd.)
Railway Arches. E10 7D 34 (off Capworth St.)
Railway Arches. E11 2G 53 (off Leytonstone High Rd.)
Railway Arches. E11 1F 53 (off Sidings, The)
Railway Arches. E17 5C 34 (off Yunus Khan Clo.)
Railway Arches. W12 2E 82 (off Shepherd's Bush Mkt.)
Railway Av. SE16 2J 87 (in two parts)
Railway Children Wlk. Brom 2J 125
Railway Cotts. SW19 4K 119
Railway Cotts. W6 2E 82 (off Sulgrave Rd.)
Railway Cotts. Twic 6E 96
Railway Gro. SE14 7B 88
Railway M. E3 3C 70 (off Wellington Way)
Railway M. W11 6G 65
Railway Pas. Tedd 6A 116
Railway Pl. SW19 6H 119
Railway Pl. Belv 3G 93
Railway Ri. SE22 4E 104
Railway Rd. Tedd 4J 115
Railway Side. SW13 3A 100 (in two parts)
Railway St. N1 2J 67
Railway St. Romf 7C 38
Railway Ter. E17 1E 34
Railway Ter. SE13 5D 106
Railway Ter. Felt 1J 113
Rainborough Clo. NW10 6J 45
Rainbow Av. E14 5D 88
Rainbow Ct. SE14 6A 88 (off Chipley St.)
Rainbow Ind. Est. W Dray 7A 58
Rainbow Quay. SE16 3A 88 (in two parts)
Rainbow St. SE5 7E 86
Raine St. E1 1H 87
Rainham Clo. SE9 6J 109
Rainham Clo. SW11 6C 102
Rainham Ho. NW1 1G 67 (off Bayham Pl.)
Rainham Rd. NW10 3E 64
Rainham Rd. N. Dag 2G 57
Rainham Rd. S. Dag 4H 57
Rainhill Way. E3 3C 70 (in two parts)
Rainsborough Av. SE8 4A 88
Rainsford Clo. Stan 4H 11
Rainsford Rd. NW10 2H 63 (in two parts)
Rainsford St. W2 6C 66 (7C 158)
Rainton Rd. SE7 5J 89
Rainville Rd. W6 6E 82
Raisins Hill. Pinn 3A 24
Raith Av. N14 3C 16
Raleana Rd. E14 1E 88
Raleigh Av. Hay 5K 59
Raleigh Av. Wall 4H 151
Raleigh Clo. NW4 5E 28
Raleigh Clo. Pinn 7B 24
Raleigh Clo. Ruis 2H 41

Raleigh Ct. SE16 1K 87
(off Clarence M.)
Raleigh Ct. W12 2E 82
(off Scott's Rd.)
Raleigh Ct. W13 5B 62
Raleigh Ct. Beck 1D 142
Raleigh Ct. Wall 6F 151
Raleigh Dri. N20 3H 15
Raleigh Dri. Surb 1J 147
Raleigh Gdns. SW2 6K 103
Raleigh Gdns. Mitc 3D 138
(in two parts)
Raleigh Ho. E14 2D 88
(off Admirals Way)
Raleigh Ho. SW1
6H 85 (7C 172)
(off Dolphin Sq.)
Raleigh M. N1 1B 68
(off Packington St.)
Raleigh Rd. N2 2C 30
Raleigh Rd. N8 4A 32
Raleigh Rd. SE20 7K 123
Raleigh Rd. Enf 4J 7
Raleigh Rd. Felt 3H 113
Raleigh Rd. Rich 3F 99
Raleigh Rd. S'hall 5C 78
Raleigh St. N1 1B 68
Raleigh Way. N14 1C 16
Raleigh Way. Felt 5A 114
Ralph Brook Ct. N1
3D 68 (1F 163)
(off Chart St.)
Ralph Ct. W2 6K 65
(off Queensway)
Ralph Perring Ct. Beck 4C 142
Ralston St. SW3 5D 84 (6E 170)
Ramac Ind. Est. SE7 4K 89
Rama Clo. SW16 7J 121
Rama Ct. Harr 2J 43
Ramac Way. SE7 4K 89
Rama La. SE19 7F 123
Ramar Ho. E1 5G 69
(off Hanbury St.)
Rambler Clo. SW16 4G 121
Rame Clo. SW17 5E 120
Ramilles Clo. SW2 6J 103
Ramillies Pl. W1 6G 67 (1A 166)
Ramillies Rd. NW7 2F 13
Ramillies Rd. W4 4K 81
Ramillies Rd. Sidc 6B 110
Ramillies St. W1 6G 67 (1A 166)
Ramones Ter. Mitc 4J 139
Rampart St. E1 6H 69
Ram Pas. King T 2D 134
Rampayne St. SW1
5H 85 (5C 172)
Ram Pl. E9 6J 51
Rampton Clo. E4 3H 19
Ramsay Ho. NW8 2C 66
(off Townshend Est.)
Ramsay M. SW3 6C 84 (7C 170)
Ramsay Pl. Harr 1J 43
Ramsay Rd. E7 4G 53
Ramsay Rd. W3 3J 81
Ramscroft Clo. N9 7K 7
Ramsdale Rd. SW17 5E 120
Ramsden Dri. Romf 1G 39
Ramsden Rd. N11 5J 15
Ramsden Rd. SW12 6E 102
Ramsden Rd. Eri 7K 93
Ramsey Clo. NW9 6B 28
Ramsey Clo. Gnfd 5H 43
Ramsey Ct. Croy 2B 152
(off Church St.)
Ramsey Ho. SW9 7A 86
Ramsey Rd. T Hth 6K 139
Ramsey St. E2 4G 69
Ramsey Wlk. N1 6D 50
(off Handa Wlk.)
Ramsey Way. N14 7B 6
Ramsfort Ho. SE16 4H 87
(off Camilla Rd.)
Ramsgate Clo. E16 1K 89
Ramsgate St. E8 6F 51
Ramsgill App. Ilf 4K 37
Ramsgill Dri. Ilf 5K 37
Rams Gro. Romf 4E 38
Ram St. SW18 5K 101
Ramulis Dri. Hay 4B 60
Rancliffe Gdns. SE9 4C 108
Rancliffe Rd. E6 2C 72
Randall Av. NW2 2A 46
Randall Clo. SW11 1C 102
Randall Clo. Eri 6J 93
Randall Ct. NW7 7H 13
Randall Pl. SE10 7E 88
Randall Rd. SE11
5K 85 (4G 173)
Randall Row. SE11
4K 85 (4G 173)
Randalls Rents. SE16 3B 88
(off Gulliver St.)
Randell's Rd. N1 1J 67
(in two parts)
Randisbourne Gdns. SE6 3D 124
Randle Rd. Rich 4C 116
Randlesdown Rd. SE6 4C 124
(in two parts)
Randolph App. E16 6A 72
Randolph Av. W9
2K 65 (4A 158)
Randolph Clo. Bexh 3J 111
Randolph Clo. King T 5J 117
Randolph Cres. W9 4A 66
Randolph Gdns. NW6 2K 65
Randolph Gro. Romf 5C 38
Randolph M. W9 4A 66
Randolph Rd. E17 5D 34
Randolph Rd. W9 4A 66
Randolph Rd. Brom 1D 156
Randolph Rd. S'hall 2D 78
Randolph St. NW1 7G 49
Randon Clo. Harr 2F 25
Ranelagh Av. SW6 3H 101
Ranelagh Av. SW13 2C 100
Ranelagh Bri. W2 5K 65
Ranelagh Clo. Edgw 4B 12
Ranelagh Dri. Edgw 4B 12
Ranelagh Dri. Twic 4B 98
Ranelagh Gdns. E11 5A 36
Ranelagh Gdns. SW6 3G 101
(in two parts)
Ranelagh Gdns. W4 7J 81
Ranelagh Gdns. W6 4B 82
Ranelagh Gdns. Ilf 1D 54
Ranelagh Gdns. Mans.
SW6 3G 101
(off Ranelagh Gdns.)
Ranelagh Gro. SW1
5E 84 (5H 171)
Ranelagh Ho. SW3
5D 84 (5E 170)
(off Elystan Pl.)
Ranelagh M. W5 2D 80
Ranelagh Pl. N Mald 5A 136
Ranelagh Rd. E6 1E 72
Ranelagh Rd. E11 4G 53
Ranelagh Rd. E15 2G 71
Ranelagh Rd. N17 3E 32
Ranelagh Rd. N22 1K 31
Ranelagh Rd. NW10 2B 64
Ranelagh Rd. SW1
5G 85 (6B 172)
Ranelagh Rd. W5 2D 80
Ranelagh Rd. S'hall 1B 78
Ranelagh Rd. Wemb 6D 44
Ranfurly Rd. Sutt 2J 149
Rangbourne Ho. N7 5J 49
Rangefield Rd. Brom 5G 125
Rangemoor Rd. N15 5F 33
Ranger's House 1F 107
Ranger's Rd. E4 1B 20
Rangers Sq. SE10 1F 107
Range Way. Shep 7C 130
Rangeworth Pl. Sidc 3K 127
Rangoon St. EC3 1J 169
Rankin Clo. NW9 3A 28
Rankine Ho. SE1 3C 86
(off Bath Ter.)
Ranleigh Gdns. Bexh 7F 93
Ranmere St. SW12 1F 121
Ranmoor Clo. Harr 4H 25
Ranmoor Gdns. Harr 4H 25
Ranmore Av. Croy 3F 153
Ranmore Path. Orp 4K 145
Ranmore Rd. Sutt 7F 149
Rannoch Clo. Edgw 2C 12
Rannoch Rd. W6 6E 82
Rannock Av. NW9 7K 27
Ransome's Dock Bus. Cen.
SW11 7C 84
Ransom Rd. SE7 4A 90
Ranston St. NW1
5C 66 (5C 158)
Ranulf Rd. NW2 4H 47
Ranwell Clo. E3 1B 70
Ranworth Rd. N9 2D 18
Ranyard Clo. Chess 3F 147
Raphael Ct. SE16 5H 87
(off Stubbs Dri.)
Raphael Dri. Th Dit 7K 133
Raphael St. SW7 2D 84 (7E 164)
Rapley Ho. E2 3G 69 (2K 163)
(off Turin St.)
Rashleigh Ct. SW8 2F 103
Rashleigh Ho. WC1
3J 67 (2E 160)
(off Thanet St.)
Rasper Rd. N20 2F 15
Rastell Av. SW2 2H 121
Ratcliff. 6A 70
Ratcliffe Clo. SE12 7J 107
Ratcliffe Cross St. E1 6K 69
Ratcliffe Ho. E14 6A 70
Ratcliffe La. E14 6A 70
Ratcliffe Orchard. E1 7K 69
Ratcliff Rd. E7 5A 54
Rathbone Ho. E16 6H 71
(off Rathbone St.)
Rathbone Ho. NW6 1J 65
Rathbone Mkt. E16 5H 71
Rathbone Pl. W1 5H 67 (6C 160)
Rathbone Point. E5 4G 51
Rathbone Sq. Croy 4C 152
Rathbone St. E16 5H 71
Rathbone St. W1
5G 67 (6B 160)
Rathcoole Av. N8 5K 31
Rathcoole Gdns. N8 5K 31
Rathfern Rd. SE6 1B 124
Rathgar Av. W13 1B 80
Rathgar Clo. N3 2H 29
Rathgar Rd. SW9 3B 104
Rathmell Dri. SW4 6H 103
Rathmore Rd. SE7 5K 89
Rattray Ct. SE6 2H 125
Rattray Rd. SW2 4A 104
Raul Rd. SE15 2G 105
Raveley St. NW5 4G 49
(in two parts)
Raven Clo. NW9 2A 28
Ravendale Rd. Sun 2H 131
Ravenet St. SW11 1F 103
Ravenfield Rd. SW17 3D 120
Ravenhill Rd. E13 2A 72
Raven Ho. SE16 4K 87
(off Tawny Way)
Ravenings Pde. Ilf 1A 56
Ravenna Rd. SW15 5F 101
Ravenor Ct. Gnfd 4F 61
Ravenor Pk. Rd. Gnfd 3F 61
Raven Rd. E18 2A 36
Raven Row. E1 5H 69
(in two parts)
Ravensbourne Av. Brom 7F 125
Ravensbourne Av. Stai 1A 112
Ravensbourne Ct. SE6 7C 106
Ravensbourne Gdns. W13 5B 62
Ravensbourne Gdns. Ilf 1E 36
Ravensbourne Ho. NW8
5C 66 (5C 158)
(off Broadley St.)
Ravensbourne Ho. Brom 5F 125
Ravensbourne Mans. SE8 6C 88
(off Berthon St.)
Ravensbourne Pk. SE6 7C 106
Ravensbourne Pk. Cres.
SE6 7B 106
Ravensbourne Pl. SE13 2D 106
Ravensbourne Rd. SE6 7B 106
Ravensbourne Rd. Brom 3J 143
Ravensbourne Rd. Twic 6C 98
Ravensbury Av. Mord 5A 138
Ravensbury Ct. Mitc 4B 138
(off Ravensbury Gro.)
Ravensbury Gro. Mitc 4B 138
Ravensbury La. Mitc 4B 138
Ravensbury Path. Mitc 4B 138
Ravensbury Rd. SW18 2J 119
Ravensbury Rd. Orp 3K 145
Ravensbury Ter. SW18 2K 119
Ravenscar. NW1 1G 67
(off Bayham St.)
Ravenscar Rd. Brom 4G 125
Ravenscar Rd. Surb 2F 147
Ravens Clo. Brom 2H 143
Ravens Clo. Enf 2K 7
Ravens Clo. Surb 6D 134
Ravens Ct. King T 5D 134
(off Uxbridge Rd.)
Ravenscourt. Sun 1H 131
Ravenscourt Av. W6 4C 82
Ravenscourt Clo. Ruis 7E 22
Ravenscourt Gdns. W6 4C 82
Ravenscourt Pk. W6 3C 82
Ravenscourt Pk. Barn 4A 4
Ravenscourt Pk. Mans.
W6 3D 82
(off Paddenswick Rd.)
Ravenscourt Pl. W6 4D 82
Ravenscourt Rd. W6 4D 82
(in two parts)
Ravenscourt Sq. W6 3C 82
Ravenscraig Rd. N11 4B 16
Ravenscroft Av. NW11 7H 29
Ravenscroft Av. Wemb 1E 44
Ravenscroft Clo. E16 5J 71
Ravenscroft Cotts. Barn 4D 4
Ravenscroft Cres. SE9 3D 126
Ravenscroft Pk. Barn 3A 4
Ravenscroft Rd. E16 5J 71
Ravenscroft Rd. W4 4J 81
Ravenscroft Rd. Beck 2J 141
Ravenscroft St. E2
2F 69 (1K 163)
Ravensdale Av. N12 4F 15
Ravensdale Gdns. SE19 7D 122
Ravensdale Rd. N16 7F 33
Ravensdale Rd. Houn 3C 96
Ravensdon St. SE11
5A 86 (6K 173)
Ravensfield Clo. Dag 4D 56
Ravensfield Gdns. Eps 5A 148
Ravenshaw St. NW6 5H 47
Ravenshill. Chst 1F 145
Ravenshurst Av. NW4 4E 28
Ravenside. King T 5D 134
(off Portsmouth Rd.)
Ravenside Clo. N18 5E 18
Ravenside Retail Pk. N18 5E 18
Ravenslea Rd. SW12 7D 102
Ravensleigh Gdns. Brom 5K 125
Ravensmead Rd. Brom 7F 125
Ravensmede Way. W4 4B 82
Ravens M. SE12 5J 107
Ravenstone. SE17 5E 86
Ravenstone Rd. N8 3A 32
Ravenstone Rd. NW9 6B 28
Ravenstone St. SW12 1E 120
Ravens Way. SE12 5J 107
Ravenswood. Bex 1E 128
Ravenswood Av. Surb 2F 147
Ravenswood Av. W Wick 1E 154
Ravenswood Ct. King T 6H 117
Ravenswood Cres. Harr 2D 42
Ravenswood Cres.
W Wick 1E 154
Ravenswood Gdns. Iswth 1J 97
Ravenswood Ind. Est. E17 4E 34
Ravenswood Rd. E17 4E 34
Ravenswood Rd. SW12 7F 103
Ravenswood Rd. Croy 3B 152
Ravensworth Ct. SW6 7H 83
(off Fulham Rd.)
Ravensworth Rd. NW10 3D 64
Ravensworth Rd. SE9 3D 126
Ravent Rd. SE11 4K 85 (3H 173)
Ravey St. EC2 4E 68 (3G 163)
Ravine Gro. SE18 6J 91
Rav Pinter Clo. N16 7E 32
Rawalpindi Ho. E16 4H 71
Rawchester Clo. SW18 1H 119
Rawlings Cres. Wemb 3H 45
Rawlings St. SW3
4D 84 (3E 170)
Rawlins Clo. N3 3G 29
Rawlins Clo. S Croy 7A 154
Rawlinson Ct. NW2 7E 28
Rawlinson Ho. SE13 4F 107
(off Mercator Rd.)
Rawlinson Point. E16 5H 71
(off Fox Rd.)
Rawlinson Ter. N17 3F 33
Rawnsley Av. Mitc 5B 138
Rawreth Wlk. N1 1C 68
(off Basire St.)
Rawson St. SW11 1E 102
(in two parts)
Rawsthorne Clo. E16 1D 90
Rawsthorne Ct. Houn 4D 96
Rawstone Wlk. E13 2J 71
Rawstorne Pl. EC1
3B 68 (1A 162)
Rawstorne St. EC1
3B 68 (1A 162)
Raybell Ct. Iswth 2K 97
Rayburne Ct. W14 3G 83
Rayburne Ct. Buck H 1F 21
Ray Clo. Chess 6C 146
Raydean Rd. New Bar 5E 4
Raydons Gdns. Dag 4E 56
Raydons Rd. Dag 5E 56
Raydon St. N19 2F 49
Rayfield Clo. Brom 6C 144
Rayford Av. SE12 7H 107
Ray Gdns. Bark 2A 74
Ray Gdns. Stan 5G 11
Ray Gunter Ho. SE17 5B 86
(off Marsland Clo.)
Ray Ho. N1 1D 68
(off Colville Est.)
Rayleas Clo. SE18 1F 109
Rayleigh Av. Tedd 6J 115
Rayleigh Clo. N13 3J 17
Rayleigh Ct. N22 1C 32
Rayleigh Ct. King T 2G 135
Rayleigh Ho. Brom 1J 143
(off Hammelton Rd.)
Rayleigh Ri. S Croy 6E 152
Rayleigh Rd. E16 1K 89
Rayleigh Rd. N13 3H 17
Rayleigh Rd. SW19 1H 137
Rayleigh Rd. Wfd G 6F 21
Ray Lodge Rd. Wfd G 6F 21
Ray Massey Way. E6 1C 72
(off High St. N.)
Raymead Av. T Hth 5A 140
Raymede Towers. W10 5F 65
(off Treverton St.)
Raymere Gdns. SE18 7H 91
Raymond Av. E18 3H 35
Raymond Av. W13 3A 80
Raymond Bldgs. WC1
5K 67 (5H 161)
Raymond Clo. SE26 5J 123
Raymond Ct. N10 7A 16
Raymond Ct. Sutt 6K 149
Raymond Postage Ct.
SE28 7B 74
Raymond Revuebar.
7H 67 (2C 166)
(off Walkers Ct.)
Raymond Rd. E13 1A 72
Raymond Rd. SW19 6G 119
Raymond Rd. Beck 4A 142

Raymond Rd. *Ilf* 7H 37
Raymond Way. *Clay* 6A 146
Raymouth Rd. *SE16* 4H 87
Raynald Ho. *SW16* 3J 121
Rayne Ct. *E18* 4H 35
Rayne Ho. W9 4K 65
(off Delaware Rd.)
Rayner Ct. W12 2E 82
(off Bamborough Gdns.)
Rayners Clo. *Wemb* 5D 44
Rayners Cres. *N'holt* 3K 59
Rayners Gdns. *N'holt* 2K 59
Rayners Lane 1D 42
Rayners La. *Pinn & Harr* 5D 24
Rayners Rd. *SW15* 5G 101
Rayner Towers. E10 7C 34
(off Albany Rd.)
Raynes Av. *E11* 7A 36
Raynes Park 4E 136
Raynes Pk. Bri. *SW20* 2E 136
Raynham. W2 6C 66 (7D 158)
(off Norfolk Cres.)
Raynham Av. *N18* 6B 18
Raynham Ho. E1 4K 69
(off Harpley Sq.)
Raynham Rd. *N18* 5B 18
Raynham Rd. *W6* 4D 82
Raynham Ter. *N18* 5B 18
Raynor Clo. *S'hall* 1D 78
Raynor Pl. *N1* 7C 50
Raynton Clo. *Harr* 1C 42
Raynton Clo. *Hay* 4H 59
Raynton Dri. *Hay* 4H 59
Ray Rd. *W Mol* 5F 133
Rays Av. *N18* 4D 18
Rays Rd. *N18* 4D 18
Rays Rd. *W Wick* 7E 142
Ray St. *EC1* 4A 68 (4K 161)
Ray St. Bri. *EC1* 4K 161
Ray Wlk. *N7* 2K 49
Raywood Clo. *Hay* 7E 76
Reachview Clo. *NW1* 7G 49
Read Clo. *Th Dit* 7A 134
Read Ct. *E17* 6C 34
Reade Ct. W3 3J 81
(off Stanley Rd.)
Reade Ho. SE10 6F 89
(off Trafalgar Gro.)
Reade Wlk. *NW10* 7A 46
Read Ho. *SE11* 7J 173
Reading Ho. SE15 6G 87
(off Friary Est.)
Reading Ho. W2 6A 66
(off Hallfield Est.)
Reading La. *E8* 6H 51
Reading Rd. *N'holt* 5F 43
Reading Rd. *Sutt* 5A 150
Reading Way. *NW7* 5A 14
Reads Clo. *Ilf* 3F 55
Reapers Clo. *NW1* 1H 67
Reapers Way. *Iswth* 5H 97
Reardon Ct. *N21* 2G 17
Reardon Ho. E1 1H 87
(off Reardon St.)
Reardon Path. *E1* 1H 87
(in two parts)
Reardon St. *E1* 1H 87
Reaston St. *SE14* 7K 87
Rebecca Ct. *Sidc* 4B 128
Reckitt Rd. *W4* 5A 82
Record St. *SE15* 6J 87
Recovery St. *SW17* 5C 120
Recreation Av. *Romf* 5J 39
Recreation Rd. *SE26* 4K 123
Recreation Rd. *Brom* 2H 143
Recreation Rd. *Sidc* 3J 127
Recreation Rd. *S'hall* 4C 78
Recreation Way. *Mitc* 3H 139
Rector St. *N1* 1C 68
Rectory Bus. Cen. *Sidc* 4B 128
Rectory Clo. *E4* 3H 19
Rectory Clo. *N3* 1H 29
Rectory Clo. *SW20* 3E 136
Rectory Clo. *Shep* 3C 130
Rectory Clo. *Sidc* 4B 128
Rectory Clo. *Stan* 5G 11
Rectory Clo. *Surb* 1C 146
Rectory Ct. *E18* 1H 35
Rectory Ct. *Felt* 4A 114
Rectory Ct. *Wall* 4G 151
Rectory Cres. *E11* 6A 36
(in two parts)
Rectory Farm Rd. *Enf* 1E 6
Rectory Fld. Cres. *SE7* 7A 90
Rectory Gdns. *N8* 4J 31
Rectory Gdns. *SW4* 3G 103
Rectory Gdns. Beck 1C 142
(off Rectory Rd.)
Rectory Gdns. *N'holt* 1D 60
Rectory Grn. *Beck* 1B 142
Rectory Gro. *SW4* 3G 103
Rectory Gro. *Croy* 2B 152
Rectory Gro. *Hamp* 4D 114
Rectory La. *SW17* 6E 120
Rectory La. *Edgw* 6B 12
Rectory La. *Sidc* 4B 128
Rectory La. *Stan* 5G 11
Rectory La. *Surb* 1B 146
Rectory La. *Wall* 4G 151
Rectory Orchard. *SW19* 4G 119
Rectory Pk. Av. *N'holt* 3D 60
Rectory Pl. *SE18* 4E 90
Rectory Rd. *E12* 5D 54
Rectory Rd. *E17* 4D 34
Rectory Rd. *N16* 2F 51
Rectory Rd. *SW13* 2C 100
Rectory Rd. *W3* 1H 81
Rectory Rd. *Beck* 2C 142
Rectory Rd. *Dag* 6H 57
Rectory Rd. *Hay* 6J 59
Rectory Rd. *Houn* 2A 96
Rectory Rd. *Kes* 7B 156
Rectory Rd. *S'hall* 3D 78
Rectory Rd. *Sutt* 3J 149
Rectory Sq. *E1* 5K 69
Rectory Way. *Uxb* 2D 40
Reculver Ho. SE15 6J 87
(off Lovelinch Clo.)
Reculver M. *N18* 4B 18
Reculver Rd. *SE16* 5K 87
Red Anchor Clo. *SW3*
6B 84 (7B 170)
Redan Pl. *W2* 6K 65
Redan St. *W14* 3F 83
Redan Ter. *SE5* 2B 104
Red Barracks Rd. *SE18* 4D 90
Redberry Gro. *SE26* 3J 123
Redbourne Av. *N3* 1J 29
Redbourne Dri. *SE28* 6D 74
Redbourne Ho. E14 6B 70
(off Norbiton Rd.)
Redbourn Ho. W10 4E 64
(off Sutton Way)
Redbridge 6B 36
Redbridge Enterprise Cen.
Ilf 2G 55
Redbridge Foyer. Ilf 2G 55
(off Sylvan Rd.)
Redbridge Gdns. *SE5* 7E 86
Redbridge La. E. *Ilf* 6B 36
Redbridge La. W. *E11* 6K 35
Redbridge Roundabout. (Junct.)
6A 36
Redburn St. *SW3*
6D 84 (7E 170)
Redburn Trad. Est. *Enf* 6E 8
Redcar Clo. *N'holt* 5F 43
Redcar St. *SE5* 7C 86
Redcastle Clo. *E1* 7J 69
Red Cedars Rd. *Orp* 7J 145
Redchurch St. *E2* 4F 69 (3J 163)
Redcliffe Clo. SW5 5K 83
(off Old Brompton Rd.)
Redcliffe Ct. E5 3H 51
(off Napoleon Rd.)
Redcliffe Gdns.
SW5 & SW10 5K 83
Redcliffe Gdns. *W4* 7H 81
Redcliffe Gdns. *Ilf* 1E 54
Redcliffe M. *SW10* 5K 83
Redcliffe Pl. *SW10* 6A 84
Redcliffe Rd. *SW10* 5A 84
Redcliffe Sq. *SW10* 5K 83
Redcliffe St. *SW10* 6K 83
Redclose Av. *Mord* 5J 137
Redclyffe Rd. *E6* 1A 72
Redclyf Ho. E1 4J 69
(off Cephas St.)
Redcourt. *Croy* 3E 152
Redcroft Rd. *S'hall* 7G 61
Redcross Way. *SE1*
2C 86 (6D 168)
Redding Ho. *SE18* 3C 90
Reddings Clo. *NW7* 4G 13
Reddings, The. *NW7* 3G 13
Reddins Rd. *SE15* 6G 87
Reddons Rd. *Beck* 7A 124
Redenham Ho. SW15 7C 100
(off Ellisfield Dri.)
Rede Pl. *W2* 6J 65
Redesdale Gdns. *Iswth* 7A 80
Redesdale St. *SW3*
6C 84 (7D 170)
Redfern Av. *Houn* 7E 96
Redfern Ho. E15 1H 71
(off Redriffe Rd.)
Redfern Rd. *NW10* 7A 46
Redfern Rd. *SE6* 7E 106
Redfield La. *SW5* 4J 83
Redfield M. *SW5* 4K 83
Redford Av. *T Hth* 4K 139
Redford Av. *Wall* 6J 151
Redford Clo. *Felt* 2H 113
Redford Ho. W10 3H 65
(off Dowland St.)
Redford Wlk. N1 1C 68
(off Popham St.)
Redgate Dri. *Brom* 2K 155
Redgate Ter. *SW15* 6F 101
Redgrave Clo. *Croy* 6F 141
Redgrave Rd. *SW15* 3F 101
Redgrave Ter. E2 3G 69
(off Derbyshire St.)
Red Hill. *Chst* 5F 127
Redhill Ct. *SW2* 2A 122
Redhill Dri. *Edgw* 2H 27
Redhill St. *NW1* 2F 67 (1K 159)
Red Ho. La. *Bexh* 4D 110
Redhouse Rd. *Croy* 6H 139
Red Ho. Sq. *N1* 6C 50
Redington Gdns. *NW3* 4K 47
Redington Ho. N1 2K 67
(off Priory Grn. Est.)
Redington Rd. *NW3* 3K 47
Redland Gdns. *W Mol* 4D 132
Redlands. *N15* 4D 32
Redlands. *Tedd* 6A 116
Redlands Ct. *Brom* 7H 125
Redlands Rd. *Enf* 1F 9
Redlands, The. *Beck* 2D 142
Redlands Way. *SW2* 7K 103
Red La. *Clay* 6A 146
Redleaf Clo. *Belv* 6G 93
Redleaves Av. *Ashf* 6D 112
Redlees Clo. *Iswth* 4A 98
Red Leys. *Uxb* 7A 40
Red Lion Bus. Pk. *Surb* 3F 147
Red Lion Clo. SE17 6D 86
(off Red Lion Row)
Red Lion Ct. *EC4* 6A 68 (1K 167)
Red Lion Ct. *SE1*
1C 86 (4D 168)
Red Lion Hill. *N2* 2B 30
Red Lion La. *SE18* 7E 90
Red Lion Pde. *Pinn* 3C 24
Red Lion Pl. *SE18* 1E 108
Red Lion Rd. *Surb* 2F 147
Red Lion Row. *SE17* 6C 86
Red Lion Sq. *SW18* 5J 101
Red Lion Sq. *WC1*
5K 67 (6G 161)
Red Lion St. *WC1*
5K 67 (5G 161)
Red Lion St. *Rich* 5D 98
Red Lion Yd. *W1* 4H 165
Red Lodge. *W Wick* 1E 154
Red Lodge Cres. *Bex* 3K 129
Red Lodge Rd. *Bex* 3K 129
Red Lodge Rd. *W Wick* 1E 154
Redman Clo. *N'holt* 2A 60
Redman Ho. EC1 5A 68 (5J 161)
(off Bourne Est.)
Redman Ho. SE1
2C 86 (7D 168)
(off Borough High St.)
Redman's Rd. *E1* 5J 69
Redmead La. *E1* 1G 87
Redmead Rd. *Hay* 4G 77
Redmill Ho. E1 4H 69
(off Headlam St.)
Redmond Ho. N1 1K 67
(off Barnsbury Est.)
Redmore Rd. *W6* 4D 82
Redo Ho. E12 5E 54
(off Dore Av.)
Red Path. *E9* 6A 52
Red Pl. *W1* 7E 66 (2G 165)
Redpoll Way. *Eri* 3D 92
Red Post Hill.
SE24 & SE21 4D 104
Red Post Ho. *E6* 7B 54
Redriffe Rd. *E13* 1H 71
Redriff Est. *SE16* 3B 88
Redriff Rd. *SE16* 4K 87
Redriff Rd. *Romf* 2H 39
Redroofs Clo. *Beck* 1D 142
Redrose Trad. Cen. *Barn* 5G 5
Red Rover. (Junct.) 4B 100
Redrup Ho. SE14 6K 87
(off John Williams Clo.)
Redruth Clo. *N22* 7E 16
Redruth Ho. *Sutt* 7K 149
Redruth Rd. *E9* 1J 69
Redstart Clo. *E6* 5C 72
Redstart Clo. *SE14* 7A 88
Redston Rd. *N8* 4H 31
Redvers Rd. *N22* 2A 32
Redvers St. *N1* 3E 68 (1H 163)
Redwald Rd. *E5* 4K 51
Redway Dri. *Twic* 7G 97
Redwing Path. *SE28* 2H 91
Redwing Rd. *Wall* 6J 151
Redwood Clo. *N14* 7C 6
Redwood Clo. *SE16* 1A 88
Redwood Clo. *Buck H* 2E 20
Redwood Clo. *Sidc* 7A 110
Redwood Clo. *Uxb* 2D 58
Redwood Ct. *N19* 7H 31
Redwood Ct. *NW6* 7G 47
Redwood Ct. *N'holt* 3C 60
Redwood Ct. *Surb* 7D 134
Redwood Est. *Houn* 6K 77
Redwood Gdns. *E4* 6J 9
Redwood Mans. W8 3K 83
(off Chantry Sq.)
Redwood M. *SW4* 3F 103
Redwoods. *SW15* 1C 118
Redwood Wlk. *Surb* 1D 146
Redwood Way. *Barn* 5A 4
Reece M. *SW7* 4B 84 (3A 170)
Reed Clo. *E16* 5J 71
Reed Clo. *SE12* 5J 107
Reede Gdns. *Dag* 5H 57
Reede Rd. *Dag* 6G 57
Reede Way. *Dag* 6H 57
Reedham Clo. *N17* 4H 33
Reedham St. *SE15* 2G 105
Reedholm Vs. *N16* 4D 50
Reed Rd. *N17* 2F 33
Reedsfield Clo. *Ashf* 4D 112
Reedsfield Rd. *Ashf* 4D 112
Reed's Pl. *NW1* 7G 49
Reedworth St. *SE11*
4A 86 (4K 173)
Reef Ho. E14 3E 88
(off Manchester St.)
Reenglass Rd. *Stan* 4J 11
Rees Dri. *Stan* 4K 11
Rees Gdns. *Croy* 6F 141
Reesland Clo. *E12* 6E 54
Rees St. *N1* 1C 68
Reets Farm Clo. *NW9* 6A 28
Reeves Av. *NW9* 7K 27
Reeves Corner. *Croy* 2B 152
Reeves Ho. SE1 2A 86 (7J 167)
(off Baylis Rd.)
Reeves M. *W1* 7E 66 (3G 165)
Reeves Path. *Hay* 4H 77
Reeves Rd. *E3* 4D 70
Reeves Rd. *SE18* 6F 91
Reflection, The. E16 2F 91
(off Woolwich Mnr. Way)
Reform Row. *N17* 2F 33
Reform St. *SW11* 2D 102
Regal Clo. *E1* 5G 69
Regal Clo. *W5* 5D 62
Regal Ct. *N18* 5A 18
Regal Cres. *Wall* 3F 151
Regal Dri. *N11* 5A 16
Regal La. *NW1* 1E 66
Regal Pl. *E3* 3B 70
Regal Pl. *SW6* 7K 83
Regal Row. *SE15* 1J 105
Regal Way. *Harr* 6E 26
Regan Ho. *N18* 6A 18
Regan Way. *N1* 2E 68 (1G 163)
Regatta Ho. *Tedd* 4A 116
Regatta Point. *Bren* 6F 81
Regency Clo. *W5* 6E 62
Regency Clo. *Hamp* 5D 114
Regency Ct. *Enf* 5J 7
Regency Ct. *Sutt* 4K 149
Regency Ct. *Tedd* 6B 116
Regency Cres. *NW4* 2F 29
Regency Dri. *Ruis* 1G 41
Regency Gdns. *W on T* 7A 132
Regency Ho. E16 1J 89
(off Pepys Cres.)
Regency Ho. NW1
4F 67 (3K 159)
(off Osnaburgh St.)
Regency Lawn. *NW5* 3F 49
Regency Lodge. NW3 7B 48
(off Adelaide Rd.)
Regency Lodge. *Buck H* 2G 21
Regency M. *NW10* 6C 46
Regency M. *SW9* 7B 86
Regency M. *Beck* 7E 124
Regency M. *Iswth* 5J 97
Regency Pl. *SW1*
4H 85 (3D 172)
Regency St. *SW1*
4H 85 (3D 172)
Regency Ter. SW7
5B 84 (5A 170)
(off Fulham Rd.)
Regency Wlk. *Croy* 6B 142
Regency Wlk. Rich 5E 98
(off Grosvenor Av.)
Regency Way. *Bexh* 3D 110
Regent Av. *Uxb* 7D 40
Regent Bus. Cen. *Hay* 2K 77
Regent Clo. *N12* 5F 15
Regent Clo. *Harr* 6E 26
Regent Clo. *Houn* 1K 95
Regent Ct. *N3* 7E 14
Regent Ct. *N20* 2F 15
Regent Ct. *NW8* 2C 158
Regent Gdns. *Ilf* 7A 38
Regent Ho. W14 4G 83
(off Windsor Way)
Regent Pl. *SW19* 5A 120
Regent Pl. *W1* 7G 67 (2B 166)
Regent Pl. *Croy* 1F 153
Regent Rd. *SE24* 6B 104
Regent Rd. *Surb* 5F 135
Regents Av. *N13* 5F 17
Regent's Bri. Gdns. *SW8* 7J 85
Regents Canal Ho. E14 6A 70
(off Commercial Rd.)
Regents Clo. *Hay* 5H 59
Regents Clo. *S Croy* 6E 152
Regents Clo. *Stan* 4K 11
Regent's College.
4D 66 (3G 159)

Regents Ct. E8 . . . 1F 69 (off Pownall Rd.)
Regents Ct. Brom . . . 7H 125
Regents Ct. King T. . . . 1E 134 (off Sopwith Way)
Regents Ct. Pinn . . . 2B 24
Regents Dri. Kes . . . 5B 156
Regents Ga. Ho. E14 . . . 7A 70 (off Horseferry Rd.)
Regents M. NW8 . . . 2A 66
Regent's Park. . . . 2F 67 (1K 159)
Regent's Pk. . . . 3D 66 (1F 159)
Regents Pk. Est. NW1 . . . 1A 160
Regent's Pk. Gdns. M. NW1 . . . 1D 66
Regent's Pk. Ho. NW8 . . . 3C 66 (2D 158) (off Park Rd.)
Regent's Pk. Open Air Theatre. . . . 3E 66 (2G 159)
Regents Pk. Rd. N3 . . . 3H 29
Regent's Pk. Rd. NW1 . . . 7D 48 (in two parts)
Regent's Pk. Ter. NW1 . . . 1F 67
Regent's Pl. SE3 . . . 2J 107
Regents Plaza. NW6 . . . 2K 65 (off Kilburn High Rd.)
Regent Sq. E3 . . . 3D 70
Regent Sq. WC1 . . . 3J 67 (2F 161)
Regent Sq. Belv . . . 4H 93
Regent's Row. E8 . . . 1G 69
Regent St. NW10 . . . 3F 65
Regent St. SW1 . . . 7H 67
Regent St. W1 . . . 6F 67 (7K 159)
Regent St. W4 . . . 5G 81
Regents Wharf. E8 . . . 1H 69 (off Wharf Pl.)
Regents Wharf. N1 . . . 2K 67
Regina Clo. Barn . . . 3A 4
Regina Ho. SE20 . . . 1K 141
Reginald Pl. SE8 . . . 7C 88 (off Deptford High St.)
Reginald Rd. E7 . . . 7J 53
Reginald Rd. SE8 . . . 7C 88
Reginald Rd. N'wd . . . 1H 23
Reginald Sq. SE8 . . . 7C 88
Regina Point. SE16 . . . 2J 87
Regina Rd. N4 . . . 1K 49
Regina Rd. SE25 . . . 3G 141
Regina Rd. W13 . . . 1A 80
Regina Rd. S'hall . . . 4C 78
Regina Ter. W13 . . . 1B 80
Regis Ct. N8 . . . 4K 31
Regis Ct. NW1 . . . 5D 66 (5E 158) (off Melcombe Pl.)
Regis Ho. W1 . . . 5E 66 (5H 159) (off Beaumont St.)
Regis Pl. SW2 . . . 4K 103
Regis Rd. NW5 . . . 5F 49
Regnart Bldgs. NW1 . . . 3B 160
Reid Clo. Pinn . . . 4J 23
Reidhaven Rd. SE18 . . . 4J 91
Reigate Av. Sutt . . . 1J 149
Reigate Rd. Brom . . . 3H 125
Reigate Rd. Ilf . . . 2K 55
Reigate Way. Wall . . . 5J 151
Reighton Rd. E5 . . . 3G 51
Reinickendorf Av. SE9 . . . 6G 109
Relay Rd. W12 . . . 1E 82
Relf Rd. SE15 . . . 3G 105
Reliance Arc. SW9 . . . 4A 104
Reliance Sq. EC2 . . . 3H 163
Relko Gdns. Sutt . . . 5B 150
Relton M. SW7 . . . 3C 84 (1D 170)
Rembold Ho. SE10 . . . 1E 106 (off Blissett St.)
Rembrandt Clo. E14 . . . 3F 89
Rembrandt Clo. SW1 . . . 4G 171
Rembrandt Ct. SE16 . . . 5H 87 (off Stubbs Dri.)
Rembrandt Ct. Eps . . . 6B 148
Rembrandt Rd. SE13 . . . 4G 107
Rembrandt Rd. Edgw . . . 2G 27
Remembrance Rd. E7 . . . 4B 54
Remington Rd. E6 . . . 6C 72
Remington Rd. N15 . . . 6D 32
Remington St. N1 . . . 2B 68 (1B 162)
Remnant St. WC2 . . . 6K 67 (7G 161)
Remsted Ho. NW6 . . . 1K 65 (off Mortimer Cres.)
Remus Building, The. EC1 . . . 3A 68 (2K 161) (off Hardwick St.)
Remus Rd. E3 . . . 7C 52
Rendle Clo. Croy . . . 5F 141
Rendlesham Rd. E5 . . . 4G 51
Rendlesham Rd. Enf . . . 1G 7
Renforth St. SE16 . . . 3J 87
Renfree Way. Shep . . . 7C 130
Renfrew Clo. E6 . . . 7E 72
Renfrew Ct. Houn . . . 2C 96
Renfrew Ho. E17 . . . 2B 34
Renfrew Rd. SE11 . . . 4B 86 (3K 173)
Renfrew Rd. Houn . . . 2B 96
Renfrew Rd. King T . . . 7H 117
Renmuir St. SW17 . . . 6D 120
Rennell St. SE13 . . . 3E 106
Rennels Way. Iswth . . . 2J 97
Renness Rd. E17 . . . 3A 34
Rennets Clo. SE9 . . . 5J 109
Rennets Wood Rd. SE9 . . . 5H 109
Rennie Cotts. E1 . . . 4J 69 (off Pemell Clo.)
Rennie Ct. SE1 . . . 4A 168
Rennie Est. SE16 . . . 4H 87
Rennie Ho. SE1 . . . 3C 86 (off Bath Ter.)
Rennie St. SE1 . . . 1B 86 (4A 168) (in two parts)
Renoir Ct. SE16 . . . 5H 87 (off Stubbs Dri.)
Renovation, The. E16 . . . 2F 91 (off Woolwich Mnr. Way)
Renown Clo. Croy . . . 1B 152
Renown Clo. Romf . . . 1G 39
Rensburg Rd. E17 . . . 5K 33
Renshaw Clo. Belv . . . 6F 93
Renters Av. NW4 . . . 6E 28
Renton Clo. SW2 . . . 6K 103
Renwick Ind. Est. Bark . . . 2B 74
Renwick Rd. Bark . . . 4B 74
Repens Way. Hay . . . 4B 60
Rephidim St. SE1 . . . 3E 86
Replingham Rd. SW18 . . . 1H 119
Reporton Rd. SW6 . . . 7G 83
Repository Rd. SE18 . . . 6D 90
Repton Av. Hay . . . 4F 77
Repton Av. Wemb . . . 4C 44
Repton Clo. Cars . . . 5C 150
Repton Ct. Beck . . . 1D 142
Repton Ct. Ilf . . . 1D 36
Repton Gro. Ilf . . . 1D 36
Repton Ho. E14 . . . 6A 70 (off Repton St.)
Repton Ho. SW1 . . . 4G 85 (4B 172) (off Charlwood St.)
Repton Rd. Harr . . . 4F 27
Repton St. E14 . . . 6A 70
Repulse Clo. Romf . . . 1G 39
Reservoir Clo. T Hth . . . 4D 140
Reservoir Rd. N14 . . . 5B 6
Reservoir Rd. SE4 . . . 2A 106
Reservoir Rd. Ruis . . . 4F 23
Reservoir Studios. E1 . . . 6K 69 (off Cable St.)
Resolution Wlk. SE18 . . . 3D 90
Restell Clo. SE3 . . . 6G 89
Restmor Way. Wall . . . 2E 150
Reston Pl. SW7 . . . 2A 84
Restons Cres. SE9 . . . 6H 109
Restoration Sq. SW11 . . . 1B 102
Restormel Clo. Houn . . . 5E 96
Restormel Ho. SE11 . . . 4J 173
Retcar Clo. N19 . . . 2F 49
Retcar Pl. N19 . . . 2F 49 (off Retcar Clo.)
Retford St. N1 . . . 2E 68 (1H 163)
Retingham Way. E4 . . . 2J 19
Retles Ct. Harr . . . 7J 25
Retreat Clo. Harr . . . 5C 26
Retreat Ho. E9 . . . 6J 51
Retreat Pl. E9 . . . 6J 51
Retreat Rd. Rich . . . 5D 98
Retreat, The. NW9 . . . 5K 27
Retreat, The. SW14 . . . 3A 100
Retreat, The. Harr . . . 7E 24
Retreat, The. Surb . . . 6F 135
Retreat, The. T Hth . . . 4D 140
Retreat, The. Wor Pk . . . 2D 148
Reubens Ct. W4 . . . 5H 81 (off Chaseley Dri.)
Reunion Row. E1 . . . 7H 69
Reveley Sq. SE16 . . . 2A 88
Revell Ri. SE18 . . . 6K 91
Revell Rd. King T. . . . 2H 135
Revell Rd. Sutt . . . 6H 149
Revelon Rd. SE4 . . . 4A 106
Revelstoke Rd. SW18 . . . 2H 119
Reventlow Rd. SE9 . . . 1G 127
Reverdy Rd. SE1 . . . 4G 87
Reverend Clo. Harr . . . 3F 43
Revesby Rd. Cars . . . 6B 138
Review Rd. NW2 . . . 2B 46
Review Rd. Dag . . . 1H 75
Rewell St. SW6 . . . 7A 84
Rewley Rd. Cars . . . 6B 138
Rex Av. Ashf . . . 6C 112
Rex Clo. Romf . . . 1H 39
Rex Pl. W1 . . . 7E 66 (3H 165)
Reydon Av. E11 . . . 5A 36
Reynard Clo. SE4 . . . 3A 106
Reynard Clo. Brom . . . 3E 144
Reynard Dri. SE19 . . . 7F 123
Reynard Mills Trad. Est. Bren . . . 5C 80
Reynard Pl. SE14 . . . 6A 88
Reynardson Rd. N17 . . . 7H 17
Reynolds Av. E12 . . . 5E 54
Reynolds Av. Chad H . . . 7C 38
Reynolds Av. Chess . . . 7E 146
Reynolds Clo. NW11 . . . 7K 29
Reynolds Clo. SW19 . . . 1B 138
Reynolds Clo. Cars . . . 1D 150
Reynolds Ct. Romf . . . 3D 38
Reynolds Dri. Edgw . . . 3F 27
Reynolds Ho. E2 . . . 2J 69 (off Approach Rd.)
Reynolds Ho. NW8 . . . 2B 66 (off Wellington Rd.)
Reynolds Ho. SW1 . . . 4H 85 (4D 172) (off Erasmus St.)
Reynolds Pl. SE3 . . . 7K 89
Reynolds Pl. Rich . . . 6F 99
Reynolds Rd. SE15 . . . 4J 105
Reynolds Rd. W4 . . . 3J 81
Reynolds Rd. Hay . . . 4A 60
Reynolds Rd. N Mald . . . 7K 135
Reynolds Way. Croy . . . 4E 152
Rheidol M. N1 . . . 2C 68
Rheidol Ter. N1 . . . 1C 68
Rheingold Way. Wall . . . 7J 151
Rhein Ho. N8 . . . 3J 31 (off Campsfield Rd.)
Rheola Clo. N17 . . . 1F 33
Rhoda St. E2 . . . 4F 69 (3K 163)
Rhodes Av. N22 . . . 1G 31
Rhodes Ho. N1 . . . 3D 68 (1E 162) (off Provost Est.)
Rhodes Ho. W12 . . . 1D 82
Rhodesia Rd. E11 . . . 2F 53
Rhodesia Rd. SW9 . . . 2J 103
Rhodesmoor Ho. Ct. Mord . . . 6J 137
Rhodes St. N7 . . . 5K 49
Rhodeswell Rd. E14 . . . 5A 70
Rhodrons Av. Chess . . . 5E 146
Rhondda Gro. E3 . . . 3A 70
Rhyl Rd. Gnfd . . . 2K 61
Rhyl St. NW5 . . . 6E 48
Rhys Av. N11 . . . 7C 16
Rialto Rd. Mitc . . . 2E 138
Ribble Clo. Wfd G . . . 6F 21
Ribblesdale Av. N11 . . . 6K 15
Ribblesdale Av. N'holt . . . 6F 43
Ribblesdale Ho. NW6 . . . 1J 65 (off Kilburn Va.)
Ribblesdale Rd. N8 . . . 4K 31
Ribblesdale Rd. SW16 . . . 6F 121
Ribbon Ct. N11 . . . 6K 15 (off Ribblesdale Av.)
Ribbon Dance M. SE5 . . . 1D 104
Ribchester Av. Gnfd . . . 3K 61
Ribston Clo. Brom . . . 1D 156
Ricardo Path. SE28 . . . 1C 92
Ricardo St. E14 . . . 6D 70
Ricards Rd. SW19 . . . 5H 119
Riccall Ct. NW9 . . . 1A 28 (off Pageant Av.)
Rice Pde. Orp . . . 5H 145
Riceyman Ho. WC1 . . . 3A 68 (2J 161) (off Lloyd Baker St.)
Richard Anderson Ct. SE14 . . . 7K 87 (off Monson Rd.)
Richard Burbidge Mans. SW13 . . . 6E 82 (off Brasenose Dri.)
Richard Clo. SE18 . . . 4C 90
Richard Fell Ho. E12 . . . 4E 54 (off Walton Rd.)
Richard Ho. SE16 . . . 4J 87 (off Silwood St.)
Richard Ho. Dri. E16 . . . 6B 72
Richard Neale Ho. E1 . . . 7H 69 (off Cornwall St.)
Richards Av. Romf . . . 6J 39
Richards Clo. Bush . . . 1C 10
Richards Clo. Harr . . . 5A 26
Richards Clo. Hay . . . 6F 77
Richards Clo. Uxb . . . 1C 58
Richards Fld. Eps . . . 7K 147
Richard Sharples Ct. Sutt . . . 7A 150
Richardson Clo. E8 . . . 1F 69
Richardson Ct. SW4 . . . 2J 103 (off Studley Rd.)
Richardson Rd. E15 . . . 2G 71
Richardson's M. W1 . . . 4A 160
Richards Pl. E17 . . . 3C 34
Richard's Pl. SW3 . . . 4C 84 (3D 170)
Richard St. E1 . . . 6H 69
Richbell Pl. WC1 . . . 5K 67 (5G 161)
Richborne Ter. SW8 . . . 7K 85
Richborough Ho. SE15 . . . 6J 87 (off Sharratt St.)
Richborough Rd. NW2 . . . 4G 47
Richens Clo. Houn . . . 2H 97
Riches Rd. Ilf . . . 2G 55
Richfield Rd. Bush . . . 1B 10
Richford Ga. W6 . . . 3E 82
Richford Rd. E15 . . . 1H 71
Richford St. W6 . . . 2E 82
Rich Ind. Est. SE15 . . . 6H 87
Richlands Av. Eps . . . 4C 148
Rich La. SW5 . . . 5K 83
Richman Ho. SE8 . . . 5B 88 (off Grove St.)
Richmond. . . . 5D 98
Richmond Av. E4 . . . 5A 20
Richmond Av. N1 . . . 1K 67
Richmond Av. NW10 . . . 6E 46
Richmond Av. SW20 . . . 1G 137
Richmond Av. Felt . . . 6G 95
Richmond Av. Uxb . . . 6D 40
Richmond Bri. Twic & Rich . . . 6D 98
Richmond Bldgs. W1 . . . 6H 67 (1C 166)
Richmond Circus. (Junct.) . . . 4E 98
Richmond Clo. E17 . . . 6B 34
Richmond Cotts. W14 . . . 4G 83 (off Hammersmith Rd.)
Richmond Ct. E8 . . . 7H 51 (off Mare St.)
Richmond Ct. NW6 . . . 7F 47 (off Willesden La.)
Richmond Ct. SW1 . . . 2D 84 (7F 165) (off Sloane St.)
Richmond Ct. Mitc . . . 3B 138
Richmond Ct. Wemb . . . 3F 45
Richmond Cres. E4 . . . 5A 20
Richmond Cres. N1 . . . 1K 67
Richmond Cres. N9 . . . 1B 18
Richmond Dri. Shep . . . 6F 131
Richmond Gdns. NW4 . . . 5C 28
Richmond Gdns. Harr . . . 7E 10
Richmond Grn. Croy . . . 3J 151
Richmond Gro. N1 . . . 7B 50 (in two parts)
Richmond Gro. Surb . . . 6F 135
Richmond Hill. Rich . . . 6E 98
Richmond Hill Ct. Rich . . . 6E 98
Richmond Ho. NW1 . . . 2F 67 (1K 159) (off Park Village E.)
Richmond Ho. SE17 . . . 5D 86 (off Portland St.)
Richmond Mans. Twic . . . 6D 98
Richmond M. W1 . . . 6H 67 (1C 166)
Richmond M. Tedd . . . 5K 115
Richmond Pde. Twic . . . 6C 98 (off Richmond Rd.)
Richmond Pk. . . . 7G 99
Richmond Pk. Rd. SW14 . . . 5J 99
Richmond Pk. Rd. King T . . . 1E 134
Richmond Pl. SE18 . . . 4G 91
Richmond Rd. E4 . . . 1A 20
Richmond Rd. E7 . . . 5K 53
Richmond Rd. E8 . . . 7F 51
Richmond Rd. E11 . . . 2F 53
Richmond Rd. N2 . . . 2A 30
Richmond Rd. N11 . . . 6D 16
Richmond Rd. N15 . . . 6E 32
Richmond Rd. SW20 . . . 1D 136
Richmond Rd. W5 . . . 2E 80
Richmond Rd. Croy . . . 3J 151
Richmond Rd. Ilf . . . 3G 55
Richmond Rd. Iswth . . . 3A 98
Richmond Rd. King T . . . 4D 116
Richmond Rd. New Bar . . . 5E 4
Richmond Rd. T Hth . . . 3B 140
Richmond Rd. Twic . . . 7B 98
Richmond R.U.F.C. . . . 4D 98
Richmond St. E13 . . . 2J 71
Richmond Ter. SW1 . . . 2J 85 (6E 166)
Richmond Way. E11 . . . 2J 53
Richmond Way. W12 & W14 . . . 2F 83
Richmount Gdns. SE3 . . . 3J 107
Rich St. E14 . . . 7B 70
Rickard Clo. NW4 . . . 4D 28
Rickard Clo. SW2 . . . 1A 122
Rickard Clo. W Dray . . . 3A 76
Rickards Clo. Surb . . . 2E 146
Rickett St. SW6 . . . 6J 83
Rickman Ho. E1 . . . 3J 69 (off Rickman St.)
Rickman St. E1 . . . 4J 69
Rickmansworth Rd. N'wd . . . 1F 23
Rickmansworth Rd. Pinn . . . 2K 23
Rick Roberts Way. E15 . . . 1E 70
Rickthorne Rd. N19 . . . 2J 49
Rickyard Path. SE9 . . . 4C 108
Riddell Ct. SE5 . . . 5F 87 (off Albany Rd.)
Ridding La. Gnfd . . . 5K 43 (in two parts)
Riddons Rd. SE12 . . . 3A 126
Rideout St. SE18 . . . 4D 90
Rider Clo. Sidc . . . 6J 109
Ride, The. Bren . . . 5B 80
Ride, The. Enf . . . 3D 8
Ridgdale St. E3 . . . 2D 70
Ridge Av. N21 . . . 7H 7
Ridgebrook Rd. SE3 . . . 3B 108
Ridge Clo. NW4 . . . 2F 29

Ridge Clo. NW9 4K 27
Ridge Clo. SE28 2H 91
Ridge Ct. SE22 7G 105
Ridge Crest. Enf 1E 6
Ridgecroft Clo. Bex 1J 129
Ridge Hill. NW11 1G 47
Ridgemead Clo. N14 2D 16
Ridgemont Gdns. Edgw 4D 12
Ridgemount. Enf 2G 7
Ridgemount Av. Croy 1K 153
Ridgemount Clo. SE20 7H 123
Ridgemount Gdns. Enf 3G 7
Ridge Rd. N8 6K 31
Ridge Rd. N21 1H 17
Ridge Rd. NW2 3H 47
Ridge Rd. Mitc 7F 121
Ridge Rd. Sutt 1G 149
Ridges Yd. Croy 3B 152
Ridge, The. Barn 5C 4
Ridge, The. Bex 7F 111
Ridge, The. Surb 5G 135
Ridge, The. Twic 7H 97
Ridgeview Clo. Barn 6A 4
Ridgeview Rd. N20 3E 14
Ridge Way. SE19 6E 122
Ridgeway. Brom 2J 155
Ridge Way. Felt 3C 114
Ridgeway. Rich 6E 98
Ridge Way. Wfd G 4F 21
Ridgeway Av. Barn 6J 5
Ridgeway Dri. Brom 4K 125
Ridgeway E. Sidc 5K 109
Ridgeway Gdns. N6 7H 31
Ridgeway Gdns. Ilf 5C 36
Ridgeway Rd. Iswth 7J 79
Ridgeway Rd. N. Iswth 7J 79
Ridgeway, The. E4 2J 19
Ridgeway, The. N3 7E 14
Ridgeway, The. N11 4J 15
Ridgeway, The. N14 2D 16
Ridgeway, The. NW7 3H 13
Ridgeway, The. NW9 4K 27
Ridgeway, The. NW11 7G 29
Ridgeway, The. W3 3G 81
Ridgeway, The. Croy 3K 151
Ridgeway, The. Enf 1E 6
Ridgeway, The. Kent 6C 26
Ridgeway, The. N Har 5D 24 (in two parts)
Ridgeway, The. Ruis 7J 23
Ridgeway, The. Stan 6H 11
Ridgeway, The. W on T 7H 131
Ridgeway Wlk. N'holt 6C 42 (off Cowings Mead)
Ridgeway W. Sidc 5J 109
Ridgewell Clo. N1 1C 68
Ridgewell Clo. SE26 4B 124
Ridgewell Clo. Dag 1H 75
Ridgmount Gdns. WC1 5H 67 (5C 160)
Ridgmount Pl. WC1 5H 67 (5C 160)
Ridgmount Rd. SW18 5K 101
Ridgmount St. WC1 5H 67 (5C 160)
Ridgway. SW19 7E 118
Ridgway Ct. SW19 6F 119
Ridgway Gdns. SW19 7F 119
Ridgway Pl. SW19 6G 119
Ridgway Rd. SW9 3B 104
Ridgway, The. Sutt 7B 150
Ridgwell Rd. E16 5A 72
Riding Ho. St. W1 5F 67 (6K 159)
Ridings Av. N21 4G 7
Ridings Clo. N6 7G 31
Ridings, The. E11 5J 35
Ridings, The. W5 4F 63
Ridings, The. Barn 7G 5
Ridings, The. Ewe 7B 148
Ridings, The. Sun 1J 131
Ridings, The. Surb 5G 135
Riding, The. NW11 7H 29
Ridler Rd. Enf 1K 7
Ridley Av. W13 3B 80
Ridley Clo. Bark 7K 55
Ridley Ct. SW16 6J 121
Ridley Rd. E7 4A 54
Ridley Rd. E8 5F 51
Ridley Rd. NW10 2C 64
Ridley Rd. SW19 7K 119
Ridley Rd. Brom 3H 143
Ridley Rd. Well 1B 110
Ridsdale Rd. SE20 1H 141
Riefield Rd. SE9 4G 109
Riesco Dri. Croy 6J 153
Riffel Rd. NW2 5E 46
Rifle Ct. SE11 6A 86 (7K 173)
Rifle St. E14 5D 70
Riga Ho. E1 5K 69 (off Shandy St.)
Rigault Rd. SW6 2G 101
Rigby Clo. Croy 3A 152
Rigby La. Hay 2E 76
Rigby M. Ilf 2E 54
Rigden St. E14 6D 70
Rigeley Rd. NW10 3C 64
Rigg App. E10 1K 51
Rigge Pl. SW4 4H 103
Riggindale Rd. SW16 5H 121
Riley Ho. SW10 7B 84 (off Riley St.)
Riley Rd. SE1 3F 87 (7H 169)
Riley Rd. Enf 1D 8
Riley St. SW10 6B 84
Rill Ho. SE5 7D 86 (off Harris St.)
Rinaldo Rd. SW12 7F 103
Ring Clo. Brom 7K 125
Ringcroft St. N7 5A 50
Ringers Ct. Brom 3J 143 (off Ringers Rd.)
Ringers Rd. Brom 3J 143
Ringford Rd. SW18 5H 101
Ring Ho. E1 7J 69 (off Sage St.)
Ringles Ct. E6 1D 72
Ringlet Clo. E16 5K 71
Ringlewell Clo. Enf 2C 8
Ringmer Av. SW6 1G 101
Ringmer Gdns. N19 2J 49
Ringmer Pl. N21 5J 7
Ringmer Way. Brom 5C 144
Ringmore Ri. SE23 7H 105
Ring Rd. W12 1E 82
Ringsfield Ho. SE17 5C 86 (off Bronti Clo.)
Ringslade Rd. N22 2K 31
Ringstead Rd. SE6 7D 106
Ringstead Rd. Sutt 4B 150
Ring, The. W2 7B 66 (2C 164) (in three parts)
Ring Way. N11 6B 16
Ringway. S'hall 5B 78
Ringwold Clo. Beck 7A 124
Ringwood Av. N2 2D 30
Ringwood Av. Croy 7J 139
Ringwood Clo. Pinn 3A 24
Ringwood Gdns. E14 4C 88
Ringwood Gdns. SW15 1C 118
Ringwood Rd. E17 6B 34
Ringwood Way. N21 1G 17
Ringwood Way. Hamp H 4E 114
Ripley Clo. Brom 5D 144
Ripley Clo. New Ad 6E 154
Ripley Ct. Mitc 2B 138
Ripley Gdns. SW14 3K 99
Ripley Gdns. Sutt 4A 150
Ripley Ho. SW1 6G 85 (7A 172) (off Churchill Gdns.)
Ripley M. E11 6G 35
Ripley Rd. E16 6A 72
Ripley Rd. Belv 4G 93
Ripley Rd. Enf 1H 7
Ripley Rd. Hamp 7E 114
Ripley Rd. Ilf 2K 55
Ripley Vs. W5 6C 62
Ripon Clo. N'holt 5E 42
Ripon Gdns. Chess 5D 146
Ripon Gdns. Ilf 6C 36
Ripon Rd. N9 7C 8
Ripon Rd. N17 3D 32
Ripon Rd. SE18 6F 91
Rippersley Rd. Well 1A 110
Ripple Rd. Bark & Dag 7G 55
Ripple Road Junction. (Junct.) 1B 74
Rippleside 1B 74
Rippleside Commercial Est. Bark 2C 74
Ripplevale Gro. N1 7K 49
Rippolson Rd. SE18 5K 91
Ripston Rd. Ashf 5F 113
Risboro' Clo. N10 3F 31
Risborough. SE17 4C 86
Risborough Dri. Wor Pk 7C 136
Risborough Ho. NW8 4C 66 (3D 158) (off Mallory St.)
Risborough St. SE1 2B 86 (6B 168)
Risdon Ho. SE16 2J 87 (off Risdon St.)
Risdon St. SE16 3J 87
Risedale Rd. Bexh 3J 111
Riseholme Ct. E9 6B 52
Riseldine Rd. SE23 6A 106
Rise Park 1K 39
Rise Pk. Pde. Romf 2K 39
Rise, The. E11 5J 35
Rise, The. N13 4F 17
Rise, The. NW7 6G 13
Rise, The. NW10 4K 45
Rise, The. Bex 7C 110
Rise, The. Buck H 1G 21
Rise, The. Edgw 5C 12
Rise, The. Gnfd 5A 44
Rise, The. Uxb 2B 58
Risinghill St. N1 2K 67
Risingholme Clo. Bush 1A 10
Risingholme Clo. Harr 1J 25
Risingholme Rd. Harr 2J 25
Risings, The. E17 4F 35
Rising Sun Ct. EC1 5B 162
Risley Av. N17 1C 32
Rita Rd. SW8 6J 85
Ritches Rd. N15 5C 32
Ritchie Ho. E14 6F 71 (off Blair St.)
Ritchie Ho. N19 1H 49
Ritchie Ho. SE16 3J 87 (off Howland Est.)
Ritchie Rd. Croy 6H 141
Ritchie St. N1 2A 68
Ritchings Av. E17 4A 34
Ritherdon Rd. SW17 2E 120
Ritson Ho. N1 1K 67 (off Barnsbury Est.)
Ritson Rd. E8 6G 51
Ritter St. SE18 6E 90
Ritz Pde. W5 4F 63
Rivaz Pl. E9 6J 51
Riven Ct. W2 6K 65 (off Inverness Ter.)
Rivenhall Gdns. E18 4H 35
River Ash Estate 7H 131
River Av. N13 3G 17
River Av. Th Dit 7A 134
River Av. Ind. Est. N13 5F 17
River Bank. N21 7H 7
River Bank. E Mol 3J 133
River Bank. Th Dit 5K 133
River Bank. W Mol 3E 132
Riverbank Rd. Brom 3J 125
Riverbank Way. Bren 6C 80
River Barge Clo. E14 2E 88
River Brent Bus. Pk. W7 3J 79
River Clo. E11 6A 36
River Clo. Ruis 6H 23
River Clo. S'hall 2G 79
River Ct. SE1 7B 68 (3A 168)
River Ct. Surb 5D 134 (off Portsmouth Rd.)
Rivercourt Rd. W6 4D 82
River Crane Way. Felt 2D 114 (off Watermill Way)
Riverdale. SE13 4E 106
Riverdale Ct. N21 5J 7
Riverdale Dri. SW18 1K 119
Riverdale Gdns. Twic 6C 98
Riverdale Rd. SE18 5K 91
Riverdale Rd. Bex 7F 111
Riverdale Rd. Eri 5H 93
Riverdale Rd. Felt 4C 114
Riverdale Rd. Twic 6C 98
Riverdale Shop. Cen. SE13 3E 106
Riverdene. Edgw 3D 12
Riverdene Rd. Ilf 3E 54
Riverfleet. WC1 3J 67 (1F 161) (off Birkenhead St.)
River Front. Enf 3K 7
River Gdns. Cars 2E 150
River Gdns. Felt 5K 95
River Gdns. Bus. Cen. Felt 5K 95
River Gro. Pk. Beck 1B 142
Riverhead Clo. E17 2K 33
Riverhill. Wor Pk 2K 147
Riverholme Dri. Eps 7K 147
Riverhope Mans. SE18 3C 90
River Ho. SE26 3H 123
River La. Rich 7D 98
Riverleigh Ct. E4 5G 19
Rivermead. E Mol 3G 133
Rivermead. King T 5D 134
Rivermead Clo. Tedd 5B 116
Rivermead Ct. SW6 3H 101
Rivermead Ho. E9 5A 52
Rivermead Rd. N18 6E 18
River Meads Av. Twic 3E 114
River Mt. W on T 7H 131
Rivernook Clo. W on T 5A 132
River Pk. Gdns. Brom 7F 125
River Pk. Rd. N22 2K 31
River Pk. Trad. Est. E14 3B 88
River Pl. N1 7C 50
River Reach. Tedd 5C 116
River Rd. Bark 2J 73
River Rd. Buck H 1H 21
River Rd. Bus. Pk. Bark 3K 73
Riversdale Rd. N5 3B 50
Riversdale Rd. Romf 1H 39
Riversdale Rd. Th Dit 5A 134
Riversfield Rd. Enf 3K 7
Rivers Ho. W4 5G 81 (off Chiswick High Rd.)
Riverside. NW4 7D 28
Riverside. SE7 3K 89 (in two parts)
Riverside. WC1 3J 67 (1F 161) (off Birkenhead St.)
Riverside. Rich 5D 98
Riverside. Shep 7G 131
Riverside. Sun 2B 132
Riverside. Twic 1B 116
Riverside Apartments. N13 5E 16
Riverside Av. E Mol 5H 133
Riverside Bus. Cen. SW18 1K 119
Riverside Clo. E5 1J 51
Riverside Clo. W7 4J 61
Riverside Clo. King T 4D 134
Riverside Clo. Wall 3F 151
Riverside Cotts. Bark 2H 73
Riverside Ct. E4 6H 9
Riverside Ct. SE3 4H 107
Riverside Ct. SW8 6H 85 (7D 172)
Riverside Ct. Felt 7G 95
Riverside Ct. Iswth 2K 97 (off Woodlands Rd.)
Riverside Dri. NW11 6G 29
Riverside Dri. W4 7K 81
Riverside Dri. Mitc 5C 138
Riverside Dri. Rich 3B 116
Riverside Gdns. N3 3G 29
Riverside Gdns. W6 5D 82
Riverside Gdns. Enf 2H 7
Riverside Gdns. Wemb 2E 62
Riverside Ho. N1 7C 50 (off Canonbury St.)
Riverside Ind. Est. Bark 3A 74
Riverside Ind. Est. Enf 6F 9
Riverside Mans. E1 1J 87 (off Milk Yd.)
Riverside M. Croy 3J 151
Riverside Pl. N11 3B 16
Riverside Pl. Stanw 6A 94
Riverside Rd. E15 2E 70
Riverside Rd. N15 6G 33
Riverside Rd. SW17 4K 119
Riverside Rd. Sidc 3E 128
Riverside Rd. Stanw 5A 94 (in two parts)
Riverside, The. E Mol 3H 133
Riverside Wlk. N12 & N20 3E 14 (in two parts)
Riverside Wlk. SE10 3G 89 (Morden Wharf Rd.)
Riverside Wlk. SE10 2F 89 (Tunnel Av.)
Riverside Wlk. SW6 3G 101
Riverside Wlk. W4 6B 82 (off Chiswick Wharf)
Riverside Wlk. Barn 6A 4 (in two parts)
Riverside Wlk. Iswth 3J 97
Riverside Wlk. King T 3D 134
Riverside Wlk. W Wick 1D 154
Riverside Works. Bark 7F 55
Riverside Workshops. SE1 1C 86 (4D 168) (off Park St.)
Riverstone Ct. King T 1F 135
River St. EC1 3A 68 (1J 161)
River Ter. W6 5E 82
River Ter. WC2 3G 167
Riverton Clo. W9 3H 65
River Vw. Enf 3H 7
Riverview Gdns. SW13 6D 82
River Vw. Gdns. Twic 2K 115
Riverview Gro. W4 6H 81
Riverview Heights. SE16 2G 87 (off Bermondsey Wall W.)
Riverview Pk. SE6 2C 124
Riverview Rd. W4 7H 81
Riverview Rd. Eps 4J 147
River Wlk. W6 7E 82
River Wlk. W on T 6J 131
Riverway. N13 5F 17
River Way. SE10 3H 89
River Way. Eps 5K 147
River Way. Twic 2F 115
River Wharf Bus. Pk. Belv 1K 93
Riverwood La. Chst 1H 145
Rivet Ho. SE1 5F 87 (off Coopers Rd.)
Rivington Av. Wfd G 2B 36
Rivington Bldgs. EC2 3E 68 (2G 163)
Rivington Ct. NW10 1C 64
Rivington Cres. NW7 7G 13
Rivington Pl. EC2 3E 68 (2H 163)
Rivington St. EC2 3E 68 (2G 163)
Rivington Wlk. E8 1G 69
Rivulet Rd. N17 7H 17
Rixon Ho. SE18 6F 91
Rixon St. N7 3A 50
Rixsen Rd. E12 5C 54
Roach Rd. E3 7C 52
Roads Pl. N19 2J 49
Roan St. SE10 6E 88
Robarts Clo. Pinn 6K 23
Robb Rd. Stan 6F 11
Robert Adam St. W1 6E 66 (7G 159)
Roberta St. E2 3G 69
Robert Bell Ho. SE16 4G 87 (off Rouel Rd.)
Robert Clo. W9 4A 66 (4A 158)

Robert Dashwood Way. SE17 4C 86
Robert Gentry Ho. W14 5G 83
(off Gledstanes Rd.)
Robert Jones Ho. SE16 4G 87
(off Rouel Rd.)
Robert Keen Clo. SE15 1G 105
Robert Lowe Clo. SE14 7K 87
Roberton Dri. Brom 1A 144
Robert Owen Ho. N22 1A 32
(off Progress Way)
Robert Owen Ho. SW6 1F 101
Robert Runcie Ct. SW9 4K 103
Roberts All. W5 2D 80
Robertsbridge Rd. Cars 1A 150
Roberts Clo. SE9 1H 127
Roberts Clo. SE16 2K 87
Roberts Clo. Sutt 7F 149
Roberts Clo. W Dray 1A 76
Roberts Ct. N1 1B 68
(off Essex Rd.)
Roberts Ct. NW10 6A 46
Roberts Ct. SE20 1J 141
(off Maple Rd.)
Roberts M. SW1 3E 84 (1G 171)
Robertson Rd. E15 1E 70
Robertson St. SW8 3F 103
Roberts Pl. EC1 4A 68 (3K 161)
Roberts Rd. E17 1D 34
Roberts Rd. NW7 6B 14
Roberts Rd. Belv 5G 93
Robert St. E16 1F 91
Robert St. NW1 3F 67 (2K 159)
Robert St. SE18 5H 91
(in two parts)
Robert St. WC2 7J 67 (3F 167)
Robert St. Croy 3C 152
Robert Sutton Ho. E1 6J 69
(off Tarling St.)
Robeson St. E3 5B 70
Robina Clo. Bexh 4D 110
Robina Clo. N'wd 1H 23
Robin Clo. NW7 3F 13
Robin Clo. Hamp 5C 114
Robin Clo. Romf 1K 39
Robin Ct. E14 2E 88
Robin Ct. SE16 4G 87
Robin Cres. E6 5B 72
Robin Gro. N6 2E 48
Robin Gro. Bren 6C 80
Robin Gro. Harr 6F 27
Robin Hill Dri. Chst 6C 126
Robin Hood. (Junct.) 3A 118
Robinhood Clo. Mitc 3G 139
Robin Hood Dri. Harr 7E 10
Robin Hood Gdns. E14 7E 70
(off Woolmore St., in two parts)
Robin Hood Grn. Orp 5K 145
Robin Hood La. E14 7E 70
Robin Hood La. SW15 3A 118
Robin Hood La. Bexh 5E 110
Robinhood La. Mitc 3G 139
Robin Hood La. Sutt 5J 149
Robin Hood Rd. SW19 & SW15 5C 118
Robin Hood Way. SW15 & SW20 3A 118
Robin Hood Way. Gnfd 6K 43
Robin Ho. NW8 2C 66
(off Barrow Hill Est.)
Robinia Cres. E10 2D 52
Robins Ct. SE12 3A 126
Robin's Ct. Beck 2F 143
Robins Ct. S Croy 4E 152
(off Birdhurst Rd.)
Robinscroft M. SE10 1E 106
Robins Gro. W Wick 3J 155
Robinson Clo. E11 3G 53
Robinson Ct. N1 1B 68
(off St Mary's Path)
Robinson Cres. Bus H 1B 10
Robinson Ho. E14 5C 70
(off Selsey St.)
Robinson Ho. W10 6F 65
(off Bramley Rd.)
Robinson Rd. E2 2J 69
Robinson Rd. SW17 & SW19 6C 120
Robinson Rd. Dag 4G 57
Robinson's Clo. W13 5A 62
Robinson St. SW3 6D 84 (7E 170)
Robinwood Pl. SW15 4K 117
Robsart St. SW9 2K 103
Robson Av. NW10 7C 46
Robson Clo. E6 6C 72
Robson Clo. Enf 2G 7
Robson Rd. SE27 3B 122
Roby Ho. EC1 4C 68 (3C 162)
(off Mitchell St.)
Roch Av. Edgw 2F 27
Rochdale Rd. E17 7C 34
Rochdale Rd. SE2 5B 92
Rochdale Way. SE8 7C 88
Roche Ho. E14 7B 70
(off Beccles St.)
Rochelle Clo. SW11 4B 102
Rochelle St. E2 3F 69 (2J 163)
(in two parts)
Rochemont Wlk. E8 1G 69
(off Pownell Rd.)
Roche Rd. SW16 1K 139
Rochester Av. E13 1A 72
Rochester Av. Brom 2K 143
Rochester Av. Felt 2H 113
Rochester Clo. SW16 7J 121
Rochester Clo. Enf 1K 7
Rochester Clo. Sidc 6B 110
Rochester Ct. E2 4H 69
(off Wilmot St.)
Rochester Ct. NW1 7G 49
(off Rochester Sq.)
Rochester Dri. Bex 6F 111
Rochester Dri. Pinn 5B 24
Rochester Gdns. Croy 3E 152
Rochester Gdns. Ilf 7D 36
Rochester Ho. SE1 2D 86 (7F 169)
(off Manciple St.)
Rochester Ho. SE15 6J 87
(off Sharratt St.)
Rochester M. NW1 7G 49
Rochester M. W5 4C 80
Rochester Pde. Felt 2J 113
Rochester Pl. NW1 6G 49
Rochester Rd. NW1 6G 49
Rochester Rd. Cars 4D 150
Rochester Rd. N'wd 3H 23
Rochester Row. SW1 4G 85 (3B 172)
Rochester Sq. NW1 7G 49
Rochester St. SW1 3H 85 (2C 172)
Rochester Ter. NW1 6G 49
Rochester Wlk. SE1 1D 86 (4E 168)
Rochester Way. SE3 & SE9 1K 107
Rochester Way. Dart 7K 111
Rochester Way Relief Rd. SE3 & SE9 1K 107
Roche Wlk. Cars 6B 138
Rochford. N17 2E 32
(off Griffin Rd.)
Rochford Av. Romf 5C 38
Rochford Clo. E6 2B 72
Rochford Wlk. E8 7G 51
Rochford Way. Croy 6J 139
Rochfort Ho. SE8 5B 88
Rock Av. SW14 3K 99
Rockbourne M. SE23 1K 123
Rockbourne Rd. SE23 1K 123
Rock Clo. Mitc 2B 138
Rockell's Pl. SE22 6H 105
Rockfield Ho. NW4 4F 29
(off Belle Vue Est.)
Rockfield Ho. SE10 6E 88
(off Welland St.)
Rockford Av. Gnfd 2A 62
Rock Gdns. Dag 5H 57
Rock Gro. Way. SE16 4G 87
(in two parts)
Rockhall Rd. NW2 4F 47
Rockhall Way. NW2 3F 47
Rockhampton Clo. SE27 4A 122
Rockhampton Rd. SE27 4A 122
Rockhampton Rd. S Croy 6E 152
Rock Hill. SE26 4F 123
(in two parts)
Rockingham Clo. SW15 4B 100
Rockingham St. SE1 3C 86
Rockland Rd. SW15 4G 101
Rocklands Dri. Stan 2B 26
Rockley Ct. W14 2F 83
(off Rockley Rd.)
Rockley Rd. W14 2F 83
Rockmount Rd. SE18 5K 91
Rockmount Rd. SE19 6D 122
Rocks La. SW13 1C 100
Rock St. N4 2A 50
Rockware Av. Gnfd 1H 61
Rockware Av. Bus. Cen. Gnfd 1H 61
Rockwell Gdns. SE19 5E 122
Rockwell Rd. Dag 5H 57
Rockwood Pl. W12 2E 82
Rocliffe St. N1 2B 68
Rocombe Cres. SE23 7J 105
Rocque Ho. SW6 7H 83
(off Estcourt Rd.)
Rocque La. SE3 3H 107
Rodale Mans. SW18 6K 101
Rodborough Ct. W9 4J 65
(off Hermes Clo.)
Rodborough Rd. NW11 1J 47
Roden Gdns. Croy 6E 140
Rodenhurst Rd. SW4 6G 103
Roden St. N7 3K 49
Roden St. Ilf 3E 54
Roden Way. Ilf 3E 54
(off Roden St.)
Roderick Ho. SE16 4J 87
(off Raymouth Rd.)
Roderick Rd. NW3 4D 48
Rodgers Ho. SW4 7H 103
(off Clapham Pk. Est.)
Rodin Ct. N1 1B 68
(off Essex Rd.)
Roding Av. Wfd G 6H 21
Roding Ho. N1 1A 68
(off Barnsbury Est.)
Roding La. Buck H 1H 21
Roding La. N. Wfd G 6H 21
Roding La. S. Ilf 4B 36
Roding M. E1 1G 87
Roding Rd. E5 4K 51
Roding Rd. E6 5F 73
Rodings Row. Barn 4B 4
(off Leecroft Rd.)
Rodings, The. Wfd G 6F 21
Roding Trad. Est. Bark 7F 55
Roding Vw. Buck H 1G 21
Rodmarton St. W1 5D 66 (6F 159)
Rodmell. WC1 3J 67 (2F 161)
(off Regent Sq.)
Rodmell Clo. Hay 4C 60
Rodmell Slope. N12 5C 14
Rodmere St. SE10 5G 89
Rodmill La. SW2 7J 103
Rodney Clo. Croy 1B 152
Rodney Clo. N Mald 5A 136
Rodney Clo. Pinn 7C 24
Rodney Ct. W9 4A 66 (3A 158)
Rodney Ct. Barn 3C 4
Rodney Gdns. Pinn 5K 23
Rodney Gdns. W Wick 4J 155
Rodney Ho. E14 4D 88
(off Cahir St.)
Rodney Ho. N1 2K 67
(off Donegal St.)
Rodney Ho. SW1 5G 85 (6B 172)
(off Dolphin Sq.)
Rodney Ho. W11 7J 65
(off Pembridge Cres.)
Rodney Pl. E17 2A 34
Rodney Pl. SE17 4C 86
Rodney Pl. SW19 1A 138
Rodney Rd. E11 4K 35
Rodney Rd. SE17 4C 86
(in two parts)
Rodney Rd. Mitc 3C 138
Rodney Rd. N Mald 5A 136
Rodney Rd. Twic 6E 96
Rodney St. N1 2K 67 (1H 161)
Rodney Way. Romf 1H 39
Rodway Rd. SW15 7C 100
Rodway Rd. Brom 1K 143
Rodwell Clo. Ruis 1A 42
Rodwell Pl. Edgw 6B 12
Rodwell Rd. SE22 6F 105
Roe. NW9 7G 13
Roebourne Way. E16 1E 90
Roebuck Clo. Felt 4K 113
Roebuck Ho. SW1 3G 85 (1A 172)
(off Palace Ho.)
Roebuck La. N17 6A 18
Roebuck La. Buck H 1F 21
Roebuck Rd. Chess 5G 147
Roedean Av. Enf 1D 8
Roedean Clo. Enf 1D 8
Roedean Cres. SW15 6A 100
Roe End. NW9 4J 27
Roe Green. 4J 27
Roe Grn. NW9 5J 27
Roehampton. 7C 100
Roehampton Clo. SW15 4C 100
Roehampton Dri. Chst 6G 127
Roehampton Ga. SW15 6A 100
Roehampton High St. SW15 7C 100
Roehampton Lane. (Junct.) 1D 118
Roehampton La. SW15 4C 100
Roehampton Va. SW15 3B 118
Roe La. NW9 4H 27
Roffey St. E14 2E 88
Rogate Ho. E5 3G 51
Roger Bannister Sports Cen., The. 6B 10
Roger Dowley Ct. E2 2J 69
Roger Harriss Almshouses. E15 1H 71
(off Gift La.)
Roger Reede's Almshouses. Romf 4K 39
Rogers Ct. E14 7C 70
(off Premiere Pl.)
Rogers Est. E2 3J 69
Rogers Gdns. Dag 5G 57
Rogers Ho. SW1 4H 85 (3D 172)
(off Page St.)
Roger's Ho. Dag 3G 57
Rogers Rd. E16 6H 71
Rogers Rd. SW17 4B 120
Rogers Rd. Dag 5G 57
Rogers Ruff. N'wd 1E 22
Roger St. WC1 4K 67 (4H 161)
Rogers Wlk. N12 3E 14
Rohere Ho. EC1 3C 68 (2C 162)
Rojack Rd. SE23 1K 123
Rokeby Gdns. Wfd G 1J 35
Rokeby Pl. SW20 7D 118
Rokeby Rd. SE4 2B 106
Rokeby Rd. Harr 3H 25
Rokeby St. E15 1F 71
Rokell Ho. Beck 5D 124
(off Beckenham Hill Rd.)
Roker Pk. Av. Uxb 4A 40
Rokesby Clo. Well 2H 109
Rokesby Pl. Wemb 5D 44
Rokesly Av. N8 5J 31
Roland Gdns. SW7 5A 84 (5A 170)
Roland Ho. SW7 5A 84 (5A 170)
(off Cranley M.)
Roland M. E1 5K 69
Roland Rd. E17 4F 35
Roland Way. SE17 5D 86
Roland Way. SW7 5A 84 (5A 170)
Roland Way. Wor Pk 2B 148
Roles Gro. Romf 4D 38
Rolfe Clo. Barn 4H 5
Rolinsden Way. Kes 5B 156
Rolland Ho. W7 5J 61
Rollesby Rd. Chess 6G 147
Rollesby Way. SE28 6C 74
Rolleston Av. Orp 6F 145
Rolleston Clo. Orp 7F 145
Rolleston Rd. S Croy 7D 152
Roll Gdns. Ilf 5E 36
Rollins St. SE15 6J 87
Rollit Cres. Houn 5E 96
Rollit St. N7 5A 50
Rolls Bldgs. EC4 6A 68 (7J 161)
Rollscourt Av. SE24 5C 104
Rolls Pk. Av. E4 5H 19
Rolls Pk. Rd. E4 5J 19
Rolls Pas. EC4 7J 161
Rolls Rd. SE1 5F 87
Rolt St. SE8 6A 88
(in two parts)
Rolvenden Gdns. Brom 7B 126
Rolvenden Pl. N17 1G 33
Roman Clo. W3 2H 81
Roman Clo. Felt 5A 96
Roman Clo. Rain 2K 75
Roman Ct. N7 6K 49
Romanfield Rd. SW2 7K 103
Roman Ho. EC2 6D 162
Romanhurst Av. Brom 4G 143
Romanhurst Gdns. Brom 4G 143
Roman Ind. Est. Croy 7E 140
Roman Ri. SE19 6D 122
Roman Rd. E2 & E3 3J 69
Roman Rd. E3 1B 70
Roman Rd. E6 4B 72
Roman Rd. N10 7A 16
Roman Rd. NW2 3E 46
Roman Rd. W4 4A 82
Roman Rd. Ilf 6F 55
Roman Sq. SE28 1A 92
Roman Way. N7 6K 49
Roman Way. SE15 7J 87
Roman Way. Croy 2B 152
Roman Way. Enf 5A 8
Roman Way Ind. Est. N7 7K 49
(off Roman Way)
Romany Gdns. E17 1A 34
Romany Gdns. Sutt 7J 137
Roma Read Clo. SW15 7D 100
Roma Rd. E17 3A 34
Romayne Ho. SW4 3H 103
Romberg Rd. SW17 3E 120
Romborough Gdns. SE13 5E 106
Romborough Way. SE13 5E 106
Romer Ho. W10 3H 65
(off Dowland St.)
Romero Clo. SW9 3K 103
Romero Sq. SE3 4A 108
Romeyn Rd. SW16 3K 121
Romford Greyhound Stadium. 6J 39
Romford Rd. E15 & E7 6G 53
Romford Rd. Romf 1F 39
Romford St. E1 5G 69
Romilly Rd. N4 2B 50
Romilly St. W1 7H 67 (2D 166)
Romily Ct. SW6 2H 101
Rommany Rd. SE27 4D 122
(in two parts)
Romney Clo. N17 1H 33
Romney Clo. NW11 1A 48
Romney Clo. SE14 7J 87
Romney Clo. Ashf 5E 112
Romney Clo. Chess 4E 146
Romney Clo. Harr 7E 24
Romney Ct. NW3 6C 48
Romney Ct. W12 2F 83
(off Shepherd's Bush Grn.)

Romney Dri. Brom. 7B 126
Romney Dri. Harr 7E 24
Romney Gdns. Bexh 1F 111
Romney M. W1 5E 66 (5G 159)
Romney Pde. Hay 2F 59
Romney Rd. SE10 6F 89
Romney Rd. Hay 2F 59
Romney Rd. N Mald 6K 135
Romney Row. NW2 2F 47 (off Brent Ter.)
Romney St. SW1 3J 85 (2E 172)
Romola Rd. SE24 1B 122
Romsey Gdns. Dag 1D 74
Romsey Rd. W13 7A 62
Romsey Rd. Dag 1D 74
Romulus Ct. Bren 7D 80
Ronald Av. E15 3G 71
Ronald Buckingham Ct. SE16 2J 87 (off Kenning St.)
Ronald Clo. Beck 4B 142
Ronald Ct. New Bar 3E 4
Ronald Ho. SE3 4A 108
Ronaldshay. N4 1A 50
Ronalds Rd. N5 5A 50 (in three parts)
Ronalds Rd. Brom 1J 143
Ronaldstone Rd. Sidc 6J 109
Ronald St. E1 6J 69
Rona Rd. NW3 4E 48
Ronart St. W'stone 3K 25
Rona Wlk. N1 6D 50 (off Ramsey Wlk.)
Rondel Ct. Bex 6E 110
Rondu Rd. NW2 5G 47
Ronelean Rd. Surb 2F 147
Ron Leighton Way. E6 1C 72
Ronver Rd. SE12 1H 125
Rood La. EC3 7E 68 (2G 169)
Rookby Ct. N21 2G 17
Rook Clo. Wemb 3H 45
Rookeries Clo. Felt 3K 113
Rookery Clo. NW9 5B 28
Rookery Cres. Dag 7H 57
Rookery Dri. Chst 1E 144
Rookery La. Brom 6B 144
Rookery Rd. SW4 4G 103
Rookery Way. NW9 5B 28
Rooke Way. SE10 5H 89
Rookfield Av. N10 4G 31
Rookfield Clo. N10 4G 31
Rooksmead Rd. Sun 2H 131
Rooks Ter. W Dray 2A 76
Rookstone Rd. SW17 5D 120
Rook Wlk. E6 6B 72
Rookwood Av. N Mald 4C 136
Rookwood Av. Wall 4H 151
Rookwood Gdns. E4 2C 20
Rookwood Ho. Bark 2H 73
Rookwood Rd. N16 7F 33
Roosevelt Way. Dag 6K 57
Rootes Dri. W10 5F 65
Ropemaker Rd. SE16 2A 88
Ropemaker's Fields. E14 7B 70
Ropemaker St. EC2 5D 68 (5E 162)
Roper La. SE1 2E 86 (7H 169)
Ropers Av. E4 5J 19
Ropers Orchard. SW3 6C 84 (off Danvers St.)
Roper St. SE9 5D 108
Ropers Wlk. SW2 7A 104
Roper Way. Mitc 2E 138
Ropery Bus. Pk. SE7 4A 90
Ropery St. E3 4B 70
Rope St. SE16 4A 88
Rope Wlk. Sun 3A 132
Rope Wlk. Gdns. E1 6G 69
Ropewalk M. E8 7G 51 (off Middleton Rd.)
Rope Yd. Rails. SE18 3F 91
Ropley St. E2 2G 69
Rosa Alba M. N5 4C 50
Rosa Av. Ashf 4C 112
Rosalind Ct. Bark 7A 56 (off Meadow Rd.)
Rosalind Ho. N1 2E 68 (off Arden Ho.)
Rosaline Rd. SW6 7G 83
Rosaline Ter. SW6 7G 83 (off Rosaline Rd.)
Rosamond St. SE26 3H 123
Rosamund Clo. S Croy 4D 152
Rosamun St. S'hall 4C 78
Rosary Clo. Houn 2C 96
Rosary Gdns. SW7 4A 84
Rosary Gdns. Ashf 4D 112
Rosaville Rd. SW6 7H 83
Roscoe St. EC1 4C 68 (4D 162) (in two parts)
Roscoe St. Est. EC1 4C 68 (4D 162)
Roscoff Clo. Edgw 1J 27
Roseacre Clo. W13 5B 62
Roseacre Clo. Shep 5C 130
Roseacre Rd. Well 3B 110
Rose All. EC2 5E 68 (6H 163) (off Bishopsgate)
Rose All. SE1 1C 86 (4D 168)
Rose & Crown Ct. EC2 7D 162
Rose & Crown Pas. Iswth 1A 98
Rose & Crown Yd. SW1 1G 85 (4B 166)
Rose Av. E18 2K 35
Rose Av. Mitc 1D 138
Rose Av. Mord 5A 138
Rosebank. SE20 7H 123
Rosebank. SW6 7E 82
Rosebank. W3 6K 63
Rosebank Av. Wemb 4K 43
Rose Bank Clo. N12 5H 15
Rosebank Clo. Tedd 6A 116
Rosebank Gdns. E3 2B 70
Rosebank Gdns. W3 6K 63
Rosebank Gro. E17 3B 34
Rosebank Rd. E17 6D 34
Rosebank Rd. W7 2J 79
Rosebank Vs. E17 4C 34
Rosebank Wlk. NW1 7H 49
Rosebank Wlk. SE18 4C 90
Rosebank Way. W3 6K 63
Rose Bates Dri. NW9 4G 27
Roseberry Av. T Hth 2C 140
Roseberry Gdns. N4 6B 32
Roseberry Pl. E8 6F 51
Roseberry St. SE1 4H 87
Rosebery Av. E12 6C 54
Rosebery Av. EC1 4A 68 (4J 161)
Rosebery Av. N17 2G 33
Rosebery Av. Harr 4C 42
Rosebery Av. N Mald 2B 136
Rosebery Av. Sidc 7J 109
Rosebery Clo. Mord 6F 137
Rosebery Ct. EC1 4A 68 (4J 161) (off Rosebery Av.)
Rosebery Gdns. N8 5J 31
Rosebery Gdns. W13 6A 62
Rosebery Gdns. Sutt 4K 149
Rosebery Ho. E2 2K 69 (off Sewardstone Rd.)
Rosebery Ind. Est. N17 2H 33
Rosebery Ind. Pk. N17 2H 33
Rosebery M. N10 2G 31
Rosebery Rd. N9 3B 18
Rosebery Rd. N10 2G 31
Rosebery Rd. SW2 6J 103
Rosebery Rd. Bush 1A 10
Rosebery Rd. Houn 5G 97
Rosebery Rd. King T 2H 135
Rosebery Rd. Sutt 6H 149
Rosebery Sq. EC1 4J 161
Rosebery Sq. King T 2H 135
Rosebine Av. Twic 7H 97
Rosebury Rd. SW6 2K 101
Rosebury Sq. Wfd G 7K 21
Rosebury Va. Ruis 2J 41
Rose Bush Ct. NW3 5D 48
Rose Ct. E1 6K 163
Rose Ct. E8 7F 51 (off Richmond Rd.)
Rose Ct. SE16 4K 87
Rose Ct. S Harr 2G 43
Rose Ct. Wemb 2E 62 (off Vicars Bri. Clo.)
Rosecourt Rd. Croy 6K 139
Rosecroft. N14 2D 16
Rosecroft Av. NW3 3J 47
Rosecroft Gdns. NW2 3C 46
Rosecroft Gdns. Twic 1H 115
Rosecroft Rd. S'hall 4E 60
Rosecroft Wlk. Pinn 5B 24
Rosecroft Wlk. Wemb 5D 44
Rosedale Av. Hay 5F 59
Rosedale Clo. SE2 3B 92
Rosedale Clo. W7 2K 79
Rosedale Clo. Stan 6G 11
Rosedale Ct. N5 4B 50
Rosedale Ct. Harr 4K 43
Rosedale Gdns. Dag 7B 56
Rosedale Ho. N16 1D 50
Rosedale Pl. Croy 7K 141
Rosedale Rd. E7 5A 54
Rosedale Rd. Dag 7B 56
Rosedale Rd. Eps 5C 148
Rosedale Rd. Rich 3E 98
Rosedale Rd. Romf 2J 39
Rosedale Ter. W6 3D 82 (off Dalling Rd.)
Rosedene. NW6 1F 65 (in three parts)
Rosedene Av. SW16 3K 121
Rosedene Av. Croy 7J 139
Rosedene Av. Gnfd 3E 60
Rosedene Av. Mord 5J 137
Rosedene Ct. Ruis 1G 41
Rosedene Gdns. Ilf 4E 36
Rosedene Ter. E10 2D 52
Rosedew Rd. W6 6F 83
Rose End. Wor Pk 1F 149
Rosefield Clo. Cars 5C 150
Rosefield Gdns. E14 7C 70
Roseford Ct. W12 2F 83 (off Shepherd's Bush Grn.)
Rose Garden Clo. Edgw 6K 11
Rose Gdns. W5 3D 80
Rose Gdns. Felt 2J 113
Rose Gdns. S'hall 4E 60
Rose Glen. NW9 4K 27
Rose Glen. Romf 1K 57
Rosehart M. W11 6J 65
Rosehatch Av. Romf 3D 38
Roseheath Rd. Houn 5D 96
Rosehill. 1A 150
Rosehill. Clay 6A 146
Rosehill. Hamp 1E 132
Rosehill. Sutt 2K 149
Rosehill Av. Sutt 1A 150
Rosehill Ct. Mord 7A 138 (off St Helier Av.)
Rosehill Ct. Pde. Mord 7A 138 (off St Helier Av.)
Rosehill Gdns. Gnfd 5K 43
Rosehill Gdns. Sutt 2K 149
Rosehill Pk. W. Sutt 1A 150
Rosehill Rd. SW18 6A 102
Rose Hill Roundabout. (Junct.) 7A 138
Roseland Clo. N17 7J 17
Rose La. Romf 3D 38
Rose Lawn. Bus H 1B 10
Roseleigh Av. N5 4B 50
Roseleigh Clo. Twic 6D 98
Rosemary Av. N2 4K 29
Rosemary Av. N3 2K 29
Rosemary Av. N9 1C 18
Rosemary Av. Enf 1K 7
Rosemary Av. Houn 2B 96
Rosemary Av. W Mol 3E 132
Rosemary Clo. Croy 6J 139
Rosemary Clo. Uxb 5C 58
Rosemary Ct. SE8 6B 88 (off Dorking Clo.)
Rosemary Dri. E14 6F 71
Rosemary Dri. Ilf 5B 36
Rosemary Gdns. SW14 3J 99
Rosemary Gdns. Chess 4E 146
Rosemary Gdns. Dag 1F 57
Rosemary Ho. N1 1D 68 (off Colville Est.)
Rosemary La. SW14 3J 99
Rosemary Rd. SE15 7F 87
Rosemary Rd. SW17 3A 120
Rosemary Rd. Well 1K 109
Rosemary St. N1 1D 68
Rosemead. NW9 7B 28
Rosemead Av. Felt 2H 113
Rosemead Av. Mitc 3G 139
Rosemead Av. Wemb 5E 44
Rose M. N18 4C 18
Rosemont Av. N12 6F 15
Rosemont Rd. NW3 6A 48
Rosemont Rd. W3 7H 63
Rosemont Rd. N Mald 3J 135
Rosemont Rd. Rich 6E 98
Rosemoor St. SW3 4D 84 (4E 170)
Rosemount Clo. Wfd G 6J 21
Rosemount Dri. Brom 4D 144
Rosemount Point. SE23 3K 123
Rosemount Rd. W13 6A 62
Rosenau Cres. SW11 1D 102
Rosenau Rd. SW11 1C 102
Rosendale Rd. SE24 & SE21 7C 104
Roseneath Av. N21 1G 17
Roseneath Rd. SW11 6E 102
Roseneath Wlk. Enf 4K 7
Rosen's Wlk. Edgw 3C 12
Rosenthal Rd. SE6 6D 106
Rosenthorpe Rd. SE15 5K 105
Rose Pk. Clo. Hay 5A 60
Rosepark Ct. Ilf 2D 36
Roserton St. E14 2E 88
Rosery, The. Croy 6K 141
Rose Sq. SW3 5B 84 (5B 170)
Roses, The. Wfd G 7C 20
Rose St. EC4 6B 68 (7B 162)
Rose St. WC2 7J 67 (2E 166) (in two parts)
Rosethorn Clo. SW12 7H 103
Rosetta Clo. SW8 7J 85 (off Kenchester Clo.)
Rosetti Ter. Dag 4B 56 (off Marlborough Rd.)
Roseveare Rd. SE12 4A 126
Roseville Av. Houn 5E 96
Roseville Rd. Hay 5J 77
Rosevine Rd. SW20 1E 136
Rose Wlk. Surb 5H 135
Rose Wlk. W Wick 2E 154
Rose Way. SE12 5J 107
Roseway. SE21 6D 104
Rose Way. Edgw 4D 12
Rosewell Clo. SE20 7H 123
Rosewood. Th Dit 2A 146
Rosewood Av. Gnfd 5A 44
Rosewood Clo. Sidc 3C 128
Rosewood Ct. E11 4F 53
Rosewood Ct. Brom 1A 144
Rosewood Dri. Shep 5B 130
Rosewood Gdns. SE13 2E 106
Rosewood Gro. Sutt 2A 150
Rosewood Ho. SW8 6K 85 (7G 173)
Rosewood Sq. W12 6C 64
Rosher Clo. E15 7F 53
Roshni Ho. SW17 6C 120
Rosina St. E9 6K 51
Roskell Rd. SW15 3F 101
Roslin Ho. E1 7K 69 (off Brodlove La.)
Roslin Rd. W3 3H 81
Roslin Way. Brom 5J 125
Roslyn Clo. Mitc 2B 138
Roslyn Rd. N15 5D 32
Rosmead Rd. W11 7G 65
Rosoman Pl. EC1 4A 68 (3K 161)
Rosoman St. EC1 3A 68 (2K 161)
Rossall Cres. NW10 3F 63
Ross Av. NW7 5B 14
Ross Av. Dag 2F 57
Ross Clo. Harr 7B 10
Ross Clo. Hay 4F 77
Ross Clo. N'holt 4H 43
Ross Ct. E5 4H 51 (off Napoleon Rd.)
Ross Ct. NW9 3A 28
Ross Ct. W13 5B 62 (off Cleveland Rd.)
Rosscourt Mans. SW1 3F 85 (1A 172) (off Buckingham Pal. Rd.)
Rossdale. Sutt 5C 150
Rossdale Dri. N9 6D 8
Rossdale Dri. NW9 1J 45
Rossdale Rd. SW15 4E 100
Rosse M. SE3 1K 107
Rossendale St. E5 2H 51
Rossendale Way. NW1 1G 67
Rossetti Ct. WC1 5H 67 (5C 160) (off Ridgmount Pl.)
Rossetti Ho. SW1 4H 85 (4D 172) (off Erasmus St.)
Rossetti M. NW8 1B 66
Rossetti Rd. SE16 5H 87
Rosshaven Pl. N'wd 1H 23
Ross Ho. E1 1H 87 (off Prusom St.)
Rossignol Gdns. Cars 2E 150
Rossindel Rd. Houn 5E 96
Rossington Clo. Enf 1C 8
Rossington St. E5 2G 51
Rossiter Fields. Barn 6C 4
Rossiter Rd. SW12 1F 121
Rossland Clo. Bexh 5H 111
Rosslyn Av. E4 2C 20
Rosslyn Av. SW13 3A 100
Rosslyn Av. Dag 7F 39
Rosslyn Av. E Barn 6H 5
Rosslyn Av. Felt 6J 95
Rosslyn Clo. Hay 5F 59
Rosslyn Clo. Sun 6G 113
Rosslyn Clo. W Wick 3H 155
Rosslyn Cres. Harr 4K 25
Rosslyn Cres. Wemb 4E 44
Rosslyn Gdns. Wemb 3E 44 (off Rosslyn Cres.)
Rosslyn Hill. NW3 4B 48
Rosslyn Mans. NW6 7A 48 (off Goldhurst Ter.)
Rosslyn M. NW3 4B 48
Rosslyn Pk. M. NW3 5B 48
Rosslyn Park R.U.F.C. 4B 100
Rosslyn Rd. E17 4E 34
Rosslyn Rd. Bark 7H 55
Rosslyn Rd. Twic 6C 98
Rossmore Clo. NW1 4C 66 (4D 158) (off Rossmore Rd.)
Rossmore Ct. NW1 4D 66 (3E 158)
Rossmore Rd. NW1 4C 66 (4D 158)
Ross Pde. Wall 6F 151
Ross Rd. SE25 3D 140
Ross Rd. Twic 1F 115
Ross Rd. Wall 5G 151
Ross Way. SE9 3C 108
Rosswood Gdns. Wall 6G 151
Ross Wyld Lodge. E17 3C 34 (off Forest Rd.)
Rostella Rd. SW17 4B 120
Rostrevor Av. N15 6F 33
Rostrevor Gdns. Hay 1G 77
Rostrevor Gdns. S'hall 5C 78
Rostrevor M. SW6 1H 101
Rostrevor Rd. SW6 1H 101

Rostrevor Rd. SW19 ..... 5J 119
Rotary St. SE1 .... 3B 86 (7A 168)
Rothay. NW1 ..... 3F 67 (1K 159)
(off Albany St.)
Rothbury Gdns. Iswth 7A 80
Rothbury Hall. SE10 ..... 4G 89
(off Azof St.)
Rothbury Rd. E9 ..... 7B 52
Rothbury Wlk. N17 ..... 7B 18
Rotheley Ho. E9 ..... 7J 51
(off Balcorne St.)
Rotherfield Ct. N1 ..... 7D 50
(off Rotherfield St., in two parts)
Rotherfield Rd. Cars 4E 150
Rotherfield St. N1 ..... 7C 50
Rotherham Wlk. SE1 ..... 5A 168
Rotherhill Av. SW16 ..... 6H 121
Rotherhithe. **2J 87**
Rotherhithe New Rd. SE16 ..... 5H 87
Rotherhithe Old Rd. SE16 ... 4K 87
Rotherhithe St. SE16 ..... 2J 87
Rother Ho. SE15 ..... 4H 105
Rothermere Rd. Croy 5K 151
Rotherwick Hill. W5 ..... 4F 63
Rotherwick Ho. E1 ..... 7G 69
(off Thomas More St.)
Rotherwick Rd. NW11 ..... 7J 29
Rotherwood Clo. SW20 .... 1G 137
Rotherwood Rd. SW15 .... 3F 101
Rothery St. N1 ..... 1B 68
(off St Marys Path)
Rothesay Av. SW20 ..... 2G 137
Rothesay Av. Gnfd 6G 43
(in two parts)
Rothesay Av. Rich 4H 99
Rothesay Ct. SE6 ..... 2H 125
(off Cumberland Pl.)
Rothesay Ct. SE11 ..... 7J 173
Rothesay Ct. SE12 ..... 3K 125
Rothesay Rd. SE25 ..... 4D 140
Rothley Ct. NW8 ... 4B 66 (3A 158)
(off St John's Wood Rd.)
Rothsay Rd. E7 ..... 7A 54
Rothsay St. SE1 ..... 3E 86
Rothsay Wlk. E14 ..... 4C 88
(off Charnwood Gdns.)
Rothschild Rd. W4 ..... 4J 81
Rothschild St. SE27 ..... 4B 122
Roth Wlk. N7 ..... 2K 49
Rothwell Ct. Harr 5K 25
Rothwell Gdns. Dag 7C 56
Rothwell Ho. Houn 6E 78
Rothwell Rd. Dag 1C 74
Rothwell St. NW1 ..... 1D 66
Rotten Row. NW3 ..... 1A 48
Rotten Row. SW7 & SW1 ..... 2C 84 (6B 164)
Rotterdam Dri. E14 ..... 3E 88
Rotunda, The. Romf 5K 39
(off Yew Tree Gdns.)
Rouel Rd. SE16 ..... 3G 87
(Old Jamaica Rd.)
Rouel Rd. SE16 ..... 4G 87
(Yalding Rd.)
Rougemont Av. Mord 6J 137
Roundabout Ho. N'wd 1J 23
Roundacre. SW19 ..... 2F 119
Roundaway Rd. Ilf 1D 36
Roundel Clo. SE4 ..... 4B 106
Round Gro. Croy 7K 141
Roundhay Clo. SE23 ..... 2K 123
Roundhedge Way. Enf 1E 6
Round Hill. SE26 ..... 2J 123
(in two parts)
Roundhill Dri. Enf 4E 6
Roundhouse Theatre, The. 7E 48
Roundshaw. **7J 151**
Roundshaw Cen. Wall 7J 151
(off Mollison Dri.)
Roundtable Rd. Brom 3H 125
Roundtree Rd. Wemb 5B 44
Roundways. Ruis 3H 41
Roundway, The. N17 ..... 1C 32
Roundway, The. Clay 6A 146
Roundwood. Chst 2F 145
Roundwood Av. Uxb 1E 76
Roundwood Clo. Ruis 7F 23
Roundwood Rd. NW10 ..... 6B 46
Rounton Rd. E3 ..... 4C 70
Roupell Ho. King T 7F 117
(off Florence Rd.)
Roupell Rd. SW2 ..... 1K 121
Roupell St. SE1 ... 1A 86 (5K 167)
Rousden St. NW1 ..... 7G 49
Rouse Gdns. SE21 ..... 4E 122
Rous Rd. Buck H 1H 21
Routemaster Clo. E13 ..... 3K 71
Routh Ct. Felt 1F 113
Routh Rd. SW18 ..... 7C 102
Routh St. E6 ..... 5D 72
Rover Ho. N1 ..... 1E 68
(off Whitmore Est.)
Rowallan Rd. SW6 ..... 7G 83
Rowallen Pde. Dag 1C 56
Rowan. N10 ..... 2F 31
Rowan Av. E4 ..... 6G 19
Rowan Clo. SW16 ..... 1G 139
Rowan Clo. W5 ..... 2E 80
Rowan Clo. Ilf 5H 55
Rowan Clo. N Mald 2A 136
Rowan Clo. Stan 6E 10
Rowan Clo. Wemb 3A 44
Rowan Ct. E13 ..... 2K 71
(off High St.)
Rowan Ct. SE15 ..... 7F 87
(off Garnies Clo.)
Rowan Ct. SW11 ..... 6D 102
Rowan Cres. SW16 ..... 1G 139
Rowan Dri. NW9 ..... 3C 28
Rowan Gdns. Croy 3F 153
Rowan Ho. SE16 ..... 2K 87
(off Woodland Cres.)
Rowan Ho. Short 2G 143
Rowan Ho. Sidc 3K 127
Rowan Lodge. W8 ..... 3K 83
(off Chantry Sq.)
Rowan Pl. Hay 7H 59
Rowan Rd. SW16 ..... 2G 139
Rowan Rd. W6 ..... 4F 83
Rowan Rd. Bexh 3E 110
Rowan Rd. Bren 7B 80
Rowan Rd. W Dray 4A 76
Rowans Bowl. N4 ..... 2A 50
Rowans, The. N13 ..... 3G 17
Rowans, The. Sun 5H 113
Rowan Ter. W6 ..... 4F 83
(off Rowan Rd.)
Rowantree Clo. N21 ..... 1J 17
Rowantree Rd. N21 ..... 1J 17
Rowantree Rd. Enf 2G 7
Rowan Wlk. N2 ..... 5A 30
Rowan Wlk. N19 ..... 2G 49
Rowan Wlk. W10 ..... 4G 65
Rowan Wlk. Barn 5E 4
Rowan Wlk. Brom 3D 156
Rowan Way. Romf 3C 38
Rowanwood Av. Sidc 1A 128
Rowanwood M. Enf 2G 7
Rowben Clo. N20 ..... 1E 14
Rowberry Clo. SW6 ..... 7E 82
Rowcross St. SE1 ..... 5F 87
Rowdell Rd. N'holt 1E 60
Rowden Pk. Gdns. E4 ..... 7H 19
(off Chingford Rd.)
Rowden Rd. E4 ..... 6J 19
Rowden Rd. Beck 1A 142
Rowden Rd. Eps 4H 147
Rowditch La. SW11 ..... 2E 102
Rowdon Av. NW10 ..... 7D 46
Rowdown Cres. New Ad 7F 155
Rowdowns Rd. Dag 1F 75
Rowe Gdns. Bark 2K 73
Rowe La. E9 ..... 5J 51
Rowena Cres. SW11 ..... 2C 102
Rowe Wlk. Harr 3E 42
Rowfant Rd. SW17 ..... 1E 120
Rowhill Rd. E5 ..... 4H 51
Rowington Clo. W2 ..... 5K 65
Rowland Av. Harr 3C 26
Rowland Ct. E16 ..... 4H 71
Rowland Gro. SE26 ..... 3H 123
Rowland Hill Almshouses. Ashf 5C 112
(off Feltham Hill Rd.)
Rowland Hill Av. N17 ..... 7H 17
Rowland Hill Ho. SE1 ..... 2B 86 (6A 168)
Rowland Hill St. NW3 ..... 5C 48
Rowlands Av. Pinn 5A 10
Rowlands Clo. N6 ..... 6E 30
Rowlands Clo. NW7 ..... 7H 13
Rowlands Rd. Dag 2F 57
Rowland Way. SW19 ..... 1K 137
Rowland Way. Ashf 7F 113
Rowley Av. Sidc 7B 110
Rowley Clo. Wemb 7F 45
Rowley Ct. Enf 5K 7
(off Wellington Rd.)
Rowley Gdns. N4 ..... 7C 32
Rowley Ho. SE8 ..... 5C 88
(off Watergate St.)
Rowley Ind. Pk. W3 ..... 3H 81
Rowley Rd. N15 ..... 5C 32
Rowley Way. NW8 ..... 1K 65
Rowlheys Pl. W Dray 3A 76
Rowlls Rd. King T 3F 135
Rowney Gdns. Dag 6C 56
Rowney Rd. Dag 6B 56
Rowntree Clifford Clo. E13 ... 4J 71
Rowntree Clo. NW6 ..... 6J 47
Rowntree Path. SE28 ..... 1B 92
Rowntree Rd. Twic 1J 115
Rowse Clo. E15 ..... 1E 70
Rowsley Av. NW4 ..... 3E 28
Rowstock Gdns. N7 ..... 5H 49
Rowton Rd. SE18 ..... 7G 91
Roxborough Av. Harr 7H 25
Roxborough Av. Iswth 7K 79
Roxborough Heights. Harr ... 6J 25
(off College Rd.)
Roxborough Pk. Harr 7J 25
Roxborough Rd. Harr 5H 25
Roxbourne Clo. N'holt 6C 42
Roxbourne Pk. Miniature Railway. 2B 42
Roxburgh Rd. SE27 ..... 5B 122
Roxburn Way. Ruis 3H 41
Roxby Pl. SW6 ..... 6J 83
Roxeth. **2H 43**
Roxeth Ct. Ashf 5C 112
Roxeth Grn. Av. Harr 3F 43
Roxeth Gro. Harr 4F 43
Roxeth Hill. Harr 2H 43
Roxford Clo. Shep 5G 131
Roxley Rd. SE13 ..... 6D 106
Roxton Gdns. Croy 5C 154
Roxwell. NW1 ..... 6F 49
(off Hartland Rd.)
Roxwell Rd. W12 ..... 2C 82
Roxwell Rd. Bark 2A 74
Roxwell Trad. Pk. E17 ..... 7A 34
Roxwell Way. Wfd G 7F 21
Roxy Av. Romf 7C 38
Royal Academy of Arts. 7G 67 (3A 166)
Royal Academy of Music. 4H 159
Royal Air Force Memorial. 1J 85 (5F 167)
Royal Albert Hall. 2B 84 (7A 164)
Royal Albert Roundabout. (Junct.) 7C 72
Royal Albert Way. E16 ..... 7B 72
Royal Arc. W1 ..... 3A 166
Royal Arsenal West. SE18 ... 3F 91
Royal Artillery Mus. of Fire Power, The. ... 3F 91
Royal Av. SW3 ... 5D 84 (5E 170)
Royal Av. Wor Pk 2A 148
Royal Av. Ho. SW3 ..... 5D 84 (5E 170)
(off Royal Av.)
Royal Belgrave Ho. SW1 ..... 4F 85 (3K 171)
(off Hugh St.)
Royal Botanic Gardens Kew, The. 1E 98
Royal Ceremonial Dress Collection, The. (Kensington Palace) 1K 83
Royal Cir. SE27 ..... 3A 122
Royal Clo. N16 ..... 1E 50
Royal Clo. SE8 ..... 6B 88
Royal Clo. SW19 ..... 2F 119
Royal Clo. Ilf 7A 38
Royal Clo. Uxb 6B 58
Royal Clo. Wor Pk 2A 148
Royal College of Art. 2B 84 (7A 164)
Royal College of Music. 3B 84 (1A 170)
Royal College of Obstetricians & Gynaecologists. 4D 66 (3E 158)
Royal College of Surgeons. 6K 67 (7H 161)
Royal College St. NW1 ..... 7G 49
Royal Connaught Apartments. E16 ..... 1B 90
(off Connaught Rd.)
Royal Ct. EC3 ..... 6D 68 (1F 169)
(off Finch La.)
Royal Ct. SE16 ..... 3B 88
Royal Ct. Enf 6K 7
Royal Courts of Justice. 6A 68 (1H 167)
Royal Court Theatre. 4E 84 (4G 171)
(off Sloane Sq.)
Royal Cres. W11 ..... 1F 83
Royal Cres. Ruis 4C 42
Royal Cres. M. W11 ..... 1F 83
Royal Docks Rd. E6 ..... 6F 73
Royal Dri. N11 ..... 5K 15
Royal Duchess M. SW12 ..... 7F 103
Royal Epping Forest & Chingford (Public) Golf Course. 6K 9
Royal Exchange ... 6D 68 (1F 169)
Royal Exchange Av. EC3 .... 1F 169
Royal Exchange Bldgs. EC3 ..... 1F 169
Royal Festival Hall. 1K 85 (5H 167)
Royal Fusiliers Mus. 3J 169
(in Tower of London, The)
Royal Gdns. W7 ..... 3A 80
Royal Herbert Pavilions. SE18 ..... 1D 108
Royal Hill. SE10 ..... 7E 88
Royal Hill Ct. SE10 ..... 7E 88
(off Greenwich High St.)
Royal Hospital Chelsea Mus. 5E 84 (6G 171)
Royal Hospital Rd. SW3 ..... 6D 84 (7E 170)
Royal La. Uxb & W Dray 5B 58
Royal London Ind. Est. NW10 ..... 2K 63
Royal M. SW1 .... 3F 85 (1K 171)
Royal Mews, The. 3F 85 (1K 171)
Royal Mint Ct. EC3 & E1 ..... 7F 69 (3K 169)
Royal Mint Pl. E1 ..... 7G 69 (2K 169)
Royal Mint St. E1 ..... 7F 69 (2K 169)
Royal National Theatre. 1K 85 (4J 167)
Royal Naval Pl. SE14 ..... 7B 88
Royal Oak Ct. N1 ... 3E 68 (1G 163)
(off Pitfield St.)
Royal Oak Pl. SE22 ..... 6H 105
Royal Oak Rd. E8 ..... 6H 51
Royal Oak Rd. Bexh 5F 111
(in two parts)
Royal Oak Yd. SE1 ..... 2E 86 (7G 169)
Royal Observatory Greenwich. 7F 89
Royal Opera Arc. SW1 ..... 1H 85 (4C 166)
Royal Opera House. 6J 67 (1F 167)
Royal Orchard Clo. SW18 ..... 7G 101
Royal Pde. SE3 ..... 2H 107
Royal Pde. SW6 ..... 7G 83
Royal Pde. W5 ..... 3E 62
Royal Pde. Chst 7G 127
Royal Pde. Dag 6H 57
(off Church St.)
Royal Pde. Rich 1G 99
(off Layton Pl.)
Royal Pde. M. SE3 ..... 2H 107
(off Royal Pde.)
Royal Pde. M. Chst 7G 127
(off Royal Pde.)
Royal Pl. SE10 ..... 7E 88
Royal Rd. E16 ..... 6B 72
Royal Rd. SE17 ... 6B 86 (7K 173)
Royal Rd. Sidc 3D 128
Royal Rd. Tedd 5H 115
Royal Route. Wemb 4G 45
Royal St. SE1 ..... 3K 85 (1H 173)
Royal Tower Lodge. E1 ..... 7G 69 (3K 169)
(off Cartwright St.)
Royalty M. W1 .... 6H 67 (1C 166)
Royalty Studios. W11 ..... 6G 65
(off Lancaster Rd.)
Royal Victoria Patriotic Building. SW18 ..... 6B 102
Royal Victoria Pl. E16 ..... 1K 89
Royal Victor Pl. E3 ..... 2K 69
Royal Wlk. Wall 2F 151
Royal Westminster Lodge. SW1 ..... 4H 85 (3C 172)
(off Elverton St.)
Roycraft Av. Bark 2K 73
Roycroft Clo. E18 ..... 1K 35
Roycroft Clo. SW2 ..... 1A 122
Roydene Rd. SE18 ..... 6J 91
Roydon Clo. SW11 ..... 2D 102
(off Battersea Pk. Rd.)
Roydon Clo. Lou 1H 21
Roy Gdns. Ilf 4J 37
Roy Gro. Hamp 6F 115
Royle Building. N1 ..... 2C 68
(off Wenlock Rd.)
Royle Cres. W13 ..... 4A 62
Roymount Ct. Twic 3J 115
Roy Rd. N'wd 1H 23
Roy Sq. E14 ..... 7A 70
Royston Av. E4 ..... 5H 19
Royston Av. Sutt 3B 150
Royston Av. Wall 4H 151
Royston Clo. Houn 1K 95
Royston Clo. W on T 7J 131
Royston Ct. E13 ..... 1J 71
(off Stopford Rd.)
Royston Ct. SE24 ..... 6C 104
Royston Ct. Rich 1F 99
Royston Gdns. Ilf 6B 36
Royston Ho. N11 ..... 4J 15
Royston Ho. SE15 ..... 6H 87
(off Friary Est.)
Royston Pde. Ilf 6B 36
Royston Rd. SE20 ..... 1K 141
Royston Rd. Rich 5E 98
Roystons, The. Surb 5H 135
Royston St. E2 ..... 2J 69
Rozel Ct. N1 ..... 1E 68
Rozel Rd. SW4 ..... 3G 103
Rozel Ter. Croy 2C 152
(off Church Rd.)
Rubastic Rd. S'hall 3A 78
Rubens Pl. SW4 ..... 4J 103
Rubens Rd. N'holt 2A 60

Rubens St. SE6 2B 124
Ruby M. E17 3C 34
Ruby Rd. E17 3C 34
Ruby St. NW10 7K 45
Ruby St. SE15 6H 87
Ruby Triangle. SE15 6H 87
Ruckholt Clo. E10 3D 52
Ruckholt Rd. E10 4D 52
Rucklidge Av. NW10 2B 64
Rucklidge Pas. NW10 2B 64
(off Rucklidge Av.)
Rudall Cres. NW3 4B 48
Rudbeck Ho. SE15 7G 87
(off Peckham Pk. Rd.)
Ruddington Clo. E5 4A 52
Ruddock Clo. Edgw 7D 12
Ruddstreet Clo. SE18 4F 91
Ruddy Way. NW7 6G 13
Rudge Ho. SE16 3G 87
(off Jamaica Rd.)
Rudgwick Ct. SE18 4C 90
(off Woodville St., in two parts)
Rudgwick Ter. NW8 1C 66
Rudland Rd. Bexh 3H 111
Rudloe Rd. SW12 7G 103
Rudolf Pl. SW8 6J 85 (7F 173)
Rudolph Rd. E13 2H 71
Rudolph Rd. NW6 2J 65
Rudyard Gro. NW7 6D 12
Ruegg Ho. SE18 6E 90
(off Woolwich Comn.)
Ruffetts Clo. S Croy 7H 153
Ruffetts, The. S Croy 7H 153
Ruffle Clo. W Dray 2A 76
Rufford Clo. Harr 6A 26
Rufford St. N1 1J 67
Rufford Tower. W3 1H 81
Rufforth Ct. NW9 1A 28
(off Pageant Av.)
Rufus Clo. Ruis 3C 42
Rufus Ho. SE1 3F 87 (7K 169)
(off Abbey St.)
Rufus St. N1 3E 68 (2G 163)
Rugby Av. N9 1A 18
Rugby Av. Gnfd 6H 43
Rugby Av. Wemb 5B 44
Rugby Clo. Harr 4J 25
Rugby Gdns. Dag 6C 56
Rugby Mans. W14 4G 83
(off Bishop King's Rd.)
Rugby Rd. NW9 4H 27
Rugby Rd. W4 2A 82
Rugby Rd. Dag 6B 56
Rugby Rd. Twic 5J 97
Rugby St. WC1 4K 67 (4G 161)
Rugg St. E14 7C 70
Rugless Ho. E14 2E 88
(off E. Ferry Rd.)
Rugmere. NW1 7E 48
(off Ferdinand St.)
Ruislip. 1G 41
Ruislip Clo. Gnfd 4F 61
Ruislip Common. 4E 22
Ruislip Ct. Ruis 2H 41
Ruislip Gardens. 3J 41
Ruislip Lido Railway. 4F 23
Ruislip Manor. 1J 41
Ruislip Rd. Gnfd 3E 60
Ruislip Rd. N'holt & S'hall 1A 60
Ruislip Rd. E. Gnfd & W7 4H 61
Ruislip St. SW17 4D 120
Rumball Ho. SE5 7E 86
(off Harris St.)
Rumbold Rd. SW6 7K 83
Rum Clo. E1 7J 69
Rumford Ho. SE1 3C 86
(off Tiverton St.)
Rumney Ct. N'holt 2B 60
(off Parkfield Dri.)
Rumsey Clo. Hamp 6D 114
Rumsey M. N4 3B 50
Rumsey Rd. SW9 3K 103
Runacres Ct. SE17 5C 86
Runbury Circ. NW9 2K 45
Runcorn Clo. N17 4H 33
Runcorn Pl. W11 7G 65
Rundell Cres. NW4 5D 28
Rundell Tower. SW8 1K 103
Runes Clo. Mitc 4B 138
Runnel Fld. Harr 3J 43
Running Horse Yd. Bren 6E 80
Runnymede. SW19 1A 138
Runnymede Clo. Twic 6F 97
Runnymede Ct. SW15 1C 118
Runnymede Cres. SW16 1H 139
Runnymede Gdns. Gnfd 2J 61
Runnymede Gdns. Twic 6F 97
Runnymede Ho. E9 4A 52
Runnymede Rd. Twic 6F 97
Runway, The. Ruis 5K 41
Rupack St. SE16 2J 87
Rupert Av. Wemb 5E 44
Rupert Ct. W1 7H 67 (2C 166)
Rupert Ct. W Mol 4E 132
(off St Peters Rd.)
Rupert Gdns. SW9 2B 104
Rupert Ho. SE11 4A 86 (4K 173)
Rupert Rd. N19 3H 49
(in two parts)
Rupert Rd. NW6 2H 65
Rupert Rd. W4 3A 82
Rupert St. W1 7H 67 (2C 166)
Rural Way. SW16 7F 121
Rusbridge Clo. E8 5G 51
Ruscoe Rd. E16 6H 71
Ruscombe Way. Felt 7H 95
Rusham Rd. SW12 6D 102
Rushbrook Cres. E17 1B 34
Rushbrook Rd. SE9 2G 127
Rushbury Ct. Hamp 1E 132
Rush Common M. SW2 7K 103
Rushcroft Rd. E4 7J 19
Rushcroft Rd. SW2 4A 104
Rushcutters Ct. SE16 4A 88
(off Boat Lifter Way)
Rushden Clo. SE19 7D 122
Rushdene. SE2 3C 92
(in two parts)
Rushdene Av. Barn 7H 5
Rushdene Clo. N'holt 2A 60
Rushdene Cres. N'holt 2K 59
Rushdene Rd. Pinn 6B 24
Rushden Gdns. NW7 6K 13
Rushden Gdns. Ilf 2E 36
Rushen Wlk. Cars 1B 150
Rushett Clo. Th Dit 1B 146
Rushett Rd. Th Dit 7B 134
Rushey Clo. N Mald 4K 135
Rushey Grn. SE6 7D 106
Rushey Hill. Enf 4E 6
Rushey Mead. SE4 5C 106
Rushford Rd. SE4 6B 106
Rush Green. 1K 57
Rush Grn. Gdns. Romf 1J 57
Rush Grn. Rd. Romf 1H 57
Rushgrove Av. NW9 5A 28
Rushgrove Pde. NW9 5A 28
Rushgrove St. SE18 4D 90
Rush Hill M. SW11 3E 102
(off Rush Hill Rd.)
Rush Hill Rd. SW11 3E 102
Rushley Clo. Kes 4B 156
Rushmead. E2 3H 69
Rushmead. Rich 3B 116
Rushmead Clo. Croy 4F 153
Rushmead Clo. Edgw 2C 12
Rushmere Ct. Wor Pk 2C 148
Rushmere Pl. SW19 5F 119
Rushmon Pl. Cheam 6G 149
Rushmon Vs. N Mald 4B 136
Rushmoor Clo. Pinn 4K 23
Rushmore Clo. Brom 3C 144
Rushmore Cres. E5 4K 51
Rushmore Ho. W14 3G 83
(off Russell Rd.)
Rushmore Rd. E5 4J 51
(in three parts)
Rusholme Av. Dag 3G 57
Rusholme Gro. SE19 5E 122
Rusholme Rd. SW15 6F 101
Rushout Av. Harr 6B 26
Rush, The. SW19 1H 137
(off Kingston Rd.)
Rushton Ho. SW8 2H 103
Rushton St. N1 2D 68
Rushworth Av. NW4 3C 28
Rushworth Gdns. NW4 3C 28
Rushworth St. SE1 2B 86 (6B 168)
Rushy Mdw. La. Cars 3C 150
Ruskin Av. E12 6C 54
Ruskin Av. Felt 6H 95
Ruskin Av. Rich 7G 81
(in two parts)
Ruskin Av. Well 2A 110
Ruskin Clo. NW11 6K 29
Ruskin Ct. N21 7E 6
Ruskin Ct. SE5 3D 104
(off Champion Hill)
Ruskin Dri. Well 3A 110
Ruskin Dri. Wor Pk 2D 148
Ruskin Gdns. W5 4D 62
Ruskin Gdns. Harr 5F 27
Ruskin Gro. Well 2A 110
Ruskin Ho. SW1 4H 85 (4D 172)
(off Herrick St.)
Ruskin Ho. S Croy 5D 152
(off Selsdon Rd.)
Ruskin Mans. W14 6G 83
(off Queen's Club Gdns.)
Ruskin Pde. S Croy 5D 152
(off Selsdon Rd.)
Ruskin Pk. Ho. SE5 3D 104
Ruskin Rd. N17 1F 33
Ruskin Rd. Belv 4G 93
Ruskin Rd. Cars 5D 150
Ruskin Rd. Croy 2B 152
Ruskin Rd. Iswth 3K 97
Ruskin Rd. S'hall 7C 60
Ruskin Wlk. N9 2B 18
Ruskin Wlk. SE24 5C 104
Ruskin Wlk. Brom 6D 144
Ruskin Way. SW19 1B 138
Rusland Heights. Harr 4J 25
Rusland Pk. Rd. Harr 4J 25
Rusper Clo. NW2 3E 46
Rusper Clo. Stan 4H 11
Rusper Ct. SW9 2J 103
(off Clapham Rd.)
Rusper Rd. N22 & N17 2B 32
Rusper Rd. Dag 6C 56
Russell Av. N22 2A 32
Russell Clo. NW10 7J 45
Russell Clo. SE7 7A 90
Russell Clo. W4 6B 82
Russell Clo. Beck 3D 142
Russell Clo. Bexh 4G 111
Russell Clo. Ruis 2A 42
Russell Ct. E10 7D 34
Russell Ct. N14 6C 6
Russell Ct. SE15 2H 105
(off Heaton Rd.)
Russell Ct. SW1 5B 166
Russell Ct. SW16 5K 121
Russell Ct. WC1 4E 160
Russell Ct. New Bar 4F 5
Russell Ct. Wall 5G 151
(off Ross Rd.)
Russell Flint Ho. E16 1K 89
(off Pankhurst Av.)
Russell Gdns. N20 2H 15
Russell Gdns. NW11 6G 29
Russell Gdns. W14 3G 83
Russell Gdns. Ilf 7H 37
Russell Gdns. Rich 2C 116
Russell Gdns. W Dray 5C 76
Russell Gdns. M. W14 2G 83
Russell Gro. NW7 5F 13
Russell Gro. SW9 7A 86
Russell Ho. E14 6C 70
(off Saracen St.)
Russell Ho. SW1 5G 85 (5A 172)
(off Cambridge St.)
Russell Kerr Clo. W4 7J 81
Russell La. N20 2H 15
Russell Lodge. E4 2K 19
Russell Lodge. SE1 3D 86
(off Spurgeon St.)
Russell Mead. Har W 1K 25
Russell Pde. NW11 6G 29
(off Golders Grn. Rd.)
Russell Pl. NW3 5C 48
Russell Pl. SE16 3A 88
Russell Pl. Sutt 7K 149
Russell Rd. E4 4G 19
Russell Rd. E10 6D 34
Russell Rd. E16 6J 71
Russell Rd. E17 3B 34
Russell Rd. N8 6H 31
Russell Rd. N13 6E 16
Russell Rd. N15 5E 32
Russell Rd. N20 2H 15
Russell Rd. NW9 6B 28
Russell Rd. SW19 7J 119
Russell Rd. W14 3G 83
Russell Rd. Buck H 1E 20
Russell Rd. Enf 1A 8
Russell Rd. Mitc 3C 138
Russell Rd. N'holt 5G 43
Russell Rd. Shep 7E 130
Russell Rd. Twic 6K 97
Russell Rd. W on T 6J 131
Russell's Footpath.
SW16 5J 121
Russell Sq. WC1 5J 67 (4E 160)
Russell St. WC2 7J 67 (2F 167)
Russell Wlk. Rich 6F 99
Russell Way. Sutt 5K 149
Russell Yd. SW15 4G 101
Russet Av. Shep 3G 131
Russet Clo. Uxb 4E 58
Russet Cres. N7 5K 49
Russet Dri. Croy 1A 154
Russets Clo. E4 4A 20
Russett Way. SE13 2D 106
Russia Ct. EC2 7D 162
Russia Dock Rd. SE16 1A 88
Russia La. E2 2J 69
Russia Row. EC2
6C 68 (1D 168)
Russia Wlk. SE16 2A 88
Russington Rd. Shep 6F 131
Rusthall Av. W4 4K 81
Rusthall Clo. Croy 6J 141
Rustic Av. SW16 7F 121
Rustic Pl. Wemb 4D 44
Rustic Wlk. E16 6K 71
(off Lambert Rd.)
Rustington Wlk. Mord 7H 137
Ruston Av. Surb 7H 135
Ruston Gdns. N14 6K 5
Ruston M. W11 6G 65
Ruston Rd. SE18 3C 90
Ruston St. E3 1B 70
Rust Sq. SE5 7D 86
Rutford Rd. SW16 5J 121
Ruth Clo. Stan 4F 27
Ruth Ct. E3 2A 70
Rutherford Clo. Sutt 6B 150
Rutherford Clo. Uxb 4B 58
Rutherford Ho. E1 4H 69
(off Brady St.)
Rutherford Ho. Wemb 3J 45
(off Barnhill Rd.)
Rutherford St. SW1
4H 85 (3C 172)
Rutherford Tower. S'hall 6F 61
Rutherford Way. Bus H 1C 10
Rutherford Way. Wemb 4G 45
Rutherglen Rd. SE2 6A 92
Rutherwyke Clo. Eps 6C 148
Ruth Ho. W10 4G 65
(off Kensal Rd.)
Ruthin Clo. NW9 6A 28
Ruthin Rd. SE3 6J 89
Ruthven St. E9 1K 69
Rutland Av. Sidc 7A 110
Rutland Clo. SW14 3H 99
Rutland Clo. SW19 7C 120
Rutland Clo. Bex 2D 128
Rutland Clo. Chess 6F 147
Rutland Ct. SE5 4D 104
Rutland Ct. SE9 2G 127
Rutland Ct. SW7 7D 164
Rutland Ct. W3 6G 63
Rutland Ct. Chst 1E 144
Rutland Ct. Enf 5C 8
Rutland Ct. King T 4D 134
(off Palace Rd.)
Rutland Dri. Mord 6H 137
Rutland Dri. Rich 1D 116
Rutland Gdns. N4 6B 32
Rutland Gdns. SW7
2C 84 (7D 164)
Rutland Gdns. W13 5A 62
Rutland Gdns. Croy 4E 152
Rutland Gdns. Dag 5C 56
Rutland Gdns. M.
SW7 2C 84 (7D 164)
Rutland Ga. SW7
2C 84 (7D 164)
Rutland Ga. Belv 5H 93
Rutland Ga. Brom 4H 143
Rutland Ga. M. SW7 7C 164
Rutland Gro. W6 5D 82
Rutland Ho. W8 3K 83
(off Marloes Rd.)
Rutland Ho. N'holt 6E 42
(off Farmlands, The)
Rutland M. NW8 1K 65
Rutland M. E. SW7 1D 170
Rutland M. S. SW7 1C 170
Rutland M. W. SW7 1C 170
Rutland Pk. NW2 6E 46
Rutland Pk. SE6 2B 124
Rutland Pk. Gdns.
NW2 6E 46
(off Rutland Pk.)
Rutland Pk. Mans.
NW2 6E 46
Rutland Pl. EC1 4B 68 (5B 162)
Rutland Pl. Bush 1C 10
Rutland Rd. E7 7B 54
Rutland Rd. E9 1K 69
Rutland Rd. E11 5K 35
Rutland Rd. E17 6C 34
Rutland Rd. SW19 7C 120
Rutland Rd. Harr 6G 25
Rutland Rd. Hay 4F 77
Rutland Rd. Ilf 3F 55
Rutland Rd. S'hall 5E 60
Rutland Rd. Twic 2H 115
Rutland St. SW7 3C 84 (1D 170)
Rutland Wlk. SE6 2B 124
Rutley Clo. SE17 6B 86 (7K 173)
Rutlish Rd. SW19 1J 137
Rutter Gdns. Mitc 4A 138
Rutters Clo. W Dray 2C 76
Rutt's Ter. SE14 1K 105
Rutts, The. Bush 1C 10
Ruvigny Gdns. SW15 3F 101
Ruxley. 6D 128
Ruxley Clo. Eps 5H 147
Ruxley Clo. Sidc 6D 128
Ruxley Corner Ind. Est.
Sidc 6D 128
Ruxley Ct. Eps 5J 147
Ruxley Cres. Clay 6B 146
Ruxley La. Eps 6H 147
Ruxley M. Eps 5H 147
Ruxley Ridge. Clay 7A 146
Ruxley Towers. Clay 7A 146
Ryalls Ct. N20 3J 15
Ryan Clo. SE3 4K 107
Ryan Clo. Ruis 1K 41
Ryan Ct. SW16 7J 121
Ryan Dri. Bren 6A 80
Rycott Path. SE22 7G 105
Rycroft Way. N17 3F 33
Ryculff Sq. SE3 2H 107
Rydal Clo. NW4 1G 29
Rydal Ct. Edgw 5A 12
Rydal Ct. Wemb 7F 27
Rydal Cres. Gnfd 3B 62
Rydal Dri. Bexh 1G 111

Rydal Dri. W Wick........2G 155
Rydal Gdns. NW9.........5A 28
Rydal Gdns. SW15.......5A 118
Rydal Gdns. Houn.........6F 97
Rydal Gdns. Wemb.........1C 44
Rydal Mt. Brom..........4H 143
Rydal Rd. SW16..........4H 121
Rydal Water. NW1
..........3G 67 (2A 160)
Rydal Way. Enf............6D 8
Rydal Way. Ruis...........4A 42
Rydens Ho. SE9..........3A 126
Rydens Rd. W on T.......7C 132
Ryde Pl. Twic............6D 98
Ryder Clo. Brom.........5K 125
Ryder Ct. E10.............2D 52
Ryder Ct. SW1............4B 166
Ryder Dri. SE16...........5H 87
Ryder Ho. E1.............4J 69
(off Colebert Av.)
Ryder M. E9..............5J 51
Ryder's Ter. NW8..........2A 66
Ryder St. SW1....1G 85 (4B 166)
Ryder Yd. SW1....1G 85 (4B 166)
Ryde Va. Rd. SW12.......2G 121
Rydon M. SW19..........7E 118
Rydons Clo. SE9.........3C 108
Rydon St. N1.............1C 68
Rydston Clo. N7...........7J 49
Rye Clo. Bex............6H 111
Ryecotes Mead. SE21.....1E 122
Ryecroft Av. Ilf...........2F 37
Ryecroft Av. Twic..........7F 97
Ryecroft Lodge. SW16.....6B 122
Ryecroft Rd. SE13........5E 106
Ryecroft Rd. SW16.......6A 122
Ryecroft Rd. Orp.........6H 145
Ryecroft St. SW6.........1K 101
Ryedale. SE22...........6H 105
Ryefield Av. Uxb..........7D 40
Ryefield Ct. N'wd..........2J 23
Ryefield Cres. N'wd........2J 23
Ryefield Path. SW15......1C 118
Ryefield Pde. N'wd.........2J 23
(off Joel St.)
Ryefield Rd. SE19........6C 122
Rye Hill Pk. SE15.........4J 105
Rye Ho. SE16.............2J 87
(off Swan Rd.)
Rye Ho. SW1......5F 85 (5J 171)
(off Ebury Bri. Rd.)
Ryeland Clo. W Dray.......6A 58
Ryelands Cres. SE12......6A 108
Rye La. SE15............1G 105
Rye Pas. SE15...........3G 105
Rye Rd. SE15............4K 105
Rye, The. N14.............7C 6
Rye Wlk. SW15...........5F 101
Rye Way. Edgw...........6A 12
Ryfold Rd. SW19.........3J 119
Ryhope Rd. N11...........4A 16
Ryland Clo. Felt..........4H 113
Rylandes Rd. NW2.........3C 46
Ryland Rd. NW5...........6F 49
Rylett Cres. W12..........2B 82
Rylett Rd. W12............2B 82
Rylston Rd. N13...........3J 17
Rylston Rd. SW6...........6H 83
Rymer Rd. Croy..........7E 140
Rymer St. SE24..........6B 104
Rymill St. E16............1E 90
Rysbrack St. SW3
..........3D 84 (1E 170)
Rythe Ct. Th Dit..........7A 134

S

Sabah Ct. Ashf.........4C 112
Sabbarton St. E16.........6H 71
Sabella Ct. E3............2B 70
Sabine Rd. SW11........3D 102
Sable Clo. Houn...........3A 96
Sable St. N1..............7B 50
Sach Rd. E5..............2H 51
Sackville Av. Brom.......1J 155
Sackville Clo. Harr.........3H 43
Sackville Gdns. Ilf.........1D 54
Sackville Ho. SW16.......3J 121
Sackville Rd. Sutt........7J 149
Sackville St. W1...7G 67 (3B 166)
Saddlebrook Pk. Sun......7G 113
Saddlers Clo. Pinn.........6A 10
Saddlers M. SW8.........1J 103
Saddlers M. King T.......1C 134
Saddlers M. Wemb........4K 43
Saddlescombe Way. N12....5D 14
Saddle Yd. W1.....1F 85 (4J 165)
Sadler Clo. Mitc..........2D 138
Sadler Ho. EC1.....3B 68 (1K 161)
(off Spa Grn. Est.)
Sadlers Ride. W Mol.....2G 133
Sadler's Wells Theatre.
........3A 68 (1K 161)
Saffron Av. E14............7F 71
Saffron Clo. NW11.........6H 29
Saffron Clo. Croy.........6J 139
Saffron Ct. E15............5G 53
(off Maryland Pk.)
Saffron Ct. Felt...........7E 94
Saffron Hill. EC1...5A 68 (5K 161)
Saffron Rd. Romf..........2K 39
Saffron St. EC1....5A 68 (5K 161)
Saffron Way. Surb........1D 146
Saffron Wharf. SE1
..........2F 87 (6K 169)
(off Shad Thames)
Sage Clo. E6..............5D 72
Sage St. E1...............7J 69
Sage Way. WC1..........2G 161
Sahara Ct. S'hall..........7C 60
Saigasso Clo. E16.........6B 72
Sailmakers Ct. SW6.......2A 102
Sail St. SE11......4K 85 (3H 173)
Saimel. NW9...............7G 13
(off Satchell Mead)
Sainfoin Rd. SW17.......2E 120
Sainsbury Rd. SE19.......5E 122
St Agatha's Dri. King T.....6F 117
St Agatha's Gro. Cars.....1D 150
St Agnes Clo. E9..........1J 69
St Agnes Pl. SE11.........6A 86
St Agnes Well. EC1.......3F 163
St Aidans Ct. Bark.........2B 74
St Aidan's Rd. SE22......6H 105
St Aidan's Rd. W13........2B 80
St Alban's Av. E6..........3D 72
St Alban's Av. W4.........4K 81
St Albans Av. Felt........5B 114
St Alban's Clo. NW11.......1J 47
St Albans Ct. EC2.........6D 162
St Alban's Cres. N22.......1A 32
St Alban's Cres. Wfd G.....7D 20
St Alban's Gdns. Tedd.....5A 116
St Alban's Gro. W8.........3K 83
St Alban's Gro. Cars......7C 138
St Alban's La. NW11.......1J 47
St Albans Mans. W8.......3K 83
(off Kensington Ct. Pl.)
St Alban's Pl. N1..........1B 68
St Albans Rd. NW5.........3E 48
St Alban's Rd. NW10.......1A 64
St Albans Rd. Barn..........1A 4
St Albans Rd. Ilf...........1K 55
St Alban's Rd. King T.....6E 116
St Alban's Rd. Sutt.......4H 149
St Alban's Rd. Wfd G.......7D 20
St Alban's St. SW1
..........7H 67 (3C 166)
(in two parts)
St Albans Ter. W6..........6G 83
St Albans Tower. E4........6G 19
St Albans Vs. NW5.........3E 48
St Alfege Pas. SE10.......6E 88
St Alfege Rd. SE7..........6B 90
St Alphage Garden.
EC2.......5C 68 (6D 162)
(in two parts)
St Alphage Highwalk.
EC2.............6D 162
St Alphage Ho. EC2.......6E 162
St Alphage Wlk. Edgw......2J 27
St Alphege Rd. N9..........7D 8
St Alphonsus Rd. SW4....4G 103
St Amunds Clo. SE6......4C 124
St Andrew's Av. Wemb.....4A 44
St Andrews Chambers.
W1.......5G 67 (6B 160)
(off Wells St.)
St Andrew's Clo. N12.......4F 15
St Andrew's Clo. NW2......3D 46
St Andrews Clo. SE16......5H 87
St Andrews Clo. SE28......6D 74
St Andrew's Clo. Iswth......1J 97
St Andrew's Clo. Ruis......2B 42
St Andrew's Clo. Shep.....4F 131
St Andrew's Clo. Stan......2C 26
St Andrew's Ct. SW18.....2A 120
St Andrews Ct. Sutt.......3C 150
St Andrews Dri. Stan.......1C 26
St Andrew's Gro. N16......1D 50
St Andrew's Hill. EC4
..........7B 68 (2B 168)
(in two parts)
St Andrews Mans. W1
..........5E 66 (6G 159)
(off Dorset St.)
St Andrews Mans. W14.....6G 83
(off St Andrews Rd.)
St Andrew's M. N16........1E 50
St Andrew's M. SE3........7J 89
St Andrews M. SW12......1H 121
St Andrew's Pl. NW1
..........4F 67 (3K 159)
St Andrew's Rd. E11.......6G 35
St Andrew's Rd. E13.......3K 71
St Andrew's Rd. E17.......2K 33
St Andrew's Rd. N9..........7D 8
St Andrew's Rd. NW9.......1K 45
St Andrew's Rd. NW10......6D 46
St Andrew's Rd. NW11......6H 29
St Andrew's Rd. W3........7A 64
St Andrews Rd. W7.........2J 79
St Andrew's Rd. W14.......6G 83
St Andrew's Rd. Cars......3C 150
St Andrew's Rd. Croy......4C 152
St Andrew's Rd. Enf..........3J 7
St Andrew's Rd. Ilf.........7D 36
St Andrew's Rd. Romf......6K 39
St Andrew's Rd. Sidc......3D 128
St Andrew's Rd. Surb.....6D 134
St Andrew's Rd. Uxb.......1A 58
St Andrews Sq. W11........6G 65
St Andrew's Sq. Surb.....6D 134
St Andrew's Tower. S'hall....7G 61
(off Baird Av.)
St Andrew St. EC1 & EC4....5A 68
St Andrews Way. E3........4D 70
St Andrew's Wharf. SE1
..........2F 87 (6K 169)
St Anna Rd. Barn............5A 4
St Anne's Clo. N6..........3E 48
St Anne's Ct. NW6..........1G 65
St Anne's Ct. W1.....6H 67 (1C 166)
St Anne's Ct. W Wick......4G 155
St Anne's Flats. NW1
..........3H 67 (1C 160)
(off Doric Way)
St Anne's Gdns. NW10......3F 63
St Anne's Pas. E14.........6B 70
St Anne's Rd. E11..........2F 53
St Anne's Rd. Wemb........5D 44
St Anne's Row. E14.........6B 70
St Anne's Trad. Est. E14.....6B 70
(off St Anne's Row)
St Anne St. E14............6B 70
St Ann's. Bark..............1G 73
St Ann's Ct. NW4...........3D 28
St Ann's Cres. SW18......6K 101
St Ann's Gdns. NW5........6E 48
St Ann's Hill. SW18.......5K 101
St Ann's Ho. WC1
..........3A 68 (2J 161)
(off Margery St.)
St Ann's La. SW1
..........3H 85 (2D 172)
St Ann's Pk. Rd. SW18....6A 102
St Ann's Pas. SW13.......3A 100
St Ann's Rd. N9.............2A 18
St Ann's Rd. N15...........5B 32
St Ann's Rd. SW13........2B 100
St Ann's Rd. W11...........7F 65
St Ann's Rd. Bark..........1G 73
St Ann's Rd. Harr...........6J 25
St Ann's Shop. Cen. Harr....6J 25
St Ann's St. SW1
..........3H 85 (1D 172)
St Ann's Ter. NW8..........2B 66
St Ann's Vs. W11...........1F 83
St Ann's Way. S Croy......6B 152
St Anselm's Pl. W1
..........7F 67 (2J 165)
St Anselm's Rd. Hay........2H 77
St Anthony's Av. Wfd G......6F 21
St Anthony's Clo. E1........1G 87
St Anthony's Clo. SW17.....2C 120
St Anthony's Flats. NW1.....2H 67
(off Aldenham St.)
St Anthony's Way. Felt......4H 95
St Antony's Rd. E7.........7K 53
St Arvan's Clo. Croy.......3E 152
St Asaph Rd. SE4.........3K 105
St Aubins Ct. N1...........1D 68
St Aubyn's Av. SW19......5H 119
St Aubyn's Av. Houn........5E 96
St Aubyn's Rd. SE19......6F 123
St Audrey Av. Bexh.......2G 111
St Augustine's Av. W5......2E 62
St Augustine's Av. Brom....5C 144
St Augustine's Av. S Croy...6C 152
St Augustine's Av. Wemb....3E 44
St Augustine's Ho. NW1
..........3H 67 (1C 160)
(off Werrington St.)
St Augustine's Mans. SW1
..........4G 85 (4B 172)
(off Bloomburg St.)
St Augustine's Path. N5.....4C 50
St Augustine's Rd. NW1.....7H 49
St Augustine's Rd. Belv.....4F 93
St Austell Clo. Edgw........2F 27
St Austell Rd. SE13.......2E 106
St Awdry's Rd. Bark........7H 55
St Awdry's Wlk. Bark........7G 55
St Barnabas Clo. SE22.....5E 104
St Barnabas Clo. Beck.....2E 142
St Barnabas Ct. Har W......1G 25
St Barnabas Gdns.
W Mol..............5E 132
St Barnabas Rd. E17........6C 34
St Barnabas Rd. Mitc......7E 120
St Barnabas Rd. Sutt......5B 150
St Barnabas Rd. Wfd G......1K 35
St Barnabas St. SW1
..........5E 84 (5H 171)
St Barnabas Ter. E9.........5K 51
St Barnabas Vs. SW8......1J 103
St Bartholomew's Clo.
SE26............4H 123
St Bartholomew's Ct. E6....2C 72
(off St Bartholomew's Rd.)
St Bartholomew's Hospital Mus.
..............6B 162
St Bartholomew's Rd. E6....2D 72
St Benedict's Clo. SW17....5E 120
St Benet's Clo. SW17......2C 120
St Benet's Gro. Cars......7A 138
St Benet's Pl. EC3
..........7D 68 (2F 169)
St Bernards. Croy........3E 152
St Bernard's Clo. SE27....4D 122
St Bernards Ho. E14........3E 88
(off Galbraith St.)
St Bernard's Rd. E6.........1B 72
St Blaise Av. Brom........2K 143
St Botolph Row. EC3
..........6F 69 (1J 169)
St Botolph St. EC3
..........6F 69 (7J 163)
St Brelades Ct. N1..........1E 68
St Bride's Av. EC4........1A 168
St Bride's Av. Edgw........1F 27
St Bride's Church.
........6B 68 (1A 168)
St Brides Clo. Eri..........2D 92
St Bride's Crypt Mus.
........6B 68 (1A 168)
(off St Bride's Church)
St Bride's Pas. EC4.......1A 168
St Bride St. EC4....6B 68 (7A 162)
St Catherines Clo. Chess....6D 146
St Catherine's Clo. SW17...2C 120
St Catherine's Ct. W4.......3A 82
St Catherines Ct. Felt......1J 113
St Catherine's Dri. SE14....2K 105
St Catherine's Farm Ct.
Ruis..............6E 22
St Catherines M. SW3
..........4D 84 (3E 170)
St Catherine's Rd. E4.......2H 19
St Catherine's Rd. Ruis.....6F 23
St Catherines Tower. E10....7D 34
St Cecilia's Clo. Sutt......1G 149
St Chads Clo. Surb.......7C 134
St Chad's Gdns. Romf......7E 38
St Chad's Pl. WC1
..........3J 67 (1F 161)
St Chad's Rd. Romf.........7E 38
St Chad's St. WC1
..........3J 67 (1F 161)
(in two parts)
St Charles Pl. W10.........5G 65
St Charles Sq. W10.........5F 65
St Christopher Rd. Uxb.....6A 58
St Christopher's Clo. Iswth...1J 97
St Christophers Dri. Hay....7K 59
St Christopher's Gdns.
T Hth............3A 140
St Christopher's Ho. NW1...2G 67
(off Bridgeway St.)
St Christopher's M. Wall...5G 151
St Christopher's Pl. W1
..........6E 66 (7H 159)
St Clair Clo. Ilf............2D 36
St Clair Dri. Wor Pk.......3D 148
St Clair Rd. E13............2K 71
St Clair's Rd. Croy........2E 152
St Clare Bus. Pk. Hamp....6G 115
St Clare St. EC3....6F 69 (1J 169)
St Clement's Ct. EC4......2F 169
St Clement's Ct. N7.........6K 49
St Clements Ct. SE14......6K 87
(off Myers La.)
St Clements Ct. W11........7F 65
(off Stoneleigh St.)
St Clement's Heights.
SE26.............3G 123
St Clement's La. WC2
..........6K 67 (1H 167)
St Clements Mans. SW6....6F 83
(off Lillie Rd.)
St Clements St. N7.........6A 50
St Clements Yd. SE22.....4F 105
St Cloud Rd. SE27........4C 122
St Columbas Ho. E17......4D 34
St Crispin's Clo. NW3.......4C 48
St Crispin's Clo. S'hall......6D 60
St Cross St. EC1...5A 68 (5K 161)
St Cuthbert's Rd. NW2......6H 47
St Cyprian's St. SW17.....4D 120
St Daniel Ct. Beck........7C 124
(off Brackley Rd.)
St Davids Clo. SE16........5H 87
(off Masters Dri.)
St David's Clo. Wemb.......3J 45
St David's Clo. W Wick....7D 142
St David's Dri. Edgw........1F 27
St Davids M. E3............3A 70
(off Morgan St.)
St David's Pl. NW4..........7D 28
St Davids Sq. E14..........5D 88
St Denis Rd. SE27.........4D 122
St Dionis Rd. SW6........2H 101
St Domingo Ho. SE18......3D 90
(off Leda Rd.)
St Donatt's Rd. SE14......1B 106
St Dunstan's. (Junct.)......6H 149

St Dunstan's All. EC3......2G 169
St Dunstans Av. W3......7K 63
St Dunstan's Clo. Hay......5H 77
St Dunstan's Ct. EC4......6A 68 (1K 167)
St Dunstan's Gdns. W3......7K 63
St Dunstans Hill. EC3......7E 68 (3G 169)
St Dunstan's Hill. Sutt......5G 149
St Dunstan's La. EC3......7E 68 (3G 169)
St Dunstan's La. Beck......6E 142
St Dunstan's Rd. E7......6K 53
St Dunstan's Rd. SE25......4F 141
St Dunstan's Rd. W6......5F 83
St Dunstan's Rd. W7......2J 79
St Dunstan's Rd. Felt......3H 113
St Dunstan's Rd. Houn......2K 95 (in two parts)
St Edmund's Av. Ruis......6F 23
St Edmund's Clo. NW8......1D 66
St Edmund's Clo. SW17......2C 120
St Edmunds Clo. Eri......2D 92
St Edmund's Ct. NW8......1D 66 (off St Edmund's Ter.)
St Edmund's Dri. Stan......1A 26
St Edmund's La. Twic......7F 97
St Edmund's Rd. N9......7B 8
St Edmund's Rd. Ilf......6D 36
St Edmunds Sq. SW13......6E 82
St Edmund's Ter. NW8......1C 66
St Edward's Clo. NW11......6J 29
St Edwards Ct. E10......7D 34
St Edwards Ct. NW11......6J 29
St Edwards Way. Romf......5K 39
St Egberts Way. E4......1K 19
St Elizabeth Ct. E10......7D 34
St Elmo Rd. W12......1B 82 (in two parts)
St Elmos Rd. SE16......2A 88
St Erkenwald M. Bark......1H 73
St Erkenwald Rd. Bark......1H 73
St Ermin's Hill. SW1......1C 172
St Ervan's Rd. W10......5H 65
St Eugene Ct. NW6......1G 65 (off Salusbury Rd.)
St Fabian Tower. E4......6G 19
St Faith's Clo. Enf......1H 7
St Faith's Rd. SE21......1B 122
St Fidelis Rd. Eri......4K 93
St Fillans Rd. SE6......1E 124
St Frances Way. Ilf......4H 55
St Francis Clo. Orp......6J 145
St Francis' Ho. NW1......2H 67 (off Bridgeway St.)
St Francis Rd. SE22......4E 104
St Francis Rd. Eri......4K 93
St Francis Tower. E4......6G 19 (off Burnside Av.)
St Frideswides M. E14......6E 70
St Gabriel's Clo. E11......1K 53
St Gabriels Mnr. SE5......1B 104 (off Cormont Rd.)
St Gabriels Rd. NW2......5F 47
St George's Av. E7......7K 53
St George's Av. N7......4H 49
St George's Av. NW9......4K 27
St George's Av. W5......2D 80
St George's Av. S'hall......7D 60
St George's Bldgs. SE1......3B 86 (off St George's Rd.)
St George's Cir. SE1......3B 86 (7A 168)
St George's Clo. NW11......6H 29
St Georges Clo. SE28......6D 74
St George's Clo. SW8......1G 103
St George's Clo. Wemb......3A 44
St George's Ct. E6......4D 72
St Georges Ct. E17......5F 35
St Georges Ct. EC4......6B 68 (7A 162)
St George's Ct. SW15......4H 101
St Georges Ct. Harr......6A 26 (off Kenton Rd.)
St George's Dri. SW1......4F 85 (4K 171)
St George's Dri. Uxb......3B 40
St George's Fields. W2......6C 66 (1D 164)
St George's Gdns. Surb......2H 147
St George's Gro. SW17......3B 120
St George's Ho. NW1......2H 67 (off Bridgeway St.)
St Georges Ind. Est. N17......7G 17
St George's Ind. Est. King T......5D 116
St George's La. EC3......2F 169
St George's Mans. SW1......5H 85 (5D 172) (off Causton St.)
St George's M. NW1......7D 48
St George's M. SE1......1K 173
St Georges Pde. SE6......2B 124
St George's Path. SE4......4C 106 (off Adelaide Av.)
St George's Pl. Twic......1A 116
St George's Rd. E7......7K 53
St George's Rd. E10......3E 52
St George's Rd. N9......3B 18
St George's Rd. N13......3E 16
St George's Rd. NW11......6H 29
St George's Rd. SE1......3A 86 (1K 173)
St George's Rd. SW19......7H 119 (in two parts)
St George's Rd. W4......2K 81
St George's Rd. W7......1K 79
St George's Rd. Beck......1D 142
St George's Rd. Brom......2D 144 (in two parts)
St George's Rd. Dag......5E 56
St George's Rd. Enf......1A 8
St George's Rd. Felt......4B 114
St George's Rd. Ilf......7D 36
St George's Rd. King T......7G 117
St George's Rd. Mitc......3F 139
St George's Rd. Orp......6H 145
St Georges Rd. Rich......3F 99
St George's Rd. Sidc......6D 128
St George's Rd. Twic......5B 98
St George's Rd. Wall......5F 151
St George's Rd. W. Brom......2C 144
St George's Shop. & Leisure Cen. Harr......6J 25
St George's Sq. E7......7K 53
St Georges Sq. E14......7A 70
St George's Sq. SE8......4B 88
St George's Sq. SW1......5H 85 (5C 172)
St George's Sq. N Mald......3A 136
St George's Sq. M. SW1......5H 85 (6C 172)
St George's Ter. NW1......7D 48
St George St. W1......7F 67 (1K 165)
St George's Wlk. Croy......3C 152
St George's Way. SE15......6E 86
St George's Wharf. SE1......2F 87 (6K 169) (off Shad Thames)
St George Wharf. SW8......6J 85 (7E 172)
St Gerards Clo. SW4......5G 103
St German's Pl. SE3......1J 107
St German's Rd. SE23......1A 124
St Giles Av. Dag......7H 57
St Giles Av. Uxb......4E 40
St Giles Cir. W1......6H 67 (7D 160)
St Giles Clo. Dag......7H 57
St Giles Ct. WC2......7E 160
St Giles High St. WC2......6H 67 (7D 160)
St Giles Ho. New Bar......4F 5
St Giles Pas. WC2......1D 166
St Giles Rd. SE5......7E 86
St Giles Ter. EC2......5C 68 (6D 162) (off Beech St.)
St Giles Tower. SE5......1E 104 (off Gables Clo.)
St Gilles Ho. E2......2K 69 (off Mace St.)
St Gothard Rd. SE27......4D 122 (in two parts)
St Gregory Clo. Ruis......4A 42
St Helena Ho. WC1......3A 68 (2J 161) (off Margery St.)
St Helena Rd. SE16......4K 87
St Helena St. WC1......3A 68 (2J 161)
St Helens. Th Dit......7K 133
St Helen's Cres. SW16......1K 139
St Helen's Gdns. W10......5F 65
St Helen's Pl. EC3......6E 68 (7G 163)
St Helen's Rd. SW16......1K 139
St Helen's Rd. W13......1B 80
St Helen's Rd. Eri......2D 92
St Helen's Rd. Ilf......6D 36
St Helier......7C 138
St Helier Av. Mord......7A 138
St Helier Ct. N1......1E 68 (off De Beauvoir Est.)
St Helier Ct. SE16......2K 87 (off Poolmans St.)
St Helier's Av. Houn......5E 96
St Helier's Rd. E10......6E 34
St Hilda's Av. Ashf......5A 112
St Hilda's Clo. NW6......7F 47
St Hilda's Clo. SW17......2C 120
St Hilda's Rd. SW13......6D 82
St Hilda's Wharf. E1......1J 87 (off Wapping High St.)
St Hubert's Ho. E14......3C 88 (off Janet St.)
St Hughes Clo. SW17......2C 120
St Hugh's Rd. SE20......1H 141
St James. SE14......1A 106
St James Apartments. E17......5A 34 (off High St.)
St James Av. N20......3H 15
St James Av. W13......1A 80
St James Av. Sutt......5J 149
St James Clo. N20......3H 15
St James Clo. SE18......5G 91
St James Clo. Barn......4G 5
St James Clo. N Mald......5B 136
St James Clo. Ruis......2A 42
St James Ct. E2......3G 69 (off Bethnal Grn. Rd.)
St James Ct. E12......2A 54
St James Ct. SE3......1K 107
St James' Ct. SW1......3G 85 (1B 172)
St James Gdns. Ilf......4B 38
St James' Gdns. Wemb......7D 44
St James Ga. Buck H......1E 20
St James Gro. SW11......2D 102
St James' Mans. NW6......7J 47 (off W. End La.)
St James M. E14......3E 88
St James M. E17......5A 34 (off St James's St.)
St James Pl. S Croy......6E 152
St James Residences. W1......7H 67 (2C 166) (off Brewer St.)
St James' Rd. E15......5H 53
St James' Rd. N9......2C 18
St James Rd. Cars......3C 150
St James Rd. Mitc......7E 120
St James' Rd. Surb......6D 134
St James Rd. Sutt......5J 149
St James's......1H 85 (5C 166)
St James's. SW1......1G 85 (4B 166)
St James's App. EC2......4E 68 (4G 163)
St James's Av. E2......2J 69
St James's Av. Beck......3A 142
St James's Av. Hamp H......5G 115
St James's Chambers. SW1......1G 85 (4B 166) (off Jermyn St.)
St James's Clo. NW8......1D 66 (off St James's Ter. M.)
St James's Clo. SW17......2D 120
St James's Cotts. Rich......5D 98
St James's Ct. N18......6A 18 (off Fore St.)
St James's Ct. Harr......6A 26
St James's Ct. King T......3E 134
St James's Cres. SW9......3A 104
St James's Dri. SW17 & SW12......1D 120
St James's Gdns. W11......1G 83 (in two parts)
St James's La. N10......4F 31
St James's Mkt. SW1......7H 67 (3C 166)
St James's Palace......2G 85 (5B 166)
St James's Pk......2H 85 (5D 166)
St James's Pk. Croy......7C 140
St James's Pas. EC3......1H 169
St James's Pl. SW1......1G 85 (5A 166)
St James's Rd. SE1 & SE16......6G 87
St James's Rd. SE16......3G 87
St James's Rd. Croy......7B 140
St James's Rd. Hamp H......5F 115
St James's Rd. King T......2D 134
St James's Sq. SW1......1G 85 (4B 166)
St James's St. E17......5A 34
St James's St. SW1......1G 85 (4A 166)
St James's Ter. NW8......1D 66 (off Prince Albert Rd.)
St James's Ter. M. NW8......1D 66
St James St. W6......5E 82
St James's Wlk. EC1......4B 68 (3A 162)
St James Ter. SW12......1E 120
St James Way. Sidc......5E 128
St Jeromes Gro. Hay......6E 58
St Joan's Rd. N9......2A 18
St John Fisher Rd. Eri......3D 92
St John's......2C 106
St John's Av. N11......5J 15
St John's Av. NW10......1B 64
St John's Av. SW15......5F 101
St Johns Chu. Rd. E9......5J 51
St Johns Clo. N14......6B 6
St John's Clo. N20......3F 15 (off Rasper Rd.)
St John's Clo. SW6......7J 83
St John's Clo. Wemb......5E 44
St John's Cotts. SE20......7J 123
St John's Ct. E1......1H 87 (off Scandrett St.)
St John's Ct. N4......2B 50
St John's Ct. N5......4B 50
St John's Ct. SE13......2E 106
St John's Ct. W6......4D 82 (off Glenthorne Rd.)
St John's Ct. Buck H......1E 20
St John's Ct. Eri......4K 93
St John's Ct. Harr......6K 25
St John's Ct. Iswth......2K 97
St John's Ct. King T......4E 134 (off Beaufort Rd.)
St John's Ct. N'wd......1G 23 (off Murray Rd.)
St John's Cres. SW9......3A 104
St Johns Dri. SW18......1K 119
St John's Est. N1......2D 68
St John's Est. SE1......6J 169
St John's Gdns. W11......7G 65
St John's Gate......4A 162
St John's Gro. N19......2G 49
St John's Gro. SW13......2B 100
St John's Gro. Rich......4E 98
St John's Hill. SW11......5B 102
St John's Hill Gro. SW11......4B 102
St John's Ho. E14......4E 88 (off Pier St.)
St Johns Ho. SE17......6D 86 (off Lytham St.)
St John's La. EC1......4B 68 (4A 162)
St John's M. W11......6J 65
St John's Pde. W13......1B 80
St Johns Pde. Sidc......4A 128 (off Sidcup High St.)
St John's Pk. SE3......7H 89
St John's Pk. Mans. N19......3G 49
St John's Pas. SW19......6G 119
St John's Path. EC1......4A 162
St Johns Pathway. SE23......1J 123
St John's Pl. EC1......4B 68 (4A 162)
St John's Rd. E4......4J 19
St John's Rd. E6......1C 72
St John's Rd. E16......6J 71
St John's Rd. E17......2D 34
St John's Rd. N15......6E 32
St John's Rd. NW11......6H 29
St John's Rd. SE20......6J 123
St John's Rd. SW11......4C 102
St John's Rd. SW19......7G 119
St John's Rd. Bark......1J 73
St John's Rd. Cars......3C 150
St John's Rd. Croy......3B 152
St John's Rd. E Mol......4H 133
St John's Rd. Eri......5K 93
St John's Rd. Felt......4C 114
St John's Rd. Hamp W......2C 134
St John's Rd. Harr......6K 25
St John's Rd. Ilf......7J 37
St John's Rd. Iswth......2K 97
St John's Rd. N Mald......3J 135
St John's Rd. Orp......6H 145
St John's Rd. Rich......4E 98
St John's Rd. Sidc......4B 128
St John's Rd. S'hall......3C 78
St John's Rd. Sutt......2K 149
St John's Rd. Well......3B 110
St John's Rd. Wemb......4D 44
St John's Sq. EC1......4B 68 (4A 162)
St John's Ter. E7......6K 53
St John's Ter. SE18......6G 91
St John's Ter. SW15......3A 118 (off Kingston Va.)
St John's Ter. W10......4F 65
St John St. EC1......2A 68 (1K 161)
St John's Va. SE8......2C 106
St John's Vs. N11......5J 15 (off Friern Barnet Rd.)
St John's Vs. N19......2H 49
St John's Vs. W8......3K 83
St John's Way. N19......2G 49
St John's Wood......2B 66
St John's Wood Ct. NW8......2B 158
St John's Wood High St. NW8......2B 66 (1C 158)
St John's Wood Pk. NW8......1B 66
St John's Wood Rd. NW8......4B 66 (3A 158)
St John's Wood Ter. NW8......2B 66
St John's Yd. N17......7A 18
St Joseph's Clo. W10......5G 65
St Josephs Ct. SE7......6K 89
St Joseph's Dri. S'hall......1C 78
St Joseph's Flats. NW1......3H 67 (1C 160) (off Drummond Cres.)
St Joseph's Gro. NW4......4D 28
St Joseph's Ho. W6......4F 83 (off Brook Grn.)
St Joseph's Rd. N9......7C 8
St Joseph's St. SW8......1F 103
St Joseph's Va. SE3......3F 107
St Jude's Rd. E2......2H 69
St Jude St. N16......5E 50
St Julian's Clo. SW16......4A 122
St Julian's Farm Rd. SE27......4A 122
St Julian's Rd. NW6......1J 65
St Katharine Docks......1G 87 (3K 169)

St Katharine's Pier. E1 .... 1F 87 (4J 169) (off Tower Bri. App.)
St Katharine's Precinct. NW1 .... 2F 67
St Katharine's Way. E1 .... 1F 87 (4K 169) (in two parts)
St Katherine's Rd. Eri 2D 92
St Katherine's Row. EC3 .... 2H 169
St Katherines Wlk. W11 .... 1F 83 (off St Ann's Rd.)
St Keverne Rd. SE9 .... 4C 126
St Kilda Rd. W13 .... 1A 80
St Kilda Rd. Orp 7K 145
St Kilda's Rd. N16 .... 1D 50
St Kilda's Rd. Harr 6J 25
St Kitts Ter. SE19 .... 5E 122
St Laurence Clo. NW6 .... 1F 65
St Lawrence Bus. Cen. Twic 2K 113
St Lawrence Clo. Edgw 7A 12
St Lawrence Cotts. E14 .... 1E 88 (off St Lawrence St.)
St Lawrence Ct. N1 .... 7D 50 (off De Beauvoir Est.)
St Lawrence Dri. Pinn 5K 23
St Lawrence Ho. SE1 .... 3E 86 (7H 169) (off Purbrook St.)
St Lawrence St. E14 .... 1E 88
St Lawrence Ter. W10 .... 5G 65
St Lawrence Way. SW9 .... 2A 104
St Leonard M. N1 .... 2E 68
St Leonard's Av. E4 .... 6A 20
St Leonard's Av. Harr 5C 26
St Leonard's Clo. Well 3A 110
St Leonard's Ct. N1 .... 1F 163
St Leonards Ct. SW14 .... 3J 99
St Leonard's Gdns. Houn 1C 96
St Leonard's Gdns. Ilf 5G 55
St Leonard's Rd. E14 .... 5D 70 (in two parts)
St Leonard's Rd. NW10 .... 4K 63
St Leonard's Rd. SW14 .... 3H 99
St Leonard's Rd. W13 .... 7C 62
St Leonard's Rd. Clay 6A 146
St Leonard's Rd. Croy 3B 152
St Leonard's Rd. Surb 5D 134
St Leonard's Rd. Th Dit 6A 134
St Leonards Sq. NW5 .... 6E 48
St Leonards Sq. Surb 5D 134
St Leonard's St. E3 .... 3D 70
St Leonard's Ter. SW3 .... 5D 84 (6E 170)
St Leonard's Wlk. SW16 .... 7K 121
St Loo Av. SW3 .... 6C 84 (7D 170)
St Louis Rd. SE27 .... 4D 122
St Loy's Rd. N17 .... 2E 32
St Lucia Dri. E15 .... 1H 71
St Luke Clo. Uxb 6A 58
St Luke's. 4C 68 (3D 162)
St Luke's Av. SW4 .... 4H 103
St Luke's Av. Enf 1J 7
St Luke's Av. Ilf 5F 55
St Luke's Clo. EC1 .... 4C 68 (3D 162)
St Luke's Clo. SE25 .... 6H 141
St Lukes Ct. E10 .... 7D 34 (off Capworth St.)
St Luke's Est. EC1 .... 3D 68 (2E 162)
St Luke's M. W11 .... 6H 65
St Luke's Pas. King T 1F 135
St Luke's Path. Ilf 5F 55
St Luke's Rd. W11 .... 5H 65
St Luke's Rd. Uxb 7A 40
St Luke's Sq. E16 .... 6H 71
St Luke's St. SW3 .... 5C 84 (5D 170)
St Luke's Yd. W9 .... 2H 65 (in two parts)
St Malo Av. N9 .... 3D 18
St Margarets. 6B 98
St Margaret's. Bark 1G 73
St Margaret's Av. N15 .... 4B 32
St Margaret's Av. N20 .... 1F 15
St Margaret's Av. Ashf 5D 112
St Margaret's Av. Harr 3G 43
St Margaret's Av. Sidc 3H 127
St Margaret's Av. Sutt 3G 149
St Margarets Av. Uxb 4C 58
St Margarets Bus. Cen. Twic 6B 98
St Margarets Clo. EC2 .... 6D 68 (7E 162) (off Lothbury)
St Margaret's Ct. N11 .... 4K 15
St Margarets Ct. SE1 .... 1C 86 (5D 168)
St Margarets Ct. SW15 .... 4D 100
St Margarets Ct. Edgw 5C 12
St Margaret's Cres. SW15 .... 5D 100
St Margaret's Dri. Twic 5B 98
St Margaret's Gro. E11 .... 3H 53
St Margaret's Gro. SE18 .... 6G 91
St Margaret's Gro. Twic 6A 98
St Margaret's La. W8 .... 3K 83
St Margaret's Pas. SE13 .... 3G 107 (in two parts)
St Margarets Path. SE18 .... 5G 91
St Margaret's Rd. E12 .... 2A 54
St Margaret's Rd. N17 .... 3E 32
St Margaret's Rd. NW10 .... 3E 64
St Margarets Rd. SE4 .... 4B 106 (in two parts)
St Margaret's Rd. W7 .... 2J 79
St Margaret's Rd. Edgw 5C 12
St Margarets Rd. Iswth & Twic 4B 98
St Margaret's Rd. Ruis 6F 23
St Margarets Roundabout. (Junct.) 6B 98
St Margaret's Ter. SE18 .... 5G 91
St Margaret St. SW1 .... 2J 85 (7E 166)
St Mark's Clo. SE10 .... 7E 88
St Marks Clo. SW6 .... 1J 101
St Marks Clo. Harr 7B 26
St Mark's Clo. New Bar 3E 4
St Marks Ct. E10 .... 7D 34 (off Capworth St.)
St Marks Ct. NW8 .... 2A 66 (off Abercorn Pl.)
St Marks Ct. W7 .... 2J 79 (off Lwr. Boston Rd.)
St Mark's Cres. NW1 .... 1E 66
St Mark's Ga. E9 .... 7B 52
St Mark's Gro. SW10 .... 7K 83
St Mark's Hill. Surb 6E 134
St Marks Ho. SE17 .... 6D 86 (off Lytham St.)
St Marks Ind. Est. E16 .... 1B 90
St Mark's Pl. SW19 .... 6H 119
St Mark's Pl. W11 .... 6G 65
St Mark's Ri. E8 .... 5F 51
St Mark's Rd. SE25 .... 4G 141
St Mark's Rd. W5 .... 1E 80
St Mark's Rd. W7 .... 2J 79
St Mark's Rd. W10 & W11 .... 5F 65
St Mark's Rd. Brom 3J 143
St Marks Rd. Enf 6A 8
St Marks Rd. Mitc 2D 138
St Mark's Rd. Tedd 7B 116
St Mark's Sq. NW1 .... 1E 66
St Mark St. E1 .... 6F 69 (1K 169)
St Martin Clo. Uxb 6A 58
St Martin-in-the-Fields Church. 3E 166
St Martin's Almshouses. NW1 .... 1G 67
St Martin's App. Ruis 7G 23
St Martin's Av. E6 .... 2B 72
St Martin's Clo. NW1 .... 1G 67
St Martin's Clo. Enf 1C 8
St Martin's Clo. Eri 2D 92
St Martins Ct. N1 .... 1E 68 (off De Beauvoir Est.)
St Martin's Ct. WC2 .... 7J 67 (2E 166)
St Martins Est. SW2 .... 1A 122
St Martin's La. WC2 .... 7J 67 (2E 166)
St Martins La. Beck 5D 142
St Martin's le-Grand. EC1 .... 6C 68 (7C 162)
St Martin's Pl. WC2 .... 7J 67 (3E 166)
St Martin's Rd. N9 .... 2C 18
St Martin's Rd. SW9 .... 2K 103
St Martin's St. WC2 .... 7H 67 (3D 166) (in two parts)
St Martins Ter. N10 .... 3E 30
St Martin's Theatre. .... 7J 67 (2E 166) (off West St.)
St Martins Way. SW17 .... 3A 120
St Mary Abbot's Ct. W14 .... 3H 83 (off Warwick Gdns.)
St Mary Abbot's Pl. W8 .... 3H 83
St Mary Abbot's Ter. W14 .... 3H 83
St Mary at Hill. EC3 .... 7E 68 (3G 169)
St Mary Av. Wall 3E 150
St Mary Axe. EC3 .... 6E 68 (1G 169)
St Marychurch St. SE16 .... 2J 87
St Mary Graces Ct. E1 .... 7F 69 (3K 169)
St Marylebone Crematorium. N2 .... 3K 29
St Mary le-Park Ct. SW11 .... 7C 84 (off Parkgate Rd.)
St Mary Newington Clo. SE17 .... 5E 86 (off Surrey Sq.)
St Mary Rd. E17 .... 4C 34
St Mary's. Bark 1H 73
St Mary's App. E12 .... 5D 54
St Mary's Av. E11 .... 7K 35
St Mary's Av. N3 .... 2G 29
St Mary's Av. Brom 3G 143
St Mary's Av. Tedd 6K 115
St Mary's Av. Central. S'hall 4F 79
St Mary's Av. N. S'hall 4F 79
St Mary's Av. S. S'hall 4F 79
St Mary's Clo. N17 .... 1F 33
St Mary's Clo. Chess 7F 147
St Mary's Clo. Eps 7B 148
St Mary's Clo. Sun 4J 131
St Mary's Ct. E6 .... 4D 72
St Mary's Ct. SE7 .... 7B 90
St Mary's Ct. W5 .... 2D 80
St Mary's Ct. W12 .... 3B 82
St Mary's Ct. Wall 4G 151
St Mary's Cres. NW4 .... 3D 28
St Mary's Cres. Hay 7H 59
St Mary's Cres. Iswth 7H 79
St Mary's Dri. Felt 7E 94
St Mary's Est. SE16 .... 2J 87 (off St Marychurch St.)
St Mary's Flats. NW1 .... 3H 67 (1C 160) (off Drummond Cres.)
St Mary's Gdns. SE11 .... 4A 86 (3K 173)
St Mary's Ga. W8 .... 3K 83
St Mary's Grn. N2 .... 2A 30
St Mary's Gro. N1 .... 6B 50
St Mary's Gro. SW13 .... 3D 100
St Mary's Gro. W4 .... 6H 81
St Mary's Gro. Rich 4F 99
St Mary's Ho. N1 .... 1B 68 (off St Mary's Path)
St Mary's Mans. W2 .... 5B 66 (5A 158)
St Mary's M. NW6 .... 7K 47 (in two parts)
St Marys M. Rich 2C 116
St Mary's Path. N1 .... 1B 68
St Mary's Pl. SE9 .... 6D 108
St Mary's Pl. W5 .... 2D 80
St Mary's Pl. W8 .... 3K 83
St Mary's Rd. E10 .... 3E 52
St Mary's Rd. E13 .... 2K 71
St Mary's Rd. N8 .... 4J 31
St Mary's Rd. N9 .... 1C 18
St Mary's Rd. NW10 .... 1A 64
St Mary's Rd. NW11 .... 7G 29
St Mary's Rd. SE15 .... 1J 105
St Mary's Rd. SE25 .... 3E 140
St Mary's Rd. SW19 .... 5G 119
St Marys Rd. W5 .... 2D 80
St Mary's Rd. Barn 7J 5
St Mary's Rd. Bex 1J 129
St Mary's Rd. Dit H 7C 134
St Mary's Rd. E Mol 5H 133
St Mary's Rd. Hay 7H 59
St Mary's Rd. Ilf 2H 55
St Mary's Rd. Surb 6D 134
St Mary's Rd. Wor Pk 2A 148
St Mary's Sq. W2 .... 5B 66 (5A 158)
St Mary's Sq. W5 .... 2D 80
St Mary's Ter. W2 .... 5B 66 (5A 158)
St Mary's Tower. EC1 .... 4C 68 (4D 162) (off Fortune St.)
St Mary St. SE18 .... 4D 90
St Mary's Vw. Harr 5C 26
St Mary's Wlk. SE11 .... 4A 86 (3K 173)
St Mary's Wlk. Hay 7H 59
St Mary's Way. Chig 5K 21
St Matthew Clo. Uxb 6A 58
St Matthew's Av. Surb 1E 146
St Matthews Ct. E10 .... 7D 34
St Matthews Ct. N10 .... 2E 30
St Matthews Ct. SE1 .... 3C 86 (off Meadow Row)
St Matthew's Dri. Brom 3D 144
St Matthews Ho. SE17 .... 6D 86 (off Phelp St.)
St Matthew's Lodge. NW1 .... 2G 67 (off Oakley Sq.)
St Matthew's Rd. SW2 .... 4K 103
St Matthew's Rd. W5 .... 1E 80
St Matthew's Row. E2 .... 3G 69
St Matthew St. SW1 .... 3H 85 (2C 172)
St Matthias Clo. NW9 .... 5B 28
St Maur Rd. SW6 .... 1H 101
St Mellion Clo. SE28 .... 6D 74
St Merryn Clo. SE18 .... 7H 91
St Merryn Ct. Beck 7C 124
St Michael's All. EC3 .... 6D 68 (1F 169)
St Michael's Av. N9 .... 7D 8
St Michael's Av. Wemb 6G 45
St Michaels Clo. E16 .... 5B 72
St Michael's Clo. N3 .... 2H 29
St Michael's Clo. N12 .... 5H 15
St Michael's Clo. Brom 3C 144
St Michael's Clo. Eri 2D 92
St Michael's Clo. Wor Pk 2B 148
St Michaels Ct. E14 .... 5E 70 (off St Leonards Rd.)
St Michael's Ct. SE1 .... 2C 86 (7D 168) (off Trinity St.)
St Michael's Cres. Pinn 6C 24
St Michael's Flats. NW1 .... 2H 67 (1C 160) (off Aldenham St.)
St Michael's Gdns. W10 .... 5G 65
St Michael's Ri. Well 1B 110
St Michael's Rd. NW2 .... 4E 46
St Michael's Rd. SW9 .... 2K 103
St Michael's Rd. Ashf 5C 112
St Michael's Rd. Croy 1C 152
St Michael's Rd. Wall 6G 151
St Michael's Rd. Well 3B 110
St Michael's St. W2 .... 6B 66 (7B 158)
St Michaels Ter. N6 .... 1E 48 (off South Gro.)
St Michael's Ter. N22 .... 1J 31
St Mildred's Ct. EC2 .... 6D 68 (1E 168)
St Mildreds Rd. SE12 .... 7G 107
St Mirren Ct. New Bar 5F 5
St Nicholas Cen. Sutt 5K 149
St Nicholas Clo. Uxb 6A 58
St Nicholas Ct. King T .... 4E 134 (off Surbiton Rd.)
St Nicholas Dri. Shep 7C 130
St Nicholas' Flats. NW1 .... 2H 67 (1C 160) (off Werrington St.)
St Nicholas Glebe. SW17 .... 5E 120
St Nicholas Ho. SE8 .... 6C 88 (off Deptford Grn.)
St Nicholas Ho. SE18 .... 7C 90 (off Shrapnel Clo.)
St Nicholas Rd. SE18 .... 5K 91
St Nicholas Rd. Sutt 5K 149
St Nicholas Rd. Th Dit 6K 133
St Nicholas St. SE8 .... 1B 106
St Nicholas Way. Sutt 4K 149
St Nicolas La. Chst 1C 144
St Ninian's Ct. N20 .... 3J 15
St Norbert Grn. SE4 .... 4A 106
St Norbert Rd. SE4 .... 5K 105
St Olaf Ho. SE1 .... 4F 169
St Olaf's Rd. SW6 .... 7G 83
St Olaf Stairs. SE1 .... 4F 169
St Olave's Ct. EC2 .... 6D 68 (1E 168)
St Olave's Est. SE1 .... 2E 86 (6H 169)
St Olave's Gdns. SE11 .... 4A 86 (3J 173)
St Olave's Mans. SE11 .... 3J 173
St Olave's Rd. E6 .... 1E 72
St Olave's Ter. SE1 .... 6H 169
St Olaves Wlk. SW16 .... 2G 139
St Olav's Sq. SE16 .... 2J 87
St Onge Pde. Enf .... 3J 7 (off Southbury Rd.)
St Oswald's Pl. SE11 .... 5K 85 (6G 173)
St Oswald's Rd. SW16 .... 1B 140
St Oswulf St. SW1 .... 4H 85 (4D 172)
St Owen Ho. SE1 .... 3E 86 (off Fendall St.)
St Pancras. 3J 67 (1E 160)
St Pancras Commercial Cen. NW1 .... 1G 67 (off Pratt St.)
St Pancras Ct. N2 .... 2B 30
St Pancras Way. NW1 .... 7G 49
St Patrick's Ct. Wfd G 7B 20
St Paul Clo. Uxb 5A 58
St Paul's Av. NW2 .... 6D 46
St Paul's Av. SE16 .... 1K 87
St Paul's Av. Harr 4F 27
St Paul's Cathedral. 6C 68 (1C 168)
St Paul's Chyd. EC4 .... 6B 68 (1B 168) (in two parts)
St Pauls Clo. SE7 .... 5B 90
St Paul's Clo. W5 .... 2F 81
St Paul's Clo. Ashf 5E 112
St Paul's Clo. Cars 1C 150
St Paul's Clo. Chess 4D 146
St Paul's Clo. Hay 5F 77
St Paul's Clo. Houn 2C 96
St Pauls Ct. SW4 .... 5H 103
St Paul's Ct. Houn 3C 96
St Pauls Courtyard. SE8 .... 7C 88 (off Crossfield St.)
St Paul's Cray Rd. Chst 1H 145
St Paul's Cres. NW1 .... 7H 49 (in two parts)
St Paul's Dri. E15 .... 5F 53
St Paul's M. NW1 .... 7H 49
St Paul's Pl. N1 .... 6D 50
St Paul's Ri. N13 .... 6G 17
St Paul's Rd. N1 .... 6B 50
St Paul's Rd. N17 .... 7B 18

St Paul's Rd. Bark 1G 73
St Paul's Rd. Bren 6D 80
St Paul's Rd. Eri 7J 93
St Paul's Rd. Rich 3F 99
St Paul's Rd. T Hth 3C 140
St Paul's Shrubbery. N1 6D 50
St Paul's Sq. Brom 2H 143
St Paul's Studios. W6 5G 83 (off Talgarth Rd.)
St Pauls Ter. SE17 6B 86
St Pauls Tower. E10 7D 34 (off Beaumont Rd.)
St Paul St. N1 1C 68 (in two parts)
St Pauls Vw. Apartments. EC1 3A 68 (2K 161) (off Amwell St.)
St Paul's Wlk. King T 7G 117
St Pauls Way. E3 5B 70
St Paul's Way. N3 7E 14
St Paul's Wood Hill. Orp 2J 145 & 7A 128
St Peter's All. EC3 6D 68 (1G 169) (off Cornhill)
St Peter's Av. E2 2G 69
St Peter's Av. E17 4G 35
St Peters Av. N2 7H 15
St Peter's Av. N18 4B 18
St Petersburgh M. W2 7K 65
St Petersburgh Pl. W2 7K 65
St Peter's Cen. E1 1H 87 (off Reardon St.)
St Peter's Chu. Ct. N1 1B 68 (off Devonia Rd.)
St Peter's Clo. E2 2G 69
St Peter's Clo. SW17 2C 120
St Peters Clo. Bus H 1C 10
St Peter's Clo. Chst 7H 127
St Peter's Clo. Ilf 4J 37
St Peter's Clo. Ruis 2B 42
St Peter's Ct. NW4 5E 28
St Peters Ct. W Mol 4E 132
St Peter's Gdns. SE27 3A 122
St Peter's Gro. W6 4C 82
St Peters Ho. SE17 6D 86
St Peter's Ho. WC1 3J 67 (2F 161) (off Regent Sq.)
St Peters Pl. W9 4K 65
St Peter's Rd. N9 1C 18
St Peter's Rd. W6 5C 82
St Peter's Rd. Croy 4D 152
St Peter's Rd. King T 2G 135
St Peter's Rd. S'hall 5E 60
St Peter's Rd. Twic 5B 98
St Peters Rd. Uxb 5A 58
St Peter's Rd. W Mol 4E 132
St Peter's Sq. E2 2G 69
St Peter's Sq. W6 4B 82
St Peter's St. N1 1B 68
St Peter's St. S Croy 5D 152
St Peter's St. M. N1 2B 68 (off St Peters St.)
St Peter's Ter. SW6 7H 83
St Peter's Vs. W6 4C 82
St Peter's Way. N1 7E 50
St Peter's Way. W5 5D 62
St Peters Way. Hay 5F 77
St Peter's Wharf. W4 5C 82
St Philip Ho. WC1 3A 68 (2J 161) (off Lloyd Baker St.)
St Philips Av. N2 7H 15
St Philip's Av. Wor Pk 2D 148
St Philip's Ga. Wor Pk 2D 148
St Philip Sq. SW8 2F 103
St Philip's Rd. E8 6G 51
St Philips Rd. Surb 6D 134
St Philip St. SW8 2F 103
St Philip's Way. N1 1C 68
St Quentin Rd. Well 3K 109
St Quintin Av. W10 5E 64
St Quintin Gdns. W10 5E 64
St Quintin Rd. E13 3K 71
St Raphael's Way. NW10 5J 45
St Regis Clo. N10 2F 31
St Regis Heights. NW3 3K 47
St Richard's Ho. NW1 3H 67 (1C 160) (off Eversholt St.)
St Ronan's Clo. Barn 1G 5
St Ronan's Cres. Wfd G 7D 20
St Rule St. SW8 2G 103
St Saviour's College. SE27 4D 122
St Saviour's Ct. N10 2F 31 (off Alexandra Pk. Rd.)
St Saviours Ct. Harr 5J 25
St Saviour's Est. SE1 2F 87 (7J 169)
St Saviour's Rd. SW2 5K 103
St Saviour's Rd. Croy 6B 140
St Saviour's Wharf. SE1 2F 87 (6K 169) (off Mill St.)
St Saviour's Wharf. SE1 2F 87 (6K 169) (off Shad Thames)
Saints Clo. SE27 4B 122
Saints Dri. E7 5B 54
St Silas Pl. NW5 6E 48
St Simon's Av. SW15 5E 100
Saints M. Mitc 3C 138
St Stephen's Av. E17 5E 34
St Stephen's Av. W12 1D 82 (in two parts)
St Stephen's Av. W13 6B 62
St Stephen's Clo. E17 5D 34
St Stephen's Clo. NW8 1C 66
St Stephen's Clo. S'hall 5E 60
St Stephens Ct. N8 6K 31
St Stephens Ct. W13 6B 62
St Stephen's Ct. Enf 6K 7 (off Park Av.)
St Stephen's Cres. W2 6J 65
St Stephen's Cres. T Hth 3A 140
St Stephen's Gdns. SW15 5H 101
St Stephen's Gdns. W2 6J 65 (in two parts)
St Stephen's Gdns. Twic 6C 98
St Stephens Gro. SE13 3E 106
St Stephens Ho. SE17 6D 86 (off Lytham St.)
St Stephens M. W2 5J 65
St Stephens Pde. E7 7A 54
St Stephen's Pas. Twic 6C 98
St Stephen's Rd. E3 1A 70
St Stephen's Rd. E6 7A 54
St Stephen's Rd. E17 5D 34
St Stephen's Rd. W13 6B 62
St Stephen's Rd. Barn 5A 4
St Stephen's Rd. Houn 6E 96
St Stephen's Rd. W Dray 1A 76
St Stephen's Row. EC4 1E 168
St Stephen's Ter. SW8 7K 85
St Stephen's Wlk. SW7 4A 84 (off Southwell Gdns.)
St Swithins La. EC4 7D 68 (2E 168)
St Swithun's Rd. SE13 6F 107
St Theresa's Rd. Felt 4H 95
St Thomas Clo. Surb 1F 147
St Thomas Ct. E10 7D 34 (off Beaumont Rd.)
St Thomas Ct. Bex 7G 111
St Thomas Ct. Pinn 1C 24
St Thomas Dri. Orp 7G 145
St Thomas Dri. Pinn 1C 24
St Thomas Gdns. Ilf 6G 55
St Thomas Ho. E1 6K 69 (off W. Arbour St.)
St Thomas Rd. E16 6J 71
St Thomas Rd. N14 7C 6
St Thomas Rd. W4 6J 81
St Thomas Rd. Belv 2J 93
St Thomas's Gdns. NW5 6E 48
St Thomas's Pl. E9 7J 51
St Thomas's Rd. N4 2A 50
St Thomas's Rd. NW10 1A 64
St Thomas's Sq. E9 7J 51
St Thomas St. SE1 1D 86 (5F 169)
St Thomas's Way. SW6 7H 83
St Timothys M. Brom 1K 143
St Ursula Gro. Pinn 5B 24
St Ursula Rd. S'hall 6E 60
St Vincent Clo. SE27 5B 122
St Vincent De Paul Ho. E1 5J 69 (off Jubilee St.)
St Vincent Ho. SE1 3F 87 (off Fendall St.)
St Vincent Rd. Twic 6G 97
St Vincent St. W1 5E 66 (6H 159)
St Wilfrid's Clo. Barn 5H 5
St Wilfrid's Rd. New Bar 5H 5
St Winefride's Av. E12 5D 54
St Winifred's Rd. Tedd 6B 116
Sala Ho. SE3 4K 107
Salamanca Pl. SE1 4K 85 (4G 173)
Salamanca St. SE1 & SE11 4K 85 (4F 173)
Salamander Clo. King T 5C 116
Salamander Quay. King T 1D 134
Salcombe Dri. Mord 1F 149
Salcombe Dri. Romf 6F 39
Salcombe Gdns. NW7 6K 13
Salcombe Rd. E17 7B 34
Salcombe Rd. N16 5E 50
Salcombe Rd. Ashf 3A 112
Salcombe Way. Hay 3G 59
Salcombe Way. Ruis 2J 41
Salcott Rd. SW11 5C 102
Salcott Rd. Croy 3J 151
Salehurst Clo. Harr 5E 26
Salehurst Rd. SE4 6B 106
Salem Pl. Croy 3C 152
Salem Rd. W2 7K 65
Sale Pl. W2 5C 66 (6C 158)
Sale St. E2 4G 69
Salford Ho. E14 4E 88 (off Seyssel St.)
Salford Rd. SW2 1H 121
Salhouse Clo. SE28 6C 74
Salisbury Av. N3 3H 29
Salisbury Av. Bark 7H 55
Salisbury Av. Sutt 6H 149
Salisbury Clo. SE17 4D 86
Salisbury Clo. Wor Pk 3B 148
Salisbury Ct. EC4 6B 68 (1A 168)
Salisbury Ct. Cars 5D 150
Salisbury Ct. Edgw 6B 12
Salisbury Ct. Enf 4J 7 (off London Rd.)
Salisbury Ct. N'holt 5F 43 (off Newmarket Av.)
Salisbury Gdns. SW19 7G 119
Salisbury Gdns. Buck H 2G 21
Salisbury Hall Gdns. E4 6H 19
Salisbury Ho. E14 6D 70 (off Hobday St.)
Salisbury Ho. EC2 5D 68 (6F 163) (off London Wall)
Salisbury Ho. N1 1B 68 (off St Mary's Path)
Salisbury Ho. SW1 5H 85 (5D 172) (off Drummond Ga.)
Salisbury Ho. SW9 7A 86 (off Cranmer Rd.)
Salisbury Ho. Stan 6F 11
Salisbury Mans. N4 5B 32
Salisbury M. SW6 7H 83
Salisbury Pas. SW6 7H 83 (off Dawes Rd.)
Salisbury Pavement. SW6 7H 83 (off Dawes Rd.)
Salisbury Pl. SW9 7B 86
Salisbury Pl. W1 5D 66 (5E 158)
Salisbury Rd. E4 3H 19
Salisbury Rd. E7 6J 53
Salisbury Rd. E10 2E 52
Salisbury Rd. E12 5B 54
Salisbury Rd. E17 5E 34
Salisbury Rd. N4 5B 32
Salisbury Rd. N9 3B 18
Salisbury Rd. N22 1B 32
Salisbury Rd. SE25 6G 141
Salisbury Rd. SW19 7G 119
Salisbury Rd. W13 2B 80
Salisbury Rd. Barn 3B 4
Salisbury Rd. Bex 1G 129
Salisbury Rd. Brom 5C 144
Salisbury Rd. Cars 6D 150
Salisbury Rd. Dag 6H 57
Salisbury Rd. Felt 1A 114
Salisbury Rd. Harr 5H 25
Salisbury Rd. Houn 3A 96
Salisbury Rd. Ilf 2J 55
Salisbury Rd. H'row A 5E 94
Salisbury Rd. N Mald 3K 135
Salisbury Rd. Pinn 4J 23
Salisbury Rd. Rich 4E 98
Salisbury Rd. S'hall 4C 78
Salisbury Rd. Wor Pk 4K 147
Salisbury Sq. EC4 6A 68 (1K 167)
Salisbury St. NW8 4C 66 (4C 158)
Salisbury St. W3 2J 81
Salisbury Ter. SE15 3J 105
Salisbury Wlk. N19 2G 49
Salix Clo. Sun 7K 113
Salix Ct. N3 6D 14
Salliesfield. Twic 6H 97
Sally Murray Clo. E12 4E 54 (off Grantham Rd.)
Salmen Rd. E13 2H 71
Salmond Clo. Stan 6F 11
Salmon La. E14 6A 70
Salmon M. NW6 5J 47
Salmon Rd. Belv 5G 93
Salmons Rd. N9 1B 18
Salmons Rd. Chess 6E 146
Salmon St. E14 6B 70
Salmon St. NW9 1H 45
Salomons Rd. E13 5A 72
Salop Rd. E17 6K 33
Saltash Clo. Sutt 4H 149
Saltash Rd. Ilf 1H 37
Saltash Rd. Well 1C 110
Saltcoats Rd. W4 2A 82
Saltcroft Clo. Wemb 1H 45
Saltdene. N4 1K 49
Salter Clo. Harr 4D 42
Salterford Rd. SW17 6E 120
Salter Rd. SE16 1K 87
Salters Ct. EC4 1D 168
Salter's Hall Ct. EC4 2E 168
Salter's Hill. SE19 5D 122
Salters Rd. E17 4F 35
Salters Rd. W10 4F 65
Salter St. E14 7B 70
Salter St. NW10 3C 64
Salterton Rd. N7 3K 49
Salt Hill Clo. Uxb 5A 40
Saltley Clo. E6 6C 72
Saltoun Rd. SW2 4A 104
Saltram Clo. N15 4F 33
Saltram Cres. W9 3H 65
Saltwell St. E14 7C 70
Saltwood Gro. SE17 5D 86
Saltwood Ho. SE15 6J 87 (off Lovelinch Clo.)
Salusbury Rd. NW6 1G 65
Salutation Rd. SE10 4G 89
Salvador. SW17 5D 120
Salvia Gdns. Gnfd 2A 62
Salvin Rd. SW15 3F 101
Salway Clo. Wfd G 7D 20
Salway Pl. E15 6F 53
Salway Rd. E15 6F 53
Samantha Clo. E17 7B 34
Sam Bartram Clo. SE7 5A 90
Sambrook Ho. E1 5J 69 (off Jubilee St.)
Sambrook Ho. SE11 4J 173
Sambruck M. SE6 1D 124
Samels Ct. W6 5C 82
Samford Ho. N1 1A 68 (off Barnsbury Est.)
Samford St. NW8 4B 66 (4C 158)
Samira Clo. E17 6C 34
Sam Manners Ho. SE10 5G 89 (off Tuskar St.)
Sam March Ho. E14 6F 71 (off Blair St.)
Samos Rd. SE20 2H 141
Sampson Av. Barn 5A 4
Sampson Clo. Belv 3D 92
Sampson Ho. SE1 1B 86 (4A 168)
Sampsons Ct. Shep 5E 130
Sampson St. E1 1G 87
Samsbrooke Ct. Enf 6K 7
Samson St. E13 2A 72
Samuda Est. E14 3E 88
Samuel Clo. E8 1F 69
Samuel Clo. SE14 6K 87
Samuel Clo. SE18 4C 90
Samuel Gray Gdns. King T 1D 134
Samuel Ho. E8 1F 69 (off Clarissa St.)
Samuel Johnson Clo. SW16 4K 121
Samuel Jones Ind. Est. SE15 7E 86 (off Peckham Gro.)
Samuel Lewis Bldgs. N1 6A 50
Samuel Lewis Trust Dwellings. N15 6E 32
Samuel Lewis Trust Dwellings. SE5 1C 104 (off Warner Rd.)
Samuel Lewis Trust Dwellings. SW3 4C 170 (in two parts)
Samuel Lewis Trust Dwellings. SW6 7J 83 (off Vanston Pl.)
Samuel Lewis Trust Dwellings. W14 4H 83 (off Lisgar Ter.)
Samuel Richardson Ho. W14 4H 83 (off N. End Cres.)
Samuel's Clo. W6 4E 82
Samuel St. SE15 7F 87
Samuel St. SE18 4D 90
Sancroft Clo. NW2 3D 46
Sancroft Ho. SE11 5H 173
Sancroft Rd. Harr 2K 25
Sancroft St. SE11 5K 85 (5H 173)
Sanctuary Rd. H'row A 6C 94
Sanctuary St. SE1 2C 86 (6D 168)
Sanctuary, The. SW1 1D 172
Sanctuary, The. Bex 6D 110
Sanctuary, The. Mord 6J 137
Sandale Clo. N16 3D 50
Sandall Clo. W5 4E 62
Sandall Ho. E3 2A 70
Sandall Rd. NW5 6G 49
Sandall Rd. W5 4E 62
Sandal Rd. N18 5B 18
Sandal Rd. N Mald 5K 135
Sandal St. E15 1G 71
Sandalwood Clo. E1 4A 70
Sandal Wood Dri. Ruis 7E 22
Sandalwood Ho. Sidc 3K 127
Sandalwood Mans. W8 3K 83 (off Stone Hall Gdns.)
Sandalwood Rd. Felt 3K 113
Sandbach Pl. SE18 4G 91
Sandbanks. Felt 1G 113

Sandbourne. NW8 . . . . 1K 65
(off Abbey Rd.)
Sandbourne. W11 . . . . 6J 65
(off Dartmouth Clo.)
Sandbourne Av. SW19 . . . . 2K 137
Sandbourne Rd. SE4 . . . . . 2A 106
Sandbrook Clo. NW7 . . . . . . 6E 12
Sandbrook Rd. N16 . . . . 3E 50
Sandby Grn. SE9 . . . . 3C 108
Sandby Ho. NW6 . . . . 1J 65
Sandcliff Rd. Eri 4K 93
Sandcroft Clo. N13 . . . . 6G 17
Sandell's Av. Ashf 4E 112
Sandell St. SE1 . . . . 2A 86 (6J 167)
Sanderling Ct. SE8 . . . . 6B 88
(off Abinger Gro.)
Sanderling Ct. SE28 . . . . 7C 74
Sanders Clo. Hamp H 5G 115
Sanders Ho. WC1
. . . . 3A 68 (1J 161)
(off Gt. Percy St.)
Sanders La. NW7 . . . . 7K 13
(in three parts)
Sanderson Clo. NW5 . . . . 4F 49
Sanderson Ho. SE8 . . . . 5B 88
(off Grove St.)
Sanderstead Av. NW2 . . . . . . 2G 47
Sanderstead Clo. SW12 . . . . . 7G 103
Sanderstead Rd. E10 . . . . 1A 52
Sanderstead Rd. S Croy 7D 152
Sanders Way. N19 . . . . 1H 49
Sandfield. WC1 . . . . 3J 67 (2F 161)
(off Cromer St.)
Sandfield Gdns. T Hth 3B 140
Sandfield Rd. T Hth 3B 140
Sandford Av. N22 . . . . 1C 32
Sandford Clo. E6 . . . . 4D 72
Sandford Ct. N16 . . . . 1E 50
Sandford Ct. New Bar 3E 4
Sandford Rd. E6 . . . . 3C 72
Sandford Rd. Bexh 4E 110
Sandford Rd. Brom 3J 143
Sandford Row. SE17 . . . . 5D 86
Sandford St. SW6 . . . . 7K 83
Sandgate Clo. Romf 7J 39
Sandgate Ho. E5 . . . . 5H 51
Sandgate Ho. W5 . . . . 5C 62
Sandgate La. SW18 . . . . 1C 120
Sandgate Rd. Well 7C 92
Sandgate St. SE15 . . . . 6H 87
Sandgate Trad. Est. SE15 . . . . 6H 87
(off Sandgate St.)
Sandham Ct. SW4 . . . . 1J 103
Sandhills. Wall 4H 151
Sandhills Mdw. Shep 7E 130
Sandhills, The. SW10
. . . . 6A 84 (7A 170)
(off Limerston St.)
Sandhurst Av. Harr 6F 25
Sandhurst Av. Surb 7H 135
Sandhurst Clo. NW9 . . . . 3G 27
Sandhurst Clo. S Croy 7E 152
Sandhurst Ct. SW2 . . . . 4J 103
Sandhurst Dri. Ilf 4K 55
Sandhurst Ho. E1 . . . . 5J 69
(off Wolsy St.)
Sandhurst Mkt. SE6 . . . . 1E 124
(off Sandhurst Rd.)
Sandhurst Rd. N9 . . . . 6D 8
Sandhurst Rd. NW9 . . . . 3G 27
Sandhurst Rd. SE6 . . . . 1F 125
Sandhurst Rd. Bex 5D 110
Sandhurst Rd. Sidc 3K 127
Sandhurst Way. S Croy 7E 152
Sandifer Dri. NW2 . . . . 3F 47
Sandiford Rd. Sutt 2H 149
Sandiland Cres. Brom 2H 155
Sandilands. Croy 2G 153
Sandilands Rd. SW6 . . . . . . 1K 101
Sandison St. SE15 . . . . 3G 105
Sandland St. WC1
. . . . 5K 67 (6H 161)
Sandling Ri. SE9 . . . . 3E 126
Sandlings Clo. SE15 . . . . . . 2H 105
Sandlings, The. N22 . . . . 3B 32
Sandmere Rd. SW4 . . . . 4J 103
Sandon Clo. Esh 7H 133
Sandow Cres. Hay 3H 77
Sandown Av. Dag 6J 57
Sandown Clo. Houn 1J 95
Sandown Ct. SE26 . . . . 3H 123
Sandown Ct. Stan 5H 11
Sandown Ct. Sutt 7K 149
Sandown Dri. Cars 7E 150
Sandown Rd. SE25 . . . . 5H 141
Sandown Way. N'holt 6C 42
Sandpiper Clo. E17 . . . . 7E 18
Sandpiper Clo. SE16 . . . . 2B 88
Sandpiper Ct. E14 . . . . 3E 88
(off New Union Clo.)
Sandpiper Ct. SE8 . . . . 6C 88
(off Edward Pl.)
Sandpiper Rd. Sutt 5H 149
Sandpit Pl. SE7 . . . . 5C 90
Sandpit Rd. Brom 5G 125
Sandpits Rd. Croy 4K 153
Sandpits Rd. Rich 2D 116
Sandra Clo. N22 . . . . 1C 32
Sandra Clo. Houn 5F 97
Sandridge Clo. Harr 4J 25
Sandridge Ct. N4 . . . . 2C 50
Sandridge St. N19 . . . . 2G 49
Sandringham Av. SW20 . . . . 1G 137
Sandringham Clo. SW19 . . . 1F 119
Sandringham Clo. Enf 2K 7
Sandringham Clo. Ilf 3G 37
Sandringham Ct. SE16 . . . . . . 1K 87
(off King & Queen Wharf)
Sandringham Ct. W1
. . . . 6G 67 (1B 166)
(off Dufour's Pl.)
Sandringham Ct. W9 . . . . 3A 66
(off Maida Va.)
Sandringham Ct. Sidc 6K 109
Sandringham Ct. Uxb 4E 58
Sandringham Cres. Harr 2E 42
Sandringham Dri. Ashf 4A 112
Sandringham Dri. Bex 2K 129
Sandringham Dri. Well 2J 109
Sandringham Flats. WC2
. . . . 7H 67 (2D 166)
(off Charing Cross Rd.)
Sandringham Gdns. N8 . . . . . 6J 31
Sandringham Gdns. N12 . . . . 6G 15
Sandringham Gdns. Houn . . . 1J 95
Sandringham Gdns. Ilf 3G 37
Sandringham Gdns.
W Mol 4E 132
Sandringham Ho. W14 . . . . . 4G 83
(off Windsor Way)
Sandringham M. W5 . . . . 7D 62
Sandringham Rd. E7 . . . . 5A 54
Sandringham Rd. E8 . . . . 5F 51
Sandringham Rd. E10 . . . . . . 6F 35
Sandringham Rd. N22 . . . . . . 3C 32
Sandringham Rd. NW2 . . . . . . 6D 46
Sandringham Rd. NW11 . . . . . 7G 29
Sandringham Rd. Bark 5K 55
Sandringham Rd. Brom 5J 125
Sandringham Rd. H'row A . . . 5A 94
Sandringham Rd. N'holt 7E 42
Sandringham Rd. T Hth 5C 140
Sandringham Rd. Wor Pk
. . . . 3C 148
Sandrock Pl. Croy 4K 153
Sandrock Rd. SE13 . . . . 3C 106
Sands End. 1A 102
Sand's End La. SW6 . . . . . . 1K 101
Sandstone Pl. N19 . . . . 2F 49
Sandstone Rd. SE12 . . . . . . 2K 125
Sands Way. Wfd G 6J 21
Sandtoft Rd. SE7 . . . . 6K 89
Sandwell Cres. NW6 . . . . 6J 47
Sandwich Ho. SE16 . . . . 2J 87
(off Swan Rd.)
Sandwich Ho. WC1
. . . . 3J 67 (2E 160)
(off Sandwich St.)
Sandwich St. WC1
. . . . 3J 67 (2E 160)
Sandwick Clo. NW7 . . . . 7H 13
Sandycombe Rd. Felt 1J 113
Sandycombe Rd. Rich 3F 99
Sandycoombe Rd. Twic 6C 98
Sandycroft. SE2 . . . . 6A 92
Sandy Dri. Felt 1G 113
Sandy Hill Av. SE18 . . . . 5F 91
Sandy Hill Rd. SE18 . . . . 4F 91
Sandyhill Rd. Ilf 4F 55
Sandy Hill Rd. Wall 7G 151
Sandy La. Harr 6F 27
Sandy La. Mitc 1E 138
(in two parts)
Sandy La. Orp 7K 145
Sandy La. Rich 2C 116
Sandy La. St P & Sidc 7D 128
Sandy La. Sutt 7G 149
Sandy La.
Tedd & Hamp W 7A 116
Sandy La. W on T 6K 131
Sandy La. N. Wall 5H 151
Sandy La. S. Wall 7G 151
Sandymount Av. Stan 5H 11
Sandy Ridge. Chst 6E 126
Sandy Rd. NW3 . . . . 2K 47
(in two parts)
Sandys Row. E1 . . . 5E 68 (6H 163)
Sandy Way. Croy 3B 154
Sandy Way. W on T 7H 131
Sanford La. N16 . . . . 3F 51
(in two parts)
Sanford St. SE14 . . . . 6A 88
Sanford Ter. N16 . . . . 3F 51
Sanford Wlk. N16 . . . . 2F 51
Sanford Wlk. SE14 . . . . 6A 88
Sanger Av. Chess 5E 146
Sangley Rd. SE6 . . . . 7D 106
Sangley Rd. SE25 . . . . 4E 140
Sangora Rd. SW11 . . . . 4B 102
Sankey Ho. E2 . . . . 2J 69
(off St James's Av.)
Sansom Rd. E11 . . . . 2H 53
Sansom St. SE5 . . . . 1D 104
Sans Wlk. EC1 . . . . 4A 68 (3K 161)
Santley Ho. SE1 . . . 2A 86 (7K 167)
Santley St. SW4 . . . . 4K 103
Santos Rd. SW18 . . . . 5J 101
Santway, The. Stan 5D 10
Sapcote Trad. Cen.
NW10 . . . . 6B 46
Saperton Wlk. SE11 . . . . . . 3H 173
Sapperton Ct. EC1 . . . . 3C 162
Sapphire Clo. E6 . . . . 6E 72
Sapphire Clo. Dag 1C 56
Sapphire Ct. E1 . . . . 7G 69
(off Cable St.)
Sapphire Rd. SE8 . . . . 4A 88
Saracen Clo. Croy 6D 140
Saracens Head Yd.
EC3 . . . . 1J 169
Saracen St. E14 . . . . 6C 70
Sarah Ct. N'holt 1D 60
Sarah Ho. E1 . . . . 6H 69
(off Commercial Rd.)
Sarah St. N1 . . . . . . 3E 68 (1H 163)
Sarah Swift Ho. SE1
. . . . 2D 86 (6F 169)
(off Kipling St.)
Sara La. Ct. N1 . . . . 2E 68
(off Stanway St.)
Saratoga Rd. E5 . . . . 4J 51
Sara Turnbull Ho.
SE18 . . . . 4D 90
Sardinia St. WC2
. . . . 6K 67 (1G 167)
Sarita Clo. Harr 2H 25
Sarjant Path. SW19 . . . . 2F 119
(off Blincoe Clo.)
Sark Clo. Houn 7E 78
Sark Ho. Enf 1E 8
Sark Tower. SE28 . . . . 2G 91
(off Erebus Dri.)
Sark Wlk. E16 . . . . 6K 71
Sarnes Ct. N11 . . . . 4A 16
(off Oakleigh Rd. S.)
Sarnesfield Ho. SE15 . . . . 6H 87
(off Pencraig Way)
Sarnesfield Rd. Enf 4J 7
Sarratt Ho. W10 . . . . 5E 64
(off Sutton Way)
Sarre Rd. NW2 . . . . 5H 47
Sarsen Av. Houn 2E 96
Sarsfeld Rd. SW12 . . . . 2D 120
Sarsfield Rd. Gnfd 2B 62
Sartor Rd. SE15 . . . . 4K 105
Sarum Ter. E3 . . . . 4B 70
Sassoon. NW9 . . . . 1B 28
Satanita Clo. E16 . . . . 6B 72
Satchell Mead. NW9 . . . . 1B 28
Satchwell Rd. E2 . . . 3G 69 (2K 163)
Satchwell St. E2 . . . 3G 69 (2K 163)
Sattar M. N16 . . . . 3D 50
(off Clissold Rd.)
Saul Ct. SE15 . . . . 6F 87
Sauls Grn. E11 . . . . 3G 53
Saunders Clo. E14 . . . . 7B 70
(off Limehouse Causeway)
Saunders Ho. SE16 . . . . 2K 87
(off Quebec Way)
Saunders Ho. W11 . . . . 1F 83
Saunders Ness Rd. E14 . . . . . 5E 88
Saunders Rd. SE18 . . . . 5K 91
Saunders Rd. Uxb 7B 40
Saunders St. SE11
. . . . 4A 86 (3H 173)
Saunders Way. SE28 . . . . 7B 74
Saunderton Rd. Wemb 5B 44
Saunton Av. Hay 7H 77
Saunton Ct. S'hall 7G 61
(off Haldane Rd.)
Savage Gdns. E6 . . . . 6D 72
Savage Gdns. EC3
. . . . 7E 68 (2H 169)
(in two parts)
Savernake Ct. Stan 6G 11
Savernake Ho. N4 . . . . 7C 32
Savernake Rd. N9 . . . . 6B 8
Savernake Rd. NW3 . . . . 4D 48
Savery Dri. Surb 7C 134
Savile Clo. N Mald 5A 136
Savile Clo. Th Dit
. . . . 7K 133 & 1A 146
Savile Gdns. Croy 2F 153
Savile Row. W1 . . . . 7G 67 (2A 166)
Saville Cres. Ashf 6F 113
Saville Rd. E16 . . . . 1C 90
Saville Rd. W4 . . . . 3K 81
Saville Rd. Romf 6F 39
Saville Rd. Twic 1K 115
Saville Row. Brom 1H 155
Saville Row. Enf 2E 8
Savill Gdns. SW20 . . . . 3C 136
Savill Ho. E16 . . . . 1F 91
(off Robert St.)
Savill Ho. SW4 . . . . 6H 103
Savill Row. Wfd G 6C 20
Savin Lodge. Sutt 7A 150
(off Walnut M.)
Savona Clo. SW19 . . . . 7F 119
Savona Ho. SW8 . . . . 7G 85
(off Savona St.)
Savona St. SW8 . . . . 7G 85
Savoy Av. Hay 5G 77
Savoy Bldgs. WC2 . . . . 3G 167
Savoy Circus. (Junct.) 7B 64
Savoy Clo. E15 . . . . 1G 71
Savoy Clo. Edgw 5B 12
Savoy Ct. NW3 . . . . 3A 48
Savoy Ct. WC2 . . . . 7K 67 (3F 167)
Savoy Hill. WC2 . . . 7K 67 (3G 167)
Savoy Pde. Enf 3K 7
Savoy Pl. WC2 . . . . . 7J 67 (3F 167)
Savoy Row. WC2 . . . . 2G 167
Savoy Steps. WC2 . . . . 3G 167
Savoy St. WC2 . . . . 7K 67 (3G 167)
Savoy Theatre. . . . 7J 67 (3F 167)
Savoy Way. WC2 . . . . 3G 167
Sawbill Clo. Hay 5B 60
Sawkins Clo. SW19 . . . . 2G 119
Sawley Rd. W12 . . . . 1B 82
Sawmill Yd. E3 . . . . 1A 70
Sawtry Clo. Cars 7C 138
Sawyer Clo. N9 . . . . 2B 18
Sawyer Ct. NW10 . . . . 7K 45
Sawyers Clo. Dag 6J 57
Sawyer's Hill. Rich 7F 99
Sawyers Lawn. W13 . . . . 6A 62
Sawyer St. SE1 . . . . 2C 86 (6C 168)
Saxby Rd. SW2 . . . . 7J 103
Saxham Rd. Bark 1J 73
Saxlingham Rd. E4 . . . . 3A 20
Saxon Av. Felt 2C 114
Saxonbury Av. Sun 3K 131
Saxonbury Clo. Mitc 3B 138
Saxonbury Ct. N7 . . . . 5J 49
Saxonbury Gdns. Surb 1C 146
Saxon Bus. Cen. SW19 . . . . 2A 138
Saxon Clo. E17 . . . . 7C 34
Saxon Clo. Surb 6D 134
Saxon Clo. Uxb 5B 58
Saxon Dri. W3 . . . . 6G 63
Saxonfield Clo. SW2 . . . . . . 1K 121
Saxon Gdns. S'hall 7C 60
Saxon Ho. Felt 2D 114
Saxon Lodge. Croy 1C 152
(off Tavistock Rd.)
Saxon Rd. E3 . . . . 2B 70
Saxon Rd. E6 . . . . 4D 72
Saxon Rd. N22 . . . . 1B 32
Saxon Rd. SE25 . . . . 5D 140
Saxon Rd. Ashf 6F 113
Saxon Rd. Brom 7H 125
Saxon Rd. Ilf 6F 55
Saxon Rd. King T 1E 134
Saxon Rd. S'hall 7C 60
Saxon Rd. Wemb 3J 45
Saxon Wlk. Sidc 6C 128
Saxon Way. N14 . . . . 6C 6
Saxony Pde. Hay 5E 58
Saxton Clo. SE13 . . . . 3F 107
Sayers Ho. N2 . . . . 2B 30
(off Grange, The)
Sayer's Wlk. Rich 7F 99
Sayesbury La. N18 . . . . 5B 18
Sayes Ct. SE8 . . . . 6B 88
Sayes Ct. St. SE8 . . . . 6B 88
Scads Hill Clo. Orp 6K 145
Scafell. NW1 . . . . . 3G 67 (1A 160)
(off Stanhope St.)
Scala St. W1 . . . . . . 5G 67 (5B 160)
Scales Rd. N17 . . . . 3F 33
Scampston M. W10 . . . . 6F 65
Scampton Rd. H'row A 6B 94
Scandrett St. E1 . . . . 1H 87
Scarba Wlk. N1 . . . . 6D 50
(off Marquess Rd.)
Scarborough Rd. E11 . . . . 1F 53
Scarborough Rd. N4 . . . . 1A 50
Scarborough Rd. N9 . . . . 7D 8
Scarborough Rd. H'row A . . . 6E 94
Scarborough St. E1
. . . . 6F 69 (1K 169)
Scarbrook Rd. Croy 3C 152
Scarle Rd. Wemb 6D 44
Scarlet Rd. SE6 . . . . 3G 125
Scarlette Mnr. Way. SW2 . . . 7A 104
Scarsbrook Rd. SE3 . . . . . . 3B 108
Scarsdale Pl. W8 . . . . 3K 83
Scarsdale Rd. Harr 3G 43
Scarsdale Vs. W8 . . . . 3J 83
Scarth Rd. SW13 . . . . 3B 100
Scawen Clo. Cars 4E 150
Scawen Rd. SE8 . . . . 5A 88
Scawfell St. E2 . . . . 2F 69
Sceaux Gdns. SE5 . . . . 1E 104
Sceptre Ct. EC3 . . . . 7F 69 (3K 169)
(off Tower Hill)
Sceptre Ho. E1 . . . . 4J 69
(off Malcolm Rd.)
Sceptre Rd. E2 . . . . 3J 69
Sceynes Link. N12 . . . . 4D 14
Schafer Ho. NW1
. . . . 3G 67 (2A 160)
Schiller International University.
. . . . 1A 86 (5J 167)

Schofield Wlk. SE3 ... 7K 89
Scholars Rd. E4 ... 1A 20
Scholars Rd. SW12 ... 1G 121
Scholefield Rd. N19 ... 1H 49
Scholey Ho. SW11 ... 3C 102
Schomberg Ho. SW1 ... 4H 85 (3D 172) (off Page St.)
Schonfeld Sq. N16 ... 2D 50
School All. Twic ... 1A 116
School App. E2 ... 3E 68 (1H 163)
Schoolbank Rd. SE10 ... 3H 89
Schoolbell M. E3 ... 2A 70
School Ho. SE1 ... 4E 86 (off Quadrangle Clo.)
School Ho. La. E1 ... 7K 69
School Ho. La. Tedd ... 7B 116
School La. Bush ... 1A 10
School La. King T ... 1C 134
School La. Pinn ... 4C 24
School La. Shep ... 6D 130
School La. Surb ... 1G 147
School La. Well ... 3B 110
School of Advanced Study. ... 5D 160 (in University of London, Senate House)
School of Hygiene & Tropical Medicine. ... 5D 160
School of Oriental & African Studies. ... 4D 160
School of Pharmacy, The. ... 3F 161
School of Slavonic & East European Studies. ... 5D 160 (in University of London, Senate House)
School Pas. King T ... 2F 135
School Pas. S'hall ... 7D 60
School Rd. E12 ... 4D 54
School Rd. NW10 ... 4K 63
School Rd. Ashf ... 6D 112
School Rd. Chst ... 1G 145
School Rd. Dag ... 1G 75
School Rd. E Mol ... 4H 133
School Rd. Hamp H ... 6G 115
School Rd. Houn ... 3G 97
School Rd. King T ... 1C 134
School Rd. Av. Hamp H ... 6G 115
School Road Junction. (Junct.) ... 6D 112
School Wlk. Sun ... 4H 131
School Way. N12 ... 6G 15
School Way. Dag ... 3C 56
Schooner Clo. E14 ... 3F 89
Schooner Clo. SE16 ... 2K 87
Schooner Clo. Bark ... 3B 74
Schubert Rd. SW15 ... 5H 101
Science Mus. ... 3B 84 (2A 170)
Sclater St. E1 ... 4F 69 (3J 163)
Scoble Pl. N16 ... 4F 51
Scoles Cres. SW2 ... 1A 122
Scope Way. King T ... 4E 134
Scoresby St. SE1 ... 1B 86 (5A 168)
Scorton Av. Gnfd ... 2A 62
Scorton Ho. N1 ... 2E 68 (off Whitmore Est.)
Scotch Comn. W13 ... 5A 62
Scotch House. (Junct.) ... 2D 84 (7E 164)
Scoter Clo. Wfd G ... 7E 20
Scoter Ct. SE8 ... 6B 88 (off Abinger Gro.)
Scot Gro. Pinn ... 1B 24
Scotia Building. E1 ... 7K 69 (off Jardine Rd.)
Scotia Ct. SE16 ... 2J 87 (off Canada Est.)
Scotia Rd. SW2 ... 7A 104
Scotland Grn. N17 ... 2F 33
Scotland Grn. Rd. Enf ... 5E 8
Scotland Grn. Rd. N. Enf ... 4E 8
Scotland Pl. SW1 ... 1J 85 (5E 166)
Scotland Rd. Buck H ... 1F 21
Scotney Clo. Orp ... 4E 156
Scotney Ho. E9 ... 6J 51
Scots Clo. Stanw ... 1A 112
Scotsdale Clo. Orp ... 4J 145
Scotsdale Clo. Sutt ... 7G 149
Scotsdale Rd. SE12 ... 5K 107
Scotson Ho. SE11 ... 4J 173
Scotswood St. EC1 ... 4A 68 (3K 161)
Scotswood Wlk. N17 ... 7B 18
Scott Clo. SW16 ... 1K 139
Scott Clo. Eps ... 5J 147
Scott Clo. W Dray ... 4B 76
Scott Ct. W3 ... 2K 81
Scott Cres. Harr ... 1F 43
Scott Ellis Gdns. NW8 ... 3B 66 (2A 158)
Scottes La. Dag ... 1D 56
Scott Farm Clo. Th Dit ... 1B 146
Scott Gdns. Houn ... 7B 78
Scott Ho. E13 ... 2J 71 (off Queens Rd. W.)
Scott Ho. E14 ... 2C 88 (off Admirals Way)
Scott Ho. N1 ... 1D 68 (off Sherborne St.)
Scott Ho. N7 ... 6K 49 (off Caledonian Rd.)
Scott Ho. NW8 ... 4C 66 (4C 158) (off Ashmill St.)
Scott Ho. NW10 ... 7K 45 (off Stonebridge Pk.)
Scott Ho. Belv ... 5F 93
Scott Lidgett Cres. SE16 ... 2G 87
Scott Russell Pl. E14 ... 5D 88
Scotts Av. Brom ... 2F 143
Scotts Av. Sun ... 7G 113
Scotts Ct. W12 ... 2E 82 (off Scott's Rd.)
Scotts Dri. Hamp ... 7F 115
Scotts Farm Rd. Eps ... 6J 147
Scott's La. Brom ... 3F 143
Scotts Pas. SE18 ... 4F 91
Scott's Rd. E10 ... 1E 52
Scott's Rd. W12 ... 2D 82
Scotts Rd. Brom ... 7J 125
Scott's Rd. S'hall ... 3A 78
Scott's Sufferance Wharf. SE1 ... 7K 169
Scott St. E1 ... 4H 69
Scotts Way. Sun ... 7G 113
Scott's Yd. EC4 ... 7D 68 (2E 168)
Scott Trimmer Way. Houn ... 2C 96
Scottwell Dri. NW9 ... 5B 28
Scoulding Ho. E14 ... 3C 88 (off Mellish St.)
Scoulding Rd. E16 ... 6J 71
Scouler St. E14 ... 7E 70
Scout App. NW10 ... 4A 46
Scout La. SW4 ... 3G 103
Scout Way. NW7 ... 4E 12
Scovell Cres. SE1 ... 7C 168
Scovell Rd. SE1 ... 2C 86 (7C 168)
Scrattons Ter. Bark ... 2D 74
Scriven Ct. E8 ... 1F 69
Scriven St. E8 ... 1F 69
Scrooby St. SE6 ... 6D 106
Scrope Ho. EC1 ... 5A 68 (5J 161) (off Bourne Est.)
Scrubs La. NW10 & W10 ... 3C 64
Scrutton Clo. SW12 ... 7H 103
Scrutton St. EC2 ... 4E 68 (4G 163)
Scudamore La. NW9 ... 4J 27
Scutari Rd. SE22 ... 5J 105
Scylla Cres. H'row A ... 6D 94
Scylla Rd. SE15 ... 3G 105 (in two parts)
Scylla Rd. H'row A ... 6D 94
Seabright St. E2 ... 3H 69
Seabrook Dri. W Wick ... 2G 155
Seabrook Gdns. Romf ... 7G 39
Seabrook Rd. Dag ... 3D 56
Seaburn Clo. Rain ... 2K 75
Seacole Clo. W3 ... 6K 63
Seacourt Rd. SE2 ... 2D 92
Seafield Rd. N11 ... 4C 16
Seaford Clo. Ruis ... 1F 41
Seaford Ho. SE16 ... 2J 87 (off Swan Rd.)
Seaford Rd. E17 ... 3D 34
Seaford Rd. N15 ... 5D 32
Seaford Rd. W13 ... 1B 80
Seaford Rd. Enf ... 4K 7
Seaford Rd. H'row A ... 5A 94
Seaford St. WC1 ... 3K 67 (2F 161)
Seaforth Av. N Mald ... 5D 136
Seaforth Cres. N5 ... 5C 50
Seaforth Gdns. N21 ... 7E 6
Seaforth Gdns. Eps ... 4B 148
Seaforth Gdns. Wfd G ... 5F 21
Seaforth Pl. SW1 ... 1B 172
Seagar Bldgs. SE8 ... 1C 106
Seagar Pl. E3 ... 5B 70
Seagrave Clo. E1 ... 5K 69
Seagrave Lodge. SW6 ... 6J 83 (off Seagrave Rd.)
Seagrave Rd. SW6 ... 6J 83
Seagry Rd. E11 ... 7J 35
Sealand Rd. H'row A ... 6C 94
Sealand Wlk. N'holt ... 3B 60
Seal Ho. SE1 ... 3D 86 (7F 169) (off Pardoner St.)
Seal St. E8 ... 4F 51
Searle Pl. N4 ... 1K 49
Searles Clo. SW11 ... 7C 84
Searles Dri. E6 ... 5F 73
Searles Rd. SE1 ... 4D 86
Searson Ho. SE17 ... 4B 86 (off Canterbury Pl.)
Sears St. SE5 ... 7D 86
Seasprite Clo. N'holt ... 3B 60
Seaton Av. Ilf ... 5K 55
Seaton Clo. E13 ... 4J 71
Seaton Clo. SE11 ... 5A 86 (5K 173)
Seaton Clo. SW15 ... 1D 118
Seaton Clo. Twic ... 6H 97
Seaton Dri. Ashf ... 2A 112
Seaton Gdns. Ruis ... 3H 41
Seaton Point. E5 ... 4G 51
Seaton Rd. Hay ... 4F 77
Seaton Rd. Mitc ... 2C 138
Seaton Rd. Twic ... 6G 97
Seaton Rd. Well ... 7C 92
Seaton Rd. Wemb ... 2E 62
Seaton St. N18 ... 5B 18
Sebastian Ho. N1 ... 2E 68 (1G 163) (off Hoxton St.)
Sebastian St. EC1 ... 3B 68 (2B 162)
Sebastopol Rd. N9 ... 4B 18
Sebbon St. N1 ... 7B 50
Sebergham Gro. NW7 ... 7H 13
Sebert Rd. E7 ... 5K 53
Sebright Ho. E2 ... 2G 69 (off Coate St.)
Sebright Pas. E2 ... 2G 69
Sebright Rd. Barn ... 2A 4
Secker Cres. Harr ... 1G 25
Secker Ho. SW9 ... 2B 104 (off Loughborough Est.)
Secker St. SE1 ... 1A 86 (5J 167)
Secombe Cen. ... 5K 149
Second Av. E12 ... 4C 54
Second Av. E13 ... 3J 71
Second Av. E17 ... 5C 34
Second Av. N18 ... 4D 18
Second Av. NW4 ... 4F 29
Second Av. SW14 ... 3A 100
Second Av. W3 ... 1B 82
Second Av. W10 ... 4G 65
Second Av. Dag ... 1H 75
Second Av. Enf ... 5A 8
Second Av. Hay ... 1H 77
Second Av. Romf ... 5C 38
Second Av. W on T ... 6K 131
Second Av. Wemb ... 2D 44
Second Clo. W Mol ... 4G 133
Second Cross Rd. Twic ... 2J 115
Second Way. Wemb ... 4H 45
Sedan Way. SE17 ... 5E 86
Sedcombe Clo. Sidc ... 4B 128
Sedcote Rd. Enf ... 5D 8
Sedding St. SW1 ... 4E 84 (3G 171)
Sedding Studios. SW1 ... 4E 84 (3G 171) (off Sedding St.)
Seddon Highwalk. EC2 ... 5C 68 (5C 162) (off Seddon Ho.)
Seddon Ho. EC2 ... 5C 162
Seddon Rd. Mord ... 5B 138
Seddon St. WC1 ... 3K 67 (2H 161)
Sedgebrook Rd. SE3 ... 2B 108
Sedgecombe Av. Harr ... 5C 26
Sedgefield Ct. N'holt ... 5F 43 (off Newmarket Av.)
Sedgeford Rd. W12 ... 1B 82
Sedgehill Rd. SE6 ... 4C 124
Sedgemere Av. N2 ... 3A 30
Sedgemere Rd. SE2 ... 3C 92
Sedgemoor Dri. Dag ... 4G 57
Sedge Rd. N17 ... 7D 18
Sedgeway. SE6 ... 1H 125
Sedgewick Av. Uxb ... 7D 40
Sedgewood Clo. Brom ... 7H 143
Sedgmoor Pl. SE5 ... 7E 86
Sedgwick Ho. E3 ... 5C 70 (off Gale St.)
Sedgwick Rd. E10 ... 2E 52
Sedgwick St. E9 ... 5K 51
Sedleigh Rd. SW18 ... 6H 101
Sedlescombe Rd. SW6 ... 6J 83
Sedley Clo. Enf ... 1C 8
Sedley Ct. SE26 ... 2H 123
Sedley Ho. SE11 ... 5K 85 (5H 173) (off Newburn St.)
Sedley Pl. W1 ... 6F 67 (1J 165)
Sedum Clo. NW9 ... 5H 27
Seeley Dri. SE21 ... 4E 122
Seelig Av. NW9 ... 7C 28
Seely Rd. SW17 ... 6E 120
Seething La. EC3 ... 7E 68 (2H 169)
Seething Wells. ... 6C 134
Seething Wells La. Surb ... 6C 134
Sefton Av. NW7 ... 5E 12
Sefton Av. Harr ... 2H 25
Sefton Clo. Orp ... 4K 145
Sefton Ct. Enf ... 2G 7 (in two parts)
Sefton Ct. Houn ... 1F 97
Sefton Rd. Croy ... 1G 153
Sefton Rd. Orp ... 4K 145
Sefton St. SW15 ... 3E 100
Segal Clo. SE23 ... 7A 106
Sekforde St. EC1 ... 4B 68 (4A 162)
Sekhon Ter. Felt ... 3E 114
Selah Dri. Swan ... 7J 129
Selan Gdns. Hay ... 5K 59
Selbie Av. NW10 ... 5B 46
Selborne Av. E12 ... 4E 54
Selborne Av. Bex ... 1E 128
Selborne Gdns. NW4 ... 4C 28
Selborne Gdns. Gnfd ... 1A 62
Selborne Rd. E17 ... 5B 34
Selborne Rd. N14 ... 3D 16
Selborne Rd. SE5 ... 2D 104
Selborne Rd. Croy ... 3E 152
Selborne Rd. Ilf ... 2E 54
Selborne Rd. N Mald ... 2A 136
Selborne Rd. Sidc ... 4B 128
Selborne Wlk. E17 ... 5B 34
Selborne Wlk. Shop. Cen. E17 ... 4B 34
Selbourne Av. Surb ... 2F 147
Selbourne Ho. SE1 ... 7E 168
Selbourne Rd. N22 ... 1K 31
Selby Chase. Ruis ... 2K 41
Selby Clo. E6 ... 5C 72
Selby Clo. Chess ... 7E 146
Selby Clo. Chst ... 6E 126
Selby Gdns. S'hall ... 4E 60
Selby Grn. Cars ... 7C 138
Selby Ho. W10 ... 3G 65 (off Beethoven St.)
Selby Rd. E11 ... 3G 53
Selby Rd. E13 ... 5K 71
Selby Rd. N17 ... 7K 17
Selby Rd. SE20 ... 2G 141
Selby Rd. W5 ... 4B 62
Selby Rd. Ashf ... 6E 112
Selby Rd. Cars ... 7C 138
Selby St. E1 ... 4G 69
Selcroft Ho. SE10 ... 5H 89 (off Glenister Rd.)
Selden Ho. SE15 ... 2J 105 (off Selden Rd.)
Selden Rd. SE15 ... 2J 105
Selden Wlk. N7 ... 2K 49
Seldon Ho. SW1 ... 5G 85 (6A 172) (off Churchill Gdns.)
Seldon Ho. SW8 ... 7G 85 (off Stewart's Rd.)
Selfridges. ... 1H 165
Selhurst. ... 6D 140
Selhurst Clo. SW19 ... 1F 119
Selhurst New Rd. SE25 ... 6E 140
Selhurst Pk. (Crystal Palace F.C. & Wimbledon F.C.) ... 4E 140
Selhurst Pl. SE25 ... 6E 140
Selhurst Rd. N9 ... 3J 17
Selhurst Rd. SE25 ... 6E 140
Selina Ho. NW8 ... 4B 66 (3B 158) (off Frampton St.)
Selinas La. Dag ... 7E 38
Selkirk Rd. SW17 ... 4C 120
Selkirk Rd. Twic ... 2G 115
Sellers Hall Clo. N3 ... 7D 14
Sellincourt Rd. SW17 ... 5C 120
Sellindge Clo. Beck ... 7B 124
Sellons Av. NW10 ... 1B 64
Selma Ho. W12 ... 6D 64 (off Du Cane Rd.)
Selsdon Av. S Croy ... 6D 152
Selsdon Clo. Romf ... 1J 39
Selsdon Clo. Surb ... 5E 134
Selsdon Ct. S'hall ... 6F 61 (off Dormers Ri.)
Selsdon Pk. Rd. S Croy & Croy ... 7K 153
Selsdon Rd. E11 ... 7J 35
Selsdon Rd. E13 ... 1A 72
Selsdon Rd. NW2 ... 2B 46
Selsdon Rd. SE27 ... 3A 122
Selsdon Rd. S Croy ... 5D 152
Selsdon Way. E14 ... 3D 88
Selsea Pl. N16 ... 5E 50
Selsey Cres. Well ... 1D 110
Selsey St. E14 ... 5C 70
Selvage La. NW7 ... 5E 12
Selway Clo. Pinn ... 4K 23
Selway Ho. SW8 ... 1J 103 (off S. Lambeth Rd.)
Selwood Dri. Barn ... 5A 4
Selwood Pl. SW7 ... 5B 84 (5A 170)
Selwood Rd. Chess ... 4D 146
Selwood Rd. Croy ... 2H 153
Selwood Rd. Sutt ... 1H 149
Selwoods. SW2 ... 7A 104
Selwood Ter. SW7 ... 5B 84 (5A 170)
Selworthy Clo. E11 ... 5J 35
Selworthy Rd. SE6 ... 3B 124
Selwyn Av. E4 ... 6K 19
Selwyn Av. Ilf ... 6K 37
Selwyn Av. Rich ... 3E 98
Selwyn Clo. Houn ... 4C 96
Selwyn Ct. E17 ... 5C 34 (off Yunus Khan Clo.)
Selwyn Ct. SE3 ... 3H 107
Selwyn Ct. Edgw ... 7C 12
Selwyn Ct. Wemb ... 3J 45
Selwyn Cres. Well ... 3B 110
Selwyn Rd. E3 ... 2B 70
Selwyn Rd. E13 ... 1K 71

Selwyn Rd. NW10 7K 45
Selwyn Rd. N Mald 5K 135
Semley Ga. E9 6B 52
Semley Ho. SW1 4F 85 (4J 171) (off Semley Pl.)
Semley Pl. SW1 4E 84 (4H 171)
Semley Rd. SW16 2J 139
Senate St. SE15 2J 105
Senators Lodge. E3 2A 70 (off Roman Rd.)
Senator Wlk. SE28 3H 91
Seneca Rd. T Hth 4C 140
Senga Rd. Wall 1E 150
Senhouse Rd. Sutt 3F 149
Senior St. W2 5K 65
Senlac Rd. SE12 1K 125
Sennen Rd. Enf 7A 8
Sennen Wlk. SE9 3C 126
Senrab St. E1 6K 69
Sentinel Clo. N'holt 4C 60
Sentinel Sq. NW4 4E 28
September Ct. S'hall 1F 79 (off Dormer's Wells La.)
September Ct. Uxb 2A 58
September Way. Stan 6G 11
Septimus Pl. Enf 5B 8
Sequoia Clo. Bus H 1C 10
Sequoia Gdns. Orp 7K 145
Sequoia Pk. Pinn 6A 10
Seraph Ct. EC1 3C 68 (1B 162) (off Moreland St.)
Serbin Clo. E10 7E 34
Serenaders Rd. SW9 2A 104
Sergeant Ind. Est. SW18 6K 101
Serica Ct. SE10 7E 88
Serjeant's Inn. EC4 6A 68 (1K 167)
Serle St. WC2 6K 67 (7H 161)
Sermon La. EC4 1C 168
Serpentine Gallery. 2B 84 (6B 164)
Serpentine Rd. W2 1C 84 (5C 164)
Serviden Dri. Brom 1B 144
Servite Ho. Wor Pk 2B 148 (off Avenue, The)
Servius Ct. Bren 7D 80
Setchell Rd. SE1 4F 87
Setchell Way. SE1 4F 87
Seth St. SE16 2J 87
Seton Gdns. Dag 7C 56
Settle Rd. E13 2J 71
Settles St. E1 5G 69
Settrington Rd. SW6 2K 101
Seven Acres. Cars 2C 150
Seven Dials. WC2 6J 67 (1E 166)
Seven Dials Ct. WC2 6J 67 (1E 166) (off Shorts Gdns.)
Sevenex Pde. Wemb 5E 44
Seven Kings. 1J 55
Seven Kings Rd. Ilf 1J 55
Seven Kings Way. King T 1E 134
Sevenoaks Clo. Bexh 4H 111
Sevenoaks Ct. N'wd 1E 22
Sevenoaks Rd. SE4 6A 106
Sevenoaks Way. Sidc & Orp 7C 128
Seven Sisters. (Junct.) 5F 33
Seven Sisters Rd. N7 & N4 3K 49
Seven Sisters Rd. N15 6D 32
Seven Stars Corner. W6 3C 82
Seventh Av. E12 4D 54
Seventh Av. Hay 1J 77
Severnake Clo. E14 4C 88
Severn Ct. King T 1D 134
Severn Dri. Esh 2A 146
Severn Way. NW10 5B 46
Severus Rd. SW11 4C 102
Seville M. N1 7E 50
Seville St. SW1 2D 84 (7F 165)
Sevington Rd. NW4 6D 28
Sevington St. W9 4K 65
Seward Rd. W7 2A 80
Seward Rd. Beck 2K 141
Sewardstone. 1K 9
Sewardstone Gdns. E4 5J 9
Sewardstone Rd. E2 2J 69
Sewardstone Rd. E4 & Wal A 7J 9
Seward St. EC1 3B 68 (3B 162)
Sewdley St. E5 3K 51
Sewell Rd. SE2 3A 92
Sewell St. E13 3J 71
Sextant Av. E14 4F 89
Sextons Ho. SE10 6E 88 (off Bardsley La.)
Seymer Rd. Romf 3K 39
Seymour Av. N17 2G 33
Seymour Av. Eps 7E 148
Seymour Av. Mord 7F 137
Seymour Clo. E Mol 5G 133
Seymour Clo. Pinn 1D 24
Seymour Ct. E4 2C 20
Seymour Ct. N10 2E 30
Seymour Ct. N21 6E 6
Seymour Ct. NW2 2D 46
Seymour Dri. Brom 1D 156
Seymour Gdns. SE4 3A 106
Seymour Gdns. Felt 4A 114
Seymour Gdns. Ilf 1D 54
Seymour Gdns. Ruis 1B 42
Seymour Gdns. Surb 5F 135
Seymour Gdns. Twic 7B 98
Seymour Ho. E16 1J 89 (off De Quincey M.)
Seymour Ho. NW1 3H 67 (2D 160) (off Churchway)
Seymour Ho. WC1 4J 67 (3E 160) (off Tavistock Pl.)
Seymour Ho. Sutt 6K 149 (off Mulgrave Rd.)
Seymour M. W1 6E 66 (7G 159)
Seymour Pl. SE25 4H 141
Seymour Pl. W1 5D 66 (6E 158)
Seymour Rd. E4 1J 19
Seymour Rd. E6 2B 72
Seymour Rd. E10 1B 52
Seymour Rd. N3 7E 14
Seymour Rd. N8 5A 32
Seymour Rd. N9 2C 18
Seymour Rd. SW18 7H 101
Seymour Rd. SW19 3F 119
Seymour Rd. W4 4J 81
Seymour Rd. Cars 5E 150
Seymour Rd. E Mol 5G 133
Seymour Rd. Hamp H 5G 115
Seymour Rd. King T 1D 134
Seymour Rd. Mitc 7E 138
Seymour St. W2 & W1 6D 66 (1E 164)
Seymour Ter. SE20 1H 141
Seymour Vs. SE20 1H 141
Seymour Wlk. SW10 6A 84
Seymour Way. Sun 7H 113
Seyssel St. E14 4E 88
Shaa Rd. W3 7K 63
Shacklegate La. Tedd 4J 115
Shackleton Clo. SE23 2H 123
Shackleton Ct. E14 5C 88 (off Maritime Quay)
Shackleton Ct. W12 2D 82
Shackleton Ho. E1 1J 87 (off Prusom St.)
Shackleton Ho. NW10 7K 45
Shackleton Rd. S'hall 7D 60
Shacklewell. 4F 51
Shacklewell Grn. E8 4F 51
Shacklewell Ho. E8 4F 51
Shacklewell La. N16 5F 51
Shacklewell Rd. N16 4F 51
Shacklewell Row. E8 4F 51
Shacklewell St. E2 3F 69 (2K 163)
Shadbolt Clo. Wor Pk 2B 148
Shad Thames. SE1 1F 87 (5J 169)
Shadwell. 7H 69
Shadwell Ct. N'holt 2D 60
Shadwell Dri. N'holt 3D 60
Shadwell Gdns. E1 7J 69 (off Sutton St.)
Shadwell Pierhead. E1 7J 69
Shadwell Pl. E1 7J 69 (off Shadwell Gdns.)
Shadybush Clo. Bush 1B 10
Shaef Way. Tedd 7A 116
Shafter Rd. Dag 6J 57
Shaftesbury Av. W1 & WC2 6J 67 (3C 166)
Shaftesbury Av. Enf 2E 8
Shaftesbury Av. Felt 6J 95
Shaftesbury Av. Harr 1F 43
Shaftesbury Av. Kent 5D 26
Shaftesbury Av. New Bar 4F 5
Shaftesbury Av. S'hall 4E 78
Shaftesbury Cen. W10 4F 65 (off Barlby Rd.)
Shaftesbury Circ. S Harr 1G 43
Shaftesbury Ct. E6 6E 72 (off Sapphire Clo.)
Shaftesbury Ct. N1 2D 68 (off Shaftesbury St.)
Shaftesbury Ct. SW6 1K 101 (off Maltings Pl.)
Shaftesbury Ct. SW16 3H 121
Shaftesbury Cres. Stai 7A 112
Shaftesbury Gdns. NW10 4A 64
Shaftesbury Lodge. E14 6D 70 (off Up. North St.)
Shaftesbury M. SE1 3D 86 (off Falmouth Rd.)
Shaftesbury M. SW4 5G 103
Shaftesbury M. W8 3J 83 (off Stratford Rd.)
Shaftesbury Pde. S Harr 1G 43
Shaftesbury Pl. EC2 5C 68 (off London Wall)
Shaftesbury Pl. W14 4H 83 (off Warwick Rd.)
Shaftesbury Point. E13 2J 71 (off High St.)
Shaftesbury Rd. E4 1A 20
Shaftesbury Rd. E7 7A 54
Shaftesbury Rd. E10 1C 52
Shaftesbury Rd. E17 6D 34
Shaftesbury Rd. N18 6K 17
Shaftesbury Rd. N19 1J 49
Shaftesbury Rd. Beck 2B 142
Shaftesbury Rd. Cars 7B 138
Shaftesbury Rd. Rich 3E 98
Shaftesburys, The. Bark 2G 73
Shaftesbury St. N1 2C 68 (in two parts)
Shaftesbury Theatre. 6J 67 (7E 160) (off Shaftesbury Av.)
Shaftesbury Way. Twic 3H 115
Shaftesbury Waye. Hay 5A 60
Shafto M. SW1 3D 84 (2F 171)
Shafton M. E9 1K 69
Shafton Rd. E9 1K 69
Shaftsbury Ct. SE5 4D 104
Shafts Ct. EC3 6E 68 (1G 169)
Shahjalal Ho. E2 2G 69 (off Pritchards Rd.)
Shakespeare Av. N11 5B 16
Shakespeare Av. NW10 1K 63
Shakespeare Av. Felt 6J 95
Shakespeare Av. Hay 6J 59 (in two parts)
Shakespeare Clo. Harr 6G 27
Shakespeare Ct. Harr 7G 27
Shakespeare Ct. New Bar 3E 4
Shakespeare Cres. E12 6D 54
Shakespeare Cres. NW10 1K 63
Shakespeare Dri. Harr 6F 27
Shakespeare Gdns. N2 4D 30
Shakespeare Ho. E9 7J 51 (off Lyme Gro.)
Shakespeare Ho. N14 2C 16
Shakespeare Rd. E17 2K 33
Shakespeare Rd. N3 1J 29
Shakespeare Rd. NW7 4G 13
Shakespeare Rd. SE24 5B 104
Shakespeare Rd. W3 1J 81
Shakespeare Rd. W7 7K 61
Shakespeare Rd. Bexh 1E 110
Shakespeare's Globe Theatre & Exhibition. 1C 86 (3C 168)
Shakespeare Tower. EC2 5D 162
Shakespeare Way. Felt 4A 114
Shakspeare M. N16 4E 50
Shakspeare Wlk. N16 4E 50
Shalbourne Sq. E9 6B 52
Shalcomb St. SW10 6A 84 (7A 170)
Shalden Ho. SW15 6B 100
Shaldon Dri. Mord 5G 137
Shaldon Dri. Ruis 3A 42
Shaldon Rd. Edgw 2F 27
Shalfleet Dri. W10 7F 65
Shalford Ct. N1 2B 68 (off Charlton Pl.)
Shalford Ho. SE1 3D 86
Shalimar Gdns. W3 7J 63
Shalimar Rd. W3 7J 63
Shallons Rd. SE9 4F 127
Shalstone Rd. SW14 3H 99
Shalston Vs. Surb 6F 135
Shamrock Rd. Croy 6K 139
Shamrock St. SW4 3H 103
Shamrock Way. N14 1A 16
Shandon Rd. SW4 6G 103
Shand St. SE1 2E 86 (6H 169)
Shandy St. E1 5K 69
Shanklin Ho. E17 2B 34
Shanklin Rd. N8 5H 31
Shannon Clo. NW2 3F 47
Shannon Clo. S'hall 5B 78
Shannon Corner. (Junct.) 4C 136
Shannon Corner Retail Pk. N Mald 4C 136
Shannon Ct. N16 3E 50
Shannon Ct. Croy 1C 152 (off Tavistock Rd.)
Shannon Gro. SW9 4K 103
Shannon Pl. NW8 2C 66
Shannon Way. Beck 6D 124
Shanti Ct. SW18 1J 119
Shap Cres. Cars 1D 150
Shapland Way. N13 5E 16
Shap St. E2 2F 69
Shapwick Clo. N11 5J 15
Shardcroft Av. SE24 5B 104
Shardeloes Rd. SE14 2B 106
Shard's Sq. SE15 6G 87
Sharland Clo. T Hth 6A 140
Sharman Ct. Sidc 4A 128 (off Carlton Rd.)
Sharnbrooke Clo. Well 3C 110
Sharnbrook Ho. W14 6J 83
Sharon Clo. Surb 1C 146
Sharon Ct. S Croy 5C 152 (off Warham Rd.)
Sharon Gdns. E9 1J 69
Sharon Rd. W4 5K 81
Sharon Rd. Enf 2F 9
Sharpe Clo. W7 5K 61
Sharp Ho. SW8 3F 103
Sharp Ho. Twic 6D 98
Sharpleshall St. NW1 7D 48
Sharpness Clo. Hay 5C 60
Sharpness Ct. SE15 7F 87 (off Daniel Gdns.)
Sharp's La. Ruis 7F 23
Sharratt St. SE15 6J 87
Sharsted St. SE17 5B 86 (6K 173)
Sharvel La. N'holt 1K 59
Sharwood. WC1 2K 67 (1H 161) (off Penton Ri.)
Shaver's Pl. SW1 3C 166
Shaw Av. Bark 2E 74
Shawbrooke Rd. SE9 5A 108
Shawbury Rd. SE22 5F 105
Shaw Clo. SE28 1B 92
Shaw Clo. Bus H 2D 10
Shaw Ct. W3 3J 81 (off All Saints Rd.)
Shaw Dri. W on T 7A 132
Shawfield Ct. W Dray 3A 76
Shawfield Pk. Brom 2B 144
Shawfield St. SW3 5C 84 (6D 170)
Shawford Ct. SW15 7C 100
Shawford Rd. Eps 6K 147
Shaw Gdns. Bark 2E 74
Shaw Ho. E16 1E 90 (off Claremont St.)
Shaw Ho. Belv 5F 93
Shaw Path. Brom 3H 125
Shaw Rd. SE22 4E 104
Shaw Rd. Brom 3H 125
Shaw Rd. Enf 1E 8
Shaws Cotts. SE23 3A 124
Shaws Path. Hamp W 1C 134 (off Bennett Clo.)
Shaw Sq. E17 1A 34
Shaw Way. Wall 7J 151
Shearing Dri. Cars 7A 138
Shearling Way. N7 6J 49
Shearman Rd. SE3 4H 107
Shears Ct. Sun 7G 113
Shears, The. (Junct.) 7G 113
Shearwater Ct. SE8 6B 88 (off Abinger Gro.)
Shearwater Rd. Sutt 5H 149
Shearwater Way. Hay 6B 60
Sheaveshill Av. NW9 4A 28
Sheaveshill Ct. NW9 4K 27
Sheaveshill Pde. NW9 4A 28 (off Sheaveshill Av.)
Sheba Ct. N17 6B 18 (off Altair Clo.)
Sheen Comn. Dri. Rich 4G 99
Sheen Ct. Rich 4G 99
Sheen Ct. Rd. Rich 4G 99
Sheendale Rd. Rich 4F 99
Sheenewood. SE26 4H 123
Sheen Ga. Gdns. SW14 4J 99
Sheengate Mans. SW14 4K 99
Sheen Gro. N1 1A 68
Sheen La. SW14 5J 99
Sheen Pk. Rich 4F 99
Sheen Rd. Orp 4K 145
Sheen Rd. Rich 5E 98
Sheen Way. Wall 5K 151
Sheen Wood. SW14 5J 99
Sheepcote Clo. Houn 7J 77
Sheepcote La. SW11 2D 102
Sheepcote Rd. Harr 6K 25
Sheepcotes Rd. Romf 4E 38
Sheephouse Way. N Mald 1K 147
Sheep La. E8 1H 69
Sheep Wlk. Shep 5C 130
Sheep Wlk. M. SW19 6F 119
Sheep Wlk., The. Shep 7B 130
Sheerness M. E16 2F 91
Sheerwater Rd. E16 5B 72
Sheffield Rd. H'row A 6E 94
Sheffield Sq. E3 3B 70
Sheffield St. WC2 6K 67 (1G 167)
Sheffield Ter. W8 1J 83
Sheffield Way. H'row A 5F 95
Shelbourne Clo. Pinn 3D 24
Shelbourne Pl. Beck 7B 124
Shelbourne Rd. N17 2H 33
Shelburne Dri. Houn 6E 96
Shelburne Rd. N7 4K 49
Shelbury Clo. Sidc 3A 128
Shelbury Rd. SE22 5H 105
Sheldon Av. N6 7C 30
Sheldon Av. Ilf 2F 37
Sheldon Clo. SE12 5K 107
Sheldon Clo. SE20 1H 141

Sheldon Ct. SW8 . . . . 1J 103 (off Lansdowne Grn.)
Sheldon Ct. Barn 4E 4
Sheldon Rd. N18 . . . . 4K 17
Sheldon Rd. NW2 . . . . 4F 47
Sheldon Rd. Bexh 1F 111
Sheldon Rd. Dag 7E 56
Sheldon St. Croy 3C 152
Sheldrake Clo. E16 . . . . 1D 90
Sheldrake Ct. E6 . . . . 2C 72 (off St Bartholomew's Rd.)
Sheldrake Ho. SE16 . . . . 4K 87 (off Tawny Way)
Sheldrake Pl. W8 . . . . 2J 83
Sheldrick Clo. SW19 . . . . . . 2B 138
Shelduck Clo. E15 . . . . 5H 53
Shelduck Ct. SE8 . . . . 6B 88 (off Pilot Clo.)
Sheldwich Ter. Brom 6C 144
Shelford Pl. N16 . . . . 3D 50
Shelford Ri. SE19 . . . . 7F 123
Shelford Rd. Barn 6A 4
Shelgate Rd. SW11 . . . . 5C 102
Shell Clo. Brom 6C 144
Shellduck Clo. NW9 . . . . 2A 28
Shelley. N8 . . . . 3J 31 (off Boyton Rd.)
Shelley Av. E12 . . . . 6C 54
Shelley Av. Gnfd 3H 61
Shelley Clo. SE15 . . . . 2H 105
Shelley Clo. Edgw 4B 12
Shelley Clo. Gnfd 3H 61
Shelley Clo. Hay 5J 59
Shelley Ct. E10 . . . . 7D 34 (off Skelton's La.)
Shelley Ct. E11 . . . . 4K 35 (off Makepeace Rd.)
Shelley Ct. N4 . . . . 1K 49
Shelley Ct. SW3 . . . 6D 84 (7F 171) (off Tite St.)
Shelley Cres. Houn 1B 96
Shelley Cres. S'hall 6D 60
Shelley Dri. Well 1J 109
Shelley Gdns. Wemb 2C 44
Shelley Ho. E2 . . . . 3J 69 (off Cornwall Av.)
Shelley Ho. SE17 . . . . 5C 86 (off Browning St.)
Shelley Ho. SW1 . . . 6G 85 (7B 172) (off Churchill Gdns.)
Shelley Rd. NW10 . . . . 1K 63
Shelley Way. SW19 . . . . 6B 120
Shellness Rd. E5 . . . . 5H 51
Shell Rd. SE13 . . . . 3D 106
Shellwood Rd. SW11 . . . . . . 2D 102
Shelmerdine Clo. E3 . . . . 5C 70
Shelson Av. Felt 3H 113
Shelton Rd. SW19 . . . . 1J 137
Shelton St. WC2 . . . 6J 67 (1E 166) (in two parts)
Shene Ho. EC1 . . . . 5A 68 (5J 161) (off Bourne Est.)
Shenfield Ho. SE18 . . . . 1B 108 (off Portway Gdns.)
Shenfield Rd. Wfd G 7E 20
Shenfield St. N1 . . . 2E 68 (1H 163) (in two parts)
Shenley Av. Ruis 2H 41
Shenley Rd. SE5 . . . . 1E 104
Shenley Rd. Houn 1C 96
Shenstone. W5 . . . . 1C 80
Shenstone Clo. Dart 4K 111
Shepherd Clo. W1 . . . . 7E 66 (2G 165) (off Lees Pl.)
Shepherd Clo. Felt 4C 114
Shepherdess Pl. N1 . . . . 3C 68 (1D 162)
Shepherdess Wlk. N1 . . . . 2C 68 (1D 162)
Shepherd Ho. E14 . . . . 6D 70 (off Annabel Clo.)
Shepherd Mkt. W1 . . . . 1F 85 (4J 165)
Shepherd's Bush 2E 82
Shepherd's Bush Grn. W12 . . . . 2E 82
Shepherd's Bush Mkt. W12 . . . . 2E 82 (in two parts)
Shepherd's Bush Pl. W12 . . . . 2F 83
Shepherd's Bush Rd. W6 . . . . 4E 82
Shepherd's Clo. N6 . . . . 6F 31
Shepherds Clo. Romf 5D 38
Shepherds Clo. Shep 6D 130
Shepherds Ct. W12 . . . . 2F 83 (off Shepherd's Bush Grn.)
Shepherds Grn. Chst 7H 127
Shepherd's Hill. N6 . . . . 6F 31
Shepherds La. E9 . . . . 6K 51
Shepherds Leas. SE9 . . . . . 4G 109
Shepherd's Path. NW3 . . . . . . 5B 48 (off Lyndhurst Rd.)
Shepherds Path. N'holt . . . . . 6C 42 (off Arnold Rd.)
Shepherds Pl. W1 . . . . 7E 66 (2G 165)
Shepherd St. W1 . . . 1F 85 (5J 165)
Shepherds Wlk. NW2 . . . . . . 2C 46
Shepherd's Wlk. NW3 . . . . . . 5B 48 (in two parts)
Shepherds Wlk. Bus H 2C 10
Shepherds Way. S Croy 7K 153
Shepiston La. Hay 4D 76
Shepley Clo. Cars 3E 150
Sheppard Clo. Enf 1C 8
Sheppard Clo. King T 4E 134
Sheppard Dri. SE16 . . . . 5H 87
Sheppard Ho. E2 . . . . 2G 69 (off Warner Pl.)
Sheppard Ho. SW2 . . . . 1A 122
Sheppards College. Brom . . . 1J 143 (off London Rd.)
Sheppard St. E16 . . . . 4H 71
Shepperton 6E 130
Shepperton Bus. Pk. Shep 5E 130
Shepperton Ct. Shep 6D 130
Shepperton Ct. Dri. Shep . . . 5D 130
Shepperton Film Studios. 3B 130
Shepperton Green 4C 130
Shepperton Rd. N1 . . . . 1C 68
Shepperton Rd. Orp 6G 145
Shepperton Rd. Stai 4A 130
Sheppey Gdns. Dag 7C 56
Sheppey Rd. Dag 7B 56
Sheppey Wlk. N1 . . . . 7C 50 (off Oronsay Wlk.)
Shepton Houses. E2 . . . . 3J 69 (off Welwyn St.)
Sherard Ct. N7 . . . . 3J 49
Sherard Ho. E9 . . . . 7J 51 (off Frampton Pk. Rd.)
Sherard Rd. SE9 . . . . 5C 108
Sheraton Bus. Cen. Gnfd 2C 62
Sheraton Ho. SW1 . . . . 6F 85 (7K 171) (off Churchill Gdns.)
Sheraton St. W1 . . . 6H 67 (1C 166)
Sherborne Av. Enf 2D 8
Sherborne Av. S'hall 4E 78
Sherborne Clo. Hay 6A 60
Sherborne Cres. Cars 7C 138
Sherborne Gdns. NW9 . . . . . . 3G 27
Sherborne Gdns. W13 . . . . . . 5B 62
Sherborne Gdns. Shep 7G 131
Sherborne Ho. SW1 . . . . 5F 85 (5K 171)
Sherborne Ho. SW8 . . . . 7K 85 (off Bolney St.)
Sherborne La. EC4 . . . . 7D 68 (2E 168)
Sherborne Rd. Chess 5E 146
Sherborne Rd. Felt . . . . 1F 113 (in two parts)
Sherborne Rd. Orp 4K 145
Sherborne Rd. Sutt 2J 149
Sherborne St. N1 . . . . 1D 68
Sherboro Rd. N15 . . . . 6F 33
Sherbourne Ct. Sutt 6A 150
Sherbourne Pl. Stan 6F 11
Sherbrooke Clo. Bexh 4G 111
Sherbrooke Ho. E2 . . . . 2J 69 (off Bonner Rd.)
Sherbrooke Rd. SW6 . . . . 7G 83
Sherbrook Gdns. N21 . . . . 7G 7
Shere Clo. Chess 5D 146
Sheredan Rd. E4 . . . . 5A 20
Shere Ho. SE1 . . . . 7E 168
Shere Rd. Ilf 5E 36
Sherfield Clo. N Mald 4H 135
Sherfield Gdns. SW15 . . . . . 6B 100
Sheridan Bldgs. WC2 . . . . 6J 67 (1F 167) (off Martlett Ct.)
Sheridan Clo. Uxb 4E 58
Sheridan Ct. NW6 . . . . 7A 48 (off Belsize Rd.)
Sheridan Ct. W7 . . . . 7K 61 (off Milton Rd.)
Sheridan Ct. Croy . . . . 4E 152 (off Coombe Rd.)
Sheridan Ct. Harr 6H 25
Sheridan Ct. Houn 5C 96
Sheridan Ct. N'holt 5F 43
Sheridan Cres. Chst 2F 145
Sheridan Gdns. Harr 6D 26
Sheridan Ho. E1 . . . . 6J 69 (off Tarling St.)
Sheridan Ho. SE11 . . . . 4A 86 (4K 173) (off Wincott St.)
Sheridan Lodge. Brom . . . . . 4A 144 (off Homesdale Rd.)
Sheridan M. E11 . . . . 6K 35 (off High St.)
Sheridan Pl. SW13 . . . . 3B 100
Sheridan Pl. Hamp 1F 133
Sheridan Rd. E7 . . . . 3H 53
Sheridan Rd. E12 . . . . 5C 54
Sheridan Rd. SW19 . . . . 1H 137
Sheridan Rd. Belv 4G 93
Sheridan Rd. Bexh 3E 110
Sheridan Rd. Rich 3C 116
Sheridan St. E1 . . . . 6H 69
Sheridan Ter. N'holt 5F 43
Sheridan Wlk. NW11 . . . . 6J 29
Sheridan Wlk. Cars 5D 150
Sheridan Way. Beck 1B 142
Sheriden Pl. Harr 7J 25
Sheringham. NW8 . . . . 1B 66
Sheringham Av. E12 . . . . 4D 54
Sheringham Av. N14 . . . . 5C 6
Sheringham Av. Felt 3J 113
Sheringham Av. Romf 6J 39
Sheringham Av. Twic 1D 114
Sheringham Ct. Enf 3G 7
Sheringham Ct. Felt . . . . 3J 113 (off Sheringham Av.)
Sheringham Dri. Bark 5K 55
Sheringham Ho. NW1 . . . . 5C 66 (5C 158) (off Lisson St.)
Sheringham Rd. N7 . . . . 6K 49
Sheringham Rd. SE20 . . . . . . 3J 141
Sheringham Tower. S'hall 7F 61
Sherington Av. Pinn 7A 10
Sherington Rd. SE7 . . . . 6K 89
Sherland Rd. Twic 1K 115
Sherlock Ct. NW8 . . . . 1B 66 (off Dorman Way)
Sherlock Holmes Mus. . . . 4F 159
Sherlock M. W1 . . . 5E 66 (5G 159)
Sherman Gdns. Romf 6C 38
Sherman Rd. Brom 1J 143
Shernhall St. E17 . . . . 3E 34
Sherrard Rd. E7 & E12 . . . . . 6A 54
Sherrards Way. Barn 5D 4
Sherren Ho. E1 . . . . 4J 69 (off Nicholas Rd.)
Sherrick Grn. Rd. NW10 . . . . 5D 46
Sherriff Rd. NW6 . . . . 6J 47
Sherringham Av. N17 . . . . 2G 33
Sherrin Rd. E10 . . . . 4D 52
Sherrock Gdns. NW4 . . . . 4C 28
Sherry M. Bark 7H 55
Sherston Ct. SE1 . . . . 4B 86 (off Newington Butts)
Sherston Ct. WC1 . . . . 2J 161
Sherwin Ho. SE11 . . . . 7J 173
Sherwin Rd. SE14 . . . . 1K 105
Sherwood. NW6 . . . . 7G 47
Sherwood Av. E18 . . . . 3K 35
Sherwood Av. SW16 . . . . 7H 121
Sherwood Av. Gnfd 6J 43
Sherwood Av. Hay 4K 59
Sherwood Av. Ruis 6G 23
Sherwood Clo. E17 . . . . 2B 34
Sherwood Clo. SW13 . . . . . . 3D 100
Sherwood Clo. W13 . . . . 1B 80
Sherwood Clo. Bex 6C 110
Sherwood Ct. SW11 . . . . . . 3A 102
Sherwood Ct. W1 . . . . 5D 66 (6E 158) (off Bryanston Pl.)
Sherwood Ct. S Croy . . . . . . 5C 152 (off Nottingham Rd.)
Sherwood Ct. S Harr 2F 43
Sherwood Gdns. E14 . . . . 4C 88
Sherwood Gdns. SE16 . . . . . . 5G 87
Sherwood Gdns. Bark 7H 55
Sherwood Pk. Av. Sidc 7A 110
Sherwood Pk. Rd. Mitc 4G 139
Sherwood Pk. Rd. Sutt 5J 149
Sherwood Rd. NW4 . . . . 3E 28
Sherwood Rd. SW19 . . . . 7H 119
Sherwood Rd. Croy 7H 141
Sherwood Rd. Hamp H 5G 115
Sherwood Rd. Harr 2G 43
Sherwood Rd. Ilf 4H 37
Sherwood Rd. Well 2J 109
Sherwood St. N20 . . . . 3G 15
Sherwood St. W1 . . . . 7G 67 (2B 166)
Sherwood Ter. N20 . . . . 3G 15
Sherwood Way. W Wick 2E 154
Shetland Rd. E3 . . . . 2B 70
Shield Dri. Bren 6A 80
Shieldhall St. SE2 . . . . 4C 92
Shield Rd. Ashf 4E 112
Shifford Path. SE23 . . . . 3K 123
Shillaker Ct. W3 . . . . 1B 82
Shillibeer Pl. W1 . . . . 6D 158
Shillingford St. N1 . . . . 7B 50
Shilling Pl. W7 . . . . 2A 80
Shillingstone Ho. W14 . . . . . . 3G 83 (off Russell Rd.)
Shinfield St. W12 . . . . 6E 64
Shingle End. Bren 7C 80
Shinglewell Rd. Eri 7G 93
Shinners Clo. SE25 . . . . 5G 141
Ship All. W4 . . . . 6G 81
Ship & Mermaid Row. SE1 . . . . 2D 86 (6F 169)
Shipka Rd. SW12 . . . . 1F 121
Shiplake Ho. E2 . . . . 3F 69 (2J 163) (off Arnold Cir.)
Ship La. SW14 . . . . 3J 99
Shipman Rd. E16 . . . . 6K 71
Shipman Rd. SE23 . . . . 2K 123
Ship St. SE8 . . . . 1C 106
Ship Tavern Pas. EC3 . . . . 7E 68 (2G 169)
Shipton Clo. Dag 3D 56
Shipton Ho. E2 . . . . 2F 69 (1K 163) (off Shipton St.)
Shipton Rd. Uxb 4B 40
Shipton St. E2 . . . . 2F 69 (1K 163)
Shipway Ter. N16 . . . . 3F 51
Shipwright Rd. SE16 . . . . 2A 88
Shipwright Yd. SE1 . . . . 1E 86 (5G 169)
Ship Yd. E14 . . . . 5D 88
Shirburn Clo. SE23 . . . . 7J 105
Shirebrook Rd. SE3 . . . . 3B 108
Shire Ct. Eps 7B 148
Shire Ct. Eri 3D 92
Shirehall Clo. NW4 . . . . 6F 29
Shirehall Gdns. NW4 . . . . 6F 29
Shirehall La. NW4 . . . . 6F 29
Shirehall Pk. NW4 . . . . 5F 29
Shire Horse Way. Iswth 3K 97
Shire La. Kes . . . . 7C 156 (in two parts)
Shire M. Whit 6G 97
Shire Pl. SW18 . . . . 7A 102
Shire Pl. Bren 7C 80
Shires, The. Ham 4E 116
Shirland M. W9 . . . . 3H 65
Shirland Rd. W9 . . . . 3H 65
Shirlbutt St. E14 . . . . 7D 70
Shirley 2J 153
Shirley Av. Bex 7D 110
Shirley Av. Croy 1J 153
Shirley Av. Sutt 4B 150
Shirley Chu. Rd. Croy 3J 153
Shirley Clo. Houn 5G 97
Shirley Ct. SW16 . . . . 7J 121
Shirley Cres. Beck 4A 142
Shirley Dri. Houn 5G 97
Shirley Gdns. W7 . . . . 1K 79
Shirley Gdns. Bark 6J 55
Shirley Gro. N9 . . . . 7D 8
Shirley Gro. SW11 . . . . 3E 102
Shirley Heights. Wall 7G 151
Shirley Hills Rd. Croy 5J 153
Shirley Ho. SE5 . . . . 7D 86 (off Picton St.)
Shirley Ho. Dri. SE7 . . . . 7A 90
Shirley Oaks 1K 153
Shirley Oaks Rd. Croy 1K 153
Shirley Pk. Croy 2J 153
Shirley Pk. Rd. Croy 1H 153
Shirley Rd. E15 . . . . 7G 53
Shirley Rd. W4 . . . . 2K 81
Shirley Rd. Croy 7H 141
Shirley Rd. Enf 3H 7
Shirley Rd. Sidc 3J 127
Shirley Rd. Wall 7G 151
Shirleys Clo. E17 . . . . 5D 34
Shirley St. E16 . . . . 6H 71
Shirley Way. Croy 3A 154
Shirlock Rd. NW3 . . . . 4D 48
Shobden Rd. N17 . . . . 1D 32
Shobroke Clo. NW2 . . . . 3E 46
Shoebury Rd. E6 . . . . 7D 54
Shoelands Ct. NW9 . . . . 3K 27
Shoe La. EC4 . . . . . 6A 68 (7K 161)
Shooters Av. Harr 4C 26
Shooters Hill 1E 108
Shooters Hill. SE18 & Well 1D 108
Shooters Hill Rd. SE3 & SE18 . . . . . . 7A 90
Shooters Hill Rd. SE10 & SE3 . . . . . . 1F 107
Shooters Rd. Enf 1G 7
Shoot Up Hill. NW2 . . . . 5G 47
Shop. Hall, The. E6 . . . . 1C 72
Shore Bus. Cen. E9 . . . . 7J 51
Shore Clo. Felt 7J 95
Shore Clo. Hamp 6C 114
Shorediche Clo. Uxb 3B 40
Shoreditch 3E 68 (2H 163)
Shoreditch Ct. E8 . . . . 7F 51 (off Queensbridge Rd.)
Shoreditch High St. E1 . . . . 4E 68 (4H 163)
Shore Gro. Felt 2E 114
Shoreham Clo. SW18 . . . . . 5K 101
Shoreham Clo. Bex 1D 128
Shoreham Clo. Croy 6J 141
Shoreham Rd. E. H'row A 5A 94
Shoreham Rd. W. H'row A . . . 5A 94
Shoreham Way. Brom 6J 143
Shore Ho. SW8 . . . . 3F 103
Shore M. E9 . . . . 7J 51 (off Shore Rd.)
Shore Pl. E9 . . . . 7J 51
Shore Rd. E9 . . . . 7J 51
Shorncliffe Rd. SE1 . . . . 5F 87
Shorndean St. SE6 . . . . 1E 124
Shorne Clo. Sidc 6B 110
Shornefield Clo. Brom 3E 144

Shornells Way. SE2 4C 92
Shorrold's Rd. SW6 7H 83
Shortcroft Mead Ct. NW10 5C 46 (off Cooper Rd.)
Shortcroft Rd. Eps 7B 148
Shortcrofts Rd. Dag 6F 57
Shorter St. EC3 & E1 7F 69 (2K 169)
Short Ga. N12 4C 14
Short Hedges. Houn 1E 96
Short Hill. Harr 1J 43
Shortlands 2G 143
Shortlands. W6 4F 83
Shortlands. Hay 6F 77
Shortlands Clo. N18 3J 17
Shortlands Clo. Belv 3F 93
Shortlands Gdns. Brom 2G 143
Shortlands Gro. Brom 3F 143
Shortlands Ho. E17 5B 34
Shortlands Rd. E10 7D 34
Shortlands Rd. Brom 3F 143
Shortlands Rd. King T 7F 117
Short La. Stai 7B 94
Short Path. SE18 6F 91
Short Rd. E11 2G 53
Short Rd. W4 6A 82
Short Rd. H'row A 6A 94
Shorts Cft. NW9 4H 27
Shorts Gdns. WC2 6J 67 (1E 166)
Shorts Rd. Cars 4C 150
Short St. NW4 4E 28
Short St. SE1 2A 86 (6K 167)
Short Wall. E15 3E 70
Short Way. N12 6H 15
Short Way. SE9 3C 108
Short Way. Twic 7G 97
Shotfield. Wall 6F 151
Shott Clo. Sutt 5A 150
Shottendane Rd. SW6 1J 101
Shottery Clo. SE9 3C 126
Shottfield Av. SW14 4A 100
Shottsford. W2 6J 65 (off Ledbury Rd.)
Shoulder of Mutton All. E14 7A 70
Shouldham St. W1 5C 66 (6D 158)
Showers Way. Hay 1J 77
Shrapnel Clo. SE18 7C 90
Shrapnel Rd. SE9 3D 108
Shrewsbury Av. SW14 4J 99
Shrewsbury Av. Harr 4E 26
Shrewsbury Clo. Surb 2E 146
Shrewsbury Ct. EC1 4D 162
Shrewsbury Cres. NW10 1K 63
Shrewsbury Ho. SW8 7H 173
Shrewsbury La. SE18 1F 109
Shrewsbury M. W2 5J 65 (off Chepstow Rd.)
Shrewsbury Rd. E7 5B 54
Shrewsbury Rd. N11 6B 16
Shrewsbury Rd. W2 6J 65
Shrewsbury Rd. Beck 3A 142
Shrewsbury Rd. Cars 7C 138
Shrewsbury Rd. H'row A 6E 94
Shrewsbury St. W10 4E 64
Shrewsbury Wlk. Iswth 3A 98
Shrewton Rd. SW17 7D 120
Shroffold Rd. Brom 4G 125
Shropshire Clo. Mitc 4J 139
Shropshire Ct. W7 6K 61 (off Copley Clo.)
Shropshire Pl. WC1 4G 67 (4C 160)
Shropshire Rd. N22 7E 16
Shroton St. NW1 5C 66 (5D 158)
Shrubberies, The. E18 2J 35
Shrubbery Clo. N1 1C 68
Shrubbery Gdns. N21 7G 7
Shrubbery Rd. N9 3B 18
Shrubbery Rd. SW16 4J 121
Shrubbery Rd. S'hall 1D 78
Shrubbery, The. E11 5K 35
Shrubbery, The. Surb 1E 146
Shrubland Clo. N20 1G 15
Shrubland Gro. Wor Pk 3E 148
Shrubland Rd. E8 1G 69
Shrubland Rd. E10 7C 34
Shrubland Rd. E17 5C 34
Shrublands Av. Croy 3C 154
Shrublands Clo. SE26 3J 123
Shrubsall Clo. SE9 1C 126
Shuna Wlk. N1 6D 50
Shurland Av. Barn 6G 5
Shurland Gdns. SE15 7F 87
Shuters Sq. W14 5H 83
Shuttle Clo. Sidc 7K 109
Shuttlemead. Bex 7F 111
Shuttle St. E1 4G 69
Shuttleworth Rd. SW11 2C 102
Sibella Rd. SW4 2H 103
Sibley Clo. Bexh 5E 110
Sibley Ct. Uxb 5E 58
Sibley Gro. E12 7C 54
Sibthorpe Rd. SE12 6K 107
Sibthorp Rd. Mitc 2D 138
Sibton Rd. Cars 7C 138
Sicilian Av. WC1 6F 161
Sickle Corner. Dag 4H 75
Sidbury St. SW6 1G 101
Sidcup. 4A 128
Sidcup By-Pass. Chst & Sidc 3H 127
Sidcup High St. Sidc 4A 128
Sidcup Hill. Sidc 4B 128
Sidcup Hill Gdns. Sidc 5C 128
Sidcup Pl. Sidc 5A 128
Sidcup Rd. SE12 & SE9 6A 108
Sidcup Technical Cen. Sidc 6D 128
Siddeley Dri. Houn 3C 96
Siddons Ho. W2 5B 66 (6B 158) (off Harbet Rd.)
Siddons La. NW1 4D 66 (4F 159)
Siddons Rd. N17 1G 33
Siddons Rd. SE23 2A 124
Siddons Rd. Croy 3A 152
Side Rd. E17 5B 34
Sidewood Rd. SE9 1H 127
Sidford Ho. SE1 2J 173
Sidford Pl. SE1 3A 86 (2H 173)
Sidgwick Ho. SW9 2K 103 (off Lingham St.)
Sidings M. N7 3A 50
Sidings, The. E11 1E 52
Sidlaw Ho. N16 1F 51
Sidmouth Av. Iswth 2J 97
Sidmouth Dri. Ruis 3J 41
Sidmouth Ho. SE15 7G 87 (off Lympstone Gdns.)
Sidmouth Ho. W1 6C 66 (7D 158) (off Cato St.)
Sidmouth Pde. NW2 7E 46
Sidmouth Rd. E10 3E 52
Sidmouth Rd. NW2 7E 46
Sidmouth Rd. Well 7C 92
Sidmouth St. WC1 3K 67 (2F 161)
Sidney Av. N22 5E 16
Sidney Boyd Ct. NW6 7J 47
Sidney Elson Way. E6 2E 72
Sidney Est. E1 6J 69 (Bromhead St.)
Sidney Est. E1 5J 69 (Jubilee St.)
Sidney Gdns. Bren 6D 80
Sidney Godley (VC) Ho. E2 3J 69 (off Digby St.)
Sidney Gro. EC1 2B 68 (1A 162)
Sidney Ho. E2 2K 69 (off Old Ford Rd.)
Sidney Miller Ct. W3 1H 81 (off Crown St.)
Sidney Rd. E7 3J 53
Sidney Rd. N22 7E 16
Sidney Rd. SE25 5G 141
Sidney Rd. SW9 2K 103
Sidney Rd. Beck 2A 142
Sidney Rd. Harr 3G 25
Sidney Rd. Twic 6A 98
Sidney Rd. W on T 7J 131
Sidney Sq. E1 5J 69
Sidney St. E1 5H 69
Sidworth St. E8 7H 51
Siebert Rd. SE3 6J 89
Siege Ho. E1 6H 69 (off Sidney St.)
Siemens Rd. SE18 3B 90
Sienna Ter. NW2 2C 46
Sigdon Pas. E8 5G 51
Sigdon Rd. E8 5G 51
Sigers, The. Pinn 6K 23
Sigmund Freud Statue. 6B 48
Signmakers Yd. NW1 1F 67 (off Delancey St.)
Sigrist Sq. King T 1E 134
Silbury Av. Mitc 1C 138
Silbury Ho. SE26 3G 123
Silbury St. N1 3D 68 (1E 162)
Silchester Rd. W10 6F 65
Silecroft Rd. Bexh 1G 111
Silesia Bldgs. E8 7H 51
Silex St. SE1 2B 86 (7B 168)
Silicone Bus. Cen. Gnfd 2C 62
Silk Clo. SE12 5J 107
Silk Ct. E2 3G 69 (off Squirries St.)
Silkfield Rd. NW9 5A 28
Silk Ho. NW9 3K 27
Silk Mills Pas. SE13 2D 106
Silk Mills Path. SE13 2D 106
Silk Mills Sq. E9 6B 52
Silks Ct. E11 1H 53
Silkstream Pde. Edgw 1J 27
Silkstream Rd. Edgw 1J 27
Silk St. EC2 5C 68 (5D 162)
Sillitoe Ho. N1 1D 68 (off Colville Est.)
Silsoe Ho. NW1 2F 67
Silsoe Rd. N22 2K 31
Silver Birch Av. E4 5G 19
Silverbirch Clo. N11 6K 15
Silverbirch Clo. SE6 3B 124
Silver Birch Clo. SE28 1A 92
Silver Birch Clo. Dart 4K 129
Silver Birch Clo. Uxb 4A 40
Silver Birch Gdns. E6 4D 72
Silverbirch Wlk. NW5 6E 48
Silverburn Ho. SW9 1B 104 (off Lothian Rd.)
Silver Chase Ct. Enf 1G 7
Silvercliffe Gdns. Barn 4H 5
Silver Clo. SE14 7A 88
Silver Clo. Harr 7C 10
Silver Cres. W4 4H 81
Silverdale. NW1 3G 67 (1A 160) (off Hampstead Rd.)
Silverdale. SE26 4J 123
Silverdale. Enf 4D 6
Silverdale Av. Ilf 5J 37
Silverdale Cen., The. Wemb 1F 63
Silverdale Clo. W7 1J 79
Silverdale Clo. N'holt 5D 42
Silverdale Clo. Sutt 4H 149
Silverdale Ct. EC1 3B 162
Silverdale Dri. SE9 2C 126
Silverdale Dri. Sun 2K 131
Silverdale Factory Cen. Hay 3J 77
Silverdale Gdns. Hay 2J 77
Silverdale Ind. Est. Hay 3J 77
Silverdale Rd. E4 6A 20
Silverdale Rd. Bexh 2H 111
Silverdale Rd. Hay 2H 77
Silverdale Rd. Pet W 4G 145
Silverdene. N12 6E 14 (off Thyra Gro.)
Silverhall St. Iswth 3A 98
Silverholme Clo. Harr 7E 26
Silver Jubilee Way. Houn 2K 95
Silverland St. E16 1D 90
Silver La. W Wick 2F 155
Silverleigh Rd. T Hth 4K 139
Silvermead. E18 1J 35
Silvermere Dri. N18 6E 18
Silvermere Rd. SE6 7D 106
Silver Pl. W1 6G 67 (2B 166)
Silver Rd. SE13 3D 106 (in two parts)
Silver Rd. W12 7F 65
Silver Spring Clo. Eri 6H 93
Silverston Way. Stan 6H 11
Silver St. N18 4J 17
Silver St. Enf 3J 7
Silverthorn. NW8 1K 65 (off Abbey Rd.)
Silverthorne Rd. SW8 2F 103
Silverthorn Gdns. E4 2H 19
Silverton Rd. W6 6F 83
Silvertown. 1B 90
Silvertown Way. E16 6G 71
Silvertree La. Gnfd 3H 61
Silver Wlk. SE16 1A 88
Silver Way. Hil 2D 58
Silver Way. Romf 3H 39
Silver Wing Ind. Est. Croy 6K 151
Silverwood Clo. Beck 7C 124
Silverwood Clo. Croy 7B 154
Silverwood Clo. N'wd 1E 22
Silvester Ho. E1 6H 69 (off Varden St.)
Silvester Ho. E2 3J 69 (off Sceptre Rd.)
Silvester Ho. W11 6H 65 (off Basing St.)
Silvester Rd. SE22 5F 105
Silvester St. SE1 2D 86 (7E 168)
Silvocea Way. E14 6F 71
Silwood Est. SE16 4J 87
Silwood St. SE16 4J 87
Simla Ho. SE1 2D 86 (7F 169) (off Kipling Est.)
Simmons Clo. N20 2H 15
Simmons Clo. Chess 6C 146
Simmons La. E4 2A 20
Simmons Rd. SE18 5F 91
Simmons Way. N20 2H 15
Simms Clo. Cars 2C 150
Simms Gdns. N2 2A 30
Simms Rd. SE1 4G 87
Simnel Rd. SE12 7K 107
Simon Clo. W11 7H 65
Simon Ct. W9 3J 65 (off Saltram Cres.)
Simonds Rd. E10 2C 52
Simone Clo. Brom 1B 144
Simone Ct. SE26 3J 123
Simon Peter Ct. Enf 2G 7
Simons Ct. N16 2F 51
Simons Wlk. E15 5F 53
Simpson Clo. N21 5D 6
Simpson Dri. W3 6K 63
Simpson Ho. NW8 3C 66 (2C 158)
Simpson Ho. SE11 5K 85 (6H 173)
Simpson Rd. Houn 6D 96
Simpson Rd. Rich 4C 116
Simpson's Rd. E14 7D 70
Simpsons Rd. Brom 3J 143
Simpson St. SW11 2C 102
Simpson Way. Surb 6C 134
Simrose Ct. SW18 5J 101
Sims Wlk. SE3 4H 107
Sinclair Ct. Croy 2E 152
Sinclair Dri. Sutt 7K 149
Sinclair Gdns. W14 2F 83
Sinclair Gro. NW11 6F 29
Sinclair Ho. WC1 3J 67 (2E 160) (off Sandwich St.)
Sinclair Mans. W12 2F 83 (off Richmond Way)
Sinclair Pl. SE4 6C 106
Sinclair Rd. E4 5G 19
Sinclair Rd. W14 2F 83
Sinclare Clo. Enf 1A 8
Singapore Rd. W13 1A 80
Singer St. EC2 3D 68 (2F 163)
Singleton Clo. SW17 7D 120
Singleton Clo. Croy 7C 140
Singleton Rd. Dag 5F 57
Singleton Scarp. N12 5D 14
Sinnott Rd. E17 1K 33
Sion Ct. Twic 1B 116
Sion Rd. Twic 1B 116
Sippetts Ct. Ilf 1H 55
Sipson. 6C 76
Sipson Clo. W Dray 6C 76
Sipson La. W Dray & Hay 6C 76
Sipson Rd. W Dray 3B 76 (in two parts)
Sipson Way. W Dray 7C 76
Sir Abraham Dawes Cotts. SW15 4G 101
Sir Alexander Clo. W3 1B 82
Sir Alexander Rd. W3 1B 82
Sir Cyril Black Way. SW19 7J 119
Sirdar Rd. N22 3B 32
Sirdar Rd. W11 7F 65
Sirdar Rd. Mitc 6E 120
Sir Henry Floyd Ct. Stan 2G 11
Sirinham Point. SW8 6K 85 (off Meadow Rd.)
Sirius Building. E1 7K 69 (off Jardine Rd.)
Sir John Soane's Mus. 6K 67 (7G 161)
Sir Nicholas Garrow Ho. W10 4G 65 (off Kensal Rd.)
Sir Oswald Stoll Foundation, The. SW6 7K 83 (off Fulham Rd.)
Sir Oswald Stoll Mans. SW6 7K 83 (off Fulham Rd.)
Sir William Powell's Almshouses. SW6 2G 101
Sise La. EC4 1E 168
Siskin Ho. SE16 4K 87 (off Tawny Way)
Sisley Rd. Bark 1J 73
Sispara Gdns. SW18 6H 101
Sissinghurst Clo. Brom 5G 125
Sissinghurst Ho. SE15 6J 87 (off Sharratt St.)
Sissinghurst Rd. Croy 7G 141
Sissulu Ct. E6 1A 72
Sister Mabel's Way. SE15 7G 87
Sisters Av. SW11 3D 102
Sistova Rd. SW12 1F 121
Sisulu Pl. SW9 3A 104
Sittingbourne Av. N21 6J 7
Sitwell Gro. Stan 5E 10
Siverst Clo. N'holt 6F 43
Sivill Ho. E2 3F 69 (1K 163) (off Columbia Rd.)
Siviter Way. Dag 7H 57
Siward Rd. N17 1D 32
Siward Rd. SW17 3A 120
Siward Rd. Brom 3K 143
Six Acres Est. N4 2K 49
Six Bridges Ind. Est. SE1 5G 87
Sixth Av. E12 4D 54
Sixth Av. W10 3G 65
Sixth Av. Hay 1H 77
Sixth Cross Rd. Twic 3G 115
Skardu Rd. NW2 5G 47
Skeena Hill. SW18 7G 101
Skeffington Rd. E6 1D 72
Skeggs Ho. E14 3E 88 (off Glengall St.)
Skegness Ho. N7 7K 49 (off Sutterton St.)
Skelbrook St. SW18 2A 120
Skelgill Rd. SW15 4H 101
Skelley Rd. E15 7H 53
Skelton Clo. E8 6F 51

Skelton Rd. E7 ... 6J 53
Skelton's La. E10 ... 7D 34
Skelwith Rd. W6 ... 6E 82
Skenfrith Ho. SE15 ... 6H 87
(off Commercial Way)
Skerne Rd. King T ... 1D 134
Skerne Wlk. King T ... 1D 134
(off Skerne Rd.)
Sketchley Gdns. SE16 ... 5K 87
Sketty Rd. Enf ... 3A 8
Skiers St. E15 ... 1G 71
Skiffington Clo. SW2 ... 1A 122
Skillen Lodge. Pinn ... 1B 24
Skinner Pl. SW1 ... 4G 171
Skinners La. EC4 ... 7C 68 (2D 168)
Skinners La. Houn ... 1F 97
Skinner's Row. SE10 ... 1D 106
Skinner St. EC1 ... 3A 68 (2K 161)
Skip La. Hare ... 1A 40
Skipper Ct. Bark ... 1G 73
Skipsey Av. E6 ... 3D 72
Skipton Clo. N11 ... 6K 15
Skipton Dri. Hay ... 3E 76
Skipton Ho. SE4 ... 4A 106
Skipwith Ho. EC1 ... 5A 68 (5J 161)
(off Bourne Est.)
Skipworth Rd. E9 ... 1J 69
Skua Ct. SE8 ... 6B 88
(off Dorking Clo.)
Skyline Plaza Building. E1 ... 6G 69
(off Commercial Rd.)
Skylines. E14 ... 2E 88
Sky Peals Rd. Wfd G ... 7A 20
Sladebrook Rd. SE3 ... 3B 108
Slade Ct. New Bar ... 3E 4
Sladedale Rd. SE18 ... 5J 91
Slade Ho. Houn ... 6D 96
Sladen Pl. E5 ... 4H 51
Slades Clo. Enf ... 3F 7
Slades Dri. Chst ... 4G 127
Slades Gdns. Enf ... 2F 7
Slades Hill. Enf ... 3F 7
Slades Ri. Enf ... 3F 7
Slade, The. SE18 ... 6J 91
Slade Tower. E10 ... 2C 52
(off Leyton Grange Est.)
Slade Wlk. SE17 ... 6B 86
Slagrove Pl. SE4 ... 5C 106
Slaidburn St. SW10 ... 6A 84
Slaithwaite Rd. SE13 ... 4E 106
Slaney Ct. NW10 ... 7E 46
Slaney Pl. N7 ... 5A 50
Slater Clo. SE18 ... 5E 90
Slatter. NW9 ... 7G 13
Slattery Rd. Felt ... 1B 114
Sleaford Ind. Est. SW8 ... 7G 85
Sleaford St. SW8 ... 7G 85
Sledmere Ct. Felt ... 1G 113
Sleigh Ho. E2 ... 3J 69
(off Bacton St.)
Slievemore Clo. SW4 ... 3H 103
Sligo Ho. E1 ... 4K 69
(off Beaumont Gro.)
Slindon Ct. N16 ... 3F 51
Slingsby Pl. WC2 ... 7J 67 (2E 166)
Slippers Pl. SE16 ... 3H 87
Slipway Ho. E14 ... 5D 88
(off Burrells Wharf Sq.)
Sloane Av. SW3 ... 4C 84 (4D 170)
Sloane Ct. E. SW3 ... 5E 84 (5G 171)
Sloane Ct. W. SW3 ... 5E 84 (5G 171)
Sloane Gdns. SW1 ... 4E 84 (4G 171)
Sloane Ho. E9 ... 7J 51
(off Loddiges Rd.)
Sloane Sq. SW1 ... 4D 84 (4F 171)
Sloane St. SW1 ... 2D 84 (7F 165)
Sloane Ter. SW1 ... 4E 84 (3G 171)
Sloane Ter. Mans. SW1 ... 4E 84 (3G 171)
Sloane Wlk. Croy ... 6B 142
Slocum Clo. SE28 ... 7C 74

Sloman Ho. W10 ... 3G 65
(off Beethoven St.)
Slough La. NW9 ... 5J 27
Sly St. E1 ... 6H 69
Smaldon Clo. W Dray ... 3C 76
Smallberry Av. Iswth ... 2K 97
Smallbrook M. W2 ... 6B 66 (1A 164)
Smalley Clo. N16 ... 3F 51
Smalley Rd. Est. N16 ... 3F 51
(off Smalley Clo.)
Smallwood Rd. SW17 ... 4B 120
Smarden Clo. Belv ... 5G 93
Smarden Gro. SE9 ... 4D 126
Smart's Pl. N18 ... 5B 18
Smart's Pl. WC2 ... 6J 67 (7F 161)
Smart St. E2 ... 3K 69
Smeaton Clo. Chess ... 6D 146
Smeaton Ct. SE1 ... 3C 86
Smeaton Rd. SW18 ... 7J 101
Smeaton Rd. Wfd G ... 5J 21
Smeaton St. E1 ... 1H 87
Smedley St. SW8 & SW4 ... 2H 103
Smeed Rd. E3 ... 7C 52
Smiles Pl. SE13 ... 2E 106
Smith Clo. SE16 ... 1K 87
Smithfield St. EC1 ... 5B 68 (6A 162)
Smith Hill. Bren ... 6E 80
Smithies Ct. E15 ... 5E 52
Smithies Rd. SE2 ... 4B 92
Smith's Ct. W1 ... 2B 166
Smithson Rd. N17 ... 1D 32
Smiths Point. E13 ... 1J 71
(off Brooks Rd.)
Smith Sq. SW1 ... 3J 85 (2E 172)
Smith St. SW3 ... 5D 84 (5E 170)
Smith St. Surb ... 6F 135
Smith's Yd. SW18 ... 2A 120
Smiths Yd. Croy ... 3C 152
(off St George's Wlk.)
Smith Ter. SW3 ... 5D 84 (6E 170)
Smithwood Clo. SW19 ... 1G 119
Smithy St. E1 ... 5J 69
Smock Wlk. Croy ... 6C 140
Smokehouse Yd. EC1 ... 5B 68 (5B 162)
(off St John St.)
Smoothfield. Houn ... 4E 96
Smugglers Way. SW18 ... 4K 101
Smyrk's Rd. SE17 ... 5E 86
Smyrna Rd. NW6 ... 7J 47
Smythe St. E14 ... 7D 70
Snakes La. Barn ... 3A 6
Snakes La. E. Wfd G ... 6F 21
Snakes La. W. Wfd G ... 5D 20
Snaresbrook ... 5J 35
Snaresbrook Dri. Stan ... 4J 11
Snaresbrook Hall. E18 ... 4J 35
Snaresbrook Rd. E11 ... 4G 35
Snarsgate St. W10 ... 5E 64
Sneath Av. NW11 ... 7H 29
Snells Pk. N18 ... 6A 18
Sneyd Rd. NW2 ... 5E 46
Snowberry Clo. E15 ... 4F 53
Snowbury Rd. SW6 ... 2K 101
Snowden Av. Uxb ... 2D 58
Snowden Dri. NW9 ... 6A 28
Snowden St. EC2 ... 4E 68 (4G 163)
Snowdon Cres. Hay ... 3E 76
Snowdon Rd. H'row A ... 6E 94
Snowdown Clo. SE20 ... 1J 141
Snowdrop Clo. Hamp ... 6E 114
Snow Hill. EC1 ... 5B 68 (6A 162)
Snow Hill Ct. EC1 ... 6B 68 (7B 162)
(in two parts)
Snowman Ho. NW6 ... 1K 65
Snowsfields. SE1 ... 2D 86 (6F 169)
Snowshill Rd. E12 ... 5C 54
Snowy Fielder Waye. Iswth ... 2B 98

Soames St. SE15 ... 3F 105
Soames Wlk. N Mald ... 1A 136
Soane Clo. W5 ... 2D 80
Soane Ct. NW1 ... 7G 49
(off St Pancras Way)
Sobraon Ho. King T ... 7F 117
(off Elm Rd.)
Socket La. Brom ... 6K 143
Soho ... 6G 67 (1B 166)
Soho Sq. W1 ... 6H 67 (7C 160)
Soho St. W1 ... 6H 67 (7C 160)
Soho Theatre & Writers Cen. ... 6H 67 (1C 166)
(off Dean St.)
Sojourner Truth Clo. E8 ... 6H 51
Solander Gdns. E1 ... 7J 69
Solar Ct. N3 ... 7E 14
Solar Ho. E6 ... 5E 72
Solarium Ct. SE1 ... 4F 87
(off Alscot Rd.)
Soldene Ct. N7 ... 5K 49
(off George's Rd.)
Solebay St. E1 ... 4A 70
Solent Ho. E1 ... 5A 70
(off Ben Jonson Rd.)
Solent Ri. E13 ... 3J 71
Solent Rd. NW6 ... 5J 47
Solent Rd. H'row A ... 6B 94
Soley M. WC1 ... 3A 68 (1J 161)
Solna Av. SW15 ... 5E 100
Solna Rd. N21 ... 1J 17
Solomon Av. N18 ... 4B 18
Solomon's Pas. SE15 ... 4H 105
Solon New Rd. SW4 ... 4J 103
Solon New Rd. Est. SW4 ... 4J 103
Solon Rd. SW2 ... 4J 103
Solway Clo. E8 ... 6F 51
(off Queensbridge Rd.)
Solway Clo. Houn ... 3C 96
Solway Ho. E1 ... 4K 69
(off Ernest St.)
Solway Rd. N22 ... 1B 32
Solway Rd. SE22 ... 4G 105
Somaford Gro. Barn ... 6G 5
Somali Rd. NW2 ... 5H 47
Somerby Rd. Bark ... 7H 55
Somercoates Clo. Barn ... 3H 5
Somer Ct. SW6 ... 6J 83
(off Anselm Rd.)
Somerfield Ho. SE16 ... 5K 87
Somerfield Rd. N4 ... 2B 50
Somerford Clo. Pinn ... 4J 23
Somerford Gro. N16 ... 4F 51
Somerford Gro. N17 ... 7B 18
(in two parts)
Somerford Gro. Est. N16 ... 4F 51
Somerford St. E1 ... 4H 69
Somerford Way. SE16 ... 2A 88
Somerhill Av. Sidc ... 7B 110
Somerhill Rd. Well ... 2B 110
Somerleyton Pas. SW9 ... 4B 104
Somerleyton Rd. SW9 ... 4A 104
Somersby Gdns. Ilf ... 5D 36
Somers Clo. NW1 ... 2H 67
Somers Cres. W2 ... 6C 66 (1C 164)
Somerset Av. SW20 ... 2D 136
Somerset Av. Chess ... 4D 146
Somerset Av. Well ... 5K 109
Somerset Clo. N17 ... 2D 32
Somerset Clo. N Mald ... 6A 136
Somerset Clo. Wfd G ... 1J 35
Somerset Ct. W7 ... 6K 61
(off Copley Clo.)
Somerset Ct. Buck H ... 2F 21
Somerset Est. SW11 ... 1B 102
Somerset Gdns. N6 ... 7E 30
Somerset Gdns. N17 ... 7K 17
Somerset Gdns. SE13 ... 2D 106
Somerset Gdns. SW16 ... 3K 139
Somerset Gdns. Tedd ... 5J 115
Somerset Hall. N17 ... 7K 17
Somerset House. ... 7K 67 (2G 167)
Somerset Lodge. Bren ... 6D 80

Somerset Rd. E17 ... 6C 34
Somerset Rd. N17 ... 3F 33
Somerset Rd. N18 ... 5A 18
Somerset Rd. NW4 ... 4E 28
Somerset Rd. SW19 ... 3F 119
Somerset Rd. W4 ... 3K 81
Somerset Rd. W13 ... 1B 80
Somerset Rd. Bren ... 6C 80
Somerset Rd. Harr ... 5G 25
Somerset Rd. King T ... 2F 135
Somerset Rd. New Bar ... 5E 4
Somerset Rd. S'hall ... 5D 60
Somerset Rd. Tedd ... 5J 115
Somerset Sq. W14 ... 2G 83
Somerset Waye. Houn ... 6C 78
Somersham Rd. Bexh ... 2E 110
Somers Pl. SW2 ... 7K 103
Somers Rd. E17 ... 4B 34
Somers Rd. SW2 ... 6K 103
Somers Town ... 3H 67 (1C 160)
Somerton Av. Rich ... 3H 99
Somerton Rd. NW2 ... 3G 47
Somerton Rd. SE15 ... 4H 105
Somertrees Av. SE12 ... 2K 125
Somervell Rd. Harr ... 5D 42
Somerville Av. SW13 ... 6D 82
Somerville Point. SE16 ... 2B 88
Somerville Rd. SE20 ... 7K 123
Somerville Rd. Romf ... 6C 38
Sonderburg Rd. N7 ... 2K 49
Sondes St. SE17 ... 6D 86
Sonia Ct. Edgw ... 7A 12
Sonia Ct. Harr ... 6K 25
Sonia Gdns. N12 ... 4F 15
Sonia Gdns. NW10 ... 4B 46
Sonia Gdns. Houn ... 7E 78
Sonning Gdns. Hamp ... 6C 114
Sonning Ho. E2 ... 3F 69 (2J 163)
(off Swanfield St.)
Sonning Rd. SE25 ... 6G 141
Sontan Ct. Twic ... 1H 115
Soper Clo. E4 ... 5G 19
Soper Clo. SE23 ... 1K 123
Soper M. Enf ... 1H 9
Sophia Clo. N7 ... 6K 49
Sophia Ho. W6 ... 5E 82
(off Queen Caroline St.)
Sophia Rd. E10 ... 1D 52
Sophia Rd. E16 ... 6K 71
Sophia Sq. SE16 ... 7A 70
(off Sovereign Cres.)
Sopwith. NW9 ... 7G 13
Sopwith Av. Chess ... 5E 146
Sopwith Clo. King T ... 5F 117
Sopwith Rd. Houn ... 7A 78
Sopwith Way. SW8 ... 7F 85
Sopwith Way. King T ... 1E 134
Sorensen Ct. E10 ... 2D 52
(off Leyton Grange Est.)
Sorrel Clo. SE28 ... 1A 92
Sorrel Gdns. E6 ... 5C 72
Sorrel La. E14 ... 6F 71
Sorrell Clo. SE14 ... 7A 88
Sorrell Clo. SW9 ... 2A 104
Sorrento Rd. Sutt ... 3J 149
Sotheby Rd. N5 ... 3B 50
Sotheran Clo. E8 ... 1G 69
Sotherby Lodge. E2 ... 2J 69
(off Sewardstone Rd.)
Sotheron Rd. SW6 ... 7K 83
Soudan Rd. SW11 ... 1D 102
Souldern Rd. W14 ... 3F 83
S. Access Rd. E17 ... 7A 34
Southacre. W2 ... 6C 66 (1C 164)
(off Hyde Pk. Cres.)
Southacre Way. Pinn ... 1A 24
South Acton ... 2H 81
S. Africa Rd. W12 ... 1D 82
Southall ... 1D 78
Southall Ct. S'hall ... 7D 60
Southall Enterprise Cen. S'hall ... 2E 78
Southall Green ... 3C 78
Southall La. Houn & S'hall ... 6K 77
Southall Pl. SE1 ... 2D 86 (7E 168)

Southampton Bldgs. WC2 ... 5A 68 (6J 161)
Southampton Gdns. Mitc ... 5J 139
Southampton M. E16 ... 1K 89
Southampton Pl. WC1 ... 5J 67 (6F 161)
Southampton Rd. NW5 ... 5D 48
Southampton Rd. H'row A ... 6A 94
Southampton Row. WC1 ... 5J 67 (5F 161)
Southampton St. WC2 ... 7J 67 (2F 167)
Southampton Way. SE5 ... 7D 86
Southampton Way. Stanw ... 6A 94
Southam St. W10 ... 4G 65
S. Audley St. W1 ... 7E 66 (3H 165)
South Av. E4 ... 7J 9
South Av. N2 ... 4K 29
South Av. NW10 ... 4E 64
South Av. Cars ... 7E 150
South Av. Rich ... 2G 99
South Av. S'hall ... 7D 60
South Av. Gdns. S'hall ... 7D 60
South Bank. Surb ... 6E 134
Southbank. Th Dit ... 7B 134
S. Bank Bus. Cen. SW8 ... 6H 85 (7D 172)
South Bank Cen. ... 1K 85 (4H 167)
S. Bank Ter. Surb ... 6E 134
South Bank University. ... 3B 86 (7B 168)
South Bank University. (New Kent Rd. Hall) ... 3C 86
(off New Kent Rd.)
South Barnet ... 1K 15
South Beddington ... 6H 151
South Bermondsey ... 5J 87
S. Birkbeck Rd. E11 ... 3F 53
S. Black Lion La. W6 ... 5C 82
South Block. SE1 ... 2K 85 (7G 167)
(off Westminster Bri. Rd.)
S. Bolton Gdns. SW5 ... 5A 84
Southborough ... 5D 144
(Bromley)
Southborough ... 1E 146
(Surbiton)
Southborough Clo. Surb ... 1D 146
Southborough Ho. SE17 ... 5E 86
(off Surrey Gro.)
Southborough La. Brom ... 5C 144
Southborough Rd. E9 ... 1K 69
Southborough Rd. Brom ... 3C 144
Southborough Rd. Surb ... 1E 146
S. Boundary Rd. E12 ... 3D 54
Southbourne. Brom ... 7J 143
Southbourne Av. NW9 ... 2J 27
Southbourne Clo. Pinn ... 7C 24
Southbourne Ct. NW9 ... 2J 27
Southbourne Cres. NW4 ... 4G 29
Southbourne Gdns. SE12 ... 5K 107
Southbourne Gdns. Ilf ... 5G 55
Southbourne Gdns. Ruis ... 1K 41
S. Branch Av. NW10 ... 4E 64
Southbridge Pl. Croy ... 4C 152
Southbridge Rd. Croy ... 4C 152
Southbridge Way. S'hall ... 2C 78
South Bromley ... 6F 71
Southbrook M. SE12 ... 6H 107
Southbrook Rd. SE12 ... 6H 107
Southbrook Rd. SW16 ... 1J 139
Southbury. NW8 ... 1A 66
(off Loudoun Rd.)
Southbury Av. Enf ... 4B 8
Southbury Rd. Enf ... 3K 7
S. Carriage Dri. SW7 & SW1 ... 2B 84 (7B 164)
South Chingford ... 5G 19
Southchurch Ct. E6 ... 2D 72
(off High St. S.)
Southchurch Rd. E6 ... 2D 72
S. Circular Rd. SW15 ... 4C 100
South Clo. N6 ... 6F 31

South Clo. Barn 3C 4
South Clo. Bexh 4D 110
South Clo. Dag 1G 75
South Clo. Mord 6J 137
South Clo. Pinn 7D 24
South Clo. Twic 3E 114
South Clo. W Dray 3B 76
S. Colonnade, The. E14 1C 88
Southcombe St. W14 4G 83
S. Common Rd. Uxb 6A 40
Southcote Av. Felt 2H 113
Southcote Av. Surb 7H 135
Southcote Ri. Ruis 7F 23
Southcote Rd. E17 5K 33
Southcote Rd. N19 4G 49
Southcote Rd. SE25 5H 141
S. Countess Rd. E17 3B 34
South Cres. E16 4F 71
South Cres. WC1 5H 67 (6C 160)
Southcroft Av. Well 3J 109
Southcroft Av. W Wick 2E 154
Southcroft Rd. SW17 & SW16 6E 120
S. Cross Rd. Ilf 5G 37
S. Croxted Rd. SE21 3D 122
South Croydon 5D 152
Southdean Gdns. SW19 2H 119
South Dene. NW7 3E 12
Southdene Ct. N11 3A 16
Southdown. N7 6J 49
Southdown Av. W7 3A 80
Southdown Cres. Harr 1G 43
Southdown Cres. Ilf 5J 37
Southdown Dri. SW20 7F 119
Southdown Rd. SW20 1F 137
Southdown Rd. Cars 7E 150
South Dri. E12 3C 54
South Dri. Ruis 1G 41
S. Ealing Rd. W5 2D 80
S. Eastern Av. N9 3A 18
South Eastern University 3K 49
S. Eaton Pl. SW1 4E 84 (3H 171)
S. Eden Pk. Rd. Beck 6D 142
S. Edwardes Sq. W8 3H 83
Southend 4F 125
South End. W8 3K 83
South End. Croy 4C 152
S. End Clo. NW3 4C 48
Southend Clo. SE9 6F 109
Southend Cres. SE9 6F 109
S. End Grn. NW3 4C 48
Southend La. SE26 & SE6 4B 124
Southend Rd. E4 & E17 5F 19
Southend Rd. E6 7D 54
Southend Rd. E18 & Wfd G 1J 35
S. End Rd. NW3 4C 48
Southend Rd. Beck 1C 142
S. End Row. W8 3K 83
Southern Av. SE25 3F 141
Southern Av. Felt 1J 113
Southerngate Way. SE14 7A 88
Southern Gro. E3 3B 70
Southern Perimeter Rd. H'row A 5A 94
Southern Rd. E13 2K 71
Southern Rd. N2 4D 30
Southern Row. W10 4G 65
Southern St. N1 2K 67
Southern Way. Romf 6G 39
Southernwood Retail Pk. SE1 5F 87
Southerton Rd. W6 3E 82
S. Esk Rd. E7 6A 54
Southey Ho. SE17 5C 86 (off Browning St.)
Southey M. E16 1J 89
Southey Rd. N15 5E 32
Southey Rd. SW9 1A 104
Southey Rd. SW19 7J 119
Southey St. SE20 7K 123
Southfield. Barn 6A 4
Southfield Clo. Uxb 4C 58
Southfield Cotts. W7 2K 79 (in two parts)
Southfield Ct. E11 3H 53
Southfield Gdns. Twic 4K 115
Southfield Pk. Harr 4F 25
Southfield Rd. N17 2E 32
Southfield Rd. W4 2K 81
Southfield Rd. Chst 3K 145
Southfield Rd. Enf 6C 8
Southfields 7J 101
Southfields. NW4 3D 28
Southfields. E Mol 6J 133
Southfields Av. Ashf 6D 112
Southfields Ct. Sutt 2J 149
Southfields M. SW18 6J 101
Southfields Pas. SW18 6J 101
Southfields Rd. SW18 6J 101
South Gdns. SW19 7B 120
South Gdns. Wemb 2G 45
Southgate 1C 16
Southgate Av. Felt 4F 113
Southgate Cir. N14 1C 16
Southgate Gro. N1 7D 50
Southgate Ind. Est. N14 7C 6
Southgate Rd. N1 1D 68
S. Gipsy Rd. Well 3D 110
S. Glade, The. Bex 1F 129
South Grn. NW9 1A 28
South Gro. E17 5B 34
South Gro. N6 1E 48
South Gro. N15 5D 32
South Gro. Ho. N6 1E 48
South Hackney 7K 51
South Hampstead 7A 48
South Harrow 3G 43
S. Harrow Ind. Est. S Harr 2G 43
South Herts Golf Course 7D 4
South Hill. Chst 6D 126
South Hill. N'wd 1G 23
S. Hill Av. Harr 3G 43
S. Hill Gro. Harr 4J 43
S. Hill Pk. NW3 4C 48
S. Hill Pk. Gdns. NW3 3C 48
S. Hill Rd. Brom 3G 143
Southholme Clo. SE19 1E 140
Southill Ct. Brom 5H 143
Southill La. Pinn 4J 23
Southill Rd. Chst 7C 126
Southill St. E14 6D 70
S. Island Pl. SW9 7K 85
South Kensington 4B 84 (3B 170)
S. Kensington Sta. Arc. SW7 4B 84 (3B 170) (off Pelham St.)
South Lambeth 7J 85
S. Lambeth Pl. SW8 5J 85 (7F 173)
S. Lambeth Rd. SW8 6J 85 (7F 173)
Southland Rd. SE18 7K 91
Southlands Dri. SW19 2F 119
Southlands Gro. Brom 3C 144
Southlands Rd. Brom 5A 144
Southland Way. Houn 5H 97
South La. King T 3D 134 (in two parts)
South La. N Mald 4K 135
South La. W. N Mald 4K 135
South Lodge. E16 1K 89 (off Audley Dri.)
South Lodge. NW8 2B 66 (1A 158)
South Lodge. SW7 2C 84 (7D 164) (off Knightsbridge)
South Lodge. Twic 6G 97
S. Lodge Av. Mitc 4J 139
S. Lodge Cres. Enf 4C 6 (in two parts)
S. Lodge Dri. N14 4C 6
South London Crematorium. Mitc 2G 139
South London Gallery 1E 104 (off Peckham Rd.)
Southly Clo. Sutt 3J 149
South Mall. N9 3B 18 (off Plevna Rd.)
South Mead. NW9 1B 28
South Mead. Eps 7B 148
South Meadows. Wemb 5F 45
Southmead Rd. SW19 1G 119
S. Molton La. W1 6F 67 (1J 165)
S. Molton Rd. E16 6J 71
S. Molton St. W1 6F 67 (1J 165)
Southmoor Way. E9 6B 52
South Mt. N20 2F 15 (off High Rd.)
South Norwood 4F 141
South Norwood Country Pk. 4J 141
S. Norwood Hill. SE25 1E 140
S. Oak Rd. SW16 4K 121
Southold Ri. SE9 3D 126
Southolm St. SW11 1F 103
Southover. N12 3D 14
Southover. Brom 5J 125
South Pde. SW3 5B 84 (5B 170)
South Pde. W4 4K 81
South Pde. Edgw 2G 27
South Pde. Wall 6G 151
S. Park Ct. Beck 7C 124
S. Park Cres. SE6 1G 125
S. Park Cres. Ilf 3H 55
S. Park Dri. Ilf 2J 55
S. Park Gro. N Mald 4J 135
S. Park Hill Rd. S Croy 5D 152
S. Park M. SW6 3K 101
S. Park Rd. SW19 6J 119
S. Park Rd. Ilf 3H 55
S. Park Ter. Ilf 3J 55
S. Park Vs. Ilf 4J 55
S. Park Way. Ruis 6A 42
South Pl. EC2 5D 68 (5F 163)
South Pl. Enf 5D 8
South Pl. Surb 7F 135
South Pl. M. EC2 5D 68 (6F 163)
Southport Rd. SE18 4H 91
S. Quay Plaza. E14 2D 88
Southridge Pl. SW20 7F 119
South Ri. W2 2D 164
South Ri. Cars 7C 150
South Ri. Way. SE18 5H 91
South Rd. N9 1B 18
South Rd. SE23 2K 123
South Rd. SW19 6A 120
South Rd. W5 4D 80
South Rd. Chad H 6E 38
South Rd. Edgw 1H 27
South Rd. Felt 5B 114
South Rd. Hamp 6C 114
South Rd. Harr 1A 44
South Rd. L Hth 5C 38
South Rd. S'hall 2D 78
South Rd. Twic 3H 115
South Rd. W Dray 3C 76
South Row. SE3 2H 107
South Ruislip 4A 42
Southsea Rd. King T 4E 134
S. Sea St. SE16 3B 88
South Side. N15 4F 33
South Side. W6 3B 82
Southside Comn. SW19 6E 118
Southside House 6E 118
Southside Ind. Est. SW8 1G 103 (off Havelock Ter.)
Southspring. Sidc 7H 109
South Sq. NW11 6K 29
South Sq. WC1 5A 68 (6J 161)
South St. W1 1E 84 (4H 165)
South St. Brom 2J 143
South St. Enf 5D 8
South St. Iswth 3A 98
South St. Rain 2J 75
S. Tenter St. E1 7F 69 (2K 169)
South Ter. SW7 4C 84 (3C 170)
South Ter. Surb 6E 134
South Tottenham 5F 33
Southvale. SE19 6E 122
South Va. Harr 4J 43
Southvale Rd. SE3 2G 107
South Vw. Brom 2A 144
Southview Av. NW10 5B 46
Southview Clo. SW17 5E 120
S. View Clo. Bex 6F 111
S. View Ct. SE19 7C 122
Southview Cres. Ilf 6F 37
S. View Dri. E18 3K 35
Southview Gdns. Wall 7G 151
Southview Pde. Rain 3K 75
S. View Rd. N8 3H 31
Southview Rd. Brom 4F 125
S. View Rd. Pinn 1K 23
South Vs. NW1 6H 49
Southville. SW8 1H 103
Southville Clo. Eps 7K 147
Southville Clo. Felt 1G 113
Southville Cres. Felt 1G 113
Southville Rd. Felt 1G 113
Southville Rd. Th Dit 7A 134
South Wlk. Hay 5F 59
South Wlk. W Wick 3G 155
Southwark 1C 86 (4D 168)
Southwark Bri. SE1 & EC4 7C 68 (3D 168)
Southwark Bri. Bus. Cen. SE1 1C 86 (5D 168) (off Southwark Bri. Rd.)
Southwark Bri. Office Village. SE1 4D 168
Southwark Bri. Rd. SE1 3B 86 (7B 168)
Southwark Cathedral 1D 86 (4E 168)
Southwark Pk. Est. SE16 3H 87
Southwark Pk. Rd. SE16 4F 87
Southwark Pl. Brom 3D 144
Southwark St. SE1 1B 86 (4A 168)
Southwater Clo. E14 6B 70
Southwater Clo. Beck 7D 124
South Way. N9 2D 18
South Way. N11 6B 16
Southway. N20 2D 14
Southway. NW11 6K 29
Southway. SW20 5E 136
South Way. Croy 3A 154
South Way. Harr 4E 24
South Way. Hayes 7J 143
Southway. Wall 4G 151
South Way. Wemb 5G 45
Southway Clo. W12 2D 82 (off Scott's Rd.)
Southways Pde. Ilf 5E 36
Southwell Av. N'holt 6E 42
Southwell Gdns. SW7 4A 84
Southwell Gro. Rd. E11 2G 53
Southwell Ho. SE16 4H 87 (off Anchor St.)
Southwell Rd. SE5 3C 104
Southwell Rd. Croy 6A 140
Southwell Rd. Kent 6D 26
S. Western Rd. Twic 6A 98
S. W. India Dock Entrance. E14 2E 88
South West Middlesex Crematorium. Felt 1C 114
Southwest Rd. E11 1F 53
S. Wharf Rd. W2 6B 66 (7A 158)
Southwick M. W2 6B 66 (7B 158)
Southwick Pl. W2 6C 66 (1C 164)
Southwick St. W2 6C 66 (7C 158)
Southwick Yd. W2 1C 164
South Wimbledon 6K 119
Southwold Dri. Bark 5A 56
Southwold Mans. W9 3J 65 (off Widley Rd.)
Southwold Rd. E5 2H 51
Southwold Rd. Bex 6H 111
Southwood Av. N6 7F 31
Southwood Av. King T 1J 135
Southwood Clo. Brom 4D 144
Southwood Clo. Wor Pk 1F 149
Southwood Ct. EC1 3B 68 (2A 162) (off Wynyatt St.)
Southwood Ct. NW11 5K 29
Southwood Dri. Surb 7J 135
South Woodford 2J 35
S. Woodford to Barking Relief Rd. E11 5B 36
Southwood Gdns. Esh 3A 146
Southwood Gdns. Ilf 4F 37
Southwood Hall. N6 6F 31
Southwood Heights. N6 7F 31
Southwood Ho. W11 7G 65 (off Avondale Pk. Rd.)
Southwood La. N6 1E 48
Southwood Lawn Rd. N6 7E 30
Southwood Mans. N6 6E 30 (off Southwood La.)
Southwood Pk. N6 7E 30
Southwood Rd. SE9 2F 127
Southwood Rd. SE28 1B 92
Southwood Smith Ho. E2 3H 69 (off Florida St.)
Southwood Smith St. N1 1B 68
S. Worple Av. SW14 3A 100
S. Worple Way. SW14 3K 99
Southwyck Ho. SW9 4B 104
Sovereign Bus. Cen. Enf 3G 9
Sovereign Clo. E1 7H 69
Sovereign Clo. W5 5C 62
Sovereign Clo. Ruis 1G 41
Sovereign Ct. Houn 3E 96
Sovereign Ct. N'wd 1J 23
Sovereign Ct. W Mol 4D 132
Sovereign Cres. SE16 7A 70
Sovereign Gro. Wemb 3D 44
Sovereign Ho. E1 4H 69 (off Cambridge Heath Rd.)
Sovereign Ho. SE18 3D 90 (off Leda Rd.)
Sovereign M. E2 2F 69
Sovereign M. Barn 3J 5
Sovereign Pk. NW10 4H 63
Sovereign Pk. Trad. Est. NW10 4H 63
Sovereign Pl. Harr 5K 25
Sovereign Rd. Bark 3C 74
Sowerby Clo. SE9 5C 108
Space Waye. Felt 5J 95
Spa Clo. SE25 1E 140
Spa Ct. SW16 4K 121
Spafield St. EC1 4A 68 (3J 161)
Spa Grn. Est. EC1 3B 68 (1K 161)
Spa Hill. SE19 1D 140
Spalding Ho. SE4 4A 106
Spalding Rd. NW4 7E 28
Spalding Rd. SW17 5F 121
Spanby Rd. E3 4C 70
Spaniards Clo. NW3 1B 48
Spaniards End. NW3 1A 48
Spaniards Rd. NW3 2A 48
Spanish Pl. W1 6E 66 (7H 159)
Spanish Rd. SW18 5A 102
Spanswick Lodge. N15 4B 32
Sparkbridge Rd. Harr 4J 25
Sparke Ter. E16 6H 71 (off Clarkson Rd.)
Sparkford Gdns. N11 5K 15
Sparks Clo. W3 6K 63
Sparks Clo. Dag 2D 56
Sparks Clo. Hamp 6C 114
Spa Rd. SE16 3F 87
Sparrick's Row. SE1 2D 86 (6F 169)
Sparrow Clo. Hamp 6C 114
Sparrow Dri. Orp 7G 145
Sparrow Farm Dri. Felt 7A 96
Sparrow Farm Rd. Eps 4C 148
Sparrow Grn. Dag 3H 57
Sparrow Ho. E1 4J 69 (off Cephas Av.)

Sparrows Herne. Bush 1A 10
Sparrows La. SE9 7G 109
Sparrows Way. Bush 1B 10
Sparsholt Clo. Bark 1J 73 (off Sparsholt Rd.)
Sparsholt Rd. N19 1K 49
Sparsholt Rd. Bark 1J 73
Sparta St. SE10 1E 106
Speaker's Corner. 7D 66 (2F 165)
Speakers Ct. Croy 1D 152
Speakman Ho. SE4 3A 106 (off Arica Rd.)
Spearman Ho. E14 6C 70 (off Up. North St.)
Spearman St. SE18 6E 90
Spear M. SW5 4J 83
Spearpoint Gdns. Ilf 5K 37
Spears Rd. N19 1J 49
Speart La. Houn 7C 78
Spectacle Works. E13 3A 72
Spedan Clo. NW3 3A 48
Speed Highwalk. EC2 5C 68 (5D 162) (off Silk St.)
Speed Ho. EC2 5D 162
Speedway Ind. Est. Hay 2F 77
Speedwell Ho. N12 4E 14
Speedwell St. SE8 7C 88
Speedy Pl. WC1 2E 160
Speer Rd. Th Dit 6K 133
Speirs Clo. N Mald 6B 136
Speke Hill. SE9 3D 126
Speke Rd. T Hth 2D 140
Speke's Monument. 1A 84 (4A 164)
Speldhurst Clo. Brom 5H 143
Speldhurst Rd. E9 7K 51
Speldhurst Rd. W4 3K 81
Spellbrook Wlk. N1 1C 68
Spelman Ho. E1 5G 69 (6K 163) (off Spelman St.)
Spelman St. E1 5G 69 (5K 163) (in two parts)
Spelthorne Gro. Sun 7H 113
Spelthorne La. Ashf 1E 130
Spence Clo. SE16 2B 88
Spencer Av. N13 6E 16
Spencer Av. Hay 5J 59
Spencer Clo. N3 2J 29
Spencer Clo. NW10 3F 63
Spencer Clo. Wfd G 5F 21
Spencer Dri. N2 6A 30
Spencer Gdns. SE9 5D 108
Spencer Gdns. SW14 5J 99
Spencer Hill Rd. SW19 7G 119
Spencer House. 5A 166
Spencer Ho. NW4 5D 28
Spencer Mans. W14 6G 83 (off Queen's Club Gdns.)
Spencer M. SW9 1K 103 (off S. Lambeth Rd.)
Spencer M. W6 6G 83
Spencer Park. 5B 102
Spencer Pk. SW18 5B 102
Spencer Pk. E Mol 5G 133
Spencer Pl. N1 7B 50
Spencer Pl. Croy 7D 140
Spencer Ri. NW5 4F 49
Spencer Rd. E6 1B 72
Spencer Rd. E17 2E 34
Spencer Rd. N8 5K 31 (in two parts)
Spencer Rd. N11 4A 16
Spencer Rd. N17 1G 33
Spencer Rd. SW11 4B 102
Spencer Rd. SW19 6G 119
Spencer Rd. SW20 1D 136
Spencer Rd. W3 1J 81
Spencer Rd. W4 7J 81
Spencer Rd. Brom 7H 125
Spencer Rd. E Mol 4G 133
Spencer Rd. Harr 2J 25
Spencer Rd. Ilf 1K 55
Spencer Rd. Iswth 1G 97
Spencer Rd. Mitc 3E 138
Spencer Rd. Mit J 7E 138
Spencer Rd. Rain 3K 75
Spencer Rd. S Croy 5E 152
Spencer Rd. Twic 3J 115
Spencer Rd. Wemb 2C 44
Spencer St. EC1 3B 68 (2A 162)
Spencer St. S'hall 2B 78
Spencer Wlk. NW3 4B 48
Spencer Wlk. SW15 4F 101
Spenlow Ho. SE16 3G 87 (off Jamaica Rd.)
Spenser Gro. N16 5E 50 (in two parts)
Spenser M. SE21 2D 122
Spenser Rd. SE24 5B 104
Spenser St. SW1 3G 85 (1B 172)
Spensley Wlk. N16 3D 50
Speranza Rd. SE18 5K 91
Sperling Rd. N17 2E 32
Spert St. E14 7A 70
Speyside. N14 6B 6
Spey St. E14 5E 70
Spey Way. Romf 1K 39
Spezia Rd. NW10 2C 64
Spice Ct. E1 7G 69
Spice Quay Heights. SE1 1F 87 (5K 169)
Spicer Clo. SW9 2B 104
Spicer Clo. W on T 6A 132
Spicer Ct. Enf 3K 7
Spice's Yd. Croy 4C 152
Spigurnell Rd. N17 1D 32
Spikes Bri. Rd. S'hall 6C 60
Spilsby Clo. NW9 1A 28
Spindle Clo. SE18 3C 90
Spindlewood Gdns. Croy 4E 152
Spindrift Av. E14 4C 88
Spinel Clo. SE18 5K 91
Spinnaker Clo. Bark 3B 74
Spinnaker Ct. Hamp W 1D 134 (off Becketts Pl.)
Spinnaker Ho. E14 2C 88 (off Byng St.)
Spinnells Rd. Harr 1D 42
Spinney Clo. Beck 4D 142
Spinney Clo. N Mald 5A 136
Spinney Clo. W Dray 7A 58
Spinney Clo. Wor Pk 2B 148
Spinney Dri. Felt 7E 94
Spinney Gdns. SE19 5F 123
Spinney Gdns. Dag 5E 56
Spinney Oak. Brom 2C 144
Spinneys, The. Brom 2D 144
Spinney, The. N21 7F 7
Spinney, The. SW13 7D 82
Spinney, The. SW16 3G 121
Spinney, The. Barn 2E 4
Spinney, The. Sidc 5E 128
Spinney, The. Stan 4K 11
Spinney, The. Sun 1J 131
Spinney, The. Sutt 4E 148
Spinney, The. Wemb 3A 44
Spire Ho. W2 7A 66 (off Lancaster Ga.)
Spires Shop. Cen., The. Barn 3B 4
Spirit Quay. E1 1G 87
Spitalfields. 5F 69 (5J 163)
Spital Sq. E1 5E 68 (5H 163)
Spital St. E1 5G 69 (5K 163)
Spital Yd. E1 5E 68 (5H 163)
Spitfire Est., The. Houn 5A 78
Spitfire Rd. H'row A 6E 94
Spitfire Rd. Wall 7J 151
Spitfire Way. Houn 5A 78
Splendour Wlk. SE16 5J 87 (off Verney Rd.)
Spode Ho. SE11 2J 173
Spode Wlk. NW6 5K 47
Spondon Rd. N15 4G 33
Spoonbill Way. Hay 5B 60
Spooner Ho. Houn 6E 78
Spooners M. W3 1K 81
Spooner Wlk. Wall 5J 151
Sportsbank St. SE6 7E 106
Spottons Gro. N17 1C 32
Spout Hill. Croy 5C 154
Spratt Hall Rd. E11 6J 35
Spray La. Twic 6J 97
Spray St. SE18 4F 91
Spreighton Rd. W Mol 4F 133
Spriggs Ho. N1 7B 50 (off Canonbury Rd.)
Sprimont Pl. SW3 5D 84 (5E 170)
Springall St. SE15 7H 87
Springalls Wharf. SE16 2G 87 (off Bermondsey Wall W.)
Spring Bank. N21 6E 6
Springbank Rd. SE13 6F 107
Springbank Wlk. NW1 7H 49
Springbourne Ct. Beck 1E 142 (in two parts)
Spring Bri. M. W5 7D 62
Springbridge Rd. W5 7D 62
Spring Clo. Barn 5A 4
Spring Clo. Dag 1D 56
Spring Clo. La. Sutt 6G 149
Spring Corner. Felt 3J 113
Spring Cotts. Surb 5D 134
Spring Ct. NW6 6H 47
Spring Ct. W7 7H 61
Spring Ct. Eps 7B 148
Spring Ct. Rd. Enf 1F 7
Springcroft Av. N2 4D 30
Springdale M. N16 4D 50
Springdale Rd. N16 4D 50
Spring Dri. Pinn 6J 23
Springfield. E5 1H 51
Springfield. Bus H 1C 10
Springfield Av. N10 3G 31
Springfield Av. SW20 3H 137
Springfield Av. Hamp 6F 115
Springfield Clo. N12 5E 14
Springfield Clo. Stan 3F 11
Springfield Ct. NW3 7C 48 (off Eton Av.)
Springfield Ct. Ilf 5F 55
Springfield Ct. King T 3E 134 (off Springfield Rd.)
Springfield Ct. Wall 5F 151
Springfield Dri. Ilf 5G 37
Springfield Gdns. E5 1H 51
Springfield Gdns. NW9 5K 27
Springfield Gdns. Brom 4D 144
Springfield Gdns. Ruis 1K 41
Springfield Gdns. W Wick 2D 154
Springfield Gdns. Wfd G 7F 21
Springfield Gro. SE7 6A 90
Springfield Gro. Sun 1H 131
Springfield La. NW6 1K 65
Springfield Mt. NW9 5A 28
Springfield Pde. M. N13 4F 17
Springfield Pl. N Mald 4J 135
Springfield Ri. SE26 3H 123 (in two parts)
Springfield Rd. E4 1B 20
Springfield Rd. E6 7D 54
Springfield Rd. E15 3G 71
Springfield Rd. E17 6B 34
Springfield Rd. N11 5A 16
Springfield Rd. N15 4G 33
Springfield Rd. NW8 1A 66
Springfield Rd. SE26 5H 123
Springfield Rd. SW19 5H 119
Springfield Rd. W7 1J 79
Springfield Rd. Ashf 5B 112
Springfield Rd. Bexh 3H 111
Springfield Rd. Brom 4D 144
Springfield Rd. Harr 6J 25
Springfield Rd. Hay 1A 78
Springfield Rd. King T 3E 134
Springfield Rd. Tedd 5A 116
Springfield Rd. T Hth 1C 140
Springfield Rd. Twic 1E 114
Springfield Rd. Wall 5F 151
Springfield Rd. Well 3B 110
Springfields. New Bar 5E 4 (off Somerset Rd.)
Springfield Wlk. NW6 1K 65
Spring Gdns. N5 5C 50
Spring Gdns. SW1 1H 85 (4D 166) (in two parts)
Spring Gdns. Romf 5J 39
Spring Gdns. Wall 5G 151
Spring Gdns. W Mol 5F 133
Spring Gdns. Wfd G 7F 21
Spring Grove. 1J 97
Spring Gro. SE19 7F 123
Spring Gro. W4 5G 81
Spring Gro. Hamp 1F 133
Spring Gro. Mitc 1E 138
Spring Gro. Cres. Houn 1G 97
Spring Gro. Rd. Houn & Iswth 1F 97
Spring Gro. Rd. Rich 5F 99
Spring Hill. E5 7G 33
Spring Hill. SE26 4J 123
Springhill Clo. SE5 3D 104
Spring Ho. WC1 2J 161
Springhurst Clo. Croy 4B 154
Spring Lake. Stan 4G 11
Spring La. E5 7H 33
Spring La. N10 3E 30
Spring La. SE25 6H 141
Spring M. W1 5D 66 (5F 159)
Spring M. Eps 7B 148
Spring Park. 3C 154
Spring Pk. Av. Croy 2K 153
Spring Pk. Dri. N4 1C 50
Springpark Dri. Beck 3E 142
Spring Pk. Rd. Croy 2K 153
Spring Pas. SW15 3F 101
Spring Path. NW3 5B 48
Spring Pl. N3 3J 29
Spring Pl. NW5 5F 49
Springpond Rd. Dag 5E 56
Springrice Rd. SE13 6F 107
Spring Rd. Felt 3H 113
Spring Shaw Rd. Orp 7A 128 & 1K 145
Spring St. W2 6B 66 (1A 164)
Spring Ter. Rich 5E 98
Spring Tide Clo. SE15 1G 105
Spring Va. Bexh 4H 111
Springvale Av. Bren 5D 80
Spring Va. Ter. W14 3F 83
Spring Villa Rd. Edgw 7B 12
Spring Wlk. E1 5G 69
Springwater. WC1 5G 161
Springwater Clo. SE18 1E 108
Springway. Harr 7H 25
Springwell Av. NW10 1B 64
Springwell Clo. SW16 4K 121
Springwell Ct. Houn 2B 96
Springwell Rd. SW16 4A 122
Springwell Rd. Houn 2B 96
Springwood Ct. S Croy 4E 152 (off Birdhurst Rd.)
Springwood Cres. Edgw 2C 12
Sprowston M. E7 6J 53
Sprowston Rd. E7 5J 53
Spruce Ct. W5 3E 80
Sprucedale Gdns. Croy 4K 153
Spruce Hills Rd. E17 2E 34
Spruce Ho. SE16 2K 87 (off Woodland Cres.)
Spruce Pk. Brom 4H 143
Sprules Rd. SE4 2A 106
Spurfield. W Mol 3F 133
Spurgeon Av. SE19 1D 140
Spurgeon Rd. SE19 1D 140
Spurgeon St. SE1 3D 86
Spurling Rd. SE22 4F 105
Spurling Rd. Dag 6F 57
Spurrell Av. Bex 4K 129
Spur Rd. N15 4D 32
Spur Rd. SE1 2A 86 (6J 167)
Spur Rd. SW1 2G 85 (7A 166)
Spur Rd. Edgw 4K 11
Spur Rd. Felt 4K 95
Spur Rd. Iswth 7A 80
Spurstowe Rd. E8 6H 51
Spurstowe Ter. E8 6H 51
Spurway Pde. Ilf 5D 36 (off Woodford Av.)
Square Rigger Row. SW11 3A 102
Square, The. W6 5E 82
Square, The. Cars 5E 150
Square, The. Ilf 7E 36
Square, The. Rich 5D 98
Square, The. Uxb 1F 77
Square, The. Wfd G 5D 20
Squarey St. SW17 3A 120
Squire Gdns. NW8 3B 66 (2A 158) (off Grove End Rd.)
Squire's Bri. Rd. Shep 4B 130
Squires Ct. SW4 1J 103
Squires Ct. SW19 4J 119
Squires La. N3 2K 29
Squires Mt. NW3 3B 48
Squire's Rd. Shep 4C 130
Squires, The. Romf 6J 39
Squires Wlk. Ashf 7F 113
Squires Way. Dart 4K 129
Squires Wood Dri. Chst 7C 126
Squirrel Clo. Houn 3A 96
Squirrel Clo. Orp 7J 145
Squirrel M. W13 7K 61
Squirrels Clo. N12 4F 15
Squirrels Clo. Uxb 7C 40
Squirrels Ct. Wor Pk 2C 148 (off Avenue, The)
Squirrels Drey. Brom 2G 143 (off Pk. Hill Rd.)
Squirrels Grn. Wor Pk 2B 148
Squirrel's La. Buck H 3G 21
Squirrels, The. SE13 3F 107
Squirrels, The. Pinn 3D 24
Squirrels Trad. Est., The. Hay 3H 77
Squirries St. E2 3G 69
Stable Clo. N'holt 2E 60
Stables Mkt., The. NW1 7F 49
Stables M. SE27 5C 122
Stables, The. Buck H 1F 21
Stables Way. SE11 5A 86 (5J 173)
Stable Wlk. N2 1B 30
Stable Way. W10 6E 64
Stable Yd. SW1 6A 166
Stable Yd. SW15 3E 100
Stable Yd. Rd. SW1 2G 85 (6B 166) (in two parts)
Stableyard, The. SW9 2K 103
Stacey Av. N18 4D 18
Stacey Clo. E10 5F 35
Stacey St. N7 3A 50
Stacey St. WC2 6H 67 (1D 166)
Stack Ho. SW1 4E 84 (4H 171) (off Cundy St.)
Stackhouse St. SW3 1E 170
Stacy Path. SE5 7E 86
Stadium Bus. Cen. Wemb 3H 45
Stadium Retail Pk. Wemb 3G 45
Stadium Rd. SE18 7D 90
Stadium Rd. E. NW4 7D 28
Stadium St. SW10 7A 84
Stadium Way. Wemb 4F 45
Staffa Rd. E10 1A 52
Stafford Clo. E17 6B 34 (in two parts)
Stafford Clo. N14 5B 6
Stafford Clo. NW6 3J 65 (in two parts)
Stafford Clo. Sutt 6G 149
Stafford Ct. SW8 7J 85
Stafford Ct. W7 6K 61 (off Copley Clo.)
Stafford Cripps Ho. E2 3J 69 (off Globe Rd.)
Stafford Cripps Ho. SW6 6H 83 (off Clem Attlee Ct.)
Stafford Cross Bus. Pk. Croy 5K 151

Stafford Gdns. *Croy* 5K **151**
Stafford Mans. SW1 *3G 85 (1A 172)*
(off Stafford Pl.)
Stafford Mans. *SW4* 4J **103**
Stafford Mans. SW11 *7D 84*
(off Albert Bri. Rd.)
Stafford Mans. W14 *3F 83*
(off Haarlem Rd.)
Stafford Pl. *SW1* 3G **85** (1A **172**)
Stafford Pl. *Rich* 7F **99**
Stafford Rd. *E3* 2B **70**
Stafford Rd. *E7* 7A **54**
Stafford Rd. *NW6* 3J **65**
Stafford Rd. *Harr* 7B **10**
Stafford Rd. *N Mald* 3J **135**
Stafford Rd. *Ruis* 4H **41**
Stafford Rd. *Sidc* 4J **127**
Stafford Rd. *Wall & Croy* 6G **151**
Staffordshire St. *SE15* 1G **105**
Stafford St. *W1* 1G **85** (4A **166**)
Stafford Ter. *W8* 3J **83**
Staff St. *EC1* 3D **68** (2F **163**)
Stag Clo. *Edgw* 2H **27**
Stag Ct. King T *1G 135*
(off Coombe Rd.)
Stag Lane. (Junct.) 2B **118**
Stag La. *SW15* 3B **118**
Stag La. *Buck H* 2E **20**
Stag La. *Edgw & NW9* 2H **27**
Stag Pl. *SW1* 3G **85** (1A **172**)
Stags Way. *Iswth* 7K **79**
Stainbank Rd. *Mitc* 3F **139**
Stainby Clo. *W Dray* 3A **76**
Stainby Rd. *N15* 4F **33**
Stainer Ho. *SE3* 4A **108**
Stainer St. *SE1* 1D **86** (5F **169**)
Staines Av. *Sutt* 2F **149**
Staines By-Pass. *Stai* 5A **112**
Staines Rd. *Felt & Houn* 1C **112**
(in two parts)
Staines Rd. *Ilf* 5G **55**
Staines Rd. *Twic* 3E **114**
Staines Rd. E. *Sun* 7J **113**
Staines Rd. W. *Ashf & Sun* 6D **112**
Staines Wlk. *Sidc* 6C **128**
Stainford Clo. *Ashf* 5F **113**
Stainforth Rd. *E17* 4C **34**
Stainforth Rd. *Ilf* 7H **37**
Staining La. *EC2* 6C **68** (7D **162**)
Stainmore Clo. *Chst* 1H **145**
Stainsbury St. *E2* 2J **69**
Stainsby Pl. *E14* 6C **70**
Stainsby Rd. *E14* 6C **70**
Stainton Rd. *SE6* 6F **107**
Stainton Rd. *Enf* 1D **8**
Stalbridge Flats. W1 *6E 66 (1H 165)*
(off Lumley St.)
Stalbridge St. *NW1* 5C **66** (5D **158**)
Stalham St. *SE16* 3H **87**
Stalham Way. *Ilf* 1F **37**
Stambourne Way. *SE19* 7E **122**
Stambourne Way. *W Wick* 2E **154**
Stamford Brook Arches. *W6* 4C **82**
Stamford Brook Av. *W6* 3B **82**
Stamford Brook Gdns. *W6* 3B **82**
Stamford Brook Mans. W6 *4B 82*
(off Goldhawk Rd.)
Stamford Brook Rd. *W6* 3B **82**
Stamford Clo. *N15* 5G **33**
Stamford Clo. NW3 *3A 48*
(off Heath St.)
Stamford Clo. *Harr* 7D **10**
Stamford Clo. *S'hall* 7E **60**
Stamford Ct. *W6* 4C **82**
Stamford Dri. *Brom* 4H **143**
Stamford Gdns. *Dag* 7C **56**
Stamford Ga. *SW6* 7K **83**
Stamford Gro. E. *N16* 1G **51**
Stamford Gro. W. *N16* 1G **51**
Stamford Hill. 1F **51**
Stamford Hill. *N16* 2F **51**
Stamford Lodge. *N16* 7F **33**
Stamford Rd. *E6* 1C **72**
Stamford Rd. *N1* 7E **50**
Stamford Rd. *N15* 5G **33**
Stamford Rd. *Dag* 1B **74**
Stamford St. *SE1* 1A **86** (5J **167**)
Stamp Pl. *E2* 2F **69** (1J **163**)
Stanard Clo. *N16* 7E **32**
Stanborough Clo. *Hamp* 6D **114**
Stanborough Pas. *E8* 6F **51**
Stanborough Rd. *Houn* 3H **97**
Stanbridge Pl. *N21* 2G **17**
Stanbridge Rd. *SW15* 3E **100**
Stanbrook Rd. *SE2* 2B **92**
Stanbury Ct. *NW3* 6D **48**
Stanbury Rd. *SE15* 2H **105**
(in two parts)
Stancroft. *NW9* 5A **28**
Standale Gro. *Ruis* 5E **22**
Standard Ind. Est. *E16* 2D **90**
Standard Pl. *EC2* 2H **163**
Standard Rd. *NW10* 4J **63**
Standard Rd. *Belv* 5G **93**
Standard Rd. *Bexh* 4E **110**
Standard Rd. *Houn* 3C **96**
Standen Rd. *SW18* 7H **101**
Standfield Gdns. *Dag* 6G **57**
Standfield Rd. *Dag* 5G **57**
Standish Ho. SE3 *4K 107*
(off Elford Clo.)
Standish Ho. W6 *4C 82*
(off St Peter's Gro.)
Standish Rd. *W6* 4C **82**
Standlake Point. *SE23* 3K **123**
Stane Clo. *SW19* 7K **119**
Stane Pas. *SW16* 5J **121**
Stanesgate Ho. SE15 *7G 87*
(off Friary Est.)
Stane Way. *SE18* 7B **90**
Stanfield Ho. NW8 *4B 66 (3B 158)*
(off Frampton St.)
Stanfield Ho. N'holt *2B 60*
(off Academy Gdns.)
Stanfield Rd. *E3* 2A **70**
Stanford Clo. *Hamp* 6D **114**
Stanford Clo. *Romf* 6H **39**
Stanford Clo. *Ruis* 6E **22**
Stanford Clo. *Wfd G* 5H **21**
Stanford Ct. *SW6* 1K **101**
Stanford Ho. *Bark* 2B **74**
Stanford Pl. *SE17* 4E **86**
Stanford Rd. *N11* 5J **15**
Stanford Rd. *SW16* 2H **139**
Stanford Rd. *W8* 3K **83**
Stanford St. *SW1* 4H **85** (4C **172**)
Stanford Way. *SW16* 2H **139**
Stangate. *SE1* 1H **173**
Stangate Gdns. *Stan* 4G **11**
Stangate Lodge. *N21* 6E **6**
Stanger Rd. *SE25* 4G **141**
Stanhill Cotts. *Dart* 7K **129**
Stanhope Av. *N3* 3H **29**
Stanhope Av. *Brom* 1H **155**
Stanhope Av. *Harr* 1H **25**
Stanhope Clo. *SE16* 2K **87**
Stanhope Gdns. *N4* 6B **32**
Stanhope Gdns. *N6* 6F **31**
Stanhope Gdns. *NW7* 5G **13**
Stanhope Gdns. *SW7* 4A **84** (3A **170**)
Stanhope Gdns. *Dag* 3F **57**
Stanhope Gdns. *Ilf* 1D **54**
Stanhope Ga. *W1* 1E **84** (5H **165**)
Stanhope Gro. *Beck* 5B **142**
Stanhope Ho. N11 *4A 16*
(off Coppies Gro.)
Stanhope Ho. SE8 *7B 88*
(off Adolphus St.)
Stanhope M. E. *SW7* 4A **84** (3A **170**)
Stanhope M. S. *SW7* 4A **84**
Stanhope M. W. *SW7* 4A **84**
Stanhope Pde. *NW1* 3G **67** (1A **160**)
Stanhope Pk. Rd. *Gnfd* 4G **61**
Stanhope Pl. *W2* 7D **66** (1E **164**)
Stanhope Rd. *E17* 5D **34**
Stanhope Rd. *N6* 6G **31**
Stanhope Rd. *N12* 5F **15**
Stanhope Rd. *Barn* 6A **4**
Stanhope Rd. *Bexh* 2E **110**
Stanhope Rd. *Cars* 7E **150**
Stanhope Rd. *Croy* 3E **152**
Stanhope Rd. *Dag* 2F **57**
Stanhope Rd. *Gnfd* 5G **61**
Stanhope Rd. *Sidc* 4A **128**
Stanhope Row. *W1* 1F **85** (5J **165**)
Stanhope St. *NW1* 2G **67** (1A **160**)
Stanhope Ter. *W2* 7B **66** (2B **164**)
Stanhope Ter. *Twic* 7K **97**
Stanier Clo. *W14* 5H **83**
Stanlake M. *W12* 1E **82**
Stanlake Rd. *W12* 1E **82**
Stanlake Vs. *W12* 1E **82**
Stanley Av. *Bark* 3K **73**
Stanley Av. *Beck* 2E **142**
Stanley Av. *Dag* 1F **57**
Stanley Av. *Gnfd* 1G **61**
Stanley Av. *N Mald* 5C **136**
Stanley Av. *Wemb* 7E **44**
Stanley Bldgs. NW1 *2J 67*
(off Stanley Pas.)
Stanley Clo. *SW8* 6K **85**
Stanley Clo. *Wemb* 7E **44**
Stanley Cohen Ho. EC1 *4C 68 (4C 162)*
(off Golden La. Est.)
Stanley Ct. *W5* 5C **62**
Stanley Ct. *Cars* 7E **150**
Stanley Ct. *Sutt* 7K **149**
Stanley Cres. *W11* 7H **65**
Stanleycroft Clo. *Iswth* 1J **97**
Stanley Gdns. *NW2* 5E **46**
Stanley Gdns. *W3* 2A **82**
Stanley Gdns. *W11* 7H **65**
Stanley Gdns. *Mitc* 6E **120**
Stanley Gdns. *Wall* 6G **151**
Stanley Gdns. M. W11 *7H 65*
(off Kensington Pk. Rd.)
Stanley Gdns. Rd. *Tedd* 5J **115**
Stanley Gro. *N17* 7A **18**
Stanley Gro. *SW8* 2E **102**
Stanley Gro. *Croy* 6A **140**
Stanley Holloway Ct. E16 *6J 71*
(off Coolfin Rd.)
Stanley Ho. E14 *6C 70*
(off Saracen St.)
Stanley Pk. Dri. *Wemb* 1F **63**
Stanley Pk. Rd. *Cars* 7D **150**
Stanley Pas. *NW1* 2J **67**
Stanley Rd. *E4* 1A **20**
Stanley Rd. *E10* 6D **34**
Stanley Rd. *E12* 5C **54**
Stanley Rd. *E15* 1F **71**
Stanley Rd. *E18* 1H **35**
Stanley Rd. *N2* 3B **30**
Stanley Rd. *N9* 1A **18**
Stanley Rd. *N10* 7A **16**
Stanley Rd. *N11* 6C **16**
Stanley Rd. *N15* 4B **32**
Stanley Rd. *NW9* 7C **28**
Stanley Rd. *SW14* 4H **99**
Stanley Rd. *SW19* 6J **119**
Stanley Rd. *W3* 3J **81**
Stanley Rd. *Ashf* 5A **112**
Stanley Rd. *Brom* 4K **143**
Stanley Rd. *Cars* 7E **150**
Stanley Rd. *Croy* 7A **140**
Stanley Rd. *Enf* 3K **7**
Stanley Rd. *Harr* 2G **43**
Stanley Rd. *Houn* 4G **97**
Stanley Rd. *Ilf* 2H **55**
Stanley Rd. *Mitc* 7E **120**
Stanley Rd. *Mord* 4J **137**
Stanley Rd. *N'wd* 1J **23**
Stanley Rd. *Orp* 7K **145**
Stanley Rd. *Sidc* 3A **128**
Stanley Rd. *S'hall* 7C **60**
Stanley Rd. *Sutt* 6K **149**
Stanley Rd. *Twic* 3H **115**
Stanley Rd. *Wemb* 6F **45**
Stanley Sq. *Cars* 7D **150**
Stanley St. *SE8* 7B **88**
Stanley Ter. *N19* 2J **49**
Stanmer St. *SW11* 1C **102**
Stanmore. 5G **11**
Stanmore Gdns. *Rich* 3F **99**
Stanmore Gdns. *Sutt* 3A **150**
Stanmore Golf Course. *7F 11*
Stanmore Hill. *Stan* 3F **11**
Stanmore Lodge. *Stan* 4G **11**
Stanmore Pl. *NW1* 1F **67**
Stanmore Rd. *E11* 1H **53**
Stanmore Rd. *N15* 4B **32**
Stanmore Rd. *Belv* 4J **93**
Stanmore Rd. *Rich* 3F **99**
Stanmore St. *N1* 1K **67**
Stanmore Ter. *Beck* 2C **142**
Stannard Cotts. E1 *4J 69*
(off Fox Clo.)
Stannard M. E8 *6G 51*
(off Stannard Rd.)
Stannard Rd. *E8* 6G **51**
Stannary Pl. *SE11* 5A **86** (6K **173**)
Stannary St. *SE11* 6A **86** (7K **173**)
Stannet Way. *Wall* 4G **151**
Stansbury Ho. W10 *3G 65*
(off Beethoven St.)
Stansfeld Rd. *E6 & E16* 5B **72**
Stansfield Ho. SE1 *4F 87*
(off Balaclava Rd.)
Stansfield Rd. *SW9* 3K **103**
Stansfield Rd. *Houn* 2K **95**
Stansgate Rd. *Dag* 2G **57**
Stanstead Clo. *Brom* 5H **143**
Stanstead Gro. *SE6* 1B **124**
Stanstead Mnr. *Sutt* 6J **149**
Stanstead Rd. *E11* 5K **35**
Stanstead Rd. *SE23 & SE6* 1K **123**
Stanstead Rd. *H'row A* 6B **94**
Stansted Cres. *Bex* 1D **128**
Stanswood Gdns. *SE5* 7E **86**
Stanthorpe Clo. *SW16* 5J **121**
Stanthorpe Rd. *SW16* 5J **121**
Stanton Av. *Tedd* 6J **115**
Stanton Clo. *Eps* 5H **147**
Stanton Clo. *Wor Pk* 1F **149**
Stanton Ct. S Croy *5E 152*
(off Birdhurst Ri.)
Stanton Ho. SE10 *6E 88*
(off Thames St.)
Stanton Ho. SE16 *2B 88*
(off Rotherhithe St.)
Stanton Rd. *SE26* 4B **124**
Stanton Rd. *SW13* 2B **100**
Stanton Rd. *SW20* 1F **137**
Stanton Rd. *Croy* 7C **140**
Stanton Sq. *SE26* 4B **124**
Stanton Way. *SE26* 4B **124**
Stanway Ct. *N1* 2E **68** (1H **163**)
Stanway Gdns. *W3* 1G **81**
Stanway Gdns. *Edgw* 5D **12**
Stanway St. *N1* 2E **68**
Stanwell Clo. *Stanw* 6A **94**
Stanwell Rd. *Ashf* 2A **112**
Stanwell Rd. *Felt* 7D **94**
Stanwick Rd. *W14* 4H **83**
Stanworth Ct. *Houn* 7D **78**
Stanworth St. *SE1* 3F **87** (7J **169**)
Stanyhurst. *SE23* 1A **124**
Stapenhill Rd. *Wemb* 3B **44**
Staple Clo. *Bex* 3K **129**
Staplefield Clo. *SW2* 1J **121**
Stapleford. N17 *2E 32*
(off Willan Rd.)
Stapleford Av. *Ilf* 5J **37**
Stapleford Clo. *E4* 3K **19**
Stapleford Clo. *SW19* 7G **101**
Stapleford Clo. *King T* 2G **135**
Stapleford Rd. *Wemb* 7D **44**
Stapleford Way. *Bark* 3B **74**
Staplehurst Rd. *SE13* 5F **107**
Staplehurst Rd. *Cars* 7C **150**
Staple Inn. *WC1* 6J **161**
Staple Inn Bldgs. *WC1* 5A **68** (6J **161**)
Staples Clo. *SE16* 1A **88**
Staples Corner. (Junct.) 1D **46**
Staples Corner Bus. Pk. *NW2* 1D **46**
Staples Ho. E6 *6E 72*
(off Savage Gdns.)
Staple St. *SE1* 2D **86** (7F **169**)
Stapleton Gdns. *Croy* 5A **152**
Stapleton Hall Rd. *N4* 1K **49**
Stapleton Ho. E2 *3H 69*
(off Ellsworth St.)
Stapleton Rd. *SW17* 3E **120**
Stapleton Rd. *Bexh* 7F **93**
Stapley Rd. *Belv* 5G **93**
Stapylton Rd. *Barn* 3B **4**
Star All. *EC3* 2H **169**
Star & Garter Hill. *Rich* 1E **116**
Starboard Way. *E14* 3C **88**
Star Bus. Cen. *Rain* 5K **75**
Starch Ho. La. *Ilf* 2H **37**
Star Clo. *Enf* 6D **8**
Starcross St. *NW1* 3G **67** (2B **160**)
Starfield Rd. *W12* 2C **82**
Star Hill. *Dart* 5K **111**
Star La. *E16* 4G **71**
Starling Clo. *Buck H* 1D **20**
Starling Clo. *Pinn* 3A **24**
Starling Ho. NW8 *2C 66*
(off Barrow Hill Est.)
Starling Wlk. *Hamp* 5C **114**
Starmans Clo. *Dag* 1E **74**
Star Path. N'holt *2E 60*
(off Brabazon Rd.)
Star Pl. *E1* 7G **69** (3K **169**)
Star Rd. *W14* 6H **83**
Star Rd. *Iswth* 2H **97**
Star Rd. *Uxb* 4E **58**
Star St. *W2* 6C **66** (7B **158**)
Starts Clo. *Orp* 3E **156**
Starts Hill Rd. *Orp* 3E **156**
Starveall Clo. *W Dray* 3B **76**
Star Yd. *WC2* 6A **68** (7J **161**)
Staten Gdns. *Twic* 1K **115**
Statham Gro. *N16* 4D **50**
Statham Gro. *N18* 5K **17**
Statham Ho. SW8 *1G 103*
(off Wadhurst Rd.)
Station App. *E4* 6A **20**
Station App. *E7* 4K **53**
Station App. *E11* 5J **35**
Station App. *E17* 5C **34**
(in two parts)
Station App. *E18* 2K **35**
Station App. *N11* 5A **16**
Station App. *N12* 4E **14**
Station App. *NW10* 3B **64**
Station App. *SE3* 3K **107**
Station App. SE12 *6J 107*
(off Burnt Ash Hill)
Station App. *SE26* 4J **123**
(Sydenham Rd.)
Station App. *SE26* 5B **124**
(Westerley Cres.)
Station App. *SW6* 3G **101**
Station App. *SW14* 3J **99**
Station App. *SW16* 6H **121**
(Estreham Rd.)
Station App. *SW16* 5H **121**
(Streatham High Rd.)
Station App. *W7* 1J **79**
Station App. *Ashf* 4B **112**

Station App. B'hurst 2J 111
Station App. Beck 1C 142
Station App. Bex 1G 129
Station App. Bexh 2E 110
Station App. Bren 6C 80 (off Sidney Gdns.)
Station App. Brom 3J 143 (off High St.)
Station App. Buck H 4G 21
Station App. Cars 4D 150
Station App. Cheam 7G 149
Station App. Chst 6C 126 (Elmstead La.)
Station App. Chst. 1E 144 (Lower Camden)
Station App. Ewe 7B 148
Station App. Gnfd 7G 43
Station App. Hamp 1E 132
Station App. Harr 7J 25
Station App. Hayes 1J 155
Station App. Hay 3H 77
Station App. High Bar 4F 5
Station App. King T 1G 135
Station App. Pinn 3C 24
Station App. Rich 1G 99
Station App. Ruis 1G 41 (Pembroke Rd.)
Station App. Ruis 5K 41 (W. End Rd.)
Station App. Shep 5E 130
Station App. S Croy 7D 152
Station App. S'leigh 5C 148
Station App. Sun 1J 131
Station App. Well 2A 110 (in three parts)
Station App. Wemb 6B 44
Station App. W Dray 1A 76
Station App. W Wick 7E 142
Station App. Wor Pk 1C 148
Station App. N. Sidc 2A 128
Station App. Rd. SE1 2A 86 (7H 167)
Station App. Rd. W4 7J 81
Station Av. SW9 3B 104
Station Av. Eps 7A 148
Station Av. Kew 1G 99
Station Av. N Mald 3A 136
Station Bldgs. King T 2E 134 (off Fife Rd.)
Station Clo. N3 1J 29
Station Clo. N12 4E 14
Station Clo. Hamp 1F 133
Station Ct. E10 7D 34 (off Kings Clo.)
Station Cres. N15 4D 32
Station Cres. SE3 5J 89
Station Cres. Ashf 4A 112
Station Cres. Wemb 6B 44
Stationer's Hall Ct. EC4 6B 68 (1B 168)
Station Est. Beck 3K 141
Station Est. Rd. Felt 1K 113
Station Garage M. SW16 6H 121
Station Gdns. W4 7J 81
Station Gro. Wemb 6E 44
Station Hill. Brom 2J 155
Station Ho. M. N9 4B 18
Station Pde. E11 5J 35
Station Pde. N14 1C 16
Station Pde. NW2 6E 46
Station Pde. SW12 1E 120
Station Pde. W3 6G 63
Station Pde. W4 7J 81
Station Pde. W5 1F 81
Station Pde. Ashf 4B 112
Station Pde. Bark 7G 55
Station Pde. Barn 4K 5
Station Pde. Bexh 2E 110 (off Pickford La.)
Station Pde. Buck H 4G 21
Station Pde. Dag 6G 57
Station Pde. Edgw 7K 11
Station Pde. Felt 1K 113
Station Pde. Harr (HA2) 4F 43
Station Pde. Harr (HA3) 2A 26
Station Pde. N Har 4F 43
Station Pde. N'holt 7E 42
Station Pde. Rich 1G 99
Station Pde. Sidc 2A 128
Station Pde. Sutt 6A 150 (off High St.)
Station Pas. E18 2K 35
Station Pas. SE15 1J 105
Station Path. E8 6H 51 (off Graham Rd.)
Station Path. SW6 3H 101
Station Pl. N4 2A 50
Station Ri. SE27 2B 122
Station Rd. E4 1A 20
Station Rd. E7 4J 53
Station Rd. E10 3E 52
Station Rd. E12 4C 54
Station Rd. E17 6A 34
Station Rd. N3 1J 29
Station Rd. N11 5A 16
Station Rd. N17 3G 33
Station Rd. N19 3G 49
Station Rd. N21 1G 17
Station Rd. N22 2J 31
Station Rd. NW4 6C 28
Station Rd. NW7 6F 13
Station Rd. NW10 2B 64
Station Rd. SE13 3E 106
Station Rd. SE20 6J 123
Station Rd. SE25 4F 141
Station Rd. SW13 2B 100
Station Rd. SW19 1A 138
Station Rd. W5 6F 63
Station Rd. W7 1J 79
Station Rd. Ashf 4B 112
Station Rd. B'side 3H 37
Station Rd. Barn 5E 4
Station Rd. Belv 3G 93
Station Rd. Bexh 3E 110
Station Rd. Brom 1J 143
Station Rd. Cars 4D 150
Station Rd. Chad H 7D 38
Station Rd. Chess 5E 146
Station Rd. Croy 1C 152
Station Rd. Edgw 6B 12
Station Rd. Hamp 1E 132
Station Rd. Hamp W 1C 134
Station Rd. Harr 4K 25
Station Rd. Hay 4G 77 (in three parts)
Station Rd. Houn 4F 97
Station Rd. Ilf 3F 55
Station Rd. King T 1G 135
Station Rd. N Mald 5D 136
Station Rd. N Har 5F 25
Station Rd. Shep 5E 130
Station Rd. Short 2G 143
Station Rd. Sidc 2A 128
Station Rd. Sun 7J 113
Station Rd. Tedd 6A 116
Station Rd. Th Dit 7K 133
Station Rd. Twic 1K 115
Station Rd. W Dray 2A 76
Station Rd. W Wick 1E 154
Station Rd. N. Belv 3H 93
Station Sq. Orp 5G 145
Station St. E16 1F 91
Station Ter. NW10 2F 65
Station Ter. SE5 1C 104
Station Ter. M. SE3 5J 89
Station Vw. Gnfd 1H 61
Station Way. SE15 2G 105
Station Way. Buck H 4F 21
Station Way. Sutt 6G 149
Station Yd. Twic 7A 98
Staunton Ho. SE17 4E 86 (off Tatum St.)
Staunton Rd. King T 6E 116
Staunton St. SE8 6B 88
Staveley. NW1 3G 67 (1A 160) (off Varndell St.)
Staveley Clo. E9 5J 51
Staveley Clo. N7 4J 49
Staveley Clo. SE15 1H 105
Staveley Gdns. W4 1K 99
Staveley Rd. W4 6J 81
Staveley Rd. Ashf 6F 113
Staverton Rd. NW2 7E 46
Stave Yd. Rd. SE16 1A 88
Stavordale Rd. N5 4B 50
Stavordale Rd. Cars 7A 138
Stayner's Rd. E1 4K 69
Stayton Rd. Sutt 3J 149
Steadfast Rd. King T 1D 134
Steadman Clo. Uxb 3C 40
Steadman Ct. EC1 4C 68 (3D 162) (off Old St.)
Steadman Ho. Dag 3G 57 (off Uvedale Rd.)
Stead St. SE17 4D 86
Steam Farm La. Felt 4H 95
Stean St. E8 1F 69
Stebbing Ho. W11 1F 83 (off Queensdale Cres.)
Stebbing Way. Bark 2A 74
Stebondale St. E14 4E 88
Stedham Pl. WC1 7E 160
Stedman Clo. Bex 3K 129
Steedman St. SE17 4C 86
Steeds Rd. N10 1D 30
Steele Ho. E15 2G 71 (off Eve Rd.)
Steele Rd. E11 4G 53
Steele Rd. N17 3E 32
Steele Rd. NW10 2J 63
Steele Rd. W4 3J 81
Steele Rd. Iswth 4A 98
Steele's M. N. NW3 6D 48
Steele's M. S. NW3 6D 48
Steele's Rd. NW3 6D 48
Steeles Studios. NW3 6D 48
Steele Wlk. Eri 7H 93
Steel's La. E1 6J 69
Steelyard Pas. EC4 3E 168
Steen Way. SE22 5E 104
Steep Hill. SW16 3H 121
Steep Hill. Croy 4E 152
Steeple Clo. SW6 2G 101
Steeple Clo. SW19 5G 119
Steeple Ct. E1 4H 69
Steeplestone Clo. N18 5H 17
Steeple Wlk. N1 1C 68 (off Basire St.)
Steerforth St. SW18 2A 120
Steers Mead. Mitc 1D 138
Steers Way. SE16 2A 88
Stelfox Ho. WC1 3K 67 (1H 161) (off Penton Ri.)
Stella Rd. SW17 6D 120
Stelling Rd. Eri 7K 93
Stellman Clo. E5 3G 51
Stembridge Rd. SE20 2H 141
Stephan Clo. E8 1G 69
Stephendale Rd. SW6 3K 101
Stephen Fox Ho. W4 5A 82 (off Chiswick La.)
Stephen M. W1 5H 67 (6C 160)
Stephen Pl. SW4 3G 103
Stephen Rd. Bexh 3J 111
Stephens Ct. E16 4H 71
Stephens Ct. SE4 3A 106
Stephens Lodge. N12 3F 15 (off Woodside La.)
Stephenson Ct. Cheam 7G 149 (off Station App.)
Stephenson Ho. SE1 3C 86
Stephenson Rd. E17 5A 34
Stephenson Rd. W7 6K 61
Stephenson Rd. Twic 7E 96
Stephenson St. E16 4G 71
Stephenson St. NW10 3A 64
Stephenson Way. NW1 4G 67 (3B 160)
Stephen's Rd. E15 1G 71
Stephen St. W1 5H 67 (6C 160)
Stepney 5K 69
Stepney Causeway. E1 6K 69
Stepney Grn. E1 5J 69
Stepney Grn. Ct. E1 5K 69 (off Stepney Grn.)
Stepney High St. E1 5K 69
Stepney Way. E1 5H 69
Sterling Av. Edgw 4A 12
Sterling Clo. NW10 7C 46
Sterling Gdns. SE14 6A 88
Sterling Ho. SE3 4K 107
Sterling Pl. W5 4E 80
Sterling Rd. Enf 1J 7
Sterling St. SW7 3C 84 (1D 170)
Sterling Way. N18 5J 17
Stern Clo. Bark 2C 74
Sterndale Rd. W14 3F 83
Sterne St. W12 2F 83
Sternhall La. SE15 3G 105
Sternhold Av. SW2 2H 121
Sterry Cres. Dag 5G 57
Sterry Dri. Eps 4A 148
Sterry Dri. Th Dit 6J 133
Sterry Gdns. Dag 6G 57
Sterry Rd. Bark 1K 73
Sterry Rd. Dag 4G 57
Sterry St. SE1 2D 86 (7E 168)
Steucers La. SE23 1A 124
Stevannie Ct. Belv 5G 93
Steve Biko La. SE6 4C 124
Steve Biko Rd. N7 3A 50
Steve Biko Way. Houn 3E 96
Stevedale Rd. Well 2C 110
Stevedore St. E1 1H 87
Stevenage Rd. E6 6E 54
Stevenage Rd. SW6 7F 83
Stevens Av. E9 6J 51
Stevens Clo. Beck 6C 124
Stevens Clo. Bex 4K 129
Stevens Clo. Hamp 5C 114
Stevens Clo. Pinn 5A 24
Stevens Grn. Bus H 1B 10
Stevens La. Clay 7A 146
Stevenson Clo. Barn 7G 5
Stevenson Cres. SE16 5G 87
Stevenson Ho. NW8 1A 66 (off Boundary Rd.)
Stevens Rd. Dag 3B 56
Stevens St. SE1 3E 86 (7H 169)
Steventon Rd. W12 7B 64
Stewards Holte Wlk. N11 4A 16
Steward St. E1 5E 68 (5H 163) (in two parts)
Stewart Av. Shep 4C 130
Stewart Clo. NW9 6J 27
Stewart Clo. Chst 5F 127
Stewart Clo. Hamp 6C 114
Stewart Quay. Hay 2G 77
Stewart Rainbird Ho. E12 5E 54 (off Parkhurst Rd.)
Stewart Rd. E15 4F 53
Stewartsby Clo. N18 5H 17
Stewart's Gro. SW3 5B 84 (5B 170)
Stewart's Rd. SW8 7G 85
Stewart St. E14 2E 88
Stew La. EC4 7C 68 (2C 168)
Steyne Ho. W3 1J 81 (off Horn La.)
Steyne Rd. W3 1H 81
Steyning Gro. SE9 4D 126
Steynings Way. N12 5D 14
Steyning Way. Houn 4A 96
Steynton Av. Bex 2D 128
Stickland Rd. Belv 4G 93
Stickleton Clo. Gnfd 3F 61
Stifford Ho. E1 5J 69 (off Stepney Way)
Stilecroft Gdns. Wemb 3B 44
Stile Hall Gdns. W4 5G 81
Stile Hall Pde. W4 5G 81
Stileman Ho. E3 5B 70 (off Ackroyd Dri.)
Stile Path. Sun 3J 131
Stiles Clo. Brom 6D 144
Stiles Clo. Eri 5H 93
Stillingfleet Rd. SW13 6C 82
Stillington St. SW1 4G 85 (3B 172)
Stillness Rd. SE23 6A 106
Stillwell Dri. Uxb 4B 58
Stilton Cres. NW10 7K 45
Stilwell Roundabout. (Junct.) 7C 58
Stilwell Roundabout. Uxb 7C 58
Stipularis Dri. Hay 4B 60
Stirling Av. Pinn 1B 42
Stirling Av. Shep 3G 131
Stirling Av. Wall 7J 151
Stirling Clo. SW16 1H 139
Stirling Ct. W13 7B 62
Stirling Gro. Houn 2G 97
Stirling Ho. SE18 5F 91
Stirling Rd. E13 2K 71
Stirling Rd. E17 3A 34
Stirling Rd. N17 1G 33
Stirling Rd. N22 1B 32
Stirling Rd. SW9 2J 103
Stirling Rd. W3 3H 81
Stirling Rd. Harr 3K 25
Stirling Rd. Hay 7K 59
Stirling Rd. H'row A 6B 94
Stirling Rd. Twic 7E 96
Stirling Rd. Path. E17 3A 34
Stirling Wlk. Surb 6H 135
Stirling Way. Croy 7J 139
Stiven Cres. Harr 3D 42
Stockbeck. NW1 2G 67 (1B 160) (off Ampthill Est.)
Stockbury Rd. Croy 6J 141
Stockdale Rd. Dag 2F 57
Stockdove Way. Gnfd 3K 61
Stocker Gdns. Dag 7C 56
Stock Exchange. 6D 68 (1F 169)
Stockfield Rd. SW16 3K 121
Stockholm Ho. E1 7G 69 (off Swedenborg Gdns.)
Stockholm Rd. SE16 5J 87
Stockholm Way. E1 1G 87
Stockhurst Clo. SW15 2E 100
Stockingswater La. Enf 2G 9
Stockland Rd. Romf 6K 39
Stockleigh Hall. NW8 2C 66 (off Prince Albert Rd.)
Stockley Clo. W Dray 2D 76
Stockley Country Pk. 7C 58
Stockley Farm Rd. W Dray 3D 76
Stockley Park 1D 76
Stockley Rd. Uxb & W Dray 6C 58
Stockley Rd. W Dray 4D 76
Stock Orchard Cres. N7 5K 49
Stock Orchard St. N7 5K 49
Stockport Rd. SW16 1H 139
Stocksfield Rd. E17 3E 34
Stocks Pl. E14 7B 70
Stocks Pl. Uxb 1C 58
Stock St. E13 2J 71
Stockton Clo. New Bar 4F 5
Stockton Gdns. N17 7H 17
Stockton Gdns. NW7 3F 13
Stockton Ho. E2 3H 69 (off Ellsworth St.)
Stockton Ho. S Harr 1E 42
Stockton Rd. N17 7H 17
Stockton Rd. N18 6B 18
Stockwell 2K 103
Stockwell Av. SW9 3K 103
Stockwell Clo. Brom 2K 143
Stockwell Gdns. SW9 1K 103
Stockwell Gdns. Est. SW9 2J 103
Stockwell Grn. SW9 2K 103
Stockwell Grn. Ct. SW9 2K 103
Stockwell La. SW9 2K 103
Stockwell M. SW9 2K 103
Stockwell Pk. Cres. SW9 2K 103
Stockwell Pk. Est. SW9 2K 103
Stockwell Pk. Rd. SW9 1K 103
Stockwell Pk. Wlk. SW9 3A 104
Stockwell Rd. SW9 2K 103

Stockwell St. SE10 . . . . 6E 88
Stockwell Ter. SW9 . . . . 1K 103
Stodart Rd. SE20 . . . . 1J 141
Stoddart Ho. SW8
. . . . 6K 85 (7H 173)
Stofield Gdns. SE9 . . . . 3B 126
Stoford Clo. SW19 . . . . 7G 101
Stokenchurch St. SW6 . . . . . 1K 101
Stoke Newington 3F 51
Stoke Newington Chu. St.
N16 . . . . 3D 50
Stoke Newington Comn.
N16 . . . . 2F 51
Stoke Newington High St.
N16 . . . . 3F 51
Stoke Newington Rd. N16 . . . 5F 51
Stoke Pl. NW10 . . . . 3B 64
Stoke Rd. King T 7J 117
Stokesby Rd. Chess 6F 147
Stokes Cotts. Ilf 1G 37
Stokes Ct. N2 . . . . 4C 30
Stokesley St. W12 . . . . 6B 64
Stokes Rd. E6 . . . . 4C 72
Stokes Rd. Croy 6K 141
Stokley Ct. N8 . . . . 4J 31
Stoll Clo. NW2 . . . . 3E 46
Stoms Path. SE6 . . . . 5C 124
Stonard Rd. N13 . . . . 3F 17
Stonard Rd. Dag 5B 56
Stondon Ho. E15 . . . . 1H 71
(off John St.)
Stondon Pk. SE23 . . . . 6A 106
Stondon Wlk. E6 . . . . 2B 72
Stonebanks. W on T 7J 131
Stonebridge 1K 63
Stonebridge Pk. NW10 . . . . . 7K 45
Stonebridge Rd. N15 . . . . 5F 33
Stonebridge Shop. Cen.
NW10 . . . . 1K 63
Stonebridge Way. Wemb 6H 45
Stone Bldgs. WC2 . . . . 6H 161
Stonechat Sq. E6 . . . . 5C 72
Stone Clo. SW4 . . . . 2G 103
Stone Clo. Dag 2F 57
Stone Clo. W Dray 1B 76
Stonecot Clo. Sutt 1G 149
Stonecot Hill. Sutt 1G 149
Stone Cres. Felt 7H 95
Stonecroft Rd. Eri 7J 93
Stonecroft Way. Croy 7J 139
Stonecrop Clo. NW9 . . . . 3K 27
Stonecutter St. EC4
. . . . 6B 68 (7A 162)
Stonefield. N7 . . . . 2K 49
Stonefield Clo. Bexh 3G 111
Stonefield Clo. Ruis 5C 42
Stonefield St. N1 . . . . 1A 68
Stonefield Way. SE7 . . . . 7B 90
Stonefield Way. Ruis 4C 42
Stonegrove 4K 11
Stonegrove. Edgw 4K 11
Stone Gro. Ct. Edgw 5A 12
Stonegrove Gdns. Edgw 5A 12
Stone Hall. W8 . . . . 3K 83
(off Stone Hall Gdns.)
Stonehall Av. Ilf 6C 36
Stone Hall Gdns. W8 . . . . 3K 83
Stone Hall Pl. W8 . . . . 3K 83
Stone Hall Rd. N21 . . . . 7E 6
Stoneham Rd. N11 . . . . 5B 16
Stonehill Bus. Pk. N18 . . . . . . 6F 19
Stonehill Clo. SW14 . . . . 5K 99
Stonehill Ct. E4 . . . . 7J 9
Stonehill Green 7J 129
Stonehill Rd. SW14 . . . . 5J 99
Stone Hill Rd. W4 . . . . 5G 81
Stonehills Ct. SE21 . . . . 3E 122
Stonehill Woods Pk. Sidc . . . 6H 129
Stonehorse Rd. Enf 5D 8
Stonehouse. NW1 . . . . 1G 67
(off Plender St.)
Stone Ho. Ct. EC3 . . . . 7H 163
Stone Lake Ind. Pk. SE7 . . . . 4A 90
Stone Lake Retail Pk. SE7 . . . 4A 90
Stoneleigh 5C 148
Stoneleigh Av. Enf 1C 8
Stoneleigh Av. Wor Pk 4C 148
Stoneleigh B'way. Eps 5C 148
Stoneleigh Ct. Ilf 3C 36
Stoneleigh Cres. Eps 5B 148
Stoneleigh M. E3 . . . . 2A 70
Stoneleigh Pk. Av. Croy 6K 141
Stoneleigh Pk. Rd. Eps 6B 148
Stoneleigh Pl. W11 . . . . 7F 65
Stoneleigh Rd. N17 . . . . 3F 33
Stoneleigh Rd. Cars 7C 138
Stoneleigh Rd. Ilf 3C 36
Stoneleigh St. W11 . . . . 7F 65
Stoneleigh Ter. N19 . . . . 2F 49
Stonell's Rd. SW11 . . . . 6D 102
Stonemasons Clo. N15 . . . . . 4D 32
Stonenest St. N4 . . . . 1K 49
Stone Pk. Av. Beck 4C 142
Stone Pl. Wor Pk 2C 148
Stone Rd. Brom 5H 143
Stones End St. SE1
. . . . 2C 86 (7C 168)
Stone St. Croy 5A 152
Stonewall. E6 . . . . 5E 72
Stonewold Ct. W5 . . . . 6D 62
Stoney All. SE18 . . . . 2E 108
Stoneyard La. E14 . . . . 7D 70
Stoneycroft Clo. SE12 . . . . . 7H 107
Stoneycroft Rd. Wfd G 6H 21
Stoneydeep. Tedd 4A 116
Stoneydown. E17 . . . . 4A 34
Stoneydown Av. E17 . . . . 4A 34
Stoneydown Ho. E17 . . . . 4A 34
(off Blackhorse Rd.)
Stoneyfields Gdns. Edgw 4D 12
Stoneyfields La. Edgw 5D 12
Stoney La. E1 . . . . . 6F 69 (7H 163)
Stoney La. SE19 . . . . 6F 123
Stoney St. SE1 . . . . 1D 86 (4E 168)
Stonhouse St. SW4 . . . . 4H 103
Stonor Rd. W14 . . . . 4H 83
Stonycroft Clo. Enf 2F 9
Stopes St. SE15 . . . . 7F 87
Stopford Rd. E13 . . . . 1J 71
Stopford Rd. SE17 . . . . 5B 86
Stopher Ho. SE1 . . . 2B 86 (7B 168)
(off Webber St.)
Store Rd. E16 . . . . 2E 90
Storers Quay. E14 . . . . 4F 89
Store St. E15 . . . . 5F 53
Store St. WC1 . . . . . 5H 67 (6C 160)
Storey Ct. NW8 . . . . 2A 158
Storey Ho. E14 . . . . 7D 70
(off Cottage St.)
Storey Rd. E17 . . . . 4B 34
Storey Rd. N6 . . . . 6D 30
Storey's Ga. SW1
. . . . 2H 85 (7D 166)
Storey St. E16 . . . . 1E 90
Stories M. SE5 . . . . 2E 104
Stories Rd. SE5 . . . . 3E 104
Stork Rd. E7 . . . . 6H 53
Storksmead Rd. Edgw 7F 13
Stork's Rd. SE16 . . . . 3G 87
Stormont Rd. N6 . . . . 7D 30
Stormont Rd. SW11 . . . . 3E 102
Stormont Way. Chess 5C 146
Stormount Dri. Hay 2E 76
Storrington. WC1 . . . 3J 67 (2F 161)
(off Regent Sq.)
Storrington Rd. Croy 1F 153
Story St. N1 . . . . 7K 49
Stothard Ho. E1 . . . . 4J 69
(off Amiel St.)
Stothard St. E1 . . . . 4J 69
Stott Clo. SW18 . . . . 6B 102
Stoughton Av. Sutt 5F 149
Stoughton Clo. SE11
. . . . 4K 85 (4H 173)
Stoughton Clo. SW15 . . . . . 1C 118
Stour Av. S'hall 3E 78
Stourcliffe Clo. W1
. . . . 6D 66 (1E 164)
Stourcliffe St. W1 . . . . 6D 66
Stour Clo. Kes 4A 156
Stourhead Clo. SW19 . . . . . . 7F 101
Stourhead Gdns. SW20 . . . . 3C 136
Stourhead Ho. SW1
. . . . 5H 85 (5C 172)
(off Tachbrook St.)
Stour Rd. E3 . . . . 7C 52
Stour Rd. Dag 2G 57
Stourton Av. Felt 4D 114
Stowage. SE8 . . . . 6C 88
Stow Cres. E17 . . . . 7F 19
Stowe Cres. Ruis 6D 22
Stowe Gdns. N9 . . . . 1A 18
Stowe Ho. NW11 . . . . 6A 30
Stowell Ho. N8 . . . . 4J 31
(off Pembroke Rd.)
Stowe Pl. N15 . . . . 3E 32
Stowe Rd. W12 . . . . 2D 82
Stoxmead. Harr 1H 25
Stracey Rd. E7 . . . . 4J 53
Stracey Rd. NW10 . . . . 1K 63
Strachan Pl. SW19 . . . . 6E 118
Stradbroke Dri. Chig 6K 21
Stradbroke Gro. Buck H 1G 21
Stradbroke Gro. Ilf 3C 36
Stradbroke Pk. Chig 6K 21
Stradbroke Rd. N5 . . . . 4C 50
Stradbrook Clo. Harr 3D 42
Stradella Rd. SE24 . . . . 6C 104
Strafford Av. Ilf 2E 36
Strafford Ho. SE8 . . . . 5B 88
(off Grove St.)
Strafford Rd. W3 . . . . 2J 81
Strafford Rd. Barn 3B 4
Strafford Rd. Houn 3D 96
Strafford Rd. Twic 7A 98
Strafford St. E14 . . . . 2C 88
Strahan Rd. E3 . . . . 3A 70
Straightsmouth. SE10 . . . . . . 7E 88
Straight, The. S'hall 2B 78
Strait Rd. E6 . . . . 7C 72
Strakers Rd. SE15 . . . . 4H 105
Strale Ho. N1 . . . . 1E 68
(off Whitmore Est.)
Strand. WC2 . . . . . . 7J 67 (3F 167)
Strand Ct. SE18 . . . . 5J 91
Strandfield Clo. SE18 . . . . 5J 91
Strand La. WC2 . . . 7K 67 (2H 167)
Strand on the Green 6G 81
Strand on the Grn. W4 . . . . . 6G 81
Strand Pl. N18 . . . . 4K 17
Strand School App. W4 . . . . . 6G 81
Strand Theatre 7K 67 (2G 167)
(off Aldwych)
Strang Ho. N1 . . . . 1C 68
Strang Print Room 3C 160
Strangways Ter. W14 . . . . 3H 83
Stranraer Rd. H'row A 6A 94
Stranraer Way. N1 . . . . 7J 49
Stranraer Way. Stanw 6A 94
Strasburg Rd. SW11 . . . . . . 1E 102
Stratfield Pk. Clo. N21 . . . . . . 7G 7
Stratford 7F 53
Stratford Av. Uxb 2B 58
Stratford Cen., The. E15 . . . . . 7F 53
Stratford Circus Arts Cen.
. . . . 6F 53
Stratford Clo. Bark 7A 56
Stratford Clo. Dag 7J 57
Stratford Ct. N Mald 4K 135
Stratford Gro. SW15 . . . . . . 4F 101
Stratford Ho. Av. Brom 3C 144
Stratford Marsh 7D 52
Stratford New Town 5E 52
Stratford Office Village, The.
E15 . . . . 7G 53
(off Romford Rd.)
Stratford Pl. W1 . . . . 6F 67 (1J 165)
Stratford Rd. E15 . . . . 1H 71
(in two parts)
Stratford Rd. NW4 . . . . 4F 29
Stratford Rd. W8 . . . . 3J 83
Stratford Rd. Hay 4K 59
Stratford Rd. H'row A 6D 94
Stratford Rd. S'hall 4C 78
Stratford Rd. T Hth 4A 140
Stratford Shop. Cen. E15 . . . . 7F 53
(off Stratford Cen., The)
Stratford Studios. W8 . . . . . . 3J 83
Stratford Vs. NW1 . . . . 7G 49
Stratham Ct. N19 . . . . 3J 49
(off Alexander Rd.)
Strathan Clo. SW18 . . . . 6G 101
Strathaven Rd. SE12 . . . . . . 6K 107
Strathblaine Rd. SW11 . . . . 5B 102
Strathbrook Rd. SW16 . . . . . 7K 121
Strathcona Rd. Wemb 2D 44
Strathdale. SW16 . . . . 5K 121
Strathdon Dri. SW17 . . . . . . 3B 120
Strathearn Av. Hay 7H 77
Strathearn Av. Twic 1F 115
Strathearn Pl. W2
. . . . 6C 66 (1C 164)
Strathearn Rd. SW19 . . . . . . 5J 119
Strathearn Rd. Sutt 5J 149
Stratheden Pde. SE3 . . . . 7J 89
Stratheden Rd. SE3 . . . . 1J 107
Strathfield Gdns. Bark 6H 55
Strathleven Rd. SW2 . . . . . . 5J 103
Strathmore Ct. NW8
. . . . 3C 66 (1C 158)
(off Park Rd.)
Strathmore Gdns. N3 . . . . 1K 29
Strathmore Gdns. W8 . . . . 1J 83
Strathmore Gdns. Edgw 2H 27
Strathmore Rd. SW19 . . . . . . 3J 119
Strathmore Rd. Croy 7D 140
Strathmore Rd. Tedd 4J 115
Strathnairn St. SE1 . . . . 4G 87
Strathray Gdns. NW3 . . . . 6C 48
Strath Ter. SW11 . . . . 4C 102
Strathville Rd. SW18 . . . . . . 2J 119
Strathyre Av. SW16 . . . . 3A 140
Stratton Clo. SW19 . . . . 2J 137
Stratton Clo. Bexh 3E 110
Stratton Clo. Edgw 6A 12
Stratton Clo. Houn 1E 96
Stratton Ct. N1 . . . . 7E 50
(off Hertford Rd.)
Stratton Ct. Pinn 1D 24
(off Devonshire Rd.)
Strattondale St. E14 . . . . 3E 88
Stratton Dri. Bark 5J 55
Stratton Gdns. S'hall 6D 60
Stratton Rd. SW19 . . . . 2J 137
Stratton Rd. Bexh 3E 110
Stratton Rd. Sun 2H 131
Stratton St. W1 . . . . 1F 85 (4K 165)
Strauss Rd. W4 . . . . 2K 81
Strawberry Hill 3K 115
Strawberry Hill. Twic 3K 115
Strawberry Hill Clo. Twic . . . 3K 115
Strawberry Hill House 3K 115
(off Strawberry Va.)
Strawberry Hill Rd. Twic . . . 3K 115
Strawberry La. Cars 3E 150
Strawberry Ter. N10 . . . . 1D 30
Strawberry Va. N2 . . . . 1B 30
Strawberry Va. Twic 3A 116
(in two parts)
Streakes Fld. Rd. NW2 . . . . . 2C 46
Streamdale. SE2 . . . . 6B 92
Stream La. Edgw 5C 12
Streamline Ct. SE22 . . . . . . 1G 123
(off Streamline M.)
Streamline M. SE22 . . . . 1G 123
Streamside Clo. N9 . . . . 1A 18
Streamside Clo. Brom 4J 143
Stream Way. Belv 6F 93
Streatfield Av. E6 . . . . 1D 72
Streatfield Rd. Harr 3C 26
Streatham 5J 121
Streatham Clo. SW16 . . . . . . 2J 121
Streatham Common 6J 121
Streatham Comn. N.
SW16 . . . . 5J 121
Streatham Comn. S.
SW16 . . . . 6J 121
Streatham Ct. SW16 . . . . 3J 121
Streatham High Rd.
SW16 . . . . 4J 121
Streatham Hill 2J 121
Streatham Hill. SW2 . . . . 2J 121
Streatham Ice Rink 5H 121
Streatham Park 5G 121
Streatham Pl. SW2 . . . . 7J 103
Streatham Rd.
Mitc & SW16 . . . . . . 1E 138
Streatham St.
WC1 . . . . 6J 67 (7E 160)
Streatham Vale 7G 121
Streatham Va. SW16 . . . . . . 1G 139
Streathbourne Rd.
SW17 . . . . 2E 120
Streatley Pl. NW3 . . . . 4A 48
Streatley Rd. NW6 . . . . 7H 47
Streeters La. Wall 3H 151
Streetfield M. SE3 . . . . 3J 107
Streimer Rd. E15 . . . . 2E 70
Strelley Way. W3 . . . . 7A 64
Stretton Mans. SE8 . . . . 5C 88
Stretton Rd. Croy 7E 140
Stretton Rd. Rich 2C 116
Strickland Ct. SE15 . . . . 3G 105
Strickland Ho. E2 . . . 3F 69 (2K 163)
(off Chambord St.)
Strickland Row. SW18 . . . . . 7B 102
Strickland St. SE8 . . . . 2C 106
Stride Rd. E13 . . . . 2H 71
Strimon Clo. N9 . . . . 2D 18
Stringer Ho. N1 . . . . 1E 68
(off Whitmore Est.)
Strode Clo. N10 . . . . 7K 15
Strode Rd. E7 . . . . 4J 53
Strode Rd. N17 . . . . 2E 32
Strode Rd. NW10 . . . . 6C 46
Strode Rd. SW6 . . . . 7G 83
Strome Ho. NW6 . . . . 2K 65
(off Carlton Va.)
Strone Rd. E7 & E12 . . . . 6A 54
Strone Way. Hay 4C 60
Strongbow Cres. SE9 . . . . . 5D 108
Strongbow Rd. SE9 . . . . 5D 108
Strongbridge Clo. Harr 1E 42
Stronsa Rd. W12 . . . . 2B 82
Strood Av. Romf 1K 57
Strood Ho. SE1 . . . . 2D 86 (7F 169)
(off Staple St.)
Stroud Cres. SW15 . . . . 3C 118
Stroudes Clo. Wor Pk 7A 136
Stroud Fld. N'holt 6C 42
Stroud Ga. Harr 4F 43
Stroud Green 7K 31
Stroud Grn. Gdns. Croy 7J 141
Stroud Grn. Rd. N4 . . . . 1K 49
Stroud Grn. Way. Croy 7H 141
Stroudley Ho. SW8 . . . . 1G 103
Stroudley Wlk. E3 . . . . 3D 70
Stroud Rd. SE25 . . . . 6G 141
Stroud Rd. SW19 . . . . 3J 119
Stroud's Clo. Chad H 5B 38
Stroud Way. Ashf 6D 112
Strouts Pl. E2 . . . . . 3F 69 (1J 163)
Strudwick Ct. SW4 . . . . 1J 103
(off Binfield Rd.)
Strutton Ground. SW1
. . . . 3H 85 (1C 172)
Strype St. E1 . . . . . . 5F 69 (6J 163)
Stuart Av. NW9 . . . . 7C 28
Stuart Av. W5 . . . . 2F 81
Stuart Av. Brom 1J 155
Stuart Av. Harr 3D 42
Stuart Av. W on T 7K 131
Stuart Clo. Uxb 6C 40
Stuart Ct. Croy 3B 152
(off St John's Rd.)
Stuart Cres. N22 . . . . 1K 31
Stuart Cres. Croy 3B 154
Stuart Cres. Hay 6E 58
Stuart Evans Clo. Well 3C 110
Stuart Gro. Tedd 5J 115
Stuart Ho. E16 . . . . 1K 89
(off Beaulieu Av.)
Stuart Ho. W14 . . . . 4G 83
(off Windsor Way)
Stuart Mantle Way. Eri 7K 93

Stuart Mill Ho. N1 . . . . 2K 67 (1G 161) (off Killick St.)
Stuart Pl. Mitc. 1D 138
Stuart Rd. NW6 . . . . 3J 65 (in two parts)
Stuart Rd. SE15 . . . . 4J 105
Stuart Rd. SW19 . . . . 3J 119
Stuart Rd. W3 . . . . 1J 81
Stuart Rd. Bark 7K 55
Stuart Rd. E Barn 7H 5
Stuart Rd. Harr 3K 25
Stuart Rd. Rich 2B 116
Stuart Rd. T Hth 4C 140
Stuart Rd. Well 1B 110
Stuart Tower. W9. . . . . 3A 66 (off Maida Va.)
Stubbs Ct. W4. . . . . 5H 81 (off Chaseley Dri.)
Stubbs Dri. SE16. . . . . 5H 87
Stubbs Ho. E2. . . . . 3K 69 (off Bonner St.)
Stubbs Ho. SW1. . . 4H 85 (4D 172) (off Erasmus St.)
Stubbs M. Dag . . . . 4B 56 (off Marlborough Rd.)
Stubbs Point. E13 . . . . 4J 71
Stubbs Way. SW19 . . . . 1B 138
Stucley Pl. NW1. . . . . 7F 49
Stucley Rd. Houn 7G 79
Studdridge St. SW6 . . . . 2J 101 (in two parts)
Studd St. N1 . . . . 1B 68
Studholme Ct. NW3. . . . . 4J 47
Studholme St. SE15 . . . . 7H 87
Studio La. W5. . . . . 1D 80
Studio Pl. SW1 . . . . 7F 165
Studios Rd. Shep 3B 130
Studland. SE17. . . . . 5D 86 (off Portland St.)
Studland Clo. Sidc. 3K 127
Studland Ho. E14 . . . . 6A 70 (off Aston St.)
Studland Rd. SE26 . . . . 5K 123
Studland Rd. W7. . . . . 6H 61
Studland Rd. King T. 6E 116
Studland St. W6 . . . . 4D 82
Studley Av. E4. . . . . 7A 20
Studley Clo. E5 . . . . 5A 52
Studley Ct. E14 . . . . 7F 71 (off Jamestown Way)
Studley Ct. Sidc. 5B 128
Studley Dri. Ilf. 6B 36
Studley Est. SW4. . . . . 1J 103
Studley Grange Rd. W7 . . . . . 2J 79
Studley Rd. E7 . . . . 6K 53
Studley Rd. SW4 . . . . 1J 103
Studley Rd. Dag 7D 56
Stukeley Rd. E7. . . . . 7K 53
Stukeley St. WC2. . . 6J 67 (7F 161)
Stumps Hill La. Beck 6C 124
Stunell Ho. SE14. . . . . 6K 87 (off John Williams Clo.)
Sturdee Ho. E2. . . . 2G 69 (1K 163) (off Horatio St.)
Sturdy Ho. E3 . . . . 2A 70 (off Gernon Rd.)
Sturdy Rd. SE15 . . . . 2H 105
Sturge Av. E17 . . . . 2D 34
Sturgeon Rd. SE17 . . . . 5C 86
Sturges Fld. Chst. 6H 127
Sturgess Av. NW4. . . . . 7D 28
Sturge St. SE1 . . . 2C 86 (6C 168)
Sturmer Way. N7. . . . . 5K 49
Sturminster Clo. Hay 6A 60
Sturminster Ho. SW8 . . . . . . 7K 85 (off Dorset Rd.)
Sturrock Clo. N15 . . . . 4D 32
Sturry St. E14. . . . . 6D 70
Sturt St. N1. . . . . 1D 162
Stutfield St. E1 . . . . 6G 69
Styles Gdns. SW9 . . . . 3B 104
Styles Ho. SE1. . . . . 6A 168
Styles Way. Beck 4E 142
Sudbourne Rd. SW2 . . . . . . 5J 103
Sudbrooke Rd. SW12 . . . . . 6D 102
Sudbrook Gdns. Rich 3D 116
Sudbrook La. Rich. 1E 116
Sudbury. 5B 44
Sudbury. E6. . . . . 5E 72
Sudbury Av. Wemb 3C 44
Sudbury Ct. E5 . . . . 4A 52
Sudbury Ct. SW8 . . . . 1H 103
Sudbury Ct. Dri. Harr. 3K 43
Sudbury Ct. Rd. Harr. 3K 43
Sudbury Cres. Brom 6J 125
Sudbury Cres. Wemb 5B 44
Sudbury Cft. Wemb 4K 43
Sudbury Gdns. Croy 4E 152
Sudbury Heights Av. Gnfd. 5K 43
Sudbury Hill. Harr 2J 43
Sudbury Hill Clo. Wemb 4K 43
Sudbury Ho. SW18 . . . . 5K 101
Sudbury Rd. Bark 5K 55
Sudeley St. N1 . . . . 2B 68
Sudlow Rd. SW18 . . . . 5J 101
Sudrey St. SE1 . . . . 2C 86 (7C 168)
Suez Av. Gnfd 2K 61
Suez Rd. Enf 4F 9
Suffield Hatch. 4K 19
Suffield Ho. SE17 . . . . 5B 86 (off Berryfield Rd.)
Suffield Rd. E4. . . . . 3J 19
Suffield Rd. N15 . . . . 5F 33
Suffield Rd. SE20. . . . . 2J 141
Suffolk Ct. E10 . . . . 7C 34
Suffolk Ct. Ilf. 6J 37
Suffolk Ho. SE20. . . . . 1K 141 (off Croydon Rd.)
Suffolk Ho. Croy . . . . 2D 152 (off George St.)
Suffolk La. EC4. . . . 7D 68 (2E 168)
Suffolk Pk. Rd. E17 . . . . 4A 34
Suffolk Pl. SW1 . . . 1H 85 (4D 166)
Suffolk Rd. E13 . . . . 3J 71
Suffolk Rd. N15. . . . . 5D 32
Suffolk Rd. NW10 . . . . 7A 46
Suffolk Rd. SE25 . . . . 4F 141
Suffolk Rd. SW13 . . . . 7B 82
Suffolk Rd. Bark 7H 55
Suffolk Rd. Dag 5J 57
Suffolk Rd. Enf 5C 8
Suffolk Rd. Harr 6D 24
Suffolk Rd. Ilf 6J 37
Suffolk Rd. Sidc 6C 128
Suffolk Rd. Wor Pk 2B 148
Suffolk St. E7. . . . . 4J 53
Suffolk St. SW1 . . . 7H 67 (3D 166)
Sugar Bakers Ct. EC3 . . . . . 1H 169
Sugar Ho. La. E15 . . . . 2E 70
Sugar Loaf Wlk. E2 . . . . 3J 69
Sugar Quay. EC3. . . . . 3H 169
Sugar Quay Wlk. EC3 . . . . 7E 68 (3H 169)
Sugden Rd. SW11. . . . . 3E 102
Sugden Rd. Th Dit. 1B 146
Sugden St. SE5. . . . . 6D 86 (off Depot St.)
Sugden Way. Bark. 2K 73
Sulby Ho. SE4 . . . . 4A 106 (off Turnham Rd.)
Sulgrave Gdns. W6 . . . . 2E 82
Sulgrave Rd. W6. . . . . 3E 82
Sulina Rd. SW2 . . . . 7J 103
Sulivan Ct. SW6. . . . . 2J 101
Sulivan Enterprise Cen. SW6. . . . . 3K 101
Sulivan Rd. SW6 . . . . 3J 101
Sulkin Ho. E2 . . . . 3K 69 (off Knottisford St.)
Sullivan Av. E16. . . . . 5B 72
Sullivan Clo. SW11 . . . . 3C 102
Sullivan Clo. Hay. 5A 60
Sullivan Clo. W Mol 3F 133
Sullivan Ct. N16. . . . . 7F 33
Sullivan Cres. Hare 2A 22
Sullivan Ho. SE11 . . . . 4K 85 (4H 173) (off Vauxhall St.)
Sullivan Ho. SW1 . . . . 6F 85 (7K 171) (off Churchill Gdns.)
Sullivan Rd. SE11 . . . . 4A 86 (3K 173)
Sullivans Reach. W on T . . . 7H 131
Sultan Rd. E11 . . . . 4K 35
Sultan St. SE5. . . . . 7C 86
Sultan St. Beck 2K 141
Sultan Ter. N22 . . . . 2A 32
Sumatra Rd. NW6 . . . . 5J 47
Sumburgh Rd. SW12. . . . . . 6E 102
Summer Av. E Mol. 5J 133
Summercourt Rd. E1 . . . . 6J 69
Summerene Clo. SW16 . . . . 7G 121
Summerfield Av. NW6. . . . . . 2G 65
Summerfield La. Surb 2D 146
Summerfield Rd. W5. . . . . . . 4B 62
Summerfields. Brom . . . . . . 1K 143 (off Freelands Rd.)
Summerfields Av. N12. . . . . . 6H 15
Summerfield St. SE12 . . . . . 7H 107
Summer Gdns. E Mol. 5J 133
Summer Hill. Chst 2E 144
Summerhill Gro. Enf 6K 7
Summerhill Rd. N15 . . . . 4D 32
Summerhill Vs. Chst . . . . . . 1E 144 (off Susan Wood)
Summerhill Way. Mitc 1E 138
Summerhouse Av. Houn 1C 96
Summerhouse Dri. Bex & Dart. 4K 129
Summerhouse Rd. N16 . . . . . 2E 50
Summerland Gdns. N10. . . . . . 3F 31
Summerland Grange. N10 . . . 3F 31
Summerlands Av. W3. . . . . . . 7J 63
Summerlands Lodge. Orp. 4E 156
Summerlee Av. N2. . . . . 4D 30
Summerlee Gdns. N2 . . . . . . 4D 30
Summerley St. SW18 . . . . . 2K 119
Summer Rd. E Mol & Th Dit 5J 133
Summersby Rd. N6 . . . . 6F 31
Summers Clo. Sutt. 7J 149
Summers Clo. Wemb 1H 45
Summerskille Clo. N9 . . . . . . 3C 18
Summers La. N12. . . . . 7G 15
Summers Row. N12 . . . . 6H 15
Summers St. EC1 . . . . 4A 68 (4J 161)
Summerstown. 3A 120
Summerstown. SW17 . . . . . 3A 120
Summerton Way. SE28. . . . . 6D 74
Summer Trees. Sun. 1K 131
Summerville Gdns. Sutt. . . . 6H 149
Summerwood Rd. Iswth 5K 97
Summit Av. NW9. . . . . 5K 27
Summit Bus. Pk. Sun. 7J 113
Summit Clo. N14. . . . . 2B 16
Summit Clo. NW2. . . . . 5G 47
Summit Clo. NW9. . . . . 4K 27
Summit Clo. Edgw. 7B 12
Summit Dri. Wfd G 2B 36
Summit Est. N16. . . . . 7G 33
Summit Rd. E17. . . . . 4D 34
Summit Rd. N'holt. 7E 42
Summit Way. N14 . . . . 2A 16
Summit Way. SE19 . . . . 7E 122
Sumner Av. SE15. . . . . 1F 105
Sumner Bldgs. SE1 . . . . . . 4C 168
Sumner Ct. SW8 . . . . 7J 85
Sumner Est. SE15 . . . . 7F 87
Sumner Gdns. Croy. 1A 152
Sumner Ho. E3 . . . . 5D 70 (off Watts Gro.)
Sumner Pl. SW7. . . 4B 84 (4B 170)
Sumner Pl. M. SW7 . . . . 4B 84 (4B 170)
Sumner Rd. SE15 . . . . 6F 87 (in two parts)
Sumner Rd. Croy. 1A 152
Sumner Rd. Harr. 7G 25
Sumner Rd. S. Croy. 1A 152
Sumner St. SE1 . . . 1B 86 (4B 168)
Sumpter Clo. NW3 . . . . 6A 48
Sun All. Rich 4E 98
Sunbeam Cres. W10 . . . . 4E 64
Sunbeam Rd. NW10 . . . . 4J 63
Sunbury. 3A 132
Sunbury Av. NW7 . . . . 5E 12
Sunbury Av. SW14 . . . . 4K 99
Sunbury Av. Pas. SW14. . . . 4A 100
Sunbury Clo. W on T 6J 131
Sunbury Common. 7H 113
Sunbury Ct. Barn. 4B 4
Sunbury Ct. Island. Sun. . . . 3B 132
Sunbury Ct. M. Sun. 2B 132
Sunbury Ct. Rd. Sun 2A 132
Sunbury Cres. Felt. 4H 113
Sunbury Cross. (Junct.). . . . 7J 113
Sunbury Cross Shop. Cen. Sun 7H 113
Sunbury Gdns. NW7 . . . . 5E 12
Sunbury Ho. E2 . . . . 3F 69 (2J 163) (off Swanfield St.)
Sunbury Ho. SE14. . . . . 6K 87 (off Myers La.)
Sunbury La. SW11 . . . . 1B 102 (in two parts)
Sunbury La. W on T. 6J 131
Sunburylock Ait. W on T . . . 4K 131
Sunbury Pk. Walled Garden. 3K 131
Sunbury Rd. Felt. 3H 113
Sunbury Rd. Sutt 3F 149
Sunbury St. SE18 . . . . 3D 90
Sunbury Way. Hanw 5A 114
Sunbury Workshops. E2 . . . . 3F 69 (2J 163) (off Swanfield St.)
Sun Ct. EC3. . . . . 1F 169
Suncroft Pl. SE26 . . . . 3J 123
Sunderland Ct. SE22 . . . . . . 7G 105
Sunderland Ct. Stanw 6A 94
Sunderland Mt. SE23. . . . . . 2K 123
Sunderland Rd. SE23. . . . . . 1K 123
Sunderland Rd. W5. . . . . 3D 80
Sunderland Rd. H'row A 6A 94
Sunderland Ter. W2. . . . . 6K 65
Sunderland Way. E12. . . . . . . 2B 54
Sundew Av. W12. . . . . 7C 64
Sundew Clo. W12 . . . . 7C 64
Sundew Ct. Wemb. . . . . 2E 62 (off Elmore Clo.)
Sundial Av. SE25 . . . . 3F 141
Sundorne Rd. SE7. . . . . 5A 90
Sundown Rd. Ashf. 5E 112
Sundra Wlk. E1 . . . . 4K 69
Sundridge. 6A 126
Sundridge Av. Brom. 1B 144
Sundridge Av. Well 2H 109
Sundridge Ho. E9 . . . . 7K 51 (off Church Cres.)
Sundridge Pde. Brom 7K 125
Sundridge Park. 7K 125
Sundridge Pl. Croy 1G 153
Sundridge Rd. Croy 7F 141
Sunfields Pl. SE3. . . . . 7K 89
Sungate Cotts. Romf 1F 39
Sun-in-the-Sands. (Junct.). . . 7K 89
Sunken Rd. Croy 5J 153
Sunkist Way. Wall 7J 151
Sunland Av. Bexh. 4E 110
Sun La. SE3 . . . . 7K 89
Sunleigh Rd. Wemb. 1E 62
Sunley Gdns. Gnfd 1A 62
Sunlight Clo. SW19. . . . . . . 6A 120
Sunlight Sq. E2. . . . . 3H 69
Sunmead Rd. Sun 3J 131
Sunna Gdns. Sun 2K 131
Sunniholme Ct. S Croy . . . . 5C 152 (off Warham Rd.)
Sunningdale. N14 . . . . 5C 16
Sunningdale. W13. . . . . 5B 62 (off Hardwick Grn.)
Sunningdale Av. W3 . . . . 7A 64
Sunningdale Av. Bark. 1H 73
Sunningdale Av. Felt 2C 114
Sunningdale Av. Ruis. 1A 42
Sunningdale Clo. E6 . . . . 3D 72
Sunningdale Clo. SE16 . . . . . 5H 87
Sunningdale Clo. SE28. . . . . . 6E 74
Sunningdale Clo. Stan 6F 11
Sunningdale Clo. Surb 2E 146
Sunningdale Ct. Houn . . . . . . 6H 97 (off Whitton Dene)
Sunningdale Ct. S'hall . . . . . . 6G 61 (off Fleming Rd.)
Sunningdale Gdns. NW9 . . . . 5J 27
Sunningdale Gdns. W8. . . . . . 3J 83 (off Stratford Rd.)
Sunningdale Lodge. Edgw . . . 5A 12 (off Stonegrove)
Sunningdale Lodge. Harr . . . . 7J 25 (off Grove Hill)
Sunningdale Rd. Brom. 4C 144
Sunningdale Rd. Sutt. 3H 149
Sunningfields Cres. NW4. . . . 2D 28
Sunningfields Rd. NW4 . . . . . 3D 28
Sunninghill Ct. W3. . . . . 2J 81
Sunninghill Rd. SE13. . . . . . 2D 106
Sunny Bank. SE25. . . . . 3G 141
Sunny Cres. NW10 . . . . 7J 45
Sunnycroft Rd. SE25. . . . . . 3G 141
Sunnycroft Rd. Houn 2F 97
Sunnycroft Rd. S'hall. 5E 60
Sunnydale. Orp 2E 156
Sunnydale Gdns. NW7. . . . . . 6E 12
Sunnydale Rd. SE12 . . . . . . 5K 107
Sunnydene Av. E4 . . . . 5A 20
Sunnydene Av. Ruis. 1J 41
Sunnydene Gdns. Wemb 6C 44
Sunnydene St. SE26 . . . . . . 4A 124
Sunnyfield. NW7. . . . . 4G 13
Sunnyfield Rd. Chst. 3K 145
Sunny Gdns. Pde. NW4. . . . . 2D 28
Sunny Gdns. Rd. NW4 . . . . . 2D 28
Sunny Hill. NW4 . . . . 3D 28
Sunnyhill Clo. E5. . . . . 4A 52
Sunny Hill Pk. 2D 28
Sunnyhill Rd. SW16. . . . . . . 4J 121
Sunnyhurst Clo. Sutt 3J 149
Sunnymead Av. Mitc 3H 139
Sunnymead Rd. NW9 . . . . . . 7K 27
Sunnymead Rd. SW15 . . . . 5D 100
Sunnymede Av. Eps. 7A 148
Sunnymede Dri. Ilf. 5F 37
Sunny Nook Gdns. S Croy 6D 152
Sunny Rd., The. Enf. 1E 8
Sunnyside. NW2. . . . . 3H 47
Sunnyside. SW19 . . . . 6G 119
Sunnyside. W on T 5A 132
Sunnyside Dri. E4 . . . . 7K 9
Sunnyside Houses. NW2. . . . . 3H 47 (off Sunnyside)
Sunnyside Pas. SW19. . . . . 6G 119
Sunnyside Rd. E10 . . . . 1C 52
Sunnyside Rd. N19. . . . . 7H 31
Sunnyside Rd. W5 . . . . 1D 80
Sunnyside Rd. Ilf. 3G 55
Sunnyside Rd. Tedd. 4H 115
Sunnyside Rd. E. N9 . . . . 3B 18
Sunnyside Rd. N. N9. . . . . . . 3A 18
Sunnyside Rd. S. N9. . . . . . . 3A 18
Sunnyside Ter. NW9 . . . . 3K 27
Sunny Vw. NW9 . . . . 5K 27
Sunny Way. N12. . . . . 7H 15
Sun Pas. SE16 . . . . 3G 87 (off Old Jamaica Rd.)
Sunray Av. SE24. . . . . 4D 104
Sunray Av. Brom. 6C 144
Sunray Av. Surb 2H 147
Sunrise Clo. Felt 3D 114
Sunrise Vw. NW7 . . . . 6G 13
Sun Rd. W14 . . . . 5H 83
Sunset Av. E4 . . . . 1J 19
Sunset Av. Wfd G 4C 20
Sunset Ct. Wfd G. 7F 21
Sunset Gdns. SE25 . . . . 2F 141
Sunset Rd. SE5. . . . . 4C 104
Sunset Rd. SE28. . . . . 1A 92
Sunset Vw. Barn 2B 4
Sunshine Way. Mitc. 2D 138

Sun St. EC2 5D 68 (5F 163) (in two parts)
Sun St. Pas. EC2 5E 68 (6G 163)
Sun Wlk. E1 7F 69 (3K 169)
Sunwell Clo. SE15 1H 105
Sun Wharf. SE8 7D 88 (off Creekside)
Surbiton. 6D 134
Surbiton Ct. Surb 6C 134
Surbiton Cres. King T. 4E 134
Surbiton Hall Clo. King T 4E 134
Surbiton Hill Pk. Surb 5F 135
Surbiton Hill Rd. Surb 4E 134
Surbiton Pde. Surb 6E 134
Surbiton Rd. King T. 4D 134
Surlingham Clo. SE28 7D 74
Surma Clo. E1 4G 69
Surmans Clo. Dag 1C 74
Surrendale Pl. W9 4J 65
Surrey Canal Rd. SE15 & SE14 6J 87
Surrey County Cricket Club (Oval Cricket Ground, The) 6K 85 (7H 173)
Surrey Ct. N3 2G 29
Surrey Cres. W4 5G 81
Surrey Gdns. N4 6C 32
Surrey Gro. SE17 5E 86
Surrey Gro. Sutt 3B 150
Surrey Ho. SE16 1K 87 (off Rotherhithe St.)
Surrey La. SW11 1C 102
Surrey La. Est. SW11 1C 102
Surrey M. SE27 4E 122
Surrey Mt. SE23 1H 123
Surrey Quays Rd. SE16 3J 87
Surrey Quays Shop. Cen. SE16 3K 87
Surrey Rd. SE15 5K 105
Surrey Rd. Bark 7J 55
Surrey Rd. Dag 5H 57
Surrey Rd. Harr 5G 25
Surrey Rd. W Wick 1D 154
Surrey Row. SE1 2B 86 (6A 168)
Surrey Sq. SE17 5E 86
Surrey Steps. WC2 7K 67 (2H 167) (off Surrey St.)
Surrey St. E13 3K 71
Surrey St. WC2 7K 67 (2H 167)
Surrey St. Croy 2C 152
Surrey Ter. SE17 5E 86
Surrey Water Rd. SE16 1K 87
Surridge Ct. SW9 2J 103 (off Clapham Rd.)
Surridge Gdns. SE19 6D 122
Surr St. N7 5J 49
Susan Clo. Romf 3J 39
Susan Constant Ct. E14 7F 71 (off Newport Av.)
Susan Lawrence Ho. E12 4E 54 (off Walton Rd.)
Susannah St. E14 6D 70
Susan Rd. SE3 2K 107
Susan Wood. Chst 1E 144
Sussex Av. Iswth 3J 97
Sussex Clo. N19 2J 49
Sussex Clo. Ilf 5D 36
Sussex Clo. N Mald 4A 136
Sussex Clo. Twic 6B 98
Sussex Ct. SE10 6E 88 (off Roan St.)
Sussex Cres. N'holt 6E 42
Sussex Gdns. N4 5C 32
Sussex Gdns. N6 5D 30
Sussex Gdns. W2 7B 66 (2A 164)
Sussex Gdns. Chess 6D 146
Sussex Ga. N6 5D 30
Sussex Lodge. W2 6B 66 (1B 164) (off Sussex Pl.)
Sussex Mans. SW7 4A 170
Sussex Mans. WC2 7J 67 (2F 167) (off Maiden La.)
Sussex M. SE6 7C 106
Sussex M. E. W2 1B 164
Sussex M. W. W2 7B 66 (2B 164)
Sussex Pl. NW1 4D 66 (3E 158)
Sussex Pl. W2 6B 66 (1B 164)
Sussex Pl. W6 5E 82
Sussex Pl. Eri 7H 93
Sussex Pl. N Mald 4A 136
Sussex Ring. N12 5D 14
Sussex Rd. E6 1E 72
Sussex Rd. Cars 7D 150
Sussex Rd. Eri 7H 93
Sussex Rd. Harr 5G 25
Sussex Rd. Mitc 5J 139
Sussex Rd. N Mald 4A 136
Sussex Rd. Sidc 5B 128
Sussex Rd. S'hall 3B 78
Sussex Rd. S Croy 6D 152
Sussex Rd. Uxb 4E 40
Sussex Rd. W Wick 1D 154
Sussex Sq. W2 7B 66 (2B 164)
Sussex St. E13 3K 71
Sussex St. SW1 5F 85 (6K 171)
Sussex Ter. SE20 7J 123 (off Graveney Gro.)
Sussex Wlk. SW9 4B 104 (in two parts)
Sussex Way. N19 & N7 1H 49 (in four parts)
Sussex Way. Barn 5A 6
Sutcliffe Clo. NW11 5K 29
Sutcliffe Rd. SE18 6J 91
Sutcliffe Rd. Well 2C 110
Sutherland Av. W9 4J 65
Sutherland Av. W13 6B 62
Sutherland Av. Hay 4J 77
Sutherland Av. Orp 6K 145
Sutherland Av. Sun 2H 131
Sutherland Av. Well 4J 109
Sutherland Clo. Barn 4B 4
Sutherland Ct. N16 3D 50
Sutherland Ct. NW9 5H 27
Sutherland Ct. W9 4J 65 (off Marylands Rd.)
Sutherland Dri. SW19 1B 138
Sutherland Gdns. SW14 3A 100
Sutherland Gdns. Sun 2H 131
Sutherland Gdns. Wor Pk 1D 148
Sutherland Gro. SW18 6G 101
Sutherland Gro. Tedd 5J 115
Sutherland Ho. W8 3K 83
Sutherland Pl. W2 6J 65
Sutherland Rd. E3 2B 70
Sutherland Rd. E17 2K 33
Sutherland Rd. N9 1C 18
Sutherland Rd. N17 7B 18
Sutherland Rd. W4 6A 82
Sutherland Rd. W13 6A 62
Sutherland Rd. Belv 3G 93
Sutherland Rd. Croy 7A 140
Sutherland Rd. Enf 6E 8
Sutherland Rd. S'hall 6D 60
Sutherland Rd. Path. E17 3K 33
Sutherland Row. SW1 5F 85 (5K 171)
Sutherland Sq. SE17 5C 86
Sutherland St. SW1 5F 85 (5J 171)
Sutherland Wlk. SE17 5C 86
Sutlej Rd. SE7 7A 90
Sutterton St. N7 6K 49
Sutton. 5K 149
Sutton Arc. Sutt 5K 149
Sutton Clo. Beck 1D 142
Sutton Clo. Lou 1H 21
Sutton Clo. Pinn 5J 23
Sutton Comn. Rd. Sutt 7H 137
Sutton Ct. SE19 7F 123
Sutton Ct. W4 6J 81
Sutton Ct. W5 1E 80
Sutton Ct. Sutt 6A 150
Sutton Ct. Rd. E13 3A 72
Sutton Ct. Rd. W4 7J 81
Sutton Ct. Rd. Sutt 6A 150
Sutton Ct. Rd. Uxb 1D 58
Sutton Cres. Barn 5A 4
Sutton Dene. Houn 1F 97
Sutton Est. EC1 2F 163
Sutton Est. W10 5E 64
Sutton Est., The. N1 7B 50
Sutton Est., The. SW3 5C 84 (5C 170)
Sutton Gdns. SE25 5F 141
Sutton Gdns. Bark 1J 73
Sutton Grn. Bark 1J 73
Sutton Gro. Sutt 4B 150
Sutton Hall Rd. Houn 7E 78
Sutton Heights. Sutt 7B 150
Sutton La. Houn 3D 96
Sutton La. N. W4 5J 81
Sutton La. S. W4 6J 81
Sutton Pde. NW4 4E 28 (off Church Rd.)
Sutton Pk. Rd. Sutt 6K 149
Sutton Pl. E9 5J 51
Sutton Rd. E13 4H 71
Sutton Rd. E17 1K 33
Sutton Rd. N10 1E 30
Sutton Rd. Bark 2J 73
Sutton Rd. Houn 1E 96
Sutton Row. W1 6H 67 (7D 160)
Suttons Bus. Pk. Rain 3K 75
Sutton Sq. E9 5J 51
Sutton Sq. Houn 1D 96
Sutton St. E1 7J 69
Sutton's Way. EC1 4C 68 (4D 162)
Sutton United F.C. 4J 149
Sutton Wlk. SE1 1K 85 (5H 167)
Sutton Way. W10 4E 64
Sutton Way. Houn 1D 96
Swaby Rd. SW18 1A 120
Swaffham Way. N22 7G 17
Swaffield Rd. SW18 7K 101
Swain Clo. SW16 6F 121
Swain Rd. T Hth 5C 140
Swains Clo. W Dray 2A 76
Swains La. N6 1E 48
Swainson Rd. W3 2B 82
Swains Rd. SW17 7D 120
Swain St. NW8 4C 66 (3C 158) (off Tresham Cres.)
Swakeleys Dri. Uxb 4C 40
Swakeleys Rd. Uxb 4A 40
Swakeleys Roundabout. (Junct.) 4A 40
Swalecliffe Rd. Belv 5H 93
Swaledale Clo. N11 6K 15
Swallands Rd. SE6 3C 124 (in two parts)
Swallow Clo. SE14 1K 105
Swallow Clo. Bush 1B 10
Swallow Clo. Eri 1K 111
Swallow Ct. SE12 7J 107
Swallow Ct. W9 5J 65 (off Admiral Wlk.)
Swallow Ct. Ilf 5F 37
Swallow Ct. Ruis 1A 42
Swallow Dri. NW10 6K 45
Swallow Dri. N'holt 2E 60
Swallowfield Rd. SE7 5K 89
Swallowfield Way. Hay 2F 77
Swallow Gdns. SW16 5H 121
Swallow Ho. NW8 2C 66 (off Barrow Hill Est.)
Swallow Pk. Cvn. Site. Surb 3F 147
Swallow Pas. W1 6F 67 (1K 165) (off Swallow Pl.)
Swallow Pl. W1 6F 67 (1K 165)
Swallow St. E6 5C 72
Swallow St. W1 7G 67 (3B 166)
Swanage Ct. N1 7E 50 (off Hertford Rd.)
Swanage Ho. SW8 7K 85 (off Dorset Rd.)
Swanage Rd. E4 7K 19
Swanage Rd. SW18 6A 102
Swanage Waye. Hay 6A 60
Swan & Pike Rd. Enf 1H 9
Swan App. E6 5C 72
Swanbourne. SE17 4C 86 (off Wansey St.)
Swanbourne Ho. NW8 4C 66 (3C 158) (off Capland St.)
Swanbridge Rd. Bexh 1G 111
Swan Cen., The. SW17 3K 119
Swan Clo. E17 1A 34
Swan Clo. Croy 7E 140
Swan Clo. Felt 4C 114
Swan Ct. E14 6B 70 (off Agnes St.)
Swan Ct. SW3 5C 84 (6D 170)
Swan Ct. SW6 7J 83 (off Fulham Rd.)
Swan Ct. Iswth 3B 98 (off Swan St.)
Swandon Way. SW18 5K 101
Swan Dri. NW9 2A 28
Swanfield St. E2 3F 69 (2J 163)
Swan Ho. N1 7D 50 (off Oakley Rd.)
Swan La. EC4 7D 68 (3F 169)
Swan La. N20 3F 15
Swanley Ho. SE17 5E 86 (off Kinglake Est.)
Swanley Rd. Well 1C 110
Swan Mead. SE1 3E 86
Swan M. SW6 1H 101
Swan M. SW9 2K 103
Swann Ct. Iswth 3A 98 (off South St.)
Swanne Ho. SE10 7E 88 (off Gloucester Cir.)
Swan Pas. E1 3K 169
Swan Pl. SW13 2B 100
Swan Rd. SE16 2J 87
Swan Rd. Felt 5C 114
Swan Rd. S'hall 6F 61
Swan Rd. W Dray 2A 76
Swanscombe Ho. W11 1F 83 (off St Ann's Rd.)
Swanscombe Point. E16 5H 71 (off Clarkson Rd.)
Swanscombe Rd. W4 5A 82
Swanscombe Rd. W11 1F 83
Swansea Ct. E16 1F 91
Swansea Rd. Enf 4D 8
Swansea Rd. H'row A 6E 94
Swansland Gdns. E17 1A 34
Swan St. SE1 3C 86 (7D 168)
Swan St. SE18 3B 90 (in two parts)
Swan St. Iswth 3B 98
Swan, The. (Junct.) 1E 154
Swanton Gdns. SW19 1F 119
Swanton Rd. Eri 7G 93
Swan Wlk. SW3 6D 84 (7E 170)
Swan Wlk. Shep 7G 131
Swan Way. Enf 2E 8
Swanwick Clo. SW15 7B 100
Swan Yd. N1 6B 50
Sward Rd. Orp 6K 145
Swathling Ho. SW15 6B 100 (off Tunworth Cres.)
Swaton Rd. E3 4C 70
Swaylands Rd. Belv 6G 93
Swaythling Clo. N18 4C 18
Swedeland Ct. E1 6H 163
Swedenborg Gdns. E1 7H 69
Sweden Ga. SE16 3A 88
Swedish Quays. SE16 3A 88 (in two parts)
Sweeney Cres. SE1 2F 87 (7K 169)
Sweet Briar Grn. N9 3A 18
Sweet Briar Gro. N9 3A 18
Sweet Briar Wlk. N18 4A 18
Sweetcroft La. Uxb 7B 40
Sweetland Ct. Dag 6B 56
Sweetmans Av. Pinn 3B 24
Sweets Way. N20 2G 15
Swell Ct. E17 6C 34
Swetenham Wlk. SE18 5G 91
Swete St. E13 2J 71
Sweyn Pl. SE3 2J 107
Swift Clo. E17 7F 19
Swift Clo. Harr 2F 43
Swift Clo. Hay 6H 59
Swift Ct. Sutt 7K 149
Swift Lodge. W9 4J 65 (off Admiral Wlk.)
Swift Rd. Felt 3C 114
Swift Rd. S'hall 3E 78
Swiftsden Way. Brom 6G 125
Swift St. SW6 1H 101
Swinbrook Rd. W10 5G 65
Swinburne Ct. SE5 4D 104 (off Basingdon Way)
Swinburne Cres. Croy 6J 141
Swinburne Ho. E2 3J 69 (off Roman Rd.)
Swinburne Rd. SW15 4C 100
Swinderby Rd. Wemb 6E 44
Swindon Clo. Ilf 2J 55
Swindon Rd. H'row A 5E 94
Swindon St. W12 1D 82
Swinfield Clo. Felt 3C 114
Swinford Gdns. SW9 3B 104
Swingate La. SE18 6J 91
Swingfield Ho. E9 1J 69 (off Templecombe Rd.)
Swinley Ho. NW1 3F 67 (1K 159) (off Redhill St.)
Swinnerton St. E9 5A 52
Swinton Clo. Wemb 1H 45
Swinton Pl. WC1 3K 67 (1G 161)
Swinton St. WC1 3K 67 (1G 161)
Swires Shaw. Kes 4B 156
Swiss Cen. W1 3C 166
Swiss Cottage. (Junct.) 7B 48
Swiss Ct. WC2 3D 166
Swiss Ter. NW6 7B 48
Swithland Gdns. SE9 4E 126
Swyncombe Av. W5 4B 80
Swynford Gdns. NW4 4C 28
Sybil M. N4 6B 32
Sybil Phoenix Clo. SE8 5K 87
Sybil Thorndike Casson Ho. SW5 5J 83 (off Old Brompton Rd.)
Sybourn St. E17 7B 34
Sycamore Av. E3 1B 70
Sycamore Av. W5 3D 80
Sycamore Av. Hay 7G 59
Sycamore Av. Sidc 6K 109
Sycamore Clo. E16 4G 71
Sycamore Clo. N9 4B 18
Sycamore Clo. SE9 2C 126
Sycamore Clo. W3 1A 82
Sycamore Clo. Barn 6G 5
Sycamore Clo. Cars 4D 150
Sycamore Clo. Edgw 4D 12
Sycamore Clo. Felt 3J 113
Sycamore Clo. N'holt 1C 60
Sycamore Clo. S Croy 5E 152
Sycamore Clo. W Dray 7B 58
Sycamore Ct. E7 6J 53
Sycamore Ct. NW6 1J 65 (off Bransdale Clo.)
Sycamore Ct. Eri 5K 93 (off Sandcliff Rd.)
Sycamore Ct. Houn 4C 96
Sycamore Ct. N Mald 3A 136
Sycamore Gdns. N15 4F 33
Sycamore Gdns. W6 2D 82
Sycamore Gdns. Mitc 2B 138
Sycamore Gro. NW9 7J 27
Sycamore Gro. SE6 6E 106
Sycamore Gro. SE20 1G 141
Sycamore Gro. N Mald 3K 135

Sycamore Hill. N11 ... 6K 15
Sycamore Ho. N2 ... 2B 30
(off Grange, The)
Sycamore Ho. SE16 ... 2K 87
(off Woodland Cres.)
Sycamore Ho. W6 ... 2D 82
Sycamore Ho. Buck H ... 2G 21
Sycamore Ho. Short ... 2G 143
Sycamore Lodge. W8 ... 3K 83
(off Stone Hall Pl.)
Sycamore M. SW4 ... 3G 103
Sycamore M. Eri ... 5K 93
(off St John's Rd.)
Sycamore Rd. SW19 ... 6E 118
Sycamore St. EC1 ... 4C 68 (4C 162)
Sycamore Wlk. W10 ... 4G 65
Sycamore Wlk. Ilf ... 4G 37
Sycamore Way. Tedd ... 6C 116
Sycamore Way. T Hth ... 5A 140
Sydcote. SE21 ... 1C 122
Sydenham. ... 4J 123
Sydenham Av. N21 ... 5E 6
Sydenham Av. SE26 ... 5H 123
Sydenham Cotts. SE12 ... 2A 126
Sydenham Ct. Croy ... 1D 152
(off Sydenham Rd.)
Sydenham Hill. SE23 & SE26 ... 1H 123
Sydenham Pk. SE26 ... 3J 123
Sydenham Pk. Mans. SE26 ... 3J 123
(off Sydenham Pk.)
Sydenham Pk. Rd. SE26 ... 3J 123
Sydenham Pl. SE27 ... 3B 122
Sydenham Ri. SE23 ... 2H 123
Sydenham Rd. SE26 ... 4J 123
Sydenham Rd. Croy ... 1C 152
Sydmons Ct. SE23 ... 7J 105
Sydner M. N16 ... 4F 51
Sydner Rd. N16 ... 4F 51
Sydney Clo. SW3 ... 4B 84 (4B 170)
Sydney Ct. Hay ... 4A 60
Sydney Cres. Ashf ... 6D 112
Sydney Gro. NW4 ... 5E 28
Sydney M. SW3 ... 4B 84 (4B 170)
Sydney Pl. SW7 ... 4B 84 (4B 170)
Sydney Rd. E11 ... 6K 35
Sydney Rd. N8 ... 4A 32
Sydney Rd. N10 ... 1E 30
Sydney Rd. SE2 ... 3C 92
Sydney Rd. SW20 ... 2F 137
Sydney Rd. W13 ... 1A 80
Sydney Rd. Bexh ... 4D 110
Sydney Rd. Enf ... 3J 7
(in two parts)
Sydney Rd. Felt ... 1J 113
Sydney Rd. Ilf ... 2G 37
Sydney Rd. Rich ... 4E 98
Sydney Rd. Sidc ... 4J 127
Sydney Rd. Sutt ... 4J 149
Sydney Rd. Tedd ... 5K 115
Sydney Rd. Wfd G ... 4D 20
Sydney St. SW3 ... 5C 84 (5C 170)
Sylvana Clo. Uxb ... 1B 58
Sylvan Av. N3 ... 2J 29
Sylvan Av. N22 ... 7E 16
Sylvan Av. NW7 ... 6F 13
Sylvan Av. Romf ... 6F 39
Sylvan Ct. N12 ... 3E 14
Sylvan Est. SE19 ... 1F 141
Sylvan Gdns. Surb ... 7D 134
Sylvan Gro. NW2 ... 4F 47
Sylvan Gro. SE15 ... 6H 87
Sylvan Hill. SE19 ... 1E 140
Sylvan Rd. E7 ... 6J 53
Sylvan Rd. E11 ... 5J 35
Sylvan Rd. E17 ... 5C 34
Sylvan Rd. SE19 ... 1F 141
Sylvan Wlk. Brom ... 3D 144
Sylvan Way. Dag ... 4B 56
Sylvan Way. W Wick ... 4G 155
Sylverdale Rd. Croy ... 3B 152
Sylvester Av. Chst ... 6D 126
Sylvester Path. E8 ... 6H 51
Sylvester Rd. E8 ... 6H 51
Sylvester Rd. E17 ... 7B 34
Sylvester Rd. N2 ... 2A 30
Sylvester Rd. Wemb ... 5C 44
Sylvestrus Clo. King T ... 1G 135
Sylvia Ct. N1 ... 2D 68
Sylvia Ct. Wemb ... 7H 45
Sylvia Gdns. Wemb ... 7H 45
Sylvia Pankhurst Ho. Dag ... 3G 57
(off Wythenshawe Rd.)
Symes M. NW1 ... 2G 67
Symington Ho. SE1 ... 3D 86
(off Deverell St.)
Symington M. E9 ... 5K 51
Symister M. N1 ... 2G 163
Symons St. SW3 ... 4D 84 (4F 171)
Symphony M. W10 ... 3G 65
Syon Ga. Way. Bren ... 7A 80
Syon House & Pk. ... 1C 98
Syon La. Iswth ... 6K 79
Syon Lodge. SE12 ... 7J 107
Syon Pk. Gdns. Iswth ... 7K 79
Syringa Ho. SE4 ... 3B 106

Tabard Ct. E14 ... 6E 70
(off Lodore St.)
Tabard Garden Est. SE1 ... 3D 86 (7E 168)
Tabard Ho. SE1 ... 3D 86 (7F 169)
(off Manciple St.)
Tabard St. SE1 ... 2C 86 (6D 168)
Tabernacle Av. E13 ... 4J 71
Tabernacle St. EC2 ... 4D 68 (4F 163)
Tableer Av. SW4 ... 5G 103
Tabley Rd. N7 ... 4J 49
Tabor Ct. Sutt ... 6G 149
Tabor Gdns. Sutt ... 6H 149
Tabor Gro. SW19 ... 7G 119
Tabor Rd. W6 ... 3D 82
Tachbrook Est. SW1 ... 5H 85 (6C 172)
Tachbrook M. SW1 ... 4G 85 (3A 172)
Tachbrook Rd. Felt ... 7H 95
Tachbrook Rd. S'hall ... 4B 78
Tachbrook Rd. W Dray ... 1A 76
Tachbrook St. SW1 ... 4G 85 (4B 172)
(in two parts)
Tack M. SE4 ... 3C 106
Tadema Ho. NW8 ... 4B 158
Tadema Rd. SW10 ... 7A 84
Tadlow. King T ... 3G 135
(off Washington Rd.)
Tadmor Clo. Sun ... 4H 131
Tadmor St. W12 ... 1F 83
Tadworth Av. N Mald ... 4B 136
Tadworth Ho. SE1 ... 7A 168
Tadworth Rd. NW2 ... 2C 46
Taeping St. E14 ... 4D 88
Taffrail Ho. E14 ... 5D 88
(off Burrells Wharf Sq.)
Taffy's Row. Mitc ... 3C 138
Taft Way. E3 ... 3D 70
Tailor Ho. WC1 ... 4J 67 (4F 161)
(off Colonnade)
Tailworth St. E1 ... 5G 69 (6K 163)
(off Chicksand St.)
Tailworth St. Houn ... 2G 97
Tait Ct. E3 ... 1B 70
(off St Stephen's Rd.)
Tait Ct. SW8 ... 1J 103
(off Lansdowne Grn.)
Tait Ho. SE1 ... 1A 86 (5K 167)
(off Greet St.)
Tait Rd. Croy ... 7E 140
Takeley Clo. Romf ... 2K 39
Takhar M. SW11 ... 2C 102
Talacre Rd. NW5 ... 6E 48
Talbot Av. N2 ... 3B 30
Talbot Clo. N15 ... 4F 33
Talbot Ct. EC3 ... 2F 169
Talbot Ct. NW9 ... 3K 45
Talbot Cres. NW4 ... 5C 28
Talbot Gdns. Ilf ... 2A 56
Talbot Gro. Ho. W11 ... 6G 65
(off Lancaster Rd.)
Talbot Ho. E14 ... 6D 70
(off Girauld St.)
Talbot Pl. SE3 ... 2G 107
Talbot Rd. E6 ... 2E 72
Talbot Rd. E7 ... 4J 53
Talbot Rd. N6 ... 6E 30
Talbot Rd. N15 ... 4F 33
Talbot Rd. N22 ... 2G 31
Talbot Rd. SE22 ... 4E 104
Talbot Rd. W11 & W2 ... 6H 65
(in two parts)
Talbot Rd. W13 ... 1A 80
Talbot Rd. Ashf ... 5A 112
Talbot Rd. Cars ... 5E 150
Talbot Rd. Dag ... 6F 57
Talbot Rd. Harr ... 2K 25
Talbot Rd. Iswth ... 4A 98
Talbot Rd. S'hall ... 4C 78
Talbot Rd. T Hth ... 4D 140
Talbot Rd. Twic ... 1J 115
Talbot Rd. Wemb ... 6D 44
Talbot Sq. W2 ... 6B 66 (1B 164)
Talbot Wlk. NW10 ... 6A 46
Talbot Wlk. W11 ... 6G 65
Talbot Yd. SE1 ... 1D 86 (5E 168)
Talcott Path. SW2 ... 1A 122
Talfourd Pl. SE15 ... 1F 105
Talfourd Rd. SE5 ... 1F 105
Talgarth Mans. W14 ... 5G 83
(off Talgarth Rd.)
Talgarth Rd. W6 & W14 ... 5F 83
Talgarth Wlk. NW9 ... 5A 28
Talia Ho. E14 ... 3E 88
(off Manchester Rd.)
Talina Cen. SW6 ... 1A 102
Talisman Clo. Ilf ... 1B 56
Talisman Sq. SE26 ... 4G 123
Talisman Way. Wemb ... 3F 45
Tallack Clo. Harr ... 7D 10
Tallack Rd. E10 ... 1B 52
Tall Elms Clo. Brom ... 5H 143
Talleyrand Ho. SE5 ... 2C 104
(off Lilford Rd.)
Tallis Clo. E16 ... 6K 71
Tallis Gro. SE7 ... 6K 89
Tallis St. EC4 ... 7A 68 (2K 167)
Tallis Vw. NW10 ... 6K 45
Tall Trees. SW16 ... 3K 139
Talma Gdns. Twic ... 6J 97
Talmage Clo. SE23 ... 7J 105
Talman Gro. Stan ... 6J 11
Talma Rd. SW2 ... 4A 104
Talwin St. E3 ... 3D 70
Tamar Clo. E3 ... 1B 70
Tamar Ho. E14 ... 2E 88
(off Plevna St.)
Tamar Ho. SE11 ... 5A 86 (5K 173)
(off Kennington La.)
Tamarind Ct. W8 ... 3K 83
(off Stone Hall Gdns.)
Tamarind Yd. E1 ... 1G 87
(off Kennet St.)
Tamarisk Sq. W12 ... 7B 64
Tamar Sq. Wfd G ... 6E 20
Tamar St. SE7 ... 3C 90
Tamar Way. N17 ... 3G 33
Tamesis Gdns. Wor Pk ... 2A 148
Tamian Ind. Est. Houn ... 4A 96
Tamian Way. Houn ... 4A 96
Tamplin Ho. W10 ... 3H 65
(off Dowland St.)
Tamworth. N7 ... 6J 49
Tamworth Av. Wfd G ... 6B 20
Tamworth La. Mitc ... 2F 139
Tamworth Pk. Mitc ... 4F 139
Tamworth Pl. Croy ... 2C 152
Tamworth Rd. Croy ... 2B 152
Tamworth St. SW6 ... 6J 83
Tamworth Vs. Mitc ... 4F 139
Tancred Rd. N4 ... 7B 32
Tandem Cen. Retail Pk. SW19 ... 1B 138
Tandem Way. SW19 ... 1B 138
Tandridge Dri. Orp ... 7H 145
Tandridge Pl. Orp ... 7H 145
Tanfield Av. NW2 ... 4B 46
Tanfield Rd. Croy ... 4C 152
Tangier Rd. Rich ... 4G 99
Tangleberry Clo. Brom ... 4D 144
Tangle Tree Clo. N3 ... 2K 29
Tanglewood Clo. Croy ... 3J 153
Tanglewood Clo. Stan ... 2D 10
Tanglewood Clo. Uxb ... 4C 58
Tanglewood Way. Felt ... 3K 113
Tangley Gro. SW15 ... 6B 100
Tangley Pk. Rd. Hamp ... 5D 114
Tanglyn Av. Shep ... 5D 130
Tangmere. N17 ... 2D 32
(off Willan Rd.)
Tangmere. WC1 ... 3K 67 (2G 161)
(off Sidmouth St.)
Tangmere Gdns. N'holt ... 2A 60
(in two parts)
Tangmere Gro. King T ... 5D 116
Tangmere Way. NW9 ... 2A 28
Tanhurst Ho. SW2 ... 7K 103
(off Redlands Way)
Tanhurst Wlk. SE2 ... 3D 92
Tankerton Houses. WC1 ... 3J 67 (2F 161)
(off Tankerton St.)
Tankerton Rd. Surb ... 2F 147
Tankerton St. WC1 ... 3J 67 (2F 161)
Tankerton Ter. Croy ... 6K 139
Tankerville Rd. SW16 ... 7H 121
Tankridge Rd. NW2 ... 2D 46
Tanner Ho. SE1 ... 2E 86 (7H 169)
(off Tanner St.)
Tanneries, The. E1 ... 4J 69
(off Cephas Av.)
Tanner Point. E13 ... 1J 71
(off Pelly Rd.)
Tanners Clo. W on T ... 6K 131
Tanners End La. N18 ... 4K 17
Tanner's Hill. SE8 ... 1B 106
Tanners La. B'side ... 3G 37
Tanner St. SE1 ... 2E 86 (7H 169)
(in two parts)
Tanner St. Bark ... 6G 55
Tannery Clo. Beck ... 5K 141
Tannery Clo. Dag ... 3H 57
Tannington Ter. N5 ... 3B 50
Tannsfeld Rd. SE26 ... 5K 123
Tansley Clo. N7 ... 5H 49
Tanswell St. SE1 ... 2A 86 (7J 167)
Tansy Clo. E6 ... 6E 72
Tantallon Rd. SW12 ... 1E 120
Tant Av. E16 ... 6H 71
Tantony Gro. Romf ... 3D 38
Tanworth Gdns. Pinn ... 2K 23
Tanyard La. Bex ... 7G 111
Tanza Rd. NW3 ... 4D 48
Tapestry Clo. Sutt ... 7K 149
Tapley Ho. SE1 ... 2G 87 (7K 169)
(off Wolseley St.)
Taplins Trad. Est. W Dray ... 7A 58
Taplow. SE17 ... 5D 86
(off Thurlow St.)
Taplow Ct. Mitc ... 4C 138
Taplow Ho. E2 ... 3F 69 (2J 163)
(off Palissy St.)
Taplow Rd. N13 ... 4H 17
Taplow St. N1 ... 2C 68 (1D 162)
Tappesfield Rd. SE15 ... 3J 105
Tapp St. E1 ... 4H 69
Tapster St. Barn ... 3C 4
Tara Ct. Beck ... 2D 142
Tara M. N8 ... 6J 31
Taranto Ho. E1 ... 5K 69
(off Master's St.)
Tarbert M. N15 ... 5E 32
Tarbert Rd. SE22 ... 5E 104
Tarbert Wlk. E1 ... 7J 69
Target Clo. Felt ... 6G 95
Target Ho. W13 ... 1B 80
(off Sherwood Clo.)
Target Roundabout. (Junct.) ... 1D 60
Tariff Cres. SE8 ... 4B 88
Tariff Rd. N17 ... 6B 18
Tarleton Ct. N22 ... 2A 32
Tarleton Gdns. SE23 ... 2H 123
Tarling Clo. Sidc ... 3B 128
Tarling Ho. E1 ... 6H 69
(off Tarling St.)
Tarling Rd. E16 ... 6H 71
Tarling Rd. N2 ... 2A 30
Tarling St. E1 ... 6H 69
Tarling St. Est. E1 ... 6J 69
Tarn Bank. Enf ... 5D 6
Tarns, The. NW1 ... 3G 67 (1A 160)
(off Varndell St.)
Tarn St. SE1 ... 3C 86
Tarnwood Pk. SE9 ... 7D 108
Tarplett Ho. SE14 ... 6J 87
(off John Williams Clo.)
Tarquin Ho. SE26 ... 4G 123
(off High Level Dri.)
Tarragon Clo. SE14 ... 7A 88
Tarragon Gro. SE26 ... 6K 123
Tarranbrae. NW6 ... 7G 47
Tarrant Ho. E2 ... 3J 69
(off Roman Rd.)
Tarrant Pl. W1 ... 5D 66 (6E 158)
Tarrington Clo. SW16 ... 3H 121
Tartan Ho. E14 ... 6E 70
(off Dee St.)
Tarver Rd. SE17 ... 5B 86
Tarves Way. SE10 ... 7D 88
Tash Pl. N11 ... 5A 16
Tasker Clo. Hay ... 7E 76
Tasker Ho. E14 ... 5B 70
(off Wallwood St.)
Tasker Ho. Bark ... 2H 73
Tasker Rd. NW3 ... 5D 48
Tasman Ct. E14 ... 4D 88
(off Westferry Rd.)
Tasman Ct. Sun ... 7G 113
Tasman Ho. E1 ... 1H 87
(off Clegg St.)
Tasmania Ter. N18 ... 6H 17
Tasman Rd. SW9 ... 3J 103
Tasman Wlk. E16 ... 6B 72
Tasso Rd. W6 ... 6G 83
Tasso Yd. W6 ... 6G 83
(off Tasso Rd.)
Tatam Rd. NW10 ... 7K 45
Tatchbury Ho. SW15 ... 6B 100
(off Tunworth Cres.)
Tate Britain. ... 4J 85 (4E 172)
Tate Ho. E2 ... 2K 69
(off Mace St.)
Tate Modern. ... 1B 86 (4B 168)
Tate Rd. E16 ... 1D 90
(in two parts)
Tate Rd. Sutt ... 5J 149
Tatnell Rd. SE23 ... 6A 106
Tatsfield Ho. SE1 ... 3D 86 (7F 169)
(off Pardoner St.)
Tattersall Clo. SE9 ... 5C 108
Tatton Cres. N16 ... 7F 33
Tatum St. SE17 ... 4D 86
Tauheed Clo. N4 ... 2C 50
Taunton Av. SW20 ... 2D 136
Taunton Clo. Bexh ... 2K 111
Taunton Clo. Sutt ... 1J 149
Taunton Dri. N2 ... 2A 30
Taunton Dri. Enf ... 3F 7
Taunton Ho. W2 ... 6A 66
(off Hallfield Est.)
Taunton M. NW1 ... 4D 66 (4E 158)
Taunton Pl. NW1 ... 4D 66 (3E 158)
Taunton Rd. SE12 ... 5G 107
Taunton Rd. Gnfd ... 1F 61
Taunton Way. Stan ... 2E 26
Tavern Clo. Cars ... 7C 138
Taverners Clo. W11 ... 1G 83
Taverners Ct. E3 ... 3A 70
(off Grove Rd.)

Taverner Sq. N5 . . . 4C 50
Taverners Way. E4 . . . 1B 20
Tavern La. SW9 . . . 2A 104
Tavern Quay. SE16 . . . 4A 88
Tavistock Av. E17 . . . 3K 33
Tavistock Av. NW7 . . . 7A 14
Tavistock Av. Gnfd . . . 2A 62
Tavistock Clo. N16 . . . 5E 50
Tavistock Clo. Stai . . . 7A 112
Tavistock Ct. WC1 . . . 4H 67 (3D 160) (off Tavistock Sq.)
Tavistock Ct. Croy . . . 1D 152 (off Tavistock Rd.)
Tavistock Cres. W11 . . . 5H 65 (in three parts)
Tavistock Cres. Mitc . . . 4J 139
Tavistock Gdns. Ilf . . . 4J 55
Tavistock Ga. Croy . . . 1D 152
Tavistock Gro. Croy . . . 7D 140
Tavistock Ho. WC1 . . . 4H 67 (3D 160)
Tavistock M. E18 . . . 4J 35
Tavistock M. W11 . . . 6H 65
Tavistock Pl. E18 . . . 4J 35
Tavistock Pl. N14 . . . 7A 6
Tavistock Pl. WC1 . . . 4J 67 (3E 160)
Tavistock Rd. E7 . . . 4H 53
Tavistock Rd. E15 . . . 6H 53
Tavistock Rd. E18 . . . 3J 35
Tavistock Rd. N4 . . . 6D 32
Tavistock Rd. NW10 . . . 2B 64
Tavistock Rd. W11 . . . 6H 65 (in two parts)
Tavistock Rd. Brom . . . 4H 143
Tavistock Rd. Cars . . . 1B 150
Tavistock Rd. Croy . . . 1D 152
Tavistock Rd. Edgw . . . 1G 27
Tavistock Rd. Uxb . . . 5F 41
Tavistock Rd. Well . . . 1C 110
Tavistock Rd. W Dray . . . 1A 76
Tavistock Sq. WC1 . . . 4H 67 (3D 160)
Tavistock St. WC2 . . . 7J 67 (2F 167) (in two parts)
Tavistock Ter. N19 . . . 3H 49
Tavistock Tower. SE16 . . . 3A 88
Tavistock Wlk. Cars . . . 1B 150
Taviton St. WC1 . . . 4H 67 (3C 160)
Tavy Bri. SE2 . . . 2C 92
Tavy Bri. Cen. SE2 . . . 2C 92
Tavy Clo. SE11 . . . 5K 173 (in two parts)
Tawney Rd. SE28 . . . 7B 74
Tawny Clo. W13 . . . 1B 80
Tawny Clo. Felt . . . 3J 113
Tawny Way. SE16 . . . 4K 87
Tayben Av. Twic . . . 6J 97
Taybridge Rd. SW11 . . . 3E 102
Tay Bldgs. SE1 . . . 7G 169
Tayburn Clo. E14 . . . 6E 70
Tayfield Clo. Uxb . . . 3E 40
Tayler Ct. NW8 . . . 1B 66
Taylor Av. Rich . . . 2H 99
Taylor Clo. N17 . . . 7B 18
Taylor Clo. SE8 . . . 6B 88
Taylor Clo. Hamp H . . . 5G 115
Taylor Clo. Houn . . . 1G 97
Taylor Ct. E15 . . . 5E 52
Taylor Ct. SE20 . . . 2J 141 (off Elmers End Rd.)
Taylor Rd. Mitc . . . 7C 120
Taylor Rd. Wall . . . 5F 151
Taylors Bldgs. SE18 . . . 4F 91
Taylors Clo. Sidc . . . 3K 127
Taylors Ct. Felt . . . 2J 113
Taylors Grn. W3 . . . 6A 64
Taylors La. NW10 . . . 7A 46
Taylor's La. SE26 . . . 4H 123
Taylors La. Barn . . . 1C 4
Taylorsmead. NW7 . . . 5H 13
Taymount Grange. SE23 . . . 2J 123
Taymount Ri. SE23 . . . 2J 123
Tayport Clo. N1 . . . 7J 49
Tayside Ct. SE5 . . . 4D 104
Tayside Dri. Edgw . . . 3C 12
Taywood Rd. N'holt . . . 3D 60
Teak Clo. SE16 . . . 1A 88
Tealby Ct. N7 . . . 5K 49 (off George's Rd.)
Teal Clo. E16 . . . 5B 72
Teal Ct. NW10 . . . 6K 45
Teal Ct. SE8 . . . 6B 88 (off Abinger Gro.)
Teal Dri. N'wd . . . 1E 22
Teale St. E2 . . . 2G 69
Tealing Dri. Eps . . . 4K 147
Teal Pl. Sutt . . . 5H 149
Teasel Clo. Croy . . . 1K 153
Teasel Way. E15 . . . 3G 71
Tea Trade Wharf. SE1 . . . 2F 87 (6K 169) (off Shad Thames)
Tebworth Rd. N17 . . . 7A 18
Technology Pk. NW9 . . . 3A 28
Teck Clo. Iswth . . . 2A 98
Tedder Clo. Chess . . . 5C 146
Tedder Clo. Ruis . . . 5J 41
Tedder Clo. Uxb . . . 7B 40
Tedder Rd. S Croy . . . 7J 153
Teddington . . . 5A 116
Teddington Bus. Pk. Tedd . . . 6K 115 (off Station Rd.)
Teddington Pk. Tedd . . . 5K 115
Teddington Pk. Rd. Tedd . . . 4K 115
Ted Roberts Ho. E2 . . . 2H 69 (off Parmiter St.)
Tedworth Gdns. SW3 . . . 5D 84 (6E 170)
Tedworth Sq. SW3 . . . 5D 84 (6E 170)
Tees Av. Gnfd . . . 2J 61
Tees Ct. W7 . . . 6H 61 (off Hanway Rd.)
Teesdale Av. Iswth . . . 1A 98
Teesdale Clo. E2 . . . 2G 69
Teesdale Gdns. SE25 . . . 2E 140
Teesdale Gdns. Iswth . . . 1A 98
Teesdale Rd. E11 . . . 6H 35
Teesdale St. E2 . . . 2H 69
Teesdale Yd. E2 . . . 2H 69 (off Teesdale St.)
Teeswater Ct. Eri . . . 3D 92
Tee, The. W3 . . . 6A 64
Teevan Clo. Croy . . . 7G 141
Teevan Rd. Croy . . . 1G 153
Teignmouth Clo. SW4 . . . 4H 103
Teignmouth Clo. Edgw . . . 2F 27
Teignmouth Gdns. Gnfd . . . 2A 62
Teignmouth Pde. Gnfd . . . 2A 62
Teignmouth Rd. NW2 . . . 5F 47
Teignmouth Rd. Well . . . 2C 110
Telcote Way. Ruis . . . 7A 24
Telecom Tower, The. . . . 5G 67 (5A 160)
Telegraph Hill. NW3 . . . 3K 47
Telegraph La. Clay . . . 5A 146
Telegraph M. Ilf . . . 1A 56
Telegraph Pas. SW2 . . . 7J 103
Telegraph Path. Chst . . . 5F 127
Telegraph Pl. E14 . . . 4D 88
Telegraph Quarters. SE10 . . . 5F 89 (off Park Row)
Telegraph Rd. SW15 . . . 7D 100
Telegraph St. EC2 . . . 6D 68 (7E 162)
Teleman Sq. SE3 . . . 4K 107
Telephone Pl. SW6 . . . 6H 83
Telfer Clo. W3 . . . 2J 81
Telfer Ho. EC1 . . . 3C 68 (2B 162) (off Lever St.)
Telferscot Rd. SW12 . . . 1H 121
Telford Av. SW2 . . . 1H 121
Telford Clo. E17 . . . 7A 34
Telford Clo. SE19 . . . 6F 123
Telford Dri. W on T . . . 7A 132
Telford Ho. SE1 . . . 3C 86 (off Tiverton St.)
Telford Rd. N11 . . . 5B 16
Telford Rd. NW9 . . . 6C 28
Telford Rd. SE9 . . . 2H 127
Telford Rd. W10 . . . 5G 65
Telford Rd. S'hall . . . 7F 61
Telford Rd. Twic . . . 7E 96
Telfords Yd. E1 . . . 7G 69
Telford Ter. SW1 . . . 6G 85 (7A 172)
Telford Way. W3 . . . 5A 64
Telford Way. Hay . . . 5C 60
Telham Rd. E6 . . . 2E 72
Tell Gro. SE22 . . . 4F 105
Tellson Av. SE18 . . . 1B 108
Temair Ho. SE10 . . . 7D 88 (off Tarves Way)
Temeraire St. SE16 . . . 2J 87
Tempelhof Av. NW4 . . . 7E 28
Temperley Rd. SW12 . . . 7E 102
Templar Ct. NW8 . . . 2A 158
Templar Dri. SE28 . . . 6D 74
Templar Ho. NW2 . . . 6H 47
Templar Pl. Hamp . . . 7E 114
Templars Av. NW11 . . . 6H 29
Templars Cres. N3 . . . 2J 29
Templars Dri. Harr . . . 6C 10
Templars Ho. E15 . . . 5D 52
Templar St. SE5 . . . 2B 104
Temple. EC4 . . . 2J 167
Temple Av. EC4 . . . 7A 68 (2K 167)
Temple Av. N20 . . . 7G 5
Temple Av. Croy . . . 2B 154
Temple Av. Dag . . . 1G 57
Temple Bar. . . . 6A 68 (1J 167) (off Strand)
Temple Chambers. EC4 . . . 2K 167
Temple Clo. E11 . . . 7G 35
Temple Clo. N3 . . . 2H 29
Temple Clo. SE28 . . . 3G 91
Templecombe Rd. E9 . . . 1J 69
Templecombe Way. Mord . . . 5G 137
Temple Ct. E1 . . . 5K 69 (off Rectory Sq.)
Temple Ct. SW8 . . . 7J 85 (off Thorncroft St.)
Templecroft. Ashf . . . 6F 113
Temple Dwellings. E2 . . . 2H 69 (off Temple St.)
Temple Fortune. . . . 5H 29
Temple Fortune Hill. NW11 . . . 5J 29
Temple Fortune La. NW11 . . . 6H 29
Temple Fortune Pde. NW11 . . . 5H 29
Temple Gdns. EC4 . . . 7A 68 (2J 167) (off Middle Temple La.)
Temple Gdns. N13 . . . 2G 17
Temple Gdns. NW11 . . . 6H 29
Temple Gdns. Dag . . . 3D 56
Temple Gro. NW11 . . . 6J 29
Temple Gro. Enf . . . 2G 7
Temple Hall Ct. E4 . . . 2A 20
Temple La. EC4 . . . 6A 68 (1K 167)
Templeman Rd. W7 . . . 5K 61
Templemead Clo. W3 . . . 6A 64
Temple Mead Clo. Stan . . . 6G 11
Templemead Ho. E9 . . . 4A 52
Temple Mill La. E10 & E15 . . . 4D 52 (in two parts)
Temple Mills. . . . 4D 52
Temple Pde. Barn . . . 7G 5 (off Netherlands Rd.)
Temple Pk. Uxb . . . 3C 58
Temple Pl. WC2 . . . 7K 67 (2H 167)
Temple Rd. E6 . . . 1C 72
Temple Rd. N8 . . . 4K 31
Temple Rd. NW2 . . . 4E 46
Temple Rd. W4 . . . 3J 81
Temple Rd. W5 . . . 3D 80
Temple Rd. Croy . . . 4D 152
Temple Rd. Houn . . . 4F 97
Temple Rd. Rich . . . 2F 99
Temple Sheen. SW14 . . . 4J 99
Temple Sheen Rd. SW14 . . . 4H 99
Temple St. E2 . . . 2H 69
Templeton Av. E4 . . . 4H 19
Templeton Clo. N15 . . . 6D 32
Templeton Clo. N16 . . . 5E 50
Templeton Clo. SE19 . . . 1D 140
Templeton Pl. SW5 . . . 4J 83
Templeton Rd. N15 . . . 6D 32
Temple Way. Sutt . . . 3B 150
Temple W. M. SE11 . . . 3B 86 (off West Sq.)
Templewood. W13 . . . 5B 62
Templewood Av. NW3 . . . 3K 47
Templewood Gdns. NW3 . . . 3K 47
Templewood Point. NW2 . . . 2H 47 (off Granville Rd.)
Tempo Ho. N'holt . . . 3B 60
Tempsford Clo. Enf . . . 3H 7
Tempsford Ct. Harr . . . 6K 25
Temsford Clo. Harr . . . 2G 25
Tenbury Clo. E7 . . . 5B 54
Tenbury Ct. SW12 . . . 1H 121
Tenby Av. Harr . . . 2B 26
Tenby Clo. N15 . . . 4F 33
Tenby Clo. Romf . . . 6E 38
Tenby Ct. E17 . . . 5A 34
Tenby Gdns. N'holt . . . 6E 42
Tenby Ho. W2 . . . 6A 66 (off Hallfield Est.)
Tenby Ho. Hay . . . 3E 76
Tenby Mans. W1 . . . 5E 66 (5H 159) (off Nottingham St.)
Tenby Rd. E17 . . . 5A 34
Tenby Rd. Edgw . . . 1F 27
Tenby Rd. Enf . . . 4D 8
Tenby Rd. Romf . . . 6E 38
Tenby Rd. Well . . . 1D 110
Tench St. E1 . . . 1H 87
Tenda Rd. SE16 . . . 4H 87
Tendring Way. Romf . . . 5C 38
Tenham Av. SW2 . . . 1H 121
Tenison Ct. W1 . . . 7G 67 (2A 166)
Tenison Way. SE1 . . . 1K 85 (5H 167)
Tenniel Clo. W2 . . . 7A 66
Tennis Ct. La. E Mol . . . 3K 133
Tennison Rd. SE25 . . . 4F 141
Tennis St. SE1 . . . 2D 86 (6E 168)
Tenniswood Rd. Enf . . . 1K 7
Tennyson. N8 . . . 3J 31 (off Boyton Clo.)
Tennyson Av. E11 . . . 7J 35
Tennyson Av. E12 . . . 7C 54
Tennyson Av. NW9 . . . 3J 27
Tennyson Av. N Mald . . . 5D 136
Tennyson Av. Twic . . . 1K 115
Tennyson Clo. Enf . . . 5E 8
Tennyson Clo. Felt . . . 6H 95
Tennyson Clo. Well . . . 1J 109
Tennyson Ct. SW6 . . . 1A 102 (off Imperial Rd.)
Tennyson Ho. SE17 . . . 5C 86 (off Browning St.)
Tennyson Ho. Belv . . . 5F 93
Tennyson Mans. W14 . . . 6H 83 (off Queen's Club Gdns.)
Tennyson Rd. E10 . . . 1D 52
Tennyson Rd. E15 . . . 7G 53
Tennyson Rd. E17 . . . 6B 34
Tennyson Rd. NW6 . . . 1H 65 (in two parts)
Tennyson Rd. NW7 . . . 5H 13
Tennyson Rd. SE20 . . . 7K 123
Tennyson Rd. SW19 . . . 6A 120
Tennyson Rd. W7 . . . 7K 61
Tennyson Rd. Ashf . . . 5A 112
Tennyson Rd. Houn . . . 2G 97
Tennyson St. SW8 . . . 2F 103
Tensing Rd. S'hall . . . 3E 78
Tentelow La. S'hall . . . 5E 78
Tenterden Clo. NW4 . . . 3F 29
Tenterden Clo. SE9 . . . 4C 126
Tenterden Dri. NW4 . . . 3F 29
Tenterden Gdns. NW4 . . . 3F 29
Tenterden Gdns. Croy . . . 7G 141
Tenterden Gro. NW4 . . . 3F 29
Tenterden Ho. SE17 . . . 5E 86 (off Surrey Gro.)
Tenterden Rd. N17 . . . 7A 18
Tenterden Rd. Croy . . . 7G 141
Tenterden Rd. Dag . . . 2F 57
Tenterden St. W1 . . . 6F 67 (1K 165)
Tenter Ground. E1 . . . 5F 69 (6J 163)
Tenter Pas. E1 . . . 6F 69 (1K 169) (off N. Tenter St.)
Tent Peg La. Orp . . . 5G 145
Tent St. E1 . . . 4H 69
Terborch Way. SE22 . . . 5E 104
Teredo St. SE16 . . . 3K 87
Terence Ct. Belv . . . 6F 93 (off Charton Clo.)
Teresa M. E17 . . . 4C 34
Teresa Wlk. N10 . . . 5F 31
Terling Clo. E11 . . . 3H 53
Terling Ho. W10 . . . 5E 64 (off Sutton Way)
Terling Rd. Dag . . . 2G 57
Terling Wlk. N1 . . . 1C 68 (off Popham St.)
Terminal Ho. Stan . . . 5J 11
Terminus Pl. SW1 . . . 3F 85 (2K 171)
Terrace Av. NW10 . . . 4E 64
Terrace Gdns. SW13 . . . 2B 100
Terrace Hill. Croy . . . 3B 152 (off Hanover St.)
Terrace La. Rich . . . 6E 98
Terrace Rd. E9 . . . 7J 51
Terrace Rd. E13 . . . 2J 71
Terrace Rd. W on T . . . 7J 131
Terraces, The. NW8 . . . 2B 66 (off Queen's Ter.)
Terrace, The. E2 . . . 3J 69 (off Old Ford Rd.)
Terrace, The. E4 . . . 3B 20 (off Newgate St.)
Terrace, The. EC4 . . . 1K 167
Terrace, The. N3 . . . 2H 29
Terrace, The. NW6 . . . 1J 65
Terrace, The. SE8 . . . 4B 88 (off Longshore)
Terrace, The. SE23 . . . 7A 106
Terrace, The. SW13 . . . 2A 100
Terrace, The. Wfd G . . . 6D 20
Terrace Wlk. SW11 . . . 7H 171
Terrace Wlk. Dag . . . 5E 56
Terrapin Rd. SW17 . . . 3F 121
Terretts Pl. N1 . . . 7B 50 (off Upper St.)
Terrick Rd. N22 . . . 1J 31
Terrick St. W12 . . . 6D 64
Terrilands. Pinn . . . 3D 24
Territorial Ho. SE11 . . . 4K 173
Terront Rd. N15 . . . 4C 32
Tersha St. Rich . . . 4F 99
Tessa Sanderson Pl. SW8 . . . 3F 103 (off Daley Thompson Way)
Tessa Sanderson Way. Gnfd . . . 5H 43
Testerton Rd. W11 . . . 7F 65
Testerton Wlk. W11 . . . 7F 65
Testwood Ct. W7 . . . 7J 61
Tetbury Pl. N1 . . . 1B 68
Tetcott Rd. SW10 . . . 7A 84 (in two parts)
Tetherdown. N10 . . . 3E 30
Tetty Way. Brom . . . 2J 143
Teversham La. SW8 . . . 1J 103
Teviot Clo. Well . . . 1B 110
Teviot Est. E14 . . . 5D 70
Teviot St. E14 . . . 4E 70
Tewkesbury Av. SE23 . . . 1H 123
Tewkesbury Av. Pinn . . . 5C 24
Tewkesbury Clo. N15 . . . 6D 32
Tewkesbury Gdns. NW9 . . . 3H 27
Tewkesbury Rd. N15 . . . 6D 32
Tewkesbury Rd. W13 . . . 1A 80
Tewkesbury Rd. Cars . . . 1B 150
Tewkesbury Ter. N11 . . . 6B 16

Tewson Rd. SE18 . . . . . 5J 91
Teynham Av. Enf 6J 7
Teynham Ct. Beck 3D 142
Teynham Grn. Brom 5J 143
Teynton Ter. N17 . . . . . 1C 32
Thackeray Av. N17 . . . . . 2G 33
Thackeray Clo. SW19 . . . . . 7F 119
Thackeray Clo. Harr 1E 42
Thackeray Clo. Iswth 2A 98
Thackeray Clo. Uxb 6D 58
Thackeray Ct. SW3 . . . . . 5D 84 (5E 170) (off Elystan Pl.)
Thackeray Ct. W14 . . . . . 3G 83 (off Blythe Rd.)
Thackeray Dri. Romf 7A 38
Thackeray Ho. WC1 . . . . . 3E 160
Thackeray Lodge. Felt 6F 95
Thackeray M. E8 . . . . . 6G 51
Thackeray Rd. E6 . . . . . 2B 72
Thackeray Rd. SW8 . . . . . 2F 103
Thackeray St. W8 . . . . . 3K 83
Thackrah Clo. N2 . . . . . 2A 30
Thakeham Clo. SE26 . . . . . 4H 123
Thalia Clo. SE10 . . . . . 6F 89
Thame Rd. SE16 . . . . . 2K 87
Thames Av. SW10 . . . . . 1A 102
Thames Av. Dag 4G 75
Thames Av. Gnfd 2K 61
Thames Bank. SW14 . . . . . 2J 99
Thamesbank Pl. SE28 . . . . . 6C 74
Thames Barrier Ind. Area. SE18 . . . . . 3B 90 (off Faraday Way)
Thames Barrier Vis. Cen. 3B 90
Thamesbrook. SW3 . . . . . 5C 84 (6C 170) (off Dovehouse St.)
Thames Circ. E14 . . . . . 4C 88
Thames Clo. Hamp 2F 133
Thames Ct. SE15 . . . . . 7F 87 (off Daniel Gdns.)
Thames Ct. W7 . . . . . 6J 61 (off Hanway Rd.)
Thames Cres. W4 . . . . . 7A 82
Thames Ditton. 6A 134
Thames Ditton Miniature Railway. 1A 146
Thames Dri. Ruis 6E 22
Thames Exchange Building. EC4 . . . . . 3D 168
Thames Eyot. Twic 1A 116
Thamesfield Ct. Shep 7E 130
Thamesfield M. Shep 7E 130
Thames Flood Barrier, The. 2B 90
Thamesgate Clo. Rich 4B 116
Thames Gateway. Dag 2F 75
Thameshill Av. Romf 2J 39
Thames Ho. EC4 . . . 7C 68 (2D 168) (off Up. Thames St.)
Thames Ho. SW1 . . . . . 4J 85 (off Millbank)
Thames Ho. King T . . . . . 4D 134 (off Surbiton Rd.)
Thameside. Tedd 7D 116
Thameside. W Mol 3F 133
Thameside Cen. Bren 6F 81
Thameside Ind. Est. E16 . . . . 2B 90
Thameside Wlk. SE28 . . . . . 6A 74
Thames Lock. Sun 3A 132
Thamesmead. 1D 92
Thames Mead. W on T 7J 131
Thamesmead Central. 7A 74
Thamesmead East. 2G 93
Thamesmead North. 6C 74
Thames Mdw. Shep 7F 131
Thames Mdw. W Mol 2E 132
Thamesmead South. 2D 92
Thamesmead South West. . . 2K 91
Thamesmead West. 3G 91
Thamesmere Dri. SE28 . . . . 7A 74
Thames Pl. SW15 . . . . . 3F 101 (in two parts)
Thamespoint. Tedd 7D 116
Thames Quay. E14 . . . . . 2D 88
Thames Quay. SW10 . . . . . 1A 102 (off Chelsea Harbour)
Thames Reach. W6 . . . . . 6E 82 (off Rainville Rd.)
Thames Rd. E16 . . . . . 1B 90
Thames Rd. W4 . . . . . 6G 81
Thames Rd. Bark 3J 73
Thames Rd. Ind. Est. E16 . . . . . 2B 90
Thames Side. King T 1D 134
Thames Side. Th Dit 6B 134
Thames St. SE10 . . . . . 6D 88
Thames St. Hamp 1F 133
Thames St. King T . . . . . 2D 134 (in two parts)
Thames St. Sun 4K 131
Thames St. W on T 7H 131
Thames Va. Clo. Houn 3E 96
Thames Valley University (Ealing Campus). . . . 1D 80
Thamesview Houses. W on T 6J 131
Thames Village. W4 . . . . . 1J 99
Thames Wlk. SW11 . . . . . 7C 84
Thames Wharf Studios. W6 . . . . . 6E 82 (off Rainville Rd.)
Thanescroft Gdns. Croy 3E 152
Thanet Ct. W3 . . . . . 6G 63
Thanet Dri. Kes 3B 156
Thanet Ho. WC1 . . . 3J 67 (2E 160) (off Thanet St.)
Thanet Ho. Croy . . . . . 4C 152 (off Coombe Rd.)
Thanet Lodge. NW2 . . . . . 6G 47 (off Mapesbury Rd.)
Thanet Pl. Croy 4C 152
Thanet Rd. Bex 7G 111
Thanet St. WC1 . . . . 3J 67 (2E 160)
Thanet Wharf. SE8 . . . . . 6D 88 (off Copperas St.)
Thane Vs. N7 . . . . . 3K 49
Thane Works. N7 . . . . . 3K 49
Thant Clo. E10 . . . . . 3D 52
Tharp Rd. Wall 5H 151
Thatcham Ct. N20 . . . . . 7F 5
Thatcham Gdns. N20 . . . . . 7F 5
Thatcher Clo. W Dray 2A 76
Thatchers Way. Iswth 5H 97
Thatches Gro. Romf 4E 38
Thavie's Inn. EC1 . . . . . 6A 68 (7K 161)
Thaxted Ct. N1 . . . . 2D 68 (1F 163) (off Fairbank Est.)
Thaxted Ho. SE16 . . . . . 4J 87 (off Abbeyfield Est.)
Thaxted Ho. Dag 7H 57
Thaxted Pl. SW20 . . . . . 7F 119
Thaxted Rd. SE9 . . . . . 3G 127
Thaxted Rd. Buck H 1H 21
Thaxton Rd. W14 . . . . . 6H 83
Thayers Farm Rd. Beck 1A 142
Thayer St. W1 . . . . . 6E 66 (6H 159)
Theatre Mus. 2F 167
Theatre Royal (Stratford). 6F 53
Theatre Sq. E15 . . . . . 6F 53
Theatre St. SW11 . . . . . 3D 102
Theberton St. N1 . . . . . 1A 68
Theed St. SE1 . . . . 1A 86 (5K 167)
Thelma Gdns. SE3 . . . . . 1B 108
Thelma Gro. Tedd 6A 116
Theobald Cres. Harr 1G 25
Theobald Rd. E17 . . . . . 7B 34
Theobald Rd. Croy 2B 152
Theobalds Av. N12 . . . . . 4F 15
Theobalds Ct. N4 . . . . . 3C 50
Theobald's Rd. WC1 . . . . . 5K 67 (5G 161)
Theobald St. SE1 . . . . . 3D 86
Theodora Way. Pinn 3H 23
Theodore Ct. SE13 . . . . . 6F 107
Theodore Rd. SE13 . . . . . 6F 107
Therapia La. Croy . . . . . 7H 139 (in two parts)
Therapia Rd. SE22 . . . . . 6J 105
Theresa Rd. W6 . . . . . 4C 82
Therfield Ct. N4 . . . . . 2C 50
Thermopylae Ga. E14 . . . . . 4D 88
Theseus Wlk. N1 . . . . . 1B 162
Thesiger Rd. SE20 . . . . . 7K 123
Thessaly Ho. SW8 . . . . . 7G 85 (off Thessaly Rd.)
Thessaly Rd. SW8 . . . . . 7G 85 (in two parts)
Thesus Ho. E14 . . . . . 6E 70 (off Blair St.)
Thetford Clo. N13 . . . . . 6G 17
Thetford Gdns. Dag 1E 74
Thetford Ho. SE1 . . . 3F 87 (7J 169) (off Maltby St.)
Thetford Rd. Ashf 4A 112
Thetford Rd. Dag 7D 56
Thetford Rd. N Mald 6K 135
Thetis Ter. Rich 6G 81
Theydon Gro. Wfd G 6F 21
Theydon Rd. E5 . . . . . 2J 51
Theydon St. E17 . . . . . 7B 34
Thicket Cres. Sutt 4A 150
Thicket Gro. SE19 . . . . . 7G 123
Thicket Gro. Dag 6C 56
Thicket Rd. SE20 . . . . . 7G 123
Thicket Rd. Sutt 4A 150
Thicket, The. W Dray 6A 58
Third Av. E12 . . . . . 4C 54
Third Av. E13 . . . . . 3J 71
Third Av. E17 . . . . . 5C 34
Third Av. W3 . . . . . 1B 82
Third Av. W10 . . . . . 3G 65
Third Av. Dag 1H 75
Third Av. Enf 5A 8
Third Av. Hay 1H 77
Third Av. Romf 6C 38
Third Av. Wemb 2D 44
Third Clo. W Mol 4G 133
Third Cross Rd. Twic 2H 115
Third Way. Wemb 4H 45
Thirleby Rd. SW1 . . . . . 3G 85 (2B 172)
Thirleby Rd. Edgw 1K 27
Thirlestane Ct. N10 . . . . . 2E 30
Thirlmere. NW1 . . . . 3F 67 (1K 159) (off Cumberland Mkt.)
Thirlmere Av. Gnfd 3C 62
Thirlmere Gdns. Wemb 1C 44
Thirlmere Ri. Brom 6H 125
Thirlmere Rd. N10 . . . . . 1F 31
Thirlmere Rd. SW16 . . . . . 4H 121
Thirlmere Rd. Bexh 2J 111
Thirsk Clo. N'holt 6E 42
Thirsk Rd. SE25 . . . . . 4D 140
Thirsk Rd. SW11 . . . . . 3E 102
Thirsk Rd. Mitc 7E 120
Thistlebrook. SE2 . . . . . 2C 92
Thistlecroft Gdns. Stan 1D 26
Thistledene. Th Dit 6J 133
Thistledene Av. Harr 3C 42
Thistlefield Clo. Bex 1D 128
Thistle Gro. SW10 . . . . . 5A 84
Thistle Ho. E14 . . . . . 6E 70 (off Dee St.)
Thistlemead. Chst 2F 145
Thistlewaite Rd. E5 . . . . . 3H 51
Thistlewood Clo. N7 . . . . . 2K 49
Thistleworth Clo. Iswth 7H 79
Thistleworth Marina. Iswth . . . . . 4B 98 (off Railshead Rd.)
Thistley Clo. N12 . . . . . 6H 15
Thistley Ct. SE8 . . . . . 6D 88
Thomas A'Beckett Clo. Wemb 4K 43
Thomas Baines Rd. SW11 . . . . . 3B 102
Thomas Burt Ho. E2 . . . . . 3H 69 (off Canrobert St.)
Thomas Cribb M. E6 . . . . . 6E 72
Thomas Darby Ct. W11 . . . . . 6G 65 (off Lancaster Rd.)
Thomas Dean Rd. SE26 . . . . 4B 124
Thomas Dinwiddy Rd. SE12 . . . . . 2K 125
Thomas Doyle St. SE1 . . . . . 3B 86 (7A 168)
Thomas England Ho. Romf . . . . . 6K 39 (off Waterloo Gdns.)
Thomas Hewlett Ho. Harr 4J 43
Thomas Hollywood Ho. E2 . . . 2J 69 (off Approach Rd.)
Thomas Ho. Sutt 7K 149
Thomas La. SE6 . . . . . 7C 106
Thomas Lodge. E17 . . . . . 5D 34
Thomas More Highwalk. EC2 . . . . . 5C 68 (6C 162) (off Beech St.)
Thomas More Ho. EC2 . . . . 6C 162
Thomas More Ho. Ruis 1G 41
Thomas More Sq. E1 . . . . . 7G 69 (off Thomas More St.)
Thomas More St. E1 . . . . . 7G 69 (3K 169)
Thomas More Way. N2 . . . . . 3A 30
Thomas Neal's Shop. Mall. WC2 . . . . 6J 67 (1E 166)
Thomas N. Ter. E16 . . . . . 5H 71 (off Barking Rd.)
Thomas Pl. W8 . . . . . 3K 83
Thomas Rd. E14 . . . . . 6B 70
Thomas Rd. Ind. Est. E14 . . . 5C 70
Thomas St. SE18 . . . . . 4F 91
Thomas Turner Path. Croy . . . . . 2C 152 (off George St.)
Thomas Wall Clo. Sutt 5K 149
Thomas Watson Cottage Homes. Barn . . . . . 4B 4 (off Leecroft Rd.)
Thompson Av. Rich 3G 99
Thompson Clo. Ilf 2G 55
Thompson Clo. Sutt 1J 149
Thompson Ho. SE14 . . . . . 6J 87 (off John Williams Clo.)
Thompson Rd. SE22 . . . . . 6F 105
Thompson Rd. Dag 3F 57
Thompson Rd. Houn 4F 97
Thompson Rd. Uxb 1A 58
Thompson's Av. SE5 . . . . . 7C 86
Thomson Cres. Croy 1A 152
Thomson Ho. E14 . . . . . 6C 70 (off Saracen St.)
Thomson Ho. SE17 . . . . . 4E 86 (off Tatum St.)
Thomson Ho. SW1 . . . . . 6D 172
Thomson Ho. S'hall . . . . . 7C 60 (off Broadway, The)
Thomson Rd. Harr 3J 25
Thorburn Sq. SE1 . . . . . 4G 87
Thorburn Way. SW19 . . . . . 1B 138
Thoresby St. N1 . . . 3C 68 (1D 162)
Thorkhill Gdns. Th Dit 1A 146
Thorkhill Rd. Th Dit 1A 146
Thornaby Gdns. N18 . . . . . 6B 18
Thornaby Ho. E2 . . . . . 3H 69 (off Canrobert St.)
Thorn Av. Bus H 1B 10
Thorn Bank. Edgw 6B 12
Thornbury. NW4 . . . . . 4D 28 (off Prince of Wales Clo.)
Thornbury Av. Iswth 7H 79
Thornbury Clo. N16 . . . . . 5E 50
Thornbury Ct. W11 . . . . . 7J 65 (off Chepstow Vs.)
Thornbury Ct. Iswth 7J 79
Thornbury Ct. S Croy . . . . . 5D 152 (off Blunt Rd.)
Thornbury Rd. SW2 . . . . . 6J 103
Thornbury Rd. Iswth 7H 79
Thornbury Sq. N6 . . . . . 1G 49
Thornby Rd. E5 . . . . . 3J 51
Thorncliffe Rd. SW4 . . . . . 6J 103
Thorncliffe Rd. S'hall 5D 78
Thorn Clo. Brom 6E 144
Thorn Clo. N'holt 3D 60
Thorncombe Rd. SE22 . . . . . 5E 104
Thorncroft Rd. Sutt 5K 149
Thorncroft St. SW8 . . . . . 7J 85
Thorndean St. SW18 . . . . . 2A 120
Thorndene. SE28 . . . . . 7B 74
Thorndene Av. N11 . . . . . 1K 15
Thorndike Av. N'holt 1B 60
Thorndike Clo. SW10 . . . . . 7A 84
Thorndike Ho. SW1 . . . . . 5H 85 (5C 172) (off Vauxhall Bri. Rd.)
Thorndike St. SW1 . . . . . 4H 85 (4C 172)
Thorndon Clo. Orp 2K 145
Thorndon Gdns. Eps 5A 148
Thorndon Rd. Orp 2K 145
Thorne Clo. E11 . . . . . 4G 53
Thorne Clo. E16 . . . . . 6J 71
Thorne Clo. Ashf 7E 112
Thorne Clo. Eri 6H 93
Thorne Ho. E2 . . . . . 3J 69 (off Roman Rd.)
Thorne Ho. E14 . . . . . 3E 88 (off Launch St.)
Thorne Ho. Clay 7B 146
Thorneloe Gdns. Croy 5A 152
Thorne Pas. SW13 . . . . . 2A 100
Thorne Rd. SW8 . . . . . 7J 85
Thornes Clo. Beck 3E 142
Thorne St. SW13 . . . . . 3A 100
Thornet Wood Rd. Brom . . . 3E 144
Thornewill Ho. E1 . . . . . 7J 69 (off Cable St.)
Thorney Ct. W8 . . . . . 2A 84 (off Palace Ga.)
Thorney Cres. SW11 . . . . . 7B 84
Thorneycroft Clo. W on T . . . 6A 132
Thorney Hedge Rd. W4 . . . . . 4H 81
Thorney St. SW1 . . . 4J 85 (3E 172)
Thornfield Av. NW7 . . . . . 1G 29
Thornfield Ct. NW7 . . . . . 1G 29
Thornfield Ho. E14 . . . . . 7C 70 (off Rosefield Gdns.)
Thornfield Pde. NW7 . . . . . 7B 14 (off Holders Hill Rd.)
Thornfield Rd. W12 . . . . . 2D 82 (in four parts)
Thornford Rd. SE13 . . . . . 5E 106
Thorngate Rd. W9 . . . . . 4J 65
Thorngrove Rd. E13 . . . . . 1K 71
Thornham Gro. E15 . . . . . 5F 53
Thornham St. SE10 . . . . . 6D 88
Thornhaugh M. WC1 . . . . . 4H 67 (4D 160)
Thornhaugh St. WC1 . . . . . 4H 67 (4D 160)
Thornhill Av. SE18 . . . . . 7J 91
Thornhill Av. Surb 2E 146
Thornhill Bri. Wharf. N1 . . . . 1K 67
Thornhill Cres. N1 . . . . . 7K 49
Thornhill Gdns. E10 . . . . . 2D 52
Thornhill Gdns. Bark 7J 55
Thornhill Gro. N1 . . . . . 7K 49
Thornhill Ho. W4 . . . . . 5A 82 (off Wood St.)
Thornhill Houses. N1 . . . . . 7A 50
Thornhill Rd. E10 . . . . . 2D 52
Thornhill Rd. N1 . . . . . 7A 50
Thornhill Rd. Croy 7C 140
Thornhill Rd. Surb 2E 146
Thornhill Rd. Uxb 4B 40
Thornhill Sq. N1 . . . . . 7K 49
Thornhill Way. Shep 5C 130
Thornicroft Ho. SW9 . . . . . 2K 103 (off Stockwell Rd.)
Thornlaw Rd. SE27 . . . . . 4A 122
Thornley Clo. N17 . . . . . 7B 18
Thornley Dri. Harr 2F 43
Thornley Pl. SE10 . . . . . 5G 89
Thornsbeach Rd. SE6 . . . . . 1E 124
Thornsett Pl. SE20 . . . . . 2H 141
Thornsett Rd. SE20 . . . . . 2H 141
Thornsett Rd. SW18 . . . . . 1K 119

Thornsett Ter. SE20 . . . 2H 141 (off Croydon Rd.)
Thorn Ter. SE15 . . . 3J 105
Thornton Av. SW2 . . . 1H 121
Thornton Av. W4 . . . 4A 82
Thornton Av. Croy . . . 6K 139
Thornton Av. W Dray . . . 3B 76
Thornton Clo. W Dray . . . 3B 76
Thornton Dene. Beck . . . 2C 142
Thornton Gdns. SW12 . . . 1H 121
Thornton Heath . . . 4C 140
Thornton Heath Pond. (Junct.) . . . 5A 140
Thornton Hill. SW19 . . . 7G 119
Thornton Ho. SE17 . . . 4E 86 (off Townsend St.)
Thornton Pl. W1 . . . 5D 66 (5E 158)
Thornton Rd. E11 . . . 2F 53
Thornton Rd. N18 . . . 3D 18
Thornton Rd. SW12 . . . 7H 103
Thornton Rd. SW14 . . . 4K 99
Thornton Rd. SW19 . . . 6F 119
Thornton Rd. Barn . . . 3B 4
Thornton Rd. Belv . . . 4H 93
Thornton Rd. Brom . . . 5J 125
Thornton Rd. Cars . . . 1B 150
Thornton Rd. Croy & T Hth . . . 7K 139
Thornton Rd. Ilf . . . 4F 55
Thornton Rd. E. SW19 . . . 6F 119
Thornton Row. T Hth . . . 5A 140
Thornton's Farm Av. Romf . . . 1J 57
Thornton St. SW9 . . . 2A 104
Thornton Way. NW11 . . . 5K 29
Thorntree Ct. W5 . . . 5E 62
Thorntree Rd. SE7 . . . 5B 90
Thornville Gro. Mitc . . . 2B 138
Thornville St. SE8 . . . 1C 106
Thornwell Ct. W7 . . . 2J 79 (off Du Burstow Ter.)
Thornwood Clo. E18 . . . 2K 35
Thornwood Ho. Buck H . . . 1H 21
Thornwood Rd. SE13 . . . 5G 107
Thornycroft Ho. W4 . . . 5A 82 (off Fraser St.)
Thorogood Gdns. E15 . . . 5G 53
Thorogood Way. Rain . . . 7K 57
Thorold Ho. SE1 . . . 2C 86 (6C 168) (off Pepper St.)
Thorold Rd. N22 . . . 7D 16
Thorold Rd. Ilf . . . 2F 55
Thorparch Rd. SW8 . . . 1H 103
Thorpebank Rd. W12 . . . 1C 82
Thorpe Clo. SE26 . . . 4K 123
Thorpe Clo. W10 . . . 6G 65
Thorpe Ct. Enf . . . 3G 7
Thorpe Cres. E17 . . . 2B 34
Thorpedale Gdns. Ilf . . . 4E 36
Thorpedale Rd. N4 . . . 2J 49
Thorpe Hall Rd. E17 . . . 1E 34
Thorpe Ho. N1 . . . 1K 67 (off Barnsbury Est.)
Thorpe Rd. E6 . . . 1D 72
Thorpe Rd. E7 . . . 4H 53
Thorpe Rd. E17 . . . 2E 34
Thorpe Rd. N15 . . . 6E 32
Thorpe Rd. Bark . . . 7H 55
Thorpe Rd. King T . . . 7E 116
Thorpewood Av. SE26 . . . 2H 123
Thorpland Av. Uxb . . . 3E 40
Thorsden Way. SE19 . . . 5E 122
Thorverton Rd. NW2 . . . 3G 47
Thoydon Rd. E3 . . . 2A 70
Thrale Rd. SW16 . . . 4G 121
Thrale St. SE1 . . . 1C 86 (5D 168)
Thrasher Clo. E8 . . . 1F 69
Thrawl St. E1 . . . 5F 69 (6K 163)
Thrayle Ho. SW9 . . . 3K 103 (off Benedict Rd.)
Threadgold Ho. N1 . . . 6D 50 (off Dovercourt Est.)
Threadneedle St. EC2 . . . 6D 68 (1F 169)
Three Barrels Wlk. EC4 . . . 7C 68 (2D 168) (off Queen St. Pl.)
Three Bridges Bus. Cen. S'hall . . . 2G 79
Three Colt Corner. E2 & E1 . . . 3K 163
Three Colts La. E2 . . . 4H 69
Three Colt St. E14 . . . 6B 70
Three Corners. Bexh . . . 2H 111
Three Cranes Wlk. EC4 . . . 3D 168
Three Cups Yd. WC1 . . . 6H 161
Three Kings Yd. W1 . . . 7F 67 (2J 165)
Three Meadows M. Harr . . . 1K 25
Three Mill La. E3 . . . 3E 70 (in two parts)
Three Oak La. SE1 . . . 2F 87 (6J 169)
Three Oaks Clo. Uxb . . . 3B 40
Three Quays. EC3 . . . 3H 169
Three Quays Wlk. EC3 . . . 7E 68 (3H 169)
Threshers Pl. W11 . . . 7G 65
Thriffwood. SE26 . . . 3J 123
Thrigby Rd. Chess . . . 6F 147
Thring Ho. SW9 . . . 2K 103 (off Stockwell Rd.)
Throckmorten Rd. E16 . . . 6K 71
Throgmorton Av. EC2 . . . 6D 68 (7F 163) (in two parts)
Throgmorton St. EC2 . . . 6D 68 (7F 163)
Throwley Clo. SE2 . . . 3C 92 (in two parts)
Throwley Rd. Sutt . . . 5K 149
Throwley Way. Sutt . . . 4K 149
Thrupp Clo. Mitc . . . 2F 139
Thrush Grn. Harr . . . 4E 24
Thrush St. SE17 . . . 5C 86
Thurbarn Rd. SE6 . . . 5D 124
Thurland Ho. SE16 . . . 4H 87 (off Camilla Rd.)
Thurland Rd. SE16 . . . 3G 87
Thurlby Clo. Harr . . . 6A 26
Thurlby Clo. Wfd G . . . 5J 21
Thurlby Cft. NW4 . . . 3E 28 (off Mulberry Clo.)
Thurlby Rd. SE27 . . . 4A 122
Thurlby Rd. Wemb . . . 6D 44
Thurleigh Av. SW12 . . . 6E 102
Thurleigh Rd. SW12 . . . 7D 102
Thurleston Av. Mord . . . 5G 137
Thurlestone Av. N12 . . . 6J 15
Thurlestone Av. Ilf . . . 4K 55
Thurlestone Clo. Shep . . . 6E 130
Thurlestone Ct. S'hall . . . 6F 61 (off Howard Rd.)
Thurlestone Pde. Shep . . . 6E 130 (off High St.)
Thurlestone Rd. SE27 . . . 3A 122
Thurloe Clo. SW7 . . . 4C 84 (3C 170)
Thurloe Ct. SW3 . . . 4C 84 (4C 170) (off Fulham Ct.)
Thurloe Pl. SW7 . . . 4B 84 (3B 170)
Thurloe Pl. M. SW7 . . . 3B 170
Thurloe Sq. SW7 . . . 4C 84 (3C 170)
Thurloe St. SW7 . . . 4B 84 (3B 170)
Thurlow Clo. E4 . . . 6K 19
Thurlow Gdns. Wemb . . . 5D 44
Thurlow Hill. SE21 . . . 1C 122
Thurlow Ho. SW16 . . . 3J 121
Thurlow Pk. Rd. SE21 . . . 2B 122
Thurlow Rd. NW3 . . . 5B 48
Thurlow Rd. W7 . . . 2A 80
Thurlow St. SE17 . . . 5D 86 (in two parts)
Thurlow Ter. NW5 . . . 5E 48
Thurlow Wlk. SE17 . . . 5E 86 (in two parts)
Thurlstone Rd. Ruis . . . 3J 41
Thurnby Ct. Twic . . . 3J 115
Thurnscoe. NW1 . . . 1G 67 (off Pratt St.)
Thursland Rd. Sidc . . . 5E 128
Thursley Cres. New Ad . . . 7E 154
Thursley Gdns. SW19 . . . 2F 119
Thursley Ho. SW2 . . . 7K 103 (off Holmewood Gdns.)
Thursley Rd. SE9 . . . 3D 126
Thurso Ho. NW6 . . . 2K 65
Thurso St. SW17 . . . 4B 120
Thurstan Dwellings. WC2 . . . 6J 67 (7F 161) (off Newton St.)
Thurstan Rd. SW20 . . . 7D 118
Thurston Ind. Est. SE13 . . . 3D 106
Thurston Rd. SE13 . . . 2D 106
Thurston Rd. S'hall . . . 6D 60
Thurtle Rd. E2 . . . 2F 69
Thwaite Clo. Eri . . . 6J 93
Thyra Gro. N12 . . . 6E 14
Tibbatt's Rd. E3 . . . 4D 70
Tibbenham Pl. SE6 . . . 2C 124
Tibbenham Wlk. E13 . . . 2H 71
Tibberton Sq. N1 . . . 1C 68
Tibbet's Clo. SW19 . . . 1F 119
Tibbet's Corner. (Junct.) . . . 7F 101
Tibbet's Ride. SW15 . . . 7F 101
Tiber Gdns. N1 . . . 1J 67
Ticehurst Clo. Orp . . . 7A 128
Ticehurst Rd. SE23 . . . 2A 124
Tickford Clo. SE2 . . . 2C 92
Tickford Ho. NW8 . . . 3C 66 (2C 158)
Tidal Basin Rd. E16 . . . 7H 71
Tidbury Ct. SW8 . . . 7G 85 (off Stewart's Rd.)
Tidelea Tower. SE28 . . . 2G 91 (off Erebus Dri.)
Tidenham Gdns. Croy . . . 3E 152
Tideside Ct. SE18 . . . 3C 90
Tideswell Rd. SW15 . . . 4E 100
Tideswell Rd. Croy . . . 3C 154
Tideway Clo. Rich . . . 4B 116
Tideway Ct. SE16 . . . 1K 87
Tideway Ho. E14 . . . 2C 88 (off Strafford St.)
Tideway Ind. Est. SW8 . . . 6G 85
Tideway Wlk. SW8 . . . 6G 85 (7B 172)
Tidey St. E3 . . . 5C 70
Tidford Rd. Well . . . 2K 109
Tidlock Ho. SE28 . . . 2H 91 (off Erebus Dri.)
Tidworth Rd. E3 . . . 4C 70
Tiepigs La. W Wick . . . 2G 155
Tierney Ct. Croy . . . 2E 152
Tierney Rd. SW2 . . . 1J 121
Tiffany Heights. SW18 . . . 7J 101
Tiger La. Brom . . . 4K 143
Tiger Way. E5 . . . 4H 51
Tigris Clo. N9 . . . 2D 18
Tilbrook Rd. SE3 . . . 3A 108
Tilbury Clo. SE15 . . . 7F 87
Tilbury Ho. SE14 . . . 6K 87 (off Myers La.)
Tilbury Rd. E6 . . . 2D 72
Tilbury Rd. E10 . . . 7E 34
Tildesley Rd. SW15 . . . 6E 100
Tilehurst Point. SE2 . . . 2D 92
Tilehurst Rd. SW18 . . . 1B 120
Tilehurst Rd. Sutt . . . 5G 149
Tile Kiln La. N6 . . . 1F 49
Tile Kiln La. N13 . . . 5H 17 (in two parts)
Tile Kiln La. Bex . . . 2J 129 (in three parts)
Tile Kiln La. Hare . . . 7D 22
Tile Kiln Studios. N6 . . . 7G 31
Tile Yd. E14 . . . 6B 70
Tileyard Rd. N7 . . . 7J 49
Tilford Av. New Ad . . . 7E 154
Tilford Gdns. SW19 . . . 1F 119
Tilford Ho. SW2 . . . 7K 103 (off Holmewood Gdns.)
Tilia Clo. Sutt . . . 5H 149
Tilia Rd. E5 . . . 4H 51
Tilia Wlk. SW9 . . . 4B 104
Tilleard Ho. W10 . . . 3G 65 (off Herries St.)
Tiller Rd. E14 . . . 3C 88
Tillett Clo. NW10 . . . 6J 45
Tillett Sq. SE16 . . . 2A 88
Tillet Way. E2 . . . 3G 69
Tillingbourne Gdns. N3 . . . 3H 29
Tillingbourne Grn. Orp . . . 4K 145
Tillingbourne Way. N3 . . . 4H 29
Tillingham Way. N12 . . . 4D 14
Tilling Rd. NW2 . . . 1E 46
Tilling Way. Wemb . . . 3D 44
Tillman St. E1 . . . 6H 69
Tilloch St. N1 . . . 7K 49
Tillotson Ct. SW8 . . . 7H 85 (off Wandsworth Rd.)
Tillotson Rd. N9 . . . 2A 18
Tillotson Rd. Harr . . . 7A 10
Tillotson Rd. Ilf . . . 7E 36
Tilney Ct. EC1 . . . 4C 68 (3D 162)
Tilney Ct. Buck H . . . 2D 20
Tilney Dri. Buck H . . . 2D 20
Tilney Gdns. N1 . . . 6D 50
Tilney Rd. Dag . . . 6F 57 (in two parts)
Tilney Rd. S'hall . . . 4A 78
Tilney St. W1 . . . 1E 84 (4H 165)
Tilson Clo. SE5 . . . 7E 86
Tilson Gdns. SW12 . . . 7J 103
Tilson Ho. SW2 . . . 7J 103
Tilson Rd. N17 . . . 1G 33
Tilston Clo. E11 . . . 3H 53
Tilton St. SW6 . . . 6G 83
Tiltwood, The. W3 . . . 7J 63
Tilt Yd. App. SE9 . . . 6D 108
Timber Clo. Chst . . . 2E 144
Timbercroft. Eps . . . 4A 148
Timbercroft La. SE18 . . . 6J 91
Timberdene. NW4 . . . 2F 29
Timberdene Av. Ilf . . . 1F 37
Timberland Clo. SE15 . . . 7G 87
Timberland Rd. E1 . . . 6H 69
Timber Mill Way. SW4 . . . 3H 103
Timber Pond Rd. SE16 . . . 1K 87
Timberslip Dri. Wall . . . 7H 151
Timbers, The. Sutt . . . 6G 149
Timber St. EC1 . . . 4C 68 (3C 162)
Timberwharf Rd. N16 . . . 6G 33
Timber Wharves Est. E14 . . . 4C 88 (off Copeland Dri.)
Timbrell Pl. SE16 . . . 1B 88
Time Sq. E8 . . . 5F 51
Times Sq. Sutt . . . 5K 149
Timor Ho. E1 . . . 4A 70 (off Duckett St.)
Timothy Clo. SW4 . . . 5G 103
Timothy Clo. Bexh . . . 5E 110
Timothy Ho. Eri . . . 2E 92 (off Kale Rd.)
Timothy Rd. E3 . . . 5B 70
Timsbury Wlk. SW15 . . . 1C 118
Tindal St. SW9 . . . 1B 104
Tinderbox All. SW14 . . . 3K 99
Tinniswood Clo. N5 . . . 5A 50
Tinsley Rd. E1 . . . 5J 69
Tintagel Cres. SE22 . . . 4F 105
Tintagel Dri. Stan . . . 4J 11
Tintagel Gdns. SE22 . . . 4F 105
Tintern Av. NW9 . . . 3H 27
Tintern Clo. SW15 . . . 5G 101
Tintern Clo. SW19 . . . 6A 120
Tintern Ct. W13 . . . 7A 62
Tintern Gdns. N14 . . . 7D 6
Tintern Ho. NW1 . . . 2F 67 (1K 159) (off Augustus St.)
Tintern Ho. SW1 . . . 4F 85 (4J 171) (off Abbots Mnr.)
Tintern Path. NW9 . . . 6A 28 (off Fryent Gro.)
Tintern Rd. N22 . . . 1C 32
Tintern Rd. Cars . . . 1B 150
Tintern St. SW4 . . . 4J 103
Tintern Way. Harr . . . 1F 43
Tinto Rd. E16 . . . 4J 71
Tinworth St. SE11 . . . 5J 85 (5F 173)
Tippett Ct. E6 . . . 2D 72
Tippetts Clo. Enf . . . 1H 7
Tipthorpe Rd. SW11 . . . 3E 102
Tipton Dri. Croy . . . 4E 152
Tiptree. NW1 . . . 7F 49 (off Castlehaven Rd.)
Tiptree Clo. E4 . . . 3K 19
Tiptree Cres. Ilf . . . 2E 36
Tiptree Dri. Enf . . . 4J 7
Tiptree Rd. Ruis . . . 4K 41
Tirlemont Rd. S Croy . . . 7C 152
Tirrell Rd. Croy . . . 6C 140
Tisbury Ct. W1 . . . 2C 166
Tisbury Rd. SW16 . . . 2J 139
Tisdall Pl. SE17 . . . 4D 86
Tissington Ct. SE16 . . . 4J 87
Titan Bus. Est. SE8 . . . 7C 88 (off Ffinch St.)
Titan Ct. Bren . . . 5F 81
Titchborne Row. W2 . . . 6C 66 (1D 164)
Titchfield Rd. NW8 . . . 1C 66
Titchfield Rd. Cars . . . 1B 150
Titchfield Wlk. Cars . . . 7B 138
Titchwell Rd. SW18 . . . 1B 120
Tite St. SW3 . . . 5D 84 (6E 170)
Tithe Barn Clo. King T . . . 1F 135
Tithe Barn Way. N'holt . . . 2K 59
Tithe Clo. NW7 . . . 1C 28
Tithe Clo. Hay . . . 5H 59
Tithe Clo. W on T . . . 6K 131
Tithe Farm Av. Harr . . . 3E 42
Tithe Farm Clo. Harr . . . 3E 42
Tithe Wlk. NW7 . . . 1C 28
Titian Av. Bus H . . . 1D 10
Titley Clo. E4 . . . 5H 19
Titmus Clo. Uxb . . . 6E 58
Titmuss Av. SE28 . . . 7B 74
Titmuss St. W12 . . . 2E 82
Tivendale. N8 . . . 3J 31
Tiverton Av. Ilf . . . 3E 36
Tiverton Clo. Croy . . . 7F 141
Tiverton Dri. SE9 . . . 1G 127
Tiverton M. Houn . . . 2G 97
Tiverton Rd. N15 . . . 6D 32
Tiverton Rd. N18 . . . 5K 17
Tiverton Rd. NW10 . . . 1F 65
Tiverton Rd. Edgw . . . 2F 27
Tiverton Rd. Houn . . . 2G 97
Tiverton Rd. Ruis . . . 3J 41
Tiverton Rd. T Hth . . . 5A 140
Tiverton Rd. Wemb . . . 2E 62
Tiverton St. SE1 . . . 3C 86
Tiverton Way. Chess . . . 5D 146
Tivoli Ct. SE16 . . . 1B 88
Tivoli Gdns. SE18 . . . 4C 90 (in two parts)
Tivoli Rd. N8 . . . 5H 31
Tivoli Rd. SE27 . . . 5C 122
Tivoli Rd. Houn . . . 4C 96
Toad La. Houn . . . 4D 96
Tobacco Dock. E1 . . . 7H 69
Tobacco Quay. E1 . . . 7H 69
Tobago St. E14 . . . 2C 88
Tobin Clo. NW3 . . . 7C 48
Toby Ct. N9 . . . 7D 8 (off Tramway Av.)
Toby La. E1 . . . 4A 70
Toby Way. Surb . . . 2H 147
Todd Ho. N2 . . . 2B 30 (off Grange, The)
Todds Wlk. N7 . . . 2K 49
Todhunter Ter. Barn . . . 4D 4
Tokenhouse Yd. EC2 . . . 6D 68 (7E 162)
Token Yd. SW15 . . . 4G 101
Tokyngton . . . 6H 45
Tokyngton Av. Wemb . . . 6G 45
Toland Sq. SW15 . . . 5C 100
Tolcairn Ct. Belv . . . 5G 93
Tolcarne Dri. Pinn . . . 2J 23

Tolchurch. W11 6H 65 (off Dartmouth Clo.)
Toley Av. Wemb 7E 26
Toll Bar Ct. Sutt 7K 149
Tollbridge Clo. W10 4G 65
Tollesbury Gdns. Ilf 3H 37
Tollet St. E1 4K 69
Tollgate Dri. SE21 2E 122
Tollgate Dri. Hay 7B 60
Tollgate Gdns. NW6 2K 65
Tollgate Ho. NW6 2K 65 (off Tollgate Gdns.)
Tollgate Rd. E16 & E6 5A 72
Tollgate Sq. E6 5D 72
Tollhouse Way. N19 2G 49
Tollington Pk. N4 2K 49
Tollington Pl. N4 2K 49
Tollington Rd. N7 4K 49
Tollington Way. N7 3J 49
Tolmers Sq. NW1 4G 67 (3B 160) (in two parts)
Tolpaide Ho. SE11 4J 173
Tolpuddle Av. E13 1A 72 (off Queens Rd.)
Tolpuddle St. N1 2A 68
Tolsford Rd. E5 5H 51
Tolson Rd. Iswth 3A 98
Tolverne Rd. SW20 1E 136
Tolworth. 2H 147
Tolworth B'way. Surb 1H 147
Tolworth Clo. Surb 1H 147
Tolworth Gdns. Romf 5D 38
Tolworth Junction (Toby Jug). (Junct.) 2H 147
Tolworth Pde. Chad H 5E 38
Tolworth Pk. Rd. Surb 2F 147
Tolworth Ri. N. Surb 1H 147
Tolworth Ri. S. Surb 2H 147
Tolworth Rd. Surb 2E 146
Tolworth Tower. Surb 2H 147
Tomahawk Gdns. N'holt 3B 60
Tom Coombs Clo. SE9 4C 108
Tom Cribb Rd. SE28 3G 91
Tom Groves Clo. E15 5F 53
Tom Hood Clo. E15 5F 53
Tom Jenkinson Rd. E16 1J 89
Tomkyns Ho. SE11 4J 173
Tomlins All. Twic 1A 116
Tomlin's Gro. E3 3C 70
Tomlinson Clo. E2 3F 69 (2K 163)
Tomlinson Clo. W4 5H 81
Tomlins Orchard. Bark 1G 73
Tomlins Ter. E14 6A 70
Tomlins Wlk. N7 2K 49
Tom Mann Clo. Bark 1J 73
Tom Nolan Clo. E15 2G 71
Tom Oakman Cen. E4 2A 20
Tompion Ho. EC1 4B 68 (2B 162) (off Percival St.)
Tompion St. EC1 3B 68 (2A 162) (in two parts)
Tom Smith Clo. SE10 6G 89
Tomson Ho. SE1 3F 87 (7J 169) (off Riley Rd.)
Tomswood Ct. Ilf 1G 37
Tomswood Hill. Ilf 6K 21 & 1F 37
Tomswood Rd. Chig 6K 21
Tom Williams Ho. SW6 6H 83 (off Clem Attlee Ct.)
Tonbridge Cres. Harr 4E 26
Tonbridge Houses. WC1 3J 67 (2E 160) (off Tonbridge St.)
Tonbridge Rd. W Mol 4D 132
Tonbridge St. WC1 3J 67 (1E 160)
Tonbridge Wlk. WC1 1E 160
Toneborough. NW8 1K 65 (off Abbey Rd.)
Tonfield Rd. Sutt 1H 149
Tonge Clo. Beck 5C 142
Tonsley Hill. SW18 5K 101
Tonsley Pl. SW18 5K 101
Tonsley Rd. SW18 5K 101
Tonsley St. SW18 5K 101
Tonstall Rd. Mitc 2E 138
Tony Cannell M. E3 3B 70
Tony Law Ho. SE20 1H 141
Tooke Clo. Pinn 1C 24
Tookey Clo. Harr 7F 27
Took's Ct. EC4 6A 68 (7J 161)
Tooley St. SE1 1D 86 (4F 169)
Toomy Cen. E16 1K 89 (off Evelyn Rd.)
Toorack Rd. Harr 2H 25
Tooting. 5C 120
Tooting Bec. 3E 120
Tooting Bec Gdns. SW16 4H 121 (in two parts)
Tooting Bec Rd. SW17 & SW16 3E 120
Tooting B'way. SW17 5C 120
Tooting Graveney. 6D 120
Tooting Gro. SW17 5C 120
Tooting High St. SW17 6C 120
Tooting Mkt. SW17 4D 120
Tootswood Rd. Brom 5G 143
Topaz Wlk. NW2 7F 29
Topham Ho. SE10 7E 88 (off Prior St.)
Topham Sq. N17 1C 32
Topham St. EC1 4A 68 (3J 161)
Top Ho. Ri. E4 7K 9
Topiary Sq. Rich 3F 99
Topley St. SE9 4A 108
Topmast Point. E14 2C 88
Top Pk. Beck 5G 143
Topp Wlk. NW2 2E 46
Topsfield Clo. N8 5H 31
Topsfield Pde. N8 5J 31 (off Tottenham La.)
Topsfield Rd. N8 5J 31
Topsham Rd. SW17 3D 120
Torbay Ct. NW1 7F 49
Torbay Mans. NW6 1H 65 (off Willesden La.)
Torbay Rd. NW6 7H 47
Torbay Rd. Harr 2C 42
Torbay St. NW1 7F 49
Torbitt Way. Ilf 5K 37
Torbridge Clo. Edgw 7K 11
Torbrook Clo. Bex 6E 110
Tor Ct. W8 2J 83
Torcross Dri. SE23 2J 123
Torcross Rd. Ruis 3K 41
Tor Gdns. W8 2J 83
Tor Ho. N6 6F 31
Tormead Clo. Sutt 6J 149
Tormount Rd. SE18 6J 91
Tornay Ho. N1 2K 67 (off Priory Grn. Est.)
Torney Ho. E9 7J 51
Toronto Av. E12 4D 54
Toronto Rd. E11 4F 53
Toronto Rd. Ilf 1F 55
Torquay Gdns. Ilf 4B 36
Torquay St. W2 5K 65
Torrance Clo. SE7 6B 90
Torrens Ct. SE5 3D 104
Torrens Rd. E15 6H 53
Torrens Rd. SW2 5K 103
Torrens Sq. E15 6H 53
Torrens St. EC1 2A 68
Torres Sq. E14 5C 88
Torre Wlk. Cars 1C 150
Torriano Av. NW5 5H 49
Torriano Cotts. NW5 5G 49
Torriano M. NW5 5G 49
Torridge Gdns. SE15 4J 105
Torridge Rd. T Hth 5B 140
Torridon Ho. NW6 2K 65 (off Randolph Gdns.)
Torridon Rd. SE6 7F 107
Torrington Av. N12 5G 15
Torrington Clo. N12 4G 15
Torrington Ct. SE26 5G 123 (off Crystal Pal. Pk. Rd.)
Torrington Dri. Harr 4F 43
Torrington Gdns. N11 6B 16
Torrington Gdns. Gnfd 1C 62
Torrington Gro. N12 5H 15
Torrington Pk. N12 5F 15
Torrington Pl. E1 1G 87
Torrington Pl. WC1 5H 67 (5C 160)
Torrington Rd. E18 3J 35
Torrington Rd. Dag 1F 57
Torrington Rd. Gnfd 1C 62
Torrington Rd. Ruis 3J 41
Torrington Sq. WC1 4H 67 (4D 160)
Torrington Sq. Croy 7D 140
Torrington Way. Mord 6J 137
Tor Rd. Well 1C 110
Torr Rd. SE20 7K 123
Tortington Ho. SE15 7G 87 (off Friary Est.)
Torver Rd. Harr 4J 25
Torwood Rd. SW15 5C 100
Tothill Ho. SW1 4H 85 (3D 172) (off Page St.)
Tothill St. SW1 2H 85 (7D 166)
Totnes Rd. Well 7B 92
Totnes Vs. N11 5B 16 (off Telford Rd.)
Totnes Wlk. N2 4B 30
Tottan Ter. E1 6K 69
Tottenhall. NW1 7E 48 (off Ferdinand St.)
Tottenhall Rd. N13 6F 17
Tottenham. 2F 33
Tottenham Ct. Rd. W1 4G 67 (4B 160)
Tottenham Grn. E. N15 4F 33
Tottenham Hale. 2G 33
Tottenham Hale Gyratory. (Junct.) 3F 33
Tottenham Hale Gyratory. N15 4G 33
Tottenham Hale Retail Pk. N15 4G 33
Tottenham Hotspur F.C. (White Hart Lane) 7B 18
Tottenham La. N8 6J 31
Tottenham M. W1 5G 67 (5B 160)
Tottenham Rd. N1 6E 50
Tottenham St. W1 5G 67 (6B 160)
Totterdown St. SW17 4D 120
Totteridge. 1C 14
Totteridge Comn. N20 2H 13
Totteridge Grn. N20 2D 14
Totteridge La. N20 2D 14
Totteridge Village. N20 1B 14
Totternhoe Clo. Harr 5C 26
Totton Rd. T Hth 3A 140
Toulmin St. SE1 2C 86 (7C 168)
Toulon St. SE5 7C 86
Toulouse Ct. SE16 5H 87 (off Rossetti Rd.)
Tourist Info. Cen. 6J 111 **(Bexley)**
Tourist Info. Cen. 4G 111 **(Bexleyheath)**
Tourist Info. Cen. 6C 68 (1C 168) **(City of London)**
Tourist Info. Cen. 3C 152 **(Croydon)**
Tourist Info. Cen. 6E 88 **(Greenwich)**
Tourist Info. Cen. 4J 25 **(Harrow)**
Tourist Info. Cen. 3D 94 **(Heathrow Airport)**
Tourist Info. Cen. 3F 97 **(Hounslow)**
Tourist Info. Cen. 2D 134 **(Kingston)**
Tourist Info. Cen. 2D 134 **(Kingston Upon Thames)**
Tourist Info. Cen. 4E 106 **(Lewisham)**
Tourist Info. Cen. 3F 55 **(Redbridge)**
Tourist Info. Cen. 5D 98 **(Richmond upon Thames)**
Tourist Info. Cen. 4F 169 **(Southwark)**
Tourist Info. Cen. 1B 116 **(Twickenham)**
Tourist Info. Cen. 2K 85 (6H 167) **(Waterloo International Terminal)**
Tournay Rd. SW6 7H 83
Tours Pas. SW11 4A 102
Toussaint Wlk. SE16 3G 87
Tovil Clo. SE20 2H 141
Tovy Ho. SE1 5G 87 (off Avondale Sq.)
Towcester Rd. E3 4D 70
Tower Bri. SE1 & E1 1F 87 (5J 169)
Tower Bri. App. E1 1F 87 (4J 169)
Tower Bri. Bus. Complex. SE16 3G 87
Tower Bri. Bus. Sq. SE16 4H 87
Tower Bridge Experience. 4J 169
Tower Bri. Plaza. SE1 1F 87 (5J 169)
Tower Bri. Rd. SE1 3E 86
Tower Bri. Sq. SE1 6J 169
Tower Bri. Wharf. E1 1G 87 (5K 169)
Tower Bldgs. E1 1H 87 (off Brewhouse La.)
Tower Clo. NW3 5B 48
Tower Clo. SE20 7H 123
Tower Ct. E5 7F 33
Tower Ct. N1 7C 50 (off Canonbury St.)
Tower Ct. NW8 2C 66 (off Mackennal St.)
Tower Ct. WC2 1E 166
Tower 42. 6E 68 (7G 163)
Tower Gdns. Clay 7B 146
Tower Gdns. Rd. N17 1C 32
Towergate Clo. Uxb 5A 40
Tower Hamlets Rd. E7 4H 53
Tower Hamlets Rd. E17 3C 34
Tower Hill. (Junct.) 1F 87 (3J 169)
Tower Hill. EC3 7E 68 (3H 169)
Tower Hill Ter. EC3 3H 169
Tower Ho. E1 5G 69 (off Fieldgate St.)
Tower La. Wemb 3D 44
Tower M. E17 4C 34
Tower of London, The. 7F 69 (3J 169)
Tower Pl. EC3 3H 169
Tower Ri. Rich 3E 98
Tower Rd. NW10 7C 46
Tower Rd. Belv 4J 93
Tower Rd. Bexh 4G 111
Tower Rd. Twic 3K 115
Tower Royal. EC4 7D 68 (2E 168)
Towers Av. Hil 3E 58
Towers Bus. Pk. Wemb 4J 45 (off Carey Way)
Towers Ct. Uxb 3E 58
Towers Pl. Rich 5E 98
Towers Rd. Pinn 1C 24
Towers Rd. S'hall 4E 60
Tower St. WC2 6J 67 (1E 166)
Tower Ter. N22 2K 31
Tower Vw. Croy 1A 154
Tower Yd. Rich 5F 99
Towfield Ct. Felt 2D 114
Towfield Rd. Felt 2D 114
Towgar Ct. N20 7F 5
Towncourt Cres. Orp 5G 145
Towncourt La. Orp 6H 145
Towncourt Path. N4 1C 50
Town End Pde. King T 3D 134 (off High St.)
Towney Mead. N'holt 2D 60
Towney Mead Ct. N'holt 2D 60
Townfield Rd. Hay 1H 77
Townfield Sq. Hay 7H 59
Town Fld. Way. Iswth 2A 98
Town Hall App. Rd. N15 4F 33
Town Hall Av. W4 5K 81
Town Hall Rd. SW11 3D 102
Town Hall Wlk. N16 4D 50 (off Church Wlk.)
Townholm Cres. W7 3K 79
Town La. Stanw 1A 112 (in two parts)
Townley Ct. E15 6H 53
Townley Rd. SE22 5E 104
Townley Rd. Bexh 5F 111
Townley St. SE17 5D 86 (in two parts)
Townmead Bus. Cen. SW6 3A 102
Town Mdw. Bren 6D 80
Town Mdw. Rd. Bren 7D 80
Townmead Rd. SW6 3K 101
Townmead Rd. Rich 2H 99
Town Quay. Bark 1F 73
Town Quay Wharf. Bark 1F 73
Town Rd. N9 2C 18
Townsend Av. N14 4C 16
Townsend Ho. SE1 4G 87 (off Strathnairn St.)
Townsend Ind. Est. NW10 2J 63
Townsend La. NW9 7K 27
Townsend Rd. N15 5F 33
Townsend Rd. Ashf 5A 112
Townsend Rd. S'hall 1C 78
Townsend St. SE17 4E 86
Townsend Way. N'wd 1H 23
Townsend Yd. N6 1F 49
Townshend Clo. Sidc 6B 128
Townshend Ct. NW8 2C 66 (off Townshend Rd.)
Townshend Est. NW8 2C 66
Townshend Rd. NW8 1C 66 (in two parts)
Townshend Rd. Chst 5F 127
Townshend Rd. Rich 4F 99
Townshend Ter. Rich 4F 99
Towns Ho. SW4 3H 103
Townson Av. N'holt 2J 59
Townson Way. N'holt 2J 59
Town Sq. Iswth 3B 98 (off Swan St.)
Town, The. Enf 3J 7
Town Tree Rd. Ashf 5C 112
Town Wharf. Iswth 3B 98
Towpath. Shep 7B 130
Towpath. W on T 5J 131
Towpath Rd. N18 6E 18
Towpath, The. SW10 1B 102
Towpath Wlk. E9 5B 52
Towpath Way. SE25 6F 141
Towton Rd. SE27 2C 122
Toynbec Clo. Chst 4F 127
Toynbee Rd. SW20 1G 137
Toynbee St. E1 5F 69 (6J 163)
Toyne Way. N6 6D 30
Tracey Av. NW2 5E 46
Tracy Ct. Stan 7H 11
Trade Clo. N13 4F 17
Trader Rd. E6 6F 73
Tradescant Ho. E9 7J 51 (off Frampton Pk. Rd.)
Tradescant Rd. SW8 7J 85
Tradewinds Ct. E1 7G 69
Trading Est. Rd. NW10 4J 63
Trafalgar Av. N17 6K 17
Trafalgar Av. SE15 5F 87
Trafalgar Av. Wor Pk 1F 149
Trafalgar Bus. Cen. Bark 4K 73
Trafalgar Clo. SE16 3A 88

Trafalgar Ct. E1 1J 87
(off Wapping Wall)
Trafalgar Gdns. E1 5K 69
Trafalgar Gdns. W8 3K 83
(off South End)
Trafalgar Gro. SE10 6F 89
Trafalgar Ho. SE17 5C 86
(off Bronti Clo.)
Trafalgar Pl. E11 4J 35
Trafalgar Pl. N18 5B 18
Trafalgar Rd. SE10 6F 89
Trafalgar Rd. SW19 7K 119
Trafalgar Rd. Twic 2H 115
Trafalgar Square. 1J 85 (4D 166)
Trafalgar Sq. WC2 1H 85 (4D 166)
Trafalgar St. SE17 5D 86
Trafalgar Ter. Harr 1J 43
Trafalgar Trad. Est. Enf 4F 9
Trafalgar Way. E14 1E 88
Trafalgar Way. Croy 2A 152
Trafford Clo. E15 5D 52
Trafford Ho. N1 2D 68
(off Cranston Est.)
Trafford Rd. T Hth 5K 139
Traitors' Gate. 4J 169
Tralee Ct. SE16 5H 87
(off Masters Dri.)
Tramsheds Ind. Est. Croy 7H 139
Tramway Av. E15 7G 53
Tramway Av. N9 7C 8
Tramway Path. Mitc 4C 138
(in three parts)
Tranley M. NW3 4C 48
Tranmere Ct. Sutt 7A 150
Tranmere Rd. N9 7A 8
Tranmere Rd. SW18 2A 120
Tranmere Rd. Twic 7F 97
Tranquil Pas. SE3 2H 107
(off Montpelier Va.)
Tranquil Va. SE3 2G 107
Transay Wlk. N1 6D 50
Transept St. NW1 5C 66 (6D 158)
Transmere Clo. Orp 6G 145
Transmere Rd. Orp 6G 145
Transom Clo. SE16 4A 88
Transom Sq. E14 5D 88
Transport Av. Bren 5A 80
Tranton Rd. SE16 3G 87
Trappes Ho. SE16 4H 87
(off Camilla Rd.)
Traps La. N Mald 1A 136
Travellers Site. E17 6G 19
Travellers Way. Houn 2A 96
Travers Clo. E17 1K 33
Travers Ho. SE10 6F 89
(off Trafalgar Gro.)
Travers Rd. N7 3A 50
Travis Ho. SE10 1E 106
Treacy Clo. Bus H 2B 10
Treadgold Ho. W11 7F 65
(off Bomore Rd.)
Treadgold St. W11 7F 65
Treadway St. E2 2H 69
Treasury Pas. SW1 6E 166
Treaty Cen. Houn 3F 97
Treaty St. N1 1K 67
Trebeck St. W1 1F 85 (4J 165)
Trebovir Rd. SW5 5J 83
Treby St. E3 4B 70
Trecastle Way. N7 4H 49
Tredegar M. E3 3B 70
Tredegar Rd. E3 2B 70
Tredegar Rd. N11 7C 16
Tredegar Sq. E3 3B 70
Tredegar Ter. E3 3B 70
Trederwen Rd. E8 1G 69
Tredown Rd. SE26 5J 123
Tredwell Clo. SW2 2K 121
Tredwell Clo. Brom 4C 144
Tredwell Rd. SE27 4B 122
Tree Clo. Rich 1D 116
Treen Av. SW13 3B 100
Tree Rd. E16 6A 72
Treeside Clo. W Dray 4A 76
Tree Top M. Dag 6K 57
Treetops Clo. SE2 5E 92
Treeview Clo. SE19 1E 140
Treewall Gdns. Brom 4K 125
Trefgarne Rd. Dag 2G 57
Trefil Wlk. N7 4J 49
Trefoil Ho. Eri 2E 92
(off Kale Rd.)
Trefoil Rd. SW18 5A 102
Trefusis Ct. Houn 1K 95
Tregaron Av. N8 6J 31
Tregaron Gdns. N Mald 4A 136
Tregarvon Rd. SW11 4E 102
Tregenna Av. Harr 4E 42
Tregenna Clo. N14 5B 6
Tregenna Ct. S Harr 4E 42
Trego Rd. E9 7C 52
Tregothnan Rd. SW9 3J 103
Tregunter Rd. SW10 6K 83
Trehearn Rd. Ilf 1H 37
Treherne Ct. SW9 1B 104
Treherne Ct. SW17 4E 120
Trehern Rd. SW14 3K 99
Trehurst St. E5 5A 52
Trelawney Est. E9 6J 51
Trelawney Ho. SE1 2C 86 (6C 168)
(off Pepper St.)
Trelawney Rd. Ilf 1H 37
Trelawn Rd. E10 3E 52
Trelawn Rd. SW2 5A 104
Trelawny Clo. E17 4D 34
Trellick Tower. W10 4H 65
(off Golborne Rd.)
Trellis Sq. E3 3B 70
Treloar Gdns. SE19 6D 122
Tremadoc Rd. SW4 4H 103
Tremaine Clo. SE4 2C 106
Tremaine Rd. SE20 2H 141
Trematon Ho. SE11 5A 86 (5K 173)
(off Kennings Way)
Trematon Pl. Tedd 7C 116
Tremlett Gro. N19 3G 49
Tremlett M. N19 3G 49
Trenance Gdns. Ilf 3A 56
Trenchard Av. Ruis 4K 41
Trenchard Clo. NW9 1A 28
Trenchard Clo. Stan 6F 11
Trenchard Ct. NW4 5C 28
Trenchard Ct. Mord 6J 137
Trenchard St. SE10 5F 89
Trenchold St. SW8 6J 85
Trendell Ho. E14 6C 70
(off Dod St.)
Trenholme Clo. SE20 7H 123
Trenholme Rd. SE20 7H 123
Trenholme Ter. SE20 7H 123
Trenmar Gdns. NW10 3D 64
Trent Av. W5 3C 80
Trent Ct. S Croy 5C 152
(off Nottingham Rd.)
Trent Gdns. N14 6A 6
Trentham St. SW18 1J 119
Trent Ho. SE15 4J 105
Trent Ho. King T 1D 134
Trent Pk. (Country Pk.) 1A 6
Trent Pk. Golf Course. 3B 6
Trent Rd. SW2 5K 103
Trent Rd. Buck H 1E 20
Trent Way. Hay 2G 59
Trent Way. Wor Pk 3E 148
Trentwood Side. Enf 3E 6
Treport St. SW18 7K 101
Tresco Clo. Brom 6G 125
Trescoe Gdns. Harr 7C 24
Tresco Gdns. Ilf 2A 56
Tresco Ho. SE11 5J 173
Tresco Rd. SE15 4H 105
Tresham Cres. NW8 4C 66 (3C 158)
Tresham Rd. Bark 7K 55
Tresham Wlk. E9 5J 51
Tresidder Ho. SW4 7H 103
Tresilian Av. N21 5E 6
Tressell Clo. N1 7B 50
Tressillian Cres. SE4 3C 106
Tressillian Rd. SE4 4B 106
Tress Pl. SE1 4A 168
Trestis Clo. Hay 4B 60
Treswell Rd. Dag 1E 74
Tretawn Gdns. NW7 4F 13
Tretawn Pk. NW7 4F 13
Trevanion Rd. W14 4G 83
Treve Av. Harr 7H 25
Trevelyan Av. E12 4D 54
Trevelyan Cres. Harr 7D 26
Trevelyan Gdns. NW10 1E 64
Trevelyan Ho. E2 3K 69
(off Morpeth St.)
Trevelyan Ho. SE5 7B 86
(off John Ruskin St.)
Trevelyan Rd. E15 4H 53
Trevelyan Rd. SW17 5C 120
Trevenna Ho. SE23 3K 123
(off Dacres Rd.)
Trevera Ct. Enf 5F 9
Treveris St. SE1 1B 86 (5B 168)
Treverton St. W10 4G 65
Treverton Towers. W10 5F 65
(off Treverton St.)
Treves Clo. N21 5E 6
Treves Ho. E1 4G 69
(off Vallance Rd.)
Treville St. SW15 7D 100
Treviso Rd. SE23 2K 123
Trevithick Clo. Felt 1H 113
Trevithick Ho. SE16 4H 87
(off Rennie Est.)
Trevithick St. SE8 6C 88
Trevone Ct. SW2 7J 103
(off Doverfield Rd.)
Trevone Gdns. Pinn 6C 24
Trevor Clo. Brom 7H 143
Trevor Clo. E Barn 6G 5
Trevor Clo. Harr 7E 10
Trevor Clo. Iswth 5K 97
Trevor Clo. N'holt 2A 60
Trevor Cres. Ruis 4H 41
Trevor Gdns. Edgw 1K 27
Trevor Gdns. N'holt 2A 60
Trevor Gdns. Ruis 4J 41
Trevor Pl. SW7 2C 84 (7D 164)
Trevor Rd. SW19 7G 119
Trevor Rd. Edgw 1K 27
Trevor Rd. Hay 2G 77
Trevor Rd. Wfd G 7D 20
Trevor Sq. SW7 2D 84 (7E 164)
Trevor St. SW7 2C 84 (7D 164)
Trevor Wlk. SW7 2C 84 (7D 164)
(off Trevor Pl.)
Trevose Ho. SE11 5K 85 (5H 173)
(off Orsett St.)
Trevose Rd. E17 1F 35
Trewenna Dri. Chess 5D 146
Trewince Rd. SW20 1E 136
Trewint St. SW18 2A 120
Trewsbury Ho. SE2 1D 92
Trewsbury Rd. SE26 5K 123
Triandra Way. Hay 5B 60
Triangle Bus. Cen., The. NW10 3B 64
Triangle Cen. S'hall 1H 79
Triangle Ct. E16 5B 72
Triangle Pas. Barn 4F 5
Triangle Pl. SW4 4H 103
Triangle Rd. E8 1H 69
Triangle, The. E8 1H 69
Triangle, The. N13 4E 16
Triangle, The. Bark 6G 55
Triangle, The. King T 2H 135
Triangle, The. Sidc 7A 110
(off Burnt Oak La.)
Trickett Ho. Sutt 7K 149
Tricycle Theatre. 7H 47
(off Kilburn High Rd.)
Trident Bus. Cen. SW17 5D 120
Trident Gdns. N'holt 3B 60
Trident Ho. E14 6E 70
(off Blair St.)
Trident St. SE16 4K 87
Trident Way. S'hall 3K 77
Trig La. EC4 7C 68 (2C 168)
Trigon Rd. SW8 7K 85
Trilby Rd. SE23 2K 123
Trillo Ct. Ilf 7J 37
Trimdon. NW1 1G 67
Trimmer Wlk. Bren 6E 80
Trim St. SE14 6B 88
Trinder Gdns. N19 1J 49
Trinder Rd. N19 1J 49
Trinder Rd. Barn 5A 4
Tring Av. W5 1F 81
Tring Av. S'hall 6D 60
Tring Av. Wemb 6G 45
Tring Clo. Ilf 5H 37
Tring Ct. Twic 4A 116
Trinidad Gdns. Dag 7K 57
Trinidad Ho. E14 7B 70
(off Gill St.)
Trinidad St. E14 7B 70
Trinity Av. N2 3B 30
Trinity Av. Enf 6A 8
Trinity Buoy Wharf. E14 7G 71
(off Orchard Pl.)
Trinity Bus. Pk. E4 6G 19
Trinity Chu. Pas. SW13 6D 82
Trinity Chu. Rd. SW13 6D 82
Trinity Chu. Sq. SE1 3C 86 (7D 168)
Trinity Clo. E8 6F 51
Trinity Clo. E11 2G 53
Trinity Clo. NW3 4B 48
Trinity Clo. SE13 4F 107
Trinity Clo. SW4 4G 103
Trinity Clo. Brom 1C 156
Trinity Clo. Houn 4C 96
Trinity Clo. S Croy 7E 152
Trinity Cotts. Rich 3F 99
Trinity Ct. N1 1E 68
(off Downham Rd.)
Trinity Ct. NW2 5E 46
Trinity Ct. SE1 3C 86
(off Brockham St.)
Trinity Ct. SE7 4B 90
Trinity Ct. SE25 6E 140
Trinity Ct. SE26 3J 123
Trinity Ct. W2 6A 66
(off Gloucester Ter.)
Trinity Ct. WC1 3G 161
Trinity Ct. Croy 2C 152
Trinity Ct. Enf 2H 7
Trinity Cres. SW17 2D 120
Trinity Gdns. E16 5H 71
Trinity Gdns. SW9 4K 103
Trinity Grn. E1 4J 69
Trinity Gro. SE10 1E 106
Trinity Hospital (Almshouses). SE10 5F 89
Trinity Ho. SE1 3C 86
(off Bath Ter.)
Trinity M. E1 5J 69
(off Redman's Rd.)
Trinity M. SE20 1H 141
Trinity M. W10 6F 65
Trinity Path. SE23 3J 123
Trinity Pl. EC3 7F 69 (2J 169)
Trinity Pl. Bexh 4F 111
Trinity Ri. SW2 1A 122
Trinity Rd. N2 3B 30
Trinity Rd. N22 7D 16
(in two parts)
Trinity Rd. SW18 & SW17 4A 102
Trinity Rd. SW19 6J 119
Trinity Rd. Ilf 3G 37
Trinity Rd. Rich 3F 99
Trinity Rd. S'hall 1C 78
Trinity Sq. EC3 7E 68 (2H 169)
Trinity St. E16 5H 71
Trinity St. SE1 2C 86 (7D 168)
(in two parts)
Trinity St. Enf 2H 7
Trinity Tower. E1 7G 69
(off Vaughan Way)
Trinity Wlk. NW3 6A 48
Trinity Way. E4 6G 19
Trinity Way. W3 7A 64
Trio Pl. SE1 2C 86 (7D 168)
Tristan Ct. SE8 6B 88
(off Dorking Clo.)
Tristan Sq. SE3 3G 107
Tristram Clo. E17 3F 35
Tristram Rd. Brom 4H 125
Triton Ho. E14 4D 88
(off Cahir St.)
Triton Sq. NW1 4G 67 (3A 160)
Tritton Av. Croy 4J 151
Tritton Rd. SE21 3D 122
Triumph Clo. Hay 1E 94
Triumph Ho. Bark 3A 74
Triumph Rd. E6 6D 72
Triumph Trad. Est. N17 6B 18
Trocadero Cen. 7H 67 (3C 166)
Trocette Mans. SE1 3E 86
(off Bermondsey St.)
Trojan Ct. NW6 7G 47
Trojan Ind. Est. NW10 6B 46
Trojan Way. Croy 3K 151
Troon Clo. SE16 5H 87
Troon Clo. SE28 6D 74
Troon Ho. E1 6A 70
(off White Horse Rd.)
Troon St. E1 6A 70
Tropical Ct. W10 3F 65
(off Kilburn La.)
Trosley Rd. Belv 6G 93
Trossachs Rd. SE22 5E 104
Trothy Rd. SE1 4G 87
Trotman Ho. SE14 1J 105
(off Pomeroy St.)
Trott Rd. N10 7J 15
Trott St. SW11 1C 102
Troughton Rd. SE7 5K 89
Troutbeck. NW1 2K 159
Troutbeck Rd. SE14 1A 106
Trout Rd. W Dray 7A 58
Trouville Rd. SW4 6G 103
Trowbridge Rd. E9 6B 52
Trowlock Av. Tedd 6C 116
Trowlock Way. Tedd 6D 116
Troy Ct. SE18 4F 91
Troy Ct. W8 3J 83
(off Kensington High St.)
Troy Ind. Est. Harr 5K 25
Troy Rd. SE19 6D 122
Troy Town. SE15 3G 105
Trubshaw Rd. S'hall 3F 79
Truesdale Rd. E6 6D 72
Trulock Ct. N17 7B 18
Trulock Rd. N17 7B 18
Truman Clo. Edgw 7C 12
Trumans Rd. N16 5F 51
Trumble Gdns. T Hth 4B 140
Trumpers Way. W7 3J 79
Trumpington Rd. E7 4H 53
Trump St. EC2 6C 68 (1D 168)
Trundlers Way. Bush 1D 10
Trundle St. SE1 2C 86 (6C 168)
Trundleys Rd. SE8 5K 87
Trundley's Ter. SE8 4K 87
Truro Gdns. Ilf 7C 36
Truro Ho. Pinn 1D 24
Truro Rd. E17 4B 34
Truro Rd. N22 7D 16
Truro St. NW5 6E 48
Truro Way. N'holt 3G 59
Truslove Rd. SE27 5A 122
Trussley Rd. W6 3E 82
Trust Wlk. SE21 1B 122
Tryfan Clo. Ilf 5B 36
Tryon Cres. E9 1J 69
Tryon St. SW3 5D 84 (5E 170)
Trystings Clo. Clay 6A 146
Tuam Rd. SE18 6H 91
Tubbs Rd. NW10 2B 64
Tucklow Wlk. SW15 7B 100

Tudor Av. Hamp 6E 114
Tudor Av. Wor Pk 3D 148
Tudor Clo. N6 7G 31
Tudor Clo. NW3 5C 48
Tudor Clo. NW7 6H 13
Tudor Clo. NW9 2J 45
Tudor Clo. SW2 6K 103
Tudor Clo. Ashf 4A 112
Tudor Clo. Chess 5E 146
Tudor Clo. Chig 4K 21
Tudor Clo. Chst 1D 144
Tudor Clo. Hamp 5G 115
Tudor Clo. Pinn 5J 23
Tudor Clo. Sutt 5F 149
Tudor Clo. Wall 7G 151
Tudor Clo. Wfd G 5E 20
Tudor Ct. E17 7B 34
Tudor Ct. N1 6E 50
Tudor Ct. N22 7D 16
Tudor Ct. SE9 4C 108
Tudor Ct. SE16 1K 87 (off Princes Riverside Rd.)
Tudor Ct. W3 2G 81
Tudor Ct. Felt 4A 114
Tudor Ct. Sidc 3A 128
Tudor Ct. Stanw 6A 94
Tudor Ct. Tedd 6K 115
Tudor Ct. N. Wemb 5G 45
Tudor Ct. S. Wemb 5G 45
Tudor Cres. Enf 1H 7
Tudor Dri. King T 5D 116
Tudor Dri. Mord 6F 137
Tudor Enterprise Pk. Harr (HA1) 3K 43
Tudor Enterprise Pk. Harr (HA3) 3H 25
Tudor Est. NW10 2H 63
Tudor Gdns. NW9 2J 45
Tudor Gdns. SW13 3A 100
Tudor Gdns. W3 5G 63
Tudor Gdns. Harr 2H 25
Tudor Gdns. Twic 1K 115
Tudor Gdns. W Wick 3E 154
Tudor Gro. E9 7J 51
Tudor Ho. E9 7J 51
Tudor Ho. E16 1K 89 (off Wesley Av.)
Tudor Ho. W14 4F 83 (off Windsor Way)
Tudor Ho. Pinn 2A 24 (off Pinner Hill Rd.)
Tudor Pde. SE9 4C 108
Tudor Pde. Romf 7D 38
Tudor Pk. Golf Course 2F 5
Tudor Pl. SE19 7F 123
Tudor Pl. Mitc 7C 120
Tudor Rd. E4 6J 19
Tudor Rd. E6 1A 72
Tudor Rd. E9 1H 69
Tudor Rd. N9 7C 8
Tudor Rd. SE19 7F 123
Tudor Rd. SE25 5H 141
Tudor Rd. Ashf 6F 113
Tudor Rd. Bark 1K 73
Tudor Rd. Barn 3D 4
Tudor Rd. Beck 3E 142
Tudor Rd. Hamp 7E 114
Tudor Rd. Harr 2H 25
Tudor Rd. Hay 6F 59
Tudor Rd. Houn 4H 97
Tudor Rd. King T 7G 117
Tudor Rd. Pinn 2A 24
Tudor Rd. S'hall 7C 60
Tudor Sq. Hay 5F 59
Tudor Stacks. SE24 4C 104
Tudor St. EC4 7A 68 (2K 167)
Tudor Wlk. Bex 6E 110
Tudor Way. N14 1C 16
Tudor Way. W3 2G 81
Tudor Way. Orp 6H 145
Tudor Way. Uxb 6C 40
Tudor Well Clo. Stan 5G 11
Tudor Works. Hay 1B 78
Tudway Rd. SE3 3K 107
Tufnell Park 4G 49
Tufnell Pk. Rd. N19 & N7 4G 49
Tufton Ct. SW1 3J 85 (2E 172) (off Tufton St.)
Tufton Gdns. W Mol 2F 133
Tufton Rd. E4 4H 19
Tufton St. SW1 3J 85 (1E 172)
Tugboat St. SE28 2J 91
Tugela Rd. Croy 6D 140
Tugela St. SE6 2B 124
Tulip Clo. E6 5D 72
Tulip Clo. Croy 1K 153
Tulip Clo. Hamp 6D 114
Tulip Clo. S'hall 2G 79
Tulip Gdns. E4 3A 20
Tulip Gdns. Ilf 6F 55
Tullis Ho. E9 7J 51 (off Frampton Pk. Rd.)
Tull St. Mitc 7D 138
Tulse Clo. Beck 3E 142
Tulse Hill 1B 122
Tulse Hill. SW2 6A 104
Tulse Hill Est. SW2 6A 104
Tulse Ho. SW2 6A 104
Tulsemere Rd. SE27 2C 122
Tumbling Bay. W on T 6J 131
Tummons Gdns. SE25 2E 140
Tunbridge Ho. EC1 1K 161
Tuncombe Rd. N18 4K 17
Tunis Rd. W12 1E 82
Tunley Grn. E14 5B 70
Tunley Rd. NW10 1A 64
Tunley Rd. SW17 1E 120
Tunmarsh La. E13 3K 71
Tunnanleys. E6 6E 72
Tunnel App. E14 7A 70
Tunnel App. SE10 2G 89
Tunnel App. SE16 2J 87
Tunnel Av. SE10 2F 89 (in three parts)
Tunnel Av. Trad. Est. SE10 2F 89
Tunnel Gdns. N11 7B 16
Tunnel Link Rd. H'row A 5C 94
Tunnel Rd. SE16 2J 87
Tunnel Rd. E. H'row A 1D 94
Tunnel Rd. W. H'row A 1C 94
Tunstall Rd. SW9 4K 103
Tunstall Rd. Croy 1E 152
Tunstall Wlk. Bren 6E 80
Tunstock Way. Belv 3E 92
Tunworth Clo. NW9 6J 27
Tunworth Cres. SW15 6B 100
Tun Yd. SW8 2F 103 (off Silverthorne Rd.)
Tupelo Rd. E10 2D 52
Tupman Ho. SE16 2G 87 (off Scott Lidgett Cres.)
Tuppy St. SE28 2G 91
Turenne Clo. SW18 4A 102
Turin Rd. N9 7D 8
Turin St. E2 3G 69 (2K 163)
Turkey Oak Clo. SE19 7E 122
Turks Clo. Uxb 3C 58
Turk's Head Yd. EC1 5B 68 (5A 162)
Turk's Row. SW3 5D 84 (5F 171)
Turle Rd. N4 2K 49
Turle Rd. SW16 2J 139
Turlewray Clo. N4 1K 49
Turley Clo. E15 1G 71
Turnagain La. EC4 7A 162
Turnage Rd. Dag 1E 56
Turnberry Clo. NW4 2F 29
Turnberry Clo. SE16 5H 87
Turnberry Quay. E14 3D 88
Turnberry Way. Orp 7H 145
Turnbull Ho. N1 1B 68
Turnbury Clo. SE28 6D 74
Turnchapel M. SW4 3F 103
Turner Av. N15 4E 32
Turner Av. Mitc 1D 138
Turner Av. Twic 3G 115
Turner Clo. NW11 6K 29
Turner Clo. SW9 7B 86
Turner Clo. Hay 2E 58
Turner Clo. Wemb 6D 44
Turner Ct. SE16 2J 87 (off Albion St.)
Turner Dri. NW11 6K 29
Turner Ho. NW8 2C 66 (off Townshend Est.)
Turner Ho. SW1 4H 85 (4D 172) (off Herrick St.)
Turner Ho. Twic 6D 98 (off Clevedon Rd.)
Turner Pl. SW11 5C 102
Turner Rd. E17 3E 34
Turner Rd. Edgw 2E 26
Turner Rd. N Mald 7K 135
Turner's All. EC3 7E 68 (2G 169)
Turners Mdw. Way. Beck 1B 142
Turners Rd. E14 & E3 5B 70
Turner St. E1 5H 69
Turner St. E16 6H 71
Turner's Way. Croy 2A 152
Turners Wood. NW11 7A 30
Turneville Rd. W14 6H 83
Turney Rd. SE21 7C 104
Turnham Green 4A 82
Turnham Grn. Ter. W4 4A 82
Turnham Grn. Ter. M. W4 4A 82
Turnham Rd. SE4 5A 106
Turnmill St. EC1 4B 68 (4A 162)
Turnour Ho. E1 6H 69 (off Walburgh St.)
Turnpike Clo. SE8 7B 88
Turnpike Ct. Bexh 4D 110
Turnpike Ho. EC1 3B 68 (2B 162)
Turnpike La. N8 4K 31
Turnpike La. Sutt 5A 150
Turnpike La. Uxb 3A 58
Turnpike Link. Croy 2E 152
Turnpike Pde. N8 3B 32 (off Green Lanes)
Turnpike Way. Iswth 1A 98
Turnpin La. SE10 6E 88
Turnstone Clo. E13 3J 71
Turnstone Clo. NW9 2A 28
Turnstone Clo. Ick 5D 40
Turpentine La. SW1 5F 85 (5K 171)
Turpington Clo. Brom 6C 144
Turpington La. Brom 7C 144
Turpin Ho. SW11 1F 103
Turpin Rd. Felt 6H 95
Turpin's La. Wfd G 5J 21
Turpin Way. N19 2H 49 (in two parts)
Turpin Way. Wall 7F 151
Turquand St. SE17 4C 86
Turret Gro. SW4 3G 103
Turton Rd. Wemb 5E 44
Turville Ho. NW8 4C 66 (3C 158) (off Grendon St.)
Turville St. E2 4F 69 (3J 163)
Tuscan Ho. E2 3J 69 (off Knottisford St.)
Tuscan Rd. SE18 5H 91
Tuscany Ho. E17 2B 34
Tuskar St. SE10 6G 89
Tustin Est. SE15 6J 87
Tuttlebee La. Buck H 2D 20
Tuttle Ho. SW1 5H 85 (6C 172) (off Aylesford St.)
Tweedale Ct. E15 5E 52
Tweed Ct. W7 6J 61 (off Hanway Rd.)
Tweeddale Gro. Uxb 3E 40
Tweeddale Rd. Cars 1B 150
Tweed Glen. Romf 1K 39
Tweed Grn. Romf 1K 39
Tweed Ho. E14 4E 70 (off Teviot St.)
Tweedmouth Rd. E13 2K 71
Tweed Way. Romf 1K 39
Tweedy Clo. Enf 5A 8
Tweedy Rd. Brom 1J 143
Tweezer's All. WC2 2J 167
Twelvetrees Cres. E3 & E16 4E 70 (in three parts)
Twentyman Clo. Wfd G 5D 20
Twickenham 1A 116
Twickenham Bri. Twic & Rich 5C 98
Twickenham Clo. Croy 3K 151
Twickenham Gdns. Gnfd 5A 44
Twickenham Gdns. Harr 7D 10
Twickenham Rd. E11 2E 52
Twickenham Rd. Felt 3D 114
Twickenham Rd. Iswth 5A 98
Twickenham Rd. Rich 4C 98
Twickenham Rd. Tedd 4A 116 (in two parts)
Twickenham Rugby Union Football Ground. 6J 97
Twickenham Stadium Tours. 6J 97 (Twickenham Rugby Union Football Ground)
Twickenham Trad. Est. Twic 6K 97
Twig Folly Clo. E2 2K 69
Twigg Clo. Eri 7K 93
Twilley St. SW18 7K 101
Twin Bridges Bus. Pk. S Croy 6D 152
Twine Clo. Bark 3B 74
Twine Ct. E1 7J 69
Twineham Grn. N12 4D 14
Twine Ter. E3 4B 70 (off Ropery St.)
Twining Av. Twic 3G 115
Twinn Rd. NW7 6B 14
Twin Tumps Way. SE28 7A 74
Twisden Rd. NW5 4F 49
Twybridge Way. NW10 7J 45
Twycross M. SE10 5G 89
Twyford Abbey Rd. NW10 3F 63
Twyford Av. N2 3D 30
Twyford Av. W3 7G 63
Twyford Ct. N10 3E 30
Twyford Ct. Wemb 2E 62 (off Vicars Bri. Clo.)
Twyford Cres. W3 1G 81
Twyford Ho. N5 3B 50
Twyford Ho. N15 6E 32 (off Chisley Rd.)
Twyford Pl. WC2 6K 67 (7G 161)
Twyford Rd. Cars 1B 150
Twyford Rd. Harr 1F 43
Twyford Rd. Ilf 5G 55
Twyford St. N1 1K 67
Tyas Rd. E16 4H 71
Tybenham Rd. SW19 3J 137
Tyberry Rd. Enf 3C 8
Tyburn La. Harr 7K 25
Tyburn Way. W1 7D 66 (2F 165)
Tyers Est. SE1 6G 169
Tyers Ga. SE1 2E 86 (7G 169)
Tyers St. SE11 5K 85 (6G 173)
Tyers Ter. SE11 5K 85 (6G 173)
Tyeshurst Clo. SE2 5E 92
Tylecroft Rd. SW16 2J 139
Tylehurst Gdns. Ilf 5G 55
Tyler Clo. E2 2F 69
Tyler Rd. S'hall 3F 79
Tylers Ct. E17 4C 34 (off Westbury Rd.)
Tyler's Ct. W1 1C 166
Tylers Ct. Wemb 2E 62
Tylers Ga. Harr 6E 26
Tylers Path. Cars 4D 150
Tyler St. SE10 5G 89 (in two parts)
Tylney Av. SE19 5F 123 (in two parts)
Tylney Ho. E1 6H 69 (off Nelson St.)
Tylney Rd. E7 4A 54
Tylney Rd. Brom 2B 144
Tynamara. King T 4D 134 (off Portsmouth Rd.)
Tynan Clo. Felt 1J 113
Tyndale Ct. E14 5D 88 (off Transom Sq.)
Tyndale La. N1 7B 50
Tyndale Mans. N1 7B 50 (off Upper St.)
Tyndale Ter. N1 7B 50
Tyndall Gdns. E10 2E 52
Tyndall Rd. E10 2E 52
Tyndall Rd. Well 3K 109
Tyne Ct. W7 6J 61 (off Hanway Rd.)
Tyneham Clo. SW11 3E 102
Tyneham Rd. SW11 2E 102
Tyne Ho. King T 1D 134
Tynemouth Clo. E6 6F 73
Tynemouth Dri. Enf 1B 8
Tynemouth Rd. N15 4F 33
Tynemouth Rd. SE18 5J 91
Tynemouth Rd. Mitc 7E 120
Tynemouth St. SW6 2A 102
Tyne St. E1 6F 69 (7K 163)
Tynsdale Clo. NW10 6A 46
Tynwald Ho. SE26 3G 123
Type St. E2 2K 69
Tyrawley Rd. SW6 1K 101
Tyre La. NW9 4A 28
Tyrell Clo. Harr 4J 43
Tyrell Ct. Cars 4D 150
Tyrell Ho. Beck 5D 124 (off Beckenham Hill Rd.)
Tyrols Rd. SE23 1K 123
Tyrone Rd. E6 2D 72
Tyron Way. Sidc 4J 127
Tyrrell Av. Well 5A 110
Tyrrell Ho. SW1 6G 85 (7B 172) (off Churchill Gdns.)
Tyrrell Rd. SE22 4G 105
Tyrrell Sq. Mitc 1C 138
Tyrrel Way. NW9 7B 28
Tyrwhitt Rd. SE4 3C 106
Tysoe St. EC1 3A 68 (2K 161)
Tyson Gdns. SE23 7J 105
Tyson Rd. SE23 7J 105
Tyssen Pas. E8 6F 51
Tyssen Rd. N16 3F 51
Tyssen St. E8 6F 51
Tyssen St. N1 2E 68
Tytherton. E2 2J 69 (off Cyprus St.)
Tytherton Rd. N19 3H 49

Uamvar St. E14 5D 70
UCI Empire Cinema. 7H 67 (2D 166) (off Leicester Sq.)
Uckfield Gro. Mitc 7E 120
Udall St. SW1 4G 85 (4B 172)
Udimore Ho. W10 5E 64 (off Sutton Way)
Udney Pk. Rd. Tedd 6A 116
Uffington Rd. NW10 1C 64
Uffington Rd. SE27 4A 122
Ufford Clo. Harr 7A 10
Ufford Rd. Harr 7A 10
Ufford St. SE1 2A 86 (6K 167)
Ufton Ct. N'holt 3B 60
Ufton Gro. N1 7D 50
Ufton Rd. N1 7D 50 (in two parts)
UGC Haymarket Cinema. 7H 67 (3C 166) (off Haymarket)
UGC Trocadero Cinema. 7H 67 (3C 166) (off Windmill St.)
Uhura Sq. N16 3E 50
Ujima Ct. SW16 4J 121
Ullathorne Rd. SW16 4G 121
Ulleswater Rd. N14 3D 16
Ullin St. E14 5E 70
Ullswater Clo. SW15 4K 117
Ullswater Clo. Brom 7G 125
Ullswater Clo. Hay 2G 59

Ullswater Ct. Harr 7E 24
Ullswater Cres. SW15 4K 117
Ullswater Ho. SE15 6J 87 (off Hillbeck Clo.)
Ullswater Rd. SE27 2B 122
Ullswater Rd. SW13 7C 82
Ulster Gdns. N13 4H 17
Ulster Pl. NW1 4F 67 (4J 159)
Ulster Ter. NW1 3H 159
Ulundi Rd. SE3 6G 89
Ulva Rd. SW15 5F 101
Ulverscroft Rd. SE22 5F 105
Ulverstone Rd. SE27 2B 122
Ulverston Rd. E17 2F 35
Ulysses Rd. NW6 5H 47
Umberston St. E1 6G 69
Umbria St. SW15 6C 100
Umfreville Rd. N4 6B 32
Undercliff Rd. SE13 3C 106
Underhill. 5D 4
Underhill. Barn 5D 4
Underhill Ct. Barn 5D 4
Underhill Ho. E14 5C 70 (off Burgess St.)
Underhill Pas. NW1 1F 67 (off Camden High St.)
Underhill Rd. SE22 5G 105
Underhill St. NW1 1F 67
Underne Av. N14 2A 16
Undershaft. EC3 6E 68 (1G 169)
Undershaw Rd. Brom 3H 125
Underwood. New Ad 5E 154
Underwood Ct. E10 1D 52 (off Leyton Grange Est.)
Underwood Ho. W6 3D 82 (off Sycamore Gdns.)
Underwood Rd. E1 4G 69
Underwood Rd. E4 5J 19
Underwood Rd. Wfd G 7F 21
Underwood Row. N1 3C 68 (1D 162)
Underwood St. N1 3C 68 (1D 162)
Underwood, The. SE9 2D 126
Undine Rd. E14 4D 88
Undine St. SW17 5D 120
Uneeda Dri. Gnfd 1H 61
Unicorn Building. E1 7K 69 (off Jardine Rd.)
Union Clo. E11 4F 53
Union Cotts. E15 7G 53
Union Ct. EC2 7G 163
Union Ct. SW4 2J 103
Union Ct. W9 5J 65 (off Elmfield Way)
Union Ct. Rich 5E 98
Union Dri. E1 4A 70
Union Gro. SW8 2H 103
Union M. SW4 2J 103
Union Rd. N11 6C 16
Union Rd. SW8 & SW4 2H 103
Union Rd. Brom 5B 144
Union Rd. Croy 7C 140
Union Rd. N'holt 2E 60
Union Rd. Wemb 6E 44
Union Sq. N1 1C 68
Union St. E15 1F 71
Union St. SE1 1B 86 (5A 168)
Union St. Barn 3B 4
Union St. King T 2D 134
Union Theatre. 5B 168
Union Wlk. E2 3E 68 (1H 163)
Union Wharf. N1 1C 68
Union Yd. W1 6F 67 (1K 165)
Unitair Cen. Felt 6E 94
Unit Workshops. E1 6G 69 (off Adler St.)
Unity Clo. NW10 6C 46
Unity Clo. SE19 5C 122
Unity Clo. New Ad 7D 154
Unity M. NW1 2H 67
Unity Trad. Est. Wfd G 2B 36
Unity Way. SE7 3B 90
Unity Wharf. SE1 2F 87 (6K 169) (off Mill St.)
University Clo. NW7 7G 13
University College. 4H 67 (4C 160)
University Gdns. Bex 7F 111
University of East London. (Docklands Campus) 7E 72
University of London Observatory. 6G 13
University of London. (Senate House) 5H 67 (5D 160)
University of London Union. 4H 67 (4D 160)
University of North London. 5C 50 (Highbury Gro.)
University of North London. 5A 50 (Holloway Rd.)
University of Westminster. (Cavendish Campus) 5F 67 (5K 159) (Bolsover St.)
University of Westminster. (Cavendish Campus) 5G 67 (5A 160) (Hanson St.)
University of Westminster. (Harrow Campus) 7A 26
University of Westminster. (Marylebone Campus) 5E 66 (5G 159)
University of Westminster. (Regent Campus) 6A 160 (Lit. Titchfield St.)
University of Westminster. (Regent Campus) 6F 67 (7K 159) (Regent St.)
University of Westminster. (Regent Campus) 6B 160 (Wells St.)
University Pl. Eri 7J 93
University Rd. SW19 6B 120
University St. WC1 4G 67 (4B 160)
University Way. E16 7E 72
Unwin Av. Felt 5F 95
Unwin Clo. SE15 6G 87
Unwin Mans. W14 6H 83 (off Queen's Club Gdns.)
Unwin Rd. SW7 3B 84 (1A 170)
Unwin Rd. Iswth 3J 97
Upbrook M. W2 6A 66 (1A 164)
Upcerne Rd. SW10 7A 84
Upchurch Clo. SE20 7H 123
Upcott Ho. E9 7J 51 (off Frampton Pk. Rd.)
Upcroft Av. Edgw 5D 12
Updale Rd. Sidc 4K 127
Upfield. Croy 3H 153
Upfield Rd. W7 5K 61
Upgrove Mnr. Way. SE24 7A 104
Uphall Rd. Ilf 5F 55
Upham Pk. Rd. W4 4A 82
Uphill Dri. NW7 5F 13
Uphill Dri. NW9 5J 27
Uphill Gro. NW7 4F 13
Uphill Rd. NW7 4F 13
Upland M. SE22 5G 105
Upland Rd. E13 4J 71
Upland Rd. SE22 5G 105
Upland Rd. Bexh 3F 111
Upland Rd. S Croy 5D 152
Upland Rd. Sutt 7B 150
Uplands. Beck 2C 142
Uplands Av. E17 2K 33
Uplands Bus. Pk. E17 3K 33
Uplands Clo. SW14 5H 99
Uplands Ct. N21 7F 7 (off Green, The)
Uplands End. Wfd G 7H 21
Uplands Pk. Rd. Enf 2F 7
Uplands Rd. N8 5K 31
Uplands Rd. E Barn 1K 15
Uplands Rd. Romf 3D 38
Uplands Rd. Wfd G 7H 21
Uplands, The. Ruis 1J 41
Uplands Way. N21 5F 7
Upnall Ho. SE15 6J 87
Upney La. Bark 5J 55
Upnor Way. SE17 5E 86
Uppark Dri. Ilf 6G 37
Up. Abbey Rd. Belv 4F 93
Up. Addison Gdns. W14 2G 83
Up. Bardsey Wlk. N1 6C 50 (off Douglas Rd. N.)
Up. Belgrave St. SW1 3E 84 (1H 171)
Up. Berenger Wlk. SW10 7B 84 (off Berenger Wlk.)
Up. Berkeley St. W1 6D 66
Up. Beulah Hill. SE19 1E 140
Up. Blantyre Wlk. SW10 7B 84 (off Blantyre Wlk.)
Up. Brighton Rd. Surb 6D 134
Up. Brockley Rd. SE4 3B 106
Up. Brook St. W1 7E 66 (2G 165)
Up. Butts. Bren 6C 80
Up. Caldy Wlk. N1 7C 50 (off Caldy Wlk.)
Up. Camelford Wlk. W11 6G 65 (off St Mark's Rd.)
Up. Cavendish Av. N3 3J 29
Up. Cheyne Row. SW3 7C 170
Upper Clapton. 2H 51
Up. Clapton Rd. E5 2H 51
Up. Clarendon Wlk. W11 6G 65 (off Clarendon Rd.)
Up. Dartrey Wlk. SW10 7A 84 (off Whistler Wlk.)
Up. Dengie Wlk. N1 1C 68 (off Baddow Wlk.)
Upper Edmonton. 5C 18
Upper Elmers End. 5B 142
Up. Elmers End Rd. Beck 4A 142
Up. Farm Rd. W Mol 4D 132
Upper Feilde. W1 7E 66 (2G 165) (off Park St.)
Upper Fosters. NW4 4E 28 (off New Brent St.)
Up. Green E. Mitc 3D 138
Up. Green W. Mitc 2D 138 (in two parts)
Up. Grosvenor St. W1 7E 66 (3G 165)
Up. Grotto Rd. Twic 2K 115
Upper Ground. SE1 1A 86 (4J 167)
Upper Gro. SE25 4E 140
Up. Grove Rd. Belv 6F 93
Up. Gulland Wlk. N1 6C 50 (off Oronsay Wlk.)
Upper Halliford. 4G 131
Up. Halliford By-Pass. Shep 5G 131
Up. Halliford Grn. Shep 4G 131
Up. Halliford Rd. Shep 3G 131
Up. Hampstead Wlk. NW3 4A 48
Up. Ham Rd. Rich 4D 116
Up. Handa Wlk. N1 6D 50 (off Handa Wlk.)
Up. Hawkwell Wlk. N1 1C 68 (off Baddow Wlk.)
Up. Hilldrop Est. N7 5H 49
Upper Holloway. 2G 49
Up. Holly Hill Rd. Belv 5H 93
Up. James St. W1 7G 67 (2B 166)
Up. John St. W1 7G 67 (2B 166)
Up. Lismore Wlk. N1 6D 50 (off Clephane St.)
Upper Mall. W6 5C 82 (in two parts)
Upper Marsh. SE1 3K 85 (1H 173)
Up. Montagu St. W1 5D 66 (5E 158)
Up. Mulgrave Rd. Sutt 7G 149
Up. North St. E14 5C 70
Upper Norwood. 1E 140
Up. Palace Rd. E Mol 3G 133
Up. Park Rd. N11 5A 16
Up. Park Rd. NW3 5D 48
Up. Park Rd. Belv 4H 93
Up. Park Rd. Brom 1K 143
Up. Park Rd. King T 6G 117
Up. Phillimore Gdns. W8 2J 83
Up. Ramsey Wlk. N1 6D 50 (off Ramsey Wlk.)
Up. Rawreth Wlk. N1 1C 68 (off Basire St.)
Up. Richmond Rd. SW15 4B 100
Up. Richmond Rd. W. Rich & SW14 4G 99
Upper Rd. E13 3J 71
Upper Rd. Wall 5H 151
Upper Ruxley. 7G 129
Up. St Martin's La. WC2 7J 67 (2E 166)
Up. Selsdon Rd. S Croy 7F 153
Up. Sheridan Rd. Belv 4G 93
Upper Shirley. 4K 153
Up. Shirley Rd. Croy 2J 153
Upper Sq. Iswth 3A 98
Upper St. N1 2A 68
Up. Sunbury Rd. Hamp 1C 132
Up. Sutton La. Houn 7E 78
Upper Sydenham. 3H 123
Up. Tachbrook St. SW1 4G 85 (3B 172)
Up. Talbot Wlk. W11 6G 65 (off Talbot Wlk.)
Up. Teddington Rd. King T 7C 116
Upper Ter. NW3 3A 48
Up. Thames St. EC4 7B 68 (2B 168)
Up. Tollington Pk. N4 1A 50 (in two parts)
Upperton Rd. Sidc 5K 127
Upperton Rd. E. E13 3A 72
Upperton Rd. W. E13 3A 72
Upper Tooting. 3D 120
Up. Tooting Pk. SW17 2D 120
Up. Tooting Rd. SW17 4D 120
Up. Town Rd. Gnfd 4F 61
Up. Tulse Hill. SW2 7K 103
Up. Vernon Rd. Sutt 5B 150
Upper Walthamstow. 4F 35
Up. Walthamstow Rd. E17 4E 34
Up. Whistler Wlk. SW10 7A 84 (off Worlds End Est.)
Up. Wickham La. Well 7B 92
Up. Wimpole St. W1 5E 66 (5H 159)
Up. Woburn Pl. WC1 3H 67 (2D 160)
Uppingham Av. Stan 1B 26
Upsdell Av. N13 6F 17
Upshire Ho. E17 2B 34
Upstall St. SE5 1B 104
Upton. 5D 110 (Bexleyheath)
Upton. 7J 53 (Plaistow)
Upton Av. E7 7J 53
Upton Clo. NW2 3G 47
Upton Clo. Bex 6F 111
Upton Ct. SE20 7J 123
Upton Dene. Sutt 7K 149
Upton Gdns. Harr 5B 26
Upton La. E7 7J 53
Upton Lodge. E7 6J 53
Upton Lodge Clo. Bush 1B 10
Upton Park. 2B 72
Upton Pk. Rd. E7 7K 53
Upton Rd. N18 5B 18
Upton Rd. SE18 6G 91
Upton Rd. Bexh 4E 110
Upton Rd. Houn 3E 96
Upton Rd. T Hth 2D 140
Upton Rd. S. Bex 6F 111
Upton Vs. Bexh 4E 110
Upway. N12 6H 15
Upwey Ho. N1 1E 68
Upwood Rd. SE12 6J 107
Upwood Rd. SW16 1J 139
Urlwin St. SE5 6C 86
Urlwin Wlk. SW9 1A 104
Urmston Dri. SW19 1G 119
Urmston Ho. E14 4E 88 (off Seyssel St.)
Urquhart Ct. Beck 7B 124
Ursula Lodges. Sidc 5B 128 (off Eynswood Dri.)
Ursula M. N4 1C 50
Ursula St. SW11 1C 102
Urswick Gdns. Dag 7E 56
Urswick Rd. E9 5J 51
Urswick Rd. Dag 7D 56
Usborne M. SW8 7K 85
Usher Rd. E3 1B 70
Usk Rd. SW11 4A 102
Usk St. E2 3K 69
Utopia Village. NW1 7E 48
Uvedale Rd. Dag 3G 57
Uvedale Rd. Enf 5J 7
Uverdale Rd. SW10 7A 84
Uxbridge Ct. King T 5D 134 (off Uxbridge Rd.)
Uxbridge Rd. W5 & W3 7E 62
Uxbridge Rd. W7 1K 79
Uxbridge Rd. W12 1B 82
Uxbridge Rd. W13 & W5 1B 80
Uxbridge Rd. Felt 2A 114
Uxbridge Rd. Hamp H 4E 114
Uxbridge Rd. Harr & Stan 7B 10
Uxbridge Rd. Hil & Hay 3C 58
Uxbridge Rd. King T 4D 134
Uxbridge Rd. Pinn 2A 24
Uxbridge Rd. S'hall 1E 78
Uxbridge St. W8 1J 83
Uxendon Cres. Wemb 1E 44
Uxendon Hill. Wemb 1F 45

Vaizeys Wharf. SE7 3K 89 (off Riverside)
Valan Leas. Brom 3G 143
Vale Clo. N2 3D 30
Vale Clo. W9 3A 66
Vale Clo. Orp 4E 156
Vale Clo. Twic 3A 116
Vale Cotts. SW15 3A 118
Vale Ct. W3 1B 82
Vale Ct. W9 3A 66
Vale Ct. New Bar 4E 4
Vale Cres. SW15 4A 118
Vale Cft. Pinn 5C 24
Vale Dri. Barn 4C 4
Vale End. SE22 4F 105
Vale Est., The. W3 1A 82
Vale Gro. N4 7C 32
Vale Gro. W3 2K 81
Vale La. W3 5G 63
Vale Lodge. SE23 2J 123
Valence Av. E4 1B 20
Valence Av. Dag 1D 56
Valence Cir. Dag 3D 56
Valence House Mus. 3E 56
Valence Rd. Eri 7K 93
Valence Wood Rd. Dag 3D 56
Valencia Rd. Stan 4H 11
Valentia Pl. SW9 4A 104
Valentine Av. Bex 2E 128
Valentine Ct. SE23 2K 123 (in two parts)
Valentine Pl. SE1 2B 86 (6A 168)
Valentine Rd. E9 6K 51
Valentine Rd. Harr 3F 43
Valentine Row. SE1 2B 86 (7A 168)
Valentines Rd. Ilf 1F 55

Valentine's Way. Romf 2K 57
Vale of Health. 3A 48
Vale of Health. NW3 3B 48
Vale Pde. SW15 3A 118
Valerian Way. E15 3G 71
Valerie Ct. Sutt 7K 149
Vale Ri. NW11 1H 47
Vale Rd. E7 6K 53
Vale Rd. N4 7C 32
Vale Rd. Brom 1E 144
Vale Rd. Eps 4B 148
Vale Rd. Mitc 3H 139
Vale Rd. Sutt 4K 149
Vale Rd. Wor Pk 3B 148
Vale Rd. N. Surb 2E 146
Vale Rd. S. Surb 2E 146
Vale Row. N5 3B 50
Vale Royal. N7 7J 49
Vale Royal Ho. WC2 7H 67 (2D 166) (off Charing Cross Rd.)
Valery Pl. Hamp 7E 114
Valeside Ct. Barn 4E 4
Vale St. SE27 3D 122
Valeswood Rd. Brom 5H 125
Vale Ter. N4 6C 32
Vale, The. N10 1E 30
Vale, The. N14 7C 6
Vale, The. NW11 3F 47
Vale, The. SW3 6B 84 (7A 170)
Vale, The. W3 1K 81
Vale, The. Croy 2K 153
Vale, The. Felt 6K 95
Vale, The. Houn 6C 78
Vale, The. Ruis 4A 42
Vale, The. Sun 6J 113
Vale, The. Wfd G 7D 20
Valetta Gro. E13 2J 71
Valetta Rd. W3 2A 82
Valette Ct. N10 4F 31 (off St James's La.)
Valette Ho. E9 6J 51
Valette St. E9 6J 51
Valiant Clo. N'holt 3B 60
Valiant Clo. Romf 2H 39
Valiant Ho. E14 2E 88 (off Plevna St.)
Valiant Ho. SE7 5A 90
Valiant Way. E6 5D 72
Vallance Rd. E2 & E1 3G 69
Vallance Rd. N10 2G 31
Vallentin Rd. E17 4E 34
Valley Av. N12 4G 15
Valley Clo. Pinn 2K 23
Valley Dri. NW9 6G 27
Valleyfield Rd. SW16 5K 121
Valley Fields Cres. Enf 2F 7
Valley Gdns. SW19 7B 120
Valley Gdns. Wemb 7F 45
Valley Gro. SE7 5A 90
Valleylink Est. Enf 6F 9
Valley M. Twic 2K 115
Valley Rd. SW16 5K 121
Valley Rd. Belv 4H 93
Valley Rd. Brom 2G 143
Valley Rd. Eri 4J 93
Valley Rd. Orp 7B 128
Valley Rd. Uxb 2A 58
Valley Side. E4 2H 19
Valley Side. SE7 5B 90
Valley Side Pde. E4 2H 19
Valley Vw. Barn 6B 4
Valley Wlk. Croy 2J 153
Valliere Rd. NW10 3C 64
Valliers Wood Rd. Sidc 1J 127
Vallis Way. W13 5A 62
Vallis Way. Chess 4D 146
Valmar Rd. SE5 1C 104
Valmar Trad. Est. SE5 1C 104
Val McKenzie Av. N7 3A 50
Valnay St. SW17 5D 120
Valognes Av. E17 1A 34
Valois Ho. SE1 3F 87 (off Grange, The)
Valonia Gdns. SW18 6H 101
Vambery Rd. SE18 6G 91
Vanbrough Cres. N'holt 1A 60
Vanbrugh Castle. SE3 6G 89 (off Maze Hill)
Vanbrugh Clo. E16 5B 72
Vanbrugh Ct. SE11 4K 173
Vanbrugh Dri. W on T 7A 132
Vanbrugh Fields. SE3 6H 89
Vanbrugh Hill. SE10 & SE3 5H 89
Vanbrugh Ho. E9 7J 51 (off Loddiges Rd.)
Vanbrugh Pk. SE3 7H 89
Vanbrugh Pk. Rd. SE3 7H 89
Vanbrugh Pk. Rd. W. SE3 7H 89
Vanbrugh Rd. W4 3K 81
Vanbrugh Ter. SE3 1H 107
Vanburgh Clo. Orp 7J 145
Vanburgh Ho. E1 5F 69 (5J 163) (off Folgate St.)
Vancouver Ho. E1 1H 87 (off Reardon Path)
Vancouver Mans. Edgw 1H 27
Vancouver Rd. SE23 2A 124
Vancouver Rd. Edgw 1H 27
Vancouver Rd. Hay 4K 59
Vancouver Rd. Rich 4C 116
Vanderbilt Rd. SW18 1K 119
Vanderville Gdns. N2 2A 30
Vandome Clo. E16 6K 71
Vandon Ct. SW1 3G 85 (1B 172) (off Petty France)
Vandon Pas. SW1 3G 85 (1B 172)
Vandon St. SW1 3G 85 (1B 172)
Van Dyck Av. N Mald 7K 135
Vandyke Clo. SW15 7F 101
Vandyke Cross. SE9 5C 108
Vandy St. EC2 4E 68 (4G 163)
Vane Clo. NW3 5B 48
Vane Clo. Harr 6F 27
Vanessa Clo. Belv 5G 93
Vanessa Way. Bex 3K 129
Vane St. SW1 4G 85 (3B 172)
Vangaurd. NW9 7F 13
Vange Ho. W10 5E 64 (off Sutton Way)
Van Gogh Clo. Iswth 3A 98
Van Gogh Ct. E14 3F 89
Vanguard Building. E14 2B 88
Vanguard Clo. E16 5J 71
Vanguard Clo. Croy 1B 152
Vanguard Clo. Romf 2G 39
Vanguard St. SE8 1C 106
Vanguard Trad. Est. E15 1E 70
Vanguard Way. H'row A 2G 95
Vanguard Way. Wall 7J 151
Vanneck Sq. SW15 5C 100
Vanoc Gdns. Brom 4J 125
Vansittart Rd. E7 4H 53
Vansittart St. SE14 7A 88
Vanston Pl. SW6 7J 83
Vantage M. E14 1E 88 (off Preston's Rd.)
Vantage Pl. W8 3J 83
Vantage W. W3 4F 81
Vantrey Ho. SE11 4J 173
Vant Rd. SW17 5D 120
Varcoe Rd. SE16 5H 87
Vardens Rd. SW11 4B 102
Varden St. E1 6H 69
Vardon Clo. W3 6K 63
Vardon Ho. SE10 1E 106
Varley Ho. NW6 1J 65
Varley Pde. NW9 4A 28
Varley Rd. E16 6K 71
Varley Way. Mitc 2B 138
Varna Rd. SW6 7G 83
Varna Rd. Hamp 1F 133
Varndell St. NW1 3G 67 (1A 160)
Varsity Dri. Twic 5J 97
Varsity Row. SW14 2J 99
Vartry Rd. N15 6D 32
Vassall Ho. E3 3A 70 (off Antill Rd.)
Vassall Rd. SW9 7A 86
Vat Ho. SW8 7J 85 (off Rita Rd.)
Vauban Est. SE16 3F 87
Vauban St. SE16 3F 87
Vaudeville Ct. N4 2A 50
Vaudeville Theatre. 7J 67 (3F 167) (off Strand)
Vaughan Almshouses. Ashf 5D 112 (off Feltham Hill Rd.)
Vaughan Av. NW4 5C 28
Vaughan Av. W6 4B 82
Vaughan Clo. Hamp 6C 114
Vaughan Est. E2 1J 163
Vaughan Gdns. Ilf 7D 36
Vaughan Ho. SE1 2B 86 (6A 168) (off Blackfriars Rd.)
Vaughan Ho. SW4 7G 103
Vaughan Rd. E15 6H 53
Vaughan Rd. SE5 2C 104
Vaughan Rd. Harr 7G 25
Vaughan Rd. Th Dit 7B 134
Vaughan Rd. Well 2K 109
Vaughan St. SE16 2B 88
Vaughan Way. E1 7G 69
Vaughan Williams Clo. SE8 7C 88
Vauxhall. 5J 85 (6F 173)
Vauxhall Bri. SW1 & SE1 5J 85 (6E 172)
Vauxhall Bri. Rd. SW1 3G 85 (2A 172)
Vauxhall Cross. (Junct.) 5J 85
Vauxhall Cross. SE1 5J 85 (6F 173)
Vauxhall Distribution Pk. SW8 7C 172
Vauxhall Gdns. S Croy 6C 152
Vauxhall Gro. SW8 6K 85 (7G 173)
Vauxhall St. SE11 5K 85 (5H 173)
Vauxhall Wlk. SE11 5K 85 (5G 173)
Vawdrey Clo. E1 4J 69
Veals Mead. Mitc 1C 138
Vectis Gdns. SW17 6F 121
Vectis Rd. SW17 6F 121
Veda Rd. SE13 4C 106
Vega Rd. Bush 1B 10
Veitch Clo. Felt 7H 95
Veldene Way. Harr 3D 42
Velde Way. SE22 5E 104
Velletri Ho. E2 2K 69 (off Mace St.)
Vellum Dri. Cars 3E 150
Venables Clo. Dag 4H 57
Venables St. NW8 4B 66 (5B 158)
Vencourt Pl. W6 4C 82
Venetian Rd. SE5 2C 104
Venetia Rd. N4 6B 32
Venetia Rd. W5 2D 80
Venice Ct. SE5 7C 86 (off Bowyer St.)
Venner Rd. SE26 6J 123
Venn Ho. N1 1K 67 (off Barnsbury Est.)
Venn St. SW4 4G 103
Ventnor Av. Stan 1B 26
Ventnor Dri. N20 3E 14
Ventnor Gdns. Bark 6J 55
Ventnor Rd. SE14 7K 87
Ventnor Rd. Sutt 7K 149
Venture Clo. Bex 7E 110
Venture Ct. SE12 7J 107
Venture Ho. W10 6F 65 (off Bridge Clo.)
Venue St. E14 5E 70
Venus Rd. SE18 3D 90
Vera Av. N21 5F 7
Vera Lynn Clo. E7 4J 53
Vera Rd. SW6 1G 101
Verbena Clo. E16 4H 71
Verbena Gdns. W6 5C 82
Verdant Ct. SE6 7G 107 (off Verdant La.)
Verdant La. SE6 7G 107
Verdayne Av. Croy 1K 153
Verdi Ho. W10 2G 65 (off Herries St.)
Verdun Rd. SE18 6A 92
Verdun Rd. SW13 6C 82
Vereker Dri. Sun 3J 131
Vereker Rd. W14 5G 83
Vere St. W1 6F 67 (1J 165)
Veritas Ho. Sidc 2A 128 (off Station Rd.)
Verity Clo. W11 7G 65
Vermeer Ct. E14 3F 89
Vermeer Gdns. SE15 4J 105
Vermont Clo. Enf 4G 7
Vermont Ho. E17 2B 34
Vermont Rd. SE19 6D 122
Vermont Rd. SW18 6K 101
Vermont Rd. Sutt 3K 149
Verne Ct. W3 3J 81 (off Vincent Rd.)
Verney Gdns. Dag 4E 56
Verney Ho. NW8 3B 158
Verney Rd. SE16 6G 87
Verney Rd. Dag 4E 56 (in two parts)
Verney St. NW10 3K 45
Verney Way. SE16 5H 87
Vernham Rd. SE18 6G 91
Vernon Av. E12 4D 54
Vernon Av. SW20 2F 137
Vernon Av. Wfd G 7E 20
Vernon Clo. Eps 6J 147
Vernon Ct. NW2 3H 47
Vernon Ct. W5 7C 62
Vernon Ct. Stan 1B 26
Vernon Cres. Barn 6K 5
Vernon Dri. Stan 1A 26
Vernon Ho. SE11 6H 173
Vernon Ho. WC1 5J 67 (6F 161) (off Vernon Pl.)
Vernon M. E17 5B 34
Vernon M. W14 4G 83
Vernon Pl. WC1 5J 67 (6F 161)
Vernon Ri. WC1 3K 67 (1H 161)
Vernon Ri. Gnfd 5H 43
Vernon Rd. E3 2B 70
Vernon Rd. E11 1G 53
Vernon Rd. E15 7G 53
Vernon Rd. E17 5B 34
Vernon Rd. N8 3A 32
Vernon Rd. SW14 3K 99
Vernon Rd. Felt 2H 113
Vernon Rd. Ilf 1K 55
Vernon Rd. Sutt 5A 150
Vernon Sq. WC1 3K 67 (1H 161)
Vernon St. W14 4G 83
Vernon Yd. W11 7H 65
Veroan Rd. Bexh 2E 110
Verona Ct. SE14 6K 87 (off Myers La.)
Verona Dri. Surb 2E 146
Verona Rd. E7 7J 53
Veronica Gdns. SW16 1G 139
Veronica Ho. SE4 3B 106
Veronica Rd. SW17 2F 121
Veronique Gdns. Ilf 5G 37
Verran Rd. SW12 7F 103
Versailles Rd. SE20 7G 123
Verulam Av. E17 6B 34
Verulam Bldgs. WC1 5H 161
Verulam Ct. NW9 7C 28
Verulam Ct. S'hall 6G 61 (off Haldane Rd.)
Verulam Ho. W6 2D 82 (off Hammersmith Gro.)
Verulam Rd. Gnfd 4E 60
Verulam St. WC1 5A 68 (5J 161)
Verwood Dri. Barn 3J 5
Verwood Ho. SW8 7K 85 (off Cobbett St.)
Verwood Lodge. E14 3F 89 (off Manchester Rd.)
Verwood Rd. Harr 2G 25
Veryan Ct. N8 5H 31
Vesage Ct. EC1 5A 68 (6K 161) (off Leather La.)
Vesey Path. E14 6D 70
Vespan Rd. W12 2C 82
Vesta Rd. SE4 2A 106
Vestris Rd. SE23 2K 123
Vestry Ct. SW1 3H 85 (2D 172) (off Monck St.)
Vestry House Mus. 4D 34
Vestry M. SE5 1E 104
Vestry Rd. E17 4D 34
Vestry Rd. SE5 1E 104
Vestry St. N1 3D 68 (1E 162)
Vevey St. SE6 2B 124
Veysey Gdns. Dag 3G 57
Viaduct Bldgs. EC1 5A 68 (6K 161)
Viaduct Pl. E2 3H 69
Viaduct Rd. N2 2B 30
Viaduct St. E2 3H 69
Viaduct, The. E18 2J 35
Viaduct, The. Wemb 1E 62
Vian St. SE13 3D 106
Viant Ho. NW10 7K 45
Vibart Gdns. SW2 7K 103
Vibart Wlk. N1 1J 67 (off Outram Pl.)
Vibia Clo. Stanw 7A 94
Vicarage Clo. Eri 6J 93
Vicarage Clo. N'holt 7D 42
Vicarage Clo. Ruis 7F 23
Vicarage Clo. Wor Pk 1A 148
Vicarage Ct. W8 2K 83
Vicarage Ct. Beck 3A 142
Vicarage Ct. Felt 7E 94
Vicarage Ct. Ilf 5F 55
Vicarage Cres. SW11 1B 102
Vicarage Dri. SW14 5K 99
Vicarage Dri. Bark 7G 55
Vicarage Dri. Beck 1C 142
Vicarage Farm Ct. Houn 7D 78
Vicarage Farm Rd. Houn 2C 96
Vicarage Fields. W on T 6A 132
Vicarage Fld. Shop. Cen. Bark 7G 55
Vicarage Gdns. SW14 5J 99
Vicarage Gdns. W8 1J 83
Vicarage Gdns. Mitc 3C 138
Vicarage Ga. W8 1K 83
Vicarage Gro. SE5 1D 104
Vicarage Ho. King T 2F 135 (off Cambridge Rd.)
Vicarage La. E6 3D 72
Vicarage La. E15 7G 53
Vicarage La. Eps 7C 148 (in two parts)
Vicarage La. Ilf 1H 55
Vicarage M. NW9 2K 45
Vicarage Pde. N15 4C 32
Vicarage Pk. SE18 5G 91
Vicarage Path. N8 7J 31
Vicarage Rd. E10 7C 34
Vicarage Rd. E15 7H 53
Vicarage Rd. N17 1G 33
Vicarage Rd. NW4 6C 28
Vicarage Rd. SE18 5G 91 (in two parts)
Vicarage Rd. SW14 5J 99
Vicarage Rd. Bex 1H 129
Vicarage Rd. Croy 3A 152
Vicarage Rd. Dag 7H 57
Vicarage Rd. Hamp W 1C 134
Vicarage Rd. King T 2D 134
Vicarage Rd. Sun 5H 113
Vicarage Rd. Sutt 4K 149
Vicarage Rd. Tedd 5A 116
Vicarage Rd. Twic 2J 115 (Green, The)
Vicarage Rd. Twic 6G 97 (Kneller Rd.)
Vicarage Rd. Wfd G 7H 21

Vicarage Wlk. SW11 . . . . . . 1B 102
Vicarage Wlk. W on T. 7J 131
Vicarage Way. NW10. . . . . . . 3K 45
Vicarage Way. Harr 7E 24
Vicars Bri. Clo. Wemb 2E 62
Vicar's Clo. E9 . . . . 1J 69
Vicars Clo. E15 . . . . 1J 71
Vicars Clo. Enf. 2K 7
Vicar's Hill. SE13. . . . . 4D 106
Vicars Moor La. N21 . . . . 7F 7
Vicars Oak Rd. SE19 . . . . . . 6E 122
Vicar's Rd. NW5 . . . . 5E 48
Vicars Wlk. Dag. 3B 56
Viceroy Clo. N2. . . . . 4C 30
Viceroy Ct. NW8 . . . . 2C 66 (off Prince Albert Rd.)
Viceroy Ct. Croy 1D 152
Viceroy Pde. N2. . . . . 4C 30 (off High Rd.)
Viceroy Rd. SW8 . . . . 1J 103
Vickers Clo. Wall 7K 151
Vickers Rd. Eri 5K 93
Vickers Way. Houn 5C 96
Vickery Ct. EC1. . . . 4C 68 (3D 162) (off Mitchell St.)
Victor Cazalet Ho. N1. . . . . . . 1B 68 (off Gaskin St.)
Victor Gro. Wemb 7E 44
Victoria & Albert Mus. 3B 84 (2B 170)
Victoria Arc. SW1 . . . . 3F 85 (2K 171) (off Victoria St.)
Victoria Av. E6. . . . . 1B 72
Victoria Av. EC2 . . . 5E 68 (6H 163)
Victoria Av. N3 . . . . 1H 29
Victoria Av. Barn 4G 5
Victoria Av. Houn. 5E 96
Victoria Av. Surb 6D 134
Victoria Av. Uxb. 6D 40
Victoria Av. Wall. 3E 150
Victoria Av. Wemb. 6H 45
Victoria Av. W Mol 3F 133
Victoria Bldgs. E8 . . . . 1H 69 (off Mare St.)
Victoria Clo. Barn 4G 5
Victoria Clo. Harr. 6K 25
Victoria Clo. Hay 6F 59
Victoria Clo. W Mol 3E 132
Victoria Colonnade. WC1 . . . . 5J 67 (6F 161) (off Southampton Row)
Victoria Cotts. E1 . . . . 5G 69 (off Deal St.)
Victoria Cotts. N10 . . . . 2E 30
Victoria Cotts. Rich 1F 99
Victoria Ct. E18. . . . . 3K 35
Victoria Ct. SE26 . . . . 6J 123
Victoria Ct. W3 . . . . 2G 81
Victoria Ct. Wemb. 6G 45
Victoria Cres. N15 . . . . 5E 32
Victoria Cres. SE19 . . . . 6E 122
Victoria Cres. SW19 . . . . . . 7H 119
Victoria Dock Rd. E16 . . . . . . 6H 71
Victoria Dri. SW19. . . . . 7F 101
Victoria Embkmt. SW1 & WC2 . . . . 2J 85 (6F 167)
Victoria Gdns. W11 . . . . 1J 83
Victoria Gdns. Houn 1C 96
Victoria Gro. N12 . . . . 5G 15
Victoria Gro. W8 . . . . 3A 84
Victoria Gro. M. W2. . . . . 7J 65
Victoria Hall. E16. . . . . 1J 89 (off Wesley Av., in two parts)
Victoria Ho. E6 . . . . 6E 72
Victoria Ho. SW1 . . . . 4G 85 (3B 172) (off Francis St.)
Victoria Ho. SW1. . . 5F 85 (3B 172) (off Ebury Bri. Rd.)
Victoria Ho. SW8. . . . . 7J 85 (off S. Lambeth Rd.)
Victoria Ho. Edgw 6C 12
Victoria Ind. Est. W3 . . . . 5A 64
Victoria La. Barn 4C 4
Victoria La. Hay. 5E 76
Victoria Mans. NW10 . . . . . . 7D 46
Victoria Mans. SW8. . . . . 7J 85 (off S. Lambeth Rd.)
Victoria M. NW6 . . . . 1J 65
Victoria M. SW4. . . . . 4F 103
Victoria M. SW18 . . . . 1A 120
Victorian Gro. N16. . . . . 4E 50
Victorian Rd. N16 . . . . 3E 50
Victoria Palace Theatre. . . . . 3G 85 (2A 172) (off Victoria St.)
Victoria Pde. Rich . . . . 1G 99 (off Sandycombe Rd.)
Victoria Pk. 1A 70
Victoria Pk. Ct. E9 . . . . 7J 51 (off Well St.)
Victoria Pk. Ind. Cen. E9 . . . . 7C 52 (off Rothbury Rd.)
Victoria Pk. Rd. E9. . . . . 1J 69
Victoria Pk. Sq. E2. . . . . 3J 69
Victoria Pas. NW8 . . . . 3B 158
Victoria Pl. Rich 5D 98
Victoria Pl. Shop. Cen. SW1. . . . . 3K 171
Victoria Point. E13. . . . . 2J 71 (off Victoria Rd.)
Victoria Retail Pk. Ruis 5B 42
Victoria Ri. SW4 . . . . 3F 103
Victoria Rd. E4 . . . . 1B 20
Victoria Rd. E11 . . . . 4G 53
Victoria Rd. E13. . . . . 2J 71
Victoria Rd. E17. . . . . 2E 34
Victoria Rd. E18 . . . . 2K 35
Victoria Rd. N4 . . . . 7K 31
Victoria Rd. N15 . . . . 4G 33
Victoria Rd. N18 & N9. . . . . . 4A 18
Victoria Rd. N22. . . . . 1G 31
Victoria Rd. NW4. . . . . 4E 28
Victoria Rd. NW6 . . . . 2H 65
Victoria Rd. NW7 . . . . 5G 13
Victoria Rd. NW10. . . . . 5K 63
Victoria Rd. SW14. . . . . 3K 99
Victoria Rd. W3. . . . . 5K 63
Victoria Rd. W5. . . . . 5B 62
Victoria Rd. W8. . . . . 3A 84
Victoria Rd. Bark 6F 55
Victoria Rd. Barn. 4G 5
Victoria Rd. Bexh 4G 111
Victoria Rd. Brom 5B 144
Victoria Rd. Buck H. 2G 21
Victoria Rd. Bush 1A 10
Victoria Rd. Chst 5E 126
Victoria Rd. Dag 5H 57
Victoria Rd. Eri . . . . 6K 93 (in two parts)
Victoria Rd. Felt. 1K 113
Victoria Rd. King T. 2F 135
Victoria Rd. Mitc 7C 120
Victoria Rd. Ruis 1J 41
Victoria Rd. Sidc 3K 127
Victoria Rd. S'hall 3D 78
Victoria Rd. Surb. 6D 134
Victoria Rd. Sutt 5B 150
Victoria Rd. Tedd. 6A 116
Victoria Rd. Twic. 7B 98
Victoria Sq. SW1 . . . 3F 85 (1K 171)
Victoria St. E15 . . . . 7G 53
Victoria St. SW1 . . . 3G 85 (2K 171)
Victoria St. Belv. 5F 93
Victoria Ter. N4 . . . . 1A 50
Victoria Ter. NW10. . . . . 4B 64
Victoria Ter. SW8. . . . . 2F 103
Victoria Ter. W5. . . . . 1D 80
Victoria Ter. Harr 1J 43
Victoria Vs. Rich 3F 99
Victoria Way. SE7 . . . . 5K 89
Victoria Way. Ruis 5B 42
Victoria Wharf. E2 . . . . 2K 69 (off Palmers Rd.)
Victoria Wharf. E14 . . . . 7A 70
Victoria Wharf. SE8. . . . . 5B 88 (off Dragoon Rd.)
Victoria Works. NW2. . . . . . . 2D 46
Victoria Yd. E1 . . . . 6G 69
Victor Rd. NW10. . . . . 3D 64
Victor Rd. SE20. . . . . 7K 123
Victor Rd. Harr 3G 25
Victor Rd. Tedd 4J 115
Victors Dri. Hamp 6C 114
Victors Way. Barn 3C 4
Victor Vs. N9. . . . . 3J 17
Victory Av. Mord 5A 138
Victory Bus. Cen. Iswth 4K 97
Victory Ct. W9. . . . . 4J 65 (off Hermes Clo.)
Victory Pk. Wemb 3D 44
Victory Pl. E14 . . . . 7A 70
Victory Pl. SE17 . . . . 4D 86
Victory Pl. SE19. . . . . 7E 122
Victory Rd. E11. . . . . 4K 35
Victory Rd. SW19 . . . . 7A 120
Victory Rd. M. SW19. . . . . . 7A 120
Victory Wlk. SE8 . . . . 1C 106
Victory Way. SE16. . . . . 2A 88
Victory Way. Houn. 5A 78
Victory Way. Romf 2H 39
Vidler Clo. Chess. 6C 146
Vienna Clo. Ilf 2B 36
View Clo. N6. . . . . 7D 30
View Clo. Harr. 4H 25
View Ct. SE12 . . . . 3A 126
View Cres. N8 . . . . 5H 31
Viewfield Clo. Harr. 7E 26
Viewfield Rd. SW18. . . . . . . 6H 101
Viewfield Rd. Bex 1C 128
Viewland Rd. SE18 . . . . 5K 91
View Rd. N6 . . . . 7D 30
View, The. SE2 . . . . 5E 92
Viga Rd. N21. . . . . 6F 7
Vigilant Clo. SE26 . . . . 4G 123
Vignoles Rd. Romf 7G 39
Vigo St. W1 . . . . . . 7G 67 (3A 166)
Viking Clo. E3 . . . . 2A 70
Viking Ct. SW6 . . . . 6J 83
Viking Gdns. E6. . . . . 4C 72
Viking Ho. SE5 . . . . 2C 104 (off Denmark Rd.)
Viking Pl. E10 . . . . 1B 52
Viking Rd. S'hall 7C 60
Viking Way. Eri 3J 93
Villacourt Rd. SE18 . . . . 7A 92
Village Arc. E4. . . . . 1A 20
Village Clo. E4. . . . . 5K 19
Village Clo. NW3 . . . . 5B 48 (off Belsize La.)
Village Ct. SE3. . . . . 3G 107 (off Hurren Clo.)
Village Heights. Wfd G. 5C 20
Village M. NW9. . . . . 2K 45
Village Pk. Clo. Enf 6K 7
Village Rd. N3. . . . . 2G 29
Village Rd. Enf. 5K 7
Village Row. Sutt 7J 149
Village, The. NW3 . . . . 2A 48
Village, The. SE7 . . . . 6A 90
Village Way. NW10 . . . . 4K 45
Village Way. SE24 . . . . 6D 104
Village Way. Ashf. 4B 112
Village Way. Beck 2C 142
Village Way. Pinn. 7C 24
Village Way E. Harr 7E 24
Villa Rd. SW9 . . . . 3A 104
Villas on the Heath. NW3. . . . 3A 48
Villas Rd. SE18 . . . . 5G 91 (in three parts)
Villa St. SE17 . . . . 5D 86
Villa Wlk. SE17 . . . . 5D 86 (off Inville Rd.)
Villiers Av. Surb 5F 135
Villiers Av. Twic. 1D 114
Villiers Clo. E10. . . . . 2C 52
Villiers Clo. Surb 4F 135
Villiers Gro. Sutt 7F 149
Villiers M. NW2. . . . . 6C 46
Villiers Path. Surb 5E 134
Villiers Rd. NW2 . . . . 6C 46
Villiers Rd. Beck 2K 141
Villiers Rd. Iswth 2J 97
Villiers Rd. King T 4F 135
Villiers Rd. S'hall. 1D 78
Villiers St. WC2 . . . . 1J 85 (3E 166)
Vincam Clo. Twic. 7E 96
Vincennes Est. SE27 . . . . . . 4D 122
Vincent Av. Surb 2J 147
Vincent Clo. SE16 . . . . 2A 88
Vincent Clo. Barn. 3E 4
Vincent Clo. Brom 4K 143
Vincent Clo. Sidc 1J 127
Vincent Clo. W Dray 6C 76
Vincent Ct. N4 . . . . 1J 49
Vincent Ct. NW4 . . . . 4F 29
Vincent Ct. SW9 . . . . 1K 103
Vincent Ct. W1 . . . . 6D 66 (7E 158) (off Seymour Pl.)
Vincent Ct. N'wd 1H 23
Vincent Dri. Shep 3G 131
Vincent Dri. Uxb 1B 58
Vincent Gdns. NW2. . . . . 3B 46
Vincent Ho. SW1 . . . . 4H 85 (4C 172) (off Vincent Sq.)
Vincent M. E3 . . . . 2C 70
Vincent Rd. E4 . . . . 6A 20
Vincent Rd. N15 . . . . 4C 32
Vincent Rd. N22 . . . . 2A 32
Vincent Rd. SE18. . . . . 4F 91
Vincent Rd. W3 . . . . 3J 81
Vincent Rd. Croy 7E 140
Vincent Rd. Dag. 7E 56
Vincent Rd. Houn 2B 96
Vincent Rd. Iswth 1H 97
Vincent Rd. King T 3G 135
Vincent Rd. Wemb. 7F 45
Vincent Row. Hamp H 6G 115
Vincents Path. N'holt . . . . 6C 42 (off Arnold Rd.)
Vincent Sq. N22 . . . . 2A 32
Vincent Sq. SW1 . . . 4H 85 (3C 172)
Vincent Sq. Mans. SW1 . . . . 4G 85 (3B 172) (off Walcott St.)
Vincent St. E16 . . . . 5H 71
Vincent St. SW1 . . . 4H 85 (3C 172)
Vincent Ter. N1 . . . . 2B 68
Vince St. EC1 . . . . . 3D 68 (2F 163)
Vine Clo. Surb 6F 135
Vine Clo. Sutt 3A 150
Vine Clo. W Dray. 4C 76
Vine Cotts. E1 . . . . 6J 69 (off Sidney Sq.)
Vine Ct. E1 . . . . 5G 69
Vine Ct. Harr 6E 26
Vinegar All. E17. . . . . 4D 34
Vine Gdns. Ilf 5G 55
Vinegar St. E1. . . . . 1H 87
Vinegar Yd. SE1 . . . 2E 86 (6G 169)
Vine Gro. Uxb 7C 40
Vine Hill. EC1 . . . . . 4A 68 (4J 161)
Vine La. SE1 . . . . . . 1E 86 (5H 169)
Vine La. Uxb 1B 58
Vine Pl. W5. . . . . 1E 80 (off St Mark's Rd.)
Vine Pl. Houn. 4F 97
Viner Clo. W on T 6A 132
Vineries Bank. NW7. . . . . 5J 13
Vineries Clo. Dag. 6F 57
Vineries Clo. W Dray 6C 76
Vineries, The. N14. . . . . 6B 6
Vineries, The. SE6. . . . . 1C 124
Vineries, The. Enf 3K 7
Vine Rd. E15. . . . . 7H 53
Vine Rd. SW13 . . . . 3B 100
Vine Rd. E Mol 4G 133
Vinery Way. W6. . . . . 3D 82
Vines Av. N3 . . . . 1K 29
Vine Sq. W14 . . . . 5H 83 (off Star Rd.)
Vine St. EC3 . . . . . . 6F 69 (1J 169)
Vine St. W1 . . . . . . 7G 67 (3B 166)
Vine St. Romf 4J 39
Vine St. Bri. EC1 . . . 4A 68 (4K 161)
Vine Yd. SE1. . . . . 6D 168
Vineyard Av. NW7. . . . . 7B 14
Vineyard Clo. SE6 . . . . 1C 124
Vineyard Clo. King T 3F 135
Vineyard Gro. N3. . . . . 1K 29
Vineyard Hill Rd. SW19. . . . 4H 119
Vineyard M. EC1 . . . . 3K 161
Vineyard Pas. Rich. 5E 98
Vineyard Path. SW14. . . . . . . 3K 99
Vineyard Rd. Felt 3J 113
Vineyard Row. Hamp W. . . . 1C 134
Vineyards, The. Felt . . . . 3J 113 (off High St.)
Vineyards, The. Sun. 3J 131
Vineyard, The. Rich 5E 98
Vineyard Wlk. EC1 . . . . 4A 68 (3J 161)
Viney Bank. Croy 7B 154
Viney Rd. SE13 . . . . 3D 106
Vining St. SW9 . . . . 4A 104
Vinlake Av. Uxb 3B 40
Vinopolis, City of Wine. 1D 86 (4E 168)
Vinson Clo. Orp. 7K 145
Vintners Ct. EC4 . . . 7C 68 (2D 168)
Vintner's Pl. EC4 . . . 7C 68 (3D 168)
Vintry M. E17 . . . . 4C 34
Viola Av. SE2. . . . . 4B 92
Viola Av. Felt 6A 96
Viola Av. Stai 1A 112
Viola Sq. W12. . . . . 7B 64
Violet Av. Enf. 1J 7
Violet Av. Uxb 5B 58
Violet Clo. E16 . . . . 4G 71
Violet Clo. SE8 . . . . 6B 88
Violet Clo. Wall 1E 150
Violet Gdns. Croy 5B 152
Violet Hill. NW8. . . . . 2A 66
Violet Hill Ho. NW8 . . . . 2A 66 (off Violet Hill, in two parts)
Violet La. Croy. 6B 152
Violet Rd. E3. . . . . 4D 70
Violet Rd. E17. . . . . 6C 34
Violet Rd. E18 . . . . 2K 35
Violet St. E2 . . . . 4H 69
V.I.P. Trading Est. SE7 . . . . . . 4A 90
Virgil Pl. W1 . . . . . . 5D 66 (6E 158)
Virgil St. SE1 . . . . . 3K 85 (1H 173)
Virginia Clo. N Mald. 4J 135
Virginia Clo. Romf. 1J 39
Virginia Ct. SE16. . . . . 2K 87 (off Eleanor Clo.)
Virginia Ct. WC1. . . 4H 67 (3D 160) (off Burton St.)
Virginia Gdns. Ilf 2G 37
Virginia Ho. E14. . . . . 7E 70 (off Newby Pl.)
Virginia Rd. E2. . . . . 3F 69 (2J 163)
Virginia Rd. T Hth 1B 140
Virginia St. E1. . . . . 7G 69
Virginia Wlk. SW2. . . . . 6K 103
Viscount Clo. N11 . . . . 6A 16
Viscount Ct. W2. . . . . 6J 65 (off Pembridge Vs.)
Viscount Dri. E6 . . . . 5D 72
Viscount Gro. N'holt 3B 60
Viscount Rd. Stanw 1A 112
Viscount St. EC1 . . . 4C 68 (4C 162)
Viscount Way. H'row A . . . . . 4G 95 (in two parts)
Vista Av. Enf 2E 8
Vista Dri. Ilf. 5B 36
Vista, The. SE9 . . . . 6B 108
Vista, The. Sidc. 5K 127
Vista Way. Harr 6E 26
Vittoria Ho. N1 . . . . 1K 67 (off High Rd.)
Viveash Clo. Hay 3H 77
Vivian Av. NW4 . . . . 5D 28
Vivian Av. Wemb. 5G 45
Vivian Comma Clo. N4. . . . . . 3B 50
Vivian Ct. N12 . . . . 5E 14
Vivian Gdns. Wemb. 5G 45
Vivian Mans. NW4. . . . . 5D 28 (off Vivian Av.)
Vivian Rd. E3. . . . . 2A 70
Vivian Sq. SE15. . . . . 3H 105
Vivian Way. N2 . . . . 5B 30

Vivien Clo. Chess 7E 146
Vivienne Clo. Twic 6D 98
Vixen M. E8 7F 51 (off Haggerston Rd.)
Voce Rd. SE18 7H 91
Voewood Clo. N Mald 6B 136
Vogans Mill. SE1 2F 87 (6K 169)
Vogler Ho. E1 7J 69 (off Cable St.)
Vogue Ct. Brom 1K 143
Vollasky Ho. E1 5G 69 (5K 163) (off Daplyn St.)
Volta Clo. N9 3D 18
Voltaire Rd. SW4 3H 103
Voltaire Way. Hay 7G 59
Volt Av. NW10 3A 64
Volta Way. Croy 1K 151
Voluntary Pl. E11 6J 35
Vorley Rd. N19 2G 49
Voss Ct. SW16 6J 121
Voss St. E2 3G 69
Voyager Bus. Est. SE16 3G 87 (off Spa Rd.)
Voyagers Clo. SE28 6C 74
Vulcan Clo. E6 6E 72
Vulcan Ga. Enf 2F 7
Vulcan Rd. SE4 2B 106
Vulcan Sq. E14 4D 88
Vulcan Ter. SE4 2B 106
Vulcan Way. N7 6K 49
Vyner Rd. W3 7K 63
Vyner St. E2 1H 69
Vyner's Way. Uxb 5C 40
Vyne, The. Bexh 3H 111

W12 Shop. Cen. W12 2F 83
Wadbrook St. King T 2D 134
Wadding St. SE17 4D 86
Waddington Clo. Enf 4K 7
Waddington Rd. E15 5F 53
Waddington St. E15 6F 53
Waddington Way. SE19 7C 122
Waddon. 3A 152
Waddon Clo. Croy 3A 152
Waddon Ct. Rd. Croy 3A 152
Waddon Marsh Way. Croy 1K 151
Waddon New Rd. Croy 3B 152
Waddon Pk. Av. Croy 4A 152
Waddon Rd. Croy 3A 152
Waddon Way. Croy 6A 152
Wade Ct. N10 7A 16
Wade Ho. SE1 2G 87 (7K 169) (off Parkers Row)
Wade Ho. Enf 5J 7
Wades Gro. N21 7F 7
Wades Hill. N21 6F 7
Wades La. Tedd 5A 116
Wadeson St. E2 2H 69
Wade's Pl. E14 7D 70
Wadeville Av. Romf 6E 38
Wadeville Clo. Belv 6G 93
Wadham Av. E17 7J 19
Wadham Clo. Shep 7E 130
Wadham Gdns. NW3 1C 66
Wadham Gdns. Gnfd 6H 43
Wadham Rd. E17 7J 19
Wadham Rd. SW15 4G 101
Wadhurst Clo. SE20 2H 141
Wadhurst Rd. SW8 1G 103
Wadhurst Rd. W4 3K 81
Wadley Rd. E11 7G 35
Wadsworth Bus. Cen. Gnfd 2C 62
Wadsworth Clo. Enf 5E 8
Wadsworth Clo. Gnfd 2C 62
Wadsworth Rd. Gnfd 2B 62
Wager St. E3 4B 70
Waggoners Roundabout. (Junct.) 1K 95
Waggon La. N17 6B 18
Waggon M. N14 1B 16
Waghorn Rd. E13 1A 72
Waghorn Rd. Harr 3D 26
Waghorn St. SE15 3G 105
Wagner St. SE15 7J 87
Wagstaff Gdns. Dag 7C 56
Wagtail Clo. NW9 2A 28
Wagtail Wlk. Beck 5E 142
Waight's Ct. King T 1E 134
Wainfleet Av. Romf 2J 39
Wainford Clo. SW19 7F 101
Wainwright Gro. Iswth 4H 97
Wainwright Ho. E1 1J 87 (off Garnet St.)
Waite Davies Rd. SE12 7H 107
Waite St. SE15 6F 87
Waithman St. EC4 6B 68 (1A 168) (off Apothecary St.)
Wakefield Ct. SE26 6J 123
Wakefield Gdns. SE19 7E 122
Wakefield Gdns. Ilf 6C 36
Wakefield Ho. SE15 1G 105
Wakefield M. WC1 3J 67 (2F 161)
Wakefield Rd. N11 5C 16
Wakefield Rd. N15 5F 33
Wakefield Rd. Rich 5D 98
Wakefield St. E6 1B 72
Wakefield St. N18 5B 18
Wakefield St. WC1 4J 67 (2F 161)
Wakeford Clo. SW4 5G 103
Wakehams Hill. Pinn 3D 24
Wakeham St. N1 6D 50
Wakehurst Rd. SW11 5C 102
Wakeling Rd. W7 5K 61
Wakeling St. E14 6A 70
Wakelin Ho. N1 7B 50 (off Sebbon St.)
Wakelin Ho. SE23 7A 106
Wakelin Rd. E15 2G 71
Wakeman Ho. NW10 3F 65 (off Wakeman Rd.)
Wakeman Rd. NW10 3E 64
Wakemans Hill Av. NW9 5K 27
Wakering Rd. Bark 6G 55 (in two parts)
Wakerings, The. Bark 6G 55
Wakerley Clo. E6 6D 72
Wakley St. EC1 3B 68 (1A 162)
Walberswick St. SW8 7J 85
Walbrook. EC4 7D 68 (2E 168) (in three parts)
Walbrook Ho. N9 2D 18 (off Huntingdon Rd.)
Walbrook Wharf. EC4 7C 68 (3D 168) (off Bell Wharf La.)
Walburgh St. E1 6H 69
Walcorde Av. SE17 4C 86
Walcot Gdns. SE11 3J 173
Walcot Rd. Enf 2G 9
Walcot Sq. SE11 4A 86 (3K 173)
Walcott St. SW1 4G 85 (3B 172)
Waldair Ct. E16 2F 91
Waldeck Gro. SE27 3B 122
Waldeck Rd. N15 4B 32
Waldeck Rd. SW14 3J 99
Waldeck Rd. W4 6G 81
Waldeck Rd. W13 6B 62
Waldeck Ter. SW14 3J 99 (off Waldeck Rd.)
Waldegrave Av. Tedd 5K 115
Waldegrave Ct. Bark 1H 73
Waldegrave Gdns. Twic 2K 115
Waldegrave Pk. Twic 4K 115
Waldegrave Rd. N8 3A 32
Waldegrave Rd. SE19 7F 123
Waldegrave Rd. W5 7F 63
Waldegrave Rd. Brom 4C 144
Waldegrave Rd. Dag 2C 56
Waldegrave Rd. Tedd & Twic 4K 115
Waldegrove. Croy 3F 153
Waldemar Av. SW6 1G 101
Waldemar Av. W13 1C 80
Waldemar Rd. SW19 5J 119
Walden Av. N13 4H 17
Walden Av. Chst 4D 126
Walden Av. Rain 2K 75
Walden Clo. Belv 5F 93
Walden Ct. SW8 1H 103
Walden Gdns. T Hth 3K 139
Walden Ho. SW1 4E 84 (4H 171) (off Pimlico Rd.)
Walden Pde. Chst 6D 126 (in two parts)
Walden Rd. N17 1D 32
Walden Rd. Chst 6D 126
Waldenshaw Rd. SE23 1J 123
Walden St. E1 6H 69
Walden Way. NW7 6A 14
Waldo Clo. SW4 5G 103
Waldo Ho. NW10 3D 64 (off Waldo Rd.)
Waldo Ind. Est. Brom 3B 144
Waldo Pl. Mitc 7C 120
Waldorf Clo. S Croy 7B 152
Waldo Rd. NW10 3C 64 (in two parts)
Waldo Rd. Brom 3B 144
Waldram Cres. SE23 1J 123
Waldram Pk. Rd. SE23 1K 123
Waldram Pl. SE23 1J 123
Waldrist Way. Eri 2F 93
Waldron Gdns. Brom 3F 143
Waldronhyrst. S Croy 4B 152
Waldron M. SW3 6B 84 (7B 170)
Waldron Rd. SW18 3A 120
Waldron Rd. Harr 1J 43
Waldron's Path. S Croy 4C 152
Waldrons, The. Croy 4B 152
Waldrons Yd. S Harr 2H 43
Waldstock Rd. SE28 7A 74
Waleran Clo. Stan 5E 10
Walerand Rd. SE13 2E 106
Waleran Flats. SE1 4E 86
Wales Av. Cars 5C 150
Wales Clo. SE15 7H 87
Wales Farm Rd. W3 5K 63
Waleton Acres. Wall 6G 151
Waley St. E1 5A 70
Walfield Av. N20 7E 4
Walford Ho. E1 6G 69
Walford Rd. N16 4E 50
Walfrey Gdns. Dag 7E 56
Walham Green. 1K 101
Walham Grn. Ct. SW6 7K 83 (off Waterford Rd.)
Walham Gro. SW6 7J 83
Walham Ri. SW19 6G 119
Walham Yd. SW6 7J 83
Walkato Lodge. Buck H 1F 21
Walkden Rd. Chst 5E 126
Walker Clo. N11 4B 16
Walker Clo. SE18 4G 91
Walker Clo. W7 1J 79
Walker Clo. Felt 7H 95
Walker Clo. Hamp 6D 114
Walker Ho. NW1 2H 67 (1C 160)
Walker's Ct. W1 2C 166
Walkerscroft Mead. SE21 1C 122
Walkers Pl. SW15 4G 101
Walkinshaw Ct. N1 7C 50 (off Rotherfield St.)
Walks, The. N2 3B 30
Walk, The. N13 3F 17 (off Fox La.)
Walk, The. Sun 7H 113
Wallace Clo. SE28 7D 74
Wallace Clo. Shep 4F 131
Wallace Clo. Uxb 2A 58
Wallace Collection. 6E 66 (7G 159)
Wallace Ct. NW1 5C 66 (6D 158) (off Old Marylebone Rd.)
Wallace Cres. Cars 5D 150
Wallace Ho. N7 6K 49 (off Caledonian Rd.)
Wallace Rd. N1 6C 50
Wallace Way. N19 2H 49 (off St John's Way)
Wallasey Cres. Uxb 2C 40
Wallbrook Bus. Cen. Houn 3K 95
Wallbutton Rd. SE4 2A 106
Wallcote Av. NW2 1F 47
Wall Ct. N4 1K 49 (off Stroud Grn. Rd.)
Wallend. 1E 72
Wall End Ct. E6 1E 72 (off Wall End Rd.)
Wall End Rd. E6 7D 54
Waller Dri. N'wd 2J 23
Waller Rd. SE14 1K 105
Wallers Clo. Dag 1E 74
Wallers Clo. Wfd G 6J 21
Waller Way. SE10 7D 88
Wallflower St. W12 7B 64
Wallgrave Rd. SW5 4K 83
Wallingford Av. W10 5F 65
Wallington. 6G 151
Wallington Clo. Ruis 6E 22
Wallington Corner. Wall 4F 151 (off Manor Rd. N.)
Wallington Ct. Wall 6F 151 (off Stanley Pk. Rd.)
Wallington Green. (Junct.) 4F 151
Wallington Rd. Ilf 7K 37
Wallington Sq. Wall 6F 151
Wallis All. SE1 6D 168
Wallis Clo. SW11 3B 102
Wallis Ho. SE14 1A 106
Wallis M. N8 3A 32 (off Courcy Rd.)
Wallis Rd. E9 6B 52
Wallis Rd. S'hall 6F 61
Wallis's Cotts. SW2 7J 103
Wallman Pl. N22 1K 31
Wallorton Gdns. SW14 4K 99
Wallside. EC2 6D 162
Wall St. N1 6D 50
Wallwood Rd. E11 7F 35
Wallwood St. E14 5B 70
Walmar Clo. Barn 1G 5
Walmer Clo. E4 2J 19
Walmer Clo. Romf 2H 39
Walmer Ct. Surb 5E 134 (off Cranes Pk.)
Walmer Gdns. W13 2A 80
Walmer Ho. W10 6F 65 (off Bramley Rd.)
Walmer Pl. W1 5E 158
Walmer Rd. W10 6E 64
Walmer Rd. W11 7G 65
Walmer St. W1 5D 66 (5E 158)
Walmer Ter. SE18 4G 91
Walmgate Rd. Gnfd 1B 62
Walmington Fold. N12 6D 14
Walm La. NW2 6E 46
Walney Wlk. N1 6C 50
Walnut Av. W Dray 3C 76
Walnut Clo. SE8 6B 88
Walnut Clo. Cars 5D 150
Walnut Clo. Hay 7G 59
Walnut Clo. Ilf 4G 37
Walnut Ct. E17 4E 34
Walnut Ct. W5 2E 80
Walnut Ct. W8 3K 83 (off St Mary's Ga.)
Walnut Fields. Eps 7B 148
Walnut Gdns. E15 5G 53
Walnut Gro. Enf 5J 7
Walnut M. Sutt 7A 150
Walnut Rd. E10 2C 52
Walnut Tree Av. Mitc 3C 138
Walnut Tree Clo. SW13 1B 100
Walnut Tree Clo. Chst 1H 145
Walnut Tree Clo. Shep 3E 130
Walnut Tree Cotts. SW19 5G 119
Walnut Tree Ho. SW10 6K 83 (off Tregunter Rd.)
Walnut Tree Rd. SE10 5G 89 (in two parts)
Walnut Tree Rd. Bren 6E 80
Walnut Tree Rd. Dag 2E 56
Walnut Tree Rd. Houn 6D 78
Walnut Tree Rd. Shep 2E 130
Walnut Tree Wlk. SE11 4A 86 (3J 173)
Walnut Way. Buck H 3G 21
Walnut Way. Ruis 6A 42
Walpole Av. Rich 2F 99
Walpole Clo. W13 2C 80
Walpole Ct. W14 3F 83 (off Blythe Rd.)
Walpole Ct. Twic 2J 115
Walpole Cres. Tedd 5K 115
Walpole Gdns. W4 5J 81
Walpole Gdns. Twic 2J 115
Walpole Ho. SE1 2A 86 (7J 167) (off Westminster Bri. Rd.)
Walpole Lodge. W5 1C 80
Walpole M. NW8 1B 66
Walpole M. SW19 6B 120
Walpole Pl. SE18 4F 91
Walpole Pl. Tedd 5K 115
Walpole Rd. E6 7A 54
Walpole Rd. E17 4A 34
Walpole Rd. E18 1H 35
Walpole Rd. N17 2C 32 (in two parts)
Walpole Rd. SW19 6B 120
Walpole Rd. Brom 5B 144
Walpole Rd. Croy 2D 152
Walpole Rd. Surb 7E 134
Walpole Rd. Tedd 5K 115
Walpole Rd. Twic 2J 115
Walpole St. SW3 5D 84 (5E 170)
Walrond Av. Wemb 5E 44
Walsham Clo. N16 1G 51
Walsham Clo. SE28 7D 74
Walsham Ho. SE14 2K 105
Walsham Ho. SE17 5D 86 (off Blackwood St.)
Walsham Rd. SE14 2K 105
Walsham Rd. Felt 7K 95
Walsingham. NW8 1B 66
Walsingham Gdns. Eps 4A 148
Walsingham Lodge. SW13 1C 100
Walsingham Mans. SW6 7K 83 (off Fulham Rd.)
Walsingham Pk. Chst 2H 145
Walsingham Pl. SW11 6E 102
Walsingham Rd. E5 3G 51
Walsingham Rd. W13 1A 80
Walsingham Rd. Enf 4J 7
Walsingham Rd. Mitc 5D 138
Walsingham Wlk. Belv 6G 93
Walston Ho. SW1 5H 85 (5C 172) (off Aylesford St.)
Walter Besant Ho. E1 3K 69 (off Bancroft Rd.)
Walter Ct. W3 6J 63 (off Lynton Ter.)
Walter Grn. Ho. SE15 1J 105 (off Lausanne Rd.)
Walter Hurford Pde. E12 4E 54
Walter Langley Ct. SE16 2J 87 (off Brunel Rd.)
Walter Rodney Clo. E6 6D 54
Walters Clo. SE17 4D 86 (off Brandon St.)
Walters Clo. Hay 2H 77
Walters Ho. SE17 6B 86 (off Otto St.)
Walters Rd. SE25 4E 140
Walters Rd. Enf 4D 8
Walter St. E2 3K 69
Walter St. King T 1E 134
Walters Way. SE23 6K 105
Walters Yd. Brom 2J 143
Walter Ter. E1 6K 69
Walterton Rd. W9 4H 65
Walter Wlk. Edgw 6D 12
Waltham Av. NW9 6G 27
Waltham Av. Hay 3E 76
Waltham Dri. Edgw 2G 27
Waltham Ho. NW8 1A 66
Waltham Pk. Way. E17 1C 34
Waltham Rd. Cars 7B 138

Waltham Rd. S'hall 3C 78
Waltham Rd. Wfd G 6H 21
Walthamstow. 4C 34
Walthamstow Av. E4 6G 19
Walthamstow Bus. Cen. E17 2E 34
Walthamstow Greyhound Stadium. 7J 19
Waltham Way. E4 3G 19
Waltheof Av. N17 1D 32
Waltheof Gdns. N17 1D 32
Walton Av. Harr 5D 42
Walton Av. N Mald 4B 136
Walton Av. Sutt 3H 149
Walton Av. Wemb 3H 45
Walton Bri. Shep & W on T 7G 131
Walton Bri. Rd. Shep 7G 131
Walton Clo. E5 3K 51
Walton Clo. NW2 2D 46
Walton Clo. SW8 7J 85
Walton Clo. Harr 4H 25
Walton Ct. New Bar 5F 5
Walton Ct. S Croy 5C 152 (off Warham Rd.)
Walton Cft. Harr 4J 43
Walton Dri. NW10 6K 45
Walton Dri. Harr 4H 25
Walton Gdns. W3 5H 63
Walton Gdns. Felt 4H 113
Walton Gdns. Wemb 2E 44
Walton Grn. New Ad 7D 154
Walton Ho. E2 4F 69 (3J 163)
Walton Ho. E4 5H 19 (off Chingford Mt. Rd.)
Walton Ho. E17 3D 34 (off Drive, The)
Walton La. Shep 7F 131
Walton-on-Thames. 7J 131
Walton Pl. SW3 3D 84 (1E 170)
Walton Rd. E12 4E 54 (in three parts)
Walton Rd. E13 2A 72
Walton Rd. N15 4F 33
Walton Rd. Harr 4H 25
Walton Rd. Romf 1F 39
Walton Rd. Sidc 2C 128
Walton Rd. W on T & W Mol 5A 132
Walton Rd. W Mol 4D 132
Walton St. SW3 4C 84 (3D 170)
Walton St. Enf 1J 7
Walton Way. W3 5H 63
Walton Way. Mitc 4G 139
Walt Whitman Clo. SE24 4B 104
Walworth. 5C 86
Walworth Pl. SE17 5C 86
Walworth Rd. SE1 & SE17 4C 86
Walwyn Av. Brom 3B 144
Wanborough Dri. SW15 1D 118
Wanderer Dri. Bark 3C 74
Wandle Bank. SW19 7B 120
Wandle Bank. Croy 3J 151
Wandle Ct. Croy 3J 151
Wandle Ct. Eps 4J 147
Wandle Ct. Gdns. Croy 3J 151
Wandle Ho. NW8 5C 66 (5C 158) (off Penfold St.)
Wandle Ho. Brom 5F 125
Wandle Pk. Trad. Est., The. Croy 1B 152
Wandle Rd. SW17 2C 120
Wandle Rd. Bedd 3J 151
Wandle Rd. Croy 3C 152
Wandle Rd. Mord 4A 138
Wandle Rd. Wall 3F 151
Wandle Side. Croy 3K 151
Wandle Side. Wall 3F 151
Wandle Way. SW18 1K 119
Wandle Way. Mitc 5D 138
Wandon Rd. SW6 7K 83 (in two parts)
Wandsworth. 5H 101
Wandsworth Bri. SW6 & SW18 3K 101
Wandsworth Bri. Rd. SW6 1K 101
Wandsworth Common. 1D 120
Wandsworth Comn. W. Side. SW18 5A 102
Wandsworth Gyratory. (Junct.) 5K 101
Wandsworth High St. SW18 5J 101
Wandsworth Plain. SW18 5K 101
Wandsworth Rd. SW8 3F 103 (7E 172)
Wandsworth Shop. Cen. SW18 6K 101
Wangey Rd. Chad H 7D 38
Wangford Ho. SW9 4B 104 (off Loughborough Pk.)
Wanless Rd. SE24 3C 104
Wanley Rd. SE5 4D 104
Wanlip Rd. E13 4K 71
Wannock Gdns. Ilf 1F 37
Wansbeck Ct. Enf 3G 7 (off Waverley Rd.)
Wansbeck Rd. E9 & E3 7B 52
Wansey St. SE17 4C 86
Wansford Rd. Wfd G 1A 36
Wanstead. 5K 35
Wanstead Clo. Brom 2A 144
Wanstead Gdns. Ilf 6B 36
Wanstead La. Ilf 6B 36
Wanstead Pk. Av. E12 1B 54
Wanstead Pk. Rd. Ilf 6B 36
Wanstead Pl. E11 6J 35
Wanstead Rd. Brom 2A 144
Wansunt Rd. Bex 1J 129
Wantage Rd. SE12 5H 107
Wantz Rd. Dag 4H 57
Wapping. 1H 87
Wapping Dock St. E1 1H 87
Wapping High St. E1 1G 87
Wapping La. E1 7H 69
Wapping Wall. E1 1J 87
Warbank La. King T 7B 118
Warberry Rd. N22 2K 31
Warboys App. King T 6H 117
Warboys Cres. E4 5K 19
Warboys Rd. King T 6H 117
Warbreck Rd. W12 1D 82
Warburg Institute. 4H 67 (4D 160)
Warburton Clo. N1 6E 50 (off Culford Rd.)
Warburton Clo. Harr 6C 10
Warburton Ct. Ruis 2J 41
Warburton Ho. E8 1H 69 (off Warburton St.)
Warburton Rd. E8 1H 69
Warburton Rd. Twic 1F 115
Warburton St. E8 1H 69
Warburton Ter. E17 2D 34
Wardalls Gro. SE14 7J 87
Wardalls Ho. SE8 6B 88 (off Staunton St.)
Ward Clo. Eri 6K 93
Ward Clo. S Croy 6E 152
Wardell Clo. NW7 7F 13
Wardell Fld. NW9 1A 28
Wardell Ho. SE10 6E 88 (off Welland St.)
Warden Av. Harr 1D 42
Warden Rd. NW5 6E 48
Wardens Gro. SE1 1C 86 (5C 168)
Wardle St. E9 5K 51
Wardley St. SW18 7K 101
Wardo Av. SW6 1G 101
Wardour M. W1 1B 166
Wardour St. W1 6G 67 (7B 160)
Ward Point. SE11 4A 86 (4J 173)
Ward Rd. E15 1F 71
Ward Rd. N19 3G 49
Ward Rd. SW19 1A 138
Wardrobe Pl. EC4 1B 168
Wardrobe Ter. EC4 2B 168
Wardrobe, The. Rich 5D 98 (off Old Pal. Yd.)
Wards Rd. Ilf 7H 37
Ware Ct. Sutt 4H 149
Wareham Clo. Houn 4F 97
Wareham Ct. N1 7E 50 (off Hertford Rd.)
Wareham Ho. SW8 7K 85
Warehouse Theatre. 2D 152
Waremead Rd. Ilf 5F 37
Warepoint Dri. SE28 2H 91
Warfield Rd. NW10 3F 65
Warfield Rd. Felt 7G 95
Warfield Rd. Hamp 1F 133
Warfield Yd. NW10 3F 65 (off Warfield Rd.)
Wargrave Av. N15 6F 33
Wargrave Ho. E2 3F 69 (2J 163) (off Navarre St.)
Wargrave Rd. Harr 3G 43
Warham Rd. N4 5A 32
Warham Rd. Harr 2K 25
Warham Rd. S Croy 5B 152
Warham St. SE5 7B 86
Waring & Gillow Est. W3 4G 63
Waring Rd. Sidc 6C 128
Waring St. SE27 4C 122
Warkworth Gdns. Iswth 7A 80
Warkworth Rd. N17 7J 17
Warland Rd. SE18 7H 91
Warley Av. Dag 7F 39
Warley Av. Hay 6J 59
Warley Clo. E10 1B 52
Warley Rd. N9 2D 18
Warley Rd. Hay 6J 59
Warley Rd. Ilf 1E 36
Warley Rd. Wfd G 7E 20
Warley St. E2 3K 69
Warlingham Rd. T Hth 4B 140
Warlock Rd. W9 4H 65
Warlters Clo. N7 4J 49
Warlters Rd. N7 4J 49
Warltersville Mans. N19 7J 31
Warltersville Rd. N19 7J 31
Warmington Clo. E5 3K 51
Warmington Rd. SE24 6C 104
Warmington St. E13 4J 71
Warmington Tower. SE14 1A 106
Warminster Gdns. SE25 2G 141
Warminster Rd. SE25 2F 141
Warminster Sq. SE25 2G 141
Warminster Way. Mitc 1F 139
Warmley Ct. SE15 6E 86 (off Newent Ct.)
Warmsworth. NW1 1G 67 (off Pratt St.)
Warndon St. SE16 4K 87
Warneford Rd. Harr 3D 26
Warneford St. E9 1H 69
Warne Pl. Sidc 6B 110
Warner Av. Sutt 2G 149
Warner Clo. E15 5G 53
Warner Clo. NW9 7B 28
Warner Clo. Hamp 5D 114
Warner Clo. Hay 7F 77
Warner Ho. NW8 3A 66
Warner Ho. SE13 2D 106 (off Russett Way)
Warner Pde. Hay 7F 77
Warner Pl. E2 2G 69
Warner Rd. E17 4A 34
Warner Rd. N8 4H 31
Warner Rd. SE5 1C 104
Warner Rd. Brom 7H 125
Warners Clo. Wfd G 5D 20
Warners La. King T 4D 116
Warners Path. Wfd G 5D 20
Warner St. EC1 4A 68 (4J 161)
Warner Ter. E14 5C 70 (off Broomfield St.)
Warner Village West End Cinema. 7H 67 (2D 166) (off Leicester Ct.)
Warner Yd. EC1 4J 161
Warnford Ho. SW15 6A 100 (off Tunworth Cres.)
Warnford Ind. Est. Hay 2G 77
Warnham. WC1 3K 67 (2G 161) (off Sidmouth St.)
Warnham Ct. Rd. Cars 7D 150
Warnham Ho. SW2 7K 103 (off Up. Tulse Hill)
Warnham Rd. N12 5H 15
Warpiner Dri. N9 3B 18
Warple M. W3 2A 82
Warple Way. W3 1A 82 (in two parts)
Warren Av. E10 3E 52
Warren Av. Brom 7G 125
Warren Av. Rich 4H 99
Warren Av. S Croy 7K 153
Warren Clo. N9 7E 8
Warren Clo. SE21 7C 104
Warren Clo. Bexh 5G 111
Warren Clo. Hay 5A 60
Warren Clo. Wemb 2D 44
Warren Ct. N17 3G 33 (off High Cross Rd.)
Warren Ct. NW1 4G 67 (3B 160) (off Warren St.)
Warren Ct. W5 5C 62
Warren Ct. Beck 7C 124
Warren Ct. Croy 1E 152
Warren Cres. N9 7A 8
Warren Cutting. King T 7K 117
Warrender Rd. N19 3G 49
Warrender Way. Ruis 7J 23
Warren Dri. Gnfd 4F 61
Warren Dri. Ruis 7B 24
Warren Dri. N. Surb 1H 147
Warren Dri. S. Surb 1J 147
Warren Dri., The. E11 7A 36
Warren Farm Cotts. Romf 4F 39
Warren Fields. Stan 4H 11
Warren Footpath. Twic 1C 116
Warren Gdns. E15 5F 53
Warren Ho. W14 4H 83 (off Beckford Clo.)
Warren La. SE18 3F 91
Warren La. Stan 2F 11
Warren M. W1 4G 67 (4A 160)
Warren Pk. King T 6J 117
Warren Pk. Rd. Sutt 6B 150
Warren Pl. E1 6K 69 (off Caroline St.)
Warren Pond Rd. E4 1C 20 (in two parts)
Warren Ri. N Mald 1K 135
Warren Rd. E4 2K 19
Warren Rd. E10 3E 52
Warren Rd. E11 6A 36 (in two parts)
Warren Rd. NW2 2B 46
Warren Rd. SW19 6C 120
Warren Rd. Ashf 7G 113
Warren Rd. Bexh 5G 111
Warren Rd. Brom 2J 155
Warren Rd. Bus H 1B 10
Warren Rd. Croy 1E 152
Warren Rd. Ilf 5H 37
Warren Rd. King T 6J 117
Warren Rd. Sidc 3C 128
Warren Rd. Twic 6G 97
Warren Rd. Uxb 4A 40
Warrens Shawe La. Edgw 2C 12
Warren St. W1 4G 67 (4A 160)
Warren Ter. Romf 4D 38 (in two parts)
Warren, The. E12 4C 54
Warren, The. Hay 6J 59
Warren, The. Houn 7D 78
Warren, The. Wor Pk 4K 147
Warren Wlk. SE7 6A 90
Warren Way. NW7 6B 14
Warren Wood Clo. Brom 2H 155
Warriner Gdns. SW11 1D 102
Warrington Ct. Croy 3B 152 (off Warrington Rd.)
Warrington Cres. W9 4A 66
Warrington Gdns. W9 4A 66
Warrington Pl. E14 1E 88 (off Yabsley St.)
Warrington Rd. Croy 3B 152
Warrington Rd. Dag 2D 56
Warrington Rd. Harr 5J 25
Warrington Rd. Rich 5D 98
Warrington Sq. Dag 2D 56
Warrior Sq. E12 4E 54
Warsaw Clo. Ruis 6K 41
Warspite Ho. E14 4D 88 (off Cahir St.)
Warspite Rd. SE18 3C 90
Warton Rd. E15 7E 52
Warwall. E6 6F 73
Warwick. W14 4H 83 (off Kensington Village)
Warwick Av. W9 & W2 4K 65
Warwick Av. Edgw 3C 12
Warwick Av. Harr 4D 42
Warwick Chambers. W8 3J 83 (off Pater St.)
Warwick Clo. Barn 5G 5
Warwick Clo. Bex 7F 111
Warwick Clo. Bus H 1D 10
Warwick Clo. Hamp 7G 115
Warwick Ct. W7 6K 61 (off Copley Clo.)
Warwick Ct. WC1 5K 67 (6H 161)
Warwick Ct. Brom 2G 143
Warwick Ct. Harr 3J 25
Warwick Ct. New Bar 5E 4 (off Station Rd.)
Warwick Ct. N'holt 5E 42 (off Newmarket Av.)
Warwick Cres. W2 5A 66
Warwick Cres. Hay 4H 59
Warwick Dene. W5 1E 80
Warwick Dri. SW15 3D 100
Warwick Est. W2 5K 65
Warwick Gdns. N4 5C 32
Warwick Gdns. W14 3H 83
Warwick Gdns. Barn 1C 4
Warwick Gdns. Ilf 1F 55
Warwick Gdns. Th Dit 5K 133
Warwick Gdns. T Hth 3A 140
Warwick Gro. E5 2H 51
Warwick Gro. Surb 7F 135
Warwick Ho. E16 1J 89 (off Wesley Av.)
Warwick Ho. SW9 2A 104
Warwick Ho. King T 1E 134 (off Acre Rd.)
Warwick Ho. St. SW1 1H 85 (4D 166)
Warwick La. EC4 6B 68 (7B 162)
Warwick Lodge. Twic 3F 115
Warwick Pde. Harr 2B 26
Warwick Pas. EC4 6B 68 (1B 168) (off Old Bailey)
Warwick Pl. W5 2D 80
Warwick Pl. W9 5A 66
Warwick Pl. Th Dit 6A 134
Warwick Pl. N. SW1 4G 85 (4A 172)
Warwick Rd. E4 5H 19
Warwick Rd. E11 5K 35
Warwick Rd. E12 5C 54
Warwick Rd. E15 6H 53
Warwick Rd. E17 1B 34
Warwick Rd. N11 6C 16
Warwick Rd. N18 4K 17
Warwick Rd. SE20 3H 141
Warwick Rd. W5 2D 80
Warwick Rd. W14 & SW5 4H 83
Warwick Rd. Ashf 5A 112
Warwick Rd. Barn 4E 4
Warwick Rd. Houn 3K 95
Warwick Rd. King T 1C 134
Warwick Rd. N Mald 3J 135
Warwick Rd. Sidc 5B 128
Warwick Rd. S'hall 3D 78
Warwick Rd. Sutt 4A 150

Warwick Rd. Th Dit 5K 133
Warwick Rd. T Hth 3A 140
Warwick Rd. Twic 1J 115
Warwick Rd. Well 3C 110
Warwick Rd. W Dray 2A 76
Warwick Row. SW1 3F 85 (1K 171)
Warwickshire Path. SE8 7B 88
Warwickshire Rd. N16 4E 50
Warwick Sq. EC4 6B 68 (7B 162)
Warwick Sq. SW1 5G 85 (5A 172)
Warwick Sq. M. SW1 4G 85 (4A 172)
Warwick St. W1 7G 67 (2B 166)
Warwick Ter. E10 5F 35 (off Lea Bri. Rd.)
Warwick Ter. SE18 6H 91
Warwick Way. SW1 5F 85 (5J 171)
Warwick Yd. EC1 4C 68 (4D 162)
Washington Av. E12 4D 54
Washington Clo. E3 3D 70
Washington Ho. E17 2B 34 (off Priory Ct.)
Washington Rd. E6 7A 54
Washington Rd. E18 2H 35
Washington Rd. SW13 7C 82
Washington Rd. King T 2G 135
Washington Rd. Wor Pk 2D 148
Wasps R.U.F.C. (Queen's Pk. Rangers F.C.) 1D 82
Wastdale Rd. SE23 1K 123
Watchfield Ct. W4 5J 81
Watch, The. N12 4F 15
Watcombe Cotts. Rich 6G 81
Watcombe Pl. SE25 5H 141
Watcombe Rd. SE25 5H 141
Waterbank Rd. SE6 3D 124
Waterbeach Rd. Dag 6C 56
Water Brook La. NW4 5E 28
Watercress Pl. N1 7E 50
Waterdale Rd. SE2 6A 92
Waterden Cres. E15 5C 52
Waterden Rd. E15 5C 52
Waterer Ho. SE6 4E 124
Waterer Ri. Wall 6H 151
Waterfall Clo. N14 3B 16
Waterfall Cotts. SW19 6B 120
Waterfall Rd. N11 & N14 4A 16
Waterfall Rd. SW19 6B 120
Waterfall Ter. SW17 6C 120
Waterfall Wlk. N14 1A 16
Waterfield Clo. SE28 1B 92
Waterfield Clo. Belv 3G 93
Waterfield Gdns. SE25 4D 140
Waterford Ho. W11 7H 65 (off Kensington Pk. Rd.)
Waterford Rd. SW6 7K 83 (in two parts)
Waterford Way. NW10 5D 46
Water Gdns. Stan 6G 11
Water Gdns., The. W2 6C 66 (7D 158)
Watergardens, The. King T 6J 117
Watergate. EC4 7B 68 (2A 168)
Watergate St. SE8 6C 88
Watergate Wlk. WC2 1J 85 (4F 167)
Waterhall Av. E4 4B 20
Waterhall Clo. E17 1K 33
Waterhead. NW1 3G 67 (1A 160) (off Varndell St.)
Waterhouse Clo. E16 5B 72
Waterhouse Clo. NW3 5B 48
Waterhouse Clo. W6 4F 83
Waterhouse Sq. EC1 5A 68 (6J 161)
Wateridge Clo. E14 3C 88
Water La. E15 6G 53
Water La. EC3 7E 68 (3H 169)
Water La. N9 1C 18
Water La. NW1 7F 49
Water La. SE14 7J 87
Water La. Ilf 3J 55
Water La. King T 1D 134
Water La. Rich 5D 98
Water La. Sidc 2F 129 (in two parts)
Water La. Twic 1A 116
Water Lily Clo. S'hall 2G 79
Waterloo Bri. WC2 & SE1 7K 67 (3G 167)
Waterloo Clo. E9 5J 51
Waterloo Clo. Felt 1H 113
Waterloo Gdns. E2 2J 69
Waterloo Gdns. Romf 6K 39
Waterloo Pas. NW6 7H 47
Waterloo Pl. SW1 1H 85 (4C 166)
Waterloo Pl. Cars 3D 150 (off Wrythe La.)
Waterloo Pl. Kew 6G 81
Waterloo Pl. Rich 4E 98
Waterloo Rd. E6 7A 54
Waterloo Rd. E7 5H 53
Waterloo Rd. E10 7C 34
Waterloo Rd. NW2 1C 46
Waterloo Rd. SE1 1K 85 (4H 167)
Waterloo Rd. Ilf 2G 37
Waterloo Rd. Romf 5K 39
Waterloo Rd. Sutt 5B 150
Waterloo Ter. N1 7B 50
Waterlow Ct. NW11 7K 29
Waterlow Rd. N19 1G 49
Waterman Building. E14 2B 88
Watermans Clo. King T 7E 116
Watermans Ct. Bren 6D 80 (off High St.)
Watermans M. W5 7E 62
Waterman St. SW15 3F 101
Waterman's Wlk. EC4 3E 168
Watermans Wlk. SE16 2A 88
Waterman Way. E1 1H 87
Watermead. Felt 1G 113
Watermead Ho. E9 5A 52
Watermead La. Cars 7D 138
Watermeadow La. SW6 2A 102
Watermead Rd. SE6 4E 124
Watermead Way. N17 3G 33
Watermen's Sq. SE20 7J 123
Water M. SE15 4J 105
Watermill Bus. Cen. Enf 2G 9
Watermill Clo. Rich 3C 116
Water Mill Ho. Felt 2E 114
Watermill La. N18 5K 17
Watermill Way. SW19 1B 138
Watermill Way. Felt 2D 114
Watermint Quay. N16 7G 33
Water Rd. Wemb 1F 63
Waters Edge. SW6 1E 100
Watersedge. Eps 4J 147
Watersfield Way. Edgw 7J 11
Waters Gdns. Dag 5G 57
Waterside. E17 6J 33
Waterside. Beck 1B 142
Waterside Bus. Cen. Iswth 4B 98
Waterside Clo. E3 1B 70
Waterside Clo. SE16 2G 87
Waterside Clo. Bark 4A 56
Waterside Clo. N'holt 3D 60
Waterside Clo. Surb 2E 146
Waterside Dri. W on T 5J 131
Waterside Ho. E14 2D 88 (off Admirals Way)
Waterside Pl. NW1 1E 66
Waterside Point. SW11 7C 84
Waterside Rd. S'hall 3E 78
Waterside Trad. Cen. W7 3J 79
Waterside Way. SW17 4A 120
Watersmeet Way. SE28 6C 74
Waterson St. E2 3E 68 (1H 163)
Waters Pl. SW15 2E 100
Watersplash Clo. King T 3E 134
Watersplash La. Hay 4J 77 (in two parts)
Watersplash Rd. Shep 5C 130
Waters Rd. SE6 3G 125
Waters Rd. King T 2H 135
Waters Sq. King T 3H 135
Water St. WC2 2J 167
Water Tower Clo. Uxb 5A 40
Water Tower Hill. Croy 4D 152
Water Tower Pl. N1 1A 68
Waterview Ho. E14 5A 70 (off Carr St.)
Waterways Bus. Cen. Enf 1G 9
Waterworks Corner. (Junct.) 2G 35
Waterworks La. E5 2K 51
Waterworks Rd. SW2 6K 103
Waterworks Yd. Croy 3C 152
Watery La. SW20 2H 137
Watery La. Hay 5G 77
Watery La. N'holt 2A 60
Watery La. Sidc 6B 128
Wates Way. Mitc 6D 138
Wateville Rd. N17 1C 32
Watford By-Pass. Edgw 4C 12
Watford By-Pass. Stan 1G 11
Watford Clo. SW11 1C 102
Watford Rd. E16 5J 71
Watford Rd. Harr 7A 26
Watford Way. NW4 4C 28
Watford Way. NW7 & NW4 4F 13
Watkin Rd. Wemb 3H 45
Watkins Ct. N'wd 1H 23
Watkins Ho. E14 2E 88 (off Manchester Rd.)
Watkinson Rd. N7 6K 49
Watling. 7E 12
Watling Av. Edgw 1J 27
Watling Ct. EC4 1D 168
Watling Farm Clo. Stan 1H 11
Watling Gdns. NW2 6G 47
Watling Ga. NW9 4A 28
Watlings Clo. Croy 6A 142
Watling St. EC4 6C 68 (1D 168)
Watling St. SE15 6E 86
Watling St. Bexh 4H 111
Watlington Gro. SE26 5A 124
Watney Cotts. SW14 3J 99
Watney Mkt. E1 6H 69
Watney Rd. SW14 3J 99
Watney's Rd. Mitc 5H 139
Watney St. E1 6H 69
Watson Av. E6 7E 54
Watson Av. Sutt 2G 149
Watson Clo. N16 5D 50
Watson Clo. SW19 6C 120
Watson's M. W1 5C 66 (6D 158)
Watsons Rd. N22 1K 31
Watsons St. SE8 7C 88
Watson St. E13 2K 71
Watsons Yd. NW2 2C 46
Wattisfield Rd. E5 3J 51
Watts Clo. N15 5E 32
Watts Gro. E3 5C 70
Watts La. Chst 1F 145
Watts La. Tedd 5A 116
Watts Point. E13 1J 71 (off Brooks Rd.)
Watts Rd. Th Dit 7A 134
Watts St. E1 1H 87
Watts St. SE15 1F 105
Wat Tyler Ho. N8 3J 31 (off Boyton Rd.)
Wat Tyler Rd. SE10 & SE3 2E 106
Wauthier Clo. N13 5G 17
Wavel Ct. E1 1J 87 (off Garnet St.)
Wavel Ct. Croy 5D 152 (off Hurst Rd.)
Wavell Dri. Sidc 6J 109
Wavel M. N8 4H 31
Wavel M. NW6 7K 47
Wavel Pl. SE26 4F 123
Wavendon Av. W4 5K 81
Waveney Av. SE15 4H 105
Waveney Clo. E1 1G 87
Waveney Ho. SE15 4H 105
Waverley Av. E4 4G 19
Waverley Av. E17 3F 35
Waverley Av. Surb 6H 135
Waverley Av. Sutt 2K 149
Waverley Av. Twic 1D 114
Waverley Av. Wemb 5F 45
Waverley Clo. E18 1A 36
Waverley Clo. Brom 5B 144
Waverley Clo. Hay 4F 77
Waverley Clo. W Mol 5E 132
Waverley Ct. NW3 6D 48
Waverley Ct. NW6 7G 47
Waverley Ct. SE26 5J 123
Waverley Ct. Enf 3H 7
Waverley Cres. SE18 5H 91
Waverley Gdns. E6 5C 72
Waverley Gdns. NW10 2F 63
Waverley Gdns. Bark 2J 73
Waverley Gdns. Ilf 2G 37
Waverley Gdns. N'wd 1J 23
Waverley Gro. N3 3G 29
Waverley Ind. Est. Harr 3H 25
Waverley Pl. N4 2B 50
Waverley Pl. NW8 2B 66
Waverley Rd. E17 3E 34
Waverley Rd. E18 1A 36
Waverley Rd. N8 6J 31
Waverley Rd. N17 7C 18
Waverley Rd. SE18 5G 91
Waverley Rd. SE25 4H 141
Waverley Rd. Enf 3G 7
Waverley Rd. Eps 5D 148
Waverley Rd. Harr 2C 42
Waverley Rd. S'hall 7E 60
Waverley Vs. N17 2F 33
Waverley Way. Cars 6C 150
Waverton Ho. E3 1B 70
Waverton Rd. SW18 7A 102
Waverton St. W1 1E 84 (4J 165)
Wavertree Ct. SW2 1J 121
Wavertree Rd. E18 2J 35
Wavertree Rd. SW2 1K 121
Waxlow Cres. S'hall 6E 60
Waxlow Ho. Hay 5B 60
Waxlow Rd. NW10 2J 63
Waxwell Clo. Pinn 2B 24
Waxwell Farm Ho. Pinn 2B 24
Waxwell La. Pinn 2B 24
Wayborne Gro. Ruis 6E 22
Waye Av. Houn 1J 95
Wayfarer Rd. N'holt 3B 60
Wayfield Link. SE9 6H 109
Wayford St. SW11 2C 102
Wayland Av. E8 5G 51
Wayland Clo. E8 5G 51
Wayland Ho. SW9 2A 104 (off Robsart St.)
Waylands. Hay 5F 59
Waylands Mead. Beck 1D 142
Waylett Ho. SE11 6J 173
Waylett Pl. SE27 3B 122
Waylett Pl. Wemb 4D 44
Wayman Ct. E8 6H 51
Wayne Kirkum Way. NW6 5H 47
Waynflete Av. Croy 3B 152
Waynflete Sq. W10 7F 65
Waynflete St. SW18 2A 120
Wayside. NW11 1G 47
Wayside. SW14 5J 99
Wayside. New Ad 6D 154
Wayside Clo. N14 6B 6
Wayside Ct. Twic 6C 98
Wayside Ct. Wemb 3G 45
Wayside Gdns. Dag 5G 57
Wayside Gro. SE9 4D 126
Wayside M. Ilf 5E 36
Weald Clo. SE16 5H 87
Weald Clo. Brom 2C 156
Weald La. Harr 2H 25
Weald Ri. Harr 7E 10
Weald Rd. Uxb 2C 58
Weald Sq. E5 2G 51
Wealdstone. 3J 25
Wealdstone Rd. Sutt 2H 149
Weald, The. Chst 6D 126
Weald Way. Hay 3G 59
Weald Way. Romf 6H 39
Wealdwood Gdns. Pinn 6A 10
Weale Rd. E4 3A 20
Weall Ct. Pinn 4C 24
Weardale Gdns. Enf 1J 7
Weardale Rd. SE13 4F 107
Wearmouth Ho. E3 5B 70 (off Joseph St.)
Wear Pl. E2 3H 69 (in two parts)
Wearside Rd. SE13 4D 106
Weatherbury. W2 6J 65 (off Talbot Rd.)
Weatherbury Ho. N19 3H 49 (off Wedmore St.)
Weatherley Clo. E3 5B 70
Weaver Clo. E6 7F 73
Weaver Clo. Croy 4F 153
Weavers Clo. Iswth 4J 97
Weavers Ho. E11 6J 35 (off New Wanstead)
Weavers La. SE1 1E 86 (5H 169)
Weavers Ter. SW6 6J 83 (off Micklethwaite Rd.)
Weaver St. E1 4G 69
Weavers Way. NW1 1H 67
Weaver Wlk. SE27 4C 122
Webb Clo. W10 4E 64
Webber Row. SE1 2B 86 (1K 173) (in two parts)
Webber St. SE1 2A 86 (6K 167)
Webb Est. E5 7G 33
Webb Gdns. E13 4J 71
Webb Ho. SW8 7H 85
Webb Ho. Dag 3G 57 (off Kershaw Rd.)
Webb Ho. Felt 3C 114
Webb Pl. NW10 3B 64
Webb Rd. SE3 6H 89
Webbscroft Rd. Dag 4H 57
Webb's Rd. SW11 4D 102
Webbs Rd. Hay 3K 59
Webb St. SE1 3E 86
Webheath. NW6 7H 47
Webster Gdns. W5 1D 80
Webster Rd. E11 3E 52
Webster Rd. SE16 3G 87
Weddell Ho. E1 4K 69 (off Duckett St.)
Wedderburn Rd. NW3 5B 48
Wedderburn Rd. Bark 1J 73
Wedgewood Ct. Bex 7F 111
Wedgewood Ct. Brom 3H 143 (off Cumberland Rd.)
Wedgewood Ho. SW1 5F 85 (6K 171) (off Churchill Gdns.)
Wedgewood M. W1 6H 67 (1D 166)
Wedgwood Ho. E2 3K 69 (off Warley St.)
Wedgwood Ho. SE11 3A 86 (2J 173) (off Lambeth Wlk.)
Wedgwood Wlk. NW6 5K 47 (off Dresden Clo.)
Wedgwood Way. SE19 7C 122
Wedlake St. W10 4G 65
Wedmore Av. Ilf 1E 36
Wedmore Ct. N19 2H 49
Wedmore Gdns. N19 2H 49
Wedmore M. N19 3H 49
Wedmore Rd. Gnfd 3H 61
Wedmore St. N19 3H 49
Weech Rd. NW6 4J 47
Weedington Rd. NW5 5E 48
Weedon Ho. W12 6C 64
Weekley Sq. SW11 3B 102
Weigall Rd. SE12 5J 107

Weighhouse St. W1 … 6E 66 (1H 165)
Weighton M. SE20 … 2H 141
Weighton Rd. SE20 … 2H 141
Weighton Rd. Harr … 1H 25
Weihurst Ct. Sutt … 5C 150
Weihurst Gdns. Sutt … 5B 150
Weimar St. SW15 … 3G 101
Weirdale Av. N20 … 2J 15
Weir Hall Av. N18 … 6J 17
Weir Hall Gdns. N18 … 5J 17
Weir Hall Rd. N18 & N17 … 5J 17
Weir Rd. SW12 … 7G 103
Weir Rd. SW19 … 3K 119
Weir Rd. Bex … 7H 111
Weir Rd. W on T … 6J 131
Weir's Pas. NW1 … 3H 67 (1D 160)
Weiss Rd. SW15 … 3F 101
Welbeck Av. Brom … 4J 125
Welbeck Av. Hay … 4K 59
Welbeck Av. Sidc … 1A 128
Welbeck Clo. N12 … 5G 15
Welbeck Clo. Eps … 7C 148
Welbeck Clo. N Mald … 5B 136
Welbeck Ct. W14 … 4H 83 (off Addison Bri. Pl.)
Welbeck Ho. W1 … 6F 67 (7J 159) (off Welbeck St.)
Welbeck Rd. E6 … 3B 72
Welbeck Rd. Barn … 6H 5
Welbeck Rd. Harr … 1F 43
Welbeck Rd. Sutt … 2B 150
Welbeck St. W1 … 5E 66 (6H 159)
Welbeck Vs. N21 … 2H 17
Welbeck Wlk. Cars … 1B 150
Welbeck Way. W1 … 6F 67 (7J 159)
Welbourne Rd. N17 … 3F 33
Welby Ho. N19 … 7H 31
Welby St. SE5 … 1B 104
Welch Pl. Pinn … 1A 24
Welcome Ct. E17 … 7C 34 (off Boundary Rd.)
Weldon Clo. Ruis … 6K 41
Weldon Ct. N21 … 5E 6
Weldon Dri. W Mol … 4D 132
Weld Pl. N11 … 5A 16 (in two parts)
Welfare Rd. E15 … 7G 53
Welford Clo. E5 … 3K 51
Welford Ct. NW1 … 7F 49 (off Castlehaven Rd.)
Welford Ct. SW8 … 2G 103
Welford Ct. W9 … 5J 65 (off Elmfield Way)
Welford Pl. SW19 … 4G 119
Welham Rd. SW17 & SW16 … 5E 120
Welhouse Rd. Cars … 1C 150
Wellacre Rd. Harr … 6B 26
Wellan Clo. Sidc … 5B 110
Welland Ct. SE6 … 2B 124 (off Oakham Clo.)
Welland Gdns. Gnfd … 2K 61
Welland Ho. SE15 … 4J 105
Welland M. E1 … 1G 87
Wellands Clo. Brom … 2D 144
Welland St. SE10 … 6E 88
Well App. Barn … 5A 4
Wellbrook Rd. Orp … 4E 156
Wellby Ct. E13 … 1A 72
Well Clo. SW16 … 4K 121
Well Clo. Ruis … 3C 42
Wellclose Sq. E1 … 7G 69
Wellclose St. E1 … 7G 69
Wellcome Cen. for Medical Science … 3C 160
Well Cottage Clo. E11 … 6A 36
Well Ct. EC4 … 6C 68 (1D 168) (in two parts)
Welldon Ct. Harr … 5J 25
Welldon Cres. Harr … 5J 25
Weller Ho. SE16 … 2G 87 (off George Row)
Wellers Ct. NW1 … 2J 67 (1E 160)
Weller St. SE1 … 2C 86 (6C 168)
Welles Ct. E14 … 7C 70 (off Premiere Pl.)
Wellesley Av. W6 … 3D 82
Wellesley Clo. SE7 … 5A 90
Wellesley Ct. NW2 … 2C 46
Wellesley Ct. W9 … 3A 66 (off Maida Va.)
Wellesley Ct. Sutt … 1G 149
Wellesley Ct. Rd. Croy … 2D 152
Wellesley Cres. Twic … 2J 115
Wellesley Gro. Croy … 2D 152
Wellesley Ho. NW1 … 3H 67 (2D 160) (off Wellesley Pl.)
Wellesley Ho. SW1 … 5F 85 (5J 171) (off Ebury Bri. Rd.)
Wellesley Lodge. Sutt … 7J 149 (off Worcester Rd.)
Wellesley Mans. W14 … 5H 83 (off Edith Vs.)
Wellesley Pde. Twic … 3J 115
Wellesley Pk. M. Enf … 2G 7
Wellesley Pas. Croy … 2C 152
Wellesley Pl. NW1 … 3H 67 (2C 160)
Wellesley Pl. NW5 … 5E 48
Wellesley Rd. E11 … 5J 35
Wellesley Rd. E17 … 6C 34
Wellesley Rd. N22 … 2A 32
Wellesley Rd. NW5 … 5E 48
Wellesley Rd. W4 … 5G 81
Wellesley Rd. Croy … 1C 152
Wellesley Rd. Harr … 5J 25
Wellesley Rd. Ilf … 2F 55
Wellesley Rd. Sutt … 6A 150
Wellesley Rd. Twic … 3H 115
Wellesley St. E1 … 5K 69
Wellesley Ter. N1 … 3C 68 (1D 162)
Wellfield Av. N10 … 3F 31
Wellfield Rd. SW16 … 4J 121
Wellfield Wlk. SW16 … 5K 121 (in two parts)
Wellfit St. SE24 … 3B 104
Wellgarth. Gnfd … 6B 44
Wellgarth Rd. NW11 … 1K 47
Well Gro. N20 … 1F 15
Well Hall Pde. SE9 … 4D 108
Well Hall Rd. SE9 … 3C 108
Well Hall Roundabout. (Junct.) … 3C 108
Wellhouse La. Barn … 4A 4
Wellhouse Rd. Beck … 4C 142
Welling … 3B 110
Welling High St. Well … 3B 110
Wellington. N8 … 4J 31 (in two parts)
Wellington Arch … 6H 165
Wellington Av. E4 … 2H 19
Wellington Av. N9 … 3C 18
Wellington Av. N15 … 6F 33
Wellington Av. SE18 … 3F 91
Wellington Av. Houn … 5E 96
Wellington Av. Pinn … 1D 24
Wellington Av. Sidc … 6A 110
Wellington Av. Wor Pk … 3E 148
Wellington Bldgs. SW1 … 5E 84 (6H 171)
Wellington Clo. SE14 … 1K 105
Wellington Clo. W11 … 6J 65
Wellington Clo. Dag … 7J 57
Wellington Clo. W on T … 7H 131
Wellington Ct. NW8 … 2B 66 (off Wellington Rd.)
Wellington Ct. SW1 … 2D 84 (7E 164) (off Knightsbridge)
Wellington Ct. SW6 … 1K 101 (off Maltings Pl.)
Wellington Ct. Hamp … 5H 115
Wellington Ct. Pinn … 1D 24 (off Wellington Rd.)
Wellington Ct. Stanw … 7A 94
Wellington Cres. N Mald … 3J 135
Wellington Dri. Dag … 7J 57
Wellington Est. E2 … 2J 69
Wellington Gdns. SE7 … 6A 90
Wellington Gdns. Twic … 4H 115
Wellington Gro. SE10 … 7F 89
Wellington Ho. E16 … 1J 89 (off Pepys Cres.)
Wellington Ho. NW3 … 6D 48 (off Eton Rd.)
Wellington Ho. W5 … 3E 62
Wellington Ho. N'holt … 7E 42 (off Farmlands, The)
Wellington Mans. E10 … 1C 52
Wellington M. N7 … 6K 49 (off Roman Way)
Wellington M. SE7 … 6A 90
Wellington M. SE22 … 4G 105
Wellington M. SW16 … 3H 121
Wellington Monument … 6H 165
Wellington Mus. … 2E 84 (6H 165)
Wellington Pde. Sidc … 5A 110
Wellington Pk. Est. NW2 … 1C 46
Wellington Pas. E11 … 5J 35 (off Wellington Rd.)
Wellington Pl. E11 … 5J 35
Wellington Pl. N2 … 5C 30
Wellington Pl. NW8 … 3B 66 (1B 158)
Wellington Rd. E6 … 1D 72
Wellington Rd. E7 … 4H 53
Wellington Rd. E10 … 1A 52
Wellington Rd. E11 … 5J 35
Wellington Rd. E17 … 4A 34
Wellington Rd. NW8 … 2B 66 (1B 158)
Wellington Rd. NW10 … 3F 65
Wellington Rd. SW19 … 2J 119
Wellington Rd. W5 … 3C 80
Wellington Rd. Ashf … 5A 112
Wellington Rd. Belv … 5F 93
Wellington Rd. Bex … 5D 110
Wellington Rd. Brom … 4A 144
Wellington Rd. Croy … 7B 140
Wellington Rd. Enf … 5K 7
Wellington Rd. Felt … 5G 95
Wellington Rd. Hamp … 5H 115
Wellington Rd. Harr … 3J 25
Wellington Rd. Pinn … 1D 24
Wellington Rd. N. Houn … 3D 96
Wellington Rd. S. Houn … 4D 96
Wellington Row. E2 … 3F 69 (1K 163)
Wellington Sq. SW3 … 5D 84 (5E 170)
Wellington St. SE18 … 4E 90
Wellington St. WC2 … 7K 67 (2G 167)
Wellington St. Bark … 1G 73
Wellington Ter. E1 … 1H 87
Wellington Ter. N8 … 3A 32 (off Turnpike La.)
Wellington Ter. W2 … 7J 65
Wellington Ter. Harr … 1H 43
Wellington Way. E3 … 3C 70
Welling United F.C. … 3C 110
Welling Way. SE9 & Well … 3G 109
Well La. SW14 … 5J 99
Wellmeadow Rd. SE13 & SE6 … 6G 107 (in two parts)
Wellmeadow Rd. W7 … 4A 80
Wellow Wlk. Cars … 1B 150
Well Pl. NW3 … 3B 48
Well Rd. NW3 … 3B 48
Well Rd. Barn … 5A 4
Wells Clo. N'holt … 3A 60
Wells Clo. S Croy … 5E 152
Wells Ct. NW6 … 2J 65 (off Cambridge Av.)
Wells Dri. NW9 … 1K 45
Wells Gdns. Dag … 5H 57
Wells Gdns. Ilf … 7C 36
Wells Ho. EC1 … 3A 68 (1K 161) (off Spa Grn. Est.)
Wells Ho. SE16 … 3J 87 (off Howland Est.)
Wells Ho. W5 … 1D 80 (off Grove Rd.)
Wells Ho. Bark … 7A 56 (off Margaret Bondfield Av.)
Wells Ho. Brom … 5K 125 (off Pike Clo.)
Wells Ho. Rd. NW10 … 5A 64
Wellside Clo. Barn … 4A 4
Wellside Gdns. SW14 … 4J 99
Wells M. W1 … 5G 67 (6B 160)
Wellsmoor Gdns. Brom … 3E 144
Wells Pk. Rd. SE26 … 3G 123
Wells Path. N'holt … 3G 59
Wells Pl. SW18 … 7A 102
Wells Ri. NW8 … 1D 66
Wells Rd. W12 … 2E 82
Wells Rd. Brom … 2D 144
Wells Sq. WC1 … 3K 67 (2G 161)
Wells St. W1 … 5G 67 (6A 160)
Wellstead Av. N9 … 7E 8
Wellstead Rd. E6 … 2E 72
Wells Ter. N4 … 2A 50
Wells, The. N14 … 7C 6
Well St. E9 … 7J 51
Well St. E15 … 6G 53
Wells Way. SE5 … 6D 86
Wells Way. SW7 … 3B 84 (1A 170)
Wells Yd. N7 … 5A 50
Well Wlk. NW3 … 4B 48
Wellwood Rd. Ilf … 1A 56
Welsby Ct. W5 … 5C 62
Welsford St. SE1 … 4G 87 (in two parts)
Welsh Clo. E13 … 3J 71
Welsh Ho. E1 … 1H 87 (off Wapping La.)
Welshpool Ho. E8 … 1G 69 (off Welshpool St.)
Welshpool St. E8 … 1G 69 (in two parts)
Welshside. NW9 … 6A 28 (off Ruthin Clo.)
Welshside Wlk. NW9 … 6A 28
Welstead Ho. E1 … 6H 69 (off Cannon St. Rd.)
Welstead Way. W4 … 4B 82
Weltje Rd. W6 … 4C 82
Welton Ct. SE5 … 1E 104
Welton Ho. E1 … 5K 69 (off Stepney Way)
Welton Rd. SE18 … 7J 91
Welwyn Av. Felt … 6H 95
Welwyn St. E2 … 3J 69
Welwyn Way. Hay … 4G 59
Wembley … 5E 44
Wembley Arena … 4G 45
Wembley Commercial Cen. Wemb … 2D 44
Wembley Conference Cen. … 4G 45
Wembley Hill Rd. Wemb … 3F 45
Wembley Park … 3G 45
Wembley Pk. Bus. Cen. Wemb … 4H 45
Wembley Pk. Dri. Wemb … 4F 45
Wembley Retail Pk. Wemb … 4H 45
Wembley Rd. Hamp … 1E 132
Wembley Stadium … 4G 45
Wembley Stadium Ind. Est. Wemb … 4H 45
Wembley Way. Wemb … 6H 45
Wemborough Rd. Stan … 1B 26
Wembury M. N6 … 7G 31
Wembury Rd. N6 … 7F 31
Wemyss Rd. SE3 … 2H 107
Wendela Ct. Harr … 2J 43
Wendell Rd. W12 … 3B 82
Wenderholme. S Croy … 5D 152 (off S. Park Hill Rd.)
Wendle Ct. SW8 … 6J 85 (7E 172)
Wendling Rd. Sutt … 1B 150
Wendon St. E3 … 1B 70
Wendover. SE17 … 5E 86 (in two parts)
Wendover Clo. Hay … 4C 60
Wendover Ct. NW2 … 3J 47
Wendover Ct. NW10 … 4H 63
Wendover Ct. W1 … 5E 66 (6G 159) (off Chiltern St.)
Wendover Ct. Brom … 3K 143 (off Wendover Rd.)
Wendover Dri. N Mald … 6B 136
Wendover Ho. W1 … 5E 66 (6G 159) (off Chiltern St.)
Wendover Rd. NW10 … 2B 64
Wendover Rd. SE9 … 3B 108
Wendover Rd. Brom … 4K 143
Wendover Way. Well … 5A 110
Wendy Clo. Enf … 6A 8
Wendy Way. Wemb … 1E 62
Wenham Ho. SW8 … 7G 85
Wenlake Ho. EC1 … 4C 68 (3C 162) (off Old St.)
Wenlock Barn Est. N1 … 2D 68 (off Wenlock St.)
Wenlock Ct. N1 … 2D 68 (1F 163)
Wenlock Gdns. NW4 … 4D 28
Wenlock Rd. N1 … 2C 68 (1D 162)
Wenlock Rd. Edgw … 7C 12
Wenlock St. N1 … 2C 68 (1D 162)
Wennington Rd. E3 … 2K 69
Wensdale Ho. E5 … 2G 51
Wensley Av. Wfd G … 7C 20
Wensley Clo. N11 … 6K 15
Wensley Clo. SE9 … 6D 108
Wensleydale Av. Ilf … 2C 36
Wensleydale Gdns. Hamp … 7F 115
Wensleydale Pas. Hamp … 1E 132
Wensleydale Rd. Hamp … 6E 114
Wensley Rd. N18 … 6C 18
Wentland Clo. SE6 … 2F 125
Wentland Rd. SE6 … 2F 125
Wentway Ct. W13 … 4K 61 (off Ruislip Rd. E.)
Wentworth Av. N3 … 7D 14
Wentworth Clo. N3 … 7E 14
Wentworth Clo. SE28 … 6D 74
Wentworth Clo. Ashf … 4D 112
Wentworth Clo. Hayes … 2J 155
Wentworth Clo. Mord … 7J 137
Wentworth Clo. Surb … 2D 146
Wentworth Ct. W6 … 6G 83 (off Paynes Wlk.)
Wentworth Ct. Twic … 3J 115
Wentworth Cres. SE15 … 7G 87
Wentworth Cres. Hay … 3F 77
Wentworth Dri. Pinn … 5J 23
Wentworth Dwellings. E1 … 6F 69 (7J 163) (off Wentworth St.)
Wentworth Fields. Hay … 2F 59
Wentworth Gdns. N13 … 3G 17
Wentworth Hill. Wemb … 1F 45
Wentworth M. E3 … 4A 70
Wentworth Pk. N3 … 7D 14
Wentworth Pl. Stan … 6G 11
Wentworth Rd. E12 … 4B 54
Wentworth Rd. NW11 … 6H 29
Wentworth Rd. Barn … 3A 4
Wentworth Rd. Croy … 7A 140
Wentworth Rd. S'hall … 4A 78
Wentworth St. E1 … 6F 69 (7J 163)
Wentworth Way. Pinn … 4C 24
Wenvoe Av. Bexh … 2H 111
Wepham Clo. Hay … 5B 60
Wernbrook St. SE18 … 6G 91
Werndee Rd. SE25 … 4G 141
Werneth Hall Rd. Ilf … 3E 36
Werrington St. NW1 … 2G 67 (1B 160)
Werter Rd. SW15 … 4G 101
Wesleyan Pl. NW5 … 4F 49
Wesley Av. E16 … 1J 89
Wesley Av. NW10 … 3K 63

Wesley Av. Houn 2C 96
Wesley Clo. N7 2K 49
Wesley Clo. SE17 4B 86
Wesley Clo. Harr 2G 43
Wesley Ct. SE16 3H 87
Wesley Rd. E10 7E 34
Wesley Rd. N2 1C 30
Wesley Rd. NW10 1J 63
Wesley Rd. Hay 7J 59
Wesley's House Chapel & Mus. of Methodism. 4D 68 (4F 163)
Wesley Sq. W11 6G 65
Wesley St. W1 5E 66 (6H 159)
Wessex Av. SW19 3J 137
Wessex Clo. Ilf 6J 37
Wessex Clo. King T 1H 135
Wessex Ct. Barn 4A 4
Wessex Ct. Beck 1A 142
Wessex Ct. Stanw 6A 94
Wessex Dri. Pinn 1C 24
Wessex Gdns. NW11 1G 47
Wessex Ho. SE1 5F 87
Wessex La. Gnfd 3H 61
Wessex Rd. H'row A 2A 94
Wessex St. E2 3J 69
Wessex Wlk. Bex 2K 129
Wessex Way. NW11 1G 47
Westacott. Hay 5G 59
Westacott Clo. N19 1H 49
West Acton. 6G 63
West App. Orp 5G 145
W. Arbour St. E1 6K 69
West Av. E17 4D 34
West Av. N2 3K 29
West Av. N3 6D 14
West Av. NW4 5F 29
West Av. Hay 7H 59
West Av. Pinn 6D 24
West Av. S'hall 7D 60
West Av. Wall 5J 151
W. Avenue Rd. E17 4C 34
West Bank. N16 7E 32
West Bank. Bark 1F 73
West Bank. Enf 2H 7
Westbank Rd. Hamp H 6G 115
West Barnes. 4D 136
W. Barnes La. N Mald & SW20 5C 136
West Beckton. 6B 72
West Bedfont. 6B 94
Westbeech Rd. N22 3A 32
Westbere Dri. Stan 5J 11
Westbere Rd. NW2 4G 47
West Block. SE1 2K 85 (7H 167) (off Addington St.)
Westbourne Av. W3 6K 63
Westbourne Av. Sutt 2G 149
Westbourne Bri. W2 5A 66
Westbourne Clo. Hay 4A 60
Westbourne Cres. W2 7B 66 (2A 164)
Westbourne Cres. M. W2 2A 164
Westbourne Dri. SE23 2K 123
Westbourne Gdns. W2 6K 65
Westbourne Green. 6H 65
Westbourne Gro. W11 & W2 7H 65
Westbourne Gro. M. W11 6J 65
Westbourne Gro. Ter. W2 6K 65
Westbourne Ho. SW1 5F 85 (5J 171) (off Ebury Bri. Rd.)
Westbourne Ho. Houn 6E 78
Westbourne Pde. Hil 4D 58
Westbourne Pk. Pas. W2 5J 65 (in two parts)
Westbourne Pk. Rd. W11 & W2 6G 65
Westbourne Pk. Vs. W2 5J 65
Westbourne Pl. N9 3C 18
Westbourne Rd. N7 6K 49
Westbourne Rd. SE26 6K 123
Westbourne Rd. Bexh 7D 92
Westbourne Rd. Croy 6F 141
Westbourne Rd. Felt 3H 113
Westbourne Rd. Uxb 4D 58
Westbourne St. W2 7B 66 (2A 164)
Westbourne Ter. SE23 2K 123 (off Westbourne Dri.)
Westbourne Ter. W2 6A 66 (1A 164)
Westbourne Ter. M. W2 6A 66
Westbourne Ter. Rd. W2 5K 65
Westbourne Ter. Rd. Bri. W2 5A 66 (off Westbourne Ter. Rd.)
Westbridge Clo. W12 2C 82
Westbridge Rd. SW11 1B 102
West Brompton. 6K 83
Westbrook Av. Hamp 7D 114
Westbrook Clo. Barn 3G 5
Westbrook Cres. Cockf 3G 5
Westbrooke Cres. Well 3C 110
Westbrooke Rd. Sidc 2H 127
Westbrooke Rd. Well 3B 110 (in two parts)
Westbrook Ho. E2 3J 69 (off Victoria Pk. Sq.)
Westbrook Rd. SE3 1K 107
Westbrook Rd. Houn 7D 78
Westbrook Rd. T Hth 1D 140
Westbrook Sq. Barn 3G 5
Westbury Av. N22 3B 32
Westbury Av. S'hall 4E 60
Westbury Av. Wemb 7E 44
Westbury Clo. Ruis 7J 23
Westbury Clo. Shep 6D 130
Westbury Ct. Bark 1H 73 (off Westbury Rd.)
Westbury Gro. N12 6D 14
Westbury Ho. E17 4B 34
Westbury La. Buck H 2F 21
Westbury Lodge Clo. Pinn 3B 24
Westbury Pl. Bren 6D 80
Westbury Rd. E7 6K 53
Westbury Rd. E17 4B 34
Westbury Rd. N11 6D 16
Westbury Rd. N12 6D 14
Westbury Rd. SE20 1K 141
Westbury Rd. W5 6E 62
Westbury Rd. Bark 1H 73
Westbury Rd. Beck 3A 142
Westbury Rd. Brom 1B 144
Westbury Rd. Buck H 2F 21
Westbury Rd. Croy 6D 140
Westbury Rd. Felt 1B 114
Westbury Rd. Ilf 2E 54
Westbury Rd. N Mald 4K 135
Westbury Rd. Wemb 7E 44
Westbury St. SW8 2G 103 (off Portslade Rd.)
Westbury Ter. E7 6K 53
W. Carriage Dri. W2 7C 66 (3C 164) (in two parts)
W. Central St. WC1 6J 67 (7E 160)
W. Centre Av. NW10 4D 64
West Chantry. Harr 1F 25
Westchester Dri. NW4 3F 29
West Clo. N9 3A 18
West Clo. Ashf 4A 112
West Clo. Cockf 4K 5
West Clo. Gnfd 2G 61
West Clo. Hamp 6C 114
West Clo. Wemb 1F 45
Westcombe Av. Croy 7J 139
Westcombe Ct. SE3 7H 89
Westcombe Dri. Barn 5D 4
Westcombe Hill. SE3 7J 89
Westcombe Lodge Dri. Hay 5G 59
Westcombe Pk. Rd. SE3 6G 89
West Comn. Rd. Brom & Kes 1J 155
West Comn. Rd. Uxb 5A 40
Westcoombe Av. SW20 1B 136
Westcote Ri. Ruis 7E 22
Westcote Rd. SW16 5G 121
West Cotts. NW6 5J 47
Westcott Clo. N15 6F 33
Westcott Clo. Brom 5D 144
Westcott Clo. New Ad 7D 154
Westcott Cres. W7 6J 61
Westcott Ho. E14 7C 70
Westcott Rd. SE17 6B 86
West Ct. E17 4C 34
West Ct. Houn 7G 79
West Ct. Wemb 2C 44
Westcroft Clo. NW2 4G 47
Westcroft Clo. Enf 1D 8
Westcroft Gdns. Mord 3H 137
Westcroft Rd. Cars 4E 150
Westcroft Sq. W6 4C 82
Westcroft Way. NW2 4G 47
W. Cromwell Rd. W14 & SW5 5H 83
W. Cross Cen. Bren 6A 80
W. Cross Route. W10 7F 65
W. Cross Way. Bren 6B 80
Westdale Pas. SE18 6F 91
Westdale Rd. SE18 6F 91
Westdean Av. SE12 1K 125
W. Dean Clo. SW18 6K 101
West Dene. Sutt 6G 149
Westdown Rd. E15 4E 52
Westdown Rd. SE6 7C 106
West Drayton. 2A 76
W. Drayton Pk. Av. W Dray 3A 76
W. Drayton Rd. Uxb 6D 58
West Dri. SW16 4G 121
West Dri. Harr 6C 10
West Dri. Sutt 7F 149
West Dri. Gdns. Harr 6C 10
West Dulwich. 2D 122
West Ealing. 7B 62
W. Ealing Bus. Cen. W13 7A 62
W. Eaton Pl. SW1 4E 84 (3G 171)
W. Eaton Pl. M. SW1 2G 171
W. Ella Rd. NW10 7A 46
West End. 2B 60
W. End Av. E10 5F 35
W. End Av. Pinn 4B 24
Westend Clo. NW10 7J 45
W. End Ct. NW6 7K 47
W. End Ct. Pinn 4B 24
W. End Gdns. N'holt 2A 60
W. End La. NW6 5J 47 (in two parts)
W. End La. Barn 4A 4
W. End La. Hay 7E 76
W. End La. Pinn 3B 24
W. End Rd. Ruis 2G 41
W. End Rd. S'hall 1C 78
Westerdale Rd. SE10 5J 89
Westerfield Rd. N15 5F 33
Westergate. W5 5E 62
Westergate Ho. King T 4D 134 (off Portsmouth Rd.)
Westergate Rd. SE2 6E 92
Westerham. NW1 1G 67 (off Bayham St.)
Westerham Av. N9 3J 17
Westerham Dri. Sidc 6B 110
Westerham Ho. SE1 3D 86 (off Law St.)
Westerham Lodge. Beck 7C 124 (off Park Rd.)
Westerham Rd. E10 7D 34
Westerham Rd. Kes 7B 156
Westerley Cres. SE26 5B 124
Western Av. NW11 6F 29
Western Av. W5 & W3 4F 63
Western Av. Dag 6J 57
Western Av. Gnfd & W5 2H 61
Western Av. Uxb & Ruis 5A 40
Western Av. Bus. Pk. W3 4H 63
Western Beach Apartments. E16 7J 71
Western Circus. (Junct.) 7B 64
Western Ct. N3 6D 14
Western Ct. NW6 2H 65
Western Ct. W3 6K 63
Western Dri. Shep 6F 131
Western Gdns. W5 7G 63
Western International Mkt. S'hall 4K 77
Western La. SW12 7E 102
Western Mans. New Bar 5E 4 (off Gt. North Rd.)
Western M. W9 4H 65
Western Pde. New Bar 5D 4
Western Pl. SE16 2J 87
Western Rd. E13 2A 72
Western Rd. E17 5E 34
Western Rd. N2 4D 30
Western Rd. N22 2K 31
Western Rd. NW10 4J 63
Western Rd. SW9 3A 104
Western Rd. SW19 & Mitc 1B 138
Western Rd. W5 7D 62
Western Rd. S'hall 4A 78
Western Rd. Sutt 5J 149
Western Ter. W6 5C 82 (off Chiswick Mall)
Western Vw. Hay 2H 77
Westernville Gdns. Ilf 7G 37
Western Way. SE28 3H 91
Western Way. Barn 6D 4
West Ewell. 7A 148
Westferry Cir. E14 1B 88
Westferry Rd. E14 7B 70
Westfield Clo. NW9 3J 27
Westfield Clo. SW10 7A 84
Westfield Clo. Enf 3F 9
Westfield Clo. Sutt 4H 149
Westfield Ct. NW10 3F 65 (off Chamberlayne Rd.)
Westfield Ct. Surb 5D 134 (off Portsmouth Rd)
Westfield Dri. Harr 4D 26
Westfield Gdns. Harr 4D 26
Westfield Gdns. Romf 6C 38
Westfield Ho. SE16 4K 87 (off Rotherhithe New Rd.)
Westfield Ho. SW18 1K 119
Westfield La. Harr 5D 26 (in two parts)
Westfield Pk. Pinn 1D 24
Westfield Pk. Dri. Wfd G 6H 21
Westfield Rd. NW7 3E 12
Westfield Rd. W13 1A 80
Westfield Rd. Beck 2B 142
Westfield Rd. Bexh 3J 111
Westfield Rd. Croy 2B 152
Westfield Rd. Dag 4E 56
Westfield Rd. Mitc 2C 138
Westfield Rd. Surb 5D 134
Westfield Rd. Sutt 4H 149
Westfield Rd. W on T 7C 132
Westfields. SW13 3B 100
Westfields Av. SW13 3A 100
Westfields Rd. W3 5H 63
Westfield St. SE18 3B 90
Westfield Way. E1 3A 70
Westfield Way. Ruis 3G 41
W. Garden Pl. W2 6C 66 (1D 164)
West Gdns. E1 7H 69
West Gdns. SW17 6C 120
Westgate. W5 3E 62
Westgate Cen., The. E8 1H 69 (off Bocking St.)
Westgate Ct. SE12 1J 125 (off Burnt Ash Hill)
Westgate Ct. SW9 3A 104 (off Canterbury Cres.)
Westgate M. W10 4G 65 (off West Row)
Westgate Rd. SE25 4H 141
Westgate Rd. Beck 2D 142
Westgate St. E8 1H 69
Westgate Ter. SW10 5K 83
Westglade Ct. Kent 5D 26
West Green. 4B 32
W. Green Pl. Gnfd 1H 61
W. Green Rd. N8 4B 32
West Gro. SE10 1E 106
West Gro. Wfd G 6F 21
Westgrove La. SE10 1E 106
W. Halkin St. SW1 3E 84 (1G 171)
West Hallowes. SE9 1B 126
W. Hall Rd. Rich 1H 99
West Ham. 1J 71
W. Ham La. E15 7F 53
West Hampstead. 6K 47
W. Hampstead M. NW6 6K 47
West Ham United F.C. (Upton Pk.) 2B 72
W. Harding St. EC4 6A 68 (7K 161)
West Harrow. 7G 25
W. Hatch Mnr. Ruis 1H 41
Westhay Gdns. SW14 5H 99
West Heath. 6D 92
W. Heath Av. NW11 1J 47
W. Heath Clo. NW3 3J 47
W. Heath Ct. NW11 1J 47
W. Heath Dri. NW11 1J 47
W. Heath Gdns. NW3 3J 47
W. Heath Rd. NW3 2J 47
W. Heath Rd. SE2 6C 92
West Hendon. 7C 28
West Hill. 6H 101
West Hill. SW15 & SW18 7F 101
West Hill. Harr 2J 43
West Hill. S Croy 7E 152
West Hill. Wemb 1F 45
W. Hill Ct. N6 3E 48
Westhill Pk. N6 2D 48 (in two parts)
W. Hill Rd. SW18 6H 101
W. Hill Way. N20 1E 14
Westholm. NW11 4K 29
West Holme. Eri 1J 111
Westholme. Orp 7J 145
Westholme Gdns. Ruis 1J 41
Westhope Ho. E2 4G 69 (off Derbyshire St.)
Westhorne Av. SE12 & SE9 7J 107
Westhorpe Gdns. NW4 3E 28
Westhorpe Rd. SW15 3E 100
West Ho. Clo. SW19 1G 119
West Ho. Cotts. Pinn 4B 24
Westhurst Dri. Chst 5F 127
W. India Av. E14 1C 88
W. India Dock Rd. E14 7B 70 (in two parts)
W. India Ho. E14 7C 70 (off W. India Dock Rd.)
West Kensington. 4H 83
W. Kensington Ct. W14 5H 83 (off Edith Vs.)
W. Kensington Mans. W14 5H 83 (off Beaumont Cres.)
West Kilburn. 3H 65
Westlake. SE16 4J 87 (off Rotherhithe New Rd.)
Westlake Clo. N13 3F 17
Westlake Clo. Hay 4C 60
Westlake Rd. Wemb 2D 44
Westland Clo. Stanw 6A 94
Westland Ct. N'holt 3B 60 (off Seasprite Clo.)
Westland Dri. Brom 2H 155
Westland Ho. E16 1E 90 (off Rymill St.)
Westland Pl. N1 3D 68 (1E 162)
Westlands Clo. Hay 4J 77
Westlands Ter. SW12 6G 103
West La. SE16 2H 87
Westlea Rd. W7 3A 80
Westleigh Av. SW15 5D 100
Westleigh Ct. E11 5J 35
Westleigh Ct. S Croy 4E 152 (off Birdhurst Rd.)
Westleigh Dri. Brom 1C 144

Westleigh Gdns. Edgw. . . . 1G 27
Westlington Clo. NW7 . . . 6C 14
West Lodge. E16 . . . 1J 89
(off Britannia Ga.)
W. Lodge Av. W3 . . . 1G 81
W. Lodge Ct. W3 . . . 1G 81
West London Crematorium.
NW10 . . . 4D 64
Westmacott Dri. Felt . . . 1H 113
Westmacott Ho. NW8
. . . 4B 66 (4B 158)
(off Hatton St.)
West Mall. W8 . . . 1J 83
(off Palace Gdns. Ter.)
Westmead. SW15 . . . 6D 100
West Mead. Eps . . . 6A 148
West Mead. Ruis . . . 4A 42
Westmead Corner.
Cars . . . 4C 150
Westmead Rd. Sutt . . . 4B 150
Westmere Dri. NW7 . . . 3E 12
W. Mersea Clo. E16 . . . 1K 89
West M. N17 . . . 7C 18
West M. SW1 . . . 4A 172
Westmill Ct. N4 . . . 2C 50
(off Brownswood Rd.)
Westminster. . . . 2J 85 (7E 166)
Westminster Abbey.
. . . 3J 85 (1E 172)
Westminster Abbey
Chapter House. . . . 1E 172
Westminster Abbey Mus.
. . . 1E 172
(in Westminster Abbey)
Westminster Abbey Pyx Chamber.
. . . 1E 172
(in Westminster Abbey)
Westminster Av. T Hth. . . . 2B 140
Westminster Bri. SW1 & SE1
. . . 2J 85 (7F 167)
Westminster Bri. Rd. SE1
. . . 2K 85 (7G 167)
Westminster Bri. Rd. SE1
. . . 3A 86 (7G 167)
Westminster Bus. Sq.
SE11 . . . 5K 85 (6G 173)
Westminster Clo. Felt . . . 1J 113
Westminster Clo. Ilf . . . 2H 37
Westminster Clo. Tedd . . . 5A 116
Westminster Ct. E11 . . . 6J 35
(off Cambridge Pk.)
Westminster Ct. SE16 . . . 1K 87
(off King & Queen Wharf)
Westminster Dri. N13 . . . 5D 16
Westminster Gdns. E4 . . . 1B 20
Westminster Gdns. SW1
. . . 4J 85 (3E 172)
(off Marsham St.)
Westminster Gdns. Bark . . . 2J 73
Westminster Gdns. Ilf . . . 2G 37
Westminster Hall. . . . 7E 166
Westminster Ho. Har W . . . 7E 10
Westminster Ind. Est. SE18
. . . 3B 90
Westminster Mans. SW1
. . . 3H 85 (2D 172)
Westminster Pal. Gdns.
SW1 . . . 2C 172
Westminster RC Cathedral.
. . . 3G 85 (2B 172)
Westminster Rd. N9 . . . 1C 18
Westminster Rd. W7 . . . 1J 79
Westminster Rd. Sutt . . . 2B 150
Westminster Theatre.
. . . 3G 85 (1A 172)
(off Palace St.)
Westmoat Clo. Beck . . . 7E 124
West Molesey. . . . 4E 132
Westmoor Gdns. Enf . . . 2E 8
Westmoor Rd. Enf . . . 2E 8
Westmoor St. SE7 . . . 3A 90
Westmoreland Av. Well . . . 3J 109
Westmoreland Dri. Sutt . . . 7K 149
Westmoreland Ho. E16 . . . 1J 89
(off Gatcombe Rd.)
Westmoreland Pl. SW1
. . . 5F 85 (6K 171)
Westmoreland Pl. W5 . . . 5D 62
Westmoreland Pl. Brom . . . 3J 143
Westmoreland Rd. NW9 . . . 3F 27
Westmoreland Rd. SE17 . . . 6D 86
(in two parts)
Westmoreland Rd. SW13 . . . 1B 100
Westmoreland Rd. Brom . . . 5G 143
Westmoreland St. W1
. . . 5E 66 (6H 159)
Westmoreland Ter. SW1
. . . 5F 85 (6K 171)
Westmoreland Wlk. SE17 . . . 6D 86
(in three parts)
Westmorland Clo. E12 . . . 2B 54
Westmorland Clo. Twic . . . 6B 98
Westmorland Ct. Surb . . . 7D 134
Westmorland Rd. E17 . . . 6C 34
Westmorland Rd. Harr . . . 5F 25
Westmorland Sq. Mitc . . . 5J 139
(off Westmorland Way)
Westmorland Ter. SE20 . . . 7H 123
Westmorland Way. Mitc . . . 4H 139
Westmount Ct. W5 . . . 6F 63
Westmount Rd. SE9 . . . 2D 108
West Norwood. . . . 4C 122
West Norwood Crematorium.
SE27 . . . 3C 122
West Oak. Beck . . . 1F 143
Westoe Rd. N9 . . . 2C 18
Weston Av. Th Dit . . . 7J 133
Weston Av. W Mol . . . 3C 132
Westonbirt Ct. SE15 . . . 6F 87
(off Ebley Clo.)
Weston Ct. N4 . . . 3C 50
Weston Ct. King T . . . 3E 134
(off Grove Cres.)
Weston Dri. Stan . . . 1B 26
West One Ho. W1
. . . 5G 67 (6A 160)
(off Wells St.)
Westone Mans. Bark . . . 7K 55
(off Upney La.)
Weston Gdns. Iswth . . . 1J 97
Weston Green. . . . 7J 133
Weston Grn. Dag . . . 4F 57
Weston Grn. Rd. Esh . . . 7J 133
Weston Gro. Brom . . . 1H 143
Weston Ho. E9 . . . 1J 69
(off King Edward's Rd.)
Weston Ho. NW6 . . . 7G 47
Weston Pk. N8 . . . 6J 31
Weston Pk. King T . . . 2E 134
Weston Pk. Th Dit . . . 7J 133
Weston Ri. WC1 . . . 3K 67 (1H 161)
Weston Rd. W4 . . . 3J 81
Weston Rd. Brom . . . 7H 125
Weston Rd. Dag . . . 4E 56
Weston Rd. Enf . . . 2J 7
Weston St. SE1 . . . 2E 86 (7F 169)
(in three parts)
Weston Wlk. E8 . . . 7H 51
Westover Hill. NW3 . . . 2J 47
Westover Rd. SW18 . . . 7A 102
Westow Hill. SE19 . . . 6E 122
Westow St. SE19 . . . 6E 122
West Pk. SE9 . . . 2C 126
W. Park Av. Rich . . . 1G 99
W. Park Clo. Houn . . . 6D 78
W. Park Clo. Romf . . . 5D 38
W. Park Rd. Rich . . . 1G 99
W. Park Rd. S'hall . . . 1G 79
West Parkside. SE10 . . . 2G 89
West Pl. SW19 . . . 5E 118
West Point. E14 . . . 7B 70
(off Grenade St.)
West Point. SE1 . . . 5G 87
Westpoint Trad. Est. W3 . . . 5H 63
Westpole Av. Barn . . . 4K 5
Westport Ct. Hay . . . 4A 60
Westport Rd. E13 . . . 4K 71
Westport St. E1 . . . 6K 69
W. Poultry Av. EC1
. . . 5B 68 (6A 162)
West Quarters. W12 . . . 6C 64
West Quay. SW10 . . . 1A 102
W. Quay Dri. Hay . . . 5C 60
West Ramp. H'row A . . . 1C 94
W. Ridge Gdns. Gnfd . . . 2G 61
West Ri. W2 . . . 2D 164
West Rd. E15 . . . 1H 71
West Rd. N2 . . . 2B 30
West Rd. N17 . . . 6C 18
West Rd. SE1 . . . 2K 85 (6H 167)
West Rd. SW3 . . . 5D 84 (6F 171)
West Rd. SW4 . . . 5H 103
West Rd. W5 . . . 5E 62
West Rd. Barn . . . 1K 15
West Rd. Chad H . . . 6D 38
West Rd. Felt . . . 6F 95
West Rd. King T . . . 1J 135
West Rd. Rush G . . . 7K 39
West Rd. W Dray . . . 3B 76
Westrow. SW15 . . . 6E 100
West Row. W10 . . . 4G 65
Westrow Dri. Bark . . . 5A 56
Westrow Gdns. Ilf . . . 2K 55
West Ruislip. . . . 2E 40
W. Ruislip Ct. Ruis . . . 2F 41
(off Ickenham Rd.)
W. Sheen Va. Rich . . . 4F 99
Westside. N2 . . . 3D 30
West Side. NW4 . . . 2D 28
W. Side Comn. SW19 . . . 5E 118
Westside Ct. W9 . . . 4J 65
(off Elgin Av.)
West Smithfield. EC1
. . . 5B 68 (6A 162)
West Sq. SE11 . . . 3B 86
West St. E2 . . . 2H 69
West St. E11 . . . 3G 53
West St. E17 . . . 5D 34
West St. WC2 . . . 6H 67 (1D 166)
West St. Bexh . . . 3F 111
West St. Bren . . . 6C 80
West St. Brom . . . 1J 143
West St. Cars . . . 3D 150
West St. Croy . . . 4C 152
West St. Eri . . . 4K 93
West St. Harr . . . 1H 43
West St. Sutt . . . 5K 149
West St. La. Cars . . . 4D 150
(in two parts)
W. Street Pl. Croy . . . 4C 152
(off West St.)
W. Temple Sheen. SW14 . . . 5H 99
W. Tenter St. E1 . . . 6F 69 (1K 169)
West Ter. Sidc . . . 1J 127
West Towers. Pinn . . . 6B 24
Westvale M. W3 . . . 2A 82
West Vw. NW4 . . . 4E 28
Westview. W7 . . . 6J 61
West Vw. Felt . . . 7E 94
W. View Clo. NW10 . . . 5B 46
Westview Clo. W10 . . . 6E 64
Westview Ct. N20 . . . 1F 15
Westview Cres. N9 . . . 7K 7
Westview Dri. Wfd G . . . 2B 36
Westville Rd. W12 . . . 2C 82
Westville Rd. Th Dit . . . 1A 146
West Wlk. W5 . . . 5E 62
West Wlk. E Barn . . . 7K 5
West Wlk. Hay . . . 1J 77
Westward Rd. E4 . . . 5G 19
(in two parts)
Westward Way. Harr . . . 6E 26
W. Warwick Pl. SW1
. . . 4G 85 (4A 172)
Westway. N18 . . . 4J 17
West Way. NW10 . . . 3K 45
Westway. SW20 . . . 3D 136
Westway. W10, W9 & W2
. . . 5H 65 (6A 158)
Westway. W12 & W10 . . . 7B 64
West Way. Croy . . . 2A 154
West Way. Edgw . . . 6C 12
West Way. Houn . . . 1D 96
Westway. Orp . . . 5H 145
West Way. Pinn . . . 4B 24
West Way. Ruis . . . 1H 41
West Way. Shep . . . 6F 131
West Way. W Wick . . . 6F 143
Westway Clo. SW20 . . . 3D 136
Westway Ct. N'holt . . . 1E 60
Westway Cross Retail Pk.
Gnfd . . . 1J 61
W. Way Gdns. Croy . . . 2K 153
Westways. Eps . . . 4B 148
West Ways. N'wd . . . 2J 23
Westwell M. SW16 . . . 6J 121
Westwell Rd. SW16 . . . 6J 121
Westwell Rd. App.
SW16 . . . 6J 121
Westwick. King T . . . 2G 135
(off Chesterton Ter.)
Westwick Gdns. W14 . . . 2F 83
Westwick Gdns. Houn . . . 2K 95
West Wickham. . . . 1E 154
Westwood Av. SE19 . . . 1C 140
Westwood Av. Harr . . . 4F 43
Westwood Bus. Cen.
NW10 . . . 4A 64
Westwood Clo. Brom . . . 2B 144
Westwood Clo. Ruis . . . 6D 22
Westwood Ct. Gnfd . . . 5H 43
Westwood Ct. Wemb . . . 4B 44
Westwood Gdns. SW13 . . . 3B 100
Westwood Hill. SE26 . . . 5G 123
Westwood Ho. W12 . . . 1E 82
(off Wood La.)
Westwood La. Sidc . . . 5A 110
Westwood La. Well . . . 3K 109
Westwood Pk. SE23 . . . 7H 105
Westwood Pk. Trad. Est.
W3 . . . 5H 63
Westwood Pl. SE26 . . . 4G 123
Westwood Rd. E16 . . . 1K 89
Westwood Rd. SW13 . . . 3B 100
Westwood Rd. Ilf . . . 1K 55
West Woodside. Bex . . . 1E 128
Wetheral Dri. Stan . . . 1B 26
Wetherby Clo. N'holt . . . 6F 43
Wetherby Gdns. SW5 . . . 4A 84
Wetherby Mans. SW5 . . . 5K 83
(off Earl's Ct. Sq.)
Wetherby M. SW5 . . . 5K 83
Wetherby Pl. SW7 . . . 4A 84
Wetherby Rd. Enf . . . 1H 7
Wetherby Way. Chess . . . 7E 146
Wetherden St. E17 . . . 7B 34
Wetherell Rd. E9 . . . 1K 69
Wetherill Rd. N10 . . . 1E 30
Wetland Cen., The. . . . 1D 100
Wevco Wharf. SE16 . . . 6H 87
Wevell Ho. N6 . . . 7E 30
(off Hillcrest)
Wexford Ho. E1 . . . 5J 69
(off Sidney St.)
Wexford Rd. SW12 . . . 7D 102
Weybourne St. SW18 . . . 2A 120
Weybridge Ct. SE16 . . . 5H 87
(off Argyle Way)
Weybridge Point.
SW11 . . . 2D 102
Weybridge Rd. T Hth . . . 4A 140
Wey Ct. Eps . . . 4J 147
Weydown Clo. SW19 . . . 1G 119
Weyhill Rd. E1 . . . 6G 69
Weylands Clo. W on T . . . 7D 132
Weylond Rd. Dag . . . 3F 57
Weyman Rd. SE3 . . . 1A 108
Weymarks, The. N17 . . . 6J 17
Weymouth Av. NW7 . . . 5F 13
Weymouth Av. W5 . . . 3C 80
Weymouth Clo. E6 . . . 6F 73
Weymouth Ct. E2 . . . 2F 69
(off Weymouth Ter.)
Weymouth Ct. Sutt . . . 7J 149
Weymouth Ho. SW8 . . . 7K 85
(off Bolney St.)
Weymouth Ho. Brom . . . 2H 143
(off Beckenham La.)
Weymouth M. W1
. . . 5F 67 (5J 159)
Weymouth Rd. Hay . . . 3G 59
Weymouth St. W1
. . . 5E 66 (6H 159)
Weymouth Ter. E2
. . . 2F 69 (1K 163)
Weymouth Wlk. Stan . . . 6F 11
Whadcoat St. N4 . . . 2A 50
Whalebone Av. Romf . . . 6F 39
Whalebone Ct. EC2 . . . 7E 162
Whalebone Gro. Romf . . . 6F 39
Whalebone La. E15 . . . 7G 53
Whalebone La. N. Romf . . . 1E 38
Whalebone La. S. Romf . . . 7F 39
Whales Yd. E15 . . . 7G 53
(off West Ham La.)
Wharfdale Clo. N11 . . . 6K 15
Wharfdale Rd. N1 . . . 2J 67
Wharfedale Ct. E5 . . . 4K 51
Wharfedale Gdns. T Hth . . . 4K 139
Wharfedale Ho. NW6 . . . 1K 65
(off Kilburn Va.)
Wharfedale St. SW10 . . . 5K 83
Wharf La. Twic . . . 1A 116
Wharf Pl. E2 . . . 1H 69
Wharf Rd. E15 . . . 1F 71
Wharf Rd. N1 . . . 2C 68 (1C 162)
Wharf Rd. NW1 . . . 1H 67
Wharf Rd. Enf . . . 6F 9
Wharf Rd. Ind. Est. Enf . . . 6F 9
Wharfside Rd. E16 . . . 5G 71
Wharf St. E16 . . . 5G 71
Wharf, The. EC3 . . . 1F 87 (4H 169)
Wharncliffe Dri. S'hall . . . 1H 79
Wharncliffe Gdns. SE25 . . . 2E 140
Wharncliffe Rd. SE25 . . . 2E 140
Wharton Clo. NW10 . . . 6A 46
Wharton Cotts. WC1
. . . 3A 68 (2J 161)
Wharton Ho. SE1 . . . 3F 87 (7J 169)
(off Maltby St.)
Wharton Rd. Brom . . . 1K 143
Wharton St. WC1
. . . 3K 67 (2H 161)
Whateley Rd. SE20 . . . 7K 123
Whateley Rd. SE22 . . . 5F 105
Whatley Av. SW20 . . . 3F 137
Whatman Ho. E14 . . . 6B 70
(off Wallwood St.)
Whatman Rd. SE23 . . . 7K 105
Wheatfields. E6 . . . 6F 73
Wheatfields. Enf . . . 1F 9
Wheatfield Way. King T . . . 2E 134
Wheathill Rd. SE20 . . . 3H 141
Wheatland Ho. SE22 . . . 3E 104
Wheatlands. Houn . . . 6E 78
Wheatlands Rd. SW17 . . . 3E 120
Wheatley Clo. NW4 . . . 2C 28
Wheatley Cres. Hay . . . 7J 59
Wheatley Gdns. N9 . . . 2K 17
Wheatley Ho. SW15 . . . 7C 100
(off Ellisfield Dri.)
Wheatley Mans. Bark . . . 7A 56
(off Bevan Av.)
Wheatley Rd. Iswth . . . 3K 97
Wheatley St. W1 . . . 5E 66 (6H 159)
Wheat Sheaf Clo. E14 . . . 4D 88
Wheatsheaf Clo. N'holt . . . 5C 42
Wheatsheaf La. SW6 . . . 7E 82
Wheatsheaf La. SW8 . . . 7J 85
(in two parts)
Wheatsheaf Ter. SW6 . . . 7H 83
Wheatstone Clo. Mitc . . . 1C 138
Wheatstone Rd. W10 . . . 5G 65
Wheatstone Rd. Eri . . . 5K 93
Wheeler Clo. Wfd G . . . 6J 21
Wheeler Gdns. N1 . . . 1J 67
(off Outram Pl.)
Wheelers Cross. Bark . . . 2H 73
Wheelers Dri. Ruis . . . 6E 22
Wheel Farm Dri. Dag . . . 3J 57
Wheel Ho. E14 . . . 5D 88
(off Burrells Wharf Sq.)
Wheelock Clo. Eri . . . 7H 93
Wheelwright St. N7 . . . 7K 49
Whelan Way. Wall . . . 3H 151

Wheler Ho. E1 ..... 4F 69 (4J 163) (off Quaker St.)
Wheler St. E1 ..... 4F 69 (4J 163)
Whellock Rd. W4 ..... 3A 82
Whenman Av. Bex 2J 129
Whernside Clo. SE28 ..... 7C 74
Whetstone 2F 15
Whetstone Clo. N20 ..... 2G 15
Whetstone Pk. WC2 ..... 6K 67 (7G 161)
Whetstone Rd. SE3 ..... 2A 108
Whewell Rd. N19 ..... 2J 49
Whidborne Bldgs. WC1 ..... 3J 67 (2F 161) (off Whidborne St.)
Whidborne Clo. SE8 ..... 2C 106
Whidborne St. WC1 ..... 3J 67 (2F 161) (in two parts)
Whimbrel Clo. SE28 ..... 7C 74
Whimbrel Way. Hay 5B 60
Whinchat Rd. SE28 ..... 3H 91
Whinfell Clo. SW16 ..... 5H 121
Whinyates Rd. SE9 ..... 3C 108
Whippendell Way. Orp 7B 128
Whipps Cross. E11 ..... 5F 35
Whipps Cross Ho. E17 ..... 5F 35 (off Wood St.)
Whipps Cross Rd. E11 ..... 5F 35 (in two parts)
Whiskin St. EC1 ..... 3B 68 (2A 162)
Whisperwood Clo. Harr 1J 25
Whistler Gdns. Edgw 2F 27
Whistler M. SE15 ..... 7F 87
Whistler M. Dag ..... 5B 56 (off Fitzstephen Rd.)
Whistlers Av. SW11 ..... 7B 84
Whistler St. N5 ..... 5B 50
Whistler Tower. SW10 ..... 7A 84 (off Worlds End Est.)
Whistler Wlk. SW10 ..... 7B 84
Whiston Ho. N1 ..... 7B 50 (off Richmond Gro.)
Whiston Rd. E2 ..... 2F 69 (in two parts)
Whitbread Clo. N17 ..... 1G 33
Whitbread Rd. SE4 ..... 4A 106
Whitburn Rd. SE13 ..... 4D 106
Whitby Av. NW10 ..... 3H 63
Whitby Ct. N7 ..... 4J 49
Whitby Gdns. NW9 ..... 3G 27
Whitby Gdns. Sutt 2B 150
Whitby Ho. NW8 ..... 1A 66 (off Boundary Rd.)
Whitby Pde. Ruis 2A 42
Whitby Rd. SE18 ..... 4D 90
Whitby Rd. Harr 3G 43
Whitby Rd. Ruis 3K 41
Whitby Rd. Sutt 2B 150
Whitby St. E1 ..... 4F 69 (3J 163) (in two parts)
Whitcher Clo. SE14 ..... 6A 88
Whitcher Pl. NW1 ..... 6G 49
Whitchurch Av. Edgw 7A 12
Whitchurch Clo. Edgw 6A 12
Whitchurch Gdns. Edgw 6A 12
Whitchurch Ho. W10 ..... 6F 65 (off Kingsdown Clo.)
Whitchurch La. Edgw 7J 11
Whitchurch Pde. Edgw 7B 12
Whitchurch Rd. W11 ..... 7F 65
Whitcomb Ct. WC2 ..... 3D 166
Whitcomb St. WC2 ..... 7H 67 (3D 166)
Whiteadder Way. E14 ..... 4D 88
Whitear Wlk. E15 ..... 6F 53
Whitebarn La. Dag 1G 75
Whitebeam Av. Brom 7E 144
Whitebeam Clo. SW9 ..... 7K 85
White Bear Pl. NW3 ..... 4B 48
White Bear Yd. EC1 ..... 4A 68 (4J 161) (off Clerkenwell Rd.)
White Bri. Av. Mitc 3B 138
Whitebridge Clo. Felt 6H 95
White Butts Rd. Ruis 3B 42
Whitechapel 5G 69 (6K 163)
Whitechapel Art Gallery ..... 6F 69 (7K 163) (off Whitechapel High St.)
Whitechapel High St. E1 ..... 6F 69 (7K 163)
Whitechapel Rd. E1 ..... 5G 69 (7K 163)
White Chu. La. E1 ..... 6G 69 (7K 163)
White Chu. Pas. E1 ..... 6G 69 (7K 163) (off White Chu. La.)
White City 7D 64
White City. (Junct.) 7D 64
White City Clo. W12 ..... 7E 64
White City Est. W12 ..... 7D 64
White City Rd. W12 ..... 7E 64
White Conduit St. N1 ..... 2A 68
Whitecote Rd. S'hall 6G 61
Whitecroft Clo. Beck 4F 143
Whitecroft Way. Beck 5E 142
Whitecross Pl. EC2 ..... 5D 68 (5F 163)
Whitecross St. EC1 ..... 4C 68 (3D 162)
Whitefield Av. NW2 ..... 1E 46
Whitefield Clo. SW18 ..... 6G 101
Whitefoot La. Brom 4E 124
Whitefoot Ter. Brom 3G 125
Whitefriars Av. Harr 2J 25
Whitefriars Ct. N12 ..... 5G 15
Whitefriars Dri. Harr 2H 25
Whitefriars St. EC4 ..... 6A 68 (1K 167)
Whitefriars Trad. Est. Harr 3H 25
White Gdns. Dag 6G 57
Whitegate Gdns. Harr 7E 10
Whitehall 6G 149
Whitehall. SW1 ..... 1J 85 (5E 166)
Whitehall Ct. SW1 ..... 1J 85 (5E 166) (in two parts)
Whitehall Cres. Chess 5D 146
Whitehall Gdns. E4 ..... 1B 20
Whitehall Gdns. SW1 ..... 5E 166
Whitehall Gdns. W3 ..... 1G 81
Whitehall Gdns. W4 ..... 6H 81
Whitehall La. Buck H 2D 20
Whitehall Lodge. N10 ..... 3E 30
Whitehall Pk. N19 ..... 1G 49
Whitehall Pk. Rd. W4 ..... 6H 81
Whitehall Pl. E7 ..... 5J 53
Whitehall Pl. SW1 ..... 1J 85 (5E 166)
Whitehall Pl. Wall 4F 151
Whitehall Rd. E4 ..... 2B 20
Whitehall Rd. W7 ..... 2A 80
Whitehall Rd. Brom 5B 144
Whitehall Rd. Harr 7J 25
Whitehall Rd. T Hth 5A 140
Whitehall St. N17 ..... 7A 18
Whitehall Theatre ..... 1J 85 (5E 166) (off Whitehall)
White Hart Clo. Hay 6F 77
White Hart Ct. EC2 ..... 6G 163
White Hart La. N22 & N17 ..... 1K 31
White Hart La. NW10 ..... 6B 46
White Hart La. SW13 ..... 3A 100
White Hart La. Romf 1G 39
White Hart Rd. SE18 ..... 4J 91
White Hart Roundabout. (Junct.) 2B 60
White Hart Roundabout. N'holt 2B 60
White Hart Slip. Brom 2J 143
White Hart St. EC4 ..... 6B 68 (7B 162)
White Hart St. SE11 ..... 5A 86 (5K 173)
White Hart Yd. SE1 ..... 1D 86 (5E 168)
Whitehaven Clo. Brom 4J 143
Whitehaven St. NW8 ..... 4C 66 (4C 158)
Whitehead Clo. N18 ..... 5J 17
Whitehead Clo. SW18 ..... 7A 102
Whiteheads Gro. SW3 ..... 4C 84 (4D 170)
White Heart Av. Uxb 5E 58
Whiteheath Av. Ruis 7E 22
White Heather Ho. WC1 ..... 3J 67 (2F 161) (off Cromer St.)
White Heron M. Tedd 6K 115
White Horse All. EC1 ..... 5A 162
White Horse Hill. Chst 4E 126
White Horse La. E1 ..... 4K 69
Whitehorse La. SE25 ..... 4D 140
Whitehorse M. SE1 ..... 3A 86 (1K 173)
White Horse Rd. E1 ..... 5A 70 (in two parts)
White Horse Rd. E6 ..... 3D 72
Whitehorse Rd. Croy & T Hth 7C 140
White Horse St. W1 ..... 1F 85 (5K 165)
White Horse Yd. EC2 ..... 6D 68 (7E 162)
White Ho. SW4 ..... 7H 103 (off Clapham Pk. Est.)
White Ho. SW11 ..... 1B 102
White Ho. Ct. N14 ..... 2D 16
White Ho. Dri. Stan 4H 11
White Ho. Dri. Wfd G 6C 20
Whitehouse Est. E10 ..... 6E 34
Whitehouse La. Enf 1H 7
White Ho., The. NW1 ..... 4F 67 (3K 159) (off Albany St.)
Whitehouse Way. N14 ..... 2A 16
Whitehurst Dri. N18 ..... 5E 18
White Kennett St. E1 ..... 6E 68 (7H 163)
Whitelands Ho. SW3 ..... 5D 84 (5F 171) (off Cheltenham Ter.)
Whiteledges. W13 ..... 6C 62
Whitelegg Rd. E13 ..... 2H 71
Whiteley Rd. SE19 ..... 5D 122
Whiteleys Cen. W2 ..... 6K 65
Whiteley's Cotts. W14 ..... 4H 83
Whiteleys Pde. Uxb 4D 58
Whiteley's Way. Hanw 3E 114
White Lion Ct. EC3 ..... 1G 169
White Lion Ct. SE15 ..... 6J 87
White Lion Ct. Iswth 3B 98
White Lion Hill. EC4 ..... 7B 68 (2B 168)
White Lion St. N1 ..... 2A 68
White Lodge. SE19 ..... 7B 122
White Lodge. W5 ..... 5C 62
White Lodge Clo. N2 ..... 6B 30
White Lodge Clo. Sutt 7A 150
White Lyon Ct. EC2 ..... 5C 162
Whiteoak Ct. Chst 6E 126
White Oak Dri. Beck 2E 142
White Oak Gdns. Sidc 7K 109
Whiteoaks La. Gnfd 3H 61
White Orchards. N20 ..... 7C 4
White Orchards. Stan 5F 11
White Post La. E9 ..... 7B 52
White Post St. SE15 ..... 7J 87
White Rd. E15 ..... 7G 53
White Rose Trad. Est. Barn ..... 5G 5 (off Margaret Rd.)
Whites Av. Ilf 6J 37
White's Grounds. SE1 ..... 2E 86 (7H 169)
White's Grounds Est. SE1 ..... 6H 169
White's Mdw. Brom 4E 144
White's Row. E1 ..... 5F 69 (6J 163)
Whites Sq. SW4 ..... 4H 103
Whitestile Rd. Bren 5C 80
Whitestone La. NW3 ..... 3A 48
Whitestone Wlk. NW3 ..... 3A 48
White St. S'hall 2B 78
Whiteswan M. W4 ..... 5A 82
Whitethorn Av. W Dray 7A 58
Whitethorn Gdns. Croy 2H 153
Whitethorn Gdns. Enf 5J 7
Whitethorn Ho. E1 ..... 1J 87 (off Prusom St.)
Whitethorn Pas. E3 ..... 4C 70 (off Whitethorn St.)
Whitethorn Pl. W Dray 1B 76
Whitethorn St. E3 ..... 5C 70
White Tower, The ..... 7F 69 (3J 169) (in Tower of London)
Whitewebbs Way. Orp 1K 145
Whitfield Ho. NW8 ..... 4C 66 (4C 158) (off Salisbury St.)
Whitfield Pl. W1 ..... 4A 160
Whitfield Rd. E6 ..... 7A 54
Whitfield Rd. SE3 ..... 1F 107
Whitfield Rd. Bexh 7F 93
Whitfield St. W1 ..... 4G 67 (4A 160)
Whitford Gdns. Mitc 3D 138
Whitgift Av. S Croy 5B 152
Whitgift Cen. Croy 2C 152
Whitgift Ct. S Croy ..... 5C 152 (off Nottingham Rd.)
Whitgift Ho. SE11 ..... 4K 85 (3G 173)
Whitgift Sq. Croy 2C 152
Whitgift St. SE11 ..... 4K 85 (3G 173)
Whitgift St. Croy 3C 152
Whiting Av. Bark 7F 55
Whitings. Ilf 5J 37
Whitings Rd. Barn 5A 4
Whitings Way. E6 ..... 5E 72
Whitland Rd. Cars 1B 150
Whitley Clo. Stanw 6A 94
Whitley Ho. SW1 ..... 6G 85 (7B 172) (off Churchill Gdns.)
Whitley Rd. N17 ..... 2E 32
Whitlock Dri. SW19 ..... 7G 101
Whitman Ho. E2 ..... 3J 69 (off Cornwall Av.)
Whitman Rd. E3 ..... 4A 70
Whitmead Clo. S Croy 6E 152
Whitmore Clo. N11 ..... 5A 16
Whitmore Est. N1 ..... 1E 68
Whitmore Gdns. NW10 ..... 2E 64
Whitmore Ho. E2 ..... 1E 68 (off Whitmore Est.)
Whitmore Rd. N1 ..... 1E 68
Whitmore Rd. Beck 3B 142
Whitmore Rd. Harr 7G 25
Whitnell Way. SW15 ..... 5E 100
Whitney Av. Ilf 4B 36
Whitney Rd. E10 ..... 7D 34
Whitney Wlk. Sidc 6E 128
Whitstable Clo. Beck 1B 142
Whitstable Clo. Ruis 2G 41
Whitstable Ho. W10 ..... 6F 65 (off Silchester Rd.)
Whitstable Pl. Croy 4C 152
Whittaker Av. Rich 5D 98
Whittaker Pl. Rich ..... 5D 98 (off Whittaker Av.)
Whittaker Rd. E6 ..... 7A 54
Whittaker Rd. Sutt 3H 149
Whittaker St. SW1 ..... 4E 84 (4G 171)
Whittaker Way. SE1 ..... 4G 87
Whitta Rd. E12 ..... 4B 54
Whittell Gdns. SE26 ..... 3J 123
Whittingham. N17 ..... 7C 18
Whittingham Ct. W4 ..... 7A 82
Whittingstall Rd. SW6 ..... 1H 101
Whittington Av. EC3 ..... 6E 68 (1G 169)
Whittington Av. Hay 5H 59
Whittington Ct. N2 ..... 5D 30
Whittington M. N12 ..... 4F 15 (off Fredericks Pl.)
Whittington Rd. N22 ..... 7D 16
Whittington Way. Pinn 5C 24
Whittlebury Clo. Cars 7D 150
Whittle Clo. E17 ..... 6A 34
Whittle Clo. S'hall 6F 61
Whittle Rd. Houn 7A 78
Whittle Rd. S'hall 2F 79
Whittlesea Clo. Harr 7B 10
Whittlesea Path. Harr 1G 25
Whittlesea Rd. Harr 7B 10
Whittlesey St. SE1 ..... 1A 86 (5J 167)
Whitton 7G 97
Whitton Av. E. Gnfd 5J 43
Whitton Av. W. N'holt & Gnfd 5F 43
Whitton Clo. Gnfd 6B 44
Whitton Dene. Houn & Iswth 5G 97
Whitton Dri. Gnfd 6A 44
Whitton Mnr. Rd. Iswth 6G 97
Whitton Rd. Houn 4F 97
Whitton Rd. Twic 6J 97
Whitton Road Roundabout. (Junct.) 6K 97
Whitton Wlk. E3 ..... 3C 70
Whitton Waye. Houn 6E 96
Whitwell Rd. E13 ..... 3J 71
Whitworth Ho. SE1 ..... 3C 86
Whitworth Rd. SE18 ..... 7E 90
Whitworth Rd. SE25 ..... 3E 140
Whitworth St. SE10 ..... 5G 89
Whorlton Rd. SE15 ..... 3H 105
Whymark Av. N22 ..... 3A 32
Whytecroft. Houn 7B 78
Whyteville Rd. E7 ..... 6K 53
Whytlaw Ho. E3 ..... 5B 70 (off Baythorne St.)
Wickersley Rd. SW11 ..... 2E 102
Wickers Oake. SE19 ..... 4F 123
Wicker St. E1 ..... 6H 69
Wicket Rd. Gnfd 3A 62
Wickets, The. Ashf 4A 112
Wicket, The. Croy 5C 154
Wickfield Ho. SE16 ..... 2H 87 (off Wilson Gro.)
Wickford Ho. E1 ..... 4J 69 (off Wickford St.)
Wickford St. E1 ..... 4J 69
Wickford Way. E17 ..... 4K 33
Wickham Av. Croy 2A 154
Wickham Av. Sutt 5E 148
Wickham Chase. W Wick 1F 155
Wickham Clo. E1 ..... 5J 69
Wickham Clo. Enf 3C 8
Wickham Clo. N Mald 6B 136
Wickham Ct. Surb ..... 5F 135 (off Cranes Pk.)
Wickham Ct. Rd. W Wick 2E 154
Wickham Cres. W Wick 2E 154
Wickham Gdns. SE4 ..... 3B 106
Wickham La. SE2 ..... 5A 92
Wickham M. SE4 ..... 2B 106
Wickham Rd. E4 ..... 7K 19
Wickham Rd. SE4 ..... 4B 106
Wickham Rd. Beck 2D 142
Wickham Rd. Croy 2J 153
Wickham Rd. Harr 2H 25
Wickham St. SE11 ..... 5K 85 (5G 173)
Wickham St. Well 2J 109
Wickham Way. Beck 4E 142
Wick Ho. King T ..... 1D 134 (off Station Rd.)
Wick La. E3 ..... 1C 70 (in two parts)
Wickliffe Av. N3 ..... 2G 29
Wickliffe Gdns. Wemb 2H 45
Wicklow Ho. N16 ..... 1F 51
Wicklow St. WC1 ..... 3K 67 (1G 161)
Wick M. E9 ..... 6A 52
Wick Rd. E9 ..... 6K 51
Wick Rd. Tedd 7B 116
Wicks Clo. SE9 ..... 4B 126

Wick Sq. E9 . . . . . 6B 52
Wicksteed Clo. Bex 3K 129
Wicksteed Ho. SE1 . . . . . 3C 86
Wicksteed Ho. Bren 5F 81
Wickway Ct. SE15 . . . . . 6F 87
(off Cator St.)
Wickwood St. SE5 . . . . . 2B 104
Widdecombe Av. S Harr. 2C 42
Widdenham Rd. N7 . . . . . 4K 49
Widdin St. E15 . . . . . 7G 53
Widecombe Gdns. Ilf 4C 36
Widecombe Rd. SE9 . . . . . 3C 126
Widecombe Way. N2 . . . . . 5B 30
Widegate St. E1 . . . 5E 68 (6H 163)
Widenham Clo. Pinn 5A 24
Wide Way. Mitc 3H 139
Widewing Clo. Tedd 7B 116
Widford. NW1 . . . . . 6F 49
(off Lewis St.)
Widford Ho. N1 . . . . . 2B 68
(off Colebrooke Rd.)
Widgeon Clo. E16 . . . . . 6K 71
Widley Rd. W9 . . . . . 3J 65
Widmer Ct. Houn 2C 96
Widmore 3A 144
Widmore Green 1A 144
Widmore Lodge Rd.
Brom 2B 144
Widmore Rd. Brom 2J 143
Widmore Rd. Uxb 4D 58
Wigan Ho. E5 . . . . . 1H 51
Wigeon Path. SE28 . . . . . 3H 91
Wigeon Way. Hay 6C 60
Wiggins La. Rich 2C 116
Wiggins Mead. NW9 . . . . . 7G 13
Wigginton Av. Wemb 6H 45
Wight Ho. King T 3D 134
(off Portsmouth Rd.)
Wightman Rd. N8 & N4 . . . . . 4A 32
Wighton M. Iswth 2J 97
Wigley Rd. Felt 2B 114
Wigmore Ct. W13 . . . . . 1A 80
(off Singapore Rd.)
Wigmore Hall 7J 159
Wigmore Pl. W1 . . . 6F 67 (7J 159)
Wigmore Rd. Cars 2B 150
Wigmore St. W1 . . . 6E 66 (7H 159)
Wigmore Wlk. Cars 2B 150
Wigram Ho. E14 . . . . . 7D 70
(off Wade's Pl.)
Wigram Rd. E11 . . . . . 6A 36
Wigram Sq. E17 . . . . . 3E 34
Wigston Clo. N18 . . . . . 5K 17
Wigston Rd. E13 . . . . . 4K 71
Wigton Gdns. Stan 1E 26
Wigton Pl. SE11 . . . 5A 86 (6K 173)
Wigton Rd. E17 . . . . . 1B 34
Wilberforce Rd. N4 . . . . . 2B 50
Wilberforce Rd. NW9 . . . . . 6C 28
Wilberforce Way. SW19 . . . . 6F 119
Wilbraham Ho. SW8 . . . . . 7J 85
(off Wandsworth Rd.)
Wilbraham Pl. SW1
. . . . . 4D 84 (3F 171)
Wilbrahams Almshouses.
Barn 2C 4
Wilbury Way. N18 . . . . . 5J 17
Wilby M. W11 . . . . . 1H 83
Wilcox Clo. SW8 . . . . . 7J 85
(in two parts)
Wilcox Gdns. Shep 3A 130
Wilcox Ho. E3 . . . . . 5B 70
(off Ackroyd Dri.)
Wilcox Pl. SW1 . . . . 3G 85 (2B 172)
Wilcox Rd. SW8 . . . . . 7J 85
Wilcox Rd. Sutt 4K 149
Wilcox Rd. Tedd 4H 115
Wild Ct. WC2 . . . . . 6K 67 (1G 167)
(in two parts)
Wildcroft Gdns. Edgw 6J 11
Wildcroft Mnr. SW15 . . . . . 7E 100
Wildcroft Rd. SW15 . . . . . 7E 100
Wilde Clo. E8 . . . . . 1G 69
Wilde Pl. N13 . . . . . 6G 17
Wilde Pl. SW18 . . . . . 7B 102
Wilder Clo. Ruis 1K 41
Wilderness M. SW4 . . . . . 4F 103
Wilderness Rd. Chst 7F 127
Wilderness, The. E Mol 5G 133
Wilderness, The. Hamp 4F 115
Wilde Rd. Eri 7H 93
Wilderton Rd. N16 . . . . . 7E 32
Wildfell Rd. SE6 . . . . . 7D 106
Wild Goose Dri. SE14 . . . . . 1J 105
Wild Hatch. NW11 . . . . . 6J 29
Wild's Rents. SE1 . . . . . 3E 86
Wild St. WC2 . . . . . 6J 67 (1F 167)
Wildwood Clo. SE12 . . . . . 7H 107
Wildwood Gro. NW3 . . . . . 1A 48
Wildwood Ri. NW11 . . . . . 1A 48
Wildwood Rd. NW11 . . . . . 6K 29
Wildwood Ter. NW11 . . . . . 1A 48
Wilford Clo. Enf 3J 7
Wilfred Ct. N15 . . . . . 5D 32
(off South Gro.)
Wilfred Owen Clo. SW19 . . . 6A 120
Wilfred St. SW1 . . . 3G 85 (1A 172)
Wilfrid Gdns. W3 . . . . . 5J 63
Wilkes Rd. Bren 6E 80
Wilkes St. E1 . . . . . 5F 69 (5K 163)
Wilkie Ho. SW1 . . . 5H 85 (5D 172)
(off Cureton St.)
Wilkins Clo. Hay 5H 77
Wilkins Clo. Mitc 1C 138
Wilkins Ho. SW1 . . . 6F 85 (7K 171)
(off Churchill Gdns.)
Wilkinson Clo. Uxb 1D 58
Wilkinson Ct. SW17 . . . . . 4B 120
Wilkinson Ho. N1 . . . . . 2D 68
(off Cranston Est.)
Wilkinson Rd. E16 . . . . . 6A 72
Wilkinson St. SW8 . . . . . 7K 85
Wilkinson Way. W4 . . . . . 2K 81
Wilkin St. NW5 . . . . . 6E 48
Wilkin St. M. NW5 . . . . . 6F 49
Wilks Gdns. Croy 1A 154
Wilks Pl. N1 . . . . . 2E 68
Willan Rd. N17 . . . . . 2D 32
Willan Wall. E16 . . . . . 7H 71
Willard St. SW8 . . . . . 3F 103
Willcocks Clo. Chess 3E 146
Willcott Rd. W3 . . . . . 1H 81
Will Crooks Gdns. SE9 . . . . 4A 108
Willenfield Rd. NW10 . . . . . 2J 63
Willenhall Av. New Bar 6F 5
Willenhall Ct. New Bar 6F 5
Willenhall Dri. Hay 7G 59
Willenhall Rd. SE18 . . . . . 5F 91
Willersley Av. Sidc 1K 127
Willersley Clo. Sidc 1K 127
Willesden 6C 46
Willesden Green 6D 46
Willesden La.
NW2 & NW6 . . . . . 6E 46
Willesden Section Ho.
NW2 . . . . . 6F 47
(off Willesden La.)
Willes Rd. NW5 . . . . . 6F 49
Willett Clo. N'holt 3A 60
Willett Clo. Orp 6J 145
Willett Ho. E13 . . . . . 2K 71
(off Queens Rd. W.)
Willett Pl. T Hth 5A 140
Willett Rd. T Hth 5A 140
Willett Way. Orp 5H 145
William Allen Ho. Edgw 7A 12
William Banfield Ho.
SW6 . . . . . 2H 101
(off Munster Rd.)
William Barefoot Dri. SE9 . . . 4E 126
William Blake Ho. SW11 . . . 1C 102
William Bonney Est.
SW4 . . . . . 4H 103
William Booth Rd. SE20 . . . 1G 141
William Carey Way. Harr 6J 25
William Caslon Ho. E2 . . . . . 2H 69
(off Patriot Sq.)
William Channing Ho. E2 . . . . 3H 69
(off Canrobert St.)
William Clo. N2 . . . . . 3B 30
William Clo. SE13 . . . . . 3E 106
William Clo. Romf 1J 39
William Clo. S'hall 2G 79
William Cobbett Ho. W8 . . . . 3K 83
(off Scarsdale Pl.)
William Ct. W5 . . . . . 5C 62
William Covell Clo. Enf 1E 6
William Dromey Ct. NW6 . . . . 7H 47
William Dunbar Ho. NW6 . . . . 2H 65
(off Albert Rd.)
William Dyce M. SW16 . . . . 4H 121
William Ellis Way. SE16 . . . . 3G 87
(off St James's Rd.)
William Evans Ho. SE8 . . . . . 4K 87
(off Bush Rd.)
William Farm La. SW15 . . . . 3D 100
William Fenn Ho. E2
. . . . . 3G 69 (1K 163)
(off Shipton Rd.)
William IV St. WC2
. . . . . 7J 67 (3E 166)
William Gdns. SW15 . . . . . 5D 100
William Gibbs Ct. SW1
. . . . . 3H 85 (2C 172)
(off Old Pye St.)
William Gunn Ho. NW3 . . . . . 5C 48
William Guy Gdns. E3 . . . . . 3D 70
William Henry Wlk. SW8
. . . . . 6H 85 (7C 172)
William Hunt Mans. SW13 . . . 6E 82
William Margrie Clo. SE15
. . . . . 2G 105
William M. SW1 . . . 2D 84 (7F 165)
William Morley Clo. E6 . . . . . 1B 72
William Morris Clo. E17 . . . . 3B 34
William Morris Gallery 3C 34
William Morris Ho. W6 . . . . . 6F 83
William Morris Way. SW6
. . . . . 3A 102
William Paton Ho. E16 . . . . . 6K 71
William Pike Ho. Romf 6K 39
(off Waterloo Gdns.)
William Pl. E3 . . . . . 2B 70
William Rathbone Ho. E2 . . . . 3H 69
(off Florida St.)
William Rd. NW1
. . . . . 3G 67 (2K 159)
William Rd. SW19 . . . . . 7G 119
William Rd. Sutt 5A 150
William Rushbrooke Ho.
SE16 . . . . . 4G 87
(off Rouel Rd.)
Williams Av. E17 . . . . . 1B 34
William Saville Ho. NW6 . . . . 2H 65
(off Denmark Rd.)
William's Bldgs. E2 . . . . . 4J 69
Williams Clo. N8 . . . . . 6H 31
Williams Clo. SW6 . . . . . 7G 83
Williams Dri. Houn 4E 96
Williams Gro. N22 . . . . . 1A 32
Williams Gro. Surb 6C 134
Williams Ho. E9 . . . . . 1H 69
(off King Edward's Rd.)
Williams Ho. NW2 . . . . . 3E 46
(off Stoll Clo.)
William's La. SW14 . . . . . 3J 99
Williams La. Mord 5A 138
William Smith Ho. Belv 3G 93
(off Ambrook Rd.)
Williamson Clo. SE10 . . . . . 5H 89
Williamson Ct. SE17 . . . . . 5C 86
Williamson Rd. N4 . . . . . 6B 32
Williamson St. N7 . . . . . 4J 49
Williamson Way. NW7 . . . . . 6B 14
William Sq. SE16 . . . . . 7A 70
(off Sovereign Cres.)
Williams Rd. W13 . . . . . 1A 80
Williams Rd. S'hall 4C 78
Williams Ter. Croy 6A 152
William St. E10 . . . . . 6D 34
William St. N17 . . . . . 7A 18
William St. SW1 . . . 2D 84 (7F 165)
William St. Bark 7G 55
William St. Cars 3C 150
Williams Way. Bex 2K 129
William White Ct. E13 . . . . . 1A 72
(off Green St.)
William Wood Ho. SE26 . . . . 3J 123
(off Shrublands Clo.)
Willifield Way. NW11 . . . . . 4H 29
Willingale Clo. Wfd G 6F 21
Willingdon Rd. N22 . . . . . 2B 32
Willingham Clo. NW5 . . . . . 5G 49
Willingham Ter. NW5 . . . . . 5G 49
Willingham Way. King T 3G 135
Willington Ct. E5 . . . . . 3A 52
Willington Rd. SW9 . . . . . 3J 103
Willis Av. Sutt 6C 150
Willis Ct. T Hth 6A 140
Willis Ho. E14 . . . . . 7D 70
(off Hale St.)
Willis Rd. E15 . . . . . 2H 71
Willis Rd. Croy 7C 140
Willis Rd. Eri 4J 93
Willis St. E14 . . . . . 6D 70
Will Miles Ct. SW19 . . . . . 7A 120
Willmore End. SW19 . . . . . 1K 137
Willoughby Av. Croy 4K 151
Willoughby Dri. Rain 7K 57
Willoughby Gro. N17 . . . . . 7C 18
Willoughby Highwalk. EC2
. . . . . 5D 68 (6E 162)
(off Moor La.)
Willoughby Ho. E1 . . . . . 1H 87
(off Reardon Path)
Willoughby Ho. EC2 . . . . . 5E 162
Willoughby La. N17 . . . . . 6C 18
Willoughby Pk. Rd. N17 . . . . 7C 18
(in two parts)
Willoughby Pas. E14 . . . . . 1C 88
(off W. India Av.)
Willoughby Rd. N8 . . . . . 3A 32
Willoughby Rd. NW3 . . . . . 4B 48
Willoughby Rd. King T 1F 135
Willoughby Rd. Twic 5C 98
(in two parts)
Willoughbys, The. SW15 . . . 3A 100
Willoughby St. WC1 . . . . . 6E 160
Willoughby Way. SE7 . . . . . 4K 89
Willow Av. SW13 . . . . . 2B 100
Willow Av. Sidc 6A 110
Willow Av. W Dray 7B 58
Willow Bank. SW6 . . . . . 3G 101
Willow Bank. Rich 3B 116
Willow Bri. Rd. N1 . . . . . 6C 50
Willowbrook. Hamp H 5F 115
Willowbrook Est. SE15 . . . . . 7G 87
Willow Brook Rd. SE15 . . . . . 7F 87
Willowbrook Rd. S'hall 3E 78
Willowbrook Rd. Stai 2A 112
Willow Bus. Cen., The.
Mitc 6D 138
Willow Bus. Pk. SE26 . . . . . 3J 123
Willow Clo. SE6 . . . . . 1H 125
Willow Clo. Bex 6F 111
Willow Clo. Bren 6C 80
Willow Clo. Brom 5D 144
Willow Clo. Buck H 3G 21
Willow Cotts. Hanw 3C 114
Willow Cotts. Rich 6G 81
Willow Ct. E11 . . . . . 2G 53
(off Trinity Clo.)
Willow Ct. EC2 . . . . . 3G 163
Willow Ct. NW6 . . . . . 7G 47
Willow Ct. W4 . . . . . 7A 82
(off Corney Reach Way)
Willow Ct. W9 . . . . . 5J 65
(off Admiral Wlk.)
Willow Ct. Edgw 4K 11
Willow Ct. Harr 1K 25
Willowcourt Av. Harr 5B 26
Willowdene. N6 . . . . . 7D 30
Willowdene. SE15 . . . . . 7H 87
Willow Dene. Bus H 1D 10
Willow Dene. Pinn 2B 24
Willowdene Clo. Twic 7G 97
Willowdene Ct. N20 . . . . . 7F 5
(off High Rd.)
Willow Dri. Barn 4B 4
Willow End. N20 . . . . . 2D 14
Willow End. Surb 1E 146
Willowfields Clo. SE18 . . . . . 5J 91
Willow Gdns. Houn 1E 96
Willow Gdns. Ruis 2H 41
Willow Grange. Sidc 3B 128
Willow Grn. NW9 . . . . . 1A 28
Willow Gro. E13 . . . . . 2J 71
Willow Gro. Chst 6E 126
Willow Gro. Ruis 2H 41
Willowhayne Dri. W on T . . . 7K 131
Willowhayne Gdns.
Wor Pk 3E 148
Willow Ho. W10 . . . . . 4F 65
(off Maple Wlk.)
Willow Ho. Short 2G 143
Willow La. SE18 . . . . . 4D 90
Willow La. Mitc 5D 138
Willow Lodge. SW6 . . . . . 1F 101
Willowmead Clo. W5 . . . . . 5D 62
Willow Mt. Croy 3E 152
Willow Pl. SW1 . . . . 4G 85 (3B 172)
Willow Rd. E12 . . . . . 3D 54
Willow Rd. NW3 . . . . . 4B 48
Willow Rd. W5 . . . . . 2E 80
Willow Rd. Enf 3K 7
Willow Rd. N Mald 4J 135
Willow Rd. Romf 6E 38
Willow Rd. Wall 7F 151
Willows Av. Mord 5K 137
Willows Clo. Pinn 2A 24
Willowside Ct. Enf 3G 7
Willows Ter. NW10 . . . . . 2B 64
(off Rucklidge Av.)
Willows, The. E6 . . . . . 7D 54
Willows, The. Beck 1C 142
Willow St. E4 . . . . . 1A 20
Willow St. EC2 . . . . 4E 68 (3G 163)
Willow St. Romf 4J 39
Willow Tree Clo. E3 . . . . . 1A 70
Willow Tree Clo. SW18 . . . . 1K 119
Willow Tree Clo. Hay 4A 60
Willowtree Clo. Uxb 3E 40
Willow Tree Ct. Sidc 5A 128
Willow Tree Ct. Wemb 5D 44
Willow Tree La. Hay 4A 60
Willow Tree Wlk. Brom 1K 143
Willowtree Way. T Hth 1A 140
Willow Va. W12 . . . . . 1C 82
Willow Va. Chst 6F 127
Willow Vw. SW19 . . . . . 1B 138
Willow Wlk. E17 . . . . . 5B 34
Willow Wlk. N2 . . . . . 2B 30
Willow Wlk. N15 . . . . . 4B 32
Willow Wlk. N21 . . . . . 6E 6
Willow Wlk. SE1 . . . . . 3E 86
Willow Wlk. Ilf 2F 55
Willow Wlk. Sutt 3H 149
Willow Way. N3 . . . . . 7E 14
Willow Way. SE26 . . . . . 3J 123
Willow Way. W11 . . . . . 7F 65
Willow Way. Eps 6K 147
Willow Way. Sun 4J 131
Willow Way. Twic 2F 115
Willow Way. Wemb 3A 44
Willow Wood Cres. SE25 . . . 6E 140
Willow Wren Wharf. S'hall . . . 4K 77
Willrose Cres. SE2 . . . . . 5B 92
Willsbridge Ct. SE15 . . . . . 6E 86
Wills Cres. Houn 6F 97
Wills Gro. NW7 . . . . . 5H 13
(in two parts)
Wilman Gro. E8 . . . . . 7G 51
Wilmar Clo. Hay 4F 59
Wilmar Gdns. W Wick 1D 154
Wilmcote Ho. W2 . . . . . 5K 65
(off Woodchester Sq.)
Wilment Ct. NW2 . . . . . 3E 46
Wilmer Clo. King T 5F 117
Wilmer Cres. King T 5F 117
Wilmer Gdns. N1 . . . . . 1E 68
(in two parts)
Wilmer Lea Clo. E15 . . . . . 7F 53
Wilmer Pl. N16 . . . . . 2F 51
Wilmers Ct. NW10 . . . . . 1K 63
(off Stacey Rd.)

Wilmer Way. N14 ... 5C 16
Wilmington Av. W4 ... 7K 81
Wilmington Ct. SW16 ... 7J 121
Wilmington Gdns. Bark ... 6H 55
Wilmington Sq. WC1 ... 3A 68 (2J 161) (in two parts)
Wilmington St. WC1 ... 3A 68 (2J 161)
Wilmot Clo. N2 ... 2A 30
Wilmot Clo. SE15 ... 7G 87
Wilmot Pl. W7 ... 1J 79
Wilmot Rd. E10 ... 2D 52
Wilmot Rd. N17 ... 3D 32
Wilmot Rd. Cars ... 5D 150
Wilmot St. E2 ... 4H 69
Wilmot St. NW1 ... 7G 49
Wilmount St. SE18 ... 4F 91
Wilna Rd. SW18 ... 7A 102
Wilsham St. W11 ... 1F 83
Wilshaw Ct. NW4 ... 3C 28
Wilshaw Ho. SE8 ... 7C 88
Wilshaw St. SE14 ... 1C 106
Wilsmere Dri. Har W ... 7D 10
Wilsmere Dri. N'holt ... 5C 42
Wilson Av. Mitc ... 1C 138
Wilson Clo. S Croy ... 5D 152
Wilson Clo. Wemb ... 7F 27
Wilson Dri. Wemb ... 7F 27
Wilson Gdns. Harr ... 7G 25
Wilson Gro. SE16 ... 2H 87
Wilson Rd. E6 ... 3B 72
Wilson Rd. SE5 ... 1E 104
Wilson Rd. Chess ... 6F 147
Wilson Rd. Ilf ... 7D 36
Wilson's Av. N17 ... 2F 33
Wilson's Pl. E14 ... 6B 70
Wilson's Rd. W6 ... 5F 83
Wilson St. E17 ... 5E 34
Wilson St. EC2 ... 5D 68 (5F 163)
Wilson St. N21 ... 7F 7
Wilson Wlk. W6 ... 4B 82 (off Prebend Gdns.)
Wilstone Clo. Hay ... 4C 60
Wiltern Ct. NW2 ... 6G 47
Wilthorne Gdns. Dag ... 7H 57
Wilton Av. W4 ... 5A 82
Wilton Clo. W Dray ... 6A 76
Wilton Ct. E1 ... 6H 69 (off Cavell St.)
Wilton Cres. SW1 ... 2E 84 (7G 165)
Wilton Cres. SW19 ... 7H 119
Wilton Dri. Romf ... 1J 39
Wilton Est. E8 ... 6G 51
Wilton Gdns. W Mol ... 3E 132
Wilton Gro. SW19 ... 1H 137
Wilton Gro. N Mald ... 6B 136
Wilton Ho. S Croy ... 5C 152 (off Nottingham Rd.)
Wilton M. SW1 ... 3E 84 (1H 171)
Wilton Pde. Felt ... 1K 113
Wilton Pl. SW1 ... 2E 84 (7G 165)
Wilton Pl. Harr ... 6K 25
Wilton Rd. N10 ... 2E 30
Wilton Rd. SE2 ... 4C 92
Wilton Rd. SW1 ... 3F 85 (2A 172)
Wilton Rd. SW19 ... 7C 120
Wilton Rd. Cockf ... 4J 5 (in two parts)
Wilton Rd. Houn ... 3B 96
Wilton Row. SW1 ... 2E 84 (7G 165)
Wilton Sq. N1 ... 1D 68
Wilton St. SW1 ... 3F 85 (1J 171)
Wilton Ter. SW1 ... 3E 84 (1G 171)
Wilton Vs. N1 ... 1D 68 (off Wilton Sq.)
Wilton Way. E8 ... 6G 51
Wiltshire Clo. NW7 ... 5G 13
Wiltshire Clo. SW3 ... 4D 84 (3E 170)
Wiltshire Ct. N4 ... 1K 49 (off Marquis Rd.)
Wiltshire Ct. Ilf ... 6G 55
Wiltshire Ct. S Croy ... 5C 152
Wiltshire Gdns. N4 ... 6C 32
Wiltshire Gdns. Twic ... 1G 115
Wiltshire La. Pinn ... 3H 23
Wiltshire Rd. SW9 ... 3A 104
Wiltshire Rd. Orp ... 7K 145
Wiltshire Rd. T Hth ... 3A 140
Wiltshire Row. N1 ... 1D 68
Wilverley Cres. N Mald ... 6A 136
Wimbart Rd. SW2 ... 7K 103
Wimbledon. ... 6H 119
Wimbledon (All England Lawn Tennis & Croquet Club) ... 4G 119
Wimbledon Bri. SW19 ... 6H 119
Wimbledon Clo. SW20 ... 7F 119
Wimbledon Common. ... 4C 118
Wimbledon Common Postmill & Mus. ... 2D 118
Wimbledon F.C. (Selhurst Pk.) ... 4E 140
Wimbledon Greyhound Stadium. ... 4A 120
Wimbledon Hill Rd. SW19 ... 6G 119
Wimbledon Lawn Tennis Mus. ... 3G 119 (Centre Court, All England Lawn Tennis & Croquet Club)
Wimbledon Mus. of Local History. ... 6G 119
Wimbledon Park. ... 3J 119
Wimbledon Pk. Rd. SW19 & SW18 ... 2G 119
Wimbledon Pk. Side. SW19 ... 3F 119
Wimbledon Rd. SW17 ... 4A 120
Wimbledon Stadium Bus. Cen. SW17 ... 3K 119
Wimbolt St. E2 ... 3G 69
Wimborne Av. Hay ... 6K 59
Wimborne Av. Orp ... 4K 145
Wimborne Av. S'hall ... 4E 78
Wimborne Clo. SE12 ... 5H 107
Wimborne Clo. Buck H ... 2E 20
Wimborne Clo. Wor Pk ... 1E 148
Wimborne Ct. SW12 ... 3G 121
Wimborne Ct. N'holt ... 6E 42
Wimborne Dri. NW9 ... 3G 27
Wimborne Dri. Pinn ... 7B 24
Wimborne Gdns. W13 ... 5B 62
Wimborne Ho. E16 ... 7H 71 (off Victoria Dock Rd.)
Wimborne Ho. NW1 ... 4C 66 (4D 158) (off Harewood Av.)
Wimborne Ho. SW8 ... 7K 85 (off Dorset Rd.)
Wimborne Rd. N9 ... 2B 18
Wimborne Rd. N17 ... 2E 32
Wimborne Way. Beck ... 3K 141
Wimbourne Ct. N1 ... 2D 68 (off Wimbourne St.)
Wimbourne St. N1 ... 2D 68
Wimpole Clo. Brom ... 4A 144
Wimpole Clo. King T ... 2F 135
Wimpole M. W1 ... 5F 67 (5J 159)
Wimpole Rd. W Dray ... 1A 76
Wimpole St. W1 ... 5F 67 (6J 159)
Wimshurst Clo. Croy ... 1J 151
Winans Wlk. SW9 ... 2A 104
Winant Ho. E14 ... 7D 70 (off Simpson's Rd.)
Wincanton Ct. N11 ... 6K 15 (off Martock Gdns.)
Wincanton Cres. N'holt ... 5E 42
Wincanton Gdns. Ilf ... 3F 37
Wincanton Rd. SW18 ... 7H 101
Winchcombe Bus. Cen. SE15 ... 6E 86
Winchcombe Ct. SE15 ... 6E 86 (off Longhope Clo.)
Winchcombe Rd. Cars ... 7B 138
Winchcomb Gdns. SE9 ... 3B 108
Winchelsea Av. Bexh ... 7F 93
Winchelsea Clo. SW15 ... 5F 101
Winchelsea Cres. W Mol ... 2G 133
Winchelsea Ho. SE16 ... 2J 87 (off Swan Rd.)
Winchelsea Rd. E7 ... 3J 53
Winchelsea Rd. N15 ... 3E 32
Winchelsea Rd. NW10 ... 1K 63
Winchelsey Ri. S Croy ... 6F 153
Winchendon Rd. SW6 ... 1H 101
Winchendon Rd. Tedd ... 4H 115
Winchester Av. NW6 ... 1G 65
Winchester Av. NW9 ... 3G 27
Winchester Av. Houn ... 6D 78
Winchester Clo. E6 ... 6D 72
Winchester Clo. SE17 ... 4B 86
Winchester Clo. Brom ... 3H 143
Winchester Clo. Enf ... 5K 7
Winchester Clo. King T ... 7H 117
Winchester Ct. W8 ... 2J 83 (off Vicarage Ga.)
Winchester Dri. Pinn ... 5B 24
Winchester Ho. SE18 ... 7B 90 (off Portway Gdns.)
Winchester Ho. SW3 ... 7B 170
Winchester Ho. SW9 ... 7A 86
Winchester Ho. W2 ... 6A 66 (off Hallfield Est.)
Winchester Ho. Bark ... 7A 56 (off Keir Hardie Way)
Winchester Pk. Brom ... 3H 143
Winchester Pl. E8 ... 5F 51
Winchester Pl. N6 ... 1F 49
Winchester Rd. E4 ... 7K 19
Winchester Rd. N6 ... 7F 31
Winchester Rd. N9 ... 1A 18
Winchester Rd. NW3 ... 7B 48
Winchester Rd. Bexh ... 2D 110
Winchester Rd. Brom ... 3H 143
Winchester Rd. Felt ... 3D 114
Winchester Rd. Harr ... 4E 26
Winchester Rd. Hay ... 7G 77
Winchester Rd. Ilf ... 3H 55
Winchester Rd. N'wd ... 2H 23
Winchester Rd. Twic ... 6B 98
Winchester Rd. W on T ... 7J 131
Winchester Sq. SE1 ... 4E 168
Winchester St. SW1 ... 5F 85 (5K 171)
Winchester St. W3 ... 1J 81
Winchester Wlk. SE1 ... 1D 86 (4E 168)
Winchet Wlk. Croy ... 6J 141
Winchfield Clo. Harr ... 6C 26
Winchfield Ho. SW15 ... 6B 100
Winchfield Rd. SE26 ... 5A 124
Winch Ho. E14 ... 3D 88 (off Tiller Rd.)
Winch Ho. SW10 ... 7A 84 (off King's Rd.)
Winchilsea Ho. NW8 ... 3B 66 (2B 158) (off St John's Wood Rd.)
Winchmore Hill. ... 7F 7
Winchmore Hill Rd. N14 & N21 ... 1C 16
Winchmore Vs. N21 ... 7E 6 (off Winchmore Hill Rd.)
Winchstone Clo. Shep ... 4B 130
Winckley Clo. Harr ... 5F 27
Wincott St. SE11 ... 4A 86 (4K 173)
Wincrofts Dri. SE9 ... 4H 109
Windall Clo. SE19 ... 1G 141
Windborough Rd. Cars ... 7E 150
Windermere. NW1 ... 3F 67 (2K 159) (off Albany St.)
Windermere Av. N3 ... 3J 29
Windermere Av. NW6 ... 1G 65
Windermere Av. SW19 ... 3K 137
Windermere Av. Ruis ... 7A 24
Windermere Av. Wemb ... 7C 26
Windermere Clo. Felt ... 1H 113
Windermere Clo. Stai ... 1A 112
Windermere Ct. SW13 ... 6B 82
Windermere Ct. Cars ... 3E 150
Windermere Ct. Wemb ... 7C 26
Windermere Gdns. Ilf ... 5C 36
Windermere Gro. Wemb ... 1C 44
Windermere Hall. Edgw ... 5A 12
Windermere Ho. E3 ... 4B 70
Windermere Ho. New Bar ... 4E 4
Windermere Point. SE15 ... 7J 87 (off Old Kent Rd.)
Windermere Rd. N10 ... 1F 31
Windermere Rd. N19 ... 2G 49
Windermere Rd. SW15 ... 4A 118
Windermere Rd. SW16 ... 1G 139
Windermere Rd. W5 ... 3C 80
Windermere Rd. Bexh ... 2J 111
Windermere Rd. Croy ... 1F 153
Windermere Rd. S'hall ... 5D 60
Windermere Rd. W Wick ... 2G 155
Windermere Way. W Dray ... 1A 76
Winders Rd. SW11 ... 2C 102 (in two parts)
Windfield Clo. SE26 ... 4K 123
Windham Rd. Rich ... 3F 99
Winding Way. Dag ... 3C 56
Winding Way. Harr ... 4J 43
Windlass Pl. SE8 ... 4A 88
Windlesham Gro. SW19 ... 1F 119
Windley Clo. SE23 ... 2J 123
Windmill. WC1 ... 5K 67 (5G 161) (off New N. St.)
Windmill Av. S'hall ... 1G 79
Windmill Bridge Ho. Croy ... 1E 152 (off Freemasons Rd.)
Windmill Bus. Cen. S'hall ... 1G 79
Windmill Bus. Village. Sun ... 1G 131
Windmill Clo. SE1 ... 4G 87 (off Beatrice Rd.)
Windmill Clo. SE13 ... 2E 106
Windmill Clo. Sun ... 7G 113
Windmill Clo. Surb ... 1C 146
Windmill Ct. NW2 ... 6G 47
Windmill Ct. W5 ... 4C 80 (off Windmill Rd.)
Windmill Dri. NW2 ... 3G 47
Windmill Dri. SW4 ... 5F 103
Windmill Dri. Kes ... 4A 156
Windmill Gdns. Enf ... 3F 7
Windmill Grn. Shep ... 7G 131 (off Walton La.)
Windmill Gro. Croy ... 6C 140
Windmill Hill. NW3 ... 3A 48
Windmill Hill. Enf ... 3G 7
Windmill Hill. Ruis ... 7H 23
Windmill La. E15 ... 6F 53
Windmill La. Bus H ... 1D 10
Windmill La. Gnfd ... 4G 61
Windmill La. S'hall & Iswth ... 1G 79
Windmill La. Surb ... 6B 134
Windmill M. W4 ... 4A 82
Windmill Pas. W4 ... 4A 82
Windmill Ri. King T ... 7H 117
Windmill Rd. N18 ... 4J 17
Windmill Rd. SW18 ... 6B 102
Windmill Rd. SW19 ... 4D 118
Windmill Rd. W4 ... 4A 82
Windmill Rd. W5 & Bren ... 4C 80
Windmill Rd. Croy ... 7C 140
Windmill Rd. Hamp H ... 5F 115
Windmill Rd. Mitc ... 5G 139
Windmill Rd. Sun ... 1G 131
Windmill Rd. W. Sun ... 2G 131
Windmill Row. SE11 ... 5A 86 (6J 173)
Windmill St. W1 ... 5H 67 (6C 160) (in two parts)
Windmill St. Bus H ... 1D 10
Windmill Ter. Shep ... 7G 131
Windmill Wlk. SE1 ... 1A 86 (5K 167)
Windmill Way. Ruis ... 1H 41
Windmore Clo. Wemb ... 5A 44
Windover Av. NW9 ... 4K 27
Windrose Clo. SE16 ... 2K 87
Windrush. SE28 ... 1B 92
Windrush. N Mald ... 4H 135
Windrush Clo. N17 ... 1E 32
Windrush Clo. SW11 ... 4B 102
Windrush Clo. W4 ... 1J 99
Windrush Clo. Uxb ... 4B 40
Windrush La. SE23 ... 3K 123
Windrush Rd. NW10 ... 1K 63
Windsock Clo. SE16 ... 4B 88
Windsor Av. E17 ... 2A 34
Windsor Av. SW19 ... 1A 138
Windsor Av. Edgw ... 4C 12
Windsor Av. N Mald ... 5J 135
Windsor Av. Sutt ... 3G 149
Windsor Av. Uxb ... 1D 58
Windsor Av. W Mol ... 3E 132
Windsor Cen., The. N1 ... 1B 68 (off Windsor St.)
Windsor Clo. N3 ... 2G 29
Windsor Clo. SE27 ... 4C 122
Windsor Clo. Bren ... 6B 80
Windsor Clo. Chst ... 5F 127
Windsor Clo. Harr ... 3E 42
Windsor Clo. N'wd ... 2J 23
Windsor Cotts. SE14 ... 7B 88 (off Amersham Gro.)
Windsor Ct. N12 ... 5J 15
Windsor Ct. N14 ... 7B 6
Windsor Ct. NW2 ... 6G 47 (off Chatsworth Rd.)
Windsor Ct. NW3 ... 4J 47
Windsor Ct. NW11 ... 6G 29 (off Golders Grn. Rd.)
Windsor Ct. SE16 ... 7K 69 (off King & Queen Wharf)
Windsor Ct. SW3 ... 5C 84 (5D 170) (off Jubilee Pl.)
Windsor Ct. SW11 ... 2B 102
Windsor Ct. W2 ... 7K 65 (off Moscow Rd.)
Windsor Ct. King T ... 4D 134 (off Palace Rd.)
Windsor Ct. Pinn ... 3B 24
Windsor Ct. Sun ... 7J 113
Windsor Cres. Harr ... 3E 42
Windsor Cres. Wemb ... 3H 45
Windsor Dri. Barn ... 6J 5
Windsor Gdns. W9 ... 5J 65
Windsor Gdns. Croy ... 3J 151
Windsor Gdns. Hay ... 3F 77
Windsor Gro. SE27 ... 4C 122
Windsor Hall. E16 ... 1K 89 (off Wesley Av., in two parts)
Windsor Ho. E2 ... 3K 69 (off Knottisford St.)
Windsor Ho. N1 ... 2C 68
Windsor Ho. NW1 ... 1K 159
Windsor Ho. N'holt ... 6E 42 (off Farmlands, The)
Windsor M. SE6 ... 1E 124
Windsor M. SE23 ... 1A 124
Windsor M. SW18 ... 7A 102 (off Wilna Rd.)
Windsor Pk. Rd. Hay ... 7H 77
Windsor Pl. SW1 ... 3G 85 (3B 172)
Windsor Rd. E4 ... 4J 19
Windsor Rd. E7 ... 5K 53
Windsor Rd. E10 ... 2D 52
Windsor Rd. E11 ... 1J 53
Windsor Rd. N3 ... 2G 29
Windsor Rd. N7 ... 3J 49
Windsor Rd. N13 ... 3F 17
Windsor Rd. N17 ... 2G 33
Windsor Rd. NW2 ... 6D 46
Windsor Rd. W5 ... 7E 62 (in two parts)
Windsor Rd. Barn ... 6A 4
Windsor Rd. Bexh ... 4E 110
Windsor Rd. Dag ... 3E 56
Windsor Rd. Harr ... 1G 25
Windsor Rd. Houn ... 2K 95
Windsor Rd. Ilf ... 4F 55
Windsor Rd. King T ... 7E 116
Windsor Rd. Rich ... 2F 99

Windsor Rd. S'hall 3D 78
Windsor Rd. Sun 6J 113
Windsor Rd. Tedd 5H 115
Windsor Rd. T Hth 2B 140
Windsor Rd. Wor Pk 2C 148
Windsors, The. Buck H 2H 21
Windsor St. N1 1B 68
Windsor Ter. N1 3C 68 (1D 162)
Windsor Wlk. SE5 2D 104
Windsor Way. W14 4F 83
Windsor Wharf. E9 6C 52
Windspoint Dri. SE15 6H 87
Windus Rd. N16 1F 51
Windus Wlk. N16 1F 51
Windy Ridge. Brom 1C 144
Windy Ridge Clo. SW19 5F 119
Wine Clo. E1 7J 69
(in two parts)
Wine Office Ct. EC4
6A 68 (7K 161)
Winery La. King T 3F 135
Winford Ct. SE15 1H 105
Winford Ho. E3 7B 52
Winford Pde. S'hall 6F 61
(off Marconi Way)
Winforton St. SE10 1E 106
Winfrith Rd. SW18 7A 102
Wingate Cres. Croy 6J 139
Wingate Rd. W6 3D 82
Wingate Rd. Ilf 5F 55
Wingate Rd. Sidc 6C 128
Wingate Trad. Est. N17 7B 18
Wingfield Ct. Sidc 2K 127
Wingfield Ho. E2 3F 69 (2J 163)
(off Virginia Rd.)
Wingfield Ho. NW6 2K 65
(off Tollgate Gdns.)
Wingfield M. SE15 3G 105
Wingfield Rd. E15 4G 53
Wingfield Rd. E17 5D 34
Wingfield Rd. King T 6F 117
Wingfield St. SE15 3G 105
Wingfield Way. Ruis 6K 41
Wingford Rd. SW2 6J 103
Wingmore Rd. SE24 3C 104
Wingrad Ho. E1 5J 69
(off Jubilee St.)
Wingrave. SE17 4D 86
(in three parts)
Wingrave Rd. W6 6E 82
Wingreen. NW8 1K 65
(off Abbey Rd.)
Wingrove. E4 7H 9
Wingrove Ct. Romf 5J 39
Wingrove Rd. SE6 2G 125
Wings Clo. Sutt 4J 149
Winicotte Ho. W2
5B 66 (5B 158)
(off Paddington Grn.)
Winifred Pl. N12 5F 15
Winifred Rd. SW19 1J 137
Winifred Rd. Dag 2E 56
Winifred Rd. Eri 5K 93
Winifred Rd. Hamp H 4E 114
Winifred St. E16 1D 90
Winifred Ter. E13 2J 71
(off Victoria Rd.)
Winifred Ter. Enf 7A 8
Winkfield Rd. E13 2K 71
Winkfield Rd. N22 1A 32
Winkley Ct. N10 4F 31
(off St James's La.)
Winkley Ct. S Harr 3E 42
Winkley St. E2 2H 69
Winkworth Cotts. E1 4J 69
(off Cephas St.)
Winlaton Rd. Brom 4F 125
Winmill Rd. Dag 3F 57
Winnett St. W1 7H 67 (2C 166)
Winningales Ct. Ilf 2C 36
Winnings Wlk. N'holt 6C 42
Winnington Clo. N2 6B 30
Winnington Ho. SE5 7C 86
(off Wyndham Est.)
Winnington Rd. N2 6B 30
Winnock Rd. W Dray 1A 76
Winn Rd. SE12 1J 125
Winns Av. E17 3B 34
Winns Comn. Rd. SE18 6J 91
Winns M. N15 4E 32
Winns Ter. E17 3C 34
Winsbeach. E17 2F 35
Winscombe Cres. W5 4D 62
Winscombe St. NW5 3F 49
Winscombe Way. Stan 5F 11
Winsford Rd. SE6 3B 124
Winsford Ter. N18 5J 17
Winsham Gro. SW11 5E 102
Winsham Ho. NW1
3H 67 (1D 160)
(off Churchway)
Winslade Rd. SW2 5J 103
Winslade Way. SE6 7D 106
Winsland M. W2 6B 66 (7A 158)
Winsland St. W2 6B 66 (7A 158)
Winsley St. W1 6G 67 (7B 160)
Winslow. SE17 5E 86
Winslow Clo. NW10 3A 46
Winslow Clo. Pinn 6K 23
Winslow Gro. E4 2B 20
Winslow Rd. W6 6E 82
Winslow Way. Felt 3B 114
Winsmoor Ct. Enf 3G 7
Winsor Park. 5F 73
Winsor Ter. E6 5E 72
Winstanley Est. SW11 3B 102
Winstanley Rd. SW11 3B 102
Winstead Gdns. Dag 5J 57
Winston Av. NW9 7A 28
Winston Churchill's Britain at War Experience. 5G 169
Winston Clo. Harr 6E 10
Winston Clo. Romf 4H 39
Winston Ct. Brom 1K 143
(off Widmore Rd.)
Winston Ct. Harr 7A 10
Winston Ho. N1 2D 68
(off Cherbury St.)
Winston Ho. W13 2A 80
(off Balfour Rd.)
Winston Ho. WC1 3D 160
Winston Rd. N16 4D 50
Winston Wlk. W4 3K 81
Winston Way. Ilf 3F 55
Winter Av. E6 1C 72
Winterbourne Ho. W11 7G 65
(off Portland Rd.)
Winterbourne Rd. SE6 1B 124
Winterbourne Rd. Dag 2C 56
Winterbourne Rd. T Hth 4A 140
Winter Box Wlk. Rich 5F 99
Winterbrook Rd. SE24 6C 104
Winterburn Clo. N11 6K 15
Winterfold Clo. SW19 2G 119
Wintergreen Clo. E6 5C 72
Winterleys. NW6 2H 65
(off Albert Rd.)
Winter Lodge. SE16 5G 87
(off Fern Wlk.)
Winter's Ct. E4 3J 19
Winterslow Ho. SE5 2C 104
(off Flaxman Rd.)
Winters Rd. Th Dit 7B 134
Winterstoke Gdns. NW7 5H 13
Winterstoke Rd. SE6 1B 124
Winterton Ct. SE20 2G 141
Winterton Ct. King T 1D 134
(off Lwr. Teddington Rd.)
Winterton Ho. E1 6J 69
(off Deancross St.)
Winterton Pl. SW10
6A 84 (7A 170)
Winterwell Rd. SW2 5J 103
Winthorpe Rd. SW15 4G 101
Winthrop Ho. W12 7D 64
(off White City Est.)
Winthrop St. E1 5H 69
Winthrop Wlk. Wemb 3E 44
Winton Av. N11 7B 16
Winton Clo. N9 7E 8
Winton Gdns. Edgw 7A 12
Winton Way. SW16 5A 122
Wirrall Ho. SE26 3G 123
Wirral Wood Clo. Chst 6E 126
Wisbeach Rd. Croy 5D 140
Wisbech. N4 1K 49
(off Lorne Rd.)
Wisborough Rd. S Croy 7F 153
Wisden Ho. SW8
6K 85 (7G 173)
Wisdom Ct. Isw th 3A 98
(off South St.)
Wisdons Clo. Dag 1H 57
Wise La. NW7 5H 13
Wise La. W Dray 4A 76
Wiseman Rd. E10 2C 52
Wise Rd. E15 1F 71
Wiseton Rd. SW17 1C 120
Wisham Wlk. N13 6D 16
Wishart Rd. SE3 2B 108
Wisley Ho. SW1 5H 85 (5C 172)
(off Rampayne St.)
Wisley Rd. SW11 5E 102
Wisley Rd. Orp 7A 128
Wisteria Clo. NW7 6G 13
Wisteria Clo. Ilf 5F 55
Wisteria Gdns. Wfd G 5D 20
Wisteria Rd. SE13 4F 107
Witanhurst La. N6 1E 48
Witan St. E2 3H 69
Witham Ct. E10 3D 52
Witham Ct. SW17 3D 120
Witham Rd. SE20 3J 141
Witham Rd. W13 1A 80
Witham Rd. Dag 5G 57
Witham Rd. Isw th 1H 97
Witherby Clo. Croy 5E 152
Witherington Rd. N5 5A 50
Withers Clo. Chess 6C 146
Withers Mead. NW9 1B 28
Withers Pl. EC1 4C 68 (3D 162)
Witherston Way. SE9 2E 126
Withycombe Rd. SW19 7F 101
Withy Ho. E1 4K 69
(off Globe Rd.)
Withy La. Ruis 5E 22
Withy Mead. E4 3A 20
Witley Ct. WC1 4E 160
Witley Cres. New Ad 6E 154
Witley Gdns. S'hall 4D 78
Witley Ho. SW2 7J 103
Witley Ind. Est. S'hall 4D 78
Witley Rd. N19 2G 49
Witney Clo. Uxb 4B 40
Witney Path. SE23 3K 123
Wittenham Way. E4 3A 20
Wittering Clo. King T 5D 116
Wittersham Rd. Brom 5H 125
Witts Ho. King T 3F 135
(off Winery La.)
Wivenhoe Clo. SE15 3H 105
Wivenhoe Ct. Houn 4D 96
Wivenhoe Rd. Bark 2A 74
Wiverton Rd. SE26 6J 123
Wixom Ho. SE3 4A 108
Wix Rd. Dag 1D 74
Wix's La. SW4 3F 103
Woburn. W13 5B 62
(off Clivedon Ct.)
Woburn Clo. SE28 6D 74
Woburn Clo. SW19 6A 120
Woburn Ct. E18 2J 35
Woburn Ct. SE16 5H 87
(off Masters Dri.)
Woburn Ct. Croy 1C 152
Woburn M. WC1 4H 67 (4D 160)
Woburn Pl. WC1 4J 67 (4E 160)
Woburn Rd. Cars 1C 150
Woburn Rd. Croy 1C 152
Woburn Sq. WC1
4H 67 (4D 160)
Woburn Tower. N'holt 3B 60
(off Broomcroft Av.)
Woburn Wlk. WC1
3H 67 (2D 160)
Wodehouse Av. SE5 1F 105
Wodehouse Ct. W3 3J 81
(off Vincent Rd.)
Woffington Clo. King T 1C 134
Woking Clo. SW15 4B 100
Wolcot Ho. NW1 2G 67 (1B 160)
(off Aldenham St.)
Woldham Pl. Brom 4A 144
Woldham Rd. Brom 4A 144
Wolds Dri. Orp 4E 156
Wolfe Clo. Brom 6J 143
Wolfe Clo. Hay 3K 59
Wolfe Cres. SE7 5B 90
Wolfe Cres. SE16 2K 87
Wolfe Ho. W12 7D 64
(off White City Est.)
Wolferton Rd. E12 4D 54
Wolffe Gdns. E15 6H 53
Wolfington Rd. SE27 4B 122
Wolfram Clo. SE13 5G 107
Wolftencroft Clo. SW11 3C 102
Wollaston Clo. SE1 4C 86
Wollett Ct. NW1 7G 49
(off St Pancras Way)
Wolmer Clo. Edgw 4B 12
Wolmer Gdns. Edgw 3B 12
Wolseley Av. SW19 2J 119
Wolseley Gdns. W4 6H 81
Wolseley Rd. E7 7K 53
Wolseley Rd. N8 6H 31
Wolseley Rd. N22 1K 31
Wolseley Rd. W4 4J 81
Wolseley Rd. Harr 3J 25
Wolseley Rd. Mitc 7E 138
Wolseley Rd. Romf 7K 39
Wolseley St. SE1 2G 87 (7K 169)
Wolsey Av. E6 3E 72
Wolsey Av. E17 3B 34
Wolsey Av. Th Dit 5K 133
Wolsey Clo. SW20 7D 118
Wolsey Clo. Houn 4G 97
Wolsey Clo. King T 1H 135
Wolsey Clo. S'hall 3G 79
Wolsey Clo. Wor Pk 4C 148
Wolsey Ct. NW6 7A 48
Wolsey Ct. SW11 1C 102
(off Westbridge Rd.)
Wolsey Cres. Mord 7G 137
Wolsey Cres. New Ad 7E 154
Wolsey Dri. King T 5E 116
Wolsey Dri. W on T 7B 132
Wolsey Gro. Edgw 7E 12
Wolsey M. NW5 6G 49
Wolsey Rd. N1 5D 50
Wolsey Rd. Ashf 4A 112
Wolsey Rd. E Mol 4H 133
Wolsey Rd. Enf 2C 8
Wolsey Rd. Hamp H 6F 115
Wolsey Rd. Sun 7H 113
Wolsey Spring. King T 7J 117
Wolsey St. E1 5J 69
Wolsey Way. Chess 5G 147
Wolstonbury. N12 5D 14
Wolvercote Rd. SE2 2D 92
Wolverley St. E2 3H 69
Wolverton. SE17 5E 86
(in two parts)
Wolverton Av. King T 1G 135
Wolverton Gdns. W5 7F 63
Wolverton Gdns. W6 4F 83
Wolverton Rd. Stan 6G 11
Wolverton Way. N14 5B 6
Wolves La. N22 & N13 7F 17
Womersley Rd. N8 6K 31
Wonersh Way. Sutt 7F 149
Wonford Clo. King T 1A 136
Wontner Clo. N1 7C 50
Wontner Rd. SW17 2D 120
Wooburn Clo. Uxb 4D 58
Woodall Clo. E14 7D 70
Woodall Clo. Chess 6D 146
Woodall Ho. N22 1A 32
Woodall Rd. Enf 6E 8
Woodbank Rd. Brom 3H 125
Woodbastwick Rd. SE26 5K 123
Woodberry Av. N21 2F 17
Woodberry Av. Harr 4F 25
Woodberry Clo. Sun 6J 113
Woodberry Cres. N10 3F 31
Woodberry Down. N4 7C 32
Woodberry Down Est. N4 7C 32
(in two parts)
Woodberry Gdns. N12 6F 15
Woodberry Gro. N4 7C 32
Woodberry Gro. N12 6F 15
Woodberry Gro. Bex 3K 129
Woodberry Way. E4 7K 9
Woodberry Way. N12 6F 15
Woodbine Clo. Twic 2H 115
Woodbine Gro. SE20 7H 123
Woodbine Gro. Enf 1J 7
Woodbine La. Wor Pk 3D 148
Woodbine Pl. E11 6J 35
Woodbine Rd. Sidc 1J 127
Woodbines Av. King T 3D 134
Woodbine Ter. E9 6J 51
Woodborough Rd. SW15 4D 100
Woodbourne Av. SW16 3H 121
Woodbourne Clo. SW16 3J 121
Woodbourne Gdns. Wall 7F 151
Woodbridge Clo. N7 2K 49
Woodbridge Clo. NW2 3C 46
Woodbridge Ct. Wfd G 7H 21
Woodbridge Ho. E11 1H 53
Woodbridge Rd. Bark 5K 55
Woodbridge St. EC1
4B 68 (3A 162)
(in two parts)
Woodbrook Rd. SE2 6A 92
Woodburn Clo. NW4 5F 29
Woodbury Clo. E11 4K 35
Woodbury Clo. Croy 2F 153
Woodbury Ho. SE26 3G 123
Woodbury Pk. Rd. W13 4B 62
Woodbury Rd. E17 4D 34
Woodbury St. SW17 5C 120
Woodchester Sq. W2 5K 65
Woodchurch Clo. Sidc 3H 127
Woodchurch Dri. Brom 7B 126
Woodchurch Rd. NW6 7J 47
Wood Clo. E2 4G 69
Wood Clo. NW9 7K 27
Wood Clo. Harr 7H 25
Woodclyffe Dri. Chst 2E 144
Woodcock Ct. Harr 7E 26
Woodcock Dell Av. Harr 7D 26
Woodcock Hill. Harr 5C 26
Woodcock Ho. E14 5C 70
(off Burgess St.)
Woodcocks. E16 5A 72
Woodcombe Cres. SE23 1J 123
Woodcote Av. NW7 6K 13
Woodcote Av. T Hth 4B 140
Woodcote Av. Wall 7F 151
Woodcote Clo. Enf 6D 8
Woodcote Clo. King T 5F 117
Woodcote Ct. Sutt 6J 149
Woodcote Dri. Orp 7H 145
Woodcote Grn. Wall 7G 151
Woodcote Ho. SE8 6B 88
(off Prince St.)
Woodcote M. Wall 6F 151
Woodcote Pl. SE27 5B 122
Woodcote Rd. E11 7J 35
Woodcote Rd. Wall 6F 151
Wood Ct. Eri 7K 93
Wood Crest. Sutt 7A 150
(off Christchurch Pk.)
Woodcroft. N21 1F 17
Woodcroft. SE9 3D 126
Woodcroft. Gnfd 6A 44
Woodcroft Av. NW7 6F 13
Woodcroft Av. Stan 1A 26
Woodcroft Cres. Uxb 1D 58
Woodcroft M. SE8 4A 88
Woodcroft Rd. T Hth 5B 140
Wood Dene. SE15 1H 105
(off Queen's Rd.)
Wood Dri. Chst 6C 126
Woodedge Clo. E4 1C 20

Wood End 5H 59 (Hayes)
Wood End 5H 43 (Northolt)
Woodend. SE19 6C 122
Wood End. Hay 6G 59
Woodend. Sutt 2A 150
Wood End Av. Harr 4F 43
Wood End Clo. N'holt 5H 43
Woodend Gdns. Enf 4D 6
Wood End Gdns. N'holt 5G 43
Wood End Green 5G 59
Wood End Grn. Rd. Hay 5F 59
Wood End La. N'holt 6F 43 (in two parts)
Woodend Rd. E17 2E 34
Wood End Rd. Harr 4H 43
Woodend, The. Wall 7F 151
Wood End Way. N'holt 5G 43
Wooder Gdns. E7 4J 53
Wooderson Clo. SE25 4E 140
Woodfall Av. Barn 5C 4
Woodfall Rd. N4 2A 50
Woodfall St. SW3 5D 84 (6E 170)
Woodfarrs. SE5 4D 104
Wood Fld. NW3 5D 48
Woodfield Av. NW9 4A 28
Woodfield Av. SW16 3H 121
Woodfield Av. W5 4C 62
Woodfield Av. Cars 6E 150
Woodfield Av. Wemb 3C 44
Woodfield Clo. SE19 7C 122
Woodfield Clo. Enf 4K 7
Woodfield Cres. W5 4C 62
Woodfield Dri. E Barn 1K 15
Woodfield Gdns. N Mald 5B 136
Woodfield Gro. SW16 3H 121
Woodfield Ho. SE23 3K 123 (off Dacres Rd.)
Woodfield La. SW16 3H 121
Woodfield Pl. W9 4H 65
Woodfield Ri. Bush 1C 10
Woodfield Rd. W5 4C 62
Woodfield Rd. W9 5H 65
Woodfield Rd. Houn 2K 95
Woodfield Way. N11 7C 16
Woodford 6E 20
Woodford Av. Ilf (IG2) 5D 36
Woodford Av. Ilf (IG4) 3B 36
Woodford Bridge 6H 21
Woodford Bri. Rd. Ilf 3B 36
Woodford Ct. W14 2F 83 (off Shepherd's Bush Grn.)
Woodford Cres. Pinn 2K 23
Woodforde Ct. Hay 5F 77
Woodford Green 6D 20
Woodford Hall Path. E18 1H 35
Woodford Ho. E18 4J 35
Woodford New Rd. E17 & E18 4G 35
Woodford Pl. Wemb 1E 44
Woodford Rd. E7 3K 53
Woodford Rd. E18 4J 35
Woodford Side 5C 20
Woodford Trad. Est. Wfd G 2B 36
Woodford Wells 3E 20
Woodgate Av. Chess 5D 146
Woodgate Dri. SW16 7H 121
Woodger Rd. W12 2E 82
Woodget Clo. E6 6C 72
Woodgrange Av. N12 6G 15
Woodgrange Av. W5 1G 81
Woodgrange Av. Enf 6B 8
Woodgrange Av. Harr 5C 26
Woodgrange Clo. Harr 5D 26
Woodgrange Gdns. Enf 6B 8
Woodgrange Mans. Harr 5D 26
Woodgrange Rd. E7 5K 53
Woodgrange Ter. Enf 6B 8
Wood Green 2K 31
Wood Green Shop. City. N22 2A 32
Woodhall. NW1 3G 67 (2A 160) (off Robert St.)
Woodhall Av. SE21 3F 123
Woodhall Av. Pinn 1C 24
Woodhall Clo. Uxb 5A 40
Woodhall Dri. SE21 3F 123
Woodhall Dri. Pinn 1B 24
Woodhall Ga. Pinn 1B 24
Woodham Ct. E18 4H 35
Woodham Rd. SE6 3E 124
Woodhatch Clo. E6 5C 72
Woodhaven Gdns. Ilf 4G 37
Woodhayes Rd. SW19 7E 118
Woodheyes Rd. NW10 5K 45
Woodhill. SE18 4C 90
Woodhill Cres. Harr 6D 26
Woodhouse Av. Gnfd 2K 61
Woodhouse Clo. Gnfd 1K 61
Woodhouse Clo. Hay 3G 77
Woodhouse Gro. E12 6C 54
Woodhouse Rd. E11 3H 53
Woodhouse Rd. N12 6G 15
Woodhurst Av. Orp 6G 145
Woodhurst Rd. SE2 5A 92
Woodhurst Rd. W3 7J 63
Woodington Clo. SE9 6E 108
Woodknoll Dri. Chst 1D 144
Woodland App. Gnfd 6A 44
Woodland Clo. NW9 6J 27
Woodland Clo. SE19 6E 122
Woodland Clo. Eps 6A 148
Woodland Clo. Ick 2D 40
Woodland Clo. Wfd G 3E 20
Woodland Ct. E11 6J 35 (off New Wanstead)
Woodland Cres. SE10 6G 89
Woodland Cres. SE16 2K 87
Woodland Gdns. N10 5F 31
Woodland Gdns. Iswth 3J 97
Woodland Hill. SE19 6E 122
Woodland Ri. N10 4F 31
Woodland Ri. Gnfd 6A 44
Woodland Rd. E4 1K 19
Woodland Rd. N11 5A 16
Woodland Rd. SE19 5E 122
Woodland Rd. T Hth 4A 140
Woodlands 2J 97
Woodlands. NW11 5G 29
Woodlands. SW20 4E 136
Woodlands. Brom 4H 143
Woodlands. Harr 4E 24
***Woodlands Art Gallery** 6J 89*
Woodlands Av. E11 1K 53
Woodlands Av. N3 7F 15
Woodlands Av. W3 1H 81
Woodlands Av. N Mald 1J 135
Woodlands Av. Romf 6E 38
Woodlands Av. Ruis 7A 24
Woodlands Av. Sidc 1J 127
Woodlands Av. Wor Pk 2B 148
Woodlands Clo. NW11 5G 29
Woodlands Clo. Brom 2D 144
Woodlands Clo. Clay 7A 146
Woodlands Ct. NW10 1F 65 (off Wrentham Av.)
Woodlands Ct. SE23 7H 105
Woodlands Ct. Brom 1H 143
Woodlands Ct. Harr 5K 25
Woodlands Dri. Stan 6E 10
Woodlands Dri. Sun 2A 132
Woodlands Gdns. E17 4G 35
Woodlands Ga. SW15 5H 101
Woodlands Gro. SE10 5G 89
Woodlands Gro. Iswth 2J 97
Woodlands Ho. NW6 7G 47
Woodlands Pde. Ashf 6E 112
Woodlands Pk. Bex 4K 129
Woodlands Pk. Rd. N15 5B 32
Woodlands Pk. Rd. SE10 6G 89 (in two parts)
Woodlands Rd. E11 2G 53
Woodlands Rd. E17 3E 34
Woodlands Rd. N9 1D 18
Woodlands Rd. SW13 3B 100
Woodlands Rd. Bexh 3E 110
Woodlands Rd. Brom 2C 144
Woodlands Rd. Enf 1J 7
Woodlands Rd. Harr 5K 25
Woodlands Rd. Ilf 3G 55
Woodlands Rd. Iswth 3H 97
Woodlands Rd. S'hall 1B 78
Woodlands Rd. Surb 7D 134
Woodlands St. SE13 7F 107
Woodlands, The. N5 4C 50
Woodlands, The. N12 6F 15
Woodlands, The. N14 1A 16
Woodlands, The. SE13 7F 107
Woodlands, The. SE19 7C 122
Woodlands, The. Harr 2J 43
Woodlands, The. Iswth 2K 97
Woodlands, The. Stan 5G 11
Woodlands, The. Wall 7F 151
Woodland St. E8 6F 51
Woodlands Way. SW15 5H 101
Woodland Ter. SE7 4C 90
Woodland Wlk. NW3 5C 48
Woodland Wlk. SE10 5G 89
Woodland Wlk. Brom 4F 125 (in two parts)
Woodland Wlk. Eps 6G 147
Woodland Way. N21 2F 17
Woodland Way. NW7 6F 13
Woodland Way. SE2 4D 92
Woodland Way. Croy 1A 154
Woodland Way. Mitc 7E 120
Woodland Way. Mord 4H 137
Woodland Way. Orp 4G 145
Woodland Way. Surb 2H 147
Woodland Way. W Wick 4D 154
Woodland Way. Wfd G 3E 20
Wood La. N6 6F 31
Wood La. NW9 7K 27
Wood La. W12 6E 64
Wood La. Dag 4C 56
Wood La. Iswth 6J 79
Wood La. Ruis 1F 41
Wood La. Stan 3F 11
Wood La. Wfd G 4C 20
Woodlawn Clo. SW15 5H 101
Woodlawn Cres. Twic 2F 115
Woodlawn Dri. Felt 2B 114
Woodlawn Rd. SW6 7F 83
Woodlawns. Eps 7K 147
Woodlea Dri. Brom 5G 143
Woodlea Rd. N16 3E 50
Woodleigh. E18 1J 35
Woodleigh Av. N12 6H 15
Woodleigh Gdns. SW16 3J 121
Woodley Clo. SW17 7D 120
Woodley La. Cars 3C 150
Wood Lodge Gdns. Brom 7C 126
Wood Lodge La. W Wick 3E 154
Woodman Pde. E16 1E 90 (off Woodman St.)
Woodmans Gro. NW10 5B 46
Woodman's M. W12 5D 64
Woodmansterne Rd. SW16 7G 121
Woodmansterne Rd. Cars 7C 150
Woodman St. E16 1E 90 (in two parts)
Wood Mead. N17 6B 18
Woodmere. SE9 1D 126
Woodmere Av. Croy 7J 141
Woodmere Clo. SW11 3E 102
Woodmere Clo. Croy 7K 141
Woodmere Ct. N14 7A 6
Woodmere Gdns. Croy 7K 141
Woodmere Way. Beck 5F 143
Woodnook Rd. SW16 5F 121
Woodpecker Clo. N9 6C 8
Woodpecker Clo. Bush 1B 10
Woodpecker Clo. Harr 1K 25
Woodpecker Mt. Croy 7A 154
Woodpecker Rd. SE14 6A 88
Woodpecker Rd. SE28 7C 74
Wood Point. E16 5J 71 (off Fife Rd.)
Woodquest Av. SE24 5C 104
Wood Retreat. SE18 7H 91
Wood Ride. Barn 1G 5
Wood Ride. Orp 4H 145
Woodridge Clo. Enf 1F 7
Woodridings Av. Pinn 1D 24
Woodridings Clo. Pinn 1C 24
Woodridings Ct. N22 1H 31
Woodriffe Rd. E11 7F 35
Wood Ri. Pinn 5J 23
Wood Rd. Shep 4C 130
Woodrow. SE18 4D 90
Woodrow Av. Hay 5H 59
Woodrow Clo. Gnfd 7B 44
Woodrow Ct. N17 7C 18
Woodrush Clo. SE14 7A 88
Woodrush Way. Romf 4D 38
Wood's Bldgs. E1 5H 69 (off Winthrop St.)
Woodseer St. E1 5F 69 (5K 163)
Woodsford. SE17 5D 86 (off Portland St.)
Woodsford Sq. W14 2G 83
Woodshire Rd. Dag 3H 57
Woodside 6G 141
Woodside. N10 3E 30
Wood Side. NW11 5J 29
Woodside. SW19 6H 119
Woodside. Buck H 2F 21
Woodside Av. N6 & N10 5D 30
Woodside Av. N12 4F 15
Woodside Av. SE25 6H 141
Woodside Av. Chst 5G 127
Woodside Av. Esh 7J 133
Woodside Av. Wemb 1E 62
Woodside Clo. Bexh 4K 111
Woodside Clo. Ruis 6F 23
Woodside Clo. Stan 5G 11
Woodside Clo. Surb 7J 135
Woodside Clo. Wemb 1E 62
Woodside Ct. E12 1A 54
Woodside Ct. N12 4E 14
Woodside Ct. W5 1E 80
Woodside Ct. Rd. Croy 7G 141
Woodside Cres. Sidc 3J 127
Woodside Dri. Dart 4K 129
Woodside End. Wemb 1E 62
Woodside Gdns. E4 6J 19
Woodside Gdns. N17 2E 32
Woodside Grange. N12 4D 14
Woodside Grange Rd. N12 4E 14
Woodside Grn. SE25 6G 141 (in two parts)
Woodside Gro. N12 3F 15
Woodside La. N12 3F 15
Woodside La. Bex 6D 110
Woodside M. SE22 5F 105
Woodside Pde. Sidc 3J 127
Woodside Park 4D 14
Woodside Pk. SE25 6H 141
Woodside Pk. Av. E17 4F 35
Woodside Pk. Rd. N12 4E 14
Woodside Pl. Wemb 1E 62
Woodside Rd. E13 4A 72
Woodside Rd. N22 7E 16
Woodside Rd. SE25 6H 141
Woodside Rd. Bexh 4K 111
Woodside Rd. Brom 5C 144
Woodside Rd. King T 7E 116
Woodside Rd. N Mald 2K 135
Woodside Rd. Sidc 3J 127
Woodside Rd. Sutt 3A 150
Woodside Rd. Wfd G 4D 20
Woodside Way. Croy 6J 141
Woodside Way. Mitc 1F 139
Woods M. W1 7E 66 (2G 165)
Woodsome Rd. NW5 3E 48
Woods Pl. SE1 3E 86
Woodspring Rd. SW19 2G 119
Woods Rd. SE15 1H 105
Woodstead Gro. Edgw 6K 11
Woods, The. Uxb 4D 40
Woodstock Av. NW11 7G 29
Woodstock Av. W13 3A 80
Woodstock Av. Iswth 5A 98
Woodstock Av. S'hall 3D 60
Woodstock Av. Sutt 7H 137
Woodstock Clo. Bex 1F 129
Woodstock Clo. Stan 2E 26
Woodstock Ct. SE11 5K 85 (5H 173)
Woodstock Ct. SE12 6J 107
Woodstock Cres. N9 6C 8
Woodstock Dri. Uxb 4A 40
Woodstock Gdns. Beck 1D 142
Woodstock Gdns. Hay 5H 59
Woodstock Gdns. Ilf 2A 56
Woodstock Grange. W5 1E 80
Woodstock Gro. W12 2F 83
Woodstock La. N. Surb 2C 146
Woodstock La. S. Clay 5B 146
Woodstock M. W1 6H 159
Woodstock Ri. Sutt 7H 137
Woodstock Rd. E7 7A 54
Woodstock Rd. E17 2F 35
Woodstock Rd. N4 1A 50
Woodstock Rd. NW11 7H 29
Woodstock Rd. W4 4A 82
Woodstock Rd. Cars 5E 150
Woodstock Rd. Croy 3D 152
Woodstock Rd. Wemb 1F 63
Woodstock St. W1 6F 67 (1J 165)
Woodstock Ter. E14 7D 70
Woodstock, The. (Junct.) 7H 137
Woodstock Way. Mitc 2F 139
Woodstone Av. Eps 5C 148
Wood Street. (Junct.) 2E 34
Wood St. E16 7K 71
Wood St. E17 3E 34
Wood St. EC2 6C 68 (7D 162)
Wood St. W4 5A 82
Wood St. Barn 4A 4
Wood St. King T 2D 134
Wood St. Mitc 7E 138
Woodsyre. SE26 4F 123
Wood Ter. NW2 3D 46
Woodthorpe Rd. SW15 4D 100
Woodthorpe Rd. Ashf 5A 112
Woodtree Clo. NW4 2F 29
Wood Va. N10 5G 31
Wood Va. SE23 1H 123
Woodvale Av. SE25 3F 141
Woodvale Ct. Brom 1K 143 (off Widmore Rd.)
Wood Va. Est. SE23 7J 105
Woodvale Wlk. SE27 5C 122
Woodvale Way. NW11 3F 47
Woodview Av. E4 4K 19
Woodview Clo. N4 7B 32
Woodview Clo. SW15 4K 117
Woodville. SE3 7K 89
Woodville Clo. SE12 5J 107
Woodville Clo. Tedd 4A 116
Woodville Ct. SE19 1F 141
Woodville Gdns. NW2 7F 29
Woodville Gdns. W5 6E 62
Woodville Gdns. Ilf 3F 37
Woodville Gdns. Ruis 7E 22
Woodville Gdns. Surb 7D 134
Woodville Gro. Well 3A 110
Woodville Ho. SE1 3F 87 (off Grange Wlk.)
Woodville Rd. E11 1H 53
Woodville Rd. E17 4B 34
Woodville Rd. E18 2K 35
Woodville Rd. N16 5E 50
Woodville Rd. NW6 2H 65
Woodville Rd. NW11 7F 29
Woodville Rd. W5 6D 62
Woodville Rd. Barn 3E 4
Woodville Rd. Mord 4J 137
Woodville Rd. Rich 3B 116
Woodville Rd. T Hth 4C 140
Woodville St. SE18 4C 90
Woodville, The. W5 6D 62 (off Woodville Rd.)
Woodward Av. NW4 5C 28
Woodward Clo. Clay 6A 146
Woodwarde Rd. SE22 6E 104
Woodward Gdns. Dag 7C 56

Woodward Gdns. Stan . . . 7E 10
Woodward Rd. Dag . . . 7B 56
Woodward's Footpath. Twic . . . 6G 97
Wood Way. Orp . . . 2E 156
Woodway Cres. Harr . . . 6A 26
Woodwell St. SW18 . . . 5A 102
Wood Wharf. SE10 . . . 6E 88
Wood Wharf Bus. Pk. E14 . . . 1D 88
Woodyard Clo. NW5 . . . 5E 48
Woodyard La. SE21 . . . 7E 104
Woodyates Rd. SE12 . . . 6J 107
Woolacombe Rd. SE3 . . . 1A 108
Woolacombe Way. Hay . . . 4G 77
Woolcombes Ct. SE16 . . . 1K 87 (off Princes Riverside Rd.)
Wooler St. SE17 . . . 5D 86
Woolf Clo. SE28 . . . 1B 92
Woolf Ct. W3 . . . 3J 81 (off Vincent Rd.)
Woolf M. WC1 . . . 4H 67 (3D 160) (off Burton Pl.)
Woolgar M. N16 . . . 5E 50 (off Gillett St.)
Woollaston Rd. N4 . . . 6B 32
Woolley Ho. SW9 . . . 3B 104 (off Loughborough Rd.)
Woollon Ho. E1 . . . 6J 69 (off Clark St.)
Woolmead Av. NW9 . . . 7C 28
Woolmer Gdns. N18 . . . 5B 18
Woolmer Rd. N18 . . . 5B 18
Woolmore St. E14 . . . 7E 70
Woolneigh St. SW6 . . . 3K 101
Woolridge Way. E9 . . . 7J 51
Wool Rd. SW20 . . . 6D 118
Woolstaplers Way. SE16 . . . 3G 87
Woolston Clo. E17 . . . 2K 33
Woolstone Rd. SE23 . . . 2A 124
Woolwich. . . . 3E 90
Woolwich Chu. St. SE18 . . . 3C 90
Woolwich Comn. SE18 . . . 6E 90
Woolwich Dockyard Ind. Est. SE18 . . . 3C 90
Woolwich High St. SE18 . . . 3E 90
Woolwich Ind. Est. SE28 . . . 3J 91 (Hadden Rd.)
Woolwich Ind. Est. SE28 . . . 3K 91 (Kellner Rd.)
Woolwich Mnr. Way. E6 & E16 . . . 4D 72
Woolwich New Rd. SE18 . . . 5E 90
Woolwich Rd. SE2 . . . 6D 92
Woolwich Rd. SE10 & SE7 . . . 5H 89
Woolwich Rd. Bexh . . . 3G 111
Wooster Gdns. E14 . . . 6F 71
Wooster M. Harr . . . 3G 25
Wooster Pl. SE1 . . . 4D 86 (off Searles Rd.)
Wootton Gro. N3 . . . 1J 29
Wootton St. SE1 . . . 1A 86 (5K 167)
Worbeck Rd. SE20 . . . 2H 141
Worcester Av. N17 . . . 7B 18
Worcester Clo. NW2 . . . 3D 46
Worcester Clo. Croy . . . 2C 154
Worcester Clo. Mitc . . . 2E 138
Worcester Ct. N12 . . . 5E 14
Worcester Ct. W7 . . . 6K 61 (off Copley Clo.)
Worcester Ct. W9 . . . 5J 65 (off Elmfield Way)
Worcester Ct. Harr . . . 3J 25
Worcester Ct. Wor Pk . . . 3A 148
Worcester Cres. NW7 . . . 3F 13
Worcester Cres. Wfd G . . . 4E 20
Worcester Dri. W4 . . . 2A 82
Worcester Dri. Ashf . . . 5D 112
Worcester Gdns. Gnfd . . . 6H 43
Worcester Gdns. Ilf . . . 7C 36
Worcester Gdns. Wor Pk . . . 3A 148
Worcester Ho. SE11 . . . 3A 86 (2J 173) (off Kennington Rd.)
Worcester Ho. SW9 . . . 7A 86 (off Cranmer Rd.)
Worcester Ho. W2 . . . 6A 66 (off Hallfield Est.)
Worcester M. NW6 . . . 6K 47
Worcester Park. . . . 1C 148
Worcester Pk. Rd. Wor Pk . . . 3K 147
Worcester Rd. E12 . . . 4D 54
Worcester Rd. E17 . . . 2K 33
Worcester Rd. SW19 . . . 5H 119
Worcester Rd. Sutt . . . 7J 149
Worcesters Av. Enf . . . 1B 8
Wordsworth Av. E12 . . . 7C 54
Wordsworth Av. E18 . . . 3H 35
Wordsworth Av. Gnfd . . . 3H 61
Wordsworth Ct. Harr . . . 7J 25
Wordsworth Dri. Cheam & Sutt . . . 4E 148
Wordsworth Ho. NW6 . . . 3J 65 (off Stafford Rd.)
Wordsworth Ho. SE18 . . . 6E 90 (off Woolwich Comn.)
Wordsworth Pde. N15 . . . 4B 32
Wordsworth Pl. NW3 . . . 5D 48
Wordsworth Rd. N16 . . . 4E 50
Wordsworth Rd. SE1 . . . 4F 87
Wordsworth Rd. SE20 . . . 7K 123
Wordsworth Rd. Hamp . . . 4D 114
Wordsworth Rd. Wall . . . 6G 151
Wordsworth Rd. Well . . . 1J 109
Wordsworth Wlk. NW11 . . . 4J 29
Wordsworth Way. W Dray . . . 4A 76
Worfield St. SW11 . . . 7C 84
Worgan St. SE11 . . . 5K 85 (5G 173)
Worgan St. SE16 . . . 4K 87
Worland Rd. E15 . . . 7G 53
World Bus. Cen. H'row A . . . 1E 94
World of Silk. . . . 5K 111 (off Bourne Ind. Pk.)
World's End. . . . 3E 6
Worlds End Est. SW10 . . . 7B 84
World's End La. N21 & Enf . . . 5E 6
World's End Pas. SW10 . . . 7B 84 (off Worlds End. Est)
World's End Pl. SW10 . . . 7B 84 (off Worlds End Est.)
Worlidge St. W6 . . . 5E 82
Worlingham Rd. SE22 . . . 4F 105
Wormholt Rd. W12 . . . 7C 64
Wormwood St. EC2 . . . 6E 68 (7G 163) (in two parts)
Wornington Rd. W10 . . . 4G 65 (in two parts)
Wornum Ho. W10 . . . 2G 65 (off Kilburn La.)
Woronzow Rd. NW8 . . . 1B 66
Worple Av. SW19 . . . 7F 119
Worple Av. Iswth . . . 5A 98
Worple Clo. Harr . . . 1D 42
Worple Rd. SW20 & SW19 . . . 2E 136
Worple Rd. Iswth . . . 4A 98
Worple Rd. M. SW19 . . . 6H 119
Worple St. SW14 . . . 3K 99
Worple Way. Harr . . . 1D 42
Worple Way. Rich . . . 5E 98
Worship St. EC2 . . . 4D 68 (4F 163)
Worslade Rd. SW17 . . . 4B 120
Worsley Bri. Rd. SE26 & Beck . . . 4B 124
Worsley Ho. SE23 . . . 2J 123
Worsley Rd. E11 . . . 4G 53
Worsopp Dri. SW4 . . . 5G 103
Worthfield Clo. Eps . . . 7K 147
Worth Gro. SE17 . . . 5D 86
Worthing Clo. E15 . . . 1G 71
Worthing Rd. Houn . . . 6D 78
Worthington Clo. Mitc . . . 4F 139
Worthington Ho. EC1 . . . 3A 68 (1K 161) (off Myddelton Pas.)
Worthington Rd. Surb . . . 1F 147
Wortley Rd. E6 . . . 7B 54
Wortley Rd. Croy . . . 7A 140
Worton Ct. Iswth . . . 4J 97
Worton Gdns. Iswth . . . 2H 97
Worton Hall Ind. Est. Iswth . . . 4J 97
Worton Rd. Iswth . . . 4H 97
Worton Way. Iswth . . . 2H 97
Wotton Ct. E14 . . . 7F 71 (off Jamestown Way)
Wotton Rd. NW2 . . . 3E 46
Wotton Rd. SE8 . . . 6B 88
Wouldham Rd. E16 . . . 6H 71
Wragby Rd. E11 . . . 3G 53
Wrampling Pl. N9 . . . 1B 18
Wrangthorn Wlk. Croy . . . 4A 152
Wray Av. Ilf . . . 3E 36
Wrayburn Ho. SE16 . . . 2G 87 (off Llewellyn St.)
Wray Cres. N4 . . . 2J 49
Wrayfield Rd. Sutt . . . 3F 149
Wray Rd. Sutt . . . 7H 149
Wraysbury Clo. Houn . . . 5C 96
Wrays Way. Hay . . . 4G 59
Wrekin Rd. SE18 . . . 7G 91
Wren Av. NW2 . . . 5E 46
Wren Av. S'hall . . . 4D 78
Wren Clo. E16 . . . 6H 71
Wren Clo. N9 . . . 1E 18
Wren Ct. Croy . . . 4D 152 (off Coombe Rd.)
Wren Cres. Bush . . . 1B 10
Wren Gdns. Dag . . . 5D 56
Wren Ho. E3 . . . 2A 70 (off Gernon Rd.)
Wren Ho. SW1 . . . 5H 85 (6C 172) (off Aylesford St.)
Wren Ho. Hamp W . . . 2D 134 (off High St.)
Wren Landing. E14 . . . 1C 88
Wrenn Ho. SW13 . . . 6E 82
Wren Path. SE28 . . . 3H 91
Wren Rd. SE5 . . . 1D 104
Wren Rd. Dag . . . 5D 56
Wren Rd. Sidc . . . 4C 128
Wren's Av. Ashf . . . 4E 112
Wren's Pk. Ho. E5 . . . 2H 51
Wren St. WC1 . . . 4K 67 (3H 161)
Wrentham Av. NW10 . . . 2F 65
Wrenthorpe Rd. Brom . . . 4G 125
Wrenwood Way. Pinn . . . 4K 23
Wrestlers Ct. EC3 . . . 7G 163
Wrexham Rd. E3 . . . 2C 70
Wricklemarsh Rd. SE3 . . . 2K 107 (in two parts)
Wrigglesworth St. SE14 . . . 7K 87
Wright Clo. SE13 . . . 4F 107
Wright Gdns. Shep . . . 5C 130
Wright Rd. N1 . . . 6E 50
Wright Rd. Houn . . . 7A 78
Wrights All. SW19 . . . 6E 118
Wrights Clo. Dag . . . 4H 57
Wrights Grn. SW4 . . . 4H 103
Wright's La. W8 . . . 3K 83
Wrights Pl. NW10 . . . 6J 45
Wright's Rd. E3 . . . 2B 70 (in two parts)
Wrights Rd. SE25 . . . 3E 140
Wrights Row. Wall . . . 4F 151
Wrights Wlk. SW14 . . . 3K 99
Wrigley Clo. E4 . . . 5A 20
Writtle Ho. NW9 . . . 2B 28
Wrotham Ho. SE1 . . . 3D 86 (off Law St.)
Wrotham Ho. Beck . . . 7B 124 (off Sellindge Clo.)
Wrotham Rd. NW1 . . . 7G 49
Wrotham Rd. W13 . . . 1C 80
Wrotham Rd. Barn . . . 2B 4
Wrotham Rd. Well . . . 1C 110
Wrottesley Rd. NW10 . . . 2C 64
Wrottesley Rd. SE18 . . . 6G 91
Wroughton Rd. SW11 . . . 5D 102
Wroughton Ter. NW4 . . . 4D 28
Wroxall Rd. Dag . . . 6C 56
Wroxham Gdns. N11 . . . 7C 16
Wroxham Rd. SE28 . . . 7D 74
Wroxham Way. Ilf . . . 1F 37
Wroxton Rd. SE15 . . . 2J 105
Wrythe Grn. Cars . . . 3D 150
Wrythe Grn. Rd. Cars . . . 3D 150
Wrythe La. Cars . . . 1A 150
Wrythe, The. . . . 3D 150
Wulfstan St. W12 . . . 5B 64 (in two parts)
Wyatt Clo. SE16 . . . 2B 88
Wyatt Clo. Bus H . . . 1C 10
Wyatt Clo. Felt . . . 1B 114
Wyatt Clo. Hay . . . 5J 59
Wyatt Ct. Wemb . . . 7E 44
Wyatt Dri. SW13 . . . 6D 82
Wyatt Ho. NW8 . . . 4B 66 (4B 158) (off Frampton St.)
Wyatt Ho. SE3 . . . 2H 107
Wyatt Ho. Twic . . . 6D 98
Wyatt Pk. Rd. SW2 . . . 2J 121
Wyatt Point. SE28 . . . 2G 91 (off Erebus Dri.)
Wyatt Rd. E7 . . . 6J 53
Wyatt Rd. N5 . . . 3C 50
Wyatts La. E17 . . . 3E 34
Wybert St. NW1 . . . 4G 67 (3A 160)
Wyborne Ho. NW10 . . . 7J 45
Wyborne Way. NW10 . . . 7J 45
Wyburn Av. Barn . . . 3C 4
Wyche Gro. S Croy . . . 7D 152
Wych Elm Lodge. Brom . . . 7H 125
Wych Elm Pas. King T . . . 7F 117
Wycherley Clo. SE3 . . . 7H 89
Wycherley Cres. New Bar . . . 6E 4
Wychombe Studios. NW3 . . . 6D 48
Wychwood Av. Edgw . . . 6J 11
Wychwood Av. T Hth . . . 3C 140
Wychwood Clo. Edgw . . . 6J 11
Wychwood Clo. Sun . . . 6J 113
Wychwood End. N6 . . . 7G 31
Wychwood Gdns. Ilf . . . 4D 36
Wychwood Way. SE19 . . . 6D 122
Wyclif Ct. EC1 . . . 3B 68 (2A 162) (off Wyclif St.)
Wycliffe Clo. Well . . . 1K 109
Wycliffe Rd. SW11 . . . 2E 102
Wycliffe Rd. SW19 . . . 6K 119
Wyclif St. EC1 . . . 3B 68 (2A 162)
Wycombe Gdns. NW11 . . . 2J 47
Wycombe Ho. NW8 . . . 4C 66 (3C 158) (off Grendon St.)
Wycombe Pl. SW18 . . . 6A 102
Wycombe Rd. N17 . . . 1G 33
Wycombe Rd. Ilf . . . 5D 36
Wycombe Rd. Wemb . . . 1G 63
Wycombe Sq. W8 . . . 1H 83
Wydehurst Rd. Croy . . . 7G 141
Wydell Clo. Mord . . . 6F 137
Wydeville Mnr. Rd. SE12 . . . 4K 125
Wye Clo. Ashf . . . 4D 112
Wye Clo. Orp . . . 7K 145
Wye Clo. Ruis . . . 6E 22
Wye Ct. W13 . . . 5B 62 (off Malvern Way)
Wyemead Cres. E4 . . . 2B 20
Wye St. SW11 . . . 2B 102
Wyevale Clo. Pinn . . . 3J 23
Wyfields. Ilf . . . 1F 37
Wyfold Ho. SE2 . . . 2D 92 (off Wolvercote Rd.)
Wyfold Rd. SW6 . . . 7G 83
Wyhill Wlk. Dag . . . 7J 57
Wyke Clo. Iswth . . . 6K 79
Wyke Gdns. W7 . . . 3A 80
Wykeham Av. Dag . . . 6C 56
Wykeham Clo. W Dray . . . 5C 76
Wykeham Ct. N11 . . . 2K 15 (off Wykeham Rd.)
Wykeham Ct. NW4 . . . 5E 28 (off Wykeham Rd.)
Wykeham Grn. Dag . . . 6C 56
Wykeham Hill. Wemb . . . 1F 45
Wykeham Ri. N20 . . . 1B 14
Wykeham Rd. NW4 . . . 4E 28
Wykeham Rd. Harr . . . 4B 26
Wyke Rd. E3 . . . 7C 52
Wyke Rd. SW20 . . . 2E 136
Wylchin Clo. Pinn . . . 3H 23
Wyldes Clo. NW11 . . . 1A 48
Wyldfield Gdns. N9 . . . 2A 18
Wyld Way. Wemb . . . 6H 45
Wyleu St. SE23 . . . 7A 106
Wylie Rd. S'hall . . . 3E 78
Wyllen Clo. E1 . . . 4J 69
Wymans Way. E7 . . . 4A 54
Wymering Mans. W9 . . . 3J 65 (off Wymering Rd., in two parts)
Wymering Rd. W9 . . . 3J 65
Wymond St. SW15 . . . 3E 100
Wynan Rd. E14 . . . 5D 88
Wynash Gdns. Cars . . . 5C 150
Wynaud Ct. N22 . . . 6E 16
Wyncham Av. Sidc . . . 1J 127
Wyncham Ho. Sidc . . . 2A 128 (off Longlands Rd.)
Wynchgate. N14 & N21 . . . 1C 16
Wynchgate. Harr . . . 7D 10
Wynchgate. N'holt . . . 5D 42
Wyncroft Clo. Brom . . . 3D 144
Wyndale Av. NW9 . . . 6G 27
Wyndcliff Rd. SE7 . . . 6K 89
Wyndcroft Clo. Enf . . . 3G 7
Wyndham Clo. Sutt . . . 7J 149
Wyndham Ct. W7 . . . 4A 80
Wyndham Cres. N19 . . . 3G 49
Wyndham Cres. Houn . . . 6E 96
Wyndham Deedes Ho. E2 . . . 2G 69 (off Hackney Rd.)
Wyndham Est. SE5 . . . 7C 86
Wyndham Ho. E14 . . . 2D 88 (off Marsh Wall)
Wyndham M. W1 . . . 5D 66 (6E 158)
Wyndham Pl. W1 . . . 5D 66 (6E 158)
Wyndham Rd. E6 . . . 7B 54
Wyndham Rd. SE5 . . . 7C 86
Wyndham Rd. W13 . . . 3B 80
Wyndham Rd. Barn . . . 1J 15
Wyndham Rd. King T . . . 7F 117 (in two parts)
Wyndhams Ct. E8 . . . 7F 51 (off Celandine Dri.)
Wyndhams Theatre. . . . 7J 67 (2E 166) (off St Martin's La.)
Wyndham St. W1 . . . 5D 66 (5E 158)
Wyndham Yd. W1 . . . 5D 66 (6E 158)
Wyneham Rd. SE24 . . . 5D 104
Wynell Rd. SE23 . . . 3K 123
Wynford Ho. N1 . . . 2K 67 (off Wynford Rd.)
Wynford Pl. Belv . . . 6G 93
Wynford Rd. N1 . . . 2K 67
Wynford Way. SE9 . . . 3D 126
Wynlie Gdns. Pinn . . . 2K 23
Wynndale Rd. E18 . . . 1K 35
Wynne Ho. SE14 . . . 1K 105
Wynne Rd. SW9 . . . 2A 104
Wynnstay Gdns. W8 . . . 3J 83
Wynter St. SW11 . . . 4A 102
Wynton Gdns. SE25 . . . 5F 141
Wynton Pl. W3 . . . 6H 63
Wynyard Ho. SE11 . . . 5H 173
Wynyard Ter. SE11 . . . 5K 85 (5H 173)
Wynyatt St. EC1 . . . 3B 68 (2A 162)
Wyre Gro. Edgw . . . 3C 12
Wyre Gro. Hay . . . 4J 77
Wyresdale Cres. Gnfd . . . 3K 61
Wyteleaf Clo. Ruis . . . 6E 22
Wythburn Ct. W1 . . . 6D 66 (7E 158) (off Wythburn Pl.)
Wythburn Pl. W1 . . . 6D 66 (1E 164)
Wythenshawe Rd. Dag . . . 3G 57

Wythens Wlk. SE9 6F 109
Wythes Clo. Brom 2D 144
Wythes Rd. E16 1C 90
Wythfield Rd. SE9 6D 108
Wyvenhoe Rd. Harr 4G 43
Wyvern Est. N Mald 4C 136
Wyvil Rd. SW8 7J 85
Wyvis St. E14 5D 70

X

Xylon Ho. Wor Pk 2D 148

Y

Yabsley St. E14 1E 88
Yalding Rd. SE16 3G 87
Yale Clo. Houn 5D 96
Yale Ct. NW6 5K 47
Yaohan Plaza. NW9 3K 27
Yarborough Rd. SW19 1B 138
Yardley Clo. E4 5J 9
Yardley Ct. Sutt 4E 148
Yardley La. E4 5J 9
Yardley St. WC1 3A 68 (2J 161) (in two parts)
Yarlington Ct. N11 5K 15 (off Sparkford Gdns.)
Yarmouth Cres. N17 5H 33
Yarmouth Pl. W1 1F 85 (5J 165)
Yarnfield Sq. SE15 1G 105
Yarnton Way. SE2 2C 92
Yarrow Cres. E6 5C 72
Yarrow Ho. E14 3E 88 (off Stewart St.)
Yarrow Ho. W10 5E 64 (off Sutton Way)
Yateley St. SE18 3B 90
Yates Ct. NW2 6F 47 (off Willesden La.)
Yates Ho. E2 3G 69 (off Roberta St.)
Yatton Ho. W10 5E 64 (off Sutton Way)
Yeading 4A 60
Yeading Av. Harr 2C 42
Yeading Ct. Hay 4A 60
Yeading Fork. Hay 5A 60
Yeading Gdns. Hay 5K 59
Yeading Ho. Hay 5B 60
Yeading La. Hay & N'holt 6K 59
Yeading Wlk. N Har 5D 24
Yeadon Ho. W10 5E 64 (off Sutton Way)
Yeames Clo. W13 6A 62
Yearby Ho. W10 4E 64 (off Sutton Way)
Yeate St. N1 7D 50
Yeatman Rd. N6 6D 30
Yeats Clo. NW10 5A 46
Yeats Clo. SE13 2F 107
Yeend Clo. W Mol 4E 132
Yeldham Ho. W6 5F 83 (off Yeldham Rd.)
Yeldham Rd. W6 5F 83
Yelverton Lodge. Twic 7C 98 (off Richmond Rd.)
Yelverton Rd. SW11 2B 102
Ye Market. S Croy 5D 152 (off Selsdon Dri.)
Yenston Clo. Mord 6J 137
Yeoman Clo. E6 7F 73
Yeoman Clo. SE27 3B 122
Yeoman Ct. SE1 5F 87 (off Cooper's Rd.)
Yeoman Ct. Houn 7D 78
Yeoman Rd. N'holt 7C 42
Yeomans Acre. Ruis 6J 23
Yeomans M. Iswth 6H 97
Yeoman's Row. SW3 3C 84 (2D 170)
Yeoman St. SE8 4A 88
Yeomans Way. Enf 2D 8
Yeoman's Yd. E1 2K 169
Yeo St. E3 5D 70
Yeovil Ho. W10 4E 64 (off Sutton Way)
Yeovilton Pl. King T 5C 116
Yerbury Rd. N19 3H 49 (in two parts)
Yester Dri. Chst 7C 126
Yester Pk. Chst 7D 126
Yester Rd. Chst 7C 126
Yetev Lev Ct. E5 1G 51
Yew Av. W Dray 7A 58
Yew Clo. Buck H 2G 21
Yewdale Clo. Brom 6G 125
Yewfield Rd. NW10 6B 46
Yew Gro. NW2 4F 47
Yew Ho. SE16 2K 87 (off Woodland Cres.)
Yews, The. Ashf 3D 112
Yew Tree Clo. N21 7F 7
Yewtree Clo. N22 1G 31
Yewtree Clo. N Har 4F 25
Yewtree Clo. Well 1A 110
Yew Tree Clo. Wor Pk 1A 148
Yew Tree Ct. NW11 5H 29 (off Bridge La.)
Yew Tree Ct. Sutt 7A 150 (off Walnut M.)
Yew Tree Gdns. Chad H 5E 38
Yew Tree Gdns. Romf 5K 39
Yew Tree Lodge. SW16 4G 121
Yew Tree Lodge. Romf 5K 39 (off Yew Tree Gdns.)
Yew Tree Rd. W12 7B 64
Yewtree Rd. Beck 3B 142
Yew Tree Rd. Uxb 1B 58
Yew Trees. Shep 4B 130
Yew Tree Wlk. Houn 5D 96
Yew Tree Way. Croy 7B 154 (in two parts)
Yew Wlk. Harr 1J 43
Yiewsley 1A 76
Yiewsley Ct. W Dray 1A 76
Yoakley Rd. N16 2E 50
Yoke Clo. N7 6J 49
Yolande Gdns. SE9 5C 108
Yonge Pk. N4 3A 50
York Av. SE17 5C 86
York Av. SW14 5J 99
York Av. W7 1J 79
York Av. Hay 5E 58
York Av. Sidc 2J 127
York Av. Stan 1B 26
York Bri. NW1 4E 66 (3G 159)
York Bldgs. WC2 7J 67 (3F 167)
York Clo. E6 6D 72
York Clo. SE5 2C 104 (off Lilford Rd.)
York Clo. W7 1J 79
York Clo. Mord 4K 137
York Ct. N14 3D 16
York Ga. N14 7D 6
York Ga. NW1 4E 66 (4G 159)
York Gro. SE15 1J 105
York Hill. SE27 3B 122
York Ho. E16 1J 89 (off De Quincey M.)
York Ho. SE1 3K 85 (2H 173)
York Ho. W1 5D 66 (5E 158) (off York St.)
York Ho. Enf 1J 7
York Ho. King T 7F 117 (off Elm Rd.)
York Ho. Wemb 4G 45
York Ho. Pl. W8 2K 83
Yorkland Av. Well 3K 109
Yorkley House. W10 4E 64 (off Sutton Way)
York Mans. SW5 5K 83 (off Earls Ct. Rd.)
York Mans. SW11 1E 102 (off Prince Of Wales Dri.)
York Mans. W1 5E 66 (5G 159) (off Chiltern St.)
York M. NW5 5F 49
York M. Ilf 3E 54
York Pde. Bren 5D 80
York Pl. SW11 3B 102
York Pl. WC2 3F 167
York Pl. Dag 6J 57
York Pl. Ilf 2E 54
York Pl. Mans. W1 5D 66 (5F 159) (off Baker St.)
York Ri. NW5 3F 49
York Rd. E4 4H 19 (in two parts)
York Rd. E7 6J 53
York Rd. E10 3E 52
York Rd. E17 5K 33
York Rd. N11 6C 16
York Rd. N18 6C 18
York Rd. N21 7J 7
York Rd. SE1 2K 85 (7H 167)
York Rd. SW18 & SW11 4A 102
York Rd. SW19 6A 120
York Rd. W3 6J 63
York Rd. W5 3C 80
York Rd. Bren 5D 80
York Rd. Croy 7A 140
York Rd. Houn 3F 97
York Rd. Ilf 3E 54
York Rd. King T 7F 117
York Rd. New Bar 5F 5
York Rd. N'wd 2J 23
York Rd. Rain 7K 57
York Rd. Rich 5F 99
York Rd. Sutt 6J 149
York Rd. Tedd 4J 115
Yorkshire Clo. N16 3E 50
Yorkshire Gdns. N18 5C 18
Yorkshire Grey (Eltham Hill). (Junct.) 6B 108
Yorkshire Grey Pl. NW3 4A 48
Yorkshire Grey Yd. WC1 6G 161
Yorkshire Rd. E14 6A 70
Yorkshire Rd. Mitc 5J 139
Yorkshire St. E14 6A 70
York Sq. E14 6A 70
York St. W1 5D 66 (6E 158)
York St. Bark 1G 73
York St. Mitc 7E 138
York St. Twic 1A 116
York St. Chambers. W1 5D 66 (6E 158) (off York St.)
York Ter. Enf 1H 7
York Ter. Eri 1J 111
York Ter. E. NW1 4E 66 (4H 159)
York Ter. W. NW1 4E 66 (4G 159)
Yorkton St. E2 2G 69
York Way. N7 & N1 6H 49 (1F 161)
York Way. N20 3J 15
York Way. Chess 7E 146
York Way. Felt 3C 114 (in two parts)
York Way Ct. N1 1J 67
York Way Est. N7 6J 49
Young Ct. NW6 7G 47
Youngmans Clo. Enf 1H 7
Young Rd. E16 6A 72
Youngs Bldgs. EC1 3D 162
Youngs Ct. SW11 1E 102
Youngs Rd. Ilf 5H 37
Young St. W8 2K 83
Young Vic Theatre, The. 6K 167
Yoxall Ho. W10 4E 64 (off Sutton Way)
Yoxley App. Ilf 6G 37
Yoxley Dri. Ilf 6G 37
Yukon Rd. SW12 7F 103
Yunus Khan Clo. E17 5C 34

Z

Zampa Rd. SE16 5J 87
Zander Ct. E2 3G 69
Zangwill Rd. SE3 1B 108
Zealand Av. W Dray 7A 76
Zealand Ho. SE5 2C 104 (off Denmark Rd.)
Zealand Rd. E3 2A 70
Zenith Lodge. N3 7E 14
Zennor Rd. SW12 1G 121
Zennor Rd. Ind. Est. SW12 1G 121
Zenoria St. SE22 4F 105
Zermatt Rd. T Hth 4C 140
Zetland Ho. W8 3K 83 (off Marloes Rd.)
Zetland St. E14 5D 70
Zion Ho. E1 6J 69 (off Jubilee St.)
Zion Pl. T Hth 4D 140
Zion Rd. T Hth 4D 140
Zoar St. SE1 1C 86 (4C 168)
Zoffany St. N19 2H 49

HOSPITALS and HOSPICES

covered by this atlas

with their map square reference

N.B. Where Hospitals and Hospices are not named on the map, the reference given is for the road in which they are situated.

ACTON HOSPITAL —2G **81**
Gunnersbury La.
LONDON
W3 8EG
Tel: 020 83831133

ASHFORD HOSPITAL —2A **112**
London Rd.
ASHFORD
Middlesex
TW15 3AA
Tel: 01784 884488

ATHLONE HOUSE —1D **48**
Hampstead La.
LONDON
N6 4RX
Tel: 020 83485231

ATKINSON MORLEY'S HOSPITAL —7D **118**
31 Copse Hill
LONDON
SW20 0NE
Tel: 020 89467711

BARKING HOSPITAL —7K **55**
Upney La.
BARKING
Essex
IG11 9LX
Tel: 0208 9838000

BARNES HOSPITAL —3A **100**
S. Worple Way
LONDON
SW14 8SU
Tel: 020 88784981

BARNET HOSPITAL —4A **4**
Wellhouse La.
BARNET
Hertfordshire
EN5 3DJ
Tel: 020 82164000

BECKENHAM HOSPITAL —2B **142**
379 Croydon Rd.
BECKENHAM
Kent
BR3 3QL
Tel: 020 82896600

BECONTREE DAY HOSPITAL —2E **56**
508 Becontree Av.
DAGENHAM
Essex
RM8 3HR
Tel: 0208 9841234

BELVEDERE DAY HOSPITAL —1C **64**
341 Harlesden Rd.
LONDON
NW10 3RX
Tel: 020 84593562

BELVEDERE PRIVATE CLINIC —5C **92**
Knee Hill
LONDON
SE2 0AT
Tel: 020 83114464

BETHLEM ROYAL HOSPITAL, THE —7C **142**
Monks Orchard Rd.
BECKENHAM
Kent
BR3 3BX
Tel: 020 87776611

BLACKHEATH BMI HOSPITAL, THE —3H **107**
40-42 Lee Ter.
LONDON
SE3 9UD
Tel: 020 83187722

BOLINGBROKE HOSPITAL —5C **102**
Bolingbroke Gro.
LONDON
SW11 6HN
Tel: 020 72237411

BRITISH HOME & HOSPITAL FOR INCURABLES —5B **122**
Crown La.
LONDON
SW16 3JB
Tel: 020 86708261

BROMLEY HOSPITAL —4K **143**
Cromwell Av.
BROMLEY
BR2 9AJ
Tel: 020 82897000

BUSHEY BUPA HOSPITAL —1E **10**
Heathbourne Rd.
Bushey Heath
BUSHEY
Hertfordshire
WD23 1RD
Tel: 020 89509090

CAMDEN MEWS DAY HOSPITAL —6G **49**
1-5 Camden M.
LONDON
NW1 9DB
Tel: 020 75304780

CARSHALTON WAR MEMORIAL HOSPITAL —6D **150**
The Park
CARSHALTON
Surrey
SM5 3DB
Tel: 020 86475534

CASSEL HOSPITAL, THE —4D **116**
1 Ham Comn.
RICHMOND
Surrey
TW10 7JF
Tel: 020 89408181

CENTRAL MIDDLESEX HOSPITAL —3J **63**
Acton La.
LONDON
NW10 7NS
Tel: 020 89655733

CHADWELL HEATH HOSPITAL —5B **38**
Grove Rd.
ROMFORD
RM6 4XH
Tel: 020 89838000

CHARING CROSS HOSPITAL —6F **83**
Fulham Pal. Rd.
LONDON
W6 8RF
Tel: 020 88461234

CHASE FARM HOSPITAL —1F **7**
127 The Ridgeway
ENFIELD
Middlesex
EN2 8JL
Tel: 020 83666600

CHELSEA & WESTMINSTER HOSPITAL —6A **84**
369 Fulham Rd.
LONDON
SW10 9NH
Tel: 020 87468000

CLAYPONDS HOSPITAL —4E **80**
Sterling Pl.
LONDON
W5 4RN
Tel: 020 85604011

CLEMENTINE CHURCHILL HOSPITAL, THE —3K **43**
Sudbury Hill, HARROW
Middlesex
HA1 3RX
Tel: 020 88723872

COLINDALE HOSPITAL —2A **28**
Colindale Av., LONDON
NW9 5HG
Tel: 020 89522381

COTTAGE DAY HOSPITAL —3C **120**
Springfield University Hospital
61 Glenburnie Rd.
LONDON
SW17 7DJ
Tel: 020 86826514

CROMWELL HOSPITAL, THE —4K **83**
162-174 Cromwell Rd.
LONDON
SW5 0TU
Tel: 020 74602000

DEVONSHIRE HOSPITAL, THE —5E **66** (5H **159**)
29-31 Devonshire St., LONDON
W1G 6PU
Tel: 020 74867131

EALING HOSPITAL —1H **79**
Uxbridge Rd.
SOUTHALL
Middlesex
UB1 3HW
Tel: 020 89675000

EAST HAM MEMORIAL HOSPITAL —7B **54**
Shrewsbury Rd.
LONDON
E7 8QR
Tel: 0208 5865000

EASTMAN DENTAL HOSPITAL & DENTAL INSTITUTE, THE —4K **67** (3G **161**)
256 Gray's Inn Rd.
LONDON
WC1X 8LD
Tel: 020 79151000

EDENHALL MARIE CURIE CENTRE —5B **48**
11 Lyndhurst Gdns.
LONDON
NW3 5NS
Tel: 020 77940066

EDGWARE COMMUNITY HOSPITAL —7C **12**
Burnt Oak B'way.
EDGWARE
Middlesex
HA8 0AD
Tel: 020 89522381

ERITH & DISTRICT HOSPITAL —6K **93**
Park Cres.
ERITH
Kent
DA8 3EE
Tel: 020 83022678

FARNBOROUGH HOSPITAL —4E **156**
Farnborough Comn.
ORPINGTON
Kent
BR6 8ND
Tel: 01689 814000

FINCHLEY MEMORIAL HOSPITAL —7F **15**
Granville Rd.
LONDON
N12 0JE
Tel: 020 83493121

FLORENCE NIGHTINGALE DAY HOSPITAL —5C **66** (5D **158**)
1B Harewood Row
LONDON
NW1 6SE
Tel: 020 7259940

FLORENCE NIGHTINGALE HOSPITAL —5C **66** (5D **158**)
11-19 Lisson Gro.
LONDON
NW1 6SH
Tel: 020 72583828

GAINSBOROUGH CLINIC, THE —3A **86** (1K **173**)
22 Barkham Ter.
LONDON
SE1 7PW
Tel: 020 79285633

GARDEN HOSPITAL, THE —3E **28**
46-50 Sunny Gdns. Rd.
LONDON
NW4 1RP
Tel: 020 84574500

GOODMAYES HOSPITAL —5A **38**
Barley La.
ILFORD
Essex
IG3 8XJ
Tel: 020 89838000

GORDON HOSPITAL —4H **85** (4C **172**)
Bloomburg St.
LONDON
SW1V 2RH
Tel: 020 87468733

GREAT ORMOND STREET HOSPITAL FOR CHILDREN —4J **67** (4F **161**)
Gt. Ormond St.
LONDON
WC1N 3JH
Tel: 020 74059200

GREENWICH & BEXLEY COTTAGE HOSPICE —5C **92**
185 Bostall Hill
LONDON
SE2 0QX
Tel: 020 83122244

GROVELANDS PRIORY HOSPITAL —1D **16**
The Bourne
LONDON
N14 6RA
Tel: 020 88828191

GUY'S HOSPITAL —1D **86** (5E **168**)
St Thomas St.
LONDON
SE1 9RT
Tel: 020 79555000

GUY'S NUFFIELD HOUSE —2D **86** (6E **168**)
Newcomen St.
LONDON
SE1 1YR
Tel: 020 79554257

HAMMERSMITH & NEW QUEEN CHARLOTTE'S HOSPITAL —6D **64**
Du Cane Rd.
LONDON
W12 0HS
Tel: 020 83831000

HARLEY STREET CLINIC, THE —5F **67** (5J **159**)
35 Weymouth St.
LONDON
W1G 8BJ
Tel: 020 79357700

HAYES GROVE PRIORY HOSPITAL —2J **155**
Prestons Rd., BROMLEY
BR2 7AS
Tel: 020 84627722

HEART HOSPITAL, THE —5E **66** (6H **159**)
16-18 Westmoreland St.
LONDON
W1G 8PH
Tel: 020 75738888

HEATHVIEW DAY CENTRE —6C **92**
Lodge Hill, LONDON
SE2 0AY
Tel: 020 83197100

HIGHGATE PRIVATE HOSPITAL —6D **30**
17 View Rd., LONDON
N6 4DJ
Tel: 020 83414182

HILLINGDON HOSPITAL —5B **58**
Pield Heath Rd.
UXBRIDGE
Middlesex
UB8 3NN
Tel: 01895 238282

HOLLY HOUSE HOSPITAL —2E **20**
High Rd.
BUCKHURST HILL
Essex
IG9 5HX
Tel: 0208 5053311

HOMERTON HOSPITAL —5K **51**
Homerton Row
LONDON
E9 6SR
Tel: 020 85105555

HORNSEY CENTRAL HOSPITAL —5H **31**
Park Rd.
LONDON
N8 8JL
Tel: 020 82191700

HOSPITAL FOR TROPICAL DISEASES —4G **67** (4B **160**)
Mortimer Mkt.
Capper St.
LONDON
WC1E 6AU
Tel: 020 73879300

HOSPITAL OF ST JOHN & ST ELIZABETH —2B **66**
60 Gro. End Rd.
LONDON
NW8 9NH
Tel: 020 72865126

KING EDWARD VII'S HOSPITAL SISTER AGNES —5E **66** (5H **159**)
5-10 Beaumont St.
LONDON
W1G 6AA
Tel: 020 74864411

KING GEORGE HOSPITAL —5A **38**
Barley La.
ILFORD
Essex
IG3 8YB
Tel: 020 89838000

KINGSBURY COMMUNITY HOSPITAL —4G **27**
Honeypot La.
LONDON
NW9 9QY
Tel: 020 89031323

KING'S COLLEGE HOSPITAL —2D **104**
Denmark Hill
LONDON
SE5 9RS
Tel: 020 77374000

KING'S COLLEGE HOSPITAL, DULWICH —4E **104**
E. Dulwich Gro.
LONDON
SE22 8PT
Tel: 020 77374000

KING'S OAK BMI HOSPITAL, THE —1F **7**
The Ridgeway
ENFIELD
Middlesex
EN2 8SD
Tel: 020 83709500

KINGSTON HOSPITAL —1H **135**
Galsworthy Rd.
KINGSTON UPON THAMES
Surrey
KT2 7QB
Tel: 020 85467711

LAMBETH HOSPITAL —3J **103**
108 Landor Rd.
LONDON
SW9 9NT
Tel: 020 74116100

LATIMER DAY HOSPITAL —5G **67** (5A **160**)
40 Hanson St.
LONDON
W1W 6UL
Tel: 020 73809187

LEWISHAM UNIVERSITY HOSPITAL —5D **106**
Lewisham High St.
LONDON
SE13 6LH
Tel: 020 83333000

LISTER HOSPITAL, THE —5F **85** (6J **171**)
Chelsea Bri. Rd.
LONDON
SW1W 8RH
Tel: 020 77303417

LONDON BRIDGE HOSPITAL —1D **86** (4F **169**)
27 Tooley St.
LONDON
SE1 2PR
Tel: 020 74073100

LONDON CHEST HOSPITAL —2J **69**
Bonner Rd.
LONDON
E2 9JX
Tel: 020 73777000

LONDON CLINIC, THE —4E **66** (4H **159**)
20 Devonshire Pl.
LONDON
W1G 6BW
Tel: 020 79354444

LONDON FOOT HOSPITAL —4G **67** (4A **160**)
33 & 40 Fitzroy Sq.
LONDON
W1P 6AY
Tel: 020 75304500

LONDON INDEPENDENT HOSPITAL —5K **69**
1 Beaumont Sq.
LONDON
E1 4NL
Tel: 020 77900990

LONDON LIGHTHOUSE —6G **65**
111-117 Lancaster Rd.
LONDON
W11 1QT
Tel: 020 77921200

LONDON WELBECK HOSPITAL —5E **66** (6H **159**)
27 Welbeck St., LONDON
W1G 8EN
Tel: 020 72242242

MAITLAND DAY HOSPITAL —4J **51**
143-153 Lwr. Clapton Rd.
LONDON
E5 8EQ
Tel: 020 89195600

MAUDSLEY HOSPITAL, THE —2D **104**
Denmark Hill
LONDON
SE5 8AZ
Tel: 020 77036333

MAYDAY UNIVERSITY HOSPITAL —6B **140**
Mayday Rd.
THORNTON HEATH
Surrey
CR7 7YE
Tel: 020 84013000

MEADOW HOUSE HOSPICE —2H **79**
Ealing Hospital, Uxbridge Rd.
SOUTHALL
Middlesex
UB1 3HW
Tel: 020 8967 5179

MEMORIAL HOSPITAL —2E **108**
Shooters Hill
LONDON
SE18 3RZ
Tel: 020 88565511

MIDDLESEX HOSPITAL, THE —5G **67** (6B **160**)
Mortimer St.
LONDON
W1N 8AA
Tel: 020 76368333

MILDMAY MISSION HOSPITAL —3F **69** (2J **163**)
Hackney Rd.
LONDON
E2 7NA
Tel: 020 76136300

MOLESEY HOSPITAL —5E **132**
High St.
WEST MOLESEY
Surrey
KT8 2LU
Tel: 020 89414481

MOORFIELDS EYE HOSPITAL —3D **68** (2E **162**)
162 City Rd.
LONDON
EC1V 2PD
Tel: 020 72533411

MORLAND ROAD DAY HOSPITAL —7G **57**
Morland Rd.
DAGENHAM
Essex
RM10 9HU
Tel: 0208 5932343

NATIONAL HOSPITAL FOR NEUROLOGY & NEUROSURGERY (FINCHLEY), THE —4C **30**
Gt. North Rd.
LONDON
N2 0NW
Tel: 020 78373611

NATIONAL HOSPITAL FOR NEUROLOGY & NEUROSURGERY, THE —4J **67** (4F **161**)
Queen Sq.
LONDON
WC1N 3BG
Tel: 020 78373611

NELSON HOSPITAL —2H **137**
Kingston Rd.
LONDON
SW20 8DB
Tel: 020 82962000

NEWHAM GENERAL HOSPITAL —4A **72**
Glen Rd.
LONDON
E13 8SL
Tel: 020 74764000

NEW VICTORIA HOSPITAL —1A **136**
184 Coombe La. W.
KINGSTON UPON THAMES
Surrey
KT2 7EG
Tel: 020 89499000

NORTH LONDON HOSPICE —3F **15**
47 Woodside Av.
LONDON
N12 8TT
Tel: 020 83438841

NORTH LONDON NUFFIELD HOSPITAL, THE —2F **7**
Cavell Dri.
ENFIELD
Middlesex
EN2 7PR
Tel: 020 83662122

NORTH MIDDLESEX HOSPITAL, THE —5K **17**
Sterling Way
LONDON
N18 1QX
Tel: 020 88872000

NORTHWICK PARK HOSPITAL —7A **26**
Watford Rd.
HARROW
Middlesex
HA1 3UJ
Tel: 020 88643232

NORTHWOOD & PINNER COMMUNITY HOSPITAL —1J **23**
Pinner Rd.
NORTHWOOD
Middlesex
HA6 1DE
Tel: 01923 824182

OBSTETRIC HOSPITAL, THE —4G **67** (4B **160**)
Huntley St.
LONDON
WC1E 6DH
Tel: 020 73879300

OLDCHURCH HOSPITAL —6K **39**
Oldchurch Rd.
ROMFORD
RM7 0BE
Tel: 01708 746090

PARKSIDE HOSPITAL —3F **119**
53 Parkside
LONDON
SW19 5NX
Tel: 020 89718000

PENNY SANGHAM DAY HOSPITAL —3D **78**
Osterley Pk. Rd.
SOUTHALL
Middlesex
UB2 4EU
Tel: 020 85719676

PLAISTOW HOSPITAL —2A **72**
Samson St.
LONDON
E13 9EH
Tel: 020 85866200

PORTLAND HOSPITAL FOR WOMEN & CHILDREN, THE —4F **67** (4K **159**)
209 Gt. Portland St.
LONDON
W1N 6AH
Tel: 020 75804400

PRINCESS GRACE HOSPITAL —4E **66** (4G **159**)
42-52 Nottingham Pl.
LONDON
W1U 5NY
Tel: 020 74861234

PRINCESS LOUISE HOSPITAL —5F **65**
St Quintin Av.
LONDON
W10 6DL
Tel: 020 89690133

QUEEN ELIZABETH HOSPITAL —7C **90**
Stadium Rd.
LONDON
SE18 4QH
Tel: 020 88366000

QUEEN MARY'S HOSPITAL —3A **48**
23 E. Heath Rd.
LONDON
NW3 1DU
Tel: 020 74314111

QUEEN MARY'S HOSPITAL —5A **128**
Frognal Av.
SIDCUP
Kent
DA14 6LT
Tel: 020 83022678

QUEEN MARY'S HOSPITAL FOR CHILDREN —1A **150**
Wrythe La.
CARSHALTON
Surrey
SM5 1AA
Tel: 020 82962000

QUEEN MARY'S UNIVERSITY HOSPITAL —6C **100**
Roehampton La.
LONDON
SW15 5PN
Tel: 020 87896611

REDFORD LODGE PSYCHIATRIC HOSPITAL —2B **18**
15 Church St.
LONDON
N9 9DY
Tel: 020 89561234

RICHARD HOUSE CHILDREN'S HOSPICE —7B **72**
Richard Ho. Dri.
LONDON
E16 3RG
Tel: 020 75110222

RICHMOND HEALTHCARE HAMLET —3E **98**
Kew Foot Rd.
RICHMOND
Surrey
TW9 2TE
Tel: 020 89403331

RODING HOSPITAL (BUPA) —3B **36**
Roding La. S.
ILFORD
Essex
IG4 5PZ
Tel: 020 85511100

ROEHAMPTON PRIORY HOSPITAL —4B **100**
Priory La.
LONDON
SW15 5JJ
Tel: 020 88768261

ROYAL BROMPTON HOSPITAL —5C **84** (5C **170**)
Sydney St.
LONDON
SW3 6NP
Tel: 020 73528121

ROYAL BROMPTON HOSPITAL (ANNEXE) —5B **84** (5B **170**)
Fulham Rd.
LONDON
SW3 6HP
Tel: 020 73528121

ROYAL FREE HOSPITAL, THE —5C **48**
Pond St.
LONDON
NW3 2QG
Tel: 020 77940500

ROYAL HOSPITAL FOR NEURO-DISABILITY —6G **101**
West Hill
LONDON
SW15 3SW
Tel: 020 87804500

ROYAL LONDON HOMOEOPATHIC HOSPITAL, THE —5J **67** (5F **161**)
Gt. Ormond St.
LONDON
WC1N 3HR
Tel: 020 78378833

ROYAL LONDON HOSPITAL (MILE END) —4K **69**
Bancroft Rd.
LONDON
E1 4DG
Tel: 020 73777920

ROYAL LONDON HOSPITAL (WHITECHAPEL) —5H **69**
Whitechapel Rd.
LONDON
E1 1BB
Tel: 020 73777000

ROYAL MARSDEN HOSPITAL (FULHAM), THE —5B **84** (5B **170**)
Fulham Rd.
LONDON
SW3 6JJ
Tel: 020 73528171

ROYAL NATIONAL ORTHOPAEDIC HOSPITAL —2G **11**
Brockley Hill
STANMORE
Middlesex
HA7 4LP
Tel: 020 89542300

ROYAL NATIONAL ORTHOPAEDIC HOSPITAL (OUTPATIENTS) —4F **67** (4K **159**)
45-51 Bolsover St.
LONDON
W1W 5AQ
Tel: 020 89542300

ROYAL NATIONAL THROAT, NOSE & EAR HOSPITAL —3K **67** (1G **161**)
330 Gray's Inn Rd.
LONDON
WC1X 8DA
Tel: 020 79151300

ROYAL NATIONAL THROAT, NOSE & EAR HOSPITAL - SPEECH & LANGUAGE UNIT —5C **62**
10 Castlebar Hill
LONDON
W5 1TD
Tel: 020 89978480

ST ANDREW'S AT HARROW —2J **43**
Bowden Ho. Clinic, London Rd.
HARROW
Middlesex
HA1 3JL
Tel: 020 89667000

ST ANDREW'S HOSPITAL —4D **70**
Devas St.
LONDON
E3 3NT
Tel: 020 74764000

ST ANN'S HOSPITAL —5C **32**
St Ann's Rd.
LONDON
N15 3TH
Tel: 020 84426000

ST ANTHONY'S HOSPITAL —2F **149**
London Rd., LONDON
SM3 9DW
Tel: 020 83376691

ST BARTHOLOMEW'S HOSPITAL —5B **68** (6B **162**)
West Smithfield, LONDON
EC1A 7BE
Tel: 020 73777000

ST BERNARD'S HOSPITAL —2H **79**
Uxbridge Rd., SOUTHALL
Middlesex
UB1 3EU
Tel: 020 89675000

ST CHARLES HOSPITAL —5F **65**
Exmoor St., LONDON
W10 6DZ
Tel: 020 89692488

ST CHRISTOPHER'S HOSPICE —5J **123**
51-59 Lawrie Park Rd.
LONDON
SE26 6DZ
Tel: 020 87789252

ST CLEMENT'S HOSPITAL —3B **70**
2A Bow Rd.
LONDON
E3 4LL
Tel: 020 73777000

ST GEORGE'S HOSPITAL (TOOTING) —5B **120**
Blackshaw Rd.
LONDON
SW17 0QT
Tel: 020 86721255

ST HELIER HOSPITAL —1A **150**
Wrythe La.
CARSHALTON
Surrey
SM5 1AA
Tel: 020 82962000

ST JOHN'S AND AMYAND HOUSE —7A **98**
Strafford Rd.
TWICKENHAM
TW1 3AD
Tel: 020 87449943

ST JOHN'S HOSPICE —2B **66** (1A **158**)
Hospital of St John & St Elizabeth
60 Gro. End Rd.
LONDON
NW8 9NH
Tel: 020 72865126

ST JOSEPH'S HOSPICE —1H **69**
Mare St.
LONDON
E8 4SA
Tel: 020 85256000

ST LUKE'S HOSPITAL FOR THE CLERGY —4G **67** (4A **160**)
14 Fitzroy Sq.
LONDON
W1T 6AH
Tel: 020 73884954

ST LUKE'S KENTON GRANGE HOSPICE —5D **26**
Kenton Grange
Kenton Rd.
HARROW
Middlesex
HA3 0YG
Tel: 020 83828000

ST LUKE'S WOODSIDE HOSPITAL —4E **30**
Woodside Av.
LONDON
N10 3HU
Tel: 020 82191800

ST MARY'S HOSPITAL —6B **66** (7B **158**)
Praed St.
LONDON
W2 1NY
Tel: 020 77256666

ST PANCRAS HOSPITAL —1H **67**
4 St Pancras Way
LONDON
NW1 0PE
Tel: 020 75303500

ST RAPHAEL'S HOSPICE —1F **149**
St Anthony's Hospital
London Rd.
SUTTON
Surrey
SM3 9DW
Tel: 020 83354575

ST THOMAS' HOSPITAL —3K **85** (1G **173**)
Lambeth Pal. Rd.
LONDON
SE1 7EH
Tel: 020 79289292

SHIRLEY OAKS HOSPITAL —7J **141**
Poppy La.
CROYDON
CR9 8AB
Tel: 020 86555500

SLOANE HOSPITAL, THE —1F **143**
125-133 Albemarle Rd.
BECKENHAM
Kent
BR3 5HS
Tel: 020 84666911

SOUTHWOOD HOSPITAL —7E **30**
70 Southwood La.
LONDON
N6 5SP
Tel: 020 83408778

SPRINGFIELD UNIVERSITY HOSPITAL —3C **120**
61 Glenburnie Rd.
LONDON
SW17 7DJ
Tel: 020 86826000

SURBITON HOSPITAL —6E **134**
Ewell Rd.
SURBITON
Surrey
KT6 6EZ
Tel: 020 83997111

TEDDINGTON MEMORIAL HOSPITAL —6J **115**
Hampton Rd.
TEDDINGTON
Middlesex
TW11 0JL
Tel: 020 84088210

THORPE COOMBE HOSPITAL —3E **34**
714 Forest Rd.
LONDON
E17 3HP
Tel: 020 85208971

TOLWORTH HOSPITAL —2G **147**
Red Lion Rd.
SURBITON
Surrey
KT6 7QU
Tel: 020 83900102

TRINITY HOSPICE —4F **103**
30 Clapham Comn. N. Side
LONDON
SW4 0RN
Tel: 020 77871000

UNITED ELIZABETH GARRETT ANDERSON & SOHO HOSPITALS FOR WOMEN —3H **67** (2D **160**)
144 Euston Rd.
LONDON
NW1 2AP
Tel: 020 73872501

UNIVERSITY COLLEGE HOSPITAL —4G **67** (4B **160**)
Gower St.
LONDON
WC1E 6AU
Tel: 020 73879300

UPTON DAY HOSPITAL —4E **110**
14 Upton Rd.
BEXLEYHEATH
Kent
DA6 8LQ
Tel: 020 83017900

WELLINGTON HOSPITAL, THE —3B **66** (1B **158**)
8a Wellington Pl.
LONDON
NW8 9LE
Tel: 0207 5865959

WESTERN OPHTHALMIC HOSPITAL —5D **66** (5E **158**)
153 Marylebone Rd.
LONDON
NW1 5QH
Tel: 020 78866666

WEST MIDDLESEX UNIVERSITY HOSPITAL —2A **98**
Twickenham Rd.
ISLEWORTH
Middlesex
TW7 6AF
Tel: 020 85602121

WHIPPS CROSS HOSPITAL —6F **35**
Whipps Cross Rd.
LONDON
E11 1NR
Tel: 020 85395522

WHITTINGTON NHS TRUST —2G **49**
Highgate Hill
LONDON
N19 5NF
Tel: 020 72723070

WILLESDEN COMMUNITY HOSPITAL —7C **46**
Harlesden Rd.
LONDON
NW10 3RY
Tel: 020 84591292

RAIL, CROYDON TRAMLINK, DOCKLANDS LIGHT RAILWAY AND LONDON UNDERGROUND STATIONS

with their map square reference

Abbey Wood Station. Rail —3C 92
Acton Central Station. Rail —1K 81
Acton Main Line Station. Rail —6J 63
Acton Town Station. Tube —2G 81
Addington Village Stop. CT —6C 154
Addiscombe Stop. CT —1G 153
Albany Park Station. Rail —2D 128
Aldgate East Station. Tube —6F 69 (7K 163)
Aldgate Station. Tube —6F 69 (1J 169)
Alexandra Palace Station. Rail —2J 31
All Saints Station. DLR —7D 70
Alperton Station. Tube —1D 62
Ampere Way Stop. CT —1K 151
Anerley Station. Rail —1H 141
Angel Road Station. Rail —5D 18
Angel Station. Tube —2A 68
Archway Station. Tube —2G 49
Arena Stop. CT —5J 141
Arnos Grove Station. Tube —5B 16
Arsenal Station. Tube —3A 50
Ashford Station. Rail —4B 112
Avenue Road Stop. CT —2K 141

Baker Street Station. Tube —4D 66 (4F 159)
Balham Station. Rail & Tube —1F 121
Bank Station. Tube & DLR —6D 68 (1E 168)
Barbican Station. Rail & Tube —5C 68 (5C 162)
Barking Station. Rail & Tube —7G 55
Barkingside Station. Tube —3H 37
Barnehurst Station. Rail —2J 111
Barnes Bridge Station. Rail —2B 100
Barnes Station. Rail —3C 100
Barons Court Station. Tube —5G 83
Battersea Park Station. Rail —7F 85
Bayswater Station. Tube —7K 65
Beckenham Hill Station. Rail —5E 124
Beckenham Junction Station. Rail & CT —1C 142
Beckenham Road Stop. CT —1A 142
Beckton Park Station. DLR —7D 72
Beckton Station. DLR —5E 72
Becontree Station. Tube —6D 56
Beddington Lane Stop. CT —6G 139
Belgrave Walk Stop. CT —4B 138
Bellingham Station. Rail —3D 124
Belsize Park Station. Tube —5C 48
Belvedere Station. Rail —3H 93
Bermondsey Station. Tube —3G 87
Berrylands Station. Rail —4H 135
Bethnal Green Station. Tube —3J 69
Bethnal Green Station. Rail —4H 69
Bexley Station. Rail —1G 129
Bexleyheath Station. Rail —2E 110
Bickley Station. Rail —3C 144
Bingham Road Stop. CT —1G 153
Birkbeck Stop. CT —3J 141
Blackfriars Station. Rail & Tube —7B 68 (2A 168)
Blackheath Station. Rail —3H 107
Blackhorse Lane Stop. CT —7G 141
Blackhorse Road Station. Rail & Tube —4K 33
Blackwall Station. DLR —7E 70
Bond Street Station. Tube —6F 67 (1J 165)
Borough Station. Tube —2C 86 (7D 168)
Boston Manor Station. Tube —4A 80
Bounds Green Station. Tube —6C 16
Bow Church Station. DLR —3C 70
Bow Road Station. Tube —3C 70
Bowes Park Station. Rail —7D 16
Brent Cross Station. Tube —7F 29
Brentford Station. Rail —6C 80
Brimsdown Station. Rail —2F 9
Brixton Station. Rail & Tube —4A 104
Brockley Station. Rail —3A 106
Bromley North Station. Rail —1J 143
Bromley South Station. Rail —3J 143
Bromley-by-Bow Station. Tube —3E 70
Brondesbury Park Station. Rail —1G 65
Brondesbury Station. Rail —7H 47
Bruce Grove Station. Rail —2F 33
Buckhurst Hill Station. Tube —2G 21
Burnt Oak Station. Tube —1J 27
Bush Hill Park Station. Rail —6A 8

Caledonian Road & Barnsbury Station. Rail —7K 49
Caledonian Road Station. Tube —6K 49
Cambridge Heath Station. Rail —2H 69
Camden Road Station. Rail —7G 49
Camden Town Station. Tube —1F 67
Canada Water Station. Tube —2J 87
Canary Wharf Station. DLR —1C 88
Canary Wharf Station. Tube —1D 88
Canning Town Station. Rail, DLR & Tube —6G 71
Cannon Street Station. Rail & Tube —7D 68 (2E 168)
Canonbury Station. Rail —5C 50
Canons Park Station. Tube —7K 11
Carshalton Beeches Station. Rail —6D 150
Carshalton Station. Rail —4D 150
Castle Bar Park Station. Rail —5K 61
Catford Bridge Station. Rail —7C 106
Catford Station. Rail —7C 106
Chadwell Heath Station. Rail —7D 38
Chalk Farm Station. Tube —7E 48
Chancery Lane Station. Tube —5A 68 (6J 161)
Charing Cross Station. Rail & Tube —1J 85 (4E 166)
Charlton Station. Rail —5A 90
Cheam Station. Rail —7G 149
Chessington North Station. Rail —5E 146
Chessington South Station. Rail —7D 146
Chingford Station. Rail —1B 20
Chislehurst Station. Rail —2E 144
Chiswick Park Station. Tube —4J 81
Chiswick Station. Rail —7J 81
Church Street Stop. CT —2C 152
City Thameslink Station. Rail —6B 68 (7A 162)
Clapham Common Station. Tube —4G 103
Clapham High Street Station. Rail —3H 103
Clapham Junction Station. Rail —3C 102
Clapham North Station. Tube —3J 103
Clapham South Station. Tube —6F 103
Clapton Station. Rail —2H 51
Clock House Station. Rail —1A 142
Cockfosters Station. Tube —4K 5
Colindale Station. Tube —3A 28
Colliers Wood Station. Tube —7B 120
Coombe Lane Stop. CT —5J 153
Covent Garden Station. Tube —7J 67 (1F 167)
Cricklewood Station. Rail —4F 47
Crofton Park Station. Rail —5B 106
Crossharbour & London Arena Station. DLR —3D 88
Crouch Hill Station. Rail —7K 31
Croydon Central Stop. CT —2C 152
Crystal Palace Station. Rail —6G 123
Custom House for ExCeL Station. Rail & DLR —7K 71
Cutty Sark Station. DLR —6E 88
Cyprus Station. DLR —7E 72

Dagenham Dock Station. Rail —3F 75
Dagenham East Station. Tube —5J 57
Dagenham Heathway Station. Tube —6F 57
Dalston Kingsland Station. Rail —5E 50
Denmark Hill Station. Rail —2D 104
Deptford Bridge Station. DLR —1C 106
Deptford Station. Rail —7C 88
Devons Road Station. DLR —4D 70
Dollis Hill Station. Tube —5C 46
Drayton Green Station. Rail —6K 61
Drayton Park Station. Rail —4A 50
Dundonald Road Stop. CT —7H 119

Ealing Broadway Station. Rail & Tube —7D 62
Ealing Common Station. Tube —1F 81
Earl's Court Station. Tube —4K 83
Earlsfield Station. Rail —1A 120
East Acton Station. Tube —6B 64
East Croydon Station. Rail & CT —2D 152
East Dulwich Station. Rail —4E 104
East Finchley Station. Tube —4C 30
East Ham Station. Tube —7C 54
East India Station. DLR —7F 71
East Putney Station. Tube —5G 101
Eastcote Station. Tube —7A 24
Eden Park Station. Rail —5C 142
Edgware Road Station. Tube —5C 66 (6C 158)
Edgware Station. Tube —6C 12
Edmonton Green Station. Rail —2B 18
Elephant & Castle Station. Rail & Tube —4C 86
Elmers End Station. Rail & CT —4K 141
Elmstead Woods Station. Rail —6C 126
Eltham Station. Rail —5D 108
Elverson Road Station. DLR —2D 106
Embankment Station. Tube —1J 85 (4F 167)
Enfield Chase Station. Rail —3H 7
Enfield Town Station. Rail —3K 7
Erith Station. Rail —5K 93
Essex Road Station. Rail —7C 50
Euston Square Station. Tube —4G 67 (3B 160)
Euston Station. Rail & Tube —3H 67 (2C 160)
Ewell West Station. Rail —7A 148

Fairlop Station. Tube —1H 37
Falconwood Station. Rail —4H 109
Farringdon Station. Rail & Tube —5B 68 (5A 162)
Feltham Station. Rail —1K 113
Fenchurch Street Station. Rail —7E 68 (2J 169)
Fieldway Stop. CT —7D 154
Finchley Central Station. Tube —1J 29
Finchley Road & Frognal Station. Rail —5A 48
Finchley Road Station. Tube —6A 48
Finsbury Park Station. Rail & Tube —2A 50
Forest Gate Station. Rail —5J 53
Forest Hill Station. Rail —2J 123
Fulham Broadway Station. Tube —7J 83
Fulwell Station. Rail —4H 115

Gallions Reach Station. DLR —7F 73
Gants Hill Station. Tube —6E 36
George Street Stop. CT —2C 152

Gipsy Hill Station. Rail —5E **122**
Gloucester Road Station. Tube —4A **84**
Golders Green Station. Tube —1J **47**
Goldhawk Road Station. Tube —2E **82**
Goodge Street Station. Tube —5H **67** (5C **160**)
Goodmayes Station. Rail —1A **56**
Gordon Hill Station. Rail —1G **7**
Gospel Oak Station. Rail —4E **48**
Grange Park Station. Rail —5G **7**
Gravel Hill Stop. CT —6A **154**
Great Portland Street Station. Tube —4F **67** (4K **159**)
Green Park Station. Tube —1G **85** (4K **165**)
Greenford Station. Rail & Tube —1H **61**
Greenwich Station. Rail & DLR —7D **88**
Grove Park Station. Rail —3K **125**
Gunnersbury Station. Rail & Tube —5H **81**

Hackbridge Station. Rail —2F **151**
Hackney Central Station. Rail —6H **51**
Hackney Downs Station. Rail —5H **51**
Hackney Wick Station. Rail —6C **52**
Hadley Wood Station. Rail —1F **5**
Hammersmith Station. Tube —4E **82**
Hampstead Heath Station. Rail —4C **48**
Hampstead Station. Tube —4A **48**
Hampton Court Station. Rail —4J **133**
Hampton Station. Rail —1E **132**
Hampton Wick Station. Rail —1C **134**
Hanger Lane Station. Tube —3E **62**
Hanwell Station. Rail —7J **61**
Harlesden Station. Rail & Tube —2K **63**
Harringay Green Lanes Station. Rail —6B **32**
Harringay Station. Rail —6A **32**
Harrington Road Stop. CT —3J **141**
Harrow & Wealdstone Station. Rail & Tube —4J **25**
Harrow-on-the-Hill Station. Rail & Tube —6J **25**
Hatton Cross Station. Tube —4H **95**
Haydons Road Station. Rail —5A **120**
Hayes & Harlington Station. Rail —3H **77**
Hayes Station. Rail —1J **155**
Headstone Lane Station. Rail —1F **25**
Heathrow Central Station. Rail —3C **94**
Heathrow Terminal 4 Station. Tube —6E **94**
Heathrow Terminals 1, 2, 3 Station. Tube —3D **94**
Hendon Central Station. Tube —5D **28**
Hendon Station. Rail —6C **28**
Herne Hill Station. Rail —6B **104**
Heron Quays Station. DLR —1C **88**
High Barnet Station. Tube —4D **4**
High Street Kensington Station. Tube —2K **83**
Highams Park Station. Rail —6A **20**
Highbury & Islington Station. Rail & Tube —6B **50**
Highgate Station. Tube —6F **31**
Hillingdon Station. Tube —5D **40**
Hither Green Station. Rail —6G **107**
Holborn Station. Tube —6K **67** (6G **161**)
Holland Park Station. Tube —1H **83**
Holloway Road Station. Tube —5K **49**
Homerton Station. Rail —6K **51**
Honor Oak Park Station. Rail —6K **105**
Hornsey Station. Rail —4K **31**
Hounslow Central Station. Tube —3F **97**
Hounslow East Station. Tube —2G **97**
Hounslow Station. Rail —5F **97**
Hounslow West Station. Tube —2C **96**
Hyde Park Corner Station. Tube —2E **84** (6H **165**)

Ickenham Station. Tube —4E **40**
Ilford Station. Rail —3F **55**
Island Gardens Station. DLR —5E **88**
Isleworth Station. Rail —2K **97**

Kennington Station. Tube —5B **86**
Kensal Green Station. Rail & Tube —3E **64**
Kensal Rise Station. Rail —2F **65**
Kensington Olympia Station. Rail & Tube —3G **83**
Kent House Station. Rail —1A **142**
Kentish Town Station. Rail & Tube —5G **49**
Kentish Town West Station. Rail —6F **49**
Kenton Station. Rail & Tube —6B **26**
Kew Bridge Station. Rail —5F **81**
Kew Gardens Station. Rail & Tube —1G **99**
Kidbrooke Station. Rail —3K **107**
Kilburn High Road Station. Rail —1K **65**
Kilburn Park Station. Tube —2J **65**
Kilburn Station. Tube —6H **47**
King's Cross St Pancras Station. Tube —3J **67** (1E **160**)
King's Cross Station. Rail —2J **67**
King's Cross Thameslink Station. Rail —3J **67** (1G **161**)
Kingsbury Station. Tube —5G **27**
Kingston Station. Rail —1E **134**
Knightsbridge Station. Tube —2D **84** (7F **165**)

Ladbroke Grove Station. Tube —6G **65**
Ladywell Station. Rail —5D **106**
Lambeth North Station. Tube —3A **86** (1J **173**)
Lancaster Gate Station. Tube —7B **66** (2A **164**)
Latimer Road Station. Tube —7F **65**
Lebanon Road Stop. CT —2E **152**
Lee Station. Rail —6J **107**
Leicester Square Station. Tube —7J **67** (2E **166**)
Lewisham Station. Rail & DLR —3E **106**
Leyton Midland Road Station. Rail —1E **52**
Leyton Station. Tube —3E **52**
Leytonstone High Road Station. Rail —2G **53**
Leytonstone Station. Tube —1G **53**
Limehouse Station. Rail & DLR —6A **70**
Liverpool Street Station. Rail & Tube —5E **68** (6G **163**)
Lloyd Park Stop. CT —4F **153**
London Arena Station. DLR —3D **88**
London Bridge Station. Rail & Tube —1D **86** (5F **169**)
London Fields Station. Rail —7H **51**
Loughborough Junction Station. Rail —3B **104**
Lower Sydenham Station. Rail —5B **124**

Maida Vale Station. Tube —3K **65**
Malden Manor Station. Rail —7A **136**
Manor House Station. Tube —7C **32**
Manor Park Station. Rail —4B **54**
Mansion House Station. Tube —7C **68** (2D **168**)
Marble Arch Station. Tube —6D **66** (1F **165**)
Maryland Station. Rail —6G **53**
Marylebone Station. Rail & Tube —4D **66** (4E **158**)
Maze Hill Station. Rail —6G **89**
Merton Park Stop. CT —1J **137**
Mile End Station. Tube —4B **70**
Mill Hill Broadway Station. Rail —6F **13**
Mill Hill East Station. Tube —7B **14**
Mitcham Junction Station. Rail & CT —5E **138**
Mitcham Stop. CT —4C **138**
Monument Station. Tube —7D **68** (2F **169**)
Moorgate Station. Rail & Tube —5D **68** (6E **162**)
Morden Road Stop. CT —2K **137**
Morden South Station. Rail —5J **137**
Morden Station. Tube —3K **137**
Mornington Crescent Station. Tube —2G **67**
Mortlake Station. Rail —3J **99**
Motspur Park Station. Rail —5D **136**
Mottingham Station. Rail —1D **126**
Mudchute Station. DLR —4D **88**

Neasden Station. Tube —5A **46**
New Barnet Station. Rail —5G **5**
New Beckenham Station. Rail —7B **124**
New Cross Gate Station. Rail & Tube —1A **106**
New Cross Station. Rail & Tube —7B **88**
New Eltham Station. Rail —1G **127**
New Malden Station. Rail —3A **136**
New Southgate Station. Rail —5A **16**
Newbury Park Station. Tube —6H **37**
Norbiton Station. Rail —1G **135**
Norbury Station. Rail —1K **139**
North Acton Station. Tube —5K **63**
North Dulwich Station. Rail —5D **104**
North Ealing Station. Tube —6F **63**
North Greenwich Station. Tube —2G **89**
North Harrow Station. Tube —5F **25**
North Sheen Station. Rail —4G **99**
North Wembley Station. Rail & Tube —3D **44**
North Woolwich Station. Rail —2E **90**
Northfields Station. Tube —3C **80**
Northolt Park Station. Rail —4F **43**
Northolt Station. Tube —6E **42**
Northumberland Park Station. Rail —7C **18**
Northwick Park Station. Tube —7B **26**
Northwood Hills Station. Tube —2J **23**
Norwood Junction Station. Rail —4G **141**
Notting Hill Gate Station. Tube —1J **83**
Nunhead Station. Rail —2J **105**

Oakleigh Park Station. Rail —7G **5**
Oakwood Station. Tube —5B **6**
Old Street Station. Rail & Tube —4D **68** (3F **163**)
Osterley Station. Tube —7H **79**
Oval Station. Tube —6A **86**
Oxford Circus Station. Tube —6G **67** (7A **160**)

Paddington Station. Rail & Tube —6B **66** (1A **164**)
Palmers Green Station. Rail —4E **16**
Park Royal Station. Tube —4G **63**
Parsons Green Station. Tube —1J **101**
Peckham Rye Station. Rail —2G **105**
Penge East Station. Rail —6J **123**
Penge West Station. Rail —6H **123**
Perivale Station. Tube —2A **62**
Petts Wood Station. Rail —5G **145**
Phipps Bridge Stop. CT —3B **138**
Piccadilly Circus Station. Tube —7H **67** (3C **166**)
Pimlico Station. Tube —5H **85** (5C **172**)
Pinner Station. Tube —4C **24**
Plaistow Station. Tube —2H **71**
Plumstead Station. Rail —4H **91**
Ponders End Station. Rail —5F **9**
Poplar Station. DLR —7D **70**
Preston Road Station. Tube —1E **44**
Prince Regent Station. DLR —7A **72**
Pudding Mill Lane Station. DLR —1D **70**
Putney Bridge Station. Tube —3H **101**
Putney Station. Rail —4G **101**

Queen's Park Station. Rail & Tube —2H **65**
Queen's Road (Peckham) Station. Rail —1J **105**
Queens Park Station. Rail & Tube —2H **65**
Queensbury Station. Tube —3F **27**
Queenstown Road (Battersea) Station. Rail —1F **103**
Queensway Station. Tube —7K **65**

Ravensbourne Station. Rail —7F **125**
Ravenscourt Park Station. Tube —4D **82**
Rayners Lane Station. Tube —7D **24**
Raynes Park Station. Rail —2E **136**
Rectory Road Station. Rail —3F **51**
Redbridge Station. Tube —6B **36**
Reeves Corner Stop. CT —2B **152**
Regent's Park Station. Tube —4F **67** (4J **159**)
Richmond Station. Rail & Tube —4E **98**
Roding Valley Station. Tube —4G **21**
Rotherhithe Station. Tube —2J **87**
Royal Albert Station. DLR —7C **72**
Royal Oak Station. Tube —5K **65**
Royal Victoria Station. DLR —7J **71**
Ruislip Gardens Station. Tube —4J **41**
Ruislip Manor Station. Tube —1J **41**

Rail, Croydon Tramlink, Docklands Light Railway & London Underground Stations

Ruislip Station. Tube —1G **41**
Russell Square Station. Tube —4J **67** (4E **160**)

St Helier Station. Rail —6J **137**
St James Street, Walthamstow Station. Rail —5A **34**
St James's Park Station. Tube —2H **85** (1C **172**)
St John's Wood Station. Tube —2B **66**
St Johns Station. Rail —2C **106**
St Margarets Station. Rail —6B **98**
St Pancras Station. Rail —3J **67** (1E **160**)
St Paul's Station. Tube —6C **68** (7C **162**)
Sanderstead Station. Rail —7D **152**
Sandilands Stop. CT —2F **153**
Selhurst Station. Rail —5E **140**
Seven Kings Station. Rail —1J **55**
Seven Sisters Station. Rail & Tube —5E **32**
Shadwell Station. DLR & Tube —7H **69**
Shepherd's Bush Station. Tube —1E **82**
Shepherd's Bush Station. Tube —2F **83**
Shepperton Station. Rail —5E **130**
Shoreditch Station. Tube —4F **69** (4K **163**)
Shortlands Station. Rail —2G **143**
Sidcup Station. Rail —2A **128**
Silver Street Station. Rail —4A **18**
Silvertown & City Airport Station. Rail —1C **90**
Sloane Square Station. Tube —4E **84** (4G **171**)
Snaresbrook Station. Tube —5J **35**
South Acton Station. Rail —3J **81**
South Bermondsey Station. Rail —5J **87**
South Croydon Station. Rail —5D **152**
South Ealing Station. Tube —3D **80**
South Greenford Station. Rail —3J **61**
South Hampstead Station. Rail —7A **48**
South Harrow Station. Tube —3G **43**
South Kensington Station. Tube —4B **84** (3B **170**)
South Kenton Station. Rail & Tube —1C **44**
South Merton Station. Rail —3H **137**
South Quay Station. DLR —2D **88**
South Ruislip Station. Rail & Tube —5A **42**
South Tottenham Station. Rail —5F **33**
South Wimbledon Station. Tube —7K **119**
South Woodford Station. Tube —2K **35**
Southall Station. Rail —2D **78**
Southbury Station. Rail —4C **8**
Southfields Station. Tube —1H **119**
Southgate Station. Tube —1C **16**
Southwark Station. Tube —1B **86** (5A **168**)
Stamford Brook Station. Tube —4B **82**
Stamford Hill Station. Rail —7E **32**
Stanmore Station. Tube —4J **11**
Stepney Green Station. Tube —4K **69**
Stockwell Station. Tube —2J **103**
Stoke Newington Station. Rail —2F **51**
Stonebridge Park Station. Rail & Tube —7H **45**
Stoneleigh Station. Rail —5C **148**
Stratford (Low Level) Station. Rail —7F **53**
Stratford Station. Rail, Tube & DLR —7F **53**
Strawberry Hill Station. Rail —3K **115**
Streatham Common Station. Rail —7H **121**
Streatham Hill Station. Rail —2J **121**
Streatham Station. Rail —5H **121**
Sudbury & Harrow Road Station. Rail —5B **44**
Sudbury Hill Station. Tube —4J **43**
Sudbury Hill, Harrow Station. Rail —4J **43**
Sudbury Town Station. Tube —6B **44**
Sunbury Station. Rail —1J **131**
Sundridge Park Station. Rail —7K **125**
Surbiton Station. Rail —6E **134**
Surrey Quays Station. Tube —4K **87**
Sutton Common Station. Rail —2K **149**
Sutton Station. Rail —6A **150**
Swiss Cottage Station. Tube —7B **48**
Sydenham Hill Station. Rail —3F **123**
Sydenham Station. Rail —4J **123**
Syon Lane Station. Rail —7A **80**

Teddington Station. Rail —6A **116**
Temple Station. Tube —7K **67** (2H **167**)
Thames Ditton Station. Rail —7K **133**
Therapia Lane Stop. CT —7J **139**
Thornton Heath Station. Rail —4C **140**
Tolworth Station. Rail —2H **147**
Tooting Bec Station. Tube —3E **120**
Tooting Broadway Station. Tube —5C **120**
Tooting Station. Rail —6D **120**
Tottenham Court Road Station. Tube —6H **67** (7D **160**)
Tottenham Hale Station. Rail & Tube —3H **33**
Totteridge & Whetstone Station. Tube —2F **15**
Tower Gateway Station. DLR —7F **69** (2J **169**)
Tower Hill Station. Tube —7F **69** (2J **169**)
Tufnell Park Station. Tube —4G **49**
Tulse Hill Station. Rail —2B **122**
Turnham Green Station. Tube —4A **82**
Turnpike Lane Station. Tube —3B **32**
Twickenham Station. Rail —7A **98**

Upney Station. Tube —7K **55**
Upper Halliford Station. Rail —2G **131**
Upper Holloway Station. Rail —2H **49**
Upton Park Station. Tube —1A **72**

Vauxhall Station. Rail & Tube —6J **85** (6F **173**)
Victoria Coach Station. Bus —4F **85** (4J **171**)
Victoria Station. Rail & Tube —3F **85** (3K **171**)

Waddon Marsh Stop. CT —2A **152**
Waddon Station. Rail —4A **152**
Wallington Station. Rail —6F **151**
Walthamstow Central Station. Rail & Tube —5C **34**
Walthamstow Queens Road Station. Rail —5C **34**
Wandle Park Stop. CT —2A **152**
Wandsworth Common Station. Rail —1D **120**
Wandsworth Road Station. Rail —2G **103**
Wandsworth Town Station. Rail —4K **101**
Wanstead Park Station. Rail —4K **53**
Wanstead Station. Tube —6K **35**
Wapping Station. Tube —1J **87**
Warren Street Station. Tube —4G **67** (3A **160**)
Warwick Avenue Station. Tube —4A **66**
Waterloo East Station. Rail —1A **86** (5K **167**)
Waterloo International Station. Rail —2K **85** (6H **167**)
Waterloo Station. Rail & Tube —2A **86** (6J **167**)
Wellesley Road Stop. CT —2D **152**
Welling Station. Rail —2A **110**
Wembley Central Station. Rail & Tube —5E **44**
Wembley Park Station. Tube —3G **45**
Wembley Stadium Station. Rail —5F **45**
West Acton Station. Tube —6G **63**
West Brompton Station. Rail & Tube —6J **83**
West Croydon Station. Rail & CT —1C **152**
West Drayton Station. Rail —1A **76**
West Dulwich Station. Rail —2D **122**
West Ealing Station. Rail —7B **62**
West Finchley Station. Tube —6E **14**
West Ham Station. Rail —3G **71**
West Ham Station. Tube —3G **71**
West Hampstead Station. Rail —6J **47**
West Hampstead Station. Tube —6K **47**
West Hampstead Thameslink Station. Rail —6J **47**
West Harrow Station. Tube —6G **25**
West India Quay Station. DLR —7C **70**
West Kensington Station. Tube —5H **83**
West Norwood Station. Rail —4B **122**
West Ruislip Station. Rail & Tube —2E **40**
West Sutton Station. Rail —4J **149**
West Wickham Station. Rail —7E **142**
Westbourne Park Station. Tube —5H **65**
Westcombe Park Station. Rail —5J **89**
Westferry Station. DLR —7C **70**
Westminster Station. Tube —2J **85** (7F **167**)
White City Station. Tube —7E **64**
White Hart Lane Station. Rail —7A **18**
Whitechapel Station. Tube —5H **69**
Whitton Station. Rail —7G **97**
Willesden Green Station. Tube —6E **46**
Willesden Junction Station. Rail & Tube —3B **64**
Wimbledon Chase Station. Rail —2G **137**
Wimbledon Park Station. Tube —3J **119**
Wimbledon Station. Rail, CT & Tube —6H **119**
Winchmore Hill Station. Rail —7G **7**
Wood Green Station. Tube —2A **32**
Wood Street, Walthamstow Station. Rail —4F **35**
Woodford Station. Tube —6E **20**
Woodgrange Park Station. Rail —5B **54**
Woodside Park Station. Tube —4E **14**
Woodside Stop. CT —6H **141**
Woolwich Arsenal Station. Rail —4F **91**
Woolwich Dockyard Station. Rail —4D **90**
Worcester Park Station. Rail —1C **148**